AF660061

Fundamentals of Mathematics

Differential Calculus

Sanjay Mishra

B.Tech.
Indian Institute of Technology, Varanasi

G K Publications (P) Ltd

Title : Fundamentals of Mathematics Differential Calculus

Language : English

Author : Sanjay Mishra

Copyright © : 2023 Sanjay Mishra

No part of this book may be reproduced in a retrieval system or transmitted, in any form or by any means, electronics, mechanical, photocopying, recording, scanning and or without the written permission of the Author/Publisher.

Typeset & Published by :

Career Launcher Infrastructure (P) Ltd.

A-45, Mohan Cooperative Industrial Area, Near Mohan Estate Metro Station, New Delhi - 110044

Marketed by :

G.K. Publications (P) Ltd.

Plot No. 63, Sector-27A, Near Sector - 28 Metro Station, Faridabad, Haryana-121003

ISBN : **978-81-93975-90-9**

Printer's Details : Printed in India, New Delhi.

For product information :
Visit ***www.gkpublications.com*** or email to ***gkp@gkpublications.com***

Preface

If I am asked to choose the most important event in the history of mathematics, I shall definitely mark the simultaneous development of calculus by two contemporary, eminent mathematicians – Isaac Newton and Gottfried Leibnitz. By developing calculus, they made mathematics the only language that can describe the physical universe around us. Calculus, the mathematical analysis of motion and change, was invented by these two great mathematicians in their process of attempting to answer the fundamental questions about the world around us and the way it operates.

As we say, the Rome was not built in a day, similarly, an event so momentous involved a basic idea too, that was so profound that an average human can only hope to comprehend it. The essential idea of calculus involving the derivative and the integrals is one among such ideas, as are the paradoxes of Zeno (500 BC) and the novel idea of Archimedes (c.a 200 BC).

Calculus has major share in the syllabus of IIT JEE and other competitive examinations. During my high-school days as an IIT aspirant, and later as a tutor of mathematics, I had always felt the need for a comprehensive textbook on this subject. This book has been written with the objective of providing a textbook as well as an exercise book that focuses on problem-solving. I feel this will not only fulfill the need of class XI and class XII students but will also meet the requirements of advanced-level students who are preparing for various entrance examinations such as IIT–JEE Mains/Advanced, BIT–SAT, and other state engineering entrance examinations. This book (*Fundamental of Mathematics*, Volume-VI) has been designed to give the students a deep insight into topics such as limits, continuity and differentiability methods of differentiation and application of derivatives in detail. I have observed in my teaching career that three topics—limits, continuity and differentiability and mean value theorem, are the most challenging but high scoring topics of mathematics in the competitive exams. One of the reasons why students dread these topics is because of their non-familiarity with the basic concepts and the lack of good books that spell out the fundamentals in a student-friendly manner. This book provides a well-arranged content list that will help students and teachers to access the chapters and sub-topics of their interest conveniently. Each chapter is divided into several topics and each topic rationalizes its theory with sufficient number of worked-out problems to enable students to imbibe the concepts and apply them as required. This is followed by a textual exercise of both objective and subjective problems. Each chapter is replete with solved examples of both objective- and subjective-type questions that entail students to apply the concepts learnt in the chapter, thus enabling them acquire masters over the newly assimilated ideas. The tutorial exercise given at the end contains ample multiple-choice problems with single and multiple correct options, comprehension passage, column-matching problems and numerical integer-type questions to help students hone their mathematical skills. For teachers, this text will serve as a repository of well-graded problems, arranged topic- and subtopic-wise, that can be used to set home assignments to their students.

Suggestions for the improvement of this book are welcome and shall be gratefully acknowledged.

Sanjay Mishra

Acknowledgements

I would like to express my gratitude to GK Publications for providing me an opportunity to share my knowledge from years of experience in teaching this comprehensive textbook. I thank all my friends and teachers for enabling me to write this book. I would like to acknowledge my pupils, without their support I would not have been able to develop new insights into the subject. I drew my inspiration to write this book in the course of my interactions with them. I feel that I have learnt more through my interaction with students than what I could have taught them. Above all I thank my parents and all my family members, who supported and encouraged me in spite of all the time it took me away from them. I am obliged to my team consisting of teachers, managers and computer operators, for their hard work and dedication in completing this task.

Sanjay Mishra

Contents

The Limit of a Function

CHAPTER 1

INTRODUCTION

We have studied about the important events that lead to the development of calculus, famous among these were sun, moon and earth problem, problem of force (tangent) and problem on energy (Area) that paved the path for invention of an amazing mathematical tool presently known as calculus. The breakthrough in the development of these concepts was the formulation of a beautiful mathematical idea called as limit. The story of development of this concept is too long to be told here but we would definetly mark some of the events those became the foundation stone of the concept of limits and continuity.

Zeno: Zeno was a Greek philosopher (Ca 500 BC) of an extraordinary intellect much ahead of his time primarily known for his famous paradoxes. He was mainly concerned with three problems.

(a) Problem of infinitesimals

(b) Problem of infinite

(c) Idea of continuity

Since then, the finest minds of each generation have attempted these problems. The problem of infinitesimal was solved by weierstrass whereas the solution of other two was initialed by Dedekind and concluded by 'cantor'.

Zeno's Paradoxes: Zeno proposed that in a race between Achilles (a legendary Greek hero), and a Tortoise if a head start is given to the tortoise (Slower) as shown in the figure 1.1. Then it is not possible for Achilles to overtake the Tortoise. He forwarded following argument to establish his proposition.

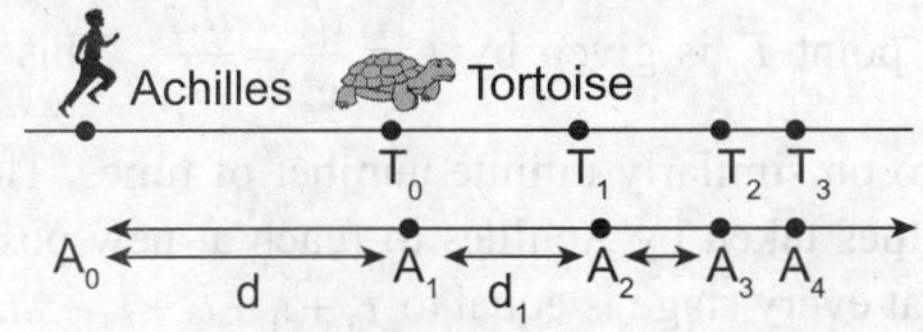

FIGURE 1.1

He said that by the time Achilles occupies the starting point of Tortoise ($A_1 = T_0$), the tortoise will have moved ahead to a new point T_1. When Achilles gets to this next position $A_2 = T_1$, the tortoise will move further ahead and occupy a new point T_2. Thus the tortoise, even though slower than Achilles, keeps moving forward. Although the distance between Achilles and the tortoise is getting smaller and smaller, the tortoise will apparently always be ahead.

By applying commonsense, one can say that Achilles must overtake the slower tortoise. But it is important to investigate that, "where is the error in Zeno's proposition"? To indicate the error in Zeno's proposition and of course to find the truth, one should sum up the infinite number of finite time intervals and prove that the summation is always finite. And this discussion shall automatically lead to the notion of limit.

Let Achilles be at point A_0 and Tortoise be at T_0 and let *d* be the distance between Achilles and Tortoise at the beginning of race i.e., Tortoise is given ahead start of distance *d*.

Corresponding	Positions of Achilles and Tortoise				
Achilles:	A_0,	A_1,	A_2,	A_3,	A_4 ....
Tortoise:		T_0,	T_1,	T_2,	T_3, T_4 ....

Let v_a and v_t be the speed of Achilles and Tortoise respectively. Therefore the time taken by Achilles to reach at point $T_0 = t_0 = \frac{d}{v_a}$. Now after time t_0 when Achilles reach at $T_0 = A_1$, the Tortoise would have reached at some other point T_1 at a distance d_1 from T_0 given by $d_1 = v_t \cdot t_0 = v_t \cdot \frac{d}{v_a}$. Now time taken by Achilles to go from T_0 to T_1 is given by $t_1 = \frac{d_1}{v_a} = \frac{dv_t}{v_a^2}$. In time t_1 when Achilles reach at T_1, tortoise would have reached at some other point T_2 traveling a distance $d_2 = v_t . t_1 = \frac{dv_t^2}{v_a^2}$. Now time taken by Achilles to reach at point T_2 is given by $t_2 = \frac{d_2}{v_a} = \frac{dv_t^2}{v_a^3}$. This process would go on similarly infinite number of times. Thus sum of the times taken by Achilles to reach at new position of tortoise at every stage is equal to $t_0 + t_1 + t_2 + t_3 + ...$

$$= \frac{d}{v_a}\left\{1 + \left(\frac{v_t}{v_a}\right) + \left(\frac{v_t}{v_a}\right)^2 + \left(\frac{v_t}{v_a}\right)^3 + ...\right\}$$

$= \frac{d}{v_a}\{1 + r + r^2 + r^3 + ...\}$; where $r = \frac{v_t}{v_a} < 1$ as $v_t < v_a$. Thus the above series is a decreasing infinite geometric progression and hence the sum converges to $\frac{d}{v_a}\left(\frac{1}{1-r}\right) = \frac{d}{v_a(1-r)} = \frac{d}{(v_a - v_t)}$ which is definitely a finite time interval.

Thus even if infinite number of processes of catching the tortoise by Achilles have been taken the sum of time taken by Achilles would be finite and hence definitely after a certain stage Achilles would over take the tortoise. Hence the Zeno's assumption that Achilles would never catch the tortoise when given a head start was wrong.

Similarly we can understand the meaning of "approaching a real number on real number line."

ILLUSTRATION 1: Imagine a child C_1 has a cake weighing 1 kg. He divides it in two equal parts, keeping one part with him, gives 2nd part to his friend C_2. He further divides his portion in two equal parts and gives one equal part to C_2 and go on continuously doing so. Show that at the end complete cake shall get transferred to C_2.

SOLUTION: It is very clear that C_2 gets $\frac{1}{2}$ kg cake in step 1, $\frac{1}{4}$ kg cake in step 2 and $\frac{1}{8}$ kg cake he receives from C_1 in step 3 and the process continue indefinitely. Consequently, the share of C_2 goes on increasing whereas cake held by C_1 continues decreasing and approaches zero. At the end of n steps,

Amount of cake with $C_2 = \frac{1}{2} + \frac{1}{4} + \frac{1}{8} + ...$ upto n terms (in a GP)

$$\therefore \quad A_n = \frac{\frac{1}{2}\left(1 - \left(\frac{1}{2}\right)^n\right)}{1 - \frac{1}{2}} = 1 - \left(\frac{1}{2}\right)^n$$

Clearly when $n \to \infty$, $\left(\frac{1}{2}\right)^n \to 0$

$\Rightarrow A_n \to 1$

FIGURE 1.2

In mathematical language we say that as n increases and approaches to ∞, the amount of cake transformed to $C_2 = \lim_{n\to\infty}(A_n) = 1kg$

This is the basic idea and important thing is to remember, however large the value of n be the whole cake (1 kg) can never reach to C_2. This can be more clearly understood by the figure 1.2. You become more clear to see the given figure.

ILLUSTRATION 2: The sequence $\frac{1}{2}, \frac{2}{3}, \frac{3}{4}, \frac{4}{5}, ...$ can be described by writing a general term $\frac{n}{n+1}$ where $n = 1$, 2, 3, 4, … Can you guess the limit, L, of this sequence?

SOLUTION: The limit is an important idea in calculus, and we discuss this concept extensively later in this chapter. We will say that L is the number that the sequence with general term $\frac{n}{n+1}$ tends towards as n becomes large and larger without bound. We will define a notation to summarize this idea:

$$L = \lim_{n \to \infty} \frac{n}{n+1}$$

As you consider larger and larger values for n, you find a sequence of fractions:

$$\frac{1}{2}, \frac{2}{3}, \frac{3}{4}, ..., \frac{1,000}{1,001}, \frac{1,001}{1,002}, ..., \frac{9,999,999}{10,000,000} ..... \text{ therefore,}$$

it is reasonable to guess that the sequence of fractions is approaching the number 1.

Archimedes and The Problem of Area

The Egyptians were the first to find area of circles over as early as 3000 B.C., but Greek philosopher Archimedes first illustrated how to derive the formula for area of circle ($A = \pi r^2$) by applying an infinite limiting process, inscribing regular polygons inside circle and increasing number of sides to infinity. He called his method as "Method of exhaustion".

Considering A_n be area of n sided regular polygon inscribed in circle of radius 'r' as shown in diagrams and conclude that the square of Areas $A_3, A_4, A_5, A_6, ..., A_n, ...$ Clearly indicates that each successive area approximates more closely to that of a circle.

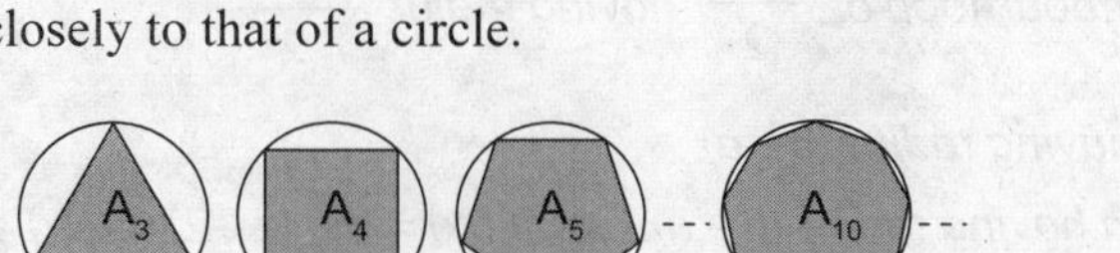

FIGURE 1.3

Based on above discussion we can define the limit of a function $f(x)$ when $x \to a$ as the real number towards which the value of function tends to approach when we approach x from left-hand side or right-hand side. So you must not confuse it with value of function at $x = a$. When x is approaching nearer and nearer to 'a' (i.e. x can be taken to as much close to 'a' as we wish), then we say that x is in neighborhood of 'a' and at that instant $f(x)$ is approaching to a real number I(say) is called limit of function. Let us study limit of a function starting from very beginning i.e. neighborhood of a point 'a'

Neighbourhood of Point '*a*'

An open interval $(a - \delta, a + \delta)$; where $\delta > 0$ is called a neighbourhood of the point 'a'. It is denoted by $N(a, \delta)$ and called as δ – *neighbourhood* of point 'a' here 'δ' specifies the radius of neighbourhood $N(a, \delta)$, and 'a' is known as its centre for any real number $x \in N(a, \delta), \Leftrightarrow x \in (a - \delta, a + \delta)$

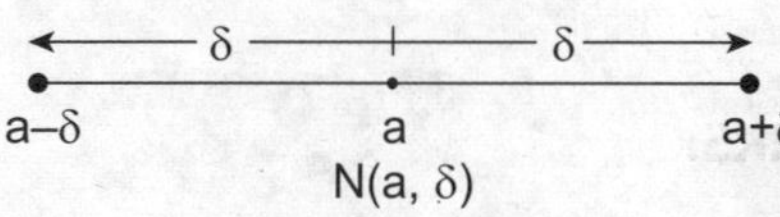

FIGURE 1.4

$$\Rightarrow a - \delta < x < a + \delta$$
$$\Rightarrow -\delta < x - a < \delta$$
$$\Rightarrow 0 \le |x - a| < \delta$$

Thus a real number x belongs to δ-neighbourhood of 'a' if and only if $0 \le |x - a| < \delta$ i.e., distance of x from 'a' is lesser than δ (may be zero) e.g., the function $f(x) = \frac{1}{\sqrt{(x-2)(3-x)}}$ has its domain $(2, 3) \equiv \left(\frac{5}{2} - \frac{1}{2}, \frac{5}{2} + \frac{1}{2}\right)$ which is 1/2-neighbourhood of 5/2 i.e., neighbourhood having its centre at 5/2 and radius = 1/2.

Deleted Neighbourhood of a Point *a*

If the real number 'a' is removed from the neighbourhood $N(a,\delta)$ of 'a' then it is called a deleted neighbourhood of 'a'. Thus $(a - \delta, a) \cup (a, a + \delta)$ is called deleted neighbourhood of 'a'.

For any real $(a - \delta, \alpha + \delta)$ number x belonging to deleted neighbourhood of 'a' we have $x \in (a - \delta, a) \cup (a, a + \delta)$

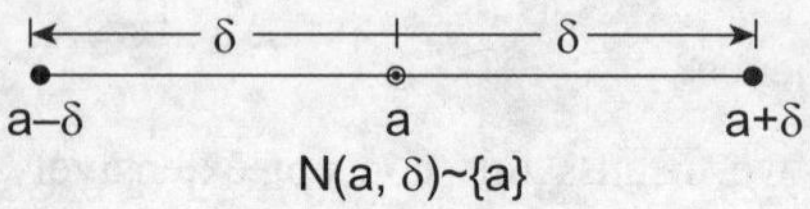

FIGURE 1.5

$\Rightarrow\ a - \delta < x < a + \delta$ and $x \neq a$

$\Rightarrow\ -\delta < x - a < \delta$ and $x - a \neq 0$

$\Rightarrow\ 0 < |x - a| < \delta$

Thus a real number x belongs to δ – *deleted* neighbourhood of 'a' if and only if $0 < |x\text{-}a| < \delta$, i.e., distance of x from a is lesser than δ but not equal to zero. e.g., $f(x) = \dfrac{1}{\sqrt{(x-2)(4-x)(x-3)}}$ has its domain (2, 4) ~ $\{3\}\ \equiv (2,3) \cup (3,4)$, i.e., deleted neighbourhood of 3 having radius '1', here $a = 3$, $\delta = 1$.

Left Deleted Neighbourhood of '*a*'

The set $\{x : a - \delta, < x < a\}$ is called left deleted neighbourhood of a. Thus $(a - \delta, a)$ is left deleted neighbourhood of 'a'. Thus if a real number x belongs to left deleted neighbourhood of 'a', then x is less than 'a' and distance of x from a is less than δ. e.g., the function $f(x) = \dfrac{1}{\sqrt{(x-2)(4-x)}}$ has its domain (2,4) which is left deleted neighbourhood of 4, having its radius '2'.

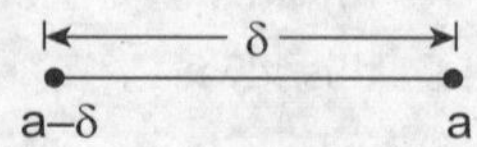

FIGURE 1.6

Right Deleted Neighbourhood of '*a*'

The set $\{x : a < x < a + \delta\}$ is called right deleted neighbourhood of a. Thus if a real number x belongs to right deleted neighbourhood of 'a', then x is greater than 'a' and its distance from 'a' is less than δ. For example the function $f(x) = \log (x - 1)(2 - x)$ has its domain (1, 2) which is right deleted neighbourhood of 1, having its radius 1.

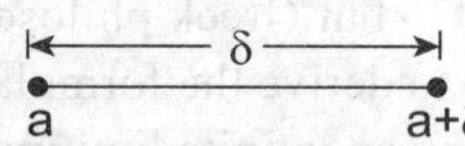

FIGURE 1.7

REMARKS:

If domain of a function f(x) is (a, b); then we can write (a, b) as

(i) $\left(\dfrac{(a+b)}{2} - \dfrac{(b-a)}{2}, \dfrac{(a+b)}{2} + \dfrac{(b-a)}{2}\right)$ *Which is the neighbourhood of* $\dfrac{a+b}{2}$ *having radius* $\dfrac{(b-a)}{2}$

(ii) (b – (b – a), b) which is left deleted neighbourhood of b having radius (b – a)

(iii) (a, a + (b – a)) which is right deleted neighbourhood of a having radius (b – a). e.g., If f(x) = log (x – 2) (4 – x), then domain of f(x) = D_f *= (2, 4) which may be defined as*

(i) Neighbourhood of 3 having radius 1

(ii) Left deleted neighbourhood of 4 with radius 2

(iii) Right deleted neighbourhood of 2 with radius 2

Meaning of '$x \to a$' (*x* tends to *a*)

$x \to a$ (*x tends to a*) means x is approaching nearer and nearer to 'a' but is never equal to 'a'. $x \to a$ does not predict about the way in which x is approaching to 'a' i.e., from left side of 'a' or from right side of 'a'. Thus depending on the way in which x is approaching to 'a' we define the following two symbols:

(a) $x \to a^-$: (*x* tends to *a* from negative side)

Means x is approaching to 'a' from negative side (left side). Here x is approaching to 'a' by taking the increasing values from left deleted neighbourhood of 'a' i.e., $x \in (a - \delta, a)$ and every value of x is greater than its previous value e.g., $x \to 2^-$ implies x takes values like 1.991, 1.992, 1.994, 1.998, 1.99901, and so on but $x < 2$ (always).

(b) $x \to a^+$: (x tends to a from positive side)

Means x is approaching to 'a' from positive side (right side). Here x is approaching to 'a' by taking the decreasing values from right deleted neighbourhood of 'a' i.e., $x \in (a, a + \delta)$ and every value of x is lesser than its previous value e.g., $x \to 2^+$ implies x takes value like 2.106, 2.102, 2.092, 2.065, 2.008 and so on but x always remains larger than 2.($x > 2$).

REMARKS:

(i) $x \to a$ is equivalent to $x = a \pm h; h \to 0^+$

(ii) $x \to a^-$ is equivalent to $x = a - h; h \to 0^+$

(iii) $x \to a^+$ is equivalent to $x = a + h; h \to 0^+$

LIMIT OF A FUNCTION

Limit of a function at $x = a$ is tendency of the value output of the function f(x) as x gets its values nearer and nearer to a. Limit of a function can be discussed for the following two cases.

Case I : Limit of a function $f(x)$ at a real finite number '$x = a$'

A real number 'ℓ' is said to be the limit of a function $f(x)$ as x tends to a if the value $f(x)$ is approaching closer & closer to ℓ as x is approaching nearer and nearer to 'a'. We can take $f(x)$, as much nearer to ℓ as we please by taking x sufficiently close to 'a'.

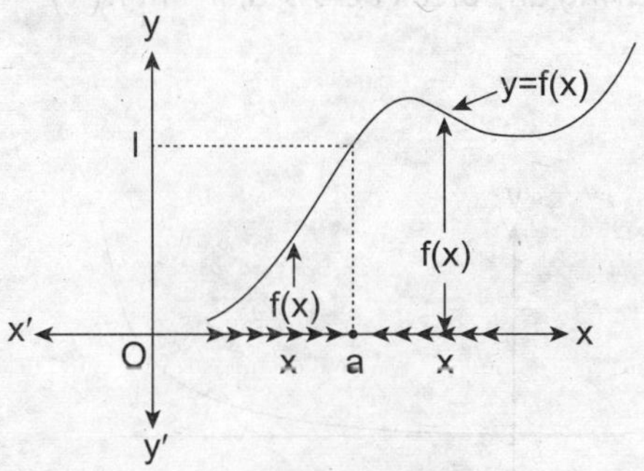

FIGURE 1.8

The above statement can be represented symbolically as $f(x) \to \ell$ as $x \to$ a and we write $\lim_{x \to a} f(x) = l$ and read as "Limit of $f(x)$ is ℓ as x tends to 'a'.

Note that $\lim_{x \to a} f(x) = l$ means $f(x)$ has the tendency to approach ℓ as x tends to 'a'. It does not ensure that $f(a) = \ell$. i.e., $f(a)$ may or may not be equal to ℓ

e.g. 1. If $f(x) = x^2$. Consider the following tables representing the values of $f(x)$ as x is approaching nearer and nearer to 2.

$x(x \to 2^-)$	1.9	1.91	1.94	1.98	1.99	1.995	1.998
$f(x)$	3.61	3.6481	3.7636	3.9204	3.9601	3.980025	3.992004

$x(x \to 2^+)$	2.05	2.04	2.02	2.01	2.005
$f(x)$	4.2025	4.1616	4.0804	4.0401	4.020025

The first one table shows that as x approaches nearer and nearer to 2 from left side, $f(x)$ is approaching nearer and nearer to 4 from left side i.e., $f(x) \to 4^-$ as $x \to 2^-$.

The second table shows that as x approaches nearer and nearer to 2 from right side $f(x)$ is approaching nearer and nearer to 4 from right side i.e., $f(x) \to 4^+$ as $x \to 2^+$.

Thus overall we conclude and say that $f(x) \to 4$ as $x \to 2$. i.e., $\lim_{x \to 2} f(x) = 4$ (Here $a = 2$, $\ell = 4$).

Graphically,

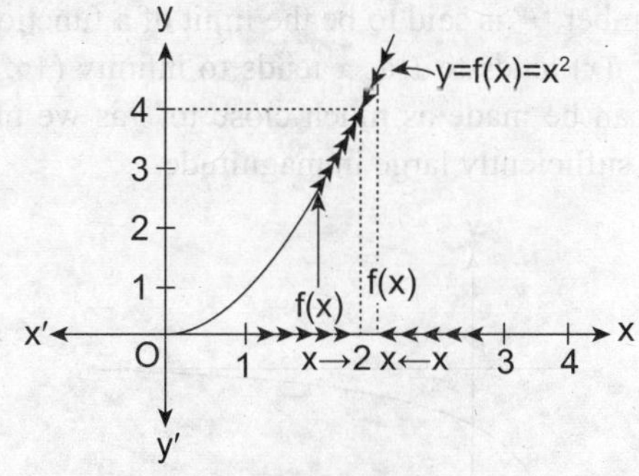

FIGURE 1.9

e.g 2. If $f(x) = \dfrac{x^2 - 9}{(x-3)} = \dfrac{(x-3)(x+3)}{(x-3)} = (x+3)$

[as $x \to 3$ implies $(x - 3)$ is non-zero and hence this factor can be cancelled out]

Consider the following tables representing the values of $f(x)$ as x is approaching nearer and nearer to 3

$x(x \to 3^-)$	2.9	2.91	2.92	2.93	2.94	2.98....
$f(x)$	5.9	5.91	5.92	5.93	5.94	5.98....

$x(x \to 3^+)$	3.05	3.04	3.03	3.02	3.01	3.004...
$f(x)$	6.05	6.04	6.03	6.02	6.01	6.004...

The first table shows that as x is approaching nearer and nearer to 3 from left side $f(x)$ is getting loser and closer to 6 from left side, i.e., $f(x) \to 6^-$ as $x \to 3^-$. The second table shows that as x is approaching nearer and nearer to 3 from right side, $f(x)$ is approaching nearer and nearer to 6 from right side i.e., $f(x) \to 6^+$ as $x \to 3^+$

Thus overall, we can say $f(x) \to 6$ as $x \to 3$. i.e., $\lim_{x \to 3} f(x) = 6$

Graphically:

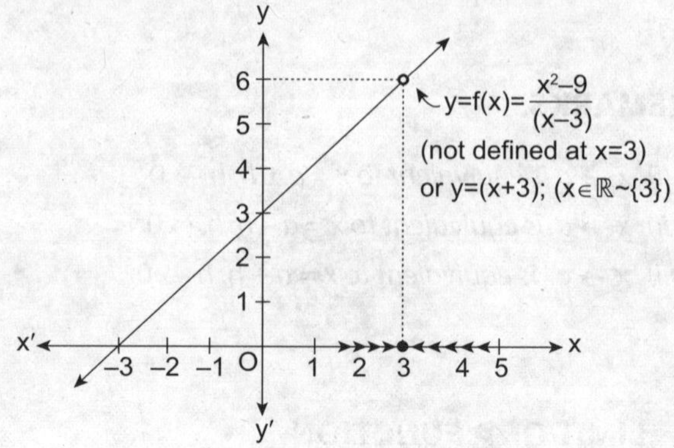

FIGURE 1.10

REMARKS:

1. *In example (1)* $\lim_{x \to 2} f(x) = 4$ *and also f(2) = 4, whereas in example (2)* $\lim_{x \to 3} f(x) = 6$ *but* $f(3) \neq 6$*, thus limit of a function f(x) equal to ℓ may or may not be equal to value f(a) as x tends 'a' does not ensure f(a) = ℓ*
2. *Conversely if f(a) = ℓ, then is it necessary that* $\lim_{x \to a} f(x) = l$ *?*

   The answer is no. For support consider the function f(x) = $\begin{cases} \dfrac{x^2-9}{x-3} & ; x \neq 3 \\ 5 & ; x = 3 \end{cases}$. *Here* $\lim_{x \to 3} f(x) = \lim_{x \to 3} \dfrac{x^2-9}{x-3} = 6$

   (As discussed earlier) and f(3) = 5. Thus f(3) = 5 but $\lim_{x \to 3} f(x) \neq 5$
3. *For the functions having their graphs continuous i.e., without having any break across 'a', if* $\lim_{x \to a} f(x) = \ell$*, then f(a) = ℓ and conversely if f(a) = ℓ, then* $\lim_{x \to a} f(x) = \ell$.

Case II: Limit of a function *f*(*x*) at infinity (Limit at infinity)

A real number 'ℓ' is said to be the limit of a function $f(x)$ at infinity if $f(x)$ tends to ℓ as x tends to infinity ($+\infty$ or $-\infty$), i.e., $f(x)$ can be made as much close to ℓ as we please by making x sufficiently large in magnitude.

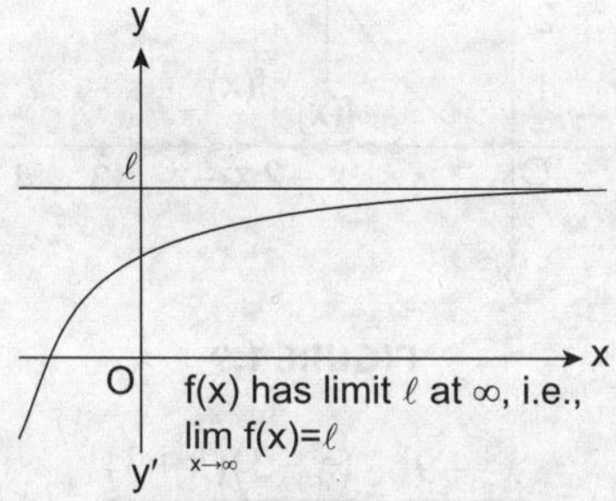

FIGURE 1.11

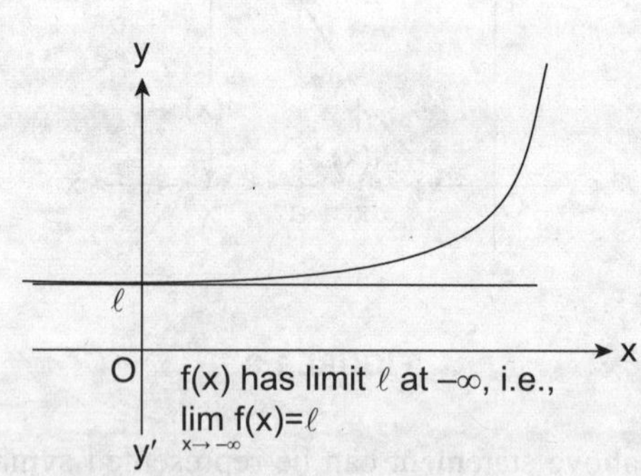

FIGURE 1.12

Illustration: Prove the following and hence draw their graph

(i) $\lim_{x \to \infty} \left(1 - \frac{1}{x}\right) = 1$

since by increasing the values of x its reciprocal $1/x$ decrease thus

As $x \to \infty \Rightarrow \frac{1}{x} \to 0$

$\Rightarrow \quad 1 - \frac{1}{x} \to 1$. Graphically, it is shown in figure 1.13

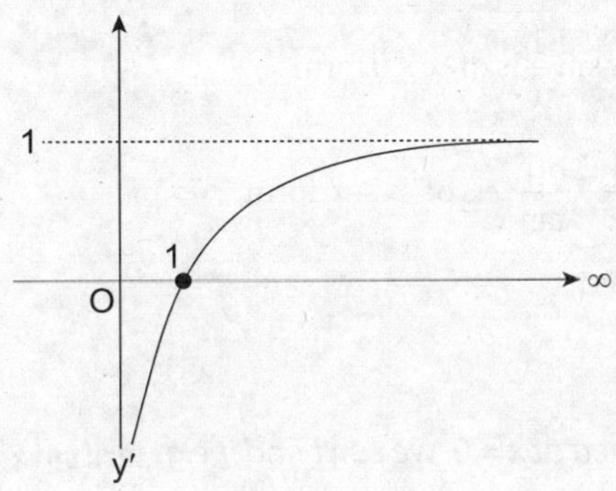

FIGURE 1.13

(ii) $\lim\limits_{x\to\infty} e^{-1/x} = 1$

when x increases from zero to infinity the reciprocal $1/x$ decreases from ∞ to zero (but takes +ve values) thus $-1/x$ increases $-\infty$ to zero taking all possible negative real values

i.e., $x \to \infty$, $\frac{1}{x} \to 0^+; \frac{-1}{x} \to 0^-$ $\Rightarrow e^{-1/x} \to 1^-$

Graphically, it is as shown below

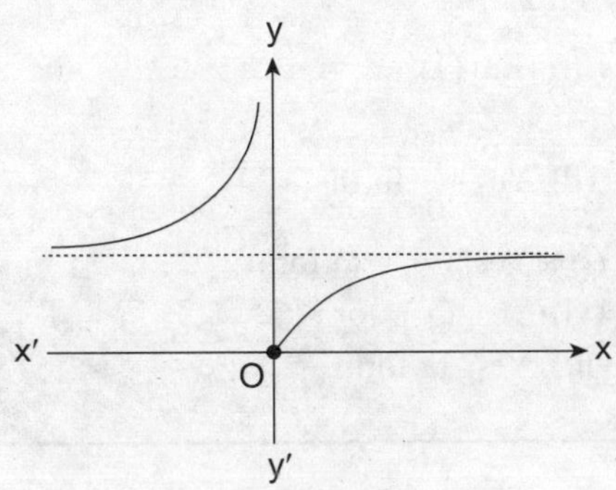

FIGURE 1.14

(iii) $\lim\limits_{x\to\pm\infty} \sin\frac{1}{x} = 0$

As $x \to \infty$, $\frac{1}{x} \to 0^+ \Rightarrow \sin\frac{1}{x} \to 0^+$

As x takes values in $\left[-\frac{1}{\pi}, \frac{1}{\pi}\right] \sim \{0\}$ the reciprocal function $\frac{1}{x} \in (-\infty, -\pi] \cup [\pi, \infty)$ therefore sin $1/x$ attains its all possible values infinitely many times as the range of $1/x$ consists of infinite periodic intervals of sine function.

And As $x \to -\infty, \frac{1}{x} \to 0^- \Rightarrow \sin\frac{1}{x} \to 0^-$

Geometrically it is shown in figure 1.15

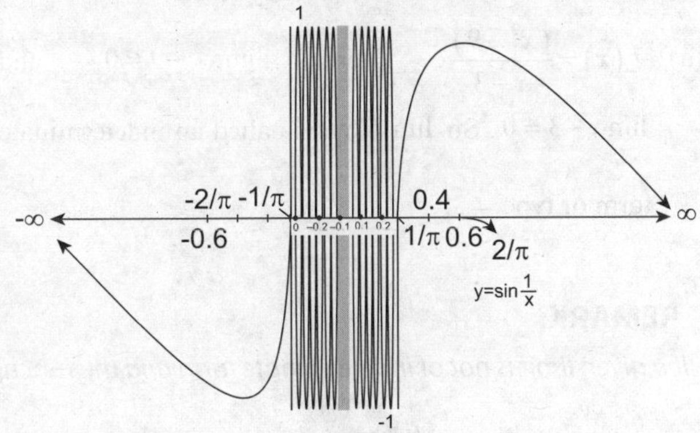

FIGURE 1.15

Why Limit of a Function is Needed?

There are some functions $f(x)$ whose values can't be determined at some real numbers (say at $x = 'a'$). For example

(i) $f(x) = \frac{\sin x}{x}$ at $x = 0$,

(ii) $f(x) = \frac{|x-2|}{x-2}$ at $x = 2$,

(iii) $f(x) = \frac{x^2 - 4}{x - 2}$ at $x = 2$,

(iv) $f(x) = x\sin\frac{1}{x}$ at $x = 0$

(v) $f(x) = \frac{1}{x} - \frac{1}{\sin x}$ at $x = 0$ etc.

These functions are not defined at indicated points. However we can predict the values of real numbers (ℓ) to which these functions tend when x tends to indicated points, through the knowledge of limit i.e., $\lim\limits_{x\to a} f(x) = \ell$. We can find limit of a function at a point only when the limit is in "indeterminate form" as discussed in the next section.

■ INDETERMINATE FORMS

Some times, we come across functions which do not have definite value corresponding to some particular value of the independent variable. (If by substituting $x = a$ in any function $f(x)$, it takes up any one of form $\frac{0}{0}, \frac{\infty}{\infty}$, $0 \times \infty$, $\infty - \infty$,

1^∞, 0^0, ∞^0, then the limit of function $f(x)$ as $x \to a$ is called indeterminate form.) There are two basic indeterminate forms $\left(\frac{0}{0}, \frac{\infty}{\infty}\right)$ and all the other forms can be converted to these two basic forms. In such cases, value of function at $x = a$ does not exist while $\lim_{x \to a} f(x)$ may exist.

(a) $f(x) = \frac{(x^2 - 9)}{x - 3}$. Here $\lim_{x \to 3} x^2 - 9 = 0$ and $\lim_{x \to 3} x - 3 = 0$. So $\lim_{x \to 3} f(x)$ is called an indeterminate form of type –.

(b) $\lim_{x \to \infty} \frac{\ln x}{x}$ is an indeterminate form of type $\frac{\infty}{\infty}$.

(c) $\lim_{x \to 0} (1 + x)^{1/x}$ is an indeterminate form of type 1^∞.

(d) $\lim_{x \to 0} (\sin x)^x$ is of indeterminate form $(0)^0$

(e) $\lim_{x \to \infty} x \sin \frac{1}{x}$ is of $\infty \times 0$ form

(f) $\lim_{x \to 0} \frac{1}{x} - \frac{1}{\tan x}$ is of $\infty - \infty$ form

REMARK:

If a given limit is not of indeterminate form and the function is not defined at x = 0, we can't find it e.g., $\lim_{x \to 0} (\sin x)^{1/x}$; $\lim_{x \to 0} \left(\frac{1}{x}\right)^{1/x}$ $\lim_{x \to 0} [\ln |x|]^{1/x}$ *are not defined.*

ILLUSTRATION 3: Which of the following limits are taking up indeterminate form? Also indicate the form.

(i) $\lim_{x \to 0} \frac{1}{x}$

(ii) $\lim_{x \to 1} \frac{1 - x}{1 - x^2}$

(iii) $\lim_{x \to 0} x(\ell n\, x)$

(iv) $\lim_{x \to 0} \left(\frac{1}{x} - \frac{1}{x^2}\right)$

(v) $\lim_{x \to 0} (\sin x)^x$

(vi) $\lim_{x \to 0} (\ell n\, x)^x$

(vii) $\lim_{x \to 0} (1 + \sin x)^{\frac{1}{x}}$

(viii) $\lim_{x \to 0} (1)^{1/x}$

SOLUTION:

(i) No

(ii) Yes, $\frac{0}{0}$ form

(iii) Yes, $0 \times \infty$ form

(iv) Yes, $(\infty - \infty)$ form

(v) Yes, $(0)^0$ form

(vi) Yes, $(\infty)^0$ form

(vii) Yes, $(1)^\infty$ form

(viii) Yes, 1^∞ form

REMARKS:

(i) *'0' doesn't mean exact zero but represents a value approaching towards zero similary to '1' and infinity.*

(ii) $\infty + \infty = \infty$

(iii) $\infty \times \infty = \infty$

(iv) $(a/\infty) = 0$ *if a is finite*

(v) $\frac{a}{0}$ *is not defined for any* $a \in R$.

(vi) $ab = 0$, *if & only if* $a = 0$ *or* $b = 0$ *and a, b are finite i.e.,* $0 \times$ *finite* $= 0$

Left-hand Limit of Function

A real number 'ℓ_1' is said to be left-hand limit of a function $f(x)$, if $f(x)$ is approaching nearer and nearer to ℓ_1 if x is approaching nearer and nearer to 'a' from left side of 'a' i.e x belongs to each left deleted neighbourhood of 'a'. Symbolically we write $f(a^-) = \ell_1$ and left-hand limit is expressed as $\lim_{x \to a^-} f(x) = \ell_1$ left-hand limit is abbreviated as L.H.L. Thus L.H.L $= \lim_{x \to a^-} f(x) = l_1$.

Geometrically, it is as shown below :

(i) (Function without any break and L.H.L $= \ell_1$ at $x = a$ and $f(a) = \ell_1$).

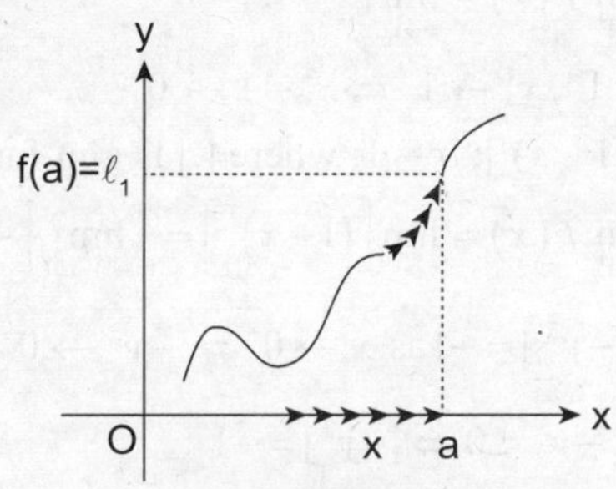

FIGURE 1.16

(ii) Function with break and L.H.L $= \ell_1$ at $x = a$ and $f(a) \neq \ell_1$.

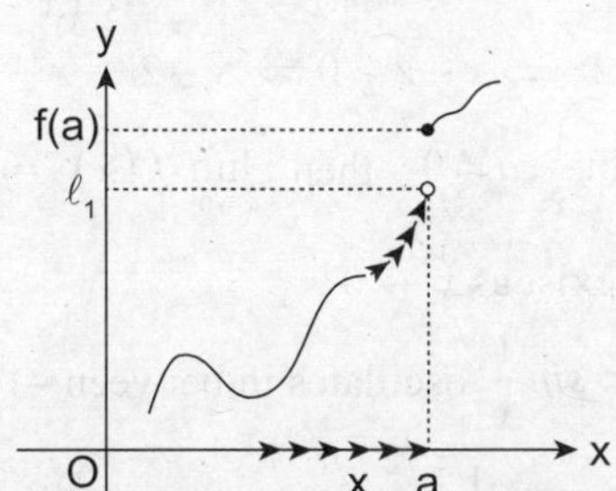

FIGURE 1.17

(iii) Function with break at $x = a$, L.H.L $= \ell_1$ at $x = a$ and $f(a) = \ell_1$.

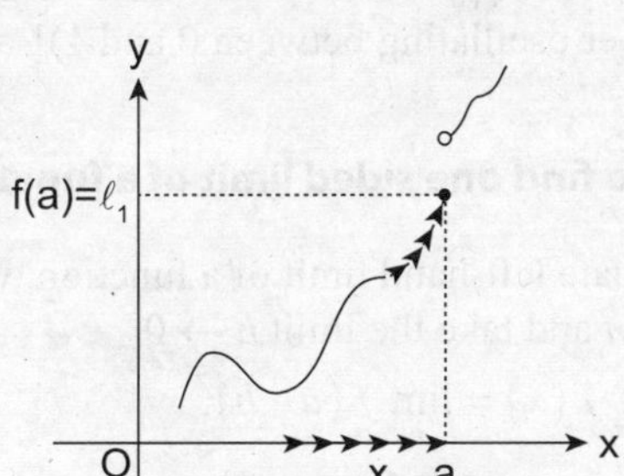

FIGURE 1.18

(iv) Function with break at $x = a$, L.H.L $= \ell_1$ at $x = a$ and $f(a) \neq \ell_1$,

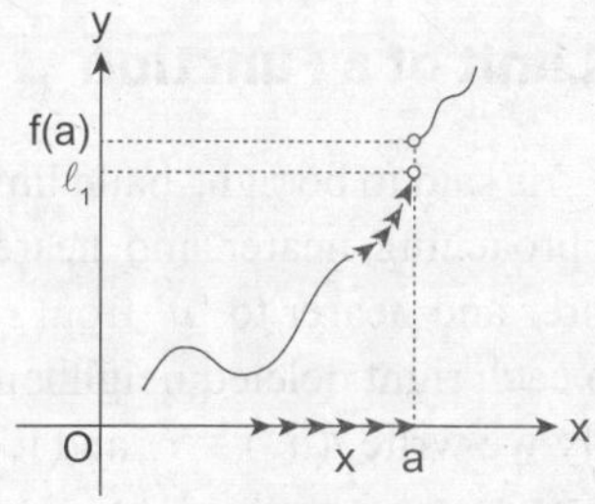

FIGURE 1.19

Example:

(i) $f(x) = (x-1)^3$; $a = 1$, then

L.H.L $= \lim_{x \to 1^-} (x-1)^3 = 0$, as x is approaching nearer and nearer to 1 from left side $(x-1)$ is approaching nearer and nearer to 0 from negative side i.e., $(x-1)^3 < 0$ and $(x-1)^3 \to 0$ i.e., $(x-1)^3 \to 0^-$

(ii) $f(x) = [(x-1)^3]$; $a = 1$; where [.] is gint. function, then

$$\text{L.H.L.} = \lim_{x \to 1^-} \left[(x-1)^3 \right] = \lim_{(x-1) \to 0^-} \left[(x-1)^3 \right]$$

$$= \lim_{y \to 0^-} \left[y^3 \right] = -1$$

As $(y \to 0^- \Rightarrow y^3 \to 0^- \Rightarrow -1 < y^3 < 0 \Rightarrow [y^3] = -1)$

(iii) $f(x) = \dfrac{x-2}{|x-2|}; a = 2$,

then L.H.L $= \lim_{x \to 2^-} \dfrac{(x-2)}{|x-2|} = \lim_{x \to 2^-} \dfrac{(x-2)}{-(x-2)} = -1$

$$\left[\begin{array}{l} \because x \to 2^- \\ \Rightarrow x < 2 \text{ and } x \to 2 \\ \Rightarrow x - 2 < 0 \\ \Rightarrow |x-2| = -(x-2) \text{ and} \neq 0 \end{array} \right]$$

(iv) $f(x) = \sin\dfrac{1}{x}; a = 0$; then L.H.L $= \lim_{x \to 0^-} \sin\dfrac{1}{x}$ would not exist, as $x \to 0^-$ $\dfrac{1}{x} \to -\infty$ and $\sin\theta$ being an oscillating function, $\sin\dfrac{1}{x}$ could not approach to a particular real number and oscillates in between –1 and 1

(v) $f(x) = \left[x\sin^2 \dfrac{1}{x} \right]; a = 0$; [.] gint function, then L.H.L

$$= \lim_{x \to 0^-} \left[x \sin^2 \frac{1}{x} \right] =$$

[(a number approaching to 0) from left side) × (a number oscillating between 0 and 1 includingly)] = –1

Right-hand Limit of a Function

A real number 'ℓ_2' is said to be right-hand limit of a function $f(x)$ if $f(x)$ is approaching nearer and nearer to ℓ_2 as x is approaching nearer and nearer to 'a' from right side of 'a' i.e., x belongs to each right deleted neighbourhood of 'a'.

Symbolically we write $f(a^+) = \ell_2$ and it is expressed as $\lim_{x\to a^+} f(x) = \ell_2$. Right-hand limit is abbreviated as R.H.L.

Thus R.H.L $= \lim_{x\to a^+} f(x) = l_2$. Geometrically, it is as shown below

(i) Function without any break and R.H.L = ℓ_2 at $x = a$ and $f(a) = \ell_2$

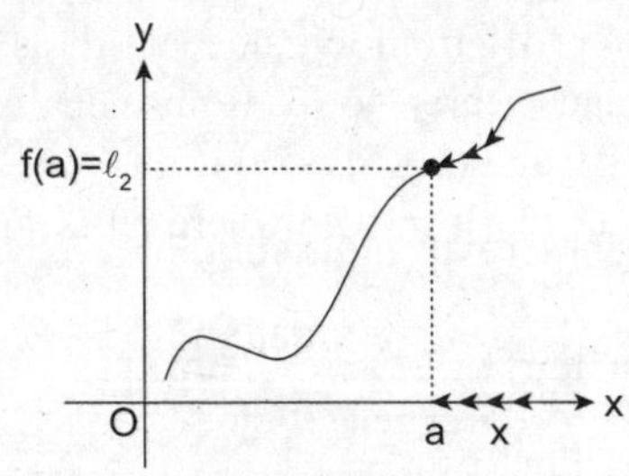

FIGURE 1.20

(ii) Function with break at $x = a$ and R.H.L = ℓ_2 at $x = a$ and $f(a) \neq \ell_2$

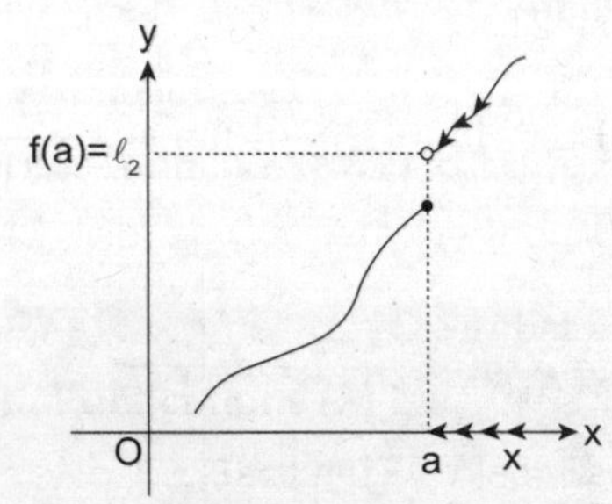

FIGURE 1.21

(iii) Function with break at $x = a$ and R.H.L = l_2 at $x = a$ and R.H.L = ℓ_2 at $x = a$ and $f(a) \neq \ell_2$

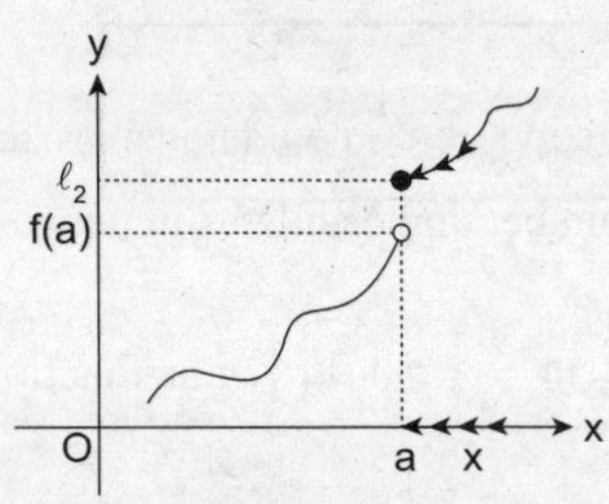

FIGURE 1.22

(iv) Function with break at $x = a$, R.H.L = ℓ_2 at $x = a$ and $f(a) \neq \ell_2$, e.g.,

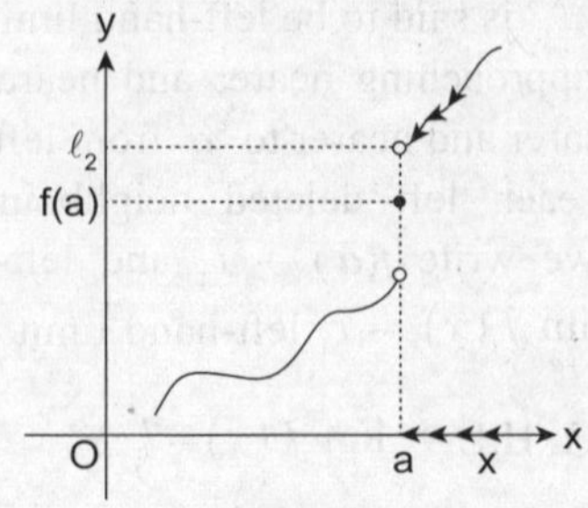

FIGURE 1.23

1. $f(x) = x^3 - 1$; $a = 1$;

   then $\lim_{x\to 1^+} f(x) = \lim_{x\to 1^+}(x^3 - 1) = 0$

   As $x \to 1^+, x^3 \to 1^+ \Rightarrow x^3 - 1 \to 0^+$

2. $f(x) = [(1 - x)^3]$; $a = 1$; where [.] is gint function

   then $\lim_{x\to 1^+} f(x) = \lim_{x\to 1^+}\left[(1-x)^3\right] = \lim_{(x-1)\to 0^+}\left[-(x-1)^3\right]$

   $= \lim_{y\to 0^+}\left[-y^3\right] = -1$ as $y \to 0^+ \Rightarrow -y^3 \to 0^-$

   $\Rightarrow -1 < -y^3 < 0 \Rightarrow [-y^3] = -1$

3. $f(x) = \dfrac{x-2}{|x-2|}; a = 2$

   Then $\lim_{x\to 2^+} f(x) = \lim_{x\to 2^+}\dfrac{x-2}{|x-2|} = \lim_{x\to 2^+}\dfrac{(x-2)}{(x-2)} = 1$

   (As $x \to 2^+ \Rightarrow x - 2 > 0 \Rightarrow |x - 2| = x - 2 \neq 0$)

4. $f(x) = \sin\dfrac{1}{x}; a = 0$; then $\lim_{x\to 0^+} f(x) = \lim_{x\to 0^+}\left(\sin\dfrac{1}{x}\right)$

   does not exist as $x \to 0^+$

   $\Rightarrow \dfrac{1}{x} \to \infty \Rightarrow \sin\dfrac{1}{x}$ oscillates in between –1 and 1)

5. $f(x) = \left[x\sin^2\dfrac{1}{x}\right]; a = 0$; [.] is gint function, then

   $\lim_{x\to 0^+} f(x) = \lim_{x\to 0^+}\left[x\sin^2\dfrac{1}{x}\right] =$

   [(a number approaching 0 from right side) × (a number oscillating between 0 and 1)] = $[0^+] = 0$

Procedure to find one sided limit of a function

1. To evaluate left-hand limit of a function, we substitute $x = a - h$ and take the limit $h \to 0^+$

   i.e., $\lim_{x\to a^-} f(x) = \lim_{h\to 0^+} f(a-h)$

   e.g., for $f(x) = \dfrac{x-2}{|x-2|}$;

$$\lim_{x\to 2^-} f(x) = \lim_{x\to 2^-} \frac{(x-2)}{|x-2|} = \lim_{h\to 0^+} \frac{(2-h-2)}{|2-h-2|}$$

$$= \lim_{h\to 0^+} \frac{(-h)}{|-h|} = \lim_{h\to 0^+} \frac{(-h)}{h} = -1$$

$(\because h \to 0^+ \Rightarrow h > 0 \Rightarrow -h < 0 \Rightarrow |-h| = h)$

2. To evaluate right-hand limit of a function, we substitute $x = a + h$ and take the limit $h \to 0^+$

i.e., $\lim_{x\to a^+} f(x) = \lim_{h\to 0^+} f(a+h)$

e.g., for $f(x) = \frac{\{x-2\}}{|2-x|}$; $\{x\}$ is fractional part of x;

$$\lim_{x\to 2^+} f(x) = \lim_{h\to 0^+} \frac{\{2+h-2\}}{|2-(2+h)|} = \lim_{h\to 0^+} \frac{\{h\}}{|-h|} = \frac{h}{h} = 1$$

$(\because 0 < h < 1 \Rightarrow \{h\} = h \text{ and } -h < 0 \Rightarrow |-h| = h)$

Existence of limit of a function

The limit of a function at $x = a$, is said to exist if

(i) $\lim_{x\to a^-} f(x) = \lim_{x\to a^+} f(x) = l$

(ii) ℓ is a finite real number

i.e., Left-hand limit and right-hand limit of function exist, equal and they are equal to finite real number. Thus existence of limit of a function at $x = a$ means "As x tends to 'a' from either way (from left or right) $f(x)$ tends to a unique finite (real number).

Geometrically it is as shown below

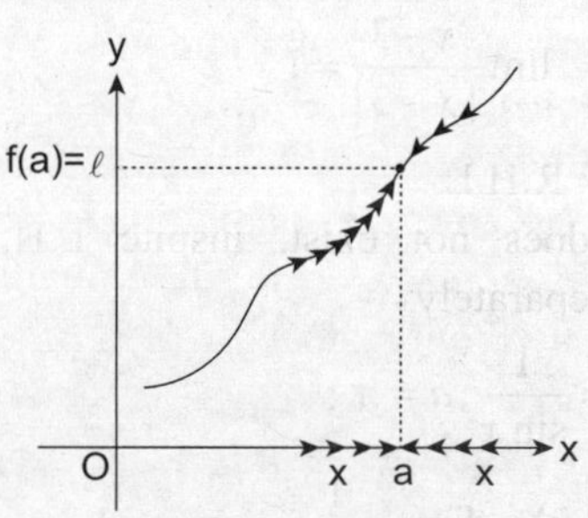

FIGURE 1.24

Function without any break at $x = a$ and L.H.L = R.H.L = ℓ at $x = a$, $f(a) = \ell$

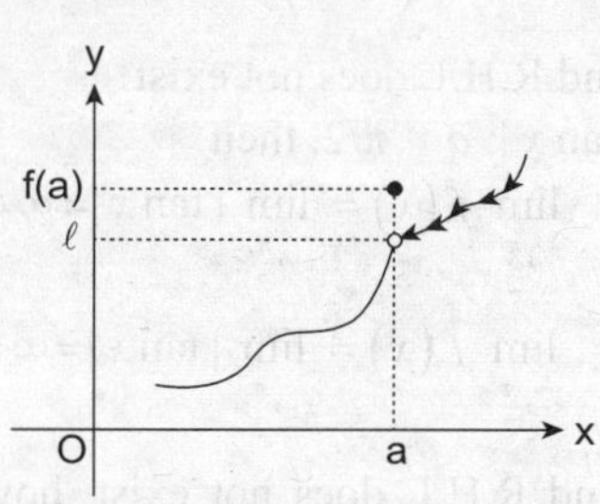

FIGURE 1.25

Function having a break at $x = a$, L.H.L = R.H.L = $\ell \neq f(a)$

Reason for non-existence of limit of a function

Any one of the following may be the reason for non-existence of limit of a function.

(i) Any one or both L.H.L and R.H.L do not exist

(ii) Both L.H.L and R.H.L exist but are unequal

(iii) $f(x)$ oscillates with large frequency near the point $x = a$

The following graphs illustrate the reasons for non-existence of limits:

(i) (L.H.L and R.H.L. exist but are not equal, x)

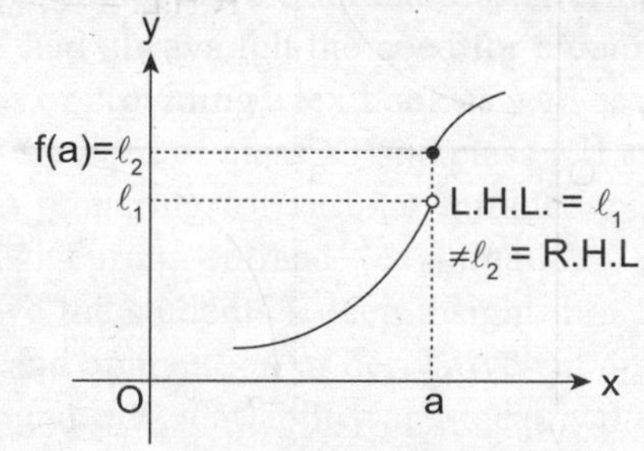

FIGURE 1.26

(ii) One of the L.H.L. and R.H.L. exist finitely and other in infinitely.

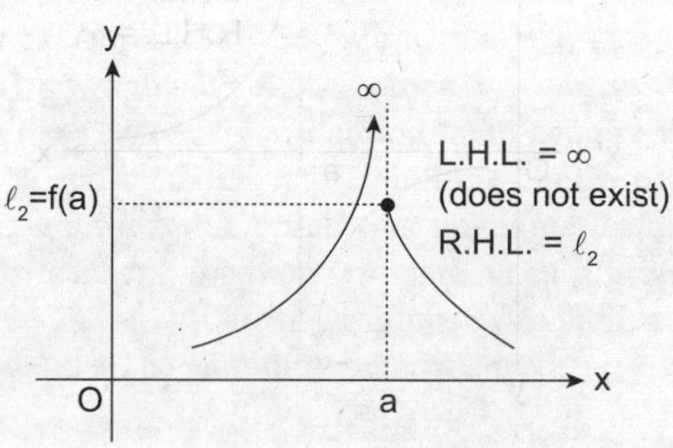

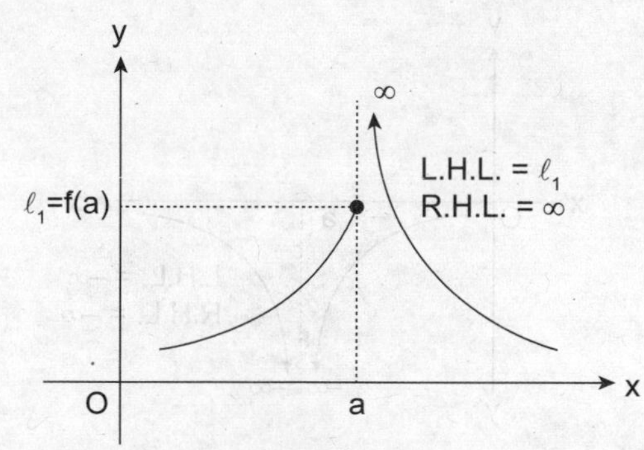

FIGURE 1.27

(iii) Both L.H.L. and R.H.L. are infinite

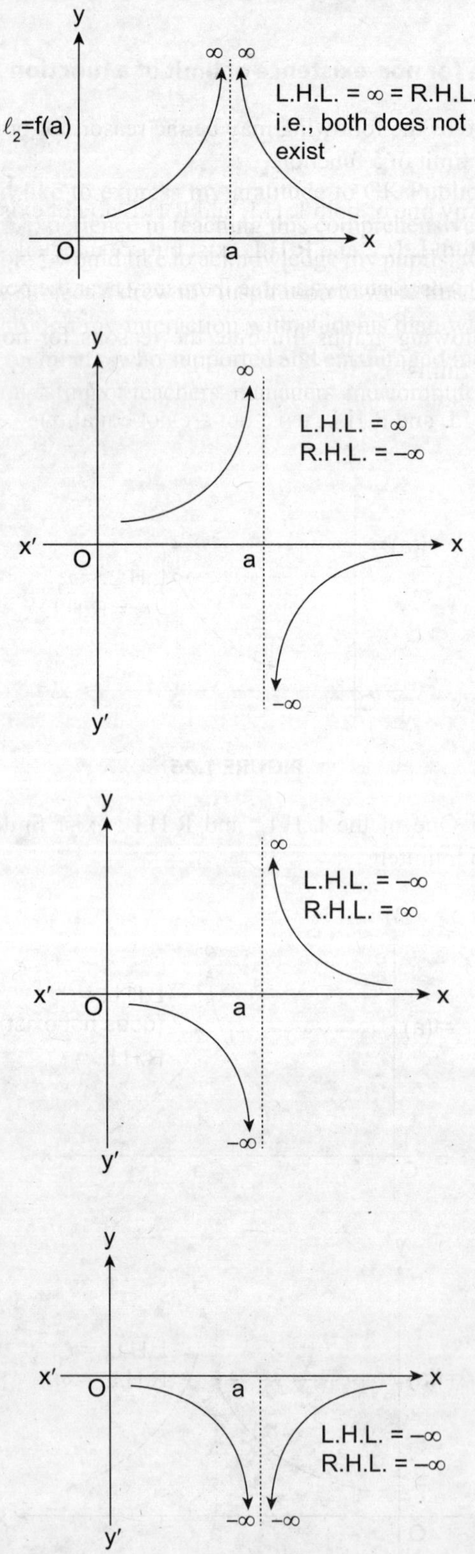

FIGURE 1.28

(iv) When the function is oscillating

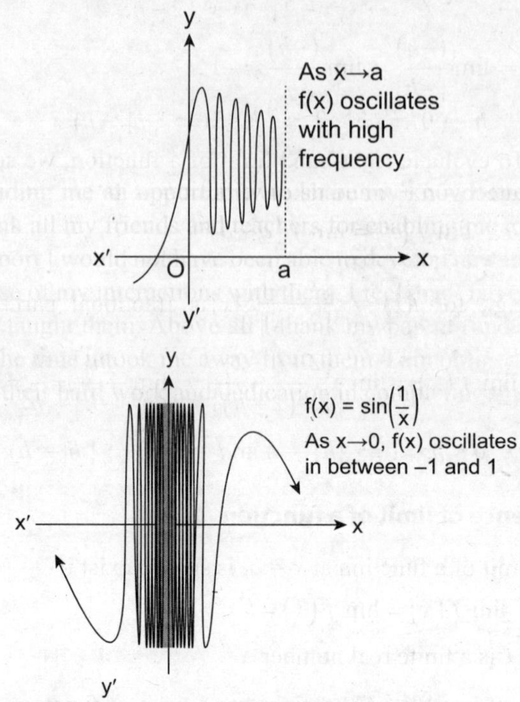

FIGURE 1.29

For example:

(i) $f(x) = \dfrac{x-3}{|x-3|}$; L.H.L $= \lim\limits_{x\to 3^-} \dfrac{x-3}{|x-3|} = -1$ and

RH.L $= \lim\limits_{x\to 3^+} \dfrac{x-3}{|x-3|} = 1$

$\therefore$ L.H.L ≠ R.H.L

$\therefore$ Limit does not exist, inspite L.H.L and R.H.L exists separately.

(ii) $f(x) = \dfrac{1}{\sin x}; a = \pi$; then

$\lim\limits_{x\to \pi^-} f(x) = \lim\limits_{x\to \pi^-} \dfrac{1}{(\sin x)} = \infty$ and

$\lim\limits_{x\to \pi^+} f(x) = \lim\limits_{x\to \pi^+} \dfrac{1}{(\sin x)} = -\infty$

$\therefore$ L.H.L and R.H.L does not exist

(iii) $f(x) = |\tan x|$; $a = \pi/2$, then

L.H.L $= \lim\limits_{x\to \frac{\pi}{2}^-} f(x) = \lim\limits_{x\to \frac{\pi}{2}^-} |\tan x| = \infty$ and

R.H.L $= \lim\limits_{x\to \frac{\pi}{2}^+} f(x) = \lim\limits_{x\to \frac{\pi}{2}^+} |\tan x| = \infty$

$\therefore$ L.H.L and R.H.L does not exist, however both are infinite.

(iv) $f(x) = \dfrac{1}{[x-1]}$; $a = 1$, where [.] is gint function. Then

L.H.L =

$$\lim_{x\to 1^-} f(x) = \lim_{x\to 1^-} \frac{1}{[x-1]} = \lim_{h\to 0^+} \frac{1}{[(1-h)-1]} = \lim_{h\to 0^+} \frac{1}{[-h]}$$

$$= \frac{1}{(-1)} = -1 \; (\because -1 < -h < 0)$$

Here domain of $f(x)$ is $R \sim [1, 2)$. Since $f(x)$ is not defined in [1,2), thus we need not to find R.H.L of $f(x)$ at $x = 1$ and $\lim_{x\to 1} f(x)$ is considered to be $\lim_{x\to 1^-} f(x)$ and is equal to – 1. Thus we in this case say limit exists and is equal to –1.

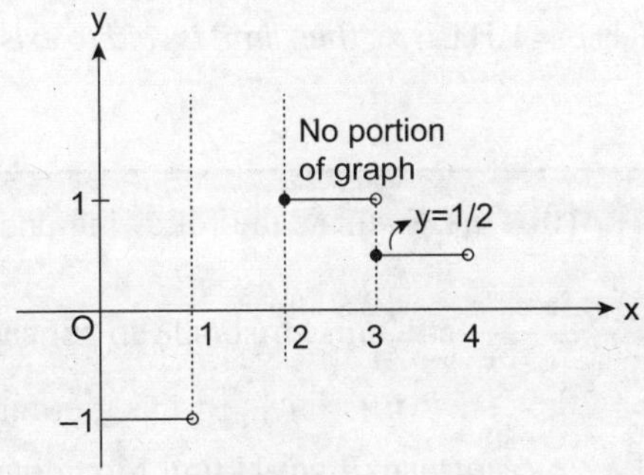

FIGURE 1.30

REMARKS:

1. *If limit of a function f(x) is to be determined at x = a first of all make sure that the function f(x) is defined in left deleted neighbourhood (a-δ, a) and right deleted neighbourhood (a, a + δ). If f(x) is defined in (a – δ, a) and is not defined in (a, a + δ), then left-hand limit is taken as the value of given limit. Similarly if f(x) is not defined in (a-δ, a) and is defined in (a, a + δ), then right-hand limit is taken as the value of given limit. For example*

   (i) $f(x) = \dfrac{1}{[x-1]}$; *([x] is gint function) is defined in (1 – δ, 1); δ > 0 but not defined in [1,1 + δ);0 < δ ≤ 1*

   $\therefore \; \lim_{x\to 1} f(x) = \lim_{x\to 1^-} f(x) = -1$

   (ii) *f(x) = sin*$^{-1}$*x; a = 1,*

   then f(x) is defined in [1 – δ, 1]; 0 < δ ≤ 2

   but f(x) is not defined in (1,1 + δ); δ > 0

   Thus $\lim_{x\to 1} f(x) = \lim_{x\to 1^-} f(x) = \lim_{x\to 1^-} \sin^{-1} x = \dfrac{\pi}{2}$

2. *If L.H.L = R.H.L = ∞ or -∞, then we say that limit does not exist. It means the limit does not exist finitely, i.e, there is no real finite number to which f(x) tends as x tends to a. In this case we say"limits exists infinitely/"*
3. ***Infinite Limits**: If f(x) tends to ∞ (or - ∞) as x → a (or ∞), then the limit is called infinite limit. Thus we can make f(x) as much large in magnitude as we please by making x sufficiently close to a.*
4. *By* $\lim_{x\to a}$ *f(x) we mean x takes values closer and closer to 'a' without being equal a.*
5. *It is evident from the definition that in order to find the limit of f(x) at x = a, the first thing is that f(x) should be well defined in the neighbourhood of x = a and not necessarily at x = a (that means x = a may or may not be in the domain of f(x)), because we have to examine its behaviour or tendency in the neighbourhood of x = a.*

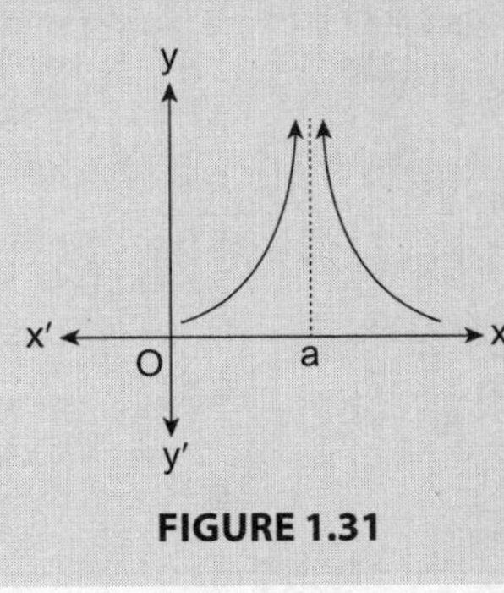

FIGURE 1.31

6. *If* $\lim_{x\to a^+} f(x) \neq \lim_{x\to a^-} f(x)$, *then limit does not exist at* $x = a$

7. *If* R.H.L. = L.H.L = ∞, *then limit is said to exist infinitely.*

ILLUSTRATION 4: Evaluate the following one sided limits:

(i) $\lim_{x\to 2^+} \frac{|x-2|}{(x-2)}$ **(ii)** $\lim_{x\to 2^-} \frac{|x-2|}{(x-2)}$

(iii) $\lim_{x\to 3^+} [x]$;[.] is gint function **(iv)** $\lim_{x\to 3^-} [x]$,[.] is gint function

(v) $\lim_{x\to -\pi/4^-} [\cot x]$. **(vi)** $\lim_{x\to -\pi/4^+} [\cot x]$

(vii) $\lim_{x\to -\pi/4^+} [\cot x]$ **(viii)** $\lim_{x\to 10^-} [\log x]$

SOLUTION: **(i)** $\lim_{x\to 2^+} \frac{|x-2|}{(x-2)}$; As $x \to 2^+ \Rightarrow x > 2$

$\therefore\ x - 2 > 0 \Rightarrow |x-2| = x - 2$ $\qquad \therefore\ \lim_{x\to 2^+} \frac{|x-2|}{(x-2)} = \lim_{x\to 2^+} \frac{(x-2)}{(x-2)} = 1$

(ii) $\lim_{x\to 2^-} \frac{|x-2|}{x-2}$; As $x \to 2^- \Rightarrow x < 2$

$\Rightarrow x - 2 < 0$ $\qquad \Rightarrow |x-2| = -(x-2)$

$\therefore\ \lim_{x\to 2^-} \frac{|x-2|}{(x-2)} = \lim_{x\to 2^-} \frac{-(x-2)}{(x-2)} = -1$

(iii) $\lim_{x\to 3^+} [x]$; As $x \to 3^+$

$\Rightarrow 3 < x < 4$ $\qquad \therefore\ [x] = 3$

$\therefore\ \lim_{x\to 3^+} [x] = 3$

(iv) $\lim_{x\to 3^-} [x]$; As $x \to 3^-$

$\Rightarrow 2 < x < 3$ $\qquad \therefore\ [x] = 2$

$\therefore\ \lim_{x\to 3^-} [x] = 2$

(v) $\lim_{x\to\left(-\frac{\pi}{4}\right)^-} [\cot x]$; As $x \to \left(-\frac{\pi}{4}\right)^-$

$\Rightarrow x < -\pi/4$

$\Rightarrow \cot x > \cot\left(-\frac{\pi}{4}\right)$ as $\cot x$ is a decreasing function

$0 > \cot x > -1$

$\therefore\ [\cot x] = -1$

$\therefore\ \lim_{x\to\left(-\frac{\pi}{4}\right)^-} [\cot x] = -1$

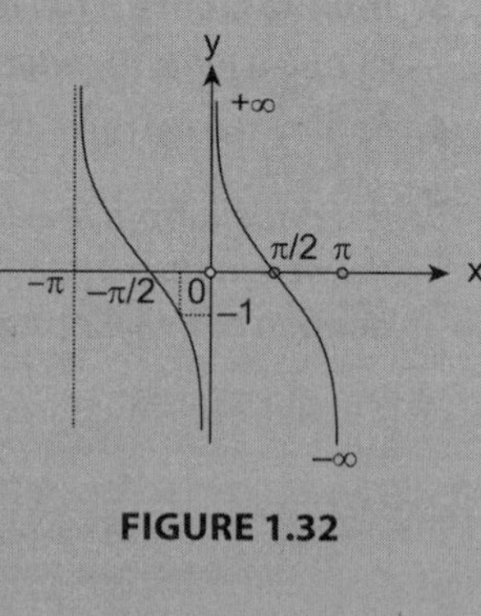

FIGURE 1.32

(vi) $\lim_{x\to\left(-\frac{\pi}{4}\right)^+} [\cot x]$; As $x \to \left(-\frac{\pi}{4}\right)^+$ $\qquad \Rightarrow x > -\frac{\pi}{4}$

$\Rightarrow \cot x < \cot(-\pi/4)$ $\Rightarrow -2 < \cot x < -1$

$\therefore\ [\cot x] = -2$ $\therefore\ \lim_{x \to \left(-\frac{\pi}{4}\right)^+} [\cot x] = -2$

(vii) $\lim_{x \to 10^-} [\log x]$; As $x \to 10^-$

$\Rightarrow 9 < x < 10$

$\Rightarrow 1 < x < 10$

As $\log_{10} x$ is an increasing function

$\Rightarrow \log_{10} 1 < \log_{10} x < \log_{10} 10$

$\Rightarrow 0 < \log x < 1$

$\Rightarrow [\log x] = 0$

$\therefore\ \lim_{x \to 10^-} [\log x] = 0$

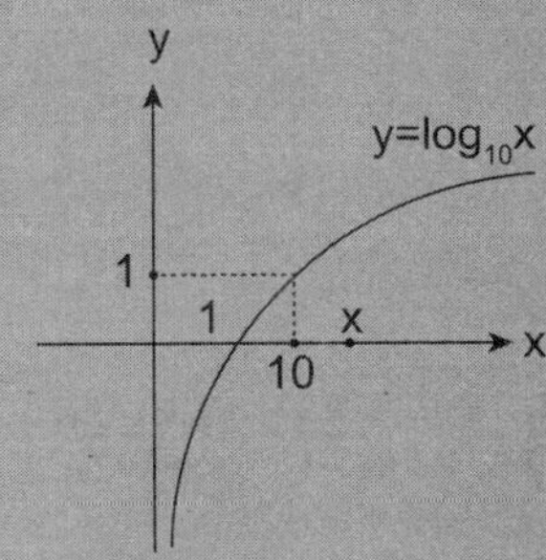

FIGURE 1.33

(viii) $\lim_{x \to 10^+} [\log x]$; As $x \to 10^+$

$\therefore\ x > 10$ but x is nearer to 10 $\therefore\ 10 < x < 100$

$\therefore\ \log_{10} 10 < \log_{10} x < \log_{10} 100$ $\Rightarrow 1 < \log_{10} x < 2$

$\therefore\ [\log x] = 1$ $\therefore\ \lim_{x \to 10^+} [\log x] = 1$

ILLUSTRATION 5: Evaluate the following one sided limit:

(i) $\lim_{x \to 2^-} |[x-2]|$; [.] is greatest integer function

(ii) $\lim_{x \to 3^+} \{x-2\}$; {.} is fractional part of x

(iii) $\lim_{x \to 2^-} \left[\sin \frac{(x^2-4)}{(x+2)}\right]$; [.] is greatest integer function

(iv) $\lim_{x \to 3^-} \left\{\tan\left(\frac{x^2-9}{x+3}\right)\right\}$; {.} is fractional part of x

(v) $\lim_{x \to 0^+} \left\{\cos\left(\frac{x-\pi/2}{x^2-\pi^2/4}\right)\right\}$; {.} is fractional part of x

SOLUTION: **(i)** $\lim_{x \to 2-} |[x-2]|$; As $x < 2$ and $x \to 2 \Rightarrow 1 < x < 2$

$\Rightarrow -1 < x - 2 < 0$ $\Rightarrow [x-2] = -1$

$\Rightarrow |[x-2]| = 1$

(ii) $\lim_{x \to 3^+} \{x-2\}$; As $x \to 3^+ \Rightarrow 3 < x < 4$

$\Rightarrow 1 < x - 2 < 2$ $\Rightarrow (x-2) = [x-2] + \{x-2\}$

$\Rightarrow (x-2) = 1 + \{x-2\}$ $\Rightarrow \{x-2\} = (x-2) - 1 = x - 3$

$\therefore\ \lim_{x \to 3^+} \{x-2\} = \lim_{x \to 3^+} (x-3) = 0$

(iii) $\lim_{x \to 2^-} \left[\sin\left(\frac{x^2-4}{x+2}\right)\right] = \lim_{x \to 2^-} [\sin(x-2)]$ $[\because x \to 2 \Rightarrow x + 2 \neq 0]$

$= \lim_{h \to 0^+} [\sin(2-h-2)] = \lim_{h \to 0^+} [\sin(-h)] = \lim_{h \to 0^+} [-\sin h] = [k]$; (where $-1 < k < 0$) $= -1$

(iv) $\lim\limits_{x\to 3^-}\left\{\tan\left(\frac{x^2-9}{x+3}\right)\right\} = \lim\limits_{x\to 3^-}\{\tan(x-3)\}$ as $x+3\neq 0$

$= \lim\limits_{h\to 0^+}\{\tan(3-h-3)\} = \lim\limits_{h\to 0^+}\{\tan(-h)\}$

$= \lim\limits_{h\to 0^+}(1-\{\tan h\})$ ($\because$ $\{x\}+\{-x\}=1$ for $x\notin\mathbb{Z}$ $=0$ for $x\notin\mathbb{Z}$)

$= \lim\limits_{h\to 0^+}(1-\tan h)$ ($\because$ $0<\tan h<1$ $\Rightarrow$ $\{\tan h\}=\tan h$)

$= 1-0=1$

(v) $\lim\limits_{x\to 0^+}\left\{\cos\left(\frac{x-\pi/2}{x^2-\pi^2/4}\right)\right\} = \lim\limits_{x\to 0^+}\left\{\cos\left(\frac{1}{x+\pi/2}\right)\right\}\left[\because x-\frac{\pi}{2}\neq 0\right]$

As $x\to 0^+$; $x+(\pi/2)\to \pi/2^+$

$\Rightarrow \frac{1}{x+(\pi/2)}\to\left(\frac{2}{\pi}\right)^+ \Rightarrow 0<\frac{1}{x+(\pi/2)}<1$ radian

$\Rightarrow 0<\cos\left(\frac{1}{x+\pi/2}\right)<1\Rightarrow\left\{\cos\left(\frac{1}{x+\pi/2}\right)\right\}=\cos\left(\frac{1}{x+\pi/2}\right)$

$\therefore \lim\limits_{x\to 0^+}\left\{\cos\left(\frac{x-\pi/2}{x^2-\pi^2/4}\right)\right\} = \lim\limits_{x\to 0^+}\cos\left(\frac{1}{x+\pi/2}\right) = \cos\left(\frac{2}{\pi}\right)$

ILLUSTRATION 6: If $f(x)=\begin{cases}x^2+1\ ; x\geq 1\\ 3x-1\ ; x<1\end{cases}$, then find the value of $\lim\limits_{x\to 1} f(x)$.

SOLUTION: L.H.L $= \lim\limits_{x\to 1^-} f(x) = \lim\limits_{x\to 1^-}(3x-1) = 3(1)-1=2$

R.H.L $= \lim\limits_{x\to 1^+} f(x) = \lim\limits_{x\to 1^+}(x^2+1) = 1^2+1=2$

$\therefore$ L.H.L = R.H.L $\Rightarrow$ limit of $f(x)$ as $x\to 1$ exists and is equal to 2

ILLUSTRATION 7: Simplify $f(x)=\begin{cases}\frac{|x^2-1|}{x-1} & ; x\neq 1\\ 0 & ; x=1\end{cases}$, and test the existence of its limit at $x=1$ and -1.

SOLUTION: Simplifying the above function, we get $f(x)=\begin{cases}x+1 & ;\ x<-1\\ -(x+1) & ;\ -1<x<1\\ 0 & ;\ x=1\\ x+1 & ;\ x>1\end{cases}$

(i) at $x=1$; Clearly L.H.L at $x=1$ is -2 while R.H.L $=2$, so $\lim\limits_{x\to 1} f(x)$ does not exist.

(ii) at $x=-1$; L.H.L = R.H.L = 0 (at $x=-1$) so $\lim\limits_{x\to -1} f(x)$ exists and it is equal, to zero.

ILLUSTRATION 8: Show that $\lim\limits_{x\to 0}\left(\frac{e^{1/x}-1}{e^{1/x}+1}\right)$ does not exist.

SOLUTION: Given function is $f(x)=\frac{e^{1/x}-1}{e^{1/x}+1}$

L.H.L $= \lim\limits_{x\to 0^-} f(x) = \lim\limits_{h\to 0} f(0-h) = \lim\limits_{h\to 0}\frac{e^{-1/h}-1}{e^{-1/h}+1} = \lim\limits_{h\to 0}\frac{(1/e^{1/h}-1)}{(1/e^{1/h}+1)} = \frac{0-1}{0+1} = -1$

$(\because h \to 0^+ \Rightarrow 1/h \to \infty \Rightarrow e^{1/h} \to \infty \Rightarrow 1/e^{1/h} \to 0)$

$$\text{R.H.L} = \lim_{x\to 0^+} f(x) = \lim_{h\to 0^+} f(0+h) = \lim_{h\to 0} \frac{e^{1/h}-1}{e^{1/h}+1} = \lim_{h\to 0} \frac{(1-1/e^{1/h})}{(1+1/e^{1/h})} = +1$$

Clearly $\lim_{x\to 0^-} f(x) \neq \lim_{x\to 0^+} f(x)$. Therefore $\lim_{x\to 0} f(x)$ does not exist.

ILLUSTRATION 9: If $f(x) = \begin{cases} x^2+x+1 & ; x \geq 0 \\ x-1 & ; x < 0 \end{cases}$, then evaluate $\lim_{x\to 0} f(x)$

SOLUTION: L.H.L. $= f(0^-) = \lim_{h\to 0^+} f(0-h) = \lim_{h\to 0} (-h-1) = -1$

R.H.L $= f(0^+) = \lim_{h\to 0^+} f(0+h) = \lim_{h\to 0} (h^2+h+1) = 1$

Since $f(0^+) \neq f(0^-)$, so $\lim_{x\to 0} f(x)$ does not exist.

ILLUSTRATION 10: Show that $[1+x+x^2]$ is defined and hence evaluate $\lim_{x\to 1/2^+} [1+x+x^2] = 1$

SOLUTION: Let $f(x) = 1+x+x^2$; $g(x) = [x]$; $R_f = \left[-\frac{D}{4a}, \infty\right) \equiv \left[\frac{3}{4}, \infty\right)$; $D_g = \mathbb{R}$

Clearly $R_f \subseteq D_g$ $\therefore$ $(gof)(x)$ is defined

$\therefore$ $(gof)(x) = g(f(x)) = g(1+x+x^2) = [1+x+x^2]$

$\therefore L = \lim_{x\to 1/2^+} [1+x+x^2] = \lim_{x\to 1/2^+} g(x^2+x+1)$

Now $\lim_{x\to 1/2^+} f(x) = \lim_{x\to 1/2^+} (1+x+x^2) = (7/4)$

$\therefore$ $L = \lim_{x\to 7/4^+} g(x) = \lim_{x\to 7/4^+} [x] = [7/4] = 1$

$\therefore$ $\lim_{x\to 1/2^+} (gof)(x) = 1$.

Hence $\lim_{x\to 1/2^+} [1+x+x^2] = 1$

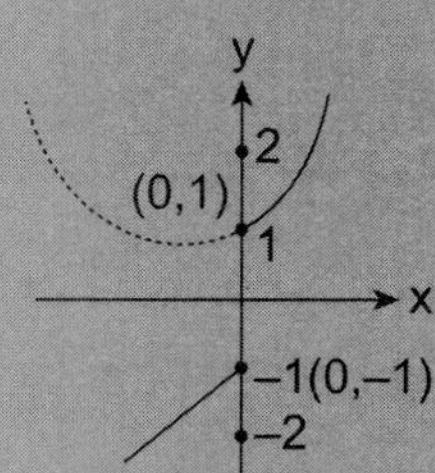

FIGURE 1.34

ILLUSTRATION 11: Evaluate the following limits if they exist

(i) $\lim_{x\to 5} \frac{x^3-125}{x^3-3x^2-7x-15}$

(ii) $\lim_{x\to 2} \frac{x^3-8}{x^3-4x^2+4x}$

(iii) $\lim_{x\to 2} \cos\left(\frac{\pi}{2-x}\right)$

(iv) $\lim_{x\to 0} \left[\sin(\pi - x)\right]$; [.] denotes greatest integer function

(v) $\lim_{x\to e} \{\ln x\}$; {.} is fractional part function

SOLUTION: **(i)** $$\lim_{x\to 5} \frac{x^3-125}{x^3-3x^2-7x-15} = \lim_{x\to 5} \frac{(x-5)(x^2+5x+25)}{(x-5)(x^2+2x+3)} = \lim_{x\to 5} \frac{x^2+5x+25}{x^2+2x+3} = \frac{25+25+25}{25+10+3} = \frac{75}{38}$$

(ii) $$\lim_{x\to 2} \frac{x^3-8}{x^3-4x^2+4x} = \lim_{x\to 2} \frac{x^3-(2)^3}{x(x^2-4x+4)} = \lim_{x\to 2} \frac{(x-2)(x^2+2x+4)}{x(x-2)^2} = \lim_{x\to 2} \frac{(x^2+2x+4)}{x(x-2)}$$

Now L.H.L $= \lim\limits_{x\to 2^-} \dfrac{x^2+2x+4}{x(x-2)} = \lim\limits_{h\to 0^+} \dfrac{(2-h)^2+2(2-h)+4}{(2-h)(-h)}$

$= \lim\limits_{h\to 0^+} \dfrac{4+h^2-4h+4-2h+4}{(h^2-2h)} = \lim\limits_{h\to 0^+} \dfrac{h^2-6h+12}{h(h-2)} = -\infty$

and R.H.L $= \lim\limits_{x\to 2^+} \dfrac{(x^2+2x+4)}{x(x-2)} = \lim\limits_{h\to 0^+} \dfrac{(2+h)^2+2(2+h)+4}{(2+h)(h)} = \infty$

∴ Limit does not exist

(iii) $\lim\limits_{x\to 2^+} \cos\left(\dfrac{\pi}{2-x}\right)$

L.H.L. $= \lim\limits_{x\to 2^-} \cos\left(\dfrac{\pi}{2-x}\right) = \lim\limits_{h\to 0^+} \cos\left(\dfrac{\pi}{2-(2-h)}\right) = \lim\limits_{h\to 0^+} \cos\left(\dfrac{\pi}{h}\right)$

and R.H.L. $= \lim\limits_{x\to 2^+} \cos\left(\dfrac{\pi}{2-x}\right) = \lim\limits_{h\to 0^+} \cos\left(\dfrac{\pi}{2-(2+h)}\right)$

$= \lim\limits_{h\to 0^+} \cos\left(\dfrac{\pi}{-h}\right) = \lim\limits_{h\to 0^+} \cos\left(\dfrac{\pi}{h}\right)$ as $\cos(-\theta) = \cos\theta$

As $h \to 0^+$, $\dfrac{\pi}{h} \to \infty$ and $\cos\left(\dfrac{\pi}{h}\right)$ oscillates from –1 to 1 and cannot attain a finite unique limit.

Therefore the limit does not exist.

(iv) $\lim\limits_{x\to 0}[\sin(\pi-x)]$; $[.]$ is a greatest integer function

L.H.L. $= \lim\limits_{x\to 0^-}[\sin(\pi-x)] = \lim\limits_{h\to 0^+}[\sin(\pi+h)] = -1$

and R.H.L $= \lim\limits_{x\to 0^+}[\sin(\pi-x)] = \lim\limits_{h\to 0^+}[\sin(\pi-h)] = 0$

∴ L.H.L ≠ R.H.L

⇒ Limit does not exist

(v) $\lim\limits_{x\to e}\{\ln x\}$; $\{.\}$ is fractional part function

L.H.L $= \lim\limits_{x\to e^-}\{\ln x\} = \lim\limits_{h\to 0^+}\{\ln(e-h)\}$ ...(i)

R.H.L $= \lim\limits_{h\to 0^+}\{\ln(e+h)\}$ ...(ii)

From figure 1.35, it is clear that $0 < \ln(e-h) < 1$ and $1 < \ln(e+h) < 2$

⇒ $\{\ln(e-h)\} = \ln(e-h)$ and $\{\ln(e+h)\} = \ln(e+h) - 1$

∴ L.H.L $= \lim\limits_{h\to 0^+} \ln(e-h) = \ln e = 1$ and R.H.L $= \lim\limits_{h\to 0^+}(\ln(e+h)-1) = \ln e - 1 = 1 - 1 = 0$

∴ L.H.L ≠ R.H.L

⇒ limit does not exist

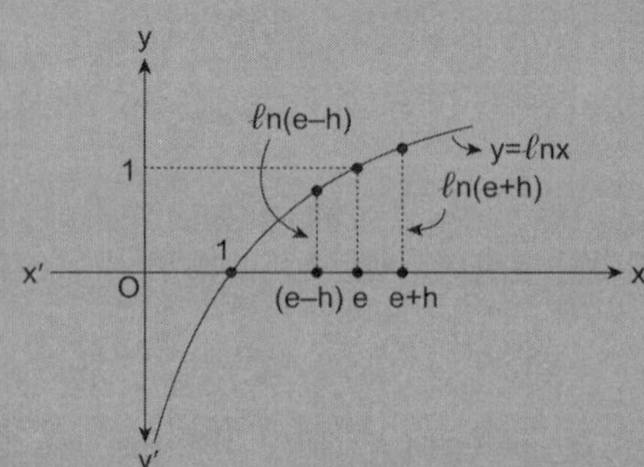

FIGURE 1.35

ILLUSTRATION 12: Does the limit of function $f(x) = \cos\left(\frac{1}{x}\right) / \cos\left(\frac{1}{x}\right)$ exists at $x = 0$?

SOLUTION: The function $f(x)$ is given by $f(x) = \begin{cases} 1 \text{ if } \cos\left(\frac{1}{x}\right) \neq 0 \\ \text{otherwise not defined} \end{cases}$

$$\Rightarrow f(x) = \begin{cases} 1 \text{ if } \cos\left(\frac{1}{x}\right) \neq 0 \\ \text{not defined for } x = \pm\frac{2}{\pi}, \frac{\pm 2}{3\pi}, \frac{\pm 2}{5\pi}, \ldots\ldots. \end{cases}$$

$\Rightarrow$ $f(x)$ is not defined at infinitely many points in each neighbourhood $(-\delta, \delta)$ of '0'

$\therefore$ Limit of function does not exist at $x = 0$.

ILLUSTRATION 13: Prove that the following limits do not exist:

(i) $\lim\limits_{x\to\pi/2} \frac{\tan x}{\sin 2x}$ **(ii)** $\lim\limits_{x\to\pi/2} \frac{e^{\tan x} - 1}{e^{\tan x} + 1}$

(iii) $\lim\limits_{x\to 0} (5)^{1/x}$ **(iv)** $\lim\limits_{x\to 1} \tan^{-1}\left(\frac{1}{x-1}\right)$

SOLUTION: **(i)** $\lim\limits_{x\to\pi/2} \frac{\tan x}{\sin 2x} = \lim\limits_{x\to\pi/2} \frac{\tan x\left(1 + \tan^2 x\right)}{2\tan x}$

$$= \lim_{x\to\pi/2} \frac{\left(1 + \tan^2 x\right)}{2} = \lim_{x\to\pi/2} \frac{\sec^2 x}{2} = \infty$$

$\therefore$ Limit does not exist, but exist infinitely

(ii) $\lim\limits_{x\to\pi/2} \frac{e^{\tan x} - 1}{e^{\tan x} + 1}$

$$\text{L.H.L} = \lim_{x\to\pi/2^-} \frac{e^{\tan x} - 1}{e^{\tan x} + 1}$$

$$= \lim_{h\to 0^+} \frac{e^{\tan\left(\frac{\pi}{2} - h\right)} - 1}{e^{\tan\left(\frac{\pi}{2} - h\right)} + 1} = \lim_{h\to 0^+} \frac{1 - e^{-\tan\left(\frac{\pi}{2} - h\right)}}{1 + e^{-\tan\left(\frac{\pi}{2} - h\right)}} = \frac{1 - e^{-\infty}}{1 + e^{-\infty}} = 1 \text{ and R.H.L} = \lim_{x\to\frac{\pi}{2}^+} \frac{e^{\tan x} - 1}{e^{\tan x} + 1}$$

$$= \lim_{h\to 0^+} \frac{e^{\tan\left(\frac{\pi}{2} + h\right)} - 1}{e^{\tan\left(\frac{\pi}{2} + h\right)} + 1} = \frac{e^{-\infty} - 1}{e^{-\infty} + 1} = \frac{-1}{1} = -1$$

$\therefore$ L.H.L $\neq$ R.H.L

$\Rightarrow$ Limit of function does not exist

(iii) $\lim\limits_{x\to 0} (5)^{1/x}$

$$\text{L.H.L} = \lim_{x\to 0^-} (5)^{1/x} = \lim_{h\to 0^+} (5)^{-1/h} = (5)^{-\infty} = 0 \text{ and}$$

$$\text{R.H.L} = \lim_{x\to 0^+} (5)^{1/x} = \lim_{h\to 0^+} (5)^{1/h} = (5)^{\infty} = \infty$$

$\therefore$ Limit of function does not exist

(iv) $\lim_{x\to 1} \tan^{-1}\left(\frac{1}{x-1}\right)$

$$\text{L.H.L} = \lim_{x\to 1^-} \tan^{-1}\left(\frac{1}{x-1}\right) = \lim_{h\to 0^+} \tan^{-1}\left(\frac{1}{1-h-1}\right)$$

$$= \lim_{h\to 0^+} \tan^{-1}\left(\frac{-1}{h}\right) = \lim_{h\to 0^+}\left(-\tan^{-1}\left(\frac{1}{h}\right)\right) \qquad [\because \tan^{-1}(-x) = -\tan^{-1}x]$$

$$= -\tan^{-1}(\infty) = -\pi/2 \text{ and R.H.L} = \lim_{x\to 1^+} \tan^{-1}\left(\frac{1}{x-1}\right) = \lim_{h\to 0^+} \tan^{-1}\left(\frac{1}{1+h-1}\right)$$

$$\lim_{h\to 0^+} \tan^{-1}\left(\frac{1}{h}\right) = \tan^{-1}(\infty) = \pi/2$$

∴ L.H.L and R.H.L both exist but are unequal

∴ Limit does not exist

ILLUSTRATION 14: Evaluate the following limits if exist

(i) $\lim_{x\to 1} \frac{\tan^{-1}x}{\cos^{-1}x}$ **(ii)** $\lim_{x\to 1} \frac{x}{\sin^{-1}x}$

(iii) $\lim_{x\to 1/\sqrt{2}} \frac{\sin^{-1}x}{\cos^{-1}\left(x-\frac{1}{\sqrt{2}}\right)}$

SOLUTION: $\lim_{x\to 1} \frac{\tan^{-1}x}{\cos^{-1}x}$; Here $f(x) = \frac{\tan^{-1}x}{\cos^{-1}x}$ and the domain of $f(x)$

$$= \mathbb{R}\cap[-1,1) = [-1,1)$$

$$\therefore \lim_{x\to 1}\frac{\tan^{-1}x}{\cos^{-1}x} = \lim_{x\to 1^-}\frac{\tan^{-1}x}{\cos^{-1}x} = \lim_{h\to 0^+}\frac{\tan^{-1}(1-h)}{\cos^{-1}(1-h)} = \frac{\pi/4}{0^+} = +\infty$$

∴ Limit does not exist

(ii) $\lim_{x\to 1} \frac{x}{\sin^{-1}x}$

Here $f(x) = \frac{x}{\sin^{-1}x}$ and the domain $f(x)$ is $[-1, 1] \sim \{0\}$

$$\therefore \lim_{x\to 1}\frac{x}{\sin^{-1}x} = \lim_{x\to 1^-}\left(\frac{x}{\sin^{-1}x}\right) = \lim_{h\to 0^+}\left(\frac{1-h}{\sin^{-1}(1-h)}\right) = \frac{1-0}{\pi/2} = \frac{2}{\pi}$$

(iii) $\lim_{x\to\left(\frac{1}{\sqrt{2}}\right)^-} \frac{\sin^{-1}x}{\cos^{-1}\left(x-\frac{1}{\sqrt{2}}\right)}$

$$\text{L.H.L} = \lim_{x\to\left(\frac{1}{\sqrt{2}}\right)^-}\frac{\sin^{-1}x}{\cos^{-1}\left[x-\left(1/\sqrt{2}\right)\right]} = \lim_{h\to 0^+}\frac{\sin^{-1}\left(\frac{1}{\sqrt{2}}-h\right)}{\cos^{-1}\left(\frac{1}{\sqrt{2}}-h-\frac{1}{\sqrt{2}}\right)}$$

$$= \lim_{h\to 0^+}\frac{\sin^{-1}\left(\frac{1}{\sqrt{2}}-h\right)}{\cos^{-1}(-h)} = \lim_{h\to 0^+}\frac{\sin^{-1}\left(\frac{1}{\sqrt{2}}-h\right)}{\pi-\cos^{-1}h}$$

$(\because \cos^{-1}(-x) = \pi - \cos^{-1}x)$

$$= \frac{\pi/4}{\pi-\pi/2} = \frac{\pi/4}{\pi/2} = \frac{1}{2} \text{ and R.H.L} = \lim_{x\to(1/\sqrt{2})^+} \frac{\sin^{-1}x}{\cos^{-1}\left(x-\frac{1}{\sqrt{2}}\right)} = \lim_{h\to0^+} \frac{\sin^{-1}\left(\frac{1}{\sqrt{2}}+h\right)}{\cos^{-1}\left(\frac{1}{\sqrt{2}}+h-\frac{1}{\sqrt{2}}\right)}$$

$$= \lim_{h\to0^+} \frac{\sin^{-1}\left(\frac{1}{\sqrt{2}}+h\right)}{\cos^{-1}h} = \frac{\pi/4}{\pi/2} = \frac{1}{2}$$

∴ L.H.L = R.H.L = 1/2

∴ Limit of $f(x)$ is 1/2

Finite Limit at Infinity

A function $f(x)$ is said to have limit ℓ as $x \to \infty$ if for each $\varepsilon > 0$, $\exists\ \delta(\varepsilon) > 0$ such that $|f(x) - \ell| < \varepsilon$ whenever $x > \delta(\varepsilon)$ and denote it by $\lim_{x\to\infty} f(x) = \ell$ and a function $f(x)$ is said to have limit ℓ as $x \to -\infty$ if for each $\varepsilon > 0\ \exists\ \delta(\varepsilon) > 0$ such that $|f(x) - l| < \varepsilon$ wherever $x < \delta(\varepsilon)$ and denote it by $\lim_{x\to-\infty} f(x) = l$.

Hence $d(\varepsilon)$ denotes a real number depending on ε.

Infinite Limit at a Finite Point

A function $f(x)$ is said to tend to infinity as $x \to a$ if for any given real number ℓ (hower lager) $\exists\ \delta > 0$ such that $f(x) > \ell$ whenever $|x - a| < \delta$. Similarly a function $f(x)$ is said to tend to $-\infty$ as $x \to a$ if for any given real number ℓ (however small) $\exists\ \delta > 0$ such that $f(x) < \ell$ whenever $|x - a| < \delta$.

Infinite Limit at Infinity

(i) a function $f(x)$ is said to have limit infinity as x tends to ∞ if for any given real number ℓ (however large) $\exists\ \delta > 0$ such that $f(x) > \ell$ whenever $x > \delta$ and denote it as $\lim_{x\to\infty} f(x) = \infty$

(ii) limit minus infinity as x tends to $-\infty$ if for any given real number ℓ (however large) $\exists\ \delta > 0$ such that $f(x) < -\ell$ whenever $x < -\delta$ and denote it as $\lim_{x\to-\infty} f(x) = -\infty$

(iii) limit infinity as x tends to $-\infty$ if for any given $\ell > 0$ (however large) $\exists\ \delta > 0$ such that $f(x)) > \ell$ whenever $x < -\delta$ and denote it by $\lim_{x\to-\infty} f(x) = \infty$

(iv) limit minus infinity as x tends to ∞ it for ℓ (however large) $\exists\ \delta > 0$ such $f(x) < -\ell$ whenever $x > \delta$ and denote it by $\lim_{x\to\infty} f(x) = -\infty$

TEXTUAL EXERCISE–1: (SUBJECTIVE)

1. Evaluate the following limits

(i) $\lim_{x\to5^+}[x]$ **(ii)** $\lim_{x\to0^-}\frac{[x]}{|x|}$

(iii) $\lim_{x\to0^-}\frac{|x|}{x}$ **(iv)** $\lim_{x\to0^+}\frac{x-[x]}{|x|}$

(v) $\lim_{x\to\left(\frac{\pi}{2}\right)^+}\frac{\{\sin x\}+1}{\cos\left(\frac{\pi}{2}-x\right)}$ **(vi)** $\lim_{x\to\pi^+}\frac{[[\sin x]+[\cos x]]}{|\sin x+\cos x|}$

(vii) $\lim_{x\to\frac{\pi}{2}^-}\frac{\sin 3x}{[\sin 3x]}$

2. Test the existence of the following limits and find them: (where [ ] represents the greatest integer function $\le x$).

(a) $\lim_{x\to1}[x]$ **(b)** $\begin{cases}\frac{1}{1+e^{-1/x}}; & x\ne0\\ 0; & x=0\end{cases}$ at $x = 0$

(c) $\lim_{x\to1/2^+}[1 + x + x^3]$ **(d)** $\lim_{x\to\pi/4^+}\cos[x]$

(e) $\lim_{x\to\pi/4^-}[\sin x]$ **(f)** $\lim_{x\to0}[x^2]^{x^2}$

(g) $\lim_{x\to0}(x^2)^{[x^2]}$ **(h)** $\lim_{x\to0}\cos\frac{1}{x}$

(i) $\lim_{x\to0}(1+\tan^2\sqrt{x})^{1/2x}$ **(j)** $\lim_{x\to2}\{x+(x-[x])^2\}$

3. Let $f(x) = \begin{cases} x^4 & ; x^2 < 1 \\ x & ; x^2 \geq 1 \end{cases}$, discuss the existence of limit at $x = -1, 1$.

4. Discuss the existence of limit of the function $f(x) = \begin{cases} \left|\frac{|x-1|}{x}\right| & ; x > 0 \\ (x+1)^{2-(1/|x|+1/x)} & ; x < 0 \end{cases}$

5. Show that $\lim\limits_{x\to 0} \frac{\{x\}^2}{x^2}$ does not exist but $\lim\limits_{x\to 0} \frac{\{x^2\}}{x^2}$ exists.

6. Evaluate the following:

(i) $\lim\limits_{x\to\infty} (3)^x$ (ii) $\lim\limits_{x\to\infty} \left(\frac{1}{4}\right)^x$

(iii) If $y = \lim\limits_{x\to\pi/4} \{\sin x\}$, then find $\lim\limits_{x\to\infty} (y)^x$

(iv) If $f(x) = e^{-x} (\sin x)$; then evaluate $\lim\limits_{x\to\infty} f(x)$

(v) If $f(x) = \left(\left\{\frac{5}{4}\right\}^x + \frac{[5/4]}{x}\right) \sin x$, then evaluate $\lim\limits_{x\to\infty} f(x)$; where {.} is fractional part of x.

7. Using $\varepsilon - \delta$ definition, prove that $\lim\limits_{x\to 0} \frac{\sin 2x}{\cos x} = 0$

8. (a) Evaluate the right-hand limit and left-hand limit of the function $f(x) = \begin{cases} \frac{|x-4|}{x-4}, & x \neq 4 \\ 0, & x = 4 \end{cases}$

(b) If $f(x) = \begin{cases} 5x - 4 & ; 0 < x \leq 1 \\ 4x^3 - 3x & ; 1 < x < 2 \end{cases}$, show that $\lim\limits_{x\to 1} f(x)$ exists.

9. Test the existence of the following limits and hence evaluate (where [.] denotes G.I.F.)

(a) $\lim\limits_{x\to 2} \frac{[x-2]\,|x-2|}{x-2}$ (b) $\lim\limits_{x\to 2} \frac{\sqrt{x^2-4x+4}}{x-2}$

(c) $\lim\limits_{x\to 2} \frac{\sqrt{x^2-3x+2}}{x-2}$ (d) $\lim\limits_{x\to \frac{\pi}{2}} \cos^{-1}(\operatorname{cosec} x)$

10. Evaluate the following limits: (where [.] denotes the greatest integer function):

(i) $\lim\limits_{x\to 1^-} [\sin^{-1} x]$ (ii) $\lim\limits_{x\to\infty} [\tan^{-1} x]$

(iii) $\lim\limits_{x\to-\infty} [\tan^{-1} x]$ (iv) $\lim\limits_{x\to 1^-} [\sin(\sin^{-1} x)]$

(v) $\lim\limits_{x\to \frac{\pi}{2}} [\sin^{-1}(\sin x)]$

11. The value of $\lim\limits_{x\to 0} \sin^{-1}\{x\}$, (where {.} denotes fractional part of x):

12. State whether the following limits exist or not. Also evaluate if they exist : ([x] denotes gint of x and {x} denotes fractional part of x)

(a) $\lim\limits_{x\to 0} x \sin\left(\frac{1}{x}\right)$ (b) $\lim\limits_{x\to\infty} \frac{\sin x}{x}$

(c) $\lim\limits_{x\to 0} |x|^{[\cos x]}$

13. (a) Evaluate the $\lim\limits_{x\to k} ([k-x]+[x-k]-x)$; where [x] denotes G.I.F. and $k \in \mathbb{Z}$.

(b) Evaluate the above limit if $k \notin \mathbb{Z}$.

(c) Evaluate $\lim\limits_{x\to k} (\{k-x\}+\{x-k\})$; where $k \in \mathbb{Z}$ and {x} denotes the fractional part of x.

Answer Keys

1. (i) 5 (ii) $-\infty$ (iii) -1 (iv) 1 (v) 2 (vi) -2 (vii) 1
2. (a) does not exist L.H.L = 0 & R.H.L = 1 (b) does not exist L.H.L = 0 & R.H.L = 1
(c) R.H.L = L.H.L = 1 (d) R.H.L = L.H.L = 1 (e) R.H.L = L.H.L = 0
(f) R.H.L = L.H.L = 0 (g) R.H.L = L.H.L = 1 (h) does not exist
(i) $(e^{1/2})$ (j) does not exist
3. At $x = -1$, L.H.L = -1, R.H.L = 1; $\lim\limits_{x\to 1} f(x) = 1$
4. R.H.L = ∞, L.H.L = 1
6. (i) ∞ (ii) 0 (iii) 0 (iv) 0 (v) 0
8. (a) L.H.L. = -1, R.H.L. = 1 limit does not exist. (b) L.H.L. = 1, R.H.L. = 1 limit exist and at $x = 1$.
9. (a) L.H.L = 1, R.H.L = 0 (b) L.H.L = -1, R.H.L = 1
(c) L.H.L = not exist, R.H.L = ∞ (d) both L.H.L & R.H.L does not exist
10. (i) 1 (ii) 1 (iii) -2 (iv) 0 (v) 1 11. does not exist
12. (a) 0 (b) 0 (c)
13. (a) $-1-k$ (b) $-k-1$ (c) 1

TEXTUAL EXERCISE–1: (OBJECTIVE)

1. The value of $\lim\limits_{x\to 2^+}[x-2]$; ([.] is gint function) is
(a) 1 (b) 2
(c) 0 (d) None of these

2. The value of $\lim\limits_{x\to n^+}\{x-2\}$; ({.} is fractional part function and $n \in \mathbb{Z}$ and $n > 2$) is
(a) 1 (b) 0
(c) – 1 (d) None of these

3. The value of $\lim\limits_{x\to n^-}\{x - 2\}$; ({.} is fractional part function; $n \in \mathbb{Z}$ and $n > 2$) is:
(a) 0 (b) –1
(c) 1 (d) None of these

4. If $f(x) = \begin{cases} x+2; x<1 \\ 4x-1; 1\le x\le 3 \\ x^2+5, \text{where } x>3 \end{cases}$; then
(a) $\lim\limits_{x\to 1^+} f(x) = 3$
(b) $\lim\limits_{x\to 1^+} f(x) =$ does not exist
(c) $\lim\limits_{x\to 3^+} f(x) = 11$
(d) $\lim\limits_{x\to 3} f(x)$ = does not exist

5. $\lim\limits_{x\to 0}\dfrac{e^{1/x}-1}{e^{1/x}+1}$, then
(a) L.H.L = –1
(b) R.H.L = 1
(c) limit does not exist
(d) None of these

6. If $\lim\limits_{x\to \frac{\pi}{4}}$ [(tan x) + 3], (where [.] is gint function), then
(a) L.H.L = 3
(b) R.H.L = 4
(c) limit does not exist
(d) None of these

7. $\lim\limits_{x\to 0}\sin\dfrac{1}{x}$
(a) does not exist (b) 0
(c) 1 (d) None of these

8. $\lim\limits_{x\to 0} x\sin\dfrac{1}{x}$
(a) does not exist (b) 0
(c) 1 (d) None of these

9. $\lim\limits_{x\to \frac{\pi}{2}^+}\cot(\pi - x)$
(a) 1 (b) does not exist
(c) 0 (d) None of these

10. $\lim\limits_{x\to 1^-}\sin^{-1}(x)$ is
(a) 1 (b) π/2
(c) – π/2 (d) None of these

11. $\lim\limits_{x\to 1^+}\sin^{-1}(x)$ is equal to
(a) π/2 (b) -π/2
(c) does not exist (d) None of these

12. $\lim\limits_{x\to 1}\cos^{-1} x = L$
(a) L.H.L = 0
(b) R.H.L = does not exist
(c) $L = 0$
(d) None of these

13. $\lim\limits_{x\to -\sqrt{3}} |\tan^{-1} x|$ is
(a) –π/3 (b) π/6
(c) π/3 (d) None of these

14. If $\sin^{-1}x + \sin^{-1}y = \pi$, then $\lim\limits_{z\to (xy)}\tan^{-1}(z)$ is
(a) π/2 (b) π/3
(c) π/4 (d) None of these

15. $\lim\limits_{x\to \infty}\dfrac{e^x+e^{-x}}{e^x-e^{-x}}$ is
(a) 1 (b) – 1
(c) ∞ (d) None of these

16. Let $\sin^{-1}(\sin x) + \cos^{-1}(\cos y)$ has k integer values for $x, y \in \{1, 2, 3, 4\}$, then $\lim\limits_{z\to k}\tan\dfrac{\pi}{z}$ is
(a) $\dfrac{1}{\sqrt{3}}$ (b) 1
(c) $\sqrt{3}$ (d) None of these

Answer Keys

1. (c) 2. (b) 3. (c) 4. (a, d) 5. (a, b, c) 6. (a, b, c) 7. (a) 8. (b) 9. (c) 10. (b)
11. (c) 12. (a, c) 13. (c) 14. (c) 15. (a) 16. (c)

■ ALGEBRA OF LIMITS

If $\lim_{x\to a} f(x) = \ell$ and $\lim_{x\to a} g(x) = m$ (where ℓ and m are finite real numbers), then following statements hold good.

(i) Sum Rule: $\lim_{x\to a} (f(x) + g(x)) = \ell + m$. e.g.,
$\lim_{x\to 2} (x+\sin x) = \lim_{x\to 2} x + \lim_{x\to 2} \sin x = 2 + \sin 2$

(ii) Difference Rule: $\lim_{x\to a} (f(x) - g(x)) = \ell - m$. e.g.,
$\lim_{x\to 3} (\tan x - 2^x) = \lim_{x\to 3} \tan x - \lim_{x\to 3} 2^x = \tan 3 - 2^3$

(iii) Product Rule: $\lim_{x\to a} (f(x).\ g(x)) = \ell.m$. e.g.,
$\lim_{x\to 3/4} x\cos x = \lim_{x\to 3/4} x\ .\ \lim_{x\to 3/4} \cos x = (3/4)\cos 3/4$

(iv) Constant Multiple Rule: $\lim_{x\to a} k.f(x) = k.\ell$; where k is a constant real number e.g., $\lim_{x\to 5} 5e^x = 5 \times \lim_{x\to 5} e^x = 5e^5$

(v) Quotient Rule: $\lim_{x\to a} \dfrac{f(x)}{g(x)} = \dfrac{\ell}{m}, m \neq 0$, e.g.,
$\lim_{x\to 1} \dfrac{e^x}{\sin x} = \dfrac{\lim_{x\to 1} e^x}{\lim_{x\to 1} \sin x} = \dfrac{e}{\sin 1}$

(vi) Power Rule: If p and q are integers, then $\lim_{x\to a} (f(x))^{\frac{p}{q}} = \ell^{\frac{p}{q}}$, provided $(\ell)^{\frac{p}{q}}$ is a real number.

(vii) Rule for Composite Functions: $\lim_{x\to a} f(g(x)) = f(\lim_{x\to a} g(x)) = f(m)$; provided '$f$' is a function continuous at $\lim_{x\to 0} g(x) = m$. e.g., $\lim_{x\to a} \ln\{f(x)\} = \ln \ell$, only if $\ell > 0$

NOTE:

$\sin \ell = \lim_{x\to a} \sin(f(x))$.

Above said is also valid for cos (f (x)), tan (f(x)), cot(f (x)), sec (f (x)), cosec (f (x)), P_n (f (x)) provided these functions are defined at these points.

ILLUSTRATION 15: Find the following limits:

(a) $\lim_{x\to \pi/2} (\sin x + [x])$;[.] is greatest integer function

(b) $\lim_{x\to 1} \sin(\sin^{-1} x + \tan^{-1} x)$

(c) $\lim_{x\to 1/2} \{\cos^{-1} x - \sin^{-1} x\}$; where {.} is fractional part functional

(d) $\lim_{x\to 0} x^2 \sin\dfrac{1}{x}$

(e) $\lim_{x\to 0} \dfrac{1}{x} \sin\dfrac{1}{x}$

(f) $\lim_{x\to 1} \left\{\sin^{-1}\left(x \sin^{-1}\left(\sin\dfrac{1}{x}\right)\right)\right\}$; {.} is fractional part function

(g) Evaluate $\lim_{x\to 1/\sqrt{2}} \sqrt{(\sin^{-1} x)/\pi}$

(h) $\lim\limits_{x\to 1}\left[\dfrac{\sin^{-1}x}{\cot^{-1}x}\right]$; [.] is greatest integer function

(i) $\lim\limits_{x\to 1}\{\tan^{-1}x\}/\pi$; {.} is fractional part of x

SOLUTION: **(a)** $\lim\limits_{x\to\pi/2}(\sin x+[x]) = \lim\limits_{x\to\pi/2}(\sin x)+\lim\limits_{x\to\pi/2}[x]=1+\left[\dfrac{\pi}{2}\right]=1+1=2$

(b) $\lim\limits_{x\to 1}\sin\left(\sin^{-1}x+\tan^{-1}x\right)$

$\because \lim\limits_{x\to 1}\left(\sin^{-1}x+\tan^{-1}x\right)=\lim\limits_{x\to 1}\left(\sin^{-1}x\right)+\lim\limits_{x\to 1}\left(\tan^{-1}x\right)$

$=\dfrac{\pi}{2}+\dfrac{\pi}{4}=\dfrac{3\pi}{4}$ ...... (i)

And sin x is a continuous function (graph of sin x is continuous without any break on $\mathbb{R}$)

$\therefore \lim\limits_{x\to 1}\sin\left(\sin^{-1}x+\tan^{-1}x\right)=\sin\left(\lim\limits_{x\to 1}\left(\sin^{-1}x+\tan^{-1}x\right)\right)$

$=\sin\left(\dfrac{3\pi}{4}\right)$ [by (i)]

$=\sin\left(\pi-\dfrac{\pi}{4}\right)=\sin\dfrac{\pi}{4}=\dfrac{1}{\sqrt{2}}$

(c) $\lim\limits_{x\to 1/2}\left\{\cos^{-1}x-\sin^{-1}x\right\}$

Here $\lim\limits_{x\to 1/2}\left(\cos^{-1}x-\sin^{-1}x\right)=\lim\limits_{x\to 1/2}\cos^{-1}x-\lim\limits_{x\to 1/2}\sin^{-1}x$

$=\dfrac{\pi}{3}-\dfrac{\pi}{6}=\dfrac{\pi}{6}$ ...... (ii)

Also the graph of $\{x\}$ is as illustrated in figure 1.36

Clearly $\{x\}$ is discontinuous (break) at only integer and $\dfrac{\pi}{6}$ is non-integer.

$\therefore$ $\{x\}$ is continuous at $x=\dfrac{\pi}{6}$

$\therefore \lim\limits_{x\to 1/2}\left\{\cos^{-1}x-\sin^{-1}x\right\}=\left\{\lim\limits_{x\to 1/2}\left(\cos^{-1}x-\sin^{-1}x\right)\right\}$

$=\left\{\dfrac{\pi}{6}\right\}=\dfrac{\pi}{6}$ as $0<\dfrac{\pi}{6}<1$

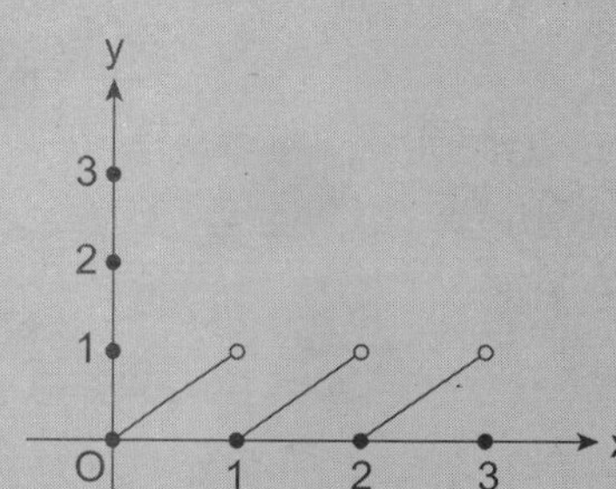

FIGURE 1.36

(d) $\lim\limits_{x\to 0}x^2\sin\dfrac{1}{x}=\left(\lim\limits_{x\to 0}x^2\right)\left(\lim\limits_{x\to 0}\sin\dfrac{1}{x}\right)$

= (0) × (a finite number oscillating between – 1 and 1 includingly) = (0)

(e) $\lim\limits_{x\to 0}\dfrac{1}{x}\sin\dfrac{1}{x}=\lim\limits_{x\to 0}\left(\dfrac{1}{x}\right)\lim\limits_{x\to 0}\left(\sin\dfrac{1}{x}\right)=(\pm\infty)\times$ (a real number between – 1 and 1, both inclusive

and does not exist uniquely

(f) $\lim\limits_{x\to 1}\left\{\left(x\sin^{-1}\left(\sin\dfrac{1}{x}\right)\right)\right\}$. Here $\lim\limits_{x\to 1}\left(x\sin^{-1}(\sin\dfrac{1}{x})\right)=\left(\lim\limits_{x\to 1}x\right).\lim\limits_{x\to 1}\sin^{-1}\left(\sin\dfrac{1}{x}\right)$

$=(1).\lim\limits_{x\to 1}\left(\dfrac{1}{x}\right)=1.\left(\dfrac{1}{1}\right)=1$

$$\left[\begin{array}{l}\because\ x\to 1\Rightarrow \dfrac{1}{x}\to 1\Rightarrow \dfrac{1}{x}\in(1-\delta,1+\delta);\delta>0\ \&\ \delta\to 0\\ \Rightarrow \dfrac{1}{x}\in\left(-\dfrac{\pi}{2},\dfrac{\pi}{2}\right)\\ \Rightarrow \sin^{-1}\left(\sin\dfrac{1}{x}\right)=\dfrac{1}{x}\end{array}\right]$$

(g) $\lim\limits_{x\to 1/\sqrt{2}}\sqrt{\dfrac{(\sin^{-1}x)}{\pi}}$

Here $\lim\limits_{x\to 1/\sqrt{2}}\dfrac{(\sin^{-1}x)}{\pi}=\dfrac{1}{\pi}\lim\limits_{x\to 1/\sqrt{2}}(\sin^{-1}x)=\dfrac{1}{\pi}\sin^{-1}\left(\dfrac{1}{\sqrt{2}}\right)=\dfrac{1}{\pi}.\dfrac{\pi}{4}=\dfrac{1}{4}$

$\therefore\ \lim\limits_{x\to 1/\sqrt{2}}\left(\dfrac{\sin^{-1}x}{\pi}\right)^{1/2}=\left(\lim\limits_{x\to 1/\sqrt{2}}\dfrac{\sin^{-1}x}{\pi}\right)^{1/2}=\left(\dfrac{1}{4}\right)^{1/2}=\dfrac{1}{2}$

[$\because\ \lim\limits_{x\to a}(f(x))^{p/q}=\left(\lim\limits_{x\to a}f(x)\right)^{p/q}$, provided $\left(\lim\limits_{x\to a}f(x)\right)^{p/q}$ is real]

(h) $\lim\limits_{x\to 1}\left[\dfrac{\sin^{-1}x}{\cot^{-1}x}\right]$; here $\lim\limits_{x\to 1}\left(\dfrac{\sin^{-1}x}{\cot^{-1}x}\right)=\dfrac{\lim\limits_{x\to 1^-}(\sin^{-1}x)}{\lim\limits_{x\to 1^-}(\cot^{-1}x)}=\dfrac{\pi/2}{\pi/4}=2$ ..... (iii)

Now $\sin^{-1}x$ is increasing and $\cot^{-1}x$ is a decreasing function and $\sin^{-1}x$, $\cot^{-1}x>0$; when $x\to 1^-$

$\Rightarrow\ \dfrac{\sin^{-1}x}{\cot^{-1}x}$ is increasing function

$\therefore\ \dfrac{\sin^{-1}x}{\cot^{-1}x}<\dfrac{\sin^{-1}1}{\cot^{-1}1}$ where $x\to 1^-$

$\Rightarrow\ \left(\dfrac{\sin^{-1}x}{\cot^{-1}x}\right)<2$ and $\lim\limits_{x\to 1^-}\left(\dfrac{\sin^{-1}x}{\cot^{-1}x}\right)=2$ [from (iii)]

$\Rightarrow\ \lim\limits_{x\to 1}\left[\dfrac{\sin^{-1}x}{\cot^{-1}x}\right]=1$

(i) $\lim\limits_{x\to 1}\dfrac{\{\tan^{-1}x\}}{\pi}=\dfrac{1}{\pi}\lim\limits_{x\to 1}\{\tan^{-1}x\}$ ...(iv)

Also $\lim\limits_{x\to 1}\tan^{-1}x=\dfrac{\pi}{4}$ = non-integer and hence at $x=\pi/4$ $\{x\}$ is continuous.

$\Rightarrow\ \lim\limits_{x\to 1}\{\tan^{-1}x\}=\{\lim\limits_{x\to 1}\tan^{-1}x\}=\left\{\dfrac{\pi}{4}\right\}=\dfrac{\pi}{4}$ as $0<\dfrac{\pi}{4}<1$

$\therefore$ From (iv)

$\Rightarrow\ \lim\limits_{x\to 1}\dfrac{\{\tan^{-1}x\}}{\pi}=\dfrac{1}{\pi}\left(\dfrac{\pi}{4}\right)=\dfrac{1}{4}$

INFINITESIMAL QUANTITY

A quantity $f(x)$ tending towards zero as $x \to$ a is called infinitesimal at $x = a \Rightarrow f(x)$ is infinitesimal at $x = a \Leftrightarrow \lim_{x\to a} f(x) = 0$.

For example:

(i) If $f(x) = \sin x$ and $a = 0$. Then $\sin x \to 0$ as $x \to 0$

$\Rightarrow$ $\sin x$ is an infinitesimal at $x = 0$

$\therefore$ $\lim_{x\to 0} \sin x = 0$

(ii) If $f(x) = \log x$ and $a = 1$. Then $\log x \to 0$ as $x \to 1$

$\therefore$ $\log x$ is an infinitesimal at $x = 1$

$\therefore$ $\lim_{x\to 1} \log x = 0$

(iii) If $f(x) = 1 - \sin x$ and $a = \pi/2$ then $f(x)$ is an infinitesimal at $x = \pi/2$

$\therefore$ $\lim_{x\to \pi/2} (1-\sin x) = 0$

PROPERTIES OF INFINITESIMAL

1. Sum of finite number of infinitesimals is always an infinitesimal.

Proof: Let $g(x) = f_1(x) + f_2(x) + \ldots + f_n(x)$, where each $f_i(x)$ is an infinitesimal.

Let $f_k(x)$ be the largest of them and $f_k(x) = m$, then $f_i(x) \le m$ for each $i \in \{1, 2, 3, \ldots n\}$

$\Rightarrow g(x) \le m + m + m + m + \ldots + m$' ($n$-times)

$\Rightarrow g(x) \le nm$ and $m \to 0 \Rightarrow g(x) \to 0$

2. Sum of infinite number of infinitesimals may not necessarily be an infinitesimal. For example

(i) $x + x^2 + x^3 + \ldots + \infty = \left(\dfrac{x}{1-x}\right)_{x\to 0} = 0$

(ii) $\dfrac{1}{n^3} + \dfrac{2}{n^3} + \ldots \dfrac{n^2}{n^3} =$

$$\frac{n^2(n^2+1)}{2n^3} = \frac{n^4+n^2}{2n^3} = \left[\frac{1+\frac{1}{n^2}}{2/n}\right] \to \infty \text{ ; as } n \to \infty$$

(iii) $\dfrac{1}{n^3} + \dfrac{2}{n^3} + \ldots + \dfrac{n}{n^3} = \dfrac{n(n+1)}{2n^3} = \dfrac{\left(1+\frac{1}{n}\right)}{2n} \to 0$ as $n \to \infty$;

(iv) $\dfrac{1}{3n^2} + \dfrac{2}{3n^2} + \ldots \dfrac{n}{3n^2} = \dfrac{n(n+1)}{6n^2} = \dfrac{\left(1+\frac{1}{n}\right)}{6} \to \dfrac{1}{6}$ as $n \to \infty$

3. Difference of two infinitesimals is also an infinitesimal.

Proof: Let $f(x)$ and $g(x)$ be two infinitesimals at $x = a$, then $\lim_{x\to a} f(x)$ $\lim_{x\to a} g(x)$

$\therefore$ $\lim_{x\to a}(f(x)-g(x)) = \lim_{x\to a} f(x) - \lim_{x\to a} g(x)$

$= 0 - 0 = 0$. For example

$f(x) = x$ and $g(x) = \sin x$, then both are infinitesimals at $x = 0$.

$\therefore$ $\lim_{x\to 0}(f(x)-g(x)) = \lim_{x\to 0}(x-\sin x) = 0 - 0 = 0$

4. Product of two infinitesimals is always an infinitesimal quantity.

Proof: proof is obvious from the fact that $\lim_{x\to 0} f(x).g(x) = \lim_{x\to 0} f(x).\lim_{x\to 0} g(x)$. e.g.,

(i) $f(x) = x$ and $g(x) = x^2$ both are infinitesimals at $x = 0$ and $h(x) = f(x).\ g(x) = x.\ x^2 = x^3 \to 0$ as $x \to 0$ is also an infinitesimal at $x = 0$.

(ii) $f(x) = x$ and $g(x) = \sin x$, both are infinitesimal at $x = 0$ and $h(x) = f(x).g(x) = x \sin x \to 0$ as $x \to 0$ is also an infinitesimal at $x = 0$

5. Quotient of two infinitesimals may or may not be an infinitesimal. For example

(i) $\dfrac{\sin x}{x} \to 1$ as $x \to 0$ ($\sin x$, x are infinitesimals at $x = 0$)

(ii) $\dfrac{x^2}{\sin x} \to 0$ as $x \to 0$ (x^2, $\sin x$, and x are infinitesimals at $x = 0$)

(iii) $\dfrac{\sin x}{x^2} \to \infty$ as $x \to 0$ (x^2, $\sin x$ are infinitesimals at $x = 0$)

$\therefore$ $\dfrac{x^2}{\sin x}$ is an infinitesimal at $x = 0$, whereas $\dfrac{\sin x}{x}$ and $\dfrac{\sin x}{x^2}$ are not infinitesimals at $x = 0$

From above we conclude that quotient of two infinitesimals may be an infinitesimal, may be finite or may tend to infinity.

REMARK:

If f(x) and g(x) are two infinitesimals at x = a such that $\lim_{x\to a}\dfrac{f(x)}{g(x)} = k$, *then*

(i) *If $k \neq 0$ finite real number, then f(x) & g(x) are called infinitesimals of same order, e.g.,* $\lim_{x\to 0}\frac{2x^2}{x^2} = 2$ *(non-zero finite real number)*

(ii) *If k = 1, then f(x) & g(x) are said to be equivalent infinitesimals, e.g.,* $\lim_{x\to 0}\frac{\sin x}{x} = 1, \lim_{x\to 0}\frac{\tan x}{x} = 1$

$\Rightarrow$ *sin x and x are equivalent infinitesimals of same order*

(iii) *if k = 0, then f(x) is said to be of higher order than g(x) e.g.,* $\lim_{x\to 0}\frac{x^2}{x} = 0 \Rightarrow$ *x^2 is infinitesimals of higher order than x*

(iv) *if $k = \infty$, then g(x) is said to be of higher order than f(x) e.g.,* $\lim_{x\to 0}\frac{x^2}{x^3} = \lim_{x\to 0}\frac{1}{x} = \infty$

$\Rightarrow$ *x^3 is of higher order infinitesimal than x^2*

List of Equivalent Infinitesimals

If $f(x)$ is an infinitesimal as $x \to a$, then given below is the list of equivalent infinitesimals.

sin (f(x))	*f(x)*	*tan (f(x))*	*f(x)*
1-cos$f(x)$	$\frac{1}{2}\{f(x)\}^2$	arc sin $f(x)$	$f(x)$

sin (f(x))	*f(x)*	*tan (f(x))*	*f(x)*
arc tan $f(x)$	$f(x)$	$a^{f(x)} - 1$ $(a > 0)$	$f(x)$ *ln a*
ln $[1 + f(x)]$	$f(x)$	$e^{f(x)} - 1$	$f(x)$
$[1 + f(x)]^p - 1$	$pf(x)$	$\sqrt[n]{1+f(x)}-1$	$\frac{f(x)}{n}$

REMARKS:

1. *Order of infinitesimal i.e., the infinitesimal having higher tendency to reach zero as compared to other infinitesimal as x → a, is said to be of higher order infinitesimal. e. g. f(x) = x and g(x) = x^2, h(x) = x^3. Their graphs are as shown in figure 1.37.*

   Clearly as x is approaching 0, y = x^3 has greater tendency to reach zero, then y = x^2 and then y = x

   ∴ *x^3 is higher order infinitesimal as compared to x^2, x^2 is of higher order infinitesimal as compared to x.*

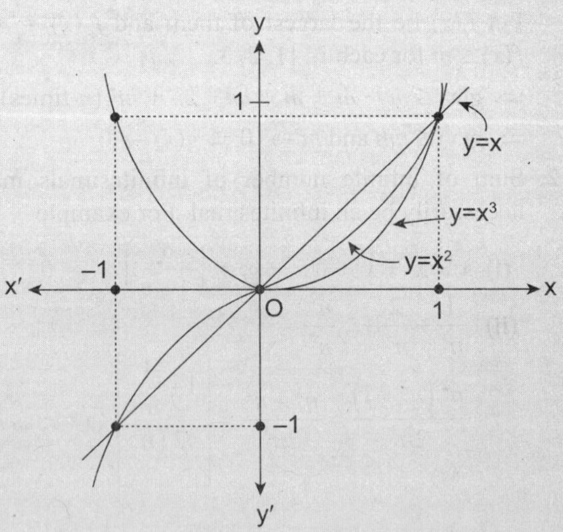

FIGURE 1.37

2. *Product of two infinitesimals is higher order infinitesimal than both the infinitesimal factors. e. g. f(x) = x and g(x) = x^2 are infinitesimals at x = 0, But h(x) = x. x^2 = x^3 is higher order infinitesimal as compared to x and x^2*
3. *Quotient of two infinitesimals becomes zero as x → a if order of numerator is greater than that of denominator and becomes infinite if order of denominator is greater than that of numerator. It remain finite non-zero if two infinitesimals in numerator and denominator are of same order. e. g.* $\lim_{x\to 0}\frac{x^2}{x} = 0; \lim_{x\to 0}\frac{x}{x^3} = \infty$ *and* $\lim_{x\to 0}\frac{3x}{x} = 3$
4. *An equivalent infinitesimal can be obtained from a given sum of infinitesimals by rejecting the higher order summand infinitesimal. e. g. $x^5 + 2x^3$ is an infinitesimal at x = 0*

⇒ $2x^3$ *is equivalent infinitesimal*

$$\because \lim_{x\to 0}\frac{x^5+2x^3}{2x^3}=\lim_{x\to 0}\left(\frac{x^2}{2}+1\right)=1$$

5. *Product of infinitesimal at x = a and a bounded function is an infinitesimal at x = a, e.g.,* $\lim_{x\to 0} x\left(\sin\frac{1}{x}\right)=0$

ILLUSTRATION 16: Replace each of the following infinitesimal with an equivalent one:

(a) $3\sin x - 5x^3$ **(b)** $\{(1-\cos x)^2 + 16x^3 + 5x^4 + 6x^5\}$

SOLUTION: **(a)** We know that the sum of two infinitesimals x & y of different orders is equivalent to the summand of the lower order, since the replacement of an infinitesimal with one equivalent to it is tantamount to the rejection of an infinitesimal of a higher order. In the given example the quantity $3\sin x$ has the order of smallness 1.

Hence $3\sin x + (-5x^3) \sim 3\sin x \sim 3x$

(b) $\{(1-\cos x)^2 + 16x^3 + 5x^4 + 6x^5\} = 4\sin^4 x/2 + 16x^3 + 5x^4 + 6x^5$

The summand $16x^3$ is of the lowest order, therefore $\{(1-\cos x)^2 + 16x^3 + 5x^4 + 6x^5\} \sim 16x^3$

ILLUSTRATION 17: Using the principle of equivalent infinitesimal, evaluate the following limits:

(a) $\lim_{x\to 0}\frac{1-\cos x}{1-\cos x/2}$ **(b)** $\lim_{x\to 0}\frac{\sqrt{1+x+x^2}-1}{\sin 4x}$

(c) $\lim_{x\to 0}\frac{\sin 2x + \arcsin 2x - \arctan 2x}{3x}$

SOLUTION: **(a)** Since $1-\cos x \sim x^2/2$ and $1-\cos x/2 \sim \frac{1}{2}\left(\frac{x}{2}\right)^2$

Therefore, $\lim_{x\to 0}\frac{1-\cos x}{1-\cos x/2}=\frac{x^2/2}{x^2/8}=4$

(b) From the equivalent infinitesimal, we find $\sqrt{1+x+x^2}-1 \sim \frac{(x+x^2)}{2} \sim \frac{(x)}{2}$, & $\sin 4x \sim 4x$

$\left(\begin{array}{l}\because [(1+f(x))^p-1]\sim pf(x)\\ \text{if } f(x) \text{ is an infinitesimal}\end{array}\right)$

Therefore $\lim_{x\to 0}\frac{\sqrt{1+x+x^2}-1}{\sin 4x}=\lim_{x\to 0}\frac{x/2}{4x}=\frac{1}{8}$

(c) Using the equivalent infinitesimal function, we obtain $\sin 2x + \arcsin 2x - \arctan 2x \sim 2x + 2x - 2x = 2x$

Hence, $\lim_{x\to 0}\frac{\sin 2x + arc\sin 2x - arc\tan 2x}{3x}=\lim_{x\to 0}\frac{2x}{3x}=\frac{2}{3}$

NOTE:

The concept of infinite functions of various orders is introduced similarly as done for infinitesimal functions.

"The function f(x) is called infinite as x → a if $\lim_{x\to a} f(x)=\infty$*. Therefore infinite is inverse quantity of infinitesimal."*

ILLUSTRATION 18: Prove that the functions given below are infinitesimal at the indicated points.

(a) $f(x) = \dfrac{2x-4}{x^2+5}$ at $x = 2$

(b) $f(x) = (x-1)^2 \sin^3 \dfrac{1}{x-1}$ at $x = 1$

SOLUTION: **(a)** It is sufficient to find $\lim\limits_{x\to 2} f(x) = \lim\limits_{x\to 2} \dfrac{2x-4}{x^2+5} = 0$

(b) First, the function $\phi(x) = (x-1)^2$ is infinitesimal as $x \to 1$; indeed,

$\lim\limits_{x\to 1}(x-1)^2 = 0$. Second, the function $\psi(x) = \sin^3\left(\dfrac{1}{x-1}\right)$; $x \neq 1$, is bounded: $\left|\sin^3 \dfrac{1}{x-1}\right| \le 1$

Hence, the given function $f(x)$ represents the product of the bounded function $\psi(x)$ by the infinitesimal $\phi(x)$, which means that $f(x)$ is an infinitesimal function as $x \to 1$.

ILLUSTRATION 19: Find $\lim\limits_{x\to 0} x \sin(1/x)$

SOLUTION: Since x is an infinitesimal as $x \to 0$ and the function $\sin(1/x)$ is bounded, the product $x \sin(1/x)$ is an infinitesimal, which means that $\lim\limits_{\to} x\sin(1/x) \;\; 0$

ILLUSTRATION 20: Determine the order of smallness of the following functions $f(x)$ with respect to the infinitesimal x at $x = 0$

(a) $f(x) = \tan x^3$ **(b)** $\sqrt{\sin}$

(c) $f(x) = \cos x - \cos 2x$

SOLUTION: **(a)** We have $\lim\limits_{x\to 0}\dfrac{\tan x^3}{x} = \lim\limits_{x\to 0}\left[\dfrac{\tan x^3}{x^3}x^2\right]$

$$= \lim_{x\to 0}\frac{\tan x^3}{x^3}\lim_{x\to 0} x^2 = 0$$

Hence $\tan x^3$ is an infinitesimal of a higher order relative to x.

(b) We have $\lim\limits_{x\to 0}\dfrac{\sqrt[3]{\sin^2 x}}{x} = \lim\limits_{x\to 0}\left[\sqrt[3]{\dfrac{\sin^2 x}{x^2}}\dfrac{1}{\sqrt[3]{x}}\right] = \infty$

Hence $\sqrt[3]{\sin^2 x}$ is an infinitesimal of a lower order as compared to x.

(c) $f(x) = \cos x - \cos 2x = 2\sin\dfrac{3}{2}x\sin\dfrac{x}{2}$.

Whence $\lim\limits_{x\to 0}\dfrac{f(x)}{x} = \lim\limits_{x\to 0}\dfrac{2\sin\left(\dfrac{3x}{2}\right)\sin\left(\dfrac{x}{2}\right)}{x}$

$$= \lim_{x\to 0}\frac{2\left(\dfrac{3x}{2}\right)\left(\dfrac{x}{2}\right)}{x} = 0.$$

Hence $f(x)$ is an infinitesimal of higher order with respect to x.

SANDWICH THEOREM AND STANDARD RESULTS ON LIMITS

If $g(x) \le f(x) \le h(x)$ for all x belonging to neighbourhood of a (i.e., $(a - \delta, a + \delta)$ may exclude $x = a$) and there exist a real and finite number ℓ such that $\lim_{x\to a} g(x) = \lim_{x\to a} h(x) = \ell$, then $\lim_{x\to a} f(x)$ is also equal to ℓ.

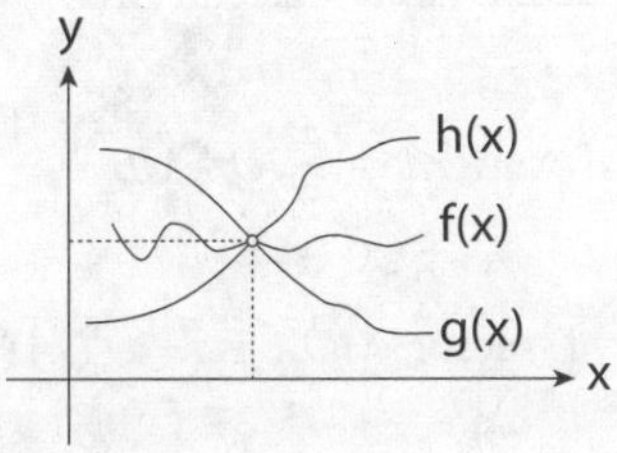

FIGURE 1.38

ILLUSTRATION 21: If $1 - \dfrac{x^2}{4} \le f(x) \le 1 + \dfrac{x^2}{2}$ for all $x \ne 0$, find $\lim_{x\to 0} f(x)$

SOLUTION: Here $\lim_{x\to 0}\left(1 - \dfrac{x^2}{4}\right) = 1$ and also $\lim_{x\to 0}\left(1 + \dfrac{x^2}{2}\right) = 1$

So $\lim_{x\to 0} f(x) = 1$ (by sandwich theorem)

ILLUSTRATION 22: If $\tan^{-1}x < f(x) < \sin^{-1}x$, for $x > 0$, then evaluate $\lim_{x\to 0^+} f(x)$

SOLUTION: $\lim_{x\to 0^+} \tan^{-1} x = 0$ and $\lim_{x\to 0^+} \sin^{-1} x = 0$ and $\tan^{-1}x < f(x) < \sin^{-1}x$ for $x > 0$

$\Rightarrow \lim_{x\to 0^+} f(x) = 0$ (by Sandwich theorem)

ILLUSTRATION 23: If $\dfrac{2x^2}{x^2+1} < f(x) < \dfrac{2x^2+4}{x^2+1}$, then evaluate $\lim_{x\to\infty} f(x)$

SOLUTION: $\lim_{x\to\infty} \dfrac{2x^2}{x^2+1} = \lim_{x\to\infty} \dfrac{2(x^2+1-1)}{x^2+1} = \lim_{x\to\infty} 2 - \dfrac{2}{(x^2+1)} = 2$ and

$\lim_{x\to\infty} \dfrac{2x^2+4}{x^2+1} = \lim_{x\to\infty} \dfrac{2(x^2+1)+2}{(x^2+1)} = \lim_{x\to\infty}\left[2 + \dfrac{2}{(x^2+1)}\right] = 2$

and $\dfrac{2x^2}{x^2+1} < f(x) < \dfrac{2x^2+4}{x^2+1}$

$\therefore \lim_{x\to\infty} f(x) = 2$

STANDARD RESULTS ON LIMITS

1. $\lim_{x\to 0} \dfrac{\sin x}{x} = 1 = \lim_{x\to 0} \dfrac{x}{\sin x}$

Proof: The function $\dfrac{\sin x}{x}$ is not defined for $x = 0$ since the numerator and denominator of the fraction becomes zero. Let us find the limit of this function as $x \to 0$. We consider circle of radius 1; denote the central angle MOB by x, $(0 < x < \pi/2)$. From the figure, it follows that

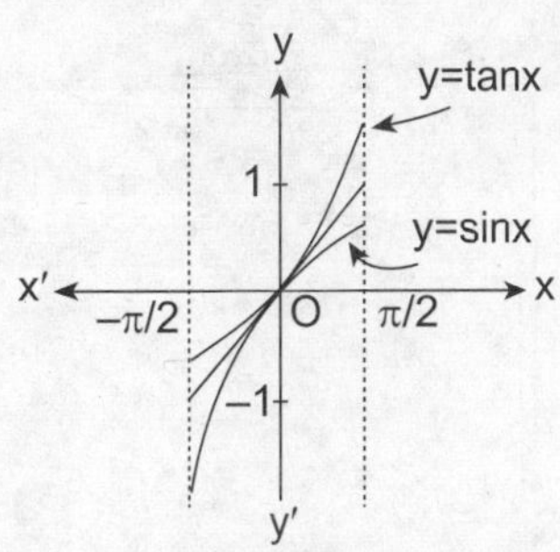

FIGURE 1.39

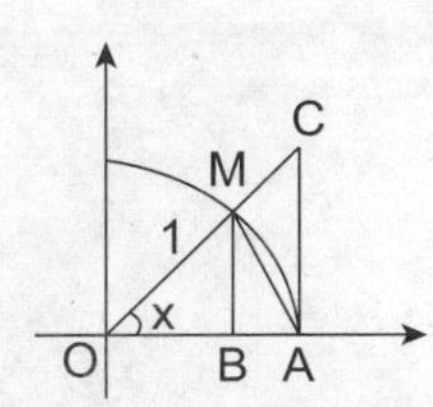

FIGURE 1.40

area of Δ *MOA* < area of sector *MOA* < area of Δ *COA* ...(i)

The area of $\Delta MOA = \frac{1}{2} OA.MB = \frac{1}{2}(1)(\sin x) = \frac{1}{2} \sin x$

The area of sector $MOA = \frac{1}{2}(OA)^2. x = \frac{1}{2}(1)^2. x = \frac{1}{2}x$

The area of $COA = \frac{1}{2} OA.AC = \frac{1}{2}.(1).(\tan x) = \frac{1}{2} \tan x$

After cancelling $\frac{1}{2}$, inequalities (i) can be rewritten as $\sin x < x < \tan x$

For $x \to 0^+$, $\sin x > 0$

Divide all terms by $\sin x$; $1 < \frac{x}{\sin x} < \frac{1}{\cos x}$

or $1 > \frac{\sin x}{x} > \cos x$

We derived this inequality on the assumption that $x > 0$; noting that $\frac{\sin(-x)}{(-x)} = \frac{\sin x}{x}$ and $\cos(-x) = \cos x$, we conclude that it holds for $x < 0$ as well. But $\lim_{x\to 0} \cos x = 1$, $\lim_{x\to 0} 1 = 1$. Hence the variable $\frac{\sin x}{x}$ lies between two quantities that have the same limit (unity).

Thus applying the sandwich theorem given in the preceding article $\lim_{x\to 0} \frac{\sin x}{x}$ comes out to be one. The graph of $\frac{\sin x}{x}$ is shown in the figure 1.41

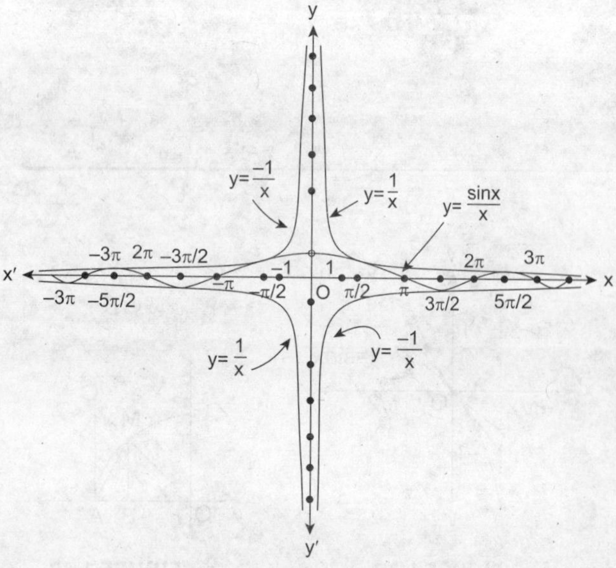

FIGURE 1.41

2. $\lim_{x\to 0} \frac{\tan x}{x} = 1 = \lim_{x\to 0} \frac{x}{\tan x}$

Proof: We have already proved $\sin x < x < \tan x$ for $x \in \left(0, \frac{\pi}{2}\right)$

Dividing each by $\tan x$ we get $\frac{\sin x}{\tan x} < \frac{x}{\tan x} < 1$

($\because \tan x > 0$)

$\Rightarrow \cos x < \frac{x}{\tan x} < 1$ ..... (ii)

$\because \lim_{x\to 0^+} \cos x = \lim_{x\to 0^+} 1 = 1$

$\therefore$ By Sandwich theorem, $\lim_{x\to 0^+} \frac{x}{\tan x} = 1$,

Also $\cos(-x) = \cos x$ and $\frac{(-x)}{\tan(-x)} = \frac{x}{\tan x}$

$\Rightarrow \cos(-x) < \frac{(-x)}{\tan(-x)} < 1$ for $x \in \left(0, \frac{\pi}{2}\right)$

$\Rightarrow \cos x < \frac{x}{\tan x} < 1$ for $x \in \left(-\frac{\pi}{2}, 0\right)$

$\therefore \lim_{x\to 0^-} \frac{x}{\tan x} = 1$

$\Rightarrow \lim_{x\to 0} \frac{\tan x}{x} = 1$

3. $\lim_{x\to 0} \frac{\sin^{-1} x}{x} = 1 = \lim_{x\to 0} \frac{x}{\sin^{-1} x}$

Proof: We know that $\sin x$ and $\sin^{-1}x$ are reflection of each other on line $y = x$ as shown below.

And $\lim_{x\to 0} \frac{\sin x}{x} = 1$ .....(i)

At point $P(x, \sin x)$, $\frac{\sin x}{x} = \frac{PL}{OL}$ .....(ii)

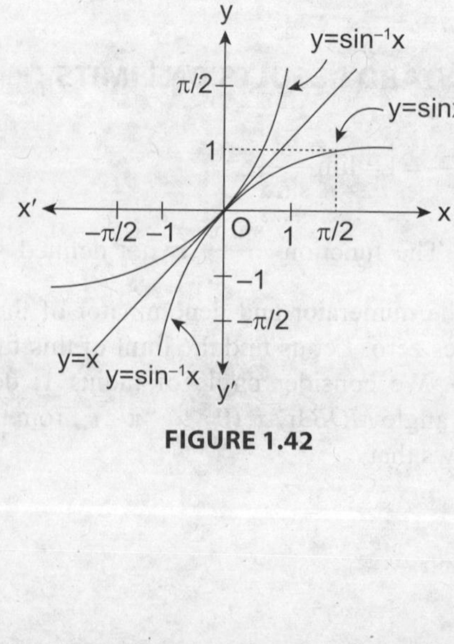

FIGURE 1.42

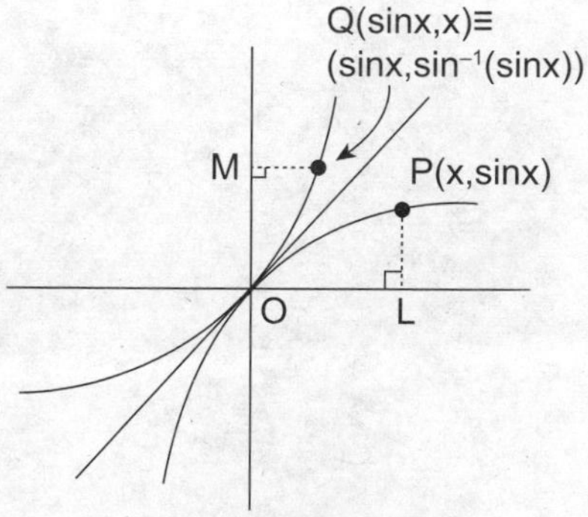

FIGURE 1.43

Now, $\frac{\sin x}{x} = \frac{PL}{OL} = \frac{MQ}{OM} = \frac{\sin x}{\sin\ (\sin\ )}$

Let $\sin x = y$, then $\frac{\sin x}{x} = \frac{y}{\sin^{-1}(y)}$ and $x \to 0$, $\sin x \to 0$

$\Rightarrow y \to 0$

$\therefore \lim\limits_{x\to 0}\frac{\sin x}{x} = \lim\limits_{y\to 0}\frac{y}{\sin y} = \lim\limits_{x\to 0}\frac{x}{\sin^{-1} x}$

$\therefore \lim\limits_{x\to 0}\frac{x}{\sin x} = 1 \qquad \left(\because \lim\limits_{x\to 0}\frac{\sin x}{x} = 1\right)$

$\Rightarrow \lim\limits_{x\to 0}\frac{\sin^{-1} x}{x} = 1$

4. $\lim\limits_{x\to 0}\frac{\tan^{-1} x}{x} = 1 = \lim\limits_{x\to 0}\frac{x}{\tan^{-1} x}$

Proof: $\tan x$ and $\tan^{-1}x$ are reflection of each other on line $y = x$ and intersect at $x = 0$

$\therefore \lim\limits_{x\to 0}\frac{\tan x}{x} = \lim\limits_{x\to 0}\frac{\tan^{-1} x}{x}$ (As proved in(3))

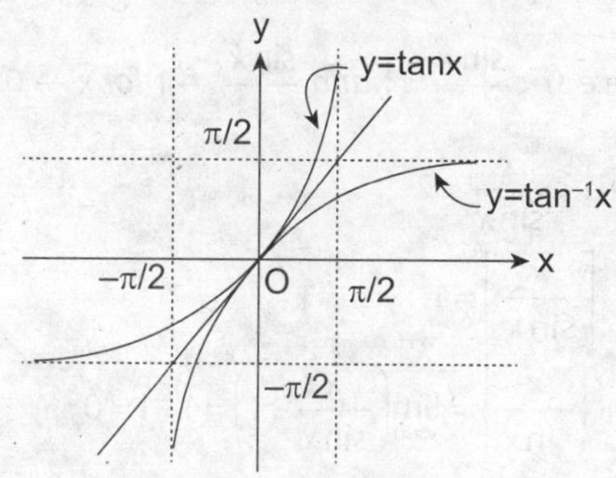

FIGURE 1.44

$\Rightarrow \lim\limits_{x\to 0}\frac{\tan^{-1} x}{x} = 1 \quad \Rightarrow \lim\limits_{x\to 0}\frac{x}{\tan^{-1} x} = 1$

REMARKS:

1. *Although* $\lim\limits_{x\to 0}\frac{\sin x}{x} = 1$ *yet* $0 < \frac{\sin x}{x} < 1$ *for* $x \in \left(-\frac{\pi}{2}, \frac{\pi}{2}\right) \sim \{0\}$ *as is clear from the graph given in figure 1.45*

For $x \in \left(0, \frac{\pi}{2}\right)$, $\sin x < x \Rightarrow \frac{\sin x}{x} < 1$

And for $x \in \left(-\frac{\pi}{2}, 0\right)$, $\sin x > x \Rightarrow \frac{\sin x}{x} < 1$ *as* $x < 0$

$\therefore 0 < \frac{\sin x}{x} < 1$ *for* $x \in \left(-\frac{\pi}{2}, \frac{\pi}{2}\right) \sim \{0\}$

$\Rightarrow \lim\limits_{x\to 0}\left\{\frac{\sin x}{x}\right\} = \lim\limits_{x\to 0}\frac{\sin x}{x} = 1$; *where {.} denotes fractional part function*

and $\lim\limits_{x\to 0}\left[\frac{\sin x}{x}\right] = 0$; *where [.] denotes integer part function*

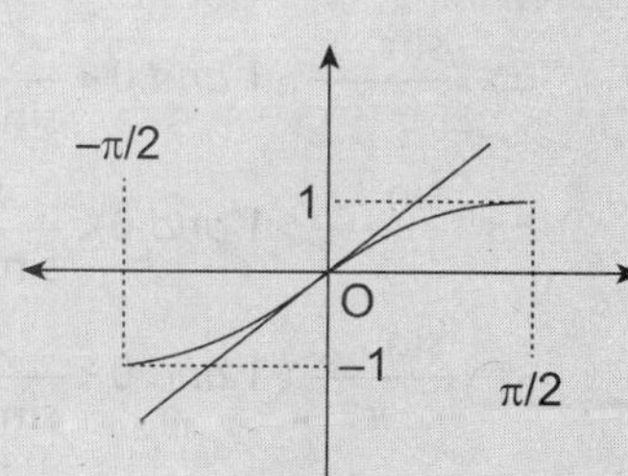

FIGURE 1.45

2. *Although* $\lim\limits_{x\to 0}\frac{\tan x}{x} = 1$, *yet* $\frac{\tan x}{x} > 1$ *for* $x \in \left(-\frac{\pi}{2}, \frac{\pi}{2}\right) \sim \{0\}$ *as i s clear from figure 1.46*

For $x \in \left(0, \frac{\pi}{2}\right)$, $\tan x > x \quad \Rightarrow \frac{\tan x}{x} > 1$

And for $x \in \left(-\frac{\pi}{2}, 0\right)$, $\tan x < x \quad \Rightarrow \frac{\tan x}{x} > 1$ *as* $x < 0$

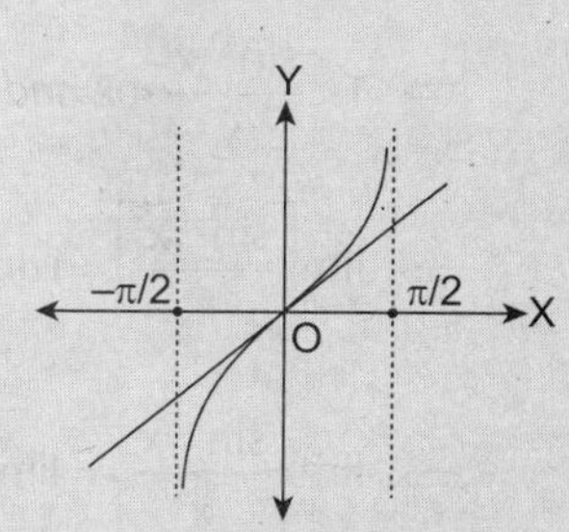

FIGURE 1.46

$$\therefore\quad 1<\frac{\tan x}{x}<2 \text{ for } x\in\left(-\frac{\pi}{2},\frac{\pi}{2}\right)\sim\{0\}$$

$$\Rightarrow\quad \lim_{x\to0}\left[\frac{\tan x}{x}\right]=1$$

$$\Rightarrow\quad \lim_{x\to0}\left\{\frac{\tan x}{x}\right\}=\frac{\tan x}{x}-1 \text{ for } x\in\left(-\frac{\pi}{2},\frac{\pi}{2}\right)\sim\{0\}$$

$$\Rightarrow\quad \lim_{x\to0}\left\{\frac{\tan x}{x}\right\}=\lim_{x\to0}\left(\frac{\tan x}{x}-1\right)=1-1=0$$

3. *Since* $0<\frac{\sin x}{x}<1$ *and* $\frac{\sin x}{x}\to1$ *for* $x\to0$

$$\Rightarrow\quad 1<\frac{x}{\sin x}<2$$

$$\Rightarrow\quad \left[\frac{x}{\sin x}\right]=1$$

$$\Rightarrow\quad \left\{\frac{x}{\sin x}\right\}=\lim_{x\to0}\left(\frac{x}{\sin x}-1\right)=1-1=0$$

4. *Since,* $\frac{\tan x}{x}>1$ *and* $\frac{\tan x}{x}\to1$ *for* $x\to0$

$$\Rightarrow\quad 1<\frac{\tan x}{x}<2 \text{ for } x\in\left(-\frac{\pi}{2},\frac{\pi}{2}\right)\sim\{0\}$$

$$\Rightarrow\quad 0<\frac{x}{\tan x}<1 \text{ for } x\in\left(-\frac{\pi}{2},\frac{\pi}{2}\right)\sim\{0\}$$

$$\Rightarrow\quad \lim_{x\to0}\left[\frac{x}{\tan x}\right]=0 \text{ and } \lim_{x\to0}\left\{\frac{x}{\tan x}\right\}=\lim_{x\to0}\left(\frac{x}{\tan x}\right)=1$$

5. *For* $x\in(0,1)$, $\sin^{-1}x>x$

$$\Rightarrow\quad \frac{\sin\ x}{}>1 \text{ and } 0<\frac{x}{\sin}<1 \text{ and for } x\in(-1,0),\ \sin^{-1}x<x$$

$$\Rightarrow\quad \frac{\sin^{-1}x}{x}>1 \text{ and } 0<\frac{x}{\sin^{-1}x}<1$$

$$\therefore\quad \frac{\sin^{-1}x}{x}>1 \text{ and } 0<\frac{x}{\sin^{-1}x}<1 \text{ for } x\in(-1,1)\sim\{0\}$$

Also $\frac{\sin^{-1}x}{x}$ *and* $\frac{x}{\sin^{-1}x}$ *have limit 1 as* $x\to0$

$$\Rightarrow\quad 1<\frac{\sin^{-1}x}{x}<2 \text{ and } 0<\frac{x}{\sin^{-1}x}<1 \text{ for } x\in(-1,1)\sim\{0\}$$

$$\Rightarrow\quad \lim_{x\to0}\left[\frac{\sin^{-1}x}{x}\right]=1 \text{ and } \lim_{x\to0}\left[\frac{x}{\sin^{-1}x}\right]=0$$

$$\Rightarrow\quad \lim_{x\to0}\left\{\frac{\sin^{-1}x}{x}\right\}=\lim_{x\to0}\left(\frac{x}{\sin^{-1}x}-1\right)=0 \text{ and } \lim_{x\to0}\left\{\frac{x}{\sin^{-1}x}\right\}=\lim_{x\to0}\left(\frac{x}{\sin^{-1}x}\right)=1$$

6. $\lim_{x\to 0}\sin x = \lim_{x\to 0}\tan x = 0$; $\lim_{x\to 0}\cos x = \lim_{x\to 0}\sec x = 1$

5. $\lim_{x\to 0}\dfrac{e^x - 1}{x} = 1$

Proof: Expansion for e^x is given by $e^x = 1 + \dfrac{x}{1!} + \dfrac{x^2}{2!} + \dfrac{x^3}{3!} + ...\infty$

$$\Rightarrow \frac{e^x - 1}{x} = \frac{1}{1!} + \frac{x}{2!} + \frac{x^2}{3!} + ...\infty$$

As $x \to 0^+$

$$\Rightarrow \frac{e^x - 1}{x} = \frac{1}{1!} + \frac{x}{2!} + \frac{x^2}{3!} + ... < 1 + x + x^2 + x^3 + ...\infty = \left\{1 + \left(\frac{x}{1-x}\right)\right\} \to 1 \text{ as } x \to 0^+$$

Also $\dfrac{e^x - 1}{x} = \dfrac{1}{1!} + \dfrac{x}{2!} + \dfrac{x^2}{3!} + ... > 1$ as $x \to 0^+$

$\to 1$ as $x \to 0^+$. Thus R.H.L. $= \lim_{x\to 0^+}\dfrac{e^x - 1}{x} = 1$.

Now for $x \to 0^-$, replacing x by $-y$ and taking limit $y \to 0+$, we get

$$\text{L.H.L} = \lim_{y\to 0^-}\frac{e^x - 1}{x} = \lim_{y\to 0^+}\frac{1 - e^y}{-ye^y}$$

$$= \lim_{y\to 0^+}\left(\frac{e^y - 1}{y}\right)\cdot\left(\frac{1}{e^y}\right) = (1)\,\frac{1}{(1)} = 1$$

As for $y \to 0^+$

$1 < e^y < 1 + y + y^2 + ...\infty$

$$\left(\because\ e^y = 1 + y + \frac{y^2}{2!} + \frac{y^3}{3!} + ...\right)$$

$$\Rightarrow 1 < e^y < \frac{1}{1-y}$$

$\therefore$ by Sandwich theorem $\lim_{y\to 0} e^y = 1$

6. $\lim_{x\to 0}\dfrac{a^x - 1}{x} = \ln a; a > 0$

Proof: $a^x = e^{\ln a^x}$ $\quad\left(\because e^{\ln f(x)} = f(x)\right)$

$= e^{(\ln a)x}$

$$\therefore \lim_{x\to 0}\frac{a^x - 1}{x} = \lim_{x\to 0}\frac{e^{x\ln a} - 1}{x} = \lim_{x\to 0}\frac{e^{x\ln a} - 1}{(\ln a)x}(\ln a)$$

$= (1)(\ln a)$ (by result (5))

7. $\lim_{x\to 0}(1 + x)^{1/x} = e$ and $\lim_{x\to\infty}\left(1 + \dfrac{1}{x}\right)^x = e$

Proof: As $x \to 0$

$\Rightarrow |x| < 1$

$$(1+x)^{1/x} = 1 + \frac{\left(\frac{1}{x}\right)(x)}{1!} + \frac{\left(\frac{1}{x}\right)\times\left(\frac{1}{x}-1\right)(x)^2}{2!} +$$

$\therefore$ By binomial theorem, $\dfrac{\left(\frac{1}{x}\right)\times\left(\frac{1}{x}-1\right)\left(\frac{1}{x}-2\right)(x)^3}{3!} + ...\infty$

$$= 1 + \frac{1}{1!} + \frac{(1)(1-x)}{2!} + \frac{(1)(1-x)(1-2x)}{3!} + ...\infty$$

$$\Rightarrow \lim_{x\to 0}(1+x)^{1/x} = 1 + \frac{1}{1!} + \frac{1}{2!} + \frac{1}{3!} + ...\infty = e$$

$$\left(\because e^x = 1 + \frac{x}{1!} + \frac{x^2}{2!} + \frac{x^3}{3!} + ...\infty\right)$$

Thus $\lim_{x\to 0}(1+x)^{1/x} = e$

$$\Rightarrow \lim_{x\to\infty}\left(1+\frac{1}{x}\right)^x = e$$

8. $\lim_{x\to 0}\dfrac{\ln(1+x)}{x} = 1$

Proof: Expression of $\ln(1 + x)$ is given by

$$\ln(1+x) = x - \frac{x^2}{2!} + \frac{x^3}{3!} - \frac{x^4}{4!} + ...\infty$$

$$\Rightarrow \frac{\ln(1+x)}{x} = 1 - \frac{x}{2!} + \frac{x^2}{3!} - \frac{x^3}{4!} + ...\infty$$

$\therefore$ For $x \to 0^+$

$$1 - x - x^2 - x^3...\infty < \frac{\ell n(1+x)}{x} < 1 + x^2 + x^4 + ...$$

$$\Rightarrow 1 - \left(\frac{x}{1-x}\right) < \frac{\ell n(1+x)}{x} < \frac{1}{1-x^2}$$

But $\lim_{x\to 0^+} 1 - \left(\dfrac{x}{1-x}\right) = 1$ and $\lim_{x\to 0^+}\dfrac{1}{1-x^2} = 1$

$\therefore \lim_{x\to 0^+}\dfrac{\ell n(1+x)}{x} = 1$ (by Sandwich theorem)

For $x \to 0^-$

$$1 < \frac{\ell n(1+x)}{x} < 1 - x + x^2 - x^3$$

$$\Rightarrow 1 < \frac{\ell n(1+x)}{x} < 1 + \frac{(-x)}{1-(-x)}$$

$$\Rightarrow 1 < \frac{\ell n(1+x)}{x} < 1 - \frac{x}{1+x} \text{ and } \lim_{x\to 0^-} 1 = 1, \lim_{x\to 0^-}\left(1 - \frac{x}{1+x}\right) = 1$$

$\therefore$ By Sandwich theorem, $\lim\limits_{x\to 0^-}\dfrac{\ell n(1+x)}{x}=1$

$\therefore$ L.H.L = R.H.L = 1

Aliter: we have $\lim\limits_{x\to 0}(1+x)^{1/x}=e$

$\Rightarrow \lim\limits_{x\to 0}\ln(1+x)^{1/x}=\ln\left(\lim\limits_{x\to 0}(1+x)^{1/x}\right)$

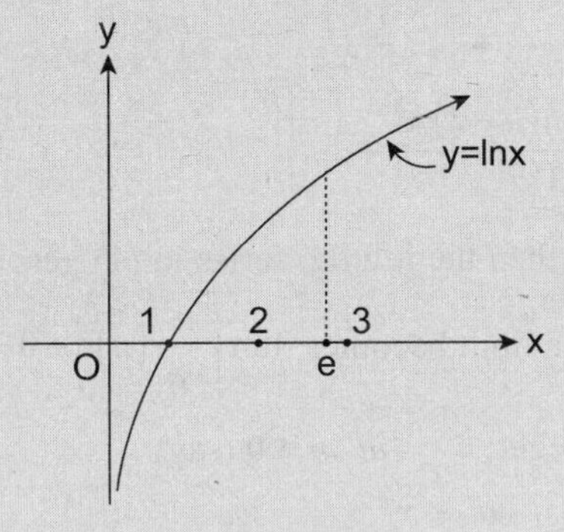

FIGURE 1.47

$\left[\begin{array}{l}\because \lim\limits_{x\to 0} f(g(x))=f\left(\lim\limits_{x\to a} g(x)\right)\\ \text{provided } f(x) \text{ is continuous at}\\ \text{limit of } g(x) \text{ at } x=a\end{array}\right]$

$=\ell n\ e=1$, as $ln(x)$ is continuous at $x=e$ as is clear from the graph of $\ell n\ x$ given above.

$\therefore \quad \lim\limits_{x\to 0}\ln(1+x)^{1/x}=1$ or $\lim\limits_{x\to 0}\dfrac{\ell n(1+x)}{x}=1$

9. $\lim\limits_{x\to\infty}\dfrac{\log_a(1+x)}{x}=\log_a e;\ a>0;\ a\neq 1$

Proof: By result (8), we have $\lim\limits_{x\to 0}\dfrac{\ln(1+x)}{x}=1$ ...(i)

$\therefore \quad \lim\limits_{x\to 0}\dfrac{\log_a(1+x)}{x}=\lim\limits_{x\to 0}\dfrac{\log_e(1+x).\log_a e}{x}$

$=\log_a e.\lim\limits_{x\to 0}\dfrac{\log_e(1+x)}{x}$

$=(\log_a e)$ (1) (By (i))

$=\log_a e$

10. $\lim\limits_{x\to a}\dfrac{x^n-a^n}{x-a}=n(a)^{n-1};n\in\mathbb{R}$

Proof: Let $x=a+h;\ h\to 0$

$\therefore\ x^n-a^n=(a+h)^n-a^n$

$=(a)^n\left[1+\dfrac{h}{a}\right]^n-a^n=(a)^n\left\{\left(1+\dfrac{h}{a}\right)^n-1\right\}$

$$= (a)^n\left\{\left(\left(1+n\left(\frac{h}{a}\right)+n\frac{(n-1)\left(\frac{h}{a}\right)^2}{2!}+\frac{n(n-1)(n-2)\left(\frac{h}{a}\right)^3}{3!}+.....\infty\right)-1\right\} = a^n\left\{n\frac{h}{a}+\frac{n(n-1)h^2}{2!(a)^2}+\frac{n(n-1)(n-2)(h)^3}{3!(a)^3}+....\right\}$$

$$\Rightarrow \lim_{x\to a}\frac{x^n-a^n}{x-a}=\lim_{h\to 0}\frac{(a+h)^n-a^n}{h}$$

$$= \lim_{x\to a}\frac{a^n}{h}\left\{n\frac{h}{a}+\frac{n(n-1)h^2}{2!\,a^2}+\frac{n(n-1)(n-2)h^3}{3!a^3}+.....\right\} \qquad ....(i)$$

Case (i): If n is a positive integer, then the infinite series in (1) gets terminated and hence the sum of finitely many infinitesimals is zero. Thus, the limit becomes $\lim_{h\to 0^-}\left(\frac{a^n}{a}(n)\right)+0=na^{n-1}$

Case (ii): When n is a negative integer; $n = -m.\ m > 0$ (say)

$$\therefore \lim_{x\to a}\frac{x^n-a^n}{x-a}=\lim_{x\to a}\frac{x^{-m}-a^{-m}}{x-a}=\lim_{x\to a}\frac{a^m-x^m}{x^m a^m(x-a)}$$

$$= \lim_{x\to a}\frac{(x^m-a^m)}{(x-a)x^m a^m}=-\lim_{x\to a}\frac{x^m-a^m}{x-a}.\lim_{x\to a}\frac{1}{x^m a^m}$$

$$= -(m)(a)^{m-1}.\frac{1}{a^{2m}}=(-m)a^{m-1-2m}=-ma^{-m-1}$$

$$= (n)a^{n-1}$$

Case (iii): $n=\dfrac{p}{q}$ (rational number)

$$\therefore \lim_{x\to a}\frac{x^{p/q}-(a)^{p/q}}{(x-a)}=\lim_{x\to a}\frac{(x^{1/q})^p-(a^{1/q})^p}{x-a}$$

Put $x^{1/q}=y$

$\Rightarrow x = y^q$; as $x\to a \Rightarrow y \to a^{1/q}$

$$\Rightarrow \lim_{y\to a^{\frac{1}{q}}}\frac{(y)^p-\left(a^{\frac{1}{q}}\right)^p}{y^q-\left(a^{\frac{1}{q}}\right)^q}=\lim_{y\to a^{\frac{1}{q}}}\frac{(y)^p-\left(a^{\frac{1}{q}}\right)^p}{\left(y-a^{\frac{1}{q}}\right)}\times\frac{\left(y-a^{\frac{1}{q}}\right)}{y^q-\left(a^{\frac{1}{q}}\right)^q}$$

$$= \frac{p\left(a^{\frac{1}{q}}\right)^{p-1}}{q\left(a^{\frac{1}{q}}\right)^{q-1}}=\frac{p}{q}\,(a)^{\frac{p}{q}-\frac{1}{q}-1+\frac{1}{q}}=\frac{p}{q}(a)^{\frac{p}{q}-1}=n(a)^{n-1}$$

$$\therefore \lim_{x\to a}\frac{x^n-a^n}{x-a}=n(a)^{n-1}\ \forall n\in\mathbb{Q}$$

REMARK:

The above standard limit (10) is also applicable when 'n' is an irrational number. But the proof is beyond the scope of this book.

ILLUSTRATION 24: Evaluate the following limits:

(i) $\lim_{x\to 0}\frac{\sin 3x}{x}$

(ii) $\lim_{x\to 0}\frac{\sin^{-1}x}{\tan x}$

(iii) $\lim_{x\to 0}\frac{\sin 3x-3\sin x}{x^3}$

(iv) $\lim_{x\to 0^-}\sqrt{\frac{1-\cos x}{x^2}}$

(v) $\frac{3\sin 3x+5\sin x-7\sin 2x}{x^2\sin x}$

(vi) $\lim_{x\to 0}\frac{\frac{\pi}{2}-\cos^{-1}x}{\tan^{-1}x}$

(vii) $\lim_{x\to 0}\frac{x-\sin^{-1}x}{\sin x}$

(viii) $\lim_{x\to 0}\frac{x^3-x^2\tan^{-1}x}{1-\cos x}$

(ix) $\lim_{x\to 0}\left[\frac{\sin^{-1}3x}{x}\right]$; where [.] is greatest integer function

(x) $\lim_{x\to 0}\left\{\frac{\tan^{-1}3x}{x}\right\}$; where {} is fractional part function

(xi) $\lim_{x\to 0}\left[\frac{\tan^{-1}x}{\sin^{-1}x}\right]$; where [] is greatest integer function

(xii) $\lim_{x\to 0}\left\{\frac{\sin^{-1}x}{\tan^{-1}x}\right\}$; where {.} is fractional part function

(xiii) $\lim_{x\to 0}\left[\frac{1-\cos x}{\sin x}\right]$; where [.] is greatest integer function

(xiv) $\lim_{x\to 0}\left[\frac{1-\cos x}{x\sin x}\right]$; where [.] is greatest integer function

SOLUTION: **(i)** $\lim_{x\to 0}\left(\frac{\sin 3x}{x}\right)=\lim_{x\to 0}3\left(\frac{\sin 3x}{3x}\right)=3(1)=3\quad\left[\text{as}\lim_{\theta\to 0}\frac{\sin\theta}{\theta}=1\right]$

(ii) $\lim_{x\to 0}\frac{\sin^{-1}x}{\tan x}=\lim_{x\to 0}\left(\frac{\sin^{-1}x}{x}\right)\left(\frac{x}{\tan x}\right)=(1)(1)=1$

(iii) $\lim\limits_{x\to 0}\dfrac{\sin 3x-3\sin x}{x^3}=\lim\limits_{x\to\infty}\dfrac{\left(3\sin x-4\sin^3 x\right)-3\sin x}{x^3}$

$=\lim\limits_{x\to 0}\dfrac{-4\sin^3 x}{x^3}=-4\lim\limits_{x\to 0}\left(\dfrac{\sin x}{x}\right)^3=-4(1)^3=-4$

(iv) $\lim\limits_{x\to 0^-}\sqrt{\dfrac{1-\cos x}{x^2}}=\lim\limits_{x\to 0^-}\sqrt{\dfrac{2\sin^2 x/2}{x^2}}=\lim\limits_{x\to 0^-}\sqrt{2}\left|\dfrac{\sin x/2}{x}\right|\left(\because\sqrt{x^2}=|x|\right)$

As $x\to 0^-\Rightarrow \sin x/2<0$ and $x<0\Rightarrow \dfrac{\sin x/2}{x}>0$

$=\lim\limits_{x\to 0^-}\sqrt{2}\left(\dfrac{\sin x/2}{x}\right)=\lim\limits_{x\to 0^-}\sqrt{2}\left(\dfrac{\sin x/2}{2x/2}\right)=\dfrac{\sqrt{2}}{2}(1)=\dfrac{1}{\sqrt{2}}$

(v) $\lim\limits_{x\to 0}\dfrac{3\sin 3x+5\sin x-7\sin 2x}{x^2\sin x}=\lim\limits_{x\to 0}\dfrac{3\left(3\sin x-4\sin^3 x\right)+5\sin x-7\left(2\sin x\cos x\right)}{x^2\sin x}$

$=\lim\limits_{x\to 0}\dfrac{9-12\sin^2 x+5-14\cos x}{x^2}=\lim\limits_{x\to 0}\dfrac{14(1-\cos x)-12\sin^2 x}{x^2}$

$=\lim\limits_{x\to 0}\dfrac{14\left(2\sin^2 x/2\right)-12\sin^2 x}{x^2}=\lim\limits_{x\to 0}\left\{\dfrac{28}{4}\left(\dfrac{\sin x/2}{x/2}\right)^2-12\left(\dfrac{\sin x}{x}\right)^2\right\}=7(1)^2-12(1)^2=-5$

(vi) $\lim\limits_{x\to 0}\dfrac{\left(\dfrac{\pi}{2}-\cos^{-1}x\right)}{\tan^{-1}x}=\lim\limits_{x\to 0}\dfrac{\sin^{-1}x}{\tan^{-1}x}$ $(\because \sin^{-1}x+\cos^{-1}x=\pi/2)$ $=\lim\limits_{x\to 0}\dfrac{\sin^{-1}x}{x}\cdot\dfrac{x}{\tan^{-1}x}=(1)(1)=1$

(vii) $\lim\limits_{x\to 0}\dfrac{x-\sin^{-1}x}{\sin x}=\lim\limits_{x\to 0}\dfrac{1-\dfrac{\sin^{-1}x}{x}}{\dfrac{\sin x}{x}}=\dfrac{1-1}{1}=0$

(viii) $\lim\limits_{x\to 0}\dfrac{x^3-x^2\tan^{-1}x}{1-\cos x}=\lim\limits_{x\to 0}\dfrac{x^3-x^2\tan^{-1}x}{2\sin^2(x/2)}$

$=\dfrac{1}{2}\lim\limits_{x\to 0}\dfrac{x^2}{\sin^2 x/2}\left(x-\tan^{-1}x\right)=\dfrac{4}{2}\lim\limits_{x\to 0}\left(\dfrac{x/2}{\sin x/2}\right)^2\left(x-\tan^{-1}x\right)=2(1)^2(0-0)=0$

(ix) $\lim\limits_{x\to 0}\left[\dfrac{\sin^{-1}3x}{x}\right]=\lim\limits_{x\to 0}\left[3\left(\dfrac{\sin^{-1}3x}{3x}\right)\right]$

$=\lim\limits_{\delta\to 0^+}\left[3(1+\delta)\right]=\lim\limits_{\delta\to 0^+}\left[3+3\delta\right]=3$

$\left(\begin{array}{l}\because \lim\limits_{x\to 0}\dfrac{\sin^{-1}3x}{3x}=\lim\limits_{y\to 0}\dfrac{\sin^{-1}y}{y};\ y=3x\\ =1 \text{ and } \dfrac{\sin^{-1}y}{y}>1 \text{ for } y\to 0\\ \Rightarrow \dfrac{\sin^{-1}y}{y}=1+\delta,\delta\to 0^+ \text{ for } y\to 0\end{array}\right)$

(x) $\lim\limits_{x\to 0}\left\{\dfrac{\tan^{-1}3x}{x}\right\}=\lim\limits_{x\to 0}\left\{3\left(\dfrac{\tan^{-1}3x}{3x}\right)\right\}$

$=\lim\limits_{\delta\to 0}\left\{3(1-\delta)\right\}$

$\left(\begin{array}{l}\because \dfrac{\tan^{-1}3x}{3x}<1 \text{ as } x\to 0 \text{ and } \dfrac{\tan^{-1}3x}{3x}\to 1\\ \Rightarrow \dfrac{\tan^{-1}3x}{3x}=1-\delta;\delta\to 0^+\end{array}\right)$

$$= \lim_{\delta\to 0}\{3-3\delta\} = \lim_{\delta\to 0}\left((3-3\delta)-[3-3\delta]\right)(\because \{x\} = x-[x])$$

$$= \lim_{\delta\to 0^+}(3-3\delta-2) = \lim_{\delta\to 0^+}(1-3\delta) = 1$$

(xi) $\lim_{x\to 0}\left[\frac{\tan^{-1}x}{\sin^{-1}x}\right] = \lim_{x\to 0}\left[\frac{\tan^{-1}x}{x}.\frac{x}{\sin^{-1}x}\right] = \lim_{x\to 0}\left[\frac{\tan^{-1}x}{x}.\frac{x}{\sin^{-1}x}\right]$

$= \text{Clearly } \frac{\tan^{-1}x}{\sin^{-1}x}\to 1, \text{ but } \frac{\tan^{-1}x}{\sin^{-1}x} < 1 \text{ for } x\in(-1,1)$

$\Rightarrow\ 0 < \frac{\tan^{-1}x}{\sin^{-1}x} < 1 \text{ for } x\in(-1,1) \Rightarrow \lim_{x\to 0}\left[\frac{\tan^{-1}x}{\sin^{-1}x}\right] = 0$

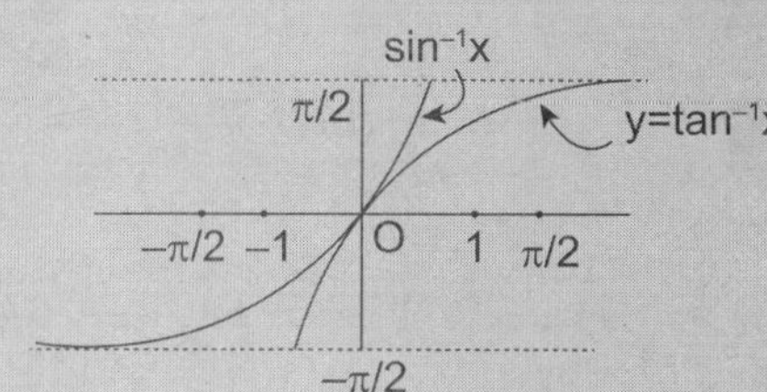

FIGURE 1.48

(xii) $\lim_{\to}\left\{\frac{\sin}{\tan}\right\}$

$\because\ \frac{\sin^{-1}x}{\tan^{-1}x} > 1 \text{ for } x\in(-1,1)$

and $\frac{\sin^{-1}x}{\tan^{-1}x} = \frac{\sin^{-1}x}{x}.\frac{x}{\tan^{-1}x}\to 1 \text{ for } x\to 0$

$\Rightarrow\ 1 < \frac{\sin^{-1}x}{\tan^{-1}x} < 2 \text{ for } x\in(-1, 1)$

$\Rightarrow\ \lim_{x\to 0}\left\{\frac{\sin^{-1}x}{\tan^{-1}x}\right\} = \lim_{x\to 0}\left(\frac{\sin x}{\tan^{-1}x} - \left[\frac{\sin^{-1}x}{\tan x}\right]\right) = \lim_{x\to 0}\frac{\sin^{-1}x}{\tan^{-1}x} - 1 = (1-1) = 0$

(xiii) $\lim_{x\to 0}\left[\frac{1-\cos x}{\sin x}\right] = \lim_{x\to 0}\left[\frac{2\sin^2 x/2}{2\sin(x/2)\cos(x/2)}\right] = \lim_{x\to 0}[\tan x/2]$

$\therefore$ L.H.L $= \lim_{x\to 0^-}[\tan x/2] = -1$ as $x\to 0^- \Rightarrow \tan(x/2)\to 0^-$

and R.H.L $= \lim_{x\to 0^+}[\tan x/2] = 0$ as $x\to 0^+ \Rightarrow \tan x/2\to 0^+$

$\therefore$ L.H.L ≠ R.H.L

$\therefore$ Limit does not exist

(xiv) $\lim_{x\to 0}\left[\frac{1-\cos x}{x\sin x}\right] = \lim_{x\to 0}\left[\frac{2\sin^2 x/2}{2x\sin\frac{x}{2}\cos\frac{x}{2}}\right] = \lim_{x\to 0}\left[\frac{\sin x/2}{x\cos x/2}\right] = \lim_{x\to 0}\left[\frac{\tan x/2}{2(x/2)}\right]$

$= \lim_{x\to 0}\left[\frac{1}{2}\left(\frac{\tan x/2}{x/2}\right)\right] = \lim_{\delta\to 0^+}\left[\frac{1}{2}(1+\delta)\right] = \lim_{\delta\to 0^+}\left[\frac{1}{2}+\frac{\delta}{2}\right] = 0$

$\left(\because \frac{\tan x/2}{x/2} > 1 \text{ and } \frac{\tan x/2}{x/2}\to 1 \text{ as } x\to 0\right)$

ILLUSTRATION 25: Evaluate the following limits:

(i) $\lim_{x\to 0}\frac{\sin 4x - \sin 2x}{x}$ **(ii)** $\lim_{x\to 0}\frac{\sin^3 x}{x}$

(iii) $\lim_{x\to 0}\frac{1-\cos x\sqrt{\cos 2x}}{x^2}$

SOLUTION: (i) $\lim_{x\to 0}\frac{\sin 4x-\sin 2x}{x}=\lim_{x\to 0}\frac{2\cos\left(\frac{4x+2x}{2}\right)\sin\left(\frac{4x-2x}{2}\right)}{x}=\lim_{x\to 0}\frac{2\cos(3x)\sin x}{x}=2(1)(1)=2$

(ii) $\lim_{x\to 0}\frac{\sin^3 x}{x}=\lim_{x\to 0}\left(\frac{3\sin x-\sin 3x}{4x}\right)=\frac{1}{4}\lim_{x\to 0}\left[\frac{3\sin x}{x}-\frac{3(\sin 3x)}{3x}\right]$

$\left[\begin{array}{l}\because \sin 3x=3\sin x-4\sin^3 x\\ \Rightarrow \sin^3 x=\dfrac{3\sin x-\sin 3x}{4}\end{array}\right]=\frac{1}{4}\lim_{x\to 0}\left[3(1)-3(1)\right]=\frac{1}{4}(0)=0$

(iii) $\lim_{x\to 0}\frac{1-\cos x\sqrt{\cos 2x}}{x^2}=\lim_{x\to 0}\frac{1-\cos x\sqrt{\cos 2x}}{x^2}\times\frac{1+\cos x\sqrt{\cos 2x}}{\left(1+\cos x\sqrt{\cos 2x}\right)}=\lim_{x\to 0}\frac{1-\cos^2 x\cos 2x}{x^2\left(1+\cos x\sqrt{\cos 2x}\right)}$

$=\lim_{x\to 0}\frac{1-\cos^2 x\left(2\cos^2 x-1\right)}{x^2\left[1+\cos x\sqrt{\cos 2x}\right]}=\lim_{x\to 0}\frac{1-2\cos^4 x+\cos^2 x}{x^2\left[1+\cos x\sqrt{\cos 2x}\right]}=-\lim_{x\to 0}\frac{\left(2\cos^4 x-\cos^2 x-1\right)}{x^2\left[1+\cos x\sqrt{\cos 2x}\right]}$

$=-\lim_{x\to 0}\frac{\left[2\cos^4 x-2\cos^2 x+\cos^2 x-1\right]}{x^2\left[1+\cos x\sqrt{\cos 2x}\right]}=-\lim_{x\to 0}\left[\frac{2\cos^2 x\left(\cos^2 x-1\right)+1\left(\cos^2 x-1\right)}{x^2\left[1+\cos x\sqrt{\cos 2x}\right]}\right]$

$=-\lim_{x\to 0}\left[\frac{\left(\cos^2 x-1\right)\left(2\cos^2 x+1\right)}{x^2\left[1+\cos x\sqrt{\cos 2x}\right]}\right]=\lim_{x\to 0}\left(\frac{\sin^2 x}{x^2}\right)\frac{\left[1+2\cos^2 x\right]}{1+\cos x\sqrt{\cos 2x}}=(1)^2\frac{[1+2]}{(1+1)}=\frac{3}{2}$

TEXTUAL EXERCISE–2: (SUBJECTIVE)

1. For $x \to 2$ determine the order of smallness, relative to the infinitesimal $\beta(x) = x - 2$ of the following infinitesimal:

   (a) $3(x-2)+2(x^2-4)$ (b) $\sqrt[3]{\sin \pi x}$

2. With the aid of the principle of substitution of equivalent quantities, find the limits of the following:

   (a) $\lim_{x\to 0}\frac{\log(\cos x)}{\sqrt[4]{1+x^2}-1}$ (b) $\lim_{x\to 0}\frac{\sin\sqrt[3]{x}\log(1+3x)}{[(\tan^{-1}\sqrt{x})^2(e^{5\sqrt[3]{x}}-1)}$

   (c) $\lim_{x\to 0}\frac{\log(1+\sin 4x)}{e^{\sin 5x}-1}$ (d) $\lim_{x\to 0}\frac{e^{\sin 3x}-1}{\log(1+\tan 2x)}$

   (e) $\lim_{x\to 0}\frac{\log(2-\cos 2x)}{\log^2[(\sin 3x)+1]}$

   (f) $\lim_{x\to 0}\frac{\sqrt{1+\sin 3x}-1}{\log(1+\tan 2x)}$

   (g) $\lim_{x\to 0}\frac{\log(1+2x-3x^2+4x^3)}{\log(1-x+2x^2-7x^3)}$

   (h) $\lim_{x\to 0}\frac{\sqrt{1+x^2}-1}{1-\cos x}$

   (i) $\lim_{x\to 0}\frac{3\sin x-x^2+x^3}{\tan x+2\sin^2 x+5x^4}$

   (j) $\lim_{x\to 0}\frac{(\sin x-\tan x)^7+(1-\cos 2x)^4+x^5}{7\tan^7 x+\sin^6 x+2\sin^5 x}$

   (k) $\lim_{x\to 0}\frac{1-\cos x+2\sin x-\sin^3 x-x^2+3x^4}{\tan^3 x-6\sin^2 x+x-5x^2}$

3. Evaluate the following limits and hence or otherwise comment over the following statements "sum of finite number of infinitesimals is always zero whereas sum of infinitely many infinitesimals may not neccessarily be zero."

   (a) $\lim_{n\to\infty}\left(\frac{1}{n^2}+\frac{2}{n^2}+.......+\frac{n-1}{n^2}\right)$

   (b) $\lim_{n\to\infty}\left(1-\frac{1}{7}+\frac{1}{49}-......+\frac{(-1)^{n-1}}{7^{n-1}}\right)$

(c) $\lim_{n\to\infty}\left(\frac{1}{n^2+1}+\frac{2}{n^2+1}+....+\frac{n-1}{n^2+1}\right)$

(d) $\text{Lt}_{n\to\infty}\frac{[x]+[2x]+[3x]+.....+[nx]}{n^2}$

4. Evaluate

(a) $\lim_{x\to\infty} f(x)$ if $\frac{2x-3}{x} < f(x) < \frac{2x^2+5x}{x^2}$

(b) $\lim_{x\to 0} f(x)$ if $\frac{\sin x}{x} < f(x) < \frac{\tan x}{x}$

5. Choosing two suitable functions and applying sandwich theorem prove the following (given that x is positive infinitesimal):

(a) $\lim_{x\to\infty} x+\frac{x^2}{2!}+\frac{x^3}{3!}+\frac{x^4}{4!}+....+\frac{x^n}{n!}=0$

(b) $\lim_{x\to\infty} x-\frac{x^2}{2}+\frac{x^3}{3}-\frac{x^4}{4}+\frac{x^5}{5}-....+(-1)^{n-1}\frac{x^n}{n}=0$

6. Examine whether the following limit exists or not. If exists, find the value of limit? (where [.] denotes greatest integer less than or equal to x and { } denotes fractional part of x).

(a) $\lim_{x\to 0}\left[\frac{\sin x}{x}\right]$ **(b)** $\lim_{x\to 0}\left[\frac{\sin^{-1} x}{x}\right]$.

(c) $\lim_{x\to 0}\left[\frac{\tan x}{x}\right]$ **(d)** $\lim_{x\to 0}\left[\frac{\ln(1+x)}{x}\right]$

(e) $\lim_{x\to 0}\left[\frac{e^x-1}{x}\right]$ **(f)** $\lim_{x\to 0}\left\{\frac{\tan^{-1} x}{x}\right\}$

7. $\lim_{x\to 0}\left[\frac{-2x}{\tan x}\right]$, where [.] denotes the greatest integer function.

8. The value of $\lim_{x\to 0}\left[\frac{|\sin x|}{|x|}\right]$, (where $|x|$, [.] denotes modulus and greatest integer function) is :

9. Evaluate the limit $\lim_{x\to 0}\left(\left[\frac{n\sin x}{x}\right]+\left[\frac{n\tan x}{x}\right]\right)$

Answer Keys

1. (a) Same order **(b)** $(x-2)$ is of higher order infinitesimal

2. (a) -2 **(b)** 3/5 **(c)** 4/5 **(d)** 3/2 **(e)** 2/9 **(f)** 3/4 **(g)** -2
(h) 1 **(i)** 3 **(j)** 1/2 **(k)** 2

3. (a) 1/2 **(b)** 7/8 **(c)** 1/2 **(d)** $x/2$

4. (a) 2 **(b)** 1

6. (a) 0 **(b)** 1 **(c)** 1 **(d)** does not exist R.H.L = 0, L.H.L = 1
(e) does not exist R.H.L = 1, L.H.L = 0 **(f)** 1

7. -2 **8.** 0 **9.** $2n-1$

TEXTUAL EXERCISE–2: (OBJECTIVE)

1. The $\lim_{x\to\infty} f(x)$ if $\frac{2x+8}{x} < f(x) < \frac{8x^2-6x}{4x^2}$, is

(a) 2
(b) 3
(c) 5
(d) None of these

2. $\lim_{x\to 1}\frac{\sqrt{1-\cos 2(x-1)}}{x-1}$

(a) exists and is equal to $\sqrt{2}$
(b) exists and is equal to $-\sqrt{2}$
(c) does not exist because $x-1\to 0$
(d) does not exist because left-hand limit is not equal to the right-hand limit.

3. $\lim_{x\to 0}\frac{\sin(\pi\cos^2 x)}{x^2}$ equals

(a) $-\pi$ (b) π
(c) $\frac{\pi}{2}$ (d) None of these

4. If $0<x<y$, then $\lim_{n\to\infty}(y^n+x^n)^{1/n}$ is equal to

(a) e (b) x
(c) y (d) None of these

5. The value of the $\lim\limits_{x\to 0}\dfrac{\cos(m+2)x-\cos mx}{\cos(m+4)x-\cos(m+2)x}$

(a) $\dfrac{m+1}{m+3}$ (b) $\dfrac{m-1}{m+3}$

(c) $\dfrac{m+1}{m-3}$ (d) None of these

6. A: $\lim\limits_{x\to\infty} x\sin\dfrac{1}{x}=1$

R: $\lim\limits_{y\to 0} y\sin\dfrac{1}{y}=1$

(a) A and R are both correct and R is correct explanation of A

(b) A and R are correct but R is not correct explanation of A

(c) A is correct R is wrong

(d) A and R are both wrong

7. $\lim\limits_{\theta\to 0^+}\dfrac{\sin\sqrt{\theta}}{\sqrt{\sin\theta}}$ is equal to

(a) 0 (b) 1

(c) – 1 (d) None of these

8. $\lim\limits_{x\to 0}\dfrac{\sin x^n}{(\sin x)^m}$ $(m<n)$ is equal to

(a) 1 (b) 0

(c) n/m (d) None of these

9. One value of k; for which $\lim\limits_{x\to 0}\dfrac{(e^x-1)^4}{\sin(x^2/k^2).\log\{1+(x^2/2)\}}=8$; is

(a) 1 (b) – 1

(c) 2 (d) 3

10. $\lim\limits_{n\to\infty}\dfrac{a^n+b^n}{a^n-b^n}$ (where $a>b>1$) is equal to

(a) – 1 (b) 1

(c) c (d) None of these

11. $\lim\limits_{x\to\infty}(1-a^4)^x\sin\dfrac{b}{(1-a^4)^x}$ $(a\in(-1,1),\ b\in\mathbb{R})$ is

(a) 0 (b) 1

(c) 2 (d) None of these

12. $\lim\limits_{x\to 1}\dfrac{\cos 2-\cos 2x}{x^2-|x|}=$

(a) 2 cos 2 (b) – 2 cos2

(c) 2 sin 2 (d) – 2 sin 2

13. If $\lim\limits_{x\to 0}(x^{-3}\sin 3x+ax^{-2}+b)$ exists and is equal to zero then:

(a) $a=-3$ and $b=0$

(b) $a=3$ and $b=9/2$

(c) $a=-3$ and $b=-9/2$

(d) $a=3$ and $b=-9/2$

14. If $\lim\limits_{x\to 0}\dfrac{\ln(3+x)-\ln(3-x)}{x}=k$, then value of k is

(a) $\dfrac{2}{3}$ (b) $-\dfrac{1}{3}$

(c) $-\dfrac{2}{3}$ (d) 0

15. Which of the following limits vanishes?

(a) $\lim\limits_{x\to\infty}x^{\frac{1}{4}}\sin\dfrac{1}{\sqrt{x}}$

(b) $\lim\limits_{x\to\pi/2}(1-\sin x).\tan x$

(c) $\lim\limits_{x\to\infty}\dfrac{2x^2+3}{x^2+x-5}\operatorname{sgn}(x)$

(d) $\lim\limits_{x\to 3^+}\dfrac{[x]^2-9}{x^2-9}$

where [ ] denotes greatest integer function.

16. $\lim\limits_{x\to 0}\dfrac{\sqrt{1-\cos 2x}}{\sqrt{2}x}$ is

(a) 1 (b) – 1

(c) zero (d) Does not exist

Answer Keys

1. (a)	**2.** (d)	**3.** (b)	**4.** (c)	**5.** (a)	**6.** (c)	**7.** (b)	**8.** (b)	**9.** (c)	**10.** (b)
11. (a)	**12.** (c)	**13.** (a)	**14.** (a)	**15.** (a,b,d)	**16.** (d)				

EVALUATION OF LIMITS

To evaluate a limit, we must always put the value where 'x' is approaching to the function. If we get a determinate form, then that value becomes the limit otherwise if an indeterminate form comes. Then apply one of the following methods to reduce the function so as to remove indeterminancy.

(i) Factorization
(ii) Rationalization or double rationalization
(iii) Substitution
(iv) Using standard limits
(v) Expansions of functions

1. By Using Factorization

The limits of some functions can be evaluated by factorizing both the numerator and the denominator. e.g., $\lim\limits_{x\to 2}\frac{x^2-4}{x-2}$ $= \lim\limits_{x\to 2}\frac{(x-2)(x+2)}{x-2} = \lim\limits_{x\to 2}(x+2)=4$, here we cancelled the factor $(x-2)$ as $x \to 2$

$\Rightarrow x \neq 2 \quad \Rightarrow x-2\neq 0$

ILLUSTRATION 26: Evaluate $\lim\limits_{x\to a}\frac{x^n - a^n}{x - a}$

SOLUTION: $\lim\limits_{x\to a}\frac{x^n - a^n}{x-a} = \lim\limits_{x\to a}\frac{(x-a)(x^{n-1}+x^{n-2}a+...+a^{n-1})}{(x-a)} = \lim\limits_{x\to a}(x^{n-1}+ax^{n-2}+.....+xa^{n-2}+a^{n-1})$

$= a^{n-1} + a^{n-1} + ... + a^{n-1}$ (n times) $= na^{n-1}$

ILLUSTRATION 27: Evaluate $\lim\limits_{x\to 1}\left[\frac{(2x-3)(\sqrt{x}-1)}{2x^2+x-3}\right]$

SOLUTION: Given $\lim\limits_{x\to 1}\left[\frac{(2x-3)(\sqrt{x}-1)}{2x^2+3x-2x-3}\right] = \lim\limits_{x\to 1}\left[\frac{(2x-3)(\sqrt{x}-1)}{(2x+3)(\sqrt{x}+1)(\sqrt{x}-1)}\right] = \lim\limits_{x\to 1}\left[\frac{(2x-3)}{(2x+3)(\sqrt{x}+1)}\right] = \frac{-1}{10}$

ILLUSTRATION 28: Evaluate $\lim\limits_{x\to 1}\left(\frac{x^7-2x^5+1}{x^3-3x^2+2}\right)$

SOLUTION: Since $x = 1$ makes both numerator and denominator zero, therefore $(x - 1)$ must be a factor of both.

$\therefore \lim\limits_{x\to 1}\left[\frac{x^6(x-1)+x^5(x-1)-x^4(x-1)-x^3(x-1)-x^2(x-1)-x(x-1)-(x-1)}{x^2(x-1)-2x(x-1)-2(x-1)}\right]$

$= \lim\limits_{x\to 1}\left[\frac{(x-1)(x^6+x^5-x^4-x^3-x^2-x-1)}{(x^2-2x-2)(x-1)}\right] = \lim\limits_{x\to 1}\left[\frac{(x^6+x^5-x^4-x^3-x^2-x-1)}{x^2-2x-2}\right] = \frac{-3}{-3} = 1$

ILLUSTRATION 29: Evaluate $\lim\limits_{x\to 2}\left[\frac{1}{x-2}-\frac{2(2x-3)}{x^3-3x^2+2x}\right]$

SOLUTION: We have $\lim\limits_{x\to 2}\left[\frac{1}{x-2}-\frac{2(2x-3)}{x^3-3x^2+2x}\right]$

$= \lim\limits_{x\to 2}\left[\frac{1}{x-2}-\frac{2(2x-3)}{x(x-1)(x-2)}\right] = \lim\limits_{x\to 2}\left[\frac{x(x-1)-2(2x-3)}{x(x-1)(x-2)}\right] = \lim\limits_{x\to 2}\left[\frac{x^2-5x+6}{x(x-1)(x-2)}\right]$

$= \lim\limits_{x\to 2}\left[\frac{(x-2)(x-3)}{x(x-1)(x-2)}\right] = \lim\limits_{x\to 2}\left[\frac{x-3}{x(x-1)}\right] = -\frac{1}{2}$

2. By Rationalization

"Meaning of rationalization is to remove radical signs from the given expression" which can be achieved either by multiplying the numerator and (or) denominator with their respective conjugates or by substitution or by application of formula $x^n - a^n$, we can evaluate the limits which involves radical signs.

e.g., $\sqrt{x}-\sqrt{a}=\dfrac{x-a}{\sqrt{x}+\sqrt{a}}$, $x^{1/3}-a^{1/3}=\dfrac{x-a}{x^{2/3}+x^{1/3}a^{1/3}+a^{2/3}}$

, $\lim\limits_{x\to 0}\dfrac{(x+p)^{1/k}-p^{1/k}}{x}$

$$\Rightarrow \lim_{z\to p^{1/k}}\frac{z-p^{1/k}}{z^k-(p^{1/k})^k}==\frac{1}{k(p^{1/k})^{k-1}}=\frac{1}{k(p)^{\frac{k-1}{k}}}$$

[putting $(x+p)^{1/k}=z$]

ILLUSTRATION 30: Evaluate the following:

(a) $\lim\limits_{x\to 0}\dfrac{\sqrt{1+x}-1}{(1+x)^{1/3}-1}$ **(b)** $\lim\limits_{x\to 0}\dfrac{\sqrt{1+x+x^2}-1}{x}$

SOLUTION: **(a)** By rationalization we get, Limit $=\lim\limits_{x\to 0}\dfrac{x\{(1+x)^{2/3}+(1+x)^{1/3}+1\}}{(\sqrt{1+x}+1).x}=3/2$

(b) By rationalization of numerator $=\lim\limits_{x\to 0}\dfrac{\sqrt{1+x+x^2}-1}{x}.\dfrac{\sqrt{1+x+x^2}+1}{\sqrt{1+x+x^2}+1}$

$$=\lim_{x\to 0}\frac{1+x+x^2-1}{x(\sqrt{1+x+x^2}+1)}=\lim_{x\to 0}\frac{x(1+x)}{x(\sqrt{1+x+x^2}+1)}=\lim_{x\to 0}\frac{(1+x)}{\sqrt{1+x+x^2}+1}=\frac{1}{2}$$

ILLUSTRATION 31: Evaluate $\lim\limits_{x\to 1^-}\dfrac{1-\sqrt{x}}{(\cos^{-1}x)^2}$

SOLUTION: Put $\cos^{-1}x=y$ and $x\to 1^-$ $\Rightarrow y\to 0^+$

$$\therefore \lim_{x\to 1^-}\frac{1-\sqrt{x}}{(\cos^{-1}x)^2}=\lim_{y\to 0^+}\frac{1-\sqrt{\cos y}}{y^2}$$

Now, by rationalizing numerator, we get $\lim\limits_{y\to 0^+}\dfrac{(1-\cos y)}{y^2(1+\sqrt{\cos y})}$

$$=\lim_{y\to 0}\frac{1-\cos y}{y^2}.\lim_{y\to 0}\frac{1}{1+\sqrt{\cos y}}=(1/2)\times(1/2)=1/4$$

ILLUSTRATION 32: $\lim\limits_{x\to 1}\dfrac{4-\sqrt{15x+1}}{2-\sqrt{3x+1}}$

SOLUTION: $\lim\limits_{x\to 1}\dfrac{4-\sqrt{15x+1}}{2-\sqrt{3x+1}}=\lim\limits_{x\to 1}\dfrac{(4-\sqrt{15x+1})(2+\sqrt{3x+1})(4+\sqrt{15x+1})}{(2-\sqrt{3x+1})(4+\sqrt{15x+1})(2+\sqrt{3x+1})}$

$$=\lim_{x\to 1}\frac{(15-15x)}{(3-3x)}\times\frac{2+\sqrt{3x+1}}{4+\sqrt{15x+1}}=\frac{5}{2}$$

ILLUSTRATION 33: Evaluate the following limits

(i) $\lim\limits_{x\to 0}\dfrac{\sqrt{1+x}-\sqrt{1-x}}{x}$ **(ii)** $\lim\limits_{x\to 1}\left[\dfrac{(2x-3)\left(\sqrt{x}-1\right)}{2x^2+x-3}\right]$

SOLUTION: **(i)** $\lim_{x\to 0}\left[\frac{\sqrt{1+x}-\sqrt{1-x}}{x}\times\frac{\sqrt{1+x}+\sqrt{1-x}}{\sqrt{1+x}+\sqrt{1-x}}\right]$

$$= \lim_{x\to 0}\left[\frac{(1+x)-(1-x)}{x\left(\sqrt{1+x}+\sqrt{1-x}\right)}\right] = \lim_{x\to 0}\left[\frac{2x}{x\left(\sqrt{1+x}+\sqrt{1-x}\right)}\right] = \lim_{x\to 0}\left[\frac{2}{\sqrt{1+x}+\sqrt{1-x}}\right] = \frac{2}{2} = 1$$

(ii) $\lim_{x\to 1}\left[\frac{(2x-3)\left(\sqrt{x}-1\right)}{2x^2+x-3}\right] = \lim_{x\to 1}\left[\frac{(2x-3)\left(\sqrt{x}-1\right)}{(2x+3)(x-1)}\right]$

$$= \lim_{x\to 1}\left[\frac{(2x-3)\left(\sqrt{x}-1\right)}{(2x+3)\left(\sqrt{x}-1\right)\left(\sqrt{x}+1\right)}\right] = \lim_{x\to 1}\left[\frac{2x-3}{(2x+3)\left(\sqrt{x}+1\right)}\right] = \frac{-1}{(5)(2)} = -\frac{1}{10}$$

ILLUSTRATION 34: Evaluate the following limits:

(i) $\lim_{x\to 2}\frac{\sqrt{6-x}-2}{(x-2)}$ **(ii)** $\lim_{x\to 2}\frac{(x-2)}{(6+x)^{1/3}-2}$

SOLUTION: **(i)** $\lim_{x\to 2}\frac{\sqrt{6-x}-2}{(x-2)}\times\frac{\sqrt{6-x}+2}{\sqrt{6-x}+2}$ [rationalizing the numerator]

$$= \lim_{x\to 2}\frac{(6-x)-4}{(x-2)\left[\sqrt{6-x}+2\right]} = \lim_{x\to 2}\frac{(2-x)}{(x-2)\left[\sqrt{6-x}+2\right]} = \frac{-1}{\sqrt{6-2}+2} = \frac{-1}{2+2} = \frac{-1}{4}$$

(ii) $\lim_{x\to 2}\frac{(x-2)}{(6+x)^{1/3}-2} = \lim_{x\to 1}\frac{(x-2)}{(6+x)^{1/3}-(8)^{1/3}}$

$$= \lim_{x\to 2}\frac{(x-2)}{\left[\frac{(6+x-8)}{(6+x)^{2/3}+(6+x)^{1/3}(8)^{1/3}+(8)^{2/3}}\right]}$$

$$= \lim_{x\to 2}(x-2)\frac{\left[(6+x)^{2/3}+(6+x)^{1/3}(2)+(8)^{2/3}\right]}{(x-2)}$$

$$= (8)^{2/3} + (8)^{1/3}(2) + (8)^{2/3} = 4 + 4 + 4 = 12$$

$$\left[\because\ a^{1/3}-b^{1/3} = \frac{(a-b)}{(a^{2/3}+a^{1/3}b^{1/3}+b^{2/3})}\right]$$

ILLUSTRATION 35: Evaluate the following limits by using the method of rationalization:

(i) $\lim_{x\to 5}\frac{\sqrt{x+20}-\sqrt{2x+15}}{\sqrt{x}-\sqrt{5}}$ **(ii)** $\lim_{x\to 5}\frac{(x+22)^{1/3}-3}{\sqrt{x+4}-3}$

SOLUTION: **(i)** $\lim_{x\to 5}\frac{(x+20)-(2x+15)}{(x-5)}\times\frac{\left(\sqrt{x}+\sqrt{5}\right)}{\left(\sqrt{x+20}+\sqrt{2x+15}\right)}$

$$\lim_{x\to 5}\frac{(5-x)}{(x-5)}\times\frac{\left(\sqrt{x}+\sqrt{5}\right)}{\left(\sqrt{x+20}+\sqrt{2x+15}\right)} = \frac{(-1)\left[2\sqrt{5}\right]}{(5+5)} = \frac{-2\sqrt{5}}{10} = \frac{-\sqrt{5}}{5} = \frac{-1}{\sqrt{5}}$$

(ii) $\lim_{x\to 5}\frac{(x+22)^{1/3}-(3)}{\sqrt{x+4}-3}=\lim_{x\to 5}\frac{(x+22)^{1/3}-(27)^{1/3}}{\sqrt{x+4}-\sqrt{9}}$

$$=\lim_{x\to 5}\frac{(x+22-27)}{\left[(x+22)^{2/3}+(x+22)^{1/3}(27)^{1/3}+(27)^{2/3}\right]}\times\frac{\sqrt{x+4}+\sqrt{9}}{(x+4-9)}$$

$$=\lim_{x\to 5}\frac{(x-5)}{[9+9+9]}\frac{(6)}{(x-5)}=\frac{6}{27}=\frac{2}{9}$$

ILLUSTRATION 36: Evaluate the following limits by using rationalization method

(i) $\lim_{x\to 64}\frac{x^{1/6}-2}{x^{1/3}-4}$ (ii) $\lim_{x\to 1}\frac{\sqrt[3]{x^2+x+6}-\sqrt[3]{x+7}}{\sqrt{x+1}-\sqrt{2}}$

SOLUTION: (i) $\lim_{x\to 64}\frac{x^{1/6}-2}{x^{1/3}-4}=\lim_{x\to 64}\frac{x^{1/6}-(64)^{1/6}}{x^{1/3}-(64)^{1/3}}$

$$=\lim_{x\to 64}\frac{(x-64)}{\left[x^{5/6}+x^{4/6}(64)^{1/6}+x^{3/6}(64)^{2/6}+x^{2/6}(64)^{3/6}+x^{1/6}(64)^{4/6}+(64)^{5/6}\right]}\times\frac{\left(x^{2/3}+x^{1/3}(64)^{1/3}+(64)^{2/3}\right)}{(x-64)}$$

$$\left[\begin{array}{l}\because a^{1/k}-b^{1/k}=\dfrac{(a-b)}{\left(a^{1-\frac{1}{k}}+a^{1-\frac{2}{k}}.b^{\frac{1}{k}}+a^{1-\frac{3}{k}}.b^{\frac{2}{k}}+....+b^{1-\frac{1}{k}}\right)}\\ \text{where } k\in\mathbb{Z}^+ \text{ and } k\ge 2\end{array}\right]$$

$$=\lim_{x\to 64}\frac{\left[x^{2/3}+x^{1/3}(64)^{1/3}+(64)^{2/3}\right]}{\left[x^{5/6}+x^{4/6}(64)^{1/6}+x^{3/6}(64)^{2/6}+x^{2/6}(64)^{3/6}+x^{1/6}(64)^{4/6}+(64)^{5/6}\right]}$$

$$=\frac{16+(4)(4)+16}{[32+(16)(2)+(8)(4)+(4)(8)+(2)(16)+32]}=\frac{48}{32\times 6}=\frac{3}{2\times 6}=\frac{1}{4}$$

(ii) $\lim_{x\to 1}\frac{\sqrt[3]{x^2+x+6}-\sqrt[3]{x+7}}{\sqrt{x+1}-\sqrt{2}}$

$$=\lim_{x\to 1}\frac{(x^2+x+6)-(x+7)}{\left[(x^2+x+6)^{2/3}+(x^2+x+6)^{1/3}(x+7)^{1/3}+(x+7)^{2/3}\right]}\times\frac{\left[\sqrt{(x+1)}+\sqrt{(2)}\right]}{(x+1-2)}$$

$$=\lim_{x\to 1}\frac{(x^2-1)\left(\sqrt{x+1}+\sqrt{2}\right)}{\left[(x^2+x+6)^{2/3}+(x^2+x+6)^{1/3}(x+7)^{1/3}+(x+7)^{2/3}\right](x-1)}$$

$$=\frac{(2)\left[2\sqrt{2}\right]}{4+(2)(2)+4}=\frac{4\sqrt{2}}{12}=\frac{\sqrt{2}}{3}$$

3. By Using Substitution

In this method we put $x = a + h$ and $h \to 0$ e.g.,

$$\lim_{x\to 3}\frac{(x^2-9)}{(x-3)} = \lim_{h\to 0}\frac{\left[(3+h)^2-9\right]}{(3+h)-3} = \lim_{h\to 0}\frac{\left[9+h^2+6h-9\right]}{h} = \lim_{h\to 0}\frac{\left[h^2+6h\right]}{h} = \lim_{h\to 0}(h+6) = 6$$

If we need to find LH.L and R.H.L, then while evaluating L.H.L we put $x = a - h$ and $h \to 0^+$ and while evaluating R.H.L, we put $x = a + h$ and $h \to 0^+$ e.g., $\lim_{x\to 2}[x-2]$; where [.] is gint function, then,

$$\text{L.H.L} = \lim_{h\to 0^+}\left[(2-h)-2\right] = \lim_{h\to 0^+}[-h] = -1$$

($\because 0 < h < 1 \Rightarrow -1 < -h < 0 \Rightarrow [-h] = -1$) and

$$\text{R.H.L} = \lim_{h\to 0^+}\left[(2+h)-2\right] = \lim_{h\to 0^+}[h] = 0$$

($\because 0 < h < 1 \Rightarrow [h] = 0$). Thus above limit does not exist.

ILLUSTRATION 37: **(i)** $\lim_{x\to 3}\frac{x^4-81}{x-3}$

(ii) $\lim_{x\to 5}\frac{|x-5|}{(x-5)}$

(iii) $\lim_{x\to 12}[x-12]$; where [.] gint function

(iv) $\lim_{x\to \frac{\pi}{4}}[\tan x]$; [.] is gint function

(v) $\lim_{x\to\left(\frac{5\pi}{4}\right)^-}\{\tan x\}$; {.} is fractional part function

(vi) $\lim_{x\to \pi/3}[\{\tan x\}]$; where {.} and [.] are fractional part and gint function respectively

SOLUTION: **(i)** $\lim_{x\to h}\frac{(3+h)^4-81}{(3+h)-3}$

$$= \lim_{x\to h}\frac{\left[{}^4C_0(3)^4(h)^0+{}^4C_1(3)^3(h)+{}^4C_2(3)^2h^2+{}^4C_3(3)h^3+{}^4C_4(3)^0h^4\right]-81}{(h)}$$

$$= \lim_{x\to h}\left[{}^4C_1(3)^3+{}^4C_2(3)^2h+{}^4C_3(3)h^2+{}^4C_4h^3\right] = {}^4C_1(3)^3 = 4(27) = 108$$

(ii) $\lim_{x\to 5}\frac{|x-5|}{(x-5)}$

$$\text{L.H.L.} = \lim_{h\to 0^+}\frac{|(5-h)-5|}{(5-h-5)} = \lim_{h\to 0^+}\frac{|-h|}{-h} = \lim_{h\to 0^+}\frac{h}{-h} = -1$$

$$\text{And R.H.L} = \lim_{h\to 0^+}\frac{|(5+h)-5|}{(5+h-5)} = \lim_{h\to 0^+}\frac{|h|}{h} = \lim_{h\to 0^+}\frac{h}{h} = 1$$

$\therefore$ Limit does not exist.

(iii) $\lim_{h\to 12}[x-12]$

$$\text{L.H.L} = \lim_{x\to 12^-}[x-12] = \lim_{h\to 0^+}\left[(12-h)-12\right] = \lim_{h\to 0^+}[-h] = -1$$

$$\text{R.H.L} = \lim_{x\to 12^+}[x+12] = \lim_{h\to 0^+}\left[(12+h)-12\right] = \lim_{h\to 0^+}[h] = 0$$

$\therefore$ Limit does not exist.

(iv) $\lim\limits_{x\to\pi/4}[\tan x]$

L.H.L. $= \lim\limits_{x\to(\pi/4)^-}[\tan x] = \lim\limits_{h\to 0^+}\left[\tan\left(\frac{\pi}{4}-h\right)\right] = 0 \quad \left[\because\ 0<\tan\left(\frac{\pi}{4}-h\right)<1\right]$

R.H.L. $= \lim\limits_{x\to(\pi/4)^+}[\tan x] = \lim\limits_{h\to 0^+}\left[\tan\left(\frac{\pi}{4}+h\right)\right] = 1 \quad \left[\because\ 1<\tan\left(\frac{\pi}{4}+h\right)<2\right]$

$\therefore$ Limits does not exist.

(v) $\lim\limits_{x\to\left(\frac{5\pi}{4}\right)^-}\{\tan x\}$

$= \lim\limits_{x\to\left(\frac{5\pi}{4}\right)^-}\{\tan x\} = \lim\limits_{h\to 0^+}\left\{\tan\left(\frac{5\pi}{4}-h\right)\right\}$ $\left[\begin{array}{l}\because\ 0<\tan\left(\frac{5\pi}{4}-h\right)<1 \\ \Rightarrow \left\{\tan\left(\frac{5\pi}{4}-h\right)\right\} = \tan\left(\frac{5\pi}{4}-h\right)\end{array}\right]$

$= \lim\limits_{h\to 0^+}\tan\left(\frac{5\pi}{4}-h\right) = \tan\left(\frac{5\pi}{4}-0\right) = 1$

(vi) $\lim\limits_{x\to\pi/3}[\{\tan x\}]$

L.H.L. $= \lim\limits_{x\to(\pi/3)^-}[\{\tan x\}] = \lim\limits_{h\to 0^+}\left[\left\{\tan\left(\frac{\pi}{3}-h\right)\right\}\right]$

$$\left[\begin{array}{l}\because\ 1<\tan\left(\frac{\pi}{3}-h\right)<\sqrt{3}=1.732 \\ \Rightarrow \left\{\tan\left(\frac{\pi}{3}-3\right)\right\} = \tan\left(\frac{\pi}{3}-h\right)-1 \\ \&\ 0<\tan\left(\frac{\pi}{3}-h\right)-1<\left(\sqrt{3}-1\right)<1\end{array}\right]$$

$= \lim\limits_{h\to 0^+}\left[\tan\left(\frac{\pi}{3}-h\right)-1\right] = 0$

And R.H.L. $\lim\limits_{x\to\left(\frac{\pi}{3}\right)^+}[\{\tan x\}] = \lim\limits_{h\to 0^+}\left[\left\{\tan\left(\frac{\pi}{3}+h\right)\right\}\right]$

$= \lim\limits_{h\to 0^+}\left[\tan\left(\frac{\pi}{3}+h\right)-1\right] = 0 \Rightarrow \lim\limits_{x\to\frac{\pi}{3}}[\{\tan x\}] = 0$

ILLUSTRATION 38: Find the value of the following limits:

(a) $\lim\limits_{x\to y}\dfrac{\cos x-\cos y}{x-y}$ **(b)** $\lim\limits_{x\to -1^+}\dfrac{\sqrt{\pi}-\sqrt{\cos^{-1}x}}{\sqrt{x+1}}$

SOLUTION: **(a)** $\lim\limits_{x\to y}\dfrac{\cos x-\cos y}{x-y} = \lim\limits_{h\to 0}\dfrac{\cos(y+h)-\cos y}{h}$ (putting $x = y + h$)

$= -\lim\limits_{h\to 0}\dfrac{\sin(y+h/2)\sin h/2}{h/2} = -\sin y$

(b) Let the given limit $= \lim_{\theta\to\pi^-} \frac{\sqrt{\pi}-\sqrt{\theta}}{\sqrt{1+\cos\theta}}$

By putting $\cos^{-1}x = \theta$, we get, $x = \cos\theta$

$$= \lim_{\theta\to\pi} \frac{\pi-\theta}{\sqrt{1+\cos\theta}}\frac{1}{\sqrt{\pi}+\sqrt{\theta}} = \lim_{\theta\to\pi} \frac{\pi-\theta}{\sqrt{2\cos^2\theta/2}}.\lim_{\theta\to\pi}\frac{1}{\sqrt{\pi}+\sqrt{\theta}}$$

$$= \lim_{k\to 0^-} \frac{-k}{\sqrt{2\cos^2[(\pi/2)+(k/2)]}}.\frac{1}{2\sqrt{\pi}} \quad \text{Putting } \theta = \pi + k;\ k \to 0^-$$

$$= \lim_{k\to 0} \frac{k/2}{\frac{\sqrt{2}}{2}\sin\frac{k}{2}}.\frac{1}{2\sqrt{\pi}} = \frac{1}{\sqrt{2\pi}}$$

ILLUSTRATION 39: Solve $\lim_{\theta\to\pi/4}\left[\frac{\sqrt{2}-\sin\theta-\cos\theta}{(4\theta-\pi)^2}\right]$

SOLUTION: Given $\lim_{\theta\to\pi/4}\left[\frac{\sqrt{2}-\sin\theta-\cos\theta}{(4\theta \quad \pi)}\right]$; Put $\theta = \pi/4 + h$;

$$= \lim_{h\to 0}\left[\frac{\sqrt{2}(2\sin^2 h/2)}{16h^2}\right] = \lim_{h\to 0}\frac{\sqrt{2}}{8}\left(\frac{\sin h/2}{h/2}\right)^2.\frac{1}{4} = \frac{1}{16\sqrt{2}}$$

ILLUSTRATION 40: Evaluate the following limits;

(a) $\lim_{\theta\to-\pi/4}\frac{\cos\theta+\sin\theta}{\theta+\pi/4}$

(b) $\lim_{n\to\infty} n^2\sqrt{\left(1-\cos\frac{1}{n}\right)\sqrt{\left(1-\cos\frac{1}{n}\right)\sqrt{\left(1-\cos\frac{1}{n}\right)\ldots\ldots\infty}}}$

SOLUTION: **(a)** Put $\theta + \pi/4 = h$ or $\theta = -\pi/4 + h$; $\lim_{h\to 0}\frac{\cos(-\frac{\pi}{4}+h)+\sin(-\frac{\pi}{4}+h)}{h}$

$$= \lim_{h\to 0}\frac{\cos(\pi/4-h)-\sin(\pi/4-h)}{h} = \lim_{h\to 0}\frac{\cos(\pi/4-h)-\cos(\pi/4+h)}{h}$$

$$= \lim_{h\to 0}\frac{2\sin(\pi/4).\sin h}{h} = \sqrt{2}$$

(b) Put $n = 1/x$; $= \lim_{x\to 0}\frac{\sqrt{(1-\cos x)\sqrt{(1-\cos x)\sqrt{(1-\cos x)\ldots..\infty}}}}{x^2}$

Let, $A = \sqrt{(1-\cos x)\sqrt{(1-\cos x)\ldots..\infty}}$

$A = \sqrt{(1-\cos x)A}$ $\Rightarrow A^2 = (1-\cos x)A \Rightarrow A = 1-\cos x$

Now, Limit $= \lim_{x\to 0}\frac{A}{x^2} = \lim_{x\to 0}\frac{1-\cos x}{x^2} = \lim_{x\to 0}\frac{2\sin^2 x/2}{x^2} = \frac{1}{2}$

By Using Standard Limits

Application of standard limits $\lim_{x\to 0}\frac{\sin x}{x}=1$

Transformation: If $\lim_{x\to a}\frac{f(x)}{g(x)}=k$, then $\lim_{x\to a}\frac{\sin f(x)}{g(x)}=k$;

where $f(x), g(x)\to 0$ as $x\to a$

Proof: $\lim_{x\to a}\frac{\sin f(x)}{g(x)}=\lim_{x\to a}\frac{\sin f(x)}{f(x)}\cdot\frac{f(x)}{g(x)}$

$=\lim_{x\to a}\frac{\sin f(x)}{f(x)}.\lim_{x\to a}\frac{f(x)}{g(x)}=(1)\,(k)=k$

[as $f(x)\to 0$ as $x\to a\Rightarrow\frac{\sin f(x)}{f(x)}\to 1$ as $x\to a$]

ILLUSTRATION 41: Evaluate $\lim_{x\to 0}\frac{\sin x}{5x}$

SOLUTION: $\lim_{x\to 0}\frac{\sin x}{5x}=\lim_{x\to 0}\frac{\sin x}{x}\cdot\frac{x}{5x}=\lim_{x\to 0}\frac{\sin x}{x}.\lim_{x\to 0}\frac{x}{5x}=(1)\left(\frac{1}{5}\right)=\frac{1}{5}$

ILLUSTRATION 42: Evaluate $\lim_{x\to 0}\frac{1-\cos x}{5x^2}$

SOLUTION: $\lim_{x\to 0}\frac{1-\cos x}{5x^2}=\lim_{x\to 0}\frac{2\sin^2 x/2}{5x^2}=\frac{2}{5}\lim_{x\to 0}\left[\frac{\sin x/2}{2(x/2)}\right]^2=\frac{2}{5}\left(\frac{1}{4}\right)(1)^2=\frac{1}{10}$

ILLUSTRATION 43: Evaluate $\lim_{x\to 0}\frac{3x-\sin 2x}{5x}$

SOLUTION: $\lim_{x\to 0}\left(\frac{3x-\sin 2x}{5x}\right)=\lim_{x\to 0}\left[\frac{3x}{5x}-\frac{\sin 2x}{5x}\right]=\lim_{x\to 0}\left(\frac{3}{5}-\frac{\sin 2x}{2x}\times\frac{2x}{5x}\right)=\frac{3}{5}-(1)\left(\frac{2}{5}\right)=\frac{1}{5}$.

ILLUSTRATION 44: Evaluate $\lim_{x\to 0}\frac{\cos 5x-\cos 3x}{3x^2}$

SOLUTION: $\lim_{x\to 0}\frac{2\sin(4x)\sin(-x)}{3x^2}=\lim_{x\to 0}\left(\frac{-2}{3}\right)\left(\frac{\sin 4x}{x}\right)\left(\frac{\sin x}{x}\right)=\lim_{x\to 0}\left(\frac{-2}{3}\right)(4)\left(\frac{\sin 4x}{4x}\right)\left(\frac{\sin x}{x}\right)$

$=-\frac{2}{3}(4)(1)(1)=-\frac{8}{3}$

ILLUSTRATION 45: Evaluate the following limits:

(i) $\lim_{x\to 0^+}\frac{\sin\{x\}}{\{x\}}$ **(ii)** $\lim_{x\to 0^-}\frac{\sin\{x\}}{\{x\}}$

(iii) $\lim_{x\to 0^+}\frac{\sin[x]}{[x]}$ **(iv)** $\lim_{x\to 0^-}\frac{\sin[x]}{[x]}$

and hence comment on $\lim_{x\to 0}\frac{\sin\{x\}}{\{x\}}$ and $\lim_{x\to 0}\frac{\sin[x]}{[x]}$; where $[x]$ and $\{x\}$ are integer part and fractional parts of x respectively.

SOLUTION: **(i)** $\lim_{x\to 0^+}\frac{\sin\{x\}}{\{x\}}$

Since $x\to 0^+$

$\Rightarrow x\in(0, 1)$ $\Rightarrow \{x\}=x$

$\therefore \lim_{x\to 0^+}\frac{\sin\{x\}}{\{x\}}=\lim_{x\to 0^+}\frac{\sin x}{x}=1$

(ii) $\lim\limits_{x\to 0^-}\dfrac{\sin\{x\}}{\{x\}}$, Since $x \to 0^-$

$\Rightarrow x \in (-1, 0)$ $\qquad \Rightarrow [x] = -1 \qquad \Rightarrow \{x\} = x+1$

$\therefore \quad \lim\limits_{x\to 0^-}\dfrac{\sin\{x\}}{\{x\}} = \lim\limits_{x\to 0^-}\dfrac{\sin(x+1)}{(x+1)} = \sin 1$

(iii) $\lim\limits_{x\to 0^+}\dfrac{\sin[x]}{[x]}$

As $x \to 0^+$

$\Rightarrow x \in (0, 1)$ $\qquad \Rightarrow [x] = 0$

$\therefore \ \sin[x] = 0$ $\qquad \therefore \quad \lim\limits_{x\to 0^+}\dfrac{\sin[x]}{[x]} = \lim\limits_{x\to 0^+}\dfrac{0}{0}$ which is not defined.

(iv) $\lim\limits_{x\to 0^-}\dfrac{\sin[x]}{[x]}$

Since $x \to 0^-$ $\qquad \Rightarrow x \in (-1, 0) \qquad \Rightarrow [x] = -1$

$\therefore \quad \lim\limits_{x\to 0^-}\dfrac{\sin[x]}{[x]} = \lim\limits_{x\to 0^-}\dfrac{\sin(-1)}{(-1)} = \lim\limits_{x\to 0^-}\sin 1 = \sin 1$

Clearly L.H.L. $\neq$ R.H.L. for $\dfrac{\sin\{x\}}{\{x\}}$ and $\dfrac{\sin[x]}{[x]}$

$\Rightarrow$ Both limits do-not exist.

ILLUSTRATION 46: $\text{Lim}_{x\to 0}\dfrac{8}{x^8}\left[1-\cos\dfrac{x^2}{2}-\cos\dfrac{x^2}{4}+\cos\dfrac{x^2}{2}\cos\dfrac{x^2}{4}\right]$

SOLUTION: $\text{Lim}_{x\to 0}\dfrac{8}{x^8}\left[\left(1-\cos\dfrac{x^2}{2}\right)-\cos\dfrac{x^2}{4}\left(1-\cos\dfrac{x^2}{2}\right)\right] = \text{Lim}_{x\to 0}\dfrac{8}{x^8}\left[\left(1-\cos\dfrac{x^2}{2}\right)\left(1-\cos\dfrac{x^2}{4}\right)\right]$

$= \text{Lim}_{x\to 0}\dfrac{8}{x^8}\left[\left\{1-\left(2\cos^2\dfrac{x^2}{4}-1\right)\right\}\left(1-\cos\dfrac{x^2}{4}\right)\right] = \text{Lim}_{x\to 0}\dfrac{8}{x^8}\left[\left(2-2\cos^2\dfrac{x^2}{4}\right)\left(1-\cos\dfrac{x^2}{4}\right)\right]$

$= \text{Lim}_{x\to 0}\dfrac{8\times 2}{x^8}\left[\left(1-\cos^2\dfrac{x^2}{4}\right)\left(1-\cos\dfrac{x^2}{4}\right)\right] = \text{Lim}_{x\to 0}\dfrac{16}{x^8}\left[\sin^2\dfrac{x^2}{4}\ \ 2\sin^2\dfrac{x^2}{8}\right]$

$= \text{Lim}_{x\to 0}\dfrac{32}{x^8}\left[\sin^2\dfrac{x^2}{4}\sin^2\dfrac{x^2}{8}\right] = \lim\limits_{x\to 0}32\left(\dfrac{\sin\dfrac{x^2}{4}}{4.\left(\dfrac{x^2}{4}\right)}\right)^2.\left(\dfrac{\sin\dfrac{x^2}{8}}{8.\left(\dfrac{x^2}{8}\right)}\right)^2 = \dfrac{32}{16}\times\dfrac{1}{64} = \dfrac{1}{32}$

ILLUSTRATION 47: Find the limiting value of $\dfrac{\tan 2x - 2\sin x}{x^3}$ as x tends to zero.

SOLUTION: $\lim\limits_{x\to 0}\dfrac{\sin 2x - 2\sin x\cos 2x}{x^3\cos 2x} = \lim\limits_{x\to 0}\dfrac{2\sin x[\cos x - \cos 2x]}{x^3\cos 2x}$

$= 2\lim\limits_{x\to 0}\dfrac{2\sin\dfrac{3x}{2}.\sin\dfrac{x}{2}}{x^2} = 2\lim\limits_{x\to 0}\dfrac{3\sin\dfrac{3x}{2}}{2\dfrac{3x}{2}}.\dfrac{\sin\dfrac{x}{2}}{\dfrac{x}{2}} = 3$

ILLUSTRATION 48: If $\ell = \text{Lim}_{n\to\infty}\sum_{r=2}^{n}\left((r+1)\sin\frac{\pi}{r+1} - r\sin\frac{\pi}{r}\right)$, then find $\{\ell\}$. (where {} denotes the fractional part function).

SOLUTION: $\ell = \lim_{n\to\infty}\sum_{r=2}^{n}\left((r+1)\sin\frac{\pi}{r+1} - r\sin\frac{\pi}{r}\right)$

$$\Rightarrow \ell = \lim_{n\to\infty}$$

$$\left(3\sin\frac{\pi}{3} - 2\sin\frac{\pi}{2} + 4\sin\frac{\pi}{4} - 3\sin\frac{\pi}{3} + 5\sin\frac{\pi}{5} - 4\sin\frac{\pi}{4} + \ldots\ldots + n\sin\frac{\pi}{n} - (n-1)\sin\frac{\pi}{n-1}\right.$$

$$\left. + (n+1)\sin\frac{\pi}{n+1} - n\sin\frac{\pi}{n}\right)$$

$$\Rightarrow \ell = \lim_{n\to\infty}\left((n+1)\sin\frac{\pi}{n+1} - 2\sin\frac{\pi}{2}\right)$$

$$\Rightarrow \ell = \lim_{n\to\infty}\left((n+1)\frac{\sin\left(\frac{\pi}{n+1}\right)}{\left(\frac{\pi}{n+1}\right)}\times\left(\frac{\pi}{n+1}\right) - 2\right)$$

$$\Rightarrow \ell = \lim_{n\to\infty}(\pi - 2) = \pi - 2$$

$$\Rightarrow [\ell] = 1$$

So, $\{\ell\} = \ell - [\ell] = \pi - 2 - 1 = \pi - 3$

APPLICATION OF STANDARD LIMITS

$$\lim_{x\to 0}\frac{\tan x}{x} = 1;\ \lim_{x\to 0}\frac{\sin^{-1}x}{x} = 1,\ \lim_{x\to 0}\frac{\tan^{-1}x}{x} = 1.$$

Transformations

(a) $\lim_{x\to a}\frac{\tan(f(x))}{g(x)} = k$; provided $\lim_{x\to a}\frac{f(x)}{g(x)} = k$ and $f(x)$, $g(x)\to 0$ as $x\to a$

(b) $\lim_{x\to a}\frac{\sin^{-1}(f(x))}{g(x)} = k$; provided $\lim_{x\to a}\frac{f(x)}{g(x)} = k$ and $f(x)$, $g(x)\to 0$ as $x\to a$

(c) $\lim_{x\to a}\frac{\tan^{-1}(f(x))}{g(x)} = k$; provided $\lim_{x\to a}\frac{f(x)}{g(x)} = k$ and $f(x)$, $g(x)\to 0$ as $x\to a$

Proof:

(a) Since $f(x)\to 0$ as $x\to a$

$$\Rightarrow \lim_{x\to a}\frac{\tan(f(x))}{f(x)} = 1$$

$$\therefore \lim_{x\to a}\frac{\tan f(x)}{g(x)} = \lim_{x\to a}\frac{\tan f(x)}{f(x)}.\frac{f(x)}{g(x)} = (1)(k) = k$$

(b) Since $f(x)\to 0$ as $x\to a$

$$\Rightarrow \lim_{x\to a}\frac{\sin^{-1}(f(x))}{f(x)} = 1$$

$$\therefore \lim_{x\to a}\frac{\sin^{-1}(f(x))}{g(x)} = \lim_{x\to a}\frac{\sin^{-1}(f(x))}{f(x)}.\frac{f(x)}{g(x)} = (1)(k) = k$$

(c) Since $f(x)\to 0$ as $x\to a$

$$\Rightarrow \lim_{x\to a}\frac{\tan^{-1}(f(x))}{f(x)} = 1$$

$$\therefore \lim_{x\to a}\frac{\tan^{-1}f(x)}{g(x)} = \lim_{x\to a}\frac{\tan^{-1}f(x)}{f(x)}.\frac{f(x)}{g(x)} = (1)(k) = k$$

ILLUSTRATION 49: Evaluate the following limits

(i) $\lim\limits_{x\to1}\dfrac{\sin^{-1}(x-1)}{\tan^{-1}(x-1)}$

(ii) $\lim\limits_{x\to2}\dfrac{\sin^{-1}(x^2-5x+6)}{(x^2-4)}$

(iii) $\lim\limits_{x\to2^+}\dfrac{\sin^{-1}\{x-2\}}{\tan\{x-2\}}$; {.} is fractional part function.

SOLUTION: **(i)** $\lim\limits_{x\to1}\dfrac{\sin^{-1}(x-1)}{\tan^{-1}(x-1)}=\lim\limits_{x\to1}\dfrac{\sin^{-1}(x-1)}{\tan(x-1)}\cdot\dfrac{(x-1)}{\tan^{-1}(x-1)}=(1)\,(1)=1.$

(ii) $\lim\limits_{x\to2}\dfrac{\sin^{-1}(x^2-5x+6)}{(x^2-4)}=\lim\limits_{x\to2}\dfrac{\sin^{-1}[(x-2)(x-3)]}{(x-2)(x+2)}=\lim\limits_{x\to2}\dfrac{\sin^{-1}[(x-2)(x-3)]}{(x-2)(x-3)}\times\dfrac{(x-3)}{(x+2)}$

$=\dfrac{(1)(2-3)}{(2+2)}=-\dfrac{1}{4}$

(iii) $\lim\limits_{x\to2^+}\dfrac{\sin^{-1}\{x-2\}}{\tan\{x-2\}}$, As $x\to2^+$

$\Rightarrow x-2\to0^+$ $\Rightarrow \{x-2\}=x-2$

$\therefore \lim\limits_{x\to2^+}\dfrac{\sin^{-1}\{x-2\}}{\tan\{x-2\}}=\lim\limits_{x\to2^+}\dfrac{\sin^{-1}(x-2)}{\tan(x-2)}=\lim\limits_{x\to2^+}\dfrac{\sin^{-1}(x-2)}{(x-2)}\cdot\dfrac{(x-2)}{\tan(x-2)}=(1)\,(1)=1$

ILLUSTRATION 50: $\lim\limits_{x\to0}\dfrac{\tan x-\sin x}{x^3}$

SOLUTION: $\lim\limits_{x\to0}\dfrac{\tan x-\sin x}{x^3}=\lim\limits_{x\to0}\dfrac{\tan x(1-\cos x)}{x^3}=\lim\limits_{x\to0}\dfrac{\tan x\,.\,2\sin^2\frac{x}{2}}{x^3}=\lim\limits_{x\to0}\dfrac{2\tan x}{x}\cdot\left(\dfrac{\sin\frac{x}{2}}{2\left(\frac{x}{2}\right)}\right)^2=\dfrac{1}{2}$

ILLUSTRATION 51: $\lim\limits_{x\to\pi/4}\dfrac{1-\tan x}{1-\sqrt{2}\sin x}$

SOLUTION: Put $x=\dfrac{\pi}{4}+h$

$\because x\to\dfrac{\pi}{4}$ $\Rightarrow h\to0$

$=\lim\limits_{h\to0}\dfrac{1-\tan\left(\frac{\pi}{4}+h\right)}{1-\sqrt{2}\sin\left(\frac{\pi}{4}+h\right)}=\lim\limits_{h\to0}\dfrac{1-\left(\frac{1+\tan h}{1-\tan h}\right)}{1-\sin h-\cos h}=\lim\limits_{h\to0}\dfrac{\frac{-2\tan h}{1-\tan h}}{2\sin^2\frac{h}{2}-2\sin\frac{h}{2}\cos\frac{h}{2}}$

$=\lim\limits_{h\to0}\dfrac{-2\tan h}{2\sin\frac{h}{2}\left[\sin\frac{h}{2}-\cos\frac{h}{2}\right]}\dfrac{1}{(1-\tan h)}=\lim\limits_{h\to0}\dfrac{-2\frac{\tan h}{h}}{\frac{\sin\frac{h}{2}}{\frac{h}{2}}\left[\sin\frac{h}{2}-\cos\frac{h}{2}\right]}\dfrac{1}{(1-\tan h)}=\dfrac{-2}{-1}=2$

ILLUSTRATION 52: $\displaystyle\lim_{x\to 0}\frac{\sec 4x-\sec 2x}{\sec 3x-\sec x}$

SOLUTION: $\displaystyle\lim_{x\to 0}\frac{\sec 4x-\sec 2x}{\sec 3x-\sec x}=\lim_{x\to 0}\frac{\frac{1}{\cos 4x}-\frac{1}{\cos 2x}}{\frac{1}{\cos 3x}-\frac{1}{\cos x}}=\lim_{x\to 0}\frac{\cos 2x-\cos 4x}{\cos x-\cos 3x}\times\frac{\cos x.\cos 3x}{\cos 4x.\cos 2x}$

$\displaystyle=\lim_{x\to 0}\frac{2\sin 3x.\sin x}{2\sin 2x.\sin x}=\lim_{\to}\frac{\sin 3x}{\sin 2x}\times\frac{2x}{3x}\times\frac{3x}{2x}=\lim_{x\to 0}\frac{3x}{2x}=\frac{3}{2}$

ILLUSTRATION 53: If $\displaystyle\lim_{x\to 0}\frac{a\sin x-\sin 2x}{\tan^3 x}$ is finite, then find the value of 'a' and the limit.

SOLUTION: $\displaystyle\lim_{x\to 0}\frac{a\sin x-\sin 2x}{\tan^3 x}$; $\displaystyle\frac{f(x)}{g(x)}=\frac{a\sin x-\sin 2x}{\tan^3 x}$

$\displaystyle\Rightarrow \frac{f'(x)}{g'(x)}=\frac{a\cos x-2\cos 2x}{3\tan^2 x\sec^2 x}$

on putting $x=0$, for existing limit, $\displaystyle\frac{a-2}{0}\Rightarrow a=2$

$\displaystyle\therefore$ Given limit $\displaystyle=\lim_{x\to 0}\frac{2\sin x-2\sin x\cos x}{\tan^3 x}=\lim_{x\to 0}\frac{2\sin x(1-\cos x)}{\tan^3 x}$

$\displaystyle=\lim_{x\to 0}\frac{2\sin x.2\sin^2(x/2)}{\tan^3 x}=\lim_{x\to 0}\frac{4\frac{\sin x}{x}.\frac{\sin^2(x/2)}{x^2}}{\frac{\tan^3 x}{x^3}}$

$\displaystyle=\lim_{x\to 0}\frac{4\left(\frac{\sin x}{x}\right).\left(\frac{\sin(x/2)}{x/2}\right)^2.\frac{1}{4}}{\left(\frac{\tan x}{x}\right)^3}=1$

■ APPLICATION OF STANDARD LIMITS

$\displaystyle\lim_{x\to\infty}\left(1+\frac{1}{x}\right)^x=e$ **OR** $\displaystyle\lim_{x\to 0}(1+x)^{1/x}=e$

The limit of function in $(1)^\infty$ forms can be transformed into the above standard form using the following transformations:

Transformation 1: To evaluate $\displaystyle\lim_{x\to a}(1+f(x))^{1/g(x)}$ where $\displaystyle\lim_{x\to a}f(x)=\lim_{x\to a}g(x)=0$.

Given limit $\displaystyle=\lim_{x\to a}\{1+f(x)\}^{1/g(x)}=e^{\lim_{x\to a}\frac{f(x)}{g(x)}}$

Note: Some particular cases are mentioned below:

(a) $\displaystyle\lim_{x\to 0}(1+x)^{1/x}=e$ **(b)** $\displaystyle\lim_{x\to\infty}(1+1/x)^x=e$

(c) $\displaystyle\lim_{x\to 0}(1+\lambda x)^{1/x}=e^{\lambda}$ **(d)** $\displaystyle\lim_{x\to\infty}(1+\lambda/x)^x=e^{\lambda}$

Transformation 2: To evaluate $\displaystyle\lim_{x\to a}(f(x))^{g(x)}$; then $\displaystyle\lim_{x\to a}f(x)=1$ and $\displaystyle\lim_{x\to a}g(x)=\infty$.

Given limit =

$\displaystyle\lim_{x\to a}\{f(x)\}^{g(x)}=\lim_{x\to a}[1+f(x)-1]^{g(x)}=e^{\lim_{x\to a}(f(x)-1)g(x)}$

ILLUSTRATION 54: Evaluate the following limits:

(a) $\lim_{x\to 0}(1+\sin x)^{1/x}$ **(b)** $\lim_{x\to 0}(1+\tan x)^{1/x^2}$

(c) $\lim_{x\to 0}(1+x^2)^{1/x}$ **(d)** $\lim_{x\to 0}(1+x^2)^{1/x^2}$

SOLUTION: **(a)** $\lim_{x\to 0}(1+\sin x)^{1/x} = \lim_{x\to 0}(1+\sin x)^{\frac{1}{\sin x}\cdot\frac{\sin x}{x}} = e^{\lim_{x\to 0}\frac{\sin x}{x}} = e$

(b) $\lim_{x\to 0}(1+\tan x)^{1/x^2} = e^{\lim_{x\to 0}\frac{\tan x}{x^2}}$

$\Rightarrow$ R.H.L $= e^{\infty} = \infty$ and L.H.L $= e^{-\infty} = 0$

Therefore limit does not exist

(c) $\lim_{x\to 0}(1+x^2)^{1/x} = e^{\lim_{x\to 0} x} = 1$

(d) $\lim_{x\to 0}(1+x^2)^{1/x^2} = e$

ILLUSTRATION 55: If a, b, c, d are positive, then evaluate $\lim_{x\to\infty}\left(1+\frac{1}{a+bx}\right)^{c+dx}$.

SOLUTION: limit $= \lim_{x\to\infty} e^{\left(\frac{1}{a+bx}\right)\times(c+dx)}$ (required limit is of the form 1^{∞} we applied the transformation (i))

$= \lim_{x\to\infty} e^{\left(\frac{d+c/x}{b+a/x}\right)} = e^{d/b}$

ILLUSTRATION 56: Find the value of $\lim_{x\to 0}\left(\frac{\sin x}{x}\right)^{\frac{\sin x}{x-\sin x}}$

SOLUTION: Given limit $= \lim_{x\to 0} e^{\left(\frac{\sin x}{x}-1\right)\frac{\sin x}{x-\sin x}} = \lim_{x\to 0} e^{\left(\frac{\sin x - x}{x}\right)\frac{\sin x}{x-\sin x}} = e^{-1}$

ILLUSTRATION 57: Find the value of

(a) $\lim_{x\to\infty}\left(\frac{x+6}{x+1}\right)^{x+4}$ **(b)** $\lim_{x\to 0}\left(\frac{1+5x^2}{1+3x^2}\right)^{1/x^2}$

SOLUTION: **(a)** $\lim_{x\to\infty}\left(1+\frac{5}{x+1}\right)^{\frac{x+1}{5}\cdot\frac{5(x+4)}{x+1}} = e^{5\lim_{x\to\infty}\left(\frac{x+4}{x+1}\right)} = e^5$

(b) $\lim_{x\to 0}\left(1+\frac{2x^2}{1+3x^2}\right)^{\frac{1+3x^2}{2x^2}\cdot\frac{2}{1+3x^2}} = e^{\lim_{x\to 0}\frac{2}{1+3x^2}} = e^2$

ILLUSTRATION 58: Evaluate $\lim_{x\to 1}(\log_3 3x)^{\log_x 3}$

SOLUTION: Given $\lim_{x\to 1}(\log_3 3x)^{\log_x 3} = \lim_{x\to 1}(\log_3 3+\log_3 x)^{\log_x 3}$

$= \lim_{x\to 1}(1+\log_3 x)^{1/\log_3 x} = e$ $\left[\because\ \log_b a = \frac{1}{\log_a b}\right]$

■ APPLICATION OF STANDARD LIMITS

(i) $\lim_{x\to 0}\frac{\ell n(1+x)}{x}=1$

(ii) $\lim_{x\to 0}\frac{a^x-1}{x}=\ell n\, a$

(iii) $\lim_{x\to 0}\frac{\log_a(1+x)}{x}=\log_a e$

(iv) $\lim_{x\to 0}\frac{e^x-1}{x}=1$

ILLUSTRATION 59: Evaluate $\lim_{x\to 0}\frac{\ell n(1+x)}{3^x-1}$

SOLUTION: $\lim_{x\to 0}\frac{\ell n(1+x)}{3^x-1}=\frac{\lim_{x\to 0}\frac{\ell n(1+x)}{x}}{\lim_{x\to 0}\left(\frac{3^x-1}{x}\right)}=\frac{1}{\ell n3}$

ILLUSTRATION 60: Solve $\lim_{x\to e}\frac{\log_e x-1}{x-e}=\lim_{x\to e}\frac{\log_e x/e}{e(x/e-1)}$

SOLUTION: Put $x/e=t\Rightarrow \lim_{t\to 1}\frac{\log_e t}{(t-1)e}$, Put $t=1+z\Rightarrow \lim_{z\to 0}\frac{\log_e(1+z)}{ez}=\frac{1}{e}$

ILLUSTRATION 61: Evaluate $\lim_{x\to 0}\frac{2^x-1}{(\sqrt{1+x}-1)}$

SOLUTION: $\lim_{x\to 0}\frac{2^x-1}{x}.(\sqrt{1+x}+1)=\lim_{x\to 0}\frac{2^x-1}{x}.\lim_{x\to 0}(\sqrt{1+x}+1)=2.\ \ell n2$ $\left\{\because \lim_{x\to 0}\frac{a^x-1}{x}=\log_e a\right\}$

ILLUSTRATION 62: Evaluate $\lim_{x\to 0}\frac{\ln(1+\sin x)}{x}$

SOLUTION: $\lim_{x\to 0}\frac{\ln(1+\sin x)}{x}=\lim_{x\to 0}\frac{\ln(1+\sin x)}{\sin x}\times\frac{\sin x}{x}=(1)\,(1)=1$

ILLUSTRATION 63: Evaluate $\lim_{x\to 0}\frac{\ln(1+x)}{\tan x}$

SOLUTION: $\lim_{x\to 0}\frac{\ln(1+x)}{\tan x}=\lim_{x\to 0}\frac{\ln(1+x)}{x}.\frac{x}{\tan x}=(1)\,(1)=1$

ILLUSTRATION 64: $\lim_{x\to 0}\frac{\ln(\cos x)}{\tan x}$

SOLUTION: $\lim_{x\to 0}\frac{\ln(\cos x)}{\tan x}=\lim_{x\to 0}\frac{\ln(1+(\cos x-1))}{\tan x}=\lim_{x\to 0}\frac{\ln[1+(\cos x-1)]}{(\cos x-1)}\left(\frac{\cos x-1}{\tan x}\right)$

$$=(1)\lim_{x\to 0}\left[\frac{-(1-\cos x)}{\tan x}\right]=-\lim_{x\to 0}\left[\frac{2\sin^2 x/2}{\sin x}.\cos x\right]$$

$$=-2\lim_{x\to 0}\left[(\sin x/2)\frac{\sin x/2}{2(x/2)}.\frac{x}{\sin x}.\cos x\right]=-2(0)\,(1/2)\,(1)(1)=0$$

ILLUSTRATION 65: $\lim\limits_{x\to 0}\left(\dfrac{2^x-3^x}{x}\right)$

SOLUTION: $\lim\limits_{x\to 0}\left[\dfrac{(2^x-1)-(3^x-1)}{x}\right] = \lim\limits_{x\to 0}\dfrac{2^x-1}{x}\quad \lim\limits_{x\to 0}\dfrac{3^x-1}{x} = \ln 2-\ln 3=\ln(2/3)$

ILLUSTRATION 66: $\lim\limits_{x\to 0}\dfrac{\ln(3^x+2^x-1)}{(\sin x)}$

SOLUTION: $\lim\limits_{x\to 0}\dfrac{\ln(3^x+2^x-1)}{(\sin x)} = \lim\limits_{x\to 0}\dfrac{\ln(1+3^x+2^x-2)}{\sin x} = \lim\limits_{x\to 0}\dfrac{\ln(1+(3^x+2^x-2))}{(3^x+2^x-2)}.\dfrac{(3^x+2^x-2)}{\sin x}$

$= \lim\limits_{x\to 0}\dfrac{\ln[1+(3^x+2^x-2)]}{(3^x+2^x-2)}.\dfrac{(3^x-1)+(2^x-1)}{x}.\dfrac{x}{\sin x} = (1)\ [\ln 3+\ln 2]=\ln 6$

ILLUSTRATION 67: Evaluate $\lim\limits_{x\to 0}\dfrac{[ln(1+\sin^{-1}x+\tan^{-1}x+x)]\sin x}{(5^x-2^x)\ell n(1+x)}$

SOLUTION: $\lim\limits_{x\to 0}\dfrac{[\ln(1+\sin^{-1}x+\tan^{-1}x+x)]\sin x}{(5^x-2^x)\ln(1+x)} = \lim\limits_{x\to 0}\dfrac{[\ln(1+\sin^{-1}x+\tan^{-1}x+x)]}{(\sin^{-1}x+\tan^{-1}x+x)}$

$\times\dfrac{(\sin^{-1}x+\tan^{-1}x+x)}{(5^x-2^x)\ell n(1+x)}.\sin x = \lim\limits_{x\to 0}\dfrac{(\sin^{-1}x+\tan^{-1}x+x)\sin x}{(5^x-2^x)\ell n(1+x)} = \lim\limits_{\to}\dfrac{\left(\dfrac{\sin^{-1}x}{x}+\dfrac{\tan^{-1}x}{x}+1\right).x.\sin x}{(5^x-2^x)\ n(1+x)}$

$= \lim\limits_{x\to 0}(1+1+1).(1)\dfrac{\sin x}{5^x-2^x} = 3\lim\limits_{x\to 0}\dfrac{\sin x}{x}.\dfrac{x}{(5^x-2^x)} = 3(1)\lim\limits_{x\to 0}\dfrac{x}{(5^x-1)-(2^x-1)}$

$= 3\left[\dfrac{1}{\ell n5-\ell n2}\right] = \dfrac{3}{\ell n(5/2)} = 3\log_{5/2}e$

ILLUSTRATION 68: Evaluate $\lim\limits_{x\to 0}\dfrac{\log_4(1+\sin x)}{\tan x}$

SOLUTION: $\lim\limits_{x\to 0}\dfrac{\log_4(1+\sin x)}{\tan x} = \lim\limits_{x\to 0}\dfrac{\log_4(1+\sin x)}{\sin x}\dfrac{\sin x}{\tan x}$

$= \lim\limits_{x\to 0}\dfrac{\log_4(1+\sin x)}{\sin x}\dfrac{\sin x}{x}\dfrac{x}{\tan x} = (\log_4 e)\ (1)\ (1) = \log_4 e \qquad \left(\because \lim\limits_{x\to 0}\dfrac{\log_a(1+x)}{x}=\log_a e\right)$

ILLUSTRATION 69: Evaluate $\lim\limits_{x\to 0}\dfrac{e^{\sin^{-1}x+\tan^{-1}x+x}+(1+x)^{2013}}{\log_{2013}(1+\tan x)}$

SOLUTION: $\lim\limits_{x\to 0}\dfrac{e^{\sin^{-1}x+\tan^{-1}x+x}-(1+x)^{2013}}{\log_{2013}(1+\tan x)} = \lim\limits_{x\to 0}\dfrac{(e^{\sin^{-1}x+\tan^{-1}x+x}-1)-((1+x)^{2013}-1)}{\log_{2013}(1+\tan x)}$

$$= \lim_{x\to 0}\left\{\frac{e^{\sin^{-1}x+\tan^{-1}x+x}-1}{\log_{2013}(1+\tan x)} - \frac{\left({}^{2013}C_1x + {}^{2013}C_2x^2+...+{}^{2013}C_{2013}\,x^{2013}\right)}{\log_{2013}(1+\tan x)}\right\}$$

$$= \lim_{x\to 0}\left\{\frac{e^{\sin^{-1}x+\tan^{-1}x+x}-1}{\left(\sin^{-1}x+\tan^{-1}x+x\right)} \times \frac{\left(\sin^{-1}x+\tan^{-1}x+x\right)}{\tan x} \times \frac{\tan x}{\log_{2013}(1+\tan x)}\right.$$

$$\left. - \frac{x\left({}^{2013}C_1 + {}^{2013}C_2x+....+{}^{2013}C_{2013}x^{2012}\right).\tan x}{(\tan x)\log_{2013}(1+\tan x)}\right\}$$

$$= (1)(3)\times\frac{1}{\log_{2013}e} - \frac{2013}{\log_{2013}e} = \frac{-2010}{\log_{2013}e} = -2010\ln(2013)$$

$(\because \log_b a = \log_a b)$

■ APPLICATION OF STANDARD LIMIT $\lim\limits_{x\to a}\dfrac{x^n-a^n}{x-a} = na^{n-1}$

ILLUSTRATION 70: Evaluate the following limits:

(a) $\lim\limits_{x\to -1}\dfrac{1+x^{1/3}}{1+x^{1/5}}$

(b) $\lim\limits_{x\to -1}\dfrac{x+1}{\sqrt[4]{x+17}-2}$

(c) $\lim\limits_{x\to 2}\dfrac{x^3-2^3}{x-2}$

SOLUTION: **(a)** Given limit $= \lim\limits_{x\to -1}\dfrac{x^{1/3}-(-1)}{x^{1/5}-(-1)} = \lim\limits_{x\to -1}\dfrac{x-(-1)}{x^{1/5}-(-1)}.\dfrac{x^{1/3}-(-1)}{x-(-1)} = 5/3$

(b) $\lim\limits_{x+1\to 0}\dfrac{x+1}{\{(x+1)+16\}^{1/4}-(16)^{1/4}} = \lim\limits_{z\to 0}\dfrac{(z+16)-16}{\{z+16\}^{1/4}-(16)^{1/4}} = 4(2)^3 = 32$

(c) $\lim\limits_{x\to 2}\dfrac{x^3-2^3}{x-2}$

$= 3\,(2)^{3-1}$

$= 3\,(2)^2 = 12$

ILLUSTRATION 71: Evaluate

(i) $\lim\limits_{x\to 2}\dfrac{\sqrt{x+2}-2}{x-2}$

(ii) $\lim\limits_{x\to 5}\dfrac{\sqrt[3]{x+3}-2}{x-5}$

(iii) $\lim\limits_{x\to 2}\dfrac{\sqrt{\log_2(x+14)}-2}{\log_2(x+14)-4}$

(iv) $\lim\limits_{x\to \pi/4}\dfrac{\sin^2 x-(1/2)}{\sin x-(1/\sqrt{2})}$

(v) $\lim\limits_{x\to \pi/4}\dfrac{\sqrt[3]{\tan x}-1}{\tan x-1}$

SOLUTION: (i) $\lim_{x\to 2}\frac{\sqrt{x+2}-2}{x-2}=\lim_{x\to 2}\frac{(x+2)^{1/2}-(4)^{1/2}}{(x+2)-(4)}=\lim_{y\to 4}\frac{y^{1/2}-(4)^{1/2}}{y-4}$; where $y = x + 2$

$=\frac{1}{2}(4)^{\frac{1}{2}-1}=\frac{1}{2}(4)^{-1/2}=\frac{1}{4}$

(ii) $\lim_{x\to 5}\frac{\sqrt[3]{x+3}-2}{x-5}=\lim_{x\to 5}\frac{(x+3)^{1/3}-(8)^{1/3}}{(x+3)-8}=\lim_{y\to 8}\frac{(y)^{1/3}-(8)^{1/3}}{y-8}$; where $y = x + 3$

$=\frac{1}{3}(8)^{-2/3}=\frac{1}{12}$

(iii) $\lim_{x\to 2}\frac{\sqrt{\log_2(x+14)}-2}{\log_2(x+14)-4}=\lim_{x\to 2}\frac{(\log_2(x+14))^{1/2}-(4)^{1/2}}{(\log_2(x+14))-(4)}$

$=\lim_{y\to 4}\frac{(y)^{1/2}-(4)^{1/2}}{y-4}$; (Where $y = \log_2(x + 14)$) $=\frac{1}{2}(4)^{\frac{1}{2}-1}=\frac{1}{2}(4)^{-1/2}=\frac{1}{4}$

(iv) $\lim_{x\to\pi/4}\frac{\sin^2 x-1/2}{\sin x-1/\sqrt{2}}=\lim_{x\to\pi/4}\frac{(\sin x)^2-(1/\sqrt{2})^2}{(\sin x)-(1/\sqrt{2})}=\lim_{y\to 1/\sqrt{2}}\frac{y^2-(1/\sqrt{2})^2}{y-1/\sqrt{2}}$; (where $y = \sin x$)

$=2\left(\frac{1}{\sqrt{2}}\right)^{2-1}=\sqrt{2}$

(v) $\lim_{x\to\pi/4}\frac{\sqrt[3]{\tan x}-1}{\tan x-1}=\lim_{x\to\pi/4}\frac{(\tan x)^{1/3}-(1)^{1/3}}{\tan x-1}=\lim_{y\to 1}\frac{(y)^{1/3}-(1)^{1/3}}{y-1}$; (where $y = \tan x$)

$=\frac{1}{3}(1)^{\frac{1}{3}-1}=\frac{1}{3}$

TEXTUAL EXERCISE–3: (SUBJECTIVE)

1. Find out the following limits using factorization:

(a) $\lim_{x\to -2}\frac{x^4+5x^3+6x^2}{x^2-3x-10}$

(b) $\lim_{x\to 0}\frac{(4+x)^3-64}{x}$

(c) $\lim_{x\to 0}\frac{(1+x)(1+2x)(1+3x)-1}{x}$

(d) $\lim_{x\to 0}\frac{(1+x)^5-(1+5x)}{x^2+x^5}$

(e) $\lim_{x\to 1}\frac{x^4-2x^2+1}{x^3-1}$

(f) $\lim_{x\to -1}\frac{x^3-2x-1}{x^5-2x-1}$

(g) $\lim_{x\to 1}\frac{x^m-1}{x^n-1}$

(h) $\lim_{x\to 0}\left(\frac{1}{x}-\frac{1}{x^2}\right)$

(i) $\lim_{x\to 0}\frac{[(1+x)^{1/k}-1]}{x}$ $\forall\ k\in I^+$

2. Evaluate the following limits.

(a) $\lim_{x\to 0}\frac{e^{2x}+e^x-2}{e^x-1}$

(b) $\lim_{x\to\pi/4}\frac{1-\tan x}{\sin x-\cos x}$

(c) $\lim_{x\to\pi/6}\frac{(2\sin^2 x+\sin x-1)}{(2\sin^2 x-3\sin x+1)}$

(d) $\lim_{x\to\tan^{-1}3}\dfrac{(\tan^2 x-2\tan x-3)}{(\tan^2 x-4\tan x+3}$

3. Evaluate the following limit using rationalization:

(a) $\lim_{x\to a}\dfrac{\sqrt{x}-\sqrt{a}}{x^2-a^2}$

(b) $\lim_{x\to a}\dfrac{\sqrt[3]{x}-\sqrt[3]{a}}{x^3-a^3}$

(c) $\lim_{x\to 4}\dfrac{\sqrt{1+2x}-3}{\sqrt{x}-2}$

(d) $\lim_{x\to -8}\dfrac{\sqrt{1-x}-3}{2+\sqrt[3]{x}}$

(e) $\lim_{x\to 1}\dfrac{\sqrt[3]{x}-1}{\sqrt{x}-1}$

(f) $\lim_{x\to 0}\dfrac{\sqrt{\cos x}-\sqrt[3]{\cos x}}{\sin^2 x}$

(g) $\lim_{x\to 0}\dfrac{\sqrt{x^2+1}-1}{\sqrt{x^2+9}-3}$

(h) $\lim_{x\to b}\dfrac{\sqrt{x-a}-\sqrt{b-a}}{x^2-b^2}$ for $b > a$

(i) $\lim_{x\to\infty} x^{3/2}\left(\sqrt{x^3+1}-\sqrt{x^3-1}\right)$

(j) $\lim_{x\to 0}\ [\sqrt{(a^2+ax+x^2)}-\sqrt{(a^2-ax+x^2)}]/[\sqrt{(a+x)}-\sqrt{(a-x)}]$

(k) $\lim_{x\to 0}\dfrac{[(1+x^5)^{1/5}-(1+x^2)^{1/5}]}{[(1-x^5)^{1/5}-(1-x^3)^{1/5}]}$

4. Evaluate the limits using the concept of rationalization or otherwise $\lim_{x\to\infty}\sqrt{(x+a)(x+b)}-x$

5. Evaluate the following limit using standard forms :

(a) $\lim_{x\to 0}\dfrac{\sin 3x}{5x}$

(b) $\lim_{x\to 0}\dfrac{\sec x-1}{x\sec x}$

(c) $\lim_{x\to 0}\dfrac{e^{-4x}-1}{e^{-2x}+e^{-x}-2}$

(d) $\lim_{x\to 0}\dfrac{\sin^{-1}x+\tan^{-1}(2x)}{x}$

(e) $\lim_{x\to 0}\dfrac{\log\cos x}{3x^2}$

(f) $\lim_{x\to 0}\dfrac{a^x-b^x}{3\sin x}$

(g) $\lim_{x\to 0}\dfrac{[\log(a+x)-\log a]}{x}$

(h) $\lim_{x\to 0}\dfrac{\log(1+x^2+x^4)}{[3x^2(1-2x)]}$

(i) $\lim_{x\to 0}\dfrac{x(e^{1/x}-e^{-1/x})}{e^{1/x}+e^{-1/x}}$

(j) $\lim_{x\to\pi/6}\dfrac{\sin\left[x-\left(\dfrac{\pi}{6}\right)\right]}{\left(\sqrt{3}-2\cos x\right)}$

(k) $\lim_{x\to\pi}\dfrac{\left[\sqrt{(2+\cos x)}-1\right]}{(\pi-x)^2}$

(l) $\lim_{x\to\pi/4}\dfrac{(1-\tan x)}{(1-\sqrt{2}\sin x)}$

(m) $\lim_{x\to\pi/4}\dfrac{[\sqrt{2}-\sin x-\cos x]}{(4x-\pi)^2}$

(n) $\lim_{x\to\pi/4}\dfrac{[2\sqrt{2}-(\cos x+\sin x)^3]}{(1-\sin 2x)}$

(o) $\lim_{x\to\pi/3}\dfrac{(\tan^3 x-3\tan x)}{\cos[x+(\pi/6)]}$

(p) $\lim_{x\to 0}\left(\dfrac{a^x+b^x}{2}\right)^{\frac{1}{x}}$, $a, b>0$

(q) $\lim_{x\to 0}\dfrac{1-\cos^3 x}{x\sin x\cos x}$

(r) $\lim_{x\to 1}(1-x)\tan\left(\dfrac{\pi x}{2}\right)$

(s) $\lim_{x\to\infty} a^x\sin\left(\dfrac{b}{a^x}\right),(a>1)$

(t) $\lim_{x\to 0}\dfrac{(8^x-4^x-2^x+1^x)}{x^2}$

6. Evaluate following limits using suitable substitution

(a) $\lim_{x\to 1}\dfrac{x^2+1-2x}{2\log^2 x}$

(b) $\lim_{x\to 1}\dfrac{2^{2x}-5.2^x+6}{(2^x-2)(2^x+3)}$

Answer Keys

1. (a) $-4/7$ (b) 48 (c) 6 (d) 10 (e) 0 (f) 1/3 (g) m/n
(h) $-\infty$ (i) 1/k
2. (a) 3 (b) $-\sqrt{2}$ (c) -3 (d) 2
3. (a) $\dfrac{1}{4.a^{3/2}}$ (b) $\dfrac{1}{9.a^{\frac{8}{3}}}$
(c) 4/3 (d) -2 (e) 2/3 (f) $-1/12$ (g) 3
(h) $\dfrac{1}{4b\sqrt{b-a}}$ (i) 1 (j) $\dfrac{1}{2\sqrt{a}}$ (k) L.H.L. $= \infty$ and R.H.L. $= -\infty$
4. $\dfrac{a+b+c}{3}$
5. (a) 3/5 (b) 0 (c) 4/3 (d) 3 (e) $-1/6$ (f) $\dfrac{1}{3}\log\left(\dfrac{a}{b}\right)$ (g) 1/a
(h) 1/3 (i) 0 (j) 1 (k) 1/4 (l) 2 (m) $\dfrac{1}{16\sqrt{2}}$ (n) $3/\sqrt{2}$ (o) -24
(p) $\sqrt{ab}$ (q) 3/2 (r) $2/\pi$ (s) b (t) $2(\log 2)^2$
6. (a) 1/2 (b) $\dfrac{-1}{5}$

TEXTUAL EXERCISE-3: (OBJECTIVE)

1. $\lim\limits_{x\to 3}\dfrac{(x^3+27)\ln(x-2)}{(x^2-9)} =$
   (a) -8 (b) 1
   (c) -1 (d) 9

2. $\lim\limits_{x\to 1}\left[\left[\dfrac{4}{x^2-x^{-1}}-\dfrac{1-3x+x^2}{1-x^3}\right]^{-1}+\dfrac{3.(x^4-1)}{x^3-x^{-1}}\right] =$
   (a) $\dfrac{1}{3}$ (b) 3
   (c) $\dfrac{1}{2}$ (d) None of these

3. Let $f:(1,2)\to R$ satisfies the inequality $\dfrac{\cos(2x-4)-33}{2} < f(x) < \dfrac{x^2|4x-8|}{x-2}$, $\forall\, x \in (1,2)$.
   Then $\lim\limits_{x\to 2^-} f(x)$ is equal to
   (a) 16
   (b) -16
   (c) cannot be determined from the given information
   (d) does not exists

4. $\lim\limits_{x\to\frac{\pi}{2}} \tan^2 x\left(\sqrt{2\sin^2 x+3\sin x+4}-\sqrt{\sin^2 x+6\sin x+2}\right)$ $(\infty \times 0)$ form is
   (a) $\dfrac{1}{12}$ (b) $\dfrac{1}{13}$
   (c) $\dfrac{1}{14}$ (d) None of these

5. $\lim\limits_{n\to\infty}\dfrac{\sqrt{n^3-2n^2+1}+\sqrt[3]{n^4+1}}{\sqrt[4]{n^6+6n^5+2}-\sqrt[5]{n^7+3n^3+1}}$
   (a) 1 (b) 2
   (c) 3 (d) None of these

6. $\lim\limits_{x\to\infty}\dfrac{(x-3)^{40}.(5x+1)^{10}}{(3x^2-2)^{25}}$
   (a) $\dfrac{5^{10}}{3^{25}}$ (b) 1001
   (c) 2000 (d) None of these

7. $\lim\limits_{x\to\pm\infty}\left(\sqrt{x^2-2x-1}-\sqrt{x^2-7x-3}\right)$

(a) $\pm\frac{3}{2}$ (b) $\pm\frac{5}{2}$

(c) $\pm\frac{7}{2}$ (d) None of These

8. $\lim\limits_{x\to\infty}\sqrt[3]{x^3+3x^2}-\sqrt{x^2-2x}$

(a) 2 (b) 3

(c) 1 (d) 0

9. $\lim\limits_{x\to 5}\frac{x^2-9x+20}{x-[x]}$

(a) LHL = RHL = 0 (b) LHL = 0, RHL =1

(c) LHL = RHL = 1 (d) Limit does not exist

10. $\lim\limits_{x\to 0}\frac{\sqrt{1+\tan x}-\sqrt{1+\sin x}}{x^3}$

(a) $\frac{1}{4}$ (b) $\frac{1}{2}$

(c) $\frac{1}{3}$ (d) None of these

11. $\lim\limits_{x\to\pi/2}\left[\frac{x-\frac{\pi}{2}}{\cos x}\right]$ is where[.] represents greatest integer function

(a) –1 (b) 0

(c) –2 (d) Does not exist

12. $\lim\limits_{x\to 2^+}\left(\frac{|x|^3}{3}-\left[\frac{x}{3}\right]^3\right)$, where $[x]$ is the greatest integer less than or equal to x is

(a) 5/3 (b) 8/3

(c) 7/9 (d) None of these

13. $\lim\limits_{x\to 0}\frac{(4^x-1)^3}{\sin\left(\frac{x}{p}\right)\ln\left(1+\frac{x^2}{3}\right)}=$

(a) $9p(\log 4)$ (b) $3p(\log 4)^3$

(c) $12p(\log 4)^3$ (d) $27p(\log 4)^2$

14. The value of $\lim\limits_{x\to 0}\frac{\sin(\ell n(1+x))}{\ell n(1+\sin x)}$ is

(a) 0 (b) 1/2

(c) 1/4 (d) 1

15. $\lim\limits_{n\to\infty} n\cos\left(\frac{\pi}{4n}\right)\sin\left(\frac{\pi}{4n}\right)$ has the value equal to

(a) $\pi/3$ (b) $\pi/4$

(c) $\pi/6$ (d) None of these

16. $\lim\limits_{x\to\infty}\left(\frac{x+2}{x-2}\right)^{x+1}=$

(a) e^4 (b) e^{-4}

(c) e^2 (d) None of these

17. $\lim\limits_{x\to 0^+}\left(1+\tan^2\sqrt{x}\right)^{5/x}=$

(a) e^5 (b) e^2

(c) e (d) None of these

18. The value of $\lim\limits_{x\to\pi/4}(1+[x])^{1/\ln(\tan x)}$ (where [.] denotes the greatest integer function) is equal to

(a) 0 (b) 1

(c) e (d) e^{-1}

19. $\lim\limits_{x\to\infty}\left(\frac{x^2-2x+1}{x^2-4x+2}\right)^x=$

(a) 1 (b) 2

(c) e^2 (d) e

20. If $\lim\limits_{x\to 0}(\cos x+a\sin bx)^{1/x}=e^2$, then the possible value of 'a' & 'b' is :

(a) $a=1, b=2$ (b) $a=2, b=1$

(c) $a=3, b=2/3$ (d) $a=2/3, b=3$

21. $\lim\limits_{x\to\pi/2}\frac{\left(1-\tan\frac{x}{2}\right)(1-\sin x)}{\left(1+\tan\frac{x}{2}\right)(\pi-2x)^3}$ is

(a) 1/16 (b) –1/16

(c) 1/32 (d) –1/32

22. Let $f(x)=\begin{cases}x\sin\left(\frac{1}{x}\right)+\sin\left(\frac{1}{x^2}\right) & x\neq 0\\ 0 & x=0\end{cases}$, then $\lim\limits_{x\to\infty} f(x)$ equals

(a) 0 (b) –1/2

(c) 1 (d) None of these

23. $\lim\limits_{x\to\infty}\left(\frac{x^2+5x+3}{x^2+x+3}\right)^x$ is equal to

(a) e^4 (b) e^2

(c) e^3 (d) e

24. Which one of the following best represents the graph of the function $f(x) = \lim\limits_{n\to\infty} \frac{2}{\pi}\tan^{-1}(nx)$?

(a) 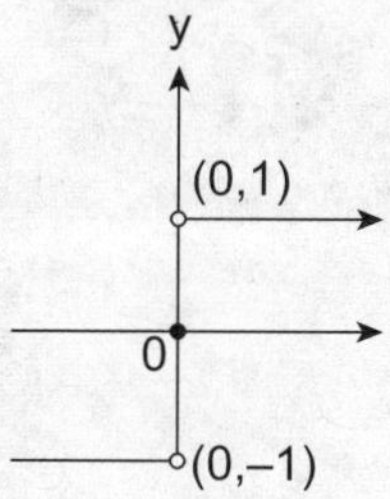

(b) 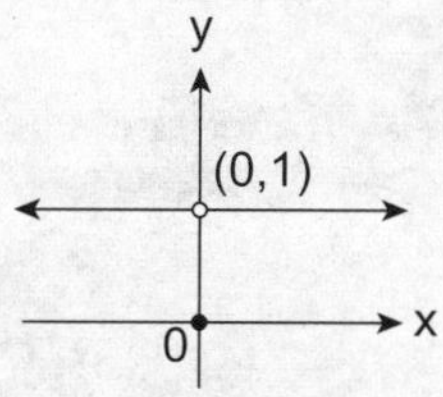

(c) 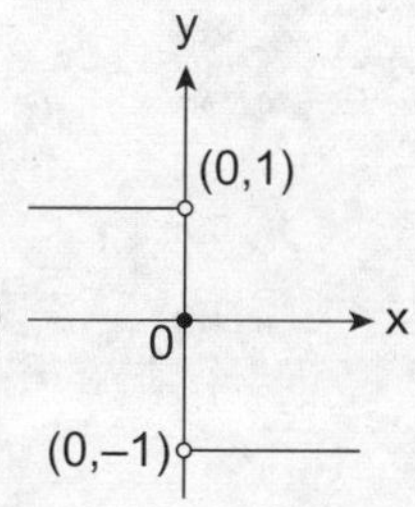

(d) 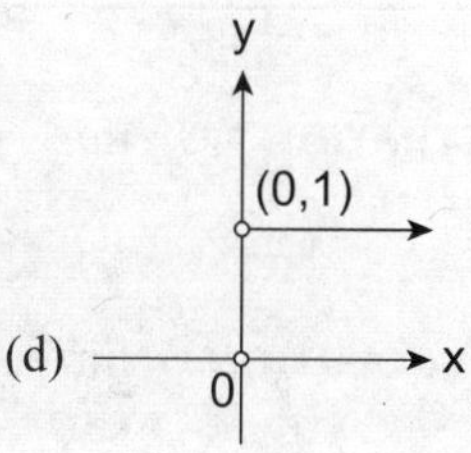

Answer Keys

1. (d) **2.** (b) **3.** (b) **4.** (a) **5.** (a) **6.** (a) **7.** (b) **8.** (a) **9.** (b), (d) **10.** (a)
11. (c) **12.** (b) **13.** (b) **14.** (d) **15.** (b) **16.** (a) **17.** (a) **18.** (b) **19.** (c)
20. (a),(b),(c),(d) **21.** (c) **22.** (c) **23.** (a) **24.** (a)

■ EVALUATION OF LIMIT USING EXPANSIONS

Limits of various functions can be evaluated by expanding the functions using the binomial, exponential and Logarithmic expansion and expansion of functions like sin*x*, cos*x*, tan*x* etc. The following results are to be remembered and can be used directly to evaluate limits, unless otherwise mentioned.

(a) $a^x = 1 + \frac{x\ln a}{1!} + \frac{x^2(\ln a)^2}{2!} + ..., a > 0$

(b) $e^x = 1 + \frac{x}{1!} + \frac{x^2}{2!} + ...$

(c) $\ln(1+x) = x - \frac{x^2}{2} + \frac{x^3}{3} .... \; -1 < x \le 1$

(d) $\sin x = x - \frac{x^3}{3!} + \frac{x^5}{5!} - \frac{x^7}{7!} + ...$

(e) $\cos x = 1 - \frac{x^2}{2!} + \frac{x^4}{4!} - \frac{x^6}{6!} + ...$

(f) $\tan x = x + \frac{x^3}{3} + \frac{2x^5}{15} + ...$

(g) $(1+x)^n = 1 + nx + \frac{n(n-1)}{2!}x^2 + ...$ (for rational *n*)

for irrational *n* rule is not applicable

(h) $(1+x)^{1/x} = e\left[1 - \frac{x}{2} + \frac{11}{24}x^2 ......\right]$

(i) $\tan^{-1}x = x - \frac{x^3}{3} + \frac{x^5}{5} - \frac{x^7}{7} + ...$

(j) $\sin^{-1}x = x + \frac{1^2}{3!}x^3 + \frac{1^2.3^2}{5!}x^5 + ...$

(k) $\sec^{-1}x = 1 + \frac{x^2}{2!} + \frac{5x^4}{4!} + \frac{61x^6}{6!} + ...$

(l) $\cos^{-1}x = \frac{\pi}{2} - \left(x + \frac{x^3}{3!} + \frac{9x^5}{5!} + ...\right)$

(m) $\sin hx = x + \frac{x^3}{3!} + \frac{x^5}{5!} + ...$

(n) $\cos hx = 1 + \frac{x^2}{2!} + \frac{x^4}{4!} + ...$

(o) $\tan hx = x - \frac{x^3}{3} + \frac{2x^5}{15} - ...$

NOTE:

where $\sin hx = \frac{e^x - e^{-x}}{2}$, $\cos hx = \frac{e^x + e^{-x}}{2}$ *and* $\tan hx = \frac{e^x - e^{-x}}{e^x + e^{-x}}$

ILLUSTRATION 72: $\lim_{x\to 0}\frac{e^x-1-x}{x^2}$

SOLUTION: $\lim_{x\to 0}\frac{e^x-1-x}{x^2} = \lim_{x\to 0}\frac{\left(1+x+\frac{x^2}{2!}.......\right)-1-x}{x^2} = \frac{1}{2}$

ILLUSTRATION 73: $\lim_{x\to 0}\frac{\tan x-\sin x}{x^3}$

SOLUTION: $\lim_{x\to 0}\frac{\tan x-\sin x}{x^3} = \lim_{x\to 0}\frac{\left(x+\frac{x^3}{3}........\right)-\left(x-\frac{x^3}{3!}.......\right)}{x^3} = \frac{1}{3}+\frac{1}{6}=\frac{1}{2}$

ILLUSTRATION 74: $\lim_{x\to 0}\frac{(7+x)^{1/3}-2}{x-1}$

SOLUTION: Put $x = 1 + h, h\to 0 = \lim_{h\to 0}\frac{(8+h)^{1/3}-2}{h} = \lim_{h\to 0}\frac{2.\left(1+\frac{h}{8}\right)^{1/3}-2}{h}$

$$= \lim_{h\to 0}\frac{2\left\{1+\frac{1}{3}.\frac{h}{8}+\frac{\frac{1}{3}\left(\frac{1}{3}-1\right)\left(\frac{h}{8}\right)^2}{1.2}+.......-1\right\}}{h} = \lim_{x\to 0} 2\times\frac{1}{24}=\frac{1}{12}$$

ILLUSTRATION 75: $\lim_{x\to 0}\frac{\ell n(1+x)-\sin x+\frac{x^2}{2}}{x\tan x\sin x}$

SOLUTION: $\lim_{x\to 0}\frac{\ell n(1+x)-\sin x+\frac{x^2}{2}}{x\tan x\sin x} = \lim_{x\to 0}\frac{\ell n(1+x)-\sin x+\frac{x^2}{2}}{x\tan x\sin x}$

$$= \lim_{x\to 0}\frac{\left(x-\frac{x^2}{2}+\frac{x^3}{3}.....\right)-\left(x-\frac{x^3}{3!}+\frac{x^5}{5!}-.....\right)+\frac{x^2}{2}}{x^3.\frac{\tan x}{x}.\frac{\sin x}{x}} = \frac{1}{3}+\frac{1}{6}=\frac{1}{2}$$

ILLUSTRATION 76: Evaluate $\lim_{x\to 0}\left(\frac{\tan^{-1}x-\sin^{-1}x}{x^3}\right)$

SOLUTION: $\lim_{x\to 0}\frac{(x-x^3/3+....)-(x+x^3/3!+...)}{x^3} = \lim_{x\to 0}\frac{(-1/3-1/6)x^3+\text{higher powers of }x}{x^3} = -\frac{1}{2}$

ILLUSTRATION 77: If $f(x)$ is integral of $\frac{2\sin x-\sin 2x}{x^3}$, $x\neq 0$, then find $\lim_{x\to 0} f'(x)$.

SOLUTION: $\lim_{x\to 0} f'(x) = \lim_{x\to 0}\frac{2\sin x-\sin 2x}{x^3} = \lim_{x\to 0}\frac{2(x-x^3/3!......)-(2x-8x^3/3!.....)}{x^3} = \frac{8-2}{3!}=1$

ILLUSTRATION 78: Evaluate the following limits:

(i) $\lim\limits_{x\to 0}\left[\dfrac{x2^x - x}{1-\cos x}\right]$ **(ii)** $\lim\limits_{x\to 0}\left(\dfrac{1}{x}-\dfrac{1}{x^2}\log(1+x)\right)$

(iii) $\lim\limits_{x\to 0}\dfrac{e^{-x^2}-1}{-x^2}$

SOLUTION: (i) $$\lim_{x\to 0}\left[\frac{x2^x - x}{1-\cos x}\right] = \lim_{x\to 0}\left[\frac{x\{e^{x\ln 2}-1\}}{1-\cos x}\right] = \lim_{x\to 0}\left[\frac{x\left\{x\log 2+\dfrac{(x\log 2)^2}{2!}+....\right\}}{1-\left(1-\dfrac{x^2}{2!}+\dfrac{x^4}{4!}.....\right)}\right] = \log 4$$

(ii) $$\lim_{x\to 0}\frac{x-\log(1+x)}{x^2} = \lim_{x\to 0}\frac{x-\left\{x-\dfrac{x^2}{2}+\dfrac{x^3}{3}......\right\}}{x^2} = \frac{1}{2}$$

(iii) $$\lim_{x\to 0}\frac{e^{-x^2}-1}{-x^2} = \lim_{x\to 0}\frac{-x^2+\dfrac{(-x^2)^2}{2!}+\dfrac{(-x^2)^3}{3!}+....\text{to}\,\infty}{-x^2}$$

$$= \lim_{x\to 0}\frac{-x^2\left(1+\dfrac{-x^2}{2!}+\dfrac{(-x^2)^2}{3!}+....to\,\infty\right)}{-x^2} = 1+0+0+0+....\text{to}\,\infty = 1$$

ILLUSTRATION 79: Evaluate $\lim\limits_{x\to 0}\dfrac{e-(1+x)^{1/x}}{\tan x}$

SOLUTION: $$\lim_{x\to 0}\frac{e-(1+x)^{1/x}}{\tan x} = \lim_{x\to 0}\frac{e-e\left(1-\dfrac{x}{2}\right)}{\tan x} = \lim_{x\to 0}\frac{e}{2}\times\frac{x}{\tan x} = \frac{e}{2}$$

ILLUSTRATION 80: The integer 'n' for which $\lim\limits_{x\to 0}\dfrac{(\cos x-1)(\cos x-e^x)}{x^n}$ is a finite non-zero number is.

(a) 1 (b) 2

(c) 3 (d) 4

SOLUTION: $$\lim_{x\to 0}\frac{(\cos x-1)(\cos x-e^x)}{x^n} = \lim_{x\to 0}\frac{-2\sin^2\dfrac{x}{2}\left\{\left(1-\dfrac{x^2}{2!}+\dfrac{x^4}{4!}-......\right)-\left(1+x+\dfrac{x^2}{2!}+.........\right)\right\}}{x^n}$$

$$= \lim_{x\to 0}\frac{-2\sin^2\dfrac{x}{2}\left[-x-\dfrac{2x^2}{2!}-\dfrac{x^3}{3!}-......\right]}{4.\left(\dfrac{x}{2}\right)^2.x^{n-2}} = \lim_{x\to 0}\frac{\sin^2\dfrac{x}{2}\left(1+x+\dfrac{x^2}{3!}+......\right)}{2.\left(\dfrac{x}{2}\right)^2.x^{n-3}}$$

This is finite if $n-3=0$. i.e., $n=3$

ILLUSTRATION 81: Find the values of a, b and c so that $\lim\limits_{x\to 0}\dfrac{ae^x - b\cos x + ce^{-x}}{x.\sin x} = 2$

SOLUTION: $\lim\limits_{x\to 0}\dfrac{ae^x - b\cos x + ce^{-x}}{x\sin x} = 2$

$$\Rightarrow \lim_{x\to 0}\frac{a\left[1+\frac{x}{1!}+\frac{x^2}{2!}+.....\right]-b\left[1-\frac{x^2}{2!}+\frac{x^4}{4!}-.....\right]+c\left[1-\frac{x}{1!}+\frac{x^2}{2!}-.....\right]}{x^2\left[\frac{\sin x}{x}\right]} = 2$$

$\Rightarrow a - b + c = 0 =$ constant

coefficient of $x = a - c = 0 \Rightarrow a = c$

coefficient of $x^2 = \dfrac{a}{2}+\dfrac{b}{2}+\dfrac{c}{2} = 2 \Rightarrow a + b + c = 4$

$\Rightarrow 2(a + c) = 4 \Rightarrow a + c = 2$

$\Rightarrow a = 1 = c$

$\Rightarrow b = 2$

Thus $a = 1$, $b = 2$, $c = 1$

ILLUSTRATION 82: $\lim\limits_{x\to 0}\dfrac{\tan^2 x - x^2}{x^2\tan^2 x}$

SOLUTION: $\lim\limits_{x\to 0}\dfrac{(\tan x - x)(\tan x + x)}{x^2\tan^2 x}$

$$= \lim_{x\to 0}\frac{\left\{\left(x+\frac{x^3}{3}+\frac{2x^5}{15}+.......\right)-x\right\}\frac{(\tan x + x)}{x}}{x.x^2\tan^2 x/x^2} = \left(\frac{1}{3}\right)(1+1) = \frac{2}{3}$$

ILLUSTRATION 83: $\lim\limits_{x\to 0}\left[\dfrac{\ell n(1+x)^{1+x}}{x^2}-\dfrac{1}{x}\right]$

SOLUTION: $\lim\limits_{x\to 0}\left[\dfrac{\ell n(1+x)^{1+x}}{x^2}-\dfrac{1}{x}\right] = \lim\limits_{x\to 0}\left\{\dfrac{\frac{(1+x)}{x}\left[\frac{x}{1}-\frac{x^2}{2}+\frac{x^3}{3}......\right]-1}{x}\right\}$

$$= \lim_{x\to 0}\frac{(1+x)\left[1-\frac{x}{2}+\frac{x^2}{3}.....\right]-1}{x} = \lim_{x\to 0}\frac{\left(-\frac{x}{2}+\frac{x^2}{3}-\frac{x^3}{4}.....\right)+x\left(1-\frac{x}{2}.....\right)}{x} = -\frac{1}{2}+1 = \frac{1}{2}$$

ILLUSTRATION 84: $f(x)$ is the function such that $\lim\limits_{x\to 0}\dfrac{f(x)}{x} = 1$. If $\lim\limits_{x\to 0}\dfrac{x(1+a\cos x)-b\sin x}{(f(x))^3} = 1$, then find the value of a and b.

SOLUTION: Given $\lim\limits_{x\to 0}\dfrac{f(x)}{x} = 1$

$$\therefore \ \lim_{x\to 0}\frac{x(1+a\cos x)-b\sin x}{(f(x))^3}=1 = \lim_{\to}\frac{x(1+a\cos x)-b\sin x}{\left[(f(x))\right]} \quad 1$$

$$\lim_{x\to 0}\frac{1+a\cos x-b\dfrac{\sin x}{x}}{x^2}=1 \quad \ldots\text{(i)}$$

$$1 + a - b = 0 \Rightarrow b = 1 + a \quad \ldots\text{(ii)}$$

$$\text{From (i) } \lim_{x\to 0}\frac{1+a\left[1-\dfrac{x^2}{2!}+\dfrac{x^4}{4!}-\dfrac{x^6}{6!}\ldots\right]-\dfrac{b}{x}\left[x-\dfrac{x^3}{3!}+\dfrac{x^5}{5!}\ldots\right]}{x^2}=1$$

$$\therefore \ \text{Coefficient of } x^2 = \frac{-a}{2}+\frac{b}{6}=1 \quad \ldots\text{(iii)}$$

$$\Rightarrow -3a + b = 6 \quad \ldots\text{(iv)}$$

$$\Rightarrow -2a + 1 = 6$$

$$\Rightarrow a = -5/2,\ b = -3/2$$

LIMIT AT INFINITY

When x tends to infinity the limit is called limit at infinity. Let us first discuss the limit of the form $\frac{\infty}{\infty}$ **i.e.,** $\lim_{x\to\infty}\frac{f(x)}{g(x)}$ to be found such that $f(x), g(x) \to \infty$ as $x \to \infty$, where $f(x)$ and $g(x)$ are polynomials of degree m and n respectively.

Let $f(x) = a_0x^m + a_1x^{m-1} + a_2x^{m-2} + \ldots + a_{m-1}x + a_m$

And $f(x) = b_0x^n + b_1x^{n-1} + b_2x^{n-2} + \ldots + b_{n-1}x + b_n$

Case (i) **when $m > n$**

Then $$\lim_{x\to\infty}\frac{\left(a_0x^m+a_1x^{m-1}+a_2x^{m-2}+\ldots+a_{m-1}x+a_m\right)}{b_0x^n+b_1x^{n-1}+b_2x^{n-2}+\ldots+b_{n-1}x+b_n}$$

Dividing numerator and denominator by x^m we get

$$\lim_{x\to\infty}\frac{a_0+\dfrac{a_1}{x}+\dfrac{a_2}{x^2}+\ldots+\dfrac{a_{m-1}}{x^{m-1}}+\dfrac{a_m}{x^m}}{\left(\dfrac{b_0}{x^{m-n}}+\dfrac{b_1}{x^{m-(n-1)}}+\dfrac{b_2}{x^{m-(n-2)}}+\ldots+\dfrac{b_{n-1}}{x^{m-1}}+\dfrac{b_n}{x^m}\right)}$$

$\to \frac{a_0}{0}=\infty$ [$\because m > m-1 > \ldots > m-(n-2) > m-(n-1) > (m-n) > 0$, denominator tends to zero.]

$$\therefore \ \lim_{x\to\infty}\frac{f(x)}{g(x)}=\infty$$

Case (ii) $m = n$

$\lim_{x\to\infty}\frac{a_0x^m+a_1x^{m-1}+a_2x^{m-2}+\ldots+a_{m-1}x+a_m}{b_0x^n+b_1x^{n-1}+b_2x^{n-2}+\ldots+b_{n-1}x+b_n}$. Dividing numerator and denominator by x^n we get

$$\lim_{x\to\infty}\frac{\left[a_0+\dfrac{a_1}{x}+\dfrac{a_2}{x^2}+\ldots+\dfrac{a_{m-1}}{x^{n-1}}+\dfrac{a_m}{x^n}\right]}{\left[b_0+\dfrac{b_1}{x}+\dfrac{b_2}{x^2}+\ldots+\dfrac{b_{n-1}}{x^{n-1}}+\dfrac{b_n}{x^n}\right]}=\frac{a_0}{b_0}$$

Case (iii) **$m < n$**

$$\lim_{x\to\infty}\frac{a_0x^m+a_1x^{m-1}+\ldots+a_{m-1}x+a_m}{b_0x^n+b_1x^{n-1}+b_2x^{n-2}+\ldots+b_{n-1}x+b_n}$$

Dividing numerator and denominator by x^n we get

$$\lim_{x\to\infty}\left[\frac{\dfrac{a_0}{x^{n-m}}+\dfrac{a_1}{x^{n-m+1}}+\ldots+\dfrac{a_{m-1}}{x^{n-1}}+\dfrac{a_m}{x^n}}{b_0+\dfrac{b_1}{x}+\dfrac{b_2}{x^2}+\ldots+\dfrac{b_{n-1}}{x^{n-1}}+\dfrac{b_n}{x^n}}\right]=\frac{0}{b_0}=0$$

$$\therefore \ \lim_{x\to\infty}\frac{f(x)}{g(x)}=0$$

Thus if degree of numerator > degree of denominator, then limit $= \infty$, if degree of numerator = degree of denominator, then limit $= \frac{a_0}{b_0}$, if degree $N_r <$ degree D_r, then limit $= 0$.

ILLUSTRATION 85: Evaluate $\lim\limits_{x\to\infty}\frac{x-2}{2x-3}$.

SOLUTION: $\lim\limits_{x\to\infty}\frac{x-2}{2x-3} = \lim\limits_{x\to\infty}\frac{1-2/x}{2-3/x}=\frac{1}{2}$

ILLUSTRATION 86: Evaluate $\lim\limits_{x\to\infty}\frac{x^2-4x+5}{3x^2-x^3+2}$

SOLUTION: $\lim\limits_{x\to\infty}\frac{x^2-4x+5}{3x^2-x^3+2} = \lim\limits_{x\to\infty}\frac{\frac{1}{x}-\frac{4}{x^2}+\frac{5}{x^3}}{\frac{3}{x}-1+\frac{2}{x^3}}=0$

ILLUSTRATION 87: Evaluate $\lim\limits_{x\to\infty}\frac{\sqrt{3x^2+2}}{x-2}$

SOLUTION: $\lim\limits_{x\to\infty}\frac{\sqrt{3x^2+2}}{x-2}$

Put $x=\frac{1}{t}$; $x\to\infty$

$$\Rightarrow t\to 0^+ = \lim_{t\to 0^+}\frac{\sqrt{3+2t^2}\cdot\frac{1}{\sqrt{t^2}}}{\frac{1-2t}{t}} = \lim_{t\to 0^+}\frac{\sqrt{3+2t^2}}{(1-2t)}\frac{t}{|t|}=\frac{\sqrt{3}}{1}=\sqrt{3}$$

ILLUSTRATION 88: $\text{Lim}_{x\to\infty}\frac{2\sqrt{x}+3x^{1/3}+5x^{1/5}}{\sqrt{3x-2}+(2x-3)^{1/3}}$

SOLUTION: $\text{Lim}_{x\to\infty}\frac{2x^{\frac{1}{2}}+3x^{\frac{1}{3}}+5x^{\frac{1}{5}}}{(3x-2)^{\frac{1}{2}}+(2x-3)^{\frac{1}{3}}}$; dividing numerator and denominator by $x^{1/2}$

$$= \text{Lim}_{x\to\infty}\frac{2+\frac{3}{x^{\frac{1}{6}}}+\frac{5}{x^{\frac{3}{10}}}}{\left(3-\frac{2}{x}\right)^{\frac{1}{2}}+x^{-\frac{1}{6}}\left(2-\frac{3}{x}\right)^{\frac{1}{3}}} \Rightarrow \frac{2+0+0}{\sqrt{3}+0}=\frac{2}{\sqrt{3}}$$

ILLUSTRATION 89: If $\lim\limits_{x\to\infty}\left(\frac{x^2+1}{x+1}-ax-b\right)=0$, find the values of a and b

SOLUTION: We have $\lim\limits_{x\to\infty}\left(\frac{x^2+1}{x+1}-ax-b\right)=0$

$$\Rightarrow \lim_{x\to\infty}\frac{x^2+1-ax^2-ax-bx-b}{x+1}=0 \qquad \Rightarrow \lim_{x\to\infty}\frac{x^2(1-a)-x(a+b)+(1-b)}{x+1}=0$$

The limit of above expression is zero

∴ degree of numerator < degree of denominator. So, numerator must be a constant. i.e., zero degree polynomial

∴ $1-a=0$ and $a+b=0$; Hence $a=1$ and $b=-1$

ILLUSTRATION 90: If $\lim_{x\to\infty}\left(\frac{x^2-1}{x+1}-ax-b\right)=2$, find the values of a and b

SOLUTION: We have $\lim_{x\to\infty}\left(\frac{x^2-1}{x+1}-ax-b\right)=2 \Rightarrow \lim_{x\to\infty}\frac{x^2(1-a)-x(a+b)+(-1-b)}{x+1}=2$

Since, limit of above expression is a finite non zero number,

$\therefore$ Degree of numerator = degree of denominator

$\Rightarrow 1-a=0 \qquad \Rightarrow a=1$

$\therefore$ Putting $a=1$ in above limit we get, $\lim_{x\to\infty}\frac{-x(1+b)+(-1-b)}{x+1}=2$

$\Rightarrow -(1+b)=2 \qquad \Rightarrow b=-3$

Hence $a=1$ and $b=-3$

ILLUSTRATION 91: Let $P_n=\frac{2^3-1}{2^3+1}\cdot\frac{3^3-1}{3^3+1}\cdot\frac{4^3-1}{4^3+1}\cdots\cdots\frac{n^3-1}{n^3+1}$. Prove that $\lim_{n\to\infty}P_n=\frac{2}{3}$

SOLUTION: $P_n=\frac{2^3-1}{2^3+1}\cdot\frac{3^3-1}{3^3+1}\cdot\frac{4^3-1}{4^3+1}\cdots\cdots\frac{n^3-1}{n^3+1}$

$$\therefore\ P_n=\frac{2^3-1}{2^3+1}\cdot\frac{3^3-1}{3^3+1}\cdots\cdots\frac{n^3-1}{n^3+1}=\frac{(2-1)(2^2+2+1)}{(2+1)(2^2-2+1)}\cdot\frac{(3-1)(3^2+3+1)}{(3+1)(3^2-3+1)}\cdots\cdots\frac{(n-1)(n^2+n+1)}{(n+1)(n^2-n+1)}$$

$$=\frac{1.7}{3.3}\cdot\frac{2.13}{4.7}\cdot\frac{3.21}{5.13}\cdots\cdots\frac{(n-1)(n^2+n+1)}{(n+1)(n^2-n+1)}=\frac{1.2.3\ldots\ldots\ldots(n-1)}{3.4.5\ldots\ldots\ldots(n+1)}\cdot\frac{7.13.21\ldots\ldots\ldots(n^2+n+1)}{3.7.13\ldots\ldots\ldots(n^2-n+1)}$$

$$=\frac{1.2}{n(n+1)}\cdot\frac{(n^2+n+1)}{3}\Rightarrow \lim_{n\to\infty}P_n=\lim_{n\to\infty}\frac{2(n^2+n+1)}{3(n^2+n)}=\lim_{n\to\infty}\frac{2}{3}\frac{\left(1+\frac{1}{n}+\frac{1}{n^2}\right)}{\left(1+\frac{1}{n}\right)}=\frac{2}{3}$$

■ USING L-HOSPITAL RULE

If $f(x)$ and $g(x)$ are functions of x such that $\frac{f(a)}{g(a)}$ is either $\left\{\frac{0}{0}\right\}$ or $\left[\frac{\infty}{\infty}\right]$ ......, then $\lim_{x\to a}\frac{f(x)}{g(x)}=\lim_{x\to a}\frac{f'(x)}{g'(x)}=\lim_{x\to a}\frac{f''(x)}{g''(x)}$ till a determinate is obtained.

Proof: If $\lim_{x\to a}\frac{f(x)}{g(x)}$ is of $\frac{0}{0}$ form, then using Taylors expansion:

$$f(x)=f(a)+(x-a)f'(a)+\frac{(x-a)^2}{2!}f''(a)+\ldots$$

$$g(x)=g(a)+(x-a)g'(a)+\frac{(x-a)^2}{2!}g''(a)+\frac{(x-a)^3}{3!}g'''(a)+\ldots$$

$\because \lim_{x\to a}\frac{f(x)}{g(x)}=\frac{0}{0}$

$\Rightarrow g(a)=0, f(a)=0$ so

$$L=\lim_{x\to a}\frac{(x-a)\left[f'(a)+\frac{(x-a)f''(a)}{2!}+\frac{(x-a)^2f'''(a)}{3!}+\ldots..\right]}{(x-a)\left[g'(a)+\frac{(x-a)g''(a)}{2!}+\frac{(x-a)^2g'''(a)}{3!}+\ldots..\right]}$$

$=\frac{f'(a)}{g'(a)}$ (if it is not of 0/0 form)

and if it is of $\frac{0}{0}$ form, then this process continuous till limit takes up determinate form.

ILLUSTRATION 92: Find the value of $\lim_{x\to 0}\frac{x\cos x-\ln(1+x)}{x^2}$

SOLUTION: This limit is of the form 0/0

Applying L.H. Rule, we get $\lim_{x\to 0}\frac{\cos x - x\sin x - \frac{1}{1+x}}{2x}$ [0/0 form]

Now, again applying L.H. Rule, $= \lim_{x\to 0}\frac{-\sin x-\sin x-x\cos x+\frac{1}{(1+x)^2}}{2}=\frac{1}{2}$

ILLUSTRATION 93: Evaluate the following:

(a) $\lim_{x\to 0}\log_{\sin x}\sin 2x$ **(b)** $\lim_{x\to 1}\sec\frac{\pi}{2^x}.\ln x$

SOLUTION: **(a)** $\lim_{x\to 0}\frac{\ln\sin 2x}{\ln\sin x}$ $\left(\frac{\infty}{\infty}\text{ form}\right)=\lim_{x\to 0}\frac{\frac{1}{\sin 2x}.2\cos 2x}{\frac{1}{\sin x}.\cos x}=\lim_{x\to 0}\frac{\cos 2x}{\cos^2 x}=1$

(b) $\lim_{x\to 1}\sec\frac{\pi}{2^x}.\ln x$ $(\infty\times 0\text{ form})=\lim_{x\to 1}\frac{\ln x}{\cos\pi/2^x}$ (0/0 form)

$=\lim_{x\to 1}\frac{1/x}{\left(-\sin\frac{\pi}{2^x}\right)\left(\pi.2^{-x}(\ln 2)(-1)\right)}=\frac{1}{(-1)\left(-\frac{\pi}{2}\ln 2\right)}=\frac{2}{\pi\ln 2}$ (By L.H. Rule)

ILLUSTRATION 94: Evaluate $\lim_{x\to 1}\frac{x^2-3x+2}{x-1}$

SOLUTION: ***Method - I:*** $\lim_{x\to 1}\frac{x^2-3x+2}{x-1}$ (0/0 form)

$\lim_{x\to 1}\frac{(x-1)(x-2)}{x-1}=\lim_{x\to 1}(x-2)$ [as x -1 $\neq$ 0] = 1 − 2 = −1

Method - II $\lim_{x\to 1}\frac{x^2-3x+2}{x-1}$ (0/0 form)

So applying L-Hospital's rule

$\lim_{x\to 1}\frac{2x-3}{1}=\frac{2-3}{1}=-1$

(i.e., differentiating numerator and denominator separately)

ILLUSTRATION 95: Evaluate $\lim_{x\to 0}\frac{\sin 5x}{x}$

SOLUTION: Here $\lim_{x\to 0}\frac{f(x)}{g(x)}=\lim_{x\to 0}\frac{\sin 5x}{x}$

$\Rightarrow \frac{f(0)}{g(0)}=\frac{0}{0}$. So $\lim_{x\to 0}\frac{\sin 5x}{x}=\lim_{x\to 0}\frac{5\cos 5x}{1}=5$ (By L.H Rule)

ILLUSTRATION 96: $\lim\limits_{x\to 1}\dfrac{x^2-\sqrt{x}}{\sqrt{x}-1}$

SOLUTION: $\lim\limits_{x\to 1}\dfrac{x^2-\sqrt{x}}{\sqrt{x}-1}$ (Applying L.H Rule)

$$\Rightarrow \lim_{x\to 1}\frac{2x-\dfrac{1}{2\sqrt{x}}}{\dfrac{1}{2\sqrt{x}}}$$

$$\Rightarrow \lim_{x\to 1}\frac{4x^{3/2}-1}{1}=3 \text{ Ans.}$$

ILLUSTRATION 97: $\lim\limits_{x\to 1}\dfrac{\sqrt[13]{x}-\sqrt[7]{x}}{\sqrt[5]{x}-\sqrt[3]{x}}$

SOLUTION: $\lim\limits_{x\to 1}\dfrac{x^{\frac{1}{13}}-x^{\frac{1}{7}}}{x^{\frac{1}{5}}-x^{\frac{1}{3}}}$ $\left(\dfrac{0}{0}\text{ form}\right)$ (Apply L.H Rule)

$$=\lim_{x\to 1}\frac{\dfrac{1}{13}x^{-1+\frac{1}{13}}-\dfrac{1}{7}x^{-1+\frac{1}{7}}}{\dfrac{1}{5}x^{\frac{1}{5}-1}-\dfrac{1}{3}x^{\frac{1}{3}-1}}=\lim_{x\to 1}\frac{\dfrac{1}{13}-\dfrac{1}{7}}{\dfrac{1}{5}-\dfrac{1}{3}}=\frac{45}{91}$$

ILLUSTRATION 98: $\lim\limits_{x\to 1}\dfrac{x^2-x\ln x+\ln x-1}{x-1}$

SOLUTION: Applying L-H Rule, $=\lim\limits_{x\to 1}\dfrac{x^2-x\ell nx+\ell nx-1}{x-1}=\lim\limits_{x\to 1}\dfrac{2x-\left(x\times\dfrac{1}{x}+\ell nx\times 1\right)+\dfrac{1}{x}-0}{1}$

$$=\lim_{x\to 1}\frac{2x-1-\ell nx+\dfrac{1}{x}-1}{1}=2$$

ILLUSTRATION 99: $\lim\limits_{x\to 1}\dfrac{\left[\sum\limits_{k=1}^{100}x^k\right]-100}{x-1}$

SOLUTION: $\lim\limits_{x\to 1}\dfrac{\sum\limits_{k=1}^{100}x^k-100}{x-1}$

$$\Rightarrow \lim_{x\to 1}\frac{x-1}{x-1}+\lim_{x\to 1}\frac{x^2-1}{x-1}+\lim_{x\to 1}\frac{x^3-1}{x-1}+.....+\lim_{x\to 1}\frac{x^{100}-1}{x-1}$$

Applying L.H Rule

$$=\lim_{x\to 1}1+\lim_{x\to 1}2x+\lim_{x\to 1}3x^2+\lim_{x\to 1}4x^3+.........+\lim_{x\to 1}100x^{99}=1+2+3+4+..........+100$$

$$=\frac{100(100+1)}{2}=50\times 101\left(\because\ 1+2+3..........+n=\frac{n(n+1)}{2}\right)=5050$$

ILLUSTRATION 100: $\lim\limits_{x\to\frac{3\pi}{4}} \dfrac{1+\sqrt[3]{\tan x}}{1-2\cos^2 x}$

SOLUTION: $\lim\limits_{x\to 3\pi/4} \dfrac{1+(\tan x)^{\frac{1}{3}}}{1-2\cos^2 x} = \lim\limits_{x\to 3\pi/4} \dfrac{1+(\tan x)^{\frac{1}{3}}}{-\cos 2x} \quad \left(\dfrac{0}{0} \text{ form}\right)$

Applying L.H Rule

$$= \lim_{x\to\frac{3\pi}{4}} \frac{\frac{1}{3}(\tan x)^{\frac{-2}{3}} \times \sec^2 x}{+2\sin 2x} = \frac{-1}{6}\left(-\sec\frac{\pi}{4}\right)^2 = \frac{-1}{6}\times 2 = -\frac{1}{3}$$

ILLUSTRATION 101: $\lim\limits_{x\to 1}\left(\dfrac{p}{1-x^p} - \dfrac{q}{1-x^q}\right); p, q \in \mathbb{Z}$

SOLUTION: $\lim\limits_{x\to 1}\left(\dfrac{p}{1-x^p} - \dfrac{q}{1-x^q}\right) \quad (\infty - \infty \text{ form})$

$$= \lim_{x\to 1}\left(\frac{p(1-x^q)-q(1-x^p)}{(1-x^p)\,(1-x^q)}\right) = \lim_{x\to 1}\left(\frac{p-px^q-q+qx^p}{1-x^q-x^p+x^{p+q}}\right) \left(\frac{0}{0} \text{ form}\right)$$

Apply L-H Rule

$$\lim_{x\to 1}\left(\frac{-pqx^{q-1}+qpx^{p-1}}{-qx^{q-1}-px^{p-1}+(p+q)x^{(p+q-1)}}\right) \left(\frac{0}{0} \text{ form}\right)$$

$$\lim_{x\to 1}\left(\frac{-pq(q-1)x^{q-2}+qp(p-1)x^{p-2}}{-q(q-1)x^{q-2}-p(p-1)x^{p-2}+(p+q)(p+q-1)x^{(p+q-2)}}\right)$$

$$= \frac{-pq^2+pq+p^2q-pq}{-q^2+q-p^2+p+p^2+pq-p+qp+q^2-q}$$

$$= \frac{p^2q-pq^2}{2pq} = \frac{pq(p-q)}{2pq} = \frac{p-q}{2}$$

ILLUSTRATION 102: $\lim\limits_{\theta\to\frac{\pi}{4}} \dfrac{\sqrt{2}-\cos\theta-\sin\theta}{(4\theta-\pi)^2}$

SOLUTION: $\lim\limits_{\theta\to\frac{\pi}{4}} \dfrac{\sqrt{2}-\cos\theta-\sin\theta}{(4\theta-\pi)^2} \quad \left(\dfrac{0}{0} \text{ form}\right)$

Apply L.H. rule

$$= \lim_{\theta\to\frac{\pi}{4}} \frac{\sin\theta-\cos\theta}{2(4\theta-\pi).4} \quad \left(- \text{ form}\right)$$

Again apply L-Hospital rule

$$= \lim_{\theta\to\frac{\pi}{4}} \frac{\cos\theta+\sin\theta}{8(4)} = \frac{\frac{1}{\sqrt{2}}+\frac{1}{\sqrt{2}}}{32} = \frac{\sqrt{2}}{32} = \frac{1}{16\sqrt{2}}$$

ILLUSTRATION 103: $\lim\limits_{x\to 0}\dfrac{1+\sin x-\cos x+\ell n(1-x)}{x\cdot\tan^2 x}$

SOLUTION: $\lim\limits_{x\to 0}\dfrac{1+\sin x-\cos x+\ell n(1-x)}{x\cdot\tan^2 x}=\text{Lim}_{x\to 0}\dfrac{1+\sin x-\cos x+\ell n(1-x)}{x^3}\left(\dfrac{0}{0}\right)=\text{Lim}_{x\to 0}\dfrac{\cos x+\sin x-\dfrac{1}{1-x}}{3x^2}$

Again apply L.H. rule

$$=\text{Lim}_{x\to 0}\frac{-\sin x+\cos x-\dfrac{1}{(1-x)^2}}{6x}=\text{Lim}_{x\to 0}\frac{-\cos x-\sin x-\dfrac{2}{(1-x)^3}}{6}=\frac{-1-2}{6}=-\frac{1}{2}$$

■ EVALUATION OF LIMITS BY USING LOGARITHM

To evaluate limit of the form $\lim\limits_{x\to a}\left(f(x)\right)^{g(x)}$ $\left(1^\infty \text{ or } 0^0 \text{ or} \infty^0 \text{ forms}\right)$. We assume limit to be 'L' and then take natural logarithm on both sides, i.e., $L=\lim\limits_{x\to a}f((x))^{g(x)}$

$\Rightarrow\ \ell nL=\lim\limits_{x\to a}g(x)\ell nf(x)\Rightarrow L=e^{\lim\limits_{x\to a}g(x)\ell nf(x)}$ .....(i)

Evaluation of Limit $\lim\limits_{x\to a}\left(f(x)\right)^{g(x)}$ When It is of the Form $(1)^\infty$.

Then from **(i)** $L=e^{\lim\limits_{x\to a}g(x)\ell n f(x)}$

$$=e^{\lim\limits_{x\to a}g(x)(f(x)-1)\cdot\frac{\ell n\left[1+(f(x)-1)\right]}{(f(x)-1)}}=e^{\lim\limits_{x\to a}g(x)(f(x)-1)}$$

Aliter: $\lim\limits_{x\to a}f(x)^{\phi(x)}=\lim\limits_{x\to a}e^{\phi(x)\,\ell n\,f(x)}$

$$=e^{\lim\limits_{x\to a}\phi(x).(f(x)-1)\frac{\ell n\,[1+(f(x)-1)]}{f(x)-1}}=e^{\lim\limits_{x\to a}\phi(x)\,(f(x)-1)}$$

ILLUSTRATION 104: Evaluate the $\lim\limits_{x\to 0}\left[\dfrac{a^x+b^x+c^x}{3}\right]^{2/x}$

SOLUTION: $\lim\limits_{x\to 0}\left[\dfrac{a^x+b^x+c^x}{3}\right]^{2/x}=\lim\limits_{x\to 0}e^{2/x\left\{\frac{a^x+b^x+c^x}{3}-1\right\}}=\lim\limits_{x\to 0}e^{\left\{\frac{2(a^x+b^x+c^x)-6}{3x}\right\}}$

$$=\lim_{x\to 0}e^{\frac{2}{3}\left\{\frac{a^x-1}{x}+\frac{b^x-1}{x}+\frac{c^x-1}{x}\right\}}=e^{\frac{2}{3}\{\ell na+\ell nb+\ell nc\}}=e^{\frac{2\ell n\,abc}{3}}=(abc)^{2/3}$$

(Can you think of! applying inequality of means A.M. ≥ G.M in this question to evaluate the limit of function? The result will give you** a **broad smile on your face)

ILLUSTRATION 105: Evaluate $\lim\limits_{x\to\infty}\left(\dfrac{2x^2-1}{2x^2+3}\right)^{4x^2+2}$

SOLUTION: Since it is in the form of 1^∞

$$\lim_{x\to\infty}\left(\frac{2x^2-1}{2x^2+3}\right)^{4x^2+2}=\exp\left(\lim_{x\to\infty}\left(\frac{2x^2-1-2x^2-3}{2x^2+3}\right)\left(4x^2+2\right)\right)=e^{-8}$$

ILLUSTRATION 106: Evaluate $\lim\limits_{x\to\frac{\pi}{4}}(\tan x)^{\tan 2x}$

SOLUTION: Since it is in the form of $1^{\infty} = e^{\lim\limits_{x\to\frac{\pi}{4}}(\tan x-1)\tan 2x} = e^{\lim\limits_{x\to\frac{\pi}{4}}(\tan x-1)\frac{2\tan x}{1-\tan^2 x}} = e^{2\times\frac{\tan\pi/4}{-1(1+\tan\pi/4)}} = e^{-1} = \frac{1}{e}$

ILLUSTRATION 107: Evaluate $\lim\limits_{x\to a}\left(2-\frac{a}{x}\right)^{\tan\frac{\pi x}{2a}}$

SOLUTION: $\lim\limits_{x\to a}\left(2-\frac{a}{x}\right)^{\tan\frac{\pi x}{2a}}$; put $x = a + h$

$$= \lim_{h\to 0}\left(1+\frac{h}{(a+h)}\right)^{\tan\left(\frac{\pi}{2}+\frac{\pi h}{2a}\right)} = \lim_{h\to 0}\left(1+\frac{h}{(a+h)}\right)^{-\cot\left(\frac{\pi h}{2a}\right)} = e^{\lim\limits_{h\to 0}-\cot\frac{\pi h}{2a}\left(1+\frac{h}{a+h}-1\right)} = e^{\lim\limits_{h\to 0}-\left(\frac{\frac{\pi h}{2a}}{\tan\frac{\pi h}{2a}}\right)\frac{\frac{2a}{\pi}}{a+h}} = e^{-2/\pi}$$

ILLUSTRATION 108: Evaluate $\lim\limits_{x\to 0^+} x^x$

SOLUTION: Let $y = \lim\limits_{x\to 0^+} x^x$

$$\Rightarrow \ell \boldsymbol{n}\, y = \lim_{x\to 0^+} x\,\ell n\, x = \lim_{x\to 0^+} -\frac{\ell n\frac{1}{x}}{\frac{1}{x}} = 0 \textbf{ as } \frac{1}{x}\to\infty \Rightarrow y = 1$$

ILLUSTRATION 109: $\lim\limits_{\to\infty}\left(\frac{x \quad c}{x \quad c}\right) \quad 4$, then find c

SOLUTION: $e^{\lim\limits_{x\to\infty}\left[\left(\frac{x+c-x+c}{x-c}\right).x\right]} = e^{2c} = 4,\ 2c = \ell n 4 \Rightarrow c = \ell n 2$

ILLUSTRATION 110: $\lim\limits_{x\to 0}\left[\frac{(1+x)^{1/x}}{e}\right]^{1/x}$

SOLUTION: $\lim\limits_{x\to 0}\left[\frac{(1+x)^{1/x}}{e}\right]^{1/x} \quad ((1)^{\infty})$

$$L = e^{\lim\limits_{x\to 0}\frac{(1+x)^{1/x}-e}{e}.\frac{1}{x}} = \lim_{x\to 0}\frac{e[e^{\frac{\ell n(1+x)}{x}-1}-1]}{\frac{e(\ell n(1+x)-x)}{x}}\cdot\left(\frac{\ell n(1+x)-x}{x^2}\right) = e^{-\frac{1}{2}}$$

ILLUSTRATION 111: $\lim\limits_{x\to 0}\left(\frac{x-1+\cos x}{x}\right)^{\frac{1}{x}}$

SOLUTION: $\lim\limits_{x\to 0}\left(\frac{x-1+\cos x}{x}\right)^{\frac{1}{x}} = \lim\limits_{x\to 0}\left(\frac{x-1+1-\frac{x^2}{2!}+\frac{x^4}{4!}+.....}{x}\right)^{1/x} = \lim\limits_{x\to 0}\left(1-\frac{x}{2}+\frac{x^3}{4!}.........\right)^{1/x}$

$$\Rightarrow e^{\lim\limits_{x\to 0}\left(\frac{-x}{2}+\frac{x^2}{4!}+.........\right)\frac{1}{x} = e^{-1/2}}$$

Aliter: $e^{\lim\limits_{x\to 0}\left(\frac{x-1+\cos x-x}{x}\right)\frac{1}{x}} = e^{\lim\limits_{x\to 0}\frac{-2\sin^2\frac{x}{2}}{\frac{4x^2}{4}} = e^{-1/2}}$

Evaluat of Limit $\lim\limits_{x\to 0^+}(f(x))^{g(x)}$ When It is of the Form $(0)^0$

Let $L = \lim\limits_{x\to a}(f(x))^{g(x)}$

$\Rightarrow \quad \ell nL = \lim\limits_{x\to a} g(x)\,\ell n\, f(x)$

$\Rightarrow \quad L = e^{\lim\limits_{x\to a} g(x)\ell n f(x)} = e^{\lim\limits_{x\to a}\frac{\ell nf(x)}{1/g(x)}}$

Now evaluating the limit $\lim\limits_{x\to a}\dfrac{\ell nf(x)}{1/g(x)}$ (being of $\dfrac{\infty}{\infty}$ form) By L.H. Rule we can evaluate L.

ILLUSTRATION 112: Find $\lim\limits_{x\to 0^+}(\sin x)^{\sin x}$ (0^0 form)

SOLUTION: Let $A = \lim\limits_{x\to 0^+}(\sin x)^{\sin x}$

$\Rightarrow \log A = \lim\limits_{x\to 0^+}(\sin x).\log\sin x = \lim\limits_{x\to 0^+}\dfrac{\log\sin x}{\cos ec\, x}\left(\dfrac{\infty}{\infty}\right) = \lim\limits_{x\to 0^+}\dfrac{\cot x}{-\text{cosec}\, x\cot x} = 0$

$\Rightarrow A = 1$

ILLUSTRATION 113: Evaluate $\lim\limits_{x\to 0}(\sin x)^{\tan x}$

SOLUTION: Let $\ell = \lim\limits_{x\to 0}(\sin x)^{\tan x}$ (0^0 form)

Taking log on both sides $\ell n\, l = \lim\limits_{x\to 0}\tan x\ \ell \text{n}(\sin x)$ $(0\times(-\infty)$ form)

$= \lim\limits_{x\to 0}\dfrac{\ln\sin x}{\cot x}$ $(-\infty/\infty$ form)

$= \lim\limits_{x\to 0}\dfrac{\frac{1}{\sin x}\times\cos x}{-\cos ec^2 x} = \lim\limits_{x\to 0}(-\sin x\cos x) = 0 \quad \therefore\ l = e^0 = 1$

Evaluate of Limit $\lim\limits_{x\to a}(f(x))^{g(x)}$ When It is of the Form $(\infty)^0$

Let $L = \lim\limits_{x\to a}(f(x))^{g(x)}$, then take natural logarithm on both sides.

i.e., $\ell n L = \lim\limits_{x\to a} g(x)\,\ell n\, f(x) = \lim\limits_{x\to a}\dfrac{\ell nf(x)}{1/g(x)}$ .... $\dfrac{\infty}{\infty}$ form

$L = e^{\lim\limits_{x\to a}\frac{\ell nf(x)}{1/g(x)}}$

Now evaluating the limit $\lim\limits_{x\to a}\dfrac{\ell nf(x)}{1/g(x)}$ (being of $\dfrac{\infty}{\infty}$ form) by L.H. rule we can evaluate L.

ILLUSTRATION 114: For $x > 0$, evaluate $\lim\limits_{x\to 0}(\sin x)^{1/x} + (1/x)^{\sin x}$

SOLUTION: for $x > 0$, $\lim\limits_{x\to 0}(\sin x)^{1/x} + \left(\dfrac{1}{x}\right)^{\sin x}$

$\lim\limits_{x\to 0}(\sin x)^{1/x} + \lim\limits_{x\to 0}\left(\dfrac{1}{x}\right)^{\sin x} = 0 + \lim\limits_{x\to 0}\left(\dfrac{1}{x}\right)^{\sin x} = e^{\lim\limits_{x\to 0}\sin x.\ell n\left(\frac{1}{x}\right)} = e^{\lim\limits_{x\to 0}\left(\frac{\ell n(x)}{-\cos ecx}\right)}$ $\left(\dfrac{\infty}{\infty}\right)$ form

$= e^{\lim\limits_{x\to 0}\frac{1/x}{(+\cos ecx\ \cot x)}} = e^{\lim\limits_{x\to 0}\frac{\sin^2 x}{x\cos x}} = e^0 = 1$

LEIBINITIZ RULES

Let us consider the definite integral $F(x) = \int_{\varphi(x)}^{\psi(x)} f(t)dt$

Newton-Leibinitz's formula states that $\frac{d}{dx}(F(x)) = f\{\psi(x)\}.\left\{\frac{d}{dx}\psi(x)\right\} - f\{\phi(x)\}\left\{\frac{d}{dx}\phi(x)\right\}$

Proof: Let $\int f(t)dt = F(x)$

$\Rightarrow F'(t) = f(t)$

$\Rightarrow I(x) = F(\psi(x)) - F(\phi(x))$

$\Rightarrow I'(x) = F'(\psi(x)).\psi'(x) - F'(\phi(x)).\phi'(x)$

$= f\{\psi(x)\}.\left\{\frac{d}{dx}\psi(x)\right\} - f\{\phi(x)\}\left\{\frac{d}{dx}\phi(x)\right\}$

ILLUSTRATION 115: Evaluate $\lim_{x\to\infty}\left\{\frac{1}{x^5}\left(\int_0^x e^{-t^2}dt\right) - \frac{1}{x^4} + \frac{1}{3x^2}\right\}$

SOLUTION: Let $\lim_{x\to\infty}\frac{3\int_0^x e^{-t^2}dt - 3x + x^3}{3x^5}$ (0/0 form)

$= \lim_{x\to\infty}\frac{3\frac{d}{dx}\int_0^x e^{-t^2}dt - 3 + 3x^2}{15x^4}$ (by applying LHR)

By applying Newton's Leibinitz's formula, we get

$\Rightarrow \frac{d}{dx}\int_0^x e^{-t^2}dt = e^{-x^2}.\frac{dx}{dx} - e^{-0}\frac{d}{dx}(0) = e^{-x^2}$

$\therefore \lim_{x\to 0}\frac{3\frac{d}{dx}\int_0^x e^{-t^2}dt - 3 + 3x^2}{15x^4} = \lim_{x\to 0}\frac{3e^{-x^2} - 3 + 3x^2}{15x^4}$

(0/0 form, now again applying LH rule)

$= \lim_{x\to 0}\frac{-3(2x)e^{-x^2} + 6x}{60x^3} = \lim_{x\to 0}\frac{-6(e^{-x^2} - 1)}{60x^2}$

$= \lim_{x\to 0}\frac{-(e^{-x^2} - 1)}{10x^2} = \frac{1}{10}\lim_{x\to 0}\left(\frac{e^{-x^2} - 1}{-x^2}\right) = \frac{1}{10}\times 1 = \frac{1}{10}$

ILLUSTRATION 116: Evaluate $\lim_{x\to 0}\frac{x - \int_0^x \cos t^2 dt}{(x^3 - 6x)}$

SOLUTION: Let $\lim_{x\to 0}\frac{x - \int_0^x \cos t^2 dt}{(x^3 - 6x)}$ (0/ 0 form), ∴ Applying L.H. rule)= $\lim_{x\to 0}\frac{1 - \cos x^2}{3x^2 - 6} = 0$

Aliter: $\lim_{x\to 0}\frac{x - \int_0^x \cos t^2 dt}{x^3 - 6x} = \lim_{x\to 0}\frac{1 - \frac{d}{dx}\int_0^x \cos t^2 dt}{3x^2 - 6}$ (Applying L.H.)

Applying Newton-Leibnitz rule to $\frac{d}{dx}\int_0^x(\cos t^2)\,dt = \cos(x^2).1 - 0$

$\therefore \lim_{x\to 0}\frac{1 - \frac{d}{dx}\int_0^x \cos t^2 dt}{3x^2 - 6} = \lim_{x\to 0}\frac{1 - \cos(x^2)}{3(x^2 - 2)} = \frac{1 - \cos(0)}{3(0 - 2)} = \frac{1 - 1}{3(-2)} = \frac{0}{-6} = 0$

■ LIMIT OF SUMMMATION OF SERIES USING DEFINITE INTEGRAL

If $f(x)$ is defined and continuous in $[a, b]$. Let this interval be divided among n subinterval and i^{th} interval be $[x_i, x_{i+1}]$ such that $\Delta x_i = x_{i+1} - x_i$ and for any $\xi_i \in [x_i, x_{i+1}]$, $m_i \le f(\xi_1) \le M_i$

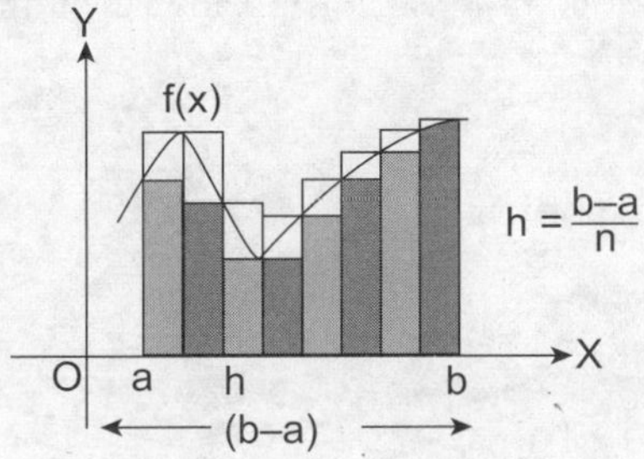

FIGURE 1.49

So we define lower limit sum as (s_n), upper limit sum as (S_n) and integral sum as $s = \sum_{i=0}^{n-1} m_i \Delta x_i$, $S = \sum_{i=0}^{n-1} M_i \Delta x_i$ and

$I = \sum_{i=0}^{n-1} f(\xi_i)\Delta x_i$ respectively. Clearly $s \le I \le S$, from here we can also say that $m(b - a) \le I \le M(b - a)$ when largest interval go to zero $(n \to \infty)$;

$$I = \int_a^b f(x)dx = \lim_{n\to\infty} \sum_{i=0}^{n-1} f(\xi_i)\Delta x_i$$

If interval be divided into n equal parts of width h, then

$$h = \frac{b-a}{n} \text{ when } n \to \infty \text{ ; } h \to 0$$

$$\therefore \quad \int_a^b f(x)dx = \lim_{n\to\infty} \sum_{r=1}^{n} hf(a+rh) = \lim_{h\to 0} \sum_{r=0}^{n-1} hf(a+rh)$$

$$= \lim_{n\to\infty} \frac{b-a}{n} \sum_{r=1}^{n} f\left[a + r\left(\frac{b-a}{n}\right)\right]$$

If we set the values of $a = 0$ and $b = 1$, then $\int_0^1 f(x)dx = \lim_{n\to\infty} \frac{1}{n} \sum f(r/n)$, hence if a series is represented as a recurring function, then its sum can be evaluated as definite integral of function as above. The method to evaluate the integral as limit of the sum of an infinite series is also known as **integration by first principle.**

■ METHOD TO EVALUATE THE LIMIT USING DEFINITE INTEGRAL

(a) Express the given series in form $\sum \frac{1}{n} f\left(\frac{r}{n}\right)$.

(b) $\lim_{n\to\infty} \sum \frac{1}{n} f\left(\frac{r}{n}\right) = \int_0^1 f(x)dx$, replacing $r/n = x$ & $1/n$ by dx and $\lim_{n\to\infty} \sum$ by sign of $\int$

(c) The lower and upper limits of integration will be the (r/n) for the $\lim_{n\to\infty} r_{\min}$ and $r_{\max}$ respectively.

ILLUSTRATION 117: Evaluate $\lim_{n\to\infty} \frac{1}{n} \sum_{r=1}^{2n} \frac{r}{\sqrt{n^2 + r^2}}$

SOLUTION: Here, $\lim_{n\to\infty} \frac{1}{n} \sum_{r=1}^{2n} \frac{r}{\sqrt{n^2 + r^2}}$, By dividing numerator and denominator by n,

we get $\lim_{n\to\infty} \frac{1}{n} \sum_{r=1}^{2n} \frac{r/n}{\sqrt{1 + (r/n)^2}}$

Put $r/n = x$, $1/n = dx$; $\lim_{n\to\infty} \sum_{r=1}^{2n} = \int_a^b$; where $a = \lim_{n\to\infty} \frac{1}{n} = 0$ and $b = \lim_{n\to\infty} \frac{2n}{n} = 2$

$$\therefore \quad \lim_{n\to\infty} \frac{1}{n} \sum_{r=1}^{2n} \frac{r/n}{\sqrt{1+(r/n)^2}} = \int_0^2 \frac{x}{\sqrt{1+x^2}} dx = \left(\sqrt{1+x^2}\right)_0^2 = \sqrt{5} - 1$$

ILLUSTRATION 118: Show that $\lim_{n\to\infty} \left(\frac{1}{n+1} + \frac{1}{n+2} + \frac{1}{n+3} + ... + \frac{1}{6n}\right) = \ln 6$

SOLUTION: Let $S_n = \sum_{r=1}^{5n} \frac{1}{n+r} = \frac{1}{n} \sum_{r=1}^{5n} \frac{1}{1 + r/n} = \int_0^5 \frac{dx}{1+x} = \ln 6$

■ GEOMETRICAL APPLICATION

When the number of dimensions of a geometrical figure tends to infinity or a process repeats infinitely or any dimension tends to zero or infinity, then to find its limiting area or circumference or any other property we use limits as illustrated in figure 1.50, with the help of examples.

ILLUSTRATION 119: A circular area AB of radius 2 subtends an angle x radians $(0 < x < \pi/2)$ at the centre C of a circle. The tangents to circular arc at B and A meet at point P as shown below, then find

(i) $ar\ \Delta ABC$

(ii) $ar\ \Delta ABP$

(iii) area of circular segment shown by shaded portion $(S(x))$ (say)

(iv) $\lim\limits_{x\to 0}\dfrac{ar\Delta ABP}{ar\Delta ABC}$

(v) $\lim\limits_{x\to 0}\dfrac{S(x)}{ar\Delta ABP}$

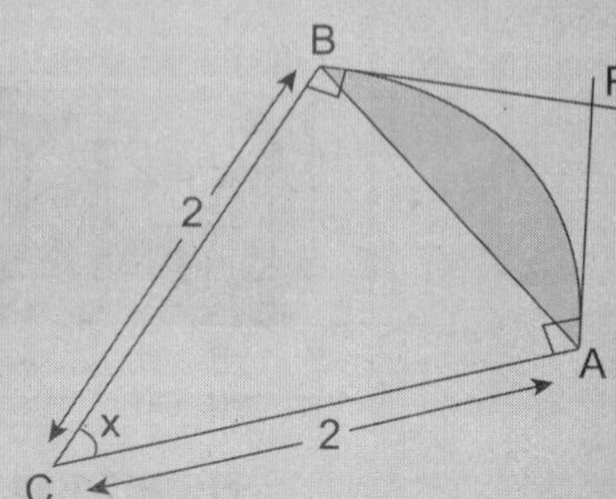

FIGURE 1.50

SOLUTION: (i) $\text{ar}\ \Delta ABC = \dfrac{1}{2}(AC)\times(BC)\sin\angle ACB$

$$= \frac{1}{2}(2)\,(2)\sin x = 2\sin x$$

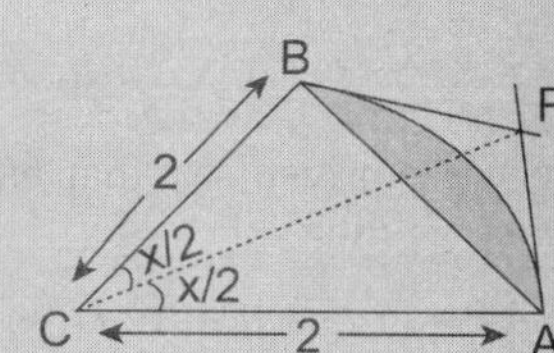

FIGURE 1.51

(ii) $\text{ar}\ \Delta ABP = \dfrac{1}{2}(AP)\times(BP)\sin\angle APB = \dfrac{1}{2}(AP)(BP)\sin(\pi - x)$

$$= \frac{1}{2}\left(2\tan\frac{x}{2}\right)\left(2\tan\frac{x}{2}\right)\sin x = 2\tan^2\frac{x}{2}\sin x$$

(iii) $ar\ S(x) = (ar.\ \text{sector}\ ACB) - (ar\ \Delta ACB)$

$$= \frac{1}{2}x(2)^2 - \frac{1}{2}(2)^2\sin x \quad = 2x - 2\sin x$$

(iv) $$\lim_{x\to 0}\frac{ar\Delta ABP}{ar\Delta ABC} = \lim_{x\to 0}\frac{2\tan^2\frac{x}{2}\sin x}{2\sin x} = \lim_{x\to 0}\tan^2\frac{x}{2} = 0$$

(v) $$\lim_{x\to 0}\frac{arS(x)}{ar\Delta ABP} = \lim_{x\to 0}\frac{2x - 2\sin x}{2\tan^2\frac{x}{2}\sin x} = \lim_{x\to 0}\frac{-2(\sin x - x)}{2\tan^2\frac{x}{2}\sin x}$$

$$= \lim_{x\to 0}\frac{-\left[\left(x - \frac{x^3}{3!} + \frac{x^5}{5!}\ldots.\right) - x\right]}{\tan^2\frac{x}{2}\sin x} = \lim_{x\to 0}\frac{\left[\frac{x^3}{3!} - \frac{x^5}{5!} + \ldots\right]}{\tan^2\frac{x}{2}\sin x}$$

$$= \lim_{x\to 0}\frac{x^3\left(\frac{1}{6} - \frac{x^2}{5!} + \ldots.\right)}{\tan^2\frac{x}{2}\sin x} = \lim_{x\to 0}\frac{x^2.x\left(\frac{1}{6} - \frac{x^2}{5!} + \ldots\right)}{\tan\frac{2x}{2}\sin x}$$

$$= 4\lim_{x\to 0}\left(\frac{x/2}{\tan x/2}\right)^2\left(\frac{x}{\sin x}\right)\left(\frac{1}{6}-\frac{x^2}{5!}+...\right)$$

$$= 4(1)^2(1)(1/6) = 2/3$$

ILLUSTRATION 120: In the figure 1.52 shown below find the limiting area of shaded portion, when the base is divided into infinitely many small subintervals.

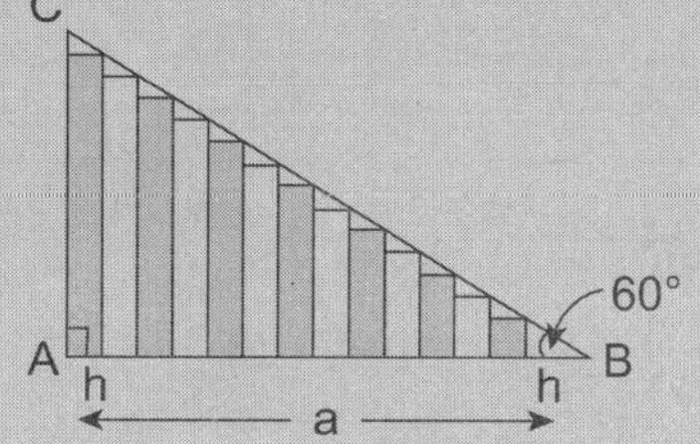

FIGURE 1.52

SOLUTION: Let the base AB be divided into n-parts

$\therefore$ Width of each subinterval of $AB = \frac{a}{n} = h(\text{say})$

Now as $n \to \infty$, $h \to 0$

Also $\angle ABC = 60°$

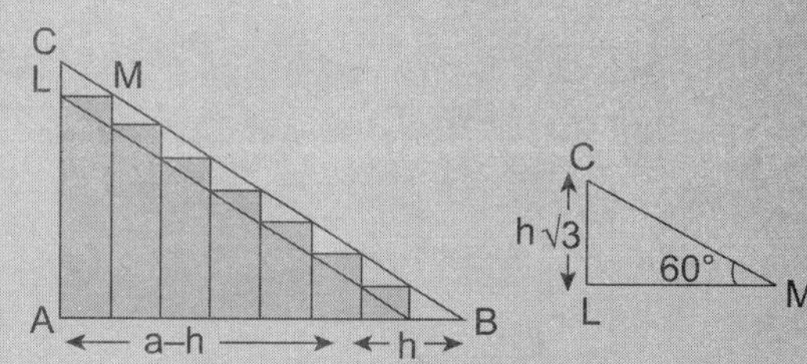

FIGURE 1.53

$\Rightarrow$ $\tan 60° = \frac{AC}{AB} \Rightarrow AC = AB \tan 60°$

$\Rightarrow$ $AC = a\sqrt{3}$

The shaded area is greater than the area of ΔAKL and less than the area of ΔABC.

$$\Rightarrow \frac{1}{2}(AK)(AL) < A < \frac{1}{2}AB \times AC$$

$$\Rightarrow \frac{1}{2}(a-h)(AC-CL) < A < \frac{1}{2}(a)(a\sqrt{3})$$

$$\Rightarrow \frac{1}{2}(a-h)(a\sqrt{3}-h\sqrt{3}) < A < \frac{1}{2}a^2(\sqrt{3})$$

$$\Rightarrow \frac{1}{2}\left(a-\frac{a}{n}\right)\left(a\sqrt{3}-\frac{a\sqrt{3}}{n}\right) < A < \frac{\sqrt{3}}{2}a^2$$

In limiting condition when $n \to \infty$, $\underset{x\to\infty}{\text{Lt}}\ \frac{1}{2}\left(a-\frac{a}{n}\right)\left(a\sqrt{3}-\frac{a\sqrt{3}}{n}\right) = \frac{1}{2}a(a\sqrt{3}) = \frac{\sqrt{3}a^2}{2}$

$$\lim_{n\to\infty}\frac{\sqrt{3}}{2}a^2 = \frac{\sqrt{3}}{2}a^2$$

$\therefore$ By sandwich theorem, when $n \to \infty$, $A \to \frac{\sqrt{3}}{2}a^2$

ILLUSTRATION 121: The circumference of a circle of radius r is divided into 'n; parts and curvilinear isosceles right angled triangles are formed on each subdivision as shown in figure 1.54. Shown that in limiting condition n tends to infinity.

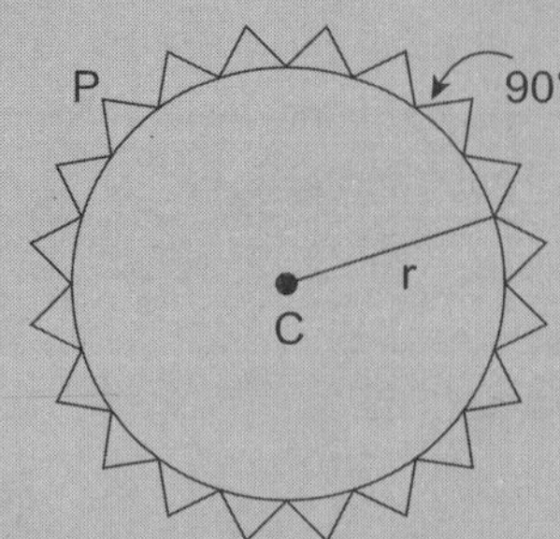

FIGURE 1.54

The sum of perimeters of isosceles triangle (except base) is different from the circumference of circle inspite when $n \to \infty$, the perimeter of curvilinear Δs coincide with circumference of circle.

SOLUTION: Consider the curvilinear triangle ABP as shown below.

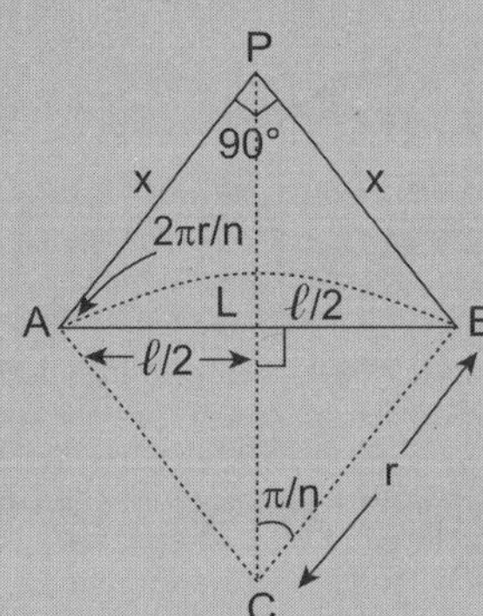

FIGURE 1.55

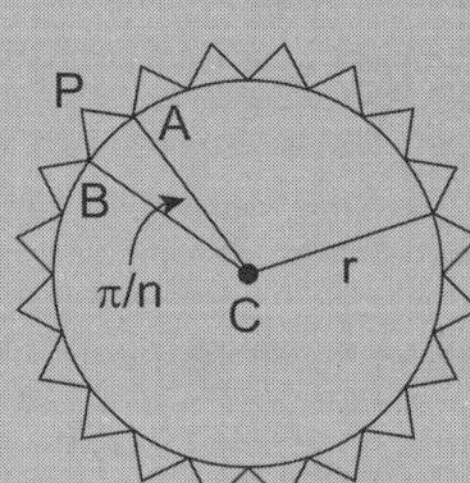

FIGURE 1.56

In ΔCLB, $\sin \pi/n = \dfrac{\ell/2}{r}$

$\Rightarrow \ell = 2\sin\pi/n$ $\qquad\qquad$ $\therefore$ In ΔAPB; $2x^2 = l^2$

$\Rightarrow x^2 = \ell^2/2 = \dfrac{4r^2 \sin^2 \pi/n}{2} = 2r^2 \sin^2 \pi/n$

$\Rightarrow x = \sqrt{2}r \sin \pi/n$

$\therefore$ Perimeter of one curvilinear Δ (excluding base)

$= 2\sqrt{2}r \sin \pi/n$

$\therefore$ Total perimeter of curvilinear Δ's

$= 2n\sqrt{2}r \sin \pi/n = 2n\sqrt{2}r \sin\dfrac{\theta}{2}$; where $\theta = \dfrac{2\pi}{n} = 2\sqrt{2}.r\left(\dfrac{2\pi}{\theta}\right)\sin\dfrac{\theta}{2} = 2\sqrt{2}r\pi\dfrac{\sin\theta/2}{\theta/2}$

$\therefore$ when $n \to \infty$, perimeter has limiting value $= \lim\limits_{\eta\to\infty}\left(2\sqrt{2}r\pi\right)\dfrac{\sin\theta/2}{\theta/2}$

$$= \lim_{\theta\to 0}\left(2\sqrt{2}r\pi\frac{\sin\theta/2}{\theta/2}\right) = 2\sqrt{2}r\pi \neq 2\pi r$$

ILLUSTRATION 122: A mass hanging by a spring is vibrating with a displacement at time t given by $S(t) = \dfrac{k}{\alpha^2 - \beta^2}(\sin \beta t - \sin \alpha t)$; where α, β, k are constants, then find

(i) distancement of mass at time when α → β

(ii) Velocity of mass at time when α → β

SOLUTION: **(i)** $S(t) = \dfrac{k}{\alpha^2 - \beta^2}(\sin \beta t - \sin \alpha t)$

When α → β, the displacement is given by

$$\lim_{\alpha\to\beta} S(t) = \lim_{\alpha\to\beta} \frac{k}{\alpha^2 - \beta^2}(\sin \beta t - \sin \alpha t)$$

$$= \lim_{\alpha-\beta\to 0} \frac{k}{(\alpha-\beta)(\alpha+\beta)}\left[2\cos\left(\frac{\beta+\alpha}{2}\right) + t\sin\left(\frac{\beta-\alpha}{2}\right)t\right]$$

$$= \lim_{(\alpha-\beta)\to 0} \frac{kt}{\frac{(\alpha-\beta)}{2}t(\alpha+\beta)}\left[-\cos\left(\frac{\alpha+\beta}{2}\right) + t\sin\left(\frac{\alpha-\beta}{2}\right)t\right]$$

$$= \frac{kt}{2\beta}(-\cos(\beta)t) = \frac{-kt\cos\beta t}{2\beta}$$

(ii) velocity when α → β is given by $\lim_{\alpha\to\beta} \dfrac{d}{dt}[s(t)]$

$$= \lim_{\alpha\to\beta} \frac{k}{\alpha^2 - \beta^2}\ [\beta \cot\beta t - \alpha \cos\alpha t] = \text{Let } \alpha = \beta + h;\ h \to 0$$

$$= \lim_{h\to 0} \frac{k}{(\beta+h)^2 - \beta^2}\ [\beta \cos \beta t - (\beta + h) \cos (\beta + h)y]$$

$$= \lim_{h\to 0} \frac{k}{(2\beta+h)(h)}\ [\beta \cos\beta\, t - (\beta + h)\,[\cos\beta t \cos ht - \sin\beta t \sin ht]]$$

$$= \lim_{h\to 0} \frac{k}{(2\beta+h)h}\ [\beta\cos \beta t - \beta\cos\beta t \cos ht + \beta \sin\beta t \sin ht - h \cos \beta t \cos ht + h \sin\beta t \sin ht]$$

$$= \lim_{h\to 0} \frac{k}{(2\beta+h)h}$$

$[\beta \cos\beta t\,(1 - \cos ht) + \beta\sin \beta t \sin ht - h \cos \beta t \cos ht + h\sin\beta t \sin ht]$

$$= \lim_{h\to 0} \frac{k}{(2\beta+h)}\left[\frac{\beta\cos\beta t\left(2\sin^2\frac{ht}{2}\right)}{h} + \frac{\beta\sin\beta t \sinh t}{h} - \cos\beta t\right]$$

$$= \frac{k}{2\beta}[\beta t\sin\beta t - \cos\beta t] = \frac{k}{2\beta}(\beta t\sin\beta t - \cos\beta t)$$

ILLUSTRATION 123: Show that the perimeter of a regular polygon of n-sides is equal to $2nr \sin\dfrac{\theta}{2}$, where $\theta = 2\pi/n$ and r is the circumradius of polygon and hence show that the circumference of circle of radius 'r' is $2\pi r$.

SOLUTION: Let the number of sides of polygon be 'n'

$\Rightarrow$ Central angle is given by $\theta = 2\pi/n$, then length $AB = 2AL = 2\,(r\sin\theta/2)$; where $\theta = \dfrac{2\pi}{n}$

$\therefore$ Perimeter of regular polygon having x – sides

$= 2xr\sin\left(\dfrac{\theta}{2}\right)$; where $\theta = \dfrac{2\pi}{x}$.

The perimeter would converter to circumference of circle if $n \to \infty$

Circumference of circle is given by

$$C = \lim_{n\to\infty} 2n\pi\sin\left(\frac{\theta}{2}\right)$$

$$= \lim_{n\to\infty} 2\left(\frac{2\pi}{\theta}\right) r\sin\left(\frac{\theta}{2}\right)\left(\because \theta = \frac{2\pi}{n} \Rightarrow n = \frac{2\pi}{\theta}\right) = \lim_{n\to\infty} 2\pi r\left[\frac{\sin\theta/2}{\theta/2}\right]$$

$[\because n \to \infty \Rightarrow \theta \to 0)$

$= 2\pi r\,(1) = 2\pi r$

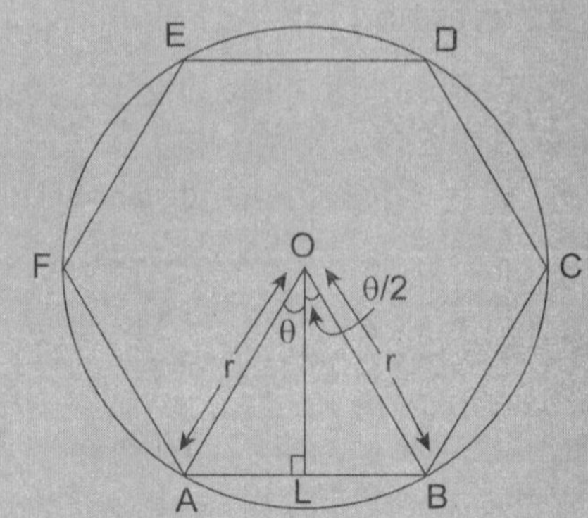

FIGURE 1.57

ILLUSTRATION 124: Find the limit of the sum of the lengths of the ordinates of the curve $y = e^{-x}\sin\dfrac{\pi x}{2}$ at the points $x = 0,1,2,3,4.........\infty$

SOLUTION: $-1 \le \sin\dfrac{\pi x}{2} \le 1$

$\Rightarrow -e^{-x} \le e^{-x}\sin\left(\dfrac{\pi x}{2}\right) \le e^{-x}$

$\therefore$ The graph of $y = e^{-x}\sin\dfrac{\pi x}{2}$ lies between the graphs of $y = -e^{-x}$ and $y = e^{-x}$ as shown in At $x = 0, 2,4,6,8.....$length of ordinates is zero and at $x = 1,3,5,7,9...$ length of ordinates are $|e^{-1}|$; $|e^{-3}|$; $|e^{-5}|$; $|e^{-7}|$;.... and so on figure 1.58.

$\therefore$ Sum of ordinates $= e^{-1} + e^{-3} + e^{-5} + e^{-7} + ...\infty$

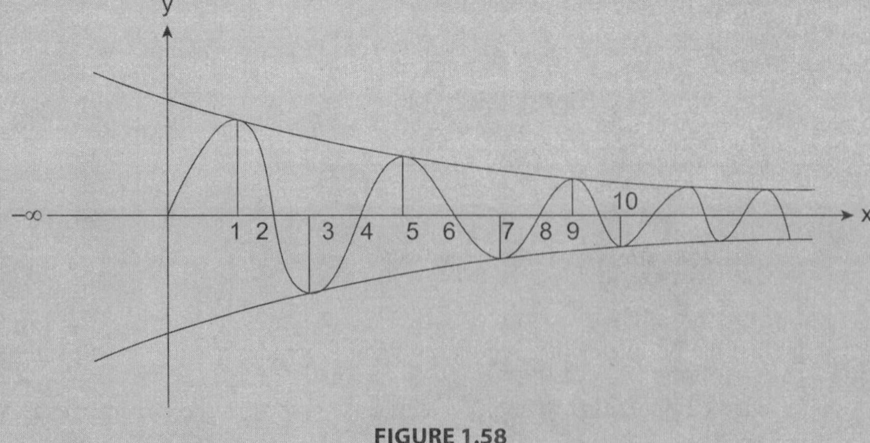

FIGURE 1.58

$$= \frac{1}{e}+\frac{1}{e^3}+\frac{1}{e^5}+\frac{1}{e^7}+\ldots\infty = \lim_{n\to\infty}\sum\left(\frac{1}{e}+\frac{1}{e^3}+\frac{1}{e^5}+\ldots+\frac{1}{e^{2n-1}}\right)$$

$$= \lim_{n\to\infty}\frac{\frac{1}{e}\left(1-\left(\frac{1}{e^2}\right)^n\right)}{\left(1-\frac{1}{e^2}\right)} = \frac{\frac{1}{e}\left(1-\frac{1}{\infty}\right)}{\left(1-\frac{1}{e^2}\right)} = \frac{1/e}{(e^2-1)/e} = \frac{1}{e^2-1}$$

ILLUSTRATION 125: At the end-points and the midpoint of a circular arc AB tangent lines are drawn, and the points A and B are joined with a chord. Prove that the ratio of the areas of the two triangles thus formed tends to 4 as the arc AB decreases infinitely.

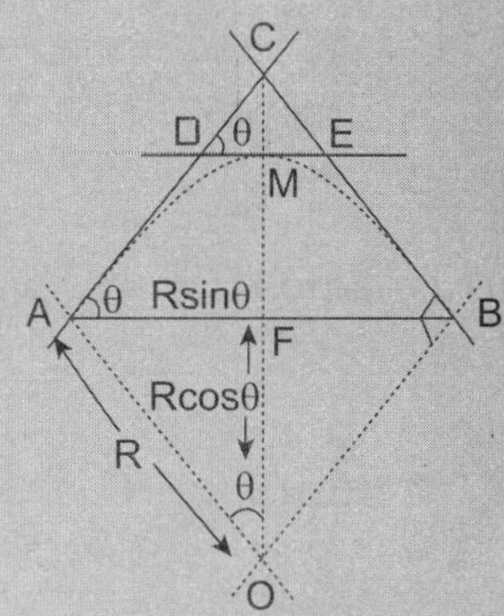

FIGURE 1.59

SOLUTION: Let Δ_1 = area of $\Delta\,ABC = R^2 \sin\theta\,(\sec\theta - \cos\theta)$

$\Delta_1 = R^2 \tan\theta\,(1-\cos^2\theta)$

And let Δ_2 = Area of $\Delta\,CDE = \dfrac{{}^2(1\quad\cos\quad)^2}{\cos\quad\theta.\tan\theta}$

$$\left[\begin{array}{l}\because\ CM = R\sec\theta R\\ DM = CM\cot\theta\end{array}\right]$$

$$\therefore\ \frac{\Delta_1}{\Delta_2} = \frac{\tan\theta(1-\cos^2\theta).\cos^2\theta.\tan\theta}{(1-\cos\theta)^2} = \ell(say)$$

as $\theta\to 0$ $\ell = \underset{\theta\to 0}{\text{Limit}}\dfrac{(\tan^2\theta)\cos^2\theta.(1-\cos\theta).(1+\cos\theta)}{(1-\cos\theta)^2} = 1.\,2\ \underset{\theta\to 0}{\text{Limit}}\dfrac{\tan^2\theta}{\theta^2}.\dfrac{\theta^2}{1-\cos\theta} = 4.$

ILLUSTRATION 126: Without using series expansion or L.H. rule evaluate $\lim\limits_{x\to 0}\dfrac{x+\ell n\left(\sqrt{1+x^2}-x\right)}{x^3}$

SOLUTION: Let $\sqrt{1+x^2}-x = t$; $\therefore x\to 0 \Rightarrow t\to 1$

Also $1+x^2 = t^2+x^2+2t\,(x)$

$$\Rightarrow x = \frac{1-t^2}{2t}.\ \text{Hence } L = \lim_{t\to 1}\frac{\frac{1-t^2}{2t}+\ell nt}{\left(1-t^2\right)^3}8t^3$$

$$= \lim_{t\to 1}\frac{2t\ell nt+1-t^2}{2t.\left(1-t^2\right)^3}8t^3 = \lim_{t\to 1}\frac{2t\ell nt+1-t^2}{(1+t)^3(1-t)^3}.4t^2 = \frac{1}{2}\lim_{t\to 1}\frac{2t\,\ell nt+1-t^2}{(1-t)^3}$$

Put $t = 1+y$; as $t\to 1$, $y\to 0$

$$\frac{1}{2}\lim_{y\to 0}\frac{2(1+y)\ell n(1+y)+1-(1+y)^2}{-y^3};\ \text{Put } 1+y = e^z \text{ as } y\to 0;\ z\to 0$$

$$= -\frac{1}{2}\lim_{z\to 0}\frac{2ze^z+1-e^{2z}}{\left(\frac{e^z-1}{z}\right)^3.z^3} = \frac{1}{2}\lim_{z\to 0}\frac{e^{2z}-2ze^z-1}{z^3} = \frac{1}{2}\lim_{z\to 0}\frac{e^z\left(e^z-e^{-z}-2z\right)}{z^3} = \frac{1}{2}.l$$

$$\Rightarrow l = \lim_{u\to 0}\frac{e^{3u}-e^{-3u}-6u}{27u^3}\ \text{when}z=3u, \therefore \lim_{u\to 0}\frac{(e^u-e^{-u})^3+3(e^u-e^{-u})-6u}{27u^3} = \lim_{u\to 0}\frac{8}{27}\left(\frac{e^{2u}-1}{2u}\right)^3+\frac{\ell}{9}$$

$$\Rightarrow \frac{8}{9}l = \frac{8}{27} \Rightarrow l = \frac{1}{3}\text{; Hence } L = \frac{1}{6}$$

Alternatively: $\ln\left(\sqrt{1+x^2}-x\right) = t$

$\sqrt{1+x^2} - x = e^t$ $\Rightarrow \sqrt{1+x^2} + x = e^{-1}$

$x = \dfrac{e^{-t}-e^t}{2}$ $\therefore\ l = \dfrac{\dfrac{e^{-t}-e^t}{2}+t}{-\left(\dfrac{e^t-e^{-1}}{2}\right)^3}$

ILLUSTRATION 127: Without using any series expansion or L Hospital's rule, evaluate $\lim\limits_{x\to 0}\dfrac{e^x-e^{-x}-2x}{x^3.\dfrac{x-\sin x}{x^3}}$

SOLUTION: Let $L = \lim\limits_{x\to 0}\dfrac{e^x-e^{-x}-2x}{x^3.\dfrac{x-sinx}{x^3}}$

Now $l_1 = \lim\limits_{x\to 0}\dfrac{x-\sin x}{x^3} = \dfrac{1}{6}(use\, x = 3t)$ and $l_2 = \lim\limits_{x\to 0}\dfrac{e^x-e^{-x}-2x}{x^3}$. Put $x = 3y$

$$= \lim_{x\to 0}\frac{e^{3y}-e^{-3y}-6y}{27y^3} = \lim_{y\to 0}\frac{\left(e^y-e^{-y}\right)^3+3\left(e^y-e^{-y}\right)-6y}{27y^3}$$

$$= \left[\lim_{y\to 0}\frac{8}{27}\frac{\left(e^{2y}-1\right)^3}{(2y)^8}+\frac{1}{9}\ell_2\right] \Rightarrow l_2 = \frac{8}{27}+\frac{\ell_2}{9} \Rightarrow l_2 = \frac{1}{3}$$

Hence $L = \dfrac{\ell_2}{\ell_1} = 2$

ILLUSTRATION 128: Without using series expansion or L.H. rule evaluate $\lim\limits_{x\to 1}\dfrac{1-x+\ln x}{1+\cos\pi x}$

SOLUTION: $\lim\limits_{x\to 1}\dfrac{1-x+\ln x}{(1+\cos\pi x)}$; Let $x = 1 + h;\ h \to 0$

$$= \lim_{h\to 0}\frac{1-(1+h)+\ln(1+h)}{1-\cos\pi h}\cdot\frac{\pi^2h^2}{\pi^2h^2}$$

$$= \frac{2}{\pi^2}\cdot\lim_{h\to 0}\frac{-h+\ln(1+h)}{h^2} \qquad \left(\text{as } \lim_{h\to 0}\frac{\pi^2h^2}{1-\cos\pi h} = 2\right)$$

Put $\ln(1 + h) = t$

$$= \frac{2}{\pi^2}\cdot\lim_{t\to 0}\frac{t-(e^t-1)}{\left(\dfrac{e^t-1}{t}\right)^2-t^2} = -\frac{2}{\pi^2}\cdot\lim_{t\to 0}\frac{e^t-1-t}{t^2} = -\frac{2}{\pi^2}\cdot\frac{1}{2} = -\frac{1}{\pi^2}.$$

ILLUSTRATION 129: A segment $AB = \ell$ (figure 1.60) is divided into n equal parts, each part serving as a base of an isosceles triangle with base angles $\alpha = 30^{\circ}$. Show that the limit of perimeter of (zig zag) line thus formed is different from the length of AB inspite the fact that in the limiting condition the zig zag line geometrically merges with the line segment.

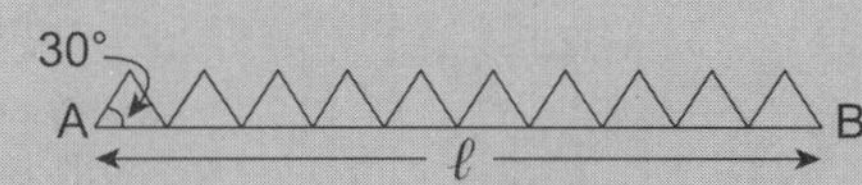

FIGURE 1.60

SOLUTION: Let the line segment AB be divided into n equal parts. Thus length of each equal part is ℓ/n.

Let us consider any small triangle formed on a sub equal part of length ℓ/n as shown in figure 1.61.

In ΔXZL, $\cos 30^0 - \dfrac{XL}{XZ} = \dfrac{\ell/2n}{x} = \dfrac{\ell}{2nx}$

$\Rightarrow \dfrac{\sqrt{3}}{2} = \dfrac{l}{2nx} \Rightarrow x = \dfrac{l}{\sqrt{3}n}$

$\Rightarrow$ Perimeter of zig-zag line $= (2x) \times n = \dfrac{2l}{\sqrt{3}}$

$\therefore$ Perimeter of zing-zag line is independent of n

$\therefore \lim\limits_{n\to\infty} \dfrac{2l}{\sqrt{3}} = \dfrac{2l}{\sqrt{3}} \neq l$. Hence proved

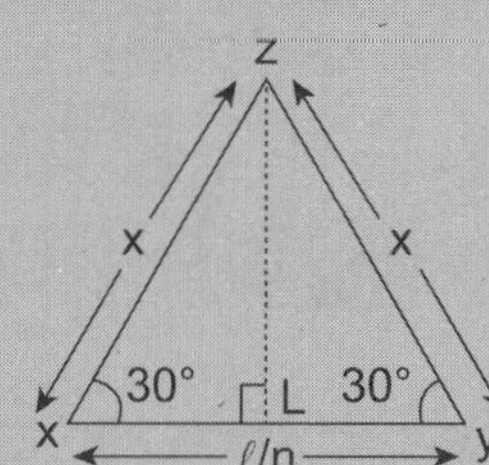

FIGURE 1.61

ILLUSTRATION 130: The circumference of circle of radius 'r' is divided into n-equal parts and on each equal part (arc), a semi-circle is drawn (shown in figure 1.62) taking the line segment joining the end points of arc as diameter. Find the total perimeter of semi-circles in limiting case as $n \to \infty$ and show that it is different from the circumference of given circle. Also find the limiting area of bounded closed figure so obtained and show that it is πr^2.

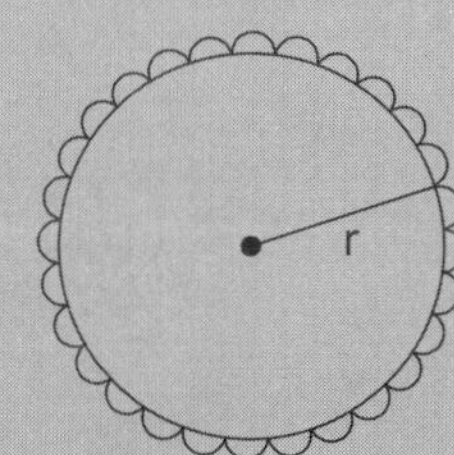

FIGURE 1.62

SOLUTION: Length of each sub-arc of circle $= \dfrac{2\pi r}{n}$ shown in figure 1.63.

In ΔCLB, $\sin\dfrac{\pi}{n} = \dfrac{l}{2r}$

$\therefore \dfrac{l}{2} = r\sin\dfrac{\pi}{n}$ .....(i)

$\therefore$ Radius of each semi-circle $= \dfrac{l}{2} = r\sin\dfrac{\pi}{n}$

$\therefore$ Perimeter of each semi circle $= \pi(\ell/2) = \pi r \sin\dfrac{\pi}{n}$

$\therefore$ Total perimeter of semi-circles drawn $= n\pi r\sin\dfrac{\pi}{n}$

$\therefore$ Limiting perimeter $\lim\limits_{n\to\infty} n\pi r\sin\dfrac{\pi}{n}$

$= \lim\limits_{n\to\infty} n\pi r\sin\theta$ (where $\theta = \pi/n$, $n = \pi/\theta$))

$= \lim\limits_{n\to\infty} \pi r\left(\dfrac{\pi}{\theta}\right)\sin\theta = \pi^2 r\lim\limits_{\theta\to 0}\left(\dfrac{\sin\theta}{\theta}\right)\begin{bmatrix}\because n\to\infty \\ \Rightarrow\theta\to 0\end{bmatrix} = \pi^2 r \neq 2\pi r$

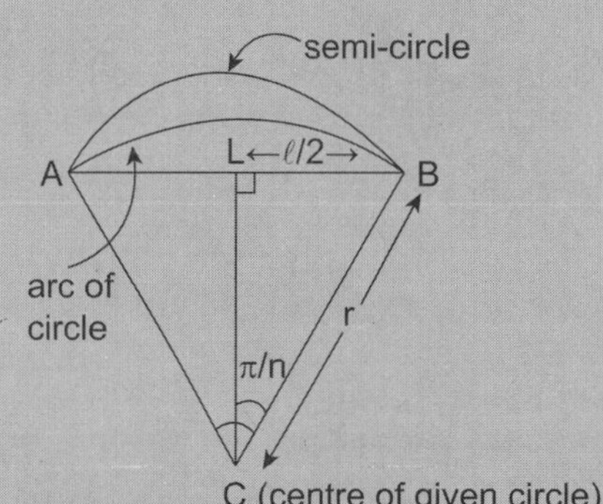

FIGURE 1.63

Now area of each semi-circle drawn out side the given circle shown by shaded portion.

Area of each shaded portion = Area of semi-circle – Area of segment ($APBLA$) of given circle

$= \frac{1}{2}\pi\left(\frac{\ell}{2}\right)^2$ – [Area of sector - area of ΔCAB]

$= \frac{1}{2}\pi\left(r\sin\frac{\pi}{n}\right)^2 - \left[\frac{2\pi/n}{2\pi}\pi r^2 - \frac{1}{2}l^2\sin\left(\frac{2\pi}{n}\right)\right]$

$= \frac{1}{2}\pi r^2\sin^2\frac{\pi}{n} - \frac{1}{n}\pi r^2 + \frac{1}{2}r^2\sin\frac{2\pi}{n}$

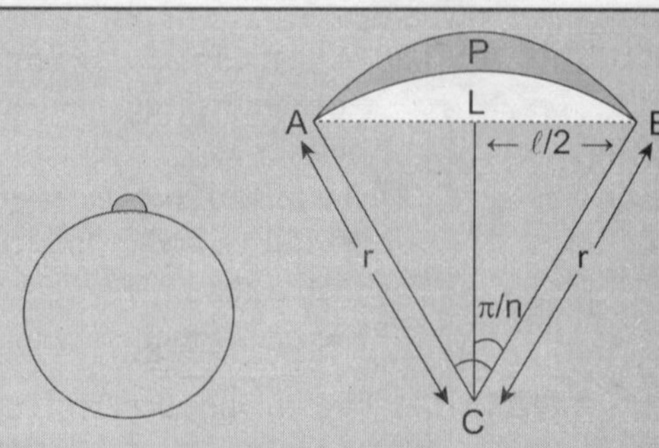

FIGURE 1.64

$\therefore$ Area of new closed figure = Area circle + n (area of shaded portion)

$= \pi r^2 + n\left[\frac{1}{2}\pi r^2\sin^2\frac{\pi}{n} - \frac{\pi r^2}{n} + \frac{1}{2}r^2\sin\frac{2\pi}{n}\right]$

In limiting condition, required area $= \lim_{x\to\infty}\left[\pi r^2 + \frac{\pi r^2}{2}n\sin^2\frac{\pi}{n} - \pi r^2 + \frac{n}{2}r^2\sin\frac{2\pi}{n}\right]$

$= \lim_{n\to\infty}\left[\frac{\pi r^2}{2}n\sin^2\frac{\pi}{n} + \frac{n}{2}r^2\sin\frac{2\pi}{n}\right] = \lim_{\theta\to\infty}\left[\frac{\pi^2 r^2}{2}\frac{\sin^2\theta}{\theta} + \frac{\pi r^2\sin 2\theta}{2\theta}\right] = 0 + \pi r^2 = \pi r^2$

ILLUSTRATION 131: In the figure 1.65 below, let $f(\theta)$ be the area of ΔPQR and $g(\theta)$ be the area of shaded portion. Then evaluate

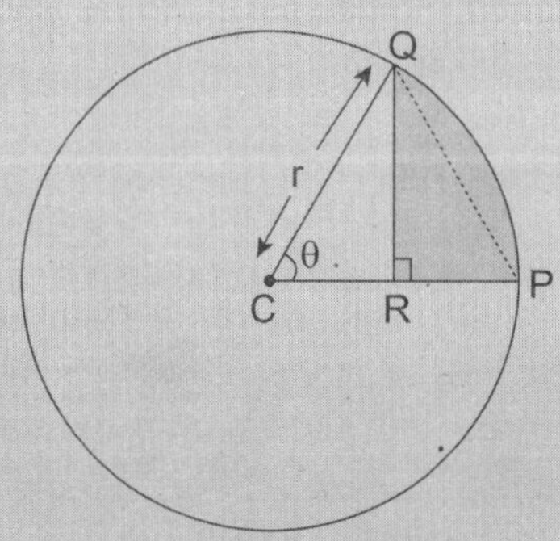

FIGURE 1.65

(i) $\lim_{\theta\to P}\frac{f(\theta)}{g(\theta)}$ **(ii)** $\lim_{\theta\to P}\frac{\text{length of } PQ(\text{minor})}{\text{length of chord } PQ}$

SOLUTION: Coordinates of Q are $(r\cos\theta, r\sin\theta)$

$\therefore$ $RP = CP - CR - r - r\cos\theta$ and $QR = r\sin\theta$

$\therefore$ Area of $\Delta PQR = f(\theta) = \frac{1}{2}RP\times RQ = \frac{1}{2}(r - r\cos\theta)(r\sin\theta) = \frac{1}{2}r^2(\sin\theta)(1-\cos\theta)$ ...(i)

and $g(\theta)$ = Area of shaded portion

= (Area of sector CPQ) – (ar ΔCRQ) $= \frac{\theta}{2\pi}(\pi r^2) - \frac{1}{2}(CR)\times(RQ)$

$$=\frac{\theta}{2}r^2-\frac{1}{2}(r\cos\theta)(r\sin\theta)=\frac{1}{2}r^2\theta-\frac{1}{2}r^2\sin\theta\cos\theta$$

(i) $$\lim_{Q\to P}\frac{f(\theta)}{g(\theta)}=\lim_{\theta\to 0}\frac{\frac{1}{2}r^2\sin\theta(1-\cos\theta)}{\frac{1}{2}r^2\theta-\frac{1}{2}r^2\sin\theta\cos\theta}\qquad\left[\begin{array}{l}\because Q\to P\\ \Rightarrow \theta\to 0\end{array}\right]$$

$$=\lim_{\theta\to 0}\frac{\sin\theta(1-\cos\theta)}{[\theta-\sin\theta\cos\theta]}=\lim_{\theta\to 0}\frac{\left(\frac{\sin\theta}{\theta}\right)\left(\frac{2\sin^2\theta/2}{4\left(\frac{\theta^2}{4}\right)}\right)}{\frac{1}{2}\left[\frac{2\theta-\sin 2\theta}{\theta^3}\right]}$$

$$=\lim_{\theta\to 0}\frac{(1)(1)^2}{\left(\frac{2\theta-\sin^2\theta}{\theta^3}\right)}=\lim_{\theta\to 0}\frac{1}{\frac{1}{\theta^3}\left[2\theta-\left(2\theta-\frac{(2\theta)^3}{3!}+\frac{(2\theta)^5}{5!}\cdots\right)\right]}=\lim_{\theta\to 0}\frac{1}{\left[\frac{8}{6}-\frac{32\theta^2}{120}+\ldots\right]}=\frac{3}{4}$$

(ii) Now $\widehat{PQ}=\theta r-\left(\because\theta=\widehat{PQ}/radius\right)$ and chord PQ is given by $2r\sin(\theta/2)$

$$=\lim_{\theta\to 0}\frac{\text{length of are }\widehat{\text{PQ}}(\text{minor})}{\text{length of chord PQ}}=\lim_{Q\to 0}\frac{r\theta}{2r\sin\theta/2}=\lim_{\theta\to 0}\frac{\theta/2}{\sin\theta/2}=1$$

ILLUSTRATION 132: Given a fixed circle C_1 having its equation $x^2+y^2+4y=0$ and a shrinking circle C_2 having its equation $x^2+y^2=r$. Let P be in variable left most point of shrinking circle. Let PQ and PR be the line segments passing through points of intersection of two circles and Q and R lying on y-axis, then find the limiting length of RQ when the radius of shrinking circles tends to zero.

SOLUTION: Fixed circle is $C_1: x^2+y^2+4y=0$ or $(x-0)^2+(y+2)^2=4$

C_1 has its centre at $(0,-2)$ and having radius $=2$, $C_2: x^2+y^2=r^2$ is a shrinking circle with its centre at origin and radius 'r'. The figure 1.66 is shown below

We are to find $\lim\limits_{r\to 0^+}(RQ)=\lim\limits_{r\to 0^+}|y_2-y_1|$; where $Q\equiv(0,-y_2);R(0,-y_1)$. Let the co-ordinates of point P (left most) on shrinking circle be $P(-r,0)$.

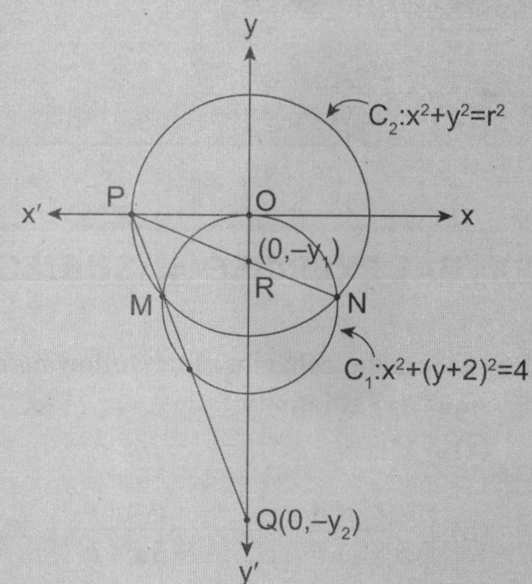

FIGURE 1.66

At the point of intersection $N\equiv\left(r\sqrt{1-\frac{r^2}{16}},\frac{-r^2}{4}\right)$

and $M\equiv\left(-r\sqrt{1-\frac{r^2}{16}},-\frac{r^2}{4}\right)$

Now P,M,Q are collinear

$\Rightarrow$ Slope of PM = slope MQ

$$\Rightarrow\quad\frac{-r^2/4-0}{-r\sqrt{1-\frac{r^2}{16}}+r}=\frac{-r^2/4+y_2}{-r\sqrt{1-\frac{r^2}{16}}-0}$$

$$\Rightarrow y_2 - \frac{r^2}{4} = \frac{\frac{r^3}{4}\sqrt{1-\frac{r^2}{16}}}{r - r\sqrt{1-\frac{r^2}{16}}}$$

$$\Rightarrow y_2 = \frac{r^2}{4} + \frac{\frac{r^2}{4}\sqrt{1-\frac{r^2}{16}}}{1-\sqrt{1-\frac{r^2}{16}}} = \frac{r^2}{4}\left[\frac{1}{1-\sqrt{1-r^2/16}}\right] = \frac{r^2/4}{1-\sqrt{1-\frac{r^2}{16}}}$$

At limiting condition, $y_2 = \lim\limits_{r\to 0^+} \frac{r^2/4}{1-\left(1-\frac{r^2}{16}\right)^{1/2}} = \lim\limits_{r\to 0^+} \frac{r^2}{1-\left[1-\frac{r^2}{32}+\left(\frac{1}{2}\right)\left(\frac{-1}{2}\right)\times\frac{\left(\frac{-r^2}{16}\right)^2}{2!}\ldots\right]}$

$$\Rightarrow y_2 = \lim_{r\to 0^+} \frac{r^2}{\left(\frac{r^2}{32}+\frac{r^4}{2048}+\ldots\right)} = 32$$

Similarly $\frac{-r^2/4}{r + r\sqrt{1-r^2/16}} = \frac{y_1 - r^2/4}{r\sqrt{1-r^2/16}} \Rightarrow y_1 = \frac{r^2}{4} - \frac{\frac{r^3}{4}\sqrt{1-r^2/16}}{r + r\sqrt{1-r^2/16}}$

And at limit condition $y_1 = \lim\limits_{r\to 0^+} \frac{r^2}{4}\left[\frac{1-\sqrt{1-\frac{r^2}{16}}}{1+\sqrt{1-r^2/16}}\right]$

$\therefore\ y_1 = \lim\limits_{r\to 0^+} \frac{r^2}{4}\left[\frac{1}{1+\left(1-\frac{r^2}{16}\right)^{1/2}}\right] = 0$ $\qquad \therefore\ RQ = \lim\limits_{r\to 0^+} |y_2 - y_1| = \lim\limits_{r\to 0^+} |32 - 0| = 32$

TEXTUAL EXERCISE–4: (SUBJECTIVE)

1. Discuss the behavior of the following rational expressions $f(x)$ at infinity:

(a) $a_n x^n + a_{n-1} x^{n-1} + \ldots + a_1 x + a_0, a_n > 0$

(b) $\left(\frac{a_n x^n + a_{n-1}x^{n-1} + .. + a_1 x + a_0}{b_n x^n + b_{n-1}x^{n-1} + .. + b_1 x + b_0}\right)$; if $a_n \neq 0$, $b_n \neq 0$

(c) $\left(\frac{a_n x^n + a_{n-1}x^{n-1} + .. + a_1 x + a_0}{b_k x^k + b_{k-1}x^{k-1} + .. + b_1 x + b_0}\right)$; $a_n > 0$, $b_k > 0, n > k$

(d) $\left(\frac{a_n x^n + a_{n-1}x^{n-1} + .. + a_1 x + a_0}{b_k x^k + b_{k-1}x^{k-1} + .. + b_1 x + b_0}\right)$; $a_n > 0$, $b_k > 0$, $n < k$

2. Evaluate the following limits:

(a) $\lim\limits_{x\to 0} \frac{1+\sin x - \cos x + \log(1-x)}{x^3}$

(b) $\lim\limits_{x\to 0} \left(\frac{\sin x - x + \frac{x^3}{6}}{x^5}\right)$

(c) $\lim\limits_{x\to 0} \frac{e^x - 1 - \frac{x^2}{2!} - x}{3x^3}$

(d) $\lim_{x\to 0}\dfrac{\sin x - x + \dfrac{x^3}{6}}{5x^4}$

(e) $\lim_{x\to 0}\dfrac{\log(1+x) - \dfrac{x}{1!} + \dfrac{x^2}{2!} - \dfrac{x^3}{3!}}{4x^3}$

3. Find the values of a, b, c when

(a) $\lim_{n\to\infty}\dfrac{1^2 - 2^2 + 3^2 - 4^2 + ... - 4n^2}{\sqrt{n^4+4} + \sqrt{9n^2+1}} = a$

(b) $\lim_{x\to\infty}\dfrac{ax^2+b}{x+1} \ge 0$ and finite.

(c) $\lim_{x\to\infty}\left(\dfrac{x^2+1}{x+1} - ax - b\right) = 0$

(d) $\lim_{x\to\infty}\left(\dfrac{x^2-1}{x+1} - ax - b\right) = 2$

(e) $\lim_{x\to\infty}\left(\dfrac{x^2+1}{x+1} - ax - b\right) = \infty$

(f) $\lim_{x\to 0}\dfrac{ae^x - b}{x} = 2$

4. Find the Integer 'n' for which the $\lim_{x\to 0}\dfrac{\cos^2 x - \cos x - e^x\cos x + e^x - \dfrac{x^3}{2}}{x^n}$ is a finite non-zero number.

5. Evaluates the limits:

(a) $\lim_{x\to 0}\dfrac{e^x - 1 - x}{x^2}$ (b) $\lim_{x\to 0}\dfrac{\sin x - x}{x^3}$

(c) $\lim_{x\to 0}\left(\dfrac{\sin x}{x}\right)^{1/x}$ (d) $\lim_{x\to .0}\dfrac{\cos(\sin x) - \cos x}{x^4}$

(e) $\lim_{x\to 0}\dfrac{1}{x^2} - \dfrac{1}{\sin^2 x}$ (f) $\lim_{x\to 0}\dfrac{1}{x^2} - \dfrac{1}{\tan^2 x}$

(g) $\lim_{x\to 0} x^x$ (h) $\lim_{x\to\pi/2}(\sin x)^{\tan x}$

6. Find the values of a and b such that $\lim_{x\to 0}\dfrac{x(1+a\cos x) - b\sin x}{x^3} = 1$

7. Evaluate the following:

(a) $\lim_{x\to a}\dfrac{a\sin x - x\sin a}{ax^2 - a^2x}$ (b) $\lim_{x\to 0}\dfrac{27^x - 9^x - 3^x + 1}{\sqrt{2} - \sqrt{(1+\cos x)}}$

8. Evaluate the following limits.

(i) $\lim_{n\to\infty}\dfrac{n!}{(n+1)! - n!}$ (ii) $\lim_{n\to\infty}\dfrac{1 + \dfrac{1}{2} + \dfrac{1}{4} + ... \dfrac{1}{2^n}}{1 + \dfrac{1}{3} + \dfrac{1}{9} + ... \dfrac{1}{3^n}}$

9. Inscribed in a circle of radius R is a square, a circle is inscribed in the square, a new square in the circle and so on for n times. Find the limit of the sum of areas of all circles and the limit of the sum of areas of all the squares as $n \to \infty$.

10. Let

$$f(x) = \left[x^x - (\cot x)^{\sin x} + (\sec x)^{\text{cosec} x} - \frac{\ell n(\sec x)}{x^2}\right],$$

evaluate $\lim_{x\to 0^+} f(x)$

11. Evaluate the following limits using L' hospitals rule

(i) $\lim_{x\to 1}\dfrac{x^x - x}{1 - x + \ell nx}$ (ii) $\lim_{x\to 0}\dfrac{(1+x)^{1/x} - e + \dfrac{xe}{2}}{x^2}$

(iii) $\lim_{x\to 0}\dfrac{e^x + \ell n\left(\dfrac{1-x}{e}\right)}{\tan x - x}$ (iv) $\lim_{x\to 1/2}\dfrac{\sec \pi x}{\tan 3\pi x}$

12. Evaluate $\lim_{x\to\infty}\left[\dfrac{2^{\frac{1}{x}} + 3^{\frac{1}{x}} + ... + 10^{\frac{1}{x}}}{9}\right]^{9x}$

13. Evaluate:

(a) $\lim_{x\to 0}\dfrac{1}{x^3}\displaystyle\int_0^x \dfrac{t^2}{t^4+1}\,dt$ (b) $\lim_{x\to 0}\dfrac{\displaystyle\int_0^x (\cos t)^{\frac{1}{t^2}}\,dt}{x}$

(c) $\dfrac{\lim_{x\to 0}\displaystyle\int_0^{\sin^2 x}\sqrt{t}\,dt}{3x^3}$

14. Let, $P_n = a^{P_{n-1}} - 1\ \forall\ n = 2, 3,......$and let $P_1 = a^x - 1$, where $a \in \mathbb{R}^+$, then evaluate $Lim_{x\to 0}\dfrac{P_n}{x}$

15. Show that the area of a regular polygon having n-sides is given by $\dfrac{nr^2}{2}\sin\theta$; where $\theta = 2\pi/n$, hence show that the area of circle of radius r is πr^2.

16. Find the limit of the sum of the lengths of ordinates of the curve $y = e^{-2x}\cos\pi x$, drawn at the points $x = 0,1,2,3,....$upto ∞.

17. From a tangent line drawn at point P on a circle of unit radius, a line segment PQ equal to length of arc PR is cut off as shown in figure 1.67. QR is joined and produced to intersect the extension of diameter through P a point T. Find the length PT in terms of θ and hence find the limiting value of length PT when R tends to P.

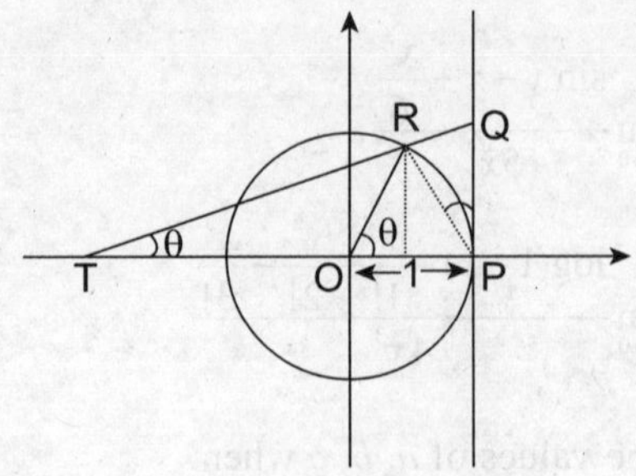

FIGURE 1.67

Answer Keys

1. **(a)** ∞ **(b)** a_n/b_n **(c)** ∞ **(d)** 0

2. **(a)** –(1/2) **(b)** 1/120 **(c)** 1/18 **(d)** 0 **(e)** 1/24

3. **(a)** $a = -2$ **(b)** $a = 0 \;\&\; b \in \mathbb{R}$ **(c)** $a = 1$ and $b = -1$ **(d)** $a = 1$ and $b = -3$

(e) $a < 1,\ b \in \mathbb{R}$ **(f)** $a = 2,\ b = 2$

4. 5

5. **(a)** 1/2 **(b)** –1/6 **(c)** 1 **(d)** –1/3 **(e)** 2/3 **(f)** 1 **(g)** 1

6. $a = -5/3$ and $b = -3/2$

7. **(a)** $\dfrac{a\cos a - \sin a}{a^2}$ **(b)** $8\sqrt{2}(\log 3)^2$

8. **(i)** 0 **(ii)** 4/3 **9.** $2\pi R^2$; $4R^2$ **10.** 1/2

11. **(i)** – 2 **(ii)** $\dfrac{11e}{24}$ **(iii)** $-\dfrac{1}{2}$ **(iv)** 3

12. 10!

13. **(a)** 1/3 **(b)** $e^{-1/2}$ **(c)** 2/9

14. $(\ln a)^n$ **16.** $-\dfrac{1}{e^2+1}$ **17.** $\text{PT} = \dfrac{\theta(1-\cos\theta)}{\theta - \sin\theta}$; $\lim\limits_{R\to P} \text{PT} = 3$

TEXTUAL EXERCISE–4: (OBJECTIVE)

1. $\lim\limits_{x\to\infty} x - x^2 \ell n\left(1+\dfrac{1}{x}\right)$ is equal to

(a) 1/2 (b) 3/2
(c) 1/3 (d) 1

2. $\lim\limits_{x\to\infty} \dfrac{e^x\left(\left(2^{x^n}\right)^{\frac{1}{e^x}} - \left(3^{x^n}\right)^{\frac{1}{e^x}}\right)}{x^n}$, $n \in \mathbb{N}$ is equal to :

(a) 0 (b) ln(2/3)
(c) ln(3/2) (d) None of these

3. For a certain value of c, $\lim\limits_{x\to-\infty} [(x^5 + 7x^4 + 2)^c - x]$ is finite and non zero. The value of c and the value of the limit is

(a) 1/5, 7 (b) 0, 1
(c) 1, 7/5 (d) None of These

4. Evaluate $\lim\limits_{x\to 0} \dfrac{a^{\tan x} - a^{\sin x}}{\tan x - \sin x}$, $a > 0$.

(a) $ln\ a$
(b) $ln\ a^2$
(c) $3ln\ a$
(d) None of These

5. The integer n for which $\lim\limits_{x\to 0} \dfrac{(\cos x - 1)(\cos x - e^x)}{x^n}$ is a finite non-zero number is

(a) 1 (b) 2
(c) 3 (d) 4

6. If $\lim\limits_{x\to 0} \dfrac{\sin(nx)[(a-n)nx-\tan x]}{x^2} = 0\ (n>0)$, then the value of '$a$' is equal to

(a) $\dfrac{1}{n}$ (b) n^2+1
(c) $\dfrac{n^2+1}{n}$ (d) None of these

7. $\lim\limits_{x\to 2} \dfrac{\sin\left(e^{x-2}-1\right)}{\ell n(x-1)}$ is equal to

(a) 0 (b) –1
(c) 2 (d) 1

8. The value of the limit $\prod\limits_{n=2}^{\infty}\left(1-\dfrac{1}{n^2}\right)$ is

(a) 1 (b) $\dfrac{1}{4}$
(c) $\dfrac{1}{3}$ (d) $\dfrac{1}{2}$

9. $\lim\limits_{n\to\infty} \dfrac{1^2\,n+2^2\,(n-1)+3^2\,(n-2)+\ldots..+n^2.1}{1^3+2^3+3^3+\ldots...+n^3}$ is equal to:

(a) $\dfrac{1}{3}$ (b) $\dfrac{2}{3}$
(c) $\dfrac{1}{2}$ (d) $\dfrac{1}{6}$

10. Let $f(x) = \dfrac{\ln(x^2+e^x)}{\ln(x^4+e^{2x})}$. If $\lim\limits_{x\to\infty} f(x) = l$ and $\lim\limits_{x\to-\infty} f(x) = m$, then:

(a) $l = m$ (b) $l = 2m$
(c) $2l = m$ (d) $l + m = 0$

11. $\lim\limits_{x\to\infty} \dfrac{2+2x+\sin 2x}{(2x+\sin 2x)e^{\sin x}}$ is:

(a) equal to zero (b) equal to 1
(c) equal to – 1 (d) Does not exist

12. Which of the following limits vanish?

(a) $\lim\limits_{x\to\infty} x^{\frac{1}{4}}\sin\dfrac{1}{\sqrt{x}}$ (b) $\lim\limits_{x\to\pi/2}(1-\sin x).\tan x$

(c) $\lim\limits_{x\to 0}\left(\dfrac{\sin 2x-2\sin x}{x^3}\right)$ (d) $\lim\limits_{x\to 0}\left(\dfrac{\cos x-1}{\sin x}\right)$

13. The value of $\lim\limits_{x\to 0}(\cos ax)^{\operatorname{cosec}^2 bx}$ is

(a) $e^{\left(-\frac{8b^2}{a^2}\right)}$ (b) $e^{\left(-\frac{8a^2}{b^2}\right)}$
(c) $e^{\left(-\frac{a^2}{2b^2}\right)}$ (d) $e^{\left(-\frac{b^2}{2a^2}\right)}$

14. $\lim\limits_{x\to 4} \dfrac{(\cos\alpha)^x-(\sin\alpha)^x-\cos 2\alpha}{x-4}$; where $0<\alpha<\dfrac{\pi}{2}$ is

(a) $\cos^4\alpha\ \ln\cos\alpha - \sin^4\alpha\ \ln\sin\alpha$
(b) $\cos^2\alpha\ \ln\cos\alpha - \sin^2\alpha\ \ln\sin\alpha$
(c) $\cos^4\alpha\ \ln\cos\alpha + \sin^4\alpha\ \ln\sin\alpha$
(d) None of these

15. $\lim\limits_{x\to 0}\ (\cos 2x)^{3/x^2}$ has the value equal to

(a) e^{-6} (b) e^2
(c) e^{-3} (d) None of these

16. If $\lim\limits_{x\to 0}\ (x^{-3}\sin 3x + ax^{-2} + b)$ exists and is equal to zero, then :

(a) $a = -3$ and $b = 9/2$
(b) $a = 3$ and $b = 9/2$
(c) $a = -3$ and $b = -9/2$
(d) $a = 3$ and $b = -9/2$

17. The limiting value of the function $f(x) = \dfrac{2\sqrt{2}-(\cos x+\sin x)^3}{1-\sin 2x}$ when $x\to\dfrac{\pi}{4}$ is

(a) $\sqrt{2}$ (b) $\dfrac{1}{\sqrt{2}}$
(c) $3\sqrt{2}$ (d) $\dfrac{3}{\sqrt{2}}$

18. ABC is an isosceles triangle inscribed in a circle of radius r. If $AB = AC$ and h is the altitude from A to BC and p be the perimeter of ABC then $\lim\limits_{h\to 0}\dfrac{\Delta}{p^3}$ equals (where Δ is the area of the triangle)

(a) $\dfrac{1}{32r}$ (b) $\dfrac{1}{64r}$
(c) $\dfrac{1}{128r}$ (d) None of these

Answer Keys

1. (b)	**2.** (a)	**3.** (a)	**4.** (a)	**5.** (c)	**6.** (c)	**7.** (d)	**8.** (d)	**9.** (a)	**10.** (a)
11. (d)	**12.** (a,b,d)	**13.** (c)	**14.** (a)	**15.** (a)	**16.** (a)	**17.** (d)	**18.** (c)		

ASYMPTOTES

A straight line at a finite distance from origin which tends to meet the given curve at infinity is called an asymptote to the curve.

Thus if P is any variable point on the given curve having co-ordinate x and y, then the perpendicular distance of point P from the asymptote tends to zero as x or y or both tend to infinity as shown figure 1.68.

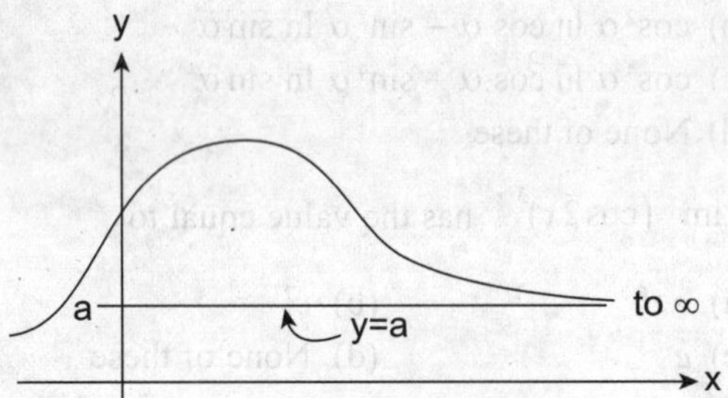

FIGURE 1.68

In figure 1.69 asymptote is parallel to x-axis and is called a horizontal asymptote.

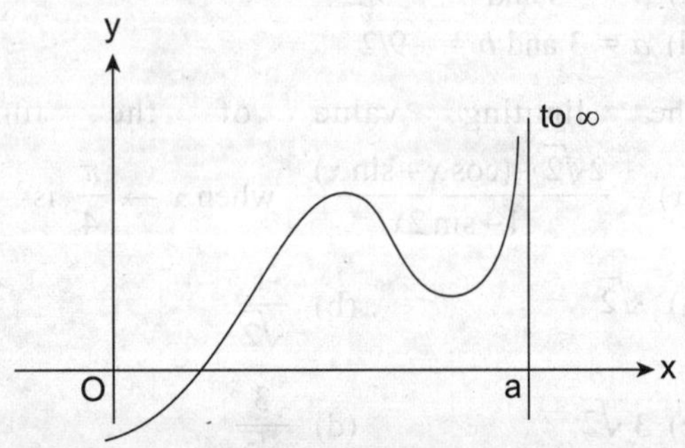

FIGURE 1.69

In figure 1.70 Asymptote is parallel to y-axis and is called a Vertical Asymptote.

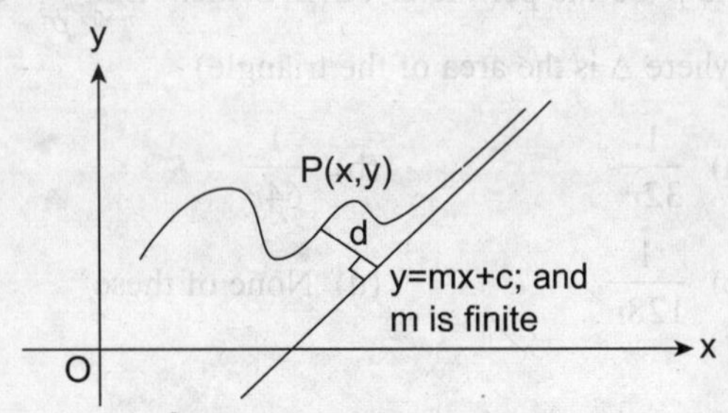

FIGURE 1.70

In figure 1.71 asymptote is not parallel to any axis and is called Oblique asymptote.

Horizontal Asymptote (Asymptotes Parallel to x-axis)

Let $y = f(x)$ be a given curve, then horizontal asymptote is/are given by $y = \operatorname*{Lt}_{x\to\infty} f(x)$ and $y = \operatorname*{Lt}_{x\to-\infty} f(x)$

At most two horizontal asymptotes are possible, one for $x \to -\infty$ and other for $x \to \infty$ as shown figure 1.71.

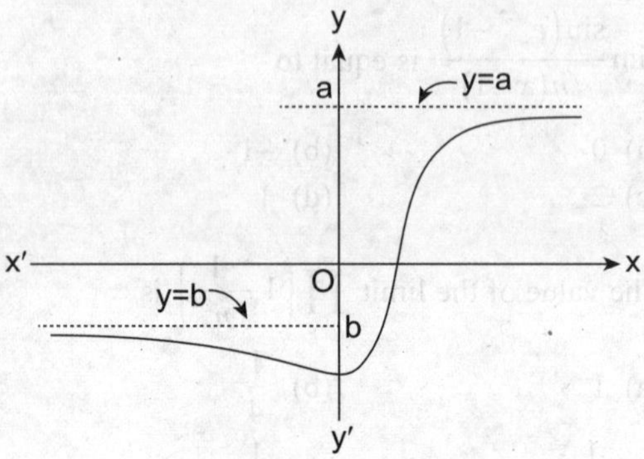

FIGURE 1.71

For example: Consider the function $f(x) = \dfrac{5x-4}{\sqrt{2x^2+3}}$ then $\operatorname*{Lt}_{x\to\infty} f(x) = \operatorname*{Lt}_{x\to\infty} \dfrac{5x-4}{\sqrt{2x^2+3}}$

$$= \operatorname*{Lt}_{x\to\infty} \frac{\frac{5x}{x}-\frac{4}{x}}{\sqrt{2+\frac{3}{x^2}}}$$ (Dividing each numerator and denominator by x)

$$= \operatorname*{Lt}_{x\to\infty} \frac{5-\frac{4}{x}}{\sqrt{2+\frac{3}{x^2}}} = \frac{5}{\sqrt{2}}$$

and $\operatorname*{Lt}_{x\to-\infty} f(x) = \operatorname*{Lt}_{x\to-\infty} \dfrac{5x-4}{\sqrt{2x^2+3}}$

$$= \operatorname*{Lt}_{x\to-\infty} \frac{5x-4}{\sqrt{x^2}\sqrt{2+x3/x^2}} = \operatorname*{Lt}_{x\to-\infty} \frac{5x-4}{|x|\sqrt{2+3/x^2}}$$

$$\left(\begin{array}{l} \because x<0 \\ \Rightarrow \sqrt{x^2} = |x| = -x \end{array}\right)$$

$$= \operatorname*{Lt}_{x\to-\infty} \frac{5-4/x}{-\sqrt{2+3/x^2}} = \frac{5}{-\sqrt{2}}$$

The two horizontal asymptotes are $y = \dfrac{5}{\sqrt{2}}$ and $y = -\dfrac{5}{\sqrt{2}}$. It is as shown below.

Procedure to find horizontal asymptote to algebraic curve

When the equation of curve is given by implicit form i.e., $f(x, y) = 0$ and is of degree n i.e., $(a_0x^n + a_1x^{n-1}y + a_2x^{n-2}y^2 + a_3x^{n-3}y^3 + ... + a_ny^n) + (b_1x^{n-1} + b_2x^{n-2}y + b_3x^{n-3}y^2 + ... + b_ny^{n-1}) + (c_2x^{n-2} + c_3x^{n-3}y + c_4x^{n-4}y^2 + ... + c_ny^{n-2}) + ... + = 0$ ...(i)

or $a_0x^n + (a_1y + b_1)x^{n-1} + (a_2y^2 + b_2y + c_2)x^{n-2} + ... + = 0$ ...(ii)

If a_0 = constant in (ii), then there will be no asymptote parallel to x-axis. If $a_0 = 0$; then

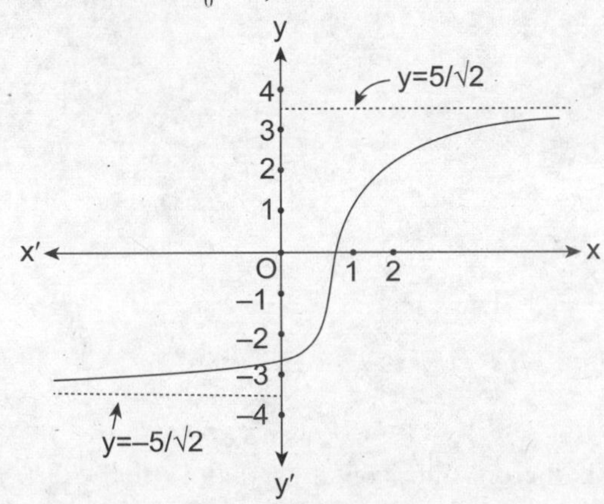

FIGURE 1.72

$$(a_1y + b_1)x^{n-1} + (a_2y^2 + b_2y + c_2)x^{n-2} + ... + = 0$$

$$\Rightarrow (a_1y + b_1) + (a_2y^2 + b_2y + c_2)\frac{1}{x} + (....)\frac{1}{x^2} + ... + = 0$$

As $x \to \infty$

$a_1y + b_1 = 0$ gives an asymptote parallel to x-axis. If $a_0 = 0$, coefficient of x^{n-1} is zero, then $(a_2y^2 + b_2y + c_2)x^{n-2} + ()\,x^{x-1} + ... + = 0$

$$\Rightarrow a_2y^2 + b_2y + c_2 + ().\frac{1}{x} + ()\frac{1}{x^2} + ... + = 0$$

$\therefore$ $x \to \infty \Rightarrow a_2y^2 + b_2y + c_2 = 0$, gives us two asymptotes $y_1 = c$ and $y_2 = d$ (say) parallel to x-axis and so on.

Algorithm

1. If the coefficient of term containing highest power of x is zero, then there will be no asymptote parallel to x-axis.
2. For finding the asymptotes parallel to x-axis put the coefficient of term containing highest power of x equal to zero.

ILLUSTRATION 133: Find the horizontal asymptotes to curves

(i) $x^2y^2 + xy - x^2 = 0$ (ii) $x^3y^2 - x^2y^3 - 5yx^3 + 6x^3 = 0$

SOLUTION: (i) Given equation is $x^2y^2 + xy - x^2 = 0$ or $x^2(y^2 - 1) + xy = 0$

Term containing highest power of x is $x^2(y^2 - 1)$ and coefficient of x^2 is $y^2 - 1$

Putting $y^2 - 1 = 0$, we get, $y + 1 = 0$ and $y - 1 = 0$

$\therefore$ $y = -1$ and $y = 1$ are two horizontal asymptotes to given curve.

(ii) Given equation is $x^3y^2 - x^2y^3 - 5yx^3 + 6x^3 = 0$

or $x^3(y^2 - 5y + 6) + x^2y^3 = 0$

Equating the coefficient of term containing highest power of x i.e., of x^3 equal to zero we get $y^2 - 5y + 6 = 0$ or $(y - 2)(y - 3) = 0$

$\Rightarrow$ $y = 2$ and $y = 3$ are two horizontal asymptotes to the given curve.

Vertical asymptotes (asymptotes parallel to y-axis). To find the vertical asymptotes to the curve $y = f(x)$, express x in terms of y i.e., $x = g(y)$ and vertical asymptotes can be obtained by applying limit $y \to \infty$ and $y \to -\infty$ on $g(y)$ i.e., $x = \underset{y\to-\infty}{\text{Lt}}\, g(y)$ and $x = \underset{y\to\infty}{\text{Lt}}\, g(y)$ gives us two vertical asymptotes.

Any curve $y = f(x)$ can have any number (or infinite number) of vertical asymptotes, as a function can be many one and hence $y \to \pm\infty$ can occur at infinitely many inputs x.

e.g., $y = \tan x$ has infinitely many vertical asymptotes at $x = (2n+1)\frac{\pi}{2}; n \in \mathbb{Z}$ as shown in figure 1.73.

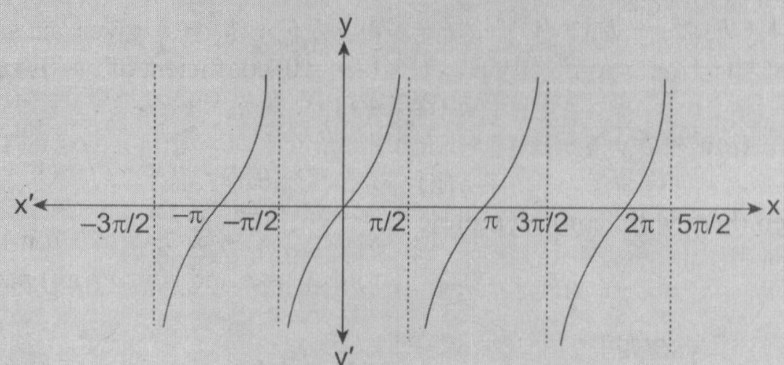

FIGURE 1.73

ILLUSTRATION 134: Find the horizontal and vertical asymptotes to curve

(i) $y = \frac{1}{x-5}$ (ii) $y = \frac{3x-4}{x+2}$

(iii) $y = \frac{1}{x(x-2)}$

SOLUTION: (i) $y = \frac{1}{(x-5)}$; clearly $y = \underset{x \to \pm\infty}{\text{Lt}} \left(\frac{1}{x-5}\right) = 0$ is the only horizontal asymptote, and $y > 0$ for $x > 5$ and $y < 0$ for $x < 5$.

$\Rightarrow x - 5 = \frac{1}{y}$ $\Rightarrow x = 5 + \frac{1}{y}$

$\therefore$ Vertical asymptotes are given by $x = \underset{y \to \infty}{\text{Lt}} \left(5 + \frac{1}{y}\right)$ and $x = \underset{y \to -\infty}{\text{Lt}} \left(5 + \frac{1}{y}\right)$

i.e., $x = 5$ and $x > 5$ when $y \to \infty$; $x < 5$ when $y \to -\infty$. Graphically as shown in figure 1.74.

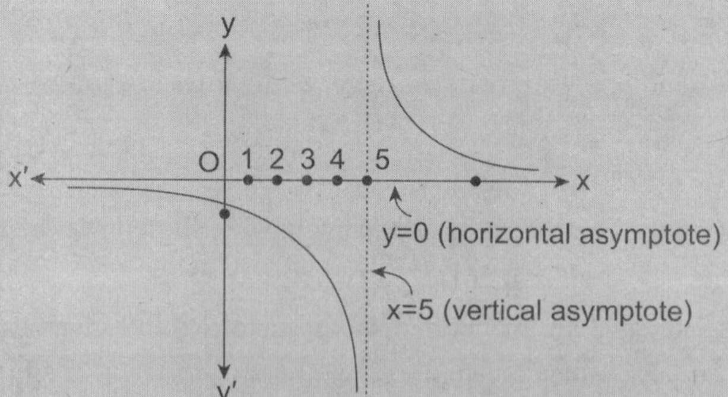

FIGURE 1.74

(ii) $y = \frac{3x-4}{x+2}$

$$y = \underset{x \to \pm\infty}{\text{Lt}} \left(\frac{3x-4}{x+2}\right) = \underset{x \to \pm\infty}{\text{Lt}} \left(\frac{3 - 4/x}{1 + 2/x}\right) = 3$$

$y = 3$ is the only horizontal asymptote, and $y > 0 \Rightarrow (3x - 4)(x + 2) > 0$

$\Rightarrow \quad x \in (-\infty, -2) \cup \left(\frac{4}{3}, \infty\right)$ and $y < 0$

$\Rightarrow \quad x \in \left(-2, \frac{4}{3}\right)$

Now, $y \to \infty$ for $x + 2 \to 0 \Rightarrow x \to -2$

$\therefore \quad x = -2$ is the only vertical asymptote when $x \to -2^{-}$; $y \to -\infty$ and when $x \to -2^{+}$; $y \to \infty$

Graphically shown in figure 1.75 below:

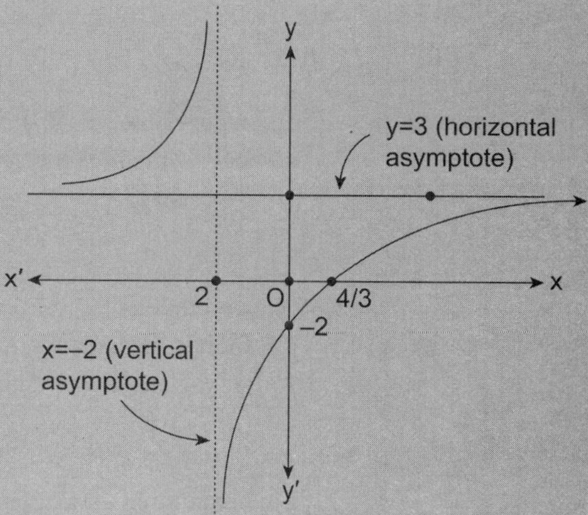

FIGURE 1.75

(iii) $y = \dfrac{1}{x(x-2)}$

$\therefore \quad y = \underset{x \to \pm\infty}{\text{Lt}} \dfrac{1}{x(x-2)} = 0$

$\therefore \quad y = 0$ is the only horizontal asymptote and $y < 0$ for $x \in (0, 2)$ and $y > 0$ for $x \in (-\infty, 0) \cup (2, \infty)$

$\therefore \quad y \to 0^{+}$ for $x \to \pm\infty$

Also $y \to -\infty$ as $x \to 0^{+}$ and $y \to \infty$ as $x \to 0^{-}$ and $y \to \infty$ ans $x \to 2^{+}$ and $y \to -\infty$ as $x \to 2^{-}$

$\therefore \quad x = 0$ and $x = 2$ are to vertical asymptotes. Graphically shown below:

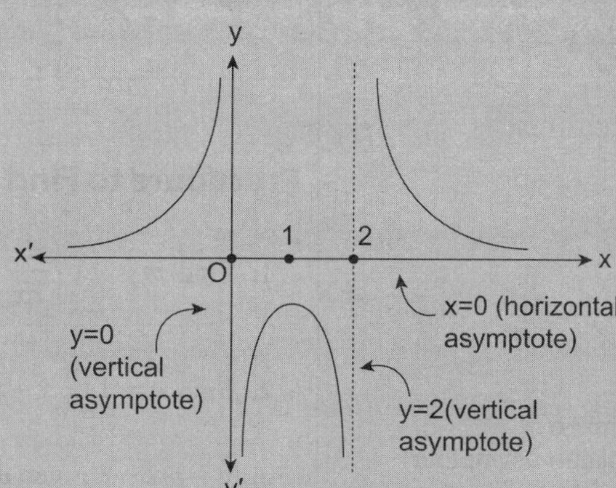

FIGURE 1.76

■ PROCEDURE TO FIND VERTICAL ASYMPTOTE

For the algebraic curves given in implicit form of degree 'n' in x and y i.e., $f(x, y) = 0$.

i.e., $(a_0x^n + a_1x^{n-1} + a_2x^{n-2}y^2 + \ldots + a_ny^n) + (b_1x^{n-1} + b_2x^{n-2}y + b_3x^{n-3}y^2 + \ldots + b_ny^{n-1}) + (c_2x^{n-2} + c_3x^{n-3}y + c_4x^{n-4}y^2 + \ldots + c_ny^{n-2}) + \ldots + = 0$

(i) If the coefficient of term containing highest power of y is zero, then there will be no asymptote parallel to y-axis.

(ii) Equating the coefficient of term containing highest power of y equal to zero gives us vertical asymptotes.

ILLUSTRATION 135: Find the vertical asymptotes to the curves

(i) $x^2y^2 - 2xy + 3y = 0$ (ii) $3y^2 - 2xy + 3y = 0$

(iii) $5x^3y^2 + 2xy - 5y^2x = 0$

SOLUTION: (i) Given curve is $x^2y^2 - 2xy + 3y = 0$. Coefficient of highest power of y i.e., of y^2 is x^2

$\therefore$ vertical asymptotes are given by $x^2 = 0$

$\Rightarrow x = 0$ (y-axis)

(ii) Given curve is $3y^2 - 2xy + 3y = 0$. Coefficient of highest power of y (i.e., y^2) is 3, which is constant. Thus there is no asymptote parallel to y-axis.

(iii) Given curve is $5x^3y^2 + 2xy - 5y^2x = 0$ or $y^2(5x^3 - 5x) + 2xy = 0$

Coefficient of highest power of y (i.e., y^2) is $5x^3 - 5x$

$\therefore$ vertical asymptotes are given by $5x^3 - 5x = 0$

$\Rightarrow 5x(x^2 - 1) = 0$

$\Rightarrow x = 0, x = -1, x = 1$

$\therefore$ There are three vertical asymptotes, namely $x = 0$, $x = -1$ and $x = 1$.

OBLIQUE ASYMPTOTES

Let $y = f(x)$ be a given curve and $P(x, y)$ be any variable point on it, then equation of tangent to curve at point $P(x, y)$ will be

$$Y - y = \frac{dy}{dx}(X - x) \text{ or } Y = y + \frac{dy}{dx}(X - x)$$

$$\text{or} \quad Y = \frac{dy}{dx}X + \left(y - x\frac{dy}{dx}\right) \quad .....(1)$$

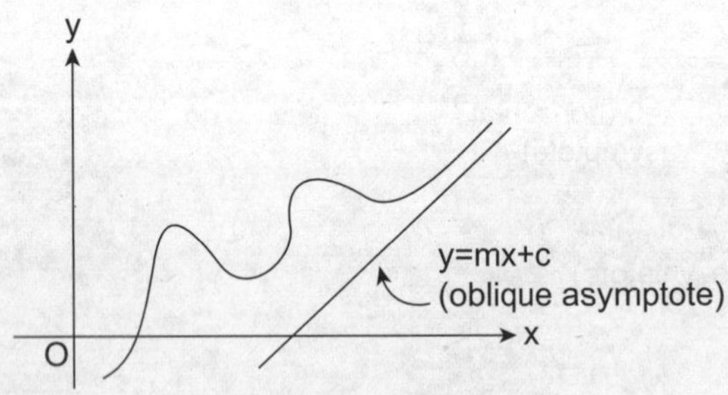

FIGURE 1.77

$\because$ There exists an oblique asymptote for the given curve, as $x, y \to \infty$, slope of tangent (m) should be finite and

Also the y – intercept should be finite

$$\Rightarrow m = \underset{\substack{x\to\infty \\ y\to\infty}}{\text{Lt}}\left(\frac{dy}{dx}\right) \text{ and } c = \underset{\substack{x\to\infty \\ y\to\infty}}{\text{Lt}}\left(y - x\frac{dy}{dx}\right)$$

$\therefore$ $y = mx + c$ is the required oblique asymptote.

Procedure to Find Oblique Asymptotes

1. Find $m = \underset{\substack{x\to\infty \\ y\to\infty}}{\text{Lt}}\left(\frac{dy}{dx}\right)$

2. Find $c = \underset{\substack{x\to\infty \\ y\to\infty}}{\text{Lt}}\left(y - x\frac{dy}{dx}\right)$

3. $y = mx + c$ given us oblique asymptote

ILLUSTRATION 136: Find the asymptotes to the given curves:

(i) $y = 2x + \frac{3}{x}$ (ii) $3y = 2\sqrt{x^2 - 9}$

SOLUTION: (i) Equation of curve is $y = 2x + \frac{3}{x}$ or $xy = 2x^2 + 3$

For horizontal asymptote:

Put coefficient of x^2 i.e., 2 equals to zero but it is constant, so, there is no asymptote parallel to x-axis. For vertical asymptote:

Put coefficient of y i.e., x equals to zero i.e., $x = 0$ (y-axis). For oblique asymptote:

$$y = \quad x + - \quad \Rightarrow \quad \frac{dy}{dx} = 2 - \frac{3}{x^2}$$

$$\therefore \quad m = \underset{\substack{x\to\infty \\ y\to\infty}}{\text{Lt}} \left(\frac{dy}{dx}\right) = \underset{\substack{x\to\infty \\ y\to\infty}}{\text{Lt}} \left(2 - \frac{3}{x^2}\right) = 2 \text{ and } c = \underset{\substack{x\to\infty \\ y\to\infty}}{\text{Lt}} \left(y - x\frac{dy}{dx}\right) = \underset{\substack{x\to\infty \\ y\to\infty}}{\text{Lt}} \left(y - x\left(2 - \frac{3}{x^2}\right)\right)$$

$$= \underset{\substack{x\to\infty \\ y\to\infty}}{\text{Lt}} \left(y - 2x + \frac{3}{x}\right) = \underset{x\to\infty}{\text{Lt}} \left(\frac{3}{x} + \frac{3}{x}\right) = \underset{x\to\infty}{\text{Lt}} \left(\frac{6}{x}\right) = 0$$

$\therefore \quad y = 2x + 0$ or $y = 2x$

$\therefore \quad$ As $x = 0$, $y = 2x$ are the asymptotes to the curve.

(ii) $3y = 2\sqrt{x^2 - 9}$, $y = \frac{2}{3}\sqrt{x^2 - 9}$ or $9y^2 = 4(x^2 - 9)$

$\Rightarrow 9y^2 = 4x^2 - 36$

$\Rightarrow$ There is no asymptote parallel to coordinate axis as coefficient of x^2 and y^2 are zeros.

Now, $y = \frac{2}{3}\sqrt{x^2 - 9} \Rightarrow \frac{dy}{dx} = \frac{2}{3}\left(\frac{1}{2}\right).\frac{1}{\sqrt{x^2 - 9}}(2x)$

$$\Rightarrow \quad \frac{dy}{dx} = \frac{2}{3}x.\frac{1}{\sqrt{x^2 - 9}}$$

$$\therefore \quad m = \underset{x\to\infty}{\text{Lt}} \frac{2}{3}\frac{x}{\sqrt{x^2 - 9}} = \underset{x\to\infty}{\text{Lt}} \frac{2}{3}\frac{x}{|x|\sqrt{1 - 9/x^2}} = \underset{x\to\infty}{\text{Lt}} \frac{2}{3}\frac{1}{\sqrt{1 - 9/x^2}} = \frac{2}{3}$$

$$\text{and } m = \underset{x\to-\infty}{\text{Lt}} \frac{2}{3}\frac{x}{|x|\sqrt{1 - 9/x^2}} = \underset{x\to-\infty}{\text{Lt}} \frac{2}{3}\frac{x}{(-x)\sqrt{1 - 9/x^2}} = -\frac{2}{3} \text{ and } c = \underset{\substack{y\to\infty \\ x\to\infty}}{\text{Lt}} \left(y - x\frac{dy}{dx}\right)$$

$$= \underset{\substack{x\to\infty \\ y\to\infty}}{\text{Lt}} \left(\frac{2}{3}\sqrt{x^2 - 9} - \frac{2}{3}x^2.\frac{1}{\sqrt{x^2 - 9}}\right) = \underset{x\to\infty}{\text{Lt}} \frac{2}{3}\left(\frac{x^2 - 9 - x^2}{\sqrt{x^2 - 9}}\right) = \underset{x\to\infty}{\text{Lt}} \frac{-6}{\sqrt{x^2 - 9}} = 0$$

$$\therefore \quad y = -\frac{2}{3}x + 0 \text{ and } y = \frac{2}{3}x + 0$$

i.e., $y = \pm\frac{2}{3}x$ are the only asymptotes to the given curve.

Another method to find oblique asymptote for second degree curve :

Let $f(x, y) = 0$ be the given curve, Let $y = mx + c$ be the oblique asymptote(s).

Put $y = mx + c$ in $f(x, y) = 0$

Putting the highest power of x equal to zero gives us the possible slopes and second highest power of x equal to zero gives us the possible values of y-intercept 'c'.

ILLUSTRATION 137: Find the asymptotes of the curve $y = \frac{x^2 + 2x + 1}{x}$.

SOLUTION: Given equation is $xy = x^2 + 2x + 1$ or $x^2 - xy + 2x + 1 = 0$

Horizontal Asymptote: As coefficient of $x^2 = 1$ (constant) there is no asymptote parallel to x-axis.

Vertical Asymptote: Coefficient of y is $x = 0$ (y-axis).

Oblique Asymptote: Let $y = mx + c$ be the oblique asymptote.

$\therefore\ x^2 - x(mx + c) + 2x + 1 = 0$

$\Rightarrow x^2(1 - m) + (2 - c)x + 1 = 0$

$\therefore$ slope of asymptote is given by $1 - m = 0$ and y-intercept is given by $2 - c = 0$

$\Rightarrow m = 1, c = 2$

$\therefore\ y = x + 2$ is the only oblique asymptote to the given curve.

REMARK:

A curve having n-degree in x and y can not have more than n-asymptotes.

Method to Find Oblique Asymptotes for Algebraic Curves of Any Degree

Let the given curve be of degree 'n' in x and y given by $(a_0x^n + a_1x^{n-1}y + a_2x^{n-2}y^2 + \ldots + a_ny^n) + (b_1x^{n-1} + b_2x^{n-2}y + b_3x^{n-3}y^2 + \ldots + b_ny^{n-1}) + (c_2x^{n-2} + c_3x^{n-3}y + \ldots + c_ny^{n-2}) + \ldots + = 0$ .....(1)

Putting $x = 1$ and $y = m$ in equation (1) we get

$(a_0 + a_1m + a_2m^2 + \ldots + a_nm^n) + (b_1 + b_2m + b_3m^2 + \ldots + b_nm^{n-1}) + (c_2 + c_3m + \ldots + c_nm^{n-2}) + \ldots + = 0$

Let us denote the polynomial of degree n in 'm' by $\phi_n(m)$

The polynomial of degree $n - 1$ in (m) by $\phi_{n-1}, (m)$, the polynomial of degree $n - 2$ in 'm' by $\phi_{n-2}(m)$ and so on.

Step I: Putting $\phi_n(m) = 0$, gives us at most n real roots $m_1, m_2, m_3, \ldots m_n$ i.e., slope of asymptotes.

Step II: Now to find y-intercept 'c' corresponding to a given slope $m_i(=m)$ we use

$c\phi_n'(m) + \phi_{n-1}(m) = 0$, if m is a non-repeated root, $\frac{c^2}{2!}\phi_n''(m) + \frac{c}{1!}\phi'_{n-1}(m) + \phi_{n-2}(m) = 0$, if m is a root twice repeated $\frac{c^3}{3!}\phi_n'''(m) + \frac{c^2}{2!}\phi''_{n-1}(m) + \frac{c}{1!}\phi'_{n-2}(m) + \phi_{n-3}(m) = 0$, if m is a root thrice repeated and so on.

Step III: Asymptotes are given by $y = mx + c$

ILLUSTRATION 138: Find all the asymptotes to the curve $(x^3y - x^2y^2) + (4x^2y + 2xy^2) - 8xy + 12x + 10 = 0$

SOLUTION: Given curve is $(x^3y - x^2y^2) + (4x^2y + 2xy^2) - 8xy + 12x + 10 = 0$

Asymptotes || to x-axis are given by $y = 0$ (equating the coefficient of highest power of x i.e., x^3 equal to 0)

Asymptotes || to y-axis are given by $2x - x^2 = 0$ (equating the coefficient of $y^2 = 0$)

$\Rightarrow x(2 - x) = 0$

$\Rightarrow x = 0$ and $x = 2$ are two asymptotes parallel to y-axis

and $\phi_4(x, y) = x^3y - x^2y^2$;

$\phi_3(x, y) = 4x^2y + 2xy^2$;

$\phi_2(x, y) = -8xy$; $\phi_1(x, y) = 12x$;

$\phi_0(x, y) = 10$

Replacing x by 1 and y by 'm' get

$\phi_4(m) = m - m^2$

$\phi_3(m) = 4m + 2m^2$

$\phi_2(m) = -8m$

$\phi_1(m) = 12,\ \phi_0(m) = 10$

Now slopes of oblique asymptotes are given by $\phi_4(m) = 0$, i.e., $m - m^2 = 0 \Rightarrow m(1-m) = 0$

$\Rightarrow m = 0$ and $m = 1$

But $m = 0$ corresponds to asymptote parallel to x-axis i.e., $y = 0$

$\therefore$ $m = 1$ corresponds to oblique asymptote not parallel to x-axis,

Corresponding y-intercept 'c' is given by $c\phi_4'(m) + \phi_3'(m) = 0$

$\Rightarrow c(1-2m) + (4m + 2m^2) = 0$ $\quad\Rightarrow c(1-2) + (4+2) = 0$

$\Rightarrow c = 6$

$\therefore$ $y = x + 6$ is the oblique asymptote

Thus $y = 0, x = 0, x = 2, y = x + 6$ are asymptotes to given curve

Asymptote by Expansion

If the equation of the curve is of the form $y = mx + c + \frac{A}{x} + \frac{B}{x^2} + \frac{C}{x^3} + \ldots\ldots\ldots$, then $y = mx + c$ will be an asymptote of the given curve.

Example: Find the asymptote for $y = x + 1/x$.

Solution: Here, $y = x + 1/x$ is of the form,

$$y = mx + c + \frac{A}{x} + \frac{B}{x^2} + \ldots..$$

$\Rightarrow$ $y = x$ is asymptote of the curve $y = x + 1/x$.

NOTE:

Above method is useful to find all asymptote. Thus, students are advised to find vertical and horizontal asymptote (i.e., asymptote parallel to x-axis and y-axis) also using this method.

ILLUSTRATION 139: Find the asymptotes to the curve $y^3 = 2x^3 + 12x^2 + x$

SOLUTION: $y^3 = x^3\left(2 + \frac{12}{x} + \frac{1}{x^2}\right)$

$$\Rightarrow y^3 = 2x^3\left[1 + \frac{6}{x} + \frac{1}{2x^2}\right] \qquad \Rightarrow y = (2)^{1/3}x\left[1 + \frac{6}{x} + \frac{1}{2x^2}\right]^{1/3}$$

$$\Rightarrow y = (2)^{1/3x}\left[1 + \frac{1}{3}\left(\frac{6}{x} + \frac{1}{2x^2}\right) + \frac{\left(\frac{1}{3}\right)\left(\frac{-2}{3}\right)\left(\frac{6}{x} + \frac{1}{2x^2}\right)^2}{2!} + \ldots.\right]$$

$$\Rightarrow y = \sqrt[3]{2}\,x\left[1 + \frac{2}{x} + \frac{1}{6x^2} - \frac{1}{9}\left(\frac{36}{x^2} + \frac{1}{4x^4} + \frac{6}{x^3}\right) + \ldots\right]$$

$$\Rightarrow y = \sqrt[3]{2}x + 2\sqrt[3]{2} + \frac{\sqrt[3]{2}}{6x} - \frac{4\sqrt[3]{2}}{x} - \frac{\sqrt[3]{2}}{36x^3} - \frac{2}{3}\frac{\sqrt[3]{2}}{x^2} + \ldots$$

$\therefore$ $y = \sqrt[3]{2}\,x + 2\sqrt[3]{2}$ is the oblique asymptote to the given curve

The Position of the Curve with Respect to An Asymptote

Let the equation of the curve is of the form;

$y = mx + c + \frac{A}{x} + \frac{B}{x^2} + \frac{C}{x^3} + \ldots..$, then.

(a) The curve lies above the asymptote if

(i) $A \neq 0$ and A and x have same signs.

(ii) $A \neq 0, B > 0$

(iii) $A = 0, B = 0, C \neq 0$ and C and x have same signs.

(b) The curve lies below the asymptote if.

(i) $A \neq 0$ and A and x have opposite signs.

(ii) $A = 0, B < 0$

(iii) $A = 0, B = 0, C \neq 0$ and C and x have opposite signs.

ILLUSTRATION 140: For the curve $y^4 - x^4 + 4x^3 = 0$

(i) show that the curve lie above asymptote $y = x - 1$ for $x < 0$

(ii) show that the curve lie below asymptote $y = x - 1$ for $x > 0$

SOLUTION: Given equation of curve is $y^4 - x^4 + 4x^3 = 0$

$\Rightarrow y^4 = x^4 - 4x^3$

$\Rightarrow y^4 = x^4\left(1 - \frac{4}{x}\right)$

$\Rightarrow y = x\left[1 - \frac{4}{x}\right]^{1/4}$

$$\Rightarrow y = x\left(1 + \frac{1}{4}\left(\frac{-4}{x}\right) + \frac{1}{4}\frac{\left(\frac{1}{4}-1\right)\left(\frac{-4}{x}\right)^2}{2!} + \frac{\left(\frac{1}{4}\right)\left(\frac{1}{4}-1\right)\left(\frac{1}{4}-2\right)\left(-\frac{4}{x}\right)^3}{3!} + \ldots.\right)$$

$\Rightarrow y = x\left(1 - \frac{1}{x} - \frac{3}{2x^2} - \frac{7}{2x^3} + \ldots\right)$

$\Rightarrow y = x - 1 - \frac{3}{2x} - \frac{7}{2x^2} + \ldots$

Comparing with $y = mx + c + \frac{A}{x} + \frac{B}{x^2} + \ldots$, we get

the oblique asymptote given by $y = x - 1, A = -3/2, B = -7/2$

∴ The curve lies above the asymptote where x and A are of same sign

Here $A = -3/2 < 0$

$\Rightarrow$ Curve lies above the asymptote for $x < 0$ and the curve lies below the asymptote where x and A are opposite sign

$\Rightarrow x > 0$

∴ The curve lies above asymptote $y = x - 1$ for $x < 0$

and the curve lies below asymptote $y = x - 1$ for $x > 0$

TEXTUAL EXERCISE–5: (SUBJECTIVE)

1. Find the horizontal and vertical asymptotes to the curve
   (i) $x^2y^2 + 2xy^3 - 4x^2 + 10 = 0$
   (ii) $2x^2y - 3xy^2 + 10x^2 - 5y = 0$
   (iii) $x^3y^2 - y^3x^2 + 4 = 0$
   (iv) $x^4y^2 - x^3y^3 - 9x^4 + 8y^3 = 0$

2. Define asymptotes of a curve and find vertical and horizontal asymptotes of the following curves:
   (a) $y = 1/x$ (b) $y = \dfrac{4x-5}{3x+2}$
   (c) $y = \dfrac{2x+3}{\sqrt{x^2-2x-3}}$ (d) $y = \sqrt{(x+1)} - \sqrt{x}$
   (e) $y = \dfrac{x^2-5x+6}{x-3}$ (f) $y = \dfrac{x^2-x+1}{x^2+x+1}$
   (g) $y = \dfrac{2x}{x^2+1}$

3. Find the asymptotes of following functions
   (i) $y = \dfrac{1}{x-5}$ (ii) $y = e^{1/x}$
   (iii) $y = x - \dfrac{1}{x}$

4. Find horizontal, vertical and oblique asymptotes of the following curves:
   (i) $x^2y + xy^2 = a^3$ (ii) $y^3 = x^2(x - a)$

5. Find all the asymptotes to the curve
   (i) $y^4 - 6x^2y^2 + 2x^4 - 3x^3y + 2x^2y + 8y^3 - 9x^2 + 7xy + 8x + 1 = 0$
   (ii) $y^3 - x^3 + 2y - 5x = 0$
   (iii) $y^2x^2 - 4x^2y + 8xy^2 - 8xy + 2x + y = 0$
   (iv) $x^3 + y^3 - 3axy = 0$

6. Find the oblique asymptotes by using expansion
   (i) $y^2 = x^2 + 4x$
   (ii) $y^2 = x^2 + \dfrac{1}{x}$
   (iii) $y = 2x + 5 + \dfrac{4}{x} + \dfrac{8}{x^2} + \ldots$
   (iv) $y^5 = x^5 + 8x^4$

7. For the curve $y^5 = x^5 + 2x^4$; show
   (i) The curve lies above the asymptote $y = x + \dfrac{2}{5}$, if $x < 0$
   (ii) The curve lies below the asymptote $y = x + \dfrac{2}{5}$, if $x > 0$

8. For the curve $y = x + \dfrac{1}{x}$ show,
   (i) The curve lies above the asymptote $y = x$ if $x > 0$
   (ii) The curve lies below the asymptote $y = x$ if $x < 0$

9. Find the horizontal and vertical asymptotes of $h(x) = \dfrac{3x+1}{x^2-4}$

10. Find the horizontal and vertical asymptotes of $y = \ell n(2x+8)$.

Answer Keys

1. H : $y = \pm 2$; $V : x = 0$; (ii) $H : y = -5$; $V : x = 0$; (iii) $H : y = 0$; $V : x = 0$; (iv) $H : y = \pm 3$; $V : x = 2$
2. (a) $x = 0$; $y = 0$ (b) $x = -2/3$; $y = 4/3$ (c) $x = -1, 3$; $y = 2$ (d) $x =$ no vertical asymptotes; $y = 0$
   (e)no horizontal and vertical asymptotes
   (f) $x =$ no vertical asymptotes; $y = 1$ (g) $x =$ no vertical asymptotes; $y = 0$
3. (i) $x = 5, y = 0$ (ii) $x = 0, y = 1$ (iii) $x = 0$, No, oblique asymptotes is $y = x$
4. (i) $x = 0, y = 0, y = -x$ (ii) $y = x - \dfrac{a}{3}$
5. (i) (ii) $-y = x$ (iii) $y = 0, y = 4, x = 0, x = -8$ (iv) $y + x + a = 0$
6. (i)$y = x + 2$ (ii) $y = x$ (iii)$y = 2x + 5$ (iv) $y = x + 8/5$ **9.** $x = 2, x = -2, y = 0$ **10.** $x = -4$

TEXTUAL EXERCISE–5: (OBJECTIVE)

1. The horizontal asymptote of the curve $x^2 - 2xy + yx^2 = 0$ is
(a) $y = 0$ (b) $y = 1$
(c) $y = -1$ (d) Does not axist

2. The vertical asymptote of the curve $yx^2 - 2xy^2 + 8y^2 + 7y = 0$
(a) $x = 0$ (b) $x = 1$
(c) $x = 4$ (d) Does not exist

3. The oblique asymptote to curve $yx^2 - 2xy^2 + 8y^2 + 7y = 0$ is/are
(a) $y = 0$ (b) $y = \frac{x}{2} + 2$
(c) $y = \frac{x}{2} - 2$ (d) None of these

4. The oblique asymptote the curve $y = 2x + 5 + \frac{8}{x} + \frac{9}{x^2} + \frac{10}{x^3} + \ldots$ is
(a) $y = 2x$ (b) $y = 2x + 5$
(c) $y = 2x - 5$ (d) None of these

5. The curve having equation $y = 2x - 4 - \frac{2}{x} + \frac{4}{x^2} + ..$ lies below its oblique asymptote $y = 2x - 4$ for
(a) $x < 0$ (b) $x > 0$
(c) $x \in [0, \infty)$ (d) $\mathbb{R}$

6. Which of the following functions has two horizontal asymptotes?
(a) $y = \frac{3x}{\sqrt{x^2+2}}$ (b) $y = \frac{|x|}{x+2}$
(c) $y = \tan^{-1}(3x - 4)$ (d) $y = \cot^{-1}(2x-1)$

7. Which of the following function has a vertical asymptotes at $x = 2$?
(a) $y = \frac{|x^2-4|}{(x-2)}$ (b) $y = \frac{x^2-5x+6}{(x-2)}$
(c) $y = \frac{x^4+1}{(x-2)}$ (d) $y = \frac{\cos(x+1)}{(x-2)}$

8. The asymptotes to the curve $xy = c^2$ are ($c \in \mathbb{R}$)
(a) $x = 0$ (b) $x = c$
(c) $y = x$ (d) $y = 0$

9. The asymptotes to the curve $x^2 - y^2 = a^2$ ($a \in R$) is /are
(a) $y - x = 0$ (b) $y + x = 0$
(c) x-axis (d) y-axis

10. $y = e^{1/x}$ has asymptotes having equations
(a) $x = 0$ (b) $y = 0$
(c) $x = 1$ (d) $y = 1$

11. Which of the following statements are false?
(a) A function can't have more than two horizontal asymptotes
(b) If $P(x)$ is a polynomial functions, then $y = \frac{P(x)}{x-2}$ has a vertical asymptote at $x = 2$
(c) A polynomial function always has a vertical asymptote
(d) A rational function always has a vertical asymptote

Answer Key

1. (c) **2.** (c) **3.** (a,b) **4.** (b) **5.** (b) **6.** (a,b,c,d) **7.** (c,d) **8.** (a,d)
9. (a,b) **10.** (a,d) **11.** (b,c,d)

MULTIPLE CHOICE QUESTIONS

SECTION–I

OBJECTIVE SOLVED EXAMPLES

1. $\lim_{x\to 2}\frac{\sqrt{x-2}+\sqrt{x}-\sqrt{2}}{\sqrt{x^2-4}}$ is equal to

(a) 1/2 (b) 1
(c) 2 (d) None of these

Solution: (a) Limit $=\lim_{x\to 2}\left\{\frac{1}{\sqrt{x+2}}+\frac{\sqrt{x}-\sqrt{2}}{\sqrt{x^2-4}}\right\}$

$=\frac{1}{2}+\lim_{x\to 2}\frac{x-2}{\sqrt{x}+\sqrt{2}}\cdot\frac{1}{\sqrt{(x+2)(x-2)}}$

$=\frac{1}{2}+\lim_{x\to 2}\frac{1}{\sqrt{x}+\sqrt{2}}\cdot\sqrt{\frac{x-2}{x+2}}=\frac{1}{2}$

2. $\lim_{x\to 1}\frac{\sum_{r=1}^{n}x^r-n}{x-1}$ is equal to

(a) $n/2$ (b) $\frac{n(n+1)}{2}$
(c) 1 (d) None of these

Solution: (b) Limit $=\lim_{x\to 1}\sum_{r=1}^{n}\frac{x^r-1^r}{x-1}$

$=\lim_{x\to 1}\sum_{r=1}^{n}r.1^{r-1}$

$\left(\because\ \lim_{x\to 0}\frac{x^n-a^n}{x-a}=n(a)^{n-1}\right)$

$=[1+2+3+....+n]=\frac{n(n+1)}{2}$

3. $\lim_{x\to 1}\frac{\sqrt{1-\cos\{2(x-1)\}}}{x-1}$ is equal to

(a) exists and it is $\sqrt{2}$
(b) exists and it is $-\sqrt{2}$
(c) does not exist because $x-1\to 0$
(d) does not exist because L.H.L ≠ R.H.L

Solution: (d) Limit $=\lim_{x\to 1}\frac{\sqrt{2}\,|\sin(x-1)|}{x-1}$

$=\lim_{h\to 0}\frac{\sqrt{2}\,|\sin h|}{h}$

$\therefore$ R.H.L. $=\lim_{h\to 0}\frac{\sqrt{2}\sin h}{h}=\sqrt{2}$ and L.H.L. $=-\sqrt{2}$

4. Let $f(x)=\begin{cases}x^2-1 & ;0<x<2\\ 2x+3 & ;2\le x<3\end{cases}$. The quadratic equation whose roots are $\lim_{x\to 2^-}f(x)$ and $\lim_{x\to 2^+}f(x)$ is

(a) $x^2-6x+9=0$
(b) $x^2-10x+21=0$
(c) $x^2-14x+49=0$
(d) None of these

Solution: (b) $\lim_{x\to 2^-}f(x)=\lim_{x\to 2^-}(x^2-1)=2^2-1=3$

$\lim_{x\to 2^+}f(x)=\lim_{x\to 2^+}(2x+3)=7$

$\therefore$ Quadratic equation is $x^2-(3+7)x+21=0$
or $x^2-10x+21=0$

5. If $\lim_{n\to\infty}\left(an-\frac{1+n^2}{1+n}\right)=b$, a finite number, then

(a) $a=1$ (b) $a=0$
(c) $b=1$ (d) $b=-1$

Solution: (a, c)

$\lim_{n\to\infty}\frac{an(1+n)-(1+n^2)}{1+n}=\lim_{n\to\infty}\frac{(a-1)n^2+an-1}{1+n}$

$=\infty$ if $a-1\neq 0$

If $a-1=0$, limit $=\lim_{n\to\infty}\frac{an-1}{n+1}=a=b$

$\therefore\ a=b=1$

6. The value of $\lim_{x\to 0}\frac{a^x-b^x}{x}$

(a) $\ell n\,(a/b)$ (b) $\ell n\,(b/a)$
(c) $\ell n\,(ab)$ (d) None of these

Solution: (a) We have,

$$\lim_{x\to 0}\frac{a^x-b^x}{x}=\lim_{x\to 0}\left[\left(\frac{a^x-1}{x}\right)-\left(\frac{b^x-1}{x}\right)\right]$$

$$=\ell n(a)-\ell n(b)=\ell n\left(\frac{a}{b}\right)$$

7. The value of $\lim_{x\to-\pi}\frac{|x+\pi|}{\sin x}$

(a) is equal to –1 (b) is equal to 1
(c) is equal to π (d) does not exist

Solution: (d) We have, $f(x)=\frac{|x+\pi|}{\sin x}$

$$\therefore \quad \lim_{x\to-\pi^-}f(x)=\lim_{h\to 0^+}f(-\pi-h)=\lim_{h\to 0^+}\frac{|-\pi-h+\pi|}{\sin(-\pi-h)}$$

$$=-\lim_{h\to 0^+}\frac{|h|}{\sin(\pi+h)}=\lim_{h\to 0^+}\frac{h}{\sinh}=1$$

and, $\lim_{x\to-\pi^+}f(x)=\lim_{h\to 0^+}f(-\pi+h)$

$$=\lim_{h\to 0}\frac{|-\pi+h+\pi|}{\sin(-\pi+h)}=\lim_{h\to 0}\frac{h}{-\sinh}=-1$$

Hence, $\lim_{x\to-\pi}f(x)$ does not exist

8. The value of $\lim_{x\to 0}x^m(\ell n\,x)^n$, $m, n\in N$ is

(a) 0 (b) m/n
(c) mn (d) None of these

Solution: (a) Given $\lim_{x\to 0}x^m(\ell nx)^n=\lim_{x\to 0}\frac{(\ell nx)^n}{x^{-m}}$

$\left(\frac{\infty}{\infty}\text{ from}\right)$

$$=\lim_{x\to 0^+}\frac{n(\ell nx)^{n-1}\frac{1}{x}}{-mx^{-m-1}}\quad\text{(By L.Hospital's Rule)}$$

$$=\lim_{x\to 0^+}\frac{n(\ell nx)^{n-1}}{-mx^{-m}}\quad\left(\frac{\infty}{\infty}\text{ from}\right)$$

$$=\lim_{x\to 0^+}\frac{n(n-1)(\ell nx)^{n-2}\frac{1}{x}}{(-m)^2x^{-m-1}}\quad\text{(By L-Hospital's Rule)}$$

$$=\lim_{x\to 0^+}\frac{n(n-1)(\log x)^{n-2}}{m^2x^{-m}}$$ (Diff. numerator and denominator n times)

$$=\lim_{x\to 0^+}\frac{n!}{(-m)^n x^{-m}}=0$$

9. $\lim_{x\to 1^-}[\sin^{-1}x]$ is

(a) 1 (b) π
(c) π/2 (d) does not exist

where [ ] represents the greatest integer function.

Solution: (a) R.H.L. = $\lim_{h\to 0^+}[\sin^{-1}(1+h)]$

= Does not exist

∴ Limit does not exist

L.H.L. = $\lim_{h\to 0^+}[\sin^{-1}(1-h)]=[\pi/2]=1$

10. The value of b; if $\lim_{x\to 0}\left[\frac{ae^x-b\cos x+ce^{-x}}{x\sin x}\right]=2$; is

(a) 1 (b) –1
(c) 0 (d) 2

Solution: (d)

$$\lim_{x\to 0}\frac{a\left(1+x+\frac{x^2}{2!}+...\right)-b\left(1-\frac{x^2}{2}+....\right)+c\left(1-x+\frac{x^2}{2!}-....\right)}{x^2}\times\underbrace{\lim_{x\to 0}\frac{x}{\sin x}}=2$$

$$\Rightarrow \lim_{x\to 0}\frac{a-b+c}{x^2}+\frac{a-c}{x}+\left(\frac{a}{2}+\frac{b}{2}+\frac{c}{2}\right)+.....=2$$

LHS can be equal to *a* finite quantity only if

$a-b+c=0$ ....(i)

and $a-c=0$ ...(ii)

When (i) and (ii) are satisfied then LHS is equal to 2 only if

$\frac{a+b+c}{2}=2$ ....(iii)

Solving (i), (ii) and (iii) $b=2$

11. If $\{x\}$ denotes the fractional part of x, then $\lim_{x\to[a]}\frac{e^{\{x\}}-\{x\}-1}{\{x\}^2}$; where $[a]$ denotes the integral part of a, is equal to

(a) 0 (b) 1/2
(c) $e-2$ (d) None of these

Solution: (d) Let $[a]=k$, then k is an integer

Now $\lim_{x\to k^-}\frac{e^{\{x\}}-\{x\}-1}{\{x\}^2}=\frac{e-1-1}{1}=e-2$

$[\because \lim_{x\to k-0}\{x\}=1]$

and $\lim\limits_{x\to k^+}\dfrac{e^{\{x\}}-\{x\}-1}{\{x\}^2}=\lim\limits_{t\to 0}\left(\dfrac{e^t-t-1}{t^2}\right)$, where $t=\{x\}$

$\left[\because \lim\limits_{x\to k^+}=\lim\limits_{t\to 0} t\right]$

$$=\frac{\left(1+\frac{t}{1!}+\frac{t^2}{2!}+.....\right)-t-1}{t^2}=\frac{1}{2}$$

Thus L.H.L. $\neq$ R.H.L.

$\therefore$ Given limit does not exist

12. $\lim\limits_{x\to 0}\left(\left[\dfrac{n\sin x}{x}\right]+\left[\dfrac{n\tan x}{x}\right]\right)$; ($n\in N$; [.] denotes the greatest integer function)

(a) is equal to $2n$ (b) is equal to $2n-1$
(c) is equal to $2n-2$ (d) does not exist

Solution: (b) $\dfrac{n\sin x}{x}\to n$ as $x\to 0$ but remains less than n

$\dfrac{n\tan x}{x}\to n$ as $x\to 0$ but remain more than n

so $\lim\limits_{x\to 0}\left(\left[\dfrac{n\sin x}{x}\right]+\left[\dfrac{n\tan x}{x}\right]\right)=n-1+n=2n-1$

13. $\lim\limits_{n\to\infty}\left(\dfrac{n!}{(mn)^n}\right)^{1/n}$; ($m\in N$) is equal to

(a) $1/em$ (b) m/e
(c) em (d) e/m

Solution: (a) Let $L=\lim\limits_{n\to\infty}\left(\dfrac{n!}{(mn)^n}\right)^{1/n}$

$$\Rightarrow \ell nL=\lim_{n\to\infty}\sum_{r=1}^{n}\frac{1}{n}\ell n\left(\frac{r}{mn}\right)=\int_0^1 \ell n\left(\frac{x}{m}\right)dx$$

$$=m\left[\frac{1}{m}\ell n\frac{1}{m}-\frac{1}{m}\right]=\ell n\frac{1}{m}-\ell ne=\ell n\left(\frac{1}{em}\right)$$

$$\Rightarrow L=\frac{1}{em}$$

14. The value of $\lim\limits_{x\to\infty}\dfrac{x^3\sin(1/x)-2x^2}{1+3x^2}$

(a) is 0 (b) is $-1/3$
(c) is -1 (d) is $-2/3$

Solution: (c) The given limit can be re-written as

$$\lim_{x\to\infty}\frac{\frac{\sin(1/x)}{1/x}-2}{1/x^2+3}=-1/3$$

15. If $f(n)=\dfrac{1}{n}\,[(n+1)(n+2)\,.......\,(n+n)]^{1/n}$.

Then $\lim\limits_{n\to\infty} f(n)$ is equal to

(a) e (b) $1/e$
(c) $2/e$ (d) $4/e$

Solution: (d) Let $A=\lim\limits_{n\to\infty}\dfrac{1}{n}\,[(n+1)(n+2)\,....\,(n+n)]^{1/n}$

$$=\lim_{n\to\infty}\left[\left(1+\frac{1}{n}\right)\left(1+\frac{2}{n}\right)......\left(1+\frac{n}{n}\right)\right]^{1/n}$$

Then $\ell n\,A=\lim\limits_{n\to\infty}\dfrac{1}{n}\sum\limits_{r=1}^{n}\ell n\left(1+\dfrac{r}{n}\right)$

$$=\int_0^1 \ell n(1+x)\,dx=\ell n\left(\frac{4}{e}\right)$$

$$\Rightarrow A=\frac{4}{e}$$

16. Let $f(x)=\left(\dfrac{e^{x\ln(2^x-1)}-(2^x-1)^x\sin x}{e^{x\ln x}}\right)^{\frac{1}{x}}$. Then right-hand limit of $f(x)$ at $x=0$

(a) is equal to ln 2 (b) is equal to $\dfrac{\ln 2}{e}$
(c) is equal to e ln 2 (d) does not exist

Solution: (b) $f(x)$ can be rewritten as

$$\left(\frac{2^x-1}{x}\right)(1-\sin x)^{\frac{1}{x}}$$

$$\therefore \lim_{x\to 0^+} f(x)=\lim_{x\to 0^+}\frac{2^x-1}{x}\lim_{x\to 0^+}(1-\sin x)^{\frac{1}{x}}=\frac{\ln 2}{e}$$

17. If α is a root of $x^2+ax+1=0$, then $\lim\limits_{x\to 1/\alpha}\dfrac{\sin(x^2+ax+1)}{(\alpha x-1)}$ is equal to

(a) $2a\alpha$ (b) $a\alpha^2$
(c) $\dfrac{1-\alpha^2}{\alpha^2}$ (d) does not exist

Solution: (c) Since coefficient of x^2+ax+1 are reciprocal, so roots will be α, $\dfrac{1}{\alpha}$

$\therefore\ L = \lim_{x\to 1/\alpha} \dfrac{\sin(x^2+ax+1)}{(\alpha x-1)}$

$= \lim_{x\to 1/\alpha} \dfrac{\sin\left[\left(x-\frac{1}{\alpha}\right)(x-\alpha)\right]}{\left(x-\frac{1}{\alpha}\right)(x-\alpha)} \cdot \dfrac{\left(x-\frac{1}{\alpha}\right)(x-\alpha)}{(\alpha x-1)}$

$= \lim_{x\to 1/\alpha} \dfrac{(x-\alpha)}{\alpha} = \dfrac{\frac{1}{\alpha}-\alpha}{\alpha} = \dfrac{1-\alpha^2}{\alpha^2}$

18. If $\lim_{x\to 1} \dfrac{a\sin(x-1)+b\cos(x-1)+4}{x^2-1} = 2$, then (a, b) is equal to

(a) (2, 3)
(b) (a, –4), a is any real number
(c) (3, –b), b is any real number
(d) (6, –2)

Solution: (b) Since $\lim_{x\to 1} (x^2 - 1) = 0$, so limit will exists only,

when $\lim_{x\to 1}$ [asin $(x - 1) + b\cos(x - 1) + 4 = 0$

$\Rightarrow b + 4 = 0 \quad\quad \Rightarrow b = -4$

Now applying L'Hospital rule, we get

$\lim_{x\to 1} \dfrac{a\cos(x-1)+4\sin(x-1)}{2x} = 2$

Again differentiating we get

$\lim_{x\to 1} \dfrac{-a\sin(x-1)+4\cos(x-1)}{2} = 2.$

which is true for any value of a.

19. The $\lim_{x\to a}\left(2-\dfrac{a}{x}\right)^{\tan\left(\frac{\pi x}{2a}\right)}$ is equal to

(a) $e^{-a/\pi}$ (b) $e^{-2a/\pi}$
(c) $e^{-2/\pi}$ (d) 1

Solution: (c) $\lim_{x\to a}\left(2-\dfrac{a}{x}\right)^{\tan\left(\frac{\pi x}{2a}\right)}$

$= \lim_{x\to a}\left[1+\left(2-\dfrac{a}{x}-1\right)\right]^{\tan\left(\frac{\pi x}{2a}\right)}$

$= \exp.\left\{\lim_{x\to a}\left[2-\dfrac{a}{x}-1\right]\tan\left(\dfrac{\pi x}{2a}\right)\right\}$

$= \exp.\left\{\lim_{x\to 0}\left(\dfrac{x-a}{x}\right)\tan\left(\dfrac{\pi x}{2a}\right)\right\}$

$= \exp.\left\{\lim_{x\to 0}\left[\dfrac{(x-a)}{\cot\frac{\pi x}{2a}}\right]\cdot\dfrac{1}{x}\right\}$ .... $\left(\dfrac{0}{0}\text{ form}\right)$

$= \exp.\left\{\dfrac{1}{a}\lim_{x\to 0}\left(\dfrac{1}{-\operatorname{cosec}^2\frac{\pi x}{2a}}\right)\times\left(\dfrac{2a}{\pi}\right)\right\}$

$= e^{\frac{1}{a}\left(\frac{1}{-1}\right)\left(\frac{2a}{\pi}\right)} = e^{-2/\pi}$

20. If $[x]$ denotes the greatest integer $\le x$, then $\lim_{n\to\infty} \dfrac{1}{n^4}([1^3x]+[2^3x]+...+[n^3x])$ equals

(a) $x/2$ (b) $x/3$
(c) $x/6$ (d) $x/4$

Solution: (d) $\lim_{n\to\infty} \dfrac{1}{n^4}([1^3x]+[2^3x]+...+[n^3x])$

$1^3 . x - 1 < [1^3 .x] \le 1^3 . x$
$2^3 . x - 1 < [2^3 .x] \le 2^3 . x$
.
.
$n^3 . x - 1 < (n^3 x) \le n^3 . x$

$\Rightarrow (1^3 + 2^3 + 3^3 \ldots.. + n^3)\, x - n < [1^3x] + [2^3x] + \ldots. [n^3x] \le (1^3 + 2^3 + \ldots. + n^3)x$

$\Rightarrow \dfrac{\frac{n^2(n+1)^2}{4}x-n}{n^4} < \dfrac{[1^3x]+[2^3x]+...+[n^3x]}{n^4} \le \dfrac{\left[\frac{n(n+1)}{2}\right]^2 x}{n^4}$

Now, $\lim_{n\to\infty}\left(\dfrac{n+1}{n}\right)^2 \dfrac{x}{4}-\dfrac{1}{n^3}=\dfrac{x}{4}$ and

$\lim_{n\to\infty}\left[\dfrac{n+1}{n}\right]^2\cdot\dfrac{x}{4}=\dfrac{x}{4}$

$\therefore$ By sandwich theorem

$\lim_{n\to\infty}\dfrac{[1^3x]+[2^2x]+.....+[n^3x]}{n^4}=\dfrac{x}{4}$

21. Let $f(x)=\dfrac{\cos 2-\cos 2x}{x^2-|x|}$, then

(a) $\lim_{x\to -1} f(x) = 2\sin 2$ (b) $\lim_{x\to 1} f(x) = 2\sin 2$
(c) $\lim_{x\to -1} f(x) = 2\cos 2$ (d) $\lim_{x\to 1} f(x) = 2\cos 2$

Solution: (a, b) Let $f(x)=\dfrac{\cos 2-\cos 2x}{x^2-|x|}$.

for $x \to -1$; $|x| = -x$

$\therefore\ f(x)=\dfrac{\cos 2-\cos 2x}{x^2+x}$, and

$$\underset{x\to -1}{\text{Lt}} f(x)=\lim_{x\to -1}\frac{\cos 2-\cos 2x}{x^2+x}\ \left(\frac{0}{0}\right)$$

$$=\lim_{x\to -1}\frac{2\sin 2x}{2x+1}=2\sin 2 \text{ (By L.H. rule)}$$

For $x \to 1$, $|x| = x$;

$$\therefore\ \underset{x\to 1}{\text{Lt}} f(x)=\lim_{x\to 1}\frac{\cos 2-\cos 2x}{x^2-x}\ \left(\frac{0}{0}\right)$$

$$=\lim_{x\to 1}\frac{2\sin 2x}{2x-1} \text{ (By L.H. rule)}$$

$= 2\sin 2$

22. If α and β be the roots of $ax^2 + bx + c = 0$, then $\lim\limits_{x\to\alpha}(1+ax^2+bx+c)^{\frac{1}{x-\alpha}}$ is

(a) $a(\alpha-\beta)$ (b) $ln\,|a(\alpha-\beta)|$

(c) $e^{a(\alpha-\beta)}$ (d) $e^{a|\alpha-\beta|}$

Solution: (c) α, β are the roots of the equation $ax^2 + bx + c = 0$

$\Rightarrow a\alpha^2 + b\alpha + c = 0$ ...(i)

and $a\beta^2 + b\beta + c = 0$ ...(ii)

Now, $\lim\limits_{x\to\alpha}(1+ax^2+bx+c)^{\frac{1}{x-\alpha}}$ [(1^∞) form]

$$=e^{\lim\limits_{x\to\alpha}\frac{ax^2+bx+c}{x-\alpha}}$$

$$=e^{\lim\limits_{x\to\alpha}\frac{2ax+b}{1}}$$

[$\because$ By (i) and (ii) $a(\alpha^2-\beta^2)+b(\alpha-\beta)=0$; $(\alpha-\beta)$ $[a\alpha+a\beta+b]=0$; $\because \alpha\neq\beta$; So $a\alpha+b=-\alpha\beta$]

$= e^{2a\alpha+b}$ $= e^{a\alpha-a\beta}$

$= e^{a(\alpha-\beta)}$

23. $\underset{x\to 0}{\text{Lim}}\left[(1-e^x)\dfrac{\sin x}{|x|}\right]$ is (where [.] represents greatest integral part function)

(a) –1 (b) 1

(c) 0 (d) None of these

Solution: (a) R.H.L. $=\lim\limits_{x\to 0^+}\left[(1-e^x)\dfrac{\sin x}{x}\right]$

when $x \in (0, h)$, then $(1-e^x) \in (-1, 0)$

when $h\to 0$, $\dfrac{\sin x}{x}<1$

So $-1<(1-e^x)\dfrac{\sin x}{x}<0$

$$=\lim_{x\to 0^+}\left[(1-e^x)\frac{\sin x}{x}\right]=-1$$

$$\text{L.H.L.}=\lim_{x\to 0^+}\left[(1-e^x)\frac{\sin x}{-x}\right]=\lim_{x\to 0^+}\left[(e^x-1)\frac{\sin x}{x}\right]$$

when $x \in (-h, 0)$, then $e^x - 1 \in (-1, 0)$

and $h\to 0$, $\dfrac{\sin x}{x}<0$

So $-1<-1(1-e^x)\dfrac{\sin x}{x}<1$

So $\lim\limits_{x\to 0^+}\left[(1-e^x)\dfrac{\sin x}{x}\right]=-1$

$\therefore$ R.H.L.= R.H.L. = –1

24. If $\ell=\lim\limits_{x\to\infty}(\sin\sqrt{x+1}-\sin\sqrt{x})$ and $m=\lim\limits_{x\to-\infty}[\sin\sqrt{x+1}-\sin\sqrt{x}]$; where [.] denotes the greatest integer function , then:

(a) $\ell = m = 0$

(b) $\ell = 0$; m is undefined

(c) ℓ, m both do not exist

(d) $\ell = 0$, $m \neq 0$ (although m exist)

Solution: (b) $\ell=\lim\limits_{x\to\infty}(\sin\sqrt{x+1}-\sin\sqrt{x})$

$m=\lim\limits_{x\to-\infty}[\sin\sqrt{x+1}-\sin\sqrt{x}]$

where [.] $\to$ G.I.F.

$\ell=\lim\limits_{x\to\infty}(\sin\sqrt{x+1}-\sin\sqrt{x})$

$$=\lim_{x\to\infty}2\cos\left(\frac{\sqrt{x+1}+\sqrt{x}}{2}\right)\sin\left(\frac{\sqrt{x+1}-\sqrt{x}}{2}\right)$$

$$=\lim_{x\to\infty}2\cos\left(\frac{\sqrt{x+1}+\sqrt{x}}{2}\right)\sin\left(\frac{x+1-x}{2\left(\sqrt{x+1}+\sqrt{x}\right)}\right)$$

$$=\lim_{x\to\infty}2\cos\left(\frac{\sqrt{x}+\sqrt{x+1}}{2}\right)\sin\left(\frac{1}{2\left(\sqrt{x}+\sqrt{x+1}\right)}\right)$$

= (oscillating value from –1 to 1) × 0 = 0

(ii) $m=\lim\limits_{x\to-\infty}|\sin\sqrt{x+1}-\sin\sqrt{x}|$

when $x\to-\infty$, then $\sqrt{x}$ undefined

$\therefore$ m is undefined

25. If $f(x)=\sum_{\lambda=1}^{n}\left(x-\frac{1}{\lambda}\right)\left(x-\frac{1}{\lambda+1}\right)$, then $\lim_{n\to\infty} f(0)$ is

(a) 1 (b) –1
(c) 2 (d) None of these

Solution: (a) $f(x)=\sum_{\lambda=1}^{n}\left(x-\frac{1}{\lambda}\right)\left(x-\frac{1}{\lambda+1}\right)$, then

$\lim_{n\to\infty} f(0)$

$$f(0)=\sum_{\lambda=1}^{n}\left(-\frac{1}{\lambda}\right)\left(-\frac{1}{\lambda+1}\right)$$

$$=\sum_{\lambda=1}^{n}\left(\frac{1}{(\lambda)(\lambda+1)}\right)=\sum_{\lambda=1}^{n}\left(\frac{1}{\lambda}-\frac{1}{\lambda+1}\right)$$

$$=1-\frac{1}{n+1}=\frac{n}{n+1}$$

$$=\lim_{n\to\infty} f(0)=\lim_{n\to\infty}\frac{n}{n+1}$$

$$=\lim_{n\to\infty}\frac{1}{1+1/n}=\frac{1}{1+0}=1$$

26. $\lim_{x\to 0}\frac{e-(1+x)^{1/x}}{\tan x}$ equals

(a) e (b) $e/2$
(c) $e/3$ (d) does not exists

Solution: (b) $\text{Lim}_{x\to 0}\frac{e-(1+x)^{1/x}}{\tan x}=L$ and let $(1+x)^{1/x}=y$

$$\Rightarrow \ell ny=\frac{\ell n(1+x)}{x}$$

$$\Rightarrow \ell ny=\frac{\left[x-\frac{x^2}{2}+\frac{x^3}{3}-....\right]}{x}$$

$$\Rightarrow y=e^{\left(1-\frac{x}{2}+\frac{x^2}{3}-....\right)}$$

$$\Rightarrow y=e.e^{\left(-\frac{x}{2}+\frac{x^2}{3}-....\right)}$$

$$\Rightarrow y=e\left[1+\frac{(-x/2+x^2/3-....)}{1!}+\frac{(-x/2+x^2/3-...)^2}{2!}+....\right]$$

$$\Rightarrow y=e\left[1-\frac{x}{2}+\frac{x^2}{3}+\frac{x^2}{8}+ \text{terms containing higher powers of } x\right]$$

Now putting $(1+x)^{1/x}$ in $\lim_{x\to 0}\frac{e-(1+x)^{1/x}}{\tan x}$, we get

$$L=\lim_{x\to 0}\frac{e-e\left[1-\frac{x}{2}+\frac{x^2}{3}+\frac{x^2}{8}+...\right]}{\left[x+\frac{x^3}{3}+\frac{2x^5}{15}+....\right]}$$

$$=\lim_{x\to 0}\frac{e\frac{x}{2}\left[1-\frac{2}{3}x+\frac{x}{4}+....\right]}{x\left[1+\frac{x^2}{3}+....\right]}=e/2$$

27. $\text{Lim}_{x\to-\infty}\frac{x^5\tan\left(\frac{1}{\pi x^2}\right)+3|x|^2+7}{|x|^3+7|x|+8}$ equals

(a) $\frac{1}{\pi}$ (b) $-\pi$
(c) $-\frac{1}{\pi}$ (d) None of these

Solution: (c) $\text{Lim}_{x\to-\infty}\frac{x^5\tan\left(\frac{1}{\pi x^2}\right)+3|x|^2+7}{|x|^3+7|x|+8}$

$$=\text{Lim}_{x\to-\infty}\frac{\frac{x^5}{|x|^3}\tan\left(\frac{1}{\pi x^2}\right)+\frac{3|x|^2}{|x|^3}+\frac{7}{|x|^3}}{1+\frac{7}{|x|^2}+\frac{8}{|x|^3}}$$

$$=\text{Lim}_{x\to\infty}\frac{\frac{-x^5}{|-x|^3}\tan\left(\frac{1}{\pi x^2}\right)+\frac{3|-x|^2}{|-x|^3}+\frac{7}{|-x|^3}}{1+\frac{7}{|-x|^2}+\frac{8}{|-x|^3}}$$

$$=\lim_{x\to\infty}\frac{\frac{-x^5}{x^3}\tan\left(\frac{1}{\pi x^2}\right)+\frac{3x^2}{x^3}+\frac{7}{x^3}}{1+\frac{7}{x^2}+\frac{8}{x^3}}$$

$$=\text{Lim}_{x\to\infty}\frac{\frac{3}{(x)}+\frac{7}{(x)^3}-x^2\tan\left(\frac{1}{\pi x^2}\right)}{1+\frac{7}{(x)^2}+\frac{8}{x^3}}$$

$$=\text{Lim}_{x\to\infty}\frac{\frac{3}{x}+\frac{7}{x^3}}{1+\frac{7}{x^2}+\frac{8}{x^3}}-\text{Lim}_{x\to\infty}\frac{x^2\tan\left(\frac{1}{\pi x^2}\right)}{1+\frac{7}{(x^2)}+\frac{8}{x^3}}$$

$$=0-1.\lim_{x\to\infty}\frac{\tan\left(\frac{1}{\pi x^2}\right)}{\frac{\pi}{\pi x^2}}=-\frac{1}{\pi}$$

28. Let $f(x)=\lim_{m\to\infty}\left\{\lim_{n\to\infty}(\cos^{2m}(n!\pi x))\right\}$; where $x\in\mathbb{R}$, then

(a) $f(x)=1$ if x is rational
(b) $f(x)=0$ if x is rational
(c) $f(x)=1$ if x is irrational
(d) $f(x)=0$ if x is irrational

Solution: (a,b) $f(x)=\lim_{m\to\infty}\left\{\lim_{n\to\infty}(\cos^{2m}(n!\pi x))\right\} x\in\mathbb{R}$

Let us discuss two cases for $x\in\mathbb{R}$

Case (i): when x is rational

Let $x=\frac{p}{q}$, when $p,q\in\mathbb{Z}, q\neq 0$

when $n\to\infty$ then $n!$ would contain q as one of its factors.

$\Rightarrow n!\pi x$ is multiple of π.

So $\cos^2(n!\pi x)=1$

$\therefore \lim_{m\to\infty}\left\{\lim_{n\to\infty}(\cos^{2m}(n!\pi x))\right\}=1$

Case (ii): when x is irrational, then $n!\,\pi x$ is not multiple of π.

So $\cos(n!\,\pi x)$ lie in between -1 to 1

So $\cos^2(n!\,\pi x)$ lie in between 0 to 1

$\Rightarrow \lim_{m\to\infty}\left\{\lim_{n\to\infty}\cos^{2m}(n!\pi x)\right\}=0$

29. $\lim_{x\to 0^+}\left\{\lim_{n\to\infty}\left(\frac{[1^2(\sin x)^x]+[2^2(\sin x)^x]+...+[n^2(\sin x)^x]}{n^3}\right)\right\}$,

where [.] denotes the greatest integer function.

(a) 0 (b) $\frac{2}{3}$

(c) $\frac{4}{3}$ (d) $\frac{1}{3}$

Solution: (d)

$$\lim_{x\to 0^+}\left\{\lim_{n\to\infty}\left(\frac{[1^2(\sin x)^x]+[2^2(\sin x)^x]+...+[n^2(\sin x)^x]}{n^3}\right)\right\}$$

we know that $x-[x]\le x$

$\therefore\ 1^2(\sin x)^x-1<[1^2(\sin x)^x]\le 1^2(\sin x)^x$

$2^2(\sin x)^x-1<[2^2(\sin x)^x]\le 2^2(\sin x)^x$

.

.

.

$n^2(\sin x)^x-1<[n^2(\sin x)^x]\le n^2(\sin x)^x$

Adding all these inequalities, we get,

$$[(\sin x)^x\Sigma n^2]-n<\sum_{k=1}^{n}[k^2(\sin x)^x]\le(\sin x)^x\Sigma n^2$$

$$\Rightarrow \frac{\left[\frac{(\sin x)^x.n(n+1)(2n+1)}{6}-n\right]}{n^3}<\frac{\sum_{k=1}^{n}[k^2(\sin x)^x]}{n^3}$$

$$\le\frac{\frac{n(n+1)(2n+1)}{6}(\sin x)^x}{n^3}$$

As $n\to\infty$,

$$\lim_{n\to\infty}\frac{(\sin x)^x n(n+1)(2n+1)-n}{6(n^3)}=\frac{(\sin x)^x}{3}$$

and $\lim_{n\to\infty}\frac{x(n+1)(2n+1)(\sin x)^x}{6n^3}=\frac{(\sin x)^x}{3}$

So $\lim_{n\to\infty}\frac{\sum_{k=1}^{n}[k^2(\sin x)^x]}{n^3}=\frac{(\sin x)^x}{3}$

(By sandwich theorem)

Now $\lim_{x\to 0^+}\left[\frac{\lim_{n\to\infty}\sum_{k=1}^{n}[k^2(\sin x)^x]}{n^3}\right]=\frac{1}{3}\lim_{x\to 0}(\sin x)^x$

Now Let $A=\lim_{x\to 0}(\sin x)^x$

$\ell nA=\lim_{x\to 0}x\ell n(\sin x)$

$=\lim_{x\to 0}\frac{\ell n\sin x}{1/x}\quad\left(\frac{\infty}{\infty}\text{ form}\right)$

$=\lim_{x\to 0}\frac{\cot x}{-1/x^2}=\lim_{x\to 0}\frac{-x^2}{\tan x}=0$

(By L.H. Rule)

$\Rightarrow A=e^0$

$\Rightarrow A=1$

$$\Rightarrow \lim_{x\to 0^+}\left[\lim_{n\to\infty}\sum_{k=1}^{n}\frac{[k^2(\sin x)^x]}{n^3}\right]=\frac{1}{3}$$

30. Let $a=\min\ [x^2+2x+3,\ x\in\mathbb{R}]$ and $b=\lim_{x\to 0}\frac{\sin x\cos x}{e^x-e^{-x}}$. Then the value of $\sum_{r=0}^{n}a^r b^{n-r}$ is

(a) $\frac{2^{n+1}+1}{3\cdot 2^n}$ (b) $\frac{2^{n+1}-1}{3\cdot 2^n}$

(c) $\frac{2^n-1}{3\cdot 2^n}$ (d) $\frac{4^{n+1}-1}{3\cdot 2^n}$

Solution: (d) $a = \min\{(x+1)^2 + 2; x \in \mathbb{R}\} \Rightarrow a = 2$

$$b = \lim_{x\to 0} \frac{\sin 2x.e^x}{\frac{2(e^{2x}-1).2x}{2x}} = \frac{1}{2}$$

$$\text{now } \sum_{r=0}^{n} a^r b^{n-r} = \sum_{r=0}^{n} 2^r \left(\frac{1}{2}\right)^{n-r} = \frac{1}{2^n}\sum_{r=0}^{n} 2^{2r}$$

$$= \frac{1}{2^n}[1 + 2^2 + 2^4 + \ldots + 2^{2n}]$$

$$= \frac{1}{2^n}\left[\frac{(2^2)^{n+1}-1}{2^2-1}\right] = \frac{1}{2^n}\left[\frac{4^{n+1}-1}{3}\right] = \frac{4^{n+1}-1}{3.2^n}$$

31. $\lim\limits_{x\to 0^-} \sin^{-1}[\tan x] = l$, then $\{l\}$ is equal to

(a) 0 (b) $1-\frac{\pi}{2}$

(c) $\frac{\pi}{2}-1$ (d) $2-\frac{\pi}{2}$

where [ ] and { } denotes greatest integer and fractional part function.

Solution: (d) As $x \to 0^-$; $\tan x \to 0^- \Rightarrow [\tan x] = -1$

$\Rightarrow \sin^{-1}(-1) = -\pi/2$

$$\therefore \lim_{x\to 0^-} \sin^{-1}[\tan x] = -\frac{\pi}{2}$$

$$\text{Hence } \{\ell\} = \left\{-\frac{\pi}{2}\right\}$$

$$= \left\{2-\frac{\pi}{2}-2\right\} = 2-\frac{\pi}{2}$$

32. The value of $\lim\limits_{x\to 0} \frac{(\tan(\{x\}-1)).\sin\{x\}}{\{x\}(\{x\}-1)}$

where $\{x\}$ denotes the fractional part function:

(a) is 1 (b) is tan 1

(c) is sin 1 (d) does not exist

Solution: (d) $\lim\limits_{x\to 0} \frac{(\tan(\{x\}-1))\ \sin\{x\}}{\{x\}(\{x\}-1)}$

$$= \lim_{x\to 0^+} f(x) = \lim_{h\to 0^+} \frac{\tan(h-1).\sinh}{h(h-1)} = \frac{\tan(-1)}{-1} = \tan 1$$

$$\text{and } \lim_{x\to 0^-} \frac{\tan((1-h)-1)\sin(1-h)}{(1-h)(1-h-1)} = \frac{\sin 1}{1} = \sin 1$$

Hence $\lim\limits_{x\to 0} f(x)$ does not exist.

SECTION–II

SUBJECTIVE SOLVED EXAMPLES

1. Evaluate $\lim\limits_{x\to 2} \frac{x^6-24x-16}{x^3+2x-12}$.

Solution: Given $\lim\limits_{x\to 2} \frac{x^6-24x-16}{x^3+2x-12}$ (0/0 form)

$$= \lim_{x\to 2} \frac{(x-2)(x^5+2x^4+4x^3+8x^2+16x+8)}{(x-2)(x^2+2x+6)}$$

$$= \lim_{x\to 2} \frac{(x^5+2x^4+4x^3+8x^2+16x+8)}{(x^2+2x+6)}$$

$$= \frac{2^5+2(2)^4+4(2)^3+8(2)^2+16(2)+8)}{(2)^2+2(2)+6} = \frac{168}{14} = 12$$

2. (a) Find

$$\lim_{x\to 0}\left\{\ell n(1+x) - x + \frac{x^2}{2} - \frac{x^3}{3} + \ldots + (-1)^n \frac{x^n}{n}\right\} \times \frac{1}{x^{n+1}}$$

(b) Evaluate $\lim\limits_{x\to 1} \frac{x^3 - x^2\ell nx + \ell nx - 1}{x^2 - 1}$

Solution: (a) Since $\ell n(1+x) = x - \frac{x^2}{2} + \frac{x^3}{3} + \ldots\infty$

We have $\ell n(1+x) - x + \frac{x^2}{2} - \frac{x^3}{3} + \ldots + \frac{(-1)^n x^n}{n} + \frac{(-1)^{n+1}x^{n+1}}{n+1} + \ldots\ldots = 0$

$$\Rightarrow \lim_{x\to 0} \frac{\log(1+x) - x + \frac{x^2}{2} - \frac{x^3}{3} + \ldots + (-1)^n \frac{x^n}{n}}{x^{n+1}}$$

$$\Rightarrow \lim_{x\to 0} x^{n+1} \left\{\frac{\frac{-(-1)^{n+1}}{n+1} + \text{terms containing higher powers of } x}{x^{n+1}}\right\}$$

$$= \frac{-(-1)^{n+1}}{n+1} = \frac{(-1)^n}{n+1}$$

(b) Let $\lim\limits_{x\to 1}\dfrac{x^3-x^2\ell nx+\ell nx-1}{x^2-1}$

$$= \lim_{x\to 1}\frac{(x^3-1)-(x^2-1)\ell nx}{x^2-1}$$

$$= \lim_{x\to 1}\frac{(x-1)\{x^2+x+1-(x+1)\ell nx^2\}}{(x-1)(x+1)}$$

$$= \lim_{x\to 1}\frac{x^2+x+1-(x+1)\ell nx^2}{(x+1)}$$

$$= \frac{1^2+1+1-(1+1)\ell n1}{(1+1)} = \frac{3}{2}$$

3. Find the value of $\lim\limits_{m\to\infty}(\cos x/m)^m$; $x\in\mathbb{R}$ and $x\neq 0$.

Solution: Since above limit is of 1^∞ form, so
$L = e^{\lim\phi(f-1)}$

$$= e^{\lim\limits_{m\to\infty}(\cos\frac{x}{m}-1)m} = e^{\lim\limits_{m\to\infty}-\frac{2x^2 m\sin^2\frac{x}{2m}}{\left(\frac{x}{2m}\right)^2 4m^2}}$$

$$= e^{\lim\limits_{m\to\infty}\frac{-x^2}{2m}} = e^0 = 1$$

4. Evaluate $\lim\limits_{n\to\infty}\left(\dfrac{\sin a/n}{\tan b/(n+1)}\right)$

Solution: Let $\lim\limits_{n\to\infty}\left(\dfrac{\sin a/n}{a/n}\right)\left(\dfrac{\frac{b}{n+1}}{\tan\frac{b}{n+1}}\right)\cdot\dfrac{a}{b}\left(\dfrac{n+1}{n}\right)$

$$= (1)(1)\frac{a}{b}\cdot\lim_{n\to\infty}\left(\frac{n+1}{n}\right) = \frac{a}{b}$$

5. Evaluate $\lim\limits_{x\to 0}\left[\dfrac{\sin[x]}{[x]}\right]$; where [ ] represents the greatest integer function.

Solution: R.H.L $= \lim\limits_{h\to 0^+}\left[\dfrac{\sin[h]}{[h]}\right] = \left[\dfrac{\sin 0}{0}\right]$

$= \left[\dfrac{0}{0}\right]$ = exactly indeterminate

L.H.L $= \lim\limits_{h\to 0^+}\left[\dfrac{\sin[-h]}{[-h]}\right] = \lim\limits_{h\to 0}\left[\dfrac{\sin(-1)}{(-1)}\right]$

$= \lim\limits_{h\to 0}[\sin 1] = 0 \quad [\because 0<\sin 1<1]$

6. Evaluate $\lim\limits_{x\to 0}\dfrac{8}{x^8}\left(1-\cos\dfrac{x^2}{2}-\cos\dfrac{x^2}{4}+\cos\dfrac{x^2}{2}\cos\dfrac{x^2}{4}\right)$

Solution: Given

$$\lim_{x\to 0}\frac{8\left(1-\cos\frac{x^2}{2}-\cos\frac{x^2}{4}+\cos\frac{x^2}{2}\cos\frac{x^2}{4}\right)}{x^8}$$

$$= \lim_{x\to 0}\frac{8\left\{\left(1-\cos\frac{x^2}{2}\right)-\cos\frac{x^2}{4}\left(1-\cos\frac{x^2}{2}\right)\right\}}{x^8}$$

$$= \lim_{x\to 0}\frac{8\left\{\left(1-\cos\frac{x^2}{2}\right)\left(1-\cos\frac{x^2}{4}\right)\right\}}{x^8}$$

$$= \lim_{x\to 0}\frac{8\left(2\sin^2\frac{x^2}{4}\right)\left(2\sin^2\frac{x^2}{8}\right)}{x^8}$$

$$= \lim_{x\to 0}\left[32\left(\frac{\sin x^2/4}{x^2/4}\right)^2\left(\frac{\sin x^2/8}{x^2/8}\right)^2\cdot\frac{1}{16}\cdot\frac{1}{64}\right] = \frac{1}{32}$$

7. Evaluate $\lim\limits_{x\to 0}\ \ell n_{\tan^2 x}\tan^2 2x$

Solution: Given $\lim\limits_{x\to 0}\ \ell n_{\tan^2 x}\tan^2 2x$

$$= \lim_{x\to 0}\left[\frac{\ell n\tan^2 2x}{\ell n\tan^2 x}\right]$$

Applying L.H. rule

$$= \lim_{x\to 0}\left[\frac{2\ell n\tan 2x}{2\ell n\tan x}\right] = \lim_{x\to 0}\left[\frac{2\sec^2 2x\tan x}{\tan 2x\sec^2 x}\right]$$

$$= \lim_{x\to 0}\left[\frac{2\sin x\cos x}{\sin 2x\cos 2x}\right] = \lim_{x\to 0}\left[\frac{\sin 2x}{\sin 2x\cos 2x}\right]$$

$$= \lim_{x\to 0}\left[\frac{1}{\cos 2x}\right] = 1$$

8. Evaluate $\lim\limits_{x\to 0}(\cot x)^{1/\ell nx}$

Solution: Let $L = \lim\limits_{x\to 0}(\cot x)^{1/\ell nx}$

$$\therefore\ \ell n L = \lim_{x\to 0}\left(\frac{\ell n\cot x}{\ell nx}\right)$$

Applying L.H. rule,

$$= \lim_{x\to 0}\left[\frac{(-\operatorname{cosec}^2 x)x}{\cot x}\right] = \lim_{x\to 0}\left[-\frac{x}{\sin x\cos x}\right]$$

again applying LH rule,

$$= \lim_{x\to 0}\left[\frac{-1}{(\cos^2 x - \sin^2 x)}\right] = -1$$

$\therefore\ L = e^{-1} = 1/e$

9. Evaluate $\lim_{x\to\infty} e^x \sin(d/e^x)$

Solution: When $x \to \infty$, $e^x \to \infty$

But angle of $\sin = \dfrac{d}{e^x} = \dfrac{\text{finite}}{\infty} = 0$

$\therefore$ The given limit $= \lim_{x\to\infty}\dfrac{\sin(d/e^x)}{1/e^x}$

$$= \lim_{x\to\infty}\frac{\sin(d/e^x)}{d/e^x}\times d$$

$$= 1\times d = d$$

10. Evaluate the following limits:

(i) $\lim_{x\to 0}\dfrac{(1+x)^5-1}{3x+5x^2}$

(ii) $\lim_{x\to 2}\dfrac{\sqrt{x+7}-3\sqrt{2x-3}}{\sqrt[3]{x+6}-2\sqrt[3]{3x-5}}$

Solution: (i) $\lim_{x\to 0}\dfrac{(1+x)^5-1}{3x+5x^2}$

Method I: On expanding $(1 + x)^5$

we get $\lim_{x\to 0}\dfrac{1+5x+10x^2+10x^3+5x^4+x^5-1}{3x+5x^2}$

$$= \lim_{x\to 0}\frac{x[5+\text{term containing } x \text{ and higher power of } x]}{x[3+5x]}$$

$$= \frac{5}{3}$$

Method II: $\dfrac{(1+x)^5-1^5}{(1+x)-1}\cdot\dfrac{x}{3x+5x^2}$

$$= 5.(1)^4.\ \frac{1}{3+0} = 5/3$$

(ii) $\lim_{x\to 2}\dfrac{\sqrt{x+7}-3\sqrt{2x-3}}{\sqrt[3]{x+6}-2\sqrt[3]{3x-5}}$

$$\Rightarrow\ \lim_{x\to 2}\frac{(x+7)^{1/2}-[9(2x-3)]^{1/2}}{(x+6)^{1/3}-[8(3x-5)^{1/3}]}$$

$$\lim_{x\to 2}\frac{(x+7-18x+27)}{(\sqrt{x+7}+\sqrt{9(2x-3)})}\times$$

$$\frac{\left[(x+6)2+[8(3x-5)]^2+(x+6).8(3x-5)\right]}{((x+6)-24x+40)}$$

$$\lim_{x\to 2}\frac{(34-17x)}{\sqrt{x+7}+\sqrt{9(2x-3)}}\times$$

$$\frac{\left[(x+6)^2+64(3x-5)^2+8(x+6)(3x-5)\right]}{(46-23x)}$$

$$= \frac{17\times 64\times 3}{23\times 6} = \frac{544}{23}$$

11. Evaluate the following limits:

(i) $\lim_{x\to-\infty}\dfrac{(3x^4+2x^2)\sin|1/x|+|x|^3+5}{|x|^3+|x|^2+|x|+1}$

(ii) $\lim_{x\to\infty}\dfrac{x\sin\alpha-\alpha\sin x}{x\text{-}\alpha}$

Solution: (i) Given is

$$\lim_{x\to-\infty}\frac{(3x^4+2x^2)\sin|1/x|+|x|^3+5}{|x|^3+|x|^2+|x|+1}$$

(as $x \to -\infty$, $|x| = -x$; $\sin\left|\dfrac{1}{x}\right| = -\sin\dfrac{1}{x}$)

$$= \lim_{x\to-\infty}\frac{-(3x^2+2)x\dfrac{\sin 1/x}{1/x}-x^3+5}{-x^3+x^2-x+1}$$

highest power of x is 3 in denominator and numerator both. Dividing numerator and denominator by x^3.

$$= \lim_{x\to-\infty}\frac{-\left(3+\dfrac{2}{x^2}\right)\dfrac{\sin(1/x)}{1/x}-1+5/x^3}{-1+1/x-1/x^2+1/x^3}$$

$$= \frac{-(3+0).1-1+0}{-1+0-0+0} = \frac{-4}{-1} = 4$$

(ii) Given $\lim_{x\to\infty}\dfrac{x\sin\alpha-\alpha\sin x}{x-\alpha}$

If x approaches to some value other than 0 (say α), then it is useful to substitute.

$x - \alpha = h;\ h \to 0$ i.e.

$$= \lim_{h\to 0}\frac{(\alpha+h)\sin\alpha(-\alpha\sin(h+\alpha))}{h}$$

$$= \lim_{h\to 0}\frac{h\sin\alpha+\alpha[\sin\alpha-\sin(h+\alpha)]}{h}$$

$$= \lim_{h\to 0}\frac{h\sin\alpha+\alpha 2\cos(\alpha+h/2)\sin[\alpha-h-\alpha]/2}{h}$$

$$= \lim_{h\to 0}\ \sin\alpha - \alpha.2\cos\cdot(\alpha+h/2)\left(\frac{\sin(h/2)}{(h.2)/2}\right)$$

$$= \sin\alpha - \alpha\cdot\cos\alpha\cdot 1 = \sin\alpha - \alpha\cos\cdot\alpha$$

12. Solve the following limits:

(i) $\lim_{x\to\infty}\frac{x^5}{5^x}$ (ii) $\lim_{x\to 1}(x)^{(\cot \pi x)}$

Solution: (i) Given $\lim_{x\to\infty}\frac{x^5}{5^x} = \lim_{x\to\infty}\frac{x^5}{e^{\ell n 5^x}} = \lim_{x\to\infty}\frac{x^5}{e^{x\ell n5}}$

$$= \lim_{x\to\infty}\frac{x^5}{1+x\ell n5+\frac{(x\ell n5)^2}{2!}+\frac{(x\ell n5)^3}{3!}+.........}$$

$$\lim_{x\to\infty}\frac{1}{\frac{1}{x^5}+\frac{1}{x^4}\ell n5+\frac{1}{x^3}(\ell n5)^2\frac{1}{2!}+\frac{1}{x^2}\frac{(\ell n5)^3}{3!}+....+}$$

$$= \frac{1}{x}\frac{(\ell n5)^4}{4!}+\frac{(\ell n5)^5}{5!}+x\frac{(\ell n5)^6}{6!}$$

term containing higher power of x

$$= \frac{1}{0+\frac{1}{5!}(\ell n5)^5+\infty} = 0$$

(ii) $\lim_{x\to 1}(x)^{(\cot \pi x)}$

Method (1): $\lim_{x\to 1}(1+(x-1))^{\frac{1}{(x-1)}\frac{(x-1)}{\tan \pi x}} = e^{\lim_{x\to 1}\frac{(x-1)}{\tan \pi x}}$

$= e^{\lim_{x\to 1}\frac{1}{\pi \sec^2 \pi x}} = e^{\frac{1}{\pi}}$ $e^{1/\pi}$

Method (2): $\lim_{x\to 1} x^{\cot \pi x}$ here put $x = (1+h)$; $h \to 0$

$= \lim_{h\to 0}(1+h)^{\cot(\pi+\pi h)} = \lim_{h\to 0}[1+h]^{\frac{1}{h}\times\frac{h}{\tan \pi h}}$

$= e^{\lim_{h\to 0}\frac{h}{\tan \pi h}} = e^{\frac{1}{\pi}\lim_{h\to 0}\left(\frac{\pi h}{\tan \pi h}\right)} = e^{\frac{1}{\pi}}$

13. Evaluate the folloiwng

(i) $\lim_{x\to 0}[\lim_{n\to\infty}(\cos(x/2)\cos(x/4)\cos(x/8)\ ....\ \cos(x/2^n)]$

(ii) $\lim_{n\to\infty}\sin^{2n} x$

Solution: (i) Let $P = \cos(x/2)\cos(x/2^2)\cos(x/2^3)$ ....$\cos(x/2^n)$

$\Rightarrow P\ \sin(x/2^n) = \cos(x/2).\cos(x/2^2).\cos(x/2^3)$........ $\cos(x/2^n).\sin(x/2^n)$

$= 1/2.\ (\cos\ x/2)\ (\cos\ x/2^2)(\cos\ x/2^3)$............ $\cos x/(2^{n-1})\ .\ \sin x/(2^{n-1})$

$= 1/2^2\ .\ (\cos x/2)\ (\cos x/2^2)\ (\cos x/2^3)$........... $\cos x/(2^{n-2}).\ \sin x/(2^{n-2})$

Proceeding similarly, we get $P.\ \sin x/2^n = 1/2^{n-1}$ $\cos x/2.\ \sin x/2 = \frac{\sin x}{2^n}$

$\therefore\ P = \frac{\sin x}{2^n \sin(x/2^n)} \Rightarrow \lim_{n\to\infty}\frac{\sin x/x}{\frac{\sin(x/2^n)}{x/2^n}} = \frac{\sin x}{x}$

$\Rightarrow \lim_{x\to 0} P = \lim_{x\to 0}\frac{\sin x}{x} = 1$

(ii) $\lim_{n\to\infty}\sin^{2n} x$

Let $L = \lim_{n\to\infty}\sin^{2n} x$

$\Rightarrow L = \lim_{n\to\infty}(0)^{2n} = 0$ (at $\sin x = 0$; i.e., $x = n\pi$)

$\Rightarrow L = \lim_{n\to\infty}(\pm 1)^{2n} = 1$

(at $\sin x = (\pm 1)$ i.e., $x = m\pi/2$ (m is odd integer))

$\Rightarrow L = \lim_{n\to\infty}(\sin^{2n} x) = 0$ (For other values of x we have $0 < \sin^2 x < 1$)

$\lim_{\substack{x\to(2\ell+1)\pi/2\\ n\to\infty}}(\sin 1)^{2n}$ = Not defined (indetermined)

where $\ell \in I$

Note: $(1.1)^1 = 1.1$; $(1.1)^2 = 1.21$; $(1.1)^3 = 1.331$; $(1.01)^3 = 1.03$

Thus we observe that $\lim_{\substack{x\to 1^+\\ y\to\infty}} x^y$ approaches one if $x \to 1+$ faster than $y\to\infty$.

And $\lim_{\substack{x\to 1^+\\ y\to\infty}} x^y$ approaches infinity if $y \to \infty$ faster than $x \to 1^+$

14. Evaluate $\lim_{x\to 0}\frac{(1+x)^{1/x} - e}{x}$

Solution: ***Method1:*** (using expansion)

$\lim_{x\to 0}\frac{e^{\ell n_e(1+x)^{1/x}} - e}{x}$ $(x = e^{\ell n_e^x})$

$$= \lim_{x\to 0}\frac{e^{1/x(x-x^2/2+x^3/3-x^4+.....)} - e}{x}$$

$[\ell n(1+x) = x - x^2/2 + x^3/3 - .....]$

$$= \lim_{x\to 0}\frac{e^{(1-x/2+x^2/3-x^3/4+.....)} - e}{(-x/2+x^2/3-x^3/4+.....)}$$

$$\lim_{x\to 0}\left(\frac{-x/2+x^2/3-x^3/4+....}{x}\right)$$

$$= \lim_{x\to 0} e \times 1 \times (-1/2)\left[\because \lim_{x\to 0}\frac{e^x-1}{x} = 1\right] = -e/2$$

Method 2: (using L.H. rule) $L = \lim_{x\to 0}\frac{(1+x)^{1/x} - e}{x}$

(0/0 form)

$$= \lim_{x\to 0}\frac{\frac{d}{dx}[(1+x)^{1/x}-e]}{\frac{d}{dx}x} \quad \text{(Applying L' Hospital's Rule)}$$

$$= \lim_{x\to 0}\frac{(1+x)^{1/x}}{1+x}\frac{(x-(1+x)\ell n(1+x))}{x^2}$$

$$\left[\begin{array}{l} \because\ k=(1+x)^{1/x} \\ \Rightarrow \ell nk = \frac{1}{x}\ell n(1+x) \\ \Rightarrow \frac{1}{k}\frac{dk}{dx} = \frac{1}{x}\cdot\frac{1}{(1+x)}+\ell n(1+x)\left(\frac{-1}{x^2}\right) \\ \Rightarrow \frac{dk}{dx} = k\left[\frac{1}{x(1+x)}-\frac{1}{x^2}\ell n(1+x)\right]\end{array}\right]$$

$$= \lim_{x\to 0}\frac{(1+x)^{1/x}}{1+x}\lim_{x\to 0}\frac{-\ell n(1+x)}{2x}$$

(Applying L 'Hospital's Rule)

$= -e/2$

15. Evaluate $\lim_{n\to\infty}\frac{2^3-1}{2^3+1}\cdot\frac{3^3-1}{3^3+1}\cdot\frac{4^3-1}{4^3+1}\cdots\cdots\frac{n^3-1}{n^3+1}$

Solution:

$$\lim_{n\to\infty}\frac{(1)(7)}{(3)(3)}\cdot\frac{(2)(13)}{(4)(7)}\cdot\frac{(3)(21)}{(5)(13)}\cdots\cdots$$

$$\frac{(n-2)[(n-1)^2+(n-1)+1]}{n[(n-1)^2-(n-1)+1]}\cdot\frac{(n-1)(n^2+n+1)}{(n+1)(n^2-n+1)}$$

$$= \lim_{n\to\infty}\frac{(1)(7)}{(3)(3)}\cdot\frac{(2)(13)}{(4)(7)}\cdot\frac{(3)(21)}{(5)(13)}\cdots\cdots$$

$$\frac{(n-2)(n^2-n+1)}{(n)(n^2-3n+3)}\cdot\frac{(n-1)(n^2+n+1)}{(n+1)(n^2-n+1)}$$

$$= \lim_{n\to\infty}\frac{(1)(2)(n^2+n+1)}{(n)(n+1)(3)} = \frac{2}{3}\lim_{n\to\infty}\frac{1+\frac{1}{n}+\frac{1}{n^2}}{1+\frac{1}{n}}$$

$= 2/3 \times 1 = 2/3$

16. Evaluate $\lim_{x\to 0}\frac{\sin^3 x-3x\sin^2 x+3x^2\sin x-x^3}{(\sin x)^9}$

Solution: Well, if you apply L' Hospital's rule or series, you will get into problem, so proceed as below

$$\text{L} = \lim_{x\to 0}\left(\frac{\sin x-x}{x^3}\right)^3\times\left(\frac{x}{\sin x}\right)^9$$

Let $L_1 = \lim_{x\to 0}\frac{\sin x-x}{x^3}$ (0/0 form)

Apply L'Hospital's Rule

$$= \lim_{x\to 0}\frac{\cos x-1}{3x^2} = \lim_{x\to 0}\frac{-\sin x}{6x} = \frac{-1}{6}$$

Required limit

$$= \left(\lim_{x\to 0}\frac{\sin x-x}{x^3}\right)^3\times\left(\lim_{x\to 0}\frac{x}{\sin x}\right)^9 = -\frac{1}{216}$$

17. Evaluate the following limits, if exists:

(a) $\lim_{x\to 4}\frac{(\cos\alpha)^x-(\sin\alpha)^x-\cos 2\alpha}{(x-4)}$

(b) $\lim_{x\to 0}\frac{|x|^\alpha}{e^x}, a\in R^+$

(c) $\lim_{x\to 3}\frac{[x]-3}{(x-3)}$

(d) $\lim_{x\to 0}\left(\frac{1^x+2^x+3^x+\ldots..+n^x}{n}\right)^{a/x}$

(e) $\lim_{x\to\infty}\frac{2.x^{1/2}+3.x^{1/3}+4.x^{1/4}+\ldots..+n.x^{1/n}}{(3x-4)^{1/2}+(3x-4)^{1/3}+\ldots..+(3x-4)^{1/n}}$

(f) $\lim_{x\to 0}\frac{e^x-e^{x\cos x}}{x+\sin x}$

Solution: (a)

$$\lim_{x\to 4}\frac{(\cos\alpha)^x-(\sin\alpha)^x-\cos 2\alpha}{(x-4)} \quad \text{(0/0 form)}$$

$$= \lim_{x\to 4}\frac{(\cos\alpha)^x-(\sin\alpha)^x-(\cos^2\alpha-\sin^2\alpha)(\cos^2\alpha+\sin^2\alpha)}{(x-4)}$$

$$= \lim_{x\to 4}\frac{(\cos\alpha)^x-(\sin\alpha)^x-\cos^4\alpha+\sin^4\alpha}{(x-4)}$$

$$= \lim_{x\to 4}\frac{(\cos\alpha)^4.((\cos\alpha)^{x-4}-1)-\sin^4\alpha((\sin\alpha)^{x-4}-1)}{(x-4)}$$

$$= \cos^4\alpha\lim_{x\to 4}\frac{(\cos\alpha)^{x-4}-1}{x-4}-\sin^4\alpha.\lim_{x\to 4}\frac{(\sin\alpha)^{x-4}-1}{x-4}$$

$= \cos^4\alpha.\ \ln(\cos\alpha) - \sin^4\alpha.\ \ln(\sin\alpha)$

(b) $\lim_{x\to 0}\frac{|x|^\alpha}{e^x} = 0$ as $\lim_{x\to 0}|x|^\alpha = 0$ and $\lim_{x\to 0}e^x = 1$

(c) Let $\lim_{x\to 3}\frac{[x]-3}{(x-3)}$ Towards the right of $x = 3$, $[x] = 3$

$\Rightarrow [x]-3 = 0$, in the right neighbourhood of $x = 3$

$\Rightarrow \lim_{x\to 3+0}\frac{[x]-3}{x-3} = 0$ Towards the left of $x = 3$, $[x] = 2$

$\Rightarrow [x]-3=-1$, in the left neighbourhood of $x=3$

$\Rightarrow \lim_{x\to 3-0}\frac{[x]-3}{x-3}=\lim_{x\to 3-0}\frac{-1}{x-3}=\infty$. Thus $\lim_{x\to 3}\frac{[x]-3}{(x-3)}$ does not exist.

(d) $\lim_{x\to 0}\left(\frac{1^x+2^x+3^x+.....+n^x}{n}\right)^{a/x}$ (1^∞ form)

$$= e^{\lim_{x\to 0}\left(\frac{1^x+2^x+3^x+.....+n^x}{n}-1\right)\frac{a}{x}} = e^{\lim_{x\to 0}\left(\frac{1^x+2^x+3^x+.....+n^x-n}{n}\right)\frac{a}{x}}$$

$$= e^{\lim_{x\to 0}\left(\frac{(1^x-1)+(2^x-1)+.....+(n^x-1)}{x}\right)\frac{a}{n}} = e^{(\ln 1+\ln 2+......+\ln(n))\frac{a}{n}}$$

$$= (e^{\ln(n!)})^{a/n} = (n!)^{a/n}$$

(e) $\lim_{x\to\infty}\frac{2.x^{1/2}+3.x^{1/3}+4.x^{1/4}+.....+n.x^{1/n}}{(3x-4)^{1/2}+(3x-4)^{1/3}+.....+(3x-4)^{1/n}}$

Divide numerator and denominator by the highest power of x. Here $x^{1/2}$ is the highest power

$$= \lim_{x\to\infty}\frac{2.+3/x^{(1/3-1/2)}+.....+n.x^{(1/n-1/2)}}{(3-4/x)^{1/2}+x^{1/3-1/2}(3-4/x)^{1/3}+.....+x^{1/n-1/2}(3-4/x)^{1/n}}=\frac{2}{\sqrt{3}}$$

(f) $\lim_{x\to 0}\frac{(e^x-1)-(e^{x\cos x}-1)}{x+\sin x}$

$$=\lim_{x\to 0}\left(\frac{(e^x-1)}{x\left(1+\frac{\sin x}{x}\right)}-\frac{(e^{x\cos x}-1)}{x\cos x\left(\sec x+\frac{\sin x}{x\cos x}\right)}\right)$$

$$=\lim_{x\to 0}\frac{(e^x-1)}{x\left(1+\frac{\sin x}{x}\right)}-\lim_{x\to 0}\frac{(e^{x\cos x}-1)}{x\cos x\left(\sec x+\frac{\sin x}{x\cos x}\right)}$$

$$=\frac{1}{2}-\frac{1}{2}=0$$

18. Evaluate $\lim_{x\to -1^+}\frac{\sqrt{\pi}-\sqrt{\cos^{-1}x}}{\sqrt{x+1}}$.

Solution: Put $\cos^{-1}x=\theta \Rightarrow x=\cos\theta$

$$\therefore \text{ Limit} = \lim_{\theta\to\pi}\frac{\sqrt{\pi}-\sqrt{\theta}}{\sqrt{1+\cos\theta}}$$

$$= \lim_{\theta\to\pi}\frac{\pi-\theta}{\sqrt{1+\cos\theta}}.\frac{1}{\sqrt{\pi}+\sqrt{\theta}}$$

$$= \lim_{\theta\to\pi}\frac{\pi-\theta}{\sqrt{2\cos^2\theta/2}}.\lim_{\theta\to\pi}\frac{1}{\sqrt{\pi}+\sqrt{\theta}}$$

$$= \lim_{k\to 0}\frac{-k}{\sqrt{2\cos^2(\pi/2+k/2)}}\frac{1}{2\sqrt{\pi}}$$

(Putting $\theta=\pi+k$)

$$= \lim_{k\to 0}\frac{-k}{2\sqrt{2}\sqrt{\pi}\left|\cos\left(\frac{\pi}{2}+\frac{k}{2}\right)\right|} = \lim_{k\to 0}\frac{k}{2\sqrt{2}\sqrt{\pi}\left(\sin\frac{k}{2}\right)}$$

$$\left[\because \left|\cos\left(\frac{\pi}{2}+\frac{k}{2}\right)\right| = -\cos\left(\frac{\pi}{2}+\frac{k}{2}\right) = -\sin\frac{k}{2}\right]$$

$$= \lim_{k\to 0}\frac{(k/2)}{\sin\frac{k}{2}}.\frac{1}{\sqrt{2}\sqrt{\pi}}=\frac{1}{\sqrt{2\pi}}$$

19. Find *a* polynomial of least degree, such that $\lim_{x\to 0}\left(1+\frac{x^2+f(x)}{x^2}\right)^{1/x}=e^2$

Solution: Now, $\lim_{x\to 0}\left(1+\frac{x^2+f(x)}{x^2}\right)^{1/x}$

$$= \lim_{x\to 0}\left(1+\frac{x^2+f(x)}{x^2}\right)^{1/x} = L \text{ (say)}$$

It exists only when $\lim_{x\to 0}\frac{x^2+f(x)}{x^2}=0$ (i.e. it converts into 1^∞ form), so the least degree of $f(x)$ would be 2. i.e., $f(x)=a_2x^2+a_3x^3+....$

Now $L=\lim_{x\to 0}\left(1+\frac{x^2+f(x)}{x^2}\right)^{1/x}=e^2$

$$\Rightarrow e^{\lim_{x\to 0}\left(\frac{x^2+f(x)}{x^2}\right)^{1/x}\times\frac{1}{x}}=e^2$$

$$\Rightarrow e^{\lim_{x\to 0}\frac{x^2+f(x)}{x^3}}=e^2 \Rightarrow \lim_{x\to 0}\frac{x^2+f(x)}{x^3}=2$$

$$\Rightarrow \lim_{x\to 0}\frac{x^2+a_2x^2+a_3x^3+....}{x^3}=2$$

$\Rightarrow a_2=-1$, $a_3=2$ and a_4, a_5 are any arbitrary constants. Since we want polynomial of least degree. Hence $f(x)=-x^2+2x^3$

20. Evaluate $\lim_{x\to 0}\frac{\sin x - x+(x^3/3)}{x^5}$

Solution: Given $\lim_{x\to 0}\frac{\sin x-x+(x^3/3)}{x^5}$ (0/0 form)

Applying L-Hospital's rule, we get

$L = \lim\limits_{x\to 0} \dfrac{\cos x - 1 + x^2}{5x^4}$ (0/0 form, hence again applying LH rule)

$= \lim\limits_{x\to 0} \dfrac{-\sin x + 2x}{20x^3}$ (0/0 form, hence again applying LH rule)

$= \lim\limits_{x\to 0} \dfrac{-\cos x + 2}{60x^2} = \infty$

21. Evaluate $\lim\limits_{x\to 0}\left(\dfrac{1}{x^2} - \dfrac{1}{\sin^2 x}\right)$ by using L' Hospital's rule or expansion.

Solution: Given limit $= \lim\limits_{x\to 0} \dfrac{(\sin^2 x - x^2)}{x^2 \sin^2 x}$

$$= \lim_{x\to 0}\left(\frac{\sin x - x}{x^3} \times \frac{\sin x + x}{x} \times \frac{x^2}{\sin^2 x}\right) \quad \text{...(i)}$$

Let $L_1 = \lim\limits_{x\to 0} \dfrac{\sin x - x}{x^3}$

Let $x = 3\theta$, as $x \to 0$, $\theta \to 0$

$\therefore\ L_1 = \lim\limits_{x\to 0} \dfrac{\sin 3\theta - 3\theta}{(3\theta)^3}$

$= \lim\limits_{\theta\to 0} \dfrac{3\sin\theta - 4\sin^3\theta - 3\theta}{27\theta^3}$

$= \lim\limits_{\theta\to 0} \dfrac{\sin\theta - \theta}{9\theta^3} - \lim\limits_{\theta\to 0} \dfrac{4}{27}\left(\dfrac{\sin\theta}{\theta}\right)^3$

$\therefore\ L_1 = \dfrac{L_1}{9} - \dfrac{4}{27}$

$\Rightarrow L_1 = -\dfrac{1}{6}$

$\therefore$ (i) becomes

$$\lim_{x\to 0} \frac{\sin x - x}{x^3} \times \lim_{x\to 0} \frac{\sin x + x}{x^3} \times \lim_{x\to 0}\left(\frac{x}{\sin x}\right)^2$$

$$= -\frac{1}{6} \times 2 \times 1 = -\frac{1}{3}$$

22. Evaluate $\lim\limits_{x\to\infty} a^x \sin\left(\dfrac{b}{a^x}\right)$.

Solution: This is an interesting problem, where value of the limit will depend on the value of the constant 'a' i.e. for same value of constant 'b' and different values of 'a' the value of the limit would be different.

Case I: when $a > 1$

$$L = \lim_{x\to\infty} a^x \sin\left(\frac{b}{a^x}\right) = \lim_{x\to\infty} \frac{\sin\left(\frac{b}{a^x}\right)}{\left(\frac{b}{a^x}\right)} \times b = 1 \times b = b$$

$(\because x \to \infty \Rightarrow a^x \to \infty \Rightarrow \dfrac{b}{a^x} \to 0)$

Case II: when $a = 1$

$\lim\limits_{x\to\infty} a^x = 1$

$\Rightarrow$ L = sin(b)

Case III: when $0 < a < 1$; $\lim\limits_{x\to\infty} a^x = 0$

$\therefore\ L = \lim\limits_{x\to\infty} a^x \sin\left(\dfrac{b}{a^x}\right)$

$= 0 \times$ (a finite real number $\in [-1, 1]$) $= 0$

Note: Well, would you mind evaluating $\lim\limits_{\substack{x\to\infty \\ a\to 1}} a^x$?

Since the two variables 'a' and 'x' are independent variables.

$\therefore$ We can not evaluate this limit.

For the evaluation of $\lim\limits_{x\to\infty} a^x$; a must be a fixed real number.

23. Evaluate a, b, c and d, if

$$\lim_{x\to\infty} \sqrt{x^4 + ax^3 + 3x^2 + bx + 2} - \sqrt{x^4 + 2x^3 - cx^2 + 3x - d} = 4$$

Solution: Here,

$$\lim_{x\to\infty} \sqrt{x^4 + ax^3 + 3x^2 + bx + 2} - \sqrt{x^4 + 2x^3 - cx^2 + 3x - d} = 4 \quad (\infty - \infty \text{ form})$$

By Rationalizing, we get

$$\lim_{x\to\infty} \frac{(a-2)x^3 + (3+c)x^2 + (b-3)x + (2+d)}{\sqrt{x^4 + ax^3 + 3x^2 + bx + 2} + \sqrt{x^4 + 2x^3 - cx^2 + 3x - d}} = 4$$

Since, limit is finite, so the degree of the numerator must be 2.

So, $a - 2 = 0$ i.e., $a = 2$.

$$\Rightarrow \lim_{x\to\infty} \frac{(3+c)x^2 + (b-3)x + (2+d)}{\sqrt{x^4 + ax^3 + 3x^2 + bx + 2} + \sqrt{x^4 + 2x^3 - cx^2 + 3x - d}} = 4$$

Dividing numerator and denominator by x^2, we get

$$\lim_{x\to\infty}\frac{(3+c)+(b-3)/x+(2+d)/x^2}{\sqrt{1+a/x+3/x^2+b/x^3+2/x^4}+\sqrt{1+2/x-c/x^2+3/x^3-d/x^4)}}=4$$

$\Rightarrow \dfrac{3+c}{2}=4$

$\Rightarrow c=5$

$\therefore\ c=5,\ a=2$

Hence $a=2$, $c=5$ and b, d may be any real numbers.

24. Solve

$$\lim_{n\to\infty}\frac{1}{n^3}\{[[1^2x+1^2]]+[[2^2x+2^2]]+\ldots+[[n^2x+n^2]]\};$$

where [.] denotes the greatest integer function.

Solution: We know $[x+I]=[x]+I$;

where $I\in\mathbb{Z}$ and $nx-1<[nx]\le nx$

$\therefore\ \lim_{n\to\infty}\frac{1}{n^3}\{[[1^2x+1^2]]+[[2^2x+2^2]]+\ldots+[[n^2x+n^2]]\}$

$\Rightarrow \lim_{n\to\infty}\frac{1}{n^3}\{[1^2x]+[2^2x]+\ldots+[n^2x]+(1^2+2^2+\ldots+n^2)\}$

(By using $[x+I]=[x]+I$

$$\Rightarrow \lim_{n\to\infty}\frac{1}{n^3}[1^2x]+[2^2x^2]+\ldots+[n^2x]+\frac{(1^2+2^2+\ldots+n^2)}{n^3} \quad \ldots\text{(i)}$$

As we know, $1^2x-1<[1^2x]\le 1^2x$

$2^2x-1<[2^2x]\le 2^2x$

....

$n^2x-1<[n^2x]\le n^2x$

$\Rightarrow (1^2+2^2+\ldots+n^2)x-n<[1^2x]+[2^2x]+\ldots+[n^2x]\le(1^2+2^2+\ldots+n^2)x$

$$\Rightarrow \frac{n(n+1)(2n+1)x}{6n^3}-\frac{n}{n^3}<\frac{[1^2x]+[2^2x]+\ldots+[n^2x]}{n^3}\le\frac{n(n+1)(2n+1)x}{6n^3}$$

Now

$$\lim_{x\to\infty}\frac{n(n+1)(2n+1)(x)}{6n^3}-\frac{n}{n^3}$$

$$\lim_{n\to\infty}\left\{\frac{1}{6}\left(1+\frac{1}{n}\right)\left(2+\frac{1}{n}\right)x-\frac{1}{n^2}\right\}=\frac{x}{3}$$

and

$$\lim_{n\to\infty}\frac{n(n+1)(2n+1)x}{6n^3}=\lim_{n\to\infty}\frac{1}{6}\left(1+\frac{1}{n}\right)\left(2+\frac{1}{n}\right)x=\frac{x}{3}$$

$\therefore$ By sandwich theorem

$$\lim_{n\to\infty}\frac{[1^2x]+[2^2x]+\ldots\ldots+[n^2x]}{n^3}=\frac{x}{3} \quad \ldots\text{(ii)}$$

$\therefore$ From (i) and (ii),

$$\lim_{n\to\infty}\frac{1}{n^3}[1^2x]+[2^2x]+\ldots+[n^2x]+\frac{1^2+2^2+\ldots+n^2}{n^3}$$

$$=\frac{x}{3}+\lim_{n\to\infty}\frac{1}{6}\left(1+\frac{1}{n}\right)\left(2+\frac{1}{n}\right)=\frac{x}{3}+\frac{1}{3}$$

25. Evaluate

$$\lim_{x\to0^+}\frac{-1+\sqrt{(\tan x-\sin x)+\sqrt{(\tan x-\sin x)+\sqrt{(\tan x-\sin x)+\ldots}}}}{-1+\sqrt{x^3+\sqrt{x^3+\sqrt{x^3+\ldots}}}}.$$

Solution: Let

$$y=\sqrt{(\tan x-\sin x)+\sqrt{(\tan x-\sin x)+\sqrt{(\tan x-\sin x)+\ldots}}}$$

$\Rightarrow y=\sqrt{(\tan x-\sin x)+y}$

$\Rightarrow y^2-y-(\tan x-\sin x)=0$

$$\Rightarrow y=\frac{1+\sqrt{1+(\tan x-\sin x)4}}{2}\quad[\text{as } y>0] \quad \ldots\text{(i)}$$

again let, $Z=\sqrt{x^3+\sqrt{x^3+\sqrt{x^3+\ldots\infty}}}$

$\Rightarrow Z=\sqrt{x^3+Z}$

$\Rightarrow Z^2-Z-x^3=0$

$$\Rightarrow Z=\frac{1+\sqrt{1+4x^3}}{2}\quad \text{as } Z>0 \quad \ldots\text{(ii)}$$

$$\therefore\ \lim_{x\to0^+}\frac{-1+\sqrt{(\tan x-\sin x)+\sqrt{(\tan x-\sin x)+\sqrt{(\tan x-\sin x)+\ldots}}}}{-1+\sqrt{x^3+\sqrt{x^3+\sqrt{x^3+\ldots\infty}}}}$$

$$=\lim_{x\to0^+}\frac{-1+\left(\dfrac{1+\sqrt{1+4(\tan x-\sin x)}}{2}\right)}{-1+\left(\dfrac{1+\sqrt{1+4x^3}}{2}\right)}$$

(From (i) and (ii))

$$=\lim_{x\to0^+}\frac{-1+\sqrt{1+4(\tan x-\sin x)}}{-1+\sqrt{1+4x^3}}$$

Rationalizing numerator and denominator we get

$$\lim_{x\to0^+}\frac{4(\tan x-\sin x)(1+\sqrt{1+4x^3})}{4x^3(1+\sqrt{1+4(\tan x-\sin x)})}$$

$$= \lim_{x\to 0^+} \frac{\left(\frac{\sin x}{\cos x} - \frac{\sin x}{1}\right)(1+\sqrt{1+4x^3})}{x^3(1+\sqrt{1+4(\tan x - \sin x)})}$$

$$= \lim_{x\to 0^+} \frac{\sin x(1-\cos x)}{x^3 \cos x} \cdot \frac{(1+\sqrt{1+4x^3})}{(1+\sqrt{1+4(\tan x - \sin x)})}$$

$$\lim_{x\to 0^+} \frac{\sin x}{x} \frac{2\sin^2(x/2)}{4(x^2/4)} \cdot \frac{1}{\cos x}$$

$$= \frac{(1+\sqrt{1+4x^3})}{(1+\sqrt{1+4(\tan x - \sin x)})} \quad = 1.\frac{1}{2}.1.\left(\frac{1+1}{1+1}\right) = \frac{1}{2}$$

26. Evaluate $\lim\limits_{x\to\infty}(x+2)\ \tan^{-1}(x+2) - (x\ \tan^{-1} x)$

Solution: Let $\lim\limits_{x\to\infty}(x+2)\tan^{-1}(x+2) - (x\tan^{-1} x)$

$$= \lim_{x\to\infty} [x\tan^{-1}(x+2) + 2\tan^{-1}(x+2) - (x\tan^{-1} x)\}$$

$$= \lim_{x\to\infty} [x\{\tan^{-1}(x+2) - \tan^{-1}(x)\} + 2\tan^{-1}(x+2)]$$

$$= \lim_{x\to\infty} [x\{\tan^{-1}(x+2) - \tan^{-1}(x)\} + 2\ \tan^{-1}(x+2)]$$

$$= \lim_{x\to\infty} x\ \tan^{-1} \frac{x+2-x}{1+(x+2)x} + 2\lim_{x\to\infty} \tan^{-1}(x+2)$$

$$= \lim_{x\to\infty} x\ \tan^{-1}\left(\frac{2}{(1+x)^2}\right) + 2.\frac{\pi}{2}$$

[as $x \to \infty$, $\tan^{-1} x \to \pi/2$]

$$= \lim_{x\to\infty} \left\{ \frac{\tan^{-1}\left(\frac{2}{(1+x)^2}\right)}{\frac{2}{(x+1)^2}} \cdot \frac{2x}{(x+1)^2} \right\} + \pi$$

$$= 1\times 0 + \pi = \pi$$

Therefore $\lim\limits_{x\to\infty}(x+2)\tan^{-1}(x+2) - (x\tan^{-1} x) = \pi$

27. Evaluate $\lim\limits_{x\to\pi/4}\left[\frac{(\cos x + \sin x)^3 - 2\sqrt{2}}{1 - \sin 2x}\right]$

Solution: Given $\lim\limits_{x\to\pi/4}\left[\frac{(\cos x + \sin x)^3 - 2\sqrt{2}}{1 - \sin 2x}\right]$

$$= \lim_{x\to\pi/4}\left[\frac{\{\sqrt{2}\cos(\pi/4 - x)\}^3 - 2\sqrt{2}}{1 - \cos(\pi/2 - 2x)}\right]$$

$$= \lim_{x\to\pi/4}\left[\frac{-2\sqrt{2}\{1 - \cos^3(\pi/4 - x)\}}{2\sin^2(\pi/4 - x)}\right]$$

let $\pi/4 - x = t$

$$= \lim_{t\to 0}\left[\frac{-2\sqrt{2}\{1-\cos^3 t\}}{2\sin^2 t}\right]$$

$$= \lim_{t\to 0}\left[\frac{-\sqrt{2}(1-\cos t)(1+\cos t + \cos^2 t)}{(1-\cos^2 t)}\right]$$

$$= \lim_{t\to 0}\left[\frac{-\sqrt{2}\,(1+\cos t + \cos^2 t)}{(1+\cos t)}\right]$$

$$= \frac{-\sqrt{2}.3}{2} = -\frac{3}{\sqrt{2}}$$

28. Show that $\left(1+\sum\limits_{k=1}^{n} \frac{2}{{}^nC_k}\right)^n \to e^2$ as $n \to \infty$ (for $n \geq 6$)

Solution: Let $a_n = 1 + 2\sum\limits_{k=1}^{n} \frac{1}{{}^nC_k}$ while for $n \geq 6$

$$\Rightarrow\ a_n = 1 + 2.\frac{1}{{}^nC_1} + 2.\frac{1}{{}^nC_2} + 2\left(\underbrace{\frac{1}{{}^nC_3} + \ldots\ldots + \frac{1}{{}^nC_n}}_{(n-2)}\right)$$

$$\Rightarrow\ a_n \leq 1 + \frac{2}{n} + \frac{4}{n(n-1)} + \frac{2(n-2)}{{}^nC_3}$$

$$\Rightarrow\ a_n \leq 1 + \frac{2}{n} + \frac{4}{n(n-1)} + \frac{12(n-2)}{n(n-1)(n-2)}$$

$$\Rightarrow\ a_n \leq 1 + \frac{2}{n} + \frac{16}{n(n-1)} \qquad \text{...(i)}$$

$$\text{also } a_n = 1 + 2\sum_{k=1}^{n} \frac{1}{{}^nC_k} \geq 1 + \frac{2}{{}^nC_1} \qquad \text{....(ii)}$$

$$\Rightarrow\ 1 + \frac{2}{n} \leq a_n \leq 1 + \frac{2}{n} + \frac{16}{n(n-1)}$$

$$\Rightarrow\ \left(1+\frac{2}{n}\right)^n \leq a^n \leq \left(1 + \frac{2}{n} + \frac{16}{n(n-1)}\right)^n;$$

$$\lim_{n\to\infty}\left(1+\frac{2}{n}\right)^n = e^2 \text{ and } \lim_{n\to\infty}\left[1 + \frac{2}{n}\left(1 + \frac{8}{(n-1)}\right)\right]$$

$\therefore$ By squeeze principle for limits, we get

$$\lim_{n\to\infty}\left(1+\sum_{k=1}^{n} \frac{2}{{}^nC_k}\right)^n = e^2$$

29. Suppose that function f; $\mathbb{R} \to \mathbb{R}$ satisfies the inequality $\left|\sum\limits_{k=1}^{n} 3^k \{f(x+ky) - f(x-ky)\}\right| \leq 1$ for every positive integer n and for all x, $y \in \mathbb{R}$. Prove that f is a constant function.

Solution: Replacing n by $(n-1)$ in

$$\left|\sum_{k=1}^{n} 3^k \{f(x+ky)-f(x-ky)\}\right| \le 1 \quad \text{...(i)}$$

we get $\left|\sum_{k=1}^{n-1} 3^k \{f(x+ky)-f(x-ky)\}\right| \le 1 \quad \text{...(ii)}$

Subtracting (i) and (ii), we get

$$\left|3^n \{f(x+ny)-f(x-ny)\}\right| \le 2$$

$$\Rightarrow \left|\{f(x+ny)-f(x-ny)\}\right| \le \frac{2}{3^n} \quad \text{...(iii)}$$

We choose x and y such that $x + ny = u$ and $x - ny = v$ where $u, v \in \mathbb{R}$ and $n \in \mathbb{N}$

$\therefore$ (iii) becomes, $|f(u)-f(v)| \le \frac{2}{3^n}$ for arbitrary $n \in \mathbb{N}$

i.e. as $n \to \infty \quad \Rightarrow |f(u)-f(v)| \le \lim_{n\to\infty} \frac{2}{3^n}$

$\Rightarrow |f(u) - f(v)| \le 0 \quad \Rightarrow f(u) = f(v)\ \forall\ u, v \in \mathbb{R}$

Hence f is *a* constant function.

30. Suppose $P(x) = a_0 + a_1x + a_2x^2 + ... + a_nx^n$. If $|P(x)| \le |e^{x-1} - 1|$ for all $x \ge 0$, prove that, $|a_1 + 2a_2 + 3a_3 + ... + na_n| \le 1$

Solution: Here, $P(x) = a_0 + a_1x + a_2x^2 + ... + a_nx^n$

$\Rightarrow P'(x) = a_1 + 2a_2x + ... + na_nx^{n-1}$

$\Rightarrow P'(1) = a_1 + 2a_2 + ... + na_n \quad \text{...(i)}$

Now $|P(x)| \le |e^{x-1} - 1|$ for all $x \ge 0$

$\Rightarrow |P(1)| \le |e^0 - 1| = |1-1| = 0$ i.e., $|P(1)| \le 0$

But $|P(1)|$ must be greater than equal to zero, so $|P(1)| = 0$

Now $|P(1+h)| \le |e^h - 1|$ for all $h > -1$, $h \ne 0$

$|P(1+h) - 0| \le |e^h - 1|$ for all $h > -1$, $h \ne 0$

$$\Rightarrow \left|\frac{P(1+h)-P(1)}{h}\right| \le \left|\frac{e^h-1}{h}\right| \quad (\because P(1) = 0)$$

Taking limits as $h \to 0$, we get

$$\lim_{h\to 0}\left|\frac{P(1+h)-P(1)}{h}\right| \le \lim_{h\to 0}\left|\frac{e^h-1}{h}\right|$$

$\Rightarrow |P(1)| \le 1$

$\Rightarrow |a_1 + 2a_2 + 3a_3 + ... + na_n| \le 1 \quad$ (from (i))

Hence $|a_1 + 2a_2 + 3a_3 + ... + na_n| \le 1$

31. Evaluate the $\lim_{x\to 1}\left(\frac{1}{x^2-1} - \frac{2}{x^4-1}\right)$

Solution: Given

$$\lim_{x\to 1}\left(\frac{\frac{x^4-1}{2} - (x^2-1)}{\frac{(x^2-1)(x^4-1}{2}}\right) \quad \left(\frac{0}{0} \text{ form}\right)$$

$$= \lim_{x\to 1} \frac{(x^4-1)-2(x^2-1)}{(x^6-x^2-x^4+1)} = \lim_{x\to 1} \frac{x^4-2x^2+1}{x^6-x^2-x^4+1}$$

$$= \lim_{x\to 1} \frac{4x^3-4x}{6x^5-2x-4x^3} \text{ (By using L.H. Rule)}$$

$$= \lim_{x\to 1} \frac{12x^2-4}{30x^4-2-12x^2} = 1/2$$

(Again using L.H. Rule)

32. Evaluate $\lim_{x\to 0}\left(\frac{\ln(\cos 3x)}{x^2} \cdot \frac{2\sin x}{e^x - e^{-x}}\right)$

Solution: $\lim_{x\to 0}\left(\frac{\ln(\cos 3x)}{x^2} \cdot \frac{2\sin x}{e^x - e^{-x}}\right)$

$$= \lim_{x\to 0}\left(\frac{\ln(1+\cos 3x - 1)}{(\cos 3x - 1)} \times \frac{\left(-2\sin^2 \frac{3x}{2}\right)}{x^2} \times \frac{2\sin x}{x} \times \frac{1}{\left(\frac{e^x-1}{x} + \frac{e^{-x}-1}{-x}\right)}\right)$$

$$= 1 \times (-2) \times \frac{9}{4} \times 2 \times 1 \times \frac{1}{1+1} = -\frac{9}{2}$$

33. Evaluate $\lim_{x\to 0} \frac{\sin x - x - x\cos x + x^2 \cot x}{x^5}$

Solution: Given $\lim_{x\to 0} \frac{\sin x - x - x\cos x + x^2 \cot x}{x^5}$

$$= \lim_{x\to 0} \frac{(\sin x - x) - x\cot x(x - \sin x)}{x^5}$$

$$= \lim_{x\to 0} \frac{(\sin x - x)(1 - x\cot x)}{x^5}$$

$$= \lim_{x\to 0} \frac{\sin x - x}{x^3} \times \frac{\tan x - x}{x^3} \times \frac{x}{\tan x}$$

Now, $\lim_{x\to 0} \frac{-\sin x + x}{x^3} = -\frac{1}{6} = \lim_{x\to 0} \frac{\tan x - x}{x^3} = \frac{1}{3}$

Hence the required limit $= -\frac{1}{18}$

34. Evaluate $\lim_{x\to 1} \sec\frac{\pi}{2^x}\ell nx$

Solution: Given $\lim_{x\to 1} \sec\frac{\pi}{2^x}\ell nx$

$$= \lim_{h\to 0} \sec\frac{\pi}{2^{1+h}}\ell n(1+h) = \lim_{h\to 0} \frac{\ell n(1+h)}{h}\frac{h}{\cos\left(\frac{\pi}{2^{1+h}}\right)}$$

$$= \lim_{h\to 0}\left[\frac{\ell n(1+h)}{h}\right]\frac{h}{\sin\left(\frac{\pi}{2}-\frac{\pi}{2.2^h}\right)}$$

$$= \lim_{h\to 0}\left[\frac{\ell n(1+h)}{h}\right]\frac{h}{\sin\left[\frac{\pi}{2}\left(1-\frac{1}{2^h}\right)\right]}$$

$$= \lim_{h\to 0}\left[\frac{\ell n(1+h)}{h}\right]\frac{\frac{\pi}{2}h\left(\frac{2^h-1}{h}\right)\frac{2^h}{2^h}}{\frac{\pi}{2}\sin\left[\frac{\pi}{2}h\left(\frac{2^h-1}{h}\right)\frac{1}{2^h}\right]\left(\frac{2^h-1}{h}\right)}$$

$$= \lim_{h\to 0}\left[\frac{\ell n(1+h)}{h}\right]\left(\frac{\frac{\pi}{2}h\left(\frac{2^h-1}{h}\right)\frac{1}{2^h}}{\sin\frac{\pi}{2}h\left(\frac{2^h-1}{h}\right)\frac{1}{2^h}}\right)\frac{2^h.2}{\left(\frac{2^h-1}{h}\right)\pi}$$

$$= \lim_{h\to 0} 1.1.\frac{2}{\pi\ell n2} = \frac{2}{\pi\ell n2}$$

35. Evaluate $\lim_{x\to 0}\left(1+\log^2_{\cos\frac{x}{2}}\cos x\right)^2$

Solution: Given $\lim_{x\to 0}\left(1+\log^2_{\cos\frac{x}{2}}\cos x\right)^2$

$$= \left[1+\lim_{x\to 0}\left(\frac{\ell n_e\cos x}{\ell n\cos x/2}\right)^2\right]^2$$

$$= \left[1+\lim_{x\to 0}\left(\frac{\ell n_e(1-2\sin^2 x/2)}{\ell n_e(1-2\sin^2 x/4)}\right)^2\right]^2$$

$$= \left[1+\lim_{x\to 0}\left[\frac{\log\left(1-2\sin^2\frac{x}{2}\right)\left(-2\sin^2\frac{x}{2}\right)\left(\frac{x}{2}\right)^2\left(-2\sin^2\frac{x}{4}\right)\left(\frac{x}{4}\right)^2}{-2\sin^2\frac{x}{2}\left(\frac{x}{2}\right)^2\log\left(1-2\sin^2\frac{x}{4}\right)\left(-2\sin^2\frac{x}{4}\right)\left(\frac{x}{4}\right)^2}\right]\right]^2$$

$$= \left[1+\left[\lim_{x\to 0}\left(\frac{\log\left(1-2\sin^2\frac{x}{2}\right)}{-2\sin^2\frac{x}{2}}\right)\left(\frac{-2\sin^2\frac{x}{4}}{\log\left(1-2\sin^2\frac{x}{4}\right)}\right)\left(\frac{\frac{x}{4}}{\sin\frac{x}{4}}\right)^2\left(\frac{\sin\frac{x}{2}}{\frac{x}{2}}\right)^2\frac{x^2\,.\,2^4}{2^2\,.\,x^2}\right]^2\right]^2$$

$$= [1+16]^2 = 289$$

36. Prove that $\lim_{n\to\infty}\sum_{k=0}^{n}\frac{{}^nC_k}{n^k(k+3)} = e-2$

Solution: Given limit is $\lim_{n\to\infty}\sum_{k=0}^{n}\frac{{}^nC_k}{n^k(k+3)} = e-2$

Coefficient of x^k in $(1+x)^n$ is ${}^nC_k$

$$\Rightarrow (1+x)^n = \sum_{k=0}^{n}{}^nC_kx^k$$

Multiplying both sides by x^2, $x^2(1+x)^n = \sum_{k=0}^{n}{}^nC_kx^{k+2}$

Integrating both sides:

$$\int x^2(1+x)^n dx = \int\sum_{k=0}^{n}{}^nC_kx^{k+2}dx$$

$$\Rightarrow \frac{(1+x)^{n+3}}{n+3}+\frac{(1+x)^{n+1}}{n+1}-\frac{2(1+x)^{n+2}}{n+2}$$

$$= \sum_{k=0}^{n}\frac{{}^nC_kx^{k+3}}{k+3}$$

Putting $x = 1/n$ we get,

$$\frac{(1+1/n)^{n+3}}{n+3}+\frac{(1+1/n)^{n+1}}{n+1}-\frac{2(1+1/n)^{n+2}}{n+2}$$

$$= \sum_{k=0}^{n}\frac{{}^nC_k}{(k+3)n^{k+3}}$$

Multiplying both sides by n^3

$$\frac{(1+1/n)^{n+3}.n^3}{n+3}+\frac{(1+1/n)^{n+1}.n^3}{n+1}-\frac{2(1+1/n)^{n+2}.n^3}{n+2}$$

$$= \sum_{k=0}^{n}\frac{{}^nC_k}{(k+3)n^k}$$

37. Evaluate the limit $\lim\limits_{x\to 0}\dfrac{27^x-9^x-3^x+1}{\sqrt{2}-\sqrt{1+\cos x}}$

Solution: Given limit is

$$\lim_{x\to 0}\frac{27^x-9^x-3^x+1}{\sqrt{2}-\sqrt{1+\cos x}}\times\frac{\sqrt{2}+\sqrt{1+\cos x}}{\sqrt{2}+\sqrt{1+\cos x}}$$

$$=\lim_{x\to 0}\frac{2\sqrt{2}(27^x-9^x-3^x+1)}{2-1-\cos x}$$

$$=\lim_{x\to 0}\frac{2\sqrt{2}(27^x-9^x-3^x+1)}{x^2(1-\cos x)}\times x^2$$

$$=\lim_{x\to 0}\frac{4\sqrt{2}(27^x-9^x-3^x+1)}{x^2}$$

$$=\lim_{x\to 0}4\sqrt{2}\left(\frac{9^x(3^x-1)-1(3^x-1)}{x^2}\right)$$

$$=\lim_{x\to 0}4\sqrt{2}\left(\frac{(9^x-1)\,(3^x-1)}{x^2}\right)$$

$$=\lim_{x\to 0}4\sqrt{2}\left(\frac{9^x-1}{x}\right)\times\lim_{x\to 0}\frac{3^x-1}{x}=8\sqrt{2}(\ell n3)^2$$

38. Let $f(x)=\begin{cases}\dfrac{x}{\sin x}; & x>0\\ 2-x; & x\le 0\end{cases}$ and

$$g(x)=\begin{cases}x+3; & 0<x<1\\ x^2-2x-2; & 1\le x<2\\ x-5; & x\ge 2\end{cases}$$

Find L.H.L and R.H.L of g(*f*(x)) at x = 0 and hence find $\lim\limits_{x\to 0} g(f(x))$.

Solution: $f(x)=\begin{cases}\dfrac{x}{\sin x} & ; & x>0\\ 2-x & ; & x\le 0\end{cases}$

and $g(x)=\begin{cases}x+3 & ; & 0<x<1\\ x^2-2x-2 & ; & 1\le x<2\\ x-5 & ; & x\ge 2\end{cases}$

$$g(f(x))=\begin{cases}f(x)+3 & ; & 0<f(x)<1\\ f^2(x)-2f(x)-2 & ; & 1\le f(x)<2\\ f(x)-5 & ; & f(x)\ge 2\end{cases}$$

$$=\begin{cases}\dfrac{x}{\sin x}+3 & ;\ \{x:x>0\}\cap\left\{x:0<\dfrac{x}{\sin x}<1\right\}\\ 2-x+3 & ;\ \{x:x\le 0\}\cap\{x:0<2-x<1\}\\ \left(\dfrac{x}{\sin x}\right)^2-2\left(\dfrac{x}{\sin x}\right)-2 & ;\ \{x:x>0\}\cap\left\{x:1\le\dfrac{x}{\sin x}<2\right\}\\ (2-x)^2-2(2-x)-2 & ;\ \{x:x\le 0\}\cap\{x:1\le 2-x<2\}\\ \dfrac{x}{\sin x}-5 & ;\ \{x:x>0\}\cap\left\{x:\dfrac{x}{\sin x}\ge 2\right\}\\ 2-x-5 & ;\ \{x:x\le 0\}\cap\{x:2-x\ge 2\}\end{cases}
=\begin{cases}\phi\\ \phi\\ \left(\dfrac{x}{\sin x}\right)^2-2\left(\dfrac{x}{\sin x}\right)-2; & \{x:x>0\}\cap\left\{x:1\le\dfrac{x}{\sin x}<2\right\}\\ \phi\\ \dfrac{x}{\sin x}-5; & \{x:x>0\}\cap\left\{x:\dfrac{x}{\sin x}\ge 2\right\}\\ 2-x-5; & x\le 0\end{cases}$$

$$\Rightarrow g(f(x))=\begin{cases}-x-3 & ; & x\le 0\\ \left(\dfrac{x}{\sin x}\right)^2-2\left(\dfrac{x}{\sin x}\right)-2 & ; & \left\{x:x>0\ \&\ 1\le\dfrac{x}{\sin x}<2\right\}\\ \dfrac{x}{\sin x}-5 & ; & \left\{x:x>0\ \&\ \dfrac{x}{\sin x}\ge 2\right\}\end{cases}$$

$\because$ $gf(0)=-0-3=-3$

$\because$ $\dfrac{x}{\sin x}$ is increasing on $\left(0,\dfrac{\pi}{2}\right)$; As $x\to 0^+$; x will be closer to 0 when $1\le\dfrac{x}{\sin x}\le 2$ as compared to instant when $\dfrac{x}{\sin x}\ge 2$

$\therefore\ g(f(x)) = \left(\frac{x}{\sin x}\right)^2 - 2\left(\frac{x}{\sin x}\right) - 2$ for $x \to 0^+$

$\therefore$ R.H.L $= \lim_{x\to 0^+} g(f(x))$

$$= \lim_{x\to 0^+}\left[\left(\frac{x}{\sin x}\right)^2 - 2\left(\frac{x}{\sin x}\right) - 2\right]$$

$$= \lim_{x\to 0^+}\left[\frac{1}{\left(\frac{\sin x}{x}\right)^2} - \frac{2}{\left(\frac{\sin x}{x}\right)} - 2\right]$$

$$= \lim_{x\to 0^+}\frac{1}{\left(\frac{\sin x}{x}\right)^2} - \lim_{x\to 0^+}\frac{2}{\left(\frac{\sin x}{x}\right)} - 2$$

$= 1 - 2 - 2 = -3$ and L.H.L. $= \lim_{x\to 0^-} g(f(x)) = \lim_{x\to 0^-} -(x+3) = -3$

$\therefore$ L.H.L = R.H.L = – 3

$\therefore\ \lim_{x\to 0} g(f(x)) = -3$

Remark: In above example we note that L.H.S. = R.H.S. = $g(f(0))$, $g(f(x))$ is continuous function at $x = 0$,

39. Let $P_n = a^{P_{n-1}} - 1, \forall n = 2, 3, \ldots\ldots..$ and Let $P_1 = a^x - 1$; where $a \in R^+$, then evaluate $\text{Lim}_{x\to 0}\frac{P_n}{x}$.

Solution: Given $P_n = a^{P_{n-1}} - 1$; $p_{n-1} = a^{P_{n-2}} - 1$

Let $P_1 = a^x - 1$; $P_2 = a^{P_1} - 1, P_3 = a^{P_2} - 1, \ldots, P_n = a^{P_{n-1}} - 1$

As $x \to 0$, $P_1 \to 0$

$\Rightarrow P_2 \to 0 \qquad \Rightarrow P_3 \to 0 \ldots..$

$\Rightarrow P_{n-1} \to 0$

Now, $\lim_{x\to 0}\frac{P_n}{x}$

$$= \lim_{x\to 0}\frac{a^{P_{n-1}} - 1}{x} \times \frac{p_{n-1}}{p_{n-1}} = \lim_{x\to 0}\frac{a^{P_{n-1}} - 1}{p_{n-1}} \times \frac{P_{n-1}}{x}$$

$$= \lim_{x\to 0} \ell na \times \frac{P_{n-1}}{x}$$

$$= \lim_{x\to 0} \ell na \times \frac{a^{P_{n-2}} - 1}{x} \times \frac{P_{n-2}}{P_{n-2}}$$

$$= \lim_{x\to 0}(\ell na)^2 \times \frac{P_{n-2}}{x} \text{ and so on.}$$

$$= \lim_{x\to 0}(\ell na)^{n-1} \times \frac{P_1}{x}$$

$$= (\ell na)^{n-1} \times \lim_{x\to 0}\frac{a^x - 1}{x}$$

$$= (\ell na)^n$$

40. If the $\text{Lim}_{x\to 0}\frac{1}{x^3}\left(\frac{1}{\sqrt{1+x}} - \frac{1+ax}{1+bx}\right)$ exists and has the value equal to ℓ, then find the value of $\frac{1}{a} - \frac{2}{\ell} + \frac{3}{b}$.

Solution: $\lim_{x\to 0}\frac{1}{x^3}\left[\frac{1}{\sqrt{1+x}} - \frac{1+ax}{1+bx}\right]$

$$= \lim_{x\to 0}\frac{1}{x^3}\left[\frac{1+bx-(1+ax)\sqrt{1+x}}{\sqrt{1+x}\ (1+bx)}\right]$$

$$= \lim_{x\to 0}\frac{1+bx-(1+ax)\ (1+x)^{1/2}}{x^3(1+x)^{1/2}(1+bx)}$$

We know that

$$(1+x)^n = 1 + nx + \frac{n(n-1)}{2!}x^2 + \frac{n(n-1)\ (n-2)}{3!}x^3 + \ldots.$$

where, $n \in Q$ and $|x| < 1$

$$= \lim_{x\to 0}\frac{1+bx-(1+ax)\left[1+\frac{1}{2}x+\frac{\frac{1}{2}\left(\frac{1}{2}-1\right)}{2!}x^2+\frac{\frac{1}{2}\left(\frac{1}{2}-1\right)\left(\frac{1}{2}-2\right)}{3!}x^3+\ldots\ldots.\right]}{x^3(1+x)^{1/2}\ (1+bx)}$$

$$= \lim_{x\to 0}\frac{1+bx-1-\frac{1}{2}x-\frac{\frac{1}{2}\left(\frac{1}{2}-1\right)}{2!}x^2-\frac{\frac{1}{2}\left(\frac{1}{2}-1\right)\left(\frac{1}{2}-2\right)}{3!}x^3-\ldots-ax\left(1+\frac{1}{2}x+\frac{\frac{1}{2}\left(\frac{1}{2}-1\right)}{2!}x^2+\frac{\frac{1}{2}\left(\frac{1}{2}-1\right)\left(\frac{1}{2}-2\right)}{3!}x^3+\ldots\right)}{x^3(1+x)^{1/2}(1+bx)}$$

$$= \lim_{x\to 0}\frac{bx-\frac{1}{2}x-\frac{\frac{1}{2}\left(\frac{1}{2}-1\right)}{2!}x^2-\frac{\frac{1}{2}\left(\frac{1}{2}-1\right)\left(\frac{1}{2}-2\right)}{3!}x^3-\ldots-ax\left(1+\frac{1}{2}x+\frac{\frac{1}{2}\left(\frac{1}{2}-1\right)}{2!}x^2+\frac{\frac{1}{2}\left(\frac{1}{2}-1\right)\left(\frac{1}{2}-2\right)}{3!}x^3+\ldots\right)}{x^3(1+x)^{1/2}(1+bx)}$$

$$= \lim_{x\to 0}\frac{b-\frac{1}{2}-\frac{\frac{1}{2}\left(\frac{1}{2}-1\right)}{2!}x-\frac{\frac{1}{2}\left(\frac{1}{2}-1\right)\left(\frac{1}{2}-2\right)x^2}{3!}-\ldots-a\left(1+\frac{1}{2}x+\frac{\frac{1}{2}\left(\frac{1}{2}-1\right)}{2!}x^2+\frac{\frac{1}{2}\left(\frac{1}{2}-1\right)\left(\frac{1}{2}-2\right)}{3!}x^3+\ldots\right)}{x^2(1+x)^{1/2}(1+bx)}$$

$$= \lim_{x\to 0}\frac{\left(b-a-\frac{1}{2}\right)-\left(\frac{a}{2}+\frac{\frac{1}{2}\left(\frac{1}{2}-1\right)}{2!}\right)x-\left(\frac{\frac{1}{2}\left(\frac{1}{2}-1\right)\left(\frac{1}{2}-2\right)}{3!}+a.\frac{\frac{1}{2}\left(\frac{1}{2}-1\right)}{2!}\right)x^2-(\ )x^3-(\ )x^4-\ldots\ldots}{x^2.1.1}$$

Limit exists finitely if

(i) $b-a-\frac{1}{2}=0$

(ii) $\frac{a}{2}+\frac{\frac{1}{2}\left(\frac{1}{2}-1\right)}{2!}=0$

$\Rightarrow \frac{a}{2}-\frac{\frac{1}{2}\cdot\frac{1}{2}}{2}=0 \qquad \Rightarrow a-\frac{1}{4}=0$

$\Rightarrow a=\frac{1}{4} \qquad \because b-a=\frac{1}{2}$

$\Rightarrow b=a+\frac{1}{2}=\frac{3}{4}$

$a=\frac{1}{4}$ & $b=\frac{3}{4}$

$$=\lim_{x\to 0}\frac{\left(-\frac{\frac{1}{2}\left(\frac{1}{2}-1\right)}{2!}a-\frac{\frac{1}{2}\left(\frac{1}{2}-1\right)\left(\frac{1}{2}-2\right)}{3!}\right)x^2-(\ )x^3-(\ )x^4-\ldots\ldots}{x^2}$$

$$=\left(\frac{a}{8}-\frac{\frac{1}{2}.\frac{1}{2}.\frac{3}{2}}{2.3}\right)$$

$$=\frac{1}{32}-\frac{1}{2}.\frac{1}{2}.\frac{1}{2}.\frac{1}{2}=-\frac{1}{16}+\frac{1}{32}=-\frac{1}{32}$$

$\Rightarrow \lim_{x\to 0}\frac{1}{x^3}\left(\frac{1}{\sqrt{1+x}}-\frac{1+ax}{1+bx}\right)=-\frac{1}{32}$

$\therefore \ \ell=-\frac{1}{32} \qquad \therefore \ \frac{1}{a}-\frac{2}{\ell}+\frac{3}{b}$

$=\frac{1}{\frac{1}{4}}-\frac{2}{\frac{-1}{32}}+\frac{3}{\frac{3}{4}}$

$= 4 + 2.32 + 4$

$= 4 + 64 + 4$

$= 72$

41. Let $\{a_n\}$, $\{b_n\}$, $\{c_n\}$ be sequences such that
(i) $a_n + b_n + c_n = 2n + 1$;
(ii) $a_nb_n + b_nc_n + c_na_n = 2n - 1$;
(iii) $a_nb_nc_n = -1$;
(iv) $a_n < b_n < c_n$ Then find the value of $\lim_{n\to\infty} na_n$.

Solution: Given: $a_n + b_n + c_n = 2n + 1$ = sum of roots
$a_nb_n + b_nc_n + c_na_n = 2n - 1$ = sum of product of roots taking two at a time.
$a_nb_nc_n = -1$ product of all three roots
$\Rightarrow a_n, b_n, c_n$ are the ℓwts of equation
$x^3 - (2n + 1)x^2 + (2n - 1)x + 1 = 0$ ...(1)
Clearly, $x = 1$ is a root of equation (1)
$\Rightarrow (x - 1)(x^2 - 2nx - 1) = 0$

$\Rightarrow x=\frac{2n\pm\sqrt{4n^2+4.1}}{2.1};1$

$\Rightarrow x = n\pm\sqrt{n^2+1};1$

Thus the three roots of cubic equation (1) are $n+\sqrt{n^2+1}, n-\sqrt{n^2+1}, 1$; As $a_n < b_n < c_n$

$\therefore$ so $\lim\limits_{n\to\infty} n\,a_n = \lim\limits_{n\to\infty} n(n-\sqrt{n^2+1})\times\dfrac{n+\sqrt{n^2+1}}{n+\sqrt{n^2+1}}$

$= \lim\limits_{n\to\infty}\dfrac{n(n^2-n^2-1)}{n+\sqrt{n^2+1}}$

$= \lim\limits_{n\to\infty}\dfrac{-n}{n\left(1+\sqrt{1+\dfrac{1}{n^2}}\right)} = -\dfrac{1}{2}$

42. If $n \in N$ and $a_n = 2^2 + 4^2 + 6^2 + \ldots + (2n)^2$ and $b_n = 1^2 + 3^2 + 5^2 + \ldots + (2n-1)^2$. Find the value $\lim\limits_{n\to\infty}\dfrac{\sqrt{a_n}-\sqrt{b_n}}{\sqrt{n}}$.

Solution: Given $a_n = 2^2\,[1^2 + 2^2 + 3^2 + \ldots + n^2]$

$\Rightarrow a_n = 2^2\left[\dfrac{n(n+1)\,(2n+1)}{6}\right]$ ...(1)

Now, $a_n + b_n = 1^2 + 2^2 + 3^2 + 4^2 + 5^2 + 6^2 + \ldots + (2n-1)^2 + (2n)^2$

$\Rightarrow a_n + b_n = \dfrac{2n(2n+1)\,(4n+1)}{6}$

$\Rightarrow b_n = \dfrac{2n(2n+1)(4n+1)}{6} - a_n$

$\Rightarrow b_n = \dfrac{2n(2n+1)\,(4n+1)}{6} - \dfrac{4(n(n+1))\,(2n+1)}{6}$

(using (1))

$\Rightarrow b_n = \dfrac{n(2n+1)}{6}\,[2(4n+1) - 4(n+1)]$

$\Rightarrow b_n = \dfrac{n(2n+1)}{6}\,[4n-2] = \dfrac{n(2n+1)(2n-1)}{3}$

$\therefore \lim\limits_{n\to\infty}\dfrac{\sqrt{a_n}-\sqrt{b_n}}{\sqrt{n}}$

$= \lim\limits_{n\to\infty}\dfrac{\sqrt{\dfrac{4n(n+1)\,(2n+1)}{6}}}{\sqrt{n}} - \sqrt{\dfrac{n(2n+1)(2n-1)}{3n}}$

$= \lim\limits_{n\to\infty}\dfrac{1}{\sqrt{3}}\left(\sqrt{4n^2+6n+2}-\sqrt{4n^2-1}\right)$

$= \lim\limits_{n\to\infty} = \dfrac{\dfrac{1}{\sqrt{3}}(6n+2+1)}{\sqrt{4n^2+6n+2}+\sqrt{4n^2-1}}$

(By rationalization)

$= \lim\limits_{n\to\infty}\dfrac{1}{\sqrt{3}}\dfrac{6+\dfrac{3}{n}}{\sqrt{4+\dfrac{6}{n}+\dfrac{2}{n^2}}+\sqrt{\dfrac{4n^2-1}{n^2}}}$

$= \dfrac{1}{\sqrt{3}}\cdot\dfrac{6}{2+2} = \dfrac{\sqrt{3}}{2}$

43. At the end points A, B of a fixed segment of length L, lines are drawn meeting in C and making angles θ and 2θ respectively with the given segment. Let D be the foot of the altitude CD and let x represents the length of AD. Find the value of x as θ tends to zero i.e. $\lim\limits_{\theta\to 0} x$.

Solution: In $\Delta\,ABC$, we have $\tan\theta = \dfrac{CD}{AD} = \dfrac{CD}{x}$ and

$\tan 2\theta = \dfrac{CD}{BD} = \dfrac{CD}{AB-AD} = \dfrac{CD}{L-x}$

Thus $\tan 2\theta = \dfrac{CD}{L-x}$

$\Rightarrow CD = (L-x)\tan 2\theta$

$\Rightarrow x\tan\theta = (L-x)\tan^2\theta$ $\quad(\because CD = x\tan\theta)$

$\Rightarrow x\tan\theta = (L-x)\left(\dfrac{2\tan\theta}{1-\tan^2\theta}\right)$

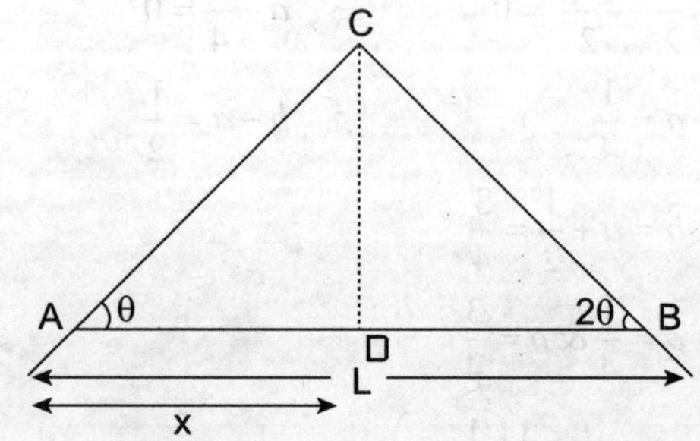

$\Rightarrow x = \dfrac{2(L-x)}{1-\tan^2\theta}$

$\Rightarrow x(1-\tan^2\theta) = 2L - 2x$

$\Rightarrow x(2+1-\tan^2\theta) = 2L$

$\Rightarrow x = \dfrac{2L}{3-\tan^2\theta}$

$\therefore \lim\limits_{\theta\to 0} x = \lim\limits_{\theta\to 0}\dfrac{2L}{3-\tan^2\theta} = \dfrac{2L}{3}$

Thus, $\lim\limits_{\theta\to 0} x = \dfrac{2L}{3}$

44. At the end-points and the midpoint of a circular arc AB tangent lines are drawn, and the points A and B are joined. Prove that the ratio of the areas of the two triangles thus formed tends to 4 as the arc AB decreases indefinitely.

Solution: Let the radius of circle is r and O be its centre.

Let $\angle AOB = 2\theta$ and the tangents at A and B intersect at C and R be the mid point of arc AB.

$\Rightarrow \angle ACB = \pi - 2\theta$

($\because$ points A, C, B, O are concyclic)

Also $\angle AOP = \angle BOP = \theta$

$\angle ACP = \angle BCP = \dfrac{\pi}{2} - \theta$

In ΔAOP, $\sin\theta = \dfrac{AP}{OA} = \dfrac{AP}{r}$

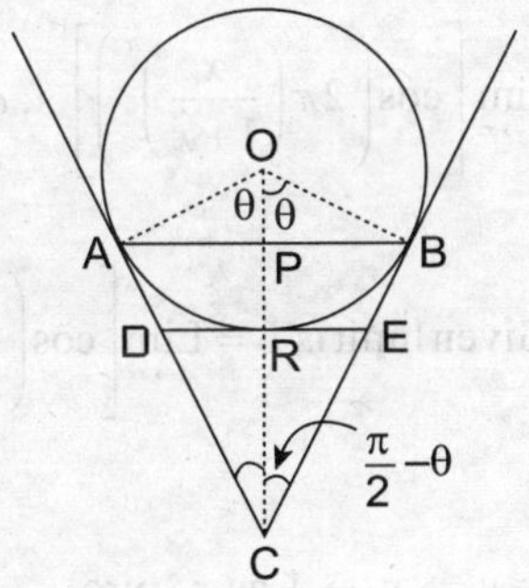

$\Rightarrow AP = r\sin\theta$ ....(1)

and $\cos\theta = \dfrac{OP}{OA} = \dfrac{OP}{r}$

$\Rightarrow OP = r\cos\theta$ ...(2)

Now, $AB = 2AP = 2r\sin\theta$ ...(3)

In ΔAOC, $\sin\left(\dfrac{\pi}{2} - \theta\right) = \dfrac{OA}{OC}$

$\Rightarrow \cos\theta = \dfrac{r}{OC}$

$\Rightarrow OC = \dfrac{r}{\cos\theta}$ ...(4)

Now, $PC = OC - OP$

$= \dfrac{r}{\cos\theta} - r\cos\theta$ (using (2) and (4))

$= r\left(\dfrac{1}{\cos\theta} - \cos\theta\right)$

$= \dfrac{r}{\cos\theta}(1 - \cos^2\theta)$

$\therefore PC = \dfrac{r}{\cos\theta}\sin^2\theta$ ...(5)

$\therefore ar(\Delta ABC) = \dfrac{1}{2} AB.PC$

$= \dfrac{1}{2} 2r\sin\theta \dfrac{r}{\cos\theta}.\sin^2\theta$ ...(From (3) and (5))

$= r^2\tan\theta \,.\, \sin^2\theta$ ...(6)

Also $RC = OC - OR$

$= \dfrac{r}{\cos\theta} - r$ (using (4) and $OR = r =$ radius)

$= \dfrac{r}{\cos\theta}(1 - \cos\theta)$ ...(7)

In ΔDRC, $\tan\left(\dfrac{\pi}{2} - \theta\right) = \dfrac{DR}{RC}$

$\Rightarrow \cot\theta = \dfrac{DR}{RC} \Rightarrow DR = RC\cot\theta$

$= \dfrac{r}{\cos\theta}(1 - \cos\theta).\cot\theta$ (using (7))

$= \dfrac{r}{\cos\theta}(1 - \cos\theta).\dfrac{\cos\theta}{\sin\theta} = \dfrac{r(1-\cos\theta)}{\sin\theta}$, thus

$DR = \dfrac{r(1-\cos\theta)}{\sin\theta}$ ...(8)

Now $DE = 2DR$

$= \dfrac{2r}{\sin\theta}(1 - \cos\theta)$ (using (8))

Now area of $(\Delta DEC) = \dfrac{1}{2} \times DE \times RC$

$= \dfrac{1}{2}\dfrac{2r(1-\cos\theta)}{\sin\theta}.\dfrac{r(1-\cos\theta)}{\cos\theta}$

$= \dfrac{r^2(1-\cos\theta)(1-\cos\theta)}{\sin\theta.\cos\theta}$

$= \dfrac{r^2.2\sin^2\dfrac{\theta}{2}\cdot 2\sin^2\dfrac{\theta}{2}}{\sin\theta.\cos\theta}$

$= \dfrac{4r^2\sin^2\dfrac{\theta}{2}\sin^2\dfrac{\theta}{2}}{\sin\theta.\cos\theta} = \dfrac{4r^2\sin^4\dfrac{\theta}{2}}{\sin\theta\cos\theta}$ ...(9)

Now, $AB = 2r\sin\theta$ (from (3))

If $AB \to 0$ i.e., $2r\sin\theta \to 0 \Rightarrow \theta \to 0$

$\therefore \lim\limits_{AB\to 0} \dfrac{ar(\Delta ABC)}{ar(\Delta CDE)}$

$$= \lim_{\theta\to 0}\left[\frac{r^2\tan\theta.\sin^2\theta}{\left(\dfrac{4r^2\sin^4\dfrac{\theta}{2}}{\sin\theta.\cos\theta}\right)}\right]$$

$$= \lim_{\theta\to 0} r^2\tan\theta\sin^2\theta\left(\frac{\sin\theta.\cos\theta}{4r^2.\sin^4\dfrac{\theta}{2}}\right)$$

$$= \lim_{\theta\to 0}\frac{\tan\theta.\sin^3\theta.\cos\theta}{4\sin^4\theta/2} = \lim_{\theta\to 0}\frac{\dfrac{\tan\theta.\sin^3\theta.\cos\theta}{\theta^4}}{4\dfrac{\sin^4\theta/2}{\theta^4}}$$

$$= \lim_{\theta\to 0}\frac{\left(\dfrac{\tan\theta}{\theta}\right).\left(\dfrac{\sin\theta}{\theta}\right)^3\cdot\cos\theta}{4\left(\dfrac{\sin\theta/2}{\theta/2}\right)^4.\dfrac{1}{2^4}}$$

$$= \frac{1.1.1}{4.1.1/16} = 4$$

45. Evaluate the limit $\lim\limits_{n\to\infty}\left(\dfrac{\sqrt{n^2+n-1}}{n}\right)^{2\sqrt{n^2+n-1}}$

Solution: $\lim\limits_{n\to\infty}\left(\dfrac{\sqrt{n^2+n-1}}{n}\right)^{2\sqrt{n^2+n-1}}$

$$= e^{\lim\limits_{n\to\infty}\left[\frac{\sqrt{n^2+n}-1-n}{n}\right](2\sqrt{n^2+n}-1)} \quad (\because 1^\infty \text{ form})$$

$$= e^{\lim\limits_{n\to\infty}\frac{[(n^2+n)-(1+n)^2]\,(2\sqrt{n^2+n}-1)}{n\left\{\sqrt{n^2+n}+(1+n)\right\}}} = e^{\lim\limits_{n\to\infty}\frac{(-n-1)(2\sqrt{n^2+n}-1)}{n\left\{\sqrt{n^2+n}+(1+n)\right\}}}$$

$$= e^{\lim\limits_{n\to\infty}\frac{\left(-1-\frac{1}{n}\right)\left(2\sqrt{1+\frac{1}{n}}-\frac{1}{n}\right)n^2}{n^2\left\{\sqrt{1+\frac{1}{n}}+\frac{1}{n}+1\right\}}=e^{-1}}$$

46. Evaluate $\lim\limits_{x\to\infty} x^2\sin\left(\ell n\sqrt{\cos\dfrac{\pi}{x}}\right)$

Solution: Given limit is $\lim\limits_{x\to\infty} x^2\sin\left(\ell n\sqrt{\cos\dfrac{\pi}{x}}\right)$

$((\infty.\ 0)$ form)

$$= \lim_{x\to\infty}\frac{x^2\sin\left(\ell n\sqrt{\cos\dfrac{\pi}{x}}\right)}{\left(\ell n\sqrt{\cos\dfrac{\pi}{x}}\right)}\left(\ell n\sqrt{\cos\frac{\pi}{x}}\right)$$

$$= \lim_{x\to\infty} x^2.\ell n\sqrt{\cos\frac{\pi}{x}} = \lim_{x\to\infty}\frac{x^2}{2}\ell n\left(\cos\frac{\pi}{x}\right)$$

$$= \lim_{x\to\infty}\frac{x^2}{2}\frac{\ell n\left[1+\left(\cos\dfrac{\pi}{x}-1\right)\right]}{\left(\cos\dfrac{\pi}{x}-1\right)}\left(-2\sin^2\frac{\pi}{2x}\right)$$

$$= \lim_{x\to\infty}\frac{x^2}{2}\frac{\left(-2\sin^2\dfrac{\pi}{2x}\right)}{\left(\dfrac{\pi}{2x}\right)^2}.\left(\frac{\pi}{2x}\right)^2 = -\frac{\pi^2}{4}$$

47. Evaluate $\lim\limits_{x\to\infty}\left[\cos\left(2\pi\left(\dfrac{x}{1+x}\right)^a\right)\right]^{x^2}$; $a\in R$

Solution: Given limit is $L = \lim\limits_{x\to\infty}\left[\cos\left(2\pi\left(\dfrac{x}{1+x}\right)^a\right)\right]^{x^2}$

$((1)^\infty$ form)

Put $\dfrac{x}{1+x} = y \Rightarrow y\to 1$ as $x\to\infty$

Now, $1 - \dfrac{1}{1+x} = y$

$$\Rightarrow 1+x = \frac{1}{1-y} \Rightarrow x = \frac{1}{1-y}-1$$

$$\Rightarrow x = \frac{y}{1-y}$$

$$= e^{\lim\limits_{y\to 1}\left[\cos 2\pi y^a-1\right]\left(\frac{y}{1-y}\right)^2} = e^{\lim\limits_{y\to 1}(-2\sin^2\pi y^a)\left(\frac{y^2}{(1-y)^2}\right)}$$

$$= e^{\lim\limits_{y\to 1}-2\left[\frac{\sin^2\pi(1-y^a)}{\pi^2(1-y^a)^2}.\frac{\pi^2(1-y^a)^2}{(1-y)^2}.y^2\right]}$$

$$= \lim_{y\to 1} e^{-2\pi^2\left(\frac{1-y^a}{1-y}\right)^2.y^2} = e^{-2\pi^2(a^2)}$$

$$\left[\because \lim_{x\to 1}\frac{x^n-1}{x-1} = n\right]$$

Aliter: Let limit = e^L where

$$L = \lim_{x\to\infty}\left[\cos\left(2\pi\left(\frac{x}{1+x}\right)^a\right)-1\right]x^2$$

Let $= \dfrac{x}{1+x} = t$

$\Rightarrow\ x = \dfrac{t}{1-t}$ and $x \to \infty$

$\Rightarrow 1 - t \to 0 \Rightarrow t \to 1$

$$\Rightarrow\ L = \lim_{t\to1}[\cos 2\pi t^a - 1]\left(\frac{t}{1-t}\right)^2$$

$$= \lim_{t\to1}\left[\frac{\cos(2\pi - 2\pi t^a) - 1}{(\pi(1-t^a))^2}\right]\frac{t^2}{(1-t)^2}\pi^2(1-t^a)^2$$

$$= \lim_{t\to1}\frac{-2\sin^2(\pi - \pi t^a)}{(\pi(1-t^a))^2}.t^2\pi^2\left(\frac{1-t^a}{1-t}\right)^2$$

$= -2(1)^2\,\pi^2a^2 = -2\pi^2a^2$

Given limit is $e^L = e^{-2\pi^2a^2}$

48. Evaluate $\lim\limits_{x\to1}\left(\tan\dfrac{\pi x}{4}\right)^{\tan\frac{\pi x}{2}}$

Solution: Given limit is $\lim\limits_{x\to1}\left[\tan\dfrac{\pi x}{4}\right]^{\tan\frac{\pi x}{2}}$ (1^∞ form)

$$= e^{\lim\limits_{x\to1}\left(\tan\frac{\pi x}{4}-1\right)\tan\frac{\pi x}{2}} = e^{\lim\limits_{x\to1}\frac{\sin\left(\frac{\pi x}{4}-\frac{\pi}{4}\right)}{\cos\frac{\pi}{4}.\cos\frac{\pi x}{4}}.\tan\frac{\pi x}{2}}$$

$$= e^{\lim\limits_{x\to1}\frac{\sin\frac{\pi}{4}(x-1)}{\frac{\pi}{4}(x-1)\cos\frac{\pi}{4}\cos\frac{\pi}{4}x}.\left(\tan\frac{\pi x}{2}\right).\left(\frac{\pi}{4}(x-1)\right)}$$

$$= e^{\lim\limits_{x\to1}2\left[\tan\left(\frac{\pi x}{2}\right)\right]\left[\frac{\pi}{4}(x-1)\right]} = e^{\lim\limits_{x\to1}\tan\left(\frac{\pi x}{2}\right)\left[\frac{\pi}{2}x-\frac{\pi}{2}\right]}$$

$$= e^{\lim\limits_{x\to1}\left[\cot\left(\frac{\pi}{2}-\frac{\pi x}{2}\right)\right]\left(\frac{\pi}{2}x-\frac{\pi}{2}\right)}$$

$$= e^{-\lim\limits_{x\to1}\left\{\frac{\left(\frac{\pi}{2}x-\frac{\pi}{2}\right)}{\tan\left(\frac{\pi}{2}x-\frac{\pi}{2}\right)}\right\}} = e^{-1}$$

59. Evaluate

$$\lim_{x\to a}\frac{1}{(a^2-x^2)^2}\left(\frac{a^2+x^2}{ax} - 2\sin\left(\frac{a\pi}{2}\right)\sin\left(\frac{\pi x}{2}\right)\right);$$

where a is an odd integer.

Solution: Given limit is

$$\lim_{x\to a}\frac{1}{(a^2-x^2)^2}\left[\frac{a^2+x^2}{ax} + \cos\frac{\pi}{2}(a+x) - \cos\left(\frac{\pi}{2}(a-x)\right)\right]$$

$$= \lim_{x\to a}\frac{1}{(a^2\quad x^2)^2}$$

$$\left[\frac{(a\quad x)}{ax} + \cos\frac{\pi}{2}(a+x) + (1+1) - \cos\frac{\pi}{2}(a-x)\right]$$

$$= \lim_{x\to a}\frac{1}{(a+x)^2ax} + \frac{1}{(a^2-x^2)^2}$$

$$\left[1+\cos\frac{\pi}{2}(a+x) + 1 - \cos\frac{\pi}{2}(a-x)\right]$$

$$= \lim_{x\to a}\frac{1}{(a+x)^2ax} + \frac{2\cos^2\frac{\pi}{4}(a+x)}{(a^2-x^2)^2} + \frac{2\sin^2\frac{\pi}{4}(a-x)}{(a^2-x^2)^2}$$

$$\left[\begin{array}{l}\because\ \cos^2\left(\dfrac{a\pi}{4}+\dfrac{\pi}{4}x\right) = \sin^2\left(\left(\dfrac{a\pi}{2}\right)-\left(\dfrac{(a+x)\pi}{4}\right)\right)\\ = \sin^2\left(\dfrac{a\pi}{4}-\dfrac{x\pi}{4}\right)\text{ as } a \text{ is an odd integer}\end{array}\right]$$

$$= \frac{1}{4a^4} + 2\lim_{x\to a}\frac{\sin^2(a-x)\frac{\pi}{4}}{(a-x)^2(a+x)^2} + 2\lim_{x\to a}\frac{\sin^2(a-x)\frac{\pi}{4}}{(a-x)^2(a+x)^2}$$

$$= \frac{1}{4a^4} + \lim_{x\to a}\frac{4\sin^2\frac{\pi}{4}(a-x)}{\frac{(a-x)^2\pi^2}{16}(a+x)^2}.\frac{\pi^2}{16}$$

$$= \frac{1}{4a^4} + \frac{\pi^2}{16a^2} = \frac{a^2\pi^2+4}{16a^4}$$

60. If $L = \lim\limits_{x\to1}\dfrac{(1-x)(1-x^2)(1-x^3)......(1-x^{2n})}{[(1-x)(1-x^2)(1-x^3).....(1-x^n)]^2}$; then show that L can be equals

(a) $\displaystyle\prod_{r=1}^{n}\frac{n+r}{r} = \frac{1}{n!}\prod_{r=1}^{n}(4r-2) = {}^{2n}C_n$

(b) the sum of the coefficients of two middle terms in the expansion of $(1+x)^{2n-1}$.

(c) the coefficient of x^n in the expansion of $(1+x)^{2n}$.

Solution: Let

$$L = \lim_{x\to1}\frac{(1-x)(1-x^2)\,(1-x^3)....(1-x^{2n})}{[(1-x)\,(1-x^2)\,(1-x^3).....(1-x^n)]^2}$$

$$= \lim_{x\to1}\frac{(1-x)(1-x^2)...(1-x^n)(1-x^{n+1})(1-x^{n+2})...(1-x^{2n})}{[(1-x)(1-x^2)(1-x^3)....(1-x^n)]^2}$$

$$= \lim_{x\to1}\frac{1-x^{n+1}}{1-x}.\frac{1-x^{n+2}}{1-x^2}.\frac{1-x^{n+3}}{1-x^3}+.....\frac{(1-x^{2n})}{(1-x^n)}$$

$$\left(\text{using the result } \underset{x\to a}{Lt}\frac{x^n-a^n}{x-a} = n(a)^{n-1}\right)$$

$$= \frac{(n+1)\,(n+2).......2n}{1.2.3....n} = \frac{2n!}{n!n!} = {}^{2n}C_n\,;$$

clearly $\displaystyle\prod_{r=1}^{n}\frac{(n+r)}{r} = \frac{(n+1)}{1}.\frac{(n+2)}{2}.\frac{(n+3)}{3}...\frac{2n}{n}$

Also $\frac{1}{n!}\prod_{r=1}^{n}(4r-2)$

$$= \frac{2.6.10.....(4n-2)}{n!} = \frac{2^n[1.3.5.....(2n-1)]}{n!}$$

$$= \frac{2^n[1.3.5.....(2n-1)]\,[1.2.3......n]}{n!.n!} = \frac{2n!}{n!n!} = {}^{2n}C_n$$

Now sum of coefficient of two middle terms in the expansion of $(1 + x)^{2n-1} = {}^{2n-1}C_{n-1} + {}^{2n-1}C_n = {}^{2n}C_n$ and the coefficient of x^n in the expansion of $(1 + x)^{2n} = {}^{2n}C_n$

62. Evaluate, $\lim_{x\to 1}\frac{1-x+\ell nx}{1+\cos\pi x}$

Solution: $\lim_{x\to 1}\frac{1-x+\ell nx}{1+\cos\pi x}$

Put $x = 1 - h$; $h \to 0^+$

$$= \lim_{h\to 0^+}\frac{h+\ell n(1-h)}{1+\cos\pi(1-h)}$$

$$= \lim_{h\to 0^+}\frac{h+\ell n(1-h)}{1-\cos\pi h}$$

$$= \lim_{h\to 0^+}\frac{-\left(\frac{h^2}{2}+\frac{h^3}{3}+\frac{x^4}{4}+...\right)}{2\left(\frac{\pi^2h^2}{4}\right)\frac{\sin^2\frac{\pi h}{2}}{\left(\frac{\pi^2h^2}{4}\right)}} = \frac{1}{\pi^2}$$

63. Evaluate

$$\lim_{y\to 0}\left[\lim_{x\to\infty}\frac{\exp\left(x\ell n\left(1+\frac{ay}{x}\right)\right)-\exp\left(x\ell n\left(1+\frac{by}{x}\right)\right)}{y}\right]$$

Solution:

$$\lim_{y\to 0}\left[\lim_{x\to\infty}\frac{\exp.\left(x\ell n\left(1+\frac{ay}{x}\right)\right)-\exp.\left(x\ell n\left(1+\frac{by}{x}\right)\right)}{y}\right]$$

$$= \lim_{y\to 0}\left[\lim_{x\to\infty}\frac{\left(1+\frac{ay}{x}\right)^x-\left(1+\frac{by}{x}\right)^x}{y}\right]$$

$$= \lim_{y\to 0}\frac{e^{ay}-e^{by}}{y} = \lim_{y\to 0}\frac{[e^{(a-b)y}-1]}{y}.e^{by}$$

$$= a - b$$

64. Let $x_0 = 2\cos\frac{\pi}{6}$ and $x_n = \sqrt{2+x_{n-1}}$, $n = 1, 2, 3,.....,$ find $\lim_{n\to\infty}2^{(n+1)}\sqrt{2-x_n}$

Solution: $x_1 = \sqrt{2+2\cos\frac{\pi}{6}} = 2\cos\frac{\theta}{2}$; where $\theta = \frac{\pi}{6}$;

$x_2 = 2\cos\frac{\theta}{4}$, ..., $x_n = 2\cos\frac{\theta}{2^n}$

$$\therefore \lim_{n\to\infty}2^{(n+1)}\sqrt{2-2\cos\frac{\theta}{2^n}} = \lim_{n\to\infty}2^{n+1}2\sin\frac{\theta}{2^{n+1}}$$

$$= \operatorname{Lt}_{n\to\infty}\frac{2\theta\sin\left(\frac{\theta}{2^{n+1}}\right)}{\left(\frac{\theta}{2^{n+1}}\right)}$$

$$= 2\theta = 2\times\frac{\pi}{6} = \frac{\pi}{3} \qquad \left(\because \theta = \frac{\pi}{6}\right)$$

65. Let $L = \prod_{n=3}^{\infty}\left(1-\frac{4}{n^2}\right)$; $M = \prod_{n=2}^{\infty}\left(\frac{n^3-1}{n^3+1}\right)$ and $N = \prod_{n=1}^{\infty}\frac{(1+n^{-1})^2}{1+2n^{-1}}$, then find the value of $L^{-1} + M^{-1} + N^{-1}$.

Solution: Given $L = \left(1-\frac{4}{3^2}\right)\left(1-\frac{4}{4^2}\right)\left(1-\frac{4}{5^2}\right)......$

$$= \left[\left(1-\frac{2}{3}\right)\left(1-\frac{2}{4}\right)\left(1-\frac{2}{5}\right)\left(1-\frac{2}{6}\right)......\right]\times\left[\left(1+\frac{2}{3}\right)\left(1+\frac{2}{4}\right)\left(1+\frac{2}{5}\right)...\right]$$

$$= \left[\frac{1}{3}\times\frac{2}{4}\times\frac{3}{5}\times\frac{4}{6}\times....\right]\times\left[\left(\frac{5}{3}\right)\left(\frac{6}{4}\right)\left(\frac{7}{5}\right).......\right]$$

$$= \frac{1}{3}\times\frac{2}{4} = \left(\frac{1}{6}\right)$$

($\because$ Remaining terms in two braces are reciprocal of each other)

Also, $M = \frac{2^3-1}{2^3+1}.\frac{3^3-1}{3^3+1}.\frac{4^3-1}{4^3+1}........$

$$\left(\text{Now } \frac{x^3-1}{x^3+1} = \frac{(x-1)(x^2+x+1)}{(x+1)(x^2-x+1)}\right)$$

$$\therefore \quad M = \left(\frac{2-1}{2+1}.\frac{3-1}{3+1}.\frac{4-1}{4+1}.\frac{5-1}{5+1}.....\right)\times$$

$$\left(\frac{2^2+2+1}{2^2-2+1}\right)\left(\frac{3^2+3+1}{3^2-3+1}\right)\left(\frac{4^2+4+1}{4^2-4+1}\right).......$$

$$M = \operatorname*{Lim}_{n\to\infty}\frac{1\times 2}{(n+1)(n)}.\frac{n^2+n+1}{3} = \frac{2}{3};$$

$$N = \prod_{n=1}^{\infty}\frac{\left(1+\frac{1}{n}\right)^2}{\left(1+\frac{2}{n}\right)} = \operatorname*{Lt}_{n\to\infty}\prod\frac{(n+1)^2/n^2}{(n+2)/n}$$

$$= \operatorname*{Lt}_{n\to\infty}\prod_{r=1}^{n}\left(\frac{(r+1)^2}{r(r+2)}\right)$$

$$= \operatorname*{Lt}_{n\to\infty}\left(\prod_{r=1}^{n}\frac{r+1}{r}.\frac{r+1}{r+2}\right)$$

$$= \operatorname*{Lt}_{n\to\infty}\left(\frac{2}{1}\times\frac{3}{2}\times\frac{4}{3}\times...\times\frac{n+1}{n}\right)\times\left(\frac{2}{3}\times\frac{3}{4}\times...\times\frac{n+1}{n+2}\right)$$

$$= \operatorname*{Lt}_{n\to\infty}\left(\frac{2(n+1)}{n+2}\right) = 2$$

$$\therefore \quad L^{-1}+M^{-1}+N^{-1} = 6+\frac{3}{2}+\frac{1}{2} = 8$$

66. Let $f(x) = \operatorname*{Lim}_{n\to\infty}\sum_{r=1}^{n}3^{r-1}\sin^3\frac{x}{3^r}$ and $g(x) = x - 4f(x)$. Evaluate $\operatorname*{Lim}_{x\to 0}(1+g(x))^{\cot x}$.

Solution: $\sin^3 x = \dfrac{3\sin x - \sin 3x}{4}$

$[\because \sin 3x = 3\sin x - 4\sin^3 x]$

$$\therefore \quad f(x) = \frac{1}{4}\sum_{n=1}^{n}\left(3\sin\frac{x}{3} - \sin x\right) +$$

$$3\left(3\sin\frac{x}{3^2} - \sin\frac{x}{3}\right) + 3^2\left(3\sin\frac{x}{3^3} - \sin\frac{x}{3^2}\right)$$

$$+ \ldots + 3^{n-1}\left(3\sin\frac{x}{3^n} - \sin\left(\frac{x}{3^{n-1}}\right)\right)$$

$$= \operatorname*{Lim}_{n\to\infty}\frac{1}{4}\left(3^n\sin.\frac{x}{3^n} - \sin x\right)$$

$$= \frac{1}{4}\left[\operatorname*{Lim}_{n\to\infty}\frac{x\sin\left(\frac{x}{3^n}\right)}{\frac{x}{3^n}} - \sin x\right]$$

$$= \frac{1}{4}[x - \sin x]$$

Now, $g(x) = x - 4\left[\dfrac{1}{4}(x - \sin x)\right]$

$(\because g(x) = x - 4f(x)$ given)

$\Rightarrow g(x) = \sin x$

$$\therefore \quad \operatorname*{Lt}_{x\to 0}(1+g(x))^{\cot x} = \operatorname*{Lt}_{x\to 0}(1+\sin x)^{\cot x} = e^{\operatorname*{Lt}_{x\to 0}(\cos x)} = e$$

67. If $f(n, \theta) = \prod_{r=1}^{n}\left(1-\tan^2\frac{\theta}{2^r}\right)$, then compute $\operatorname*{Lim}_{n\to\infty} f(n,\theta)$

Solution: $f(n,\theta) = \prod_{r=1}^{n}\left(1-\tan^2\dfrac{\theta}{2^r}\right)$

$$\left[\left(\text{use } \tan 2\theta = \frac{2\tan\theta}{1-\tan^2\theta}\right)\right]$$

$$\Rightarrow f(n,\theta) = \left(1-\tan^2\frac{\theta}{2}\right)\left(1-\tan^2\frac{\theta}{2^2}\right)...\left(1-\tan^2\frac{\theta}{2^n}\right)$$

$$= \frac{2\tan\frac{\theta}{2}}{\tan\theta}.\frac{2\tan\frac{\theta}{2^2}}{\tan\frac{\theta}{2}}.\frac{2\tan\frac{\theta}{2^3}}{\tan\frac{\theta}{2^2}}........$$

$$\Rightarrow f(n,\theta) = \frac{2^n\tan\frac{\theta}{2^n}}{\tan\theta}$$

($\because$ other terms cancel out)

$$\therefore \quad \operatorname*{Lt}_{n\to\infty} f(n,\theta) = \operatorname*{Lim}_{n\to\infty}\frac{\theta\tan\frac{\theta}{2^n}}{(\tan\theta)\left(\frac{\theta}{2^n}\right)} = \frac{\theta}{\tan\theta}$$

68. $\operatorname*{Lim}_{x\to\infty}\left(\dfrac{\cosh(\pi/x)}{\cos(\pi/x)}\right)^{x^2}$; where $\cosh t = \dfrac{e^t+e^{-t}}{2}$

Solution: Let $L = \operatorname*{Lim}_{x\to\infty}\left[\dfrac{\cosh(\pi/x)}{\cos(\pi/x)}\right]^{x^2}$

put $\dfrac{\pi}{x} = t$

As $x\to\infty$, $t\to 0$

$$\therefore \quad L = \operatorname*{Lim}_{t\to 0}\left(\frac{e^t+e^{-t}}{2\cos t}\right)^{\pi^2/t^2} \quad ((1)^\infty \text{ form})$$

$$\Rightarrow \quad L = \operatorname*{Lim}_{t\to 0}\left[1+\left(\frac{e^t+e^{-t}}{2\cos t}\right)-1\right]^{\pi^2/t^2}$$

$$= e^{\operatorname*{Lim}_{t\to 0}\left(\frac{e^t+e^{-t}-2\cos t}{2\cos t}\right).\frac{\pi^2}{t^2}}$$

$$= e^{\lim\limits_{t\to 0}\left(\frac{e^t+e^{-t}-2+2(1-\cos t)}{2\cos t}\right)\cdot\frac{\pi^2}{t^2}}$$

$$= e^{\left\{\lim\limits_{t\to 0}\frac{\pi^2(e^t+e^{-t}-2)}{2t^2\cos t}+\lim\limits_{t\to 0}\frac{\pi^2}{t^2}\frac{(1-\cos t)}{\cos t}\right\}}$$

$$= e^{\left\{\lim\limits_{t\to 0}\frac{\pi^2}{2}\left(\frac{e^t+e^{-t}-2}{t^2}\right)+\pi^2\ \mathop{Lt}\limits_{t\to 0}\frac{2\sin^2 t/2}{4(t^2/4)}\right\}}$$

$$= e^{\lim\limits_{t\to 0}\left\{\frac{\pi^2}{2}(1)+\frac{\pi^2}{2}\right\}} = e^{\pi^2} \qquad \text{(By using L.H. Rule)}$$

69. Through a point A on *a* circle, *a* chord AP is drawn and on the tangent at A a point T is taken such that $AT = AP$. If TP produced meet the diameter through A at Q, prove that the limiting value of AQ, when P moves upto A is double the diameter of the circle.

Solution:

Let 'r' be the radius of given circle and $\angle ATP = \theta$

$\because\ AT = AP$ (given),

$\angle APT = \angle ATP = \theta$

$\Rightarrow\ \angle APQ = \pi - \theta$ and $\angle AQP = \dfrac{\pi}{2} - \theta$

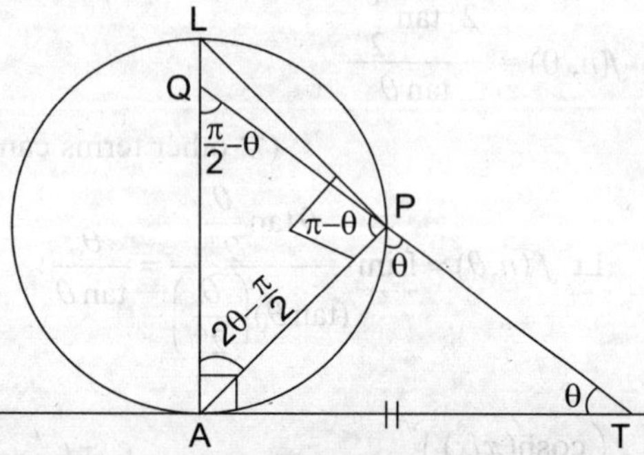

$\therefore$ In ΔAPQ, by sine formula $\dfrac{AQ}{\sin(\pi-\theta)} = \dfrac{AP}{\sin\left(\dfrac{\pi}{2}-\theta\right)}$

$$\Rightarrow\ AQ = \frac{AP\sin\theta}{\cos\theta} \qquad \ldots(1)$$

Also in rt. angled $\angle APL$

$$\cos\left(2\theta-\frac{\pi}{2}\right) = \frac{AP}{AL} = \frac{AP}{2r}$$

$$\Rightarrow\ AP = 2r\cos\left(\frac{\pi}{2}-2\theta\right) = 2r\sin 2\theta \qquad \ldots(2)$$

from (1) and (2) $AQ = \dfrac{2r\sin 2\theta.\sin\theta}{\cos\theta} = 4r\sin^2\theta$

Now, when $P \to A$, $AP = AT \Rightarrow T \to A$

$$\Rightarrow\ \theta \to \frac{\pi}{2}$$

$$\therefore\ AQ = \mathop{\text{Lt}}\limits_{\theta\to\pi/2}(4r\sin^2\theta) = 4r = 2(\text{diameter})$$

70. Using Sandwich theorem, evaluate

(a) $\lim\limits_{n\to\infty}\dfrac{1}{1+n^2}+\dfrac{2}{2+n^2}+\ldots..+\dfrac{n}{n+n^2}$

(b) $\lim\limits_{n\to\infty}\left(\dfrac{1}{\sqrt{n^2}}+\dfrac{1}{\sqrt{n^2+1}}+\dfrac{1}{\sqrt{n^2+2}}+\ldots+\dfrac{1}{\sqrt{n^2+2n}}\right)$

Solution: (a)

Let $S_n = \dfrac{1}{1+n^2}+\dfrac{2}{2+n^2}+\dfrac{3}{3+n^2}+\ldots+\dfrac{n}{n+n^2}$

We have $\dfrac{1}{n+n^2} \le \dfrac{1}{1+n^2} \le \dfrac{1}{1+n^2}$;

$$\frac{2}{n+n^2} \le \frac{2}{2+n^2} \le \frac{2}{1+n^2};$$

$$\frac{3}{n+n^2} \le \frac{3}{3+n^2} \le \frac{3}{1+n^2};\ldots..\frac{n}{n+n^2} \le \frac{n}{n+n^2} \le \frac{n}{1+n^2};$$

Adding we get, $\dfrac{n(n+1)}{2(n+n^2)} \le Sn \le \dfrac{n(n+1)}{2(1+n^2)}$;

Now $\lim\limits_{n\to\infty}\dfrac{n^2+n}{2n^2+2n} = \dfrac{1}{2}$ and $\mathop{\text{Lt}}\limits_{n\to\infty}\dfrac{n^2+n}{2n^2+2} = \dfrac{1}{2}$

$\therefore$ By sandwich theorem $\mathop{\text{Lt}}\limits_{n\to\infty} Sn = \dfrac{1}{2}$

(b) We have $\dfrac{1}{\sqrt{n^2+2n}} \le \dfrac{1}{\sqrt{n^2}} \le \dfrac{1}{\sqrt{n^2}}$;

$$\frac{1}{\sqrt{n^2+2n}} \le \frac{1}{\sqrt{n^2+1}} \le \frac{1}{\sqrt{n^2}};$$

....

$$\frac{1}{\sqrt{n^2+2n}} \le \frac{1}{\sqrt{n^2+2n}} \le \frac{1}{\sqrt{n^2}}$$

$$\Rightarrow\ \frac{2n}{\sqrt{n^2+2n}} \le Sn \le \frac{2n}{\sqrt{n^2}} \quad \text{(Adding vertically)}$$

But $\mathop{\text{Lt}}\limits_{n\to\infty}\dfrac{2n}{\sqrt{n^2+2n}} = \mathop{\text{Lt}}\limits_{n\to\infty}\dfrac{2n}{\sqrt{n^2}} = 2$

$\therefore$ By sandwich theorem $\lim\limits_{n\to\infty} Sn = 2$

71. If $L = \lim\limits_{x\to 0}\left(\dfrac{1}{\ell n(1+x)} - \dfrac{1}{\ell n(x+\sqrt{1+x^2})}\right)$, then find the value of $\dfrac{L+15}{L}$.

Solution: $L = \lim_{x\to 0}\left[\frac{1}{\ell n(1+x)} - \frac{1}{\ell n(x+\sqrt{1+x^2})}\right]$

put $x = -x$ ($\because x \to 0$, we can put $x = -x$)

$$L = \lim_{x\to 0}\left[\frac{1}{\ell n(1-x)} - \frac{1}{\ell n\sqrt{1+x^2}-x}\right]$$

Adding both, we get

$$2L = \lim_{x\to 0}\frac{1}{\ell n(1+x)} + \frac{1}{\ell n(1-x)} - \frac{1}{\ell n(x+\sqrt{1+x^2})} - \frac{1}{\ell n\sqrt{1+x^2}-x}$$

$$\Rightarrow\ 2L = \lim_{x\to 0}\frac{\ell n(1-x^2)}{\ell n(1+x)\ell n(1-x)} - \left\{\frac{\ell n(1+x^2-x^2)}{\ell n(x+\sqrt{1+x^2})\ell n(\sqrt{1+x^2}-x)}\right\}$$

$$\Rightarrow\ 2L = \lim_{x\to 0}\left(\frac{\ell n(1-x^2)}{-x^2}\right)\Big/\left(\frac{\ell n(1+x)}{x}\right)\cdot\left(\frac{\ell n(1-x)}{(-x)}\right)$$

$$\Rightarrow\ 2L = \frac{1}{(1)(1)}$$

$$\Rightarrow\ L = \frac{1}{2}$$

$$\therefore\ \frac{L+15}{L} = \frac{\frac{1}{2}+15}{\frac{1}{2}} = \frac{\frac{31}{2}}{\frac{1}{2}} = 31$$

72. Determine the value of a, b and c so that $\lim_{x\to 0}\frac{(a+b\cos x)x - c\sin x}{x^5} = 1$

Solution: Let $\ell = \lim_{x\to 0}\frac{(a+b\cos x)x - c\sin x}{x^5}$

$$= \lim_{x\to 0}\frac{ax + bx\cos x - c\sin x}{x^5}\quad\left(\frac{0}{0}\ form\right)$$

$$= \lim_{x\to 0}\left(\frac{a+b\cos x - bx\sin x - c\cos x}{5x^4}\right)$$

(By L.H.Rule)

$= a + b - c = 0$ …(1)

($\because$ Denominator $\to 0$)

$$\Rightarrow\ \ell = \lim_{x\to 0}\frac{-b\sin x - b\sin x - bx\cos x + c\sin x}{20x^3}$$

(By L.H.Rule)

$$= \lim_{x\to 0}\frac{a\sin x - b\sin x - bx\cos x}{20x^3}$$

($\because c - b = a$ by (i))

$$= \lim_{x\to 0}\frac{a\cos x - b\cos x + bx\sin x - b\cos x}{60x^2}$$

(By L.H. Rule)

$\therefore$ For finite limit

Limit of numerator $= a - 2b = 0$ …(2)

$$\therefore\ \ell = \lim_{x\to 0}\frac{bx\sin x}{60x^2}$$

$$= \lim_{x\to 0}\frac{b\sin x}{60x} = 1\quad\text{(Given)}$$

$\Rightarrow b = 60$

$\therefore$ From (2); $a = 120$ and from (1) $c = a + b = 180$

$\therefore$ $a = 120$, $b = 60$, $c = 180$

73. Using L' Hospital rule or otherwise, evaluate limit $\lim_{x\to 0}\frac{3x\,\ell n\left(\frac{\sin x}{x}\right)^2 + x^3}{(x-\sin x)(1-\cos x)}$

Solution: $\ell = \lim_{x\to 0}\frac{6x[\ell n\ \sin x - \ell nx] + x^3}{\left(\frac{x-\sin x}{x^3}\right)x^3\left(\frac{1-\cos x}{x^2}\right)x^2}$

$$\because\left[\begin{array}{l}\lim_{x\to 0}\frac{x-\sin x}{x^3} = \frac{1}{6}\\ \&\lim_{x\to 0}\frac{1-\cos x}{x^2} = \frac{1}{2}\end{array}\right]$$

$$= 12\lim_{x\to 0}\left\{\frac{6x(\ell n\sin x - \ell nx) + x^3}{x^5}\right\}$$

$$= 12\lim_{x\to 0}\left\{\frac{6(\ell n\sin x - \ell nx) + x^2}{x^4}\right\}$$

(Using L' hospital rule)

$$= 12\lim_{x\to 0}\frac{6\left(\cot x - \frac{1}{x}\right) + 2x}{4x^3}$$

$$= 6\lim_{x\to 0}\frac{3(x-\tan x) + x^2\tan x}{x^4\,\frac{\tan x}{x}\,x}\quad\text{(By L.H rule)}$$

$$= 6\lim_{x\to 0}\frac{3(x-\tan x) + x^2\tan x}{x^5}$$

$$= 6\lim_{x\to0}\frac{3\left(1-\sec^2 x\right)+x^2\sec^2 x+2x\tan x}{5x^4}$$

(Using L' Hospital rule)

$$= 6\lim_{x\to0}\frac{-3\tan^2 x+x^2\sec^2 x+2x\tan x+x\tan x-x\tan x}{5x^4}$$

(add and subtract x tan x)

$$= 6\lim_{x\to0}\frac{3\tan x\left(x-\tan x\right)+x^2\sec^2 x-x\tan x}{5x^4}$$

$$= \frac{18}{5}\lim_{x\to0}\frac{\tan x}{x}.\frac{x-\tan x}{x^3}+6\lim_{x\to0}\frac{x^2\sec^2 x-x\tan x+x^2-x^2}{5x^4}$$

$$= -\frac{18}{5}.\frac{1}{3}+6\lim_{x\to0}\frac{x^2\left(\sec^2 x-1\right)+x\left(x-\tan x\right)}{5x^4}$$

$$= -\frac{6}{5}+6\lim_{x\to0}\frac{x^2\tan^2 x+x\left(x-\tan x\right)}{5x^4}$$

$$= -\frac{6}{5}+\frac{6}{5}+\frac{6}{5}\left(\frac{x-\tan x}{x^3}\right)\left(\because \lim_{x\to0}\frac{\tan x-x}{x^3}=\frac{1}{3}\right)$$

$$= \frac{6}{5}\left(-\frac{1}{3}\right)=\frac{-2}{5}$$

Comprehension Type:

A: Consider two functions $f\left(x\right)=\lim_{n\to\infty}\left(\cos\frac{x}{\sqrt{n}}\right)^n$ and $g(x) = -x^{4b}$; where $b = \lim_{x\to\infty}\left(\sqrt{x^2+x+1}-\sqrt{x^2+1}\right)$.

Then

74. $f(x)$ is

(a) e^{-x^2} (b) $e^{\frac{-x^2}{2}}$

(c) e^x (d) $e^{\frac{x^2}{2}}$

75. $g(x)$ is

(a) $-x^2$ (b) x^2

(c) x^4 (d) $-x^4$

76. Number of solutions of $f(x) + g(x) = 0$ is

(a) 2 (b) 4

(c) 0 (d) 1

Ans. **74.** (b) **75.** (b) **76.** (a)

Solution: $f\left(x\right)=\lim_{n\to\infty}\left(\cos\frac{x}{\sqrt{n}}\right)^n = e^{\lim_{n\to\infty}\left(\cos\frac{x}{\sqrt{n}}-1\right).n}$

Substituting, $n=\frac{1}{t^2}$,

we get; $f\left(x\right)=e^{\lim_{t\to0}\left(\frac{\cos tx-1}{t^2}\right)}$

$= e^{\lim_{t\to0}-x^2\left(\frac{1-\cos tx}{t^2x^2}\right)} = e^{\lim_{t\to0}-x^2\left(\frac{2\sin^2(tx/2)}{4(t^2x^2/4)}\right)} = e^{-\frac{1}{2}x^2}$

Now, $g(x) = -x^{4b}$ (Given);

Where $b = \lim_{x\to\infty}\left(\sqrt{x^2+x+1}-\sqrt{x^2+1}\right)$

$$= \lim_{x\to\infty}\left(\frac{x^2+x+1-x^2-1}{\sqrt{x^2+x+1}+\sqrt{x^2+1}}\right)=\frac{1}{2}$$

$\therefore\ g(x) = -x^{4\left(\frac{1}{2}\right)} = -x^2$

$\therefore\ f(x) + g(x) = 0 \Rightarrow f(x) = -g(x)$

$\Rightarrow\ e - x^2/2 = x^2$

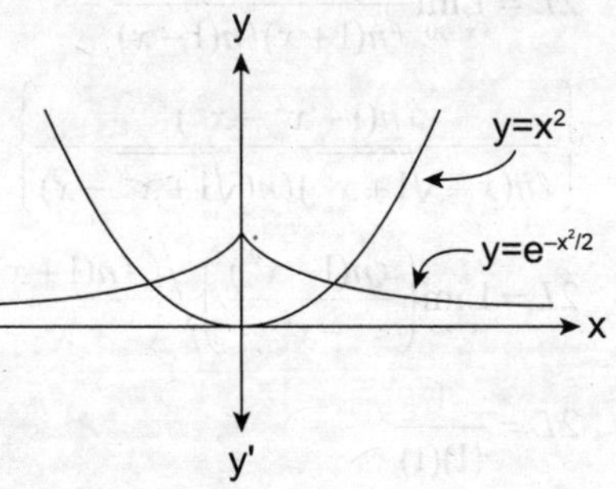

By observation, graphs of $f(x)$ and $-g(x)$ intersect each other at two points.

$\therefore$ Number of solutions is 2

B. Let $f(x) = \frac{\tan^{-1}\left(1-\{x\}\right).\cos^{-1}\left(1-\{x\}\right).\sin^{-1}\left(1-\{x\}\right)}{\sqrt{2\{x\}}\left(1-\{x\}\right)^2}$, $\{x\}$ denotes fractional part of x, then

77. $P = \lim_{x\to0^+} f\left(x\right)$, then which is/are correct?

(a) $\sin\left(\frac{2P}{\pi}\right)=\frac{1}{2}$ (b) $\cos\left(\frac{2P}{\pi}\right)=\frac{1}{\sqrt{2}}$

(c) $\tan\left(\frac{2P}{\pi}\right)=1$ (d) None of these

78. $Q = \lim_{x\to0^-} f\left(x\right)$, then which is/are correct?

(a) $\sin\sqrt{2}Q=0$ (b) $\sin\sqrt{2}Q=1$

(c) $\tan\sqrt{2}Q=1$ (d) $\cos\sqrt{2}Q=0$

79. Which of the following is/are true?

(a) $Q^2 = P$ (b) $P = Q$

(c) $P^2 = Q$ (d) $P{:}Q = Q$

Ans. **77.** (b, c) **78.** (b, d) **79.** (a, d)

77. $f(x)=\dfrac{\tan^{-1}(1-\{x\})\cos^{-1}(1-\{x\}).\sin^{-1}(1-\{x\})}{\sqrt{2\{x\}}(1-\{x\})^2}$

$\therefore \quad P=\lim_{x\to 0^+} f(x)$

$=\lim_{x\to 0^+}\dfrac{\tan^{-1}(1-x)\cos^{-1}(1-x)\sin^{-1}(1-x)}{\sqrt{2x}(1-x)^2}$

$(\because x\to 0^+ \Rightarrow \{x\}=x)$

$=\lim_{x\to 0^+}\dfrac{\tan^{-1}(1-x)}{(1-x)}.\dfrac{\sin^{-1}(1-x)}{(1-x)}\dfrac{\cos^{-1}(1-x)}{\sqrt{2x}}$

$=\dfrac{\pi}{4}.\dfrac{\pi}{2}\times\lim_{x\to 0^+}\dfrac{\cos^{-1}(1-x)}{\sqrt{2}\sqrt{x}}$

$=\dfrac{\pi^2}{8}\times\lim_{\theta\to 0^+}\dfrac{\theta}{\sqrt{2}\sqrt{1-\cos\theta}}$

$\left(\begin{array}{l}\text{Assuming } \cos^{-1}(1-x)=\theta\\ \text{As } x\to 0^+, 1-x\in(0,1)\\ \Rightarrow \theta\in(0,\pi/2)\\ \Rightarrow \sin\theta>0\end{array}\right)$

$=\dfrac{\pi^2}{8\sqrt{2}}\times\lim_{\theta\to 0^+}\dfrac{\theta}{\sqrt{2\sin^2\theta/2}}$

$=\dfrac{\pi^2}{8\sqrt{2}}\lim_{\theta\to 0^+}\dfrac{\theta}{\sqrt{2}\,|\sin(\theta/2)|}$

$=\dfrac{\pi^2}{16}\lim_{\theta\to 0^+}\dfrac{\theta}{\sin\theta/2} \qquad \left(\because \sin\left(\dfrac{\theta}{2}\right)>0\right)$

$=\dfrac{\pi^2}{16}\lim_{\theta\to 0^+}2\left(\dfrac{\theta/2}{\sin\theta/2}\right)$

$=\dfrac{\pi^2}{8}(1)=\dfrac{\pi^2}{8}$

$\Rightarrow \quad P=\dfrac{\pi^2}{8}\Rightarrow\dfrac{2P}{\pi}=\dfrac{\pi}{4}$

$\Rightarrow \quad \cos\left(\dfrac{2P}{\pi}\right)=\dfrac{1}{\sqrt{2}};\tan\left(\dfrac{2P}{\pi}\right)=1$

78. Now $Q=\lim_{x\to 0^-} f(x)$

$=\lim_{x\to 0^-}\dfrac{\tan^{-1}(1-\{x\})\cos^{-1}(1-\{x\})\sin^{-1}(1-\{x\})}{\sqrt{2\{x\}}(1-\{x\})^2}$

$(\because x\to 0^- \Rightarrow \{x\}=1+x)$

$=\lim_{x\to 0^-}\tan^{-1}\dfrac{(1-(1+x))\cos^{-1}(1-(1+x))\sin^{-1}(1-(1+x))}{\sqrt{2(1+x)}(1-(1+x))^2}$

$=\lim_{x\to 0^-}\dfrac{\tan^{-1}(-x)\cos^{-1}(-x)\sin^{-1}(-x)}{\sqrt{2}\sqrt{1+x}(-x)^2}$

$=\lim_{x\to 0^+}\dfrac{(\tan^{-1}x)\cos^{-1}(x)\sin^{-1}x}{\sqrt{2}\sqrt{1-x}\,x^2}$

(Replacing x by $-x$ and limit $x\to 0^+$)

$=\lim_{x\to 0^+}\dfrac{\tan^{-1}x}{x}.\dfrac{\sin^{-1}x}{x}\dfrac{\cos^{-1}x}{\sqrt{2}\sqrt{1-x}}$

$=(1)(1);\ \dfrac{\pi/2}{\sqrt{2}(1)}=\dfrac{\pi}{2\sqrt{2}}\Rightarrow Q=\dfrac{\pi}{2\sqrt{2}}\Rightarrow\sqrt{2}Q=\dfrac{\pi}{2}$

$\sin\sqrt{2}Q=1$ and $\cos\sqrt{2}Q=0$

79. Clearly $P=\dfrac{\pi^2}{8}, Q=\dfrac{\pi}{2\sqrt{2}}$

$\Rightarrow \quad Q^2=\dfrac{\pi^2}{8}=P$

$\therefore \quad Q^2=P$ and $\dfrac{P}{Q}=\dfrac{Q}{1}$

C: If $\lim_{x\to 0}\left[\dfrac{\sin 2x+a\cos x+be^x+ce^{-x}+c\,\ell n(1+x)}{x^3}\right]=L$

(finite real)

80. The value of L is

(a) 0 (b) 1

(c) –1 (d) None of these

81. The value of $a+2b+4c$ equals

(a) –20

(b) 10

(c) 24

(d) None of these

82. The roots of equation $ax^2+bx+c=0$ are

(a) Real and distinct

(b) Real and equal

(c) Imaginary

(d) Real roots having opposite signs

Ans. 81. (c) **81.** (b) **82.** (a, d)

Solution:

$L=\lim_{x\to 0}\dfrac{\sin 2x+a\cos x+be^x+ce^{-x}+c\ell n(1+x)}{x^3}$

$\because$ L is finite and real and denominator $\to 0$

$\Rightarrow \sin 0+a\cos 0+b+c+c\,(0)\to 0$

$\Rightarrow a+b+c=0$ …(1)

$$\therefore\ L = \lim_{x\to 0}\frac{\sin 2x + a\cos x + be^{x} + (-a-b)e^{-x} + (-a-b)\ell n(1+x)}{x^3}$$

$$= \lim_{x\to 0}\frac{\sin 2x + a\left(\cos x - e^{-x} - \ell n(1+x)\right) + b\left(e^{x} - e^{-x} - \ell n(1+x)\right)}{x^3}$$

$$= \lim_{x\to 0}\frac{2\cos 2x + a\left(-\sin x + e^{-x} - \frac{1}{1+x}\right) + b\left(e^{x} + e^{-x} - \frac{1}{1+x}\right)}{3x^2} \qquad \text{(By L.H.rule)}$$

$\Rightarrow 2 + a\,(0) + b\,(1) = 0$ $\qquad\qquad \Rightarrow b = -2$

$$\therefore\ L = \lim_{x\to 0}\frac{2\cos 2x + a\left(-\sin x + e^{-x} - \frac{1}{1+x}\right) - 2\left(e^{x} + e^{-x} - \frac{1}{1+x}\right)}{3x^2}$$

$$= \lim_{x\to 0}\frac{-4\sin 2x + a\left(-\cos x - e^{-x} + \frac{1}{(1+x)^2}\right) - 2\left[e^{x} - e^{-x} + \frac{1}{(1+x)^2}\right]}{6x}$$

$\Rightarrow a(-1 - 1 + 1) - 2\,(1 - 1 + 1) = 0$ as denominator $6x \to 0$.

$\Rightarrow -a - 2 = 0$ $\qquad\qquad \Rightarrow a = -2$

$\therefore$ from (1), $c = +4$

$$\therefore\ L = \lim_{x\to 0}\frac{-4\sin 2x - 2\left(-\cos x - e^{-x} + \frac{1}{(1+x)^2}\right) - 2\left[e^{x} - e^{-x} + \frac{1}{(1+x)^2}\right]}{6x}$$

$$= \lim_{x\to 0}\frac{-8\cos 2x - 2\left[\sin x + e^{-x} - \frac{2}{(1+x)^3}\right] - 2\left[e^{x} + e^{-x} - \frac{2}{(1+x)^3}\right]}{6}$$

$$= \frac{-8 - 2[0+1-2] - 2[1+1-2]}{6} = \frac{-8+2-0}{6} = \frac{-6}{6} = -1$$

Clearly $L = -1$, $a + 2b + 4c$

$= (-2) + 2\,(-2) + 4(4) = 10$

Now, $ax^2 + bx + c = 0$ is equivalent to

$-2x^2 - 2x + 4 = 0;$

Disc $= (-2)^2 - 4\,(-2)\,(+4) = 36$

$\Rightarrow$ The roots are real and distinct.

Also product of roots $= \frac{c}{a} = \frac{4}{-a} = -2 < 0$

$\Rightarrow$ roots are of opposite signs

Column-Matching Type

83. Column-I

(i) $\lim_{x\to\infty}\left(3 - \sqrt[3]{x^3 + x^2 - 1} + \sqrt[3]{x^3 - x^2 + 1}\right)$ equals

(ii) $\lim_{m\to\infty}\lim_{n\to\infty}\sum_{k=1}^{m}\frac{\sqrt[n]{(k-1)^n + k^n}}{m^2}$

(iii) $\lim_{n\to\infty}\left(\frac{n}{n^2 - 4} + \frac{(4)^n(-1)^n}{2^n - 1}\right)^{-1}$ equals

(iv) $\lim_{x\to-\infty}\left\{x + \sqrt{x^2 + 5x\cos\frac{1}{|x|}}\right\}$ equals

Column-II

(a) 7/3

(b) 0

(c) –5/2

(d) $\frac{1}{2}$

Ans. (i) → (a);
(ii) → (d);
(iii) → (b);
(iv) → (c)

Solution:

(i) $\lim_{x\to\infty}\left[3-\left(x^3+x^2-1\right)^{1/3}+\left(x^3-x^2+1\right)^{1/3}\right]$

$= \lim_{x\to\infty}\left[(x^3-x^2+1)^{1/3}-(x^3+x^2-1)^{1/3}+3\right]$

$= \lim_{t\to 0^+}\left[\left(\frac{1}{t^3}-\frac{1}{t^2}+1\right)^{1/3}-\left(\frac{1}{t^3}+\frac{1}{t^2}-1\right)^{1/3}+3\right]$

(Substituting $x=\frac{1}{t}$).

$= \lim_{t\to 0^+}\left[\frac{\left(1-t+t^3\right)^{1/3}}{t}-\frac{\left(1+t-t^3\right)^{1/3}}{t}+3\right]$

$= \lim_{x\to 0^+}\frac{1}{t}\left[3t+\left\{1+\frac{1}{3}\left(t^3-t\right)+\frac{\left(\frac{1}{3}\right)\left(\frac{-2}{3}\right)\left(t^3-t\right)^2}{2!}+...\right\}\right.$

$\left.-\left\{1+\frac{1}{3}\left(t-t^3\right)+\frac{\frac{1}{3}\left(\frac{-2}{3}\right)\left(t-t^3\right)^2}{2!}+....\right\}\right]$

$= \lim_{t\to 0^+}\frac{1}{t}\left[\frac{2}{3}\left(t^3-t\right)+3t+\text{terms containing higher power of } t\right]$

$= \lim_{t\to 0^+}\frac{2}{3}(t^2-1)+3+$ terms containing higher powers of $t = -\frac{2}{3}+3=\frac{7}{3}$

(ii) $\lim_{m\to\infty}\lim_{n\to\infty}\sum_{k=1}^{m}\frac{\sqrt[n]{(k-1)^n+k^n}}{m^2}$

$= \lim_{m\to\infty}\lim_{n\to\infty}\left\{\left[\begin{matrix}1+\sqrt[n]{(1)^n+2^n}+\sqrt[n]{(2)^n+(3)^n}+... \\ ....+\sqrt[n]{(m-1)^n+m^n}\end{matrix}\right]\div m^2\right\}$

$= \lim_{m\to\infty}\lim_{n\to\infty}\left\{\left[\begin{matrix}1+2\sqrt[n]{1+\left(\frac{1}{2}\right)^n}+3\sqrt[n]{1+\left(\frac{2}{3}\right)^n}+... \\ .....+m\sqrt[n]{1+\left(\frac{m-1}{m}\right)^n}\end{matrix}\right]\div m^2\right\}$

$= \lim_{m\to\infty}\left[\frac{1+2+3+...+m}{m^2}\right]$

$= \lim_{m\to\infty}\frac{m(m+1)}{2m^2}=\lim_{m\to\infty}\frac{1}{2}\left[1+\frac{1}{m}\right]=\frac{1}{2}$

(iii) $\lim_{n\to\infty}\left[\frac{n}{n^2-4}+\frac{(4)^n(-1)^n}{(2)^n-1}\right]^{-1}$

$= \lim_{n\to\infty}\left[\frac{1/n}{1-4/n^2}+\frac{(4)^n(-1)^n}{(2)^n-1}\right]^{-1}$

$= \lim_{n\to\infty}\frac{1}{\left(\frac{1/n}{1-4/n^2}+\frac{(4)^n(-1)^n}{(2)^n-1}\right)}$

$= \lim_{n\to\infty}\frac{1}{\left[\frac{(4)^n(-1)^n}{(2)^n-1}\right]}=\lim_{n\to\infty}\frac{1}{\left[\frac{4^n-1+1}{(2^n-1)}\right](-1)^n}$

$= \lim_{n\to\infty}\frac{1}{\left(2^n+1+\frac{1}{2^n-1}\right)(-1)^n}=\frac{1}{\infty+0}=0$

(iv) $\lim_{x\to-\infty}\left\{x+\sqrt{x^2+5x\cos\frac{1}{|x|}}\right\}$

$= \lim_{x\to-\infty}\left\{x+\sqrt{x^2+5x\cos\frac{1}{x}}\right\}$

$\left(\because x\to-\infty\Rightarrow|x|=-x \text{ and } \cos\left(\frac{1}{|x|}\right)=\cos\left(\frac{1}{-x}\right)=\cos\frac{1}{x}\right)$

$= \lim_{x\to-\infty}\left[\frac{x^2-\left(x^2+5x\cos\frac{1}{x}\right)}{x-\sqrt{x^2+5x\cos\frac{1}{x}}}\right]$

$= \lim_{x\to-\infty}\left[\frac{-5x\cos\frac{1}{x}}{x-|x|\sqrt{1+\frac{5}{x}\cos\frac{1}{x}}}\right]$

$= \lim_{x\to-\infty}\left[\frac{-5x\cos\frac{1}{x}}{x+x\sqrt{1+\frac{5}{x}\cos\frac{1}{x}}}\right]=\lim_{x\to-\infty}\left[\frac{-5\cos\frac{1}{x}}{1+\sqrt{1+\frac{5}{x}\cos\frac{1}{x}}}\right]$

$= \frac{-5}{1+1}=-\frac{5}{2}$

84. **Column-I**

(i) $\lim_{x\to\infty}\frac{(1+a^3)+8e^{1/x}}{2+(1-b^3)e^{1/x}}=2$, then (a^3, b^3) lie on line

(ii) If $\lim_{x\to\infty}\sqrt{x^2+x+1}-(ax+b)=0$, then (a, b); $a>0$ lies on the line

(iii) If $\lim_{x\to\infty} \sqrt{x^4+x^2-1}-ax^2+b=0, a>0;$ then (a, b) lies on the line

(iv) If $\lim_{x\to 0} \dfrac{\int_0^x \left(\dfrac{t^2}{\sqrt{b+t}}\right)dt}{ax-\sin x} = 1; (b \neq 0)$, then (a, b) lies on the line

Column-II

(a) $x - y + 3 = 0$

(b) $3x + 4y - 5 = 0$

(c) $x + 6y + 2 = 0$

(d) $x + 2y + 3 = 0$

Ans. (i) → (d); (ii) → (d); (iii) → (c); (iv) → (a)

Solution: (i) $\lim_{x\to\infty} \dfrac{(1+a^3)+8e^{1/x}}{2+(1-b^3)e^{1/x}} = 2$

As $x \to \infty$, $\dfrac{1}{x} \to 0 \Rightarrow e^{1/x} \to e^0 \to 1$

$\Rightarrow \dfrac{(1+a^3)+8}{2+(1-b^3)} = 2$

$\Rightarrow \dfrac{a^3+9}{3-b^3} = 2$

$\Rightarrow a^3 + 9 = 6 - 2b^3$

$\Rightarrow a^3 + 2b^3 + 3 = 0$

$\Rightarrow (a^3, b^3)$ satisfy the line $x + 2y + 3 = 0$

(ii) $\lim_{x\to\infty} \sqrt{x^2+x+1}-(ax+b) = 0$

$\Rightarrow \lim_{x\to\infty} \dfrac{(x^2+x+1)-(ax+b)^2}{\sqrt{x^2+x+1}+(ax+b)} = 0$

$\Rightarrow \lim_{x\to\infty} \dfrac{x^2(1-a^2)+x(1-2ab)+(1-b^2)}{\sqrt{x^2+x+1}+(ax+b)} = 0$

$\Rightarrow a^2 - 1 = 0$

$\Rightarrow a = \pm 1$ but $a > 0$

$\Rightarrow a = 1$

$\Rightarrow \lim_{x\to\infty} \dfrac{x(1-2b)+(1-b^2)}{\sqrt{x^2+x+1}+(x+b)} = 0$

$\Rightarrow \lim_{x\to\infty} \dfrac{(1-2b)+\left(\dfrac{1-b^2}{x}\right)}{\sqrt{1+\dfrac{1}{x}+\dfrac{1}{x^2}}+\left(1+\dfrac{b}{x}\right)} = 0$

$\Rightarrow \dfrac{1-2b}{1+1} = 0 \Rightarrow b = \dfrac{1}{2}$

$\therefore (a,b) \equiv \left(1, \dfrac{1}{2}\right)$ which lies on line $3x + 4y - 5 = 0$

(iii) $\lim_{x\to\infty} \sqrt{x^4+x^2-1}-ax^2+b=0$

$\Rightarrow \lim_{x\to\infty} \dfrac{x^4+x^2-1-(ax^2-b)^2}{\sqrt{x^4+x^2-1}+(ax^2-b)} = 0$

$\Rightarrow \lim_{x\to\infty} \dfrac{x^4(1-a^2)+x^2(1+2ab)+(-1-b^2)}{\sqrt{x^4+x^2-1}+(ax^2-b)} = 0$

$\Rightarrow (1 - a^2) = 0 \Rightarrow a = \pm 1$; but $a > 0 \Rightarrow a = 1$

$\Rightarrow \lim_{x\to\infty} \dfrac{(1+2b)-\left(\dfrac{1+b^2}{x^2}\right)}{\sqrt{1+\dfrac{1}{x^2}-\dfrac{1}{x^4}}+\left(1-\dfrac{b}{x^2}\right)} = 0$

$\Rightarrow \dfrac{1+2b}{2} = 0 \Rightarrow b = -1/2$

$\Rightarrow (a, b) \equiv \left(1, \dfrac{-1}{2}\right)$ which lies on line $x + 6y + 2 = 0$

(iv) $\lim_{x\to 0} \dfrac{\int_0^x \dfrac{t^2}{\sqrt{b+t}}dt}{ax-\sin x} = 1$

$\Rightarrow \lim_{x\to 0} \dfrac{\int_0^x \dfrac{t^2}{\sqrt{b+t}}dt}{ax-\sin x} = 1 \quad \left(\text{limit is of } \dfrac{0}{0} \text{ form}\right)$

$\Rightarrow \lim_{x\to 0} \dfrac{\dfrac{d}{dx}\int_0^x \dfrac{t^2}{\sqrt{b+t}}dt}{(a-\cos x)} = 1$ (By L–Hospital 's rule)

$\Rightarrow \lim_{x\to 0} \dfrac{\dfrac{x^2}{\sqrt{b+x}}(1)-0}{a-\cos x} = 1$ (By Leibinitz's rule)

$\Rightarrow \lim_{x\to 0} \dfrac{x^2}{\sqrt{b+x}\,(a-\cos x)} = 1$

$\Rightarrow \sqrt{b}\,(a-1) = 0$

$\Rightarrow a = 1\ (\because b \neq 0)$

$\Rightarrow \lim_{x\to 0} \dfrac{x^2}{\sqrt{b+x}\,(1-\cos x)} = 1$

$\Rightarrow \lim_{x\to 0} \dfrac{x^2}{\sqrt{b+x}\,(2\sin^2 x/2)} = 1$

$$\Rightarrow \lim_{x\to 0}\frac{4\left(\dfrac{x}{2}\right)^2}{2\sqrt{b+x}\,\sin^2\dfrac{x}{2}}=1$$

$$\Rightarrow \frac{1}{2\sqrt{b}}(4)(1)^2=1$$

$$\Rightarrow \sqrt{b}=2\Rightarrow b=4$$

Thus $a = 1$, $b = 4$

$\therefore$ $(a, b) \equiv (1, 4)$ which satisfy the line $x - y + 3 = 0$

85. **Column-I**

(i) $\lim_{x\to 0}\left(\left[200\dfrac{\tan x}{x}\right]+\left[200\dfrac{\sin x}{x}\right]\right)$ equals

(ii) $\lim_{x\to 0}\left\{100\dfrac{\tan x}{x}\right\}+\left\{100\dfrac{\sin x}{x}\right\}$ equals

(iii) $\lim_{x\to 0}\left(100\left[\dfrac{\sin x}{x}\right]+200\left[\dfrac{x}{\tan^{-1}}\right]\right)$ equals

(iv) $\lim_{x\to 0}\left\{\dfrac{\sin x^{-1}}{x}\right\}+\left[200\dfrac{\tan^{-1}x}{x}\right]$

Column-II

(a) 1

(b) 399

(c) 199

(d) 200

Here [.] and $\{x\}$ are respectively greatest integer function and fractional part functions

Solution: (i) $\dfrac{\tan x}{x}>1$ and $\dfrac{\tan x}{x}\to 1$ for $x\to 0$

$$\Rightarrow \frac{\tan x}{x}=1+h;\ h\to 0^+$$

$$\Rightarrow 200\frac{\tan x}{x}=200+200h;\ h\to 0^+$$

$$\Rightarrow \left[200\frac{\tan}{x}\right]=200$$

Also $\dfrac{\sin x}{x}<1$ and $\dfrac{\sin x}{x}\to 1$ for $x\to 0$

$$\Rightarrow \frac{\sin x}{x}=1-h;\ h\to 0^+$$

$$\Rightarrow 200\left(\frac{\sin x}{x}\right)=200-200h;\ h\to 0^+$$

$$\Rightarrow \left[200\frac{\sin x}{x}\right]=199$$

$$\therefore\ \lim_{x\to 0}\left(\left[200\frac{\tan x}{x}\right]+\left[200\frac{\sin x}{x}\right]\right)=399$$

(ii) $100\dfrac{\tan x}{x}=100\ (1+h)=100+100h;\ h\to 0^+$

$$\therefore\ \left\{100\frac{\tan x}{x}\right\}=100\ \ h\to 0 \text{ as } h\to 0^+$$

Also $\left\{100\dfrac{\sin x}{x}\right\}=\{100(1-h)\}=\{100-100h\}$

$=\{99+(1-100h)\}=1-100h\to 1 \text{ as } h\to 0^+$

$$\therefore\ \lim_{x\to 0}\left\{100\frac{\tan x}{x}\right\}+\left\{100\frac{\sin x}{x}\right\}=0+1=1$$

(iii) $\dfrac{\sin x}{x}=1-h;\ h\to 0^+ \text{ as } x\to 0^+$

$$\Rightarrow \left[\frac{\sin x}{x}\right]=[1-h]=0 \text{ and } \frac{x}{\tan^{-1}x}>1 \text{ for } x\to 0$$

$$\Rightarrow \frac{x}{\tan^{-1}x}=1+h;\ h\to 0^+$$

$$\Rightarrow \left[\frac{x}{\tan^{-1}x}\right]=1$$

$$\therefore\ \lim_{x\to 0}\left(100\left[\frac{\sin x}{x}\right]+200\left[\frac{x}{\tan^{-1}x}\right]\right)=0+200=200$$

(iv) As $x\to 0$, $\dfrac{\sin^{-1}x}{x}>1$ and $\dfrac{\sin^{-1}x}{x}\to 1$ as $x\to 0$

$$\Rightarrow \frac{\sin^{-1}x}{x}=1+h;\ h\to 0^+$$

$$\therefore\ \left\{\frac{\sin^{-1}x}{x}\right\}=h\to 0 \text{ as } h\to 0^+$$

Also $\dfrac{\tan^{-1}x}{x}<1$ and $\dfrac{\tan^{-1}x}{x}\to 1$ as $x\to 0$

$$\Rightarrow 200\frac{\tan^{-1}x}{x}=200(1-h);\ h\to 0^+$$

$$\Rightarrow \left[200\frac{\tan^{-1}x}{x}\right]=[200-200h]=199$$

$$\therefore\ \lim_{x\to 0}\left\{\frac{\sin^{-1}x}{x}\right\}+\left[200\frac{\tan^{-1}x}{x}\right]=0+199=199$$

TUTORIAL EXERCISE

SECTION–III

ONLY ONE CORRECT ANSWER

1. For $\lim_{x\to1}\frac{\sin[x]}{[x]}$

(a) R.H.L does not exist and L.H.L = sin1
(b) L.H.L= 0; R.H.L = sin1
(c) L.H.L does not exist and R.H.L = sin1
(d) None of these

2. $\lim_{n\to\infty}\frac{1-2+3-4+....-2n}{\sqrt{n^2+1}+\sqrt{4n^2-1}}$ equals

(a) –1/5 (b) 1/3
(c) 1 (d) None of these

3. The value of $\lim_{x\to a}\left(\frac{\cos x-\cos a}{\cot x-\cot a}\right)$ is

(a) (1/2) $\sin^3 a$ (b) (1/2) $\operatorname{cosec}^3 a$
(c) $\sin^3 a$ (d) $\operatorname{cosec}^3 a$

4. The value of k; for which $\lim_{x\to0}\frac{(e^x-1)^4}{\sin(x^2/k^2).\ell n\{1+(x^2/2)\}}=8$ is equal to

(a) 1 (b) –1
(c) 2 (d) 4

5. $\lim_{h\to0}\frac{\left(e^{\sin h}-1\right).\sin h}{\left(\tan^{-1}(\sin h)\right)^2}$ is

(a) 1 (b) 1/2
(c) 2 (d) None of these

6. $\lim_{x\to\infty}(1-a^4)^x\sin\frac{b}{(1-a^4)^x}$, $(a\in(-1,1)\sim\{0\}, b\in\mathbb{R})$ is

(a) 0 (b) 1
(c) 2 (d) None of these

7. $\lim_{x\to\infty}\frac{(x+1)^{10}+(x+2)^{10}+....+(x+100)^{10}}{x^{10}+10^{10}}$ is equal to

(a) 50 (b) 100
(c) 70 (d) 80

8. $\lim_{x\to1}\left(\frac{x+x^2.....+x^n-n}{x-1}\right)$ is equal to

(a) $\frac{(n+1)}{2}$ (b) $\frac{(n-1)}{2}$
(c) $\frac{n(n+1)}{2}$ (d) None of these

9. $\lim_{x\to1}\frac{x^{p+1}-(p+1)x+p}{(x-1)^2}$ is equal to

(a) $\frac{p(p-1)}{2}$ (b) $\frac{p(p+1)}{2}$
(c) $\frac{(p+1)}{2}$ (d) None of these

10. The value of $\lim_{x\to\infty}\left[\frac{2\sqrt{x}+3.\sqrt[3]{x}+5.\sqrt[5]{x}}{\sqrt{3x-2}+\sqrt[3]{2x-3}}\right]$ is

(a) 1/√3 (b) 2/√3
(c) 8 (d) None of these

11. $\lim_{x\to0}(\cos x+a\sin bx)^{1/x}$ is

(a) e^{ab} (b) $a\,e^b$
(c) be^a (d) ab

12. What is the value of the $\left[\left\{4\sum_{r=1}^{n}(r+1)(r+2)(r+3)\right\}^{\frac{1}{4}}-n\right]$ is

(a) 0 (b) Does not exist
(c) 2/5 (d) 5/2

13. If α is a root of $x^2+ax+1=0$, then $\lim_{x\to1/\alpha}\frac{\sin(x^2+ax+1)}{(\alpha x-1)}$ is equal to

(a) $2a\alpha$ (b) $a\alpha^2$
(c) $\frac{1-\alpha^2}{\alpha^2}$ (d) does not exist

14. If $f(x)$ is a polynomial satisfying $2+f(x)f(y)=f(x)+f(y)+f(xy)$ for all real x and y and $f(2)=5$. Then $\lim_{x\to2}f(x)$ is

(a) 5 (b) 25
(c) 4 (d) None of these

15. $\lim_{h\to 0}\dfrac{2\left[\sqrt{3}\sin\left(\dfrac{\pi}{6}+h\right)-\cos\left(\dfrac{\pi}{6}+h\right)\right]}{\sqrt{3}h(\sqrt{3}\cos h-\sin h)}$ is equal to

(a) $-\dfrac{2}{3}$ (b) $-\dfrac{3}{4}$
(c) $-2\sqrt{3}$ (d) $\dfrac{4}{3}$

16. If $\underset{x\to\infty}{\text{Lt}}(a^x+e^x)^{1/x}=a;\ (a>0)$ then

(a) $a\in(1,\infty)$ (b) $a\in(e,\infty)$
(c) $a\in(1,e)$ (d) None of these

17. $\lim_{n\to\infty}(e.a^2.e^3.a^4.....e^{n-1}a^n)^{\frac{1}{n^2+1}}$; when n is even, equals

(a) $e^{1/4}a^{1/2}$ (b) $e^{1/2}a^{1/2}$
(c) $e^{1/4}a^{1/4}$ (d) $e^{1/2}a^{1/4}$

18. $\lim_{x\to\frac{\pi}{2}}\left\{\dfrac{\sqrt[3]{\sin^4 x+\cos^2 x+\sin^2 3x}}{\sin^4 x-\sin^4 2x-\sin^2 3x}-\dfrac{\sqrt[3]{\cos^2 x+\sin^4 2x+2\sin^2 3x}}{\sin^4 x-\sin^4 2x-\sin^2 3x}\right\}$ is equal to

(a) 2 (b) 0
(c) $\dfrac{1}{2\sqrt{2}}$ (d) $\dfrac{1}{3.2^{2/3}}$

19. If $f(n+1)=\dfrac{1}{2}\left\{f(n)+\dfrac{9}{f(n)}\right\}, n\in N$ and $f(n)>0$ for all $n\in\mathbb{N}$, then the $\lim_{n\to\infty}f(n)$ is equal to

(a) 3 (b) –3
(c) 1/12 (d) None of these

20. If $\lim_{x\to 0}\dfrac{x^n\sin^n x}{x^n-\sin^n x}$ is zero, then the least positive integral value of n is

(a) 1 (b) 2
(c) 3 (d) 4

21. $\underset{x\to 0}{\text{Lt}}\dfrac{\sin x^4-x^4\cos x^4+x^{20}}{x^4(e^{2x^4}-1-2x^4)}$ is equal to

(a) 0 (b) 1/6
(c) 1/12 (d) does not exist

22. $\lim_{x\to 0}\left[m\dfrac{\sin x}{x}\right]$, where $m\in\mathbb{Z}$ and [.] denotes greatest integer function, is

(a) m if $m\le 0$ (b) $m-1$ if $m>0$
(c) $m-1$ if $m<0$ (d) m if $m>0$

23. The value of $\lim_{x\to 0}\left[\dfrac{x^2}{\sin x\tan x}\right]$, (where [.] denotes the greatest integer function.) is equal to

(a) 1 (b) 0
(c) Does not exist (d) None of these

24. Let $f(x)=\dfrac{ax+b}{cx+d},\ x\ne\dfrac{-d}{c}$, $g(x)=f(f(x))$. If $d=-a$, then the value of $\lim_{x\to 0}\dfrac{e^{\tan x}-e^{g(x)}}{\tan x-g(x)}$ is equal to

(a) 0 (b) 1
(c) –1 (d) does not exist

25. The value of limit; $\lim_{x\to -1}\dfrac{\int_{-1}^{x}(t^2+2t)(t^2-1)}{x^3+1}$ is equal to.

(a) 1 (b) 0
(c) -1 (d) None of these

26. The value of

$$\lim_{x\to 1}\dfrac{x-\ell nx+\left\{\int_1^x\left(\dfrac{1}{z}-2-2\cos(4z)\right)dz\right\}-1}{x-1}$$ is equal to.

(a) 2 cos 4 (b) 1 – 2 cos 4
(c) –1 + 2 cos 4 (d) –1 – 2 cos 4

27. The value of $\lim_{x\to 0}\sqrt{\dfrac{x\sin x}{x+\sin^2 x}}$ is equal to

(a) 1 (b) 0
(c) ∞ (d) None of these

28. $\lim_{x\to\infty}\dfrac{\sqrt{x^2+1}-\sqrt[3]{x^3-1}}{\sqrt[4]{x^4+1}-\sqrt[5]{x^4+1}}$ equals

(a) 1 (b) 0
(c) –1 (d) None of these

29. The $\lim_{x\to\infty}\left(\dfrac{3x^2+1}{4x^2-1}\right)^{\frac{x^3}{1+x}}$ is

(a) 0 (b) 1
(c) $e^{7/2}$ (d) None of these

30. $\lim_{n\to\infty}\left(1+\sin\frac{a}{n}\right)^n$ is equal to

(a) $e^{a/2}$ (b) e^a
(c) e (d) e^{2a}

31. $\lim_{x\to 2}\frac{\sin(e^{x-2}-1)}{\ln(x-1)}$ is equal to

(a) –2 (b) –1
(c) 0 (d) 1

32. If $[x]$ denotes the greatest integer less than or equal to x, then the value of $\lim_{x\to 1}(1-x+[x-1]+[1-x])$ is

(a) 0 (b) 1
(c) –1 (d) None of these

33. The value of $\lim_{x\to 1}(1-x)\tan\left(\frac{\pi}{2}(2-x)\right)$ is

(a) $-2/\pi$ (b) $-\pi/2$
(c) 1 (d) 0

34. If $f(x)=\left[\frac{x^2+5x+3}{x^2+x+2}\right]$, then $\lim_{x\to 0}f(x)$ is; (where [ ] is greatest integer function)

(a) 1 (b) 0
(c) e (d) None of these

35. $\lim_{x\to 0}\left(\frac{\log(1-x^2)}{\log\cos x}\right)$; ($n \in \mathbb{N}$) is equal to

(a) 2 (b) 0
(c) 1 (d) –2

36. $\lim_{x\to 0}\frac{x\sqrt{y^2-(y-x)^2}}{(\sqrt{8xy-4x^2}+\sqrt{8xy})^3}$ is equal to

(a) 1/4 (b) 1/2
(c) $1/(2\sqrt{2})$ (d) None of these

37. Let r^{th} term of a series be given by $t_r=\frac{r}{1-3r^2+r^4}$.

Then $\lim_{n\to\infty}\sum_{r=1}^{n}t_r$ is

(a) 3/2 (b) 1/2
(c) –1/2 (d) –3/2

38. Let $f(x)=\lim_{n\to\infty}\frac{1}{((3/\pi)\tan^{-1}2x)^{2n}+5}$. Then the set of values of x for which $f(x) = 0$ is

(a) $|2x|>\sqrt{3}$ (b) $|2x|<\sqrt{3}$
(c) $|2x|\geq\sqrt{3}$ (d) $|2x|\leq\sqrt{3}$

39. Let $f(x)$ be defined for all $x\in\mathbb{R}$ such that $\lim_{x\to 0}\left[f(x)+\ell n\left(1-\frac{1}{e^{f(x)}}\right)-\ell n(f(x))\right]=0$; then $f(0)$ is equal to

(a) 0 (b) 1
(c) 2 (d) 3

40. The value of $\lim_{x\to 0}\frac{\sin|\sec^2 x|}{1+[\cos x]}$; where [.] denotes greatest integer function is

(a) –sin 1 (b) sin2
(c) sin 1 (d) ± sin1

41. $\lim_{x\to\infty}\left|1-a^4\right|^x\sin\frac{b}{\left|1-a^4\right|^x}$ ($a, b \in \mathbb{R}$) and $a^2 \neq 1$, 0 is

(a) 0 (b) 1
(c) 2 (d) None of these

42. The value of $\lim_{x\to\infty}\left(\frac{1+x}{2+x}\right)^{\frac{1-\sqrt{x}}{1-x}}$ is

(a) 1/2 (b) $\sqrt{2/3}$
(c) 1 (d) None of these

43. The value of the $\lim_{x\to 0}\left(\sin\frac{x}{m}+\cos\frac{3x}{m}\right)^{2m/x}$ is

(a) 1 (b) e^2
(c) e^{6m} (d) $\ell n\ 6m$

44. The value of the $\lim_{x\to 0}\left\{\sin^2\left(\frac{\pi}{2-ax}\right)\right\}^{\sec^2\frac{\pi}{2-bx}}$ is equal to

(a) e^{a^2/b^2} (b) e^{-a^2/b^2}
(c) 1 (d) 0

45. The value of $\lim_{n\to\infty}\{(1.5)^n+([(1+0.0001])^n\}^{1/n}$ is where [ ] = G.I.F.

(a) 1.5 (b) 2
(c) 3 (d) None of these

46. The value of the limit $\lim_{x\to 0}\frac{\sqrt[m]{1+ax}\sqrt[n]{1+bx}-1}{x}$ ($m, n \in \mathbb{N}$) is

(a) $a/m + b/n$ (b) $a/m - b/n$
(c) ab/mn (d) None of these

47. The value of the limit $\lim_{x\to\infty}n^2\left(\sqrt[n]{a}-\sqrt[n+1]{a}\right)$ ($a > 0$) is

(a) $\ln a$ (b) e^a
(c) e^{-a} (d) None of these

SECTION–IV

MORE THAN ONE CORRECT ANSWER

1. Which of the following limits tend to unity?

(a) $\lim\limits_{t\to 0}\dfrac{\sin(\tan t)}{\sin t}$ (b) $\lim\limits_{x\to \pi/2}\dfrac{\sin(\cos x)}{\cos x}$

(c) $\lim\limits_{x\to 0}\dfrac{\sqrt{1+x}-\sqrt{1-x}}{x}$ (d) $\lim\limits_{x\to 0}\dfrac{\sqrt{x^2}}{x}$

2. If $f(x)=\begin{cases}2x-3 & ;-3\le x<0\\ 4-x^2 & ;0\le x\le 5\end{cases}$ and

$g(x)=\begin{cases}2x+3 & ;-10\le x<0\\ -1-x & ;0\le x\le 3\end{cases}$; then

(a) $\lim\limits_{x\to 0+} f(g(x))=-5$ (b) $\lim\limits_{x\to 0-} f(g(x))=-5$

(c) $\lim\limits_{x\to 0} f(g(x))=-5$ (d) $\lim\limits_{x\to 0} f(g(x))$ exists

3. Which of the following is/are true?

(a) If $\lim\limits_{x\to a}\{f(x)+g(x)\}$ exists, then both $\lim\limits_{x\to a} f(x)$ and $\lim\limits_{x\to a} g(x)$ exist

(b) If $\lim\limits_{x\to a} f(x)$ and $\lim\limits_{x\to a} g(x)$ exists, then $\lim\limits_{x\to a}\{f(x)+g(x)\}$ exists

(c) If $\lim\limits_{x\to a}\{f(x)\,g(x)\}$ exists, then both $\lim\limits_{x\to a} f(x)$ and $\lim\limits_{x\to a} g(x)$ exist

(d) If $\lim\limits_{x\to a} f(x)$ and $\lim\limits_{x\to a} g(x)$ exists, then $\lim\limits_{x\to a} f(x)\,g(x)$ exists

4. $\lim\limits_{n\to\infty}\cos^{2n}x$ is equal to;

(a) 0 if $x=m\pi$; $m\in\mathbb{Q}$ (b) 1 if $x=m\pi$; $m\in\mathbb{Q}$

(c) 1 if $x\ne m\pi$; $m\in\mathbb{Q}$ (d) 0 if $x\ne m\pi$; $m\in\mathbb{Q}$

5. $\lim\limits_{\to\infty}\tan^{2n}x$ is equal to;

(a) 1 if $x=2n\pi+\pi/4$

(b) 1 if $x=n\pi+\pi/4$

(c) 0 if $n\pi-\pi/4<x<n\pi+\pi/4$

(d) 0 if $x\ne n\pi+\pi/4$

6. If $a<0$, $b<0$, then $\lim\limits_{x\to 0+}\dfrac{\sqrt{1-\cos 2ax}}{\sin bx}$ equal to

(a) $\dfrac{\sqrt{2}a}{b}$ (b) $\dfrac{-\sqrt{2}a}{b}$

(c) $\dfrac{-\sqrt{2}|a|}{|b|}$ (d) $\dfrac{\sqrt{2}|a|}{|b|}$

7. If $f(x)=\left(\dfrac{|x|}{|x|+2}\right)^{-x}$, then

(a) $\lim\limits_{x\to-\infty} f(x)=0$ (b) $\lim\limits_{x\to 0} f(x)=1$

(c) $\lim\limits_{x\to\infty} f(x)=e^2$ (d) $\lim\limits_{x\to-\infty} f(x)=e^{-2}$

8. If $\lim\limits_{x\to\infty}\sqrt{x^4+ax^3+3x^2+bx+2}-\sqrt{x^4+2x^3-cx^2+3x-d}=4$, then

(a) $a=2$ (b) b is any real number

(c) $c=5$ (d) $d\ne 0$

9. If $f(x)=\dfrac{(1+x)^{1/x}-e}{x}$, then

(a) $\lim\limits_{x\to 0} f(x)<-1$ (b) $\lim\limits_{x\to\infty} f(x)=e/2$

(c) $\lim\limits_{x\to 0} f(x)=-e/2$ (d) $\lim\limits_{x\to 0} f(x)>1$

10. If $\lim\limits_{x\to 0}\left(\dfrac{a^x+b^x+c^x}{3}\right)^{k/x}$ $(a, b, c, k>0)$

(a) equals 1 if $k=1$

(b) equals abc if $k=3$

(c) equals abc if $k=1$

(d) equals $(a^2b^2c^2)^{1/3}$ if $k=2$

SECTION–V

ASSERTION AND REASON TYPE

The questions given below consist of an assertion (A) and the reason (R). Use the following key to choose the appropriate answer.

(a) If both assertion and reason are correct and reason is the correct explanation of the assertion.

(b) If both assertion and reason are correct but reason is not correct explanation of the assertion.

(c) If assertion is correct, but reason is incorrect.

(d) If assertion is incorrect, but reason is correct.

Now consider the following statements:

1. A: $\lim\limits_{x\to 0}\frac{\sqrt{1-\cos 2x}}{x}$ does not exist

R: $|\sin x| = \begin{cases} \sin x, 0 < x \le \frac{\pi}{2} \\ -\sin x, -\frac{\pi}{2} \le x < 0 \end{cases}$

2. A: $\text{Lim}_{x\to 0}\frac{[\sin x]}{\tan x} = 0$, where [] = Greatest integer function

R: If $0 \le f(x) < 1$ and $g(x)$ is such that $\text{Lim}_{x\to a^+} g(x) = 0$, then $\text{Lim}_{x\to a^+}\frac{[f(x)]}{g(x)} = 0$

3. A: $\text{Lim}_{x\to 0}\frac{x-\sin x}{x^3} = \text{Lim}_{x\to 0}\left(\frac{1}{x^2} - \frac{\sin x}{x}\cdot\frac{1}{x^2}\right)$

$= \text{Lim}_{x\to 0}\left(\frac{1}{x^2} - \frac{1}{x^2}\right) = 0$

R; $\text{Lim}_{x\to 0}\frac{\sin x}{x} = 1$

4. A: $\text{Lim}_{x\to\infty}\frac{2x^4+3x^3+7x}{3x^4+2x^2+3x} = \frac{2}{3}$

R: If $P(x)$ and $Q(x)$ are two polynomials with rational coefficients, then

$$\text{Lim}_{x\to\infty}\frac{P(x)}{Q(x)} = \frac{\text{leading coefficient of } P(x)}{\text{leading coefficient of } Q(x)}$$

5. A: $\lim\limits_{x\to 0}\left[\frac{\sin x}{x}\right] \ne \left[\lim\limits_{x\to 0}\frac{\sin x}{x}\right]$; where [.] respect greatest integer function

R: $\lim\limits_{x\to 0} h(g(x)) = h\left(\lim\limits_{x\to\infty} g(x)\right)$, if $h(x)$ = is continuous at $x = \lim\limits_{x\to\infty} g(x)$

6. A: $\lim\limits_{x\to 0}\frac{\frac{\sqrt{1-\cos 2x}}{2}}{x}$ does not exist.

R; $\lim\limits_{x\to 0}\frac{\sin x}{x} = 1$

7. A: $\lim\limits_{x\to 0}\left(\tan\left(\frac{\pi}{4}+x\right)\right)^{\frac{1}{x}} = e^2$

R: $\lim\limits_{x\to a}(1+f(x))^{g(x)} = e^{\lim\limits_{x\to a} f(x).g(x)}$. If $\lim\limits_{x\to a} f(x) = 0$ and $\lim\limits_{x\to a} g(x) = \infty$

SECTION–VI

COMPREHESION TYPE QUESTION

A: Consider $f(x) = \frac{\sin x + ae^x + be^{-x} + c\ell n(1+x)}{x^3}$, where a, b, c are real numbers

1. If $\lim\limits_{x\to 0^+} f(x)$ is finite, then value of $a + b + c$ is

(a) 0 (b) 1
(c) 2 (d) –2

2. If $\lim\limits_{x\to 0^+} f(x) = \ell$ (finite), then the value of ℓ is

(a) –2 (b) $-\frac{1}{2}$
(c) –1 (d) $-\frac{1}{3}$

B: If $\lim\limits_{x\to 0}\frac{axe^x - b\log(1+x) + cxe^{-x}}{x^2\sin x} = 2$, then answer the following questions.

3. Which one is/are correct?

(a) $a = 3$ (b) $b = 12$
(c) $c = 10$ (d) $b = 4$

4. Roots of equation $ax^2 + bx + c = 0$ are

(a) Real and unequal (b) Imaginary
(c) Rational (d) Irrational

5. Domain of $f(x) = \sqrt{\frac{ax^2 - b}{c}}$ is

(a) [–2, 2] (b) $(-\infty, -2] \cup [2, \infty)$
(c) [–3. 3] (d) None of these

C: Let $\lim_{n\to\infty}\left[\frac{2}{\pi}(1+n)\cos^{-1}\left(\frac{1}{n}\right)-n\right]=\lim_{n\to\infty} n\left(f\left(\frac{1}{n}\right)\right)$,

then

6. $f'(0)$ equals

(a) $\frac{\pi-1}{\pi}$

(b) $\frac{\pi-2}{\pi}$

(c) $\pi-3$

(d) None of these

7. $\lim_{x\to0} f(x)$ equals

(a) 1 (b) 2

(c) 0 (d) None of these

8. $\left|\lim_{x\to\frac{1}{2}} f(x-1)\right|$ equals

(a) $\frac{1}{2}$ (b) $\frac{1}{\sqrt{2}}$

(c) $\frac{1}{3}$ (d) None of these

SECTION–VII

COLUMN-MATCHING PROBLEMS

1. **Column-I:** $\lim_{x\to0} f(x) =$; where

(i) $f(x)=\frac{\tan\left[e^2\right]x^2-\tan\left[-e^2\right]x^2}{\sin^2 x}$;

where $[x]$ is the greatest integer function

(ii) $f(x)=\frac{\left[(5/2)+\tan x+\tan^2 x\right]-[5/2]}{\tan x}$

(iii) $f(x)=\frac{\sqrt[3]{1+x^2}-\sqrt[4]{1-2x}}{x+x^2}$

(iv) $f(x)=\frac{\sqrt{2}-\sqrt{1+\cos x}}{\sin^2 x}$

Column-II

(a) $\sqrt{2}/8$

(b) 15

(c) 0

(d) 1/2

2. Let $\phi(x)=\frac{a_0x^m+a_1x^{m+1}+\ldots+a_kx^{m+k}}{b_0x^n+b_1x^{n+1}+\ldots+b_\ell x^{n+\ell}}$; where $a_0\neq0$, $b_0\neq0$, then $\lim_{x\to0}\phi(x)$ is equal

Column-I

(i) $m>n$

(ii) $m=n$

(iii) $m<n$ and $n-m$ is even, $a_0/b_0>0$

(iv) $m<n$ and $n-m$ is even $a_0/b_0<0$

Column-II

(a) ∞

(b) $-\infty$

(c) a_0/b_0

(d) 0

3. **Column-I**

(i) $\lim_{x\to0}\frac{\sin 2x+\text{arc}\sin^2 x-\text{arc}\tan^2 x}{3x}$ equals

(ii) $\lim_{x\to0}\frac{(\sin x-\tan x)^2+\left(1-\cos^2 x\right)^4+x^5}{7\tan^7 x+\sin^6 x+2\sin^5 x}$ equals

(iii) $\lim_{x\to0}\frac{\sin\sqrt[3]{x}\,\ell n(1+3x)}{\left(arc\tan\sqrt{x}\right)^2\left(e^{5\sqrt[3]{x}}-1\right)}$ equals

(iv) $\lim_{x\to0}\frac{1-\cos x+2\sin x-\sin^3 x-x^2+3x^4}{\tan^3 x-6\sin^2 x+x-5x^3}$

Column-II

(a) 1/2

(b) 2/3

(c) 2

(d) 3/5

SECTION–VIII

INTEGER TYPE

1. The value

$\lim_{x\to\pi/2} \tan^2 x\left(\sqrt{2\sin^2 x+3\sin x+4}-\sqrt{\sin^2 x+6\sin x+2}\right)$

$=\frac{1}{p}$, then evaluate $\sqrt{p-3}$

2. If $\lim_{x\to\infty}\frac{x^3\sin\frac{1}{x}+x+1}{x^2+x+1} = \ell$, then evaluate $\sqrt{\ell\sqrt{\ell\sqrt{\ell........\infty}}}$

3. $\lim_{n\to\infty}\frac{-3n+(-1)^n}{4n-(-1)^n}=\frac{r}{t}$ (lowest form), then evaluate $\sqrt{r^2+t^2}$

4. If $\lim_{x\to\infty} x - x^2\,\ell n\left(1+\frac{1}{x}\right) = \ell$, then evaluate $(25)^\ell$

5. If $\lim_{x\to0^+}\left(1+\tan^2\sqrt{x}\right)^{5/x}$ = p, then evaluate $\frac{(p)^{1/5}}{e}$

6. If $\ell = \lim_{x\to0}\frac{x(1+a\cos x)-b\sin x}{x^3}=\lim_{x\to0}\frac{1+a\cos x}{x^2}$,

then, evaluate $a + b + 4\ell$

7. If $\lim_{x\to1}\left(1+ax+bx^2\right)^{\frac{c}{x-1}}=e^3$, then find $a^2 - b^2 + 2bc$

8. If $\lim_{n\to\infty}\frac{\sqrt{n^3-2n^2+1}+\sqrt[3]{n^4+1}}{\sqrt[4]{n^6+6n^5+2}-\sqrt[5]{n^7+3n^3+1}}$ = k, then evaluate $(k)^{2013}$

9. If $\lim_{x\to2}\frac{(x+6)^{1/3}-2}{2-x}=\frac{p}{q}$ (in lowest form), then evaluate $\sqrt{|q|+4|p|}$

10. If $\lim_{x\to1}\frac{\sqrt{5-x}-2}{\sqrt{2-x}-1}=\frac{p}{q}$ (lowest form), then evaluate $p+q$

11. If $\lim_{x\to0}\frac{\ln(2+x)+\ln 0.5}{x}=\frac{p}{q}$, gcd (p, q) = 1, then evaluate $(16)^{p/q}$

12. If $\lim_{x\to0}\frac{e^{\tan x}-e^x}{\tan x - x}=\ell$, then evaluate $(\ell)^{2016}$

13. If $\lim_{x\to\infty}\left(\sqrt{(x+a)(x+b)}-x\right)=f(a,b)$, then evaluate $f(9,7)$

14. If $\lim_{n\to\infty}\frac{(n+2)!+(n+1)!}{(n+3)!}, n\in\mathbb{N}$ = ℓ, then evaluate $(2016)^\ell$

15. If $\lim_{x\to0}\frac{((a-n)nx-\tan x)\sin nx}{x^2}$ = 0, where n is a non-zero real number, then $a = f(n)$, then evaluate f(1)

16. $\lim_{x\to\frac{\pi}{2}}\frac{\left[1-\tan\left(\frac{x}{2}\right)\right][1-\sin x]}{\left[1+\tan\left(\frac{x}{2}\right)\right][\pi-2x]^3}=\frac{1}{p}$, then evaluate $(p)^{1/5}$

17. If $\lim_{x\to0}\frac{\ell n(3+x)-\ell n(3-x)}{x}=k$ (lowest from), then evaluate 6 k.

18. $\lim_{x\to\infty}\frac{1+2^4+3^4+....+n^4}{n^5}-\lim_{n\to\infty}\frac{1+2^3+3^3+....+n^3}{n^5}$

$=\frac{p}{q}$ (in lowest from), then evaluate $(3125)^{p/q}$

19. If $\lim_{x\to0}\frac{x\tan 2x-2x\tan x}{(1-\cos 2x)^2}=\ell$, then evaluate $(9)^\ell$,

Answer Keys

SECTION–III

1. (c)	**2.** (a)	**3.** (c)	**4.** (c)	**5.** (a)	**6.** (a)	**7.** (b)	**8.** (c)	**9.** (b)	**10.** (b)
11. (a)	**12.** (d)	**13.** (c)	**14.** (a)	**15.** (d)	**16.** (b)	**17.** (c)	**18.** (d)	**19.** (a)	**20.** (b)
21. (b)	**22.** (a, b)	**23.** (b)	**24.** (b)	**25.** (b)	**26.** (d)	**27.** (b)	**28.** (b)	**29.** (a)	**30.** (b)
31. (d)	**32.** (c)	**33.** (a)	**34.** (a)	**35.** (a)	**36.** (d)	**37.** (c)	**38.** (a)	**39.** (a)	**40.** (c)
41. (d)	**42.** (c)	**43.** (b)	**44.** (b)	**45.** (a)	**46.** (a)	**47.** (a)			

SECTION–IV

1. (a,b,c)	**2.** (a,b,c,d)	**3.** (b,d)	**4.** (b,d)	**5.** (a,b,c)	**6.** (b,c)	**7.** (b,c,d)	**8.** (a,b,c)	**9.** (a,c)
10. (b,d)								

SECTION–V

1. (a)	**2.** (d)	**3.** (d)	**4.** (c)	**5.** (a)	**6.** (b)	**7.** (a)

SECTION–VI

1. (a)	**2.** (d)	**3.** (a,b)	**4.** (a,c)	**5.** (b)	**6.** (b)	**7.** (c)	**8.** (c)

SECTION–VII

1. (i) → (b) (ii) → (c) (iii) → (d) (iv) → (a)
2. (i) → (d) (ii) → (c) (iii) → (a) (iv) → (b)
3. (i) → (b) (ii) → (a) (iii) → (d) (iv) → (c)

SECTION–VIII

1. 3	**2.** 1	**3.** 5	**4.** 5	**5.** 1	**6.** 1	**7.** 6	**8.** 1	**9.** 4	**10.** 3
11. 4	**12.** 1	**13.** 8	**14.** 1	**15.** 2	**16.** 2	**17.** 4	**18.** 5	**19.** 3	

HINTS AND SOLUTIONS

TEXTUAL EXERCISE-1: (SUBJECTIVE)

1. (i) $\lim_{x\to 5^+}[x]$

This limit can be expressed as: $\lim_{h\to 0^+}[5+h]$

Clearly, $5 < 5 + h < 6$

$\Rightarrow [5 + h] = 5$

$\Rightarrow \lim_{h\to 0^+}[5+h] = 5$

(ii) $\lim_{x\to 0^-}\frac{[x]}{|x|} = \lim_{h\to 0^+}\frac{[0-h]}{|0-h|}$

Clearly, $0 < h < 1$

$\Rightarrow \lim_{h\to 0^+}\frac{[0-h]}{|0-h|} = \lim_{h\to 0^+}\frac{-1}{h}$

$\Rightarrow \lim_{x\to 0^-}\frac{[x]}{|x|} = -\infty$

(iii) $\lim_{x\to 0^-}\frac{|x|}{x} = \lim_{h\to 0^+}\frac{|0-h|}{(0-h)}$

Clearly, $0 < h < 1 = \lim_{h\to 0^+}\frac{h}{-h} = -1$

(iv) $\lim_{x\to 0^+}\frac{x-[x]}{|x|}$

The limit can be written as $\lim_{h\to 0^+}\frac{(0+h)-[0+h]}{|0+h|}$

Clearly, $0 < h < 1$

$\Rightarrow \lim_{h\to 0^+}\frac{h-0}{h} = 1$

(v) $\lim_{x\to\left(\frac{\pi}{2}\right)^+}\frac{\{\sin x\}+1}{\cos\left[\frac{\pi}{2}-x\right]}$

$\Rightarrow \lim_{h\to 0^+}\frac{\left\{\sin\left(\frac{\pi}{2}+h\right)\right\}+1}{\cos\left(\frac{\pi}{2}-\left(\frac{\pi}{2}+h\right)\right)}$

Clearly, $0 < h < 1$

$\Rightarrow \frac{\pi}{2} < \frac{\pi}{2}+h < \frac{\pi}{2}+1$

$\Rightarrow 1 > \sin\left(\frac{\pi}{2}+h\right) > \sin\left(\frac{\pi}{2}+1\right) > 0$

$\Rightarrow \left\{\sin\left(\frac{\pi}{2}+h\right)\right\} = \sin\left[\frac{\pi}{2}+h\right] - \left[\sin\left(\frac{\pi}{2}+h\right)\right] = \sin\left[\frac{\pi}{2}+h\right]$

The limit becomes $\lim_{h\to 0^+}\frac{\sin\left(\frac{\pi}{2}+h\right)+1}{\cos(-h)} = 2$

(vi) $\lim_{x\to\pi^+}\frac{[[\sin x]+[\cos x]]}{|\sin x+\cos x|}$

$\Rightarrow \lim_{h\to\pi^+}\frac{[\sin(\pi+h)]+[\cos(\pi+h)]}{|\sin(\pi+h)+\cos(\pi+h)|}$

$\Rightarrow 0 < h < 1$

$\Rightarrow \pi < \pi + h < \pi + 1$

$\Rightarrow \sin(\pi) > \sin(\pi + h) > \sin(\pi + 1) > -1$

$\Rightarrow 0 > \sin(\pi + h) > -1$

$\Rightarrow [\sin(\pi + h)] = -1$

Similarly, $-1 < \cos(\pi + h) < 0$

$\Rightarrow [\cos(\pi + h)] = -1$

Expression reduces to $\lim_{h\to 0^+}\frac{[-1+(-1)]}{|\sin(\pi+h)+\cos(\pi+h)|}$

$= \lim_{h\to 0^+}\frac{-2}{1} = -2$

(vii) $\lim_{x\to\frac{\pi}{2}^-}\frac{\sin 3x}{[\sin 3x]}$

This can be written as $\lim_{h\to 0^+}\frac{\sin 3\left(\frac{\pi}{2}-h\right)}{\left[\sin 3\left(\frac{\pi}{2}-h\right)\right]}$

Clearly, $0 < h < 1$

$\Rightarrow 0 > -h > -1$

$\Rightarrow -1 < -h < 0$

$\Rightarrow -3 < -3h < 0$

$\Rightarrow \frac{3\pi}{2}-3 < \frac{3\pi}{2}-3h < \frac{3\pi}{2}$

$\Rightarrow \left[\sin\left(\frac{3\pi}{2}-3h\right)\right] = -1$

$\Rightarrow \lim_{h\to 0^+}\frac{\sin\left(\frac{3\pi}{2}-3h\right)}{-1} = \frac{-1}{-1} = 1$

2. (a) $\lim_{x\to 1}[x]$

$\text{L.H.L} = \lim_{x\to 1^-}[x]$

$\Rightarrow 0 < x < 1$

$\Rightarrow \lim_{x\to 1^-}[x] = 0$

$\text{R.H.L} = \lim_{x\to 1^+}[x]$

$\Rightarrow 1 < x < 2$

$\Rightarrow \lim_{x\to 1^+}[x] = 1$

Since LHL ≠ RHL ⇒ limit does not exist

(b) $f(x) = \begin{cases}\frac{1}{1+e^{-1/x}}; & x\neq 0\\ 0 & ; x=0\end{cases}$

$\text{L.H.L} = \lim_{x\to 0^-}f(x) = \frac{1}{1+\infty} = 0$

$\text{R.H.L} = \lim_{x\to 0^+}f(x) = \frac{1}{1+0} = 1$

$\Rightarrow$ LHL $\neq$ RHL

$\Rightarrow$ Hence limit does not exist.

(c) $\lim\limits_{\to-} [1 + x + x^3]$

$\Rightarrow \lim\limits_{x\to\frac{1}{2}^+} (1+x+x^3)=\dfrac{13}{8}$

$\Rightarrow \lim\limits_{x\to\frac{13}{8}^+} [x]=\left[\dfrac{13}{8}\right]=1$

(d) $\lim\limits_{x\to\frac{\pi}{4}^+} \cos[x]$

$\Rightarrow \lim\limits_{h\to0^+} \cos\left[\dfrac{\pi}{4}+h\right]$

Clearly, $0 < h < 1$

$\Rightarrow \dfrac{\pi}{4} < \dfrac{\pi}{4}+h<\dfrac{\pi}{4}+1$

$\Rightarrow \left[\dfrac{\pi}{4}+h\right]=0$

$\Rightarrow \lim\limits_{x\to\frac{\pi}{4}^+} \cos[x] = 1$

(e) $\lim\limits_{x\to\frac{\pi}{4}^-} [\sin(x)]$

Limit can be written as $\lim\limits_{h\to0^+}\left[\sin\left(\dfrac{\pi}{4}-h\right)\right]$

Clearly, $0 < h < 1$

$\Rightarrow -1 < -h < 0$ or $-\dfrac{\pi}{4}<-h<0$

$\Rightarrow \dfrac{\pi}{4}-\dfrac{\pi}{4}<\dfrac{\pi}{4}-h<\dfrac{\pi}{4}$

$\Rightarrow 0<\dfrac{\pi}{4}-h<\dfrac{\pi}{4}$

$\Rightarrow \sin(0) < \sin\left(\dfrac{\pi}{4}-h\right)<\dfrac{1}{\sqrt{2}}$

$\Rightarrow 0< \sin\left(\dfrac{\pi}{4}-h\right)<\dfrac{1}{\sqrt{2}}$

$\Rightarrow \lim\limits_{h\to0^+}\left[\sin\left(\dfrac{\pi}{4}-h\right)\right]=0$

(f) $\lim\limits_{x\to0}[x^2]^{x^2}$

L.H.L = $\lim\limits_{x\to0^-}[x^2]^{x^2}$

Clearly, $-1 < x < 0$

$\Rightarrow 0 < x^2 < 1$

$\Rightarrow \lim\limits_{x\to0^-}[x^2]^{x^2}=0$

Similarly R.H.L = $\lim\limits_{x\to0^+}[x^2]^{x^2}$

$\Rightarrow 0 < x < 1$

$\Rightarrow 0 < x^2 < 1$

$\Rightarrow \lim\limits_{x\to0^+}[x^2]^{x^2}=0$

$\Rightarrow$ LHL = RHL = 0

(g) $\lim\limits_{x\to0}(x^2)^{[x^2]}$

$\Rightarrow \lim\limits_{x\to0^-}(x^2)^{[x^2]}=1$

$\Rightarrow \lim\limits_{x\to0^+}(x^2)^{[x^2]}=1$

$\Rightarrow$ L.H.L = R.H.L = 1

(h) $\lim\limits_{x\to0}\cos\left(\dfrac{1}{x}\right)$

L.H.L = $\lim\limits_{x\to0^-}\cos\left(\dfrac{1}{x}\right)$

When $x\to0^-$ $\Rightarrow \dfrac{1}{x}\to-\infty$

$\Rightarrow \lim\limits_{x\to0^-}\cos\left(\dfrac{1}{x}\right)=\cos(-\infty)$ = some finite number between –1 and 1

Similarly, $\lim\limits_{x\to0^+}\cos\left(\dfrac{1}{x}\right)=\cos(\infty)$ = some finite number between –1 and 1

$\Rightarrow$ Limit does not exist (no particular number)

(i) $\lim\limits_{x\to0}\left(1+\tan^2\sqrt{x}\right)^{\frac{1}{2x}}$

L.H.L = $\lim\limits_{x\to0^-}\left(1+\tan^2\sqrt{x}\right)^{\frac{1}{2x}}$

$\sqrt{x}$ is not defined for $x < 0$

$\Rightarrow$ L.H.L does not exist

So $\lim\limits_{x\to0}\left(1+\tan^2\sqrt{x}\right)^{\frac{1}{2x}}=\lim\limits_{x\to0^+}\left(1+\tan^2\sqrt{x}\right)^{1/2x}$

$=\lim\limits_{x\to0^+}\left\{\left(1+\tan^2\sqrt{x}\right)^{\frac{1}{\tan^2\sqrt{x}}}\right\}^{\frac{\tan^2\sqrt{x}}{2x}}$

$=e^{\lim\limits_{x\to0}\frac{1}{2}\frac{\tan^2\sqrt{x}}{x}}=e^{\frac{1}{2}(1)}=e^{\frac{1}{2}}$

Hence limit does not exist

(j) $\lim\limits_{x\to2}\{x+(x-[x]^2\}$

L.H.L. = $\lim\limits_{h\to0^+}\left\{(2-h)+(2-h-[2-h])^2\right\}$

$=\lim\limits_{h\to0^+}\left\{(2-h)+(2-h-1)^2\right\}$

$=\lim\limits_{h\to0^+}\left\{(2-h)+(1-h)^2\right\}$

$=\lim\limits_{h\to0^+}\left\{2-h+1+h^2-2h\right\}$

$=\lim\limits_{h\to0^+}\left\{h^2-3h+3\right\}=3$

R.H.L. = $\lim\limits_{h\to0^+}\left\{(2+h)+(2+h-[2+h])^2\right\}$

$=\lim\limits_{h\to0^+}\left\{(2+h)+(2+h-2)^2\right\}$

$=\lim\limits_{\to}\left\{(2+h)+h\right\}=2$

$\because$ L.H.L $\neq$ R.H.L. Hence limit does not exist

3. $f(x)=\begin{cases}x^4; & x^2<1\\ x; & x^2\geq1\end{cases}$

At $x = 1$

L.H.L = $\lim\limits_{x\to1^-}f(x)=\lim\limits_{x\to1^-}x^4=1$

R.H.L = $\lim\limits_{x\to1^+}f(x)=\lim\limits_{x\to1^+}x=1$

$\Rightarrow$ L.H.L = R.H.L = 1

At $x = -1$

L.H.L = $\lim_{x\to -1^-} f(x) = -1$

R.H.L = $\lim_{x\to -1^+} f(x) = 1$

$\Rightarrow$ At $x = -1$ limit does not exist

4. $f(x) = \begin{cases} \dfrac{|x-1|}{x}; x>0 \\ (x+1)^{2-\left(\frac{1}{|x|}+\frac{1}{x}\right)}; x<0 \end{cases}$

The function is continuous at all points except at $x = 0$

Let us discuss the continuity at $x = 0$

L.H.L at x= 0

$\Rightarrow \lim_{x\to 0^-} f(x) = \lim_{x\to 0^-} (x+1)^{2-\frac{1}{|x|}-\frac{1}{x}} = \lim_{x\to 0^+} (x+1)^{2+\frac{1}{x}-\frac{1}{x}} = (1)^2 = 1$

R.H.L = $\lim_{x\to 0^+} f(x) = \lim_{x\to 0^+}\left(\dfrac{|x-1|}{x}\right)$

Clearly, $0 < x < 1$

$\Rightarrow -1 < x - 1 < 0$

$\Rightarrow \lim_{x\to 0^+}\left(\dfrac{1-x}{x}\right) = \infty$

$\Rightarrow$ Limit does not exist at $x = 0$

$\Rightarrow$ L.H.L = 1 and R.H.L = ∞

5. $\lim_{x\to 0} \dfrac{\{x\}^2}{x^2}$

$\Rightarrow$ L.H.L = $\lim_{x\to 0^-} \dfrac{\{x\}^2}{x^2} = \lim_{x\to 0^-} \dfrac{(x-(-1))^2}{x^2} = \lim_{x\to 0^-} \dfrac{(x+1)^2}{x^2} = \infty$

$\Rightarrow$ R.H.L = $\lim_{x\to 0^+} \dfrac{\{x\}^2}{x^2} = \lim_{x\to 0^+} \dfrac{(x-0)^2}{x^2} = 1$

$\because$ L.H.L $\neq$ R.H.L

$\Rightarrow$ Limit does not exist

For $\lim_{x\to 0} \dfrac{\{x^2\}}{x^2}$, L.H.L = $\lim_{x\to 0^-} \dfrac{\{x^2\}}{x^2} = \lim_{x\to 0^-} \dfrac{x^2-[x^2]}{x^2}$

$= \lim_{x\to 0^-} \dfrac{x^2-0}{x^2} = 1$

$\Rightarrow$ R.H.L = $\lim_{x\to 0^+} \dfrac{\{x^2\}}{x^2} = \lim_{x\to 0^+} \dfrac{x^2-[x^2]}{x^2} = \lim_{x\to 0^+} \dfrac{x^2-0}{x^2} = 1$

$\Rightarrow$ L.H.L = R.H.L

$\Rightarrow$ Limit exist

6. (i) $\lim_{x\to\infty} (3)^x$

$\because 3 > 1 \quad \Rightarrow \quad \lim_{x\to\infty} (3)^x = \infty$

(ii) $\lim_{x\to\infty} \left(\dfrac{1}{4}\right)^x \quad \because \dfrac{1}{4} < 1$

$\Rightarrow \lim_{x\to\infty} \left(\dfrac{1}{4}\right)^x = 0$

(iii) $y = \lim_{x\to\frac{\pi}{4}} \{\sin x\}$

L.H.L = $\lim_{x\to\left(\frac{\pi}{4}\right)^-} \{\sin x\} = \lim_{h\to 0^+} \left\{\sin\left(\dfrac{\pi}{4}-h\right)\right\}$

Clearly, $0 < h < \pi/4$

$\Rightarrow -\pi/4 < -h < 0$

$\Rightarrow \dfrac{\pi}{4}-\dfrac{\pi}{4} < \dfrac{\pi}{4}-h < \dfrac{\pi}{4}$

$\Rightarrow 0 < \sin\left(\dfrac{\pi}{4}-1\right) < \sin\left(\dfrac{\pi}{4}-h\right) < \dfrac{1}{\sqrt{2}}$

$\Rightarrow \left[\sin\left(\dfrac{\pi}{4}-h\right)\right] = 0$

$\Rightarrow \lim_{x\to\frac{\pi}{4}^-} \{\sin x\} = \lim_{h\to 0^+}\left(\sin\dfrac{\pi}{4}-h\right) = \dfrac{1}{\sqrt{2}}$

R.H.L = $\lim_{x\to\frac{\pi}{4}^+} \{\sin(x)\}$

$\Rightarrow \lim_{h\to 0^+} \left\{\sin\left(\dfrac{\pi}{4}+h\right)\right\}$

Clearly, $0 < h < \pi/4$

$\Rightarrow \dfrac{\pi}{4} < \dfrac{\pi}{4}+h < \dfrac{\pi}{4}+\dfrac{\pi}{4}$

$\Rightarrow \sin\dfrac{\pi}{4} = \dfrac{1}{\sqrt{2}} < \sin\left(\dfrac{\pi}{4}+h\right) < \sin\dfrac{\pi}{2} = 1$

$\Rightarrow \left[\sin\left(\dfrac{\pi}{4}+h\right)\right] = 0$

$\Rightarrow \lim_{x\to\frac{\pi}{4}^+} \{\sin(x)\} = \dfrac{1}{\sqrt{2}}$

By the question, $\lim_{x\to\infty}\left(\dfrac{1}{\sqrt{2}}\right)^x = 0$ as in the part (ii)

(iv) $f(x) = e^{-x} (\sin x)$

$\Rightarrow \lim_{x\to\infty} f(x) = \lim_{x\to\infty} e^{-x}(\sin x) = 0 \times$ (some finite number) $= 0$

(v) $f(x) = \left[\left(\dfrac{5}{4}\right)^x + \dfrac{[5/4]}{x}\right]\sin x \quad \because [5/4] = 1$

$\Rightarrow f(x) = \left[\left\{\dfrac{5}{4}\right\}^x + \dfrac{1}{x}\right]\sin x$

$\Rightarrow \lim_{x\to\infty}\left[\left\{\dfrac{5}{4}\right\}^x \sin x + \dfrac{\sin x}{x}\right] \quad \because \left\{\dfrac{5}{4}\right\} = 0.25$

$\Rightarrow \lim_{x\to\infty}\left((0.25)^x \sin x + \dfrac{\sin x}{x}\right) = 0$

7. $\lim_{x\to 0} \dfrac{\sin 2x}{\cos x} = 0 = \lim_{x\to 0}\left(\dfrac{2\sin x.\cos x}{\cos x}\right) = \lim_{x\to 0} (2\sin x)$;

$\because \ell = 0; a = 0$

$|f(x) - \ell| = |2 \sin x| < 2|x| < \varepsilon$

if $|x| < \dfrac{\varepsilon}{2}$

For $\varepsilon > 0$ select $\delta = \dfrac{\varepsilon}{2}$

$|f(x) - l| < \varepsilon$

Whenever $|x - 0| < \delta$

Hence existence of δ has been ensured.

8. (a) $f(x) = \begin{cases} \dfrac{|x-4|}{x-4}; & x \neq 4 \\ 0 & ; x = 4 \end{cases}$

$$\text{L.H.L} = \lim_{x\to 4^-} f(x) = \lim_{x\to 4^-} \frac{|x-4|}{x-4} = -1$$

$$\text{R.H.L} = \lim_{x\to 4^+} f(x) = \lim_{x\to 4^+} \frac{|x-4|}{x-4} = 1$$

⇒ Limit does not exist

(b) $f(x) = \begin{cases} 5x-4; & 0 < x \le 1 \\ 4x^3 - 3x; & 1 < x < 2 \end{cases}$

$$\text{L.H.L} = \lim_{x\to 1^-} f(x) = \lim_{x\to 1^-} (5x-4) = 1$$

$$\text{R.H.L} = \lim_{x\to 1^+} f(x) = \lim_{x\to 1^+} (4x^3 - 3x) = 1$$

⇒ Limit exists and equals 1

9. (a) $\lim\limits_{x\to 2} \dfrac{[x-2]|x-2|}{x-2}$

$$\text{L.H.L} = \lim_{x\to 2^-} \frac{[x-2]|x-2|}{x-2} = \lim_{h\to 0^+} \frac{[2-h-2]|2-h-2|}{2-h-2}$$

$$= \lim_{h\to 0^+} \frac{[-h]|-\text{h}|}{-h} = \lim_{h\to 0^+} -[-h] = 1$$

$$\text{R.H.L} = \lim_{x\to 2^+} \frac{[x-2]\ |x-2|}{x-2}$$

$$= \lim_{h\to 0^+} \frac{[2+h-2]|2+\text{h}-2|}{2+n-2} = \lim_{h\to 0^+} \frac{[h]|h|}{h} = 0$$

⇒ L.H.L ≠ R.H.L, limit does not exist.

(b) $\lim\limits_{x\to 2} \dfrac{\sqrt{x^2-4x+4}}{x-2}$

$$\text{L.H.L} = \lim_{x\to 2^-} \frac{\sqrt{(\quad 2)}}{x-2} \quad \lim_{x\to 2^-} \frac{|\quad 2|}{x-2} = -1$$

$$\text{R.H.L} = \lim_{x\to 2^+} \frac{|x-2|}{x-2} = 1$$

⇒ L.H.L ≠ R.H.L limit does not exist.

(c) $\lim\limits_{x\to 2} \dfrac{\sqrt{x^2-3x+2}}{x-2} = \lim\limits_{x\to 2} \dfrac{\sqrt{(x-2)(x-1)}}{x-2} = \lim\limits_{x\to 2} \sqrt{\dfrac{x-1}{x-2}}$

$$\text{L.H.L} = \lim_{x\to 2^-} \sqrt{\frac{x-1}{x-2}} = \lim_{h\to 0^+} \sqrt{\frac{2-h-1}{2-h-2}} = \lim_{h\to 0^+} \sqrt{\frac{1-h}{-h}}$$

L.H.L does not exist

$$\text{R.H.L} = \lim_{x\to 2^+} \sqrt{\frac{x-1}{x-2}} = \lim_{h\to 0^+} \sqrt{\frac{2+h-1}{2+h-2}} = \lim_{h\to 0^+} \sqrt{\frac{1+h}{h}}$$

$$= \lim_{h\to 0^+} \sqrt{\frac{1}{h} + 1} = \infty$$

(d) $\lim\limits_{x\to \frac{\pi}{2}} \cos^{-1}(\operatorname{cosec} x)$

$$\text{R.H.L} = \lim_{x\to \frac{\pi}{2}^+} \cos^{-1}(\operatorname{cosec} x)$$

$$= \lim_{h\to 0^+} \cos^{-1}\left(\operatorname{cosec}\left(\frac{\pi}{2}+h\right)\right) = \lim_{h\to 0^+} \cos^{-1}\left(\frac{1}{\sin\left(\frac{\pi}{2}+h\right)}\right)$$

Clearly $\dfrac{1}{\sin\left(\dfrac{\pi}{2}+h\right)} > 1$

⇒ R.H.L does not exist as domain of $\cos^{-1} f(x)$ is [–1, 1].

$$\text{L.H.L} = \lim_{x\to \frac{\pi}{2}^-} \cos^{-1}(\operatorname{cosec} x) = \lim_{h\to 0^+} \cos^{-1}\left(\frac{1}{\sin\left(\frac{\pi}{2}-h\right)}\right)$$

Again limit inside gets outside the domain of inverse cosine function.

⇒ Both L.H.L and R.H.L does not exist.

10. (i) $\lim\limits_{x\to 1^-} [\sin^{-1} x] = \lim\limits_{h\to 0^+} \left[\sin^{-1}(1-h)\right] = \lim\limits_{h\to 0^+} \left[\dfrac{\pi}{2}\right] = 1$

(ii) $\lim\limits_{x\to \infty} [\tan^{-1} x] = \lim\limits_{x\to \infty} \left[\dfrac{\pi}{2}\right] = 1$

(iii) $\lim\limits_{x\to -\infty} [\tan^{-1} x] = \lim\limits_{x\to -\infty} \left[\dfrac{-\pi}{2}\right] = -2$

(iv) $\lim\limits_{x\to 1^{-1}} \left[\sin\left(\sin^{-1} x\right)\right] = \lim\limits_{h\to 0^+} \left[\sin\left(\sin^{-1}(1-h)\right)\right]$

$= \lim\limits_{h\to 0^+} [(1-h)] = 0$

(v) $\lim\limits_{x\to \frac{\pi}{2}} [\sin^{-1}(\sin x)] = [\sin^{-1}(1)] = \left[\dfrac{\pi}{2}\right] = 1$

11. $\lim\limits_{x\to 0} \sin^{-1}\{x\}$

$$\text{L.H.L} = \lim_{x\to 0^-} \sin^{-1}\{x\} = \lim_{h\to 0^+} \sin^{-1}\{-h\}$$

$$= \lim_{h\to 0^+} \sin^{-1}(-h-(-1)) = \lim_{\to} \sin\ (-\ +1)$$

$$= \sin^{-1}(1) = \frac{\pi}{2}$$

$$\text{R.H.L} = \lim_{x\to 0^+} \sin^{-1}\{x\} = \lim_{h\to 0^+} \sin^{-1}(h-(0))$$

$$= \lim_{h\to 0^+} \sin^{-1}(h) = 0$$

∴ L.H.L ≠ R.H.L

⇒ Limit does not exist

12. (a) $\lim\limits_{x\to 0} \sin\left(\dfrac{1}{x}\right)$ = A number between –1 and 1

⇒ $\lim\limits_{x\to 0} x \sin\left(\dfrac{1}{x}\right)$ = 0 × a number oscillating between –1 and 1 = 0

(b) $\lim\limits_{x\to \infty} \dfrac{\sin x}{x} = \lim\limits_{x\to \infty} \dfrac{1}{x} (\sin x)$

⇒ 0 × (a number between –1 and 1)

= 0

(c) $\lim\limits_{x\to 0} |x|^{[\cos x]}$

$\text{R.H.L} = \lim\limits_{x\to 0^+} |x|^{[\cos x]}$

⇒ $\lim\limits_{x\to 0^+} x^{[\cos x]}$ = (a non-zero number)^0 = 1

$\text{R.H.L} = \lim\limits_{x\to 0^-} |x|^{[\cos x]}$

⇒ $\lim\limits_{x\to 0^-} (-x)^{[\cos x]}$

⇒ (a non-zero number)^0 = 1

13. **(a)** $\lim\limits_{x\to k}([k-x]+[x-k]-x)$

We know that $[x] + [-x] = 0$

if $x \in \mathbb{Z}$ and $= -1$ if $x \notin \mathbb{Z}$

$\therefore$ We can reduce our limit to $\lim\limits_{x\to k}(-1-x) = -1-k$

(b) Even if $k \notin \mathbb{Z}$ and $k - x$ is a non-integer

$\Rightarrow$ limit will remain the same

$\Rightarrow \lim\limits_{x\to k}([k-x] + [x-k] - x) = -1 - k$

(c) $\lim\limits_{x\to k}(\{k-x\} + \{x-k\})$; $k \in \mathbb{Z} \Rightarrow k - x \notin \mathbb{Z}$

$\therefore$ $\{-x\} + \{x\} = 1$ for $x \notin \mathbb{Z}$ and $= 0$ for $x \in \mathbb{Z}$

Hence, $\{k-x\} + \{x-k\} = 1$ for $(x-k) \notin \mathbb{Z}$

$\Rightarrow \lim\limits_{x\to k}(\{k-x\} + \{x-k\}) = 1$

TEXTUAL EXERCISE–1: (OBJECTIVE)

1. **(c)** $\lim\limits_{x\to 2^+}[x-2]$

Clearly, x will take values slightly greater than 2

$\Rightarrow 0 < x - 2 < 1$

$\Rightarrow \lim\limits_{x\to 2^+}[x-2] = 0$

2. **(b)** $\lim\limits_{x\to n^+}\{x-2\} = \lim\limits_{h\to 0^+}\{n+h-2\} = \lim\limits_{h\to 0^+}\{h\}[\because \{n+h\} = \{h\}]$

$\therefore \lim\limits_{h\to n^+}\{x-2\} = \lim\limits_{h\to 0^+}\{h\} = \lim\limits_{h\to 0^+}(h) = 0$

3. **(c)** $\lim\limits_{x\to n}\{x-2\}; n<2, n\in\mathbb{Z}$

$= \lim\limits_{h\to 0^+}\{n-h-2\} = \lim\limits_{h\to 0^+}\{-h\} = \lim\limits_{h\to 0^+}1-\{h\} = \lim\limits_{h\to 0^+}1-h = 1$

4. **(a), (d)** $f(x) = \begin{cases} x+2; x<1 \\ 4x-1; 1\le x\le 3 \\ x^2+5; x>3 \end{cases}$

$\Rightarrow \lim\limits_{x\to 1^+}(f(x)) = 4(1) - 1 = 3$

$\Rightarrow \lim\limits_{x\to 3^-} f(x) = 4(3) - 1 = 11$

$\Rightarrow \lim\limits_{x\to 3^+}(f(x)) = (3)^2 + 1 = 10$

$\Rightarrow$ L.H.L $\ne$ R.H.L

$\Rightarrow \lim\limits_{x\to 3} f(x)$ does not exist

5. **(a), (b), (c)** $\lim\limits_{x\to 0}\dfrac{e^{1/x}-1}{e^{1/x}+1}$; L.H.L $= \lim\limits_{x\to 0^-}\dfrac{e^{1/x}-1}{e^{1/x}+1}$

$\therefore \lim\limits_{x\to 0^-} e^{1/x} = e^{-\infty} = 0$

$\Rightarrow \lim\limits_{x\to 0^-}\dfrac{e^{1/x}-1}{e^{1/x}+1} = -1$

R.H.L $= \lim\limits_{x\to 0^+}\dfrac{1-e^{-1/x}}{1+e^{-1/x}} = \dfrac{1-0}{1+0} = 1$

$\because$ L.H.L $\ne$ R.H.L

$\Rightarrow$ Limit does not exist

6. **(a), (b), (c)** $\lim\limits_{x\to \frac{\pi}{4}}[(\tan x) + 3]$

L.H.L $= \lim\limits_{x\to \frac{\pi}{4}^-}[(\tan x) + 3]$

Clearly $\tan x$ is increasing in $(0, \pi/2)$, when $x \to \pi/4$ from left hand side.

$\Rightarrow \tan x < 1$

$\Rightarrow \lim\limits_{x\to \frac{\pi}{4}^-}[\tan(x) + 3] = 3$

R.H.L $= \lim\limits_{x\to \frac{\pi}{4}^+}[(\tan x) + 3]$

In this case $x \to \dfrac{\pi}{4}$ by taking values greater than $\dfrac{\pi}{4}$

$\Rightarrow (\tan x) > 1$

$\Rightarrow \lim\limits_{x\to \frac{\pi}{4}^+}[(\tan x) + 3] = 4$

$\because$ L.H.L $\ne$ R.H.L

$\Rightarrow$ Limit does not exist

7. **(a)** $L = \lim\limits_{x\to 0}\sin\left(\dfrac{1}{x}\right)$

$\therefore$ $L = \lim\limits_{x\to 0}\sin\left(\dfrac{1}{x}\right)$ = a number lying between –1 and 1 not fixed i.e., limit L is not unique

$\Rightarrow$ Limit does not exist.

8. **(b)** $\lim\limits_{x\to 0}\left(x\sin\dfrac{1}{x}\right) = \lim\limits_{x\to 0}x.\lim\limits_{x\to 0}\left(\sin\dfrac{1}{x}\right) = 0\times$ (finite real number between –1 and 1, not unique $= 0$

9. **(c)** $\lim\limits_{x\to \frac{\pi}{2}^+}\cot(\pi - x) = \lim\limits_{h\to 0^+}\cot\left(\pi - \left(\dfrac{\pi}{2}+h\right)\right)$

$= \lim\limits_{h\to 0^+}\cot\left(\dfrac{\pi}{2}-h\right) = 0$

10. **(b)** $\lim\limits_{x\to 1^-}\sin^{-1}(x)$

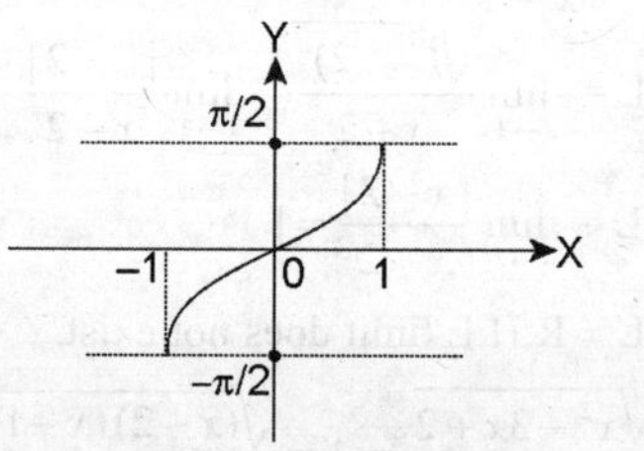

$\lim\limits_{x\to 1^-}\sin^{-1}(x)$

$\Rightarrow$ x is approaching 1 by taking values less than 1

$\Rightarrow \lim\limits_{x\to 1^-}\left(\sin^{-1}(x)\right) = \dfrac{\pi}{2}$

11. **(c)** $\lim\limits_{x\to 1^+}\sin^{-1}(x)$

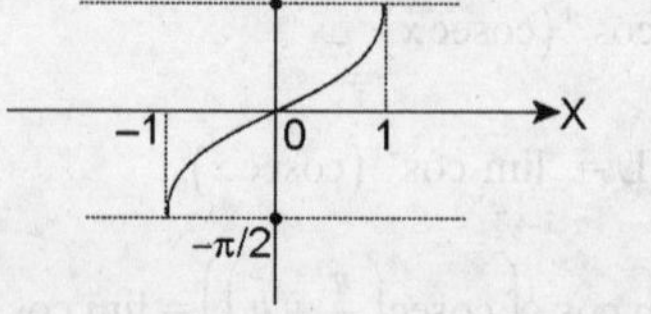

$\lim\limits_{x\to 1^+}\sin^{-1}(x)$

⇒ x is approaching 1 by taking values greater than 1

⇒ Limit does not exist.

12. (a), (c) $L = \lim\limits_{x\to 1}\cos^{-1}x = L$; $\cos^{-1}x$ is defined for $x \in [-1, 1]$, R.H.L. is not defined.

⇒ $L = \lim\limits_{x\to 1^-}\cos^{-1}(x)$ = L.H.L.

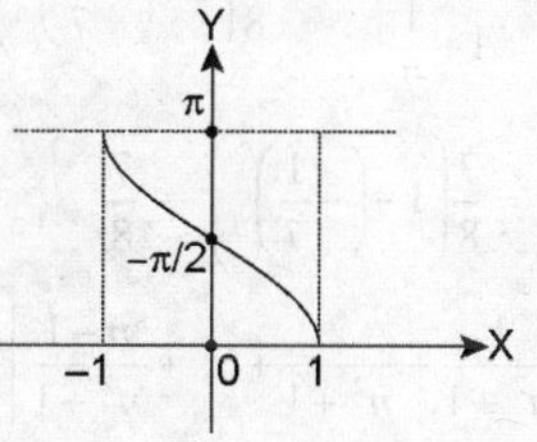

⇒ $L = \lim\limits_{x\to 1^-}\cos^{-1}(x) = 0$

⇒ L.H.L = 0, L = 0, R.H.L = does not exist.

13. (c) $L = \lim\limits_{x\to -\sqrt{3}}|\tan^{-1}x|$; $\tan^{-1}x < 0$ for $x \in (-\infty, 0)$,

$|\tan^{-1}x| = -\tan^{-1}x$

∴ $L = \lim\limits_{x\to -\sqrt{3}} -\tan^{-1}x = -\left(\tan^{-1}\left(-\sqrt{3}\right)\right) = \frac{\pi}{3}$

14. (c) Given $\sin^{-1}x + \sin^{-1}y = \pi$

Let $\sin^{-1}x = A$

⇒ $x = \sin A$

Similarly, $\sin^{-1}y = B$

⇒ $\sin B = y$

By the question, $A + B = \pi$

⇒ $A = \pi - B$

⇒ $\sin A = \sin B$

⇒ $x = y = \sin\left(\frac{\pi}{2}\right) = 1$

⇒ $xy = 1$

⇒ $L = \lim\limits_{z\to 1}\tan^{-1}(z) = \frac{\pi}{4}$

15. (a) $L = \lim\limits_{x\to\infty}\frac{e^x + e^{-x}}{e^x - e^{-x}}$

This can be rewritten as $\lim\limits_{x\to\infty}\left(\frac{1+e^{-2x}}{1-e^{-2x}}\right) = \frac{(1+0)}{(1-0)} = 1$

16. (c) Let $E(x, y) = \sin^{-1}(\sin x) + \cos^{-1}(\cos y)$; $x, y \in \{1, 2, 3, 4\} \in \left(0, \frac{3\pi}{2}\right)$; where

$$\sin^{-1}(\sin x) = \begin{cases} x & \text{for } \frac{-\pi}{2} \le x \le \frac{\pi}{2} \\ \pi - x & \text{for } \frac{\pi}{2} < x \le \frac{3\pi}{2} \end{cases} \text{ and}$$

$$\cos^{-1}(\cos y) = \begin{cases} y & \text{for } 0 \le y \le \pi \\ 2\pi - y & \text{for } \pi < y \le 2\pi \end{cases}$$

⇒ $E(1,1) = 2 \in \mathbb{Z}, E(1,2) = 3 \in \mathbb{Z}$, E(1, 3) = 4 are the only integer values

⇒ $k = 3$

⇒ $\lim\limits_{z\to 3}\tan\frac{\pi}{z} = \sqrt{3}$

TEXTUAL EXERCISE–2: (SUBJECTIVE)

1. (a) $3(x-2) + 2(x^2-4) = f(x)$ say to determine the order of small ness

Let us evaluate $\lim\limits_{x\to 2}\frac{3(x-2)+2(x^2-4)}{x-2} = \lim\limits_{x\to 2} 3 + 2(x + 2) = 3 + 8 = 11$ = a finite number

⇒ $f(x)$ has the same order of smallness as $\beta(x)$

(b) Let $f(x) = (\sin \pi x)^{1/3}$

To determine the order of smallness

Let us evaluate $\lim\limits_{x\to 2}\frac{(\sin\pi x)^{1/3}}{x-2}$

This can be written as $\lim\limits_{x\to 2}\left(\frac{\sin\pi x}{x-2}\right)^{1/3}\frac{1}{(x-2)^{2/3}}$

$= \lim\limits_{h\to 0}\left(\frac{\sin\pi(2+h)}{h}\right)^{1/3}.\frac{1}{(h)^{2/3}} = \lim\limits_{h\to 0}\left(\frac{\sin\pi h}{h}\right)^{1/3}.\frac{1}{(h)^{2/3}}$

$= \lim\limits_{h\to 0}(\pi)^{1/3}\left(\frac{\sin\pi h}{\pi h}\right)^{1/3}.\frac{1}{(h)^{2/3}} = (\pi)^{1/3}(1).\lim\limits_{h\to 0}\frac{1}{(h)^{2/3}} = \infty$

⇒ $\beta(x)$ is of higher order infinitesimal

2. (a) $\lim\limits_{x\to 0}\frac{\log(\cos x)}{\sqrt[4]{(1+x^2)}-1} = \lim\limits_{x\to 0}\frac{\cos x - 1}{x^2/4} = \lim\limits_{x\to 0}\frac{\frac{-1}{2}x^2}{\frac{x^2}{4}} = -2$

(b) $\lim\limits_{x\to 0}\frac{\sin\sqrt[3]{x}\,\log(1+3x)}{\left(\tan^{-1}\sqrt{x}\right)^2\left(e^{5\sqrt[3]{x}}-1\right)}$

Replacing by infinitesimals of the equivalent order

$\lim\limits_{x\to 0}\frac{3x.x^{\frac{1}{3}}}{x.5.\sqrt[3]{x}}$

⇒ $\lim\limits_{x\to 0}\frac{3}{5} = \frac{3}{5}$

(c) $\lim\limits_{x\to 0}\frac{\log(1+\sin 4x)}{e^{\sin 5x}-1}$

Replacing by infinitesimal of equivalent order

$\lim\limits_{x\to 0}\frac{\sin 4x}{\sin 5x}$

⇒ $\lim\limits_{x\to 0}\frac{4\left(\frac{\sin 4x}{4x}\right)}{5\left(\frac{\sin 5x}{5x}\right)}$ ⇒ $\frac{\lim\limits_{x\to 0}4\left(\frac{\sin 4x}{4x}\right)}{\lim\limits_{x\to 0}5\left(\frac{\sin 5x}{x}\right)} = \frac{4}{5}$

(d) $\lim\limits_{x\to 0}\frac{e^{\sin 3x}-1}{\log(1+\tan 2x)} = \lim\limits_{x\to 0}\frac{\sin 3x}{\tan 2x} = \frac{\lim\limits_{x\to 0}3\frac{\sin 3x}{3x}}{\lim\limits_{x\to 0}2.\frac{\tan 2x}{2x}} = \frac{3}{2}$

(e) $\lim\limits_{x\to 0}\frac{\log(2-\cos 2x)}{\log^2[(\sin 3x)+1]} = \lim\limits_{x\to 0}\frac{\log[2-(1-2\sin^2 x)]}{\log^2[1+\sin 3x]}$

$= \lim\limits_{x\to 0}\frac{\log[1+2\sin^2 x]}{\log^2[1+\sin 3x]} = \lim\limits_{x\to 0}\left(\frac{2\sin^2 x}{\sin^2 3x}\right) = 2\lim\limits_{x\to 0}\left[\frac{\sin x}{\sin 3x}\right]^2$

$= 2\left[\frac{1}{3}\right]^2 = \frac{2}{9}$

(f) $\lim\limits_{x\to 0}\dfrac{\sqrt{1+\sin 3x}-1}{\log(1+\tan 2x)}$

$$=\lim_{x\to 0}\frac{\sin 3x}{\left(\sqrt{1+\sin 3x}+1\right)}\times\frac{1}{\log(1+\tan 2x)}$$

$$=\lim_{x\to 0}\frac{1}{2}\left(\frac{3x}{2x}\right)=\frac{3}{4}$$

(g) $\lim\limits_{x\to 0}\dfrac{\log\left(1+2x-3x^2+4x^3\right)}{\log\left(1-x+2x^2-7x^3\right)}$

$$=\lim_{x\to 0}\frac{(2x-3x^2+4x^3)}{(-x+2x^2-7x^3)}=\lim_{x\to 0}\frac{(2-3x+4x^2)}{(-1+2x-7x^2)}=-2$$

(h) $\lim\limits_{x\to 0}\dfrac{\sqrt{1+x^2}-1}{1-\cos x}$

This can be reduced as $\lim\limits_{x\to 0}\dfrac{\frac{1}{2}x^2}{2\sin^2\frac{x}{2}}=\lim\limits_{x\to 0}\dfrac{2\left(\frac{x}{2}\right)^2}{2\left(\sin\frac{x}{2}\right)^2}$

$$=\lim_{x\to 0}\left(\frac{\frac{x}{2}}{\sin\frac{x}{2}}\right)^2=1$$

(i) $\lim\limits_{x\to 0}\dfrac{3\sin x-x^2+x^3}{\tan x+2\sin^2 x+5x^4}$

Replacing by equivalent infinitesimals

$$=\lim_{x\to 0}\frac{3x-x^2+x^3}{x+2x^2+5x^4}=\lim_{x\to 0}\left(\frac{3-x+x^2}{1+2x+5x^3}\right)=3$$

(j) $\lim\limits_{x\to 0}\dfrac{(\sin x-\tan x)^7+(1-\cos 2x)^4+x^5}{7\tan^7 x+\sin^6 x+2\sin^5 x}$

Replacing by equivalent infinitesimal

$$=\lim_{x\to 0}\frac{(x-x)^7+(2x^2)^4+x^5}{7x^7+x^6+2x5}=\lim_{x\to 0}\frac{x^5(1+16x^8)}{x^5(2+x+7x^2)}=\frac{1}{2}$$

(k) $\lim\limits_{x\to 0}\dfrac{1-\cos x+2\sin x-\sin^3 x-x^2+3x^4}{\tan^3 x-6\sin^2 x+x-5x^2}$

Replacing infinitesimals of equivalent order

$$=\lim_{x\to 0}\frac{2\frac{x^2}{4}+2x-x^3-x^2+3x^4}{x^3-6x^2+x-5x^2}$$

$$=\lim_{x\to 0}\frac{x\left(2-\frac{x}{2}-x^2+3x^3\right)}{x\left(1-11x+x^2\right)}=2$$

3. (a) $\lim\limits_{n\to\infty}\left[\dfrac{1}{n^2}+\dfrac{2}{n^2}+....+\dfrac{n-1}{n^2}\right]=\lim\limits_{n\to\infty}\left(\dfrac{(n-1)(n)}{2n^2}\right)$

$$=\lim_{n\to\infty}\left(\frac{(n-1)n}{2n^2}\right)=\lim_{n\to\infty}\left(\frac{n-1}{2n}\right)=\lim_{n\to\infty}\left(\frac{1}{2}-\frac{1}{2n}\right)=\frac{1}{2}$$

Sum of infinite number of infinitesimals may not necessarily be infinitesimals.

(b) $\lim\limits_{n\to\infty}\left[1-\dfrac{1}{7}+\dfrac{1}{49}-....+\dfrac{(-1)^{n-1}}{7^{n-1}}\right]$

$$\Rightarrow\ 1-\frac{1}{7}+\frac{1}{49}-.....+\frac{(-1)^{n-1}}{7^{n-1}}=S_n$$

This is a G.P. with common ratio $=-\dfrac{1}{7}$ and first term 1.

$$\Rightarrow\ S_n=\frac{\left(1-\left(-\frac{1}{7}\right)^n\right)}{1+\frac{1}{7}}=\frac{7}{8}\left(1-\left(-\frac{1}{7}\right)^n\right)$$

$$\Rightarrow\ \lim_{n\to\infty}S_n=\frac{7}{8}\left(1-\left(-\frac{1}{7}\right)^n\right)=\frac{7}{8}$$

(c) $\lim\limits_{n\to\infty}\left[\dfrac{1}{n^2+1}+\dfrac{2}{n^2+1}+....+\dfrac{n-1}{n^2+1}\right]$

$$=\lim_{n\to\infty}\left[\frac{1+2+....+n-1}{n^2+1}\right]=\lim_{n\to\infty}\left(\frac{n(n-1)}{2\left(n^2+1\right)}\right)$$

$$=\lim_{n\to\infty}\frac{n^2-n}{2n^2+2}$$

Dividing numerator and denominator by n^2, we get

$$\lim_{n\to\infty}\left(\frac{1-\frac{1}{n}}{2+\frac{2}{n^2}}\right)=\frac{1}{2}$$

(d) $\lim\limits_{\to\infty}\dfrac{[x]+[2x]+[3x]+.....+[nx]}{}$

We know that $x-1<[x]\le x$

$2x-1<[2x]\le 2x$

$3x-1<[3x]\le 3x$

....

....

$nx-1<[nx]\le nx$

Adding all from above, we get $(x+2x+....+nx)-n<[x]+....+[nx]\le(x+2x+...+nx)$

$$\Rightarrow\ \frac{xn(n+1)}{2}-n<\sum_{r=1}^{n}[rx]\le\frac{nx(n+1)}{2}$$

$$\Rightarrow\ \left[\frac{x\left(1+\frac{1}{n}\right)}{2}-\frac{1}{n}\right]<\sum_{r=1}^{n}\frac{[rx]}{n^2}\le\frac{x\left(1+\frac{1}{n}\right)}{2}$$

$$\Rightarrow\ \frac{x}{2}<\sum_{r=1}^{n}\frac{[rx]}{n^2}\le\frac{x}{2}\ \text{ as } n\to\infty$$

$$\Rightarrow\ \lim_{n\to\infty}\sum_{r=1}^{n}\frac{[rx]}{n^2}=\frac{x}{2}$$

4. (a) $\lim\limits_{x\to\infty}f(x)$

$\therefore\ \lim\limits_{x\to\infty}\left(2-\dfrac{3}{x}\right)=2$ and $\lim\limits_{x\to\infty}\left(2+\dfrac{5}{x}\right)=2$

By Sandwich theorem, $\lim\limits_{x\to\infty}f(x)=2$

(b) $\lim\limits_{x\to 0}\left(\dfrac{\sin x}{x}\right)=1$ and $\lim\limits_{x\to 0}\left(\dfrac{\tan x}{x}\right)=1$

By sandwich theorem, we get $\lim\limits_{x\to 0}f(x)=1$

5. (a) $\because$ x > 0; $L = \lim_{x\to 0^+}\left(x+\frac{x^2}{2!}+\frac{x^3}{3!}+....+\frac{x^n}{n!}\right)$

$\because$ $e^x = 1 + x + \frac{x^2}{2!}+....+\frac{x^n}{n}+\frac{x^{n+1}}{(n+1)!}+.....$

$\Rightarrow$ $e^x - 1 = x+\frac{x^2}{2!}+\frac{x^3}{3!}+....+\frac{x^n}{n!}+\frac{x^{n+1}}{(n+1)!}+....$

$\therefore$ $L < \lim_{x\to 0^+}\left(e^x-1\right)=0$

Also $L > \lim_{x\to 0^+}(x) = 0$

$\Rightarrow$ L = 0

(b) $\lim_{x\to 0^+}\left(x-\frac{x^2}{2}+\frac{x^3}{3}.....+(-1)^{n-1}\frac{x^n}{n}\right)$

$\Rightarrow$ $\lim_{x\to 0^+}\left(-x-\frac{x^2}{2}-\frac{x^3}{3}-.....-\frac{x^n}{n}\right)$

$=-\lim_{x\to 0^+}\left(x+\frac{x^2}{2}+\frac{x^3}{3}+....+\frac{x^n}{n}\right)$

$>-\lim_{x\to 0^+}\left(x+x^2+x^3+....+x^n\right)=-\lim_{x\to 0^+}\frac{x\left(1-x^n\right)}{(1-x)}=0$

Also, $L < \lim_{x\to 0^+}\left(x+\frac{x^2}{2}+\frac{x^3}{3}+....+\frac{x^n}{n}\right)$

$<\lim_{x\to 0^+}\left(x+x^2+x^3+....+x^n\right)=\lim_{x\to 0^+}\frac{x\left(1-x^n\right)}{(1-x)}=0$

$\Rightarrow$ L = 0

6. (a) $\lim_{x\to 0}\left[\frac{\sin x}{x}\right]$

$\sin x = x - \frac{x^3}{3!}+\frac{x^5}{5!}-\frac{x^7}{7!}+....$

$\frac{\sin x}{x}=1-\frac{x^2}{3!}+\frac{x^4}{5!}-\frac{x^6}{7!}+....$

$=1-x^2\underbrace{\left(\frac{1}{3!}-\frac{x^2}{5!}\right)}_{+ve}-x^6\underbrace{\left(\frac{1}{7!}-\frac{x^2}{9!}\right)}_{+ve}.........<1$

Also $\frac{\sin x}{x}=\underbrace{\left(1-\frac{x^2}{3!}\right)}_{+ve}+\left(x^4\right)\underbrace{\left(\frac{1}{5!}-\frac{x^2}{7!}\right)}_{+ve}+....>0$

$0<\frac{\sin x}{x}<1$

$\Rightarrow$ $\lim_{\to}\left[\frac{\sin}{\ }\right]\ \ 0$

(b) $\lim_{x\to 0}\left[\frac{\sin^{-1}x}{x}\right]=L$ (Say)

Let $\sin^{-1}x = \theta$

$\Rightarrow$ $\sin(\sin^{-1}x) = \sin\theta$

$\Rightarrow$ $x = \sin\theta, x\to 0$

$\Rightarrow$ $x\to 0$

$\therefore$ $L=\lim_{\theta\to 0}\left[\frac{\theta}{\sin\theta}\right]$ $\quad\therefore$ For $\theta\to 0$, $0<\frac{\sin\theta}{\theta}<1$

$\Rightarrow$ $\frac{\theta}{\sin\theta}>1$

$\Rightarrow$ $L=\lim_{\theta\to 0}\left[\frac{\theta}{\sin\theta}\right]=1$ $\quad\therefore$ $\lim_{x\to 0}\left[\frac{\sin^{-1}x}{x}\right]=1$

(c) $\lim_{x\to 0}\left[\frac{\tan x}{x}\right]$

Also $\frac{\tan x}{x}>1$ $\quad$ ($\because$ For $x\to 0^+$, $y = \tan x$ is above $y = x$ and $y = \tan x$ is below $y = -x$ for $x\to 0^-$)

$\Rightarrow$ $\frac{\tan x}{x}\to 1$ for $x\to 0$ $\Rightarrow$ $\lim_{x\to 0}\left[\frac{\tan x}{x}\right]=1$

(d) $\lim_{x\to 0}\left[\frac{\ell n(1+x)}{x}\right]$

$\Rightarrow$ $\ell n(1+x)=x-\frac{x^2}{2}+\frac{x^3}{3}-\frac{x^4}{4}+.....$

$\Rightarrow$ $\frac{\ell n(1+x)}{x}=1-\frac{x}{2}+\frac{x^2}{3}-\frac{x^3}{4}+.......$

$\Rightarrow$ 1^+ for $x\to 0^-$ and $(1)-x\underbrace{\left(\frac{1}{2}-\frac{x}{3}\right)}_{+ve}-x^2\underbrace{\left(\frac{1}{3}-\frac{x}{y}\right)}_{+ve}....<1$ for $x\to 0^+$

$=\left(1-\frac{x}{2}\right)+x^2\left(\frac{1}{3}-\frac{x}{4}\right)+....>0$ for $x\to 0^+$

$\Rightarrow$ $\lim_{x\to 0^+}\left[\frac{\ell n(1+x)}{x}\right]=0$

$\Rightarrow$ $\lim_{x\to 0^-}\left[\frac{\ell n(1+x)}{x}\right]=1$

$\Rightarrow$ Limit does not exist.

(e) $\lim_{x\to 0}\left[\frac{e^x-1}{x}\right]$

$\Rightarrow$ $e^x = 1 + x + \frac{x^2}{2!}+\frac{x^3}{3!}$

$\Rightarrow$ $ex - 1 = x + \frac{x^2}{2!}+\frac{x^3}{3!}+\frac{x^4}{4!}+......$

$\Rightarrow$ $\frac{e^x-1}{x}=\left(1+\frac{x}{2!}+\frac{x^2}{3!}+\frac{x^3}{4!}+....\right)\to 1^+$ as $x\to 0^+$

$\Rightarrow$ $\lim_{x\to 0^+}\left[\frac{e^x-1}{x}\right]=1$ and $\left(1+\frac{x}{2!}\right)+x^2\left(\frac{1}{3!}+\frac{x}{4!}\right)+....>0$;

for $x\to 0^+$ and let $x = -y$; $y\to 0^+$ as $x\to 0^-$.

$\Rightarrow$ $\frac{e^x-1}{x}=1-\frac{y}{2!}+\frac{y^2}{3!}-\frac{y^3}{4!}+....=1$

$-y\underbrace{\left(\frac{1}{2!}-\frac{y}{3!}\right)}_{+ve}-y^3\underbrace{\left(\frac{1}{4!}-\frac{y}{5!}\right)}_{+ve}....<1$

$\Rightarrow \lim\limits_{x\to 0^-}\left[\dfrac{e^x-1}{x}\right]=0$

$\Rightarrow$ Limit does not exist.

(f) $\lim\limits_{x\to 0}\left(\dfrac{\tan^{-1}x}{x}-\left[\dfrac{\tan^{-1}x}{x}\right]\right)$

For $x \to 0^+$, $0 < \tan^{-1}x < x$

$\Rightarrow \dfrac{\tan^{-1}x}{x} \in (0,1)$

$\Rightarrow \left[\dfrac{\tan^{-1}x}{x}\right]=0$

$$\text{R.H.L} = \lim_{x\to 0^+}\left\{\frac{\tan^{-1}x}{x}\right\} = \lim_{x\to 0^+}\left(\frac{\tan^{-1}x}{x}-\left[\frac{\tan^{-1}x}{x}\right]\right)=1-0=1$$

Also for $x \to 0^-$, $x < \tan^{-1}x < 0$

$\Rightarrow 0<\dfrac{\tan^{-1}x}{x}<1 \qquad \Rightarrow \left[\dfrac{\tan^{-1}x}{x}\right]=0$

$\Rightarrow$ L.H.L. = 1 – 0 = 1

$\therefore$ Limit = 1

7. $\lim\limits_{x\to 0}\left[\dfrac{-2x}{\tan x}\right] \quad \because \quad 0<\dfrac{x}{\tan x}<1\,\forall x\in\left[\dfrac{-\pi}{2},\dfrac{\pi}{2}\right]$

$\Rightarrow -2<\dfrac{-2x}{\tan x}<0$; but $\dfrac{-2x}{\tan x}\to 2$ as $x\to 0$

$\Rightarrow \lim\limits_{x\to 0}\left[\dfrac{-2x}{\tan x}\right]=-2$

8. $\lim\limits_{x\to 0}\left[\dfrac{|\sin x|}{|x|}\right]$

$\Rightarrow 0 < |\sin x| < |x|$

$\Rightarrow 0<\left|\dfrac{\sin x}{x}\right|<1$

$\Rightarrow \lim\limits_{x\to 0}\left[\dfrac{|\sin x|}{|x|}\right]=0$

9. $\lim\limits_{x\to 0}\left(\left[\dfrac{n\sin x}{x}\right]+\left[\dfrac{n\tan x}{x}\right]\right)$; $0<\dfrac{\sin x}{x}<1$ for $x\to 0$

Which is equivalent to writing $0<\dfrac{n\sin x}{x}<n$ but $\dfrac{n\sin x}{x}\to$ n for $x\to 0$

$\Rightarrow \lim\limits_{x\to 0}\left[\dfrac{n\sin x}{x}\right]=n-1$

Also $n<\dfrac{n\tan x}{x}<0\ \forall\ x\in\left(\dfrac{-\pi}{2},\dfrac{\pi}{2}\right)$ and $\dfrac{n\tan x}{x}\to n$ as $x\to 0$

$\Rightarrow \lim\limits_{x\to 0}\left[\dfrac{n\tan x}{x}\right]=(n)$

$\Rightarrow \lim\limits_{x\to 0}\left(\left[\dfrac{n\sin x}{x}\right]+\left[\dfrac{n\tan x}{x}\right]\right)=n-1+n=2n-1$

TEXTUAL EXERCISE–2: (OBJECTIVE)

1. (a) Given that $\dfrac{2x+8}{x}<f(x)<\dfrac{8x^2-6x}{4x^2}$

Let us consider the limit $\lim\limits_{x\to\infty}\left(2+\dfrac{8}{x}\right)=2$

$\Rightarrow \lim\limits_{x\to\infty}\left(2-\dfrac{6}{4x}\right)=2$

By sandwich theorem $\lim\limits_{x\to\infty}f(x)=2$

2. (d) $\lim\limits_{\to}\dfrac{\sqrt{1-\cos 2(\ \ -1)}}{\ }$

The limit reduces to $\lim\limits_{x\to 1}\dfrac{\sqrt{2}\,|\sin(x-1)|}{x-1}$

L.H.L. $=\lim\limits_{x\to 1^-}\left(\dfrac{-\sqrt{2}\,(\sin(x-1))}{x-1}\right)=-\sqrt{2}$ and

R.H.L. $=\lim\limits_{x\to 1^+}\left(\dfrac{\sqrt{2}\,(\sin(x-1))}{x-1}\right)=\sqrt{2}$

$\Rightarrow$ L.H.L $\neq$ R.H.L

$\Rightarrow$ Limit does not exist

3. (b) $\dfrac{\sin\left(\pi\cos^2 x\right)}{x^2}$

By L-Hospital rule, we get $\dfrac{-\cos\left(\pi\cos^2 x\right).2\pi.\cos x\sin x}{2x}$

$\Rightarrow \lim\limits_{x\to 0}\dfrac{-\cos\left(\pi\cos^2 x\right).\pi.\sin 2x}{2x}=-(-1)\,\pi\,(1)=\pi$

4. (c) $0<x<y$, then $\lim\limits_{n\to\infty}\left(y^n+x^n\right)^{1/n}$

$\Rightarrow \lim\limits_{n\to\infty}\left[y\left(1+\left(\dfrac{x}{y}\right)^n\right)^{1/n}\right]$

By the question $x<y$

$\Rightarrow \dfrac{x}{y}<1$

$\Rightarrow \lim\limits_{n\to\infty}\left(\dfrac{x}{y}\right)^n=0$

$\Rightarrow \lim\limits_{n\to\infty}\left[y(1+0)^{1/n}\right]=y$

5. (a) $\lim\limits_{x\to 0}\dfrac{\cos(m+2)x-\cos mx}{\cos(m+4)x-\cos(m+2)x}$

$$=\lim_{x\to 0}\frac{-2\sin\left(\dfrac{2mx+2x}{2}\right).\sin\left(\dfrac{2x}{2}\right)}{-2\sin\left(\dfrac{2mx+6x}{2}\right)\sin\left(\dfrac{2x}{2}\right)}$$

Which can be further written as $\lim\limits_{x\to 0}\dfrac{\sin(mx+x)}{\sin(mx+3x)}$

$\Rightarrow \lim\limits_{x\to 0}\dfrac{\sin(x(m+1))}{\sin(x(m+3))}=\dfrac{(m+1)}{(m+3)}$

6. (c) **A:** $\lim_{x\to\infty}\left(x\sin\frac{1}{x}\right)=1$

This is equal to $\lim_{x\to\infty}\left(\frac{\sin\frac{1}{x}}{\frac{1}{x}}\right)=\lim_{h\to 0}\left(\frac{\sinh}{h}\right)=1$, where $h=\frac{1}{x}$

$\Rightarrow$ Assertion is correct

R: $\lim_{y\to 0} y.\sin\left(\frac{1}{y}\right)$

When $y\to 0 \Rightarrow \frac{1}{y}\to\infty$ but sin (∞) will still be a finite in the interval [–1,1]

$\Rightarrow \lim_{y\to 0} y\sin\left(\frac{1}{y}\right)=0$

$\Rightarrow$ Reason is incorrect

7. (b) $\lim_{\theta\to 0^+}\frac{\sin\sqrt{\theta}}{\sqrt{\sin\theta}}$

which can be written as -: $\lim_{\theta\to 0^+}\frac{\left(\frac{\sin\sqrt{\theta}}{\sqrt{\theta}}\right)\sqrt{\theta}}{\sqrt{\theta}.\sqrt{\frac{\sin\theta}{\theta}}}$

$\Rightarrow \lim_{\theta\to 0^+}\frac{\frac{\sin\sqrt{\theta}}{\sqrt{\theta}}}{\sqrt{\frac{\sin\theta}{\theta}}}=1$

8. (b) $\lim_{x\to 0}\frac{\sin x^n}{(\sin x)^m}$

which can be written as-: $\lim_{x\to 0}\frac{\left(\frac{\sin x^n}{x^n}\right)x^n}{\left(\frac{\sin x}{x}\right)^m .x^m}$

which hence reduces to $\lim_{x\to 0}(x)^{n-m}$

Given n > m $\quad\Rightarrow n-m>0$

$\Rightarrow \lim_{x\to 0}(x)^{n-m}=0$

9. (c) $\lim_{x\to 0}\frac{(e^x-1)^4}{\sin\left(\frac{x^2}{k^2}\right)\log\left(1+\frac{x^2}{2}\right)}$

Replacing by infinitesimals of equivalent order we get

$\lim_{x\to 0}\frac{x^4}{\frac{x^2}{k^2}.\frac{x^2}{2}}=\lim_{x\to 0}(2k^2)$

Given in the equation $\lim_{x\to 0}(2k^2)=8$

$\Rightarrow 2k^2=8 \quad\Rightarrow k^2=4$

$\Rightarrow$ k = 2 or – 2

10. (b) $\lim_{n\to\infty}\left(\frac{a^n+b^n}{a^n-b^n}\right)$

which can be re-written as-: $\lim_{n\to\infty}\left[\frac{a^n\left(1+\left(\frac{b}{a}\right)^n\right)}{a^n\left(1-\left(\frac{b}{a}\right)^n\right)}\right]$

Given in the question a > b > 1

$\Rightarrow 1 > b/a$

$\Rightarrow \lim_{n\to\infty}\left(\frac{b}{a}\right)^n=0$

The limit reduces to -: $\lim_{n\to\infty}\left[\frac{a^n}{a^n}\right]=1$

11. (a) $\lim_{x\to\infty}(1-a^4)^x.\sin\frac{b}{(1-a^4)^x}; a\in(-1,1)$

Here $a^4\in(0,1)$

$\Rightarrow -a^4\in(-1,0)$

$\Rightarrow (1-a^4)\in(0,1)$

$\Rightarrow (1-a^4)^x\to 0$ as $x\to\infty$ and $\frac{b}{(1-a^4)^x}$ oscillates on ℝ

$\Rightarrow \sin\left(\frac{b}{(1-a^4)^x}\right)$ Oscillates on [–1, 1]

$\Rightarrow \lim_{x\to\infty}(1-a^4)^x\sin\left(\frac{b}{(1-a^4)^x}\right)=0$

12. (c) $\lim_{x\to 1}\frac{\cos 2-\cos 2x}{x^2-|x|}=\lim_{x\to 1}\frac{-2\sin(1+x)\sin(1-x)}{x^2-|x|}$

$\Rightarrow \lim_{x\to 1}\frac{2\sin(1+x)\sin(x-1)}{|x|(|x|-1)}$

$\Rightarrow$ 2 sin 2

13. (a) $\lim_{x\to 0}(x^{-3}\sin 3x+ax^{-2}+b)=\lim_{x\to 0}\left(\frac{\sin 3x}{x^3}+\frac{a}{x^2}+b\right)$

$\Rightarrow \lim_{x\to 0}\left(\frac{3}{x^2}\frac{\sin 3x}{3x}+\frac{a}{x^2}+b\right)$

Since the limit exists and is equal to zero.

$\Rightarrow$ a = – 3, b = 0

14. (a) $\lim_{x\to 0}\frac{\ell n(3+x)-\ell n(3-x)}{x}=k$

$=\lim_{x\to 0}\left(\frac{\ell n(3+x)}{x}-\frac{\ell n(3-x)}{x}\right)=k$

which can be written as $\lim_{x\to 0}\frac{\ell n\left(\frac{3+x}{3-x}\right)}{x}=k$

$=\lim_{x\to 0}\frac{\ell n\left(1+\frac{2x}{3-x}\right)}{x}=k$

$=\lim_{x\to 0}\frac{2}{3-x}\frac{\ell n\left(1+\frac{2x}{3-x}\right)}{\frac{2x}{3-x}}=k$

$=\lim_{x\to 0}\left(\frac{2}{3-x}\right)=k$

$\Rightarrow k=\frac{2}{3}$

15. (a), (b), (d)

(a) $\lim_{x\to\infty}\sqrt[4]{x}.\sin\left(\frac{1}{\sqrt{x}}\right)=\lim_{x\to\infty}\frac{\left(x^{-\frac{1}{4}}\right)\sin\left(\frac{1}{\sqrt{x}}\right)}{\left(\frac{1}{\sqrt{x}}\right)}=\lim_{x\to\infty}\left(\frac{1}{x}\right)^{\frac{1}{4}}=0$

⇒ limit vanishes

(b) $\lim_{x\to\frac{\pi}{2}}(1-\sin x)\tan x=\lim_{h\to0}\left(1-\sin\left(\frac{\pi}{2}+h\right)\right)\tan\left(\frac{\pi}{2}+h\right)$

$=\lim_{h\to0}\left(\frac{2\sin^2\frac{h}{2}}{1}\right)\left(\frac{-\cos h}{\sin h}\right)=\lim_{h\to0}\frac{-2h^2}{4(h)}=0$

(c) $\lim_{x\to\infty}\left(\frac{2x^2+3}{x^2+x-5}\right)\left(\frac{|x|}{x}\right)=\lim_{x\to\infty}\left(\frac{2+\frac{3}{x^2}}{1+\frac{1}{x}-\frac{5}{x^2}}\right)\left(\frac{|x|}{x}\right)=2$

which is a finite number

(d) $\lim_{x\to3^+}\frac{[x]^2-9}{x^2-9}$

$x\to3^+$

⇒ x is slightly greater than 3

⇒ $[x]=3$

$=\lim_{h\to0^+}\frac{[3+h]^2-9}{(3+h)^2-9}=\lim_{h\to0^+}\frac{[3+h]^2-9}{9+h^2+6h-9}$

$=\lim_{h\to0^+}\frac{0}{h^2+6h}=0$

16. (d) $\lim_{x\to0}\frac{\sqrt{1-\cos2x}}{\sqrt{2}x}=\lim_{x\to0}\frac{\sqrt{2}\,|\sin x|}{\sqrt{2}x}=\lim_{x\to0}\frac{|\sin x|}{x}$

⇒ Limit does not exist, as, L.H.L = –1 ≠ R.H.L = 1

TEXTUAL EXERCISE–3: (SUBJECTIVE)

1. (a) $\lim_{x\to-2}\frac{x^4+5x^3+6x^2}{x^2-3x-10}$

which can be re-written as $=\lim_{x\to-2}\frac{x^2(x+2)(x+3)}{(x-5)(x+2)}=$

$\lim_{x\to-2}\frac{x^2(x+3)}{(x-5)}=\frac{4(1)}{-7}=-\frac{4}{7}$

(b) $\lim_{x\to0}\frac{(4+x)^3-4^3}{x}=\lim_{x\to0}(4+x)^2+(4+x).4+4^2$

$=\lim_{x\to0}((4+x)^2+4(4+x)+4^2)$

$=16+16+16=48$

(c) $\lim_{x\to0}\frac{(1+x)(1+2x)(1+3x)-1}{x}$

$=\lim_{x\to0}\frac{(1+2x+x+2x^2)(1+3x)-1}{x}$

$=\lim_{x\to0}\frac{(1+3x+2x^2+3x+9x^2+6x^3)-1}{x}$

$=\lim_{x\to0}\left(\frac{6x+11x^2+6x^3}{x}\right)=6$

(d) $\lim_{x\to0}\frac{(1+x)^5-(1+5x)}{x^2+x^5}$

$=\lim_{x\to0}\frac{({}^5C_0.x^0+{}^5C_1.x^1+{}^5C_2.x^2+...+{}^5C_5.x^5-1-5x)}{x^2+x^5}$

$=\lim_{x\to0}\frac{\left({}^5C_2x^2+{}^5C_3x^3+{}^5C_4x^4+x^5\right)}{x^2+x^5}$

$=\lim_{x\to0}\left(\frac{{}^5C_2+{}^5C_3x+{}^5C_4x^2+x^3}{1+x^3}\right)$

$={}^5C_2=\frac{5!}{3!2!}=10$

(e) $\lim_{x\to1}\frac{x^4-2x^2+1}{x^3-1}$

$=\lim_{x\to1}\frac{x^2(x^2-1)-(x^2-1)}{x^3-1}=\lim_{x\to1}\frac{(x^2-1)(x^2-1)}{x^3-1}$

$=\lim_{x\to1}\frac{(x^2-1)(x+1)}{(x^2+1-x)}=0$

(f) $\lim_{x\to-1}\frac{x^3-2x-1}{x^5-2x-1}=\lim_{x\to-1}\frac{3x^2-2}{5x^4-2}=\frac{1}{3}$

(g) $\lim_{x\to1}\frac{x^m-1^m}{x^m-1}=\lim_{x\to1}\frac{(x-1)(x^{m-1}+...+1)}{(x-1)(x^{n-1}+.....+1)}$

Cancelling factors $(x-1)$ from both numerator and denominator, given limit $=\frac{m}{n}$

(h) $\lim_{x\to0}\left(\frac{1}{x}-\frac{1}{x^2}\right)=\lim_{x\to0}\left(\frac{x-1}{x^2}\right)=-\infty$

(i) $\lim_{x\to0}\frac{[(1+x)^{\frac{1}{k}}-1]}{x};k\in\mathbb{Z}^+$

which is similar to writing

$\lim_{x\to0}\frac{(x+1)-1}{x\left((x+1)^{1-\frac{1}{k}}+(x+1)^{1-\frac{2}{k}}+......+1\right)}=\frac{1}{k}$

2. (a) $\lim_{x\to0}\frac{e^{2x}+e^x-2}{e^x-1}=\lim_{x\to0}\frac{e^{2x}-1}{e^x-1}+1$

$=\lim_{x\to0}\left[2\left[\frac{\frac{e^{2x}-1}{2x}}{\frac{e^x-1}{x}}\right]+1\right]=2+1=3$

(b) $\lim_{x\to\frac{\pi}{4}}\frac{1-\tan x}{\sin x-\cos x}=\lim_{x\to\frac{\pi}{4}}\frac{(\cos x-\sin x)}{\cos x(\sin x-\cos x)}$

$=\lim_{x\to\frac{\pi}{4}}\left(\frac{1}{-\cos x}\right)=\lim_{x\to0}(-\sec x)=-\sqrt{2}$

(c) $\lim_{x\to\frac{\pi}{6}}\frac{(2\sin^2x+\sin x-1)}{(2\sin^2x-3\sin x+1)}$

$$= \lim_{x\to\frac{\pi}{6}}\left(\frac{2\sin^2 x+2\sin x-\sin x-1}{2\sin^2 x-2\sin x-\sin x+1}\right)$$

$$= \lim_{x\to\frac{\pi}{x}}\left(\frac{2\sin x(\sin x+1)-(\sin x+1)}{2\sin x(\sin x-1)-(\sin x-1)}\right)$$

$$= \lim_{x\to\frac{\pi}{6}}\left(\frac{(\sin x+1)(2\sin x-1)}{(\sin x-1)(2\sin x-1)}\right) = \lim_{x\to\frac{\pi}{6}}\left(\frac{\sin x+1}{\sin x-1}\right) = -3$$

(d) $\lim_{x\to\tan^{-1}3}\left(\frac{\tan^2 x-2\tan x-3}{\tan^2 x-4\tan x+3}\right)$

On factorizing, we get $\lim_{x\to\tan^{-1}3}\left(\frac{(\tan x-3)(\tan x+1)}{(\tan x-3)(\tan x-1)}\right)$

$$= \lim_{x\to\tan^{-1}3}\left(\frac{\tan x+1}{\tan x-1}\right) = 2$$

3. (a) $\lim_{x\to a}\frac{x^{\frac{1}{2}}-a^{\frac{1}{2}}}{(x+a)(x-a)} = \lim_{x\to a}\frac{\sqrt{x}-\sqrt{a}}{(x+a)(\sqrt{x}-\sqrt{a})(\sqrt{x}+\sqrt{a})}$

$$= \lim_{x\to a}\frac{1}{(x+a)(\sqrt{x}+\sqrt{a})} = \frac{1}{4a^{3/2}}$$

(b) $\lim_{x\to a}\frac{x^{\frac{1}{3}}-a^{\frac{1}{3}}}{(x^3-a^3)}$

$$= \lim_{x\to a}\frac{x-a}{(x-a)(x^2+a^2+ax)\left(x^{\frac{2}{3}}+x^{\frac{1}{3}}.a^{\frac{1}{3}}+a^{\frac{2}{3}}\right)}$$

$$= \frac{1}{9.a^{\frac{8}{3}}}$$

(c) $\lim_{x\to 4}\frac{(1+2x)^{\frac{1}{2}}-3}{\sqrt{x}-2}$

$$= \lim_{x\to 4}\frac{(2x-8)(\sqrt{x}+2)}{(x-4)(\sqrt{1+2x}+3)} = \frac{(2)(4)}{(6)} = \frac{4}{3}$$

(d) $\lim_{x\to -8}\frac{\sqrt{1-x}-3}{2+x^{1/3}}$

$$= \lim_{x\to -8}\frac{(1-x)-9}{\sqrt{1-x}+3}\times\frac{(4-2(x)^{1/3}+x^{2/3})}{(8+x)} = -2$$

(e) $\lim_{x\to 1}\frac{x^{\frac{1}{3}}-1^{\frac{1}{3}}}{x^{\frac{1}{2}}-1^{\frac{1}{2}}}$

$$= \lim_{x\to 1}\frac{x-1}{(x^{2/3}+x^{1/3}.(1)^{1/3}+(1)^{2/3})}\times\frac{x^{1/2}+(1)^{1/2}}{(x-1)} = \frac{2}{3}$$

(f) $\lim_{x\to 0}\frac{\sqrt{\cos x}-\sqrt[3]{\cos x}}{\sin^2 x} = \lim_{x\to 0}\frac{(\cos x)^{1/2}-(\cos x)^{1/3}}{1-\cos^2 x}$

$$= \lim_{x\to 0}\frac{(\cos^3 x)^{1/6}-(\cos^2 x)^{1/6}}{(1-\cos^2 x)} = \lim_{t\to 1}\frac{(t^3)^{1/6}-(t^2)^{1/6}}{(1-t^2)}$$

$$= \lim_{t\to 1}\frac{(t^3-t^2)}{(1-t^2)(t^{15/6}+t^{14/6}+t^{13/6}+(t)^{12/6}+(t)^{11/6}+(t)^{10/6})}$$

$$= \lim_{t\to 1}\frac{-t^2(1-t)}{(1-t)(1+t)(6)} = \frac{-1}{12}$$

(g) $\lim_{x\to 0}\frac{\sqrt{x^2+1}-1}{\sqrt{x^2+9}-3}$

Upon rationalization, we get

$$\lim_{x\to 0}\frac{x^2+1-1}{(\sqrt{x^2+1}+1)}\frac{\sqrt{x^2+9}+3}{(x^2+9-9)}$$

$$= \lim_{x\to 0}\left(\frac{x^2(\sqrt{x^2+9}+3)}{x^2(\sqrt{x^2+1}+1)}\right) = 3$$

(h) $\lim_{x\to b}\frac{\sqrt{x-a}-\sqrt{b-a}}{x^2-b^2}$; $b > a$

which is same as $\lim_{x\to b}\frac{(x-a)^{\frac{1}{2}}-(b-a)^{\frac{1}{2}}}{(x+b)(x-b)}$

$$= \lim_{x\to b}\frac{(x-b)}{(\sqrt{x-a}+\sqrt{b-a})(x+b)(x-b)} = \frac{1}{4b\sqrt{b-a}}$$

(i) $\lim_{x\to\infty} x^{\frac{3}{2}}\left(\sqrt{x^3+1}-\sqrt{x^3-1}\right)$

$$= \lim_{x\to\infty}\left(x^{\frac{3}{2}}\sqrt{x^3+1}-x^{\frac{3}{2}}\sqrt{x^3-1}\right)$$

By rationalization, we get $\lim_{x\to\infty}\frac{x^{\frac{3}{2}}(x^3+1-x^3+1)}{(\sqrt{x^3-1}+\sqrt{x^3+1})}$

$$= \lim_{x\to\infty}\frac{2x^{\frac{3}{2}}}{(\sqrt{x^3-1}+\sqrt{x^3+1})}$$

$$= \lim_{x\to\infty}\frac{2x^{\frac{3}{2}}}{x^{\frac{3}{2}}\left(\sqrt{1-\frac{1}{x^3}}+\sqrt{1+\frac{1}{x^3}}\right)} = \lim_{x\to\infty}\frac{2}{\sqrt{1-\frac{1}{x^3}}+\sqrt{1+\frac{1}{x^3}}}$$

$$= 1$$

(j) $\lim_{x\to 2a}\frac{\sqrt{x-2a}+\sqrt{x}-\sqrt{2a}}{\sqrt{x^2-4a^2}}$

$$= \lim_{x\to 2a}\frac{\sqrt{x-2a}+\sqrt{x}-\sqrt{2a}}{\sqrt{x-2a}\sqrt{x+2a}}$$

which is same as

$$\lim_{x\to 2a}\frac{1}{\sqrt{x+2a}}+\frac{x-2a}{(\sqrt{x^2-4a^2})(\sqrt{x}+\sqrt{2a})}$$

$$= \lim_{x\to 2a}\frac{1}{\sqrt{x+2a}}+\frac{\sqrt{x-2a}}{(\sqrt{x+2a})(\sqrt{x}+\sqrt{2a})}$$

$$= \frac{1}{\sqrt{4a}} = \frac{1}{2\sqrt{a}}$$

(k) $\lim_{x\to 0}\dfrac{\left[(1+x^5)^{\frac{1}{5}}-(1+x^2)^{\frac{1}{5}}\right]}{\left[(1-x^5)^{\frac{1}{5}}-(1-x^3)^{\frac{1}{5}}\right]}$

$$= \lim_{x\to 0}\frac{(x^5-x^2)}{(x^3-x^5)}\cdot\frac{\sum_{r=1}^{5}(1-x^5)^{\left(1-\frac{r}{5}\right)}.(1-x^3)^{\left(\frac{r-1}{5}\right)}}{\sum_{r=1}^{5}(1+x^5)^{\left(1-\frac{r}{5}\right)}.(1+x^2)^{\left(\frac{r-1}{5}\right)}}$$

$$= \lim_{x\to 0}\frac{-x^2(1-x^3)}{x^3(1-x^2)}\cdot\frac{5}{5} = \lim_{x\to 0}\frac{-1}{x}\cdot\frac{(1+x+x^2)}{(1+x)}$$

⇒ L.H.L. = ∞, R.H.L. = −∞

Using $a^{\frac{1}{k}} - b^{\frac{1}{k}} = \dfrac{(a-b)}{a^{1-\frac{1}{k}} + a^{1-\frac{2}{k}}.b^{\frac{1}{k}} + ...+ b^{1-\frac{1}{k}}} = -\infty$

4. $\lim_{x\to\infty}\sqrt{(x+a)(x+b)}-x$

On rationalization, we get

$$\lim_{x\to\infty}\frac{\left(\sqrt{(x+a)(x+b)}-x\right)\left(\sqrt{(x+a)(x+b)}+x\right)}{\sqrt{(x+a)(x+b)}+x)}$$

$$= \lim_{x\to\infty}\frac{(x+a)(x+b)-x^2}{\left(\sqrt{(x+a)(x+b)}+x\right)}$$

$$= \lim_{x\to\infty}\frac{ax+bx+ab}{x\left(\sqrt{\left(1+\frac{a}{x}\right)\left(1+\frac{b}{x}\right)}+1\right)}$$

$$= \lim_{x\to\infty}\frac{a+b+ab/x}{\sqrt{\left(1+\frac{a}{x}\right)\left(1+\frac{b}{x}\right)}+1} = \frac{a+b}{2}$$

5. (a) $\lim_{x\to 0}\dfrac{\sin 3x}{5x}$

which can be re-written as $\dfrac{-1}{5}\lim_{x\to 0}\left(\dfrac{\sin 3x}{3x}\times 3\right) = \dfrac{3}{5}$

(b) $\lim_{x\to 0}\dfrac{\sec x-1}{x\sec x} = \lim_{x\to 0}\dfrac{1-\cos x}{x}$

$$= \lim_{x\to 0}\left(\frac{2\sin^2\frac{x}{2}}{x}\right) = \lim_{x\to 0}\sin\frac{x}{2}\left(\frac{\sin\frac{x}{2}}{\frac{x}{2}}\right) = 0$$

(c) $\lim_{x\to 0}\dfrac{e^{-4x}-1}{e^{-2x}+e^{-x}-2}$; which can be written as

$$\lim_{x\to 0}\frac{e^{-4x}-1}{e^{-2x}-1+e^{-x}-1}$$

$$= \lim_{x\to 0}\frac{\left(\frac{e^{-4x}-1}{-4x}\right)(-4)}{\left(\frac{e^{-2x}-1}{-2x}\right)(-2)+\left(\frac{e^{-x}-1}{-x}\right)(-1)} = \frac{4}{3}$$

(d) $\lim_{x\to 0}\dfrac{\sin^{-1}x+\tan^{-1}(2x)}{x}$

which can be written as $\lim_{x\to 0}\left(\dfrac{\sin^{-1}x}{x}+\dfrac{2.\tan^{-1}(2x)}{2x}\right)$

Distributing the limits, we get = 1 + 2.(1) = 3

(e) $\lim_{x\to 0}\dfrac{\log\cos x}{3x^2} = \lim_{x\to 0}\dfrac{\log(1+\cos x-1)}{3x^2(\cos x-1)}.(\cos x-1)$

which can be written as

$$\lim_{x\to 0}\left(\frac{\log(1+(\cos x-1))}{(\cos x-1)}\cdot\left(\frac{-2\sin^2\frac{x}{2}}{4.3\left(\frac{x^2}{4}\right)}\right)\right)$$

which is equal to $\dfrac{-2}{12} = -\dfrac{1}{6}$ (by standard limits)

(f) $\lim_{x\to 0}\dfrac{a^x-b^x}{3\sin x} = \lim_{x\to 0}\dfrac{b^x\left(\left(\frac{a}{b}\right)^x-1\right)}{3\left(\frac{\sin x}{x}\right)^x}$

$$= \lim_{x\to 0}\frac{b^x\ln\left(\frac{a}{b}\right)}{3} = \frac{1}{3}\ln\left(\frac{a}{b}\right)$$

$$\left(\because \lim_{x\to 0}\frac{a^x-1}{x} = \ell na\right)$$

(g) $\lim_{x\to 0}\dfrac{[\log(a+x)-\log a]}{x}$

which can be written as $\lim_{x\to 0}\dfrac{\log\left(1+\frac{x}{a}\right)}{x}$

$$= \lim_{x\to 0}\frac{\log\left(1+\frac{x}{a}\right)}{a.\frac{x}{a}} = \frac{1}{a}$$

(h) $\lim_{x\to 0}\dfrac{\log(1+x^2+x^4)}{3x^2(1-2x)}$. Dividing both numerator and denominator by $x^4 + x^2$, we get $\lim_{x\to 0}\dfrac{\frac{\log(1+x^2+x^4)}{x^2+x^4}}{\frac{3(x^2-2x^3)}{x^2(1+x^2)}} =$

$$\lim_{x\to 0}\frac{1}{\frac{3-6x}{1+x^2}} = \frac{1}{3}$$

(i) $\lim_{x\to 0}\dfrac{x\left(e^{\frac{1}{x}}-e^{-\frac{1}{x}}\right)}{e^{\frac{1}{x}}+e^{-\frac{1}{x}}}$

⇒ L.H.L. $= \lim_{x\to 0^-}x\dfrac{\left(e^{\frac{2}{x}}-1\right)}{\left(e^{\frac{2}{x}}+1\right)} = \dfrac{0(0-1)}{(0+1)} = 0$ and R.H.L.

$$= \lim_{x\to 0^+}x\frac{\left(1-e^{\frac{-2}{x}}\right)}{\left(1+e^{\frac{-2}{x}}\right)} = \frac{0(0-1)}{(0+1)} = 0$$

$\Rightarrow$ Given limit = 0

(j) $\lim\limits_{x\to\frac{\pi}{6}} \dfrac{\sin\left[x-\left(\frac{\pi}{6}\right)\right]}{\left(\sqrt{3}-2\cos x\right)} = L = \lim\limits_{h\to 0}\dfrac{\sin(h)}{\sqrt{3}-2\cos\left(h+\frac{\pi}{6}\right)}$

$= \lim\limits_{h\to 0}\dfrac{\sin h}{\sqrt{3}-\sqrt{3}\cos h+\sin h}$

$= \lim\limits_{h\to 0}\dfrac{\frac{\sin h}{h}}{\left[\sqrt{3}\left(\dfrac{2\sin^2\frac{h}{2}}{h}\right)+\left(\dfrac{\sin h}{h}\right)\right]} = \dfrac{1}{0+1} = 1$

(k) $\lim\limits_{x\to\pi}\dfrac{\left[\sqrt{2+\cos x}-1\right]}{(\pi-x)^2} = \lim\limits_{x\to\pi}\dfrac{(1+\cos x)}{(\pi-x)^2\left(\sqrt{2+\cos x}+1\right)}$

$= \lim\limits_{x\to\pi}\dfrac{2\cos^2\frac{x}{2}}{2.(\pi-x)^2} = = \lim\limits_{h\to 0}\dfrac{\sin^2\left(\frac{h}{2}\right)}{(h^2)} = \dfrac{1}{4}$

(l) $\lim\limits_{x\to\frac{\pi}{4}}\dfrac{(1-\tan x)}{\left(1-\sqrt{2}\sin x\right)} = \lim\limits_{h\to 0}\dfrac{\left(1-\tan\left(\frac{\pi}{4}+h\right)\right)}{\left(1-\sqrt{2}\sin\left(\frac{\pi}{4}+h\right)\right)}$

$= \lim\limits_{h\to 0}\left(\dfrac{-2\tan h}{1-\cos h-\sin h}\right) = \lim\limits_{h\to 0}\left(\dfrac{-2\tan h}{2\sin^2\frac{h}{2}-\sin h}\right) = \dfrac{-2}{-1} = 2$

(m) $\lim\limits_{x\to\frac{\pi}{4}}\dfrac{\left[\sqrt{2}-\sin x-\cos x\right]}{(4x-\pi)^2} = \lim\limits_{x\to\frac{\pi}{4}}\dfrac{\left[\sqrt{2}-\sin x-\cos x\right]}{16\left(x-\frac{\pi}{4}\right)^2}$

$= \lim\limits_{x\to\frac{\pi}{4}}\left[\dfrac{\sqrt{2}-\sqrt{2}\left(\frac{\sin x}{\sqrt{2}}+\frac{\cos x}{\sqrt{2}}\right)}{16\left(x-\frac{\pi}{4}\right)^2}\right]$

$= \lim\limits_{x\to\frac{\pi}{4}}\left(\dfrac{\sqrt{2}-\sqrt{2}\cos\left(x-\frac{\pi}{4}\right)}{16.\left(x-\frac{\pi}{4}\right)^2}\right)$

$= \lim\limits_{h\to 0}\left(\dfrac{(1-\cosh)}{16h^2}.\dfrac{(1+\cosh)}{(1+\cosh)}\right)\times\sqrt{2} = \lim\limits_{h\to 0}\dfrac{\sin^2 h}{h^2}.\dfrac{\sqrt{2}}{32}$

$= \dfrac{1}{16\sqrt{2}}$

(n) $\lim\limits_{x\to\frac{\pi}{4}}\dfrac{\left[2\sqrt{2}-(\cos x+\sin x)^3\right]}{(1-\sin 2x)}$

$= \lim\limits_{x\to\frac{\pi}{4}}\dfrac{\left[2\sqrt{2}-(\cos x+\sin x)^3\right]}{(\cos x-\sin x)^2}$

$= \lim\limits_{x\to\frac{\pi}{4}}\left[\dfrac{2\sqrt{2}-2\sqrt{2}\left(\sin\left(x+\frac{\pi}{4}\right)\right)^3}{(\cos x-\sin x)^2}\right]$

$= \lim\limits_{x\to\frac{\pi}{4}}\left[\dfrac{2\sqrt{2}\left(1-\sin\left(x+\frac{\pi}{4}\right)\right)}{2\sin^2\left(\frac{\pi}{4}-x\right)}\right]$

$= \lim\limits_{x\to\frac{\pi}{4}}\left[\dfrac{\sqrt{2}\left(1-\sin^3\left(x+\frac{\pi}{4}\right)\right)}{\sin^2\left(x-\frac{\pi}{4}\right)}\right] = \lim\limits_{h\to 0}\dfrac{\sqrt{2}(1-\cos^3 h)}{\sin^2 h}$

$= \lim\limits_{h\to 0}\dfrac{\sqrt{2}(1-\cos h)(1+\cos h+\cos^2 h)}{\sin^2 h}$

$= \lim\limits_{h\to 0}\dfrac{\sqrt{2}(1+\cos h+\cos^2 h)}{(1+\cos h)} = \dfrac{3}{\sqrt{2}}$

(o) $\lim\limits_{x\to\frac{\pi}{3}}\dfrac{\tan^3 x-3\tan x}{\cos\left(x+\frac{\pi}{6}\right)} = \lim\limits_{x\to\frac{\pi}{3}}\dfrac{-(1-3\tan^2 x)\tan 3x}{\cos\left(x+\frac{\pi}{6}\right)}$

$= \lim\limits_{h\to 0}\dfrac{-\left(1-3\tan^2\left(\frac{\pi}{3}+h\right)\right)\tan(\pi+3h)}{-\sin h}$

$= \lim\limits_{h\to 0}\dfrac{\left[1-3\tan^2\left(\frac{\pi}{3}+h\right)\right]\tan 3h}{3h}.\dfrac{3h}{\sin h} = -8\times 3 = -24$

(p) $\lim\limits_{x\to 0}\left(\dfrac{a^x+b^x}{2}\right)^{\frac{1}{x}}$; $a, b > 0$

This we can write as $\lim\limits_{x\to 0}\left(\dfrac{2+a^x+b^x-2}{2}\right)^{\frac{1}{x}}$

which further gives as $\lim\limits_{x\to 0}\left(1+\dfrac{a^x+b^x-2}{2}\right)^{\frac{1}{x}}$

Let us now compare it with the form

$\lim\limits_{x\to a}\{1+f(x)\}^{\frac{1}{g(x)}} = e^{\lim\limits_{x\to a}\left[\frac{f(x)}{g(x)}\right]}$

where $\lim\limits_{x\to a} f(x) = \lim\limits_{x\to a} g(x) = 0$, we get $e^{\left(\lim\limits_{x\to 0}\frac{a^x+b^x-2}{2x}\right)} =$

$e^{\frac{1}{2}(\ell na+\ell nb)} = e^{\ell n(ab)^{\frac{1}{2}}} = (ab)^{1/2} = \sqrt{ab}$

(q) $\lim\limits_{x\to 0}\dfrac{1-\cos^3 x}{x\sin x.\cos x}$

which is equivalent to $\lim\limits_{x\to 0}\dfrac{\left(2\sin^2\frac{x}{2}\right)(1+\cos^2 x+\cos x)}{\frac{x^2}{4}\cdot\frac{\sin 2x}{2x}.4}$

$= \lim\limits_{x\to 0} 2\left(\dfrac{\sin\frac{x}{2}}{\frac{x}{2}}\right)^2\left(\dfrac{1+\cos^2 x+\cos x}{\frac{\sin 2x}{2x}.4}\right)$

Putting limit $x \to 0$, we get $2\times\frac{3}{4}=\frac{3}{2}$

(r) $\lim_{x\to1}(1-x)\tan\left(\frac{\pi x}{2}\right)$

Let $1-x=y$

$\Rightarrow x=1-y$

Hence the given limit reduces to $\lim_{y\to0} y\left(\tan\left(\frac{\pi}{2}(1-y)\right)\right)$

$= \lim_{y\to0} y\left(\tan\left(\frac{\pi}{2}-\frac{\pi y}{2}\right)\right)$

Which can be written as $\lim_{y\to0} y.\cot\frac{\pi y}{2}$

$= \lim_{y\to0}\left[\frac{\frac{\pi}{2}y}{\tan\frac{\pi}{2}y}\right].\frac{2}{\pi}=\frac{2}{\pi}$

(s) $\lim_{x\to\infty} a^x \sin\left(\frac{b}{a^x}\right);(a>1)$

Let $\frac{b}{a^x}=y$

as $x\to\infty$ since $a>1 \Rightarrow a^x\to\infty$

$\Rightarrow y\to0$

Hence the limit reduces to $\lim_{y\to0}\frac{b}{y}\sin y$

Rearranging this gives us $\lim_{y\to0} b\left(\frac{\sin y}{y}\right)=b$

(t) $\lim_{x\to0}\left(\frac{8^x-4^x-2^x+1^x}{x^2}\right)$

Which can be written as $\lim_{x\to0}\left(\frac{4^x.2^x-4^x-2^x+1^x}{x^2}\right)$

$= \lim_{x\to0}\left(\frac{4^x(2^x-1)-(2^x-1)}{x^2}\right)$

$= \lim_{x\to0}\left(\frac{(2^x-1)(4^x-1)}{x.x}\right)=(\ell n\,2)(\ell n\,4)=2(\ell n\,2)^2$

6. (a) $\lim_{x\to1}\frac{x^2+1-2x}{2\log^2 x}=\lim_{x\to1}\frac{(x-1)^2}{2(\log x)^2}$

Let $x-1=y$

$\Rightarrow 1+y=x \qquad \Rightarrow y\to0$

Hence the limit reduces to $\lim_{y\to0}\frac{y^2}{2(\log(y+1))^2}$

$= \lim_{y\to0}\frac{1}{2\left[\frac{\log(y+1)}{y}\right]^2}=\frac{1}{2}$

(b) $\lim_{x\to1}\frac{2^{2x}-5.2^x+6}{(2^x-2)(2^x+3)}=\lim_{x\to1}\frac{2^x.2^x-2.2^x-3.2^x+6}{(2^x-2)(2^x+3)}$

$= \lim_{x\to1}\frac{2^x(2^x-2)-3(2^x-2)}{(2^x-2)(2^x+3)}$

Which is equal to $\lim_{x\to1}\frac{(2^x-2)(2^x-3)}{(2^x-2)(2^x+3)}$

$= \lim_{x\to1}\frac{2^x-3}{2^x+3}=-\frac{1}{5}$

TEXTUAL EXERCISE–3: (OBJECTIVE)

1. (d) $\lim_{x\to3}\frac{(x^3+27)\ell n(x-2)}{(x^2-9)}$

$= \lim_{x\to3}\frac{(x+3)(x^2+9-3x)\ell n(x-2)}{(x+3)(x-3)}$

$= \lim_{x\to3}(x^2+9-3x)\frac{\ell n(1+(x-3))}{(x-3)}=9-9+9=9$

2. (b) $\lim_{x\to1}\left[\left[\frac{4}{x^2-x^{-1}}-\frac{1-3x+x^2}{1-x^3}\right]^{-1}+\frac{3(x^4-1)}{x^3-x^{-1}}\right]$

$= \lim_{x\to1}\left[\left[\frac{4x}{x^3-1}-\frac{1-3x+x^2}{1-x^3}\right]^{-1}+\frac{3(x^4-1).x}{x^4-1}\right]$

which on simplification gives us

$\lim_{x\to1}\left[\left(\frac{4x+1-3x+x^2}{x^3-1}\right)^{-1}+3x\right]$

$= \lim_{x\to1}\left[\left(\frac{x^2+x+1}{x^3-1}\right)^{-1}+3x\right]$

$\Rightarrow \lim_{x\to1}\left[\left[\frac{1}{x-1}\right]^{-1}+3x\right]=\lim_{x\to1}(x-1+3x)=\lim_{x\to1}(4x-1)=3$

3. (b) Given $\frac{\cos(2x-4)-33}{2}<f(x)<\frac{x^2|4x-8|}{x-2}\forall x\in(1,2)$

In view of applying sandwich theorem

$\lim_{x\to2^-}\left(\frac{\cos(2x-4)-33}{2}\right)=\frac{\cos(4-4)-33}{2}$

$= \frac{-32}{2}=-16$

Similarly, $\lim_{x\to2^-}\left(\frac{x^2|4x-8|}{x-2}\right)=\lim_{x\to2^-}\left(\frac{4x^2|x-2|}{x-2}\right)=$

$\lim_{x\to2^-}(-4x^2)=-16$

Hence by sandwich theorem $\lim_{x\to2^-}f(x)=-16$

4. (a) $\lim_{x\to\frac{\pi}{2}}\tan^2 x\left(\sqrt{2\sin^2 x+3\sin x+4}-\sqrt{\sin^2 x+6\sin x+2}\right)$

$= \lim_{x\to\frac{\pi}{2}}\frac{\tan^2 x\left(\left(\sqrt{2\sin^2 x+3\sin x+4}\right)^2-\left(\sqrt{\sin^2 x+6\sin x+2}\right)^2\right)}{\sqrt{2\sin^2 x+3\sin x+4}+\sqrt{\sin^2 x+6\sin x+2}}$

$= \lim_{x\to\frac{\pi}{2}}\frac{\tan^2 x(2\sin^2 x+3\sin x+4-\sin^2 x-6\sin x-2)}{\sqrt{2\sin^2 x+3\sin x+4}+\sqrt{\sin^2 x+6\sin x+2}}$

$$= \lim_{x\to\frac{\pi}{2}} \frac{\tan^2 x\left(\sin^2 x - 3\sin x + 2\right)}{\sqrt{2\sin^2 x + 3\sin x + 4} + \sqrt{\sin^2 x + 6\sin x + 2}}$$

$$= \lim_{x\to\frac{\pi}{2}} \frac{\tan^2 x((\sin x - 1)(\sin x - 2))}{\sqrt{2\sin^2 x + 3\sin x + 4} + \sqrt{\sin^2 x + 6\sin x + 2}}$$

Let $x - \pi/2 = y$

$x \to \pi/2$

$\Rightarrow y \to 0$

Hence the limit becomes

$$\lim_{y\to 0} \frac{\left[\tan\left(y+\frac{\pi}{2}\right)\right]^2\left(\sin\left(y+\frac{\pi}{2}\right)-1\right)\left(\sin\left(y+\frac{\pi}{2}\right)-2\right)}{\sqrt{2\sin^2\left(y+\frac{\pi}{2}\right)+3\sin\left(y+\frac{\pi}{2}\right)+4}+\sqrt{\sin^2\left(y+\frac{\pi}{2}\right)+6\sin\left(y+\frac{\pi}{2}\right)+2}}$$

which gives us

$$\lim_{y\to 0} \frac{(\cot y)^2(\cos y - 1)(\cos y - 2)}{\sqrt{2\cos^2 y + 3\cos y + 4} + \sqrt{\cos^2 y + 6\cos y + 2}}$$

$$\Rightarrow \lim_{y\to 0} \frac{(\cot y)^2\left(-2\sin^2\frac{y}{2}\right)(\cos y - 2)}{\sqrt{2\cos^2 y + 3\cos y + 4} + \sqrt{\cos^2 y + 6\cos y + 2}}$$

$$= \lim_{y\to 0} \frac{\left(\frac{\cos^2 y}{\sin^2 y}.\left(-2\sin^2\frac{y}{2}\right).(\cos y - 2)\right)}{3+3}$$

$$= \lim_{y\to 0} \frac{\left(\frac{\cos^2 y}{4.\sin^2\frac{y}{2}.\cos^2\frac{y}{2}}.\left(-2\sin^2\frac{y}{2}\right)(\cos y - 2)\right)}{6}$$

$$= \lim_{y\to 0} \frac{\left(\frac{-2.\cos^2 y}{4.\cos^2\frac{y}{2}}(\cos y - 2)\right)}{6} = \frac{1}{2}\times\frac{1}{6} = \frac{1}{12}$$

5. (a) $\displaystyle \lim_{n\to\infty} \frac{\sqrt{n^3 - 2n^2 + 1} + \sqrt[3]{n^4 + 1}}{\sqrt[4]{n^6 + 6n^5 + 2} - \sqrt[5]{n^7 + 3n^3 + 1}}$

$$= \lim_{n\to\infty} \frac{n^{\frac{3}{2}}\sqrt{1 - \frac{2}{n} + \frac{1}{n^3}} + n^{\frac{4}{3}}\sqrt[3]{1 + \frac{1}{n^4}}}{n^{\frac{6}{4}}\sqrt[4]{1 + \frac{6}{n} + \frac{2}{n^6}} - n^{\frac{7}{5}}\sqrt[5]{1 + \frac{3}{n^4} + \frac{1}{n^7}}}$$

$$= \lim_{n\to\infty} \frac{n^{\frac{3}{2}}\left(\sqrt{1 - \frac{2}{n} + \frac{1}{n^3}} + n^{-\frac{1}{6}}\sqrt[3]{1 + \frac{1}{n^4}}\right)}{n^{\frac{3}{2}}\left(\sqrt[4]{1 + \frac{6}{n} + \frac{2}{n^6}} - n^{-\frac{1}{10}}\sqrt[5]{1 + \frac{3}{n^4} + \frac{1}{n^7}}\right)}$$

$$= \frac{\sqrt{1 - 0 + 0} + 0(1 + 0)}{\sqrt{1 + 0 + 0} - 0(1 + 0 + 0)} = 1$$

6. (a) $\displaystyle \lim_{x\to\infty} \frac{(x-3)^{40}(5x+1)^{10}}{(3x^2-2)^{25}}$

Separating out term of x, so as to obtain negative powers of x

$$= \lim_{x\to\infty} \frac{x^{40}\left(1 - \frac{3}{x}\right)^{40}.x^{10}\left(5 + \frac{1}{x}\right)^{10}}{x^{50}\left(3 - \frac{2}{x^2}\right)^{25}}$$

Hence the limit reduces to $\displaystyle \lim_{x\to\infty} \frac{\left(1 - \frac{3}{x}\right)^{40}\left(5 + \frac{1}{x}\right)^{10}}{\left(3 - \frac{2}{x^2}\right)^{25}}$

$$= \frac{(1)^{40}(5)^{10}}{(3)^{25}} = \frac{5^{10}}{3^{25}}$$

7. (b) $\displaystyle \lim_{x\to\pm\infty} \left(\sqrt{x^2 - 2x - 1} - \sqrt{x^2 - 7x - 3}\right)$

Upon rationalizing, we get

$$\lim_{x\to\pm\infty} \frac{x^2 - 2x - 1 - x^2 + 7x + 3}{\sqrt{x^2 - 2x - 1} + \sqrt{x^2 - 7x - 3}}$$

$$= \lim_{x\to\pm\infty} \frac{5x + 2}{\sqrt{x^2 - 2x - 1} + \sqrt{x^2 - 7x - 3}}$$

$$= \lim_{x\to\pm\infty} \frac{x\left(5 + \frac{2}{x}\right)}{x\sqrt{1 - \frac{2}{x} - \frac{1}{x^2}} + x\sqrt{1 - \frac{7}{x} - \frac{3}{x^2}}}$$

$$= \lim_{x\to\pm\infty} \frac{\left(5 + \frac{2}{x}\right)}{\sqrt{1 - \frac{2}{x} - \frac{1}{x}} + \sqrt{1 - \frac{7}{x} - \frac{3}{x^2}}} = \pm\frac{5}{2}$$

8. (a) $\displaystyle \lim_{x\to\infty} \left(\sqrt[3]{x^3 + 3x^2} - \sqrt{x^2 - 2x}\right)$

$$= \lim_{x\to\infty} \left(\left[\left(x^3 + 3x^2\right)^2\right]^{1/6} - \left[\left(x^2 - 2x\right)^3\right]^{1/6}\right)$$

$$= \lim_{x\to\infty} \frac{\left(x^3 + 3x^2\right)^2 - \left(x^2 - 2x\right)^3}{\sum_{r=1}^{6}\left(x^3 + 3x^2\right)^{2-\frac{r}{3}}\left(x^2 - 2x\right)^{\frac{r-1}{2}}}$$

$$= \lim_{x\to\infty} \frac{x^6\left(1 + \frac{3}{x}\right)^2 - x^6\left(1 - \frac{2}{x}\right)^3}{x^5\sum_{r=1}^{6}\left(1 + \frac{3}{x}\right)^{2-\frac{r}{3}}\left(1 - \frac{2}{x}\right)^{\frac{r-1}{2}}}$$

$$= \lim_{x\to\infty} \frac{x\left(\frac{9}{x^2} + \frac{6}{x} + \frac{8}{x^3} + \frac{6}{x} - \frac{12}{x^2}\right)}{6}$$

$$= \lim_{x\to\infty} \frac{\left(\frac{9}{x} + 6 + \frac{8}{x^2} + 6 - \frac{12}{x}\right)}{6} = 2$$

9. (b), (d) $\displaystyle \lim_{x\to 5} \frac{x^2 - 9x + 20}{x - [x]}$

$$\text{L.H.L} = \lim_{x\to 5^-} \frac{x^2 - 9x + 20}{x - 4} = \left(\lim_{x\to 5^-} \frac{(x-5)(x-4)}{(x-4)}\right)$$

$$= \lim_{h\to 0} \frac{(-h)(1-h)}{(1-h)} = \lim_{h\to 0} (-h) = 0$$

$$\text{R.H.L} = \lim_{x\to 5^+}\frac{x^2-9x+20}{x-5} = \lim_{x\to 5^+}\frac{(x-5)(x-4)}{(x-5)}$$

$$= \lim_{h\to 0}\frac{h(1+h)}{h} = \lim_{h\to 0}(1+h) = 1$$

⇒ L.H.L = 0, R.H.L = 1

⇒ limit does not exist.

10. (a) $\lim_{x\to 0}\frac{\sqrt{1+\tan x}-\sqrt{1+\sin x}}{x^3}$

$$= \frac{\left(\sqrt{1+\tan x}-\sqrt{1+\sin x}\right)\left(\sqrt{1+\tan x}+\sqrt{1+\sin x}\right)}{x^3\left(\sqrt{1+\tan x}+\sqrt{1+\sin x}\right)}$$

$$= \lim_{x\to 0}\frac{1+\tan x-1-\sin x}{x^3\left(\sqrt{1+\tan x}+\sqrt{1+\sin x}\right)}$$

$$= \lim_{x\to 0}\frac{\sin x(1-\cos x)}{x^3.\cos x\left(\sqrt{1+\tan x}+\sqrt{1+\sin x}\right)}$$

$$= \lim_{x\to 0}\frac{\sin x.\left(2.\sin^2\frac{x}{2}\right)}{x^3.\cos x.\left(\sqrt{1+\tan x}+\sqrt{1+\sin x}\right)}$$

$$= \lim_{x\to 0}\frac{\left(\frac{\sin x}{x}\right).\left(2\sin^2\frac{x}{2}\right)}{4\cos x.\left(\frac{x^2}{4}\right)\left(\sqrt{1+\tan x}+\sqrt{1+\sin x}\right)} = \frac{2}{4.(2)}$$

$$= \frac{1}{4}$$

11. (c) $\lim_{x\to\frac{\pi}{2}}\left[\frac{x-\frac{\pi}{2}}{\cos x}\right]$

$$\text{R.H.L.} = \lim_{h\to 0^+}\left[\frac{\frac{\pi}{2}+h-\frac{\pi}{2}}{\cos\left(\frac{\pi}{2}+h\right)}\right];\ \{x = \pi/2 + h\}$$

$$= \lim_{h\to 0^-}\left[\frac{h}{-\sin h}\right] = -2$$

$$\left(\because \text{ For } h\to 0, \frac{h}{\sin h}\to 1^+ \Rightarrow \frac{-h}{\sin h}\to -1^-\right)$$

$$\text{R.H.L.} = \lim_{h\to 0^+}\left[\frac{\frac{\pi}{2}-h-\frac{\pi}{2}}{\cos\left(\frac{\pi}{2}-h\right)}\right] = \lim_{h\to 0^+}\left[\frac{-h}{\sin h}\right] = -2$$

⇒ Given limit = – 2

12. (b) $\lim_{x\to 2^+}\left(\frac{|x|^3}{3}-\left[\frac{x}{3}\right]^3\right)$

which is same as $\lim_{h\to 0^+}\left(\frac{|2+h|^3}{3}-\left[\frac{2+h}{3}\right]^3\right) = \frac{8}{3}$

13. (b) $\lim_{x\to 0}\frac{(4^x-1)^3}{\sin\left(\frac{x}{p}\right)\ell n\left(1+\frac{x^2}{3}\right)} = \lim_{x\to 0}\left[\frac{\left(\frac{4^x-1}{x}\right)^3}{\frac{\sin\left(\frac{x}{p}\right)\ell n\left(1+\frac{x^2}{3}\right)}{x^3}}\right]$

$$= \lim_{x\to 0}\frac{\left(\frac{4^x-1}{x}\right)^3}{\left[\frac{\sin\left(\frac{x}{p}\right)}{p.\frac{x}{p}}.\frac{\ell n\left(1+\frac{x^2}{3}\right)}{3\left(\frac{x^2}{3}\right)}\right]} = \frac{(\ln 4)^3}{\left[\frac{1}{p}(1).\frac{1}{3}(1)\right]} = 3p(\ln 4)^3$$

14. (d) $\lim_{x\to 0}\frac{\sin(\ell n(1+x))}{\ell n(1+\sin x)} = \lim_{x\to 0}\frac{\frac{\sin(\ell n(1+x))}{\ell n(1+x)}}{\frac{\ell n(1+\sin x)}{\ell n(1+x)}}$

$$= \frac{1}{\lim_{x\to 0}\left[\frac{\ell n(1+\sin x)}{\ell n(1+x)}\right]} = \frac{1}{\lim_{x\to 0}\left[\frac{\frac{\ell n(1+\sin x).\sin x}{\sin x}}{\frac{\ell n(1+x)}{x}.x}\right]}$$

$$= \lim_{x\to 0}\left(\frac{x}{\sin x}\right) = 1$$

15. (b) $\lim_{x\to\infty} n\cos\left(\frac{\pi}{4n}\right)\sin\left(\frac{\pi}{4n}\right)$

which is same as $\lim_{n\to\infty}\frac{n}{2}\left[\sin\left(\frac{\pi}{2n}\right)\right]$

Multiplying and dividing by $\frac{\pi}{2n}$, we get

$$\lim_{n\to\infty}\left[\frac{\frac{n}{2}\sin\left(\frac{\pi}{2n}\right).\frac{\pi}{2n}}{\frac{\pi}{2n}}\right] = \lim_{n\to\infty}\left[\frac{\frac{\pi}{4}\sin\left(\frac{\pi}{2n}\right)}{\frac{\pi}{2n}}\right] = \frac{\pi}{4}$$

16. (a) $\lim_{x\to\infty}\left(\frac{x+2}{x-2}\right)^{x+1}$

which can be re-written as $\lim_{x\to\infty}\left(\frac{4+x-2}{x-2}\right)^{x+1} =$

$$\lim_{x\to\infty}\left(1+\frac{4}{x-2}\right)^{x+1} = e^{\left\{\lim_{x\to\infty}\left[\frac{4(x+1)}{(x-2)}\right]\right\}} = e^4$$

17. (a) $\lim_{x\to 0^+}\left(1+\tan^2\sqrt{x}\right)^{\frac{5}{x}}$

As in the previous question, again comparing it with the standard format $\lim_{x\to 0}(1+f(x))^{\frac{1}{g(x)}}$

Hence the limit reduces to $e^{\lim_{x\to 0}\frac{\tan^2\sqrt{x}.5}{x}} = e^5$

18. (b) $\lim_{x\to\frac{\pi}{4}}(1+[x])^{\frac{1}{\ell n(\tan x)}} = \lim_{x\to\frac{\pi}{4}}(1+0)^{\frac{1}{\ln(\tan x)}} = (1)$

19. (c) $\lim_{x\to\infty}\left[\frac{x^2-2x+1}{x^2-4x+2}\right]^x = \lim_{x\to\infty}\left(\frac{x^2-4x+2+2x-1}{x^2-4x+2}\right)^x$

$= \lim_{x\to\infty}\left(1+\frac{2x-1}{x^2-4x+2}\right)^x$

which can be written as $\lim_{x\to\infty}\left(1+\frac{2-\frac{1}{x}}{x-4+\frac{2}{x}}\right)^x$

$= e^{\lim_{x\to\infty}\left(\frac{2-\frac{1}{x}}{x-4+\frac{2}{x}}\right)x} = e^{\lim_{x\to\infty}\left(\frac{2x-1}{x-4+\frac{2}{x}}\right)} = e^2$

20. (a), (b), (c), (d)

$\lim_{x\to 0}(\cos x + a\sin bx)^{\frac{1}{x}} = \lim_{x\to 0}(1+(\cos x + a\sin bx - 1))^{1/x}$

$= e^{\lim_{x\to 0}\frac{\cos x + a\sin bx - 1}{x}} = e^{ab} = e^2$ (given)

$\Rightarrow$ All given cases are possible

21. (c) $\lim_{x\to\frac{\pi}{2}}\frac{\left(1-\tan\frac{x}{2}\right)(1-\sin x)}{\left(1+\tan\frac{x}{2}\right)(\pi-2x)^3} = \lim_{x\to\frac{\pi}{2}}\frac{\tan\left(\frac{\pi}{4}-\frac{x}{2}\right)(1-\sin x)}{(\pi-2x)^3}$

$= \lim_{y\to 0}\frac{\tan\left(\frac{y}{2}\right)(1-\cos y)}{8y^3} = \lim_{y\to 0}\frac{\left(\tan\frac{y}{2}\right)}{16\left(\frac{y}{2}\right)}\cdot\frac{\left(2\sin^2\frac{y}{2}\right)}{4\left(\frac{y^2}{4}\right)} = \frac{1}{32}$

22. (c) $f(x) = \begin{cases} x\sin\left(\frac{1}{x}\right)+\sin\left(\frac{1}{x^2}\right); & x\neq 0 \\ 0 & ; x=0 \end{cases}$

For $x \neq 0$

$f(x) = \frac{\sin\left(\frac{1}{x}\right)}{\frac{1}{x}} + \sin\left(\frac{1}{x^2}\right)$

$\lim_{x\to\infty} f(x) = 1 + \sin(0) = 1$

23. (a) $\lim_{x\to\infty}\left(\frac{x^2+x+3+4x}{x^2+x+3}\right)^x = \lim_{x\to\infty}\left(1+\frac{4x}{x^2+x+3}\right)^x$

$= e^{\left(\lim_{x\to\infty}\left(\frac{4x^2}{x^2+x+3}\right)\right)} = e^4$

24. (a) $f(x) = \lim_{n\to\infty}\frac{2}{\pi}\tan^{-1}(nx)$

For $x > 0$, $n \to \infty$

$\Rightarrow \tan^{-1}(nx) \to \frac{\pi}{2}$ and

For $x < 0$, $n \to \infty$

$\Rightarrow \tan^{-1}(nx) \to -\frac{\pi}{2}$

$\Rightarrow f(x) = \frac{2}{\pi}\cdot\frac{\pi}{2} = 1$ for $x > 0$ and -1 for $x < 0$

TEXTUAL EXERCISE-4: (SUBJECTIVE)

1. (a) $f(x) = a_n x^n + a_{n-1}x^{n-1} + \ldots + a_0$, $a_n > 0$

Since $a_n > 0$

$\Rightarrow x \to \infty \qquad \Rightarrow f(x) \to \infty$

Hence at infinity this function will find towards infinity.

(b) $f(x) = \frac{a_n x^n + a_{n-1}x^{n-1} + \ldots\ldots + a_0}{b_n x^n + b_{n-1}x^{n-1} + \ldots\ldots + b_0}$

Taking x^n common from both numerator and denominator, we get $f(x) = \frac{a_n + \frac{a_{n-1}}{x} + \ldots\ldots + \frac{a_0}{x^n}}{b_n + \frac{b_{n-1}}{x} + \ldots\ldots + \frac{b_0}{x_n}}$

$\therefore \lim_{x\to\infty} f(x) = \frac{a_n}{b_n}$

Hence at ∞ this function will tend to a_n / b_n (constant)

(c) $f(x) = \left[\frac{a_n x^n + a_{n-1} + \ldots\ldots + a_0}{b_k x^k + \ldots\ldots + b_0}\right]$; $a_n > 0$, $b_k > 0$, $n > k$

$\lim_{x\to\infty} f(x) = \infty$

(d) $f(x) = \left[\frac{a_n x^n + \ldots\ldots + a_0}{b_k x^k + \ldots\ldots + b_0}\right]$; $a_n > 0$; $b_k > 0$; $n < k$

$\Rightarrow \lim_{x\to\infty} f(x) = 0$

2. (a) $\lim_{x\to 0}\frac{1+\sin x - \cos x + \log(1-x)}{x^3}$

Putting $\sin x = x - \frac{x^3}{3!} + \frac{x^5}{5!} - \frac{x^7}{7!}$

$\cos x = 1 - \frac{x^2}{2!} + \frac{x^4}{4!} - \frac{x^6}{6!} + \ldots\ldots$

$\log(1-x) = -x - \frac{x^2}{2} - \frac{x^3}{3} - \ldots\ldots$

Hence the limits reduces to

$\lim_{x\to 0}\frac{\left(1+x-\frac{x^3}{3!}+\ldots\right) - 1 + \frac{x^2}{2!} - \frac{x^4}{4!} + \ldots\ldots + \left(-x-\frac{x^2}{2}-\frac{x^3}{3}\ldots\right)}{x^3}$

$= \lim_{x\to 0}\frac{x^3\left(-\frac{1}{6}-\frac{1}{3}\right)}{x^3} = \frac{-1}{2}$

(b) $\lim_{x\to 0}\left[\frac{\sin x - x + \frac{x^3}{6}}{x^5}\right]$

Using the expression of $\sin x$, we get $\sin x = x - \frac{x^3}{3!} + \frac{x^5}{5!} - \frac{x^7}{7!} + \ldots\ldots = x - \frac{x^3}{3!} + \frac{x^5}{5!} - \frac{x^7}{7!} + \ldots\ldots$

Hence the limit reduces to $\lim_{x\to 0}\dfrac{\dfrac{x^5}{5!}-\dfrac{x^7}{7!}+.....}{x^5}=\dfrac{1}{5!}=\dfrac{1}{120}$

(c) $\lim_{x\to 0}\dfrac{e^x-1-\dfrac{x^2}{2!}-x}{3x^3}$

Putting $e^x=1+x+\dfrac{x^2}{2!}+\dfrac{x^3}{3!}+......$

Hence the limit reduces to

$$\lim_{x\to 0}\left[\dfrac{\left(1+x+\dfrac{x^2}{2!}+\dfrac{x^3}{3!}\right)-1-x-\dfrac{x^2}{2!}}{3x^3}\right]$$

which gives us $\lim_{x\to 0}\left[\dfrac{\dfrac{x^3}{3!}+\dfrac{x^4}{4!}+....}{3x^3}\right]=\dfrac{1}{3!}\cdot\dfrac{1}{3}=\dfrac{1}{18}$

(d) $\lim_{x\to 0}\dfrac{\sin x-x+\dfrac{x^3}{6}}{5x^4}$

Putting $\sin x=x-\dfrac{x^3}{3!}+\dfrac{x^5}{5!}-\dfrac{x^7}{7!}+......$

Hence the limit reduces to

$$\lim_{x\to 0}\left[\dfrac{\left[x-\dfrac{x^3}{3!}+\dfrac{x^5}{5!}....\right]-x+\dfrac{x^3}{3!}}{5x^4}\right]$$

Which is same as $\lim_{x\to 0}\left[\dfrac{\dfrac{x^5}{5!}-\dfrac{x^7}{7!}+\dfrac{x^9}{9!}-......}{5x^4}\right]$

$=\lim_{x\to 0}\left[\dfrac{x}{5.5!}-\dfrac{x^3}{5.7!}+.....\right]=0$

(e) $\lim_{x\to 0}\left[\dfrac{\log(1+x)-x+\dfrac{x^2}{2!}-\dfrac{x^3}{3!}}{4x^3}\right]$

Using the standard expression log (1 + *x*)

$=x-\dfrac{x^2}{2}+\dfrac{x^3}{3}-......$

Hence the limit reduces to

$$\lim_{x\to 0}\left[\dfrac{\left[x-\dfrac{x^2}{2}+\dfrac{x^3}{3}-\dfrac{x^4}{4}+....\right]-x+\dfrac{x^2}{2}-\dfrac{x^3}{3!}}{4x^3}\right]$$

which gives us $\lim_{x\to 0}\left[\dfrac{\dfrac{x^2}{2}-\dfrac{x^2}{2}+\dfrac{x^3}{3}-\dfrac{x^3}{6}-\dfrac{x^4}{4}+\dfrac{x^5}{5}.....}{4x^3}\right]$

$=\dfrac{1}{4}\left[\dfrac{1}{3}-\dfrac{1}{6}\right]=\dfrac{1}{4}\left[\dfrac{1}{6}\right]=\dfrac{1}{24}$

3. (a) $\lim_{n\to\infty}\dfrac{1^2-2^2+3^2-4^2+......-4n^2}{\sqrt{n^4+4}+\sqrt{9n^2+1}}=\text{a}$

$=\lim_{n\to\infty}\dfrac{(1^2-2^2)+(3^2-4^2)+(5^2-6^2)......+((2n-1)^2-(2n)^2))}{\sqrt{n^4+4}+\sqrt{9n^2+1}}$

$=\lim_{n\to\infty}\dfrac{(-1)[3+7+11+....+(4n-1)]}{\sqrt{n^4+4}+\sqrt{9n^2+1}}$

$=\lim_{n\to\infty}\dfrac{(-1)\left[\dfrac{n}{2}[3+4n-1]\right]}{\sqrt{n^4+4}+\sqrt{9n^2+1}}$

$=\lim_{n\to\infty}\dfrac{(-1)(2n+1)n}{\sqrt{n^4+4}+\sqrt{9n^2+1}}$

$=\lim_{n\to\infty}\dfrac{-(2n^2+n)}{\sqrt{n^4+4}+\sqrt{9n^2+1}}$

$=-\lim_{n\to\infty}\dfrac{\left(2+\dfrac{1}{n}\right)}{\sqrt{1+\dfrac{4}{n^4}}+\sqrt{\dfrac{9}{n^2}+\dfrac{1}{n^2}}}=-2=\text{a}$

(b) $\lim_{x\to\infty}\dfrac{ax^2+b}{x+1}\geq 0$ and finit

Here the order of numerator is grater than the order of denominator, for finite limit, $a=0$, $\lim_{x\to\infty}\dfrac{b}{x+1}\geq 0$

$\Rightarrow\ \lim_{x\to\infty}\dfrac{b}{x+1}=0$

$\Rightarrow\ \text{b}\in\mathbb{R}$

(c) $\lim_{x\to\infty}\left[\dfrac{x^2+1}{x+1}-ax-b\right]=0$

$\Rightarrow\ \lim_{x\to\infty}\left[\dfrac{x^2(1-a)-(a+b)x+(1-b)}{(x+1)}\right]=0$

⇒ Degree of numerator must be less than that of denom.

$\Rightarrow\ a=1,\ -(a+b)=0,\ 1-b\neq 0$

$\Rightarrow\ a=1,\ b=-1$

(d) $\lim_{x\to\infty}\left[\dfrac{x^2-1}{x+1}-ax-b\right]=2$

$\Rightarrow\ \lim_{x\to\infty}\left(\dfrac{x^2-1-ax^2-ax-bx-1}{x+1}\right)=2$

⇒ degree of numerator = degree of denom.

$\Rightarrow\ a=1,\ -a-b=2$

$\Rightarrow\ a=1,\ b=-3$

(e) $\lim_{x\to\infty}\left[\frac{x^2+1}{x+1}-ax-b\right]=\infty$

$\Rightarrow \lim_{x\to\infty}\left[\frac{x^2(1-a)-(a+b)x-b}{(x+1)}\right]=\infty$

We need make the order of numerator greater than denominator $a<1$ and $b\in\mathbb{R}$

(f) $\lim_{x\to 0}\frac{ae^x-b}{x}=2$

which can be written as $\lim_{x\to 0}\frac{ae^x-a-b+a}{x}=$

$\lim_{x\to 0}a\left(\frac{e^x-1}{x}\right)+\frac{a-b}{x}=\text{a}+\lim_{x\to 0}\frac{a-b}{x}=2$

$\Rightarrow$ a = b = 2

4. $L=\lim_{x\to 0}\left[\frac{\cos^2 x-\cos x-e^x\cos x+e^x-\frac{x^3}{2}}{x^n}\right]$

$\Rightarrow \lim_{x\to\infty}\left[\frac{(1-\cos x)(e^x-\cos x)-\frac{x^3}{2}}{x^n}\right]$

$\because (1-\cos x)=\frac{x^2}{2!}-\frac{x^4}{4!}-\frac{x^6}{6!}+\ldots,$

$e^x-\cos x=\left(\frac{x}{1!}\right)+\left(\frac{x^3}{3!}\right)+\left(\frac{x^5}{5!}\right)$

$\Rightarrow (1-\cos x)(e^x-\cos x)-\frac{x^3}{2}$

$=\left(\frac{1}{2}\times\frac{1}{1}-\frac{1}{2}\right)x^3+\left(\frac{1}{12}-\frac{1}{24}\right)x^5+\ldots$

$\Rightarrow L=\lim_{x\to\infty}\frac{\left(\frac{1}{24}x^5+ax^7+bx^9+\ldots\right)}{x^n}$

$\therefore$ For finite $x\geq 5$ but for finite non-zero limit $n=5$

5. (a) $\lim_{x\to 0}\frac{e^x-1-x}{x^2}=\lim_{x\to 0}\left[\frac{\left(1+x+\frac{x^2}{2!}+\frac{x^3}{3!}+\ldots\right)-1-x}{x^2}\right]$

$=\lim_{x\to 0}\left[\frac{\frac{x^2}{2!}+\frac{x^3}{3!}+\frac{x^4}{5!}+\ldots}{x^2}\right]=\frac{1}{2!}=\frac{1}{2}$

(b) $\lim_{x\to 0}\left[\frac{\sin x-x}{x^3}\right]=\lim_{x\to 0}\frac{\left[\frac{-x^3}{3!}+\frac{x^5}{5!}-\frac{x^7}{7!}+\ldots\right]}{x^3}=-\frac{1}{3!}$

$=-\frac{1}{6}$

(c) $\lim_{x\to 0}\left[\frac{\sin x}{x}\right]^{\frac{1}{x}}=\lim_{x\to 0}\left[1+\left(\frac{\sin x}{x}-1\right)\right]^{\frac{1}{x}}=e^{\lim_{x\to 0}\left(\frac{\sin x-x}{x}\right)\cdot\frac{1}{x}}$

$=e^{\lim_{x\to 0}\left[\frac{\frac{-x^2}{3!}+\frac{x^4}{4!}-\frac{x^6}{7!}}{x}\right]}=e^0=1$

(d) $\lim_{x\to 0}\left[\frac{1}{x^2}-\frac{1}{\sin^2 x}\right]=\lim_{x\to 0}\left[\frac{\sin^2 x-x^2}{x^2\sin^2 x}\right]$

$=\lim_{x\to 0}\frac{\left(x-\frac{x^3}{3!}+\frac{x^5}{5!}\right)^2-x^2}{x^2\left(x-\frac{x^3}{3!}+\frac{x^5}{5!}-\ldots\right)^2}$

$\Rightarrow \lim_{x\to 0}\left[\frac{-\frac{2}{6}x^4+\text{ terms containing higher power of x}}{x^2\left(x^2-\frac{2}{6}x^4+\ldots\right)}\right]=-\frac{1}{3}$

(e) $\lim_{x\to 0}\left(\frac{1}{x^2}-\frac{1}{\tan^2 x}\right)$

Proceeding as in part (*f*), we get $\lim_{x\to 0}\left(\frac{\tan^2 x-x^2}{x^2\tan^2 x}\right)$

Here $\left(\frac{1}{x^2}-\frac{1}{\tan^2 x}\right)=\left(\frac{\sin^2 x-x^2\cos^2 x}{x^2\sin^2 x}\right)$

$=\frac{\left(x-\frac{x^3}{3!}+\frac{x^5}{5!}-\ldots\right)^2-x^2\left(1-\frac{x^2}{2!}+\frac{x^4}{4!}\ldots\right)^2}{x^2\left(x-\frac{x^3}{3!}+\frac{x^5}{5!}-\ldots\right)^2}$

$\Rightarrow \lim_{x\to 0}\left(\frac{1}{x^2}-\frac{1}{\tan^2 x}\right)=\frac{1-\frac{1}{3}}{1}=\frac{2}{3}$

(f) $\lim_{x\to 0}x^x$

$\Rightarrow y=x^x \qquad \Rightarrow \log y=x\log x$

$\Rightarrow y=e^{x\log x} \qquad \Rightarrow \lim_{x\to 0}y=1$

(g) $\lim_{x\to\frac{\pi}{2}}(\sin x)^{\tan x}$

which can be written as $\lim_{x\to\frac{\pi}{2}}(1+(\sin x-1))^{\frac{1}{\left(\frac{1}{\tan x}\right)}}$

$=e^{\left(\lim_{x\to\pi/2}(\sin x-1).\tan x\right)}=e^{\lim_{h\to 0}\left[\sin\left(\frac{\pi}{2}-h\right)-1\right].\tan\left(\frac{\pi}{2}-h\right)}=e^{\lim_{h\to 0}[\cos h-1]\cot h}$

$=e^{-\lim_{h\to 0}\left[2\sin^{2h/2}\right]\frac{1}{\tan h}}=e^{-\lim_{h\to 0}\left[\frac{2\left(\frac{h^2}{4}\right)}{h}\right]}=e^0=1$

6. $\lim_{x\to 0}\frac{x(1+a\cos x)-b\sin x}{[f(x)]^3}=1$

$\Rightarrow \lim_{x\to 0}\frac{x(1+a\cos x)-b\sin x}{x^3}=1$

$$\therefore \quad \cos x = \left\{1-\frac{x^2}{2!}+\frac{x^4}{4!}-......\right\}$$

$$\sin x = \left\{x-\frac{x^3}{3!}+\frac{x^5}{5!}-......\right\}$$

Using these expressions the limit reduces to

$$\lim_{x\to 0}\frac{\left[x\left\{1+a\left(1-\frac{x^2}{2!}+\frac{x^4}{4!}-....\right)\right\}-\left\{b.\left(x-\frac{x^3}{3!}+\frac{x^5}{5!}........\right)\right\}\right]}{x^3}=1$$

$$\Rightarrow \lim_{x\to 0}\frac{x(1+a-b)+x^3\left(\frac{-a}{2!}+\frac{b}{3!}\right)+x^5\left(\frac{a}{4!}-\frac{b}{5!}\right)+....}{x^3}$$

$$\Rightarrow \lim_{x\to 0}\frac{(1+a-b)}{x^2}+\lim_{x\to 0}\left[\frac{-a}{2!}+\frac{b}{3!}\right]+\lim_{x\to 0}\left[\frac{a}{4!}-\frac{b}{5!}\right]x^2-.....=1$$

$\Rightarrow$ $1 + a - b = 0$

$\Rightarrow$ $b = 1 + a$ and $\frac{-a}{2!}+\frac{b}{3!}=1$

$\Rightarrow$ $-3a + b = 6$

$\Rightarrow$ $a = -5/2$ and $b = -3/2$

7. (a) $\lim_{x\to a}\frac{a\sin x - x\sin a}{ax^2-a^2x}$

It would be complicated to put expansion in this limit.

Clearly, on application of the limit the format is $\frac{0}{0}$.

Applying L.H. rule $\lim_{x\to a}\frac{a\cos x-\sin a}{2xa-a^2}$

$$=\frac{a\cos a-\sin a}{a^2}$$

(b) $\lim_{x\to 0}\frac{27^x-9^x-3^x+1}{\sqrt{2}-\sqrt{1+\cos x}}$

which can be written as $\lim_{x\to 0}\frac{3^{3x}-3^{2x}-3^x+1}{\sqrt{2}-\sqrt{1+\cos x}}$

Multiplying numerator and denominator by $\sqrt{2}+\sqrt{1+\cos x}$

$$=\lim_{x\to 0}\frac{(3^{3x}-3^{2x}-3^x+1)(\sqrt{2}+\sqrt{1+\cos x})}{1-\cos x}$$

$$=\lim_{x\to 0}\frac{(3^{3x}-3^{2x}-3^x+1)(\sqrt{2}+\sqrt{1+\cos x})}{2\sin^2\frac{x}{2}}$$

$$=\lim_{x\to 0}\frac{(3^{2x}-1)(3^x-1)(\sqrt{2}+\sqrt{1+\cos x})}{2\frac{\sin^2\frac{x}{2}}{\frac{x^2}{4}}\cdot\frac{x^2}{4}}$$

$$=\lim_{x\to 0}\frac{\frac{((3^{2x}-1)(3^x-1))}{2x\ .\ x}(\sqrt{2}+\sqrt{1+\cos x}).2}{\frac{1}{4}\left(\frac{\sin\frac{x}{2}}{\left(\frac{x}{2}\right)}\right)^2.2}$$

$$=(\ln 3)^2\left(4\sqrt{2}\right)(2) = 8\sqrt{2}\ (\log 3)^2$$

8. (i) $\lim_{n\to\infty}\frac{n!}{(n+1)!-n!}=\lim_{n\to\infty}\frac{1}{(n+1)-1}=\lim_{n\to\infty}\left(\frac{1}{n}\right)=0$

(ii) $\lim_{n\to\infty}\frac{1+\frac{1}{2}+\frac{1}{4}+......\frac{1}{2^n}}{1+\frac{1}{3}+\frac{1}{9}+.....\frac{1}{3^n}}=\lim_{n\to\infty}\frac{\left(1-\left(\frac{1}{2}\right)^n\right).\frac{2}{3}}{\frac{1}{2}.\left(1-\left(\frac{1}{3}\right)^n\right)}=\frac{4}{3}$

9. To start with consider a circle C_1 of radius R

$A_1 = \pi R^2$

Now the diagonal of the square inscribed in this circle (C_1) $= 2R$

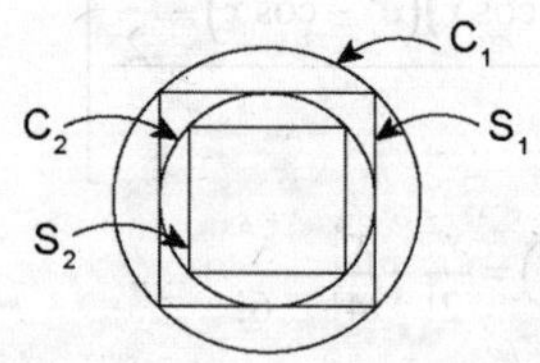

$\Rightarrow$ Side length of square $S_1 = \sqrt{2}$ R and radius of $C_2 = \frac{R}{\sqrt{2}}$

Area of square $S_1 = 2R^2$ and area of $C_2 = \frac{\pi R^2}{2}$

$\Rightarrow$ Diagonal of S_2 = 4 diameter $C_2 = \sqrt{2}$ R

$\Rightarrow$ Side of square $S_2 = \sqrt{R}$

$\Rightarrow$ Area of $S_2 = R^2$

Sum of areas of squares $2R^2 + R^2 + \frac{R^2}{2}+\frac{R^2}{4}+..... = R^2$

$\left(2+\frac{1}{2}+\frac{1}{4}+\frac{1}{8}+....\right) = R^2\ (2 + 2) = 4R^2$

Sum of areas of all circles

$$=\left(\pi R^2+\frac{\pi R^2}{2}+\frac{\pi R^2}{4}+\frac{\pi R^2}{8}+.....\right)$$

$$=\pi R^2\left(1+\frac{1}{2}+\frac{1}{4}+\frac{1}{8}+......\right)=\frac{\pi R^2}{\frac{1}{2}}=2\pi R^2$$

10. $f(x) = \left[x^x-(\cot x)^{\sin x}+(\sec x)^{\cos ecx}-\frac{\ell n(\sec x)}{x^2}\right]$

Let us consider all the summands of $f(x)$ as discrete terms.

$g(x) = x^x$

$h(x) = (\cot x)^{\sin x}$

$i(x) = (\sec x)^{\text{cosec } x}$

$j(x) = \dfrac{\ell n(\sec x)}{x^2}$

$\lim\limits_{x\to 0^+} g(x) = \lim\limits_{x\to 0^+} x^x = 1$

$\lim\limits_{x\to 0}\left(\dfrac{\ell n(\sec x)}{x^2}\right)$

$= \lim\limits_{x\to 0}\dfrac{\tan x}{2x}$

$= \lim\limits_{x\to 0}\dfrac{1}{2}\left(\dfrac{\tan x}{x}\right) = \dfrac{1}{2}$

$\lim\limits_{x\to 0} i(x) = \lim\limits_{x\to 0}(\sec x)^{\operatorname{cosec} x}$

$k = (\sec x)^{\operatorname{cosec} x}$

$\log k = \operatorname{cosec} x \,.\, \log(\sec)\, x$

Applying L.H. Rule, we get $\lim\limits_{x\to 0} \ell nk = \lim\limits_{x\to 0}\dfrac{\tan x}{\cos x} = 0$

$\Rightarrow \lim\limits_{x\to 0}\ i(x) = e^0 = 1$

$h(x) = (\cot x)^{\sin x}$

$\ell n\, h(x) = \sin x \,.\, \ell n(\cot x)$

$\lim\limits_{x\to 0}(\ell n h(x)) = \lim\limits_{x\to 0}\dfrac{\ell n(\cot x)}{\operatorname{cosec} x}$

Applying L.H. Rule, we get $\lim\limits_{x\to 0} \ell n h(x) \Rightarrow \lim\limits_{x\to 0}\dfrac{\operatorname{cosec}^2 x.\tan x}{\cot x.\operatorname{cosec} x}$

$= \lim\limits_{x\to 0}\dfrac{\sin x}{\cos^2 x} = 0$

$\Rightarrow \lim\limits_{x\to 0} h(x) = e^0 = 1$

Hence, $\lim\limits_{x\to 0^{-1}} f(x) = 1 - 1 + 1 - \dfrac{1}{2} = \dfrac{1}{2}$

11. (i) $\lim\limits_{x\to 1}\dfrac{x^x - x}{1 + \ell n x - x}$

Hence Applying L.H. rule, we get $\lim\limits_{x\to 1}\dfrac{(\ell nx + 1)x^x - 1}{\dfrac{1}{x} - 1}$

Again applying L.H. rule, we get

$\lim\limits_{x\to 1}\dfrac{\dfrac{1}{x}.x^x + \ell nx(\ell nx + 1)x^x + (\ell nx + 1)x^x}{-\dfrac{1}{x^2}} = -2$

(ii) $\lim\limits_{x\to 0}\dfrac{(1+x)^{\frac{1}{x}} - e + \dfrac{xe}{2}}{x^2}$

The original limit is 0/0 format. L.H. rule applying twice, we get $\lim\limits_{x\to 0}\dfrac{(1+x)^{\frac{1}{x}} - e + \dfrac{xe}{2}}{x^2} = \dfrac{11e}{24}$

(iii) $\lim\limits_{x\to 0}\dfrac{e^x + \ell n\left(\dfrac{1-x}{e}\right)}{\tan x - x}$

which can be written as $\lim\limits_{x\to 0}\left(\dfrac{e^x - 1 + \ell n(1-x)}{\tan x - x}\right)$

By L.H. rule $\lim\limits_{x\to 0}\left[\dfrac{e^x + \dfrac{1}{1-x}(-1)}{\sec^2 x - 1}\right] = \lim\limits_{x\to 0}\left[\dfrac{e^x - \dfrac{1}{1-x}}{\sec^2 x - 1}\right]$

$= \lim\limits_{x\to 0}\left[\dfrac{e^x - \dfrac{1}{(1-x)^2}}{2\sec x.\sec x.\tan x}\right]$

Applying L.H. rule again a putting limit $x \to 0$

$= \dfrac{-2}{4} = -\dfrac{1}{2}$

(iv) $\lim\limits_{x\to\frac{1}{2}}\left[\dfrac{\sec \pi x}{\tan 3\pi x}\right]$

$= \lim\limits_{x\to\frac{1}{2}}\left[\dfrac{\sec \pi x.\cos 3\pi x}{\sin 3\pi x}\right] = \lim\limits_{x\to\frac{1}{2}}\left[\dfrac{\sec \pi x(4\cos^3 \pi x - 3\cos \pi x)}{\sin 3\pi x}\right]$

$= \dfrac{-3}{(-1)} = 3$

12. $\lim\limits_{x\to\infty}\left[\dfrac{2^{\frac{1}{x}} + 3^{\frac{1}{x}} + \ldots\ldots + 10^{\frac{1}{x}}}{9}\right]^{9x}$

$= \lim\limits_{x\to\infty}\left[1 + \left(\dfrac{2^{\frac{1}{x}} + 3^{\frac{1}{x}} + \ldots. + 10^{\frac{1}{x}}}{9} - 1\right)\right]^{9x} = e^{\lim\limits_{x\to\infty}\left(\frac{2^{\frac{1}{x}} + 3^{\frac{1}{x}} + \ldots. + 10^{\frac{1}{x}}}{9}\right)_9 (9x)}$

$= e^{\lim\limits_{x\to\infty}\frac{(2^{1/x} + 3^{1/x} + \ldots + 10^{1/x} - 9)}{1/x}} = e^{\lim\limits_{x\to\infty}\left[2^{1/x}.\ln 2 + 3^{1/x}.\ln x + \ldots + 10^{1/x}\ln 4\right]}$

$= e^{\ln 2 + \ln 3 + \ldots + \ln 10} = e^{\ln(2.3.4\ldots.10)} = (10)!$

13. (a) $\lim\limits_{x\to 0}\dfrac{1}{x^3}\displaystyle\int_0^x\left(\dfrac{t^2}{t^4+1}\right)dt = \lim\limits_{x\to 0}\left[\dfrac{\int_0^x \frac{t^2}{t^4+1}dt}{x^3}\right]$

$= \lim\limits_{x\to 0}\left[\dfrac{\dfrac{x^2}{x^4+1}}{3x^2}\right] = \lim\limits_{x\to 0}\left[\dfrac{1}{3(x^4+1)}\right] = \dfrac{1}{3}$

(b) $\lim\limits_{x\to 0}\left[\dfrac{\int_0^x (\cos t)^{\frac{1}{t^2}}.dt}{x}\right] = \lim\limits_{x\to 0}\left[\dfrac{(\cos x)^{\frac{1}{x^2}}}{1}\right]$

$= \lim\limits_{x\to 0}(1 + (\cos x - 1))^{\frac{1}{x^2}} = e^{\lim\limits_{x\to 0}\frac{\cos x - 1}{x^2}} = e^{\lim\limits_{x\to 0}\frac{-\sin x}{2x}} = e^{-\frac{1}{2}}$

(c) $\lim\limits_{x\to 0}\dfrac{\int_0^{\sin^2 x}\sqrt{t}\,dt}{3x^3} = \lim\limits_{x\to 0}\dfrac{|\sin x|.\sin 2x}{9x^2} = \lim\limits_{x\to 0}\dfrac{|\sin x|.\sin 2x}{\dfrac{9}{2}x.2x}$

$= \frac{2}{9}$ $(\because\ x \to 0^+$ as $\sqrt{t}$ is there)

14. Clearly $P_n \to 0$ as $x \to 0\ \forall n \in \mathbb{N}$;

$\therefore\ \lim\limits_{x\to 0}\frac{P_n}{x} = \lim\limits_{x\to 0} P'_n(x) = \lim\limits_{x\to 0}\left(a^{P_{n-1}(x)} - 1\right)'$

$= \lim\limits_{x\to 0}(\ln a)\, a^{P_{n-1}(x)}\cdot(P_{n-1}(x))'$ and so an

$= \lim\limits_{x\to 0}\ln(a).a^{P_{n-1}(0)}.\ln(a).^{P_{n-2}(0)}....\ln(a).a^{P_2(0)}\ln a.a^{P_1(0)}P_1'(0)$

$= (\ln a)^{n-1}.\lim\limits_{x\to 0}\frac{d}{dx}\left(a^x - 1\right) = (\ln a)^n.\lim\limits_{x\to 0}\left(a^x\right) = (\ln a)^n$

15. $\sin\theta = \frac{a/2}{r}$

$\Rightarrow\ \frac{a}{2} = r\sin\theta$

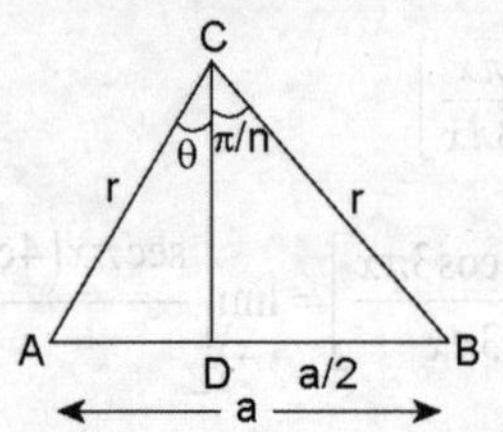

$\Rightarrow\ a = 2r\sin\theta$ ...(1)

Also, $\cos\theta = \frac{CD}{r}$

$\Rightarrow$ CD = $r\cos\theta$ ...(2)

$\therefore$ Area of $\Delta\ ABC = \frac{1}{2}(a)\ (CD) = \frac{1}{2}\ (2r\sin\theta)\ (r\cos\theta)$

$= \frac{1}{2}r^2.\sin 2\theta$

$\therefore$ Area of poygon $= \frac{nr^2}{2}\sin\frac{2\pi}{n}$

$\therefore$ Area of circle $= \lim\limits_{n\to\infty}\frac{nr^2}{2}\sin\frac{2r\pi}{n} = \lim\limits_{n\to\infty}\frac{nr^2}{2}\sin\left(\frac{2\pi}{n}\right) =$

$\frac{r^2}{2}\lim\limits_{n\to\infty}\left[\frac{\sin\left(\frac{2\pi}{n}\right)}{\frac{1}{n}}\right]$

Multiplying and dividing by 2π, we get

$\pi r^2\lim\limits_{n\to\infty}\left[\frac{\sin\left(\frac{2\pi}{n}\right)}{\frac{2\pi}{n}}\right] = \pi r^2$

16. $\lim\limits_{n\to\infty}\sum\limits_{r=1}^{n} e^{-2r}.\cos(r\pi)$

$= \lim\limits_{n\to\infty}\sum\limits_{r=1}^{n}(-1)^r e^{-2r} = \left[-e^{-2} + e^{-4} - e^{-6} + ...\right]$

$= \left[\frac{-e^{-2}}{1+(e^{-2})}\right] = \frac{-1}{(e^2+1)}$

17. $\because\ \theta = \frac{l(PR)}{\text{radius}} = \frac{PQ}{1}$

$\Rightarrow\ PQ = \theta$ ...(1)

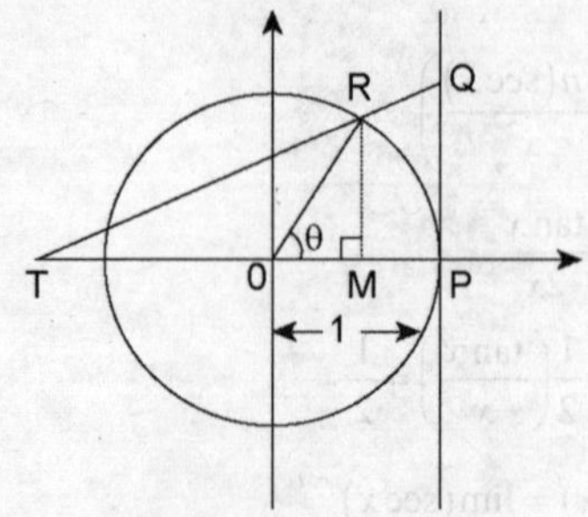

Also coordinates of R are (cosθ, sinθ)

$\Rightarrow$ OM = cosθ, RM = sinθ

$\Rightarrow$ MP = 1 − cosθ and TM = PT − (MP)

$\Rightarrow$ TM = PT − (1 − cosθ) ...(2)

Now in similarΔ's TRM and TQP, $\frac{RM}{QP} = \frac{TM}{TP}$

$\Rightarrow\ \frac{\sin\theta}{\theta} = \frac{PT - (1-\cos\theta)}{TP}$

$\Rightarrow$ TP sin θ = TP. θ − θ(1 − cosθ)

$\Rightarrow\ TP = \frac{\theta(1-\cos\theta)}{(\theta - \sin\theta)}$

Now $\lim\limits_{R\to P} TP = \lim\limits_{\theta\to 0}\frac{\theta(1-\cos\theta)}{(\theta-\sin\theta)} = \lim\limits_{\theta\to 0}\frac{1+\theta\sin\theta-\cos\theta}{(1-\cos\theta)}$

$= \lim\limits_{\theta\to 0}\frac{\theta\cos\theta+\sin\theta+\sin\theta}{\sin\theta} = \lim\limits_{\theta\to 0}\left(\frac{\theta}{\tan\theta}\right) + 2 = 3$

TEXTUAL EXERCISE-4: (OBJECTIVE)

1. (b) $\lim\limits_{x\to\infty}\frac{e^x\left(\left(2^{x^n}\right)^{\frac{1}{e^x}} - \left(3^{x^n}\right)^{\frac{1}{e^x}}\right)}{x^n}$

which can be written as $\lim\limits_{x\to\infty}\left[\frac{\left(\left(2^{x^n}\right)^{\frac{1}{e^x}} - \left(3^{\frac{x^n}{e^x}}\right)\right)}{\frac{x^n}{e^x}}\right]$

$= \lim\limits_{x\to\infty}\frac{3^{\frac{x^n}{e^x}}\left(\left(\frac{2}{3}\right)^{\frac{x^n}{e^x}} - 1\right)}{\frac{x^n}{e^x}}$

Consider $\lim\limits_{x\to\infty}\frac{x^n}{e^x} =$

$\lim\limits_{x\to\infty}\left(\frac{x^n}{1+x+\frac{x^2}{2!}+\frac{x^3}{3!}+....+\frac{x^n}{n!}+\frac{x^{n+1}}{(n+1)!}+....}\right) = \frac{1}{\infty} = 0$

Let $x^n/e^x = y$

$$\lim_{y\to 0}\frac{3^y\left(\left(\frac{2}{3}\right)^y-1\right)}{y}=\ell n\,(2/3)$$

2. (a) $\lim\limits_{x\to\infty}\left[x-x^2\ell n\left(1+\frac{1}{x}\right)\right]=\lim\limits_{x\to\infty}\left[x-x^2\{\ln(x+1)-\ln x\}\right]$

$=\lim\limits_{x\to\infty}\left[x+\ln x-x^2\ln(1+x)\right]$

Let us assume $\ell n\left(1+\frac{1}{x}\right)=y$

$\Rightarrow\ 1+\frac{1}{x}=e^y \qquad \Rightarrow \frac{1}{x}=e^y-1$

$\Rightarrow\ x=\frac{1}{e^y-1}$

$=\lim\limits_{x\to\infty}\left[x-x^2\left(\frac{1}{x}-\frac{1}{2x^2}+\frac{1}{3x^3}-\frac{1}{4x^4}+....\right)\right]$

$=\lim\limits_{x\to\infty}\left[x-x+\frac{1}{2}-\frac{1}{3x}+\frac{1}{4x^2}-....\right]=\frac{1}{2}$

3. (a) $\lim\limits_{x\to-\infty}\ [(x^5+7x^4+2)^c-x]$ = finite, for the limit to finitely exist $\lim\limits_{x\to-\infty}\left[x^{5c}\left(1+\frac{7}{x}+\frac{2}{x^5}\right)-x\right]$

$\Rightarrow\ x^{5c}=x \qquad \Rightarrow\ 5c=1$

$\Rightarrow\ c=\frac{1}{5}$

$\Rightarrow$ Limit = 7

4. (a) $\lim\limits_{x\to 0}\frac{a^{\tan x}-a^{\sin x}}{\tan x-\sin x}=\lim\limits_{x\to 0}\frac{a^{\sin x}\left[\frac{a^{\tan x}}{a^{\sin x}}-1\right]}{\tan x-\sin x}$

$=\lim\limits_{x\to 0}\frac{a^{\sin x}\left(a^{\tan x-\sin x}-1\right)}{(\tan x-\sin x)}=\ell na$

5. (c) $\lim\limits_{x\to 0}\frac{(\cos x-1)(\cos x-e^x)}{x^n}$

$=\lim\limits_{x\to 0}\frac{-2\sin^2\frac{x}{2}\left(-\frac{x^2}{2!}-\frac{x}{1!}-\frac{x^2}{2!}+\frac{x^4}{4!}-\frac{x^3}{3!}+....\right)}{x^n}$

$=\lim\limits_{x\to 0}\frac{\left(-2\sin^2\frac{x}{2}\right)}{x^2}\frac{\left[-x-x^2-\frac{x^3}{3!}+....\right]}{x^{n-2}}$

$\Rightarrow\ n-2=1 \qquad \Rightarrow\ n=3$

6. (c) $\lim\limits_{x\to 0}\left(\frac{\sin(nx)[(a-n)nx-\tan x]}{x^2}\right)=0\ ;\ n>0$

$\Rightarrow\ \lim\limits_{x\to 0}n\left(\frac{\sin(nx)}{nx}\right)\left[(a-n)n-\frac{\tan x}{x}\right]=0$

$\Rightarrow\ (a-n)\,n=1 \qquad \Rightarrow\ a-n=\frac{1}{n}$

$\Rightarrow\ a=n+\frac{1}{n}=\frac{n^2+1}{n}$

7. (d) $\lim\limits_{x\to 2}\left[\frac{\sin\left(e^{x-2}-1\right)}{\ell n(x-1)}\right]=\lim\limits_{x\to 2}\left[\frac{\left(\frac{\sin\left(e^{x-2}-1\right)}{e^{x-2}-1}\right).\left(e^{x-2}-1\right)}{\frac{\ell n(1+(x-2))}{(x-2)}.(x-2)}\right]$

Clearly as $x\to 2$

$\Rightarrow\ e^{x-2}-1\to 0$

Hence the limit reduces to $\lim\limits_{x\to 2}\left[\frac{e^{x-2}-1}{x-2}\right]=1$

8. (d) $\prod\limits_{n=2}^{\infty}\left(1-\frac{1}{n^2}\right)=\left(1-\frac{1}{2^2}\right)\left(1-\frac{1}{3^2}\right)\left(1-\frac{1}{4^2}\right)......\left(1-\frac{1}{n^2}\right)$

$=\left(\frac{2^2-1}{2^2}\right)\left(\frac{3^2-1}{3^2}\right)\left(\frac{4^2-1}{4^2}\right)....\left(\frac{n^2-1}{n^2}\right)$

$=\frac{(1.3)(2.4)(3.5).........[(n-1)(n+1)]}{2^2.3^2.4^2.......n^2}=\lim\limits_{n\to\infty}\left[\frac{1}{2}\left(1+\frac{1}{n}\right)\right]$

$=\frac{1}{2}$

9. (a) $\lim\limits_{n\to\infty}\frac{1^2n+2^2(n-1)+3^2(n-2)+....n^2-1.(n-(n-1))}{1^3+2^3+.....+n^3}$

$=\lim\limits_{n\to\infty}\frac{n\left(1^2+2^2+...+n^2\right)-1.2^2-2.3^2-3.4^2...-(n-1).n^2}{\left[\frac{n(n+1)}{2}\right]^2}$

$=\lim\limits_{n\to\infty}\left[\frac{\frac{n(n(n+1)(2n+1)}{6}-\sum\limits_{r=1}^{n-1}r(r+1)^2}{\frac{n^2(n+1)^2}{4}}\right]$

$=\lim\limits_{n\to\infty}\left[\frac{\frac{\left(1+\frac{1}{n}\right)\left(2+\frac{1}{n}\right).n^4}{6}-\sum\limits_{r=1}^{n-1}(r+1)^3-(r+1)^2}{n^4.\frac{1}{4}\left(1+\frac{1}{n}\right)^2}\right]$

$=\lim\limits_{n\to\infty}\left[\frac{\frac{n^4\left(1+\frac{1}{n}\right)\left(2+\frac{1}{n}\right)-\left\{\sum\limits_{r=1}^{n}\left(r^3-r^2\right)\right\}}{6}}{\frac{n^4}{4}\left(1+\frac{1}{n}\right)^2}\right]$

$=\lim\limits_{n\to\infty}\left[\frac{\frac{n^4}{6}\left(1+\frac{1}{n}\right)\left(2+\frac{1}{n}\right)-\left[\left[\frac{n(n+1)}{2}\right]^2-\frac{n(n+1)(2n+1)}{6}\right]}{\frac{n^4}{4}\left(1+\frac{1}{n}\right)^2}\right]$

$=\frac{\frac{(1)}{6}(2)-\frac{1}{4}(1)}{\frac{1}{4}}=\frac{1}{3}$

10. (a) $l = \lim_{x\to\infty}\dfrac{\ln(x^2+e^x)}{\ln(x^4+e^{2x})} = \lim_{x\to\infty}\dfrac{1}{(x^2+e^x)}\dfrac{(2x+e^x)(x^4+e^{2x})}{(4x^3+2e^{2x})}$

$= \lim_{x\to\infty}\dfrac{(2x+e^x)(x^4+e^{2x})}{(x^2+e^x)(4x^3+2e^{2x})}$

$= \lim_{x\to\infty}\dfrac{\left(\dfrac{2x}{e^x}+1\right)\left(\dfrac{x^4}{e^{2x}}+1\right)}{\left(\dfrac{x^2}{e^x}+1\right)\left[\left(\dfrac{4x^3}{e^{2x}}\right)+2\right]}$

$= \lim_{x\to\infty}\dfrac{\left(\dfrac{\dfrac{2}{e^x}+1}{x}\right)\left(\dfrac{\dfrac{1}{e^{2x}}+1}{x^4}\right)}{\left(\dfrac{\dfrac{1}{e^x}+1}{x^2}\right)\left(\dfrac{\dfrac{4}{e^{2x}}+2}{x^3}\right)} = \dfrac{1}{2}$ and $m = \lim_{x\to-\infty}\dfrac{\ln(x^2+e^x)}{\ln(x^4+e^{2x})}$

$= \lim_{x\to-\infty}\dfrac{(2x+e^x)(x^4+e^{2x})}{(x^2+e^x)(4x^3+2e^{2x})}$

$= \lim_{x\to-\infty}\dfrac{\left(2+\dfrac{e^x}{x}\right)\left(1+\dfrac{e^{2x}}{x^4}\right)}{\left(1+\dfrac{e^x}{x^2}\right)\left(4+2\dfrac{e^{2x}}{x^3}\right)} = \dfrac{2}{4} - \dfrac{1}{2}$

$\Rightarrow \quad l = m = \dfrac{1}{2}$

11. (d) $\lim_{x\to\infty}\left[\dfrac{2+2x+\sin 2x}{(2x+\sin 2x)e^{\sin x}}\right] = \lim_{x\to\infty}\left[\dfrac{\dfrac{2}{x}+2+\dfrac{\sin 2x}{x}}{\left(2+\dfrac{\sin 2x}{x}\right)e^{\sin x}}\right]$

$= \lim_{x\to\infty}\dfrac{2}{2e^{\sin x}} = \lim_{x\to\infty}\dfrac{1}{e^{\sin x}}$

which oscillates between 1/e and e

$\Rightarrow$ limit does not exists.

12. (a), (b), (d)

Let us obtain the limits first

(a) $\lim_{x\to\infty}\left(x^{\frac{1}{4}}\sin\dfrac{1}{\sqrt{x}}\right) = \lim_{x\to\infty}\left[x^{-\frac{1}{4}}\dfrac{\sin\dfrac{1}{\sqrt{x}}}{\dfrac{1}{\sqrt{x}}}\right] = 0$

Hence limit vanishes.

(b) $\lim_{x\to\frac{\pi}{2}}(1-\sin x).\tan x = \lim_{x\to\frac{\pi}{2}}\dfrac{(1-\sin x)}{\cot x}$

By L.H rule $= \lim_{x\to\frac{\pi}{2}}\dfrac{-\cos x}{-\text{cosec}^2 x} = 0$

Hence limit vanishes.

(c) $\lim_{x\to 0}\left[\dfrac{\sin 2x - 2\sin x}{x^3}\right]$

By L.H. rule $= \lim_{x\to 0}\left[\dfrac{2\cos 2x - 2\cos x}{3x^2}\right]$

$= \lim_{x\to 0}\left[\dfrac{-4\sin 2x + 2\sin x}{6x}\right] = \lim_{x\to 0}\dfrac{-8\cos 2x + 2\cos x}{6}$

$= \dfrac{-8+2}{6} = -1$

$\Rightarrow$ It does not vanishes

(d) $\lim_{x\to 0}\left(\dfrac{\cos x - 1}{\sin x}\right) = \lim_{x\to 0}\left(\dfrac{-\sin x}{\cos x}\right) = 0$

$\Rightarrow$ Hence limit vanishes.

13. (c) $\lim_{x\to 0}(\cos ax)^{\text{cosec}^2 bx}$

The limit can be written as $\lim_{x\to 0}(1+\cos ax - 1)^{\text{cosec}^2 bx}$

$= e^{\lim_{x\to 0}\left(\frac{\cos ax - 1}{\sin^2 bx}\right)} = e^{\lim_{x\to 0}\frac{-a.\sin ax}{2\sin bx.\cos bx.b}} = e^{\lim_{x\to 0}\left[\frac{-a\frac{\sin ax}{ax}.ax}{2b.b.\frac{\sin bx}{bx}.\cos bx.x}\right]}$

$= e^{-\frac{a^2}{2b^2}}$

14. (a) $\lim_{x\to 4}\left[\dfrac{(\cos\alpha)^x - (\sin\alpha)^x - \cos 2\alpha}{x-4}\right];\ 0 < \alpha < \dfrac{\pi}{2}$

Consider $g(x) = (\cos\alpha)^x - (\sin\alpha)^x - \cos 2\alpha$

$\lim_{x\to 4}(g(x)) = (\cos^2\alpha + \sin^2\alpha)(\cos^2\alpha - \sin^2\alpha) - \cos 2\alpha$

$= \cos 2\alpha(\cos^2\alpha + \sin^2\alpha - 1) = 0$

Hence the original limit is of the form $\dfrac{0}{0}$

$\therefore$ By L.H. rule, we get $\lim_{x\to 4}[(\cos\alpha)^x.\ \ell n(\cos\alpha) - (\sin\alpha)^x.\ \ell n(\sin\alpha)]$

$= [(\cos\alpha)^4\ \ell n(\cos x) - \sin^4\alpha\ \ell n(\sin\alpha)]$

15. (a) $\lim_{x\to 0}(\cos 2x)^{\frac{3}{x^2}} = \lim_{x\to 0}(1+(\cos 2x - 1))^{\frac{3}{x^2}} = e^{\lim_{x\to 0}\left(\frac{\cos 2x - 1}{x^2}\right)(3)}$

$= e^{\lim_{x\to 0}\left(\frac{-2\sin^2 x}{x^2}\right)(3)} = e^{-6}$

16. (a) $\lim_{x\to 0}(x^{-3}\sin 3x + ax^{-2} + b) = \lim_{x\to 0}\left(\dfrac{\sin 3x}{x^3} + \dfrac{a}{x^2} + b\right)$

$= \lim_{x\to 0}\left(\dfrac{\sin 3x + ax + bx^3}{x^3}\right)$

$\therefore$ By L.H rule, we get $\lim_{x\to 0}\left(\dfrac{3\cos 3x + a + 3bx^2}{3x^2}\right)$

$\Rightarrow$ For limit to exist, $a = -3$

$\therefore$ By L.H rule again, we get $\lim_{x\to 0}\left(\dfrac{-9\sin 3x + 6bx}{6x}\right)$

$= \lim_{x\to 0}\left(\dfrac{-27\cos 3x + 6b}{6}\right) = 0$ (given)

$\Rightarrow -27 + 6b = 0$

$\Rightarrow b = \dfrac{27}{6} = \dfrac{9}{2}$

17. (d) $f(x)=\left[\dfrac{2\sqrt{2}-(\cos x+\sin x)^3}{1-\sin 2x}\right]$

$$=\lim_{x\to\frac{\pi}{4}} f(x)=\lim_{x\to\frac{\pi}{4}}\left[\frac{2\sqrt{2}-2\sqrt{2}\left(\frac{\cos x}{\sqrt{2}}+\frac{\sin x}{\sqrt{2}}\right)^3}{1-\cos\left(\frac{\pi}{2}-2x\right)}\right]$$

$$=\lim_{x\to\frac{\pi}{4}}\left[\frac{2\sqrt{2}\left(1-\cos^3\left(x-\frac{\pi}{4}\right)\right)}{2\left(\sin^2\left(x-\frac{\pi}{4}\right)\right)}\right]$$

Let $x-\frac{\pi}{4}=y\to 0$

Hence the limit becomes $\lim\limits_{y\to 0}\left[\dfrac{\sqrt{2}(1-\cos^3 y)}{\sin^2 y}\right]$

Applying L.H rule, we get $\lim\limits_{y\to 0}\left(\dfrac{\sqrt{2}.3.\cos^2 y.\sin y}{2\sin y.\cos y}\right)$

$=\dfrac{3}{\sqrt{2}}$

18. (c) $AD = h$; $BC = 2BD$; $AD = h$; $OD = h - r$

$BC = 2\sqrt{r^2-(h-r)^2}=2\sqrt{2hr-h^2}$; $AB^2 = h^2 + BD^2 =$

$h^2 + r^2 - (h - r)^2 = zhr$

$\Rightarrow AB=\sqrt{2hr}$

$\Rightarrow p = 2AB + BC = 2\sqrt{2hr}+2\sqrt{2hr-h^2}$

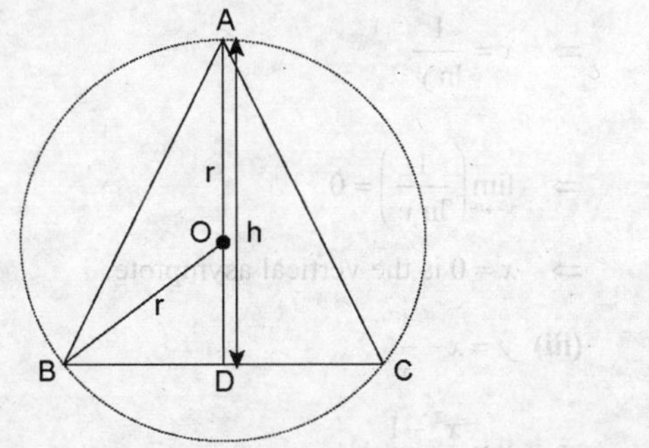

Also, Δ = area of $\Delta ABC = BD \times AD = h\sqrt{2hr-h^2}$

$$\Rightarrow \frac{\Delta}{p^3}=\frac{h\sqrt{2hr-h^2}}{8\left(\sqrt{2r-h}+\sqrt{2r}\right)^3 h^{3/2}}=\frac{\sqrt{2r-h}}{8\left(\sqrt{2r-h}+\sqrt{2r}\right)^3}$$

$$\Rightarrow \lim_{h\to 0}\frac{\Delta}{p^3}=\frac{\sqrt{2r}}{8\times\left(2\sqrt{2r}\right)^3}=\frac{1}{128r}$$

TEXTUAL EXERCISE–5: (SUBJECTIVE)

1. (i) $x^2y^2+2xy^3-4x^2+10=0$

Horizontal Asymptote-:

Put coefficient of highest power of $x = 0$ in $x^2(y^2-4)+2xy^3+10=0$

$\Rightarrow y^2-4=0 \qquad \Rightarrow y=\pm 2$

Vertical Asymptote-:

Put coefficient of highest power of $y = 0$ in $2xy^3+x^2y^2-4x^2+10=0$

$\Rightarrow 2x=0 \qquad \Rightarrow x=0$

(ii) $2x^2y-3xy^2+10x^2-5y=0$

Horizontal Asymptote-:

$x^2(2y+10)-3xy^2-5y=0$

$\Rightarrow 2y+10=0 \qquad \Rightarrow y=-5$

Vertical Asymptote-: $-3xy^2 + (2x^2 - 5)y + 10x^2 = 0$

$\Rightarrow x=0$ is the vertical asymptote

(iii) $x^3y^2-y^3x^2+4=0$

Horizontal Asymptote-: $y^2=0$

$\Rightarrow y=0$ is the horizontal asymptote.

Vertical asymptote-: $x^2=0$

$\Rightarrow x=0$ is the vertical asymptote

(iv) $x^4y^2-x^3y^3-9x^4+8y^3=0$

Horizontal Asymptote-:

Coefficient of highest power of x is given by $x^4(y^2-9)-x^3y^3+8y^3=0$

$\Rightarrow y^2-9=0$

$\Rightarrow y=\pm 3$; gives the two horizontal asymptote to the curve

Vertical Asymptote-:

Coefficient of highest power of y is given by-: $y^3(-x^3+8)+y^2x^4-9x^4=0$

$\Rightarrow x^3-8=0$

$\Rightarrow x=2$ is the vertical asymptote

2. Asymptote: A straight line at a finite distance from origin which tends to meet the curve at infinity

(a) $y=\dfrac{1}{x}$

Horizontal asymptote $y=\lim\limits_{x\to\infty}\left(\dfrac{1}{x}\right)=0$ i.e., $y=0$

Similarly vertical asymptote is $x=\lim\limits_{y\to 0}\left(\dfrac{1}{y}\right)=0$ i.e., $x = 0$

(b) $y=\dfrac{4x-5}{3x+2}=\dfrac{4-\frac{5}{x}}{3+\frac{2}{x}}$

Horizontal asymptote-: $y=\lim\limits_{x\to\infty}\left(\dfrac{4-\frac{5}{x}}{3+\frac{2}{x}}\right)=\dfrac{4}{3}$

i.e., $y=\dfrac{4}{3}$

Now $y=\dfrac{4x-5}{3x+2}$

$\Rightarrow y(3x)+2y-4x+5=0$

$\Rightarrow x(3y-4)+2y+5=0$

$\Rightarrow x=\dfrac{-2y-5}{3y-4}$

$\Rightarrow$ Vertical asymptote is, $x = \lim\limits_{y\to\infty}\left(\dfrac{-2y-5}{3y-4}\right)$

$\Rightarrow \lim\limits_{y\to\infty}\left(\dfrac{-2-\dfrac{5}{y}}{3-\dfrac{4}{y}}\right) = -\dfrac{2}{3}$

$\Rightarrow x = -\dfrac{2}{3}$ is the vertical asymptote.

(c) $y = \dfrac{2x+3}{\sqrt{x^2-2x-3}}$

$\Rightarrow y = \dfrac{2+\dfrac{3}{x}}{\sqrt{1-\dfrac{2}{x}-\dfrac{3}{x^2}}}$

$\Rightarrow$ Horizontal asymptote is $y = \lim\limits_{x\to\infty}\left(\dfrac{2+\dfrac{3}{x}}{\sqrt{1-\dfrac{2}{x}-\dfrac{3}{x^2}}}\right) = 2$

$\Rightarrow y = 2$ is the horizontal asymptote.

Vertical Asymptote is given by $x = \lim\limits_{y\to\infty}(x)$

Now, $y \to \infty$

$\Rightarrow x^2 - 2x - 3 \to 0$

$\Rightarrow (x-3)(x+1) \to 0$

$\Rightarrow x \to -1$ or 3

$\therefore$ $x = -1$ and $x = 3$ are two vertical asymptotes.

(d) $y = \sqrt{x+1} - \sqrt{x}$

On rationalizing $y = \dfrac{x+1-x}{\sqrt{x+1}+\sqrt{x}}$

$\Rightarrow y = \dfrac{1}{\sqrt{x}+\sqrt{x+1}}$

$\Rightarrow y = 0$ is the horizontal asymptote

Vertical Asymptote-: $y = \dfrac{1}{\sqrt{x}+\sqrt{x+1}}$

Clearly $y \to \infty$

$\Rightarrow \sqrt{x}+\sqrt{x+1} \to 0$ which is impossible

$\Rightarrow$ Curve has no vertical asymptote.

(e) $y = \dfrac{x^2-5x+6}{x-3} = \dfrac{(x-2)(x-3)}{(x-3)}$

$\Rightarrow y = (x-2); x \neq 3$

Since the coefficient of highest power of x and y are both constants.

Hence the curve has no horizontal and vertical asymptotes.

(f) $y = \dfrac{x^2-x+1}{x^2+x+1}$

$\Rightarrow y = \dfrac{1-\dfrac{1}{x}+\dfrac{1}{x^2}}{1+\dfrac{1}{x}+\dfrac{1}{x^2}}$; Now as $x \to \infty$

$\Rightarrow y \to 1$

$y = 1$ is the horizontal asymptote.

No vertical asymptote is there as (coefficient of y) = 0

$\Rightarrow x^2 + x + 1 = 0$ which has no real solution.

(g) $y = \dfrac{2x}{x^2+1}$ or $x^2y - 2x + y = 0$ or $(x^2+1)y - 2x = 0$

$\Rightarrow y = 0$ is horizontal asymptote and vertical asymptote are given by $x^2 + 1 = 0$.

$\Rightarrow$ No vertical asymptote (as $x^2+1=0$ has no solution)

3. (i) $y = \dfrac{1}{x-5}$

$\Rightarrow \lim\limits_{x\to\infty}\left(\dfrac{1}{x-5}\right) = 0$

$\Rightarrow y = 0$ (x-axis) is the horizontal asymptote

Now $y = \dfrac{1}{x-5}$

$\Rightarrow x = \dfrac{1}{y}+5$

$\Rightarrow \lim\limits_{y\to\infty}\left(\dfrac{1}{y}+5\right) = 5$

$\Rightarrow x = 5$ is the vertical asymptote

(ii) $y = e^{\frac{1}{x}}$

$\Rightarrow \lim\limits_{x\to\infty}\left(e^{\frac{1}{x}}\right) = 1$

$\Rightarrow y = 1$ is the horizontal asymptote.

$\Rightarrow \ln y = \dfrac{1}{x}$

$\Rightarrow x = \dfrac{1}{\ln y}$

$\Rightarrow \lim\limits_{y\to\infty}\left(\dfrac{1}{\ln y}\right) = 0$

$\Rightarrow x = 0$ is the vertical asymptote

(iii) $y = x - \dfrac{1}{x}$

$\Rightarrow y = \dfrac{x^2-1}{x}$

$\Rightarrow x^2 - 1 - yx = 0$

$\Rightarrow x = 0$ is the vertical asymptote and no horizontal asymptote.

Now, $y = x - \dfrac{1}{x}$

$\Rightarrow$ Oblique asymptote are given by $y = mx + c$; where

$m = \lim\limits_{\substack{x\to\infty\\y\to\infty}}\left(\dfrac{dy}{dx}\right); c = \lim\limits_{\substack{x\to\infty\\y\to\infty}}\left(y - x\dfrac{dy}{dx}\right)$

$\Rightarrow \dfrac{dy}{dx} = 1 + \dfrac{1}{x^2}$

$\Rightarrow m = \lim\limits_{\substack{x\to\infty\\y\to\infty}}\left(1+\dfrac{1}{x^2}\right) = 1$

$\Rightarrow \quad c = \lim\limits_{\substack{x\to\infty \\ y\to\infty}} \left(y - x\left(1+\frac{1}{x^2}\right)\right)$

$\Rightarrow \quad c = \lim\limits_{\substack{x\to\infty \\ y\to\infty}} \left(y - x - \frac{1}{x^2}\right) = \lim\limits_{\substack{x\to\infty \\ y\to\infty}} \left(-\frac{1}{x} - \frac{1}{x^2}\right) = 0$

$\Rightarrow \quad c = 0$

$\Rightarrow \quad y = x$ is the oblique asymptote

4. (i) $x^2y + xy^2 = a^3$

Horizontal Asymptote-: $y = 0$

Vertical Asymptote-: $x = 0$

Oblique Asymptote-: $x^2y + xy^2 = a^3$

$\Rightarrow x^2y + xy^2 - a^3 = 0$

$\Rightarrow \phi_3(x, y) = x^2y + xy^2$

$\Rightarrow m^2 + m - a^3 = 0$

$\Rightarrow \phi_2(x, y) = 0, \phi_1(x, y) = 0, \phi_0(x, y) = -a^3$

Now, $\phi_3(m) = m + m^2 = 0$

$\Rightarrow m = 0$ or $m = -1$

$\therefore \; c\phi'_3(m) + \phi_2(m) = 0$

$\Rightarrow c(1 + 2m) = 0$

$\therefore$ For $m = 0$, $c = 0$ and for $m = -1$, $c = 0$

$\Rightarrow y = -x$ is the oblique asymptote.

(ii) $y^3 = x^2(x-a)$

$\Rightarrow \quad y^3 = x^3 - x^2a$ or $y^3 - x^3 + x^2a = 0$

There are no horizontal and no vertical asymptotes.

$\Rightarrow \quad 3y^2\frac{dy}{dx} = 3x^2 - 2xa$

$\Rightarrow \quad \frac{dy}{dx} = \frac{3x^2 - 2xa}{3y^2}$

$\Rightarrow \quad \phi_3(x\, y) = y^3 - x^3$

$\Rightarrow \quad \phi_2(x, y) = x^2a, \phi_1(x, y) = 0$

$\Rightarrow \quad \phi_3(m) = m^3 - 1, \phi_2(m) = m^2a, \phi_1(m) = 0$

Slopes of asymptote are given by $\phi_3(m) = 0$

$\Rightarrow m = 1$ and $c\phi'_3(m) + \phi_2(m) = 0$

$\Rightarrow c(3m^2) + m^2a = 0$

$\Rightarrow 3c + a = 0$ for $m = 1$

$\Rightarrow \quad c = \frac{-a}{3}$

$\therefore \quad y = mx + c = x - \frac{a}{3}$ is the oblique asymptote.

5. (i) $y^4 - 6x^2y^2 + 2x^4 - 3x^3y + 2x^2y + 8y^3$
$-9x^2 + 7xy + 8x + 1 = 0$

Coefficient of highest power of x i.e., x^4 = constant

$\Rightarrow$ No horizontal asymptote.

Coefficient of highest power of y i.e., y^4 = constant

$\Rightarrow$ No Vertical Asymptote.

Now, $\phi_4(x, y) = y^4 - 6x^2y^2 + 2x^4 - 3x^3y$

$\phi_3(x, y) = 8y^3 + 2x^2y$,

$\phi_2(x, y) = -9x^2 + 7xy$,

$\phi_1(x, y) = 8x$,

$\phi_0(x, y) = 1$,

Put $x = 1$ & $y = m$

$\Rightarrow \quad \phi_4(m) = m^4 - 6m^2 + 2 - 3m = 0$

For $m = -1$, $1 - 6 + 2 + 3 = 0$

$\therefore \quad \phi_4(m) = 0$

$\Rightarrow \quad (m + 1)(m^3 - m^2 - 5m + 2) = 0$

Also $m = -2$

$\Rightarrow \quad -8 - 4 + 10 + 2 = 0$

$\Rightarrow \quad (m + 1)(m + 2)/(m^2 - 3m + 1) = 0$

$\Rightarrow \quad m = -1, -2, \frac{3\pm\sqrt{5}}{2}$

$\Rightarrow \quad c\phi'_4(m) + \phi_3(m) = 0$

$\Rightarrow \quad c.[4m^3 - 6m - 3] + (8m^3 + 2m) = 0$

$\Rightarrow \quad c = \frac{-(8m^3 + 2m)}{(4m^3 - 6m - 3)}$

$\therefore \quad$ For $m = -1$, $c = 10$, for $m = -2$, $c = -68/23$

$\Rightarrow \quad$ Oblique asymptotes are given by $y = -x + 10$, $y = -2x - \frac{68}{23}$ and $y = \left(\frac{3\pm\sqrt{5}}{2}\right)x + c$;

where $c = \frac{-(8m^3 + 2m)}{(4m^3 - 6m - 3)}; m = \frac{3\pm\sqrt{5}}{2}$

(ii) $y^3 - x^3 + 2y - 5x = 0$

There are no horizontal or vertical asymptotes.

Oblique asymptotes-: $\phi_3(x, y) = y^3 - x^3$, $\phi_2(x, y) = 0$

Putting $x = 1$ & $y = m$

$\Rightarrow \quad \phi_3(m) = m^3 - 1$

$\Rightarrow \quad m = 1 \qquad \therefore \quad c\phi'_3(m) + \phi_2(m) = 0$

$\Rightarrow \quad 3cm^2 = 0$

$\Rightarrow \quad c = 0$

$\Rightarrow \quad y = x$ is an oblique asymptote.

(iii) $y^2x^2 - 4x^2y + 8xy^2 - 8xy + 2x + y = 0$

Horizontal asymptote-:

$y \;\; - 4y = 0$

$\Rightarrow \quad y(y - 4) = 0$

$\Rightarrow \quad y = 0, y = 4$ are horizontal asymptote

Vertical asymptote-:

$x^2 + 8x = 0$

$\Rightarrow \quad x(x + 8) = 0$

$\Rightarrow \quad x = 0, x = -8$ are vertical asymptotes

Oblique Asymptote-:

$\phi_4(x, y) = x^2y^2$

$\Rightarrow \quad \phi_3(x, y) = -4x^2y + 8xy^2$

$\Rightarrow \phi_2(x, y) = -8xy$

$\phi_1(x, y) = 2x + y$

$\Rightarrow \phi_0(x, y) = 0$

Putting $x = 1$ and $y = m$ in $\phi_4(x, y)$, we get $\phi_4(m) = m^2$,

$\phi_3(m) = -4m + 8m^2$

$\therefore \quad m^2 = 0$

$\Rightarrow$ $m = 0$ which gives us horizontal asymptotes

i.e., horizontal asymptote are the only oblique asymptote.

(iv) $x^3 + y^3 - 3axy = 0$

There are no horizontal or vertical asymptotes.

$\phi_3(m) = 1 + m^3$

$\phi_2(m) = -3am$

$\Rightarrow \quad m = -1$

$c\phi'_3 m + \phi_2(m) = 0$

$\Rightarrow \quad c(3m^2) - 3am = 0$

$\Rightarrow \quad c = -a$

The only asymptote is $y + x + a = 0$

6. (i) $y^2 = x^2 + 4x$

$$\Rightarrow \quad y^2 = x^2\left(1 + \frac{4}{x}\right)$$

$$\Rightarrow \quad y = x\left(1 + \frac{4}{x}\right)^{\frac{1}{2}} = x\left[1 + \frac{1}{2}\left(\frac{4}{x}\right) + \frac{\frac{1}{2}\left(\frac{-1}{2}\right)\left(\frac{4}{x}\right)^2}{2!} + \ldots\right]$$

$\Rightarrow \quad y = x + 2 + \ldots\ldots\ldots\ldots$

$y = x + 2$ is the oblique asymptote for the curve

(ii) $y^2 = x^2 + \frac{1}{x}$

$$\Rightarrow \quad y^2 = x^2\left(1 + \frac{1}{x^3}\right)$$

$$\Rightarrow \quad y = x\left(1 + \frac{1}{x^3}\right)^{\frac{1}{2}}$$

$$\Rightarrow \quad y = x\left(1 + \frac{1}{2}\left(\frac{1}{x^3}\right) + \frac{\frac{1}{2}\left(-\frac{1}{2}\right)\left(\frac{1}{x^3}\right)^2}{2!} + \ldots\right)$$

$\Rightarrow \quad y = x$ is the oblique asymptote.

(iii) $y = 2x + 5 + \frac{4}{x} + \frac{8}{x^2} + \ldots$

$\Rightarrow \quad y = 2x + 5$ is the oblique asymptote.

(iv) $y^5 = x^5 + 8x^4$

$$\Rightarrow \quad y^5 = x^5\left(1 + \frac{8}{x}\right)$$

$$\Rightarrow \quad y = x\left(1 + \frac{8}{x}\right)^{\frac{1}{5}}$$

$$\Rightarrow \quad y = x\left(1 + \frac{1}{5}\left(\frac{8}{x}\right) + \frac{1}{5}\;\frac{\frac{4}{5}\left(\frac{8}{x}\right)^2}{2!} + \ldots\right)$$

$\Rightarrow \quad y = x + \frac{8}{5}$ is the oblique asymptote

7. $y^5 = x^5 + 2x^4$

$$\Rightarrow \quad y^5 = x^5\left(1 + \frac{2}{x}\right)$$

$$\Rightarrow \quad y = x\left(1 + \frac{2}{x}\right)^{\frac{1}{5}} = x\left(1 + \frac{2}{5}\left(\frac{1}{x}\right) + \frac{\left(\frac{1}{5}\right)\left(\frac{-4}{5}\right)\left(\frac{4}{x^2}\right)}{2!} + \ldots\right)$$

or $y = x + \frac{2}{5} - \frac{8}{25x}$

Asymptote $= y = x + \frac{2}{5}$ and $A = \frac{-8}{25}$

Curve lies above the asymptote if $x < 0$ as in this case x and A will have the same signs.

Similarly (*i*) if $x > 0$, then A and x will have opposite signs

$\Rightarrow$ curve will lies below the asymptote.

8. $y = x + \frac{1}{x}$

Clearly, $y = x$ is the asymptote, for the curve $A = 1$

$\Rightarrow \quad x > 0$

$\Rightarrow$ A and x have the same signs

$\Rightarrow$ curve lies above the asymptote

$\Rightarrow \quad x < 0$

$\Rightarrow$ curve lies below the asymptote.

9. Vertical Asymptote $x^2 - 4 = 0$

$\Rightarrow \quad x = 2$ and $x = -2$ are vertical asymptote and $y = 0$ is the only horizontal asymptote

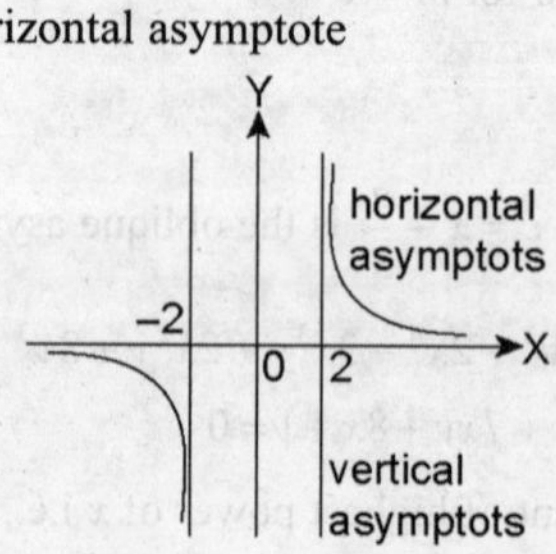

10. The logarithmic function will have a vertical asymptote at $2x + 8 = 0$

$\Rightarrow \quad 2x + 8 = 0$

$\Rightarrow \quad x = -4$, there is no horizontal asymptote for the curve.

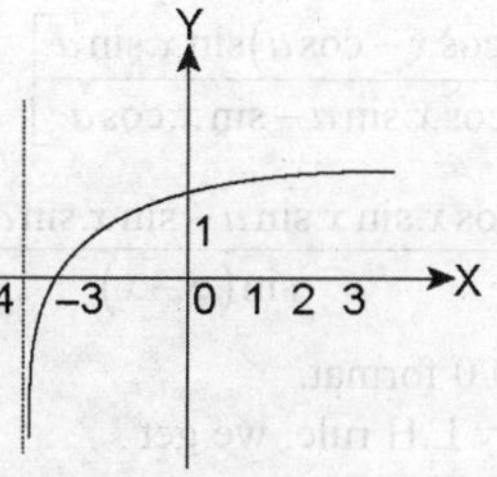

TEXTUAL EXERCISE–5 : (OBJECTIVE)

1. (c) $x^2 - 2xy + yx^2 = 0$

which can be written as-: $x^2(1+y) - 2xy = 0$

$y = -1$ is the horizontal asymptote.

2. (c) $yx^2 - 2xy^2 + 8y^2 + 7y = 0$

$\Rightarrow \quad y^2(8-2x) + 7y + yx^2 = 0$

$\Rightarrow \quad x = 4$ is the vertical asymptote.

3. (a), (b) $yx^2 - 2xy^2 + 8y^2 + 7y = 0$

$\phi_3(x,y) = x^2y - 2xy^2$

$\phi_2(x,y) = 8y^2$

$\phi_1(x,y) = 7y$

Put $x = 1, y = m$

$\Rightarrow \quad \phi_3(m) = m - 2m^2$,

$\phi_2(m) = 8m^2$,

$\phi_1(m) = 7m$,

$\phi_3(m) = 0$

$\Rightarrow \quad m(1-2m) = 0$

$\Rightarrow \quad m = 0, m = \frac{1}{2}$

$\therefore \quad c\phi'_3(m) + \phi_2(m) = 0$

$\Rightarrow \quad c(1-4m) + 8m^2 = 0$

$\Rightarrow \quad c - 4mc + 8m^2 = 0$

$\Rightarrow$ c = 0 for $m = 0$ and $c = 2$ for $m = \frac{1}{2}$

$\Rightarrow \quad y = 0$ and $y = \frac{x}{2} + 2$

4. (b) $y = 2x + 5 + \frac{8}{x} + \frac{9}{x^2} + ...$

$\Rightarrow \quad y = 2x + 5$ is the oblique asymptote.

5. (b) $y = 2x - 4 - \frac{2}{x} + \frac{4}{x^2}$

Asymptote $2x - 4$

$\Rightarrow \quad A = -2$

The curve lies below the asymptote if $x > 0$

6. (a), (b), (c), (d)

(a) $y = \frac{3x}{\sqrt{x^2+2}}$

$\Rightarrow \quad y^2 = \frac{9x^2}{x^2+4}$

This clearly has 2 horizontal asymptote $y = 3, y = -3$

(b) $y = \frac{|x|}{x+2}$

$\Rightarrow \quad y^2 = \frac{x^2}{x^2+4+4x}$ which has two horizontal asymptotes, $y = \pm 1$

(c) $y = \tan^{-1}(3x+4)$ has two horizontal asymptotes $y = \pm \pi/2$

(d) $y = \cot^{-1}(2x-1)$ has two horizontal asymptote $y = 0$ and $y = \pi$

7. (c), (d)

(a) $\lim\limits_{x\to 2} y = \lim\limits_{x\to 2} \frac{|x^2-4|}{(x-2)}$

$\Rightarrow \quad \lim\limits_{x\to 2^-} \frac{-(x-2)|x+2|}{(x-2)} - 4$ and $\lim\limits_{x\to 2^+} \frac{(x-2)|x+2|}{(x-2)} = 4$

(b) $y = \frac{x^2-5x+6}{x-2} = x - 3$ has no asymptote at $x = 2$

$\Rightarrow$ x = 2 is not a vertical asymptote

(c) $y(x-2) = x^4 + 1$

$\Rightarrow$ has a vertical asymptote $x = 2$

(d) $\lim\limits_{x\to 2} y = \lim\limits_{x\to 2} \frac{\cos(x+1)}{(x-2)} = \pm\infty$

$\Rightarrow$ x = 2 is a vertical asymptote

8. (a), (d)

$xy = c^2$, clearly $x = 0, y = 0$ are the asymptote this is basically a rectangular hyperbola.

9. (a), (b)

$x^2 - y^2 = a^2$

$\Rightarrow \quad \phi_2(x,y) = x^2 - y^2; \phi_2(m) = 1 - m^2$.

Thus $\phi_2(m) = 0$

$\Rightarrow$ m = ± 1 and $c\phi'_2(m) + \phi_1(m) = 0$

$\Rightarrow$ $c(-2m) = 0$

$\Rightarrow$ c = 0

$\Rightarrow \quad y = x, y = -x$ are the asymptotes.

10. (a), (d)

Consider $y = e^{\frac{1}{x}}$

$\lim\limits_{x\to\infty}(y) = \lim\limits_{x\to\infty}\left(e^{\frac{1}{x}}\right) \to 1$

$\Rightarrow$ y = 1 is horizontal asymptote and $x = \frac{1}{\ln y}$

$\therefore \quad \lim\limits_{y\to\infty}(x) = \lim\limits_{y\to\infty}\left(\frac{1}{\ln y}\right) \to 0$

$\Rightarrow$ x = 0 is the vertical asymptote

11. (b), (c), (d)

(a) $\because$ An algebraic curve of degree 'n' can have maximum n-asymptote, but a function can't have more then two horizontal asymptotes.

$\Rightarrow$ option (*a*) has true statement

(*b*) $y = \dfrac{p(x)}{x-2}$

Since p(*x*) is a function of *x*.

Hence it not necessary that is a vertical asymptote. e.g., if $P(x) = (x^2 - 3x + 2)$, then

$$\lim_{x\to 2}\frac{P(x)}{(x-2)} = \lim_{(x\to 2)}\frac{(x-2)(x-1)}{(x-2)} = 1$$

$\Rightarrow x = 2$ is not a vertical asymptote

(*c*) False

e.g., $F(x) = x^3 - 9x^2 + 15x + 30$ has no vertical asymptote.

(*d*) False

e.g., $y = x$ has no asymptote.

SECTION–III: (ONLY ONE ANSWER CORRECT)

1. (c) $\lim\limits_{x\to 1}\left(\dfrac{\sin[x]}{[x]}\right)$

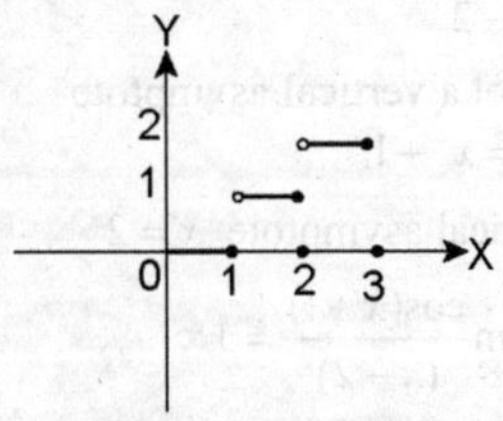

L.H.L. $= \lim\limits_{x\to 1^-}\left(\dfrac{\sin[x]}{[x]}\right) = \lim\limits_{x\to 1^-}\left(\dfrac{\sin(0)}{0}\right)$

$\Rightarrow$ L.H.L does not exist.

R.H.L $= \lim\limits_{x\to 1^+}\left[\dfrac{\sin[x]}{[x]}\right] = \sin 1$

$\Rightarrow$ L.H.L does not exist, R.H.L = sin 1

2. (a) $\lim\limits_{n\to\infty}\left[\dfrac{1-2+3-4+....+-2n}{\sqrt{n^2+1}+\sqrt{4n^2-1}}\right]$

$$= \lim_{n\to\infty}\left[\frac{(1+3+5.....+2n-1)-2(1+2+....+n)}{\sqrt{n^2+1}+\sqrt{4n^2-1}}\right]$$

$$= \lim_{n\to\infty}\left[\frac{n^2-2\dfrac{(n(n+1))}{2}}{n\left(\sqrt{1+\dfrac{1}{n^2}}+\sqrt{4-\dfrac{1}{n^2}}\right)}\right]$$

$$= \lim_{n\to\infty}\left[\frac{-n}{n\sqrt{1+\dfrac{1}{n^2}}+\sqrt{4-\dfrac{1}{n^2}}}\right] = -\frac{1}{5}$$

3. (c) $\lim\limits_{x\to a}\left[\dfrac{\cos x-\cos a}{\cot x-\cot a}\right] = \lim\limits_{x\to a}\left[\dfrac{\cos x-\cos a}{\dfrac{\cos x}{\sin x}-\dfrac{\cos a}{\sin a}}\right]$

$$= \lim_{x\to a}\left[\frac{(\cos x-\cos a)\sin x.\sin a}{\cos x.\sin a-\sin x.\cos a}\right]$$

$$= \lim_{x\to a}\left(\frac{\cos x.\sin x.\sin a-\sin x.\sin a.\cos a}{\sin(a-x)}\right)$$

This is 0/0 format.

Hence by L.H rule, we get

$$\frac{1}{2}\lim_{x\to a}\left[\frac{2.\sin a.\cos 2x-\cos x.\sin 2a}{-\cos(a-x)}\right]$$

$= -\dfrac{1}{2}$ (2 cos 2*a* .sin *a* – cos *a*.sin 2*a*)

$= \dfrac{1}{2}$ (cos *a*.sin 2*a* – 2 cos 2*a*.sin *a*)

$= \dfrac{1}{2}$ [2 sin *a*.cos² *a* – 2 (cos²α – sin²α) sin *a*]

$= \dfrac{1}{2}$ (2 sin ³ *a*) = sin³ *a*

4. (c) $\lim\limits_{x\to 0}\dfrac{(e^x-1)^4}{\sin\left(\dfrac{x^2}{k^2}\right).\ell n\left(1+\dfrac{x^2}{2}\right)} = 8$

$$\Rightarrow \lim_{x\to 0}\frac{\left[\dfrac{(e^x-1)}{x}\right]^4.(x^4)}{\dfrac{x^2}{k^2}\dfrac{\sin\left(\dfrac{x^2}{k^2}\right)}{\dfrac{x^2}{k^2}}.\dfrac{\ell n\left(1+\dfrac{x^2}{2}\right)}{\dfrac{x^2}{2}}.\dfrac{x^2}{2}} = 8$$

$$\Rightarrow \lim_{x\to 0}\left[\frac{\left(\dfrac{e^x-1}{x}\right)^4}{\dfrac{1}{2k^2}\left(\dfrac{\sin\left(\dfrac{x^2}{k^2}\right)}{\dfrac{x^2}{k^2}}.\dfrac{\ell n\left(1+\dfrac{x^2}{2}\right)}{\dfrac{x^2}{2}}\right)}\right] = 8$$

$\Rightarrow 2k^2 = 8$ $\qquad\Rightarrow k = 2$ or $k = -2$

5. (a) $\lim\limits_{h\to 0}\left[\dfrac{(e^{\sin h}-1)\sin h}{(\tan^{-1}(\sin h))^2}\right]$

Dividing numerator as well as denominator by sin² *h*,

we get $\lim\limits_{h\to 0}\left[\dfrac{\dfrac{(e^{\sin h}-1)}{\sin h}}{\left[\dfrac{\tan^{-1}(\sin h)}{\sin h}\right]^2}\right] = 1$

6. (a) $\lim\limits_{x\to\infty}(1-a^4)^x\sin\left(\dfrac{b}{(1-a^4)^x}\right)$; 0 < |a| < 1 but (1 – a^4) ∈ (0, 1)

$\Rightarrow \lim_{x\to\infty} (1-a^4)^x = 0$

$\therefore$ Given limit $= \lim_{x\to\infty} \left(1-a^4\right)^x \sin\left(\dfrac{b}{\left(1-a^4\right)^x}\right)$

$= 0.$ (Finite oscillating quantity) $= 0$

7. (b) $\lim_{x\to\infty}\left[\dfrac{(x+1)^{10}+(x+2)^{10}+......+(x+100)^{10}}{x^{10}+10^{10}}\right]$

This can also be written as

$$\lim_{x\to\infty}\left[\frac{x^{10}\left(\left(1+\frac{1}{x}\right)^{10}+\left(1+\frac{2}{x}\right)^{10}+......+\left(1+\frac{100}{x}\right)^{10}\right)}{x^{10}\left(1+\frac{10^{10}}{x^{10}}\right)}\right]$$

$$= \lim_{x\to\infty}\left(\frac{\left(1+\frac{1}{x}\right)^{10}+\left(1+\frac{2}{x}\right)^{10}+....+\left(1+\frac{100}{x}\right)^{10}}{\left(1+\frac{10^{10}}{x^{10}}\right)}\right)$$

$= \dfrac{100}{1} = 100$

8. (c) $\lim_{x\to 1}\left(\dfrac{x+x^2+....+x^n-n}{x-1}\right)$

This achieves a 0/0 format.

Hence by L.H rule, we get $\lim_{x\to 1}\left(\dfrac{1+2x+3x+....+nx^{n-1}}{1}\right)$

$= \dfrac{n(n+1)}{2}$

9. (b) $\lim_{x\to 1}\left[\dfrac{x^{p+1}-(p+1)x+p}{(x-1)^2}\right]$

This tends to a 0/0 format.

Hence by L.H rule, we get $\lim_{x\to 1}\left[\dfrac{(p+1)x^p-p-1}{2(x-1)}\right]$

Applying L.H rule again, we get $\lim_{x\to 1}\left[\dfrac{p(p+1)x^{p-1}}{2}\right]$

$= \dfrac{p(p+1)}{2}$

10. (b) $\lim_{x\to\infty}\left[\dfrac{2\sqrt{x}+3.\sqrt[3]{x}+5.\sqrt[5]{x}}{\sqrt{3x-2}+(2x-3)^{\frac{1}{3}}}\right]$

$$= \lim_{x\to\infty}\left[\frac{2x^{\frac{1}{2}}+3.x^{\frac{1}{3}}+5.x^{\frac{1}{5}}}{(3x-2)^{\frac{1}{2}}+(2x-3)^{\frac{1}{3}}}\right]$$

Taking $(x)^{\frac{1}{2}}$ common from numerator as well as denominator

$$= \lim_{x\to\infty}\frac{x^{\frac{1}{2}}\left(2+3.x^{-\frac{1}{6}}+5.x^{-\frac{3}{10}}\right)}{x^{\frac{1}{2}}\left(\left(3-\frac{2}{x}\right)^{\frac{1}{2}}+\left(2-\frac{3}{x}\right)^{\frac{1}{3}}.x^{-\frac{1}{6}}\right)}$$

$$= \lim_{x\to\infty}\left[\frac{\left(2+3x^{-\frac{1}{6}}+5x^{-\frac{3}{10}}\right)}{\left(\left(3-\frac{2}{x}\right)^{\frac{1}{2}}+x^{-\frac{1}{6}}\left(2-\frac{3}{x}\right)^{\frac{1}{3}}\right)}\right]$$

Upon putting the limit, we get $\dfrac{2}{\sqrt{3}}$

11. (a) $\lim_{x\to 0}(\cos x + a\sin bx)^{1/x}$

This can be written as $\lim_{x\to 0}(1+\cos x + a\sin bx - 1)^{1/x}$

Comparing it with the standard format, we get $\lim_{x\to 0}(1+f(x))^{\frac{1}{g(x)}}$

Hence the limit becomes $e^{\lim_{x\to 0}\left(\frac{\cos x + a\sin bx - 1}{x}\right)}$

$= e^{\lim_{x\to 0}(-\sin x + ab\cos bx)} = e^{ab}$

12. (d) $\lim_{n\to\infty}\left[\left\{4\sum_{r=0}^{n}(r+1)(r+2)(r+3)\right\}^{\frac{1}{4}}-n\right]$

$$= \lim_{n\to\infty}\left[\left\{\frac{4(n+1)(n+2)(n+3)(n+4)}{4}\right\}^{1/4}-n\right]$$

$$= \lim_{n\to\infty}\left[\{(n+1)(n+2)(n+3)(n+4)\}^{1/4}-n\right]$$

$$= \lim_{n\to\infty}\left[n\left\{\left(1+\frac{1}{n}\right)\left(1+\frac{2}{n}\right)\left(1+\frac{3}{n}\right)\left(1+\frac{4}{n}\right)\right\}^{1/4}-n\right]$$

$$= \lim_{n\to\infty}\left[\frac{\left\{\left(1+\frac{1}{n}\right)\left(1+\frac{2}{n}\right)\left(1+\frac{3}{n}\right)\left(1+\frac{4}{n}\right)\right\}^{1/4}-1}{\frac{1}{n}}\right]$$

$$= \lim_{x\to 0}\left[\frac{\{(1+x)(1+2x)(1+3x)(1+4x)\}^{1/4}-1}{x}\right]$$

$$= \lim_{x\to 0}\left[\frac{(1+10x+35x^2+50x^3+24x^4)^{1/4}-1}{x}\right] = \frac{10}{4} = \frac{5}{2}$$

(By L.H. Rule)

13. (c) α is a root of $x^2 + ax + 1 = 0$

$\Rightarrow \alpha^2 + a\alpha + 1 = 0$ ...(*i*)

$\Rightarrow \lim_{x\to\frac{1}{a}}\left(\dfrac{\sin(x^2+ax+1)}{\alpha x-1}\right)$

$= \lim_{x\to\frac{1}{\alpha}}\left[\dfrac{\sin(x^2+ax+1)}{(x^2+ax+1)}.\dfrac{x^2+ax+1}{(\alpha x-1)}\right] = \lim_{x\to\frac{1}{\alpha}}\left(\dfrac{2x+a}{\alpha}\right)$

$$= \left(\frac{2}{\alpha}+a\right)\frac{1}{\alpha} = \frac{2+a\alpha}{\alpha^2} = \frac{1-\alpha^2}{\alpha^2} \text{ (using (i))}$$

14. (a) $2+f(x)f(y)=f(x)+f(y)+f(xy)\,;\, y \to x$

$\Rightarrow \; 2+[f(x)]^2 = 2f(x)+f(x^2)$

Put $x = 1$;

$\Rightarrow \; 2+(f(1))^2 = 3f(1)$

$\Rightarrow \; (f(1))^2 - 3f(1)+2 = 0$

$\Rightarrow \; (f(1)-1)(f(1)-2) = 0$

$\Rightarrow \; f(1) = 1$ or $f(1) = 2$, Replacing y by $\frac{1}{x}$

$\Rightarrow \; 2+f(x).f\left(\frac{1}{x}\right) = f(x)+f\left(\frac{1}{x}\right)+f(1)$

$\Rightarrow \; 2+f(x).f\left(\frac{1}{x}\right) = f(x)+f\left(\frac{1}{x}\right)+f(1)$

If $f(1) = 2$

$\Rightarrow \; f(x)+f\left(\frac{1}{x}\right) = f(x).f\left(\frac{1}{x}\right)$

$\Rightarrow \; f(x) = 1 \pm x^2$ but $f(2) = 5$

$\Rightarrow \; 1 \pm (2)^n$

$\Rightarrow \; n = 2$ and $f(x) = 1+x^2$

If $f(1) = 1$, then $2+f(x)(1) = f(x)+1+f(x)$

$\Rightarrow \; f(x) = 1 \;\forall x \in \mathbb{R}$

But $f(2) = 5$

$\Rightarrow \; f(1) \neq 1$

$\therefore \; f(x);1+x^2$ which is a continuous function

$\Rightarrow \; \lim\limits_{x\to z} f(x) = f(2) = 5$

15. (d) $\lim\limits_{h\to 0} 2\dfrac{\left[\sqrt{3}\sin\left(\frac{\pi}{6}+h\right)-\cos\left(\frac{\pi}{6}+h\right)\right]}{\sqrt{3}h\left(\sqrt{3}\cosh - \sin h\right)}$

which can be written as

$$\lim_{h\to 0}\frac{\left[4\left(\frac{\sqrt{3}}{2}\sin\left(\frac{\pi}{6}+h\right)-\frac{1}{2}\cos\left(\frac{\pi}{6}+h\right)\right)\right]}{2h\left(\sqrt{3}\left(\frac{\sqrt{3}}{2}\cos\text{h}-\frac{1}{2}\sin\text{h}\right)\right)}$$

$$= \lim_{h\to 0}\left[\frac{2\sin\left(\frac{\pi}{6}+h-\frac{\pi}{6}\right)}{\sqrt{3}\,h\cos\left(\frac{\pi}{6}+h\right)}\right]$$

$$= \lim_{h\to 0}\left[\frac{4}{3}\right] = \frac{4}{3}$$

16. (b) $\lim\limits_{x\to\infty}\left(a^x+e^x\right)^{\frac{1}{x}} = a; a>0$

$a = \lim\limits_{x\to\infty}(a^x+e^x)^{1/x}$

$\Rightarrow \; \ell na = \lim\limits_{x\to\infty}\dfrac{\ell n(a^x+e^x)}{x}$

This gives as ∞/∞ format.

Hence by L.H. rule, we get $\lim\limits_{x\to\infty}\ell na = \left[\dfrac{a^x\ell na+e^x}{a^x+e^x}\right]$

$\Rightarrow \; \left[\dfrac{\ell na+\left(\frac{e}{a}\right)^x}{1+\left(\frac{e}{a}\right)^x}\right]$

$\Rightarrow \; a \in (e, \infty)$

17. (c) $\lim\limits_{n\to\infty}\left(e.a^2.e^3.....e^{n-1}a^n\right)^{\frac{1}{n^2+1}}$

which is same as $\lim\limits_{n\to\infty}\left(e^{1+3+5....+n-1}.a^{2+4...n}\right)^{\frac{1}{n^2+1}}$

$$= \lim_{n\to\infty}\left(e^{\left(\frac{n}{2}\right)^2}.a^{\frac{2\left(\frac{n}{2}\left(\frac{n}{2}+1\right)\right)}{2}}\right)^{\frac{1}{n^2+1}} = \lim_{n\to\infty}\left(e^{\frac{\left(\frac{n}{2}\right)^2}{n^2+1}}.a^{\frac{(n^2+2n)}{4(n^2+1)}}\right)$$

$$= \lim_{n\to\infty}\left(e^{\frac{\left(\frac{1}{2}\right)^2}{1+\frac{1}{n^2}}}.a^{\frac{1+\frac{2}{n}}{4\left(1+\frac{1}{n^2}\right)}}\right) = \lim_{n\to\infty}\left(e^{\frac{1}{4}}.a^{\frac{1}{4}}\right) = e^{\frac{1}{4}}.a^{\frac{1}{4}}$$

18. (d) $\lim\limits_{x\to\frac{\pi}{2}}\left\{\dfrac{(\sin^4 x+\cos^2 x+\sin^2 3x)^{\frac{1}{3}}}{\sin^4 x-\sin^4 2x-\sin^2 3x} - \dfrac{(\cos^2 x+\sin^4 2x+2\sin^2 3x)^{\frac{1}{3}}}{\sin^4 x-\sin^4 2x-\sin^2 3x}\right\}$

$$= \lim_{x\to\frac{\pi}{2}}\left\{\frac{a^{1/3}-b^{1/3}}{c}\right\}\text{(say)}$$

$$= \lim_{x\to\frac{\pi}{2}}\left\{\frac{a-b}{c(a^{2/3}+a^{1/3}b^{1/3}+b^{2/3})}\right\}$$

$$= \lim_{x\to\frac{\pi}{2}}\left\{\frac{\sin^4 x-\sin^4 2x-\sin^2 3x}{(c)(a^{1/3}+a^{1/3}+b^{1/3}+b^{1/3})}\right\}$$

$$= \lim_{x\to\frac{\pi}{2}}\left\{\frac{1}{a^{2/3}+a^{1/3}+b^{1/3}+b^{2/3}}\right\} = \frac{1}{3(2)^{2/3}}$$

19. (a) $f(n+1) = \dfrac{1}{2}\left\{f(n)+\dfrac{9}{f(n)}\right\}$

$\Rightarrow \; f(n+1) = \dfrac{1}{2}\left(\dfrac{(f(n))^2+9}{f(n)}\right)$

$\Rightarrow \; 2.f(n).f(n+1) = [f(n)]^2+9$

$\Rightarrow \; 9 = 2f(n+1).f(n) - [f(n)]^2$

$\Rightarrow \; 9 = f(n)[2f(n+1) - f(n)]$

$\Rightarrow \; f(n) = \dfrac{9}{2f(n+1)-f(n)}$ ...(*i*)

Let $\lim\limits_{n\to\infty} f(n) = L$

By equation (*i*), we get $L = \dfrac{9}{2L-L}$

$\Rightarrow\ L^2 = 9$

$\Rightarrow\ L = 3$ or -3 but since $f(n) > 0$

$\Rightarrow\ L = 3$

20. (b) $\lim_{x\to 0}\left(\dfrac{x^n \sin^n x}{x^n - \sin^n x}\right) = \lim_{x\to 0}\dfrac{x^n\left(x-\frac{x^2}{2!}+\frac{x^3}{3!}+\frac{x^4}{4!}+....\right)^n}{x^n-\left(x-\frac{x^2}{2!}+\frac{x^3}{3!}+\frac{x^4}{4!}+....\right)^n}$

$= \lim_{x\to 0}\left[\dfrac{x^{2n}\left(1-\frac{x}{2!}+\frac{x^2}{3!}-\frac{x^3}{4!}+....\right)^n}{x^n\left[1-\left(1-\frac{x}{2!}+\frac{x^2}{3!}-\frac{x^3}{4!}+....\right)^n\right]}\right]$

$\Rightarrow$ Degree of numerator $= 2n$ and degree of denominator $= (n+1)$

$\therefore$ For limit to be come finite $2n \geq n + 1$

$\Rightarrow\ n \geq 1$

But for $n = 1$; given limit

$= \lim_{x\to 0}\left(\dfrac{x\sin x}{x-\sin x}\right) = \lim_{x\to 0}\dfrac{x\left(x-\frac{x^2}{2!}+\frac{x^3}{3!}....\right)}{x-x\left(x-\frac{x^2}{2!}+\frac{x^3}{3!}....\right)}$

$= \lim_{x\to 0}\dfrac{x^2\left(1-\frac{x}{2!}+\frac{x^2}{3!}+....\right)}{x^2\left(\frac{1}{2!}-\frac{x}{3!}+....\right)} = 2$

But limit will be come zero if $2n > n + 1$

$\Rightarrow\ n > 1$

$\Rightarrow\ n \geq 2$

$\therefore$ Least value of $n = 2$ for which given limit $t = 0$

21. (b) $\lim_{x\to 0}\dfrac{\sin x^4 - x^4.\cos x^4 + x^{20}}{x^4.\left(e^{2x^4}-1-2x^4\right)}$

Let $x^4 = y$

$x \to 0$

$\Rightarrow\ y \to 0$

$\Rightarrow\ \lim_{y\to 0}\dfrac{\sin y - y\cos y + y^5}{y(e^{2y}-1-2y)}$

$= \lim_{y\to 0}\dfrac{\left(y-\frac{y^3}{3!}+\frac{y^5}{5!}-....\right)-y\left(1-\frac{y^2}{2!}+\frac{y^4}{4!}-....\right)+y^5}{y\left(\frac{4y^2}{2!}+\frac{8y^3}{3!}+....\right)}$

$= \lim_{y\to 0}\dfrac{\left(\frac{1}{2}-\frac{1}{6}\right)y^3+\left(1+\frac{1}{120}-\frac{1}{24}\right)y^5+....}{y^3\left(2+\frac{3}{4}y+....\right)} = \dfrac{(6-2)}{12}\times\dfrac{1}{2} = \dfrac{1}{6}$

22. (a), (b) $\lim_{x\to 0}\left[\left(m\dfrac{\sin x}{x}\right)\right]$

$\therefore\ 0 < \dfrac{\sin x}{x} < 1\ \forall\ x \in \left[-\dfrac{\pi}{2},\dfrac{\pi}{2}\right]-\{0\}$

Further $\lim_{x\to 0}\left(\dfrac{m\sin x}{x}\right)$

By L.H rule, we get $\lim_{x\to 0}((m)\cos x) = m$ (assuming m > 0) and $\dfrac{m\sin x}{x} \in (0, m)$

$\Rightarrow\ \lim_{x\to 0}\left[m\dfrac{\sin x}{x}\right] = m - 1$

Also for $m < 0$, $\dfrac{m\sin x}{x} \in (m, 0)$

$\Rightarrow\ \lim_{x\to 0}\left[m.\dfrac{\sin x}{x}\right]^x = m$

23. (b) $\lim_{x\to 0}\left[\dfrac{x^2}{\sin x\tan x}\right] = \lim_{x\to 0}\left[\dfrac{x^2\cos x}{\sin^2 x}\right]$

Clearly $\dfrac{x^2\cos x}{\sin^2 x} \to 1$ as $x \to 0$

Also for $x \to 0$, $\dfrac{x^2}{\sin^2 x} > 1$

Which can be written as $\lim_{x\to 0}\left[\dfrac{1}{\left(\frac{\sin x}{x}\right)\left(\frac{\tan x}{x}\right)}\right] = 0$

24. (b) $\lim_{x\to 0}\left[\dfrac{e^{\tan x}-e^{g(x)}}{\tan x - g(x)}\right]$

which can be written as $\lim_{x\to 0}\left[\dfrac{e^{g(x)}.\left(e^{\tan x - g(x)}-1\right)}{(\tan x - g(x))}\right]$

Given $f(x) = \left(\dfrac{ax+b}{cx+d}\right)$ and $g(x) = f(f(x))$

$= \dfrac{a^2x+ab+cbx+bd}{cax+cd+dcx+d^2}$

Let us consider the limit $\lim_{x\to 0}(g(x)) = \left[\dfrac{b(a+d)}{d(c+d)}\right]$

Given $a = -d$

$\Rightarrow\ \lim_{x\to 0}[g(x)] = 0$

Hence the original limit $\lim_{x\to 0}\left(\dfrac{e^{g(x)}\left(e^{\tan x - g(x)}-1\right)}{\tan x - g(x)}\right) = 1$

25. (b) $\lim_{x\to -1}\left[\dfrac{\int_{-1}^{x}(t^2+2t)(t^2-1)}{x^3+1}\right]$

By Leibinitiz formula and L.H rule, we get

$\lim_{x\to -1}\left(\dfrac{(x^2+2x)(x^2-1)}{3x^2}\right) = 0$

26. (d) $\lim_{x\to 1}\left[\dfrac{\left\{x-\ell n x+\left\{\int_1^x \frac{1}{z}-2-2\cos(4z)dz\right\}-1\right.}{x-1}\right]$

The format goes to 0/0.

Hence by L.H rule, we get $\lim_{x\to 1}\left[\dfrac{1-\frac{1}{x}+\frac{1}{x}-2-2\cos 4x}{1}\right]$

$= -1 - 2\cos 4$

27. (b) $\lim_{x\to 0}\sqrt{\dfrac{x\sin x}{x+\sin^2 x}}$

which is same as evaluating, we get

$$\lim_{x\to 0}\left[\left(\frac{\sin x+x\cos x}{1+\sin 2x}\right)\right]^{\frac{1}{2}}=0$$

28. (b) $\lim_{x\to\infty}\dfrac{(x^2+1)^{\frac{1}{2}}-(x^3-1)^{\frac{1}{3}}}{(x^4+1)^{\frac{1}{4}}-(x^4+1)^{\frac{1}{5}}}$

which is same as $\lim_{x\to\infty}\dfrac{x\left(1+\dfrac{1}{x^2}\right)^{\frac{1}{2}}-x\left(1-\dfrac{1}{x^3}\right)^{\frac{1}{3}}}{x\left(1+\dfrac{1}{x^4}\right)^{\frac{1}{4}}-x^{4/5}\left(1+\dfrac{1}{x^4}\right)^{\frac{1}{5}}}$

Dividing numerator and denominator by x, we get

$$\lim_{x\to\infty}\left(\frac{\left(1+\dfrac{1}{x^2}\right)^{\frac{1}{2}}-\left(1-\dfrac{1}{x^3}\right)^{\frac{1}{3}}}{\left(1+\dfrac{1}{x}\right)^{\frac{1}{4}}-x^{-\frac{1}{5}}\left(1+\dfrac{1}{x^4}\right)^{\frac{1}{5}}}\right)=0$$

29. (a) $\lim_{x\to\infty}\left[\dfrac{3x^2+1}{4x^2-1}\right]^{\frac{x^3}{1+x}}=\lim_{x\to\infty}\left[\dfrac{3+\dfrac{1}{x^2}}{4-\dfrac{1}{x^2}}\right]^{\frac{x^3}{1+x}}=\left(\dfrac{3}{4}\right)^{\infty}=0$

30. (b) $\lim_{n\to\infty}\left(1+\sin\left(\dfrac{a}{n}\right)\right)^n \; e^{\lim_{n\to\infty} n\left(\sin\frac{a}{n}\right)}=e^{\lim_{n\to\infty} a.\frac{\left(\sin\frac{a}{n}\right)}{\left(\frac{a}{n}\right)}}=e^a$

31. (d) $\lim_{x\to 2}\dfrac{\sin\left(e^{x-2}-1\right)}{\ell n(1+(x-2))}=\lim_{x\to 2}\dfrac{\sin(e^{x-2}-1)}{(e^{x-2}-1)}\times\dfrac{(e^{x-2}-1)(x-2)}{\ln(1+(x-2))}$

$=(1)\times(1)\times(1)=1$

32. (c) $\lim_{x\to 1}(1-x+[x-1]+[1-x])$

L.H.L $=\lim_{x\to 1^-}(0-1+0)=-1$

R.H.L $=\lim_{x\to 1^+}(0+0-1)=-1$

$\Rightarrow$ Limit exists and equals -1

33. (a) $\lim_{x\to 1}(1-x)\tan\left(\dfrac{\pi}{2}(2-x)\right)$

which can be written as $\lim_{x\to 1}\dfrac{\tan\left(\dfrac{\pi}{2}(2-x)\right)}{\left(\dfrac{1}{1-x}\right)}$

By L.H. rule, we get $\lim_{x\to 1}\dfrac{-\dfrac{\pi}{2}\sec^2\left(\dfrac{\pi}{2}(2-x)\right)}{\dfrac{1}{(1-x)^2}.(-1)}$

which can be written as $\lim_{x\to 1}\left[\dfrac{(1-x)^2}{\cos^2\left(\dfrac{\pi}{2}(2-x)\right)}\right]\left(-\dfrac{\pi}{2}\right)$

Applying L.H rule again, we get $\lim_{x\to 1}\left[\dfrac{2(1-x)}{\sin(\pi(2-x))}\right]$

$=\lim_{x\to 1}\left[\dfrac{2(1-x)}{\sin[\pi+\pi-\pi x]}\right]=\lim_{x\to 1}\left[\dfrac{2(1-x)}{-\sin\pi(1-x)}\right]$

Multiplying and dividing the numerator by π, we get $-\dfrac{2}{\pi}$

34. (a) $f(x)=\left[\dfrac{x^2+5x+3}{x^2+x+2}\right]$. As $x\to 0, \dfrac{x^2+5x+3}{x^2+x+2}\to\dfrac{3}{2}$

$\Rightarrow \lim_{x\to 0}\left[\dfrac{x^2+5x+3}{x^2+x+2}\right]=1$

35. (a) $\lim_{x\to 0}\left(\dfrac{\log(1-x^2)}{\log\cos x}\right)$

This gives 0/0 format. Hence by L H rule, we get

$$\lim_{x\to 0}\left[\frac{\dfrac{-2x}{1-x^2}}{-\dfrac{\sin x}{\cos x}}\right]=\lim_{x\to 0}\left[\frac{2}{1-x^2}.\frac{x}{\tan x}\right]$$

$=\left(\lim_{x\to 0}\dfrac{2}{1-x^2}\right)\left(\lim_{x\to 0}\dfrac{x}{\tan x}\right)$

$=2\times 1$

$=2$

36. (d) $\lim_{x\to 0}\dfrac{x\sqrt{y^2-(y-x)^2}}{\left(\sqrt{8xy-4x^2}+\sqrt{8xy}\right)^3}$

$=\lim_{x\to 0}\dfrac{x\sqrt{2xy-x^2}}{x^{3/2}\left(\sqrt{8y-4x}+\sqrt{8y}\right)^3}$

$=\lim_{x\to 0}\dfrac{3^{3/2}\sqrt{2y-x}}{x^{3/2}\left(\sqrt{8y-4x}+\sqrt{8y}\right)^3}$

$=\lim_{x\to 0}\dfrac{\sqrt{2y-x}}{\left(\sqrt{8y-4x}+\sqrt{8y}\right)^3}=\dfrac{\sqrt{2y}}{\left(4\sqrt{2y}\right)^3}=\dfrac{1}{(4)^3(2y)}$

$=\dfrac{1}{128y}$

37. (c) $\sum_{r=1}^{n}t_r=\sum_{r=1}^{n}\dfrac{r}{1-3r^2+r^4}=\sum_{r=1}^{n}\dfrac{r}{\left[(r^2-1)^2-r^2\right]}$

$=\sum_{r=1}^{n}\dfrac{r}{(r^2-1-r)(r^2-1+r)}$

$=\sum_{r=1}^{n}\dfrac{1}{2}\dfrac{(r^2+r-1)-(r^2-r-1)}{(r^2-r-1)(r^2+r-1)}$

$$=\frac{1}{2}\sum_{r=1}^{n}\left[\frac{1}{r^2-r-1}-\frac{1}{r^2+r-1}\right]=\frac{1}{2}\left[-1-\frac{1}{(n^2+n-1)}\right]$$

$$=\frac{1}{2}\left[\frac{-n^2-n+1-1}{n^2+n-1}\right]=\frac{1}{2}\left[\frac{-n^2-n}{n^2+n-1}\right]\therefore\ \lim_{n\to\infty}\sum_{r=1}^{n}tr=\frac{-1}{2}$$

38. (a) Here $\left|\frac{3}{\pi}\tan^{-1}2x\right|>1$

$\Rightarrow\quad |\tan^{-1}(2x)|>\frac{\pi}{3}\quad\Rightarrow\quad |2x|>\sqrt{3}$

$\therefore\quad$ For $|2x|>\sqrt{3},\left|\left(\frac{3}{\pi}\tan^{-1}2x\right)\right|>1$

$\Rightarrow\quad \left(\frac{3}{\pi}\tan^{-1}2x\right)^{2n}\to\infty$ as $n\to\infty$

$$\Rightarrow\quad \lim_{n\to\infty}\frac{1}{\left(\frac{3}{\pi}\tan^{-1}(2x)\right)^{2n}+5}=0$$

$\Rightarrow\quad f(x)=0$ for $|2x|>\sqrt{3}$

39. (a) $\lim_{x\to 0}\left[f(x)+\ln\left(1-\frac{1}{e^{f(x)}}\right)-\ln(f(x))\right]$

$=\lim_{x\to 0}\left[f(x)+\ln(e^{f(x)}-1)-\ln e^{f(x)}-\ln f(x)\right]$

$=\lim_{x\to 0}\left[\ln(e^{f(x)}-1)-\ln f(x)\right]=\lim_{x\to 0}\left[\ln\left(\frac{e^{f(x)}-1}{f(x)}\right)\right]$

$=0$ if $f(x)\to 0$ as $x\to 0$

As $f(x)$ is defined $\forall x\in\mathbb{R}$

$\Rightarrow\quad f(x)$ is continuous $\quad\Rightarrow\quad f(0)=0$

40. (c) $\lim_{x\to 0}\frac{\sin|\sec^2 x|}{1+[\cos x]}=\lim_{x\to 0}\left(\frac{\sin\left|\frac{1}{\cos^2 x}\right|}{1+[\cos x]}\right)$

$\lim_{x\to 0}[\cos x]=0$

$\Rightarrow\quad \lim_{x\to 0}\left(\frac{\sin\left|\frac{1}{\cos^2 x}\right|}{1+[\cos x]}\right)=\sin(1)$

41. (d) $L=\lim_{x\to\infty}|1-a^4|^x\sin\frac{b}{|1-a^4|^x}$

This can be written as $\lim_{x\to\infty}\left[\frac{\sin\left(\frac{b}{|1-a^4|^x}\right)}{\frac{b}{|1-a^4|^x}}\right].b$

Now the limit is governed by value of a.

Case (i): $0<|1-a^4|<1$

$\Rightarrow\quad |1-a^4|\to 0$ as $x\to\infty$ and $\sin\frac{b}{|1-a^4|^x}\in[-1,1]$

$\Rightarrow\quad L=0$

Case (ii): If $|1-a^4|>1$

$\Rightarrow\quad |1-a^4|^x\to\infty$ as $x\to\infty$

$\Rightarrow\quad L=b$

42. (c) $\lim_{x\to\infty}\left(\frac{1+x}{2+x}\right)^{\frac{1-\sqrt{x}}{1-x}}$

This can be written as $\lim_{x\to\infty}\left(1-\frac{1}{2+x}\right)^{\frac{1}{1+\sqrt{x}}}=(1)^0=1$

43. (b) $\lim_{x\to 0}\left(\sin\frac{x}{m}+\cos\frac{3x}{m}\right)^{\frac{2m}{x}}$

This can be written as $\lim_{x\to 0}\left(1+\left(\sin\frac{x}{m}+\cos\frac{3x}{m}-1\right)\right)^{\frac{2m}{x}}$

$=e^{\left(\lim_{x\to 0}\frac{\sin\frac{x}{m}+\cos\frac{3x}{m}-1}{\frac{x}{2m}}\right)}=e^2$ (By L.H. rule)

44. (b) $\lim_{x\to 0}\left(\sin^2\left(\frac{\pi}{2-ax}\right)\right)^{\sec^2\frac{\pi}{2-bx}}$

Let $k=\lim_{x\to 0}\left(\sin^2\left(\frac{\pi}{2-ax}\right)\right)^{\sec^2\frac{\pi}{2-bx}}$

Taking ℓn both sides, ℓnk

$=\sec^2\frac{\pi}{2-bx}\,\ell n\left(\sin^2\left(\frac{\pi}{2-ax}\right)\right)$

$=\ell nk=\lim_{x\to 0}\left[\frac{\ell n\left(\sin^2\left(\frac{\pi}{2-ax}\right)\right)}{\cos^2\left(\frac{\pi}{2-bx}\right)}\right]$

By L.H rule, we get ℓnk $=-\frac{a^2}{b^2}$

$\Rightarrow\quad k=e^{-\frac{a^2}{b^2}}$

45. (a) $\lim_{n\to\infty}\left((1.5)^n+([1+0.0001])^n\right)^{1/n}=\lim_{n\to\infty}(1.5)\left(1+\left(\frac{1}{1.5}\right)^n\right)^{1/n}$

$=(1.5).e^{\lim_{n\to\infty}\left(\frac{1}{1.5}\right)^n\frac{1}{n}}=(1.5).e^{\lim_{n\to\infty}\frac{1}{n(1.5)^n}}=(1.5)e^0=(1.5)$

46. (a) $\lim_{x\to 0}\left(\frac{(1+ax)^{\frac{1}{m}}.(1+bx)^{\frac{1}{n}}-1}{x}\right)$

This is 0/0 format.

Applying L.H rule, we get Limit $=\frac{an+bm}{mn}=\frac{a}{m}+\frac{b}{n}$

47. (a) $\lim_{n\to\infty}n^2\left((a)^{\frac{1}{n}}-a^{\frac{1}{n+1}}\right)=\lim_{n\to\infty}n^2.a^{\frac{1}{n+1}}\left(a^{\frac{1}{n(n+1)}}-1\right)$

$=\lim_{n\to\infty}n^2.a^{\frac{1}{n+1}}\left(\frac{a^{\frac{1}{n(n+1)}}-1}{\frac{1}{n(n+1)}.n(n+1)}\right)$

$=(a)^0.\ln a.\lim_{n\to\infty}\frac{n^2}{n^2+n}=(1)(\ln a)(1)=\ln(a)$

SECTION–IV: (MORE THAN ONE CORRECT ANSWER)

1. (a), (b), (c)

(a) $\lim_{t\to 0}\frac{\sin(\tan t)}{\sin t,} = \lim_{t\to 0}\frac{\sin(\tan t)}{\tan t}\times\frac{\tan t}{\sin t}$

$= \lim_{t\to 0}\frac{1}{\cos t}\left[\frac{\sin(\tan t)}{\tan t}\right] = (1)(1) = 1$

(b) $\lim_{t\to\frac{\pi}{2}}\frac{\sin(\cos x)}{\cos x} = 1$

(c) $\lim_{x\to 0}\frac{\sqrt{1+x}-\sqrt{1-x}}{x} = \lim_{x\to 0}\frac{1+x-1+x}{x\left[\sqrt{1+x}+\sqrt{1-x}\right]} = \frac{2}{2} = 1$

(d) $\lim_{x\to 0}\frac{\sqrt{x^2}}{x} = \lim_{x\to 0}\frac{|x|}{x}$

⇒ L.H.L. = –1, R.H.L. = 1

⇒ limit does not exist.

2. (a), (b), (c), (d)

$f(x) = \begin{cases} 2x-3; & -3\le x<0 \\ 4-x^2; & 0\le x\le 5 \end{cases}$ and

$g(x) = \begin{cases} 2x+3; & -10\le x<0 \\ -1-x; & 0\le x\le 3 \end{cases}$

$\lim_{x\to 0^+} f(g(x)) = \lim_{x\to 0^+} f(-1-x)$

$= \lim_{x\to 0^+} 2(-1-x)-3 = -5$ and

$\lim_{x\to 0^-} f(g(x)) = \lim_{x\to 0^-} f(2x+3)$

$= \lim_{x\to 0^-}\left[4-(2x+3)^2\right] = 4-9 = -5$

∴ $\lim_{x\to 0^+} f(g(x)) = \lim_{x\to 0^-} f(g(x)) = \lim_{x\to 0} f(g(x)) = -5$

⇒ $\lim_{x\to 0} f(g(x))$ exists

3. (b), (d)

(a) $f(x) = \frac{\sqrt{2+x}}{x}, g(x) = \frac{-\sqrt{2-x}}{x}$, then

$\lim_{x\to 0}\left[\frac{\sqrt{2+x}}{x}+\frac{\left(-\sqrt{2-x}\right)}{x}\right] = \lim_{x\to 0}\left[\frac{\sqrt{2+x}-\sqrt{2-x}}{x}\right]$

$= \lim_{x\to 0}\left[\frac{2+x-2+x}{x\left[\sqrt{2+x}+\sqrt{2-x}\right]}\right]$

$= \lim_{x\to 0}\left[\frac{2}{\sqrt{2+x}+\sqrt{2-x}}\right] = \frac{1}{\sqrt{2}}$

∴ $\lim_{x\to 0}[f(x)+g(x)]$ exists, but neither $\lim_{x\to 0}\frac{\sqrt{2+x}}{x}$ not $\lim_{x\to 0}\frac{-\sqrt{2-x}}{x}$ exists

∴ (a) is false.

(b) If $\lim_{x\to a^-} f(x) = \lim_{x\to a^+} f(x) = \ell_1$ and

$\lim_{x\to a^-} g(x) = \lim_{x\to a^+} g(x) = \ell_2$, then

$\lim_{x\to a^-}[f(x)+g(x)] = \ell_1+\ell_2 = \lim_{x\to a^+}[f(x)+g(x)]$

⇒ $\lim_{x\to a}[f(x)+g(x)]$ exists

⇒ (b) is true

(c) Let $f(x) = \frac{|x|}{x}, g(x) = |x|$, then $\lim_{x\to 0^-} f(x) = \lim_{x\to 0^-}\frac{|x|}{x} = -1$

and $\lim_{x\to 0^+} f(x) = \lim_{x\to 0^+}\frac{|x|}{x} = 1$

⇒ $\lim_{x\to 0} f(x)$ does not exists and $\lim_{x\to 0} g(x) = \lim_{x\to 0}|x| = 0$

⇒ $\lim_{x\to 0} g(x)$ exists. But

$\lim_{x\to 0} f(x).g(x) = \lim_{x\to 0}\frac{|x|^2}{x} = \lim_{x\to 0}\frac{x^2}{x} = \lim_{x\to 0}(x) = 0$

⇒ $\lim_{x\to 0} f(x).g(x)$ exists. Thus (c) is false

(d) If $\lim_{x\to a} f(x) = \ell_1, \lim_{x\to a} g(x) = \ell_2$, then

$\lim_{x\to a} f(x).g(x) = \ell_1.\ell_2$

⇒ (d) is true.

4. (b), (d)

$\lim_{x\to\infty}\cos^{2n} x = \lim_{x\to\infty}(\cos^2 x)^n$

As n → ∞, $\cos^2 x \in [0, 1)$ for $x \ne m\pi$.

⇒ $(\cos^2 x)^n \to 0$ for $x \ne m\pi$, $n\to\infty$.

∴ $\lim_{n\to\infty}\cos^{2n} x = 0$ for $x \ne m\pi, m\in\mathbb{Z}$ and

$\lim_{n\to\infty}(\cos(m\pi))^{2n} = 1$

∴ $\lim_{n\to\infty}\cos^{2n} x = 1$ for $x = m\pi, m\in\mathbb{Z}$

5. (a), (b), (c)

$L = \lim_{n\to\infty}\tan^{2n} x = \lim_{n\to\infty}\left(\tan^2 x\right)^n = \begin{cases} 0 \text{ for } \tan^2 x\in[0,1) \\ 1 \text{ for } \tan^2 x = 1 \\ \infty \text{ for } \tan^2 x>1 \end{cases}$

⇒ $L = \begin{cases} 0 \text{ for } x\in\left(n\pi-\frac{\pi}{4}, n\pi+\frac{\pi}{4}\right) \\ 1 \text{ at } x = n\pi\pm\frac{\pi}{4} \\ \infty \text{ for } x<\left(n\pi-\frac{\pi}{2}, n\pi-\frac{\pi}{4}\right)\cup\left(n\pi+\frac{\pi}{4}, n\pi+\frac{\pi}{2}\right) \end{cases}$

6. (b), (c)

$L = \lim_{x\to 0^+}\frac{\sqrt{1-\cos 2ax}}{\sin bx}; a<0, b<0$

$= \lim_{x\to 0^+}\frac{\sqrt{2\sin^2 ax}}{\sin bx} = \lim_{x\to 0^+}\frac{\sqrt{2}|\sin ax|}{\sin bx}$

∵ $a<0, x\to 0^+$

$\Rightarrow\ ax<0$ and $ax\to 0^-$

$\Rightarrow\ \sin ax\to 0^-$

$\Rightarrow\ |\sin ax|=-\sin ax$

$$\Rightarrow\ \text{L}=\lim_{x\to 0^+}\frac{-\sqrt{2}\sin ax}{\sin bx}=\lim_{x\to 0^+}\left(-\sqrt{2}\right)\frac{\sin ax}{ax}\cdot\frac{bx}{\sin bx}\cdot\frac{a}{b}$$

$$=-\sqrt{2}\frac{a}{b}=\frac{\sqrt{2}(-a)}{b}=\frac{\sqrt{2}|a|}{b}(\because a<0)$$

$$=\frac{\sqrt{2}(-a)}{(-b)}=\frac{-\sqrt{2}|a|}{|b|}(\because a<0,b<0)$$

7. (b), (c), (d)

(a) $\lim\limits_{x\to-\infty}f(x)=\lim\limits_{x\to-\infty}\left(\dfrac{|x|}{|x|+2}\right)^{-x}=\lim\limits_{x\to-\infty}\left(\dfrac{-x}{-x+2}\right)^{-x}$

$$=\lim_{y\to\infty}\left(\frac{y}{y+2}\right)^{y};y=-x$$

$$=\lim_{y\to\infty}\left(1+\left(\frac{-2}{y+2}\right)\right)^{y}=e^{\left(\lim\limits_{y\to\infty}\frac{-2y}{y+2}\right)}=e^{-2}$$

(b) $\lim\limits_{x\to 0}f(x)=\lim\limits_{x\to 0}\left(\dfrac{|x|}{|x|+2}\right)^{-x}$

$$\Rightarrow\ \text{L.H.L.}=\lim_{x\to 0^-}\left(\frac{-x}{-x+2}\right)^{-x}=\lim_{h\to 0^+}\left(\frac{h}{h+2}\right)^{h}=\text{L}_1\text{ (say)}$$

$$\Rightarrow\ \ell nL_1=\lim_{h\to 0^+}h\ln\left(\frac{h}{h+2}\right)=\lim_{h\to 0^+}\left[\frac{\ln\left(\frac{h}{h+2}\right)}{\left(\frac{1}{h}\right)}\right]$$

$$=\lim_{h\to 0^+}\left(\frac{h+2}{h}\right)\left(\frac{h+2-h}{(h+2)^2}\right)\left(\frac{-h^2}{1}\right)=\lim_{h\to 0^+}\frac{-2h}{(h+2)}=0$$

$\Rightarrow\ L_1=e^0=1$

Also, R.H.L. $=\lim\limits_{x\to 0^+}\left(\dfrac{x}{x+2}\right)^{-x}=\lim\limits_{x\to 0^+}\left(\dfrac{x+2}{x}\right)^{x}=\text{L}_2$ (say)

$$\Rightarrow\ \ln\text{L}_2=\lim_{x\to 0^+}x\ln\left(\frac{x+2}{x}\right)=\lim_{x\to 0^+}\frac{\ln\left(\frac{x+2}{x}\right)}{\left(\frac{1}{x}\right)}$$

$$=\lim_{x\to 0^+}\left(\frac{x}{x+2}\right)\times\left(\frac{-2}{x^2}\right)\times\left(\frac{-x^2}{1}\right)=\lim_{x\to 0^+}\left(\frac{2x}{x+2}\right)=0$$

$\Rightarrow\ \text{L}_2=1\qquad\therefore\ \lim\limits_{x\to 0}f(x)=1$

$\Rightarrow$ (b) is correct

(c) $\lim\limits_{x\to\infty}f(x)=\lim\limits_{x\to\infty}\left(\dfrac{|x|}{|x|+2}\right)^{-x}=\lim\limits_{x\to\infty}\left(\dfrac{x}{x+2}\right)^{-x}$

$$=\lim_{x\to\infty}\left(1-\frac{2}{x+2}\right)^{-x}=e^{\lim\limits_{x\to\infty}\left(\frac{-2}{x+2}\right)(-x)}=e^{\lim\limits_{x\to\infty}\left(\frac{2x}{x+2}\right)}=e^{2}$$

$\Rightarrow$ option(c) is correct

8. (a), (b), (c)

$$\lim_{x\to\infty}\left(\sqrt{x^4+ax^3+3x^2+bx+2}-\sqrt{x^4+2x^3-cx^2+3x-d}\right)=4$$

$$\lim_{x\to\infty}\frac{(a-2)x^3+(3+c)x^2+(b-3)x+(2+d)}{\sqrt{x^4+ax^3+3x^2+bx+2}+\sqrt{x^4+2x^3-cx^2+3x-d}}=4$$

$\because$ For finite limit, degrees of numerator and denominator must be same.

$\Rightarrow\ (a-2)=0\qquad\Rightarrow\ a=2$

$$\lim_{x\to 0}\frac{\left[(3+c)x^2+(b-3)x+(2+d)\right]}{x^2\left[\sqrt{1+\frac{2}{x}+\frac{3}{x^2}+\frac{b}{x^3}+\frac{2}{x^4}}+\sqrt{1+\frac{2}{x}-\frac{c}{x^2}+\frac{3}{x^3}-\frac{d}{x^4}}\right]}=4$$

$$\Rightarrow\ \frac{3+c}{2}=4$$

$\Rightarrow$ c = 5 and b and d can be any real numbers.

9. (a), (c) $f(x)=\dfrac{(1+x)^{1/x}-e}{x}$

(a) $\lim\limits_{x\to 0}f(x)=\lim\limits_{x\to 0}\dfrac{(1+x)^{1/x}-e}{x}$

$$=\lim_{x\to 0}(1+x)^{1/x}\left[\frac{1}{x(1+x)}-\frac{\ln(1+x)}{x^2}\right]$$

$$=\lim_{x\to 0}(1+x)^{1/x}\left[\frac{x-(1+x)\ln(1+x)}{x^2(1+x)}\right]$$

$$=\lim_{x\to 0}(1+x)^{1/x}\left[\frac{x-(1+x)\left\{x-\frac{x^2}{2}+\frac{x^3}{3}....\right\}}{x^2(1+x)}\right]$$

$$=\lim_{x\to 0}(1+x)^{1/x}\frac{\left[-\frac{x^2}{2}+\frac{x^3}{6}-\frac{x^4}{12}+....\right]}{x^2(1+x)}$$

$$=\lim_{x\to 0}(1+x)^{1/x}\frac{\left[-\frac{1}{2}+\frac{x}{6}-\frac{x^2}{12}+....\right]}{(1+x)}=-\frac{e}{2}<-1$$

$\Rightarrow$ option (a) and (c) are correct and (d) incorrect

Let $\text{L}=\lim\limits_{x\to\infty}(1+x)^{1/x}$

$$\Rightarrow\ \ln\text{L}=\lim_{x\to\infty}\frac{1}{x}\ln(1+x)=\lim_{x\to\infty}\frac{1}{(1+x)}=0$$

$\Rightarrow\ \text{L}=1\qquad\Rightarrow\ \lim\limits_{x\to\infty}f(x)=\dfrac{1-e}{\infty}=0$

10. (b), (d) $\text{L}=\lim\limits_{x\to 0}\left(\dfrac{a^x+b^x+c^x}{3}\right)^{k/x};a,b,c,k>0$

$$=\lim_{x\to 0}\left[1+\left(\frac{a^x+b^x+c^x}{3}-1\right)\right]^{k/x}=e^{\lim\limits_{x\to 0}\left(\frac{a^x+b^x+c^x}{3}-1\right)\left(\frac{k}{x}\right)}$$

$$=e^{\lim\limits_{x\to 0}\left[\frac{(a^x-1)}{x}+\frac{(b^x-1)}{x}+\frac{(c^x-1)}{x}\right]\left(\frac{k}{3}\right)}=e^{\frac{k}{3}[\ln a+\ln b+\ln c]}=e^{\frac{k}{3}\ln(abc)}=(abc)^{k/3}$$

$$\Rightarrow\ \text{L}=\begin{cases}abc & \text{if } k=3,\\ \left(a^2b^2c^2\right) & \text{if } k=2\end{cases}$$

SECTION–V : (ASSERTION AND REASON)

1. (a)

A: $\lim\limits_{x\to 0}\dfrac{\sqrt{1-\cos 2x}}{x}$

$\Rightarrow \lim\limits_{x\to 0}\dfrac{\sqrt{2}\,|\sin x|}{x}$

Now L.H.L = $-\sqrt{2} \neq$ R.H.L = $\sqrt{2}$

$\Rightarrow$ Limit does not exist

R: Reason is correct as $\sin x > 0$ for $x \in \left(0, \dfrac{\pi}{2}\right]$ and < 0 for $x \in \left(-\dfrac{\pi}{2}, 0\right]$

2. (d)

A: $\because \lim\limits_{x\to 0^-}(\tan x) = 0^-; \lim\limits_{x\to 0^+}(\tan x) = 0^+$ and

$\lim\limits_{x\to 0^-}[\sin x] = -1$ and $\lim\limits_{x\to 0^+}[\sin x] = 0$

$\therefore$ L.H.L. $= \lim\limits_{x\to 0^-}\dfrac{[\sin x]}{\tan x} = \dfrac{-1}{0^-} = \infty$, R.H.L.

$= \lim\limits_{x\to 0^+}\dfrac{[\sin x]}{\tan x} = \dfrac{0}{0^+} = 0$

$\Rightarrow$ Limit does not exist

$\Rightarrow$ A is incorrect clearly reason is correct as numerator is exact zero and denominator is non-zero infinitesimal.

3. (d)

A: $\lim\limits_{x\to 0}\left(\dfrac{x-\sin x}{x^3}\right) = \lim\limits_{x\to 0}\left(\dfrac{x-\left(x-\dfrac{x^3}{3!}+\dfrac{x^5}{5!}-....\right)}{x^3}\right) = \dfrac{1}{6}$

$\Rightarrow$ Assertion is incorrect as given is not the accurate process obviously, reason being standard result is correct

4. (c)

A: $\lim\limits_{x\to\infty}\left(\dfrac{2x^4+3x^3+7x}{3x^4+2x^2+3x}\right)$

Dividing numerator and denominator by x^4, we get

$\lim\limits_{x\to\infty}\left(\dfrac{2+\dfrac{3}{x}+\dfrac{7}{x^3}}{3+\dfrac{2}{x^2}+\dfrac{3}{x^3}}\right) = \dfrac{2}{3}$

$\Rightarrow$ A is correct.

R: $\lim\limits_{x\to\infty}\dfrac{p(x)}{Q(x)} = \dfrac{\text{leading coefficent of P(x)}}{\text{leading coefficient of } Q(x)}$, which is not true till degrees of P(x), Q(x) are same

5. (a)

A: $\because\ 0 < \dfrac{\sin x}{x} < 1$ for $x \to 0$

$\Rightarrow \lim\limits_{x\to 0}\left[\dfrac{\sin x}{x}\right] = 0$ where as $\lim\limits_{x\to 0}\dfrac{\sin x}{x} = 1$

$\Rightarrow \left[\lim\limits_{x\to 0}\dfrac{\sin x}{x}\right] = [1] = 1$

$\therefore \lim\limits_{x\to 0}\left[\dfrac{\sin x}{x}\right] \neq \left[\lim\limits_{x\to 0}\dfrac{\sin x}{x}\right]$

$\Rightarrow$ Assertion is correct

R: $\lim\limits_{x\to 0} h(g(x)) = h\left(\lim\limits_{x\to\infty} g(x)\right)$

which is possible only when h(x) is continuous at $\lim\limits_{x\to\infty} g(x)$.

$\Rightarrow$ R is correct.

Note that [] is not continuous at $x = 0$ (or any other integer).

6. (b)

A: $\lim\limits_{x\to 0}\left[\dfrac{\sqrt{\dfrac{1-\cos 2x}{2}}}{x}\right] = \lim\limits_{x\to 0}\left[\dfrac{|\sin x|}{\sqrt{2}x}\right]$

$\Rightarrow$ L.H.L. $= \dfrac{-1}{\sqrt{2}}$ and R.H.L. $= \dfrac{1}{\sqrt{2}}$

$\Rightarrow$ L.H.L $\neq$ R.H.L

$\Rightarrow$ Limit does not exist

$\Rightarrow$ *A* is correct.

R: $\lim\limits_{x\to 0}\left(\dfrac{\sin x}{x}\right) = 1$, which is true but reason does not support the assertion.

7. (a)

A: $\lim\limits_{x\to 0}\left(\tan\left(\dfrac{\pi}{4}+x\right)\right)^{\frac{1}{x}}$

This we can be written as $\lim\limits_{x\to 0}\left(1+\left(\tan\left(\dfrac{\pi}{4}+x\right)-1\right)\right)^{\frac{1}{x}}$

$= e^{\lim\limits_{x\to 0}\left(\frac{\tan\left(\frac{\pi}{4}+x\right)-1}{x}\right)} = e^{\lim\limits_{x\to 0}\left(\frac{\frac{1+\tan x}{1-\tan x}-1}{x}\right)} = e^{\lim\limits_{x\to 0}\left(\frac{2\tan x}{x(1-\tan x)}\right)} = e^2$

$\Rightarrow$ A is correct.

R: $\lim\limits_{x\to 0}(1+f(x))^{g(x)} = \lim\limits_{x\to 0}(1+f(x))^{\frac{1}{f(x)}f(x).g(x)}$

$= \left[\lim\limits_{x\to 0}(1+f(x))^{1/f(x)}\right]^{\lim\limits_{x\to 0} f(x).g(x)} = e^{\lim\limits_{x\to 0} f(x).g(x)}$

$\Rightarrow$ Reason is correct and supports the assertion.

SECTION–VI: (PASSAGE)

A:

1. (a) $\lim\limits_{x\to 0^+} f(x) = \lim\limits_{x\to 0^+}\dfrac{\sin x + ae^x + be^{-x} + c\ln(1+x)}{x^3}$

For above limit to be finite $(a+b) = 0$, $c \in \mathbb{R}$ ...(1)

$\Rightarrow \lim\limits_{x\to 0^+} f(x) = \lim\limits_{x\to 0^+}\dfrac{\cos x + ae^x - be^{-x} + \dfrac{c}{1+x}}{3x^2}$

$\Rightarrow 1 + a - b + c = 0$ ...(2)

$\Rightarrow \lim\limits_{x\to 0^+} f(x) = \lim\limits_{x\to 0^+}\dfrac{(-\sin x) + ae^x + be^{-x} - \dfrac{c}{(1+x)^2}}{6x}$ ...(3)

$\Rightarrow\ a + b - c = 0$

$\Rightarrow\ 0 - c = 0$

$\Rightarrow\ c = 0$ ...(4)

$\therefore\ (a + b) + c = 0 \quad [\because\ a + b = 0, c = 0]$

2. (d) Again from equation (3)

$$\lim_{x\to 0^+} f(x) = \lim_{x\to 0^+} \frac{-\cos x + ae^x - be^{-x} + \frac{2c}{(1+x)^3}}{6}$$

$$= \frac{-1+a-b+2c}{6} = \frac{-1+a-b}{6} = l \quad ...(5)$$

From (2), $1 + a - b + c = 0$

$\Rightarrow\ a - b = -1 \quad (\because\ c = 0)$

Also, $a + b = 0$

$\Rightarrow\ a = \frac{-1}{2}, b = \frac{1}{2}$

$\therefore\ a = \frac{-1}{2}, b = \frac{1}{2}, c = 0$

$\therefore$ From (5), $\frac{-1-\frac{1}{2}-\frac{1}{2}}{6} = \frac{-1}{3}$

B: $\lim_{x\to 0} \frac{axe^x - b\log(1+x) + cxe^{-x}}{x^2 \sin x} = 2$

$$\Rightarrow\ \lim_{x\to 0} \frac{axe^x + ae^x - \frac{b}{(1+x)} + ce^{-x} - cxe^{-x}}{x^2\cos x + 2x\sin x} = 2$$

$\Rightarrow\ a - b + c = 0$ ...(1)

$$\Rightarrow\ \lim_{x\to 0} \frac{2ae^x + axe^x + \frac{b}{(1+x)^2} - 2ce^{-x} + cxe^{-x}}{-x^2\sin x + 2x\cos x + 2\sin x + 2x\cos x} = 2$$

$\Rightarrow\ 2a + b - 2c = 0$ ...(2)

$$\Rightarrow\ \lim_{x\to 0} \frac{2ae^x + ae^x + axe^x - \frac{2b}{(1+x)^3} + 3ce^{-x} - cxe^{-x}}{(-x^2\cos x - 2x\sin x + 6\cos x - 4x\sin x)} = 2$$

$\Rightarrow\ \frac{3a - 2b + 3c}{6} = 2$

$\Rightarrow\ 3a - 2b + 3c = 12$ ...(3)

Equation (1) + (2) gives, $3a - c = 0$

Equation (2) × (2) + (3) gives, $7a - c = 12$

$\Rightarrow\ a = 3, c = 9, b = 12$

3. From above, clearly options (*a*) and (*b*) are correct

4. (a), (c) $ax^2 + bx + c = 0$

$\Rightarrow\ 3x^2 + 12x + 9 = 0$

$\Rightarrow\ x^2 + 4x + 3 = 0$

$\Rightarrow\ (x + 1)(x + 3) = 0$

$\Rightarrow\ x = -1, -3$ which are real, unequal and rational

5. (b) $f(x) = \sqrt{\frac{ax^2 - b}{c}}$

$\Rightarrow\ \frac{ax^2 - b}{c} \geq 0$

$\Rightarrow\ \frac{3x^2 - 12}{9} \geq 0$

$\Rightarrow\ \frac{x^2 - 4}{3} \geq 0$

$\Rightarrow\ x^2 - 4 \geq 0$

$\Rightarrow\ x \in (-\infty, -2] \cup [2, \infty)$

C: $\lim_{n\to\infty}\left[\frac{2}{\pi}(1+n)\cos^{-1}\left(\frac{1}{n}\right) - n\right]$

$$= \lim_{\to\infty}\left[\frac{2}{\pi}(1+n)\left[\frac{\pi}{2} - \sin^{-1}\left(\frac{1}{n}\right)\right] - n\right]$$

$$= \lim_{n\to\infty}\left[1 + n - \frac{2}{\pi}(1+n)\sin^{-1}\frac{1}{n} - n\right]$$

$$= \lim_{n\to\infty}\left[1 - \frac{2}{\pi}(1+n)\sin^{-1}\frac{1}{n}\right] = \lim_{n\to\infty}\left[1 - \frac{2}{\pi}(1+n).\frac{\sin^{-1}\frac{1}{n}}{\frac{1}{n}}\left(\frac{1}{n}\right)\right]$$

$$= \lim_{n\to\infty}\left[1 - \frac{2}{\pi}\left(1 + \frac{1}{n}\right)\left(\frac{\sin^{-1}\left(\frac{1}{n}\right)}{\left(\frac{1}{n}\right)}\right)\right] \quad ...(1)$$

$$= \left[1 - \frac{2}{\pi}(1+0)(1)\right] = 1 - \frac{2}{\pi} \quad ...(2)$$

Given, $\lim_{n\to\infty} n\left(f\left(\frac{1}{n}\right)\right) = 1 - \frac{2}{\pi}$

$$\Rightarrow\ \lim_{n\to\infty} \frac{f\left(\frac{1}{n}\right)}{\left(\frac{1}{n}\right)} = 1 - \frac{2}{\pi}$$

$$\Rightarrow\ f\left(\frac{1}{n}\right) = \frac{1}{n} - \frac{2}{\pi}\left(1 + \frac{1}{n}\right).\sin^{-1}\left(\frac{1}{n}\right) \quad (\because \text{ of (1)})$$

$\Rightarrow\ f(x) = x - \frac{2}{\pi}(1+x)\sin^{-1}(x)$

6. (b) $f'(x) = 1 - \frac{2}{\pi}(1+x).\frac{1}{\sqrt{1-x^2}} - \frac{2}{\pi}\sin^{-1} x$

$\Rightarrow\ f'(0) = 1 - \frac{2}{\pi} = \frac{\pi - 2}{\pi}$

7. (c) $\lim_{x\to 0} f(x) = \lim_{x\to 0} x - \frac{2}{\pi}(1+x)\sin^{-1} x = 0$

8. (c) $\left|\lim_{x\to\frac{1}{2}} f(x-1)\right| = \left|\lim_{x\to\frac{1}{2}}\left\{(x-1) - \frac{2}{\pi}(1+x-1)\sin^{-1}(x-1)\right\}\right|$

$$= \left|\lim_{x\to\frac{1}{2}}\left\{(x-1) - \frac{2}{\pi}x.\sin^{-1}(x-1)\right\}\right|$$

$$= \left|-\frac{1}{2} - \frac{2}{\pi}\left(\frac{1}{2}\right)\sin^{-1}\left(\frac{-1}{2}\right)\right| = \left|-\frac{1}{2} + \frac{1}{\pi}\sin^{-1}\left(\frac{1}{2}\right)\right|$$

$$= \left|-\frac{1}{2} + \frac{1}{\pi}\left(\frac{\pi}{6}\right)\right| = \left|-\frac{1}{2} + \frac{1}{6}\right| = \left|\frac{-2}{6}\right| = \frac{1}{3}$$

SECTION– VII: (COLUMN MATCHING)

1. (i) → (b); (ii) → (c); (iii) → (d); (iv) → (a)

(i) $f(x)=\dfrac{\tan[e^2]x^2-\tan[-e^2]x^2}{\sin^2 x}=\dfrac{\tan 7x^2+\tan 8x^2}{\sin^2 x}$

$\Rightarrow \lim\limits_{x\to 0} f(x)=\lim\limits_{x\to 0}\dfrac{7x^2+8x^2}{x^2}=15$

$\therefore$ **(i) → (b)**

(ii) $f(x)=\dfrac{\left[\dfrac{5}{2}+\tan x+\tan^2 x\right]-\left[\dfrac{5}{2}\right]}{\tan x}$

$\because \tan^2 x+\tan x+\dfrac{5}{2}=\tan^2 x+\tan x+\dfrac{1}{4}+\dfrac{9}{4}$

$=\left(\tan x+\dfrac{1}{2}\right)^2+\dfrac{9}{4}\to\dfrac{5}{2}$ as $x\to 0$

$\Rightarrow \dfrac{\left[\dfrac{5}{2}+\tan x+\tan^2 x\right]-\left[\dfrac{5}{2}\right]}{\tan x}=\dfrac{2-2}{\tan x}=0$ for $x\to 0$

$\therefore$ **(ii) → (c)**

(iii) $f(x)=\dfrac{\sqrt[3]{1+x^2}-\sqrt[4]{1-2x}}{x-x^2}$

$\Rightarrow \lim\limits_{x\to 0} f(x)=\lim\limits_{x\to 0}\dfrac{(1+x^2)^{1/3}-(1-2x)^{1/4}}{x(1+x)}$

$=\lim\limits_{x\to 0}\dfrac{\left[1+\dfrac{1}{3}x^2+\left(\dfrac{1}{3}\right)\left(\dfrac{-2}{3}\right)\dfrac{x^4}{2!}+....\right]-\left[1-\dfrac{1}{4}(2x)+\dfrac{1}{4}\left(\dfrac{-3}{4}\right)\left(\dfrac{4x^2}{2!}\right).....\right]}{(x^2+x)}$

$=\lim\limits_{x\to 0}\left[\dfrac{\dfrac{1}{2}x+\dfrac{11}{24}x^2+....}{(x^2+x)}\right]=\dfrac{1}{2}$

$\therefore$ **(iii) → (d)**

(iv) $\lim\limits_{x\to 0}\dfrac{\sqrt{2}-\sqrt{2}\left|\sin\dfrac{x}{2}\right|}{\sin^2 x}=\lim\limits_{x\to 0}\dfrac{1-\cos x}{\left(\sqrt{2}+\sqrt{1+\cos x}\right)(1-\cos^2 x)}$

$=\dfrac{1}{\left(2\sqrt{2}\right)(2)}=\dfrac{\sqrt{2}}{8}\quad\therefore$ **(iv) → (a)**

2. (i) → (d); (ii)→ (c); (iii)→ (a); (iv)→ (b)

$\phi(x)=\dfrac{a_0x^m+a_1x^{m+1}+.....+a_kx^{m+k}}{b_0x^n+......+b_\ell x^{\ell+e}}$

$\Rightarrow \phi(x)=\left(\dfrac{a_0+a_1x+.....+a_k.x^k}{b_0+b_1x+....+b_\ell x^\ell}\right).x^{(m-n)}$

(i) m > n

$\Rightarrow \lim\limits_{x\to 0}(\phi(x))$

$\Rightarrow \dfrac{a_0}{b_0}(0)^{m-n}=0\ (\because m>n)$

$\therefore$ **(i) → (d)**

(ii) $m=n$

$\Rightarrow \lim\limits_{x\to 0}\phi(x)=\dfrac{a_0}{b_0}\qquad\therefore$ **(ii)→ (c)**

(iii) $m<n$

$\Rightarrow \lim\limits_{x\to 0}\phi(x)=\dfrac{a_0}{b_0}\left(\dfrac{1}{(0)^{n-m}}\right)=\infty$ if $\dfrac{a_0}{b_0}>0, n-m=$ even

$\therefore$ **(iii)→ (a)**

(iv) By the similar logic $\lim\limits_{x\to 0}\phi(x)=-\infty;\left(\dfrac{a_0}{b_0}<0\right)$ and n – m is even

$\therefore$ **(iv)→ (b)**

3. (i)→ (b); (ii)→ (a); (iii)→ (d); (iv)→ (c)

(i) $\lim\limits_{x\to 0}[\dfrac{\left(\sin 2x+\sin^{-1}\left(\sin^2 x\right)-\tan^{-1}\left(\tan^2 x\right)\right)}{3x}$

$=\lim\limits_{x\to 0}\left[\dfrac{\sin 2x}{3x}+\dfrac{\sin^{-1}(\sin^2 x)}{3x}-\dfrac{\tan^{-1}(\tan^2 x)}{3x.\tan^2 x}.\tan^2 x\right]$

$=\lim\limits_{x\to 0}\left[\dfrac{2\sin 2x}{3(2x)}+\dfrac{1}{3}\dfrac{\sin^{-1}(\sin^2 x)}{\sin^2 x}.\dfrac{\sin^2 x}{x}-\dfrac{1}{3}\dfrac{\tan^{-1}(\tan^2 x)}{\tan^2 x}.\dfrac{\tan^2 x}{x}\right]$

$=\dfrac{2}{3}+\dfrac{1}{3}(1)(0)(1)-\dfrac{1}{3}(1)(1)(0)=\dfrac{2}{3}$

$\therefore$ **(i)→ (b)**

(ii) $\lim\limits_{x\to 0}\dfrac{(\sin x)^2\left[1-\dfrac{1}{\cos^2 x}\right]^2+\sin^8 x+x^5}{\tan^7 x+\sin^6 x+2\sin^5 x}$

$=\lim\limits_{x\to 0}\dfrac{\dfrac{\sin^6 x}{\cos^4 x}+\sin^8 x+x^5}{7\tan^7 x+\sin^6 x+2\sin^5 x}$

Replacing by equivalent infinitesimals, we get

$\lim\limits_{x\to 0}\dfrac{x^6+x^8+x^5}{7(x^7)+x^6+2x^5}=\lim\limits_{x\to 0}\dfrac{x^5(x+x^3+1)}{x^5(7x^2+x+2)}=\dfrac{1}{2}$

$\therefore$ **(ii)→ (a)**

(iii) $\lim\limits_{x\to 0}\dfrac{\sin(x)^{\frac{1}{3}}.\ell n(1+3x)}{\left(\tan^{-1}\left(\tan\sqrt{x}\right)^2\left(e^{5x^{1/3}}-1\right)\right)}$

$=\lim\limits_{x\to 0}\left[\dfrac{x^{\frac{1}{3}}\left(\dfrac{\sin x^{\frac{1}{3}}}{x^{\frac{1}{3}}}\right).\dfrac{\ell n(1+3x)}{3x}.3x}{\dfrac{x\tan^2\sqrt{x}}{x}.\left(\dfrac{\tan^{-1}\left(\tan\sqrt{x}\right)}{\tan\sqrt{x}}\right)^2.\left(\dfrac{e^{5x^{1/3}}-1}{5.x^{1/3}}\right).5x^{1/3}}\right]=\dfrac{3}{5}$

$\therefore$ **(iii)→ (d)**

(iv) $\lim\limits_{x\to 0}\dfrac{1-\cos x+2\sin x-\sin^3 x-x^2+3x^4}{\tan^3 x-6\sin^2 x+x-5x^3}$

$=\lim\limits_{x\to 0}\dfrac{2\left(\dfrac{x}{2}\right)^2+2x-x^3-x^2+3x^4}{x^3-6x^2+x-5x^3}=2\quad\therefore$ **(iv)→ (c)**

SECTION–VIII: (INTEGER TYPE:)

1. $\lim\limits_{x\to\frac{\pi}{2}} \tan^2 x\left(\sqrt{2\sin^2 x+3\sin x+4}-\sqrt{\sin^2 x+6\sin x+2}\right)$

Multiplying the numerator and denominator by $\sqrt{2\sin^2 x+3\sin x+4}+\sqrt{\sin^2 x+6\sin x+2}$

$\Rightarrow \lim\limits_{x\to\frac{\pi}{2}} \dfrac{\tan^2 x\left(2\sin^2 x+3\sin x+4-\sin^2 x-6\sin x-2\right)}{\sqrt{2\sin^2 x+3\sin x+4}+\sqrt{\sin^2 x+6\sin x+2}}$

$\Rightarrow \lim\limits_{x\to\frac{\pi}{2}} \dfrac{\tan^2 x(\sin^2 x-3\sin x+2)}{\sqrt{2\sin^2 x+3\sin x+4}+\sqrt{\sin^2 x+6\sin x+2}}$

$\Rightarrow \lim\limits_{x\to\frac{\pi}{2}} \dfrac{\tan^2 x\left((\sin x-1)(\sin x-2)\right)}{\sqrt{2\sin^2 x+3\sin x+4}+\sqrt{\sin^2 x+6\sin x+2}}$

$\Rightarrow \lim\limits_{x\to\frac{\pi}{2}} \dfrac{(\sin^2 x)(\sin x-1)(\sin x-2)}{(1-\sin^2 x)\left[\sqrt{2\sin^2 x+3\sin x+4}+\sqrt{\sin^2 x+6\sin x+2}\right]}$

$\Rightarrow \lim\limits_{x\to\frac{\pi}{2}} \dfrac{(\sin^2 x)(\sin x-2)}{-(\sin x+1)\left[\sqrt{2\sin^2 x+3\sin x+4}+\sqrt{\sin^2 x+6\sin x+2}\right]}$

$= \dfrac{(1)(-1)}{-(2)[6]} = \dfrac{1}{12}$

$\Rightarrow p = 12 \qquad \Rightarrow \sqrt{p-3}=\sqrt{12-3}=3$

2. $\lim\limits_{x\to\infty}\left(\dfrac{x^3\sin\frac{1}{x}+x+1}{x^2+x+1}\right) = \lim\limits_{x\to\infty}\left(\dfrac{x^2\dfrac{\sin\left(\frac{1}{x}\right)}{\frac{1}{x}}+x+1}{x^2+x+1}\right)$

Dividing numerator and denominator by x^2 we get-:

$\lim\limits_{x\to\infty}\left(\dfrac{\dfrac{\sin\left(\frac{1}{x}\right)}{\frac{1}{x}}+\frac{1}{x}+\frac{1}{x^2}}{1+\frac{1}{x}+\frac{1}{x^2}}\right)$

$\Rightarrow l = 1$

Hence clearly $\sqrt{1\sqrt{1\sqrt{1........\infty}}} = 1$

3. $\lim\limits_{n\to\infty}\dfrac{-3n+(-1)^n}{4n-(-1)^n}=\dfrac{r}{t}$ can be written as $\lim\limits_{n\to\infty} = \dfrac{-3+\frac{(-1)^n}{n}}{4-\frac{(-1)^n}{n}}$

Consider $\lim\limits_{n\to\infty}\dfrac{(-1)^n}{n}$ which is equal to $\lim\limits_{n\to\infty}\dfrac{(\pm1)}{n}=0$

$\Rightarrow \lim\limits_{n\to\infty}\dfrac{-3+\frac{(-1)^n}{n}}{4-\frac{(-1)^n}{n}} = -\dfrac{3}{4}=\dfrac{r}{t}$

$\Rightarrow r=\pm3,\ t=\mp4$

$\Rightarrow \sqrt{r^2+t^2}=\sqrt{3^2+4^2}=5$

4. $\lim\limits_{x\to\infty}\left(x-x^2\ln\dfrac{(1+x)}{x}\right)=\lim\limits_{x\to\infty}\left(x-x^2\ln\left(1+\dfrac{1}{x}\right)\right)$

$=\lim\limits_{x\to\infty}\left[x-x^2\left(\dfrac{1}{x}-\dfrac{1}{2x^2}+\dfrac{1}{3x^3}-....\right)\right]$

$=\lim\limits_{x\to\infty}\left[\dfrac{1}{2}-\dfrac{1}{3x}+\dfrac{1}{4x^2}-....\right]=\dfrac{1}{2}=l$

$\Rightarrow (25)^l = 5$

5. $\lim\limits_{x\to0^+}\left(1+\tan^2\sqrt{x}\right)^{\frac{5}{x}}$

This can be compared with the format

$\lim\limits_{x\to a}(1+f(x))^{\frac{1}{g(x)}}=e^{\lim\limits_{x\to a}\frac{f(x)}{g(x)}}$; where $\lim\limits_{x\to0}f(x)=\lim\limits_{x\to a}g(x)=0$

$\Rightarrow \lim\limits_{x\to a^+}\left(1+\tan^2\sqrt{x}\right)^{\frac{5}{x}}$

$=e^{\lim\limits_{x\to0^+}\frac{(\tan^2\sqrt{x}).5}{x}}=e^{\lim\limits_{x\to0^+}\left(\frac{\tan\sqrt{x}}{\sqrt{x}}\right)^2.(5)}=e^5=p$

$\Rightarrow \dfrac{(p)^{\frac{1}{5}}}{e}=\dfrac{(e^5)^{\frac{1}{5}}}{e}=\dfrac{e}{e}=1$

6. (i) $L=\lim\limits_{x\to0}\left(\dfrac{x(1+a\cos x)-b\sin x}{x^3}\right)$

$=\dfrac{x\left[1+a\left(1-\dfrac{x^2}{2!}+\dfrac{x^4}{4!}-...\right)\right]-b\left(x-\dfrac{x^3}{3!}+\dfrac{x^5}{5!}-...\right)}{x^3}$

$=\lim\limits_{x\to0}\left[\dfrac{x(1+a-b)+x^3\left[-\dfrac{a}{2!}+\dfrac{b}{3!}\right]+....}{x^3}\right]$

$=\left[\lim\limits_{x\to0}\dfrac{(1+a-b)}{x^2}\right]+\left[\dfrac{-a}{2}+\dfrac{b}{6}\right]$ Which is finite if $1+a-b=0$

$\therefore$ Limit $=\dfrac{-a}{2}+\dfrac{b}{6}$

$\Rightarrow l=-\dfrac{a}{2}+\dfrac{b}{6}$

(ii) $L=\lim\limits_{x\to0}\dfrac{1+a\cos x}{x^2}=\dfrac{1+a\left(1-\dfrac{x^2}{2!}+\dfrac{x^4}{4!}+...\right)}{x^2}$

$=\lim\limits_{x\to0}\dfrac{1+a-\frac{a}{2}x^2}{x^2}=\dfrac{-a}{2}+\lim\limits_{x\to0}\dfrac{(1+a)}{x^2}$ Where exists finitely if $1+a=0$

$\Rightarrow a=-1$

$\Rightarrow l=\dfrac{1}{2}=\dfrac{-a}{2}+\dfrac{b}{6}$

$\Rightarrow\quad \frac{1}{2}=\frac{1}{2}+\frac{b}{6}$

$\Rightarrow\quad b=0$

Also $1 + a - b = 0$ holds for above values.

$\therefore\quad a+b+41=-1+0+4\left(\frac{1}{2}\right)=1$

7. $\lim_{x\to1}(1+ax+bx^2)^{\frac{c}{x-1}}=e^3$ (Given)

$\Rightarrow\quad \lim_{x\to1}(ax+bx^2)=0, c\neq0$

$\Rightarrow\quad a+b=0, c\neq0$

In such a case, we get

$\lim_{x\to1}\left(1+ax+bx^2\right)^{\frac{c}{x-1}}=e^{\lim_{x\to1}\frac{x(a+bx).c}{(x-1)}}=e^3$

$\Rightarrow\quad \lim_{x\to1}\frac{x(a+bx)c}{x-1}=3$

$\Rightarrow\quad c\,(bx^2+ax)=(bcx+d)\,(x-1)$

$\Rightarrow\quad \lim_{x\to1}(bcx+d)=3$

$\Rightarrow\quad bc+d=3$ and $d-bc=a, d=0$

$\Rightarrow\quad bc=3, a=-3, b=3, c=1$

$\Rightarrow\quad a^2-b^2+2bc=6$

8. $\lim_{n\to\infty}\frac{\sqrt{n^3-2n^2+1}+\sqrt[3]{n^4+1}}{\sqrt[4]{n^6+6n^5+2}-\sqrt[5]{n^7+3n^3+1}}=k$

which is equal to $\lim_{n\to\infty}\frac{n^{\frac{3}{2}}\sqrt{1-\frac{2}{n}+\frac{1}{n^3}}+n^{\frac{4}{3}}\sqrt[3]{1+\frac{1}{n^4}}}{n^{\frac{3}{2}}\sqrt[4]{1+\frac{6}{n}+\frac{2}{n^6}}-n^{\frac{7}{5}}\sqrt[5]{1+\frac{3}{n^4}+\frac{1}{n^7}}}$

$\Rightarrow\quad \lim_{n\to\infty}\frac{\sqrt{1-\frac{2}{n}+\frac{1}{n^3}}+n^{-\frac{1}{6}}\sqrt{1+\frac{1}{n^4}}}{\sqrt{1+\frac{6}{n}+\frac{2}{n^6}}+n^{-\frac{1}{10}}\sqrt{1+\frac{3}{n^4}+\frac{1}{n^7}}}=1$

$\Rightarrow\quad k=1$

$\Rightarrow\quad (k)^{2013}=1$

9. $\lim_{\to}\frac{(x+6)^{-}-2}{x}\quad\frac{p}{q}$

This can be written as $\lim_{x\to2}\frac{(x+6)^{\frac{1}{3}}-2}{(2-x)}$

$\Rightarrow\quad \lim_{x\to2}\frac{(x+6)^{\frac{1}{3}}-(8)^{\frac{1}{3}}}{(8-(x+6))}$

$\Rightarrow\quad \lim_{y\to8}\frac{y^{\frac{1}{3}}-8^{\frac{1}{3}}}{-(y-8)}=\frac{p}{q}=-\frac{1}{12}$

$\Rightarrow\quad |p|=1, |q|=12$

$\Rightarrow\quad \sqrt{|q|+4|p|}$

$\Rightarrow\quad \sqrt{12+4}=\sqrt{16}=4$

10. $\lim_{x\to1}\left(\frac{\sqrt{5-x}-2}{\sqrt{2-x}-1}\right)$

which can be written as-: $\lim_{x\to1}\left(\frac{\frac{\sqrt{5-x}-(4)^{\frac{1}{2}}}{5-x-4}}{\frac{\sqrt{2-x}-1}{2-x-1}}\right)$

$=\lim_{x\to1}\left(\frac{\frac{\sqrt{5-x}-(4)^{\frac{1}{2}}}{1-x}}{\frac{\sqrt{2-x}-1}{1-x}}\right)=\lim_{x\to1}\left(\frac{\frac{\sqrt{5-x}-(4)^{\frac{1}{2}}}{1-x}}{\frac{\sqrt{2-x}-1}{1-x}}\right)=\frac{1}{2}=\frac{p}{q}$

(lowest from) $\Rightarrow p=1, q=1$

$=p+q=3$

11. $\lim_{x\to0}\left(\frac{\ln(2+x)+\ln0.5}{x}\right)=\lim_{x\to0}\left(\frac{\ln\left(1+\frac{x}{2}\right)}{2.\frac{x}{2}}\right)$

$=\frac{1}{2}\lim_{x\to0}\ln\left(\frac{\left(1+\frac{x}{2}\right)}{\frac{x}{2}}\right)=\frac{1}{2}$

$\Rightarrow\quad \frac{1}{2}=\frac{p}{q}\qquad\Rightarrow\quad (16)^{\frac{p}{q}}=(16)^{\frac{1}{2}}=4$

12. $\lim_{x\to0}\frac{e^{\tan x}-e^x}{\tan x-x}=l$

which can be written as: $\lim_{x\to0}\left(\frac{e^x\left(\frac{e^{\tan x}}{e^x}-1\right)}{(\tan x-x)}\right)=l$

$\Rightarrow\quad \lim_{x\to0}\left(\frac{e^x\left(e^{\tan x-x}-1\right)}{\tan x-x}\right)=l$

Since $\lim_{x\to0}\frac{e^x-1}{x}=1$

$\Rightarrow\quad l=1\qquad\Rightarrow\quad (l)^{2016}=1$

13. $\lim_{x\to\infty}\left(\sqrt{(x+a)(x+b)}-x\right)=f(a,b)$

which can be written as

$\lim_{x\to\infty}\left(\frac{\left(\sqrt{(x+a)(x+b)}-x\right)}{\sqrt{(x+a)(x+b)}+x}\right)\left(\sqrt{(x+a)(x+b)}+x\right)$

$=\lim_{x\to\infty}\left(\frac{x^2+(a+b)x+ab-x^2}{\sqrt{(x+a)(x+h)}+x}\right)$

$\Rightarrow\quad \lim_{x\to\infty}\left(\frac{x(a+b)+ab}{x\sqrt{1+\frac{a}{x}+\frac{b}{x}+\frac{ab}{x^2}}+x}\right)=\lim_{x\to\infty}\left(\frac{a+b}{1+1}\right)=\frac{a+b}{2}$

$\Rightarrow\quad f(9,7)=\frac{9+7}{2}=\frac{16}{2}=8$

14. $\lim_{n\to\infty}\frac{(n+2)!+(n+1)!}{(n+3)!}=\lim_{n\to\infty}\frac{(n+2)(n+1)!+(n+1)!}{(n+3)!}$

$$=\lim_{n\to\infty}\frac{(n+1)!(n+3)}{(n+3)!}=\lim_{n\to\infty}\frac{(n+1)!}{(n+2)!}=\lim_{n\to\infty}\frac{1}{(n+2)}=0$$

$\Rightarrow\ l=0$

$\Rightarrow\ (2016)^l=1$

15. $\lim_{x\to0}\frac{((a-n)nx-\tan x)\sin nx}{x^2}=0$

$$=\lim_{x\to0}\left\{\frac{(a-n)nx.(\cos x-\sin x)}{x\cos x}.\frac{\sin nx}{nx}.n\right\}=0$$

$$\Rightarrow\ n\lim_{x\to0}\left\{\frac{(a-n)(nx)\left(1+\frac{x^2}{2!}+\frac{x^4}{4!}-....\right)-\left(x-\frac{x^3}{3!}+....\right)}{x\left(1-\frac{x^2}{2!}+\frac{x^4}{4!}-....\right)}\right\}=0$$

$$\Rightarrow\ \lim_{x\to0}\left\{\frac{(a-n)n\left(1-\frac{x^2}{2!}+\frac{x^4}{4!}-....\right)-\left(1-\frac{x^3}{3!}+....\right)}{\left(1-\frac{x^2}{2!}+\frac{x^4}{4!}-....\right)}\right\}=0$$

$$\Rightarrow\ \lim_{x\to0}\frac{[(a-n)(n)-1]-\left[\frac{(a-n)n}{2}-\frac{1}{6}\right]x^2+....}{\left(1-\frac{x^2}{2!}+\frac{x^4}{4!}-....\right)}$$

$=(a-n)n-1=0$

$\Rightarrow\ (a-1)n=1$

$\Rightarrow\ a-1=\frac{1}{n}$

$\Rightarrow\ a=1+\frac{1}{n}=f(n)$

$\Rightarrow\ f(1)=1+\frac{1}{1}=2$

16. $\lim_{x\to\frac{\pi}{2}}\frac{\left[1-\tan\left(\frac{x}{2}\right)\right][1-\sin x]}{\left[1+\tan\left(\frac{x}{2}\right)\right][\pi-2x]^3}$

$$=\lim_{x\to\frac{\pi}{2}}\frac{\tan\left(\frac{\pi}{4}-\frac{x}{2}\right)\left(1-\cos\left(\frac{\pi}{2}-x\right)\right)}{(\pi-2x)^3}$$

$$=\lim_{x\to\frac{\pi}{2}}\frac{\tan\left(\frac{\pi-2x}{4}\right)}{4\left(\frac{\pi-2x}{4}\right)}.\frac{2\sin^2\left(\frac{\pi}{4}-\frac{x}{2}\right)}{16\left(\frac{\pi}{4}-\frac{x}{2}\right)^2}=\frac{1}{32}=\frac{1}{p}$$

$\Rightarrow\ p=32$

$\Rightarrow\ (p)^{\frac{1}{5}}=2$

17. $\lim_{x\to0}\frac{\ln(3+x)-\ln(3-x)}{x}$

By L.H. Rule, we get $\lim_{x\to0}\left(\frac{1}{3+x}+\frac{1}{3-x}\right)=\frac{2}{3}=k$

$\Rightarrow\ 6k=4$

18. $\lim_{n\to\infty}\left(\frac{1+2^4+3^4+....+n^4}{n^5}\right)-\lim_{n\to\infty}\left(\frac{1^3+2^3+....+n^3}{n^5}\right)$

$$=\lim_{n\to\infty}\frac{1}{n}\sum_{r=1}^{n}\left(\frac{r}{n}\right)^4-\lim_{n\to\infty}\left[\frac{n(n+1)}{2}\right]^2.\frac{1}{n^5}$$

$$=\lim_{n\to\infty}\left(\frac{\frac{n^5}{5}+\frac{n^4}{2}+\frac{n^3}{3}-\frac{n}{30}}{n^5}\right)-\lim_{n\to\infty}\left(\frac{\frac{n^4}{4}+\frac{n^3}{2}+\frac{n^2}{4}}{n^5}\right)$$

$$=\int_0^1x^4dx-\lim_{n\to\infty}\frac{1}{4}\times\frac{1}{n}\left[1+\frac{1}{n}\right]^2=\left[\frac{x^5}{5}\right]_0^1-0=\frac{1}{5}=\frac{p}{q}$$

$\Rightarrow\ (3125)^{\frac{1}{5}}=5$

19. $\lim_{x\to0}\frac{(x\tan2x-2x\tan x)}{(1-\cos2x)^2}=\lim_{x\to0}\left(\frac{x\left(\frac{2\tan x}{1-\tan^2x}-2\tan x\right)}{\left(2\sin^2x\right)^2}\right)$

$$=\lim_{x\to0}\left(\frac{\frac{x\tan x}{1-\tan^2x}(1-1+\tan^2x)}{2\sin^4x}\right)$$

$$=\lim_{x\to0}\frac{x\tan^3x}{(1-\tan^2x)(2\sin^4x)}$$

$$=\lim_{x\to0}\frac{x^4\left(\frac{\tan^3x}{x^3}\right)}{(1-\tan^2x)(2\sin^4x)}=\frac{1}{2}=l$$

$\Rightarrow\ (9)^l=(9)^{\frac{1}{2}}=3$

Continuity and Differentiability

CHAPTER 2

CONTINUITY

■ INTRODUCTION

In ordinary language, continuous means any process, which goes on without interruption or without abrupt changes. In mathematics also the word continuous has much the same meaning i.e., continuous function means continuous arrangement of ordered pairs, which further means sufficiently small change in one variable leads to an infinitesimally small change in other variable.

We know that function f is defined as a machine that takes an input c and produces an output $f(c)$. If it is a good machine (a continuous one) a small variation in input must result into a correspondingly small variation in output i.e., a continuous function $f(x)$ produces $f(x)$ near $f(c)$ as x is taken near to c. For example length of metal rod as a function of temperature is a continuous function of temperature.

A very good example of discontinuous machine is postage machine say charging ₹ 2 for letters weighing 10 gm but ₹ 5 for letters weighing little over 10 gms. So the continuity of function also means the connectedness of graph of function at each point from both left and right hand side. Qualitatively the graph of a function is said to be continuous at $x = a$. If while traveling along the graph of the function and in crossing over the point at $x = a$ either from left to right or from right to left one does not have to lift his pen as shown figure 2.1.

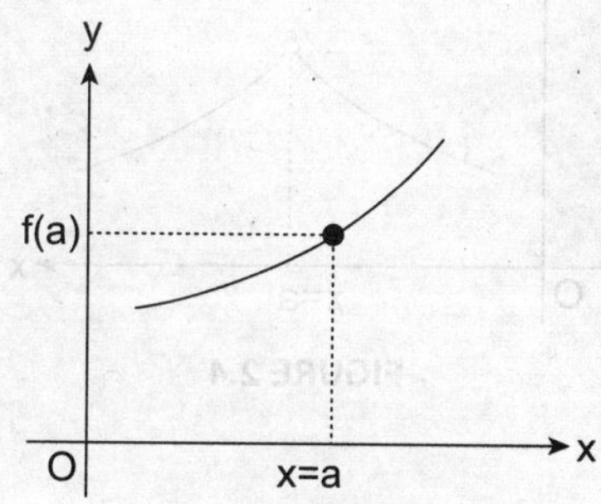

FIGURE 2.1

Graph of a function continuous at $x = a$

In case one has to lift his pen the graph of the function is said to have a break or discontinuity at $x = a$ as shown figure 2.2.

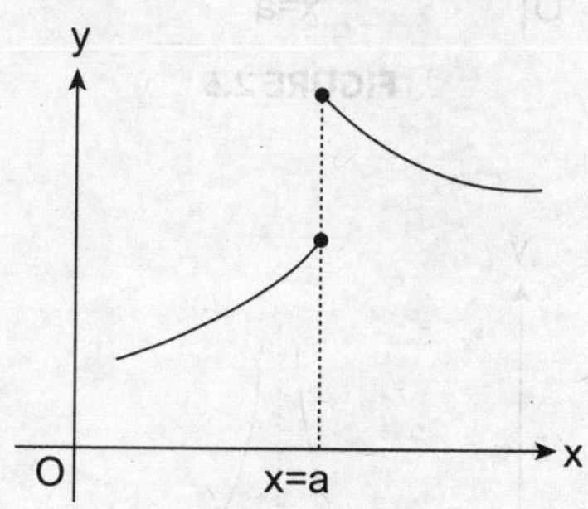

FIGURE 2.2

Graph of a function discontinuous at $x = a$

Different Situations of Discontinuity at $x = a$

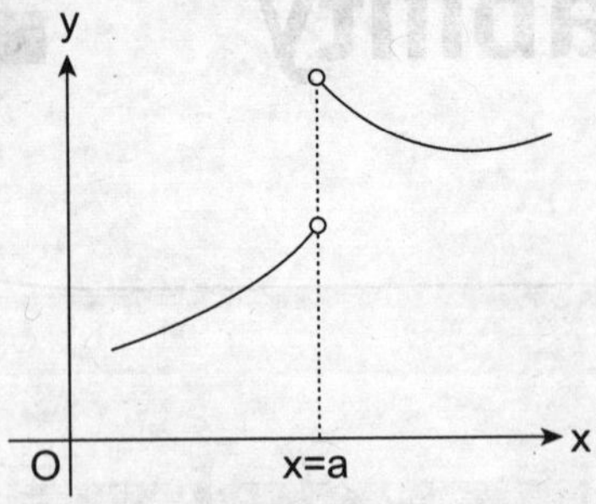

FIGURE 2.3

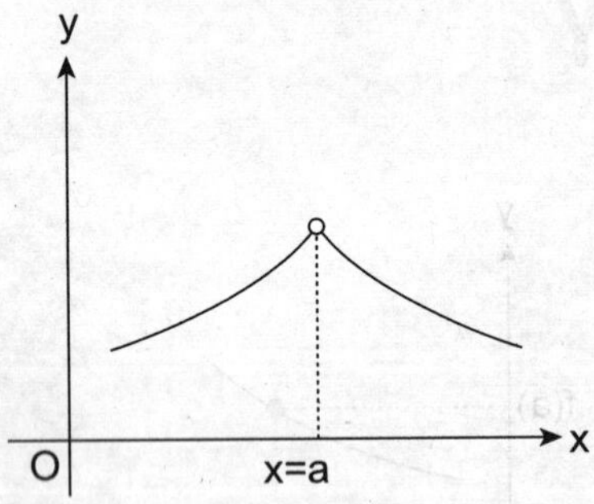

FIGURE 2.4

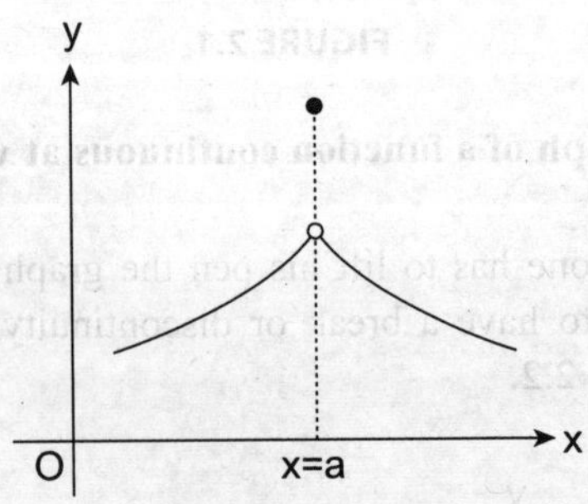

FIGURE 2.5

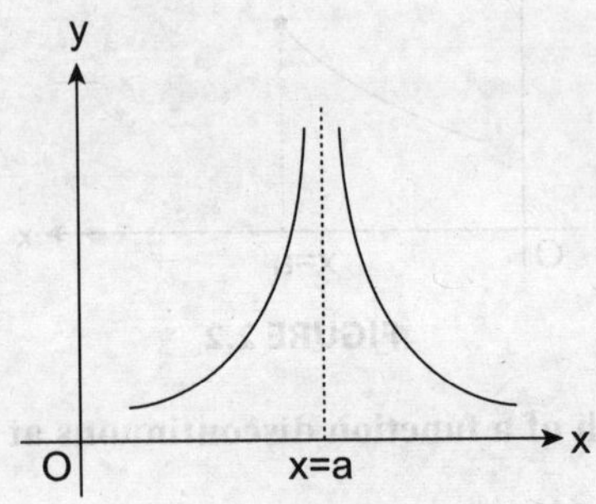

FIGURE 2.6

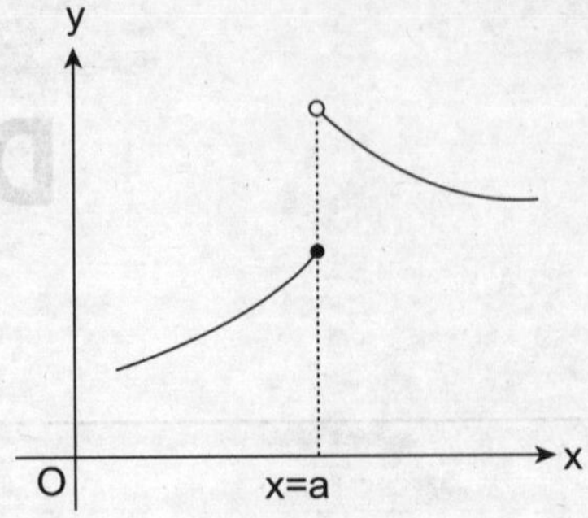

FIGURE 2.7

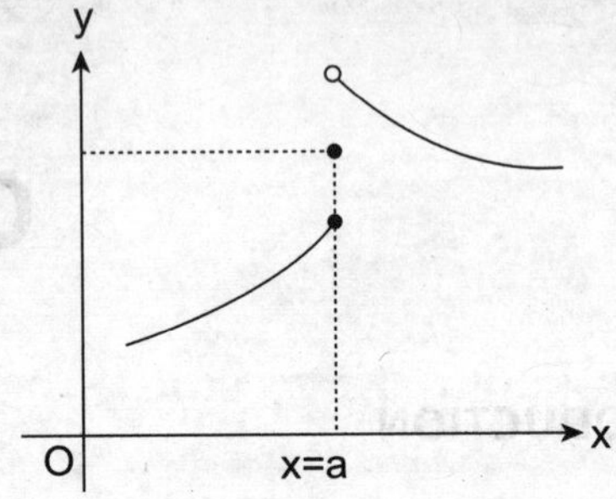

FIGURE 2.8

■ CONTINUITY OF A FUNCTION AT A POINT

A function $f(x)$ is said to be continuous at a given point $x = a$ if its graph is both left and right connected with the point $(a, f(a))$ which is possible if $f(a)$ is real and finite. i.e., if $f(x)$ satisfies the following three conditions:

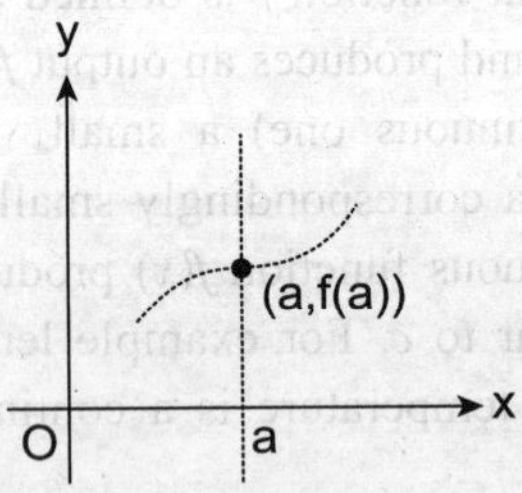

Continuous at x = a

FIGURE 2.9

(i) $f(a)$ exists ($a \in$ domain of $f(x)$)

(ii) $\lim_{x \to a} f(x)$ exists (i.e., f has a limit as $x \to a$)

(iii) $\lim_{x \to a} f(x) = f(a)$ (i.e., the limit equals the value of function at $x = a$)

e.g., If $f(x) = \dfrac{x^2 - 4}{x + 2}$; then

$$\lim_{x \to 2} f(x) = \lim_{x \to 2} \frac{(x+2)(x-2)}{(x+2)} = \lim_{x \to 2}(x+2) = 4$$

and $f(2)=\frac{4-4}{2+2}=\frac{0}{4}=0$; thus

$\lim_{x\to 2} f(x)=f(2) \Rightarrow f(x)$ is continuous at $x = 2$

Mathematical Definition

The dictionary meaning of continuity is regularity or no breakage and, it is applied with same meaning in mathematics also, i.e., the function $f(x)$ is said to be continuous at $x = a$ if its limit at $x = a$ exists and is equal to value of function at $x = a$

i.e., $\lim_{x\to a} f(x)$ = (value of $f(x)$ at $x = a$)

$\Rightarrow \left(\lim_{x\to a^-} f(x)\right) = \left(\lim_{x\to a^+} f(x)\right) = f(a)$

$\Rightarrow$ [i.e., L.H.L = R.H.L = $f(a)$]

i.e., $\lim_{h\to 0^+} f(a-h) = \lim_{h\to 0^+} f(a+h) = f(a)$

Geometric Significance

Graphically a function is continuous at 'a' point $x = a$, if its graph can be drawn across the point $(a, f(a))$ on co-ordinates plane without raising the tip of pencil i.e., it is made up of an unbroken line at $x = a$. (otherwise it is said to be discontinuous at that point.)

Functions continuous from one side (one sided continuity)

A function $f(x)$ is said to be left t continuous (right discontinuous) at $x = a$ if $\lim_{x\to a} f(x) = f(a) \neq \lim_{x\to a^+} f(x)$

Similarly, a function $f(x)$ is said to be right continuous (left discontinuous) at $x = a$ if $\lim_{x\to a^+} f(x) = f(a) \neq \lim_{x\to a^-} f(x)$

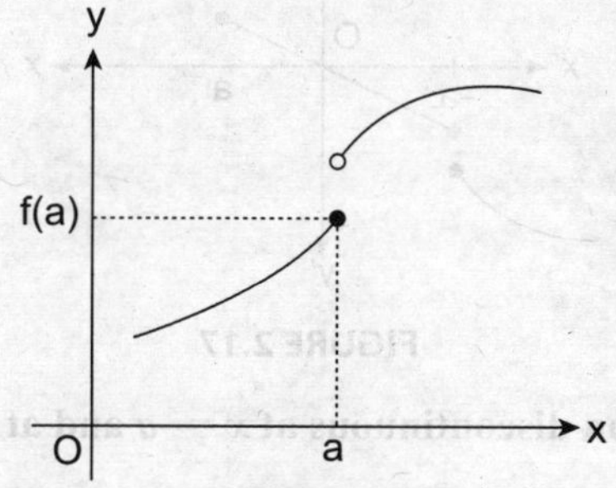

FIGURE 2.10

Function left is continuous, but right is discontinuous at $x = a$

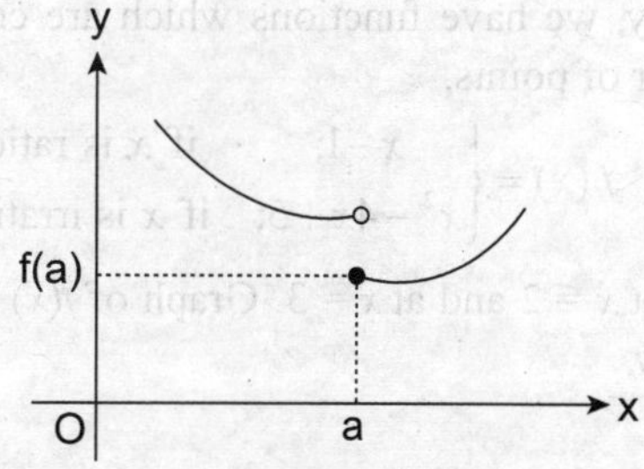

FIGURE 2.11

Function right continuous but left discontinuous at $x = a$

For example, if $f(x)=\begin{cases} x^2+1; & x<1 \\ x+2; & x\geq 1\end{cases}$

then L.H.L. $=\lim_{x\to 1^-} f(x)=\lim_{x\to 1^-}(x^2+1)=2$

and R.H.L. $=\lim_{x\to 1^+} f(x)=\lim_{x\to 1^+}(x+2)=3$

and $f(1) = 1 + 2 = 3$

R.H.L. $= f(1) \neq$ L.H.L $\Rightarrow f(x)$ is left discontinuous and right continuous at $x = 1$, graphically shown in figure 2.12.

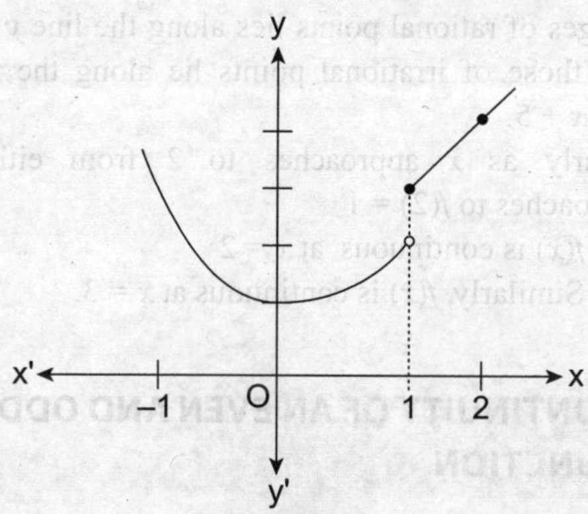

FIGURE 2.12

Single point continuity

There are some functions which are continuous only at single point. Such functions are called single point continuous functions.

Example:

1. $f(x)=\begin{cases} x; & \text{if } x \text{ is rational} \\ -x; & \text{if } x \text{ is irrational}\end{cases}$ is continuous only at $x = 0$

2. $f(x)=\begin{cases} 2x; & \text{if } x \text{ is rational} \\ x-2; & \text{if } x \text{ is irrational}\end{cases}$ is continuous only at $x = -2$

Similarly, we have functions which are continuous at finite number of points.

e.g. $f(x)=\begin{cases} x-1; & \text{if } x \text{ is rational} \\ x^2-4x+5; & \text{if } x \text{ is irrational} \end{cases}$ is continuous at $x = 2$ and at $x = 3$. Graph of $f(x)$ would be as shown below.

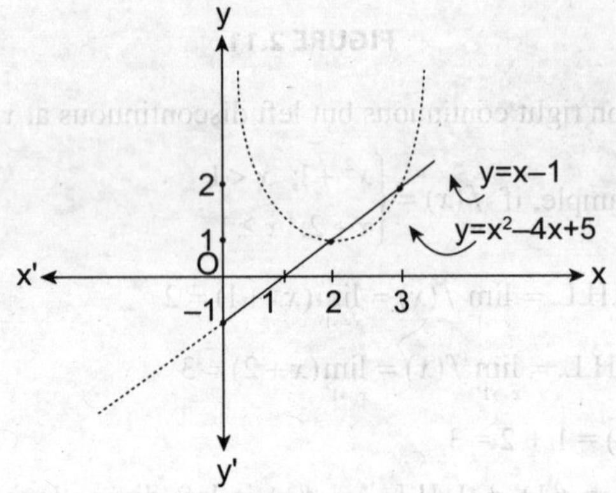

FIGURE 2.13

Images of rational points lies along the line $y = x - 1$, whereas those of irrational points lie along the parabola $y = x^2 - 4x + 5$.

Clearly as x approaches to 2 from either side $f(x)$ approaches to $f(2) = 1$

$\therefore$ $f(x)$ is continuous at $x = 2$

Similarly, $f(x)$ is continuous at $x = 3$.

■ CONTINUITY OF AN EVEN AND ODD FUNCTION

If f is an even or odd function having portion of graph in neighborhood of $x = -a$, and $x \to a$ then f is continuous/discontinuous at $x = a$ means f is continuous/discontinuous. at $x = -a$.

Since for even function $f(-a^+) = f(a^-)$; $f(-a^-) = f(a^+)$; $f(-a) = f(a)$ and for odd function $f(a^+) = -f(-a)^-$ and $f(a^-) = -f(-a^+)$; $f(a) = -f(-a)$

Thus if $f(x)$ is an even continuous function at $x = a$, then $f(a^-) = f(a^+) = f(a)$

$\Rightarrow$ $f(-a^+) = f(-a^-) = f(-a)$

$\Rightarrow$ $f(x)$ is also continuous at $x = -a$

Similarly if $f(x)$ is an odd continuous function at $x = a$; then $f(a^-) = f(a^+) = f(a)$

$\Rightarrow$ $-f(-a^+) = -f(-a^-) = -f(-a)$

$\Rightarrow$ $f(-a^+) = f(-a^-) = f(-a)$

$\Rightarrow$ $f(x)$ is also continuous at $x = -a$

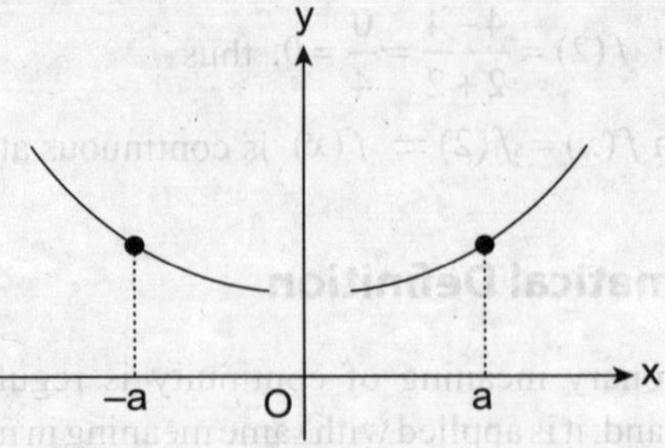

FIGURE 2.14

Even function continuous at $x = a$ and at $x = a$

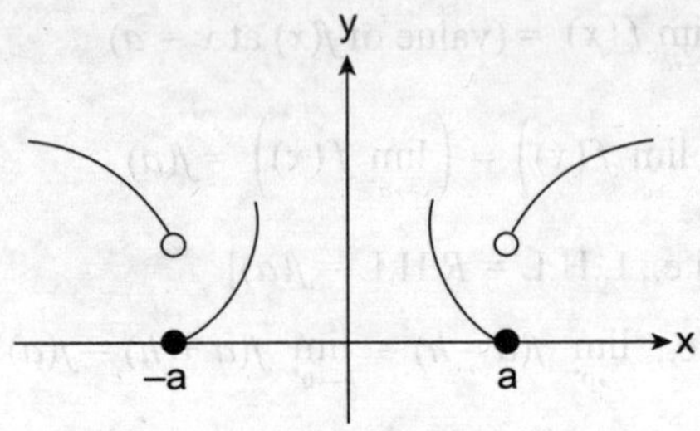

FIGURE 2.15

Even function discontinuous at $x = a$ and at $x = a$

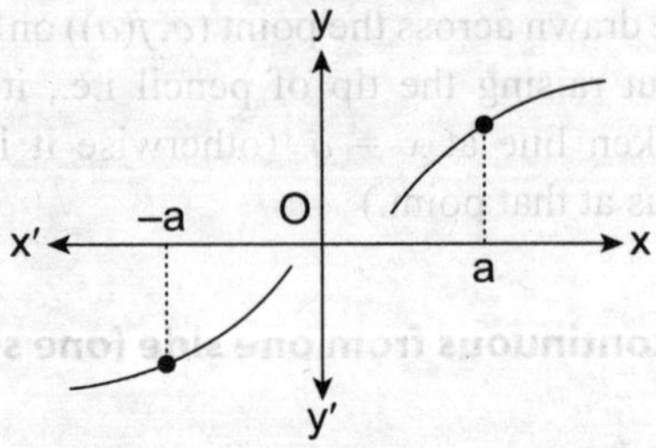

FIGURE 2.16

Odd function continuous at $x = -a$ and at $x = a$

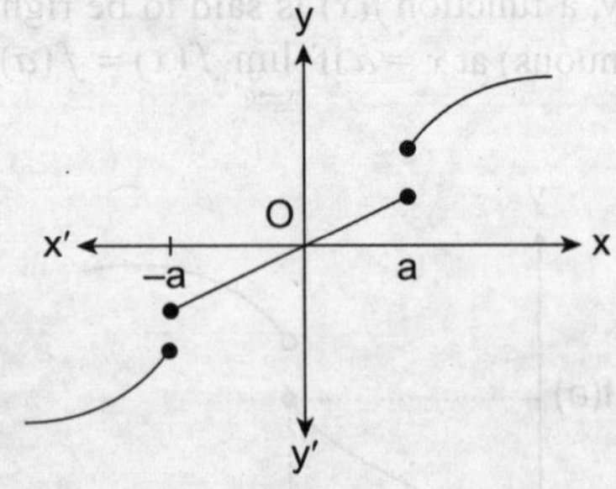

FIGURE 2.17

Odd function discontinuous at $x = -a$ and at $x = a$

Note that if $f(x)$ is an even or odd function having portion of its graph in neighborhood of $x = -a$ and $x = a$, then $f(x)$ is left continuous (discontinuous) at $x = a$ implies $f(x)$ is right continuous (discontinuous) at $x = -a$.

ILLUSTRATION 1: Suppose that $f(x) = x^3 - 3x^2 - 4x + 12$ and $h(x) = \begin{bmatrix} \dfrac{f(x)}{x-3} & ; & x \neq 3 \\ k & ; & x = 3 \end{bmatrix}$, then

(a) Find all zeros of $f(x)$

(b) Find the value of k that makes h continuous at $x = 3$.

(c) Using the value of k found in (b), determine whether h is an even function.

SOLUTION: (a) $f(x) = x^3 - 3x^2 - 4x + 12$

$= x^2(x - 3) - 4(x - 3) = (x - 3)(x^2 - 4)$

hence zeros are $-2, 2, 3$

(b) $\lim\limits_{x\to 3^+} h(x) = \dfrac{x^3 - 3x^2 - 4x + 12}{x - 3}$

($\because f(x)$ is continuous at $x = 3$, both sided limits are equal, we can take any one)

$= \lim\limits_{x\to 3^+} \dfrac{(x-3)(x^2-4)}{(x-3)} = \lim\limits_{x\to 3^+}(x^2 - 4) = 5 = f(3) = k$

$\Rightarrow k = 5.$

(c) Given function becomes $h(x) = \begin{cases} \dfrac{f(x)}{x-3}; & x \neq 3 \\ 5; & x = 3 \end{cases}$ For even function $h(-x) = h(x)$

Now, $h(x) = \dfrac{x^3 - 3x^2 - 4x + 12}{(x-3)}; x \neq 3$

$\Rightarrow h(x) = x^2 - 4;\ x \neq 3$ and $h(x) = 5$ for $x = 3$

$\Rightarrow h(-x) = h(x)$ " $x \in \mathbb{R}$

$\Rightarrow h(x)$ is an even function.

ILLUSTRATION 2: Test the continuity of the function $f(x) = \begin{cases} (2-x)\tan\dfrac{\pi x}{4} \text{ if } x \neq 2 \\ \dfrac{4}{\pi}; \text{if } x = 2 \end{cases}$; at $x = 2$

SOLUTION: As $x \to 2, x \neq 2$

$\therefore$ While taking left hand limit and right hand limit, we shall take $f(x) = (2-x)\tan\dfrac{\pi x}{4}$

$\therefore$ L.H.L $= \lim\limits_{x\to 2^-} f(x) = \lim\limits_{h\to 0^+} f(2-h)$

$= \lim\limits_{h\to 0^+}\left[2-(2-h)\right]\tan\dfrac{\pi(2-h)}{4} = \lim\limits_{h\to 0^+} h\left[\tan\dfrac{\pi(2-h)}{4}\right]$

$= \lim\limits_{h\to 0^+} h\tan\left[\dfrac{\pi}{2} - \dfrac{\pi h}{4}\right] = \lim\limits_{h\to 0^+} h\cot\left(\dfrac{\pi h}{4}\right)$

$= \lim\limits_{h\to 0^+} \cos\left(\dfrac{\pi h}{4}\right) \cdot \dfrac{\left(\dfrac{\pi h}{4}\right)\cdot\dfrac{4}{\pi}}{\sin\left(\dfrac{\pi h}{4}\right)} = (1)(1)\dfrac{4}{\pi}$

and R.H.L $= \lim\limits_{x\to 2^+} f(x) = \lim\limits_{h\to 0^+} f(2+h)$

$$= \lim_{h\to 0^+}[2-(2+h)]\tan\frac{\pi}{4}(2+h) = \lim_{h\to 0^+}[-h]\tan\left[\frac{\pi}{2}+\frac{\pi h}{4}\right]$$

$$= \lim_{h\to 0^+} h\cot\left(\frac{\pi h}{4}\right) = \lim_{h\to 0^+}\frac{h}{\sin\left(\frac{\pi h}{4}\right)}.\cos\left(\frac{\pi h}{4}\right) = \lim_{h\to 0^+}\frac{\frac{\pi h}{4}\times\frac{4}{\pi}}{\sin\left(\frac{\pi h}{4}\right)}.\cos\left(\frac{\pi h}{4}\right) = \frac{4}{\pi}$$

Also $f(2) = \dfrac{4}{\pi}$

$\therefore$ L.H.L = R.H.L = $f(2)$

$\Rightarrow$ $f(x)$ is continuous at $x = 2$

ILLUSTRATION 3: Discuss the continuity of the function $f(x)=\begin{cases}\dfrac{5^{1/x}-7}{5^{1/x}+4} & \text{if } x\neq 0\\ \dfrac{-7}{4} & \text{if } x=0\end{cases}$; at $x = 0$

SOLUTION: L.H.L $= \lim_{x\to 0^-}\dfrac{5^{1/x}-7}{5^{1/x}+4}$

As $x \to 0^-$; $\dfrac{1}{x}\to -\infty \Rightarrow (5)^{1/x} \to 5^{-\infty} \to 0$

$\therefore$ L.H.L $= \dfrac{0-7}{0+4} = \dfrac{-7}{4}$ and R.H.L $= \lim_{x\to 0^+}\dfrac{5^{1/x}-7}{5^{1/x}+4} = \lim_{x\to 0^+}\dfrac{1-7(5)^{-1/x}}{1+4(5)^{-1/x}}$

(Dividing Numerator and Denominator by $(5)^{1/x}$)

As $x \to 0^+$; $\dfrac{-1}{x}\to -\infty \Rightarrow 5^{-1/x} \to 5^{-\infty} \to 0$

$\therefore$ R.H.L $= \dfrac{1-7(0)}{1+4(0)} = 1$; Also $f(0) = \dfrac{-7}{4}$

$\therefore$ L.H.L $= f(0) = \dfrac{-7}{4} \neq 1$ = R.H.L

$\therefore$ $f(x)$ is discontinuous at $x = 0$

ILLUSTRATION 4: Discuss the continuity of the function $f(x)=\begin{cases}\dfrac{[x^2]-9}{x^2-9} & \text{if } x^2\neq 9\\ 0 & \text{if } x^2=9\end{cases}$, at $x = \pm 3$; where [.] is greatest integer function.

SOLUTION: $f(x)=\begin{cases}\dfrac{[x^2]-9}{x^2-9}; & x^2\neq 9\\ 0 & ; x^2=9\end{cases}$

Let us discuss the continuity of $f(x)$ at $x = 3$

L.H.L $= \lim_{x\to 3^-} f(x)$

$$= \lim_{h\to 0^+} f(3-h) = \lim_{h\to 0^+} \frac{\left[(3-h)^2\right]-9}{(3-h)^2-9} = \lim_{h\to 0^+} \frac{\left[9+\left(h^2-6h\right)\right]-9}{9+h^2-6h-9}$$

$$= \lim_{h\to 0^+} \frac{[9-(6-h)h]-9}{h^2-6h} = \lim_{h\to 0^+} \frac{8-9}{-h(6-h)} = \frac{-1}{0^-} = \infty$$

$$\begin{pmatrix} \because\ 6-h>0, h>0 \text{ as } h\to 0^+ \\ \Rightarrow (6-h)h \to 0^+ \\ \Rightarrow 8 < 9-(6-h)h < 9 \end{pmatrix}$$

$$\text{R.H.L} = \lim_{x\to 3^+} f(x) = \lim_{x\to 3^+} f(3+h)$$

$$= \lim_{h\to 0^+} \frac{\left[(3+h)^2\right]-9}{(3+h)^2-9} = \lim_{h\to 0^+} \frac{\left[9+h^2+6h\right]-9}{(9+h^2+6h)-9}$$

$$= \lim_{h\to 0^+} \frac{\left[9+h(6+h)\right]-9}{(h^2+6h)} \text{ as } < 9+9+h(6+h) < 10$$

$$= \lim_{h\to 0^+} \frac{9-9}{h(6+h)} = 0 \qquad \begin{pmatrix} \because \text{ Numerator is perfect zero,} \\ \text{where as demoninator approaches} \\ \text{to zero} \end{pmatrix}$$

Also $f(x = 3) = 0$

$\therefore$ L.H.L $= \infty \neq f(3) = R$.H.L $= 0$

$\therefore$ $f(x)$ is discontinuous at $x = 3$

Let us discuss continuity of $f(x)$ at $x = -3$

$$\text{L.H.L} = \lim_{x\to -3^-} f(x) = \lim_{h\to 0^+} f(-3-h) = \lim_{h\to 0^+} \frac{\left[(-3-h)^2\right]-9}{(-3-h)^2-9}$$

$$= \lim_{h\to 0^+} \frac{\left[9+h^2+6h\right]-9}{(9+h^2+6h-9)}$$

$$= \lim_{h\to 0^+} \frac{9-9}{h^2+6h} = 0 \text{ as } 9 < 9 + h^2 + 6h < 10$$

$$\text{R.H.L} = \lim_{h\to -3^+} f(x) = \lim_{h\to 0^+} f(-3+h) = \lim_{h\to 0^+} \frac{\left[(-3+h)^2\right]-9}{(-3+h)^2-9}$$

$$= \lim_{h\to 0^+} \frac{[9+h^2-6h]-9}{9+h^2-6h-9} = \lim_{h\to 0^+} \frac{[9-h(6-h)]-9}{-h(6-h)}$$

$$= \lim_{h\to 0^+} \frac{8-9}{-h(6-h)} = \frac{-1}{0^-} = \infty \text{ as } 8 < 9 - h(6-h) < 9$$

Also $f(-3) = 0$

$\therefore$ L.H.L $= 0 = f(-3) \neq$ R.H.L $= \infty$

$\therefore$ $f(x)$ is discontinuous at $x = 0$

DISCONTINUITY OF A FUNCTION *F*(*X*) AT *X* = *A*

A function $f(x)$ is said to be discontinuous at $x = a$ if it is not continuous at $x = a$ and this happens if at least one of the following conditions holds

(i) $f(a)$ does not exist

(ii) L.H.L $= f(a^-) = \lim_{h \to a^-} f(x)$ does not exist (i.e., either not defined or is infinite)

(iii) R.H.L $= f(a^+) = \lim_{h \to a^+} f(x)$ does not exist. It may happen that both L.H.L. and R.H.L. are not finite.

(iv) L.H.L and R.H.L both exist finitely, but L.H.L $\neq$ R.H.L

(v) L.H.L = R.H.L (a finite real number) $\neq f(a)$

(vi) L.H.L and R.H.L or any one of them oscillates i.e., does not tend to a unique real number.

Depending on the above reasons of discontinuity of a function $f(x)$ at a point $x = a$, let us discuss the types of discontinuity of a function at a point $x = a$.

Types of Discontinuity of a Function *f*(*x*) at *x* = *a*

Depending on the fact whether the discontinuity of $f(x)$ observed at $x = a$ can be removed or not we classify discontinuity at a point $x = a$ into the two main categories following

(i) Removable discontinuity
(ii) Non-removable discontinuity

(i) Removable discontinuity

In this type of discontinuity at $x = a$, $\lim_{x \to a} f(x)$ necessarily exists, but is either not equal to $f(a)$ or $f(a)$ is not defined. Therefore it is possible to redefine the function in such a manner that $\lim_{x \to a} f(x) = f(a)$ and thus making the function continuous. Further removable

Discontinuity is of two types

(a) Missing point removable discontinuity
(b) Isolated point removable discontinuity

(a) Missing point discontinuity: If $\lim_{x \to a^-} f(x) = \lim_{x \to a^+} f(x) = a$ finite real number but $f(a)$ is not defined i.e., image of point $x = a$ does not exist, then $f(x)$ is said to have missing point discontinuity at $x = a$. Graphically it is shown below.

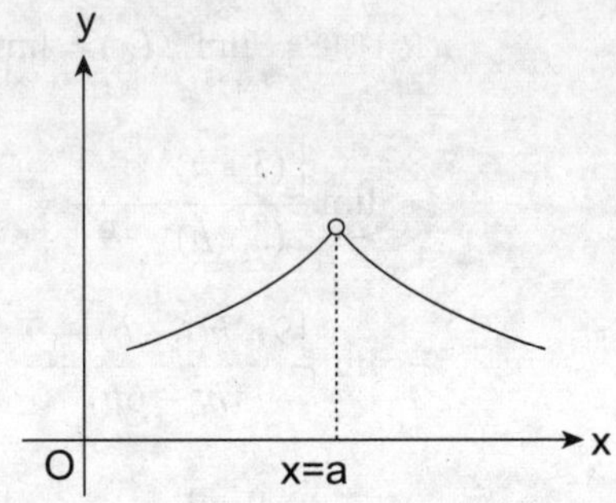

FIGURE 2.18

(b) Isolated point discontinuity: If $\lim_{x \to a^-} f(x) = \lim_{x \to a^+} f(x) = a$ finite real number but $\lim_{x \to a} f(x) \neq f(a) =$ a finite real number then $f(x)$ is said to have isolated point discontinuity at $x = a$, as the image $f(a)$ is isolated from the remaining graph. Graphically it is shown below.

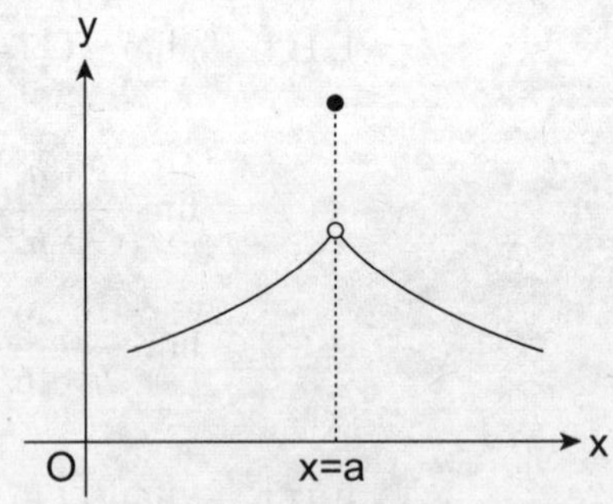

FIGURE 2.19

ILLUSTRATION 5: Show that the following functions have removable discontinuity at the referred point. Also name the type of removable discontinuity.

(a) $f(x) = \dfrac{(x-2)(9-x^2)}{(x-2)}$ at $x = 2$

(b) $f(x) = [x] + [-x]$ at $x = 2$

SOLUTION: (a) $\lim\limits_{x\to 2} f(x) = \lim\limits_{x\to 2}\dfrac{(x-2)(9-x^2)}{(x-2)} = 5$ and $f(2) = \dfrac{0}{0}$ = not defined

Thus at $x = 2$ we have removable discontinuous

The above removable discontinuity is missing point discontinuity

(b) $f(x) = [x]+[-x] = \begin{cases} -1; x \notin \mathbb{Z} \\ 0; x \in \mathbb{Z}\end{cases}$

$\therefore$ L.H.L $= \lim\limits_{x\to 2^-} f(x) = \lim\limits_{x\to 2^-}([x]+[-x]) = -1$

$= \left(\because x \to 2^- \Rightarrow x \in (1,2) \Rightarrow x \notin \mathbb{Z} \Rightarrow f(x) = -1\right)$

Similarly R.H.L. = –1, but $f(2) = 0$

$\therefore$ L.H.L = R.H.L = $-1 \neq f(2) = 0$

$\therefore$ $f(x)$ has removable discontinuity at $x = 2$. The above removable discontinuity is isolated point discontinuity.

ILLUSTRATION 6: Test the continuity of $f(x) = \begin{cases} (1-x)^{4-\left(\frac{1}{|x|}+\frac{1}{x}\right)} & ; x<0, \text{ at } x=0 \\ 0 & ; x=0 \\ (1+x)^{-2/x}(1-x)^{2-\left(\frac{1}{|x|}+\frac{1}{x}\right)} & ; x>0 \end{cases}$, at $x = 0$

SOLUTION: $f(x) = \begin{cases} (1-x)^{4-\left(\frac{1}{|x|}+\frac{1}{x}\right)} & ; x<0 \\ 0 & ; x=0 \\ (1+x)^{-2/x}(1-x)^{2-\left(\frac{1}{|x|}+\frac{1}{x}\right)} & ; x>0 \end{cases}$

L.H.L $= \lim\limits_{x\to 0^-} f(x) = \lim\limits_{x\to 0^+} f(0-h) = \lim\limits_{h\to 0^+}(1-(-h))^{4-\left(\frac{1}{|-h|}+\frac{1}{(-h)}\right)} = \lim\limits_{h\to 0^+}(1+h)^{4-\left(+\frac{1}{h}-\frac{1}{h}\right)}$

$= \lim\limits_{h\to 0^+}(1+h)^{4-\left(+\frac{1}{h}-\frac{1}{h}\right)} = \lim\limits_{h\to 0^+}(1+h)^4 = (1+0)^4 = 1$

R.H.L $= \lim\limits_{h\to 0^+} f(x) = \lim\limits_{h\to 0^+} f(0+h)$

$= \lim\limits_{h\to 0^+}(1+h)^{-2/h}(1-h)^{2-\left(\frac{1}{|h|}+\frac{1}{h}\right)}$

$= \lim\limits_{h\to 0^+}(1+h)^{-2/h}\lim\limits_{h\to 0^+}(1-h)^2\lim\limits_{h\to 0^+}(1-h)^{\frac{-2}{h}} = e^{-2}(1)e^{+2} = 1$

Also $f(0) = 0$

$\therefore$ L.H.L = R.H.L = $1 \neq f(0) = 0$

$\therefore$ $f(x)$ has a removable discontinuity at $x = 0$ and it is isolated point discontinuity

ILLUSTRATION 7: Let $f(x) = \begin{cases} \dfrac{\ell n(2-\cos 2x)}{\ell n^2(1+\sin 3x)} \text{ for } x<0 \\ \dfrac{e^{\sin 2x}-1}{\ell n(1+\tan 9x)} \text{ for } x>0 \end{cases}$; Show that $f(x)$ has a removable discontinuity at $x = 0$. Also find $f(0)$ so that function $f(x)$ becomes continuous at $x = 0$

SOLUTION: $\text{L.H.L} = \lim_{x\to 0^-} f(x) = \lim_{h\to 0^+} f(0-h)$

$$= \lim_{h\to 0^+} \frac{\ell n(2-\cos(-2h))}{\ell n^2(1+\sin 3(-h))} = \lim_{h\to 0^+} \frac{\ell n[2-\cos 2h]}{\ell n^2[1-\sin 3h]}$$

$$= \lim_{h\to 0^+} \frac{\ell n[1+2\sin^2 h]}{\ell n^2[1-\sin 3h]} = \lim_{h\to 0^+} \frac{\ell n\left[1+2\sin^2 h\right]}{2\sin^2 h}.2\sin^2 h.\frac{(-\sin 3h)^2}{(-\sin 3h)^2\,\ell n^2(1-\sin 3h)}$$

$$= \lim_{h\to 0^+} (1)(1).\frac{2\sin^2 h}{\sin^2 3h} = \frac{2}{9}\lim_{h\to 0^+}.\frac{\sin^2 h}{h^2}.\frac{9h^2}{\sin^2 3h} = \frac{2}{9}(1)^2(1)^2 = \frac{2}{9}$$

Now $\text{R.H.L} = \lim_{x\to 0^+} f(x) = \lim_{x\to 0^+} \frac{e^{\sin 2x}-1}{\ell n(1+\tan 9x)}$

$$= \lim_{x\to 0^+} \frac{e^{\sin 2x}-1}{\sin 2x}.\frac{\sin 2x}{\tan 9x}.\frac{\tan 9x}{\ell n(1+\tan 9x)} = \lim_{x\to 0^+} \frac{\sin 2x}{\tan 9x} = \frac{2}{9}$$ 1800266121

$\therefore$ L.H.L = R.H.L = 2/9

But $f(0)$ is not defined

So $f(x)$ has a removable discontinuity at $x = 0$.The discontinuity is missing point discontinuity and $f(x)$ can be made continuous by redefining the function only at $x = 0$. i.e., $f(0) = 2/9$

(ii) Non-removable discontinuity

A function $f(x)$ is said to have non-removable discontinuity at $x = a$ if $\lim_{x\to a} f(x)$ does not exist and therefore it is not possible to redefine the function in any manner to make it continuous. These are further classified into three catagories.

(a) Jump discontinuity (b) Infinite discontinuity

(c) Oscillatory discontinuity

(a) Jump discontinuity: If both the limits at $x = a$ exist finitely, but are unequal irrespective of the nature of $f(a)$, then $f(x)$ is said to have jump discontinuity at $x = a$.

Difference of L.H.L and R.H.L. is called jump of discontinuous function at $x = a$. The graph of such a function is given figure 2.20

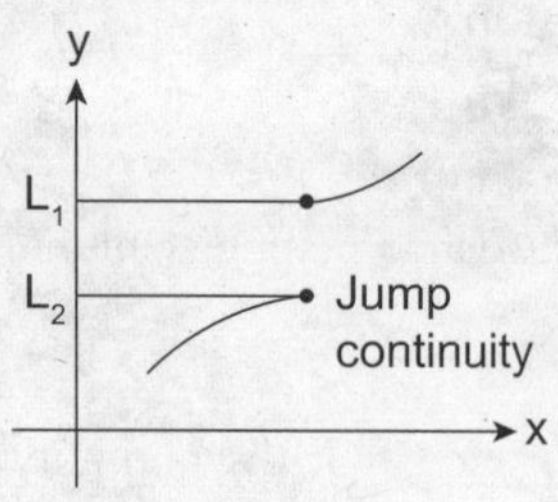

FIGURE 2.20

For example if $f(x) = \tan^{-1}\frac{1}{x}$ then

$\text{L.H.L.} = \underset{x\to 0^-}{\text{Lt}} \tan^{-1}\frac{1}{x} = \frac{-\pi}{2}$ and $\text{R.H.L.} = \underset{x\to 0^+}{\text{Lt}} \tan^{-1}\frac{1}{x} = \frac{\pi}{2}$

but $f(0)$ is not defined and L.H.L $\neq$ R.H.L.

(b) Infinite discontinuity: If at least one of the two sided limits of $f(x)$ at $x = a$ becomes infinite, then the function $f(x)$ is said to have infinite discontinuity at $x = a$. The graphs of some of such function are given below.

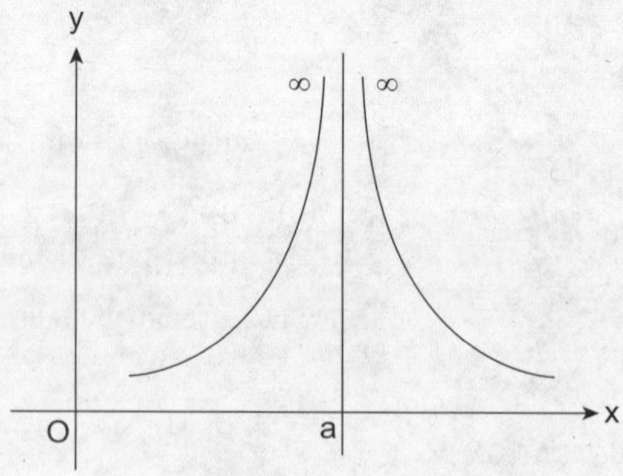

FIGURE 2.21

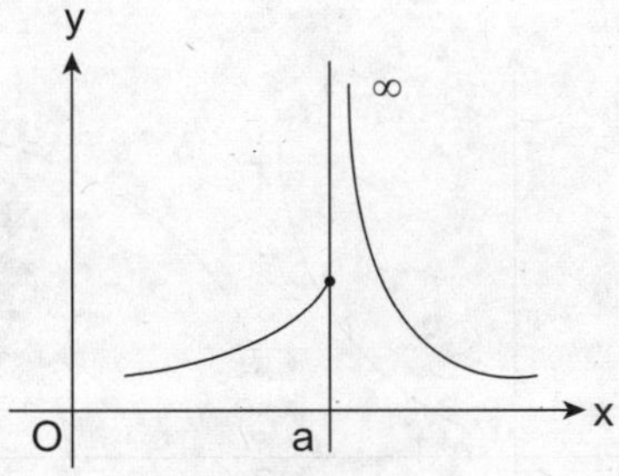

FIGURE 2.22

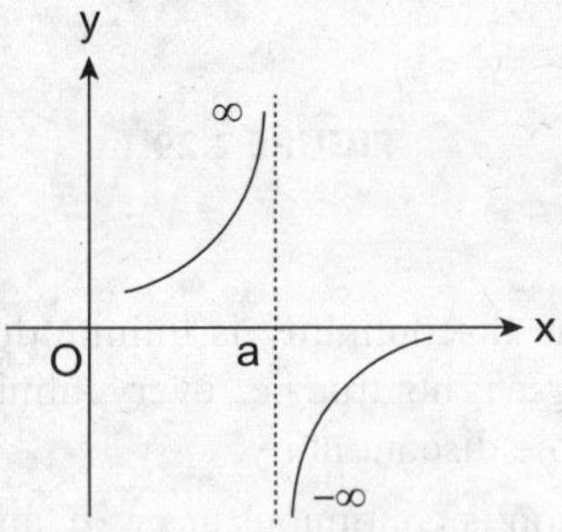

FIGURE 2.23

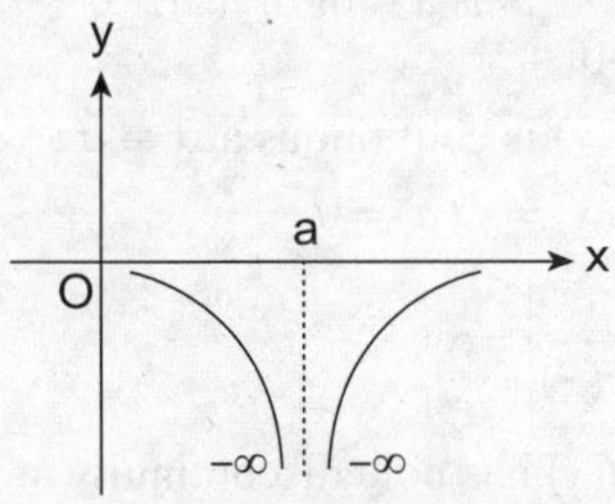

FIGURE 2.24

for example if $f(x)=\dfrac{x}{1-x}$,

then L.H.L. $= \lim\limits_{x\to 1^-}\dfrac{x}{1-x} = \lim\limits_{h\to 0^+}\dfrac{(1-h)}{1-(1-h)}$

$= \lim\limits_{h\to 0^+}\dfrac{1-h}{h} = \dfrac{1}{0^+} = \infty$

and R.H.L. $= \lim\limits_{x\to 1^+}\dfrac{x}{1-x} = \lim\limits_{h\to 0^+}\dfrac{(1+h)}{1-(1+h)} = \dfrac{1}{0^-} = -\infty$

$\therefore$ $f(x)$ has infinite discontinuity at $x = 1$

(c) Oscillatory discontinuity: If at least one of the two limits oscillates between two finite real numbers, then the function $f(x)$ cannot attain a unique limit at $x = a$ and the function $f(x)$ is said to have oscillatory discontinuity at $x = a$.

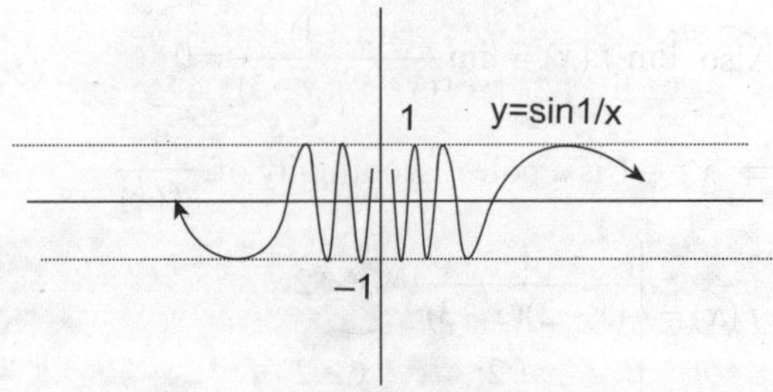

FIGURE 2.25

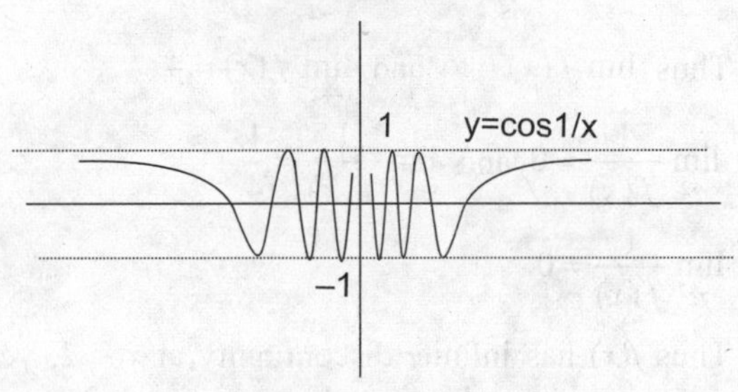

FIGURE 2.26

$\sin\dfrac{1}{x}$ and $\cos\dfrac{1}{x}$ are discontinuous at $x = 0$ because their values oscillates with infinite frequency in the neighbourhood of '0' in between −1 and 1. Thus limit does not exist at $x = 0$. i.e., $f(x)$ has oscillatory discontinuity at $x = 0$.

POLE DISCONTINUITY

Pole discontinuity of a function is an infinite discontinuity, when both left hand limit and right hand limit becomes infinite (positive or negative).

A function $f(x)$ is said to have pole discontinuity at $x = a$ if its numerical value becomes infinitely large as x tends to a. Mathematically $\lim\limits_{x\to a}\dfrac{1}{f(x)} = 0$ or $\left|\lim\limits_{x\to a} f(x)\right| = \infty$

Example

1. $f(x)=\dfrac{2}{(x-2)}$ has pole discontinuity at $x = 2$ as

$\lim\limits_{x\to 2}\dfrac{1}{f(x)} = \lim\limits_{x\to 2}\dfrac{(x-2)}{2} = 0$

2. $f(x)=\dfrac{x+1}{(x-2)(x-3)}$ has pole discontinuity at $x = 2$ and at $x = 3$ as

$\lim\limits_{x\to 2}\dfrac{1}{f(x)} = \lim\limits_{x\to 2}\dfrac{(x-2)(x-3)}{(x+1)} = 0$ and

$\lim\limits_{x\to 3}\dfrac{1}{f(x)} = \lim\limits_{x\to 3}\dfrac{(x-2)(x-3)}{(x+1)} = 0$

Also $\lim\limits_{x\to -1} f(x) = \lim\limits_{x\to -1} \dfrac{(x+1)}{(x-2)(x-3)} = 0$

$\Rightarrow x = -1$ is a pole discontinuity of $\dfrac{1}{f(x)}$

3. $f(x) = \begin{cases} \dfrac{1}{(x-2)(x-3)}; & x < 2 \\ x+2; & x \geq 2 \end{cases};$

Then $\lim\limits_{x\to 2^-} f(x) = \infty$ and $\lim\limits_{x\to 2^+} f(x) = 4$

Thus $\lim\limits_{x\to 2^-} f(x) = \infty$ and $\lim\limits_{x\to 2^+} f(x) = 4$

$\Rightarrow \lim\limits_{x\to 2^-} \dfrac{1}{f(x)} = 0$ and $\lim\limits_{x\to 2^+} \dfrac{1}{f(x)} = \dfrac{1}{4}$

$\Rightarrow \lim\limits_{x\to 2} \dfrac{1}{f(x)} \neq 0$

Thus $f(x)$ has infinite discontinuity at $x = 2$, yet $f(x)$ does not has pole discontinuity at $x = 2$, as when x tends to 2 from left side, $f(x)$ tends to ∞ and when x tends to 2 from right side $f(x)$ tends to finite real number 4.

The graph given below clarifies the distinction between infinite discontinuity and pole discontinuity.

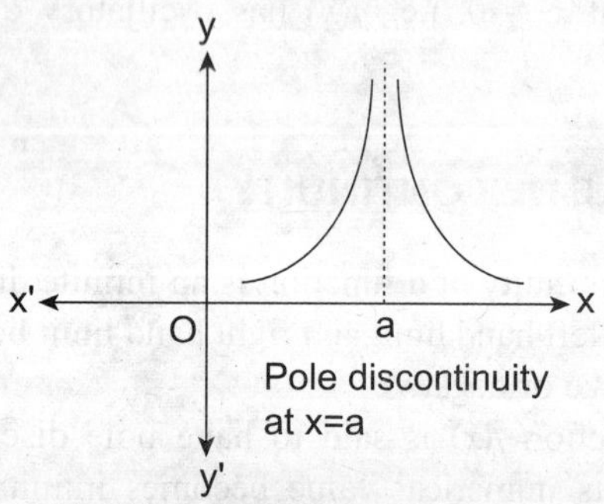

FIGURE 2.27

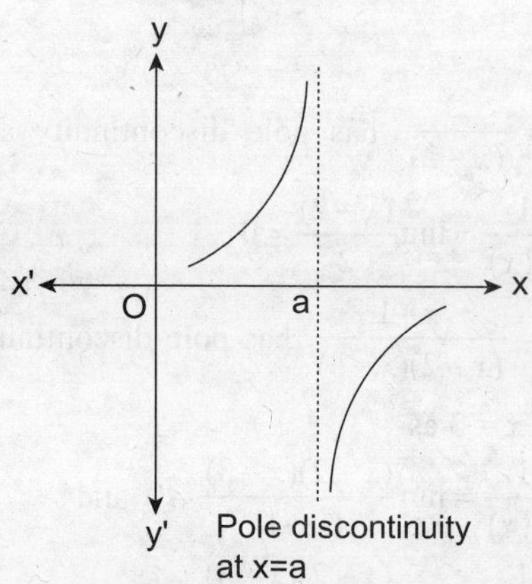

FIGURE 2.28

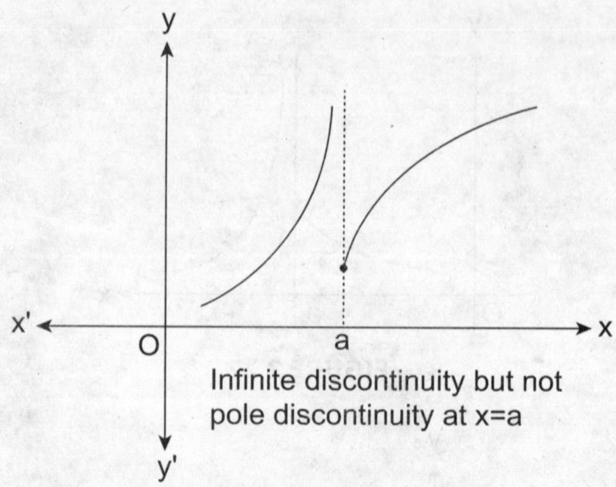

FIGURE 2.29

Remarks:

1. Every pole discontinuity is infinite discontinuity, but the converse is not true i.e., every infinite discontinuity is not a pole discontinuity.
2. If a function is continuous at $x = a$, and 'a' is a root of $f(x) = 0$, then $x = a$ is a pole discontinuity of reciprocal of $f(x)$.

   Proof: $\because$ 'a' is a root of $f(x) = 0$

   $\Rightarrow f(a) = 0$

   Also $f(x)$ is continuous at $x = a$

   $\Rightarrow \lim\limits_{x\to a} f(x) = f(a) = 0$

   $\Rightarrow \left|\lim\limits_{x\to a} \dfrac{1}{f(x)}\right| = \infty$

   Thus $f(x)$ has pole discontinuity at $x = a$
3. Zeros of all polynomial functions are poles of their reciprocal functions
4. Zeros of $\sin x$, $\cos x$ and $\tan x$ are poles of cosec x, sec x and cot x respectively.
5. If a function $f(x)$ does not has any zero, then its reciprocal function cannot have any pole.

■ DISCONTINUITY OF FIRST AND SECOND KIND

Discontinuity of First Kind

A function $f(x)$ is said to have discontinuity of first kind at $x = a$ if both L.H.L. as well as R.H.L. exist but the condition of continuity is not satisfied.

Thus following may be the causes of a function to have discontinuity of first kind at $x = a$

(i) $\lim\limits_{x\to a^-} f(x) = \lim\limits_{x\to a^+} f(x) \neq f(a)$

(ii) $\lim\limits_{x\to a^-} f(x) \neq \lim\limits_{x\to a^+} f(x)$

For example

(i) $f(x)=\begin{cases} x-2 & \text{for } x<1 \\ 0 & \text{for } x=1 \\ 2x-3 & \text{for } x>1 \end{cases}$

Clearly $\lim_{x\to 1^-} f(x)=\lim_{x\to 1^+} f(x)=-1\neq 0=f(1)$

$\therefore$ $f(x)$ has first kind of discontinuity at $x = 1$.

Discontinuity of Second Kind

A function $f(x)$ is said to have discontinuity of second kind at $x = a$ if at least one of two one sided limits either does not exist or becomes infinite.

Thus following may be the reasons of second kind of discontinuity of a function $f(x)$ at $x = a$.

(i) $\left|\lim_{x\to a^-} f(x)\right|=\infty;\ \lim_{x\to a^+} f(x)$ is finite

(ii) $\left|\lim_{x\to a^+} f(x)\right|=\infty;\ \lim_{x\to a^-} f(x)$ is finite

(iii) $\lim_{x\to a^-} f(x)$ or $\lim_{x\to a^+} f(x)$ or both does not exist (neither finitely nor infinitely).

For example

(i) $f(x)=\sin\frac{1}{x}$, then $\lim_{x\to 0} f(x)=\lim_{x\to 0}\sin\frac{1}{x}$ does not exist as it oscillates in between –1 and 1.

(ii) $f(x)=\frac{x+3}{x-2}$

$\lim_{x\to 2^-} f(x)=\lim_{x\to 2^-}\frac{x+3}{x-2}=-\infty$

and $\lim_{x\to 2^+} f(x)=\lim_{x\to 2^+}\frac{x+3}{x-2}=\infty$

Thus $f(x)$ has second kind of discontinuity at $x = 2$.

ILLUSTRATION 8: Mention the nature of discontinuity in the following functions:

(a) $f(x) = 3^{\tan x}$ at $x=(2n+1)\frac{\pi}{2}; n\in\mathbb{Z}$

(b) $f(x)=\frac{1}{x^4}$ at $x=0$

(c) $f(x)=\frac{|\sin 3x|}{x}$ at $x=0$

(d) $f(x)=\frac{\{x\}}{x}$ at $x=0$

(e) $f(x)=\frac{[x]}{x}$ at $x=3$

SOLUTION: (a) $f(x) = 3^{\tan x}$ at $x=\left((2n+1)\frac{\pi}{2}\right)^-; n\in\mathbb{Z}$

As $x\to\left((2n+1)\frac{\pi}{2}\right)^-$; $\tan x\to\infty$

$\Rightarrow 3^{\tan x}\to 3^{\infty}=\infty$

$\therefore$ L.H.L $=\lim_{x\to\left((2n+1)\frac{\pi}{2}\right)^-} f(x)=\lim_{x\to\left((2n+1)\frac{\pi}{2}\right)^-}(3)^{\tan x}=\infty$

As $x\to\left((2n+1)\frac{\pi}{2}\right)^+$; $\tan x\to-\infty$

$\Rightarrow 3^{\tan x}\to 3^{-\infty}\to 0$

$\therefore$ R.H.L $=\lim_{x\to\left((2n+1)\frac{\pi}{2}\right)^+} f(x)=\lim_{x\to\left((2n+1)\frac{\pi}{2}\right)^+}(3)^{\tan x}=0$ and $f\left((2n+1)\frac{\pi}{2}\right)=3^{\infty}=\infty$

$\therefore$ $f(x)$ has an infinite discontinuity and hence non-removable discontinuity at $x=(2n+1)\frac{\pi}{2}$

(b) $f(x)=\frac{1}{x^4}$ at $x=0$

L.H.L $=\lim_{h\to 0^-} f(x)=\lim_{h\to 0^+} f(0-h)$

$= \lim_{h\to 0^+}\left(\frac{1}{(-h)^4}\right) = \lim_{h\to 0^+}\frac{1}{(h)^4} = \infty$

Also R.H.L $= \lim_{x\to 0^+} f(x) = \lim_{h\to 0^+} f(0+h)$

$= \lim_{x\to 0^+}\frac{1}{x^4} = \infty$ and $f(0) = \frac{1}{0}$ which is not defined

∴ L.H.L = R.H.L = ∞ and $f(0)$ is not defined

∴ $f(x)$ has an infinite discontinuity and hence non-removable discontinuity at $x = 0$

(c) $f(x) = \frac{|\sin 3x|}{x}$ at $x = 0$

L.H.L $= \lim_{x\to 0^-}\frac{|\sin 3x|}{x} = \lim_{x\to 0^-}\frac{-\sin 3x}{x} = -3$

and R.H.L $= \lim_{x\to 0^+}\frac{|\sin 3x|}{x} = \lim_{x\to 0^+}\frac{|\sin 3x|}{x} = 3$

And $f(0) = \frac{0}{0}$ which is not defined

∴ L.H.L and R.H.L both exist but are unequal

∴ $f(x)$ has a jump discontinuity at $x = 0$ and hence non-removable discontinuity

(d) $f(x) = \frac{\{x\}}{2}$ at $x = 0$

L.H.L $\lim_{x\to 0^-} f(x) = \lim_{h\to 0^+} f(0-h) = \lim_{h\to 0^+}\frac{\{-h\}}{-h} = \lim_{h\to 0^+}\frac{1-\{-h\}}{-h} = \frac{1-h}{-h} = -\infty$

and R.H.L $\lim_{x\to 0^+} f(x) = \lim_{x\to 0^+}\frac{\{x\}}{x} = \lim_{x\to 0^+}\frac{x}{x} = 1$

∴ $f(x)$ has infinite discontinuity at $x = 0$ and hence is non-removable

(e) $f(x) = \frac{[x]}{x}$ at $x = 3$

L.H.L $= \lim_{x\to 3^-}\frac{[x]}{x} = \lim_{h\to 0^+}\frac{[3-h]}{(3-h)} = \lim_{h\to 0^+}\frac{2}{(3-h)} = \frac{2}{3}$

and R.H.L $= \lim_{x\to 0^+} f(x) = \lim_{h\to 0^+} f(3+h) = \lim_{h\to 0^+}\frac{[3+h]}{(3+h)} = \lim_{h\to 0^+}\frac{3}{3} = 1$ and $f(3) = \frac{[3]}{3} = 1$

∴ L.H.L and R.H.L are finite and unequal. Thus the function is discontinuous and the function has jump discontinuity at $x = 3$. Also R.H.L. $= f(3) = 1 \neq$ L.H.L. $= \frac{2}{3}$ Thus $f(x)$ is right continuous and left discontinuous.

ILLUSTRATION 9: Mention the nature of discontinuity in the following functions.

(a) $f(x) = \frac{x^2-9}{x+3}$ at $x = -3$

(b) $\frac{\tan x}{x}$ at $x = (2x+1)\frac{\pi}{2}; n \in \mathbb{Z}$

(c) $f(x) = \text{sgn}(\cos 2x - 3\cos x - 4)$ at $x = (2n + 1)\pi$; $n \in \mathbb{Z}$ and at $x = 0$

SOLUTION: (a) $f(x) = \dfrac{x^2-9}{x+3}$ and at $x \in \mathbb{R} \sim \{(2n+1)\pi;\ n \in \mathbb{Z}\}$

Clearly $f(x)$ is not defined at $x = -3$

and $\lim_{x\to -3} f(x) = \lim_{x\to -3} \dfrac{x^2-9}{(x+3)} = \lim_{x\to -3} \dfrac{(x+3)(x-3)}{(x+3)}$

$= \lim_{x\to -3}(x-3) = -6$

$\therefore \lim_{x\to -3} f(x) = -6 \neq f(-3)$ which is not defined

$\therefore$ $f(x)$ has a missing point removable discontinuity at $x = -3$

(b) $f(x) = \dfrac{\tan x}{x}$, which is not defined at $x = (2n+1)\pi/2;\ n \in \mathbb{Z}$ and at $x = 0$

At $x = (2n+1)\dfrac{\pi}{2}; n \in \mathbb{Z}; x \neq 0$ and $x \to (2n+1)\dfrac{\pi}{2} \Rightarrow \tan x \to \pm\infty$

$\therefore$ $f(x) \to \pm\infty$ and hence $\lim_{x\to (2x+1)\frac{\pi}{2}} f(x) = \pm\infty$

At $x = 0$

$\lim_{x\to 0} \dfrac{\tan x}{x} = 1;\ f(0) = \dfrac{0}{0}$ which is not defined

$\therefore$ $f(x)$ has a missing point removable discontinuity at $x = 0$

(c) $f(x) = \text{sgn}(\cos 2x - 3\cos x - 4)$

$= \text{sgn}(2\cos^2 x - 1 - 3\cos x - 4)$

$= \text{sgn}(2\cos^2 x - 3\cos x - 5)$

$= \text{sgn}[2\cos^2 x - 5\cos x + 2\cos x - 5] = \text{sgn}[\cos x(2\cos x - 5) + 1(2\cos x - 5)]$

$= \text{sgn}[(2\cos x - 5)(\cos x + 1)]$

We know that $f(x) = \sin(x) = \begin{cases} -1 \text{ for } x < 0 \\ 0 \text{ for } x = 0 \\ 1 \text{ for } x > 0 \end{cases}$

$\therefore$ $f(x) = \text{sgn}[(2\cos x - 5)(\cos x + 1)] = \begin{cases} -1 \text{ for } (2\cos x - 5)(\cos x + 1) < 0 \\ 0 \text{ for } (2\cos x - 5)(\cos x + 1) = 0 \\ 1 \text{ for } (2\cos x - 5)(\cos x + 1) > 0 \end{cases}$

$= \begin{cases} -1 \text{ for } -1 < \cos x < \dfrac{5}{2} \\ 0 \text{ for } \cos x = -1, \dfrac{5}{2} \\ 1 \text{ for } \cos x < -1 \text{ or } \cos x > \dfrac{5}{2} \end{cases}$

But $\cos x \in [-1,.1]$

$\therefore \quad f(x)=\begin{cases}-1 \text{ for } -1<\cos x\le 1\\ 0 \text{ for } \cos x=-1\end{cases}$

$\Rightarrow \quad f(x)=\begin{cases}-1 \text{ for } x\in\mathbb{R}\sim\{(2n+1)\pi; n\in\mathbb{Z}\}\\ 0 \text{ for } x=(2n+1)\pi; n\in\mathbb{Z}\end{cases}$

$\therefore \quad \lim_{x\to(2n+1)\pi} f(x)=\lim_{x\to(2x+1)\pi}(-1)=-1$ but $f(2n+1)$

$\pi = 0$ and if $k\in\mathbb{R}\sim\{(2n+1)\pi;\ n\in\mathbb{Z}\}$; then $\lim_{x\to k} f(x)=\lim_{x\to k} f(x)=-1$ and $f(k)=-1$

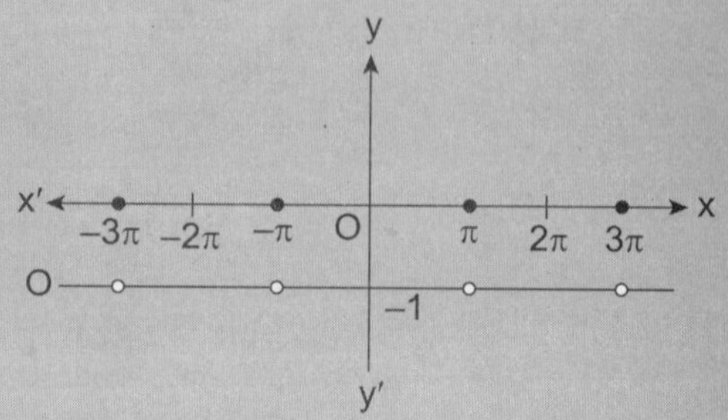

FIGURE 2.30

$\therefore$ $f(x)$ is continuous everywhere except for the points $x=(2n+1)\pi$; $n\in\mathbb{Z}$

and At $x=(2n+1)\pi$; L.H.L = R.H.L = $-1\ne f(2n+1)\pi)=0$

$\therefore$ $f(x)$ has isolated point removable discontinuity at $x=(2n+1)\pi$ i.e., odd integral multiple of π

ILLUSTRATION 10: Observe the following graph and state the type of discontinuity at the following points:

(i) At $x=-1$

(ii) At $x=1$

(iii) At $x=2$

(iv) At $x=3$; where $f(x)$ is defined in domain $[-2, 5]$

(v) At $x=-2$

(vi) At $x=5$

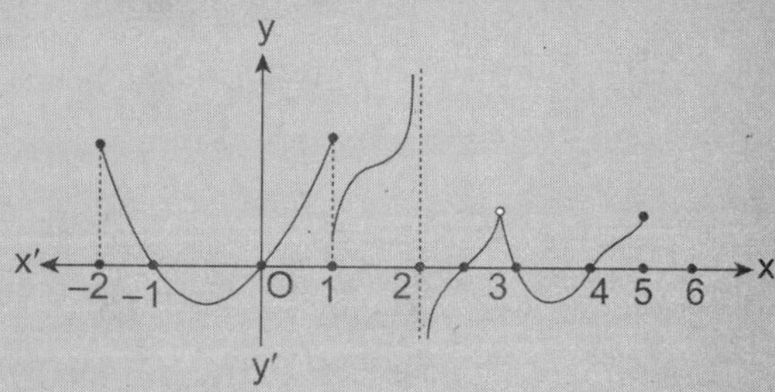

FIGURE 2.31

SOLUTION: (i) At $x=-1$, $f(-1^-)=f(-1^+)\ne f(-1)$

As image of $f(-1)$ does not exist Thus function has a missing point removable discontinuity at $x=-1$

(ii) At $x=1$, $f(1^-)=f(1)\ne f(1^+)$

$\therefore$ Function has a jump discontinuity at $x=1$, which is non-removable. Hence $f(x)$ is left continuous but right discontinuous at $x=1$

(iii) At $x=2$; $f(2^-)=\infty$ and $f(2^+)=-\infty$

$\therefore$ Function has an infinite discontinuity at $x=2$ and which is non-removable

(iv) At $x=3$; $f(3^-)=f(3^+)\ne f(3)$

$\therefore$ $f(x)$ has isolated removable discontinuity at $x=3$

(v) Since no portion of graph lies on the left of $x=-2$ therefore we do not talk about the left hand limit at $x=-2$

Clearly $\lim_{x\to(-2)^+} f(x)\ne f(-2)$

$\therefore$ $f(x)$ is discontinuous at $x=-2$ and has isolated point removable discontinuity at $x=-2$

(vi) Since no portion of graph lies on the right of $x=5$ therefore we do not talk about the right hand limit at $x=5$. Clearly $\lim_{x\to 5} f(x)=f(5)$. Thus $f(x)$ is continuous at $x=5$

Note that if a function is defined on [a, b], then $f(x)$ is said to be continuous at $x=a$ if $f(x)$ is right continuous at $x=a$ and is said to be continuous at $x=a$, if $f(x)$ is left continuous at $x=b$

ILLUSTRATION 11: Find the values of a, b, c for which the function $f(x)$ defined by $f(x)=\begin{cases}\frac{\sin 3ax}{2bx} & \text{if } x<0\\ c & \text{if } x=0\\ \frac{|x|}{x}+\frac{x^3-1}{x-1} & \text{if } 0<x<1\\ a & \text{if } x\ge 1\end{cases}$

be continuous at $x = 0$ and $x = 1$

SOLUTION: For continuity at $x = 0$

$$\text{L.H.L} = \lim_{x\to 0^-} f(x) = \lim_{x\to 0^-}\frac{\sin 3ax}{2bx} = \lim_{x\to 0^-}\frac{1}{2b}\frac{\sin 3ax}{3ax}(3a) = \frac{1}{2b}(1).(3a) = \frac{3a}{2b}$$

$$\text{R.H.L.} = \lim_{x\to 0^+} f(x) = \lim_{x\to 0^+}\frac{|x|}{x}+\frac{x^3-1}{x-1} = \lim_{x\to 0^+}\left(\frac{x}{x}+(x^2+x+1)\right) = \lim_{x\to 0^+}(1+x^2+x+1) = 2 \text{ and } f(0) = c$$

$$\Rightarrow \frac{3a}{2b} = 2 = c \qquad \text{...(1)}$$

For continuity at $x = 1$

$$\text{L.H.L} = \lim_{x\to 1^-} f(x) = \lim_{h\to 0^+}\left(\frac{|1-h|}{(1-h)}+\frac{(1-h)^3-1}{(1-h-1)}\right)$$

$$= \lim_{h\to 0^+}\left(\frac{1-h}{1-h}+\frac{1-h^3-3h+3h^2-1}{-h}\right) = \lim_{h\to 0^+}\left[1+(h^2+3-3h)\right] = 4$$

$$\text{R.H.L} = \lim_{x\to 1^+} f(x) = \lim_{x\to 1^+}(a) = a$$

Also $f(1) = a$

$$\Rightarrow 4 = a \qquad \text{...(2)}$$

$\therefore$ from (1) $a = 4$, $b = 3$, $c = 2$;

ILLUSTRATION 12: Define a function $f(x)$ by $f(x)=\begin{cases}\frac{2\cos x-\sin 2x}{(\pi-2x)^3} & \text{for } x<\frac{\pi}{2}\\ \frac{1}{6} & \text{for } x=\frac{\pi}{2}\\ \frac{e^{-\cos x}-1}{6x-3\pi} & \text{for } x>\frac{\pi}{2}\end{cases}$; then show that $f(x)$ is discontinuous at $x = \pi/2$. Also find the type of discontinuity

SOLUTION: $\text{L.H.L} = \lim_{x\to\frac{\pi}{2}} f(x) = \lim_{x\to\left(\frac{\pi}{2}\right)^-}\frac{2\cos x-\sin 2x}{(\pi-2x)^3}$

$$= \lim_{x\to\left(\frac{\pi}{2}\right)^-}\frac{2\cos x(1-\sin x)}{(\pi-2x)^3} = \lim_{h\to 0^+}\frac{2\cos\left(\frac{\pi}{2}-h\right)[1-\sin\left(\frac{\pi}{2}-h\right)]}{(2h)^3} = \lim_{h\to 0^+}\frac{2\sin h[1-\cos h]}{(2h)^3}$$

$$= \lim_{h\to 0^+}\frac{2}{8}\frac{\sin h}{h}.\frac{2\sin^2 h/2}{4\left(\frac{h^2}{4}\right)} = \lim_{h\to 0^+}\frac{1}{8}(1)(1)^2 = \frac{1}{8}$$

$$\text{R.H.L} = \lim_{x\to\frac{\pi}{2}^+} f(x) = \lim_{x\to\left(\frac{\pi}{2}\right)^+} \frac{e^{-\cos x}-1}{6x-3\pi} = \lim_{h\to 0^+} \frac{e^{-\cos\left(\frac{\pi}{2}+h\right)}-1}{(6h)} = \lim_{h\to 0^+} \frac{e^{\sin h}-1}{6h} = \frac{1}{6}$$

$\therefore$ L.H.L $\neq$ R.H.L

$\therefore$ $f(x)$ has a jump non-removable discontinuity at $x = \pi/2$

Also $f\left(\frac{\pi}{2}\right) = \frac{1}{6}$

$\therefore$ R.H.L. $= f\left(\frac{\pi}{2}\right) \neq$ L.H.L.

$\Rightarrow$ $f(x)$ is left discontinuous and right continuous.

TEXTUAL EXERCISE–1: (SUBJECTIVE)

1. Discuss the continuity of the following functions $f(x)$ at referred points:

(a) $f(x) = \begin{cases} \dfrac{e^{1/x}-1}{e^{1/x}+1}; & x \neq 0 \\ -1 \quad ; & x = 0 \end{cases}$, at $x = 0$

(b) $f(x) = \begin{cases} \dfrac{[x^2]-1}{x^2-1}; & x^2 \neq 1 \\ 0 & ; x^2 = 1 \end{cases}$, at $x = \pm 1$

(c) $f(x) = \begin{cases} \dfrac{a^{2[x]+\{x\}}-1}{2[x]+\{x\}}; & x \neq 0 \\ \log_e a & ; x = 0 \end{cases}$ at $x = 0$; $[x]$ denotes integer part of x.

2. Find p and $f(0)$ if $f(x) = \begin{cases} \dfrac{(\sin(3p-1)x)}{3x}; & x < 0 \\ \dfrac{(\tan(3p+1)x)}{2x}; & x > 0 \end{cases}$ is continuous at $x = 0$.

3. Let $f(x) = \begin{cases} \dfrac{1-\sin \pi x}{1+\cos 2\pi x} & ; \ x < \dfrac{1}{2} \\ p & ; \ x = \dfrac{1}{2} \\ \dfrac{\sqrt{2x-1}}{\sqrt{4+\sqrt{2x-1}}-2} & ; \ x > \dfrac{1}{2} \end{cases}$. Determine the value of p, if possible, so that the function is continuous at $x = 1/2$.

4. Let $[x]$ denote the greatest integer function and $f(x)$ be defined in a neighbourhood of 2 by

$$f(x) = \begin{cases} \dfrac{(\exp\{(x+2)\ell n 4\})^{\frac{[x+1]}{4}} - 16}{4x-16} & ; x < 2 \\ a\dfrac{1-\cos(x-2)}{(x-2)\tan(x-2)} & ; x > 2 \end{cases};$$

Find the values of a and $f(2)$ in order that $f(x)$ may be continuous at $x = 2$.

5. The function

$$f(x) = \begin{cases} \left(\dfrac{6}{5}\right)^{\frac{\tan 6x}{\tan 5x}} & \text{if } 0 < x < \dfrac{\pi}{2} \\ b+2 & \text{if } x = \dfrac{\pi}{2} \\ \left(1+|\cos x|\right)^{\left(\frac{a|\tan x|}{b}\right)} & \text{if } \dfrac{\pi}{2} < x < \pi \end{cases};$$

Determine the values of $'a'$ and $'b'$, if f is continuous at $x = \pi/2$.

6. Let $f(x) = \begin{cases} x^2 \sin\dfrac{1}{x} & \text{if } x \neq 0 \\ 0 & \text{if } x = 0 \end{cases}$. Use squeeze play theorem to prove that f is continuous at $x = 0$.

7. Determine a and b so that f is continuous at $x=\dfrac{\pi}{2}$;

$$f(x)=\begin{cases}\dfrac{1-\sin^3 x}{3\cos^2 x} & \text{if } x<\dfrac{\pi}{2}\\ a & \text{if } x=\dfrac{\pi}{2}\\ \dfrac{b(1-\sin x)}{(\pi-2x)^2} & \text{if } x>\dfrac{\pi}{2}\end{cases}$$

8. Determine the values of a, b and c for which the function $f(x)=\begin{cases}\dfrac{\sin(a+1)x+\sin x}{x} & \text{for } x<0\\ c & \text{for } x=0\\ \dfrac{(x+bx^2)^{1/2}-x^{1/2}}{bx^{3/2}} & \text{for } x>0\end{cases}$ is continuous at $x = 0$.

9. Find the locus of (a, b) for which the function $f(x)=\begin{cases}ax-b & \text{for } x\le 1\\ 3x & \text{for } 1<x<2\\ bx^2-a & \text{for } x\ge 2\end{cases}$ is continuous at $x = 1$ but discontinuous at $x = 2$.

10. The function $f(x)=\left(\dfrac{2+\cos x}{x^3\sin x}-\dfrac{3}{x^4}\right)$ is not defined at $x = 0$. How should the function be defined at $x = 0$ to make it continuous at $x = 0$?

11. Let

$$f(x)=\begin{cases}\dfrac{\left(\dfrac{\pi}{2}-\sin^{-1}(1-\{x\}^2)\right).\sin^{-1}(1-\{x\})}{\sqrt{2}(\{x\}-\{x\}^3)} & \text{for } x\neq 0\\ \dfrac{\pi}{2} & \text{for } x=0\end{cases}$$

where $\{x\}$ is the fractional part of x. Consider another function $g(x)$; such that $g(x)=\begin{cases}f(x) & \text{for } x\ge 0\\ 2\sqrt{2}f(x) & \text{for } x<0\end{cases}$. Discuss the continuity of the functions $f(x)$ and $g(x)$ at $x = 0$.

12. State the type of discontinuity of the following function and at $x = 0$

(i) $f(x)=\dfrac{1}{1+2^{\cot x}}$ (ii) $f(x)=\cos\left(\dfrac{|\sin x|}{x}\right)$

(iii) $f(x)=x\sin\dfrac{\pi}{x}$ (iv) $f(x)=\dfrac{1}{\ell n|x|}$

13. Determine the constants a, b and c for which the function $f(x)=\begin{cases}(1+ax)^{1/x} & \text{for } x<0\\ b & \text{for } x=0\\ \dfrac{(x+c)^{1/3}-1}{(x+1)^{1/2}-1} & \text{for } x>0\end{cases}$ is continuous at $x = 0$.

14. Discuss the continuity of the function $f(x)=\begin{cases}\dfrac{e^{1/(x-1)}-2}{e^{1/(x-1)}+2}; & x\neq 1\\ 1 & ; x=1\end{cases}$; at $x = 1$.

Answer Keys

1. (a) function is not continuous at $x = 0$ (b) function is not continuous at $x = 1$
   (c) function is not continuous at $x = 0$
2. $p = -5/3$ and $f(0) = -2$
3. p is not possible
4. $a = 1$ and $f(2) = 1/2$
5. $a = 0$ and $b = -1$
7. $a = 1/2$ and $b = 4$
8. $a = -3/2$, $b \neq 0$, $c = 1/2$
9. locus of (a, b) is $y = x - 3$ excluding the points where $y = 3$ intersects it
10. 1/60
11. $f(0^+)=\dfrac{\pi}{2}; f(0^-)=\dfrac{\pi}{4\sqrt{2}} \Rightarrow f$ is discontinuous at $x = 0$

    $g(0^+)=g(0^-)=g(0)=\dfrac{\pi}{2} \Rightarrow g$ is continuous at $x = 0$
12. (i) Non- removable (ii) Removable (iii) Removable (iv) Removable
13. $a=\ell n\dfrac{2}{3}; b=\dfrac{2}{3}; c=1$
14. Discontinuous at $x = 1$; $f(1^+) = 1$ and $f(1^-) = -1$

TEXTUAL EXERCISE–1: (OBJECTIVE)

1. Which of the following cannot be the reason of discontinuity of a function at a point $x = c$?

(a) $\lim\limits_{x\to c} f(x)$ doesn't exist i.e., $\lim\limits_{x\to c^-} f(x) \neq \lim\limits_{x\to c^+} f(x)$ or at least one is infinite

(b) $f(x)$ is not defined at $x = c$

(c) $\lim\limits_{x\to c} f(x) \neq f(c)$

(d) $f(x)$ is a polynomial of very extremely large degree

2. A function $f(x)$ is defined as $f(x) = \dfrac{\cos(\sin x) - \cos x}{x^2}$, $x \neq 0$, $f(0) = a$. If $f(x)$ is continuous at $x = 0$, then 'a' is equal to

(a) 0 (b) 4

(c) 5 (d) 6

3. The function $f(x) = [x]^2 - [x^2]$ (where $[y]$ is the greatest integer less than or equal to y), is discontinuous at

(a) all integers

(b) all integers except 0 and 1

(c) all integers except 0

(d) all integers except 1

4. Let $f(x) = \left|\left(x + \dfrac{1}{2}\right)[x]\right|$ when $-2 \leq x \leq 2$, then

(a) $f(x)$ is continuous at $x = 2$

(b) $f(x)$ is continuous at $x = 1$

(c) $f(x)$ is continuous at $x = -1$

(d) $f(x)$ is discontinuous at $x = 0$

5. If $f(x) = \lim\limits_{m\to\infty} \dfrac{x^m f(1) + h(x) + 1}{2x^m + 3x + 3}$ and $g(1) = \lim\limits_{x\to 1}\{\log_e(ex)\}^{2/\log_e x}$ and it is assumed that $f(x)$ and $h(x)$ are continuous at $x = 1$, then $2g(1) + 2f(1) - h(1)$ equals

(a) $2e^2 - 1$ (b) $2e^2 + 1$

(c) $1 + 2e^2$ (d) $2 + e^2$

6. If $f(x) = \begin{cases} 1 - 2x; x < 0 \\ 2; x = 0 \\ x^2 + 2; x > 0 \end{cases}$, then at $x = 0$

(a) f is continuous

(b) f is continuous from left

(c) f has a jump discontinuity

(d) f has a removable discontinuity

7. Let $f(x) = \begin{cases} \tan\dfrac{\pi x}{2}; x < 1 \\ x - 1; 1 \leq x < 2 \\ \dfrac{1}{2 - x}; x \geq 2 \end{cases}$, then at $x = 1$, f has a

(a) Jump discontinuity

(b) Removable discontinuity

(c) Infinite discontinuity

(d) No discontinuity

8. Let $f(x) = \begin{cases} x^2; x \leq 0 \\ 2; 0 < x < 1 \\ \dfrac{\sin(x-1)}{x-1}; x \geq 1 \end{cases}$; Then at $x = 0$, f has

(a) Finite irremovable discontinuity (or jump discontinuity)

(b) Removable discontinuity

(c) Infinite discontinuity

(d) No discontinuity

9. The function $f(x) = |2 \sin 2x| + 2$ has at $x = 0$

(a) Jump discontinuity

(b) Removable discontinuity

(c) Infinite discontinuity

(d) No discontinuity

10. Let $f(x) = \sin\dfrac{1}{x}$, then at $x = 0$, f has

(a) Finite irremovable discontinuity

(b) Removable discontinuity

(c) Oscillatory discontinuity

(d) No discontinuity

11. The jump of discontinuity of the function at the point of discontinuity i.e., $x = -2$ of the function $f(x) = \dfrac{|x+2|}{\tan^{-1}(x+2)}$ is

(a) 2 (b) –2

(c) 0 (d) 1

12. Indicate the correct alternative(s): The function defined as $f(x) = \lim\limits_{n\to\infty} \dfrac{\cos \pi x - x^{2n} \sin(x-1)}{1 + x^{2n+1} - x^{2n}}$

(a) is discontinuous at $x = 1$ because $f(1^+) \neq f(1^-)$

(b) is discontinuous at $x = 1$ because $f(1)$ is not defined

(c) is discontinuous at $x = 1$ because $f(1^+) = f(1^-) \neq f(1)$

(d) is continuous at $x = 1$

13. Let $g(x) = \tan^{-1}|x| - \cot^{-1}|x|$, $f(x) = \frac{[x]}{[x+1]}\{x\}$, $h(x) = |g(f(x))|$, where $\{x\}$ denotes fractional part and $[x]$ denotes the integral part, then which of the following holds good?

(a) h is continuous at $x = 0$

(b) h is discontinuous at $x = 0$

(c) $h(0) = \frac{\pi}{2}$

(d) $h(0^+) = -\frac{\pi}{2}$

14. Consider $f(x) = \underset{n\to\infty}{Limit}\ \frac{x^n - \sin x^n}{x^n + \sin x^n}$ for $x > 0$, $x \neq 1$; $f(1) = 0$, then

(a) f is continuous at $x = 1$

(b) f has a finite discontinuity at $x = 1$

(c) f has an infinite or oscillatory discontinuity at $x = 1$

(d) f has a removable type of discontinuity at $x = 1$

15. Given $f(x) = \begin{cases} \dfrac{[\{|x|\}]\, e^{x^2}\{[x+\{x\}]\}}{\left(e^{\frac{1}{x^2}} - 1\right)\operatorname{sgn}(\sin x)} & \text{for } x \neq 0 \\ 0 & \text{for } x = 0 \end{cases}$;

where $\{x\}$ is the fractional part function; $[x]$ is the step up function and $\operatorname{sgn}(x)$ is the signum function of x then, $f(x)$

(a) is continuous at $x = 0$

(b) is discontinuous at $x = 0$

(c) has a removable discontinuity at $x = 0$

(d) has an irremovable discontinuity at $x = 0$

16. Consider $f(x) = \begin{cases} x[x]^2 \log_{(1+x)} 2 & \text{for } -1 < x < 0 \\ \dfrac{\ln\left(e^{x^2} + 2\sqrt{\{x\}}\right)}{\tan\sqrt{x}} & \text{for } 0 < x < 1 \end{cases}$;

where [*] and {*} are the greatest integer function and fractional part function respectively, then

(a) $f(0) = ln2 \Rightarrow f$ is continuous at $x = 0$

(b) $f(0) = 2 \Rightarrow f$ is continuous at $x = 0$

(c) $f(0) = e^2 \Rightarrow f$ is continuous at $x = 0$

(d) f has an irremovable discontinuity at $x = 0$

17. Consider $f(x) = \frac{\sqrt{1+x} - \sqrt{1-x}}{\{x\}}$ for $x \neq 0$;

$g(x) = \cos 2x$ for $-\frac{\pi}{4} < x < 0$ and

$h(x) = \begin{cases} \frac{1}{\sqrt{2}} f(g(x)) & \text{for } x < 0 \\ 1 & \text{for } x = 0 \\ f(x) & \text{for } x > 0 \end{cases}$; where $\{x\}$

denotes fractional part function, then which of the following holds good.

(a) 'h' is continuous at $x = 0$

(b) 'h' is discontinuous at $x = 0$

(c) $f(g(x))$ is an even function

(d) $f(x)$ is an even function

18. Consider the function $f(x) = \begin{cases} \frac{x}{[x]} & \text{if } 1 \le x < 2 \\ 1 & \text{if } x = 2 \\ \sqrt{6-x} & \text{if } 2 < x \le 3 \end{cases}$;

where $[x]$ denotes step up function, then at $x = 2$ function

(a) has missing point removable discontinuity

(b) has isolated point removable discontinuity

(c) has non-removable discontinuity finite type

(d) is continuous

19. For the function $f(x) = \frac{1}{x + 2^{\frac{1}{(x-2)}}}$, $x \neq 2$ which of the following holds?

(a) $f(2) = 1/2$ and f is continuous at $x = 2$

(b) $f(2) \neq 0$, $1/2$ and f is continuous at $x = 2$

(c) f cannot be continuous at $x = 2$

(d) $f(2) = 0$ and f is continuous at $x = 2$.

20. The function $f(x)$ is defined by

$f(x) = \begin{cases} \log_{(4x-3)}(x^2 - 2x + 5) & \text{if } \frac{3}{4} < x < 1 \text{ or } x > 1 \\ 4 & \text{if } x = 1 \end{cases}$

(a) is continuous at $x = 1$

(b) is discontinuous at $x = 1$ since $f(1^+)$ does not exist though $f(1^-)$ exists.

(c) is discontinuous at $x = 1$ since $f(1^-)$ does not exist though $f(1^+)$ exists.

(d) is discontinuous since neither $f(1^-)$ nor $f(1^+)$ exists.

Answer Keys

1. (d)	**2.** (a)	**3.** (d)	**4.** (d)	**5.** (c)	**6.** (c)	**7.** (c)	**8.** (a)	**9.** (d)	**10.** (c)
11. (a)	**12.** (a)	**13.** (b)	**14.** (b)	**15.** (a)	**16.** (d)	**17.** (a)	**18.** (b)	**19.** (c)	**20.** (d)

■ ALGEBRA OF CONTINUITY

If $f(x)$ and $g(x)$ are two continuous functions i.e., $f(a^+) = f(a^-) = f(a)$; $g(a^+) = g(a^-) = g(a)$, then following results always hold good.

1. $kf(x)$ is continuous at $x = a$ (k is finite real constant)
2. $f(x) \pm g(x)$ is continuous at $x = a$
3. $f(x) . g(x)$ is also continuous at $x = a$
4. $\dfrac{f(x)}{g(x)}$ is also continuous at $x = a$ iff $g(a) \neq 0$
5. The sum of a finite number of functions continuous at a point is a continuous function at that point.

Proof: Let $f_1, f_2 \ldots\ldots f_n$ be n – continuous functions at a point $x = a$. We have to prove that their sum $g = f_1 + f_2 + \ldots + f_n$ is a continuous function at $x = a$. The functions $f_1 f_2, \ldots. f_n$ being continuous at $x = a$ we have,

$$\lim_{x\to a} f_1(x) = f_1(a); \lim_{x\to a} f_2(x) = f_2(a), \ldots, \lim_{x\to a} f_n(x) = f_n(a)$$

Now, $\lim_{x\to a} g(x) = \lim_{x\to a}(f_1 + f_2 + \ldots\ldots + f_n)(x)$

$$= \lim_{x\to a}\{f_1(x) + f_2(x) + \ldots\ldots + f_n(x)\}$$

$$= \lim_{x\to a} f_1(x) + \lim_{x\to a} f_2(x) + \ldots\ldots + \lim_{x\to a} f_n(x)$$

($\because$ limit of sum = sum of limits)

$= f_1(a) + f_2(a) + \ldots + f_n(a) = (f_1 + f_2 + f_3 + \ldots. + f_n)(a) = g(a)$

Thus $\lim_{x\to a} g(x) = g(a)$. Hence $g(x)$ is continuous at $x = a$.

Thus we can definitely say $f(x) = \sin x + e^x + x^2$; $f(x) = x^3 + 2x^2 + x$ are continuous at each real number since $\sin x$, e^x, x^2, x^3, x all are continuous at each real number.

> **REMARK:**
>
> *From the above theorem it is obvious that difference of finite number of continuous functions at x = a, is also continuous at x = a.*

6. The product of a finite number of functions continuous at a point is a continuous function at that point.

   Proof: Let $g(x) = (f_1.f_2.f_3 \ldots\ldots. f_n)(x)$; where $f_1(x)$, $f_2(x) \ldots.., f_n(x)$ are continuous functions at $x = a$

   $\therefore \lim_{x\to a} f_1(x) = f_1(a); \lim_{x\to a} f_2(x) = f_2(a), \ldots..,$

   $\lim_{x\to a} f_n(x) = f_n(a)$

   $\therefore \lim_{x\to a} g(x) = \lim_{x\to a} f_1(x). \lim_{x\to a} f_2(x) \ldots\ldots. \lim_{x\to a} f_n(x)$

   (By theorem of product of limits)

   $= f_1(a).f_2(a) \ldots f_n(a)$

   $= (f_1 f_2 f_3 \ldots f_n)(a) = g(a)$

   Thus $g(x)$ is continuous at $x = a$

7. If $\{f_1, f_2, f_3, \ldots.., f_n\}$ and $\{g_1, g_2, g_3, \ldots\ldots\ldots., g_n\}$ are two sets of continuous functions at $x = a$, such that $g_i(a) \neq 0$ for any i, then $\dfrac{f_{k_1}}{g_{m_1}}.\dfrac{f_{k_2}}{g_{m_2}}.\dfrac{f_{k_3}}{g_{m_3}}\ldots..\dfrac{f_{k_n}}{g_{m_n}}$ is continuous at $x = a$, where $k_i, m_i \in \{1, 2, 3, \ldots, n\}$

   Proof: Let $h_{t_i} = \dfrac{f_{k_i}}{g_{m_i}}$; then

   $$\lim_{x\to a} h_{t_i}(x) = \lim_{x\to a}\left(\frac{f_{k_i}}{g_{m_i}}\right)(x) = \lim_{x\to a}\frac{f_{k_i}(x)}{g_{m_i}(x)}$$

   $$= \frac{\lim_{x\to a} f_{k_i}(x)}{\lim_{x\to a} g_{m_i}(x)} = \frac{f_{k_i}(a)}{g_{m_i}(a)} = \left(\frac{f_{k_i}}{g_{m_i}}\right)(a) = h_{t_i}(a)$$

   ($\because$ By limit of quotient equals quotient of limits provided limit of denominator is not zero)

   Thus h_{t_i} is continuous $\forall_i$

   $\therefore$ By continuity of product of finitely many functions at $x = a$, $(h_{t_1}.h_{t_2}.h_{t_3} \ldots\ldots. h_{t_n})$ is continuous at $x = a$.

8. (Chain rule for continuity or continuity of composite functions). If $f(x)$ is continuous at $x = a$ and $g(y)$ is continuous at $y = f(a)$, then the composite function $(gof)(x)$ is continuous at $x = a$

Proof: Let $u = f(x)$, thus $y = gof(x) = g(f(x)) = g(u)$, where $f(x)$ is continuous at $x = a$ and $g(u)$ is continuous at $u = b = f(a)$. We have to prove that $y = gof(x))$ is continuous at the point a.

$\lim_{x\to a} gof(x) = \lim_{u\to b} g(u)$, as $f(x)$ is continuous at $x = a$

thus $x \to a \Rightarrow f(x) \to f(a)$ i.e., $u \to b$

$\therefore$ $\lim_{x\to a} gof(x) = g(b) = g(f(a)) = gof(a)$; as $g(u)$ is continuous at $u = b$

$\therefore$ $x \to a \Rightarrow gof(x) \to gof(a)$

$\Rightarrow$ gof is continuous at $x = a$

For example, $f(x) = \cos x$ is continuous at $x = \pi/2$ and $g(x) = \begin{cases} x^2 - 4, & x \le 0 \\ x - 4, & x > 0 \end{cases}$ is continuous at $x = f(\pi/2) = 0$. Hence the composite function $(gof)(x)$ is continuous at $x = \pi/2$

REMARKS:

(i) *Let a function f(x) be continuous at all points in the interval [a,b] and let its range be the interval [m, M] and further the function g(x) be contininuous in the interval [m, M], then the composite function (gof) (x) is continuous in the interval [a, b].*

(ii) *If the function f is continuous everywhere and the function g is continuous everywhere, then the composition gof is continuous everywhere.*

(iii) *All polynomials, trigonometric functions, inverse trigonometric functions exponential and logarithmic functions are continuous at all points in their respective domains.*

(iv) *If f(x) is continuous at x = a, then |f(x)| is also continuous at x = a.*

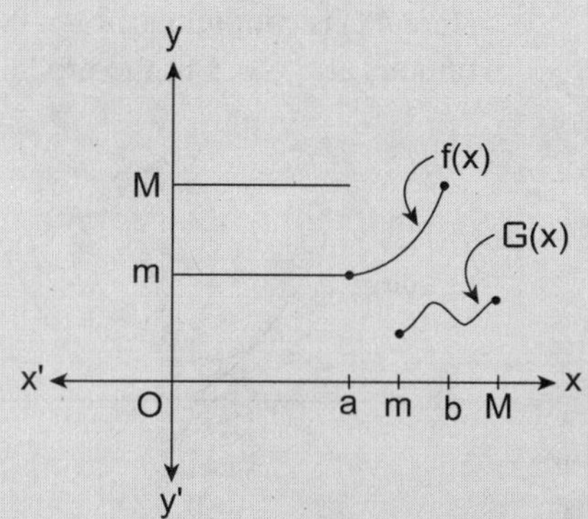

FIGURE 2.32

Proof: *Let* $\lim_{x\to a} f(x) = f(a)$

Then $\lim_{x\to a} |f(x)| = \lim_{f(x)\to f(a)} |f(x)|$ *(∵ f(x) continuous at x = a, x → a ⇒ f(x) → f(a))*

$= \lim_{u\to f(a)} |u|$ *; where u = f(x)*

= |f(a)| as |x| is a continuous function at every real number

For example, $f(x) = \dfrac{e^x \cos x}{x^2+4}$ *and g(x) = |x| are continuous for all x. Hence the composite function (gof)* $(x) = \left|\dfrac{e^x \cos x}{x^2+4}\right|$ *is also continuous for all x.*

9. Sum of the two discontinuous functions may be continuous.

Proof: $f(a^-) = l_1, f(a^+) = l_2$

$g(a^-) = l_3$ and $g(a^+) = l_4$

If $l_1 + l_3 = l_2 + l_4$ then this is possible

e.g., $f(x) = \{x\}$, $g(x) = [x]$ are both discontinuous at $x = 2$ as $\text{Lt}_{x\to 2^-} f(x) = \text{Lt}_{x\to 2^-} \{x\} = 1$; $\text{Lt}_{x\to 2^+} \{x\} = 0$ and

$\text{Lt}_{x\to 2^-} g(x) = \text{Lt}_{x\to 2^-} [x] = 1$; $\text{Lt}_{x\to 2^+} [x] = 2$

but $f(x) + g(x) = [x] + \{x\} = x$

i.e., $\text{Lt}_{x\to 2^-} (f+g)x = \text{Lt}_{x\to 2^+} (f+g)(x) = 2$

10. Summation of a continuous and a discontinuous function is always discontinuous.

If $f(a^-) = f(a^+) = f(a) = l$ and $g(a^-) = l_1$, $g(a^+) = l_2 = g(a)$

Let $h(x) = f(x) + g(x)$, then $h(a^-) = l + l_1$, and $h(a^+) = l + l_2$ clearly $h(a)$ is discontinuous.

For example, consider $f(x) = x$ and $g(x) = \{x\}$. Here $f(x)$ is continuous at $x = 0$ and $g(x)$ is discontinuous at $x = 0$. Both the sum function $x + \{x\}$ and the difference function $x - \{x\}$ are discontinuous at $x = 0$.

11. Product of a continuous function with a discontinuous function may be continuous and this is possible only when the continuous function attains zero at that point.

Proof: Let $f(x)$ be continuous and $g(x)$ be discontinuous at $x = a$

$\Rightarrow f(a^-) = l, f(a^+) = l; g(a^-) = l_1, g(a^+) = l_2$ and $l_1 \neq l_2$

Let $h(x) = f(x) \,.\, g(x) \Rightarrow h(a^+) = f(a^+) \,.\, g(a^+) = l\,l_2$

and $h(a^-) = f(a^-) \,.\, g(a^-) = l\,l_1$

Now, $\ell\, l_2 = l\,l_1$ gives $l(l_2 - l_1) = 0$

But $l_2 \neq l_1 \Rightarrow l = 0$. Thus the product of a continuous and discontinuous function can be continuous, provided the limit of continuous function is zero.

For example:

(i) Consider, $f(x) = x^3$ and $g(x) = \text{sgn}(x)$
Here $f(x)$ is continuous at $x = 0$, and $g(x)$ is discontinuous at $x = 0$. But the product function

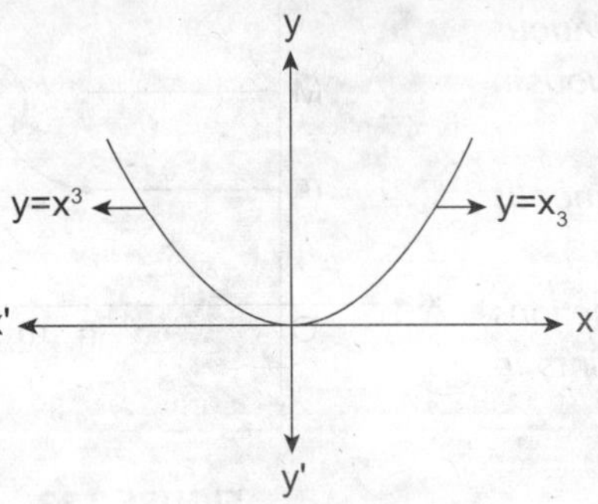

FIGURE 2.33

$$h(x) = f(x).g(x) = \begin{cases} x^3, & x > 0 \\ 0, & x = 0 \\ -x^3, & x < 0 \end{cases}$$ is continuous at $x = 0$ as shown in graph given below

(ii) Product of $f(x)$ and $g(x)$ where $f(x) = x$ and $$g(x) = \begin{cases} \sin\dfrac{1}{x} \,; & x \neq 0 \\ 0 \,; & x = 0 \end{cases}$$ is continuous at $x = 0$ even when $f(x)$ is continuous at $x = 0$ and $g(x)$ is discontinuous at $x = 0$

(iii) However, the product of the function $f(x) = x$ and $g(x) = [x]$ is discontinuous at $x = 1$

$\because \lim\limits_{x\to 1^-} x[x] = (1)(0) = 0; \& \lim\limits_{x\to 1^+} x[x] = (1)(1) = 1$

12. Quotient of a continuous and discontinuous function may be continuous, may be discontinuous

For example

(i) $f(x) = x(x^2 - 4)$ and $g(x) = \begin{cases} x+2, & x \geq 0 \\ x-2, & x < 0 \end{cases}$;

$$\lim_{x\to 0^-} \frac{f(x)}{g(x)} = \lim_{x\to 0^-} x(x+2) = 0;$$

$$\lim_{x\to 0^+} \frac{f(x)}{g(x)} = \lim_{x\to 0^-} x(x-2) = 0. \text{ Also } \frac{f}{g}(0) = 0$$

Therefore $\dfrac{f}{g}(x)$ is continuous at $x = 0$

(ii) $f(x) = (x^2 - 4)$ and $g(x) = \begin{cases} x+2; x \geq 0 \\ x-2; x < 0 \end{cases}$

Clearly $f(x)$ is continuous and $g(x)$ is discontinuous at $x = 0$,

But $$\lim_{x\to 0^-} \frac{f}{g}(x) = \frac{\lim\limits_{x\to 0^-} f(x)}{\lim\limits_{x\to 0^-} g(x)} = \lim_{x\to 0^-} \frac{x^2 - 4}{(x-2)} = 2$$ and

$$\lim_{x\to 0^+} \frac{f}{g}(x) = \lim_{x\to 0^+} \frac{f(x)}{g(x)} = \lim_{x\to 0^+} \frac{x^2 - 4}{x+2} = -2$$

$\therefore$ f/g is discontinuous at $x = 0$

ILLUSTRATION 13: Given the function $f(x) = \dfrac{1}{1-x}$. Find the points of discontinuity of the composite function $y = f\{f[f(x)]\}$

SOLUTION: The point $x = 1$ is a discontinuity of the function $v = f(x) = \dfrac{1}{1-x}$

If $x \neq 1$, then $u = f[f(x)] = \dfrac{1}{1 - 1/(1-x)} = \dfrac{(x-1)}{x}$

Hence, the point $x = 0$ is discontinuity of the function $u = f[f(x)]$

If $x \neq 0, x \neq 1$, then $y = f\{f[f(x)]\} = \dfrac{1}{1-(x-1)/x} = x$ is continuous everywhere

Thus , the points of discontinuity of this composite function are $x = 0$, $x = 1$, both of them being removable.

ILLUSTRATION 14: Let $f(x) = \begin{cases} 1+x; & 0 \le x \le 2 \\ 3-x; & 2 < x \le 3 \end{cases}$. Determine the form of $g(x) = f(f(x))$ and hence find the point of discontinuity of g, if any.

SOLUTION: $g(x) = f(f(x)) = \begin{cases} 1+x; & 0 \le x \le 2 \\ 3-x; & 2 < x \le 3 \end{cases} = \begin{cases} f(1+x); & 0 \le x \le 1 \\ f(1+x); & 1 \le x \le 2 \\ f(3-x); & 2 < x \le 3 \end{cases}$

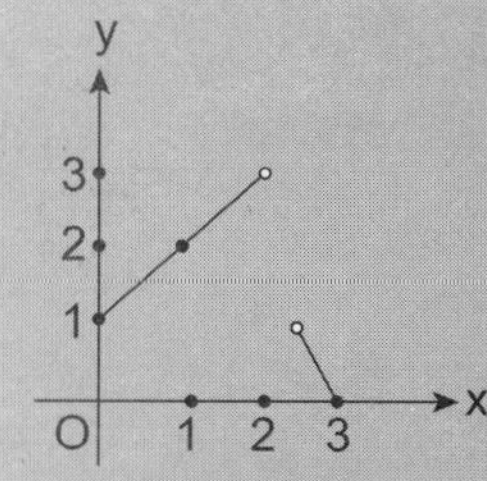

FIGURE 2.34

$x \in [0, 1] \quad \Rightarrow (1 + x) \in [1, 2]$

$x \in [1, 2] \quad \Rightarrow (1 + x) \in [2, 3]$

$x \in [2, 3] \quad \Rightarrow (3 + x) \in [0, 1]$

Hence, $g(x) = \begin{cases} f(1+x); & 0 \le x \le 1 \Rightarrow 1 \le x+1 \le 2 \\ f(1+x); & 1 \le x \le 2 \Rightarrow 2 \le x+1 \le 3 \\ f(3-x); & 2 < x \le 3 \Rightarrow 0 \le 3-x \le 1 \end{cases}$

Now if $(1 + x) \in [1, 2]$ then $f(1+x) = 1 + (1 + x) = 2 + x$ ..(i)

(from original definition of $f(x)$]

Similarly if $(1+x) \in (2, 3)$ then $f(1+x) = 3 - (1 + x) = 2 - x$ ...(ii)

if $(3 - x) \le (0, 1)$ then $f(3 - x) = 1 + (3 - x) = 4 - x$ ...(iii)

Using (i), (ii) and (iii), we get $g(x) = \begin{cases} 2+x; & 0 \le x < 1 \\ 2-x; & 1 < x \le 2 \\ 4-x; & 2 < x \le 3 \end{cases}$

Now we will check the continuity of $g(x)$ at $x = 1, 2$

At $x = 1$; LHL $= \lim\limits_{x \to 1^-} g(x) = \lim\limits_{x \to 1^-}(2+x) = 3$

RHL $= \lim\limits_{x \to 1^+} g(x) = \lim\limits_{x \to 1^+}(2-x) = 1$

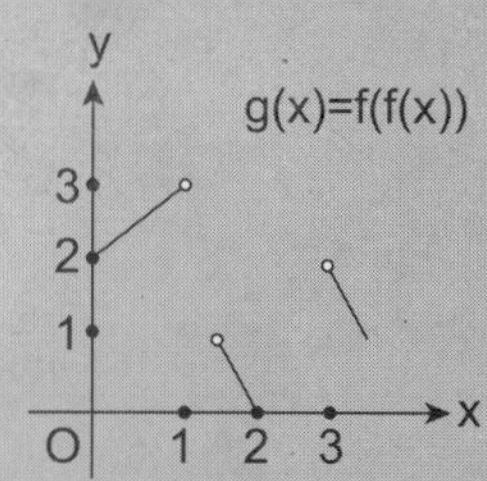

FIGURE 2.35

As LHL ≠ RHL, $g(x)$ is discontinuous at $x = 1$

At $x = 2$; LHL $= \lim\limits_{x \to 2^-} g(x) = \lim\limits_{x \to 2^-}(2-x) = 0$

RHL $= \lim\limits_{x \to 2^+} g(x) = \lim\limits_{x \to 2^+}(4-x) = 2$

As LHL ≠ RHL, $g(x)$ is discontinuous at $x = 2$

Thus , $g(x)$ is discontinuous at $x = 1$ and 2

Aliter Method:

$g(x) = \begin{cases} f(1+x); & 0 \le x \le 1 \Rightarrow 1 \le x+1 \le 2 \\ f(1+x); & 1 \le x \le 2 \Rightarrow 2 \le x+1 \le 3 \\ f(3-x); & 2 < x \le 3 \Rightarrow 0 \le 3-x \le 1 \end{cases}$

$g(x) = \left\{\begin{matrix} 2+x, & 0 \le x \le 1 \\ 2-x, & 1 \le x \le 2 \\ 4-x, & 2 < x \le 3 \end{matrix}\right\}$

ILLUSTRATION 15: Find the points of discontinuity of $y = \frac{1}{u^2 + u - 2}$ where $u = \frac{1}{x-1}$.

SOLUTION: The function $u = f(x) = \frac{1}{x-1}$ is discontinuous at this point $x = 1$ ....(i)

The function $y = g(x) = \frac{1}{u^2 + u - 2} = \frac{1}{(u+2)(u-1)}$ is discontinuous at $u = -2$ and $u = 1$,

when $u = -2$, $\frac{1}{x-1} = u = 2$

$\Rightarrow x - 1 = -1/2$ $\Rightarrow x = 1/2$ ....(ii)

when $u = 1$, $\frac{1}{x-1} = u = 1$

$\Rightarrow x - 1 = 1$ $\Rightarrow x = 2$ ....(iii)

Hence the composite function $y = g(f(x))$ is discontinuous at three points $x = 1/2, 1, 2$

ILLUSTRATION 16: If $f(x) = \frac{x+1}{x-1}$ and $g(x) = \frac{1}{x-2}$, then discuss the continuity of $f(x)$, $g(x)$ and log (x)

SOLUTION: $f(x) = \frac{x+1}{x-1}$. $f(x)$ is a rational function it must be continuous in its domain and f is not defined at $x = 1$

$\therefore$ f is discontinuous at $x = 2$

$g(x) = \frac{1}{x-2}$, $g(x)$ is also a rational function. It must be continuous in its domain and g s not defined at $x = 2$

$\therefore$ g is discontinuous at $x = 2$.

Now fog (x) will be discontinuous at

(i) $x = 2$ (point of discontinuity of $g(x)$)

(ii) $g(x) = 1$ (when $g(x)$ = point of discontinuity of $f(x)$)

$\Rightarrow \frac{1}{x-2} = 1 \quad \Rightarrow x = 3$

$\therefore$ Discontinuity of fog (x) should be checked at $x = 2$ and $x = 3$ fog $(x) = \dfrac{\frac{1}{x-2}+1}{\frac{1}{x-2}-1}$

fog(2) is not defined

$$\lim_{x\to 2} \text{fog}(x) = \lim_{x\to 2} \frac{\frac{1}{x-2}+1}{\frac{1}{x-2}-1} = \lim_{x\to 2} \frac{1+x-2}{1-x+2} = 1$$

$\therefore$ fog (x) is discontinuous at $x = 2$ and it is removable discontinuity at $x = 2$fog (3) = not defined

$$\lim_{x\to 3^+} fog(x) = \lim_{x\to 3^+} \frac{\frac{1}{x-2}+1}{\frac{1}{x-2}-1} = \infty \qquad \lim_{x\to 3^-} fog(x) = \lim_{x\to 3^-} \frac{\frac{1}{x-2}+1}{\frac{1}{x-2}-1} = -\infty$$

$\therefore$ fog (x) is discontinuous at $x = 3$ and it is non-removable discontinuity of second kind.

ILLUSTRATION 17: If $f(x) = \dfrac{1}{(x-1)(x-2)}$ and $g(x) = \dfrac{1}{x^2}$, then find the points of discontinuity of $f(g(x))$.

SOLUTION: B. $f(g(x)) = \dfrac{}{\left(\dfrac{1}{x^2}-1\right)\left(\dfrac{1}{x^2}-2\right)}\quad \dfrac{}{(1-x^2)(1-2x^2)} = f(g(x))$ is discontinuous at

$x = \pm 1, = \pm\dfrac{1}{\sqrt{2}}$ and $x = 0$. Since $g(x)$ is discontinuous at $x = 0$.

$\therefore$ The point of discontinuity of $f(g(x))$ is $\pm\dfrac{1}{\sqrt{2}}, \pm 1, 0$

■ CONTINUITY OF A FUNCTION ON A SET

So far we studied continuity of a function $f(x)$ at a point $x = a$. Now we shall study continuity of a function on a set. A function $f(x)$ is said to be continuous on a set A if $f(x)$ is continuous at every point of set A.

For example, if $f(x) = x^2$ and $A = \mathbb{Z}$ = set of integers, then $f(x)$ is continuous at every integer point. Then $f(x)$ is continuous on set A $(=\mathbb{Z})$.

If a function has discontinuity even at single point of set A, then $f(x)$ is said to be discontinuous on set A.

For example, $f(x) = \text{sgn}(x) = \begin{cases} 1 \text{ for } x > 0 \\ 0 \text{ for } x = 0 \\ -1 \text{ for } x < 0 \end{cases}$

Then $f(x)$ is discontinuous only at single real number $x = 0$, so $f(x)$ is discontinuous on $\mathbb{R}$. A function $f(x)$ continuous on one set can be discontinuous on other set. For example, (i) If we consider fractional part the function $\{x\}$, then $\{x\}$ is continuous on (0, 1), but $\{x\}$ is discontinuous on (0, 2), as it is discontinuous at $x = 1$ and $1 \in (0, 2)$.

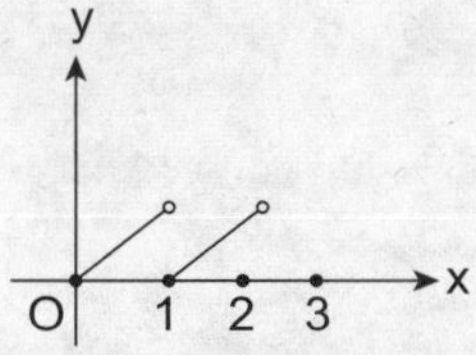

{x} continuous on (0, 1)
but discontinuous on (0, 2)

FIGURE 2.36

$\{x\}$ continuous on (0, 1) but discontinuous on (0,2)

(ii) $f(x) = \tan x$ is continuous on $\left(-\dfrac{\pi}{2}, \dfrac{\pi}{2}\right)$ but is discontinuous on $\left(-\dfrac{\pi}{2}, \dfrac{3\pi}{2}\right)$ as $\tan x$ discontinuous at $x = \pi/2$ and $\pi/2 \in \left(-\dfrac{\pi}{2}, \dfrac{3\pi}{2}\right)$.

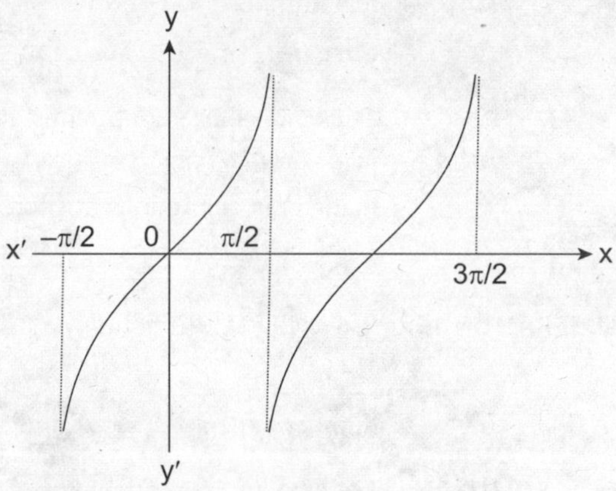

FIGURE 2.37

Domain of Continuity of Function

The set of all those points where the function $f(x)$ is continuous is called Domain of continuity of function $f(x)$. Every function is continuous on its domain of continuity.

For example:

(1) $f(x) = \tan x$, then $f(x)$ is continuous on $\mathbb{R} \sim \left\{(2n+1)\dfrac{\pi}{2}; n \in \mathbb{Z}\right\}$. Thus the set of all real numbers except for odd integer multiple of $\pi/2$ is the domain of continuity of tan x.

(2) $f(x) = \text{sgn}(x)$, then $f(x)$ is continuous at every real number except for $x = 0$. Thus $\mathbb{R} \sim \{0\}$ is the domain of continuity of sgn (x).

ILLUSTRATION 18: Prove that the function $f(x)$ defined by $f(x)=\begin{cases} x^2 & \text{for } x \le 0 \\ x & \text{for } x > 0 \end{cases}$ is continuous at each real number

SOLUTION: Let $k \in \mathbb{R}$

Case (i) $k < 0$ then $\lim\limits_{x \to k^-} f(x) = \lim\limits_{x \to k^-} x^2 = k^2$ and $\lim\limits_{x \to k^+} f(x) = \lim\limits_{x \to k^+} x^2 = k^2$. Also $f(k) = k^2$

Thus $f(x)$ is continuous at k. Since k was choosen arbitrarily, $f(x)$ is continuous at each negative real number

Case (ii) $k > 0$, then $\lim\limits_{x \to k^-} f(x) = \lim\limits_{x \to k^-} x = k$ and $\lim\limits_{x \to k^+} f(x) = \lim\limits_{x \to k^+} x = k$

Also $f(k) = k$

Thus $f(x)$ is continuous at k. Since k was choosen arbitrarily, $f(x)$ is continuous at each positive real number

Case (iii) $k = 0$, Then, $\lim\limits_{x \to k^-} f(x) = \lim\limits_{x \to 0^-} x^2 = 0$. And $\lim\limits_{x \to 0^+} f(x) = \lim\limits_{x \to 0^+} x = 0$, also $f(0) = (0)^2 = 0$

Thus $f(x)$ is also continuous at $x = 0$

From above three cases we conclude that $f(x)$ is continuous. From above three cases we conclude that $f(x)$ is continuous at each real number. Thus domain of continuity of $f(x)$ is $\mathbb{R}$

ILLUSTRATION 19: Prove that the function $f(x)$ defined by $f(x)=\begin{cases} x^2+2; -\infty < x \le 1 \\ x+1 \ ; 1 < x \le 2 \\ \sin x; 2 < x < \infty \end{cases}$ is continuous at each real number except for $x = 1$ and 2 and hence find its domain of continuity.

SOLUTION: Let k be any real number. Let us discuss following the cases depending on the nature of k

Case (i) $-\infty < k < 1$

Then $\lim\limits_{x \to k^-} f(x) = \lim\limits_{x \to k^-} x^2 + 2 = k^2 + 2$ and $\lim\limits_{x \to k^+} f(x) = \lim\limits_{x \to k^+} x^2 + 2 = k^2 + 2$

Also $f(k) = k^2 + 2$

$\therefore$ $f(x)$ is continuous at each real number less than 1

Case (ii) $1 < k < 2$ $\lim\limits_{x \to k^-} f(x) = \lim\limits_{x \to k^-} (x+1) = k+1$ and $\lim\limits_{x \to k^+} f(x) = \lim\limits_{x \to k^+} (x+1) = k+1$

Also $f(k) = k + 1$

$\therefore$ $f(x)$ is continuous at each real number between 1 and 2

Case (iii) $k > 2$; $\lim\limits_{x \to k^-} f(x) = \lim\limits_{x \to k^-} \sin x = \sin k$ and $\lim\limits_{x \to k^+} f(x) = \lim\limits_{x \to k^+} \sin x = \sin k$

and also $f(k) = \sin k$

$f(x)$ is continuous at each real number greater than 2

Case (iv) $k = 1$; then L.H.L = $\lim\limits_{x \to 1^-} f(x) = \lim\limits_{x \to 1^-} x^2 + 2 = 3$

and R.H.L = $\lim\limits_{x \to 1^+} f(x) = \lim\limits_{x \to 1^+} x + 1 = 2$, also $f(1) = (1)^2 + 2 = 3$

$\therefore$ $f(x)$ is discontinuous at $x = 1$

Case (v) $k = 2$, then L.H.L $\lim\limits_{x \to 2^-} f(x) = \lim\limits_{x \to 2^-} (x+1) = 3$

and R.H.L = $\lim\limits_{x \to 2^+} f(x) = \lim\limits_{x \to 2^+} \sin x = \sin 2$, also $f(2) = 3$

Clearly $\sin 2 \ne 3$, thus $f(x)$ is discontinuous at $k = 2$

Thus $f(x)$ is continuous at all real numbers except for $x = 1$ and $x = 2$

Thus graph of $f(x)$ is as shown below:

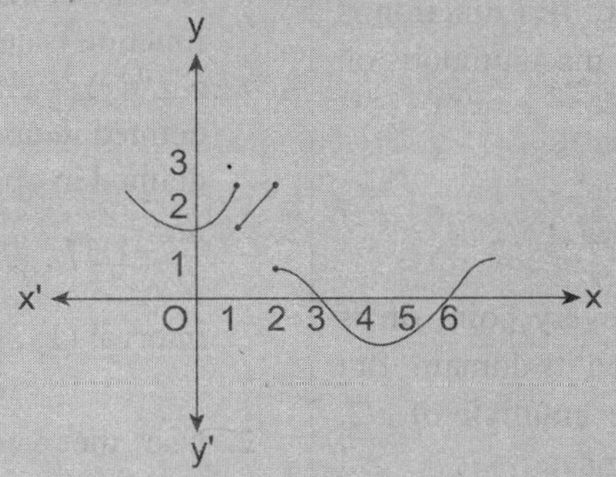

FIGURE 2.38

REMARKS:

1. *It is not necessary that every point of domain of function may belong to domain of continuity of function. For example; x = 0 is in the domain of function, but it does not belong to domain of continuity of function which is* $\mathbb{R} \sim \{0\}$
2. *As we do not talk about the continuity of function at isolated points,(i.e., point having no portion of graph in its left and right neighborhood), we never discuss about the domain of continuity of a function having each point of its domain an isolated point*

   For example, if $f(x) = \begin{cases} 2 \text{ if } x \text{ is rational} \\ -2 \text{ if } x \text{ is irrational} \end{cases}$
3. *Also we cannot discuss about the continuity of single point function (i.e., function having single point and single point in its domain and range or function defined only at single point) and domain of continuity of single point function*

   For example, if $f(x) = \sqrt{x-1} + \sqrt{1-x}$, *then domain of f(x) = {1} and range of f(x) = {0}*

Domain of Continuity of Some Standard Function

f(x)	Domain of continuity	f(x)	Domain of continuity
Polynomial $P(x)$	$\mathbb{R}$	$\sec x$	$\mathbb{R} - \{(2n+1).\frac{\pi}{2}; n \in \mathbb{Z}\}$
$\frac{P(x)}{Q(x)}$	$\mathbb{R} - \{x : Q(x) = 0\}$	$\text{cosec } x$	$\mathbb{R} - \{n\pi; n \in \mathbb{Z}\}$
$a^x; a > 0$	$\mathbb{R}$	$\sin^{-1} x$	$[-1, 1]$
$\log x$	$(0, \infty)$	$\cos^{-1} x$	$[-1, 1]$
$\sin x$	$\mathbb{R}$	$\tan^{-1} x$	$\mathbb{R}$
$\cos x$	$\mathbb{R}$	$\cot^{-1} x$	$\mathbb{R}$
$\tan x$	$\mathbb{R} - \{(2n+1).\frac{\pi}{2}; n \in \mathbb{Z}\}$	$\sec^{-1} x$	$(-\infty, -1] \cup [1, \infty)$
$\cot x$	$\mathbb{R} - \{n\pi; n \in \mathbb{Z}\}$	$\text{cosec}^{-1} x$	$(-\infty, -1] \cup [1, \infty)$

Continuity of a Function on its Domain

A function $f(x)$ is said to be continuous on its domain if it is continuous at every point of its domain. If a function is continuous on its domain, then it may be discontinuous on any other set or on real number set.

For example: (i) $f(x) = \tan x$

Domain of $f(x)$ $\mathbb{R} \sim \left\{(2n+1)\frac{\pi}{2}; n \in \mathbb{Z}\right\}$

Then $f(x) = \tan x$ is continuous at every point of its domain i.e., $\tan x$ is continuous function on its domain. But $\tan x$ is discontinuous at every odd integer multiple of $\pi/2$, thus $\tan x$ is discontinuous on real number set.

Continuity in an Open Interval

A function $f(x)$ is said to be continuous in (a, b) when $f(x)$ is continuous at each point $c \in (a, b)$. i.e., $f(c^-) = f(c^+) = f(c)$ $\forall\ c \in (a, b)$

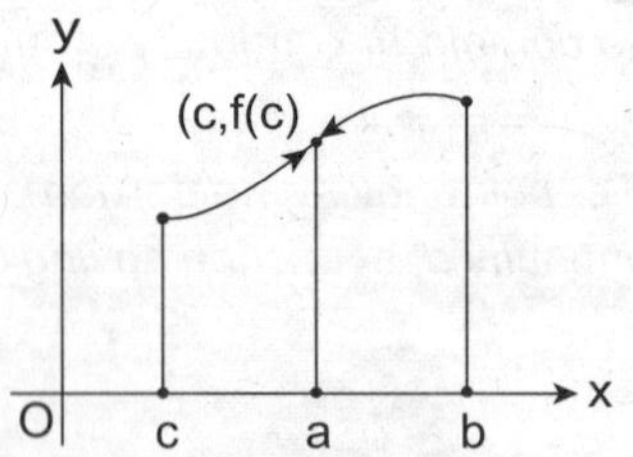

FIGURE 2.39

Method of testing

1. First of all make sure that every point of open interval is in the domain of given function i.e., each constituent function is defined at each point of open interval (a, b), e.g, $f(x) = x^2 + \sin x - \tan x$, then x^2, $\sin x$, $\tan x$ each is defined in open interval $(0, 1)$ but same function is not defined in open interval $(1, 2)$ as $\tan x$ is not defined at $\frac{\pi}{2} \simeq 1.57$. Thus $f(x)$ cannot be continuous in open interval $(1, 2)$, due to discontinuity at $x = \frac{\pi}{2}$.

2. Use the knowledge of domain of continuity of standard constituent functions involved and algebra of continuity e.g., If $f(x)\begin{cases} x\sin x; & 0 < x \le 1 \\ x^2 + 2; & 1 < x < 4 \end{cases}$

   Now x and $\sin x$ have their domain of continuity $\mathbb{R}$ and the product of two continuous functions at a point is also continuous at that point, thus $x \sin x$ is continuous in $(0, 1)$.

   Also $(x^2 + 2)$ being a polynomial function is also continuous at each real number, $x^2 + 2$ is also continuous on $(1, 4)$.

3. Test the continuity of $f(x)$ at suspesious points (i.e., points splitting the function into two different definitions) For example, in above step (2), $x = 1$ is the suspesious point.

ILLUSTRATION 20: If $f(x) = \begin{cases} x^2 & ; \quad 0 < x < 1 \\ 2x - 1; & 1 \le x < 2 \end{cases}$ then discuss the continuity of $f(x)$ on $(0, 2)$

SOLUTION: $f(x) = x^2$ is a polynomial function which is always continuous on $\mathbb{R}$ and hence on $(0, 1)$.

$f(x) = 2x - 1$ is a linear functions, which is also continuous on $\mathbb{R}$ and hence on $(1, 2)$. Also $x = 1$ is a suspesious point. Now L.H.L. at $x = 1$

$f(1^-) = \lim\limits_{h \to 0} (1 - h)^2 = 1.$ and $f(1^+) = \lim\limits_{h \to 0} 2(1 + h) - 1 = 2 - 1 = 1$

Also $f(1) = 2(1) - 1 = 2 - 1 = 1$

$\therefore$ LHL = RHL = $f(1) = 1$, Hence it is continuous function on $(0, 2)$

ILLUSTRATION 21: Check the continuity of function $f(x) = \begin{cases} \sin x: & 0 < x \le \pi/2 \\ \{x\}: & \pi/2 < x < \pi \end{cases}$ in $(0, \pi)$

SOLUTION: L.H.L. $= f(\pi/2^-) = \underset{x \to \frac{\pi}{2}}{\text{Lt}} \sin x = \underset{x \to 0^+}{\text{Lt}} \sin\left(\frac{\pi}{2} - h\right) = 1;$

Also R.H.L. $= f(\pi/2^+) = \lim\limits_{h \to 0^+} \{\pi/2 + h\} = \lim\limits_{h \to 0} (\pi/2 + h) - [\pi/2 + h]$

$= \lim\limits_{h \to 0} (\pi/2 - 1) + h = \pi/2 - 1 \cong 0.57$

$f(\pi/2) = \sin \pi/2 = 1$; Thus $f(x)$ is discontinuous at $x = \frac{\pi}{2}$ sin x is always continuous. Also we know that $\{x\}$ is discontinuous at each integer point.

There are two integers 2 and 3 between $\pi/2$ and π.

$\Rightarrow$ $\{x\}$ is discontinuous at 2 and 3

Therefore, there are three points of discontinuity which are $\pi/2$, 2 and 3.

■ CONTINUITY OF A FUNCTION ON A CLOSED INTERVAL

A function $f(x)$ is said to be continuous on closed interval $[a, b]$ if

(i) $f(x)$ is continuous in (a, b)
(ii) $f(x)$ is right continuous at $x = a$
(iii) $f(x)$ is left continuous at $x = b$

Thus $f(x)$ is continuous on $[a, b]$ if

(i) $f(c^-) = f(c^+) = f(c)\ \forall\ c \in (a, b)$
(ii) $f(a) = f(a^+)$
(iii) $f(b^-) = f(b)$

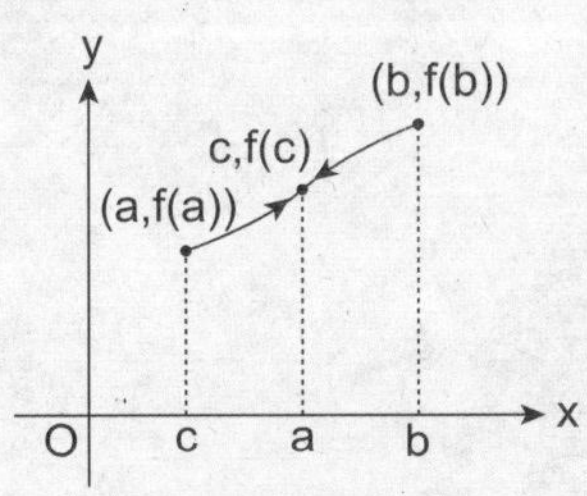

FIGURE 2.40

Function continuous on $[a, b]$

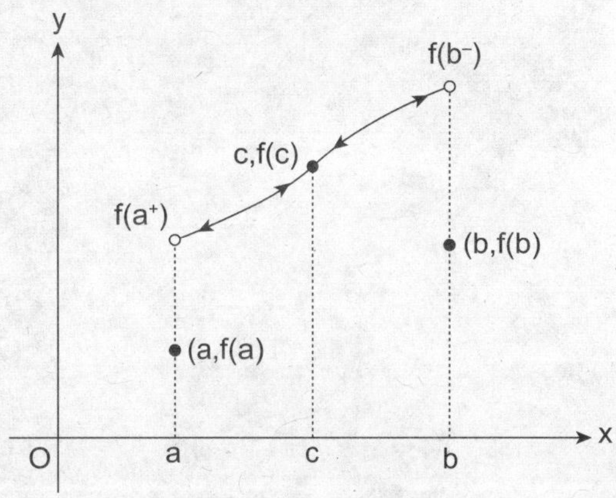

FIGURE 2.41

Function discontinuous on $[a, b]$ due to discontinuing at extreme points

ILLUSTRATION 22: Find the values of a and b so that the function $f(x)$ is continuous on $[0, \pi]$; where a and b.

$$f(x) = \begin{cases} x + a\sqrt{2}\sin x;\ 0 \le x < \pi/4 \\ 2x\cot x + b; \frac{\pi}{4} \le x \le \frac{\pi}{2} \\ a\cos 2x - b\sin x; \frac{\pi}{2} < x \le \pi \end{cases}$$

SOLUTION: Clearly $x + a\sqrt{2}\sin x$ being sum of two continuous functions x and $a\sqrt{2}\sin x$ with domain of continuity $\mathbb{R}$, is continuous on $\left(0, \frac{\pi}{4}\right)$. Similarly $2x \cot x + b$ is also continuous on $\left(\frac{\pi}{4}, \frac{\pi}{2}\right)$ Also $a \cos 2x + - b \sin x$ is continuous on $\left(\frac{\pi}{2}, \pi\right)$.

Thus for continuity of function $f(x)$ defined above, it must be right continuous at $x = 0$, continuous at $x = \pi/4$, $\pi/2$ (suspicious points), left continuous at $x = \pi$

At $x = 0$

R.H.L = $\lim_{x\to 0^+} x + a\sqrt{2}\sin x = 0$ and $f(0) = 0 + a\sqrt{2}\sin 0 = 0$

$\therefore$ R.H.L at $x = 0 = f(0)$

$\Rightarrow$ $f(x)$ is right continuous at $x = 0$

At $x = \pi/4$

L.H.L = $\lim_{x\to\frac{\pi}{4}} f(x) = \lim_{x\to\frac{\pi}{4}^-} (x + a\sqrt{2}\sin x) = \frac{\pi}{4} + a\sqrt{2}\frac{1}{\sqrt{2}} = \frac{\pi}{4} + a;$

R.H.L = $\lim_{x\to\frac{\pi}{4}^+} f(x) = \lim_{x\to\frac{\pi}{4}^+} 2x\cot x + b = 2\left(\frac{\pi}{4}\right)\cot\frac{\pi}{4} + b = \frac{\pi}{2}(1) + b = \frac{\pi}{2} + b$

$\therefore$ Also $f(\pi/4) = 2\left(\frac{\pi}{4}\right)\cot\frac{\pi}{4} + b = \frac{\pi}{2} + b$

$\therefore$ For continuity at $x = \pi/4$; $a + \frac{\pi}{4} = b + \frac{\pi}{2}$

$\Rightarrow$ $a = b + \frac{\pi}{4}$ ...(1)

At $x = \pi/2$

L.H.L = $\lim_{x\to\frac{\pi}{2}} f(x) = \lim_{x\to\frac{\pi}{2}^-} (2x\cot x + b) = 2\left(\frac{\pi}{2}\right)\cot\frac{\pi}{2} + b = b;$

R.H.L = $\lim_{x\to\frac{\pi}{2}^+} f(x) = \lim_{x\to\frac{\pi}{2}^+} (a\cos 2x - b\sin x) = a\cos 2\left(\frac{\pi}{2}\right) - b\sin\frac{\pi}{2} = a(-1) - b = -a - b$

= also $f(\pi/2) = 2\left(\frac{\pi}{2}\right)\cot\frac{\pi}{2} + b = b$

$\therefore$ For continuity at $x = \pi/2$, $-a - b = b \Rightarrow a + 2b = 0$ ...(2)

$\therefore$ From (1) and (2), $b = \frac{-\pi}{12}; a = \frac{\pi}{6}$

ILLUSTRATION 23: Find the value of p for which the function $f(x) = \begin{cases} \frac{\sqrt{1+px} - \sqrt{1-px}}{x} & ; -1 \le x < 0 \\ \frac{2x+1}{x-2} & ; 0 \le x < 1 \end{cases}$ is continuous in the interval $[-1, 1]$

SOLUTION: $f(x)$ will be continuous in interval $[-1, 1]$ if

(i) $f(x)$ is right continuous at $x = -1$;

(ii) $f(x)$ is continuous at $x = 0$; (suspicious point);

(iii) $f(x)$ is left continuous at $x = 1$

At $x = -1$, R.H.L = $\lim_{x\to(-1)^+} f(x) = \lim_{x\to(-1)^+} \frac{\sqrt{1+px} - \sqrt{1-px}}{x} = \sqrt{1+p} - \sqrt{1-p} = f(-1)$

At $x = 0$, L.H.L = $\lim_{x\to 0^-} f(x) = \lim_{x\to 0^-} \frac{\sqrt{1+px} - \sqrt{1-px}}{x}$

$= \lim_{x\to 0^-} \frac{1 + px - 1 + px}{x} \times \frac{1}{(\sqrt{1+px} + \sqrt{1-px})} = \lim_{x\to 0^-} \frac{2p}{\sqrt{1+px} + \sqrt{1-px}} = \frac{2p}{2} = p$

R.H.L = $\lim_{x\to 0^+} f(x) = \lim_{x\to 0^+} \frac{2x+1}{x-2} = \frac{-1}{2}$

$\therefore$ For continuity at $x = 0$, $p = -1/2$

TEXTUAL EXERCISE–2: (SUBJECTIVE)

1. Show that the function $f(x)$ defined as
$$f(x)=\begin{cases}3x+2; & x\in(-3,-2)\\ 2x\ ; & x\in[-2,1]\\ x+2\ ; & x\in(1,2)\end{cases}$$ is discontinuous at $x=1$ and continuous at every other point of the open interval (–3, 2). Draw a rough sketch of the function.

2. (a) Prove that every odd continuous function has its value zero at $x = 0$.

 (b) Let a function $f: R \to R$ satisfying the equation $f(x + y) = f(x) + f(y)$. $\forall x, y\in\mathbb{R}$ Show that

 (i) if f is continuous at the point $x = a$, then it is continuous for all $x\in R$

 (ii) if f is continuous at $x = 0$, then it is continuous for all $x\in R$

3. Discuss the continuity of $f(x)=\begin{cases}[\cos \pi x] & ; x\le 1\\ |2x-3|[x-2]; & x>1\end{cases}$ in the interval [0, 2] If $[x]$ is the integer part and $\{x\}$ is the fractional part of x.

4. Find the function $f(x)$ and discuss its continuity if $f(x)$ is defined as

 (a) $f(x)=\lim\limits_{n\to\infty}\dfrac{\left[x^{2n+2}-\cos x\right]}{\left(x^{2n}+1\right)}$

 (b) $f(x)=\lim\limits_{n\to\infty}\dfrac{\left[\ln(2+x)-x^{2n}\sin x\right]}{\left(x^{2n}+1\right)};\ 0\le x\le\pi/2$

5. (a) Find the values of a and b so that the functions given below are continuous in their indicated domain.

 (i) $$f(x)=\begin{cases}a\tan^{-1}\left[\dfrac{1}{(x-4)}\right] & ;\ 0\le x<4\\ \pi/2 & ;\ x=4\\ b\tan^{-1}\left[\dfrac{2}{x-4}\right] & ;\ 4<x<6\\ \sin^{-1}(7-x)+a\pi/4; & 6\le x\le 8\end{cases}$$

 (ii) $$f(x)=\begin{cases}\left(1-\sin^3 x\right)/3\cos^2 x & ;x<\dfrac{\pi}{2}\\ a & ;x=\dfrac{\pi}{2};x\in(0,\pi)\\ \left[b(1-\sin x)/(\pi-2x)^2\right. & ;x>\dfrac{\pi}{2}\end{cases}$$

 (iii) $$f(x)=\begin{cases}(1+|\sin x|)^{a/|\sin x|} & ;\dfrac{-\pi}{6}<x<0\\ b & ;x=0\\ e^{\tan 2x/\tan 3x} & ;0<x<\dfrac{\pi}{6}\end{cases}$$

 (b) Determine the values of a, b, c etc. for which the following functions $f(x)$ are continuous at their indicated domain:

 (i) $$f(x)=\begin{cases}\dfrac{(ae^{1/|x+2|}-1)}{(2-e^{1/|x+2|})}; & -3<x<-2\\ b & ;\ x=-2\\ \dfrac{\sin(x^4-16)}{(x^5+32)} & ;-2<x<0\end{cases}$$

 (ii) $$f(x)=\begin{cases}[\sin(a+1)x+\sin x]/x\ ; & x<0\\ c & ;\ x=0\\ \dfrac{\sqrt{x+bx^2}-\sqrt{x}}{bx^{3/2}} & ;\ x>0\end{cases}$$

6. Let f be a continuous function and g be a discontinuous function. Prove that $f + g$ is a discontinuous function.

7. Let $f(x.\ y) = f(x)\ .\ f(y)$ for all $x, y \in \mathbb{R}$. If the function f is continuous at $x = 1$, then prove that it is continuous for all $x\ne 0$.

8. Three cylinders having the radii of the base circles equal to 3, 2 and 1m respectively and equal altitudes (5m) are mounted on each other to form a single solid. Express the volume of the solid thus obtained as a function of the distance between any cross section and the lower base of the lower cylinder. Will this function be continuous?

9. Let $$f(x)=\begin{cases}\left(\left(1+|\cos x|\right)^{\frac{ab}{|\cos x|}}\right) & ,n\pi<x<(2n+1)\dfrac{\pi}{2}\\ e^a e^b & ,x=(2n+1)\dfrac{\pi}{2}\\ e^{\frac{\cot 2x}{\cot 8x}} & ,(2n+1)\dfrac{\pi}{2}<x<(n+1)\pi\end{cases};$$

 If $f(x)$ is continuous in $(n\pi, (n + 1)\pi)$ $n \in \mathbb{N}$, then find the values of a and b.

Answer Keys

2. (b) Function is cont. at $x = a$

3. Cont. in $x \in [0, 2] - \{0, 1/2, 2\}$

4. (a) $f(x) = \begin{cases} -\cos x & ; x \in (-1,1) \text{ or } |x| < 1 \\ \dfrac{1-\cos 1}{2} & ; x = \pm 1 \\ x^2 & ; |x| > 1 \end{cases}$, Not continuous at $x = \pm 1$ (b) $f(x) = \begin{cases} \ell n(2+x) \text{ for } 0 \le x < 1 \\ \dfrac{\ell n 3 - \sin 1}{2} \text{ at } x = 1 \\ -\sin x \text{ for } x > 1 \end{cases}$,

Not continuous at $x = 1$

5. (a) (i) $a = -1$; $b = 1$ (ii) $a = 1/2$, $b = 4$ (iii) $a = 2/3$, $b = e^{2/3}$
(b) (i) $a = 2/5$; $b = -2/5$ (ii) $a = -3/2$, $b \in \mathbb{R} - \{0\}$, $c = 1/2$

8. $f(x) = \begin{cases} 9\pi x & , 0 \le x \le 5 \\ 45\pi + 4\pi(x-5) & , 5 < x \le 10 \\ 65\pi + \pi(x-10) & , 10 < x \le 15 \end{cases}$; $f(x)$ will be continuous function

9. $a = b = 2$

TEXTUAL EXERCISE-2: (OBJECTIVE)

1. Points of discontinuity of $f(x) = [x] \sin \dfrac{\pi}{[x+1]}$ where [.] denotes the greatest integer function, are

(a) $x \in \mathbb{Z} - \{-1, 0\}$ (b) $x \in \mathbb{Z} - \{0\}$
(c) $x \in \mathbb{Z} - \{-1\}$ (d) None of these

2. All points of discontinuity of the function fog where $g(x) = \dfrac{1}{x-1}$ and $f(x) = \dfrac{1}{x^2 + x - 2}$ are

(a) $\dfrac{1}{2}, 2, 1$ (b) 2, 1
(c) 2 (d) None of these

3. The set of points of discontinuity of the function $f(x) \dfrac{\tan x . \tan^{-1}\left(\dfrac{1}{x-1}\right)}{x(x-3)(x-5)}$ is equal to

(a) $\{0, 3, 5\}$
(b) $\left\{(2n+1)\dfrac{\pi}{2}, n \in Z\right\}$
(c) $\{0,1,3,5\} \cup \left\{(2n+1)\dfrac{\pi}{2} : n \in \mathbb{Z}\right\}$
(d) none of these

4. The set of points of discontinuities of the function $f(x) = \sqrt{x} - [\sqrt{x}]$; where $[x]$ denotes the greatest integer less than or equal to x contains the set

(a) $\{1, 4, 9, ..., 100\}$ (b) $\{n^2 : n \in \mathbb{N}\}$
(c) $\mathbb{N}$ (d) $\{2n : n \in \mathbb{N}\}$

5. If $f(x) = \begin{cases} -2\sin x & \text{for } -\pi \le x < -\dfrac{\pi}{2} \\ a \sin x + b & \text{for } -\dfrac{\pi}{2} \le x < \dfrac{\pi}{2} \\ \cos x & \text{for } \dfrac{\pi}{2} \le x \le \pi \end{cases}$ is continuous in the interval $[-\pi, \pi]$, then $(a, b) =$

(a) $(1, -1)$ (b) $(-1, -1)$
(c) $(1, 1)$ (d) $(-1, 1)$

6. Graph of a function $f(x)$ is given. Which of the following is not correct?

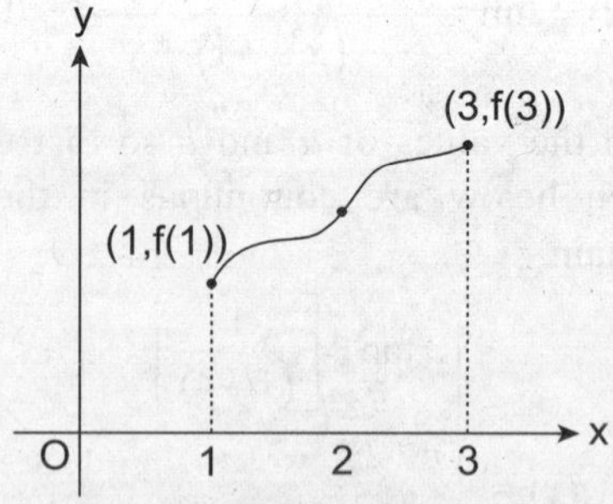

FIGURE 2.42

(a) $f(x)$ is continuous on $(1, 3)$
(b) $f(x)$ is continuous on $(1, 3]$
(c) $f(x)$ is continuous on $[1, 3]$
(d) None of these

7. Let $[x]$ denotes the integral part of $x \in \mathbb{R}$. $g(x) = x - [x]$. Let $f(x)$ be any continuous function with $f(0) = f(1)$, then the function $h(x) = f(g(x))$:

(a) has finitely many discontinuities
(b) is discontinuous at some $x = c$
(c) is continuous on $\mathbb{R}$
(d) is a constant function.

8. The number of points where $f(x) = [\sin x + \cos x]$; (where [ ] denotes the greatest integer function), $x \in (0, 2\pi)$ is not continuous is:
(a) 3 (b) 4
(c) 5 (d) 6

9. Let $f(x) = [2 + 3 \sin x]$; (where [] denotes the greatest integer function); $x \in (0, \pi)$. Then number of points at which $f(x)$ is discontinuous is:
(a) 0 (b) 4
(c) 5 (d) infinite

10. Let $f(x)=\begin{cases}\dfrac{x^3+x^2-16x+20}{(x-2)^2}; & \text{if } x \neq 2\\ k & ; \text{if } x=2\end{cases}$. If $f(x)$ is continuous for all x and $k = a^2 - b^2$, where $a, b \in \mathbb{R}$, then b is equal to
(a) 4 (b) 7
(c) 3 (d) None of these

11. 'f' is a continuous function on the real line. Given that $x^2+(f(x)-2)x-\sqrt{3}.f(x)+2\sqrt{3}-3=0$. Then the value of $f\left(\sqrt{3}\right)$ is
(a) Cannot be determined
(b) $2\left(1-\sqrt{3}\right)$
(c) Zero
(d) $\dfrac{2\left(\sqrt{3}-2\right)}{\sqrt{3}}$

12. The function $f(x)=\begin{cases}\dfrac{x^2}{a} & ;0\le x<1\\ a & ;1\le x<\sqrt{2}\\ \dfrac{(2b^2-4b)}{x^2} & ;\sqrt{2}\le x<\infty\end{cases}$ is continuous for $0 \le x < \infty$, then the most suitable values of a and b are
(a) $a = 1, b = -1$
(b) $a = -1, b = 1 + \sqrt{2}$
(c) $a = -1, b = 1$
(d) None of these

13. The function $f(x)=\begin{cases}[x]+\sqrt{x-[x]} & \text{for } x\ge 0\\ \sin x & \text{for } x<0\end{cases}$ is:
(a) Continuous only for all non-negative integers
(b) Continuous only for all positive integers
(c) Discontinuous only for all negative integers
(d) Continuous for all real numbers

14. $y = f(x)$ is a continuous function such that its graph passes through $(a, 0)$. Then $\lim\limits_{x\to a}\dfrac{\ln(1+3f(x))}{2f(x)}$ is :
(a) 1
(b) 0
(c) 3/2
(d) 2/3

15. $\lim\limits_{n\to\infty}\dfrac{x^n f(x)+g(x)}{x^n+1}$; ($x \in \mathbb{R}$, $f(x)$ and $g(x)$ are continuous functions) does not exists if :
(a) $|x| < 1$
(b) $|x| > 1$
(c) $x = 1$
(d) $x = -1$

16. Let $f(x)$ be a function on [0, 1] such that $f(x)=\begin{cases}x & ; x\in\mathbb{Q}\\ 1-x & ; x\notin\mathbb{Q}\end{cases}$, then $fof(x)$ is
(a) Continuous for all x is $\in [0, 1]$
(b) Continuous for only one value of x
(c) Not possible to define
(d) None of these

17. Given: $f(x)=\begin{cases}x & \text{for } |x|\le 1\\ 1 & \text{for } |x|>1\end{cases}$;

$g(x)=\begin{cases}\cos\left(\dfrac{\pi}{2}x\right) & \text{for} |x|\le 1\\ |x-1| & \text{for} |x|>1\end{cases}$;

$h(x)=\begin{cases}\dfrac{(|x|-1)}{\log_a|x|} & \text{for} |x|\ne 1\\ \ell n a & \text{for } |x|=1,\ a>0, a\ne 1\end{cases}$. If ℓ m, n denotes the number of points of discontinuity of the functions f, g and h in their domains respectively, then (ℓ, m, n) is
(a) (0, 0, 0) (b) (1, 1, 1)
(c) (2, 2, 2) (d) (1, 1, 0)

18. Let $f(x)=\begin{cases}x^2-4x+3; & x<3\\ x-4 & ; x\geq 3\end{cases}$ and $g(x)=\begin{cases}x-3\ ; & x\geq 4\\ x^2-x; & 1<x<4\\ 1 & ; x=1\end{cases}$; then function $f(x).g(x)$ is discontinuous at

(a) exactly 1 point (b) exactly 2 points
(c) exactly 3 points (d) None of these

19. The function $f(x)=\dfrac{4-x^2}{|4x-x^3|}$ is

(a) Discontinuous at only one point
(b) Discontinuous at exactly two points
(c) Discontinuous at exactly three points
(d) None of these

20. Let f be function defined by

$$f(x)=\begin{cases}\dfrac{x^2-1}{x^2-2|x-1|-1} & \text{if } x\neq 1\\ \dfrac{1}{2} & \text{if } x=1\end{cases}$$

(a) The function is continuous for all values of x
(b) The function is continuous only for $x>1$
(c) The function is continuous at $x=1$
(d) The function is not continuous at $x=1$

21. In [1, 3] the function $[x^2+1]$, $[x]$ denoting the greatest integer function, is continuous

(a) for all $x\in\mathbb{R}$
(b) for all reals except at nine points
(c) for all reals except at seven points
(d) for all reals except at eight points

Answer Keys

1. (c)	**2.** (a)	**3.** (c)	**4.** (a, b)	**5.** (d)	**6.** (c)	**7.** (c)	**8.** (c)	**9.** (c)	**10.** (c)
11. (b)	**12.** (c)	**13.** (d)	**14.** (c)	**15.** (d)	**16.** (a)	**17.** (d)	**18.** (a)	**19.** (c)	**20.** (d)
21. (d)									

■ PROPERTIES OF CONTINUOUS FUNCTION

P1 (Fermat's Theorem)

Every function $f(x)$ which is continuous in $[a, b]$ is always bounded

Proof: Since $f(x)$ is continuous $\forall\ c\in[a, b]$

$\therefore$ f cannot attain infinite value in $[a, b]$

$\Rightarrow f(c^+)=f(c^-)=f(c)$

which is real and finite $\forall\ c\in[a, b]$

Therefore by property of order of real numbers, there exist real numbers m and M.

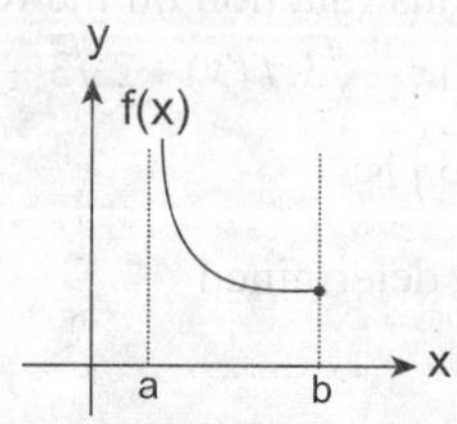

FIGURE 2.43

Such that $m=\min\{f(c): a\leq c\leq b\}$ and $M=\max\{f(c): a\leq c\leq b\}$. Thus $m\leq f(x)\leq M\ \forall\ x\in[a, b]$

Thus $f(x)$ is a bounded function.

REMARK:

If a function is continuous in open interval then it is not necessarily bounded.

e.g., $\tan x\ \forall\ x\in\left(-\dfrac{\pi}{2},\dfrac{\pi}{2}\right)$ *is continuous but not bounded as its range is* $(-\infty,\infty)$

$f(x)=\dfrac{4}{|x-2|}\forall x\in(0,2)$ *is continuous but not bounded as its range is* $(2,\infty)$

ILLUSTRATION 24: Let $f(x) = \begin{cases} \dfrac{1+a\cos 2x+b\cos 4x}{x^2 \sin^2 x} & ; x \neq 0 \\ c & ; x = 0 \end{cases}$

Then find the values of a, b and c so that $f(x)$ is bounded in the interval $\left[-\dfrac{\pi}{2}, \dfrac{\pi}{2}\right]$

SOLUTION: It is obvious that $f(x)$ may attain infinitely large value as x tends to zero. At all other points $f(x)$ has finite values

Let us assume that $\lim\limits_{x\to 0} f(x)$ be finite

i.e., $\lim\limits_{x\to 0} \dfrac{1+a\cos 2x+b\cos 4x}{x^2 \sin^2 x}$ = finite = ℓ (say)

$\Rightarrow \lim\limits_{x\to 0} \dfrac{(1+a\cos 2x+b\cos 4x)}{x^4\left(\dfrac{\sin^2 x}{x^2}\right)} = \ell$

$\Rightarrow \lim\limits_{x\to 0} \dfrac{1+a\cos 2x+b\cos 4x}{x^4} = \ell$ ...(1)

As $x \to 0$, denominator $x^4 \to 0$, for the existence of finite limit, numerator must approach to zero

$\Rightarrow 1 + a + b = 0$

$\Rightarrow 1 = -a - b$ ...(2)

Using (2) in (1) we get, $\lim\limits_{x\to 0} \dfrac{a\cos 2x+b\cos 4x-a-b}{x^4} = \ell$

$\Rightarrow \lim\limits_{x\to 0} \dfrac{-a(1-\cos 2x)-b(1-\cos 4x)}{x^4} = \ell$ ...(3)

$\Rightarrow \lim\limits_{x\to 0} \dfrac{-a(2\sin^2 x)-b(2\sin^2 2x)}{x^4} = \ell$

$\Rightarrow \lim\limits_{x\to 0} \dfrac{\dfrac{-2a\sin^2 x}{x^2} - \dfrac{-2b\sin^2 2x}{x^2}}{x^2} = \ell$ ...(4)

Numerator $\to 0$, denominator $-2a - 8b = 0$

$\Rightarrow a + 4b = 0$

Also $-a - b = 1$

$\Rightarrow 3b = 1 \Rightarrow b = 1/3$

Again form (2) $a = -1 - b = -1 - 1/3 = -4/3$

$\therefore$ Form (3), required limit

$= \lim\limits_{x\to 0} \dfrac{\dfrac{4}{3}(1-\cos 2x)-\dfrac{1}{3}(1-\cos 4x)}{x^4}$

$= \lim\limits_{x\to 0} \dfrac{\dfrac{4}{3}(2\sin^2 x)-\dfrac{1}{3}(2\sin^2 2x)}{x^4} = \lim\limits_{x\to 0} \dfrac{\dfrac{8}{3}\sin^2 x-\dfrac{8}{3}\sin^2 x\cos^2 x}{x^4}$

$$= \lim_{x\to 0} \frac{\frac{8}{3}\sin^2 x\left(1-\cos^2 x\right)}{x^4} = \lim_{x\to 0} \frac{8}{3}\,\frac{\sin^2 x}{x^2}\,\frac{\sin^2 x}{x^2}$$

$$= \frac{8}{3}(1)\,(1) = \frac{8}{3}$$

$\therefore$ It we take $c = 8/3$, then the function will be continuous at all real points in $\left[-\frac{\pi}{2}, \frac{\pi}{2}\right]$

$\therefore$ By Fermat's theorem, $f(x)$ is bounded in $\left[-\frac{\pi}{2}, \frac{\pi}{2}\right]$

$\therefore$ for $a = \frac{-4}{3}, b = \frac{1}{3}$ and $c = 8/3$

P2: Intermediate Value Theorem

If f is continuous on $[a, b]$ and $f(a) \neq f(b)$, then for any value c lying in between $f(a)$ and $f(b)$ there exist at least one number x_0 in $[a, b]$ for which $f(x_0) = c$.

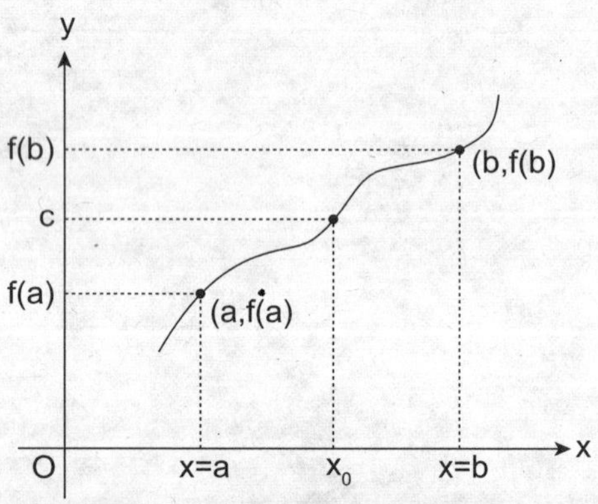

FIGURE 2.44

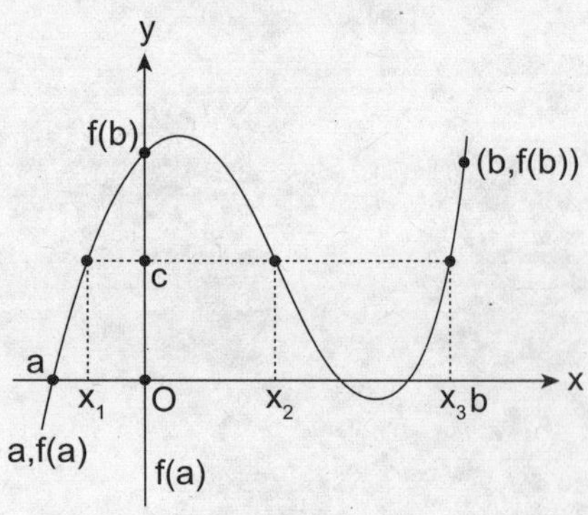

FIGURE 2.45

for $c \in [f(a), f(b)]$, exactly one x_0 exist for which $f(x_0) = c$

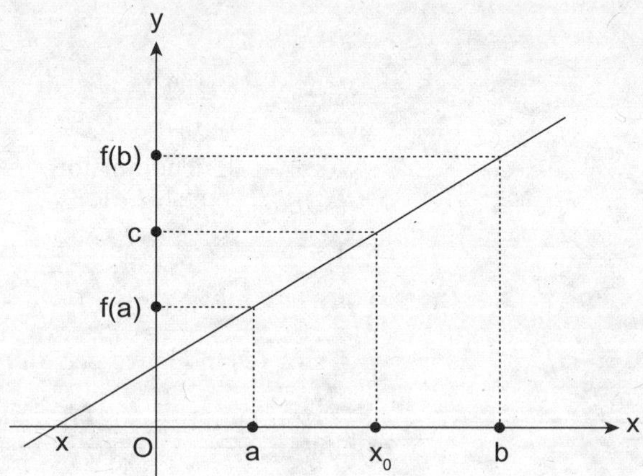

FIGURE 2.46

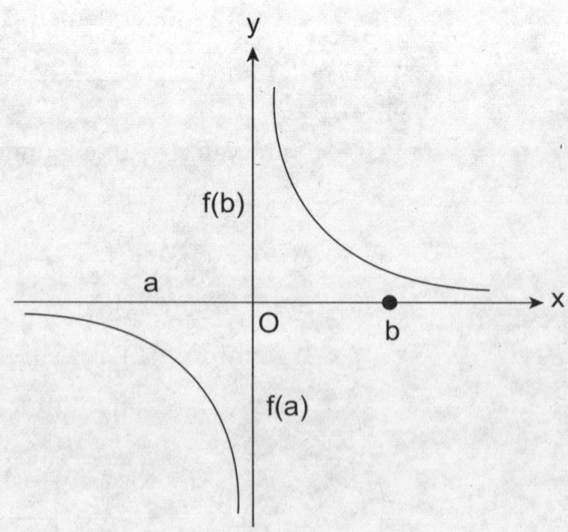

FIGURE 2.47

$f(x)$ discontinuous on $[a, b]$ does not at tain $f(x) = 0 \in [f(a), f(b)]$

ILLUSTRATION 25: Show that function $f(x) = (x - a)^2 (x - b)^2 + x$, takes the value $\frac{a+b}{2}$ for some $x \in [a, b]$

SOLUTION: We know that the polynomial functions are continuous on $\mathbb{R}$

$\therefore$ $f(x)$ is also continuous on $[a, b]$

Also $f(a) = a$ and $f(b) = b$

$\therefore$ By intermediate value theorem, $f(x)$ would attain each value in between $f(a)$ and $f(b)$ i.e., between a and b

$\therefore$ $f(x)$ would also attain the value $\frac{a+b}{2}$ for some $x \in [a, b]$

ILLUSTRATION 26: Show that the function $f(x) = 1 - \sin\frac{\pi}{2}x$ attains value 1 in $[-1, 1]$

SOLUTION: $f(x) = 1 - \sin\frac{\pi}{2}x$ is continuous as 1 being constant is continuous, $\sin\frac{\pi}{2}x$ is continuous and $1 - \sin\frac{\pi}{2}x$ being the difference of two continuous functions is also continuous.

Further, $f(-1) = 1 - \sin\left(-\frac{\pi}{2}\right) = 2$ and $f(1) = 1 - \sin\left(-\frac{\pi}{2}\right) = 0$

$\therefore$ by intermediate value theorem, $f(x)$ would attain each and every value between $f(-1)$ and $f(1)$ i.e., of interval $[0, 2]$

$\therefore$ $f(x)$ also attains value 1 in $[-1, 1]$

ILLUSTRATION 27: Show that the polynomial equation $x^3 - 5x^2 - 17x = 20$ has a solution in $[1, 2]$

SOLUTION: Let $P(x) = x^3 - 5x^2 + 17x$

$P(x)$ being a polynomial function is continuous in $[1, 2]$ and $f(1) = 1 - 5 + 17 = 13$; $f(2) = 8 - 20 + 34 = 22$

By intermediate value theorem, $f(x)$ would attain each value between 13 and 22 and hence it would also attain value 20 in $[1, 2]$. Thus the equation $x^3 - 5x^2 + 17x = 20$ has a solution in $[1, 2]$.

ILLUSTRATION 28: Show that the converse of intermediate value theorem is not true by giving a suitable example.

SOLUTION: Consider the functions $f(x) = \begin{cases} -x^2 + 2x + 4 & ; -2 \le x \le 0 \\ x^3 + 3 & ; 0 < x \le 2 \\ 2 + x & ; 2 < x \le 6 \end{cases}$

$$\text{L.H.L} = \lim_{x\to 0^-} f(x) = \lim_{x\to 0^-} (-x^2 + 2x + 4) = 4$$

$$\text{R.H.L} = \lim_{x\to 0^+} f(x) = \lim_{x\to 0^+} (x^3 + 3) = 3$$

$\therefore$ $f(x)$ is discontinues at $x = 0$. Similarly, L.H.L at $x = 2$ is 11 and R.H.L at $x = 2$ is 4

$\therefore$ $f(x)$ is discontinuous at $x = 2$. The graph of $f(x)$ is as shown in figure 2.48.

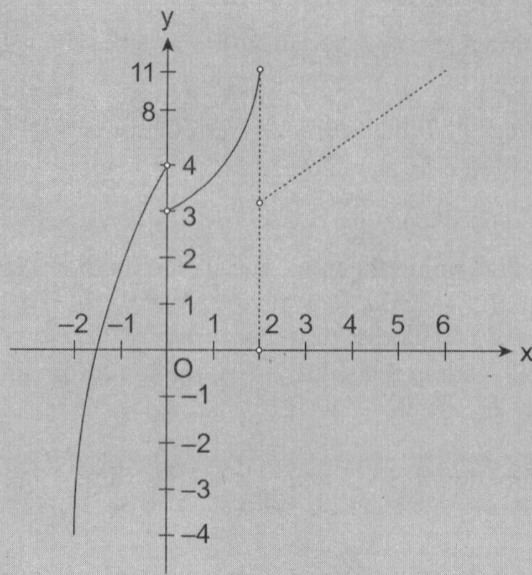

FIGURE 2.48

Clearly $f(x)$ attains each value from $f(-2)$ to $f(6)$ even when the function $f(x)$ is discontinuous in $[-2, 6]$.

Thus the converse of intermediate value theorem is not true.

ILLUSTRATION 29: Show that there is a real number x such that $x^{2008} + \dfrac{1}{1+\sin^2 x} = 2008$

SOLUTION: Clearly $f(x) = x^{2008} + \dfrac{1}{1+\sin^2 x}$ being sum of two continuous function is also continuous on $\mathbb{R}$

$\therefore$ In particular $f(x)$ is also continuous on $[1, 2]$

But $f(1) = 1 + \dfrac{1}{1+\sin^2 1} \in (1,2); f(2) = (2)^{2008} + \dfrac{1}{1+\sin^2 2} > 2008$,

as $f(2) > (2)^{11} = 2048$

Thus $f(x)$ would attain each value from $f(1)$ to $f(2)$ and hence it would also attain 2008 at some real x.

ILLUSTRATION 30: Show that $4^x + 8^x = 3.6^x$ has a solution.

SOLUTION: Given equation is $4^x + 8^x = 3.6^x$ ...(1)

$\Rightarrow \dfrac{4^x}{6^x} + \dfrac{8^x}{6^x} = 3 \qquad \Rightarrow \left(\dfrac{2}{3}\right)^x + \left(\dfrac{4}{3}\right)^x = 3$ ...(2)

$\Rightarrow f(x) = 3$; where $f(x) = \left(\dfrac{2}{3}\right)^x + \left(\dfrac{4}{3}\right)^x$

Clearly $f(x)$ being a sum of two continuous (exponential) functions is also continuous

Also $f(1) = \dfrac{2}{3} + \dfrac{4}{3} = 2$ and $f(4) = \left(\dfrac{2}{3}\right)^4 + \left(\dfrac{4}{3}\right)^4 = \dfrac{16}{81} + \dfrac{256}{81} = \dfrac{272}{81} \simeq 3.358$

Since $f(x)$ is continuous on $\mathbb{R}$ and hence also in $[1, 4]$, therefore by Fermat's theorem, $f(x)$ would attain each value from $f(1)$ to $f(4)$ i.e., from 2 to 3.358.Thus $f(x)$ would also attain value 3. That means equation (2) and hence equation (1) would have a real solution.

P3: Weierstrass Theorem (Extreme Value Theorem)

If f is continuous on $[a, b]$ then f takes on a least value m and a greatest value M on this interval

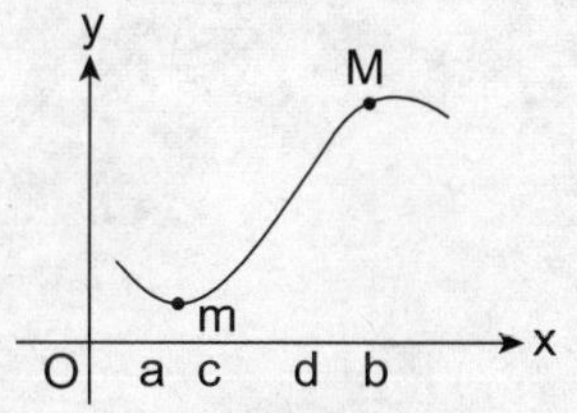

FIGURE 2.49

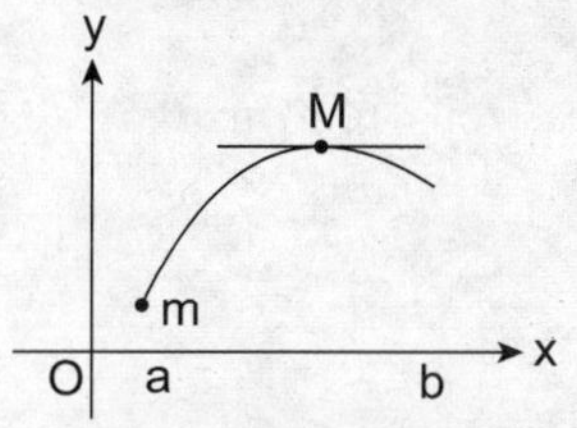

FIGURE 2.50

Proof: Since $f(x)$ is continuous on $[a, b]$ by Fermat's theorem $f(x)$ is bounded on $[a, b]$. Let m and M be the minimum and maximum value of functions respectively. Then $m \le f(x) \le M$ "$x \in [a, b]$

As m and M are selected from images $f(x)$; $x \in [a, b]$; naturally there exist α, β, $\in [a, b]$ for which $f(\alpha) = m$ and $f(\beta) = M$. Further if the function is many-one, then there may exist more than one real numbers at which least and greatest values occus.

For example

(i) $f(x) = \sin^{-1}x$ is continuous on $[-1, 1]$ having its minimum value $-\pi/2$ and maximum value $\pi/2$ such that $f(-1) = \frac{\pi}{2}$ and $f(1) = \frac{\pi}{2}$

(ii) $f(x) = \sin x$ in continuous on $[0, 4\pi]$; then, least value of $f(x) = -1$ occurs at $x = \frac{3\pi}{2}, \frac{7\pi}{2}$ and the maximum value of $f(x) = 1$ occurs at $x = \frac{\pi}{2}, \frac{5\pi}{2}$.

REMARK:

Continuity is necessary for the extreme values theorem to be true.
Because from the graph shown given below; clearly f(x) has

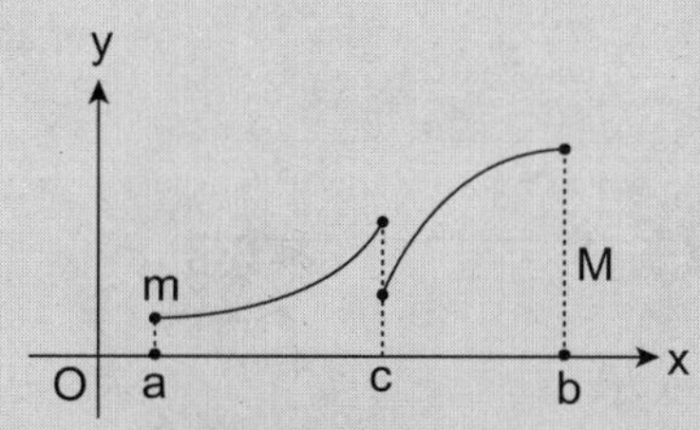

FIGURE 2.51

a discontinuity at $x = c$, even when least and greatest values m and M are attain in [a, b].

P4: Bolzanos Theorem

If $f(a)$ and $f(b)$ possesses opposite signs then $\exists$ at least one solution of the equation $f(x) = 0$ in the open interval (a, b) provided f is continuous in $[a, b]$.

Proof: Since $f(a)$ and $f(b)$ are of opposite signs without loss of generality let $f(a) < 0$ and $f(b) > 0$ as shown below

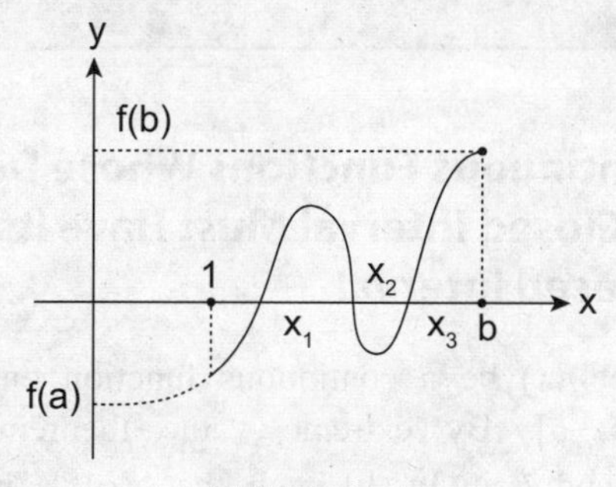

FIGURE 2.52

∴ By intermediate value theorem $f(x)$ would attain each real number inbetween $f(a)$ and $f(b)$ at least once in $[a, b]$. But $f(a)$, $f(b)$ are non-zeros, thus I at least one root of $f(x) = 0$ in (a, b). Hence the proof.

ILLUSTRATION 31: Show that $f(x) = x^2 - 9x^2 + 12x + 8 = 0$ has

(i) At least one root in the interval (0, 6)

(ii) Exactly one root in $\left(-\infty, 3-\sqrt{5}\right)$

(iii) Exactly one root in $\left(3+\sqrt{5}, \infty\right)$

(iv) Exactly one root in $\left(3-\sqrt{5}, 3+\sqrt{5}\right)$

SOLUTION: $f(x) = x^3 - 9x^2 + 12x + 8$ being a polynomial function is continuous $f(0) = 8$; $f(6) = 216 - 324 + 72 + 8 = -28$

∴ $f(0)$ and $f(6)$ are of opposite signs

Thus by Bolzanos theorem, $f(x)$ must have at least one root in (0,6) i.e., $f(x) = 0$ for some $x \in (0,6)$

Now $f'(x) = 3x^2 - 18x + 12 = 3(x^2 - 6x + 4)$

$= 3\left[x-(3-\sqrt{5})\right]\left[x-\left(3+\sqrt{5}\right)\right] = 0$

Now $f'(x) < 0 \Rightarrow x \in \left(3-\sqrt{5}, 3+\sqrt{5}\right)$

∴ $f(x)$ is a decreasing function in $\left(3-\sqrt{5}, 3+\sqrt{5}\right)$ and increasing on $\left(-\infty, 3-\sqrt{5}\right)$ and $\left(3+\sqrt{5}, \infty\right)$. Also $f(-\infty) = -\infty$ and $f(\infty) = \infty$

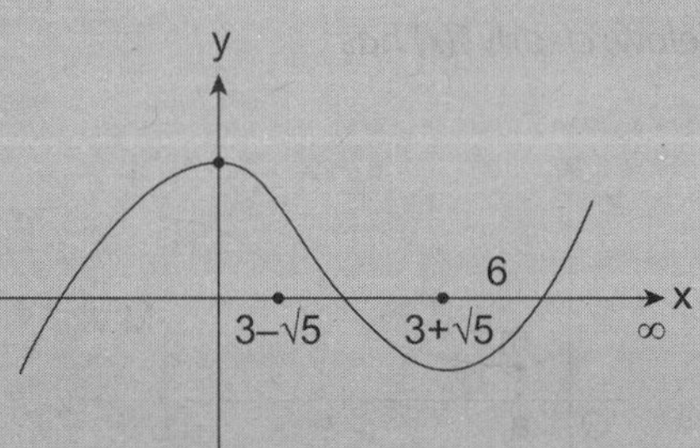

FIGURE 2.53

The graph of $f(x)$ would be as shown in figure 2.53. Clearly $f(x)$ has exactly one root each in $\left(-\infty, 3-\sqrt{5}\right)$, in $\left(3-\sqrt{5}, 3+\sqrt{5}\right)$ and in $\left(3+\sqrt{5}, \infty\right)$.

P5: A Continuous Functions Whose Domain is Some Closed Interval Must Have Its Range Also a Closed Interval

Proof: Let $f(x)$ be a continuous function on a closed interval $[a, b]$. By extreme value theorem ∃ real number α and β in [a, b] such that $f(\alpha) = min. \{f(x); x \in [a, b]\}$ and $f(\beta) = max\ \{f(x)\ ;\ x \in [a, b]\}$. Also $f(x)$ is continuous on $[\alpha, \beta]$, thus by intermediate value theorem $f(x)$ would attain each and every real number from $f(\alpha)$ to $f(\beta)$.

Thus range of $f(x) = [f(\alpha), f(\beta)]$ which is a closed interval.

REMARKS:

(i) If a function f(x) is continuous on an open interval (a, b) or on Real number line R, and m and M are, respectively, the greatest lower bound and least upper bounds of f(x), then Range of f(x) = [m, M] if f(x) attains m and M, and it is (m, M) if f(x) does not attain its bounds m or M are included in range if m or M are attained by the function.

P6: Continuity of Inverse Function

If the function $y = f(x)$ is defined, continuous and strictly monotonic on the domain of function $f(x)$, then there exists a single-valued inverse function $x = \phi(y)$ defined, continuous and also strictly monotonic in the range of the function $y = f(x)$.

Proof: Let $y = f(x)$ be continuous, and monotonic on the interval I. Let a $\in I$, then $\lim_{x\to a} f(x) = f(a) = b$ (say) ...(i)

Let $g(x)$ be the inverse of $f(x)$

$\therefore$ $g(b) = a$ ....(2)

Now $\lim_{x\to b} g(x) = \lim_{y\to b} f^{-1}(y) = \lim_{f(x)\to(b)} f^{-1}(f(x))$

[$\because f(x)$ is continuous at $x = a$ so $x \to a \Rightarrow f(x) \to f(a)$]

$= \lim_{f(x)\to f(a)} (x)$

[$\because f(x)$ being monotonic is one-one]

$= a$ [$\because f(x) \to f(a) \Rightarrow x \to a$] $= g(b)$

$\therefore$ $\lim_{x\to b} g(x) = g(b)$

$\Rightarrow$ $f^1(x)$ is continuous at $x = b$

$\therefore$ Inverse of a continuous and monotonic function $f(x)$ is also continuous on the range of function $f(x)$.

P7: If a Function *f(x)* is Integrable on [*a*, *b*], Then $\int_a^x f(t)\,dt; x \in [a, b]$ is Continuous Function

Proof: For each $x \in [a, b]$ $\int_a^x f(t)dt$ is a function of x(say) $F(x)$.

Thus $F(x) = \int_a^x f(t)\,dt; x \in [a,b]$ ...(1)

We are to prove that $F(x)$ is continuous on $[a, b]$

Let $x_0 \in [a, b]$

We shall prove that $\lim_{x\to x_0} F(x) = F(x_0)$ i.e., $x \to x_0$

$\Rightarrow$ $F(x) - F(x_0) \to 0$

i.e., $\int_a^x f(t)\,dt - \int_a^{x_0} f(t)\,dt \to 0$

i.e., $\int_{x_0}^x f(t)\,dt \to 0$ ...(2)

$\because$ $f(x)$ is continuous on $[a, b]$ by Fermat's theorem $f(x)$ is bounded on $[a, b]$

$\Rightarrow$ $\exists$ a real number M such that $|f(t)| \le M$

$\Rightarrow$ $-M \le f(t) \le M$

$\Rightarrow$ $\int_{x_0}^x (-M)dt \le \int_{x_0}^x f(t)\,dt \le \int_{x_0}^x Mdt$

$\Rightarrow$ $-M(x - x_0) \le \int_{x_0}^x f(t)\,dt \le M(x - x_0)$

Thus clearly by Sandwich theorem, $\lim_{x\to x_0} \int_{x_0}^x f(t)\,dt = 0$ as $x - x_0 \to 0$

Hence the result.

Corollary: Integral $\int_a^x f(t)\,dt$ of a continuous function $f(x)$ on $[a, b]$ is also continuous on $[a, b]$

Proof: We know that every continuous function on a closed interval $[a, b]$ is integrable, hence by above theorem, its integration is continuous on $[a, b]$.

ILLUSTRATION 32: Examine the continuity of $\int_0^x f(t)\,dt$ on [0,2] defined

by $f(t) = \begin{cases} \dfrac{\sin(t-1)}{(t-1)} & \text{for } t \ne 1 \\ 1 & \text{for } t = 1 \end{cases}$

SOLUTION: Here $f(t) = \dfrac{\sin(t-1)}{(t-1)}$;

$\therefore \lim\limits_{t\to 1} \dfrac{\sin(t-1)}{(t-1)} = \lim\limits_{h\to 0} \dfrac{\sin h}{h} = 1 = f(1)$

$\therefore$ $f(t)$ is continuous on [0,2]

$\therefore$ By above theorem, $\int_0^x f(t)dt$ is also continuous on [0, 2]

To Find the Range of Function Using the Properties of Continuous Functions

By using the earlier discussed theorem, Fermat's theorem, intermediate value theorem, extreme value theorem, we can find the range of functions by finding the intervals of their continuity and the points of their discontinuity. Some of such problems are discussed below in the form of illustrations.

ILLUSTRATION 33: Find the range of functions $f(x) = 2x^2 + 6x + 7$

SOLUTION: $f(x) = 2x^2 + 6x + 7 = 2(x^2 + 3x) + 7$

$= 2\left(x^2 + 3x + \dfrac{9}{4}\right) - \dfrac{9}{2} + 7$

$= 2\left(x + \dfrac{3}{2}\right)^2 + \dfrac{5}{2} \ge \dfrac{5}{2} \; \forall x \in \mathbb{R}$

We know that $f(x)$ being a polynomial function is continuous on $\mathbb{R}$. Also we find the minimum possible value of $f(x) = 5/2$, which the function attains at $x = -3/2$. But $f(x)$ tends to ∞ as $x \to \infty$

$\therefore$ each and every real number from $\dfrac{5}{2}$ to ∞ are attained by $f(x)$

$\therefore$ Range of $f(x) = \left[\dfrac{5}{2}, \infty\right)$

ILLUSTRATION 34: Find the range of function $f(x)$ defined by $f(x) = \begin{cases} \max\left\{\sqrt{4-x^2}, \sqrt{1+x^2}\right\} & ; -2 \le x \le 0 \\ \min\left\{\sqrt{4-x^2}, \sqrt{1+x^2}\right\} & ; 0 < x \le 2 \end{cases}$

SOLUTION: $\sqrt{1+x^2}$ is defined "x$\in\mathbb{R}$ But $\sqrt{4-x^2}$ is defined for $x \in [-2, 2]$

$\therefore$ Domain of function $f(x)$ is [–2,2]

$y = \sqrt{4-x^2} \Rightarrow y^2 = 4 - x^2 \Rightarrow x^2 + y^2 = 4$

Which is a circle with centre at origin and radius = 2

$\therefore$ $y = \sqrt{4-x^2}$ represents semi-circle of circle $x^2 + y^2 = 4$ on and above x –axis

Again $y = \sqrt{1+x^2} \Rightarrow y^2 = 1 + x^2$

$\Rightarrow y^2 - x^2 = 1$

which represents rectangular hyperbola with centre at origin and transverse axis along y – axis and conjugate axis along x – axis.

Thus $y = \sqrt{1+x^2}$ represents positive branch of hyperbola $y^2 - x^2 = 1$ as shown below

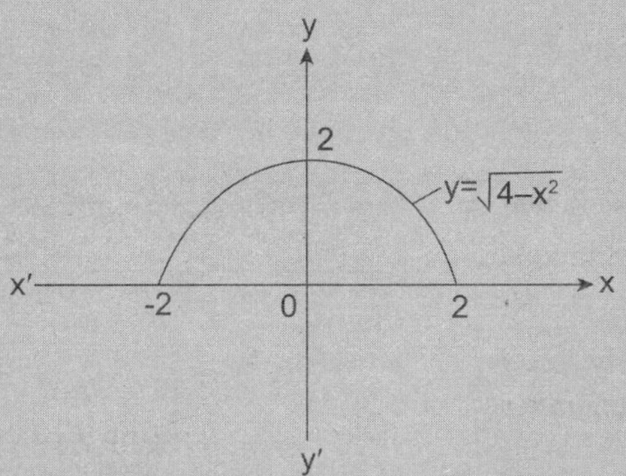

FIGURE 2.54

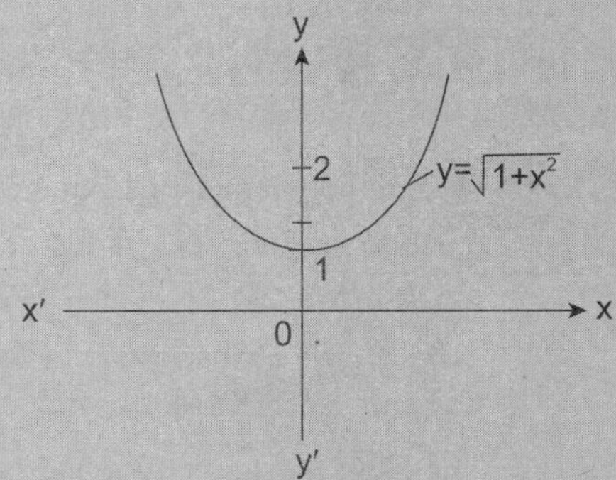

FIGURE 2.55

At the point of intersection of two functions

$\sqrt{4-x^2} = \sqrt{1+x^2} \Rightarrow 4-x^2 = 1+x^2 \Rightarrow 2x^2 = 3 \Rightarrow x = \pm\sqrt{3/2}$

$\therefore$ The graph of $f(x)$ is as shown in figure 2.56.

Clearly $f(x)$ is continuous on $[-2, 2]$ except for the point $x = 0$, where $f(x)$ has a jump discontinuity.

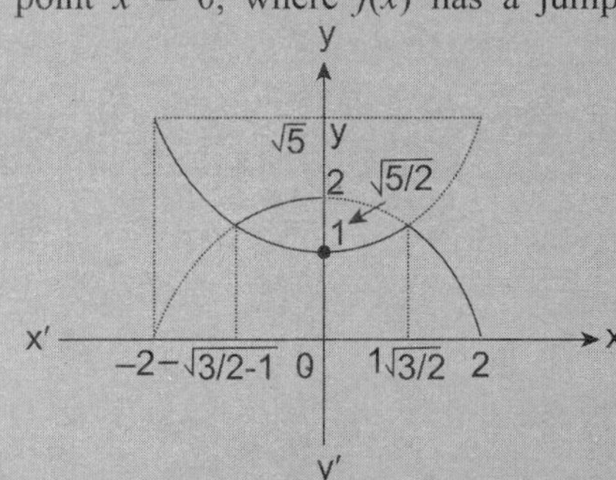

FIGURE 2.56

$\therefore$ $f(x)$ is continuous on $[-2, 0]$ and on $(0, 2]$

In $[-2, 0]$, minimum value of $f(x)$ is $\sqrt{\frac{5}{2}}$ and maximum value of $f(x)$ is $\sqrt{5}$

$\therefore$ Range of $f(x)$ in $[-2, 0]$ is $\left[\sqrt{\frac{5}{2}}, \sqrt{5}\right]$

Similarly $f(x)$ is continuous in $(0,2]$

Having its minimum value 0 and maximum value $\sqrt{\frac{5}{2}}$.

$\therefore$ Range of $f(x)$ in $(0, 2]$ is $\left[0, \sqrt{\frac{5}{2}}\right]$

$\therefore$ Range of $f(x) = \left[0, \sqrt{\frac{5}{2}}\right] \cup \left[\sqrt{\frac{5}{2}}, \sqrt{5}\right] \equiv \left[0, \sqrt{5}\right]$

ILLUSTRATION 35: Find the range of $f(x) = \dfrac{x-2}{x^3+2x^2-4x-8}$

SOLUTION: $f(x) = \dfrac{x-2}{x^3+2x^2-4x-8} = \dfrac{x-2}{(x^3-8)+(2x^2-4x)}$

$$= \frac{x-2}{(x-2)(x^2+4+2x)+2x(x-2)} = \frac{(x-2)}{(x-2)(x^2+4x+4)}$$

$\therefore\ f(x) = \dfrac{(x-2)}{(x-2)(x+2)^2}$; Domain of $f(x) = \mathbb{R} \sim \{-2,2\}$

$\therefore\ f(x) = \dfrac{1}{(x+2)^2}\ \forall x \in \mathbb{R} \sim \{-2,2\}$

Clearly $f(x)$ being rational function (polynomial/polynomial) i.e., quotient of two continuous functions is also continuous on $\mathbb{R} \sim \{-2, 2\}$. As $x \to -2$, $f(x) \to +\infty$

And as $x \to \pm\infty$, $f(x) \to 0^+$. Clearly $f(x) > 0$, being a perfect square of a real number

$\therefore$ Range of $f(x)$ is $(0, \infty)$

Graph of $f(x)$ shown below verifies the range of $f(x)$

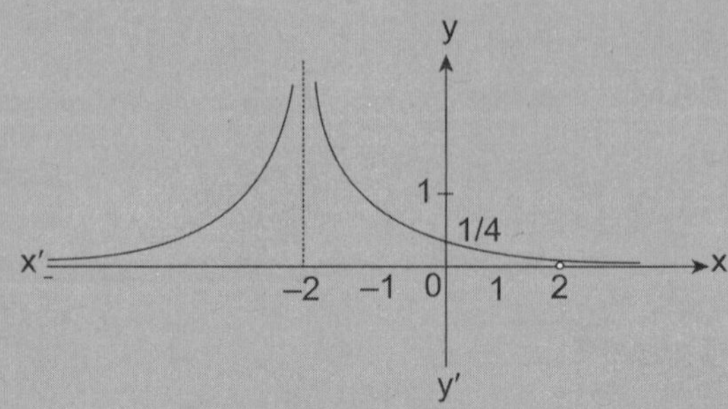

FIGURE 2.57

ILLUSTRATION 36: Prove that the inverse of discontinuous function $f(x) = (1+x^2)$ sgn x is a continuous functions. Also find the range of $f(x)$ and $f^{-1}(x)$

SOLUTION: $f(x) = (1+x^2)\operatorname{sgn} x = \begin{cases} 1+x^2 \text{ for } x>0 \\ 0 \ \ for\ x=0 \\ -(1+x^2) \text{ for } x<0 \end{cases}$.

The graph of $f(x)$ is as shown below

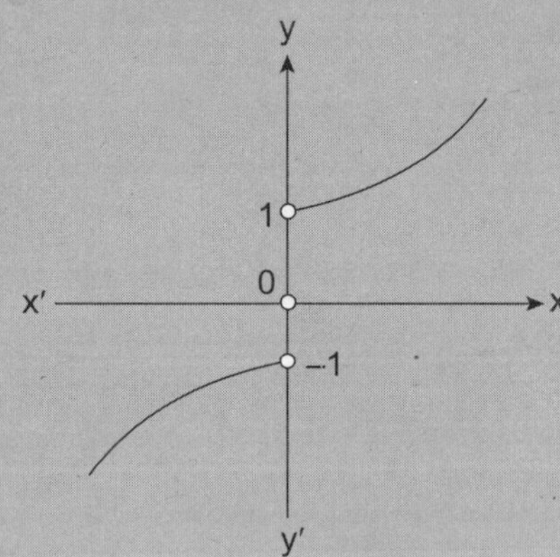

FIGURE 2.58

Clearly $f(x)$ is discontinuous at $x = 0$. But continuous on $(-\infty, -1)$ and $(0, \infty)$.

$\therefore$ Range of $f(x) = (-\infty,-1) \cup (1,\infty) = \mathbb{R} \sim [-1, 1]$

Now $f(x)^{-1} = \begin{cases} \sqrt{x-1} & ;x>1 \\ 0 & ;x=0 \\ -\sqrt{-(1+x)} & ;x<-1 \end{cases}$

$\therefore$ Domain of $f^{-1}(x)$ is $(-\infty,-1)\cup(1,\infty) \cup \{0\}$, in which $f^{-1}(x)$ is continuous. Here we do not discuss about the continuity of $f(x)$ at $x = 0$, as no portion of graph exists in neighbourhood of $x = 0$. Thus the range of function $f(x)$ is $(-\infty, \infty) \equiv \mathbb{R}$.

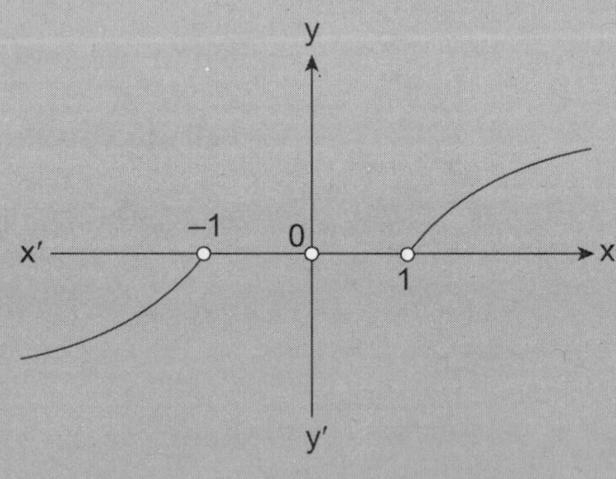

FIGURE 2.59

ILLUSTRATION 37: Let $f(x) = x - x^2$ and $g(x) = \begin{cases} -x+1 & ;\ x<0 \\ \max\{f(t); 0 \le t \le x,\ 0 \le x \le 1\} \\ \sin \pi x, x>1 \end{cases}$. Then find the points of discontinuity of function $f(x)$ and find the range of $f(x)$

SOLUTION: $f(x) = x - x^2 \qquad \Rightarrow\ f'(x) = 1-2x$

$\therefore\ f'(x) < 0$ for $x \in \left(\dfrac{1}{2},1\right]$ and $f'(x) > 0$ for $x \in \left[0,\dfrac{1}{2}\right)$

i.e., $f(x)$ in increasing in $\left[0,\dfrac{1}{2}\right)$ and decreasing in $\left(\dfrac{1}{2},1\right]$

$$g(x)=\begin{cases}-x+1 & ;x<0\\ f(x) & ;0\le x\le\frac{1}{2}\\ \frac{1}{4} & ;\frac{1}{2}\le x\le 1\\ \sin\pi x & ;x>1\end{cases}=\begin{cases}-x+1 & ;x<0\\ x-x^2 & ;0\le x\le\frac{1}{2}\\ \frac{1}{4} & ;\frac{1}{2}\le x\le 1\\ \sin\pi x & ;x>1\end{cases}$$

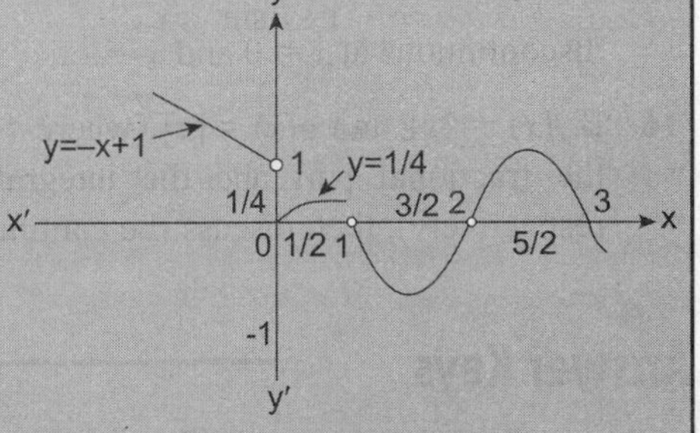

The graph of function $g(x)$ is shown in Figure 2.60

Clearly $f(x)$ is discontinuous at $x = 0, 1$

i.e., $f(x)$ is continuous in $(-\infty, 0)$ and $(0, 1)$ and $(1, \infty)$

$\therefore$ Range of $f(x)$ would be $(1,\infty)\cup\left[0,\frac{1}{4}\right]\cup[-1,1]=[-1,1]\cup(1,\infty)=[-1,\infty)$

FIGURE 2.60

TEXTUAL EXERCISE–3: (SUBJECTIVE)

1. A function $f(x) = x^3 - 3x - 5$, then state whether the following statements are True/False.

(a) It has at least one root $\in (0, 5)$

(b) It has exactly one root $\in (0, 5)$

(c) It has exactly one root $\in (1, 5)$

2. Prove that $f(x) = x^3 + 3x - 5$ has exactly one root $\in (0, 5)$.

3. Prove that $2^x + 3^x + 5^x = 7^x$ has exactly one solution.

4. Let f: $[0, 1] \to [0, 1]$ be continuous function. Show that there exists a point $x \in [0, 1]$ such that $f(x) = x$.

5. Let f be a continuous function defined for $1 \le x \le 3$. If $f(x)$ takes rational values for all x and $f(2) = 10$, then find $f(5/2)$.

6. Prove that the function $f(x) = \left(\frac{x^3}{4}\right)-\sin\left(\frac{\pi}{x}\right)+3$ takes the value $\frac{7}{3}$ in the interval $[-2, 2]$.

7. If $f(x) = x + \{-x\} + [x]$, where $[x]$ is the integral part and $\{x\}$ is the fractional part of x discuss the continuity of f in $[-2, 2]$.

8. Prove that the inverse of the discontinuous function $y = (1 + x^2)\ \text{sgn}\ x$ is a continuous function in its domain.

9. If g: $[a, b]$ onto $[a, b]$ is continuous show that there is some $c \in [a, b]$ such that $g(c) = c$.

10. (a) Let $f(x + y) = f(x) + f(y)$ for all x, y and if the function $f(x)$ is continuous at $x = 0$, then show that $f(x)$ is continuous at all x.

(b) If $f(x \cdot y) = f(x) \cdot f(y)$ for all x, y and $f(x)$ is continuous at $x = 1$ prove that $f(x)$ is continuous for all x except at $x = 0$. Given $f(1) \ne 0$.

11. Let f be continuous on the interval $[0, 1]$ to R such that $f(0) = f(1)$. Prove that there exists a point c in $\left[0, \frac{1}{2}\right]$ such that $f(c)=f\left(c+\frac{1}{2}\right)$.

12. Suppose that $f(x) = x^3 - 3x^2 - 4x + 12$ and $h(x)=\begin{cases}\frac{f(x)}{x-3} & ,x\ne 3\\ k & ,x=3\end{cases}$; then

(a) Find all zeros of f

(b) Find the values of k that makes h continuous at $x = 3$

(c) Using the value of k found in (b), determine whether h is an even function.

13. Find points at which the function given by the following expressions are continuous.

(a) $f(x)=\frac{3x+7}{x^2-5x+6}$ (b) $f(x)=\frac{1}{|x|-1}-\frac{x^2}{2}$

(c) $f(x)=\frac{\sqrt{x^2+1}}{1+\sin^2 x}$ (d) $f(x)=\tan\left(\frac{x}{2}\right)$

14. Examine the continuity at $x = 0$ of the sum function of the infinite series

$$f(x)=\left(\frac{x}{x+1}+\frac{x}{(x+1)(2x+1)}+\frac{x}{(2x+1)(3x+1)}+\ldots\infty\right)$$

$$=\lim_{x\to\infty}\sum S_n=f(x)=1$$

15. Let $f(x) = \lim_{n\to\infty} \frac{x^2 + nx\sin^2 \pi x}{1+n\sin^3 \pi x}$, prove that $f(x)$ is discontinuous at $x = 0$ and $x = -1$.

16. If $f(x) = \{x\}$ and $g(x) = [x]$ (where {} and [] denotes the fractional part and the integral part functions respectively), then discuss the continuity of

(a) $h(x) = f(x)\, g(x)$, $x = 1$ and 2
(b) $h(x) = f(x) + g(x)$, $x = 1$
(c) $h(x) = f(x) - g(x)$, $x = 1$
(d) $h(x) = g(x) + \sqrt{f(x)}$, $x = 1$ and 2

Answer Keys

1. (a) T (b) T (c) T
5. 10
7. discontinuous at all integral values in [–2, 2]
12. (a) –2, 2, 3 (b) $k = 5$ (c) even
13. (a) $x \in \mathbb{R} - \{2, 3\}$ (b) $x \in \mathbb{R} - \{-1, 1\}$ (c) $x \in \mathbb{R}$ (d) $x \in \mathbb{R}^{*} - \{(2n + 1), n \in \mathbb{Z}\}$
14. discontinuous
16. (a) continuous at $x = 1$ (b) continuous (c) discontinuous (d) continuous at $x = 1, 2$

TEXTUAL EXERCISE–3: (OBJECTIVE)

1. Let $f(x) = \text{sgn}(x)$ and $g(x) = x\,(x^2 - 5x + 6)$. The function $f(g(x))$ is discontinuous at
(a) infinitely many points
(b) exactly one points
(c) exactly three points
(d) no points

2. If $y = \frac{1}{t^2+t-2}$ where $t = \frac{1}{x-1}$, then the number of points of discontinuities of $y = f(x)$, $x \in \mathbb{R}$ is
(a) 1 (b) 2
(c) 3 (d) infinite

3. The equation $2\tan x + 5x - 2 = 0$ has
(a) no solution in $[0, \pi/4]$
(b) at least one real solution in $[0, \pi/4]$
(c) two real solution in $[0, \pi/4]$
(d) None of these

4. Let $f(x) = [x] + \sqrt{x-[x]}$; where $[x]$ denotes the greatest integer function. Then
(a) $f(x)$ is continuous on R^+
(b) $f(x)$ is continuous on R
(c) $f(x)$ is continuous on $R - \{1\}$
(d) discontinuous at $x = 1$

5. The function $f(x) = [x]\cos\left(\frac{2x-1}{2}\right)\pi$, [.] denotes the greatest integer function, is discontinuous at
(a) all x (b) all integer points
(c) no x (d) x which is not an integer

6. Function $f(x) = (|x-1| + |x-2| + \cos x)$, where $x \in [0, 4]$ is not continuous at number of points
(a) 3 (b) 2
(c) 1 (d) 0

7. If $f(x) = \begin{cases} \frac{1-|x|}{1+x} & ,x \neq -1 \\ 1 & ,x = -1 \end{cases}$, then $f([2x])$ is; where [] represent greatest integer function, then which is/are false
(a) continuous at $x = -1$
(b) continuous at $x = 0$
(c) discontinuous at $x = 1/2$
(d) continuous at $x = 1/2$

8. The range of the function
$$f(x) = \frac{e^x \ell n\, x\, 5^{(x^2+2)}(x^2 - 7x + 10)}{2x^2 - 11x + 12}$$ is
(a) $(-\infty, \infty)$ (b) $[0, \infty)$
(c) $\left(\frac{3}{2}, \infty\right)$ (d) $\left(\frac{3}{2}, 4\right)$

9. The range of the function $f(x) = \tan^{-1}\frac{1+x}{1-x} - \tan^{-1} x$ is
(a) $\left\{\frac{\pi}{4}\right\}$ (b) $\left\{-\left(\frac{\pi}{4}\right), \frac{3\pi}{4}\right\}$
(c) $\left\{\frac{\pi}{4}, -\left(\frac{3\pi}{4}\right)\right\}$ (d) $\frac{3\pi}{4}$

10. Range of the function $f(x)=\left[\frac{1}{\ell n(x^2+e)}\right]+\frac{1}{\sqrt{1+x^2}}$ is, where [*] denotes the greatest integer function and $e=\lim_{\alpha\to 0}(1+\alpha)^{1/\alpha}$

(a) $\left(0,\frac{e+1}{e}\right)\cup\{2\}$ (b) (0, 1)

(c) $(0,1]\cup\{2\}$ (d) $(0, 1) \cup \{2\}$

11. The range of the function, $f(x) = \cot^{-1}\log_{0.5}(x^4-2x^2+3)$ is

(a) (0, π) (b) $\left(0,\frac{3\pi}{4}\right]$

(c) $\left[\frac{3\pi}{4},\pi\right)$ (d) $\left[\frac{\pi}{2},\frac{3\pi}{4}\right]$

12. The function, $f(x) = [|x|] - |[x]|$; where $[x]$ denotes greatest integer function

(a) is continuous for all positive integers

(b) is discontinuous for all non-positive integers

(c) has finite number of elements in its range

(d) is such that its graph does not lie above the x-axis.

13. Total number of points of discontinuity of $f(x) = [3 + 4\sin x]$, where [.] denotes the greatest integer function, in [π, 2 π] is equal to

(a) 9 (b) 6

(c) 8 (d) 5

14. If $f(x) = \frac{1}{x+[x]}$, where [ ] is the greatest integer function, then $f(x)$ is discontinuous at

(a) no point (b) only one point

(c) infinite points (d) None of these

15. Number of points where $f(x) = \frac{1}{\ln[x^2-3x+3]}$ is discontinuous is

(a) 2 (b) 4

(c) 6 (d) 0

16. If $f(x) = \frac{2}{2+x}$, the number of points of discontinuity of $f(f(f(x)))$ is :

(a) 1 (b) 2

(c) 3 (d) 4

17. Number of points of discontinuity of the function $f(x)=\lim_{n\to\infty}\frac{2\sin x}{3^n+(2\cos x)^{2n}}$ are given by

(a) 0 (b) 1

(c) infinite (d) None of these

18. The function $f(x)=\begin{cases}[x]+\sqrt{x-[x]} & \text{for } x\ge 0\\ \sin x & \text{for } x<0\end{cases}$ is

(a) Continuous only for all non-negative integers

(b) Continuous only for all positive integers

(c) Discontinuous only for all negative integers

(d) Continuous for all real numbers.

19. The function $f(x)=\begin{cases}(1-\operatorname{sgn} x)\operatorname{sgn} x & ;x\le 1\\ \frac{1}{1-e^{x/(1-x)}} & ;x>1\end{cases}$ is discontinuous at

(a) $x = 0$ (b) $x = 2$

(c) $x = 1$ (d) $x = 3$

20. The function $f(x)=\frac{4-x^2}{|4x-x^3|}$ is

(a) Discontinuous at only one point

(b) Discontinuous at exactly two points

(c) Discontinuous at exactly three points

(d) None of these

Answer Keys

1. (c)	**2.** (c)	**3.** (b)	**4.** (a,b,c)	**5.** (c)	**6.** (d)	**7.** (d)	**8.** (a)	**9.** (c)	**10.** (d)
11. (c)	**12.** (a,b,c,d)	**13.** (c)	**14.** (c)	**15.** (a)	**16.** (c)	**17.** (a)	**18.** (d)	**19.** (a,c)	**20.** (c)

DIFFERENTIABILITY

INTRODUCTION

A check of the rate of arbitrarily small change in other variable with respect to sufficiently small change in one variable is called the differentiability of set of ordered pairs or differentiability of function. On the other hand, geometrically differentiability means smoothness of function with no sharp edge or corners in its graph.

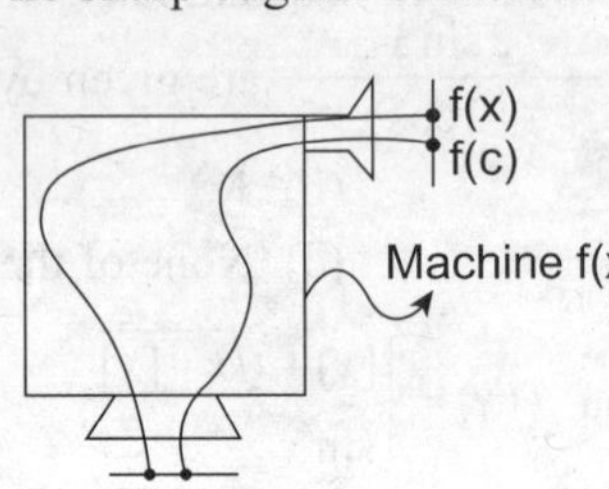

FIGURE 2.61

In this chapter we will discuss the basics of the differential calculus in detail and build up the base to determine the approximate nature of the curves represented by a function and it's various properties.

Differentiability at a Point

A function $f(x)$ is said to be differentiable at a point

$$x = a \text{ iff } \underbrace{\lim_{h\to 0^+}\left(\frac{f(a-h)-f(a)}{-h}\right)}_{\text{slope of left hand tangent at }(a,f(a))} = f'(a^-)$$

$$= \underbrace{\text{left hand derivative}}_{\substack{\text{instantaneous rate of change in}\\ \text{left neighbourhood of a}}} \text{(L.H.D)}$$

$$= \underbrace{\lim_{h\to 0^+}\left(\frac{f(a+h)-f(a)}{h}\right)}_{\text{slope of right hand tangent at }(a,f(a))} = f'(a^+)$$

$$= \underbrace{\text{right hand derivative}}_{\substack{\text{instantaneous rate of change in}\\ \text{right neighbourhood of a}}} \text{(R.H.D)} = \text{a finite real number}$$

Let $P(a, f(a))$ be any arbitrary point on the curve of function $y = f(x)$. Further let $C(a - h, f(a - h))$ and $B(a + h, f(a + h))$ be two points in left and right neighbourhood of P respectively as shown in figure 2.62. Then slope of left secant $AC = \dfrac{f(a)-f(a-h)}{h} = \dfrac{f(a-h)-f(a)}{-h}$ and the slope of right secant $AB = \dfrac{f(a+h)-f(a)}{h}$.

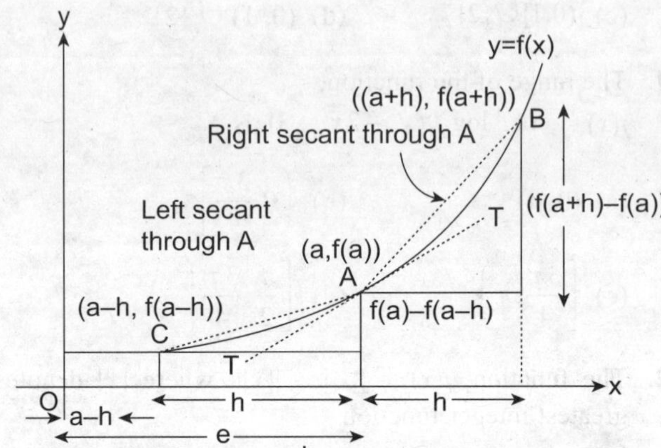

FIGURE 2.62

Now as C and B tends to A i.e., $h \to 0$, secants AC and AB tend to become left and right tangent to curve at P.

Thus $\lim\limits_{h\to 0^+}\dfrac{f(a-h)-f(a)}{-h} = \lim\limits_{h\to 0^+}\dfrac{f(a+h)-f(a)}{h} = a$ finite real number ensures the unique tangent at P having finite slope.

Physical Significance

Since $\dfrac{f(x)-f(a)}{x-a}$ is an average rate of change of $f(x)$ w.r.t 'x' in $[a, x]$, therefore $x \to a$, the interval $[a, x]$ converts to an instant and $\lim\limits_{x\to a}\dfrac{f(x)-f(a)}{x-a}$ becomes instantaneous rate of change of $f(x)$ w.r.t x at $x = a$ .So differentiability physically signifies that no sudden change in the instantaneous rate of change at $x = a$.

Geometrical Significance

Differentiability of $f(x)$ at $x = a$, implies LHD = RHD. This geometrically means that a unique tangent with finite slope can be drawn at $x = a$. Therefore, graph of $f(x)$ must be smooth without any sharp edge/corner at $x = a$ and tangent line at $x = a$ is not vertical.

ILLUSTRATION 38: Comment on the differentiability of $f(x) = \begin{cases} x, & x<1 \\ x^2, & x \ge 1 \end{cases}$ at $x = 1$

SOLUTION: R.H.D $= f'(1^+) = \lim_{h\to 0}\frac{f(1+h)-f(1)}{h} = \lim_{h\to 0}\frac{(1+h)^2-1}{h} = \lim_{h\to 0}\frac{1+h^2+2h-1}{h} = \lim_{h\to 0}(h+2) = 2$

L.H.D $= f'(1^-) = \lim_{h\to 0}\frac{f(1-h)-f(1)}{-h} = \lim_{h\to 0}\frac{1-h-1}{-h} = 1$

As L.H.D $\neq$ R.H.D. Hence $f(x)$ is not differentiable at $x = 1$

Remark: Whenever are we use $h \to 0$ it should be understood that $h \to 0^+$

ILLUSTRATION 39: If $f(x) = \begin{cases} f(x) = a + bx^2; & x<1 \\ 3ax - b + 2; & x \ge 1 \end{cases}$, then find a and b so that $f(x)$ becomes differentiable at $x = 1$

SOLUTION: R.H.D. $= f'(1^+) = \lim_{h\to 0}\frac{f(1+h)-f(1)}{h} = \lim_{h\to 0}\frac{3a(1+h)-b+2-3a+b-2}{h} = \lim_{h\to 0}\frac{3ah}{h} = 3a$

L.H.L $= f'(1^-) = \lim_{h\to 0}\frac{f(1-h)-f(1)}{-h} = \lim_{h\to 0}\frac{a+b(1-h)^2-3a+b-2}{-h}$

$= \lim_{h\to 0}\frac{(-2a+2b-2)+bh^2-2bh}{-h}$

Hence for this limit to be defined $-2a + 2b - 2 = 0$

i.e., $b = a + 1$

$\therefore\ f'(1^-) = = \lim_{h\to 0} -(bh-2b) = 2b$ $\qquad\qquad$ $\therefore\ f'(1^-) = f'(1^+)$

$\Rightarrow\ 3a = 2b = 2(a + 1)$ $\qquad\qquad$ $\Rightarrow\ a = 2,\ b = 3$

ILLUSTRATION 40: If $f(x) = |\sin x|$ and $g(x) = x^3$, discuss about the continuity and differentiability of $f(g(x))$ at $x = 0$.

SOLUTION: $f(x) = |\sin x|$

$g(x) = x^3$

$f(g(x)) = |\sin x^3|$

To check continuity at $x = 0$

LHL $= \lim_{x\to 0^-}(-\sin x^3) = 0$, and RHL $= \lim_{x\to 0^+}\sin x^3 = 0$

Thus at $x = 0$, L.H.L. = R.H.L. = 0

To check differentiability at $x = 0$

LHD $= \lim_{h\to 0}\frac{f(0-h)-f(0)}{-h} = \lim_{h\to 0}\frac{-\sin h^3-0}{-h} = \text{Lt}_{h\to 0}(h^2) = 0$

and RHD $= \lim_{h\to 0}\frac{f(0+h)-f(0)}{h} = \lim_{h\to 0}\frac{\sin h^3-0}{h} = \text{Lt}_{h\to 0}(h^2) = 0$

Thus LHD = RHD so function is derivable at $x = 0$

ILLUSTRATION 41: For the function $f(x) = \begin{cases} [\cos \pi x]; & x \le 1 \\ 2\{x\} - 1; & x > 1 \end{cases}$ comment on the derivability at $x = 1$; where [.] and {.} stnds for integer part function and fractional part function.

SOLUTION: $f'(1^-) = \lim_{h\to 0}\frac{f(1-h)-f(1)}{-h} = \lim_{h\to 0}\frac{[\cos(\pi-\pi h)]+1}{-h} = \lim_{h\to 0}\frac{-1+1}{-h} = 0$

$f'(1^+) = \lim_{h\to 0}\frac{f(1+h)-f(1)}{h} = \lim_{h\to 0}\frac{2\{1+h\}-1+1}{h} = \lim_{h\to 0}\frac{2h}{h} = 2$

$\therefore$ $f(x)$ is not differentiable at $x = 1$

ILLUSTRATION 42: Test the differentiability at $x = 0$ for the function $f(x)=\begin{cases} x^2 & ; x<0 \\ \sin x; & x\ge 0\end{cases}$

SOLUTION: $\text{LHD} = \lim_{h\to 0}\frac{f(0)-f(0-h)}{h} = \lim_{h\to 0}\frac{\sin(0)-(-h)^2}{h} = \lim_{h\to 0}\frac{0-(h)^2}{h} = 0$

and $\text{RHD} = \lim_{h\to 0}\frac{\sin(0+h)-\sin(0)}{h} = \lim_{h\to 0}\frac{\sin h}{h} = 1$

$\therefore$ LHD $\neq$ RHD

$\Rightarrow$ $f(x)$ is not differentiable at $x = 0$

ILLUSTRATION 43: Check the differentiability of the function $f(x) = \cos x + |\cos x|$ at $x = \frac{\pi}{2}$

SOLUTION: $f(x) = \cos x + |\cos x|$ at $x = \pi/2$

Now, $\cos x + |\cos x| + \begin{cases} 2\cos x \text{ if } \frac{-\pi}{2} < x < \frac{\pi}{2} \\ 0 \quad \text{ if } \frac{\pi}{2} \le x < \frac{3\pi}{2}\end{cases}$

$\Rightarrow \text{ R.H.D} = f'\left(\frac{\pi^+}{2}\right) = \lim_{x\to\frac{\pi^+}{2}}\frac{f(x)-f\left(\frac{\pi}{2}\right)}{x-\frac{\pi}{2}} = \lim_{h\to 0^+}\frac{f\left(\frac{\pi}{2}+h\right)-f\left(\frac{\pi}{2}\right)}{h} = \lim_{h\to 0^+}\frac{0-0}{h} = 0$

$\Rightarrow \text{ and L.H.D.} = f'\left(\frac{\pi^-}{2}\right) = \lim_{h\to 0^+}\frac{f\left(\frac{\pi}{2}-h\right)-f\left(\frac{\pi}{2}\right)}{-h} = \frac{2\cos\left(\frac{\pi}{2}-h\right)-0}{-h} = -2$

ILLUSTRATION 44: If the function $f(x)$ is defined as $f(x)=\begin{cases} -\frac{x^2}{2} \text{ for } x\le 0 \\ x^n \sin\frac{1}{x} \text{ for } x>0\end{cases}$ is continuous but not derivable at $x = 0$, then find the range of n.

SOLUTION: Given $f(x) = \begin{bmatrix} -\frac{x^2}{2} \text{ for } x\le 0 \\ x^n \sin\frac{1}{x} \text{ for } x>0\end{bmatrix}$ and $f(x)$ is continuous at $x = 0$ clearly $f(0) = 0$

Now $\text{L.H.L.} = \lim_{x\to 0^-} f(x) = \lim_{x\to 0^-}\left(\frac{-x^2}{2}\right) = 0$

and $\text{R.H.L.} = \lim_{x\to 0^+} f(x) = \lim_{x\to 0^+} x^n \sin\frac{1}{x}$

$\therefore$ For continuity at $x = 0$

$$\lim_{x\to 0^+} f(x) = \lim_{x\to 0^-} f(x) = f(0)$$

$$\Rightarrow \quad \lim_{x\to 0^+} x^n \sin\left(\frac{1}{x}\right) = 0$$

$\Rightarrow$ limit is defined only when $n > 0$ .... (i)

since $f(x)$ is non-differentiable at $x = 0$, L.H.D $\neq$ R.H.D

$$\text{Now L.H.D} = f'(0^-) = \lim_{h\to 0^+} \frac{f(0-h)-f(0)}{-h} = \lim_{h\to 0^+} \frac{-\frac{h^2}{2} - 0}{-h} = 0$$

$$\text{and R.H.D} = f'(0^+) = \lim_{h\to 0^+} \frac{f(0+h)-f(0)}{h} = \lim_{h\to 0^+} \frac{h^n \sin\frac{1}{h}}{h} = \lim_{h\to 0^+} h^{n-1} \sin\frac{1}{h}$$

Now L.H.D $\neq$ R.H.D

$$\Rightarrow \quad \lim_{h\to 0^+} h^{n-1} \sin\left(\frac{1}{h}\right) \neq 0, \text{ which is possible only when } n - 1 \leq 0$$

$\Rightarrow n \leq 1$ .....(ii)

$\therefore$ from equation (i) and (ii) $n \in (0, 1]$

CONCEPT OF TANGENT AND ITS ASSOCIATION WITH DERIVABILITY

Tangent: The tangent is defined as the limiting case of a chord or a secant

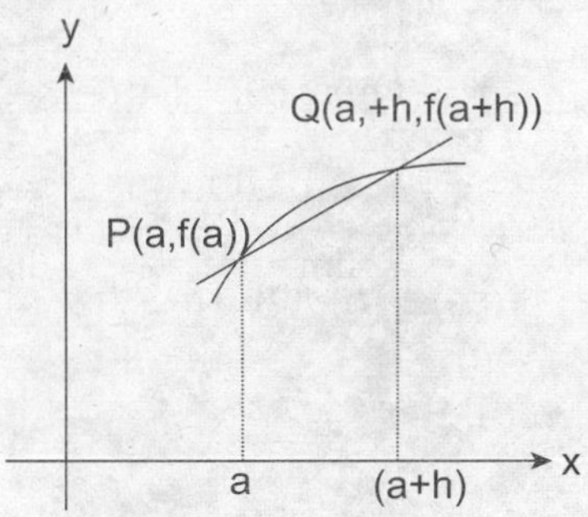

FIGURE 2.63

Slope of the line joining $P(a, f(a))$ and $Q(a + h, f(a + h)) = \dfrac{f(a+h)-f(a)}{h}$

Slope of tangent at $P = f(a) = \lim\limits_{h\to 0} \dfrac{f(a+h)-f(a)}{h}$

The tangent to the graph of a continuous function f at the point P (a, $f(a)$) is

(i) the line through P with slope $f(a)$ if $f(a)$ exists :

(ii) the line $x = a$ if $= \lim\limits_{h\to 0} \left|\dfrac{f(a+h)-f(a)}{h}\right| = \infty$

If neither (i) nor (ii) holds, then the graph of f does not have a tangent at the point P

In case (i) the equation of tangent is $(y - f(a)) = f(a)(x - a)$

In case (ii) it is $x = a$

REMARKS:

(i) tangent is also defined as the line joining two infinitely small close points on a curve

(ii) A function is said to be derivable at x = a if there exists a tangent *of finite slope at that point i.e.,* $f'(a^+) = f'(a^-)$ = *finite real number*

(iii) $y = x^3$ *has x-axis as tangent at origin*

(iv) $y = |x|$ *does not have* tangent *at x = 0 as* L.H.D $\neq$ R.H.D

ILLUSTRATION 45: If $f(x) = |x-1|.([x]-[-x])$, then find $f'(1^+)$ and $f'(1^-)$ where $[x]$ denotes greatest integer function. Also discuss the differentiability of $f(x)$ at $x = 1$.

SOLUTION: Given $f(x) = |x-1|.([x]-[-x])$

clearly $f(1) = 0$

$$\text{Now L.H.D} = \lim_{h\to0^+}\frac{f(1-h)-f(1)}{-h} = \lim_{h\to0^+}\frac{f(1-h)}{-h} = \lim_{h\to0^+}\frac{|1-h-1|([1-h]-[-(1-h)])}{-h}$$

$$= \lim_{h\to0^+}\frac{h(0-(-1))}{-h} = -1$$

$$\text{and R.H.D} = \lim_{h\to0^+}\frac{f(1+h)-f(1)}{h} = \lim_{h\to0^+}\frac{|1+h-1|([1+h]-[-(1+h)])}{h} = \lim_{h\to0^+}\frac{h(1-(-2))}{h} = 3$$

$\therefore\ f'(1^-) = -1 \neq f'(1^+) = 3$ $\therefore$ $f(x)$ is not differentialle at $x = 1$

ILLUSTRATION 46: If $f(x) = \begin{cases} ax^2 - b & \text{if } |x|<1 \\ -\dfrac{1}{|x|} & \text{if } |x|\geq 1 \end{cases}$ is derivable and continuous at $x = 1$. Find the values of a and b.

SOLUTION: Given $f(x) = \begin{cases} ax^2 - b & \text{if } |x|<1 \\ -\dfrac{1}{|x|} & \text{if } |x|\geq 1 \end{cases}$

$\because$ $f(x)$ is continuous at $x = 1$

$\therefore\ \lim_{x\to1} f(x) = f(1) \Rightarrow \lim_{x\to1^-} f(x) = f(1) \Rightarrow \lim_{x\to1^-} ax^2 - b = -1$

$\Rightarrow a - b = -1$ ...(i)

Also $f(x)$ is differentiable at $x = 1$

$$\text{Now L.H.D} = f'(1) = \lim_{h\to0^-}\frac{f(1-h)-f(1)}{-h} = \lim_{h\to0^+}\frac{a(1-h)^2-b+1}{-h}$$

$$= \lim_{h\to0^+}\frac{a+ah^2-2ah-b+1}{-h} = \lim_{h\to0^+}\frac{ah^2-2ah}{-h}\ (\because\ a-b=-1 \text{ from } (i)) = \lim_{h\to0^+}(-ha+2a) = 2a$$

$$\text{and R.H.D} f'(1^+) = \lim_{h\to0^+}\frac{f(1+h)-f(1)}{h} = \lim_{h\to0^+}\frac{\dfrac{-1}{|h+1|}+1}{h} = \lim_{h\to0^+}\frac{\dfrac{-1+1+h}{1+h}}{h} = \lim_{h\to0^+}\frac{1}{1+h} = 1$$

$\therefore\ f'(1^-) = f'(1^+)$

$\Rightarrow 2a = 1$ $\Rightarrow a = 1/2$

$\Rightarrow b = 3/2$ $(\because a - b = -1)$

ILLUSTRATION 47: Given $f(x) = \cos^{-1}\left(\text{sgn}\left(\dfrac{2[x]}{3x-[x]}\right)\right)$; where sgn. $(\cdot)$ denotes the signum function and $[\cdot]$ denotes the greatest integer function. Discuss the continuity and differentiability of $f(x)$ at $x = \pm 1$.

SOLUTION: Continuity at $x = 1$

$$\lim_{x\to1^-} f(x) = \lim_{x\to1^-}\cos^{-1}\left(\text{sgn}\left(\frac{O}{3x-0}\right)\right) = \lim_{x\to1^-}\cos^{-1}(0) = \frac{\pi}{2}$$

$\Rightarrow \lim_{x\to1^+} f(x) = \lim_{x\to1^+}\cos^{-1}\left(\text{sgn}\left(\dfrac{2}{3x-1}\right)\right)$. As $x \to 1^+ \Rightarrow 3x-1 \to 2^+$

$\therefore \quad \dfrac{2}{3x-1} \to 1^-$

$\Rightarrow \quad \dfrac{2}{3x-1} \in (0, 1) \qquad\qquad \Rightarrow \quad \text{sgn}\left(\dfrac{2}{3x-1}\right) = 1$

$\therefore \quad \lim\limits_{x\to1^+} f(x) = \cos^{-1}(1) = 0 \qquad\qquad \therefore$ $f(x)$ is discontinuous at $x = 1$

continuity at $x = -1$

$$\lim_{x\to-1^-} f(x) = \lim_{x\to-1^-} \cos^{-1}\left(\text{sgn}\left(\frac{2[x]}{3x-[x]}\right)\right) = \lim_{x\to-1} \cos^{-1}\left(\text{sgn}\left(\frac{-4}{3x+2}\right)\right)$$

Now $-2 < x < -1 \Rightarrow -4 < 3x + 2 < -1$

$\Rightarrow \quad 1 < \dfrac{-4}{3x+2} < 4 \qquad\qquad \Rightarrow \quad \text{sgn}\left(\dfrac{-4}{3x+2}\right) = 1$

R.H.L $= \cos^{-1}(1) = 0$

Now $\lim\limits_{x\to-1^+} f(x) = \lim\limits_{x\to-1^+} \cos^{-1}\left(\text{sgn}\left(\dfrac{-4}{3x+2}\right)\right)$

Now $x \to -1^+ \Rightarrow 3x \to -3^+$

$\Rightarrow \quad 3x + 2 \Rightarrow -1^+ \qquad\qquad \Rightarrow \quad 3x + 2 < 0$

$\Rightarrow \quad \dfrac{-4}{3x+2} > 0$

$\therefore \quad \text{sgn}\left(\dfrac{-4}{3x+2}\right) = 1 \qquad\qquad \therefore \quad$ R.H.L $= \cos^{-1}(1)$

Also $f(-1) = \cos^{-1}\left(\text{sgn}\left(\dfrac{-2}{-3+1}\right)\right) = \cos^{-1}(1) = 0$

Thus $f(x)$ is continuous at $x = 01$

Differentiability at $x = 1$

$\because$ $f(x)$ is discontinuous at $x = 1$, $f(x)$ cannot be differentiable $x = 1$

(we shall prove it in our next topic)

Differentibility at $x = -1$

$$\text{L.H.D} = \lim_{h\to0^+} \frac{f(-1-h) - f(-1)}{-h} = \lim_{h\to0^+} \cos^{-1} \frac{\left(\text{sgn}\left(\dfrac{2[-1-h]}{3(-1-h)}\right) - [-1-h]\right)}{-h}$$

$$= \lim_{h\to0^+} \frac{\cos^{-1}\left(\text{sgn}\left(\dfrac{-4}{-3-3h+2}\right)\right)}{-h} = \lim_{h\to0^+} \frac{\cos^{-1} 1}{-h} = 0$$

$$\text{R.H.D} = \lim_{h\to0^+} \frac{f(-1+h) - f(-1)}{h} = \lim_{h\to0^+} \frac{\cos^{-1}\left(\text{sgn}\left(\dfrac{2[-1+h]}{3(-1+h)-[-1+h]}\right)\right)}{h}$$

$$= \lim_{h\to0^+} \frac{\cos^{-1}\left(\text{sgn}\left(\dfrac{-2}{-3+3h+1}\right)\right)}{h} = \lim_{h\to0^+} \frac{\cos^{-1}\left(\text{sgn}\left(\dfrac{-2}{-2+3h}\right)\right)}{h} = \frac{0}{h} = 0$$

$\therefore$ $f(x)$ is differentiable at $x = 1$

ILLUSTRATION 48: If the function $g(x)$ is differentiable at $x = 2$, then find values of a and b; where
$$g(x)=\begin{cases} a\sqrt{x+2} & ; \quad 0<x<2 \\ bx+2 & ; \quad 2\le x<5 \end{cases}$$

SOLUTION: $$g(x)=\begin{cases} a\sqrt{x+2} & ; \quad 0<x<2 \\ bx+2 & ; \quad 2\le x<5 \end{cases}$$

Now L.H.D. $= g'(2^-) = \lim\limits_{h\to 0^+}\dfrac{g(2+h)-g(2)}{-h} = \lim\limits_{h\to 0^-}\dfrac{a\sqrt{2-h+2}-2b-2}{-h} = \lim\limits_{h\to 0^+}\dfrac{a\sqrt{4-h}-2b-2}{-h}$

Above limit is defined if $\lim\limits_{h\to 0} a\sqrt{4-h}-2b-2=0$

$\Rightarrow 2a-2b-2=0$

$\Rightarrow a=b+1$ ...(i)

$\therefore \quad g'(2^-) = \lim\limits_{h\to 0^+}\dfrac{a\sqrt{4-h}-2a}{-h} = \lim\limits_{h\to 0^+}\dfrac{a(2-\sqrt{4-h})}{h}$

$= \lim\limits_{h\to 0^+}\dfrac{a}{2+\sqrt{4-h}} = \dfrac{a}{4}$ ...(ii)

Now R.H.D $= g'(2^+) = \lim\limits_{h\to 0^-}\dfrac{f(2+h)-f(2)}{h} = \lim\limits_{h\to 0^+}\dfrac{b(2+h)+2-2b-2}{h} = \lim\limits_{h\to 0^+}\dfrac{bh}{h} = b$

$\because$ $g(x)$ is differentiable at $x = 2$

$\Rightarrow g'(2^-) = g'(2^+) \qquad \Rightarrow \dfrac{a}{4} = b$

$\Rightarrow a = 4b$ ...... (iii)

Solving equation, (i) and (iii) we get $b = \dfrac{1}{3}$, $a = \dfrac{4}{3}$

ILLUSTRATION 49: If $f(x) = x.\left(\dfrac{e^{[x]+|x|}-2}{[x]+|x|}\right)$, $x \neq 0$ and $f(0) = -1$; where $[x]$ denotes greatest integer less than or equal to x. Test the differentiability of $f(x)$ at $x = 0$.

SOLUTION: Given $f(x) = \begin{cases} x.\left(\dfrac{e^{[x]+|x|}-2}{[x]+|x|}\right) & ; \quad x\neq 0 \\ -1 & ; \quad x=0 \end{cases}$

R.H.D $= \lim\limits_{h\to 0^+}\dfrac{f(0+h)-f(0)}{h} = \lim\limits_{h\to 0^+}\dfrac{f(h)+1}{h}$

$= \lim\limits_{h\to 0^+}\dfrac{h\left(\dfrac{e^{[h]+|h|}-2}{[h]+|h|}\right)+1}{h} = \lim\limits_{h\to 0^+}\dfrac{\dfrac{h(e^h-2)}{h}+1}{h} = \lim\limits_{h\to 0^+}\dfrac{e^h-1}{h} = 1$

and L.H.D $= \lim\limits_{h\to 0^+}\dfrac{f(-h)-f(0)}{-h} = \lim\limits_{h\to 0^+}\dfrac{-h\left(\dfrac{e^{[-h]+|-h|}-2}{[-h]+|-h|}\right)+1}{-h}$

$= \lim\limits_{h\to 0^+}\dfrac{-h\left(\dfrac{e^{-1+h}-2}{-1+h}\right)+1}{-h} = \lim\limits_{h\to 0^+}\dfrac{-he^{-1+h}+2h-1+h}{-h(-1+h)} = \lim\limits_{h\to 0^+}\dfrac{-he^{-1+h}+3h-1}{-h(-1+h)}$

which does not exist.

Hence function is non-differentiable at $x = 0$

ILLUSTRATION 50: Find the equation of tangent $y = (x)^{1/3}$ at $x = 1$ and $x = 0$

SOLUTION: At $x = 1$. Here $f(x) = (x)^{1/3}$

$$\text{L.H.D} = f'(1^-) = \lim_{h\to 0}\frac{f(1-h)-f(1)}{-h} = \lim_{h\to 0}\frac{(1-h)^{1/3}-1}{-h} = \frac{1}{3}$$

$$\text{R.H.D} = f'(1^+) = \lim_{h\to 0}\frac{f(1+h)-f(1)}{h} = \lim_{h\to 0}\frac{(1+h)^{1/3}-1}{h} = \frac{1}{3}$$

As R.H.D = L.H.D = 1/3

∴ Slope of tangent = 1/3

∴ Equation of tangent is given by $y - f(1) = (1/3)(x - 1)$, i.e., $y - 1 = (1/3)(x - 1)$

⇒ $3y - x = 2$ is tangent to $y = x^{1/3}$ at (1, 1)

At $x = 0$; $\text{L.H.D} = \lim_{h\to 0}\frac{(0-h)^{1/3}-0}{-h} = +\infty$ and $\text{R.H.D} = \lim_{h\to 0}\frac{(0+h)^{1/3}-0}{h} = +\infty$

As L.H.D and R.H.D are infinite, $y = f(x)$ will have a vertical tangent at origin. Thus $x = 0$ is the tangent to $y = x^{1/3}$ at origin.

ILLUSTRATION 51: If $f(x)=\begin{cases}\dfrac{\sin x^2}{x}; \text{at } x\neq 0\\ 0 \quad ; \text{at } x=0\end{cases}$. Find tangent and normal at $x = 0$ if they exist.

SOLUTION: $\text{R.H.D} = f'(0^+) = \lim_{h\to 0}\frac{f(0+h)-f(0)}{h} = \lim_{h\to 0}\frac{\sin h^2}{h^2} = 1$

and $\text{L.H.D} = f'(0^-) = \lim_{h\to 0}\frac{f(0-h)-f(0)}{-h} = \lim_{h\to 0}\frac{\sin h^2}{+h^2} = 1$

∴ Slope of tangent at $x = 0$ is $f'(0) = 1$, the corresponding point on the curve is (0, 0)

∴ Equation of tangent is $(y - 0) = f'(0)(x - 0)$, i.e., $y = x$

Now slope of normal at $x = 0$ is $\frac{-1}{f'(0)} = \frac{-1}{1} = -1$

∴ Equation of normal will be $(y - 0) = -1(x - 0)$, i.e., $y = -x$

Theorem Relating Continuity and Differentiability

Differentiability ⇒ Continuity:

If a function f is derivable at $x = a$, then f is continuous at $x = a$

Proof: Let f is derivable at $x = a$

$$\Rightarrow f'(a) = \lim_{h\to 0}\frac{f(a+h)-f(a)}{h} \text{ exist finitely}$$

$$\because f(a+h) - f(a) = \frac{f(a+h)-f(a)}{h}.h \text{ ; where } (h\neq 0)$$

$$\Rightarrow \lim_{h\to 0}[(f(a+h)-f(a)] = 0$$

$$= \lim_{h\to 0}\frac{f(a+h)-f(a)}{h}.h = \lim_{h\to 0}f'(a).h = f'(a).(0) = 0$$

$$\Rightarrow \lim_{h\to 0}f(a+h) = f(a) \quad \Rightarrow \lim_{h\to a}f(x) = f(a)$$

⇒ $f(x)$ is continuous at $x = a$

∴ If a function is discontinuous at a point, then it must be non-differentiable.

Reasons of Non-differentiability of *a* Function at *x* = *a*

In our previous discussion we studied how to check the differentiability of a function at a point. This is done by verifying the equality of left hand derivative and right hand derivative and both should be finite.

Now we shall study what makes the left hand derivative and right hand derivative unequal or why they do not exist?

What should be the reason behind it? What should be the nature of graph of functions which are 'non-differentiable? In our last chapter we studied that differentiable functions are continuous i.e differentiability of a function at $x = a$ implies the continuity of function at $x = a$, clearly if a function is discontinuous at $x = a$, then surely it will be non-differentiable at $x = a$. Thus we reach to one of the reasons of non-differentiability i.e., discontinuity. Let us explain the various other reasons of non-differentiability in detail.

1. Discontinuity of function at $x = a$

Case (i) When function has a jump discontinuity at $x = a$ such that $f(x)$ is left continuous but right discontinuous or left discontinuous but right continuous

$$\text{Let}\begin{cases} f(a^+) = L_1 \\ f(a^-) = L_2 = f(a) \end{cases}$$

$$\Rightarrow \quad \text{RHD} = \lim_{h\to 0}\frac{f(a+h)-f(a)}{h} = \lim_{h\to 0}\frac{L_1 - L_2}{h} = \infty$$

$$\text{and LHD} = \lim_{h\to 0}\frac{f(a-h)-f(a)}{-h} = f'(a^-)$$

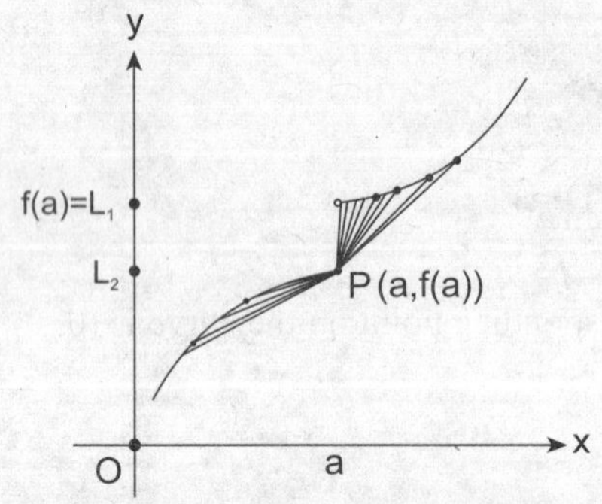

FIGURE 2.64

R.H.D $= \infty$

$\Rightarrow$ $f(x)$ is non-differentiable at $x = a$

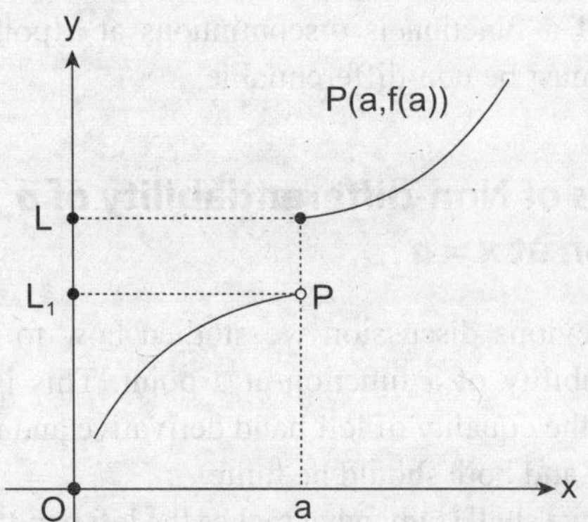

FIGURE 2.65

Case (ii): When the function has a jump discontinuity at $x = a$ such that $f(x)$ is left as well as right discontinuous at $x = a$

$$Let\begin{cases} f(a^-) = L_1 \\ f(a) = L \\ f(a^+) = L_2 \end{cases}$$

$$\text{Then, L.H.D} = \lim_{x\to 0^+}\frac{f(a-h)-f(a)}{-h} = \lim_{x\to 0^+}\frac{L_1 - L}{-h} = \infty$$

$$\text{and R.H.D} = \lim_{x\to 0^+}\frac{f(a+h)-f(a)}{h} = \lim_{x\to 0^+}\frac{L_2 - L}{h} = \infty$$

$$L.H.D. = \lim_{h\to 0}\frac{L_1 - L}{-h} = \infty\ ;\ R.H.D. = \lim_{h\to 0}\frac{L_2 - L}{h} = \infty$$

L.H.D and R.H.D both are infinite thus $f(x)$ is non-differential at $x = a$.

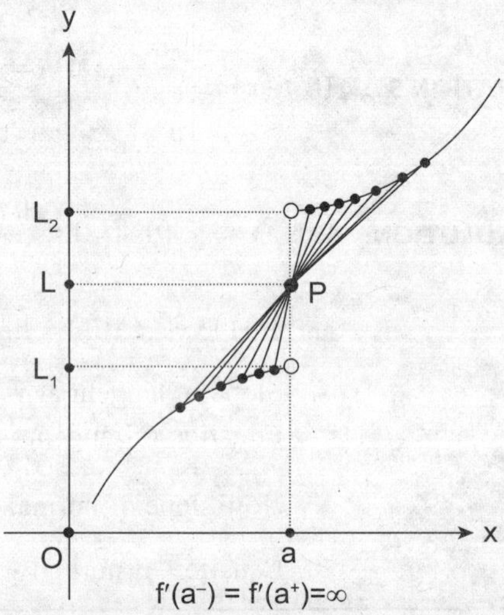

FIGURE 2.66

Similarly for the figure given below

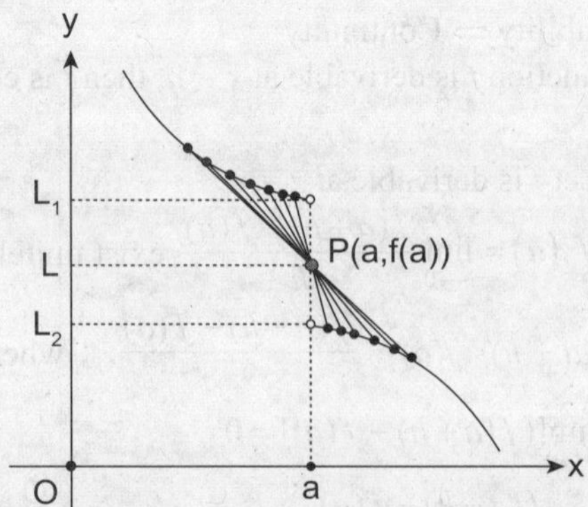

FIGURE 2.67

$$\text{L.H.D.} = \lim_{h\to 0^+}\frac{L_1 - L}{-h} = -\infty \text{ and}$$

$$\text{R.H.D.} = \lim_{h\to 0^+}\frac{L_2 - L}{h} = -\infty$$

∴ L.H.D and R.H.D both are infinite. Thus $f(x)$ is non-differentiable at $x = a$.

Case (iii) When the function $f(x)$ has removable discontinuity at $x = a$

$$\text{Let}\begin{cases} f(a^-) = L_1 = f(a^+) \\ f(a) = L \end{cases}$$

then from figure 2.68

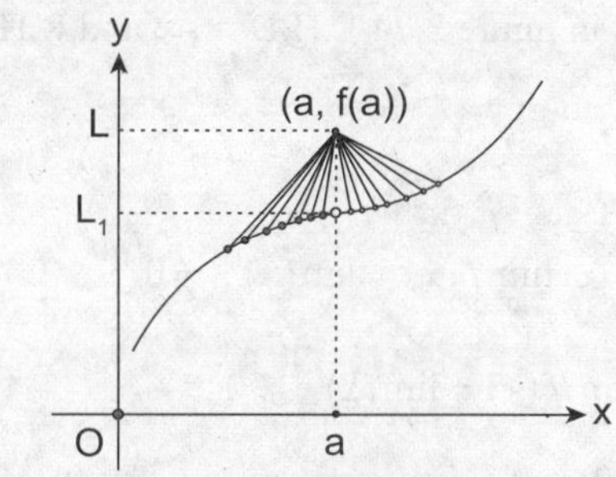

FIGURE 2.68

$$\text{L.H.D} = \lim_{h\to 0^+}\frac{f(a-h)-f(a)}{-h}$$

$$= \lim_{h\to 0^+}\frac{L_1 - L}{-h} = \infty$$

$$\text{And R.H.D} = \lim_{h\to 0^+}\frac{f(a+h)-f(a)}{h} = \lim_{h\to 0^+}\frac{L_1 - L}{h} = -\infty$$

and for the figure given below

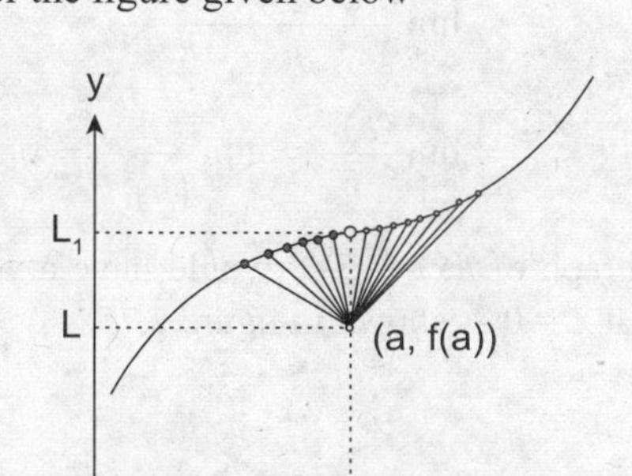

FIGURE 2.69

$$\text{L.H.D} = \lim_{h\to 0^+}\frac{L_1 - L}{-h} = -\infty$$

$$\text{And R.H.D} = \lim_{h\to 0^+}\frac{L_1 - L}{h} = \infty$$

Hence from above four cases we observe that due to discontinuity of a function at a given point whatever it may be (jump on removable) at least one of the two one-sided derivatives becomes infinite. Due to which function becomes non-differentiable at that point.

2. **Sharp points on graph:** It may happen that a function $f(x)$ is continuous at $x = a$, still the function is non-differentiable at $x = a$. This situation may arise due to sharp point on the graph of function at $P(a, f(a))$ as shown below

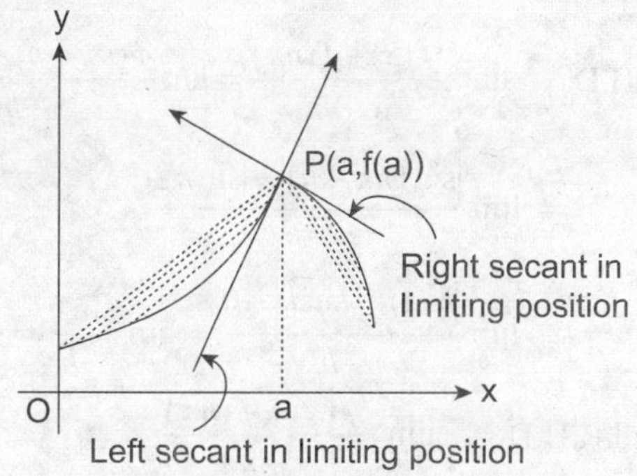

FIGURE 2.70

The point P on graph is called sharp corner or kink. At such points the graph changes its direction abruptly.

Example

(i) The function $f(x) = |x|$ is non-differentiable at $x = 0$

$$\text{L.H.D} = \lim_{x\to 0^-}\frac{f(x)-f(0)}{x-0} = \lim_{x\to 0^-}\frac{|x|-|0|}{x-0} = \lim_{x\to 0^-}\frac{-x}{x} = -1$$

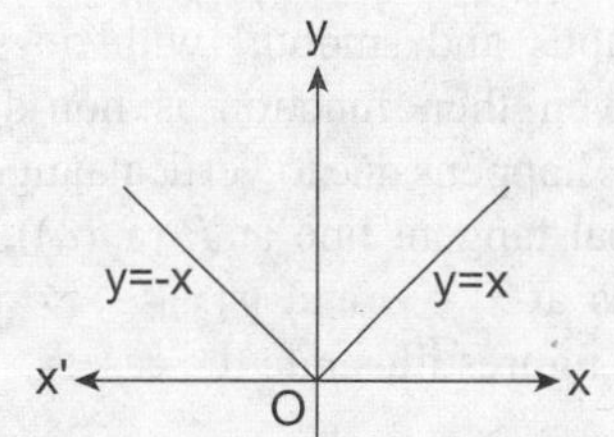

FIGURE 2.71

And

$$\text{R.H.D} = \lim_{x\to 0^+}\frac{f(x)-f(0)}{x-0} = \lim_{x\to 0^+}\frac{|x|-|0|}{x-0} = \lim_{x\to 0^+}\frac{x}{x} = 1$$

∴ L.H.D $= -1$ = slope of $y = -x$

≠ R.H.D $= 1$ = slope of $y = x$

∴ $f(x) = |x|$ is continuous at $x = 0$, but is non-differentiable at $x = 0$

(ii) The function $f(x) = |\sin x|$ is non-differentiable at $x = n\pi$; $n \in \mathbb{Z}$

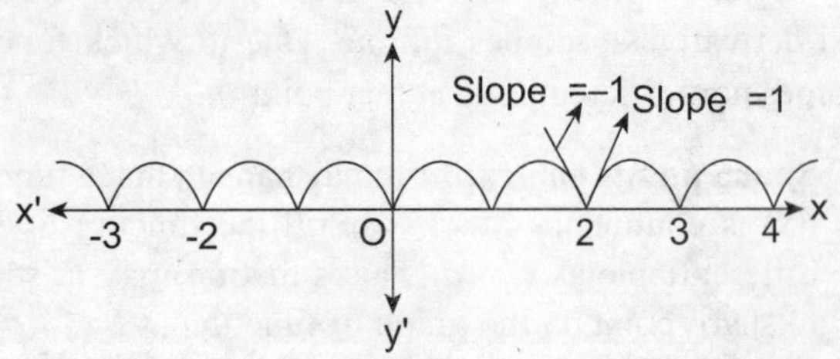

FIGURE 2.72

$$\text{L.H.D} = \lim_{x\to(n\pi)^-} \frac{f(x)-f(n\pi)}{x-n\pi} = \lim_{h\to 0^+} \frac{f(n\pi-h)-f(n\pi)}{-h}$$

$$= \lim_{h\to 0^+} \frac{|\sin(n\pi-h)|-|\sin n\pi|}{-h}$$

$$= \lim_{h\to 0^+} \frac{|(-1)^{n+1}\sin h|-0}{-h} = \lim_{h\to 0^+} \frac{\sin h}{-h} = -1$$

$$\text{and R.H.D} = \lim_{x\to(n\pi)^+} \frac{f(x)-f(n\pi)}{x-n\pi}$$

$$\lim_{h\to 0^+} \frac{f(n\pi+h)-f(n\pi)}{h}$$

$$= \lim_{h\to 0^+} \frac{|\sin(n\pi+h)-|\sin(n\pi)||}{h}$$

$$= \lim_{h\to 0^+} \frac{|(-1)^n\sin h|-0}{h} = \lim_{h\to 0^+} \frac{\sin h}{h} = 1$$

$\therefore$ L.H.D $\neq$ R.H.D

3. **Vertical tangent:** It may happen that a function is continuous and smooth (with no sharp point) at $x = a$, even then function is non-differentiable at $x = a$. This happens due to vertical tangent at $P(a, f(a))$. For vertical tangent line at $P(a, f(a))$, $f(x)$ should be continuous at $x = a$ and $|f'(x)| \to \infty$ as $x \to a$. The following figures illustrate the case:

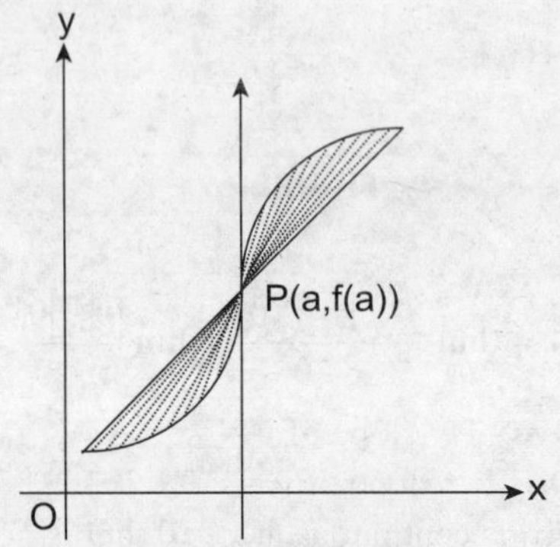

FIGURE 2.73

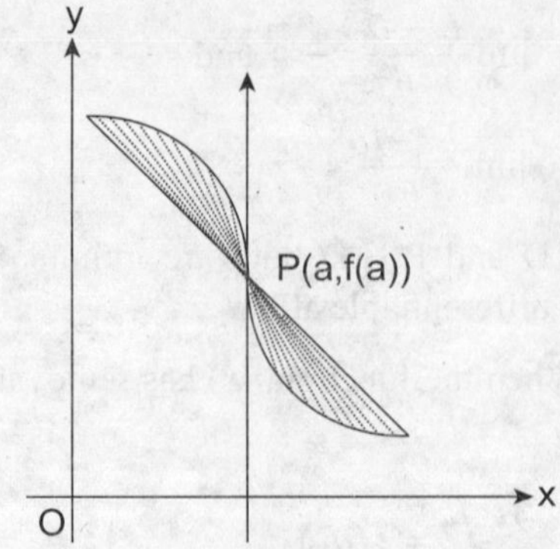

FIGURE 2.74

In figure 2.73 L.H.D = ∞ and R.H.D = ∞
Whereas in figure 2.74 L.H.D = $-\infty$ and R.H.D = $-\infty$

For example:

(i) $f(x) = x^{1/5}$

At $x = 0$, $\lim_{x\to 0^-} f(x) = \lim_{x\to 0^-}(x)^{1/5} = 0$

And $\lim_{x\to 0^+} f(x) = \lim_{x\to 0^+}(x)^{1/5} = 0$

Also $f(0) = 0$
Thus $f(x)$ is continuous at $x = 0$

$$\text{Now L.H.D} = \lim_{h\to 0^+} \frac{f(-h)-0}{-h} = \lim_{h\to 0^+} \frac{(-h)^{1/5}}{-h}$$

$$= \lim_{h\to 0^+} \frac{1}{(-h)^{4/5}} = +\infty$$

$$\text{And R.H.D} = \lim_{h\to 0^+} \frac{f(0+h)-f(0)}{h}$$

$$= \lim_{h\to 0^+} \frac{f(h)-f(0)}{h}$$

$$= \lim_{h\to 0^+} \frac{(h)^{1/5}}{h} = \lim_{h\to 0^+} \frac{1}{(h)^{4/5}} = \infty$$

$\therefore$ The graph of $f(x) = (x)^{1/5}$ would have a vertical tangent at $x = 0$ as shown in figure 2.75.

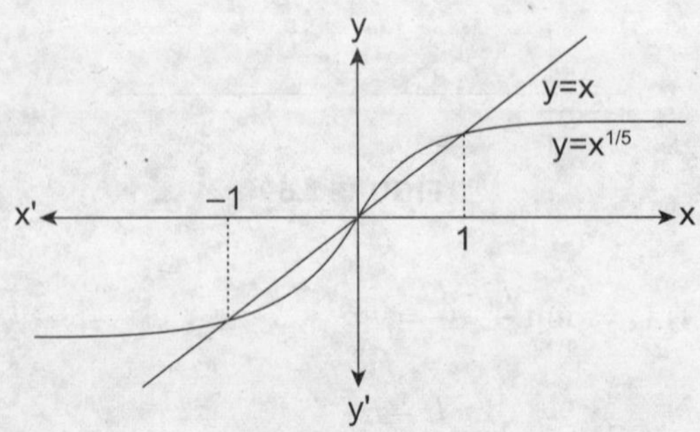

FIGURE 2.75

(ii) For $f(x) = (x)^{2/3}$

$\lim_{x\to 0^-} f(x) = \lim_{x\to 0^+} f(x) = f(0) = 0$

$\therefore$ $f(x)$ is continuous at $x = 0$

Now L.H.D $= \lim_{h\to 0^+} \dfrac{f(0-h)-f(0)}{-h} = \lim_{h\to 0^+} \dfrac{f(-h)}{-h}$

$= \lim_{h\to 0^+} \dfrac{(-h)^{2/3}}{(-h)} = \lim_{h\to 0^+} \dfrac{1}{(-h)^{1/3}} = -\infty$

and R.H.D $= \lim_{h\to 0^+} \dfrac{f(0+h)-f(0)}{h} = \lim_{h\to 0^+} \dfrac{f(h)}{h}$

$= \lim_{h\to 0^+} \dfrac{(h)^{2/3}}{h} = \lim_{h\to 0^+} \dfrac{1}{(h)^{1/3}} = +\infty$

$\therefore$ The graph of $f(x) = (x)^{2/3}$ would have a vertical tangent at $x = 0$ as shown in figure 2.76.

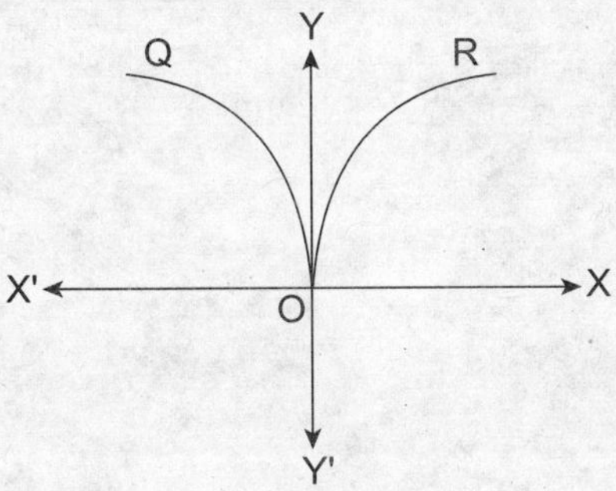

FIGURE 2.76

Thus slope of OQ approaches to $-\infty$ as $x \to 0^-$ and the slope of OR approaches to ∞ as $x \to 0^+$ such a function is said to have cusp at the point under consideration. Hence it is $x = 0$.

4. **Oscillation point:** If a function $f(x)$ is continuous but left and right derivative do not exist at $x = a$ due to high frequency oscillations in neighbourhood of $x = a$, then the function $f(x)$ is non-differentiable at $x = a$ and such a point is called oscillation point.

For example

(i) Consider the function $f(x)$ defined by

$$f(x) = \begin{cases} x\sin\dfrac{1}{x}; x \neq 0 \\ 0; x = 0 \end{cases}$$

$\sin\dfrac{1}{x} \in [-1,1]$

then, $x\sin\dfrac{1}{x}$ lies in between $y = -x$ and $y = x$

and $\lim_{x\to 0} f(x) = \lim_{x\to 0} x\sin\dfrac{1}{x} = 0 \times$ (a finite real number) $= 0 = f(0)$

Thus $f(x)$ is continuous at $x = 0$

Now L.H.D $= \lim_{x\to 0^-} \left(\dfrac{x\sin\frac{1}{x} - 0}{-x}\right) = \lim_{x\to 0^-}\left(-\sin\dfrac{1}{x}\right)$

which oscillates between -1 and 1.

Similarly R.H.D $= \lim_{x\to 0^+}\left(\sin\dfrac{1}{x}\right)$ which also oscillates in between -1 and 1.

Thus L.H.D and R.H.D do not exist at $x = 0$. The graph $f(x)$ is as shown below:

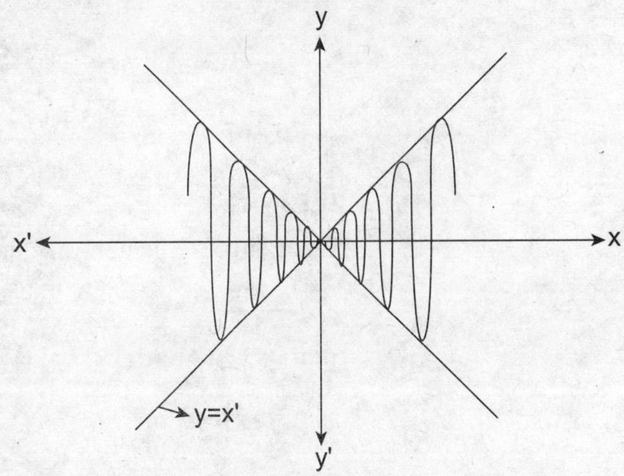

FIGURE 2.77

(ii) $f(x) = \begin{cases} x\left|\sin\dfrac{1}{x}\right|, x \neq 0 \\ 0 \quad ; x = 0 \end{cases}$

The graph of $f(x)$ is as shown below:

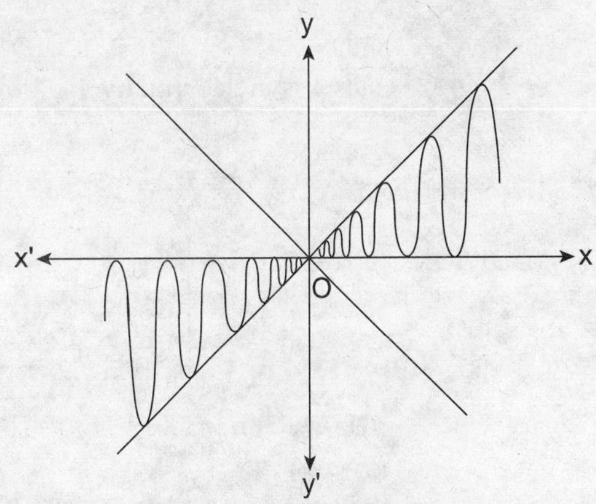

FIGURE 2.78

Clearly $f(x)$ is non-differentiable at $x = 0$.

ILLUSTRATION 52: Examine for continuity and differentiability at the points $x = 1$ and $x = 2$, the function f defined by $f(x) = \begin{cases} x[x], & 0 \le x < 2 \\ (x-1)[x], & 2 \le x \le 3 \end{cases}$; where $[x]$ = greatest integer less than or equal to x.

SOLUTION: Given $f(x) = \begin{cases} x[x], & 0 \le x < 2 \\ (x-1)[x], & 2 \le x \le 3 \end{cases}$

L.H.L. $= \lim\limits_{x \to 1^-} f(x) = \lim\limits_{x \to 1^-} x\,[x] = 0$ and R.H.L. $= \lim\limits_{x \to 1^+} f(x) = \lim\limits_{x \to 1^+} x[x] = 1$

$\therefore \quad \lim\limits_{x \to 1^-} f(x) \ne \lim\limits_{x \to 1^+} f(x)$

$\therefore$ function is discontinuous as well as non-diff. at $x = 1$

Also $f(2) = (2 - 1).2 = 2$

Now L.H.D $= \lim\limits_{h \to 0^+} \dfrac{f(2-h) - f(2)}{-h} = \lim\limits_{h \to 0^+} \dfrac{(2-h)[2-h]-2}{-h} = \lim\limits_{h \to 0^+} \dfrac{(2-h)(1)-2}{-h} = 1$

and R.H.D $= \lim\limits_{h \to 0^+} \dfrac{f(2+h) - f(2)}{h} = \lim\limits_{h \to 0^+} \dfrac{(2+h-1)[2+h]-2}{h} = \lim\limits_{h \to 0^+} \dfrac{(1+h)(2)-2}{h} = 2$

$\therefore \quad f'(2^-) \ne f'(2^+)$

hence function is non-diff. at $x = 2$

Also $\lim\limits_{x \to 2^-} f(x) = \lim\limits_{x \to 2^-} x[x] = 2 \times 1 = 2$

$\lim\limits_{x \to 2^+} f(x) = \lim\limits_{x \to 2^+} (x - 1)\,[x] = (2 - 1).\,2 = 2$

$\therefore \quad \lim\limits_{\to} f(x) = \lim\limits_{x \to 2^+} f(x) = f(2) = 2$

$\therefore$ Function is continuous at $x = 2$

Thus $f(x)$ has a sharp corner point at $x = 2$

ILLUSTRATION 53: A function f is defined as follows: $f(x) = \begin{cases} 1 & \text{for} \quad -\infty < x < 0 \\ 1 + |\sin x| & \text{for} \quad 0 \le x < \dfrac{\pi}{2} \\ 2 + \left(x - \dfrac{\pi}{2}\right) & \text{for} \quad \dfrac{\pi}{2} \le x < +\infty \end{cases}$

Discuss the continuity and differentiability at $x = 0$ and $x = \pi/2$.

SOLUTION: Given $f(x) = \begin{cases} 1 & \text{for} \quad -\infty < x < 0 \\ 1 + |\sin x| & \text{for} \quad 0 \le x < \dfrac{\pi}{2} \\ 2 + \left(x - \dfrac{\pi}{2}\right) & \text{for} \quad \dfrac{\pi}{2} \le x < +\infty \end{cases}$

Clearly $\lim\limits_{x \to 0} f(x) = 1 = f(0)$ so $f(x)$ is continuous at $x = 0$

$f(0) = 1;\ f\left(\dfrac{\pi}{2}\right) = 2$

$$\text{L.H.D} = f'(0^-) = \underset{h\to 0^+}{\text{Lt}} \frac{f(0-h)-f(0)}{-h} = \underset{h\to 0^+}{\text{Lt}} \frac{f(-h)-1}{-h} = \underset{h\to 0^+}{\text{Lt}} \frac{1-1}{-h} = 0$$

$$\text{and R.H.D} = f'(0^+) = \lim_{h\to 0^+} \frac{f(h+0)-f(0)}{h} = \lim_{h\to 0^+} \frac{1+|\sin h|-1}{h} = \lim_{h\to 0^+} \frac{|\sin h|}{h} = \lim_{h\to 0^+} \frac{\sin h}{h} = 1$$

$\therefore\ f'(0^+) \neq f'(0^-)$

hence $f(x)$ is non-differentiable at $x = 0$

$\Rightarrow$ $f(x)$ has a corner point/sharp point at $x = 0$

At $x = \dfrac{\pi}{2}$

$$\text{R.H.D} = f'\left(\frac{\pi^+}{2}\right) = \lim_{h\to 0^+} \frac{f\left(h+\frac{\pi}{2}\right) - f\left(\frac{\pi}{2}\right)}{h} = \lim_{h\to 0^+} \frac{2+\left(h+\frac{\pi}{2}-\frac{\pi}{2}\right)^2 - 2}{h} = \lim_{h\to 0^+} \frac{h^2}{h} = 0$$

$$\text{and L.H.D} = f'\left(\frac{\pi^-}{2}\right) = \lim_{h\to 0^+} \frac{f\left(\frac{\pi}{2}-h\right) - f\left(\frac{\pi}{2}\right)}{h} = \lim_{h\to 0^+} \frac{1+\left|\sin\left(\frac{\pi}{2}-h\right)\right| - 2}{-h}$$

$$= \lim_{h\to 0^+} \frac{|\cos h|-1}{-h} = \lim_{h\to 0^+} \frac{\cos h - 1}{-h} = \lim_{h\to 0^+} \frac{2\sin^2 h/2}{h} = 0$$

$$\therefore\ f'\left(\frac{\pi^-}{2}\right) = f'\left(\frac{\pi^+}{2}\right) = 0$$

$\Rightarrow$ $f(x)$ is differentiable at $x = \dfrac{\pi}{2}$

$\Rightarrow$ $f(x)$ is also continuous at $x = \dfrac{\pi}{2}$

ILLUSTRATION 54: Examine for continuity and derivability at origin in case of the function f defined by $f(x) = x \tan^{-1}(1/x)$, $x \neq 0$ and $f(0) = 0$.

SOLUTION: Given $f(x) = \begin{cases} x\tan^{-1}(1/x) & ; \ x \neq 0 \\ 0 & ; \ x = 0 \end{cases}$

$$\text{Hence } f'(0) = \lim_{h\to 0} \frac{f(h+0)-f(0)}{h} = \lim_{h\to 0} \frac{h\tan^{-1}\frac{1}{h} - 0}{h} = \lim_{h\to 0} \tan^{-1}\left(\frac{1}{h}\right)$$

$$\Rightarrow \begin{cases} \text{R.H.D.} \\ \text{L.H.D.} \end{cases} = \begin{cases} \lim\limits_{h\to 0^+} \tan^{-1}\left(\frac{1}{h}\right) \\ \lim\limits_{h\to 0^-} \tan^{-1}\left(\frac{1}{h}\right) \end{cases} = \begin{cases} \pi/2 \\ -\pi/2 \end{cases}$$

$\therefore\ f'(0^+) \neq f'(0^-) \Rightarrow$ function is non-diff. at $x = 0$

Also $\lim\limits_{x\to 0} f(x) = \lim\limits_{x\to 0} x\tan^{-1}\left(\dfrac{1}{x}\right) = 0 = f(0)$

$\Rightarrow$ function is continuous at $x = 0$

Thus function has a sharp point at $x = 0$

ILLUSTRATION 55: Let $f(x) = xe^{-\left(\frac{1}{|x|}+\frac{1}{x}\right)}$; $x \neq 0$ $f(0) = 0$, test the continuity and differentiability at $x = 0$

SOLUTION: Given $f(x) = \begin{cases} xe^{-\left(\frac{1}{|x|}+\frac{1}{x}\right)} & ; \ x \neq 0 \\ 0 & ; \ x = 0 \end{cases}$

for diff., $f'(0) = \lim\limits_{h \to 0} \dfrac{f(h+0) - f(0)}{h} = \lim\limits_{h \to 0} \dfrac{he^{-\left(\frac{1}{|h|}+\frac{1}{h}\right)} - 0}{h}$

$= \lim\limits_{h \to 0} e^{-\left(\frac{1}{|h|}+\frac{1}{h}\right)} = \begin{cases} \text{L.H.D} \\ \text{R.H.D} \end{cases} = \begin{cases} \lim\limits_{h \to 0^-} e^{-\left(-\frac{1}{h}+\frac{1}{h}\right)} \\ \lim\limits_{h \to 0^+} e^{-\left(\frac{1}{h}+\frac{1}{h}\right)} \end{cases} = \begin{cases} \lim\limits_{h \to 0^-} e^0 \\ \lim\limits_{h \to 0^+} e^{-2/h} \end{cases} = \begin{cases} 1 \\ 0 \end{cases}$

$\therefore$ $f'(0^+) \neq f'(0^-) \Rightarrow$ hence function is non-diff. at $x = 0$

for continuity, $\lim\limits_{x \to 0} f(x) = \lim\limits_{x \to 0} xe^{-\left(\frac{1}{|x|}+\frac{1}{x}\right)} = 0$

$\therefore$ Function is continuous at $x = 0$

$\therefore$ Function has a sharp point at $x = 0$

TEXTUAL EXERCISE–4: (SUBJECTIVE)

1. Check the continuity and differentiability of $f(x) = \begin{cases} x\sin(\log x^2); & x \neq 0 \\ 0 & ; \ x = 0 \end{cases}$ at $x = 0$.

2. (a) Show that the value of the derivative of $|x - 1| + |x - 3|$ at $x = 2$ is 0.

   (b) If $f(x) = |x|/[x]$, $x \notin (0, 1)$, then find $f'(2)$. Here [ ] denotes greatest integer function.

3. A function $f(x)$ is defined as $f(x) = \begin{cases} \dfrac{|x-1|}{x-1}; & x \neq 1 \\ 0 & ; \ x = 1 \end{cases}$ then discuss the continuity and differentiability of $f(x)$ and mention the direction of tangent at the point $x = 1$.

4. If $f(x) = |\sin x - \cos x|$, find $f'(\pi/2)$, if it exists.

5. Does $f'(1)$ and $f'(2)$ exists for the function

   $f(x) = \begin{cases} x[x]; & 0 \leq x < 2 \\ x^2 - x; & 2 \leq x \leq 3 \end{cases}$; where $[x]$ denotes greatest integer $\leq x$.

6. If $f(x)$ is defined as $f(x) = \begin{cases} (x)^p \cos\left[\dfrac{1}{x}\right]; & x \neq 0 \\ 0 & ; \ x = 0 \end{cases}$, find the condition that can be imposed on p such that f can be

   (i) continuous

   (ii) differentiable at $x = 0$.

7. Let $f(x) = \begin{cases} (x-1)^2 \sin\left[\dfrac{1}{(x-1)}\right] - |x| & ; \ x \neq 1 \\ -1 & ; \ x = 1 \end{cases}$, then prove that the above function is differentiable at $x = 1$.

8. Find the values of a, b and c. If $f(x) = a\,|\sin x| + b\,e^{|x|} + c\,|x|^3$ is differentiable at $x = 0$.

9. Check the continuity and differentiability of $f(x) = x^2 \sin 1/x$ if $x \neq 0$ and x if $x = 0$ and show that "differentiability of function not necessarily implies continuity of its derivative."

10. Prove that the derivative of an even derivable function is always an odd function.

11. If $f(x)$ be an even function and $f'(0)$ exists, then show that $f'(0) = 0$.

12. Examine the function $f(x) = x.\dfrac{a^{1/x} - a^{-1/x}}{a^{1/x} + a^{-1/x}}, x \neq 0$ $(a > 0)$ and $f(0) = 0$ for continuity and existence of the derivative at origin.

13. A function 'f' is defined by $f(x) = \begin{cases} \dfrac{1}{[x]} & \text{if } |x| \geq \dfrac{1}{2} \\ ax^2 + bx + c & \text{if } |x| < \dfrac{1}{2} \end{cases}$. If '$f$' is differentiable at $x = 1$ and $x = -1/2$, then find the values of a, b and c if possible.

14. Check the differentiability of $f(x) = \begin{cases} (x-e)2^{-2\left(\frac{1}{e-x}\right)} & ; x \neq e \\ 0 & ; x = e \end{cases}$ at $x = e$

15. Let $f(x) = \dfrac{xg(x)}{|x|}$, $g(0) = g'(0) = 0$ and $f(x)$ be continuous at $x = 0$. Find $f'(0)$, if it exists.

16. Prove that $f(x) = \dfrac{x}{1+|x|^n}$ is differentiable at $x = 0$ for all $n \in [0, \infty)$.

17. $f(x) = \begin{cases} a + (x-b)^2 & , |x-b| \leq k \\ c + |x-b| & , |x-b| > k \end{cases}$ Find the value of 'k', so that $f(x)$ becomes differentiable at $x = b - k$, $b + k$ and prove that $a - c = 1/4$.

Answer Keys

1. Continuous but non-differentiable

2. (b) does not exist **3.** $f(x)$ is discontinuous and non-differentiable at $x = 1$, At $x = 1$, tangent is vertical

4. $f'\left(\dfrac{\pi}{2}\right) = 1$ **5.** No differentiable at $x = 1, 2$ **6.** (i) $p > 0$, (ii) $p > 1$

8. $a + b = 0$; $c \in \mathbb{R}$ **9.** Continuous and differentiable at $x = 0$

12. Continuous but not differentiable at origin **13.** $(a,b,c) \in \left\{\left(k, k, \dfrac{k-4}{4}\right); k \in \mathbb{R}\right\}$ **14.** non-diff

15. 0 **17.** $k = 1/2$

TEXTUAL EXERCISE–4: (OBJECTIVE)

1. If $y = |x - a| + |x - b|$, then:
(a) $f(x)$ is continuous and differentiable at $x = a, b$
(b) $f(x)$ is continuous but not differentiable at $x = a, b$
(c) $f(x)$ is neither differentiable nor continuous at $x = a, b$
(d) None of these

2. $y = ||x - 1| - 1| + 1$ is NOT differentiable at the points :
(a) (0, 0), (1, 1), (0, 2)
(b) (0, – 1), (1, 0), (2, 1)
(c) (1, 0), (1, 2), (1, – 2)
(d) (0, 1), (1, 2), (2, 1)

3. If $f(x) = \sin|x| - e^{|x|}$, then at $x = 0$, $f(x)$ is :
(a) Continuous but not differentiable
(b) Neither continuous nor differentiable
(c) Both continuous and differentiable
(d) None of these

4. Number of points where $f(x) = |\text{Max }\{x^2 - 2, x\}|$ is not differentiable is :
(a) 1 (b) 2
(c) 3 (d) 4

5. Let $f(x) = \dfrac{\sin x}{|x|}$, where $x \neq 0$ and $f(x) = 1$, where $x = 0$, then
(a) $f(x)$ is differentiable at $x = 0$
(b) $f(x)$ is continuous but not differentiable at $x = 0$
(c) $f(x)$ is not continuous at $x = 0$
(d) $\lim_{x \to 0^{+}} f(x) = 0$

6. $\sin^{-1}(\sin x)$ is NOT differentiable at $x =$
(a) $\pi/4$ (b) $\pi/2$
(c) $\pi/6$ (d) π

7. The left hand derivative of $f(x) = [x] \sin \pi x$ at $x = k$, k an integer and [ ] is the greatest integer function is:
(a) $(-1)^k (k-1)\pi$ (b) $(-1)^{k-1} (k-1)\pi$
(c) $(-1)^k k\pi$ (d) $(-1)^{k-1} k\pi$

8. Number of points where $f(x) = \text{Max}\ \{9-4x, 2x^2+3, 4x+1\}$ is NOT differentiable is:
(a) 2 (b) 3
(c) 1 (d) differentiable at all points

9. $y = Max\ \{e^{|x|}, \ln |x|\}$ is non-differentiable at
(a) all values of x
(b) No value of x
(c) only three value of x
(d) only two values of x

10. The domain of derivative of the function:
$$f(x)=\begin{cases}\tan^{-1}x & if\ |x|\le 1\\ \frac{1}{2}(|x|-1) & if\ |x|>1\ is\end{cases}$$
(a) $R - \{0\}$ (b) $R - \{1\}$
(c) $R - \{-1\}$ (d) $R - \{-1, 1\}$

11. If $|f(x) - f(y)| \le |x-y|^{2n+1}$ $(n \in N)$ then $f'(x)$ is equal to :
(a) 0 (b) n
(c) nx (d) 1

12. At the points where $y = |\cos x|$ is differentiable, $\frac{dy}{dx}$ equals:
(a) $|\sin x|$ (b) $-|\sin x|$
(c) $-|\sin x| \cot x$ (d) $-|\cos x| \tan x$

13. The points of non-differentiability of the function $f(x) = |||x-1|-1|-1|$ are:
(a) $\{0, 1, 2, 3, 4\}$ (b) $\{-1, 0, 1, 2, 3\}$
(c) $\{-1, 0, 1\}$ (d) None of these

14. If $f(x) = 1 - |x|$, the number of points where $f(f(x))$ ceases to be differentiable is:
(a) 0 (b) 1
(c) 2 (d) 3

15. Which of the following is/are true?
(a) If f is continuous, then $|f|$ is also continuous
(b) If $|f|$ is continuous, then f is also continuous
(c) If f is differentiable, then $|f|$ is also differentiable
(d) If $|f|$ is differentiable, then f is also differentiable

16. Which of the following functions is differentiable at $x = 0$?
(a) $\cos(|x|) + |x|$ (b) $\cos(|x|) - |x|$
(c) $\sin(|x|) + |x|$ (d) $\sin(|x|) - |x|$

17. Let [ ] denotes the greatest integer functions and $f(x) = [\tan^2 x]$, then
(a) $\lim_{x\to 0} f(x)$ does not exist
(b) $f(x)$ is continuous at $x = 0$
(c) $f(x)$ is not differentiable at $x = 0$
(d) $f'(0) = 1$

18. The function $f(x) = |2x-3|\ [x]$, $x \ge 1$; and $f(x) = \sin \frac{\pi x}{2}$, $x < 1$; ([ ] denotes the greatest integer function)
(a) is continuous at $x = 2$
(b) is differentiable at $x = 2$
(c) continuous and differentiable at $x = 1$
(d) is continuous but not differentiable at $x = 3/2$

19. If $f(x)=\begin{cases}\frac{x^2-1}{x^2+1} & ;\ 0<x\le 2\\ \frac{1}{4}(x^3-x^2) & ;\ 2<x\le 3\\ \frac{9}{4}(|x-4|+|2-x|) & ;\ 3<x<4\end{cases}$, then
(a) $f(x)$ is differentiable at $x = 2$ and $x = 3$
(b) $f(x)$ is non-differentiable at $x = 2$ and $x = 3$
(c) $f(x)$ is differentiable at $x = 3$ but not at $x = 2$
(d) $f(x)$ is differentiable at $x = 2$ but not at $x = 3$

20. A function $f(x)$ is defined as $f(x)=\begin{cases}x^m \sin\frac{1}{x}; & x\ne 0,\ m\in \mathbb{N}\\ 0\ ; & \text{if } x=0\end{cases}$. The least value of m for which $f'(x)$ is continuous at $x = 0$ is
(a) 1 (b) 2
(c) 3 (d) None of these

21. Let the function f, g and h be defined as follows:
$$f(x)=\begin{cases}x\sin\left(\frac{1}{x}\right) & \text{for } -1\le x\le 1 \text{ and } x\ne 0\\ 0 & \text{for } x=0\end{cases}$$
$$g(x)=\begin{cases}x^2\sin\left(\frac{1}{x}\right) & \text{for } -1\le x\le 1 \text{ and } x\ne 0\\ 0 & \text{for } x=0\end{cases}$$
$h(x) = |x|^3$ for $-1 \le x \le 1$
Which of these functions are differentiable at $x = 0$?
(a) f and g only (b) f and h only
(c) g and h only (d) None of these

22. The function $g(x)=\begin{cases} x+b, & x<0 \\ \cos x, & x\geq 0 \end{cases}$ can be made differentiable at $x = 0$.

(a) if b is equal to zero
(b) if b is not equal to zero
(c) if b takes any real value
(d) for no value of b

23. Let f be differentiable at $x = 0$ and $f'(0) = 1$. Then $\lim\limits_{h\to 0}\dfrac{f(h)-f(-2h)}{h}$ equals

(a) 3 (b) 2
(c) 1 (d) – 1

24. If $f(3) = 6$ and $f'(3) = 2$, then $\lim\limits_{x\to 3}\dfrac{x f(3) - 3 f(x)}{x - 3}$ is given by :

(a) 6 (b) 4
(c) 0 (d) none of these

25. Consider $f(x) = \left[\dfrac{2\left(\sin x - \sin^3 x\right) + \left|\sin x - \sin^3 x\right|}{2\left(\sin x - \sin^3 x\right) - \left|\sin x - \sin^3 x\right|}\right]$, $x \neq \dfrac{\pi}{2}$ for $x \in (0, \pi)$; $f(\pi/2) = 3$, where [ ] denotes the greatest integer function, then,

(a) f is continuous and differentiable at $x = \pi/2$
(b) f is continuous but not differentiable at $x = \pi/2$
(c) f is neither continuous nor differentiable at $x = \pi/2$
(d) None of these

26. Given the function $f(x) = 2x\sqrt{x^3 - 1} + 5\sqrt{x}\sqrt{1 - x^4} + 7x^2\sqrt{x - 1} + 3x + 2$ then:

(a) the function is continuous but not differentiable at $x = 1$
(b) the function is discontinuous at $x = 1$
(c) the function is both continuous and differentiable at $x = 1$
(d) the range of $f(x)$ is R^+

27. If $f(x)=\begin{cases} \dfrac{x\,.\,\ell n(\cos x)}{\ell n\left(1+x^2\right)}; & x\neq 0 \\ 0 \quad ; & x=0 \end{cases}$, then:

(a) f is continuous at $x = 0$
(b) f is continuous at $x = 0$ but not differentiable at $x = 0$
(c) f is differentiable at $x = 0$
(d) f is not continuous at $x = 0$

28. The function $f(x)=\begin{cases} |x-3|, & x\geq 1 \\ \left(\frac{x^2}{4}\right)-\left(\frac{3x}{2}\right)+\left(\frac{13}{4}\right), & x<1 \end{cases}$ is:

(a) Continuous at $x = 1$
(b) Differentiable at $x = 1$
(c) Continuous at $x = 3$
(d) Differentiable at $x = 3$

29. The function $f(x) = \sqrt{1-\sqrt{1-x^2}}$

(a) has its domain $-1 \leq x \leq 1$
(b) has finite one sided derivative at the point $x = \pm 1$
(c) is continuous and differentiable at $x = 0$
(d) is continuous but not differentiable at $x = 0$

Answer Keys

1. (b)	**2.** (d)	**3.** (c)	**4.** (d)	**5.** (c)	**6.** (b)	**7.** (a)	**8.** (a)	**9.** (c)	**10.** (d)
11. (a)	**12.** (d)	**13.** (b)	**14.** (d)	**15.** (a)	**16.** (d)	**17.** (b)	**18.** (d)	**19.** (b)	**20.** (c)
21. (c)	**22.** (d)	**23.** (a)	**24.** (c)	**25.** (a)	**26.** (a)	**27.** (a,c)	**28.** (a,b,c)	**29.** (a,b,d)	

ALGEBRA OF DIFFERENTIABILITY

If $f(x)$ and $g(x)$ are differentiable functions at $x = a$, then following holds good

1. $kf(x)$ is always differentiable (k is finite) at $x = a$

Proof: Since $f(x)$ is differentiable at $x = a$

$$\Rightarrow \lim_{h\to 0^+}\frac{f(a-h)-f(a)}{-h} = \lim_{h\to 0^+}\frac{f(a+h)-f(a)}{h} = f'(a),$$

finite and real

Now $\lim\limits_{h\to 0^+}\dfrac{kf(a-h)-kf(a)}{-h} = \lim\limits_{h\to 0^+} k\left[\dfrac{f(a-h)-f(a)}{-h}\right]$

$= kf(a)$

and $\lim\limits_{h\to 0^+}\dfrac{kf(a+h)-kf(a)}{h} = \lim\limits_{h\to 0^+}\dfrac{k\left[f(a+h)-f(a)\right]}{h}$

$= kf(a)$

$\therefore$ kf is differentiable at $x = a$

2. $f(x) \pm g(x)$ is always differentiable at $x = a$

Proof: Let $\psi(x) = f(x) + g(x)$

$$\text{L.H.D} = \lim_{h\to 0^+} \frac{\psi(a-h)-\psi(a)}{-h}$$

$$= \lim_{h\to 0^+} \frac{[f(a-h)+g(a-h)]-[f(a)+g(a)]}{-h}$$

$$= \lim_{h\to 0^+} \frac{f(a-h)-f(a)}{-h} + \lim_{h\to 0^+} \frac{g(a-h)-g(a)}{-h}$$

$$= \underbrace{f'(a^-)}_{\text{finite}} + \underbrace{g'(a^-)}_{\text{finite}} = \text{finite}$$

$$\text{R.H.D} = \lim_{h\to 0^+} \frac{\psi(a+h)-\psi(a)}{h}$$

$$= \lim_{h\to 0^+} \frac{[f(a+h)+g(a+h)]-[f(a)+g(a)]}{h}$$

$$= \lim_{h\to 0^+} \frac{f(a+h)-f(a)}{h} + \lim_{h\to 0^+} \frac{g(a+h)-g(a)}{h}$$

$$= f'(a^+) + g'(a^+) = \text{finite}$$

$\because f'(a^-) = f'(a^+)$ and $g'(a^-) = g'(a^+)$

$\therefore$ L.H.D = R.H.D at $x = a$ for $\psi(x)$

Thus $(f + g)$ is differentiable at $x = a$

Similarly, we can show that $(f-g)$ is differentiable at $x = a$

3. $f(x) \,.\, g(x)$ is always differentiable at $x = a$

Proof: Let $\psi(x) = f(x)\, g(x)$

$$\text{L.H.D} = \lim_{h\to 0^+} \frac{\psi(a-h)-\psi(a)}{-h}$$

$$= \lim_{h\to 0^+} \frac{f(a-h)g(a-h)-f(a).g(a)}{-h}$$

$$= \lim_{h\to 0^+} \frac{f(a-h)g(a-h)-f(a)g(a-h)+f(a)g(a-h)-f(a)g(a)}{-h}$$

$$= \lim_{h\to 0^+} \frac{g(a-h)[f(a-h)-f(a)]}{-h} + \lim_{h\to 0^+} \frac{f(a)[g(a-h)-g(a)]}{-h}$$

$= g(a).f'(a^-) + f(a)\, g'(a^-)$ …(i)

$$\text{R.H.D} = \lim_{h\to 0^+} \frac{\psi(a+h)-\psi(a)}{h}$$

$$= \lim_{h\to 0^+} \frac{f(a+h)g(a+h)-f(a).g(a)}{h}$$

$$= \lim_{h\to 0^+} \frac{f(a+h).g(a+h)-f(a)g(a+h)+f(a)g(a+h)-f(a)g(a)}{h}$$

$$= \lim_{h\to 0^+} g(a+h)\left\{\frac{f(a+h)-f(a)}{h}\right\} + \lim_{h\to 0^+} f(a).\left\{\frac{g(a+h)-g(a)}{h}\right\}$$

$= g(a)f'(a^+) + f(a).g'(a^+)$ …(ii)

$\because f'(a^-) = f'(a^+)$ and $g'(a^-) = g'(a^+)$

$\therefore$ from (i) and (ii)

L.H.D = R.H.D at $x = a$ for $\psi(x)$

$\therefore$ $(f.g)$ is differentiable at $x = a$

4. $\dfrac{f(x)}{g(x)}$ is differentiable at $x = a$, provided $g(a) \neq 0$

Proof: Let $\phi(x) = \dfrac{f(x)}{g(x)}; g(a) \neq 0$

$$\text{Then, L.H.D} = \lim_{h\to 0^+} \frac{\phi(a-h)-\phi(a)}{-h}$$

$$= \lim_{h\to 0^+} \frac{\dfrac{f(a-h)}{g(a-h)} - \dfrac{f(a)}{g(a)}}{-h}$$

$$= \lim_{h\to 0^+} \frac{f(a-h)g(a)-f(a)g(a-h)}{-h\,g(a-h)g(a)}$$

$$= \lim_{h\to 0^+} \frac{f(a-h)g(a)-f(a)g(a)+f(a)g(a)-f(a)g(a-h)}{-hg(a-h)g(a)}$$

$$= \frac{\lim\limits_{h\to 0^+}\left\{\dfrac{g(a)[f(a-h)-f(a)]}{-h} - f(a)\dfrac{[g(a-h)-g(a)]}{-h}\right\}}{g(a-h)g(a)}$$

$$= \frac{g(a)f'(a^-)-f(a)g'(a^-)}{[g(a)]^2} \quad \text{…(i)}$$

$$\text{Also R.H.D} = \lim_{h\to 0} \frac{\phi(a+h)-\phi(a)}{h}$$

$$= \lim_{h\to 0} \frac{\dfrac{f(a+h)}{g(a+h)} - \dfrac{f(a)}{g(a)}}{h}$$

$$= \lim_{h\to 0} \frac{f(a+h)g(a)-g(a+h)f(a)}{hg(a+h).g(a)}$$

$$= \lim_{h\to 0} \frac{f(a+h)g(a)-f(a)g(a)+f(a)g(a)-g(a+h)f(a)}{h\,g(a+h).g(a)}$$

$$= \frac{\lim\limits_{h\to 0}\left\{g(a)\dfrac{[f(a+h)-f(a)]}{h} - f(a)\dfrac{[g(a+h)-g(a)]}{h}\right\}}{g(a+h)g(a)}$$

$$= \frac{g(a)f'(a^+)-f(a)g'(a^+)}{[g(a)]^2} \quad \text{…(ii)}$$

$f'(a^-) = f'(a^+)$ and $g'(a^-) = g(a^+)$ and $g(a) \neq 0$

$\therefore$ from (i) and (ii) we have $\phi'(a^-) = \phi'(a^+)$

5. $f(g(x))$ is differentiable at $x = a$ if f is differentiable at $x = g(a)$ and $g(x)$ is differenable at $x = a$.

Proof: Given $g(x)$ is differentiable at $x = a$, and $f(x)$ is differentiable at $x = g(a) = u$ (say)

Let $\phi(x) = (fog)(x)$

$$\Rightarrow \lim_{h\to 0^+}\frac{g(a-h)-g(a)}{-h} = \frac{\lim g(a+h)-g(a)}{h} = g'(a) \quad ..(i)$$

and

$$\lim_{h\to 0^+}\frac{f(u-h)-f(u)}{-h} = \lim_{h\to 0^+}\frac{f(u+h)-f(u)}{h} = f(u) \quad ..(ii)$$

At $x = a$, let us discuss differentiability of $\phi(x) = fog(x)$.

$$\text{L.H.D} = \lim_{h\to 0^+}\frac{\phi(a-h)-\phi(a)}{-h}$$

$$= \lim_{h\to 0^+}\frac{(fog)(a-h)-(fog)(a)}{-h}$$

$$\lim_{h\to 0^+}\frac{f(g(a-h))-f(g(a))}{-h}$$

$$= \lim_{h\to 0^+}\frac{f(g(a-h))-f(u)}{-h}$$

$\therefore$ $g(a) = u \Rightarrow g(a-h) = u - \delta;\ \delta \to 0$

$$\text{as } g'(a) = \lim_{h\to 0^+}\frac{g(a-h)-g(a)}{-h} \Rightarrow g(a-h) \to g(a) = u$$

$\therefore$ $g(a-h) = u - \delta,\ \delta \to 0$ as $h \to 0$

$$\therefore \text{ L.H.D.} = \lim_{h\to 0^+}\frac{f(u-\delta)-f(u)}{-h(\delta)}$$

$$= \lim_{\delta,h\to 0^+}\frac{f(u-\delta)-f(u)}{-\delta}\times\frac{\delta}{h}$$

$$= f'(u^-)\lim_{\delta,h\to 0^+}\frac{\delta}{h} = f'(u^-).\lim_{h\to 0^+}\frac{u-g(a-h)}{h}$$

$$= f'(u^-)\lim_{h\to 0^+}\frac{g(a-h)-g(a)}{-h}$$

$$= f'(u^-)g'(a^-) = f'(u).g'(a) = f'(g(a).g'(a)$$

$$\text{Similarly R.H.D} = \lim_{h\to 0^+}\frac{\phi(a+h)-\phi(a)}{h}$$

$$= \lim_{h\to 0^+}\frac{f(g(a+h)-f(g(a))}{h}$$

$$= \lim_{h\to 0^+}\frac{f(g(a+h))-f(u)}{h}$$

$\therefore$ $g(a) = u \Rightarrow g(a+h) = u + \delta$

$$\text{as } g'(a) = \lim_{h\to 0}\frac{g(a+h)-g(a)}{h} \Rightarrow g(a+h) \to g(a) = u$$

$\Rightarrow$ $g(a+h) = u + \delta$ for some $\delta \to 0$ as $h \to 0$

$$\therefore \text{ R.H.D} = \lim_{h\to 0^+}\frac{f(u+\delta)-f(u)}{h}$$

$$\lim_{\delta,h\to 0}\frac{f(u+\delta)-f(u)}{\delta}.\frac{\delta}{h}$$

$$= \lim_{\delta\to 0}\frac{f(u+\delta)-f(a)}{\delta}\lim_{\delta,x\to\infty}\frac{\delta}{h}$$

$$= f'(u^+).\lim_{h\to 0^+}\frac{g(a+h)-g(a)}{h}$$

$= f'(u^+).\ g'(a^+)$

$= f'(u)\ g'(a) = f'(g(a)).g'(a)$

Thus L.H.D = R.H.D = $f'(g(a)).g'(a)$. Hence $fog(x)$ is differentiable at $x = a$ if $f(x)$ is differentiable at $x = g$ (a) and $g(x)$ is differentiable at $x = a$.

6. Sum of two non-differentiable functions can be differentiable

Proof: Let $f(x)$ and $g(x)$ be two non-differentiable functions at $x = a$ and let $h(x) = f(x) + g(x)$.

Let $f'(a^-) = l_1, f'(a^+) = l_2$; l_1, l_2 finite but $l_1 \neq l_2$

And $g'(a^-) = m_1$, $g'(a^+) = m_2$; $m_1\ m_2$ finite but $m_1 \neq m_2$

Now $f'(a^-) + g'(a^-) = l_1 + m_1$

And $f'(a^+) + g'(a^+) = l_2 + m_2$

Now, it may happen that $l_1 + m_1 = l_2 + m_2$

For example, (i) $f(x) = \begin{cases} x \text{ for } x > 0 \\ -x \text{ for } x \le 0 \end{cases}$

and $g(x) = \begin{cases} 2x \text{ for } x > 0 \\ 4x \text{ for } x < 0 \end{cases}$

Clearly $f'(0^-) = -1$; $f'(0^+) = 1$

And $g'(0^-) = 4$; $g'(0^+) = 2$

$\therefore$ $f(x)$ and $g(x)$ are non-differentiable at $x = 0$

But $f(x) + g(x) = 3x \forall\ x \in$

and $f'(0^-) + g'(0^-) = 3$ and $f'(0^+) + g'(0^+) = 3$

$\Rightarrow$ $f(x) + g(x)$ is differentiable at $x = 0$

(ii) $f(x) = 2 + |x|$ and $g(x) = 3 - |x|$ are non-diff at $x = 0$ But, $f(x) + g(x) = 5 \Rightarrow$ always iff

Also $f(x) = [x]$; $g(x) = \{x\}$; $f(x) + g(x) = x \Rightarrow$ diff

7. Sum of differentiable function and non-differentiable function is always non-differentiable

Proof: Let $f(x)$ be differentiable at $x = a$, and $g(x)$ be non-differentiable at $x = a$

So, let $f'(a^-) = f'(a^+)$ & $g'(a^-) \neq g'(a^+)$

Clearly $f'(a^-) + g'(a^-) \neq f'(a^+) + g'(a^+)$

Thus $f(x) + g(x)$ is always non-differentiable

8. Product of two non-diff functions may be differentiable.

e.g., $f(x) = |x|$ and $g(x) = |x|$ $f(x).g(x) = (|x|)^2 = |x^2| = x^2$ which is always differentiable

9. Product of a diff and non-differentiable function may be differentiable $f(x) = |x|$ and $g(x) = x$

e.g. $f(x) = x|x| = \begin{cases} x^2 & x > 0 \\ -x^2 & x < 0 \end{cases}$

Domain of Differentiability

The set containing all the points at which the function is differentiable is called domain of differentiability of a given function, for example if $f(x) = ||x| - 1|$; then its graph is given below

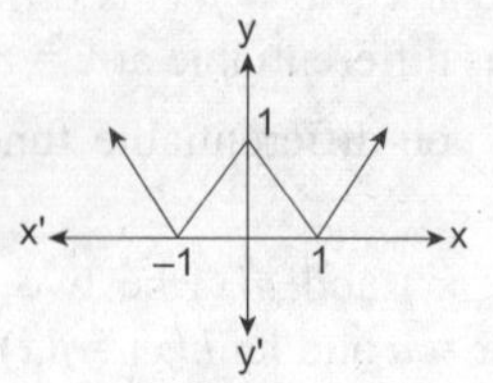

FIGURE 2.79

The graph of $f(x)$ has corner points at $x = -1$, 0 and 1. Except for all these points, $f(x)$ has smooth and continuous graph at all real points. Thus domain of differentiability of $f(x)$ is $\mathbb{R} \sim \{-1, 0, 1\}$.

DOMAIN OF DIFFERENTIABILITY OF SOME STANDARD FUNCTIONS

f(x)	Domain of differentiability	f(x)	Domain of differentiability
Polynomial $P(x)$	$\mathbb{R}$	$\sec x$	$\mathbb{R} - \{(2n+1).\pi/2;\ n\in\mathbb{Z}\}$
$\dfrac{P(x)}{Q(x)}$	$\mathbb{R} - \{x : Q(x) = 0\}$	$\operatorname{cosec} x$	$\mathbb{R} - \{n\pi;\ n\in\mathbb{Z}\}$
a^x	$\mathbb{R}$	$\sin^{-1} x$	$(-1, 1)$
$\log x$	$(0,\infty)$	$\cos^{-1} x$	$(-1, 1)$
$\sin x$	$\mathbb{R}$	$\tan^{-1} x$	$\mathbb{R}$
$\cos x$	$\mathbb{R}$	$\cot^{-1} x$	$\mathbb{R}$
$\tan x$	$\mathbb{R} - \{(2n+1).\pi/2;\ n\in\mathbb{Z}\}$	$\sec^{-1} x$	$(-\infty,-1)\cup(1,\infty)$
$\cot x$	$\mathbb{R} - \{n\pi;\ n\in\mathbb{Z}\}$	$\operatorname{cosec}^{-1} x$	$(-\infty,-1)\cup(1,\infty)$

Differentiability in Open and Closed Interval

A function is differentiable in open interval (a, b) if $f'(c^-) = f'(c^+)$ real and finite $\forall\ c \in (a, b)$. A function is differentiable in closed interval $[a, b]$ if f is differentiable in (a, b) and RHD at $x = a$ and LHD at $x = b$ should be real and finite. i.e., $f'(c^+) = f'(c^-)$ = real and finite $\forall\ c \in (a, b)$ and RHD at $x = a$ i.e., $\lim\limits_{h\to 0}\dfrac{f(a+h)-f(a)}{h}$ as well as LHD at $x = b$ i.e., $\lim\limits_{h\to 0}\dfrac{f(b-h)-f(b)}{-h}$ are real and finite.

METHOD TO CHECK THE DIFFERENTIABILITY OF A GIVEN FUNCTION ON A SET OR TO FIND DOMAIN OF DIFFERENTIABILITY

1. From the graph theory or using standard function's domain of continuity, find all those points where the function is discontinuous (say) $x = x_1, x_2, x_3 \ldots, x_n$. Then $f(x)$ will be non-differentiable at these points.
2. Find all those points where the function $f(x)$ takes a sharp turn i.e., have kink points. At these points function will be non-differentiable.
3. Also find all those points where the function $f(x)$ has vertical tangent. At such points $f(x)$ will be non-differentiable.
4. Find all points where $f(x)$ oscillates with infinite frequency. At such points $f(x)$ will be non-differentiable.
5. The set $\mathbb{R}$ except for the points of non-differentiability will be the domain of differentiability of given function.
6. If $f(x)$ is a multi formula function, then remove the sign of equality at the points where the definition of function changes. Find the corresponding derivative functions. The continuity of function at the point of separation of two different branches and continuity of derivative function implies the differentiability of function at that point.

ILLUSTRATION 56: Discuss the differentiability of $f(x) = x + |x|$

SOLUTION: $f(x) = x + |x| = \begin{cases} 2x; & x \ge 0 \\ 0; & x < 0 \end{cases}$

The graph of given function is as shown below:

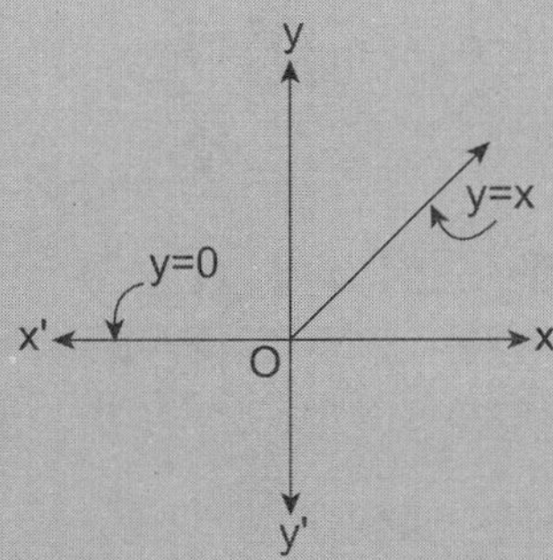

FIGURE 2.80

Clearly $f(x)$ has a sharp corner point at $x = 0$, Thus $f(x)$ is differentiahle at all real points except for $x = 0$. Thus domain of differentiability of $f(x)$ is $\mathbb{R} \sim \{0\}$

ILLUSTRATION 57: Discuss of differentiability of $f(x) = x|x|$

SOLUTION: $f(x) = \begin{cases} x^2 & ,x \geq 0 \\ -x^2 & ,x < 0 \end{cases}$

Now, $f'(x) = \begin{cases} 2x & ;x > 0 \\ -2x^2 & ;x < 0 \end{cases}$

Now $f'(0^+) = f'(0^-) = -2$

Also $f(0^+) = f(0^-) = 0$

Thus $f(x)$ is differentiable at each real number. Thus $\mathbb{R}$ is the domain of differentiability of given function.

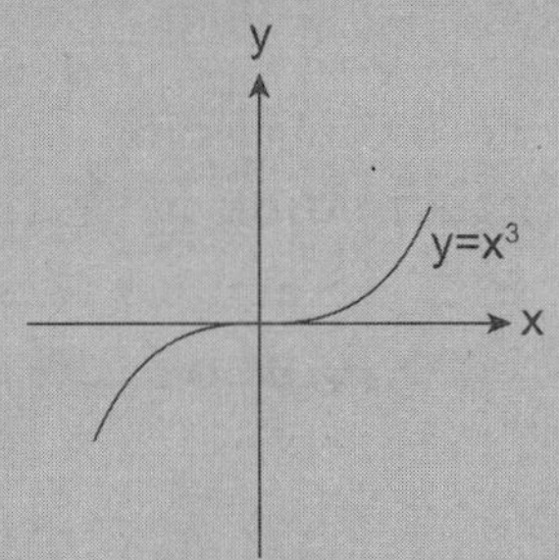

FIGURE 2.81

ILLUSTRATION 58: If $f(x) = \begin{cases} x-3 & ,x < 0 \\ x^2 - 3x + 2 & ,x \geq 0 \end{cases}$; $g(x) = f(|x|) + |f(x)|$, then comment on the continuity and differentiability of $g(x)$ by drawing the graph of $(f|x|)$ and $|f(x)|$

SOLUTION: The graph of given function $f(x)$ is as shown below:

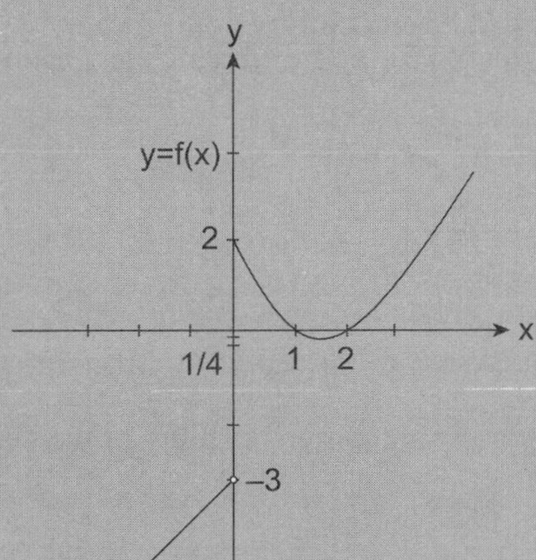

Graph of f(|x|) and |f(x)|

FIGURE 2.82

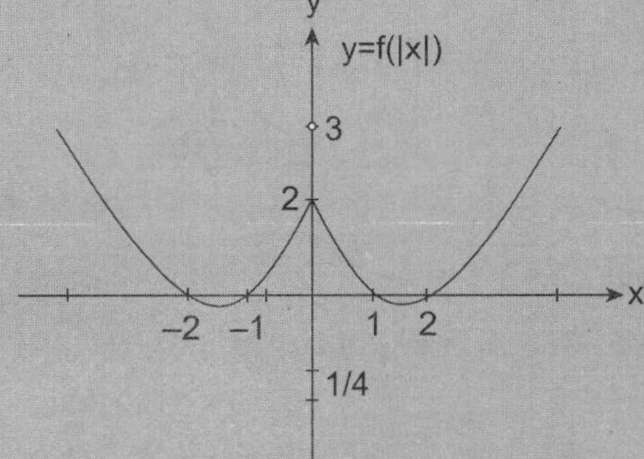

FIGURE 2.83

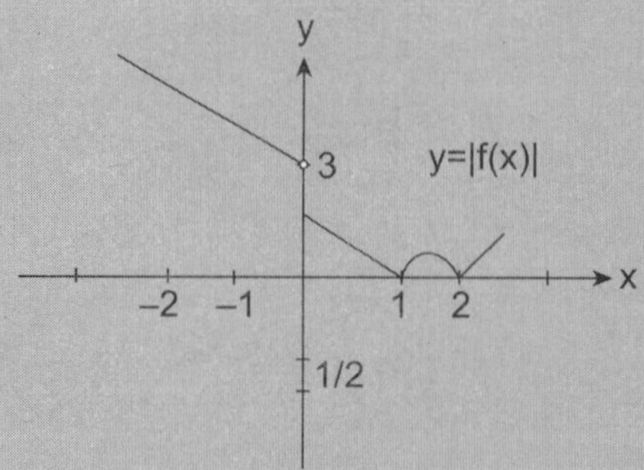

FIGURE 2.84

If $f(|x|)$ and $|f(x)|$ are continuous, then $g(x)$ is continuous. At $x = 0$, $f(|x|)$ is continuous , and $|f(x)|$ is discontinuous therefore $g(x)$ is discontinuous at $x = 0$.

$\therefore$ $g(x)$ is non-differentiable at $x = 0$. Futher $f(|x|)$ is differentiable at $x = 1$ and $x = 2$ whereas $|f(x)|$ is non-differentiable at $x = 1$ and $x = 2$. But the sum of a differentiable and non-differentiable function is also non-differentiable so $g(x)$ is non-differentiable at $x = 0, 1, 2$.

ILLUSTRATION 59: Let $f(x)$ = maximum $\{2\sin x, 1 - \cos x\}$ for all $x \in (0, \pi)$, then discuss the differentiability of $f(x)$ in $(0, \pi)$.

SOLUTION: We know $f(x)$ = maximum $\{2 \sin x, 1 - \cos x)$ can be plotted as shown in figure 2.85.

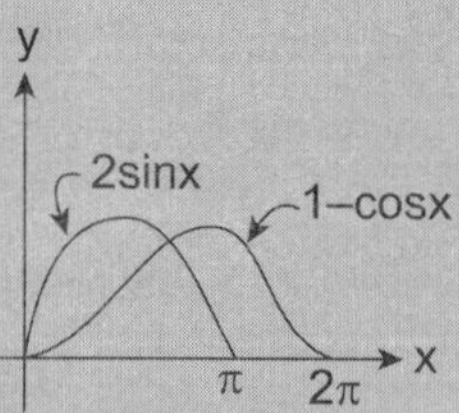

FIGURE 2.85

Thus $f(x)$ = maximum $\{2 \sin x, 1 - \cos x\}$ is not differentiable when, $2 \sin x = 1 - \cos x$

or $4\sin^2 x = (1 - \cos x)^2$ or $4(1 + \cos x) = (1 - \cos x)$

or $4 + 4 \cos x = 1 - \cos x$ or $\cos x = -3/5$

$\Rightarrow x = \cos^{-1}(-3/5)$

$\therefore$ $f(x)$ is not differentiable at $x = \pi - \cos^{-1}(3/5)$, and differentiable for all remaining real numbers of $(0, \pi)$.

Remark: One must remember the formula we can write

$$\max\{f(x), g(x)\} = \frac{f(x)+g(x)}{2} + \left|\frac{f(x)-g(x)}{2}\right|$$

$$\min\{f(x), g(x)\} = \frac{f(x)+g(x)}{2} - \left|\frac{f(x)-g(x)}{2}\right|$$

ILLUSTRATION 60: Let $f(x) = |x - 1| + |x + 1|$. Discuss the continuity and differentiability of the function.

SOLUTION: Here $f(x) = |x - 1| + |x + 1|$

$$\Rightarrow f(x) = \begin{cases} (x-1)+(x+1); & \text{when } x > 1 \\ -(x-1)+(x+1); & \text{when } -1 \le x \le 1 \\ -(x-1)-(x+1); & \text{when } x < -1 \end{cases}$$

$$\Rightarrow f(x)=\begin{cases}2x, & \text{when} \quad x>1\\ 2, & \text{when} \quad -1\le x\le 1\\ -2x, & \text{when} \quad x<-1\end{cases}$$

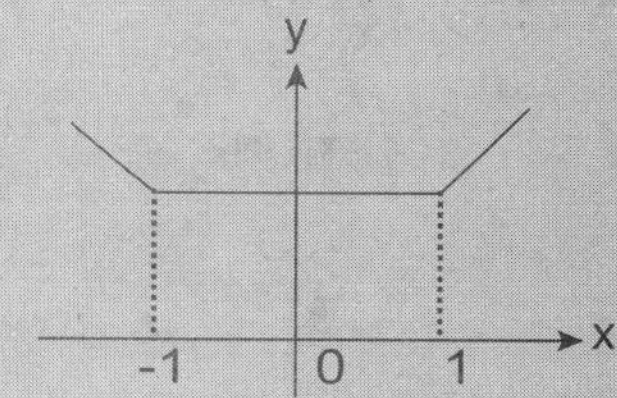

FIGURE 2.86

Graphical method: From the graph it is clear that function is continuous at all real x, also differentiable at all real x except at $x = \pm 1$; Since sharp edges at $x = -1$ and $x = 1$. At $x = 1$ we see that the slope is from the right.

i.e., RHD = 2, while slope from the left i.e., LHD = 0. Similarly at $x = -1$ it is clear that RHD = 0, while LHD = -2

Shortcut Method: In this method, first of all, we differentiate the function and on the derivative equality sign should be removed from doubtful points.

$$\text{Here, } f'(x)=\begin{cases}-2; & x<-1\\ 0; & -1<x<1 \quad (\text{no equality on } -1 \text{ and } +1)\\ 2; & x>1\end{cases}$$

Now, at $x = 1$ $f'(1^+) = 2$ while $f'(1^-) = 0$ and at $x = -1$, $f(-1^+) = 0$ while $f'(-1^-) = -2$

Thus $f(x)$ is not differentiable at $x = \pm 1$

ILLUSTRATION 61: Discuss the continuity and differentiability of the function $f(x) = \sin x + \sin |x|$, $x \in R$. Draw a rough sketch of the graph of $f(x)$.

SOLUTION: $$f(x) = \underbrace{\sin x}_{\text{different } f.\forall\, x\in R} + \underbrace{\sin|x|}_{\text{different. } \forall x\in R\sim\{0\}}$$

We have to check differentiability at $x = 0$.

$f(0) = 0$

$$f'(0^+) = \lim_{h\to 0^+}\frac{f(h+0)-f(0)}{h} = \lim_{h\to 0^+}\frac{\sin h+\sin|h|}{h} = \lim_{h\to 0^+}\frac{\sin h+\sin h}{h} = 2$$

$$f'(0^-) = \lim_{h\to 0^+}\frac{f(0-h)-f(0)}{-h} = \lim_{h\to 0^+}\frac{-\sin h+\sin|-h|}{-h} = \lim_{h\to 0^+}\frac{\sin h-\sin h}{h} = 0$$

$\therefore$ $f'(0^+) \neq f(0^-)$

hence the function is non-differentiable at $x = 0$

for continuity at $x = 0$

$$\lim_{x\to 0} f(x) = \lim_{x\to 0}(\sin x+\sin|x|)$$

$$= \begin{cases}\lim\limits_{x\to 0^+}(\sin x+\sin x)\\ \lim\limits_{x\to 0^-}(\sin x-\sin x)\end{cases} = \begin{cases}0\\0\end{cases}$$

$\therefore$ $\lim\limits_{x\to 0} f(x) = f(0)$

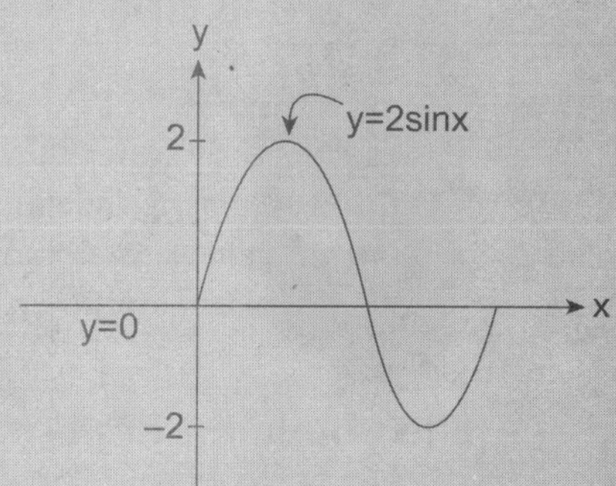

FIGURE 2.87

hence function is continuous at $x = o$

$f(x) = \sin x = \sin |x|$

$$=\begin{cases}\sin x-\sin x & ; \; x<0\\ 0 & ; \; x=0\\ \sin x+\sin x & ; \; x>0\end{cases} = \begin{cases}0 & ; \; x\le 0\\ 2\sin x & ; \; x>0\end{cases}$$

ILLUSTRATION 62: Examine the continuity and differentiability of $f(x) = |x| + |x - 1| + |x - 2|$; $x \in R$. Also draw the graph of $f(x)$.

SOLUTION: $f(x) = \underbrace{|x|}_{\text{different. } \forall x \in R-\{0\}} + \underbrace{|x-1|}_{\text{different. } \forall x \in R-\{1\}} + \underbrace{|x-2|}_{\text{different } \forall x \in R-\{2\}}$

$\therefore$ $f(x)$ can be non-differentiable only at $x = 0, 1, 2$

$$f(x) = \begin{cases} -x-x+1-x+2 & ; \quad x \le 0 \\ x-x+1-x+2 & ; \quad 0 \le x \le 1 \\ x+x-1-x+2 & ; \quad 1 \le x \le 2 \\ x+x-1+x-2 & ; \quad x \ge 2 \end{cases}$$

$$= \begin{cases} -3x+3 & ; \quad x \le 0 \\ -x+3 & ; \quad 0 \le x \le 1 \\ x+1 & ; \quad 1 \le x \le 2 \\ 3x-3 & ; \quad x \ge 2 \end{cases}$$

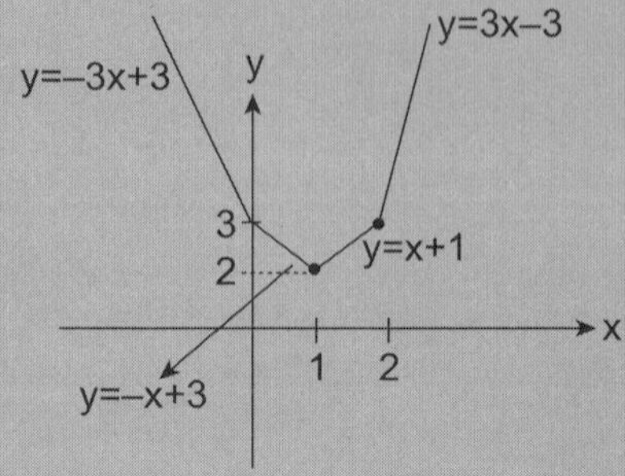

FIGURE 2.88

Clearly $f(x)$ has corner sharp points at $x = 0$, 1, and 2. At all other points the graph of function is smooth. So $f(x)$ is non-differentiable only at $x = 0$, 1, and $x = 2$.

ILLUSTRATION 63: Let $f(x)$ be defined in the interval $[-2, 2]$ such that $f(x) = \begin{cases} -1\,; & -2 \le x \le 0 \\ x-1; & 0 < x \le 2 \end{cases}$ and $g(x) = f(|x| + |f(x)|)$. Test the differentiability of $g(x)$ in $(-2, 2)$.

SOLUTION: $f(x) = \begin{cases} -1, & -2 \le x \le 0 \\ x-1, & 0 < x \le 2 \end{cases}$

$\text{f}(|\text{x}|) = \begin{cases} -1\,; -2 \le |x| \le 0 \\ |x|-1; 0 < |x| \le 2 \end{cases}$ and $|f(x)| = \begin{cases} |-1|\,; -2 \le x \le 0 \\ |x-1|;\ 0 < x \le 2 \end{cases}$

$\therefore\ \text{f}(|\text{x}|) = \begin{cases} -1 \ \text{ for } x = 0 \\ |x|-1;\ 0 < |x| \le 2 \end{cases}$ and $|f(x)| = \begin{cases} 1 & ; \ -2 \le x \le 0 \\ |x-1| & ; \ 0 < x \le 2 \end{cases}$

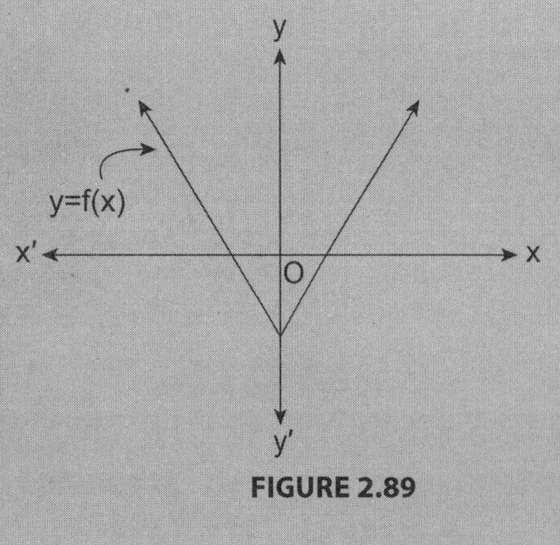

FIGURE 2.89

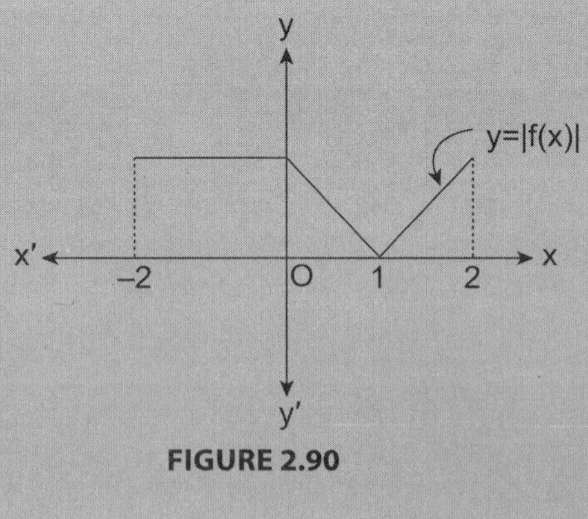

FIGURE 2.90

Thus $y = f(|x|) = \begin{cases} -x-1 & ; \ -2 \le x < 0 \\ -1 & ; \ x = 0 \\ x-1 & ; \ 0 < x \le 2 \end{cases}$ and $|f(x)| = \begin{cases} 1 & ; \ -2 < x \le 0 \\ -x+1 & ; \ 0 < x < 1 \\ x-1 & ; \ 1 < x \le 2 \end{cases}$

Also $g(x) = f(|x|) + |f(x)|$

$$= \begin{cases} -x-1+1 & ; \ -2 \le x \le 0 \\ x-1-x+1 & ; \ 0 < x < 1 \\ x-1+x-1 & ; \ 1 \le x \le 2 \end{cases}$$

$$= \begin{cases} -x & ; \ -2 \le x \le 0 \\ 0 & ; \ 0 < x < 1 \\ 2x-2 & ; \ 1 \le x \le 2 \end{cases}$$

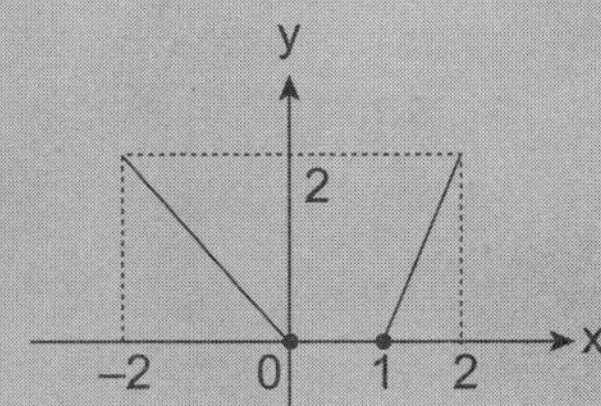

FIGURE 2.91

$\therefore$ $g(x)$ is non. diff. at $x = 0, 1$

ILLUSTRATION 64: For $f(x) = \begin{cases} 1-x & ; \ (0 \le x \le 1) \\ x+2 & ; \ (1 < x < 2) \\ 4-x & ; \ (2 \le x \le 4) \end{cases}$, discuss the continuity and differentiability of $y = f[f(x)]$ for $0 \le x \le 4$.

SOLUTION: Given $f(x) = \begin{cases} 1-x & ; \ (0 \le x \le 1) \\ x+2 & ; \ (1 < x < 2) \\ 4-x & ; \ (2 \le x \le 4) \end{cases}$

$$f(f(x)) = \begin{cases} 1-f(x) & ; \ 0 \le f(x) \le 1 \\ f(x)+2 & ; \ 1 < f(x) < 2 \\ 4-f(x) & ; \ 2 \le f(x) \le 4 \end{cases}$$

$$= \begin{cases} 1-1+x & ; \ \{x : 0 \le 1-x \le 1\} \cap \{x \le 1-x \le 1\} \Rightarrow 0 \le x \le 1 \\ 1-x-2 & ; \ (1 < x < 2) \cap (0 \le x+2 \le 1) \Rightarrow -2 \le x \le -1) \\ 1-4+x & ; \ (2 \le x \le 4) \cap (0 \le 4-x \le 1 \Rightarrow 3 \le x \le 4) \\ 1-x+2 & ; \ (0 \le x \le 1) \cap (1 < 1-x < 2 \Rightarrow -1 < x < 0) \\ x+2+2 & ; \ (1 < x < 2) \cap (1 < x+2 < 2 \Rightarrow -1 < x < 0) \\ 4-x+2 & ; \ (2 \le x \le 4) \cap (1 < 4-x < 2 \Rightarrow 2 < x < 3) \\ 4-1+x & ; \ (0 \le x \le 1) \cap (2 \le 1-x \le 4 \Rightarrow -3 \le x \le -1) \\ 4-x-2 & ; \ (1 < x < 2) \cap (2 \le x+2 \le 4 \Rightarrow 0 \le x \le 2) \\ 4-4+x & ; \ (2 \le x \le 4) \cap (2 \le 4-x \le 4 \Rightarrow 0 \le x \le 2) \end{cases} = \begin{cases} x & ; \ 0 \le x \le 1 \\ x-3 & ; \ 3 \le x \le 4 \\ -x+6 & ; \ 2 < x < 3 \\ -x+2 & ; \ 1 < x < 2 \\ x & ; \ x = 2 \end{cases}$$

$$f(f(x)) = \begin{cases} x & ; \ 0 \le x \le 1 \\ -x+2 & ; \ 1 < x < 2 \\ x & ; \ x = 2 \\ -x+6 & ; \ 2 < x < 3 \\ x-3 & ; \ 3 \le x \le 4 \end{cases}$$

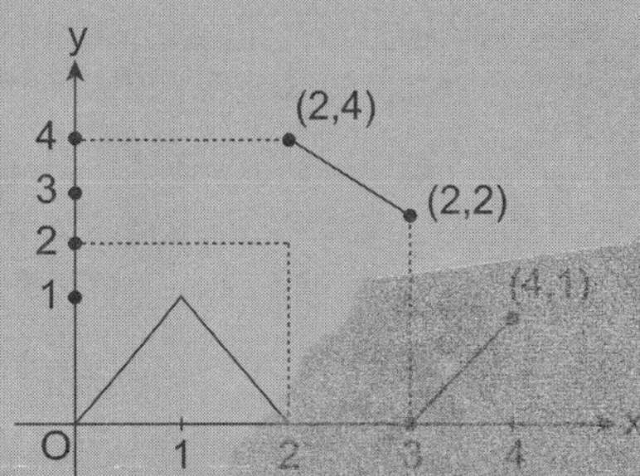

FIGURE 2.92

Graph of $f(f(x))$ is as shown below.

$\therefore$ $f(x)$ is continuous at $x = 1$ and discontinuous at $x = 2, 3$ and non-diff. at $x = 1, 2, 3$

ILLUSTRATION 65: Discuss the continuity and the derivability in [0, 2] of $f(x) = \begin{bmatrix} |2x-3|[x] & \text{for } x \ge 1 \\ \sin\frac{\pi x}{2} & \text{for } x < 1 \end{bmatrix}$ where [ ] denote greatest integer function.

SOLUTION: $f(x)=\begin{cases}|2x-3|[x] & ; \; x\geq 1 \\ \sin\dfrac{\pi x}{2} & ; \; x<1\end{cases}$

$f(1) = 1$

$$f'(1) = \lim_{h\to 0}\frac{f(h+1)-f(1)}{h} = \begin{cases}\displaystyle\lim_{h\to 0^-}\frac{\sin\frac{\pi}{2}(h+1)-1}{h} \\ \displaystyle\lim_{h\to 0^+}\frac{|2(h+1)-3|[h+1]-1}{h}\end{cases}$$

$$= \begin{cases}\displaystyle\lim_{h\to 0^-}\frac{\cos\left(\frac{\pi}{2}h\right)-1}{h} \\ \displaystyle\lim_{h\to 0^+}\frac{|2h-1|.1-1}{h}\end{cases} = \begin{cases}\displaystyle\lim_{h\to 0^-}\frac{\pi}{2}\left(-\sin\frac{\pi}{2}h\right) \\ \displaystyle\lim_{h\to 0^+}\frac{1-2h-1}{h}\end{cases} = \begin{cases}0 \\ \displaystyle\lim_{h\to 0^+}\frac{-2h}{h}\end{cases} = \begin{cases}0 \\ -2\end{cases}$$

$f'(1^-)\neq f'(1^+) \Rightarrow$ hence function is non-diff. at $x=1$

$$\lim_{x\to 1^-} f(x) = \lim_{x\to 1^-}\sin\left(\frac{\pi}{2}x\right) = 1$$

$$\lim_{x\to 1^+} f(x) = \lim_{x\to 1^+} f(x) = \lim_{x\to 1^+}|2x-3|\,[x] = \lim_{x\to 1^-}(3-2x) = 1$$

Function is continuous at $x = 1$

for $x < 1$

$f(x) = \sin\left(\dfrac{\pi x}{2}\right)$ which is cont. and diff. " x, for $x > 1$

$f(x) = |2x - 3| \times [x]$

(i) non-diff. at $x = 3/2$ (i) non-diff. at $x = 2$

(ii) cont. " x (ii) discont. at $x = 2$

checking diff. at $x = 3/2$ and cont. at $x = 3/2$

$$f'(3/2) = \lim_{h\to 0}\frac{f\left(h+\frac{3}{2}\right)-f\left(\frac{3}{2}\right)}{h} = \lim_{h\to 0}\frac{(2h+3-3)-0}{h} = \lim_{h\to 0}\frac{2|h|}{h} = \begin{cases}\displaystyle\lim_{h\to 0^+}\frac{2|h|}{h} \\ \displaystyle\lim_{h\to 0^-}\frac{2|h|}{h}\end{cases} = \begin{cases}2 \\ -2\end{cases}$$

$f'(3^+/2) = 1$ and $f'(3^-/2) = -2$

non-diff. at $x = 3/2$

$$\lim_{x\to 3/2} f(x) = \lim_{x\to 3/2}|2x-3|\,[x] = \lim_{x\to 3/2}|2x-3|.\,1 = 0$$

$f(3/2) = 0$

$$\lim_{x\to 3/2} f(x) = f(3/2)$$

Hence continuous at $x = 3/2$, checking continuity and diff. at $x = 2$

$f(2) = |2\times 2 - 3|\,[2] = 2$

$$\lim_{x\to 2} f(x) = \lim_{\to}|2x-3|\,[x] = \begin{cases}\displaystyle\lim_{x\to 2^+}(2x-3).2 \\ \displaystyle\lim_{x\to 2^-}(2x-3).1\end{cases} = \begin{cases}1.2 \\ 1.1\end{cases} = \begin{cases}2 \\ 1\end{cases}$$

$$\lim_{x\to 2^-} f(x) \neq \lim_{x\to 2^+} f(x) = f(2)$$

So, function is discontinuous at $x = 2$ and hence function is non-diff. at $x = 2$

ILLUSTRATION 66: For what triplets of real numbers (a, b, c) with $a \neq 0$ the function $f(x) = \begin{cases} x \ ; & x \leq 1 \\ ax^2 + bx + c \ ; & \text{otherwise} \end{cases}$ is differentiable for all real x?

(a) $\{(a, 1 - 2a, a) \mid a \in R, a \neq 0\}$
(b) $\{(a, 1 - 2a, c) \mid a, c \in R, a \neq 0\}$
(c) $\{(a, b, c) \mid a, b, c \in R, a + b + c = 1\}$
(d) $\{(a, 1 - 2a, 0) \mid a \in R, a \neq 0\}$

SOLUTION: $f(x) = \begin{cases} x \ ; & x \leq 1 \\ ax^2 + bx + c \ ; & \text{otherwise} \end{cases}$

At $x = 1$

LHL $= \lim_{x \to 1^-} f(x) = 1$

RHL $= \lim_{x \to 1^+} f(x) = a + b + c$

$\therefore$ $f(x)$ is differentiable at $x = 1$

$\Rightarrow$ $f(x)$ must be continuous at $x = 1$

Now $f(1) = 1$; $\therefore$ $f(1^-) = f(1^+) = f(1)$

$\Rightarrow$ $1 = a + b + c$ ...(1)

Also $f'(x) = \begin{cases} 1 \ ; & x < 1 \\ 2ax + b \ ; & \text{otherwise} \end{cases}$. At $x = 1$

LHD $= \lim_{x \to 1^{-1}} f'(x) = 1$

RHD $= \lim_{x \to 1^+} f'(x) = 2a + b$, for derivability at $x = 1$, LHD = RH.D.

$\Rightarrow$ $(2a + b = 1)$ ...(2)

$\therefore$ $a + b + c = 1 \Rightarrow a + (1 - 2a) + c = 1 \Rightarrow c = a$

$\therefore$ $a = a, b = 1 - 2a, c = a$

$\therefore$ $\{(a, 1 - 2a, a); a \in \mathbb{R}\}$ is the triplets possible.

ILLUSTRATION 67: Discuss the continuity and differentiability of the function, $f(x) = \begin{cases} \dfrac{x}{1+|x|}; & |x| \geq 1 \\ \dfrac{x}{1-|x|}; & |x| < 1 \end{cases}$

SOLUTION: Given $f(x) = \begin{cases} \dfrac{x}{1+|x|}; & |x| \geq 1 \\ \dfrac{x}{1-|x|}; & |x| < 1 \end{cases}$. Clearly $f(-1) = f(1) = \dfrac{1}{1+|1|} = \dfrac{1}{2}$; $f(0) = 0$

Clearly $f(x)$ is differentiable every where possibly except for $x = 0, \pm 1$. So have to check differentiability only at points $x = 0, \pm 1$

At $x = 0$,

$$f'(0) = \lim_{h \to 0} \frac{f(h+0) - f(0)}{h} = \lim_{h \to 0} \frac{\frac{h}{1-|h|} - 0}{h} = \lim_{h \to 0} \frac{h}{h(1-|h|)} = \lim_{h \to 0} \frac{1}{1-|h|}$$

$$\Rightarrow \begin{cases} \text{L.H.D} \\ \text{R.H.D} \end{cases} = \begin{cases} \lim_{h \to 0^-} \dfrac{1}{1+h} \\ \lim_{h \to 0^+} \dfrac{1}{1-h} \end{cases} = \begin{cases} \dfrac{1}{1+0} \\ \dfrac{1}{1-0} \end{cases} = \begin{cases} 1 \\ 1 \end{cases}$$

$\therefore\ f'(0^-) = f'(0^+) = 1$

So, function is differentiable at $x = 0$ and hence it is also continuous at $x = 0$

At $x = 1$,

$$f'(1^-) = \lim_{h\to 0^-}\frac{f(1-h)-f(1)}{-h} = \lim_{h\to 0^+}\frac{\frac{1-h}{1-|1-h|}-\frac{1}{2}}{-h} = \lim_{h\to 0^+}\frac{\frac{1-h}{1-1+h}-\frac{1}{2}}{-h} = \lim_{h\to 0^+}\frac{\frac{1-h}{+h}-\frac{1}{2}}{-h}$$

$$= \lim_{h\to 0^+}\frac{2-2h-h}{-2h^2} = \lim_{h\to 0^+}\frac{2-3h}{-2h^2}\text{ which do not exist}$$

Hence $f(x)$ is non-differentiable at $x = 1$

$$\lim_{x\to 1^-} f(x) = \lim_{x\to 1^-}\frac{x}{1-|x|} = \lim_{x\to 1^-}\frac{x}{1-x} = \infty$$

So $f(x)$ is discontinuous at $x = 1$

Also $\lim_{x\to(-1)^-} f(x) = \lim_{x\to(-1)^-}\frac{x}{|-1x|} = \lim_{x\to(-1)^-} -\frac{x}{1+x} = \infty$

So function is discontinuous at $x = -1$ and hence it is non-differentiable at $x = -1$

MISCELLANEOUS RESULTS ON DIFFERENTIABILITY

1. Differentiability of a function does not imply the continuity of derivative function

For example: $f(x) = \begin{cases} x^2\sin\frac{1}{x}; x \neq 0 \\ 0 \text{ if } x = 0 \end{cases}$

Now $\lim_{x\to 0} f(x) = \lim_{x\to 0} x^2 \sin\frac{1}{x} = 0\times(\text{a real number}$ oscillating in between –1 and 1)

$= 0 = f(0)$

$\therefore$ $f(x)$ is continuous at $x = 0$

Now $f'(0^-) = \lim_{h\to 0^+}\frac{-h^2\sin\frac{1}{h}}{-h} = \lim_{h\to 0^+}\left(h\sin\frac{1}{h}\right) = 0$

and $f'(0^+) = \lim_{h\to 0^+}\frac{h^2\sin\frac{1}{h}-0}{h} = \lim_{h\to 0^+} h\sin\frac{1}{h} = 0$

$\therefore$ $f(x)$ is differentiable at $x = 0$

Further, $f'(x) = \begin{cases} -\cos\frac{1}{x}+\left(\sin\frac{1}{x}\right)(2x); x\neq 0 \\ 0;\ x = 0 \end{cases}$

$\therefore\ \lim_{x\to 0} f'(x) = \lim_{x\to 0}\left(2x\sin\frac{1}{x}-\cos\frac{1}{x}\right)$, which does not exist

$\therefore$ $f'(x)$ is discontinuous at $x = 0$

2. Continuity of derivative function does not imply differentiability of function

e.g., $f(x) = \begin{cases} \tan x; & x < \frac{\pi}{4} \\ (\tan x)+1; & \frac{\pi}{4} \leq x < \frac{\pi}{2} \end{cases}$

then L.H.L $= \lim_{x\to\left(\frac{\pi}{4}\right)^-} f(x) = \lim_{x\to\left(\frac{\pi}{4}\right)^-}\tan x = 1$

R.H.L $= \lim_{x\to\left(\frac{\pi}{4}\right)^+} f(x) = \lim_{x\to\left(\frac{\pi}{4}\right)^+}\{(\tan x)+1\} = 2 = f\left(\frac{\pi}{4}\right)$

$\therefore$ $f(x)$ is left discontinuous at $x = \pi/4$, but right continuous at $x = \pi/4$

Thus $f(x)$ is non-differentiable at $x = \pi/4$

Now, $f'(x) = \begin{cases} \sec^2 x; & x < \pi/4 \\ \sec^2 x; & \frac{\pi}{4} < x < \frac{\pi}{2} \end{cases}$

$\therefore\ f'\left(\frac{\pi^-}{4}\right) = f'\left(\frac{\pi^+}{4}\right) = \sec^2\frac{\pi}{4} = 2$

In such case we take $f'\left(\frac{\pi}{4}\right) = f'\left(\frac{\pi^-}{4}\right) = f'\left(\frac{\pi^+}{4}\right)$

Thus derivative function $f'(x)$ is continuous at $\pi/4$

Graphically

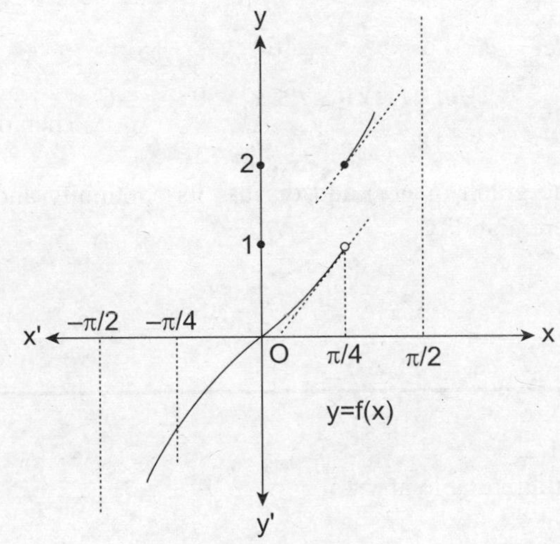

FIGURE 2.93

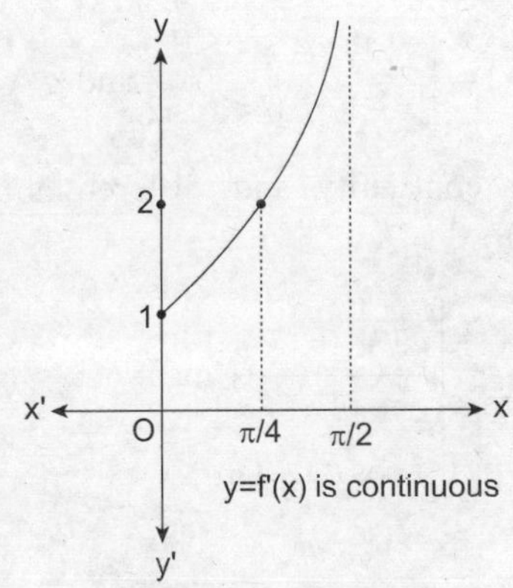

FIGURE 2.94

Thus continuity of derivative function does not imply differentiability of function; however continuity of derivative of continuous function which are non-oscillating implies differentiability of function.

TEXTUAL EXERCISE–5: (SUBJECTIVE)

1. Discuss the differentiability of the function $f(x) = (x^2 - 1)\,|x^2 - 3x + 2| + \cos(|x|)$.

2. If $f(x) = \begin{cases} \left|1-4x^2\right| & ; \quad 0 \le x < 1 \\ \left[x^2 - 2x\right]; & 1 \le x < 2 \end{cases}$, then discuss the differentiability of f in (0, 2). Here [] denotes the greatest integer function.

3. Find a, b for which the function $f(x) = \begin{cases} \sin x & ; x < \pi \\ ax + b & ; x \ge \pi \end{cases}$ is differentiable for all x.

4. Discuss the continuity of $f(x)$ and $f'(x)$ on [0, 2] when $f(x) = \begin{cases} x^5/5 & 0 \le x \le 1 \\ 2x^2 - 3x + 3/2 & 1 < x \le 2 \end{cases}$ and comment over the statement "continuity of derivative implies the differentiability of function".

5. Find the values of a, b s.t. function $f(x) = \begin{cases} ax^2 - b & ; \ |x| < 1 \\ -1/|x| & ; \ |x| \ge 1 \end{cases}$ is differentiable $\forall\, x$.

6. Discuss the differentiability of functions given below: (here below $[y]$ denotes greatest integer $\le y$)

(a) $\sin(\pi\,[x])$

(b) $\sin(\pi\{x\})$ for all $x \in (-\pi/2, \pi/2)$

7. If $f(x) = \min\{|x|, |x-2|, 2-|x-1|\}$ Then draw the graph of $f(x)$ and also discuss its continuity and differentiability.

8. If $f(x) = -1 + |x - 2|$; $0 \le x \le 4$ and $g(x) = 2 - |x|$, $-1 \le x \le 3$, then find $(fog)(x)$ and $(gof)(x)$. Draw rough sketch of the graphs of $(fog)(x)$ and $(gof)(x)$. Discuss the continuity of $(fog)x$ at $x = 0$.

9. Let $f(x)$ is defined in the interval [− 2, 2] such that $f(x) = \begin{cases} -1 & ; \ -2 \le x < 0 \\ x - 1 & ; \ 0 \le x \le 2 \end{cases}$ and $g(x) = f(|x|) + |f(x)|$. Test the differentiability of $g(x)$ in [−2, 2]

10. Let $f(x) = \sin x$,

$$g(x) = \begin{cases} \{\max. f(t) \ \ 0 \le t \le x\} & \text{for } 0 \le x \le \pi \\ (1 - \cos x)/2 & \text{for } x > \pi \end{cases}.$$

Discuss the continuity and differentiability of $g(x)$ in $(0, \infty)$.

11. Let $f(x) = \begin{cases} \left[1-4x^2\right]; & 0 \le x < 1 \\ \left[x^2 - 2x\right]; & 1 \le x < 2 \end{cases}$, where [.] denotes the greatest integer function. Then discuss the differentiability of $f(x)$ in (0, 2).

12. Let $f(x)=\begin{cases}-1 \text{ if } -2\le x\le 0\\ |x-1| \text{ if } 0<x\le 2\end{cases}$ and $g(x)=\int_{-2}^{x} f(t)\,dt.$

Test the continuity and differentiability of $g(x)$ in $(-2, 2)$.

13. If $f(x) = \begin{cases}\dfrac{\sin\left[x^2\right]\pi}{x^2-3x+8}+ax^3+b\ ; & 0\le x\le 1\\ 2\cos\pi x+\tan^{-1}x\ ; & 1<x\le 2\end{cases}$ is differentiable in $[0, 2]$, find $'a'$ and $'b'$. Here $[x]$ stands for the greatest integer function.

14. Let $f(x) = x^3 - 9x^2 + 15x + 6$ and $g(x)=\begin{cases}Min.\{f(t); 0\le t\le x\}\ ; & 0\le x\le 6\\ x-18\ ; & x>6\end{cases}$. Then drawn the graph of $g(x)$ and discuss its continuity and differentiability.

Answer Keys

1. Not differentiable at $x = 2$ **2.** Not differentiable at $x = 1/2, 1$
3. $a = -1, b = \pi$ **4.** Discontinuous and non-differentiable at $x = 1$
5. $a = 1/2, b = 3/2$
6. (a) always differentiable (b) continuous and not differentiable at x = -1,0,1

8. fog(x)=$\begin{cases}-1-x & -1\le x\le 0\\ x-1 & 0<x\le 2\end{cases}$; gof(x)=$\begin{cases}1+x & 0\le x<1\\ 3-x & 1<x\le 2\\ x-1 & 2<x\le 3\\ 5-x & 3<x\le 4\end{cases}$ continuous at $x = 0$. **9.** Not differentiable at $x = 0$ and 1.

10. Continuous and differentiable for all values of x **11.** non-derivable at $x = 1/2$ and $x = 1$
12. $g(x)$ is cont. in $(-2, 2)$; $g(x)$ is der. At $x = 1$ and non-der. At $x = 0$

Note that $g(x) = f(x) = \begin{cases}-x-2 \text{ if } -2\le x\le 0\\ -2+x-\dfrac{x^2}{2} \text{ for } 0<x<1\\ \dfrac{x^2}{2}-x-1 \text{ for } 1\le x\le 2\end{cases}$ **13.** $a=\dfrac{1}{6};\ b=\dfrac{\pi}{4}-\dfrac{13}{6}$

14. $g(x)$ is discontinuous and non-differentiable at $x = 1$ and $x = 6$

TEXTUAL EXERCISE–5: (OBJECTIVE)

1. If $f(x) = \sin^{-1}(\sin x)$; $x \in \mathbb{R}$, then f is
(a) Continuous and differentiable for all x
(b) Continuous for all x but not differentiable for all $x = (2k+1)\dfrac{\pi}{2}, k \in \mathbb{Z}$
(c) Neither continuous nor differentiable for $x = (2k-1)\dfrac{\pi}{2}, k \in \mathbb{Z}$
(d) Neither continuous nor differentiable for $x \in \mathbb{R} - [-1, 1]$

2. The functions defined by $f(x) = \max\{x^2, (x-1), 2x(1-x)\}, 0 \le x \le 1$
(a) is differentiable for all x
(b) is differentiable for all x except at one point
(c) is differentiable for all x except at two points
(d) is not differentiable at more than two points

3. Which one of the following functions is continuous everywhere in its domain but has atleast one point where it is not differentiable?
(a) $f(x) = x^{1/3}$ (b) $f(x)=\dfrac{|x|}{x}$
(c) $f(x) = e^{-x}$ (d) $f(x) = \tan x$

4. The number of points at which the function, $f(x) = |x - 0.5| + |x - 1| + \tan x$ does not have a derivative in the interval; (0, 2) is

(a) 1 (b) 2
(c) 3 (d) 4

5. Let f be a differentiable function on the open interval (a, b). Which of the following statements must be true?

I f is continuous on the closed interval $[a, b]$
II f is bounded on the open interval (a, b)
III If $a < a_1 < b_1 < b$ and $f(a_1) < 0 < f(b_1)$, then there is a number c such that $a_1 < c < b_1$ and $f(c) = 0$

(a) I and II only. (b) I and III only
(c) II and III only (d) only III

6. The function $f(x) = \begin{cases} 2x+1 & ; x \in \mathbb{Q} \\ x^2 - 2x + 5; & x \notin \mathbb{Q} \end{cases}$ is

(a) Continuous no-where
(b) Differentiable no-where
(c) Continuous but not differentiable exactly at one point
(d) Differentiable and continuous only at one point and discontinuous elsewhere

7. A function f defined as $f(x) = x[x]$ for $-1 \le x \le 3$; where $[x]$ defines the greatest integer $\le x$ is:

(a) Continuous at all points in the domain of f but non-derivable at a finite number of points
(b) Discontinuous at all points and hence non-derivable at all points in the domain of $f(x)$
(c) Discontinuous at a finite number of points but not derivable at all points in the domain of $f(x)$
(d) Discontinuous and also non-derivable at a finite number of points of $f(x)$.

8. $[x]$ denotes the greatest integer less than or equal to x. If $f(x) = [x] [\sin \pi x]$ in $(-1, 1)$, then $f(x)$ is:

(a) Continuous at $x = 0$
(b) Continuous in $(-1, 1)$
(c) Non-differentiable in $(-1, 1)$
(d) None of these

9. The set of all points where the function $f(x) = \dfrac{x}{1+|x|}$ is differentiable is:

(a) $(-\infty, \infty)$ (b) $[0, \infty)$
(c) $(-\infty, 0) \cup (0, \infty)$ (d) $(0, \infty)$

10. If $f(x) = \min. \{1, x^2, x^3\}$, then

(a) $f(x)$ is continuous $\forall x \in \mathbb{R}$
(b) $f'(x) > 0, \forall x > 1$
(c) $f(x)$ is not differentiable but continuous $\forall x \in \mathbb{R}$
(d) $f(x)$ is not differentiable for two values of x

11. The number of point where function $f(x)$ = minimum $\{x^3 - 1, -x + 1, \text{sgn}(-x)\}$ is continuous but differentiable is

(a) One (b) Two
(c) Zero (d) None of these

12. Number of points where the function $f(x)$ = max $\{|\tan x|, \cos |x|\}$ is non-differentiable in the interval $(-\pi, \pi)$ is

(a) 4 (b) 6
(c) 3 (d) 2

13. The function $1 + |\sin x|$ is

(a) not differentiable at infinite no. of points
(b) continuous everywhere
(c) differentiable now here
(d) not differentiable at $x = 0$

14. Let $f(x) = \begin{cases} \displaystyle\int_0^x \{1 + |1 - t|\} dt & \text{if } x > 2 \\ 5x - 7 & \text{if } x \le 2 \end{cases}$

(a) f is not continuous at $x = 2$
(b) f is continuous but not differentiable at $x = 2$
(c) f is differentiable every where
(d) $f'(2+)$ does not exist

15. Let f and g be two functions defined as follows $f(x) = \dfrac{x+|x|}{2}$ for all x and $g(x) = \begin{cases} x \text{ for } x < 0 \\ x^2 \text{ for } x \ge 0 \end{cases}$, then:

(a) (gof) (x) and (fog) (x) are both continuous for all $x \in \mathbb{R}$
(b) (gof) (x) and (fog) (x) are unequal functions
(c) (gof) (x) is differentiable at $x = 0$
(d) (fog) (x) is not differentiable at $x = 0$

16. Let $f: [0,1] \to [0,1]$ be a continuous function. Then

(a) $f(x) = x$ for atleast one $0 \le x \le 1$
(b) $f(x)$ will be differentiable in $[0,1]$
(c) $f(x) + x = 0$ for atleast one x such that $0 \le x \le 1$
(d) None of these

17. Let $[x]$ denotes the greatest integer $\leq x$. If $f(x) = [x \sin \pi x]$, then $f(x)$ is
(a) continuous at $x = 0$
(b) continuous in $(-1, 0)$
(c) differentiable at $x = 1$
(d) differentiable in $(-1, 1)$

18. $f(x) = |\sin x| + [\cos x]$, $x \in [0, 2\pi]$, where [.] denotes the greatest integer functions. Total number of points where $f(x)$ is non-differentiable is equal to
(a) 2 (b) 3
(c) 5 (d) 4

Answer Keys

1. (b)	**2.** (b)	**3.** (a)	**4.** (c)	**5.** (d)	**6.** (d)	**7.** (d)	**8.** (c)	**9.** (a)
10. (a, c)	**11.** (a)	**12.** (a)	**13.** (a,b,d)	**14.** (b)	**15.** (a, c)	**16.** (a)	**17.** (a, b, c, d)	**18.** (c)

■ MISCELLANEOUS CONCEPTS ABOUT DIFFERENTIABILITY AND DERIVATIVE OF FUNCTION

Alternative Limit Form of the Derivative

We know that the derivative of a function $f(x)$ at $x = a$ is given by $f'(a) = \lim\limits_{h \to 0} \dfrac{f(a+h) - f(a)}{h}$

On substituting $a + h = x$; $x \to a$, we get $f'(a) = \lim\limits_{x \to a} \dfrac{f(x) - f(a)}{x - a}$ and we have, L.H.D $= f'(a^-) = \lim\limits_{x \to a^-} \dfrac{f(x) - f(a)}{x - a}$ and R.H.D $= f'(a^+) = \lim\limits_{x \to a^+} \dfrac{f(x) - f(a)}{x - a}$

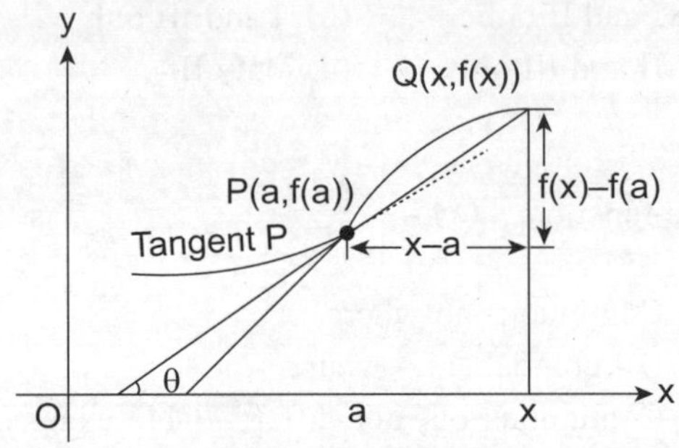

FIGURE 2.95

$$f'(a) = \lim_{x \to a} \frac{f(x) - f(a)}{x - a} = \lim_{x \to a} \tan \theta = \tan \phi$$

= slope of tangent to curve at $P(a, f(a))$

ILLUSTRATION 68: If $f(x)$ and $g(x)$ are two monotonically increasing and differentiable functions such that $[f'(2)]^2 - 4[g'(2)]^2 = 0$ then evaluate $\lim\limits_{x \to 2} \dfrac{f(x) - f(2)}{g(x) - g(2)}$

SOLUTION: $\lim\limits_{x \to 2} \dfrac{f(x) - f(2)}{g(x) - g(2)} = \lim\limits_{x \to 2} \dfrac{f(x) - f(2)}{x - 2} \cdot \dfrac{x - 2}{g(x) - g(2)} = \dfrac{f'(2)}{g'(2)}$ ...(1)

Also given $[f'(2)]^2 - 4[g'(2)]^2 = 0$

$\Rightarrow (f'(2) - 2g'(2))(f'(2) + 2g'(2)) = 0$ $\Rightarrow f'(2) = 2g'(2)$ or $f'(2) = -2g'(2)$

$\Rightarrow \dfrac{f'(2)}{g'(2)} = 2 \text{ or } -2$

But $f(x)$ and $g(x)$ both are increasing functions

$\Rightarrow \dfrac{f'(2)}{g'(2)} > 0 \Rightarrow \dfrac{f'(2)}{g'(2)} = 2$

$\therefore$ from (1) $\lim\limits_{x \to 2} \dfrac{f(x) - f(2)}{g(x) - g(2)} = 2$

ILLUSTRATION 69: If $f(x)$ is a differentiable function and $f'(3) = (3)^{1/3}$, then evaluate $\lim_{x\to 3} \frac{f(x)-f(3)}{x^{1/3}-(3)^{1/3}}$

SOLUTION: $\lim_{x\to 3} \frac{f(x)-f(3)}{x^{1/3}-(3)^{1/3}} = \lim_{x\to 3} \frac{f(x)-f(3)}{(x-3)}.\left[x^{2/3}+x^{1/3}.(3)^{1/3}+(3)^{2/3}\right]$

$\left[\because x^{1/3}-(3)^{1/3} = \frac{x-3}{x^{2/3}+x^{1/3}(3)^{1/3}+(3)^{2/3}}\right] = f'(3)\lim_{x\to 3}\left[x^{2/3}+x^{1/3}(3)^{1/3}+(3)^{2/3}\right]$

$= 3\,(3)^{2/3} f'(3) = 3\,(3)^{2/3}.(3)^{1/3} = (3)\,(3) = 9$

Another Alternative form of Derivative by Using Centered Difference Quotient

Let $(a-h, a+h)$ be neighbourhood of 'a' of radius 'h' and centre 'a' Then the quotient

$\frac{f(a+h)-f(a-h)}{(a+h)-(a-h)} = \frac{f(a+h)-f(a-h)}{2h}$ is called

centered difference quotient

Consider the limit $\lim_{h\to 0} \frac{f(a+h)-f(a-h)}{2h}$

$$= \lim_{h\to 0} \frac{f(a+h)-f(a)+f(a)-f(a-h)}{2h}$$

$$= \lim_{h\to 0} \frac{[f(a+h)-f(a)]-[f(a-h)-f(a)]}{2h}$$

$$= \frac{1}{2}\left\{\lim_{h\to 0}\frac{[f(a+h)-f(a)]}{h} \quad \lim_{h\to 0}\frac{f(a-h)-f(a)}{h}\right\}$$

If $f(x)$ is differentiable $x = a$, then

$$\lim_{h\to 0}\frac{f(a+h)-f(a)}{h} = \lim_{h\to 0}\frac{f(a-h)-f(a)}{-h} = f'(a)$$

$$\therefore \quad \lim_{h\to 0}\frac{f(a+h)-f(a-h)}{2h} = \frac{1}{2}\{f'(a)+f'(a)\} = f'(a)$$

Thus $\lim_{h\to 0}\frac{f(a+h)-f(a-h)}{2h} = f'(a)$

Geometrically

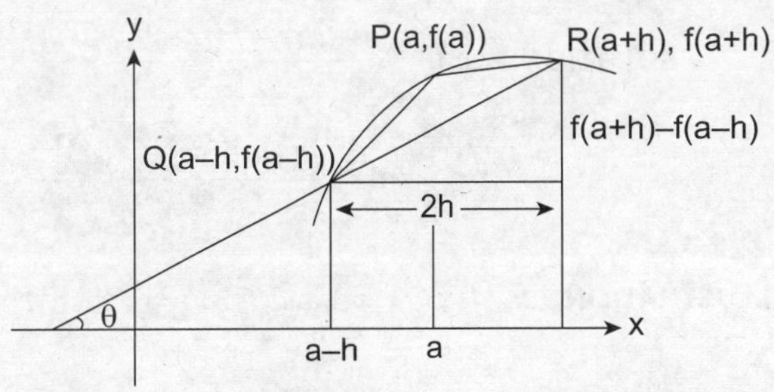

FIGURE 2.96

As $h \to 0$, Q and R gets closer and closer to P and hence chord QR tends to coincide with tangent at P i.e., limit becomes $f'(a)$.

REMARKS:

1. $\lim_{h\to 0}\frac{f(a+g(h))-f(a)}{g(h)} = f'(a)$; *provided* $g(h)\to 0$ *as* $h\to 0$
2. $\lim_{h\to 0}\frac{f(a+g(h))-f(a+\phi(h))}{g(h)-\phi(h)} = f'(a)$; *provided* $g(h), \phi(h) \to$ *as* $h\to 0$

ILLUSTRATION 70: If $f'(2) = 4$, then evaluate $\lim_{h\to 0}\frac{f(2+h)-f(2-h)}{\sin h}$

SOLUTION: $= \lim_{h\to 0}\frac{f(2+h)-f(2-h)}{h}.\frac{h}{\sin h} = 2\lim_{h\to 0}\frac{f(2+h)-f(2-h)}{2h}.\lim_{h\to 0}\frac{h}{\sin h}$

$= 2(f'(2).(1) = 2(4) = 8 \quad \left[\because \lim_{h\to 0}\frac{f(a+h)-f(a-h)}{2h} = f'(a)\right]$

ILLUSTRATION 71: If $f'(3) = 7$, then evaluate $\lim_{h\to 0}\dfrac{f(3+\sin h)-f(3+\tan h)}{(\sin h-\tan h)}$

SOLUTION: $\lim_{h\to 0}\dfrac{f(3+\sin h)-f(3+\tan h)}{(\sin h-\tan h)}$

$$\lim_{h\to 0}\frac{[f(3+\sin h)-f(3)]-[f(3+\tan h)-f(3)]}{(\sin h-\tanh)}$$

$$=\lim_{h\to 0}\frac{\dfrac{f(3+\sin h)-f(3)}{\sin h}\times\sin h-\dfrac{f(3+\tan h)-f(3)}{\tan h}}{\sin h-\tan h}$$

$$=\lim_{h\to 0}\frac{f'(3).\sin h-f'(3)\tan h}{(\sin h-\tan h)}=f'(3)\lim_{h\to 0}\left(\frac{\sin h-\tan h}{\sin h-\tan h}\right)=f'(3)(1)=7$$

ILLUSTRATION 72: If $f'(a) = 5$, then evaluate $\lim_{h\to 0}\dfrac{f(a+3h)-f(a+2h)}{5h}$

SOLUTION: $\lim_{h\to 0}\dfrac{f(a+3h)-f(a+2h)}{5h}=\dfrac{1}{5}\lim_{h\to 0}\left\{\dfrac{[f(a+3h)-f(a)]}{h}-\dfrac{[f(a+2h)-f(a)]}{h}\right\}$

$$=\frac{1}{5}\lim_{h\to 0}\left\{3\frac{[f(a+3h)-f(a)]}{3h}-\frac{2[f(a+2h)-f(a)]}{2h}\right\}=\frac{1}{5}\{3f'(a)-2f'(a)\}=\frac{f'(a)}{5}=\frac{5}{5}=1$$

ILLUSTRATION 73: If $f'(2) = 3$ and $f'(3) = 4$; then evaluate $\lim_{h\to 0}\dfrac{f(2+h^2+3h)-f(2+2h-h^2)}{f(3+h^2-h)-f(3+h-2h^2)}$

SOLUTION: $\lim_{h\to 0}\dfrac{f(2+h^2+3h)-f(2+2h-h^2)}{f(3+h^2-h)-f(3+h-2h^2)}$

$$=\lim_{h\to 0}\left\{\frac{f(2+h^2+3h)-f(2+2h-h^2)}{(2+h^2+3h-2-2h+h^2)}\times(2h^2+h)\right.$$

$$\left.\times\frac{(3+h^2-h-3-h+2h^2)}{f(3+h^2-h)-f(3+h-2h^2)}\times\frac{1}{(3h^2-2h)}\right\}$$

$$=\lim_{h\to 0}\frac{f\left(2+h^2+3h\right)-f(2+2h-h^2)}{(2h^2+h)}$$

$$\times\lim_{h\to 0}\frac{(3h^2-2h)}{f(3+h^2-h)-f(3+h-2h^2)}\times\lim_{h\to 0}\frac{2h^2+h}{3h^2-2h}$$

$$=\frac{f'(2)}{f'(3)}\times\lim_{h\to 0}\frac{h(2h+1)}{h(3h-2)}=\frac{f'(2)}{f'(3)}\left(\frac{-1}{2}\right)=\frac{3}{4}\left(\frac{-1}{2}\right)=\frac{-3}{8}$$

ILLUSTRATION 74: If $f'(1) = 6$, then evaluate $\lim_{h\to 0}\dfrac{f(1+h^2)-f(2-\cos h)}{h^2}$

SOLUTION: $\lim_{h\to 0}\dfrac{f(1+h^2)-f(2-\cos h)}{h^2}=\lim_{h\to 0}\dfrac{f(1+h^2)-f\left(1+(1-\cos h)\right)}{h^2}$

$$= \lim_{h\to 0} \frac{f(1+h^2) - f\left(1+(1-\cos h)\right)}{(1h^2 - 1 + \cos h)} \times (h^2 - 1 + \cos h)$$

$$= \lim_{h\to 0} \frac{f(1+h^2) - f(1+1-\cos h)}{[(h^2 - (1-\cos h))]} \times \frac{-(1-\cos h - h^2)}{h^2}$$

$$= -f'(1)\lim_{h\to 0} \frac{1-\cos h - h^2}{h^2} = -f'(1)\lim_{h\to 0}\left[\frac{2\sin^2\frac{h}{2}}{h^2} - 1\right] = -f'(1)\lim_{h\to 0}\left[\frac{1}{2}\frac{\sin^2\frac{h}{2}}{\frac{h^2}{4}} - 1\right]$$

$$= -f'(1)\left(\frac{1}{2} - 1\right) = \frac{1}{2}f'(1) = \frac{1}{2}(6) = 3.$$

DIFFERENTIABILITY OF PARAMETRIC FUNCTIONS

Let the function $y = f(x)$ be defined parametrically as $x = \phi(t)$ and $y = \psi(t)$. Then derivative of y w.r.t x i.e., $\frac{dy}{dx}$ is defined by $f'(x) = \frac{dy}{dx} = \frac{dy/dt}{dx/dt} = \frac{\psi'(t)}{\phi'(t)}$ ...(i)

Now, $f'(x) = \frac{\psi'(t)}{\phi'(t)} = \lim_{h\to 0} \frac{[\psi(t+h) - \psi(t)]/h}{[\phi(t+h) - \phi(t)]/h}$ ...(2)

$\therefore$ L.H.D $= f'(x^-) = \lim_{h\to 0^+} \frac{[\psi(t-h) - \psi(t)]/-h}{[\phi(t-h) - \phi(t)]/-h}$

$= \lim_{h\to 0^+} \frac{[\psi(t-h) - \psi(t)]}{[\phi(t-h) - \phi(t)]}$ ....(3)

Similarly R.H.D $= f'(x^+) = \lim_{h\to 0^+} \frac{[\psi(t+h) - \psi(t)]/h}{[\phi(t+h) - \phi(t)]/h}$

$= \lim_{h\to 0^+} \frac{[\psi(t+h) - \psi(t)]}{[\phi(t+h) - \phi(t)]}$

Thus for differentiability of $f(x)$ at $x = \phi(t)$ or at t $\lim_{h\to 0^+} \frac{[\psi(t-h) - \psi(t)]}{[\phi(t-h) - \phi(t)]} = \lim_{h\to 0^+} \frac{[\psi(t+h) - \psi(t)]}{[\phi(t+h) - \phi(t)]}$ ...(4)

= a finite real number

REMARKS:

(i) If $x = \phi(t)$ is an increasing function of t i.e., x increases with t increasing, then (3) and (4) represent L.H.D and R.H.D respectively. However if $x = \phi(t)$ is a decreasing function of t i.e x decreases with increase in t, then (3) and (4) represent R.H.D and L.H.D respectively

(ii) Alternatively, we can eliminate the parameter 't' and get y = f(x) and then we can investigate the differentiability at x

ILLUSTRATION 75: Check the differentiability of function $y = f(x)$ parametrically defined by $x = t^2 - 1$; $y = 2t$ at $t = 2$; where $t > 0$

SOLUTION: ***Method I:*** Given $x = t^2 - 1 = \phi(t)$ and $y = 2t = \psi(t)$

$\Rightarrow \frac{dx}{dt} = 2t > 0$ for $t > 0$ $\quad\therefore$ x is an increasing functions of t

$\because$ LH.D $\lim_{h\to 0^+} \frac{\psi(t-h) - \psi(t)}{\phi(t-h) - \phi(t)} = \lim_{h\to 0^+} \frac{2(t-h) - 2t}{(t-h)^2 - 1 - (t^2 - 1)}$

$= \lim_{h\to 0^+} \frac{-2h}{(t^2 + h^2 - 2th - 1 - t^2 + 1)} = \lim_{h\to 0^+} \frac{-2h}{h^2 - 2th} = \lim_{x\to 0^+} \frac{-2}{h - 2t} = \frac{1}{t}$

$\therefore$ L.H.D $= \dfrac{1}{t} \Rightarrow f'(\phi(2)^-) = \dfrac{1}{2}$

Now R.H.D $= \lim\limits_{h\to0^+} \dfrac{\psi(t+h)-\psi(t)}{\phi(t+h)-\phi(t)} = \lim\limits_{h\to0^+} \dfrac{2(t+h)-2t}{(t+h)^2-1-(t^2-1)}$

$= \lim\limits_{h\to0^+} \dfrac{2h}{t^2+h^2+2th-1-t^2+1} = \lim\limits_{h\to0^+} \dfrac{2h}{h^2+2th} = \lim\limits_{h\to0^+} \dfrac{2}{(h+2t)} = \dfrac{1}{t}$

$\therefore$ $f'(\phi(t)^+) = \dfrac{1}{t} \Rightarrow f''\phi(2)^+ = \dfrac{1}{2}$

$\therefore$ L.H.D = R.H.D $= \dfrac{1}{2}$

$\Rightarrow$ given function is derivable at $t = 2$

Method II: We have $x = t^2 - 1$, $y = 2t$

$\Rightarrow$ $x = \left(\dfrac{y}{2}\right)^2 - 1$ (eliminating t)

$\Rightarrow$ $x = \dfrac{y^2}{4} - 1$ $\Rightarrow$ $y^2 = 4(x+1)$

$\Rightarrow$ $y = \pm 2\sqrt{x+1}$ $\Rightarrow$ $f(x) = y = 2\sqrt{x+1}$

At $t = 2$, $x = (2)^2 - 1 = 3$

$\Rightarrow$ L.H.D $= f'(3^-) = \lim\limits_{h\to0^+} \dfrac{f(3-h)-f(3)}{-h}$

$= \lim\limits_{h\to0^+} \dfrac{2\sqrt{3-h+1}-2\sqrt{4}}{-h} = \lim\limits_{h\to0^+} \dfrac{2\left(\sqrt{4-h}-2\right)}{-h} = \lim\limits_{h\to0^+} \dfrac{2(4-h-4)}{-h(\sqrt{4-h}+2)}$

$= \lim\limits_{\to} \dfrac{2}{\left(\sqrt{4-\ }+2\right)}\quad \dfrac{1}{\ }$

Also R.H.D $= f'(3^+) = \lim\limits_{h\to0^+} \dfrac{f(3+h)-f(3)}{h}$

$= \lim\limits_{h\to0^+} \dfrac{2\sqrt{3+h+1}-2\sqrt{3+1}}{h} = \lim\limits_{h\to0^+} \dfrac{2\left(\sqrt{4+h}-2\right)}{h}$

$= \lim\limits_{h\to0^+} \dfrac{2(4+h-4)}{h\left(\sqrt{4+h}+2\right)} = \lim\limits_{h\to0^+} \dfrac{2}{\left(\sqrt{4+h}+2\right)} = \dfrac{1}{2}$

$\therefore$ $f(x)$ is differentiable at $x = 3$ or at $t = 2$

■ DERIVATIVES OF HIGHER ORDERS AND REPEATEDLY DIFFERENTIABLE FUNCTIONS

Let a function $f(x)$ is differentiable in an interval I (open or closed) and $f'(x)$ denotes its derivative function. If $f'(x)$ is differentiable at x, then the derivate of $f'(x)$ is denoted by $f''(x)$ and is called second derivate or derivative of second order and $f''(x) = \lim\limits_{h\to0} \dfrac{f'(x+h)-f'(x)}{h}$. Further if $f''(x)$ is differentiable at x, then it can be differentiated again and its derivative is denoted by $f'''(x)$ and is called derivative of 3rd order or third derivative. Thus we can get derivatives of a functions of higher orders until the previous one derivative function is differentiable

Thus $f'''(x) = \lim\limits_{h\to0} \dfrac{f''(x+h)-f''(x)}{h}$

and $f^{(n)}(x) = \lim\limits_{h\to0} \dfrac{f^{(n-1)}(x+h)-f^{(n-1)}(x)}{h}$

A function $f(x)$ is said to be twice differentiable at $x = a$ if $f(x)$ is also differentiable at $x = a$. i.e., $\lim_{h\to 0}\frac{f'(a+h)-f'(a)}{h}$ exists finitely or $\lim_{x\to a}\frac{f'(x)-f'(a)}{x-a}$ exists finitely. Similarly, a functions $f(x)$ is said to be thrice differentiable at $x = a$ if $f''(x)$ is differentiable at $x = a$. i.e., $\lim_{h\to 0}\frac{f''(a+h)-f''(a)}{h}$ or $\lim_{x\to a}\frac{f''(x)-f''(a)}{x-a}$ exist finitely.

In general $f(x)$ is said to be differentiable n-times at $x = a$ if $\lim_{h\to 0}\frac{f^{(n-1)}(a+h)-f^{(n-1)}(a)}{h}$ or $\lim_{x\to a}\frac{f^{(n-1)}(x)-f^{(n-1)}(a)}{x-a}$ exists finitely.

REMARKS:

1. *Note that $f^n(x)$ stands for function f applied n-times whereas $f^{(n)}(x)$ stands for nth derivative of f(x).*
2. *If a function f(x) is such that derivative function f'(x) is not defined at x = a, then it is possible that f(x) is differentiable at x = a*

   e.g. If $f(x) = (x)^{1/5}\tan x$, *then* $f'(x) = x^{1/5}(\sec^2 x) + (\tan x)\left(\frac{1}{5}(x)^{-4/5}\right) = x^{1/5}\sec^2 x + \frac{1}{5(x)^{4/5}}\tan x$

   Clearly f'(x) is not defined at x = 0, but $\lim_{h\to 0}\frac{f(0+h)-f(0)}{h} = \lim_{h\to 0}\frac{f(h)-(0)}{h}$

   $= \lim_{h\to 0}\frac{h^{1/5}\tan h - 0}{h} = \lim_{h\to 0}\frac{h^{1/5}\tan h}{h} = 0.1 = 0$

   $\therefore$ $f'(0) = 0$ *i.e., f(a) is differentiable at x = 0*
3. *If limit of a derivative function exists and is equal to the value of derivative, then the function is called continuously differentiable or f'(x) is continuous i.e., continuity of derivative function and differentiability of function.*
4. *It may happen that a function f(x) is differentiable, but not continuously differential*

   e.g. $f(x) = \begin{cases} x^2\sin\frac{1}{x} & ; x \neq 0 \\ 0 & ; x = 0 \end{cases}$

   $f'(x) = 2x\sin\frac{1}{x} - \cos\frac{1}{x}; x \neq 0$

   Now $f'(0) = \lim_{x\to 0}\frac{f(x)-f(0)}{x-0} = \lim_{x\to 0}\frac{x^2\sin\frac{1}{x} - 0}{x} = \lim_{x\to 0} x\sin\frac{1}{x} = 0$

   $\therefore\ f'(x) = \begin{cases} 2x\sin\frac{1}{x} - \cos\frac{1}{x}; x \neq 0 \\ 0 \text{ for } x = 0 \end{cases}$

   $\therefore$ *f(x) is differentiable* $\forall x \in \mathbb{R}$

   Now $\lim_{x\to 0} f'(x) = \lim_{x\to 0}\left(2x\sin\frac{1}{x} - \cos\frac{1}{x}\right)$ *which does not exist as* $2x\sin\frac{1}{x} \to 0$ *and* $\cos\frac{1}{x}$ *oscillates*

   $\therefore$ *f'(x) is discontinuous at x = 0*

   $\therefore$ *f(x) is differentiable* $\forall x \in \mathbb{R}$, *but f' (x) (derivative function is discontinuous). Thus f(x) is not continuously differentiable.*

ILLUSTRATION 76: Show that $f''(x)$ is not continuous at $x = 0$ but $f(x)$ is twice differentiable at $x = 0$ for the function $f(x) = (x)^{3/2}$ sinx

SOLUTION: $f(x) = x^{3/2} \sin x$

$f'(x) = x^{3/2} \cos x + 3/2\,(x)^{1/2} \sin x$

$f''(x) = -x^{3/2} \sin x + 3/2\, x^{1/2} \cos x + 3/2\,(x)^{1/2} \cos x + 3/4\, x^{-1/2} \sin x$

$$\text{Now } \lim_{x\to0} f''(x) = \lim_{x\to0}\left(x^{-3/2}\sin x + \frac{3}{2}x^{1/2}\cos x + \frac{3}{2}x^{1/2}\cos x + \frac{3}{4}x^{-1/2}\sin x\right)$$

$$= \lim_{x\to0}\left[\frac{3}{4}\frac{\sin x}{x^{1/2}}\right] = \lim_{x\to0}\left[\frac{3}{4}x^{1/2}\frac{\sin x}{x}\right] = 0$$

Thus $f''(x)$ is not defined at $x = 0$ but $\lim_{x\to0} f''(x) = 0$

$\therefore$ $f''(x)$ is discontinuous at $x = 0$

$$\text{Again at } x = 0, f''(0) = \lim_{x\to0}\frac{f'(x) - f'(0)}{(x-0)}$$

$$= \lim_{x\to0}\frac{x^{3/2}\cos x + \frac{3}{2}x^{1/2}\sin x - 0}{x} = \lim_{x\to0} x^{1/2}\cos x + \frac{3}{2}\frac{\sin x}{x^{1/2}}$$

$$= \lim_{x\to0}\left(x^{1/2}\cos x + \frac{3}{2}x^{1/2}\frac{\sin x}{x}\right) = 0 + \frac{3}{2}(0)(1) = 0$$

$\therefore$ $f''(x)$ is discontinuous at $x = 0$, but $f(x)$ is twice differentiable at $x = 0$

ILLUSTRATION 77: Find whether $f(x) = \begin{cases} 3x^2 - 4x; x < 0 \\ \sin^2 2x + 3x^2; x \ge 0 \end{cases}$ is twice differentiable and find the second derivative of $f(x)$

SOLUTION: $f(x) = \begin{cases} 3x^2 + x, x < 0 \\ \sin x + 3x^2; x \ge 0 \end{cases}$

$\Rightarrow$ $f'(x) = \begin{cases} 6x + 1, x < 0 \\ \cos x + 6x; x > 0 \end{cases}$

we exclude equality from $x \ge 0$ as $x = 0$ is in doubt for differentiability

$$\text{Now } f'(0^-) = \lim_{x\to0^-}\frac{f'(x) - f(0)}{x - 0} = \lim_{x\to0}\frac{3x^2 + x - 0}{x} = 1$$

$$\text{and } f'(0^+) = \lim_{x\to0^+}\frac{f'(x) - f(0)}{x - 0} = \lim_{x\to0^+}\frac{\sin x + 3x^2 - 0}{x} = 1$$

$\therefore$ $f(0) = 1$

$\therefore$ $f(x) = \begin{cases} 6x + 1\ ; & x < 0 \\ \cos x + 6x; & x \ge 0 \end{cases}$

Now $f''(x)$ $\begin{cases} 6 & ; x < 0 \\ \sin x + 6; & x > 0 \end{cases}$

$$\text{Now } f''(0^+) = \lim_{x\to0^-}\frac{f'(x) - f'(0)}{x - 0} = \lim_{x\to0^-}\frac{(6x+1) - 1}{x} = 6$$

and $f''(0^+) = \lim_{x \to 0^+} \frac{f'(x) - f'(0)}{x - 0} = \lim_{x \to 0^+} \frac{\cos x + 6x - 1}{x}$

$= 6 - \lim_{x \to 0^+} \frac{(1 - \cos x)}{x} = 6 - \lim_{x \to 0^+} \frac{2\sin^2 \frac{x}{2}}{x^2}.x = 6 - 0 = 6$

$\therefore\ f''(0^-) = f''(0^+) = 6 \Rightarrow f''(0) = 6$

$\therefore$ $f(x)$ is twice differentiable at $x = 0$ and the second derivative function is given by

$$f''(x) = \begin{cases} 6; x < 0 \\ \sin x + 6; x \geq 0 \end{cases}$$

TEXTUAL EXERCISE–6: (SUBJECTIVE)

1. Let $f(x) = \begin{cases} 2x^2 \sin \pi x \ ; & x \leq 1 \\ x^3 + ax^2 + b ; & x > 1 \end{cases}$ be a differential function. Examine whether it is twice differentiable in R

2. Identify whether True or False

(a) The function $f(x) = x^2 |x|$ is twice differentiable at $x = 0$

(b) If f: $R \to R$ has a root in $[0,1]$ and $f(x) = -x^2 + x + 2$, then f has only one root in $[0,1]$

(c) If f is continuous at $x = 5$ and $f(5) = 2$, then $\lim_{x \to 2} f(4x^2 - 11)$ exist.

(d) If $\lim_{x \to a} [f(x) + g(x)] = 2$ and $\lim_{x \to a} [f(x) - g(x)] = 1$, then $\lim_{x \to a} f(x).g(x)$ need not exist

3. If f and f' are differentiable at each point of the interval $[a, b]$, then match the statements given in column-I with the corresponding correct statement given in column-II

Column-I

(a) $f''(x) > 0$ for $\forall\ x \in (a, b)$, then

(b) $f(a) f(b) < 0$, then

Column-II

(p) there exists $c \in (a, b)$ such that $f(c) = 0$

(q) $f(x) \neq 0$ for all $x \in (a, b)$

(r) there is at most one $c \in (a, b)$ such that $f(c) = 0$

4. If $f(x)$ is derivable at $x = 3$ and $f'(3) = 2$, then find $\lim_{h \to 0} \frac{f(3 + h^2) - f((3 - h^2)}{2h^2}$

5. Prove that the inverse of the discontinuous function $y = (1 + x^2)$ sgn x is a continuous functions

Answer Keys

1. $f(x)$ is twice differentiable for all x except at $x = 1$

2. (a) T (b) T (c) T (d)

3. (a) → r, (b) → p

4. 2

TEXTUAL EXERCISE–6: (OBJECTIVE)

1. Which of the following functions is/are continuous on $(0, \pi)$?

(a) $\tan x$

(b) $\int_0^x t \sin 1/t \ dt$

(c) $\begin{cases} 1, \ 0 < x \leq 3\pi/4 \\ 2\sin(2x/9), \frac{3\pi}{4} < x \leq \pi \end{cases}$

(d) $\begin{cases} x \sin x, \ 0 < x \leq \pi/2 \\ \pi/2 \sin(\pi + x), \pi/2 < x < \pi \end{cases}$

2. If $f(x) = (4 + x)^n$, $n \in \mathbb{N}$ and $f(0)$ represents the rth derivative of $f(x)$ at $x = 0$, then the value of $\sum_{r=0}^{\infty} \frac{f^{(r)}(0)}{r!}$ is equal to

(a) 2^n (b) e^n

(c) 5^n (d) None of these

3. If the prime sign (') represents differentiation w.r.t 'x' and $f(x)$ = sin x + sin $4x$. cos x, then $f'\left(2x^2 + \frac{\pi}{2}\right)$ at $x = \sqrt{\frac{\pi}{2}}$ is equal to

(a) 0 (b) –1

(c) $-2\sqrt{2\pi}$ (d) None of these

4. If $f(x)$ is differentiable at x = 4 and $f'(4)$ = 5, then $\lim_{h\to 0} \frac{\left|f\left(4\left(1+h^2\right)\right)\right| - |f(4)|}{2h^2}$

(a) equals 10 if and only if $f(4) \neq 0$

(b) equals 10 iff $f(4) \geq 0$

(c) does not exist if $f(4) = 0$

(d) equals 10

5. If $f(x)$ is a twice differentiable function, then between two consecutive roots of the equation $f'(x)$ = 0, there exists :

(a) atleast one root of $f(x) = 0$

(b) atmost one root of $f(x) = 0$

(c) exactly one root of $f(x) = 0$

(d) almost one root of $f''(x) = 0$

6. Let $f(x)$ be a quadratic expression which is positive for all real x. If $g(x) = f(x) + f'(x) + f''(x)$, then for any real x, which one is correct?

(a) $g(x) < 0$

(b) $g(x) > 0$

(c) $g(x) = 0$

(d) $g(x) \geq 0$

7. Let $f''(x)$ be continuous at $x = 0$ and $f''(0) = 4$, then the value of $\lim_{x\to 0} \frac{2f(x) - 3f(2x) + f(4x)}{x^2}$ equals

(a) 11 (b) 2

(c) 12 (d) None of these

Answer Keys

1. (b, c) **2.** (c) **3.** (c) **4.** (b) **5.** (b) **6.** (b) **7.** (c)

■ FUNCTIONAL EQUATION

An equation involving unknown functions is called a functional equation. For examples

(i) $f(x) = f(-x)$ holds for every even function $f(x)$. e.g., $f(x) = x^2$, $f(x) = |x|$; $f(x) = \cos x$, $f(x) = \sin^2 x$ etc.

(ii) $f(-x) = -f(x)$ holds for every odd function. e.g., $f(x) = x^3$, $f(x) = x|x|$; $f(x) = \sin x$, $f(x) = \tan^3 x$ etc.

(iii) $fof(x) = x$ holds for every self invertible function. e.g. $f(x) = -x + k$; $k \in \mathbb{R}$

$\therefore$ $fof(x) = f(f(x)) = -f(x) + k = -(-x + k) + k = x$

(iv) $fog(x) = x$ holds when $g(x) = f^{-1}(x)$

$\because$ $fog(x) = f(f^{-1}(x))$

[let $f(y) = x \Rightarrow f^{-1}(x) = y$]

$= f(y)$

$= x$

e.g., $f(x) = \sin(\sin^{-1} x) = x\ \forall\ x \in [-1, 1]$

$f(x) = \exp.(\ln x) = x\ \forall\ x > 0$.

Solution of a Functional Equation

By solution of a functional equation we mean to find a function satisfying the given functional equation. Usually a given functional equation has more than one solution as is clear from above illustrations. Unique solution can exist when some additional conditions are given like continuity, differentiability at a point, values of functions at some particular points. For example let the given functional equation be $f(x + y) = f(x) + f(y)$ $\forall\ x, y \in \mathbb{R}$ and $f(x)$ is a differentiable function " $x \in \mathbb{R}$ and $f(2) = 8$,

$$\text{Now, } f'(x) = \lim_{h\to 0} \frac{f(x+h) - f(x)}{h}$$

$$= \lim_{h\to 0} \frac{f(x) + f(h) - f(x)}{h} = \lim_{h\to 0} \frac{f(h)}{h}$$

$$= \lim_{h\to 0} \frac{f(h) - f(0)}{h} = f'(0) = k(\text{say}).$$

$$\begin{bmatrix} \because f(x+y)=f(x)+f(y) \\ \Rightarrow for\ x=y=0 \\ \Rightarrow f(0)=2f(0) \\ \Rightarrow f(0)=0 \end{bmatrix}$$

$\therefore$ $f'(x) = k$

$\Rightarrow$ $\int f'(x)dx = \int k\,dx + C$

$\Rightarrow$ $f(x) = kx + C$

Now $f(0) = 0$

$\Rightarrow$ $C = 0$

$\Rightarrow$ $f(x) = kx$ (family of straight lines through origin)

$\therefore$ $f(2) = 8$

$\Rightarrow$ $f(2) = 2k = 8$

$\Rightarrow$ $k = 4$

$\therefore$ $f(x) = 4x$

$\therefore$ Solution is $f(x) = 4x$

Some Famous Functional Equations in Two Variable and their Corresponding Solutions

(a) $f(x + y) = f(x) + f(y) \Rightarrow f(x) = kx;\ k \in \mathbb{R}$.

(b) $f(x + y) = f(x) . f(y) \Rightarrow f(x) = 0$ or $f(x) = a^{kx};\ a > 0; \neq 1$

(c) $f(xy) = f(x) + f(y)\ \forall\ x, y \in \mathbb{R} \sim \{0\}$, then $f(x) = k \log_a |x|;\ a > 0$, or $f(x) = 0$.

(d) $f(xy) = f(x) . f(y);\ x > 0, y > 0 \Rightarrow f(x) = x^n;\ n \in \mathbb{R}$

Proof: (a) Already proved in last topic

(b) $f'(x) = \lim_{h\to 0}\dfrac{f(x+h)-f(x)}{h} = \lim_{h\to 0}\dfrac{f(x).f(h)-f(x)}{h}$

$\lim_{h\to 0}\dfrac{f(x)[f(h)-1]}{h}$ .... (1)

If we let $x = y = 0$, then $f(0) = [f(0)]^2$

$\Rightarrow f(0) = 0$ or $f(0) = 1$

But for $f(0) = 0$, $f(x + y) = f(x) . f(y)$

$\Rightarrow f(x + 0) = f(x) . f(0)\ \forall\ x \in \mathbb{R}$.

$\Rightarrow f(x) = 0\ \forall\ x \in \mathbb{R}$.

So let $f(0) \neq 0$ and $f(0) = 1$

from (1) $f(x) = \lim_{h\to 0}\dfrac{f(x)[f(h)-f(0)]}{h} = f(x) . f'(0)$

$\Rightarrow \dfrac{f'(x)}{f(x)} = f'(0) = k_1$ (say)

$\Rightarrow \dfrac{f'(x)}{f(x)} = k_1 \Rightarrow \ln f(x) = k_1x + C$

$\Rightarrow \ln f(0) = C \Rightarrow \ln(1) = C \Rightarrow C = 0$

$\therefore \ln f(x) = = k_1x \Rightarrow f(x) = e^{k1x}$

or $\log_a f(x) . \log_e a = kx$

$\Rightarrow \log_a f(x) = kx$

$\Rightarrow f(x) = a^{kx}$.

(c) Given $f(xy) = f(x) + f(y)\ \forall$ x, $y \in \mathbb{R} \sim \{0\}$

Now,

$$f'(x) = \lim_{h\to 0}\frac{f(x+h)-f(x)}{h} = \lim_{h\to 0}\frac{f\left(x.\left(\frac{x+h}{x}\right)\right)-f(x)}{h}$$

$$= \lim_{h\to 0}\frac{f(x)+f\left(1+\frac{h}{x}\right)-f(x)}{h} = \lim_{h\to 0}\frac{\left[f\left(1+\frac{h}{x}\right)-0\right]}{h} \quad .....(1)$$

$\therefore$ from (1)

$$f'(x) = \lim_{h\to 0}\frac{\left[f\left(1+\frac{h}{x}\right)-f(1)\right]}{h}$$

$$\begin{bmatrix} \because f(xy)=f(x)+f(y) \\ \Rightarrow for\ x=y=1,\ f(1)=2f(1) \\ \Rightarrow f(1)=0 \end{bmatrix}$$

$$= \lim_{h\to 0}\frac{\left[f\left(1+\frac{h}{x}\right)-f(1)\right]}{x,(h/x)} = \frac{1}{x}f'(1)$$

$\therefore f'(x) = k_1 . (1/x)$; where $f'(1) = k_1$ (say)

$\Rightarrow f(x) = k_1 \ln |x| + C$

for $x = 1$; $f(1) = k_1 \ln 1 + C$

$\Rightarrow C = 0$ $\quad (f(1) = 0)$

$\therefore f(x) = k_1 \ln |x|$

$\Rightarrow f(x) = k_1 . (\log_a |x|) (\log_e a)$

$\Rightarrow f(x) = k \log_a |x|$; where $k_1 \log_e a = k$ (say)

Also clearly $f(x + y) = f(x) . f(y)$ " $x, y \in \mathbb{R} \sim \{0\}$ holds for $f(x) = 0$

$\therefore f(x) = k \log_a |x|$ or $f(x) = 0$

(d) Given $f(xy) = f(x) . f(y);\ x > 0, y > 0$

$\Rightarrow f(x) = x^n;\ n \in \mathbb{R}$

Let $x = e^u$; $y = e^v$

$\therefore f(e^u . e^v) = f(e^u) . f(e^v)$

$\Rightarrow f(e^{u+v}) = f(e^u) . f(e^v)$ .... (1)

Let $g(u) = f(e^u)$

$\therefore g(u + v) = g(u) . g(v)$ .... [from (1)]

$\Rightarrow g(u) = e^{ku}$ (By p art (b))

$\therefore f(e^u) = (e^u)^k$ $\Rightarrow f(x) = x^k$

$\therefore f(x) = x^n;\ n \in \mathbb{R}$ for $x > 0$.

Jensen's Functional Equation

$$f\left(\frac{x+y}{2}\right)=\frac{f(x)+f(y)}{2} \Rightarrow f(x) = ax + b$$

Proof: Let $y = 0$ and $f(0) = a$ (say)

$\Rightarrow f\left(\frac{x}{2}\right)=\frac{f(x)+a}{2} \ \forall x \in \mathbb{R}$ .... (1)

$\therefore f\left(\frac{x+y}{2}\right)=\frac{f(x+y)+a}{2}=\frac{f(x)+f(y)}{2}$ [From given functional equation]

$\Rightarrow f(x + y) + a = f(x) + f(y)$

$\therefore f(x + y) = f(x) + f(y) – a$

Let $g(x) = f(x) – a$ ... (A)

$\therefore g(x + y) = f(x + y) – a = [f(x) + f(y) – a] – a$ .. (2)

Now $g(x) = f(x) – a$

and $g(y) = f(y) – a$

$\therefore g(x) + g(y) = f(x) + f(y) – 2a$ ... (3)

$\therefore$ From (2) and (3) $g(x + y) = g(x) + g(y)$

$\Rightarrow g(x) = kx$

$\therefore f(x) = g(x) + a$ $(\because g(x) = f(x) – a]$

$\Rightarrow f(x) = kx + a$ or $f(x) = ax + b$.

Using calculus:

$$f'(x)=\lim_{h\to 0}\frac{f(x+h)-f(x)}{h}$$

$$=\lim_{h\to 0}\frac{f\left(\frac{2x+2h}{2}\right)-f\left(\frac{2x+0}{2}\right)}{h}$$

$$=\lim_{h\to 0}\left[\frac{\frac{f(2x)+f(2h)}{2}-\frac{f(2x)+f(0)}{2}}{h}\right]$$

$$=\lim_{h\to 0}\left[\frac{f(2h)-f(0)}{2h}\right]=f'(2h)=k_1(say)$$

$\therefore f(x) = k_1x + c$ or $f(x) = ax + b$.

D' Alambert's Functional Equation

$f(x + y) + f(x – y) = 2f(x) . f(y)$

$\Rightarrow f(x) = 0 \ \forall x$

or $f(x) = \cos kx$

or $f(x) = \cos h\, kx$ (cos hyperbolic kx)

Proof: Given functional equation is $f(x + y) + f(x – y) = 2f(x) f(y)$ .... (1)

Differentiating both sides partially w.r.t. x, we get $f'(x + y) + f'(x – y) = 2f'(x) f(y)$

Differentiating again both sides partially w.r.t. x we get $f''(x + y) + f''(x – y) = 2f''(x) f(y)$ .... (2)

Now differentiating (1) partially w.r.t. y we get $f'(x + y) – f'(x – y) = 2f(x) f'(y)$

Differentiating again both sides partially w.r.t. y we get $f''(x + y) + f''(x – y) = 2f(x) f''(y)$ .... (3)

$\therefore$ From (2) and (3)

$2f''(x) f(y) = 2f(x) f''(y)$

$\Rightarrow \frac{f''(x)}{f(x)}=\frac{f''(y)}{f(y)}=c$ (say)

$\Rightarrow f''(x) = cf(x)$

$\Rightarrow \frac{d^2y}{dx^2}-cy=0$

Auxiliary equation is $D^2 – c = 0$

$\Rightarrow D = \pm \sqrt{c}$

Let for $c = –\omega^2 \Rightarrow D = \pm i\omega$

$\therefore$ sol. is $f(x) = c_1 \cos\omega x + c_2 \sin \omega x$ ... (4)

and for $c = \omega^2$, $D = \pm \omega$

$\therefore$ sol. is $f(x) = c_3e^{\omega x} + c_4e^{-\omega x}$ ... (5)

from (1) for $x = y = 0$; $2f(0) = 2[f(0)]^2$

$\Rightarrow f(0) = 0$ or $f(0) = 1$.

But for $f(0) = 0$; $f(x) + f(x) = 2f(x) f(0)$ (taking $y = 0$)

$\Rightarrow f(x) = 0$ " $x \in \mathbb{R}$

So, Let $f(0) = 1$.

$\therefore$ From (4) $f(0) = 1 = C_1$

Also for $x = 0$

we have $f(y) + f(– y) = 2f(0) f(y)$ [By given functional equation]

$\Rightarrow f(y) + f(–y) = 2f(y)$

$\Rightarrow f(–y) = f(y)$ " $y \in \mathbb{R}$

$\Rightarrow f(x)$ is an even function.

$\Rightarrow C_2 = 0$

$\therefore$ from (4) $f(x) = \cos \omega x$

from (5) $f(x) = C_3 e^{\omega x} + C_4 e^{-\omega x}$

for $x = 0$; $f(0) = C_3 + C_4 = 1$

$\Rightarrow C_4 = 1 – C_3$

$\therefore f(x) = C_3 e^{\omega x} + (1 – C_3) e^{-\omega x}$

$= C_3[e^{\omega x} – e^{-\omega x}] + e^{-\omega x}$

$f(x) = f(–x)$

$\Rightarrow f(x) = C_3(e^{-\omega x} – e^{\omega x}) + e^{\omega x}$

$= C_3(e^{\omega x} – e^{-\omega x}) + e^{-\omega x}$

$\Rightarrow 2C_3[e^{-\omega x} – e^{\omega x}] = [e^{-\omega x} – e^{\omega x}]$

$\Rightarrow C_3 = 1/2$

$$\therefore f(x)=\frac{1}{2}\left(e^{\omega x}-e^{-\omega x}\right)+e^{-\omega x}$$

$$=\frac{1}{2}\left(e^{\omega x}+e^{-\omega x}\right)=\cosh \omega x$$

$\therefore \quad f(x) = 0 \qquad$ or $f(x) = \cos \omega x$

or $\quad f(x) = \cos h\omega x$.

7. (a) $g(x + y) = g(x) \,.\, f(y) + f(x) \,.\, g(y)$

(b) $f(x + y) = f(x) \,.\, f(y) - g(x) \,.\, g(y)$

(c) $g(x - y) = g(x) \,.\, f(y) - g(y) \,.\, f(x)$

(d) $f(x - y) = f(x) \,.\, f(y) + g(x) \,.\, g(y)$

These four functional equations represent the addition and subtraction theorem for the trigonometric functions $f(x) = \cos kx$ and $g(x) = \sin kx$

For first three functional equations the converse is not true i.e., if we start from given functional equation, then there may be a lot of continuous and differentiable functions.

Other than $f(x) = \cos kx$ and $g(x) = \sin kx$. However for the fourth functional equation the only solution continuous on $\mathbb{R}$ is $f(x) = \cos kx$ and $g(x) = \sin kx$ as proved below.

Given functional equation is $f(x - y) = f(x) \,.\, f(y) + g(x) \,.\, g(y)$ .... (1)

If we take $f(x) = c$ and $g(x) = \sqrt{c(1-c)}$

i.e., both constant functions; $c \in [0, 1]$, then (1) holds.

Now let us suppose that $f(x)$ is not identically constant functions.

Interchanging x and y in (1) we get

$f(x - y) = f(y - x)$

$\Rightarrow f(x) = f(-x)\ \forall\ x \in \mathbb{R}$

$\Rightarrow f(x)$ is an even function.

Let us suppose that $g(x)$ is an even function

$\Rightarrow g(-y) = g(y)$

$\therefore$ from (1) $f(x + y) = f(x)\, f(-y) + g(x)\, g(-y)$ [Replacing x by $-x$ and y by $-y$]

$= f(x)\, f(y) + g(x)\, g(y)$

$\therefore f(x + y) = f(x - y)$

$\Rightarrow f(x + x) = f(x - x)$

$\Rightarrow f(2x) = f(0) = \text{constant}\ \forall\ x \in \mathbb{R}$.

$\Rightarrow f(x)$ is constant function contrary to our assumption that $f(x)$ is not a constant function.

$\Rightarrow g(x)$ is not an even function

$\Rightarrow g(x)$ cannot be a constant function.

$\therefore$ If $f(x)$ is not constant, then $g(x)$ is also not constant.

Let $f(x)$ is even function and $g(x)$ is odd function.

$\therefore g(-x) = -g(x)$

$\Rightarrow g(0) = -g(0)$

$\Rightarrow g(0) = 0$

from given functional equation, taking $y = 0$, we get $f(x - 0) = f(x)\, f(0) + g(x)\, g(0)$

$\Rightarrow f(x) = f(x)\, f(0)$

$\Rightarrow f(x)\,[1 - f(0)] = 0$

$\Rightarrow f(x) = 0$

or $\quad f(0) = 1$

but $f(x) \neq 0$ identically

$\Rightarrow f(0) = 1$.

From given functional equation $f(x - y) = f(x) \,.\, f(y) + g(x) \,.\, g(y)$ .... (2)

Putting $y = x$,

$\Rightarrow f(0) = f(x) \,.\, f(x) + g(x) \,.\, g(x)$

$\Rightarrow [f(x)]^2 + [g(x)]^2 = 1$

$\Rightarrow |f(x)| \leq 1$ and $|g(x)| \leq 1\ \forall\ x \in \mathbb{R}$

replacing y by $-y$ in given functional equation we get $f(x + y) = f(x)\, f(-y) + g(x)\, g(-y)$

$\Rightarrow f(x + y) = f(x)\, f(y) - g(x)\, g(y)$ .... (3)

(2) + (3) gives, $f(x + y) + f(x - y) = 2f(x)\, f(y)$

which is D' Alembart's functional equation having solution $f(x) = \cos kx$ or

$f(x) = \cos h\omega x$

however the condition $|f(x)| \leq 1$

$\Rightarrow f(x) = \cos kx$ .... (4)

$\because g(x)$ is not a constant function, we get some $\alpha \in \mathbb{R}$ for which $g(\alpha) \neq 0$

$\therefore$ from given functional equation we have $f(x + \alpha) = f(x)\, f(\alpha) + g(x)\, g(\alpha)$

$\Rightarrow f(x + \alpha) = f(x)\, f(\alpha) + g(x)\, g(\alpha)$

$\Rightarrow \cos(x + \alpha) = \cos kx \cos k\alpha + g(x)g(\alpha)$

$\Rightarrow \cos kx \cos k\alpha - \sin kx \sin k\alpha = \cos kx \cos k\alpha + g(x)\, g(\alpha)$

$\Rightarrow g(x)\, g(\alpha) = -\sin k\alpha \sin kx$

$$\Rightarrow g(x) = \left[\frac{-\sin k\alpha}{g(\alpha)}\right] \sin kx$$

$\Rightarrow g(x) = \lambda \sin kx$. .... (5)

where $\lambda = \dfrac{-\sin k\alpha}{g(\alpha)}$

but $f^2(x) + g^2(x) = 1$

$\Rightarrow \cos^2 kx + \lambda^2 \sin^2 kx = 1$

$\Rightarrow \lambda^2 \sin^2 kx = \sin^2 kx$

$\Rightarrow \lambda^2 = 1$

$\Rightarrow \lambda = \pm 1$.

$$\therefore \left.\begin{array}{l} f(x) = \cos kx \\ \text{and } g(x) = \sin kx \end{array}\right\} \text{ and } \left\{\begin{array}{l} f(x) = \cos(-k)x \\ g(x) = \sin(-k)x \end{array}\right.$$

$\therefore f(x) = \cos kx$ and $g(x) = \sin kx$ is the only continuous solution of functional Equation $f(x - y) = f(x)\, f(y) + g(x)\, g(y)$

ILLUSTRATION 78: If f is a function of x satisfying the functional equation $f(x + y) = f(x) + f(y)$ for all rational numbers x and y, then show that $f(x) = kx$, where k is a constant.

SOLUTION: ***Case (i)*** $x = y = 0$

$\Rightarrow f(0) = 2f(0)$ $\Rightarrow f(0) = 0$

$\therefore f(0) = k(0)$

Case (ii) If $x = n \in \mathbb{N}; (n \neq 1)$

then $f(n) = f(1 + 1 + ... + 1) = f(1) + f(1) + ... + f(1) = nf(1)\ kn$; where $f(1) = k$

for $n = 1; f(1) = f(1 + 0) = f(1) + f(0) = f(1) = k = k(1)$

$\therefore f(x) = kx$ for $x \in \mathbb{N}$.

Case (iii) If $x = -n; n \in \mathbb{N}$

from given functional equation $f(x + y) = f(x) + f(y)$, replacing y by $-x$

$\Rightarrow f(0) = f(x) + f(-x)$ $\Rightarrow 0 = f(x) + f(-x)$

$\Rightarrow f(-x) = -f(x)$ $\Rightarrow f(x) = -f(-x)$

$\Rightarrow f(-n) = -f(-(-n)) = -f(n) = -kn; k = f(1)$ by case (ii) $= k(-n) = kx$

$\therefore f(x) = kx$ for $x = -n; n \in \mathbb{N}$

Case (iv) $If\ x = \frac{p}{q}; p, q \in \mathbb{Z}; q \neq 0$

Now $f(p) = f\left(q.\frac{p}{q}\right) = f\left(\frac{p}{q}\right) + f\left(\frac{p}{q}\right) + ... + f\left(\frac{p}{q}\right)$ (q times, setting q = +ve)

$= q.f\left(\frac{p}{q}\right)$

$\Rightarrow f\left(\frac{p}{q}\right) = \frac{1}{q} f(p) = \frac{1}{q}(kp) = k.\frac{p}{q}.$ (by case (iii) and (iv))

$\therefore$ In view of above four cases we note that $f(x) = kx\ \forall\ x \in \mathbb{Q}$ (set of rationals)

Where $k = f(1)$.

ILLUSTRATION 79: If a function f satisfies the functional equation $f(x + y) = f(x) . f(y)\ \forall\ x, y$ rationals, show that either $f(x) = 0$ or $f(x) = e^{\alpha x}$ for all rational numbers x.

SOLUTION: For $x = y = 0$, we get $f(0) = [f(0)]^2$ $\Rightarrow f(0) = 0$ or $f(0) = 1$

for $f(0) = 0$; taking $x = x$ and $y = 0$ in given functional equation

we get $f(x) = f(x) f(0)\ \forall\ x \in \mathbb{R}$

$\Rightarrow f(x) = 0\ \forall\ x \in \mathbb{R}$ $\Rightarrow f(x) = 0$ identically

So let $f(0) = 1$

Case (i) $x = 0$

$\Rightarrow f(0) = 1 = e^{\alpha(0)}$; α is some constant

Case (ii) $x = n \in \mathbb{N}\ (\neq 1)$

$\Rightarrow f(n) = f(1 + 1 + 1 + ... +1) = \underbrace{[f(1).f(1)...f(1)]}_{n\text{-times}}$

$= [f(1)]^n = e^{\ln[f(1)]^n} = e^{n[\ln f(1)]}$

$= e^{\alpha n}$; where $\alpha = \ln f(1)$

for $x = 1$; $f(1) = e^{\ln f(1)} = e^{1.\ln f(1)} = e^{1.\alpha}$

$\therefore\ f(x) = e^{\alpha x}\ \forall\ x \in \mathbb{N}$

Case (iii) If $x = -n;\ n \in \mathbb{N}$

Let $y = x$, we get $f(x - x) = f(x)\,f(-x)$

$\Rightarrow f(0) = f(x)\,f(-x)$

$$\Rightarrow\ f(-x) = \frac{1}{f(x)}\ \Rightarrow\ f(x) = \frac{1}{f(-x)}$$

$$\Rightarrow f(-n) = \frac{1}{f(n)} = \frac{1}{e^{\alpha n}} = e^{-\alpha n} = e^{-n\alpha} = e^{\alpha x}$$

Case (iv) If x is any rational number $= \dfrac{p}{q}(say)$; where $p, q \in \mathbb{Z}$ and $q \neq 0$

$$f(p) = f\left(q.\frac{p}{q}\right)\ [let\ q > 0]$$

$$= f\left(\frac{p}{q}\right).f\left(\frac{p}{q}\right)....f\left(\frac{p}{q}\right) \qquad (q \text{ times})$$

$$= \left[f\left(\frac{p}{q}\right)\right]^q$$

$$\therefore\ f(p) = \left[f\left(\frac{p}{q}\right)\right]^q$$

$$\therefore\ f\left(\frac{p}{q}\right) = [f(p)]^{1/q} = [e^{\alpha p}]^{1/q} = e^{\alpha.p/q}$$

$\therefore\ f(x) = e^{\alpha x}\ \forall\ x \in \mathbb{Q}$; where $\alpha = \ln f(1)$

or $f(x) = 0\ \forall\ x \in \mathbb{Q}$ (set of rational numbers).

ILLUSTRATION 80: If $f(xy) = xf(y) + yf(x)\ \forall\ x, y > 0$, then show that $f(x) = kx \ln x$, $x > 0$.

SOLUTION: Let $g(x) = \dfrac{f(x)}{x}$ ...... (i)

$\therefore\ \dfrac{f(xy)}{xy} = \dfrac{f(y)}{y} + \dfrac{f(x)}{x}$ (dividing the given functional equation by $x.y$)

$\Rightarrow g(xy) = g(x) + g(y)$ $\Rightarrow g(x) = k \ln x$

$\therefore$ from (i) $k \ln x = \dfrac{f(x)}{x}$ $\Rightarrow f(x) = k\,x \ln x$.

ILLUSTRATION 81: If $f(x+y) = \dfrac{f(x).f(y)}{f(x)+f(y)}\ \forall x, y \in \mathbb{R} \sim \{0\}$, then show that $f(x) = \dfrac{\alpha}{x}\ \forall x \in \mathbb{R}$; where α is any constant

SOLUTION: Let $g(x) = \dfrac{1}{f(x)}$

$$\therefore\ g(x+y) = \frac{1}{f(x+y)} = \frac{f(x)+f(y)}{f(x).f(y)} = \frac{1}{f(x)} + \frac{1}{f(y)}$$

$\Rightarrow g(x + y) = g(x) + g(y)$

$\Rightarrow g(x) = kx$ [By cauchy's functional equation]

$\Rightarrow f(x) = \frac{1}{kx} = \frac{\alpha}{x}$; where $\alpha = \frac{1}{k}$

$\therefore f(x) = \frac{\alpha}{x} \forall x \in \mathbb{R} \sim \{0\}$

ILLUSTRATION 82: If $f(x + y) = f(x) + f(y) + xy(x + y)$ $\forall x, y \in \mathbb{R}$; then show that $f(x) = kx + \frac{x^3}{3}$ $\forall x \in \mathbb{R}$.

SOLUTION: Let $g(x) = f(x) - \frac{x^3}{3} \Rightarrow f(x) = g(x) + \frac{x^3}{3}$ ...(1)

$\Rightarrow g(x+y) = f(x+y) - \frac{(x+y)^3}{3} = f(x) + f(y) + xy(x+y) - \frac{x^3}{3}$

$\frac{-y^3}{3} - \frac{1}{3}(3xy)(x+y) = f(x) - \frac{x^3}{3} + f(y) - \frac{y^3}{3} = g(x) + g(y)$

Thus $g(x + y) = g(x) + g(y)$

$\Rightarrow g(x) = kx$ [By Cauchy's functional equation]

$\therefore f(x) = kx + \frac{x^3}{3} \forall x \in \mathbb{R}$.

ILLUSTRATION 83: A function $f : (0, \infty) \to (0, \infty)$ satisfy the functional equation $\alpha x^2 f\left(\frac{1}{x}\right) + f(x) = \frac{x}{1+x}$ $\forall x \in (0, \infty)$; where $\alpha \in \mathbb{R}$. Then find the function $f(x)$.

SOLUTION: Given functional equation is $\alpha x^2 f\left(\frac{1}{x}\right) + f(x) = \frac{x}{1+x}$ .... (1)

Replacing x by $\frac{1}{x}$ we get $\frac{\alpha}{x^2} f(x) + f\left(\frac{1}{x}\right) = \frac{1/x}{1+1/x} = \frac{1}{x+1}$

$\Rightarrow \alpha^2 f(x) + \alpha x^2 f\left(\frac{1}{x}\right) = \frac{\alpha x^2}{1+x}$ .... (2)

Eliminating $f\left(\frac{1}{x}\right)$ from (1) and (2), we get $\frac{x}{1+x} - f(x) = \frac{\alpha x^2}{x+1} - \alpha^2 f(x)$

$\Rightarrow (\alpha^2 - 1) f(x) = \frac{\alpha x^2 - x}{x+1}$ $\Rightarrow f(x) = \frac{\alpha x^2 - x}{(\alpha^2 - 1)(x+1)}$

$\Rightarrow f(x) = \frac{x(1-\alpha x)}{(x+1)(1-\alpha^2)}$ *if* $\alpha^2 \neq 1$ and no solution if $\alpha^2 = 1$.

ILLUSTRATION 84: If $f(x + y) + f(x - y) = 2f(x)$, then show that $f(x) = ax + b$.

SOLUTION: Differentiating given functional equation w.r.t. x, we get $f'(x + y) + f'(x - y) = 2f'(x)$ .... (1)

Differentiating given functional equation w.r.t. y, we get $f'(x + y) - f'(x - y) = 0$ .... (2)

(1) + (2) gives, $2f'(x + y) = 2f'(x)$

$\Rightarrow f'(x + y) = f'(x)$ $x, y \in \mathbb{R}$

$\Rightarrow f'(x) = a =$ constant $\Rightarrow f(x) = ax + b$

ILLUSTRATION 85: If $f(x) : (0, \infty) \to (0, \infty)$ satisfies the functional equation $f(x + y) f(x - y) = [f(x)]^2$, then show that $f(x) = e^{ax+b}$; $a, b \in \mathbb{R}$

SOLUTION: Given functional equation is $f(x + y) f(x - y) = [f(x)]^2$

Taking log both sides we get $\ln f(x + y) + \ln f(x - y) = 2\ln f(x)$

Let $\ln f(x) = g(x)$, then we have $g(x + y) + g(x - y) = 2g(x)$

Its solution is $g(x) = ax + b$ (By previous Illustration)

$\Rightarrow \ln f(x) = ax + b$

$\Rightarrow f(x) = e^{ax+b}$.

ILLUSTRATION 86: Function $f(x)$ satisfies the functional equation $f(x) + f(x + 2y) = 2f(x + y)$. Show that $f(x) = ax + b$.

SOLUTION: Given functional equation is $f(x) + f(x + 2y) = 2f(x + y)$

$\Rightarrow f((x + y) - y) + f((x + y) + y) = 2f(x + y)\ \forall\ x, y \in \mathbb{R}$

Replacing $x + y$ by z

we get $f(z - y) + f(z + y) = 2f(z)\ \forall\ z, y \in \mathbb{R}$

$\Rightarrow f(x) = ax + b$ (by above Illustration)

ILLUSTRATION 87: If $f(x + y) = f(x) . f(y) + f(x) + f(y)$, then show that $f(x) = a^x - 1$; $a > 0 \neq 1$ or $f(x) = -1\ \forall\ x \in \mathbb{R}$ or $f(x) = 0\ \ \forall\ x \in \mathbb{R}$

SOLUTION: Given functional equation is $f(x + y) = f(x) . f(y) + f(x) + f(y)$

$= f(x) [f(y) + 1] + f(y)$

$= f(x) [f(y) + 1] + (f(y) + 1) - 1$

$= (f(x) + 1) (f(y) + 1) - 1$

$\Rightarrow (f(x + y) + 1) = (f(x) + 1) (f(y) + 1)$

Let $g(x) = f(x) + 1$

$\Rightarrow g(x + y) = g(x) . g(y)$ $\Rightarrow g(x) = 0$

or $g(x) = a^x$; $a > 0$; $a \neq 1$

$\Rightarrow f(x) = -1$ or $g(x) = a^x$; $a > 0$; $a \neq 1$

$\therefore f(x) = a^x - 1$ or $f(x) = -1$; $a > 0$; $a \neq 1$

Clearly $f(x) = 0\ \forall\ x \in \mathbb{R}$ is also a solution.

ILLUSTRATION 88: Find all continuous solutions of functional equation $f(x + y) = g(x) + h(y)$; $x, y \in \mathbb{R}$.

SOLUTION: Given functional equation is $f(x + y) = g(x) + h(y)$ ... (1)

Putting $y = 0$

$\Rightarrow f(x) = g(x) + h(0)$

Let $h(0) = b$

$\Rightarrow f(x) = g(x) + b$

$\Rightarrow g(x) = f(x) - b$ ... (2)

Again in (1) put $x = 0$

$\Rightarrow f(y) = g(0) + h(y)$

Let $g(0) = a$

$\Rightarrow f(y) = a + h(y)$

$\Rightarrow h(y) = f(y) - a$ .... (3)

Using (2) and (3) in (1) we get $f(x + y) = f(x) + f(y) - a - b$ .... (4)

let $\phi(x) = f(x) - a - b$ ... (5)

$\therefore$ From (4) we get $\phi(x + y) + a + b = \phi(x) + a + b + \phi(y) + a + b - a - b$

$\Rightarrow \phi(x + y) = \phi(x) + \phi(y)$

$\Rightarrow \phi(x) = 0$ identically

or $\phi(x) = kx \; \forall \; x \in \mathbb{R}$

$\therefore$ from (5) $f(x) = kx + a + b$

from (2) $g(x) = kx + a$

from (3) $h(x) = kx + b$.

ILLUSTRATION 89: Let f be a real valued function defined for all real numbers x such that for some positive constant a, the equation $f(x+a) = \frac{1}{2} + \sqrt{f(x) - f^2(x)}$ holds $\forall x \in \mathbb{R}$. Then

(a) Prove that the function f is periodic

(b) for a=1, give an example of a non-constant function with given properties.

SOLUTION: (a) $f(x+a) = \frac{1}{2} + \sqrt{f(x) - f^2(x)} \; \forall x \in \mathbb{R}$ .... (1)

$\Rightarrow f(x + a) \geq 1/2 \; \forall \; x \in \mathbb{R}$

$\Rightarrow f(x) = f((x - a) + a) \geq 1/2 \; \forall \; x \in \mathbb{R}$

$\therefore \; f(x) \geq 1/2 \; \forall \; x \in \mathbb{R}$

let $g(x) = f(x) - 1/2$

$\Rightarrow g(x) \geq 0.$

$\therefore$ from (1) $g(x+a) = \sqrt{\left(g(x)+\frac{1}{2}\right) - \left(g(x)+\frac{1}{2}\right)^2}$

$= \sqrt{g(x)+\frac{1}{2} - [g(x)]^2 - \frac{1}{4} - g(x)}$

$\therefore \; g(x+a) = \sqrt{\frac{1}{4} - [g(x)]^2}$ .... (2)

Squaring we get $[g(x+a)]^2 = \frac{1}{4} - [g(x)]^2$ .... (3)

$\Rightarrow [g(x+2a)]^2 = \frac{1}{4} - [g(x+a)]^2$ .... (4)

$\therefore \; g(x) \geq 0$

$\Rightarrow g(x + 2a) = g(x)$

$\Rightarrow f(x+2a) - \frac{1}{2} = f(x) - \frac{1}{2}$

$\Rightarrow f(x + 2a) = f(x)$

$\Rightarrow f(x)$ is periodic function with period $2a$.

(b) For $a = 1$, we want to find a function $f(x)$ with period $2a = 2$

Such that $f(x) \ge \frac{1}{2}$

If we let $g(x) = k\left|\sin\frac{\pi}{2}x\right|$, then it is a periodic function with period '2' and $k > 0$ as $g(x) \ge 0$

$\Rightarrow [g(x + a)]^2 = \frac{1}{4} - [g(x)]^2$ [from (2)]

$\Rightarrow k^2\left|\sin\frac{\pi}{2}(x+1)\right|^2 = \frac{1}{4} - k^2\left|\sin\frac{\pi}{2}x\right|^2$

$\Rightarrow k^2\cos^2\frac{\pi}{2}x + k^2\sin^2\frac{\pi}{2}x = \frac{1}{4}$ $\Rightarrow k^2 = 1/4 \Rightarrow k = \pm 1/2$

$\therefore\ g(x) = \frac{1}{2}\left|\sin\frac{\pi}{2}x\right|$ $(\because k > 0)$

$\therefore\ f(x) = g(x) + \frac{1}{2}$ $\Rightarrow f(x) = \frac{1}{2}\left|\sin\frac{\pi}{2}x\right| + \frac{1}{2}$.

ILLUSTRATION 90: The function $f(x)$ is defined $\forall\ x > 0$ and satisfies the condition

(a) $f(x)$ is strictly increasing on $(0, \infty)$

(b) $f(x) \cdot f(f(x) + 1/x) = 1\ \forall\ x > 0$; then find $f(1)$ and hence find $f(x)$.

SOLUTION: (a) Let $f(1) = m$

we are given $f(x) \cdot f(f(x) + 1/x) = 1\ \forall\ x > 0$ .... (1)

$\Rightarrow f(1) \cdot f(f(1) + 1/1) = 1$ $\Rightarrow m \cdot f(m + 1) = 1$

$\Rightarrow f(m + 1) = 1/m$ .... (2)

Now in (1) put $x = (m + 1)$

$\Rightarrow f(m+1)f\left(f(m+1) + \frac{1}{m+1}\right) = 1$

$\Rightarrow f(m+1)f\left(\frac{1}{m} + \frac{1}{m+1}\right) = 1$

$\Rightarrow \frac{1}{m}f\left(\frac{1}{m} + \frac{1}{m+1}\right) = 1$ $\Rightarrow f\left(\frac{1}{m} + \frac{1}{m+1}\right) = m = f(1)$

$\because$ f is a strictly increasing function (one-one)

$\Rightarrow \frac{1}{m} + \frac{1}{m+1} = 1$ $\Rightarrow m + 1 + m = m^2 + m$

$\Rightarrow m = \frac{1 \pm \sqrt{1 - 4(1)(-1)}}{2(1)}$

$\Rightarrow m = \frac{1 \pm \sqrt{5}}{2}$ $\Rightarrow m = \frac{1+\sqrt{5}}{2}$ or $\frac{1-\sqrt{5}}{2}$

If $m = \frac{1+\sqrt{5}}{2}$ $\Rightarrow m > 1$

$\Rightarrow 1 < m < m + 1$ $\Rightarrow f(1) < f(m + 1)$ [$\because f(x)$ is S.I. ()]

$\Rightarrow\ m < \frac{1}{m}$ $\qquad \Rightarrow\ m^2 < 1 \qquad (\because m > 1 \Rightarrow m > 0)$

$\Rightarrow\ m \in (-1, 1)$

Which is a contradiction as $m > 1$

$\therefore\ m = \frac{1-\sqrt{5}}{2} \qquad \Rightarrow\ f(1) = \frac{1-\sqrt{5}}{2}$

Given functional equation is $f(x).\left(f(x)+\frac{1}{x}\right)=1$ for $x > 0$

Let $f(x) = k$

$\Rightarrow\ k.f\left(k+\frac{1}{x}\right)=1 \qquad \Rightarrow\ f\left(k+\frac{1}{x}\right)=\frac{1}{k}$

Now in given functional equation put $x = k + 1/x$

$$\Rightarrow\ f\left(k+\frac{1}{x}\right).f\left(f\left(k+\frac{1}{x}\right)+\frac{1}{k+1/x}\right)=1$$

$\Rightarrow\ \frac{1}{k}f\left(\frac{1}{k}+\frac{x}{kx+1}\right)=1 \qquad \Rightarrow\ f\left(\frac{1}{k}+\frac{x}{kx+1}\right)=k=f(x)$

$\therefore$ $f(x)$ being S.I. (one-one)

$\Rightarrow\ \frac{1}{k}+\frac{x}{kx+1}=x$

$\Rightarrow\ kx + 1 + kx = kx(kx + 1)$

$\Rightarrow\ 2kx + 1 = k^2x^2 + kx$

$\Rightarrow\ k^2x^2 - kx - 1 = 0$

$$k=\frac{x\pm\sqrt{x^2-4x^2(-1)}}{2x^2}=\frac{x\pm\sqrt{5}\,x}{2x^2}=\frac{1\pm\sqrt{5}}{2}.\frac{1}{x}$$

$\Rightarrow\ f(x)=\frac{(1+\sqrt{5})}{2x}$ or $\frac{1-\sqrt{5}}{2x}$

$\because\ f(1)=\frac{1-\sqrt{5}}{2} \qquad \Rightarrow\ f(x)=\left(\frac{1-\sqrt{5}}{2x}\right).$

ILLUSTRATION 91: Let $f : \mathbb{Q}^+ \to \mathbb{Q}^+$ which satisfies the functional equation $f(xf(y))=\frac{f(x)}{y}$, then show that $f(x)$ satisfies the equations

(i) $f(f(x))=\frac{1}{x}$ (ii) $f(x.t) = f(x) . f(t)$

SOLUTION: Given functional equation is $f(xf(y))=\frac{f(x)}{y}$ ... (1)

put $x = 1$

$\Rightarrow\ f(f(y))=\frac{f(1)}{y}$ .... (2)

$\therefore\ f(f(y_1))=\frac{f(1)}{y_1}$ .... (3)

And $f\left(f(y_2)\right)=\dfrac{f(1)}{y_2}$ .... (4)

Now $f(y_1) = f(y_2)$

$\Rightarrow f(f(y_1)) = f(f(y_2))$ [By definition of function i.e., unique image for every input]

$\Rightarrow \dfrac{f(1)}{y_1}=\dfrac{f(1)}{y_2}$ [from (3) and (4)]

$\Rightarrow y_1 = y_2$

$\therefore f(y_1) = f(y_2) \Rightarrow y_1 = y_2$

$\Rightarrow$ Function is one-one

Now in (1) put $y = 1$

$\Rightarrow f(x\,.\,f(1)) = f(x)$

$\Rightarrow x.f(1) = x$ [$\because f$ is one-one]

$\Rightarrow f(1) = 1$

$\therefore$ From (2) we have $f\left(f(y)\right)=\dfrac{1}{y}\ \forall\, y\in\mathbb{R}$,

This prove part (1)

Now let $f(y) = t$

$\therefore$ From (1) $f(x.\,t)=\dfrac{f(x)}{y}=f(x).\dfrac{1}{y}=f(x).f\left(f(y)\right)$ [$\because f(f(y)) = 1/y$]

$= f(x)\,.\,f(t)$

$\therefore f(x\,.\,t) = f(x)\,.\,f(t)$. This proves part (ii)

TEXTUAL EXERCISE–7: (SUBJECTIVE)

1. If $f(x) + f(y) = f\left(x\sqrt{1-y^2}+y\sqrt{1-x^2}\right)\forall\, x, y\in[-1,1]$ then find out the function $f(x)$ and hence or otherwise prove that

(i) $3f(x) = f(3x - 4x^3)$ only if $x\in\left[-\dfrac{1}{\sqrt{2}},\dfrac{1}{\sqrt{2}}\right]$

(ii) $2f(x)=f\left(2x\sqrt{1-x^2}\right)$

2. If $f(x.\,y) = f(x) + f(y)$ for all positive real numbers x, y, then prove that $\dfrac{f(y)}{f(x)}=\log_x y$, $x\neq 1$

3. Let $f(x)$ be a polynomial satisfying $f(x)\,.f(1/x) = f(x) + f(1/x)$ for all $x \in \mathbb{R} \sim \{0\}$ and $f(5) = 126$. Then find $f(x)$ and the value of $f(3)$.

4. Find the domain and range of a real valued function $f(x)$ satisfying $2f(\sin x) + f(\cos x) = x$.

5. If f is a polynomial function satisfying $2 + f(x).\,f(y) = f(x) + f(y) + f(xy)$ for all $x, y \in \mathbb{R}$ and if $f(2) = 5$, then evaluate $f(f(2))$.

6. If $f(x + y) = f(x) + f(y) - xy - 1$ for all real x, y and $f(1) = 1$, then find the number of solutions of $f(x) = -n$, for all $n \in \mathbb{N}$ and also show that $x = -1$ is one root of $f(x) = 0$.

7. Let $f(x) = x^2 - 2x$, $x \in \mathbb{R}$ and $g(x) = f(f(x) - 1) + f(5 - f(x))$. Show that $g(x) \geq 0$ for all $x \in \mathbb{R}$.

8. Let $f: \mathbb{N} \to \mathbb{N}$ be a function such that: (where [.] denotes the greatest integer function.)

(i) $x - f(x) = 19\left[\frac{x}{19}\right] - 90\left[\frac{f(x)}{90}\right]$ for all $x \in \mathbb{N}$

(ii) $1900 < f(1990) < 2000$. Find the possible values of $f(1990)$

9. Let f and g be real valued functions such that $f(x + y) + f(x - y) = 2f(x).g(y)$ for all $x, y \in \mathbb{R}$. Prove that if f is not identically zero and $|f(x)| \le 1$ for all $x \in \mathbb{R}$ then $|g(y)| \le 1$ for all $y \in \mathbb{R}$.

10. If p and q are positive integers, f is a function defined for positive numbers and attains only positive values such that $f(x(f(y))) = x^p y^q$, then prove that $q = p^2$.

11. If $f(x+y+1) = (\sqrt{f(x)} + \sqrt{f(y)})^2$ and $f(0) = 1\ \forall\ x, y \in \mathbb{R}$. Determine $f(x)$.

12. If $f(x + y) = f(x).f(y)$ for all real x, y and $f(0) \neq 0$, then prove that the function $F(x) = \frac{f(x)}{1+\{f(x)\}^2}$ is an even function.

13. Determine all continuous functions f satisfying the functional relation $f(x + y) = g(x) + h(y)$.

14. Find all polynomials p satisfying $p(x + 1) = p(x) + 2x + 1$.

15. Find all real not identically vanishing functions f with the property $f(x) f(y) = f(x - y)$ for all x, y.

16. Find a function f defined for $x > 0$, so that $f(xy) = xf(y) + yf(x)$; $x, y > 0$

17. Find all tame solutions of $f(x+y) = \frac{f(x)f(y)}{f(x)+f(y)}$

18. Find all tame solutions of $f^2(x) = f(x + y) f(x - y)$.

19. Find the function f which satisfies the functional equation $f(x) + f\left(\frac{1}{1-x}\right) = x$ for all $x \neq 0, 1$

20. Find all tame solutions of $f(x + y) + f(x - y) = 2[f(x) + f(y)]$

21. Find all tame solutions of $f(x + y) - f(x - y) = 2f(y)$

22. Find all tame solutions of $f(x + y) + f(x - y) = 2f(x)$

23. Find all continuous functions satisfying $f(x + y) f(x - y) = [f(x) - f(y)]^2$.

24. Find all functions f which are defined for all $x \in \mathbb{R}$ and, for any x, y satisfy $x f(y) + yf(x) = (x + y) f(x) f(y)$.

Answer Keys

1. $f(x) = \frac{2}{\pi}\sin^{-1}(x); x \in [-1,1]$ **3.** $f(3) = 28$; $f(x) = x^3 + 1$

4. $f(x) = \sin^{-1} x - \pi/6$, $x \in [-1, 1]$, Range $f(x) = [-2\pi/3, \pi/3]$

5. $f(x) = x^2 + 1$; 26 **6.** 2 solutions **8.** 1904, 1994 **11.** $f(x) = (x + 1)^2$ **14.** $p(x) = x^2 + c$

15. $f(x) = \pm 1$ **16.** $cx.\log x$ **17.** $\left[\frac{1}{kx}\right]$ **18.** $k.a^x$ where k is positive **19.** $f(x) = \frac{1}{2}\left(1 + x - \frac{1}{x} - \frac{1}{1-x}\right)$

20. $f(x) = ax^2$ **21.** $f(x) = ax$ **22.** $f(x) = ax + b$ **23.** $f(x) = ax^2$ **24.** 0 and 1

TEXTUAL EXERCISE–7: (OBJECTIVE)

1. Select the true information about the solutions of following equations (continuous and differentiable)

(i) $f(x + y) = f(x) + f(y)$

(a) The function solution of above equation is $f(x) = kx$, where k is constant.

(b) The function solution of above equation is $f(x) = x^k$, where k is constant.

(c) If $f(1) = 2$, then $f(5) = 10$

(d) None of these

(ii) $f(x + y) = f(x) . f(y)$

(a) The function solution of above solution is $f(x) = ax$, where a is constant

(b) The function solution of above equation is $f(x) = a^k$, where $a > 0$.

(c) If $f(2) = 25$, then $f(3) = 125$

(d) None of these

(iii) $f(xy) = f(x) + f(y)$

(a) The function solution of above equation is $f(x) = a^x$, where a is constant.
(b) The function solution of above equation is $f(x) = \log_a x$ where $a > 0$ and $a \neq 1$.
(c) If $f(25) = 2$ then $f(625) = 4$
(d) None of these

2. If $f(x) = x + 1/x$, then $[f(x)]^3 + 5/2$ equals
(a) $f(x^3) + 3f(1/x)$
(b) $f(x^3) + 3f(x) + f(2)$
(c) $f(x^3) + 3f(1/x) + f(1/2)$
(d) None of these

3. If $f(x) = \dfrac{3^x + 3^{-x}}{2}$, then $f(x + y).f(x - y)$ equals
(a) $\frac{1}{4}[f(2x)+f(2y)]$
(b) $-[f(2x)\ \ f(2y)]$
(c) $\frac{1}{2}[f(2x)+f(-2y)]$
(d) $\frac{1}{2}[f(-2x)+f(2y)]$

4. If f is an even function defined on $(-5, 5)$, then the real values of x satisfying the equation $f(x)=f\left(\dfrac{x+1}{x+2}\right)$ are
(a) $\dfrac{-1\pm\sqrt{5}}{2}, \dfrac{-3\pm\sqrt{5}}{2}$ (b) $\dfrac{-1\pm\sqrt{3}}{2}, \dfrac{-3\pm\sqrt{3}}{2}$
(c) $\dfrac{-2\pm\sqrt{5}}{2}$ (d) None of these

5. If $f(x)=\dfrac{x-1}{x+1}$, then value of x for which $f(x) + f(f(x)) = 0$ is
(a) $1\pm\sqrt{2}$ (b) $\pm\sqrt{2}$
(c) $3\pm\sqrt{2}$ (d) None of these

6. A function $f(x)$ satisfying the equation $f(x + y) + f(x - y) = 0\ \forall\ x, y \in \mathbb{R}$
(a) is even function
(b) is odd function
(c) Neither even nor odd
(d) does not exist

7. A continuous and differentiable function $f(x)$ satisfying the equation $f(x + y) = f(x) + f(y)\ \forall\ x, y \in \mathbb{R}$, then $f(x)$ may be
(a) an even function (b) an odd function
(c) even as well as odd (d) A periodic function

8. A continuous and differentiable function $f(x)$ satisfying the functional equation $f(x.\ y) = f(x) + f(y)\ \forall\ x, y \in \mathbb{R}^+$, then
(a) $f(x) = 0\ \forall\ x, y \in \mathbb{R}^+$
(b) $f(1) = 0$
(c) $f(x) = \log_a x;\ a > 0 \neq 1$
(d) All above

9. A continuous and differentiable function $f(x)$ satisfying the equation $f(x + y) = f(x).\ f(y)\ \forall\ x, y \in \mathbb{R}$ and $f(2) = 9$; then $f(4)$ equals
(a) 16 (b) 81
(c) 4 (d) None of these

10. A continuous and differentiable function $f(x)$ satisfy the functional equation $f(x + y) = f(x)\ f(y)$; then the solution of $f(x) + f(-x) = 2$ is
(a) $x = 1$ (b) $x = -1$
(c) $x = 0$ (d) None of these

11. A continuous and differentiable function $f(x)$ satisfies the functional equation $f(x+y)=\dfrac{f(x)\,f(y)}{f(x)\ \ f(y)}$; $f(1) = 32$, then $f(8)$ equals
(a) 2 (b) 4
(c) 6 (d) None of these

Answer Keys

1. **(i)** (a), (c) **(ii)** (b), (c) **(ii)** (b), (c) **2.** (b, c) **3.** (b, c, d) **4.** (a) **5.** (a) **6.** (a, b)
7. (a, b, c, d) **8.** (d) **9.** (b) **10.** (c) **11.** (b)

MULTIPLE CHOICE QUESTIONS

SECTION–I

OBJECTIVE SOLVED EXAMPLES

1. Let $f(x)$ be a twice-differentiable function and $f''(0) = 2$, then $\lim_{x\to 0}\frac{2f(x)-3f(2x)+f(4x)}{x^2}$ is

(a) 6 (b) 3
(c) 12 (d) None of these

Solution: (a) Given $\lim_{x\to 0}\frac{2f'(x)-6f'(2x)+4f'(4x)}{2x}$

$= \lim_{x\to 0}\frac{2f''(x)-12f''(2x)+16f''(4x)}{2}$

$= \frac{6f''(0)}{2} = 6$

2. The function f defined by $f(x)=\begin{cases}\frac{\sin x^2}{x}, & x\neq 0\\ 0, & x=0\end{cases}$ is

(a) Continuous and derivable at $x = 0$
(b) Neither continuous nor derivable at x
(c) Continuous but not derivable at $x = 0$
(d) None of these

Solution: (a) We have

$\lim_{x\to 0} f(x) = \lim_{x\to 0}\frac{\sin x^2}{x}$

$= \lim_{x\to 0}\left(\frac{\sin x^2}{x^2}\right)x = 1\times 0 = 0 = f(0)$

So, $f(x)$ is continuous at $x = 0$. $f(x)$ is also derivable at $x = 0$, because $\lim_{x\to 0}\frac{f(x)-f(0)}{x-0} = \lim_{x\to 0}\frac{\sin x^2}{x^2} = 1$ exists finitely.

3. The value of $f(0)$, so that the function $f(x) = \frac{(27-2x)^{1/3}-3}{9-3(243+5x)^{1/5}}(x\neq 0)$ is continuous, is given by

(a) 2/3 (b) 6
(c) 2 (d) 4

Solution: (c) Since $f(x)$ is continuous at $x = 0$, therefore $f(0) = \lim_{x\to 0} f(x) = \lim_{x\to 0}\frac{(27-2x)^{1/3}-3}{9-3(243+5x)^{1/5}}$ $\left(\text{form}\frac{0}{0}\right)$

$= \lim_{x\to 0}\frac{\frac{1}{3}(27-2x)^{-\frac{2}{3}}(-2)}{-\frac{3}{5}(243+5x)^{-\frac{4}{5}}(5)} = \left(-\frac{2}{3}\right)\left(-\frac{1}{3}\right)\frac{3^4}{3^2} = 2$

4. The set of points where the function $f(x) = |x-1|\,e^x$ is differentiable is

(a) R (b) $R - \{1\}$
(c) $R - \{-1\}$ (d) $R - \{0\}$

Solution: (b) Since $|x - 1|$ is not differentiable at $x = 1$. So, $f(x) = |x-1|\,e^x$ is not differentiable at $x = 1$. Hence, the required set is $R - \{1\}$

5. If $f(x) = \begin{cases}1-2x; & x<0\\ 2\ ; & x=0\\ x^2+2; & x>0\end{cases}$, then at $x = 0$

(a) f is Continuous
(b) f is Continuous from left
(c) f is Continuous from right
(d) f has removable discontinuity

Solution: (c) At $x = 0$

LHL $= \lim_{h\to 0} f(0 - h) = \lim_{h\to 0} 1 - 2(-h) = \lim_{h\to 0} 1 + 2h = 1$

RHL $= \lim_{h\to 0} f(0 + h) = \lim_{h\to 0} (h)^2 + 2 = 2$ and $f(0) = 2$

$\therefore$ LHL $\neq$ RHL $= f(0)$

$\Rightarrow$ f is continuous from right but discontinuous from left

$\therefore$ only (c) is correct

6. $f + g$ may be a continuous function if

(a) f is continuous and g is discontinuous
(b) f is discontinuous and g is continuous
(c) f and g both are discontinuous
(d) None of these

Solution: (c) Consider $h(x) = f(x) + g(x)$

If $f(x)$ is continuous and $g(x)$ is discontinuous, then let us assume that $h(x)$ is continuous.

Now, $g(x) = \underbrace{h(x)}_{cont.fn.} - \underbrace{f(x)}_{cont.fn.}$

$\Rightarrow$ $g(x)$ is a continuous function (by theorem 1)

Which is contradictory to the given fact that $g(x)$ is a discontinuous function.

Hence our assumption that $h(x)$ is continuous is wrong.

i.e., if f is continuous and g is discontinuous then $f + g$ cannot be a continuous function.

i.e., (a) is wrong.

Similarly (b) is wrong.

For (c) we take $f(x) = x - [x]$ (discontinuous function)

$g(x) = x + [x]$ (discontinuous function)

$(f + g)(x) = (x - [x]) + (x + [x]) = 2x$ (continuous function)

$\therefore$ (c) is correct

7. The equation $2 \tan x + 5x - 2 = 0$ has

(a) no solution in $[0, \pi/4]$

(b) at least one real solution in $[0,\pi/4]$

(c) two real solutions in $[0,\pi/4]$

(d) None of these

Solution: (b) Let $f(x) = 2 \tan x + 5x - 2$

$$f(0) = -2,\ f(\pi/4) = 2\tan\frac{\pi}{4} + \frac{5\pi}{4} - 2 = \frac{5\pi}{4}$$

Now $0 \in \left[-2, \frac{5\pi}{4}\right]$ and $f(x)$ is continuous on $[0,\pi/4]$

$\therefore$ By intermediate value theorem $\exists\ c \in [0, \pi/4]$ for which $f(c) = 0$

$\therefore$ (b) is correct

8. The left hand derivative of $f(x) = [x] \sin(\pi x)$ at $x = k$, k is an integer, is:

(a) $(-1)^k (k - 1)\pi$

(b) $(-1)^{k-1} (k - 1)\pi$

(c) $(-1)^k k\pi$

(d) $(-1)^{k-1} k\pi$

Solution: (a) $f(x) = [x] \sin(\pi x)$

If x is just less than k, $[x] = k - 1$

$\therefore$ $f(x) = (k - 1) \sin(\pi x)$, when $k - 1 < x < k\ \forall\ k \in I$

Now LHD at $x = k$,

$$= \lim_{x\to k}\frac{(k-1)\sin(\pi x) - k\sin(\pi k)}{x-k}$$

$$= \lim_{x\to k}\frac{(k-1)\sin(\pi x)}{(x-k)}$$

[as $\sin(\pi k) = 0$ as $k \in$ integer]

$$= \lim_{x\to k}\frac{(k-1)\sin(\pi(k-h))}{-h} \quad [\text{Let } x = (k-h)]$$

$$= \lim_{x\to k}\frac{(k-1)(-1)^{k-1}\sin(h\pi)}{-h} = \lim_{x\to k}$$

$$(k-1)(-1)^{k-1}\frac{\sinh \pi}{h\pi} x(-\pi)$$

$= (k - 1)(-1)^k \pi$ Therefore, (a) is the answer.

9. Which of the following function is differentiable at $x = 0$?

(a) $\cos(|x|) + |x|$ (b) $\cos(|x|) - |x|$

(c) $\sin(|x|) + |x|$ (d) $\sin(|x|) - |x|$

Solution: (d) Here RHD of $\sin(|x|) - |x|$

$$= \lim_{h\to 0}\frac{(\sin|h| - |h|) - (0-0)}{h}$$

$$= \lim_{h\to 0}\frac{\sin h}{h} - \frac{h}{h} = 1 - 1 = 0$$

Also LHD of $\sin(|x|) - |x|$

$$= \lim_{h\to 0}\frac{(\sin|h| - |h|) - (0-0)}{-h}$$

$$= \lim_{h\to 0}\frac{\sin h}{-h} + \frac{h}{h} = -1 + 1 = 0$$

Thus, $\sin(|x| - |x|$ is differentiable at $x = 0$).

10. Let $f(x) = \min.\{\tan x, \cot x\}\ \forall\ x \in R$. Then which of the following is true?

(a) Range of $f(x) = (-\infty, -1] \cup [0,1]$

(b) Period (if periodic) is π

(c) Points of discontinuity of $f(x)$ are $0, \pm\frac{\pi}{2}, \pm\pi, \pm\frac{3\pi}{2}, \ldots$

(d) Points of non-differentiability of $f(x)$ are $0, \pm\frac{\pi}{4}, \pm\frac{\pi}{2}, \frac{3\pi}{4}, \pm\pi, \ldots$

Solution: (a, b, c, d) We know; $f(x) = \min.\{\tan x, \cot x\}$ can be plotted in two steps.

(i) We should plot the graph of $\tan x$ and $\cot x$

(ii) We should find their point of intersection and neglect the area above their point of intersection.

Graph of $f(x) = \min, \{\tan x, \cot x\}$ is given below:

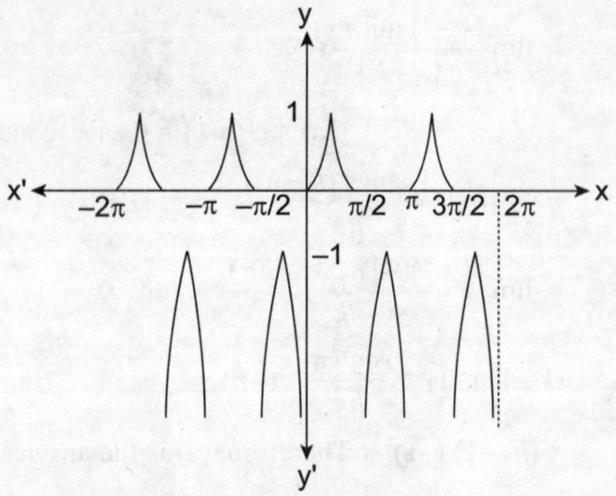

FIGURE 2.97

Clearly, (a) range of $f(x) = (-\infty, -1] \cup [0,1]$

(b) period of $f(x) = \pi$

(c) point of discontinuity are $0, \pm\frac{\pi}{2}, \pm\pi, \pm\frac{3\pi}{2}, ...$

(d) also the points of non-differentiability are $0, \pm\frac{\pi}{4}, \pm\frac{\pi}{2}, \pm\frac{3\pi}{2}, \pm\pi, ...$

11. Indicate all correct alternatives if, $f(x) = \frac{x}{2} - 1$, then on the interval $[0, \pi]$

(a) $\tan(f(x))$ and $\frac{1}{f(x)}$ are both continuous

(b) $\tan(f(x))$ and $\frac{1}{f(x)}$ are both discontinuous

(c) $\tan(f(x))$ and $f^{-1}(x)$ are both continuous

(d) $\tan(f(x))$ is continuous but $\frac{1}{f(x)}$ is not

Solution: (c) $f(x) = \frac{x}{2} - 1 \; x \in [0, \pi]$

$$\Rightarrow \frac{1}{f(x)} = \frac{2}{x-2}; x \neq 2$$

$$\Rightarrow \frac{1}{f(x)} \text{ is discontinuous in } [0, \pi]$$

Now, $\tan f(x) = \tan\left(\frac{x}{2} - 1\right)$;

$\left(\frac{x}{2} - 1\right) \in \left[-1, \frac{\pi}{2} - 1\right]$ in which $\tan f(x)$ is continuous let $f(x) = \frac{x}{2} - 1 = y$

$\Rightarrow 2y = x - 2$

$\Rightarrow x = 2y + 2$

$\Rightarrow f^{-1}(x) = 2x + 2$

$\Rightarrow c$ in given involve.

$\Rightarrow f^{-1}(x)$ is continuous in $[0, \pi]$

12. For $x > 0$, let $h(x) = \begin{cases} \frac{1}{q} & \text{if } x = \frac{p}{q} \\ 0 & \text{if } x \text{ is irrational} \end{cases}$; where p and $q > 0$ are relatively prime integers then which one does not hold good?

(a) $h(x)$ is discontinuous for all x in $(0, \infty)$

(b) $h(x)$ is continuous for each irrational in $(0, \infty)$

(c) $h(x)$ is discontinuous for each rational in $(0, \infty)$

(d) $h(x)$ is not derivable for all x in $(0, \infty)$.

Solution: (a) Let $x = \frac{2}{3}$ which is rational

$$\Rightarrow h\left(\frac{2}{3}\right) = \frac{1}{3}$$

$$\lim_{\to} h\left(-+t\right) = 0$$

$\Rightarrow$ Discontinuous at $x \in Q$

Let $x = \sqrt{2} \notin Q$

$h(\sqrt{2}) = 0$; Consider $\sqrt{2} = 1.41401235839\ 0$

$$h(\sqrt{2}) = h\left(\frac{1414023583}{10^{10}}\right) = \frac{1}{10^{10}} \to 0.$$

Hence h is continuous for all irrationals

$\Rightarrow$ (a) is correct option.

13. The graph of function f contains the point $P(1, 2)$ and $Q(s, r)$. The equation of the secant line through P and Q is $y = \left(\frac{s^2 + 2s - 3}{s - 1}\right) x - 1 - s$. The value of $f'(1)$, is

(a) 2 (b) 3

(c) 4 (d) Non-existent

Solution: (c) **I:** By definition $f'(1)$ is the limit of the slope of the secant line when $s \to 1$.

$$\text{Thus } f'(1) = \lim_{s \to 1} \frac{s^2 + 2s - 3}{s - 1}$$

$$= \lim_{s \to 1} \frac{(s-1)(s+3)}{s-1}$$

$$= \lim_{s \to 1} (s+3) = 4$$

$\Rightarrow$ (d) is correct answer

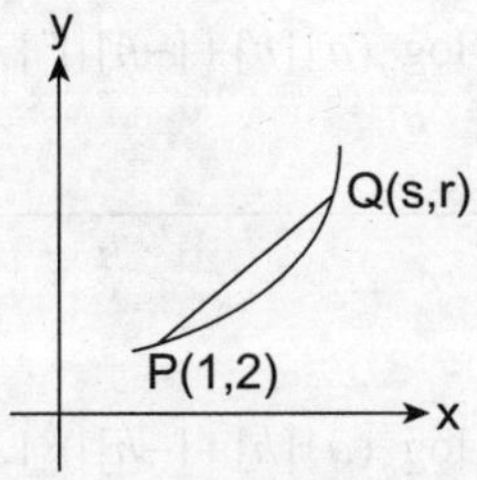

FIGURE 2.98

II: By substituting $x = s$ into the equation of the secant line, and canceling by $s - 1$ again, we get $y = s^2 + 2s - 1$. This is $f(s)$, and its derivative is $f'(s) = 2s + 2$, so $f'(1) = 4$.]

14. Which one of the following is not bounded on the intervals as indicated?

(a) $f(x) = 2^{\frac{1}{x-1}}$ on $(0, 1)$

(b) $g(x) = x \cos\frac{1}{x}$ on $(-\infty, \infty)$

(c) $h(x) = xe^{-x}$ on $(0, \infty)$

(d) $l(x) = \text{arc}\tan 2^x$ on $(-\infty, \infty)$

Solution: (b)

(a) $\lim\limits_{x\to 0^+} f(x) = \lim\limits_{h\to 0} 2^{\frac{1}{h-1}} = \frac{1}{2}$;

$\lim\limits_{x\to 1^-} f(x) = \lim\limits_{h\to 0} 2^{-\frac{1}{h}} = 0$

$\Rightarrow f(x) \in \left(0, \frac{1}{2}\right)$

$\Rightarrow f(x)$ is bounded

(b) $\cos\frac{1}{x} \in (-1, 1)$

$\Rightarrow x\cos\frac{1}{x} \in (-x, x)$ for $x > 0$

$\therefore \quad \cos - \in (-\infty, \infty)$ for $x \in (-\infty, \infty)$

$\Rightarrow g(x)$ is unbounded function.

(c) $\lim\limits_{h\to 0} x\ e^{-x} = \lim\limits_{h\to 0} h\ e^{-h} = 0$; $\lim\limits_{x\to\infty} x\ e^{-x} =$

$\lim\limits_{x\to\infty}\frac{x}{e^x} = \lim\limits_{x\to\infty}\frac{1}{e^x} = \frac{1}{e^\infty} = 0$

$\Rightarrow$ Also $y = \frac{x}{e^x} \Rightarrow y' = \frac{e^x - xe^x}{e^{2x}} = e^{-x(1-x)}$

$= 0$ at $x = 1$, also $h(1) = 1/e$

$\Rightarrow$ Range of $h(x) = \left[0, \frac{1}{e}\right]$, graphically shown below

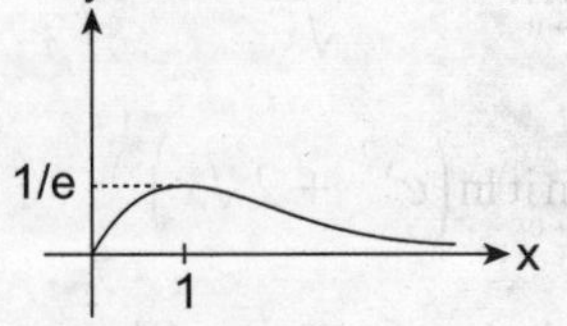

FIGURE 2.99

$\Rightarrow h(x)$ is bounded

Also $l(x) = \text{arc}(\tan 2^x)$; $x \in (-\infty, \infty) = \tan^{-1}(2^x)$

When $x \to (-\infty, \infty)$, $2^x \in (0, \infty)$

Also $\tan^{-1} x$ is a increasing on $(-\infty, \infty)$

$\Rightarrow \tan^{-1}(2^x)$ increases on $(-\infty, \infty)$

$\Rightarrow \tan^{-1}(2^x) \in (\tan^{-1} 0, \tan^{-1}, \infty) = \left(0, \frac{\pi}{2}\right)$

$\Rightarrow l(x)$ is bounded,

15. Given $f(x) = b([x]^2 + [x]) + 1$ for $x \geq -1$
$= \sin(\pi(x + a))$ for $x < -1$
where $[x]$ denotes the integral part of x, then for what values of a, b the function is continuous at $x = -1$?

(a) $a = 2n + (3/2)$; $b \in R$; $n \in I$

(b) $a = 4n + 2$; $b \in R$; $n \in I$

(c) $a = 4n + (3/2)$; $b \in R^+$; $n \in I$

(d) $a = 4n + 1$; $b \in R^+$; $n \in I$

Solution: (a) $f(-1) = b(1 - 1) + 1 = 1$

and $\lim\limits_{h\to 0} f(-1-h) = 1$

$\Rightarrow \lim\limits_{h\to 0} f(-1-h) = \lim\limits_{h\to 0} \sin(\pi(-1-h) + \pi a) = 1$

As $f(x)$ is continuous at $x = -1$

$\Rightarrow \sin \pi a = -1 = \sin\left(2n\pi + \frac{3\pi}{2}\right)$

$\Rightarrow \pi a = 2n\pi + \frac{3\pi}{2}$

$\Rightarrow a = 2n + \frac{3}{2}$.

Hence $a = 2n + \frac{3}{2}$, $n \in I$ and $b \in R$

16. If $f(x) = \dfrac{\ell n\left(e^{x^2} + 2\sqrt{x}\right)}{\tan\sqrt{x}}$ is continuous at $x = 0$, then $f(0)$ must be equal to:

(a) 0 (b) 1

(c) e^2 (d) 2

Solution: (d) For continuous at $x = 0$

$$f(0) = \underset{x\to 0}{\text{Limit}}\frac{\ell n\left(e^{x^2}+2\sqrt{x}\right)}{\sqrt{x}}$$

$$= \underset{x\to 0}{\text{Limit}}\ln\left(e^{x^2}+2\sqrt{x}\right)^{\frac{1}{\sqrt{x}}}$$

$$= \lim_{x\to 0}\ln(1+e^{x^2}+2\sqrt{x}-1)^{1/\sqrt{x}}$$

$$= \lim_{x\to 0}\frac{1}{\sqrt{x}}\left(e^{x^2}+2\sqrt{x}-1\right)$$

$$= \underset{x\to 0}{\text{Limit}}\left(\frac{e^{x^2}-1}{\sqrt{x}}+2\right) = 2.$$

17. Given $f(x) =$

$$\begin{cases}\log_a(a\,|[x]+[-x]|)^x\left(\dfrac{a^{\frac{2}{\left(\frac{[x]+[-x]}{|x|}\right)}-5}}{3+a^{\frac{1}{|x|}}}\right); & |x|\neq 0; a>1\\[2ex] 0 & ; \quad x=0\end{cases};$$

where [ ] represents the integral part function, then:

(a) f is continuous but not differentiable at $x = 0$

(b) f is cont. and diff. at $x = 0$

(c) the differentiability of 'f' at $x = 0$ depends on the value of a

(d) f is cont. and diff. at $x = 0$ and for $a = e$ only

Solution: (b) $f(x) =$

$$\begin{cases}\{\log_a(a\,|[x]+[-x]|)^x\}\left(\dfrac{a^{\frac{2}{\left(\frac{[x]+[-x]}{|x|}\right)}-5}}{3+a^{\frac{1}{|x|}}}\right); & |x|\neq 0; a>1\\[2ex] 0 \quad ; & x=0\end{cases}$$

$$f'(0) = \underset{h\to 0}{\text{Lim}}\frac{f(h+0)-f(0)}{h}$$

$$= \underset{h\to 0}{\text{Lim}}\frac{\{\log_a(a\,|[h]|+[-h])^h\}.\dfrac{a^{\frac{2}{\left(\frac{[h]+[-h]}{|h|}\right)}-5}}{3+a^{\frac{1}{|h|}}}-0}{h}$$

$$= \begin{cases}\underset{h\to 0^-}{\text{Lim}}\dfrac{\{\log_a(a\,|[h]+[-h]|)^h\}.\left(\dfrac{a^{\frac{2}{\left(\frac{[h]+[-h]}{|h|}\right)}-5}}{3+a^{\frac{1}{|h|}}}\right)}{h}\\[3ex] \underset{h\to 0^+}{\text{Lim}}\dfrac{\{\log_a(a\,|[h]+[-h]|)^h\}.\left(\dfrac{a^{\frac{2}{\left(\frac{[h]+[-h]}{|h|}\right)}-5}}{3+a^{\frac{1}{|h|}}}\right)}{h}\end{cases}$$

$$= \begin{cases}\underset{h\to 0^-}{\text{Lim}}\dfrac{\{h.\log_a(a\,|-1+0|)\}\left(\dfrac{a^{\frac{2}{\frac{-1+0}{-h}}-5}}{3+a^{-1/h}}\right)}{h}\\[3ex] \underset{h\to 0^+}{\text{Lim}}\dfrac{\{h.\log_a(a\,|0-1|)\}\left(\dfrac{a^{\frac{2}{\frac{0-1}{h}}-5}}{3+a^{1/h}}\right)}{h}\end{cases}$$

$$= \begin{cases}\underset{h\to 0^-}{\text{Lim}}\{\log_a a\}\left(\dfrac{a^{2h-5}}{3+a^{-1/h}}\right)\\[2ex] \underset{h\to 0^+}{\text{Lim}}\{\log_a a\}\left(\dfrac{a^{(-2h-5)}}{3+a^{1/h}}\right)\end{cases} = \begin{cases}\underset{h\to 0^-}{\text{Lim}}\dfrac{a^{2h-5}}{3+a^{-1/h}}\\[2ex] \underset{h\to 0^+}{\text{Lim}}\dfrac{a^{-2h-5}}{3+a^{-1/h}}\end{cases}$$

$$= \begin{cases}0\\ 0\end{cases}\quad\left(\begin{matrix}\because\ (\underset{h\to 0^-}{\text{Lim}}(3+a^{-1/h})=\infty)\\ (\underset{h\to 0^+}{\text{Lim}}(3+a^{1/h})=\infty)\end{matrix}\right)$$

$\therefore\quad f'(0) = f'(0^-) = f'(0^+) = 0$

Hence $f(x)$ is differentiable at $x = 0$ and also continuous at $x = 0$

18. Let $f(x) = [n + p \sin x]$, $x \in (0, \pi)$, $n \in \mathbb{Z}$ and p is a prime number. The number of points where $f(x)$ is not differentiable is

(a) $p - 1$ (b) $p + 1$

(c) $2p + 1$ (d) $2p - 1$

Solution: (d) $f(x) = [n + p \sin x]$; $x \in (0, \pi)$ and $n \in \mathbb{Z}$

$\Rightarrow f(x) = n + [p \sin x]$

In $\left(0, \dfrac{\pi}{2}\right)$ $\sin x \in (0,1)$

$\Rightarrow p \sin x$ takes integer values 1, 2, 3 …. $p - 1$

i.e., $(p - 1)$ integer values

$\Rightarrow f(x) = n + [p \sin x]$ is discontinuous and hence non-differentiable in $\left(0, \dfrac{\pi}{2}\right)$ at exactly $(p - 1)$ points. Similarly $f(x)$ is non-differentiable in $\left(\dfrac{\pi}{2}, \pi\right)$ at exactly $(p - 1)$ points.

Also $f(x)$ is non-differentiable at $x = \dfrac{\pi}{2}$

Thus $f(x)$ is non-differentiable in $(0, \pi)$ at $2(p - 1) + 1 = (2p - 1)$ points.

19. Let $f(x)$ be defined in $[-2, 2]$ by $f(x) = \begin{cases} \max.(4-x^2, 1+x^2); & -2 \le x \le 0 \\ \min.(4-x^2, 1+x^2); & 0 < x \le 2 \end{cases}$. Then $f(x)$

(a) is continuous at all points
(b) has a point of discontinuity
(c) is not differentiable only at one point
(d) is not differentiable at more than one point

Solution: (b), (d)

$$f(x) = \begin{cases} \max.(4-x^2, 1+x^2); & -2 \le x \le 0 \\ \min.(4-x^2, 1+x^2); & 0 < x \le 2 \end{cases}$$

Graph of $f(x)$ is as shown in figure below

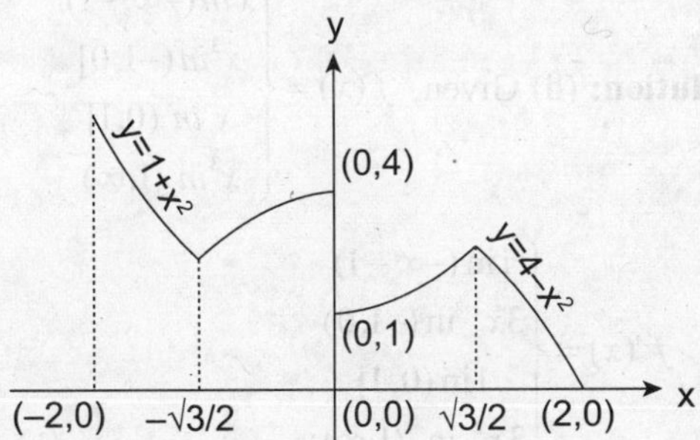

FIGURE 2.100

Clearly $f(x)$ is discontinuous at $x = 0$ and non-differentiable at $x = \pm\dfrac{\sqrt{3}}{2}$

20. The function $f(x) = \text{sgn}x.\sin x$ is

(a) discontinuous no where
(b) an even function
(c) an odd function
(d) differentiable for all x

Solution: (a), (b) $f(x) = \begin{cases} \sin x; & x \ge 0 \\ -\sin x; & x < 0 \end{cases}$

$\therefore$ Graph of $f(x)$ is as shown below.

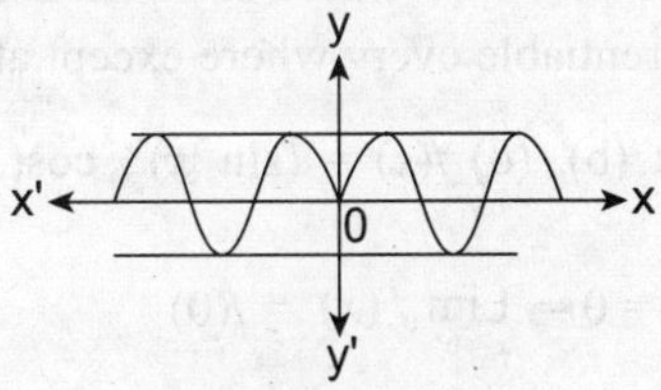

FIGURE 2.101

Clearly $f(x)$ is discontinuous nowhere, but non-differentiable only at $x = 0$.
Also $f(x)$ is even.

21. $f(x) = |x[x]|$ in $-1 \le x \le 2$, where $[x]$ is greatest integer $\le x$, then $f(x)$ is:

(a) continuous at $x = 0$
(b) discontinuous at $x = 0$
(c) not differentiable at $x = 2$
(d) differentiable at $x = 2$

Solution: (a, c) $f(x) = |x[x]|; -1 \le x \le 2$

Now, $\lim\limits_{x\to 0^+} f(x) = \lim\limits_{x\to 0^+} |x(0)| = 0$;

and $\lim\limits_{x\to 0^-} f(x) = \lim\limits_{x\to 0^-} |x(-1)| = \lim\limits_{x\to 0^-} (-x) = 0$;

$\Rightarrow f(x)$ is continuous at $x = 0$

$\lim\limits_{x\to 2^+} f(x) = \lim\limits_{x\to 2^+} |x(2)| = \lim\limits_{x\to 2^+} 2x = 4$;

$\lim\limits_{x\to 2^-} f(x) = \lim\limits_{x\to 2^-} |x(1)| = \lim\limits_{x\to 2^-} x = 2$

$\Rightarrow f(x)$ is discontinuous at $x = 2$

22. $f(x) = 1 + x. [\cos x]$ in $0 < x \le \pi/2$, where [ ] denotes greatest integer function then,

(a) It is continuous in $0 < x < \pi/2$
(b) It is differentiable in $0 < x < \pi/2$
(c) Its maximum value is 2
(d) It is not differentiable in $0 < x < \pi/2$

Solution: (a, b) $f(x) = 1 + x [\cos x];\ 0 < x \le \dfrac{\pi}{2}$

$f(x) = 1 + 0 = 1$

$\Rightarrow f(x)$ is constant in $\left(0, \dfrac{\pi}{2}\right]$

$\Rightarrow f(x)$ is continuous and differentiable $\forall x \in \left(0, \dfrac{\pi}{2}\right]$

23. $f(x) = (\sin^{-1}x)^2 . \cos(1/x)$ if $x \neq 0$; $f(0) = 0$, then, $f(x)$ is:

(a) continuous no where in $-1 \leq x \leq 1$
(b) continuous every where in $-1 \leq x \leq 1$
(c) differentiable no where in $-1 \leq x \leq 1$
(d) Differentiable every where except at $x = 0$

Solution: (b), (d) $f(x) = (\sin^{-1}x)^2 . \cos(1/x)$ if $x \neq 0$; $f(0) = 0$

$\lim_{x\to 0^-} f(x) = 0 = \lim_{x\to 0^+} f(x) = f(0)$

$\Rightarrow f(x)$ is continious in $[-1, 1]$

$$f'(0^+) = \lim_{h\to 0}\frac{(\sin^{-1}h)^2\cos^{-1}\frac{1}{h} - 0}{h}$$

$$= \lim_{h\to 0}\frac{\sin^{-1}(h)}{h} . \sin^{-1}(h)\cos^{-1}(1/h)$$

which does not exist as $\frac{1}{h} \to \infty$ as $h \to 0^+$ for which $\cos^{-1}\left(\frac{1}{h}\right)$ is not defined.

$\therefore f(x)$ is differentiable every where except at $x = 0$.

24. If $f(x) = |x| + |\sin x|$ in $\left(-\frac{\pi}{2}, \frac{\pi}{2}\right)$, then $f(x)$ is

(a) Continuous no where
(b) Continuous every where
(c) Differentiable no where
(d) Differentiable every where except at $x = 0$

Solution: (b, d) $f(x) = |x| + |\sin x|$

$$= \begin{cases} -x - \sin x \text{ for } x \in \left(\frac{-\pi}{2}, 0\right) \\ x + \sin x \text{ for } x \in \left[0, \frac{\pi}{2}\right) \end{cases}$$

$$\therefore f'(0^+) = \lim_{h\to 0}\frac{h + \sin h - 0}{h} = 2$$

$$\text{and } f'(0^-) = \lim_{h\to 0}\frac{h + \sin h - 0}{-h} = -2$$

$\Rightarrow f(x)$ is non-differentiable at $x = 0$, but $f(x)$ being the sum of two continuous functions $|x|$ and $|\sin x|$ is continuous every where.

25. Let $f : R \to R$ be any function. Define $g : R \to R$ by $g(x) = |f(x)|$ for all x. Then g is

(a) onto if f is onto
(b) one-one if f is one one
(c) continuous if f is continuous
(d) differentiable if f is differentiable.

Solution: (c) Let $h(x) = |x|$,
then $g(x) = |f(x)| = h\{f(x)\}$
Since, composition of two continuous function is continuous, g is continuous if f is continuous. So, answer is (c).

(a) is wrong answer. Let $f(x) = x$
$\Rightarrow g(x) = |x|$
Now, f (x) is an onto function. Since, co-domain of x is R and range of x is R. But $g(x)$ is into function. Since, range of $g(x)$ is $[0, \infty)$ but co-domain is given R.

(b) Let $f(x) = x \Rightarrow g(x) = |x|$. Now, $f(x)$ is one-one function but $g(x)$ is many-one function.
Hence, (b) is wrong.

(d) Let $f(x) = x \Rightarrow g(x) = |x|$. Now, $f(x)$ is differentiable for all $x \in R$ but $g(x) = |x|$ is not differentiable at $x = 0$.
Hence, (d) is wrong.

26. Let f: $R \to R$ be a function defined by , $f(x) = \max [x, x^3]$. The set of all points where $f(x)$ is NOT differentiable is:

(a) $\{-1, 1\}$ (b) $\{-1, 0\}$
(c) $\{0, 1\}$ (d) $\{-1, 0, 1\}$

Solution: (d) Given, $f(x) = \begin{cases} x \text{ in } (-\infty, -1) \\ x^3 \text{ in } (-1, 0] \\ x \text{ in } (0, 1] \\ x^3 \text{ in } (1, \infty) \end{cases}$

$$\Rightarrow f'(x) = \begin{cases} 1 \text{ in } (-\infty - 1) \\ 3x^2 \text{ in } (-1, 0) \\ 1 \text{ in } (0, 1] \\ 3x^2 \text{ in } (1, \infty) \end{cases}$$

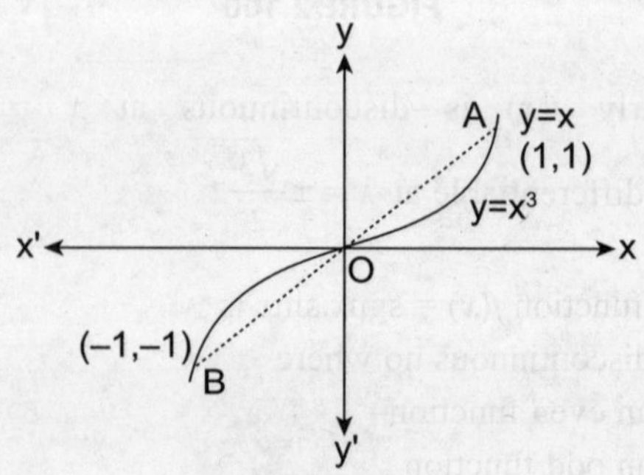

FIGURE 2.102

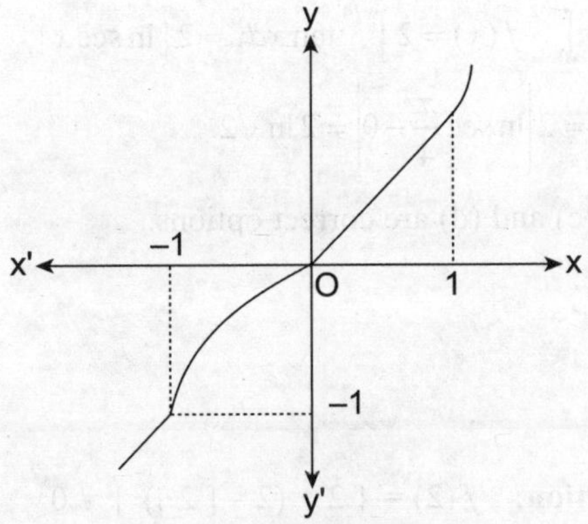

FIGURE 2.103

Above graphs represents $f(x)$. First one shows the graph of both $f(x) = x$ and $f(x) = x^3$ and the second one shows the graph $f(x) = \max\{x, x^3\}$

$\therefore$ The points for consideration are $x = -1, 0, 1$ (doubtful points)

At the point of consideration

$f'(-1^-) = 1$ and $f'(-1^+) = 3$

$f'(-0^-) = 0$ and $f'(0^+) = 1$

$f'(1^-) = 1$ and $f'(1^+) = 3$

Hence, f is not differentiable at $-1, 0, 1$.

27. If f (x) is continuous in $[0,2]$ and f $(0) = f(2)$, then the equation $f(x) = f(x+1)$ has

(a) non-real root in [0.2]

(b) at least one real root in [0, 1]

(c) at least one real root in [0,2]

(d) at least one real root in [1, 2]

Solution: (b) Let $g(x) = f(x) - f(x+1)$

$\therefore$ $g(0) = f(0) - f(1)$

and $g(1) = f(1) - f(2)$

$\Rightarrow g(0) + g(1) = 0$

$\Rightarrow g(0)$ and $g(1)$ are of opposite signs

$\Rightarrow f(x) = f(x+1)$ at least once in [0, 1].

28. Let $S(x) = \int_{x^2}^{x^3} \ell n t dt (x > 0)$ and $H(x) = \dfrac{S(x)}{x}$,

Then $H(x)$ is

(a) Continuous but not derivable in its domain

(b) Derivable and continuous in its domain

(c) Neither derivable nor continuous in its domain

(d) Derivable but not continuous in its domain

Solution: (b) $S(x) = \ln(x^3)\, 3x^2 - \ln x^2\,(2x)$

$= 9x^2 \ln x - 4x \ln x$

$= (9x^2 - 4x)\ln x$

$= (9x - 4)\, x \ln x$

$\therefore \quad \dfrac{S(x)}{x} = (9x-4)\ln x$

$\Rightarrow H(x) = (9x - 4)\ln x$

Which is clearly continuous and differentiable in its domain.

29. Given

$$f(x) = \begin{cases} x^2 e^{2(x-1)} \text{ for } 0 \le x \le 1 & ;\ 0 \le x \le 1 \\ a \text{ sgn}(x+1)\cos(2x-2) + bx^2; & 1 < x \le 2 \end{cases}$$

(a) $a = -1, b = 2$ (b) $a = 1, b = -2$

(c) $a = -3, b = 4$ (d) None of these

Solution: (a) $L.H.L. \lim\limits_{x \to 1^-} f(x) = \lim\limits_{x \to 1^-} x^2 e^{2(x-1)} = 1$

Also, $f(1) = 1$

Now R.H.L. $= \lim\limits_{x \to 1^-} f(x) = \lim\limits_{x \to 1^+} a$ sgn $(x+1)$ cos2 $(x-1) + bx^2 = a.1.1 + b$

For continuity $a + b = 1$

Also, LHD $(x = 1)$ is

$$\lim_{h \to 0} \frac{(1-h)^2 e^{-2h} - 1}{h} = \lim_{h \to 0} 2e^{-2h} + he^{-2h}\left(\frac{e^{-2h} - 1}{h}\right)$$

$= 2 + 0 + 2 = 4$

RHD $(x = 1)$ is $\lim\limits_{h \to 0} \dfrac{a \text{sgn}(2+h)\cos 2h + b(1+h)^2 - 1}{h}$

$$= \lim_{h \to 0} \frac{a\cos 2h + b + bh^2 + 2bh - (a+b)}{h}$$

$$= \lim_{h \to 0}\left(\frac{\cos 2h - 1}{h}\right) + bh + 2b = 2b$$

$(\because a + b = 1)$

$f(x)$ is differentiable at $x = 1$ if $2b = 4$

$\Rightarrow b = 2; a = -1$

30. If $f(x) = $ Min. $(\tan x, \cot x)$ then:

(a) $f(x)$ is discontinuous at $x = 0, \dfrac{\pi}{4}$ and $\dfrac{5\pi}{4}$

(b) $f(x)$ is continuous at $x = \dfrac{\pi}{2}$ and $\dfrac{3\pi}{2}$

(c) $\int_0^{\pi/2} f(x) dx = 2\ell n\sqrt{2}$

(d) $f(x)$ is periodic with period π.

Solution: (c, d) From the graph of (see figure example 10) min $\{\tan x, \cot x\}$, it is clear that $f(x)$ is discontinuous at $x = 0, \pm\frac{\pi}{2}, \pm\pi, \pm\frac{3\pi}{2}, ...$ and $f(x)$ is non-differentiable at $x = 0, \pm\frac{\pi}{4}, \pm\frac{\pi}{2}, \pm\frac{3\pi}{4}, \pm\pi, ...$

Also $f(x)$ is periodic with period π

and $\int_0^{\pi/2} f(x) = 2\int_0^{\pi/4} \tan x dx = 2\,|\ln\sec x|_0^{\pi/4}$

$= 2\left|\ln\sec\frac{\pi}{4} - 0\right| = 2\ln\sqrt{2}$

$\therefore$ (c) and (d) are correct options.

SECTION–II

SUBJECTIVE SOLVED EXAMPLES

1. If $f(x) = \{|x| - |x-1|\}^2$, draw the graph of $f(x)$ and discuss its continuity and differentiability.

Solution: We know that

$$|x| - |x-1| = \begin{cases} -x + x - 1; & x < 0 \\ x + x - 1\ ; & 0 \le x < 1 \\ x - (x-1); & x \ge 1 \end{cases}$$

$$\Rightarrow |x| - |x-1| = \begin{cases} -1\ ; & x < 0 \\ 2x - 1; & 0 \le x < 1 \\ 1,\ ; & 1 \le x \end{cases}$$

$$\therefore\ f(x) = \{|x| - |x-1|\}^2$$

$$= \begin{cases} 1, & \text{when } 0 > x \text{ or } x \ge 1 \\ (2x-1)^2 & \text{when } 0 \le x < 1 \end{cases}$$

Graphically $f(x)$ could be shown as;

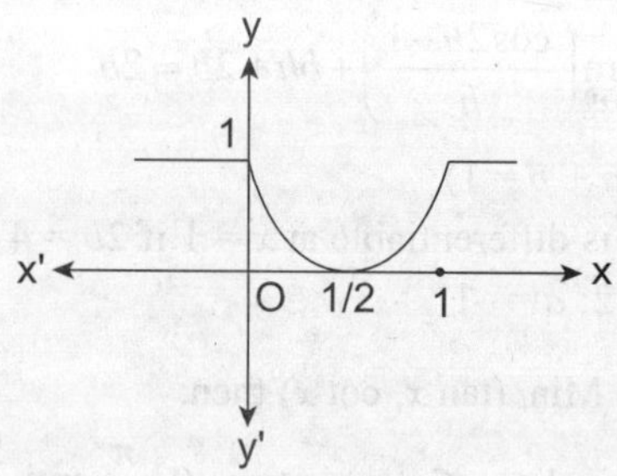

From above figure it is clear that $f(x)$ is continuous for $x \in R$; but $f(x)$ is not differentiable at $x = 0,1$

$\Rightarrow f(x)$ is continuous for all $x \in R$

$\Rightarrow f(x)$ is differentiable for all $x \in R - \{0, 1\}$

2. Discuss the continuity of $f(x) = \{x + (x - [x]^2\}$ at $x = 2$ and $x = 2.5$, where { } stands for fraction part of x and [ ] is greatest integer function.

Solution: $f(2) = \{2 + (2 - [2])^2\} = 0,$

L.H.L. $= \lim_{x\to 2^+} f(x) = \lim_{h\to 0}\{h + 2 + (h)^2\} = 0$

LHL $= \lim_{h\to 0}\{(2-h) + (1-h)^2\} = 0$

Clearly $f(x)$ is continuous at $x = 2$

At $x = 2.5$; $f(2.5) = \{2.5 + (.5)^2\} = .75$

RHL $= \lim_{h\to 0}\{(2.5+h) + (.5+h)^2\} = .75$

LHL $= \lim_{h\to 0}\{(2.5-h) + (.5-h)^2\} = .75$

$\therefore f(x)$ is continuous at $x = 2.5$

3. Let $f(x)$ is defined as follows

$$f(x) = \begin{cases} (\cos x - \sin x)^{\text{cosec}\,x}, & -\frac{\pi}{2} < x < 0 \\ a, & x = 0 \\ \dfrac{e^{1/x} + e^{2/x} + e^{3/x}}{ae^{2/x} + bx^{3/x}} & 0 < x < \pi/2 \end{cases}$$

If $f(x)$ is continuous at $x = 0$, find a and b

Solution: Here, $f(x)$ is continuous at $x = 0$

$\Rightarrow$ RHL (at $x = 0$) = LHL (at $x = 0$) = $f(0)$

$\therefore$ R.H.L (at $x = 0$)

$$\lim_{x\to 0^+}\frac{e^{1/x} + e^{2/x} + e^{3/x}}{ae^{2/x} + bx^{3/x}} = \lim_{h\to 0}\frac{e^{3/h}\left\{\frac{1}{e^{2/h}} + \frac{1}{e^{1/h}} + 1\right\}}{e^{3/h}\left\{\frac{a}{e^{1/h}} + b\right\}}$$

$= 1/b$ ..(i)

$\left\{\text{as } \lim_{h\to 0}\frac{1}{e^{1/h}} \to 0\right\}$

again LHL (at $x = 0$) $= \lim_{x\to 0^-}(\cos x - \sin x)^{\text{cosec}\,x}$

$= \lim_{h\to 0^+}(\cosh - \sin h)^{\text{cosec}\,h}$

$= \lim_{h\to 0^+}\{1 + (\cos h + \sin h - 1)\}^{-1/\sin h}$ [i.e., $(1)^\infty$ form]

$= e^{\lim_{h\to 0}\{\cos h + \sin h - 1\}\left(-\frac{1}{\sin h}\right)}$

$= e^{\lim_{h\to 0}\left\{-\sin^2\frac{h}{2}+2\sin\frac{h}{2}\cos\frac{h}{2}\right\}\left(-\frac{1}{2\sin h/2\cos h/2}\right)}$

$= e^{\lim_{h\to 0}\frac{\sin h/2-\cos h/2}{\cos h/2}} = e^{-1}$ ...(ii)

and, $f(0) = a$

$\Rightarrow a = e^{-1} = 1/b$

$\Rightarrow a = \frac{1}{e}; b = e$

4. Discuss the continuity of the function, $g(x) = [x] + [-x]$.

Solution: Let us simplify the definition of the function

(i) If x is an integer $[x] = x$ and $[-x] = -x$

$\Rightarrow g(x) = x - x = 0$

(ii) If x is not an integer:

Let $x = n + f$ where n is an integer and $f \in (0,1)$

$\Rightarrow [x] = [n + f] = n$

and $[-x] = [-n - f] = [(-n-1) + (1-f)]$

$= -n - 1$

Hence $g(x) = [x] + [-x] = n + (-n-1) = -1$

$\therefore g(x) = \begin{cases} 0 & \text{if x is an integer} \\ -1 & \text{if x is not an integer}\end{cases}$

Let us discuss the continuity of $g(x)$ at a point $x = a$ where $a \in \mathbb{Z}$

L.H.L. $= \lim_{x\to a^-} g(x) = -1$ *as* $\to a^-$, x is not an integer

and R.H.L. $= \lim_{x\to a^+} g(x) = -1$ *as* $x \to a^+$, x is not an integer.

But $g(a) = 0$ as a is an integer.

Hence $g(x)$ has a removable discontinuity at integer value of x.

Let us check the continuity at $x = b \in \mathbb{Z}$. (b is not an integer)

Now, $\lim_{x\to b^+} g(x) = -1$ and $\lim_{x\to b^-} g(x) = -1$ and

$g(b) = -1$

$\therefore$ $g(x)$ is continuous for all $x = b \in \mathbb{Z}$

5. If $f(x) = (x + [x^3+1])^{x^2+\sin x}$, find the derivative when $x \in (1, 3/2)$ and indicate the points where it does not exists. (where [.] denotes the greatest integer function)

Solution: Here $f(x) = (x + [x^3+1])^{x^2+\sin x}$

$\Rightarrow f(x) = \begin{cases} (x+2)^{x^2+\sin x}, & 1 < x < 2^{1/3} \\ (x+3)^{x^2+\sin x}, & 2^{1/3} \le x < 3^{1/3} \\ (x+4)^{x^2+\sin x}, & 3^{1/3} \le x < 3/2 \end{cases}$

As $[x^3+1] = \begin{cases} 2; & 1 < x < 2^{1/3} \\ 3; & 2^{1/3} \le x < 3^{1/3} \\ 4; & 3^{1/3} \le x < 3/2\end{cases}$

which shows $f(x)$ is discontinuous at $x = 2^{1/3}$ and $3^{1/3}$ and so not differentiable at $x = 2^{1/3}$ and $3^{1/3}$.

Also $f'(x) =$

$$\begin{cases} (x+2)^{x^2+\sin x}\left\{\begin{matrix}(2x+\cos x)\ln(x+2) \\ +\dfrac{x^2+\sin x}{x+2}\end{matrix}\right\}; & x \in (1, 2^{1/3}) \\ (x+3)^{x^2+\sin x},\left\{\begin{matrix}(2x+\cos x)\ln(x+3) \\ +\dfrac{x^2+\sin x}{x+3}\end{matrix}\right\}; & x \in (2^{1/3}, 3^{1/3}) \\ (x+4)^{x^2+\sin x},\left\{\begin{matrix}(2x+\cos x)\ln(x+4) \\ +\dfrac{x^2+\sin x}{x+4}\end{matrix}\right\}; & x \in (3^{1/3}3/2)\end{cases}$$

as $\frac{d}{dx}(f(x)g(x))$

$$= f(x)g(x)\left\{\frac{g(x)}{g(x)}f'(x) + g'(x)\ln f(x)\right\}$$

Clearly $f'(x)$ is discontinuous at $x = 2^{1/3}$ and $x = 3^{1/3}$

6. Let $f(x)$ be a continuous function defined for $1 \le x < 3$. If $f(x)$ takes rational values for all x and $f(2) = 10$. Then find the value of f(1.5).

Solution: As $f(x)$ is continuous in [1, 3], therefore by intermediate theorem $f(x)$ will attain all values between $f(1)$ and $f(3)$. As $f(x)$ takes rational values for all x and there are innumerable irrational values between $f(1)$ and $f(3)$ which implies that $f(x)$ can take rational values for all x if $f(x)$ has a constant rational values at all points between $x = 1$ and $x = 3$

So $f(2) = f(1.5) = 10$

7. Examine the continuity of the function $f(x) = \lim_{n\to\infty} \cos^{2n} x$

Solution: $f(x) = \lim_{n\to\infty} (\cos^2 x)^n$

Case (i): When $\cos^2 x = 0$ then $\lim_{n\to\infty}(\cos^2 x)^n = 0$

Case (ii): When $0 < \cos^2 x < 1$, $\lim_{n\to\infty} (\cos^2 x)^n = 0$

as $\lim_{n\to\infty} a^n = 0$ if $0 < a < 1$

Case (iii): when $\cos^2 x = 1$, then $\lim_{n\to\infty} (\cos^2 x)^n = 1$;

We have to check continuity of function at $x = k\pi$ ($k \in \mathbb{Z}$) and at $x = k\pi/2$ (k is odd) as changes are only at these values of x. $\cos^2 x = 0$ when $x = k\pi/2$ (k is odd) while $\cos^2 x = 1$ when $x = k\pi$ ($k \in \mathbb{Z}$).

At $x - \dfrac{k\pi}{2}, k \in \mathbb{Z}$

L.H.L. $= f(k\pi^-/2) = \lim_{h\to 0}\lim_{n\to\infty} [\cos^2 (k\pi/2 - h)]^n =$

$\lim_{h\to 0}\lim_{n\to\infty} [0]^n = 0$

R.H.L. $= f(k\pi^+/2) = \lim_{h\to 0}\lim_{n\to\infty} [\cos^2 (k\pi/2 + h)] =$

$\lim_{h\to 0}\lim_{n\to\infty} [0]^n = 0$

and $f(k\pi/2) = \lim_{n\to\infty} [\cos^2 k\pi/2]^n = 0$

Hence function is continuous at $x = k\pi/2$, where k is odd

At $x = k\pi$ ($k \in \mathbb{Z}$)

L.H.L. $= f(k\pi^-) = \lim_{h\to 0}\lim_{n\to\infty} [\cos^2 (k\pi - h)]^n =$ (indetermined)

and R.H.L. $= f(k\pi^+) = \lim_{h\to 0}\lim_{n\to\infty} [\cos^2 (k\pi + h)]^n =$ (indetermined), and $f(k\pi) = \lim_{n\to\infty}[\cos^2 k\pi]^n = 1$

Hence function is discontinuous at $x = k\pi$ ($k \in \mathbb{Z}$)

8. Let $f(x)$ be defined in the interval $[-2, 2]$, such that

$$f(x) = \begin{cases} -1 & ; -2 \le x \le 0 \\ x-1 & ; 0 < x \le 2 \end{cases}$$

and $g(x) = f(|x|) + |f(x)|$. Test the differentiability of $g(x)$ in $[-2, 2]$.

Solution: Let us find $f(x)$ in $[-2, 2]$ i.e., $-2 \le x \le 2$

$\Rightarrow 0 \le |x| \le 2$

Hence $f(|x|) = |x| - 1, -2 \le |x| \le 2$

$$\text{Now } |f(x)| = \begin{bmatrix} |-1|; & -2 \le x \le 0 \\ |x-1|; & 0 < x \le 2 \end{bmatrix} \quad \text{......(1)}$$

$$\Rightarrow |f(x)| = \begin{cases} 1 & ; -2 \le x \le 0 \\ |x-1| & ; 0 < x \le 2 \end{cases} \quad \text{...... (2)}$$

Adding (1) and (2), we get

$$f(|x|) + |f(x)| = \begin{cases} |x|-1+1 & ; -2 \le x \le 0 \\ |x|-1+|x-1| & ; 0 < x \le 2 \end{cases}$$

$$\Rightarrow g(x) = \begin{cases} |x| & ; -2 \le x \le 0 \\ |x|-1+|x-1| & ; 0 < x \le 2 \end{cases}$$

on further simplification

$$g(x) = \begin{cases} -x & ; -2 \le x \le 0 \\ x-1+1-x = 0 & ; 0 < x \le 1 \\ x-1+x-1 = 2(x-1) & ; 1 \le x \le 2 \end{cases}$$

$$= \begin{cases} -x & ; \quad -2 \le x \le 0 \\ 0 & ; \quad 0 < x \le 1 \\ 2(x-1); & \quad 1 \le x \le 2 \end{cases}$$

clearly $g(x)$ may be non-differentiable at $x = 0$ and $x = 1$

Now, $Lg'(0) = \lim_{\to} \dfrac{g(-h) - g(0)}{-h} = \lim_{h\to 0} \dfrac{-(-h)}{-h} = -1$

and $Rg'(0) = \lim_{h\to 0} \dfrac{g(0+h) - g(0)}{h} = \lim_{h\to 0} \dfrac{0-0}{h} = 0$

$\therefore$ $g(x)$ is non-differentiable at $x = 0$

Also $Lg'(1) = \lim_{h\to 0} \dfrac{g(1-h) - g(1)}{-h} = \lim_{h\to 0} \dfrac{0-0}{-h} = 0$

and $Rg'(1) = \lim_{h\to 0} \dfrac{g(1+h) - g(1)}{h} = \lim_{h\to 0} \dfrac{2h-0}{h} = 0$

$\Rightarrow Lg'(1) \ne Rg'(1)$

Therefore $g(x)$ is not differentiable at $x = 1$

Hence $g(x)$ is not differentiable at $x = 0$ and $x = 1$ in $[-2, 2]$.

9. If $f(x)$ be a continuous function in $[0, 2\pi]$ and $f(0) = f(2\pi)$ then prove that there exists point $c \in (0, \pi)$ such that $f(c) = f(c + \pi)$.

Solution: Let $g(x) = f(x) - f(x + \pi)$ ... (i)

at $x = \pi$; $g(\pi) = f(\pi) - f(2\pi)$ ... (ii)

at $x = 0$; $g(0) = f(0) - f(\pi)$ ... (iii)

Adding (ii) and (iii), $g(0) + g(\pi) = f(0) - f(2\pi)$

$\Rightarrow g(0) + g(\pi) = 0$ [$\because$ Given $f(0) = f(2\pi)$]

$\Rightarrow g(0) = -g(\pi)$

$\Rightarrow g(0)$ and $g(\pi)$ are opposite in sign.

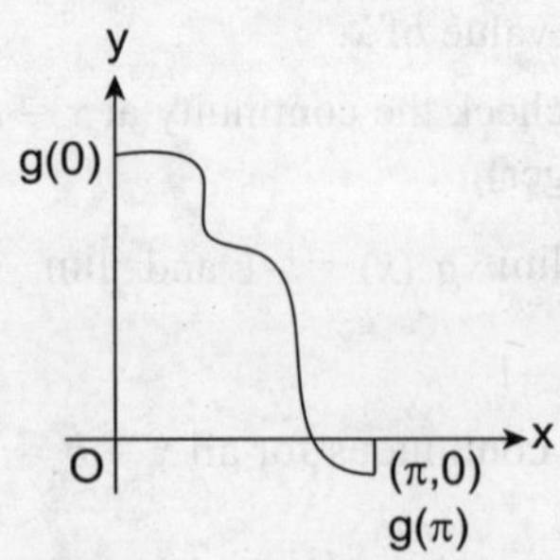

$\Rightarrow$ There exists a point c between 0 and π such that $g(c) = 0$ as shown in graph;

From (i) putting $x = c$; $g(c) = f(c) - f(c + \pi) = 0$

Hence, $f(c) = f(c + \pi)$ for some $c \in (0, \pi)$

10. If $f(x)=||x|-1|$, then draw the graph of $f(x)$ and $fof(x)$ and also discuss their continuity and differentiability. Also find derivative of $(fof)^2$ at $x = 3/2$.

Solution: The graph of $f(x)$ is shown as in the figure. It is clear from the graph that $f(x)$ is continuous for all x but $f(x)$ is not differentiable at $x \in \{-1, 0, 1\}$.

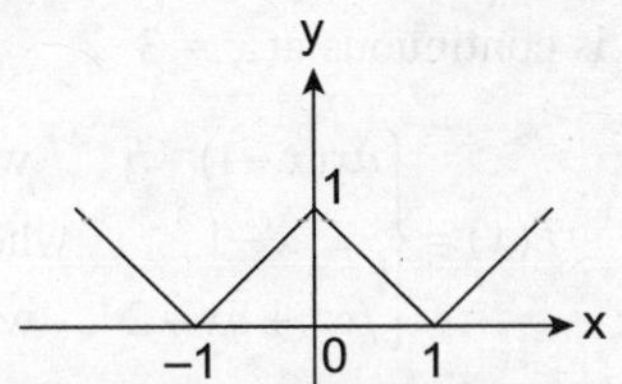

Now $fof(x) = ||f(x)| - 1| = |f(x) - 1|$ { as $f(x) \geq 0$ for all x}

Now if $f(x) \to f(x)-1$, i.e., shift the graph one unit below x-axis as shown as

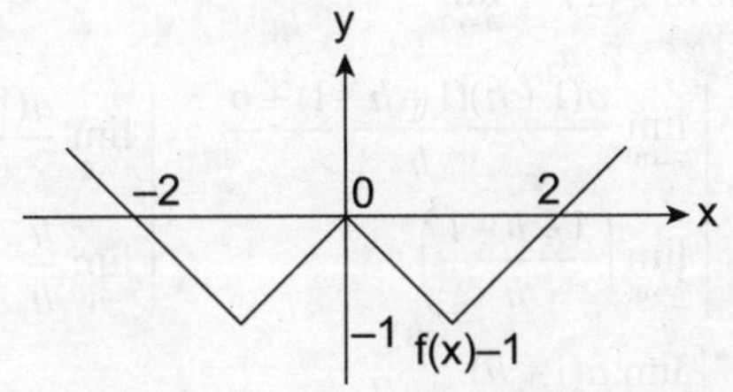

Thus for graph of $fof(x) = |f(x) - 1|$ is taking image of the graph of $f(x) - 1$ below x-axis and keeping the portion above y-axis as it is

∴ Graph for $fof(x)$ will be as shown below

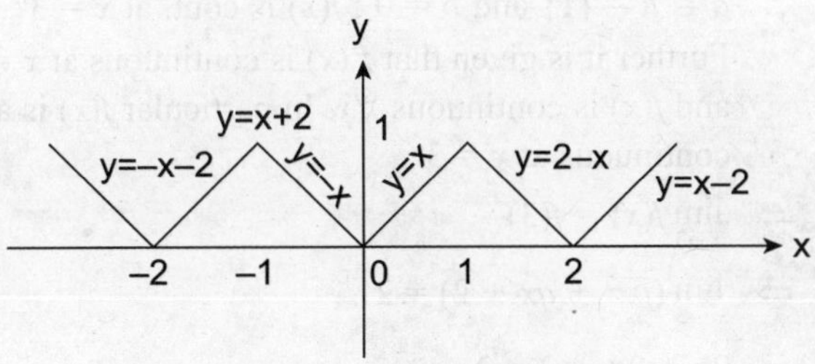

which is clearly continuous for all $x \in R$, but not differentiable at $x = \{-2, -1, 0, 1, 2\}$

which shows $fof(x) = 2-x,\ 1 \leq x \leq 2$

$\therefore\ (fof)^2 = (2-x)^2,\quad 1 \leq x \leq 2$

$\Rightarrow\ \dfrac{d}{dx}(fof)^2 = 2(2-x)(-1),\quad 1 \leq x \leq 2$

$\therefore\ \dfrac{d}{dx}(fof)^2$ (when $x = 3/2$) $= -2(2 - 3/2) = -1$

$\Rightarrow\ \dfrac{d}{dx}\{(fof)^2\}_{at\ x=3/2} = -1$

11. Let $f(0) = 0$ and $f'(0) = 1$. For a positive integer k, show that $\displaystyle \lim_{x\to 0}\frac{1}{x}\left(f(x)+f\left(\frac{x}{2}\right)+.....+f\left(\frac{x}{k}\right)\right)$ $=1+\dfrac{1}{2}+\dfrac{1}{3}+.......+\dfrac{1}{k}$

Solution: $\displaystyle \lim_{x\to 0}\frac{1}{x}\left[f(x)+f\left(\frac{x}{2}\right)+......+f\left(\frac{x}{k}\right)\right]$

$$=\lim_{x\to 0}\frac{f(x)}{x}+\frac{f\left(\frac{x}{2}\right)}{x}+....+\frac{f\left(\frac{x}{k}\right)}{x}$$

$$=\lim_{x\to 0}\frac{f(x+0)-f(0)}{x}+\lim_{x\to 0}\frac{f\left(\frac{x}{2}+0\right)-f(0)}{\frac{x}{2}}\cdot\frac{1}{2}+...+$$

$$\lim_{x\to 0^+}\frac{f\left(\frac{x}{k}+0\right)-f(0)}{\frac{x}{k}}\cdot\frac{1}{k}$$

$$= f(0) + \frac{1}{2}f'(0)+.....+\frac{1}{k}f'(0) = 1+\frac{1}{2}+....+\frac{1}{k};$$

Hence proved

12. If a function $f:[-2a,2a]\to\mathbb{R}$ is an odd function such that $f(x)=f(2a-x)$ for $x \in [a, 2a]$ and the left hand derivative at $x = a$ is 0, then find the left hand derivative at $x = -a$.

Solution: It is given that , (L.HD. at $x = a$) = 0

$$\therefore\ \lim_{h\to 0}\frac{f(a-h)-f(a)}{-h}=0$$

$$\Rightarrow\ \lim_{h\to 0}\frac{f(a-h)-f(a)}{h}=0 \qquad ...(i)$$

Now (L.H.D. at $x = -a$)

$$=\lim_{h\to 0}\frac{f(-a-h)-f(-a)}{-h}=\lim_{h\to 0}\frac{-f(a+h)+f(a)}{-h}$$

{as $f(-x) = -f(x)$ given}

$$=\lim_{h\to 0}\frac{f(a+h)-f(a)}{h}$$

$$=\lim_{h\to 0}\frac{f[2a-(a+h)]-f(a)}{h}$$

{as $f(x) = f(2a - x)$ for $x \in [a, 2a]$}

$$=\lim_{h\to 0}\frac{f(a+h)-f(h)}{h}=0 \text{ (using (i))}$$

∴ LHD at $x = -a = 0$)

13. Let $f(x) = \begin{cases} x+a & \text{if } x<0 \\ |x-1| & \text{if } x \ge 0 \end{cases}$ and $g(x) = \begin{cases} x+1 & \text{if } x<0 \\ (x-1)^2+b & \text{if } x\ge 0 \end{cases}$; where a and b are non-negative real numbers. Determine the composite function gof. If (gof) (x) is continuous for all real x, then determine the values of a and b. Further for these values of a and b, is gof differentiable at $x = 0$. Justify your answer.

Solution: Here $f(x) = \begin{cases} x+a & \text{if } x<0 \\ |x-1| & \text{if } x\ge 0 \end{cases}$ and

$$g(x) = \begin{cases} x+1 & \text{if } x<0 \\ (x-1)^2+b & \text{if } x\ge 0 \end{cases}$$

$$\therefore \quad gof(x) = g\{f(x)\} = \begin{cases} g(x+a) & ; x<0 \\ g(|x-1|) & ; x\ge 0 \end{cases}$$

$$= \begin{cases} x+a+1 & ; x+a<0;\ x<0 \\ (x+a-1)^2+b & ; x+a\ge 0;\ x<0 \\ \{|x-1|-1\}^2+b; & x\ge 0 \end{cases}$$

$$= \begin{cases} x+a+1 & ; x<-a \\ (x+a-1)^2+b & ; -a\le x<0 \\ x^2+b & ; 0\le x<1 \\ (x-2)^2+b & ; x\ge 1 \end{cases}$$

∵ gof(x) is continuous for all real x (given)

∴ It must be continuous at $x = -a$, 0, 1

Since got is continuous at $x = -a$

$\Rightarrow \lim_{x\to -a^-} gof(x) = \lim_{x\to -a^+} gof(x) = gof(-a)$

$\Rightarrow \lim_{x\to -a^-} (x+a+1) = \lim_{x\to -a^+} (x+a-1)^2 + b$

$= (-a + a - 1)^2 + b$

$\Rightarrow -a+a+1 = (-a+a-1)^2 + b$

$\Rightarrow 1 = 1 + b \Rightarrow b = 0$

And gof(x) is continuous at $x = 0$

$\Rightarrow \lim_{x\to 0^-} gof(x) = \lim_{x\to 0^+} gof(x) = gof(0)$

$\Rightarrow (a - 1)^2 + b = b \Rightarrow a = 1$

Now, (L.H.D. at $x = 0$) $= \frac{d}{dx}\{(x+a-1)^2+b\}_{at\ x=0}$

$= 2(a - 1) = 0$ {as $a = 1$}

Again (R.H.D at $x = 0$) $= \frac{d}{dx}\{(x^2+b)\}_{at\ x=0} = 0$

($\because b = 0$)

∴ gof(x) is differentiable at $x = 0$.

14. The function $f(x) = \begin{cases} ax(x-1)+b & \text{when } x<1 \\ x-1 & \text{when } 1\le x\le 3 \\ px^2+qx+2 & \text{when } x>3 \end{cases}$.

Find the values of the constants a, b, p, q so that
(i) $f(x)$ is continuous for all x
(ii) $f'(1)$ does not exist
(iii) $f'(x)$ is continuous at $x = 3$

Solution: $f(x) = \begin{cases} ax(x-1)+b & \text{when } x<1 \\ x-1 & \text{when } 1\le x\le 3 \\ px^2+qx+2 & \text{when } x>3 \end{cases}$

$f(x)$ is continuous at $x = 1$

$\Rightarrow \lim_{x\to 1^-} f(x) = f(1) = \lim_{x\to 1^+} f(x)$

$\Rightarrow \lim_{x\to 1^-} ax(x-1) + b = 0$

$\Rightarrow b = 0$ and a ∈ R

Now, $f'(1) = \lim_{h\to 0} \frac{f(1+h)-f(1)}{h}$

$$= \begin{cases} \lim_{h\to 0^-} \frac{a(1+h)(1+h-1)+b}{h} \\ \lim_{h\to 0^+} \left(\frac{1+h-1}{h}\right) \end{cases} = \begin{cases} \lim_{h\to 0^-} \frac{a(1+h)h+0}{h} \\ \lim_{h\to 0^+} \frac{h}{h} \end{cases}$$

$$= \begin{cases} \lim_{h\to 0^-} a(1+h) \\ 1 \end{cases} = \begin{cases} a \\ 1 \end{cases}$$

∵ $f'(1)$ = does not exist

$\Rightarrow a \ne 1$

∴ $a \in R - \{1\}$ and $b = 0$; $f(x)$ is cont. at $x = 3$

Further it is given that $f'(x)$ is continuous at $x = 3$, and $f(x)$ is continuous ∀x. In particular $f(x)$ is also continuous at $x = 3$

$\Rightarrow \lim_{x\to 3^+} f(x) = f(3)$

$\Rightarrow \lim_{x\to 3} (px^2 + qx + 2) = 2$

$\Rightarrow 9p + 3q + 2 = 2$

$\Rightarrow 9p + 3q = 0$ ....(i)

∵ $f'(x)$ is continuous at $x = 3$, hence $f(x)$ is must be differentiable at $x = 3$ as $f'(x)$ is continuous at $x = 3$

$$\therefore \quad f'(3) = \lim_{h\to 0} \frac{f(3+h)-f(3)}{h}$$

$$= \begin{cases} \lim_{h\to 0^-} \frac{h+3-1-2}{h} \\ \lim_{h\to 0^+} \frac{p(3+h)^2+q(3+h)+2-2}{h} \end{cases}$$

$$= \begin{cases} \lim\limits_{h\to 0^-} \dfrac{h}{n} \\ \lim\limits_{h\to 0^+} \dfrac{ph^2+6ph+qh+9p+3q}{h} \end{cases}$$

$$= \begin{cases} 1 \\ \lim\limits_{h\to 0^+} \dfrac{ph^2+6ph+qh}{h} \end{cases}$$

$\{\because$ from equation (i) $9p + 3q = 0\}$

$$= \begin{cases} 1 \\ \lim\limits_{h\to 0^+}(ph+6p+q) \end{cases} = \begin{cases} 1 \\ 6p+q \end{cases}$$

$\therefore\ f'(3^+) = f'(3^-)$

$\Rightarrow\ 6p + q = 1$ ...(ii)

Solving equation (i) and (ii) $p = 1/3$, $q = -1$

Thus $a \in \mathbb{R} - \{1\}$; $b = 0$; $p = 1/3$; $q = -1$

15. Discuss the continuity on $0 \le x \le 1$ and differentiability at $x = 0$ for the function.

$$f(x) = x\,.\,\sin\frac{1}{x}\,.\,\sin\frac{1}{x.\sin\frac{1}{x}} \text{ where } x \neq 0,\ x \neq 1/r\pi$$

and $f(0) = f(1/r\pi) = 0$, $r = 1, 2, 3,......$

Solution: Given

$$f(x)\begin{cases} x.\sin\dfrac{1}{x}.\sin\dfrac{1}{x.\sin\frac{1}{x}}; x\neq 0, 1/r\pi;\ r=1,2,3 \\ 0 \text{ for } x=0, x=\dfrac{1}{r\pi};\ r=1,2,3... \end{cases}$$

$$f'(0) = \mathit{Lim}_{h\to 0}\frac{f(h+0)-f(0)}{h}$$

$$= \mathit{Lim}_{h\to 0}\frac{h\sin\left(\frac{1}{h}\right).\sin\left(\dfrac{1}{h\sin\left(\frac{1}{h}\right)}\right)-0}{h}$$

$$= \mathit{Lim}_{h\to 0}\frac{h\sin\left(\frac{1}{h}\right).\sin\left(\dfrac{1}{h\sin\left(\frac{1}{h}\right)}\right)}{h}$$

$$= \mathit{Lim}_{h\to 0}\sin\left(\frac{1}{h}\right).\sin\left(\frac{1}{h\sin\left(\frac{1}{h}\right)}\right)$$

$$= \text{Lim}_{h\to 0}\ \underbrace{\sin\left(\frac{1}{h}\right)}_{\text{both belong to}[-1,1]}\ \underbrace{\sin\left(\frac{1}{h\sin(1/h)}\right)}_{\text{both belong to}[-1,1]}$$

which does not exist uniquely.

so $f(x)$ is not differentiable at $x = 0$

$$\text{Lim}_{x\to 0} f(x) = \text{Lim}_{x\to 0}\, x\sin\left(\frac{1}{x}\right).\sin\left(\frac{1}{x\sin(1/x)}\right)$$

$$= \text{Lim}_{x\to 0}\ \underset{\to 0}{x}\ .\ \underbrace{\sin(1/x)}_{\text{both belong to}[-1,1]}\ .\ \underbrace{\sin\left(\frac{1}{n\sin(1/x)}\right)}_{\text{both belong to}[-1,1]} = 0 = f(0)$$

$\Rightarrow f(x)$ is continuous at $x = 0$

$$\text{Lim}_{x\to\frac{1}{r\pi}} f(x) = \text{Lim}_{x\to\frac{1}{\pi r}}\, x\sin\left(\frac{1}{x}\right).\sin\left(\frac{1}{x\sin\left(\frac{1}{x}\right)}\right)$$

$$= \mathit{Lim}_{x\to\frac{1}{r\pi}}\ \underbrace{x.\sin\left(\frac{1}{x}\right)}_{\to 0}.\underbrace{\sin\left(\frac{1}{x\sin\left(\frac{1}{x}\right)}\right)}_{\text{both belong to}[-1,1]}$$

$$= 0 = f\left(\frac{1}{r\pi}\right)$$

Hence function is continuous $\forall\ x \in [0, 1]$

16. Consider the function, $f(x) = \begin{cases} x^2\left|\cos\dfrac{\pi}{2x}\right| & \text{if } x\neq 0 \\ 0 & \text{if } x = 0 \end{cases}$

(a) Show that $f'(0)$ exists and find its value

(b) Show that $f'(1/3)$ does not exist

(c) For what values of x, $f'(x)$ fails to exist

Solution: $f(x) = \begin{cases} x^2\left|\cos\dfrac{\pi}{2x}\right| & \text{if } x\neq 0 \\ 0 & \text{if } x = 0 \end{cases}$

(a) $f'(0) = \lim\limits_{h\to 0}\dfrac{f(h+0)-f(0)}{h}$

$$= \lim_{h\to 0}\frac{h^2\left|\cos\left(\frac{\pi}{2h}\right)\right|-0}{h}$$

$$= \lim_{h\to 0} h\ \underbrace{\left|\cos\left(\frac{\pi}{2h}\right)\right|}_{\text{belong to }[-1,1]} = 0 = 0$$

(b) $f'(1/3) = \lim\limits_{h\to 0}\dfrac{f\left(h+\frac{1}{3}\right)-f\left(\frac{1}{3}\right)}{h}$

$$= \lim_{h\to 0}\frac{\left(h+\frac{1}{3}\right)^2\left|\cos\left(\frac{\pi}{2\left(h+\frac{1}{3}\right)}\right)\right|}{h} \quad \{\because f(1/3)=0\}$$

$$= \lim_{h\to 0}\frac{\left(h+\frac{1}{3}\right)^2\left|\cos\left(\frac{3\pi}{2(3h+1)}\right)\right|}{h}$$

$$= \begin{cases}\lim\limits_{h\to 0^-}\dfrac{\left(h+\frac{1}{3}\right)^2.\cos\left(\frac{3\pi}{2(3h+1)}\right)}{h}\\ \lim\limits_{h\to 0^+}\dfrac{-\left(h+\frac{1}{3}\right)^2\cos\left(\frac{3\pi}{2(3h+1)}\right)}{h}\end{cases}$$

$f'(1/3)$

$$= \begin{cases}\lim\limits_{h\to 0^-}\left[2\left(h+\frac{1}{3}\right).\cos\frac{3\pi}{2(3h+1)}-\sin\frac{3\pi}{2(3h+1)}.\frac{3\pi}{2}.\frac{-3}{(3h+1)^2}.\left(h+\frac{1}{3}\right)^2\right]\\ \lim\limits_{h\to 0^+}\left[-2\left(h+\frac{1}{3}\right).\cos\frac{3\pi}{2(3h+1)}+\sin\frac{3\pi}{2(3h+1)}.\frac{3\pi}{2}.\frac{-3}{(3h+1)^2}.\left(h+\frac{1}{3}\right)^2\right]\end{cases}$$

$$= \begin{cases}\lim\limits_{h\to 0^-}\left[0-\sin\left(\frac{3\pi}{2}\right).\frac{3\pi}{2}(-3).\frac{1}{9}\right]\\ \lim\limits_{h\to 0^+}-\left[0-\sin\left(\frac{3\pi}{2}\right).\frac{3\pi}{2}(-3)\frac{1}{9}\right]\end{cases} = \begin{cases}-\pi/2\\ \pi/2\end{cases}$$

$\therefore$ $f'(1/3^-) = -\pi/2$ and $f'(1/3^+) = \pi/2$

17. Discuss the continuity and the derivability of 'f' at $x=\sqrt{2}$ where $f(x)$ = degree of $(u^{x^2}+u^2+2u-3)$

Solution: $f(x)$ = degree of $(u^{x^2}+u^2+2u-3)$

$$= \begin{cases}2 \ ; & x\le\sqrt{2}\\ x^2 \ ; & x>\sqrt{2}\end{cases}$$

$$f'(\sqrt{2}) = \lim_{h\to o}\frac{f(\sqrt{2}+h)-f(\sqrt{2})}{h}$$

$$= \begin{cases}\lim\limits_{h\to o^+}\dfrac{f(h+\sqrt{2})-f(\sqrt{2})}{h}\\ \lim\limits_{h\to o^-}\dfrac{f(h+\sqrt{2})-f(\sqrt{2})}{h}\end{cases} = \begin{cases}\lim\limits_{h\to o^+}\dfrac{(h+\sqrt{2})^2-2}{h}\\ \lim\limits_{h\to o^-}\dfrac{2-2}{h}\end{cases}$$

$$= \begin{cases}\lim\limits_{h\to o^+}\dfrac{2+2\sqrt{2}h+h^2-2}{h}\\ 0\end{cases} = \begin{cases}\lim\limits_{h\to o^+}\dfrac{h^2+2\sqrt{2}h}{h}\\ 0\end{cases}$$

$$= \begin{cases}\lim\limits_{h\to o^+}(h+2\sqrt{2})\\ 0\end{cases} = \begin{cases}2\sqrt{2}\\ 0\end{cases}$$

$\therefore$ $f'(\sqrt{2}^-) \ne f'(\sqrt{2}^+)$

Hence $f(x)$ is non-differentiable at $x=\sqrt{2}$

$\lim\limits_{x\to\sqrt{2}^+} f(x) = \lim\limits_{x\to\sqrt{2}} x^2 = 2 = f(\sqrt{2}) = \lim\limits_{x\to\sqrt{2}^-}(2)$

$\Rightarrow$ $f(\sqrt{2}) = \lim\limits_{x\to\sqrt{2}} f(x)$

Hence $f(x)$ is continuous at $x=\sqrt{2}$

18. If $f(x) = \begin{cases}x^2\,\text{sgn}[x]+\{x\}, & 0\le x<2\\ \sin x+|x-3|, & 2\le x<4\end{cases}$, comment on the continuity and differentiability of $f(x)$ at x = 1,2

Solution: continuity at x = 1

L.H.L. = $\lim\limits_{x\to 1^-} f(x) = \lim\limits_{x\to 1^-}(x^2\,\text{sgn}[x]+\{x\}) = 0+1 = 1$

R.H.L. = $\lim\limits_{x\to 1^+} f(x) = \lim\limits_{x\to 1^+}(x^2\,\text{sgn}[x]+\{x\}) = 1(1)+0 = 1$

Also $f(1) = 1$

$\therefore$ L.H.L = R.H.L = $f(1)$. Hence $f(x)$ is continuous at x =1

R.H.D = $f'(1^+) = \lim\limits_{h\to 0}\dfrac{f(1+h)-f(1)}{h}$

$= \lim\limits_{h\to 0}\dfrac{(1+h)^2+h-1}{h} = \lim\limits_{h\to 0}\dfrac{1+h^2+2h+h-1}{h}$

$= \lim\limits_{h\to 0}\dfrac{h^2+3h}{h} = 3$

and L.H.D = $f'(1^-)$

$= \lim\limits_{h\to 0}\dfrac{(1-h)^2\,\text{sgn}[1-h]+\{1-h\}-1}{-h} = 1$

$= \lim\limits_{h\to^+}\dfrac{(1+h^2-2h)(0)+1-h-1}{-h}$

$= \lim\limits_{h\to 0^+}\dfrac{-h}{-h} = 1$

$\therefore$ $f'(1^+) \ne f'(1^-)$

Hence $f(x)$ is non-differentiable at x = 1

now at $x = 2$

$$\lim_{x\to 2^-} f(x) = \lim_{x\to 2^-} x^2 \operatorname{sgn}[x] + \{x\} = 4.1 + 1 = 5$$

$$\lim_{x\to 2^+} f(x) = \lim_{x\to 2^+} \left(\sin x + |x-3|\right) = 1 + \sin 2$$

Hence L.H.L≠ R.H.L

19. $f(x) = \begin{bmatrix} b\sin^{-1}\left(\dfrac{x+c}{2}\right); & -\dfrac{1}{2} < x < 0 \\ \dfrac{1}{2}; & \text{at } x = 0 \\ \dfrac{e^{ax/2}-1}{x}; & 0 < x < \dfrac{1}{2} \end{bmatrix}$

If $f(x)$ is differentiable at $x = 0$. Find the value of a and also prove that $64b^2 = 4 - c^2$

Solution:

$$\text{RHD} = \lim_{h\to 0}\frac{f(0+h)-f(0)}{h} = \lim_{h\to 0}\frac{\dfrac{e^{ah/2}-1}{h} - \dfrac{1}{2}}{h}$$

$$\lim_{h\to 0}\frac{1+\dfrac{ah}{2}+\dfrac{a^2h^2}{2^2}\cdot\dfrac{1}{2}\ldots -1-\dfrac{h}{2}}{h^2}$$

$$= \lim_{h\to 0}\frac{\left(\dfrac{a}{2}+\dfrac{a^2h}{2^2.2}+\ldots+-\dfrac{1}{2}\right)}{h}$$

For the limit to exist $a = 1$;

$$\text{Hence RHD} = \lim_{h\to 0}\left(\frac{a^2}{8} + \tan x \text{ containing } h\right)$$

$$= \frac{a^2}{8} = \frac{1}{8}$$

Aliter: $\text{LHD} = \lim_{h\to 0}\dfrac{f(0-h)-f(0)}{-h}$

$$= \lim_{h\to 0}\frac{b\sin^{-1}\left(\dfrac{c-h}{2}\right) - \dfrac{1}{2}}{-h}$$

$$= \lim_{h\to 0}\frac{b\left\{\dfrac{c-h}{2}+\dfrac{1^2}{3!}\left(\dfrac{c-h}{2}\right)^3+\dfrac{1^23^2}{5!}\left(\dfrac{c-h}{2}\right)^5\ldots\right\}-\dfrac{1}{2}}{-h}$$

As function is differentiable so this limit is equal to $\dfrac{1}{8}$

For this constant part must be zero and coefficient of h in the numerator must be equal to $-\dfrac{1}{8}$ Coefficient of h in numerator is equal to

$$-\frac{b}{2}\left[1+\frac{1^2}{3!}3\left(\frac{c}{2}\right)^2+\frac{1^2.3^2}{5!}\times 5\left(\frac{c}{2}\right)^4+\ldots\right] = -\frac{1}{8} \quad (1)$$

Clearly left hand side is derivative of

$-b\sin^{-1}\dfrac{x}{2}$ at $x = c$

$\Rightarrow$ Left hand side of equation (1) is $-b\dfrac{1}{\sqrt{1-\dfrac{c^2}{4}}}\cdot\dfrac{1}{2} = -\dfrac{1}{8}$

$\Rightarrow$ Squaring both side and $64b^2 = 4 - c^2$

20. Let $f(x)$ be a function defined on $(-a, a)$ with $a > 0$. Asumme that $f(x)$ is continuous at $x = 0$ and $\lim\limits_{x\to 0}\dfrac{f(x)-f(kx)}{x} = \alpha$, where $k \in (0, 1)$, then compute $f'(0^+)$ and $f'(0^-)$, and comment upon the differentiability of f at $x = 0$.

Solution: $\because \lim\limits_{x\to 0}\dfrac{f(x)-f(kx)}{x} = \alpha$

$$\Rightarrow \lim_{x\to o}\frac{f(x)-f(0)+f(0)+(kx)}{x} = \alpha$$

$$\Rightarrow \lim_{x\to o}\frac{f(x)-f(0)-f(kx)+f(0)}{x} = \alpha$$

$$\Rightarrow \lim_{x\to o}\left(\frac{f(x)-f(0)}{x}-\frac{f(kx)-f(0)}{x}\right) = \alpha$$

$$\Rightarrow \left(\lim_{x\to 0}\frac{f(x)-f(0)}{x}\right)-\left(\lim_{x\to 0}\frac{f(kx)-f(0)}{kx}\right)k = \alpha$$

$$\Rightarrow \begin{cases}\lim\limits_{x\to 0^-}\dfrac{f(x)-f(0)}{x}-\lim\limits_{x\to 0^-}\dfrac{f(kx)-f(0)}{kx}.k = \alpha \\ \lim\limits_{x\to 0^+}\dfrac{f(x)-f(0)}{x}-\lim\limits_{x\to 0^+}\dfrac{f(kx)-f(0)}{kx}.k = \alpha\end{cases}$$

$$= \begin{cases} f'(0^-)-kf'(0^-) = \alpha \\ f'(0^+)-kf'(0^+) = \alpha\end{cases}$$

$$\Rightarrow \begin{cases}(1-k)f'(0^-) = \alpha \\ (1-k)f'(0^+) = \alpha\end{cases}$$

$$\Rightarrow \begin{cases} f'(0^-) = \dfrac{\alpha}{1-k} \\ f'(0^+) = \dfrac{\alpha}{1-k}\end{cases}$$

$\therefore f'(0) = f'(0^-) = f'(0^+) = \dfrac{\alpha}{1-k}$

$\therefore f(x)$ is differentiable at $x = 0$

21. If $f(x) = ax^2 + bx + c$ is such that $|f(0)| \le 1$, $|f(1)| \le 1$ and $|f(-1)| \le 1$, prove that $|f(x)| \le 5/4 \ \forall \ x \in [-1, 1]$.

Solution: We have $f(x) = ax^2 + bx + c$

$\Rightarrow f(-1) = a - b + c$, ... (i);

$f(0) = c$, ... (ii)

and $f(1) = a + b + c$ ... (iii)

From (i), (ii) and (iii) we get,

$$a = \frac{1}{2}[f(-1) + f(1) - 2f(0)];$$

$$b = \frac{1}{2}[f(1) - f(-1)] \text{ and } c = f(0)$$

$$\Rightarrow f(x) = \frac{1}{2}[f(-1) + f(1) - 2f(0)]x^2 + \frac{1}{2}[f(1) - f(-1)]x + f(0)$$

$$f(x) = \frac{x(x+1)}{2}f(1) - (x+1)(x-1)f(0) + \frac{(x-1)x}{2}f(-1) \quad ...(iv)$$

Since, $|f(\ 1)|, |f(0)|$ and $|f(1)|$ are ≤ 1, we have

$$2|f(x)| \le |x(x+1)| + 2|x^2 - 1| + |x(x-1)| \quad ...(v)$$

In the interval $x \in |-1, 1|$

$0 \le 1 + x \le 2$, $0 \le 1 - x \le 2$ and $0 \le 1 - x^2 \le 1$

$\Rightarrow 2|f(x)| \le |x|(1 - x + 1 + x) + 2(1 - x^2)$

$2|f(x)| \le 2(|x| + 1 - x^2)$

$$\Rightarrow |f(x)| \le (-|x|^2 + |x| + 1) = \frac{5}{4} - \left(|x| - \frac{1}{2}\right)^2 \le \frac{5}{4}$$

Thus $|f(x)| \le \frac{5}{4} \forall x \in [-1, 1]$

22. Discuss the continuity and differentiability of the function $y = f(x)$ defined parametrically; $x = 2t - |t - 1|$ and $y = 2t^2 + t|t|$

Solution: Here $x = 2t - |t - 1|$ and $y = 2t^2 + t|t|$

Now when $t < 0$; $x = 2t - \{-(t - 1)\} = 3t - 1$.

and $y = 2t^2 - t^2 = t^2 \quad \Rightarrow \quad y = \frac{1}{9}(x+1)^2$

when $0 \le t < 1$; $x = 2t - (-(t - 1)) = 3t - 1$

and $y = 2t^2 + t^2 = 3t^2 \quad \Rightarrow \quad y = \frac{1}{3}(x-1)^2$

when $t \ge 1$; $x = 2t - (t - 1) = t + 1$

and $y = 2t^2 + t^2 = 3t^2$

$\Rightarrow y = 3(x - 1)^2$

$$\text{Thus, } y = f(x) = \begin{cases} \frac{1}{9}(x+1)^2; & x < -1 \\ \frac{1}{3}(x+1)^2; & -1 \le x < 2 \\ 3(x-1)^2; & x \ge 2 \end{cases}$$

Now to check continuity at $x = -1$ and 2.

Continuity at $x = -1$;

$$\text{LHL} = \lim_{h\to 0} f(-1-h) = \lim_{h\to 0}\frac{1}{9}(-1-h+1)^2 = 0$$

$$\text{and RHL} = \lim_{h\to 0} f(-1+h) = \lim_{h\to 0}\frac{1}{3}(-1+h+1)^2 = 0;$$

$f(-1) = 0$;

$\therefore$ $f(x)$ is continuous at $x = -1$.

Now to check continuity at $x = 2$;

$$\text{LHL} = \lim_{h\to 0} f(2-h) = \lim_{h\to 0}\frac{1}{3}(2-h+1)^2 = 3$$

$$\text{and RHL } \lim_{h\to 0} f(2+h) = \lim_{h\to 0} 3(2+h-1)^2 = 3;$$

and $f(2) = 3$. Thus $f(x)$ is continuous at $x = 2$.

Now to check differentiability at $x = -1$ and 2.

Differentiability at $x = -1$;

LHD $Lf'(-1)$

$$= \lim_{h\to 0}\frac{f(-1-h) - f(-1)}{-h} = \lim_{h\to 0}\frac{\frac{1}{9}(-1-h+1)^2 - 0}{-h} = 0$$

and RHD = $Rf'(-1)$

$$= \lim_{h\to 0}\frac{f(-1+h) - f(-1)}{h} = \lim_{h\to 0}\frac{\frac{1}{3}(-1+h+1)^2 - 0}{h} = 0$$

Hence $f(x)$ is differentiable at $x = -1$.

Differentiability at $x = 2$;

$$\text{LHD } Lf'(2) = \lim_{h\to 0}\frac{f(2-h) - f(2)}{-h}$$

$$= \lim_{h\to 0}\frac{\frac{1}{3}(2-h+1)^2 - 3}{-h} = 2$$

$$\text{RHD } Rf'(2) = \lim_{h\to 0}\frac{f(2+h) - f(2)}{h}$$

$$= \lim_{h\to 0}\frac{3(2+h-1)^2 - 3}{h} = 6$$

Hence $f(x)$ is not differentiable at $x = 2$.

$\therefore$ $f(x)$ is continuous for all x and differentiable for all x except for $x = 2$.

23. Let $g(x)=\int_0^x f(t)\,dt,$ where f is such that $1/2 \le f(t) \le 1$ for $t \in [0, 1]$ and $0 \le f(t) \le 1/2$ for $t \in [1, 2]$. Then find the interval in which $g(2)$ lies.

Solution: $g(x)=\int_0^x f(t)\,dt$

$\Rightarrow g(2)=\int_0^2 f(t)\,dt$

$\Rightarrow g(2)=\int_0^1 f(t)\,dt+\int_1^2 f(t)\,dt$ ... (i)

Now, $1/2 \le f(t) \le 1$ for $t \in [0, 1]$

$\Rightarrow \int_0^1 \frac{1}{2}dt \le \int_0^1 f(t)\,dt \le \int_0^1 1\,dt$ for $t \in [0, 1]$

we get $\frac{1}{2} \le \int_0^1 f(t)\,dt \le 1$ ... (ii)

again, $0 \le f(t) \le \frac{1}{2}$ for $t \in [1, 2]$

$\Rightarrow \int_1^2 0\,dt \le \int_1^2 f(t)\,dt \le \int_1^2 \frac{1}{2}dt$

$\Rightarrow 0 \le \int_1^2 f(t)\,dt \le \frac{1}{2}$ ... (iii)

from (ii) and (iii), we get

$0+\frac{1}{2} \le \int_0^1 f(t)\,dt+\int_1^2 f(t)\,dt \le 1+\frac{1}{2}$

or $\frac{1}{2} \le g(2) \le \frac{3}{2} \Rightarrow g(2) \in \left[\frac{1}{2},\frac{3}{2}\right]$

24. Let $f: R \to R$ satisfying $|f(x)| \le x^2$, for all $x \in R$, then show that $f(x)$ is differentiable at $x = 0$.

Solution: Since $|f(x)| \le x^2$, for all $x \in R$

$\therefore$ at $x = 0$, $|f(0)| \le 0$

$\Rightarrow f(0) = 0$ ...(i)

$\therefore f'(0)=\lim_{h\to 0}\frac{f(h)-f(0)}{h}=\lim_{h\to 0}\frac{f(h)}{h}$ ..(ii)

$\{f(0) = 0$ from (i)$\}$

Now $\left|\frac{f(h)}{h}\right| \le |h|$

$\Rightarrow -|h| \le \frac{f(h)}{h} \le |h|$

$\Rightarrow \lim_{h\to 0}\frac{f(h)}{h}=0$ ..(iii)

(using Cauchy-Squeeze theorem)

$\therefore$ from (ii) and (iii), we get $f'(0) = 0$.

i.e., $f(x)$ is differentiable at $x = 0$

25. Discuss the continuity of $f(x)$ = maximum $\{\sin t;\ 0 \le t \le x\};\ 0 \le x \le 2\pi$

Solution: Given $f(x)$ = *maximum* $(\sin t,\ 0 \le t \le x)$, $0 \le x \le 2\pi$

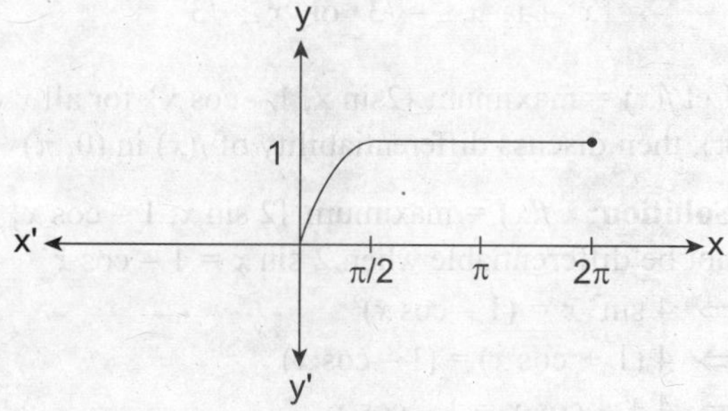

If $x \in \left[0,\frac{\pi}{2}\right]$, $\sin t$ is increasing function

Hence if $t \in [0,x]$, $\sin t$ will attain its maximum value at $t = x$

$f(x) = \sin x$ if $x \in \left[0,\frac{\pi}{2}\right]$

If $x \in \left(\frac{\pi}{2},2\pi\right]$ and $t \in [0,x]$

then $\sin t$ will attain its maximum value when $t = \frac{\pi}{2}$

$f(x)=\sin\frac{\pi}{2}=1$ if $x\in\left(\frac{\pi}{2},2\pi\right]$

$$\therefore\ f(x)=\begin{cases}\sin x\ , & \text{if } x\in\left[0,\frac{\pi}{2}\right]\\ 1\ , & \text{if } x\in\left(\frac{\pi}{2},2\pi\right]\end{cases}$$

Now $f\left(\frac{\pi}{2}\right)=1$

$\therefore \lim_{x\to\frac{\pi}{2}^-} f(x)=\lim_{x\to\frac{\pi}{2}^-}\sin x=1$

and $\lim_{x\to\frac{\pi}{2}^+} f(x)=\lim_{x\to\frac{\pi}{2}^-} 1=1$

as $f(\pi/2)$ = L.H.L = R.H.L

$\therefore f(x)$ is continuous at $x = \frac{\pi}{2}$

Hence $f(x)$ is discontinuous at $x = 2$ and then $f(x)$ will also be non-differentiable at $x = 2$.

26. Let $f(x)$ = maximum $\{4,\ 1 + x^2,\ x^2 - 1\}$ for all $x \in R$. Then find the total number of points, where $f(x)$ is not differentiable.

Solution: $f(x)$ = maximum $\{4,\ 1 + x^2,\ x^2 - 1\}$ as or Thus from above graph we can simply say, $f(x)$ is not differentiable at $x=\pm\sqrt{3}$

And it could be defined as :

$$f(x)=\begin{cases}4 & ;\ -\sqrt{3}\le x\le\sqrt{3}\\ x^2+1; & x\le-\sqrt{3}\ \text{ or }\ x\ge\sqrt{3}\end{cases}$$

27. Let $f(x)$ = maximum {2sin x, 1 – cos x} for all $x \in (0, \pi)$, then discuss differentiability of $f(x)$ in $(0, \pi)$

Solution: $f(x)$ = maximum {2 sin x, 1 – cos x} may not be differentiable when $2\sin x = 1 - \cos x$

$\Rightarrow 4\sin^2 x = (1-\cos x)^2$

$\Rightarrow 4(1+\cos x) = (1-\cos x)$

$\Rightarrow 4 + 4\cos x = 1 - \cos x$

$\Rightarrow 4(1-\cos^2 x) - (1-\cos x)^2 = 0$

$\Rightarrow (1-\cos x)[4 + 4\cos x - 1 + \cos x] = 0$

$\Rightarrow \cos x = 1$ or $\cos x = -\dfrac{3}{5}$

But for $x \in (0, \pi)$, $\cos x \ne 1$

$\Rightarrow x = \cos^{-1}\left(-\dfrac{3}{5}\right)$

$\Rightarrow x = \pi - \cos^{-1}\left(\dfrac{3}{5}\right)$

Graphically $f(x)$ maximum {2 sin x, 1 – cos x} can be represented as shown below (thick curve)

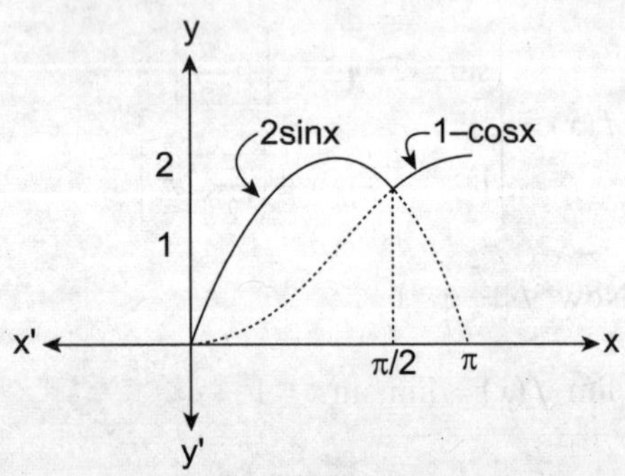

clearly $f(x)=\begin{cases}2\sin x; & 0<x<\theta;\\ 1-\cos x; & 0\le x<\pi\end{cases}$ where

$\theta = \pi - \cos^{-1}\left(\dfrac{3}{5}\right)$

$\therefore\ f'(x)=\begin{cases}2\cos x; & 0<x<\theta\\ \sin x; & \theta<x<\pi\end{cases}$

$\therefore\ f'(\theta^-) = 2\cos\theta = -\dfrac{6}{5}$

and $f'(\theta^+) = \sin\theta = \sin\left(\cos^{-1}\dfrac{3}{5}\right)$

$= \sin\left(\sin^{-1}\dfrac{4}{5}\right) = \dfrac{4}{5}$

$\therefore$ L.H.D. $\ne$ R.H.D. at $x = -\cos^{-1}\left(\dfrac{3}{5}\right)$

Thus $f(x)$ is differentiable at all $x \in (0, \pi)$ except for $x = \pi - \cos^{-1}\left(\dfrac{3}{5}\right)$

28. Let $f(x) = x^3 - x^2 + x + 1$ and

$$g(x)=\begin{cases}\max f(t); & 0\le t\le x\ \text{ for }\ 0\le x\le 1\\ 3-x; & 1<x\le 2\end{cases}$$

Discuss the continuity and differentiability of $g(x)$ in (0, 2).

Solution: Here $f(x) = x^3 - x^2 + x + 1$

$\Rightarrow f'(x) = 3x^2 - 2x + 1$ which is strictly increasing in (0, 2)

$\therefore\ g(x)=\begin{cases}f(x); & 0\le x\le 1\\ 3-x; & 1<x\le 2\end{cases}$

[as $f(x)$ is increasing so, $f(x)$ is maximum when $t = x$]

So $g(x)=\begin{cases}x^3-x^2+x+1; & 0\le x\le 1\\ 3-x; & 1<x\le 2\end{cases}$

Also $g'(x)=\begin{cases}3x^2-2x+1; & 0\le x<1\\ -1; & 1<x\le 2\end{cases}$

which clearly shows $g(x)$ is continuous for all $x \in [0, 2]$ but $g(x)$ is not differentiable at $x = 1$

29. Let $f(x) = 1 + 4x - x^2$ for all $x \in R$;

$$g(x)=\begin{cases}\max.\{f(t);\ x\le t\le(x+1);\ 0\le x<3\}\\ \min.\{(x+3);\ 3\le x\le 5\}\end{cases},$$

Verify continuity of $g(x)$ for all $x \in [0, 5]$.

Solution: Here $f(t) = 1 + 4t - t^2$

$\Rightarrow f'(t) = 4 - 2t$ when $f'(t) = 0$

$\Rightarrow t = 2$; at $t = 2$ $f(t)$ has a maxima

Since

$g(x) = \max.\{f(t)\ \ for\ t\in[x,\ x+1],\ 0\le x<3\}$

$$\therefore\ g(x)=\begin{cases}f(x+1); & \text{if } t\in[x,\ x+1]<2\\ f(2) & ;\ \text{if } x\le t=2\le x+1\\ f(x) & ;\ \text{if } t\in[x,x+1]\\ 6 & ;\ \text{if } 3\le x\le 5\end{cases}$$

$$\therefore\ g(x)=\begin{cases}4+2x-x^2, & \text{if } 0\le x\le 1\\ 5, & \text{if } 1\le x\le 2\\ 1+4x-x^2 & \text{if } 2<x<3\\ 6, & \text{if } 3\le x\le 5\end{cases}$$

which is clearly continuous for all $x \in [0, 5]$ except for $x = 3$

$\therefore$ $g(x)$ is continuous on $[0, 3)$ and on $(3, 5]$

30. If $f(x) = x^2 - 2|x|$ and

$$g(x) = \begin{cases} \min.\{f(t): -2 \le t \le x, -2 \le x < 0\} \\ \max.\{f(t): \quad 0 \le t \le x, \quad 0 \le x \le 2\} \\ f(x) \quad ; \quad x > 2 \end{cases}$$

(a) Draw the graph of $f(x)$ and discuss its continuity and differentiability.

(b) Find and draw the graph of $g(x)$. Also discuss the continuity and differentiability.

Solution: (a) $f(x) = \begin{cases} x^2 - 2x; & x \ge 0 \\ x^2 + 2x; & x < 0 \end{cases}$

The graph of $f(x)$ is shown below

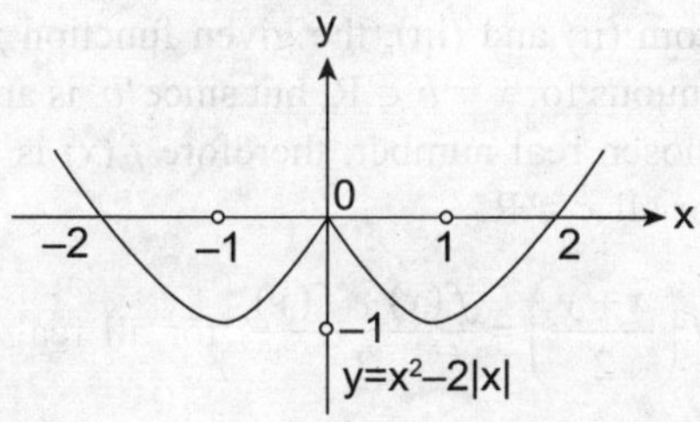

which shows $f(x)$ is continuous for all $x \in R$ but not differentiable at $x = 0$ i.e., differentiable an $\mathbb{R} \sim \{0\}$

(b) If $f(x)$ is an increasing function on [a, b], then

$\max.\{f(t): \quad a \le t \le x, \quad a \le x \le b\} = f(x)$

$\min.\{f(t): \quad a \le t \le x, \quad a \le x \le b\} = f(a)$

If $f(x)$ is decreasing function on [a, b], then

$\max.\{f(t): \quad a \le t \le x, \quad a \le x \le b\} = f(a)$

$\min.\{f(t): \quad a \le t \le x, \quad a \le x \le b\} = f(x)$

clearly $f(x)$ decreases on $(-\infty, -1]$ and $[0, 1]$, where as increase on $[-1, 0]$ and $[1, \infty)$

$$\therefore \quad g(x) = \begin{cases} f(x) \ ; & -2 \le x \le -1 \\ f(-1) \ ; & -1 \le x < 0 \\ f(0) \ ; & 0 \le x \le 2 \\ f(2) \ ; & 1 \le x \le 2 \end{cases}$$

$$\Rightarrow \quad g(x) \begin{cases} x + 2x \ ; & -2 \le x \le -1 \\ -1 \ ; & -1 \le \ < 0 \\ 0 \ ; & 0 \le \ < 2 \\ x - 2x \ ; & x > 2 \end{cases}$$

$$\Rightarrow g'(x) = \begin{cases} 2x + 2 \ ; & -2 \le x < -1 \\ -1 \ ; & -1 < x < 0 \\ 0 \ ; & 0 < x < 2 \\ 2x - 2; & x > 2 \end{cases}$$

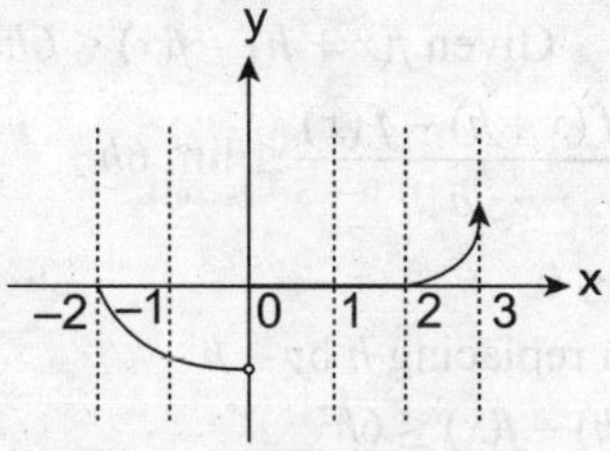

Thus graph of $g(x)$ is as shown above

From above figure it is clear that $g(x)$ is not continuous at $x = 0$, and from $g'(x)$, $g(x)$ is non-differentiable at $x = -1$, 0, and 2.

31. Let $f(x) = x^4 - 8x^3 + 22x^2 - 24x$ and $g(x) = \begin{cases} \min f(t); \ x \le t \le x+1, -1 \le x \le 1 \\ x - 10; \quad x > 1 \end{cases}$. Discuss the continuity and differentiability of $g(x)$ in $[-1, \infty)$.

Solution: Here $f(x) = x^4 - 8x^3 + 22x^2 - 24x$

$\Rightarrow f'(x) = 4x^3 - 24x^2 + 44x - 24$

or $f'(x) = 4(x - 1)(x - 2)(x - 3)$

$= 4((x^3 - 6x^2 + 11x - 6)$

Which shows $f(x)$ is increasing in $[1, 2] \cup [3, \infty)$ and decreasing in $(-\infty, 1] \cup [2, 3]$

Thus, minimum $f(t)$; $x \le t \le x + 1$, $-1 \le x \le 1$ is given by

$$\Rightarrow \text{minimum } f(t) = \begin{cases} f(x+1); & -1 \le x \le 0 \\ f(1) \quad ; & 0 < x \le 1 \end{cases}$$

$$\text{Thus, } g(x) = \begin{cases} f(x+1); & -1 \le x \le 0 \\ f(1) \quad ; & 0 < x \le 1 \\ x - 10 \quad ; & x > 1 \end{cases}$$

$$= \begin{cases} (x+1)^4 - 8(x+1)^3 + \\ \quad 22(x+1)^2 - 24(x+1); & -1 \le x \le 0 \\ 1 - 8 + 22 - 24 & ; \ 0 < x \le 1 \\ x - 10 & ; \ x > 1 \end{cases}$$

$$g(x) = \begin{cases} x^4 - 4x^3 + 4x^2 - 9; & -1 \le x \le 0 \\ -9 & ; \ 0 < x \le 1 \\ x - 10 & ; \ x > 1 \end{cases}$$

$$\text{Also, } g'(x) = \begin{cases} 4x^3 - 12x^2 + 8x; & -1 \le x \le 0 \\ 0 & ; \ 0 < x \le 1 \\ +1 & ; \ x > 1 \end{cases}$$

$\Rightarrow$ $g(x)$ is continuous on $[-1, \infty)$ but non-differentiable at $x = 1$

32. Given function $f(x)$ defined for all real x, and is such that $f(x + h) - f(x) < 6h^2$ for all real h and x. Show that $f(x)$ is constant

Solution: Given $f(x + h) - f(x) < 6h^2$ ...(1)

$$\Rightarrow \lim_{h\to 0^+} \frac{f(x+h)-f(x)}{h} \le \lim_{h\to 0^+} 6h$$

$\therefore f'(x^+) \le 0$ ...(2)

Again replacing h by $-h$

$f(x - h) - f(x) \le 6h^2$

$$\frac{f(x-h)-f(x)}{-h} \ge \frac{6h^2}{-h}$$

$$\lim_{h\to 0}\frac{f(x-h)-f(x)}{-h} \ge \lim_{h\to 0} -6h$$

$\therefore f'(x^-) \ge 0$ ... (3)

From (2) and (3) $f'(x) = 0$

Hence $f(x)$ is constant

33. **(a)** Let f be a function such that $f(x) + f(y) = f(x) + y$ for all $x, y \in R$, then find $f(0)$.

(b) Now if it is given that there exists a positive real δ, such that $f(h) = h$ for $0 < h < \delta$, then find $f'(x)$ and hence $f(x)$.

Solution: **(a)** Let $x = 0$, $y = 0$ in $f(x) + f(y) = f(x) + y$

$\Rightarrow f(0) + f(0) = f(0) + 0$

$\Rightarrow 2f(0) = f(0) \qquad \Rightarrow f(0) = 0$

(b) Given $f(h) = h$ for $0 < h < \delta$

Then, $f'(x) = \lim_{h\to 0}\dfrac{f(x+h)-f(x)}{h}$ for $0 < h < \delta$

$\Rightarrow f'(x) = \lim_{h\to 0}\dfrac{f(x)+f(h)-f(x)}{h}$ ($\because$ given $f(h)$. h)

$\Rightarrow f'(x) = \lim_{h\to 0}\dfrac{f(x+f(h))-f(x)}{h}$ (given $f(h)$ =h)

$\Rightarrow f'(x) = \lim_{h\to 0}\dfrac{h}{h}$ ($\because f(h) = h$)

$\Rightarrow$ integrating both sides we get,

$\Rightarrow f(x) = x + c$ where $f(0) = 0 \Rightarrow c = 0$

So, $f(x) = x$. Thus $f'(x) = 1$ and $f(x) = x$

34. Let a function $f : \mathbb{R} \to \mathbb{R}$ satisfy the equation $f(x + y) = f(x) + f(y)$ for all $x, y \in \mathbb{R}$, show that if f is continuous at $x = a$, $a \in R$, then it is continuous for all $x \in R$.

Solution: It is given that $f(x)$ is continuous at $x = a$

$\Rightarrow \lim_{x\to a^-} f(x) = \lim_{x\to a^+} f(x) = f(a)$

$\Rightarrow \lim_{h\to 0} f(a+h) = \lim_{h\to 0} f(a-h) = f(a)$

$\Rightarrow \lim_{h\to 0^+} f(a+h) = \lim_{h\to 0} f(a + (-h)) = f(a)$ [using property of function $f(x+y) = f(x) + f(y)$; (given)]

$\Rightarrow \lim_{h\to 0^+} f(h) = \lim_{h\to 0} f(-h) = 0$ ....(i)

Now let us check the continuity at $x = b$, $b \in R$, ba

$\lim_{x\to b^+} f(x) = \lim_{h\to 0} f(b+h)$

$= \lim_{h\to 0} (f(b) + f(h)) = f(b) + 0 = f(b)$ ....(ii) [using (i)]

Also L.H.L. $= \lim_{x\to b^-} f(x) = \lim_{h\to 0} f(b-h)$

$= \lim_{h\to 0} f(b + (-h))$

$= \lim_{h\to 0} (f(b) + f(-h)) = f(b) + 0$ .... (iii) [using (i)]

$\therefore$ from (ii) and (iii), the given function $f(x)$ is continuous for $x = b \in R$, but since 'b' is an arbitrarily chosen real number, therefore $f(x)$ is continuous for all $x \in R$.

35. Let $f\left(\dfrac{x+y}{2}\right) = \dfrac{f(x)+f(y)}{2}$ for all real x and y. If $f'(0)$ exists and equals -1 and $f(0) = 1$. Find $f(x)$ and have $f(2)$

Solution: $f'(x) = \lim_{h\to 0}\dfrac{f(x+h)-f(x)}{h}$

$$= \lim_{h\to 0}\frac{f\left(\frac{2x+2h}{2}\right)-f(x)}{h}$$

$$= \lim_{h\to 0}\frac{\left(\frac{f(2x)+f(2h)}{2}\right)-f(x)}{h}$$

$= \lim_{h\to 0}\dfrac{f(2x)+f(2h)-2f(x)}{2h}$ [Let x =2x and $y = 0$, in the given equation]

$$= \lim_{h\to 0}\frac{(2f(x)-1+f(2h)-2f(x)}{2h} = \lim_{h\to 0}\frac{f(2h)-1}{2h}$$

$= \lim_{h\to 0}\dfrac{f(2h)-f(0)}{2h-0} = f'(0) = -1$, thus $f'(x) = -1$

$\Rightarrow f(x) = -x + c$. Also, $f(0) = 1 \Rightarrow c = 1$

$\Rightarrow f(x) = 1 - x \qquad \Rightarrow f(2) = -1$

36. A function $f : R \to R$ satisfies the equation $f(x + y) = f(x). f(y)$ for all values of x and y and for any $x \in \mathbb{R}$,

$f(x) \neq 0$. Suppose the function is differentiable at $x = 0$ and $f'(0) = 2$, prove that for all $x \in \mathbb{R}, f'(x) = 2f(x)$

Solution: $f'(x) = \lim_{h\to 0}\frac{f(x+h)-f(x)}{h}$

$= \lim_{h\to 0}\frac{f(x)\times f(h)-f(x)}{h}$ (Using the given functional equation)

$= f(x)\lim_{h\to 0}\frac{f(h)-1}{h}$ ......(1)

Our aim is to evaluate $\lim_{h\to 0}\left(\frac{f(h)-1}{h}\right)$

We are given $f'(0) = 2$

$\Rightarrow \lim_{h\to 0}\frac{f(0+h)-f(0)}{h} = 2$

$\Rightarrow \lim_{h\to 0}\frac{f(h)-f(0)}{h} = 2$ ......(2)

From the equation (1) and (2), we observe that we need to find the value of $f(0)$.

Let $x = y = 0$

$\Rightarrow f(0+0) = f(0).f(0) \Rightarrow f(0) = f^2(0)$

$\Rightarrow f(0) = 0$ *or* $f(0) = 1 \Rightarrow f(0) = 1$ ......(3)

$\because f(x) \neq 0$ for any $x \in R$, given)

From equation (1), (2) and (3), we have

$f'(x) = 2f(x)$. Hence proved.

37. Obtain all functions satisfying

(i) $f(x + y) = f(x) + f(y)$, $x \in R, y \in R$

(ii) $f(xy) = f(x).f(y)$; $x > 0, y > 0$; $f(x) \neq 0$ for any x, for which the derivative of f exists wherever f is defined

Solution: (i) $f'(x^+) = \lim_{h\to 0}\frac{f(x+h)-f(x)}{h}$

$= \lim_{h\to 0}\frac{f(x)+f(h)-f(x)}{h}$

$= \lim_{h\to 0}\frac{f(h)-0}{h}$

(Let $x = y = 0$ (in given equation $\Rightarrow f(0) = 0$))

$= f'(0)$

Similarly, $f'(x^-) = f'(0)$

$\Rightarrow f'(x) = f'(0) = k$ (constant -say)

$\Rightarrow f(x) = kx + c$

But $f(0) = 0 + c$

$\Rightarrow c = 0$

$\Rightarrow f(x) = kx$, where k is an arbitrary constant.

(ii) $f'(x^+) = \lim_{h\to 0}\frac{f(x+h)-f(x)}{h} =$

$\lim_{h\to 0}\frac{f(x(1+h/x)-f(x)}{h} = f(x)\lim_{h\to 0}\frac{f(1+h/x)-1}{h}$

Substituting $x = y = 1$ in the given equation, we have

$\Rightarrow f(1) = (f(1))^2$

$\Rightarrow (f(1))^2 - f(1) = 0$

$\Rightarrow (f(1)(f(1) - 1) = 0$

$\Rightarrow f(1) = 1$ $(\because f(x) \neq 0$ *for any* $x)$

(i) becomes: $f'(x^+) = f'(x)$.

$\lim_{h\to 0}\frac{f(1+h/x)-f(1)}{h/x}.1/x = \frac{f(x)}{x}.f'(1)$ ....*(ii)*

Similarly, $f'(x^-) = \frac{f(x)}{x}f'(1)$ ....*(iii)*

$\therefore$ From equation *(ii)* and equation *(iii)*, we get

$f'(x) = \frac{f(x)}{x}.f'(1)$

$\Rightarrow f'(x) = \frac{f(x)}{x}.K$ (where $K = f'(1)$ = constant)

$\Rightarrow \frac{f'(x)}{f(x)} = \frac{K}{x}$

Integrating $In\,|f(x)| = K\,In\,|x| + In\,c$

$\Rightarrow |f(x)| = c\,|x|^K$ ......*(iv)*

Let $x = 1 \Rightarrow c = 1$

Equation (iv) becomes, $|f(x)| = |x|^k$

But $x > 0$ and $y > 0$

$\Rightarrow f(x) = x^k$

38. Let $f : R \to R$ be a function satisfying $f\left(\frac{xy}{2}\right) = \frac{f(x)\cdot f(y)}{2}$, $\forall\ x, y \in R$ and $f(1) = f(1) \neq 0$.

Show that $f(x) + f(1 - x)$ is constant, for all non-zero real values of x.

Solution: Here, $f\left(\frac{xy}{2}\right) = \frac{f(x)\cdot f(y)}{2}$

Putting $\frac{xy}{2} = 1$, , we get $2f(1) = f(x)\cdot f\left(\frac{2}{x}\right)$ ...(i)

Now, $f'(x) = \lim_{h\to 0}\frac{f(x+h)-f(x)}{h}$

$= \lim_{h\to 0}\frac{f(x+h)-\frac{2f(1)}{f(2/x)}}{h}$

$$= \lim_{h\to 0}\frac{f(x+h).f(2/x)-2f(1)}{h.f(2/x)}$$

$$= \lim_{h\to 0}\frac{2f\left(\frac{(x+h).2}{2x}\right)-2f(1)}{h.f(2/x)}$$

$$= \frac{2}{f(2/x)}\lim_{h\to 0}\frac{f\left(1+\frac{h}{x}\right)-f(1)}{\frac{h}{x}.x}$$

$$= \frac{2}{f(2/x)}.\frac{f'(1)}{x} = \frac{f(x)}{f(1)}.\frac{f'(1)}{x} \quad \text{(By using (i))}$$

$$\Rightarrow f'(x) = \frac{f(x)}{x} \qquad \{\text{ as } f'(1) = f(1)\ \}$$

$$\Rightarrow x f'(x) - f(x) = 0 \Rightarrow \frac{f(x)-xf'(x)}{f^2(x)} = 0$$

$$\Rightarrow \frac{d}{dx}\left(\frac{x}{f(x)}\right)$$

$$\left\{as;\ \frac{d}{dx}\left(\frac{x}{f(x)}\right) = \frac{f(x)\cdot 1 - x\cdot f'(x)}{f^2(x)}\right\}$$

$$\Rightarrow \frac{x}{f(x)} = \lambda\,(\text{constant}) \qquad \{\text{as; diff. (constant)} = 0\}$$

$$\Rightarrow \frac{f(x)}{x} = \frac{1}{\lambda}$$

$$\text{or} \quad f(x) = \frac{x}{\lambda} \text{ and } f(1-x) = \frac{1-x}{\lambda}$$

Adding the above two we get,

$$f(x)+f(1-x) = \frac{x}{\lambda}+\frac{1-x}{\lambda} = \frac{1}{\lambda}$$

$\therefore$ $f(x) + f(1-x) = 1/\lambda$

$\Rightarrow$ which is clearly constant.

39. If $f(x)+f(y) = f\left(\frac{x+y}{1-xy}\right)$ for all $x, y \in R$, $(xy \neq 1)$ and $\lim_{x\to 0}\frac{f(x)}{x} = 2$. Find $f\left(\frac{1}{\sqrt{3}}\right)$ and $f'(1)$

Solution: $f(x) + f(y) = f\left(\frac{x+y}{1-xy}\right)$ ..... (i)

Putting $x = y = 0$, we get $f(0) = 0$

Putting $y = -x$

we get $f(+x) + f(-x) = f(0)$ .... (ii)

$$\Rightarrow f(-x) = -f(x) \text{ also } \lim_{x\to 0}\frac{f(x)}{x} = 2$$

$$\text{Now } f'(x) = \lim_{h\to 0}\frac{f(x+h)-f(x)}{h}$$

$$= \lim_{h\to 0}\frac{f(x+h)+f(-x)}{h} \quad [\text{using (ii)} - f(x) = f(-x)]$$

$$f'(x) = \lim_{h\to 0}\frac{f\left(\frac{x+h-x}{1-(x+h)(-x)}\right)}{h} \quad [\text{using (i)}]$$

$$\Rightarrow f'(x) = \lim_{h\to 0}\frac{f\left(\frac{h}{1+x(x+h)}\right)}{h}$$

$$\Rightarrow f'(x) = \lim_{h\to 0}\frac{f\left(\frac{h}{1+xh+x^2}\right)}{\left(\frac{h}{1+xh+x^2}\right)}\times\left(\frac{1}{1+xh+x^2}\right)$$

$$\Rightarrow f'(x) = 2\times\frac{1}{1+x^2} \Rightarrow f'(x) = \frac{2}{1+x^2}$$

Integrating both sides, $f(x) = 2\tan^{-1}(x) + c$ where $f(0) = 0$

$\Rightarrow c = 0$

Thus $f(x) = 2\tan^{-1} x$

$$\text{Hence } f\left(\frac{1}{\sqrt{3}}\right) = 2\tan^{-1}\left(\frac{1}{\sqrt{3}}\right) = 2.\frac{\pi}{6} = \frac{\pi}{3} \text{ and}$$

$$f'(1) = \frac{2}{1+1^2} = \frac{2}{2} = 1$$

40. Let $f: R \to R$ is a function satisfies condition $f(x + y^3) = f(x) + [f(y)]^3$ for all $x, y \in R$. If $f'(0) \geq 0$. Find f(10).

Solution: Given $f(x + y^3) = f(x) + [f(y)]^3$ ...(i)

and $f'(0) \geq 0$ ...(ii)

Replacing x, y by 0

$f(0) = f(0) + f(0)^3$

$\Rightarrow f(0) = 0$ ...(iii)

$$\text{also } f'(0) = \lim_{h\to 0}\frac{f(0+h)-f(0)}{h} = \lim_{h\to 0}\frac{f(h)}{h}$$

$$\text{Let } I = f'(0) = \lim_{h\to 0}\frac{f(0+(h^{1/3})^3)-f(0)}{(h^{1/3})^3}$$

$$= \lim_{h\to 0}\frac{f(0)+[f(h^{1/3})^3]-f(0)}{(h^{1/3})^3}$$

$$= \lim_{h\to 0}\frac{f(h^{1/3})^3-f(0)}{(h^{1/3})^3} = \lim_{h\to 0}\left(\frac{f(h^{1/3})}{(h^{1/3})}\right)^3 = I^3$$

$\Rightarrow I = I^3$

or $I = 0, 1, -1$ as $f'(0) \geq 0$

$\therefore$ $f'(0) = 0,1$ .....(v)

Thus

$$f'(x)=\lim_{h\to 0}\frac{f(x+h)-f(x)}{h}=\lim_{h\to 0}\frac{f(x+(h^{1/3})^3)-f(x)}{(h^{1/3})^3}$$

$$f'(x)=\lim_{h\to 0}\frac{f(x)+(f(h^{1/3}))^3-f(x)}{(h^{1/3})^3} \quad \text{(using (i))}$$

$$\Rightarrow\ f'(x)=\lim_{h\to 0}\left(\frac{f(h^{1/3})}{(h^{1/3})}\right)^3=(f'(0))^3$$

$\Rightarrow f'(x) = 0,1$ [as $f'(0) = 0,1$ using (v)]

Integrating both sides $f(x) = c$ or $x + c$

as $f(0) = 0 \Rightarrow c = 0$

$\Rightarrow f(x) = O$ or $x \Rightarrow f(10) = 0$ or 10

41. Let f be a real function satisfying $f(x+y+z)=f(x)\ f(y)\ f(z)$ for all real x, y, z. If $f(2) = 4$ and $f'(2) = 3$. Then find $f(0)$ and $f'(4)$.

Solution: Here $f(x+y+z)=f(x)\ f(y)\ f(z)$ for all $x, y, z \in R$ ....(i)

Put $x = y = z = 0$

$f(0) = (f(0))^3 \quad \Rightarrow f(0) = 0, \pm 1$ ...(ii)

Putting $y = z = -1$ in (i) we get $f(x-2) = f(x)\ \{f(-1)\}^2$

$\Rightarrow f(0) = f(2)\ \{f(-1)\}^2$

$\Rightarrow f(0) = 4\ \{f(-1)\}^2 \quad \Rightarrow f(0) \geq 0$ ....(iii)

$\therefore$ from (ii) and (iii), $f(0) = O$ or 1

Again $f(x-2) = f(x)\ \{f(-1)\}^2$

from (iii) $f(0) = 0$ for $f(-1) = 0$

$\Rightarrow f(x-2) = 0\ \forall\ x \in \mathbb{R}$

$\Rightarrow f(x) = 0\ \forall\ x \in \mathbb{R}$

which contradicts the fact $f(2) = 4$ so $f(0) \neq 0$

$\therefore f(0) = 1$

Now putting $y = 2$ and $z = 0$ in (i), we get $f(x+2) = f(x) f(2) f(0)$

$\Rightarrow f(x+2) = 4 f(x)$

$\Rightarrow f'(x+2) = 4 f'(x)$; putting $x = 2$

$\Rightarrow f'(4) = 4, f'(2) = 12$. Thus $f(0) = 1$ and $f'(4) = 12$

42. Let f be a one-one function such that $f(x).f(y)+2=f(x)+f(y)+f(xy)$ for all $x, y \in R - \{0\}$ and $f(0) = 1$, $f'(1)=2$. Prove that $3\left(\int f(x)dx\right)-x(f(x)+2)$ is constant.

Solution: We have

$f(x).f(y)+2=f(x)+f(y)+f(xy)$ ...(i)

Replacing x, y by 1, we get $(f(1))^2+2=3f(1)$

$\Rightarrow f^2(1)-3f(1)+2=0$

$\Rightarrow f(1) = 2, 1$

But $f(1)$ cannot be equal to one as $f(0) = 1$ and f is one-one function

$\Rightarrow f(1) = 2$ ...(ii)

Replacing y by $1/x$ in (i), we get

$f(x).f(1/x)+2=f(x)+f(1/x)+f(1)$

$\Rightarrow f(x).f(1/x)+2=f(x)+f(1/x)+2$ (using (ii))

$\Rightarrow f(x).f(1/x)=f(x)+f(1/x)$

$$\Rightarrow f(x)=\frac{f(1/x)}{f(1/x)-1} \text{ and } f(1/x)=\frac{f(x)}{f(x)-1} \quad \text{...(iii)}$$

$$\text{Now, } f'(x)=\lim_{h\to 0}\frac{f(x+h)-f(x)}{h}$$

$$=\lim_{h\to 0}\frac{f(x+h)+\dfrac{f(1/x)}{\left(1-f\left(\dfrac{1}{x}\right)\right)}}{h}$$

$$=\lim_{h\to 0}\frac{f(x+h)-f(x+h).f(1/x)+f(1/x)}{h\{1-f(1/x)\}}$$

$$=\lim_{h\to 0}\frac{f(x+h)-f(x+h)-f(1/x)-f\left(\dfrac{x+h}{x}\right)+2+f(1/x)}{h\{1-f(1/x)\}}$$

$$\left(\begin{array}{l}\because f(x).f(y)=f(x)+f(y)+f(xy)-2\\ \therefore f(x+h).f\left(\dfrac{1}{x}\right)=f(x+h)+f\left(\dfrac{1}{x}\right)+f\left(\dfrac{x+h}{x}\right)-2\end{array}\right)$$

$$=\lim_{h\to 0}\frac{f(1+h/x)-2}{h\{f(1/x)-1\}}=\lim_{h\to 0}\frac{f(1+h/x)-f(1)}{\dfrac{h}{x}.x\ \{f(1/x)-1\}}$$

$(\because f(1) = 2$ by (ii))

$$=\frac{f'(1)}{x\{f(1/x)-1\}}$$

$$\left\{\text{from (iii), } f(x).f(1/x)=\frac{f(x)f(1/x)}{\{f(1/x)-1\}\ \{f(x)-1\}}\right\}$$

$$\Rightarrow f'(x)=\frac{2\{f(x)-1\}}{x}$$

$\Rightarrow x f'(x)=2\{f(x)-1\}$

Integrating above expression both sides, we get

$$xf(x)-\int f(x)\ dx=2\int f(x)dx-2x+\lambda$$

(λ is the constant of integration)

$$\Rightarrow 3\int f(x)\ dx=x\{2+f(x)\}-\lambda$$

Hence $3\int f(x)\ dx-x\{2+f(x)\}=-\lambda$ (constant)

43. Let $f : R \to R$, such that $f'(0) = 1$ and $f(x + 2y) = f(x) + f(2y) + e^{x+2y}(x + 2y) - xe^x - 2ye^{2y} + 4xy$, $\forall$ $x, y \in R$. Find $f(x)$.

Solution: We have, $f(x + 2y) = f(x) + f(2y) + e^{x+2y}(x + 2y) - xe^x - 2ye^{2y} + 4xy$

Replacing $x, y \to 0$, we get,

$f(0) = f(0) + f(0) + 0 - 0 - 0 + 0$

$\Rightarrow f(0) = 0$

Replacing $2y \to -x$, we get,

$f(0) = f(x) + f(-x) - xe^x + x\,e^{-x} - 2x^2$

$\Rightarrow -f(x) = f(-x) - xe^x + xe^{-x} - 2x^2$ ... (i)

Now,

$$f'(x) = \lim_{h\to 0}\frac{f(x+h)-f(x)}{h}$$

$$= \lim_{h\to 0}\frac{f(x+h)+f(-x)-xe^x+xe^{-x}-2x^2}{h}$$

$$\Rightarrow f'(x) = \lim_{h\to 0}\frac{f(h)-e^h h+(x+h)e^{(x+h)}-xe^{-x}+2(x+h)x-xe^x+xe^{-x}-2x^2}{h}$$

$$= \lim_{h\to 0}\frac{f(h)-e^h h+xe^xe^h+he^xe^h+2hx-xe^x}{h}$$

$$= \lim_{h\to 0}\frac{f(h)-f(0)}{h}-\frac{h(e^x-1)}{h}e^h+\frac{xe^x(e^h-1)}{h}+\frac{2hx}{h}$$

$= f'(0) + (e^x - 1) + xe^x + 2x$

$\Rightarrow f'(x) = 1 + e^x - 1 + xe^x + 2x$

or $f'(x) = e^x(x + 1) + 2x$ ... (ii)

Integrating (ii) both sides,

$$f(x) = \int e^x(x+1)\,dx + 2\int x\,dx$$

$$= (x + 1)\,e^x - \int 1.e^x\,dx + 2\frac{x^2}{2} + c$$

$= (x + 1)\,e^x - e^x + x^2 + c$

$\Rightarrow f(x) = x^2 + xe^x + c$

But $f(0) = 0$ $\Rightarrow c = 0$,

So, $f(x) = x^2 + xe^x$

44. Let $f: R^+ \to R$ satisfies the functional equation $f(xy) = e^{xy-x-y}\{e^y f(x) + e^x f(y)\}$ $\forall$ $x, y \in R^+$. If $f'(1) = e$, determine $f(x)$.

Solution: Given that, $f(xy) = e^{xy-x-y}\{e^y f(x) + e^x f(y)\}$ $\forall$ $x, y \in R^+$ ... (i)

Putting $x = y = 1$, we get $f(1) = e^{-1}\{e^1 f(1) + e^1 f(1)\}$

$\Rightarrow f(1) = 0$ ... (ii)

Now, applying the concept of derivative of function, we have

$$f'(x) = \lim_{h\to 0}\frac{f(x+h)-f(x)}{h} = \lim_{h\to 0}\frac{f\left\{x\left(1+\frac{h}{x}\right)\right\}-f(x)}{h}$$

$$= \lim_{h\to 0}\frac{e^{x\left(1+\frac{h}{x}\right)-x-\left(1+\frac{h}{x}\right)}\left\{e^{1+\frac{h}{x}}f(x)+e^xf\left(1+\frac{h}{x}\right)\right\}-f(x)}{h}$$

$$= \lim_{h\to 0}\frac{e^hf(x)+e^{h-1-\frac{h}{x}+x}\left\{f\left(1+\frac{h}{x}\right)-f(1)\right\}-f(x)}{h}$$

[$\because f(1) = 0$]

$$= \lim_{h\to 0}\frac{f(x)(e^h-1)+e^{h-1-\frac{h}{x}+x}\left\{f\left(1+\frac{h}{x}\right)-f(1)\right\}}{h}$$

$$= \lim_{h\to 0}\frac{f(x)(e^h-1)}{h}+\lim_{h\to 0}\frac{e^{h-1-\frac{h}{x}+x}\left\{f\left(1+\frac{h}{x}\right)-f(1)\right\}}{\frac{h}{x}.x}$$

$$= f(x)+\frac{e^{x-1}.f'(1)}{x}$$

$$\left\{\because \lim_{h\to 0}\frac{f\left(1+\frac{h}{x}\right)-f(1)}{\frac{h}{x}} = f'(1) \text{ and } \lim_{h\to 0}\frac{e^h-1}{h}=1\right\}$$

$$= f(x)+\frac{e^x}{ex}.f'(1) \qquad \{\because f'(1) = e\}$$

$\therefore$ $f'(x) = f(x) + \dfrac{e^x}{x}$

$\Rightarrow \dfrac{e^x}{x} = f'(x) - f(x)$

$\Rightarrow \dfrac{1}{x} = \dfrac{e^x f'(x) - f(x).e^x}{e^{2x}}$

$$\left\{\begin{array}{l}\text{as by quotient rule we can write}\\ \dfrac{e^xf'(x)-f(x).e^x}{(e^x)^2}=\dfrac{d}{dx}\left\{\dfrac{f(x)}{e^x}\right\}\end{array}\right\}$$

$\therefore$ $\dfrac{1}{x} = \dfrac{d}{dx}\left\{\dfrac{f(x)}{e^x}\right\}$

Integrating both sides, w.r.t. 'x', we get

$\ln|x| + c = \dfrac{f(x)}{e^x}$

or $f(x) = e^x\{\ln|x| + c\}$

Since $f(1) = 0$ $\Rightarrow c = 0$

Thus $f(x) = e^x \ln|x|$

Matrix Match Type

45. Let [.] denotes greatest integer function

Column-I

(a) If $P(x) = [2 \cos x]$, $x \in [-\pi, \pi]$, then $P(x)$

(b) If $Q(x) = [2 \sin x]$, $x \in [-\pi, \pi]$, then $Q(x)$

(c) If $R(x) = [2 \tan x/2]$, $x \in \left[-\frac{\pi}{2}, \frac{\pi}{2}\right]$, then $R(x)$

(d) If $S(x) = \left[3\,\text{cosec}\frac{x}{3}\right], x \in \left[\frac{\pi}{2}, 2\pi\right]$, then $S(x)$

Column-II

(p) is discontinuous at exactly 7 points

(q) is discontinuous at exactly 4 points

(r) has non-removable discontinuous

(s) is continuous at infinitely many values

(t) continuous at some odd integer multiple of $\pi/2$.

Ans. (a) → (p, r, s), (b) → (p, r, s, t), (c) → (q, r, s), (d) →(r, s, t)

Solution: **(a)** Graph of $2\cos x$ in $[-\pi, \pi]$ is shown below:

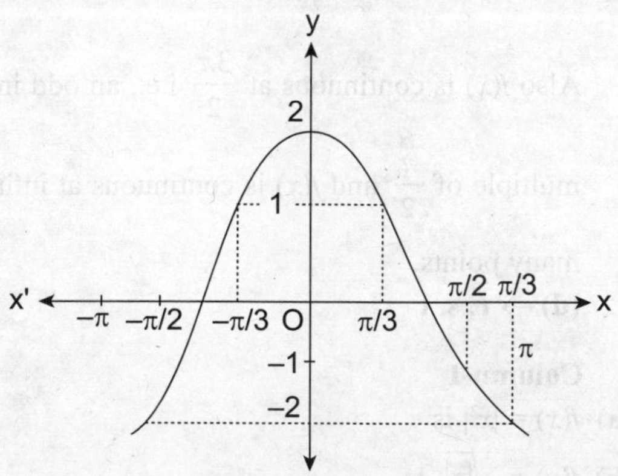

The graph of $P(x) = [2 \cos x]$ in $[-\pi, \pi]$ is given below

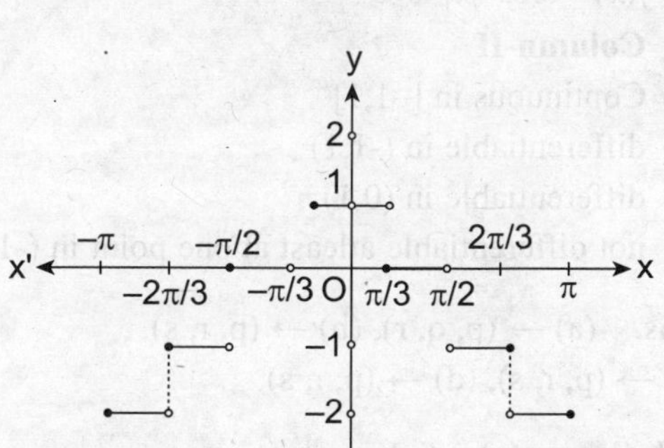

Clearly $P(x)$ is discontinuous at 7 points i.e.,

$$-\frac{2\pi}{3}, -\frac{\pi}{2}, -\frac{\pi}{3}, 0, \frac{\pi}{3}, \frac{\pi}{2}, \frac{2\pi}{3}$$

and hence non-differentiable at 7 points. Also $P(x)$ is continuous at infinitely many points except for the above seven points.

$\therefore$ **(a) → p, r, s**

(b) Graph of $2 \sin x$ in $[-\pi, \pi]$ is shown below:

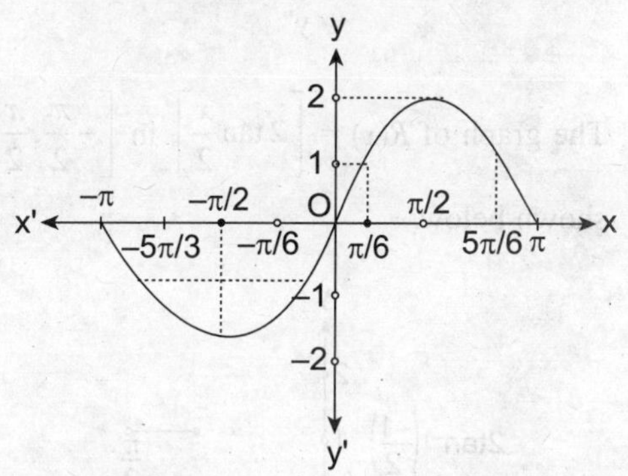

The graph of $Q(x) = [2 \sin x]$ is as shown below:

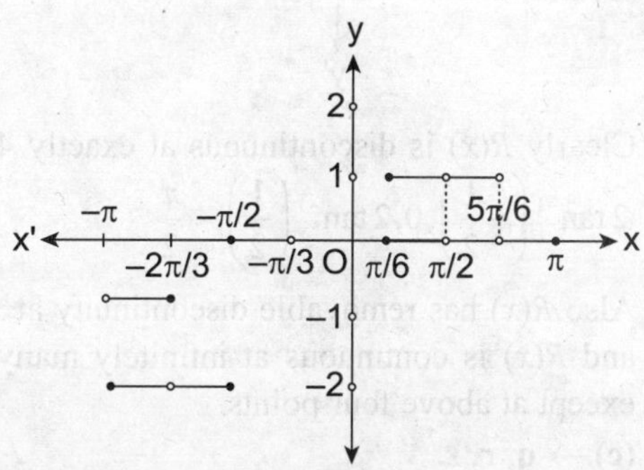

$f(x)$ is discontinuous at 7 points i.e.,

$$-\pi, \frac{-5\pi}{6}, -\frac{\pi}{6}, 0, \frac{\pi}{6}, \frac{\pi}{2}, \frac{5\pi}{6}$$

Also $f(x)$ has removable discontinuity at $x = \pi/2$ and $f(x)$ is continuous at infinitely many points in $[-\pi, \pi]$ except for above seven points.

Also $f(x)$ is continuous *at* $-\pi/2$ i.e., an odd integer multiple of $\pi/2$.

$\therefore$ **(b) → p, r, s, t**

(c) The graph of $2\tan\frac{x}{2}$ in $\left[-\frac{\pi}{2}, \frac{\pi}{2}\right]$ is as shown below:

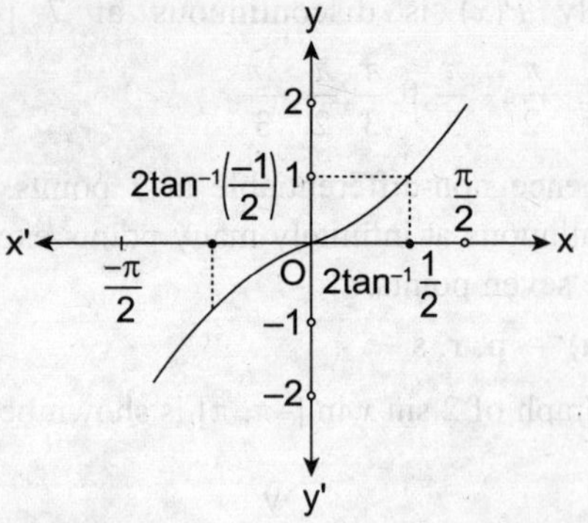

The graph of $R(x) = \left[2\tan\frac{x}{2}\right]$ in $\left[-\frac{\pi}{2},\frac{\pi}{2}\right]$ is as shown below.

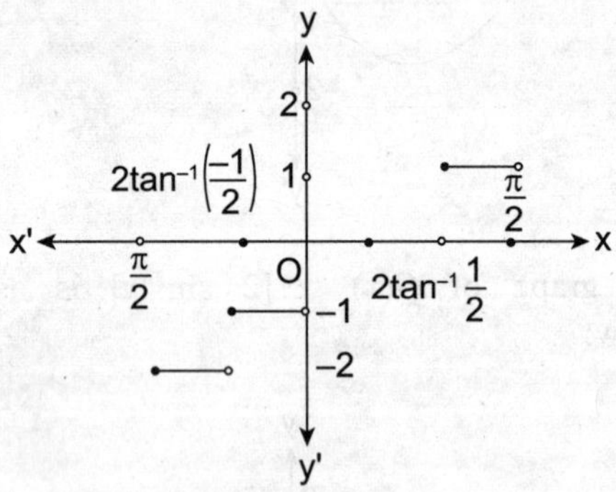

Clearly $R(x)$ is discontinuous at exactly 4 points $2\tan^{-1}\left(-\frac{1}{2}\right), 0, 2\tan^{-1}\left(\frac{1}{2}\right), -\frac{\pi}{2}$

Also $R(x)$ has removable discontinuity at $x = \pi/2$ and $R(x)$ is continuous at infinitely many points except at above four points.

$\therefore$ **(c) → q, r, s.**

(d) The graph of $3\operatorname{cosec}\frac{x}{3}$ in $\left[\frac{\pi}{2}, 2\pi\right]$ is as shown below:

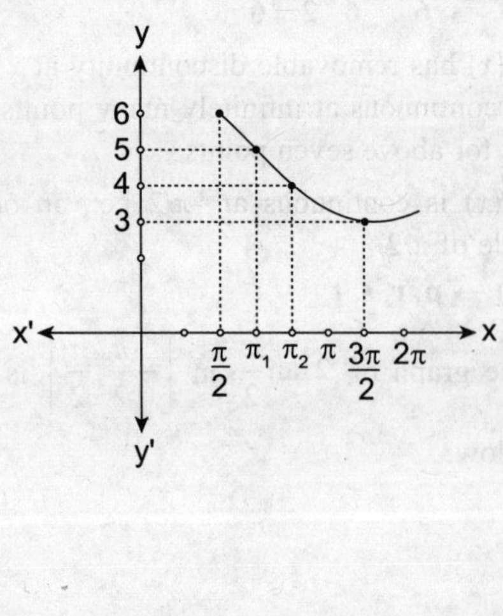

The graph of $S(x)$ $\left[3\operatorname{cosec}\frac{x}{3}\right]$ in $\left[\frac{\pi}{2}, 2\pi\right]$ is as shown below

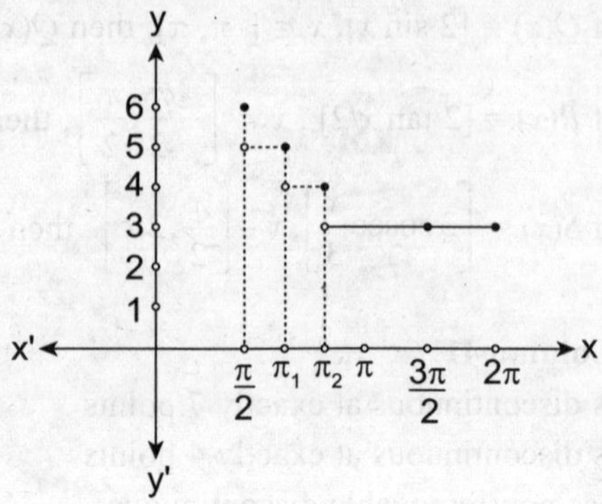

Clearly $S(x)$ is discontinuous at $x = \frac{\pi}{4}$,

$x_1 = 3\operatorname{cosec}^{-1}\left(\frac{5}{3}\right)$; $x_2 = 3\operatorname{cosec}^{-1}\left(\frac{4}{3}\right)$

i.e., at 3 points

Also $f(x)$ has removable discontinuity at $x = \frac{\pi}{4}$

Also $f(x)$ is continuous at $\frac{3\pi}{2}$ i.e., an odd integer multiple of $\frac{\pi}{2}$ and $f(x)$ is continuous at infinitely many points.

$\therefore$ **(d) → r, s, t**

46. **Column-I**

(a) $f(x) = |x^3|$ is

(b) $f(x) = \sqrt{|x|}$ is

(c) $f(x) = |\sin^{-1}x|$ is

(d) $f(x) = \cos^{-1}|x|$ is

Column-II

(p) Continuous in [–1,1]

(q) differentiable in (-1,1)

(r) differentiable in (0,1)

(s) not differentiable atleast at one point in (-1,1)

Ans. (a) → (p, q, r), (b) → (p, r, s), (c) → (p, r, s), (d) → (p, r, s)

Solution: **(a)** $f(x) = |x^3|$

Graph of x^3 is as shown below

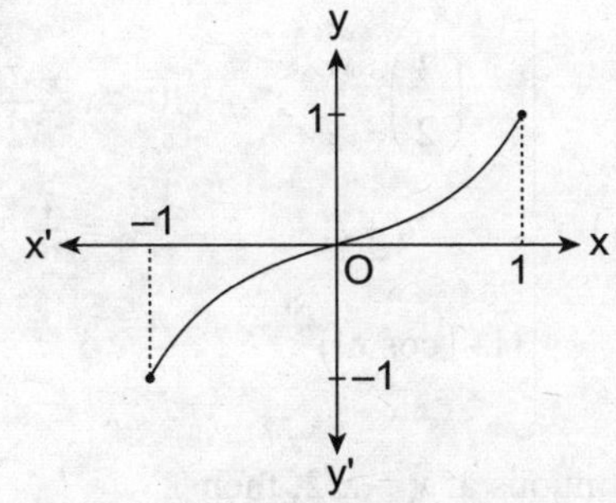

Graph of $|x^3|$ is as shown below:

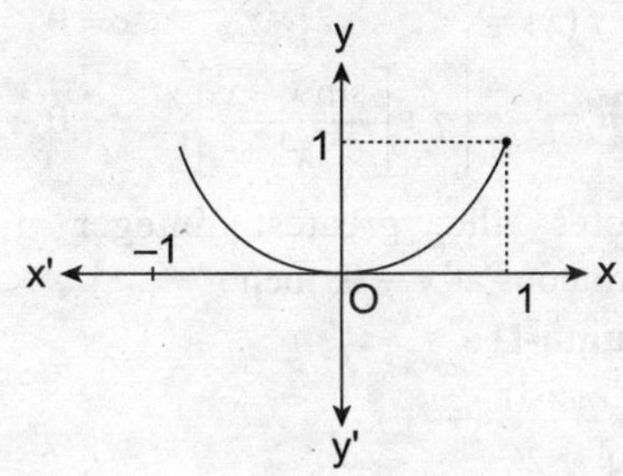

$\therefore\ f(x) = |x^3| = \begin{cases} x^3; & \text{for } x \geq 0 \\ -x^3 & \text{for } x < 0 \end{cases};$

$f(0^+) = f(0^-) = f(0) = 0$

$\Rightarrow f(x)$ is continuous at $x = 0$

$\Rightarrow f'(x) = \begin{cases} 3x^2 \text{ for } x > 0 \\ -3x^2 \text{ for } x < 0 \end{cases}$

$\therefore$ L.H.D $= f'(0^-) = 0$ and R.H.D $= f'(0^+) = 0$

$\therefore\ f(x)$ is differentiable at $x = 0$

Thus $|x^3|$ is continuous and differentiable in $[-1, 1]$

$\therefore$ (a) → p,q,r

(b) $f(x) = \sqrt{|x|} = \begin{cases} \sqrt{x} \text{ for } x \geq 0 \\ \sqrt{-x} \text{ for } x < 0 \end{cases};$

$f'(0^-) = f'(0^+) = 0 = f(0)$

$\Rightarrow f'(x) = \begin{cases} \dfrac{1}{2\sqrt{x}} \text{ for } x > 0 \\ \dfrac{-1}{2\sqrt{-x}} \text{ for } x < 0 \end{cases}$

$\Rightarrow$ L.H.D $= -\infty$ and R.H.D $= \infty$

$\Rightarrow f(x)$ is non-differentiable at $x = 0$

Graph of $f(x) = \sqrt{|x|}$ is as shown below

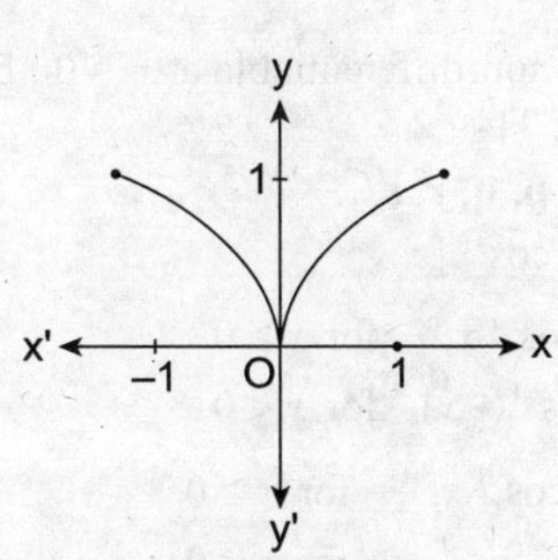

Note that $f(x)$ has a cusp at $x = 0$

$\therefore\ f(x)$ is continuous in $[-1, 1]$; non-differentiable in $(-1, 1)$; differentiable in $(0, 1)$

$\therefore$ **(b) → p, r, s**

(c) $F(x) = |\sin x|$

Graph of $g(x) = \sin^{-1}(x)$ is as shown below

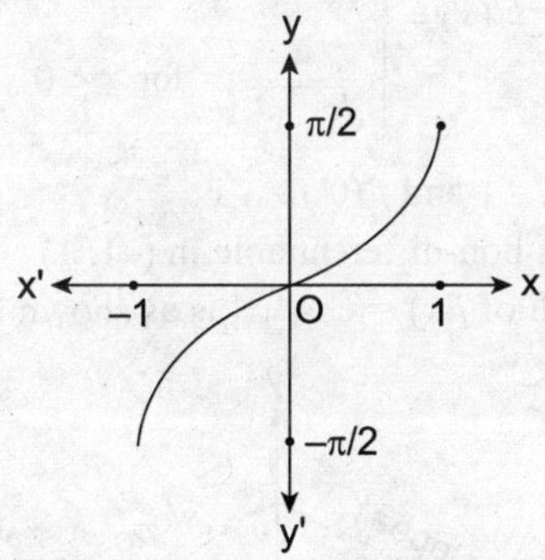

and graph of $f(x) = |\sin^{-1}x|$ is as shown below

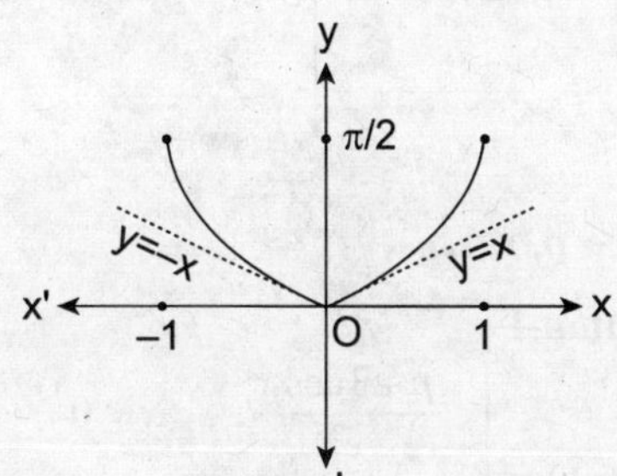

Also $f(x) = \begin{cases} \sin^{-1} x; & \text{for } x \geq 0 \\ -\sin^{-1} x; & \text{for } x < 0 \end{cases};$

$f(0^-) = f(0^+) = f(0) = 0$

$f'(x) = f'(x) = \begin{cases} \dfrac{1}{\sqrt{1-x^2}} & \text{for } x > 0 \\ \dfrac{-1}{\sqrt{1-x^2}} & \text{for } x < 0 \end{cases}$

$\therefore\ f'(0^-) = -1$ and $f'(0^+) = 1$

$\therefore$ $f(x)$ is non-differentiable at $x = 0$, but continuous in $[-1, 1]$

$\therefore$ **(c) → p, q, r, s**

(d) $f(x) = \cos^{-1}|x|$

$$= \begin{cases} \cos^{-1}x; & \text{for } x \geq 0 \\ \cos^{-1}(-x) & \text{for } x < 0 \end{cases}$$

$$= \begin{cases} \cos^{-1}x; & \text{for } x \geq 0 \\ \pi - \cos^{-1}x; & \text{for } x < 0 \end{cases}$$

$f(0^-) = \pi - \cos^{-1}0 = \pi - \pi/2 = \pi/2$

$f(0^+) = \cos^{-1}0\frac{\pi}{2}$ and $f(0) = \cos^{-1}0 = \frac{\pi}{2}$

$\therefore$ $f(x)$ is continuous in $[-1, 1]$

Also $f'(x) = \begin{cases} \dfrac{-1}{\sqrt{1-x^2}}; & \text{for } x > 0 \\ \dfrac{1}{\sqrt{1-x^2}}; & \text{for } x < 0 \end{cases}$

$\Rightarrow f'(0^-) = 1$ and $f'(0^+) = -1$

$\therefore$ $f(x)$ is non-differentiable in $(-1, 1)$

$\therefore$ Graph of $f(x) = \cos^{-1}|x|$ is as shown below:

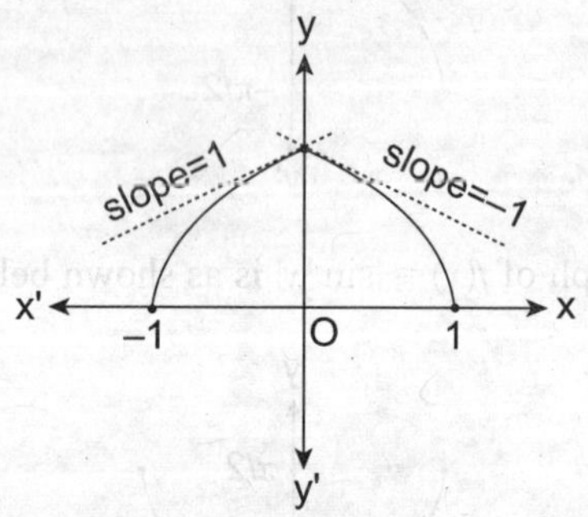

$\therefore$ **(d) → p, r, s.**

47. **Column-I**

(a) If $f(x) = \begin{cases} \dfrac{p+3\cos x}{x^2}; & x < 0 \\ q\tan\left(\dfrac{\pi}{[x+3]}\right); & x \geq 0 \end{cases}$ is continuous at $x = 0$, where [.] denotes the greatest integer function, then

(b) If $f(x) = \begin{cases} -2\sin x, & -\pi \leq x \leq -\frac{\pi}{2} \\ p\sin x + q, & \frac{-\pi}{2} < x < \frac{\pi}{2} \\ \cos x, & \frac{\pi}{2} \leq x \leq \pi \end{cases}$ is continuous in $[-\pi, \pi]$, then

(c) $f(x) = \begin{cases} \left(\frac{3}{2}\right)^{\left(\frac{\cos 3x}{\cot 2x}\right)}; & 0 < x < \frac{\pi}{2} \\ q + 3; & x = \frac{\pi}{2} \\ (1 + |\cos x|)^{\frac{p|\tan x|}{q}}; & \frac{\pi}{2} < x < \pi \end{cases}$ is continuous at $x = \pi/2$, then

(d) If $f(x) = \begin{cases} p + \dfrac{\sin[x]}{x}; & x > 0 \\ 2; & x = 0 \\ q + \left[\dfrac{\sin x - x}{x^3}\right]; & x < 0 \end{cases}$ where [.] denotes the greatest integer function is continuous at $x = 0$, then

Column-II

(p) $|p + q| = 0$

(q) $|p - q| = 2$

(r) $[p + 2q] = -2$

(s) $[p + 2q] = 4$

(t) $|p - q| = 1$

Solution: **(a)** $f(x) = \begin{cases} \dfrac{p+3\cos x}{x^2}; & x < 0 \\ q\tan\left(\dfrac{\pi}{[x+3]}\right); & x \geq 0 \end{cases}$

L.H.L. $= f(0^-) = \lim_{x\to 0^-} f(x) = \lim_{x\to 0^-}\left(\dfrac{p+3\cos x}{x^2}\right)$

$\therefore$ denominator tends to zero, numerator must also tend to zero. This implies $p = -3$

$\therefore$ L.H.L. $= \lim_{x\to 0^-}\dfrac{-3+3\cos x}{x^2} = \lim_{x\to 0^-}\dfrac{-3(1-\cos x)}{x^2}$

$$= \lim_{x\to 0^-}\frac{-3\left(2\sin^2\frac{x}{2}\right)}{x^2} = -\frac{3}{2}$$

R.H.L. $= f(0^+) = \lim_{x\to 0^+} f(x) = \lim_{x\to 0^+} q\tan\left(\dfrac{\pi}{[x+3]}\right)$

$$= q\tan\left(\frac{\pi}{3}\right) = q\sqrt{3}$$

Also $f(0) = q\sqrt{3}$

$\therefore$ For continuity at $x = 0$,

$$q\sqrt{3} = \frac{-3}{2}$$

$\Rightarrow \quad q = \dfrac{-\sqrt{3}}{2}$

$\therefore \quad p = -3,\ q = \dfrac{-\sqrt{3}}{2}$

$\therefore \quad [p - 2q] = [-3 + \sqrt{3}] = [-3 + 1.732]$
$= [-1.268] = -2$

$\therefore$ **(a) → (r)**

(b) Possibly $f(x)$ can be discontinuous at $x = \dfrac{-\pi}{2}$ and $\dfrac{\pi}{2}$

So we shall make $f(x)$ continuous only at $x = -\dfrac{\pi}{2}$ and $x = \dfrac{\pi}{2}$

Now at $x = -\dfrac{\pi}{2}$,

L.H.L. $= \lim\limits_{x \to \left(-\frac{\pi}{2}\right)^-} f(x) = \lim\limits_{x \to \left(\frac{-\pi}{2}\right)^-} (-2\sin x)$

$= -2\sin\left(-\dfrac{\pi}{2}\right) = 2$

R.H.L. $= \lim\limits_{x \to \left(-\frac{\pi}{2}\right)^+} f(x) = \lim\limits_{x \to \left(-\frac{\pi}{2}\right)^+} (p\sin x + q) = -p + q$

At $x = \dfrac{\pi}{2}$,

L.H.L. $= \lim\limits_{x \to \left(\frac{\pi}{2}\right)^-} f(x) = \lim\limits_{x \to \left(\frac{\pi}{2}\right)^-} (p\sin x + q) = p + q$

R.H.L. $= \lim\limits_{x \to \left(\frac{\pi}{2}\right)^+} f(x) = \lim\limits_{x \to \left(\frac{\pi}{2}\right)^+} \cos x = 0$

$\therefore$ For continuity at $x = -\dfrac{\pi}{2}$ and $\dfrac{\pi}{2}$

$-p + q = 2$ and $p + q = 0$

$\Rightarrow q = 1\ ;\ p = -1$

$\therefore \quad |p + q| = 0;\ |p - q| = |-1 - 1| = 2$

$[p - 2q] = [-1-2(-1)] = [1] = 1$

$[p + 2q] = [-1 + 2(-1)] = [-3] = -3$

$\therefore$ **(b) → p, q**

(c) At $x = \dfrac{\pi}{2}$

L.H.L. $= \lim\limits_{x \to \left(\frac{\pi}{2}\right)^-} f(x) = \lim\limits_{x \to \left(\frac{\pi}{2}\right)^-} \left(\dfrac{3}{2}\right)^{\frac{\cos 3x}{\cot 2x}}$

$= \left(\dfrac{3}{2}\right)^{\lim\limits_{x \to \left(\frac{\pi}{2}\right)^-} (\cos 3x)(\tan 2x)} = \left(\dfrac{3}{2}\right)^0 = 1$

R.H.L. $= \lim\limits_{x \to \left(\frac{\pi}{2}\right)^+} f(x) = \lim\limits_{x \to \left(\frac{\pi}{2}\right)^+} (1 + |\cos x|)^{\frac{p}{q}|\tan x|}$

$= \lim\limits_{x \to \left(\frac{\pi}{2}\right)^+} (1 + |\cos x|)^{\frac{1}{|\cos x|} \cdot \frac{p}{q}|\sin x|} = e^{\frac{p}{q} \cdot 1} = e^{\frac{p}{q}}$

and $f\left(\dfrac{\pi}{2}\right) = q + 3$

$\therefore$ For continuity at $x = \dfrac{\pi}{2}$,

$e^{\frac{p}{q}} = 1 = q + 3 \Rightarrow p = 0\ ;\ q = -2$

$\therefore \quad |p - q| = 2;\ |p + 2q| = 4$

$\therefore$ **(c) → (q), (s)**

(d) AT $x = 0$

L.H.L. $= \lim\limits_{x \to 0^-} f(x) = \lim\limits_{x \to 0^-} q + \left[\dfrac{\sin x - x}{x^3}\right]$

$= \lim\limits_{x \to 0^-} q + \left[\dfrac{\left(x - \dfrac{x^3}{3!} + \dfrac{x^5}{5!} - .....\right) - x}{x^3}\right]$

$= \lim\limits_{x \to 0^-} q + \left[-\dfrac{1}{3!} + \dfrac{x^2}{5!} - \dfrac{x^4}{7!} + \dfrac{x^6}{9!} - \dfrac{x^8}{11!} + ...\right]$

$= \lim\limits_{x \to 0^-} q + \left[-\dfrac{1}{6} + h\right] = q - 1$

R.H.L. $= \lim\limits_{x \to 0^+} f(x) = \lim\limits_{x \to 0^+} p + \dfrac{\sin[x]}{x}$

$= \lim\limits_{x \to 0^+} \left(p + \dfrac{\sin x}{x}\right) = p$

Also $f(0) = 2$

$\therefore$ For continuity at $x = 0,\ p = q - 1 = 2$

$\Rightarrow p = 2,\ q = 3$

$\therefore \quad |p - q| = 1$

$\Rightarrow$ **(d) → (t)**

48. **Column-I**

(a) The number of whole numbers less than the fundamental period of $\cos^2 x + \operatorname{cosec}^2 x - \cot^2 x$ is

(b) The number of points of discontinuity of the function $g(x) = [x] + \{2x\} + [3x]$ for $x \in [0, 1)$ where [.] and {.} represent greatest integer and fractional part function is

(c) If $L = \lim\limits_{x \to 0} \dfrac{\tan x(1 + \cos x)}{x \sec x}$ and [.] represents greatest integer function then [L] equals

(d) The number of solutions of the equation $\sin^{-1}x = 2\cos^{1}(x+1)$ is

Column-II

(p) 3

(q) 1

(r) 4

(s) 2

Solution: (a) $\cos^2x + \text{cosec}^2x - cot^2x = \cos^2x + 1$

$\therefore$ $f(x) = \cos^2x + 1$ and $f(\pi + x) = \cos^2(\pi + x) + 1 = \cos^2x + 1$

$\therefore$ Fundamental period of $f(x)$ is π

$\therefore$ The whole numbers less that $p(\simeq 3.14)$ are 0, 1, 2, 3 i.e., 4 in counting

$\Rightarrow$ **(a) → (r)**

(b) $g(x) = [x] + \{2x\} + [3x]$; $x \in [0, 1)$

For $x \in [0, 1)$; $[x] = 0$

$\therefore$ $g(x) = \{2x\} + [3x]$

$$\Rightarrow g(x) = \begin{cases} 2x; & 0 \le x < \frac{1}{3} \\ 2x+1; & \frac{1}{3} \le x < \frac{1}{2} \\ 2x-1+1; & \frac{1}{2} \le x < \frac{2}{3} \\ 2x-1+2; & \frac{2}{3} \le x < 1 \end{cases}$$

$$\Rightarrow g(x) = \begin{cases} 2x; & 0 \le x < \frac{1}{3} \\ 2x+1; & \frac{1}{3} \le x < \frac{1}{2} \\ 2x; & \frac{1}{2} \le x < \frac{2}{3} \\ 2x+1; & \frac{2}{3} \le x < 1 \end{cases}$$

Clearly $f(x)$ is discontinuous at $x = \frac{1}{3}, \frac{1}{2}$ and $\frac{2}{3}$

$\therefore$ **(b) → (p)**

(c) $L = \lim_{x\to 0}\dfrac{\tan x(1+\cos x)}{x\sec x} = \lim_{x\to 0}\left(\dfrac{\tan x}{x}\right)\left(\dfrac{1+\cos x}{\sec x}\right)$

$= (1)\left(\dfrac{2}{1}\right) = 2$

$\therefore$ [L] = [2] = 2

$\therefore$ **(c) → (r), (s)**

(d) $\sin^{-1}x = 2\cos^{-1}(x+1)$; for domain of equation $x \in [-1, 1] \cap [-2, 0] = [-1, 0]$

Also $\sin^{-1}x \in \left[-\frac{\pi}{2}, 0\right]$ for $x \in [-1, 0]$ and

$2\cos^{-1}(x+1) \in [0, \pi]$ for $x \in [-1, 0]$

$\therefore$ $\sin^{-1}x = 2\cos^{-1}(x+1)$ when each equals 0

$\Rightarrow$ $x = 0$

$\therefore$ There will be only one solution $x = 0$

$\therefore$ **(d) → (q)**

49. **Column-I**

(a) If $f(xy) = f(x).f(y)$ and f is differentiable at $x = 1$, such that $f'(1) = 1$ also $f(1) \neq 0$, then $f'(7)$ equals

(b) The number of points where $f(x) = |x^2 - 3x + 2| + |\sin x| - [x - 1/2]$; $-\pi \le x \le \pi$ is non-differentiable is ([.] is gint function)

(c) The number of points at which $f(x) = [a + 7\sin x]$; $x \in [0, \pi]$, $a \in \mathbb{Z}$ is non–differentiable is ([.] is gint function)

(d) If for a continuous function f, $f(0) = f(1) = 0, f'(1) = 2$ and $g(x) = f(e^x) \cdot e^{f(x)}$, then $g'(0)$ equals

Column-II

(p) 13

(q) 9

(r) 2

(s) 3

(t) 1

Solution:

$$f'(x) = \lim_{h\to 0}\frac{f(x+h)-f(x)}{h} = \lim_{h\to 0}\frac{f\left[x\left(1+\frac{h}{x}\right)\right]-f(x)}{h}$$

$$= \lim_{h\to 0}\frac{f(x)f\left(1+\frac{h}{x}\right)-f(x)}{h}$$

$$= \lim_{h\to 0} f(x)\left\{\frac{f\left(1+\frac{h}{x}\right)-1}{h}\right\}$$

$\therefore$ $f'(1) = f(1).\lim_{h\to 0}\left\{\dfrac{f(1+h)-1}{h}\right\}$

$\because$ $f'(1)$ exist finitely and $f(1) \neq 0$ and denominator is approaching to zero, numerator must approach to zero

$\Rightarrow$ $\lim_{h\to 0}\{f(1+h)-1\} = 0$

$\Rightarrow f(1) = 1$

$$f'(x) = f(x)\lim_{h\to 0}\left\{\frac{f\left(1+\frac{h}{x}\right)-1}{h}\right\}$$

$$\Rightarrow f'(x) = f(x)\lim_{h\to 0}\left\{\frac{f\left(1+\frac{h}{x}\right)-f(1)}{h}\right\}$$

$$= f(x)\lim_{h\to 0}\left\{\frac{1}{x}\cdot\frac{f\left(1+\frac{h}{x}\right)-f(1)}{h/x}\right\}$$

$$f'(x) = \frac{f(x)}{x}.f'(1) = \frac{f(x)}{x} \quad (\because f'(1) = 1)$$

$\therefore \quad \frac{f'(x)}{f(x)} = \frac{1}{x}$

$\Rightarrow \ln|f(x)| = \ln|x| + C$

$\Rightarrow \ln|f(1)| = \ln 1 + C$

$\Rightarrow \ln 1 = \ln 1 + C \quad \Rightarrow C = 0$

$\therefore \ln|f(x)| = \ln|x| \quad \Rightarrow f(x) = \pm x$

But $f(1) = 1 \quad \Rightarrow f(x) = x$

$\therefore f'(x) = 1$

$\Rightarrow f'(7) = 1$

$\Rightarrow$ **(a) → (t)**

(b) $f(x) = \left|x^2 - 3x + 2\right| + |\sin x| - \left[x - \frac{1}{2}\right]; \ -\pi \le x \le \pi$

$= |(x-1)(x-2)| + |\sin x| - \left[x - \frac{1}{2}\right];$

Clearly $|(x-1)(x-2)|$ is non-differentiable at $x = 1, x = 2$

$|\sin x|$ non-differentiable at $n\pi$; $n \in \mathbb{Z}$

But here $x \in [-\pi, \pi]$

$\Rightarrow |\sin x|$ is non-differentiable only at $x = 0$

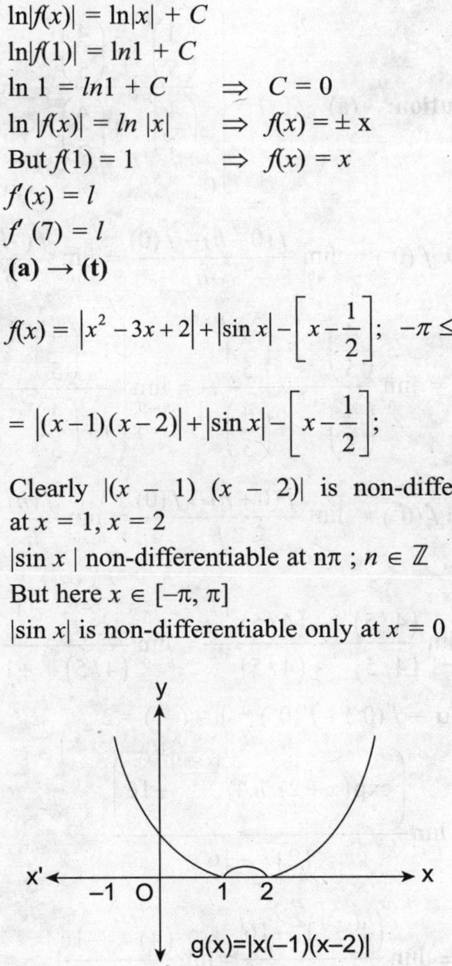

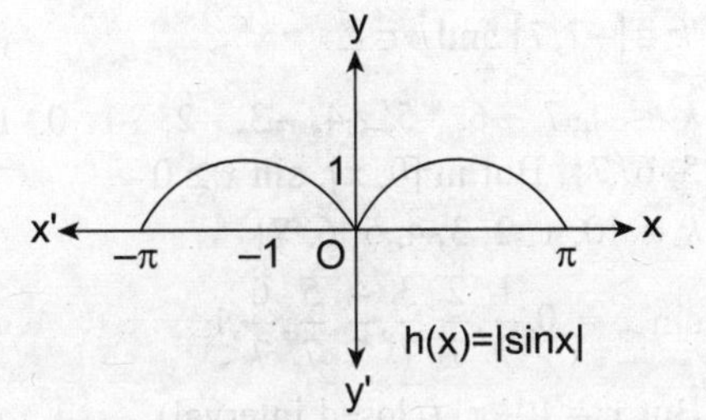

Also $[x - 1/2]$ is non-differentiable at integer points for $x \in [-\pi, \pi]$

i.e., for $\left(x - \frac{1}{2}\right) \in \left[-\pi - \frac{1}{2}, \pi - \frac{1}{2}\right]$

i.e., for $x - \frac{1}{2} = -3, -2, -1, 0, 1, 2$

$\Rightarrow \quad x = \frac{-5}{2}, \frac{-3}{2}, \frac{-1}{2}, \frac{1}{2}, \frac{3}{2}, \frac{5}{2}$

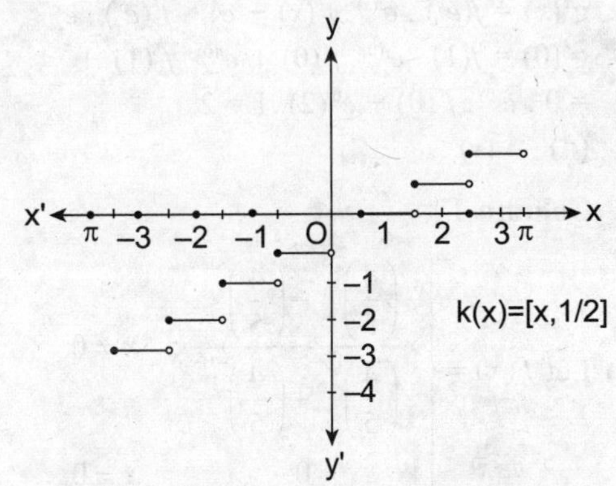

We observe that among the given three functions, no two have any common point of non-differentiability and by algebra of differentiability we know that the sum of a differentiable and non-differentiable function is non-differentiable so,.

$\frac{-5}{2}, \frac{-3}{2}, \frac{-1}{2}, 0, \frac{1}{2}, 1, \frac{3}{2}, 2, \frac{5}{2}$ are the points where $f(x)$ is non-differentiable at exactly 9 points

$\therefore$ **(b) → (q)**

(c) $f(x) = [a + 7\sin x]$; $x \in [0, \pi]$; $a \in \mathbb{Z}$ (fixed integer) for non-differentiability

$a + 7\sin x$ must be an integer

As $a \in \mathbb{Z}$, $7\sin x \in \mathbb{Z}$

$\Rightarrow 7\sin x = k; k \in \mathbb{Z}$

$\Rightarrow \sin x = k/7; k \in \mathbb{Z}$

But $\sin x$ has its range $[-1, 1]$

$\Rightarrow \quad -1 \le \frac{k}{7} \le 1$

$\Rightarrow$ $k \in [-7, 7]$ and $k \in \mathbb{Z}$

$\Rightarrow$ $k \in \{-7, -6, -5, -4, -3, -2, -1, 0, 1, 2, 3, 4, 5, 6, 7\}$. But in $[0, \pi]$, $\sin x \geq 0$

$\Rightarrow$ $k \in \{0, 1, 2, 3, 4, 5, 6, 7\}$

$\Rightarrow$ $\sin x = 0, \frac{1}{7}, \frac{2}{7}, \frac{3}{7}, \frac{4}{7}, \frac{5}{7}, \frac{6}{7}, 1$

But $x \in [0, \pi]$ (closed interval)

$\Rightarrow$ $\sin x = \frac{1}{7}, \frac{2}{7}, \frac{3}{7}, \frac{4}{7}, \frac{5}{7}, \frac{6}{7}, 1$

And $\sin x$ would repeat these values twice, once in $[0, \pi/2]$ and secondly in $[\pi/2, \pi]$, but 1 is common value in two quadrants.

Thus total number of points of non-differentiability will be $7 \times 2 - 1 = 13$

$\therefore$ **(c) → (p)**

(d) $g(x) = f(e^x) \cdot e^{f(x)}$

$g'(x) = f(e^x) \cdot e^{f(x)} \cdot f'(x) + e^{f(x)} \cdot f'(e^x) \cdot e^x$

$\Rightarrow$ $g'(0) = f(1) \cdot e^{f(0)} \cdot f'(0) + e^{f(0)} \cdot f'(1) \cdot 1$

$= 0 \cdot e^{(0)} \cdot f'(0) + e^0 (2) \cdot 1 = 2$

$\therefore$ **(d) → (r)**

50. **Column-I**

(a) Let $f(x) = \begin{cases} x\dfrac{\left(\frac{4}{5}\right)^{1/x} - \left(\frac{4}{5}\right)^{-1/x}}{\left(\frac{4}{5}\right)^{1/x} + \left(\frac{4}{5}\right)^{-1/x}}; & x \neq 0 \\ 0; & x = 0 \end{cases}$.

If $\alpha = f'(0^-) - f'(0^+)$, then $\lim\limits_{x \to \alpha} \dfrac{\left(\exp((x+2)\ell n 4)\right)^{\frac{[x+0.5]}{4}} - 16}{(2)^{2x} - 16}$ is less than or equal to

(b) If $f(x) = [2 + 5|n| \sin x]$; where $n \in \mathbb{Z}$ has exactly 19 points of non-differentiability in $(0, \pi)$, then the possible Values of n are ([.] is gint function)

(c) If $f(x) =$

$$\begin{cases} \dfrac{\left(\frac{\pi}{2} - \sin^{-1}\left(1 - \{x\}^2\right)\right)\sin^{-1}\left(1 - \{x\}\right)}{\sqrt{2}\left(\{x\} - \{x\}^3\right)}; & x > 0 \\ \lambda; & x = 0 \\ \dfrac{\mu \sin^{-1}\left(1 - \{x\}\right)\cos^{-1}\left(1 - \{x\}\right)}{\sqrt{2\{x\}}.\left(1 - \{x\}\right)} & x < 0 \end{cases}$$

is continuous at $x = 0$, then the value of $\sin^2 \lambda + \cos^2\left(\frac{\mu\pi}{\sqrt{2}}\right)$ is ({.} denotes fractional part function)

(d) If $f(x) = \dfrac{1}{1 + \frac{2}{x}}$, then the number of points in $\mathbb{R}$ at which $g(x) = \dfrac{1}{1 + \frac{3}{f(x)}}$ is non-differentiable is

Column-II

(p) 3

(q) 2

(r) –3

(s) 5

(t) –2

Solution: (a) $f(x) = \begin{cases} x\dfrac{\left(\frac{4}{5}\right)^{1/x} - \left(\frac{4}{5}\right)^{-1/x}}{\left(\frac{4}{5}\right)^{1/x} + \left(\frac{4}{5}\right)^{-1/x}}; & x \neq 0 \\ 0 & ; x = 0 \end{cases}$

Now $f'(0^-) = \lim\limits_{h \to 0^+} \dfrac{f(0-h) - f(0)}{-h} = \lim\limits_{h \to 0^+} \dfrac{f(-h)}{-h}$

$$= \lim_{h \to 0^+} \frac{\left(\frac{4}{5}\right)^{-1/h} - \left(\frac{4}{5}\right)^{1/h}}{\left(\frac{4}{5}\right)^{-1/h} + \left(\frac{4}{5}\right)^{1/h}} = \lim_{h \to 0^+} \left(\frac{1 - \left(\frac{4}{5}\right)^{2/h}}{1 + \left(\frac{4}{5}\right)^{2/h}}\right) = 1$$

And $f'(0^+) = \lim\limits_{h \to 0^+} \dfrac{f(0+h) - f(0)}{h} = \lim\limits_{h \to 0^+} \dfrac{f(h)}{h}$

$$= \lim_{h \to 0^+} \frac{(4/5)^{1/h} - (4/5)^{-1/h}}{(4/5)^{1/h} + (4/5)^{-1/h}} = \lim_{h \to 0^+} \frac{\left(\frac{4}{5}\right)^{2/h} - 1}{(4/5)^{2/h} + 1} = -1$$

$\therefore$ $\alpha = f'(0^-) - f'(0^+) = 1 - (-1) = 2$

$$\therefore \quad \lim_{x \to 2} \frac{\left(\exp(x+2)\ell n 4\right)^{\frac{[x+0.5]}{4}} - 16}{(2)^{2x} - 16}$$

$$= \lim_{x \to 2} \frac{\left(4^{(x+2)}\right)^{\frac{2}{4}} - 16}{(4)^x - 16} = \lim_{x \to 2} \frac{(4)^{\frac{x+2}{2}} - 16}{4^x - 16}$$

$$= \lim_{x\to 2}\frac{(4)^{\frac{x}{2}+1-2}-1}{4^{x-2}-1} = \lim_{x\to 2}\frac{(4)^{\frac{x}{2}-1}-1}{(4)^{x-2}-1}$$

$$= \lim_{x\to 2}\frac{(4)^{\frac{x}{2}-1}-1}{4^{x-2}-1}\times\frac{(x-2)}{\left(\frac{x}{2}-1\right)} = \frac{\ell n(4)}{\ell n(4)}.(2) = 2$$

which is less than or equal to 2, 3 and 5.

$\therefore$ **(a) → p, q, s**

(b) $f(x) = [2 + 5\,|n|\,\sin x|]$; $n \in \mathbb{Z}$ and $x \in (0, \pi)$. For non-differentiability of $f(x)$ $2 + 5\,|n|\sin x \in \mathbb{Z}$

$\Rightarrow 5\,|n|\sin x \in \mathbb{Z}$

$\Rightarrow 5\,|n|\sin x = k;\ k \in \mathbb{Z}$ …(i)

$\Rightarrow \sin x = \dfrac{k}{5|n|};\ k \in \mathbb{Z}$

But $\sin x \in (0, 1]$ for $x \in \left(0, \dfrac{\pi}{2}\right]$

$\Rightarrow 0 < \dfrac{k}{5|n|} < 1$

$\Rightarrow k \in (0, 5|n|]$

$\because$ $f(x)$ is non-differentiable at exactly 10 points in $\left(0, \dfrac{\pi}{2}\right)$

$\Rightarrow k \in \{1, 2, 3, 4, .., 5|n|\}$ and $k = 10$ and $\dfrac{k}{5|n|} = 1$

$\Rightarrow 5|n| = 10 \quad \Rightarrow |n| = \dfrac{10}{5} = 2$

$\Rightarrow n = \pm 2.$

(In $(0, \pi)$; $\sin x = 1$ at $x = \pi/2$ common value in $\left(0, \dfrac{\pi}{2}\right]$ and $\left[\dfrac{\pi}{2}, \pi\right)$ and hence non-differentiability at exactly 19 points means differentiability at 9 points in each quadrant $\left(0, \dfrac{\pi}{2}\right)$ and $\left(\dfrac{\pi}{2}, \pi\right)$ and once at $x = \dfrac{\pi}{2}$)

$\therefore$ **(b) → (q), (t)**

(c) $f'(0^-) = \lim_{x\to 0^-} f(x)$

$$= \lim_{x\to 0^-}\frac{\mu\sin^{-1}(1-\{x\})\cos^{-1}(1-\{x\})}{\sqrt{2\{x\}}(1-\{x\})}$$

$$= \lim_{x\to 0^-}\frac{\mu\sin^{-1}(\{-x\})\cos^{-1}(-\{x\})}{\sqrt{2(1-\{x\})(\{-x\})}}$$

$$= \lim_{h\to 0^+}\frac{\mu\sin^{-1}h.\cos^{-1}h}{\sqrt{2(1-h)(h)}} = \frac{\mu\cos^{-1}(0)}{\sqrt{2}} = \frac{\mu\pi}{2\sqrt{2}}$$

($\because \{x\} + \{-x\} = 1$ for $x \notin \mathbb{Z}$)

and $f'(0^+) = \lim_{x\to 0^+} f(x)$

$$= \lim_{x\to 0^+}\frac{\left(\frac{\pi}{2}-\sin^{-1}\left(1-\{x\}^2\right)\right)\sin^{-1}\left(1-\{x\}\right)}{\sqrt{2}\left(\{x\}-\{x\}^3\right)}$$

$$= \lim_{x\to 0^+}\frac{(\cos^{-1}(1-x^2)).\sin^{-1}(1-x)}{\sqrt{2}\,x(1-x^2)}$$

$$= \lim_{x\to 0^+}\frac{\cos^{-1}\left(1-x^2\right)}{x}.\frac{1}{\sqrt{2}}.\frac{\sin^{-1}(1-x)}{(1-x^2)}$$

$$= \lim_{x\to 0^+}\frac{-1}{\sqrt{1-\left(1-x^2\right)^2}}(-2x).\frac{\pi}{2\sqrt{2}} \text{ (By L.H. rule)}$$

$$= \lim_{x\to 0^+}\frac{2x}{\sqrt{2x^2-x^4}}\frac{\pi}{\sqrt{2.2}}$$

$$= \lim_{x\to 0^+}\frac{\pi}{\sqrt{2-x^2}}\frac{1}{\sqrt{2}} = \frac{\pi}{\sqrt{2}}\frac{1}{\sqrt{2}} = \frac{\pi}{2}$$

$\therefore$ for continuity at $x = 0$; $f'(0^-) = f'(0^+) = f(0) = \lambda$

$\Rightarrow \dfrac{\mu\pi}{2\sqrt{2}} = \dfrac{\pi}{2} = \lambda$

$\Rightarrow \lambda = \dfrac{\pi}{2};\ \mu = \sqrt{2}$

$\therefore \sin^2\lambda + \cos^2\left(\mu\dfrac{\pi}{\sqrt{2}}\right)$

$= \sin^2\dfrac{\pi}{2} + \cos^2(\pi) = 1 + 1 = 2$

$\therefore$ **(c) → (q)**

(d) $g(x) = \dfrac{1}{1+\dfrac{3}{f(x)}};\ f(x) = \dfrac{1}{1+\dfrac{2}{x}}$

$\Rightarrow g(x) = \dfrac{x}{6+4x}$

$g(x)$ being a rational expression can be non-differentiable only where $g(x)$ is not defined i.e., where $f(x) = 0, -3$ and $f(x)$ is not defined

But $f(x) = \dfrac{1}{1+\dfrac{2}{x}} \neq 0\ \ \forall\ x \in \mathbb{R}$ and $f(x)$ is not defined at $x = 0$ and at $x = -2$; $f(x) = -3$

$\Rightarrow \dfrac{x}{2+x} = -3$

$\Rightarrow x = -6 - 3x$

$\Rightarrow 4x = -6$

$\Rightarrow x = -3/2$

$\therefore$ Domain of $g(x) = \mathbb{R} \sim \{0, -2, -3/2\}$

$\therefore$ $g(x)$ is non-differentiable at exactly 3 real number

$\therefore$ **(d) → (p)**

Comprehension Type Passage

A: Let $f(x) = \begin{cases} xg(x) & , x \le 0 \\ x + ax^2 - x^3 & , x > 0 \end{cases}$, where

$g(t) = \lim\limits_{x\to 0}(1 + a\tan x)^{t/x}$, a is positive constant , then

51. If a is even prime number, then $g(2)$ =

(a) e^2 (b) e^3

(c) e^4 (d) none of these

52. Set of all values of a for which function $f(x)$ is continuous at $x = 0$

(a) (-1,10) (b) $(-\infty, \infty)$

(c) $(0,\infty)$ (d) none of these

53. If $f(x)$ is differentiable at $x = 0$, then a ∈

(a) (–5,–1) (b) (–10,3)

(c) $(0, \infty)$ (d) none of these

Solution: Given $g(t) = \lim\limits_{x\to 0}(1 + a\tan x)^{t/x}$

$= \lim\limits_{x\to 0}(1 + a\tan x)^{\frac{1}{a\tan x}\cdot\frac{t}{1}\cdot\frac{a\tan x}{x}}$

$= e^{a\lim\limits_{x\to 0}\left(\frac{\tan x}{x}\right)t}$

$= e^{at}; a > 0$

51. $\because$ a is even prime number

$\Rightarrow a = 2$

$\therefore$ $g(t) = e^{2t}$

$\therefore$ $g(2) = e^4$

$\therefore$ Ans (c)

52. $f(x) = \begin{cases} xg(x); & x \le 0 \\ x + ax^2 - x^3; & x > 0 \end{cases} = \begin{cases} xe^{ax}; & x \le 0 \\ x + ax^2 - x^3; & x > 0 \end{cases}$

Now $f(0^-) = \lim\limits_{x\to 0^-} xe^{ax} = 0;$

$f(0^+) = \lim\limits_{x\to 0^+}(x + ax^2 - x^3) = 0$ and $f(0) = 0$

$\therefore$ $f(x)$ is continuous at $x = 0\ \forall$ a > 0

$\therefore$ $a \in (0, \infty)$ $\therefore$ Ans (c)

53. L.H.D. at $x = 0 = f'(0^-) = \lim\limits_{h\to 0^+}\dfrac{f(-h) - f(0)}{-h}$

$= \lim\limits_{h\to 0^+}\dfrac{-he^{-ah} - 0}{-h} = 1$

R.H.D. at $x = 0 = f'(0^+) = \lim\limits_{h\to 0^+}\dfrac{f(h) - f(0)}{h}$

$= \lim\limits_{h\to 0^+}\dfrac{h + ah^2 - h^3}{h} = 1$

$\therefore$ $f(x)$ is differentiable at $x = 0\ \forall$ a > 0

$\therefore$ $a \in (0, \infty)$

$\therefore$ Ans. (c)

B: Let f: $R \to R$ be a differentiable function satisfying $f\left(\dfrac{x+y}{3}\right) = \dfrac{2 + f(x) + f(y)}{3}\ \forall x, y \in \mathbb{R}$ and $f(2) = 2$, then answer the following questions:

54. The range of $g(x) = \left|f\left|\dfrac{x}{2}\right|\right|$ is

(a) $[1,\infty)$ (b) $[2,\infty)$

(c) $[0,\infty)$ (d) None of these

55. The function $h(x) = |f(|x|) - 4|$ is

(a) non-differentiable and discontinuous at –1,0,1

(b) differentiable for all real numbers

(c) non-differentiable but continuous at –1, 0, 1

(d) non-differentiable only at –1 and 1

56. If $g(x) = x^4 - f(|x|)^2 - 6$; then the value of $g(k-1)$, where k denotes the solution as well as number of solutions of equation $g(x) = 0$ is

(a) –9 (b) 8

(c) 55 (d) None of these

57. Area bounded by the graph of relation $|y| = h(x)$; $x = -2$ and; where $h(x) = |f(|x|) - 4|$ is

(a) 6 square units (b) 10 sq.units

(c) 8 sq units (d) none of these

Solution: Putting $x = 3x$, $y = 0$ in

$f\left(\dfrac{x+y}{2}\right) = \dfrac{2 + f(x) + f(y)}{3}$, we get

$f\left(\dfrac{3x+0}{3}\right) = \dfrac{2 + f(3x) + f(0)}{3}$

$\Rightarrow f(x) = \dfrac{2 + f(3x) + f(0)}{3}$ ...(1)

Put $x = y = 0$

$\Rightarrow f(0) = \dfrac{2 + f(0) + f(0)}{3}$

$\Rightarrow 3f(0) = 2 + 2f(0)$

$\Rightarrow f(0) = 2$ ...(2)

$\therefore$ from (1); $f(x) = \dfrac{2 + f(3x) + 2}{3}$

$\Rightarrow 3f(x) = f(3x) + 4$ ......(3)

Now, $f'(x) = \lim\limits_{h\to 0} \dfrac{f(x+h) - f(x)}{h}$

$= \lim\limits_{h\to 0} \dfrac{f\left(\dfrac{3x+3h}{3}\right) - f(x)}{h}$

$= \lim\limits_{h\to 0} \left\{\dfrac{\dfrac{2 + f(3x) + f(3h)}{3} - f(x)}{h}\right\}$

$= \lim\limits_{h\to 0} \left[\dfrac{2 + f(3x) + f(3h) - 3f(x)}{3h}\right]$

$= \lim\limits_{h\to 0} \left[\dfrac{2 + 3f(x) - 4 + f(3h) - 3f(x)}{3h}\right]$

$f'(x) = \lim\limits_{h\to 0} \left[\dfrac{f(3h) - 2}{3h}\right]$

Since $f(x)$ is differentiable $\forall\, x$; $\lim\limits_{h\to 0} f(3h) = 2$

$\Rightarrow f(0) = 2$

$\Rightarrow f'(x) = \lim\limits_{h\to 0} \dfrac{3f'(3h)}{3} = f'(0) = k$ (say)

$\Rightarrow f'(x) = k$

$\Rightarrow f(x) = kx + C$

$\Rightarrow f(x) = k$

$\Rightarrow f'(2) = k$

But $f'(2) = 2 \Rightarrow k = 2$

$\therefore f(x) = 2x + C$

Also $f(0) = 2 \Rightarrow C = 2$

$\therefore f(x) = 2x + 2$

54. $\therefore f(x) = 2x + 2$

$\Rightarrow f(|x|) = 2|x| + 2$

$\Rightarrow f\left(\left|\dfrac{x}{2}\right|\right) = 2\left|\dfrac{x}{2}\right| + 2 = |x| + 2$;

$\Rightarrow g(x) = \left|f\left|\dfrac{x}{2}\right|\right| = ||x| + 2| = |x| + 2 \begin{cases} x+2 \text{ for } x \ge 0 \\ -x+2 \text{ for } x < 0 \end{cases}$

Graph of $||x| + 2||$ is shown below

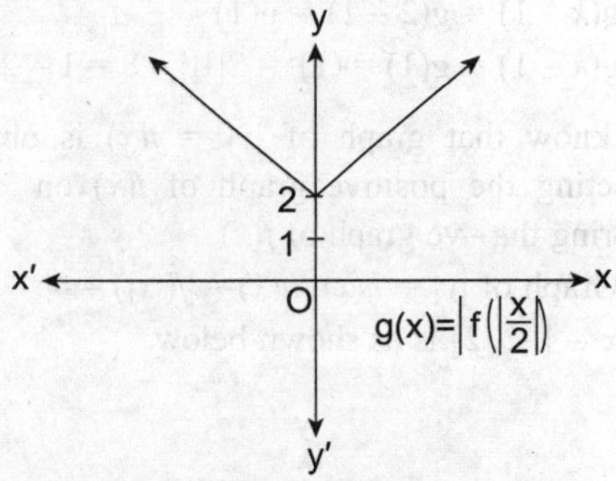

Clearly the range of $g(x)$ is $[2, \infty)$

55. $h(x) = |f(|x|) - 4| = |2|x| + 2 - 4| = |2|x| - 2|$

$= 2||x| - 1| = \begin{cases} 2|x-1| \text{ for } x \ge 0 \\ 2|-x-1| \text{ for } x < 0 \end{cases}$

$= \begin{cases} 2(x-1) \text{ for } x \ge 1 \\ 2(-x+1) \text{ for } 0 \le x < 1 \\ 2(x+1) \text{ for } -1 \le x < 0 \\ 2(-x-1) \text{ for } x < -1 \end{cases}$

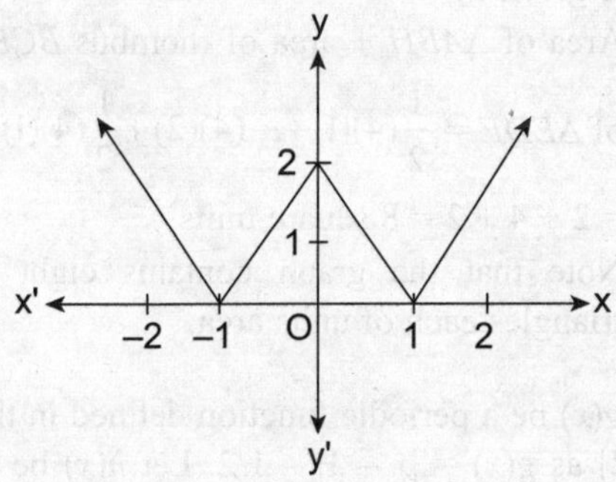

56. $g(x) = x^4 - f(|x|)^2 - 6$

$= x^4 - (2|x|^2 + 2) - 6$

$= x^4 - 2|x|^2 - 8$

$= |x|^4 - 2|x|^2 - 8$

$= (|x|^2 - 4)(|x|^2 + 2)$

$\therefore g(x) = 0$

$\Rightarrow |x|^2 = 4$ or $|x|^2 = -2$

$\Rightarrow |x|^2 = 4$ $(\because |x| \ge 0)$

$\Rightarrow |x| = \pm 2$ $(\because |x| \ne -2)$

$\Rightarrow |x| = 2$

$\Rightarrow x = \pm 2$

$\therefore$ Solution of equation $g(x) = 0$ are 2 and –2

$\Rightarrow$ there are two solutions of equation $g(x) = 0$

$\because$ K is the value of solutions as well as number of solutions

$\Rightarrow k = 2$

$\therefore\ g(k-1) = g(2-1) = g(1)$

$\therefore\ g(k-1) = g(1) = (1)^4 - 2|1|^2 - 8 = 1 - 2 - 8 = -9$

57. We know that graph of $|y| = f(x)$ is obtained by reflecting the positive graph of $f(x)$ on x-axis and ignoring the –ve graph of $f(x)$

$\therefore$ Graph of $|y| = h(x)$; $h(x) = |f(|x|) - 4|$; $x \in [-2, 2]$ is as shown below

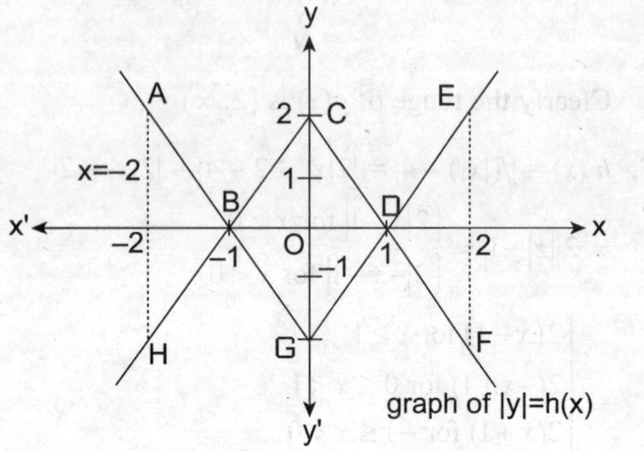

graph of |y|=h(x)

$\therefore$ The area bounded by $|y| = h(x)$; $x = -2$ and $x = 2$ is given by

Area of ΔABH + area of rhombus $BCDG$ + area of $\Delta EDF = \frac{1}{2}(4)(1) + \frac{1}{2}(4)(2) + \frac{1}{2}(4)(1)$

$= 2 + 4 + 2 = 8$ square units

Note that the graph contains eight congruent triangles each of units area.

C: Let $g(x)$ be a periodic function defined in the interval $[0, 2]$ as $g(x) = |x-1| - 1/2$. Let $h(x)$ be a periodic function with period 2 defined as $h(x) = g(x) + \sin \pi x$

Further define a composite function $\psi(x) = f(g(x))$ such that $f(x)$ satisfies the functional equation $f(mx + ny) = (f(x))^m . (f(y))^n\ \forall x, y, m, n \in \mathbb{R}$ and $f'(0) = -\ell n2 f(0)$.

Based on the above information answer the following questions?

58. The value of $\lim_{n\to\infty} \int_{-2}^{2} \frac{1}{1+(f(x))^n}dx$ is

(a) 0 (b) 1

(c) 2 (d) 4

59. The range of $\psi(x)$ is given by

(a) $[e^{-1/2}, e^{1/2}]$ (b) $[2^{-1/2}, 2^{1/2}]$

(c) $[-1, 1]$ (d) $[-2, 2]$

60. If the value of $\int_a^{a+b} \psi(x)\, dx$ does not depend upon $'a'$, then b can be

(a) –1 (b) 1

(c) 2 (d) None of these

61. Number of points where $f(x)$ and $g(x)$ intersect in $[-2, 9]$ is

(a) 4 (b) 5

(c) 6 (d) 7

62. If $\psi(x) < f(x)$, then x must belong to

(a) $(-\infty, 1/4)$ (b) $(1/4, \infty)$

(c) $(1/2, \infty)$ (d) $(-\infty, 1/2)$

63. The value of $\int_{-20}^{20} |g(x)|\, dx$ is

(a) 20 sq. units (b) 40 sq. units

(c) 10 sq. units (d) None of these

Solution: Given $\psi(x) = f(g(x))$ ...(1)

$f(mx + ny) = (f(x))^m (f(y))^n \quad \forall\ x, y, m, n \in \mathbb{R}$ ...(2)

$f'(0) = -\ln 2\, f(0)$ ...(3)

$g(x)$ is periodic function given by

$g(x) = |x-1| - 1/2;\ 0 \le x \le 2$ ...(4)

$h(x) = g(x) + \sin\pi x$ is periodic with period 2

$\Rightarrow h(x + 2) = h(x)$

$\Rightarrow g(x + 2) + \sin\pi\,(x + 2) = g(x) + \sin\pi x$

$\Rightarrow g(x + 2) + \sin\pi x = g(x) + \sin\pi x$

$\Rightarrow g(x + 2) = g(x)$

$\Rightarrow g(x)$ must be a periodic function with period 2

$$\therefore\ g(x) = \begin{cases} |x-1| - 1/2 & ; 0 \le x \le 2 \\ |x-3| - 1/2 & ; 2 \le x \le 4 \\ |x-5| - 1/2 & ; 4 \le x \le 6 \\ \text{and so on....} \end{cases}$$

Now $f(mx + hy) = (f(x))^m (f(y))^n$

$\forall\ x, y, m, n \in \mathbb{R}$

for $m = n = 0$

$f(0) = 1$; for $m = n = 1$; $f(x + y) = f(x).f(y)$

$$\therefore\ f'(a) = \lim_{h\to 0}\frac{f(x+h) - f(x)}{h} = \lim_{h\to 0}\frac{f(x).f(h) - f(x)}{h}$$

$$= \lim_{h\to 0} f(x)\left[\frac{f(h)-1}{h}\right] = \lim_{h\to 0} f(x)\left[\frac{f(h)-f(0)}{h}\right]$$

$(\because f(0) = 1)$

$= f(x) f'(0) = f(x)\,(-\ln 2\,.\,f(0)) = (-\ln 2)(f(x))$

$\therefore \quad \dfrac{f'(x)}{f(x)} = -\ln 2$

$\Rightarrow \ln f(x) + C = (\ln 2)\, x$

$\Rightarrow \ln f(x) + x \ln 2 = -C$

$\Rightarrow \ln 2^x . f(x) = -C$

for $x = 0$, $\ln 1 = -C \Rightarrow C = 0$

$\therefore \ln 2^x f(x) = 0$

$\Rightarrow 2^x f(x) = 1 \Rightarrow f(x) = 2^{-x}$

$\Rightarrow \psi(x) = (f(g(x)) = 2^{-g(x)} = 2^{1/2 - |x-1|} = \sqrt{2}.2^{-|x-1|}$

58. $f(x) = 2^{-x}$

$\therefore \lim\limits_{n\to\infty} \displaystyle\int_{-2}^{2} \frac{1}{1+2^{-nx}}\, dx = \lim\limits_{n\to\infty} \int_{-2}^{2} \frac{2^{nx}}{2^{nx}+1}\, dx$

$\Rightarrow$ put $2^{nx} + 1 = t$

$\Rightarrow 2^{nx}.(\ln 2) n\, dx = dt$

$\Rightarrow 2^{nx}\, dx = \dfrac{dt}{n \ln 2}$

when $x = -2$, $t = 2^{-2n} + 1$

when $x = 2$, $t = 2^{2n} + 1$

$$\therefore \quad I = \lim_{n\to\infty} \int_{1+2^{-2n}}^{1+2^{2n}} \frac{dt}{t\, n \ln 2}\, dx = \lim_{n\to\infty} \frac{1}{n \ln 2} \left|\ln t\right|_{1+2^{-2n}}^{1+2^{2n}}$$

$$= \lim_{n\to\infty} \frac{1}{n \ln 2} \left| \ln \left(\frac{1+2^{2n}}{1+2^{-2n}} \right) \right|$$

$$= \lim_{n\to\infty} \frac{1}{n \ln 2} \left| \ln 2^{2n} \right| = \lim_{n\to\infty} \frac{1}{n \ln 2} \times 2n \ln 2 = 2$$

$\therefore$ **Ans. (c)**

59. $\psi(x) = 2^{-g(x)} = \left(\dfrac{1}{2}\right)^{g(x)}$ and $g(x) = |x-1| - \dfrac{1}{2}$; $0 \le x \le 2$ and $g(x)$ is periodic with period 2. Clearly

$g(x) \in \left[-\dfrac{1}{2}, \dfrac{1}{2}\right]$

Here $\psi(x)$ is an exponential function with base less than 1 and hence is *a* decreasing function for

$g(x) \in \left[-\dfrac{1}{2}, \dfrac{1}{2}\right]$ and also $\psi(x)$ is periodic.

$\therefore$ Range of $\psi(x) = \left[\left(\dfrac{1}{2}\right)^{1/2}, \left(\dfrac{1}{2}\right)^{-1/2}\right]$

$= \left[\dfrac{1}{\sqrt{2}}, \sqrt{2}\right] = \left[2^{-1/2}, 2^{1/2}\right]$

Ans. (b)

60. $\displaystyle\int_a^{a+b} \psi(x)\, dx = \int_a^{a+b} 2^{-g(x)}\, dx$

$\because \displaystyle\int_a^{a+2} \psi(x)\, dx$ has same value " $a \in \mathbb{R}$ as $\psi(x)$ is periodic with period 2.

$\therefore \ b = 2$

Ans. (c)

61. $f(x) = 2^{-x}$ and $g(x) = |x-1| - \dfrac{1}{2}$; $0 \le x \le 2$ and $g(x)$ is periodic with period 2. The graphs of $f(x)$ and $g(x)$ in $0 \le x \le 2$ is shown below.

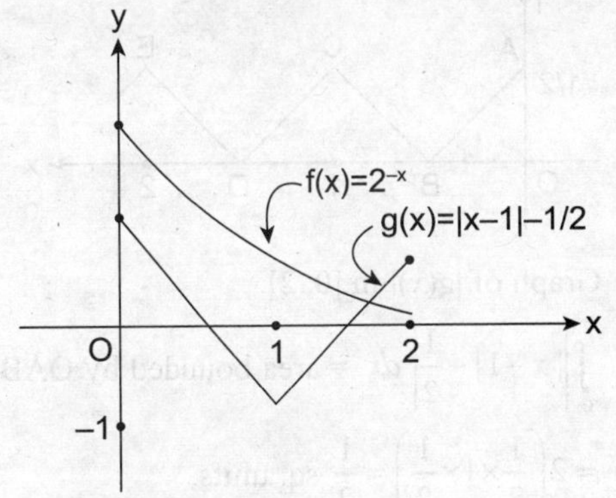

$\therefore$ In [0, 2], $f(x)$ and $g(x)$ intersect only at one point.

$\therefore$ In [–2, 9], $f(x)$ and $g(x)$ would intersect in [–2, 0]; [0, 2]; [4, 6]; [6, 4]; [6, 8]

i.e., at 5 points

$\therefore$ **Ans. (b)**

62. $\psi(x) < f(x)$

$\Rightarrow 2^{-g(x)} < 2^{-x} \Rightarrow \left(\dfrac{1}{2}\right)^{g(x)} > \left(\dfrac{1}{2}\right)^{x}$

$\Rightarrow g(x) > x$

($\because a^x$ is *a* decreasing function for $x \in (0, 1)$

$\because$ Range of $g(x)$ is $\left[-\dfrac{1}{2}, \dfrac{1}{2}\right]$;

Graph of $g(x)$ and x are shown below

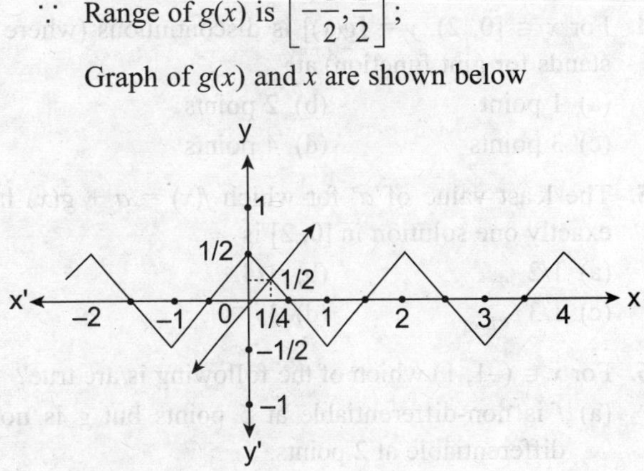

$\therefore\ g(x) > x$ for $x \in \left(-\infty, \frac{1}{4}\right)$.

$\therefore$ **Ans. (a)**

63. $\int_{-20}^{20} |g(x)|\, dx = 2\int_{0}^{20} \left| |x-1| - \frac{1}{2} \right| dx$

$= 2 \times 10 \int_{0}^{2} \left| |x-1| - \frac{1}{2} \right| dx$

Graph of $|g(x)| = \left| |x-1| - \frac{1}{2} \right|$; is shown below

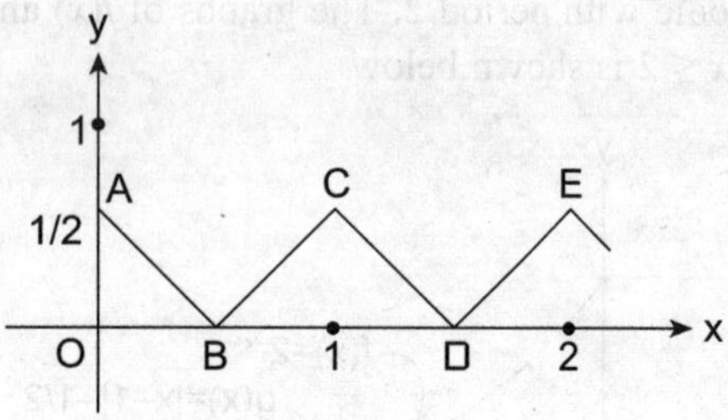

Graph of $|g(x)|$ in $[0, 2]$

$\therefore \int_{0}^{2} \left| |x-1| - \frac{1}{2} \right| dx$ = area bounded by OABCDEF

$= 2\left(\frac{1}{2} \times 1 \times \frac{1}{2}\right) = \frac{1}{2}$ sq. units.

$\therefore \int_{-20}^{20} |g(x)|\, dx = 20\left(\frac{1}{2}\right) = 10$ sq. units.

$\therefore$ **Ans. (c)**

D: Let $h(x) = x^2$; $\phi(x) = (x-1)^2$; $\psi(x) = 2x(1-x)$
Suppose $f(x) = \max.\ \{h(x), \phi(x), \psi(x)\}$; $0 \le x \le 1$
and $g(x) = \min.\ \{h(x), \phi(x), \psi(x)\}$; $0 \le x \le 1$
Further let $f(x+1) = f(x)$ and $g(x+2) = g(x)$;
$g(-x) = g(x)\ \forall\ x \in \mathbb{R}$.
On the above given information answer the following questions.

64. For $x \in [0, 2)$, $y = [g(x)]$ is discontinuous (where [] stands for gint function) at

(a) 1 point (b) 2 points
(c) 3 points (d) 4 points

65. The least value of 'a' for which $f(x) = a + g(x)$ has exactly one solution in $[0, 2]$ is

(a) 1/2 (b) 1/4
(c) 1/3 (d) 1

66. For $x \in (-1, 1)$ which of the following is/are true?

(a) f is non-differentiable at 5 points but g is non-differentiable at 2 points.
(b) f is non-differentiable at 7 points but g is non-differentiable at 2 points.
(c) $f(x) + g(x)$ is non-differentiable at 7 points.
(d) $f(x) + g(x)$ is non-differentiable at 9 points.

67. Which of the following is/are true?

(a) $f(x) \cdot g(x)$ is non-differentiable at $x = 0, \frac{1}{3}, \frac{2}{3}$
(b) $f(x) \cdot g(x)$ is non-differentiable at $x = \frac{1}{3}, \frac{1}{2}, \frac{2}{3}$
(c) $f(x) \cdot g(x)$ is non-differentiable at $x = 0, x = 1$
(d) $f(x) \cdot g(x)$ is differentiable at each integer x.

Solution: $f(x) = \max.\ \{h(x), \phi(x)\}$; $0 \le x \le 1$ ...(1)
$f(x+1) = f(x)$ " $x \in \mathbb{R}$. ...(2)
$g(x) = \min.\ \{h(x), \phi(x), \psi(x)\}$ for $0 \le x \le 1$ ...(3)
$g(-x) = -g(x)$ ...(4)
and $g(x+2) = g(x)$ " $x \in \mathbb{R}$. ...(5)
where $h(x) = x^2$; $\phi(x) = (x-1)^2$, $\psi(x) = 2x(1-x)$
Here $f(x)$ and $g(x)$ are defined for $x \in [0, 1]$ and $f(x)$ and $g(x)$ are given periodic with periods 1 and 2 respectively and $g(x)$ is an odd function.
Let us draw the graphs of given functions

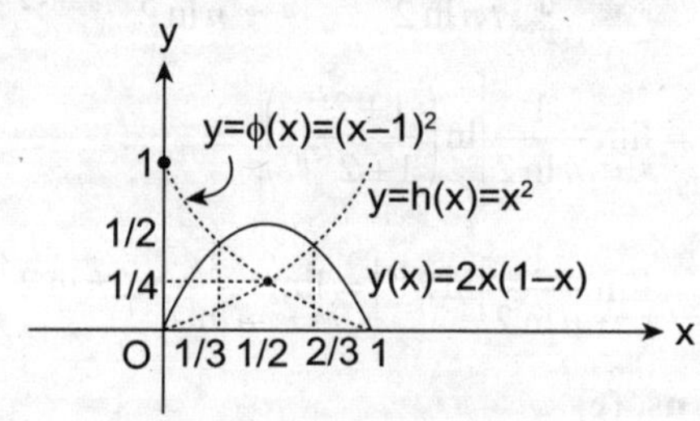

$\therefore$ Graph of $f(x)$ and $g(x)$ would be as shown below

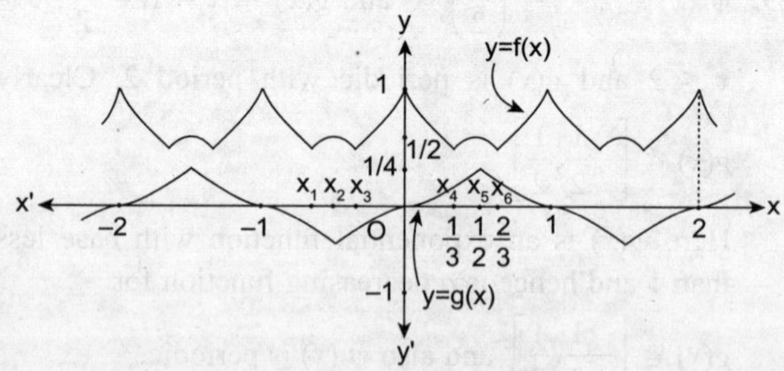

64. Range of $g(x)$ is $\left[-\frac{1}{4}, \frac{1}{4}\right]$ which contains only integer value 0.
In (0, 2), $g(x)$ takes integer value 0 at $x = 1$ (only point)
Thus $[g(x)]$ is discontinuous only at one point in (0, 2)
$\therefore$ Ans. (a)

65. Range of $f(x) = \left[\frac{4}{9}, 1\right]$ and range of $g(x) = \left[-\frac{1}{4}, \frac{1}{4}\right]$

$a = f(x) - g(x)$

least value of 'a' is the minimum difference of $f(x)$ and $g(x)$

$= \min\left\{2x(1-x) - x^2; \frac{1}{3} \le x \le \frac{1}{2}\right\}$ (from graph)

$= \min\left\{2x - 3x^2; \frac{1}{3} \le x \le \frac{1}{2}\right\}$

Let $k(x) = 2x - 3x^2$

$\Rightarrow k'(x) = 2 - 6x$

For $x \in \left[\frac{1}{3}, \frac{1}{2}\right]$, $6x \in [2, 3]$

$\Rightarrow -6x \in [-3, -2] \quad \Rightarrow 2 - 6x \in [-1, 0]$

$\Rightarrow k'(x) \le 0$ for $x \in \left[\frac{1}{3}, \frac{1}{2}\right]$

$\Rightarrow k'(x)$ is a decreasing function in $\left[\frac{1}{3}, \frac{1}{2}\right]$

$\therefore$ $k(x)$ would have least value at $x = |$

i.e., $a = k\left(\frac{1}{2}\right) = 1 - \frac{3}{4} = \frac{1}{4}$.

$\therefore$ **Ans. (b)**

66. In (–1, 1) $f(x)$ is non-differentiable at sharp turns which are 5 points

i.e., $x_1, x_3, 0, x_4, x_6$ whereas $g(x)$ is non-differentiable at 2 sharp turning points which are x_2 and x_5.

Further there is no common point of non-differentiability of $f(x)$ and $g(x)$. We know that the sum of a differentiable and non-differentiable function is always non-differentiable,

So $f(x) + g(x)$ are non-differentiable at exactly 7 points, which are $x_1, x_2, x_3, 0, x_4, x_5$ and x_6.

Ans. (a), (c).

67. If $f(x)$ and $g(x)$ are two functions such that $f(x)$ is differentiable at $x = a$ and $g(x)$ is non-differentiable at x = a, then the product function $f(x) \,.\, g(x)$ can be differentiable if the derivative of differentiable function is zero.

$f(x)$ is non-differentiable at each integer x, also at

$$x = n + \frac{1}{3},\ n + \frac{1}{2},\ n + \frac{2}{3}\ \ \forall n \in \mathbb{Z}.$$

Also $g(x)$ has its derivative 0 at each integer x.

So $f(x) \,.\, g(x)$ is differentiable at each integer x and non-differentiable at

$$x = n + \frac{1}{3},\ n + \frac{1}{2},\ n + \frac{2}{3}\ \ \forall n \in \mathbb{Z}.$$

$\therefore$ (b), (c), (d) should be correct options.

Assertion and Reason Type

The questions given below consist of an assertion (A) and the reason (R). Use the following key to choose the appropriate answer.

(a) If both assertion and reason are correct and reason is the correct explanation of the assertion.

(b) If both assertion and reason are correct but reason is not correct explanation of the assertion.

(c) If assertion is correct, but reason is incorrect

(d) If assertion is incorrect, but reason is correct

Now consider the following statements:

68. Consider the functions $f(x) = x^2 - 2x$ and $g(x) = -|x|$

A: The composite function $F(x) = f(g(x))$ is not derivable at $x = 0$.

R: $f'(0^+) = 2$ and $f'(0^-) = -2$.

Ans. (a)

Solution: $f(x) = f(g(x)) = (g(x))^2 - 2g(x) = |x|^2 + 2|x|$

$$= \begin{cases} x^2 + 2x; & x \ge 0 \\ x^2 - 2x; & x < 0 \end{cases}$$

$$\Rightarrow f'(x) = \begin{cases} 2x + 2; & x \ge 0 \\ 2x - 2; & x < 0 \end{cases}$$

Clearly $F(x)$ is continuous at $x = 0$ but $f'(0^-) = -2$ and $f'(0^+) = 2$

$\therefore$ $F(x) = f(g(x))$ is non-differentiable at $x = 0$

$\therefore$ Assertion as well as reason both are correct and reason explains the assertion.

69. Consider the function $f(x) = x^2 - |x^2 - 1| + 2\,||x| - 1| + 2\,|x| - 7$.

A: f is not differentiable at $x = 1, -1$ and 0.

R: $|x|$ is not differentiable at $x = 0$ and $|x^2 - 1|$ is not differentiable at $x = 1$ and -1.

Ans. (d)

Solution: $|x|$ is not differentiable at $x = 0$ and $|x^2 - 1|$ is not differentiable at $x = \pm 1$

So reason is correct

Now

$$f(x) = \begin{cases} x^2 - x^2 + 1 - 2x - 2 - 2x - 7; & x \le -1 \\ x^2 + x^2 - 1 + 2x + 2 - 2x - 7; & -1 < x \le 0 \\ x^2 + x^2 - 1 - 2x + 2 + 2x - 7; & 0 < x \le 1 \\ x^2 - x^2 + 1 + 2x - 2 + 2x - 7 & x > 1 \end{cases}$$

$$\Rightarrow f(x)=\begin{cases}-4x-8; & x\le -1\\ 2x^2-6; & -1<x\le 0\\ 2x^2-6; & 0<x\le 1\\ 4x-8; & x>1\end{cases}$$

$$\Rightarrow f'(x)=\begin{cases}-4; & x<-1\\ 4x; & -1<x<1\\ 4: & x>1\end{cases}$$

Clearly $f(x)$ is continuous at " $x \in \mathbb{R}$

$\therefore$ $f(x)$ is derivable at $x = -1$ and 1

$\therefore$ Assertion is wrong but reason is correct.

70. Consider the function $f(x)=\lim\limits_{n\to\infty}\dfrac{\sin \pi x - x^{2n}\sin(x-1)}{1+x^{2n+1}-x^{2n}}$; where $n \in \mathbb{N}$

A: $f(x)$ is discontinuous at $x = 1$.

R: $f(1) = 0$.

Ans. **(b)**

Solution: $\begin{cases}\sin \pi x; & x<1\\ 0; & x=1\end{cases}$; and for $x > 1$;

$$f(x)=\frac{x^{-2n}\sin \pi x-\sin(x-1)}{x^{-2n}+x-1}=\frac{\sin(x-1)}{1-x}$$

$$\Rightarrow \lim_{x\to 1^-}\sin(\pi x)=0 \text{ and } \lim_{x\to 1^+}\frac{\sin(x-1)}{-(x-1)}=-1$$

$\Rightarrow$ L.H.L. $\neq$ R.H.L.

$\therefore$ $f(x)$ is discontinuous at $x = 1$, Also $f(1) = 0$, but it does not explains the reason.

Thus (b) should be the correct option.

71. Consider the functions $f(x) = \text{sgn}(x - 1)$ and $g(x) = \cot^{-1}[x - 1]$

A: The function $F(x) = f(x).\ g(x)$ is discontinuous at $x = 1$.

R: If $f(x)$ is discontinuous at $x = a$ and $g(x)$ is also discontinuous at $x = a$ then the product function $f(x).\ g(x)$ is discontinuous at $x = a$.

Ans. **(c)**

Solution: $f(x) = \text{sgn}(x - 1)$; $g(x) = \cot^{-1}[x - 1]$

$$\therefore F(x) = f(x)\ .\ g(x) = \begin{cases}-\cot^{-1}[x+1]; & x<1\\ 0; & x=1\\ \cot^{-1}[x-1]; & x>1\end{cases}$$

$$=\begin{cases}-\cot^{-1}(-1); & x<1\\ 0; & x=1\\ \cot^{-1}(0); & x>1\end{cases}=\begin{cases}-(\pi-\cot^{-1}1); & x<1\\ 0; & x=1\\ \pi/2; & x>1\end{cases}$$

$$=\begin{cases}-\dfrac{3\pi}{4}; & x<1\\ 0; & x=1\\ \dfrac{\pi}{2}; & x>1\end{cases}$$

$$\Rightarrow f(1^-)=-\frac{3\pi}{4};\ F(1^+)=\frac{\pi}{2} \text{ and } F(1)=0$$

$\Rightarrow$ $f(x)$ is discontinuous at $x = 1$

$\therefore$ **Assertion is correct but product of two discontinuous functions may be *a* continuous function. So reason is wrong.**

72. A: If the series represented by function $f(x) = x^2 + x^4 + x^6 + x^8 + \ldots$ converges, then function $g(x) = [x]$ (gint function) is continuous at one fixed point of $f(x)$.

R: $f(x) = x$

$\Rightarrow$ $x^2 + x - 1 = 0$ which gives two fixed points.

Ans. **(c)**

Solution: Given infinite series is $f(x) = x^2 + x^4 + x^6 + x^8 + \ldots = \dfrac{x^2}{1-x^2}$

($\because$ series converges $\Rightarrow |x^2| < 1 \Rightarrow -1 < x < 1$)

Now at fixed points $f(x) = x$

$$\Rightarrow \frac{x^2}{1-x^2}=x$$

$\Rightarrow x^2 = x - x^3$ $\quad\Rightarrow x^3 + x^2 - x = 0$

$\Rightarrow x(x^2 + x - 1) = 0$ $\quad\Rightarrow x = 0$ or $x^2 + x - 1 = 0$

$$\Rightarrow x=\frac{-1\pm\sqrt{1+4}}{2}=\frac{-1\pm\sqrt{5}}{2}$$

$$\Rightarrow x=\frac{\sqrt{5}-1}{2}\quad\left(\because \frac{-1-\sqrt{5}}{2}<-1\right)$$

$\therefore$ there are two fixed points $x = \dfrac{\sqrt{5}-1}{2} \notin \mathbb{Z}$ and $x = 0$.

$\therefore$ $g(x) = [x]$ is continuous only at one fixed point $\dfrac{\sqrt{5}-1}{2}$ and discontinuous at $x = 0$

$\therefore$ **Assertion is correct, reason is incorrect.**

$\therefore$ Ans. (c)

73. A: There is no polynomial function f such that $f(x + y) = f(x) + yf(f(x))$ " $x, y \in \mathbb{R}$

R: $f'(x) = f(f(x))$. If f is of degree n, then the equation $n\ 1 = n^2$ has no positive integer solution

Ans. **(a)**

Solution: $f'(x) = \lim_{h\to 0} \dfrac{f(x+h)-f(x)}{h}$

$= \lim_{h\to 0} \dfrac{f(x)+hf(f(x))-f(x)}{h}$

$= \lim_{h\to 0} \dfrac{hf(f(x))}{h} = f(f(x))$ ...(i)

Let $f(x)$ be of degree n and let $f(x) = a_0x^n + a_1x^{n-1} + a_2x^{n-2} + \ldots + a_{n-1}x + a_n$

$f'(x) = na_0x^{n-1} + a_1(n-1)x^{n-2} + \ldots + a_{n-1}$ and

$f(f(x)) = a_0(f(x))^n + a_1(f(x))^{n-1} + \ldots + a_{n-1} f(x) + a_n$

$\therefore$ If $f((x)) = f'(x)$, then degree of both polynomials must be same

$\Rightarrow n - 1 = n^2 \qquad \Rightarrow n^2 - n + 1 = 0$

which has no root as disc. $= -3$

$\therefore$ Reason and assertion both are correct.

Solved Integer Type

74 Let $f(x) = [3 + 4 \sin x]$ (where [ ] denotes the greatest integer function). If sum of all the values of 'x' in $[\pi, 2\pi]$ where $f(x)$ fails to be differentiable, is $\dfrac{k\pi}{2}$, then find the value of k.

Solution: $f(x) = [3 + 4 \sin x] = 3 + [4 \sin x]$

For $\pi \le x \le 3\pi$; $-1 \le \sin x \le 0 \quad 4 \le 4 \sin x \le 0$

$\therefore$ [4 sin x] and hence $f(x)$ is possibly non-differentiable, where 4 sin x takes integer values

i.e., when $4 \sin x = -4, -3, -2, -1, 0$

i.e., when $\sin x = -1, -\dfrac{3}{4}, \dfrac{-1}{2}, \dfrac{-1}{4}, 0$

Graph of [4 sin x] for $x \in [\pi, 2\pi]$ is as shown below

$\therefore f(x)$ is non-differentiable $x_0 = \pi$,

$x_1 = \pi + \sin^{-1}\left(\dfrac{-1}{4}\right) \qquad x_2 = \pi + \sin^{-1}\left(\dfrac{1}{2}\right)$

$x_3 = \pi + \sin^{-1}\left(\dfrac{3}{4}\right) \qquad x_4 = 2\pi - \sin^{-1}\left(\dfrac{3}{4}\right)$

$x_5 = 2\pi - \sin^{-1}\left(\dfrac{1}{2}\right) \qquad x_6 = 2\pi - \sin^{-1}\left(\dfrac{1}{4}\right)$

$x_7 = 2\pi$

$\therefore$ Sum of points of non-differentiability $= 12\pi = \dfrac{\pi k}{2}$ (given)

$\Rightarrow k = 24.$

75. If $f(x) = \cos x + |\cos x|$; then evaluate $\left|f'\left(\dfrac{\pi^+}{2}\right) + f'\left(\dfrac{\pi^-}{2}\right)\right|$.

Solution: $f(x) = \cos x + |\cos x|$

$$= \begin{cases} 2\cos x; & for\ \dfrac{-\pi}{2} < x \le \dfrac{\pi}{2} \\ 0; & for\ \dfrac{\pi}{2} \le x \le \dfrac{3\pi}{2} \end{cases}$$

$\therefore$ L.H.D. $= f'\left(\dfrac{\pi^-}{2}\right) = \lim_{h\to 0^+} \dfrac{f\left(\dfrac{\pi}{2}-h\right) - f\left(\dfrac{\pi}{2}\right)}{-h}$

$= \lim_{h\to 0^+} \dfrac{2\cos\left(\dfrac{\pi}{2}-h\right) - 0}{-h} = \lim_{h\to 0^+} \dfrac{2\sin h}{-h} = -2$

and R.H.D. $= f'\left(\dfrac{\pi^+}{2}\right) = \lim_{h\to 0^+} \dfrac{f\left(\dfrac{\pi}{2}+h\right) - f\left(\dfrac{\pi}{2}\right)}{h}$

$= \lim_{h\to 0^+} \dfrac{0-0}{h} = 0$

$\therefore$ |L.H.D. + R.H.D.|

$= \left|f'\left(\dfrac{\pi^-}{2}\right) + f'\left(\dfrac{\pi^+}{2}\right)\right| = |-2+0| = 2$

76. For the function

$$f(x) = \begin{cases} \ln\left(e\left|[x]+[-x]\right|\right)\left(\dfrac{2^{\frac{\{x\}+\{-x\}}{||}}\quad 5}{\overline{||}}\right); & \text{for } x < 0 \\ 0; & \text{for } x = 0 \\ x.\dfrac{^{|x|\ \ \{x\}}}{|x|\ \ \{x\}}; & \text{for } x \quad 0 \end{cases};$$

evaluate $\dfrac{|f'(0^-)|}{|f'(0^+)|}$.

Solution: L.H.D $=$ f'(0⁻) $= \lim_{h\to 0^+} \dfrac{f(-h)-f(0)}{-h}$

$= \lim_{h\to 0^+} \dfrac{f(-h)}{-h}$

$= \lim_{h\to 0^+} \dfrac{\ln\left(e|[-h]+[h]|\right)^{-h}\left(\dfrac{2e^{\frac{\{-h\}+\{h\}}{h}}-5}{3+e^{1/h}}\right)}{-h}$

$= \lim_{h\to 0^+} \dfrac{\ln\left(e|-1|\right)^{-h}\left(\dfrac{2e^{1/h}-5}{3+e^{1/h}}\right)}{-h}$

$\{\because [h] + [-h] = -1$ for $h \notin \mathbb{Z}$

and $\{h\} + \{-h\} = 1$ for $h \notin \mathbb{Z}$ }

$$= \lim_{h\to 0^+} \frac{-h \ln e\left(\frac{2e^{1/h}-5}{3+e^{1/h}}\right)}{-h} = \lim_{h\to 0^+}\left(\frac{2e^{1/h}-5}{3+e^{1/h}}\right)$$

$$= \lim_{h\to 0^+}\left(\frac{2-5e^{-1/h}}{3e^{-1/h}+1}\right) = 2$$

Now, RHD. $= f'(0^+) = \lim_{h\to 0^+} \frac{f(h)-f(0)}{h} = \lim_{h\to 0^+} \frac{f(h)}{h}$

$$= \lim_{h\to 0^+} \frac{h.\frac{1-e^{|h|+\{h\}}}{|h|+\{h\}}}{h} = \lim_{h\to 0^+} \frac{1-e^{h+h}}{h+h} = \lim_{h\to 0^+} \frac{1-e^{2h}}{2h} = -1$$

$$\therefore \frac{|f'(0^-)|}{|f'(0^+)|} = \frac{2}{1} = 2.$$

77. Find the number of points at which the function $f(x) = [x-1] + [x-2]$ is not differentiable in the interval $[0, 3]$.

Solution: $f(x) = [x-1] + |x-2|$

Here $|x-2|$ is *a* continuous function, where as $[x-1]$ is discontinuous at $x = 0, 1, 2$, in $[0, 3]$

Further the sum of *a* continuous and *a* discontinuous function is again *a* discontinuous function.

So $f(x)$ is discontinuous as well as non-differentiable at $x = 0, 1, 2$.

Also $|x-2|$ is non-differentiable at $x = 2$ only point in $[0, 3]$.

Also $[x-1]$ is non-differentiable at $x = 2$.

But sum of two non-differentiable functions may be differentiable, but here due to discontinuity, $f(x)$ definitely has *a* non-differentiability. So $f(x)$ is non-differentiable in $[0, 3]$ at exactly 3 points.

78. Find the total number of points of discontinuity and non-differentiability of function $f(x) = \frac{1}{2} - x + \frac{1}{2}[2x] - \frac{1}{2}[1-2x]$ in $[0, 1]$.

Solution: $f(x) = \frac{1}{2} - x + \frac{1}{2}[2x] - \frac{1}{2}[1-2x]$

for $x \in [0, 1]$, $2x \in [0, 2]$

and $2x$ takes integer values 0, 1, 2 at $x = 0, \frac{1}{2}, 1$

Also for $x \in [0, 1]$; $(1-2x) \in [-1, 1]$ and $(1-2x)$ takes integer values $-1, 0, 1$ at $x = 1, \frac{1}{2}$ and 0 respectively.

So, we shall break the interval $[0, 1]$ at $x = |$

$$\therefore f(x) = \begin{cases} \frac{1}{2} - 0 + 0 - \frac{1}{2}; & x = 0 \\ \frac{1}{2} - x + \frac{1}{2}(0) - \frac{1}{2}(0); & 0 < x < \frac{1}{2} \\ \frac{1}{2} - \frac{1}{2} + \frac{1}{2}(1) - \frac{1}{2}(0); & x = \frac{1}{2} \\ \frac{1}{2} - x + \frac{1}{2}(1) - \frac{1}{2}(-1); & \frac{1}{2} < x < 1 \\ \frac{1}{2} - 1 + \frac{1}{2}(2) - \frac{1}{2}(-1); & x = 1 \end{cases}$$

$$\Rightarrow f(x) = \begin{cases} 0; & x = 0 \\ \frac{1}{2} - x; & 0 < x < \frac{1}{2} \\ \frac{1}{2}; & x = \frac{1}{2} \\ \frac{3}{2} - x; & \frac{1}{2} < x < 1 \\ 1; & x = 1 \end{cases}$$

$\therefore f(x)$ is discontinuous at $x = 0, \frac{1}{2}$ and 1 and

$$f'(x) = \begin{cases} -1; & 0 < x < \frac{1}{2} \\ -1; & \frac{1}{2} < x < 1 \end{cases}$$

$\Rightarrow f(x)$ is non-differentiable and discontinuous at $x = 0, \frac{1}{2}$ and 1 i.e., at 3 points.

79. Let f be *a* continuous function on $\mathbb{R}$. If $f\left(\frac{1}{5^n}\right) = (\cos e^n)5^{-n^2} + \frac{n^2}{n^2+n+5}$, then find $f(0)$.

Solution: $\because f(x)$ is continuous at $x = 0$

$$\Rightarrow f(0) = \lim_{n\to 0} f(x) = \lim_{n\to\infty} f\left(\frac{1}{5^n}\right)$$

$$= \lim_{n\to\infty}\left\{(\cos e^n)5^{-n^2} + \frac{n^2}{n^2+n+5}\right\}$$

$$= \lim_{n\to\infty}\left\{(k).\frac{1}{5^\infty} + \frac{1}{1+\frac{1}{n}+\frac{5}{n^2}}\right\}; \text{ where } k \in [-1, 1]$$

$= k(0) + 1 = 1$

TUTORIAL EXERCISE

SECTION–III

ONLY ONE CORRECT ANSWER

1. A function $f(x)$ is defined as $f(x) = \dfrac{\cos(\sin x) - \cos x}{x^2}$, $x \neq 0$, $f(0) = a$. If $f(x)$ is continuous at $x = 0$, then a is equal to
(a) 0 (b) 4
(c) 5 (d) 6

2. Among the following, which is false
(a) If f, g are any two continuous functions, then max, $\{f, g\}$; min. $\{f, g\}$ is also continuous
(b) If 'f' is continuous and g is discontinuous, then $f + g$ is discontinuous,
(c) If f is continuous and periodic in $[a, b]$, then it is bounded.
(d) A periodic function which is discontinuous cannot have its period of discontinuity as period of the function

3. If $f(x) = \begin{cases} -2\sin x & \text{for } -\pi \le x < -\dfrac{\pi}{2} \\ a\sin x + b & \text{for } -\dfrac{\pi}{2} \le x < \dfrac{\pi}{2} \\ \cos x & \text{for } \dfrac{\pi}{2} \le x \le \pi \end{cases}$ is continuous in the interval $[-\pi, \pi]$, then $(a, b) =$
(a) (1,– 1) (b) (–1,–1)
(c) (1,1) (d) (–1,1)

4. Let $[x]$ denotes the integral part of x, $g(x) = x - [x]$. Let $f(x)$ be any continuous function with $f(0) = f(1)$, then the function $h(x) = f(g(x))$:
(a) has finitely many discontinuities
(b) is discontinuous at some $x = c$
(c) is continuous on $\mathbb{R}$
(d) is a constant function

5. The number of points, where $f(x) = [\sin x + \cos x]$ (where [ ] denotes the greatest integer function), $x \in (0, 2\pi)$ is not continuous is:
(a) 3 (b) 4
(c) 5 (d) 6

6. A function $f(x) = e^{2x} + e^{x} - e$ is defined in interval [0, 1], then which of the following is true.
(a) $f(x) = 0$ has no root in [0,1]
(b) $f(x) = 0$ must have only one root in [0, 1]
(c) $f(x) = 0$ has more than one root in [0, 1]
(d) none of these

7. The jump of discontinuity of the function at the point of discontinuity i.e., $x = -2$ of the function $f(x) = \dfrac{|x+2|}{\tan^{-1}(x+2)}$ is
(a) 2 (b) 3
(c) 0 (d) 1

8. $f(x) = \dfrac{x^3}{4} - a\sin \pi x + 3$; $-4 \le x \le 4$; $a \in (0, 1)$. The value of $f(x)$ is $\dfrac{1999}{199}$ for some $x \in [-4, 4]$. This statement is
(a) true (b) false
(c) true only if $a \ge 0$ (d) true only if $a \in [-4, 4]$

9. If $f(x) = \begin{cases} x^2; & \text{if } x \text{ is rational} \\ -x^2 & \text{if } x \text{ is irrational} \end{cases}$; then
(a) f is continuous at $x = 0$
(b) f is continuous at $x = 2$
(c) f is discontinuous at $x = 0$
(d) f is continuous at $x = 1$

10. $f(x) = [x]$ and $g(x) = \begin{cases} 1, & x > 1 \\ 2, & x \le 1 \end{cases}$, (where [.] represents the greatest integer function). Then $g(f(x))$ is discontinuous at
(a) $x = 1$ (b) $x = 2$
(c) $x = 0$ (d) None of these

11. If $f(x) = \begin{cases} x+2; & x < 0 \\ -x^2 - 2; & 0 \le x < 1 \\ x; & x \ge 1 \end{cases}$, then the number of points of discontinuity of $|f(x)|$ is
(a) 1 (b) 2
(c) 3 (d) None of these

12. The correct statement for the function $f(x) = \begin{cases} x; & x \in Q \\ -x; & x \notin Q \end{cases}$ is

(a) continuous everywhere
(b) $f(x)$ is a periodic function
(c) Discontinuous every where except at $x = 0$
(d) $f(x)$ is an even function

13. Number of points of discontinuity of the function $f(x) = \lim_{n\to\infty} \dfrac{2\sin x}{3^n + (2\cos x)^{2n}}$ are given by

(a) 0 (b) 1
(c) infinite (d) None of these

14. If $f(x)$, $g(x)$ be differentiable functions and $f(1) = g(1) = 2$, then $\lim_{x\to 1} \dfrac{f(1)g(x) - f(x)g(1) - f(1) + g(1)}{g(x) - f(x)}$ is equal to

(a) 0 (b) 1
(c) 2 (d) None of these

15. If $f(3) = 6$ and $f'(3) = 2$, then $\lim_{x\to 3} \dfrac{x\, f(3) - 3f(x)}{x-3}$ is given by :

(a) 6 (b) 4
(c) 0 (d) None of these

16. $\lim_{h\to 0} \dfrac{\sin\sqrt{x+h} - \sin\sqrt{x}}{h}$ is equal to

(a) $\dfrac{\cos\sqrt{x}}{2\sqrt{x}}$ (b) $\sin\sqrt{x}$
(c) $\dfrac{1}{2\sin\sqrt{x}}$ (d) $\cos\sqrt{x}$

17. The function defined by $f(x) = \max\{x^2, (x-1)^2, 2x(1-x)\}$, $0 \le x \le 1$

(a) is differentiable for all x
(b) is differentiable for all x except at one point
(c) is differentiable for all x except at two points
(d) is not differentiable at more than two points

18. If both $f(x)$ and $g(x)$ are differentiable functions at $x = x_0$, then the function defined as, $h(x) = \text{maximum } \{f(x), g(x)\}$

(a) is always differentiable at $x = x_0$
(b) is never differentiable at $x = x_0$
(c) is differentiable at $x = x_0$ if $f(x_0) \ne g(x_0)$
(d) cannot be differentiable at $x = x_0$ if $f(x_0) = g(x_0)$

19. Let $f(x) = |x|$ and $g(x) = |x^3|$, then

(a) $f(x)$ and $g(x)$ both are continuous at $x = 0$
(b) $f(x)$ and $g(x)$ both are differentiable at $x = 0$
(c) $f(x)$ is differentiable but $g(x)$ is not differentiable at $x = 0$
(d) $f(x)$ and $g(x)$ both are not differentiable at $x = 0$

20. If $f(x)$ is twice differentiable function, then between two consecutive roots of the equation $f'(x) = 0$; then there exists

(a) more than one root of $f(x) = 0$
(b) at most one root of $f(x) = 0$
(c) exactly one root of $f(x) = 0$
(d) at most one root of $f''(x) = 0$

21. If $f(x) = \begin{cases} \sqrt{2}; & x \text{ is rational} \\ 1; & x \text{ is irrational} \end{cases}$; and $\phi(x) = [f(x)]$; ([ ] = G.I.F.); then which one is not true about $\phi(x)$.

(a) discontinuous $\forall\, x$
(b) continuous $\forall\, x$
(c) is differentiable $\forall\, x$
(d) is a periodic function

22. A mathematical minded scientist researched on the heart diseases of dolphins and recorded his finding in the coded language as "maximum number of heart attacks a dolphin can survive is equal to the number of sharp turns without jump in the graph of $f(x) = \dfrac{\tan x + \cot x}{2} - \left|\dfrac{\tan x - \cot x}{2}\right|$" (where $0 < x < 2\pi$). Try to decode his message and find the minimum number of heart attacks that will definitely result in the death of a dolphin.

(a) 2 (b) 3
(c) 4 (d) 5

23. $\lim_{h\to 0} \dfrac{2\left[\sqrt{3}\sin\left(\frac{\pi}{6}+h\right) - \cos\left(\frac{\pi}{6}+h\right)\right]}{\sqrt{3}h\left(\sqrt{3}\cos h - \sin h\right)}$ is equal to

(a) $-\dfrac{2}{3}$ (b) $-\dfrac{3}{4}$
(c) $-2\sqrt{3}$ (d) $\dfrac{4}{3}$

24. $f(x) = \begin{cases} a + \sin^{-1}(x+b), & x \ge 1 \\ x, & x < 1 \end{cases}$ is differentiable at $x = 1$, then

(a) $a = 1, b = 1$ (b) $a = -1, b = -1$
(c) $a = 1, b = -1$ (d) None of these

25. $f(x) = a\sin|x| + be^{|x|}$ is differentiable at $x = 0$, if and only if

(a) $a - b = 0$ (b) $a = 0$
(c) $a + b = 0$ (d) $b = 0$

26. Let $f(x) = x^3 - x^2 + x + 1$ and $g(x) = \begin{cases} \max\{f(t) \text{ for } 0 \le t \le x\}; & \text{for } 0 \le x \le 1 \\ 3 - x + x^2; & \text{for } 1 < x \le 2 \end{cases}$, then:

(a) $g(x)$ is cont. and derivable at $x = 1$
(b) $g(x)$ is cont. but not derivable at $x = 1$
(c) $g(x)$ is neither continuous nor derivable at $x = 1$
(d) $g(x)$ is derivable but not continuous at $x = 1$

27. If $H'(1) = 1$, $g'(1) = 2$; $H(1) = 1$, $g(1) = 2$, then $\lim_{x\to1} \dfrac{H(x) \cdot g(1) - g(x) \cdot H(1)}{\sin(x-1)}$ is equal to

(a) 1 (b) 0
(c) 1/2 (d) 2

28. Number of points where the function $f(x) = \max(|\tan x|, \cos|x|)$ is non-differentiable in the interval $(-\pi, \pi)$ is

(a) 4 (b) 6
(c) 3 (d) 2

29. The function $f(x) = \text{maximum}\left\{\sqrt{x(2-x)}, 2-x\right\}$ is non-differentiable at x equal to:

(a) 1 (b) 0, 2
(c) 0, 1 (d) 1,2

30. A function $f: \mathbb{R} \to \mathbb{R}$ is defined as $f(x) = 15 - |x - 10|$. The number of points at which the function $g(x) = f(f(x))$ is not differentiable is

(a) 0 (b) 1
(c) 2 (d) 3

31. A function $f(x) = x\,[1 + (1/3)\sin(\ln x^2)]$, $x \ne 0$. [ ] = integral part; $f(0) = 0$. Then the function:

(a) is continuous at $x = 0$
(b) is monotonic
(c) is derivable at $x = 0$
(d) cannot be defined for $x < -1$

32. If $f(x) = 3(2x + 3)^{2/3} + 2x + 3$, then which is false?

(a) $f(x)$ is cont. but not diff. at $x = -3/2$
(b) $f(x)$ is diff. at $x = 0$
(c) $f(x)$ is cont. at $x = 0$
(d) $f(x)$ is discontinuous and non-differentiable at $x = 0$

33. If $\sin^{-1}x + |y| = 2y$, then which one is false about y as a function of x.

(a) defined for $-1 \le x \le 1$
(b) continuous at $x = 0$
(c) differentiable for all x
(d) such that $\dfrac{dy}{dx} = \dfrac{1}{3\sqrt{1-x^2}}$ for $-1 < x < 0$

34. Which of the following functions is differentiable at $x = 0$?

(a) $\cos(|x|) + |x|$ (b) $\cos(|x|) - |x|$
(c) $\sin(|x|) + |x|$ (d) $\sin(|x|) - |x|$

35. Domain of the derivative of the function $f(x) = \begin{cases} \tan^{-1} x & \text{if } |x| \le 1 \\ \frac{1}{2}(|x| - 1) & \text{if } |x| > 1 \end{cases}$ is

(a) $\mathbb{R} - \{0\}$ (b) $\mathbb{R} - \{1\}$
(c) $\mathbb{R} - \{-1\}$ (d) $\mathbb{R} - \{-1, 1\}$

36. Let $f: \mathbb{R} \to \mathbb{R}$ be such that $f(1) = 3$ and $f'(1) = 6$. The $\lim_{x\to0}\left(\dfrac{f(1+x)}{f(1)}\right)^{1/x}$ equals

(a) 1 (b) $e^{1/2}$
(c) e^2 (d) e^3

37. If $|f(x_1) - f(x_2)| \le (x_1 - x_2)^2$, for all $x_1, x_2 \in \mathbb{R}$. The equation of tangent to the curve $y = f(x)$ at the point (1, 2) is

(a) $y = 1$ (b) $y = 3$
(c) $y = 2$ (d) none of these

38. If $f(x) = (1+x)(2+x)^{1/2}(3+|x^5|)^{1/5}$, then $f'(-1)$ is

(a) $(4)^{1/5}$ (b) $3^{1/5}.\sqrt{2}$
(c) 0 (d) does not exist

39. If $y = |x - a| + |x - b|$, then:

(a) $f(x)$ is continuous and differentiable at $x = a, b$
(b) $f(x)$ is continuous but not differentiable at $x = a, b$
(c) $f(x)$ is neither differentiable nor continuous at $x = a, b$
(d) None of these

40. If $f(x) = \int_{-1}^{x} |t|\,dt, x \ge -1$, then:

(a) f and f' are continuous for $x + 1 > 0$
(b) f is continuous but f' is not so for $x + 1 > 0$

(c) f and f' are not continuous at $x = 0$
(d) f is continuous at $x = 0$, but f' is not so

41. $y = ||x - 1| - 1| + 1$ is not differentiable at the points :
(a) (0, 0); (1, 1); (0, 2)
(b) (0, – 1); (1, 0); (2, 1)
(c) (1, 0); (1, 2); (1, – 2)
(d) (0, 1); (1, 2); (2, 1)

42. If $f(x) = \sin|x| - e^{|x|}$, then at $x = 0$, $f(x)$ is:
(a) Continuous but not differentiable
(b) Neither continuous nor differentiable
(c) Both continuous and differentiable
(d) None of these

43. The left hand derivative of $f(x) = [x] \sin \pi x$ at $x = k$, k an integer and [ ] is the greatest integer function is:
(a) $(-1)^k (k-1)\pi$ (b) $(-1)^{k-1}(k-1)\pi$
(c) $(-1)^k k\pi$ (d) $(-1)^{k-1} k\pi$

44. If $|f(x) - f(y)| \le |x - y|^{2n+1}$ ($n \in \mathbb{N}$), then $f'(x)$ is equal to:
(a) 0 (b) n
(c) nx (d) 1

45. The points of non-differentiability of the function $f(x) = |||x - 1| - 1| - 1|$ are :
(a) {0, 1, 2, 3, 4} (b) {– 1, 0, 1, 2, 3}
(c) {– 1, 0, 1} (d) None of these

46. If $f(x) = 1 - |x|$, the number of points where $f(f(x))$ ceases to be differentiable is :
(a) 0 (b) 1
(c) 2 (d) 3

47. The function $f(x) = \dfrac{|x| - x(3^{1/x} + 1)}{3^{1/x} - 1}$; $x \neq 0$, $f(0) = 0$ is:
(a) discontinuous at $x = 0$
(b) continuous at $x = 0$ but not differentiable there
(c) both continuous and differentiable at $x = 0$
(d) differentiable but not continuous at $x = 0$

48. Let [ ] denotes the greatest integer function and $f(x) = [\tan^2 x]$, then
(a) $\lim_{x\to 0} f(x)$ does not exist
(b) $f(x)$ is continuous at $x = 0$
(c) $f(x)$ is not differentiable at $x = 0$
(d) $f'(0) = 1$

49. Let $f(x) = \begin{cases} x^3; & x^2 < 1 \\ x; & x^2 \ge 1 \end{cases}$. Domain of $f'(x)$ is
(a) $(-\infty, \infty) - \{1\}$
(b) $(-\infty, \infty) - \{1, -1\}$
(c) $(-\infty, \infty) - \{1, -1, 0\}$
(d) $(-\infty, \infty) - \{-1\}$

50. $f(x) = \max.\{2 \sin x, 1 - \cos x\}$ $\forall x \in (0, \pi)$, then $f'(x)$ becomes zero at
(a) $x = \dfrac{5\pi}{12}$
(b) $x = x_0$, where $2\sin x_0 + \cos x_0 = 1$
(c) $x = \dfrac{\pi}{12}$
(d) $x = \dfrac{\pi}{2}$

51. Total number of critical points belonging to $[0, 2\pi]$ for the function $f(x) = \max.\{\sin x, \cos x, 1 - \cos x\}$ is
(a) 3 (b) 4
(c) 5 (d) 6

52. $f(x) = \begin{cases} xe^{-\left(\frac{1}{x}+\frac{1}{|x|}\right)}; & x \neq 0 \\ a; & x = 0 \end{cases}$. Value of '$a$' such that $f(x)$ is differentiable at $x = 0$, is equal to
(a) 1
(b) –1
(c) 0
(d) $f(x)$ cannot be made differentiable at $x = 0$

53. A function $f : \mathbb{R} \to \mathbb{R}^+$ satisfies $f(x + y) = f(x).f(y)$ $\forall x, y \in \mathbb{R}$. If $f'(0) = 2$, then $f'(x)$ is always equal to
(a) $f(x)$ (b) $2f(x)$
(c) $\dfrac{1}{f(x)}$ (d) $\dfrac{2}{f(x)}$

54. If $f(n+1) = \dfrac{1}{2}\left\{f(n) + \dfrac{9}{f(n)}\right\}$, $n \in \mathbb{N}$ and $f(n) > 0$ $\forall n \in \mathbb{N}$, then $\lim_{n\to\infty} f(n)$ is equal to
(a) 3
(b) –3
(c) 1/12
(d) None of these

SECTION–IV

MULTIPLE ANSWER CORRECT

1. State which of the following statements are true?
(a) All polynomials, trigonometrical functions, exponential and logarithmic functions are continuous in their domains.
(b) If $f(x)$ is continuous and $g(x)$ is discontinuous at $x = a$, then the product function $\phi(x) = f(x).g(x)$ is not necessarily be discontinuous at $x = a$.
(c) If $f(x)$ and $g(x)$ both are discontinuous at $x = a$, then the product function $\phi(x) = f(x).\ g(x)$ is not necessarily be discontinuous at $x = a$.
(d) None of these

2. The function $f(x) = \begin{cases} 1, & |x| \geq 1 \\ \frac{1}{n^2}, & \frac{1}{n} < |x| < \frac{1}{n-1}, n = 2, 3, ... \\ 0, & x = 0 \end{cases}$
(a) is discontinuous at many points
(b) is continuous every where
(c) is discontinuous at $x = \frac{1}{n}$, $n \in \mathbb{Z}-\{0\}$.
(d) $f(x)$ is continuous at $x = 0$

3. Which of the following function(s) has/have removable discontinuity at $x = 1$?
(a) $f(x) = \frac{1}{\ell n|x|}$ (b) $f(x) = \frac{x^2-1}{x^3-1}$
(c) $f(x) = 2^{-2^{\frac{1}{1-x}}}$ (d) $f(x) = \frac{\sqrt{x+1}-\sqrt{2x}}{x^2-x}$

4. Which of the following functions is/are continuous on $(0, \pi)$?
(a) $\tan x$
(b) $\int_0^x t \sin 1/t\ dt$
(c) $f(x) = \begin{cases} 1; & 0 < x < \frac{3\pi}{4} \\ 2\sin\left(\frac{2x}{9}\right); & \frac{3\pi}{4} \leq x \leq \pi \end{cases}$
(d) $f(x) = \begin{cases} x\sin x; & 0 < x \leq \frac{\pi}{2} \\ \frac{\pi}{2}\sin(\pi + x); & \frac{\pi}{2} < x < \pi \end{cases}$

5. Let $f(x) = \left[\frac{1}{x}[x]\right]$; $x \neq 0$, $f(0) = 0$, then ([ ] is the greatest integer function)
(a) f is not continuous at $x = 0$
(b) f is continuous at $x = 0$
(c) f is discontinuous at $x = 1$
(d) f is continuous at $x = 1$

6. If $f(x) = 0$ for $x < 0$ and $f(x)$ is differentiable at $x = 0$, then for $x > 0$, $f(x)$ may be
(a) x^2 (b) x
(c) $-x$ (d) $-x^{3/2}$

7. For the function $f(x) = (\pi - x)\frac{\cos x}{|\sin x|}$; $x \neq \pi$, $f(\pi) = 1$, which of the following statements are true?
(a) $f(\pi^-) = -1$
(b) $f(\pi^+) = 1$
(c) $f(x)$ is continuous at $x = \pi$
(d) $f(x)$ is differentiable at $x = \pi$

8. State which of the following statements are true.
(a) If $f(x)$ and $g(x)$ are derivable at $x = a$, then the functions $f(x) + g(x)$, $f(x) - g(x)$, $f(x).\ g(x)$ will also be derivable at $x = a$ and if $g(a) \neq 0$, then the function $f(x) / g(x)$ will also be derivable at $x = a$
(b) If $f(x)$ is differentiable at $x = a$ and $g(x)$ is not differentiable at $x = a$, then the product function $F(x) = f(x).g(x)$ can still be differentiable at $x = a$
(c) If $f(x)$ and $g(x)$ both are not differentiable at $x = a$, then the product function; $F(x) = f(x).\ g(x)$ can still be differentiable at $x = a$
(d) If $f(x)$ and $g(x)$ both are non-derivable at $x = a$, then the sum function $F(x) = f(x) + g(x)$ may be differentiable at $x = a$.
(e) If $f(x)$ is derivable at $x = a \Rightarrow f'(x)$ is continuous at $x = a$.

9. Given that the derivative $f'(a)$ exists. Indicate which of the following statements is/are always true
(a) $f'(a) = \lim_{h\to a}\frac{f(h)-f(a)}{h-a}$
(b) $f'(a) = \lim_{h\to 0}\frac{f(a)-f(a-h)}{h}$

(c) $f'(a) = \lim_{t\to 0} \frac{f(a+2t)-f(a)}{t}$

(d) $f'(a) = \lim_{t\to 0} \frac{f(a+2t)-f(a+t)}{2t}$

10. Let $f(x) = \cos x$ and

$$H(x) = \begin{cases} \min.\{f(t): 0 \le t \le x\}; & \text{for } 0 \le x \le \frac{\pi}{2} \\ \frac{\pi}{2} - x; & \text{for } \frac{\pi}{2} < x \le 3 \end{cases}, \text{ then}$$

(a) $H(x)$ is continuous and derivative in [0, 3]
(b) $H(x)$ is continuous but not derivable at $x = \pi/2$
(c) $H(x)$ is neither continuous nor derivable at $x = \pi/2$
(d) Maximum value of $H(x)$ in [0,3] is 1

11. $f(x) = |[x]x|$ in $-1 \le x \le 2$, where $[x]$ is greatest integer $\le x$, then $f(x)$ is:
(a) continuous at $x = 0$
(b) discontinuous $x = 0$
(c) non-differentiable at $x = 2$
(d) differentiable at $x = 2$

12. If $f(x) = \begin{cases} \frac{x \ln \cos x}{\ln(1+x^2)}; & x \ne 0 \\ 0; & x = 0 \end{cases}$; then
(a) $f(x)$ is not continuous at $x = 0$
(b) $f(x)$ is continuous at $x = 0$
(c) $f(x)$ is continuous at $x = 0$ but not differentiable at $x = 0$
(d) $f(x)$ is differentiable at $x = 0$

13. If $f(x) = [x \sin \pi x]$, then $f(x)$ is:
(a) continuous at $x = 0$
(b) continuous in $(-1, 0)$
(c) differentiable at $x = 0$
(d) differentiable at $(-1, 1)$

14. The function $f(x) = \begin{cases} |x-3|\,[x] & ; x \ge 1 \\ \sin\left(\frac{\pi x}{2}\right) & ; x < 1 \end{cases}$ ([.] denotes the greatest integer function)
(a) is continuous at $x = 0$
(b) is differentiable at $x = 0$
(c) is continuous but not differentiable at $x = 1$
(d) is continuous but not differentiable at $x = 3/2$

15. $f(x) = \frac{[x]+1}{\{x\}+1}$ for f: $[0, 5/2) \to (1/2, 3]$, where [.] represents greatest integer function and {.} represents fractional part of x, then which of the following is true?
(a) $f(x)$ is injective discontinuous function
(b) $f(x)$ is surjective non-differentiable function
(c) max. $\left(\lim_{x\to 1^-} f(x), \lim_{x\to 1^+} f(x)\right) = f(1)$
(d) min{x : x is *a* point of discontinuity} = 1

16. If $f(x) = \begin{cases} \max\{x, x^2\}; & x \ge 0 \\ \min\{2x, x^2-1\}; & x < 0 \end{cases}$
(a) $f(x)$ is not differentiable at $x = 1 - \sqrt{2}$
(b) $f(x)$ is not differentiable at $x = 1$
(c) $f(x)$ is continuous everywhere
(d) None of these

17. If $f(x) = \begin{cases} x^n \cdot \frac{e^{1/x}}{1+e^{1/x}}; & x \ne 0 \\ 0; & x = 0 \end{cases}$; then
(a) if $n = 1$, function is continuous and differentiable
(b) if $n = 2$, function is continuous and differentiable
(c) if $n = 0$, function is discontinuous and non-differentiable
(d) None of these

18. The function $f(x) = [\sin x] \cos x$ is, ([ ] is the greatest integer function) :
(a) continuous function
(b) differentiable every where
(c) not differentiable at $x = 0$
(d) not differentiable at infinite points

19. The function $f(x) = (x - [x])\sin \pi x$ is :
(a) continuous everywhere
(b) differentiable every where
(c) differentiable at $x = 0$
(d) not differentiable at infinite number of points

20. Let $f(x) = \cos x$,

$$g(x) = \begin{cases} \min\{f(t): 0 \le t \le x\}; & x \in [0, \pi] \\ \sin x - 1; & x > \pi \end{cases}, \text{ then}$$

(a) $g(x)$ is discontinuous at $x = \pi$
(b) $g(x)$ is continuous for $x \in [0, \infty)$
(c) $g(x)$ has infinitely many critical points
(d) $g(x)$ is differentiable for $x \in [0, \infty) \sim \{\pi\}$

21. A function $f(x)$ satisfies the relation $f(x + y) = f(x) + f(y) + xy(x + y)\ \forall\ x, y \in \mathbb{R}$. If $f'(0) = -1$, then
(a) $f(x)$ is a polynomial function
(b) $f(x)$ is an exponential function
(c) $f(x)$ is twice differentiable for all $x \in \mathbb{R}$
(d) $f'(3) = 8$

SECTION–V

ASSERTION AND REASON TYPE

1. **A :** $f(x) = \sin^{-1}x + \text{cosec}^{-1}x$ is not continuous
R : If domain of $f(x)$ consists of finite number of points, then $f(x)$ is discontinuous.

2. **A :** Let $f(x) = x(x-1)$ and $g(x) = \text{sgn}(x)$, then $gof(x)$ is discontinuous at $x = 0, 1$
R : If $f(x)$ is continuous and $g(x)$ is continuous at all points except at $x = a$ and b, then $g(f(x))$ is discontinuous at all those points for which $f(x) = a$ and at all those points for which $f(x) = b$.

3. **A :** $|x^3|$ is differentiable at $x = 0$
R : If $f(x)$ is differentiable at $x = a$, then $|f(x)|$ is also differentiable at $x = a$

4. **A :** $f(x) = |x|. \sin x$ is differentiable at $x = 0$
R : If $f(x)$ is not differentiable and $g(x)$ is differentiable at $x = a$, then $f(x) . g(x)$ can still be differentiable at $x = a$.

5. **A :** Sum of left hand derivative and right hand derivative of $f(x) = |x^2 - 5x + 6|$ at $x = 2$ is equal to zero.
R : Sum of left hand derivative and right hand derivative of $f(x) = |(x-a)(x-b)|$ at $x = a$ (or b) is equal to zero, (where $a, b \in \mathbb{R}$)

6. Consider the following statements S and R:
A : $\tan x$ is decreasing function in the interval $\left(\frac{\pi}{2}, \pi\right)$
R : If $f(x)$ is a differentiable function with $f'(x) \neq 0$ in (a, b) and $f(x)$ is positive and increasing in (a, b) and $f'(x)$ is decreasing, then $\frac{f(x)}{f'(x)}$ is also increasing in (a, b).

SECTION–VI

COMPREHENSION TYPE

A : Among various properties of continuous, we have if f is continuous function on $[a, b]$ and $f(a)f(b) < 0$, then there exists a point c in (a, b) such that $f(c) = 0$ equivalently if continuous on $[a, b]$ and $x \in \mathbb{R}$ is such that $f(a) < x < f(b)$, then there is $c \in (a,b)$ such that $x = f(c)$. It follows from the above result that the image of a closed interval under a continuous function is a closed interval.

1. The number of continuous functions on $\mathbb{R}$ which satisfy $(f(x))^2 = x^2$ for all $x \in \mathbb{R}$ is
(a) 1 (b) 2
(c) 4 (d) 8

2. Suppose that $f(1/2) = 1$ and f is continuous on $[0, 1]$ assuming only rational value in the entire interval. The number of such functions is
(a) infinite (b) 2
(c) 4 (d) 1

3. Let f be a continuous function on $[-1, 1]$ satisfying $(f(x))^2 + x^2 = 1$ for all $x \in [-1, 1]$. The number of such functions is
(a) 2 (b) 1
(c) 4 (d) infinitely many

4. Let $f(x) = x, x \neq 0$ and $f(0) = 1$. Then
(a) f is a continuous function
(b) Range of f is an interval
(c) Range of f is $\mathbb{R}$
(d) None of these

B : A function $f(x)$ is said to have a jump discontinuity at a point $x = a$, if both of the limits L.H.L and R.H.L exists and finite at $x = a$ but not equal and $f(a)$ may be equal to either of these limits.
The value of |LHL – RHL| is known as jump of discontinuity.

5. Jump of discontinuity of $y = 2[x]$ at $x = 2$ is, (where [.] represents greatest integer function)
(a) 1 (b) 3
(c) 2 (d) –2

6. If $f(x) = \begin{cases} x^2 + 2; & x \leq 1 \\ 2x + 5; & x > 1 \end{cases}$, then jump of discontinuity of $f(x)$ at $x = 1$ is
(a) 4 (b) 3
(c) 7 (d) None of these

7. Number of jump discontinuities in $y = f(x) \cdot g(x)$, where $f(x) = \begin{cases} x+1; & x \ge 0 \\ x^2; & x < 0 \end{cases}$ and $g(x) = \begin{cases} \sin x; & x < 0 \\ 2x^2; & x \ge 0 \end{cases}$ is

(a) 1 (b) 2
(c) 3 (d) None of these

C: Let a function f be defined as
$$f(x) = \begin{cases} [x]; & -2 \le x \le -\frac{1}{2} \\ 2x^2 - 1; & -\frac{1}{2} < x \le 2 \end{cases}$$
, where [.] denotes greatest integer function . Answer the following question by using the above information

8. The number of points of discontinuity of $f(x)$ is

(a) 1 (b) 2
(c) 3 (d) None of these

9. The function $f(x - 1)$ is discontinuous at the points

(a) $-1, -\frac{1}{2}$ (b) $-\frac{1}{2}, 1$
(c) $0, \frac{1}{2}$ (d) 0, 1

10. Number of points where $|f(x)|$ is not differentiable is

(a) 1 (b) 2
(c) 3 (d) 4

D: In certain problem the differentiation of $\{f(x) \cdot g(x)\}$ appears. One student commits mistake and differentiates as $\frac{df}{dx} \cdot \frac{dg}{dx}$ but he gets correct result if $f(x) = x^3$ and $g(x)$ is a decreasing function for which $g(0) = 1/3$.

11. The function $g(x)$ is

(a) $\frac{3}{(x-3)^3}$ (b) $\frac{4}{(x-3)^3}$
(c) $\frac{-9}{(x-3)^3}$ (d) $\frac{27}{(x-3)^3}$

12. Derivative of $\{f(x - 3) \cdot g(x)\}$ with respect to x at $x = 100$ is

(a) 0 (b) 1
(c) – 1 (d) 2

13. $\lim\limits_{x \to 0} \frac{f(x).g(x)}{x(1+g(x))}$ will be

(a) 0 (b) –1
(c) 1 (d) 2

E: Left hand derivative and Right hand derivative of a function $f(x)$ at a point $x = a$ are defined as

$$f'(a^-) = \lim_{h \to 0^+} \frac{f(a) - f(a-h)}{h} = \lim_{h \to 0^-} \frac{f(a+h) - f(a)}{h} = \lim_{x \to a^-} \frac{f(x) - f(a)}{x - a}$$

and

$$f'(a^-) = \lim_{h \to 0^+} \frac{f(a+h) - f(a)}{h} = \lim_{h \to 0^-} \frac{f(a) - f(a-h)}{h} = \lim_{x \to a^+} \frac{f(a) - f(x)}{a - x}$$

respectively. Let f be a twice differentiable function. Then answer the following questions.

14. If f is odd, which of the following is right hand derivative of f at $x = -a$?

(a) $\lim\limits_{h \to 0^-} \frac{f(a-h) - f(a)}{-h}$

(b) $\lim\limits_{h \to 0^-} \frac{f(h-a) - f(a)}{h}$

(c) $\lim\limits_{h \to 0^+} \frac{f(a) + f(a-h)}{-h}$

(d) $\lim\limits_{h \to 0^-} \frac{f(-a) - f(-a-h)}{-h}$

15. If f is even, which of the following is right hand derivative of f' at $x = a$?

(a) $\lim\limits_{h \to 0^-} \frac{f'(a) + f'(-a+h)}{h}$

(b) $\lim\limits_{h \to 0^+} \frac{f'(a) + f'(-a-h)}{h}$

(c) $\lim\limits_{h \to 0^+} \frac{-f'(-a) + f'(-a-h)}{-h}$

(d) $\lim\limits_{h \to 0^+} \frac{f'(a) + f'(-a+h)}{-h}$

16. If $\lim\limits_{h \to 0} \frac{f(-x) - f(-x-h)}{h} = \lim\limits_{h \to 0} \frac{f(x) - f(x-h)}{-h}$; where h is real, then

(a) f is odd
(b) f is even
(c) f is neither odd nor even
(d) nothing can be concluded

F. Let us define $f : [-\pi, \pi] \to \mathbb{R}, g : [-\pi, \pi] \to \mathbb{R}$ by
$f(x) = \min. \{\sin x, \cos 2x\}$
$g(x) = \max. \{\sin x, \cos 2x\}$
Answer the following questions

17. Number of points where $f(x)$ is continuous but not differentiable is

(a) 2 (b) 3
(c) 1 (d) 0

18. Number of points where $|g(x)|$ is continuous but not differentiable is
(a) 2 (b) 3
(c) 4 (d) None of these

19. Range of $f(x)$ is
(a) $[-1/2, 1]$ (b) $[-1, 1/2]$
(c) $[-1, 1]$ (d) $[1/2, 1]$

20. Range of $g(x)$ is
(a) $[-1/2, 1]$ (b) $[-1, 1/2]$
(c) $[-1, 1]$ (d) $[1/2, 1]$

21. $f(x)$ is increasing in the interval
(a) $[-\pi, -\pi/2]$ (b) $[-\pi/2, \pi/6]$
(c) $[\pi/2, 5\pi/6]$ (d) $[-\pi/2, \pi/2]$

22. $g(x)$ is decreasing in the interval
(a) $[-\pi, -\pi/2]$ (b) $[0, \pi/6]$
(c) $[\pi/2, 5\pi/6]$ (d) $[-\pi, \pi/2]$

G: A function $f(x)$ having the following properties
(i) $f(x)$ is continuous except at $x = 3$
(ii) $f(x)$ is differentiable except at $x = -2$ and $x = 3$
(iii) $f(0) = 0, \lim_{x\to 3} f(x) \to -\infty, \lim_{x\to -\infty} f(x) = 3, \lim_{x\to\infty} f(x) = 0$
(iv) $f'(x) > 0\ \forall\ x \in (-\infty, 2) \cup (3, \infty)$ and $f'(x) \le 0\ \forall\ x \in (-2, 3)$
$f''(x) > 0\ \forall\ x \in (-\infty, -2) \cup (-2, 0)$ and $f''(x) < 0\ \forall\ x \in (0, 3) \cup (3, \infty)$, then answer the following questions

23. Maximum possible number of solutions of $f(x) = |x|$ is
(a) 2 (b) 1
(c) 3 (d) 4

24. Graph of function $y = f(-|x|)$ is
(a) differentiable for all x, if $f'(0) = 0$
(b) continuous but not differentiable at two points , if $f'(0) = 0$
(c) continuous but not differentiable at one points if $f'(0) = 0$
(d) discontinuous at two points if $f'(0) = 0$

25. $f(x) + 3x = 0$ has five solutions if
(a) $f(-2) > 6$
(b) $f'(0) < -3$ and $f(-2) > 6$
(c) $f'(0) > -3$
(d) $f'(0) > -3$ and $f(-2) > 6$

SECTION–VII

COLUMN-MATCHING TYPE

1. **Column-I**
For $x \in \mathbb{R}$
(i) $f(x) = \{\sin(\pi x)\}$ is discontinuous $\forall x \in$
(ii) $g(x) = \left\{\frac{\sin x}{x}\right\}$ is discontinuous $\forall x \in$
(iii) $h(x) = \left\{\frac{\sin x}{x}\right\}$ is continuous $\forall x \in$
(iv) $u(x) = \left\{\frac{\sin x}{x}\right\}$ is discontinuous function on set

Column-II
(a) $[0, 1)$
(b) $\{1,2\}$
(c) $\{0\}$
(d) $\left\{\frac{1}{2}\right\}$

2. List-I below gives functions while List-II gives their behavior at $x = 0$. Match the function in List-I with its behavior in List-II [….] denotes the greatest integer function

Column-I
(i) $[x]\,[1 + x]$
(ii) $[x]\,[1 - x]$
(iii) $[\text{sgn}\, x][2 - x]\,[1 + |x|]$
(iv) $[\cos x]$
(v) $[-x]\,[1 + x]$

Column-II
(a) Left continuous at $x = 0$
(b) Continuous at $x = 0$
(c) Right continuous at $x = 0$
(d) $\lim_{x\to 0} f(x)$ exists but $f(x)$ is discontinuous at $x = 0$
(e) $\lim_{x\to 0} f(x)$ does not exist and $f(x)$ is neither left continuous nor right continuous at $x = 0$.

3. **Column-I**
(i) Point of discontinuity of $y = \frac{1}{t^2 - t - 2}$; where $t = \frac{1}{x+1}$ is/are
(ii) Points of discontinuity of $y = [x] + [-x]$ is/are
(iii) $y = [\sin(\pi x)]$ is non-differentiable at

(iv) $f(x) = |2x + 1| + |x + 2| - |x + 1| - |x - 4|$ is non-differentiable at

Column-II

(a) $-\frac{1}{2}$

(b) -2

(c) -1

(d) 4

4. **Column-I**

(i) f; $[0, 2] \to [0, 8]$ is continuous, then the number of roots of equation $f(x) - x^3 = 0$ is

(ii) If $f(x)$ is derivable, then between the two consecutive roots of $f'(x) = 0$, the number of roots of $f(x) = 0$ is

(iii) The number of values of x at which $|2 - |x - 2||$ is not differentiable

(iv) If $f(x) = \begin{cases} x^2 \text{ if } x \text{ is rational} \\ 5x - 6 \text{ if } x \text{ is irrational} \end{cases}$ then the number of values of x at which $f(x)$ is continuous

Column-II

(a) exactly two

(b) at least one

(c) at most one

(d) exactly three

(e) more than one

5. **Column-I**

(i) Given $f(u) = \frac{1}{u + 2u - 3}$ where $u = \frac{1}{x+1}$, then f as a function of x is

(ii) If $f(x) = \text{sgn}(x - 1)(4 - x^2)$, then $f(x)$ is

(iii) If $\lim_{x\to 0} \frac{f(x)}{x}$ exists and $f(0) = 0$, then $f(x)$ is

(iv) The function $f(x) = \lim_{n\to\infty} \frac{nx - \text{sgn}\, x}{2 - n}$ *is*

Column-II

(a) a continuous function

(b) discontinuous at $x = -\frac{4}{3}, 0, -1$

(c) continuous at $x = 0$

(d) discontinuous function

(e) discontinuous at $x = 1, 2, -2$

6. **Column-I**

(i) The function $f(x) = |x^2 + (\lambda - 1)|x| - \lambda|$ is non-differentiable at five points for λ equals

(ii) The function defined by $f(x) = \begin{cases} \min.\left(|x|, \sqrt{1-x^2}\right); & -1 \le x \le 1 \\ \left(|x|\right); & 1 < |x| < 2 \end{cases}$ is non-differentiable at

(iii) $f(x) = |x + 1|(|x| + |x - 1|)$ is non-differentiable in interval $[-2, 2]$ at the points x equals

(iv) If $f\left(\frac{x+y}{2}\right) = \frac{f(x)+f(y)}{2}$ $\forall\, x, y \in \mathbb{R}$. If $f'(0) = -1$ and $f(0) = 1$, then $f(2)$ is less than or equal to

Column-II

(a) -1

(b) $-1/\sqrt{2}$

(c) $1/\sqrt{2}$

(d) 1

(t) 0

SECTION–VIII

SINGLE INTEGER TYPE

1. If $f(x) = \cos x + |\cos x|$, then evaluate $\left|f'\left(\frac{\pi^-}{2}\right) + f'\left(\frac{\pi^+}{2}\right)\right|$.

2. If $f(x) = \cos x$ and $g(x) = \begin{cases} \min.\{f(t); 0 \le t \le x\}; & \text{for } 0 \le x \le \frac{\pi}{2} \\ \frac{\pi}{2} - x; & \text{for } \frac{\pi}{2} < x \le 3 \end{cases}$; then answer

$\begin{cases} 1; \text{if } g(x) \text{ is continuous but not differentiable on } [0,3] \\ 2; \text{if } g(x) \text{ is discontinuous on } [0,3] \\ 3; \text{if } g(x) \text{ is discontinuous but derivative function is continuous on } [0,3] \\ 4; \text{ if } g(x) \text{ is differentiable on } [0,3] \end{cases}$

3. Find the greatest value of 'm' for which the function $f(x) = \begin{cases} x^{m/2} \sin\left(\frac{1}{x}\right); x \ne 0 \\ 0 \text{ if } x = 0 \end{cases}$ is continuous but not differentiable at $x = 0$

4. If a function $f(x)$ is such that $f(x+h) - f(x) \le 2h^2 \ \forall \ h$ and x real, and $f(2) = 7$, then evaluate $f(7)$

5. If $x = x_1, x_2, x_3$ are the points of discontinuity of function $f(u) = \dfrac{1}{u^2+u-2}$, where $u = \dfrac{1}{x-1}$, then evaluate $2|x_1 + x_2 + x_3|$

6. If $f(x) = x^2 - 2|x|$, then 'm' denotes the number of points of discontinuity of functions $g(x)$ and 'n' denotes the number of points of non-differentiability of $g(x)$, where $g(x) = \begin{cases} \min.\{f(t); -2 \le t \le x\}; -2 \le x < 0 \\ \max.\{f(t); 0 \le t \le x\}; 0 \le x \le 3 \end{cases}$, then evaluate $(m + n)$

7. If the graph of the function $y = f(x)$ has a unique tangent at point $(e^a, 0)$ (not vertical, non-horizontal) on the graph, then evaluate $\lim\limits_{x \to e^a} \dfrac{\ell n(1+9f(x)) - \tan(f(x))}{2f(x)}$.

8. If $f(x) = \dfrac{x^2 - bx + 25}{x^2 - 7x + 10}$; for $x \ne 5$ and f is continuous at $x = 5$, then evaluate $f(5)$:

9. Let $g(x) = \dfrac{(x-1)^n}{\ell n \cos^m (x-1)}; 0 < x < 2$, m and n are integers, $m \ne 0$, $n > 0$ and let p be the left hand derivative of $|x - 1|$ at $x = 1$. If $\lim\limits_{x \to 1^+} g(x) = p$, then evaluate $(m)^n$

10. Let $f(x) = \begin{cases} \dfrac{a|x^2 - x - 2|}{2 + x - x^2}; & \text{for } x < 2 \\ b; & \text{for } x = 2 \\ \dfrac{x - [x]}{x - 2}; & \text{for } x > 2 \end{cases}$ where [] denotes greatest integer function is continuous at $x = 2$, then evaluate $(1 - a)^2 + (1 - b)^2$

11. Let $[x]$ denotes the greatest integer function and $f(x)$ be defined as $f(x) = \begin{cases} \dfrac{(\exp\{(x+2)\ell n 4\})^{\frac{[x+1]}{4}} - 16}{4^x - 16}; & x < 2 \\ a.\dfrac{1 - \cos(x-2)}{(x-2)\tan(x-2)}; & x > 2 \end{cases}$

Find the value of a for which $f(x)$ may be continuous at $x = 2$

12. If $f(x) = \begin{cases} |4x - 5|[x]; \text{ for } x > 1 \\ [\cos \pi x] \text{ for } x \le 1 \end{cases}$; where [.] is gint function, then 'm' is the number of points of discontinuity of $f(x)$ and 'n' is the number of points of non-differentiability in [0,2], then evaluate $(m + n)$

13. If $f(x) = x + \{-x\} + [x]$, where $[x]$ and $\{x\}$ denotes greatest integer function and fractional part function respectively, then find the number of points at which $f(x)$ is both discontinuous and non-differentiable in $[-2, 2]$

14 Find the number of points at which the function $f(x) = \max.\{a - x, a + x, b\}; -\infty < x < \infty, 0 < a < b$ cannot be differentiable.

15. If $f(x)$ is derivable at $x = 5$; $f'(5) = 4$; then evaluate $\lim\limits_{h \to 0} \dfrac{f(5+h^3) - f(5-h^3)}{2h^3}$.

16. If $f(x) = \begin{cases} (\cos x - \sin x)^{\operatorname{cosec} x}; & \dfrac{-\pi}{2} < x < 0 \\ a & ; x = 0 \\ \dfrac{e^{1/x} + e^{2/x} + e^{3/x}}{ae^{2/x} + be^{3/x}} & ; 0 < x < \dfrac{\pi}{2} \end{cases}$ is continuous $\left(-\dfrac{\pi}{2}, \dfrac{\pi}{2}\right)$; then evaluate $(\ell nb - \ell na)$

17. If $f(x) = \dfrac{1 + \sin x - \cos x}{1 - \sin x - \cos x}, x \ne 0$ is continuous at $x = 0$, then find $|f(0)|$

18. Let $f(x)$ be a continuous function defined for $0 \le x \le 3$, If $f(x)$ takes irrational values for all x and $f(1) = \sqrt{2}$, then evaluate $f(1.5) . f(2.5)$

19. A function $f : \mathbb{R} \to \mathbb{R}$ is defined as $f(x) = \lim\limits_{n \to \infty} \dfrac{ax^2 + bx + c + e^{nx}}{1 + ce^{nx}}$, where $f(x)$ is continuous on $\mathbb{R}$. Then find the value of c.

20. Let the derivative function $f'(x)$is continuous on [2, 10]. If $f'(x)$ takes only rational values $\forall \ x$ and $f'(4) = 3$, then evaluate $f(5) - f(4)$

21. Let $f(x)$ is a differentiable function on [7, 10] and takes only irrational values, given $f(8) = \sqrt{3}$, then evaluate $\prod\limits_{k=7}^{10} f(k)$

22. Find the number of points where $f(x) = \dfrac{1}{\ell n[x^2 - 3x + 3]}$ is discontinuous.

23. If $g(x) = \begin{cases} \dfrac{1 - a^x + xa^x . \ell na}{x^2 a^x}, & x < 0 \\ \dfrac{(2a)^x - x\ell n 2a - 1}{x^2}, & x > 0 \end{cases}$; (where $a > 0$) is continuous at $x = 0$, and $a = \dfrac{1}{\sqrt{p}}, g(0) = \dfrac{1}{p^3}(\ell np)^2$, then evaluate p.

24. If $f(x)=\dfrac{\sin 3\pi x + A\sin 5\pi x + B\sin \pi x}{(x-1)^5}$ for $x \neq 1$ is continuous at $x = 1$, and $f(1) = \dfrac{p^2\pi^5}{(p+1)}$; then evaluate p.

25. If $f(x)=\begin{cases} a+\dfrac{\sin[x]}{x}; & x>0 \\ 2; & x=0 \\ b+\left[\dfrac{\sin x - x}{x^3}\right]; & x<0 \end{cases}$ (where [.] denotes the greatest integer function). If $f(x)$ is continuous at $x = 0$ and $b - a = k$, then evaluate k.

Answer Keys

SECTION-III

1. (a)	**2.** (d)	**3.** (d)	**4.** (c)	**5.** (c)	**6.** (b)	**7.** (a)	**8.** (a)	**9.** (a)	**10.** (b)
11. (a)	**12.** (c)	**13.** (a)	**14.** (c)	**15.** (c)	**16.** (a)	**17.** (c)	**18.** (c)	**19.** (a)	**20.** (b)
21. (a)	**22.** (c)	**23.** (d)	**24.** (c)	**25.** (c)	**26.** (c)	**27.** (b)	**28.** (a)	**29.** (a)	**30.** (d)
31. (a)	**32.** (d)	**33.** (c)	**34.** (d)	**35.** (d)	**36.** (c)	**37.** (c)	**38.** (a)	**39.** (b)	**40.** (a)
41. (d)	**42.** (c)	**43.** (a)	**44.** (a)	**45.** (b)	**46.** (d)	**47.** (c)	**48.** (b)	**49.** (b)	**50.** (d)
51. (d)	**52.** (d)	**53.** (b)	**54.** (a)						

SECTION-IV

1. (a,b,c)	**2.** (a,c,d)	**3.** (b,d)	**4.** (b,c)	**5.** (a,c)	**6.** (a,d)	**7.** (a,b)	**8.** (a,b,c,d,e)
9. (a,b)	**10.** (a,d)	**11.** (a,c)	**12.** (b,d)	**13.** (a,b,c,d)		**14.** (a,b)	**15.** (a,b,c,d)
16. (a,b)	**17.** (b,c)	**18.** (c,d)	**19.** (a,d)	**20.** (b,c,d)	**21.** (a,c,d)		

SECTION-V

1. (a)	**2.** (a)	**3.** (c)	**4.** (a)	**5.** (a)	**6.** (d)

SECTION-VI

1. (a)	**2.** (d)	**3.** (a)	**4.** (d)	**5.** (c)	**6.** (a)	**7.** (d)	**8.** (b)	**9.** (c)	**10.** (c)
11. (c)	**12.** (a)	**13.** (a)	**14.** (a)	**15.** (c)	**16.** (b)	**17.** (a)	**18.** (c)	**19.** (b)	**20.** (c)
21. (b,c)	**22.** (a,b,c)	**23.** (c)	**24.** (b)	**25.** (d)					

SECTION-VII

1. (i) → (b, c, d), (ii) → (c), (iii) → (b, d), (iv) → (a, c)

2. (i) → (a, b, c), (ii) → (c), (iii) → (e), (iv) → (d), (v) → (a)

3. (i) → (a, b), (ii) → (b, c, d), (iii) → (b, c, d), (iv) → (a, b, c, d)

4. (i) → (b), (ii) → (c), (iii) → (d, e), (iv) → (a, e)

5. (i) → (b, d), (ii) → (c, d, e), (iii) → (c), (iv) → (a, c)

6. (i) → (a, b), (ii) → (a,b,c,d), (iii) → (a,d,e) (iv) → (a,b,c,d,e)

SECTION-VIII

1. 2	**2.** 4	**3.** 2	**4.** 7	**5.** 7	**6.** 3	**7.** 4	**8.** 0	**9.** 4	**10.** 0
11. 1	**12.** 9	**13.** 5	**14.** 2	**15.** 4	**16.** 2	**17.** 1	**18.** 2	**19.** 1	**20.** 3
21. 9	**22.** 2	**23.** 2	**24.** 4	**25.** 1					

HINTS AND SOLUTIONS

TEXTUAL EXERCISE-1: (SUBJECTIVE)

1. (a) $f(x)\begin{cases} \dfrac{e^{1/x}-1}{e^{1/x}+1} & ; x \neq 0 \\ -1 & ; x=0 \end{cases}$

$$f(0^-) = \lim_{x\to 0^-} f(x) = \lim_{x\to 0^-}\left(\frac{e^{1/x}-1}{e^{1/x}+1}\right) = \frac{0-1}{0+1} = -1$$

$$f(0^+) = \lim_{x\to 0^+} f(x) = \lim_{x\to 0^+}\left(\frac{e^{1/x}-1}{e^{1/x}+1}\right) = \lim_{x\to 0^+}\left(\frac{1-e^{-1/x}}{1+e^{-1/x}}\right)$$

$$= \frac{1-0}{1+0} = 1$$

$\therefore$ L.H.L ≠ R.H.L

⇒ $f(x)$ has jump discontinuity at $x = 0$

(b) $f(x) = \begin{cases} \dfrac{[x^2]-1}{x^2-1} & ; x^2 \neq 1 \\ 0 & ; x^2 = 1 \end{cases}$

At $x = -1$

$$\text{L.H.L.} = \lim_{x\to -1^-} f(x) = \lim_{x\to(-1)^-}\frac{[x^2]-1}{x^2-1} = \lim_{x\to(-1)^-}\frac{1-1}{(x^2-1)} = 0$$

$$\text{R.H.L.} = \lim_{x\to(-1)^+} f(x) = \lim_{x\to(-1)^+}\frac{[x^2]-1}{x^2-1} = \lim_{h\to 0^+}\frac{[(-1+h)^2]-1}{(-1+h)^2-1}$$

$$= \lim_{h\to 0^+}\frac{[1+h^2-2h]-1}{h^2-2h} = \lim_{h\to 0^+}\frac{0-1}{h^2-2h} = 0$$

$$= \lim_{h\to 0^+}\frac{-1}{h(h-2)} = +\infty$$

$f(x)$ has infinite discontinuity at $x = -1$

At $x = 1$

$$\text{L.H.L.} = \lim_{x\to 1^-} f(x) = \lim_{x\to 1^-}\frac{[x^2]-1}{x^2-1} = \lim_{h\to 0^+}\frac{[(0-h)^2]-1}{(h^2-1)}$$

$$= \lim_{h\to 0^+}\frac{[h^2]-1}{(h^2-1)} = \frac{0-1}{0-1} = 1$$

$$\text{R.H.L.} = \lim_{x\to 1^+} f(x) = \lim_{x\to 1^+}\frac{[x^2]-1}{x^2-1}$$

$$= \lim_{h\to 0^+}\frac{[h^2]-1}{(h^2-1)} = \frac{0-1}{0-1} = 1 \text{ and } f(1) = 0$$

⇒ L.H.L. = R.H.L. ≠ $f(x)$

⇒ $f(x)$ has a removable discontinuity at $x = 1$

(c) $f(x) = \begin{cases} \dfrac{a^{2[x]+\{x\}}-1}{2[x]+\{x\}} & ; x \neq 0 \\ \ln a & ; x = 0 \end{cases}$

$$\text{L.H.L.} = \lim_{x\to 0^-} f(x) = \lim_{x\to 0^-}\frac{a^{2[x]+\{x\}}-1}{2[x]+\{x\}}$$

$$= \lim_{x\to 0^-}\frac{a^{-2+x-[x]}-1}{2(-1)+x-[x]} = \lim_{x\to 0^-}\frac{a^{-1+x}-1}{(-1+x)} = \frac{a^{-1}-1}{-1} = 1-a^{-1}$$

$$\text{R.H.L.} = \lim_{x\to 0^+} f(x) = \lim_{x\to 0^+}\frac{a^{x+[x]}-1}{x+[x]} = \lim_{x\to 0^+}\frac{a^x-1}{x} = \ln a$$

Thus L.H.L. ≠ R.H.L. = $f(x)$

⇒ $f(x)$ is a discontinuous function but right continuous at $x = 0$

2. $f(x) = \begin{cases} \dfrac{\sin(3p-1)x}{3x} & ; x < 0 \\ \dfrac{\tan(3p+1)x}{2x} & ; x > 0 \end{cases}$

$$\text{L.H.L.} = \lim_{x\to 0^-} f(x) = \lim_{x\to 0^-}\frac{\sin(3p-1)x}{3x}$$

$$= \lim_{x\to 0^-}\frac{\sin(3p-1)x}{(3p-1)x}\cdot\frac{(3p-1)}{3} = \frac{3p-1}{3}$$

$$\text{R.H.L.} = \lim_{x\to 0^+} f(x) = \lim_{x\to 0^+}\frac{\tan(3p+1)x}{2x}$$

$$= \lim_{x\to 0^+}\frac{\tan(3p+1)x}{(3p+1)x}\cdot\frac{(3p+1)}{2} = \frac{3p+1}{2}$$

For continuity at $x = 0$, L.H.L. = R.H.L.= $f(0)$

⇒ $\dfrac{3p-1}{3} = \dfrac{3p+1}{2}$ ⇒ $6p - 2 = 9p + 3$

⇒ $3p = -5$ ⇒ $p = -5/3$

$\therefore$ L.H.L. = R.H.L. = $f(0)$ $= \dfrac{3p+1}{2} = \dfrac{-5+1}{2} = -2$

3. $f(x) = \begin{cases} \dfrac{1-\sin\pi x}{1+\cos 2\pi x} & ; x < \dfrac{1}{2} \\ p & ; x = \dfrac{1}{2} \\ \dfrac{\sqrt{2x-1}}{\sqrt{4+\sqrt{2x-1}-2}} & ; x > \dfrac{1}{2} \end{cases}$

$$\text{L.H.L.} = \lim_{x\to\left(\frac{1}{2}\right)^-} f(x) = \lim_{x\to\left(\frac{1}{2}\right)^-}\frac{1-\sin\pi x}{1+\cos 2\pi x}$$

$$= \lim_{h\to 0^+}\frac{1-\sin\pi\left(\frac{1}{2}-h\right)}{1+\cos 2\pi\left(\frac{1}{2}-h\right)} = \lim_{h\to 0^+}\frac{1-\sin\left(\frac{\pi}{2}-\pi h\right)}{1+\cos(\pi-2\pi h)}$$

$$= \lim_{h\to 0^+}\frac{1-\cos\pi h}{1-\cos 2\pi h} = \lim_{h\to 0^+}\frac{2\sin^2\pi h/2}{2\sin^2\pi h}$$

$$= \lim_{h\to 0^+}\frac{\pi^2 h^2/4}{\pi^2 h^\pi} = \frac{1}{4}$$

$$\text{R.H.L.} = \lim_{x\to\left(\frac{1}{2}\right)^+} f(x) = \lim_{x\to\left(\frac{1}{2}\right)^+}\frac{\sqrt{2x-1}}{\sqrt{4+\sqrt{2x-1}-2}}$$

$$= \lim_{h\to 0^+}\frac{\sqrt{2\left(\frac{1}{2}+h\right)-1}}{\sqrt{4+\sqrt{2\left(\frac{1}{2}+h\right)-1}-2}}$$

$$= \lim_{h\to 0^+} \frac{\sqrt{1+2h-1}}{\sqrt{4+\sqrt{1+2h-1}-2}} = \lim_{h\to 0^+} \frac{\sqrt{2h}}{\sqrt{2h+4}-2}$$

$$= \lim_{h\to 0^+} \frac{\sqrt{2h}\left(\sqrt{\sqrt{2h}+4}+2\right)}{\sqrt{2h}} = 4$$

$\therefore$ For continuity at $x = \frac{1}{2}$; L.H.L = R.H.L = p

$\Rightarrow \quad \frac{1}{4} = 4 = p$; but it is impossible

$\therefore$ No value of p is possible

4. $$f(x) = \begin{cases} \dfrac{\left(\exp\{x+2\}\ln 4\right)^{\frac{[x+1]}{4}} - 16}{4x-16}; x<2 \\ a.\dfrac{1-\cos(x-2)}{(x-2)\tan(x-2)}; x>2 \end{cases}$$

$$\lim_{x\to 2^-} f(x) = \lim_{h\to 0^+}\left[\frac{\left(\exp.\{(4-h)\ln 4\}\right)^{\frac{[3-h]}{4}} - 16}{(4(2-h)-16)}\right]$$

$$= \lim_{h\to 0^+}\left[\frac{\left(\exp.\{(4-h)\ln 4\}\right)^{\frac{1}{2}} - 16}{-4(h+2)}\right]$$

$$= \lim_{h\to 0^+}\left[\frac{2^{(4-h)} - 16}{-4(h+2)}\right] = 0 \text{ and}$$

$$\lim_{x\to 2^+} f(x) = \lim_{h\to 0^+} a.\frac{1-\cos(h)}{h.\tan\ h} = \lim_{h\to 0^+} a\frac{\left(2\sin^2\frac{h}{2}\right)}{4.\frac{h^2}{4}.\frac{\tan\ h}{h}} = \lim_{h\to 0^+}\frac{2a}{4} = \frac{a}{2}$$

$\Rightarrow \quad \frac{a}{2} = 0$

$\Rightarrow \quad a = 0$ for continuity at $x = 2$ and $f(2) = 0$

5. $$f(x) = \begin{cases} \left(\dfrac{6}{5}\right)^{\frac{\tan 6x}{\tan 5x}} & \text{if } 0 < x < \dfrac{\pi}{2} \\ b+2 & \text{if } \quad x = \dfrac{\pi}{2}; \\ \left(1+|\cos x|\right)^{\left(\frac{a|\tan x|}{b}\right)} & \text{if } \dfrac{\pi}{2} < x < \pi \end{cases}$$

$$\lim_{x\to\left(\frac{\pi}{x}\right)^-} f(x) = \lim_{x\to\left(\frac{\pi}{2}\right)^-}\left(\frac{6}{5}\right)^{\frac{\tan 6x}{\tan 5x}} = \text{L}_1 \text{ (say)}$$

$$\Rightarrow \log_{\frac{6}{5}} \text{L}_1 = \lim_{x\to\frac{\pi}{2}^-}\left(\frac{\tan 6x}{\tan 5x}\right) = 0$$

$\Rightarrow \text{L}_1 = 1$

$$\lim_{x\to\left(\frac{\pi}{2}\right)^+} = \lim_{x\to\frac{\pi}{2}^+}\left(1+|\cos x|\right)^{\left(\frac{a|\tan x|}{b}\right)}$$

$$= e^{\lim_{x\to\left(\frac{\pi}{2}\right)^+}\left(|\cos x| \times \frac{a|\tan x|}{b}\right)} = e^{\lim_{x\to\frac{\pi}{2}^+}\frac{a}{b}\left(\frac{\sin x}{\cos x}\right).(\cos x)} = e^{\frac{b}{a}} \text{ and}$$

$$f\left(\frac{\pi}{2}\right) = b+2$$

$\Rightarrow$ For continuity at $x = \frac{\pi}{2}$; $b+2 = e^{\frac{a}{b}} = 1$

$\Rightarrow \quad a = 0,\ b \neq 2$ and $b = -1$

$\therefore \quad a = 0,\ b = -1$

6. $$f(x) = \begin{cases} x^2\sin\dfrac{1}{x} & \text{if } x \neq 0 \\ 0 & \text{if } x = 0 \end{cases}$$

$\because \quad x^{2/3} > x^2$ for $x \to 0$

$$\Rightarrow \quad -x^{2/3} < -x^2 \leq x^2\sin\frac{1}{x} \leq x^2\left|\sin\frac{1}{x}\right|$$

$\therefore$ Let $g(x) = -x^{2/3}; x \in (-1,1)$ and

$$h(x) = \begin{cases} x^2\left|\sin\dfrac{1}{x}\right|; x\in(-1,1); x\neq 0 \\ 0 \quad ; \quad x = 0 \end{cases}$$

Clearly $g(x) \leq f(x) \leq h(x)\ \forall x \in (-1,1)$;

Now $\lim_{x\to 0} g(x) = \lim_{x\to 0}\left(-x^{2/3}\right) = 0$ and

$$\lim_{x\to 0} h(x) = \lim_{x\to 0} x^2\left|\sin\frac{1}{x}\right| = 0$$

$\therefore$ By squeeze play theorem, $\lim_{x\to 0} f(x) = 0 = f(0)$

$\Rightarrow \quad f(x)$ is continuous at $x = 0$

7. $$f\left(\frac{\pi^-}{2}\right) = \lim_{x\to\left(\frac{\pi}{2}\right)^+}\left(\frac{1-\sin^3 x}{3\cos^2 x}\right)$$

$$= \lim_{x\to\left(\frac{\pi}{2}\right)^-}\left(\frac{(1-\sin x)(1+\sin^2 x+\sin x)}{3(1-\sin x)(1+\sin x)}\right)$$

$$= \frac{1}{3}\lim_{x\to\frac{\pi}{2}^-}\left(\frac{1+\sin^2 x+\sin x}{(1+\sin x)}\right) = \frac{1}{2} \text{ and}$$

$$f\left(\frac{\pi^+}{2}\right) = \lim_{x\to\frac{\pi}{2}^+}\left(\frac{b(1-\sin x)}{(\pi-2x)^2}\right)$$

Put $x = \frac{\pi}{2} + h \qquad \Rightarrow \qquad \pi - 2x = -2h;$

$$= \lim_{h\to 0^+}\frac{b\left(1-\sin\left(\frac{\pi}{2}+h\right)\right)}{4h^2} = \lim_{h\to 0^+}\frac{b(1-\cosh)}{4h^2}$$

$$= b\lim_{h\to^+}\left[\frac{2\sin^2\frac{h}{2}}{4\times\frac{h^2}{4}\times 4}\right] = \frac{b}{8}\lim_{h\to 0^+}\left(\frac{\sin\frac{h}{2}}{\frac{h}{2}}\right)^2 = \frac{b}{8}$$

Also $f\left(\frac{\pi}{2}\right)=a$,

$\therefore$ For continuity at, $x=\frac{\pi}{2}$, $\frac{1}{2}=\frac{b}{a}=a$

$\Rightarrow\ a=\frac{1}{2}, b=4$

8. $f(x)=\begin{cases}\dfrac{\sin(a+1)x+\sin x}{x} & \text{for } x<0\\ c & \text{for } x=0\\ \dfrac{\left(x+bx^2\right)^{1/2}-x^{1/2}}{bx^{3/2}} & \text{for } x>0\end{cases}$

$f(0^-)=\lim\limits_{x\to 0^-}\dfrac{\sin(a+1)x+\sin x}{x}$

$=\lim\limits_{x\to 0^-}(a+1)\cos(a+1)x+\cos x=a+2$

$f(0^+)=\lim\limits_{x\to 0^+}\dfrac{\left(x+bx^2\right)^{1/2}-x^{1/2}}{bx^{3/2}}(b\neq 0)$

$=\lim\limits_{x\to 0^+}\dfrac{bx^2}{bx^{3/2}\left[\sqrt{x+bx^2}+\sqrt{x}\right]}=\lim\limits_{x\to 0^+}\dfrac{1}{\left[\sqrt{1+bx}+1\right]}=\dfrac{1}{2}$

Also $f(0)=c$

$\therefore$ For continuity at $x=0, a+2=\frac{1}{2}=c$

$\Rightarrow\ a=-\frac{3}{2}, c=\frac{1}{2}, b\neq 0$

9. $f(x)=\begin{cases}ax-b & \text{for } x\le 1\\ 3x & \text{for } 1<x<2\\ bx^2-a & \text{for } x\ge 2\end{cases}$

$f(1^-)=a-b, f(1^+)=3$ and $f(1)=a-b$

$\therefore$ For continuity at a = 1, a – b = 3 …(i)

$f(2^-)=6; f(2^+)=4b-a$ and $f(2)=4b-a$

$\therefore$ For discontinuity at x = 2, $4b-a\neq 6$

$\Rightarrow$ $3b+(b-a)\neq 6$

$\Rightarrow$ $3b+(-3)\neq 6$ $\Rightarrow$ $3b\neq 9$

$\Rightarrow$ $b\neq 3$

$\therefore$ $a=b+3;\ b\neq 3$

$\therefore$ Locus of (a, b) is $y=x-3$ excluding the point (6, 3)

10. $f(x)=\left(\dfrac{2+\cos x}{x^3\sin x}-\dfrac{3}{x^4}\right)$

$\lim\limits_{x\to 0}f(x)=\lim\limits_{x\to 0}\left(\dfrac{2x+x\cos x-3\sin x}{x^4\sin x}\right)$

$=\lim\limits_{x\to 0}\left(\dfrac{2+(-x\sin x)+\cos x-3\cos x}{x^4\cos x+4x^3\sin x}\right)$

$=\lim\limits_{x\to 0}\left(\dfrac{2-x\sin x-2\cos x}{x^4\cos x+4x^3\sin x}\right)$

$=\lim\limits_{x\to 0}\left(\dfrac{-x\cos x-\sin x+2\sin x}{-x^4\sin x+(\cos x)4x^3+4x^3\cos x+4\sin x\left(3x^2\right)}\right)$

$=\lim\limits_{x\to 0}\left(\dfrac{-x\cos x+\sin x}{-x^4\sin x+8x^3\cos x+12x^2\sin x}\right)$

$=\lim\limits_{x\to 0}\left[\dfrac{x\sin x}{-x^4\cos x-12x^3\sin x+36x^2\cos x+24x\sin x}\right]$

$=\lim\limits_{x\to 0}\left[\dfrac{x\cos x+\sin x}{x^4\sin x-24x^3\cos x-4x^2(\cos x+9\sin x)+24(\sin x+4x\cos x)}\right]$

$=\dfrac{(1)+(1)}{72+24+24}=\dfrac{2}{120}=\dfrac{1}{60}$

$\Rightarrow$ For continuity at x = 0, $f(0)=\dfrac{1}{60}$

11. $\lim\limits_{x\to 0^-}f(x)=\lim\limits_{x\to 0^-}\dfrac{\cos^{-1}\left(1-\{x\}^2\right).\sin^{-1}(1-\{x\})}{\sqrt{2}(\{x\})(1+\{x\})(1-\{x\})}$

$=\dfrac{\cos^{-1}(0).(1)}{\sqrt{2}(1)(1+1)}=\dfrac{\pi}{4\sqrt{2}}$ and $\lim\limits_{x\to 0^+}f(x)$

$=\lim\limits_{x\to 0^+}\dfrac{\cos^{-1}\left(1-\{x\}^2\right)\sin^{-1}(1-\{x\})}{\sqrt{2}\{x\}(1+\{x\})(1-\{x\})}$

$=\lim\limits_{x\to 0^+}\dfrac{\cos^{-1}\left(1-\{x\}^2\right)}{\sqrt{2}\{x\}.2}\dfrac{\pi}{2(1)(1)}=\dfrac{\pi}{2\sqrt{2}}\lim\limits_{x\to 0^+}\dfrac{\cos^{-1}\left(1-\{x\}^2\right)}{\{x\}}$

$=\dfrac{\pi}{2\sqrt{2}}\lim\limits_{x\to 0^+}\dfrac{\cos^{-1}\left(1-x^2\right)}{x}=\dfrac{\pi}{2\sqrt{2}}\lim\limits_{x\to 0^+}\dfrac{-1}{\sqrt{1-\left(1-x^2\right)^2}}\cdot\left(\dfrac{-2x}{1}\right)$

$=\dfrac{\pi}{\sqrt{2}}\lim\limits_{x\to 0^+}\dfrac{x}{\sqrt{2x^2-x^4}}=\dfrac{\pi}{2}$

$\therefore$ L.H.L $=\dfrac{\pi}{4\sqrt{2}}$, R.H.L. $=\dfrac{\pi}{2}$, f is discontinuous at x = 0

Next, $g(x)=\begin{cases}f(x); & x\ge 0\\ 2\sqrt{2}f(x); & x<0\end{cases}$

Clearly $g\left(0^+\right)=f\left(0^+\right)=\dfrac{\pi}{2}$ and $g\left(0^-\right)=2\sqrt{2};f\left(0^-\right)=\dfrac{\pi}{2}$

and $g(0)=f(0)=\dfrac{\pi}{2}$ (Given)

$\Rightarrow$ $f(x)$ is continuous at, x = 0

12. **(i)** $\lim\limits_{x\to 0}f(x)=\lim\limits_{x\to 0}\dfrac{1}{1+2^{\cot x}}$

$\lim\limits_{x\to 0^+}\dfrac{1}{1+2^{\cot x}}=0,\ \lim\limits_{x\to 0^-}\dfrac{1}{1+2^{\cot x}}=1$

$\Rightarrow$ $f(x)$ has a jump or non removable discontinuity at x = 0

(ii) $f(x)=\cos\left(\left|\dfrac{\sin x}{x}\right|\right)=\cos\left(\dfrac{\sin x}{x}\right)$

$\lim\limits_{x\to 0}f(x)=\cos\left(\lim\limits_{x\to 0}\left(\dfrac{\sin x}{x}\right)\right)=\cos 1$; but $f(0)$ is not

discontinuity at x = 0

(iii) $f(x) = x\sin\frac{\pi}{x}$

$\lim_{x\to0} f(x) = \lim_{x\to0} x\sin\left(\frac{\pi}{x}\right) = 0\times$ (Finite number between -1 and 1) = 0;
$f(0)$ = Not defined

$\Rightarrow$ Removable discontinuity at $x = 0$

(iv) $f(x) = \frac{1}{\ln|x|}$

$\lim_{x\to0} f(x) = \lim_{x\to0}\frac{1}{\ln|x|} = 0$, but $f(0)$ is not defined

$\Rightarrow$ Removable discontinuity at $x = 0$

13. $f(x) = \begin{cases}(1+ax)^{\frac{1}{x}} & ;x<0\\ b & ;x=0\\ \dfrac{(x+c)^{\frac{1}{3}}-1}{(x+1)^{\frac{1}{2}}-1} & ;x>0\end{cases}$

$f(0^-) = \lim_{x\to0^-}(1+ax)^{\frac{1}{x}} = e^a;$

$f(0^+) = \lim_{x\to0^-}\frac{(x+c)^{\frac{1}{3}}-1}{(x+1)^{\frac{1}{2}}-1}$ = Finite

$\Rightarrow c = 1$

$\Rightarrow f(0^+) = \lim_{x\to0^+}\frac{(x+1)^{\frac{1}{3}}-(1)^{\frac{1}{3}}}{(x+1)^{\frac{1}{2}}-(1)^{\frac{1}{2}}} = \frac{\left(\frac{1}{3}\right)}{\frac{1}{2}} = \frac{2}{3}$

$\therefore$ For continuity at $x = 0$, $e^a = b = \frac{2}{3}$

$\Rightarrow a = \ln\left(\frac{2}{3}\right), b = \frac{2}{3}, c = 1$

14. $f(x)\begin{cases}\dfrac{e^{\frac{1}{(x-1)}}-2}{e^{\frac{1}{(x-1)}}+2} & ;x\ne1\\ 1 & ;x=1\end{cases}$; $f(1^-) = \lim_{h\to0^+}\frac{e^{-\frac{1}{h}}-2}{e^{-\frac{1}{h}}+2} = -1,$

$f(1^+) = \lim_{x\to0}\frac{e^{\frac{1}{h}}-2}{e^{\frac{1}{h}}+2} = \frac{1-2e^{-\frac{1}{h}}}{1+2e^{-\frac{1}{h}}} = 1$ and $f(1) = 1$

$\Rightarrow f(x)$ is discontinuous at $x = 1$

TEXTUAL EXERCISE–1: (OBJECTIVE)

1. (d) $\because$ discontinuity exists due to

(i) Non-existence of limit i.e., Either L.H.L $\neq$ R.H.L or any one of these are infinite or does not exist uniquely.

(ii) $\lim_{x\to a} f(x) \neq f(a)$ and all polynomials are continuous function whatever may be its degree.

2. (a) $f(0^-) = f(0^+) = f(0) = a$

$\Rightarrow \lim_{x\to0}\frac{\cos(\sin x)-\cos x}{x^2} = a$

$= \lim_{x\to0}\frac{-\sin(\sin x).\cos x+\sin x}{2x}$

$= \lim_{x\to0}\frac{\left[\sin x.\sin(\sin x)-\cos^2 x\cos(\sin x)+\cos x\right]}{2} = 0$

$\Rightarrow a = 0$

3. (d) $f(x) = [x]^2 - [x^2]$ and let $k\in\mathbb{Z}$, then

$f(k^-) = (k-1)^2 - \lim_{n\to k^-}[x^2]$ and $f(k^+) = k^2 - \lim_{h\to0^+}[x^2]$

$\Rightarrow f(k^-) = (k-1)^2 - \lim_{h\to0^+}\left[(k-h)^2\right]$

and $f(k^+) = k^2 - \lim_{h\to0^+}\left[(k+h)^2\right]$ and

$f(k) = k^2 - [k^2] = k^2 - k^2 = 0$

$\therefore$ For continuity at k;

$(k-1)^2 - \lim_{h\to0^+}\left[(k-h)^2\right] = k^2$

$-\lim_{h\to0^+}\left[(k+h)^2\right] = k^2 - [k^2] = 0$

$\Rightarrow (k-1)^2 = \lim_{h\to0^+}\left[(k-h)^2\right]$ and $(k)^2 = \lim_{h\to0^+}\left[(k+h)^2\right]$

$\Rightarrow (k-1)^2 < (k+h)^2 < (k-1)^2 + 1$ and $k^2 < (k+h)^2 < k^2 + 1$ for $h\to0^+$

$\Rightarrow 1-2k < h^2 - 2kh < 2 - 2k$ and $0 < h^2 + 2kh < 1$ for $h\to0^+$

$\Rightarrow 1 < (h^2 - 2kh + 2k) < 2$ and $k\geq0$; $h\to0^+$

For $k = 1$, $1 < h^2 - 2h + 2 < 2$

i.e., $1 < (h-1)^2 + 1 < 2$ which is true.

For $k = 2$, $1 < h^2 - 4h + 4 < 2$

i.e., $1 < (h-2)^2 < 2$ which is false as $(h-2)^2\in(3, 4)$

$\therefore k \not> 2 \qquad \Rightarrow k = 1$

$\Rightarrow f(x)$ is discontinuous us at all integers except for $k = 1$

4. (d) $f(x) = \left|\left(x+\frac{1}{2}\right)[x]\right|; -2\leq x\leq 2,$

Let $k\in\mathbb{Z}$ and $k\in\{-2, -1, 0, 1, 2\}$

$f(k^+) = \lim_{x\to k^-}\left|\left(x+\frac{1}{2}\right)(k-1)\right| = \left|\left(k+\frac{1}{2}\right)(k-1)\right|$

$f(k^+) = \lim_{x\to k^+}\left|\left(x+\frac{1}{2}\right)k\right| = \left|\left(k+\frac{1}{2}\right)k\right|$ and $f(k)$

$= \left|\left(k+\frac{1}{2}\right)k\right|$

For continuity at $x = -2$,

$\left|\left(-2+\frac{1}{2}\right)(-2)\right| = \left|\left(-2+\frac{1}{2}\right)(-2)\right|$; Which is true.

For continuity at $x = 2$,

$\left|\left(2+\frac{1}{2}\right)(2-1)\right| = \left|\left(2+\frac{1}{2}\right)(2)\right|$; Which is false

$\Rightarrow f(x)$ is discontinuous at $x = 2$

For continuity *at* – 1, 0, or 1

$\left|\left(k+\frac{1}{2}\right)(k-1)\right| = \left|\left(k+\frac{1}{2}\right)(k)\right|$

$\Rightarrow |(k-1)| = |k| \qquad \Rightarrow (k-1) = \pm k$

$\Rightarrow 2k = 1$ i.e., $k = 1/2 \notin \mathbb{Z}$

$\therefore f(x)$ is discontinuous at $x = -1, 0, 1, 2$

5. (c) $f(x) = \lim\limits_{m\to\infty} \dfrac{x^m f(1) + h(x) + 1}{2x^m + 3x + 3}$

$g(1) = \lim\limits_{x\to 1}\{1 + \ell n x\}^{\frac{2}{\ell n x}} = e^2$

$= \lim\limits_{x\to 1^-} f(x) = \lim\limits_{\substack{x\to 1\\ m\to\infty}} \dfrac{x^m f(1) + h(x) + 1}{(2x^m + 3x + 3)} = \dfrac{h(1)+1}{6} = f(1)$

Also $\lim\limits_{x\to 1^+} f(x) = \dfrac{f(1)}{2}$

$\Rightarrow f(1) = 0, h(1) = -1$

$\therefore 2g(1) + 2f(1) - h(1) = 2e^2 + 2(0) - (-1) = 2e^2 + 1$

6. (c) $f(0^-) = 1$; $f(0) = 2$; $f(0^+) = 2$

$\Rightarrow f(x)$ is right continuous at $x = 0$, but left discontinuous at $x = 0$.

Also $f(x)$ has a jump discontinuity.

7. (c) $f(x) = \begin{cases} \tan\dfrac{\pi x}{2}; x < 1 \\ x - 1; 1 \le x < 2, \\ \dfrac{1}{2-x}; x \ge 2 \end{cases}$

$f(1^-) = \lim\limits_{x\to 1^-} \dfrac{\tan \pi x}{2} = \infty$

$f(1^+) = \lim\limits_{x\to 1^+} (x - 1) = 0$

$f(1) = 0$

$\Rightarrow f(x)$ has an infinite discontinuity at $x = 1$

8. (a) $f(x) = \begin{cases} x^2; x \le 0 \\ 2; 0 < x < 1 \\ \dfrac{\sin(x-1)}{(x-1)}; x \ge 1 \end{cases}$

$f(0^-) = 0; f(0^+) = 2; f(0) = 0$

$\Rightarrow f(x)$ is discontinuous at $x = 0$ having jump discontinuity at $x = 0$.

Also $f(1^-) = 2, f(1^+) = 1$ and not defined at $x = 1$

$\Rightarrow f(x)$ has a jump discontinuity at $x = 1$

9. (d) $f(x) = |2 \sin x| + 2$ function is continuous

10. (c) $f(x) = \sin \dfrac{1}{x}$

$\lim\limits_{x\to 0} f(x)$ does not exist as it is not unique as it oscillates between -1 and 1 i.e., having oscillatory discontinuity.

11. (a) $f(-2^-) = \lim\limits_{x\to(-2)^-} f(x) = \lim\limits_{x\to 2^-} \dfrac{|x+2|}{\tan^{-1}(x+2)}$

$= \lim\limits_{h\to 0^+} \dfrac{|(-2-h+2)|}{\tan^{-1}(-2-h+2)} = \lim\limits_{h\to 0^+} \dfrac{h}{\tan^{-1}(-h)} = -1$

$= f(-2^+) = \lim\limits_{x\to(-2)^+} f(x) = \lim\limits_{h\to 0^+} \dfrac{|-2+h+2|}{\tan^{-1}(h)} = 1$

$\Rightarrow f(x)$ has a jump discontinuity at $x = -2$ having jump $= |1 - (-1)| = 2$

12. (a) $f(x) = \lim\limits_{n\to\infty} \dfrac{\cos \pi x - x^{2n}\sin(x-1)}{1 + x^{2n+1} - x^{2n}}$

$\Rightarrow f(1^-) = \lim\limits_{\substack{x\to 1^-\\ n\to\infty}} \dfrac{\cos \pi x - x^{2n}\sin(x-1)}{1 + x^{2n+1} - x^{2n}}$

$\Rightarrow f(1^+) = \lim\limits_{\substack{x\to 1^+\\ n\to\infty}} \dfrac{\cos \pi x - x^{2n}\sin(x-1)}{1 + x^{2n+1} - x^{2n}}$

$= \lim\limits_{\substack{h\to 0^+\\ n\to\infty}} \dfrac{\cos \pi(1+h) - (1+h)^{2n}\sin(h)}{1 + (1+h)^{2n+1} - (1+h)^{2n}}$

$= \lim\limits_{\substack{h\to 0^+\\ n\to\infty}} \dfrac{-\cos \pi h - (1+h)^{2n}\sinh}{1 + (1+h)^{2n}(1+h-1)}$

$= \lim\limits_{\substack{h\to 0^+\\ n\to\infty}} \dfrac{-\cos \pi h - (\sin h)(1+h)^{2n}}{1 + h(1+h)^{2n}} = \lim\limits_{\substack{h\to 0^+\\ n\to\infty}}$

13. (b) $g(x) = \tan^{-1}|x| - \cot^{-1}|x|$,

$f(x) = \dfrac{[x]}{[x+1]}\{x\}$, $h(x) = |g(f(x))|$

Note that $h(x) = |g(f(x))|$ is not defined for $[x + 1] = 0$

$\Rightarrow [x] \ne -1$ i.e., $x \notin [-1, 0)$

Also $h(0) = |g(f(0))| = |g(0)| = \tan^{-1} 0 - \cot^{-1} 0 = 0 - \dfrac{\pi}{2} = -\dfrac{\pi}{2}$; $h(0^+) = \lim\limits_{x\to 0^+} |g(f(x))|$

$= \lim\limits_{x\to 0^+} |\tan^{-1}|f(x)| - \cot^{-1}|f(x)||$

$= \lim\limits_{x\to 0^+} \left|\tan^{-1}\left|\dfrac{[x]}{[x+1]}\{x\}\right| - \cot^{-1}\left|\dfrac{[x]}{[x+1]}\{x\}\right|\right|$

$= |\tan^{-1} 0 - \cot^{-1} 0| = |0 - \dfrac{\pi}{2}| = \dfrac{\pi}{2}$

$\Rightarrow h(0) = -\dfrac{\pi}{2}, h(0^+) = \dfrac{\pi}{2}$

$\Rightarrow h(x)$ is discontinuous at $x = 0$ and $h(0^+) = \dfrac{\pi}{2}$

14. (b) $f(x) = \lim\limits_{n\to\infty} \left(\dfrac{x^n - \sin x^n}{x^n + \sin x^n}\right)$

$f(1^-) = \lim\limits_{\substack{x\to 1^-\\ n\to\infty}} \left(\dfrac{x^n - \sin x^n}{x^n + \sin x^n}\right) = \lim\limits_{\substack{x\to 1^-\\ n\to\infty}} \left(\dfrac{1 - \dfrac{\sin x^n}{x^n}}{1 + \dfrac{\sin x^n}{x^n}}\right)$

$= \lim\limits_{h\to 0^+} \left(\dfrac{1 - \dfrac{\sin h}{h}}{1 + \dfrac{\sin h}{h}}\right) = \dfrac{1-1}{1+1} = 0$

$f(1^+) = \lim\limits_{\substack{x\to 1^+\\ n\to\infty}} \left(\dfrac{x^n - \sin x^n}{x^n + \sin x^n}\right) = \lim\limits_{\substack{x\to 1^+\\ n\to\infty}} \left(\dfrac{1 - \dfrac{\sin x^n}{x^n}}{1 + \dfrac{\sin x^n}{x^n}}\right) = \dfrac{1-0}{1+0} = 1$

and $f(1) = 0 \Rightarrow f(x)$ has a finite discontinuity at $x = 1$

15. (a) $f(x) = \begin{cases} \dfrac{[\{|x|\}]e^{x^2}\{[x+\{x\}]\}}{\left(e^{\frac{1}{x^2}}-1\right)\operatorname{sgn}(\sin x)}; x \neq 0 \\ 0 \qquad ; x = 0 \end{cases}$

$f(0^-) = 0$ and $f(0^+) = 0$ and $f(0) = 0$

$\Rightarrow f(x)$ is continuous at $x = 0$

16. (d) $f(x) = \begin{cases} x[x]^2 \log_{(1+x)} 2; -1 < x < 0 \\ \dfrac{\ell n\left(e^{x^2} + 2\sqrt{\{x\}}\right)}{\tan\sqrt{x}}; 0 < x < 1 \end{cases}$

$f(0^-) = \lim_{x \to 0^-} x[x^2]\log_{(1+x)} 2 = \lim_{x \to 0^-} x\log_{(1+x)} 2 = 0$, as $\log_{(1+x)} 2$ is finite;

$f(0^+) = \lim_{x \to 0^+}\left[\dfrac{\ell n\left(e^{x^2}+2\sqrt{\{x\}}\right)}{\tan\sqrt{x}}\right] = \lim_{x \to 0^+}\left[\dfrac{\ell n\left(e^{x^2}+2\sqrt{x}\right)}{\tan\sqrt{x}}\right]$

$= \lim_{x \to 0^+}\left[\dfrac{1}{e^{x^2}+2\sqrt{x}}\dfrac{\left(2xe^{x^2}+\dfrac{1}{\sqrt{x}}\right)}{\left(\sec^2\sqrt{x}\right)\left(\dfrac{1}{2}\sqrt{x}\right)}\right]$

$= \lim_{x \to 0^+}\left[\dfrac{1}{e^{x^2}+2\sqrt{x}}\cdot\dfrac{2.\left(2x\sqrt{x}e^{x^2}+1\right)}{\sec^2\sqrt{x}}\right]$

$= \lim_{x \to 0^+}\left[\dfrac{2(1)}{(1)(1)}\right] = 2$

$\therefore\ f(0^-) \neq f(0^+)$

$\Rightarrow f(x)$ has an irremovable discontinuity at $x = 0$.

17. (a) $f(x) = \dfrac{\sqrt{1+x}-\sqrt{1-x}}{\{x\}}$ for $x \neq 0$;

$g(x) = \cos 2x$ for $\dfrac{-\pi}{4} < x < 0$;

$h(x) = \begin{cases} \dfrac{1}{\sqrt{2}} f(g(x)); x < 0 \\ 1 \quad ; x = 0 \\ f(x) \ ; x > 0 \end{cases}$

Domain function $(-1, 1) - \{0\}$

$f(-x) = \dfrac{\sqrt{1-x}-\sqrt{1+x}}{\{-x\}} \qquad (\because x \in (-1,1))$

$= \dfrac{-\left(\sqrt{1+x}-\sqrt{1-x}\right)}{1-\{x\}} \neq f(x)$

$f(g(x)) = \dfrac{\sqrt{1+g(x)}-\sqrt{1-g(x)}}{\{g(x)\}}$

$= \dfrac{\sqrt{1+\cos 2x}-\sqrt{1-\cos 2x}}{\{\cos 2x\}}; \dfrac{-\pi}{2} < 2x < 0$

$\therefore \quad \cos 2x \in (0, 1) \qquad \Rightarrow \{\cos 2x\} = \cos 2x$

$= \dfrac{\sqrt{2\cos^2 x}-\sqrt{2\sin^2 x}}{\cos 2x} = \dfrac{\sqrt{2}(|\cos x|-|\sin x|)}{\left(\cos^2 x-\sin^2 x\right)}$

$= \dfrac{\sqrt{2}}{(\cos x-\sin x)}$ for $x \in \left(\dfrac{-\pi}{4}, 0\right)$

$\Rightarrow f(g(x))$ is not even.

$h(0) = 1$;

$h(0^+) = \lim_{x \to 0^+} f(x) = \lim_{x \to 0^+}\dfrac{\sqrt{1+x}-\sqrt{1-x}}{x}$

$= \lim_{x \to 0^+}\dfrac{2}{\sqrt{1+x}+\sqrt{1-x}} = 1$;

$h(0^-) = \lim_{x \to 0^-}\dfrac{1}{\sqrt{2}} f(g(x))$

$= \lim_{x \to 0^-}\dfrac{1}{\sqrt{2}}\left[\dfrac{\sqrt{2}}{\cos x-\sin x}\right] = 1$

Thus $h(0^+) = h(0^-) = h(0) = 1$

$\Rightarrow h(x)$ is continuous at $x = 0$

18. (b) $f(x) = \begin{cases} \dfrac{x}{[x]}; 1 \le x < 2 \\ 1 \ ; x = 2; \\ \sqrt{6-x} \ ; 2 < x \le 3 \end{cases}$

$f(2^-) = \lim_{x \to 2^-}\dfrac{x}{[x]} = \lim_{x \to 2^-} x = 2$;

$f(2) = 1; f(2^+) = \lim_{x \to 2^+}\sqrt{6-x} = 2$

$\therefore\ f(x)$ has a isolated point removable discontinuity.

19. (c) $f(x) = \dfrac{1}{x+(2)^{\frac{1}{x-2}}}, x \neq 2$

$f(2^-) = \lim_{x \to 2^-}\dfrac{1}{x+(2)^{\frac{1}{x-2}}} = \lim_{h \to 0^+}\dfrac{1}{(2-h)+(2)^{\frac{1}{2-h-2}}}$

$= \lim_{h \to 0^+}\dfrac{1}{(2-h)+(2)^{-1/h}} = \dfrac{1}{2}$;

$f(2^+) = \lim_{x \to 2^+}\dfrac{1}{x+(2)^{\frac{1}{x-2}}} = \lim_{h \to 0^+}\dfrac{1}{(2+h)+(2h)^{\frac{1}{h}}} = 0$

$f(x)$ can't be continuous at $x = 2$

20. (d) $f(x) = \begin{cases} \log_{(4x-3)}\left(x^2-2x+5\right); \dfrac{3}{4} < x < 1 \text{ or } x > 1 \\ 4 \qquad ; x = 1 \end{cases}$

$f(1^-) = \lim_{x \to 1^-}\log_{(4x-3)}\left(x^2-2x+5\right) = \lim_{h \to 0^+}\log_{1-4h}\left(h^2+4\right)$

Which does not exist uniquely. Also $f(1^+)$

$= \lim_{x \to 1^+}\log_{4x-3}\left(x^2-2x+5\right) = \lim_{x \to 0^+}\log_{1+4h}\left(h^2+4\right)$

Which also does not exist uniquely.

Thus $f(x)$ is discontinuous at $x = 1$

Since $f(1^-)$ and (1^+) does not exist.

TEXTUAL EXERCISE–2: (SUBJECTIVE)

1. $f(-2^-) = 3(-2) + 2 = -4;$
$f(-2^+) = f(-2) = -4;$
$f(1^-) = 2;\ f(1^+) = 3$
$\Rightarrow f(x)$ is continuous every where in $(-3, 2)$ expect at $x = 1$

2. **(a)** $\because f(x)$ is continuous at $x = 0$
$\Rightarrow f(0) = \lim_{h\to 0^+} f(-h) = \lim_{h\to 0^+} f(h)$
$\Rightarrow f(0) = -\lim_{h\to 0^+} f(h) = \lim_{h\to 0^+} f(h) = L$ $\quad (\because f(x)$ is odd$)$
$\Rightarrow f(0) = -L = L$
$\Rightarrow f(0) = L = 0$
$\Rightarrow f(0) = 0$

(b) **(i)** $f : \mathbb{R} \to \mathbb{R}$; such that $f(x + y) = f(x) + f(y)\ \forall\ x, y \in \mathbb{R}$
$\because f(x)$ is continuous at 'a'
$\Rightarrow \lim_{h\to 0} f(a+h) = f(a)$
$\Rightarrow \lim_{h\to 0} f(a) + f(h) = f(a)$
$\Rightarrow \lim_{h\to 0} f(h) = 0$
Let $x = k \in \mathbb{R}$, then $\lim_{h\to 0} f(k+h) = \lim_{h\to 0}(f(k) + f(h))$
$= \lim_{h\to 0} f(k) + \lim_{h\to 0} f(h) = f(k)$
$\Rightarrow f(x)$ is continuous at $x = k$
$\therefore f(x)$ is continuous $\forall\ x \in \mathbb{R}$
(ii) As a special case of part (i), $a = 0$ concludes the result.

3. $f(x) = \begin{cases} [\cos \pi x]; x \le 1 \\ |2x-3|[x-2]; x > 1 \end{cases}$

$\Rightarrow f(x) = \begin{cases} 1 \text{ at } x = 0 \\ 0 \text{ for } x \in \left(0, \frac{1}{2}\right] \\ -1 \text{ for } x \in \left(\frac{1}{2}, 1\right] \\ |2x-3|[x-2]; x > 1 \end{cases}$

$= \begin{cases} 1 \text{ at } x = 0 \\ 0 \text{ for } x \in \left(0, \frac{1}{2}\right] \\ -1 \text{ for } x \in \left(\frac{1}{2}, 1\right] \\ -(2x-3)(-1) \text{ for } x \in \left(1, \frac{3}{2}\right) \\ (2x-3)(-1) \text{ for } x \in \left[\frac{3}{2}, 2\right) \\ 0 \text{ at } x = 2 \end{cases}$

Clearly $f(x)$ is discontinuous at $x = 0, \frac{1}{2}, 2$ i.e., $f(x)$ is continuous on $[0, 2] - \left\{0, \frac{1}{2}, 2\right\}$

4. **(a)** $f(x) = \lim_{n\to\infty} \frac{\left[x^{2n+2} - \cos x\right]}{\left(x^{2n}+1\right)} = \lim_{n\to\infty} \frac{\left[\left(x^2\right)^{n+1} - \cos x\right]}{\left(\left(x^2\right)^n + 1\right)}$

$= \begin{cases} -\cos x; x \in (-1, 1) \\ \dfrac{1-\cos x}{2} \text{ at } x = \pm 1 \\ x^2; x \in \mathbb{R} - (-1, 1) \end{cases}$

$\Rightarrow f(-1^-) = 1,\ f(-1^+) = -\cos 1, f(1^-) = -\cos 1, f(1^+) = 1,$
$f(-1) = \frac{|-\cos|}{2}, f(1) = \frac{|-\cos|}{2}$
$\Rightarrow f(x)$ is discontinuous at $x = -1, 1$

(b) $f(x) = \lim_{x\to\infty} \frac{\left[\ell n(2+x) - x^{2n}\sin x\right]}{\left(x^{2n}+1\right)};\ 0 \le x \le \pi/2$

$f(x) = \begin{cases} \ell n(2+x) \text{ for } 0 \le x < 1 \\ \dfrac{\ell n 3 - \sin 1}{2} \text{ at } x = 1 \\ -\sin x \text{ for } x > 1 \end{cases}$

$\Rightarrow f(1^-) = ln\ 3, f(1^+) = -\sin 1$
$\Rightarrow f(x)$ is discontinuous at $x = 1$

5. **(a)** **(i)** $\lim_{x\to 4^-} f(x) = \lim_{h\to 0^+} a\tan^{-1}\left[\frac{1}{-h}\right]$

$= -a \lim_{h\to 0^+} \tan^{-1}\left(\frac{1}{h}\right) = \frac{-a\pi}{2}$

$\lim_{x\to 4^+} f(x) = \lim_{h\to 0^+} b\tan^{-1}\left(\frac{2}{h}\right) = b\frac{\pi}{2}$ and $f(4) = \frac{\pi}{2}$

$\therefore$ For continuity at $x = 4$, $-\frac{a\pi}{2} = \frac{b\pi}{2} = \frac{\pi}{2}$
$\Rightarrow a = -1, b = 1$

Also $f(6^-) = \lim_{h\to 0^+} \tan^{-1}\left(\frac{2}{6-h-4}\right) = \frac{\pi}{4}$

Also $f(6^+) = \frac{\pi}{2} + \left(\frac{-\pi}{4}\right) = \frac{\pi}{4} = f(6)$

Clearly $f(x)$ is continuous for $a = -1, b = 1$

(ii) $f(x) = \begin{cases} \dfrac{\left(1-\sin^3 x\right)}{3\cos^2 x}; x < \dfrac{\pi}{2} \\ a \quad ; x = \dfrac{\pi}{2}; \\ \dfrac{b(1-\sin x)}{(\pi - 2x)^2}; x > \dfrac{\pi}{2} \end{cases}$

$= f\left(\frac{\pi}{2}^-\right) = \lim_{h\to 0^+} \left(\frac{1-\sin^3\left(\frac{\pi}{2}-h\right)}{3\cos^2\left(\frac{\pi}{2}-h\right)}\right)$

$= \lim_{h\to 0^+} \left(\frac{1-\cos^3 h}{3\sin^2 h}\right)$

$= \lim_{h\to 0^+} \frac{(1+\cos h+\cos^2 h)}{3(1+\cos h)} = \frac{1}{2}$ and

$$f\left(\frac{\pi}{2}^+\right) = \lim_{h\to 0^+} \frac{b\left(1-\sin\left(\frac{\pi}{2}+h\right)\right)}{\left[\pi - 2\left(\frac{\pi}{2}+h\right)\right]^2}$$

$$= \lim_{h\to 0^+} \frac{b(1-\cos h)}{4h^2} = \lim_{h\to 0^+} \frac{b\left(2\sin^2\frac{h}{2}\right)}{4h^2} = \frac{b}{8}; f\left(\frac{\pi}{2}\right) = a$$

$\therefore$ For continuity of function, $a = \frac{b}{8} = \frac{1}{2} \Rightarrow a = \frac{1}{2}, b = 4$

(iii) $f(x) = \begin{cases} (1+|\sin x|)^{\frac{a}{|\sin x|}} & ; \frac{-\pi}{6} < x < 0 \\ b & ; x = 0 \\ e^{\frac{\tan 2x}{\tan 3x}} & ; 0 < x < \frac{\pi}{6} \end{cases}$

$f(0^-) = \lim_{x\to 0^-} (1+(-\sin x))^{\frac{-a}{\sin x}} = e^a$

$f(0) = b;$

$f(0^+) = \lim_{x\to 0^+} e^{\frac{\tan 2x}{\tan 3x}} = e^{\lim_{x\to 0^+}\left(\frac{\tan 2x}{\tan 3x}\right)} = e^{2/3}$

$\therefore$ For continuity of $f(x)$, $e^a = b = e^{2/3}$

$\Rightarrow a = \frac{2}{3}$, $b = e^{2/3}$

(b) (i) $f(x) = \begin{cases} \frac{\left(ae^{\frac{1}{|x+2|}} - 1\right)}{\left(2 - e^{\frac{1}{|x+2|}}\right)} & ; -3 < x < -2 \\ b & ; x = -2 \\ \frac{\sin(x^4-16)}{x^5+32} & ; -2 < x < 0 \end{cases}$

$$f(-2^-) = \lim_{x\to(-2)^-} \left[\frac{ae^{\frac{-1}{(x+2)}} - 1}{2 - e^{\frac{-1}{(x+2)}}}\right] = \lim_{h\to 0^+}\left[\frac{ae^{\frac{1}{h}} - 1}{2 - e^{\frac{1}{h}}}\right]$$

$$= \lim_{h\to 0^+}\left[\frac{a - e^{-\frac{1}{h}}}{2e^{-\frac{1}{h}}}\right] = -a,$$

$f(-2) = b;$

$$f(-2^+) = \lim_{x\to -2^+} \frac{\sin(x^4-16)}{x^5 - (-2)^5}$$

$$= \lim_{x\to -2^+} \frac{\cos(x^4-16).4x^3}{5x^4} = \frac{-2}{5}$$

$\Rightarrow -a = b = \frac{-2}{5} \Rightarrow a = \frac{2}{5}, b = \frac{-2}{5}$

$$\Rightarrow f(0^+) = \lim_{x\to 0^+}\left[\frac{\sqrt{x+bx^2} - \sqrt{x}}{bx^{3/2}}\right]$$

$$= \lim_{x\to 0^+}\left[\frac{bx^2}{bx^{3/2}\left[\sqrt{x+bx^2}+\sqrt{x}\right]}\right]$$

$$= \lim_{x\to 0^+} \frac{\sqrt{x}}{\sqrt{x}\left[\sqrt{1+bx}+1\right]} = \frac{1}{2}$$

$\therefore$ For continuity of $f(x)$, $a+2 = c = \frac{1}{2} \Rightarrow a = \frac{-3}{2}, c = \frac{1}{2}, b \neq 0$

6. $\because$ f is continuous function at $a \in \mathbb{R}$

$\Rightarrow \lim_{x\to a} f(x) = f(a)$ and g is discontinuous function at 'a'

$\Rightarrow$ Following cases arise.

Case (i): $\lim_{x\to a^-} g(x) = \lim_{x\to a^+} = \ell \neq g(a)$

Case (ii): $\lim_{x\to 0^-} g(x) \neq \lim_{x\to a^+} g(x)$ (i.e., $\ell_1 \neq \ell_2$)

Case (iii): $\lim_{x\to a} g(x)$ does not exist (i.e., infinite or not unique), then

Case (i): $(f+g)(a^-) = f(a) + \ell$, $(f+g)(a^+) = f(a) + \ell$, $(f+g)(a) = f(a) + g(a) \neq f(a) + \ell$

Case (ii): $(f+g)(a^-) = \ell + \ell_1$ and $(f+g(a^+) = \ell + \ell_2$

$\Rightarrow (f+g)(a^-) \neq (f+g)(a^+)$ as $\ell_1 \neq \ell_1$

Case (iii): $\lim_{x\to a} (f(x) + g(x))$ does not exists as $\lim_{x\to a} f(x) = \ell$ and $\lim_{x\to a} g(x)$ does not exists.

Thus $(f+g)$ is discontinuous.

7. $f(x.y) = f(x) . f(y)\ \forall\ x, y \in \mathbb{R}$

$\because$ f is continuous at $x = 1$

$\Rightarrow \lim_{h\to 0} f(1+h) = f(1) \quad \Rightarrow \quad \lim_{h\to 0}(f(1)+f(h)) = f(1)$

$\Rightarrow \lim_{h\to 0} f(h) = 0$

Now, let $x = a \in \mathbb{R}$

$\therefore \lim_{h\to 0} f(a+h) = \lim_{h\to 0} f\left(a + \left(1+\frac{h}{a}\right)\right)$

$= \lim_{h\to a} f(a).f\left(1+\frac{h}{a}\right) = f(a).\lim_{h\to a} f\left(1+\frac{h}{a}\right) = f(a).f(1)$

$= f(a.1) = f(a)$

$\Rightarrow f(x)$ is continuous at $a \in \mathbb{R}$

$\Rightarrow f(x)$ is continuous $\forall\ x \in \mathbb{R}$

8. $f(x) = \begin{cases} 9\pi x; 0 \le x \le 5 \\ 45\pi + \pi(4)(x-5); 5 < x \le 10 \\ 45\pi + 20\pi + \pi(1)(x-10); 10 < x \le 15 \end{cases}$

$\Rightarrow f(x) = \begin{cases} 9\pi x; 0 \le x \le 5 \\ 4\pi x + 25\pi; 5 < x \le 10 \\ 55\pi + \pi x; 10 < x \le 15 \end{cases}$

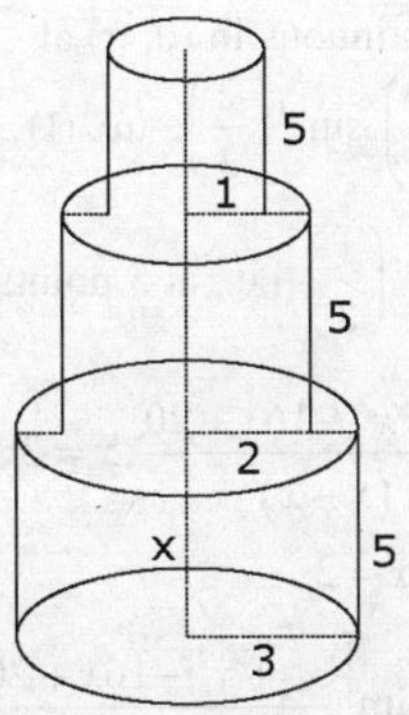

$\Rightarrow$ $f(5^-) = 45\pi$, $f(5^+) = 45\pi$, $f(5) = 45\pi$ and $f(10^-) = 65\pi$,

$f(10^+) = 65\pi$, $f(10) = 65\pi$

$\Rightarrow$ $f(x)$ is a continuous function.

9. $f(x) = \begin{cases} 1+|\cos x|^{\frac{ab}{|\cos x|}} & \text{for } n\pi < x < (2n+1)\frac{\pi}{2} \\ e^a.e^b, & x = (2n+1)\frac{\pi}{2} \\ e^{\frac{\cot 2x}{\cot 8x}}, & (2n+1)\frac{\pi}{2} < x < (n+1)\pi \end{cases}$

$$f\left((2n+1)\frac{\pi}{2}^-\right) = \lim_{x\to(2n+2)\frac{\pi}{2}^-} (1+|\cos x|)^{\frac{ab}{|\cos x|}} = e^{ab};$$

$$f\left((2n+1)\frac{\pi}{2}\right) = e^a.e^b$$

$$f\left((2n+1)\frac{\pi}{2}^+\right) = \lim_{x\to(2n+1)\frac{\pi}{2}^+} e^{\frac{\cot 2x}{\cot 8x}} = e^{\lim_{x\to(2n+1)\frac{\pi}{2}}\left(\frac{\tan 8x}{\tan 2x}\right)}$$

$$= e^{\lim_{x\to(2n+1)\frac{\pi}{2}}\left(\frac{8\sec^2 x8x}{2\sec^2 2x}\right)} = e^4$$

$\therefore$ For continuity of $f(x)$, $e^{ab} = e^a . e^b = e^4$

$\Rightarrow$ $ab = 4$; $a + b = 4$

$\Rightarrow$ $a = 2$, $b = 2$

TEXTUAL EXERCISE–2: (OBJECTIVE)

1. **(c)** $f(x) = [x] \sin \dfrac{\pi}{[x+1]}$

For $x \in (k, k+1)$, $k \neq -1$, $x \neq -1$

$f(x) = k \sin \dfrac{\pi}{(k+1)}$ and $f(k) = k \sin \dfrac{\pi}{(k+1)}$; $k \neq -1$

$\Rightarrow$ $f(x)$ is continuous for $x \in (k, k+1)$

For $k \neq -1$, and $f(x)$ has domain $\mathbb{R} - [-1, 0)$ and $(k^-) =$

$(k-1)\sin\dfrac{\pi}{k}$; $k \neq -1$, $f(k^+) = k\sin\dfrac{\pi}{k+1}$, $f(k) = k \sin$

$\dfrac{\pi}{(k+1)}$

$\Rightarrow$ $f(x)$ is discontinuous at every integer expect for $x = -1$

2. **(a)** $g(x) = \dfrac{1}{(x-1)}$ and $f(x) = \dfrac{1}{x^2+x-2}$

$$\Rightarrow \text{fog}(x) = \frac{1}{\left(\frac{1}{x-1}\right)^2 + \frac{1}{(x-1)} - 2}$$

$$= \frac{(x-1)^2}{1+(x-1)-2(x-1)^2}; x \neq 1 \text{ and } x-1 \neq \frac{-1}{2}, 1$$

$\Rightarrow$ $x \neq 1, \dfrac{1}{2}, 2$

$$\Rightarrow \text{fog}(x) = \frac{-(x-1)^2}{(x-2)(2x-1)}$$

$\Rightarrow$ All points of discontinuity are $\dfrac{1}{2}, 2, 1$

3. **(c)** $f(x) = \dfrac{\tan x.\tan^{-1}\left(\frac{1}{x-1}\right)}{x(x-3)(x-5)}$

$$f(1^-) = \frac{(\tan 1)\left(\frac{-\pi}{2}\right)}{(1)(-2)(-4)} = \frac{-\pi}{16}\tan 1$$

$$f(1^+) = \frac{(\tan 1)\left(\frac{\pi}{2}\right)}{(1)(-2)(-4)} = \frac{\pi}{16}\tan 1$$

Also $f(x)$ has infinite discontinuity at $x = 0, 3, 5$ and at $x = (2n+1)\dfrac{\pi}{2}$; $n \in \mathbb{Z}$

4. **(a), (b)** $f(x) = \sqrt{x} - \left[\sqrt{x}\right]$; $D_f = [0, \infty)$

Case (i): For $x \in (k^2, (k+1)^2)$; $k \in \mathbb{Z}$

$\Rightarrow$ $\sqrt{x} \in (k, k+1)$

$\Rightarrow$ $\left[\sqrt{x}\right] = k$

$\Rightarrow$ $f(x) = \sqrt{x} - k$, which is continuous

Case (ii): For $x = k^2$

$\Rightarrow$ $f(k^2) = k - k = 0$ $\quad\Rightarrow$ $f\left(k^{2^-}\right) = k - (k-1) = 1$

$\Rightarrow$ $f\left(k^{2^+}\right) = k - k = 0$

$\Rightarrow$ $f(x)$ is continuous at $x = 0$ and discontinuous at n^2, $n \in \mathbb{N}$.

5. **(d)** $f(x) = \begin{cases} -2\sin x; & -\pi \le x < \frac{\pi}{2} \\ a\sin x + b; & \frac{-\pi}{2} \le x < \frac{\pi}{2} \\ \cos x; & \frac{\pi}{2} \le x \le \pi \end{cases}$

$f\left(\dfrac{-\pi}{2}^-\right) = 2$, $f\left(\dfrac{-\pi}{2}^+\right) = -a + b$, $f\left(\dfrac{-\pi}{2}\right) = -a + b$,

$f\left(\dfrac{\pi}{2}^-\right) = a + b$, $f\left(\dfrac{\pi}{2}^+\right) = 0$

∴ For continuity in the interval $[-\pi, \pi]$, $-a+b=2$, $a+b=0$

⇒ $b=1, a=-1$ ⇒ $(a, b)=(-1, 1)$

6. (c) ∵ $f(1)=f(1+h)$ when $h \to 0+$ and $f(3)=f(3-h)$ when $h \to 0^+$

⇒ $f(x)$ is continuous at $x=1$ and at $x=3$ and continuity in $(1, 3)$ is obvious.

⇒ $f(x)$ is continuous on $[1, 3]$

7. (c) $g(x)=x-[x]$; $h(x)=f(g(x))=f(x-[x])=f(\{x\})$

⇒ $f(x)$ is a periodic function with period 1 and $f(0)=f(1)$ and $f(x)$ is continuous on $[0,1]$

⇒ $h(x)$ is continuous on $\mathbb{R}$

8. (c) $f(x)=[\sin x+\cos x]=\left[\sqrt{2}\sin\left(\frac{\pi}{4}+x\right)\right]$

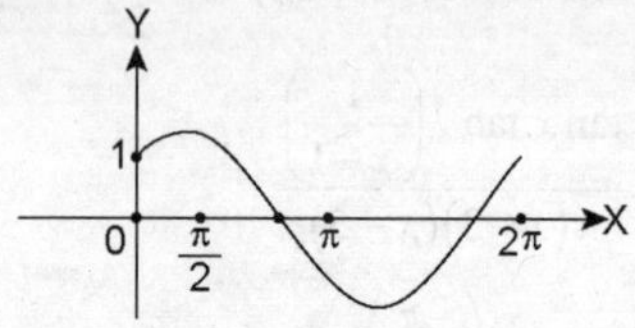

$$=\begin{cases} 1 \text{ for } x \in \left[0, \frac{\pi}{2}\right] \cup \{2\pi\} \\ 0 \text{ for } x \in \left(\frac{\pi}{2}, \frac{3\pi}{4}\right] \cup \left(\frac{7\pi}{4}, 2\pi\right) \\ -1 \text{ for } x \in \left(\frac{3\pi}{4}, \pi\right) \\ -2 \text{ for } x \in \left(\pi, \frac{3\pi}{2}\right) \\ -1 \text{ for } \left[\frac{3\pi}{2}, \frac{7\pi}{4}\right) \end{cases}$$

⇒ $f(x)$ is discontinuous at $x=\frac{\pi}{2}, \frac{3\pi}{4}, \pi, \frac{3\pi}{2}, \frac{7\pi}{4}, 2\pi$

In $(0, 2\pi)$; $f(x)$ is discontinuous at $x=\frac{\pi}{2}, \frac{3\pi}{4}, \pi, \frac{3\pi}{2}$ and $\frac{7\pi}{4}$ i.e., at 5 points

9. (c) $f(x)=[2+3\sin x]=2+[3\sin x]$; $x \in (0, \pi)$

$$=\begin{cases} 2 \text{ for } 0<x<\sin^{-1}\left(\frac{1}{3}\right) \\ 3 \text{ for } \sin^{-1}\frac{1}{3} \le x < \sin^{-1}\left(\frac{2}{3}\right) \\ 4 \text{ for } \sin^{-1}\frac{2}{3} \le x < \sin^{-1} 1 \\ 5 \text{ at } x=\sin^{-1} 1=\frac{\pi}{2} \\ 4 \text{ for } \frac{\pi}{2} < x \le \pi \sin^{-1}\left(\frac{2}{3}\right) \\ 3 \text{ for } \pi-\sin^{-1}\left(\frac{2}{3}\right) < x \le \pi-\sin^{-1}\frac{1}{3} \\ 2 \text{ for } \pi \sin^{-1}\left(\frac{1}{3}\right) < x < \pi \end{cases}$$

⇒ $f(x)$ is discontinuous in $(0, \pi)$ at

$$x=\sin^{-1}\left(\frac{1}{3}\right), \sin^{-1}\left(\frac{2}{3}\right), \sin^{-1}(1), \pi-\sin^{-1}\left(\frac{2}{3}\right),$$

$$\pi-\sin^{-1}\left(\frac{1}{3}\right) \text{ i.e., at 5 points}$$

10. (c) $f(x)=\begin{cases} \frac{x^3+x^2-16x+20}{(x-2)^2}; x \ne 2 \\ k \ ; x=2 \end{cases}$

$$\lim_{x\to 2} f(x)=\lim_{x\to 2}\left[\frac{x^3+x^2-16x+20}{(x-2)^2}\right]$$

$$=\lim_{x\to 2}\frac{(x-2)^2(x+5)}{(x-2)^2}=7 \text{ and } f(2)=k$$

∴ For continuity on $\mathbb{R}$; $k=7$, $a, b \in \mathbb{N}$

⇒ $a^2-b^2=7$ ⇒ $a^2=7+b^2$

⇒ $a=4, b=3$

11. (b) $x^2+(f(x)-2)x-\sqrt{3}.f(x)+2\sqrt{3}-3=0$

$x^2+(f(x)-2)x-\sqrt{3}(f(x)-2)=3$

⇒ $(f(x)-2)\left(x-\sqrt{3}\right)=3-x^2$

⇒ $f(x)-2=\frac{-\left(x-\sqrt{3}\right)\left(x+\sqrt{3}\right)}{\left(x-\sqrt{3}\right)}$

∴ $f(x)$ is continuous

⇒ $f(x)-2$ is also continuous

⇒ $f\left(\sqrt{3}\right)-2=\lim_{x\to\sqrt{3}}\frac{-\left(x-\sqrt{3}\right)\left(x+\sqrt{3}\right)}{\left(x-\sqrt{3}\right)}=-2\sqrt{3}$

⇒ $f\left(\sqrt{3}\right)=2\left(1-\sqrt{3}\right)$

12. (c) $f(x)=\begin{cases} \frac{x^2}{a}; 0 \le x < 1 \\ a \ ; 1 \le x < \sqrt{2} \\ \frac{2b^2-4b}{x^2}; \sqrt{2} \le x < \infty \end{cases}$

$f(1^-)=\frac{1}{a}$; $f(1^+)=a, f(1)=a$

$f\left(\left(\sqrt{2}\right)^-\right)=a, f\left(\left(\sqrt{2}\right)^+\right)=b^2-2b, \ f\left(\sqrt{2}\right)=b^2-2b$

∴ For continuity in $(0, \infty)$,

$\frac{1}{a}=a$; $b^2-2b=a$

⇒ $a^2=1$; $b^2-2b=a$

⇒ $a=\pm 1$; $b^2-2b \pm 1$

⇒ $a=\pm 1$; $b^2-2b \pm 1=0$

⇒ $b^2-2b+1-2=0$ for $a=1$ and $b^2-2b+1=0$ for $a=-1$

⇒ $(b-1)^2=2$ for $a=1$ and $(b-1)^2=0$ for $a=-1$

⇒ $a=1, b=1\pm\sqrt{2}$, $a=-1, b=1$

13. (d) $f(x) = \begin{cases} [x]+\sqrt{\{x\}}; x \ge 0 \\ \sin x \text{ for } x<0 \end{cases}$

Clearly $f(x)$ is continuous for $x < 1$.

Let $x = k \in \mathbb{N}$, then $\lim_{x\to k^-} f(x) = (k-1)+\sqrt{k-(k-1)} = k$,

$\lim_{x\to k^+} = k+\sqrt{k-k} = k; f(k) = k$

$\Rightarrow f(x)$ is continuous at $x = k \in \mathbb{N}$

$\Rightarrow f(a^-) = k + \sqrt{a-k}$; $f(a^+) = k + \sqrt{a-k}$; $f(a) = k + \sqrt{a-k}$

$\Rightarrow f(x)$ is continuous $\forall x \in \mathbb{R}$

14. (c) Given $f(a) = 0$ and $f(x)$ is a continuous function.

$\therefore \lim_{x\to a}\frac{\ell n(1+3f(x))}{2f(x)} = \lim_{x\to a}\frac{\ell n(1+3f(x))}{\frac{2}{3}.3f(x)} = \frac{3}{2}(1) = \frac{3}{2}$

15. (d) $\lim_{n\to\infty}\frac{x^n f(x)+g(x)}{x^n+1} = L$ (say)

For $x = 1$, $L = \lim_{n\to\infty}\frac{x^n f(x)+g(x)}{x^n+1} = \frac{f(1)+g(1)}{2}$

Which exists uniquely as $f(x)$ and $g(x)$ are continuous functions.

For $x = -1$, $L = \lim_{n\to\infty}\frac{(-1)^n f(-1)+g(-1)}{(-1)^n+1}$

$\therefore (-1)^n = \begin{cases} 1 \text{ for } n = \text{even and} \\ -1 \text{ for } n = \text{odd} \end{cases}$

$\Rightarrow$ L does not exist uniquely.

For $|x| < 1$, $L = \lim_{n\to\infty}\frac{x^n f(x)+g(x)}{x^n+1} = g(x)$ which is continuous $\forall x \in \mathbb{R}$.

For $|x| > 1$

$L = \lim_{n\to\infty}\frac{x^n f(x)+g(x)}{x^n+1} = \lim_{n\to\infty}\frac{f(x)+\frac{g(x)}{x^n}}{1+\frac{1}{x^n}} = f(x)$

which is also continuous $\forall x \in \mathbb{R}$

$\Rightarrow$ Limit does not exist for $x = -1$

16. (a) $f(x) = \begin{cases} x; x\in\mathbb{Q} \\ 1-x; x\notin\mathbb{Q} \end{cases}$;

$fof(x) = \begin{cases} f(x); f(x)\in\mathbb{Q} \\ 1-f(x) f(x)\notin\mathbb{Q} \end{cases} = \begin{cases} x; x\in\mathbb{Q} \\ 1-(1-x); x\notin\mathbb{Q} \end{cases}$

$\Rightarrow fof(x) = x \ \forall x \in [0, 1]$

$\Rightarrow fof(x)$ is continuous $\forall x \in [0, 1]$

17. (d) $f(x) = \begin{cases} x \text{ for } |x|\le 1 \\ 1 \text{ for } |x|>1 \end{cases}$; $g(x) = \begin{cases} \cos\left(\frac{\pi}{2}\right) \text{for } |x|\le 1 \\ |x-1| \text{ for } |x|>1 \end{cases}$;

$h(x) = \begin{cases} \frac{(|x|-1)}{log_a|x|} \text{ for } |x|\ne 1 \\ \ell n\, a \text{ for } |x|=1, a>0, a\ne 1 \end{cases}$

Clearly $f(-1^-) = 1, f(-1) = -1$

$\Rightarrow f(x)$ is discontinuous at $x = -1$

$g(1^-) = \cos\frac{\pi}{2} = 0 = g(1); g(1^+) = 0; g(-1^-) = 2 = g(-1);$

$g(-1^+) = \cos\frac{-\pi}{2} = 0$

$\Rightarrow g(x)$ is discontinuous at $x = -1$,

$h(-1^-) = \lim_{t\to 0^+}\frac{(1+t-1)}{\log_a(-1-t)} = \lim_{t\to 0^+}\frac{t}{\log_a(1+t)}$

$= \lim_{t\to 0^+}\frac{1}{\left(\frac{1}{1+t}\right)\log_a e} = \log_e a = \ell n\, a$

$h(-1) = ln$ a,

$h(-1^+) = \lim_{t\to 0^+}\frac{(1-t-1)}{\log_a(1-t)} = \lim_{t\to 0^+}\frac{-t}{\log_a(1-t)}$

$= \lim_{t\to 0^+}\frac{-1}{\left(\frac{1}{1-t}\right).\log_a e(-1)} = ln$ a

$\Rightarrow \ell = 1, m = 1, n = 0$

$\Rightarrow (\ell, m, n) \equiv (1, 1, 0)$

18. (a) $f(x) = \begin{cases} x^2-4x+3; x<3 \\ x-4 \ ; x\ge 3 \end{cases}$ and $g(x) = \begin{cases} x-3; x\ge 4 \\ x \ \ -x; 1<x<4; \\ 1 \ ; \ \ 1 \end{cases}$

Not that domain of $y = f(x) . g(x)$ is $[1, \infty)$.

$G(x) = f(x) . g(x) = \begin{cases} (x^2-4x+3); x=1 \\ (x^2-x)(x^2-4x+3); 1<x<3 \\ (x-4)(x^2-x); 3\le x<4 \\ (x-4)(x-3); x\ge 4 \end{cases}$

$= \begin{cases} (x-1)(x-3); x=1 \\ x(x-1)^2(x-3); 1<x<3 \\ x(x-1)(x-4); 3\le x<4 \\ (x-3)(x-4); x\ge 4 \end{cases}$

$\therefore G(1) = 0; G(1^+) = 0; G(3^-) = 0; G(3^+) = G(3) = -6; G(4^-) = 0; G(4) = G(4^+) = 0$

$\Rightarrow f(x).g(x)$ is discontinuous only at $x = 3$ i.e., exactly at 1 point

19. (c) $f(x) = \frac{4-x^2}{|4x-x^3|}$,

$4x - x^3 = x(4 - x^2) = x(2 - x)(2 + x) = -x(x + 2)(x - 2)$

$\Rightarrow 4x - x^3 < 0$ for $x(x + 2)(x - 2) > 0$

$\Rightarrow x \in (-2, 0) \cup (0, 2)$ and $4x - x^3 > 0$ for $x \in (-\infty, -2) \cup (0, 2)$ and $4x - x^3 = 0$ at $x = 0, -2, 2$

$\Rightarrow f(x) = \begin{cases} \frac{4-x^2}{4x-x^3} \text{for } x\in(-\infty,-2)\cup(0,2) \\ \frac{4-x^2}{(4x-x^3)} \text{for } x\in(-2,0)\cup(2,\infty) \end{cases}$

$\Rightarrow f(x) = \begin{cases} \frac{1}{x} \text{ for } x \in (-\infty,-2) \cup (0,2) \\ -\frac{1}{x} \text{ for } x \in (-2,0) \cup (2,\infty) \end{cases}$

$\Rightarrow y = f(x)$ is discontinuous at $x = 0, -2, 2$

20. **(d)** $f(x) = \begin{cases} \frac{x^2-1}{x^2-2|x-1|-1} \text{ if } x \neq 1 \\ \frac{1}{2} \text{ if } x = 1 \end{cases}$

$f(1^-) = \lim_{x\to 1^-}\left(\frac{x^2-1}{x^2-2(-x+1)-1}\right) = \lim_{x\to 1^-}\left(\frac{x^2-1}{x^2+2x-3}\right)$

$= \lim_{x\to 1^-}\left(\frac{x+1}{x+3}\right) = \frac{1}{2}$

$f(1^+) = \lim_{x\to 1^+}\frac{x^2-1}{x^2-2(x-1)-1} = \lim_{x\to 1^+}\left(\frac{x^2-1}{x^2-2x+1}\right)$

$= \lim_{x\to 1^+}\left(\frac{x+1}{x-1}\right) = \infty$ and $f(1) = \frac{1}{2}$

$\Rightarrow f(x)$ is discontinuous for $x = 1$

21. **(d)** For $x \in [1, 3]$, $(x^2 + 1) \in [2, 10]$

$\Rightarrow f(x)$ can be discontinuous at $x = \sqrt{1}, \sqrt{2}, \sqrt{3}, \sqrt{4} \ldots\ldots \sqrt{9}$

$\because$ if k be $\sqrt{n}$; $n \in \{1, 2, 3, \ldots.., 9\}$, then $f(k^-) = n$; $f(k) = n + 1$, $f(k^+) = n + 1$

$\Rightarrow f(x)$ is discontinuous at $\sqrt{1}, \sqrt{2}, \sqrt{3}, \ldots\ldots. \sqrt{8}$ i.e., at 8 points

TEXTUAL EXERCISE–3: (SUBJECTIVE)

1. $f(x) = x^3 - 3x - 5$, $f(0).f(5) = (-5)(105) < 0$

$\Rightarrow$ There is at least one root in (0, 5)

$f'(x) = 3x^2 - 3 = 3(x^2 - 1)$

$\Rightarrow f'(x) > 0$ for $x \in (-\infty, -1) \cup (1, \infty)$ and $f'(x) < 0$ for $x \in (-1, 1)$, $f(-1) = -1 + 3 - 5 = -3$; $f(1) = -7$

The graph of $f(x)$ will be as shown below.

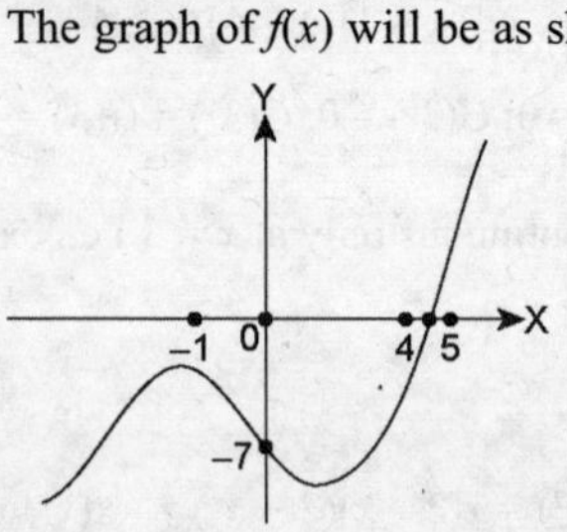

Clearly $f(x) = 0$ has exactly one root in (0, 5) as well as in (1, 5)

$\Rightarrow$ (a), (b) and (c) are true.

2. $f(x) = x^2 + 3x - 5$

$\Rightarrow f'(x) = 3x^2 + 3 > 0 \ \forall x \in \mathbb{R}$ and $f(0) = -5$, $f(5) = 135$

$\Rightarrow f(x) = 0$ has exactly one root in (0, 5) as $f(x)$ is continuous and injective.

3. $2^x + 3^x + 5^x = 7^x$ ……..(i)

$\Rightarrow \left(\frac{2}{7}\right)^x + \left(\frac{3}{7}\right)^x + \left(\frac{5}{7}\right)^x = 1$

$\Rightarrow \left(\frac{2}{7}\right)^x + \left(\frac{3}{7}\right)^x + \left(\frac{5}{7}\right)^x - 1 = 0$

Let $f(x) = \left(\frac{2}{7}\right)^x + \left(\frac{3}{7}\right)^x + \left(\frac{5}{7}\right)^x - 1$

$\Rightarrow f'(x) = \left(\frac{2}{7}\right)^x \ell n\left(\frac{2}{7}\right) + \left(\frac{3}{7}\right)^x \ell n\left(\frac{3}{7}\right) + \left(\frac{5}{7}\right)^x \ell n\left(\frac{5}{7}\right) < 0$

$\Rightarrow f(x)$ is a decreasing function, also continuous

$\Rightarrow f(x) = 0$ has exactly one root, Hence the given equation has exactly one solution .

4. $f: [0, 1] \to [0, 1]$

$\because$ f is a continuous function from [0, 1] to [0, 1] .

$\Rightarrow \exists\, x_1, x_2 \in [0, 1]$ such that $f(x_1) = 0$, $f(x_2) = 1$.

Let $g(x) = f(x) - x$

$\Rightarrow g(x_1) = f(x_1) - x_1 = 0 - x_1 = -x_1 < 0$ and $g(x_2) = f(x_2) - x_2 = 1 - x_2 > 0$

Also, $y = f(x)$, $y = x$ being continuous function on [0, 1], $f(x) - x = g(x)$ also continuous, s.t $g(x_1) = -x_1 < 0$

$g(x_2) = 1 - x_2 > 0$, $x_1, x_2 \in [0, 1]$

$\Rightarrow$ By intermediate value theorem $g(x) = 0$ for some $x \in [0, 1]$ i.e., $f(x) = x$ for some $x \in [0, 1]$

5. $f: [1, 3] \to \mathbb{R}$ is a continuous function and takes only rational values and $f(2) = 10$

$\Rightarrow f(x)$ must be a constant function

$\Rightarrow f(5/2) = 10$

6. $f(x) = \left(\frac{x^3}{4}\right) - \sin\left(\frac{\pi}{x}\right) + 3$

$f(-2) = -2 + 1 + 3 = 2$,

$f(2) = 2 - 1 + 3 = 4$

Clearly $f(x)$ is a continuous function in [–2, 2].

$\Rightarrow$ By intermediate theorem, $f(x)$ will attain all values in between 2 and 4 and $\frac{7}{3} \in (2, 4)$.

7. $f(x) = x + \{-x\} + [x]$;

$= \begin{cases} 2x \text{ for } x \in \mathbb{Z} \\ 2[x]+1 \text{ for } x \notin \mathbb{Z} \end{cases}$

Clearly $f(x)$ is continuous for $x \in (k - 1, k)$ where $k \in \mathbb{Z}$ as $f(x) = 2k - 1 \ \forall x \in (k - 1, k)$

$f(k^-) = 2(k - 1) + 1 = 2k - 1$,

$f(k^+) = 2(k) + 1 = 2k + 1$,

$f(k) = 2k$

$\therefore f(x)$ is discontinuous at each integer point i.e., at $x = -2, -1, 0, 2$

8. $y = f(x) = (1 + x^2)\ \text{sgn}\ x = \begin{cases} -(1+x^2); & x<0; y<-1 \\ 0; & x=0 \\ (1+x^2); & x>0; y>1 \end{cases}$

$\Rightarrow f(0^-) = -1$; $f(0) = 0$; $f(0^+) = 1$

$\Rightarrow f(x)$is discontinuous at $x = 0$

$\Rightarrow\ x = \begin{cases} -\sqrt{-1-y}\ ; y<-1 \\ 0 \quad ;y=0 \\ \sqrt{y-1} \quad ;y>1 \end{cases}$

$\Rightarrow\ f^{-1}(x) = \begin{cases} -\sqrt{1-x} \quad ;x<-1 \\ 0 \quad ; x=0 \\ \sqrt{x-1} \quad ;x>1 \end{cases}$

$\Rightarrow$ $f^{-1}(x)$ is continuous for $x < -1$, for $x > 1$ and at $x = 0$ (isolated point continuity) (as there exists no neighborhood of $x = 0$).

Hence $f^{-1}(x)$ is continuous in its domain.

9. $g: [a, b] \to [a, b]$

Let $x_1, x_2 \in [a, b]$ such that $g(x_1) = a$, $g(x_2) = b$, then $f(x) = g(x) - x$

$\Rightarrow$ $f(x_1) = g(x_1) - x_1 = a - x_1 \le 0$ and $f(x_2) = g(x_2) - x_2 = b - x_2 \ge 0$

$\Rightarrow$ $f(x)$ is continuous and hence will attain all values from $f(x_1)$ to $f(x_2)$ i.e., at some $x \in [a, b]$

$f(x) = 0$

$\Rightarrow$ $g(x) = x$ or $g(c) = c$ for some $c \in [a ,b]$

10. (a) $f(x + y) = f(x) + f(y)\ \forall\ x, y \in \mathbb{R}$

For $x = y = 0$, $f(0) = f(0) + f(0)$

$\Rightarrow$ $f(0) = 0$ …(1)

Now, $f(x)$ is continuous at $x = 0$

$\Rightarrow$ $\lim\limits_{x\to 0} f(x) = f(0) = 0$ …(2)

Let $a \in \mathbb{R}$, then $\lim\limits_{x\to a} f(x) = \lim\limits_{h\to 0} f(a+h)$

$= \lim\limits_{h\to 0} (f(a) + f(h))$

$[\because f(x + y) = f(x) + f(y)\ \forall\ x, y \in \mathbb{R}]$

$= f(a) + \lim\limits_{h\to 0} f(h)$

$= f(a) + 0 = f(a)$ ……(By (2))

$\therefore\ \lim\limits_{h\to a} f(x) = f(a)$

$\Rightarrow$ $f(x)$ is continuous at $a\ \forall a \in \mathbb{R}$

(b) $f(xy) = f(x).f(y)\ \forall\ x, y \in \mathbb{R}$

For $x = y = 1$, $f(1) = (f(1))^2$

$\Rightarrow$ $f(1) = 1$ as $f(1) \ne 0$ (given)

Since $f(x)$ is continuous at $x = 1$,

$\Rightarrow$ $\lim\limits_{x\to 1} f(x) = f(1) = 1$ …(1)

Now for $a \in \mathbb{R}$ and $a \ne 0$

$$\lim_{x\to a} f(x) = \lim_{h\to 0} f(a+h) = \lim_{h\to 0} f\left(a\left(1+\frac{h}{a}\right)\right)$$

$$= \lim_{h\to 0} f(a).f\left(1+\frac{h}{a}\right)$$

$$= f(a).\ \lim_{h\to 0} f\left(1+\frac{h}{a}\right) = f(a).\ \lim_{h\to 1} f(x)$$

$= f(a).\ f(1)$ ($\because$ of (1))

$= f(a).1 = f(a)$

Thus $\lim\limits_{x\to a} f(x) = f(a)\ \forall\ a \in \mathbb{R} - \{0\}$

$\Rightarrow$ $f(x)$ is continuous $\forall\ x \in \mathbb{R} - \{0\}$

11. Consider a function $g(x) = f\left(x+\frac{1}{2}\right) - f(x)$ …(1)

As $f(x)$ is continuous on $[0, 1]$

$\Rightarrow$ $f\left(x+\frac{1}{2}\right)$ is continuous on $\left[\frac{-1}{2},\frac{1}{2}\right]$

$\Rightarrow$ $g(x)$ is continuous on $\left[0,\frac{1}{2}\right]$

Now, $g(0) = f\left(\frac{1}{2}\right) - f(0) = k$ (say) and $g\left(\frac{1}{2}\right) = f(1) - f\left(\frac{1}{2}\right) = -k$

As $f(0) = f(1)$ $\Rightarrow$ $g(0).\ g\left(\frac{1}{2}\right) = -k^2 \le 0$

$\Rightarrow$ By in intermediate there $g(x) = 0$ has at least one root in $\left[0,\frac{1}{2}\right]$.

$\Rightarrow$ $g(c) = 0$ for some $c \in \left[0,\frac{1}{2}\right]$

$\Rightarrow$ $f\left(c+\frac{1}{2}\right) = f(c)$ for some $c \in \left[0,\frac{1}{2}\right]$

12. $f(x) = x^3 - 3x^2 - 4x + 12$

$h(x) = \begin{cases} \dfrac{f(x)}{x-3} \ ;x \ne 3 \\ k\ ,\ x = 3 \end{cases}$

(a) $f(x) = x^3 - 3x^2 - 4x + 12$

$= x^2(x - 3) - 4(x - 3)$

$= (x + 2)(x - 2)(x - 3)$

$\Rightarrow$ Zeros of $f(x)$ are -2, 2 and 3

(b) $\lim\limits_{x\to 3} h(x) = \lim\limits_{x\to 3} \dfrac{f(x)}{(x-3)} = \lim\limits_{x\to 3} (x + 2)(x - 2) = (5)(1) = 5$ and $h(3) = k$

$\therefore$ For continuity at $x = 3$, $k = 5$

(c) $h(x) = \begin{cases} (x+2+(x-2);x \ne 3 \\ 5\ ;x=3 \end{cases}$

$h(-x) = (-x + 2)(-x - 2)$ for $x \ne 3$

$= (x + 2)(x - 2) = h(x)$

$h(3) = 5$, $h(-3) = (-3 + 2)(-3 - 2) = 5$

Thus $h(-x) = h(x)\ \forall\ x \in \mathbb{R}$

$\Rightarrow$ $h(x)$ is an even function .

13. (a) $f(a) = \dfrac{3x+7}{(x-2)(x-3)}$

Continuous $\forall\ x \in \mathbb{R} - \{2, 3\}$

(b) $f(x) = \dfrac{1}{|x|-1} - \dfrac{x^2}{2}$

$\Rightarrow\ f(x) = \begin{cases} \dfrac{1}{x-1} - \dfrac{x^2}{2} \text{ for } x \ge 0; \ne 1 \\ \dfrac{1}{-x-1} - \dfrac{x^2}{2} \text{ for } x \le 0, \ne -1 \\ \text{Not defined at } x = \pm 1 \end{cases}$

$\Rightarrow$ $f(x)$ is continuous on $\mathbb{R} - \{-1, 1\}$

(c) $f(x) = \dfrac{\sqrt{x^2+1}}{1+\sin^2 x}$

Continuous $\forall\ x \in \mathbb{R}$ as $\sqrt{x^2+1}$ and $(1 + \sin^2 x)$ are continuous $\forall\ x \in \mathbb{R}$ and $1 + \sin^2 x \neq 0\ \forall\ x \in \mathbb{R}$.

(d) $f(x) = \tan\left(\dfrac{x}{2}\right)$ not defined where $\dfrac{x}{2} = (2n+1)\dfrac{\pi}{2}; n \in \mathbb{Z}$

or $x = (2n + 1)\pi$; $n \in \mathbb{Z}$

$\Rightarrow$ $f(x)$ is continuous on $\mathbb{R} - \{(2n + 1)\pi\ ;\ n \in \mathbb{Z}\}$

14. $f(x) = \left[\dfrac{(x+1)-1}{(x+1)}\right] + \left[\dfrac{(2x+1)-(x+1)}{(x+1)(2x+1)}\right] + \left[\dfrac{(3x+1)-(2x+1)}{(2x+1)(3x+1)}\right] + \ldots\ldots = \infty$

$= \left(-\dfrac{1}{x+1}\right) + \left(\dfrac{1}{x+1} - \dfrac{1}{2x+1}\right) + \dfrac{1}{2x+1} - \dfrac{1}{2x+1} = 1$

and $f(0) = 0$

$\Rightarrow$ $f(x)$ is discontinuous at $x = 0$

15. $f(x) = \lim\limits_{n\to\infty} \dfrac{x^2 + nx\sin^2 \pi x}{1 + n\sin^3 \pi x} = \dfrac{x\sin^2 \pi x}{\sin^3 \pi x} = \dfrac{x}{\sin \pi x}$; for $\sin \pi x \neq 0$

$\therefore$ $\lim\limits_{x\to 0} f(x) = \lim\limits_{x\to 0} \dfrac{x}{\sin \pi x} = \dfrac{1}{\pi}$ and $f(0)$ is not defined

Next, $\lim\limits_{x\to -1} f(x) = \lim\limits_{x\to -1} \dfrac{x}{\sin \pi x} = \pm\infty$

$\Rightarrow$ $f(x)$ is discontinuous at $x = 0$ and $x = -1$

16. $f(x) = \{x\}$ and $g(x) = [x]$

(a) $h(x) = f(x) \cdot g(x) = \{x\}\ [x]$

$\Rightarrow$ $\lim\limits_{x\to 1^-} h(x) = \lim\limits_{x\to 1^-} \{x\}\ [x] = (1)\ (0) = 0$ and $\lim\limits_{x\to 1^+} h(x) = \lim\limits_{x\to 1^+}$

$\{x\}[x] = (0)\ (1) = 0$

$h(1) = \{1\}[1] = 0$

$\Rightarrow$ $h(x)$ is continuous at $x = 1$

$\lim\limits_{x\to 2^-} h(x) = \lim\limits_{x\to 2^-} \{x\}\ [x] = (1)\ (1) = 1$, $\lim\limits_{x\to 2^+} h(x) = \lim\limits_{x\to 2^+}$

$\{x\}[x] = (0)\ (2) = 0$.

$\Rightarrow$ $h(x)$ is discontinuous at $x = 2$

(b) $h(x) = f(x) + g(x)$

$= \{x\} + [x] = x$

Which is continuous at $x = 1$

(c) $h(x) = f(x) - g(x)$

$= \{x\} - [x]$

$= x - [x] - [x] = x - 2[x]$

$h(1^-) = 1 - 2(0) = 1$,

$h(1^+) = 1 - 2(1) = -1$

$\Rightarrow$ Discontinuous at $x = 1$.

(d) $h(x) = g(x) + \sqrt{f(x)}$

$\Rightarrow$ $h(x) = [x] + \sqrt{\{x\}}$

$\Rightarrow$ $h(1^-) = 0 + \sqrt{1} = 1$, $h(1^+) = 1 + \sqrt{0} = 1$, $h(1) = 1 + \sqrt{0} = 1$

$\therefore$ $h(x)$ is continuous at $x = 1$ and $h(2^-) = 1 + \sqrt{1} = 2$, $h(2^+)$

$= 2 + \sqrt{0} = 2$, $h(2) = 2 + \sqrt{0} = 2$

$\Rightarrow$ $h(x)$ is continuous at $x = 2$.

TEXTUAL EXERCISE-3: (OBJECTIVE)

1. (c) $f(x) = \text{sgn}(x)$ and $g(x) = x(x^2 - 5x + 6)$

$f(g(x)) = sgn = \begin{cases} -1 \text{ for } g(x) < 0 \\ 0 \text{ for } g(x) = 0 \\ 1 \text{ for } g(x) > 0 \end{cases}$

$= \begin{cases} -1 \text{ for } x \in (-\infty, 0) \cup (2,3) \\ 0 \text{ at } x = 0, 2, 3 \\ 1 \text{ for } x \in (0,2) \cup (3,\infty) \end{cases}$

Clearly $f(g(x))$ is discontinuous at $x = 0$, 2 and 3 i.e., at exactly 3 points.

2. (c) $y = \dfrac{1}{(t^2+t-2)} = \dfrac{1}{(t+2)(t-1)}$

$\Rightarrow$ y is discontinuous at $t = 1$ *and* -2 i.e., at $\dfrac{1}{x-1} = 1$ and $\dfrac{1}{x-1} = -2$ and y is not defined at $x = 1$

$\Rightarrow$ $x = 2, \dfrac{1}{2}, 1$ are 3 points of discontinuities.

3. (b) The given equation is $2\tan x + 5x - 2 = 0$

$\Rightarrow$ $2\tan x = -5x + 2$

Let $f(x) = 2\tan x$, $g(x) = -5x + 2$

$\Rightarrow$ $f'(x) = 2\sec^2 x$, $g'(x) = -5$

$\Rightarrow$ $f(x)$ is $\uparrow$ and $g(x)$ is $\uparrow$ and both are continuous functions with range $(-\infty, \infty)$ and domain $(-\infty, \infty)$

$\Rightarrow$ Both will intersect exactly once

For $x < 0$, $2\tan x < 0$, $-5x + 2 > 0$

At $x = \dfrac{\pi}{4}$; $2\tan x = 2$ and $-5x + 2 = \dfrac{-5\pi}{4} + 2 = \dfrac{-5}{4} \times 3.14 + 2$

$= -1.9$

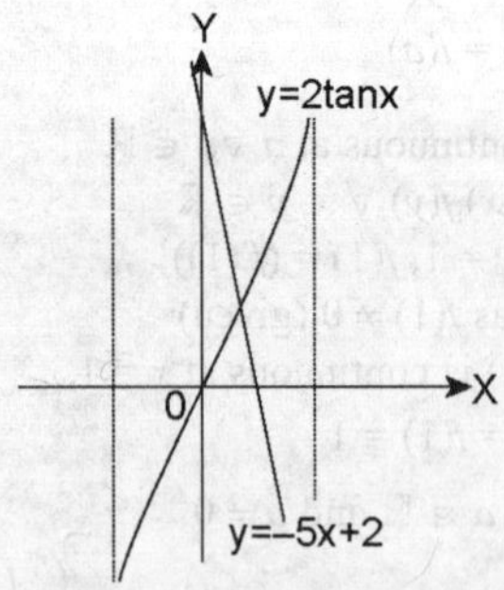

Thus $2\tan x + 5x - 2 = 0$ has exactly one root in $[0, \pi/4]$

4. (a), (b), (c)

$f(x) = [x] + \sqrt{x - [x]}$

Let $x = k \in \mathbb{Z}$, then $f(k^-) = (k - 1) + \sqrt{k - (k-1)}$

$= (k - 1) + 1 = k$; $f(k^+) = k + \sqrt{k - (k-)} = k + 0 = k$

Also $f(k) = [k] + \sqrt{k - k} = k$

$\Rightarrow$ $f(x)$ is continuous at every integer point x.

Further, let $x \in (k, k + 1)$; $k \in \mathbb{Z}$

$\Rightarrow f(x^-) = k + \sqrt{k-k} = k$

$\Rightarrow f(x^+) = k + \sqrt{k-k} = k$

$\Rightarrow f(x) = k + \sqrt{k-k} = k$

Thus $f(x)$ is continuous at $x \notin \mathbb{Z}$ i.e., $f(x)$ is a continuous function on $\mathbb{R}$

5. (c) $f(x) = [x] \cos\left(\frac{2x-1}{2}\right)\pi$

Let $x = k \in \mathbb{Z}$, then $f(k^-) = (k-1)\cos\left(\frac{2k-1}{2}\right)\pi = 0$

$f(k^+) = (k)\cos\left(\frac{2k-1}{2}\right)\pi = 0$

$f(k) = k\cos\left(\frac{2k-1}{2}\right)\pi = 0$

$\Rightarrow f(x)$ is continuous at all integer points.

Let $x \in (k, k+1)$; $k \in \mathbb{Z}$

$\Rightarrow f(x^-) = k\cos\left(\frac{2x-1}{2}\right)\pi$ and $f(x^+) = k\cos\left(\frac{2x-1}{2}\right)\pi$

$f(x) = k\cos\left(\frac{2x-1}{2}\right)\pi$

$\Rightarrow f(x)$ is continuous $\forall x \in \mathbb{R}$

6. (d) $f(x) = (|x-1| + |x-2| + \cos x)$;

Clearly $f(x)$ being the sum of continuous functions is also continuous.

7. (d) $f(x) = \begin{cases} \frac{1-|x|}{1+x}; x \neq -1 \\ 1\ ; x = -1 \end{cases};$

$\Rightarrow f([2x]) = \begin{cases} \frac{1-|[2x]|}{1+[2x]}; [2x] \neq -1 \\ 1\ ; [2x] = -1 \end{cases}$

$= \begin{cases} \frac{1-|[2x]|}{1+[2x]}; x \notin \left[\frac{-1}{2}, 0\right) \\ 1\ ; x \in \left[\frac{-1}{2}, 0\right) \end{cases}$

For $[2x] < 0 \quad \Rightarrow x < 0$

$\Rightarrow 2x < 0 \quad \Rightarrow x < 0$

$\Rightarrow f([2x]) = \begin{cases} 1 \text{ for } x < \frac{1}{2} \\ 0 \text{ for } x = \frac{1}{2} \end{cases}$

$\Rightarrow f([2x])$ is continuous at $x = -1$, $x = 0$, discontinuous at $x = 1/2$

8. (a) $f(x) = \frac{e^x \ell n x . 5^{(x^2+2)}\left(x^2 - 7x + 10\right)}{2x^2 - 11x + 12}$

$2x^2 - 11x + 12 = 0 \quad \Rightarrow x = \frac{3}{2}, 4$

Also {ℓn x is defined for $x > 0$

$\therefore D_f = (0, \infty) - \left\{\frac{3}{2}, 4\right\}$ and $f(x) = \frac{e^x \ell n x . 5^{(x^2+2)}(x-2)(x-5)}{(2x-3)(x-4)}$

$f(x)$ is discontinuous at $x = 0$ as $f(0^+)$

$= \frac{(1)(-\infty)(25)(10)}{12} = -\infty$ i.e., having infinite discontinuity.

Also $f(x)$ is discontinuous at $x = \frac{3}{2}$ and

$f\left(\frac{3^-}{2}\right) = \frac{e^{3/2}\ell n\left(\frac{3}{2}\right)(5)^{17/4}\cdot\left(\frac{-1}{2}\right)\left(\frac{-7}{2}\right)}{(0^-)(-4)} = \infty$ i.e., infinite discontinuity

But $f(x)$ is continuous in $\left(0, \frac{3}{2}\right)$

$\Rightarrow$ Range of $f(x) = (-\infty, \infty)$

9. (c) $f(x) = \tan^{-1}\left(\frac{1+x}{1-x}\right) - \tan^{-1} x$

$= \begin{cases} \tan^{-1}\left(\frac{\frac{1+x}{1-x} - x}{1 + \left(\frac{1+x}{1-x}\right).x}\right) \text{for } x < 1 \\ \text{Not defined at } x = 1 \\ -\pi + \tan^{-1}\left(\frac{\frac{1+x}{1-x} - x}{1 + \left(\frac{1+x}{1-x}\right).x}\right) \text{for } x > 1 \end{cases}$

$= \begin{cases} \tan^{-1}(1) \text{ for } x < 1 \\ \text{Not defined at } x = 1 \\ -\pi + \tan^{-1}(1) \text{ for } x > 1 \end{cases} = \begin{cases} \frac{\pi}{4} \text{ for } x < 1 \\ \text{Not defined at } x < 1 \\ -\frac{3\pi}{4} \text{ for } x > 1 \end{cases}$

$\Rightarrow$ Range of $f(x) = \left\{\frac{\pi}{4}, \frac{-3\pi}{4}\right\}$

10. (d) $f(x) = \left[\frac{1}{\ell n\left(x^2 + e\right)}\right] + \frac{1}{\sqrt{1+x^2}}$ i.e., $= \lim_{\alpha \to 0}(1+\alpha)^{1/\alpha}$

Here, $x^2 + e \geq e \quad \Rightarrow \ell n\,(x^2 + e) \geq 1$

$\Rightarrow 0 \leq \frac{1}{\ell n\left(x^2 + e\right)} \leq 1\ \forall x \in \mathbb{R}$

$\Rightarrow \left[\frac{1}{\ell n\left(x^2 + e\right)}\right] \in \{0, 1\}$ and $f(x) = \begin{cases} \frac{}{\sqrt{\ }} \text{ for } \neq 0 \\ 2 \text{ for } 0 \end{cases}$

$\Rightarrow$ Range $f(x) = (0, 1) \cup \{2\}$

11. (c) $f(x) = \cot^{-1} \log_{0.5}(x^4 - 2x^2 + 3)$

$\because$ Disc. of $(x^4 - 2x^2 + 3) = -8 < 0$

$\Rightarrow D_f = \mathbb{R}$ and $\log_{0.5}(x^4 - 2x^2 + 3)$

$= \log_{0.5}((x^2-1)^2 + 2) \in (-\infty, -1]$

$\Rightarrow f(x) \in [\cot^{-1}(-1), \cot^{-1}(-\infty))$

$\Rightarrow R_f = \left[\frac{3\pi}{4}, \pi\right)$

12. (a), (b), (c), (d)

$f(x) = [|x|] - |[x]|$

Let $x = k \in \mathbb{Z}$ and $k > 0$

$\Rightarrow k \geq 1$

$\Rightarrow f(k^-) = (k-1) - (k-1) = 0,$

$\Rightarrow f(k^+) = (k) - (k) = 0, f(k) = k - k = 0.$

$\Rightarrow f(x)$ is continuous at all $+ve$ integers.

If $x = k \in \mathbb{Z}$ and $k \leq -1$

$\Rightarrow f(k^-) = (-k) - (-(k-1)) = -1,$

$f(k^+) = (-k-1) - (-k) = -1; f(k) = -k - (-k) = 0$

$\Rightarrow f(x)$ is discontinuous at –ve integers.

$f(0^-) = 0 - 1 = -1, f(0^+) = 0 - 0 = 0.$

$\Rightarrow f(x)$ is discontinuous at $x = 0$

Let $x \in (k-1, k)$; $k \in \mathbb{Z}$ and $k \leq 0$

$\Rightarrow f(x^-) = [-x] - |k-1| = (-k) - (-k+1) = -1,$

$\Rightarrow f(x^+) = [-x] - |k-1| = (-k) - (-k+1) = -1, f(x) = -1$

$\Rightarrow f(x)$ is continuous at $x \ \forall \ \mathbb{Z}$ and Range = $\{0, -1\}$

13. (c) $f(x) = [3 + 4 \sin x]; x \in [0, 2\pi]$

$= 3 + [4 \sin x]$ which is discontinuous for which ($4 \sin x$) is an integer

$\Rightarrow 4 \sin x = \pm 4, \pm 3, \pm 2, \pm 1, 0$

$\Rightarrow \sin x = \pm 1, \pm\frac{3}{4}, \pm\frac{1}{2}, \pm\frac{1}{4}, 0$

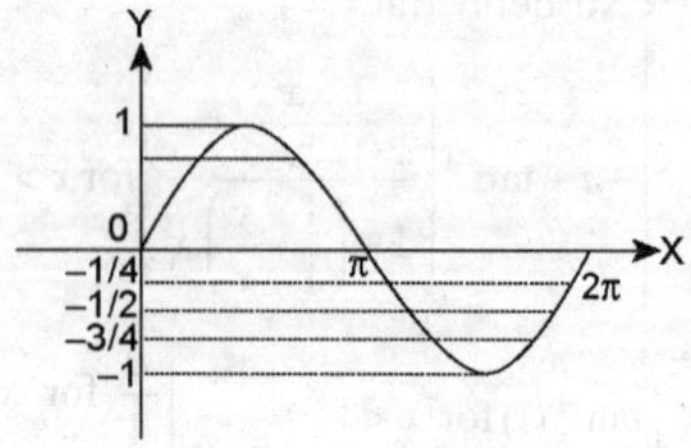

$f(\pi) = 3, f(\pi^+) = 3 + (-1) = 2,$

$f\left(\frac{3\pi^-}{2}\right) = 3 + (-4) = -1, f\left(\frac{3\pi^+}{2}\right) = 0, -1$

$f\left(\frac{3\pi}{2}\right) = 3 + (-4) = -1,$

$f(2\pi^-) = 3 + (-1) = 2, f(2\pi) = 3$

$\Rightarrow f(x)$ is discontinuous at $x = \pi, x = \pi + \sin^{-1}\left(\frac{1}{4}\right), \pi + \sin^{-1}\left(\frac{1}{2}\right), \pi + \sin^{-1}\left(\frac{3}{4}\right), 2\pi - \sin^{-1}\left(\frac{3}{4}\right), 2\pi - \sin^{-1}\left(\frac{1}{2}\right),$

$2\pi - \sin^{-1}\left(\frac{1}{4}\right), 2\pi$ i.e., at 8 points.

14. (c) $f(x) = \frac{1}{x + [x]}$; $D_f = \mathbb{R} - \{0\}$

Let $k \in \mathbb{Z}$; $f(k^-) = \frac{1}{k+k-1}$ $\frac{1}{2k-1}$ and $f(k^+) = \frac{1}{k+k} = \frac{1}{2k} = f(k)$

$\Rightarrow f(x)$ is discontinuous at all integers i.e., at infinitely many points.

15. (a) $f(x) = \frac{1}{\ell n\left[x^2 - 3x + 3\right]}$

$(x^2 - 3x + 3) \in \left[-\left(\frac{-3}{4}\right), \infty\right) = \left[\frac{3}{4}, \infty\right)$

$\Rightarrow (x^2 - 3x + 3) = 1$

$\Rightarrow x^2 - 3x + 2 = 0$

$\Rightarrow x = 1, 2$

$\therefore$ At $x = 1$ or $2, f(x) = \frac{1}{\ell n 1} \to \infty$

$\Rightarrow f(x)$ is discontinuous at Exactly 2 points

16. (c) $f(x) = \frac{2}{2+x}$; $x \neq -2$

$f(f(x)) = \frac{2}{2 + \left(\frac{2}{2+x}\right)} = \frac{2+x}{3+x} \Rightarrow x \neq -3$

$\Rightarrow f(f(f(x)) = \frac{2}{2 + \left(\frac{2+x}{3+x}\right)} = \frac{6+2x}{8+3x}$

$\Rightarrow x \neq -8/3$

$\Rightarrow f(x)$ is discontinuous at $x = -2, -3, -8/3$

17. (a) $f(x) = \lim\limits_{n \to \infty} \frac{2 \sin x}{3^n + (2\cos x)^{2n}} = \lim\limits_{n \to \infty} \frac{2 \sin x}{3^n + (4)^n (\cos^2 x)^n}$

For $x = m\pi$; $\cos^2 x = 1$, $\sin x = 0$

$\lim\limits_{n \to \infty} \frac{0}{(3)^n + (4)^n} = 0$

For $x \neq m\pi$; $\cos^2 x \in [0, 1)$

$f(x) = \lim\limits_{n \to \infty} \frac{\sin x}{(3)^n + (4)^n (\cos^2 x)^n}$

$= \lim\limits_{n \to \infty} \frac{\sin x}{(3)^n + \left(\frac{4}{\sec^2 x}\right)^n} = 0$

18. (d) $f(x) = \begin{cases} [x] + \sqrt{x - [x]}; x \geq 0 \\ \sin x \quad ; x < 0 \end{cases}$

Let $k \in \mathbb{N}$, then $f(k) = k + \sqrt{k - k} = k,$

$f(k^-) = (k-1) + \sqrt{k - (k-1)} = k$

$f(k^+) = k + \sqrt{k - k} = k$

$\Rightarrow f(x)$ is continuous at each +ve integer point.

$f(0^-) = 0; f(0^+) = 0; f(0) = 0$

Also $f(x)$ is continuous $\forall \ x < 0$

Now let $x \in (k-1, k)$; $k \in \mathbb{N}$, then

$f(x^-) = (k-1) + \sqrt{x - (k-1)}, f(x^+) = (k-1) + \sqrt{x - (k-1)},$

$f(x) = (k-1) + \sqrt{x - (k-1)},$

$\Rightarrow f(x)$ is continuous $\forall \ x \in \mathbb{R}$

19. (a), (c) $f(x) = \begin{cases} (1-\operatorname{sgn} x).\operatorname{sgn} x; x \le 1 \\ \dfrac{1}{1-e^{x/(1-x)}}; x > 1 \end{cases}$

$$= \begin{cases} -2 \text{ if } x < 0 \\ 0 \text{ if } 0 \le 1 \\ \dfrac{1}{1-e^{x/1-x}}; x > 1 \end{cases}$$

Clearly $f(x)$ is discontinuous at $x = 0$, let us examine for discontinuity at $x = 1$

$f(1^-) = f(1) = 0$; $f(1^+) = \lim_{x\to 1^+} \dfrac{1}{1-e^{x/1-x}} = \lim_{h\to 0^+} \dfrac{1}{1-e^{\frac{1+h}{-h}}} =$

$\lim_{h\to 0^+} \dfrac{1}{\left(1-e^{-\frac{1}{h}}.e^{-1}\right)} = 1$

$\Rightarrow f(x)$ is discontinuous at $x = 1$

20. (c) $f(x) = \dfrac{4-x^2}{|4x-x^3|} = \dfrac{(4-x^2)}{|x||4-x^2|}$

$\Rightarrow f(x)$ is not defined at $x = 0, \pm 2$

$$\therefore f(x) = \begin{cases} \dfrac{1}{|x|} \text{ for } 4-x^2 > 0 \\ -\dfrac{1}{|x|} \text{ for } 4-x^2 < 0 \end{cases}$$

$$= \begin{cases} -\dfrac{1}{x} \text{ for } -2 < x < 0 \text{ or } x > 2 \\ \dfrac{1}{2} \text{ for } 0 < x < 2 \text{ or } -\infty < x < -2 \end{cases}$$

$\Rightarrow f(x)$ is discontinuous at exactly three points, $x = -2$, $x = 0$ and $x = 2$.

TEXTUAL EXERCISE–4: (SUBJECTIVE)

1. $f(x) = \begin{cases} x\sin(\log x^2); x \ne 0 \text{ at } x = 0 \\ 0 \ ; x = 0 \end{cases}$

$f(0) = 0$ and $\lim_{x\to 0} f(x) = \lim_{x\to 0} x\sin(\log x^2) = 0$ as $\sin(\log x^2)$ oscillates in between -1 and 1.

$\Rightarrow f(x)$ is continuous $\forall x \in \mathbb{R}$.

$\Rightarrow f'(0) = \lim_{x\to 0} \dfrac{f(x)-f(0)}{x-0}$

$= \lim_{x\to 0} \sin(\log x^2)$ which does not exist uniquely.

Thus $f(x)$ is not differentiable at $x = 0$

2. (a) $f(x) = |x-1| + |x-3|$

$$\Rightarrow f(x) = \begin{cases} -2x+4 \text{ for } x < 1 \\ 2 \text{ for } 1 \le x < 3 \\ 2x-4 \text{ for } x \ge 3 \end{cases}$$

$\therefore f(x) = 2$ for $1 \le x \le 3$

$\Rightarrow f'(x) = 0 \ \forall x \in (1, 3) \quad \Rightarrow f'(2) = 0$

(b) $f(x) = \dfrac{|x|}{[x]}$; $x \notin (0, 1)$

$\Rightarrow f(2^-) = \dfrac{2}{1} = 2, f(2^+) = \dfrac{2}{2} = 1$ and $f(2) = \dfrac{2}{2} = 1$

$\Rightarrow f(x)$ is discontinuous at $x = 2$

$\Rightarrow f'(2)$ does not exist.

3. $f(x) = \begin{cases} \dfrac{|x-1|}{x-1}; x \ne 1 \\ 0 \ ; x = 1 \end{cases}$

$f(1^-) = -1, f(1^+) = 1, f(1) = 0$

$\Rightarrow f(x)$ is discontinuous at $x = 1$ and hence non-differentiable at $x = 1$

$$\therefore f(x) = \begin{cases} -1 \text{ for } x < 1 \\ 0 \text{ at } x = 1 \\ 1 \text{ for } x > 1 \end{cases}$$

$\Rightarrow f(x)$ has horizontal tangent at $x < 1$ and $x > 1$ and vertical tangent at $x = 1$

4. $f(x) = |\sin x - \cos x|$

$$f\left(\frac{\pi}{2}^-\right) = \left(\sin\frac{\pi}{2} - \cos\frac{\pi}{2}\right) = 1$$

$$f\left(\frac{\pi}{2}^+\right) = \left(\sin\frac{\pi}{2} - \cos\frac{\pi}{2}\right) = 1 = f\left(\frac{\pi}{2}\right)$$

$$\left(\because \sin x > \cos x \text{ for } x \in \left(\frac{\pi}{2}-8, \frac{\pi}{2}+8\right)\right)$$

$\Rightarrow f(x)$ is continuous at $x = \dfrac{\pi}{2}$

$\therefore f(x) = (\sin x - \cos x)$ for $\dfrac{\pi}{4} \le x < \dfrac{5\pi}{4}$

$\Rightarrow f'(x) = \cos x + \sin x$ for $\dfrac{\pi}{4} < x < \dfrac{5\pi}{4}$

$\Rightarrow f'\left(\dfrac{\pi}{2}\right) = \cos\dfrac{\pi}{2} + \sin\dfrac{\pi}{2} = 1$

5. $f(x) = \begin{cases} x[x], 0 \le x < 2 \\ x^2 - x, 2 \le x \le 3 \end{cases}$

$f(1^-) = 0; f(1) = 1; f(1^+) = 1$

$\Rightarrow f(x)$ is discontinuous at $x = 1$

$f(2^-) = 2, f(2) = 2, f(2^+) = 2$

$\Rightarrow f(x)$ is continuous at $x = 2$

$$f(x) = \begin{cases} 0 \ ; 0 \le x < 1 \\ x; 1 \le x < 2 \\ x^2 - x \ ; 2 \le x \le 3 \end{cases}$$

$$\Rightarrow f'(x) = \begin{cases} 0 \ ; 0 < x < 1 \\ 1 \ ; 1 < x < 2 \\ 2x-1; 2 < x < 3 \end{cases}$$

$\Rightarrow f'(2^-) = 1; f'(2^+) = 2(2) - 1 = 3$

$\Rightarrow f(x)$ is non–differentiable at $x = 1$ and $x = 2$

6. $f(x) = \begin{cases} (x)^p \cos\left[\frac{1}{x}\right]; x \neq 0 \\ 0\ ; x = 0 \end{cases}$

(i) For continuity at $x = 0$;
$f(0^-) = 0 = f(0^+)$

$\Rightarrow \lim_{x\to 0^-} (x)^p \cos\left(\frac{1}{x}\right) = \lim_{x\to 0^+} x^p \cos\left(\frac{1}{x}\right) = 0$

$\Rightarrow$ p > 0

(ii) For differentiable at $x = 0$

$$\lim_{x\to 0^+} \frac{f(x)-f(0)}{x-0} = \lim_{x\to 0^+} \frac{f(-x)-f(0)}{-x}$$

$$\Rightarrow \lim_{x\to 0^+} \frac{(x)^p \cos\left(\frac{1}{x}\right)}{x} = \lim_{x\to 0^+} \frac{(-x)^p\left(-\frac{1}{x}\right)}{-x}$$

$$\Rightarrow \lim_{x\to 0^+} (x)^{p-1}.\cos\left(\frac{1}{x}\right) = \lim_{x\to 0^+} (-x)^{p-1}\left(\frac{1}{x}\right) = 0$$

For existence of limit uniquely, $p - 1 > 0$

$\Rightarrow p > 1$

7. $f(x) = \begin{cases} (x-1)^2 \sin\left[\frac{1}{(x-1)}\right] - |x|; x \neq 1 \\ -1; \quad x = 1 \end{cases}$

$$\lim_{x\to 1} f(x) = \lim_{x\to 1}\left\{(x-1)^2 \sin\left[\frac{1}{(x-1)}\right] - |x|\right\}$$

$= (0 - 1) = -1$ and $f(1) = -1$

$\Rightarrow f(x)$ is continuous at $x = 1$.

$$\text{Now, } \lim_{x\to 1^+} \frac{f(x)-f(1)}{(x-1)} = \lim_{x\to 1^+} \frac{(x-1)^2 \sin\left(\frac{1}{x-1}\right) - x + 1}{(x-1)}$$

$= 0 - 1 = -1$

$$\text{Also } \lim_{x\to 1^-} \frac{f(x)-f(1)}{(x-1)} = \lim_{x\to 1^-} \frac{(x-1)^2 \sin\left[\frac{1}{(x-1)}\right] - x + 1}{(x-1)}$$

$= -1$

Thus L.H.D = R.H.D = – 1

$\Rightarrow f(x)$ is differentiable at $x = 1$

8. $f(x) = a\,|\sin x| + be^{|x|} + c|x|^3$

$f(0^-) = b, f(0^+) = b = f(0)$

Thus $f(x)$ is continuous $x = 0$

$$\text{L.H.D} = \lim_{x\to 0^-} \frac{f(x)-f(0)}{x-0} = \lim_{x\to 0^-} \frac{a|\sin x| + be^{|x|} + c|x|^3 - b}{x}$$

$$= \lim_{x\to 0^-} \frac{-a\sin x + be^{-x} - cx^3 - b}{x}$$

$$= \lim_{x\to 0^-} \frac{-a\cos x - be^{-x} - c(3x^2)}{1}$$

$\Rightarrow -a - b = 0 \qquad \Rightarrow a + b = 0 \qquad$ ...(i)

$$\text{R.H.D} = \lim_{x\to 0^+} \frac{f(x)-f(0)}{x-0} = \lim_{x\to 0^+} \frac{a|\sin x| + be^{|x|} + c|x|^3 - b}{x}$$

$$= \lim_{x\to 0^+} \frac{a\sin x + be^{x} + cx^3 - b}{x} = \lim_{x\to 0^+} \frac{a\cos x + be^{x} + 3cx^2}{1}$$

$\Rightarrow a + b = 0$ ...(ii)

$\therefore f(x)$ will be differentiable at $x = 0$ for $a + b = 0, c \in \mathbb{R}$

9. $f(x) = \begin{cases} x^2 \sin\frac{1}{x};\ x \neq 0 \\ 0; \quad x = 0 \end{cases}$

$f(0^-) = f(0^+) = f(0) = 0$

$\Rightarrow f(x)$ is continuous at $x = 0$

$$\text{L.H.D} = \lim_{x\to 0^-} \frac{f(x)-f(0)}{x-0} = \lim_{x\to 0^-} \frac{x^2 \sin\frac{1}{x}}{x} = 0$$

$$\text{R.H.D} = \lim_{x\to 0^+} \frac{f(x)-f(0)}{x-0} = \lim_{x\to 0^+} \frac{x^2 \sin\frac{1}{x} - 0}{x} = 0$$

$\Rightarrow f(x)$ is differentiable at $x = 0$ and $f'(x)$

$$= \left\{x^2\left(-\frac{1}{x^2}\right)\cos\frac{1}{x} + 2x\sin\frac{1}{x} \text{ for } x \neq 0\right.$$

$$\Rightarrow f'(x) = \left\{-\cos\frac{1}{x} + 2\sin x\frac{1}{x} \text{ for } x \neq 0\right.$$

$\Rightarrow \lim_{x\to 0} f'(x)$ does not exist uniquely .

$\Rightarrow$ Derivate function $f'(x)$ is not continuous at $x = 0$
Hence the differentiable of a function not necessarily of implies continuity of its derivate function.

10. Let $f(x) =$ be an even derivate function

$$\Rightarrow f'(x) = \lim_{h\to 0^+} \frac{f(x+h)-f(x)}{h} = \lim_{h\to 0^+} \frac{f(x-h)-f(x)}{-h} =$$

$g(x)$ (say)

$$\Rightarrow g(-x) = \lim_{h\to 0^+} \frac{f(-x+h)-f(-x)}{h} = \lim_{h\to 0^+} \frac{f(x-h)-f(x)}{h}$$

(As f is even function)

$$= -\lim_{h\to 0^+} \frac{f(x+h)-f(x)}{-h} = -g(x)$$

$\Rightarrow g(x) = f'(x)$ is an odd function.

11. Let $f(x)$ be an even function and $f'(0)$ exists.

$$f'(0) = \lim \frac{(h) \quad f(0)}{}$$

$$= \lim_{h\to 0^+} \frac{f(-h)-f(0)}{-h} \qquad \text{...(i)}$$

$$= \lim_{h\to 0^+} \frac{f(h)-f(0)}{-h} \qquad (\because \text{ f is even})$$

$$= -\left(\lim_{h\to 0^+} \frac{f(h)-f(0)}{h}\right) = -f'(0)$$

$\Rightarrow 2f'(0) = 0 \qquad \Rightarrow f'(0) = 0$

12. $f(x) = \begin{cases} x.\dfrac{a^{1/x} - a^{-1/x}}{a^{1/x} + a^{-1/x}}, x \neq 0 \\ 0\ , x = 0 \end{cases}$; where a > 0

Case (i): 0 < a < 1

$$\lim_{x\to 0^-} f(x) = \lim_{x\to 0^-} x.\left(\frac{1-a^{-2/x}}{1+a^{-2/x}}\right) = 0\left(\frac{1-0}{1+0}\right) = 0$$

$$\lim_{x\to 0^+} f(x) = \lim_{x\to 0^+} x.\left(\frac{a^{2/x}-1}{a^{2/x}+1}\right) = 0\left(\frac{0-1}{0+1}\right) = 0$$

Case (ii): 1 < a < ∞

$$\lim_{x\to 0^-} f(x) = \lim_{x\to 0^-} x.\left(\frac{a^{2/x}-1}{a^{2/x}+1}\right) = 0\left(\frac{0-1}{0+1}\right) = 0$$

$$\lim_{x\to 0^+} f(x) = \lim_{x\to 0^+} x.\left(\frac{1-a^{-2/x}}{1+a^{-2/x}}\right) = 0\left(\frac{1-0}{1+0}\right) = 0$$

∴ $f(0^-) = f(0^+) = f(0) = 0$

⇒ $f(x)$ is continuous at $x = 0$

$$f'(0) = \lim_{h\to 0^+} \frac{f(-h) - f(0)}{-h} = \lim_{h\to 0^+} \frac{(-h)}{(-h)}\left[\frac{a^{-1/h} - a^{1/h}}{a^{-1/h} + a^{1/h}}\right]$$

$$= \lim_{h\to 0^+}\left[\frac{a^{-1/h} - a^{1/h}}{a^{-1/h} + a^{1/h}}\right]$$

For 0 < a < 1

$$= \lim_{h\to 0^+}\left[\frac{1-a^{2/h}}{1+a^{2/h}}\right] = 1$$

For a > 1

$$= \lim_{h\to 0^+}\left[\frac{a^{-2/h}-1}{a^{-2/h}+1}\right] = -1$$

$$f'(0^+) = \lim_{h\to 0^+} \frac{f(h) - f(0)}{h} = \lim_{h\to 0^+} \frac{a^{1/h} - a^{-1/h}}{a^{1/h} + a^{-1/h}}$$

For 0 < a < 1, $= \lim_{h\to 0^+}\left(\dfrac{a^{2/h}-1}{a^{2/h}+1}\right) = -1$

For a > 1, $= \lim_{h\to 0^+}\left(\dfrac{1-a^{-2/h}}{1+a^{-2/h}}\right) = 1$

⇒ $f'(0^-) \neq f'(0^+)$

⇒ $f(x)$ is not differentiable at $x = 0$

13. $f(x) = \begin{cases} \dfrac{1}{[x]}; |x| \geq \dfrac{1}{2} \\ ax^2 + bx + c; |x| < \dfrac{1}{2} \end{cases}$

$$\Rightarrow f(x) = \begin{cases} ax^2 + bx + c; \dfrac{-1}{2} < x < \dfrac{1}{2} \\ \dfrac{1}{[x]}; x \leq \dfrac{-1}{2} \text{ or } x \geq 1 \\ \text{Not defined for } \dfrac{1}{2} \leq x < 1 \end{cases}$$

∴ Continuity at $x = 1$

⇒ $f(1^+) = f(1)$ which is true

Continuity at $x = -1/2$

$$\Rightarrow f\left(\frac{-1^-}{2}\right) = f\left(\frac{-1^+}{2}\right) = f\left(\frac{-1}{2}\right)$$

$$\Rightarrow -1 = \frac{a}{4} - \frac{b}{2} + c$$

⇒ $a - 2b + 4c = -4$ …(i)

Also $f'(x) = \begin{cases} 2ax + b; \dfrac{-1}{2} < x < \dfrac{1}{2} \\ 0 \text{ for } x < \dfrac{-1}{2} \text{ or } x > 1 x \notin \mathbb{Z} \end{cases}$

Differentiability at $x = 1$

⇒ $f'(1^+)$ exists finitely which is true as it is 0.

Differentiability at $x = \dfrac{-1}{2}$

$$\Rightarrow f'\left(\frac{-1^-}{2}\right) = f'\left(\frac{-1^+}{2}\right)$$

⇒ $0 = -a + b$ ⇒ $a = b$

∴ From (1), $-a + 4c = -4$

⇒ $4c = a - 4$

⇒ $(a, b, c) \in \left\{\left(k, k, \dfrac{\quad}{\quad}\right); k \in \mathbb{R}\right\}$

14. $f(x) = \begin{cases} (x-e)(2)^{2\left(\frac{1}{x-e}\right)}; x \neq e \\ 0\ ; x = e \end{cases}$

$$\lim_{x\to e^+} = \lim_{t\to 0^+} t(2)^{2/t} = \lim_{t\to 0^+} \frac{(2)^{2/t}}{1/t}$$

$$= \lim_{t\to 0^+} \frac{(4)^{1/t}}{1/t} = \lim_{z\to\infty} \frac{(4)^z}{z} = \lim_{z\to\infty} \frac{(4)^z \ell n4}{(1)} = \infty \text{ and}$$

$$\lim_{x\to e^-} f(x) = \lim_{t\to 0^-} (t)(2)^{2/t} = \lim_{t\to 0^-} \frac{(2)^{2/t}}{1/t}$$

$$= \lim_{z\to -\infty} \frac{(4)^z}{z} = \lim_{z\to -\infty} \frac{(4)^z \ell n4}{(1)} = 0$$

∴ L.H.L ≠ R.H.L

⇒ $f(x)$ is discontinuous and hence non-differentiable at $x = e$

15. $f(x) = \dfrac{xg(x)}{|x|}$, $g(0) = g'(0) = 0$

⇒ $f(x) = g(x)$ for $x > 0$ and $f(x) = -g(x)$ for $x < 0$

∴ $\lim_{x\to 0^-} f(x) = \lim_{x\to 0^-} -g(x) = -\lim_{x\to 0^-} g(x)$ …(i)

And $\lim_{x\to 0^+} f(x) = \lim_{x\to 0^+} g(x)$ …(ii)

∴ $g'(0)$ exists

⇒ $g(x)$ is continuous at $x = 0$

⇒ $\lim_{x\to 0^-} f(x) = \lim_{x\to 0^+} f(x) = f(0) = 0$ [∵ of (i) and (ii)]

Now $\lim_{x\to 0^+} \dfrac{f(x) - f(0)}{x} = \lim_{x\to 0^+} \dfrac{f(x)}{x} = \lim_{x\to 0^+} \dfrac{g(x)}{x}$

$= \lim_{x\to 0^+} \dfrac{g(x) - g(0)}{x} = g'(0^+) = 0$ and

$$\lim_{x\to 0^-}\frac{f(x)-f(0)}{x}=\lim_{x\to 0^-}\frac{f(x)}{x}=\lim_{x\to 0^-}\frac{(-g(x))}{x}=-g'(0^-)=0$$

$\Rightarrow f'(0)=0$

16. $\forall\, x \in [0, \infty)$; when $x \to 0$, $1+|x|^n > 1$

$\Rightarrow f(0^-)=f(0^+)=0=f(0)$

$\Rightarrow f(x)$ is continuous at $x = 0$

Now L.H.D $=\lim\limits_{x\to 0^-}\dfrac{f(x)-f(0)}{x-0}=\lim\limits_{x\to 0^-}\dfrac{1}{1+|x|^n}$ and

R.H.D $=\lim\limits_{x\to 0^+}\dfrac{f(x)-f(0)}{x-0}=\lim\limits_{x\to 0^+}\dfrac{1}{1+|x|^n}$

Clearly L.H.D and R.H.D are equal and finite $\forall\, x \in [0, \infty)$

$\Rightarrow f(x)$ is differentiable at $x = 0$

17. Clearly k is non- negative.

$\lim\limits_{x\to(b-k)^-} f(x)=\lim\limits_{x\to(b+k)^-} c+|x-b|$

$(\because x<b-k \Rightarrow x-b<-k\le 0 \Rightarrow |x-b|<k)$

$= c + |b - k - b| = c + k$ and

$\lim\limits_{x\to(b-k)^+} = \lim\limits_{x\to(b-k)^+}\left(a+(x-b)^2\right)=a+\left(k^2\right)$ and $f(b-k) = a +$

$(k)^2$ $(\because x>b-k \Rightarrow x-b>-k \Rightarrow |x-b|<k)$

$\therefore$ For continuity at $x = b - k$, $a + k^2 = c + k$.(i)

R.H.D $=\lim\limits_{x\to(b-k)^+}\dfrac{f(x)-f(b-k)}{x-(b-k)}$

$=\lim\limits_{x\to(b-k)^+}\dfrac{a+(x-b)^2-a-k^2}{x-b+k}=\lim\limits_{x\to(b-k)^+}\dfrac{(x-b)^2-k^2}{(x-b)+k}$

$=\lim\limits_{x\to(b-k)^+}(x-b)-k=-2k$

L.H.D $=\lim\limits_{x\to(b-k)^-}\dfrac{f(x)-f(b-k)}{x-(b-k)}$

$=\lim\limits_{x\to(b-k)^-}\dfrac{c+|x-b|-(a+k^2)}{x-(b-k)}$

$=\lim\limits_{x\to(b-k)^-}\dfrac{c+|x-b|-c-k}{x-(b-k)}$

$=\lim\limits_{x\to(b-k)^-}\dfrac{-x+b-k}{x-(b-k)}=-1$

$\therefore$ For differentiable at $x = b - k$, $-2k = -1$

$\Rightarrow k=\dfrac{1}{2}$ $\qquad \Rightarrow a-c=k-k^2=\dfrac{1}{4}$ (using (i))

TEXTUAL EXERCISE–4: (OBJECTIVE)

1. (b) $y = |x - a| + |x - b|$,

$f(x)$ being the sum of two continuous is also continuous at $x = a, b$. (Let $a < b$)

$$f(x)=\begin{cases}-x+a-x+b \text{ for } x<a\\ x-a-x+b \text{ for } a<x<b\\ x-a+x-b \text{ for } x>b\end{cases}=\begin{cases}-2x+a+b \text{ for } x<a\\ -a+b \text{ for } a\le x<b\\ 2x-a-b \text{ for } x\ge b\end{cases}$$

$$\Rightarrow f'(x)=\begin{cases}-2 \text{ for } x<a\\ 0 \text{ for } a<x<b\\ 2 \text{ for } x>b\end{cases}$$

$\Rightarrow f(x)$ is non-differentiable at $x = a$ and at $x = b$

2. (d) $f(x) = ||x - 1| -1| + 1$

$$=\begin{cases}|-x+1-1|+1 \text{ for } x<1\\ |x-1-1|+|+1 \text{ for } x\ge 1\end{cases}$$

$$=\begin{cases}|-x|+1 \text{ for } x<1\\ |x-2|+1 \text{ for } x\ge 1\end{cases}$$

$$=\begin{cases}-x+1 \text{ for } x<0\\ x+1 \text{ for } 0\le x<1\\ -x+3 \text{ for } 1\le x<2\\ x-1 \text{ for } x\ge 2\end{cases}$$

$$\Rightarrow f'(x)=\begin{cases}-1 \text{ for } x<0\\ 1 \text{ for } 0<x<1\\ -1 \text{ for } 1<x<2\\ 1 \text{ for } x>2\end{cases}$$

$\Rightarrow f(x)$ is non-differentiable at $x = 0$, $x = 1$ and $x = 2$

i.e., at (0, 1), (1, 2), (2, 1)

3. (c) $f(x) = \sin|x| - e^{|x|}$

Both $\sin|x|$ and $e^{|x|}$ being continuous

$\Rightarrow f(x)$ is also a continuous function.

$$f(x)=\begin{cases}-\sin x-e^{-x} \text{ for } x<0\\ \sin x-e^{x} \text{ for } x\ge 0\end{cases}$$

$$\Rightarrow f'(x)=\begin{cases}-\cos x+e^{-x} \text{ for } x<0\\ \cos x-e^{x} \text{ for } x>0\end{cases}$$

$\Rightarrow f(0^-) = f(0^+) = -1, f'(0^-) = 0, f'(0^+) = 0$

$\Rightarrow f(x)$ is differentiable at $x = 0$

4. (d) $f(x) = |\text{Max.}\{x^2 - 2, x\}| = |g(x)|$

The graph of $g(x)$ is as shown below.

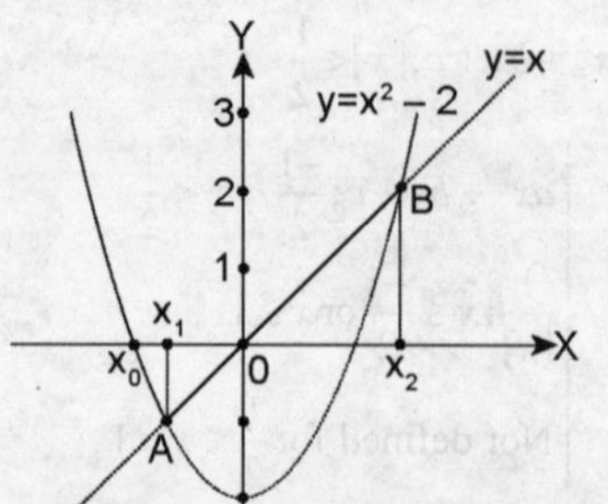

The graph of $f(x) = |g(x)|$ is as shown below.

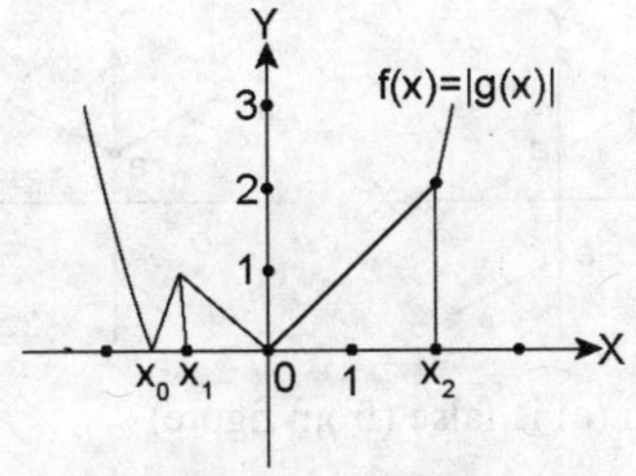

Clearly $f(x)$ is non-differentiable at $x = x_0$, $x = x_1$, $x = 0$ (origin), $x = x_2$ i.e., at 4 points.

5. (c) $f(x) = \begin{cases} \dfrac{\sin x}{|x|}; x \neq 0 \\ 1; x = 0 \end{cases} = \begin{cases} \dfrac{\sin x}{-x}; x < 0 \\ \dfrac{\sin x}{x}; x > 0 \\ 1; x = 0 \end{cases}$

$f(0^-) = -1$; for $(0^+) = 1, f(0) = 1$

$\Rightarrow$ $f(x)$ is discontinuous and hence non-differentiable at $x = 0$.

6. (b) $f(x) = \sin^{-1}(\sin x) = \begin{cases} x; -\dfrac{\pi}{2} \leq x \leq \dfrac{\pi}{2} \\ -x + \pi; \dfrac{\pi}{2} \leq x \leq \dfrac{3\pi}{2} \end{cases}$

Graphically shown below.

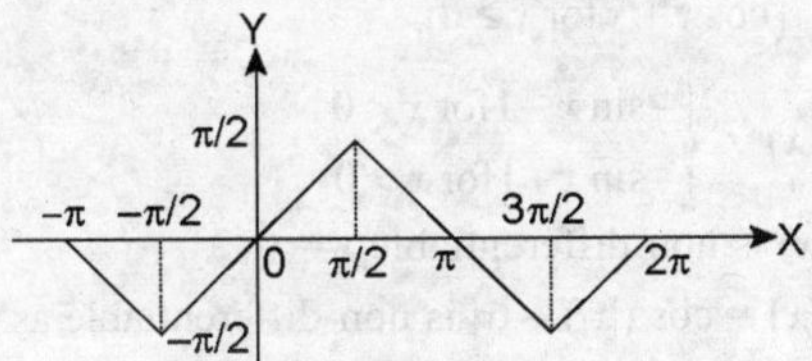

Clearly $f(x)$ is non-differentiable at $x = \pi/2$

7. (a) $f(x) = [x] \sin \pi x$

$$\text{L.H.D} = \lim_{h \to 0^+} \frac{f(k-h) - f(k)}{-h}$$

$$= \lim_{h \to 0^+} \frac{[k-h]\sin \pi(k-h) - [k]\sin \pi k}{-h}$$

$$= \lim_{h \to 0^+} \frac{(k-h)(-1)^k \sin(-h\pi) - 0}{-h} = \lim_{h \to 0^+} \frac{(-1)^k (k-1)\sin \pi h}{h}$$

$$= (-1)^k \pi (k-1)$$

8. (a) $f(x) = \text{Max.} \{9 - 4x, 2x^2 + 3, 4x + 1\}$

$g(x) = 2x^2 + 3$

$\Rightarrow$ $g'(x) = 4x$ and $2x^2 + 3 = 4x + 1$

$\Rightarrow$ $2x^2 - 4x + 2 = 0$

$\Rightarrow$ $(x - 1)^2 = 0$

$\Rightarrow$ $y = 2x^2 + 3$ and $y = 4x + 1$ touch each other at $x = 1$.

The graph of $f(x)$ will be as shown below.

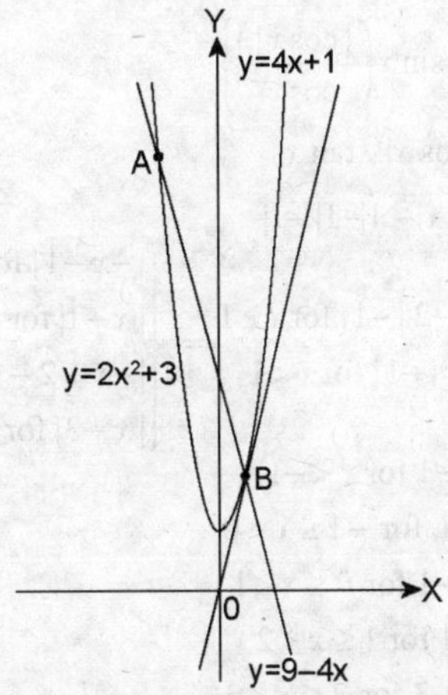

Clearly $f(x)$ has 2 point of non-differentiability.

9. (c) $y = \text{Max.} \{e^{|x|}, \ell n\,|x|\}$

The graph of above function is as shown below.

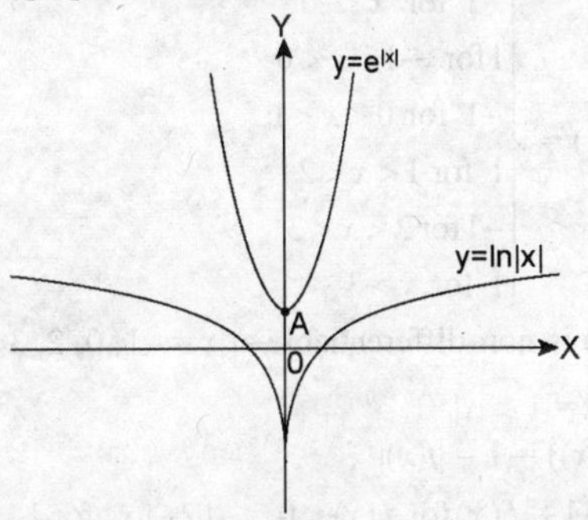

$\Rightarrow$ $f(x)$ is non-differentiable only at 1 values of x corresponding to points A.

10. (d) $f(x) = \begin{cases} \tan^{-1} x; |x| \leq 1 \\ \dfrac{1}{2}(|x| - 1); |x| > 1 \end{cases} = \begin{cases} \tan^{-1} x; -1 \leq x \leq 1 \\ \dfrac{1}{2}(-x-1); x < -1 \\ \dfrac{1}{2}(x-1); x > 1 \end{cases}$

$\Rightarrow$ $f(x)$ is discontinuous as well as non-differentiable at $x = -1, 1$

$\Rightarrow$ Domain of derivate of function is $\mathbb{R} - \{-1, 1\}$

11. (a) $|f(x) - f(y)| \leq |x - y|^{(2n+1)}; n \in \mathbb{N}$.

$\Rightarrow$ $\left|\dfrac{f(x) - f(y)}{x - y}\right| \leq |x - y|^{2n}$

$\Rightarrow$ $\left|\lim\limits_{x \to y}\left(\dfrac{f(x) - f(y)}{x - y}\right)\right| \leq \left|\lim\limits_{x \to y}(x - y)\right|^{2n}$

$\Rightarrow$ $|f'(y)| \leq 0\ \forall\ y \in \mathbb{R}$

$\Rightarrow$ $f'(y) = 0\ \forall\ y \in \mathbb{R}$ or $f'(x) = 0\ \forall\ x \in \mathbb{R}$

12. (d) $y = |\cos x| = \begin{cases} \cos x; \cos x \geq 0 \\ -\cos x; \cos x < 0 \end{cases}$

$\Rightarrow$ $y' = \begin{cases} -\sin x; \cos x > 0 \\ \sin x; \cos x < 0 \end{cases}$

$\Rightarrow\ y' = \left\{-\sin x\left(\frac{|\cos x|}{\cos x}\right)\right\}$

$\Rightarrow\ y' = -|\cos x| \,.\, \tan x$

13. (b) $f(x) = |||x-1|-1|-1|$

$$= \begin{cases} ||x-2|-1| \text{ for } x \geq 1 \\ ||-x|-1| \text{ for } x < 1 \end{cases} = \begin{cases} |-x-1| \text{ for } x < 0 \\ |x-1| \text{ for } 0 \leq x < 1 \\ |-x+2-1| \text{ for } 1 \leq x < 2 \\ |x-3| \text{ for } x \geq 2 \end{cases}$$

$$= \begin{cases} -x-1 \text{ for } x < -1 \\ x+1 \text{ for } -1 \leq x < 0 \\ -x+1 \text{ for } 0 \leq x < 1 \\ x-1 \text{ for } 1 \leq x < 2 \\ -x+3 \text{ for } 2 \leq x < 3 \\ x-3 \text{ for } x \geq 3 \end{cases}$$

$\Rightarrow$ $f(x)$ is continuous $\forall\ x \in \mathbb{R}$

$$\Rightarrow f'(x) = \begin{cases} -1 \text{ for } x < -1 \\ 1 \text{ for } -1 < x < 0 \\ -1 \text{ for } 0 < x < 1 \\ 1 \text{ for } 1 < x < 2 \\ -1 \text{ for } 2 < x < 3 \\ 1 \text{ for } x > 3 \end{cases}$$

$\Rightarrow$ $f(x)$ is non-differentiable at $x = -1, 0, 2, 3$

14. (d) $f(x) = 1 - |x|$

$f(f(x)) = 1 - |f(x)|$

$$= \begin{cases} 1+f(x) \text{ for } f(x) < 0 \\ 1-f(x) \text{ for } f(x) \geq 0 \end{cases} = \begin{cases} 2-|x| \text{ for } 1-|x| < 0 \\ |x| \text{ for } 1-|x| \geq 0 \end{cases}$$

$$= \begin{cases} 2+x \text{ for } x < -1 \\ -x \text{ for } -1 \leq x < 0 \\ x \text{ for } 0 \leq x \leq 1 \\ 2-x \text{ for } x > 1 \end{cases}$$

$$\Rightarrow f'(x) = \begin{cases} 1 \text{ for } x < -1 \\ -1 \text{ for } -1 < x < 0 \\ 1 \text{ for } 0 < x < 1 \\ -1 \text{ for } x > 1 \end{cases}$$

$\Rightarrow$ $f(x)$ is non-differentiable at $x = -1, 0, 1$ i.e., at 3 points

15. (a)

$\because\ |f(x)| = \begin{cases} f(x) \text{ for } f(x) \geq 0 \\ -f(x) \text{ for } f(x) < 0 \end{cases}$

Let $f(x) = 0$ at $x = \ell$ and $f(x) < 0$ for $x \in (\ell - \delta, \ell)\delta \to 0^+$

$f(x) > 0$ for $x \in (\ell, \ell + \in)$, $\in \to 0^+$, then $g(x) = |f(x)| =$

$\begin{cases} f(x) \text{ for } x \in [\ell, \ell + \in) \\ -f(x) \text{ for } x \in (\ell - \delta, \ell) \end{cases}$

$\Rightarrow$ $g(\ell^-) = -f(\ell^-) = f(\ell) = 0$ and $g(\ell^+) = f(\ell^+) = f(\ell) = 0$

As $f(x)$ is continuous at $x = \ell$

$\Rightarrow$ $g(x) = |f(x)|$ is continues function.

Option (b) is false (from figure)

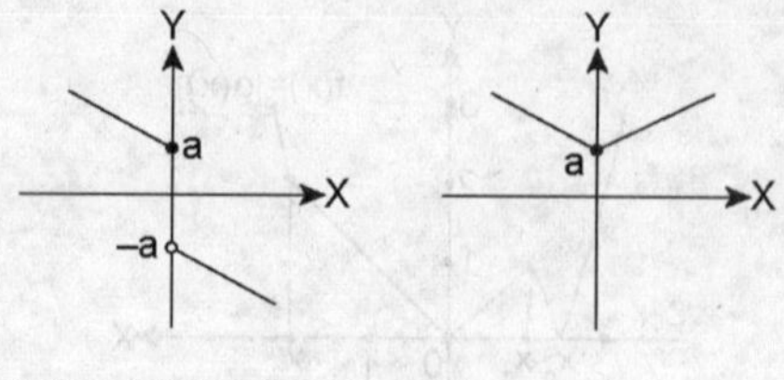

Option (c) is false (from figure)

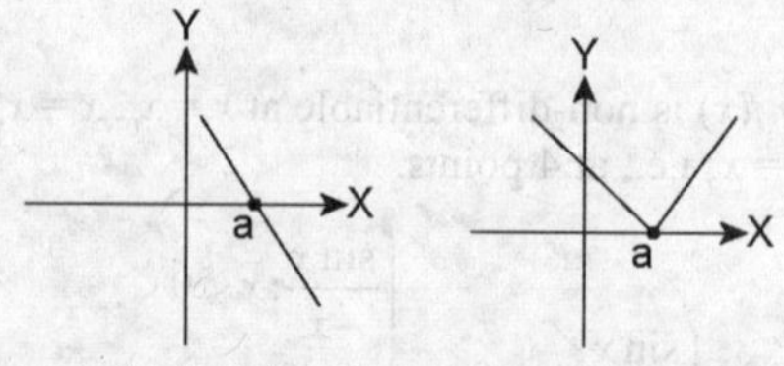

Option (d) is false (from figure)

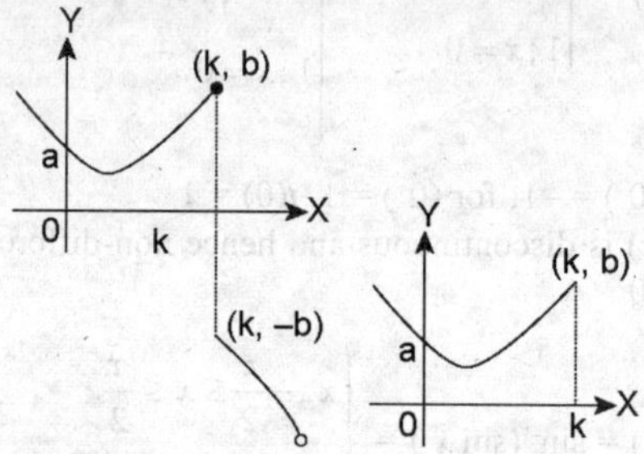

16. (d) (a) $f(x) = \cos(|x|) + |x|$

$$= \begin{cases} \cos x - x \text{ for } x < 0 \\ \cos x + x \text{ for } x \geq 0 \end{cases}$$

$\Rightarrow\ f'(x) = \begin{cases} -\sin x - 1 \text{ for } x < 0 \\ -\sin x + 1 \text{ for } x > 0 \end{cases}$

$f(x)$ is non-differentiable $x = 0$

(b) $g(x) = \cos(|x|) - |x|$ is non-differentiable as in case (a)

(c) $h(x) = \sin(|x|) + |x| = \begin{cases} -\sin x - x \text{ for } x < 0 \\ \sin x + x \text{ for } x \geq 0 \end{cases}$

$\Rightarrow\ h'(x) = \begin{cases} -\cos x - 1 \text{ for } x < 0 \\ -\cos x + 1 \text{ for } x > 0 \end{cases}$

$\Rightarrow$ $h(x)$ is non-differentiable at $x = 0$

(d) $k(x) = \sin(|x|) - |x| = \begin{cases} -\sin x + x \text{ for } x < 0 \\ \sin x - x \text{ for } x \geq 0 \end{cases}$

$\Rightarrow\ k'(x) = \begin{cases} -\cos x + 1 \text{ for } x < 0 \\ \cos x - 1 \text{ for } x > 0 \end{cases}$

$\Rightarrow$ $k(x)$ is differentiable at $x = 0$

17. (b) $f(x) = [\tan^2 x]$

$\lim\limits_{x \to 0^-} f(x) = \lim\limits_{x \to 0^-}\left[\tan^2 x\right] = 0$, $\lim\limits_{x \to 0^+} f(x) = \lim\limits_{x \to 0^+}\left[\tan^2 x\right] = 0$

$f(0) = [\tan^2 0] = 0$

$\Rightarrow$ $f(x)$ is continuous at $x = 0$

Clearly, $f(x) = 0$ for $x \in \left(\frac{-\pi}{4}, \frac{\pi}{4}\right)$

$\Rightarrow$ $f'(x) = 0$ at $x = 0$ i.e., $f(x)$ is differentiable at $x = 0$ and $f'(0) = 0$

18. **(d)** $f(x)=\begin{cases}|2x-3|[x];x\ge 1\\ \sin\left(\frac{\pi x}{2}\right);x<1\end{cases}=\begin{cases}(-2x+3);1\le x<\frac{3}{2}\\ (2x-3)[x];x\ge\frac{3}{2}\\ \sin\left(\frac{\pi x}{2}\right);x<1\end{cases}$

Clearly $f(x)$ is continuous function at $x = 1$ and $x=\frac{3}{2}$, $f(2^-) = 1; f(2^+) = 2$

$\Rightarrow$ $f(x)$ is discontinuous and non- differentiable at $x = 2$.

Also $f'(1^-) = 0; f'(1^+) = -2; f'\left(\frac{3^-}{2}\right)=2; f'\left(\frac{3^+}{2}\right)=2$

$\Rightarrow$ $f(x)$ is non-differentiable at x= 1 and $x = 3/2$.

19. **(b)** $f(x)=\begin{cases}\frac{x^2-1}{x^2+1};0<x\le 2\\ \frac{1}{4}(x^3-x^2);2<x\le 3\\ \frac{9}{4}(|x-4|+|2-x|);3<x<4\end{cases}$

$=\begin{cases}\frac{x^2-1}{x^2+1};0<x\le 2\\ \frac{1}{4}(x^3-x^2);2<x\le 3\\ \frac{9}{4}(-x+4-2+x);3<x<4\end{cases}$

$=\begin{cases}\frac{x^2-1}{x^2+1};0<x\le 2\\ \frac{1}{4}(x^3-x^2);2<x\le 3\\ \frac{9}{2};3<x<4\end{cases}$

$f(x)$ is discontinuous at $x = 2$ and continuous at $x = 3$

$f'(x)=\begin{cases}\frac{1}{4}(3x^2-2x);2<x<3\\ 0;\ 3<x<4\end{cases}$

$\Rightarrow f'(3^-)=\frac{21}{4}$, $f'(3^+) = 0$

$\Rightarrow$ $f(x)$ is non-differentiable at $x = 2$ and $x = 3$.

20. **(c)** $f(x)=\begin{cases}x^m\sin\frac{1}{x};x\ne 0,m\in\mathbb{N}\\ 0\ ;x=0\end{cases}$

$\lim\limits_{x\to 0^-}f(x)=\lim\limits_{h\to 0^+}(-h)^m\sin\left(\frac{-1}{h}\right)$

$\lim\limits_{h\to 0^+}-(-h)^m.\sin\left(\frac{-1}{h}\right)$

$\Rightarrow m>0$ ...(i)

Also $\lim\limits_{x\to 0^+}f(x)=\lim\limits_{h\to 0^+}h^m\sin\frac{1}{h}\Rightarrow m>0$

$\Rightarrow f(0^-) = f(0^+) = f(0) =$ for m > 0

Now $f'(x)=\left\{-x^{-2}.x^m\cos\left(\frac{1}{x}\right)+\left(\sin\frac{1}{x}\right)mx^{m-1};\ x\ne 0\right.$

$\Rightarrow f'(x)=\left\{-x^{m-2}.\cos\left(\frac{1}{x}\right)+m.x^{m-1}\sin\left(\frac{1}{x}\right);x\ne 0\right.$

$\Rightarrow$ $f'(x)$ is continuous at $x = 0$

If $m - 2, m - 1 > 0$

$\Rightarrow m > 2$, m > 1

$\Rightarrow m \ge 3$

21. **(c)** $f(x)=\begin{cases}x\sin\left(\frac{1}{x}\right);-1\le x\le 1;x\ne 0\\ 0\ ;x=0\end{cases}$

$g(x)=\begin{cases}x^2\sin\left(\frac{1}{x}\right);-1\le x\le 1;x\ne 0\\ 0\ ;x=0\end{cases}$

$h(x) = |x|^3; -1 \le x \le 1$

$f(0^-) = f(0^+) = f(0) = 0;\ g(0^-) = g(0^+) = g(0) = h(0^-) = h(0^+) = h(0) = 0$

$\Rightarrow$ $f(x), g(x), h(x)$ are continuous at $x = 0$.

$f'(x)=\begin{cases}-x^{-2}.x\cos\left(\frac{1}{x}\right)+\sin\frac{1}{x};-1<x<1,\\ x\ne 0\end{cases}$

$\Rightarrow$ $f'(0)$ does not exist .

$h'(x)=\begin{cases}-3x^2\ ;x<0\\ 3x^2\ ;x>0\end{cases}$

$\Rightarrow h'(0^-) = h'(0^+) = 0$

$\Rightarrow$ $h(x)$ is differentiable at $x = 0$

$g'(0)=\lim\limits_{x\to 0}\frac{g(x)-g(0)}{x-0}=\lim\limits_{x\to 0}\frac{g(x)}{x}=\lim\limits_{x\to 0}x\sin\frac{1}{x}=0$

$\Rightarrow$ $g(x)$ is differentiable at $x = 0$

22. **(d)** $g(x)=\begin{cases}x+b\ ,x<0\\ \cos x,x\ge 0\end{cases}$

$\Rightarrow g(0^-) = b; g(0^+) = 1, g(0) = 1$

$\Rightarrow$ $g(x)$ is continuous at $x = 0$ for $b = 1$ and $g'(x)$

$=\begin{cases}1,x<0\\ -\sin x,x>0\end{cases}$

$\Rightarrow g'(0^-) = 1, g'(0^+) = 0$

$\Rightarrow$ $g(x)$ is non-differentiable $\forall$ b $\in \mathbb{R}$

23. **(a)** f is differentiable at $x = 0$ and $f'(0) = 1$.

$\Rightarrow\ \lim\limits_{h\to 0}\frac{f(h)-f(0)}{h}=1$

$\therefore\ \lim\limits_{h\to 0}\frac{f(h)-f(-2h)}{h}$

$=\lim\limits_{h\to 0}\frac{[f(h)-f(0)]}{h}+2\lim\limits_{h\to 0}\left[\frac{f(-2h)-f(0)}{-2h}\right]$

$= f'(0) + 2f'(0) = 3f'(0) = 3$

24. (c) $f(3) = 6, f'(3) = 2, \lim_{x\to 3}\dfrac{xf(3)-3f(x)}{x-3}$

$= \lim_{x\to 3}\dfrac{xf(3)-3f(3)+3f(3)-3f(x)}{x-3}$

$= \lim_{x\to 3}\left[f(3)+3\left(\dfrac{f(3)-f(x)}{x-3}\right)\right]$

$= f(3) - 3f'(3) = 6 - 6 = 0$

25. (a) $f(x) = \left[\dfrac{2(\sin x-\sin^3 x)+|\sin x-\sin^3 x|}{2(\sin x-\sin^3 x)-|\sin x-\sin^3 x|}\right]$

∴ In deleted neighborhood of $\pi/2$, $\sin x > \sin^3 x$

$\Rightarrow f(x) = \dfrac{3(\sin x-\sin^3 x)}{(\sin x-\sin^3 x)}$

$\Rightarrow f\left(\dfrac{\pi^-}{2}\right) = f\left(\dfrac{\pi^+}{2}\right) = 3; f\left(\dfrac{\pi}{2}\right) = 3$

$\Rightarrow f(x)$ is continuous at $x = \dfrac{\pi}{2}$

Also $f(x) = 3$ for $x \in (0, \pi)$

$\Rightarrow f'(x) = 0\ \forall\ x \in (0, \pi)$

$\Rightarrow f(x)$ is continuous and differentiable at $x = \dfrac{\pi}{2}$

26. (a) $f(x) = 2x\sqrt{x^3-1}+5\sqrt{x}\sqrt{1-x^4} + 7x^2\sqrt{x-1}+3x+2$

$f(x)$ is defined only at $x = 1$

$\Rightarrow f(x) = 5; x = 1$

$\Rightarrow f(x)$ is an isolated point function.

By Cauchy's definition of continuity at a point $f(x)$ is continuous at $x = 1$

$$\left(\begin{array}{lll}\because & |x-c|<\delta \Rightarrow & |f(x)-f(c)|<\in \forall x\in D_f, \\ \text{here} & x=c & \Rightarrow \quad 0=|c-c|<\delta \\ \Rightarrow & |f(c)-f(c)|=0<\in & \end{array}\right)$$

But differentiability at isolated point is not defined.

27. (a), (c) $f(x) = \begin{cases}\dfrac{x.\ell n(\cos x)}{\ell n(1+x^2)}; x\neq 0\\ 0\ ; x=0\end{cases}$

$\lim_{x\to 0} f(x) = \lim_{x\to 0}\left\{\dfrac{x\ell n(\cos x)}{x^2.\dfrac{\ell n(1+x^2)}{x^2}}\right\} = \lim_{x\to 0}\dfrac{\ell n\left[(\cos x)\right]^{\frac{1}{x}}}{\left[\dfrac{\ell n(1+x^2)}{x^2}\right]}$

$= \lim_{x\to 0}\dfrac{\ell n(1+(\cos x-1))^{\frac{1}{(\cos x-1)}\cdot\frac{\cos x-1}{x}}}{\left[\dfrac{\ell n(1+x^2)}{x^2}\right]} = \dfrac{e^{\lim_{x\to 0}\frac{\cos x-1}{x}}}{e}$

$= \dfrac{1}{e}.e^{\lim_{x\to 0}\left(\frac{-2\sin^2 x/2}{x^2/4}\right)\left(\frac{x}{4}\right)} = \dfrac{1}{e}(-2(1)(0)) = 0 = f(0) = 0$

$\Rightarrow f(x)$ is continuous at $x = 0$

$f'(0) = \lim_{x\to 0}\dfrac{f(x)-f(0)}{x-0} = \lim_{x\to 0}\dfrac{x\ell n\cos x}{x\ell n(1+x^2)}$

$= \lim_{x\to 0}\dfrac{\ell n\cos x}{\ell n(1+x^2)} = \lim_{x\to 0}\dfrac{-\tan x}{\dfrac{1}{(1+x^2)}(2x)} = -\dfrac{1}{2}$

28. (a), (b), (c) $f(x) = \begin{cases}|x-3|; x\geq 1\\ \left(\dfrac{x^2}{4}\right)-\left(\dfrac{3x}{2}\right)+\left(\dfrac{13}{4}\right), x<1\end{cases}$

$\lim_{x\to 1^-} f(x) = \lim_{x\to 1^-}\left(\dfrac{x^2}{4}-\dfrac{3x}{2}+\dfrac{13}{4}\right)$

$= \dfrac{1}{4}-\dfrac{3}{2}+\dfrac{13}{4} = \dfrac{1-6+13}{4} = 2,$

$\lim_{x\to 1^+} f(x) = \lim_{x\to 1^+}|x-3| = \lim_{x\to 1^+}(-x+3) = 2$

$f(1) = |1 - 3| = 2$

∴ $f(x)$ is continuous at $x = 1$.

$f'(1^-) = \lim_{h\to 0^+}\dfrac{f(1-h)-f(1)}{-h}$

$= \lim_{h\to 0^+}\dfrac{\dfrac{(1-h)^2}{4}-\dfrac{3}{2}(1-h)+\dfrac{13}{4}-2}{-h}$

$= \lim_{h\to 0^+}\dfrac{\dfrac{-1}{2}(1-h)+\dfrac{3}{2}}{-1} = -1,$

$f'(1^+) = \lim_{h\to 0^+}\dfrac{f(1+h)-f(1)}{h} = \lim_{h\to 0^+}\dfrac{|1+h-3|-2}{h}$

$= \lim_{h\to 0^+}\dfrac{|h-2|-2}{h} = \lim_{h\to 0^+}\dfrac{-h+2-2}{h} = -1$

$\Rightarrow f(x)$ is differentiable at $x = 1$, Obviously, differentiable at $x = 3$.

29. (a), (c) $f(x) = \sqrt{1-\sqrt{1-x^2}}$

For domain, $\sqrt{1-x^2} \leq 1; x^2 \leq 1$

$\Rightarrow x \in [-1, 1]$

$\lim_{x\to 0^-} f(x) = \lim_{x\to 0^-}\sqrt{1-\sqrt{1-x^2}} = 0,$

$\lim_{x\to 0^+} f(x) = \lim_{x\to 0^+}\sqrt{1-\sqrt{1-x^2}}\ 0; f(0) = 0$

$\Rightarrow f(x)$ is continuous at $x = 0$

$f'(0^-) = \lim_{h\to 0^+}\dfrac{f(-h)-f(0)}{-h} = \lim_{x\to 0^+}\dfrac{f(-h)}{-h}$

$= \lim_{h\to 0^+}\dfrac{\sqrt{1-\sqrt{1-h^2}}}{-h}\times\dfrac{\sqrt{1+\sqrt{1-h^2}}}{\sqrt{1+\sqrt{1-h^2}}}$

$= \lim_{h\to 0^+}\dfrac{h^2}{-h\sqrt{1+\sqrt{1-h^2}}} = 0,$

$f'(0^+) = \lim_{h\to 0^+}\dfrac{f(h)-f(0)}{h} = \lim_{h\to 0^+}\dfrac{\sqrt{1-\sqrt{1-h^2}}}{h}$

$$= \lim_{h\to 0^+} \frac{\sqrt{1-\sqrt{1-h^2}} \times \sqrt{1+\sqrt{1-h^2}}}{h\sqrt{1+\sqrt{1-h^2}}}$$

$$= \lim_{h\to 0^+} \frac{h}{\sqrt{1+\sqrt{1-h^2}}} = 0$$

$\Rightarrow f(x)$ is differentiable at $x = 0$

TEXTUAL EXERCISE–5: (SUBJECTIVE)

1. $f(x) = (x^2 - 1)\,|x^2 - 3x + 2| + \cos(|x|)$
$= (x^2 - 1)\,|(x - 1)(x - 2)| + \cos(|x|)$

$$= \begin{cases} (x^2-1)(x-1)(x-2) + \cos x \text{ for } x \in (-\infty, 1] \cup [2, \infty) \\ -(x^2-1)(x-1)(x-2) + \cos x \text{ for } x \in (1,2) \end{cases}$$

$f(1^-) = \cos 1 = f(1^+) = f(1);\ f(2^-) = f(2^+) = f(2) = \cos 2$

$\Rightarrow f(x)$ is continuous at $x = 1$ and 2

$$\Rightarrow f'(x) = \begin{cases} 4x^3 - 9x^2 + 2x + 3 - \sin x \text{ for } x < 1 \text{ or } x > 2 \\ -4x^3 + 9x^2 - 2x - 3 - \sin x \text{ for } x \in (1,2) \end{cases}$$

$\Rightarrow f'(1^-) = -\sin 1,\ f'(1^+) = -\sin 1;\ f'(2^+) = 3 - \sin 2;\ f'(2^-) = -3 - \sin 2,$

$f(x)$ is not differentiable at $x = 2$

2. $$f(x) = \begin{cases} |1-4x^2|; 0 \le x < 1 \\ [x^2 - 2x]; 1 \le x < 2 \end{cases} = \begin{cases} 1-4x^2; 0 \le x \le \frac{1}{2} \\ -1+4x^2; \frac{1}{2} < x < 1 \\ -1; 1 \le x < 2 \end{cases}$$

$$\Rightarrow f\left(\frac{1^-}{2}\right) = 0, f\left(\frac{1^+}{2}\right) = 0, f\left(\frac{1}{2}\right) = 0, f(1^-) = 3;\ f(1^+) = -1$$

$\Rightarrow f(x)$ is discontinuous at $x = 1$

$$\Rightarrow f'(x) = \begin{cases} -8x; 0 < x < \frac{1}{2} \\ 8x; \frac{1}{2} < x < 1 \\ 0; 1 < x < 2 \end{cases}$$

$$\Rightarrow f'\left(\frac{1^-}{2}\right) = -4, f'\left(\frac{1^+}{2}\right) = 4$$

$\Rightarrow f(x)$ is non-differentiable at $x = 1$ and at $x = \frac{1}{2}$

3. $$f(x) = \begin{cases} \sin x; x < \pi \\ ax + b; x \ge \pi \end{cases}$$

$f(\pi^-) = \sin \pi = 0, f(\pi^+) = a\pi + b = f(\pi)$

$\therefore$ For continuity at $x = \pi$, $a\pi + b = 0$.

$$\Rightarrow f'(x) = \begin{cases} \cos x; x < \pi \\ a; x > \pi \end{cases}$$

$\therefore\ f'(\pi^-) = \cos \pi = -1;\ f'(\pi^+) = a$

$\therefore\ f(x)$ will be differentiable at $x = \pi$,
if $a = -1 \quad \Rightarrow \quad b = -a\pi = \pi$

4. $$f(x) = \begin{cases} x^{\frac{5}{5}}; 0 \le x \le 1 \\ 2x^2 - 3x + \frac{3}{2}; 1 < x \le 2 \end{cases}$$

$$f(1) = f(1^-) = \frac{1}{5};\ f(1^+) = \frac{1}{2}$$

$$\Rightarrow f'(x) = \begin{cases} x^4; 0 < x < 1 \\ 4x - 3; 1 < x < 2 \end{cases}$$

$\Rightarrow f'(1^-) = 1;\ f'(1^+) = 1$

$\Rightarrow f'(x)$ is a continuous function, but $f(x)$ being discontinuous is non-differentiable at $x = 1$

Thus continuity of derivate does not implies the differentiability of the function.

5. $$f(x) = \begin{cases} ax^2 - b; |x| < 1 \\ -\frac{1}{|x|}; |x| \ge 1 \end{cases}$$

$$f(x) = \begin{cases} \frac{1}{x}; x \le -1 \\ ax^2 - b; -1 < x < 1 \\ -\frac{1}{x}; x \ge 1 \end{cases}$$

$\Rightarrow f(-1^-) = -1;\ f(-1^+) = a - b;\ f(-1) = -1, f(1^-) = a - b;\ f(1^+) = -1$

$\therefore$ For continuity of $f(x)$; $a - b = -1$ …(i);

$$\Rightarrow f'(x) = \begin{cases} -\frac{1}{x^2}; x < -1 \\ 2ax; -1x < x < 1 \\ \frac{1}{x^2}; x > 1 \end{cases}$$

$\Rightarrow f'(-1^-) = -1, f'(-1^+) = -2a$ and $f'(1^-) = 2a, f'(1^+) = 1$

$\therefore$ For differentiability at $x - 1, 1$;

$2a = 1 \quad \Rightarrow \quad a = \frac{1}{2} \Rightarrow b = \frac{3}{2}$ (from (i))

6. (a) $\sin(\pi[x]) = 0\ \forall\ x \in \mathbb{R}$

$f(x)$ is a constant function, hence differentiable $\forall\ x \in \mathbb{R}$

(b) $f(x) = \sin(\pi\{x\});\ x \in \left(-\frac{\pi}{2}, \frac{\pi}{2}\right)$

$$= \begin{cases} \sin(\pi(x-(-2))) \text{ for } \frac{-\pi}{2} < x < -1 \\ \sin(\pi(x-(-1))) \text{ for } -1 \le x < 0 \\ \sin \pi x \text{ for } 0 \le x < 1 \\ \sin \pi(x-1) \text{ for } 1 \le x < \frac{\pi}{2} \end{cases}$$

$$= \begin{cases} \sin(\pi x) \text{ for } \frac{-\pi}{2} < x < -1 \\ -\sin \pi x \text{ for } -1 \le x < 0 \\ \sin \pi x \text{ for } 0 \le x < 1 \\ \sin \pi x \text{ for } 1 \le x < \frac{\pi}{2} \end{cases}$$

$\Rightarrow f(-1^-) = 0; f(-1^+) = 0 = f(-1);$

$f(0^-) = f(0^+) = f(0) = 0;$

$f(1^-) = 0; f(1^+) = 0$

$\Rightarrow f(x)$ is discontinuous at $x = -1$, 0 and $x = 1$ and hence non-differentiable at $= -1, 0, 1$

7. If $f(x) = min\{|x|, |x-2|, 2-|x-1|\}$

The graph of $f(x)$ is as shown below.

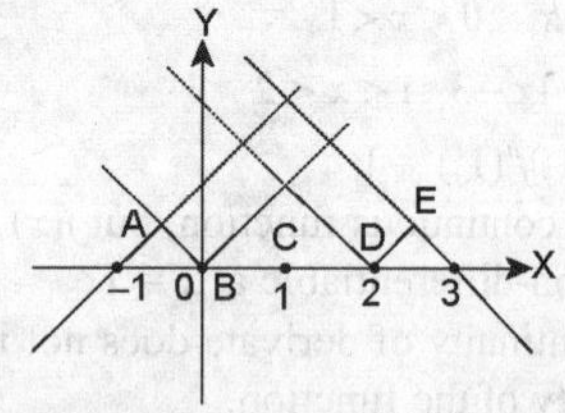

Clearly, $f(x)$ is non-differentiable at $x = A$, 0, C, D and E i.e., at 5 points.

i.e., at $x = -\frac{1}{2}$, $x = 0$, $x = 1$, $x = 2$, $x = 5/2$, but continuous everywhere.

8. $f(x) = -1 + |x-2|;\ 0 \le x \le 4$ and $g(x) = 2 - |x|;\ -1 \le x \le 3.$

$fog(x) = (g(x);\ 0 \le g(x) \le 4$

$= -1 + |g(x) - 2|;\ 0 \le 2 - |x| \le 4$

$= -1 + |-|x||;\ -2 \le -|x| \le 2$

$= -1 + |x|;\ -2 \le -|x| \le 0$

$= |x| - 1;\ -2 \le x \le 2$

But domain of $g(x)$ is $[-1, 3]$

$\Rightarrow fog\,(x) = |x| - 1;\ x \in [-1, 2]$

$$= \begin{cases} x-1;0\le x\le 2 \\ -x-1;-1\le x<0 \end{cases}$$

Now, $gof\,(x) = g(f(x));\ -1 \le f(x) \le 3$

$= 2 - |f(x)|;\ -1 \le -1 + |x-2| \le 3$

$= 2 - |-1 + |x-2||;\ 0 \le |x-2| \le 4$

$$= \begin{cases} 2-|x-2|+1;1\le|x-2|\le 4 \\ 2+|x-2|-1;0\le|x-2|<1 \end{cases}$$

$$= \begin{cases} 3-x+2;3\le x\le 6 \\ x+1;-2\le x\le 1 \\ 2-x+2-1;1<x<2 \\ 2+x-2-1;2\le x\le 3 \end{cases} = \begin{cases} 5-x;3\le x\le 6 \\ x+1;-2\le x\le 1 \\ 3-x;1<x<2 \\ x-1;1\le x<3 \end{cases}$$

But $x \in [0, 4]$

$$gof(x) = \begin{cases} x+1;0\le x\le 1 \\ 3-x;1<x<2 \\ x-1;2\le x<3 \\ 5-x;3\le x\le 4 \end{cases}$$

Graph of fog (x) is as shown below.

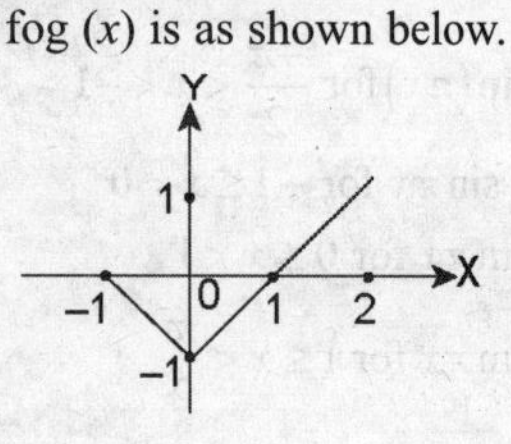

Graph of go $f(x)$ is as shown below.

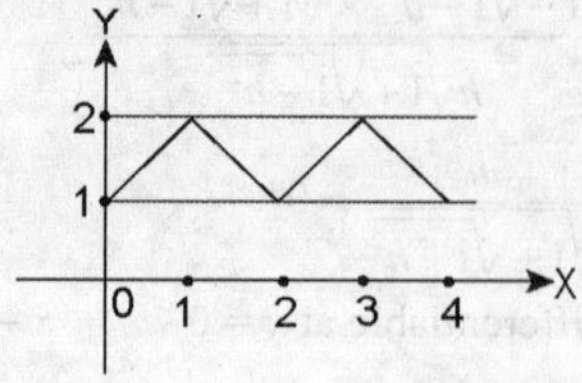

9. $f(x) = \begin{cases} -1;-2\le x<0 \\ x-1;0\le x\le 2 \end{cases}$; $g(x) = f(|x|) + |f(x)|$ and $f(|x|) = |x| - 1$

for $0 \le |x| \le 2$

$\Rightarrow f(|x|) = |x| - 1$ for $-2 \le x \le 2$ and $|f(x)| = \begin{cases} 1\text{ for } -2\le x<0 \\ |x-1| \text{ for } 0\le x\le 2 \end{cases}$

$$= \begin{cases} 1\text{ for } -2\le x<0 \\ -x+1 \text{ for } 0\le x<1 \\ x-1 \text{ for } 1\le x\le 2 \end{cases}$$

$$\therefore\ g(x) = \begin{cases} |x|\text{ for } -2\le x<0 \\ |x|-x \text{ for } 0\le x<1 \\ |x|+x-2 \text{ for } 1\le x\le 2 \end{cases} = \begin{cases} -x\text{ for } -2\le x<0 \\ 0 \text{ for } 0\le x<1 \\ 2x-2 \text{ for } 1\le x\le 2 \end{cases}$$

$\Rightarrow g(0^-) = g(0^+) = g(0);\ g(1^-) = g(1^+) = g(1) = 0$ and $g'(x) =$

$$\begin{cases} -1 \text{ for } -2<x<0 \\ 0 \text{ for } 0<x<1 \\ 2 \text{ for } 1<x<2 \end{cases}$$

$\Rightarrow g(x)$ is non-differentiable at $x = 0$ and $x = 1$

10. $f(x) = \sin x;\ g(x) = \begin{cases} \max.f(t);\ 0\le t\le x \\ \quad \text{for } 0\le x\le \pi \\ \dfrac{(1-\cos x)}{2} \text{ for } x>\pi \end{cases}$

$\because$ For $t \in [0, x] \subseteq [0, \pi]$ in which $f(t) = \sin t$ increase for $t \in [0, \pi/2]$ and sin decrease for $t \in [\pi/2, \pi]$

$$\Rightarrow\ g(x) = \begin{cases} f(x)=\sin x;\ x\in\left[0,\dfrac{\pi}{2}\right) \\ 1;\quad x\in\left[\dfrac{\pi}{2},\pi\right] \\ \sin^2\dfrac{x}{2};\ x>\pi \end{cases}$$

$$\Rightarrow\ g\left(\frac{\pi}{2}^-\right) = g\left(\frac{\pi}{2}^+\right) = g\left(\frac{\pi}{2}\right) = 1;$$

$\Rightarrow g(\pi^-) = 1;\ g(\pi^+) = 1 = g(\pi)$

$$\Rightarrow\ g'(x) = \begin{cases} \cos x;x\in\left(0,\dfrac{\pi}{2}\right) \\ 0;x\in\left(\dfrac{\pi}{2},\pi\right) \\ \cos\dfrac{x}{2};x>\pi \end{cases}$$

$\Rightarrow f'(\pi/2) = g'(\pi/2^+) = 0,\ g'(\pi^-) = g'(\pi^+) = 0$

$\Rightarrow g(x)$ is continuous and differentiable $\forall\ x \in (0, \infty)$

11. $f(x) = \begin{cases} |1-4x^2|; 0 \le x < 1 \\ |x^2 - 2x|; 1 \le x < 2 \end{cases} = \begin{cases} 1-4x^2;\ 0 \le x \le \frac{1}{2} \\ -1+4x^2;\ \frac{1}{2} < x < 1 \\ -x^2+2x;\ 1 \le x < 2 \end{cases}$

$f\left(\frac{1}{2}\right) = 0; f\left(\frac{1}{2}^+\right) = 0, f\left(\frac{1}{2}\right) = 0;$

$f(1^-) = 3; f(1^+) = 1, f(1) = 1$ and $f'(x) = \begin{cases} -8x;\ 0 < x < \frac{1}{2} \\ 8x;\ \frac{1}{2} < x < 1 \\ -2x+2; 1 < x < 2 \end{cases}$

$f(x)$ is non-differentiable at $x = \frac{1}{2}$ and at $x = 1$

12. $f(x) = \begin{cases} -1; -2 \le x \le 0 \\ |x-1|; 0 < x \le 2 \end{cases} = \begin{cases} -1; -2 \le x \le 2 \\ -x+1; 0 < x < 1 \\ x-1; 1 \le x \le 2 \end{cases}$

Case (i): For $-2 \le x \le 0$

$g(x) = \int_{-2}^{x} (-1)\,dx = -(x+2)$

Case (ii): For $0 < x < 1$

$g(x) = \int_{-2}^{0} (-1)\,dx + \int_{0}^{x} (-x+1)\,dx$

$= (-2) + \left(\frac{-x^2}{2} + x\right) = -\frac{x^2}{2} + x - 2$

Case (iii): For $1 \le x \le 2$

$g(x) = \int_{-2}^{0} (-1)\,dx + \int_{0}^{1} (-x+1)\,dx + \int_{1}^{x} (x-1)\,dx$

$= -2 + \left[\frac{-x^2}{2} + x\right]_0^1 + \left[\frac{x^2}{2} - x\right]_1^x$

$= -2 + \left[\frac{-1}{2} + 1\right] + \left[\left(\frac{x^2}{2} - x\right) - \left(\frac{1}{2} - 1\right)\right]$

$= -2 + \frac{1}{2} + \frac{x^2}{2} - x + \frac{1}{2} = \frac{x^2}{2} - x - 1$

$\therefore\ g(x) = \begin{cases} -x+2 \text{ for } -2 \le x \le 0 \\ \frac{-x^2}{2} + x - 2 \text{ for } 0 < x < 1 \\ \frac{x^2}{2} - x - 1 \text{ for } 1 \le x \le 2 \end{cases}$

$\Rightarrow\ g(0^-) = -2,\ g(0^+) = -2,\ g(0) = -2;\ g(1^-) = \frac{-3}{2};\ g(1^+) = \frac{-3}{2},\ g(1) = \frac{-3}{2}$

$\Rightarrow\ g'(x) = \begin{cases} -1; -2 < x < 0 \\ -x+1; 0 < x < 1 \\ x-1; 1 < x < 2 \end{cases}$

$\Rightarrow\ g'(0^-) = -1,\ g'(0^+) = 1;\ g'(1^-) = 0,\ g'(1^+) = 0$

$\Rightarrow\ g(x)$ is continuous in $(-2, 2)$, but non-differentiable at $x = 0$

13. $f(x) = \begin{cases} \frac{\sin[x^2]\pi}{x^2 - 3x + 8} + ax^3 + b; 0 \le x \le 1 \\ 2\cos \pi x + \tan^{-1} x; 1 < x \le 2 \end{cases}$

$\Rightarrow\ f(x) = \begin{cases} ax^3 + b; 0 \le x \le 1 \text{ as } x^2 - 3x + 8 > 0\ \forall\ x \in [0, 1] \\ 2\cos \pi x + \tan^{-1} x; 1 < x \le 2 \end{cases}$

$\Rightarrow\ f(1^-) = a + b;\ f(1^+) = \frac{\pi}{4} - 2 \Rightarrow a + b = \frac{\pi}{4} - 2$ ...(i)

$\Rightarrow\ f'(x) = \begin{cases} 3ax^2;\ 0 < x < 1 \\ -2\pi \sin \pi x + \frac{1}{1+x^2}; 1 < x < 2 \end{cases}$

$\Rightarrow\ f'(1^-) = 3a;\ f'(1^+) = \frac{1}{2} \Rightarrow 3a = \frac{1}{2}$ ...(ii)

$\therefore$ For differentiability in [0, 2], $a = \frac{1}{6}, b = \frac{\pi}{4} - 2 - \frac{1}{6}$ i.e., $a = \frac{1}{6}, b = \frac{\pi}{4} - \frac{13}{6}$

14. $f(x) = x^3 - 9x^2 + 15x + 6$

$\Rightarrow\ f'(x) = 3x^2 - 18x + 15 = 3(x^2 - 6x + 5) = 3(x-1)(x-5)$

$\Rightarrow\ f'(x) \ge 0$ for $x \in (-\infty, 1] \cup [5, \infty)$ and $f'(x) < 0$ for $x \in (1, 5)$

$\Rightarrow\ g(x) = \begin{cases} f(0) \text{ for } 0 \le x \le 1 \\ f(x) \text{ for } 1 < x < 5 \\ f(x) \text{ for } 5 \le x \le 6 \\ x - 18 \text{ for } x > 6 \end{cases}$

$= \begin{cases} 6 \text{ for } 0 \le x \le 1 \\ x^3 - 9x^2 + 15x + 6; 1 < x < 5 \\ -19 \text{ for } 5 \le x \le 6 \\ x - 18 \text{ for } x > 6 \end{cases}$

$\Rightarrow\ g(1^-) = 6;\ f(1^+) = 13;\ f(5^-) = f(5^+) = -19;\ f(6^-) = 19;\ f(6^+) = -12$

$\Rightarrow\ g(x)$ is discontinuous and non-differentiable at $x = 1$ and $x = 6$

$\Rightarrow\ g'(x) = \begin{cases} 0; 0 < x < 1 \\ 3x^2 - 18x + 15; 1 < x < 5 \\ 0 \text{ for } 5 < x < 6 \\ 1 \text{ for } x > 6 \end{cases}$

$\Rightarrow\ g(x)$ is non-differentiable at $x = 1$ and at $x = 6$

TEXTUAL EXERCISE–5: (OBJECTIVE)

1. (b) $f(x) = \sin^{-1}(\sin x);\ x \in \mathbb{R}$

$= \begin{cases} x & \text{for } \frac{-\pi}{2} \le x \le \frac{\pi}{2} \\ -x + \pi & \text{for } \frac{\pi}{2} < x \le \frac{3\pi}{2} \end{cases}$ and so on .

$\Rightarrow\ f(x)$ is non-differentiable at $x = (2n+1)\frac{\pi}{2}\ \forall\ x \in \mathbb{Z}$ and continuous $\forall\ x \in \mathbb{R}$.

2. (b) $f(x) = \max.\{x^2, (x-1), 2x(1-x)\}; 0 \le x \le 1$

The graph of $y = f(x)$ is as shown below.

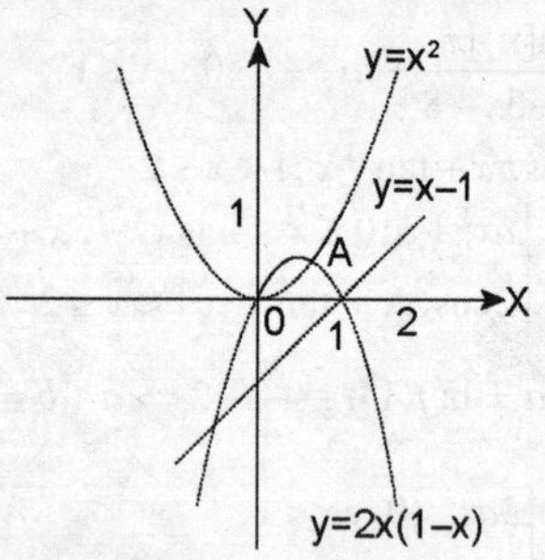

$\Rightarrow$ $f(x)$ is non-differentiable only at A

$\Rightarrow$ option (b) is correct.

3. (a) (a) $f(x) = x^{1/3}$ is continuous $\forall\ x \in \mathbb{R}$ and $f'(x) = \dfrac{1}{3}x^{-2/3}$

$\Rightarrow$ $f(x)$ has vertical tangent at $x = 0$

$\Rightarrow$ $f(x)$ is non-differentiable at $x = 0$

(b) $f(x) = \dfrac{|x|}{x} = \begin{cases} 1 \text{ for } x > 0 \\ -1 \text{ for } x < 0 \\ \text{not defined at } x = 0 \end{cases}$

$\Rightarrow$ $f(x)$ is discontinuous and hence non-differentiable at $x = 0$

(c) $f(x) = e^{-x}$, which is continuous $\forall\ x \in \mathbb{R}$.

$f'(x) = -e^{-x}$ which is also continuous $\forall\ x \in \mathbb{R}$.

(d) $f(x) = \tan x$ is discontinuous at $x = (2n+1)\dfrac{\pi}{2}$; $n \in \mathbb{Z}$ and hence non-differentiable there at

4. (c) $f(x) = |x - 0.5| + |x - 1| + \tan x$

$$\Rightarrow f(x) = \begin{cases} -2x + 1.5 + \tan x \text{ for } x < 0.5 \\ 0.5 + \tan x \text{ for } 0.5 \le x < 1 \\ 2x - 1.5 + \tan x \text{ for } 1 \le x < 2; x \ne \dfrac{\pi}{2} \end{cases}$$

$\Rightarrow$ $f(0.5^-) = 0.5 + \tan(0.5)$,

$f(0.5^+) = 0.5 + \tan(0.5) = f(0.5)$;

$f(1^-) = 0.5 + \tan 1$;

$f(1^+) = 0.5 + \tan 1 = f(1)$

$\Rightarrow$ $f(x)$ is a continuous function $\forall\ x \in (0, 2) - \left\{\dfrac{\pi}{2}\right\}$

$$f'(x) = \begin{cases} -2 + \sec^2 x; x < 0.5 \\ \sec^2 x; 0.5 < x < 1 \\ 2 + \sec^2 x; x > 1 \end{cases}$$

$\Rightarrow$ $f'(0.5^-) = -2 + \sec^2(0.5)$;

$\Rightarrow$ $f'(0.5^+) = \sec^2(0.5)$;

$f'(1^-) = \sec^2 1$;

$f'(1^+) = 2 + \sec^2 1$

$\Rightarrow$ $f(x)$ is non-differentiable at $x = 0.5$ at $x = 1$ and at $x = \dfrac{\pi}{2}$

5. (d) $\because f$ is differentiable in (a, b)

$\Rightarrow$ f is continuous in (a, b) but need not in $[a, b]$. Also f need be bounded e.g., $\tan x$ in $(0, \pi/2)$.

$\because$ $f(a_1).f(b_1) < 0$ and f is continuous in $[a, b] \supset [a_1, b_1]$

$\Rightarrow$ $f(c) = 0$ for some $c \in (a_1, b_1)$ (By intermediate value theorem).

6. (d) $f(x) = \begin{cases} 2x + 1; x \in \mathbb{Q} \\ x^2 - 2x + 5; x \notin \mathbb{Q} \end{cases}$

At the point of continuity $x^2 - 2x + 5 \to 2x + 1$

$\Rightarrow$ $x^2 - 4x + 4 \to 0$

$\Rightarrow$ $(x-2)^2 \to 0$ $\quad\Rightarrow$ $x \to 2$ and $f(2) = 5$.

$\Rightarrow$ $f(x)$ is continuous at $x = 2$

$f'(x)$ does not Exist at $x \in \mathbb{R} - \{2\}$,

$$f'(2^-) = \lim_{h\to 0^+} \frac{f(2-h) - f(2)}{-h} = \lim_{h\to 0^+} \frac{f(2-h) - 5}{-h}$$

$$\Rightarrow f'(2^-) = \lim_{h\to 0^+} \frac{2(2-h) + 1 - 5}{-h}; h \in \mathbb{Q}$$

$$= \lim_{h\to 0^+} \frac{-2h}{-h} = 2 \text{ and } f'(2^-)$$

$$= \lim_{h\to 0^+} \frac{(2-h)^2 - 2(2-h) + 5 - 5}{-h}; h \notin \mathbb{Q}$$

$$= \lim_{h\to 0^+} \frac{h^2 - 4h + 2h}{-h} = 2$$

$$f'(2^+) = \lim_{h\to 0^+} \frac{2(2+h) + 1 - 5}{h}; h \in \mathbb{Q}$$

$$= \lim_{h\to 0^+} \frac{2h}{h} = 2$$

$$f'(2^+) = \lim_{h\to 0^+} \frac{(2+h)^2 - 2(2+h) + 5 - 5}{-h}; h \notin \overline{\mathbb{Q}}$$

$$= \lim_{h\to 0^+} \frac{h^2 + 2h}{h} = 2$$

Thus $f(x)$ is continuous and differentiable at only one point $x = 2$ and discontinuous everywhere

7. (d) $f(x) = x[x]\ \forall -1 \le x \le 3$

$$= \begin{cases} -x\ \forall -1 \le x < 0 \\ 0\ \forall\ 0 \le x < 1 \\ x\ \forall\ 1 \le x < 2 \\ 2x\ \forall\ 2 \le x < 3 \\ 9 \text{ at } x = 3 \end{cases}$$

$\Rightarrow$ $f(0^-) = 0, f(0^+) = 0 = f(0)$;

$f(1^-) = 0; f(1^+) = 1; f(2^-) = 2, f(2^+) = 4, f(3^-) = 6, f(3) = 9$

$\Rightarrow$ $f(x)$ is discontinuous at $x = 1, 2,$ and 3

$$\Rightarrow f'(x) = \begin{cases} -1\ \forall -1 < x < 0 \\ 0\ \forall\ 0 < x < 1 \\ 1\ \forall\ 1 < x < 2 \\ 2\ \forall\ 2 < x < 3 \end{cases}$$

$\Rightarrow$ $f(x)$ is non-differentiable at $x = 0, x = 1, x = 2, x = 3$

8. (c) $f(x) = [x]\,[\sin \pi x]$; $x \in (-1, 1)$

$= \begin{cases} -[\sin \pi x]; -1 < x < 0 \\ 0\ ;\ 0 \le x < 1 \end{cases}$ for $x \in (-1, 0)$, $\pi x \in (-\pi, 0)$

$\Rightarrow$ $(\sin \pi x) \in [-1, 0)$

$\Rightarrow$ $[\sin \pi x] = -1$ $\quad\Rightarrow$ $-[\sin x] = 1$

$\therefore$ $f(x) = \begin{cases} 1 ; x \in (-1, 0) \\ 0 ; x \in ;[0,1) \end{cases}$

$\Rightarrow$ $f(x)$ is discontinuous and non-differentiable at $x = 0$

9. (a) $f(x) = \dfrac{x}{1+|x|} = \begin{cases} \dfrac{x}{1+x} ; x \geq 0 \\ \dfrac{x}{1-x} ; x < 0 \end{cases}$

$\Rightarrow$ $f(0^-) = f(0^+) = f(0) = 0$

$\Rightarrow$ $f(x)$ is continuous $\forall\ x \in \mathbb{R}$

and $f'(x) = \begin{cases} \dfrac{1}{(1+x)^2} ; x > 0 \\ \dfrac{1}{(1-x)^2} ; x < 0 \end{cases}$

$\Rightarrow$ $f'(0^-) = 1;\ f'(0^+) = 1$

$\Rightarrow$ $f(x)$ is differentiable on $(-\infty, \infty)$

10. (a), (c) $f(x) = \min. \{1, x^2, x^3\}$

The graph of $f(x)$ is as shown below.

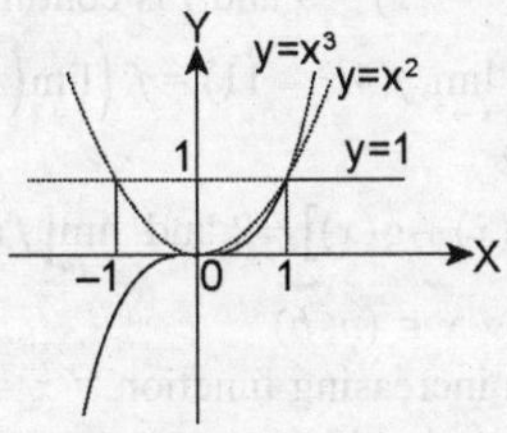

Clearly $f(x) = \begin{cases} x^3 ; -\infty < x < 1 \\ x ; x \geq 1 \end{cases}$

$\Rightarrow$ $f(1^-) = f(1^+) = f(1) = 1$ and $f'(x) = \begin{cases} 3x^2 ; -\infty < x < 1 \\ 1 ; x > 1 \end{cases}$

$\Rightarrow$ $f'(1^-) = 3, f'(1^+) = 1$

$\Rightarrow$ $f(x)$ is non-differentiable at $x = 1$

11. (a) $f(x) = \min. \{x^3 - 1, -x + 1, \text{sgn}(-x)\}$

The graph of $f(x)$ is as shown below.

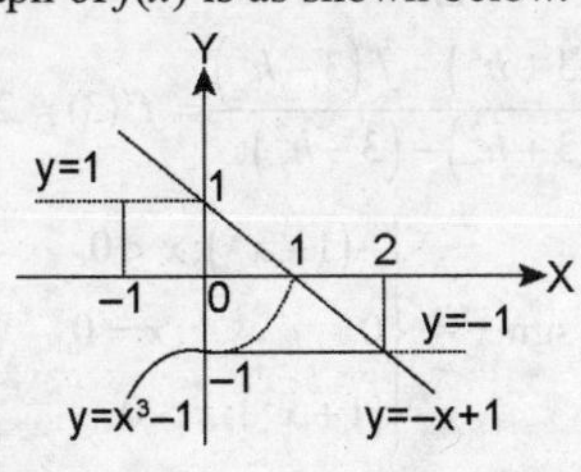

Clearly $f(x) = \begin{cases} x^3 - 1 ; -\infty < x \leq 0 \\ -1 ; 0 < x \leq 2 \\ -x + 1 ; x > 2 \end{cases}$

$\Rightarrow$ $f(x)$ is a continuous function $\forall\ x \in \mathbb{R}$ and $f'(x) =$

$\begin{cases} 3x^2 ; -\infty < x < 0 \\ 0 ; < x < 2 \\ -1 ; x > 2 \end{cases}$

$\Rightarrow$ $f(x)$ is non-differentiable at $x = 2$

12. (a) $f(x) = \max. \{|\tan x|, \cos |x|\}$

The graph of $f(x)$ is as shown below.

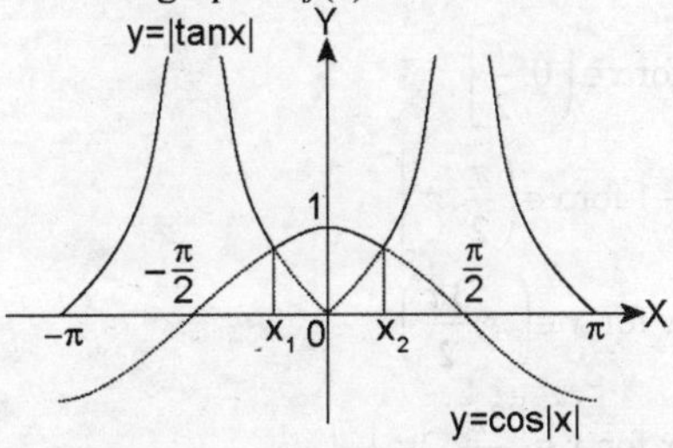

$\therefore$ $f(x)$ is non-differentiable at $x = \dfrac{-\pi}{2}, x_1, x_2, \dfrac{\pi}{2}$ i.e., at 4 points.

13. (a), (b), (d) $f(x) = 1 + |\sin x|$ being sum of two continuous function is continuous $\forall\ x \in \mathbb{R}$ and $|\sin x|$ is non-differentiable at $x = n\pi;\ n \in \mathbb{Z}$

14. (b) $f(x) = \begin{cases} \int_0^x \{1 + |1 - t|\} dt ; x > 2 \\ 5x - 7 \quad ; x \leq 2 \end{cases}$

$= \begin{cases} \int_0^1 (2 - t) dt + \int_1^x t dt ; x > 2 \\ 5x - 7 \quad ; x \leq 2 \end{cases} = \begin{cases} 1 + \dfrac{x^2}{2} ; x > 2 \\ 5x - 7 ; x \leq 2 \end{cases}$

$\Rightarrow$ $f(x)$ is continuous at $x = 2$

15. (a), (b), (c), (d)

$f(x) = \dfrac{x + |x|}{2}\ \forall x \in \mathbb{R}$

$= \begin{cases} 0 \text{ for } x < 0 \\ x \text{ for } x \geq 0 \end{cases}$ and $g(x) = \begin{cases} x \text{ for } x < 0 \\ x^2 \text{ for } x \geq 0, \end{cases}$

$gof(x) = \{x^2\ \forall\ x \in \mathbb{R}$

And fog $(x) = \begin{cases} 0 \text{ for } g(x) < 0 \\ g(x) \text{ for } g(x) \geq 0 \end{cases} = \begin{cases} 0 \text{ for } x < 0 \\ x^2 \text{ for } x \geq 0 \end{cases}$

$\Rightarrow$ $gof(x)$ is continuous $\forall\ x \in \mathbb{R}$ and also so is $fog(x)$.

16. (a) $f : [0, 1] \to [0, 1]$

Consider $g(x) = f(x) - x$

Clearly $f(x), x$ is continuous on $[0, 1]$.

$\Rightarrow$ $g(x)$ is continuous on $[0, 1]$

Now $g(0) = f(0) \geq 0$ and $g(1) = f(1) - 1 \leq 0$

$\therefore$ $g(0).g(1) \leq 0$, hence by intermediate theorem, $g(x) = 0$ has at least one root in$[0, 1]$

Further, if $h(x) = f(x) + x;\ x \in [0, 1]$

Clearly $h(x) \geq$ as $f(x), x$ are non- negative.

$\therefore$ $h(x) = 0$ if $f(0) = 0$ i.e., $f(x) + x = 0$ has root $x = 0$ provided $f(0) = 0$

17. (a), (b), (c), (d) $f(x) = [x \sin \pi x]$ for $x \in (-1, 1)$; $\sin \pi x \in [-1, 1]$

$\Rightarrow$ $x \sin \pi x \in (-1, 1)$

$\Rightarrow$ $[x \sin \pi x] \in \{-1, 0\}$

$\Rightarrow$ $f(x) = 0$ for $x \in [-1, 1]$

$\Rightarrow$ $f(x)$ is a continuous and differentiable function $\forall\ x \in [-1, 1]$

18. (c) $f(x) = |\sin x| + [\cos x];\ x \in [0, 2\pi]$

$$= \begin{cases} 1 \text{ at } x = 0 \\ \sin x \text{ for } x \in \left(0, \frac{\pi}{2}\right] \\ \sin x - 1 \text{ for } x \in \left(\frac{\pi}{2}, \pi\right] \\ -\sin x \text{ for } x \in \left(\pi, \frac{3\pi}{2}\right) \\ -\sin x \text{ for } x \in \left[\frac{3\pi}{2}, 2\pi\right) \\ 1 \text{ at } x = 2\pi \end{cases}$$

$\Rightarrow$ $f(x)$ is discontinuous at $x = 0, \frac{\pi}{2}, \frac{3\pi}{2}, 2\pi$ and $f'(x)$

$$= \begin{cases} \cos x \text{ for } x \in \left(0, \frac{\pi}{2}\right) \\ \cos x \text{ for } x \in \left(\frac{\pi}{2}, \pi\right) \\ -\cos x \text{ for } x \in \left(\pi, \frac{3\pi}{2}\right) \\ -\cos x \text{ for } x \in \left(\frac{3\pi}{2}, 2\pi\right) \end{cases}$$

$\Rightarrow$ $f(x)$ is non-differentiable at $x = 0, \frac{\pi}{2}, \pi, \frac{3\pi}{2}$ and 2π i.e., 5 points

TEXTUAL EXERCISE–6: (SUBJECTIVE)

1. $f(x) = \begin{cases} 2x^2 \sin \pi x; x \le 1 \\ x^3 + ax^2 + b; x > 1 \end{cases}$

$f(1^-) = 0;\ f(1^+) = 1 + a + b$

$\Rightarrow\ a + b = -1$ ....(i)

and $f'(x) = \begin{cases} 2x^2 \pi \cos \pi x + 4x \sin \pi x; x < 1 \\ 3x^2 + 2ax;\ x > 1 \end{cases}$

$f'(1^-) = -2\pi;\ f'(1^+) = 3 + 2a$ for $f(x)$ to be differentiable,

$3 + 2a = -2\pi$

$\Rightarrow\ a = \dfrac{-2\pi - 3}{2} = -\pi - \dfrac{3}{2}$ and $b = -1 - a$

$= -1 + \pi + \dfrac{3}{2} = \pi + \dfrac{1}{2}$

$\Rightarrow\ f'(x) = \begin{cases} 2x^2 \pi \cos \pi x + 4x \sin \pi x; x \le 1 \\ 3x^2 + (-2\pi - 3)x; x > 1 \end{cases}$

$\Rightarrow\ f''(x) = \begin{cases} -2x^2\pi^2 \sin \pi x + 4\pi x \cos \pi x + 4\pi x \cos \pi x + 4 \sin \pi x; x < 1 \\ 6x - 2\pi - 3; x > 1 \end{cases}$

$\Rightarrow\ f''(1^-) = -8\pi;\ x < 1$ and $f''(1^+) = 3 - 2\pi$

$\Rightarrow\ f'(1)$ does not exist

$\Rightarrow\ f(x)$ is twice differentiable $\forall\ x$ expect at $x = 1$

2. (a) $f(x) = x^2\,|x| = \begin{cases} -x^3 \text{ for } x < 0 \\ x^3 \text{ for } x \ge 0 \end{cases} \Rightarrow f(0^-) = f(0^+) = f(0) = 0$

$\Rightarrow$ $f(x)$ is continuous at $x = 0$ and $f'(x) = \begin{cases} -3x^2 \text{ for } x < 0 \\ 3x^2 \text{ for } x > 0 \end{cases}$

$\Rightarrow\ f'(0^-) = f'(0^+) = 0$

$\Rightarrow$ $f(x)$ is differentiable and $f''(x) = \begin{cases} -6x \text{ for } x < 0 \\ 6x \text{ for } x > 0 \end{cases}$

$\Rightarrow\ f''(0^-) = f''(0^+) = 0$

$\Rightarrow$ $f'(x)$ is differentiable

$\Rightarrow$ $f(x)$ is twice differentiable .

(b) $f: \mathbb{R} \to \mathbb{R}$

$f'(x) = -x^2 + x + 2 = -(x - 2)(x + 1)$

$f''(x) = -2x + 1$

$\Rightarrow$ $f(x)$ has a point of local minima at $x = -1$ and a point of local maxima at $x = 2$.

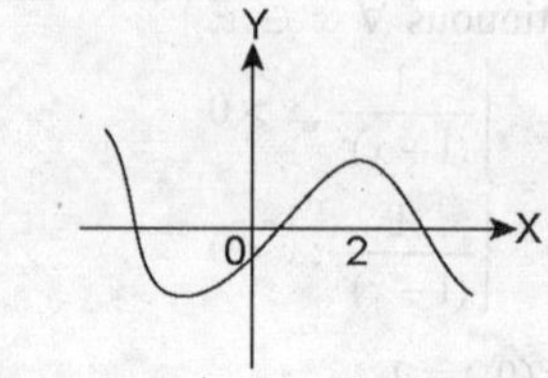

If $f(x)$ has two roots in [0, 1], then $f(x)$ has a point of local maxima in [0, 1] which is not true.

Hence $f(x)$ has only one root in [0, 1]

(c) $\because\ \lim\limits_{x\to 2} (4x^2 - 11) = 5$ and f is continuous at $x = 5$,

We have $\lim\limits_{x\to 2} f(4x^2 - 11) = f\left(\lim\limits_{x\to 2}(4x^2 - 11)\right)$

$= f(5) = 2$

(d) If $\lim\limits_{x\to a}[f(x) + g(x)] = 2$ and $\lim\limits_{x\to a}[f(x) - g(x)] = 1$

3. (a) $f''(x) > 0\ \forall\ x \in (a, b)$

$\Rightarrow$ $f'(x)$ is an increasing function $\forall\ x \in (a, b)$

$\Rightarrow$ $f'(x) = 0$ can hold at most one point in (a, b) .

$\therefore$ $(a) \to (r)$

(b) $f'(a).f'(b) < 0$

$\Rightarrow$ $f'(a)$ and $f'(b)$ are of opposite sign and $f(x)$ being differentiable is continuous in (a, b)

$\Rightarrow$ $\exists$ at atleast one c $\in (a, b)$ such that $f'(c) = 0$ $\therefore$ $(b) \to (p)$

4. $f'(3) = 2$ ...(i)

$$\lim_{h\to 0} \frac{f(3 + h^2) - f(3 - h^2)}{2h^2}$$

$$\Rightarrow \lim_{h\to 0} \frac{f(3 + h^2) - f(3 - h^2)}{(3 + h^2) - (3 - h^2)} = f'(3) = 2$$

5. $y = (1 + x^2)$ sgn $x = \begin{cases} -(1 + x^2); x < 0 \\ 0 \qquad ; x = 0 \\ (1 + x^2); x > 0 \end{cases}$

Graphically shown below

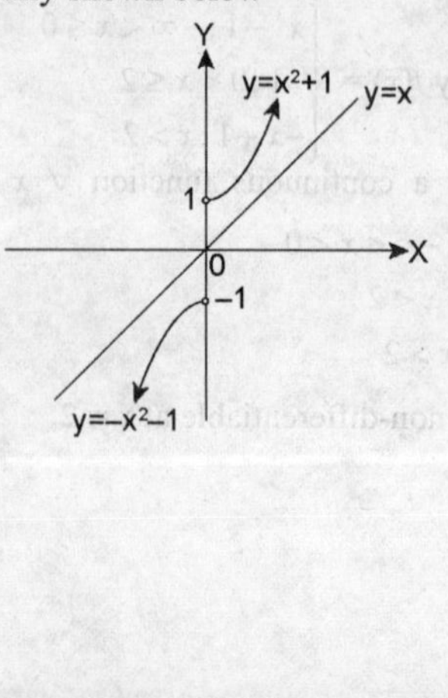

Clearly $f(x)$ is discontinuous at $x = 0$

$y = f^{-1}(x)$ will be as shown below.

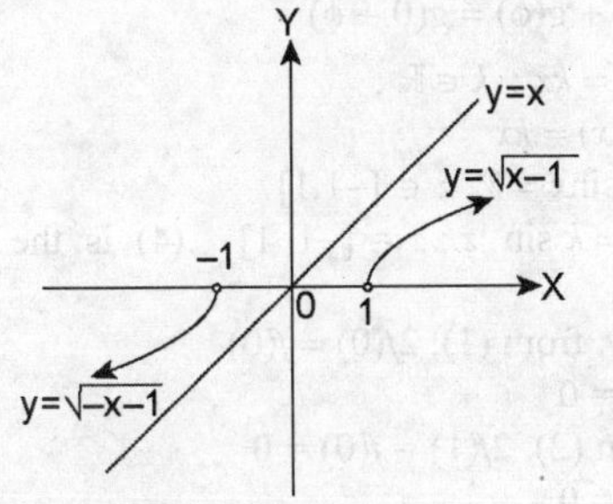

Clerkly, f^{-1} is continuous for $x < -1$, $x > 1$ and at $x = 0$, the isolated point continuity.

TEXTUAL EXERCISE– 6: (OBJECTIVE)

1. (b), (c)

(a) $\tan x$ is discontinuous at $x = \pi/2$.

(b) $\int_0^x t\sin\left(\frac{1}{t}\right)dt$

$\because\ t\sin\left(\frac{1}{t}\right)$ is continuous in $(0, \pi)$

So its integral is continuous.

(c) $f(x) = \begin{cases} 1; 0 < x \le \frac{3\pi}{4} \\ 2\sin\left(\frac{2x}{9}\right); \frac{3\pi}{4} < x \le \pi \end{cases}$

$f\left(\left(\frac{3\pi}{4}\right)^-\right) 1; f\left(\frac{3\pi}{4}^+\right) = 2\sin\left(\frac{2}{9} \times \frac{3\pi}{4}\right)$

$= 2\sin\frac{\pi}{6} = 1$

Also $f\left(\frac{3\pi}{4}\right) = 1$

$\Rightarrow f(x)$ is continuous in $(0, \pi)$.

(d) $f(x) = \begin{cases} x\sin x, 0 < x \le \frac{\pi}{2} \\ \frac{\pi}{2}\sin(\pi + x), \frac{\pi}{2} < x < \pi \end{cases}$

$\Rightarrow\ f\left(\frac{\pi}{2}^-\right) = \frac{\pi}{2}; f\left(\frac{\pi}{2}\right) = \frac{\pi}{2}$ and

$f\left(\frac{\pi}{2}^+\right) = \frac{\pi}{2}\sin\left(\frac{3\pi}{2}\right) = \frac{-\pi}{2}$

$\therefore\ f(x)$ is discontinuous in $(0, \pi)$

2. $f(x) = f(y) = f\left(x\sqrt{1-y^2} + y\sqrt{1-x^2}\right)\ \forall$ x, y$\in [-1, 1]$

put $y = 1$

$\Rightarrow f(x) + f(1) = f\left(\sqrt{1-x^2}\right)$

put $x = y = 0$

$\Rightarrow 2f(0) = f(0) \qquad \Rightarrow f(0) = 0$

Put $x = y = 1$

$\Rightarrow 2f(1) = f(0) = 0 \Rightarrow f(1) = 0$

$\Rightarrow f(x) = f\left(\sqrt{1-x^2}\right)$

$\Rightarrow f'(x) = f'\left(\sqrt{1-x^2}\right).\frac{1}{2\sqrt{1-x^2}}.(-2x)$

$\Rightarrow f'(x) = \frac{-x f'\left(\sqrt{1-x^2}\right)}{\sqrt{1-x^2}}$

3. (c) $f'(x) = \sin x + \sin 4x.\cos x$

$f'\left(2x^2 + \frac{\pi}{2}\right)$ at $x = \sqrt{\frac{\pi}{2}}$

$\because\ f'\left(2x^2 + \frac{\pi}{2}\right)$ = *derivates* of $f\left(2x^2 + \frac{\pi}{2}\right) = f(g(x))$;

$g(x) = 2x^2 + \frac{\pi}{2}$

$\Rightarrow\ f'\left(2x^2 + \frac{\pi}{2}\right) = f'(g(x)).g'(x)$

$= [\sin(g(x)) + \sin 4.\ g(x).\cos(g(x))].g'(x)$

$= \left[\sin\left(2x^2 + \frac{\pi}{2}\right) + \sin 4\left(2x^2 + \frac{\pi}{2}\right).\cos\left(2x^2 + \frac{\pi}{2}\right)\right](4x)$

At $x = \sqrt{\frac{\pi}{2}}$,

$f'\left(2x^2 + \frac{\pi}{2}\right) = \left[\sin\left(\frac{3\pi}{2}\right) + \sin 6\pi.\cos\left(\frac{3\pi}{2}\right)\right]\left(2\sqrt{2\pi}\right)$

$= -2\sqrt{2\pi}$

4. (b) $\lim_{h\to 0}\frac{\left|f\left(4(1+h^2)\right)\right| - |f(4)|}{2h^2}$

$= 2\lim_{h\to 0}\left(\frac{\left|f(4+4h^2)\right| - |f(4)|}{4h^2}\right)$

$= 2(|f(4)|)' = \left\{2\left[\frac{|f(x)|}{f(x)}\right].f'(x)\right.$

$= 2\left(\frac{|f(4)|}{f(4)}\right).f'(4)$

$= 2(1).f'(4)$ if $f(4) > 0$

$= 2(5) = 10$ if $f(4) > 0$

5. (b) Since $f(x)$ is twice differentiable

$\Rightarrow f(x)$ is differentiable

$\Rightarrow f(x)$ is continuous and if we suppose α , β are roots of $f(x) = 0$

$\Rightarrow f(\alpha) = f(\beta) = 0$ and $f(x)$ is continuous on $[\alpha, \beta]$ and differentiable on (α, β)

$\Rightarrow$ By Rolle's theorem $f''(x) = 0$ has at least one root in (α, β). Also either there is no root of $f(x) = 0$ in (α, β).

OR if there is a root of $f(x) = 0$, then it is impossible to have second root in (α, β).

6. (b) Let $f(x) = ax^2 + bx + c > 0\ \forall\ x \in \mathbb{R}$; $a > 0, b^2 - 4ac < 0$
$g(x) = f(x) + f'(x) + f''(x)$
$= ax^2 + bx + c + 2ax + b + 2a$
$= ax^2 + (b + 2a)x + (c + b + 2a)$
Disc. of $g(x) = (b + 2a)^2 - 4a(c + b + 2a)$
$= b^2 + 4a^2 + 4ab - 4ac - 4ab - 8a^2$
$= (b^2 - 4ac) - 4a^2 < 0$ (as $b^2 - 4ac < 0$, $-4a^2 < 0$)
$\Rightarrow g(x) > 0\ \forall\ x \in \mathbb{R}$

7. (c) $\because f'(0) = 4$

$$\Rightarrow \lim_{x\to 0}\frac{f'(x)-f'(0)}{x}=4 \quad \ldots(i)$$

Now, $\lim_{x\to 2}\dfrac{2f(x)-3f(2x)+f(4x)}{x^2}\left(\dfrac{0}{0}\text{ form}\right)$

$$= \lim_{x\to 0}\frac{2f'(x)-6f'(2x)+4f'(4x)}{2x}\left(\frac{0}{0}\text{form}\right)$$

$$= \lim_{x\to 0}\frac{2f''(x)-12f''(2x)+16f''(4x)}{2}$$

$$= \frac{1}{2}[2f''(0) - 12f''(0) + 16f''(0)]$$

$= 3f''(0) = 3(4) = 12$

TEXTUAL EXERCISE–7: (SUBJECTIVE)

1. Given functional equation is

$$f(x)+f(y)=f\left(x\sqrt{1-y^2}+y\sqrt{1-x^2}\right)\ \forall x,y\in[-1,1] \quad \ldots(1)$$

Put $y = x$ in (1), we get $2f(x)=f\left(2x\sqrt{1-x^2}\right)$ ...(2)

Put $y=2x\sqrt{1-x^2}$ in (1), we get $f(x)+f\left(2x\sqrt{1-x^2}\right)$

$$=f\left[\left(x\sqrt{1-4x^2+4x^4}\right)+2x\left(1-x^2\right)\right]$$

$$\Rightarrow f(x)+2f(x)=f\left[x\sqrt{\left(2x^2-1\right)^2}+2x\left(1-x^2\right)\right]$$

$$\Rightarrow 3f(x)=f\left[x\left|2x^2-1\right|+2x\left(1-x^2\right)\right]$$

Now, $2x^2 - 1 \geq 0 \Rightarrow x^2 \geq \frac{1}{2}$

$\Rightarrow x\in\left(-\infty,-\frac{1}{\sqrt{2}}\right]\cup\left[\frac{1}{\sqrt{2}},\infty\right)$ and $2x^2 - 1 \leq 0$ for

$$x\in\left[\frac{-1}{\sqrt{2}},\frac{1}{\sqrt{2}}\right]$$

$$\Rightarrow 3f(x)=f\left[-x\left(2x^2-1\right)+2x-2x^3\right] \text{ for } x\in\left[\frac{-1}{\sqrt{2}},\frac{1}{\sqrt{2}}\right]$$

or $3f(x)=f\left(3x-4x^3\right)$ for $x\in\left[\frac{-1}{\sqrt{2}},\frac{1}{\sqrt{2}}\right]$ ...(3)

Thus equations (2) and (3) proves the part (ii) and (i) respectively. Now, it remains to find the function $f(x)$. In original equation, put $x = \sin\theta$, $y = \sin\phi$; $x, y \notin [-1, 1]$
$\Rightarrow f(\sin\theta) + f(\sin\phi) = f(\sin\theta\cos\phi + \cos\theta\sin\phi)$
$\Rightarrow f(\sin\theta) + f(\sin\phi) = f(\sin(\theta + \phi))$
Consider, $f(\sin\theta) = g(\theta)$
$\Rightarrow g(\theta) + g(\phi) = g(\theta + \phi)$
$\Rightarrow g(x) = kx$; $k \in \mathbb{R}$;
$\Rightarrow f(\sin x) = kx$
Put $\sin x = \mathbb{Z}$, $z \in [-1,1]$
$\Rightarrow f(z) = k\sin^{-1}z$; $z \in [-1, 1]$ ...(4) is the required solution.
Now, from (1), $2f(0) = f(0)$
$\Rightarrow f(0) = 0$
$\therefore$ From (2), $2f(1) = f(0) = 0$
$\Rightarrow f(1) = 0$
$\therefore$ From (1), $0 = k\sin^{-1}(1)$
$\Rightarrow k = \frac{2}{\pi}$

$\therefore f(z)=\frac{2}{\pi}\sin^{-1}(z)$ or $f(x)=\frac{2}{\pi}\sin^{-1}(x)$; $x \notin [-1, 1]$ is the required solution.

2. Given functional equation is $f(x.y)=f(x)+f(y); x,y>0$ ...(1)

Putting $y = x$ in (1)
$\Rightarrow f(x^2)=2f(x)$ ...(2)
Putting, $y = x^2$ in (1), we get $f(x^3)=f(x)+f(x^2)$
$\Rightarrow f(x^3)=f(x)+2f(x)$
$\Rightarrow f(x^3)=3f(x)$ And so on,
$\Rightarrow f(x\ )\ \ nf(x)$ ...(3)
Put $x^n = z$ or $\log_x z-n; x\neq 1$
$\Rightarrow f(z)=(\log_x z).f(x); x\neq 1$

$$\Rightarrow \frac{f(z)}{f(x)}=\log_x z; x\neq 1 \text{ or } \frac{f(y)}{f(x)}=\log_x y; x\neq 1 \quad \ldots(4)$$

Also from (1), put $x = 1$,
$\Rightarrow f(y)=f(1)+f(y)$
$\Rightarrow f(1) = 0$ ...(5)
$\therefore$ From (4) and (5), we get $\frac{f(y)}{f(x)}=\log_x y; x,y>0, x\neq 1$

3. Given that $f(x)$ is a polynomial function such that $f(x)+f\left(\frac{1}{x}\right)=f(x).f\left(\frac{1}{x}\right); x\in\mathbb{R}-\{0\}$

$$\Rightarrow f(x)=f(x).f\left(\frac{1}{x}\right)-f\left(\frac{1}{x}\right)$$

$$\Rightarrow f(x)=\left(f(x)-1\right).f\left(\frac{1}{x}\right)$$

$$\Rightarrow f\left(\frac{1}{x}\right)=\frac{f(x)}{\left(f(x)-1\right)} \quad \ldots(1)$$

$$\text{and } f(x)=\frac{f\left(\frac{1}{x}\right)}{\left(f\left(\frac{1}{x}\right)-1\right)} \quad \ldots(2)$$

Multiplying (1) and (2), we get

$$f(x).f\left(\frac{1}{x}\right)=\frac{f(x).f\left(\frac{1}{x}\right)}{(f(x)-1)\left(f\left(\frac{1}{x}\right)-1\right)}$$

$\Rightarrow$ $f(x).f\left(\frac{1}{x}\right)=0$ identically or $(f(x)-1)\left(f\left(\frac{1}{x}\right)-1\right)=1$

$\Rightarrow$ $f(x) = 0$ identically or $(f(x)-1)\left(f\left(\frac{1}{x}\right)-1\right)=1$

But $f(x)$ is a polynomial function such that $f(5) = 126$.

$\Rightarrow$ $f(x)$ is not identically zero.

$\Rightarrow$ $(f(x)-1)\left(f\left(\frac{1}{x}\right)-1\right)=1$

$\Rightarrow$ $g(x).g\left(\frac{1}{x}\right)=1; x\in\mathbb{R}-\{0\}$

$\Rightarrow$ $g(x)=\frac{1}{g\left(\frac{1}{x}\right)}$ $\forall x\in\mathbb{R}-\{0\}$

$\Rightarrow$ $g(x)$ must be a monomial

$\Rightarrow$ $g(x) = ax^n$; $n \in W$ and $g(x).g\left(\frac{1}{x}\right)=ax^n.\frac{a}{x^n}=a^2=1$

$\Rightarrow$ $a = \pm 1$

$\Rightarrow$ $g(x) = \pm x^n$ $\Rightarrow$ $f(x) - 1 = \pm x^n$

$\Rightarrow$ $f(x) = (1 \pm x^n)$; $n \in$ W

$\Rightarrow$ $126 = 1 \pm (5)^n$ $\Rightarrow$ $5^n = \pm (5)^3$

$\because$ $f(5) = 126$

$\Rightarrow$ $n = 3$, $f(x) = x^3 + 1$ and $f(3) = 28$

4. Given functional equation is $2f(\sin x) + f(\cos x) = x$ ...(1)

Let $f(\sin x) = A$, $f(\cos x) = B$

$\Rightarrow$ $2A + B = x$ ...(2)

Replacing x by $\frac{\pi}{2}-x$ in (1),

$\Rightarrow$ $2f(\cos x) + f(\sin x) = \frac{\pi}{2}-x$ ...(3)

$\Rightarrow$ $2B + A = \frac{\pi}{2}-x$ ...(4)

Equation (2) + (4) gives, $3A + 3B = \frac{\pi}{2}$

$\Rightarrow$ $\mathrm{B}=\frac{\pi}{6}-\mathrm{A}$ ...(5)

$\therefore$ From (2) and (5), we get $2\mathrm{A}+\frac{\pi}{6}-\mathrm{A}=x$

$\Rightarrow$ $\mathrm{A}=x-\frac{\pi}{6}$ $\Rightarrow$ $f(\sin x)=x-\frac{\pi}{6}$

$\Rightarrow$ $f(z)=\sin^{-1}z-\frac{\pi}{6}$ $\Rightarrow$ $f(x)=\sin^{-1}x-\frac{\pi}{6}$

$\Rightarrow$ Domain of $f(x) = [-1, 1]$ and Range of $f(x)=\left[\frac{-2\pi}{3},\frac{\pi}{3}\right]$

5. $f(x)$ is a polynomial function satisfying the functional equation $2 + f(x). f(y) = f(x) + f(y) + f(xy)$, $\forall x, y \in \mathbb{R}$ ...(1)

Replacing y by x in (1), we get $2+[f(x)]^2=2f(x)+f(x^2)$

Putting $x = 1$, we get $2+(f(1))^2-2f(1)+f(1)$

$\Rightarrow$ $(f(1))^2-3f(1)+2=0$

$\Rightarrow$ $(f(1)-1)-(f(1)-2)=0$

$\Rightarrow$ $f(1) = 1$ or $f(1) = 2$

Case-(i): If $f(1) = 2$; From (1) replacing y by $\frac{1}{x}$, we get

$2+f(x).f\left(\frac{1}{x}\right)=f(x)+f\left(\frac{1}{x}\right)+f(1)$

$\Rightarrow$ $f(x).f\left(\frac{1}{x}\right)=f(x)+f\left(\frac{1}{x}\right)$ $[\because f(1)=2]$

$\Rightarrow$ $f(x) = 1 \pm x^n$ but $f(1) = 2$

$\Rightarrow$ $2 = 1 \pm (1)^n$

$\Rightarrow$ $f(x) = 1 + x^n$

Also $f(2) = 5$

$\Rightarrow$ $f(2) = 5 = 1 + (2)^n$

$\Rightarrow$ $n = 2$

$\Rightarrow$ $f(x) = 1 + x^2$

$\Rightarrow$ $f(f(x))=f(5)=1+25=26$

Case-(ii): $f(1) = 1$;

Replacing y by 1 in (1), we get

$2+f(x).f(1)=f(x)+f(1)+f(x)$

$\Rightarrow$ $2+f(x)=2f(x)+f(1)$ $[\because f(1)=1]$

$\Rightarrow$ $2 = f(x) + 1$

$\Rightarrow$ $f(x) = 1$ i.e., $f(x)$ is a constant function, but $f(2) = 5$ given.

$\Rightarrow$ $f(1) \neq 1$.

$\therefore$ By case (i), $f(x) = x^2 + 1$ and $f(f(2))=26$

6. Given functional equation is $f(x + y) = f(x) + f(y) - xy - 1$; $x, y \in \mathbb{R}$ ...(1)

Putting $y = 0$, $x = 1$, we get $f(1) = f(1) + f(0) - 1$

$\Rightarrow$ $f(0) = 1$

Now, $f'(x)=\lim_{h\to 0}\frac{f(x+h)-f(x)}{h}$

$$=\lim_{h\to 0}\frac{f(x)+f(h)-xh-1-f(x)}{h}=\lim_{h\to 0}\frac{f(h)-1-xh}{h}$$

$$=\left[\lim_{h\to 0}\frac{f(h)-f(0)}{h}\right]-x=f'(0)-x=k-x;$$

where $f'(0) = k$ (say)

$\therefore$ $f'(x) = k - x$

$\Rightarrow$ $f(x)=kx-\frac{x^2}{2}+\mathrm{C}$ but $f(0) = 1$

$\Rightarrow$ $1 = C$ $\Rightarrow$ $f(x)=kx-\frac{x^2}{2}+1$

Also $f(1) = 1$ (given)

$\Rightarrow$ $1=k-\frac{1}{2}+1$ $\Rightarrow$ $k=\frac{1}{2}$

$\Rightarrow$ $f(x)=-\frac{x^2}{2}+\frac{1}{2}x+1$ $\Rightarrow$ $f(x)=-\frac{1}{2}(x^2-x-2)$

$\Rightarrow$ $f(x)=\frac{-1}{2}(x-2)(x+1)$ ...(2)

$\Rightarrow$ $x = -1$ is a root of $f(x) = 0$

Function (2) represents a downwards parabola, which would intersect every horizontal line $y = -n$; $n \in \mathbb{N}$ at exactly 2 different points. Hence $f(x) = -n$, $n \in \mathbb{N}$ has exactly 2 solutions.

7. Given $f(x) = x - 2x$; $x \in \mathbb{R}$ or $f(x) = x(x-2)$; $x \in \mathbb{R}$

$$g(x) = f(f(x)-1) + f(5 - f(x))$$
$$= (f(x)-1)(f(x)-3) + (5-f(x))(3-f(x))$$
$$= (f(x)-1)(f(x)-3) + (f(x)-3)(f(x)-5)$$
$$= (f(x)-3)(2f(x)-6)$$
$$= 2(f(x)-3)^2 = 2(x^2-2x-3)^2 \geq 0 \ \forall x \in \mathbb{R}$$

8. By condition (ii), $\because 1900 < f(1990) < 2000$

$$\Rightarrow \frac{1900}{90} < \frac{f(1990)}{90} < \frac{2000}{90}$$
$$\Rightarrow \frac{190}{9} < \frac{f(1990)}{90} < \frac{200}{9}$$
$$\Rightarrow 21.1 < \frac{f(1990)}{90} < 22.3$$
$$\Rightarrow \left[\frac{f(1990)}{90}\right] \in \{21, 22\}$$

Case-(i): $\left[\frac{f(1990)}{90}\right] = 21$, by condition (i), put $x = 1990$

$$\Rightarrow 1990 - f(1990) = 19\left[\frac{1990}{19}\right] - 90(21)$$

$\Rightarrow$ $1990 - f(1990) = 19(104) - 1890$

$\Rightarrow$ $f(1990) = 1990 + 1890 - 1976$

$\Rightarrow$ $f(1990) = 1890 + 14 = 1904$

Case-(ii): $\left[\frac{f(1990)}{90}\right] = 22$, By condition (i), put $x = 1990$

$$\Rightarrow 1990 - f(1990) = 19\left[\frac{1990}{19}\right] - 90(22)$$

$\Rightarrow$ $1990 - f(1990) = 19(104) - 1980$

$\Rightarrow$ $f(1990) = 1990 + 1980 - 1976$

$\Rightarrow$ $f(1990) = 1994$

$\therefore$ 1904, 1994

9. Given $|f(x)| \leq 1 \ \forall x \in \mathbb{R}$

$\Rightarrow$ $f(x)$ is a bounded function.

Let M be its least upper bound.

$\Rightarrow$ $|f(x)| \leq \text{M} \ \forall x \in \mathbb{R}$

Let $x_0 \in \mathbb{R}$ such that $f(x_0) = M > 0$

Now, $2f(x).g(y) = f(x+y) + f(x-y) \ \forall x, y \in \mathbb{R}$

$\Rightarrow$ $2f(x_0) \cdot g(y) = f(x_0 + y) + f(x_0 - y) \ \forall y \in \mathbb{R}$ and fixed number

$$\Rightarrow |2f(x_0).g(y)| = |f(x_0+y) + f(x_0-y)|$$

$\Rightarrow$ $2|f(x_0)|.|g(y)| \leq |f(x_0+y)| + |f(x_0-y)|$ (By triangle in equality)

$$\Rightarrow 2|\text{M}||g(y)| \leq |\text{M}| + |\text{M}|$$
$$\Rightarrow 2\text{M}|g(y)| \leq 2\text{M} \ (\because \text{M} > 0)$$
$$\Rightarrow |g(y)| \leq 1 \ \forall y \in \mathbb{R} \text{ or } |g(x)| \leq 1 \forall x \in \mathbb{R}$$

10. Given equation $\forall x, y \in \mathbb{R}$ is

$$f(x(f(y))) = x^p, y^q \ ; \ p, q \in \mathbb{N} \quad \ldots(1)$$

Let $f(y_0) = \frac{1}{x}$, for $y_0 \in \mathbb{R}$, $x \in \mathbb{R}$

$$\Rightarrow f\left(x.\frac{1}{x}\right) = \left(\frac{1}{f(y_0)}\right)^p .{y_0}^q$$
$$\Rightarrow f(1) = \frac{{y_0}^q}{(f(y_0))^p}$$
$$\Rightarrow (f(y_0))^p = \frac{{y_0}^q}{f(1)}$$
$$\Rightarrow f(y_0) = \frac{{y_0}^{q/p}}{(f(1))^{1/p}} \quad \ldots(2)$$
$$\Rightarrow f(y_0) = k(y_0)^{q/p}; \ k = \frac{1}{(f(1))^{1/p}} = \text{Constant}$$
$$\therefore f(x(f(y))) = x^p.y^q \text{ (Given)}$$
$$\Rightarrow f(x.f(y_0)) = x^p.{y_0}^q$$
$$\Rightarrow f(x.\,k.(y_0)^{q/p}) = x^p.{y_0}^q$$
$$\Rightarrow k\left(x.\,k(y_0)^{q/p}\right)^{q/p} = x^p.{y_0}^q$$
$$\Rightarrow k.\,k^{q/p}.x^{q/p}.{y_0}^{q^2/p^2} = x^p.{y_0}^q$$
$$\Rightarrow k = 1, \frac{q}{p} = p, \frac{q^2}{p^2} = q$$
$$\Rightarrow q = p^2$$

11. $f(x+y+1) = \left(\sqrt{f(x)} + \sqrt{f(y)}\right)^2; f(0) = 1 \ \forall x, y \in \mathbb{R}$

Put $x = y = 0$

$$\Rightarrow f(1) = \left(\sqrt{f(0)} + \sqrt{f(0)}\right)^2$$
$$\Rightarrow f(1) = \left(2\sqrt{f(0)}\right)^2$$

$\Rightarrow$ $f(1) = 4f(0) = 4.$

Put $x = 0$, $y = 1$;

$$\Rightarrow f(2) = \left(\sqrt{f(0)} + \sqrt{f(1)}\right)^2$$

$\Rightarrow$ $f(2) = (1 + 2)^2 = (3)^2$

Parallely, put $x = 1$, $y = 1$,

$$\Rightarrow f(3) = \left(\sqrt{f(1)} + \sqrt{f(1)}\right)^2$$

$\Rightarrow$ $f(3) = (2)^2 f(1) = 4(4) = 16$

$\therefore$ By induction, $f(n) = (n+1)^2$

$\therefore$ $f(x) = (x+1)^2$; $x \in \mathbb{R}$

12. $f(x+y) = f(x).f(y) \ \forall x, y \in \mathbb{R}, f(0) \neq 0 \quad \ldots(1)$

Put $x = y = 0$

$$\Rightarrow f(0) = (f(0))^2$$

$\Rightarrow$ $f(0) \neq 0$ or 1 but $f(0) \neq 0$ (given)

$\Rightarrow$ $f(0) \neq 0$ ...(2)

Now replacing y by $-x$ in (1), we get $f(0) = 0\, f(x).f(-x)$

$\Rightarrow \quad f(-x) = \dfrac{1}{f(x)} \quad [\because f(0) = 1]$

Now, $F(-x) = \dfrac{f(-x)}{1+(f(-x))^2}$

$= \dfrac{\frac{1}{f(x)}}{\left[1+\frac{1}{(f(x))^2}\right]} = \dfrac{f(x)}{(f(x))^2+1} = F(x)$

$\Rightarrow$ $F(x)$ is an even function

13. Given functional equation is $f(x + y) = g(x) + h(y)$.

Put $y = 0$

$\Rightarrow$ $f(x) = g(x) + h(0)$ ...(1)

Let $h(0) = a$

$\Rightarrow$ $f(x) = g(x) + a$

$\Rightarrow$ $f(x) = g(x) - a$ ...(2)

Put $x = 0$

$\Rightarrow$ $f(y) = g(0) + h(y)$ or $f(x) = g(0) + h(x)$ ...(3)

Let $g(0) = b$

$\Rightarrow$ $h(x) = f(x) - b$ ...(4)

$\therefore$ $f(x + y) = f(x) + f(y) - a - b$ ...(5)

Let $F(x) = f(x) - a - b$ ...(6)

$\Rightarrow$ $F(x + y) = f(x + y) - a - b = f(x) + f(y) - 2a - 2b$ (using (5))

$= [f(x) - a - b] + [f(y) - a - b] = F(x) + F(y)$

$\Rightarrow$ $F(x + y) = F(x) + F(y)$ which is a cauchy's I[st] equation.

$\Rightarrow$ $F(x) = mx$

$\therefore$ From (6), $mx = f(x) - a - b$

$\Rightarrow$ $f(x) = mx + a + b$

$\therefore$ $g(x) = f(x) - a$ (From (2))

$\Rightarrow$ $g(x) = mx + b$ and $h(x) = f(x) - b = mx + a$

Thus, $\left.\begin{aligned} f(x) &= mx + a + b \\ g(x) &= mx + b, \\ h(x) &= mx + a \end{aligned}\right\}$

14. $p(x + 1) = p(x) + 2x + 1$

$\Rightarrow$ $p'(x + 1) = p'(x) + 2$

$\Rightarrow$ $p''(x + 1) = p''(x) \ \forall x \in \mathbb{R}$ ...(1)

$\Rightarrow$ $p''(x + 1) = p''(x + 1) = p''(x + 2) = p''(x + 3) + \ldots\ldots\ldots\ldots$

$\Rightarrow$ $p''(x) = \text{constant} = k$ (say).

$\Rightarrow$ $p'(x) = kx + k_1$

$\Rightarrow$ $p(x) = \dfrac{kx^2}{2} + k_1 x + k_2$

$\Rightarrow$ $p(x + 1) = \dfrac{k(x+1)^2}{2} + k_1(x + 1) + k_2$ ...(2)

But $p(x + 1) = p(x) + 2x + 1$

$\Rightarrow$ $\dfrac{kx^2}{2} + k_1 x + k_2\, 2x + 1 = \dfrac{kx^2}{2} + (k_1 + 2)x + k_2 + 1$ ...(3)

Comparing (2) and (3), we have, $k + k_1 = k_1 + 2$ and $\dfrac{k}{2} + k_1 + k_2 = k_2 + 1$

$\Rightarrow$ $k = 2,\ k_1 = 0$

$\Rightarrow$ $p(x) = x^2 + k_2$ or $p(x) = x^2 + C$ are all positive solutions.

15. Given functional equation is $f(x).\,f(y) = f(x - y)\ \forall x, y \in \mathbb{R}$

Put $x = y = 0$

$\Rightarrow$ $(f(x))^2 = f(0)$ ...(1)

Also putting $x = y = 0$

$\Rightarrow$ $(f(0))^2 - f(0) = 0$

$\Rightarrow$ $(f(0))(f(0) - 1) = 0$

$\Rightarrow$ $f(0) = 0$ or $f(0) = 1$ ...(2)

$\therefore$ From (1) and (2), we get $(f(x))^2 = \begin{cases} 0 & \text{if } f(0) = 0 \\ \text{or} \\ 1 & \text{if } f(0) = 1 \end{cases}$

$\Rightarrow$ $f(x) = \begin{cases} 0 & \text{if } f(0) = 0 \\ \pm 1 & \text{if } f(0) = 1 \end{cases}$

But given that $f(x)$ is not identically zero

$\Rightarrow$ $f(x) = \pm 1$

16. Given functional equation is $f(xy) = x f(y) + y\, f(x)$

$\Rightarrow$ $\dfrac{f(xy)}{xy} = \dfrac{f(y)}{y} + \dfrac{f(x)}{x}$ ...(1)

Let $g(x) = \dfrac{f(x)}{x}$

$\therefore$ From (1), $g(xy) = g(x) + g(y)$ ...(2)

$\therefore$ It is couchy's 3rd equation.

$\Rightarrow$ $g(x) = c \log x$

$\Rightarrow$ $f(x) = cx \log x$

17. Given functional equation is $f(x+y) = \dfrac{f(x).f(y)}{f(x)+f(y)}$

$\Rightarrow$ $f(x+y) = \dfrac{1}{\left[\frac{1}{f(x)} + \frac{1}{f(y)}\right]}$

$\Rightarrow$ $\dfrac{1}{f(x+y)} = \dfrac{1}{f(x)} + \dfrac{1}{f(y)}$ ...(2)

Let $g(x) = \dfrac{1}{f(x)}$

$\Rightarrow$ $g(x + y) = g(x) + g(y)$, but it is cauchy's Ist equation.

$\Rightarrow$ $g(x) = kx \qquad \Rightarrow \quad f(x) = \dfrac{1}{kx}$

18. Given functional equation is $f^2(x) = f(x + y)\, f(x - y)$

Taking log both sides, $2 \log f(x) = \log f(x + y) + \log f(x - y)$

$\Rightarrow$ $\log f(x) = \dfrac{1}{2} \log f(x + y) + \dfrac{1}{2} \log f(x - y)$

$\Rightarrow$ $\log f\left(\dfrac{x+y}{2} + \dfrac{x-y}{2}\right) = \dfrac{1}{2}\log f(x+y) + \dfrac{1}{2}\log f(x-y)$

Put $x + y = u,\ x - y = v$

$\Rightarrow$ $\log f\left(\dfrac{u+v}{2}\right) = \dfrac{1}{2}\log f(u) + \dfrac{1}{2}\log f(v)$

Put $\log f(x) = g(x)$

$\Rightarrow$ $g\left(\dfrac{u+v}{2}\right) = \dfrac{1}{2} g(u) + \dfrac{1}{2} g(v)$

$\Rightarrow g\left(\frac{u+v}{2}\right)=\frac{g(u)+g(v)}{2}$, It is jensen's functional equation

$\Rightarrow g(x) = mx + c \qquad \Rightarrow \log_a f(x) = mx + c$

$\Rightarrow f(x) = a^{mx+c} = a^c.\, a^{mx}$

$\Rightarrow f(x) = k.a^{mx} = k(a^m)^x$ or $f(x) = k(\alpha)^x;\ \alpha > 0$

19. Given functional equation is

$$f(x)+f\left(\frac{1}{1-x}\right)=x;\ x\neq 0,1 \qquad \ldots(1)$$

Replacing x by $\frac{1}{1-x}$, we get

$$f\left(\frac{1}{1-x}\right)+f\left(\frac{1-x}{1-\left(\frac{1}{1-x}\right)}\right)=\frac{1}{1-x}$$

$$\Rightarrow f\left(\frac{1}{1-x}\right)+f\left(\frac{1-x}{-x}\right)=\frac{1}{1-x}$$

$$\Rightarrow f\left(\frac{1}{1-x}\right)+f\left(\frac{1-x}{x}\right)=\frac{1}{1-x} \qquad \ldots(2)$$

Again replacing x by $\frac{1}{1-x}$, we get

$$f\left(\frac{1}{1-\left(\frac{1}{1-x}\right)}\right)+f\left(\frac{\frac{1}{1-x}-1}{\frac{1}{1-x}}\right)=\frac{1}{1-\left(\frac{1}{1-x}\right)}$$

$$\Rightarrow f\left(\frac{1-x}{-x}\right)+f(x)=(x-1)$$

$$\text{or } f\left(\frac{x-1}{x}\right)+f(x)=\frac{(x-1)}{x} \qquad \ldots(3)$$

$\therefore$ (1) + (3) – (2) gives,

$$2f(x)=x+\frac{(x-1)}{x}-\frac{1}{1-x}=x+1-\frac{1}{x}-\frac{1}{(1-x)}$$

$$\Rightarrow f(x)=\frac{1}{2}\left(1+x-\frac{1}{x}-\frac{1}{(1-x)}\right)$$

20. Given functional equation is

$f(x + y) + f(x - y) = 2\,[f(x) + f(y)]$ ...(1)

Differentiating (1) partially w.r.t. x,

we get $f'(x + y) + f'(x - y) = 2\,f'(x)$ ...(2)

Differentiating (2) partially w.r.t. x,

we get $f'(x + y) - f'(x - y) = 2\,f'(x)$ ...(3)

Equation (2) + (3) gives,

$2f'(x + y) = 2\,[f'(x) + f'(y)]$ or $f'(x + y) = f'(x) + f'(y)$ ...(4)

Let $f'(x) = g(x)$

$\Rightarrow g(x + y) = g(x) + g(y)$, It is cauchy's first equation.

$\Rightarrow g(x) = kx \qquad \Rightarrow f'(x) = kx$

$$\Rightarrow f(x)=\frac{kx^2}{2}+k_1 \qquad \ldots(5)$$

From (1), Putting $x = y$, we get $f(2x) + f(0) = 4f(x)$

Putting $x = 0$, we get $2f(0) = 4f(0)$

$\Rightarrow f(0) = 2$

$\therefore$ From (5), $k_1 = 0$

$\Rightarrow f(x) = ax^2$

21. Given functional equation is

$f(x + y) - f(x - y) = 2\,f(y)$ ...(1)

Differentiating (1), partially w.r.t. x,

we get $f'(x + y) - f'(x - y) = 0$ ...(2)

Differentiating (1), partially w.r.t. x,

we get $f'(x + y) - f'(x - y) = 2\,f'(y)$ ...(3)

Equation (2) + (3) gives, $2f'(x + y) = 2\,f'(y)$

$\Rightarrow f'(x + y) = 2\,f'(y)\ \forall x, y \in \mathbb{R}$

In particular, $f'(x) = f'(0)\ \forall x \in \mathbb{R}$

$\Rightarrow f'(x) = k$; where $f'(0) = k$

$\Rightarrow f(x) = kx + k_1\ \forall x, y \in \mathbb{R}$ ...(4)

From (1), $x = y = 0$

$\Rightarrow f(0) - f(0) = 2f(0) \qquad \Rightarrow f(0) = 0$

$\therefore$ From (4), we get $k_1 = 0$

$\Rightarrow f(x) = kx;\ x \in \mathbb{R}$

22. Given functional equation is $f(x + y) - f(x - y) = 2\,f(x)$ ...(1)

Differentiating (1) partially w.r.t. x,

we get $f'(x + y) - f'(x - y) = 2f'(x)$ ...(2)

Differentiating (1) partially w.r.t. y,

we get $f'(x + y) - f'(x - y) = 0$ ...(3)

Adding (2) and (3), we get $2f'(x + y) = 2f'(x)$

$\Rightarrow f'(x + y) = f'(x)\ \forall x, y \in \mathbb{R}$

$\Rightarrow f'(y) = f'(0)\ \forall y \in \mathbb{R}$

$\Rightarrow f(x) = a\ \forall x \in \mathbb{R} \qquad \Rightarrow f(x) = (ax + b)\ \forall x \in \mathbb{R}$

23. Given $f(x+y).f(x-y)=[f(x).f(y)]^2$ ...(1)

Without loss of generality let us assume that $f(x) \geq 0\ \forall x \in \mathbb{R}$.

Put $y = 0$

$$\Rightarrow [f(x)]^2=[f(x).f(0)]^2 \ \Rightarrow\ (f(x))^2\left[1-(f(0))^2\right]=0$$

$\Rightarrow f(x) \equiv 0\ \forall x \in \mathbb{R}$ or $(f(0))^2 = 1$

$\Rightarrow f(0) = \pm 1$

$\Rightarrow f(0) = 1$ ...(2)

Taking log both sides of (1), we get

$\ln f(x + y) + \ln f(x - y) = 2[\ln f(x) + \ln f(y)]$ ...(3)

Let $\ln f(x) = g(x)$

$\Rightarrow g(x + y) + g(x - y) = 2g(x) + 2g(y)$ ...(4)

Putting $y = x$, we get $g(2x) + g(0) = 2g(x) + 2g(x)$

$\Rightarrow g(2x) = 4g(x) \qquad \left[\because g(0) = \ln f(0) = \ln(1) = 0\right]$

$\Rightarrow g(x) = ax^2\ \forall x \in \mathbb{R}$

$\Rightarrow \ln f(x) = ax^2 \qquad \Rightarrow f(x) = e^{ax^2}$

Clearly if $y = f(x)$ is a solution, then $y = -f(x)$ is also a solution.

$\therefore\ f(x) = \pm\, e^{ax^2}$ is the require solution.

24. Given functional equation is

$x\,f(y) + y\,f(x) = (x + y).\,f(x).\,f(y)$ ...(1)

Put $y = 0$

$\Rightarrow x f(0) + 0 = x f(x) f(0)$

$\Rightarrow x (f(x) - 1) f(0) = 0 \ \forall x \in \mathbb{R}$

$\Rightarrow f(x) = 1 \ \forall x \in \mathbb{R}$ or $f(x) = 0$ ...(2)

From (1), for $x = y$, $2x f(x) = 2x (f(x))^2 \ \forall x \in \mathbb{R}$

$\Rightarrow 2x f(x) = [f(x) - 1] = 0 \ \forall x \in \mathbb{R}$

$\Rightarrow \left.\begin{array}{l} f(x)=0 \ \forall x\in\mathbb{R} \\ \text{or } f(x)=1 \ \forall x\in\mathbb{R}\end{array}\right\}$

TEXTUAL EXERCISE–7: (OBJECTIVE)

1. (i) (a), (c)

The functional equation $f(x + y) = f(x) + f(y)$ is Cauchy's first equation having its solution, $f(x) = kx$; k = constant

Now $f(1) = k = 2$ (given)

$\Rightarrow f(x) = 2x \quad \Rightarrow f(5) = 10$

(ii) (b), (c) $f(x + y) = f(x) \cdot f(y)$ is cauchy's second equation having solution, $f(x) = a^x$; a = constant > 0

Now $f(2) = 25$

$\Rightarrow a^2 = 25 \quad \Rightarrow a = 5$

$\Rightarrow f(x) = 5^x \quad \Rightarrow f(3) = 125$

(iii) (b), (c) $f(xy) = f(x) + f(y)$ is cauchy's third equation having solution, $f(x) = k \log_a x$;

Now, $f(25) = 2 \quad \Rightarrow 2 = k \log_a 25$

$\Rightarrow (a)^2 = (25)^k = (5^k)^2 \quad \Rightarrow a = 5^k$

$\therefore f(x) = k \log_{\left(\frac{k}{5}\right)}(x)$

$\Rightarrow f(625) = k \log_{\left(\frac{k}{5}\right)} 625 = k \times \frac{1}{k} \log_5 625 = \log_5 625 = 4$

2. (b), (c) $f(x) = x + \frac{1}{x}$; $f\left(\frac{1}{x}\right) = \frac{1}{x} + x = f(x)$

$$(f(x))^3 + \frac{5}{2} = \left(x + \frac{1}{x}\right)^3 + \frac{5}{2} = x^3 + \frac{1}{x^3} + 3\left(x + \frac{1}{x}\right) + \frac{5}{2}$$

$$= f(x^3) + 3f(x) + \frac{5}{2} = f(x^3) + 3f(x) + f(2)$$

$$= f(x^3) + 3f\left(\frac{1}{x}\right) + f\left(\frac{1}{2}\right)$$

3. (b), (c), (d)

$$f(x) = \frac{3^x + 3^{-x}}{2}; f(-x) = f(x)$$

$$\Rightarrow f(x+y).f(x-y) = \left[\frac{3^{x+y} + 3^{-x-y}}{2}\right]\left[\frac{3^{x-y} + 3^{-x+y}}{2}\right]$$

$$= \frac{3^{2x} + 3^{2y} + 3^{-2y} + 3^{-2x}}{4} = \frac{3^{2x} + 3^{-2x}}{4} + \frac{3^{2y} + 3^{-2y}}{4}$$

$$= \frac{1}{2}f(2x) + \frac{1}{2}f(2y) = \frac{1}{2}[f(2x) + f(2y)]$$

$$= \frac{1}{2}[f(2x) + f(-2y)] = \frac{1}{2}[f(-2x) + f(2y)]$$

$(\because f(-x) = f(x))$

4. (a) f is an even function on (–5, 5), Such that

$$f(x) = f\left(\frac{x+1}{x+2}\right)$$

$\Rightarrow \pm x = \frac{x+1}{x+2} \quad \Rightarrow x = \frac{x+1}{x+2}$ or $-x = \frac{x+1}{x+2}$

$\Rightarrow x^2 + x - 1 = 0$ or $x^2 + 3x + 1 = 0$

$\Rightarrow x = \frac{-1 \pm \sqrt{1+4}}{2}$ or $\frac{-3 \pm \sqrt{9-4}}{2}$

$\Rightarrow x = \frac{-1 \pm \sqrt{5}}{2}$ or $\frac{-3 \pm \sqrt{5}}{2}$

All above values $\in (-5, 5)$

5. (a) $f(x) = \frac{x-1}{x+2}$ ...(1)

Clearly $D_f = \mathbb{R} - \{-1\}$

$\therefore \ f(x) + f(f(x)) = 0 \Rightarrow f(x) + \frac{f(x)-1}{f(x)+1} = 0$

$\Rightarrow [f(x)]^2 + 2f(x) - 1 = 0$

$\Rightarrow \left(\frac{x-1}{x+1}\right)^2 + 2\left(\frac{x-1}{x+2}\right) - 1 = 0$

$\Rightarrow (x-1)^2 + (x^2-1) - (x+1)^2 = 0$

$\Rightarrow [x^2 - 2x + 1] + [2x^2 - 2 - x^2 - 1 - 2x] = 0$

$\Rightarrow 2x^2 - 4x - 2 = 0 \quad \Rightarrow x^2 - 2x - 1 = 0$

$\Rightarrow x = \frac{2 \pm \sqrt{4+4}}{2} \quad \Rightarrow x = 1 \pm \sqrt{2} \in D_f$

6. (a), (b) $f(x + y) + f(x - y) = 0 \ \forall x, y \in \mathbb{R}$

Put $y = 0 \quad \Rightarrow 2f(x) = 0$

$\Rightarrow f(x) = 0 \ \forall x \in \mathbb{R}$

$\Rightarrow f(x)$ is identically zero function.

$\Rightarrow f(x)$ is even as well as odd function.

7. (a), (b), (c), (d)

Given functional equation is $f(x + y) = f(x) + f(y) \ \forall x, y \in \mathbb{R}$

It is couchy's first equation having its solution, $f(x) = kx$; k = constant

If $k = 0$, then $f(x) = 0$ which is continuous and differentiable and both even as well as odd.

If $k = 1$, then $f(x) = x$, which is an odd function.

Clearly $f(x) = kx$ can be periodic for $k = 0$ i.e., $f(x) = 0$ is a periodic function with no fundamental period.

i.e., $f(x + T) = f(x) = 0 \ \forall x \in \mathbb{R}$

8. (d) Given functional equation is $f(x.y) = f(x) + f(y) \ \forall x, y \in \mathbb{R}^+$

It is cauchy's 3rd equation, having its solution, $f(x) = k \log_a x$, $a > 0, \neq 1$ or $f(1) = 0 \ \forall x, y \in \mathbb{R}^+$

$\Rightarrow f(1) = 0$

9. (b) Given functional equation is $f(x + y) = f(x) \cdot f(y) \ \forall x, y \in \mathbb{R}$

It is cauchy's 2nd equation, having its solution $f(x) = 0 \ \forall x \in \mathbb{R}$ or $f(x) = a^x$; $a > 0$

Given $f(2) = 9$

$\Rightarrow 9 = a^2 \quad \Rightarrow a = 3$

$\Rightarrow f(x) = 3^x \quad \Rightarrow f(4) = (3)^4 = 81$

10. (c) Given functional equation is $f(x+y) = f(x) \cdot f(y)$ $\forall x, y \in \mathbb{R}$

$\Rightarrow f(x) = a^x; a > 0 \qquad \therefore f(x) + f(-x) = 2$

$\Rightarrow a^x + a^{-x} = 2 \qquad \Rightarrow a^x = 1$

$\Rightarrow x = 0$

11. (b) Given functional equation is $f(x+y) = \dfrac{f(x).f(y)}{f(x)+f(y)}$

$$\Rightarrow f(x+y) = \frac{1}{\dfrac{1}{f(y)} + \dfrac{1}{f(x)}}$$

$$\Rightarrow \frac{1}{f(x+y)} = \frac{1}{f(x)} + \frac{1}{f(y)} \qquad \ldots(1)$$

Let $\dfrac{1}{f(x)} = g(x)$

$\Rightarrow g(x+y) = g(x) + g(y)\ \forall x, y \in \mathbb{R}$

But it is cauchy's first equation, having its solution, $g(x) = kx$; k = constant.

$\Rightarrow \dfrac{1}{f(x)} = kx \qquad \Rightarrow f(x) = \dfrac{1}{kx}$

But $f(1) = 32$ (given)

$\Rightarrow 32 = \dfrac{1}{k} \qquad \Rightarrow f(x) = \dfrac{32}{x}$

$\Rightarrow f(8) = \dfrac{32}{8} = 4$

SECTION–III: (SINGLE CORRECT ANSWER)

1. (a) $f(x) = \dfrac{\cos(\sin x) - \cos x}{x^2}$

$\lim_{x\to 0} f(x) = f(0) = a$

$$\Rightarrow \lim_{x\to 0}\left[\frac{\cos(\sin x) - \cos x}{x^2}\right] = a$$

$$\Rightarrow \lim_{x\to 0}\left[\frac{-2\sin\left(\dfrac{\sin x + x}{2}\right)\sin\left(\dfrac{\sin x - x}{2}\right)}{x^2}\right] = a$$

$$\Rightarrow -2\lim_{x\to 0}\left[\frac{\sin\left(\dfrac{\sin x + x}{2}\right)\sin\left(\dfrac{\sin x - x}{2}\right)}{\left(\dfrac{\sin x + x}{2}\right)\left(\dfrac{\sin x - x}{2}\right)} \times \left(\frac{\sin x + x}{2}\right)\left(\frac{\sin x - x}{2}\right)\cdot\frac{1}{x^2}\right] = a$$

$$\Rightarrow -2(1).(1).\left(\frac{1}{2}(1+1)\frac{1}{2}(1-1)\right) = a$$

$\Rightarrow a = 0$

2. (d)
(a) Max $\{f, g\} = \dfrac{f(x)+g(x)}{2} + \dfrac{|f(x)-g(x)|}{2}$ and Min $\{f, g\} = \dfrac{f(x)+g(x)}{2} - \dfrac{|f(x)-g(x)|}{2}$ i.e., $F(x) \pm G(x)$;

where $F(x) = \dfrac{f(x)+g(x)}{2}, G(x) = \dfrac{|f(x)+g(x)|}{2}$ are continuous functions.

$\Rightarrow$ Max. $\{f, g\}$ and Min $\{f, g\}$ are also continuous. Thus (a) is true

(b) Let f is continuous and g is discontinuous at $x = a$, then $\lim_{x\to a^-} f(x) = \ell(say) = \lim_{x\to a^+} f(x) = f(a)$ and

$\lim_{x\to a^-} f(x) = \ell_1, \lim_{x\to a^+} = \ell_2$

$\Rightarrow \lim_{x\to a^-} (f(x) + g(x)) = \ell + \ell_1$ and

$\lim_{x\to a^+} (f(x) + g(x)) = \ell + \ell_2)$

$\Rightarrow f(x) + g(x)$ is discontinuous as $\ell_1 \neq \ell_2$ implies $\ell + \ell_1$

$\Rightarrow$ (b) is true.

(c) A continuous function if periodic in $[a, b]$ will be bounded as if it is unbounded i.e., goes to infinitely, then it is impossible to repeat the previous values. Thus (c) is true.

(d) $f(x) = \tan x$ is discontinuous and periodic and its period is π which is same as the period of discontinuity.
Hence the statement (d) is false.

3. (d) $f(x) = \begin{cases} -2\sin x \text{ for } -\pi \le x < \dfrac{-\pi}{2} \\ a\sin x + b \text{ for } \dfrac{-\pi}{2} \le x < \dfrac{\pi}{2} \\ \cos x \text{ for } \dfrac{\pi}{2} \le x \le \pi \end{cases}$

For continuity in $[-\pi, \pi]$, $f(x)$ must be continuous at $x = \dfrac{-\pi}{2}$ and at $x = \dfrac{\pi}{2}$

$\Rightarrow \lim_{x\to\left(\frac{-\pi}{2}\right)} (-2\sin x) = -a + b$ and $\lim_{x\to\left(\frac{\pi}{2}\right)} (a\sin x + b) = 0$

$\Rightarrow 2 = -a + b$ and $a + b = 0$

$\Rightarrow a = -1, b = 1 \qquad \Rightarrow (a, b) \equiv (-1, 1)$

4. (c) $g(x) = x - [x] = \{x\}$,
$f(x)$ is continuous with $f(0) = f(1)$, $h(x) = f(g(x)) = f(\{x\})$

$\Rightarrow h(x) \in \{f(x): x \in [0, 1]\}$ and $h(0) = h(1) = h(2) \ldots\ldots$

$\Rightarrow h(x)$ is a continuous function on $\mathbb{R}$

5. (c) $f(x) = [\sin x + \cos x]; x \in (0, 2\pi)$

$\because (\sin x + \cos x) \in \left[-\sqrt{2}, \sqrt{2}\right]$

$\Rightarrow [\sin x + \cos x]$ has discontinuity at integer point in $\left[-\sqrt{2}, \sqrt{2}\right]$

i.e., -1, 0 and 1 i.e., at $x = \dfrac{\pi}{2}, \dfrac{3\pi}{4}, \pi, \dfrac{3\pi}{2}, \dfrac{7\pi}{4}$, points of discontinuity i.e., at 5 points

6. (b) $f(x) = e^{2x} + e^x - e; x \in [0, 1]$

$\Rightarrow f'(x) = 2e^{2x} + e^x > 0\ \forall x \in [0, 1]$

Also $f(x)$ is continuous and $f(0) = 2 - e < 0, f(1) = e^2 > 0$

$\Rightarrow f(x) = 0$ has exactly one root is $[0, 1]$

7. (a) |L.H.L – R.H.L| = Jump of discontinuity .

$$= \left|\lim_{x\to -2^-}\frac{-(x+2)}{\tan^{-1}(x+2)} - \lim_{x\to -2^+}\frac{(x+2)}{\tan^{-1}(x+2)}\right| = |-1-1| = 2$$

8. (a) Clearly $f(x)$ is a continuous function. Let $f(x) = g(x) - a\sin \pi x$; $g(x) = \frac{x^3}{4} + 3$ for $x \in [-4, 4]$; $g(x) \in [-13, 19]$ and for $x \in [-4, 4]$; $a \in (0, 1)$; $\sin\pi x \in [-1, 1]$, $a \in (0, 1)$

$\Rightarrow$ $a\sin x \in (-1, 1)$ $\Rightarrow$ $-a\sin\pi x \in (-1, 1)$

$\therefore$ $f(x) = g(x) - a\sin\pi x$ for $x \in [-4, 4]$ attains all values in $(-12, 18)$ which contains $\frac{1999}{199}$.

Thus $f(x)$ attains $\frac{1999}{199}$ at least once in $[-4, 4]$

$\Rightarrow$ The given statement is true.

9. (a) $f(x) = \begin{cases} x^2; & x \in \mathbb{Q} \\ -x^2; & x \notin \mathbb{Q}\end{cases}$

$\therefore$ $x^2 \to -x^2$ $\Rightarrow$ $2x^2 \to 0$

$\Rightarrow$ $x \to 0 = f(0)$

Thus $f(x)$ is continuous at $x = 0$

10. (b) $f(x) = [x]$ and $g(x) = \begin{cases} 1, & x > 1 \\ 2, & x \le 1\end{cases}$

$\Rightarrow$ $g(f(x)) = \begin{cases} 1, & f(x) > 1 \\ 2, & f(x) \le 2\end{cases} = \begin{cases} 1, & [x] > 1 \text{ i.e.,} [x] \ge 2 \\ 2, & [x] \le 1\end{cases}$

$= \begin{cases} 1, & x \ge 2 \\ 2, & x < 2\end{cases}$

$\Rightarrow$ $g(f(x))$ is discontinuous at $x = 2$

11. (a) $f(x) = \begin{cases} x+2\,; & x<0 \\ -x^2-2; & 0 \le x < 1, \\ x; & x \ge 1\end{cases}$

$\Rightarrow$ $|f(x)| = \begin{cases} -(x+2)\,; & x<-2 \\ (x+2)\,; & -2 \le x < 0 \\ x^2+2\,; & 0 \le x < 1 \\ x\,; & x \ge 1\end{cases}$

$\Rightarrow$ $|f(x)|$ can be discontinuous at $x = -2$ or $x = 0$ or $x = 1$

<u>At $x = -2$:</u> L.H.L = 0 = R.H.L = $|f(-2)|$

<u>At $x = 0$:</u> L.H.L = 2 = R.H.L = $f(0)$

<u>At $x = 1$:</u> L.H.L = 3 $\ne$ R.H.L = 1

$\therefore$ $|f(x)|$ is discontinuous only at 1 point i.e., at $x = 1$

12. (c) $f(x) = \begin{cases} x\,; & x \in \mathbb{Q} \\ -x\,; & x \notin \mathbb{Q}\end{cases}$

At the point of continuity, $x \to -x$

$\Rightarrow$ $2x \to 0$ $\Rightarrow$ $x \to 0$

Thus $f(x)$ is continuous at $x = 0$

$f(x)$ oscillates about 0 but oscillations are not periodic .

$\Rightarrow$ $f(x)$ is not a periodic function.

If $x \in \mathbb{Q}$, then $f(x) = x$ and $-x \in \mathbb{Q}$

$\Rightarrow$ $f(-x) = -x$

$\Rightarrow$ $f(-x) = -f(x)$

$\Rightarrow$ $f(x)$ is an odd function.

13. (a) $f(x) = \lim_{n\to\infty}\frac{2\sin x}{3^n + (2\cos x)^{2n}} = \lim_{n\to\infty}\frac{2\sin x}{3^n + (4\cos^2 x)^n}$

$\Rightarrow$ $f(x) = \lim_{n\to\infty}\left\{\frac{2\sin x}{3^n + 4^n(\cos^2 x)^n}\right\} = 0$ for $x \in \mathbb{R}$

$\Rightarrow$ $f(x)$ has no point of discontinuity .

14. (c) $\lim_{x\to 1}\frac{f(1).g(x) - f(x).g(1) - f(1) + g(1)}{g(x) - f(x)}$ ……$\left(\frac{0}{0} \text{ form}\right)$

BY L.H. Rule $= \lim_{x\to 1}\frac{f(1)g'(x) - f'(x).g(1)}{g'(x) - f'(x)}$

$= \lim_{x\to 1}(2)\frac{(g'(x) - f'(x))}{(g'(x) - f'(x))} = 2$

15. (c) $\lim_{x\to 3}\frac{x\,f(3) - 3f(x)}{x-3} = \lim_{x\to 3}\frac{6x - 3f(x)}{x-3}$.....$\left[\frac{0}{0} \text{ form}\right]$

$= \lim_{x\to 3}\frac{6 - 3f'(x)}{1}$ (By L.H Rule)

$= 6 - 3f'(3) = 6 - 3(2) = 0$

16. (a) $\lim_{h\to 0}\frac{\sin\sqrt{x+h} - \sin\sqrt{x}}{h}$

$$= \lim_{h\to 0}\frac{2\cos\left(\frac{\sqrt{x+h}+\sqrt{x}}{2}\right)\sin\left(\frac{\sqrt{x+h}-\sqrt{x}}{2}\right)}{h}$$

$$= 2\cos\sqrt{x}\lim_{h\to 0}\sin\left(\frac{\sqrt{x+h}-\sqrt{x}}{2}\right).\frac{1}{h}$$

$$= 2\cos\sqrt{x}\,.\lim_{h\to 0}\frac{\sin\left(\frac{\sqrt{x+h}-\sqrt{x}}{2}\right)}{2\left(\frac{\sqrt{x+h}-\sqrt{x}}{2}\right).(\sqrt{x+h}+\sqrt{x})}$$

$$= \frac{\cos\sqrt{x}}{2\sqrt{x}}$$

17. (c) $f(x) = \max\{x^2, (x-1)^2, 2x(1-x)\}$, $0 \le x \le 1$

Graph of $f(x)$ is as shown below

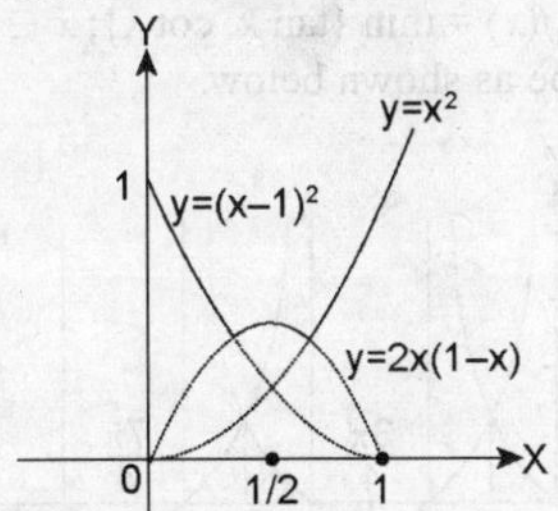

$f(x)$ is differentiable for all x expect at two points i.e., $x = \frac{1}{3}$ and $x = \frac{2}{3}$

18. (c) $h(x) = Max.\ \{f(x), g(x)\}$

Clearly, if at $x = x_0$, $f(x_0) = g(x_0)$ and $h(x)$ has a sharp point, then $f(x)$ is non-differentiable at $x = x_0$.

If $f(x_0) > g(x_0)$ or $f(x_0) < g(x_0)$), then $h(x_0) = f(x_0) = f(x_0)$ or $h(x) = g(x)) \Rightarrow h(x)$ is differentiable at $x = x_0$

However if $f(x) = g(x)$ for $x \in (x_0 - h, x_0 + h)$; $h \to 0$, then $h(x) = f(x)$ or $g(x)$ for $x \in (x_0 - h, x_0 + h)$

$\Rightarrow$ $h(x)$ is differentiable at $x = x_0$

19. (a) $f(x) = |x|$ and $g(x) = |x^3|$

$$f(x) = \begin{cases} x; x \geq 0 \\ -x; x < 0 \end{cases}$$

$$\Rightarrow f'(x) = \begin{cases} 1; x > 0 \\ -1; x < 0 \end{cases}$$

$\Rightarrow$ $f(x)$ is non-differentiable at $x = 0$

$$\text{Also } g(x) = \begin{cases} x^3; x \geq 0 \\ -x^3; x < 0 \end{cases}$$

$$\Rightarrow g'(x) = \begin{cases} 3x^2; x > 0 \\ -3x^2; x < 0 \end{cases}$$

$\Rightarrow$ $g'(x)$ is differentiable at $x = 0$

20. (b) If α, β are two roots of $f'(x) = 0$, then either there is no root of $f(x) = 0$ between α and β or exactly one root of $f(x) = 0$ as shown below.

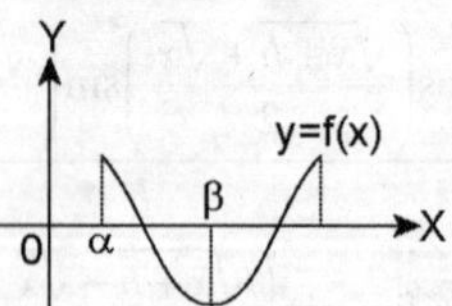

i.e., at most one root of $f(x) = 0$

21. (a) $$f(x) = \begin{cases} \sqrt{2}; x \in \mathbb{Q} \\ 1; x \in \overline{\mathbb{Q}} \end{cases}$$

$$[f(x)] = \begin{cases} 1; x \in \mathbb{Q} \\ 1; x \in \overline{\mathbb{Q}} \end{cases}$$

$\Rightarrow$ $[f(x))] = 1\ \forall\ x \in \mathbb{R}$ $\Rightarrow$ $\phi(x) = 1\ \forall\ x \in \mathbb{R}$

$\Rightarrow$ $\phi(x)$ is continuous $\forall\ x$ and differentiable $\forall\ x \in \mathbb{R}$

22. (c) Clearly, $f(x) = \min\ \{\tan x, \cot x\}$; $x \in (0, 2\pi)$. The graph of $f(x)$ will be as shown below.

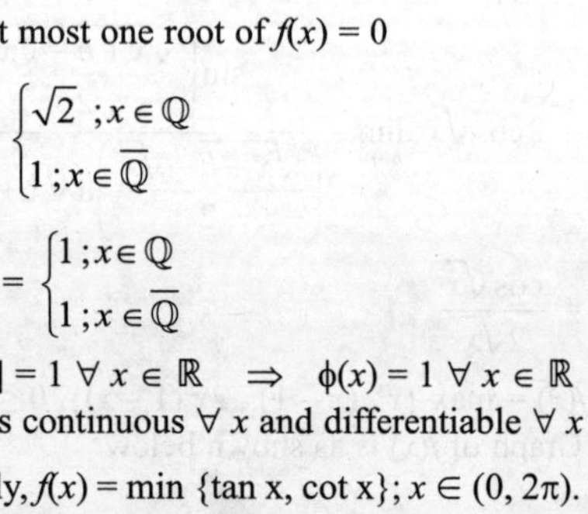

Clearly $\alpha_1 = \dfrac{\pi}{4}, \alpha_2 = \dfrac{3\pi}{4}, \alpha_3 = \dfrac{5\pi}{4}, \alpha_4 = \dfrac{7\pi}{4}$ are four sharp points

$\Rightarrow$ Minimum number of heat attacks = 4

23. (d) $$\lim_{h\to 0} \frac{2\left[\dfrac{\sqrt{3}}{2}\cosh + \dfrac{3}{2}\sinh - \dfrac{\sqrt{3}}{2}\cosh + \dfrac{1}{2}\sinh\right]}{\sqrt{3}h\left(\sqrt{3}\cos h - \sinh\right)}$$

$$= \lim_{h\to 0} \frac{4\sinh}{\sqrt{3}\,h\left(\sqrt{3}\cosh - \sinh\right)} = \frac{4}{3}$$

24. (c) $$f(x) = \begin{cases} a + \sin^{-1}(x+b), x \geq 1 \\ x, \quad x < 1 \end{cases}$$

$f(x)$ is differentiable at $x = 1$

$\Rightarrow$ L.H.L = R.H.L at $x = 1$ $\quad\Rightarrow$ $a + \sin^{-1}(1 + b) = 1$

$\Rightarrow$ $\sin^{-1}(1 + b) = (1 - a)$ $\quad$ ...(1)

Also L.H.D = R.H.D at $x = 1$

$\Rightarrow$ $\dfrac{1}{\sqrt{1-(1+b)^2}} = 1$ $\quad\Rightarrow$ $1 - (1 + b)^2 = 1$

$\Rightarrow$ $1 - (1 + b)^2 = 1$ $\quad\Rightarrow$ $b = -1$ $\quad$ ...(2)

Using $b = -1$ in (1), $\sin^{-1}(1 + b) = 1 - a$

$\Rightarrow$ $\sin^{-1} 0 = 1 - a$ $\quad\Rightarrow$ $a = 1$

25. (c) $f(x) = a \sin |x| + b\, e^{|x|}$

$f(x)$ is differentiable at $x = 0$

$\Rightarrow$ L.H.L = R.H.L at $x = 0$, which is true as $f(x)$ is continuous $\forall\ x \in \mathbb{R}$

Also L.H.D = R.H.D at $x = 0$

$\Rightarrow$ $-a - b = a + b$ $\quad\Rightarrow$ $a + b = 0$

26. (c) $f(x) = x^3 - x^2 + x + 1$ $\quad$ ...(1)

$$\text{And } g(x) = \begin{cases} \max\{f(t); 0 \leq t \leq x\}; 0 \leq x \leq 1 \\ 3 - x + x^2; 1 < x \leq 2 \end{cases}$$

$f'(x) = 3x^2 - 2x + 1 > 0\ \forall\ x \in \mathbb{R}$

$\Rightarrow$ $f(x)$ is an increasing function $\forall\ x \in \mathbb{R}$

$$\Rightarrow g(x) = \begin{cases} f(x); 0 \leq x \leq 1 \\ 3 - x + x^2; 1 < x \leq 2 \end{cases}$$

$$\Rightarrow g(x) = \begin{cases} x^3 - x^2 + x + 1; 0 \leq x \leq 1 \\ x^2 - x + 3; 1 < x \leq 2 \end{cases} \text{ and } g'(x)$$

$$= \begin{cases} 3x^2 - 2x + 1; 0 < x < 1 \\ 2x - 1; \quad 1 < x < 2 \end{cases}$$

At $x = 1$,

L.H.L = 2, R.H.L = 3

$\Rightarrow$ $g(x)$ is discontinuous at $x = 1$ and hence non-differentiable at $x = 1$.

27. (b) $H'(1) = 1$, $g'(1) = 2$; $H(1) = 1$, $g(1) = 2$,

$$\lim_{x\to 1} \frac{H(x).g(1) - g(x).H(1)}{\sin(x-1)} \left(\frac{0}{0}\ form\right)$$

$$= \lim_{x\to 1} \frac{H'(x).g(1) - g'(x) + 1(1)}{\cos(x-1)} \text{ (By L. H. Rule)}$$

$= H'(1).g(1) - g'(1).H(1) = 0$

28. **(a)** $f(x) = \max.(|\tan x|, |\cos x|)$

The graph of $f(x)$ is as shown below.

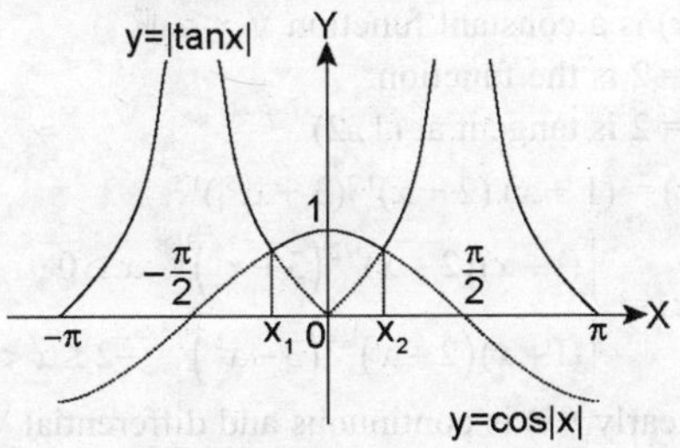

Clearly $f(x)$ is discontinuous at $x = \dfrac{-\pi}{2}$ and $\pi/2$ and has sharp points at $x = \alpha$ and β

$\Rightarrow$ $f(x)$ has 4 points of non-differentiability .

29. **(a)** $f(x) = \text{maximum}\left\{\sqrt{x(2-x)}, 2-x\right\}$

The graph of $f(x)$ is as shown below.

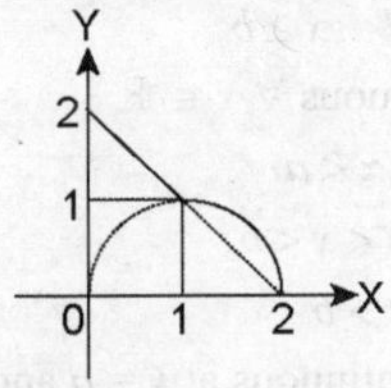

Clearly, $f(x)$ is non-differentiable at $x = 1$

30. **(d)** $f(x) = 15 - |x - 10|$

$g(x) = f(f(x)) = 15 - |f(x) - 10|$

$= 15 - |(15 - |x - 10|) - 10|$

$= 15 - |5 - |x - 10||$

$= \begin{cases} 10 + |x-10| \text{ for } 5 \geq |x-10| \\ 20 - |x-10| \text{ for } 5 < |x-10| \end{cases}$

$= \begin{cases} x \text{ for } x \geq 10 ; 5 \geq |x-10| \\ 20 - x \text{ for } x < 10 ; 5 \geq |x-10| \\ 30 - x \text{ for } x \geq 10 ; 5 < |x-10| \\ 10 + x \text{ for } x < 10 ; 5 < |x-10| \end{cases}$

$= \begin{cases} x ; 10 \leq x \leq 15 \\ 20 - x ; 5 \leq x < 10 \\ 30 - x ; x > 15 \\ 10 + x ; x < 5 \end{cases} \Rightarrow g'(x) = \begin{cases} 1 ; 10 < x < 15 \\ -1 ; 5 < x < 10 \\ -1 ; x > 15 \\ 1 ; x < 5 \end{cases}$

Clearly, $g(x)$ is continuous every where but derivate function has discontinuity at $x = 5$, $x = 10$, $x = 15$, thus non-differentiable at 3 points.

31. **(a)** $f(x) = x[1 + (1/3)\sin(\ell n\, x^2)]$, $x \neq 0$, $f(0) = 0$

$x^2 \in (0, \infty) \Rightarrow \ell n\, x^2 \in (-\infty, \infty)$

$\Rightarrow \frac{1}{3}\sin\left(\ell n x^2\right) \in \left[-\frac{1}{3}, \frac{1}{3}\right]$

$\Rightarrow 1 + \frac{1}{3}\sin\left(\ell n x^2\right) \in \left[\frac{2}{3}, \frac{4}{3}\right]$

$\Rightarrow \left[1 + \frac{1}{3}\sin\left(\ell n x^2\right)\right] \in \{0, 1\}$

$\Rightarrow$ $f(x) \in \{0, x\}$ and $f(x)$ takes value 0 for $\sin(\ell n\, x^2) \in [-1, 0)$ and takes value x for $\sin(\ell n\, x^2) \in [0, 1]$

$\Rightarrow$ $f(x)$ is non-monotomic . Also for $x \in (0, h)$; $h \to 0^+$, $\ell n (x^2) \to -\infty$

$\Rightarrow$ $\sin(\ell n\, x^2)$ oscillates between -1 and 1

$\Rightarrow$ $f(x) \to 0$ or x

$\therefore$ As $x \to 0$, $f(x) \to 0$ and $f(0) = 0$

$\Rightarrow$ $f(x)$ is continuous at $x = 0$

Also R.H.D at $x = 0$

$= \lim\limits_{h \to 0^+} \dfrac{f(h) - f(0)}{h} = \lim\limits_{h \to 0^+} \dfrac{f(h)}{h} = 0$ or $\lim\limits_{h \to 0^+} \dfrac{h}{h} \Rightarrow 0$ or 1

$\Rightarrow$ $f'(0)$ is not unique

$\Rightarrow$ $f(x)$ is non-differentiable at $x = 0$

32. **(d)** $f(x) = 3(2x + 3)^{2/3} + 2x + 3$, when $x \to -\frac{3}{2}$

$\Rightarrow$ $2x + 3 \to 0$

$\therefore$ $f(x) = g(h) = 3(h)^{2/3} + h$, when $x \to 0$, $h \to 0$

$\because$ $g(h)$ is continuous at $h = 0$

$\Rightarrow$ $f(x)$ is continuous at $x = 0$

$\Rightarrow$ $f'(x) = 3\left(\frac{2}{3}\right)(2)(2x + 3)^{-1/3} + 2$

$\Rightarrow$ $f'(x) = \dfrac{4}{(2x+3)^{1/3}} + 2$ which is discontinuous at $x = -3/2$

$\Rightarrow$ $f(x)$ is continuous, but non-differentiable at $x = -3/2$

Also $f(x)$ is continuous and differentiable at $x = 0$

33. **(c)** $\sin^{-1} x - |y| = 2y$

$\Rightarrow$ $\sin^{-1} x = y$ for $y \geq 0$ and $\sin^{-1} x = 3y$ for $y < 0$

$\Rightarrow f(x) = \begin{cases} \sin^{-1} x ; \text{for } f(x) \geq 0 \\ \frac{1}{3}\sin^{-1} x \text{ for } f(x) < 0 \end{cases}$

$\Rightarrow f(x) = \begin{cases} \sin^{-1} x \text{ for } x \in [0,1] \\ \frac{1}{3}\sin^{-1} x \text{ for } x \in [-1,0) \end{cases}$

$\Rightarrow f'(x) = \begin{cases} \dfrac{1}{\sqrt{1-x^2}} \text{ for } x \in (0,1) \\ \dfrac{1}{3\sqrt{1-x^2}} \text{ for } x \in (-1,0) \end{cases}$

$\Rightarrow$ $f'(x)$ is discontinuous at $x = 0$ but $f(x)$ is continuous at $x = 0$

$\Rightarrow$ $f(x)$ is non-differentiable at $x = 0$

34. **(d)**

(a) $f(x) = \cos(|x|) + |x| = \begin{cases} \cos x + x ; x \geq 0 \\ \cos x - x ; x < 0 \end{cases}$

$\Rightarrow$ $f(x)$ is continuous at $x = 0$

$\Rightarrow f'(x) = \begin{cases} -\sin x + 1 ; x > 0 \\ -\sin x - 1 ; x < 0 \end{cases}$ which is discontinuous at $x = 0$

$\Rightarrow$ $f(x)$ is non-differentiable at $x = 0$

(b) $g(x) = \cos(|x|) - |x| \Rightarrow g(x) = \begin{cases} \cos x - x ; x \geq 0 \\ \cos x + x ; x < 0 \end{cases}$

$\Rightarrow$ $g(x)$ is continuous at $x = 0$ and $g'(x) = \begin{cases} -\sin x - 1 ; x > 0 \\ -\sin x + 1 ; x < 0 \end{cases}$ which is discontinuous at $x = 0$

$\Rightarrow$ $g(x)$ is non-differentiable at $x = 0$

(c) $h(x) = \sin(|x|) + |x|$

$\Rightarrow h(x)$ is continuous at $x = 0$ and $h'(x) = \begin{cases} \cos x + 1; x > 0 \\ -\cos x - 1; x < 0 \end{cases}$

$\Rightarrow h(x)$ is non-differentiable at $x = 0$

(d) $k(x) = \sin(|x|) - |x| = \begin{cases} \sin x - x; x \geq 0 \\ -\sin x + x; x < 0 \end{cases}$

$\Rightarrow k(x)$ is continuous at $x = 0$ and $k'(x) = \begin{cases} \cos x - 1; x > 0 \\ -\cos x + 1; x < 0 \end{cases}$

$\Rightarrow k'(x)$ is differentiable at $x = 0$

35. (d) $f(x) = \begin{cases} \tan^{-1} x; |x| \leq 1 \\ \frac{1}{2}(|x| - 1); |x| > 1 \end{cases} = \begin{cases} \tan^{-1} x; -1 \leq x \leq 1 \\ -\frac{1}{2}(x+1); x < -1 \\ \frac{1}{2}(x-1); x > 1 \end{cases}$

$\Rightarrow f(x)$ is discontinuous at $x = -1$ and $x = 1$ and $f'(x) = \begin{cases} -\frac{1}{2}; x < -1 \\ \frac{1}{1+x^2}; -1 < x < 1 \\ \frac{1}{2}; x > 1 \end{cases}$

Which is discontinuous at $x = -1$ but continuous at $x = 1$

$\Rightarrow f(x)$ is non-differentiable at $x = -1, 1$

$\Rightarrow$ Domain of derivate of function $= \mathbb{R} - \{-1, 1\}$

36. (c) $f: \mathbb{R} \to \mathbb{R}$; $f(1) = 3$ and $f'(1) = 6$, $\lim_{x\to 0}\left(\frac{f(1+x)}{f(1)}\right)^{\frac{1}{x}}$

Let $L = \lim_{x\to 0}\left(\frac{f(1+x)}{f(1)}\right)^{1/x}$

$\Rightarrow \ell n\, L = \lim_{x\to 0}\frac{1}{x}\ell n\left(\frac{f(1+x)}{f(1)}\right) = \lim_{x\to 0}\frac{\ell n(f(1+x)) - \ell n f(1)}{x}$

$= \lim_{x\to 0}\frac{\ell n[f(1+x)] - \ell n[f(1)]}{x}$

$= \frac{d}{dx}[\ell n(f(x))]_{x=1} = \left[\frac{1}{f(x)}.f'(x)\right]_{x=1}$

$= \frac{f'(1)}{f(1)} = \frac{6}{3} = 2$

$\Rightarrow L = e^2$

37. (c) $|f(x_1) - f(x_2)| \leq (x_1 - x_2)^2\ \forall\ x_1, x_2 \in \mathbb{R}$,

Equation of tangent to the curve $y = f(x)$ at point $(1, 2)$ is given by $(y - 2) = f'(1) = (x - 1)$ …(1)

$f'(x) = \lim_{h\to 0}\frac{f(x+h) - f(x)}{(x+h) - x}$

$\Rightarrow |f'(x)| = \lim_{h\to 0}\left|\frac{f(x+h) - f(x)}{(x+h) - x}\right| \leq \frac{[(x+h) - x]^2}{|(x+h) - x|}$ (By given condition) $= \lim_{h\to 0}|h| = 0$

$\Rightarrow |f'(x)| \leq 0\ \forall\ x \in \mathbb{R}$

$\Rightarrow f'(x) = 0\ \forall\ x \in \mathbb{R}$

$\Rightarrow f(x)$ is a constant function $\forall\ x \in \mathbb{R}$

$\Rightarrow y = 2$ is the function.

$\Rightarrow y = 2$ is tangent at $(1, 2)$

38. (a) $f(x) = (1 + x)(2 + x)^{1/2}(3 + |x^5|)^{1/5}$

$\Rightarrow f(x) = \begin{cases} (1+x)(2+x)^{1/2}\left(3+x^5\right)^{1/5}; x \geq 0 \\ (1+x)(2+x)^{1/2}\left(3-x^5\right)^{1/5}; -2 \leq x < 0 \end{cases}$

Clearly $f(x)$ is continuous and differential $\forall\ -2 < x < 0$

$\Rightarrow f'(-1) = [f'(x)]_x = -1$

$\Rightarrow f'(-1) = (2 - 1)^{1/2}(3 + 1)^{1/5} = (4)^{1/5}$

39. (b) Without loss of generality let $a < b$

$f(x) = |x - a| + |x - b|$

$= \begin{cases} -2x + a + b; x < a \\ b - a; a \leq x < b \\ 2x - a - b; x \geq b \end{cases}$

$\Rightarrow f(x)$ is continuous $\forall\ x \in \mathbb{R}$

$\Rightarrow f'(x) = \begin{cases} -2; x < a \\ 0; a < x < b \\ 2; x > b \end{cases}$

$\Rightarrow f'(x)$ is discontinuous at $x = a$ and at $x = b$

$\Rightarrow f(x)$ is non-differentiable at $x = a, b$

40. (a) If $f(x) = \int_{-1}^{x}|t|\,dt, x \geq -1$

$= \int_{-1}^{0} -t\,dt + \int_{0}^{x} t\,dt$

$= -\frac{1}{2}[t^2]_{-1}^{0} + \left[\frac{t^2}{2}\right]_0^x$

$= \frac{1}{2} + \frac{1}{2}x^2;\ x \geq -1$

$\therefore f(x) = \frac{1}{2}(x^2 + 1); x \geq -1$

$\Rightarrow f'(x) = x; x > -1$

$\Rightarrow f(x)$ and $f'(x)$ are continuous $\forall\ x > -1$

41. (d) $y = ||x - 1| - 1| + 1$

$= \begin{cases} |x-1| \text{ for } |x-1| \geq 1 \\ 2 - |x-1| \text{ for } |x-1| < 1 \end{cases} = \begin{cases} x - 1 \text{ for } x \geq 1; |x-1| \geq 1 \\ -x + 1 \text{ for } x < 1; |x-1| \geq 1 \\ 3 - x \text{ for } x \geq 1; |x-1| < 1 \\ x + 1 \text{ for } x < 1; |x-1| < 1 \end{cases}$

$= \begin{cases} x - 1 \text{ for } x \geq 2; \\ -x + 1 \text{ for } x \leq 0 \\ 3 - x \text{ for } x \leq 0 \\ x + 1 \text{ for } 0 < x < 1 \end{cases}$

$\Rightarrow$ Clearly $f(x)$ is continuous $\forall\ x \in \mathbb{R}$ and $f'(x) = \begin{cases} -1 \text{ for } x < 0 \\ 1 \text{ for } 0 < x < 1 \\ -1 \text{ for } 1 < x < 2 \\ 1 \text{ for } x > 2 \end{cases}$

$\Rightarrow f(x)$ is non-differentiable at $x = 0$, 1 and 2

42. (c) $f(x) = \sin|x| - e^{|x|}$

$$= \begin{cases} \sin x - e^x \ ; x \ge 0 \\ -\sin x - e^{-x} \ ; x < 0 \end{cases}$$

$\Rightarrow$ $f(x)$ is continuous at $x = 0$ and $f'(x) = \begin{cases} \cos x - e^x \ ; x > 0 \\ -\cos x + e^{-x} \ ; x < 0 \end{cases}$

$\Rightarrow$ $f(x)$ is differentiable at $x = 0$

43. (a) L.H.D = $\lim\limits_{h \to 0^+} \dfrac{f(k-h) - f(k)}{-h}$ at $x = k$

$$= \lim_{h \to 0^+} \frac{[k-h]\sin \pi(k-h) - [k]\sin \pi k}{-h}$$

$$= \lim_{h \to 0^+} \frac{(k-1)(-1)^{k+1}\sin \pi h - k(0)}{-h}$$

$$= \lim_{h \to 0^+} \frac{(-1)^{k+1}(k-1)\pi}{(-1)} \cdot \left(\frac{\sin \pi h}{\pi h}\right)$$

$= (-1)^k (k-1)\pi$

44. (a) $|f(x) - f(y)| \le |x-y|^{2x+1}$; $(x \in \mathbb{N})$

$$|f'(x)| = \lim_{h \to 0^+} \frac{f(x+h) - f(x)}{h} \le \lim_{h \to 0^+} \frac{|x+h-x|^{(2n+1)}}{|h|}$$

$\Rightarrow$ $|f'(x)| \le \lim\limits_{h \to 0^+} |h|^{2n} = 0$

$\Rightarrow$ $f'(x) = 0$

$\Rightarrow$ $f(x)$ is a costant function.

45. (b) $f(x) = ||x-1|-1|-1|$

Graph of f (x) is as shown below.

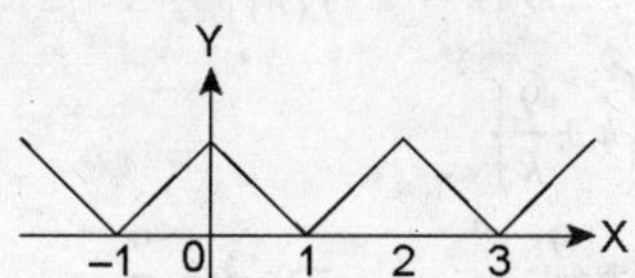

$\Rightarrow$ $f(x)$ has points of non-differentiability in set {–1, 0, 1, 2, 3}

46. (d) $f(x) = 1 - |x| = \begin{cases} 1 - x \ ; x \ge 0 \\ 1 + x \ ; x < 0 \end{cases}$

$\Rightarrow$ $f(f(x)) = \begin{cases} 1 - f(x); f(x) \ge 0 \\ 1 + f(x); f(x) < 0 \end{cases}$

$$= \begin{cases} 1-(1-x); (1-x) \ge 0; x \ge 0 \\ 1-(1+x); (1+x) \ge 0; x < 0 \\ 1+(1-x); (1-x) < 0; x \ge 0 \\ 1+(1+x); (1+x) < 0; x < 0 \end{cases} = \begin{cases} x \ ; 0 \le x \le 1 \\ -x \ ; -1 \le x < 0 \\ 2 - x; x > 1 \\ 2 + x \ ; x < -1 \end{cases}$$

$\Rightarrow$ $f(f(x))$ is continuous $\forall\ x \in \mathbb{R}$

$\Rightarrow$ $[f(f(x))]' = \begin{cases} 1 ; 0 < x < 1 \\ -1 ; -1 < x < 0 \\ 1 ; x < -1 \end{cases}$

$\Rightarrow$ $f(f(x))$ has non-differentiable at $x = 0$, $x = -1$ i.e., at 3 points

47. (c) $f(x) = \dfrac{|x| - x\left(3^{1/x} + 1\right)}{3^{1/x} - 1}$; $x \ne 0, f(0) = 0$

$\Rightarrow$ $f(x) = \begin{cases} \dfrac{-x(3)^{\frac{1}{x}}}{3^{\frac{1}{x}} - 1}; x > 0 \\[2ex] \dfrac{-2x - x(3)^{\frac{1}{x}}}{3^{\frac{1}{x}} - 1}; x < 0 \end{cases}$

Now, $\lim\limits_{x \to 0^-} f(x) = \lim\limits_{x \to 0^-} \dfrac{-2x - x(3)^{\frac{1}{x}}}{3^{\frac{1}{x}} - 1} = \lim\limits_{x \to 0^-} \dfrac{-x\left(2 + 3^{\frac{1}{x}}\right)}{\left(3^{\frac{1}{x}} - 1\right)}$

$= \dfrac{(-0)(2+0)}{(0-1)} = 0$ and $\lim\limits_{x \to 0^+} f(x) = \lim\limits_{x \to 0^+} \dfrac{-x(3)^{\frac{1}{x}}}{3^{\frac{1}{x}} - 1}$

$= \lim\limits_{x \to 0^+} (-x) \dfrac{1}{\left(1 - \dfrac{1}{3^{\frac{1}{x}}}\right)} = 0$ and f (0) = 0

$\Rightarrow$ $f(x)$ is continuous at $x = 0$

Also, $f(x) = \begin{cases} -x - \dfrac{x}{3^{\frac{1}{x}} - 1}; x > 0 \\[2ex] \dfrac{-3x}{3^{\frac{1}{x}} - 1} - x ; x < 0 \end{cases}$

$\Rightarrow$ $f'(x) = \begin{cases} -1 - \left(\dfrac{\left(3^{\frac{1}{x}}(1 - x\ell n3)\right)}{\left(3^{\frac{1}{x}} - 1\right)^2}\right); x > 0 \\[3ex] -3\left[\dfrac{3^{\frac{1}{x}}(1 - x\ell n3)}{\left(3^{\frac{1}{x}} - 1\right)^2}\right] - 1; x < 0 \end{cases}$

$\Rightarrow$ R.H.$L = \lim\limits_{x \to 0^+} f'(x) = -1$ and L.H.$L = \lim\limits_{x \to 0^-} f'(x) = -1$

$\Rightarrow$ $f(x)$ is differentiable at $x = 0$

48. (b) $f(x) = [\tan^2 x]$

$\because$ $[\tan^2 x] = 0$ for $x \in (-h, h); h \to 0$

$\Rightarrow$ $\lim\limits_{x \to 0} f(x) = 0 = f(0)$ and $f'(x) = 0\ \forall\ x \in (-h, h); h \to 0$

$\Rightarrow$ $f(x)$ is differentiable at $x = 0$

49. (b) $f(x) = \begin{cases} x^3 \ ; x^2 < 1 \\ x \ ; x^2 \ge 1 \end{cases}$

$\Rightarrow$ $f(x) = \begin{cases} x^3 \ ; -1 < x < 1 \\ x \ ; x \le -1 \text{ or } x \ge 1 \end{cases}$

$\Rightarrow$ $f(x)$ is continuous $\forall\ x \in \mathbb{R}$

$\Rightarrow$ $f'(x) = \begin{cases} 3x^2 ; -1 < x < 1 \\ 1 \ ; x < -1 \text{ or } x > 1 \end{cases}$

$\Rightarrow$ $f(x)$ is non-differentiable at $x = -1$ and $x = 1$

$\Rightarrow$ Domain of $f'(x)$ i.e., set in which $f(x)$ is differentiable $= \mathbb{R} - \{-1, 1\}$

50. (d) $f(x) = max\ \{2 \sin x, 1 - \cos x\}\ \forall\ x \in (0, \pi)$

Graph of $f(x)$ is as shown below.

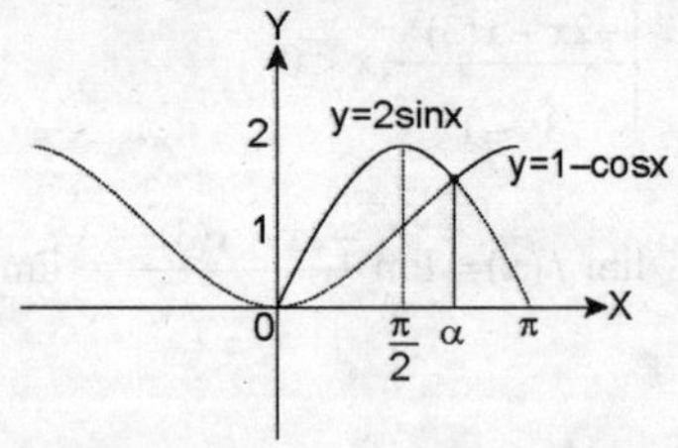

$$\Rightarrow f(x) = \begin{cases} 2\sin x\ ; 0 < x \le \alpha; \alpha > \dfrac{\pi}{2} \\ 1 - \cos x; \alpha \le x < \pi \end{cases}$$

$$\Rightarrow f'(x) = \begin{cases} 2\cos x;\ 0 < x < \alpha; \alpha > \dfrac{\pi}{2} \\ \sin x\ ; \alpha < x < \pi \end{cases}$$

$\Rightarrow f'(x) = 0$ at $x = \dfrac{\pi}{2}$

51. (d) $f(x) = \max.\{\sin x, \cos x, 1 - \cos x\}$

The graph of $f(x)$is as shown below.

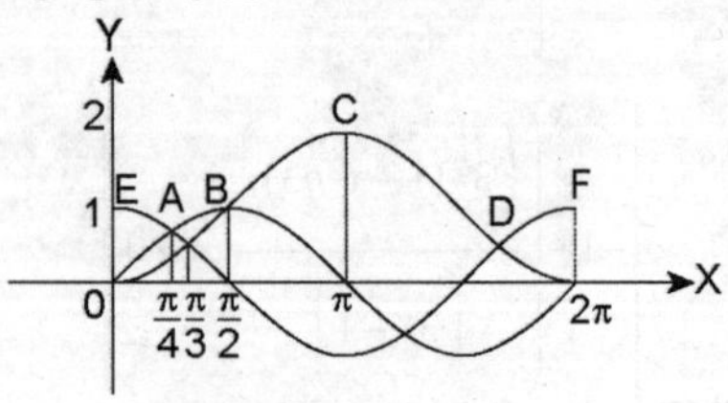

Derivate of $f(x)$ does not exist at $x = A$, B and D i.e., $x = \dfrac{\pi}{4}, x = \dfrac{\pi}{2}$ and $x = \dfrac{5\pi}{3}$.

Derivate of $f(x) = 0$ at $x = E$, C and F

$\Rightarrow$ There are 6 critical points.

52. (d) $f(x) = \begin{cases} xe^{-\left(\frac{1}{x}+\frac{1}{|x|}\right)}; x \ne 0 \\ a\ ;\ x = 0 \end{cases}$

$$\Rightarrow f(x) = \begin{cases} xe^{-\frac{2}{x}}; x > 0 \\ a\ ; x = 0 \\ x\ ; x < 0 \end{cases}$$

For $f(x)$ to be continuous L.H.L = R.H.L = $f(0) = a$ at $x = 0$

$\Rightarrow a = 0$

$$\therefore f'(x) = \begin{cases} xe^{-\frac{2}{x}}\left(\dfrac{2}{x^2}\right) + e^{-\frac{2}{x}}; x > 0 \\ 1\ ; x < 0 \end{cases}$$

$$\Rightarrow f'(x) = \begin{cases} e^{-\frac{2}{x}}\left(\dfrac{2}{x} + 1\right); x > 0 \\ 1\ ; x < 0 \end{cases}$$

$$\Rightarrow f'(x) = \begin{cases} \dfrac{(x+2)}{xe^{2/x}}; x > 0 \\ 1\ ; x < 0 \end{cases} = \begin{cases} \dfrac{1}{e^{2/x}}\left(1 + \dfrac{2}{x}\right); x > 0 \\ 1\ ; x < 0 \end{cases}$$

$$\therefore \lim_{x \to 0^+} f'(x) = \lim_{x \to 0^+} \left(\frac{1 + \frac{2}{x}}{e^{2/x}}\right) = \lim_{t \to \infty} \left(\frac{1+t}{e^t}\right) = \lim_{t \to \infty} \frac{1}{e^t} = 0 \text{ and}$$

$\lim\limits_{x \to 0^-} f'(x) = 1$

$\Rightarrow f(x)$ is not differentiable at $x = 0$

53. (b) $f'(x) = \lim\limits_{h \to 0^+} \dfrac{f(x+h) - f(x)}{h} = \lim\limits_{h \to 0^+} \dfrac{f(x).f(h) - f(h)}{h} =$

$\lim\limits_{h \to 0^+} f(x) \dfrac{[f(h) - 1]}{h}$ ...(1)

Also $f(x + y) = f(x).f(y)\ \forall$ x, $y \in \mathbb{R}$

$\Rightarrow f(0) = (f(0))^2$

$\Rightarrow f(0) = 0$ or $f(0) = 1$ but range is $\mathbb{R}^+$

$\Rightarrow f(0) = 1$

$\therefore$ From (1), we get $f'(x) = \lim\limits_{h \to 0^+} \left[\dfrac{f(h) - f(0)}{h}\right] f(x) = f(x)$

$f'(0) = 2f(x)$

$\Rightarrow f'(x) = 2f(x)$

54. (a) Let $\lim\limits_{n \to \infty} f(n) = k$

$\therefore f(n + 1) = \dfrac{1}{2}\left\{f(n) + \dfrac{1}{f(n)}\right\}$

$\Rightarrow k = \dfrac{1}{2}\left\{k + \dfrac{9}{k}\right\}$

$\Rightarrow 2k = k + \dfrac{9}{k}$ $\qquad \Rightarrow k = \dfrac{9}{k}$

$\Rightarrow k^2 = 9$ $\qquad \Rightarrow k = \pm 3$, but $f(x) > 0\ \forall \in \mathbb{N}$

$\Rightarrow k = 3$

SECTION–IV: (MORE THAN ONE ARE CORRECT)

1. (a), (b), (c)

Clearly, standard (a) is true as contains standard results.

For (b), if we let $f(x) = 0\ \forall\ x \in \mathbb{R}$ and $g(x) = \{x\}\ \forall\ x \in \mathbb{R}$

Clearly $f(x)$ is continuous and $g(x)$ is discontinuous function.

Here $\phi(x) = f(x).g(x) = 0\ \forall\ x \in \mathbb{R}$

$\Rightarrow \phi(x)$ is a continuous function.

For (c), let $\lim\limits_{x \to a^-} f(a) = \ell_1$ and $\lim\limits_{x \to a^+} f(x) = \ell_2$ and $f(a) = \ell_2$ (say),

$\lim\limits_{x \to a^-} g(x) = \ell_2$, $\lim\limits_{x \to a^+} g(x) = \ell_1$ and $g(a) = \ell_1$, then $\lim\limits_{x \to a^-} f(x).g(x) = \ell_1\ \ell_2$ and f $(x).g(x) = \ell_1\ \ell_2$

Clearly $\phi(x)$ is continuous at $x = a$

2. (a), (c), (d)

$$f(x) = \begin{cases} 1\ ; |x| \ge 1 \\ \dfrac{1}{n^2}\ ; \dfrac{1}{n} < |x| < \dfrac{1}{n-1}, n = 2, 3.... \end{cases}$$

$$= \begin{cases} 1 & ; x \le -1 \text{ or } x \ge 1 \\ \frac{1}{n^2} & ; \frac{-1}{n-1} < x < \frac{-1}{n} \text{ or } \frac{1}{n} < x < \frac{1}{n-1}; n = 2,3,.... \\ 0 & ; n = 0 \end{cases}$$

Clearly $f(x)$ if discontinuous, then the discontinuities lies at points $\pm\frac{1}{n}; n \in \mathbb{N}$, then

$\lim_{x\to -1^-} f(x) = 1,\ \lim_{x\to -1^+} f(x) = \frac{1}{(2)^2} = \frac{1}{4}$

Also $f(-1) = 1$

$\Rightarrow$ $f(x)$ is discontinuous at $x = 1$

Now, $\lim_{x\to 1^-} f(x) = \frac{-1}{(2)^2} = \frac{1}{4}$ as $x \in \left(\frac{1}{2}, 1\right)$

$\lim_{x\to 1^+} f(x) = 1$

$\Rightarrow$ $f(x)$ is discontinuous at $x = 1$

Let $x = -\frac{1}{n}; n \ge 2$, then $x \to \left(\frac{-1}{n}\right) \Rightarrow x = -\frac{1}{n} - h$; h $\to$

$0^+ \in \left(\frac{-1}{(n-1)}, \frac{-1}{n}\right)$ and $x \to \left(\frac{-1}{n}\right)^+ \Rightarrow x = \frac{-1}{n} + h$; h $\to$

$0^+ \in \left(\frac{-1}{n}, \frac{-1}{n+1}\right)$

$\Rightarrow \lim_{x\to\left(\frac{-1}{n}\right)^-} f(x) = \frac{1}{n^2},\ \lim_{x\to\left(\frac{-1}{n}\right)^+} f(x) = \frac{1}{(n+1)^2}$

$\Rightarrow$ $f(x)$ is discontinuous t $x = \frac{-1}{n}$

Let $x = \frac{1}{n}$n; $n \ge 2$; x $\to \left(\frac{1}{n}\right)^- \Rightarrow x = \frac{1}{n} - h$; h $\to 0^+$

$\Rightarrow$ x $\in \left(\frac{1}{n+1}, \frac{1}{n}\right)$ and $x \to \left(\frac{1}{n}\right)^+$

$\Rightarrow x = -$; h $\to 0^+$

$\Rightarrow x \in \left(\frac{1}{n}, \frac{1}{n-1}\right)$

$\Rightarrow \lim_{x\to\left(\frac{1}{n}\right)^-} = \frac{1}{(n+1)^2}$ and $\lim_{x\to\left(\frac{1}{n}\right)^+} = \frac{1}{n^2}$

$\Rightarrow$ $f(x)$ is discontinuous at $x = \frac{1}{n}$,

Also $x \to 0$

$\Rightarrow x \in \left(-\frac{1}{n}, \frac{-1}{n+1}\right); n \to \infty$ or $x \in \left(\frac{1}{n+1}, \frac{1}{n}\right); n \to \infty$

$\Rightarrow f(x) \to \frac{1}{(n+1)^2} \to 0,\ f(0) = 0$

$\Rightarrow$ $f(x)$ is continuous at $x = 0$

$\therefore$ $f(x)$ is discontinuous at $x = \frac{1}{n}$; n $\in \mathbb{Z} - \{0\}$

3. (b), (d)

(a) $\lim_{x\to 1^-} f(x) = \lim_{x\to 1^-} \frac{1}{\ell n|x|} = \lim_{x\to 1^-} \frac{1}{\ell nx} = -\infty$ and

$\lim_{x\to 1^+} f(x) = \lim_{x\to 1^+} \frac{1}{\ell n|x|} = \lim_{x\to 1^+} \frac{1}{\ell nx}$

$\Rightarrow$ $f(x)$ has infinite discontinuity at $x = 1$

(b) $\lim_{x\to 1} f(x) = \lim_{x\to 1}\left(\frac{x^2-1}{x^3-1}\right) = \lim_{x\to 1}\frac{(x+1)}{(x^2+x+1)} = \frac{2}{3}$; $f(1)$ is not defined

$\Rightarrow$ $f(x)$ has a removable discontinuity at $x = 1$.

(c) $\lim_{x\to 1^-} f(x) = \lim_{x\to 1^-} (2)^{-2^{\left(\frac{1}{1-x}\right)}} = \lim_{x\to 1^-}\left(\frac{1}{(2)^{2^{\left(\frac{1}{1-x}\right)}}}\right) = 0$ and

$\lim_{x\to 1^+} f(x) = \lim_{x\to 1^+} (2)^{-2^{\left(\frac{1}{1-x}\right)}} = \lim_{x\to 1^+} \frac{1}{(2)^{2^{\left(\frac{1}{1-x}\right)}}} = 1$

$\Rightarrow$ $f(x)$ has a jump discontinuity at $x = 1$

(d) $\lim_{x\to 1} f(x) = \lim_{x\to 1} \frac{\sqrt{x+1} - \sqrt{2x}}{x^2 - x}$

$= \lim_{x\to 1} \frac{1-x}{(-x)(1-x)} \times \frac{1}{\sqrt{x+1} + \sqrt{2x}} = \frac{1}{2\sqrt{2}}$; $f(1)$ is not defined

$\Rightarrow$ $f(x)$ has a removable discontinuity at $x = 1$

4. (b), (c)

(a) tan x is discontinuous at $x = \frac{\pi}{2}$

(b) Clearly $t\sin\frac{1}{t}$ is continuous on (0, π)

If $f(x)$ is continuous on (a, b) and $\int f(x)dx = G(x)$

$\Rightarrow \int_0^x f(x)dx = G(x)$

(c) $\lim_{x\to\left(\frac{3\pi}{4}\right)^-} f(x) = 1;\ \lim_{x\to\left(\frac{3\pi}{4}\right)^+} f(x) = \lim_{x\to\left(\frac{3\pi}{4}\right)^+} 2\sin\left(\frac{2x}{9}\right) = 2$ sin

$\left(\frac{2}{9}\times\frac{3\pi}{4}\right) = 1 = f\left(\frac{3\pi}{4}\right)$

$\Rightarrow$ $f(x)$ is continuous at $x = 3\pi/4$.

(d) $\lim_{x\to\left(\frac{\pi}{2}\right)^-} f(x) = \lim_{x\to\left(\frac{\pi}{2}\right)^-} x\sin x = \frac{\pi}{2} = f\left(\frac{\pi}{2}\right)$ and

$\lim_{x\to\left(\frac{\pi}{2}\right)^+} f(x) = \lim_{x\to\left(\frac{\pi}{2}\right)^+} \frac{\pi}{2}\sin(\pi + x) = \frac{-\pi}{2} \lim_{x\to\left(\frac{\pi}{2}\right)^+} \sin x$

$= \frac{-\pi}{2}$

5. (a), (c) $f(x) = \left[\frac{1}{x}[x]\right]$; $x \ne 0, f(0) = 0$,

$\lim_{x\to 0^-} f(x) = \lim_{x\to 0^-}\left[\frac{1}{x}[x]\right] = \lim_{x\to 0^-}\left[\frac{1}{x}(-1)\right]$

$= \lim_{x\to 0^-}\left[\frac{-1}{x}\right] = \lim_{x\to 0^-}\left(-1-\left[\frac{1}{x}\right]\right) = -\infty$ and

$\lim_{x\to 0^+} f(x) = \lim_{x\to 0^+}\left[\frac{1}{x}[x]\right] = 0$

$\Rightarrow f(x)$ is discontinuous at $x = 0$

Also, $\lim_{x\to 1^-} f(x) = \lim_{x\to 1^-}\left[\frac{1}{x}[x]\right] = \lim_{x\to 1^-}[0] = 0$ and

$\lim_{x\to 1^+} f(x) = \lim_{x\to 0^+}\left[\frac{1}{x}[x]\right] = 0$

$= \lim_{x\to 1^+}\left[\frac{1}{x}\right] = \lim_{x\to 0^+}\left[\frac{1}{1+h}\right] = 0$ and $f(1) = 1$

$\Rightarrow f(x)$ is discontinuous at $x = 1$

6. (a), (d) As $f(x) = 0$ for $x < 0$ and $f(x)$ is differentiable at $x = 0$

$\Rightarrow f(x)$ is continuous at $x = 0$

$\Rightarrow f(0) = 0$ as $f(0^-) = 0$, and $f'(x) = 0$ for $x < 0$

$\Rightarrow f'(0^+) = 0$ $\qquad \Rightarrow f(x) = x^2$ or $-x^{3/2}$

7. (a), (b) $f(x) = (\pi - x)\dfrac{\cos x}{|\sin x|}; x \neq \pi$

$f(\pi^-) = \lim_{x\to(\pi)^-} f(x) = \lim_{h\to 0^+} f(\pi - h) = \lim_{h\to 0^+} h\dfrac{\cos(\pi-h)}{|\sin(\pi-h)|}$

$= \lim_{h\to 0^+}\dfrac{-h\cos h}{|\sin h|} = \lim_{h\to 0^+}\left(\dfrac{h}{\sin h}\right).(\cos h)$

$= (-1)(1) = -1$ and $f(\pi^+) = \lim_{x\to\pi^+} f(x) = \lim_{h\to 0^+} f(\pi + h)$

$= \lim_{h\to 0^+} -h\dfrac{\cos(\pi+h)}{|\sin(\pi+h)|} = \lim_{h\to 0^+}\dfrac{h\cos h}{\sin h} = 1$

$\Rightarrow f(x)$ is discontinuous at $x = \pi$

$\Rightarrow f(x)$ is non-differentiable at $x = \pi$

8. (a), (b), (c), (d), (e)

Options (a) contain standard result and hence stand true.

Let $f(x) = 0$ and $g(x) = |x|$, then $f(x)$ is differentiable at $x = 1$ and $g(x)$ is non-different table at $x = 1$

But $f(x).g(x) = 0\ \forall\ x \in \mathbb{R}$

$\Rightarrow f(x).g(x) = F(x)$ is differentiable at $x = 1$

$\Rightarrow$ options (b) is correct.

For (c) Let $f(x) = |x - 1|$ and $g(x) = -|x - 1|$, then $f(x)$ and $g(x)$ are non-differentiable at $x = 1$, but $f(x).g(x) = -(x - 1)^2$ i.e., $y = -(x - 1)^2$ which is differentiable.

For (d) if $f(x) = [x]$ and $g(x) = \{x\}$

$\Rightarrow F(x) = [x] + \{x\} = x$

$\Rightarrow F(x)$ is derivable

$\Rightarrow$ Option (d) correct

Clearly if $f(x)$ is derivable at $x = a$, then

L.H.D = $\lim_{x\to a^-} f'(x)$ = R.H.D = $\lim_{x\to a^+} f'(x) = f'(a)$

$\Rightarrow f'(x)$ is continuous at $x = a$

$\Rightarrow$ (d) is correct

9. (a), (b) Clearly by definition of derivate at $x = a$, Option (a) is correct. Also option (b) is correct.

Option (c) is incorrect, as it should be $f'(a) = \lim_{t\to 0}\dfrac{f(a+2t)-f(a+t)}{t}$

Option (d) is incorrect, as it should be

$f'(a) = \lim_{t\to 0}\dfrac{f(a+2t)-f(a+t)}{t}$

$\Rightarrow$ Options (a) and (b) are correct

10. (a), (d) $f(x) = \cos x$ and $H(x)$

$= \begin{cases} \min.\{f(t): 0 \le t \le x\}; 0 \le x \le \dfrac{\pi}{2} \\ \dfrac{\pi}{2} - x; \text{for } \dfrac{\pi}{2} < x \le 3 \end{cases}$

In $[0, \pi/2]$, $f(x)$ is a decreasing function.

$\Rightarrow H(x) = \begin{cases} f(x); 0 \le x \le \dfrac{\pi}{2} \\ \dfrac{\pi}{2} - x; \dfrac{\pi}{2} < x \le 3 \end{cases}$

$\Rightarrow H'(x) = \begin{cases} f'(x); 0 < x < \dfrac{\pi}{2} \\ -1; \dfrac{\pi}{2} < x < 3 \end{cases}$

$\lim_{x\to\left(\frac{\pi}{2}\right)^-} H(x) = \lim_{x\to\left(\frac{\pi}{2}\right)^-} f(x) = \lim_{x\to\left(\frac{\pi}{2}\right)^-} \cos x = 0$ and

$\lim_{x\to\left(\frac{\pi}{2}\right)^+} H(x) = \lim_{x\to\left(\frac{\pi}{2}\right)^+}\left(\dfrac{\pi}{2} - x\right) = 0$

Also $H(\pi/2) = f(\pi/2) = \cos \pi/2 = 0$

Thus $H(x)$ is continuous at $x \in [0, 3]$

Also $H'(\pi/2^-) = f'(\pi/2^-) = -(1)$ and $H'(\pi/2^+) = -1$

$\Rightarrow H(x)$ is differentiable for $x \in [0, 3]$

Clearly $H(x)$ is a decreasing function in $[0, 3]$

Maximum value of $H(x)$ in $[0, 3] = H(0) = f(0) = \cos 0 = 1$

11. (a), (c) $f(x) = |[x]\,x|; -1 \le x \le 2,$

$\lim_{x\to 0^-} f(x) = \lim_{h\to 0^+}|[-h](-h)| = \lim_{h\to 0^+}|h| = 0$

$\lim_{x\to 0^+} f(x) = \lim_{h\to 0^+}|[h]h| = 0$ and $f(0) = 0$

$\Rightarrow f(x)$ is continuous at $x = 0$

$\lim_{x\to(2)^-} f(x) = \lim_{x\to 2^-}|[x]x| = \lim_{x\to 2^-}|1.x| = 2$ and $f(2) = |[2]2|$

$= 4$

$\Rightarrow f(x)$ is discontinuous at $x = 2$

$\Rightarrow$ non-differentiable at $x = 2$

12. (b), (d) $f(x) = \begin{cases} \dfrac{x\ell n\cos x}{\ell n(1+x^2)}; x \neq 0 \\ 0\ ; \qquad x = 0 \end{cases}$

$\lim_{x\to 0} f(x) = \lim_{x\to 0}\dfrac{x\ell n\cos x}{\ell n(1+x)^2}\left(\dfrac{0}{0}\text{form}\right)$

$= \lim_{x\to 0}\dfrac{x(-\tan x) + \ell n(\cos x)}{\left(\dfrac{1}{1+x^2}\right)(2x)}\left(\dfrac{0}{0}\text{form}\right)$

$$= \lim_{x\to 0}\frac{-x\sec^2 x-\tan x+(-\tan x)}{2\left[\frac{(1+x^2)(1)-x(2x)}{(1+x^2)^2}\right]}$$

$$= \lim_{x\to 0}\frac{-x\sec^2 x-2\tan x}{2\left[\frac{1-x^2}{(1+x^2)^2}\right]} = 0 \text{ and } f(0)=0$$

⇒ $f(x)$ is continuous at $x = 0$. Also

$$f'(x)=\left\{\frac{\ell n(1+x^2)[-x\tan x+\ell n\cos x]}{[\ell n(1+x^2)]^2}-\frac{\left[\frac{x\ell n\cos x}{(1+x^2)}(2x)\right]}{[\ell n(1+x)]^2}\right\}\text{for } x\neq 0$$

$\therefore \lim_{x\to 0} f'(x) = 0$

13. (a), (b), (c), (d) $f(x) = [x \sin \pi x]$

For $x \in \left(-1,\frac{-1}{2}\right), \pi x \in \left(-\pi,\frac{-\pi}{2}\right)$

⇒ $\sin \pi x \in (-1, 0)$

⇒ $x \sin x = |x \sin \pi x| = |x||\sin \pi x| \in (0, 1)$

$\left(\because \begin{array}{l}\frac{1}{2}<|x|<1\\ 0<|\sin\pi|<1\end{array}\right)$

⇒ $[x \sin \pi x] = 0$ for $x \in \left(-1,\frac{-1}{2}\right)$

At $x=\frac{-1}{2}$, $\sin \pi x = -1$

⇒ $[x \sin \pi x] = \left[\frac{1}{2}\right]=0$

For $x \in \left(\frac{-1}{2},0\right), \pi x\in\left(\frac{-\pi}{2},0\right)$

⇒ $\sin \pi x \in (-1, 0)$

⇒ $[x \sin \pi x] = 0$

At $x = 0$, $f(0) = 0$

For $x \in \left(0,\frac{1}{2}\right), \pi x \in \left(0,\frac{\pi}{2}\right)$

⇒ $\sin \pi x \in (0, 1)$

⇒ $x \sin \pi x \in \left(0,\frac{1}{2}\right)$

⇒ $[x \sin \pi x] = 0$

At $x=\frac{1}{2}$; $[x \sin \pi x] = 0$

At $x \in \left(\frac{1}{2},1\right); \pi x \in \left(\frac{\pi}{2},\pi\right)$

⇒ $\sin \pi x \in (0, 1)$ ⇒ $[x \sin \pi x] = 0$

Thus $[x \sin \pi x] = 0\ \forall\ x \in (-1, 1)$

14. (a), (b) $f(0^-) = f(0^+) = f(0) = 0$

⇒ $f(x)$ is continuous at $x = 0$

⇒ $f'(x)=\frac{\pi}{2}\cos\left(\frac{\pi x}{2}\right)$ and $f(x)=\sin\left(\frac{\pi x}{2}\right)$ for $x < 1$

⇒ $f(x)$ is differentiable for $x < 1$

$f(1^-) = \sin\frac{\pi}{2}=1$

$f(1^+) = \lim_{h\to 0^+} |1 + h - 3|\,[1 + h] = \lim_{h\to 0^+} (2 - h)(1) = 2$

⇒ $f(x)$ is discontinuous and hence non-differentiable at $x = 1$

⇒ $f\left(\frac{3^-}{2}\right)=\lim_{h\to 0^+}\left|\frac{3}{2}-h-3\right|\left[\frac{3}{2}-h\right]$

$=\lim_{h\to 0^+}\left|-h-\frac{3}{2}\right|\left[\frac{3}{2}-h\right]=\lim_{h\to 0^+}\left(h+\frac{3}{2}\right)(1)=\frac{3}{2}$

⇒ $f\left(\frac{3^+}{2}\right)=\lim_{x\to 0^+}\left|\frac{3}{2}+h-3\right|\left[\frac{3}{2}+h\right]$

$=\lim_{h\to 0^+}\left|\frac{-3}{2}+h\right|\left[\frac{3}{2}+h\right]=\lim_{x\to 0^+}\left(\frac{3}{2}-h\right)(1)=\frac{3}{2}$

⇒ $f(x)$ is continuous at $x = 3/2$

⇒ $f'\left(\frac{3^-}{2}\right)=\lim_{h\to 0^+}\frac{f\left(\frac{3}{2}-h\right)-f\left(\frac{3}{2}\right)}{-h}$

$=\lim_{h\to 0^+}\frac{\left|\frac{3}{2}-h-3\right|\left[\frac{3}{2}-h\right]-\left|\frac{3}{2}-3\right|\left[\frac{3}{2}\right]}{-h}$

$=\lim_{h\to 0^+}\frac{\left(h+\frac{3}{2}\right)(1)-\left(\frac{3}{2}\right)(1)}{-h}=-1$

⇒ $f'\left(\frac{3^+}{2}\right)=\lim_{h\to 0^+}\frac{f\left(\frac{3}{2}+h\right)-f\left(\frac{3}{2}\right)}{h}$

$=\lim_{h\to 0^+}\frac{\left|\frac{3}{2}+h-3\right|\left[\frac{3}{2}+h\right]-\left(\frac{3}{2}\right)}{h}=-1$

15. (a), (b), (c), (d)

$f(x) = \frac{[x]+1}{\{x\}+1}$; $x \in [0, 5/2)$

$$=\begin{cases}\frac{1}{x+1} & ;x\in[0,1)\\ \frac{2}{x} & ;x\in[1,2)\\ \frac{3}{x-1} & ;x\in\left[2,\frac{5}{2}\right)\end{cases}$$

$$\Rightarrow f'(x)=\begin{cases}\frac{-1}{(x+1)^2};x\in(0,1)\\ \frac{-2}{x^2};x\in(1,2)\\ \frac{-3}{(x-1)^2};x\in\left(2,\frac{5}{2}\right)\end{cases}$$

⇒ $f(x)$ is discontinuous at $x = 1, 2$ and $f'(x) < 0$ for $x \in (0, 1), (1, 2)$ and $(2, 5/2)$

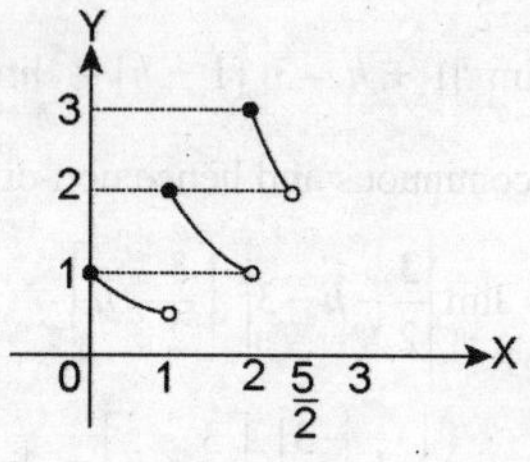

⇒ $f(1^-) = \frac{1}{2}, f(1^+) = 2 = f(1)$

⇒ $f(2^-) = 1, f(2^+) = 3, f(2) = 3, f(0) = 1, f(5/2) = 2$

Clearly $f(x)$ is decreasing and injective and having range $= \left(\frac{1}{2}, 3\right]$ and hence subjective and being discontinuous, its non-differentiable.

16. (a), (b) $f(x) = \begin{cases} \max.\{x, x^2\}; x \geq 0 \\ \min.\{2x, x^2 - 1\}; x < 0 \end{cases}$

The graph of f (x) is as shown below.

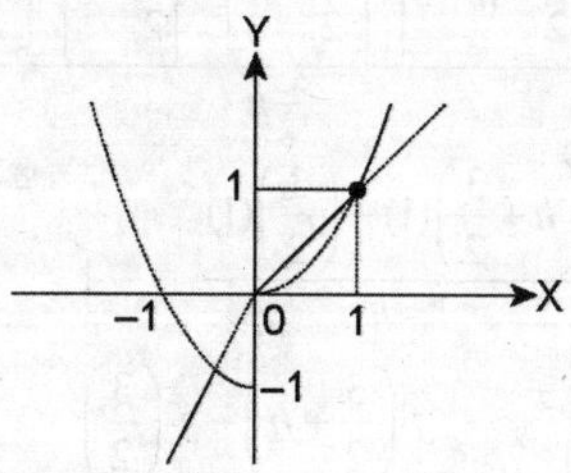

$f(x)$ is discontinuous at $x = 0$ and non-differentiable at $x = 1 - \sqrt{2}, x = 0, x = 1$

17. (b), (c) $f(x) = \begin{cases} x^n . \dfrac{e^{1/x}}{1 + e^{1/x}}; x \neq 0 \\ 0\ ; x = 0 \end{cases}$

For n = 0: $f(x) = \dfrac{e^{\frac{1}{x}}}{1 + e^{\frac{1}{x}}}$ for $x \neq 0$

$\therefore \lim_{x \to 0^-} f(x) = \lim_{x \to 0^-} \dfrac{e^{\frac{1}{x}}}{1 + e^{\frac{1}{x}}} = 0$ and $\lim_{x \to 0^+} \dfrac{e^{\frac{1}{x}}}{1 + e^{\frac{1}{x}}}$

$= \lim_{x \to 0^+} \dfrac{1}{e^{-\frac{1}{x}} + 1} = 1$

⇒ $f(x)$ is discontinuous at $x = 0$

For $n = 1$, $f(x) = \dfrac{xe^{\frac{1}{x}}}{1 + e^{\frac{1}{x}}}$ for $x \neq 0$

$\therefore \lim_{x \to 0^-} f(x) = 0; \lim_{x \to 0^+} f(x) = 0; f(0) = 0$

⇒ $f(x)$ is continuous at $x = 0$

$$\Rightarrow f(x) = \frac{x\left(e^{\frac{1}{x}} + 1 - 1\right)}{\left(1 + e^{\frac{1}{x}}\right)}$$

$$\Rightarrow f(x) = x - \frac{x}{\left(1 + e^{\frac{1}{x}}\right)}$$

$$\Rightarrow f'(x) = 1 - \left[\frac{\left(1 + e^{\frac{1}{x}}\right) - x\left[e^{\frac{1}{x}}\left(\frac{-1}{x^2}\right)\right]}{\left(1 + e^{\frac{1}{x}}\right)^2}\right] = 1 - \left[\frac{1 + e^{\frac{1}{x}} + \frac{e^{\frac{1}{x}}}{x}}{\left(1 + e^{\frac{1}{x}}\right)^2}\right]$$

$\therefore \quad \lim_{x \to 0^-} f'(x) =$

18. (c), (d) $f(x) = [\sin x].\cos x$

$$= \begin{cases} 0 \text{ for } x \in [2n\pi, (2n+1)\pi] \\ -1 \text{ for } x \in ((2n+1)\pi, (2n+1)\pi) \\ 0 \text{ for } x = \left(2n + \frac{3}{2}\right)\pi \end{cases}$$

$f(x)$ is discontinuous at $x = (2n + 1)\pi, \left(2n + \frac{3}{2}\right)\pi;\ 2n\pi;$ $n \in \mathbb{Z}$

19. (a), (d) $f(x) = \{x\} \sin \pi x$

Let $x = k \in \mathbb{Z}$, then $f(k) = \{k\} \sin k\pi = 0$

$\lim_{x \to k^-} f(x) = \lim_{h \to 0^+} \{k - h\} \sin\pi\,(k - h)$

$= \lim_{x \to 0^+} \{k - h\}(-1)^{k+1} \sin \pi h = 0$

$= \lim_{x \to 0^+} ((k - h) - (k - 1)) \sin \pi h = 0$

$= \lim_{x \to k^+} = \lim_{h \to 0^+} \{k + h\} \sin\pi\,(k + h)$

$= \lim_{h \to 0^+} ((k + h) - k)\,(-1)^k \sin \pi h = 0 = f(k)$

Also $\{x\}$ and $\sin \pi x$ being continuous of non-integral points, $f(x)$ being their product is also continuous $\forall\, x \in \mathbb{R}$

Let $x = k \in \mathbb{Z}$, then $f'(k^-) = \lim_{h \to 0^+} \dfrac{f(k-h) - f(k)}{-h}$

$$= \lim_{h \to 0^+} \frac{\{k-h\} \sin \pi(k-h) - 0}{-h}$$

$$= \lim_{h \to 0^+} \frac{((k-h) - (k-1))(-1)^{k-1} \sin \pi h}{-h}$$

$$\lim_{h \to 0^+} \frac{(-h+1)(-1)^{k-1} \sin \pi h}{-h} = (-1)^k\,\pi(1) = (-1)^k\,\pi\,.$$

$$f'(k^+) = \lim_{h \to 0^+} \frac{f(k+h) - f(k)}{h}$$

$$= \lim_{h \to 0^+} \frac{\{k+h\} \sin \pi(k+h) - 0}{h}$$

$= \lim_{h\to 0^+} \dfrac{((k+h)-k)(-1)^k \sin \pi h}{h} = \lim_{h\to 0^+} (-1)^k \sin$

$\pi h = 0$

$\Rightarrow f(x)$ is non-differentiable at $x = k \in \mathbb{Z}$

20. (b), (c), (d) $f(x) = \cos x$,

$g(x) = \begin{cases} \min.\{f(t); 0 \le t \le x\}; x \in [0,\pi] \\ \sin x - 1; x > \pi \end{cases}$

for $x \in [0, \pi]$, $f(x) = \cos x$ is a decreasing function.

$\therefore\ g(x) = \begin{cases} f(x); x \in [0,\pi] \\ \sin x - 1; x > \pi \end{cases} = \begin{cases} \cos x; x \in [0,\pi] \\ \sin x; x \in [0,\pi] \end{cases}$

$g(\pi^-) = -1; g(\pi^+) = -1; g(\pi) = -1$

$\Rightarrow g(x)$ is a continuous function $\forall x \in [0, \infty)$

$\Rightarrow g'(x) = \begin{cases} -\sin x; 0 < x < \pi \\ \cos x; x > \pi \end{cases}$

$\Rightarrow g'(\pi^-) = -\sin \pi$, $g'(\pi^+) = \cos \pi = -1$

$\Rightarrow g(x)$ is non-differentiable at $x = \pi$ and differentiable at any other points.

Also for $x > \pi$, $g'(x) = \cos x$

$\Rightarrow g'(x) = 0$ for $x\ (2n+1)\dfrac{\pi}{2}; n \in \mathbb{N}$

$\Rightarrow$ Critical points belong to set $\left\{\pi, (2n+1)\dfrac{\pi}{2}, n \in \mathbb{N}\right\}$

21. (a), (c), (d) $f(x + y) = f(x) + f(y) + xy(x + y)\ \forall x, y \in \mathbb{R}$

Put $x = y = 0$

$\Rightarrow f(0) = 2f(0) \qquad \Rightarrow f(0) = 0$

$\Rightarrow f'(x) = \lim_{x\to 0^+} \dfrac{f(x+h)-f(x)}{h} = \lim_{h\to 0^+} \dfrac{f(h)+xh(x+h)}{h}$

$= \lim_{h\to 0^+}\left[\dfrac{f(h)}{h} + x(x+h)\right] = \lim_{h\to 0^+} \dfrac{f(h)-f(0)}{h} + x^2$

$= f'(0) + x^2 = x^2 - 1$

$\therefore\ f'(x) = x^2 - 1$

$\Rightarrow f(x) = \int (x^2 - 1)\,dx = \dfrac{x^3}{3} - x + c$

Also $f(0) = 0$

$\Rightarrow 0 = c \qquad \Rightarrow f(x) = \dfrac{x^3}{3} - x$

$f'(x) = 2x$ and $f'(3) = (3)^2 - 1 = 8$

SECTION–V: (ASSERTION AND REASON)

1. (a) $f(x) = \sin^{-1} x + \operatorname{cosec}^{-1} x$

Domain of $\sin^{-1} x = [-1, 1]$ and Domain of $\operatorname{cosec}^{-1} x = (-\infty, -1] \cup [1, \infty)$

$\Rightarrow$ Domain of $f(x) = \{-1, 1\}$

$\Rightarrow f(x)$ is discontinuous function

$\Rightarrow$ Assertion is correct .

Clearly Reason is correct as for the continuity to be defined at $x = a$,

$f(x)$ should be defined in neighborhood of 'a' i.e., $(a-h, a+h)$ which contains infinitely many points.

2. (a) $f(x) = x(x - 1)$ and $g(x) = \text{sgn}(x)$, $gof(x) = \text{sgn}[f(x)]$

$= \begin{cases} -1 \text{ for } f(x) < 0 \\ 0 \text{ for } f(x) = 0 \\ 1 \text{ for } f(x) > 0 \end{cases} = \begin{cases} -1 \text{ for } x \in (0,1) \\ 0 \text{ for } x = 0,1 \\ 1 \text{ for } x < 0 \text{ or } x > 1 \end{cases}$

$gof(0^-) = 1; gof(0^+) = -1; gof(1^-) = -1; gof(1^+) = 1$

$\Rightarrow gof(x)$ is discontinuous at $x = 0$ and $x = 1$ *and* hence non-differentiable at these points too.

$gof'(x) = 0$ for $x \in \mathbb{R} - \{0, 1\}$

Also reason is correct and correctly explains the assertion

3. (c) $f(x) = |x^3| = \begin{cases} x^3; x \ge 0 \\ -x^3; x < 0 \end{cases}$

Clearly it is continuous and $f'(x) = \begin{cases} 3x^2; x > 0 \\ -3x^2; x < 0 \end{cases}$

$\Rightarrow f'(0^-) = 0; f'(0^+) = 0$

$\Rightarrow f(x)$ is continuous and differentiable function $\forall x \in \mathbb{R}$

$\Rightarrow$ Assertion is correct, but reason is incorrect as for instance, $f(x) = (x - 1)$ is differentiable at $x = 1$,

However $|f(x)| = |x - 1|$ is non-differentiable at $x = 1$

4. (a) $f(x) = |x|.\sin x = x \sin x$ for $x \in (-\pi, \pi)$

$\Rightarrow f'(x) = x \cos x + \sin x$ which begin continuous on $(-\pi, \pi)$ implies $f(x)$ is differentiable in $(-\pi, \pi)$.

Thus $f(x)$ is differentiable at $x = 0$. Also reason is standard result.

5. (a) $f(x) = |(x - a)(x - b)| = \begin{cases} (x-a)(x-b); x \le a \text{ or } x \ge b \\ -(x-a)(x-b); a < x < b \end{cases}$

$\Rightarrow f'(x) = \begin{cases} 2x-(a+b); x < a \text{ or } x > b \\ -2x+(a+b); a < x < b \end{cases}$

$\Rightarrow f'(a^-) = a - b$, $f'(a^+) = b - a$ and $f'(b^-) = a - b$, $f'(b^+) = b - a$

$\Rightarrow f'(a^-) + f'(a^+) = f'(b^-) = f'(b^+) = 0$

$\Rightarrow$ Reasons is correct and explain the assertion.

6. (d) $\because f(x)$ is differentiable

$\Rightarrow f(x)$ as well as $f'(x)$ are continuous, $f'(x) \ne 0$

Let $g(x) = \dfrac{f(x)}{f'(x)}$

$\Rightarrow g(x)$ is continuous.

$\Rightarrow g'(x) = \dfrac{(f'(x))^2 - f(x).f''(x)}{[f'(x)]^2}$

$\Rightarrow$ If $f(x) \le 0$ and $f''(x) \ge 0$, $f'(x) \ne 0$ or $f(x) \ge 0$, $f''(x) \le 0$, $f'(x) \ne 0$, for $x \in (a, b)$,then $g(x)$ is increasing in (a, b)

$\Rightarrow$ Reason is correct.

Let $\tan x = \dfrac{\sin x}{\cos x} = \dfrac{f(x)}{f'(x)}; x \in \left(\dfrac{\pi}{2}, \pi\right)$

Clearly $f(x) \sin x > 0$, $f'(x) = \cos x < 0$ in $\left(\dfrac{\pi}{2}, \pi\right)$

$\Rightarrow g(x) = \tan x = \dfrac{\cos^2 x + \sin^2 x}{\cos^2 x} > 0$

$\Rightarrow g(x)$ is increasing

$\Rightarrow$ Assertion incorrect and reason correct

SECTION–VI: (PASSAGE)

PASSAGE A:

1. **(c)** $(f(x))^2 = x^2 \ \forall \ x \in \mathbb{R}$
$\Rightarrow f(x) = \pm |x|$ i.e., $|x|$ or $-|x|$ or $f(x) = \pm x$ i.e., $y = x$ or $y = -x$
$\Rightarrow$ There are 4 such continuous functions

2. **(d)** $\because f(1/2) = 1$ and f is continuous on [0, 1] and f assumes only rational values,
$\Rightarrow f(x) = 1 \ \forall \ x \in [0, 1]$

3. **(a)** $D_f = [-1, 1]; f(f(x))^2 + x^2 = 1 \Rightarrow y^2 = 1 - x^2$
$\Rightarrow y = \pm\sqrt{1-x^2}$; which is defined $\forall \ x \in [-1, 1]$

4. **(d)** $f(x) = \begin{cases} x; x \neq 0 \\ 1; x = 0 \end{cases}$
$\Rightarrow f(x)$ is discontinuous function having only $x = 0$ as the point of discontinuity ;
$R_f = \mathbb{R} - \{0\}$ which is not an interval

PASSAGE B:

5. **(c)** L.H.L $= \lim\limits_{h\to 0^+} 2[2 - h] = 2$
R.H.L $= \lim\limits_{h\to 0^+} 2\,[2 + h] = 4$
$\Rightarrow$ Jump $= |2 - 4| = 2$

6. **(a)** $f(1^-) = 3; f(1^+) = 7$
$\Rightarrow$ Jump $= |3 - 7| = 4$

7. **(d)** $h(x) = f(x).g(x) = \begin{cases} x^2 \sin x \text{ for } x < 0 \\ 2x^2(x+1) \text{ for } x \geq 0 \end{cases}$
$h(0^-) = 0; h(0^+) = 0 \quad \Rightarrow \quad h(x)$ is continuous $\forall \ x \in \mathbb{R}$.
$\Rightarrow$ There is no jump discontinuity.

PASSAGE C:

8. **(b)** $f(x) = \begin{cases} [x]; -2 \leq x \leq \dfrac{-1}{2} \\ 2x^2 - 1; \dfrac{-1}{2} < x \leq 2 \end{cases}$

$\Rightarrow f(x) = \begin{cases} -2; -2 \leq x < -1 \\ -1; -1 \leq x \leq \dfrac{-1}{2} \\ 2x^2 - 1; \dfrac{-1}{2} < x \leq 2 \end{cases}$

$\Rightarrow f(-1^-) = -2, f(-1^+) = -1$

$f\left(-\dfrac{1}{2}^-\right) = -1;\ f\left(-\dfrac{1}{2}^+\right) = \dfrac{-1}{2}$

$\Rightarrow f(x)$ is discontinuous at $x = -1$ and at $x = \dfrac{-1}{2}$

9. **(c)** $\because f(x)$ is discontinuous at $x = -1$ and at $x = \dfrac{-1}{2}$
$\Rightarrow f(x-1)$ is discontinuous at $x - 1 = -1$ and at $x - 1 = \dfrac{-1}{2}$
$\Rightarrow x = 0$ and $x = \dfrac{1}{2}$

10. **(c)** $g(x) = |f(x)| = \begin{cases} 2; -2 \leq x < -1 \\ 1; -1 \leq x \leq \dfrac{-1}{2} \\ |2x^2 - 1|; \dfrac{-1}{2} < x \leq 2 \end{cases}$

$$= \begin{cases} 2; -2 \leq x < -1 \\ 1; -1 \leq x \leq \dfrac{-1}{2} \\ 2x^2 - 1; x \leq \dfrac{-1}{\sqrt{2}} \text{ or } x \geq \dfrac{1}{\sqrt{2}} \\ -2x^2 + 1; x \in \left(\dfrac{-1}{\sqrt{2}}, \dfrac{1}{\sqrt{2}}\right) \end{cases} = \begin{cases} 2; -2 \leq x < -1 \\ 1; -1 \leq x \leq \dfrac{-1}{2} \\ -2x^2 + 1; \dfrac{-1}{2} < x < \dfrac{1}{\sqrt{2}} \\ 2x^2 - 1; \dfrac{1}{\sqrt{2}} \leq x \leq 2 \end{cases}$$

$|f(-1^-)| = 2; |f(-1^+) = 1;$

$\left|f\left(\dfrac{-1}{2}^-\right)\right| = 1, \left|f\left(\dfrac{-1}{2}^+\right)\right| = \dfrac{1}{2}$

$\left|f\left(\dfrac{1}{\sqrt{2}}^-\right)\right| = 0; \left|f\left(\dfrac{1}{\sqrt{2}}^+\right)\right| = 0$

$\Rightarrow |f(x)|$ is discontinuous at $x = -1$, at $x = \dfrac{-1}{2}$ i.e., non-differentiable at $x = -1, \dfrac{-1}{2}$

Also $f'(x) = \begin{cases} 0; -2 < x < -1 \\ 0; -1 < x \dfrac{-1}{2} \\ -4x; \dfrac{-1}{2} < x < \dfrac{1}{\sqrt{2}} \\ 4x; \dfrac{1}{\sqrt{2}} < x < 2 \end{cases}$

$\Rightarrow f'\left(\dfrac{1}{\sqrt{2}}^-\right) = -4\left(\dfrac{1}{\sqrt{2}}\right) = -2\sqrt{2}$ and

$f'\left(\dfrac{1}{\sqrt{2}}^+\right) = 4\left(\dfrac{1}{\sqrt{2}}\right) = 2\sqrt{2}$

$\Rightarrow |f(x)|$ is non-differentiable at $x = -1, \dfrac{-1}{2}, \dfrac{1}{\sqrt{2}}$ i.e., at 3 points

PASSAGE D:

Let $F(x) = f(x).g(x)$

$\Rightarrow F'(x) = f(x).g'(x) + g(x).f'(x) = x^3.g'(x) + g(x).(3x^2)$

$= \dfrac{df}{dx}.\dfrac{dg}{dx}$ (given)

$= 3x^2.\dfrac{dg}{dx} = 3x^2.g'(x)$

$\therefore (x^3 - 3x^2)\,g'(x) = -3x^2.g(x)$

$\Rightarrow \displaystyle\int \frac{g'(x)}{g(x)}dx = \int \frac{-3x^2}{x^3 - 3x^2}dx = -3\int \frac{1}{x-3}dx$

$\Rightarrow \ell n\,|g(x)| = -3\ell n\,|x - 3| + \ell n\,C$

$\Rightarrow \ell n\,|g(x).(x-3)^3| = \ell n\, C$

$\Rightarrow g(x).(x-3)^3 = C \quad \Rightarrow g(x) = \dfrac{C}{(x-3)^3}$

Given $g(0) = \dfrac{1}{3} \Rightarrow \dfrac{1}{3} = \dfrac{C}{-27}$

$\Rightarrow C = -9 \quad \Rightarrow g(x) = \dfrac{-9}{(x-3)^3}$

11. **(c)** From above $g(x) = \dfrac{-9}{(x-3)^3}$

12. **(a)** Let $G(x) = f(x-3).g(x) = (x-3)^3 \cdot \left(\dfrac{-9}{(x-3)^3}\right) = -9$

$\therefore G(x) = -9 \quad \Rightarrow G'(x) = 0$

$\Rightarrow G'(100) = 0$

13. **(a)** $\lim\limits_{x\to 0} \dfrac{f(x).g(x)}{x(1+g(x))} = \lim\limits_{x\to 0} \dfrac{-9x^3}{x(x-3)^3\left(1-\dfrac{9}{(x-3)^3}\right)}$

$= \lim\limits_{x\to 0} \dfrac{-9x^2}{\left[(x-3)^3-9\right]} = 0$

PASSAGE E:

14. **(a)** R.H.D = $f'(-a^+)$

$= \lim\limits_{h\to 0^+} \dfrac{f(-a+h)-f(-a)}{h} = \lim\limits_{h\to 0^+} \dfrac{-f(a-h)+f(a)}{h}$

($\because f$ is odd)

$= \lim\limits_{h\to 0^+} \dfrac{f(a-h)-f(a)}{-h}$

15. **(c)** $\because f$ is even

$\Rightarrow f'$ is odd $\qquad \therefore f'(a^+)$

$= \lim\limits_{h\to 0^+} \dfrac{f'(a+h)+f'(-a)}{h} = \lim\limits_{h\to 0^+} \dfrac{-f'(-a-h)+f'(-a)}{h}$

$= \lim\limits_{h\to 0^+} \dfrac{-f'(-a)+f'(-a-h)}{-h}$

16. **(b)** $\lim\limits_{h\to 0} \dfrac{f(-x)-f(-x-h)}{h} = \lim\limits_{h\to 0} \dfrac{f(x)-f(x-h)}{-h}$ (Given)

$= -\lim\limits_{h\to 0} \dfrac{f(x+h)-f(x)}{-h}$

$\Rightarrow f'(-x) = -f'(x) \quad \Rightarrow f'(x)$ is odd

$\Rightarrow f(x)$ is an even function

PASSAGE F:

$f: [-\pi, \pi] \to \mathbb{R}$, $g: [-\pi, \pi] \to \mathbb{R}$

$f(x) = \min. \{\sin x, \cos 2x\}$;

$g(x) = \max. \{\sin x, \cos 2x\}$

The graph of $f(x)$ and $g(x)$ are as shown below.

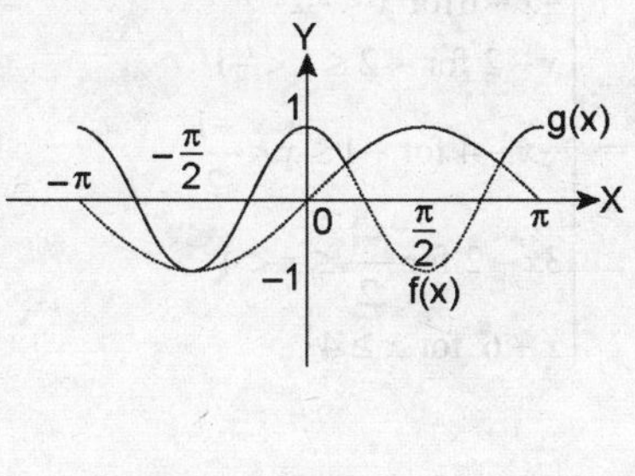

17. **(a)** Clearly, $f(x)$ is continuous and non-differentiable at $x = \dfrac{\pi}{6}, x = \dfrac{5\pi}{6}$ i.e., at two points.

18. **(c)** The graph of $|g(x)|$ is as shown below.

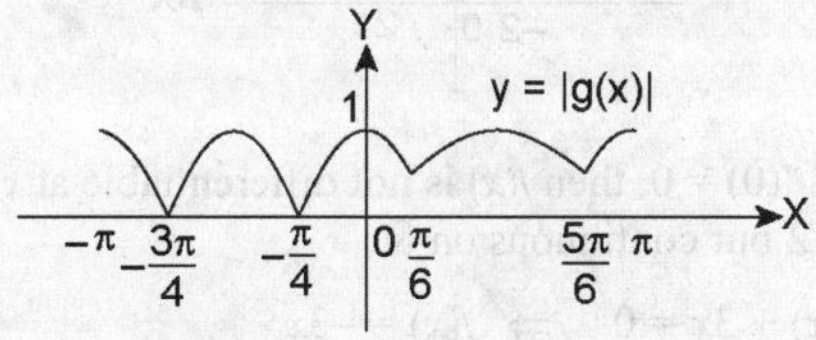

Clearly, $|g(x)|$ is non-differentiable at $x = \dfrac{-3\pi}{4}, \dfrac{-\pi}{4}, \dfrac{\pi}{6}, \dfrac{5\pi}{6}$

19. **(b)** From graph it is clear that

$f(x) \in \left[-1, \dfrac{1}{2}\right]$ = Range of $f(x)$

20. **(c)** From graph it is clear that

$g(x) \in [-1,1] =_{Range}$ of $g(x)$

21. **(b), (c)** Clearly $f(x)$ increase in the intervals

$\left[\dfrac{-\pi}{2}, \dfrac{\pi}{6}\right], \left[\dfrac{\pi}{2}, \dfrac{5\pi}{6}\right]$

22. **(a), (b), (c)** Clearly $g(x)$ decrease in the intervals

$\left[-\pi, \dfrac{-\pi}{2}\right], \left[0, \dfrac{\pi}{6}\right], \left[\dfrac{\pi}{2}, \dfrac{5\pi}{6}\right]$

PASSAGE G:

(i) $f(x)$ is continuous on $\mathbb{R} - \{3\}$ and $f(x)$ has a sharp turning point at $x = -2$.

(ii) $f(x)$ increase on $(-\infty, -2)$ and on $(3, \infty)$, decrease on $(-2, 3)$

(iii) $f'(x)$ does not exist at $x = -2$, but $f(x)$ is continuous at $x = -2$, $f'(x)$ does not exist at $x = 3$ due to infinite discontinuity ,

(iv) $f(x)$ is con cave upwards on $(-\infty, -2)$ and on $(-2, 0)$, concave downwards on $(0, 3)$ and on $(3, \infty)$

(v) $f(x)$ has a point of inflexion at $x = 0$ and $f(0) = 0$.

(vi) $f(x)$ has $x = 3$ and $x = 0$ as two horizontal asymptotes.

From above conclusions, we can draw the rough Sketch of $y = f(x)$ as shown below.

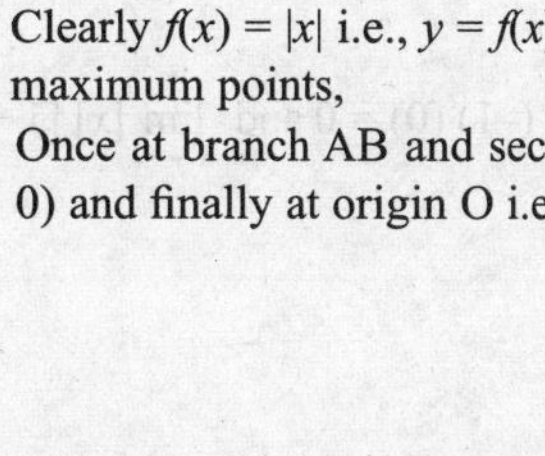

23. **(c)** Clearly $f(x) = |x|$ i.e., $y = f(x)$ and $y = |x|$ can intersect at maximum points,

Once at branch AB and secondly at branch BO (not at 0) and finally at origin O i.e., at maximum 3 points.

24. (b) Graph of $y = f(-|x|)$ is as shown below.

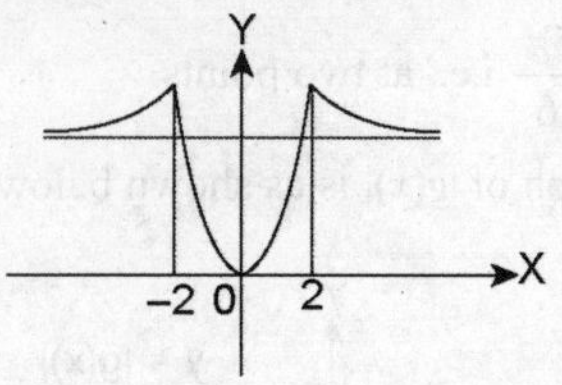

If $f'(0) = 0$, then $f(x)$ is not differentiable at $x = -2$ and $x = 2$ but continuous on $\mathbb{R}$.

25. (d) $f(x) + 3x = 0 \Rightarrow f(x) = -3x$

$\Rightarrow$ $y = f(x)$ and $y = -3x$

Clearly $y = f(x)$ and $y = -3x$ can intersect at maximum five points i.e., at branch AB at branch BO, at origin, at branch OC, at branch DE.

If $f(-2) > 6$, $f'(0) > -3$ i.e., tangent at origin to $f(x)$ should be below line $y = -3x$

SECTION VII (COLUMN – MATCHING TYPE)

1. **(i)→(b), (c), (d);(ii) →(c);(iii) →(b), (d);(iv) →(a), (c)**

(i) $f(x) = \{\sin(\pi x)\}$

Clearly, $f(x)$ is discontinuous whenever $\sin(\pi x)$ is an integer i.e., $\sin(\pi x) \in \{-1, 0, 1\}$

$\Rightarrow x \in \left\{\frac{n}{2}; n \in \mathbb{Z}\right\}$

(ii) $g(x) = \left\{\frac{\sin x}{x}\right\}$

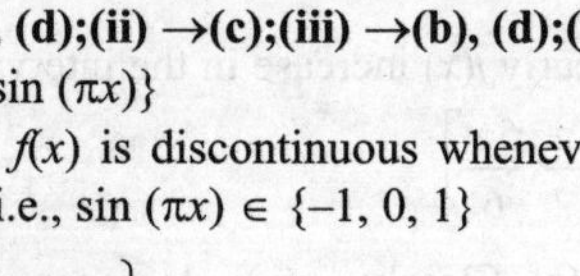

Clearly $\frac{\sin x}{x} < 1 \ \forall \ x \neq 0$ and $|\sin x| < |x| \ \forall \ x \neq 0$

$\Rightarrow 0 \le \left|\frac{\sin x}{x}\right| < 1 \ \forall \ x \neq 0$

$\Rightarrow \frac{\sin x}{x}$ can take only integer value 0 at $x = n\pi$; $n \in \mathbb{Z}$

$\Rightarrow$ $g(x)$ is discontinuous for $x \in \{0\}$

(iii) From above, $g(x)$ is continuous for $x \in \{1, 2\}, \left\{\frac{1}{2}\right\}$

(iv) $u(x) = \left\{\frac{\sin x}{x}\right\}$ is discontinuous on set [0, 1) and {0} as both contain the point of discontinuity 0

2. **(i)→(a), (b), (c);(ii) →(c);(iii) →(e);(iv) →(d);(v) →(a)**

(i) $[x]\,[1 + x]$

$\Rightarrow \lim\limits_{x \to 0^-} [x]\,[1 + x] = (-1)\,(0) = 0$ and $\lim\limits_{x \to 0^+} [x]\,[1 + x] = (0)\,(1) = 0, f(0) = 0$

$\Rightarrow$ $f(x)$ is continuous at $x = 0$

(ii) $[x], [1 - x]$

$\Rightarrow \lim\limits_{x \to 0^-} [x]\,[1 - x] = (-1)\,(1) = -1$ and $\lim\limits_{x \to 0^+} [x]\,[1 - x] = (0)\,(0) = 0, f(0) = 0$

$\Rightarrow$ Right continuous and left discontinuous at $x = 0$

(iii) $f(x) = [\text{sgn}\, x]\,[2 - x]\,[1 + |x|]$

$\lim\limits_{x \to 0^-} f(x) = (-1)\,(2)\,(1) = -2,$

$\lim\limits_{x \to 0^+} = (1)\,(1)\,(1) = 1$ and $f(0) = (0)\,(2)\,(1) = 0$

$\Rightarrow$ $f(x)$ is neither left continuous nor right continuous at $x = 0$

(iv) $f(x) = [\cos x]$

$\lim\limits_{x \to 0^-} f(x) = 0;\ \lim\limits_{x \to 0^+} f(x) = 0; f(0) = 1$

$\Rightarrow \lim\limits_{x \to 0} f(x) = 0 \neq f(0) = 1$

$\Rightarrow$ Limit exists but discontinuous at $x = 0$

(v) $f(x) = [-x]\,[1 + x]$

$\therefore \lim\limits_{x \to 0^-} f(x) = (0)\,(0) = 0$

$\lim\limits_{x \to 0^+} f(x) = (-)(1) = -1; f(0) = 0$

$\Rightarrow$ Left continuous, right discontinuous

3. **(i)→(a), (b);(ii) →(b), (c), (d);(iii) →(b), (c), (d);(iv) →(a), (b), (c), (d)**

(i) $y = \frac{1}{t^2 - t - 2} = \frac{1}{(t-2)(t+1)}$

$\Rightarrow$ y is discontinuous at $t = -1$, $t = 2$ i.e., where $\frac{1}{x+1} = -1$ or 2 i.e., $x + 1 = -1$ or $x + 1 = \frac{1}{2}$ i.e., $x = -2$ or $x = \frac{-1}{2}$

(ii) $y = [x] + [-x] = \begin{cases} 0 \text{ for } x \in \mathbb{Z} \\ -1 \text{ for } x \notin \mathbb{Z} \end{cases}$

$\Rightarrow f(k^-) = -1 = f(k^+); f(k) = 0$ for $k \in \mathbb{Z}$

$\Rightarrow$ $f(x)$ is discontinuous at each integer

(iii) $y = [\sin(\pi x)]$

y will be non-differentiable where it is discontinuous i.e., where $\sin(\pi x)$ takes integer values, except -1

$\Rightarrow \sin \pi x = 0$ or 1

$\Rightarrow x = -2, -1, 4$ all are possible

(iv) $f(x) = |2x + 1| + |x + 2| - |x + 1| - |x - 4|$ possible points of non-differentiable are $x = -\frac{1}{2}, -2, -1, 4$

$$\therefore f(x) = \begin{cases} -x - 6 \text{ for } x < -2 \\ x - 2 \text{ for } -2 \le x < -1 \\ -x - 4 \text{ for } -1 \le x < \frac{-1}{2} \\ 3x - 2 \text{ for } \frac{-1}{2} \le x < 4 \\ x + 6 \text{ for } x \ge 4 \end{cases}$$

$$\Rightarrow f'(x) = \begin{cases} -1 \text{ for } x < -2 \\ 1 \text{ for } -2 < x < -1 \\ -1 \text{ for } -1 < x < \dfrac{-1}{2} \\ 3 \text{ for } \dfrac{-1}{2} < x < 4 \\ 1 \text{ for } x > 4 \end{cases}$$

$\Rightarrow$ $f(x)$ is non-differentiable at $x = -2, -1, \dfrac{-1}{2}, 4$

4. (i)→(b);(ii) →(c);(iii) →(d), (e);(iv) →(a), (e)

(i) f: [0, 2] → [0, 8]

$f(x) - x^3 = 0 \qquad \Rightarrow f(x) = x^3 \qquad$ ...(i)

Let $y = f(x)$ and $y = g(x)$

$\therefore$ (i)

$\Rightarrow$ Number of points of intersection of $y = f(x)$ and $y = g(x)$ for $x \in [0, 2]$

In [0, 2] range of $f(x)$ as well as that of $g(x) = x^3$ i.e., [0, 8] and both are continuous function,

Thus at least once $f(x)$ has to meet with the curve of $g(x)$ i.e., $f(x) - x^3 = 0$ has at least one root.

(ii) Two consecutive roots of $g(x)$ means between two consecutive turning points, there can be at most one root of $f(x) = 0$

(iii) $f(x) = |2 - |x - 2|| = \begin{cases} |2-(x-2)| \text{for } x \geq 2 \\ |2+(x-2)| \text{for } x \leq 2 \end{cases}$

$$= \begin{cases} 4 - x \text{ for } 2 \leq x \leq 4 \\ x - 4 \text{ for } x \geq 4 \\ x \text{ for } 0 \leq x \leq 2 \\ -x \text{ for } x < 0 \end{cases}$$

$$\Rightarrow f'(x) = \begin{cases} -1 \text{ for } x < 0 \\ 1 \text{ for } 0 < x < 2 \\ -1 \text{ for } 2 < x < 4 \\ 1 \text{ for } x > 4 \end{cases}$$

$\Rightarrow$ $f(x)$ is non-differentiable at $x = 0$, 2 and 4 i.e., at exactly 3 points.

(iv) $f(x) = \begin{cases} x^2 \text{ if } x \in \mathbb{Q} \\ 5x - 6 \text{ if } x \notin \mathbb{Q} \end{cases}$

At the point of continuity, $x^2 \to 5x - 6$

$\Rightarrow x^2 - 5x + 6 \to 0$

$\Rightarrow x \to 2$ or $x \to 3$

5. (i)→(b), (d);(ii) →(c), (d), (e);(iii) →(c);(iv) →(a), (c)

(i) $f(u) = \dfrac{1}{u^2 + 2u - 3}; u = \dfrac{1}{x+1} = \dfrac{1}{(u+3)(u-1)}$

$\Rightarrow$ $f(u)$ is discontinuous at $u = -3$, $u = 1$

$\Rightarrow \dfrac{1}{x+1} = -3; \dfrac{1}{x+1} = 1$

$\Rightarrow x = -4/3; x = 0$

But $f(x) = \dfrac{1}{\left(\dfrac{1}{x+1}+3\right)\left(\dfrac{1}{x+1}-1\right)}$

$\Rightarrow$ $f(x)$ is also not continuous at x= –1

(ii) $f(x) = sgn\,(x - 1)(4 - x^2)$,

$f(x)$ is discontinuous where $(x - 1)(4 - x^2) = 0$

$\Rightarrow x = 1, -2, 2$

(iii) $\lim\limits_{x\to 0} \dfrac{f(x)}{x}$ ..... $\left[\dfrac{0}{0} \text{ form as } f(0) = 0\right]$

$= \lim\limits_{x\to 0} f'(x)$ (By L.H.Rule)

$f'(0) = k$ (as $\lim\limits_{x\to 0} \dfrac{f(x)}{x}$ exists given)

$f(x)$ is derivable at $x = 0$

$\Rightarrow$ $f(x)$ is continuous at $x = 0$

(iv) $f(x) = \lim\limits_{n\to\infty} \dfrac{(nx - \text{sgn}\,x)}{2 - n} = \lim\limits_{n\to\infty} \left(\dfrac{x - \dfrac{\text{sgn}\,x}{n}}{\dfrac{2}{n} - 1}\right) = -x$

$\Rightarrow$ $f(x)$ is a continuous function.

6. (i)→(a), (b);(ii) →(a), (b), (c), (d);(iii) →(a), (d), (e);(iv) → (a), (b), (c), (d), (e)

(i) $f(x) = |x^2 + (\lambda - 1)|x| - \lambda|$

$x^2 + (\lambda - 1)|x| - \lambda = 0$

$\Rightarrow |x| = 1$ or $-\lambda$ ($\Rightarrow \lambda \leq 0$)

$\Rightarrow f(1) = 0, f(-1) = 0$ and $f(0) = |\lambda|$

$\Rightarrow$ Graph of $f(x)$ will be of the from as shown below.

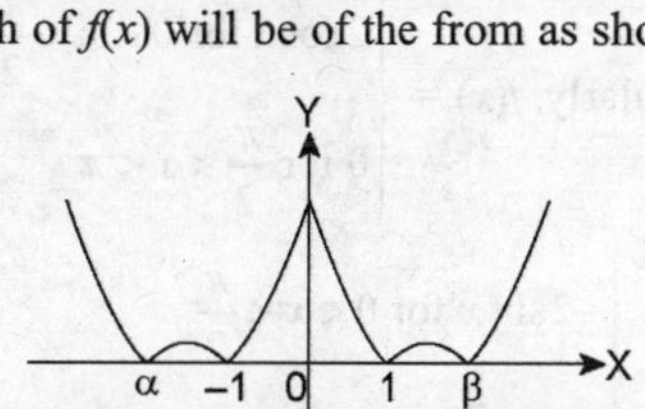

$\Rightarrow$ $f(x)$ is non-differentiable at five points for $\lambda < 0$

(ii) $f(x) = \begin{cases} \min.\left(|x|; \sqrt{1-x^2}\right); -1 \leq x \leq 1 \\ [|x|]; 1 < |x| < 2 \end{cases}$

The graph of $f(x)$ is as shown below.

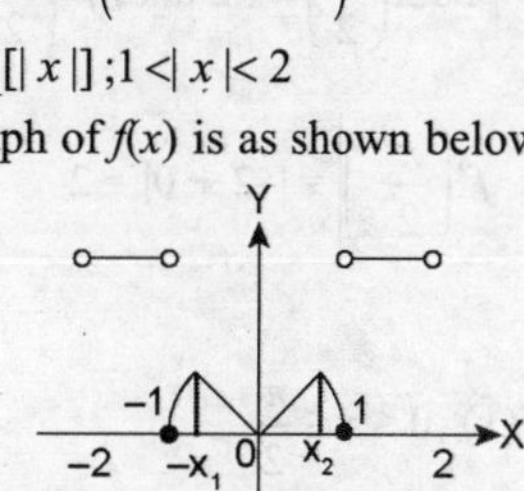

Clearly $f(x)$ is non-differentiable at $x = -1, x_1 = \dfrac{-1}{\sqrt{2}}$,

$0, x_2 = \dfrac{-1}{\sqrt{2}}, 1$

(iii) $f(x) = |x + 1|\,(|x| + |x - 1|)$

$$\Rightarrow f(x) = \begin{cases} (x+1)(2x-1) \text{for } x < -1, \\ -(x+1)(2x-1) \text{ for} -1 \leq x < 0 \\ (x+1) \text{for } 0 \leq x < 1 \\ (x+1)(2x-1) \text{ for } x \geq 1 \end{cases}$$

$$\Rightarrow f(x)=\begin{cases}4x+1 \text{ for } x<-1\\ -4x-1 \text{ for } -1<x<0\\ 1 \text{ for } 0<x<1\\ 4x+1 \text{ for } x>1\end{cases}$$

$\Rightarrow$ $f(x)$ is non-differentiable at $x=-1, x=0$ and $x=1$

(iv) $f\left(\frac{x+y}{2}\right)=\frac{f(x)+f(y)}{2}\forall x,\ y\in\mathbb{R}$

Differentiating partially w.r.t x, we get

$$\frac{1}{2}f'\left(\frac{x+y}{2}\right)=\frac{1}{2}f'(x)\forall x,y\in\mathbb{R}$$

$$\Rightarrow f'\left(\frac{x+y}{2}\right)=f(x)=\forall\ x,y\in\mathbb{R}$$

$$\Rightarrow f'\left(\frac{y}{2}\right)=f'(0)=-1\ \forall\ y\in\mathbb{R}$$

$\Rightarrow$ $f(x)=-1,\ \forall\ x\in\mathbb{R}$ $\Rightarrow$ $f(x)=-x+k$ but $f(0)=1$

$\Rightarrow$ $k=1$ $\Rightarrow$ $f(x)=-x+1$

$$\Rightarrow f(2)=-1<\frac{-1}{\sqrt{2}},0\frac{1}{\sqrt{2}},1$$

SECTION–VIII: (INTEGER TYPE)

1. $f(x)=\cos x+|\cos x|$

Particularly, $f(x)=\begin{cases}2\cos x \text{ for } 0<x<\frac{\pi}{2}\\ 0 \text{ for } \frac{\pi}{2}<x<\pi\end{cases}$

$$\Rightarrow f'(x)=\begin{cases}-2\sin x \text{ for } 0<x<\frac{\pi}{2}\\ 0 \text{ for } \frac{\pi}{2}<x<\pi\end{cases}$$

$$\Rightarrow f'\left(\frac{\pi^-}{2}\right)=-2\sin\left(\frac{\pi}{2}\right)=-2 \text{ and } f'\left(\frac{\pi^+}{2}\right)=0$$

$$\Rightarrow \left|f'\left(\frac{\pi^-}{2}\right)+f'\left(\frac{\pi^+}{2}\right)\right|=|-2+0|=2$$

2. $f(x)=\cos x;$

$$g(x)=\begin{cases}f(x);0\le x\le\frac{\pi}{2}\\ \frac{\pi}{2}-x;\frac{\pi}{2}<x\le 3\end{cases}$$

$$\Rightarrow g(x)=\begin{cases}\cos x;\ 0\le x\le\frac{\pi}{2}\\ \frac{\pi}{2}-x;\frac{\pi}{2}<x\le 3\end{cases}$$

$$\Rightarrow g\left(\frac{\pi^-}{2}\right)=0;g\left(\frac{\pi^+}{2}\right)=0;g\left(\frac{\pi}{2}\right)=0$$

$\Rightarrow$ $g(x)$ is continuous on [0, 3]

$$\Rightarrow g'(x)=\begin{cases}-\sin x;0<x<\frac{\pi}{2}\\ -1;\frac{\pi}{2}<x<3\end{cases}$$

$$\Rightarrow g'\left(\frac{\pi^-}{2}\right)=-1;g'\left(\frac{\pi^+}{2}\right)=-1$$

$\Rightarrow$ $g(x)$ is differentiable on [0, 3]

$\Rightarrow$ Ans : 4

3. $f(x)=\begin{cases}x^{\frac{m}{2}}\sin\left(\frac{1}{x}\right);x\ne 0\\ 0 \text{ if } x=0\end{cases}$

For continuity at $x=0$:

$$\lim_{x\to 0^-}f(x)=\lim_{x\to 0^+}f(x)=f(0)=0$$

$\Rightarrow$ 'm' must be an even integer

$\Rightarrow$ $m\ge 2$

For differentiability at $x=0$:

$$f'(x)=\left\{(x)^{\frac{m}{2}}\left(\frac{-1}{x^2}\right)\cos\frac{1}{x}+\sin\left(\frac{1}{x}\right).\frac{m}{2}(x)^{\frac{m}{2}-1}\right. \text{ for } x\ne 0$$

For differentiability at $x=0$

$\lim_{x\to 0^-}f'(x)=\lim_{x\to 0^+}f'(x)=\lim_{x\to 0}f'(x)=$ finite real.

$$\lim_{x\to 0^-}f'(x)=\lim_{x\to 0^-}\left(-x^{\frac{m}{2}-2}.\cos\frac{1}{x}+\frac{m}{2}(x)^{\frac{m}{2}-1}.\sin\frac{1}{x}\right)$$

$$\Rightarrow \frac{m}{2}-2\ge 0;\frac{m}{2}-1\ge 0$$

$\Rightarrow$ $m\ge 4;\ m\ge 2$

$\therefore$ For continuity and differentiability $m\ge 4$

$\Rightarrow$ Greatest value of m for which $f(x)$ is continuous but non-differentiable is 2.

4.

$\because$ $f(x+h)-f(x)\le 2h^2\ \forall\ h,x\in\mathbb{R}$

$\Rightarrow$ $f(x+h)-f(x)\le 0\ \forall\ x,h\in\mathbb{R}$

$\Rightarrow$ $f(x+h)\le f(x)\ \forall\ x,h\in\mathbb{R}$

$\Rightarrow$ $f(x+h)\le f(x)\le f(x-h)\ \forall\ x,h\in\mathbb{R}$

$\Rightarrow$ $f(x)$ must be a constant function

$\Rightarrow$ $f(7)=7$ as $f(2)=7$ (given)

5. $f(u)=\dfrac{1}{u^2+u-2};u=\dfrac{1}{x-1}$

$\Rightarrow$ $f(x)$ is not defined at $x=1$

$$f(u)=\frac{1}{u^2+u-2}=\frac{1}{(u+2)(u-1)}$$

$\Rightarrow$ $f(u)$ is not defined at $u=-2,\ 1$ i.e., $\dfrac{1}{x-1}=-2,\dfrac{1}{x+1}=1$

$$\Rightarrow x-1=\frac{-1}{2},\ x-1=1$$

$$\Rightarrow x=\frac{1}{2},\ x=2$$

$\therefore$ Points of discontinuity are 1, 2, $\frac{1}{2}$

$$\Rightarrow 2|x_1+x_2+x_3|=2|1+2+\frac{1}{2}|=2\left(\frac{7}{2}\right)=7$$

6. $f(x) = x^2 - 2|x| = \begin{cases} x^2 - 2x; x \geq 0 \\ x^2 + 2x ; x < 0 \end{cases}$

$\Rightarrow\ f'(x) = \begin{cases} 2x+2 ; x<0 \\ 2x-2 ; x>0 \end{cases}$

$\Rightarrow$ $f(x)$ is non-differentiable but continuous at $x = 0$

$\Rightarrow$ $f(x) \downarrow$ for $x \in (-\infty, -1)$, $(0, 1)$ and $f(x)$ for $x \in (-1, 0)$, $(1, \infty)$

$\therefore\ g(x) = \begin{cases} \min.\{f(t); -2 \leq t \leq x\}; -2 \leq x < 0 \\ \max.\{f(t); 0 \leq t \leq x\}; 0 \leq x \leq 3 \end{cases}$

$= \begin{cases} f(x) ; -2 \leq x < -1 \\ f(-1); -1 \leq x < 0 \\ f(0) ; 0 \leq x < 2 \\ f(x) ; 2 \leq x \leq 3 \end{cases}$

$\Rightarrow\ g(x) = \begin{cases} x^2+2x;\ -2 \leq x < -1 \\ -1 ; -1 \leq x < 0 \\ 0 ; 0 \leq x < 2 \\ x^2 - 2x ; 2 \leq x \leq 3 \end{cases}$

$\Rightarrow$ $g(x)$ is discontinuous at $x = 0$

$\Rightarrow\ g'(x) = \begin{cases} 2x+2 ; -2 < x < -1 \\ 0 ; -1 < x < 0 \\ 0 ; 0 < x < 2 \\ 2x-2 ; 2 < x < 3 \end{cases}$

$\Rightarrow$ $g'(x)$ is discontinuous at $x = 2$

$\Rightarrow$ $g(x)$ is non-differentiable at $x = 0, 2$

$\Rightarrow$ $m = 1, n = 2$

$\Rightarrow$ $(m + n) = 3$

7. According to question $f'(e^a)$ ($\neq 0$) exists finitely and $f(e^a) = 0$.

$$\Rightarrow \lim_{x \to e^a} \frac{\ell n(1 + 9f(x)) - \tan(f(x))}{2f(x)}$$

$$= \lim_{x \to e^a} \frac{\frac{1}{(1+9f(x))}(9f'(x)) - \sec^2(f(x))f'(x)}{2f'(x)}$$

$$= \lim_{x \to e^a} \frac{9f'(e^a) - f'(e^a)}{2f'(e^a)} = 4 \qquad (\because f(e^a) \neq 0, \infty)$$

8. $f(x) = \dfrac{x^2 - bx + 25}{x^2 - 7x + 10} = \dfrac{x^2 - bx + 25}{(x-2)(x-5)}; x \neq 5$

Also $f(x)$ is given to be continuous at $x = 5$,

$\Rightarrow\ f(5) = \lim\limits_{x \to 5} \dfrac{(x^2 - bx + 5)}{(x-2)(x-5)}$ and for continuity limit must exist

$\Rightarrow$ $(x - 5)$ must be a factor of $x^2 - bx + 5$

$\Rightarrow$ $(5)^2 - 5(b) + 25 = 0 \Rightarrow b = 10$

$$\Rightarrow f(5) = \lim_{x \to 5} \frac{(x^2 - 10x + 25)}{(x-2)(x-5)}$$

$$= \lim_{x \to 5} \frac{(x-5)^2}{(x-2)(x-5)} = \lim_{x \to 5} \frac{(x-5)}{(x-2)} = 0$$

9. $g(x) = \dfrac{(x-1)^n}{\ell n \cos^m (x-1)}; 0 < x < 2$

$$\Rightarrow \lim_{x \to 1^+} g(x) = \lim_{x \to 1^+} \frac{(x-1)^n}{\ell n \cos^m (x-1)}$$

$$= \lim_{h \to 0^+} \frac{(h)^n}{\ell n \cos^m (h)} \ldots \left(\frac{0}{0} \text{ form}\right)$$

$$= \lim_{h \to 0^+} \frac{n(h)^{n-1}}{\frac{1}{\cos^m(h)} . m \cos^{m-1} h (-\sinh)}$$

$$= \lim_{h \to 0^+} \frac{n.\cos h}{(-m)} . \frac{h^{n-2}}{1} \left(\frac{h}{\sin h}\right) = p \text{ (given) and p} = L.H.D$$

of $|x - 1|$ at $x = 1$

$\Rightarrow$ $p = -1$

$$\therefore \lim_{h \to 0^+} \left(\frac{n \cos h}{-m}\right) . \frac{h^{n-2}}{1} \left(\frac{h}{\sin h}\right) = -1$$

$\Rightarrow$ $n = 2, m = 2$

$\Rightarrow$ $(m)^n = 4$.

10. $f(x) = \begin{cases} \dfrac{a|x^2 - x - 2|}{2 + x - x^2}; x < 2 \\ b; x = 2 \\ \dfrac{x - [x]}{x - 2}; x > 2 \end{cases}$

$$\lim_{x \to 2^-} = \lim_{x \to 2^-} \frac{a|(x-2)(x+1)|}{-(x-2)(x+1)} = a = f(2) = b$$

$$\lim_{x \to 2^+} f(x) = \lim_{x \to 2^+} \frac{x - [x]}{x - 2} = \lim_{x \to 2^+} \frac{x-2}{x-2} = 1$$

$\Rightarrow$ a = b = 1

$\Rightarrow$ $(1 - a)^2 + (1 - b)^2 = 0$

11. $f(x) = \begin{cases} \dfrac{\left(4^{(x+2)}\right)^{\frac{[x+1]}{4}} - 16}{4^x - 16}; x < 2 \\ a.\dfrac{1 - \cos(x-2)}{(x-2)\tan(x-2)}; x > 2 \end{cases}$

$$\Rightarrow \lim_{x \to 2^-} f(x) = \lim_{x \to 2^-} \frac{(4)^{(x+2)\frac{2}{4}} - 16}{4^x - 16}$$

$$= \lim_{x \to 2^-} \frac{(4)^{\frac{x+2}{2}} - 16}{4^x - 16} = \lim_{x \to 2^-} \frac{4(2^x - 4)}{(4^x - 16)} = 4$$

$$\lim_{x \to 2^-} \frac{1}{(2^x + 4)} = \frac{1}{2}$$

$$= \lim_{x \to 2^+} f(x) = \lim_{x \to 2^+} a.\frac{1 - \cos(x-2)}{(x-2)\tan(x-2)} = a$$

$$\lim_{x\to 2^+}\frac{2\sin^2\left(\frac{x-2}{2}\right)}{(x-2)^2.\left[\frac{\tan(x-2)}{(x-2)}\right]}=\frac{a}{4}\lim_{x\to 2^+}\frac{2.\left[\frac{\sin\left(\frac{x-2}{2}\right)}{\left(\frac{x-2}{2}\right)}\right]^2}{\left[\frac{\tan(x-2)}{(x-2)}\right]}=\frac{a}{2}$$

$\therefore$ For the function $f(x)$ to be continuous at $x = 2$, $\frac{a}{2}=\frac{1}{2}$

$\Rightarrow a = 1$

12. $f(x)=\begin{cases}|4x-5|[x] \text{ for } x>1\\ [\cos\pi x] \text{ for } x\le 1\end{cases}=\begin{cases}(-4x+5)\text{for}\,1<x<\frac{5}{4}\\ (4x-5)[x] \text{ for } x\ge\frac{5}{4}\\ [\cos\pi x] \text{ for } x\le 1\end{cases}$

For $x \in [0, 2]$,

$$f(x)=\begin{cases}1 \text{ at } x=0\\ 0 \text{ for } 0<x\le\frac{1}{2}\\ -1 \text{ for } \frac{1}{2}<x\le 1\\ (-4x+5)\text{for}\,1<x<\frac{5}{4}\\ (4x-5)\text{for}\,\frac{5}{4}\le x<2\\ 2(4x-5)\text{at}\,x=2\end{cases}$$

$\Rightarrow f(x)$ is discontinuous at $x = \frac{1}{2}$, $x = 1$, $x = 0$ and $x = 2$

$\Rightarrow m = 4$

$$\Rightarrow f'(x)=\begin{cases}0 \text{ for } 0<x<\frac{1}{2}\\ 0 \text{ for } \frac{1}{2}<x<1\\ -4 \text{ for } 1<x<1\\ 4 \text{ for } \frac{5}{4}<x<2\end{cases}$$

$\Rightarrow f(x)$ is non-differentiable at $x = 0, \frac{1}{2}, 1, \frac{5}{4}, 2$

$\Rightarrow n = 5$

$\therefore$ $(m + n) = 9$

13. $f(x) = x + \{-x\} + [x] = \begin{cases}x+0+x \text{ if } x\in\mathbb{Z}\\ x+1-\{x\}+[x] \text{ if } x\notin\mathbb{Z}\end{cases}$

$=\begin{cases}2x \text{ if } x\in\mathbb{Z}\\ 1+2[x] \text{ if } x\notin\mathbb{Z}\end{cases}$

Let $x = k \in \mathbb{Z}$, then $f(k^-) = 1 + 2(k - 1) = 2k - 1$, $f(k^+) = 1 + 2(k) = 2k + 1$,

$\Rightarrow f(x)$ is discontinuous and non-differentiable at each integer point

Let $a \in (k - 1, k)$; $k \in \mathbb{Z}$, $f(a^-) = 1 + 2(k - 1) = 2k - 1$, $f(a^+) = 2k - 1$, $f(a) = 2k - 1$

$\Rightarrow f(x)$ is continuous at non-integer points.

Thus $f(x)$ is discontinuous and non-differentiable in $[-2, 2]$ at $x = -2, -1, 0, 1, 2$ i.e., at 5 points.

14. $f(x) = \max.\{a - x, a + x, b\}$; $-\infty < x < \infty$, $0 < a < b$

The graph of $f(x)$ is as shown below.

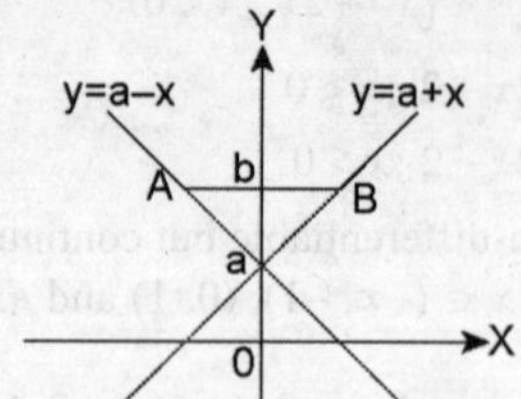

$\therefore$ $f(x)$ can't be differentiable at points A and B i.e., at 2 points.

15. $\lim_{h\to 0}\frac{f(5+h^3)-f(5-h^3)}{2h^3}$

$=\lim_{h\to 0}\frac{f(5+h^3)-f(h^3)+f(h^3)-f(5-h^3)}{2h^3}$

$=\lim_{h\to 0}\frac{f(5+h^3)-f(h^3)}{2h^3}+\lim_{h\to 0}\frac{f(5-h^3)-f(h^3)}{-2h^3}$

$=\frac{1}{2}f'(5)+\frac{1}{2}f'(5)=f'(5)=4$

16. $f(x)=\begin{cases}(\cos x-\sin x)^{\operatorname{cosec} x};\frac{-\pi}{2}<x<0\\ a\;;x=0;\\ \frac{e^{1/x}+e^{2/x}+e^{3/x}}{a.e^{2/x}+be^{3/x}};0<x<\frac{\pi}{2}\end{cases}$

$\lim_{x\to 0^-}f(x)=\lim_{x\to 0^-}\left[1+(\cos x-\sin x-1)\right]^{\operatorname{cosec} x}$

$=e^{\lim_{x\to 0}\operatorname{cosec} x(\cos x-\sin x-1)}$

$=e^{\lim_{x\to 0}(\cot x-1-\operatorname{cosec} x)}$

$=e^{\lim_{x\to 0}\left(-\tan\frac{x}{2}-1\right)}$

Also $\lim_{x\to 0^+}\frac{\left(1+\frac{1}{e^{1/x}}+\frac{1}{e^{2/x}}\right)}{\left(b+\frac{a}{e^{1/x}}\right)}=\frac{1}{b}=f(0)=a$

$\therefore$ For continuous, $a = \frac{1}{b} = e^{-1}$

$\Rightarrow$ $a = e^{-1}$; $b = e$

$\Rightarrow$ $(\ell n\, b - \ell n\, a) - (\ell n\, e - \ell n\, e^{-1}) = 2$

17. $f(x)=\frac{1+\sin x-\cos x}{1-\sin x-\cos x};x\ne 0$

$\lim_{x\to 0}f(x)=\lim_{x\to 0}\frac{2\sin^2\frac{x}{2}+2\sin\frac{x}{2}\cos\frac{x}{2}}{2\sin^2\frac{x}{2}-2\sin\frac{x}{2}\cos\frac{x}{2}}$

$=\lim_{x\to 0}\left(\frac{\sin\frac{x}{2}+\cos\frac{x}{2}}{\sin\frac{x}{2}-\cos\frac{x}{2}}\right)=-1$

$= f(0)$ for continuity at $x = 0$

$\Rightarrow |f(0)| = 1$

18. $\because$ $f(x)$ is continuous and takes only irrational values which is possible only when $f(x)$ is a constant function and $f(1) = \sqrt{2}$

$\Rightarrow f(x) = \sqrt{2}\ \forall\ x \in [0, 3]$

$\Rightarrow f(1.5).f(2.5) = \left(\sqrt{2}\right)\left(\sqrt{2}\right) = 2$

19. $f(x) = \lim\limits_{n\to\infty} \dfrac{ax^2 + bx + c + e^{nx}}{1 + ce^{nx}}$

For $x < 0$, $f(x) = \lim\limits_{n\to\infty} \dfrac{ax^2 + bx + c + e^{nx}}{1 + ce^{nx}} = ax^2 + bx + c$

For $x > 0$, $f(x) = \lim\limits_{n\to\infty} \dfrac{\frac{ax^2}{e^{nx}} + \frac{bx}{e^{nx}} + \frac{c}{e^{nx}} + 1}{\left(\frac{1}{e^{nx}} + c\right)} = \dfrac{1}{c}$

At $x = 0$, $f(x) = 1$

$$\therefore\ f(x) = \begin{cases} ax^2 + bx + c; x < 0 \\ 1; x = 0 \\ \dfrac{1}{c} \text{ for } x > 0 \end{cases}$$

$\therefore$ $f(x)$ will be continuous $\forall\ x \in \mathbb{R}$

If $\lim\limits_{x\to0^-} f(x) = c = 1 = \dfrac{1}{c}$

$\Rightarrow c = 1$

20. $\because$ $f'(x)$ is continuous on [2, 10] and takes only rational values,

$\Rightarrow f'(x)$ must be a constant function $\forall\ x \in [2, 10]$ and $f'(4) = 3$

$\Rightarrow f'(x) = 3\ \forall\ x \in [2, 10]$

$\Rightarrow f(x) = 3x + c\ \forall\ x \in [2, 10]$

$\Rightarrow f(5) - f(4) = 3(5) - 3(4) = 3$

21. $f(x)$ is differentiable on [7, 10]

$\Rightarrow f(x)$ is continuous on [7, 10] and $f(x)$ takes only irrational values and $f(8) = \sqrt{3}$

$\Rightarrow f(x) = \sqrt{3}\ \forall\ x \in [7, 10]$

$\therefore\ \prod\limits_{k=7}^{10} f(k) = \prod\limits_{k=7}^{10}\left(\sqrt{3}\right) = \left(\sqrt{3}\right)^4 = 9$

22. $f(x) = \dfrac{1}{\ell n[x^2 - 3x + 3]}$

$f(x)$ is discontinuous where $\ell n\,[x^2 - 3x + 3]$ equals zero.

Clearly, $x^2 - 3x + 3 > 0\ \forall\ x \in \mathbb{R}$ as Disc < 0

Now denominator vanishes where $x^2 - 3x + 3 = 1$

$\Rightarrow x^2 - 3x + 2 = 0$

$\Rightarrow (x - 1)(x - 2) = 0$

$\Rightarrow x = 1; 2$

$\therefore$ $f(x)$ is discontinuous at exactly 2 points .

23. $\lim\limits_{x\to0^-} g(x) = \lim\limits_{x\to0^-} \dfrac{1 - a^x + xa^x \ell na}{x^2.a^x}\left(\dfrac{0}{0}\text{ form}\right)$

$= \lim\limits_{x\to0^-} \dfrac{-a^x \ell na + \ell na\left(xa^x \ell na + a^x\right)}{x^2 a^x \ell na + a^x(2x)}$ (By L.H. Rule)

$= \lim\limits_{x\to0^-} \dfrac{xa^x(\ell na)^2}{x^2 a^x \ell na + 2xa^x} = \lim\limits_{x\to0^-} \dfrac{(\ell na)^2}{x\ell na + 2} = \dfrac{(\ell na)^2}{2}$ and

$\lim\limits_{x\to0^+} g(x) = \lim\limits_{x\to0^+} \dfrac{(2a)^x - x\ell n2a - 1}{x^2}$

$= \lim\limits_{x\to0^+} \dfrac{(2a)^x \ell n2a - \ell n2a}{2x}$ (By L.H. Rule)

$= \lim\limits_{x\to0^+} \dfrac{(2a)^x(\ell n2a)^2}{2} = \dfrac{(\ell n2a)^2}{2}$

$\therefore$ For continuity at $x = 0$,

$\dfrac{(\ell na)^2}{2} = \dfrac{(\ell n2a)^2}{2} \Rightarrow \ell n\, a = \pm\, \ell n\, 2a$

$\Rightarrow a = 0$ (impossible), $\ell n\, 2a^2 = 0$

$\Rightarrow 2a^2 = 1$

$\Rightarrow a^2 = \dfrac{1}{2} \Rightarrow a = \dfrac{1}{\sqrt{2}}$ as $a > 0$ and $g(0)$

$= \dfrac{\left(\ell n\sqrt{2}\right)^2}{2} = \dfrac{1}{(2)^3}(\ell n2)^2$

$\therefore$ By comparison, $p = 2$

24. $\lim\limits_{h\to0} \dfrac{\sin 3\pi(1+h) + A\sin 5\pi(1+h) + B\sin \pi(1+h)}{h^5}$

$= \lim\limits_{h\to0} \dfrac{-\sin 3\pi h - A\sin 5\pi h - B\sin \pi h}{h^5}$

$= \lim\limits_{h\to0} \dfrac{-3\pi\cos 3\pi h - 5\pi A\cos 5\pi h - B\pi\cos \pi h}{5h^4}$

$\Rightarrow -3\pi - 5\pi A - B\pi = 0$

$\Rightarrow 5A + B = -3$ ...(1)

$= \lim\limits_{h\to0} \dfrac{9\pi^2\sin 3\pi h + 25\pi^2 A\sin 5\pi h + B\pi^2\sin \pi h}{20h^3}$

$= \lim\limits_{h\to0} \dfrac{27\pi^3\cos 3\pi h + 125\pi^3 A\cos 5\pi h + B\pi^3\cos \pi h}{60h^2}$

$\Rightarrow 27\pi^3 + 125\pi^3 A + B\pi^3 = 0$

$\Rightarrow 125A + B = -27$ ...(2)

Solving (1) and (2), we get, $120\,A = -24$

$\Rightarrow A = \dfrac{-1}{5}$

$\Rightarrow B = -3 - 5A = -3 - 5\left(\dfrac{-1}{5}\right) = -2$

$\therefore\ B = -2$

$= \lim\limits_{h\to0} \dfrac{-81\pi^4\sin 3\pi h - 625\pi^4 A\sin 5\pi - B\pi^4\sin \pi h}{120h}$

$= \lim\limits_{h\to0} \dfrac{-243\pi^5\cos 3\pi h - 3125\pi^5 A\cos 5\pi h - B\pi^5\cos \pi h}{120}$

$$= \frac{-243\pi^5 - 3125\pi^5 A - B\pi^5}{120}$$

$$= \frac{-243\pi^5 + 625\pi^5 + 2\pi^5}{120} = \frac{348\pi^5}{120} = f(1) = \frac{p^2\pi^5}{(p+1)}$$

$\Rightarrow p = 4$

25. $f(x) = \begin{cases} a + \dfrac{\sin[x]}{x}; x > 0 \\ 2\ ; x = 0 \\ b + \left[\dfrac{\sin x - x}{x^3}\right]; x < 0 \end{cases}$

$$\lim_{x\to 0^-} f(x) \lim_{x\to 0^-}\left(b + \left[\frac{\sin x - x}{x^3}\right]\right)$$

$$\because \quad \lim_{x\to 0^-}\left(\frac{\sin x - x}{x^3}\right) = \lim_{x\to 0^-}\left(\frac{\cos x - 1}{3x^2}\right)$$

$$= \lim_{x\to 0^-}\left(\frac{-\sin x}{6x}\right) = \frac{-1}{6}$$

$$\Rightarrow \quad \lim_{x\to 0^-} f(x) = b - 1 \text{ and } \lim_{x\to 0^+} f(x) = \lim_{x\to 0^+}\left(a + \frac{\sin[x]}{x}\right)$$

$$= \lim_{x\to 0^+}\left(a + \frac{\sin 0}{x}\right) = a$$

$\therefore$ For continuity at $x = 0$, $b - 1 = a = f(0) = 2$

$\Rightarrow a = 2, b = 3$

$\Rightarrow b - a = 1$

$\Rightarrow k = 1 \qquad (\because\ b - a = k \text{ (given)})$

CHAPTER 3

Method of Differentiation

■ INTRODUCTIONS

In the history of mathematics two names are prominent to share the credit for inventing calculus, Issac Newton (1642–1727) and G.W. Leibntiz (1646–1717). Both of them independently invented calculus around the seventeenth century.

One of the most important problem in mathematics was to find the equation of tangent to a curve at a given point. Now finding the equation of tangent for a circle or even for any conic was easy, even without the help of differentiation but unfortunately the same cannot be said for any arbitrary curve. And the second problem was the Kepler's conclusion that the orbits of planets around the sun are elliptical, but he was unable to provide a logical explanation for his claim. Although any one familiar with the calculus can provide the answer to the above two problems now.

It was Leibnitz who solved the problem of tangents and Newton settled the Kepler's problem mathematically. And during their efforts both of them invented Differential Calculus independently. Leibnitz applied the geometrical approach while Newton used the physical approach.

Normally a dependent variable is expressed in terms of independent variable by means of an equation. Now when we find the differential coefficient of the dependent variable with respect to the independent variable, what we are doing is to try to find out another equation by which the change in the dependent variable (for any infinitesimal change in independent variable) is related to the independent variable, whatever be the value of the independent variable.

Derivatives Using First Principle (Ab-initio) Method

Derivative function or slope function of a given function $f(x)$ is defined as a function whose value generates the slope of $f(x)$ wherever it is defined and $f(x)$ is differentiable. There is a variety of notations for the differential coefficient or derivatives, such as, $\frac{df(x)}{dx}$, $\frac{df}{dx}$, $D\,f(x)$, $f'(x)$, f', $\dot{f}$, y', $\dot{y}$, y_1. Out of all these $\frac{d\,f(x)}{dx}$, $f'(x)$, y' and y_1 are the most prominent.

Also known as differential co-efficient of function, there can be considered as co-efficient of differential (dx).

e.g., $y = f(x) = x^2$

$\Rightarrow\ y + \Delta y = f(x + \Delta x) = (x + \Delta x)^2$

$\Rightarrow\ \Delta y = f(x + \Delta x) - f(x) = 2x\,\Delta x + (\Delta x)^2$

$$\Rightarrow\ \frac{\Delta y}{\Delta x} = \frac{f(x+\Delta x) - f(x)}{\Delta x} = 2x + \Delta x$$

$$\Rightarrow\ \lim_{\Delta x \to 0} \frac{\Delta y}{\Delta x} = 2x \text{ called as } \frac{dy}{dx} \text{ for } y = x^2$$

So derivative of $f(x)$ is obtained as

$$f'(x) = \lim_{h \to 0} \frac{f(x+h) - f(x)}{h} = \lim_{h \to 0} \frac{f(x-h) - f(x)}{-h}$$

NOTE:

The function $f'(x)$ is known as the derivative of '$f(x)$' because it has been derived from '$f(x)$' by using the limits.

Algorithm to Differentiate One variable w.r.t. Another

Step I: Let $y = f(x)$ be a function

And by substituting x by $x + \Delta x$ in $f(x)$; we will try to calculate $y + \Delta y$ i.e., $f(x + \Delta x)$.

Step II: Subtract y from '$y + \Delta y$'; thus obtaining Δy in terms of x and Δx

$\therefore \quad \Delta y = f(x + \Delta x) - f(x)$

Step III: Divide Δy by Δx, thus obtaining the value of $\dfrac{\Delta y}{\Delta x}$

Step IV: Find $\lim\limits_{\Delta x \to 0} \dfrac{\Delta y}{\Delta x}$, and this is called the value of $\dfrac{dy}{dx}$ or $f'(x)$

Caution:

If $f'(x)$ is not defined on $x = c$, then it is wrong to conclude that $f(x)$ has no derivative at $x = c$

e.g. Let $f(x) = x^{2/3} \tan x$ at $x = 0$

$\therefore \quad f'(x) = x^{2/3} \sec^2 x + \dfrac{2}{3x^{1/3}} \tan x$

Clearly $f'(x)$ seems to undefined at $x = 0$. But before coming to the conclusion, let us try to find the left hand and the right hand derivative.

$$\text{LHD}: f'(0^-) = \lim_{h \to 0^+} \frac{f(x-h) - f(x)}{-h}$$

$$= \lim_{h \to 0^-} \frac{\left((-h)^{2/3} \sec^2(-h)\right) - 0}{-h}$$

$$= \lim_{h \to 0^-} -\frac{\sec^2 h}{h^{1/3}} = 0 \text{ and}$$

$$\text{RHD}: f'(0^+) = \lim_{h \to 0^+} \frac{f(x+h) - f(x)}{h}$$

$$= \lim_{h \to 0^+} \frac{\sec^2 h - 0}{h^{1/3}} = \lim_{h \to 0^+} \frac{\sec^2 h}{h^{1/3}} = 0$$

and since, both LHD and RHD = 0

$\therefore \quad f(x)$ has a derivative at $x = 0$

ILLUSTRATION 1: Find the derivate of the following functions by Ab- initio method

(a) $f(x) = x^4$ (b) $f(x) = e^{mx+n}$

(c) $f(x) = \log(ax + b)$ (d) $f(x) = \tan x$

(e) $f(x) = \sec x$ (f) $f(x) = x^2 \cos x$

(g) $f(x) = \tan\sqrt{2x^3 - 3}$ (h) $f(x) = \cos^2\sqrt{x}$

(i) $f(x) = e^{\sin\sqrt{x}}$ (j) $f(x) = \log(\cos x)$

(k) $f(x) = \dfrac{3x-2}{4x+5}$ (l) $f(x) = \tan^{-1}x$

(m) $f(x) = \sec^{-1}x$

SOLUTION: (a) $f(x) = x^4$

$\Delta y = f(x + \Delta x) - f(x)$

$\Rightarrow \Delta y = (x + \Delta x)^4 - x^4$

$\Rightarrow \Delta y = x^4 + 4x^3(\Delta x) + 6x^2(\Delta x)^2 + 4x(\Delta x)^3 (\Delta x)^4 - x^4$

$\Rightarrow \dfrac{\Delta y}{\Delta x} = 4x^3 + 6x^2(\Delta x) + 4x(\Delta x^2) + (\Delta x)^3$

Taking $\lim\limits_{\Delta x \to 0}$; we get $\lim\limits_{\Delta x \to 0} \dfrac{\Delta y}{\Delta x} = \dfrac{dy}{dx} = 4x^3$

(b) $y = f(x) = e^{mx+n}$

$\Rightarrow \Delta y = f(x + \Delta x) - f(x)$

$\Rightarrow \Delta y = e^{mx + m(\Delta x) + n} - e^{mx+n}$

$\Rightarrow \Delta y = e^{mx+n}(e^{m(\Delta x)} - 1)$

$$\Rightarrow \frac{\Delta y}{\Delta x} = e^{mx+n} \frac{\left(e^{m(\Delta x)}-1\right)}{(\Delta x)}$$

Taking $\lim\limits_{\Delta x \to 0}$; we get $\lim\limits_{\Delta x \to 0} \frac{\Delta y}{\Delta x} = e^{mx+n} \times \lim\limits_{\Delta x \to 0} \frac{\left(e^{m(\Delta x)}-1\right)}{m\Delta x} m$

$$\Rightarrow \frac{dy}{dx} \quad m\left(e^{mx \quad n}\right)$$

(c) $y = \log(ax + b)$

$\Rightarrow \Delta y = f(x + \Delta x) - f(x)$

$\Rightarrow \Delta y = \log(ax + a(\Delta x) + b) - \log(ax + b)$

$$\Rightarrow \Delta y = \log\left(\frac{ax+b+a(\Delta x)}{ax+b}\right) \Rightarrow \frac{\Delta y}{\Delta x} = \log\frac{\left(1+\frac{a(\Delta x)}{ax+b}\right)}{\left(\frac{a\Delta x}{ax+b}\right)\times\frac{ax+b}{a}}$$

Taking $\lim\limits_{\Delta x \to 0}$; we get $\lim\limits_{\Delta x \to 0} \frac{\Delta y}{\Delta x} = \frac{dy}{dx} = \frac{1}{\frac{ax+b}{a}} = \frac{a}{ax+b}$

(d) Let $f(x) = \tan x$ then $f'(x) = \lim\limits_{\Delta x \to 0} \frac{\tan(x+\Delta x)-\tan x}{\Delta x} = \lim\limits_{\Delta x \to 0} \frac{1}{\Delta x}\left[\frac{\sin(x+\Delta x)}{\cos(x+\Delta x)} - \frac{\sin x}{\cos x}\right]$

$$= \lim_{\Delta x \to 0}\left[\frac{\sin(x+\Delta x)\cos x - \cos(x+\Delta x)\sin x}{\Delta x \cos(x+\Delta x)\cos x}\right] = \lim_{\Delta x \to 0}\left[\frac{\sin(x+\Delta x - x)}{\Delta x \cos(x+\Delta x)\cos x}\right]$$

$$= \lim_{\Delta x \to 0}\left(\frac{\sin \Delta x}{\Delta x}\right) \lim_{\Delta x \to 0} \frac{1}{\cos(x+\Delta x)\cos x} = 1.\frac{1}{\cos^2 x} = \sec^2 x$$

Thus $\frac{d}{dx}(\tan x) = \sec^2 x$

(e) Let $f(x) = \sec x$ then $f'(x) = \lim\limits_{\Delta x \to 0} \frac{\sec(x+\Delta x)-\sec x}{\Delta x} = \lim\limits_{\Delta x \to 0} \frac{1}{\Delta x}\left[\frac{1}{\cos(x+\Delta x)} - \frac{1}{\cos x}\right]$

$$= \lim_{\Delta x \to 0}\left[\frac{\cos x - \cos(x+\Delta x)}{\Delta x \cos(x+\Delta x)\cos x}\right] = \lim_{\Delta x \to 0}\left[\frac{2\sin(x+\Delta x/2)\sin \Delta x/2}{\Delta x \cos(x+\Delta x)\cos x}\right]$$

$$= \lim_{\Delta x \to 0} \frac{\sin(x+\Delta x/2)}{\cos(x+\Delta x)\cos x} \lim_{\Delta x \to 0} \frac{\sin \Delta x/2}{\Delta x/2} = \frac{\sin x}{\cos^2 x}.1 \text{ [since } \lim_{\theta \to 0} \frac{\sin\theta}{\theta} = 1\text{]}$$

$= \tan x \sec x$. Thus $\frac{d}{dx}(\sec x) = \sec x \tan x$

(f) $y = f(x) = x^2 \cos x$

$\Delta y = f(x + \Delta x) - f(x)$

$= (x+\Delta x)^2 \cos(x+\Delta x) - x^2 \cos x$

$\Rightarrow \Delta y = x^2(\cos(x + \Delta x) - \cos x) + 2x\,\Delta x \cos(x + \Delta x) + (\Delta x)^2 \cos(x + \Delta x)$

$$\Rightarrow \frac{\Delta y}{\Delta x} = \frac{x^2 \times \left(-2\sin\left(\frac{\Delta x}{2}\right)\sin\left(\frac{2x+\Delta x}{2}\right)\right) + 2x(\Delta x)\cos(x+\Delta x) + (\Delta x)^2\cos(x+\Delta x)}{\Delta x}$$

Taking $\lim\limits_{\Delta x \to 0}$; we get $\lim\limits_{\Delta x \to 0} \frac{\Delta y}{\Delta x} = x^2(-\sin x) + 2x \cos x = \frac{dy}{dx}$

(g) $y = f(x) = \tan\sqrt{2x^3 - 3}$

$$\Rightarrow \Delta y = f(x + \Delta x) - f(x)$$

$$\Rightarrow \Delta y = \left(\tan\sqrt{2(x+\Delta x)^3 - 3}\right) - \left(\tan\sqrt{2x^3 - 3}\right)$$

$$\Rightarrow \Delta y = \frac{\sin\left(\sqrt{2(x+\Delta x)^3} - \sqrt{2x^3 - 3}\right)}{\cos\sqrt{2(x+\Delta x)^3 - 3}.\cos\sqrt{2x^3 - 3}}$$

$$\Rightarrow \frac{\Delta y}{\Delta x} = \frac{1}{\cos^2\sqrt{2x^3-3}}\left[\left(\frac{\sin\left(2\sqrt{2(x+\Delta x)^3 - 3} - \sqrt{2x^3-3}\right)}{\sqrt{2(x+\Delta x)^3 - 3} - \sqrt{2x^3-3}}\right) \times \left(\frac{\sqrt{2(x+\Delta x)^3 - 3} - \sqrt{2x^3-3}}{\Delta x}\right)\right.$$

$$\Rightarrow \frac{\Delta y}{\Delta x} = \frac{1}{\cos^2\sqrt{2x^3-3}}\left[\left(\frac{\sin\left(2\sqrt{2(x+\Delta x)^3 - 3} - \sqrt{2x^3-3}\right)}{\sqrt{2(x+\Delta x)^3 - 3} - \sqrt{2x^3-3}}\right)\right.$$

Taking $\lim\limits_{\Delta x \to 0}$; we get

$$\Rightarrow \lim_{\Delta x \to 0}\frac{\Delta y}{\Delta x} = \lim_{\Delta x \to 0}\sec^2\sqrt{2x^3-3} \times 1 \times \left(\frac{\left(2(x+\Delta x)^3 - 3\right) - \left(2x^3 - 3\right)}{(\Delta x)\left[\sqrt{2(x+\Delta x)^3 - 3} + \sqrt{2x^3-3}\right]}\right)$$

$$\Rightarrow \lim_{\Delta x \to 0}\frac{\Delta y}{\Delta x} = \lim_{\Delta x \to 0}\sec^2\sqrt{2x^3-3} \times \left(\frac{2(\Delta x)^3 - 6x^2(\Delta x) + 6(\Delta x)^2 x}{(\Delta x) \times 2\left(\sqrt{2x^3-3}\right)}\right)$$

$$\Rightarrow \lim_{\Delta x \to 0}\frac{\Delta y}{\Delta x} = \lim_{\Delta x \to 0}\sec^2\sqrt{2x^3-3} \times \frac{6x^2}{2\left(\sqrt{2x^2-3}\right)}$$

(h) $y = f(x) = \cos^2\sqrt{x}$

$$\Rightarrow \Delta y = f(x + \Delta x) - f(x) = \cos^2\sqrt{x+\Delta x} - \cos^2\sqrt{x}$$

$$\Rightarrow \Delta y = \sin\left(\sqrt{x+\Delta x} + \sqrt{x}\right)\sin\left(\sqrt{x+\Delta x} - \sqrt{x}\right)$$

$$\Rightarrow \frac{\Delta y}{\Delta x} = \sin\left(2\sqrt{x}\right) \times \sin\left(\sqrt{x+\Delta x} - \sqrt{x}\right)$$

Taking $\lim\limits_{\Delta x \to 0}$; we get

$$\Rightarrow \lim_{\Delta x \to 0}\frac{\Delta y}{\Delta x} = \lim_{\Delta x \to 0}\sin\left(2\sqrt{\ }\right) \times \left(\frac{\sin\left(\sqrt{x+\Delta x} - \sqrt{x}\right)}{\left(\sqrt{x+\Delta x} - \sqrt{x}\right)}\right) \times \left(\frac{\sqrt{x+\Delta x} - \sqrt{x}}{\Delta x}\right)$$

$$\Rightarrow \lim_{\Delta x \to 0}\frac{\Delta y}{\Delta x} = \lim_{\Delta x \to 0}\sin\left(2\sqrt{x}\right) \times \frac{\sqrt{x+\Delta x} - \sqrt{x}}{\Delta x} \times \frac{\sqrt{x+\Delta x} + \sqrt{x}}{\sqrt{x+\Delta x} + \sqrt{x}}$$

$$\Rightarrow \lim_{\Delta x \to 0}\left(\frac{\Delta y}{\Delta x}\right) = \lim_{\Delta x \to 0}\sin\left(2\sqrt{x}\right) \times \frac{1}{2\sqrt{x}}$$

$$\Rightarrow \frac{dy}{dx} = \frac{\sin\sqrt{x} \times \cos\sqrt{x}}{\sqrt{x}}$$

(i) $y = f(x) = e^{\sin\sqrt{x}}$

$\Rightarrow \Delta y = f(x+\Delta x) - f(x) = e^{\sin\sqrt{x+\Delta x}} - e^{\sin\sqrt{x}}$

$\Rightarrow \Delta y = e^{\sin\sqrt{x}}\left(e^{\sin\sqrt{x+\Delta x}-\sin\sqrt{x}} - 1\right)$

$$\Rightarrow \Delta y = e^{\sin\sqrt{x}} \times \left(\frac{e^{\sin\sqrt{x+\Delta x}-\sin\sqrt{x}} - 1}{\sin\sqrt{x+\Delta x} - \sin\sqrt{x}}\right) \times (\sin\sqrt{x+\Delta x} - \sin\sqrt{x})$$

Taking $\lim\limits_{\Delta x\to 0}$; we get

$$\Rightarrow \lim_{\Delta x\to 0}\frac{\Delta y}{\Delta x} = \frac{\lim\limits_{\Delta x\to 0} e^{\sin\sqrt{x}} \times 1 \times 2\sin\left(\frac{\sqrt{x+\Delta x}-\sqrt{x}}{2}\right)\times\cos\left(\frac{\sqrt{x+\Delta x}+\sqrt{x}}{2}\right)}{\Delta x}$$

$$= \lim_{\Delta x\to 0} 2e^{\sin\sqrt{x}} \times \frac{\sin\left(\frac{\sqrt{x+\Delta x}-\sqrt{x}}{2}\right)}{\left(\frac{\sqrt{x+\Delta x}-\sqrt{x}}{2}\right)} \times \frac{\frac{\sqrt{x+\Delta x}-\sqrt{x}}{2}}{\Delta x} \times \left(\cos\sqrt{x}\right)$$

$$= \lim_{\Delta x\to 0} 2e^{\sin\sqrt{x}} \times 1 \times \frac{\sqrt{x+\Delta x}-\sqrt{x}}{2\Delta x} \times \left(\frac{\sqrt{x+\Delta x}+\sqrt{x}}{\sqrt{x+\Delta x}+\sqrt{x}}\right) \times \cos\sqrt{x}$$

$$= e^{\sin\sqrt{x}} \times \frac{1}{2\sqrt{x}} \times \cos\sqrt{x}$$

(j) $y = f(x) = \log(\cos x)$

$\Delta y = f(x+\Delta x) - f(x)$

$\Rightarrow \Delta y = \log(\cos(x+\Delta x)) - \log(\cos x)$

$$\Rightarrow \Delta y = \log\left(\frac{\cos(x+\Delta x)}{\cos x}\right)$$

$$\Rightarrow \Delta y = \log\left(\frac{\cos x\cos\Delta x - \sin x\sin\Delta x}{\cos x}\right)$$

$\Rightarrow \Delta y = \log\left(1 + \left((\cos\Delta x - 1) - \tan x\sin(\Delta x)\right)\right)$

$$\Rightarrow \Delta y = \frac{\log\left(1 + \left[\left(-2\sin^2\left(\frac{\Delta x}{2}\right)\right) - (\tan x\sin\Delta x)\right]\right)}{-2\sin^2(\Delta x/2) - \tan\sin(\Delta x)} \times \frac{-2\sin^2(\Delta x/2) - \tan x\sin(\Delta x)}{\Delta x}$$

Taking $\lim\limits_{\Delta x\to 0}$; we get $\lim\limits_{\Delta x\to 0}\frac{\Delta y}{\Delta x} = \frac{dy}{dx} = -\tan x$

(k) $y = f(x) = \frac{3x-2}{4x+5}$

$$\Delta y = f(x+\Delta x) - f(x) = \frac{3(x+\Delta x)-2}{4(x+\Delta x)+5} - \frac{3x-2}{4x+5}$$

$$= \frac{\left[12(x^2 + x\Delta x) - 8x + 15(x+\Delta x) - 10\right] - \left[12(x^2 + x\Delta x) + 15(x) - 8(x+\Delta x) - 10\right]}{(4x+5)(4(x+\Delta x)+5)}$$

$$= \frac{23(\Delta x)}{(4x+5)(4(x+\Delta x)+5)}$$

$$\Rightarrow \frac{\Delta y}{\Delta x} = \frac{23}{(4x+5)(4(x+\Delta x)+5)}$$

Taking $\lim\limits_{\Delta x \to 0}$; we get $\lim\limits_{\Delta x \to 0} \frac{\Delta y}{\Delta x} = \frac{dy}{dx} = \frac{23}{(4x+5)^2}$

(l) $y = f(x) = \tan^{-1}x$

Let $\tan^{-1}x = \theta;\ \theta \in \left(-\frac{\pi}{2}, \frac{\pi}{2}\right)$

$\Rightarrow x = \tan\theta$

and $\tan^{-1}(x + \Delta x) = \theta + \Delta\theta$ ...(1)

$\Rightarrow x + \Delta x = \tan(\theta + \Delta\theta)$ ...(2)

$$\frac{\Delta y}{\Delta x} = \frac{f(x+\Delta x) - f(x)}{\Delta x} = \frac{\tan^{-1}(x+\Delta x) - \tan^{-1}x}{x + \Delta x - x}$$

$$= \frac{(\theta+\Delta\theta)-(\theta)}{\tan(\theta+\Delta\theta) - \tan\theta} = \frac{\Delta\theta \times \cos(\theta+\Delta\theta)\cos\theta}{\sin(\Delta\theta)}$$

Taking $\lim\limits_{\Delta\theta \to 0^+}$ on RHS; we get

$$\text{RHS} = \lim_{\Delta\theta \to 0^+}\left(\frac{\Delta\theta}{\sin\Delta\theta}\right) \times \cos^2\theta$$

$$= \cos^2\theta = \frac{1}{\sec^2\theta} = \frac{1}{1+\tan^2\theta} = \frac{1}{1+x^2} = \frac{dy}{dx}$$

(m) $y = \sec^{-1}x$

Let $\sec^{-1}x = \theta\ \forall \theta \in [0, \pi] \sim \left\{\frac{\pi}{2}\right\}$

$\Rightarrow x = \sec\theta$ and $\sec^{-1}(x + \Delta x) = (\theta + \Delta\theta)$

$\Rightarrow x + \Delta x = \sec(\theta + \Delta\theta)$

$$\frac{\Delta y}{\Delta x} = \frac{f(x+\Delta x) - f(x)}{\Delta x} = \frac{f(x+\Delta x) - f(x)}{(x+\Delta x) - (x)}$$

$$= \frac{(\theta+\Delta\theta)-(\theta)}{\sec(\theta+\Delta\theta) - \sec\theta} = \frac{\Delta\theta\cos\theta\,\cos(\theta+\Delta\theta)}{\cos\theta - \cos(\theta+\Delta\theta)} = \frac{\Delta\theta\,\cos\theta\,\cos(\theta+\Delta\theta)}{-2\sin\left(\frac{\theta+\theta+\Delta\theta}{2}\right)\sin\left(\frac{-\Delta\theta}{2}\right)}$$

Taking $\lim\limits_{\Delta\theta \to 0}$ on RHS; we get

$$\frac{dy}{dx} = \lim_{\Delta\theta \to 0} \frac{\cos^2\theta(-\Delta\theta/2)}{(\sin\theta)\sin(-\Delta\theta/2)} = \frac{\cos^2\theta}{\sin\theta} = \frac{1}{\sec\theta\tan\theta}$$

Case I: When $\theta = 0$; $\sec^{-1}x = 0 \Rightarrow x = 1$

But slope of $\sec^{-1}x$ at $x = 1$ is infinite, therefore the function $\sec^{-1}x$ is non-differentiable at $x = 0$

Now, for $\theta \in (0, \pi/2)$ i.e., $x \in (1, \infty)$ $\tan\theta$ is positive and $\sec\theta$ is positive and $\tan\theta = \sqrt{\sec^2\theta - 1}$

$\Rightarrow \text{RHS} = \frac{1}{\sec\theta\tan\theta} = \frac{1}{x\sqrt{x^2-1}}$ ...(1)

Case II: When $\theta = \pi$; $\sec^{-1} x = \pi$; $x = -1$. But slope of $\sec^{-1} x$ at $x = -1$ is infinite, therefore the function $\sec^{-1} x$ is non-differentiable at $x = \pi$. Now, for $\theta \in (\pi/2, \pi)$ i.e., $x \in (-\infty, -1)$

$\tan\theta$ is negative and therefore $\tan\theta = -\sqrt{\sec^2\theta - 1}$

$\Rightarrow \tan\theta = -\sqrt{x^2-1}$

$$\therefore \text{ RHS} = \frac{1}{\sec\theta\tan\theta} = \frac{1}{-x\sqrt{x^2-1}} \quad \ldots(2)$$

$$\therefore \text{ Form (1) and (2) } dy/dx = \frac{1}{|x|\sqrt{x^2-1}}$$

Aliter:

Proof: Let $f(x) = \sec^{-1} x$. Then, $f(x) = \begin{cases} \tan^{-1}\sqrt{x^2-1}, & \text{if } x \geq 1 \\ \pi - \tan^{-1}\sqrt{x^2-1}, & \text{if } x \leq -1 \end{cases}$

Case I: When $x > 1$, We have, $f(x) = \tan^{-1}\sqrt{x^2-1}$ and $f(x + \Delta x) = \tan^{-1}\sqrt{(x+\Delta x)^2-1}$

$$\therefore \frac{d}{dx}(f(x)) = \lim_{\Delta x \to 0}\frac{f(x+\Delta x)-f(x)}{\Delta x}$$

$$\Rightarrow \frac{d}{dx}(f(x)) = \lim_{\Delta x \to 0}\frac{\tan^{-1}\sqrt{(x+\Delta x)^2-1} - \tan^{-1}\sqrt{x^2-1}}{\Delta x}$$

$$\Rightarrow \frac{d}{dx}(f(x)) = \lim_{\Delta x \to 0}\frac{1}{\Delta x}\tan^{-1}\left\{\frac{\sqrt{(x+\Delta x)^2-1}-\sqrt{x^2-1}}{1+\sqrt{(x+\Delta x)^2-1}\times\sqrt{x^2-1}}\right\}$$

$$\Rightarrow \frac{d}{dx}(f(x)) = \lim_{\Delta x \to 0}\left\{\frac{\tan^{-1}\left\{\frac{\sqrt{(x+\Delta x)^2}-\sqrt{x^2-1}}{1+\sqrt{(x+\Delta x)^2-1}\times\sqrt{x^2-1}}\right\}}{\frac{\sqrt{(x+\Delta x)^2-1}-\sqrt{x^2-1}}{1+\sqrt{(x+\Delta x)^2-1}\times\sqrt{x^2-1}}}\right\}\times\frac{\sqrt{(x+\Delta x)^2-1}-\sqrt{x^2-1}}{\Delta x\{1+\sqrt{(x+\Delta x)^2-1}\times\sqrt{x^2-1}\}}$$

$$\Rightarrow \frac{d}{dx}(f(x)) = \lim_{\Delta x \to 0}\frac{1}{\Delta x}\left\{\frac{(x+\Delta x)^2-1-(x^2-1)}{1+\sqrt{(x+\Delta x)^2-1}\times\sqrt{x^2-1}}\right\}\times\frac{1}{\sqrt{(x+\Delta x)^2-1}+\sqrt{x^2-1}}$$

$$\Rightarrow \frac{d}{dx}(f(x)) = \lim_{\Delta x \to 0}\frac{1}{\Delta x}\left\{\frac{2nx\Delta x+\Delta x^2}{1+\sqrt{(x+\Delta x)^2-1}\times\sqrt{x^2-1}}\right\}\times\frac{1}{\sqrt{(x+\Delta x)^2-1}+\sqrt{x^2-1}}$$

$$\Rightarrow \frac{d}{dx}(f(x)) = \frac{2x}{1+x^2-1}\times\frac{1}{\sqrt{(x+\Delta x)^2-1}+\sqrt{x^2-1}}$$

$$\Rightarrow \frac{d}{dx}(f(x)) = \frac{1}{x\sqrt{x^2-1}}$$

Case II: When $x < -1$.

Proceeding as in Case I, we have $\frac{d}{dx}(\sec^{-1}x) = -\frac{1}{x\sqrt{x^2-1}}$

Hence, $\frac{d}{dx}(\sec^{-1}x) = \frac{1}{|x|\sqrt{x^2-1}}$

TRY YOURSELF

Differentiate the following functions w.r.t x using the first principle of differentiation

(i) e^{2x} (ii) $e^{\sqrt{x}}$ (iii) e^{x^2} (iv) $e^{\sin x}$ (v) $\log \sin x$
(vi) $x\tan^{-1}x$ (vii) xe^x (viii) $\cos^{-1}(ax+b)$ (ix) $\log \sec x$ (x) x^2e^x

ANSWER KEYS

(i) $2e^{2x}$ (ii) $\frac{e^{\sqrt{x}}}{2\sqrt{x}}$ (iii) $2xe^{x^2}$ (iv) $e^{\sin x}.\cos x$ (v) $\cot x$

(vi) $\frac{x}{1+x^2}+\tan^{-1}x$ (vii) $(x+1)e^x$ (viii) $\frac{-a}{\sqrt{1-(ax+b)^2}}$ (ix) $\tan x$ (x) $(2x+x^2)e^x$

Derivatives of Some Standard Functions

The following formulas can be derived by using the Ab-initio method, similar to the example in Illustration 1.

Algebraic functions

1. $\frac{d}{dx}(x^n)=nx^{n-1} \quad ;n\in\mathbb{R}$

e.g. $\frac{d}{dx}(\sqrt{x})=\frac{d}{dx}(x^{1/2})=\frac{1}{2}x^{(1/2)-1}=\frac{1}{2\sqrt{x}}$;

$$\frac{d}{dx}(x^{-3})=-3(x)^{-3-1}=\frac{-3}{x^4}$$

$$\frac{d}{dx}\left(\frac{1}{x^p}\right)=\frac{d}{dx}(x^{-p})=-p\times x^{-p-1}=\frac{-p}{x^{p+1}}$$

$$\frac{d}{dx}(x^0)=0\times x^{0-1}=0 \;\therefore\; \frac{d}{dx}(\text{constant})=0$$

ILLUSTRATION 2: Find the derivative of the following functions

(a) $\text{cosec}^2 x-\cot^2 x$ (b) $x^{\sqrt{5}}$
(c) $|x|$ (d) $x\,|x|$

SOLUTION: (a) $y-\text{cosec}^2 x-\cot^2 x=1 \quad \therefore \frac{dy}{dx}=\frac{d(1)}{dx}=0$

(b) $\frac{dy}{dx}=\frac{d\left(x^{\sqrt{5}}\right)}{dx}=\sqrt{5}\,x^{(\sqrt{5}-1)}$

(c) $y=|x|=\begin{cases}x; & x\geq 0\\ -x; & x<0\end{cases}$ $\therefore$ For $x\geq 0$; $\frac{dy}{dx}=1$ and For $x<0$; $\frac{dy}{dx}=-1$

$\therefore$ we can say $\frac{d(|x|)}{dx}=\begin{cases}\frac{|x|}{x} & ;\ x\neq 0\\ \text{Non-differentiable}; & x=0\end{cases}$

(d) $y=x|x|=\begin{cases}x^2; x\geq 0\\ -x^2; x<0\end{cases}$ $\therefore$ For $x\geq 0$; $\frac{dy}{dx}=2x$ and For $x<0$; $\frac{dy}{dx}=-2x$

$\therefore$ We can say that $\frac{d(x|x|)}{dx}=\begin{cases}2|x| & \forall\, x\neq 0\\ 0 & \forall\, x=0\end{cases}$

Logarithmic and exponential functions:

1. $\dfrac{d}{dx}(e^x) = e^x$
2. $\dfrac{d}{dx}(a^x) = a^x \log a; a > 0$
3. $\dfrac{d}{dx}(\log_e |x|) = \dfrac{1}{x}$
4. $\dfrac{d}{dx}(\log_a |x|) = \dfrac{1}{x \log_e a}; a > 0, a \neq 1$

ILLUSTRATION 3: Find the derivative of the following functions

(a) $x^7 + \log_e x^3$

(b) $e^{5\log_e x}$

(c) $3^{\log_3 x^7}$

(d) $e^x + 3^x + \log_4 x$

(e) $3^{\log_{27} x} + \log_{e^4} x$

SOLUTION: (a) $y = x^7 + \log_e x^3$

$\Rightarrow y = x^7 + 3\log_e \text{x} \Rightarrow \dfrac{dy}{dx} = 7x^6 + \dfrac{3}{x}$

(b) $y = e^{5\log_e x} = e^{\log_e x^5} = x^5 \Rightarrow \dfrac{dy}{dx} = 5x^4$

(c) $y = 3^{\log_3 x^7} = x^7 \Rightarrow \dfrac{dy}{dx} = 7x^6$

(d) $y = e^x + 3^x + \log_4 x \Rightarrow \dfrac{dy}{dx} = e^x + 3^x \log_e 3 + \dfrac{1}{x \log_e 4}$

(e) $y = 3^{\log_{27} x} + \log_{e^4} x \Rightarrow y = 3^{\log_{3^3} x} + \log_{e^4} x \Rightarrow y = 3^{\frac{1}{3}\log_3 x} + \dfrac{1}{4}\log_e x$

$\Rightarrow y = 3^{\log_3 x^{1/3}} + \dfrac{1}{4}\log_e x \Rightarrow y = x^{1/3} + \dfrac{1}{4}\log_e x \Rightarrow \dfrac{dy}{dx} = \dfrac{1}{3}\dfrac{1}{x^{2/3}} + \dfrac{1}{4} \times \dfrac{1}{x}$

Trigonometric functions

1. $\dfrac{d}{dx}(\sin x) = \cos x$
2. $\dfrac{d}{dx}(\cos x) = -\sin x$
3. $\dfrac{d}{dx}(\tan x) = \sec^2 x$
4. $\dfrac{d}{dx}(\cot x) = -\operatorname{cos} ec^2 x$
5. $\dfrac{d}{dx}(\sec x) = \sec x \tan x$
6. $\dfrac{d}{dx}(\operatorname{cos} ecx) = -\operatorname{cos} ec\, x \cot x$

ILLUSTRATION 4: Find the derivative of the following functions:

(a) a $\tan x - b \sec x + x^3$

(b) $7x^3 - \operatorname{cosec} x + \sin x$

(c) $3 \cot x - 5\tan x$

(d) $\dfrac{\tan x + \sec x - 1}{\tan - \sec x + 1}$

(e) $(1 + \cot x - \operatorname{cosec} x) \times (1 + \tan x + \sec x)$

(f) $\dfrac{4\tan(x/4) - 4\tan^3(x/4)}{1 - 6\tan^2(x/4) + \tan^4(x/4)} + \dfrac{1 - \cot^2 x/2}{2\cot x/2}$

(g) $1 + \tan x \tan x/2$

SOLUTION: (a) $y = a\tan x - b\sec x + x^3$

$$\frac{dy}{dx} = a\sec^2 x - b\sec x\tan x + 3x^2$$

(b) $y = 7x^3 - \operatorname{cosec} x + \sin x$

$$\frac{dy}{dx} = 21x^2 + \cos ecx \cot x + \cos x$$

(e) $y = 3\cot x - 5\tan x$

$$\frac{d}{dx} = -3\operatorname{cosec}^2 x - 5\sec^2 x$$

(d) $y = \dfrac{\tan x + \sec x - 1}{\tan x - \sec x + 1} = \dfrac{(\tan x + \sec x) - (\sec^2 x - \tan^2 x)}{\tan x - \sec x + 1}$

$$= \frac{(\tan x + \sec x) - (\sec x - \tan x)(\sec x + \tan x)}{\tan x - \sec x + 1} = \frac{(\sec x + \tan x)(1 + \tan x - \sec x)}{1 + \tan x - \sec x}$$

$= \sec x + \tan x$

$$\frac{dy}{dx} = \sec x \tan x + \sec^2 x$$

(e) $y = (1 + \cot x - \operatorname{cosec} x) \times (1 + \tan x + \sec x)$

$$\Rightarrow y = \left(1 + \frac{\cos x}{\sin x} - \frac{1}{\sin x}\right) \times \left(1 + \frac{\sin x}{\cos x} + \frac{1}{\cos x}\right)$$

$$\Rightarrow y = \frac{(\sin x + \cos x - 1)(\sin x + \cos x + 1)}{\sin x \cos x}$$

$$\Rightarrow y = \frac{(\sin x + \cos x)^2 - 1}{\sin x \cos x} = \frac{\sin^2 x + \cos^2 x + 2\sin x\cos x - 1}{\sin x \cos x}$$

$\Rightarrow y = 2$

$$\Rightarrow \frac{dy}{dx} = \frac{d(2)}{dx} = 0$$

(f) $y = \dfrac{4\tan(x/4) - 4\tan^3(x/4)}{1 - 6\tan^2(x/4) + \tan^4(x/4)} + \dfrac{1 - \cot^2(x/2)}{2\cot(x/2)}$

$$= \tan(4(x/4)) - \cot(2(x/2)) = \tan x - \cot x$$

$$\frac{dy}{dx} = \sec^2 x + \operatorname{cosec}^2 x$$

(g) $y = 1 + \tan x . \tan x/2$

$$= 1 + \frac{\sin x \sin x/2}{\cos x \cos x/2}$$

$$= \frac{\cos(x - x/2)}{\cos x \cos x/2} = \frac{\cos x/2}{\cos x \cos x/2} = \frac{1}{\cos x} = \sec x$$

$$\therefore \frac{dy}{dx} = \sec x \tan x$$

Inverse circular functions

1. $\frac{d}{dx}(\sin^{-1}x) = \frac{1}{\sqrt{1-x^2}}$

   $-1 < x < 1$ or $|x| < 1$

2. $\frac{d}{dx}(\cos^{-1}x) = \frac{-1}{\sqrt{1-x^2}}$

   $-1 < x < 1$ or $|x| < 1$

3. $\frac{d}{dx}(\tan^{-1}x) = \frac{1}{1+x^2}$

   $-\infty < x < \infty$ or $x \in R$

4. $\frac{d}{dx}(\cot^{-1}x) = \frac{-1}{1+x^2}$

   $-\infty < x < \infty$

5. $\frac{d}{dx}(\sec^{-1}x) = \frac{+1}{|x|\sqrt{x^2-1}}$

   $|x| > 1$ or $x \in R-[-1, 1]$

6. $\frac{d}{dx}(\text{cosec}^{-1}x) = \frac{-1}{|x|\sqrt{x^2-1}}$

   $|x| > 1$ or $x \in R-[-1, 1]$

ILLUSTRATION 5: Find the derivatives of the following functions:

(a) $\sin^{-1}\left(\frac{x-3}{2x-5}\right) + \sec^{-1}\left(\frac{2x-5}{x-3}\right)$

(b) $2\sin^{-1}\sqrt{\frac{1-x}{2}}$

(c) $2\tan^{-1}\left(\text{cosec}\tan^{-1}x - \tan\cot^{-1}x\right)$

(d) $\cos^{-1}\sqrt{\frac{\sqrt{1+x^2}+1}{2\sqrt{1+x^2}}}$

(e) $\tan^{-1}\frac{1}{x^2+x+1} + \tan^{-1}\frac{1}{x^2+3x+3} + \tan^{-1}\frac{1}{x^2+5x+7} + \ldots n$ terms

SOLUTION: (a) $y = \sin^{-1}\left(\frac{x-3}{2x-5}\right) + \sec^{-1}\left(\frac{2x-5}{x-3}\right)$

$\Rightarrow y = \sin^{-1}\left(\frac{x-3}{2x-5}\right) + \cos^{-1}\left(\frac{x-3}{2x-5}\right) = \frac{\pi}{2}$

$\Rightarrow dy/dx = 0$

(b) Let $\sin^{-1}\sqrt{\frac{1-x}{2}} = \theta \Rightarrow \sin\theta = \sqrt{\frac{1-x}{2}}$

$\Rightarrow \cos 2\theta = 1 - 2\sin^2\theta = 1 - 2\left(\frac{1-x}{2}\right) = x$

$\therefore 2\theta = \cos^{-1}x$

or $2\sin^{-1}\sqrt{\frac{1-x}{2}} = \cos^{-1}x$ $\qquad \frac{dy}{dx} = \frac{d\left(\cos^{-1}x\right)}{dx} = \frac{-1}{\sqrt{1-x^2}}$

(c) Let $\tan^{-1}x = \theta$ $\qquad \Rightarrow \cot^{-1}x = \pi/2 - \theta$

$y = 2\tan^{-1}(\text{cosec}\tan^{-1}x - \tan\cot^{-1}x) = 2\tan^{-1}(\text{cosec}\theta - \tan(\pi/2-\theta))$

$= 2\tan^{-1}\left(\frac{1}{\sin\theta} - \frac{\cos\theta}{\sin\theta}\right) = 2\tan^{-1}\left(\frac{2\sin^2\theta/2}{2\sin\theta/2\cos\theta/2}\right)$

$= 2\tan^{-1}\tan\theta/2 = 2 \times \theta/2 = \theta = \tan^{-1}x$

$\therefore \frac{dy}{dx} = \frac{d\left(\tan^{-1}x\right)}{dx} = \frac{1}{1+x^2}$

(d) $y = \cos^{-1}\sqrt{\frac{\sqrt{1+x^2}+1}{2\sqrt{1+x^2}}}$

Lets put $x = \tan\theta \Rightarrow \theta = \tan^{-1}x$

$\therefore\ y = \cos^{-1}\sqrt{\dfrac{\sqrt{1+\tan^2\theta}+1}{2\sqrt{1+\tan^2\theta}}}$

$= \cos^{-1}\sqrt{\dfrac{\sec\theta+1}{2\sec\theta}} = \cos^{-1}\sqrt{\dfrac{1+\cos\theta}{2}} = \cos^{-1}\sqrt{\dfrac{2\cos^2\theta/2}{2}} = \cos^{-1}\cos\theta/2 = \dfrac{\theta}{2} = \dfrac{\tan^{-1}x}{2}$

$\therefore\ \dfrac{dy}{dx} = \dfrac{1}{2\left(1+x^2\right)}$

(e) $y = \tan^{-1}\dfrac{1}{x^2+x+1} + \tan^{-1}\dfrac{1}{x^2+3x+3} + \tan^{-1}\dfrac{1}{x^2+5x+7} + \ldots.\ n$ terms

Let $t_1 = \tan^{-1}\dfrac{1}{x^2+x+1} = \tan^{-1}\dfrac{1}{1+x(x+1)} = \tan^{-1}\dfrac{(x+1)-(x)}{1+x(x+1)} = \tan^{-1}(x+1) - \tan^{-1}x$

Similarly $t_2 = \tan^{-1}\dfrac{1}{x^2+3x+3} = \tan^{-1}(x+2) - \tan^{-1}(x+1)$

and $t_3 = \tan^{-1}\dfrac{1}{x^2+5x+7} = \tan^{-1}(x+3) - \tan^{-1}(x+2)$

.

.

.

$t_n = \tan^{-1}(x+n) - \tan^{-1}(x+n-1)$

$\therefore\ y = t_1 + t_2 + t_3 + \ldots\ldots t_n$

$= \tan^{-1}(x+n) - \tan^{-1}x$

$\therefore\ \dfrac{dy}{dx} = \dfrac{1}{1+(x+n)^2} - \dfrac{1}{1+x^2}$

Algebra of Differentiation

Rule 1: The differential coefficient or derivative of a constant is equal to zero; i.e., $\dfrac{d(\text{constant})}{dx} = 0$

Proof: Let $y = f(x) = C$ be a function, where C is a constant.

Now, we increase the variables x and y by Δx and Δy respectively. Since, the function y retains the value C for all values of x, we have $y + \Delta y = f(x + \Delta x) = C$

$\therefore\ \Delta y = f(x + \Delta x) - f(x) = 0$, the ratio of the increment of the function to the increment of argument $\dfrac{\Delta y}{\Delta x} = 0$

$$\Rightarrow\ \frac{dy}{dx} = 0$$

Now, let us observe the geometrical interpretation. The graph of the function $y = C$ is the straight line parallel to the x-axis. Obviously, the tangent to the graph at any one of its points coincides with this straight line and hence, forms a zero angle with the x-axis which means that slope is zero.

Addition and Subtraction Rule

Derivative of sum of two functions is equal to sum of their derivatives as: $\dfrac{d}{dx}[u(x) \pm v(x)] = \dfrac{d}{dx}u(x) \pm \dfrac{d}{dx}v(x)$

The d.c. of the sum of a finite number of differentiable functions is equal to the corresponding sum of the derivatives of those functions i.e., if we have $y = u(x) + v(x) + w(x)$ then $\dfrac{dy}{dx} = u'(x) + v'(x) + w'(x)$

Proof: For the increment of the argument x by Δx we have, $y + \Delta y = (u + \Delta u) + (v + \Delta v) + (w + \Delta w)$

Where Δu, Δv, Δw and Δy are the corresponding increments of the function u, v, w and y

Hence, $\dfrac{\Delta y}{\Delta x} = \dfrac{\Delta u}{\Delta x} + \dfrac{\Delta v}{\Delta x} + \dfrac{\Delta w}{\Delta x}$

$$\therefore\ \lim_{\Delta x\to 0}\frac{\Delta y}{\Delta x} = \lim_{\Delta x\to 0}\left[\frac{\Delta u}{\Delta x} + \frac{\Delta v}{\Delta x} + \frac{\Delta w}{\Delta x}\right]$$

i.e., $\dfrac{dy}{dx} = u'(x) + v'(x) + w'(x)$

Rule 2: A constant factor may be taken outside the derivative sign, i.e., if $y = k.f(x)$ [K = constant], then $\frac{dy}{dx} = K.f'(x)$

Proof: Using the reasoning as in the proof of Rule 1, we have $y = K.f(x)$

$$y + \Delta y = K.f(x + \Delta x)$$

$$\Delta y = K.f(x + \Delta x) - K.f(x) = K[f(x + \Delta x) - f(x)]$$

$$= \frac{\Delta y}{\Delta x} = K\left[\frac{f(x+\Delta x)-f(x)}{\Delta x}\right]$$

$$\lim_{\Delta x \to 0}\frac{\Delta y}{\Delta x} = \lim_{\Delta x \to 0} K\left[\frac{f(x+\Delta x)-f(x)}{\Delta x}\right] = K.f'(x)$$

i.e., $\frac{dy}{dx} = K.f'(x)$

Product Rule

If $y = u.v$ where u and v are two differentiable functions of x. Then $y + \Delta y = (u + \Delta u)(v + \Delta v)$

Therefore

$$\Delta y = (u+\Delta u)(v+\Delta v) - u.v = u\Delta u + v\Delta u + \Delta u\Delta v$$

Thus $\frac{dy}{dx} = \lim_{\Delta x\to 0}\frac{\Delta y}{\Delta x}$

$$= \lim_{\Delta x\to 0}\left[\frac{u.\Delta v + v\Delta u + \Delta u.\Delta v}{\Delta x}\right]$$

$$= \lim_{\Delta x\to 0}\left[u.\frac{\Delta v}{\Delta x} + v.\frac{\Delta u}{\Delta x} + \frac{\Delta u}{\Delta x}.\Delta v\right]$$

$$= \lim_{\Delta x\to 0} u.\frac{\Delta v}{\Delta x} + \lim_{\Delta x\to 0} v.\frac{\Delta u}{\Delta x} + \lim_{\Delta x\to 0}\frac{\Delta u}{\Delta x}.\Delta v$$

$$= u\frac{dv}{dx} + v.\frac{du}{dx} + \frac{du}{dx}.0\,.$$

Hence $\frac{d}{dx}(u.v) = u.\frac{dv}{dx} + v\frac{du}{dx}$

or $(u.v)' = u.v' + v.u'$

It can be remembered as " Derivative of the product of two functions = first function × derivative of second function + second function × derivative of first function.

In case of the product of three functions. i.e., $y = u.\ v.\ w$

Then, $\frac{dy}{dx} = u'\ (v.w) + u.v'.w + (u.v).w'$

In this way we obtain a similar formula for the derivative of the product of any finite number of function

For example if $y = u_1u_2 \ldots.. u_n$, then

$y' = u_1'u_2 \ldots u_{n-1}\, u_n + u_1u'_2 \ldots u_{n-1}u_n + \ldots + u_1u_2 .. u_{n-1}\, u'_n$

Quotient Rule

If $y = \frac{u}{v}$, where u and v are two functions then $\frac{d}{dx}\left(\frac{u}{v}\right)$

$$= \frac{v.\frac{d}{dx}u - u.\frac{d}{dx}v}{v^2}$$

Proof: Let $y = u/v$, where u, v are differentiable functions at all points in its domain and $v(x) \neq 0$.

Therefore $y + \Delta y = \frac{u+\Delta u}{v+\Delta v}$ or $\Delta y = \frac{u+\Delta u}{v+\Delta v} - \frac{u}{v}$

or $\frac{v\Delta u - u\Delta v}{v(v+\Delta v)}$

$$\Rightarrow \lim_{\Delta x\to 0}\frac{\Delta y}{\Delta x} = \frac{v\lim_{\Delta x\to 0}\frac{\Delta u}{\Delta x} - u\lim_{\Delta x\to 0}\frac{\Delta v}{\Delta x}}{v\lim_{\Delta x\to 0}(v+\Delta v)}$$

i.e., $\frac{dy}{dx} = \frac{v.\frac{du}{dx} - u.\frac{dv}{dx}}{v^2}$

Thus $\frac{d}{dx}\left(\frac{u}{v}\right) = \frac{v.\frac{du}{dx} - u.\frac{dv}{dx}}{v^2}$

or $\left(\frac{u}{v}\right)' = \frac{v.u' - u.v'}{v^2}$

ILLUSTRATION 6: Find $f'(x)$ where $f(x)$ is defined as

(i) $5\sqrt{x} + 7 + 3x^{-1/3} + 4\tan x + 5\operatorname{cosec}^{-1}x$

(ii) $\frac{\log_5 x}{\log_8 x}$

(iii) $\frac{e^x - x}{\tan x}$

(iv) $\frac{a^x + \sec x}{\tan x + x^n}$

(v) $x^2\tan x + \frac{e^x}{1+\tan x}$

(vi) $\frac{2x^3 - 7x^2 + 4x + 1}{4x^2 - 3x - 1}$

(viii) $xe^x - \frac{\sin x}{\log x}$

(ix) $\frac{\sin 8x + 3\sin 6x + 4\sin 4x - 3\sin 2x}{\cos 7x + 4\cos 5x + 8\cos 3x + 5\cos x}$

SOLUTION: (i) $y = 5\sqrt{x} + 7 + 3x^{-1/3} + 4\tan x + 5\operatorname{cosec}^{-1} x$

$$\frac{dy}{dx} = \frac{5d\left(\sqrt{x}\right)}{dx} + \frac{d(7)}{dx} + 3\frac{d\left(x^{-1/3}\right)}{dx} + 4\frac{d(\tan x)}{dx} + 5\frac{d\left(\operatorname{cosec}^{-1} x\right)}{dx}$$

$$= 5\times\left(\frac{1}{2}\times\frac{1}{\sqrt{x}}\right) + 0 + 3\times\left(\frac{-1}{3}\times\frac{1}{x^{4/3}}\right) + 4\times\sec^2 x + 5\times\frac{-1}{|x|\sqrt{x^2-1}}$$

$$= \frac{5}{2\sqrt{x}} - \frac{1}{x^{4/3}} + 4\sec^2 x - \frac{5}{|x|\sqrt{x^2-1}}$$

(ii) $y = \frac{\log_5 x}{\log_8 x} = \frac{\log_e x}{\log_e 5} \times \frac{\log_e 8}{\log_e x} = \log_5 8$

$$= \frac{dy}{dx} = \frac{d(\log_5 8)}{dx} = 0$$

(iii) $y = \frac{e^x - x}{\tan x}$

$$\Rightarrow \frac{dy}{dx} = \frac{\left(\frac{d}{dx}(e^x - x)\right)(\tan x) - \left(\frac{d}{dx}(\tan x)\right)\left(e^x - x\right)}{(\tan x)^2}$$

$$\Rightarrow \frac{dy}{dx} = \frac{\left(e^x - 1\right)\tan x - \sec^2 x\left(e^x - x\right)}{\tan^2 x}$$

(iv) $y = \frac{a^x + \sec x}{\tan x + x^n}$

$$\frac{dy}{dx} = \frac{\left(\frac{d}{dx}\left(a^x + \sec x\right)\right)\left(\tan x + x^n\right) - \left(\frac{d}{dx}\left(\tan x + x^n\right)\right) \times a^x + \sec x}{\left(\tan x + x^n\right)^2}$$

$$\Rightarrow \frac{dy}{dx} = \frac{\left(a^x \log a + \sec x \tan x\right)\left(\tan x + x^n\right) - \left(\sec^2 x + nx^{n-1}\right)\left(a^x + \sec x\right)}{\left(\tan x + x^n\right)^2}$$

(v) $y = x^2 \tan x + \frac{e^x}{1 + \tan x}$

$$\frac{dy}{dx} = \left(\frac{d\left(x^2\right)}{dx}\right)\tan x + \left(\frac{d}{dx}(\tan x)\right)x^2 + \frac{\left(\frac{d}{dx}\left(e^x\right)\right)(1 + \tan x) - \left(\frac{d}{dx}(1 + \tan x)\right)e^x}{(1 + \tan x)^2}$$

$$= 2x\tan x + x^2\sec^2 x + \frac{e^x + e^x\tan x - e^x\sec^2 x}{(1 + \tan x)^2}$$

(vi) $y = \frac{2x^3 - 7x^2 + 4x + 1}{4x^2 - 3x - 1}$

$$y = \frac{(x-1)\left(2x^2 - 5x - 1\right)}{(x-1)(4x+1)} = \frac{2x^2 - 5x - 1}{4x + 1}$$

$$\frac{dy}{dx}=\frac{\left(\frac{d}{dx}\left(2x^2-5x-1\right)\right)(4x+1)-\left(\frac{d}{dx}(4x+1)\right)\times\left(2x^2-5x-1\right)}{(4x+1)^2}$$

$$=\frac{(4x-5)(4x+1)-4\left(2x^2-5x-1\right)}{(4x+1)^2}=\frac{\left(16x^2-20x+4x-5\right)+\left(-8x^2+20x+4\right)}{(4x+1)^2}$$

$$=\frac{8x^2+4x-1}{(4x+1)^2}$$

(vii) $y=\dfrac{\sin x+\cos x}{\cos x-\sin x}+\dfrac{\sec x-\tan x}{\sec x+\tan x}$

$$\frac{dy}{dx}=\frac{d}{dx}\left(\frac{\sin x+\cos x}{\cos x-\sin x}\right)+\frac{dy}{dx}\left(\frac{\sec x-\tan x}{\sec x-\tan x}\right)$$

$$=\frac{\left(\frac{d}{dx}(\sin x+\cos x)\right)\times(\cos x-\sin x)-\left(\frac{d}{dx}(\cos x-\sin x)\right)\times(\sin x+\cos x)}{(\cos x-\sin x)^2}$$

$$+\frac{\left(\frac{d}{dx}(\sec x-\tan x)\right)\times(\sec x+\tan x)-\left(\frac{d}{dx}(\sec x+\tan x)\right)\times(\sec x-\tan x)}{(\sec x+\tan x)^2}$$

$$=\frac{(\cos x-\sin x)^2-(-\sin x-\cos x)(\sin x+\cos x)}{(\cos x-\sin x)^2}$$

$$+\frac{\left(\sec x\tan x-\sec^2 x\right)(\sec x+\tan x)-\left(\sec x\tan x+\sec^2 x\right)(\sec x-\tan x)}{(\sec x+\tan x)^2}$$

$$=\frac{(1-\sin 2x)+(1+sin2x)}{(\cos x-\sin x)}+\frac{-2\sec^3 x+2\sec x\tan^2 x}{(\sec x+\tan x)^2}$$

$$=\frac{2}{(\cos x-\sin x)^2}-\frac{2\sec x\left(\sec^2-\tan^2 x\right)}{(\sec x+\tan x)^2}=\frac{2}{(\cos x-\sin x)^2}+\frac{-2\sec x}{(\sec x+\tan x)^2}$$

(viii) $y=xe^x-\dfrac{\sin x}{\log x}$

$$\frac{dy}{dx}=\left(\frac{d}{dx}x\right)\times e^x+\left(\frac{d}{dx}e^x\right)x-\left(\frac{\left(\log x.\frac{d}{dx}\sin x\right)-\left(\sin x.\frac{d}{dx}(\log x)\right)}{(\log x)^2}\right)$$

$$=\left(e^x+xe^x\right)-\left(\frac{\cos x\log x-\frac{\sin x}{x}}{(\log x)^2}\right)$$

(ix) $y=\dfrac{\sin 8x+3\sin 6x+4\sin 4x-3\sin 2x}{\cos 7x+4\cos 5x+8\cos 3x+5\cos x}$

$$y=\frac{N^r}{D^r}$$

Considering N^r

$N^r = \sin 8x + 3\sin 6x + 4\sin 4x - 3\sin 2x$

$= (\sin 8x - \sin 6x) + (4\sin 6x - 4\sin 4x) + (8\sin 4x - 8\sin 2x) + 5\sin 2x$

$= 2\sin x \cos 7x + 4 \times 2\sin x \times \cos 5x + 8 \times 2\sin x \cos 3x + 5 \times 2\sin x \cos x$

$= 2\sin x\,[\cos 7x + 4\cos 5x + 8\cos 3x + 5\cos x]$

$\therefore\quad y = \dfrac{N^r}{D^r} = 2\sin x,\ \dfrac{dy}{dx} = 2\cos x$

ILLUSTRATION 7: Criticize the following proof that 4 = 3

We can write $x^4 = x.\,x^3 = x^3 + x^3 + \ldots\ldots x^3$ (x summands)

Differentiate to obtain $4x^3 = 3x^2 + 3x^2 + \ldots\ldots 3x^2$ (x summands)

$\Rightarrow\ 4x^3 = 3x^2 \cdot x = 3x^3$ and therefore, we get $4 = 3$

SOLUTION: We can write $x^4 = x.x^3 = x^3 + x^3 + \ldots\ldots x^3$ only for $x \in \mathbb{N}$

Therefore the above equation is not an identity of $\mathbb{R}$

$\therefore$ The LHS and RHS functions are not identical functions

Consequently, their derivatives cannot be identically equal

ILLUSTRATION 8: Consider an equation $x^2 + x - 12 = 0. \Rightarrow x^2 - 1 = 11 - x$

Differentiating both sides, we get

$2x = -1$. Again differentiating, we get $2 = 0$. Find the fallacy in the procedure.

SOLUTION: The roots of the equation $x^2 + x - 12 = 0$ are $x = 3$ and $x = -4$

When we have $x^2 - 1 = 11 - x$; we can clearly see that the above equation is not an identity and is only valid for $x = 3$ and $x = -4$. Let $f(x) = x^2 - 1$ and $g(x) = 11 - x$

Now, since the functions $f(x)$ and $g(x)$ are not identical, consequently the derivatives of the two functions are not identical.

Slope of tangent on $f(x)$ at $x = 3$ is $\left.\dfrac{d(f(x))}{dx}\right|_{x=3} = 2x\big|_{x=3} = 6$

Slope of tangent on $g(x)$ at $x = 3$ is $\left.\dfrac{d(g(x))}{dx}\right|_{x=3} = -1$

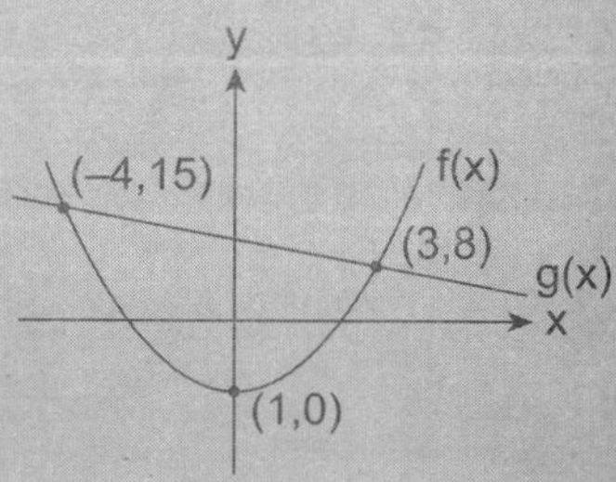

FIGURE 3.1

Similarly slope of tangent at $x = -4$ on $f(x) = -8$ and on $g(x) = -1$. Also; $f'(x) = g'(x)$

$\Rightarrow\ 2x = -1 \Rightarrow x = -1/2$

$\therefore$ At $x = -1/2$; the derivatives of $f(x)$ and $g(x)$ are same but clearly $f(x) = g(x)$ is not satisfied for $x = -1/2$

ILLUSTRATION 9: If f and g are functions whose graphs are shown,

let $u(x) = f(x).g(x)$ and $v(x) = \dfrac{f(x)}{g(x)}$. Then find

(i) $u(2)$

(ii) $v'(6)$

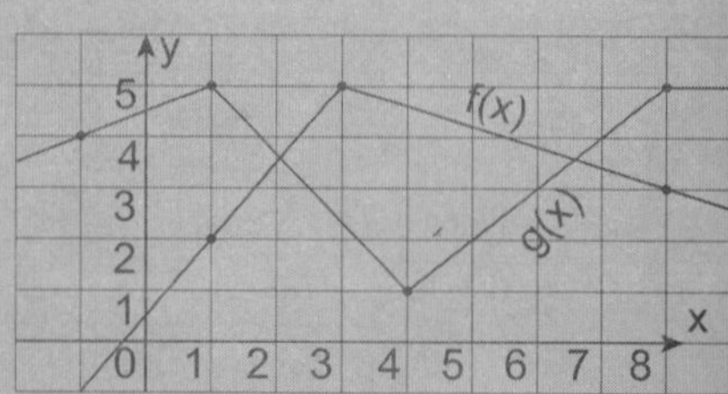

FIGURE 3.2

SOLUTION: $g(x)=\begin{cases}\dfrac{x}{2}+\dfrac{9}{2} & ;x<1\\ -\dfrac{4}{3}x+\dfrac{19}{3} & ;x\in[1,4)\\ x-3 & ;x\in[4,8)\\ 5 & ;x>8\end{cases}$; $g'(x)=\begin{cases}\dfrac{1}{2} & ;x<1\\ -\dfrac{4}{3} & ;x\in[1,4)\\ 1 & ;x\in[4,8)\\ 0 & ;x>8\end{cases}$

$f(x)=\begin{cases}\dfrac{3}{2}x+\dfrac{1}{2} & ;x<3\\ \dfrac{-2x}{5}+\dfrac{31}{5} & ;x\geq 3\end{cases}$; $f'(x)=\begin{cases}\dfrac{3}{2} & ;x<3\\ -\dfrac{2}{5} & ;x\geq 3\end{cases}$

(i) $u(x)=f(x).\,g(x)$

$\Rightarrow u'(x)=f(x).g'(x)+g(x).f'(x)$

$\Rightarrow u'(2)=f(2).\,g'(2)+g(2).\,f'(2)$

$$=\left(\frac{3}{2}\times 2+\frac{1}{2}\right)\left(-\frac{4}{3}\right)+\left(-\frac{4}{3}\times 2+\frac{19}{3}\right)\times\left(\frac{3}{2}\right)=\left(\frac{7}{2}\times-\frac{4}{3}\right)+\left(\frac{11}{3}\times\frac{3}{2}\right)=\frac{5}{6}$$

(ii) $v'(x)=\dfrac{f(x)}{g(x)}$

$$\Rightarrow v'(x)=\frac{(f'(x))g((x))-(g'(x))\times f(x)}{(g(x))^2}\qquad\Rightarrow v'(6)=\frac{f'(6)\times g(6)-g'(6)\times f(6)}{g((6))^2}$$

$$=\frac{\left(\left(-\frac{2}{5}\right)\times(6-3)\right)-\left(1\times\left(-\frac{2}{5}\times 6+\frac{31}{5}\right)\right)}{(6-3)^2}=\frac{\left(-\frac{6}{5}\right)-\left(\frac{19}{5}\right)}{9}=-\frac{25}{45}=-\frac{5}{9}$$

ILLUSTRATION 10: Find the derivative with respect to x of the function:

$(\log_{\cos x}\sin x)(\log_{\sin x}\cos x)^{-1}+\arcsin\dfrac{2x}{1+x^2}$ at $x=\dfrac{\pi}{4}$

SOLUTION: $y=(\log_{\cos x}\sin x)(\log_{\sin x}\cos x)^{-1}+\arcsin\dfrac{2x}{1+x^2}$

$$=\frac{\ell n\sin x}{\ell n\cos x}.\left(\frac{\ell n\cos x}{\ell n\sin x}\right)^{-1}+2\tan^{-1}x$$

$$y=\left(\frac{\ell n\sin x}{\ell n\cos x}\right)^2+2\tan^{-1}x$$

$$\frac{dy}{dx}=2\left(\frac{\ell n\sin x}{\ell n\cos x}\right)\frac{(\ell n\cos x)\dfrac{\cos x}{\sin x}+(\ell n\sin x)-\dfrac{\sin x}{\cos x}}{(\ell n\cos x)^2}+\frac{2}{1+x^2}$$

$$=\left.\frac{dy}{dx}\right|_{\frac{\pi}{4}}=2\frac{(1+1)}{\left(\ell n\frac{1}{\sqrt{2}}\right)}+\frac{2}{1+\left(\frac{\pi}{4}\right)^2}=\frac{2\times 2}{\left(\frac{-1}{2}\right)\ell n2}+\frac{2}{1+\left(\frac{\pi}{4}\right)^2}=-\frac{8}{\ell n2}+\frac{32}{16+\pi^2}$$

ILLUSTRATION 11: Let $P(x)$ be a polynomial of degree 4 such that $P(1) = P(3) = P(5) = P'(7) = 0$. If the real number $x \neq 1, 3, 5$ is such that $P(x) = 0$ can be expressed as $x = p/q$ where 'p' and 'q' are relatively prime, then $(p + q)$ equals

SOLUTION: $P(x) = a(x-1)(x-3)(x-5)(x-b)$

$P'(x) = a[(x-3)(x-5)(x-b) + (x-1)(x-5)(x-b) + (x-1)(x-3)(x-5) + (x-1)(x-3)(x-b)]$

$P'(7) = a[4 \times 2(7-b) + 6 \times 2 \times (7-b) + 6 \times 4 \times (7-b) + 6 \times 4 \times 2]$

$\Rightarrow (7-b)(8+12+24) + 48 = 0$

$\Rightarrow (7-b)(44) = -48$

$\Rightarrow b - 7 = \dfrac{48}{44}$

$\Rightarrow b = 7 + \dfrac{48}{44} = 7 + \dfrac{12}{11} = \dfrac{89}{11} = \dfrac{p}{q}$ where $p = 89$ and $q = 11$

$\therefore\ p + q = 89 + 11 = 100$

ILLUSTRATION 12: Find $\dfrac{dy}{dx}$ for the following functions $y = \cos^{-1}\left[\dfrac{2\cos x + 3\sin x}{\sqrt{13}}\right]$

SOLUTION: $y = \cos^{-1}\left[\dfrac{2\cos x + 3\sin x}{\sqrt{13}}\right]$

$= \cos^{-1}\left[\dfrac{2}{\sqrt{13}}\cos x + \dfrac{3}{\sqrt{13}}\sin x\right]$ Let $\dfrac{2}{\sqrt{13}} = \cos\theta$ and $\dfrac{3}{\sqrt{13}} = \sin\theta$

$\therefore y = \cos^{-1}[\cos\theta\cos x + \sin\theta\sin x]$

$= \cos^{-1}[\cos(x-\theta)]$

$y = x - \theta$; θ is a constant w.r.t. 'x'

$\dfrac{dy}{dx} = 1 - 0 = 1$

ILLUSTRATION 13: Let $f(x)$ be a polynomial function of second degree. If $f(1) = f(-1)$ and a_1, a_2, a_3 are in A.P. Then show $f'(a_1), f'(a_2), f'(a_3)$ are in A.P.

SOLUTION: Let $f(x) = \lambda x^2 + \mu x + \nu$. Then $f'(x) = 2\lambda x + \mu$ also $f(1) = f(-1)$

$\Rightarrow \lambda + \mu + \nu = \lambda - \mu + \nu$

$\Rightarrow \mu = 0$ $\therefore\ f'(x) = 2\lambda x$

$\therefore\ f'(a_1) = 2\lambda a_1,\ f'(a_2) = 2\lambda a_2,\ f'(a_3) = 2\lambda a_3$ as a_1, a_2, a_3 are in A.P.

$f'(a_1), f'(a_2), f'(a_3)$ are in A.P.

ILLUSTRATION 14: Differentiate the following functions

(i) $\sin^{-1}(\sin x)$ (ii) $\sin(\sin^{-1} x)$

(iii) $\cos^{-1}(\cos x)$ (iv) $\cos(\cos^{-1} x)$

(v) $\tan^{-1}(\tan x)$ (vi) $\tan(\tan^{-1} x)$

SOLUTION: (i) As we know $y=\sin^{-1}(\sin x)$ is defined for $x \in R$ and $y \in \left[-\frac{\pi}{2},\frac{\pi}{2}\right]$

$$\therefore \quad y=\begin{cases} -(\pi+x), & -\frac{3\pi}{2}\le x\le -\frac{\pi}{2} \\ x, & -\frac{\pi}{2}\le x\le \frac{\pi}{2} \\ \pi-x & \frac{\pi}{2}\le x\le \frac{3\pi}{2} \end{cases} \quad \text{and so on}$$

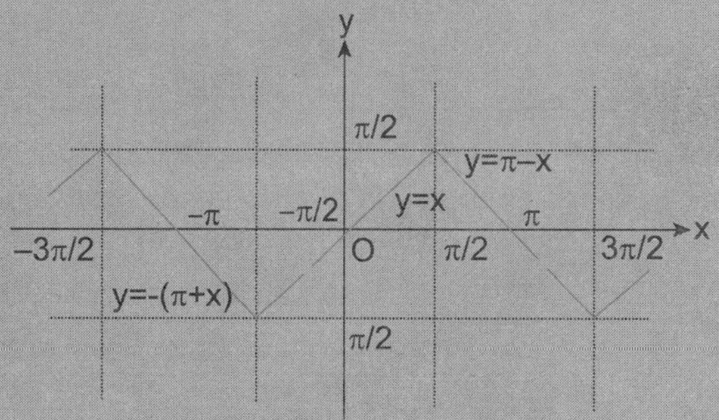

FIGURE 3.3

Graphically shown in Figure 3.3.

$$\text{Thus } \frac{dy}{dx}=\begin{cases} 1, & x\in\left(-\frac{\pi}{2},\frac{\pi}{2}\right)\cup\left(\frac{3\pi}{2},\frac{5\pi}{2}\right)\cup\ldots.. \\ -1, & x\in\left(\frac{\pi}{2},\frac{3\pi}{2}\right)\cup\left(\frac{5\pi}{2},\frac{7\pi}{2}\right)\cup\ldots. \end{cases}$$

(ii) As we know

$y=\sin(\sin^{-1}x)$ is defined for $x \in [-1, 1]$ and $y \in [-1, 1]$

$\therefore \; y=x$ for all $x \in [-1, 1]$

$\Rightarrow \; \frac{dy}{dx}=1$ for all $x \in [-1, 1]$

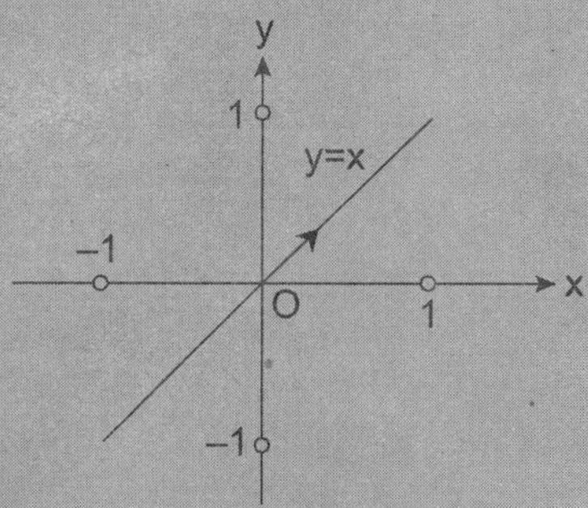

FIGURE 3.4

(iii) As we know,

$$y=\cos^{-1}(\cos x)=\begin{cases} -x, & -\pi\le x\le 0 \\ x & 0\le x\le \pi \\ 2\pi-x & \pi\le x\le 2\pi \end{cases}$$

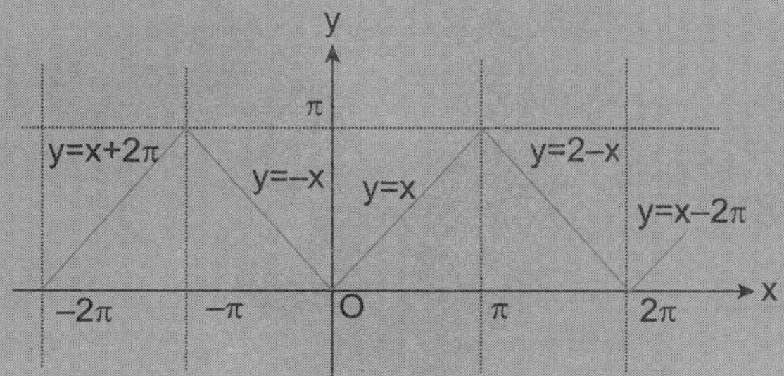

FIGURE 3.5

and so on Shown as; Thus,

$$\frac{dy}{dx}=\begin{cases} 1, & x\in(2n\pi,(2n+1)\pi) \\ -1, & x\in((2n+1)\pi,(2n+2)\pi) \end{cases}$$

(iv) $y=\cos(\cos^{-1}x)=x$

for all $x \in [-1, 1]$

Shown as;

$\Rightarrow \; \frac{dy}{dx}=1$ for all $x \in [-1, 1]$

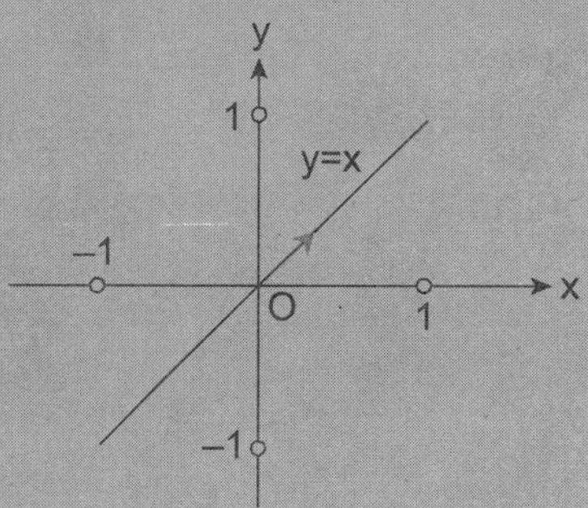

FIGURE 3.6

(v) Here, $y = \tan^{-1}(\tan x) = \begin{cases} -\pi + x, & -\dfrac{3\pi}{2} < x < -\dfrac{\pi}{2} \\ x, & -\dfrac{\pi}{2} < x < \dfrac{\pi}{2} \\ \pi + x & \dfrac{\pi}{2} < x < \dfrac{3\pi}{2} \end{cases}$ and so on

shown as

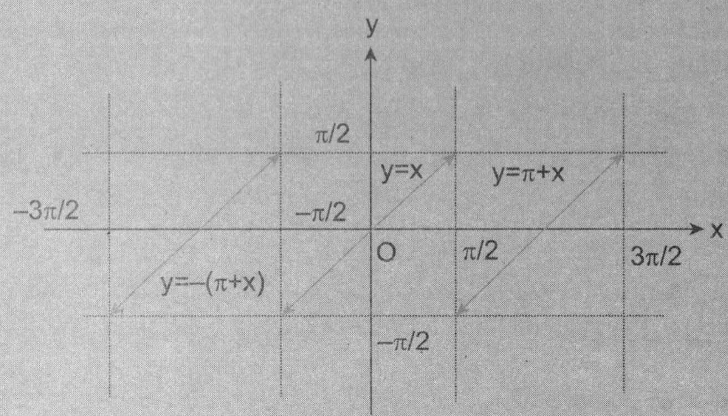

FIGURE 3.7

Thus, $\dfrac{dy}{dx} = 1$

for all $x \in R - \left\{(2n+1)\dfrac{\pi}{2}\right\}$

(vi) Here $y = \tan(\tan^{-1} x) = x$ for all $x \in R$ shown as

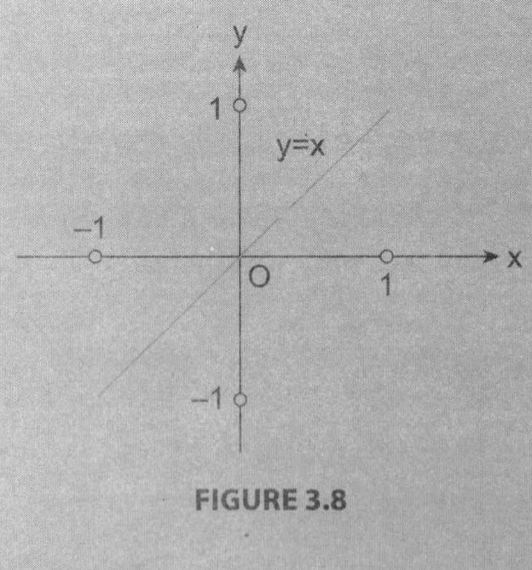

FIGURE 3.8

$\Rightarrow \quad \dfrac{dy}{dx} = 1$ for all $x \in$ R

TEXTUAL EXERCISE–1: (SUBJECTIVE)

1. Find a and b if given

$$y=\frac{5^{\log_{5^{1/4}} x}-9^{\log_{729}(x+1)^6}}{49^{4\log_{2401} x}-x-1}\ \&\ \frac{dy}{dx}=2ax-b$$

2. Prove that derivative of $y = e^x f(x)$ is $e^x(f(x) + f'(x))$ and thus evaluate the derivative of the following:
   (i) $y=e^x\left(\log_e x-\frac{1}{x}\right)$
   (ii) $y = e^x (\tan x + \cos x)$
   (iii) $y = e^x (x^3 + \sin x)$

3. A student made the mistake in writing quotient rule of differentiation and writes $\frac{d}{dx}\left(\frac{f(x)}{g(x)}\right)=\frac{f(x).g'(x)-g(x)f'(x)}{(g(x))^2}$ and still gets correct answer. Let $F(n)=\frac{f(n)}{g(n)}, n\in\mathbb{N}$ then prove that
   (a) $F(n) = F(n + 1)$
   (b) $F(n) = F(n + 2)$
   (c) $\sum_{n=1}^{20} F(n)=\sum_{n=1}^{20} F(2n-1)$
   (d) $F(1), F(2), F(3)$…. From a G.P.

4. Find the values of 'x' for which the rate of change of $\frac{x^5}{7}+\frac{x^3}{3}-x$ is more than that of $\frac{x^5}{7}$.

5. If $f(x) = x^3 g(x)$ where $g(2) = 3$ and $g'(2) = 1$. Find $f'(2)$

Answer Keys

1. $a = 1, b = -1$

2. (i) $y'=e^x\left(\log_e x+\frac{1}{x^2}\right)$ (ii) $y' = e^x (\tan x + \sec^2 x + \cos x - \sin x)$
   (iii) $y' = e^x (x^3 + 3x^2 + \sin x + \cos x)$

4. $x \in (-\infty, -1) \cup (1, \infty)$ 5. 44

TEXTUAL EXERCISE–1: (OBJECTIVE)

1. If $y = (1 - 2 \tan x) (5 + 4\sin x)$ then $\frac{dy}{dx}$ is
   (a) $4 \cos x (1 - 2 \tan x) - 2\sec^2 x (5 + 4\sin x)$
   (b) $4 \sin x (1 - 2 \tan x) + 2\sec^2 x (5 + 4\sin x)$
   (c) $4 \sin x - 8 \sin^2 x \sec x + 10 \sec^2 x + 8 \sin x \sec^2 x$
   (d) None of these

2. If $y=\frac{\sin x}{1+\tan x}$, then $\frac{dy}{dx}$ is equal to
   (a) $\frac{\cos x}{(1+\tan x)^2}$ (b) $\frac{\cos x-\tan^2 x}{(1+\tan x)^2}$
   (c) $\frac{\cos x(1-\tan^3 x)}{(1+\tan x)^2}$ (d) $\frac{\cos x-\tan^3 x}{(1+\tan x)^2}$

3. If $f(x) = \cos x. \cos 2x.\cos 4x.\cos 8x. \cos 16x$, then $f'(\pi/4)$ is
   (a) $\sqrt{2}$ (b) $\frac{1}{\sqrt{2}}$
   (c) 1 (d) None of these

4. If $y=\frac{1}{1+x^{n-m}+x^{p-m}}+\frac{1}{1+x^{m-n}+x^{p-n}}+\frac{1}{1+x^{m-p}+x^{n-p}}$ then dy/dx is equal to
   (a) 1
   (b) 0
   (c) $m + n + p$
   (d) $m - n + p$

5. If $y=\frac{x^4+4}{x^2-2x+2}$ then $\left.\frac{dy}{dx}\right]_{x=1/2}$ is:
   (a) 3 (b) -1
   (c) 4 (d) None of these

6. If $y=\tan^{-1}\left(\frac{\sqrt{1+x^2}-1}{x}\right)$ then
   (a) $y'(0) = 1$ (b) $y'(0) = 1/2$
   (c) $y'(0) = 0$ (d) None of these

7. If $y = \dfrac{\cos 6x + 6\cos 4x + 15\cos 2x + 10}{\cos 5x + 5\cos 3x + 10\cos x}$, then $\dfrac{dy}{dx} =$

(a) $2\sin x + \cos x$ (b) $-2\sin x$

(c) $\cos 2x$ (d) $\sin 2x$

8. Differential coefficient of

$\left(\dfrac{x^{\ell+m}}{x^{m-n}}\right)^{\frac{1}{n-\ell}} \cdot \left(\dfrac{x^{m+n}}{x^{n-\ell}}\right)^{\frac{1}{\ell-m}} \cdot \left(\dfrac{x^{n+\ell}}{x^{\ell-m}}\right)^{\frac{1}{m-n}}$ w.r.t. x is

(a) 1 (b) 0

(c) -1 (d) $X^{\ell mn}$

9. Let $f(x) = \dfrac{\sqrt{x-2\sqrt{x-1}}}{\sqrt{x-1}-1}.x$ then:

(a) $f'(10) = 1$

(b) $f'(3/2) = -1$

(c) domain of $f(x)$ is $x \geq 1$

(d) None of these

10. If $f(x) = \left(\dfrac{x^a}{x^b}\right)^{a+b} \cdot \left(\dfrac{x^b}{x^c}\right)^{b+c} \cdot \left(\dfrac{x^c}{x^a}\right)^{c+a}$, then $f'(x)$ is equal to:

(a) 1 (b) 0

(c) x^{a+b+c} (d) None of these

11. If $y = (1 + x)(1 + x^2)(1 + x^4) \ldots\ldots (1+x^{2^n})$, then $\dfrac{dy}{dx}$ at $x = 0$ is:

(a) 1 (b) -1

(c) 0 (d) None of these

Answer Keys

1. (a)	**2.** (c)	**3.** (a)	**4.** (b)	**5.** (a)	**6.** (b)	**7.** (b)	**8.** (b)	**9.** (a,b,c)	**10.** (b)
11. (a)									

■ CHAIN RULE

If 'y' is a function of 'u' and 'u' is a function of 'x' i.e., let us say $y = f(u)$ and $u = g(x)$ i.e., $y = f(g(x))$

then $\dfrac{dy}{dx} = \dfrac{dy}{du}.\dfrac{du}{dx} = f'(u) \times g'(x) = f'(g(x)) \times g'(x)$

Proof: We have $\dfrac{dy}{dx} = \lim\limits_{h \to 0} \dfrac{y\{u(x+h)\} - y\{u(x)\}}{h}$

$$= \lim_{h \to 0} \frac{y\{u(x+h)\} - y\{u(x)\}}{u(x+h) - u(x)}.\frac{u(x+h) - u(x)}{h} = \frac{dy}{du}.\frac{du}{dx}$$

The above method is called chain rule of differentiation. The chain rule can also be generalized to some extent as

$$\frac{df(g(h(\phi(x))))}{dx} = f'(g(h(\phi(x)))) \times g'(h(\phi(x))) \times h'\phi(x)) \times \phi'(x)$$

REMARK:

It is important to realize that the cancellation is valid because, the chain rule is incomplete in the sense that it does not say clearly, at what points to evaluate the derivatives. We can add this information by writing

$$\left(\frac{dy}{dx}\right)_{x=a} = \left(\frac{dy}{dg}\right)_{g=g(h(a))} \left(\frac{dg}{dh}\right)_{h=h(a)} \left(\frac{dh}{dx}\right)_{x=a}$$

While applying chain rule we work from the outside to inside $\dfrac{d}{dx}\underbrace{f}_{\text{outter function}}\underbrace{(g(x))}_{\text{evaluated at inner function}} = \left(\underbrace{f'}_{\text{derivative of outter function}}\underbrace{(g(x))}_{\text{evaluated at inner function}}\right)\left(\underbrace{(g'(x))}_{\text{derivative of inner function}}\right)$

■ DIFFERENTIATION OF A FUNCTION WITH RESPECT TO ANOTHER FUNCTION

So far we have discussed derivative of one variable, say, y with respect to other variable say, x. In this section, we still discuss derivative of a function with respect to another function

Let $u = f(x)$ and $\upsilon = g(x)$ be two functions of x. Then, to find the derivative of $f(x)$ w.r.t $g(x)$ i.e., to find $\dfrac{du}{d\upsilon}$ we use the following formula $\dfrac{du}{d\upsilon} = \dfrac{du/dx}{d\upsilon/dx}$

(Thus, to find the derivative of $f(x)$ w.r.t $g(x)$ we first differentiate both w.r.t x and then divide the derivative of $f(x)$ w.r.t x by the derivative of $g(x)$ w.r.t. x). Following example will illustrate the procedure.

ILLUSTRATION 15: If $y = \log(\sin x)$ find $\frac{dy}{dx}$

SOLUTION: Given $y = \log(\sin x)$ differentiating w.r. to x.

we get, $\frac{dy}{dx} = \frac{d[\log(\sin x)]}{d(\sin x)} \times \frac{d}{dx}(\sin x) = \frac{1}{\sin x} \times \cos x$

Hence $\frac{dy}{dx} = \cot x$

ILLUSTRATION 16: If $y = e^{(\tan^{-1} x)^3}$ find $\frac{dy}{dx}$

SOLUTION: Given $y = e^{(\tan^{-1} x)^3}$ differentiating w.r. to x.

we get $\frac{dy}{dx} = \frac{d\{e^{(\tan^{-1} x)^3}\}}{d\{(\tan^{-1} x)^3\}} \cdot \frac{d\{(\tan^{-1} x)^3\}}{d(\tan^{-1} x)} \cdot \frac{d(\tan^{-1} x)}{dx}$

$\Rightarrow \frac{dy}{dx} = e^{(\tan^{-1} x)^3}\, 3\,(\tan^{-1} x)^2 \cdot \frac{1}{1+x^2}$.

ILLUSTRATION 17: Find the derivative of the following:

(a) $y = \sin \log e^{3x^3}$ at $x = \sqrt[3]{\pi/2}$

(b) $y = \log \sin x^2$ at $x = \sqrt{\pi/4}$

(c) $y = \sin(\cos x) + \cos(\sin x)$ at $\pi/4$

(d) $y = \log\sqrt{1-x^2}$ at $x = 1/\sqrt{2}$

SOLUTION: (a) $y = \sin \log e^{3x^3} = \sin(3x^3)$

$= \cos 3x^3.9x^2 = 9\times\left(\frac{\pi}{2}\right)^{2/3}.\cos\left(3\times\left(\frac{\pi}{2}\right)\right) = 0$

(b) $y' = \frac{2x}{\sin x^2}.\cos x^2 = 2\left(\sqrt{\pi/4}\right) = \sqrt{\pi}$

(c) $y' = \cos(\cos x)(-\sin x) + (-\sin(\sin x).\cos x)$

$= -\cos\left(\frac{1}{\sqrt{2}}\right)\frac{1}{\sqrt{2}} + \frac{-1}{\sqrt{2}}\sin\frac{1}{\sqrt{2}} = \frac{1}{\sqrt{2}}\left(-\cos\frac{1}{\sqrt{2}} - \sin\frac{1}{\sqrt{2}}\right)$

(d) $y' = \frac{1}{\sqrt{1-x^2}}\frac{1}{2}\frac{-2x}{\sqrt{1-x^2}} = \frac{-x}{1-x^2} = \frac{x}{x^2-1} = \frac{1/\sqrt{2}}{-1/2} = -\sqrt{2}$

ILLUSTRATION 18: If $y = \log_e(\tan^{-1}\sqrt{1+x^2})$ find $\frac{dy}{dx}$?

SOLUTION: Let $y = \log_e(\tan^{-1}\sqrt{1+x^2})$, differentiating w.r.t x, we get

$$\frac{dy}{dx} = \frac{d[\log_e(\tan^{-1}\sqrt{1+x^2})]}{d(\tan^{-1}\sqrt{1+x^2})} \cdot \frac{d(\tan^{-1}\sqrt{1+x^2})}{d(\sqrt{1+x^2})} \cdot \frac{d(\sqrt{1+x^2})}{d(1+x^2)} \cdot \frac{d(1+x^2)}{dx}$$

$$= \frac{1}{(\tan^{-1}\sqrt{1+x^2})} \cdot \frac{1}{1+(\sqrt{1+x^2})^2} \cdot \frac{1}{2\sqrt{1+x^2}}.2x$$

$$= \frac{x}{(\tan^{-1}\sqrt{1+x^2})\{1+(\sqrt{1+x^2})^2\}\sqrt{1+x^2}} = \frac{x}{(\tan^{-1}\sqrt{1+x^2})(2+x^2)\sqrt{1+x^2}}$$

ILLUSTRATION 19: If $y = \cos^{-1}(\cos x)$ then $\frac{dy}{dx}$ find at $x = \frac{5\pi}{4}$

SOLUTION: ***Ist Method:*** Here $x = 5\pi/4 \Rightarrow \pi < x < 2\pi$

$\Rightarrow -2\pi < -x < -\pi \Rightarrow 0 < 2\pi - x < \pi \Rightarrow y = \cos^{-1}\cos x = 2\pi - x$

On differentiating with respect to x, we get $\frac{dy}{dx} = -1$

IInd Method: Here $y = \cos^{-1}(\cos x) \Rightarrow y = \cos^{-1}(\cos 2\pi - x)$

We know when x is around $5\pi/4$ i.e., in third quadrant

$\Rightarrow \{\cos(2\pi - x)\}$ is in the second quadrant

$\therefore \cos^{-1}(\cos(2\pi - x)) = 2\pi - x \Rightarrow y = 2\pi - x$

Hence, on differentiating with respect to x, we get $\frac{dy}{dx} = -1$

ILLUSTRATION 20: If the prime sign (') represents differentiation w.r.t. x and $f'(x) = \sin x + \sin 4x.\cos x$. Then find $f'(2x^2 + \pi/2)$

SOLUTION: Here, $f'(x) = \sin x + \sin 4x.\cos x$

$$\Rightarrow f'\left(2x^2 + \frac{\pi}{2}\right) = \frac{d\{f(2x^2 + \pi/2)\}}{dx} = \frac{df\left(2x^2 + \frac{\pi}{2}\right)}{d\left(2x^2 + \frac{\pi}{2}\right)} \cdot \frac{d\left(2x^2 + \frac{\pi}{2}\right)}{dx}$$

$$\text{Here } \frac{df\left(2x^2 + \frac{\pi}{2}\right)}{d\left(2x^2 + \frac{\pi}{2}\right)} = \left\{\sin\left(2x^2 + \frac{\pi}{2}\right) + \sin 4\left(2x^2 + \frac{\pi}{2}\right).\cos\left(2x^2 + \frac{\pi}{2}\right)\right\} \& \frac{d\left(2x^2 + \frac{\pi}{2}\right)}{dx} = 4x$$

$$f'\left(2x^2 + \frac{\pi}{2}\right) = \{\cos(2x^2) + \sin(8x^2).(-\sin(2x^2))\}.4x$$

$$\therefore f'\left(2x^2 + \frac{\pi}{2}\right) = [(\cos(2x^2) - \sin 8x^2.\sin 2x^2].4x$$

ILLUSTRATION 21: If $y = \tan^{-1}\sqrt{\frac{x+1}{x-1}}$ find $\frac{dy}{dx}$

SOLUTION: Here $\tan^{-1}\sqrt{\frac{x+1}{x-1}}$, put $x = \sec\theta \Rightarrow y = \tan^{-1}\sqrt{\frac{\sec\theta + 1}{\sec\theta - 1}}$,

$= \tan^{-1}\sqrt{\frac{1+\cos\theta}{1-\cos\theta}} = \tan^{-1}(\cot\theta/2)$ $\quad\therefore y = \tan^{-1}\left\{\tan\left(\frac{\pi}{2} - \frac{\theta}{2}\right)\right\}$

$y = \frac{\pi}{2} - \frac{1}{2}\sec^{-1}x$ $\quad\therefore \frac{dy}{dx} = -\frac{1}{2|x|\sqrt{x^2-1}}$

ILLUSTRATION 22: Find the $\frac{dy}{dx}$ for $y = \log_2 \log_3 \log_4 x$

SOLUTION: $y = \log_2 \log_3 \log_4 x = (\log_e \log_3 \log_4 x)(\log_2 e)$

$$y' = \left[\frac{1}{\log_3 \log_4 x} \times \frac{d}{dx}(\log_3 \log_4 x)\right] \times \log_2 e$$

$$= \frac{\log_2 e}{\log_3 \log_4 x}\frac{d}{dx}.(\log_3 e.(\log_e \log_4 x) = \frac{\log_2 e}{\log_3 \log_4 x} \times \frac{\log_3 e}{\log_4 x} \times \frac{d}{dx}(\log_4 x)$$

$$= \frac{\log_2 e.\log_3 e}{(\log_3 \log_4 x)\log_4 x} \times \frac{d}{dx}(\log_4 e \log_e x) = \frac{\log_2 e.\log_3 e.\log_4 e}{(\log_3 \log_4 x)(\log_4 x)(x)}$$

ILLUSTRATION 23: Find the differential coefficient of 'y' with respect to 'x'

(i) $y = \frac{1}{\log \cos x}$ (ii) $\frac{8^x}{x^8}$

SOLUTION: (i) Given $y = \frac{1}{\log \cos x}$.

Let $\log \cos x = \mu$ $\Rightarrow y = \frac{1}{\mu}$ (diffrentiating w.r.t. μ)

$\frac{dy}{d\mu} = -\frac{1}{\mu^2}$, $\mu = \log \cos x$; Let $\cos x = t$

$\Rightarrow \frac{d\mu}{dt} = \frac{1}{t}$ $\Rightarrow \frac{d\mu}{dx} = \frac{d\mu}{dt}.\frac{dt}{dx}$

$\Rightarrow \frac{1}{t}(-\sin x) = -\frac{\sin x}{\cos x} = -\tan x$

$\Rightarrow \frac{dy}{dx} = \frac{dy}{d\mu}.\frac{d\mu}{dx} = \frac{1}{\mu^2}(-\tan x) = \frac{\tan x}{(\log \cos x)^2}$

(ii) $y = \frac{8^x}{x^8}$ Taking log on both sides, we get

$\log y = \log 8^x - \log x^8$ or $\log y = x \log 8 - 8 \log x$

Differentiating w.r.t. x, $\frac{1}{y}\frac{dy}{dx} = \log 8 - \frac{8}{x}$

$\frac{dy}{dx} = \frac{8^x}{x^8}\left[\log 8 - \frac{8}{x}\right]$ or $\frac{dy}{dx} = \frac{8^x}{x^9}[x \log 8 - 8]$

ILLUSTRATION 24: If $y = \frac{\log x}{x} + e^x \sin x + \log_5 x$, find $\frac{dy}{dx}$

SOLUTION: Given is $y = \frac{\log x}{x} + e^x \sin x + \log_5 x$

On differentiating we get

$$\Rightarrow \frac{dy}{dx} = \frac{d}{dx}\left(\frac{\log x}{x}\right) + \frac{d}{dx}(e^x \sin x) + \frac{d}{dx}(\log_5 x)$$

$$= \frac{\left\{\frac{d}{dx}(\log x)\right\}.x - \log x\left\{\frac{d}{dx}x\right\}}{x^2} + \left\{\frac{d}{dx}e^x\right\}.\sin x + e^x\left\{\frac{d}{dx}\sin x\right\} + \frac{1}{x \log_e 5}$$

$$= \frac{\frac{1}{x}.x - \log x.1}{x^2} + e^x \sin x + e^x.\cos x + \frac{1}{x \log_e 5}$$

Hence $\frac{dy}{dx} = \left(\frac{1 - \log x}{x^2}\right) + e^x(\sin x + \cos x) + \frac{1}{x \log_e 5}$

ILLUSTRATION 25: If $y=\frac{x^2}{2}+\frac{1}{2}x\sqrt{x^2+1}+\ln\sqrt{x+\sqrt{x^2+1}}$ prove that $2y = xy' + \ln y'$. Where (') denotes the derivative.

SOLUTION: $y=\frac{x^2}{2}+\frac{1}{2}x\sqrt{x^2+1}+\ln\sqrt{x+\sqrt{x^2+1}}$

$$y'=x+\frac{1}{2}\left[\frac{x^2}{\sqrt{x^2+1}}+\sqrt{x^2+1}\right]+\frac{1}{2\left(x+\sqrt{x^2+1}\right)}\times\left(1+\frac{2x}{2\sqrt{x^2+1}}\right)$$

$$= x+\frac{1}{2}\left[\frac{2x^2+1}{\sqrt{x^2+1}}\right]+\frac{1}{2\sqrt{x^2+1}} = x+\frac{1}{2\sqrt{x^2+1}}[2(x^2+1)]$$

$$y'=x+\sqrt{x^2+1}$$

Also $2y=x^2+x\sqrt{x^2+1}+\ln(x+\sqrt{x^2+1})$

$$= x(x+\sqrt{x^2+1})+\ln(x+\sqrt{x^2+1}) = xy' + \ln y'$$

ILLUSTRATION 26: Differentiate $\frac{\sqrt{1+x^2}+\sqrt{1-x^2}}{\sqrt{1+x^2}-\sqrt{1-x^2}}$ w. r. t. $\sqrt{1-x^4}$

SOLUTION: $v=\frac{\sqrt{1+x^2}+\sqrt{1-x^2}}{\sqrt{1+x^2}-\sqrt{1-x^2}}$

$x^2 = \cos 2\theta$

$$v=\frac{\sqrt{1+\cos 2\theta}+\sqrt{1-\cos 2\theta}}{\sqrt{1+\cos 2\theta}-\sqrt{1-\cos 2\theta}}=\frac{(\cos\theta+\sin\theta)}{(\cos\theta-\sin\theta)}\times\frac{\cos\theta+\sin\theta}{\cos\theta+\sin\theta}=\frac{1+\sin 2\theta}{\cos 2\theta}$$

$v=\frac{1+\sin 2\theta}{\cos 2\theta}$ $\qquad$ $u=\sqrt{1-x^2}$

$v = \sec 2\theta + \tan 2\theta$ $\qquad$ $u=\sqrt{1-\cos^2 2\theta}$

$\frac{dv}{d\theta} = 2\sec 2\theta \tan 2\theta + 2\sec^2 2\theta$ $\qquad$ $\frac{du}{d\theta} = 2\cos 2\theta$

$= 2\sec 2\theta (\tan 2\theta + \sec 2\theta)$

$$\frac{dv}{du}=\frac{2\sec 2\theta(\tan 2\theta+\sec 2\theta)}{2\cos 2\theta}=\frac{\left(\frac{\sin 2\theta}{\cos 2\theta}+\frac{1}{\cos 2\theta}\right)}{\cos^2 2\theta}$$

$$=\frac{(1+\sin 2\theta)}{\cos^3 2\theta}=\frac{1+\sqrt{1-x^4}}{x^6}$$

ILLUSTRATION 27: Differentiate log sin x w.r.t $\sqrt{\cos x}$

SOLUTION: Let u = log sin x and $\upsilon = \sqrt{\cos x}$ Then,

$$\frac{du}{dx}=\cot x \text{ and } \frac{d\upsilon}{dx}=-\frac{\sin x}{2\sqrt{\cos x}}$$

$$\therefore\ \frac{du}{dx}=\frac{du/dx}{d\upsilon/dx}=\frac{\frac{\cos x}{\sin x}}{-\frac{\sin}{2\sqrt{\cos x}}}=-2\sqrt{\cos x}.\cot x.\text{cosec}\, x.$$

ILLUSTRATION 28: Differentiate $\tan^{-1}\left(\frac{1+2x}{1-2x}\right) w.r.t \sqrt{1+4x^2}$

SOLUTION: Let $u = \tan^{-1}\left(\frac{1+2x}{1-2x}\right)$ and $\upsilon = \sqrt{1+4x^2}$. Then,

$u = \tan^{-1} 1 + \tan^{-1} 2x$ and $\upsilon = \sqrt{1+4x^2}$

$$\Rightarrow \frac{du}{dx} = \frac{2}{1+4x^2} \text{ and } \frac{d\upsilon}{dx} = \frac{1}{2\sqrt{1+4x^2}} \times 8x = \frac{4x}{\sqrt{1+4x^2}}$$

$$\therefore \frac{du}{d\upsilon} = \frac{\frac{du}{dx}}{\frac{d\upsilon}{dx}} = \frac{\frac{2}{1+4x^2}}{\frac{4x}{\sqrt{1+4x^2}}} = \frac{1}{2x\sqrt{1+4x^2}}$$

ILLUSTRATION 29: Differentiate x^x with respect to $x \log x$

SOLUTION: Let $u = x^x$ and $\upsilon = x \log x$. Then,

$u = x^x$

$$\Rightarrow u = e^{\log x^x} = e^{x \log x} \qquad \Rightarrow \frac{du}{dx} = e^{x\log x} \times \frac{d}{dx}(x \log x)$$

$$\Rightarrow \frac{du}{dx} = x^x(1+\log x) \text{ and, } \upsilon = x \log x \Rightarrow \frac{d\upsilon}{dx} = x.\frac{1}{x} + \log x = (1+\log x)$$

$$\therefore \frac{du}{d\upsilon} = \frac{du/dx}{d\upsilon/dx} = \frac{x^x(1+\log x)}{(1+\log x)} = x^x$$

Aliter, we have $u = x^x$

$\Rightarrow \log u = x \log x = \upsilon \Rightarrow u = e^{\upsilon}$

$$\therefore \frac{du}{d\upsilon} = e^{\upsilon} = u \Rightarrow \frac{du}{d\upsilon} = x^x$$

ILLUSTRATION 30: If $-\frac{1}{\sqrt{3}} < x < \frac{1}{\sqrt{3}}$, differentiate $\tan^{-1}\left(\frac{3x-x^3}{1-3x^2}\right)$ with respect to $\tan^{-1}\left(\frac{2x}{1-x^2}\right)$

SOLUTION: Let $u = \tan^{-1}\left(\frac{3x-x^3}{1-3x^2}\right)$ and $u = \tan^{-1}\left(\frac{2x}{1-x^2}\right)$

Putting $x = \tan\theta$, we have $u = \tan^{-1}(\tan 3\theta)$ and $v = \tan^{-1}(\tan 2\theta)$

$\Rightarrow u = 3\theta$ and $v = 2\theta$

$$\left[\begin{array}{l} \because -\frac{1}{\sqrt{3}} < x < \frac{1}{\sqrt{3}} \Rightarrow -\frac{1}{\sqrt{3}} < \tan\theta < \frac{1}{\sqrt{3}} \Rightarrow -\frac{\pi}{6} < \theta < \frac{\pi}{6} \\ \Rightarrow -\frac{\pi}{2} < 3\theta < \frac{\pi}{2} \text{ and} -\frac{\pi}{3} < 2\theta < \frac{\pi}{3} \end{array}\right]$$

$$\Rightarrow u = 3\tan^{-1} x \text{ and } \upsilon = 2\tan^{-1} x \qquad \Rightarrow \frac{du}{dx} = \frac{3}{1+x^2} \text{ and } \upsilon = \frac{2}{1+x^2}$$

$$\Rightarrow \frac{du}{d\upsilon} = \frac{\frac{du}{dx}}{\frac{d\upsilon}{dx}} = \frac{\frac{3}{1+x^2}}{\frac{2}{1+x^2}} = \frac{3}{2}$$

TEXTUAL EXERCISE–2: (SUBJECTIVE)

1. Find the derivatives of the following functions w.r.t. 'x'.

   (i) $f(x)=\frac{3x-2}{2x+3}$ (ii) $f(x) = \ln(3x^2 + 4)$

   (iii) $f(x) = \sin^2 x^2$ (iv) $f(x)=x^{x^2}$

   (v) $f(x) = (ax + b)^n$ (vi) $f(x) = x^2 \cos x$

   (vii) $f(x)=\sqrt{\sec x}$ (viii) $f(x) = \cos(\ln x)$

   (ix) $f(x)=\tan\sqrt{x}$

2. If $y = \cos^{-1}(8x^4 - 8x^2 + 1)$ then prove that $\frac{dy}{dx}\pm\frac{4}{\sqrt{1-x^2}}=0$.

3. If $y=\frac{x\sin^{-1}x}{\sqrt{1-x^2}}+\ln\sqrt{1-x^2}$, then prove that $\frac{dy}{dx}=\frac{\sin^{-1}x}{(1-x^2)^{3/2}}$.

4. If $f(x) = |x|^{|\sin x|}$; then find $f'\left(-\frac{\pi}{4}\right)$.

5. If $y=\frac{\sqrt{a^2+x^2}+\sqrt{a^2-x^2}}{\sqrt{a^2+x^2}-\sqrt{a^2-x^2}}$, show that $\frac{dy}{dx}=\frac{2a^2x}{\sqrt{a^4-x^4}.\left(a^2-\sqrt{a^4-x^4}\right)}$.

6. Find $\frac{dy}{dx}$ in each of the following cases.

   (i) $y=\ln\sqrt{\frac{1+\sin x}{1-\sin x}}$ (ii) $y = \ln\{\cot^{-1}(a^{5x+3})\}$

   (iii) $y=\cos^{-1}\left(e^{\sqrt{\tan x}}\right)$ (iv) $y=[\ell n\{\ell n(\sin x^\circ)\}]^7$

   (v) $y=\sin^{-1}\left(\frac{a+b\cos x}{b+a\cos x}\right), b>a$

   (vi) $y=e^{\sqrt{\sin^{-1}(x^2)}}$

   (vii) $y = \tan(a^{1/x})$

   (viii) $y=\frac{e^{2x}+e^{-2x}}{e^{2x}-e^{-2x}}$

   (ix) $y=\cos^{-1}\left(\frac{x-x^{-1}}{x+x^{-1}}\right)$

   (x) $y=\tan^{-1}\left\{\frac{\sqrt{a^2+x^2}+\sqrt{a^2-x^2}}{\sqrt{a^2+x^2}-\sqrt{a^2-x^2}}\right\}$

   (xi) $y=\tan^{-1}\left(\frac{5ax}{a^2-6x^2}\right)$

7. Find the derivative of the following functions:

   (i) $y = 5x^{2/3} - 3x^{5/2} + 2x^{-3}$

   (ii) $y=\frac{\sin x+\cos x}{\sin x-\cos x}$

   (iii) $y = (x^2 + 1)$ arc tan x;

   (iv) $y=\frac{e^x+\sin x}{xe^x}$

   (v) $y=\sin^2\sqrt{1/(1-x)}$

   (vi) $y=\sqrt[3]{\sin^2 x+1/\cos^2 x}$

   (vii) $y=\sqrt[3]{2e^x+2^x+1}+\ell n^5 x$;

   (viii) $y=\sqrt{x+\sqrt{x+\sqrt{x}}}$

8. If $y=\sqrt{\frac{1+e^x}{1-e^x}}$, then show that $\frac{dy}{dx}=\frac{e^x}{(1-e^x)\sqrt{1-e^{2x}}}$

9. Find the differential coefficient of the function $f(x)=\log_x \sin x^2+(\sin x^2)^{\log_e x}$ w.r.t. $\sqrt{x+1}$.

10. Find differential co-efficient of $\tan^{-1}\left(\frac{\sqrt{1+x^2}-1}{x}\right)$ w.r.t. $\cos^{-1}\left(\sqrt{\frac{1+\sqrt{1+x^2}}{2\sqrt{1+x^2}}}\right)$ if $x \neq 0$

Answer Keys

1. (i) $\frac{13}{(2x+3)^2}$ (ii) $\frac{6x}{(3x^2+4)}$ (iii) $2x\sin(2x^2)$ (iv) $x^{x^2+1}\left(1+\ell n x^2\right)$

   (v) $an(ax + b)^{n-1}$ (vi) $2x\cos x - x^2 \sin x$ (vii) $\frac{\sqrt{\sec x}.\tan x}{2}$

(viii) $-\dfrac{\sin(\ell nx)}{x}$ (ix) $\dfrac{\sec^2(\sqrt{x})}{2\sqrt{x}}$

4. $\left(\dfrac{\pi}{4}\right)^{1/\sqrt{2}}\left(\dfrac{\sqrt{2}}{2}\ell n\dfrac{4}{\pi}-\dfrac{2\sqrt{2}}{\pi}\right)$

6. (i) sec x (ii) $\dfrac{-5.a^{5x+3}\ell na}{\cot^{-1}(a^{5x+3})\{1+a^{2\{5x+3\}}\}}$ (iii) $\dfrac{-1.e^{\sqrt{\tan x}}\sec^2 x}{2\sqrt{1-e^{2\sqrt{\tan x}}}(\sqrt{\tan x})}$

(iv) $\dfrac{7\pi}{180}[\ell n\{\ell n(\sin x°)\}]^6\dfrac{\cot x°}{\ell n\sin x°}$ (v) $\dfrac{-\sqrt{b^2-a^2}}{b+a\cos x}$ (vi) $\dfrac{x.e^{\sqrt{\sin^{-1}x^2}}}{\sqrt{\sin^{-1}x^2}.\sqrt{1-x^4}}$

(vii) $\dfrac{-\sec^2(a^{1/x}).a^{1/x}.\ln a}{x^2}$ (viii) $\dfrac{-8}{(e^{2x}-e^{-2x})^2}$ (ix) $-\dfrac{2}{1+x^2}$

(x) $-\dfrac{x}{\sqrt{a^4-x^4}}$ (xi) $\dfrac{2a}{a^2+4x^2}+\dfrac{3a}{a^2+9x^2}$

7. (i) $y'=\dfrac{10}{3\sqrt[3]{x}}-\dfrac{15}{2}x\sqrt{x}-\dfrac{6}{x^4}$ (ii) $y'=-\dfrac{2}{(\sin x-\cos x)^2}$ (iii) $y' = 2x$ arc tan $x + 1$

(iv) $y'=\dfrac{x(\cos x-\sin x)-\sin x-e^x}{x^2e^x}$ (v) $y'=\sin\dfrac{2}{\sqrt{1-x}}.\dfrac{1}{2(1-x)^{3/2}}$ (vi) $y'=\dfrac{2\cos x}{3\sin^{1/3}x}+\dfrac{2\sin x}{\cos^3 x}$

(vi) $y'=\dfrac{2e^x+2^x\ell n2}{3\sqrt[3]{(2e^x+2^x+1)^2}}+\dfrac{5\log^4 x}{x}$ (viii) $y'=\dfrac{1}{2\sqrt{x+\sqrt{x+\sqrt{x}}}}\left[1+\dfrac{1}{2\sqrt{x+\sqrt{x}}}\right]\left[\left(1+\dfrac{1}{2\sqrt{x}}\right)\right]$

9. $\dfrac{2\sqrt{x+1}}{x\ell n^2x}\left[\ell n^2(x).(\sin x^2)^{\ell nx}(2x^2\ell nx.\cot x^2+(\sin x^2))+2x^2.\ell nx(\cot x^2)-\ell n(\sin x^2)\right]$

10. 1

TEXTUAL EXERCISE-2: (OBJECTIVE)

1. The differential coefficient of $e^{2x}.\sin 3x$ is
(a) e^{2x} [3 cos 3x + 2 sin 3x]
(b) e^{2x} [3 cos 3x – 2 sin 3x]
(c) e^{2x} [3 cos$x$ (4cos²x – 3) + 2sin$x$ (3 + 4sin²x)]
(d) None of these

2. If $y = \log_2\{\log_2(x)\}$, then $\dfrac{dy}{dx}$ is
(a) $\dfrac{2\log_2 e}{x\log_e x}$ (b) $\dfrac{1}{x\log_e x\log_e 2}$
(c) $\dfrac{1}{\log_e(2x)^x}$ (d) None of these

3. If $y = e^x\cos^3 x\sin^2 x$, then $\dfrac{dy}{dx}$ is
(a) $e^x\cos^3x.\sin^2x$
(b) $e^x\cos^3x.\sin^2x$ [1 – 3 tan$x$ + 2cot$x$]
(c) $e^x\sin x.\cos^2x$ [sin$x$ cos$x$ – 3 sin²x + 2cos² x]
(d) None of these

4. If $y = \text{cosec}(1 + x^2)$, then $\dfrac{dy}{dx}$ is
(a) $-2x$. cosec $(1 + x^2)$. cot$(1 + x^2)$
(b) $2x$. cosec $(1 + x^2)$. cot$(1 + x^2)$
(c) $2x$. cosec² $(1 + x^2)$. cot$(1 + x^2)$
(d) None of these

5. If $y = \dfrac{1}{\sin x-\cos x}$, then $\dfrac{dy}{dx}$ is
(a) $-\dfrac{(\cos x+\sin x)}{(\sin x-\cos x)^2}$ (b) $-\dfrac{(\cos x+\sin x)}{1-\sin 2x}$
(c) $\dfrac{(\cos x+\sin x)}{(\sin x-\cos x)^2}$ (d) $\dfrac{\cos x+\sin x}{(1-\sin 2x)}$

6. The differential coefficient of cos (log x) is:
(a) $-\sin(\log x)$ (b) $\dfrac{\sin x\log x}{x}$
(c) $\dfrac{\sin x(\log x)}{x}$ (d) None of these

7. If $f'(x) = \sqrt{2x^2 - 1}$ and $y = f(x^2)$, then $\frac{dy}{dx}$ at $x = 1$ is

(a) 2 (b) 1

(c) –2 (d) None of these

8. A differentiable function is defined $\forall\ x > 0$ and satisfies $f(x^2) = x^3\ \forall x > 0$, then $f'(16)$ is equal to

(a) 64 (b) 16

(c) 32 (d) None of these

9. If $f(x) = \tan^{-1}\left(\frac{\sqrt{1+x^2}+\sqrt{1-x^2}}{\sqrt{1+x^2}-\sqrt{1-x^2}}\right)$, then $f'(x)$ equals:

(a) $-\frac{x}{\sqrt{1-x^4}}$ (b) $\frac{x}{\sqrt{1-x^4}}$

(c) $\frac{-x^2}{\sqrt{1-x^4}}$ (d) $\sqrt{1-x^4}$

10. If $y = f\left(\frac{2x-1}{x^2+1}\right)$ and $f'(x) = \sin x$, then $\frac{dy}{dx}$ is

(a) $\frac{1+x-x^2}{(1+x^2)^2}.\sin\left(\frac{2x-1}{x^2+1}\right)$

(b) $\frac{2(1+x-x^2)}{(1+x^2)^2}\sin\left(\frac{2x-1}{x^2+1}\right)$

(c) $\frac{1-x+x^2}{(1+x^2)^2}\sin\left(\frac{2x-1}{x^2+1}\right)$

(d) None of these

11. If $f(x) = 2\tan^{-1}x + \sin^{-1}\left(\frac{2x}{1+x^2}\right)$, then $f'(x) = 0$ in the interval:

(a) $x \in [-1, 1]$

(b) $x \in (-1, 0)$

(c) $x \in [-\infty, -1) \cup (1, \infty)$

(d) None of these

12. If $y = \tan^{-1}\sqrt{\frac{x+1}{x-1}}$, then $\frac{dy}{dx}$ is equal to:

(a) $\frac{-1}{2|x|\sqrt{x^2-1}}$ (b) $\frac{-1}{2x\sqrt{x^2-1}}$

(c) $\frac{1}{2x\sqrt{x^2-1}}$ (d) None of these

13. If $y = \sec(\tan^{-1}x)$, then $\frac{dy}{dx}$ at $x = 1$ is equal to:

(a) $\frac{1}{\sqrt{2}}$ (b) $-\frac{1}{\sqrt{2}}$

(c) 1 (d) None of these

14. If $y = \tan^{-1}\frac{2^x}{1+2^{2x+1}}$ then $\frac{dy}{dx}$ at $x = 0$ is:

(a) 1 (b) 2

(c) $-\frac{1}{10}\ln 2$ (d) None of these

15. If $y = 2\sin^{-1}\sqrt{1-x} + \sin^{-1}2\sqrt{x(1-x)}$, then for $x \in \left(0, \frac{1}{2}\right)$, $\frac{dy}{dx} =$.

(a) $\frac{2}{x\sqrt{1-x}}$ (b) $\sqrt{\frac{1-x}{x}}$

(c) $\frac{-1}{\sqrt{x(1-x)}}$ (d) Zero

16. The derivative of $\sec^{-1}\left(\frac{1}{2x^2-1}\right)$ w.r.t. $\sqrt{1-x^2}$ at $x = \frac{1}{2}$ is:

(a) 4 (b) 1/4

(c) 1 (d) None of these

17. The differential coefficient of $f(\log_e x)$ with respect to x where $f(x) = (\log_e x)$ is

(a) $\frac{x}{\log_e x}$ (b) $\frac{\log_e x}{x}$

(c) $\frac{1}{x\log_e x}$ (d) None of these

18. Differential co-efficient of $e^{\sin^{-1}x}$ w.r.t. $e^{-\cos^{-1}x}$ is equal to

(a) $e^{\pi/2}$ (b) $e^{-\pi/2}$

(d) e^{π} (d) None of these

19. The differential coefficient of $\sin^{-1}\frac{t}{\sqrt{1+t^2}}$ w.r.t. $\cos^{-1}\frac{1}{\sqrt{1+t^2}}$ is

(a) $-1\ \forall\ t > 0$ (b) $-1\ \forall\ t < 0$

(c) $1\ \forall\ t \in \mathbb{R}$ (d) None of these

20. The derivative of the function $f(x) = \cos^{-1}\left\{\frac{1}{\sqrt{13}}(2\cos x - 3\sin x)\right\} + \sin^{-1}\left\{\frac{1}{\sqrt{13}}(2\cos x + 3\sin x)\right\}$ w.r.t. $\sqrt{1+x^2}$ at $x = \frac{3}{4}$ is

(a) $\frac{3}{2}$ (b) $\frac{5}{2}$

(c) $\frac{10}{3}$ (d) 0

21. What is the derivative of $\tan^{-1}\dfrac{\sqrt{1+x^2}-1}{x}$ with respect to $\cot^{-1}\sqrt{\dfrac{1+\sqrt{1+x^2}}{2\sqrt{1+x^2}}}$ is

(a) 2/3 (b) 1/4
(c) 1 for $x > 0$ (d) -1 for $x < 0$

Answer Keys

1. (a)	**2.** (b)	**3.** (b,c)	**4.** (a)	**5.** (a,b)	**6.** (a)	**7.** (a)	**8.** (d)	**9.** (a)	**10.** (b)
11. (c)	**12.** (a)	**13.** (a)	**14.** (c)	**15.** (d)	**16.** (a)	**17.** (c)	**18.** (a)	**19.** (b)	**20.** (c)
21. (c,d)									

ORDER OF DERIVATIVE AND HIGHER DIFFERENTIAL COEFFICIENT

If $f(x)$ is a function, then the derivative of $f(x)$ w.r.t x; i.e $f'(x)$ is also a function and because the derivative of a function is a function, the process of differentiation can be applied over and over, till the derivative becomes a non-differentiable function.

To get the proper understanding of the higher order differential coefficients. We shall call $\dfrac{dy}{dx}$ as the first order derivative of y with respect to x and the derivative of $\dfrac{dy}{dx}$ w.r.t x as the second order derivative of y w.r.t. x and will be denoted by $\dfrac{d^2y}{dx^2}$. Similarly the derivative of $\dfrac{d^2y}{dx^2}$ w.r.t x will be termed as the third order derivative of y w.r.t and will be denoted by $\dfrac{d^3y}{dx^3}$ and so on. The nth order derivative of $\dfrac{d^{n-1}y}{dx^{n-1}}$ w.r.t x will be denoted by $\dfrac{d^ny}{dx^n}$.

For example, consider $y = x \cos x$. Then $y' = f'(x) = -x \sin x + \cos x$ and $y'' = f''(x) = \dfrac{d}{dx}\left(\dfrac{dy}{dx}\right) = \dfrac{d^2y}{dx^2}$

$= -x\cos x - \sin x - \sin x = -x\cos x - 2\sin x$

Similarly $y''' = x\sin x - \cos x - 2\cos x$

$= x\sin x - 3\cos x$

NOTE:

1. *$\dfrac{d}{dx}\left(\dfrac{dy}{dx}\right)$ does not mean multiplication of $\dfrac{d}{dx}$ and $\dfrac{dy}{dx}$. It means the second order derivative of y w.r.t x i.e., "the derivative of the derivative"*
2. *$\dfrac{d}{dx}\left(\dfrac{d}{dx}\right)$ can also be represented as y_2 or y'' or $\dfrac{d^2y}{dx^2}$ or $f''(x)$ (where $y = f(x)$)*
3. *Note that $\dfrac{d^2y}{dx^2}$ and $\left(\dfrac{dy}{dx}\right)^2$ are two different things. Similarly $f^2(x)$ and $(f(x))^2$ represent the second order derivative and the square of the first order derivative of y w.r.t x respectively.*

As we already know that $\dfrac{dy}{dx}$ represents the rate of change of y w.r.t x and hence $\dfrac{d^2y}{dx^2}$ represents the rate of change of $\left(\dfrac{dy}{dx}\right)$ i.e the rate of change of the rate of change or we can also say, that it is the rate of change of slope

For example: If the position function of a car that moves in a straight line is given by $s = s(t)$; then $\dfrac{ds}{dt} = s'(t) = v(t)$ i.e velocity as a function of (t). Similarly

$$\frac{d^2s}{dt^2} = \frac{d}{dt}\left(\frac{ds}{dt}\right) = \frac{d}{dt}(s'(t)) = s''(t)$$

$= \dfrac{d}{dt}(v(t)) = v'(t) = a(t)$ i.e., the acceleration as a function of 't' and there by $\dfrac{d^3s}{dt^3} = \dfrac{d}{dt}\left(\dfrac{d^2s}{dt^2}\right) = \dfrac{d}{dt}(a) = j$ known as the jerk i.e rate of change of acceleration w.r.t time

Rules of Higher Order Derivative

1. If k is a constant then $\frac{d^2}{dx^2}(k(f(x))) = k\frac{d^2}{dx^2}(f(x))$

Proof: LHS: $\frac{d^2}{dx^2}(k(f(x))) = \frac{d}{dx}\left(\frac{d}{dx}(kf(x))\right)$

$= \frac{d}{dx}\left(k\left(\frac{d}{dx}f(x)\right)\right) = k\left(\frac{d}{dx}\left(\frac{d}{dx}(f(x))\right)\right)$

$= k\frac{d^2}{dx^2}(f(x))$

2. $\frac{d^2}{dx^2}(f(x) \pm g(x)) = \frac{d^2}{dx^2}(f(x)) \pm \frac{d^2}{dx^2}(g(x))$

Proof: LHS $= \frac{d}{dx}\left(\frac{d}{dx}(f(x) \pm g(x))\right)$

$= \frac{d}{dx}\left(\frac{d}{dx}(f(x)) \pm \frac{d}{dx}(g(x))\right)$

$= \frac{d^2}{dx^2}f(x) \pm \frac{d^2}{dx^2}(g(x))$

3. $\frac{d^2}{dx^2}(uv) = u\frac{d^2v}{dx^2} + 2\times\frac{du}{dx}\times\frac{dv}{dx} + v\frac{d^2u}{dx^2}$ where u, v are function of 'x'

Proof: LHS: $\frac{d}{dx}\left(\frac{d}{dx}(u.v)\right) = \frac{d}{dx}(u.v' + v.u')$

$= \frac{d}{dx}(u.v') + \frac{d}{dx}(v.u')$

$= (u'v' + u.v'') + (v'.u' + v.u'')$

$= u.v'' + 2u'v' + v.u''$

$= u\times\frac{d^2v}{dx^2} + 2\times\frac{du}{dx}\times\frac{dv}{dx} + v\times\frac{d^2u}{dx^2}$

4. $\frac{d^3(uv)}{dx^3} = u\frac{d^3v}{dx^3} + 3\times\frac{du}{dx}\times\frac{d^2v}{dx^2} + 3\times\frac{dv}{dx}\times\frac{d^2u}{dx^2} + v\times\frac{d^3u}{dx^3}$

Where u,v are functions of 'x'

Proof: LHS: $\frac{d}{dx}\left(\frac{d}{dx}\left(\frac{d}{dx}(uv)\right)\right)$

$= \frac{d}{dx}\left(\frac{d}{dx}(u.v' + v.u')\right) = \frac{d}{dx}(u.v'' + 2u'v' + v.u'')$

$= \frac{d}{dx}(u.v'') + 2\frac{d}{dx}(u'v') + \frac{d}{dx}(v.u'')$

$= (u'.v'' + u.v''') + 2(u'v'' + v'u'') + (v'.u'' + v.u''')$

$= uv''' + 3uv'' + 3vu'' + vu'''$ = RHS

5. If $y = f(u)$ and $u = g(x)$; then $\frac{d^2y}{dx^2} = \frac{d^2y}{du^2}\left(\frac{du}{dx}\right)^2 + \frac{dy}{du}\times\frac{d^2u}{dx^2}$

Proof: LHS $= \frac{d}{dx}\left(\frac{dy}{dx}\right) = \frac{d}{dx}\left(\frac{dy}{du}\times\frac{du}{dx}\right)$

$= \left(\left(\frac{d}{dx}\left(\frac{dy}{du}\right)\right)\times\left(\frac{du}{dx}\right)\right) + \left(\left(\frac{d}{dx}\times\left(\frac{du}{dx}\right)\right)\times\frac{dy}{du}\right)$

$= \left(\left(\frac{d}{du}\left(\frac{dy}{du}\right)\times\frac{du}{dx}\right)\times\left(\frac{du}{dx}\right)\right) + \left(\frac{d^2u}{dx^2}\times\frac{dy}{du}\right)$

$= \frac{d^2y}{du^2}\times\left(\frac{du}{dx}\right)^2 + \frac{d^2u}{dx^2}\times\frac{dy}{du}$ = R.H.S.

ILLUSTRATION 31: If $f(x) = (\cos x + i \sin x)(\cos 3x + i \sin 3x)....(\cos(2n-1)x + i\sin(2n-1)x)$ then $f''(x)$ is equal to

(a) $n^2f(x)$ (b) $-n^4f(x)$

(c) $-n^2f(x)$ (d) $n^4f(x)$

SOLUTION: (b) We have, $f(x) = \cos(x + 3x + ...+(2n-1)x) + i\sin(x + 3x + ...+(2n-1)x)$
$= \cos n^2x + i\sin n^2x$

$\Rightarrow f'(x) = -n^2(\sin n^2x) + n^2(i\cos n^2x)$

$\Rightarrow f''(x) = -n^4\cos n^2x - n^4 i\sin n^2x = -n^4 f(x)$

ILLUSTRATION 32: If $f: R \to R$ is a function such that $f(x) = x^3 + x^2f'(1) + xf''(2) + f'''(3)$ for all $x \in R$ then prove that $f(2) = f(1) - f(0)$.

SOLUTION: $f(x) = x^3 + x^2f'(1) + xf''(2) + f'''(3)$

$f(x) = x^3 + ax^2 + bx + c$ where $f'(1) = a$, $f'(2) = b$ and $f'''(3) = c$

$\Rightarrow f'(x) = 3x^2 + 2ax + b$ $\Rightarrow f'(1) = 3 + 2a + b$

$\therefore\ a = 3 + 2a + b$ $\Rightarrow\ a + b + 3 = 0$ ...(1)

Now, $f''(x) = 6x + 2a$ $\Rightarrow f''(2) = 12 + 2a$

$\therefore\ b - 12 = 2a$ $\Rightarrow\ 2a - b + 12 = 0$ ...(2)

Again, $f'''(x) = 6$ $\Rightarrow f'''(3) = 6$

$\Rightarrow c = 6$

Simultaneously solving (1) and (2); we get $a = -5$ and $b = 2$

$f(x) = x^3 - 5x^2 + 2x + 6$

Now, $f(0) = 6$

and $f(1) = 1 - 5 + 2 + 6 = 4$

and $f(2) = 8 - 20 + 4 + 6 = -2$

$\therefore\ f(2) = f(1) - f(0)$

ILLUSTRATION 33: The function $f: R \to R$ satisfies $f(x^2).\,f''(x) = f'(x).\,f'(x^2)$ for all real x. Given that $f(1) = 1$ and $f'''(1) = 8$, compute the value of $f'(1) + f''(1)$.

SOLUTION: $f(x^2).\,f''(x) = f'(x).\,f'(x^2)$ ...(1)

$\Rightarrow\ 2xf'(x^2)\,f''(x) + f(x^2)\,f'''(x) = f''(x)\,f(x^2) + 2f''(x^2)\,f(x)$ ...(2)

Putting $x = 1$ in equation (2), we get

$2f'(1)\,f''(1) + f(1)\,f'''(1) = f''(1) + f(1) + f''(1)$

$\Rightarrow\ 2f'(1)\,f''(1) + 1 \times 8 = 3f''(1)\,f'(1)$

$\Rightarrow\ f'(1)\,f''(1) = 8$ ...(3)

Putting $x = 1$ in (1), we get, $f(1)\,f''(1) = f'(1)\,f'(1)$

$\Rightarrow f''(1) = (f'(1))^2$

$\Rightarrow f'(1).\,(f'(1))^2 = 8 \Rightarrow f'(1) = 2 \Rightarrow f''(1) = 4 \Rightarrow f'(1) + f''(1) = 6$

ILLUSTRATION 34: If $y = \dfrac{2}{\sqrt{a^2 - b^2}}\left(\tan^{-1}\left(\sqrt{\dfrac{a-b}{a+b}}\tan\dfrac{x}{2}\right)\right)$, then show $\dfrac{d^2y}{dx^2} = \dfrac{b\sin x}{(a+b\cos)^2}$

SOLUTION: $y = A\tan^{-1}\left(B\tan\dfrac{x}{2}\right)$; where $A = \dfrac{2}{\sqrt{a^2-b^2}}; B = \sqrt{\dfrac{a-b}{a+b}}$

$$AB = \frac{2}{\sqrt{(a-b)(a+b)}}\sqrt{\frac{a-b}{a+b}} \Rightarrow AB = \frac{2}{a+b}$$

$$\frac{dy}{dx} = \frac{A\,B\sec^2\frac{x}{2}\frac{1}{2}}{1 + B^2\tan^2\frac{x}{2}} = \frac{1}{a+b}\frac{(a+b)}{(a+b)\cos^2\frac{x}{2} + (a-b)\sin^2\frac{x}{2}}$$

$$\frac{dy}{dx} = \frac{1}{a + b\cos x} \quad \text{...(i)}$$

$$\Rightarrow \frac{d\ y}{dx^2} \quad \frac{b\sin x}{(a\quad b\cos x)^2}$$

TEXTUAL EXERCISE–3: (SUBJECTIVE)

1. Find the second order derivatives of each of the following functions
   (i) $\sin(\log x)$ (ii) $\log(\log x)$

2. If $y = x^3 \log x$, prove that $\frac{d^4y}{dx^4} = \frac{6}{x}$

3. If $y = \frac{\log x}{x}$, show that $\frac{d^2y}{dx^2} = \frac{2\log x - 3}{x^3}$

4. Find $\frac{d^2y}{dx^2}$; where $y = \log\left(\frac{x^2}{e^2}\right)$

5. If $y = x\log\frac{x}{a+bx}$, then show that $x^3\frac{d^2y}{dx^2} = \left(x\frac{dy}{dx} - y\right)^2$

6. If $y = \sin^{-1} x$, show that $\frac{d^2y}{dx^2} = \frac{x}{\left(1-x^2\right)^{3/2}}$

7. If $y = A\cos(\log x) + B\sin(\log x)$, prove that $x^2\frac{d^2y}{dx^2} + x\frac{dy}{dx} + y = 0$.

8. If $y = \tan x + \sec x$, prove that $\frac{d\ y}{dx}\quad \frac{\cos x}{(1\ \ \sin\ )}$

9. If $y = \tan x$, prove that $y_2 = 2yy_1$

10. If $e^y(x + 1) = 1$, show that $\frac{d^2y}{dx^2} = \left(\frac{dy}{dx}\right)^2$

Answer Keys

1. (i) $\frac{-\sin(\log x) - \cos\log x}{x^2}$ (ii) $\frac{-(1+\log x)}{(x\log x)^2}$

4. $\frac{-2}{x^2}$

TEXTUAL EXERCISE–3: (OBJECTIVE)

1. If $y = \frac{1}{2x^2+3x+1}$, then $\frac{d^2y}{dx^2}$ at $x = -2$ is
   (a) $\frac{38}{27}$ (b) $-\frac{38}{27}$
   (c) $\frac{27}{38}$ (d) None of these

2. If $y = x + e^x$ then $\frac{d^2x}{dy^2}$ is:
   (a) e^x (b) $-\frac{e^x}{(1+e^x)^3}$
   (c) $-\frac{e^x}{(1+e^x)^2}$ (d) $\frac{1}{(1+e^x)^2}$

3. If $y = ae^{mx} + be^{-mx}$ then y_2 is equal to
   (a) y^2 (b) my
   (c) m^2y (d) my^2

4. If $y = \tan^{-1}\left(\frac{\ell n\left(\frac{e}{x^2}\right)}{\ell n\left(ex^2\right)}\right) + \tan^{-1}\frac{3+2\ell nx}{1-6\ell nx}; x \in \left(\frac{1}{\sqrt{e}}, \sqrt[6]{e}\right)$, then $\frac{d^2y}{dx^2}$ equal to
   (a) 2 (b) 1
   (c) 1 (d) –1

5. Let $f(x)$ be a quadratic expression which is positive for all real x. If $g(x) = f(x) + f'(x) + f''(x)$, then for any real x, which one is correct
   (a) $g(x) < 0$ (b) $g(x) > 0$
   (c) $g(x) = 0$ (d) $g(x) \geq 0$

6. If $x^2y + y^3 = 2$, then the value of $\frac{d^2y}{dx^2}$ at the point (1, 1) is
   (a) $-\frac{3}{4}$ (b) $-\frac{3}{8}$
   (c) $-\frac{5}{12}$ (d) None of these

7. Let $f(x)$ be a polynomial in x. Then the second derivative of $f(e^x)$ is:
   (a) $f''(e^x).\ e^x + f'(e^x)$
   (b) $f''(e^x).\ e^{2x} + f'(e^x).\ e^{2x}$
   (c) $f''(e^x).e^{2x}$
   (d) $f''(e^x).\ e^{2x} + f'(e^x).e^x$

Answer Keys

1. (a) **2.** (b) **3.** (b) **4.** (c) **5.** (b) **6.** (b) **7.** (d)

LOGARITHMIC AND EXPONENTIAL DIFFERENTIATION

Differentiation of function which are either product of a number of functions or are in the form $(f(x))^{g(x)}$ is usually done by application of logarithms

Case I: Differentiation of a function which is the product of a number of functions

Let $u_1\, u_2\, u_3$ .... Where u_k represent $f_k(x)$ then, taking $\log_e$ on both sides, we get $\log_e y = (\log_e(u_1) + \log_e(u_2) + \log_e(u_3) + \ldots)$

Differentiating, both sides w.r.t x; we get

$$\frac{1}{y}\times\frac{dy}{dx}=\left(\frac{1}{u_1}\times\frac{du_1}{dx}+\frac{1}{u_2}\times\frac{du_2}{dx}+\frac{1}{u_3}\times\frac{du_3}{dx}+\ldots\right)$$

$$\Rightarrow \frac{dy}{dx}=f(x).\left(\frac{u'_1}{u_1}+\frac{u'_2}{u_2}+\frac{u'_3}{u_3}+\ldots\right)$$

Algorithm to Find Logarithmic Differentiation

1. Take natural logarithms of both sides of the equation $y = f(x)$
2. Simplify the equation by using the laws of logarithm.
3. Differentiate both sides with respect to x
4. Solve the resulting equation for $\frac{dy}{dx}$

If $f(x)$ in not a positive valued function for all x belonging to the domain of $f(x)$, then $\ln(f(x))$ is not defined through the domain of $(f(x))$.

When $f(x) > 0$ then consider $y = f(x)$ ...(1)

And $f(x) < 0$ then consider $-y = -f(x)$ ...(2)

Taking log on both sides of equation (i) we get, $ln(y) = \ln f(x)$

Differentiating, we get $\frac{1}{y}\times y'=\frac{1}{f(x)}\times f'(x)$

$$\Rightarrow y'=y\left(\frac{f'(x)}{f(x)}\right)$$

And similarly taking $\log_e$ on both sides of equation (2), we get $\ln(-y) = \ln(-f(x))$

Differentiating, we get $\frac{1}{-y}\times(-y')=\frac{1}{-f(x)}\times(f'(x))$

$$\Rightarrow y'=y\left(\frac{f'(x)}{f(x)}\right)$$

Now, instead of taking two cases, every time, we can simply take the modulus on both sides of equation (1)

And there by after taking $\log_e$, we get

$\ln|y| = \ln|f(x)|$

$$\Rightarrow \frac{1}{|y|}\times\frac{|y|}{y}\times y'=\frac{1}{|f(x)|}\times\frac{|f(x)|}{f(x)}\times f'(x)$$

$$\Rightarrow y'\left(\frac{f'(x)}{f(x)}\right)\sigma$$

The above argument can be illustrated better, using the following example

Example: Let $y = f(x) = x^2 - 5x - 6$

Now $f(x) = (x - 2)(x - 3)$ and

$f(x) > 0\ \forall x \in (-\infty, 2) \cup (3, \infty)$

$f(x) \le 0\ \forall x \in [2, 3]$

$\therefore$ For $x \in [-\infty, 2] \cup (3, \infty)$, consider $y = f(x)$

$\Rightarrow y = x^2 - 5x - 6$

$\Rightarrow \ln(y) = \ln(x^2 - 5x - 6)$

Differentiation, we get $\frac{1}{y}\ y'=\frac{1}{x^2-5x-6}\times 2x-5$

$\Rightarrow y'\ 2x - 5$ ...(1)

Again for $x \in [2, 3]$

Consider $-y = -f(x) \Rightarrow -y = -(x^2 - 5x - 6)$

$\Rightarrow \ln(-y) = \ln(-x^2 + 5x + 6)$

Differentiating, we get

$$\frac{1}{-y}\times -y'=\frac{1}{-x^2+5x+6}\times 2x+5$$

$\Rightarrow y' = 2x - 5$ ...(2)

$\therefore$ From (1) and (2); we get $y' = 2x - 5$

Although, all these efforts could have been saved, if we had instead taken the modulus on both sides in the very first step only.

$|y| = |x^2 - 5x - 6|$

$\Rightarrow |y| = |x^2 - 5x - 6|$

$\Rightarrow \ln|y| = \ln|x^2 - 5x - 6|$

$$\Rightarrow \frac{1}{|y|}\times\frac{|y|}{y}\times y'=\frac{1}{|x^2+5x+6|}\times\frac{|x^2-5x-6|}{x^2-5x-6}\times 2x-5$$

$$\Rightarrow y'=\frac{y}{x^2-5x-6}\times 2x-5=2x-5$$

NOTE:

Here, to explain the above procedure, we have considered a very simple example, which can be differentiated very easily, even without using logarithmic differentiation. It is however important to note that the above procedure can be used for complex functions as well.

Case II: Differentiation of function of the form $(f(x))^{g(x)}$

So far we have discussed derivatives of the functions of the form $[f(x)]^n$, $n^{f(x)}$ and n^n, where $f(x)$ is a function of x and n is a constant. In this section, we will be mainly discussing derivatives of the function of form $\left[f(x)\right]^{g(x)}$ where $f(x)$ and $g(x)$ are function of x. To find the derivative of this type of functions we proceed as follow:

Let $y = \left[f(x)\right]^{g(x)}$. Taking logarithm of both the sides, we have $\log y = g(x).\log|f(x)|$

Differentiating w.r.t x, we get

$$\frac{1}{y}\frac{dy}{dx} = g(x).\frac{1}{f(x)}\frac{df(x)}{dx} + \log|f(x)|.\frac{dg(x)}{dx}$$

$$\therefore \quad \frac{dy}{dx} = y\left\{\frac{g(x)}{f(x)}.\frac{df(x)}{dx} + \log|f(x)|.\frac{dg(x)}{dx}\right\}$$

Alternatively, we many write

$$y = \left[f(x)\right]^{g(x)} = e^{g(x).\log|f(x)|}$$

Differentiating with respect to x, we get

$$\frac{dy}{dx} = e^{g(x)\log|f(x)|}\left\{g(x)\frac{1}{f(x)}\frac{df(x)}{dx} + \log|f(x)|.\frac{dg(x)}{dx}\right\}$$

$$\Rightarrow \quad \frac{dy}{dx} = \left[f(x)\right]^{g(x)}\left\{\frac{g(x)}{f(x)}.\frac{df(x)}{dx} + \log|f(x)|.\frac{dg(x)}{dx}\right\}$$

ILLUSTRATION 35: Differentiate $y = \dfrac{x^{1/2}(1-2x)^{2/3}}{(2-3x)^{3/4}(3-4x)^{4/5}}$ with respect to x.

SOLUTION: Taking logarithms, we obtain $\log y = \frac{1}{2}\log x + \frac{2}{3}\log(1-2x) - \frac{3}{4}\log(2-3x) - \frac{4}{5}\log(3-4x)$

Differentiating with respect to x, we obtain $\frac{1}{y}.\frac{dy}{dx} = \frac{1}{2}.\frac{1}{x} + \frac{2}{3}.\frac{-2}{1-2x} - \frac{3}{4}.\frac{-3}{2-3x} - \frac{4}{5}.\frac{-4}{3-4x}$

$$\Rightarrow \quad \frac{1}{y}.\frac{dy}{dx} = \frac{1}{2x} - \frac{4}{3(1-2x)} + \frac{9}{4(2-3x)} + \frac{16}{5(3-4x)}$$

$$\Rightarrow \quad \frac{dy}{dx} = y\left[\frac{1}{2x} - \frac{4}{3(1-2x)} + \frac{9}{4(2-3x)} + \frac{16}{5(3-4x)}\right]$$

ILLUSTRATION 36: Find the derivative of the following

(a) $y = x^x$ (b) $y = \sin x^{\tan x}$

(c) $(e^x)^{\sin x}$

SOLUTION: (a) $y = x^x \Rightarrow \log y = x \log x$

$$\frac{1}{y}\frac{dy}{dx} = x\frac{1}{x} + \log x \qquad \Rightarrow \quad \frac{dy}{dx} = x^x(1 + \log x)$$

(b) $y = \sin x^{\tan x}$ $\Rightarrow \log y = \tan x \log \sin x$

$$\frac{d}{dy}\log y.\frac{dy}{dx} = \tan x\frac{\cos x}{\sin x} + \log\sin x(\sec^2 x)$$

$$\frac{dy}{dx} = \sin^{\tan x}(1 + \sec^2 x\log\sin x)$$

(c) $y = (e^x)^{\sin x}$ $\Rightarrow \log y = \sin x \log e^x$

$\Rightarrow \dfrac{dy}{dx} = e^{x \sin x}(x \cos x + \sin x)$

ILLUSTRATION 37: Find the derivative of $y = x^{\sin x}$.

SOLUTION: Given $y = x^{\sin x}$ taking log on both side, $\log y = \log(x^{\sin x}) = \sin x \log x$

Differentiating w.r.t.x, we get $\dfrac{1}{y}\dfrac{dy}{dx} = \cos x \log x + \sin x \dfrac{1}{x}$

$\Rightarrow \dfrac{dy}{dx} = x^{\sin x}\left(\cos x \log x + \dfrac{\sin x}{x}\right)$

ILLUSTRATION 38: Differentiate $y = [x^{\tan x} + (\sin x)^{\cos x}]$

SOLUTION: Let $u = x^{\tan x}$, $v = (\sin x)^{\cos x} \Rightarrow y = u + v$

By taking logarithms, we may show that $\dfrac{du}{dx} = x^{\tan x}\left(\sec^2 x \log x + \dfrac{\tan x}{x}\right)$

$\Rightarrow \dfrac{dv}{dx} = (\sin x)^{\cos x}\left(-\sin x \log \sin x + \dfrac{\cos^2 x}{\sin x}\right)$. Now $\dfrac{dy}{dx} = \dfrac{du}{dx} + \dfrac{dv}{dx}$

ILLUSTRATION 39: Find the derivative of $x^2 \sin x.\, e^x$

SOLUTION: Taking log of both side we get, $\log y = 2\log x + \log \sin x + \log e^x$

$\dfrac{1}{y}\dfrac{dy}{dx} = \left[\dfrac{2}{x} + \dfrac{\cos x}{\sin x} + 1\right]$ $\Rightarrow \dfrac{dy}{dx} = (x^2 \sin x.\, e^x)\left(\dfrac{2}{x} + \cot x + 1\right)$

ILLUSTRATION 40: Find $\dfrac{dy}{dx}$ of $x^y = y^x$

SOLUTION: $x^y = y^x$ taking logarithm, we get $y \log_e x = x \log_e y$

Differentiating w.r.t. x, we get, $\log_e x \dfrac{dy}{dx} + y.\dfrac{1}{x} = 1.\log_e y + x\dfrac{1}{y}.\dfrac{dy}{dx}$

$\left(\log_e x - \dfrac{x}{y}\right)\dfrac{dy}{dx} = \log_e y - \dfrac{y}{x}$ or $\dfrac{y\log_e x - x}{y}.\dfrac{dy}{dx} = \dfrac{x\log_e y - y}{x} \Rightarrow \dfrac{dy}{dx} = \dfrac{y}{x}.\dfrac{x\log_e y - y}{y\log_e x - x}$

ILLUSTRATION 41: find $\dfrac{dy}{dx}$ in each of the following cases

(a) If $y = (\cos x)^{\ln x} + (\ln x)^x$ (b) If $y = e^{x^{e^x}} + e^{x^{x^e}} + x^{e^{e^x}}$.

SOLUTION: (a) $y = (\cos x)^{\ln x} + (\ln x)^x$

Let us take $y = u + v$

Where $u = (\cos x)^{\log x}$

$\Rightarrow \log u = \log x \log(\cos x)$

$\Rightarrow \dfrac{1}{u}\dfrac{du}{dx} = \dfrac{1}{x}\log(\cos x) + (\log x)\dfrac{1}{\cos x}(-\sin x)$ and $v = (\log x)^x$

$\Rightarrow \dfrac{du}{dx} = (\cos x)^{\log x}\left(\dfrac{\log(\cos x)}{x} - \tan x \log x\right)$ ...(1)

$\Rightarrow \log v = x \log(\log x)$

$$\frac{dv}{dx} = (\log x)^x \left(\frac{1}{\log x} + \log\log x\right) \qquad ...(2)$$

$$\Rightarrow \frac{1}{v}\frac{dv}{dx} = \left(\log(\log x) + \frac{x}{\ell n} \times \frac{1}{x}\right)$$

$\therefore$ equation (1) + (2) then gives

$$\Rightarrow \frac{dy}{dx} = (\cos x)^{\log x}\left(\log\frac{\cos x}{x} - \tan x \log x\right) + (\log x)^x\left(\frac{1}{\log x} + \log\log x\right)$$

(b) $y = e^{x^{e^x}} + e^{x^{x^e}} + x^{e^{e^x}}$

$y = u + v + w$

$u = e^{x^{e^x}}$

$\Rightarrow \log u = x^{e^x}$

$\Rightarrow \log\log u = e^x \log x$

$$\Rightarrow \frac{1}{\log u} \times \frac{1}{u}\frac{du}{dx} = e^x \log x + \frac{e^x}{x}$$

$$\Rightarrow \frac{du}{dx} = e^{x^{e^x}} x^{e^x} e^x \left(\log x + \frac{1}{x}\right)$$

Now, $v = e^{x^{x^e}}$

$\log v = x^{x^e}$

$\log\log v = x^e \log x$

$$\frac{1}{\log v}\frac{1}{v}\frac{dv}{dx} = (ex^{e-1}\log x + x^{e-1})$$

$$\frac{dv}{dx} = x^{x^e} e^{x^{x^e}} x^{e-1}(e\log v + 1)$$

And $w = x^{e^{e^x}}$

$\log w = e^{e^x}\ e \log x$

$\log\log w = \log\ e^{e^x} + \log x$

$= e^x + \log\log x$

$$\frac{1}{\log w} \times \frac{1}{w}\frac{dw}{dx} = e^x + \frac{1}{x\log x}$$

$$\frac{dw}{dx} = e^{e^x} \log x\ x^{e^{e^x}}\left(e^x + \frac{1}{x\log x}\right)$$

$$\frac{dy}{dx} = e^{x^{e^x}} x^{e^x} e^x \left(\log x + \frac{1}{x}\right) + x^{x^e} e^{x^{x^e}} x^{e-1}(e\log x + 1) + x^{e^{e^x}} e^{e^x}\left(e\log x + \frac{1}{x}\right)$$

ILLUSTRATION 42: If $y = \ln\left(x^{e^x \cdot a^y}\right)^{y^x}$ find $\frac{dy}{dx}$

SOLUTION: $y = \ln\left(x^{e^x \cdot a^y}\right)^{y^x} = \ell n(x^{e^x \cdot a^y \cdot y^x})$

$y = e^x a^y . y^x \ell nx$

$\log = x + y \log a + x\log y + \ell n\, \ell n\, x$

$\frac{1}{y}\frac{dy}{dx} = 1\ \frac{dy}{dx} + \ell na + \log y + \frac{x}{y}\frac{dy}{dx} + \frac{1}{\ell n} \times \frac{1}{x}$

$\left(\frac{1}{y} - \ell na - \frac{x}{y}\right)\frac{dy}{dx} = 1 + \log y + \frac{1}{x\ell nx}$

$\frac{(1 - y\log a - x)}{y}\frac{dy}{dx} = l + \log y + \frac{1}{x\ell nx}$

$\frac{(1 - y\log a - x)}{y}\frac{dy}{dx} = \frac{(x\ell nx + x\ell nx\ \ell ny + 1)}{x\ell n x}$

$\frac{dy}{dx} = \frac{y}{x}\frac{(x\ell nx + x\ell nx\ \ell ny + 1)}{\ell nx(1 - y\log a - x)}$

ILLUSTRATION 43: If $y = x^{(\ell n x)^{\ell n(\ell n x)}}$, then $\frac{dy}{dx}$ is equal to

(a) $\frac{y}{x}\left(\ell nx^{\ell nx - 1} + 2\ell nx\ \ell n(\ell nx)\right)$

(b) $\frac{y}{x}\left(\left(lnx^{lnx(\ln x)}\right)2ln(\ln x) + 1\right)$

(c) $\frac{y}{x\ell nx}\left((lnx)^2 + 2ln(\ln x)\right)$

(d) $\frac{y\ell ny}{x\ell nx}(2\ \ln(\ln\ x) + 1)$

SOLUTION: $y = x^{(\ell n x)^{\ell n(\ell n x)}}$

$\Rightarrow\ \ell ny = (\ell nx)^{\ell n(\ell nx)}.\ell nx$ ...(i)

$\Rightarrow\ \ell n(\ell ny) = \ell n(\ell nx).\ell n(\ell nx) + \ell n(\ell nx)$

$\Rightarrow\ \frac{1}{\ell n y}.\frac{1}{y}\frac{dy}{dx} = \frac{2\ell n(\ell nx)}{\ell nx}\frac{1}{x} + \frac{1}{x\ell nx} = \frac{2\ell n(\ell nx) + 1}{x\ell nx}\quad \therefore\ \frac{dy}{dx} = \frac{y}{x}.\frac{\ell ny}{\ell n x}(2\ell n(\ell nx) + 1)$

Substituting the value of y from (1), we get

$\frac{dx}{dy} = \frac{y}{x}(\ell nx)^{\ell n(\ell nx)}\ (2\ell n(\ell nx) + 1) \Rightarrow B$

ILLUSTRATION 44: If $x^y + y^x = 2$ then find $\frac{dy}{dx}$

SOLUTION: Let $u = x^y$ and $v = y^x$

$u + v = 2$

$\Rightarrow\ \frac{du}{dx} + \frac{dv}{dx} = 0$ ...(i)

$\Rightarrow\ \ell n\, u = y\ \ell nx$ and $\ell n\, v = x\ \ell ny$

$\Rightarrow\ \frac{1}{u}\frac{du}{dx} = \frac{y}{x} + \ell n x\frac{dy}{dx}$ and $\frac{1}{v}\frac{dv}{dx} = \ell n\, y + \frac{x}{y}\frac{dy}{dx}$

$\Rightarrow\ \frac{du}{dx} = x^y\left(\frac{y}{x} + \ell nx\frac{dy}{dx}\right)$ and $\frac{dv}{dx} = y^x\left(\ell ny + \frac{x}{y}\frac{dy}{dx}\right)$

Now equation (i) becomes $x^y\left(\frac{y}{x} + \ell n x\frac{dy}{dx}\right) + y^x\left(\ell ny + \frac{x}{y}\frac{dy}{dx}\right) = 0$

$\Rightarrow\ \frac{dy}{dx} = \frac{-x^y\left(\frac{y}{x}\right) - y^x\ell ny}{x^y\ell nx + y^x\left(\frac{x}{y}\right)}$

ILLUSTRATION 45: If $y=\left(\frac{1}{x}\right)^x$ then find $y''(1)$

SOLUTION: $\ell n\, y = -x\ \ell n\, x$ when $x = 1 \Rightarrow y = 1$

$\Rightarrow \frac{y'}{y} = -(1+\ell nx)$ $\Rightarrow y' = -y\,(1 + \ln x)$ ...(i)

Again diff. w.r.t to x,

$y'' = -y'(1 + \ln x) - y\,\frac{1}{x}$ $\Rightarrow y'' = y(1 + \ln x)^2 - \frac{y}{x}$ (using (i))

$\Rightarrow y'' = 1(1+0)^2 - \frac{1}{1} = 0$

ILLUSTRATION 46: Differentiate the following functions w.r.t x:

(i) $x^{\cos^{-1}x}$ (ii) $(\sin x)^{\cos^{-1}x}$

SOLUTION: Let $y = x^{\cos^{-1}x}$, Then, $y = e^{\cos^{-1}x.\log x}$

On differentiating both sides w.r.t x, we get $\frac{dy}{dx} = e^{\cos^{-1}x.\log x}\frac{d}{dx}\left(\cos^{-1}x.\log x\right)$

$$\Rightarrow \frac{dy}{dx} = x^{\cos^{-1}x}\left\{\log x.\frac{d}{dx}\left(\cos^{-1}x\right)+\cos^{-1}x.\frac{d}{dx}(\log x)\right\}$$

$$\Rightarrow \frac{dy}{dx} = x^{\cos^{-1}x}\left\{\frac{-\log x}{\sqrt{1-x^2}}+\frac{\cos^{-1}x}{x}\right\}.$$

(ii) Let $y = (\sin x)^{\cos^{-1}x}$. Then, $y = e^{\cos^{-1}x.\log\sin x}$

On differentiating both sides w.r.t. x, we get

$$\frac{dy}{dx} = e^{\cos^{-1}x.\log\sin x}\frac{d}{dx}\left(\cos^{-1}x.\log\sin x\right)$$

$$\Rightarrow \frac{dy}{dx} = (\sin x)^{\cos^{-1}x}\left\{\cos^{-1}x.\frac{d}{dx}(\log\sin x)+\log\sin x\frac{d}{dx}\left(\cos^{-1}x\right)\right\}$$

$$\Rightarrow \frac{dy}{dx} = (\sin x)^{\cos^{-1}x}\left\{\cos^{-1}x.\frac{1}{\sin x}.\cos x+\log\sin x.\left(\frac{-1}{\sqrt{1-x^2}}\right)\right\}$$

$$\Rightarrow \frac{dy}{dx} = (\sin x)^{\cos^{-1}x}\left\{\cos^{-1}x.\cot x-\frac{\log\sin x}{\sqrt{1-x^2}}\right\}$$

ILLUSTRATION 47: Differentiate the function w.r.t x where $f(x) = x^{x^x}$

SOLUTION: Let $y = x^{x^x}$ .Then

$\log y = \log x \,.\, \log x$ on differentiating both sides w.r.t x, we get $\frac{dy}{dx} = e^{x^x}\,.\,\log x\ \frac{d}{dx}\ (x^{x}\,\log x)$

$$\Rightarrow \frac{dy}{dx} = x^{x^x}\frac{d}{dx}\left(e^{x\log x}.\log x\right)$$

$$\Rightarrow \frac{dy}{dx} = x^{x^x}\left\{\log x.\frac{d}{dx}\left(e^{x\log x}\right)+e^{x\log x}.\frac{d}{dx}(\log x)\right\}$$

$$\Rightarrow \frac{dy}{dx} = x^{x^x}\left\{\log x.e^{x\log x}\frac{d}{dx}(x\log x)+e^{x\log x}.\frac{1}{x}\right\}$$

$$\Rightarrow \frac{dy}{dx} = x^{x^x}\left\{\log x . x^x\left(x.\frac{1}{x} + \log x\right) + x^x . \frac{1}{x}\right\}$$

$$\Rightarrow \frac{dy}{dx} = x^{x^x}\left\{x^x(1+\log x).\log x + \frac{x^x}{x}\right\}$$

$$\Rightarrow \frac{dy}{dx} = x^{x^x} . x^x\left\{(1+\log x).\log x + \frac{1}{x}\right\}$$

TEXTUAL EXERCISE–4: (SUBJECTIVE)

1. Differentiate the following functions with respect to x

(a) $y = \sqrt{x}^{\sqrt{x}^{\sqrt{x}\ldots\ldots to\infty}}$ (b) $y = (\cos x)^{(\cos x)^{(\cos x)\ldots\ldots to\infty}}$

(c) $y = e^{x+e^{x+e^{x+\ldots\ldots to\infty}}}$

2. Find $\dfrac{dy}{dx}$ of the following:

(a) $x^y + y^x = c$ (b) $(\cos x)^y = (\sin y)^x$

(c) $y = (x^x)^x$ (d) $y = e^{(x)^x}$

(e) $y = (1+1/x)^{x^2}$

3. Find the derivative of the following functions:

(a) $y = (\cos x)^{\sin x}$ (b) $y = \sqrt[3]{\dfrac{\sin 3x}{1-\sin 3x}}$

(c) $y = \dfrac{\sqrt{x-1}}{\sqrt[3]{(x+2)^2}\sqrt{(x+3)^3}}$

4. If $x^y = e^{x-y}$, then prove that $\dfrac{dy}{dx} \quad \dfrac{y(1 \quad y)}{x}$

5. Differentiate the given functions w.r.t. x

(a) $(\ell nx)^{\cos x}$ (b) $y = (x\ell nx)^{\ell n \ell nx}$

6. Find dy/dx, if $(\tan^{-1}x)^y + y^{\cot x} = 1; x > 0$

7. Differentiate the given functions w.r.t x

(i) $x^{x \cos x} + \dfrac{x^2+1}{x^2-1}$

(ii) $(x \cos x)^x + (x \sin x)^{1/x}$

(iii) $e^{\sin x} + (\tan x)^x$

(iv) $(\cos x)^x + (\sin x)^{1/x}$

8. Differentiate y w.r.t x where $y = x^{\sin x} + (\sin x)^x$

9. Differentiate y w.r.t x where $y = (\log x)^x + x^{\log x}$

Answer Keys

1. (a) $\dfrac{y^2}{2x(1-y\log\sqrt{x})}$ (b) $\dfrac{y^2 \tan x}{[y\log(\cos x)-1]}$ (c) $\dfrac{y}{1-y}$

2. (a) $\dfrac{-(yx^{y-1}+y^x\log y)}{x^y\log x + xy^{x-1}}$ (b) $\dfrac{\log\sin y + y\tan x}{\log\cos x - x\cot y}$ (c) $x^{(x^2+1)}\log(ex^2)$

(d) $x^x.e^{x^x}(\ln e^x)$ (e) $\left(1+\dfrac{1}{x}\right)^{x^2}\left[2x\log(1+1/x) - \dfrac{x}{1+x}\right]$

3. (a) $(\cos x)^{\sin x}(\cos x \ln\cos x - \tan x.\sin x)$ (b) $\dfrac{\cos 3x}{\sqrt[3]{\sin^2 3x(1-3x)^4}}$ (c) $\dfrac{5x^2+x-24}{3(x-1)^{\frac{1}{2}}(x+2)^{\frac{5}{2}}(x+3)^{\frac{5}{2}}}$

5. (a) $(\ell nx)^{\cos}\left(\dfrac{\cos}{x \quad nx} \quad \sin x\ell n(\ell nx)\right)$ (b) $(x\ell nx)^{\ell n\ell n x}.\dfrac{1}{x}\left(1+\ell n(\ell nx)\left(1+\dfrac{2}{\ell nx}\right)\right)$

6. $\dfrac{(\log y)\operatorname{cosec}^2 x\, y^{\cot x} - y\left(\tan^{-1} x\right)^{y-1}\left(1+x^2\right)^{-1}}{\left(\tan^{-1} x\right)^y \log\left(\tan^{-1} x\right) + y^{\cot x - 1}\cot x}$

7. (i) $x^{x\cos x}\{(1+\log x)\cos x - x\log x\sin x\} - \dfrac{4x}{(x^2-1)^2}$

(ii) $(x\cos x)^x\{1 - x\tan x + \log(x\cos x)\} + (x\sin x)^{\frac{1}{x}}.\dfrac{\{1+x\cot x - \log(x\sin x)}{x^2}$

(iii) $e^{\sin x}\cos x + (\tan x)^x\{\log\tan x + x\sec x\operatorname{cosec} x\}$

(iv) $(\cos x)^x(\log\cos x - x\tan x) + (\sin x)^{\frac{1}{x}}\left(-\dfrac{1}{x^2}\log\sin x + \dfrac{\cot x}{x}\right)$

8. $x^{\sin x}\left\{\cos x\log x + \dfrac{\sin x}{x}\right\} + (\sin x)^x\{\log\sin x + x\cot x\}$

9. $\left(x^{\log x}\left(\dfrac{2\log x}{x}\right) + (\log x)^x\left(\log(\log x) + \dfrac{1}{\log x}\right)\right)$

TEXTUAL EXERCISE–4: (OBJECTIVE)

1. If $[x+y]^{a+b} = x^a . y^b$ then $dy/dx =$
   (a) y/x (b) x/y
   (c) $\dfrac{y}{a+x}$ (d) $\dfrac{x}{(b+y)}$

2. If $y = \sqrt{[\ln x + \sqrt{\{\ln x + \sqrt{(\ln x + ...\infty)}\}]}}$, then $\dfrac{dy}{dx}$ is equal to
   (a) $\dfrac{1}{x[2y-1]}$ (b) $\dfrac{1}{x[2y+1]}$
   (c) $\dfrac{x}{[2y-1]}$ (d) $\dfrac{x}{[2y+1]}$

3. Let $y = \sqrt{x + \sqrt{x + \sqrt{x + ...\infty}}}$ then $\dfrac{dy}{dx}$ is equal to
   (a) $\dfrac{1}{2y-1}$ (b) $\dfrac{x}{x+2y}$
   (c) $\dfrac{1}{\sqrt{1+4x}}$ (d) $\dfrac{y}{2x+y}$

4. Let $f(x) = \left(x^x\right)^x$ and $g(x) = \left(x^x\right)^x$ then:
   (a) $f'(1) = 1$ and $g'(1) = 2$
   (b) $f'(1) = 2$ and $g'(1) = 1$
   (c) $f'(1) = 1$ and $g'(1) = 0$
   (d) $f'(1) = 1$ and $g'(1) = 1$

5. If $y = \dfrac{a+bx^{3/2}}{x^{5/4}}$ & $\dfrac{dy}{dx}$ vanishes when $x = 5$, then $\dfrac{a}{b} =$
   (a) $\sqrt{3}$
   (b) 2
   (c) $\sqrt{5}$
   (d) None of these

6. If $f(x) = |x|^{|\sin x|}$ then $f'(\pi/4)$ equals
   (a) $\left(\dfrac{\pi}{4}\right)^{1/\sqrt{2}}\left(\dfrac{\sqrt{2}}{2}\ell n\dfrac{4}{\pi} - \dfrac{2\sqrt{2}}{\pi}\right)$
   (b) $\left(\dfrac{\pi}{4}\right)^{1/\sqrt{2}}\left(\dfrac{\sqrt{2}}{2}\ell n\dfrac{4}{\pi} + \dfrac{2\sqrt{2}}{\pi}\right)$
   (c) $\left(\dfrac{\pi}{4}\right)^{1/\sqrt{2}}\left(\dfrac{\sqrt{2}}{2}\ell n\dfrac{4}{\pi} - \dfrac{2\sqrt{2}}{\pi}\right)$
   (d) $\left(\dfrac{\pi}{4}\right)^{1/\sqrt{2}}\left(\dfrac{\sqrt{2}}{2}\ell n\dfrac{\pi}{4} + \dfrac{2\sqrt{2}}{\pi}\right)$

Answer Keys

1. (a) 2. (a) 3. (a,c,d) 4. (d) 5. (c) 6. (d)

■ DIFFERENTIATION OF INVERSE FUNCTIONS

If $f(x)$ is any one-one onto function, then its inverse function (say $g^{-1}(x)$) is also a differentiable function (except where its tangents are parallel to y-axis).

$y = f(x) \Leftrightarrow x = g(y)$.

Differentiating both sides of $f(x)$ w.r.t; x we get $\frac{dy}{dx} = f'(x)$

And differentiating both sides of $x = g(y)$ w.r.t; y' we get $\frac{dx}{dy} = g'(y)$

$$\frac{dy}{dx} = \lim_{\Delta x \to o} \times \frac{\Delta y}{\Delta x} \text{ if it exists finitely}$$

$$= \lim_{\Delta x \to 0} \frac{\Delta y}{\Delta x} \quad (\because \Delta x \to 0 \Rightarrow \Delta y \to 0)$$

$$= \lim_{\Delta y \to 0} \left(\frac{1}{\frac{\Delta x}{\Delta y}} \right) = \frac{1}{\lim_{\Delta y \to 0} \left(\frac{\Delta x}{\Delta y} \right)} = \frac{1}{\frac{dx}{dy}}$$

$$\therefore \quad f'(x) = \frac{1}{g'(y)} \text{ (provided } g'(y) \neq 0)$$

This is more evident by taking differentiation of two composite functions. If $g(x) = f^{-1}(x)$

$\Rightarrow f(g(x)) = f(f^{-1}(x)) = x$

Differentiation both sides w.r.t x;

we get $f'(g(x)) \times g'(x) = 1$

$\Rightarrow g'(x) = \frac{1}{f'(g(x))}$. i.e., derivative of f^{-1} at $x = x_0$

is equal to reciprocal of the derivative of $f(x)$ at $x = f^{-1}(x_0)$

Geometrical Interpretation

If the tangent T_1 (tangent to $y = f(x)$ at $x = (a, f(a))$) makes an angle of α with positive x-axis, then the line T_2 (tangent to $y = f^{-1}(x)$ or $x = f(y)$ at $(f(a), a)$) makes an angle α with positive y axis.

For $0 < \alpha < \pi/2$

As is evident from the diagram: 'β', i.e., the angle that the line T_2 makes with positive x-axis is equal to $\pi/2 - \alpha$

$\therefore \quad f'(x) = \tan\alpha$ and $g'(y) = \tan\beta$

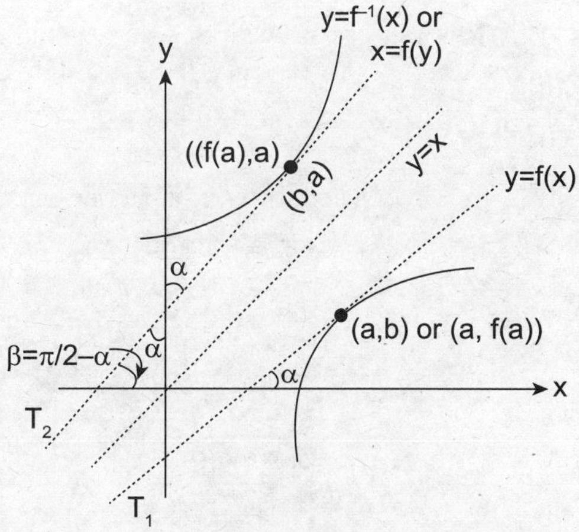

FIGURE 3.9

We need to prove that $\tan\alpha = \frac{1}{\tan\beta}$ or $\tan\alpha . \tan\beta = 1$

or $\tan\alpha \tan\left(\frac{\pi}{2} - \alpha\right) = 1$ or $\tan\alpha . \cot\alpha = 1$ which is obviously true and hence $\tan\alpha = \frac{1}{\tan\beta}$

or $\frac{dy}{dx} = \frac{1}{\frac{dx}{dy}}$ or $f'(x) = \frac{1}{g'(y)}$

Similarly, For $\pi/2 < \alpha < \pi$, $\beta = 3\pi/2 - \alpha$

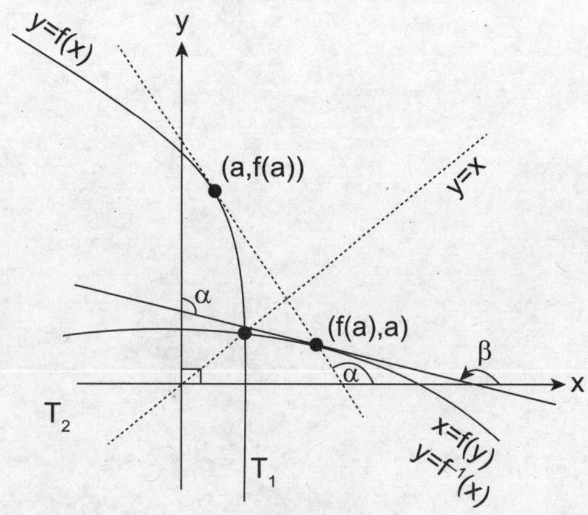

FIGURE 3.10

$$\therefore \quad \tan\alpha . \tan\beta = \tan\alpha \times \tan\left(\frac{3\pi}{2} - \alpha\right) = \tan\alpha \times \cot\alpha = 1$$

$$\therefore \quad \tan\alpha = \frac{1}{\tan\beta}$$

And hence, again, we get that $f'(x) = \frac{1}{g'(y)}$

ILLUSTRATION 48: If $y = f(x) = x + x^3 + x^5$ and g is the inverse function of f, then find $g'(3)$

SOLUTION: $\frac{dy}{dx} = 1 + 3x^2 + 5x^4 > 0$

Therefore $f(x)$ is an one-one function

Now, $g'(y) = \frac{dx}{dy} = \frac{1}{\frac{dy}{dx}} = \frac{1}{1+3x^2+5x^4}$

When $y = 3$, then $3 = x + x^3 + x^5 \Rightarrow x = 1$

$$\therefore\ g'(3) = \left.\frac{dx}{dy}\right|_{\substack{x=1\\y=3}} = \frac{1}{\left.\frac{dy}{dx}\right|_{\substack{x=1\\y=3}}} = \frac{1}{1\left(3x^2+5x^4\right)\big|_{x=1}} = \frac{1}{1+3+5} = \frac{1}{9}$$

aliter: $g(f(x)) = x \Rightarrow g'(f(x)) \times f'(x) = 1$

Now when $f(x) = 3$; $x = 1$

$\Rightarrow g'(3) \times f'(1) = 1$

$\Rightarrow g'(3) = \frac{1}{f'(1)} = \frac{1}{1+3+5} = \frac{1}{9}$

ILLUSTRATION 49: If the function $f(x) = \frac{7}{4}e^{\frac{2-x}{3}} + 3x + 5x^2$ and $f(x) = g^{-1}(x)$, then find the values of $g'\left(\frac{111}{4}\right)$

SOLUTION: $y = \frac{7}{4}e^{\frac{2-x}{3}} + 3x + 5x^2$

Now $y = \frac{111}{4}$ when $x = 2$

$\frac{dy}{dx} = \frac{-7}{12}e^{\frac{2-x}{3}} + 3 + 10x$

$g'(y) = \frac{dx}{dy} = \frac{1}{\frac{dy}{dx}} = \frac{1}{\frac{-7}{12}e^{\frac{2-x}{3}} + 3 + 10x}$

$$\therefore\ g'\left(\frac{111}{4}\right) = \frac{1}{\left.\frac{dy}{dx}\right|_{x=2}} = \frac{1}{\frac{-7}{12}e^{\frac{2-2}{3}} + 3 + 10\times 2} = \frac{1}{\frac{-7}{12} + 3 + 20} = \frac{1}{\frac{269}{12}} = \frac{12}{269}$$

ILLUSTRATION 50: (a) Let $f(x) = x^2 - 4x - 3$, $x > 2$ and let g be the inverse of f. Find the value of g' where $f(x) = 2$.

(b) Let $f: R \to R$ be defined as $f(x) = x^3 + 3x^2 + 6x - 5 + 4e^{2x}$ and $g(x) = f^{-1}(x)$, then find $g'(-1)$

SOLUTION: (a) $f(x) = x^2 - 4x - 3 = x^2 - 4x + 4 - 7 = (x-2)^2 - 7$

Now $f(x) = 2$

$\Rightarrow (x-2)^2 - 7 = 2$

$\Rightarrow (x-2)^2 = 9$

$\Rightarrow x - 2 = -3, 3$

$\Rightarrow x = -1, 5$

Given that $x > 2 \Rightarrow x = -1$ is not possible

Hence, (x, y) is (5, 2)

Now, $f'(x) = 2(x-2)$

$\Rightarrow f'(5) = 2(5-2) = 6$

If slope of $y = f(x)$ at (5, 2) is m_1 and slope of $y = g(x)$ at (2, 5) is m_2, then the lines with slope m_1 and m_2 makes equal angles with the line $y = x$ and hence $\frac{1-m_1}{1+m_1} = -\left(\frac{1-m_2}{1+m_2}\right)$

$\Rightarrow \frac{1-6}{1+6} = \frac{m_2-1}{m_2+1}$ $\qquad \Rightarrow -5m_2 - 5 = 7m_2 - 7$

$\Rightarrow 12m_2 = 2$ $\qquad \Rightarrow m_2 = \frac{1}{6}$ Ans $\Rightarrow g'(2) = \frac{1}{6}$

(b) $f(x) = x^3 + 3x^2 + 6x - 5 + 4e^{2x}$

$\Rightarrow f'(x) = 3x^2 + 6x + 6 + 8e^{2x}$

$= 3(x^2 + 2x + 2) + 8e^{2x}$

$= 3((x+1)^2 + 1) + 8e^{2x}$

$= 3(x+1)^2 + 3 + 8e^{2x} > 0$

On Putting $x = 0$, we get, $f(0) = -5 + 4 + 0 = -1$

And since $f'(x) = 3x^2 + 6x + 6 + 8e^{2x}$

$\therefore\ f'(0) = 6 + 8e^{o} = 14$

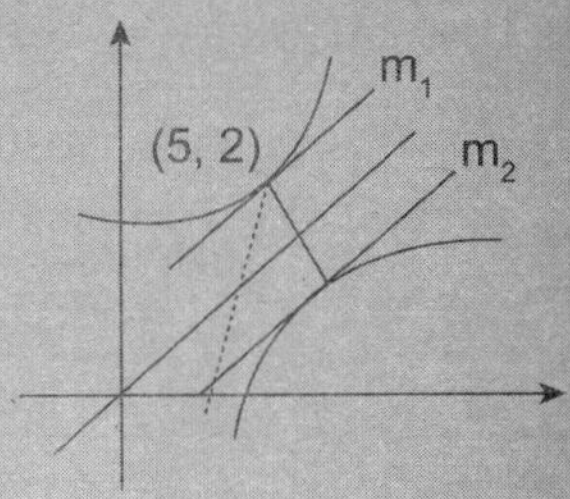

FIGURE 3.11

Now, if m_1 is the slope of tangent to $y = f(x)$ at (0, –1) and m_2 is the slope of the tangent to $y = g(x)$ at (–1, 0), then $\frac{1-m_1}{1+m_1} = -\left(\frac{1-m_2}{1+m_2}\right)$

$\Rightarrow \frac{1-14}{1+14} = \frac{m_2-1}{m_2+1}$ $\qquad \Rightarrow \frac{-13}{15} = \frac{m_2-1}{m_2+1}$

$\Rightarrow -13m_2 - 13 = 15m_2 - 15$ $\qquad \Rightarrow 28m_2 = 2$

$\Rightarrow m_2 = 1/14$

ILLUSTRATION 51: $\frac{d^2x}{dy^2}$ is equal to

(a) $\left(\frac{d^2y}{dx^2}\right)^{-1}$ $\qquad$ (b) $\left(\frac{d^2y}{dx^2}\right)^{-1}\left(\frac{dy}{dx}\right)^{-3}$

(c) $\left(\frac{d^2y}{dx^2}\right)\left(\frac{dy}{dx}\right)^{-2}$ $\qquad$ (d) $-\left(\frac{d^2y}{dx^2}\right)\left(\frac{dy}{dx}\right)^{-3}$

SOLUTION : (d) $\frac{dx}{dy} = \frac{1}{\left(\frac{dy}{dx}\right)}$

$$\frac{d^2x}{dy^2} = \frac{d}{dy}\frac{1}{\left(\frac{dy}{dx}\right)} = \frac{d}{dx}\frac{1}{\left(\frac{dy}{dx}\right)}.\frac{dx}{dy} = -\frac{1}{\left(\frac{dy}{dx}\right)^2}.\frac{d^2y}{dx^2}.\frac{1}{\left(\frac{dy}{dx}\right)} = -\frac{1}{\left(\frac{dy}{dx}\right)^3}\frac{d^2y}{dx^2}$$

ILLUSTRATION 52: Let g be the inverse function of f and $f'(x) = \dfrac{x^{10}}{\left(1+x^2\right)}$. If g(2) = a then g'(2) is equal to

(a) $\dfrac{5}{2^{10}}$ (b) $\dfrac{1+a^2}{a^{10}}$

(c) $\dfrac{a^{10}}{1+a^2}$ (d) $\dfrac{1+a^{10}}{a^2}$

SOLUTION: $f[g(x)] = x \Rightarrow f'[g(x)].g'(x) = 1 \Rightarrow f'(a).g'(2) = 1$ [Putting $x = 2$ and given g(2) = a]

Given $f'(a) = \dfrac{a^{10}}{1+a^2} \Rightarrow g'(2) = \dfrac{1+a^2}{a^{10}}$

ILLUSTRATION 53: $y = f(x)$ and $x = g(y)$ are inverse functions of each other than express $g'(y)$ and $g''(y)$ in terms of derivative of $f(x)$

SOLUTION: $\dfrac{dy}{dx} = f'(x)$ *and* $\dfrac{dx}{dy} = g'(y)$

$$\Rightarrow g'(y) = \frac{1}{f'(x)} \qquad \ldots\text{(i)}$$

Again differentiating w.r.t to y

$$g''(y) = \frac{d}{dy}\left(\frac{1}{f'(x)}\right) = \frac{d}{dx}\left(\frac{1}{f'(x)}\right).\frac{dx}{dy} = -\frac{f''(x)}{f'(x)^2}.g'(y)$$

$$= g''(y) = -\frac{f''(x)}{[f'(x)]^3} \qquad \ldots\text{(ii)}$$

Which can also can remembered as $\dfrac{d^2x}{dy^2} = -\dfrac{\dfrac{d^2y}{dx^2}}{\left(\dfrac{dy}{dx}\right)^3}$

ILLUSTRATION 54: Let $f(x) = x^2 - x - 6, x > \dfrac{1}{2}$ and let g be the inverse of f. The value of g' when $f(x) = 14$ is

(a) 1/9 (b) 1/3

(c) 1/6 (d) None of these

SOLUTION: Let g' |γ| = $\dfrac{dx}{dy}$ hence $f(x)$ 1 = $2x.\dfrac{dx}{dy} - \dfrac{dx}{dy}$

$\Rightarrow \dfrac{dx}{dy} = \dfrac{1}{2x-1}$; when $f(x) = 14$ (given)

$\Rightarrow x^2 - x - 20 = 0$ $\Rightarrow x = 5$ or $x = -4$

Now, $x = -4$ is rejected because it is given that $x > 1/2$.

TEXTUAL EXERCISE–5: (SUBJECTIVE)

1. If $f(x)=\dfrac{x^2-x}{x^2+2x}$, find the function $\dfrac{df^{-1}(x)}{dx}$ and its domain.
2. If g is the inverse of f and $f'(x)=\dfrac{1}{1+x^5}$ then prove that $g'(x) = 1 + [g(x)]^5$
3. If $y^{\frac{1}{m}}+y^{-\frac{1}{m}}=2x$, then prove that the value of $\dfrac{(x^2-1)y''+xy'}{y}$ is equal to m^2
4. Let $e^{f(x)} = \ln x$. If $g(x)$ is the inverse function of $f(x)$, then prove that $g'(x)$ equals to $e^{(e^x+x)}$.
5. The function $f(x) = e^x + x$, being differentiable and one one function, has a differentiable inverse $f^{-1}(x)$. Then find the value of $\dfrac{d}{dx}f^{-1}(x)$ at the point $f(\ell n3)$.

Answer Keys

1. $\dfrac{d}{dx}\left[f^{-1}(x)\right]=\dfrac{3}{(1-x)^2}$ Domain of $f^{-1}(x) = R - \{-1/2, 1\}$

5. $\dfrac{1}{4}$

■ IMPLICIT DIFFERENTIATION

Explicit functions are those functions in which y can be directly written in terms of x. e.g., $y = x\sin x$, $y = \sin^{-1}(x^2 + 1)$ etc.

Implicit functions are those in which y cannot be expressed exclusively in terms of x. i.e., if the relation between the variables x and y are given by an equation containing both, and this equation is not immediately solvable for y, then y is called an implicit function of x. e.g. $y^2 + x^2 + 2xy - 3x^2y = 0$ or $x^2y = \sin xy$ etc.

It is important to observe that the terms "explicit function" and "implicit function" are merely the way that the functions are defined and in no sense do they characterize the nature of the function. Every explicit function $y = f(x)$ can also be represented as an implicit function $y - f(x) = 0$ for example let us consider the equation $x^3 + y^3 = 8$ here the function is defined implicitly whereas we can rearrange the above equation to get $y = \sqrt[3]{8-x^3}$

Similarly the function of the form $y = \sqrt{x+\sqrt{x+\sqrt{x+....\infty}}}$ may be called an explicit function, but $y = \sqrt{x+y}$ will be called an implicit function, whereas there is no difference between the two.

In order to obtain dy/dx when function is written in implicit form, one should observe the steps given below:

Steps:

(a) To get $\dfrac{dy}{dx}$, differentiate entire function with respect to x, treating y as a function of x

(b) Collect the coefficient of $\dfrac{dy}{dx}$ at one place and transfer the remaining terms to the right hand side.

(c) Find $\dfrac{dy}{dx}$ in terms of x and y.

Shortcut for Implicit Functions

For implicit function put; $\dfrac{d}{dx}\{f(x,y)\}=\dfrac{-\partial f/\partial x}{\partial f/\partial y}$, where $\dfrac{\partial f}{\partial x}$ is partial differential of a given function with respect to x (i.e differentiating f with respect to x keeping, y constant) and $\dfrac{\partial f}{\partial y}$ means partial differential of a given function with respect to y (i.e., differentiating f with respect to y, keeping x constant).

Caution: Careless application of implicit differentiation may lead to errors, For eg.,: consider $x^2 + y^2 = 0$, through implicit differentiation, we get $2x + 2y\dfrac{dy}{dx}=0 \Rightarrow \dfrac{dy}{dx}=-1.$ But there is only one value of (x, y) which satisfy the equation i.e., the origin only. Hence it is wrong to find dy/dx in this case. Hence it is important to note that implicit differentiation is merely a technique to find the derivative and is applicable only if the function is differentiable.

ILLUSTRATION 55: If $x^2 + y^2 + xy = 2$ find $\frac{dy}{dx}$

SOLUTION: $x^2 + y^2 + xy = 2$

Differentiating both sides we get $\frac{d}{dx}(x^2)+\frac{d}{dx}(y^2)+\frac{d}{dx}(xy)=\frac{d}{dx}(2)$

$\Rightarrow 2x+2y\frac{dy}{dx}+\left\{\frac{dx}{dx}\right\}y+x\left\{\frac{d}{dx}y\right\}=0 \qquad \Rightarrow 2x+2y\frac{dy}{dx}+1.\,y+x\frac{dy}{dx}=0$

$\Rightarrow (2y+x)\frac{dy}{dx}=-(2x+y) \qquad \Rightarrow \frac{dy}{dx}=-\frac{(2x+y)}{(2y+x)}$

Alternate method: Put $f = x^2 + y^2 + xy - 2$

Now, $\frac{dy}{dx}=\frac{-\partial f/\partial x}{\partial f/\partial y}$ ...(i)

where $\frac{\partial f}{dx}=2x+0+y-0 \left\{\frac{\partial y^2}{\partial x}=0, \frac{\partial xy}{\partial x}=y\right\}$

and $\frac{\partial f}{\partial y}=2y+x \qquad \left\{as\frac{\partial x^2}{\partial y}=0, \frac{\partial xy}{\partial y}=x\right\}$

Substituting in (i) we get $\frac{dy}{dx}=-\frac{(2x+y)}{(2y+x)}$

ILLUSTRATION 56: Find the expression for $\frac{dy}{dx}$ for the implicit function $x^3 + y^3 - 3xy = 1$

SOLUTION: Differentiating with respect to x

$$3x^2+3y^2\frac{dy}{dx}-3\left[x\frac{dy}{dx}+y.1\right]=0 \Rightarrow \frac{dy}{dx}=\frac{y-x^2}{y^2-x}$$

ILLUSTRATION 57: Differentiate the following

(a) $y^2 + x^2 + 2xy - 3x^2y = 0$ (b) $y = x^y$

SOLUTION: (a) $y^2 + x^2 + 2xy - 3x^2 y = 0$

$$2y\frac{dy}{dx}+2\left[x\frac{dy}{dx}+y\right]+2x-3\left[x^2\frac{dy}{dx}+y(2x)\right]=0$$

$\Rightarrow \frac{dy}{dx}(2y+2x-3x^2)=-2y-2x+6xy \qquad \Rightarrow \frac{dy}{dx}=\frac{2(y+x-3xy)}{3x^2-2y-2x}$

(b) $y = x^y$, by taking log on both sides, we get $\log y = y \log x$

$$\frac{1}{y}\frac{dy}{dx}=y\frac{1}{x}+\log x\frac{dy}{dx} \Rightarrow \frac{dy}{dx}=\frac{y^2}{x}+y\log x\frac{dy}{dx}$$

$(1-y\log x)\frac{dy}{dx}=\frac{y^2}{x} \qquad \Rightarrow \frac{dy}{dx}=\frac{y^2}{(1-y\log x)x}$

ILLUSTRATION 58: If $\sin y = x\sin(a+y)$, prove that $\frac{dy}{dx}=\frac{\sin^2(a+y)}{\sin a}$

SOLUTION: We have $x=\frac{\sin y}{\sin(a+y)} \qquad \Rightarrow \frac{dx}{dy}=\frac{\cos y\sin(a+y)-\cos(a+y)\sin y}{\sin^2(a+y)}$

$$= \frac{\sin(a+y-y)}{\sin^2(a+y)} = \frac{\sin a}{\sin^2(a+y)} \qquad \Rightarrow \frac{dy}{dx} = \frac{\sin^2(a+y)}{\sin a}$$

ILLUSTRATION 59: If $y = x\cos y + y\cos x$, find $\frac{dy}{dx}$

SOLUTION: ***Method 1:*** Given $y = x\cos y + y\cos x$,

Differentiating both sides with respect to x, we get

$$\frac{dy}{dx} = \left\{\frac{d}{dx}x\right\}\cos y + x\left\{\frac{d}{dx}\cos y\right\} + y\left\{\frac{d}{dx}\cos x\right\} + \left\{\frac{d}{dx}y\right\}.\cos x$$

$$\frac{dy}{dx} = 1.\cos y + x(-\sin y)\frac{dy}{dx} + y(-\sin x) + \frac{dy}{dx}(\cos x)$$

$$\frac{dy}{dx}(1 + x\sin y - \cos x) = \cos y - y\sin x \qquad \Rightarrow \frac{dy}{dx} = \frac{\cos y - y\sin x}{1 + x\sin y - \cos x}$$

Method 2: Shortcut method: $y = x\cos y + y\cos x$. Let $f = x\cos y + y\cos x - y$

$$\Rightarrow \frac{\partial f}{\partial x} = \cos y - y\sin x \text{ and } \frac{\partial f}{\partial y} = -x\sin y + \cos x - 1$$

$$\therefore \frac{dy}{dx} = \frac{-\left(\frac{\partial f}{\partial x}\right)}{\left(\frac{\partial f}{\partial y}\right)} = \frac{-(\cos y - y\sin x)}{(-x\sin y + \cos x - 1)} \quad \text{or} \quad \frac{dy}{dx} = \frac{\cos y - y\sin x}{1 + x\sin y - \cos x}$$

ILLUSTRATION 60: If $y = a^{x^{a^{x^{a^{x^{\cdots\text{to }\infty}}}}}}$ then dy/dx is

(a) $\frac{y^2\log y}{x(1 - y\log x\log y)}$ (b) $\frac{y^2\log x}{x(1 - y\log x\ \log y)}$

(c) 0 (d) None of these

SOLUTION: (a) $y = a^{x^{a^{x^{a^{x^{\cdots\text{to }\infty}}}}}}$ $\Rightarrow y = a^{x^y}$

Taking log on both sides

$\Rightarrow \log y = x^y.\log a$ $\Rightarrow \log(\log y) = y\log x + \log(\log a)$

Differentiating w.r.t. x

$$\Rightarrow \frac{1}{\log y}.\frac{1}{y}.\frac{dy}{dx} = \frac{dy}{dx}.\log x + \frac{y}{x} \qquad \Rightarrow \frac{dy}{dx} = \frac{y^2\log y}{x(1 - y\log x\ \log y)}$$

ILLUSTRATION 61: Find the $\frac{dy}{dx}$ of the function $xy = x^3 + y^3$

SOLUTION: $xy = x^3 + y^3$

Differentiating w.r.t x, we get; $\frac{d}{dx}(xy) = \frac{d}{dx}x^3 + \frac{d}{dx}y^3$

$$x\frac{dy}{dx} + y.1 = 3x^2 + 3y^2\frac{dy}{dx} \qquad \text{or } (x - 3y^2)\frac{dy}{dx} = 3x^2 - y$$

$$\therefore \frac{dy}{dx} = \frac{3x^2 - y}{x - 3y^2}$$

ILLUSTRATION 62: Find $\frac{dy}{dx}$ for the functions $y = x^{x^{x^{x^{\infty}}}}$

SOLUTION: $y = x^{x^{x^{x^{\infty}}}}$

$y = x^y$; Since powers go up to infinity.

$\log y = y \log x$

$\frac{1}{y}\frac{dy}{dx} = \frac{y}{x} + \log x.\frac{dy}{dx}$ or $\frac{dy}{dx}\left(\frac{1}{y} - \log x\right) = \frac{y}{x}$; $\frac{dy}{dx} = \frac{y^2}{x(1 - y\log x)}$

ILLUSTRATION 63: If $e^y + xy = e$, then $\left.\frac{d^2y}{dx^2}\right|_{x=0}$ is

(a) $1/e^2$

(b) e^{-1}

(c) e

(d) None of these

SOLUTION: (a) We have $e^y + xy = e$ ...(1)

Differentiating w.r.t. x; we get

$$e^y\frac{dy}{dx} + y + x\frac{dy}{dx} = 0 \quad ...(i)$$

Differentiating again w.r.t. x; we get

$$e^y\frac{d^2y}{dx^2} + e^y\left(\frac{dy}{dx}\right)^2 + 2\frac{dy}{dx} + x\frac{d^2y}{dx^2} = 0 \quad ...(ii)$$

Put $x = 0$ in $e^y + xy = e$, we get $y = 1$

Putting $x = 0$, $y = 1$ in (i) we get $e\frac{dy}{dx} + 1 = 0$

$\Rightarrow \frac{dy}{dx} = -\frac{1}{e}$

Putting $x = 0$, $y = 1$, $\frac{dy}{dx} = -\frac{1}{e}$ in (ii) we get $\frac{d^2y}{dx^2} = \frac{1}{e^2}$

ILLUSTRATION 64: If $y = \cfrac{\sin x}{1 + \cfrac{\cos x}{1 + \cfrac{\sin x}{1 + \cos x........\infty}}}$ prove that $\frac{dy}{dx} = \frac{(1+y)\cos x + \sin x}{1 + 2y + \cos x - \sin x}$

SOLUTION: Given function is $y = \cfrac{\sin x}{1 + \cfrac{\cos x}{1+y}} = \frac{(1+y)\sin x}{1 + y + \cos x}$

Or $y + y^2 + y\cos x = (1+y)\sin x$

On differentiating both sides w.r.t.x we get

$$\frac{dy}{dx} + 2y\frac{dy}{dx} + y(-\sin x) + \cos x.\frac{dy}{dx} = (1+y)\cos x + \frac{dy}{dx}.\sin x$$

or $\frac{dy}{dx}\{1 + 2y + \cos x - \sin x\} = (1+y)\cos x + y\sin x$

or $\frac{dy}{dx} = \frac{(1+y)\cos x + \sin x}{1 + 2y + \cos x - \sin x}$

ILLUSTRATION 65: If $y=\cfrac{x}{x+\cfrac{\sqrt[3]{x}}{x+\cfrac{\sqrt[3]{x}}{x+\sqrt[3]{x}+.......\infty}}}$, find $\frac{dy}{dx}$.

SOLUTION: Given $y=\cfrac{x}{x+\cfrac{\sqrt[3]{x}}{x+\cfrac{\sqrt[3]{x}}{x+\sqrt[3]{x}+.......\infty}}}$ $\Rightarrow y=\cfrac{x}{x+\cfrac{x.x^{-2/3}}{x+\cfrac{\sqrt[3]{x}}{x+\sqrt[3]{x}+.......\infty}}}$

or $y=\frac{x}{x+y.x^{-2/3}}$ $\Rightarrow y\{x^{5/3}+y\}=x^{5/3}$

or $x^{5/3}y+y^2=x^{5/3}$

Differentiating both sides w.r.t. x,

$$x^{5/3}\frac{dy}{dx}+\frac{5}{3}x^{2/3}.y+2y\frac{dy}{dx}=\frac{5}{3}x^{2/3}$$

or $(x^{5/3}+2y)\frac{dy}{dx}=\frac{5}{3}x^{2/3}-\frac{5}{3}x^{2/3}y$ or $\frac{dy}{dx}=\frac{\frac{5}{3}x^{2/3}(1-y)}{(x^{5/3}+2y)}$

ILLUSTRATION 66: If $y=x+\cfrac{1}{x+\cfrac{1}{x+\cfrac{1}{x+..............}}}$, prove that $\frac{dy}{dx}=\cfrac{1}{2-\cfrac{x}{x+\cfrac{1}{x+\cfrac{1}{x+....................}}}}$.

SOLUTION: $y=x+\frac{1}{y}$ ...(i)

$1=\frac{x}{y}+\frac{1}{y^2}$

Differentiating w.r.t x, we get $\frac{dy}{dx}=1+\frac{-1}{y^2}\frac{dy}{dx}$

$\Rightarrow \left(1+\frac{1}{y^2}\right)\frac{dy}{dx}=1$

[from (i); $y=x+1/y \Rightarrow 1=\frac{x}{y}+\frac{1}{y^2} \Rightarrow \frac{1}{y^2}=1-\frac{x}{y}$]

$\Rightarrow \left(1+1-\frac{x}{y}\right)\frac{dy}{dx}=1$

$\Rightarrow \left(2-\frac{x}{y}\right)\frac{dy}{dx}=1$ $\Rightarrow \frac{dy}{dx}=\frac{1}{2-\frac{x}{y}}$

$\Rightarrow \frac{dy}{dx}=\cfrac{1}{2-\cfrac{x}{x+\cfrac{1}{x+\cfrac{1}{x+....................}}}}$

ILLUSTRATION 67: Let $f(x) = x + \cfrac{1}{2x + \cfrac{1}{2x + \cfrac{1}{2x + \ldots\ldots\infty}}}$. Compute the value of $f(100).f'(100)$.

SOLUTION: $f(x) = x + \cfrac{1}{2x + \cfrac{1}{2x + \cfrac{1}{2x + \ldots\ldots\infty}}}$

$\Rightarrow y = x + \dfrac{1}{x+y} = \dfrac{x^2 + xy + 1}{x+y}$ $\qquad \Rightarrow xy + y^2 = xy + x^2 + 1$

$\Rightarrow y^2 = 1 + x^2$ $\qquad \Rightarrow y = \pm\sqrt{1+x^2}$

$\Rightarrow y = \sqrt{1+x^2}$ $\qquad$ ($\because$ y cannot be negative as x is positive)

$$\Rightarrow \frac{dy}{dx} = \frac{2x}{2\sqrt{1+x^2}} = \frac{x}{\sqrt{1+x^2}}$$

$$\Rightarrow \left.\frac{dy}{dx}\right|_{100} = \frac{100}{\sqrt{1+100^2}} \text{ and } y|_{100} = \sqrt{1+100^2}$$

$\therefore$ $f(100) f'(100) = 100$

ILLUSTRATION 68: If $\sqrt{x^2+y^2} = e^{\sin^{-1}\frac{y}{\sqrt{x^2+y^2}}}$. Prove that $\dfrac{d^2y}{dx^2} = \dfrac{2(x^2+y^2)}{(x-y)^3}$, $x > 0$

SOLUTION: Given $\sqrt{x^2+y^2} = e^{\sin^{-1}\frac{y}{\sqrt{x^2+y^2}}}$

Taking $\log_e$ on both sides, we get $-\log(x^2+y^2) = \sin^{1}\dfrac{}{\sqrt{x^2 \quad y^2}}$

$$\Rightarrow \log(x^2+y^2) = 2\tan^{-1}\left(\frac{y}{x}\right)$$

Differentiating both side, we get $\dfrac{1}{(x^2+y^2)}\left(2x + 2y\dfrac{dy}{dx}\right) = \dfrac{2}{1+\dfrac{y^2}{x^2}} \times \left(\dfrac{x\dfrac{dy}{dx} - y}{x^2}\right)$

$\Rightarrow \dfrac{\left(x + y\dfrac{dy}{dx}\right)}{x^2+y^2} = \dfrac{\left(x\dfrac{dy}{dx} - y\right)}{(x^2+y^2)}$ $\qquad \Rightarrow x + y\dfrac{dy}{dx} = x\dfrac{dy}{dx} - y$

$\Rightarrow (x+y) = (x-y)\dfrac{dy}{dx}$ $\qquad \Rightarrow \dfrac{dy}{dx} = \dfrac{(x+y)}{(x-y)}$

$$\frac{d^2y}{dx^2} = \frac{(x-y)\left(1+\frac{dy}{dx}\right) - (x+y)\left(1-\frac{dy}{dx}\right)}{(x-y)^2} = \frac{(x-y)\left(1+\frac{x+y}{x-y}\right) - (x+y)\left(1-\frac{x+y}{x-y}\right)}{(x-y)^2}$$

$$= \frac{\frac{2x(x-y)}{x-y} + \frac{2y(x+y)}{x-y}}{(x-y)^2} = \frac{2(x^2 - xy + xy + y^2)}{(x-y)^3} = 2\frac{(x^2+y^2)}{(x-y)^3}$$

ILLUSTRATION 69: The equation $y^2e^{xy} = 9e^{-3}x^2$ defines y as a differentiable function of x. The value of $\frac{dy}{dx}$ for $x = -1$ and $y = 3$

(a) $-\frac{15}{2}$ (b) $-\frac{9}{5}$

(c) 3 (d) 15

SOLUTION: $y^2\left(e^{xy}\left(x\frac{dy}{dx}+y\right)\right)+e^{xy}.2y\frac{dy}{dx}=9e^{-3}.2x$

Put $x = -1$ and $y = 3$

$$9\left(e^{-3}\left(-1\frac{dy}{dx}+3\right)\right)+e^{-3}.6\frac{dy}{dx}=-9e^{-3}.2$$

$$\Rightarrow -9\left(\frac{dy}{dx}-3\right)+6\frac{dy}{dx}=-18 \qquad \Rightarrow 3\frac{dy}{dx}=45 \Rightarrow \frac{dy}{dx}=15$$

TEXTUAL EXERCISE–6: (SUBJECTIVE)

1. Differentiate the following functions
   (a) $x^3 + ax^2y + bxy^2 + y^2 = 0$
   (b) $\sin(xy) + \cos(xy) = \tan(x + y)$
2. Differentiate the following w.r.t x:
   (a) $2^x + 2^y = 2^{x+y}$
   (b) $y \sin x - \cos(x - y) = 0$
3. If $y\sqrt{1-x^2}+x\sqrt{1-y^2}=1$, find $\frac{dy}{dx}$.
4. Differentiate $y = x+\sqrt{x+\sqrt{x+\sqrt{x+}}}$ ....∞
5. If $xe^{xy} - y = \sin^2 x$, then find dy/dx at $x = 0$.
6. Differentiate the following implicit functions w.r.t x
   (a) Where $x^py^q = (x + y)^{p+q}$ and hence prove that $\frac{dy}{dx}=\frac{y}{x}$
   (b) Where $x = x^{y^x}$, and hence show that $\frac{dy}{dx}=\frac{y\ln y}{x\ln x}\left(\frac{1+x\ln x\ln y}{1-x\ln y}\right)$
7. $x^3 + y^3 - 3axy = 0$, find $\frac{dy}{dx}$
8. If $y = \ln\left(x^{e^x}.a^y\right)^{y^x}$ find $\frac{dy}{dx}$
9. If $x^4 + 7x^2y^2 + 9y^4 = 24xy^3$, show that one of the possibility of $\frac{dy}{dx}=\frac{y}{x}$
10. If $(a - b\cos y)(a + b\cos x) = a^2 - b^2$, then show that $\frac{dy}{dx}=\frac{\sqrt{a^2-b^2}}{(a+b\cos x)}$
11. If $(x + y) = e^{x-y}$, prove that $\frac{d^2y}{dx^2}=\frac{4(x+y)}{(x+y+1)^3}$

Answer Keys

1. (a) $-\frac{3x^2+2axy+by^2}{ax^2+2bxy+2y}$ (b) $-\frac{[y\cos^2(x+y)\{\cos(xy)-\sin(xy)\}-1]}{[x\cos^2(x+y)\{\cos(xy)-\sin(xy)\}-1]}$

2. (a) $2^{x-y}\frac{2^y-1}{1-2^x}$ (b) $\frac{y\cos x+\sin(x-y)}{\sin(x-y)-\sin x}$ 3. $-\frac{\sqrt{1-y^2}}{\sqrt{1-x^2}}$

4. $\left(\frac{2\sqrt{y}}{2\sqrt{y}-1}\right)$ 5. 1 7. $\frac{x^2-ay}{ax-y^2}$ 8. $\frac{xy\ell ny+y^xe^x(\ell nx+1)}{x[1-x-y^x\ell na]}$

TEXTUAL EXERCISE–6: (OBJECTIVE)

1. If $x^3 + 3x^2y - 6xy^2 + 2y^3 = 0$, then the value of $\frac{dy}{dx}$ at (1, 1) is

(a) 1 (b) –1
(c) 6 (d) None of these

2. If $x^2y + y^3 = 2$, then the value of $\frac{d^2y}{dx^2}$ at the point (1, 1) is

(a) $-\frac{3}{4}$ (b) $-\frac{3}{8}$
(c) $-\frac{5}{12}$ (d) None of these

3. $y = \sqrt{\sin x + \sqrt{\sin x + \sqrt{\sin x + ...\infty}}}$, then $\frac{dy}{dx}$ equals

(a) $\frac{\cos x}{2y-1}$ (b) $\frac{y}{2\tan x + y\sec x}$
(c) $\frac{1}{\sqrt{2+4\sin x}}$ (d) $\frac{2\cos x}{\sin x + 2y}$

4. If $\sin(x + y) = \log(x + y)$, then $\frac{dy}{dx} =$

(a) 2 (b) –2
(c) 1 (d) –1

5. If $e^{x+y} = xy$, then $\frac{d^2y}{dx^2}$ is equal to

(a) $\frac{x\left[(x+1)^2+(y+1)^2\right]}{y^2(x+1)^3}$

(b) $\frac{y\left[(x+1)^2+(y+1)^2\right]}{x^2(y+1)^3}$

(c) $-\frac{y\left[(x-1)^2+(y-1)^2\right]}{x^2(y-1)^3}$

(d) None of these

6. If $ax^2 + 2hxy + by^2 = 0$, then $\frac{dy}{dx}$ is equal to

(a) $\frac{y}{x}$ (b) $-\frac{y}{x}$
(c) $-\frac{x}{y}$ (d) $-\frac{ax+hy}{hx+by}$

7. If $\sin^{-1}\left(\frac{x^2-y^2}{x^2+y^2}\right) = \log a$, then $\frac{dy}{dx}$ is

(a) $\frac{xy}{\sqrt{x^2-y^2}}$ (b) $-x/y$
(c) y/x (d) None of these

8. If $y = \cfrac{x}{a+\cfrac{x}{b+\cfrac{x}{a+...\infty}}}$ then $\frac{dy}{dx} =$

(a) $\frac{a}{ab+2ay}$ (b) $\frac{b}{ab+2by}$
(c) $\frac{a}{ab+2by}$ (d) $\frac{b}{ab+2ay}$

9. If $\ln(x + y) = 2xy$, then y' at (0, 1) is equal to

(a) 1 (b) –1
(c) 2 (d) 0

10. If $\sin(xy) + \cos(xy) = 0$, then $\frac{dy}{dx} =$

(a) $\frac{y}{x}$ (b) $-\frac{y}{x}$
(c) $-\frac{x}{y}$ (d) $\frac{x}{y}$

11. If $x\sqrt{1+y} + y\sqrt{1+x} = 0$, then $\frac{dy}{dx} =$

(a) $\frac{1}{(1+x)^2}$ (b) $-\frac{1}{(1+x)^2}$
(c) $\frac{1}{(1+x)^2}$ (d) $\frac{1}{(1+x)}$

Answer Keys

1. (a) **2.** (b) **3.** (a) **4.** (d) **5.** (c) **6.** (a,b) **7.** (c) **8.** (d) **9.** (a) **10.** (b)
11. (b)

PARAMETRIC DIFFERENTIATION

In our book of co-ordinate geometry, we have already learnt that the Cartesian equation of the conics can also be given in the parametric form. For example the parabola $y^2 = 4ax$; the parametric from is given by $y = 2at$ and $x = at^2$. Therefore having established that a function 'y' of 'x' can be represented by the parametric equations as well. Lets say $x = g(t)$ and $y = h(t)$ are the parametric equations of $y = f(x)$.

Now, let us assume that these functions are differentiable and the inverse of the functions $x = g(t)$ is given by $t = G(x)$.

$f(x) = y = h(t)$ and $t = G(x)$

$\therefore\ f(x) = y = h(G(x))$

Differentiating w.r.t x; we get

$$\frac{dy}{dx} = \frac{d}{dx}\left(h\left(G(x)\right)\right) = \frac{d\left(h\left(G(x)\right)\right)}{d\left(G(x)\right)} \times \frac{d\left(G(x)\right)}{dx} = \frac{d\left(h(t)\right)}{dt} \times \frac{d\left(G(x)\right)}{dx} \qquad \text{...(i)}$$

Also, Since $x = g(t)$ and $t = G(x)$ are the inverse functions of each other, Therefore $\dfrac{d\left(G(x)\right)}{dx} = \dfrac{1}{\dfrac{d\left(g(t)\right)}{dt}}$

Substituting this value of $\dfrac{d\left(G(x)\right)}{dx}$ in (1); we get

$$\frac{dy}{dx} = \frac{d\left(h(t)\right)}{dt} \times \frac{1}{\dfrac{d\left(g(t)\right)}{dt}} = \frac{\dfrac{d\left(h(t)\right)}{dt}}{\dfrac{d\left(g(t)\right)}{dt}}$$

The above formula, allows us to find the differentiation of y w.r.t x without having to actually find y as a function of 'x'

$$\therefore\ \frac{dy}{dx} = \frac{dy}{dt} \times \frac{dt}{dx} = \frac{dy/dt}{dx/dt} = \frac{h'(t)}{g'(t)}$$

Similarly, differentiating again w.r.t x; we get

$$\frac{d^2y}{dx^2} = \frac{d}{dx}\left(\frac{dy}{dx}\right) = \frac{d}{dt}\left(\frac{dy}{dx}\right) \times \left(\frac{dt}{dx}\right) = \frac{d}{dt}$$

$$= \frac{d}{dt}\left(\frac{h't}{g't}\right) \times \frac{1}{dx/dt}$$

$$= \frac{h''(t) \times g'(t) - g''(t) \times h'(t)}{\left(g'(t)\right)^3}$$

ILLUSTRATION 70: Find the $\dfrac{dy}{dx}$ for the following parametric functions:

(a) $x = a\,(t + \sin t)$; $y = a(1 - \cos t)$ (b) $x = 2 \ln \cot t$; $y = \tan t + \cot t$

SOLUTION: (a) The derivative of x and y with respect to the parameter t;

$$\frac{dx}{dt} = a(1 - \cos t); \quad \frac{dy}{dt} = a \sin t$$

whence, $\dfrac{dy}{dx} = \dfrac{a \sin t}{a(1 - \cos t)} = \cot \dfrac{t}{2}$ $\quad (t \neq 2k\pi)$

(b) $\dfrac{dx}{dt} = \dfrac{-2\,\text{cosec}^2 t}{\cot t} = -\dfrac{4}{\sin 2t}$ $\quad \Rightarrow \dfrac{dy}{dt} = \sec^2 - \text{cosec}^2 t = -\dfrac{4 \cos 2t}{\sin^2 2t}$

$\Rightarrow \dfrac{dy}{dx} = \dfrac{4 \cos 2t \sin 2t}{4 \sin^2 2t} = \cot 2t$ $\quad (t \neq k\pi/2)$

ILLUSTRATION 71: Let the function $y = f(x)$ be given by $x = t^5 - 5t^3 - 20t + 7$ and $y = 4t^3 - 3t^2 - 18t + 3$, where $t \in (-2, 2)$. Then $f'(x)$ at $t = 1$ is

(a) $\dfrac{5}{2}$ (b) $\dfrac{2}{5}$

(c) $\dfrac{7}{5}$ (d) None of these

SOLUTION: (b) Let $f(x) = \frac{dy}{dx} = \frac{12t^2 - 6t - 18}{5t^4 - 15t^2 - 20}$

$$\therefore \quad f'(x)\Big]_{t=1} = \frac{12t^2 - 6t - 18}{5t^4 - 15t^2 - 20} = \frac{2}{5}$$

ILLUSTRATION 72: If $x = e^{-t^2}$ and $y = \tan^{-1}(2t+1)$, find $\frac{dy}{dx}$

SOLUTION: Here $x = e^{-t^2}$

On differentiating both sides, we get

$$\Rightarrow \frac{dx}{dt} = e^{-t^2}.(-2t) \quad \text{And } y = \tan^{-1}(2t+1)$$

On differentiating both sides, we get

$$\Rightarrow \frac{dy}{dt} = \frac{1}{1+(2t+1)^2}(2) \qquad \therefore \frac{dy}{dx} = \frac{\frac{dy}{dt}}{\frac{dx}{dt}} = \frac{\frac{2}{1+(4t^2+4t+1)}}{-\frac{2t}{e^{t^2}}}$$

Hence $\frac{dy}{dx} = \frac{-e^{t^2}}{2t(2t^2+2t+1)}$

ILLUSTRATION 73: Let $y = 3t^2 + 2t - 1$, $x = t^3 - 1$, find $\frac{dy}{dx}$ and $\frac{d^2y}{dx^2}$

SOLUTION: $\frac{dy}{dt} = 6t + 2; \quad \frac{dx}{dt} = 3t^2$

$$\frac{dy}{dx} = \frac{dy/dt}{dx/dt} = \frac{6t+2}{3t^2}$$

For second order derivative, we differentiate with respect to x

$$\frac{d}{dx}\left(\frac{dy}{dx}\right) = \frac{d^2y}{dx^2} = \frac{d}{dx}\left(\frac{6t+2}{3t^2}\right) \qquad \Rightarrow \frac{d^2y}{dx^2} = \frac{d}{dt}\left(\frac{6t+2}{3t^2}\right) \times \frac{dt}{dx}$$

$$= \frac{1}{3}\left[\frac{t^2(6) - (6t+2).2t}{t^4}\right] \times \frac{1}{3t^2} = \frac{-6t^2 - 4t}{9t^6} = \frac{-2(2+3t)}{9t^5}$$

ILLUSTRATION 74: If $u = f(x\geq)$, $v = g(x^2)$, $f'(x) = \cos x$, $g'(x) = \sin x$ then $\frac{du}{dv}$ is

(a) $\frac{3}{2}x \cos x^3 \cdot \operatorname{cosec} x^2$ (b) $\frac{2}{3}x \sin x^3 \cdot \sec x^2$

(c) $\tan x$ (d) None of these

SOLUTION: (a) $\frac{du}{dv} = \frac{\frac{du}{dx}}{\frac{dv}{dx}} = \frac{f'(x^3).3x^2}{g'(x^2).2x} = \frac{\cos x^3.3x^2}{\sin x^2.2x} = \frac{3}{2}x\cos x^3.\text{cosec}\, x^2.$

ILLUSTRATION 75: If $y = \sec 4x$ and $x = \tan^{-1}(t)$, prove that $\frac{dy}{dt} = \frac{16t(1-t^4)}{(1-6t^2+t^4)^2}$

SOLUTION: $y = \frac{1}{\cos 4x} = \frac{1+\tan^2 2x}{1-\tan^2 2x}$ ....(1)

using $\tan x = t$ (given)

$\tan 2x = \frac{2t}{1-t^2}$; substituting in (1)

$$y = \frac{1+\frac{4t^2}{(1-t^2)^2}}{1-\frac{4t^2}{(1-t^2)^2}} = \frac{(1+t^2)^2}{(1-t^2)^2-4t^2} = \frac{(1+t^2)^2}{1-6t^2+t^4}$$

$$\frac{dy}{dt} = \frac{(1-6t^2+t^4)\cdot 2(1+t^2)\cdot 2t-(1+t^2)(4t^3-12t)}{(1-6t^2+t^4)^2}$$

$$= \frac{4t(1+t^2)[(1-6t^2+t^4)-(1+t^2)(t^2-3)]}{\left(1-(t^2+t^4)^2\right)} = \frac{4t(1+t^2)(1-t^2)}{(1-6t^2+t^4)^2} = \frac{4t(1-t^4)}{(1-6t^2+t^4)^2}$$

ILLUSTRATION 76: If $x = 2\cos t - \cos 2t$ and $y = 2\text{sint} - \sin 2t$, find the value of (d^2y/dx^2) when $t = (\pi/2)$.

SOLUTION: $x = 2\cos t - \cos 2t$ $y = 2\sin t - \sin 2t$

$\frac{dx}{dt} = -2\sin t + 2\sin 2t$ $\frac{dy}{dt} = 2\cos t - 2\cos 2t$

$\frac{dx}{dt} = -2(\sin t - \sin 2t)$ $\frac{dx}{dt} = 2(\cos t - \cos 2t)$

$$\frac{dy}{dx} = \frac{\cos 2t - \cos t}{\sin t - \sin 2t}$$

$$\frac{d^2y}{dx^2} = \frac{(\sin t - \sin 2t)(-2\sin 2t + \sin t) - (\cos 2t - \cos t)(\cos t - 2\cos 2t)}{(\sin t - \sin 2t)^2} \times \frac{dt}{dx}$$

$$\left.\frac{d^2y}{dx^2}\right|_{t=\frac{\lambda}{2}} = \frac{1(1)-(-1)(+2)}{(1)^2} \times \frac{1}{-2(1)} = -\frac{3}{2} \text{ Ans.}$$

ILLUSTRATION 77: Find $\frac{d^2y}{dx^2}$ of following parametric functions:

(a) $x = a\cos^3 t$ and $y = b\sin^3 t$ (b) $x = e^t$ cost and $y = e^t \sin t$

SOLUTION: (a) $\frac{dx}{dt} = -3a\cos^2 t \sin t$ $\frac{dy}{dt} = 3b\sin^2 t \cos t$

$$\frac{dy}{dx} = -\frac{3b\sin^2 t\cos t}{3a\cos^2 t\sin t} = -\frac{b}{a}\tan t \qquad \left(t \neq (2k+1)\frac{\pi}{2}\right)$$

$$\frac{d^2y}{dx^2} = -\frac{b}{a\cos^2 t(-3a\cos^2 t\sin t)} = \frac{b}{3a^2\cos^4 t\sin t}$$

(b) $\frac{dx}{dt} = e^t \cos t - e^t \sin t = e^t(\cos t - \sin t)$

$\frac{dy}{dt} = e^t \sin t + e^t \cos t = e^t(\cos t + \sin t)$

$$\frac{dy}{dx} = \frac{\cos t + \sin t}{\cos t - \sin t} \Rightarrow \frac{d^2y}{dx^2} = \frac{\frac{d}{dt}\left(\frac{\cos t + \sin t}{\cos t - \sin t}\right)}{e^t(\cos t - \sin t)} = \frac{2}{e^t(\cos t - \sin t)^3}$$

ILLUSTRATION 78: If $y = \tan^{-1}\dfrac{u}{\sqrt{1-u^2}}$ and $x = \sec^{-1}\dfrac{1}{2u^2-1}$, $u \in \left(0, \dfrac{1}{\sqrt{2}}\right) \cup \left(\dfrac{1}{\sqrt{2}}, 1\right)$ prove that $2\dfrac{dy}{dx} + 1 = 0.$

SOLUTION: $y = \tan^{-1}\dfrac{u}{\sqrt{1-u^2}}$

$y = \sin^{-1}u$

$x = \sec^{-1}\dfrac{1}{2u^2-1} = \cos^{-1}(2u^2 - 1)$

$y = \sin^{-1} u$

$$\frac{dy}{du} = \frac{1}{\sqrt{1-u^2}}$$

$$\frac{dx}{du} = \frac{-1}{\sqrt{1-(2u^2-1)^2}}(4u)$$

$$= -\frac{4u}{\sqrt{1-4u^4-1+4u^2}} = -\frac{4u}{\sqrt{4u^2(1-u^2)}} = -\frac{2}{\sqrt{1-u^2}}$$

$$\frac{dy}{dx} = -\frac{1}{2}$$

$$\Rightarrow 2\left(\frac{dy}{dx}\right) + 1 = 0$$

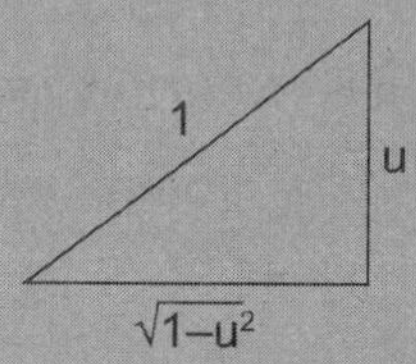

FIGURE 3.12

ILLUSTRATION 79: If $x = at^3$, $y = bt^2$ (t a parameter), find

(i) $\dfrac{d^3y}{dx^3}$ (ii) $\dfrac{d^3x}{dy^3}$

SOLUTION: (i) $x = at^3 \Rightarrow \dfrac{dx}{dt} = 3at^2$

$y = bt^2 \Rightarrow \dfrac{dy}{dt} = 2bt$

$$\Rightarrow \frac{dy}{dx} = \frac{dy/dt}{dx/dt} = \frac{2bt}{3at^2} = \frac{2b}{3at}$$

$$\Rightarrow \frac{d^2y}{dx^2} = \frac{2b}{3a}\frac{d}{dx}\left(\frac{1}{t}\right) = \frac{2b}{3a}.\frac{-1}{t^2}.\frac{dt}{dx} = \frac{-2b}{3at^2}.\frac{1}{3at^2} = \frac{-2b}{9a^2t^4}$$

Again differentiating both sides with respect to x

$$\frac{d^3y}{dx^3} = \frac{d}{dt}\left(\frac{d^2y}{dx^2}\right).\frac{dt}{dx} = -\frac{2b}{9a^2}\frac{d}{dt}\left(\frac{1}{t^4}\right).\frac{dt}{dx}$$

$$= -\frac{2b}{9a^2}.\frac{-4}{t^5}.\frac{1}{3at^2} = \frac{8b}{27a^3t^7}$$

(ii) $x = at^3, y = bt^2 \Rightarrow \dfrac{dx}{dt} = 3at^2; \dfrac{dy}{dt} = 2bt$

$$\Rightarrow \frac{dx}{dy} = \frac{dx/dt}{dy/dt} = \frac{3at^2}{2bt} = \frac{3at}{2b} \qquad \Rightarrow \frac{d^2x}{dy^2} = \frac{3a/2b}{dy/dt} = \frac{3a}{2b}.\frac{1}{2bt} = \frac{3a}{4b^2t}$$

$$\Rightarrow \frac{d^3x}{dy^3} = \frac{d}{dy}\left(\frac{3a}{4b^2t}\right) = \frac{3a}{4b^2}.\frac{d}{dt}\left(\frac{1}{t}\right).\frac{1}{dy/dt} = \left(\frac{3a}{4b^2}\right)\left(-\frac{1}{t^2}\right).\left(\frac{1}{2bt}\right) = \frac{-3a}{8b^3t^3}$$

ILLUSTRATION 80: Find $\frac{dy}{dx}, \frac{d^2y}{dx^2}$ and hence find the values of the parameter for which $y = f(x)$ increases or decreases. Also find $\frac{d^3y}{dx^3}$, where $y = f(x)$ is represented parametrically as

(i) $x = at^2, y = 2at$ (ii) $x = a\cos\theta, y = b\sin\theta$

SOLUTION: (i) For $x = at^2, y = 2at$

$$\frac{dy}{dx} = \frac{dy/dt}{dx/dt} = \frac{2a}{2\text{at}} = \frac{1}{t}$$

$$\frac{d^2y}{dx^2} = \frac{d}{dx}\left(\frac{dy}{dx}\right) = \frac{d}{dt}\left(\frac{dy}{dx}\right) \times \frac{dt}{dx} = \frac{d}{dt}\left(\frac{dy}{dx}\right) \times \frac{1}{\frac{dx}{dt}} = \frac{-1}{t^2} \times \frac{1}{2\text{at}} = -\frac{1}{2\text{at}^3}$$

Now for $t > 0$; $\frac{1}{t} > 0 \Rightarrow \frac{dy}{dx} > 0$

$\therefore$ $y = f(x)$ is increasing and $\frac{d^2y}{dx^2} = \frac{-1}{2at^3} < 0$

hence concave downward

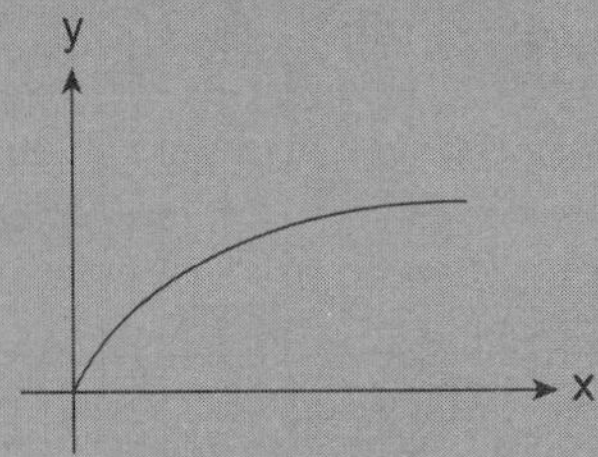

FIGURE 3.13

And for $t < 0$; $\frac{1}{t} < 0 \Rightarrow \frac{dy}{dx} < 0$

$y = f(x)$ is decreasing and $\frac{d^2y}{dx^2} = \frac{-1}{2at^3} > 0$ hence concave upwards

Now, we need to find $\frac{d^3y}{dx^3}$

$$\frac{d^3y}{dx^3} = \frac{d}{dx}\left(\frac{d^2y}{dx^2}\right) = \frac{d}{dt}\left(\frac{d^2y}{dx^2}\right) \times \frac{dt}{dx} = \frac{d}{dt}\left(\frac{d^2y}{dx^2}\right) \times \frac{1}{dx/dt}$$

$$= \frac{d}{dt}\left(\frac{-1}{2at^3}\right) \times \frac{1}{2at} = \frac{3}{2at^4} \times \frac{1}{2at} = \frac{3}{4a^2t^5}$$

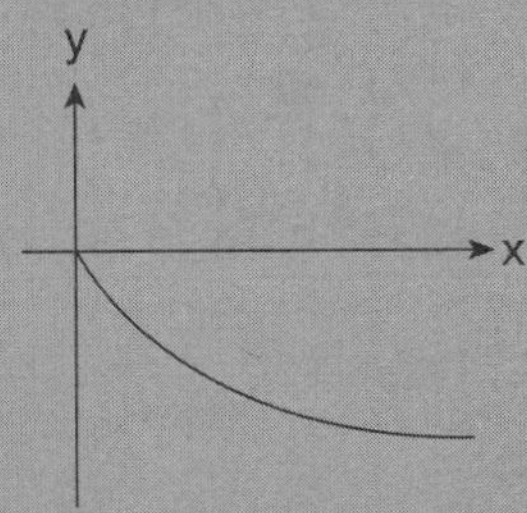

FIGURE 3.14

(ii) For $x = a\cos\theta, y = b\sin\theta$

$$\frac{dy}{dx} = \frac{dy/d\theta}{dx/d\theta} = \frac{b\cos\theta}{-a\sin\theta} = \frac{-b}{a}\cot\theta$$

$$\frac{d^2y}{dx^2} = \frac{dy}{dx}\left(\frac{dy}{dx}\right) = \frac{d}{d\theta}\left(-\frac{b}{a}\cot\theta\right) \times \frac{1}{dx/d\theta}$$

$$= \frac{-b}{a}\left(-\text{cosec}^2\theta\right) \times \frac{1}{-a\sin\theta}$$

$$= \frac{-b}{a^2}\text{cosec}^3\theta$$

For $\theta \in (0, \pi/2)$; $\frac{dy}{dx} < 0$ and $\frac{d^2y}{dx^2} < 0$

$\therefore$ $y = f(x)$ is decreasing and is concave down

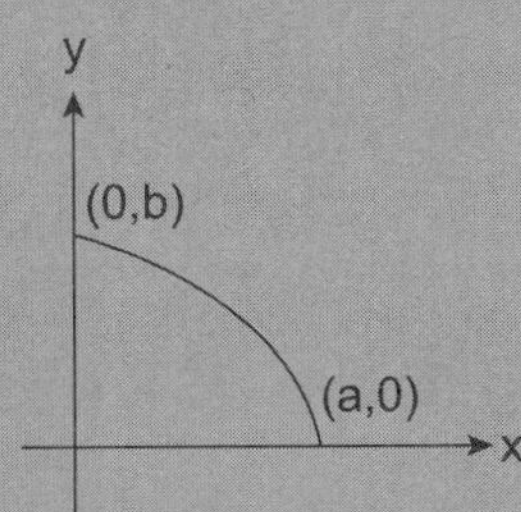

FIGURE 3.15

For $\theta \in (\pi/2,\pi)$; $\frac{dy}{dx} > 0$ & $\frac{d^2y}{dx^2} < 0$

$y = f(x)$ is increasing and is concave downwards.

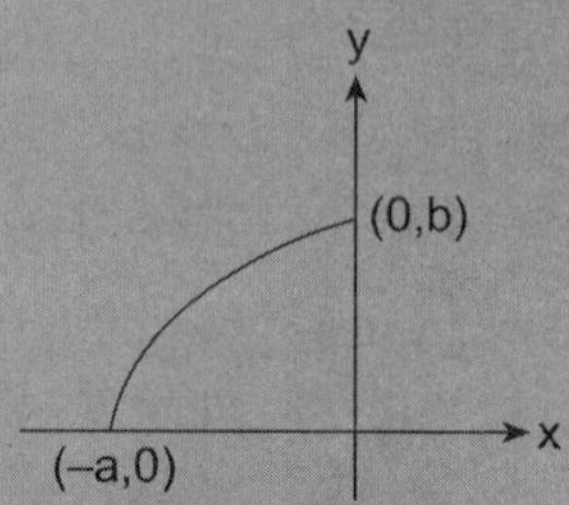

FIGURE 3.16

For $\theta \in (\pi,3\pi/2)$; $\frac{dy}{dx} < 0$ and $\frac{d^2y}{dx^2} > 0$

$\therefore$ $y f(x)$ is decreasing and is concave upwards

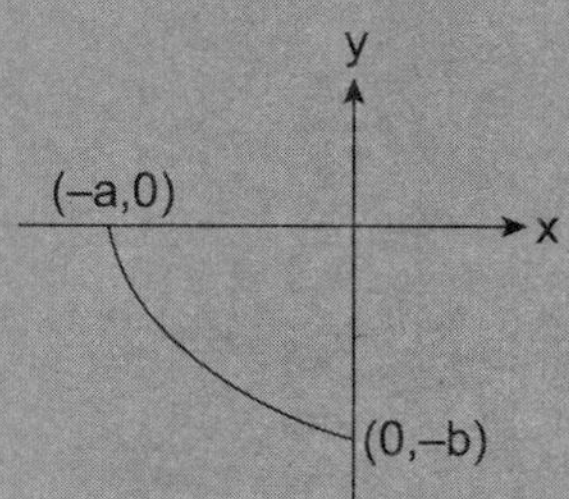

FIGURE 3.17

For $\theta \in (3\pi/2\pi)$; $\frac{dy}{dx} > 0$ and $\frac{d^2y}{dx^2} > 0$

$\therefore$ $y = f(x)$ is an increasing function and is concave upwards

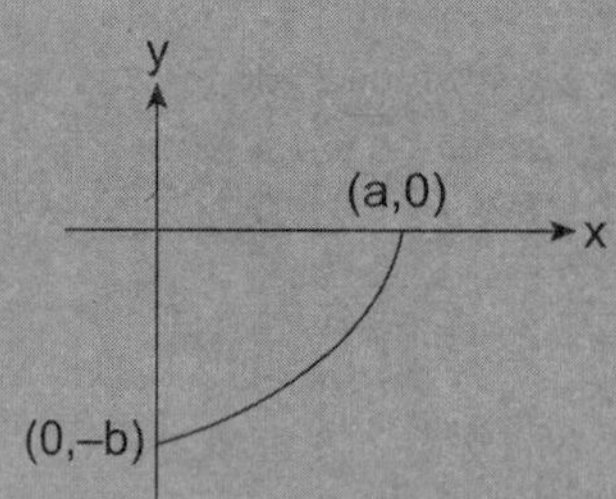

FIGURE 3.18

Now, we need to find $\frac{d^3y}{dx^3}$

$$\frac{d^3y}{dx^3} = \frac{d}{dx}\left(\frac{d^2y}{dx^2}\right) = \frac{d}{d\theta}\left(\frac{d^2y}{dx^2}\right) \times \frac{1}{\frac{dx}{d\theta}} = \frac{d}{d\theta}\left(\frac{-b}{a^2}\text{cosec}^2\theta\right) \times \frac{1}{-a\sin\theta}$$

$$= -\frac{b}{a^2} \times 3\text{cosec}^2\theta\left(-\text{cosec}\,\theta\cot\theta\right) \times \frac{-1}{a\sin\theta} = \frac{3b}{a^2}\text{cosec}^3\theta\cot\theta \times \frac{-1}{a\sin\theta} = \frac{-3b}{a^3}\text{cosec}^4\theta\cot\theta$$

TEXTUAL EXERCISE–7: (SUBJECTIVE)

1. Differentiate the following
(a) $x = a(\cos t + t\sin t);\ y = a(\sin t - t\cos t)$
(b) $x = a\dfrac{1-t^2}{1+t^2};\ y = b\dfrac{2t}{1+t^2}$
(c) $x = \dfrac{2at^2}{1+t^2};\ y = \dfrac{2at^3}{1+t^2}$
(d) $x = a\sqrt{\left(\dfrac{t^2-1}{t^2+1}\right)};\quad y = at\sqrt{\left(\dfrac{t^2-1}{t^2+1}\right)}$
(e) $x = a\left(\cos t + \log\tan\dfrac{1}{2}t\right);\ y = a\sin t$
(f) $x = \sin\sqrt{\cos 2t};\ y = \cos\sqrt{\cos 2t}$

2. If $x = t + \dfrac{1}{t}$ and $y = t - \dfrac{1}{t}$; then prove that $\dfrac{dy}{dx} = \dfrac{x}{y}$

3. Find the derivative of the functions which are defined parametrically.
(a) $\begin{cases} x = a\cos^3 t \\ y = b\sin^2 t \end{cases}$ (b) $\begin{cases} x = e^t\cos t \\ y = e^t\sin t \end{cases}$

4. Find $\dfrac{dy}{dx}$, where $x = \dfrac{\sin^3 t}{\sqrt{\cos 2t}};\ y = \dfrac{\cos^3 t}{\sqrt{\cos 2t}}$ for $t = \pi/6$

5. If $u = \sin^{-1} x$ and $v = x^3$; prove that $\dfrac{dv}{du} = 3\sqrt{v\left(v^{1/3} - v\right)}$

6. If $x = a(\cos t + t\sin t)$, $y = a(\sin t - t\cos t)$. Then find the value of $\dfrac{d^2y}{dx^2}$ when $t = \dfrac{\pi}{4}$

Answer Keys

1. (a) $\tan t$ (b) $\dfrac{(t^2-1)}{2at}$ (c) $\dfrac{3t+t^3}{2}$ (d) $\dfrac{t^4+2t^2-1}{2t}$ (e) $\tan t$ (f) $-\tan\left(\sqrt{\cos 2t}\right)$

3. (a) $\left(\dfrac{-2}{3}\sec t\right)\dfrac{b}{a}$ (b) $\dfrac{\cos t + \sin t}{\cos t - \sin t}$ 4. 0 6. 2

TEXTUAL EXERCISE–7: (OBJECTIVE)

1. If $x = 2\sin t - \sin 2t$, $y = 2\cos t - \cos 2t$, then the value of $\dfrac{d^2y}{dx^2}$ at $t = \dfrac{\pi}{2}$ is
(a) 2 (b) $-\dfrac{1}{2}$
(c) $-\dfrac{3}{4}$ (d) $-\dfrac{3}{2}$

2. If $y = \dfrac{\sqrt{(1+t^2)} - \sqrt{(1-t^2)}}{\sqrt{(1+t^2)} + \sqrt{(1-t^2)}}$ and $x = \sqrt{(1-t^4)}$ then $\dfrac{dy}{dx}$ is
(a) $\dfrac{-1}{t^2\left[1+\sqrt{(1-t^4)}\right]}$ (b) $\dfrac{\left[\sqrt{(1-t^4)}-1\right]}{t^6}$
(c) $\dfrac{1}{t^2\left[1+\sqrt{(1-t^4)}\right]}$ (d) $\dfrac{\left[1-\sqrt{(1-t^4)}\right]}{t^6}$

3. If $x = a[\cos t + \log\tan(t/2)]$, $y = a\sin t$ then:
(a) $\left(\dfrac{dy}{dx}\right) = 0$
(b) $\left(\dfrac{dy}{dx}\right)_{t=\pi/2} = \infty$
(c) $\left(\dfrac{d^2y}{dx^2}\right)_{t=\pi/4} = \dfrac{2\sqrt{2}}{a}$
(d) None of these

4. If $x = a\cos^3\theta$, $y = a\sin^3\theta$, then $\sqrt{\left[1+\left(\dfrac{dy}{dx}\right)^2\right]}$ is equal to
(a) $\tan^2\theta$ (b) $\sec^2\theta$
(c) $\sec\theta$ (d) $|\sec\theta|$

5. Let the function $y = f(x)$ be given by $x = t^5 - 5t^3 - 20t + 7$ and $y = 4t^3 - 3t^2 - 18t + 3$ where $t \in (-2, 2)$ then $f'(x)$ at $t = 1$ is

(a) 5/2 (b) 2/5
(c) 7/5 (d) None of these

6. If $x = t^3 + t + 5$ and $y = \sin t$, then $\frac{d^2y}{dx^2}$ is equal to

(a) $-\frac{(3t^2+1)\sin t + 6t\cos t}{(3t^2+1)^3}$

(b) $\frac{(3t^2+1)\sin t + 6t\cos t}{(3t^2+1)^2}$

(c) $-\frac{(3t^2+1)\sin t + 6t\cos t}{(3t^2+1)^2}$

(d) $\frac{\cos t}{3t^2+1}$

7. If $x = \frac{1+t}{t^3}, y = \frac{3}{2t^2} + \frac{2}{t}$ then, $x\left(\frac{dy}{dx}\right)^3 - \frac{dy}{dx} =$

(a) 0 (b) –1
(c) 1 (d) 2

Answer Keys

1. (d) **2.** (a,b) **3.** (b,c) **4.** (d) **5.** (b) **6.** (a) **7.** (c)

■ DETERMINANT FORMS OF DIFFERENTIATION

If y is a function of x given in determinant form as

$$y = \begin{vmatrix} f(x) & g(x) \\ u(x) & v(x) \end{vmatrix} = f(x)v(x) - u(x)g(x)$$

$$\Rightarrow \frac{dy}{dx} = f(x)\,u'(x) + v(x)f'(x) - u(x)g'(x) - g(x)u'(x)$$

$$= f'(x)v(x) - u(x)g'(x) + v'(x)f(x) - u'(x)g(x)$$

$$= \begin{vmatrix} f'(x) & g'(x) \\ u(x) & v(x) \end{vmatrix} + \begin{vmatrix} f(x) & g(x) \\ u'(x) & v'(x) \end{vmatrix}$$

Similarly $y = \begin{vmatrix} u(x) & v(x) & w(x) \\ p(x) & q(x) & r(x) \\ \lambda(x) & \mu(x) & \gamma(x) \end{vmatrix}$ then

$$\frac{dy}{dx} = \begin{vmatrix} u'(x) & v'(x) & w'(x) \\ p(x) & q(x) & r(x) \\ \lambda(x) & \mu(x) & \gamma(x) \end{vmatrix} + \begin{vmatrix} u(x) & v(x) & w(x) \\ p'(x) & q'(x) & r'(x) \\ \lambda(x) & \mu(x) & \gamma(x) \end{vmatrix} + \begin{vmatrix} u(x) & v(x) & w(x) \\ p(x) & q(x) & r(x) \\ \lambda'(x) & \mu'(x) & \gamma'(x) \end{vmatrix}$$

The differentiation can also be done Column-wise

ILLUSTRATION 81: If $f(x) = \begin{vmatrix} x^2 & x^3 & x^4 \\ 2x & 3x^2 & 4x^3 \\ 2 & 6x & 12x^2 \end{vmatrix}$ find $f'(x)$.

SOLUTION: On differentiating the given function, we get

$$\Rightarrow f'(x) = \begin{vmatrix} \frac{d}{dx}(x^2) & \frac{d}{dx}(x^3) & \frac{d}{dx}(x^4) \\ 2x & 3x^2 & 4x^3 \\ 2 & 6x & 12x^2 \end{vmatrix} + \begin{vmatrix} x^2 & x^3 & x^4 \\ \frac{d}{dx}(2x) & \frac{d}{dx}(3x^2) & \frac{d}{dx}(4x^3) \\ 2 & 6x & 12x^2 \end{vmatrix} + \begin{vmatrix} x^2 & x^3 & x^4 \\ 2x & 3x^2 & 4x^3 \\ \frac{d}{dx}(2) & \frac{d}{dx}(6x) & \frac{d}{dx}(12x^2) \end{vmatrix}$$

$$\text{or } f'(x) = \begin{vmatrix} 2x & 3x^2 & 4x^3 \\ 2x & 3x^2 & 4x^3 \\ 2 & 6x & 12x^2 \end{vmatrix} + \begin{vmatrix} x^2 & x^3 & x^4 \\ 2 & 6x & 12x^2 \\ 2 & 6x & 12x^2 \end{vmatrix} + \begin{vmatrix} x^2 & x^3 & x^4 \\ 2x & 3x^2 & 4x^3 \\ 0 & 6 & 24x \end{vmatrix}$$

As we know if any two rows and columns are identical, then value of determinant is zero.

$$\text{Therefore } f'(x) = 0 + 0 + \begin{vmatrix} x^2 & x^3 & x^4 \\ 2x & 3x^2 & 4x^3 \\ 0 & 6 & 24x \end{vmatrix}$$

$\therefore\ f'(x) = 24x^5 - 12x^5 \qquad \Rightarrow f'(x) = 12x^5$

ILLUSTRATION 82: If $f(x) = \begin{vmatrix} (x-a)^4 & (x-a)^3 & 1 \\ (x-b)^4 & (x-b)^3 & 1 \\ (x-c)^4 & (x-c)^3 & 1 \end{vmatrix}$ then $f'(x) = \lambda \begin{vmatrix} (x-a)^4 & (x-a)^2 & 1 \\ (x-b)^4 & (x-b)^2 & 1 \\ (x-c)^4 & (x-c)^2 & 1 \end{vmatrix}$. Find the value of λ.

SOLUTION: $f(x) = \begin{vmatrix} (x-a)^4 & (x-a)^3 & 1 \\ (x-b)^4 & (x-b)^3 & 1 \\ (x-c)^4 & (x-c)^3 & 1 \end{vmatrix}$

$$f'(x) = \begin{vmatrix} 4(x-a)^3 & (x-a)^3 & 1 \\ 4(x-b)^3 & (x-b)^3 & 1 \\ 4(x-c)^3 & (x-c)^3 & 1 \end{vmatrix} + \begin{vmatrix} (x-a)^4 & 3(x-a)^2 & 1 \\ (x-b)^4 & 3(x-b)^2 & 1 \\ (x-c)^4 & 3(x-c)^2 & 1 \end{vmatrix} + \begin{vmatrix} (x-a)^4 & (x-a)^3 & 0 \\ (x-b)^4 & (x-b)^3 & 0 \\ (x-c)^4 & (x-c)^3 & 0 \end{vmatrix}$$

$$= 3\begin{vmatrix} (x-a)^4 & (x-a)^2 & 1 \\ (x-b)^4 & (x-b)^2 & 1 \\ (x-c)^4 & (x-c)^2 & 1 \end{vmatrix}$$

$\lambda = 3$

ILLUSTRATION 83: If $f(x) = \begin{vmatrix} \cos(x+x^2) & \sin(x+x^2) & -\cos(x+x^2) \\ \sin(x-x^2) & \cos(x-x^2) & \sin(x-x^2) \\ \sin 2x & 0 & \sin 2x^2 \end{vmatrix}$ then find $f'(x)$.

SOLUTION: $f(x) = \begin{vmatrix} \cos(x+x^2) & \sin(x+x^2) & -\cos(x+x^2) \\ \sin(x-x^2) & \cos(x-x^2) & \sin(x-x^2) \\ \sin 2x & 0 & \sin 2x^2 \end{vmatrix}$

$= \sin 2x\,[\sin(x + x^2)\sin(x - x^2) + \cos(x - x^2)\cos(x + x^2)]$

$+ \sin 2x^2\,[\cos(x + x^2)\cos(x - x^2) - \sin(x + x^2) + \sin(x - x^2)]$

$= \sin 2x \cos(x + x^2 - x + x^2) + \sin 2x^2 \cos 2x = \sin 2x.\cos 2x^2 + \sin 2x^2.\cos 2x$

$\Rightarrow f(x) = \sin(2x + 2x^2)$

$\Rightarrow f'(x) = \cos(2x + 2x^2)(2 + 4x)$

ILLUSTRATION 84: If α be a repeated root of a quadratic equation $f(x) = 0$ and $A(x)$, $B(x)$, $C(x)$ be the polynomials of degree 3, 4 and 5 respectively, then show that $\begin{vmatrix} A(x) & B(x) & C(x) \\ A(\alpha) & B(\alpha) & C(\alpha) \\ A'(\alpha) & B'(\alpha) & C'(\alpha) \end{vmatrix}$ is divisible by $f(x)$, where dash denotes the derivative.

SOLUTION: $f(x) = a\,(x-\alpha)^2$

Let $g(x) = \begin{vmatrix} A(x) & B(x) & C(x) \\ A(\alpha) & B(\alpha) & C(\alpha) \\ A'(\alpha) & B'(\alpha) & C'(\alpha) \end{vmatrix}$

$$g(\alpha) = \begin{vmatrix} A(\alpha) & B(\alpha) & C(\alpha) \\ A(\alpha) & B(\alpha) & C(\alpha) \\ A'(\alpha) & B'(\alpha) & C'(\alpha) \end{vmatrix} = 0$$

$\Rightarrow$ α is the root of $g'(x)$

$$\text{and } g(\alpha) = \begin{vmatrix} A'(\alpha) & B'(\alpha) & C'(\alpha) \\ A(\alpha) & B(\alpha) & C(\alpha) \\ A'(\alpha) & B'(\alpha) & C'(\alpha) \end{vmatrix} = 0$$

$\Rightarrow$ α is the root of $g'(x)$

$\Rightarrow$ α is the repeated root of $g(x)$ and hence $g(x)$ is divisible by $f(x)$.

ILLUSTRATION 85: Let $f(x) = \begin{vmatrix} a+x & b+x & c+x \\ \ell+x & m+x & n+x \\ p+x & q+x & r+x \end{vmatrix}$. Show that $f''(x) = 0$ and that $f(x) = f(0) + k\,x$ where k denotes the sum of all the co-factors of the elements in $f(0)$.

SOLUTION: $f(x) = \begin{vmatrix} a+x & b+x & c+x \\ \ell+x & m+x & n+x \\ p+x & q+x & r+x \end{vmatrix}$

$$\Rightarrow f'(x) = \begin{vmatrix} 1 & 1 & 1 \\ \ell+x & m+x & n+x \\ p+x & q+x & r+x \end{vmatrix} + \begin{vmatrix} a+x & b+x & c+x \\ 1 & 1 & 1 \\ p+x & q+x & r+x \end{vmatrix} + \begin{vmatrix} a+x & b+x & c+x \\ \ell+x & m+x & n+x \\ 1 & 1 & 1 \end{vmatrix}$$

$$\Rightarrow f''(x) = \begin{vmatrix} 0 & 0 & 0 \\ \ell+x & \ell+x & n+x \\ p+x & q+x & r+x \end{vmatrix} + \begin{vmatrix} 1 & 1 & 1 \\ 1 & 1 & 1 \\ p+x & q+x & r+x \end{vmatrix} + \begin{vmatrix} 1 & 1 & 1 \\ \ell+x & m+x & n+x \\ 1 & 1 & 1 \end{vmatrix} +$$

$$\begin{vmatrix} 1 & 1 & 1 \\ 1 & 1 & 1 \\ p+x & q+x & r+x \end{vmatrix} + \begin{vmatrix} a+x & b+x & c+x \\ 0 & 0 & 0 \\ p+x & q+x & r+x \end{vmatrix} + \begin{vmatrix} a+x & b+x & c+x \\ 1 & 1 & 1 \\ 1 & 1 & 1 \end{vmatrix} +$$

$$\begin{vmatrix} 1 & 1 & 1 \\ l+x & m+x & n+x \\ 1 & 1 & 1 \end{vmatrix} + \begin{vmatrix} a+x & b+x & c+x \\ 1 & 1 & 1 \\ 1 & 1 & 1 \end{vmatrix} + \begin{vmatrix} a+x & b+x & c+x \\ l+x & m+x & n+x \\ 0 & 0 & 0 \end{vmatrix}$$

$\Rightarrow f''(x) = 0$

$\therefore$ $f'(x)$ is a constant. (Let's say $f'(x) = a$) $\quad\therefore$ $f(x) = ax + b$ where 'b' is another constant.

Now, putting $x = 0 \Rightarrow b = f(0)$

$\therefore$ $f(x) = f(0) + ax;$ $\quad$ Now, we need to find $a = f'(x)$

$$= \begin{vmatrix} 1 & 1 & 1 \\ \ell+x & m+x & n+x \\ p+x & q+x & r+x \end{vmatrix} + \begin{vmatrix} a+x & b+x & c+x \\ 1 & 1 & 1 \\ p+x & q+x & r+x \end{vmatrix} + \begin{vmatrix} a+x & b+x & c+x \\ \ell+m & m+x & n+x \\ 1 & 1 & 1 \end{vmatrix}$$

$$\therefore \quad f'(0) = \begin{vmatrix} 1 & 1 & 1 \\ \ell & m & n \\ p & q & r \end{vmatrix} + \begin{vmatrix} a & b & c \\ 1 & 1 & 1 \\ p & q & r \end{vmatrix} + \begin{vmatrix} a & b & c \\ \ell & m & n \\ 1 & 1 & 1 \end{vmatrix}$$

$$= \begin{vmatrix} m & n \\ q & r \end{vmatrix} - \begin{vmatrix} \ell & n \\ p & r \end{vmatrix} + \begin{vmatrix} \ell & m \\ p & q \end{vmatrix} - \begin{vmatrix} b & c \\ q & r \end{vmatrix} + \begin{vmatrix} a & c \\ p & r \end{vmatrix} - \begin{vmatrix} a & b \\ p & q \end{vmatrix} + \begin{vmatrix} b & c \\ m & n \end{vmatrix} - \begin{vmatrix} a & c \\ \ell & n \end{vmatrix} + \begin{vmatrix} a & b \\ \ell & m \end{vmatrix}$$

= sum of cofactors of the elements of $f(0)$.

ILLUSTRATION 86: If $Y = SX$ and $Z = tX$, where all the letters denotes the functions of x and suffixes denotes the differentiation w.r.t. x, then prove that $\begin{vmatrix} X & Y & Z \\ X_1 & Y_1 & Z_1 \\ X_2 & Y_2 & Z_2 \end{vmatrix} = X^3 \begin{vmatrix} S_1 & t_1 \\ S_2 & t_2 \end{vmatrix}$

SOLUTION: $Y = SX$; $Z = tX$

$Y_1 = S_1X + SX_1$; $Z_1 = t_1x + tx_1$ $\qquad$ $Y_2 = S_2X + 2S_1X_1 + SX_2$; $Z_2 = t_2x + tx_2 + 2t_1x_1$

$$\text{Now} \begin{vmatrix} X & Y & Z \\ X_1 & Y_1 & Z_1 \\ X_2 & Y_2 & Z_2 \end{vmatrix} = \begin{vmatrix} X & SX & tX \\ X_1 & S_1X + SX_1 & t_1X + tX_1 \\ X_2 & S_2X + SX_2 + 2S_1X_1 & t_2X + tX_2 + 2t_1X_1 \end{vmatrix}$$

On applying the transformation $\begin{cases} C_2 \Rightarrow C_2 - SC_1 \\ C_3 \Rightarrow C_3 - SC_1 \end{cases}$;

$$\text{we get} \begin{vmatrix} X & 0 & 0 \\ X_1 & S_1X & t_1x \\ X_2 & S_2X + 2S_1X_1 & t_2X + 2t_1X_1 \end{vmatrix} = X \begin{vmatrix} S_1X & t_1X \\ S_2X + 2S_1X_1 & t_2X + 2t_1X_1 \end{vmatrix}$$

Again applying the transformation, $R_2 \to R_2 - 2X_1.R_1$

$$= X^2 \begin{vmatrix} S_1 & t_1 \\ 2S_1X_1 + S_2X & 2t_1X_1 + t_2X \end{vmatrix}$$

$|R_2 \to R_2 - 2X_1 R_1|$

$$= X^2 \begin{vmatrix} S_1 & t_1 \\ S_2X & t_2X \end{vmatrix} = X^3 \begin{vmatrix} S_1 & t_1 \\ S_2 & t_2 \end{vmatrix}$$

ILLUSTRATION 87: If $f(x) = \begin{vmatrix} (1+x)^a & (1+2x)^b & 1 \\ 1 & (1+x)^a & (1+2x)^b \\ (1+2x)^b & 1 & (1+x)^a \end{vmatrix}$, then find

(a) constant term $\qquad$ (b) coefficient of x

SOLUTION: Here $f(x) = \begin{vmatrix} (1+x)^a & (1+2x)^b & 1 \\ 1 & (1+x)^a & (1+2x)^b \\ (1+2x)^b & 1 & (1+x)^a \end{vmatrix} = A + Bx + Cx^2 +$ .... (i)

Putting $x = 0$, we get $f(0) = \begin{vmatrix} 1 & 1 & 1 \\ 1 & 1 & 1 \\ 1 & 1 & 1 \end{vmatrix} = A + B(0) + C(0)^2 + ...$

$\Rightarrow A = 0$

Again differentiating (i) w.r.t. x we get

$$f'(x) = \begin{vmatrix} a(1+x)^{a-1} & 2b(1+2x)^{b-1} & 0 \\ 1 & (1+x)^a & (1+2x)^b \\ (1+2x)^b & 1 & (1+x)^a \end{vmatrix} + \begin{vmatrix} (1+x)^a & (1+2x)^b & 1 \\ 0 & a(1+x)^{a-1} & 2b(1+2x)^{b-1} \\ (1+2x)^b & 1 & (1+x)^a \end{vmatrix}$$

$$+ \begin{vmatrix} (1+x)^a & (1+2x)^b & 1 \\ 1 & (1+x)^a & (1+2x)^b \\ 2b(1+2x)^{b-1} & 0 & a(1+x)^{a-1} \end{vmatrix} = B + 2Cx + ...$$

$$f'(0) = \begin{vmatrix} a & 2b & 0 \\ 1 & 1 & 1 \\ 1 & 1 & 1 \end{vmatrix} + \begin{vmatrix} 1 & 1 & 1 \\ 0 & a & 2b \\ 1 & 1 & 1 \end{vmatrix} + \begin{vmatrix} 1 & 1 & 1 \\ 1 & 1 & 1 \\ 2b & 0 & a \end{vmatrix} = B$$

$\Rightarrow B = 0$ .....(ii)

$\therefore$ Coefficient of constant term = coefficient of $x = 0$

TEXTUAL EXERCISE–8: (SUBJECTIVE)

1. If $f(x) = \begin{vmatrix} x^3 & \sin x & \cos x \\ 6 & -1 & 0 \\ p & p^2 & p^3 \end{vmatrix}$, then prove that $\dfrac{d^3}{dx^3}[f(x)]$ $= 0$ at $x = 0$ (where p is constant)

2. If $y = \cos ax$ prove that $\begin{vmatrix} y & y_1 & y_2 \\ y_3 & y_4 & y_5 \\ y_6 & y_7 & y_8 \end{vmatrix} = 0$, where $y_r = \dfrac{d^r y}{dx^r}$

3. If $f(x) = \begin{vmatrix} 2x & x^2 & 3 \\ x^2 & x & 1 \\ 2 & 1 & x \end{vmatrix}$, then show that the coefficient of x in $f(x)$ is -8

4. If $p(x)$, $q(x)$ and $r(x)$ are polynomials of degree not greater than 3, show that $\begin{vmatrix} p(x) & q(x) & r(x) \\ p'(x) & q'(x) & r'(x) \\ p''(x) & q''(x) & r''(x) \end{vmatrix}$ is a polynomial of degree not greater than 3.

5. If $\begin{vmatrix} e^x & \sin x \\ \cos x & \log(1+x^2) \end{vmatrix} = A + Bx + Cx^2 + ...$, then $A =$ ____________ and $B =$ ____

6. If $\Delta_1 = \begin{vmatrix} x & b & b \\ a & x & b \\ a & a & x \end{vmatrix}$ and $\Delta_2 = \begin{vmatrix} x & b \\ a & x \end{vmatrix}$ are given, then prove that $\dfrac{d}{dx}\Delta_1 = 3\Delta_2$

7. If $\Delta = \begin{vmatrix} x & 1 & x^2 \\ x+2 & 2x+3 & x \\ x^2 & x^3+1 & 2x^4+1 \end{vmatrix}$ find the value of $\dfrac{d\Delta}{dx}$ at $x = 0$

8. If $y = \dfrac{u}{v}$, where u and v are functions of 'x' show that,

$$v^3 \frac{d^2 y}{dx^2} = \begin{vmatrix} u & v & 0 \\ u' & v' & v \\ u'' & v'' & 2v' \end{vmatrix}$$

9. If f, g and h are differentiable functions of x and $\Delta(x) = \begin{vmatrix} f & g & h \\ (xf)' & (xg)' & (xh)' \\ (x^2 f)'' & (x^2 g)'' & (x^2 h)'' \end{vmatrix}$, then prove that

$$\Delta'(x) = \begin{vmatrix} f & g & h \\ f' & g' & h' \\ (x^3 f'')' & (x^3 g'')' & (x^3 h'')' \end{vmatrix}$$

Answer Keys

5. $A = 0, B = -1$ **7.** 2

TEXTUAL EXERCISE–8: (OBJECTIVE)

1. The coefficient of x in the expansion of

$$f(x) = \begin{vmatrix} (x+2)^2 & (x+3)^2 & (x+4)^2 \\ x & x^2 & x^3 \\ 1 & 2x & 3x^2 \end{vmatrix}$$

(a) 1 (b) 2
(c) 3 (d) 0

2. If $\Delta(x) = \begin{vmatrix} x & 1+x^2 & x^3 \\ \log(1+x^2) & e^x & \sin x \\ \cos x & \tan x & \sin^2 x \end{vmatrix}$, then

(a) $\Delta(x)$ is divisible by x
(b) $\Delta(x) = 0$
(c) $\Delta'(x) = 0$
(d) None of the above

3. If $f(x) = \begin{vmatrix} x^n & \sin x & -\cos x \\ n! & \sin(n\pi/2) & \cos(n\pi/2) \\ a & a^2 & a^3 \end{vmatrix}$ then the value of $\dfrac{d^n}{dx^n}(f(x))$ at $x = 0$ for $n = 2m + 1$ is

(a) –1
(b) 0
(c) 1
(d) independent of a

4. If $f(x)$, $g(x)$, $h(x)$ are polynomials in x of degree 2 and $F(x) = \begin{vmatrix} f & g & h \\ f' & g' & h' \\ f'' & g'' & h'' \end{vmatrix}$, then $F'(x)$ is equal to

(a) 1 (b) 0
(c) –1 (d) $f(x), g(x), h(x)$

5. If $f(x) = \begin{vmatrix} \cos(x+x^2) & \sin(x+x^2) & -\cos(x+x^2) \\ \sin(x-x^2) & \cos(x-x^2) & \sin(x-x^2) \\ \sin 2x & 0 & \sin 2x^2 \end{vmatrix}$ then

(a) $f(-2) = 0$ (b) $f'(-1/2) = 0$
(c) $f'(-1) = 2$ (d) $f''(0) = 4$

6. Let $f(x) = \begin{vmatrix} \cos x & x & 1 \\ 2\sin x & x^2 & 2x \\ \tan x & x & 1 \end{vmatrix}$. Then $\lim\limits_{x\to 0} \dfrac{f'(x)}{x} =$

(a) 2 (b) –2
(c) –1 (d) 1

7. Let $f(x) = \begin{vmatrix} \cos x & \sin x & \cos x \\ \cos 2x & \sin 2x & 2\cos 2x \\ \cos 3x & \sin 3x & 3\cos 3x \end{vmatrix}$, then $f'\left(\dfrac{\pi}{2}\right) =$

(a) 0 (b) –12
(c) 4 (d) 12

Answer Keys

1. (d) **2.** (a) **3.** (b, d) **4.** (b) **5.** (b, d) **6.** (b) **7.** (c)

■ SOME STANDARD SUBSTITUTION

In many functions, direct differentiation becomes very tedious, whereas some suitable substitution may reduce the calculation considerably. Following are some substitutions which are useful in finding the derivatives

Expression Substitution

$a^2 + x^2$ or $\sqrt{a^2+x^2}$; $x = a \tan\theta$ where $-\pi/2 < \theta < \pi/2$ or $x = a \cot\theta$ where $0 < \theta < \pi$

$a^2 - x^2$ or $\sqrt{a^2-x^2}$; $x = a \sin\theta$ where $-\pi/2 \le \theta \le \pi/2$ $x = a \cos\theta$ where $0 \le \theta \le \pi$

$x^2 - a^2$ or $\sqrt{x^2-a^2}$; $x = a \sec\theta$ where $\theta \in [0, \pi] \sim \{\pi/2\}$ $x = a \operatorname{cosec}\theta$ where $0 \in [-\pi/2, \pi/2]$

$\sqrt{2ax-x^2}$; $x = a(1-\cos\theta)$ where $0 \le \theta \le \pi$

$\sqrt{\dfrac{a+x}{a-x}}$ or $\sqrt{\dfrac{a-x}{a+x}}$; $x = a \cos 2\theta$ where $0 < \theta \le \pi/2$

$\sqrt{\dfrac{a^2-x^2}{a^2+x^2}}$ or $\sqrt{\dfrac{a^2+x^2}{a^2-x^2}}$; $x^2 = a^2 \cos\theta$ where $0 < \theta \le \pi/2$

NOTE:

1. *Take care of the fact that substitution may sometimes violate the domain restrictions. Therefore one need to be careful while applying these substitution.*
2. *All concepts of inverse circular functions are nicely incorporated.*

ILLUSTRATION 88: Find $\frac{dy}{dx}$ if $y = \tan^{-1}\left(\frac{a\cos x - b\sin x}{b\cos x + a\sin x}\right)$ when $x \in \left(-\pi + \tan^{-1}\left(\frac{a}{b}\right), \tan^{-1}\left(\frac{a}{b}\right)\right)$

SOLUTION: Let $y = \tan^{-1}\left(\frac{a/b - \tan x}{1 + a/b\tan x}\right)$

$$= \tan^{-1}\tan\left(\tan^{-1}\left(\frac{a}{b}\right) - \tan^{-1}(\tan x)\right) = \tan^{-1}\left(\frac{a}{b}\right) - x \qquad \because \left[\tan^{-1}\left(\frac{a}{b}\right) - x \in (0, \pi)\right]$$

$$\Rightarrow \frac{dy}{dx} = \frac{d}{dx}\left(\tan^{-1}\frac{a}{b} - x\right) = 0 - 1 = -1$$

ILLUSTRATION 89: Show that $\frac{dy}{dx} = 1$ if $y = \cos^{-1}\left(\frac{\cos x + 4\sin x}{\sqrt{17}}\right)$ when

(i) $x \in \left(\tan^{-1}4, \pi + \tan^{-1}4\right)$ (ii) $x \in \left(\pi + \tan^{-1}4, 2\pi + \tan^{-1}4\right)$

SOLUTION: We can write $\cos x + 4\sin x = \sqrt{17}\left[\frac{1}{\sqrt{17}}\cos x + \frac{4}{\sqrt{17}}\sin x\right] = \sqrt{17}\cos(x - \tan^{-1}4)$

Hence $y = \cos^{-1}\left(\frac{\sqrt{17}\cos(x - \tan^{-1}4)}{\sqrt{17}}\right) = \cos^{-1}\cos(x - \tan^{-1}4)$

Case I: when $x \in \left(\tan^{-1}4, \pi + \tan^{-1}4\right)$

$\Rightarrow x - \tan^{-1}4 \in (0, \pi)$

$\Rightarrow \cos^{-1}\cos(x - \tan^{-1}4) = x - \tan^{-1}4 \qquad \therefore \frac{dy}{dx} = 1$

Case II: when $x \in \left(\pi + \tan^{-1}4, 2\pi + \tan^{-1}4\right)$

$\Rightarrow x - \tan^{-1}4 \in (\pi, 2\pi)$

$\Rightarrow \cos^{-1}\cos(x - \tan^{-1}4) = 2\pi - (x - \tan^{-1}4) \quad \therefore \frac{dy}{dx} = -1$

ILLUSTRATION 90: Find the differential co-efficient of $\tan^{-1}\frac{2x}{1-x^2}$ w.r.t $\sin^{-1}\frac{2x}{1+x^2}$ where $x \in \left[0, \frac{\pi}{4}\right)$

SOLUTION: Let $y = \tan^{-1}\frac{2x}{1-x^2}$, $z = \sin^{-1}\frac{2x}{1+x^2}$. Putting $x = \tan\theta$, we see that

$$y = \tan^{-1}\frac{2\tan\theta}{1-\tan^2\theta} = \tan^{-1}(\tan 2\theta) = 2\theta = 2\tan^{-1}x$$

$$z = \sin^{-1}\frac{2\tan\theta}{1+\tan^2\theta} = \sin^{-1}(\sin 2\theta) = 2\theta = 2\tan^{-1}x$$

$$\therefore \frac{dy}{dx} = \frac{2}{1+x^2}, \frac{dz}{dx} = \frac{2}{1+x^2} \qquad \therefore \frac{dz}{dx} = \frac{dy}{dx}.\frac{dz}{dx} = 1$$

ILLUSTRATION 91: Find the differential coefficient of 'y' with respect to 'x'; $y=\tan^{-1}\left(\sqrt{1+x^2}-x\right)$

SOLUTION: $y=\tan^{-1}\left(\sqrt{1+x^2}-x\right)$. Substituting $x=\tan\theta$

$$\Rightarrow y=\tan^{-1}\left(\sqrt{1+\tan^2\theta}-\tan\theta\right)=\tan^{-1}(\sec\theta-\tan\theta)$$

$$=\tan^{-1}\left(\frac{1-\sin\theta}{\cos\theta}\right)=\tan^{-1}\left[\frac{1-\cos(\pi/2-\theta)}{\sin(\pi/2-\theta)}\right]$$

$$=\tan^{-1}\left[\frac{\sin^2\frac{1}{2}\left(\frac{\pi}{2}-\theta\right)}{\sin\frac{1}{2}\left(\frac{\pi}{2}-\theta\right)\cos\frac{1}{2}\left(\frac{\pi}{2}-\theta\right)}\right]=\tan^{-1}\left(\tan\frac{1}{2}\left(\frac{\pi}{2}-\theta\right)\right)=\frac{\pi}{4}-\frac{\theta}{2}$$

$y=\frac{\pi}{4}-\frac{1}{2}\tan^{-1}x$; by putting the value of θ

Differentiating w.r.t. x, we get $\frac{dy}{dx}=\frac{-1}{2(1+x^2)}$

ILLUSTRATION 92: If $\sqrt{1-x^6}+\sqrt{1-y^6}=a^{3.}(x^3-y^3)$, prove that $\frac{dy}{dx}=\frac{x^2}{y^2}\sqrt{\frac{1-y^6}{1-x^6}}$.

SOLUTION: $\sqrt{1-x^6}+\sqrt{1-y^6}=a^{3.}(x^3-y^3)$

Lets put $x^3=\cos\theta$ and $y^3=\cos\phi$

$\therefore$ we get $\sqrt{1-\cos^2\theta}+\sqrt{1-\cos^2\phi}=a^3(\cos\theta-\cos\phi)$

$$2\sin\left(\frac{\theta+\phi}{2}\right)\cos\left(\frac{\theta-\phi}{2}\right)=a^3\left(-2\sin\left(\frac{\theta+\phi}{2}\right)\sin\left(\frac{\theta-\phi}{2}\right)\right)$$

$$\Rightarrow \sin\left(\frac{\theta+\phi}{2}\right)\left(\cos\left(\frac{\theta-\phi}{2}\right)+a^3\sin\left(\frac{\theta-\phi}{2}\right)\right)=0$$

$$\Rightarrow \sin\left(\frac{\theta+\phi}{2}\right)=0 \text{ or } \cos\left(\theta\ \phi\right)=-a^3\sin\left(\theta\ '\phi\right)$$

$0<\theta<\pi$ $\quad \tan\left(\frac{\theta-\phi}{2}\right)=-\frac{1}{a^3}$ and $0<\phi<\pi$

$\Rightarrow \theta-\phi=2\tan^{-1}\left(\frac{-1}{a^3}\right)$ $\qquad 0<\frac{\theta+\phi}{2}<\pi$

$\Rightarrow \cos^{-1}x^3-\cos^{-1}y^3=2\tan^{-1}\left(\frac{-1}{a^3}\right)$ $\qquad \therefore \sin\left(\frac{\theta+\phi}{2}\right)\neq 0$

$$\Rightarrow \frac{dy}{dx}=\frac{x^2}{y^2}\sqrt{\frac{1-y^6}{1-x^6}}$$

ILLUSTRATION 93: If $y=\tan^{-1}\frac{x}{1+\sqrt{1-x^2}}+\sin\left(2\tan^{-1}\sqrt{\frac{1-x}{1+x}}\right)$, then find $\frac{dy}{dx}$ for $x\in(-1,1)$

SOLUTION: $y=\tan^{-1}\frac{x}{1+\sqrt{1-x^2}}+\sin\left(2\tan^{-1}\sqrt{\frac{1-x}{1+x}}\right)$

Put $x = \sin\theta$

To simplify $y_1 = \tan^{-1}\dfrac{x}{1+\sqrt{1-x^2}}$; we put $x = \sin\theta$ where $-\dfrac{\pi}{2}<\theta<\dfrac{\pi}{2}$

$\therefore\ y_1 = \tan^{-1}\left(\dfrac{\sin\theta}{1+\cos\theta}\right)$

$\Rightarrow y_1 = \tan^{-1}\dfrac{2\sin\frac{\theta}{2}\cos\frac{\theta}{2}}{2\cos^2\frac{\theta}{2}} = \tan^{-1}\tan\dfrac{\theta}{2} = \left(\dfrac{\theta}{2}\right) \quad \Rightarrow y_1 = \left(\dfrac{1}{2}\sin^{-1}x\right)$

Similarly for $y_2 = \sin\left(2\tan^{-1}\sqrt{\dfrac{1-x}{1+x}}\right)$; we put $x = \cos\phi$ where $0<\phi<\pi$

$\therefore\ y_2 = \sin\left(2\tan^{-1}\sqrt{\dfrac{1-\cos\phi}{1+\cos\phi}}\right) = \sin\left(2\tan^{-1}\left(\dfrac{\sin\phi/2}{\cos\phi/2}\right)\right) = \sin\left(2\times\dfrac{\phi}{2}\right) = \sin\phi = \sqrt{1-x^2}$

Hence $y = \dfrac{1}{2}\sin^{-1}x+\sqrt{1-x^2}$

$\Rightarrow \dfrac{dy}{dx} = \dfrac{1}{2\sqrt{1-x^2}}+\dfrac{(-2x)}{2\sqrt{1-x^2}} = \dfrac{1-2x}{2\sqrt{1-x^2}}$

ILLUSTRATION 94: Differentiate $y = \tan^{-1}.\left(\dfrac{\sqrt{1+x^2}-1}{x}\right)$

SOLUTION: Let $x = \tan\theta$

$\Rightarrow \theta = \tan^{-1}x;$ $\quad\theta \in \left(-\dfrac{\pi}{2},\dfrac{\pi}{2}\right)$

$y = \tan^{-1}\left(\dfrac{|\sec\theta|-1}{\tan\theta}\right)$ $\quad[\ |\sec\theta| = \sec\theta\ \forall\ \theta \in \left(-\dfrac{\pi}{2},\dfrac{\pi}{2}\right)]$

$\Rightarrow y = \tan^{-1}\left(\dfrac{1-\cos\theta}{\sin\theta}\right)$ $\quad\Rightarrow y = \tan^{-1}\left(\tan\dfrac{\theta}{2}\right)$

$\Rightarrow y = \dfrac{\theta}{2}$ $[\tan^{-1}(\tan x) = x$ for $x \in\left(-\dfrac{\pi}{2},\dfrac{\pi}{2}\right)]$

$\Rightarrow y = \dfrac{1}{2}\tan^{-1}x$ $\quad\Rightarrow \dfrac{dy}{dx} = \dfrac{1}{2(1+x^2)}$

ILLUSTRATION 95: If $f(x) = \sin^{-1}\left(\dfrac{2x}{1+x^2}\right)$ then find

(i) $f'(2)$ **(ii)** $f'\left(\dfrac{1}{2}\right)$ **(iii)** $f'(1)$

SOLUTION: $x = \tan\theta$

$\Rightarrow \theta = \tan^{-1}(x); -\dfrac{\pi}{2}<\theta<\dfrac{\pi}{2}$ $\quad\Rightarrow y = \sin^{-1}(\sin 2\theta)$

$$y = \begin{cases} \pi-2\theta & \dfrac{\pi}{2}<2\theta<\pi \\ 2\theta & -\dfrac{\pi}{2}\le 2\theta\le\dfrac{\pi}{2} \\ -(\pi+2\theta) & -\pi<2\theta<-\dfrac{\pi}{2} \end{cases}$$

$$\Rightarrow f(x) = \begin{cases} \pi - 2\tan^{-1} x & x > 1 \\ 2\tan^{-1} x & -1 \le x \le 1 \\ -(\pi + 2\tan^{-1} x) & x < -1 \end{cases} \qquad \Rightarrow f'(x) = \begin{cases} -\dfrac{2}{1+x^2} & x > 1 \\ \dfrac{2}{1+x^2} & -1 < x < 1 \\ \dfrac{-2}{1+x^2} & x < -1 \end{cases}$$

(i) $f'(2) = -\dfrac{2}{5}$ **(ii)** $f'\left(\dfrac{1}{2}\right) = \dfrac{8}{5}$

(iii) $f'(1^+) = -1$ and $f'(1^-) = +1$

$\Rightarrow f'(1)$ does not exist.

Aliter: Above problem can also be solved without any substution also, but in a little tedious way.

$$f(x) = \sin^{-1}\left(\frac{2x}{1+x^2}\right)$$

$$f'(x) = \frac{1}{\sqrt{1-\dfrac{4x^2}{(1+x^2)^2}}} \cdot \frac{2\{(1+x^2)-2x^2\}}{(1+x^2)^2} = \frac{(1+x^2)}{\sqrt{(1-x^2)^2}} \cdot \frac{2(1-x^2)}{(1+x^2)^2}$$

$$f'(x) = \frac{2}{(1+x^2)} \cdot \frac{(1-x^2)}{|1-x^2|}$$

$$\text{thus } f'(x) = \begin{cases} \dfrac{2}{1+x^2} & |x| < 1 \\ \dfrac{-2}{1+x^2} & |x| > 1 \end{cases}$$

ILLUSTRATION 96: If $\sqrt{1-x^2} + \sqrt{1-y^2} = a(x-y)$, then prove that $\dfrac{dy}{dx} = \sqrt{\dfrac{1-y^2}{1-x^2}}$.

SOLUTION: Put $x = \sin\alpha \Rightarrow \alpha = \sin^{-1}(x)$

$y = \sin\beta \Rightarrow \beta = \sin^{-1}(y)$

$\Rightarrow \cos\alpha + \cos\beta = a(\sin\alpha - \sin\beta)$

$$\Rightarrow 2\cos\left(\frac{\alpha+\beta}{2}\right)\cos\left(\frac{\alpha-\beta}{2}\right) = 2a\cos\left(\frac{\alpha+\beta}{2}\right)\sin\left(\frac{\alpha-\beta}{2}\right)$$

$$\Rightarrow \cot\left(\frac{\alpha-\beta}{2}\right) = a$$

$\Rightarrow \alpha - \beta = 2\cot^{-1}(a)$

$\Rightarrow \sin^{-1} x - \sin^{-1} y = 2\cot^{-1}(a)$

differentiating w.r.t. to x; we get $\dfrac{1}{\sqrt{1-x^2}} - \dfrac{1}{\sqrt{1-y^2}}\dfrac{dy}{dx} = 0$

$$\Rightarrow \frac{dy}{dx} = \sqrt{\frac{1-y^2}{1-x^2}}$$

TEXTUAL EXERCISE–9: (SUBJECTIVE)

1. If $y = \sqrt{(a-x)(x-b)} - (a-b)\tan^{-1}\sqrt{\dfrac{a-x}{x-b}}$, $a > b$ then prove that $\dfrac{dy}{dx} = \sqrt{\dfrac{a-x}{x-b}}$

2. If $y = \sqrt{a^2-x^2} + \dfrac{a}{2}\log\left(\dfrac{a-\sqrt{a^2-x^2}}{a+\sqrt{a^2-x^2}}\right)$, then show that $\dfrac{dy}{dx} = \dfrac{\sqrt{a^2-x^2}}{x}$

TEXTUAL EXERCISE–9: (OBJECTIVE)

1. $e^x = \dfrac{\sqrt{1+t}-\sqrt{1-t}}{\sqrt{1+t}+\sqrt{1-t}}$ and $\tan\dfrac{y}{2} = \sqrt{\dfrac{1-t}{1+t}}$, then $\dfrac{dy}{dx}$ at $t = \dfrac{1}{2}$ is

(a) –1/2 (b) 1/2
(c) 0 (d) None of these

2. If $y = \dfrac{(a-x)\sqrt{a-x}-(b-x)\sqrt{x-b}}{\sqrt{a-x}+\sqrt{x-b}}$, then $\dfrac{dy}{dx}$ wherever it is defined is equal to

(a) $\dfrac{x+(a+b)}{\sqrt{(a-x)(x-b)}}$

(b) $\dfrac{2x-(a+b)}{2\sqrt{(a-x)(x-b)}}$

(c) $\dfrac{(a+b)}{2\sqrt{(a-x)(x-b)}}$

(d) $\dfrac{2x+(a+b)}{2\sqrt{(a-x)(x-b)}}$

3. If $x \in$ (-1,1); then differentiation of $\tan^{-1}\left(\dfrac{2x}{1-x^2}\right)$ $w.r.t \sin^{-1}\left(\dfrac{2x}{1+x^2}\right)$ is

(a) -1
(b) 1
(c) 3/2
(d) None of these

4. In the above question, what if $x \in (1, \infty)$

(a) -1
(b) 1
(c) 3/2
(d) None of these

5. And if $x \in (-\infty, -1)$; then differentiation is equal to

(a) -1 (b) 1
(c) 3/2 (d) None of these

6. If $\dfrac{-1}{\sqrt{3}} < x < \dfrac{1}{\sqrt{3}}$ then find the derivative of $\tan^{-1}\left(\dfrac{3x-x^3}{1-3x^2}\right)$ w.r.t x

(a) $\pi - \dfrac{3}{1+x^2}$ (b) $\dfrac{3}{1+x^2}$

(c) $\pi + \dfrac{3}{1+x^2}$ (d) None of these

7. Differentiate $\sin^{-1}\left(4x\sqrt{1-4x^2}\right)$ with respect to $\sqrt{1-4x^2}$, if $x \in \left(-\dfrac{1}{2\sqrt{2}}, \dfrac{1}{2\sqrt{2}}\right)$

(a) $1/x$ (b) $-1/x^2$
(c) $1/x^2$ (d) None of these

8. Differentiate $\sin^{-1}\left(4x\sqrt{1\quad 4x}\right)$ with respect to $\sqrt{1-4x^2}$, if $x \in \left(\dfrac{1}{2\sqrt{2}}, \dfrac{1}{2}\right)$

(a) $1/x$ (b) $-1/x^2$
(c) $1/x^2$ (d) $-1/x^2$

9. Differentiate $\sin^{-1}\left(4x\sqrt{1-4x^2}\right)$ with respect to $\sqrt{1-4x^2}$, if $x \in \left(-\dfrac{1}{2}, -\dfrac{1}{2\sqrt{2}}\right)$

(a) $1/x$ (b) $-1/x^2$
(c) $1/x^2$ (d) $-1/x^2$

10. Differentiate $\sin^{-1}\left(2ax\sqrt{1-a^2x^2}\right)$ with respect to $\sqrt{1-a^2x^2}$, if $-\frac{1}{\sqrt{2}} < ax < \frac{1}{\sqrt{2}}$

(a) $-2/a$ (b) $-2a$
(c) $-2/a$ (d) $-2/ax$

Answer Keys

1. (a)	**2.** (b)	**3.** (b)	**4.** (a)	**5.** (a)	**6.** (b)	**7.** (a)	**8.** (a)	**9.** (a)	**10.** (d)

■ SUCCESSIVE DIFFERENTIATION:

Having learnt the derivatives of elementary functions and establishing the fact that the derivative of a function is a function and hence is further differentiable, we can try to generate the general formulae for the derivative of the nth order of a given function for any arbitrary positive integral value of 'n'. For our own convenience, we will use some notations, such as $\frac{d^n y}{dx^n}$ as y_n

$$\frac{d^n u}{dx^n} = u_n \text{ and } \frac{d^n v}{dx^n} = v_n$$

NOTE:

If f and g are functions differentiable n times, then for their linear combination $\alpha f + \beta g$ (α, β are constant), we have the following formula: $(\alpha f + \beta g)_n = \alpha f_n + \beta g_n$ e.g., If $y = x^m$; then $y_1 = m x^{m-1}$

$y_2 = m(m-1)x^{m-2}$; $y_3 = m(m-1)(m-2)x^{m-3}$ and hereby generalizing, we say that if $n < m$ then $y_n = m(m-1)(m-2)\ldots(m-n+1).x^{m-n}$. similarly $y_m = m!$; $y_{m+1} = 0 = y_{m+2} = y_{m+3} = \ldots$

ILLUSTRATION 97: Find y_n if

(i) $y = \sin x$ **(ii)** $y = \cos x$

(iii) $y = e^{x+a}$ **(iv)** $y = a^x$

(v) $y = e^{ax+b}$ **(vi)** $y = \frac{1}{x+a}$

(vii) $y = \frac{1}{ax+b}$ **(viii)** $y = \ln(x+a)$

(ix) $y = \ln(ax+b)$ **(ix)** $\frac{x}{x^2 - 7x + 12}$

(xi) $y = \frac{3x^2 - 1}{x^3 - x}$

SOLUTION: **(i)** $y = \sin x \Rightarrow y_1 = \cos x = \sin(x + \pi/2)$

$\Rightarrow y_2 = -\sin x = \sin x = (x + 2\pi/2)$

$\Rightarrow y_3 = -\cos x = \sin x = (x + 3\pi/2)$

$\Rightarrow y_4 = \sin x = \sin(x + 2\pi)$

....

$\Rightarrow y_n = -\sin(x + n\pi/2)$

(ii) $y = \cos x \Rightarrow y_1 = -\sin x = \cos(x + \pi/2)$

$\Rightarrow y_2 = -\cos x = \cos (x + 2.\ \pi/2)$

$\Rightarrow y_3 = \sin x = \cos (x + 3.\ \pi/2)$

$\Rightarrow y_4 = \cos x = \cos (x + 4.\ \pi/2)$

....

$\Rightarrow y_n = \cos (x + n\pi/2)$

(iii) $y = e^{x+a}$ $\Rightarrow y_1 = e^{x+a}$

$\Rightarrow y_2 = e^{x+a}$ $\Rightarrow y_n = e^{x+a}$

(iv) $y = a^x$ $\Rightarrow y_1 = a^x(\ln a)$

$\Rightarrow y_2 = a^x(\ln a)^2$ $\Rightarrow y_n = a^x(\ln a)^n$

(v) $y = e^{ax+b}$ $\Rightarrow y_n = ae^{ax+b}$

$\Rightarrow y_2 = a^2e^{ax+b}$ $\Rightarrow y_n = a^n e^{ax+b}$

(vi) $y = \dfrac{1}{x+a}$ $\Rightarrow y = \dfrac{-1}{(x+a)^2}$

$\Rightarrow y_2 = \dfrac{-1-2}{(x+a)^3}$ $\Rightarrow y_3 = \dfrac{-1\times 2\times -3}{(x+a)^4}$

$$\Rightarrow y_n = \frac{-1\times 2\times -3\times \ldots -n}{(x+a)^{n+1}} = \frac{(1)^n \times n!}{(x+a)^{n+1}}$$

(vii) $y = \dfrac{1}{ax+b} \Rightarrow y_1 = \dfrac{-1\times a}{(ax+b)^2}$

$$\Rightarrow y_2 = \frac{-1\times -2\times a^2}{(ax+b)^3} \Rightarrow y_n = \frac{(-1)^n \times n!\times a^n}{(ax+b)^{n+1}}$$

(viii) $y = \ln(x+a)$ $\Rightarrow y_1 = \dfrac{1}{x+a}$

$$\Rightarrow y_2 = \frac{-1}{(x+a)^2} \Rightarrow y_3 = \frac{-1\times -2}{(x+a)^3}$$

$$\Rightarrow y_n = \frac{(-1)^{n-1}\times (n-1)!}{(x+a)^n}$$

(ix) $y = \ln(ax+b) \Rightarrow y_1 = \dfrac{a}{ax+b}$

$$\Rightarrow y_2 = \frac{-1\times a^2}{(ax+b)^2} \Rightarrow y_n = \frac{(-1)^{n-1}\times (n-1)!\times a^n}{(ax+b)^n}$$

(x) $y = \dfrac{x}{x^2-7x+12} = \dfrac{x}{(x-4)(x-3)}$

Now $\dfrac{x}{(x-4)(x-3)} = \dfrac{A}{x-4} + \dfrac{B}{x-3} = \dfrac{A(x-3)+B(x-4)}{(x-3)(x+4)}$

$\Rightarrow x = (A + B)x + (-3A - 4B)$

$\Rightarrow A + B = 1$ and $3A + 4B = 0$

Solving we get, $A = 4$ and $B = -3$

$$\Rightarrow y = \frac{4}{x-4} + \frac{-3}{x-3}$$

$$\Rightarrow y_1 = 4\times\frac{-1}{(x-4)^2} + (-3)\times\frac{-1}{(x-3)^2}$$

$$\Rightarrow y_2 = 4\times\frac{-1\times-2}{(x-4)^3} + (-3)\times\frac{-1\times-2}{(x-3)^3}$$

....

$$\Rightarrow y_n = 4\times\frac{(-1)^n\times n!}{(x-4)^{n+1}} + (-3)\times\frac{(-1)^n\times n!}{(x-3)^{n+1}}$$

$$\Rightarrow y_n = (-1)^n .n!\left[\frac{4}{(x-4)^{n+1}} + \frac{-3}{(x-3)^{n+1}}\right]$$

(xi) $y = \dfrac{3x^2-1}{x^3-x} = \dfrac{3x^2-1}{(x-1)x(x+1)} = \dfrac{A}{x-1} + \dfrac{B}{x} + \dfrac{C}{x+1}$

$\Rightarrow 3x^2 - 1 = Ax(x + 1) + B(x - 1)(x + 1) + c(x - 1)x$

Solving; we get $A = B = C = 1$

$$\Rightarrow y = \frac{1}{x-1} + \frac{1}{x} + \frac{1}{x+1}$$

$$\Rightarrow y_1 = \frac{-1}{(x-1)^2} + \frac{-1}{x^2} + \frac{-1}{(x+1)^2}$$

$$\Rightarrow y_2 = \frac{-1\times-2}{(x-1)^3} + \frac{-1\times-2}{x^3} + \frac{-1\times-2}{(x+1)^3}$$

....

$$\Rightarrow y_n = (-1)^n .n!\left[\frac{1}{(x-1)^n} + \frac{1}{x^n} + \frac{1}{(x+1)^n}\right]$$

LEIBNITZ'S THEOREM FOR THE n^{TH} DERIVATIVE OF THE PRODUCT OF TWO FUNCTIONS OF X

The Leibnitz's theorem is used when a function can be written as the product of two functions where it is easy to determine the nth derivative of the two functions separately. In such a case, the nth derivative of the product can be written by using Leibnitz's theorem as follows:

Theorem: If $y = fg$, where f and g are functions of x having derivatives of nth order, then $y_n = \sum_{r=0}^{n} {}^nC_r f_{n-r} g_r$

i.e., $y_n = f_n g + {}^nC_1 f_{n-1} g_1 + {}^nC_{n-2} f_{n-2} g_2 + \ldots\ldots {}^nC f_{n-r} g_r + \ldots\ldots {}^nC_n f g_n$

where suffixes denote order of derivatives with respect to x.

Proof: We shall prove the theorem by induction on n. We know that if $y = fg$, then $y_1 = f_1 g + g_1 f$.

Again, taking derivatives, we get

$y_2 = f_2g + f_1g_1 + g_1f_1 + g_2f = f_2g + {}^2C_1f_1g_1 + {}^2C_2fg_2$

Thus, the theorem is true for $n = 1$ and for $n = 2$.

Suppose the theorem is also true for $n = m$ i.e.,

$(fg)_m = f_mg + {}^mC_1f_{m-1}g_1 + {}^mC_2f_{m-2}g_2 + \ldots + {}^mC_{r-1}f_{m-r+2}g_2 + \ldots$
${}^mC_{r-1}f_{m-r+1}g_{r-1} + \ldots {}^mCf_{m-r}g_r + \ldots + {}^mC_mfg_m$ ...(1)

We now show that the theorem is also true for $n = m+1$. Taking derivative of both sides of (1), we get

$(fg)_{m+1} = f_{m+1}g + f_m + g_1 + {}^mC_1g_1 + {}^mC_1f_{m-1}g_2 + {}^mC_2f_{m-1}g_2 + {}^mC_2f_{m-2}g_3 + \ldots\ldots + {}^mC_{r-1}f_{m-r+2}g_{r-1} + {}^mC_{r-1}f_{m-r+1}g_r$

${}^mC_rf_{m-r+1}g_r + {}^mC_rf_{m-r}g_{r+1} + \ldots {}^mC_1g_1 + {}^mC_mfg_{m+1}$

$= f_{m+1}g + (1 + {}^mC_1)f_mg_1 + ({}^mC_1 + {}^mC_2)f_{f-1}g_2 + \ldots + ({}^mC_{r-1} + {}^mC_r)f_{m-r+1}g_r + \ldots + {}^mC_mfg_{m+1}$

Since ${}^mC_{r-1} + {}^mC_r = {}^{m+1}C_r$,

$1 + {}^mC_1 = 1 + m = {}^{m+1}C_1$ and ${}^mC_m = {}^{m+1}C_{m+1}$,

Therefore $(fg)_{m+1} = f_{m+1} = f_{m+1}g + {}^{m+1}C_1f_mg_1 + {}^mC_2f_{m-1}G_2 + \ldots + {}^{m+1}C_rf_{m-r+1}g_r + \ldots\ldots + {}^{m+1}C_{m+1}fg_{m+1}$

Thus, if the theorem is true for $n = m$, it is also true for $n = m+1$

ILLUSTRATION 98: Find the general expressions for derivatives of order n of the following functions:

(i) $y = e^{-x}$ (ii) $y = \sin^2 x$

(iii) $y = x\ln x$ (iv) $y = \sin^4 x + \cos^4 x$

SOLUTION: (i) Given $y = e^{-x}$ $\Rightarrow \frac{dy}{dx} = (-1)e^{-x}$ $\Rightarrow \frac{d^n y}{dx^n} = (-1)^n e^{-x}$

(ii) Let $y = \sin^2 x$ $\Rightarrow \frac{dy}{dx} = 2\sin x\cos x = \sin 2x$

$\Rightarrow \frac{d^2y}{dx^2} = 2\cos 2x = 2\sin\left(2x + \frac{t\pi}{2}\right)$ $\Rightarrow \frac{d^3y}{dx^3} = 4\sin\left(2x + 2.\frac{\pi}{2}\right)$

$\Rightarrow \frac{d^n y}{dx^n} = 2^{n-1}\left(2x + (n-1)\frac{\pi}{2}\right)$

(iii) Let $y = x\ln x$ $\Rightarrow \frac{dy}{dx} = x.\frac{1}{x} + \ln x = 1 + \ln x$

$\Rightarrow \frac{d^2y}{dx^2} = \frac{1}{x}$ and $\frac{d^3y}{dx^3} = -\frac{1}{x^2}$ $\Rightarrow \frac{d^n y}{dx^n} = \frac{(-1)(-2)\ldots\ldots(n-2)}{x^{n-1}};\ n \geq 2 = \frac{(-1)^n(n-2)!}{x^{n-1}};\ n \geq 2$

(IV) $y = \sin^4 x + \cos^4 x = (\sin^2 x + \cos^2 x)^2 - 2\sin^2 x\cos^2 x$

$y = 1 - \frac{1}{2}\sin^2 2x \Rightarrow \frac{dy}{dx} = -\frac{1}{2}.2.\sin 2x.\cos 2x$

$\Rightarrow \frac{dy}{dx} = -\frac{1}{2}.\sin 4x$ $\Rightarrow \frac{d^n y}{dx^n} = -\frac{1}{2}\cos\left(4x + \frac{n\pi}{2}\right)$

ILLUSTRATION 99: Prove that the function $y = e^x \sin x$ satisfies the relationship $y'' - 2y' + 2y = 0$; whereas $y = e^{-x}$ sinx satisfies the relationship $y'' + 2y' + 2y = 0$.

SOLUTION: Let $y = e^x \sin x$ $\Rightarrow y' = e^x\sin x + e^x\cos x$

$\Rightarrow y'' = e^x\sin x + e^x\cos x + e^x\cos x - e^x\sin x$

$y'' = 2e^x\cos x$ ...(i)

$\Rightarrow 2y' = 2e^x\sin x + 2e^x\cos x$ ...(ii)

$\Rightarrow 2y = 2e^x\sin x$ ...(iii)

(i) – (ii) + (iii)

$\Rightarrow$ y'' $-2y' + 2y = 2e^x \cos x - 2e^x \sin x - 2e^x \cos x + 2e^x \sin x = 0$

Hence proved, now let, $y = e^{-x} \sin x$

$\Rightarrow y' = e^{-x} \cos x - e^{-x} \sin x$

$\Rightarrow y' = -e^{-x} \sin x - e^{-x} \cos x + e^{-x} \sin x - e^{-x} \cos x$

$\Rightarrow y'' = -2e^{-x} \cos x$ $\qquad \Rightarrow 2y'' = 2e^{-x} \cos x - 2e^{-x} \sin x$

$\Rightarrow 2y = 2e^{-x} \sin x$

By adding (i) + (ii) + (iii), we get $y'' + 2y' + 2y = 0$

TEXTUAL EXERCISE–10: (SUBJECTIVE)

1. Find the derivatives of order n of the following functions:

(i) $y = \sin ax + \cos bx$ **(ii)** $y = \dfrac{1}{ax+b}$

(iii) $y = \log_a x$ **(iv)** $y = \ln (ax + b)$

(v) $y = e^{kx}$ **(vi)** $y = \sin x \cos x$

2. Evaluate $\dfrac{d^{100}}{dx^{100}}(x^{205})$

3. If $y = \sin 2x$, then find $\dfrac{d^6 y}{dx^6}$ at $x = \pi/4$

Answer Keys

1. (i) $a^n \sin\left(ax + \dfrac{n\pi}{2}\right) + b^n \cos\left(bx + \dfrac{n\pi}{2}\right)$ **(ii)** $\dfrac{(-1)^n . n! a^n}{(ax+b)^{n+1}}$ **(iii)** $\dfrac{(-1)^{n-1}.(n-1)!\, a^n}{(ax+b)^n}$ **(iv)** $\dfrac{(-1)^{n-1}.(n-1)!}{x^n}.\dfrac{1}{(\log_e a)}$

(iv) $k^n e^{kx}$ **(v)** $2^{n-1} \sin\left(2x + n.\dfrac{\pi}{2}\right)$ **2.** $\dfrac{(205)!}{(105)!}x^{105}$ **3.** –64

■ FORMATION OF DIFFERENTIAL EQUATION

Any equation consisting of x, y and the derivatives $\dfrac{dy}{dx}, \dfrac{d^2y}{dx^2}, \left(\dfrac{dy}{dx}\right)$,...... etc. is known as differential equation and it can be obtained for any family of curve of the type $f(x, y, c_1, c_2, ...c_n) = 0$, where c_i (i varies from 1 to n) is an arbitrary constant, by differentiating the family of curves in required number of times and eliminating the arbitrary constants.

ILLUSTRATION 100: If $y = e^{mx}(ax + b)$, where a, b, m are constants, show that $\dfrac{d^2y}{dx^2} - 2m\dfrac{dy}{dx} + m^2 y = 0$

SOLUTION: Let $y = e^{mx}(ax + b)$ ...(1)

$\Rightarrow \dfrac{dy}{dx} = (a)e^{mx} + m\,(ax+b)e^{mx}$

using (i) $\dfrac{dy}{dx} = (a)e^{mx} + my$ ...(2)

Again differentiating with respect to x; $\frac{d^2y}{dx^2} = ame^{mx} + m\frac{dy}{dx}$

Substituting for $a\,e^{mx}$ from (ii) we get $\frac{d^2y}{dx^2} = m\left(\frac{dy}{dx} - my\right) + m\frac{dy}{dx}$

$\Rightarrow \frac{d^2y}{dx^2} - 2m\frac{dy}{dx} + m^2y = 0$

ILLUSTRATION 101: If $y = (\sin^{-1}x)^2$, then show that $(1 - x^2)\frac{d^2y}{dx^2} - x\frac{dy}{dx} - 2 = 0$

SOLUTION: $y = (\sin^{-1}x)^2$ $\Rightarrow \frac{dy}{dx} = \frac{d}{dx}(\sin^{-1}x)^2$

$\Rightarrow 2(\sin^{-1}x)\frac{d}{dx}(\sin^{-1}x) = \frac{2\sin^{-1}x}{\sqrt{1-x^2}}$ $(\forall -1 < x < 1) \Rightarrow \sqrt{1-x^2}\frac{dy}{dx} = 2\sin^{-1}x$

differentiating again, with respect to x, we get $\sqrt{1-x^2}\frac{d^2y}{dx^2} + \frac{-2x}{2\sqrt{1-x^2}}\frac{dy}{dx} = \frac{2}{\sqrt{1-x^2}}$

$\Rightarrow (1 - x^2)\frac{d^2y}{dx^2} - x\frac{dy}{dx} - 2 = 0$

ILLUSTRATION 102: $y = x\log\left(\frac{x}{a+bx}\right)$, then show that $x^3\frac{d^2y}{dx^2} = \left[x\frac{dy}{dx} - y\right]^2$

SOLUTION: $y = x\log x - x\log(a + bx)$

Differentiating w.r.t. x, we get $\frac{dy}{dx} = \frac{x}{x} + \log x - \frac{x(b)}{a+bx} - \log(a+bx)$

$= 1 - \frac{bx}{a+bx} + \log x - \log(a+bx)$ or $\frac{dy}{dx} = \frac{a}{a+bx} + \frac{y}{x}$ .....(i)

Again differentiating w.r.t. x, we get $x\frac{d^2y}{dx^2} + \frac{dy}{dx} = a\left[\frac{(a+bx) - x(b)}{(a+bx)^2}\right] + \frac{dy}{dx}$

$x\frac{d^2y}{dx^2} = \frac{a^2}{(a+bx)^2} = \left[\frac{dy}{dx} - \frac{y}{x}\right]^2$ $\left[\because \text{from }(i);\ \frac{a}{a+bx} = \frac{dy}{dx} - \frac{y}{x}\right]$

$x^3\frac{d^2y}{dx^2} = \left[x\frac{dy}{dx} - y\right]^2$

ILLUSTRATION 103: Find the differential equation if the independent variable x is changed to θ in the equation $\frac{d^2y}{dx^2} + \frac{2x}{1+x^2}\cdot\frac{dy}{dx} + \frac{y}{(1+x^2)^2} = 0$ by means of the transformation $x = \tan\theta$

SOLUTION: Given, $x = \tan\theta \Rightarrow \frac{dx}{d\theta} = \sec^2\theta$

Now, $\frac{dy}{dx} = \frac{\frac{dy}{d\theta}}{\frac{dx}{d\theta}} = \cos^2\theta\frac{dy}{d\theta}$

Differentiating again w.r.t. 'x', we get $\frac{d^2y}{dx^2} = -2\cos\theta\sin\theta\frac{d\theta}{dx}.\frac{dy}{d\theta} + \cos^2\theta.\frac{d^2y}{d\theta^2}.\frac{d\theta}{dx}$

$= -2\cos\theta.\ \sin\theta.\cos^2\theta.\frac{dy}{d\theta} + \cos^2\theta\frac{d^2y}{d\theta^2}.\cos^2\theta$ $\quad\left[\because\ \frac{d\theta}{dx} = \cos^2\theta\right]$

$= -2\sin\theta.\cos^3\theta.\frac{dy}{d\theta} + \cos^4\theta.\frac{d^2y}{d\theta^2}$

Putting the values of x, $\frac{dy}{dx}$ and $\frac{d^2y}{dx^2}$ in the given equation $\frac{d^2y}{dx^2} + \frac{2x}{1+x^2}\frac{dy}{dx} + \frac{y}{(1+x^2)^2} = 0$ we get

$$-2\sin\theta.\ \cos^3\theta\frac{dy}{d\theta} + \cos^4\theta\frac{d^2y}{d\theta^2} + \frac{2\tan\theta}{1+\tan^2\theta}\cos^2\theta.\frac{dy}{d\theta} + \frac{y}{(1+\tan^2\theta)^2} = 0$$

$$\Rightarrow -2\sin\theta.\ \cos^3\theta\frac{dy}{d\theta} + \cos^4\theta\frac{d^2y}{d\theta^2} + 2\sin\theta\cos^3\theta\frac{dy}{d\theta} + y\cos^4\theta = 0$$

$$\Rightarrow \frac{d^2y}{d\theta^2} + y = 0$$

ILLUSTRATION 104: If $x = \frac{1+\ell nt}{t^2}$ and $y = \frac{3+2\ell nt}{t}$. Show that $y\frac{dy}{dx} = 2x\left(\frac{dy}{dx}\right)^2 + 1$

SOLUTION: $x = \frac{1+\ell nt}{t^2}$ $\quad y = \frac{3+2\ell nt}{t}$.

$\frac{dx}{dt} = \frac{t^2\times\frac{1}{t} - (1+\ell nt)2t}{(t^2)^2}$ $\qquad \frac{dy}{dt} = \frac{t\left(\frac{2}{t}\right) - (3+2\ell nt)}{t^2}$

$= \frac{t-2t(1+\ell nt)}{t^4} = \frac{t(1-2-2\ell n)}{t^4} = -\frac{(1+2\ell nt)}{t^3}$ $\qquad = \frac{t(1-2-2\ell nt)}{t^4} = -\frac{(1+2\ell nt)}{t^3}$

$$\Rightarrow \frac{dy}{dx} = \frac{-\frac{(1+2\ell nt)}{t^2}}{-\frac{(1+2\ell nt)}{t^3}} = t$$

$\Rightarrow y\left(\frac{dy}{dx}\right) = 2x\left(\frac{dy}{dx}\right)^2 + 1$ $\qquad \Rightarrow \frac{3+2\ell nt}{t}\times t = 2\frac{(1+\ell nt)}{t^2}\times t^2 + 1$

$\Rightarrow 3 + 2\ell nt = 2 + 2\ell nt + 1$; which is obviously true.

ILLUSTRATION 105: Let $y = x\sin kx$. Find the possible value of k for which the differential equation $\frac{d^2y}{dx^2} + y = 2k\cos kx$ holds true for all $x \in R$.

(a) 0 (b) 1

(c) –1 (d) All of the above

SOLUTION: (a,b,c,d) $y = x\sin kx$

Differentiating w.r.t x, we get, $\frac{dy}{dx} = \sin kx + kx\cos kx$

Again differentiating w.r.t. x, we get, $\frac{d^2y}{dx^2} = k\cos kx + k\cos kx - k^2x\sin kx$

$\Rightarrow \dfrac{d^2y}{dx^2} = 2\text{ k}\cos kx - k^2y$ $\Rightarrow \dfrac{d^2y}{dx^2} + k^2y = 2k\cos kx$

Comparing the above equation with $\dfrac{d^2y}{dx^2} + y = 2k\cos kx$, we get, $k^2 = 1$

$\Rightarrow k = \pm 1$

Also when $k = 0$ $\Rightarrow y = 0$. So its also true

Hence the possible answer are $k = 0, 1, -1$

ILLUSTRATION 106: If y is a function of x and $\dfrac{d^2y}{dx^2} + y\dfrac{dy}{dx} = 0$. If x is a function of y then the equation becomes:

(a) $\dfrac{d^2x}{dy^2} + x\dfrac{dx}{dy} = 0$ (b) $\dfrac{d^2x}{dy^2} + y\left(\dfrac{dx}{dy}\right)^3 = 0$

(c) $\dfrac{d^2x}{dy^2} - y\left(\dfrac{dx}{dy}\right)^2 = 0$ (d) $\dfrac{d^2x}{dy^2} - x\left(\dfrac{dx}{dy}\right)^2 = 0$

SOLUTION: Given $\dfrac{d^2y}{dx^2} + y\dfrac{dy}{dx} = 0$ .....(i)

Now $\dfrac{dy}{dx} = \dfrac{1}{\dfrac{dx}{dy}}$

$$\therefore \frac{d^2y}{dx^2} = \frac{d}{dx}\left(\frac{1}{\frac{dx}{dy}}\right) = \frac{d}{dy}\left(\frac{1}{\frac{dx}{dy}}\right)\frac{dy}{dx} = -\frac{1}{\left(\frac{dx}{dy}\right)^2}\cdot\frac{d^2x}{dy^2}\cdot\frac{1}{\frac{dx}{dy}}$$

$$\Rightarrow \frac{d^2y}{dx^2} = -\frac{\frac{d^2x}{d^2y}}{\left(\frac{dx}{dy}\right)^3} \text{ (Putting in (1)), we get } \frac{-\frac{d^2x}{d^2y}}{\left(\frac{dx}{dy}\right)^3} + y\frac{dy}{dx} = 0 \Rightarrow y\left(\frac{dy}{dx}\right)^2 - \frac{d^2x}{dy^2} = 0$$

TEXTUAL EXERCISE–11: (SUBJECTIVE)

1. $y = \dfrac{1-x^4}{1+x^4}$. Express $\dfrac{dy}{dx}$ in terms of x and $\dfrac{dx}{dy}$ in terms of y. And hence show that the relation $\dfrac{dy}{dx}\cdot\dfrac{dx}{dy} = 1$ is valid.

2. Make sure that the function y defined by the equation $xy - \ln y = 1$ also satisfies the relationship $y^2 + (xy - 1)\dfrac{dy}{dx} = 0$

3. Make sure that the function represented parametrically by the equations $x = 2t + 3t^2$, $y = t^2 + 2t^3$ satisfies the relationship $y = y'^2 + 2y'^3$ (where $y' = \dfrac{dy}{dx}$, i.e., differentiation with respect to x)

4. If $y = x\ell n[(ax)^{-1} + a^{-1}]$, prove that. $x(x+1)\dfrac{d^2y}{dx^2} + x\dfrac{dy}{dx} = y - 1$

5. If $y = \sin(2\sin^{-1}x)$, show that $(1 - x^2)\dfrac{d^2y}{dx^2} = x\dfrac{dy}{dx} - 4y$

6. If $y = A\,e^{-kt}\cos(pt + k)$, then prove that $\dfrac{d^2y}{dt^2} + 2k\dfrac{dy}{dt} + n^2y = 0$, where $n^2 = p^2 + k^2$

7. If $y=\left(x+\sqrt{1+x^2}\right)^m$, then prove that $\left(1+x^2\right)\frac{d^2y}{dx^2}+x\frac{dy}{dx}-m^2y=0$

8. If 'y' is a twice differentiable function of x, transform the expression $(1-x^2)\frac{d^2y}{dx^2}-x\frac{dy}{dx}+y$ by means of the transformation, $x = \sin t$, in terms of the independent variable 't'.

Answer Keys

1. $\frac{dy}{dx}=\frac{-8x^3}{(1+x^4)^2};\frac{dx}{dy}=\frac{1}{2(1+y)^{5/4}(1-y)^{3/4}}$

8. $\frac{d^2y}{dt^2}+y$

TEXTUAL EXERCISE–11: (OBJECTIVE)

1. If $y = a\cos(\log x) + b\sin(\log x)$, then $x^2\frac{d^2y}{dx^2}+x\frac{dy}{dx}+y$ is equal to

(a) 0 (b) 1

(c) –1 (d) None of these

2. If $y = x + \cot x$, then $\sin^2 x\,\frac{d^2y}{dx^2} - 2y + 2x =$

(a) 0 (b) 1

(c) –1 (d) None of these

3. If $y = x + e^x$, then $\frac{d^2x}{dy^2}$ is

(a) e^x (b) $-\frac{e^x}{\left(1+e^x\right)^3}$

(c) $-\frac{e^x}{\left(1+e^x\right)^2}$ (d) $\frac{1}{\left(1+e^x\right)^2}$

4. If $x = t^3 + t + 5$ and $y = \sin t$, then $\frac{d^2y}{dx^2}=$

(a) $-\frac{\left(3t^2+1\right)\sin t+6t\cos t}{\left(3t^2+1\right)^3}$

(b) $\frac{\left(3t^2+1\right)\sin t+6t\cos t}{\left(3t^2+1\right)^2}$

(c) $-\frac{\left(3t^2+1\right)\sin t+6t\cos t}{\left(3t^2+1\right)^2}$

(d) $\frac{\cos t}{3t^2+1}$

5. If $y = (\sin^{-1}x)^2 + (\cos^{-1}x)^2$, then $(1-x^2)\frac{d^2y}{dx^2}-x\frac{dy}{dx}$

(a) 4 (b) 3

(c) 1 (d) 0

6. Prove that if $(a + bx)e^{y/x} = x$ and $x^k\frac{d^2y}{dx^2}=\left(x\frac{dy}{dx}-y\right)^2$. Then find the value of k

(a) 3 (b) 1

(c) 2 (d) None of these

7. If $p = a^2\cos^2\theta + b^2\sin^2\theta$ and if $p+\frac{d^2p}{d\theta^2}=2a^2+2b^2-kp$. Then find the value of k.

(a) 1 (b) 2

(c) 3 (d) None of these

8. If $(x + y) = e^{x-y}$, and if $\frac{d^2y}{dx^2}=\frac{k(x+y)}{(x+y+1)^3}$. Then find the value of k.

(a) 2 (b) 4

(c) 6 (d) None of these

9. If $y=\left[\ell n\left(\frac{x+\sqrt{x^2-a^2}}{a}\right)\right]+k\ell n\left(x+\sqrt{x^2-a^2}\right)$, then find the value of $\left(x^2-a^2\right)\frac{d^2y}{dx^2}+x\frac{dy}{dx}$

(a) 1 (b) 2

(c) 3 (d) None of these

Answer Keys

1. (a) **2.** (a) **3.** (b) **4.** (a) **5.** (a) **6.** (a) **7.** (c) **8.** (b) **9.** (d)

MULTIPLE CHOICE QUESTIONS

SECTION–I

OBJECTIVE SOLVED EXAMPLE

1. The function $u = e^x.\sin x$ and $v = e^x \cos x$ satisfies the equation

(a) $v\dfrac{du}{dx} - u\dfrac{dv}{dx} = v^2 + u^2$

(b) $\dfrac{d^2u}{dx^2} = 2v$

(c) $\dfrac{d^2v}{dx^2} = -2u$

(d) None of these

Solution: (a, b and c)

$$\frac{du}{dx} = e^x \sin x + e^x \cos x = u + v \quad \ldots(i)$$

$$\frac{dv}{dx} = e^x \cos x - e^x \sin x = v - u \quad \ldots(ii)$$

$$\therefore \quad v\frac{du}{dx} - u\frac{dv}{dx} = v(u+v) - u(v-u) = u^2 + v^2$$

From (i),

we get $\dfrac{d^2u}{dx^2} = \dfrac{du}{dx} + \dfrac{dv}{dx} = u + v + v - u = 2v$

From (ii), we can get $\dfrac{d^2v}{dx^2} = \dfrac{dv}{dx} - \dfrac{du}{dx} = (v - u)$

$-(v+u) = -2u$

$\therefore$ (a), (b) and (c) are correct.

3. If $\dfrac{\cos^4\theta}{x} + \dfrac{\sin^4\theta}{y} = \dfrac{1}{x+y}$ then $\dfrac{dy}{dx} =$

(a) xy (b) $\tan^2\theta$

(c) 0 (d) $(x^2 + y^2)\sec^2\theta$

Solution: (b)

$$(x+y)\left(\frac{\cos^4\theta}{x} + \frac{\sin^4\theta}{y}\right) = [\cos^2\theta + \sin^2\theta]^4$$

$$\therefore \quad \frac{y}{x}\cos^4\theta + \frac{x}{y}\sin^4\theta - 2\sin^2\theta\cos^2\theta = 0$$

$$\text{or} \quad \left(\sqrt{\frac{y}{x}}\cos^2\theta - \sqrt{\frac{x}{y}}\sin^2\theta\right)^2 = 0$$

$\therefore \tan^2\theta = \dfrac{y}{x}$ or $y = x\tan^2\theta$ $\therefore \dfrac{dy}{dx} = \tan^2\theta$

4. If $\sqrt{x+y} + \sqrt{y-x} = \lambda$ then $\dfrac{d^2y}{dx^2}$ equals

(a) $\dfrac{-2}{\lambda^2}$ (b) $\dfrac{2}{\lambda^2}$

(c) $\dfrac{2}{\lambda}$ (d) None of these

Solution: (b) $\sqrt{x+y} + \sqrt{y-x} = \lambda \quad \ldots(i)$

But $(x+y) - (y-x) = 2x \quad \ldots(ii)$

Dividing (ii) by (i); we get

$$\sqrt{x+y} - \sqrt{y-x} = \frac{2x}{\lambda} \quad \ldots(iii)$$

$$\because \quad \frac{a^2 - b^2}{a+b} = a - b$$

Adding (i) and (3); we get $2\sqrt{x+y} = \lambda + \dfrac{2x}{\lambda}$

Squaring both sides, we get $4x + 4y = \lambda^2 + 4x + \dfrac{4x^2}{\lambda^2}$

$$\therefore \quad y = \frac{\lambda^2}{4} + \frac{x^2}{\lambda^2} \qquad \therefore \quad \frac{dy}{dx} = \frac{2x}{\lambda^2}$$

$$\therefore \quad \frac{d^2y}{dx^2} = \frac{2}{\lambda^2}$$

5. If $f(x) = e^x - e^{-x} - 2\sin x - \dfrac{2}{3}x^3$, then the least value of n for which $\dfrac{d^n}{dx^n}f(x)$ at $x = 0$ in non-zero is

(a) 2 (b) 1

(c) 7 (d) either 1 or 2

Solution: (c) $f(x) = e^x - e^{-x} - 2\sin x - \dfrac{2}{3}x^3$

Now, $e^x = 1 + \dfrac{x}{1!} + \dfrac{x^2}{2!} + \dfrac{x^3}{3!} + \dfrac{x^4}{4!} + \ldots\ldots\ldots\infty$

$e^{-x} = 1 - \dfrac{x}{1!} + \dfrac{x^2}{2!} - \dfrac{x^3}{3!} + \dfrac{x^4}{4!} + \ldots\ldots\ldots\infty$

$$\Rightarrow f(x) = 2\left[x + \frac{x^3}{3!} + \frac{x^5}{5!} + \frac{x^7}{7!} + ...\right]$$

$$-2\left[x - \frac{x^3}{3!} + \frac{x^5}{5!} - \frac{x^7}{7!}...\right] - \frac{2}{3}x^3$$

$$\therefore\ f(x) = 4\left(\frac{x^7}{7!} + \frac{x^{11}}{11!} + \frac{x^{15}}{15!} + ...\infty\right)$$

$$f'(x) = 4\left(\frac{7\times x^6}{7!} + \frac{11x^{10}}{11!} + ...\right)$$

$$f''(x) = 4\left(\frac{6\times x^5}{6!} + \frac{10\times x^9}{10!} + ...\right)$$

....

....

$$f^7(x) = 4\left(x^\circ + \frac{x^4}{4!} + \frac{x^8}{8!} + ...\right)$$

$f'(0) = 4$ i.e., a non-zero constant.

Hence at $x = 0$, it will be non zero

$\therefore\ n = 7$

6. If $t(1 + x^2) = x$ and $x^2 + t^2 = y$, then at $x = 2$, the value of $\frac{dy}{dx}$

(a) $\frac{488}{125}$ (b) $\frac{88}{125}$

(c) $\frac{101}{125}$ (d) None of these

Solution: (a) $\frac{dy}{dx} = 2x + 2t.\frac{dt}{dx}$ .....(i)

$t = \frac{x}{1+x^2}$ $\therefore\ \frac{dt}{dx} = \frac{1-x^2}{(1+x^2)^2}$

Putting these value of t and $\frac{dt}{dx}$ in (1)

we get $\frac{dy}{dx} = 2x + \frac{2x}{1+x^2}\frac{1-x^2}{(1+x^2)^2}$

on putting $x = 2$ in $\frac{dy}{dx}$;

we get $\frac{dy}{dx} = \frac{488}{125}$

7. Given the parametric equations $x = f(t).\ y = g(t)$. Then $\frac{d^2y}{dx^2}$ equals

(a) $\dfrac{\frac{d^2y}{dt^2}.\frac{dx}{dt} - \frac{dy}{dt}.\frac{d^2x}{dt^2}}{(dx/dt)^2}$

(b) $\dfrac{\frac{dx}{dt}.\frac{d^2y}{dt^2} - \frac{d^2x}{dt^2}\frac{dy}{dt}}{(dx/dt)^3}$

(c) $\dfrac{\frac{d^2y}{dt^2}}{\frac{d^2x}{dt^2}}$

(d) None of these

Solution: (b) we have $\frac{dy}{dx} = \frac{dy/dt}{dx/dt}$

Again differentiating both sides w.r.t x,

we get $\frac{d^2y}{dx^2} = \frac{d}{dt}\left(\frac{dy/dt}{dx/dt}\right)\frac{dt}{dx}$

$$= \frac{\frac{d^2y}{dt^2}\left(\frac{dx}{dt}\right) - \left(\frac{d^2x}{dt^2}\right)\frac{dy}{dt}}{(dt/dt)^2} \times \frac{1}{dx/dt}$$

$$= \frac{\frac{d^2y}{dt^2}.\left(\frac{dx}{dt}\right) - \left(\frac{d^2x}{dt^2}\right).\left(\frac{dy}{dt}\right)}{(dx/dt)^3}$$

8. If for a continuous function f, $f(0) = f(1) = 0$, $f'(1) = 2$ and $g(x) = f(e^x)e^{f(x)}$, then $g'(0)$ is equal to

(a) 1 (b) 2

(c) 0 (d) None of these

Solution: (b) Given $g(x) = f(e^x)\,e^{f(x)}$

Differentiating both sides w.r.t. x;

we get $g'(x) = f'(e^x).e^x\,e^{f(x)} + f(e^x).e^{f(x)}.f'(x)$ ...(i)

Now, Since we already know that $f(0) = 0$, $f'(1) = 2$

Putting $x = 0$ in (i), we get $g'(0) = 2.1.1 + 0 = 2$

9. Let $F(x) = \left(f\left(\frac{x}{2}\right)\right)^2 + \left(g\left(\frac{x}{2}\right)\right)^2$, $F(5) = 5$ and $f''(x) = -f(x)$, $g(x) = f'(x)$, then $F(10)$ is equal to:

(a) 5 (b) 10

(c) 0 (d) 3

Solution: (a)

$F'(x) = 2\times f\left(\frac{x}{2}\right)\times f'\left(\frac{x}{2}\right)\times\frac{1}{2}+2\times g\left(\frac{x}{2}\right)\times$

$g'\left(\frac{x}{2}\right)\times\frac{1}{2}$

$= f\left(\frac{x}{2}\right)\times f'(x)+g(x)\times g'(x)$

And since $g(x) = f'(x) \Rightarrow g'(x) = f''(x)$

$\Rightarrow g'(x) = -f(x) \qquad (\because f''(x) = -f(x))$

$\therefore \quad F'(x) = \left(f\left(\frac{x}{2}\right)\times f'\left(\frac{x}{2}\right)\right)+$

$\left(f'\left(\frac{x}{2}\right)\times -f\left(\frac{x}{2}\right)\right)=0$

$\therefore$ $F(x)$ is fixed constant function

$\therefore$ $F(10) = F(5) = 5$

10. If $y \cos x + x \cos y = \pi$, then $y''(0)$ is

(a) 1 (b) π

(c) 0 (d) $-\pi$

Solution: (b) $y \cos x + x \cos y = \pi$ ...(i)

Differentiating (i) w.r.t x

$-y \sin x + y' \cos x + \cos y - (x \sin y)\, y' = 0$

or $-y \sin x + \cos y + y'(\cos x - x \sin y) = 0$ ...(2)

Again differentiate (2) w.r.t x

$-y \cos x - y' \sin x - (-\sin y)\, y' + y''\,[\cos x - x \sin y]$
$+ y'\,(-\sin x - 1.\sin y - x \cos y.y'] = 0$ ...(3)

Putting $x = 0$ in (1), we get, $y = \pi$

Putting $x = 0$ and $y = \pi$ in (2), we get $0 + \cos\pi +$ $y'\,(-1 - \pi \sin \pi)$

or $-1\, y' = 0 \quad \therefore \quad y' = -1$

Putting $x = 0$ and $y = \pi$ and $y' = 1$ in (3), we get, $y''(0) = 0$.

11. If $f(x + y) = f(x) + f(y)\ \forall, x, y$ and $f'(0)$ exists., then

(a) $f'(x) = f'(0)\ \forall\ x$

(b) $f(x) = cx$, where c is a constant

(c) $f(x) = xf(1)$

(d) $f(x) = \frac{x}{2}f(2)$

Solution: **(a), (b), (c), (d)**

(a) Given $f(x + y) = f(x) + f(y)$ for all x and y

Since, the above equation is valid for $x, y \in \mathbb{R}$

Hence 'y' is independent of x and therefore $\frac{dy}{dx} = 0$

Differentiating both sides of (1) w.r.t x we get

$f(x + y)\left(1+\frac{dy}{dx}\right) = f'(x)+f'(y)\frac{dy}{dx}$

$\Rightarrow f'(x+y) = f'(x) \qquad \left[\because \frac{dy}{dx}=0\right]$

Putting $y = 0$, we get $f'(x) = f'(0)$ for all x.

(b) If $f'(0) = k$, then $f'(x) = k$

Integrating w.r.t x, we get $f(x) = kx + c$

$f(x + y) = f(x) + f(y)$,

Putting $x = y = 0$, we get

$f(0) = f(0) + f(0) \quad \Rightarrow f(0) = 0$

$\Rightarrow f(0) = k.0 + c \quad \Rightarrow c = 0$

$\therefore f(x) = k(x) + c$

(c) Putting $x = 1$ in $f(x) = kx$, we get $f(1) = k$

$\Rightarrow f(x) = x.f(1) \quad \therefore \quad y = kx$

(d) Putting $x = 2$ in $y = kx$, we get $f(2) = 2k$

$\therefore \quad k = \frac{f(2)}{2}$, Hence $f(x) = \frac{f(2)}{2}.x$

12. If $\prod_{r=1}^{n}\cos\left(\frac{x}{2^r}\right) = \frac{\sin x}{2^n \sin\left(\frac{x}{2^n}\right)}$, then which of the following statement(s) is/are correct.

(a) $\sum_{r=1}^{n}\frac{1}{2^r}\tan\left(\frac{x}{2^r}\right) = \frac{1}{2^n}\cot\left(\frac{x}{2^n}\right) - \cot x$

(b) $\sum_{r=1}^{n}\frac{1}{2^r}\tan\left(\frac{x}{2^r}\right) = \frac{1}{2^n}\cot\left(\frac{x}{2^n}\right)$

(c) $\sum_{r=1}^{n}\frac{1}{2^{2r}}\sec^2\left(\frac{x}{2^r}\right) = \frac{1}{2^n}\operatorname{cosec}^2\left(\frac{x}{2^n}\right) - \operatorname{cosec}^2 x$

(d) $\sum_{r=1}^{n}\frac{1}{2^{2r}}\sec^2\left(\frac{x}{2^r}\right) = \operatorname{cosec}^2 x - \frac{1}{2^{2n}}\operatorname{cosec}^2\left(\frac{x}{2^n}\right)$

Solution: **(a), (d)**

We have $\prod_{r=1}^{n}\cos\left(\frac{x}{2^r}\right) = \frac{\sin x}{2^n \sin\left(\frac{x}{2^n}\right)}$

$\Rightarrow \cos\frac{x}{2}.\cos\frac{x}{2^2}.\cos\frac{x}{2^3}....\cos\frac{x}{2^n} = \frac{\sin x}{2^n \sin\left(\frac{x}{2^n}\right)}$

Taking log on both the sides, we get

$\log_e \cos\frac{x}{2}+\log_e\frac{x}{2^2}+\log_e \cos\frac{x}{2^3}+...\log_e \cos\frac{x}{2^n}$

$= \log_e \sin x - (\log_e 2^n + \log_e \sin\frac{x}{2^n})$

Differentiating w.r.t. x, we get

$$\frac{1}{\cos\frac{x}{2}}\left(-\sin\frac{x}{2}\right)\frac{1}{2}+\frac{1}{\cos\frac{x}{2^2}}\left(-\sin\frac{x}{2^2}\right)\frac{1}{2^2}+$$

$$\frac{1}{\cos\frac{x}{2^3}}\left(-sin\frac{x}{2^3}\right)\frac{1}{2^3}+\ldots+$$

$$\frac{1}{\cos\frac{x}{2^n}}\left(-\sin\frac{x}{2^n}\right).\frac{1}{2^n}=\frac{1}{\sin x}.$$

$$\cos x - 0 - \frac{1}{2^n}.\frac{1}{\sin\frac{x}{2^n}}.\cos\frac{x}{2^n}$$

$$\Rightarrow -\frac{1}{2}\tan\frac{x}{2}-\frac{1}{2^2}\tan\frac{x}{2^2}-\frac{1}{2^3}\tan\frac{x}{2^3}-\ldots.-\frac{1}{2^n}\tan\frac{x}{2^n}$$

$$= \cot x - \frac{1}{2^n}\cot\frac{x}{2^n}$$

$$\Rightarrow \frac{1}{2}\tan\left(\frac{x}{2}\right)+\frac{1}{2^2}\tan\left(\frac{x}{2^2}\right)-\frac{1}{2^3}\tan\left(\frac{x}{2^3}\right)+\ldots.+$$

$$\frac{1}{2^n}\tan\left(\frac{x}{2^n}\right)=\frac{1}{2^n}\cot\left(\frac{x}{2^n}\right)-\cot x \quad \ldots(1)$$

$$\Rightarrow \sum_{r=1}^{n}\frac{1}{2^r}\tan\left(\frac{x}{2^r}\right)=\frac{1}{2^n}.\cot\left(\frac{x}{2^n}\right)-\cot x$$

Differentiating (1) w.r.t.x we get

$$\frac{1}{2^2}\sec^2\left(\frac{x}{2}\right)+\frac{1}{2^4}\sec^2\left(\frac{x}{2^2}\right)+\frac{1}{2^6}\sec^2\left(\frac{x}{2^3}\right)+\ldots+$$

$$\frac{1}{2^{2n}}\sec\left(\frac{x}{2^{2n}}\right)$$

$$= \operatorname{cosec}^2 x - \frac{1}{2^{2n}}\operatorname{cosec}^2\left(\frac{x}{2^n}\right)$$

$$\therefore \sum_{r=1}^{n}\frac{1}{2^{2r}}\sec^2\left(\frac{x}{2^r}\right)=\operatorname{cosec}^2 x-\frac{1}{2^{2n}}.\operatorname{cosec}^2\left(\frac{x}{2^n}\right)$$

13. Let f be a differentiable function such that $f(x) = f(4 - x)$ and $g(x) = f(2 + x)$ for all $x \in R$, then

(a) graph of $f(x)$ is symmetric about the line $x = 2$

(b) $f'(2) = 0$

(c) graph of $g(x)$ is symmetric about x-axis

(d) $g'(0) = 0$

Solution: (a), (b), (c), (d)

Given $f(x) = f(4 - x)$ ...(1)

And $g(x) = f(2 + x)$ ...(2)

Putting $2 + x$ in place of x in (1),

we get $f(2 + x) = f(2 - x)$

$\Rightarrow$ graph of $f(x)$ is symmetric about the line $x = 2$...(3)

From (2) and (3), $g(x) = f(2 - x)$

Putting $(-x)$ in place of x in (2), we get $g(-x) = f(2 - x)$

From (4) and (5), $g(-x) = g(x)$, therefore $g(x)$ is an even function

Hence graph of $g(x)$ is symmetric about y-axis

Differentiating both sides of (3) w.r.t x, we get

$f'(2 + x) = -f'(2 - x)$

Putting $x = 0$, we get $f'(2) = 0$

Again $g(x)= g(-x)$

Differentiating w.r.t. x we get' $g'(x) = -g'(-x)$

Putting $x = 0$, we get $2g'(0) = 0 \Rightarrow g'(0)= 0$

14. If $f(0) = 0$, $f'(0) = 3$ then the derivative of $y = f(f(f(x)))$ at $x = 0$ is

(a) 2 (b) 8

(c) 16 (d) 4

Solution:

$$y'(x) = f'\left(f\left(f\left(f(x)\right)\right)\right)f'\left(f\left(f(x)\right)\right)f'\left(f(x)\right)f'(x)$$

So

$$y'(0) = f'\left(f\left(f\left(f(0)\right)\right)\right)f'\left(f\left(f(0)\right)\right)f'\left(f(0)\right)f'(0)$$

$$= f'\left(f\left(f(0)\right)\right)f'\left(f(0)\right)f'(0)f'(0)$$

$$= (f'(x))^4 = 3^4 = 81$$

15. Let f and g be differentiable function such that $f'(x) = 2g(x)$ and $g'(x) = -f(x)$, and let $T(x) = (f(x))^2 - (g(x))^2$. Then $T'(x)$ is equal to

(a) $T(x)$ (b) 0

(c) $2f(x)\,g(x)$ (d) $6f(x)\,g(x)$

Solution: (d) $T'(x) = 2\left(f(x)f'(x) - g(x)g'(x)\right)$

$= 2(2g(x)\,f(x) + f(x)\,g(x)) = 6f(x)\,g(x)$

16. Let f be a twice differentiable function such that $f''(x) = -f(x)$ and $f'(x) = g(x)$. If $h'(x) = [f(x)]^2 + [g(x)]^2$, $h(1) = 6$ and $h(0) = 4$ then $h(4)$ is equal to

(a) 16 (b) 12

(c) 13 (d) None of these

Solution: (b) Given $h'(x) = [f(x)]^2 + [g(x)]^2$

Differentiating both side w.r.t x, we get

$h''(x)=2f(x)f'(x)+2g(x)g'(x)$

$=2f(x)g(x)+2g(x)g''(x)$

$[\because f'(x)=g(x)]$

$=2f(x)g(x)-2g(x)f(x)=0$

$[\because f''(x)=-f(x)]$

Thus $h'(x)=k$, a constant for all $x \in \mathbf{R}$. Hence $h(x) = ax + b$, so that from $h(0) = 4$, we get $b = 4$ and from $h(1) = 6$ we get $a = 2$ Therefore, $h(4) = 12$.

17 If $y^2 = P(x)$ is a polynomial of degree 3, then $2\frac{d}{dx}\left(y^3\frac{d^2y}{dx^2}\right)$ is equal to

(a) $P(x)+P'(x)$ (b) $P(x)P'(x)$

(c) $P(x)P'''(x)$ (d) a constant

Solution: **(c)** Given $y^2 = P(x)$,

Differentiating both sides w.r.t. x,

we get $2yy_1 = P'(x)$, i.e., $2y_1 = \frac{p'(x)}{y}$

Again differentiating w.r.t. x,

we get $2y_2=\frac{yP''(x)-P'(x)y_1}{y^2}$

$=\frac{yP''(x)-P'(x).P'(x)/2y}{2y^3}$

$=\frac{2y^2P''(x)-(P'(x))^2}{2y^3}=\frac{2P(x)P''(x)-(p'x)^2}{2y^3}$

$\Rightarrow 2y_2y^3=\frac{1}{2}\left[2P(x)P''(x)-(P'(x))^2\right]$

$\Rightarrow 2\frac{d}{dx}\left(y^3\frac{d^2y}{dx^2}\right)$

$=\frac{1}{2}\left[2\{P'(x)P''(x)+P(x)P'''(x)\}-2P'(x)P''(x)\right]$

$=\frac{1}{2}(2P(x)P'''(x))=P(x)P'''(x)$.

18. The value of $y''(1)$ if $x^3 - 2x^2y^2 + 5x + y - 5 = 0$ when $y(1) > 1$, is equal to

(a) $\frac{22}{7}$ (b) $-7\frac{21}{28}$

(c) 8 (d) $-8\frac{22}{27}$

Solution: (d)

Given expression is $x^3 - 2x^2y^2 + 5x + y - 5 = 0$ ...(i)

Differentiating the given expression,

we get $3x^2 - 4xy^2 - 4x^2yy' + 5 + y' = 0$ ...(ii)

Putting $x = 1$ in the given expression, we get

$3 - 2y^2 + 5 + y - 5 = 0$

$\Rightarrow 2y^2 - y - 1 = 0$

$\Rightarrow y = 1$ or $y = -1/2$

Now $\because y(1) > 0 \Rightarrow y(1) = 1$

Differentiating again we get, $6x - 4y^2 - 8xyy' - 8xyy' - 4x2y'^2 - 4x^2yy'' + y'' = 0$

Putting $x = 1$, $y = 1$ and $y'(1) = 4/3$, we get

$6-4-8\left(\frac{4}{3}\right)-8\left(\frac{4}{3}\right)-4\left(\frac{16}{9}\right)-3y''(1)=0$

$\Rightarrow y''(1)=-8\frac{22}{27}$

19. If $f(x)=\cot^{-1}\left(\frac{x^x-x^{-x}}{2}\right)$, then $f'(1)$ equals

(a) -1 (b) 1

(c) log 2 (d) $-$ log 2

Solution: (a) If $u = x^x$ and using logarithmic differentiation, we get $\log u = x \log x$.

$\Rightarrow \frac{1}{u}\frac{du}{dx}=x.\frac{1}{x}+\log x \Rightarrow \frac{du}{dx}=x^x(1+\log x)$

Similarly, if $v = x^{-x}$, we get $\frac{dv}{dx}=-x^{-x}(1+\log x)$

$f'(x)=\frac{1}{1+\left(\frac{x^x-x^{-x}}{2}\right)^2}\frac{d}{dx}\left(\frac{x^x-x^{-x}}{2}\right)$

$=-\frac{4}{x^{2x}+x^{-2x}+2}\left[\frac{1}{2}(x^x+x^{-x})(1+\log x)\right]$

$\Rightarrow f'(1)=-\frac{2}{1+1+2}[2(1+\log 1)]=-1$

20. The solution set of $f'(x)>g'(x)$ where $f(x) = (1/2)5^{2x+1}$ and $g(x) = 5^x + 4x \log 5$ is

(a) $(1, \infty)$ (b) $(0, 1)$

(c) $[0, \infty)$ (d) $(0, \infty)$

Solution: (d)

$f'(x)=\left(\frac{1}{2}\right)5^{2x+1}(\log 5)\times 2=(\log 5).5^{2x+1}$

Also $g'(x) = 5x \log 5 + 4 \log 5$

Solving $f'(x) > g'(x) = \log 5.\ 5^{2x+1} > (\log 5)\ 5^x + 4 \log 5$

$\Rightarrow 5^{2x+1} > 5^x + 4$

Putting $5^x = t$, we get, $5x : 5t^2 - t - 4 > 0$

$\Rightarrow (5t + 4)(t - 1) > 0$

$\Rightarrow t > 1$ or $t < -4/5$

But since $t = 5^x$;

$\therefore\ t > 1$

$x = (0, \infty)$

21 If $f''(x) = \dfrac{\cos(\log x)}{x}, f'(1) = 0$ and $y = f\left(\dfrac{2x+3}{3-2x}\right)$ then $\dfrac{dy}{dx}$ is equal to

(a) $(\sin(\log x))\dfrac{1}{\cos x}$

(b) $\sin\left(\log\left(\dfrac{2x+3}{3-2x}\right)\right)$

(c) $\dfrac{12}{(3-2x)^2}\sin\left(\log\left(\dfrac{2x+3}{3-2x}\right)\right)$

(d) None of these

Solution: (c)

$$f''(x) = \frac{\cos(\log x)}{x} = \frac{d}{dx}(\sin(\log x) + C)$$

So, $f'(x) = \sin(\log x) + C$ but $f'(1) = 0$ so $C = 0$.

Thus $f'(x) = \sin(\log x)$.

$$\text{Now } \frac{dy}{dx} = f'\left(\frac{2x+3}{3-2x}\right)\frac{d}{dx}\left(\frac{2x+3}{3-2x}\right)$$

$$= \sin\left(\log\left(\frac{2x+3}{3-2x}\right)\right).\left(\frac{2(3-2x)-(2)(2x+3)}{(3-2x)^2}\right)$$

$$= \frac{12}{(3-2x)^2}\sin\left(\log\left(\frac{2x+3}{3-2x}\right)\right)$$

22. If $y = e^{\sqrt{x}} + e^{-\sqrt{x}}$ then $xy_2 + (1/2)y_1$ is equal to

(a) y (b) $x\left(e^{\sqrt{x}} + e^{-\sqrt{x}}\right)$

(c) $(1/4)y$ (d) $\sqrt{xy}$

Solution: (c) Given $y = e^{\sqrt{x}} + e^{-\sqrt{x}}$.

Differentiating both sides w.r.t x,

we get $y_1 = \dfrac{1}{2\sqrt{x}}e^{\sqrt{x}} - \dfrac{1}{2\sqrt{x}}e^{-\sqrt{x}}$

$\Rightarrow 2\sqrt{x}y_1 = e^{\sqrt{x}} - e^{-\sqrt{x}}$.

Differentiating again, we get

$$2\sqrt{x}y_2 + \frac{1}{\sqrt{x}}y_1 = \frac{1}{2\sqrt{x}}e^{\sqrt{x}} + \frac{1}{2\sqrt{x}}e^{-\sqrt{x}} = \frac{1}{2\sqrt{x}}y$$

$$\Rightarrow xy_2 + \left(\frac{1}{2}\right)y_1 = \left(\frac{1}{4}\right)y.$$

23. If $y = \cos^{-1}\dfrac{x^n - x^{-n}}{x^n + x^{-n}}$ then $y'(x)$ is equal to

(a) $\dfrac{2nx^{n-1}}{x^{2n}+1}$ n is even

(b) $\dfrac{2nx^n}{|x|(x^{2n}+1)}$ if n is odd

(c) $-\dfrac{2nx^n}{|x|(x^{2n}+1)}$ if n is odd

(d) $\dfrac{2nx^{n-1}}{(x^{2n}+1)}$

Solution: (c) Given $y = \cos^{-1}\dfrac{x^n - x^{-n}}{x^n + x^{-n}}$

Differentiating both sides w.r.t. x, we get

$$y'(x) = -\frac{1}{\sqrt{1-\left(\dfrac{x^{2n}-1}{x^{2n}+1}\right)^2}}\frac{d}{dx}\left(\frac{x^{2n}-1}{x^{2n}+1}\right)$$

$$= \frac{x^{2n}+1}{\sqrt{(x^{2n}+1)^2-(x^{2n}-1)^2}}\times$$

$$\frac{2nx^{2n-1}(x^{2n}+1)-2nx^{2n-1}(x^{2n}-1)}{(x^{2n}+1)^2}$$

$$= -\frac{1}{\sqrt{4x^{2n}}}.\frac{4nx^{2n-1}}{(x^{2n}+1)} = \frac{-2n\,x^{2n-1}}{|x^n|(x^{2n}+1)}$$

$$= -\frac{2n(|x|^2)^n}{x|x|^n(x^{2n}+1)} = -\frac{2n|x|^n}{x(x^{2n}+1)}$$

$$= \begin{cases} -\dfrac{2nx^{n-1}}{x^{2n}+1} & \text{if } n \text{ is even} \\ -\dfrac{2nx^n}{|x|(x^{2n}+1)} & \text{if } n \text{ is odd} \end{cases}$$

24. If $y(n) = e^x e^{x^2} \ldots e^{x^n}, 0 < x < 1$ then $\lim\limits_{n\to\infty}\dfrac{dy(n)}{dx}$ at $x = \dfrac{1}{2}$ is

(a) e (b) $4e$

(c) $2e$ (d) $3e$

Solution: **(b)** $y(n) = e^{x+x^2+...+x^n} = e^{\frac{x(1-x^n)}{1-x}}$

So $\dfrac{dy(n)}{dx} = e^{\frac{x(1-x^n)}{1-x}} \times \dfrac{d}{dx}\left(\dfrac{x(1-x^n)}{1-x}\right)$

$\lim\limits_{n\to\infty} \dfrac{dy(n)}{dx} = \lim\limits_{n\to\infty} e^{\frac{x}{1-x}-\frac{x^{n+1}}{1-x}} \dfrac{d}{dx}\left[\lim\limits_{n\to\infty} \dfrac{x}{1-x} - \dfrac{x^{n+1}}{1-x}\right]$

$= e^{\frac{x}{1-x}} \times \dfrac{d}{dx}\left(\dfrac{x}{1-x}\right) = e^{\frac{x}{1-x}} \dfrac{d}{dx}\left(-1+\dfrac{1}{1-x}\right)$

$= e^{\frac{x}{1-x}} . \dfrac{d}{dx} \dfrac{1}{(1-x)^2}$ $\left[\begin{array}{l} \because \text{ for } x \in (0,1); x^n \to 0 \\ \therefore \lim\limits_{n\to\infty} \dfrac{x^{n+1}}{1-x} = 0 \end{array}\right]$

$\Rightarrow \lim\limits_{n\to\infty} \left(\dfrac{dy(n)}{dx}\right)_{x=1/2} = 4e$

25. If $\cos^{-1}\left(\dfrac{x^2-y^2}{x^2+y^2}\right) = \log a$ then $\dfrac{dy}{dx}$ is equal to

(a) y/x (b) x/y
(c) x^2/y^2 (d) y^2/x^2

Solution: **(a)** Given $\cos^{-1}\left(\dfrac{x^2-y^2}{x^2+y^2}\right) = \log a$

$\Rightarrow \dfrac{x^2-y^2}{x^2+y^2} = \cos \log a = A$ (say)

Putting $u = y/x$ and applying componendo and dividendo, we have $\left(\dfrac{y}{x}\right)^2 = u^2 = \left(\dfrac{1-A}{1+A}\right)$

$\Rightarrow \dfrac{y}{x} = \sqrt{\dfrac{1-A}{1+A}}$ $\Rightarrow x\dfrac{dy}{dx} - y = 0$

$\Rightarrow \dfrac{dy}{dx} = \dfrac{y}{x}$.

27. If $x = \cos\theta$, $y = \sin^3\theta$, then $\left(\dfrac{dy}{dx}\right)^2 + y\dfrac{d^2y}{dx^2}$ at $\theta = \dfrac{\pi}{2}$ is

(a) 1 (b) 2
(c) –2 (d) –3

Solution: **(d)** $\dfrac{dx}{d\theta} = -\sin\theta, \dfrac{dy}{d\theta} = 3\sin^2\theta\cos\theta$

So that $\dfrac{dy}{dx} = -3\sin\theta\cos\theta = -\dfrac{3}{2}\sin 2\theta$.

Differentiating again, we have

$\dfrac{d^2y}{dx^2} = -3\cos 2\theta . \dfrac{d\theta}{dx} = \dfrac{3\cos 2\theta}{\sin\theta}$

Now, $\left(\dfrac{dy}{dx}\right)^2 + y\dfrac{d^2y}{dx^2} = 9\sin^2\theta\cos^2\theta + \sin^3\theta\dfrac{3\cos 2\theta}{\sin\theta}$

$= 9\sin^2\theta\cos^2\theta + 3\sin^2\theta\cos 2\theta$

Putting $\theta = \pi/2$; we get $\left(\dfrac{dy}{dx}\right)^2 + y\dfrac{d^2y}{dx^2} = -3$

28. **(d)** $\dfrac{d^2x}{dy^2}$ equals

(a) $\left(\dfrac{d^2y}{dx^2}\right)^{-1}$ (b) $\left(\dfrac{d^2y}{dx^2}\right)^{-1}\left(\dfrac{dy}{dx}\right)^{-3}$
(c) $\left(\dfrac{d^2y}{dx^2}\right)\left(\dfrac{dy}{dx}\right)^{-2}$ (d) $-\left(\dfrac{d^2y}{dx^2}\right)\left(\dfrac{dy}{dx}\right)^{-3}$

Solution: $\dfrac{dx}{dy} = \dfrac{1}{\left(\dfrac{dy}{dx}\right)}$

$\dfrac{d^2x}{dy^2} = \dfrac{d}{dy}\left(\dfrac{1}{\left(\dfrac{dy}{dx}\right)}\right) = \dfrac{d}{dx}\left(\dfrac{1}{\left(\dfrac{dy}{dx}\right)}\right) \times \dfrac{dx}{dy}$

$= -\dfrac{1}{\left(\dfrac{dy}{dx}\right)^2} . \dfrac{d^2y}{dx^2} . \dfrac{1}{\left(\dfrac{dy}{dx}\right)} = -\dfrac{1}{\left(\dfrac{dy}{dx}\right)^3}\dfrac{d^2y}{dx^2}$

29. Let $g(x) = \ell n\, f(x)$ where $f(x)$ is twice differentiable positive function on $(0, \infty)$ such that $f(x + 1) = x f(x)$.

Then for $N = 1, 2, 3$. $g''\left(N+\dfrac{1}{2}\right) - g''\left(\dfrac{1}{2}\right) =$

(a) $-4\left\{1+\dfrac{1}{9}+\dfrac{1}{25}+...+\dfrac{1}{(2N+1)}\right\}$

(b) $4\left\{1+\dfrac{1}{9}+\dfrac{1}{25}+...+\dfrac{1}{(2N+1)^2}\right\}$

(c) $-4\left\{1+\dfrac{1}{9}+\dfrac{1}{25}+...+\dfrac{1}{(2N+1)^2}\right\}$

(d) $4\left\{1+\dfrac{1}{9}+\dfrac{1}{25}+...+\dfrac{1}{(2N+1)^2}\right\}$

Solution: **(a)** $g(x) = \log f(x)$

$g(x + 1) = \log f(x + 1) = \log (xf(x))$

$= \log (x\, e^{g(x)}) = \log x + g(x)$

$g(x + 1) - g(x) = \log x$

replaces $x \to x - \frac{1}{2}$; we get $g\left(x+\frac{1}{2}\right) - g\left(x-\frac{1}{2}\right)$

$= \log\left(x - \frac{1}{2}\right) = \log(2x-1) - \log 2$

Differentiating w.r.t. x,

we get $g'\left(x+\frac{1}{2}\right) - g'\left(x-\frac{1}{2}\right) = \frac{2}{(2x-1)}$

Again differentiating w.r.t. x,

we get $g''\left(x+\frac{1}{2}\right) - g''\left(x-\frac{1}{2}\right) = -4\,\frac{1}{(2x-1)^2}$

$\Rightarrow\ g''\left(x+\frac{1}{2}\right) - g''\left(x-\frac{1}{2}\right) = -4\,\frac{1}{(2x-1)^2}$

putting $x = 1, 2, 3$; we get

$g''\left(\frac{3}{2}\right) - g''\left(\frac{1}{2}\right) = -4\left(\frac{1}{1^2}\right)$

$g''\left(\frac{5}{2}\right) - g''\left(\frac{3}{2}\right) = -4\left(\frac{1}{2^2}\right)$

$g''\left(\frac{7}{2}\right) - g''\left(\frac{5}{2}\right) = -4\left(\frac{1}{3^2}\right)$

$g''\left(N+\frac{1}{2}\right) - g''\left(N-\frac{1}{2}\right) = -4\left(\frac{1}{(2N-1)^2}\right)$

Adding, we get

$$g''\left(N+\frac{1}{2}\right) - g''\left(\frac{1}{2}\right) = -4\left(\frac{1}{1}+\frac{1}{4}+\frac{1}{9}+....+\frac{1}{(2N-1)^2}\right)$$

30. The derivative of $\tan^{-1}\left(\frac{2x}{1-x^2}\right)$ with respect to $\cos^{-1}\sqrt{1-x^2}$ is

(a) $\frac{\sqrt{1-x^2}}{1+x^2}$ (b) $\frac{1}{\sqrt{1-x^2}}$

(c) $\frac{2}{\sqrt{1-x^2}\,(1+x^2)}$ (d) $\frac{2\sqrt{1-x^2}}{1+x^2}$

Solution: (d) Let $u = \tan^{-1}\left(\frac{2x}{1-x^2}\right)$

and $v = \cos^{-1}\sqrt{1-x^2}$

On differentiating w.r.t x, respectively, we get

$$\frac{du}{dx} = \frac{1}{1+\left(\frac{2x}{1-x^2}\right)^2}\left[\frac{(1-x^2)2 - 2x(-2x)}{(1-x^2)^2}\right]$$

$$= \frac{2+2x^2}{(1+x^2)^2} = \frac{2}{1+x^2}$$

and $\frac{dv}{dx} = -\frac{1}{\sqrt{1-(1-x^2)}}\left[\frac{(-2x)}{2\sqrt{1-x^2}}\right]$

$$= \frac{1}{\sqrt{x^2}}\left[\frac{x}{\sqrt{1-x^2}}\right] = \frac{1}{\sqrt{1-x^2}}$$

$$\therefore\ \frac{du}{dv} = \frac{\frac{2}{1+x^2}}{\frac{1}{\sqrt{1-x^2}}} = \frac{2\sqrt{1-x^2}}{1+x^2}$$

Aliter: Let $u = \tan^{-1}\left(\frac{2x}{1-x^2}\right) = 2\tan^{-1}x$

$\Rightarrow\ \frac{du}{dx} = \frac{2}{1+x^2}$ and let $v = \cos^{-1}\sqrt{1-x^2} = \sin^{-1}x$

$\Rightarrow\ \frac{dv}{dx} = \frac{1}{\sqrt{1-x^2}}$

Now, $\frac{du}{dv} = \frac{2}{1+x^2} / \frac{1}{\sqrt{1-x^2}} = \frac{2\sqrt{1-x^2}}{1+x^2}$

31. If $8f(x) + 6f\left(\frac{1}{x}\right) = x + 5$ and $y = x^2f(x)$, then $\frac{dy}{dx}$ at $x = -1$ is equal to

(a) 0 (b) 1/14

(c) –1/14 (d) 1

Solution: (c) We have, $8f(x) + 6f\left(\frac{1}{x}\right)x = 5$ for all x ...(i)

Substituting x by $1/x$ in the equation (i),

we get, $8f\left(\frac{1}{x}\right) + 6f(x) = \frac{1}{x} + 5$ .....(ii)

From equation (i) and (ii),

we have $f(x) = \frac{1}{28}\left(8x - \frac{6}{x} + 10\right)$

Now, $y = x^2 f(x)$

$\Rightarrow\ y = \frac{1}{28}(8x^3 - 6x + 10x^2)$

$\Rightarrow\ \frac{dy}{dx} = \frac{1}{28}(24x^3 + 20 - 6)$

$\Rightarrow\ \left(\frac{dy}{dx}\right)_{x=-1} = \frac{1}{28}(24 - 20 - 6) = -\frac{1}{14}$

32. If $y = x - x^2$, then the derivatives of y^2 w.r.t x^2 is

(a) $2x^2 + 3x - 1$ (b) $2x^2 - 3x + 1$

(c) $2x^2 + 3x + 1$ (d) $2x^2 - 3x - 1$

Solution: **(b)** Given $y = x - x^2$

$\Rightarrow \frac{y}{x} = 1 - x^2$ Also $\frac{dy}{dx} = 1 - 2x$

Now $\frac{d(y^2)}{d(x^2)} = \frac{\frac{d(y^2)}{dx}}{\frac{d(x^2)}{dx}}$

$= \frac{2y\frac{dy}{dx}}{2x} = \frac{y}{x}(1-2x) = (1-x)(1-2x)$

$= 1 - 3x + 2x^2 = 2x^2 - 3x + 1$

33. If $f(x) = \frac{x-1}{4} + \frac{(x-1)^3}{12} + \frac{(x-1)^5}{20} + \frac{(x-1)^7}{28} + \ldots\ldots$ where $0 < x < 2$, then $f'(x)$ is equal to

(a) $\frac{1}{4x(2-x)}$ (b) $\frac{1}{4(x-2)^2}$

(c) $\frac{1}{2-x}$ (d) $\frac{1}{2+x}$

Solution: **(a)** Given, $0 < x < 2$

$\Rightarrow -1 < x - 1 < 1$ $\Rightarrow |x - 1| < 1$

and

$$f(x) = \frac{1}{4}\left[\frac{x-1}{1} + \frac{(x-1)^3}{3} + \frac{(x-1)^5}{5} + \frac{(x-1)^7}{7} + \ldots\right]$$

$$\Rightarrow f(x) = \frac{1}{4}\left[\frac{1}{2}\log\left(\frac{1+(x-1)}{1-(x-1)}\right)\right] = \frac{1}{8}\log\left(\frac{x}{2-x}\right)$$

$$\Rightarrow f'(x) = \frac{1}{8} \times \frac{1}{\left(\frac{x}{2-x}\right)}\left[\frac{(2-x)1 - x(-1)}{(2-x)^2}\right] = \frac{1}{4x(2-x)}$$

34. If $f(x + y) = 2f(x)f(y)$, $f'(5) = 1024$ (log2) and $f(2) = 8$, then the value of $f'(3)$ is

(a) 64 (log 2) (b) 128 (log 2)

(c) 256 (d) 256 (log 2)

Solution: **(a)** $f'(5) = \lim_{h\to 0}\frac{f(5+h) - f(5)}{h}$

$$= \lim_{h\to 0}\frac{2f(5)f(h) - f(5)}{h} = \lim_{h\to 0} 2f(5)\left[\frac{f(h) - \frac{1}{2}}{h}\right]$$

$\Rightarrow 1024 \log 2 = 2 f(5) f'(0)$

Also since $f(x + y) = 2f(x) f(y)$

Now, putting $x = 2$ and $y = 3$,

we get $f(2 + 3) = 2f(2) f(3)$

$\Rightarrow \frac{1024\log 2}{2f'(0)} = 2 \times 8 \times f(3)$

$\Rightarrow f(3) = \frac{32\log 2}{f'(0)}$ ...(i)

$\therefore f'(3) = \lim_{h\to 0}\frac{f(3+h) - f(3)}{h}$

$= \lim_{h\to 0}\frac{2f(3)f(h) - f(3)}{h} = 2f(3) f'(0)$

$= 2 \times \frac{(32\log 2)}{f'(0)}.f'(0)$

$\left[\because \text{ from equation } (i),\ f(3) = \frac{32\log 2}{f'(0)}\right] = 64 \log 2$

35. If $y = 1 + \frac{1}{x} + \frac{1}{x^2} + \frac{1}{x^3} + \ldots.\infty$ with $|x| > 1$, then $\frac{dy}{dx}$ is

(a) $\frac{x^2}{y^2}$ (b) x^2y^2

(c) $\frac{y^2}{x^2}$ (d) $-\frac{y^2}{x^2}$

Solution: **(d)**

Given, $y = 1 + \frac{1}{x} + \frac{1}{x^2} + \frac{1}{x^3} + \ldots.\infty = \frac{1}{1 - \frac{1}{x}}$

(sum of a G.P.)

$\Rightarrow y = \frac{x}{x-1}$

$\frac{dy}{dx} = \frac{1(x-1) - x.1}{(x-1)^2} = -\frac{1}{(x-1)^2}$

$\Rightarrow \frac{dy}{dx} = -\frac{y^2}{x^2}$

36. If $r = [2\phi + \cos^2(2\phi + \pi/4)]^{1/2}$, then what is the value of the derivative $dr/d\phi$ at $\phi = \pi/4$?

(a) $2\left(\frac{1}{\pi+1}\right)^{1/2}$ (b) $2\left(\frac{2}{\pi+1}\right)^2$

(c) $\left(\frac{2}{\pi+1}\right)^{1/2}$ (d) $2\left(\frac{2}{\pi+1}\right)^{1/2}$

Solution: (d) Given, $r=\left[2\phi+\cos^2\left(2\phi+\frac{\pi}{4}\right)\right]^{1/2}$

Differentiating both side is w.r.t. ϕ, we get

$$\frac{dr}{d\phi}=\frac{\left[2-2\cos\left(2\phi+\frac{\pi}{4}\right)\sin\left(2\phi+\frac{\pi}{4}\right).2\right]}{2\sqrt{2\phi+\cos^2\left(2\phi+\frac{\pi}{4}\right)}}$$

$$=\frac{\left[1-\sin\left(4\phi+\frac{\pi}{4}\right)\right]}{\sqrt{2\phi+\cos^2\left(2\phi+\frac{\pi}{4}\right)}}$$

$$\Rightarrow\left(\frac{dr}{d\phi}\right)_{\phi=\pi/4}=\frac{\left[1-\sin\left(\pi+\frac{\pi}{2}\right)\right]}{\sqrt{2.\frac{\pi}{4}+\cos^2\left(\frac{\pi}{2}+\frac{\pi}{4}\right)}}$$

$$=\frac{1+1}{\sqrt{\frac{\pi}{2}+\frac{1}{2}}}=2\sqrt{\frac{2}{1+\pi}}$$

37. If $y=e^{a\sin^{-1}x}$, then find the value of $(1-x^2)y_{n+2}-(2n+1)xy_{n+1}$

(a) $-(n^2+a^2)y_n$ (b) $(n^2-a^2)y_n$

(c) $(n^2+a^2)y_n$ (d) $-(n^2-a^2)y_n$

Solution: (c) Given, $y=e^{a\sin^{-1}x}$

On differentiating both side w.r.t x,

we get $y_1=e^{a\sin^{-1}x}\,a.\frac{1}{\sqrt{1-x^2}}$

$\Rightarrow y_1\sqrt{1-x^2}=ay$

Squaring both side, we get $\left(1-x^2\right)y_1^2=a^2y^2$

Again, differentiating w.r.t x,

we get $(1-x^2)2y_1y_2-2xy_1^2=a^2 2yy_1$

$\Rightarrow (1-x^2)y_2-xy_1-a^2y=0$

Using Leibnitz's rule of differentiating, we get $(1-x^2)y_{n+2}+C_1y_{n+1}(-2x)+{}^nC_2y_n(-2)-xy_{n+1}-{}^nC_1y_n-a^2y_n=0$

$\Rightarrow (1-x^2)y_{n+2}+xy_{n+1}(-2n-1)+y_n[-n(n-1)-n-a^2]=0$

$\Rightarrow (1-x^2)y_{n+2}-(2n-1).\,xy_{n+1}=(n^2+a^2)y_n$

38. If $x=\cos\theta$, $y=\sin5\theta$ then the value of $(1-x^2)\frac{d^2y}{dx^2}-x\frac{dy}{dx}$ is given by

(a) $-5y$ (b) $5y$

(c) $-9y$ (d) $-25y$

Solution: (d) Given $x=\cos\theta$, $y=\sin5\theta$

$$\Rightarrow\frac{dx}{d\theta}=-\sin\theta,\ \frac{dy}{d\theta}=5\cos5\theta$$

$$\therefore\ \frac{dy}{dx}=\frac{dy/d\theta}{dx/d\theta}=-\frac{5\cos5\theta}{\sin\theta}$$

Differentiating again w.r.t. x, we get

$$\frac{d^2y}{dx^2}=\frac{d}{d\theta}\left(\frac{dy}{dx}\right)\frac{d\theta}{dx}$$

$$==\frac{d}{d\theta}\left(\frac{-5\cos5\theta}{\sin\theta}\right)\frac{1}{-\sin\theta}$$

$$=\left(\frac{\sin\theta\sin5\theta.25+5\cos5\theta\cos\theta}{\sin^2\theta}\right)\frac{1}{-\sin\theta}$$

$$=-\frac{25\sin5\theta}{\sin^2\theta}-\frac{5\cos5\theta\cos\theta}{\sin^3\theta}$$

$$\therefore\ \left(1-x^2\right)\frac{d^2y}{dx^2}-x\frac{dy}{dx}$$

$$=\left(1-\cos^2\theta\right)\left(\frac{-25\sin5\theta}{\sin^2\theta}-\frac{5\cos5\theta\cos\theta}{\sin^3\theta}\right)-\cos\theta\left(\frac{-5\cos5\theta}{\sin\theta}\right)$$

$$=\sin^2\theta\left(\frac{-25\sin5\theta}{\sin^2\theta}-\frac{5\cos\theta\cos5\theta}{\sin^3\theta}\right)+\frac{5\cos\theta\cos5\theta}{\sin\theta}$$

$$=-25\sin5\theta-\frac{5\cos\theta\cos5\theta}{\sin\theta}+\frac{5\cos\theta\cos5\theta}{\sin\theta}=-25\,y$$

39 If $f(x)=x^n$, then the value of $f(1)-\frac{f'(1)}{1!}+\frac{f''(1)}{2!}-\frac{f'''(1)}{3!}+\ldots+\frac{(-1)^nf^n(1)}{n!}$ is

(a) 2^n (b) 2^{n-1}

(c) 0 (d) 1

Solution: (c) $f(x)=x^n\Rightarrow f(1)=1$

$f'(x)=nx^{n-1}\Rightarrow f'(1)=n$

$f''(x)=n(n-1)x^{n-2}\Rightarrow f''(1)=n(n-1)$

....

....

$f^n(x)=n(n-1)(n-2)\ldots2.1$

$\Rightarrow f^n(1) = n(n-1)(n-2)\ldots 2.1$

Now

$$f(1)-\frac{f'(1)}{1!}+\frac{f''(1)}{2!}-\frac{f'''(1)}{3!}+\ldots+\frac{(-1)^n f^n(1)}{n!}$$

$$= 1-\frac{n}{1!}+\frac{n(n-1)}{2!}-\frac{n(n-1)(n-2)}{3!}+\ldots+$$

$$\frac{(1)^n n(n-1)(n-2)\ldots 2.1}{n!} = (1-1)^n = 0$$

40 If $y = \int_0^x f(t)\sin\{p(x-t)\}dt$, $\frac{d^2y}{dx^2}+p^2y$ equals

(a) 0 (b) y

(c) $k.f(x)$ (d) $k^2 f(x)$

Solution: $y = \int_0^x f(t)\sin\{p(x-t)\}dt$

Considering, $\cos\{p(x-t)\}+i\sin\{p(x-t)\} = e^{i\{p(x-t)\}}$,

we can say that $\sin\{p(x-t)\} = \text{Im}(e^{i\{p(x-t)\}})$

And hence $f(t).\sin\{p(x-t)\} = \text{Im}\left(f(t).e^{ip(x-t)}\right)$

$$\Rightarrow y = \text{Im}\int_0^x f(t)e^{ip(x-t)}dt$$

$$= \text{Im}\left\{e^{ipx}\int_0^x f(t)e^{-ipt}dt\right\} \quad \ldots\text{(i)}$$

$$\therefore \frac{dy}{dx} = Im\left\{e^{ipx}.f(x).e^{-ipx}+ik.e^{ipx}.\int_0^x f(t)e^{-ipt}dt\right\}$$

$$= 0+\text{Im}\left\{ip.e^{eip}.\int_0^x f(t)e^{-ipt}dt\right\} \quad \ldots\text{(i)}$$

Now, $\frac{d^2y}{dx^2}$

$$= \text{Im}\left\{ip.\left(e^{ip}.f(x).e^{-ipx}+\int_0^x f(t).e^{-ipt}dt\times ipe^{ipx}\right)\right\}$$

$= k f(x) - k^2 y$

$$\therefore \frac{d^2y}{dx^2}+k^2y = k.f(x)$$

41. If $F(x) = \frac{1}{x^2}\int_1^x (4t^2-2F'(t))\,dt$, then $F'(1)$ equals

(a) 4/3

(b) 4/9

(c) 8/3

(d) None of these

Solution: **(a)** Given $F(x) = \frac{1}{x^2}\int_1^x \{4t^2-2F'(t)\}dt$

or $x^2F(x) = \int_1^x \{4t^2-2F'(t)\}dt$

Differentiating both sides w.r.t x, then $x^2F'(x) + F(x).2x = 4x^2 - 2F'(x)$

Putting $x = 1$ in the above equation, we get $F'(1) + 2F(1) = 4 - 2F'(1)$

$\therefore 3F'(1) + 0 = 4$

$$\left[\because F(1) = \frac{1}{1^2}\int_1^1 (4t^2-2F'(t))dt = 0\right]$$

$$\therefore F'(1) = \frac{4}{3}$$

42 If $\int_{\pi/2}^x \sqrt{(5+2\sin^2 t)}+\int_0^y \cos t\,dt = 0$, then $\left(\frac{dy}{dx}\right)_{\pi,\pi}$ equal to

(a) –5 (b) 0

(c) $\sqrt{5}$ (d) None of these

Solution: Differentiating both sides w.r.t x, then

$$\sqrt{(5+2\sin^2 x)}.1+\cos y\frac{dy}{dx} = 0$$

$$\therefore \frac{dy}{dx} = -\frac{\sqrt{(5+2\sin^2 x)}}{\cos y}$$

$$\therefore \left.\frac{dy}{dx}\right|_{(\pi,\pi)} = \frac{-\sqrt{5}}{(-1)} = \sqrt{5}$$

43. Let $f(x) = x^3 + 3x^2 - 33x - 33$ for $x > 0$ and 'g' be its inverse then the value of 'k' such that $kg'(2) = 1$ is

(a) –36 (b) –42

(c) 12 (d) all of the above

Solution: **(a)** $g(f(x)) = x \Rightarrow g'(f(x))\, f'(x) = 1$

$$\Rightarrow g'(f(x)) = \frac{1}{f'(x)}$$

Now $f(x) = 2 \Rightarrow x^3 + 3x^2 - 33x - 33 = 2 \Rightarrow x^3 + 3x^2 - 33x - 35 = 0$

$\Rightarrow x^3 - 5x^2 + 8x^2 - 40x + 7x - 35 = 0$ or $(x-5)(x^2 + 8x + 7) = 0$

$\Rightarrow (x-5)(x+1)(x+7) = 0$

$\Rightarrow x = -7, -1, 5$

Now, since g is the inverse function of f

$\therefore f(g(x)) = x$

Differentiating both sides w.r.t. x, we get $f(g(x)).g'(x) = 1$

$$\Rightarrow g'(x) = \frac{1}{f'(g(x))}$$

Also putting $x = 2$; we get $g'(2) = \frac{1}{f'(g(2)}$

Also, since $f(x) = 2$ has solutions $x = -7, -1, 5$

$\therefore$ $x = f^{-1}(x)$ or $x = g(2)$ also has solutions $x = -7, -1, 5$

$\therefore$ $f(g(2))$ is equal to either $f(-7)$ or $f(-1)$ or $f(5)$

Now, $f(-1) = 3(1)^2 + 6(-1) - 33 = 3 - 6 - 33 = -36$

$f(-7) = 3(7)^2 + 6(-7)^2 + 6(-7) - 33 = 147 - 63 - 33 - 51$

$f(5) = 3.5^2 + 6.5 - 33 = 75 + 30 - 33 = 72$

Now, $kg'(2) = 1 \Rightarrow g'(2) = \frac{1}{k}$

$$\Rightarrow \frac{1}{k} = \frac{1}{f'(g(2))} \Rightarrow k = f(g(2))$$

$\Rightarrow$ k is equal to either $f(-7)$ or $f'(-1)$ or $f'(5)$

$\Rightarrow k \in \{36, -51, 72\}$

44. Let $g(x)$ be the inverse of an invertible function $f(x)$, which is differentiable for all real x, then $g''(f''(x))$ equals

(a) $-\frac{f''(x)}{(f'(x))^3}$

(b) $\frac{f''(x)f''(x) - (f'(x))^3}{f'(x)}$

(c) $\frac{f'(x)f''(x) - (f'(x))^2}{(f'(x))^2}$

(d) None of these

Solution: **(a)** Given that $g^{-1}(x) = f(x)$

$\Rightarrow x = g(f(x))$

Differentiating both sides w.r.t. x, we get $g'(f(x))$ $f'(x) = 1$

$$\Rightarrow g'(f(x)) = \frac{1}{f'(x)}$$

Differentiating again w.r.t. x, we get $g''(f(x))$.

$$f'(x) = \frac{-f''(x)}{[f'(x)]^2}$$

$$\Rightarrow g''f((x)) = \frac{f''(x)}{[f'(x)]^3}$$

45. If $x < 1$, then find the value of $\frac{1-2x}{1-x+x^2} + \frac{2x-4x^3}{1-x^2+x^4} + \frac{4x^3-8x^7}{1-x^4+x^8} + \ldots\infty$

(a) $\frac{1}{1+x+x^2}$ (b) $\frac{1+2x}{1+x+x^2}$

(c) $\frac{1-x+x^2}{1+x+x^2}$ (d) 1

Solution: **(b)** We have $(1 + x + x^2)(1 - x + x^2) = (1+x^2)^2 - x^2 = 1 + x^2 + x^4$

and $(1 + x + x^2)(1 - x + x^2)(1 - x^2 + x^4) = (1 + x^2 + x^4)(1 - x^2 + x^4) = 1 + x^4 + x^8$

Moving on in this manner, we get

$(1 + x + x^2)(1 - x + x^2)(1 - x^2 + x^4)(1 - x^4 + x^8)$

$$\ldots\ldots\left(1 - x^{2^{n-1}} + x^{2^n}\right) = \left(1 + x^{2^n} + x^{2^{n+1}}\right)$$

Now for $x < 1$, $x^\infty = 0$. Then limit $n \to \infty$ in (1), we get

$\ln(1 + x + x^2) + \ln(1 - x + x^2) + \ln(1 - x^2 + x^4) + \ln(1 - x^4 + x^8) + \ldots$

$$= \lim_{n\to\infty} \ell n\left(1 + x^{2^n} + x^{2^{n+1}}\right) = \ell n(1) = 0$$

Differentiating both sides w.r.t we get

$$\Rightarrow \frac{1+2x}{1+x+x^2} + \frac{-1+2x}{1-x+x^2} + \frac{-2x+4x^3}{1-x^2+x^4} + \frac{4x^3+8x^7}{1-x^4+x^8} + .. = 0$$

Hence

$$\frac{1-2x}{1-x+x^2} + \frac{2x-4x^3}{1-x^2+x^4} + \frac{4x^3-8x^7}{1-x^4+x^8} + .. = \frac{1+2x}{1+x+x^2}$$

46. Let $f(x) = x^2 + xg'(1) + g''(2)$ and $g(x) = f(1)x^2 + xf'(x) + f''(x)$, then $f(2)$ and $g(x)$ are respectively given by

(a) $x^2 + x + 2, x^2 + x + 1$

(b) $x^2 - 3x + 2, x^2 + 2$

(c) $x^2 - 3x, -3x + 2$

(d) $x^2 + 2, -3x + 2$

Solution: **(c)** Let us support $g'(1) = a$, $g''(2) = b$ ...(i)

Then $f(x) = x^2 + ax + b$,

Putting $x = 1$, we get $f(1) = a + b + 1$

$\therefore$ $g(x) = (1 + a + b)x^2 + (2x + a).x + 2$

$\Rightarrow g'(x) = x^2(3 + a + b) + ax + 2$

Differentiating both sides w.r.t. x, we get $g'(x) = 2x(3 + a + b) + a$ and $g''(x) = 2(3 + a + b)$

Hence $g'(1) = 2(3 + a + b) + a$ ...(ii)
and $g''(2) = 2(3 + a + b)$ .....(iii)
From (i), (ii) and (iii), we have $a = 2(3 + a + b) + a$ and $b = 2(3 + a + b)$

i.e. $3 + a + b = 0$ and $b + 2a + 6 = 0$
Hence, solving the above two equations simultaneously, we get, $b = 0$ and $a = -3$
Substituting these values of 'a' and 'b' in $f(x)$ and $g(x)$, we get $f(x) = x^2 - 3x$ and $g(x) = -3x + 2$

47. A function $f(x)$ satisfies the condition, $f(x) = f'(x) + f''(x) + f'''(x) + \ldots\ldots\infty$ where $f(x)$ is an indefinitely differentiable function and dash denotes the order of derivatives. If $f(0) = 1$, then $f(x)$ is

(a) $e^{x/2}$ (b) e^x
(c) e^{2x} (d) e^{4x}

Solution: (a) $f(x) = f'(x) + f''(x) + f'''(x) + \ldots\ldots\infty$

$F'(x) = f''(x) + f'''(x) + f''''(x) + \ldots\ldots\infty$

$\therefore\ 2f'(x) = f'(x) + f''(x) + f'''(x) + \ldots.$

$\Rightarrow\ 2f'(x) = f(x) \Rightarrow \dfrac{f'(x)}{f(x)} = \dfrac{1}{2}$

on integrating w.r.t. x; we get $\ell nf(x) = \dfrac{1}{2}x + c$

If $x = 0$; $f(0) = 1$

$\Rightarrow c = 0$

hence $\ell nf(x) = \dfrac{x}{2}$

$\Rightarrow f(x) = e^{\frac{x}{2}}$

SECTION–II

SUBJECTIVE SOLVED EXAMPLE

1. *If* $x = \tan(y/2) - \log\left[\dfrac{\left(1+\tan\dfrac{y}{2}\right)^2}{\tan\left(\dfrac{y}{2}\right)}\right]$ then find $\dfrac{dy}{dx}$.

Solution:

If $x = \tan(y/2) - 2\log(1+\tan y/2) + \log(\tan y/2)$

$$\frac{dx}{dy} = \frac{1}{2}\sec^2\left(\frac{y}{2}\right) + \frac{-2}{\left(1+\tan\frac{y}{2}\right)}\left(\frac{1}{2}\sec^2\frac{y}{2}\right) + \frac{\sec^2\frac{y}{2}}{2\tan\frac{y}{2}}$$

$$\frac{dx}{dy} = \sec^2\left(\frac{y}{2}\right)\left[\frac{1}{2} - \frac{1}{1+\tan\frac{y}{2}} + \frac{1}{2\tan\frac{y}{2}}\right]$$

$$= \sec^2\left(\frac{y}{2}\right)\left[\frac{\tan(y/2) + \tan^2(y/2) - 2\tan(y/2) + 1 + \tan(y/2)}{2\tan(y/2)\left(1+\tan(y/2)\right)}\right]$$

$$\frac{dx}{dy} = \frac{\sec^4(y/2)}{2\tan(y/2)\left(1+\tan(y/2)\right)}$$

$$\Rightarrow \frac{dy}{dx} = 2\tan\left(\frac{y}{2}\right)\left(1+\tan\frac{y}{2}\right)\cos^4\left(\frac{y}{2}\right)$$

$$= \frac{2\sin(y/2)}{\cos(y/2)}\left(\frac{\sin(y/2)+\cos(y/2)}{\cos(y/2)}\right)\cos^4\frac{y}{2}$$

$$= \frac{1}{2}\sin y\left(2\sin(y/2)\cos(y/2) + 2\cos^2(y/2)\right)$$

$$= \frac{1}{2}\sin y\,(1+\sin y+\cos y)$$

2. Let f, g and h are differentiable functions. If $f(0) = 1$; $g(0) = 2$; $h(0) = 3$ and the derivatives of their pair wise products at $x = 0$ are $f\,g)'(0) = 6$; $(g\,h)'(0) = 4$ and $(h\,f)'(0) = 5$ then compute the value of $(fgh)'(0)$.

Solution: $y = fgh$

$\dfrac{dy}{dx} = f'gh + fg'h + fgh'$

$= \dfrac{1}{2}(2f'gh + 2fg'h + 2fgh')$

$= \dfrac{1}{2}(h(f'g + g'f) + g(f'h + fh') + f(g'h + gh'))$

$= \dfrac{1}{2}[h.(fg)' + g.(fh)' + f.(gh)']$

$(fgh)'0 = \dfrac{1}{2}[h(0)(fg)'(0) + g(0)(fh)'(0) + f(0)(gh)'(0)]$

$= \dfrac{1}{2}(3\times 6 + 2\times 5 + 1\times 4)$

$= \dfrac{1}{2}(18 + 10 + 4) = \dfrac{32}{2} = 16$

3 Find the value of the expression $y^3\dfrac{d^2y}{dx^2}$ on the ellipse $3x^2 + 4y^2 = 12$.

Solution: $3x^2 + 4y^2 = 12$; Differentiating both side, we get $6x + 8y\dfrac{dy}{dx} = 0$

$$\Rightarrow \frac{dy}{dx} = -\frac{6x}{8y} = -\frac{3x}{4y}$$

Differentiating again w.r.t. x, we get

$$\frac{d^2y}{dx^2} = -\frac{3}{4}\left(\frac{y - x\dfrac{dy}{dx}}{y^2}\right)$$

$$= -\frac{3}{4}\left(\frac{y - x\left(-\dfrac{3}{4}\right)\dfrac{x}{y}}{y^2}\right) = -\frac{3}{4}\left(\frac{y^2 + \dfrac{3}{4}x^2}{y^3}\right)$$

$$= -\frac{3}{16}\left(\frac{3x^2 + 4y^2}{y^3}\right) = -\frac{3}{16}\times\frac{12}{y^3} = -\frac{9}{4y^3}$$

$$\Rightarrow y^3 \times \frac{d^2y}{dx^2} = -\frac{9}{4}$$

4. If $y = \dfrac{ax^2}{(x-a)(x-b)(x-c)} + \dfrac{bx}{(x-b)(x-c)} + \dfrac{c}{x-c} + 1$,

prove that $\dfrac{dy}{dx} = \dfrac{y}{x}\left\{\dfrac{a}{a-x} + \dfrac{b}{b-x} + \dfrac{c}{c-x}\right\}$

Solution: We have

$$y = \frac{ax^2}{(x-a)(x-b)(x-c)} + \frac{bx}{(x-b)(x-c)} + \frac{c}{x-c} + 1$$

$$\Rightarrow y = \frac{ax^2}{(x-a)(x-b)(x-c)} + \frac{bx}{(x-b)(x-c)} + \left(\frac{c + x - x}{x-c}\right)$$

$$\Rightarrow y = \frac{ax^2}{(x-a)(x-b)(x-c)} + \frac{bx}{(x-b)(x-c)} + \frac{x}{x-c}$$

$$\Rightarrow y = \frac{ax^2}{(x-a)(x-b)(x-c)} + \frac{bx + x(x-b)}{(x-b)(x-c)}$$

$$\Rightarrow y = \frac{ax^2}{(x-a)(x-b)(x-c)} + \frac{x^2}{(x-b)(x-c)}$$

$$\Rightarrow y = \frac{ax^2 + x^2(x-a)}{(x-a)(x-b)(x-c)}$$

$$\Rightarrow y = \frac{x^3}{(x-a)(x-b)(x-c)}$$

$$\Rightarrow \log y = \log\left\{\frac{x^3}{(x-a)(x-b)(x-c)}\right\}$$

$\Rightarrow \log y = 3\log x - \{\log(x-a) + \log(x-b) + \log(x-c)\}$

On differentiating w.r.t to x, we get

$$\frac{1}{y}\frac{dy}{dx} = \frac{3}{x} - \left\{\frac{1}{x-a} + \frac{1}{x-b} + \frac{1}{x-c}\right\}$$

$$\Rightarrow \frac{dy}{dx} = y\left\{\left(\frac{1}{x} - \frac{1}{x-a}\right) + \left(\frac{1}{x} - \frac{1}{x-b}\right) + \left(\frac{1}{x} - \frac{1}{x-c}\right)\right\}$$

$$\Rightarrow \frac{dy}{dx} = y\left\{\frac{-a}{x(x-a)} - \frac{b}{x(x-b)} - \frac{c}{x(x-c)}\right\}$$

$$\Rightarrow \frac{dy}{dx} = \frac{y}{x}\left\{\frac{a}{a-x} + \frac{b}{b-x} + \frac{c}{x-c}\right\}$$

5. If $f(x) = (2 + 3x)^6$, then find the value of $f(0) + \dfrac{f'(0)}{1!} + \dfrac{f''(0)}{2!} + \dfrac{f'''(0)}{3!} + ... \dfrac{f^{VI}(0)}{6!}$

Solution: $f(x) = (2x + 3x)^6 \Rightarrow f(0) = 2^6 = {}^6C_0 \times 2^6$

$f'(x) = 3 \times 6(2 + 3x)^5 \Rightarrow f'(0) = 3 \times 6 \times 2^5 = {}^6C_1 \times 2^5 \times 3^1$

$f''(x) = 3^2 \times 6 \times 5 \times (2 + 3x)^4 \Rightarrow f''(0) = 3^2 \times 6 \times 5 \times 2^4 = 2^1 \times {}^6C_2\, 2^4 \times 3^2$

$f'''(x) = 3^3 \times 6 \times 5 \times 4 \times (2 + 3x)^3 \Rightarrow f'''(0) = 3^3 \times 6 \times 5 \times 4 \times 2^3 = 3! \times {}^6C_3 \times 2^3 \times 3^3$

Similarly

$f'''' = 4! \times {}^6C_4 \times 2^2 \times 3^4$

$f^{(v)} = 5! \times {}^6C_5 \times 2 \times 3^5$

$f^{(vi)} = 6! \times {}^6C_6 \times 2^0 \times 3^6$

$$\therefore\quad S = f(0) + \frac{f'(0)}{1!} + \frac{f''(0)}{2!} + ... + \frac{f^{(vi)}(0)}{6!}$$

$$= {}^6C_0 \times 2^6 + \frac{{}^6C_1 \times 2^5 \times 3^1}{1!} + \frac{{}^6C_2 \times 2! \times 2^4 \times 3^2}{2!} + ... + \frac{{}^6C_6 \times 6! \times 2^0 \times 3^6}{6!}$$

$= {}^6C \times 2^6 + {}^6C_1 2^5 \times 3^2 + ...{}^6C_6 \times 2^0 \times 3^6$

$= (2 + 3)^6 = 5^6 = 15625$

6. If $x = \text{cosec}\theta - \sin\theta$ and $y = \text{cosec}^n\theta - \sin^n\theta$ then show that $(x^2 + 4)\left(\dfrac{dy}{dx}\right)^2 - n^2\left(y^2 + 4\right) = 0$

Solution: $\dfrac{dx}{d\theta} = -\text{cos}ec\theta\cot\theta - \cos\theta$

$$= -\cos\theta\left(\frac{1}{\sin^2\theta} + 1\right)$$

$$\frac{dy}{d\theta} = n\ \text{cosec}^{n-1}\theta\,(-\text{cosec}\theta\cot\theta) - n\sin^{n-1}\theta\cos\theta$$

$$= -n\cos\theta\left(\frac{1}{\sin^{n+1}\theta} + \sin^{n-1}\theta\right)$$

$$\frac{dy}{dx} = \frac{dy/d\theta}{dx/d\theta} = n\left(\frac{1+\sin^{2n}\theta}{\sin^{n+1}\theta}\right)\times\left(\frac{\sin^2\theta}{1+\sin^2\theta}\right)$$

$$\therefore\quad (x^2+4)\left(\frac{dy}{dx}\right)^2 - n^2(y^2+4) = 0$$

$$\left(\left(\frac{1}{\sin\theta} - \sin\theta\right)^2 + 4\right)n^2\left(\frac{1+\sin^{2n}\theta}{1+\sin^2\theta}\right)^2 \times$$

$$\left(\frac{1}{\sin^{n-1}\theta}\right)^2 - n^2\left(\left(\frac{1}{\sin^n\theta} - \sin^n\theta\right)^2 + 4\right)$$

$$= \left(\frac{1+\sin^2\theta}{\sin\theta}\right)^2 \times n^2\frac{\left(1+\sin^{2n}\theta\right)^2}{\left(1+\sin^2\theta\right)^2}\times\left(\frac{1}{\sin^{n-1}\theta}\right)^2$$

$$-n^2\left(\frac{\left(1+\sin^n\theta\right)^2}{\sin^{2n}\theta}\right)$$

$$= n^2\left(1+\sin^{2n}\theta\right)^2$$

$$\left[\frac{1}{\sin^2\theta}\times\left(\frac{1}{\sin^{(n-1)}\theta}\right)^2 - \frac{1}{\sin^{2n}\theta}\right] = 0$$

7. If $f(x) = u(x).\ v(x)$ and $u'(x)\ v'(x) = k$, prove that $\frac{f''}{f} = \frac{u''}{u} + \frac{v''}{v} + \frac{2k}{uv}$ and $\frac{f'''}{f} = \frac{u'''}{u} + \frac{v'''}{v}$

Solution: Given $f(x) = u(x).\ v(x)$

Differentiation g both sides w.r.t x,

we get $f'(x) = u'(x).v(x) + v'(x).u(x)$

Again differentiating both sides w.r.t x we get

$f''(x) = u''(x)v(x) + v''(x), u(x) + 2u'(x)\,v'(x)$

$\Rightarrow f''(x) = u''(x).v(x) + v''(x), u(x) + 2k$

Dividing both sides by $F(x) = f(x).\ g(x)$

we get $\frac{f''(x)}{f(x)} = \frac{u''(x)}{u(x)} + \frac{v''(x)}{v(x)} + \frac{2k}{u(x)v(x)}$

or Again $u'(x)\ v'(x) = k$

Differentiating both sides w.r.t.x we get

$f''(x) = u''(x)v(x) + v''(x), u(x) + 2u'(x)\,v'(x)$

$\Rightarrow f''(x) = u''(x).v(x) + v''(x), u(x) + 2k$

Differentiation both sides w.r.t.x, we get

$f'''(x) = u''(x).\ v'(x) + u'''(x).v(x) + v''(x).u'(x) + u(x).v'''(x) + 0$

Now, $u'(x).v(x) = k$

Differentiating both sides w.r.t. x, we get $u''(x).v'(x) + v''(x).u'(x) = 0$

Now dividing both sides by $f(x) = u(x)\ v(x)$,

we get $\frac{f'''}{f(x)} = \frac{u'''(x)}{u(x)} + \frac{v'''(x)}{v(x)}$ or $\frac{f'''}{f} = \frac{u'''}{u} + \frac{v'''}{v}$

8. If the function $f(x) = x^3 + e^{x/2}$ and $g(x) = f^{1}(x)$, then the value of $g'(1)$ is

Solution: Since $g(x) = f^{1}(x)$ so $f(g(x)) = x$ for all x.

Differentiating both sides of $f(g(x) = x$;

we get, $f'(g(x))\,g'(x) = 1$

Putting $x = 0$ in $f(a) = x^3 + e^{x/2}$; we get $f(0) = 1$

Now, (0, 1) lies on $y = g(x)$

$\because$ The graph of $f(x)$ and $g(x)$ are mirror image w.r.t. $y = x$

$\therefore\ g(1) = 0$

Now, Putting $x = 1$ in (i), we get $f'(0)\,g'(1) = 1$.

But $f'(x) = 3x^2 + \left(\frac{1}{2}\right)e^{x/2}$

$\Rightarrow f'(0) = \frac{1}{2}\qquad \therefore \left(\frac{1}{2}\right)g'(1) = 1$

$\Rightarrow g'(1) = 2$.

9. If $x\,e^{xy} = y + \sin^2 x$, then at $x = 0$, $\frac{dy}{dx}$ is equal to

Solution: Putting $x = 0$ in the given equation, we get $y = 0$.

Differentiating both the sides,

We have $e^{xy} + xe^{xy}\left[x\frac{dy}{dx} + y\right] = \frac{dy}{dx} + 2\sin x\cos x$

Putting $x = 0$, $y = 0$,

we have $e^0 + 0.e^0\left[0.\frac{dy}{dx} + 0\right] = \left.\frac{dy}{dx}\right|_{x=0} + 0$

$\Rightarrow \left.\frac{dy}{dx}\right|_{x=0} = 1$.

10. Given a function g which has derivative $h'(x)\ \forall\, x$ satisfying $h'(0) = 2$ and $h(x+y) = e^y h(x) + e^x h(y)\ \forall\, x, y \in \mathbb{R}$, $h(5) = 32$. The value of $h'(5) - 2e^5$ is

Solution: Putting $x = y = 0$ in $h(x + y) = e^y h(x) + e^x h(y)$

We get $h(0) = 2h(0) \quad \Rightarrow h(0) = 0$

So $2 = h'(0) = \lim_{h\to 0} \frac{g(h)-g(0)}{h} = \lim_{h\to 0} \frac{g(h)}{h}$

Also

$$g'(x) = \lim_{h\to 0} \frac{g(x+h)-g(0)}{h}$$

$$= \lim_{h\to 0} \frac{e^x g(h)+e^h g(x)-g(x)}{h}$$

$$= \lim_{h\to 0}\left(e^x \frac{g(h)}{h}+\frac{e^h-1}{h}g(x)\right) = e^x \lim_{h\to 0}\frac{g(h)}{h}+1.g(x)$$

Thus $g'(5)-2e^5 = 32$.

11. If the transformation $z = \log \tan(x/2)$ reduces the differential equation $\frac{d^2y}{dx^2}+\cot x+\frac{dy}{dx}+4y\cos ec^2 x = 0$ into $\frac{d^2y}{dz^2}+Ay=0$ then the value of A is

Solution: We have

$$\frac{dz}{dx}=\frac{1}{2}\frac{\sec^2(x/2)}{\tan(x/2)}=\frac{1}{\sin x}=\operatorname{cosec} x$$

$$\frac{dz}{dx}=\frac{dy}{dz}.\frac{dz}{dx}=\operatorname{cosec} x\frac{dy}{dz}$$

$$\frac{d^2y}{dx^2}=\frac{d}{dx}\left(\frac{dy}{dx}\right)=\frac{d}{dz}\left(\frac{dy}{dx}\right)\frac{dy}{dz}$$

$$\frac{d}{dz}\left(\operatorname{cosec} x\frac{dy}{dz}\right)\operatorname{cosec} x$$

$$=\left(\operatorname{cosec} x\frac{d^2y}{dz^2}-\operatorname{cosec} x\cot x\frac{dx}{dz}\frac{dy}{dz}\right)\operatorname{cosec} x$$

Putting these values in the given differential equation, we have

$$\frac{d^2y}{dx^2}+\cot x\frac{dy}{dx}+4y\operatorname{cosec}^2 x=0$$

$$\Leftrightarrow \operatorname{cosec}^2 x\frac{d^2y}{dz^2}-\operatorname{cosec} x\cot x\frac{dy}{dz}+$$

$$\cot x\operatorname{cosec} x\frac{dy}{dz}+4\operatorname{cosec}^2 x=0$$

$$\Leftrightarrow \operatorname{cosec}^2 x\left(\frac{d^2y}{dz^2}+4y\right)m=0 \Leftrightarrow \frac{d^2y}{dz^2}+4y=0$$

12. If the transformation $x = \cos\theta$ reduces the differential equation $(1-x^2)\frac{d^2y}{dx^2}-x\frac{dy}{dx}+y=0$ into $\frac{d^2y}{d\theta^2}+ky=0$; then the value of k is

Solution: Given $x = \cos\theta$

$$\therefore \quad \frac{dx}{d\theta}=-\sin\theta,$$

so $\frac{dy}{dx}=\frac{dy}{d\theta}\frac{d\theta}{dx}=-\operatorname{cosec}\theta\frac{dy}{d\theta}$

Also

$$\frac{d^2y}{dx^2}=\frac{d}{dx}\left(\frac{dy}{dx}\right)=\frac{d}{d\theta}\left(\frac{dy}{dx}\right)\frac{d\theta}{dx}$$

$$=\frac{d}{d\theta}\left(-\operatorname{cosec}\theta\frac{dy}{d\theta}\right)(-\operatorname{cosec}\theta)$$

Putting these values of $\frac{dy}{dx}$ and $\frac{d^2y}{dx^2}$ in the given differential equation,

the equation $(1-x^2)\frac{d^2y}{dx^2}-x\frac{dy}{dx}+y=0$ transforms to

$$(1-\cos^2\theta)\left(-\operatorname{cosec}^2\theta\cot\theta\frac{dy}{d\theta}+\operatorname{cosec}^2\theta\frac{d^2y}{d\theta^2}\right)-$$

$$\cos\theta\left(-\operatorname{cosec}\theta\frac{dy}{d\theta}\right)+y=0$$

$$\Rightarrow -\cot\theta\frac{dy}{d\theta}+\frac{d^2y}{d\theta^2}+\cot\theta\frac{dy}{d\theta}+y=0$$

$$\Rightarrow \frac{d^2y}{d\theta^2}+y=0$$

$$\Rightarrow \frac{d^2y}{d\theta^2}+ky=0\text{; we get } k=1$$

13. If $y = 1 + \frac{x_1}{x-x_1} + \frac{x_2 . x}{(x-x_1)(x-x_2)} + \frac{x_3 . x^2}{(x-x_1)(x-x_2)(x-x_3)}$ +..... upto $(n + 1)$ terms then prove that

$$\frac{dy}{dx}=\frac{y}{x}\left[\frac{x_1}{x_1-x}+\frac{x_2}{x_2-x}+\frac{x_3}{x_3-x}+...+\frac{x_n}{x_n-x}\right]$$

Solution: $y = 1+\frac{x_1}{x-x_1}+\frac{x_2 .x}{(x-x_1)\,(x-x_2)}+.........$

$$+\frac{x_n x^{n-1}}{(x-x_1)\,(x-x_2).......(x-xn)}$$

$$= \frac{x}{x-x_1} + \frac{x_2 x}{(x-x_1)(x-x_2)} = \ldots\ldots\ldots\ldots +$$

$$\frac{x_n x^{n-1}}{(x-x_1)(x-x_2)\ldots\ldots(x-x_n)}$$

$$= \frac{x(x)}{(x-x_1)(x-x_2)} + \frac{x_2 x^2}{(x-x_1)(x-x_2)(x-x_3)}$$

$$+\ldots\ldots+ \frac{x_n x^{n-1}}{(x-x_1)(x-x_2)\ldots\ldots(x-xn)}$$

$$= \frac{x^n}{(x-x_1)(x-x_2)\ldots\ldots\ldots(x-x_n)}$$

$$\Rightarrow y = \frac{x^n}{(x-x_1)(x-x_2)\ldots\ldots\ldots(x-x_n)}$$

Taking $\log_e$ on both sides, we get

$\ell n\, y = n\ell nx - \ell n(x-x_1) - \ell(x-x_2)\ldots\ldots\ldots\ell(x-x_n)$

$$\Rightarrow \frac{1}{y}\frac{dy}{dx} = \left(\frac{n}{x} - \frac{1}{x-x_1} - \frac{1}{x-x_2} + \ldots\ldots + \frac{1}{x-x_n}\right)$$

$$= \left(\frac{n}{x} + \frac{1}{x_1-x} + \frac{1}{x_2-x} + \ldots\ldots + \frac{1}{x_n-x}\right)$$

$$= \left(\left(\frac{1}{x}+\frac{1}{x_1-x}\right)+\left(\frac{1}{x}+\frac{1}{x_2-x}\right)+\ldots\ldots\ldots+\left(\frac{1}{x}+\frac{1}{x_n-x}\right)\right)$$

$$= \frac{1}{x}\left(\frac{x_1}{x_1-x}+\frac{x_2}{x_2-x}+\frac{x_3}{x_3-x}+\ldots\ldots+\frac{x_n}{x_{n-x}}\right)$$

$$\Rightarrow \frac{dy}{dx} = \frac{y}{x}\left(\frac{x_1}{x_1-x}+\frac{x_2}{x_2-x}+\frac{x_3}{x_3-x}+\ldots\ldots+\frac{x_n}{x_n-x}\right)$$

14. Let $g(x)$ be a polynomial, of degree one and $f(x)$ be defined by $f(x) = \begin{cases} g(x) & , x \le 0 \\ \left(\frac{1+x}{2+x}\right)^{1/x} & , x > 0 \end{cases}$. Find the continuous function $f(x)$ satisfying $f'(1) = f(-1)$

Solution: $g(x) = ax + b$

$\because$ The function is continuous

$\Rightarrow$ LHL = RHL

$$\Rightarrow a \times 0 + b = \lim_{x\to 0}\left(\frac{1+x}{2+x}\right)^{\frac{1}{x}} = \left(\frac{1}{2}\right)^{\infty} = 0$$

$\Rightarrow b = 0$

Now, for $x > 0$; $f(x) = \left(\frac{1+x}{2+x}\right)^{1/x}$

$$\Rightarrow \ell n(f(x)) = \frac{1}{x}(\ell n(1+x) - \ell n(2+x))$$

$$\Rightarrow \frac{1}{f(x)} f'(x)$$

$$= \left[\frac{-1}{x^2}\left(\log\frac{(1+x)}{(2+x)}\right) + \frac{1}{x}\left(\frac{1}{1+x} - \frac{1}{2+x}\right)\right]$$

$$\Rightarrow f'(1) = f(1)\left(-1\,\ell n\frac{2}{3} + 1\left(\frac{1}{2}-\frac{1}{3}\right)\right)$$

$$\Rightarrow f'(1) = \left(\frac{2}{3}\right)\left(-\ell n\frac{2}{3}+\frac{1}{6}\right)$$

Also, for $x < 0$; $f(x) = g(x)$

$\Rightarrow f(-1) = g(-1) = -a + b = -a$

$\Rightarrow f(-1) = -a$

$$\text{so } a = -\frac{2}{3}\left(\frac{1}{6} - \ell n\frac{3}{2}\right)$$

$$f(x) = \begin{cases} \frac{2}{3}\left(\ell n\frac{2}{3} - \frac{1}{6}\right)^x & ; x \le 0 \\ \left(\frac{1+x}{2+x}\right)^{1/x} & ; x > 0 \end{cases}$$

15. If $y = \cot^{-1}\frac{\sqrt{1+\sin x}+\sqrt{1-\sin x}}{\sqrt{1+\sin x}-\sqrt{1-\sin x}}$, find $\frac{dy}{dx}$ if $x \in \left(0, \frac{\pi}{2}\right) \cup \left(\frac{\pi}{2}, \pi\right)$.

Solution: $0 < x < \pi$; $x \ne \frac{\pi}{2}$

$$0 < \frac{x}{2} < \frac{\pi}{2};\ x \ne \frac{\pi}{4}$$

$$\cot^{-1}\left(\frac{\left|\sin\frac{x}{2}+\cos\frac{x}{2}\right| + \left|\sin\frac{x}{2}-\cos\frac{x}{2}\right|}{\left|\sin\frac{x}{2}+\cos\frac{x}{2}\right| - \left|\sin\frac{x}{2}-\cos\frac{x}{2}\right|}\right)$$

(i) $0 < \frac{x}{2} < \frac{\pi}{4}$; $\sin\frac{x}{2} - \cos\frac{x}{2} < 0$

$$\cot^{-1}\left(\frac{\sin\frac{x}{2}+\cos\frac{x}{2}-\sin\frac{x}{2}+\cos\frac{x}{2}}{\sin\frac{x}{2}+\cos\frac{x}{2}+\sin\frac{x}{2}-\cos\frac{x}{2}}\right)$$

$$\Rightarrow \cot^{-1}\left(\cot\frac{x}{2}\right) = \frac{x}{2}$$

$$\Rightarrow y = \frac{x}{2} \qquad \Rightarrow \frac{dy}{dx} = \frac{1}{2}$$

(ii) $\frac{\pi}{4} < \frac{x}{2} < \frac{\pi}{2}$; $\sin\frac{x}{2} - \cos\frac{x}{2} > 0$

$$y = \cot^{-1}\left(\frac{\sin\frac{x}{2}+\cos\frac{x}{2}+\sin\frac{x}{2}-\cos\frac{x}{2}}{\sin\frac{x}{2}+\cos\frac{x}{2}-\sin\frac{x}{2}+\cos\frac{x}{2}}\right)$$

$$= \cot^{-1}\left(\tan\frac{x}{2}\right)$$

$$= \cot^{-1} = \cot\left(\frac{\pi}{2}-\frac{x}{2}\right) = \left(\frac{\pi}{2}-\frac{x}{2}\right)$$

$$\Rightarrow \frac{dy}{dx} = -\frac{1}{2}$$

16. If $y = y(x)$ and it follows the relation $e^{xy} + y\cos x = 2$, then find (i) $y'(0)$ and (ii) $y''(0)$

Solution: $e^{xy} + y\cos x = 2$

Putting $x = 0$ in $e^0 + y\cos x = 2$; we get $y = 1$

Differentiating w.r.t. x;

we get $e^{xy}\left(x\frac{dy}{dx}+y\right) - y\sin x + \cos x\,\frac{dy}{dx} = 0$

$$\Rightarrow (xe^{xy} + \cos x)\,\frac{dy}{dx} = y(\sin x - e^{xy}) \qquad \text{........(i)}$$

$$\frac{dy}{dx} = \frac{y\sin x - ye^{xy}}{xe^{xy}+\cos x}$$

$$\left.\frac{dy}{dx}\right|_{(0,1)} = \frac{1\sin 0 - 1e^0}{e^0+\cos 0} = -\frac{1}{1} = -1$$

Again differentiating (i), w.r.t. x; we get

$$(xe^{xy}+\cos x)\,\frac{d^2y}{dx^2} + \left[e^{xy} + xe^{xy}\left(x\frac{dy}{dx}+y\right) - \sin x\right]\frac{dy}{dx}$$

$$= \left[\frac{dy}{dx}(\sin x - e^{xy}) + y\left(\cos x - e^{xy}\left(y + x\frac{dy}{dx}\right)\right)\right]$$

$$(0+1)\,\frac{d^2y}{dx^2} + (e^0)(-1) = 1$$

$$\frac{d^2y}{dx^2} - 1 = 1 \quad \frac{d^2y}{dx^2} = 2$$

17. Find a polynomial function $f(x)$ such that $f(2x) = f'(x)f''(x)$.

Solution: $f(2x) = f'(x)f''(x)$

Let $f(2x)$ is of order $- n$

$\Rightarrow$ order of $f'(x) = n - 1$ and order of $f''(x) = n - 2$

$\therefore$ order of LHS $= n$ and order of RHS $= (n - 1) + (n - 2)$

$\therefore$ $n = 2n - 3$ $\qquad \Rightarrow n = 3$

so $f(x)$ is a polynomial of order 3.

Let $f(x) = ax^3 + bx^2 + cx + d$

$\Rightarrow f'(x) = 3ax^2 + 2bx + c$

$\Rightarrow f''(x) = 6ax + 2b$

Given $f(2x) = f'(x)f''(x)$

$\Rightarrow 8ax^3 + 4bx^2 + 2cx + d = (3ax^2 + 2bx + c)(6ax + 2b)$

$= 18a^2x^3 + (12ab + 6ab)x^2 + (6ac + 4b^2)x + 2bc$

$18a^2 = 8a \qquad 12ab + 6ab = 4b$

$6ac + (4b^2) = 2c$; $18ab = 4b$; $6ac = 2c$

$a = \frac{8}{18} \quad 18 \times \frac{4}{9} \times b = 4b$

$\qquad 8b = 4b$

$3ac = c \Rightarrow c = 0\ (\because a \neq 0) \quad b = 0$

and $2bc = d$, $d = 0 \qquad f(x) = -$

18. (a) Show that the substitution $z = \ln\left(\tan\frac{x}{2}\right)$ changes the equation $\frac{d^2y}{dx^2} + \cot x\frac{dy}{dx} + 4y\,\mathrm{cosec}^2 x = 0$ to $(d^2y/dz^2) + 4y = 0$.

(b) If the dependent variable y is changed to 'z' by the substitution $y = \tan z$ then the differential equation $\frac{d^2y}{dx^2} = 1 + \frac{2(1+y)}{1+y^2}\left(\frac{dy}{dx}\right)^2$ is changed to $\frac{d^2z}{dx^2} = \cos x^2 z + k\left(\frac{dz}{dx}\right)^2$, then find the value of k.

Solution: (a) $z = \log\left(\tan\frac{x}{2}\right)$

$$\frac{dz}{dx} = \frac{1}{2}\frac{\sec^2\frac{x}{2}}{\tan\frac{x}{2}}$$

$$= \frac{1}{2}\frac{\cos\frac{x}{2}}{\sin\frac{x}{2}} \times \frac{1}{\cos^2\frac{x}{2}} = \frac{1}{(\sin x)}$$

$$\frac{dy}{dz} = \frac{dy}{dx}\left(\frac{dx}{dz}\right) = \sin x\,\frac{dy}{dx}$$

$$\frac{dy}{dx} = \left(\frac{dy}{dz}\right)\cdot\left(\frac{dz}{dx}\right) = \frac{1}{\sin x}\frac{dy}{dz}$$

Now, $\frac{d^2y}{dz^2} = \sin x\frac{d}{dz}\left(\frac{dy}{dx}\right) + \cos x\frac{dx}{dz}\frac{dy}{dx}$

$= \sin x\ \frac{d^2y}{dx^2}.\frac{dx}{dz} + \cos x \sin x\ \frac{dy}{dx}$

$= \sin^2 x.\frac{d^2y}{dx^2} + \sin x.\ \cos x \times \frac{1}{\sin x}.\frac{dy}{dz}$

$\Rightarrow \frac{d^2y}{dz^2} - \cos x\ \frac{dy}{dz} = \sin^2 x\left(\frac{d^2y}{dx^2}\right)$ ...(i)

Now given $\frac{d^2y}{dx^2} + \cot x\frac{dy}{dx} + 4y\ \text{cosec}^2 x = 0$

$\Rightarrow \sin^2 x\ \frac{d^2y}{dx^2} + \sin x \cos x\ \frac{dy}{dx} + 4y = 0$ ...(2)

$\therefore$ from (1) and (2), we get $\frac{d^2y}{dx^2} - \cos x.\frac{dy}{dz} + \sin x$

$\cos x.\ \frac{1}{\sin x}\frac{dy}{dz} + 4y = 0$

$\frac{d^2y}{dz^2} + 4y = 0$ Ans.

(b) $y = \tan z$

$\frac{dy}{dx} = \left(\sec^2\right)\frac{dz}{dx}$

$\frac{d^2y}{dx^2} = \frac{d}{dx}\left(\sec^2 z.\frac{dz}{dx}\right)$

$= \sec^2 z.\frac{d^2z}{dx^2} + 2\sec^2 z \tan z\left(\frac{dz}{dx}\right)^2$ ...(i)

$\Rightarrow \frac{d^2y}{dx^2} = 1 + \frac{2(1+y)}{1+y^2}\left(\frac{dy}{dx}\right)^2$ ...(ii)

From (i) and (ii); we get $\sec^2 z \times$

$\left(\frac{d^2z}{dx^2} + 2\tan z\left(\frac{dz}{dx}\right)^2\right) = 1 + \frac{2(1+\tan z)}{\sec^2 z}\times\left(\frac{dz}{dx}\right)^2$

$\times \sec^4 x$

$\Rightarrow \sec^2 z\left(\frac{d^2z}{dx^2} + 2\tan z\left(\frac{dz}{dx}\right)^2\right) = 1 + 2(1 + \tan z)$

$\sec^2 z\left(\frac{dz}{dx}\right)^2$

$\Rightarrow \sec^2 z\left(\frac{d^2z}{dx^2}\right) = 1 + 2\sec^2 z\left(\frac{dz}{dx}\right)^2$

$\Rightarrow k = 2$

19. Show that $R = \frac{\left[1+\left(\frac{dy}{dx}\right)^2\right]^{3/2}}{\frac{d^2y}{dx^2}}$ can be reduced to the form $R^{2/3} = \frac{1}{\left(\frac{d^2y}{dx^2}\right)^{2/3}} + \frac{1}{\left(\frac{d^2x}{dy^2}\right)^{2/3}}$.

Solution: $R^{2/3} = \frac{1}{\left(\frac{d^2y}{dx^2}\right)^{2/3}} + \frac{1}{\left(\frac{d^2x}{dy^2}\right)^{2/3}}$

Now $\frac{dx}{dy} = \frac{1}{\left(\frac{dy}{dx}\right)}$

$$\frac{d^2x}{dy^2} = \frac{d}{dy}\left(\frac{1}{\left(\frac{dy}{dx}\right)}\right) = \frac{d}{dx}\left(\frac{1}{\left(\frac{dy}{dx}\right)}\right)\times\frac{dx}{dy}$$

$$= -\frac{1}{\left(\frac{dy}{dx}\right)^2}\times\frac{d^2y}{dx^2}\times\left(\frac{dx}{dy}\right)$$

$$\frac{d^2x}{dy^2} = -\frac{1}{\left(\frac{dy}{dx}\right)^3}\times\frac{d^2y}{dx^2}$$

$$\left(\frac{dy}{dx}\right) = \left(\frac{-\frac{d^2y}{dx^2}}{\frac{d^2x}{dy^2}}\right)^{1/3}$$

$\therefore$ we get $1+\left(\frac{dy}{dx}\right)^2 = 1 + \left(\frac{-\frac{d^2y}{dx^2}}{\frac{d^2x}{dy^2}}\right)^{2/3}$

$$\text{So } R_{2/3} = \frac{1+\left(\frac{dy}{dx}\right)^2}{\left(\frac{d^2y}{dx^2}\right)^{2/3}} = \frac{1}{\left(\frac{d^2y}{dx^2}\right)^{2/3}} + \frac{\left(\frac{d^2y}{dx^2}\right)^{2/3}}{\left(\frac{d^2y}{dx^2}\right)^{2/3}\left(\frac{d^2x}{dy^2}\right)^{2/3}}$$

$$= \frac{1}{\left(\frac{d^2y}{dx^2}\right)^{2/3}} + \frac{1}{\left(\frac{d^2x}{dy^2}\right)^{2/3}}$$

20. Find $\left.\dfrac{dy}{dx}\right|_{x=1}$ if

$$y=\frac{{}^nC_0+2\,{}^nC_1x+3\,{}^nC_2x^2+...+(n+1)\,{}^nC_nx^n}{{}^nC_1+(2^2)\,{}^nC_2x+(3^2)\,{}^nC_3x^2+....(n^2)\,{}^nC_n\,x^{n-1}}$$

Solution: First all, let us try the simplify the RHS

Now, $N^r = {}^nC_0 + 2\,{}^nC_1x + 3\,{}^nC_2x^2 + ...+ (n+1)\,{}^nC_n x^n$

We already know that

$(1+x)^n = {}^nC_0 + {}^nC_1 x + {}^nC_2 x^2 .....+ {}^nC_n x^n$

Multiplying both sides by x;

we get $x(1+x)^n = C_0 x + C_1 x^2 + C_2 x^3 + ...+ C_n x^{n+1}$

Differentiating both sides, we get x.

$n(1+x)^{n-1} + (1+n)^n\cdot 1 = C_0 + 2C_1 x + 3C_2 x^2 + ...C_n x^n$

$\therefore$ $N^r = x.\ n(1+x)^{n-1} + (1+x)^n\cdot 1$

$= (1+x)^{n-1}[nx + 1 + x] = (1+x)^{n-1}[(1+(n+1)x]$

Similarly for D^r; we have $(1+x)^n = {}^nC_0 + {}^nC_1 x + {}^nC_2 x^2 + ...+ {}^nC_n x^n$

Differentiating both sides w.r.t x, we get $n(1+x)^{n-1} = C_1 + 2C_2 x + 3C_3 x^2 + ...+ nC_n x^{n-1}$

multiplying both sides by x, we get $nx(1+x)^{n-1} = C_1 x + 2C_2 x^2 + 3C_3 x^3 + ...+ nC_n x^n$

Again differentiating w.r.t. x, we get

$nx(1+x)^{n-1} + n(n-1)x(1+x)^{n-2} = C_1 + 2^2C_2 x + 3^2 C_3 x^2 + ...+ n^2 C_n x^{n-1}$

$\therefore$ $D^r = n(1+x)^{n-1} + n(n-1)x(1+x)n-2$

$= n(1+x)^{x-2}[(1+x) + (n-1)x]$

$= n(1+x)^{n-2}[1+nx]$

$$\therefore\ \ y=\frac{N^r}{D^r}=\frac{(1+x)^{n-1}\left[1+(n+1)x\right]}{n(1+x)^{n-2}\left[1+n^x\right]}$$

$$=\frac{(1+x)(1+(n+1)x)}{n(1+nx)}$$

To obtain $\dfrac{dy}{dx}$; we differentiate both sides w.r.t x

$$\Rightarrow\ \frac{dy}{dx}=\frac{\left[(1+(n+1)x)+((n+1)(1+x))\right](n(1+nx))-\left[n^2(1+x)(1+(n+1)x)\right]}{(n(1+nx))^2}$$

Substituting $x = 1$, we get

$$\frac{dy}{dx}=\frac{(2+n)\times 2(n+1)\times n(n+1)-2n^2\times(2+n)}{n^2(1+n)^2}$$

$$=\frac{2(2+n)\left[n(n+1)^2-n^2\right]}{n^2(1+n)^2}$$

$$=\frac{2(2+n)\times n\left[n^2+1+2n-n\right]}{n^2(1+n)^2}$$

$$=\frac{2(2+n)(n^2+n+1)}{n(1+n)^2}$$

21. Find the possible value(s) of 'a' so that the equation $2x^3 + 9x^2 + 6x + a = 0$ may have two roots equal.

Solution: Let $f(x) = 2x^3 + 9x^2 + 6x + a$ ...(i)

Now let roots of $f(x)$ be α, α, β

$\Rightarrow$ $f(x) = 2(x-\alpha)2(x-\beta)$.

Differentiating both sides, we get $f'(x) = 4(x-\alpha)(x-\beta) + 2(x-\alpha)^2$

$= (x-\alpha)[4x - 4\beta + 2x - 2\alpha]$

$$=(x-\alpha)\times\left[x-\left(\frac{2\alpha+4\beta}{6}\right)\right]\times 6 \quad ...(ii)$$

$\therefore$ From (2) and (3); it is very obvious that $(x-\alpha)$ is a root of $f(x) = 0$ as well as $f'(x) = 0$

Now, Differentiating both sides of (1),

we get $f'(x) = 6x^2 + 18x + 6 = 0$

$\therefore$ $2x^2 + 6x + 2 = 0$ ...(iii)

On operating (i) – x (iv); we get

$3x^2 + 4x + a = 0$ ....(iv)

Since (iv) and (v) equations have a common root i.e., $x = \alpha$;

$$\therefore\ \ \frac{\alpha^2}{6a-8}=\frac{\alpha}{6-2a}=\frac{1}{-10}$$

Now; eliminating α; we get $\left(\dfrac{6-2a}{-10}\right)^2=\left(\dfrac{6a-8}{-10}\right)$

$$\Rightarrow\ \frac{4(3-a)^2}{100}=\frac{2(3a-4)}{-10}$$

$\Rightarrow$ $(3-a)^2 = -5(3a-4)$

$\Rightarrow$ $9 + a^2 - 6a = -15a + 20$

$\Rightarrow$ $a^2 + 9a - 11 = 0$

$\Rightarrow$ $a = \dfrac{-9\pm\sqrt{81+44}}{2}=\dfrac{9\pm5\sqrt{5}}{2}$ are the possible values of 'a'

22. Let $P(x)$ be a polynomial of degree 5 with $p(3) = -2$, $p'(3) = 0$, $p''(3) = 4$, $p'''(3) = -9$, $p^{iv}(3) = 15$. Find the value of $p''(2)$

Solution: Let us assume that $P(x) = a(x-3)^4 + b(x-3)^3 + c(x-3)^2 + d(x-3) + e$ ...(1)

Putting $x = 3$; we get $p(3) = e \Rightarrow e = -2$

Differentiating both sides of (i); w.r.t. x, we get $p'(x) = 4a(x-3)^3 + 3b(x-3)^2 + 2c(x-3) + d$ ...(2)

Putting $x = 3$; we get $p'(3) = d \Rightarrow d = 0$

Differentiating both sides of (2) w.r.t x, we get

$P''(x) = 12a(x-3)^2 + 6b(x-3) + 2c$ ...(3)

Putting $x = 3$, we get $p''(3) = 2c \Rightarrow c = 2$

Again differentiating (3) w.r.t x, we get

$P'''(x) = 24a(x-3) + 6b$ ...(4)

Putting $x = 3$; we get $p'''(x) = 6b = -9 \Rightarrow b = -3/2$

Differentiating both sides of (4) w.r.t x, we get $p^{iv}(x) = 24a$

Putting $x = 3$; we get $24a = -15 \Rightarrow a = -5/8$

Now, substituting these values of a,b,c,d,e in (3); we get

$$P''(x) = 12\times\left(\frac{-5}{8}\right)(x-3)^2 + 6\left(\frac{-3}{2}\right)(x-3) + 2\times 2$$

$$P''(2) = 12\times\left(\frac{-5}{8}\right)\times(1)^2 + 6\times\left(\frac{-3}{2}\right)\times(-1) + 4$$

$$= -\frac{15}{2} + 9 + 4 = \frac{11}{2}$$

23. If $x = b\cos^{-1}\sqrt{\frac{y}{b}} + \sqrt{by - y^2}$, then prove that $\frac{dy}{dx} + \sqrt{\frac{b}{y} - 1} = 0$

Solution: $x = b\cos^{-1}\sqrt{\frac{y}{b}} + \sqrt{by - y^2}$

Putting $y = b\cos^2\theta$, we get $\frac{dy}{d\theta} = -b\sin 2\theta$

And, putting this value of y in x, we get $x = b\cos^{-1}(\cos\theta) + \sqrt{b^2\cos^2\theta - b^2\cos^4\theta} = b\theta + b\cos\theta\sin\theta$

$$\therefore \frac{dx}{d\theta} = b + b(\cos^2\theta - \sin^2\theta)$$

Now, $\frac{dy}{dx} = \frac{dy}{d\theta}\cdot\frac{d\theta}{dx} = -b\sin 2\theta \frac{1}{b(1+\cos 2\theta)}$

$$= -\frac{2\sin\theta\cos\theta}{2\cos^2\theta} = -\tan\theta$$

$$= -\sqrt{\sec^2\theta - 1} = -\sqrt{\frac{b}{y} - 1}$$

24. Find the sum of $\frac{1}{1+x} + \frac{2x}{1+x^2} + \frac{4x^3}{1+x^4} + \ldots \frac{2^n x^{2^n - 1}}{1+x^{2^n}}$

Solution: If $S = \frac{1}{1+x} + \left(\frac{2x}{1+x^2} + \frac{4x^3}{1+x^4} + \ldots + \frac{2^n x^{2^n-1}}{1+x^{2^n}}\right)$

Then, subtracting $\frac{1}{1-x}$ from both sides, we get

$$S - \frac{1}{1-x} = \frac{1}{1+x} - \frac{1}{1-x} + \left(\frac{2x}{1+x^2} + \frac{4x^3}{1+x^4} + \ldots + \frac{2^n x^{2^n-1}}{1+x^{2^n}}\right)$$

$$= -\frac{2x}{1-x^2} + \frac{2x}{1+x^2} + \left(\frac{4x^3}{1+x^4} + \frac{8x^4}{1+x^8} + \ldots + \frac{2^n x^{2^n-1}}{1+x^{2^n}}\right)$$

$$= -\frac{4x^3}{1-x^4} + \frac{4x^3}{1+x^4} + \left(\frac{8x^4}{1+x^8} + \ldots + \frac{2^n x^{2^n-1}}{1+x^{2^n}}\right)$$

$$= -\frac{2^{n+1}.x^{2^{n+1}-1}}{1-x^{2^{n+1}}}$$

$$S = \frac{1}{1-x} + \frac{2^{n+1}.x^{2^{n+1}-1}}{x^{2^{n+1}} - 1}$$

Aliter

Let $f(x) = \log(1+x) + \log(1+x^2) + \log(1+x^4) + \ldots \log\left(1+x^{2^n}\right)$

Differentiating both sides w.r.t x, we get

$$f'(x) = \frac{1}{1+x} + \frac{2x}{1+x^2} + \frac{4x^3}{1+x^4} + \ldots \frac{2^n.x^{2^n-1}}{1+x^{2^n}}$$

Now $f(x) = \log\{(1+x^2)(1+x^4)\ldots\left(1+x^{2^n}\right)\}$

$$= \log\left\{\frac{(1-x^2)}{(1-x)}(1+x^2)(1+x^4)\ldots\ldots\ldots\left(1+x^{2^n}\right)\right\}$$

$$= \log\left\{\frac{(1-x^4)}{(1-x)}(1+x^4)(1+x^8)\ldots\ldots\ldots\left(1+x^{2^n}\right)\right\}$$

$$= \log\left\{\frac{1}{1-x}\left(1-x^{2^{n+1}}\right)\right\}$$

$$\Rightarrow f'(x) = \frac{-2^{n+1}(x^{2^{n+1}-1})}{(1-x^{2^{n+1}})} + \frac{1}{(1-x)}$$

$$= \frac{1}{(1-x)} - \frac{2^{n+1}.\left(x^{2^{n+1}-1}\right)}{\left(1-x^{2^{n+1}}\right)}$$

25. If $x = \sqrt{a^{\sin^{-1}t}}, y = \sqrt{a^{\cos^{-1}t}}$, $a > 0$ and $-1 < t < 1$, show that $\frac{dy}{dx} = -\frac{y}{x}$

Solution: We have $x = \sqrt{a^{\sin^{-1}t}}$ *and* $y = \sqrt{a^{\cos^{-1}t}}$

$$\Rightarrow \frac{dx}{dt} = \frac{1}{2}\left(a^{\sin^{-1}t}\right)^{-1/2} \frac{d}{dt}\left(a^{\sin^{-1}t}\right) \text{ and}$$

$$\frac{dy}{dx} = \frac{1}{2}\left(a^{\cos^{-1}t}\right)^{-1/2} .\frac{d}{dt}\left(a^{\cos^{-1}t}\right)$$

$$\Rightarrow \frac{dx}{dt} = \frac{1}{2}\left(a^{\sin^{-1}t}\right)^{-1/2} \left(a^{\sin^{-1}t}\log a\right).\frac{d}{dt}\left(\sin^{-1}t\right)$$

$$\text{And } \frac{dx}{dt} = \frac{1}{2}\left(a^{\sin^{-1}t}\right)^{1/2} (\log_e a) \times \frac{1}{\sqrt{1-t^2}} = \frac{x\log_e a}{2\sqrt{1-t^2}}$$

Similarly,

$$\frac{dy}{dt} = \frac{1}{2}\left(a^{\cos^{-1}t}\right)^{-1/2} \left(a^{\cos^{-1}t}\log_e a\right).\frac{d}{dt}\left(\cos^{-1}t\right)$$

$$\text{And } \frac{dy}{dt} = \frac{1}{2}\left(a^{\cos^{-1}t}\right)^{1/2} (\log_e a) \times \frac{-1}{\sqrt{1-t^2}} = \frac{-y\log_e a}{2\sqrt{1-t^2}}$$

$$\text{Now, } \frac{dy}{dx} = \frac{\frac{dy}{dt}}{\frac{dx}{dt}}$$

$$\Rightarrow \frac{dy}{dx} = \frac{-y\log_e a}{2\sqrt{1-t^2}} \times \frac{2\sqrt{1-t^2}}{x\log_e a} = \frac{-y}{x}$$

Aliter: $x^2y^2 = a^{\sin^{-1}t+\cos^{-1}t} \quad \Rightarrow x^2y^2 = a^{\pi/2}$

Differentiating with respect to x, we get

$2xy^2 + 2x^2y\frac{dy}{dx} = 0 \quad \Rightarrow \frac{dy}{dx} = \frac{y}{x}$

26. If $2x = y^{1/5} + y^{-1/5}$ then $(x^2-1)\frac{d^2y}{dx^2} + x\frac{dy}{dx} = ky$, then find the value of 'k'.

Solution: $2x = y^{1/5} + \frac{1}{y^{1/5}}$

$(y^{1/5})^2 - (2x)(y^{1/5}) + 1 = 0$

$$y^{1/5} = \frac{2x \pm \sqrt{4x^2-4}}{2} = x \pm \sqrt{x^2-1}$$

$$y = (x \pm \sqrt{x^2-1})^5$$

Case-I: $y = (x + \sqrt{x^2-1})^5$

$$\frac{dy}{dx} = 5(x+\sqrt{x^2-1})^4\left(1+\frac{x}{\sqrt{x^2-1}}\right)$$

$$= 5\frac{(x+\sqrt{x^2-1})^5}{\sqrt{x^2-1}} = \frac{5y}{\sqrt{x^2-1}}$$

$$\Rightarrow (x^2-1)\frac{dy}{dx} = 5y\sqrt{x^2-1}$$

Again differentiating w.r.t. x, we get $(x^2-1)\frac{d^2y}{dx^2} + 2x\frac{dy}{dx} = 5\sqrt{x^2-1}\frac{dy}{dx} + \frac{5xy}{\sqrt{x^2-1}}$

$$\Rightarrow (x^2-1)\frac{d^2y}{dx^2} + x\frac{dy}{dx} + x \times \frac{5y}{\sqrt{x^2-1}} = 5\ (5y) + \frac{5xy}{\sqrt{x^2-1}}$$

$$\Rightarrow (x^2-1)\frac{d^2y}{dx^2} + x\frac{dy}{dx} = 25y \Rightarrow k = 25$$

Case-II: $y = (x + \sqrt{x^2-1})^5$

$$\Rightarrow \frac{dy}{dx} = 5\left(x-\sqrt{x^2-1}\right)^4 \times \left(1-\frac{x}{\sqrt{x^2-1}}\right)$$

$$= \frac{-5\left(x-\sqrt{x^2-1}\right)^5}{\sqrt{x^2-1}} = \frac{-5y}{\sqrt{x^2-1}}$$

$$\Rightarrow (x^2-1)\frac{dy}{dx} = -5y\sqrt{x^2-1}$$

Again differentiating w.r.t. x, we get

$$(x^2-1)\frac{d^2y}{dx^2} + 2x\frac{dy}{dx}$$

$$= -5\left[\left(y \times \frac{x}{\sqrt{x^2-1}}\right) + \sqrt{x^2-1}\frac{dy}{dx}\right]$$

$$\Rightarrow (x^2-1)\frac{d^2y}{dx^2} + x\frac{dy}{dx} + x\frac{dy}{dx}$$

$$= -5\left[x \times \left(\frac{y}{\sqrt{x^2-1}}\right) + \left(\sqrt{x^2-1}\right) \times \left(\frac{dy}{dx}\right)\right]$$

$$\Rightarrow (x^2-1)\frac{d^2y}{dx^2}+x\frac{dy}{dx}+x\frac{dy}{dx}$$

$$= x\times\frac{dy}{dx}+(-5)\left(\sqrt{x^2-1}\right)\times\left(\frac{-5y}{\sqrt{x^2-1}}\right)$$

$$\Rightarrow (x^2-1)\frac{d^2y}{dx^2}+x\frac{dy}{dx}=25y$$

$\Rightarrow k = 25$

27. If $x=\frac{1}{z}$ and $y = f(x)$, show that:

$$\frac{d^2y}{dx^2}=2z^3\frac{dy}{dz}+z^4\frac{d^2y}{dz^2}$$

Solution: $\frac{dy}{dx}=f'(x);\frac{dx}{dz}=-\frac{1}{z^2}$

$$\frac{dy}{dx}=\frac{dy}{dz}.\frac{dz}{dx}=-\frac{dy}{dz}.z^2$$

$$\frac{d^2y}{dx^2}=-\frac{d}{dz}\left[\frac{dy}{dz}.z^2\right]\frac{dz}{dx}=\left[z^2\frac{d^2y}{dz^2}+\frac{dy}{dz}.2z\right]z^2$$

$$\frac{d^2y}{dx^2}=z^4\frac{d^2y}{dz^2}+2z^3\frac{dy}{dz}$$

28. If $y=\frac{1}{\sqrt{a^2-b^2-c^2}}\cos^{-1}\left\{\frac{a\theta-a^2+b^2+c^2}{\theta\sqrt{b^2+c^2}}\right\}$ and

$\theta = a + b\cos x + c\sin x$; prove that $\frac{dy}{dx}=\frac{1}{\theta}$

Solution: $\frac{1}{A}\cos^{-1}\left(\frac{a\theta-A^2}{B\theta}\right)$,

where $A=\sqrt{a^2-b^2-c^2}$ and $B=\sqrt{b^2+c^2}$

$$\frac{dy}{d\theta}=\frac{1}{A}\left[\frac{-1}{\sqrt{1-\left(\frac{a\theta-A^2}{B\theta}\right)^2}}.\frac{B\theta a-\left(a\theta-A^2\right)B}{B^2\theta^2}\right]$$

$$=-\frac{1}{A}\left[\frac{B\theta}{\sqrt{B^2\theta^2-(a\theta-A^2)^2}}.\frac{A^2B}{B^2\theta^2}\right]$$

$$\frac{dy}{d\theta}=\frac{-A}{\theta\sqrt{B^2\theta^2-(a\theta-A^2)^2}} \quad \text{...(i)}$$

$$\frac{d\theta}{dx}=-b\sin x+c\cos x \quad \text{...(ii)}$$

$$\frac{dy}{dx}=\frac{dy}{d\theta}\frac{d\theta}{dx}=\frac{-A}{\theta\sqrt{B^2\theta^2-(a\theta-A^2)^2}}$$

from (i) and (ii)

$$\left[\frac{A(-c\cos x+b\sin x)}{\sqrt{B^2\theta^2-a^2\theta^2-A^4+2aA^2\theta}}\right]\frac{1}{\theta}$$

$$\left[\frac{A(-c\cos x+b\sin x)}{\sqrt{(b^2+c^2)\theta^2-a^2\theta^2-(a^2-b^2-c^2)^2+2a\theta(a^2-b^2-c^2)}}\right]\frac{1}{\theta}$$

$$\left[\frac{A(-c\cos x+b\sin x)}{\sqrt{-(a^2+b^2-c^2)(\theta^2+a^2-b^2-c^2)+2a\theta(a^2-b^2-c^2)}}\right]\frac{1}{\theta}$$

$$\left[\frac{A(-c\cos x+b\sin x)}{\sqrt{a^2-b^2-c^2}\sqrt{(b^2-c^2)-(\theta^2-2a\theta+a^2)}}\right]\frac{1}{\theta}$$

$$\left[\frac{A(-c\cos x+b\sin x)}{\sqrt{a^2-b^2-c^2}\sqrt{(b^2-c^2)-(\theta-a)^2}}\right]\frac{1}{\theta}$$

Now $(\theta - a)^2 = b^2\cos^2x + c^2\sin^2x + 2bc\sin x\cos x$

$(b^2 + c^2) - (\theta - a)^2 = b^2\sin^2x + c^2\cos^2x - 2bc\sin x\cos x$

$= (c\cos x - b\sin x)^2$

$$\therefore \frac{dy}{dx}=\left\{\frac{A(-c\cos x+b\sin x}{A(-c\cos x+b\sin x}\right\}\frac{1}{\theta}$$

$$\frac{dy}{dx}=\frac{1}{\theta}$$

29. If $y^2 + x^2 = R^2$ and $k = 1/R$, then prove that k is equal to $\frac{|y''|}{\sqrt{(1+y'^2)^3}}$

Solution: Differentiating $y^2 + x^2 = R^2$, we get $2yy' + 2x = 0 \Rightarrow y' = -x/y$

And again differentiating, we get

$$y''=-\left(\frac{y-xy'}{y^2}\right)=-\left(\frac{y-x\times\left(\frac{x}{y}\right)}{y^2}\right)$$

$$=-\left(\frac{x^2+y^2}{y^3}\right)=\frac{-1}{k^2y^3}$$

Substituting these value of y'' and y' in the given expression; we get

$$\frac{|y''|}{\sqrt{\left(1+(y')^2\right)^3}} \frac{\left|\frac{-1}{k^2y^3}\right|}{\sqrt{\left(1+\left(-\frac{x}{y}\right)^2\right)^3}}$$

$$= \frac{1}{k^2y^3} \times \frac{1}{\sqrt{\left(\frac{x^2+y^2}{y^2}\right)^3}} = \frac{1}{k^2y^3} \times \frac{1}{\frac{R^3}{y^3}}$$

$$= \frac{1}{k^2R^3} = \frac{1}{k^2} \times k^3 = k$$

30. If $R \to R$ is a function which satisfies $f(x)) = x^3 + x^2 f'(3) + x f''(2) + f'''(1)$.Then find $f(1)$

Solution: Given $f(x) = x^3 + x^2 f'($ On putting $x = 1$ in (1); we get $f(1) = 1 + f'(3) + f''(2) + f'''$ ...(1)

Differentiating both sides f (1); we get

$f'(x) = 3x^2 + 2xf'(3) + f''(2)$ ...(2)

Again differencing both sides gives

$f''(x) = 6x + 2f'(3)$ ...(3)

and differentiating again w.r.t x, we get

$f'''(x) = 6$

$\therefore$ $f'''(1) = 6 \Rightarrow f(0) = 6$ $\quad (\because f'''(1) = f(0))$

Putting $x = 2$ in (3); we get

$f''(2) = 12 + 2f'(3)$ ...(4)

and purring $x = 3$ in (2); we get

$f'(3) = 27 + 6f'(3) + f''(2)$ ...(5)

Solving (4) and (5); we get

$f'(3) = -\frac{39}{3}, f'(3) = \frac{6}{7}$

$\therefore$ $f(x) = x^3 - \frac{39}{7}x^2 + \frac{6}{7}x + 6$

$= \frac{1}{7}\left(7x^3 - 39x^2 + 6x + 42\right)$

Putting $x = 1$, we get:

$f(1) = \frac{1}{7}(7 - 39 + 6 + 42) = \frac{16}{7}$.

Passage Type Questions

A: Sometimes a function can be written as the product of two functions such that it is easy to determine the n-the derivative of two functions separately. In such cases, the nth derivative of the product can be written by applying Leibnitz's theorem which can be stated as below.

If u and v are functions of x having derivatives of nth order, and $y = f.g$ then

$y_n = fg + {}^nC_1 f_{n-1} g_1 + {}^nC_2 f_{n-2} g_2 + \ldots\ldots + {}^nC_k f_{n-k} g_k + \ldots\ldots + {}^nC_n f g_n$ where suffixes denote derivative w.r.t. x.

31. If $y = x^5 e^{2x}$ then $y^{10}(0)$ is equal to

(a) 2^{10} (b) 315×2^{10}

(c) 195×2^{10} (d) 315×2^{12}

32. If $y = x^2 \cos x$ then $y_7\left(\frac{\pi}{2}\right)$

(a) $\frac{\pi^2}{2} - 72$ (b) $\frac{\pi^2}{4} - 56$

(c) 0 (d) $\frac{\pi^2}{4} + 56$

33. If $y = \frac{\sin^{-1} x}{\sqrt{1-x^2}}$ then $y_n(0)$ is equal to

(a) $(n + 1)^2 y_{n-2}$ (0) (b) $n^2 y_{n-2}$ (0)

(c) $(n - 1)^2 y_{n-2}$ (0) (b) $(n - 1)^2 y_{n-2}$ (0)

Solution:

31. Take $f = e^{2x}$ and $g = x^5$

$y_{10} = (e^{2x})_{10}x^5 + {}^{10}C_1 (e^{2x})_9 5x^4 + {}^{10}C_2 (e^{2x})_8 20x^4 + {}^{10}C_3 (e^{2x})_7 80x^2 + {}^{10}C_4 (e^{2x})_6 160x + {}^{10}C_5(e^{2x})_5.160$

Now putting $x = 0$; we get $y_{10}(0) = 2^{12} \times 315$

Ans. (d)

32. Take $f = \cos x$, $g = x^2$

$$Y_7 = x^2 \cos\left(x + 7\frac{\pi}{2}\right) + {}^7C_1.2x\cos\left(x + 6\frac{\pi}{2}\right) + {}^8C_2.2\cos\left(x + 5\frac{\pi}{2}\right)$$

$$\text{So } y_7\left(\frac{\pi}{2}\right) = \left(\frac{\pi}{2}\right)^2 \cos 4\pi + 7.2.\left(\frac{\pi}{2}\right) \cos\left(\frac{7\pi}{2}\right) + \frac{8\times 7}{2} \times 2 \times \cos(3\pi)$$

$$y_7\left(\frac{\pi}{2}\right) = \frac{\pi^2}{4} - 56$$

Ans. (b)

33. $(1-x^2)y^2 = (\sin^{-1}x)^2$

$\Rightarrow -2xy^2 + (1-x^2)2yy_1 = \dfrac{2\sin^{-1}x}{\sqrt{1-x^2}} = 2y$

$\Rightarrow -xy + (1-x^2)y_1 = 1$

$\Rightarrow (1-x^2)y_2 - 2xy_1 - xy_1 - y = 0$

$\Rightarrow (1-x^2)y_2 - 3xy_1 - y = 0$ ...(i)

Differentiating (i); w.r.t x, we get

$(1-x^2)y_3 - 2xy_2 - 3xy_2 - 3y_1 - y_1 = 0$

$(1-x^2)y_3 - (2+3)xy_2 - 4y_1 = 0$ ...(ii)

Differentiating both side of (ii) w.r.t. x, we get

$(1-x^2)y_4 - (2.2+3)xy_3 - 9y_2 = 0$

Similarly, differentiating n times, we obtain

$(1-x^2)\,y_{n+2} - (2n+3)xy_{n+1} - (n+1)^2\,y_n = 0$

Now, putting $x = 0$, we get $y_{n+2}(0) = (n+1)^2\,y_n(0)$.

Ans. (c)

Column-Matching

34. Column-I

(i) If $y = \sin 2x$, then $\dfrac{d^6y}{dx^6}$ at $x = \dfrac{\pi}{2}$ is equal to

(ii) If $x = e^{y+ey+\ldots\infty}$, then $\dfrac{dy}{dx}$ at $x = 1$ is

(iii) If $y = 2t^2$, $x = 4t$, then $\dfrac{d^2y}{dx^2}$ at $x = \dfrac{1}{2}$ is

(iv) If $x = t^2 + 3t - 8$, $y = 2t^2 - 2t - 5$, then $\dfrac{dy}{dx}$ at $(2, -1)$ is

Column-II

(a) 0

(b) $\dfrac{16}{343}$

(c) $\dfrac{1}{4}$

(d) None of these

Ans. (i) (a) (ii) (a) (iii) (c) (iv) (b)

Solution: (i) $y = \sin 2x$ $\quad \dfrac{dy}{dx} = 2\cos 2x$

$\dfrac{d^2y}{dx^2} = -4\sin 2x \quad \dfrac{d^3y}{dx^3} = -8\cos 2x$

$\dfrac{d^4y}{dx^4} = 16\sin 2x \quad \dfrac{d^5y}{dx^5} = -32\cos 2x$ and

$\dfrac{d^6y}{dx^6} = -64\sin 2x$

$\therefore \dfrac{d^6y}{dx^6}$ at $x = \dfrac{\pi}{2}$ is $= 0$ $\therefore$ Statement is false.

(ii) $x = e^{y+e^{y+\ldots\infty}} = e^{y+x}$

$\therefore 1 = e^{y+x}\left(1+\dfrac{dy}{dx}\right) = x\left(1+\dfrac{dy}{dx}\right)$

$\therefore \dfrac{dy}{dx} = \dfrac{1}{x} - 1$

$\therefore \left.\dfrac{dy}{dx}\right|_{at\ x=1} = 0$ $\quad \therefore$ Statement is true.

$S_3 : y = 2t^2 \qquad x = 4t$

$y = 2\left(\dfrac{x}{4}\right)^2 = \dfrac{x^2}{8}$

Statement is false.

$S_4 : x = t^2 + 3t - 8,\ y = 2t^2 - 2t - 5$

$\dfrac{dx}{dt} = 2t + 3; \qquad \dfrac{dy}{dt} = 4t - 2$

$\dfrac{dy}{dx} = \dfrac{4t-2}{2t+3}$

$\dfrac{d^2y}{dx^2} = \dfrac{(2t+3)4-(4t-2)2}{(2t+3)^2}.$

$\dfrac{dt}{dx} = \dfrac{16}{(2t+3)^2} \times \dfrac{1}{(2t+3)}$

$\dfrac{d^2y}{dx^2} = \dfrac{16}{(2t+3)^3}$

When $x = 2$ and $y = -1$ then $t = 2$

$\dfrac{d^2y}{dx^2}$ at $(2, -1)$ is $= \dfrac{16}{7^3}$

35. Column-I

(i) If $y = \cos^{-1}(\cos x)$ then y' at $x = 5$ is equal to

(ii) The value of $\dfrac{1}{39.2^6}\sum\limits_{0\le i\le j\le 8} \Sigma i\,.{}^8C_j$ is

(iii) The derivative of $\tan^{-1}\left(\dfrac{1+x}{1-x}\right)$ at $x = 1$ is

(iv) The derivative of $\dfrac{\log|x|}{x}$ at $x = -1$ is

Column-II

(a) –1

(b) –1/2

(c) 1/2

(d) 1

Ans. (i) → (b), (ii) → (a), (iii) → (c), (iv) → (d)

Solution:

(i) $y = \cos^{-1}(\cos x)$

$$y' = \frac{-1}{\sqrt{1-\cos^2 x}} . (-\sin x) = \frac{\sin x}{|\sin x|}, \; y' \text{ at } x = 5 \text{ is } -1$$

(ii) $$\frac{1}{39.2^6} \sum \sum_{0 \le i \le j \le 8} ; \left({}^8C_j\right)$$

$$= \frac{1}{2^{11}} \sum_{0 \le j \le 8} \frac{j(j+1)}{2} \, {}^8C_j = \frac{1}{39.2^7} \sum_{0 \le j \le 8} \left(j^2 + j\right) {}^8C_j$$

We know that $(1 + x)^8 = {}^8C_0 + {}^8C_1 x + {}^8C_2 x + \ldots {}^8C_8 x^8$

Differentiating both sides, we get

$8\,(1 + 7)^7 = {}^8C_1 + 2\,{}^8C_2 x + \ldots 8\,{}^8C_8 x^7$

Multiplying both sides by x, we get

$8x\,(1 + x)^7 = {}^8C_1 x + 2\,{}^8C_2 x^2 + \ldots 8\,{}^8C_8 x^8$

Differentiating both sides, we get

$8\,((1+x)^7 + 7x\,(1 + x)^6) = {}^8C_1 + 2^2\,{}^8C_2 x + \ldots + 8^2\,{}^8C_8 x^7$

Putting $x = 1$, we get ${}^8C_1 + 2C_2 + \ldots {}^8C_8 = 8 \times 2^7$ and

${}^8C_1 + 2^2 . {}^8C_2 + \ldots + 8^2 . {}^8C_8 = 8 \times 2^7 + 7 \times 2^6 = 2^6\,(23)$

$$\frac{1}{39.2^7}\left[2^6 \times 23 + 2^7 \times 8\right] = \frac{1}{2} \frac{(23+16)}{39} = \frac{1}{2}$$

(iii) Let $y = \tan^{-1}\left(\frac{1+x}{1-x}\right)$

$$\frac{dy}{dx} = \frac{1}{1+\left(\frac{1+x}{1-x}\right)^2} \times \frac{(1-x)-(1+x)(-1)}{(1-x)^2}$$

$$= \frac{1}{(1-x)^2 + (1+x)^2} \times 2$$

$$\left.\frac{dy}{dx}\right|_{x=1} = \frac{1}{2^2} = \frac{1}{2}$$

(iv) Let $y = \frac{\log|x|}{x}$

$$\therefore \quad \frac{dy}{dx} = \frac{\left(\frac{1}{|x|} \times \frac{|x|}{x}\right) - (\log|x|) \times 1}{x^2}$$

Putting $x = -1$, we get $\left.\frac{dy}{dx}\right|_{x=-1} = \frac{1-\log 1}{(-1)^2} = 1$

TUTORIAL EXERCISE

SECTION–III

ONLY ONE CORRECT ANSWER

1. If $y = \sin^{-1}(x\sqrt{1-x} + \sqrt{x}\sqrt{1-x^2})$ and $\frac{dy}{dx} = \frac{1}{2\sqrt{x(1-x)}} + p'$, then p is equal to

(a) 0 (b) $\sin^{-1}x + c$
(c) $\sin^{-1}\sqrt{x} + c$ (d) None of these

2. The derivative of the function $\cot^{-1}[(\cos 2x)]^{1/2}$ at $x = \pi/6$ is

(a) $(2/3)^{1/2}$ (b) $(1/3)^{1/2}$
(c) $3^{1/2}$ (d) $6^{1/2}$

3. If $\sin^{-1}\left[\sqrt{x-ax} - \sqrt{a-ax}\right]$, then $\frac{dy}{dx} =$

(a) $\frac{1}{\sin\sqrt{a-ax}}$ (b) $\sin\sqrt{x}\sin\sqrt{a}$
(c) $\frac{1}{2\sqrt{x}\sqrt{1-x}}$ (d) 0

4. If $x = 2\log\cot t$ and $y = \tan t + \cot t$, then $(\sin 2\ )\frac{dy}{dx}\ \ 1$

(a) $\cos^2 t$ (b) $\sin^2 t$
(c) $\cos 2t$ (d) $2\cos^2 t$

5. If $y^{1/m} = [x + \sqrt{1+x^2}]$, then $(1 + x^2)\, y_2 + xy_1$ is equal to

(a) $m^2 y$ (b) my^2
(c) x^2y^2 (d) None of these

6. If $x^2 e^y + 2xye^x + 13 = 0$, then $dy/dx =$

(a) $-\frac{2xe^{y-x} + 2y(x+1)}{x(xe^{y-x}+2)}$

(b) $\frac{2xe^{x-y} + 2y(x+1)}{x(xe^{y-x}+2)}$

(c) $-\frac{2xe^{x-y} + 2y(x+1)}{x(xe^{x-y}+2)}$

(d) None of these

7. If $y = ((\tan x)^{\tan x})^{\tan x}$, then at $x = \frac{\pi}{4}, \frac{dy}{dx}$

(a) 0 (b) 1
(c) 2 (d) None of these

8. If $y = \sin^{-1}\left(\frac{\sin\alpha\sin x}{1-\cos\alpha\sin x}\right)$, then $y'(0)$ is

(a) 1 (b) $2\tan\alpha$
(c) $1/2\tan\alpha$ (d) $\sin\alpha$

9. If $f:(-1, 1) \to \mathbb{R}$ be a differentiable function with $f(0) = -1$ and $f'(0) = 1$. Let $g(x) = [f(2f(x) + 2)]^2$. Then $g'(0)$ is equal to

(a) 4 (b) –4
(c) 0 (d) –2

10. If $f(x) = |x-2| + |x+1| - x$, then $f(-10)$ is equal to

(a) –3 (b) –2
(c) 1 (d) 0

11. If $x^y = e^{2(x-y)}$, then $\frac{dy}{dx}$ is equal to

(a) $\frac{2(1+\log x)}{(2+\log x)^2}$ (b) $\frac{1+\log x}{(2+\log x)^2}$

(c) $\frac{2}{2+\log x}$ (d) $\frac{2(1-\log x)}{(2+\log x)^2}$

12. Let y be an implicit function of x defined by $x^{2x} - 2x^x\cot y - 1 = 0$. Then $y'(1)$ equals

(a) –1 (b) 1
(c) log2 (d) –log2

13. If $y = (\log_{\cos x}\sin x)(\log_{\sin x}\cos x) + \sin^{-1}\frac{2x}{1+x^2}$, then $\frac{dy}{dx}$ at $x = \frac{\pi}{2}$ is equal to

(a) $\frac{8}{(4+\pi^2)}$ (b) 0

(c) $-\frac{8}{(4+\pi^2)}$ (d) Not defined

14. Let $f(x) = 2^{2x-1}$ and $\phi(x) = -2^x + 2x\log 2$. If $f'(x) > \phi'(x)$, then

(a) $0 < x < 1$ (b) $0 \le x < 1$

(c) $x < 0$ (d) $x \ge 0$

15. If $f(x) = \dfrac{g(x)+g(-x)}{2} + \dfrac{2}{\left[h(x)+h(-x)\right]^{-1}}$; where g and h are differentiable function, then $f'(0)$ is

(a) 1 (b) 1/2

(c) 3/2 (d) 0

16. If $y = \sec^{-1}[\operatorname{cosec} x] + \operatorname{cosec}^{-1}[\sec x] + \sin^{-1}[\cos x] + \cos^{-1}[\sin x]$, then $\dfrac{dy}{dx}$ for x in first quadrant is equal to

(a) 0 (b) 2

(c) –2 (d) –4

17. If $y = \cos^{-1}(\cos x)$, then $\dfrac{dy}{dx}$ is

(a) 1 in the whole plane

(b) –1 in the whole plane

(c) 1 in the 2nd and 3rd quadrants.

(d) –1 in the 3rd and 4th quadrants.

18. Find $\dfrac{dy}{dx}$, if $x = 2\cos\theta - \cos 2\theta$ and $y = 2\sin\theta - \sin 2\theta$

(a) $\tan\dfrac{3\theta}{2}$ (b) $-\tan\dfrac{3\theta}{2}$

(c) $\cot\dfrac{3\theta}{2}$ (d) $-\cot\dfrac{3\theta}{2}$

19. The derivative of $f(\tan x)$ w.r.t $g(\sec x)$ at $x = \dfrac{\pi}{4}$, where $f'(1) = 2$ and $g'(\sqrt{2}) = 4$, is

(a) $\dfrac{1}{\sqrt{2}}$ (b) $\sqrt{2}$

(c) 1 (d) None of these

20. If $= \left(1+\dfrac{1}{x}\right)\left(1+\dfrac{2}{x}\right)\left(1+\dfrac{3}{x}\right).....\left(1+\dfrac{}{x}\right)$ and $x \ne 0$, then $\dfrac{dy}{dx}$ when $x = -1$ is

(a) $n!$ (b) $(n-1)!$

(c) $(-1)^n(n-1)!$ (d) $(1)^n\, n!$

21. If $y = \log^n x$, where $\log^n$ means log log log…..(repeated n times), then $x \log x \log^2 x \log^3 x \ldots \log^{n-1} x \log^n x \dfrac{dy}{dx}$ is equal to

(a) $\log x$ (b) x

(c) $\dfrac{1}{\log x}$ (d) $\log^n x$

22. If $x = a(1 + \cos\theta)$, $y = a(\theta + \sin\theta)$, then $\dfrac{d^2y}{dx^2}$ at $\theta = \dfrac{\pi}{2}$ is

(a) $-\dfrac{1}{a}$ (b) $\dfrac{1}{a}$

(c) –1 (d) –2

23. If $y = \sin^{-1}\left(\dfrac{5x+12\sqrt{1-x^2}}{13}\right)$, then $\dfrac{dy}{dx}$ is equal to

(a) $-\dfrac{1}{\sqrt{1-x^2}}$ (b) $\dfrac{1}{\sqrt{1-x^2}}$

(c) $\dfrac{3}{\sqrt{1-x^2}}$ (d) $\dfrac{x}{\sqrt{-x^2}}$

24. If $f(x) = 1 + nx + \dfrac{n(n-1)}{2}x^2 + \dfrac{n(n-1)(n-2)}{6}x^3 + \ldots + x^n$, then $f''(1)$ is equal to

(a) $n(n-1)2^{n-1}$ (b) $(n-1)2^{n-2}$

(c) $n(n-1)2^{n-2}$ (d) $n(n-1)2^n$

25. Let $y = t^{10} + 1$ and $x = t^8 + 1$, then $\dfrac{d^2y}{dx^2}$ is equal to

(a) $\dfrac{5}{2}t$ (b) $20t^8$

(c) $\dfrac{5}{16t^6}$ (d) None of these

26. If $f: \mathbb{R} \to \mathbb{R}$ is an even function which is twice differentiable on R and $f''(\pi) = 1$, then $f''(-\pi)$ is equal to

(a) –1 (b) 0

(c) 1 (d) 2

27. Let $y = e^{2x}$. Then $\left(\dfrac{d^2y}{dx^2}\right)\left(\dfrac{d^2x}{dy^2}\right)$ is

(a) 1 (b) e^{-2x}

(c) $2e^{-2x}$ (d) $-2e^{-2x}$

28. If $y = 2\sin^{-1}\sqrt{1-x} + \sin^{-1} 2\sqrt{x(1-x)}$, then for $x \in (0,1/2)$ $\dfrac{dy}{dx} =$

(a) $\dfrac{2}{x\sqrt{1-x}}$ (b) $\sqrt{\dfrac{1-x}{x}}$

(c) $\dfrac{-1}{\sqrt{x(1-x)}}$ (d) zero

29. Let $f(x) = \lambda + \mu|x| + v|x^2|$, where λ, μ, v are real constants. Then $f'(0)$ exist if

(a) $\mu = 0$ (b) $v = 0$

(c) $\lambda = 0$ (d) $\mu = v$

30. If g is the inverse function of f and $f'(x) = \sin x$, then $g'(x)$ is

(a) cosec $\{g(x)\}$ (b) $\sin\{g(x)\}$

(c) $-\dfrac{1}{\sin\{g(x)\}}$ (d) None of these

31. If $x = \dfrac{1+t}{t^3}$; $y = \dfrac{3}{2t^2}+\dfrac{2}{t}$ satisfies $f(x).(y')^3 = 1 + y'$, then $f(x)$ is

(a) $\dfrac{x^2}{1+x^2}$ (b) $\dfrac{x^2+1}{x^2}$

(c) $x+\dfrac{1}{x}$ (d) x

32. If $f(x) = x + \tan x$ and f is inverse of g, then $g'(x)$ is equal to

(a) $\dfrac{1}{1+(g(x)-x)^2}$ (b) $\dfrac{1}{1-(g(x)-x)^2}$

(c) $\dfrac{1}{2+(g(x)-x)^2}$ (d) $\dfrac{1}{2-(g(x)-x)^2}$

33. If $5f(x) + 3f\left(\dfrac{1}{x}\right) = x + 2$ and $y = x f(x)$, then $\left(\dfrac{dy}{dx}\right)_{x=1}$ is equal to.

(a) 14 (b) 7/8

(c) 1 (d) None of these

34. If $y = Ae^{x^2} + Be^{x^2/2}$ satisfies the relation $\dfrac{d^2y}{dx^2}+\left(kx-\dfrac{1}{x}\right)\dfrac{dy}{dx}+2x^2y=0$, then find the value of 'k'.

(a) 2 (b) 1

(c) –3 (d) None of these

35. If $y=\dfrac{x^2}{2}+\dfrac{1}{2}x\sqrt{x^2+1}+\ln\sqrt{x+\sqrt{x^2+1}}$ satisfies the relation $ky = x\dfrac{dy}{dx}+\ln\left(\dfrac{dy}{dx}\right)$, then find the value of 'k'.

(a) 2 (b) 1

(c) 3 (d) None of these

36. If $g(x) = (ax^2 + bx + c)\sin x + (dx^2 + ex + f)\cos x$ is such that $g'(x) = x^2 \sin x$., then find the values of a, b, c, d, e and f respectively.

(a) 0, 2, 0, –1, 0, 2 (b) 0, 2, 1, –1, 0, 2

(c) 0, 2, 0, –1, –1, 2 (d) None of these

37. If $2f(x) + 3f(-x) = x^2 - x + 1$, then find the value of $f'(1)$.

(a) $\dfrac{5}{7}$ (b) $\dfrac{3}{2}$

(c) $-\dfrac{7}{5}$ (d) None of these

38. In a triangle if the sides a, b be constant and the base angles A and B vary, then $\dfrac{dA}{dB}$ can be written as

(a) $\sqrt{\dfrac{a^2-b^2\sin^2 A}{b^2+a^2\sin^2 B}}$ (b) $\sqrt{\dfrac{a^2-b^2\sin^2 A}{b^2-a^2\sin^2 B}}$

(c) $\sqrt{\dfrac{a^2+b^2\sin^2 A}{b^2+a^2\sin^2 B}}$ (d) None of these

39. If $f(x) =$

$$\tan^{-1}\left(\frac{1}{\cos^2 x+\cos x+1}\right)+\tan^{-1}\left(\frac{1}{\cos^2 x+3\cos x+3}\right)$$

$$\tan^{-1}\left(\frac{1}{\cos^2 x+5\cos x+7}\right)+\tan^{-1}\left(\frac{1}{\cos^2 x+7\cos x+13}\right)$$

+.... to n terms, then find $f'(x)$.

(a) $-\dfrac{\sin x}{1+\cos^2 x}+\dfrac{\sin x}{1+(\cos(x+n))^2}$

(b) $\dfrac{\sin x}{1+\cos^2 x}-\dfrac{\sin x}{1+(\cos x+n)^2}$

(c) $\dfrac{\sin x}{1+\cos^2 x}-\dfrac{\sin(x+n-1)}{1+\cos^2(x+n-1)}$

(d) None of these

40. If a, b, c are the angles of a triangle such that sin B. sin C + sin C. sin A + sin A. sin $B = k$ (where k is a constant), then $\dfrac{dB}{dA}$ can be written as

(a) $\dfrac{\sin(C+A)+\sin B(\cos A+\cos C)}{\sin(B+C)+\sin A(\cos C+\cos B)}$

(b) $\dfrac{\sin(C-A)+\sin B(\cos A-\cos C)}{\sin(B-C)+\sin A(\cos C-\cos B)}$

(c) $\dfrac{\sin(C+A)+\sin B(\cos A-\cos C)}{\sin(B+C)+\sin A(\cos C-\cos B)}$

(d) None of these

41. If $y = sx$, $z = tx$, $s = \sin x + \cos x$ and $t = \sin x - \cos x$, and it is also given that $\begin{vmatrix} x & y & z \\ x' & y' & z' \\ x'' & y'' & z'' \end{vmatrix} = kx^3$, then find the value of 'k'.

(a) 2 (b) 1

(c) 3 (d) None of these

SECTION–IV

MORE THAN ONE CORRECT ANSWER

1. If $f_k(x) = \log_e(f_{k+1}(x))$ for all $n \in \mathbb{N}$ and $f_1(x) = x$, then $\frac{d}{dx}\{f_n(x)\}$ is equal to

(a) $f_n(x) \frac{d}{dx}\{f_{n-1}(x)\}$
(b) $f_n(x).f_{n-1}(x)$
(c) $f_n(x).f_{n-1}(x)\ldots f_2(x).f_1(x)$
(d) $\prod_{i=1}^{n} f_i(x)$

2. Let $f(t) = \log_3 t$. Then $\frac{d}{dx}\left\{\int_{x^2}^{x^3} f(t)dt\right\}$

(a) has a value 0 when $x = 0$
(b) has value of 0 when $x = 1, x = 4/9$
(c) has a value $\frac{9e^2 - 4e}{\ln 3}$ when $x = e$
(d) has a differential coefficient $\frac{(27e-8)}{\ln 3}$ when $x = e$

3. If $y = \cos^{-1} 2x + \cot^{-1} 5x + \sin^{-1} 2x + \tan^{-1} 5x$, then

(a) $y'(0) = 0$ (b) $y_2 = y_4$
(c) $y_5 = y_6$ (d) $y_1 = y_3$

4. Let $f(x) = e^{ax}\sin(bx + c)$ and $f''(x) = r^2 e^{ax}\sin(bx + \theta)$ then

(a) $r = a^2 + b^2$
(b) $r = \sqrt{a^2 + b^2}$
(c) $\theta = c + 2\tan^{-1}\left(\frac{b}{a}\right)$
(d) $\theta = 2a\tan^{-1}\left(\frac{b}{a}\right)$

5. If $y = \tan x \tan 2x \tan 3x$, then $\frac{dy}{dx}$ has the value equal to

(a) $3\sec^2 3x \tan x \tan 2x + \sec^2 x \tan 2x \tan 3x + 2\sec^2 2x \tan 3x \tan x$
(b) $2y(\operatorname{cosec} 2x + 2\operatorname{cosec} 4x + 3\operatorname{cosec} 6x)$
(c) $3\sec^2 3x - 2\sec^2 2x - \sec^2 x$
(d) $\sec^2 x + 2\sec^2 2x + 3\sec^2 3x$

6. If $y = \frac{(\sec x + \tan x)}{(\sec x - \tan x)}$, then $\frac{dy}{dx}$ is

(a) $2\sec x[\sec x + \tan x]^2$
(b) $2\cos^3 x(1 + \sin x)^2$
(c) $2\sec x[\sec x - \tan x]^2$
(d) $2\sec^3 x(1 + \sin x)^2$

7. Let $f(x) = x^n$, n being a non-negative integer, the value of n for which the equality $f'(a + b) = f'(a) + f'(b)$ is valid for all $a, b > 0$ is.

(a) 0 (b) 1
(c) 2 (d) None of these

8. Let $f(x) = (ax + b)\cos x + (cx + d)\sin x$ and $f'(x) = x\cos x$ be an identity in x, then

(a) $a = 0$ (b) $b = 1$
(c) $c = 1$ (d) $d = 0$

9. If 1 is a twice repeated root of the equation $ax^3 + bx^2 + bx + d = 0$, then.

(a) $a = b = d$ (b) $a + b = 0$
(c) $b + d = 0$ (d) $a = d$

10. Which of the following statements is/are correct?

(a) If $f(x) = |x - 2|$, then $f(f(x))' = 1$ for $x > 20$
(b) If $f(x) = \frac{x}{1+|x|}$, then $f'(-1) = \frac{1}{4}$
(c) If $f(0) = a$, $f'(0) = b$, $g(0) = 0$ and $(fog)'(0) = c$, then $g'(0) = \frac{c}{b}$
(d) Differential coefficient of $2\tan^{-1}x$ w.r.t $\sin^{-1}\frac{2x}{1+x^2}$ at $x = \frac{1}{2}$ is 1

11. Which of the following statements is/are correct?

(a) The differential coefficient of $f(\log x)$, where $f(x) = \log x$ is $\frac{1}{x\log x}$
(b) If $y = \log x^x$, then $\frac{dy}{dx} = \log(ex)$; base of log is e
(c) Differential coefficient of $\log_{10} x$ w.r.t. $\log_x 10$ is $-\frac{(\log x)^2}{(\log 10)^2}$
(d) If g is the inverse function of f and $f'(x)$ is $\sin x$, then $g'(x) = \frac{1}{\sin(g(x))}$

SECTION–V

ASSERTION AND REASON

1. A: Let $f : [0, \infty) \to [0, \infty]$, be a function defined by $y = f(x) = x^2$, then $\left(\frac{d^2y}{dx^2}\right)\left(\frac{d^2x}{dy^2}\right) = 1$

R: $\left(\frac{dy}{dx}\right) \cdot \left(\frac{dx}{dy}\right) = 1$

2. A: Let $f(x)$ be a polynomial function satisfying $f(x)$. $f\left(\frac{1}{x}\right) = f(x) + f\left(\frac{1}{x}\right)$. If $f(4) = 65$ and l_1, l_2, l_3 are in G.P., then $f(l_1), f(l_2), f(l_3)$, are also in G.P.

R: $f(x) = x^n + 1$

3. A: If $f(x) = (\cos x + i \sin x) (\cos 2x + i \sin 2x) (\cos 3x + i \sin 3x)$....... $(\cos nx + i \sin nx)$ and $f(1) = 1$ then $f''(1)$ is equal to $-\left(\frac{n(n+1)}{2}\right)^2$

R : $f(x) = \cos\frac{n(n-1)}{2}x + i \sin\frac{n(n-1)}{2}x$

4. A: If the parametric equation of a curve is given by $x = \cos\theta + \log \tan \theta/2$ and $y = \sin\theta$, then the points for which $\frac{d^2y}{dx^2} = 0$ are given by $\theta = n\pi$, $n \in Z$.

R: $\frac{d^2y}{dx^2} = \frac{\sin\theta}{\cos^4\theta}$.

5. A: For $x < 0$, $\frac{d}{dx}(\ln|x|) = -\frac{1}{x}$

R: For $x < 0$, $|x| = -x$

SECTION–VI

COMPREHENSION

A: In certain problem the differentiation of $(f(x). g(x))$ appears. One student commits mistake and differentiates as $\frac{df}{dx}\cdot\frac{dg}{dx}$ but he gets correct result if $f(x) = x^3$ and $g(x)$ is a decreasing function for which $g(0) = 1/3$

1. The function $g(x)$ is

(a) $\frac{3}{(x-3)^3}$ (b) $\frac{4}{(x-3)^3}$

(c) $\frac{9}{(x-3)^3}$ (d) $\frac{27}{(x-3)^3}$

2. Derivate of $\{f(x-3).\ g(x)\}$ with respect to x at $x = 100$ is

(a) 0 (b) 1

(c) –1 (d) 2

3. $\lim_{x\to 0}\frac{f(x).g(x)}{x(1+g(x))}$ will be

(a) 0

(b) –1

(c) 1

(d) 2

B: If $D^*\ f(x) = \lim_{h\to 0}\frac{f^2(x+h)-f^2(x)}{h}$ where $f^2(x) = \{f(x)\}^2$

On the basis of above information, answer the following questions:

4. If $u = f(x)$, $v = g(x)$, then the value of $D^*(uv)$ is.

(a) $(D^*u)\, v = (D^*\, v)\, u$

(b) $u^2D^*\, v + v^2\, D^*u$

(c) $D^*u + D^*v$

(d) $uvD^*\,(u + v)$

5. If $u = f(x)$, $v = g(x)$, then the value of $D^*\left\{\frac{u}{v}\right\}$ is.

(a) $\frac{u^2D^*v - v^2D^*u}{v^4}$ (b) $\frac{uD^*v - vD^*u}{v^2}$

(c) $\frac{v^2D^*u - u^2D^*v}{v^4}$ (d) $\frac{vD^* - uD^*v}{v^2}$

6. $D^*(\tan x)$ is equal to

(a) $\sec^2 x$ (b) $2 \sec^2 x$

(c) $\tan x \sec^2 x$ (d) $2 \tan x \sec^2 x$

7. The value of D^* at the point on the curve $y = f(x)$ such that tangent to it are parallel to x-axis, then.

(a) $f(x)$ (b) zero
(c) $2f(x)$ (d) $xf(x)$

8. The value of $D^* c$, where c is constant is.
(a) non-zero constant
(b) 2 constant
(c) does not exist
(d) zero

C: The successive derivative of certain functions follow a pattern. We can find the derivative of any order by following this pattern. Methods of induction can also be used in finding nth derivative of functions.

9. The nth derivative of $\log x$ must be.

(a) $\dfrac{(-1)^{n-1}(n-1)!}{x^{n+1}}$ (b) $\dfrac{(-1)^n(n!)}{x^n}$

(c) $\dfrac{(-1)^n(n-1)!}{x^{n+1}}$ (d) $\dfrac{(-1)^{n-1}(n-1)!}{x^n}$

10. The fifth derivative of $\dfrac{1}{1-5x+6x^2}$ must be

(a) 0

(b) $\dfrac{120}{(1-5x+6x^2)^6}$

(c) $120\left[\dfrac{3^5}{1-3x}-\dfrac{2^5}{1-2x}\right]$

(d) $120\left[\dfrac{3^6}{(1-3x)^6}-\dfrac{2^6}{(1-2x)^6}\right]$

11. If n leaves remainder 3 when divided by 4, then value of nth derivative of $\tan^{-1} x$ at $x = 0$ must be.
(a) 0 (b) $n!$
(c) $(n-1)!$ (d) $-(n-1)!$

D: If y is a differentiable function of x and let δy be increment in y for a small increment δx in x then we know that $\lim\limits_{\delta x\to 0}\dfrac{\delta y}{\delta x}=\dfrac{dy}{dx}$. For small values of δx, we must have $\dfrac{\delta y}{\delta x}=\dfrac{dy}{dx}$ approximately or $\delta y = \dfrac{dy}{dx}\delta x$.

At times δx is called an absolute error $\dfrac{\delta x}{x}$, is called relative error and $100\dfrac{\delta x}{x}$ is called percentage error.

12. Given $\log_e 4 = 1.3863$ then $\log_e 4.01$ must be approximately equal to.
(a) 1.3963 (b) 1.3763
(c) 1.3888 (d) None of these

13. If there is an error of 2 per cent in measurement of l, then the error in measurement of T, where $T = 2\pi\sqrt{\dfrac{l}{g}}$ must be.

(a) 0.5% (b) 0.2%
(c) 0.3% (d) 1%

14. If Δ is the area of triangle ABC and suppose a small error occurs in measurement of C, then $\delta\Delta$ is given by

(a) $\dfrac{1}{4}\Delta\left[\dfrac{1}{s}+\dfrac{1}{s-b}+\dfrac{1}{s-a}-\dfrac{1}{s-c}\right]\delta c$

(b) $-\dfrac{\Delta}{2}\left[\dfrac{1}{s}+\dfrac{1}{s-a}+\dfrac{1}{s-b}+\dfrac{1}{s-c}\right]\delta c$

(c) $\dfrac{\Delta}{4}\left[\dfrac{1}{s-c}-\dfrac{1}{s}+\dfrac{1}{s-a}-\dfrac{1}{s-b}\right]\delta c$

(d) None of these

E: When higher order derivatives are required in implicit cases, there are many computational difficulties we may come across. Non standard methods may work out in such situations.

15. If $s = 1 + t.\,e^s$, then $\dfrac{d^2s}{dt^2}$ is.

(a) $\dfrac{(3-s)e^{2s}}{(2-s)^3}$ (b) $\dfrac{e^s(e^s+1)}{(2-s)^2}$

(c) $\dfrac{3-s}{(3-s)^2}e^{3s}$ (d) None of these

16. If $x^2 + y^2 = r^2$, then $\dfrac{d^3y}{dx^3}$ is equal to

(a) $\dfrac{3r^2x}{y^3}$ (b) $\dfrac{3r^2x}{y^4}$

(c) $\dfrac{-3r^3x}{y^5}$ (d) $-\dfrac{3r^2x}{y^5}$

SECTION–VII

COLUMN-MATCHING

1. Column-A

(i) The function y defined by the equation $xy - \log y = 1$ satisfies $x(yy'' + y'^2) - y'' + k\,yy' = 0$. The value of k is

(ii) If the function $y(x)$ represented by $x = \sin t$, $y = ae^{t\sqrt{2}} + be^{-t\sqrt{2}}$, $t \in \left(-\frac{\pi}{2}, \frac{\pi}{2}\right)$ satisfies the equation $(1 - x^2)y'' - xy' = ky$, then k is equal to

(iii) Let $F(x) = f(x)\,g(x)\,h(x)$ for all real x, where $f(x)$, $g(x)$ and $h(x)$ are differentiable functions. At some point x_0, if $F'(x_0) = 21\,F(x_0)$, $f'(x_0) = 4\,f(x_0)$, $g'(x_0) = -7g(x_0)$ and $h'(x_0) = kh(x_0)$, then k is equal to

(iv) Let $f(x) = x^n$, n being a non-negative integer. The number of values of n for which the equality $f'(a + b) = f'(a) + f'(b)$ is valid for all, $a, b > 0$, is.

Column-B

(a) 24 (b) 2

(c) 4 (d) 3

2. Column-A

(i) The derivative of $f(\tan x)$ w.r.t. $g(\sec x)$ at $x = \frac{\pi}{4}$, where $f'(1) = 2$ and $g'(\sqrt{2}) = 4$, is.

(ii) Let $y = x^3 - 8x + 7$ and $x = f(t)$. If $\frac{dy}{dt} = 2$ and $x = 3$ at $t = 0$, then $f'(t)$ at $t = 0$ is

(iii) Let $f(x) = \sin x$, $g(x) = 2x$ and $h(x) = \cos x$. If $\phi(x) = [go\,(fh)]\,(x)$, then $\phi''\left(\frac{\pi}{4}\right)$ is equal to

(iv) If $f(x) = \cos^2 x + \cos^2\left(x + \frac{\pi}{3}\right) + \sin x \sin\left(x + \frac{\pi}{3}\right)$ and $g\left(\frac{5}{4}\right) = 3$, then $(g\,o\,f)\,(x)$ is equal to

Column-B

(a) 3 (b) –4

(c) $\frac{2}{19}$ (d) $\frac{1}{\sqrt{2}}$

SECTION–VIII

INTEGER TYPE

1. The derivatives of $\sec^{-1}\left[\frac{1}{2x^2 - 1}\right]$ with respect to $\sqrt{1 - x^2}$ at $x = \frac{1}{2}$, is

2. If f and g are two functions having derivative of order three for all x satisfying $f(x)\,g(x) = C$ (constant) and $\frac{f'''}{f'} - A\frac{f''}{f} - \frac{g'''}{g'} + \frac{3g''}{g} = 0$. Then A is equal to

3. If $\int_0^y \cos t^2\,dt \int_0^{x^2} \frac{\sin t}{t}\,dt$, and if $\frac{dy}{dx} = \frac{k \sin x^2}{x \cos y^2}$, then find the value of k.

4. If $\int_e^x t\,f(t)\,dt = \sin x - x\cos x - \frac{x^2}{2}$ for all $x \in \mathbb{R} - \{0\}$, and if the value of $f\left(\frac{\pi}{6}\right)$ is given by $-\frac{1}{k}$, then find the value of k.

5. If $y = \sin^{-1} \ln\left(\frac{x^2}{2}\right)$, then find the value of $(xy')^2 \left\{\left(\ln\frac{x^2}{2}\right)^2 - 1\right\}$.

6. If $\frac{d^2x}{dy^2}\left(\frac{dy}{dx}\right)^3 + \frac{d^2y}{dx^2} = k$, then find the value of k.

7. If $y = (\cot^{-1}x)^2$, and given that $y_2\,(x^2 + 1)^2 + 2x\,(x^2 + 1)\,y_1 = k$ where y_1 and y_2 respectively represents the first and the second order derivative of y w.r.t x, then find the value of k.

Answer Keys

SECTION–III

1. (b) **2.** (a) **3.** (c) **4.** (d) **5.** (a) **6.** (a) **7.** (c) **8.** (d) **9.** (b) **10.** (a)
11. (a) **12.** (a) **13.** (a) **14.** (c) **15.** (d) **16.** (d) **17.** (d) **18.** (a) **19.** (a) **20.** (c)
21. (d) **22.** (a) **23.** (b) **24.** (c) **25.** (c) **26.** (c) **27.** (d) **28.** (d) **29.** (a) **30.** (a)
31. (d) **32.** (c) **33.** (b) **34.** (c) **35.** (a) **36.** (a) **37.** (c) **38.** (b) **39.** (b) **40.** (b)
41. (a)

SECTION–IV

1. (a,c,d) **2.** (b,c,d) **3.** (a,b,c,d) **4.** (b,c) **5.** (a,b,c) **6.** (a,d) **7.** (a,c) **8.** (a,b,c,d)
9. (b,c) **10.** (a,b,c,d) **11.** (a,b,c,d)

SECTION–V

1. (d) **2.** (a) **3.** (c) **4.** (a) **5.** (d)

SECTION–VI

1. (c) **2.** (a) **3.** (a) **4.** (b) **5.** (c) **6.** (d) **7.** (b) **8.** (d) **9.** (d) **10.** (d)
11. (d) **12.** (c) **13.** (d) **14.** (a) **15.** (b) **16.** (b)

SECTION–VII

1. (i) → (d) (ii) → (b) (iii) → (a) (iv) → (b)
2. (i) → (d) (ii) → (c) (iii) → (b) (iv) → (a)

SECTION–VIII

1. 4 **2.** 3 **3.** 2 **4.** 2 **5.** –4 **6.** 0 **7.** 3

HINTS AND SOLUTIONS

TEXTUAL EXERCISE–1: (SUBJECTIVE)

1. $y = \dfrac{5^{\log_{\sqrt[4]{5}} x} - 9^{\log_{729}(x+1)^6}}{49^{4\log_{2401} x} - x - 1}$

$\Rightarrow y = \dfrac{x^4 - (x+1)^2}{x^2 - x - 1}$

$\Rightarrow y = x^2 + x + 1$

$\Rightarrow \dfrac{dy}{dx} = 2x + 1 = 2ax - b$ (Given)

$\Rightarrow a = 1$ and $b = -1$

2. If $y = e^x f(x)$

By product rule, we get $\dfrac{dy}{dx} = e^x f'(x) + ex.f(x)$

$= e^x(f(x) + f'(x))$

(i) $y = e^x\left(\log_e x - \dfrac{1}{x}\right)$

$\Rightarrow y = e^x \log_e x - \dfrac{e^x}{x}$

$\Rightarrow \dfrac{dy}{dx} = e^x\left(\log_e x + \dfrac{1}{x}\right) - e^x\left(\dfrac{1}{x} - \dfrac{1}{x^2}\right) = e^x (\log_e x + \dfrac{1}{x^2})$

(ii) $y = e^x (\tan x + \cos x)$

$y = e^x \tan x + ex \cos x$

$\Rightarrow \dfrac{dy}{dx} = e^x (\tan x + \sec^2 x) + ex (\cos x - \sin x)$

$\Rightarrow \dfrac{dy}{dx} = e^x (\tan x + \sec^2 x + \cos x - \sin x)$

(iii) $y = e^x (x^3 + \sin x)$

$y = e^x.x^3 + ex.\sin x$

$\Rightarrow \dfrac{dy}{dx} = e^x (x^3 + 3x^2) + ex (\sin x + \cos x)$

$= e^x (x^3 + 3x^2 + \sin x + \cos x)$

3. $\dfrac{d}{dx}\left(\dfrac{f(x)}{g(x)}\right) = \dfrac{f'(x).g(x) - f(x).g'(x)}{(g(x))^2}$

Mistaken formula, $\dfrac{d}{dx}\left(\dfrac{f(x)}{g(x)}\right) = \dfrac{g'(x).f(x) - f'(x).g(x)}{(g(x))^2}$

By the question $f'(x)\, g(x) - f(x).g'(x) = g'(x)\, f(x) - f'(x).g(x)$

$\Rightarrow 2g'(x)\, f(x) = 2f'(x).g(x)$

$\Rightarrow f(x).g'(x) = f'(x)\, g(x) \Rightarrow \dfrac{g'(x)}{g(x)} = \dfrac{f'(x)}{f(x)}$

$\Rightarrow \ln g(x) = \ln f(x) + \ln c$

$\Rightarrow g(x) = c.f(x)$

$\Rightarrow \dfrac{f(x)}{g(x)} = \dfrac{f(x)}{g(x)} = C =$ Constant

$\Rightarrow F(n) = \dfrac{f(x)}{g(x)} = C =$ Constant

$\therefore$ (a) $F(n) = F(n + 1)$ and

(b) $F(n) = F(n + 2) = c$

(c) $\sum_{n=1}^{20} F(n) = \sum_{n=1}^{20} c = 20c$ and $\sum_{n=1}^{20} F(2n-1) = \sum_{n=1}^{20} c = 20c$

$\Rightarrow \sum_{n=1}^{20} F(n) = \sum_{n=1}^{20} F(2n-1) = 20c$

(d) $F(1) = F(2) = F(3) = \ldots. = c$

$\Rightarrow$ They form G.P. (constant G.P.)

4. Let $f(x) = \dfrac{x^5}{7} + \dfrac{x^3}{3} - x$ and $g(x) = \dfrac{x^5}{7}$

$\Rightarrow \dfrac{df(x)}{dx} = \dfrac{5x^4}{7} + x^2 - 1$ and $\dfrac{dg(x)}{dx} = \dfrac{5x^4}{7}$

By the question $\dfrac{df(x)}{d(x)} > \dfrac{dg(x)}{dx}$

$\Rightarrow x^2 - 1 > 0$

$\Rightarrow x \in (-\infty, -1) \cup (1, \infty)$

5. $f(x) = x^3 g(x)$; $g(2) = 3$; $g'(2) = 1$ (given)

$\Rightarrow f'(x) = 3x^2\, g(x) + x^3\, g'(x)$

$\Rightarrow f'(2) = 12\, g(2) + 8g'(2)$

$= 12.(3) + 8.(1) = 36 + 8 = 44$

TEXTUAL EXERCISE–1: (OBJECTIVE)

1. (a) $y = (1 - 2 \tan x) (5 + 4 \sin x)$

$\Rightarrow \dfrac{dy}{dx} = (1 - 2 \tan x) (4 \cos x) + (5 + 4 \sin x) (-2 \sec^2 x)$

$= 4 \cos x (1 - 2 \tan x) - 2 \sec^2 x (5 + 4 \sin x)$

$= 4 \cos x (1 - 2 \tan x) - 2 \sec^2 x (5 + 4 \sin x)$

2. (c) $y = \dfrac{\sin x}{1 + \tan x}$

$\Rightarrow \dfrac{dy}{dx} = \dfrac{\cos x(1+\tan x) - \sin x(\sec^2 x)}{(1+\tan x)^2}$

$= \dfrac{\cos x + \sin x - \sec x \tan x}{(1+\tan x)^2}$

$= \dfrac{\cos x + \sin x - \sin x(1+\tan^2 x)}{(1+\tan x)^2}$

$= \dfrac{(\cos x + \sin x - \sin x - \sin x.\tan^2 x)}{(1+\tan x)^2}$

$= \dfrac{\cos x(1-\tan^3 x)}{(1+\tan x)^2}$

3. (a) $f(x) = \cos x.\cos 2x.\cos 4x.\cos 8x.\cos 16x$

Multiply and divide by 2 sin x, we get $f(x)$

$$= \frac{\sin 2x.\cos 2x.\cos 4x.\cos 8x.\cos 16x}{2\sin x}$$

$$= \frac{\sin 4x.\cos 4x..\cos 8x.\cos 16x}{4\sin x}$$

$$= \frac{\sin 8x.\cos 8x.\cos 16x}{8\sin x} = \frac{\sin 16x.\cos 16x}{16\sin x} = \frac{\sin 32x}{32\sin x}$$

$$\Rightarrow f'(x) = \frac{1}{32}\left(\frac{\sin x.32.\cos 32x - \sin 32x.\cos x}{(\sin x)^2}\right)$$

$$\Rightarrow f'\left(\frac{\pi}{4}\right) = \frac{1}{32}\left(\frac{\frac{1}{\sqrt{2}}.32.\cos 8\pi - \sin 8\pi.\frac{1}{\sqrt{2}}}{\frac{1}{2}}\right) = \sqrt{2}$$

4. (b) $y = \dfrac{1}{1+x^{n-m}+x^{p-m}} + \dfrac{1}{1+x^{m-n}+x^{p-n}} + \dfrac{1}{1+x^{m-p}+x^{n-p}}$

$$\Rightarrow y = \frac{1}{1+\frac{x^n}{x^m}+\frac{x^p}{x^m}} + \frac{1}{1+\frac{x^m}{x^n}+\frac{x^p}{x^n}} + \frac{1}{1+\frac{x^m}{x^p}+\frac{x^n}{x^p}}$$

$$\Rightarrow y = \frac{x^m}{x^m+x^n+x^p} + \frac{x^n}{x^m+x^p+x^n} + \frac{x^p}{x^p+x^m+x^n}$$

$$\Rightarrow y = \frac{x^m+x^n+x^p}{x^m+x^n+x^p} = 1$$

$$\Rightarrow \frac{dy}{dx} = 0$$

5. (a) $y = \dfrac{x^4+4}{x^2-2x+2}$

$$\Rightarrow \frac{dy}{dx} = \frac{4x^3(x^2-2x+2)-(x^4+4)(2x-2)}{(x^2-2x+2)^2}$$

$$\Rightarrow \frac{dy}{dx} = \frac{4x^5-8x^4+8x^3-2x^5+2x^4-8x+8}{(x^2-2x+2)^2}$$

$$= \frac{2x^5-6x^4+8x^3-8x+8}{(x^2-2x+2)^2}$$

Putting $x = 1/2$, we get $\left(\dfrac{dy}{dx}\right)_{x=1/2} = 3$

6. (b) $y = \tan^{-1}\left(\dfrac{\sqrt{1+x^2}-1}{x}\right)$

$$\Rightarrow \frac{dy}{dx} = \frac{1}{1+\left(\frac{\sqrt{1+x^2}-1}{x}\right)^2} \times \left[\frac{x.\frac{x}{\sqrt{1+x^2}} - \sqrt{1+x^2}+1}{x^2}\right]$$

$$= \frac{1}{2\sqrt{(1+x^2)}} = y'(x) \text{ (Derivative function)}$$

$$\Rightarrow y'(0) = \frac{1}{2}$$

7. (b) $y = \dfrac{\cos 6x + 6\cos 4x + 15\cos 2x + 10}{\cos 5x + 5\cos 3x + 10\cos x}$

Rewriting it as

$$y = \frac{\cos 6x + \cos 4x + 5\cos 4x + 5\cos 2x + 10(1+\cos 2x)}{\cos 5x + 5\cos 3x + 10\cos x}$$

$$\Rightarrow y = \frac{2\cos x.\cos 5x + 5.2.\cos 3x.\cos x + 2.10\cos^2 x}{\cos 5x + 5\cos 3x + 10\cos x}$$

Taking 2 cos x common from the numerator, we get

$$y = \frac{2\cos x(\cos 5x + 5\cos 3x + 10\cos x)}{\cos 5x + 5\cos 3x + 10\cos x}$$

$$\Rightarrow y = 2\cos x \qquad \Rightarrow \frac{dy}{dx} = -2\sin x$$

8. (b) $\left(x^{\frac{\ell+m}{m-n}}\right)^{\frac{1}{n-\ell}} . \left(x^{\frac{m+n}{n-\ell}}\right)^{\frac{1}{\ell-m}} . \left(x^{\frac{n+\ell}{\ell-m}}\right)^{\frac{1}{m-n}}$

which is equal to $x^{\frac{(\ell+m)}{(m-n)(n-\ell)}+\frac{m+n}{(n-\ell)(\ell-m)}+\frac{n+\ell}{(\ell-m)(m-n)}}$

$$= x^{\frac{\ell^2-m^2+m^2-n^2+n^2-\ell^2}{(m-n)(n-\ell)(\ell-m)}} = x^0 = 1$$

$$\Rightarrow y = 1 \qquad \Rightarrow \frac{dy}{dx} = 0$$

9. (a), (b), (c)

$$f(x) = \left(\frac{\sqrt{x-2\sqrt{x-1}}}{\sqrt{x-1}-1}\right).x\ ;\ D_f = [1, \infty)$$

$$\Rightarrow f(x) = \left(\frac{\sqrt{(x-1)+1-2\sqrt{x-1}}}{\sqrt{x-1}-1}\right)x$$

$$\Rightarrow f(x) = \left(\frac{\sqrt{(\sqrt{x-1}-1)^2}}{\sqrt{x-1}-1}\right)x = \left(\frac{|\sqrt{x-1}-1|}{\sqrt{x-1}-1}\right)x$$

$$\Rightarrow f(x) = \begin{cases} x \text{ if } x \ge 2 \\ -x \text{ if } x \in [1,2) \end{cases}$$

$$\Rightarrow f'(x) = \begin{cases} 1;\ x \in (2,\infty) \\ -1;\ x \in (1,2) \end{cases}$$

10. (b) $f(x) = x^{a(a+b)-b(a+b)} \times x^{b(b+c)-c(b+c)} \times x^{c(c+a)-a(a+c)}$

$$\Rightarrow f(x) = x^{a^2+ab-ab-b^2} \times x^{b^2+bc-bc-c^2} \times x^{c^2+ac-a^2-ac}$$

$$\Rightarrow f(x) = x^{a^2-b^2} \times x^{b^2-c^2} \times x^{c^2-a^2}$$

$$\Rightarrow f(x) = x^0 = 1$$

$$\Rightarrow f'(x) = 0$$

11. (a) $y = (1+x)(1+x^2)\ ....\left(1+x^{2^n}\right)$

$$= 1+x+x^2+x^3+....+x^{1+2+3+....+2^n}$$

$$= \left(1+x+x^2+x^3+....+x^{\frac{2^n(2^n+1)}{2}}\right)$$

$$\Rightarrow \frac{dy}{dx} = 1+2x+3x^2+....+2^{n-1}.(2^n+1)x^{2^{n-1}(2^n+1)-1}$$

$$\Rightarrow \left(\frac{dy}{dx}\right)_{x=0} = 1$$

TEXTUAL EXERCISE–2: (SUBJECTIVE)

1. (i) $f(x) = \dfrac{3x-2}{2x+3} \Rightarrow f'(x) = \dfrac{3(2x+3)-(3x-2)(2)}{(2x+3)^2}$

$\Rightarrow f'(x) = \dfrac{6x+9-6x+4}{(2x+3)^2}$

$\Rightarrow f'(x) = \dfrac{13}{(2x+3)^2}$

(ii) $f(x) = \ell n\,(3x^2+4)$

Using chain rule, we get

$\dfrac{d(f(x))}{dx} = \dfrac{1}{(3x^2+4)}\cdot\dfrac{d}{dx}(3x^2+4) = \dfrac{6x}{3x^2+4}$

(iii) $f(x) = \sin^2(x^2)$

which can be written as $f(x) = [\sin(x^2)]^2$

$\Rightarrow \dfrac{d(f(x))}{dx} = 2\,(\sin(x^2)).\cos(x^2).2x$

$= 4x.\sin(x^2).\cos(x^2) = 2x.\sin(2x^2)$

(iv) $f(x) = x^{x^2}$

Let $y = x^{x^2}$

$\Rightarrow \ln y = x^2 \ln x$

Differentiating both sides w.r.t. x, we get $\dfrac{1}{y}.\dfrac{dy}{dx} = \dfrac{x^2}{x} + 2x\ell nx$

$\Rightarrow \dfrac{1}{y}\dfrac{dy}{dx} = x\,(1 + \ell n\, x^2)$

$\Rightarrow \dfrac{dy}{dx} = x^{x^2+1}\left(1+\ell nx^2\right)$

(v) $f(x) = (ax+b)^n$

$\Rightarrow \dfrac{df(x)}{dx} = n\,(ax+b)^{n-1}.a$

$\Rightarrow \dfrac{df(x)}{dx} = an(ax+b)^{n-1}$

(vi) $f(x) = x^2 \cos x$

$\Rightarrow f'(x) = \dfrac{df(x)}{dx} = -x^2 \sin x + 2x \cos x = x(2\cos x - x\sin x)$

(vii) $f(x) = \sqrt{\sec x}$

$\Rightarrow \dfrac{df(x)}{dx}\ \dfrac{1}{}(\sec\ )^{1/2}.\ \sec x\,.\,\tan x$

$= \dfrac{\sec x.\tan x}{2\sqrt{\sec x}} = \dfrac{\sqrt{\sec x}.\tan x}{2}$

(viii) $f(x) = \cos(\ell n\, x)$

$\Rightarrow \dfrac{df(x)}{dx} = f'(x) = -\sin(\ell nx)\dfrac{1}{x}$

$\Rightarrow f'(x) = \dfrac{-\sin(\ell nx)}{x}$

(ix) $f(x) = \left(\tan\sqrt{x}\right)$

$\Rightarrow \dfrac{df(x)}{dx} = f'(x) = \sec^2\sqrt{x}.\dfrac{1}{2}.x^{-1/2}$

$\Rightarrow f'(x) = \dfrac{\sec^2\sqrt{x}}{2\sqrt{x}}$

2. $y = \cos^{-1}(8x^4 - 8x^2 + 1)$

$\Rightarrow -1 \le 8x^4 - 8x^2 + 1 \le 1$

$\Rightarrow 8x^4 - 8x^2 + 2 \ge 0$ and $8x^4 - 8x^2 \le 0$

$\Rightarrow 4x^4 - 4x^2 + 1 \ge 0$ and $x \in [-1, 1]$

$\Rightarrow (2x^2-1)^2 \ge 0$ and $x \in [-1, 1]$

$\Rightarrow x \in [-1, 1]$

$\Rightarrow \dfrac{dy}{dx} = \dfrac{-\dfrac{d}{dx}(8x^4-8x^2+1)}{\sqrt{1-(8x^4-8x^2+1)^2}}$

$\Rightarrow \dfrac{dy}{dx} = \dfrac{-(32x^3-16x)}{\sqrt{(2+8x^4-8x^2)(8x^2-8x^4)}}$

$\Rightarrow \dfrac{dy}{dx} = \dfrac{-16x(2x^2-1)}{\sqrt{(2\sqrt{2}x^2-\sqrt{2})^2}\ \sqrt{8x^2(1-x^2)}}$

$$= \frac{-16x(2x^2-1)}{4|x||2x^2-1|\sqrt{1-x^2}} = \begin{cases} \dfrac{-4}{\sqrt{1-x^2}} & \text{for } x \in \left(\dfrac{1}{2},0\right) \\ \dfrac{4}{\sqrt{1-x^2}} & \text{for } x \in \left(0,\dfrac{1}{2}\right) \\ \dfrac{-4}{\sqrt{1-x^2}} & \text{for } x \in \left(\dfrac{-1}{2},0\right) \\ \dfrac{4}{\sqrt{1-x^2}} & \text{for } x \in \left(-1,\dfrac{-1}{2}\right) \end{cases}$$

$\Rightarrow \dfrac{dy}{dx} = \dfrac{-4}{\sqrt{1-x^2}}$ or $\dfrac{4}{\sqrt{1-x^2}}$

$\Rightarrow \dfrac{dy}{dx} \pm \dfrac{4}{\sqrt{1-x^2}} = 0$

$\Rightarrow \dfrac{dy}{dx} + \dfrac{4}{\sqrt{1-x^2}} = 0$ for $x \in \left(\dfrac{-1}{2},0\right) \cup \left(\dfrac{1}{2},1\right)$ and

$\dfrac{dy}{dx} - \dfrac{4}{\sqrt{1-x^2}} = 0$ for $x \in \left(-1,\dfrac{-1}{2}\right) \cup \left(0,\dfrac{1}{2}\right)$

3. $y = \left[\dfrac{x\sin^{-1}x}{\sqrt{1-x^2}} + \ell n\sqrt{1-x^2}\right]$

$\Rightarrow \dfrac{dy}{dx} = \dfrac{\left(\sqrt{1-x^2}\right)\left[x.\dfrac{1}{\sqrt{1-x^2}} + \sin^{-1}x\right] - \left(x\sin^{-1}x\right)\left(\dfrac{-x}{\sqrt{1-x^2}}\right)}{(1-x^2)}$

$+ \dfrac{1}{\sqrt{1-x^2}} \times \left(\dfrac{-x}{\sqrt{1-x^2}}\right)$

$\Rightarrow \dfrac{x}{1-x^2} + \dfrac{\sin^{-1}x}{\sqrt{1-x^2}} + \dfrac{x^2\sin^{-1}x}{(1-x^2)^{3/2}} - \dfrac{x}{1-x^2}$

$= \dfrac{(1-x^2)\sin x + x^2\sin^2 x}{(1-x^2)^{3/2}} = \dfrac{\sin^{-1}x}{(1-x^2)^{3/2}}$

4. $f(x) = |x|^{\sin x|}$

$\Rightarrow f(x) = \begin{cases} x^{\sin x} & ; x \in (0,\pi) \\ (-x)^{-\sin x} & ; x \in (-\pi,0) \end{cases}$

$\Rightarrow f(x) = (-x)^{-}\sin^x\ ; x < 0$

Taking log on both sides, we get $\ell n\, f(x) = \ell n\, [(-x)^{-\sin x}]$
$= -\sin x.\ell n\,(-x)$

$$\Rightarrow \frac{1}{f(x)}.\frac{df(x)}{d(x)} = -\cos x.\ell n\,(-x) + \frac{-\sin x}{x}$$

$$\Rightarrow f'\left(\frac{-\pi}{4}\right) = f\left(\frac{-\pi}{4}\right)\left[\frac{-4}{\pi\sqrt{2}} - \ell n\left(\frac{\pi}{4}\right)\frac{1}{\sqrt{2}}\right]$$

$$= \left(\frac{\pi}{4}\right)^{1/\sqrt{2}}\left[\frac{\sqrt{2}}{2}\ell n\frac{4}{\pi} - \frac{2\sqrt{2}}{\pi}\right]$$

5. $y = \dfrac{\sqrt{a^2+x^2} + \sqrt{a^2-x^2}}{\sqrt{a^2+x^2} - \sqrt{a^2-x^2}}$

Put $x^2 = a^2\cos 2\theta; 2\theta \in \left[0, \frac{\pi}{2}\right]$

$$\Rightarrow y = \frac{\cos\theta + \sin\theta}{\cos\theta - \sin\theta} \quad \Rightarrow y = \frac{1+\tan\theta}{1-\tan\theta}$$

$$\Rightarrow y = \tan\left(\frac{\pi}{4}+\theta\right)$$

$$\Rightarrow \frac{dy}{d\theta} = -\sec^2\left(\frac{\pi}{4}+\theta\right) = \frac{-1}{\cos^2\left(\frac{\pi}{4}+\theta\right)}$$

$$= \frac{-2}{1+\cos\left(\frac{\pi}{2}+2\theta\right)} = \frac{-2}{1-\sin 2\theta} = \frac{-2}{1-\sqrt{1-\left(\frac{x^2}{a^2}\right)^2}}$$

$$= \frac{-2a^2}{a^2-\sqrt{a^4-x^4}}$$

Also, $\dfrac{d\theta}{dx} = \dfrac{x}{a^2\sin 2\theta} = \dfrac{-xa^2}{a^2\sqrt{a^4-x^4}} = \dfrac{-x}{\sqrt{a^4-x^4}}$

$$\therefore \frac{dy}{dx} = \frac{dy}{d\theta}\times\frac{d\theta}{dx} = \frac{2a^2x}{\sqrt{a^4-x^4}.\left(a^2-\sqrt{a^4-x^4}\right)}$$

6. (i) $y = \ell n\sqrt{\dfrac{1+\sin x}{1-\sin x}}$

$$\Rightarrow \frac{dy}{dx} = \frac{1}{\sqrt{\frac{1+\sin x}{1-\sin x}}}.\frac{1}{2}.\left(\frac{1+\sin x}{1-\sin x}\right)^{-1/2}\frac{d}{dx}.\left(\frac{1+\sin x}{1-\sin x}\right)$$

Let us consider $\dfrac{d}{dx}\left(\dfrac{1+\sin x}{1-\sin x}\right)$

$$= \frac{(1-\sin x)\cos x + (1+\sin x)\cos x}{(1-\sin x)^2}$$

$$\Rightarrow \frac{2\cos x}{(1-\sin x)^2}$$

Hence the expression for $\dfrac{dy}{dx}$ becomes

$$\frac{dy}{dx} = \frac{1-\sin x}{2(1+\sin x)}.\frac{2\cos x}{(1-\sin x)^2} = \frac{\cos x}{(1+\sin x)(1-\sin x)} =$$

$$\frac{\cos x}{1-\sin^2 x} = \frac{\cos x}{\cos^2 x} = \frac{1}{\cos x} = \sec x$$

(ii) $y = \ell n\,\{\cot^{-1}(a^{5x+3})\}$

$$\Rightarrow \frac{dy}{dx} = \frac{\ln a(-1)}{\cot^{-1}\left(a^{5x+3}\right)}.\frac{-1}{1+a^{2(5x+3)}}.a^{5x+3}.5$$

$$= \frac{-5\ell n a}{\cot^{-1}\left(a^{5x+3}\right)}.\frac{(a)^{5x+3}}{\left(1+a^{2(5x+3)}\right)}$$

(iii) $y = \cos^{-1}\left(e^{\sqrt{\tan x}}\right)$

$$\Rightarrow \frac{dy}{dx} = \frac{-1}{\sqrt{1-e^{2\sqrt{\tan x}}}}.e^{\sqrt{\tan x}}.\frac{1}{2}.(\tan x)^{-1/2}.\sec^2 x$$

$$\Rightarrow \frac{dy}{dx} = \left[\frac{-1.\sec^2 x.e^{\sqrt{\tan x}}}{2.\sqrt{\tan x}.\sqrt{1-e^{2\sqrt{\tan x}}}}\right]$$

(iv) $y = [\ell n\{\ell n(\sin x^0)\}]^7$

$$\Rightarrow \frac{dy}{dx} = \frac{7\left(\ell n\left(\ell n\left(\sin x^0\right)\right)\right)^6}{\ell n\left(\sin x^0\right)\sin x^0}.\cos x^0.\left(\frac{\pi}{180}\right)$$

$$\Rightarrow \frac{dy}{dx} = \frac{7\pi}{180}\,[\ell n(\ell n\,(\sin x^0))]^6.\frac{\cot x^0}{\ell n \sin x^0}$$

(v) $y = \sin^{-1}\left[\dfrac{a+b\cos x}{b+a\cos x}\right]; b > a$

$$\Rightarrow \frac{dy}{dx} = \frac{1}{\sqrt{1-\left(\frac{a+b\cos x}{b+a\cos x}\right)^2}}.\left(\frac{a+b\cos x}{b+a\cos x}\right)'$$

$$\left(\frac{b+a\cos x}{\sqrt{b^2-a^2}.\sin x}\right).$$

$$= \left[\frac{(b+a\cos x).(-b\sin x)-(a+b\cos x).(-a\sin x)}{(b+a\cos x)^2}\right]$$

$$\Rightarrow \frac{dy}{dx} = \frac{-(b^2-a^2)\sin x}{\sqrt{b^2-a^2}\sin x(b+a\cos x)}$$

$$\Rightarrow \frac{dy}{dx} = \frac{-\sqrt{b^2-a^2}}{(b+a\cos x)}$$

(vi) $y = e^{\left(\sin^{-1}(x^2)\right)^{1/2}}$

$$\Rightarrow \frac{dy}{dx} = \frac{e^{\sqrt{\sin^{-1}(x^2)}}.\frac{1}{2}.\left(\sin^{-1}(x^2)\right)^{-1/2}}{\sqrt{1-x^4}}.2x$$

$$\Rightarrow \frac{dy}{dx} = \frac{x\sqrt{e^{\sin^{-1}(x^2)}}}{\sqrt{\sin^{-1}(x^2)}.\sqrt{1-x^4}}$$

(vii) $y = \tan(a^{1/x})$

$$\Rightarrow \frac{dy}{dx} = \sec^2(a^{1/x}).a^{1/x}.\ell na.\left(\frac{-1}{x^2}\right)$$

$$\Rightarrow \frac{dy}{dx} = \frac{-\sec^2(a^{1/x}).a^{1/x}.\ell na}{x^2}$$

(viii) $y = \dfrac{e^{2x}+e^{-2x}}{e^{2x}-e^{-2x}}$

$$\Rightarrow y = \frac{1+e^{-4x}}{1-e^{-4x}}$$

$$\Rightarrow \frac{dy}{dx}=\frac{(1-e^{-4x})(-4e^{-4x})-(1+e^{-4x})4e^{-4x}}{(1-e^{-4x})^2}$$

$$=\frac{-4e^{-4x}+4e^{-8x}-4e^{-4x}-4e^{-8x}}{(1-e^{-4x})^2}=\frac{-8e^{-4x}}{(1-e^{-4x})^2}$$

$$=\frac{-8}{(e^{2x}-e^{-2x})^2}$$

(ix) $y=\cos^{-1}\left(\dfrac{x-\frac{1}{x}}{x+\frac{1}{x}}\right)$

$$\Rightarrow y=\cos^{-1}\left(\frac{x^2-1}{x^2+1}\right)$$

$$\Rightarrow \frac{dy}{dx}=\frac{-1}{\sqrt{1-\left(\frac{x^2-1}{x^2+1}\right)^2}}\cdot\left(\frac{x^2-1}{x^2+1}\right)'$$

But $\left(\dfrac{x^2-1}{x^2+1}\right)'=\dfrac{(x^2+1)(2x)-(x^2-1)(2x)}{(x^2+1)^2}$

$$=\frac{2x(x^2+1-x^2+1)}{(x^2+1)^2}=\frac{4x}{(x^2+1)^2}$$

And $\sqrt{1-\left(\dfrac{x^2-1}{x^2+1}\right)^2}=\sqrt{\dfrac{(x^2+1)^2-(x^2-1)^2}{(x^2+1)^2}}$

$$=\frac{1}{(x^2+1)}\left(\sqrt{2x^2.(2)}\right)=\frac{2x}{x^2+1}$$

Hence the overall derivative becomes $\dfrac{dy}{dx}=\dfrac{-1}{\frac{2x}{x^2+1}}\cdot\dfrac{4x}{(x^2+1)^2}$

$$=\frac{-2}{1+x^2}$$

(x) $y=\tan^{-1}\left\{\dfrac{\sqrt{a^2+x^2}+\sqrt{a^2-x^2}}{\sqrt{a^2+x^2}-\sqrt{a^2-x^2}}\right\}$

Let $x^2=a^2\cos 2\theta$

$$\Rightarrow y=\tan^{-1}\left[\frac{\sqrt{a^2+a^2\cos 2\theta}+\sqrt{a^2-a^2\cos 2\theta}}{\sqrt{a^2+a^2\cos 2\theta}-\sqrt{a^2-a^2\cos 2\theta}}\right]$$

$$=\tan^{-1}\left(\frac{\sqrt{1+\cos 2\theta}+\sqrt{1-\cos 2\theta}}{\sqrt{1+\cos 2\theta}-\sqrt{1-\cos 2\theta}}\right)=\tan^{-1}\left(\frac{1+\sin 2\theta}{\cos 2\theta}\right)$$

$$\Rightarrow \frac{dy}{d\theta}=\frac{1}{1+\left(\frac{1+\sin 2\theta}{\cos 2\theta}\right)^2}\cdot\left(\frac{1+\sin 2\theta}{\cos 2\theta}\right)'$$

Now, $\left(\dfrac{1+\sin 2\theta}{\cos 2\theta}\right)'=\dfrac{\cos 2\theta.2\cos 2\theta+2(1+\sin 2\theta).\sin 2\theta}{(\cos 2\theta)^2}$

$$=\frac{2\cos^2 2\theta+2\sin 2\theta+2\sin^2 2\theta}{(\cos 2\theta)^2}=\frac{2+2\sin 2\theta}{(\cos 2\theta)^2}$$

$$\Rightarrow \frac{dy}{d\theta}=\frac{1}{\frac{2+2\sin 2\theta}{(\cos 2\theta)^2}}\times\frac{(2+2\sin 2\theta)}{(\cos 2\theta)^2}$$

$$\Rightarrow \frac{dy}{d\theta}=1$$

By the substitution $x^2=a^2\cos 2\theta$

$$\Rightarrow \cos 2\theta=\frac{x^2}{a^2} \quad \Rightarrow -2\sin 2\theta=\frac{2x}{a^2}\cdot\frac{dx}{d\theta}$$

$$\Rightarrow -2\left(\sqrt{1-\frac{x^4}{a^4}}\right)=\frac{2x}{a^2}\frac{dx}{d\theta}$$

$$\Rightarrow \frac{d\theta}{dx}=\frac{x}{a^2\sqrt{\frac{a^4-x^4}{a^4}}}=\frac{x}{\sqrt{a^4-x^2}}$$

$$\Rightarrow \frac{dy}{dx}=\frac{dy}{d\theta}\cdot\frac{d\theta}{dx}=\frac{x}{\sqrt{a^4-x^4}}$$

(xi) $y=\tan^{-1}\left(\dfrac{5ax}{a^2-6x^2}\right)$

$$\Rightarrow \frac{dy}{dx}=\frac{1}{1+\left(\frac{5ax}{a^2-6x^2}\right)^2}\cdot\left(\frac{5ax}{a^2-6x^2}\right)'$$

But, $\left(\dfrac{5ax}{a^2-6x^2}\right)'=\dfrac{5a(a^2-6x^2)+5ax(12x)}{(a^2-6x^2)^2}$

$$=\frac{5a(a^2-6x^2+12x^2)}{(a^2-6x^2)^2}=\frac{5a(a^2+6x^2)}{(a^2-6x^2)^2}$$

$$\Rightarrow \frac{dy}{dx}=\frac{(a^2-6x^2)^2}{(a^2-6x^2)^2+25a^2x^2}\times\frac{5a(a^2+6x^2)}{(a^2-6x^2)^2}$$

$$\Rightarrow \frac{dy}{dx}=\frac{5a(a^2+6x^2)}{a^4+36x^4-12a^2x^2+25a^2x^2}$$

$$\Rightarrow \frac{dy}{dx}=\frac{5a(a^2+6x^2)}{a^4+36x^4+13a^2x^2}$$

$$\Rightarrow \frac{dy}{dx}=\frac{2a}{a^2+4x^2}+\frac{3a}{a^2+9x^2}$$

7. (i) $y=5x^{2/3}-3x^{5/2}+2x^{-3}$

$$\Rightarrow \frac{dy}{dx}=\frac{5.2}{3}x^{\frac{2}{3}-1}-\frac{3.5}{2}.x^{\frac{3}{2}}-6x^{-4}=\frac{10}{3}x^{-\frac{1}{3}}-\frac{15}{2}x^{3/2}-6x^{-4}$$

$$=\frac{10}{3\sqrt[3]{x}}-\frac{15}{2}x\sqrt{x}-\frac{6}{x^4}$$

(ii) $y=\dfrac{\sin x+\cos x}{\sin x-\cos x}$

$$\Rightarrow \frac{dy}{dx}=\frac{(\sin x-\cos x)(\cos x-\sin x)-(\sin x+\cos x)(\cos x+\sin x)}{(\sin x-\cos x)^2}$$

$$\Rightarrow \frac{dy}{dx}=\frac{-2}{(\sin x-\cos x)^2}$$

(iii) $y=(x^2+1)\tan^{-1}(x)$

$$\Rightarrow \frac{dy}{dx}=2x.\tan^{-1}x+(x^2+1)\left(\frac{1}{1+x^2}\right)$$

$$\Rightarrow \frac{dy}{dx} = 1 + 2x\tan^{-1}x = 1 + 2x\,(arc\tan x)$$

(By product rule)

(iv) $y = \dfrac{e^x + \sin x}{e^x . x}$

$$\Rightarrow \frac{dy}{dx} = \frac{xe^x\left(e^x + \cos x\right) - \left(e^x + \sin x\right).\left(e^x + xe^x\right)}{\left(e^x x\right)^2}$$

$$= \frac{xe^{2x} + x\cos x e^x - e^{2x} - xe^{2x} - e^x\sin x - xe^x\sin x}{\left(e^x . x\right)^2}$$

$$= \frac{x\cos x - e^x - \sin x - x\sin x}{x^2.e^x}$$

$$= \frac{x\left(\cos x - \sin x\right) - \sin x - e^x}{x^2.e^x}$$

(v) $y = \sin^2\sqrt{\dfrac{1}{(1-x)}}$

$$\Rightarrow \frac{dy}{dx} = 2\sin\left(\sqrt{\frac{1}{1-x}}\right).\cos\left(\sqrt{\frac{1}{1-x}}\right)\times\frac{1}{2}\left(\frac{1}{1-x}\right)^{-1/2}.\frac{1}{(1-x)^2}$$

$$\Rightarrow \frac{dy}{dx} = \sin\left(\frac{2}{(1-x)^{1/2}}\right).\frac{1}{(1-x)^{3/2}}$$

(vi) $y = \left(\sin^2 x\right)^{1/3} + \sec^2 x$

$$\Rightarrow \frac{dy}{dx} = \frac{1}{3}\left(\sin^2 x\right)^{-2/3}.2\sin x.\cos x + 2\sec x.\sec x.\tan x$$

$$\Rightarrow \frac{dy}{dx} = \frac{2\cos x}{3(\sin x)^{1/3}} + \frac{2\sin x}{\cos^3 x}$$

(vii) $y = \sqrt{2e^x + 2^x + 1} + \ell n 5x$

$$\Rightarrow \frac{dy}{dx} = \frac{1}{3}\left(2e^x + 2^x + 1\right)^{-2/3}.\left(2e^x + 2^x\,\ell n2\right) + 5\ell n^4 x\frac{1}{x}$$

$$= \frac{\left(2e^x \quad 2^x \quad n2\right)}{3\left(2\ ^x + 2^x + 1\right)^{2/3}} \quad \frac{5\log 4}{}$$

(viii) $y = \sqrt{x + \sqrt{x + \sqrt{x}}} \quad \Rightarrow \quad y^2 = x + \sqrt{x + \sqrt{x}}$

$$\Rightarrow y^2 - x = \sqrt{x + \sqrt{x}}$$

$$\Rightarrow y^2 + x^2 - 2y^2x = x + \sqrt{x}$$

Differentiating the entire equation, we get

$$2y\frac{dy}{dx} + 2x - 2y^2 - 4y.\frac{dy}{dx}x = 1 + \frac{1}{2\sqrt{x}}$$

$$\Rightarrow \frac{dy}{dx}(2y - 4yx) + 2x - 2y^2 = 1 + \frac{1}{2\sqrt{x}}$$

$$\Rightarrow \frac{dy}{dx} = \frac{1 + \dfrac{1}{2\sqrt{x}} - 2x + 2y^2}{2y - 4yx}$$

$$= \frac{1}{2\sqrt{x + \sqrt{x + \sqrt{x}}}}\left(\frac{1 + \dfrac{1}{2\sqrt{x}} - 2x + 2x + 2\sqrt{x + \sqrt{x}}}{1 - 2x}\right)$$

$$= \frac{1}{2\sqrt{x + \sqrt{x + \sqrt{x}}}}\left(\frac{1 + \dfrac{1}{2\sqrt{x}} + 2\sqrt{x + \sqrt{x}}}{1 - 2x}\right)$$

$$= \frac{1}{2\sqrt{x + \sqrt{x + \sqrt{x}}}}\left[1 + \frac{2x + 2\sqrt{x + \sqrt{x}} + \dfrac{1}{2\sqrt{x}}}{1 - 2x}\right]$$

8. $y = \left(\dfrac{1 + e^x}{1 - e^x}\right)^{1/2}$

$$\Rightarrow \frac{dy}{dx} = \frac{1}{2}\left(\frac{1 + e^x}{1 - e^x}\right)^{-1/2}\left(\frac{(1 - e^x)(e^x) + (1 + e^x)(e^x)}{(1 - e^x)^2}\right)$$

$$= \frac{1}{2}\left(\frac{1 + e^x}{1 - e^x}\right)^{-1/2}\left(\frac{e^x - e^{2x} + e^x + e^{2x}}{\left(1 - e^x\right)^2}\right)$$

$$= \frac{1}{2}\left(\frac{1 + e^x}{1 - e^x}\right)^{-1/2}\left(\frac{2e^x}{\left(1 - e^x\right)^2}\right) = \frac{1(1 + e^x)^{-1/2}e^x}{(1 - e^x)^{-1/2}(1 - e^x)^2}$$

$$= \frac{e^x}{(1 - e^x)(1 - e^{2x})^{1/2}}$$

9. Let $y = \log_x \sin x^2 + (\sin x^2)^{\ln x}$ ...(1)

$z = \sqrt{x + 1}$ ...(2)

$$u = \frac{\ln\sin x^2}{\ln x};\ v = (\sin x^2)^{\ln x}$$

$$\therefore \frac{du}{dx} = \frac{(\ln x).\dfrac{\cos x^2}{\sin x^2}(2x) - \ln(\sin x^2).\dfrac{1}{x}}{(\ln x)^2}$$

$$= \frac{2x^2\cot x^2\ln x - \ln\sin x^2}{x(\ln x)^2}$$

$v = (\sin x^2)^{\ln x}$ ...(3)

$$\Rightarrow \ln v = (\ln x)(\sin x^2)$$

$$\Rightarrow \frac{1}{v}\frac{dv}{dx} = (\ln x)(2x)\cos x^2 + (\sin x^2)\frac{1}{x}$$

$$\Rightarrow \frac{dv}{dx} = (\sin x^2)^{\ln x}\left[\frac{2x^2\cos x^2\ln x + \sin x^2}{x}\right]$$

$$\therefore \frac{dy}{dx} = \frac{du}{dx} + \frac{dv}{dx};\ \frac{dz}{dx} = \frac{1}{2\sqrt{x + 1}} \text{ and}$$

$$\frac{dy}{dz} = \frac{\dfrac{dy}{dx}}{\dfrac{dz}{dx}} = \frac{\left(\dfrac{du}{dx} + \dfrac{dv}{dx}\right)}{\left(\dfrac{dz}{dx}\right)}$$

$$=\frac{\frac{2x^2\cot x^2\ln x-\ln\sin x^2}{x(\ln x)^2}+(\sin x^2)^{\ln x}.\left[\frac{2x^2\cot^2\ln x+\sin x^2}{x}\right]}{\left(2\sqrt{x+1}\right)^{-1}}$$

$$=\frac{2\sqrt{x+1}}{2(\ln x)^2}\left[\begin{matrix}(\ln x)^2(\sin x^2)^{\ln x}(2x^2\cot x^2\ln x+\sin x^2)\\+2x^2\ln x(\cot x^2)-\ln(\sin x^2)\end{matrix}\right]$$

10. $f=\tan^{-1}\left(\frac{\sqrt{1+x^2}-1}{x}\right)$ and $g=\cos^{-1}\left(\sqrt{\frac{1+\sqrt{1+x^2}}{2.\sqrt{1+x^2}}}\right)$

Consider $f=\tan^{-1}\left(\frac{\sqrt{1+x^2}-1}{x}\right)$ and $\tan^{-1}x=y$

$\Rightarrow x=\tan y$ and $y\in\left(\frac{-\pi}{2},\frac{\pi}{2}\right)$

$$\Rightarrow f=\tan^{-1}\left[\left(\frac{\sqrt{1+\tan^2 y}-1}{\tan y}\right)\right]=\tan^{-1}\left(\frac{1-\cos y}{\sin y}\right)$$

$$=\tan^{-1}\left(\frac{2\sin^2\frac{1}{2}y}{2\sin\frac{1}{2}y.\cos\frac{1}{2}y}\right)=\tan^{-1}\left(\frac{\sin\frac{1}{2}y}{\cos\frac{1}{2}y}\right)$$

$$=\tan^{-1}\left(\tan\left(\frac{1}{2}y\right)\right)=\frac{1}{2}y$$

$\Rightarrow f=\frac{1}{2}y$ ....(i)

Consider $g=\cos^{-1}\left(\sqrt{\frac{1+\sqrt{(1+x^2)}}{2\sqrt{1+x^2}}}\right)$

Again, Let $\tan^{-1}x=y$.

$\Rightarrow x=\tan y$ and $y\in\left(\frac{-\pi}{2},\frac{\pi}{2}\right)$

$$\Rightarrow g=\cos^{-1}\left(\sqrt{\frac{1+\sqrt{(1+\tan^2 y)}}{2\sqrt{1+\tan^2 y}}}\right)=\cos^{-1}\left(\sqrt{\frac{1+\sec y}{2\sec y}}\right)$$

$$=\cos^{-1}\left(\sqrt{\frac{1+\cos y}{2}}\right)=\cos^{-1}\left(\cos\frac{y}{2}\right)=\frac{y}{2}$$

$\Rightarrow g=y/2$ ....(ii)

By (i), we get $\frac{df}{dy}=\frac{1}{2}$ and By (ii), we get $\frac{dg}{dy}=\frac{1}{2}$

$$\Rightarrow \frac{df}{dg}=\frac{df}{dy}\times\frac{dy}{dg}=1$$

TEXTUAL EXERCISE–2: (OBJECTIVE)

1. (a) $y=e^{2x}.\sin 3x$

$\Rightarrow \frac{dy}{dx}=e^{2x}.(\cos 3x.3)+(\sin 3x.2.e^{2x})=e^{2x}(3\cos 3x+2\sin 3x)$

2. (b) $y=\log_2(\log_2(x))$

$$\Rightarrow \frac{dy}{dx}=\frac{1}{\log_2 x}.\log_2 e.\frac{1}{x}\log_2 e=\frac{1}{x\ln x\ln 2}$$

3. (b), (c) $y=e^x\cos^3 x.\sin^2 x$

$$\Rightarrow \frac{dy}{dx}=e^x\left[\begin{matrix}\cos^3 x\sin^2 x+\cos^3 x(2\sin x\cos x)\\+\sin^2 x.3\cos^2 x(-\sin x)\end{matrix}\right]$$

$$\left(\because\left[e^x f(x)\right]'=e^x\left(f(x)+f'(x)\right)\right)$$

$=e^x\cos^3 x.\sin^2 x(1-3\tan x+2\cot x)$

4. (a) $y=\text{cosec}(1+x^2)$

$\Rightarrow \frac{dy}{dx}=-\text{cosec}(1+x^2)\cot(1+x^2).2x=-2x\,\text{cosec}(1+x^2)\cot(1+x^2)$

5. (a), (b) $y=\frac{1}{\sin x-\cos x}$

$$\Rightarrow \frac{dy}{dx}=\frac{-(\cos x+\sin x)}{(\sin x-\cos x)^2}=\frac{-(\cos x+\sin x)}{\sin^2 x+\cos^2 x-2\sin x.\cos x}$$

$$=\frac{-(\cos x+\sin x)}{(1-\sin 2x)}$$

6. (a) $y=\cos(\log x)$

$$\Rightarrow \frac{dy}{dx}=-\sin(\log x).\frac{1}{x}=\frac{-\sin(\log x)}{x}$$

7. (a) $f'(x)=(2x^2-1)^{1/2}$

$y=f(x^2)$

$$\Rightarrow \frac{dy}{dx}=\frac{df(x^2)}{dx}.2x=f'(x^2).2x|_{x=1}=f'(1).2=(2(1)-1)^{1/2}.2=2$$

8. (d) $f(x^2)=x^3\ \forall\ x>0$

Differentiation on both sides, we get $f'(x^2).2x=3x^2$

$$\Rightarrow f'(x^2)=\frac{3x^2}{2x}=\frac{3x}{2}\quad\Rightarrow f'(16)=\frac{3(16)}{2}=24$$

9. (a) $y=f(x)=\tan^{-1}\left(\frac{\sqrt{1+x^2}+\sqrt{1-x^2}}{\sqrt{1+x^2}-\sqrt{1-x^2}}\right)$; clearly $0\le x^2\le 1$

Let $2\theta=\cos^{-1}x^2 \Rightarrow \theta\in\left[0,\frac{\pi}{4}\right]$ and $\cos 2\theta=x^2$

$$\Rightarrow y=\tan^{-1}\left(\frac{\sqrt{1+\cos 2\theta}+\sqrt{1-\cos 2\theta}}{\sqrt{1+\cos 2\theta}-\sqrt{1-\cos 2\theta}}\right)$$

$$=\tan^{-1}\left(\frac{\cos\theta+\sin\theta}{\cos\theta-\sin\theta}\right)=\tan^{-1}\left(\frac{1+\tan\theta}{1-\tan\theta}\right)$$

$$=\tan^{-1}\left(\tan\left(\frac{\pi}{4}+\theta\right)\right)=\frac{\pi}{4}+\theta$$

$$\left(\because 0\le\ \le\frac{\pi}{4}\Rightarrow\frac{\pi}{4}\le\left(\ +\frac{\pi}{4}\right)\le\frac{\pi}{2}\right)$$

$$\Rightarrow y=\frac{1}{4}\pi+\frac{1}{2}\cos^{-1}x^2\quad\Rightarrow\frac{dy}{dx}=\frac{-1}{2}\frac{1}{\sqrt{1-x^4}}.2x$$

$$\Rightarrow \frac{dy}{dx}=\frac{-x}{\sqrt{1-x^4}}$$

10. **(b)** $y = f\left(\frac{2x-1}{x^2+1}\right)$ and $f'(x) = \sin x$

$$\Rightarrow \frac{dy}{dx} = f'\left(\frac{2x-1}{x^2+1}\right)\cdot\left(\frac{2x-1}{x^2+1}\right)'$$

$$= \sin\left(\frac{2x-1}{x^2+1}\right)\cdot\left(\frac{(x^2+1)2-(2x-1)(2x)}{(x^2+1)^2}\right)$$

$$= \sin\left(\frac{2x-1}{x^2+1}\right)\left(\frac{2x^2+2-4x^2+2x}{(x^2+1)^2}\right)$$

$$= \sin\left(\frac{2x-1}{x^2+1}\right)\left(\frac{-2x^2+2x+2}{(x^2+1)^2}\right)$$

11. **(c)** $f(x) = 2\tan^{-1} x + \sin^{-1}\left(\frac{2x}{1+x^2}\right)$

$$\text{Since, } 2\tan^{-1}x = \begin{cases} \sin^{-1}\left(\frac{2x}{1+x^2}\right) & \text{for } x\in[-1,1] \\ \pi - \sin^{-1}\left(\frac{2x}{1+x^2}\right) & \text{for } x \geq 1 \\ -\pi - \sin^{-1}\left(\frac{2x}{1+x^2}\right) & \text{for } x \leq -1 \end{cases}$$

$$\Rightarrow f(x) = 2\tan^{-1}x + \sin^{-1}\left(\frac{2}{1+x^2}\right) = \begin{cases} \pi \text{ for } x \geq 1 \\ -\pi \text{ for } x \leq -1 \\ 4\tan^{-1}x \text{ for } x\in[-1,1] \end{cases}$$

$\Rightarrow$ f'(x) = 0 for $x \in (-\infty, -1) \cup (1, \infty)$ and $f'(x) = \frac{4}{1+x^2}$ for $x \in (-1,1)$

12. **(a)** $\tan^{-1}\sqrt{\frac{x+1}{x-1}}$; $x \in (-\infty, -1) \cup (1, \infty)$

$$\Rightarrow \frac{dy}{dx} = \frac{1}{1+\left(\frac{x+1}{x-1}\right)} \times \left[\frac{(x-1)(1)-(x+1)(1)}{(x-1)^2}\right] \times \frac{1}{2}\left(\frac{x+1}{x-1}\right)^{-1/2}$$

$$= \left(\frac{x-1}{x-1+x+1}\right) \times \left[\frac{-2}{(x-1)^2}\right] \times \frac{1}{2}\left[\frac{x-1}{x+1}\right]^{1/2}$$

$$= \frac{(x-1)}{2x}\left(\frac{-1}{(x-1)^2}\right)\left(\frac{x-1}{x+1}\right)^{1/2} = \frac{-1}{2x(x-1)}\cdot\left(\frac{x-1}{x+1}\right)^{1/2}$$

$$= \frac{-1}{2x(x-1)}\sqrt{\frac{x-1}{(x+1)}}$$

Case (i): for $x - 1 > 0$; $x > 1$

$\Rightarrow x > -1 \qquad \Rightarrow x + 1 > 0$

$$\Rightarrow \frac{dy}{dx} = \frac{-1}{2|x|\sqrt{x-1}}\left(\frac{\sqrt{x-1}}{\sqrt{x+1}}\right) = \frac{-1}{2|x|\sqrt{x^2-1}} \quad \text{...(i)}$$

Case (ii): for $x - 1 < 0$; $x < 1$

$\Rightarrow x < -1 \qquad \Rightarrow x + 1 < 0$

$$\Rightarrow \frac{dy}{dx} = \frac{-1}{2x(x-1)}\frac{\sqrt{-(x-1)}}{\sqrt{-(x+1)}} = \frac{1}{2x[-(x-1)]} \times \frac{\sqrt{-(x-1)}}{\sqrt{-(x+1)}}$$

$$= \frac{1}{2x\sqrt{-(x-1)}} \times \frac{1}{\sqrt{-(x+1)}} = \frac{1}{2x\sqrt{x^2-1}} = \frac{-1}{2|x|\sqrt{x^2-1}} \quad \text{...(ii)}$$

$\therefore$ From (i) and (ii), $\frac{dy}{dx} = \frac{-1}{2|x|\sqrt{x^2-1}}$

13. **(a)** $y = \sec(\tan^{-1} x)$

$$\Rightarrow \frac{dy}{dx} = \frac{\sec\left(\tan^{-1}x\right)\tan\left(\tan^{-1}x\right)}{1+x^2} = \frac{x\sqrt{1+x^2}}{(1+x^2)} = \frac{x}{\sqrt{1+x^2}}$$

$$\Rightarrow \left(\frac{dy}{dx}\right)_{x=1} = \frac{1}{\sqrt{2}}$$

14. **(c)** $y = \tan^{-1}\left[\frac{2^x}{1+2(2^{2x})}\right]$

$$\Rightarrow y = \tan^{-1}\left[\frac{2(2^x)-2^x}{1+2.2^x.2^x}\right] = \tan^{-1}(2.2^x) \quad \tan^{-1}(2^x)$$

$$y = \tan^{-1}(2^{x+1}) - \tan^{-1}(2^x)$$

$$\Rightarrow \frac{dy}{dx} = \frac{1}{1+(2)^{(2x+2)}}.2^{x+1}.\ln 2 - \frac{1}{1+(2^x)^2}.2^x.\ln 2$$

$$= \frac{1}{5}(2)\ln 2 - \frac{1}{2}\ln 2$$

$$= \ln 2\left(\frac{2}{5}-\frac{1}{2}\right) = \ln 2\left(\frac{4-5}{10}\right) = -\frac{1}{10}\ln 2$$

15. **(d)** $y = 2\sin^{-1}\sqrt{1-x} + \sin^{-1}\left(2\sqrt{x(1-x)}\right)$; $x \in \left[0, \frac{1}{2}\right]$

Differentiating both sides, we get

$$\frac{dy}{dx} = \frac{2}{\sqrt{1-(1-x)}}.\frac{1}{2}(1-x)^{-1/2}.(-1)$$

$$+ \frac{1.(x(1-x))^{-1/2}}{\left(\sqrt{1-4(x(1-x))}\right)}.(1-2x)$$

which reduces to $\frac{dy}{dx} = \frac{-(1-x)^{-1/2}}{\sqrt{x}} + \frac{(1-2x)(x(1-x))^{-1/2}}{|1-2x|}$

$$(\because 0 \leq 2x < 1 \Rightarrow 1-2x > 0) = \frac{-1}{\sqrt{x}\sqrt{1-x}} + \frac{1}{\sqrt{x}\sqrt{1-x}} = 0$$

16. **(a)** $y = \sec^{-1}\left(\frac{1}{2x^2-1}\right)$; $z = \sqrt{1-x^2}$

Clearly $x \in [-1,1] \sim \left\{\pm\frac{1}{\sqrt{2}}\right\}$ and

$\text{è} = \cos^{-1}x, \text{è} \in [0,\pi] \sim \left\{\frac{\pi}{4}, \frac{3\pi}{4}\right\}$

$\Rightarrow y = \sec^{-1}(\sec 2\theta)$; $z = \sin\theta$

$\Rightarrow y = 2\theta$, $z = \sin\theta$

$$\Rightarrow \frac{dy}{dz} = \frac{\frac{dy}{d\theta}}{\frac{dz}{d\text{è}}} = \frac{2}{\text{èos}} = \frac{2}{x} \Rightarrow \left(\frac{dy}{dz}\right)_{x=1/2} = 4$$

17. **(c)** $f(x) = \log_e x$

Let us write $f(x) = \ell n\, x$

$\Rightarrow f(\ell n\, x) = \ell n(\ell n\, x)$

$\Rightarrow \dfrac{df(\ell nx)}{dx} = \dfrac{1}{\ell nx}.\dfrac{1}{x} = \dfrac{1}{x\log_e x}$

18. **(a)** Let $P = e^{\sin^{-1}x}$ and $Q = e^{-\cos^{-1}x}$

$\Rightarrow \dfrac{dP}{dx} = \dfrac{e^{\sin^{-1}x}.1}{\sqrt{1-x^2}}$

$\Rightarrow \dfrac{dQ}{dx} = \dfrac{+e^{-\cos^{-1}x}}{\sqrt{1-x^2}}$

The required value of $\dfrac{dP}{dQ} = \dfrac{dP/dx}{dQ/dx}$

$\Rightarrow \dfrac{dP}{dQ} = \dfrac{e^{\sin^{-1}x}}{+e^{-\cos^{-1}x}} = +\left(e^{\sin^{-1}x+\cos^{-1}x}\right) = e^{\pi/2}$

19. **(b)** Let $y = \sin^{-1}\dfrac{t}{\sqrt{1+t^2}}$ and $z = \cos^{-1}\left(\dfrac{1}{\sqrt{1+t^2}}\right)$

Put $x = \tan^{-1}t$ $\Rightarrow$ $t = \tan x$ and $x \in \left(\dfrac{-\pi}{2}, \dfrac{\pi}{2}\right)$

$\Rightarrow y = \sin^{-1}(\sin x) = x \;\; \forall x \in \left(-\dfrac{\pi}{2}, \dfrac{\pi}{2}\right)$

$\Rightarrow z = \cot^{-1}(\cos x) = \begin{cases} x & \text{for } x \in \left[0, \dfrac{\pi}{2}\right) \\ -x & \text{for } x \in \left(\dfrac{-\pi}{2}, 0\right) \end{cases}$

$\Rightarrow \dfrac{dy}{dz} = \dfrac{\frac{dy}{dz}}{\frac{dz}{dx}} = 1$ for $x \in \left[0, \dfrac{\pi}{2}\right)$ and $= -1$ for $x \in \left(\dfrac{-\pi}{2}, 0\right)$

$\Rightarrow \dfrac{dy}{dz} = 1$ for $t > 0$, -1 for $t < 0$

20. **(c)** $f(x) = \cos^{-1}\left\{\dfrac{1}{\sqrt{13}}(2\cos x - 3\sin x)\right\} + \sin^{-1}\left\{\dfrac{2\cos x + 3\sin x}{\sqrt{13}}\right\}$

$g(x) = \sqrt{1+x^2}$

Let $\dfrac{2}{\sqrt{13}} = \cos\phi;\;\; \phi \in \left(0, \dfrac{\pi}{2}\right)$

$\Rightarrow \sin\phi = \sqrt{1-\cos^2\phi} = \sqrt{1-\dfrac{4}{13}} = \dfrac{3}{\sqrt{13}}$

$\Rightarrow f(x)$ can be re-written as $f(x) = \cos^{-1}(\cos\phi\cos x - \sin\phi\sin x) + \sin^{-1}(\cos\phi.\cos x + \sin\phi.\sin x)$

$\Rightarrow f(x) = \cos^{-1}(\cos(\phi + x) + \sin^{-1}(\cos(\phi - x))$

$= \cos^{-1}(\cos(\phi+x)) + \sin^{-1}\left(\sin\left(\dfrac{\pi}{2}-(\phi-x)\right)\right)$

$\Rightarrow (\phi+x) + \dfrac{\pi}{2} - (\phi-x)$ for $(\phi+x) \in [0,\pi]$ and

$\dfrac{\pi}{2} - (\phi-x) \in \left[\dfrac{-\pi}{2}, \dfrac{\pi}{2}\right]$

Here $\phi \in \left(0, \dfrac{\pi}{2}\right)$; at $x = \dfrac{3}{4}, (\phi+x) \in \left(\dfrac{3}{4}, \dfrac{\pi}{2}+\dfrac{3}{4}\right) \subset (0,\pi)$ and

$\dfrac{\pi}{2} - \phi + x$ at $x = \dfrac{3}{4} \in \left(\dfrac{3}{4}, \dfrac{\pi}{2}+\dfrac{3}{4}\right) \subset (0,\pi)$

$\therefore f(x) = \dfrac{\pi}{2} + 2x$

$\Rightarrow f'(2) = x$ at $x = \dfrac{3}{4}; g(x) = \dfrac{x}{\sqrt{1+x^2}}$

$\Rightarrow g'(x) = \dfrac{3}{5}$ $\Rightarrow$ $\dfrac{f'(x)}{g'(x)} = \dfrac{3}{3/5} = \dfrac{10}{3}$

21. **(c), (d)** Let $y = \tan^{-1}\left(\dfrac{\sqrt{1+x^2}-1}{x}\right)$ and $t = \cot^{-1}\sqrt{\dfrac{1+\sqrt{1+x^2}}{2\sqrt{1+x^2}}}$

Let $\theta = \tan^{-1}x$

$\Rightarrow x = \tan\theta$ and $\theta \in \left(\dfrac{-\pi}{2}, \dfrac{\pi}{2}\right) \sim \{0\}$

$y = \tan^{-1}\left(\dfrac{\sec\theta - 1}{\tan\theta}\right) = \tan^{-1}\left(\dfrac{1-\cos\theta}{\sin\theta}\right)$

$\Rightarrow y = \tan^{-1}(\tan\theta/2) = \theta/2 \quad \left(\because \dfrac{\theta}{2} \in \left(\dfrac{-\pi}{4}, \dfrac{\pi}{4}\right)\right)$

And $t = \cos^{-1}\sqrt{\dfrac{1+\sec\theta}{2\sec\theta}} = \cos^{-1}\sqrt{\dfrac{1+\cos\theta}{2}}$

$\Rightarrow t = \cos^{-1}\left(\cos\dfrac{\theta}{2}\right)$

$= \left\{\text{for } \dfrac{\theta}{2} \in \left(0, \dfrac{\pi}{4}\right) - \dfrac{\theta}{2} \text{ for } \dfrac{\theta}{2} \in \left(-\dfrac{\pi}{4}, 0\right)\right\}$

$\Rightarrow \dfrac{dy}{dt} = \begin{cases} 1 & \text{for } x > 0 \\ -1 & \text{for } x < 0 \end{cases}$

TEXTUAL EXERCISE–3: (SUBJECTIVE)

1. **(i)** $f(x) = \sin(\log x)$ $\Rightarrow$ $f'(x) = \cos(\log x).\dfrac{1}{x}$

$\Rightarrow f''(x) = \cos(\log x)\left(\dfrac{-1}{x^2}\right) + \dfrac{1}{x}(-\sin(\log x))\dfrac{1}{x}$

$\Rightarrow f''(x) = \dfrac{-\sin(\log x) - \cos(\log x)}{x^2}$

(ii) $f(x) = y = \log(\log x)$

$\Rightarrow f'(x) = \dfrac{1}{\log x}.\dfrac{1}{x} = \dfrac{1}{x\log x}$

$\Rightarrow f''(x) = \dfrac{-1}{(x\log x)^2}(x.\dfrac{1}{x} + \log x - 1)$

$\Rightarrow f''(x) = \dfrac{-(1+\log x)}{(x\log x)^2}$

2. $y = x^3 \log x$

Differentiating both sides, we get $\dfrac{dy}{dx} = 3x^2\log x + x^2$

$\Rightarrow \dfrac{d^2y}{dx^2} = 6x\log x + 3x + 2x = 6x\log x + 5x$

$\Rightarrow \dfrac{d^3y}{dx^3} = 6 \log x + 6 + 5$

$\Rightarrow \dfrac{d^3y}{dx^3} = 6 \log x + 11$

Differentiating again, we get $\dfrac{d^4y}{dx^4} = \dfrac{6}{x}$

3. $y = \dfrac{\log x}{x}$

Differentiating on both sides, we get $\dfrac{dy}{dx} = \dfrac{1-\log x}{x^2}$

Differentiating again, we get $\dfrac{d^2y}{dx^2} = \dfrac{x^2\left(-\dfrac{1}{x}\right) - 2x(1-\log x)}{x^4}$

$\Rightarrow \dfrac{d^2y}{dx^2} = \dfrac{-x-2x+2x\log x}{x^4}$

$\Rightarrow \dfrac{d^2y}{dx^2} = \dfrac{2x\log x - 3x}{x^4} = \dfrac{2\log x - 3}{x^3}$

4. By the question $y = log\left(\dfrac{x^2}{e^2}\right)$

Differentiating once on both sides, we get $\dfrac{dy}{dx} = \dfrac{e^2}{x^2}.\dfrac{2x}{e^2} = \dfrac{2}{x}$

Differentiating again, we get $\dfrac{d^2y}{dx^2} = \dfrac{-2}{x^2}$

5. $y = x\log\left(\dfrac{x}{a+bx}\right)$ …(1)

$\Rightarrow \dfrac{dy}{dx} = \left(\dfrac{a}{a+bx}\right) + \log\left(\dfrac{x}{a+bx}\right)$

$\Rightarrow \dfrac{dy}{dx} = \dfrac{a}{a+bx} + \dfrac{y}{x}$ …(2)

$\Rightarrow \left(x\dfrac{dy}{dx} - y\right)^2 = \dfrac{a^2x^2}{(a+bx)^2}$ …(3)

From (2), $\dfrac{d^2y}{dx^2} = \dfrac{-ab}{(a+bx)^2} - \dfrac{y}{x^2} + \dfrac{1}{x}\dfrac{dy}{dx}$

$\Rightarrow \dfrac{d^2y}{dx^2} = \dfrac{-ab}{(a+bx)^2} - \dfrac{y}{x^2} + \dfrac{1}{x}\left[\dfrac{a}{a+bx} + \dfrac{y}{x}\right]$

$\Rightarrow \dfrac{d^2y}{dx^2} = \dfrac{-ab}{(a+bx)^2} + \dfrac{a}{x(a+bx)}$

$\Rightarrow \dfrac{d^2y}{dx^2} = \dfrac{-abx + a^2 + abx}{x(a+bx)^2} = \dfrac{a^2}{x(a+bx)^2}$

$\Rightarrow x^3\dfrac{d^2y}{dx^2} = \dfrac{a^2x^2}{(a+bx)^2}$ …(4)

$\therefore$ From (3) and (4), $x^3\dfrac{d^2y}{dx^2} = \left(x\dfrac{dy}{dx} - y\right)^2$

6. $y = \sin^{-1} x$

Differentiating both sides, we get $\dfrac{dy}{dx} = \dfrac{1}{\sqrt{1-x^2}}$

Differentiating again, we get $\dfrac{d^2y}{dx^2} = \dfrac{-\dfrac{1}{2}(1-x^2)^{-1/2}(-2x)}{(1-x^2)} = \dfrac{x}{(1-x^2)^{3/2}}$

7. $y = A\cos(\log x) + B\sin(\log x)$

$\Rightarrow \dfrac{dy}{dx} = \dfrac{-A\sin(\log x)}{x} + \dfrac{B\cos(\log x)}{x}$

$= \dfrac{B\cos(\log x) - A\sin(\log x)}{x}$

$\Rightarrow \dfrac{d^2y}{dx^2}$

$= \dfrac{x\left(\dfrac{-B\sin(\log x)}{x} - \dfrac{A\cos(\log x)}{x}\right) - (B\cos(\log x) - A\sin(\log x))}{x^2}$

$\Rightarrow x^2\dfrac{d^2y}{dx^2}$ = A [sin log$x$ – cos log$x$] –B [sin log$x$ + cos log$x$]

$= -B\sin(\log x) - A\cos(\log x) - B\cos(\log x)$
$- A\sin(\log x) + B\cos(\log x) + A\sin\log x$
$= -B\sin(\log x) - A\cos(\log x) = -y$

$\Rightarrow x^2\dfrac{d^2y}{dx^2} + \dfrac{xdy}{dx} + y = 0$

8. By the question, $y = \tan x + \sec x$

$\Rightarrow \dfrac{dy}{dx} = \sec^2 x + \sec x.\tan x$

Differentiating again, we get $\dfrac{d^2y}{dx^2} = 2\sec x.\sec x.\tan x$ $+ \sec x.\sec^2 x + \tan x . \sec x.\tan x$

$= 2\sec x^2 . \tan x + \sec^3 x + \tan^2 x \sec x$

$\Rightarrow \dfrac{d^2y}{dx^2} = \dfrac{2\sin x}{\cos^3 x} + \dfrac{1}{\cos^3 x} + \dfrac{\sin^2 x}{\cos^3 x} = \dfrac{2\sin x + 1 + \sin^2 x}{\cos^3 x}$

$= \dfrac{(1+\sin x)^2}{(\cos x)^3}$

$\Rightarrow \dfrac{d^2y}{dx^2} = \dfrac{(1+\sin x)^2}{(1-\sin^2 x)^{3/2}}$

$\Rightarrow \dfrac{d^2y}{dx^2} = \dfrac{(1+\sin x)^2}{(1+\sin x)^{3/2}(1-\sin x)^{3/2}}$

$\Rightarrow \dfrac{d^2y}{dx^2} = \dfrac{\sqrt{1+\sin x}}{(1-\sin x)^{3/2}}$

Multiplying numerator & denominator by $\sqrt{1-\sin x}$, we get $\dfrac{d^2y}{dx^2} = \dfrac{\sqrt{1-\sin^2 x}}{(1-\sin x)^2} = \dfrac{\cos x}{(1-\sin x)^2}$

9. $y = \tan x$

$\Rightarrow \dfrac{dy}{dx} = \sec^2 x$

$\Rightarrow y^2 = \tan^2 x$

$\Rightarrow 2y.\dfrac{dy}{dx} = 2\tan x . \sec^2 x$ ……..(i)

$\therefore \quad \dfrac{d^2y}{dx^2} = 2\sec x \,.\, \sec x \,.\, \tan x = 2\sec^2 x \tan x$ ....(ii)

By (i) and (ii), we get $\dfrac{d^2y}{dx^2} = 2y\dfrac{dy}{dx}$

$\Rightarrow \; y_2 = 2y\,y_1$

10. $e^y(x + 1) = 1$

Differentiating the whole equation, we get

$e^y.\dfrac{dy}{dx}(x + 1) + ey = 0$ ...(i)

$\Rightarrow \; \dfrac{dy}{dx}(x+1)+1=0$

$\Rightarrow \; \dfrac{dy}{dx} = \dfrac{-1}{x+1}$ ...(ii)

$\Rightarrow \; \dfrac{d^2y}{dx^2} = \dfrac{1}{(x+1)^2}$ ...(iii)

By (ii) and (iii), we get $\dfrac{d^2y}{dx^2} = \left(\dfrac{dy}{dx}\right)^2$

Note that (i); $ey = 0$ has no solution hence $\dfrac{dy}{dx}(x+1)+1=0$

$\Rightarrow \; dy/dx = -1/x + 1$

TEXTUAL EXERCISE–3: (OBJECTIVE)

1. (a) $y = \dfrac{1}{2x^2+3x+1}$

Differentiating once, we get $\dfrac{dy}{dx} = \dfrac{(2x^2+3x+1)0-(4x+3)}{(2x^2+3x+1)^2}$

$\Rightarrow \; \dfrac{dy}{dx} = \dfrac{-(4x+3)}{(2x^2+3x+1)^2}$

Differentiating once again, we get

$$\frac{d^2y}{dx^2} = \frac{(2x^2+3x+1)^2.(-4)+2(4x+3)(2x^2+3x+1)(4x+3)}{(2x^2+3x+1)^4}$$

Putting $x = -2$, we get

$$\frac{d^2y}{dx^2} = \frac{(8-6+1)^2(-4)+2(-8+3)(3)(-8+3)}{(8-6+1)^4}$$

$\Rightarrow \; \dfrac{d^2y}{dx^2} = \dfrac{114}{81} \qquad \Rightarrow \; \dfrac{d^2y}{dx^2} = \dfrac{38}{27}$

2. (a) $y = x + ex$

Differentiating once, we get $\dfrac{dy}{dx} = 1 + ex$

Differentiating again, we get $\dfrac{d^2y}{dx^2} = e^x$

3. (c) $y = aemx + be^{-mx}$

Differentiating once, we get $\dfrac{dy}{dx} = maemx - mbe^{-mx}$

Differentiating again, we get $\dfrac{d^2y}{dx^2} = m^2a\, emx + m^2\, be^{-mx}$

$= m^2\,(aemx + be^{-m}x)$

$= m^2\, y$

4. (c) $y = \tan^{-1}\left(\dfrac{\ell n\left(\dfrac{e}{x^2}\right)}{\ell n(ex^2)}\right) + \tan^{-1}\left(\dfrac{3+2\ell nx}{1-6\ell nx}\right); x \in \left(\dfrac{1}{\sqrt{e}}, \sqrt[6]{e}\right)$

$\Rightarrow \; y = \tan^{-1}\left(\dfrac{1-\ln x^2}{1+\ln x^2}\right) + \tan^{-1}\left(\dfrac{3+2\ln x}{1-3(2\ln x)}\right)$

$\because \quad x > \dfrac{1}{\sqrt{e}} \qquad \Rightarrow \; x^2 > \dfrac{1}{e}$

$\Rightarrow \; \ln x^2 > -1$ and $x < (^e)^{1/6}$

$\Rightarrow \; \ln x < \dfrac{1}{6}\ln e \qquad \Rightarrow \; 6\ln x < 1$

$\Rightarrow \; y = \tan^{-1} 1 - \tan^{-1}(\ln x^2) + \tan^{-1}(3) + \tan^{-1}(2\ln x)$

$\Rightarrow \; \dfrac{dy}{dx} = -\dfrac{1}{1+(\ln x^2)^2}.\dfrac{1}{x^2}(2x) + \dfrac{1}{1+4(\ln x)^2}.\left(\dfrac{2}{x}\right)$

$\Rightarrow \; \dfrac{dy}{dx} = \dfrac{2}{x[1+4(\ln x)^2]} - \dfrac{2}{x[1+(\ln x^2)]} = 0$

5. (b) $f(x)$ be a quadratic expression which is positive for all real x

$\Rightarrow \; f(x) > 0, f'(x) < 0$, Disc. $< 0 \;\; \forall x \in \mathbb{R}$

$g(x) = f(x) + f'(x) + f''(x) = (ax^2 + bx + c) + (2ax + b) + 2a$

(Taking $f(x) = ax^2 + bx + c$, $a > 0$, $b^2 - 4ac < 0$)

$\Rightarrow \; g(x) = ax^2 + (2a + b) + (2a + b + c)$

Disc. of $g(x) = (2a + b)^2 - 4a\,(2a + b + c)$

$= 4a^2 + b^2 + 4ab - 8a^2 - 4ab - 4ac = (b^2 - 4ac) - 4a^2 < 0$

Thus $a > 0$, Disc of $g(x) < 0$

$\Rightarrow \; g(x) > 0 \;\; \forall x \in \mathbb{R}$

6. (b) Given, $x^2\, y + y^3 = 2$

Differentiating both sides, we get $2xy + x^2\dfrac{dy}{dx} + 3y^2\dfrac{dy}{dx} = 0$

$\Rightarrow \; 2xy + \dfrac{dy}{dx}(x^2+3y^2) = 0$

$\Rightarrow \; \dfrac{dy}{dx} = \left(\dfrac{-2xy}{x^2+3y^2}\right)$

$\Rightarrow \; \left.\dfrac{dy}{dx}\right|_{(1,1)} = \dfrac{-2}{1+3} = -\dfrac{1}{2}$ ...(i)

$\Rightarrow \; \dfrac{d^2y}{dx^2} = \dfrac{(x^2+3y^2)\left(-2x\dfrac{dy}{dx}-2y\right)+(2xy)\left(2x+6y\dfrac{dy}{dx}\right)}{(x^2+3y^2)^2}$

$\Rightarrow \; \left.\dfrac{d^2y}{dx^2}\right|_{(1,1)} = \dfrac{(4)\left(-2\left(-\dfrac{1}{2}\right)-2\right)+(2)\left(2+6\left(-\dfrac{1}{2}\right)\right)}{(1+3)^2}$

$= \dfrac{4(-1)+2(-1)}{16} = \dfrac{-4-2}{16} = -\dfrac{6}{16} = -\dfrac{3}{8}$

7. (d) $f(x)$: polynomial in x, $f(ex)$

Differentiating $f(ex)$, we get $[f(ex)]' = f'(ex)\,.e^x$

Differentiating again, we get $[f(ex)]'' = f'(ex)\ ex + f''(ex).e^{2x}$
Hence the second derivative of $f(ex) = f''(ex)\ .e^2x + f'(ex).(ex)$

TEXTUAL EXERCISE-4: (SUBJECTIVE)

1. (a) $y = \sqrt{x}^{\sqrt{x}^{\sqrt{x}\ldots\text{to }\infty}} = \sqrt{x}^{y}$

We can write by taking logarithm on both sides, we get

$\ell n\, y = y\ \ell n\left(\sqrt{x}\right)$

$\ell n\, y = \dfrac{y}{2}\ \ell n\, x$

$\Rightarrow \dfrac{1}{y}.\dfrac{dy}{dx} = \dfrac{1}{x}.\dfrac{y}{2} + \dfrac{1}{2}\dfrac{dy}{dx}.\ell nx$

$\Rightarrow \dfrac{dy}{dx}\left(\dfrac{1}{y} - \dfrac{\ell nx}{2}\right) = \dfrac{y}{2x}$

$\Rightarrow$ dy/dx = $\dfrac{\dfrac{y}{2x}}{\left(\dfrac{1}{y} - \dfrac{\ell nx}{2}\right)} = \dfrac{y^2}{x(2 - y\,\ell nx)}$

$\Rightarrow \dfrac{dy}{dx} = \dfrac{y^2}{2x\left(1 - y\ell n\sqrt{x}\right)}$

(b) $y = (\cos x)^{(\cos x)^{(\cos x)^{(\cos x)\ldots\text{to }\infty}}} = (\cos x)^y$

Proceed in part (a), $\ell n\, y = y.\ \ell n\ \cos x$
Differentiating both sides, we get

$\dfrac{1}{y}.\dfrac{dy}{dx} = \dfrac{dy}{dx}\ell n\cos x + \dfrac{y}{\cos x}(-\sin x)$

$\Rightarrow \dfrac{dy}{dx}\left(\dfrac{1}{y} - \ell n\cos x\right) = \dfrac{-y\sin x}{\cos x}$

$\Rightarrow \dfrac{dy}{dx} = \dfrac{-y\dfrac{\sin x}{\cos x}}{\left(\dfrac{1 - y\,\ell n\cos x}{y}\right)} = \dfrac{-y^2\tan x}{(1 - y\ell n\cos x)}$

$= \dfrac{y^2\tan x}{(y\ell n\cos x - 1)}$

(c) $y = e^{x+e^{x+e^{x+e^{x}\ldots\infty}}} = e^{x+y}$

$\Rightarrow \ell n\, y = x + y$ ...(i)

Differentiating (i) on both sides, we gets $\dfrac{1}{y}.\dfrac{dy}{dx} = 1 + \dfrac{dy}{dx}$

$\Rightarrow \dfrac{dy}{dx}\left(\dfrac{1}{y} - 1\right) = 1 \quad \Rightarrow \dfrac{dy}{dx} = \dfrac{1}{\left(\dfrac{1}{y} - 1\right)} = \dfrac{y}{1-y}$

2. (a) Let $u = xy$ and $v = y^x$

$\Rightarrow$ $\ln u = y\ln x$ and $\ln v = x\ \ln y$

$\Rightarrow \dfrac{1}{u}\dfrac{du}{dx} = \dfrac{x}{y} + \ln x\dfrac{dy}{dx}$ and $\dfrac{1}{v}\dfrac{dv}{dx} = \dfrac{x}{y}\dfrac{dy}{dx} + \ln y$

$\Rightarrow \dfrac{du}{dx} = x^y\left(\dfrac{y}{x} + \ln x\dfrac{dy}{dx}\right)$ and $\dfrac{dv}{dx} = y^x\left(\dfrac{x}{y}\dfrac{dy}{dx} + \ln y\right)$

Now, $u + v = c$

$\Rightarrow \dfrac{du}{dx} + \dfrac{dv}{dx} = 0$

$\Rightarrow x^y\left(\dfrac{y}{x} + \ln x\dfrac{dy}{dx}\right) + y^x\left(\dfrac{x}{y}\dfrac{dy}{dx} + \ln y\right) = 0$

$\Rightarrow (y.x^{y-1} + y^x\ln y) + \dfrac{dy}{dx}(x^y\ln x + xy^{x-1}) = 0$

$\Rightarrow \dfrac{dy}{dx} = \dfrac{-(y.x^{y-1} + y^x\ln y)}{(x^y\ln x + xy^{x-1})}$

(b) $(\cos x)y = (\sin y)^x$

Let $(\cos x)y = P$ and and $(\sin y)^x = Q$

Given $P = Q$

$\Rightarrow \dfrac{dP}{dx} = \dfrac{dQ}{dx}$ ...(i)

Taking $P = (\cos x)^y$

$\Rightarrow \ell n\, P = y\ \ell n\ (\cos x)$

$\Rightarrow \dfrac{1}{P}\dfrac{dP}{dx} = \dfrac{y}{\cos x}(-\sin x) + \ell n(\cos x)\dfrac{dy}{dx}$

$\Rightarrow \dfrac{dP}{dx} = (\cos x)^y\left(\dfrac{dy}{dx}\ell n(\cos x) - \dfrac{y\sin x}{\cos x}\right)$ ...(ii)

Similarly $Q = (\sin y)^x$

$\Rightarrow \ell n\, Q = x\ \ell n(\sin y)$

$\Rightarrow \dfrac{1}{Q}.\dfrac{dQ}{dx} = \left(\ell n(\sin y) + \dfrac{x}{\sin y}.\cos y.\dfrac{dy}{dx}\right)$

$\Rightarrow \dfrac{dQ}{dx} = (\sin y)^x\left(\ell n(\sin y) + x.\cot y.\dfrac{dy}{dx}\right)$ ...(iii)

Putting (ii) and (iii) in (i) we get, $(\cos x)^y.(\dfrac{dy}{dx}.\ell n(\cos x)$
$- y.\tan x)$
$= (\sin y)^x\ (\ell n\ (\sin y) + x.\ \cot y\ .\ (\sin y)^x\ .\ \dfrac{dy}{dx})$

$\Rightarrow \dfrac{dy}{dx}$ [cos $x)^y$. ℓn (cos x) – x cot $y(\sin y)^x$] = $(\sin y)^x$ ℓn (sin y) + $(\cos x)^y$. y tan x

$\Rightarrow \dfrac{dy}{dx} = \dfrac{\ell n(\sin y)(\sin y)^x + y(\cos x)^y\tan x}{(\cos x)^y\ell n(\cos x) - x\cot y(\sin y)^x}$, but $(\sin y)^x$ $= (\cos x)^y$

$\Rightarrow \dfrac{dy}{dx} = \dfrac{\ell n(\sin y) + y\tan x}{\ell n(\cos x) - x\cot y}$

(c) $y = (xx)^x$

$\Rightarrow \ell n\, y = x\ \ell n\ (xx) \quad \Rightarrow \ell n\, y = x^2\ \ell n\ (x)$

$\Rightarrow \dfrac{1}{y}.\dfrac{dy}{dx} = 2x\ \ell n\ (x) + \dfrac{x^2}{x}$

$\Rightarrow \dfrac{dy}{dx} = x^{x^2}(2x\ell n(x) + x)$

$\Rightarrow \dfrac{dy}{dx} = x^{x^2+1}\left(\ell n(x^2) + \ell ne\right)$

$\Rightarrow \frac{dy}{dx} = x^{x^2+1}\left(\ell n\left(ex^2\right)\right) \Rightarrow \frac{dy}{dx} = x^{x^2+1}.\ell n(ex^2)$

(d) $y = e^{(x)^x}$

$\ell n\, y = x^x.\ell n\, e$

$\Rightarrow \ell n\, y = x^x \qquad \Rightarrow \frac{1}{y}.\frac{dy}{dx} = \frac{dp}{dx}$; where $p = x^x$

$\Rightarrow$ Let $p = x^x \qquad \Rightarrow \ell n\, p = x\, \ell n\, x$

$\Rightarrow \frac{1}{p}.\frac{dp}{dx} = \ell n\, x + 1$

$\Rightarrow \frac{dp}{dx} = x^x\left(\ell nx + 1\right) \qquad \Rightarrow \frac{dy}{dx} = e^{(x)^x}.x^x\left(\ell nx + 1\right)$

$= x^x\, e^{x^x}\, (\ell n\, x + \ell n\, e) = x^x\, e^{x^x}\, (\ell n(ex))$

(e) $y = \left(1+\frac{1}{x}\right)^{x^2} \Rightarrow \ell n\, y = x^2\, \ell n\left(1+\frac{1}{x}\right)$

Differentiating both sides, we get

$\frac{1}{y}.\frac{dy}{dx} = 2x\ell n\left(\frac{x+1}{x}\right) + \frac{x^2.x}{(x+1)}.\left(\frac{-1}{x^2}\right)$

$\Rightarrow \frac{dy}{dx} = y\left(2x\ell n\left(1+\frac{1}{x}\right) + \frac{-x}{x+1}\right)$

Hence $\frac{dy}{dx} = \left(1+\frac{1}{x}\right)^{x^2}\left(2x.\ell n\left(1+\frac{1}{x}\right) - \frac{x}{x+1}\right)$

3. (a) $y = (\cos x)^{\sin x}$

Taking log on both sides, we get $\ell n\, y = \sin x\, \ell n\, (\cos x)$

$\Rightarrow \frac{1}{y}.\frac{dy}{dx} = \cos x\, \ell n(\cos x) + \frac{\sin x}{\cos x}(-\sin x)$

$\Rightarrow \frac{dy}{dx} = y\, [\cos x\, .\ell n(\cos x\,) + \tan x(-\sin x)]$

$= (\cos x)^{\sin x}\, [\cos x\, \ell n(\cos x) - \tan x.\sin x]$

(b) $y = \left(\frac{\sin 3x}{1-\sin 3x}\right)^{1/3}$

$\Rightarrow \ell ny = \frac{1}{3}\ell n\left(\frac{\sin 3x}{1-\sin 3x}\right)$

$\Rightarrow \frac{1}{y}\frac{dy}{dx} = \frac{1}{3}\left(\frac{1-\sin 3x}{\sin 3x}\right)\left(\frac{(1-\sin 3x)\cos 3x.3 + \sin 3x \cos 3x.3}{(1-\sin 3x)^2}\right)$

$\Rightarrow \frac{dy}{dx} = \frac{(1-\sin 3x)}{3(\sin 3x)}.\left(\frac{\sin 3x}{1-\sin 3x}\right)^{1/3}$

$\left(\frac{3\cos 3x(1-\sin 3x) + 3\sin 3x.\cos 3x}{(1-\sin 3x)^2}\right)$

$= \left(\frac{\sin 3x}{1-\sin 3x}\right)^{-2/3}\left(\frac{\cos 3x}{(1-\sin 3x)^2}\right)$

$= \frac{(\sin 3x)^{-2/3}.\cos 3x}{(1-\sin 3x)^{4/3}} = \frac{\cos 3x}{\sqrt[3]{\sin^2 3x(1-\sin 3x)^4}}$

(c) $y = \frac{\sqrt{x-1}}{\sqrt[3]{(x+2)^2}\sqrt{(x+3)^3}}$

$\Rightarrow \frac{dy}{dx}$

$= \frac{(x+2)^{2/3}.(x+3)^{3/2}\left(\sqrt{x-1}\right)' - \left((x+2)^{2/3}.(x+3)^{3/2}\right)'.(x-1)^{1/2}}{\left((x+2)^{2/3}(x+3)^{3/2}\right)^2}$

$= \frac{\frac{(x+2)^{2/3}.(x+3)^{3/2}}{2\sqrt{x-1}} - \sqrt{x-1}\left(\frac{2(x+3)^{3/2}}{3(x+2)^{1/3}} + \frac{3(x+2)^{2/3}.\sqrt{x+3}}{2}\right)}{(x+2)^{4/3}(x+3)^3}$

Simplifying, we get $\frac{-(5x^2+x-24)}{3(x-1)^{1/2}(x+2)^{5/3}(x+3)^{5/2}}$

4. $xy = ex - y$

$\Rightarrow$ y $\ell n\, x = (x - y)\, \ell ne \Rightarrow$ y $\ell nx = (x - y)$

$\Rightarrow \frac{dy}{dx}\ell nx + \frac{y}{x} = 1 - \frac{dy}{dx}$

$\Rightarrow \frac{dy}{dx}(1+\ell nx) = 1 - \frac{y}{x} \Rightarrow \frac{dy}{dx} = \frac{1-\frac{y}{x}}{1+\ell nx}$

Putting $\ell n\, x = \frac{x-y}{y} = \frac{x}{y} - 1$

$\Rightarrow \frac{dy}{dx} = \frac{1-\frac{y}{x}}{1+\frac{x}{y}-1} = \frac{1-\frac{y}{x}}{\frac{x}{y}} \Rightarrow \frac{y(1-y)}{x^2}$

5. (a) $(\ell nx)^{\cos x}$

Let $y = (\ell nx)^{\cos x}$

$\Rightarrow \ell ny = \cos x\, \ell n(\ell n(x))$

Differentiating both sides, we get $\frac{1}{y}.\frac{dy}{dx} = \frac{\cos x}{\ell nx}.\frac{1}{x} + \ell n$ $(\ell n\, x)\, (-\sin x)$

$\Rightarrow \frac{dy}{dx} = y\left(\frac{\cos x}{x\ell nx} + \ell n(\ell nx)(-\sin x)\right) = (\{n\, x)^{\cos x}$

$\left(\frac{\cos x}{x\ell nx} + \ell n(\ell nx)(-\sin x)\right)$

(b) $y = (x\, \ell n\, x)^{\ell n\, \ell n\, x}$

$\ell n\, y = \ell n(\ell nx)\, \ell n(x\, \ell nx)$

$\Rightarrow \frac{1}{y}.\frac{dy}{dx} = \left(\frac{1}{\ell nx}.\frac{1}{x}.\ell n(x\ell nx) + \frac{\ell n(\ell nx)}{x\ell n(x)}(1+\ell nx)\right)$

$\Rightarrow \frac{dy}{dx} = y\left(\frac{\ell n(x\ell nx)}{x\ell nx} + \frac{\ell n(\ell nx)}{x\ell n(x)}(1+\ell nx)\right)$

$= \frac{(x\ell nx)^{\ell n(\ell nx)}}{x}.\left(\frac{\ell n(x\ell nx)}{\ell nx} + \frac{\ell n(\ell nx)}{\ell nx}(1+\ell nx)\right)$

$= \frac{(x\ell nx)^{\ell n(\ell nx)}}{x}\left(\frac{\ell n(\ell nx)}{\ell nx} + \frac{\ell n(\ell nx).\ell nx}{\ell nx} + \frac{\ell n(x\ell nx)}{\ell nx}\right)$

$= \frac{(x\ell nx)^{\ell n(\ell nx)}}{x}\left[1 + \ell n(\ell nx)\left(1+\frac{2}{\ell nx}\right)\right]$

6. Given $(\tan^{-1}x)y + yc^{otx} = 1; x > 0$

Let $u = (\tan^{-1}x)^y$; $v = (y)^{cotx}$

$\Rightarrow u + v = 1$

$$\Rightarrow \frac{du}{dx}+\frac{dv}{dx}=0 \quad \ldots(i)$$

$\Rightarrow \ln u = y \ln(\tan^{-1}x)$; $\ln v = \cot x \ln y$

$$\Rightarrow \frac{1}{u}\frac{du}{dx}=\frac{y}{\tan^{-1}x}.\frac{1}{(1+x^2)}+\frac{dy}{dx}.\ln(\tan^{-1}x) \quad \ldots(ii)$$

$$\text{and } \frac{1}{v}\frac{dv}{dx}=\frac{\cot x}{y}\frac{dy}{dx}+\ln y(-\text{cosec}^2x) \quad \ldots(iii)$$

Using (ii) and (iii) in (i), we get

$$(\tan^{-1}x)^y\left[\frac{y}{(1+x^2)\tan^{-1}x}+\frac{dy}{dx}.\ln(\tan^{-1}x)\right]$$

$$+(y)^{\cot x}\left[\frac{\cot x}{y}\frac{dy}{dx}-\text{cosec}^2x.\ln y\right]=0$$

$$\Rightarrow \frac{dy}{dx}=\frac{y^{\cot x}.\text{cosec}^2x.\ln y-\dfrac{y(\tan^{-1}x)^y}{(1+x^2).\tan^{-1}x}}{(\tan^{-1}x)^y\ln(\tan^{-1}x)+\cot x.y^{\cot x-1}}$$

7. (i) $y = x^{\cos x}+\dfrac{x^2+1}{x^2-1}$

Let $u = x^x\cos^x$

$\ell n\, u = (x \cos x)\, \ell n\, x$

$$\Rightarrow \frac{1}{u}.\frac{du}{dx} = \cos x + \ell n\, x(\cos x - x \sin x)$$

$$\Rightarrow \frac{du}{dx} = x^x\cos^x(\cos x + \ell nx(\cos x - x\sin x))$$

$$\Rightarrow \frac{dy}{dx}=\frac{d}{dx}\left(x^{x\cos x}+\frac{x^2+1}{x^2-1}\right)=\frac{d}{dx}\left(x^{x\cos x}\right)+\frac{d}{dx}\left(\frac{x^2+1}{x^2-1}\right)$$

$$=\frac{d}{dx}\left(x^{x\cos x}\right)+\frac{(x^2-1)(2x)-(x^2+1)(2x)}{(x^2-1)^2}$$

$$=\frac{d}{dx}\left(x^{x\cos x}\right)+\frac{-2x-2x}{(x^2-1)^2}$$

$$= x^x\cos^x((1+\log x)\cos x - x\log x\sin x) - \frac{4x}{(x^2-1)^2}$$

(ii) $y = (x \cos x)x + (x \sin x)^{1/x}$

Let $u = (x \cos x)^x$

$\Rightarrow \ell n\, u = x\, \ell n\, (x \cos x) = x\, \ell n\, x + x\, \ell n(\cos x)$

Differentiating both sides, we get $\dfrac{1}{u}.\dfrac{du}{dx} = 1 + \ell n\, x + \ell n\, (\cos x) - \dfrac{x\sin x}{\cos x}$

$$\Rightarrow \frac{du}{dx}=(x\cos x)^x\left(1+\ell nx+\ell n(\cos x)-x\frac{\sin x}{\cos x}\right) \quad \ldots(i)$$

Let $v = (x \sin x)^{1/x}$

Taking log on both sides, we get $\ell n\, v = \dfrac{1}{x}\ell n\,(x \sin x)$

$$\Rightarrow \ell n\, v=\frac{\ell nx}{x}+\frac{\ell n(\sin x)}{x}$$

Differentiating both sides, we get

$$\frac{1}{v}.\frac{dv}{dx}=\frac{1}{x^2}-\frac{\ell nx}{x^2}-\frac{\ell n(\sin x)}{x^2}+\frac{(\cos x)}{\sin x.x}$$

$$\Rightarrow \frac{dv}{vdx}=\left[\frac{1-\ell nx-\ell n(\sin x)}{x^2}+\frac{(\cos x)}{x\sin x}\right]$$

$$\Rightarrow \frac{dv}{dx}=(x\sin x)^{1/x}\left(\frac{1+x\cot x-\log(x\sin x)}{x^2}\right)$$

$$\Rightarrow \frac{dy}{dx}=\frac{d}{dx}((x\cos x)x + (x\sin x)^{1/x})$$

$= (x \cos x)^x (1 - x \tan x + \log (x \cos x)) + (x \sin x)^{1/x}$ $\left(\dfrac{1+x\cot x-\log(x\sin x)}{x^2}\right)$

(iii) $y = e\sin x + (\tan x)^x$

Let $u = e\sin x$

$\Rightarrow \ell nu = \sin x\, \ell n\, e$

$$\Rightarrow \frac{1}{u}.\frac{du}{dx} = \cos x$$

$$\Rightarrow \frac{du}{dx} = u\cos x = e\sin^x\cos x \quad \ldots(i)$$

Let $v = (\tan x)^x$

$\Rightarrow \ell n\, v = x\, \ell n\, (\tan x)$

Differentiating both sides, we get

$$\frac{1}{v}.\frac{dv}{dx}=\ell n(\tan x)+\frac{x(\sec^2 x)}{\tan x}$$

$$\Rightarrow \frac{dv}{dx}=v\left(\ell n(\tan x)+\frac{x(\sec^2 x)}{\tan x}\right) \quad \ldots(ii)$$

By (i) and (ii), we get $\dfrac{d}{dx}(e\sin x + (\tan x)x)$

$$= e\sin^x\cos x + (\tan x)^x\left(\ell n(\tan x)+x\frac{\sec^2 x}{\tan x}\right)$$

$= e\sin^x \cos x + (\tan x)^x (\ell n\, (\tan x) + x \sec x \text{ cosec } x)$

(iv) $y = (\cos x)x + (\sin x)^{1/x}$

Let $u = (\cos x)^x$

$\Rightarrow \ell n\, u = x\, \ell n\, (\cos x)$

$$\Rightarrow \frac{1}{u}.\frac{du}{dx}=\ell n(\cos x)+\frac{x}{\cos x}(-\sin x) \quad \ldots(i)$$

$$\Rightarrow \frac{du}{dx}=u\left(\ell n(\cos x)-\frac{x\sin x}{\cos x}\right) \quad \ldots(ii)$$

Similarly $v = (\sin x)^{1/x}$

$$\Rightarrow \ell n\, v=\frac{1}{x}\ell n(\sin x)$$

$$\Rightarrow \frac{1}{v}\frac{dv}{dx}=\frac{-\ell n(\sin x)}{x^2}+\frac{\cos x}{x\sin x} \quad \ldots(iii)$$

$$\Rightarrow \frac{dv}{dx}=(\sin x)^{1/x}\left(\frac{\cos x}{x\sin x}-\frac{\ell n(\sin x)}{x^2}\right) \quad \ldots(iv)$$

By (ii) and (iv), we get $\dfrac{d}{dx}[(\cos x)x + (\sin x)^{1/x}]$

$$=(\cos x)^x(\log(\cos x)-x\tan x)+(\sin x)^{1/x}\left(-\frac{\log\sin x}{x^2}+\frac{\cot x}{x}\right)$$

8. $y = (x\sin x) + (\sin x)^x$

Let $P = x\sin^x$

$\Rightarrow \ell n\, P = \sin x\, \ell n\, x \quad \Rightarrow \quad \frac{1}{P}.\frac{dP}{dx} = \cos x\, \ell nx + \frac{\sin x}{x}$

$\Rightarrow \frac{dP}{dx} = P\left(\frac{\sin x}{x} + \cos x\, \ell nx\right)$ ...(i) and let $Q = (\sin x)^x$

$\Rightarrow \ell n\, Q = x\, \ell n\, (\sin x)$

$\Rightarrow \frac{1}{Q}.\frac{dQ}{dx} = \left(\ell n(\sin x) + \frac{x\cos x}{\sin x}\right)$

$\Rightarrow \frac{dQ}{dx} = Q[\ell n\, (\sin x) + x\cot x]$

$\Rightarrow \frac{dy}{dx} = \left((\sin x)^x(\ell n \sin x + x\cot x) + x^{\sin x}\left(\cos x \log x + \frac{\sin x}{x}\right)\right)$

9. $y = (\log x)x + x^{logx}$

Let $P = (\log x)^x$

$\Rightarrow \ell n\, P = x\, \ell n\, (\log x)$

Differentiating both sides, we get

$\frac{1}{P}.\frac{dP}{dx} = \left(\ell n(\log x) + \frac{x}{x\log x}\right)$

$\Rightarrow \frac{dP}{dx} = P\left(\ell n(\log x) + \frac{1}{\log x}\right)$ and let $Q = x^{logx}$

$\Rightarrow \ell n\, Q = \log x.\, \ell n\, x \quad \Rightarrow \quad \frac{1}{Q}.\frac{dQ}{dx} = \frac{\ell nx}{x} + \frac{\log x}{x}$

$\Rightarrow \frac{dQ}{dx} = Q\left(\frac{2\ell nx}{x}\right)$

$\Rightarrow \frac{dy}{dx} = \left(x^{\log x}\left(\frac{2\log x}{x}\right) + (\log x)^x\left(\log(\log x) + \frac{1}{\log x}\right)\right)$

TEXTUAL EXERCISE-4: (OBJECTIVE)

1. (a) $[x + y]a + b = x^a.y^b$

$\ell n\,(x+y).(a+b) = a\,\ell n\, x + b\,\ell n\, y$.

Differentiating both sides, we get

$\frac{(a+b)}{(x+y)}\left(1 + \frac{dy}{dx}\right) = \frac{a}{x} + \frac{b}{y}.\frac{dy}{dx}$

$\Rightarrow \left(\frac{a+b}{x+y}\right) + \frac{(a+b)}{(x+y)}\frac{dy}{dx} = \frac{a}{x} + \frac{b}{y}.\frac{dy}{dx}$

$\Rightarrow \frac{dy}{dx}\left(\frac{a+b}{x+y} - \frac{b}{y}\right) = \frac{a}{x} - \left(\frac{a+b}{x+y}\right)$

$\Rightarrow \frac{dy}{dx} = \frac{\frac{a}{x} - \left(\frac{a+b}{x+y}\right)}{\left(\frac{a+b}{x+y}\right) - \frac{b}{y}} = \frac{\frac{ax+ay-ax-bx}{x(x+y)}}{\frac{ay+by-bx-by}{y(x+y)}}$

$\Rightarrow \frac{dy}{dx} = \frac{(ay-bx)y}{x(ay-bx)} = \frac{y}{x}$

2. (a) $y = \sqrt{\ell nx + \sqrt{\ell nx + \sqrt{\ell nx + ...\infty}}}$

Squaring both sides, we get $y^2 = \ell n\, x + y$

$\Rightarrow y^2 - y = \ell n\, x$

Differentiating both sides, we get $2y\frac{dy}{dx} - \frac{dy}{dx} = \frac{1}{x}$

$\Rightarrow \frac{dy}{dx} = \frac{1}{x(2y-1)}$

3. (a), (c), (d)

$y = \sqrt{z + \sqrt{x + \sqrt{x + ...\infty}}}$

Squaring both sides, we get $y^2 = x + y$

$\Rightarrow y^2 - y = x$

$\Rightarrow 2y\frac{dy}{dx} - \frac{dy}{dx} = 1 \quad \Rightarrow \quad \frac{dy}{dx} = \frac{1}{2y-1}$ ...(i)

Also $y^2 - y = x$

$\Rightarrow y = \frac{1+\sqrt{1+4x}}{2} \quad \Rightarrow \quad 2y = 1 + \sqrt{4x}$

$\Rightarrow 2y - 1 = \sqrt{1+4x} \quad \Rightarrow \quad \frac{1}{2y-1} = \frac{1}{\sqrt{1+4x}}$

$\Rightarrow \frac{dy}{dx} = \frac{1}{\sqrt{1+4x}}$ ...(2)

Also $\frac{dy}{dx} = \frac{1}{2y-1} \quad \Rightarrow \quad \frac{dy}{dx} = \frac{y}{2y^2 - y}$

$\Rightarrow \frac{dy}{dx} = \frac{y}{2(y+x) - y} \quad \Rightarrow \quad \frac{dy}{dx} = \frac{y}{2x + y}$ ...(3)

$\therefore$ From (1) (2) and (3) $\Rightarrow$ option (a), (c) and (d) are correct.

4. (d) $f(x) = (xx)^x$

$\Rightarrow \ln f(x) = x\ln x^x = x2\ln x$

$\Rightarrow \frac{1}{f(x)}.f'(x) = x + 2x\ln x$

$\Rightarrow f'(x) = (xx)^x(1 + 2\ln x).x$ ...(1)

$\Rightarrow f'(1) = 1$ and $g(x) = (x)^{x^x}$

$\Rightarrow \ln g(x) = x^x \ln x$

$\Rightarrow \ln(\ln g(x)) = \ln xx + \ln(\ln x)$

$\Rightarrow \frac{1}{\ln g(x)}.\frac{1}{g(x)}.g'(x) = 1 + \ln x + \frac{1}{x\ln x}$

$\Rightarrow g'(x) = g(x).\ln g(x).\left(1 + \ln x + \frac{1}{x\ln x}\right)$

$= (x)^{x^x}.x^x\left[\ln x + (\ln x)^2 + \frac{1}{x}\right]$

$\Rightarrow g'(1) = 1$

5. (c) $y = \frac{a + bx^{3/2}}{x^{5/4}}$

Given $\left.\frac{dy}{dx}\right|_{x=5} = 0$

Differentiating both sides, we get

$$\frac{dy}{dx}=\left[\frac{x^{5/4}\left(\frac{3}{2}bx^{1/2}\right)-\frac{5}{4}\left(a+bx^{3/2}\right).x^{1/4}}{x^{5/2}}\right]$$

Put $x = 5$, we get $\frac{dy}{dx}=\left[\frac{5^{5/4}\left(\frac{3}{2}b5^{1/2}\right)-\frac{5}{4}\left(a+b5^{3/2}\right).5^{1/4}}{5^{5/2}}\right]$

$\Rightarrow \frac{3}{2}b5^{1/2}-\frac{a}{4}-\frac{b}{4}5^{3/2}=0$

$\Rightarrow \left(\frac{3}{2}b-\frac{5b}{4}\right)5^{1/2}-\frac{a}{4}=0$

$\Rightarrow \left(\frac{b}{4}\right)\sqrt{5}=\frac{a}{4}$ $\quad\Rightarrow\quad \frac{a}{b}=\sqrt{5}$

6. (d) $f(x) = |x|^{|\sin x|}$; $\frac{\pi}{4}\in\left(0,\frac{\pi}{2}\right)$

$f(x)=x^{\sin x}$ for $x\in\left(0,\frac{\pi}{2}\right)$

$\Rightarrow \ln f(x) = (\sin x) \ln x$

$\Rightarrow \frac{1}{f(x)}.f'(x)=\frac{\sin x}{x}+(\ln x)(\cos x)$

$\Rightarrow f'(x)=f(x)\left[\frac{\sin x}{x}+\cos x.\ln x\right]$

$\Rightarrow f'(x)=(x)^{\sin x}\left[\frac{\sin x}{x}+\cos x.\ln x\right]$

$\Rightarrow f'\left(\frac{\pi}{4}\right)=\left(\frac{\pi}{4}\right)^{1/\sqrt{2}}\left[\frac{\frac{1}{\sqrt{2}}}{\left(\frac{\pi}{4}\right)}+\frac{1}{\sqrt{2}}\ln\frac{\pi}{4}\right]$

$=\left(\frac{\pi}{4}\right)^{1/\sqrt{2}}\left[\frac{2\sqrt{2}}{\pi}+\frac{\sqrt{2}}{2}\ln\frac{\pi}{4}\right]$

TEXTUAL EXERCISE–5:(SUBJECTIVE)

1. $f(x)=\frac{x^2-x}{x^2+2x}\Rightarrow f(x)=\frac{x-1}{x+2}\ (x\neq 0)$

$\Rightarrow y=\frac{x-1}{x+2}$ $\quad\Rightarrow yx+2y=x-1$

$\Rightarrow x(y-1)=-2y-1$ $\quad\Rightarrow x=\frac{-2y-1}{y-1}$

$\Rightarrow g(y)=\frac{-2y-1}{y-1}$ $\quad\Rightarrow g'(y)=\frac{3}{(1-y)^2}$

$\Rightarrow \frac{d}{dx}\left(f^{-1}(x)\right)=\frac{3}{(1-x)^2}$

$\Rightarrow \frac{d}{dx}(g(x))=\frac{-3}{(1-x)^2}$

$\Rightarrow$ Domain of $f^{-1}(x)$

$\because D_f=\mathbb{R}-\{0,-2\}$ $\quad\Rightarrow x\neq 0,-2$

$\Rightarrow \frac{-2y-1}{y-1}\neq 0,-2$ $\quad\Rightarrow y\neq-\frac{1}{2},1$

$\Rightarrow D_{f^{-1}}=\mathbb{R}-\left\{\frac{-1}{2},1\right\};D_{g'(x)}=\left\{\frac{-1}{2},1\right\}$

2. $\because f(f^{-1}(x))=x\Rightarrow f'(f^{-1}(x))\frac{d}{dx}(f^{-1}(x))=1$

$\Rightarrow \frac{d}{dx}(f^{-1}(x))=\frac{1}{f'(f^{-1}(x))}$

$\Rightarrow \frac{d}{dx}(g(x))=\frac{1}{f'(g(x))}$; where $g(x)=f^{-1}(x)$ But given,

$f'(x)$ ——

$\Rightarrow g'(x)=\frac{1}{\left(\frac{1}{[1+(g(x))^5]}\right)}$

$\Rightarrow g'(x)=[1+(g(x))^5]$

3. $y^{\frac{1}{m}}+y^{\frac{-1}{m}}=2x$ ...(i)

Differentiating once, we get $2=\left(\frac{y^{\frac{1}{m}-1}}{m}-\frac{y^{\frac{-1}{m}-1}}{m}\right)\frac{dy}{dx}$

$\Rightarrow 2my=(y^{1/m}-y^{-1/m})\,dy/dx$

Squaring both sides, we get

$4m^2y^2=\left(\frac{dy}{dx}\right)^2(y^{2/m}+y^{-2/m}-2)$ ...(ii)

Squaring (i), we get

$y^{2/m}+y^{-2/m}+2=4x^2$ ...(iii)

Putting (iii) into (ii), we get $4m^2y^2=\left(\frac{dy}{dx}\right)^2.4(x^2-1)$

$\Rightarrow 2m^2y.\frac{dy}{dx}=\frac{2dy}{dx}.\frac{d^2y}{dx^2}(x^2-1)+2x\left(\frac{dy}{dx}\right)^2$

$\Rightarrow m^2y=(x^2-1)\frac{d^2y}{dx^2}+\frac{xdy}{dx}$

$\Rightarrow \frac{(x^2-1)y''+xy'}{y}=m^2$

4. Given $g(x)\ \ f\ \ (x)$

$\therefore f(f^{-1}(x))=x$ $\quad\Rightarrow f(g(x))=x$

$\Rightarrow f'(g(x)).g'(x)=1$

$\Rightarrow f'(g(x))=\frac{1}{g'(x)}$ or $g'(x)=\frac{1}{f'(g(x))}$ ...(1)

Now $e^{f(x)}=\ln x$ $\quad\Rightarrow e^{f(x)}.f'(x)=\frac{1}{x}$

$\Rightarrow f'(x)=\frac{1}{xe^{f(x)}}$ $\quad\Rightarrow \frac{1}{f'(x)}=xe^{f(x)}=x\ln x$

$\Rightarrow g'(x)=\frac{1}{f'(g(x))}=g(x)\ln g(x)$ ...(2)

Now $x = e^{e^{f(x)}} = e^{e^y}$

$\Rightarrow$ $g(x) = e^{e^x}$

$\Rightarrow$ $g'(x) = e^{e^x}.\ln e^{e^x} = e^{e^x}.e^x = e^{(e^x+x)}$

5. $f(x) = ex + x \Rightarrow y = ex + x$

Here f is one-one $\Rightarrow f^{-1}(f(\ln 3)) = \ln 3$

Thus to find $\frac{d}{dx}(f^{-1}(x))$ at $x=\ln 3$ i.e., $\frac{1}{f'(f\ln(3))} = \frac{1}{f'(\ln 3)}$

$\Rightarrow \frac{d}{dx}(f^{-1}(x)) = \frac{1}{(e^{\ln 3}+1)} = \frac{1}{4}$

TEXTUAL EXERCISE–6: (SUBJECTIVE)

2. (a) $x^3 + ax^2 y + bxy^2 + y^2 = 0$

Differentiating both side, we get $3x^2 + 2axy + ax^2 \frac{dy}{dx} + by^2 + bx\, 2y \frac{dy}{dx} + 2y \frac{dy}{dx} = 0$

$\Rightarrow 3x^2 + 2axy + by^2 + \frac{dy}{dx}(ax^2 + 2bxy + 2y) = 0$

$\Rightarrow \frac{dy}{dx} = \frac{-(3x^2+2axy+by^2)}{(ax^2+2bxy+2y)}$

(b) sin(xy) + cos (xy) = tan(x + y)

Differentiating both side, we get

$\cos xy\left(x\frac{dy}{dx}+y\right) - \sin(xy)\left(x\frac{dy}{dx}+y\right) = \sec^2(x+y)$

(1 + dy/dx)

Arranging terms & simplifying, we get

$\frac{dy}{dx} = \frac{-[y\cos^2(x+y)\{\cos(xy)-\sin(xy)\}-1]}{[x\cos^2(x+y)\{\cos xy-\sin(xy)\}-1]}$

3. (a) $2x + 2y = 2^x \cdot 2^y$

Differentiating the entire equation, we get $2^x \ell n\, 2 + 2^y\, y'\, \ell n\, 2 = 2^x \ell n 2.\, 2y + 2^x.2^y\, y' \ell n\, 2$

$\Rightarrow y'(2^y \ell n\, 2 - 2x + y\, \ell n\, 2) = 2^x \ell n\, 2.\, 2y - 2^x \ell n\, 2$

$\Rightarrow \frac{dy}{dx} = \frac{2^{x+y}\ell n2 - 2^x \ell n2}{2^y \ell n2 - 2^{x+y}\ell n2} = \frac{2^x.2^y - 2^x}{2^y - 2^x.2^y} = \frac{2^x(2^y-1)}{2^y(1-2^x)}$

$= 2^{x-y}\frac{(2^y-1)}{(1-2^x)}$

(b) y sin x – cos (x – y) = 0

Differentiating on both sides, we get $y \cos x + y' \sin x + \sin(x-y)(1 - dy/dx) = 0$

$\Rightarrow$ y cos x + sin (x – y) + y′ sin x – sin (x – y) y′ = 0

$\Rightarrow y' = \frac{y\cos x + \sin(x-y)}{\sin(x-y) - \sin x}$

4. $y\sqrt{1-x^2} + x\sqrt{1-y^2} = 1$

$\Rightarrow y\left(\frac{1}{2\sqrt{1-x^2}}(-2x)\right) + \sqrt{1-x^2}.y' + x\left(\frac{-y.y'}{\sqrt{1-y^2}}\right) + \sqrt{1-y^2} = 0$

$\Rightarrow \frac{-xy}{\sqrt{1-x^2}} + \sqrt{1-y^2} + \left(\sqrt{1-x^2} - \frac{xy}{\sqrt{1-y^2}}\right)y' = 0$

$\Rightarrow y' = \frac{-\left(-xy+\sqrt{1-x^2}\sqrt{1-y^2}\right)}{\left(\sqrt{1-x^2}.\sqrt{1-y^2}-xy\right)}.\frac{\sqrt{1-y^2}}{\sqrt{1-x^2}} = \frac{-\sqrt{1-y^2}}{\sqrt{1-x^2}}$

5. $y = x + \sqrt{x + \sqrt{x + \sqrt{x + ...\infty}}}$

$\Rightarrow y = x + \sqrt{y} \quad \Rightarrow \frac{dy}{dx} = 1 + \frac{1}{2\sqrt{y}}.\frac{dy}{dx}$

$\Rightarrow \frac{dy}{dx}\left(1 - \frac{1}{2\sqrt{y}}\right) = 1 \quad \Rightarrow \frac{dy}{dx} = \frac{2\sqrt{y}}{2\sqrt{y}-1}$

6. $xe^{xy} - y = \sin^2 x$ ...(i)

By (i), we get $x\left(e^{xy}\left(y + x\frac{dy}{dx}\right)\right) + e^{xy} - \frac{dy}{dx} = 2 \sin x.\cos x$

$\Rightarrow xye^{xy} + x2^{exy}.\frac{dy}{dx} + e^{xy} - \frac{dy}{dx} = \sin 2x$

$\Rightarrow \frac{dy}{dx}(x^2e^{xy} - 1) = \sin 2x - e^{xy} - xye^{xy}$

$\Rightarrow \frac{dy}{dx} = \frac{\sin 2x - e^{xy} - xye^{xy}}{(x^2e^{xy}-1)}$

$\Rightarrow \left.\frac{dy}{dx}\right|_{x=0} = 1$

7. (a) $x^p.\, y^q = (x + y)^{p+q}$

$\Rightarrow x^p.\, q.\, y^{q-1}.\, y' + yq.\, p.x^{p-1} = (p + q)(x + y)^{p+q-1}.(1 + y')$

$\Rightarrow y'(q.\, x^p.\, y^{q-1} - (p + q)(x + y)^{p+q-1}) = (p + q)(x + y)^{p+q-1} - p.\, x^{p-1}.\, y^q$

$\Rightarrow y' = \left[\frac{\frac{(p+q)(x^p.y^q)}{(x+y)} - p.x^{p-1}.y^q}{qx^p.y^{q-1} - \frac{(p+q)x^p.y^p}{(x+y)}}\right]$

$= x^{p-1}.y^q\left[\frac{(p+q)x - p(x+y)}{x^py^{q-1}(q(x+y)-y(p+q))}\right]$

$= \frac{x}{y}\left[\frac{qx-py}{qx-py}\right] = \frac{y}{x}$

(b) $y = x^{y^x}$

$\Rightarrow \ln y = y^x.\ln x$ ...(1)

$\Rightarrow \frac{1}{y}\frac{dy}{dx} = y^x.\frac{1}{x} + \ln x.\frac{d}{dx}(y^x)$ ...(2)

Let $u = y^x$

$\Rightarrow \ln u = x \ln y \quad \Rightarrow \frac{1}{u}\frac{du}{dx} = x.\frac{1}{y}y' + \ln y$

$\Rightarrow \frac{dy}{dx} = y^x\left[\frac{x}{y}.y' + \ln y\right]$ ...(3)

∴ From (3) and (2), we get

$$\frac{dy}{dx}=y\left[\frac{y^3}{x}+\ln x.y^x\left[\frac{x}{y}y'+\ln y\right]\right]$$

$$\Rightarrow \frac{dy}{dx}=\frac{y^{x+1}}{x}+y^{x+1}.\ln x.\frac{x}{y}.\frac{dy}{dx}+y^{x+1}.\ln x.\ln y$$

$$\Rightarrow \frac{dy}{dx}(1-xy^x\ln x)=y^{x+1}.\ln x.\ln y+\frac{y^{x+1}}{x}$$

$$\Rightarrow \frac{dy}{dx}=\frac{y^{x+1}.(x\ln x\ln y+1)}{x(1-xy^x\ln x)}=\frac{y^x\ln x.y}{x\ln x}\left(\frac{1+x\ln x\ln y}{1-x\ln y}\right)$$

$$=\frac{y\ln y}{x\ln x}\left(\frac{1+x\ln x\ln y}{1-x\ln y}\right)\text{(using (1))}$$

8. $x^3+y^3-3axy=0$

Differentiating the whole, we get $3x^2+3y^2\frac{dy}{dx}-3ay-3ax\frac{dy}{dx}=0$

$$\Rightarrow \frac{dy}{dx}(3y^2-3ax)=3ay-3x^2$$

$$\Rightarrow \frac{dy}{dx}=\left(\frac{3ay-3x^2}{3y^2-3ax}\right)$$

$$\Rightarrow \frac{dy}{dx}=\frac{ay-x^2}{y^2-ax}\text{ or }\frac{x^2-ay}{ax-y^2}$$

9. $y=\ln(x^{e^x}.a^y)^{y^x}$

$$\Rightarrow \ln y=y^x\ln(x^{e^x}.a^y)$$

$$\Rightarrow y=y^x[\ln x^{e^x}+\ln a^y]$$

$$\Rightarrow y=y^x[e^x\ln x+y\ln a]$$

$$\Rightarrow y=e^x.y^x.\ln x+(\ln a).y^{x+1} \quad \text{...(1)}$$

$$\Rightarrow \frac{dy}{dx}=y^x\ln xe^x+e^x\ln x.\frac{d}{dx}(y^x)+e^x.y^x.\frac{1}{x}+\ln a\frac{d}{dx}(y^{x+1}) \quad \text{...(2)}$$

Let $u=y^x$

$\Rightarrow \ln u=x\ln y$

$$\Rightarrow \frac{1}{u}\frac{du}{dx}=\frac{x}{y}\frac{dy}{dx}+\ln y$$

$$\Rightarrow \frac{du}{dx}=y^x\left[\frac{x}{y}\frac{dy}{dx}+\ln y\right] \quad \text{...(3)}$$

and $v=yx+{}^1$

$$\text{Similarly }\frac{dv}{dx}=y^{x+1}\left(\frac{x+1}{y}.\frac{dy}{dx}+\ln y\right) \quad \text{...(4)}$$

∴ From (1),

$$\frac{dy}{dx}=y^xe^x.\ln x+\frac{e^x.y^x}{x}+e^x$$

$$\ln x.y^x\left[\frac{x}{y}\frac{dy}{dx}+\ln y\right]+\ln a.y^{x+1}\left[\frac{x+1}{y}\frac{dy}{dx}+\ln y\right]$$

$$\Rightarrow \frac{dy}{dx}(1-xy^{x-1}e^x\ln x-(x+1)y^x\ln a)=y^{x+1}$$

$$\ln a\ln y+e^x\ln x.y^x.\ln y+y^xe^x\ln x+\frac{e^xy^x}{x}$$

$$\Rightarrow \frac{dy}{dx}=\frac{y^x(y\ln a+e^x\ln x)\ln y+y^xe^x\ln x+\frac{e^xy^x}{x}}{1-xy^{x-1}e^x\ln x-y^x(x+1)\ln a}$$

$$=\frac{y\ln y+y^x.e^x\ln x+\frac{e^xy^x}{x}}{1-xy^{x-1}.e^x\ln x-y^x(x+1)\ln a}$$

$$=\frac{y[xy\ln y+y^xe^xx\ln x+e^xy^x]}{x[y-xy^xe^x\ln x-y.y^x(x+1)\ln a]}$$

$$=\frac{y[xy\ln y+y^xe^x\ln x+e^xy^x]}{x[y-x(y^xe^x\ln x+y^{x+1}.\ln a)-y^{n+1}\ln a]}$$

$$=\frac{y[xy\ln y+y^xe^x\ln x+e^xy^x]}{x[y-xy-y^{x+1}.\ln a]}$$

$$=\frac{[xy\ln y+y^xe^x\ln x+e^xy^x]}{x[1-x-y^x.\ln a]}$$

10. $x^4+7x^2y^2+9y^4=24xy^3$

Dividing the whole equation by

x^4, we get $1+7\left(\frac{y}{x}\right)^2+9\left(\frac{y}{x}\right)^4-24\left(\frac{y}{x}\right)^3=0$

Let $y/x=z$

$\Rightarrow 1+7z^2+9z^4-24z^3=0$

Where $z=y/x$

Let us differentiate it $(14z+36z^3-72z^2)(y/x)'=0$

$$\Rightarrow (14+36z^2-72z)\left(\frac{xy'-y}{x^2}\right)=0$$

$$\Rightarrow 14+36z2-72z=0\text{ or }\frac{xy'-y}{x^2}=0$$

$$\therefore \frac{xy'-y}{x^2}=0 \quad \Rightarrow xy'-y=0$$

$\Rightarrow y'=dy/dx=y/x$

11. Given $(a-b\cos y)(a+b\cos x)=a^2-b^2$

$$\Rightarrow (a-b\cos y)=\frac{a^2-b^2}{a+b\cos x}$$

$$\Rightarrow b\cos y=a-\frac{(a^2-b^2)}{a+b\cos x}$$

$$\Rightarrow b\cos y=\frac{a^2+ab\cos x-a^2+b^2}{a+b\cos x}$$

$$\Rightarrow b\cos y=\frac{ab\cos x+b^2}{a+b\cos x}$$

$$\Rightarrow \cos y=\frac{a\cos x+b}{a+b\cos x} \quad \text{...(i)}$$

Differentiating both sides, we get

$$-\sin y.\frac{dy}{dx}=\frac{(a+b\cos x)(-a\sin x)+(a\cos x+b)(b\sin x)}{(a+b\cos x)^2}$$

$$\Rightarrow \quad -\sin y\frac{dy}{dx}=\sin x\left(\frac{-a^2-ab\cos x+ab\cos x+b^2}{(a+b\cos x)^2}\right)$$

$$\Rightarrow \quad -\sin y\frac{dy}{dx}=\sin x\left(\frac{b^2-a^2}{(a+b\cos x)^2}\right)$$

$$\Rightarrow \quad \frac{dy}{dx}=\frac{\sin x}{\sin y}\left(\frac{a^2-b^2}{(a+b\cos x)^2}\right) \quad \text{...(ii)}$$

Consider eq^n (i), we get $\cos^2 y=\frac{a^2\cos^2 x+b^2+2ab\cos x}{a^2+b^2\cos^2 x+2ab\cos x}$

$$\Rightarrow \quad 1-\cos^2 y=\frac{a^2-b^2+\cos^2 x(b^2-a^2)}{(a+b\cos x)}$$

$$\Rightarrow \quad \sin^2 y=\frac{(a^2-b^2)(\sin^2 x)}{(a+b\cos x)^2}$$

$$\Rightarrow \quad \frac{\sin x}{\sin y}=\frac{a+b\cos x}{\sqrt{a^2-b^2}} \quad \text{...(iii)}$$

Putting (iii) in (ii), we get $\frac{dy}{dx}=\frac{\sqrt{a^2-b^2}}{a+b\cos x}$

12. $x+y=e^{x-y}$

$\Rightarrow$ $1+y'=e^{x-y}.(1-y')$

$\Rightarrow$ $1+y'=(x+y)(1-y')$ ...(1)

$\Rightarrow$ $1+y'=x+y-xy'-yy'$

$\Rightarrow$ $y'=1+y'-xy'-y'-yy'-(y')^2$

$\Rightarrow$ $y'(1+x+y)=1-(y')^2$

$\Rightarrow$ $y''\frac{1-(y')^2}{1+x+y}$ ...(2)

From (1), $y'(1+x+y)=x+y-1$

$\Rightarrow$ $y'=(x+y-1)/(1+x+y)$ ...(3)

Using (3) in (2), we get $y''=\frac{4(x+y)}{(1+x+y)^3}$

TEXTUAL EXERCISE– 6: (OBJECTIVE)

1. (a) $x^3+3x^2y-6xy^2+2y^3=0$

Differentiating once, we get $3x^2+6xy+$

$$3x^2\frac{dy}{dx}-6y^2-2.6xy\frac{dy}{dx}+6y^2\frac{dy}{dx}=0$$

$$\Rightarrow \quad 3x^2-6y^2+6xy+3x^2\frac{dy}{dx}-12xy\,y'+6y^2\frac{dy}{dx}=0$$

$\Rightarrow$ $3x^2-6y^2+6xy+(3x^2+6y^2-12xy)\,y'=0$ ...(i)

Putting $x=y=1$

$\Rightarrow$ $y'=1$

2. (b) $x^2y+y^3=2$

Differentiating, we get $2xy+x^2\frac{dy}{dx}+3y^2\frac{dy}{dx}=0$ ...(i)

$$\Rightarrow \quad \frac{dy}{dx}(x^2+3y^2)=-2xy$$

$$\Rightarrow \quad \frac{dy}{dx}=\frac{-2xy}{x^2+3y^2}$$

At (1, 1), $\frac{dy}{dx}=\frac{-2}{1+3}=-\frac{1}{2}$

Differentiating (i), we get $2y+2x\frac{dy}{dx}+2x\frac{dy}{dx}+x^2\frac{d^2y}{dx^2}+$ $6y.\left(\frac{dy}{dx}\right)^2+3y^2\frac{d^2y}{dx^2}=0$

Put $x=1$, $y=1$, $\frac{dy}{dx}=-\frac{1}{2}$

$\Rightarrow$ $2-1-1+y''+\frac{6}{4}+3y''=0$

$\Rightarrow$ $\frac{6}{4}=-4y''$

$\Rightarrow$ $y''=-3/8$

3. (a) $y=\sqrt{\sin x+\sqrt{\sin x+\sqrt{\sin x+......\infty}}}$

Squaring both sides, we get $y^2=\sin x+y$

$\Rightarrow$ $y^2-y-\sin x=0$ $\quad\Rightarrow$ $2yy'-y'-\cos x=0$

$\Rightarrow$ $y'(2y-1)=\cos x$ $\quad\Rightarrow$ $y'=\frac{\cos x}{2y-1}$

4. (d) $\sin(x+y)=\log(x+y)$

Differentiating both sides, we get $\cos(x+y)$ $\left(1+\frac{dy}{dx}\right)=\frac{\left(1+\frac{dy}{dx}\right)}{x+y}$

which means $\left(1+\frac{dy}{dx}\right)\left(\cos(x+y)-\frac{1}{x+y}\right)=0$

$$\Rightarrow \quad \frac{dy}{dx}=-1$$

5. (c) $e^{x+y}=xy$

$\Rightarrow$ $e^{x+y}.(1+y')=xy'+y$ $\quad\Rightarrow$ $xy(1+y')=xy'+y$

$\Rightarrow$ $y'(xy-x)=y-xy$ $\quad\Rightarrow$ $y'=\frac{y(1-x)}{x(y-1)}$

$$\Rightarrow \quad y''=\frac{x(y-1)[y'-y-xy']-y(1-x)[xy'+y-1]}{x^2(y-1)^2}$$

Solving after substituting value of y' in above expression for y', we get $y''=\frac{-y[(x-1)^2+(y-1)^2]}{x^2(y-1)^3}$

6. (a), (d) $ax^2+2hxy+by^2=0$

Differentiating, we get $2ax+2hy+2hx\frac{dy}{dx}+2by\frac{dy}{dx}=0$

$$\Rightarrow \quad \frac{dy}{dx}(2hx+2by)=-2ax-2hy$$

$\Rightarrow$ $\frac{dy}{dx}=\frac{-ax-hy}{hx+by}$ $\quad\Rightarrow$ Option (d) is correct.

Which same as $\frac{y}{x}=\frac{-ax-hy}{hx+by}$

7. (c) $\sin^{-1}\left(\frac{x^2-y^2}{x^2+y^2}\right) = \log a$

Differentiating both sides, we get

$$\frac{1}{\sqrt{1-\left(\frac{x^2-y^2}{x^2+y^2}\right)^2}}\left(\frac{x^2-y^2}{x^2+y^2}\right)' = 0$$

$$\Rightarrow \frac{d}{dx}\left(\frac{x^2-y^2}{x^2+y^2}\right) =$$

$$\frac{(x^2+y^2)\left(2x-2y\frac{dy}{dx}\right)-(x^2-y^2)\left(2x+2y\frac{dy}{dx}\right)}{(x^2+y^2)^2} = 0$$

$$\Rightarrow (x^2+y^2)\left(x-y\frac{dy}{dx}\right) = (x^2-y^2)\left(x+y\frac{dy}{dx}\right)$$

$$\Rightarrow x^3 - x^2y\frac{dy}{dx} + y^2x - y^3\frac{dy}{dx} = x^3 + x^2y\frac{dy}{dx} - y^2x - y^3\frac{dy}{dx}$$

$$\Rightarrow 2y^2x = 2x^2y\,(dy/dx) \Rightarrow \frac{dy}{dx} = \frac{y^2x}{x^2y} = \frac{y}{x}$$

8. (d) $y = \cfrac{x}{a+\cfrac{x}{b+\cfrac{x}{a+\ldots\infty}}}$

$$\Rightarrow y = \cfrac{x}{a+\cfrac{x}{b+y}}$$

$$\Rightarrow y = \frac{x(b+y)}{a(b+y)+x} \qquad \Rightarrow a(b+y)y + xy = x(b+y)$$

$$\Rightarrow a[by' + 2yy'] + y + xy' = b + y + xy'$$

$$\Rightarrow y'(ab + 2ay) = b$$

$$\Rightarrow y' \frac{b}{(ab+2ay)}$$

9. (a) $\ln(x + y) = 2xy$

Differentiating both sides, we get

$$\frac{1}{(x+y)}\left(1+\frac{dy}{dx}\right) = 2y + 2x\frac{dy}{dx}$$

$$\Rightarrow \frac{1}{x+y} + \frac{dy}{dx}\left(\frac{1}{x+y}\right) = 2y + 2x\frac{dy}{dx}$$

$$\Rightarrow \frac{dy}{dx}\left(\frac{1}{x+y} - 2x\right) = 2y - \frac{1}{x+y}$$

$$\Rightarrow \frac{dy}{dx} = \left(\frac{2y-\frac{1}{x+y}}{\frac{1}{x+y}-2x}\right)$$

$$\Rightarrow \frac{dy}{dx} = \frac{(2xy+2y^2-1)}{1-2x^2-2xy}$$

$$\Rightarrow \frac{dy}{dx} = \left(\frac{2xy+2y^2-1}{1-2x^2-2xy}\right)$$

At (0, 1)

$$\Rightarrow \frac{dy}{dx} = \left(\frac{0+2-1}{1-0-0}\right) = 1$$

10. (b) $\sin(xy) + \cos(xy) = 0$

$= \sin(xy) = -\cos(xy)$

Differentiating both sides, we get $\cos(xy)$

$$\left(y+x\frac{dy}{dx}\right) = \sin(xy)\left(y+x\frac{dy}{dx}\right)$$

$$\Rightarrow y + x\frac{dy}{dx} = 0$$

$$\Rightarrow dy/dx = -y/x$$

11. (b) $x\sqrt{1+y} + y\sqrt{1+x} = 0$

$$\Rightarrow x\sqrt{1+y} = -y\sqrt{1+x}$$

Squaring both sides, we get $x^2(1 + y) = y^2(1 + x)$

$\Rightarrow x^2 - y^2 + x^2y - xy^2 = 0$

$\Rightarrow (x + y)(x - y) + xy(x - y) = 0$

$\Rightarrow (x - y)(x + y + xy) = 0$

Either $x = y$ or $x + y + xy = 0$

$x \neq y$

$\Rightarrow x + y + xy = 0$

$\Rightarrow y = -x/(1+x)$

$\Rightarrow dy/dx = -1/(1 + x)^2$

TEXTUAL EXERCISE-7: (SUBJECTIVE)

1. (a) $x = a(\cos t + t\sin t)$ ...(i)

$y = a(\sin t - t\cos t)$ ...(ii)

By (i), we get $\frac{dx}{dt} = (-a\sin t + a\sin t + at(\cos t))$

$= (at\cos t)$ ...(iii)

Differentiating (ii), we get $\frac{dy}{dt} = a\cos t - a\cos t + at\sin$

$t = at\sin t$

$$\Rightarrow \frac{dy}{dx} = \frac{dy/dt}{dx/dt} = \tan t$$

(b) $x = a\frac{1-t^2}{1+t^2};\ y = b\frac{2t}{1+t^2}$

$$\frac{dx}{dt} = \frac{a\left[(1+t^2)(-2t)-(1-t^2)(2t)\right]}{(1+t^2)^2}$$

$$= a\left(\frac{-2t-2t^3-(2t-2t^3)}{(1+t^2)^2}\right)$$

$$= a\left(\frac{-2t-2t^3-2t+2t^3}{(1+t^2)^2}\right) = a\left(\frac{-4t}{(1+t^2)^2}\right)$$

Similarly $\frac{dy}{dt} = \frac{b\left[(1+t^2)2-2(2-t)t\right]}{(1+t^2)^2} = \frac{b(2+2t^2-4t^2)}{(1+t^2)^2}$

$= \frac{b(2-2t^2)}{(1+t^2)^2}$

$\Rightarrow \frac{dy}{dx} = \frac{\frac{dy}{dt}}{\frac{dx}{dt}} = \frac{2b(1-t^2)}{-4ta} = \frac{b(t^2-1)}{2at}$

(c) $x = \frac{2at^2}{1+t^2}; y = \frac{2at^3}{1+t^2}$

$\Rightarrow \frac{dx}{dt} = \frac{(1+t^2)(4at)-(2at^2)(2t)}{(1+t^2)^2} = \left(\frac{4at+4at^3-4at^3}{(1+t^2)^2}\right)$

$= \frac{4at}{(1+t^2)^2}$

$\Rightarrow \frac{dy}{dt} = \frac{(1+t^2)6at^2-2at^3(2t)}{(1+t^2)^2} = \frac{6at^2+6at^4-4at^4}{(1+t^2)^2}$

$= \frac{6at^2+2at^4}{(1+t^2)^2} = \frac{2at^2(3+t^2)}{(1+t^2)^2}$

$\Rightarrow \frac{dy}{dx} = \frac{t(3+t^2)}{2}$

(d) $x = a\sqrt{\frac{t^2-1}{t^2+1}}; y = at\sqrt{\frac{t^2-1}{t^2+1}} = t_x$

$\Rightarrow \frac{dx}{dt} = \frac{a}{2}\left(\sqrt{\frac{t^2+1}{t^2-1}}\right)\left(\frac{(t^2+1)(2t)-(t^2-1)(2t)}{(t^2+1)^2}\right)$

$= \frac{a}{2}\sqrt{\frac{t^2+1}{t^2-1}}\left(\frac{2t^3+2t-2t^3+2t}{(t^2+1)^2}\right) = \frac{a}{2}\sqrt{\frac{t^2+1}{t^2-1}}\left(\frac{4t}{(t^2+1)^2}\right)$

$= \frac{2at}{\sqrt{t^2-1}(t^2+1)^{3/2}}$

Now, $\frac{dy}{dt} = \frac{tdx}{dt} + x = \frac{2at^2}{\sqrt{t^2-1}(t^2+1)^{3/2}} + a\sqrt{\frac{t^2-1}{t^2+1}}$

$= \frac{2at^2+(t^2-1)(t^2+1)a}{\sqrt{t^2-1}(t^2+1)^{3/2}}$

$\Rightarrow \frac{dy}{dt} = \frac{at^4+2at^2-a}{\sqrt{(t^2-1)}\,(t^2+1)^{3/2}}$

$\Rightarrow \frac{at^4+2at^2-a}{2at} = \frac{t^4+2t^2-1}{2t}$

(e) $x = a\left(\cos t + \log\tan\frac{t}{2}\right)$

$y = a\sin t$

$\Rightarrow \frac{dy}{dt} = a\cos t$ and $\frac{dx}{dt} = -a\sin t + \frac{a}{\tan\frac{t}{2}}.\sec^2\left(\frac{t}{2}\right)\left(\frac{1}{2}\right)$

$= -a\sin t + \frac{a}{\sin t}$

$\Rightarrow \frac{dy}{dx} = \frac{dy/dt}{dx/dt} \qquad \Rightarrow \frac{dy}{dx} = \frac{a\cos t}{-a\sin t + \frac{a}{\sin t}}$

$\Rightarrow \frac{dy}{dx} = \frac{\cos t.\sin t}{-(-1+\sin^2 t)} = \tan t$

(f) $x = \sin\sqrt{\cos 2t}; y = \cos\sqrt{\cos 2t}$

$\Rightarrow \frac{dy}{dt} = \frac{\sin\left(\sqrt{\cos 2t}\right)}{2\sqrt{\cos 2t}}.\sin 2t.2 = \frac{\sin 2t\sin\left(\sqrt{\cos 2t}\right)}{\sqrt{\cos 2t}}$ and

$\frac{dx}{dt} = \frac{\cos\sqrt{\cos 2t}}{2\sqrt{\cos 2t}}(-\sin 2t)\,2 = \frac{-\sin 2t.\cos\sqrt{\cos 2t}}{\sqrt{\cos 2t}}$

$\therefore \frac{dy}{dx} = \frac{\frac{\sin 2t\sin\left(\sqrt{\cos 2t}\right)}{\sqrt{\cos 2t}}}{\frac{-\sin 2t\cos\sqrt{\cos 2t}}{\sqrt{\cos 2t}}} = \frac{-\sin\left(\sqrt{\cos 2t}\right)}{\cos\left(\sqrt{\cos 2t}\right)}$

$= -\tan\left(\sqrt{\cos 2t}\right)$

2. $x = t + \frac{1}{t}; y = t - \frac{1}{t}$

$\Rightarrow \frac{dx}{dt} = 1 - \frac{1}{t^2} \;\&\; \frac{dy}{dt} = 1 + \frac{1}{t^2}$

$\Rightarrow \frac{dy}{dx} = \frac{t^2+1}{t^2-1} = \frac{t+\frac{1}{t}}{t-\frac{1}{t}} = \frac{x}{y}$

3. (a) $x = a\cos^3 t; y = b\sin^2 t$

$\Rightarrow \frac{dx}{dt} = 3a\cos^2 t(-\sin t)$ and $\frac{dy}{dt} = 2b\sin t(\cos t)$

$\Rightarrow \frac{dy}{dx} = \frac{dy/dt}{dx/dt} = \frac{2b\sin t.\cos t}{-3a\cos^2 t\sin t} = \frac{-2b}{3a\cos t}$

$= \left(\frac{-2}{3}\sec t\right)\frac{b}{a}$

(b) $x = e^t\cos t; y = e^t\sin t$

$\Rightarrow \frac{dx}{dt} = -e^t\sin t + et\cos t$ and $\frac{dy}{dt} = e^t\cos t + et\sin t$

$\Rightarrow \frac{dy}{dx} = \frac{\cos t+\sin t}{\cos t-\sin t}$

4. $x = \frac{\sin^3 t}{\sqrt{\cos 2t}}, y = \frac{\cos^3 t}{\sqrt{\cos 2t}}$

$\Rightarrow \frac{dx}{dt} = \frac{\sqrt{\cos 2t}\left(3\sin^2 t.\cos t\right) + \frac{\sin^3 t.2\sin 2t}{2\sqrt{\cos 2t}}}{\cos 2t}$

and $\frac{dy}{dt} = \frac{-\sqrt{\cos 2t}\,.3\cos^2 t.\sin t + \frac{\cos^3 t.\sin 2t}{\sqrt{\cos 2t}}}{\cos 2t}$

$\Rightarrow \frac{dy}{dx} = \frac{-3\cos^2 t.\sin t\sqrt{\cos 2t} + \frac{\cos^3 t}{\sqrt{\cos 2t}}.\sin 2t}{\sqrt{\cos 2t}\left(3\sin^2 t\cos t\right) + \frac{\sin^3 t}{\sqrt{\cos 2t}}\sin 2t}$

$= \frac{-3\sin t\cos^2 t\cos 2t + \cos^3 t\sin 2t}{3\sin^2 t\cos t\cos 2t + \sin^3 t\sin 2t}$

At t = π/6, $\frac{dy}{dx} = \frac{-3\left(\frac{1}{2}\right)\left(\frac{3}{4}\right)\left(\frac{1}{2}\right) + \left(\frac{3\sqrt{3}}{8}\right)\left(\frac{\sqrt{3}}{2}\right)}{3\left(\frac{1}{2}\right)^2\left(\frac{\sqrt{3}}{2}\right)\left(\frac{1}{2}\right) + \left(\frac{1}{2}\right)^3\left(\frac{\sqrt{3}}{2}\right)} = 0$

5. $u = \sin^{-1} x \quad \Rightarrow \quad \frac{du}{dx} = \frac{1}{\sqrt{1-x^2}}$

$v = x^3 \quad \Rightarrow \quad \frac{dv}{dx} = 3x^2$

$\Rightarrow \frac{dv}{du} = 3x^2\sqrt{1-x^2}$

Put $x = v^{1/3}$

$\Rightarrow \frac{dv}{du} = 3.v^{2/3}\sqrt{1-v^{2/3}} = 3\sqrt{v^{4/3}\left(1-v^{2/3}\right)} = 3\sqrt{v\left(v^{1/3}-v\right)}$

6. $x = a(\cos t + t\sin t)$, $y = a(\sin t - t\cos t)$

$\Rightarrow \frac{dx}{dt} = -a\sin t + at\cos t + a\sin t = at\cos t \quad \ldots(i)$

And $\frac{dy}{dx} = a\cos t + at\sin t - a\cos t = at\sin t \quad \ldots(ii)$

$\therefore \frac{dy}{dx} = \frac{at\sin t}{at\cos t} = \tan t \Rightarrow \frac{d^2y}{dx^2} = \sec^2 t$

$\Rightarrow \left.\frac{d^2y}{dx^2}\right|_{t=\frac{\pi}{4}} = \sec^2\frac{\pi}{4} = 2$

TEXTUAL EXERCISE–7: (OBJECTIVE)

1. **(d)** $x = 2\sin t - \sin 2t$, $y = 2\cos t - \cos 2t$

$\Rightarrow \frac{dx}{dt} = 2\cos t - 2\cos 2t = \left(4\sin\frac{3t}{2}.\sin\frac{t}{2}\right)$ and $\frac{dy}{dt} = -$
$2\sin t + 2\sin 2t$

$\Rightarrow \frac{dy}{dx} = \frac{dy/dt}{dx/dt} = \frac{-\sin t + \sin 2t}{\cos t - \cos 2t}$

$= \frac{2\cos\left(\frac{3t}{2}\right)\sin\left(\frac{t}{2}\right)}{2\sin\left(\frac{3t}{2}\right)\sin\left(\frac{t}{2}\right)} = \cot\left(\frac{3t}{2}\right)$

$\therefore \frac{d^2y}{dx^2} = \frac{d}{dx}\left(\frac{dy}{dx}\right) = \frac{d}{dx}\left(\cot\frac{3t}{2}\right) = \frac{d}{dt}\left(\cot\frac{3t}{2}\right).\frac{dt}{dx}$

$= -\frac{3}{2}\operatorname{cosec}^2\left(\frac{3t}{2}\right) \times \frac{1}{4\sin\frac{3t}{2}\sin\frac{t}{2}}$

$= -\frac{3}{8}\left(\frac{1}{\sin^3\left(\frac{3t}{2}\right).\sin\frac{t}{2}}\right)$

$\therefore \left(\frac{d^2y}{dx^2}\right)_{\pi/2} = \frac{\frac{-3}{8}}{\left(\frac{1}{\sqrt{2}}\right)^3.\left(\frac{1}{\sqrt{2}}\right)} = \frac{-3}{2}$

2. **(a), (b)** $y = \frac{\sqrt{1+t^2} - \sqrt{1-t^2}}{\sqrt{1+t^2} + \sqrt{1-t^2}}$

Let $t^2 = \cos 2\theta$; $2\theta \in \left[0, \frac{\pi}{2}\right]$

$\Rightarrow y = \frac{\sqrt{1+\cos 2\theta} - \sqrt{1-\cos 2\theta}}{\sqrt{1+\cos 2\theta} + \sqrt{1-\cos 2\theta}} = \frac{|\cos\theta| - |\sin\theta|}{|\cos\theta| + |\sin\theta|}$

$\Rightarrow y = \frac{1-\sin 2\theta}{\cos 2\theta} = \sec 2\theta - \tan 2\theta$

$\Rightarrow \frac{dy}{d\theta} = 2\sec 2\theta.\tan 2\theta - 2\sec^2 2\theta$

$= 2\sec 2\theta(\tan 2\theta - \sec 2\theta) \quad \ldots\ldots..(i)$

$x = \sqrt{1-t^4}$

$\Rightarrow x = \sqrt{1-\cos^2 2\theta} = \sin 2\theta$

$\Rightarrow \frac{dx}{d\theta} = 2\cos 2\theta$

$\Rightarrow \frac{dy}{dx} = \frac{2\sec 2\theta\left(\tan 2\theta - \sec 2\theta\right)}{2\cos 2\theta} = \frac{\tan 2\theta - \sec 2\theta}{\cos^2 2\theta}$

Also, $\tan 2 = \frac{\sin 2}{\cos 2} = \frac{\sqrt{1}}{}$ and $\sec 2\theta = 1/t^2$

$\Rightarrow \frac{dy}{dx} = \frac{\sqrt{1-\frac{t^4}{t^2}} - \frac{1}{t^2}}{t^4} = \frac{\sqrt{1-t^4}-1}{t^6} = \frac{-1}{t^2\left(1+\sqrt{1-t^4}\right)}$

3. **(b), (c)** $x = a[\cos t + \log\tan(t/2)]$ and $y = a\sin t$

$\Rightarrow \frac{dy}{dt} = \left[-a\sin t + \frac{a}{\tan\left(\frac{t}{2}\right)}.\sec^2\left(\frac{t}{2}\right)\frac{1}{2}\right]$

$= \left[-a\sin t + \frac{a\sec\left(\frac{t}{2}\right)}{\sin\left(\frac{t}{2}\right)}\frac{1}{2}\right] = \left[-a\sin t + \frac{a}{\sin t}\right]$

and $\frac{dy}{dt} = a\cos t$

$$\Rightarrow \frac{dy}{dx}=\left(\frac{a\cos t}{\frac{a}{\sin t}-a\sin t}\right) \Rightarrow \frac{dy}{dx}=\left(\frac{\cos t(\sin t)}{(1-\sin^2 t)}\right)=\tan t$$

$$\Rightarrow \frac{dy}{dx}=\tan t=\cot x=\pi/2 \text{ and } \frac{d^2y}{dx^2}=\frac{d}{dx}(\tan t)=\sec^2 t\frac{dt}{dx}$$

$$=\sec^2 t\left[\frac{\sin t}{a(\cos^2 t)}\right]=\frac{\sin t\sec^4 t}{a}$$

$$\Rightarrow \left(\frac{d^2y}{dx^2}\right)_{t=\frac{\pi}{4}}=\frac{\frac{1}{\sqrt{2}}(\sqrt{2})^4}{a}=\frac{2\sqrt{2}}{a}$$

4. (d) $x = a\cos^3\theta$ and $y = a\sin^3\theta$

$$\Rightarrow \frac{dx}{d\theta}=-3a\cos^2\theta\sin\theta \text{ and } \frac{dy}{d\theta}=3a\sin^2\theta.\cos\theta$$

$$\Rightarrow \frac{dy}{dx}=\frac{3a\sin^2\theta.\cos\theta}{-3a\cos^2\theta.\sin\theta}=\frac{-\sin\theta}{\cos\theta}=-\tan\theta$$

$$\Rightarrow \sqrt{1+\tan^2\theta}=|\sec\theta|$$

5. (b) $y=f(x)$

$x = t^5 - 5t^3 - 20t + 7,\ y = 4t^3 - 3t^2 - 18t + 3$

$$\Rightarrow \frac{dx}{dt}=5t^4-15t^2-20 \text{ and } \frac{dy}{dt}=12t^2-6t-18$$

$$\Rightarrow \frac{dy}{dx}=\frac{12t^2-6t-18}{5t^4-15t^2-20}$$

At $t = 1$;

$$\Rightarrow \frac{dy}{dx}=\frac{12-6-18}{5-35}=\frac{-12}{-30}=\frac{2}{5}$$

6. (a) $x = t^3 + t + 5$ and $y = \sin t$

$$\Rightarrow \frac{dx}{dt}=3t^2+1 \text{ and } \frac{dy}{dt}=\cos t \Rightarrow \frac{dy}{dx}=\frac{\cos t}{3t^2+1}$$

$$\Rightarrow \frac{d^2y}{dx^2}=\frac{d}{dx}\left(\frac{\cos t}{3t^2+1}\right)=\left(\frac{(3t^2+1)(-\sin t)-\cos t(6t)}{(3t^2+1)^2}\right)\frac{dt}{dx}$$

$$=\left[\frac{-(3t^2+1)\sin t-6t\cos t}{(3t^2+1)^2}\right].\frac{1}{(3t^2+1)}$$

$$=-\left[\frac{(3t^2+1)\sin t+6t\cos t}{(3t^2+1)^3}\right]$$

7. (c) $x=\frac{1+t}{t^3},\ y=\frac{3t+4t^2}{2t^3}$

$$\Rightarrow \frac{dx}{dt}=\frac{t^3-3t^2(1+t)}{t^6}=\frac{t^3-3t^2-3t^3}{t^6}=\frac{-3t^2-2t^3}{t^6}$$

$$\text{and } \frac{dy}{dt}=\frac{2t^2(4)-(3+4t)(4t)}{4t^4}=\frac{-(3+2t)(4t)}{4t^4}=\frac{-(3+2t)}{t^3}$$

$$\therefore \frac{dy}{dx}=\frac{-(3+2t)}{t^3}\times\frac{t^6}{-t^2(3+2t)}=t$$

$$\therefore x\left(\frac{dy}{dx}\right)^3-\left(\frac{dy}{dx}\right)=\left(\frac{1+t}{t^3}\right)(t)^3-t=1$$

TEXTUAL EXERCISE–8:(SUBJECTIVE)

1. $f(x)=\begin{vmatrix} x^3 & \sin x & \cos x \\ 6 & -1 & 0 \\ p & p^2 & p^3 \end{vmatrix}$

$f(x) = x^3(-p^3) - \sin x\,(6p^3) + \cos x\,(6p^2 + p)$

$\Rightarrow f(x) = -x^3p^3 - 6\sin x\, p^3 + 6p^2\cos x + p\cos x$

Differentiating once, we get $f'(x) = -3x^2 p^3 - 6\cos x\, p^3 - 6p^2\sin x - p\sin x$

$\Rightarrow f''(x) = -6xp^3 + 6\sin x\, p^3 - 6p^2\cos x - p\cos x$

$\Rightarrow f'''(x) = -6p^3 + 6\cos x\, p^3 + 6p^2\sin x + p\sin x = 0$ at $x = 0$

2. $y = \cos ax,\ y_1 = -a\sin ax,\ y_2 = -a^2\cos ax,\ y_3 = a^3\sin ax,\ y_4 = a^4\cos ax,\ y_5 = -a^5\sin ax,\ y_6 = -a^6\cos ax,\ y_7 = a^7\sin ax,\ y_8 = a^8\cos ax$

$$\Rightarrow \Delta=\begin{vmatrix} \cos ax & -a\sin ax & -a^2\cos ax \\ a^3\sin ax & a^4\cos ax & -a^5\sin ax \\ -a^6\cos ax & a^7\sin ax & a^8\cos ax \end{vmatrix}$$

$$=(\cos ax)a^{12}(1)+(a\sin ax)a^{11}(0)-(a^2\cos ax)(a^{10})(1)$$

$$=a^{12}\cos ax-a^{12}\cos ax=0$$

3. $f(x)=\begin{vmatrix} 2x & x^2 & 3 \\ x^2 & x & 1 \\ 2 & 1 & x \end{vmatrix}$

Let $f(x) = A + Bx + Cx^2 + Dx^3 + Ex^4 + Fx^5$

$\Rightarrow$ Coefficient of x in $f(x) = B$

$\Rightarrow f'(x) = B + 2Cx + 3Dx^2 + 4Ex^3 + 5Fx^4$

$\Rightarrow f'(0) = B$

$\Rightarrow f'(x) = 2x(x^2 - 1) - x^2(x^3 - 2) + 3(x^2 - 2x)$

$\Rightarrow f(x) = (2x^3 - 2x - x^5 + 2x^2 + 2x^2 + 3x^2 - 6x) = (-x^5 + 2x^3 + 5x^2 - 8x)$

$\Rightarrow f'(x) = -5x^4 + 6x^2 + 10x - 8$

$\Rightarrow f'(0) = -8 = B$

4. Given that p(x), q(x), r(x) are polynomials of degree not greater than 3.

$p_4(x) = 0;\ q_4(x) = 0;\ r_4(x) = 0$

$y_r = r^{th}$ derivative of y.

Let $p(x) = a_0x^3 + a_1x^2 + a_2x + a_3;\ q(x) = b_0x^3 + b_1x^2 + b_2x + b_3;\ r(x) = c_0x^3 + c_1x^2 + c_2x + c_3$

Let $f(x)=\begin{vmatrix} p(x) & q(x) & r(x) \\ p'(x) & q'(x) & r'(x) \\ p''(x) & q''(x) & r''(x) \end{vmatrix}$

$$\Rightarrow f'(x)=\begin{vmatrix} p'(x) & q'(x) & r'(x) \\ p'(x) & q'(x) & r'(x) \\ p''(x) & q''(x) & r''(x) \end{vmatrix}+\begin{vmatrix} p(x) & q(x) & r(x) \\ p''(x) & q''(x) & r''(x) \\ p''(x) & q''(x) & r''(x) \end{vmatrix}$$

$$+\begin{vmatrix} p(x) & q(x) & r(x) \\ p'(x) & q'(x) & r'(x) \\ p'''(x) & q'''(x) & r'''(x) \end{vmatrix}=\begin{vmatrix} p(x) & q(x) & r(x) \\ p'(x) & q'(x) & r'(x) \\ p'''(x) & q'''(x) & r'''(x) \end{vmatrix}$$

$$\Rightarrow f''(x) = \begin{vmatrix} p(x) & q(x) & r(x) \\ p''(x) & q''(x) & r''(x) \\ p'''(x) & q'''(x) & r'''(x) \end{vmatrix}$$

$(\because p^{iv}(x) = q^{iv}(x) = r^{iv}(x) = 0)$

$$\Rightarrow f'''(x) = \begin{vmatrix} p'(x) & q'(x) & r'(x) \\ p''(x) & q''(x) & r''(x) \\ p'''(x) & q'''(x) & r'''(x) \end{vmatrix}$$

$\Rightarrow f''''(x) = 0$

$\Rightarrow f(x)$ is of degree not greater than 3

5. $f(x) = \begin{vmatrix} e^x & \sin x \\ \cos x & \log(1+x^2) \end{vmatrix} = A + Bx + Cx^2 + \ldots$ and $f'(x) = B + 2cx + \ldots$

$\Rightarrow A = f(0)$ and $B = f'(0)$

$\Rightarrow A = \begin{vmatrix} 1 & 0 \\ 1 & 0 \end{vmatrix} = 0 \quad \Rightarrow A = 0$

And $f'(x) = \begin{vmatrix} e^x & \cos x \\ \cos x & \log(1+x^2) \end{vmatrix} + \begin{vmatrix} e^x & \sin x \\ -\sin x & \dfrac{2x}{1+x^2} \end{vmatrix}$

$\Rightarrow f'(0) = \begin{vmatrix} 1 & 1 \\ 1 & 0 \end{vmatrix} + \begin{vmatrix} 1 & 0 \\ 0 & 0 \end{vmatrix} = -1 \Rightarrow B = -1$

6. $\Delta_1 = \begin{vmatrix} x & b & b \\ a & x & b \\ a & a & x \end{vmatrix}$ and $\Delta_2 = \begin{vmatrix} x & b \\ a & x \end{vmatrix} = (x^2 - ab)$

$$\Rightarrow \frac{d}{dx}\Delta_1 = \begin{vmatrix} 1 & 0 & 0 \\ a & x & b \\ a & a & x \end{vmatrix} + \begin{vmatrix} x & b & b \\ 0 & 1 & 0 \\ a & a & x \end{vmatrix} + \begin{vmatrix} x & b & b \\ a & x & b \\ 0 & 0 & 1 \end{vmatrix}$$

$= (x^2 - ab) + (x^2 - ab) + (x^2 - ab) = 3(x^2 - ab)$

$= 3\,\Delta_1$

7. $\Delta = \begin{vmatrix} x & 1 & x^2 \\ x+2 & 2x+3 & x \\ x^2 & x^3+1 & 2x^4+1 \end{vmatrix}$

$$\Rightarrow \frac{d\Delta}{dx} = \begin{vmatrix} 1 & 0 & 2x \\ x+2 & 2x+3 & x \\ x^2 & x^3+1 & 2x^4+1 \end{vmatrix} + \begin{vmatrix} x & 1 & x^2 \\ 1 & 2 & 1 \\ x^2 & x^3+1 & 2x^4+1 \end{vmatrix} + \begin{vmatrix} x & 1 & x^2 \\ x+2 & 2x+3 & x \\ 2x & 3x^2 & 8x^3 \end{vmatrix}$$

Putting $x = 0$, we get $\begin{vmatrix} 1 & 0 & 0 \\ 2 & 3 & 0 \\ 0 & 1 & 1 \end{vmatrix} + \begin{vmatrix} 0 & 1 & 0 \\ 1 & 2 & 1 \\ 0 & 1 & 1 \end{vmatrix} + \begin{vmatrix} 0 & 1 & 0 \\ 2 & 3 & 0 \\ 0 & 0 & 0 \end{vmatrix} = 3 - 1 = 2$

8. $y = \dfrac{u}{v} \Rightarrow \dfrac{dy}{dx} = \dfrac{vu' - uv'}{v^2}$

$$\Rightarrow \frac{d^2y}{dx^2} = \frac{v^2(vu'' + v'u' - uv'' - u'v') - 2vv'(vu' - uv')}{(v^2)^2}$$

$$\Rightarrow v^3\frac{d^2y}{dx^2} = v(vu'' + v'u' - uv'' - u'v') - 2v'(vu' - uv')$$

$= v\,(vu' - uv') - 2v'(v'u - uv')$

Also $\begin{vmatrix} u & v & 0 \\ u' & v' & v \\ u'' & v'' & 2v' \end{vmatrix} = u(2v'^2 - vv'') - v(2u'v' - u''v) = v(vu' - uv') - 2v'(u'v - uv')$

$$\therefore\quad v^3\frac{d^2y}{dx^2} = \begin{vmatrix} u & v & 0 \\ u' & v' & v \\ u'' & v'' & 2v' \end{vmatrix}$$

9. $\Delta(x) = \begin{vmatrix} f & g & h \\ (xf)' & (xg)' & (xh)' \\ (x^2f)'' & (x^2g)'' & (x^2h)'' \end{vmatrix}$

$$\Rightarrow \Delta(x) = \begin{vmatrix} f & g & h \\ xf' + f & xg' + g & xh' + h \\ x^2f'' + 2xf & x^2g'' + 2xg & x^2h'' + 2xh \end{vmatrix}$$

$$= x^3\begin{vmatrix} f & g & h \\ f' & g' & h' \\ f'' & g'' & h'' \end{vmatrix}$$

$\Rightarrow$ (Operating, $R_2 \to R_2 - R_1$ and $R_3 \to R_3 - 2xR_1$ and then taking x and x^2 respectively from R_2 and R_3)

$$= \begin{vmatrix} f & g & h \\ f' & g' & h' \\ x^3f'' & x^3g'' & x^3h'' \end{vmatrix}$$

$$\Rightarrow \frac{d\Delta(x)}{d\Delta} = \begin{vmatrix} f & g & h \\ f' & g' & h' \\ (x^3f'')' & (x^3g'') & (x^3h'')' \end{vmatrix}$$

TEXTUAL EXERCISE–8: (OBJECTIVE)

1. (d) $f(x) = \begin{vmatrix} (x+2)^2 & (x+3)^2 & (x+4)^2 \\ x & x^2 & x^3 \\ 1 & 2x & 3x^2 \end{vmatrix} = A + Bx + Cx^2 + \ldots$

$\Rightarrow B = f'(0) \qquad \Rightarrow f'(x) = \begin{vmatrix} 2x+4 & 2x+6 & 2x+8 \\ x & x^2 & x^3 \\ 1 & 2x & 3x^2 \end{vmatrix}$

$$+ \begin{vmatrix} (x+2)^2 & (x+3)^2 & (x+4)^2 \\ 1 & 2x & 3x^2 \\ 1 & 2x & 3x^2 \end{vmatrix}$$

$$+ \begin{vmatrix} (x+2)^2 & (x+3)^2 & (x+4)^2 \\ x & x^2 & x^3 \\ 0 & 2 & 6x \end{vmatrix} \Rightarrow f'(0) = 0 = B$$

2. (a) $\Delta(x) = \begin{vmatrix} x & 1+x^2 & x^3 \\ \log(1+x^2) & e^x & \sin x \\ \cos x & \tan x & \sin^2 x \end{vmatrix}$

$\Rightarrow \Delta(0) = \begin{vmatrix} 0 & 1 & 0 \\ 0 & 1 & 0 \\ 1 & 0 & 0 \end{vmatrix} = 0$

$\Rightarrow$ $\Delta(x)$ has no constant term

$\Rightarrow$ $\Delta(x)$ is divisible x

Also, $\Delta'(x) = \begin{vmatrix} 1 & 2x & 3x^2 \\ \log(1+x^2) & e^x & \sin x \\ \cos x & \tan x & \sin^2 x \end{vmatrix}$

$+ \begin{vmatrix} x & 1+x^2 & x^3 \\ \frac{2x}{1+x^2} & e^x & \cos x \\ \cos x & \tan x & \sin^2 x \end{vmatrix} + \begin{vmatrix} x & 1+x^2 & x^3 \\ \log(1+x^2) & e^x & \sin x \\ -\sin x & \sec^2 x & \sin 2x \end{vmatrix}$

$\Rightarrow \Delta'(0) = \begin{vmatrix} 0 & 1 & 0 \\ 0 & 1 & 1 \\ 1 & 0 & 0 \end{vmatrix} = 1 \Rightarrow \Delta'(x) \neq 0$

3. (b), (d) $f(x) = \begin{vmatrix} x^n & \sin x & -\cos x \\ n! & \sin\left(\frac{n\pi}{2}\right) & \cos\left(\frac{n\pi}{2}\right) \\ a & a^2 & a^3 \end{vmatrix}$

$\Rightarrow \frac{d^n f(x)}{dx^n} = \begin{vmatrix} n! & \sin\left(x+\frac{n\pi}{2}\right) & -\cos\left(x+\frac{n\pi}{2}\right) \\ n! & \sin\left(\frac{n\pi}{2}\right) & \cos\left(\frac{n\pi}{2}\right) \\ a & a^2 & a^3 \end{vmatrix}$

At $x = 0$, we get $\begin{vmatrix} n! & \sin\left(\frac{n\pi}{2}\right) & -\cos\left(\frac{n\pi}{2}\right) \\ n! & \sin\left(\frac{n\pi}{2}\right) & \cos\left(\frac{n\pi}{2}\right) \\ a & a^2 & a^3 \end{vmatrix}$

$= \begin{vmatrix} n! & \sin\frac{n\pi}{2} & 0 \\ n! & \sin\frac{\pi}{2} & 0 \\ a & a^2 & a^3 \end{vmatrix}$ for $n = (2m + 1)$

$\Rightarrow \left.\frac{d^n f(x)}{dx^n}\right|_{x=0} = 0$ for $n = (2m + 1)$

4. (b) $F(x) = \begin{vmatrix} f & g & h \\ f' & g' & h' \\ f'' & g'' & h'' \end{vmatrix}$

$\Rightarrow F'(x) = \begin{vmatrix} f' & g' & h' \\ f' & g' & h' \\ f'' & g'' & h'' \end{vmatrix} + \begin{vmatrix} f & g & h \\ f'' & g'' & h'' \\ f'' & g'' & h'' \end{vmatrix} + \begin{vmatrix} f & g & h \\ f' & g' & h' \\ f''' & g''' & h''' \end{vmatrix} = 0$ as

$f(x)$, $g(x)$, $h(x)$ being of degree 2,

$f'''(x) = 0 = g'''(x) = h'''(x)$

5. (b), (d) $f(x) = \begin{vmatrix} \cos(x+x^2) & \sin(x+x^2) & -\cos(x+x^2) \\ \sin(x-x^2) & \cos(x-x^2) & \sin(x-x^2) \\ \sin 2x & 0 & \sin 2x^2 \end{vmatrix}$

Solving $f(x)$ by expand along R_3, we get $f(x) = \sin(2x + 2x^2)$

$\Rightarrow f(-2) = \sin 4$

$\Rightarrow f'(x) = (2 + 4x)\cos(2x + 2x^2)$

$\Rightarrow f'(-1) = -2;\ f'(-1/2) = 0;$

$\Rightarrow f'(x) = (2 + 4x)^2(-\sin(2x + 2x^2)) + (4)\cos(2x + 2x^2)$

$\Rightarrow f'(0) = 4$

6. (b) $f(x) = \begin{vmatrix} \cos x & x & 1 \\ 2\sin x & x^2 & 2x \\ \tan x & x & 1 \end{vmatrix}$; (Operating $R_1 \to R_2 \to R_3$)

$\Rightarrow f(x) = \begin{vmatrix} \cos x - \tan x & 0 & 0 \\ 2\sin x & x^2 & 2x \\ \tan x & x & 1 \end{vmatrix}$

$\Rightarrow f(x) = (\cos x - \tan x)(x^2 - 2x^2) = x^2(\tan x - \cos x)$

$\Rightarrow f'(x) = 2x(\tan x - \cos x) - x^2(\sec^2 x + \sin x)$

$\Rightarrow \frac{f'(x)}{x} = 2\tan x - 2\cos x - x\sec^2 x - x\sin x$

$\Rightarrow \lim_{x\to 0}\left(\frac{f'(x)}{x}\right) = 0 - 2 = -2$

7. (c) $f(x) = \begin{vmatrix} \cos x & \sin x & \cos x \\ \cos 2x & \sin 2x & 2\cos 2x \\ \cos 3x & \sin 3x & 3\cos 3x \end{vmatrix}$

$\Rightarrow f'(x) = \begin{vmatrix} -\sin x & \cos x & -\sin x \\ \cos 2x & \sin 2x & 2\cos 2x \\ \cos 3x & \sin 3x & 3\cos 3x \end{vmatrix}$

$+ \begin{vmatrix} \cos x & \sin x & \cos x \\ -2\sin 2x & 2\cos 2x & -4\sin 2x \\ \cos 3x & \sin 3x & 3\cos 3x \end{vmatrix}$

$+ \begin{vmatrix} \cos x & \sin x & \cos x \\ \cos 2x & \sin 2x & 2\cos 2x \\ -3\sin 3x & 3\cos 3x & -9\sin 3x \end{vmatrix}$

$\Rightarrow f'\left(\frac{\pi}{2}\right) = \begin{vmatrix} -1 & 0 & -1 \\ -1 & 0 & -2 \\ 0 & -1 & 0 \end{vmatrix} + \begin{vmatrix} 0 & 1 & 0 \\ 0 & -2 & 0 \\ 0 & -1 & 0 \end{vmatrix} + \begin{vmatrix} 0 & 1 & 0 \\ -1 & 0 & -2 \\ 3 & 0 & 9 \end{vmatrix} = 4$

TEXTUAL EXERCISE-9: (SUBJECTIVE)

1. $y=\sqrt{(a-x)(x-b)}-(a-b)\tan^{-1}\sqrt{\dfrac{a-x}{x-b}}$

Let $x = a\cos^2\theta + b\sin^2\theta$, $\theta \in [0, \pi/2]$

$(a-x) = (a-b)\sin^2\theta$, $(x-b) = (a-b)\cos^2\theta$

$y = (a-b)\sin\theta\,.\cos\theta - (a-b)[\tan^{-1}(\tan\theta)]$

$$=\left(\frac{a-b}{2}\right)\sin 2\theta-(a-b)\theta$$

$$\Rightarrow \frac{dy}{d\theta}=(a-b)[\cos 2\theta-1] \text{ and } \frac{dx}{d\theta}=(b-a)\sin 2\theta$$

$$\Rightarrow \frac{dy}{dx}=\frac{1-\cos 2\theta}{\sin 2\theta}=\tan\theta=\sqrt{\frac{a-x}{x-b}}$$

2. $y=\sqrt{a^2-x^2}+\dfrac{a}{2}\log\left(\dfrac{a-\sqrt{a^2-x^2}}{a+\sqrt{a^2-x^2}}\right)$

Let $x = a\sin\theta$

$$\Rightarrow y=\sqrt{a^2-a^2\sin^2\theta}+\frac{a}{2}\log\left(\frac{a-a\sqrt{\cos^2\theta}}{a+a\sqrt{\cos^2\theta}}\right)$$

$$\Rightarrow y=a\cos\theta+\frac{\theta}{2}\log\left(\frac{1-\cos\theta}{1+\cos\theta}\right)=a\cos\theta+\frac{a}{2}\left(2\log\tan\frac{\theta}{2}\right)$$

$$\Rightarrow \frac{dy}{d\theta}=-a\sin\theta+\frac{1}{2}a\cot\frac{\theta}{2}\sec^2\frac{\theta}{2}$$

$$=-a\sin\theta+\frac{a}{\sin\theta}=\frac{a\cos^2\theta}{\sin\theta} \text{ and } \frac{dx}{d\theta}=a\cos\theta$$

$$\Rightarrow \frac{dy}{dx}=\frac{dy/d\theta}{dx/d\theta}=\cot\theta \Rightarrow \frac{dy}{dx}=\frac{\sqrt{a^2-x^2}}{x}$$

TEXTUAL EXERCISE-9: (OBJECTIVE)

1. (a) $e^x=\dfrac{\sqrt{1+t}-\sqrt{1-t}}{\sqrt{1+t}+\sqrt{1-t}}$

$$\Rightarrow e^x=\frac{1-\sqrt{\frac{1-t}{1+t}}}{1+\sqrt{\frac{1-t}{1+t}}}=\frac{1-\tan y/2}{1+\tan y/2}$$

$$\Rightarrow e^x=\tan\left(\frac{\pi}{4}-\frac{y}{2}\right)$$

$$\Rightarrow e^x=\sec^2\left(\frac{\pi}{4}-\frac{y}{2}\right)\left(\frac{-1}{2}\right)\frac{dy}{dx}$$

$$\Rightarrow \frac{dy}{dx}=-2e^x\cos^2\left(\frac{\pi}{4}-\frac{y}{2}\right) \quad \ldots(1)$$

When $t = 1/2$, $\tan y/2=\dfrac{1}{\sqrt{3}}$

$$\Rightarrow \frac{y}{2}=\frac{\pi}{6}$$

$\therefore$ From (1), $\dfrac{dy}{dx}=-2[e^x]_{t=1/2}.\cos^2\left(\dfrac{\pi}{4}-\dfrac{\pi}{6}\right)$

$$=-2\left[\frac{\sqrt{3/2}-\sqrt{1/2}}{\sqrt{3/2}+\sqrt{1/2}}\right]\left[\frac{1}{\sqrt{2}}.\frac{\sqrt{3}}{2}+\frac{1}{\sqrt{2}}.\frac{1}{2}\right]^2$$

$$=-2\left[\frac{\sqrt{3}-1}{\sqrt{3}+1}\right]\left[\frac{\sqrt{3}+1}{2\sqrt{2}}\right]^2=\frac{-2}{8}(3-1)=\frac{-1}{2}$$

2. (b) $y=\dfrac{(a-x)^{3/2}+(x-b)^{3/2}}{(a-x)^{1/2}+(x-b)^{1/2}}$

$$y=\frac{\left[(a-x)^{1/2}\right]^3+\left[(x-b)^{1/2}\right]^3}{(a-x)^{1/2}+(x-b)^{1/2}}$$

or $y=\dfrac{u^3+v^3}{u+v}=u^2+v^2-uv$

$\therefore$ $y = (a-x) + (x-b) - (a-x)^{1/2}(x-b)^{1/2}$

$\Rightarrow$ $y = (a-b) - (a-x)^{1/2}(x-b)^{1/2}$

$$\Rightarrow \frac{dy}{dx}=-(a-x)^{1/2}.\frac{1}{2\sqrt{x-b}}-(x-b)^{1/2}.\frac{1}{2\sqrt{a-x}}(-1)$$

$$=\frac{\sqrt{x-b}}{2\sqrt{a-x}}-\frac{\sqrt{a-x}}{2\sqrt{x-b}}=\frac{(x-b)-(a-x)}{2\sqrt{a-x}.\sqrt{x-b}}$$

$$\Rightarrow \frac{dy}{dx}=\frac{2x-(a+b)}{2\sqrt{a-x}.\sqrt{x-b}}$$

3. (b) Let $y=\tan^{-1}\left(\dfrac{2x}{1-x^2}\right)$ and $V=\sin^{-1}\left(\dfrac{2x}{1+x^2}\right)$ and $x \in (-1, 1)$

We know that $2\tan^{-1}x=\left\{\tan^{-1}\left(\dfrac{2x}{1-x^2}\right)\right.$ for $x\in(-1,1)$

and $2\tan^{-1}x=\left\{\sin^{-1}\left(\dfrac{2x}{1+x^2}\right)\right.$ for $x\in[-1,1]$

$\therefore$ $y = 2\tan^{-1}x$ and $V = 2\tan^{-1}x$

$$\therefore \frac{dy}{dV}=1$$

4. (a) For $x\in(1,\infty)$; $2\tan^{-1}x=\left\{\pi+\tan^{-1}\left(\dfrac{2x}{1-x^2}\right)\right.$ for $x>1$

and also $2\tan^{-1}x=\left\{\pi-\sin^{-1}\left(\dfrac{2x}{1+x^2}\right)\right.$ for $x>1$

$\Rightarrow$ $y = 2\tan^{-1}x - \pi$ and $V = \pi - 2\tan^{-1}x$

$\Rightarrow$ $y = -V$

$$\Rightarrow \frac{dy}{dV}=-1$$

5. (a) $2\tan^{-1}x=\left\{-\pi+\tan^{-1}\left(\dfrac{2x}{1-x^2}\right)\right.$ for $x<-1$ and

$2\tan^{-1}x=\left\{-\pi-\sin^{-1}\left(\dfrac{2x}{1+x^2}\right)\right.$ for $x<-1$

$\Rightarrow$ $y = 2\tan^{-1}x + \pi$ and $V = -\pi - 2\tan^{-1}x$

$\Rightarrow$ $y = -V$

$$\Rightarrow \frac{dy}{dx}=-1$$

6. (b) We know, that

$$3\tan^{-1}x=\left\{\tan^{-1}\left(\frac{3x-x^3}{1-3x^2}\right)\text{for } x\in\left(\frac{-1}{\sqrt{3}},\frac{1}{\sqrt{3}}\right)\right.$$

$\Rightarrow\ y=3\tan^{-1}x \qquad \Rightarrow\ \frac{dy}{dx}=\frac{3}{1+x^2}$

7. (a) Let $y=\sin^{-1}\left(4x\sqrt{1-4x^2}\right)$ and $V=\sqrt{1-4x^2}$;

$x\in\left(-\frac{1}{2\sqrt{2}},\frac{1}{2\sqrt{2}}\right)$

We know that, $2\sin^{-1}x=\left\{\sin^{-1}\left(2x\sqrt{1-x^2}\right)\text{for}\frac{-1}{\sqrt{2}}\le x\le\frac{1}{\sqrt{2}}\right.$

$\Rightarrow\ y=\sin^{-1}\left(4x\sqrt{1-4x^2}\right)=2\sin^{-1}(2x)$ for $\frac{-1}{\sqrt{2}}\le 2x\le\frac{1}{\sqrt{2}}$

$\Rightarrow\ y=2\sin^{-1}(2x)$ for $x\in\left[\frac{-1}{\sqrt{2}},\frac{1}{\sqrt{2}}\right]$

$\Rightarrow\ \frac{dy}{dx}=\frac{4}{\sqrt{1-4x^2}}$ and $\frac{dV}{dx}=\frac{1(-8x)}{2\sqrt{1-4x^2}}$

$\Rightarrow\ \frac{dy}{dV}=\frac{4}{\sqrt{1-4x^2}}\times\frac{\sqrt{1-4x^2}}{-4x}=\frac{-1}{x}$ for $x\in\left(\frac{-1}{\sqrt{2}},\frac{1}{\sqrt{2}}\right)$

8. (a) $y=\sin^{-1}\left(4x\sqrt{1-4x^2}\right)$, $V=\sqrt{1-4x^2}$

We know that,

$$2\sin^{-1}x=\left\{\pi-\sin^{-1}\left(2x\sqrt{1-x^2}\right)\text{for } 1\ge x>\frac{1}{\sqrt{2}}\right.$$

$\Rightarrow\ y=\sin^{-1}\left(4x\sqrt{1-4x^2}\right)=\pi-2\sin^{-1}2x$ for $\frac{1}{2}\ge x>\frac{1}{2\sqrt{2}}$

$\Rightarrow\ \frac{dy}{dx}=\frac{-4}{\sqrt{1-4x^2}}$ and $\frac{dV}{dx}=\frac{-4x}{\sqrt{1-4x^2}}$

$\Rightarrow\ \frac{dy}{dV}=\frac{1}{x}$ for $\frac{1}{2}>x>\frac{1}{2\sqrt{2}}$

9. (a) $y=\sin^{-1}\left(4x\sqrt{1-4x^2}\right);V=\sqrt{1-4x^2}$

We know that

$$2\sin^{-1}x=\left\{-\pi-\sin^{-1}\left(2x\sqrt{1-x^2}\right)\text{for}\frac{-1}{\sqrt{2}}<x<-1\right.$$

$\Rightarrow\ y=\sin^{-1}\left(4x\sqrt{1-4x^2}\right)=-\pi-2\sin^{-1}(2x)$

$\Rightarrow\ \frac{dy}{dx}=\frac{-4}{\sqrt{1-4x^2}}$ and $\frac{dV}{dx}=\frac{-4x}{\sqrt{1-4x^2}}$

$\Rightarrow\ \frac{dy}{dV}=\frac{1}{x}$

10. (d) Let

$y=\sin^{-1}\left(2ax\sqrt{1-a^2x^2}\right)$; $V=\sqrt{1-a^2x^2}$; $\frac{-1}{\sqrt{2}}<ax<\frac{1}{\sqrt{2}}$

We know that $2\sin^{-1}x=\sin^{-1}\left(2x\sqrt{1-x^2}\right)$ for

$\frac{-1}{\sqrt{2}}\le x\le\frac{1}{\sqrt{2}}$

$\therefore\ y=\sin^{-1}\left(2ax\sqrt{1-a^2x^2}\right)=2\sin^{-1}(ax)$ for

$\frac{-1}{\sqrt{2}}\le ax\le\frac{1}{\sqrt{2}}$

$\Rightarrow\ \frac{dy}{dx}=\frac{2a}{\sqrt{1-a^2x^2}}$ for $\frac{-1}{\sqrt{2}}<ax<\frac{1}{\sqrt{2}}$ and

$\frac{dV}{dx}=\frac{-2a^2x}{\sqrt{1-a^2x^2}}$

$\therefore\ \frac{dy}{dx}=\frac{-2}{ax}$

TEXTUAL EXERCISE–10: (SUBJECTIVE)

1. (i) $y=\sin ax+\cos bx$

$\Rightarrow\ \frac{dy}{dx}=a\cos ax-b\sin bx=a\sin\left(\frac{\pi}{2}+ax\right)+b\cos\left(\frac{\pi}{2}+bx\right)$

$\Rightarrow\ \frac{d^2y}{dx^2}=a^2\cos\left(\frac{\pi}{2}+ax\right)-b^2\sin\left(\frac{\pi}{2}+bx\right)$

$=a^2\sin\left(\frac{\pi}{2}+\left(\frac{\pi}{2}+ax\right)\right)+b^2\cos\left(\frac{\pi}{2}+\left(\frac{\pi}{2}+bx\right)\right)$

$\Rightarrow\ a^2\sin\left[2\left(\frac{\pi}{2}\right)+ax\right]+b^2\cos\left[2\left(\frac{\pi}{2}\right)+bx\right]$

Similarly, $\frac{d^ny}{dx^n}=a^n\sin\left(ax+\frac{n\pi}{2}\right)+b^n\cos\left(bx+\frac{n\pi}{2}\right)$

(ii) $y=(ax+b)^{-1}$

$y_1=-(ax+b)^{-2}\cdot a=(-1)(a)(ax+b)^{-2}$

$y_2=(-1)(-2)(a)^2(ax+b)^{-3}$

$y_3=(-1)(-2)(-3)(a)^3(ax+bx)^{-4}$ and so on

$y_n=(-1)(-2)(-3)\ .....\ (-n)(a)^n(ax+b)^{-(n+1)}$

$\Rightarrow\ y_n=\frac{(-1)^n.n!(a)^n}{(ax+b)^{n+1}}$

(iii) $y=\log ax$

$\Rightarrow\ \frac{dy}{dx}=\frac{1}{\log_a e}=x^{-1}\log_a e$

$\Rightarrow\ \frac{d^2y}{dx^2}=(-1)x^{-2}\log_a e$

$\Rightarrow\ \frac{d^3y}{dx^2}=(-1)(-2).x^{-3}\log_a e$ and so on.

$\Rightarrow\ \frac{d^ny}{dx^n}=(-1)(-2)....(-(n-1)).x^{-n}\log_a e$

$=\frac{(-1)^{n-1}.(n-1)!}{x^n\ln a}$

(iv) $y=\ell n(ax+b)$

$\Rightarrow\ \frac{dy}{dx}=\frac{a}{ax+b}=a(ax+b)^{-1}$

$\Rightarrow\ \frac{d^2y}{dx^2}=-a^2(ax+b)^{-2}$

$\Rightarrow \dfrac{d^3y}{dx^3} = (-1)(-2)a^3(ax+b)^{-3}$ and so on.

$\Rightarrow \dfrac{d^ny}{dy^n} = \dfrac{(-1)^{n-1}(n-1)!a^n}{(ax+b)^n}$

(v) $y = e^{kx}$

$\Rightarrow \dfrac{dy}{dx} = k.e^{kx}$

$\Rightarrow \dfrac{d^2y}{dx^2} = k^2e^{kx}$

$\Rightarrow \dfrac{d^3y}{dx^3} = k^3e^{kx}$

$\Rightarrow \dfrac{d^ny}{dx^n} = k^ne^{kx}$

(vi) $y = \sin x \,.\, \cos x$

$\Rightarrow y = \dfrac{\sin 2x}{2}$

$\Rightarrow \dfrac{dy}{dx} = \cos 2x = \sin\left(2x+\dfrac{\pi}{2}\right)$

$\Rightarrow \dfrac{d^2y}{dx^2} = 2\cos\left(2x+\dfrac{\pi}{2}\right) = 2\sin\left(2x+2.\dfrac{\pi}{2}\right)$

$\Rightarrow \dfrac{d^3y}{dx^2} = (2)^2\cos\left(2x+2.\dfrac{\pi}{2}\right) = (2)^2\sin\left(2x+3.\dfrac{\pi}{2}\right)$ and so on.

$\Rightarrow \dfrac{d^3y}{dx^2} = 2^{n-1}\sin\left(2x+n.\dfrac{\pi}{2}\right)$

2. $y_1 = \dfrac{d}{dx}(x^{205}) = 205.x^{204}$

$\Rightarrow y_2 = (205)(204).\, x^{203}$

$\Rightarrow y_3 = (205)(204)(203).\, x^{202}$ and so on.

$\Rightarrow y_n = (205)(204)(203) \ldots [205-(n-1)].\, x^{205-n}$

$\therefore\ y_{100} = (205)(204)(203) \ldots (106).\, x^{105} = \dfrac{(205)!}{(105)!}x^{105}$

3. $y = \sin 2x$

$\because\ y_n = (2)^n \sin\left(2x+n.\dfrac{\pi}{2}\right)$

$\Rightarrow y_6 = 64\sin(2x+3\pi) = -64\sin 2x$

$\Rightarrow y_6\Big|_{x=\frac{\pi}{4}} = -64\sin\dfrac{\pi}{2} = -64$

TEXTUAL EXERCISE–11:(SUBJECTIVE)

1. $y = \dfrac{1-x^4}{1+x^4}$ …(i)

$\Rightarrow \dfrac{dy}{dx} = \dfrac{-8x^3}{(x^4+1)^2}$ …(ii)

By (i), we get $y + yx^4 + x^4 = 1$

$\Rightarrow x^4 = \dfrac{1-y}{1+y} \qquad \Rightarrow x = \left(\dfrac{1-y}{1+y}\right)^{\frac{1}{4}}$

$\Rightarrow \dfrac{dx}{dy} = \dfrac{1}{4}\left(\dfrac{1-y}{1+y}\right)^{-3/4}\left[\dfrac{(1+y)(-1)-(1-y)(1)}{(1+y)^2}\right]$

$= \dfrac{1}{4}\left(\dfrac{1+y}{1-y}\right)^{3/4}\cdot\left[\dfrac{-2}{(1+y)^2}\right]$

$= \dfrac{1}{4}\left(\dfrac{1}{x^4}\right)^{3/4}\left[\dfrac{-2}{\left[1+\left(\dfrac{1-x^4}{1+x^2}\right)\right]^2}\right] = \dfrac{-1}{2x^3}\left[\dfrac{(1+x^4)^2}{4}\right]$

$= \dfrac{-1}{8x^3}(1+x^4)^2$ …(iii)

$\therefore$ From (i) and (iii), $\dfrac{dy}{dx}.\dfrac{dx}{dy} = 1$

2. $xy - \ell ny = 1$

Differentiating the whole equation $x\dfrac{dy}{dx} + y - \dfrac{1}{y}.\dfrac{dy}{dx} = 0$

$\Rightarrow y^2 + (xy-1)\, dy/dx = 0$

3. $x = 2t + 3t^2$

$y = t^2 + 2t^3$

$\Rightarrow \dfrac{dx}{dt} = 2 + 6t \qquad \Rightarrow \dfrac{dy}{dt} = 2t + 6t^2$

$\Rightarrow \dfrac{dy}{dx} = \dfrac{2t+6t^2}{2+6t} = t \qquad \Rightarrow (y')^2 + (2y')^3 = t^2 + 2t^3 = y$

Hence $(y') + 2(y')^3 = y$, which is true

4. $y = x\,\ell n\,[(ax)^{-1} + (a)^{-1}]$

$\Rightarrow y = x\ell n\left(\dfrac{1}{ax}+\dfrac{1}{a}\right)$

$\Rightarrow y' = \dfrac{1}{\dfrac{1}{ax}+\dfrac{1}{a}}\left(\dfrac{1}{ax}+\dfrac{1}{a}\right)'.x + \ell n\left(\dfrac{1}{a}+\dfrac{1}{ax}\right)$

$= \ell n\left(\dfrac{1}{ax}+\dfrac{1}{a}\right) - \dfrac{1}{a\left(\dfrac{1}{ax}+\dfrac{1}{a}\right).x}$

$\Rightarrow \ln\left(\dfrac{1}{ax}+\dfrac{1}{a}\right) - \dfrac{1}{ax}\left(\dfrac{ax}{1+x}\right) = \ln\left(\dfrac{1+x}{ax}\right) - \left(\dfrac{1}{1+x}\right)$

$= \dfrac{y}{x} - \dfrac{1}{1+x}$

$\Rightarrow y'' = \dfrac{ax}{1+x}.\dfrac{1}{a}\left(\dfrac{x-(1+x)}{x^2}\right) + \dfrac{1}{(1+x)^2}$

$= \dfrac{-1}{x(1+x)} + \dfrac{1}{(1+x)^2} = \dfrac{-1-x+x}{x(1+x)^2} = \dfrac{-1}{x^3+2x^3+x}$

$\Rightarrow x(x+1)\left(\dfrac{-1}{x(x+1)^2}\right) + y - \dfrac{1}{x+1} = \dfrac{-1}{x+1} + y - \dfrac{x}{x+1} = y - 1$

5. $y = \sin(2 \text{ arc} \sin(x))$

$\Rightarrow \dfrac{dy}{dx} = \dfrac{2\cos(2.arc\sin(x))}{\sqrt{1-x^2}}$

$$\Rightarrow \frac{d^2y}{dx^2} = \frac{2x\cos(2.arc\sin(x))}{(1-x^2)^{3/2}} - \frac{4\sin(2.\sin^{-1}x)}{1-x^2}$$

$$\Rightarrow (1-x^2)\frac{d^2y}{dx^2} = \frac{2x\cos(2.\sin^{-1}x)}{\sqrt{1-x^2}} - 4\sin(2\sin^{-1}x)$$

$$= x\frac{dy}{dx} - 4y. \text{ Thus } (1-x^2)\frac{d^2y}{dx^2} = x\frac{dy}{dx} - 4y$$

6. $y = A\,e^{-kt}\cos(pt+k)$

$$\Rightarrow \frac{dy}{dt} = A\frac{d}{dt}\left(e^{-kt}\cos(pt+k)\right)$$

$$= A\left(-pe^{-kt}\sin(pt+k) - ke^{-kt}.\cos(pt+k)\right)$$

$$= -e^{-kt}\ (ap\sin(pt+k) + ak\cos(pt+k)) \quad \text{........(i)}$$

$$\Rightarrow \frac{d^2y}{dt^2} = e^{-kt}(2akp\sin(pt+k) + (ak^2 - ap^2)\cos(pt+k))$$

$\Rightarrow \frac{d^2y}{dt^2} + 2k\frac{dy}{dt} + (p^2+k^2)\,y$ is given by $e^{-kt}\,2akp\sin(pt+k)$ $-\,2kape^{-kt}\sin(pt+k) + e^{-kt}(ak^2 - ap^2) - e^{-kt}ak\,.\,2k\cos(pt+k) + p^2y + k^2y = 0$

7. $y = \left(x + \sqrt{x^2+1}\right)^m$

$$\Rightarrow \frac{dy}{dx} = m\left(\frac{x}{\sqrt{x^2+1}} + 1\right)\left(\sqrt{x^2+1} + x\right)^{m-1}$$

$$= \frac{m\left(\sqrt{x^2+1}+x\right)^m}{\sqrt{x^2+1}} = \frac{my}{\sqrt{x^2+1}}$$

$$\Rightarrow \sqrt{x^2+1}\frac{dy}{dx} = my$$

$$\Rightarrow \frac{x}{\sqrt{x^2+1}}\frac{dy}{dx} + \frac{d^2y}{dx^2}\sqrt{x^2+1} = m\frac{dy}{dx}$$

$$\Rightarrow (x^2+1)\frac{dy}{dx} + x\frac{dy}{dx} = m\sqrt{x^2+1}\frac{dy}{dx}$$

$$\text{or } (x^2+1)\frac{dy}{dx} + x\frac{dy}{dx} = m^2y$$

8. $x = \sin t \quad \Rightarrow \quad dx/dt = \cos t$

$$\Rightarrow \frac{dy}{dx} = \frac{dy/dt}{dx/dt} = \frac{dy}{dt}.\sec t$$

$$\Rightarrow \frac{d^2y}{dx^2} = \frac{d}{dt}\left(\frac{dy}{dt}.\sec t\right).\frac{dt}{dx} = \sec^2 t\frac{d^2y}{dt^2} + \frac{dy}{dt}.\sec^2 t.\tan t$$

$$\Rightarrow (1-x^2)\frac{d^2y}{dx^2} - x\frac{dy}{dx} + y$$

$$= \cos^2 t\left(\sec^2 t\frac{d^2y}{dt^2} + \frac{dy}{dt}\sec^2 t.\tan t\right) - \sin t\sec t\frac{dy}{dt} + y$$

$$= \frac{d^2y}{dt^2} + \tan t\frac{dy}{dt} - t\tan t\frac{dy}{dt} + y = \frac{d^2y}{dt^2} + y$$

TEXTUAL EXERCISE–11: (OBJECTIVE)

1. (a) $y = a\cos(\log x) + b\sin(\log x)$

$$\Rightarrow \frac{dy}{dx} = \left(\frac{-a\sin(\log x)}{x} + \frac{b\cos(\log x)}{x}\right)$$

$$\Rightarrow \frac{d^2y}{dx^2} = \frac{a\sin(\log x)}{x^2} - \frac{a}{x^2}\cos(\log x) - \frac{b}{x^2}\sin(\log x) - \frac{b\cos(\log x)}{x^2}$$

$$\Rightarrow x^2\frac{d^2y}{dx^2} = a\sin(\log x) - a\cos(\log x) - b\sin(\log x) - b\cos(\log x)$$

$$= -x\frac{dy}{dx} - y$$

$$\Rightarrow x^2\frac{d^2y}{dx} + x\frac{dy}{dx} + y = 0$$

2. (a) $y = x + \cot x$

$\Rightarrow dy/dx = 1 - \text{cosec}^2 x$

$$\Rightarrow \frac{d^2y}{dx^2} = 2\text{ cosec } x.\text{ cosec } x.\cot x = 2\text{ cosec}^2 x.\cot x$$

$$\Rightarrow \sin^2 x\frac{d^2y}{dx^2} + 2x - 2y = 2\cot x + 2x - 2x - 2\cot x = 0$$

3. (b) $y = x + ex$

$$\Rightarrow y' = 1 + ex \qquad \Rightarrow \frac{dx}{dy} = \frac{1}{1+e^x} \text{ and } \frac{d^2y}{dx^2} = e^x$$

$$\text{Now, } \frac{d\,x}{dy} = \frac{d}{dy}\left(\frac{dx}{dy}\right) = \frac{d}{dy}\left(\frac{}{e}\right)$$

$$= \frac{d}{dx}\left((1+e^x)^{-1}\right).\frac{dx}{dy}\frac{-e^x}{(1+e^x)^2}\left(\frac{1}{1+e^x}\right) = \frac{-e^x}{(1+e^x)^3}$$

4. (a) $x = t^3 + t + 5$ and $y = \sin t$

$$\Rightarrow \frac{dx}{dt} = 3t^2+1 \text{ and } \frac{dy}{dx} = \cos t$$

$$\Rightarrow \frac{dy}{dx} = \frac{\cos t}{3t^2+1}$$

$$\Rightarrow \frac{d^2y}{dx^2} = \frac{d}{dt}\left(\frac{dy}{dx}\right).\frac{dt}{dx}$$

$$= \left[\frac{(3t^2+1)(-\sin t) - \cos t(6t)}{(3t^2+1)^2}\right]\left(\frac{1}{3t^2+1}\right)$$

$$= -\frac{\left[(3t^2+1)\sin t + 6t\cos t\right]}{(3t^2+1)^3}$$

5. (a) $y = (\sin^{-1} x)^2 + (\cos^{-1} x)^2$

$$\Rightarrow \frac{dy}{dx} = \frac{2\sin^{-1}x}{\sqrt{1-x^2}} - \frac{2\cos^{-1}x}{\sqrt{1-x^2}}$$

$$\Rightarrow \frac{d^2y}{dx^2} = \frac{-\sin^{-1}x(-2x)}{(1-x^2)^{3/2}} + \frac{2}{(1-x^2)} + \frac{\cos^{-1}x(-2x)}{(1-x^2)^{3/2}} + \frac{2}{(1-x^2)}$$

$$= \frac{\left(\cos^{-1}x - \sin^{-1}x\right)(-2x)}{(1-x^2)^{3/2}} + \frac{4}{(1-x^2)}$$

$\Rightarrow \quad (1-x^2)\dfrac{d^2y}{dx^2}=2\left(\dfrac{\sin^{-1}x-\cos^{-1}x}{\sqrt{1-x^2}}\right)x+4$

$\Rightarrow \quad (1-x^2)\dfrac{d^2y}{dx^2}-x\dfrac{dy}{dx}=4$

6. (a) Given: $(a + bx)e^{y/x} = x$ ...(i)

and $x^k\dfrac{d^2y}{dx^2}=\left(x\dfrac{dy}{dx}-y^2\right)$ ...(ii)

From (i); $e^{y/x}=\dfrac{x}{a+bx}$

$\Rightarrow \quad \dfrac{y}{x}=\ln\left(\dfrac{x}{a+bx}\right) \quad \Rightarrow \quad y=x\ln\left(\dfrac{x}{a+bx}\right)$

$\Rightarrow \quad \dfrac{dy}{dx}=\ln\left(\dfrac{x}{a+bx}\right)+x\left(\dfrac{a+bx}{x}\right)\left(\dfrac{a+bx-xb}{(a+bx)^2}\right)$

$\Rightarrow \quad \dfrac{dy}{dx}=\ln\left(\dfrac{x}{a+bx}\right)+\dfrac{a}{(a+bx)}$

$\Rightarrow \quad \dfrac{dy}{dx}=\dfrac{y}{x}+\dfrac{a}{a+bx}$ ...(iii)

$\Rightarrow \quad x\dfrac{dy}{dx}-y=\dfrac{ax}{a+bx}$

$\Rightarrow \quad \left(x\dfrac{dy}{dx}-y\right)^2=\left(\dfrac{ax}{a+bx}\right)^2$ ...(iv)

Also, form (iii), $\dfrac{d^2y}{dx^2}=y\left(\dfrac{-1}{x^2}\right)+\dfrac{1}{x}\dfrac{dy}{dx}+\dfrac{-ab}{(a+bx)^2}$

$\Rightarrow \quad \dfrac{d^2y}{dx^2}=\dfrac{-y}{x^2}+\dfrac{1}{x}\left(\dfrac{y}{x}+\dfrac{a}{a+bx}\right)-\dfrac{ab}{(a+bx)^2}$

$\Rightarrow \quad \dfrac{d^2y}{dx^2}=\dfrac{a}{(a+bx)x}-\dfrac{ab}{(a+bx)^2}$

$\Rightarrow \quad \dfrac{d^2y}{dx^2}=\dfrac{a^2+abx-abx}{x(a+bx)^2}=\dfrac{a^2}{x(a+bx)^2}$

$\Rightarrow \quad x^3\dfrac{d^2y}{dx^2}=\dfrac{ax}{(a+bx)^2}=\left(x\dfrac{dy}{dx}-y\right)^2$

$\Rightarrow \quad k = 3$

7. (c) $p = a^2\cos^2\theta + b^2\sin^2\theta$

$\Rightarrow \quad \dfrac{dp}{d\theta}=2a^2\cos\theta(-\sin\theta)+2b^2(\sin\theta.\cos\theta)$

$= -a^2\sin 2\theta + b^2\sin 2\theta = (\sin 2\theta)(b^2-a^2)$

$\Rightarrow \quad \dfrac{d^2p}{d\theta^2}=2(b^2-a^2)\cos 2\theta$

$\Rightarrow \quad p+\dfrac{d^2p}{d\theta^2}=a^2\cos^2\theta+b^2\sin^2\theta+2(b^2-a^2)(\cos^2\theta-\sin^2\theta)$

$= (2a^2\cos^2\theta + 2a^2\sin^2\theta) - a^2\cos^2\theta + (2b^2\sin^2\theta + 2b^2\cos^2\theta) - b^2\sin^2\theta - 2b^2\sin^2\theta - 2a^2\cos^2\theta$

$= 2a^2 + 2b^2 - 3(a2\cos^2\theta + b^2\sin^2\theta) = 2a^2 + 2b^2 - 3p$

$\Rightarrow k = 3$

8. (b) Given: $(x+y)=e^{x-}y$ ...(1) and $\dfrac{d^2y}{dx^2}=\dfrac{k(x+y)}{(x+y+1)^3}$ ...(2)

From, (1), $(x - y) = \ln(x + y)$

$\Rightarrow \quad 1-\dfrac{dy}{dx}=\dfrac{1}{(x+y)}\left(1+\dfrac{dy}{dx}\right)$

$\Rightarrow \quad \dfrac{dy}{dx}\left[\dfrac{1}{x+y}+1\right]=1-\dfrac{1}{x+y}$

$\Rightarrow \quad \dfrac{dy}{dx}=\dfrac{x+y-1}{1+x+y}$

$\Rightarrow \quad \dfrac{d^2y}{dx^2}=\dfrac{(x+y+1)\left[1+\dfrac{dy}{dx}\right]-(x+y-1)\left(1+\dfrac{dy}{dx}\right)}{(x+y+1)^2}$

$=\dfrac{(x+y+1-x-y+1)+\dfrac{dy}{dx}(x+y+1-x-y+1)}{(x+y+1)^2}$

$=\dfrac{2+(2)\dfrac{dy}{dx}}{(x+y+1)^2}=\dfrac{2\left[1+\left(\dfrac{x+y-1}{x+y+1}\right)\right]}{(x+y+1)^2}$

$=2\left[\dfrac{x+y+1+x+y-1}{(x+y+1)^3}\right]=\dfrac{4(x+y)}{(x+y+1)^3}$

$\Rightarrow \quad k = 4$ (using (2))

9. (d) $y=\left[\ln\left(\dfrac{x+\sqrt{x^2-a^2}}{a}\right)\right]+k\ln\left(x+\sqrt{x^2-a^2}\right)$

$\Rightarrow \quad \dfrac{dy}{dx}=\dfrac{a}{x+\sqrt{x^2-a^2}}.\left(1+\dfrac{x}{\sqrt{x^2-a^2}}\right)+\dfrac{k}{x+\sqrt{x^2-a^2}}\left(1+\dfrac{x}{\sqrt{x^2-a^2}}\right)$

$\Rightarrow \quad \dfrac{dy}{dx}=\dfrac{a}{\sqrt{x^2-a^2}}+\dfrac{k}{\sqrt{x^2-a^2}}=(a+k).\dfrac{1}{\sqrt{x^2-a^2}}$ ...(1)

$\Rightarrow \quad \dfrac{d^2y}{dx^2}=(a+k)\left(\dfrac{-1(2x)}{2(x^2-a^2)^{3/2}}\right)=\dfrac{-x(a+k)}{(x^2-a^2)^{3/2}}$

$\Rightarrow \quad (x^2-a^2)\dfrac{d^2y}{dx^2}=\dfrac{-x(a+k)}{\sqrt{x^2-a^2}}$

$\Rightarrow \quad (x^2-a^2)\dfrac{d^2y}{dx^2}=-\dfrac{xdy}{dx}$

$\Rightarrow \quad (x^2-a^2)\dfrac{d^2y}{dx^2}+\dfrac{xdy}{dx}=0$

SECTION–III: (ONLY ONE CORRECT ANSWER)

1. (b) $y=\sin^{-1}\left(x\sqrt{1-x}+\sqrt{x}\sqrt{1-x^2}\right)$

Clearly, $0 \le x \le 1$

Now, $y=\sin^{-1}\left(x\sqrt{1-\left(\sqrt{x}\right)^2}+\sqrt{x}\sqrt{1-x^2}\right)$

Put $\sqrt{x}=y\in[0,1]$

$\Rightarrow \quad y=\sin^{-1}\left(x\sqrt{1-y^2}+y\sqrt{1-x^2}\right)$

$=\sin^{-1}x+\sin^{-1}y=\sin^{-1}x+\sin^{-1}\sqrt{x}$

$\Rightarrow \dfrac{dy}{dx} = \dfrac{1}{\sqrt{1-x^2}} + \dfrac{1}{\sqrt{1-x}}.\dfrac{1}{2\sqrt{x}} = \dfrac{1}{\sqrt{1-x^2}} + \dfrac{1}{2\sqrt{x(1-x)}}$

$= p' + \dfrac{1}{2\sqrt{x(1-x)}}$ (Given)

Also $\dfrac{dy}{dx} = \dfrac{d}{dx}(\sin^{-1} x + c) + \dfrac{1}{2\sqrt{x(1-x)}}$

$\Rightarrow p = \sin^{-1}x + c$

2. (a) $y = \cot^{-1}(\cos 2x)^{1/2})$

$\Rightarrow \dfrac{dy}{dx} = \dfrac{-1}{(1+\cos 2x)} \times \dfrac{1}{2\sqrt{\cos 2x}}(-2\sin 2x)$

$= \dfrac{\sin 2x}{(1+\cos 2x)\sqrt{\cos 2x}} = \dfrac{\tan x}{\sqrt{\cos 2x}}$

$\Rightarrow \left.\dfrac{dy}{dx}\right|_{x=\frac{\pi}{6}} = (2/3)^{1/2}$

3. (c) $y = \sin^{-1}\left[\sqrt{x-ax} - \sqrt{a-ax}\right]$

which can be written as $\sin^{-1}\left(\sqrt{x}\sqrt{1-a} - \sqrt{a}\sqrt{1-x}\right)$

Substituting $x = \sin^2\theta$ and $a = \sin^2\phi$; $\phi \in \left[0, \dfrac{\pi}{2}\right]$

The expression becomes $\sin^{-1}\sin(\theta - \phi)$ i.e., $\theta - \phi$

$\left(\because \theta - \phi \in \left[\dfrac{-\pi}{2}, \dfrac{\pi}{2}\right]\right)$

$\Rightarrow \dfrac{dy}{dx} = \dfrac{d}{dx}(\theta - \phi) = \dfrac{d}{dx}\left(\sin^{-1}\sqrt{x} - \sin^{-1}\sqrt{a}\right)$

$= \dfrac{1}{2\sqrt{x}\sqrt{1-x}}$

4. (d) $x = 2\log\cot t$ and $y = \tan t + \cot t$

$\Rightarrow \dfrac{dx}{dt} = 2\tan t(-\text{cosec}^2 t) = -\dfrac{4}{\sin 2t}$

and $\dfrac{dy}{dt} = \sec^2 t - \text{cosec}^2 t = \dfrac{1}{\cos^2 t} - \dfrac{1}{\sin^2 t} = \dfrac{\sin^2 t - \cos^2 t}{\sin^2 t\cos^2 t}$

$= \dfrac{-4(\cos 2t)}{\sin^2 2t}$

$\Rightarrow \dfrac{dy}{dx} = \dfrac{dy/dt}{dx/dt} = \dfrac{-4\cos 2t}{\sin^2 2t} \times \dfrac{-\sin 2t}{4}$

$\Rightarrow \dfrac{dy}{dx} = \cot 2t \qquad \Rightarrow \sin 2t\dfrac{dy}{dx} = \cos 2t$

$\Rightarrow (\sin 2t)\dfrac{dy}{dx} + 1 = 1 + \cos 2t = 2\cos^2 t$

5. (a) $y = \left(x + \left(\sqrt{1+x^2}\right)\right)^m$

$\Rightarrow y_1 = \dfrac{m\left(x+\sqrt{x^2+1}\right)^m}{\sqrt{x^2+1}} = \dfrac{my}{\sqrt{x^2+1}}$ ...(i)

$\Rightarrow y_1.\sqrt{x^2+1} = my$

$\Rightarrow \dfrac{y_1 x}{\sqrt{x^2+1}} + \sqrt{x^2+1}.y_2 = my_1$

$\Rightarrow (x^2+1)y_2 + xy_1 - m\left(\sqrt{x^2+1}\right)y_1 = 0$

$\Rightarrow (x^2+1)y_2 + xy_1 = m^2 y$ (using(i))

6. (a) $x^2 ey + 2xyex + 13 = 0$

Differentiating the equation, we get $2xey + x^2 e^y . \dfrac{dy}{dx}$

$+ 2xe^x\dfrac{dy}{dx} + y\left(2e^x + 2xe^x\right) = 0$

$\Rightarrow \dfrac{dy}{dx}\left(x^2e^y + 2xe^x\right) = -y\left(2xe^x + 2e^x\right) - 2xe^y$

$\Rightarrow \dfrac{dy}{dx} = \dfrac{-y\left(e^x 2x + 2e^x\right) - 2xe^y}{\left(2xe^x + x^2e^y\right)}$

$\Rightarrow \dfrac{dy}{dx} = -\dfrac{2xe^{y-x} + 2y(x+1)}{\left(2x + x^2.e^{y-x}\right)}$

7. (c) $y = (\tan x \tan x)\tan^x$

$\Rightarrow \ell n y = \tan x.\ \ell n(\tan x)\tan x)$

$\Rightarrow \ell n y = \tan^2 x.\ \ell n \tan x$

Differentiating the whole equation, we get $\dfrac{1}{y}.\dfrac{dy}{dx} = 2$

$\tan x.\sec^2 x\ \ell n \tan x + \dfrac{\tan^2 x}{\tan x}.\sec^2 x$

$\Rightarrow \dfrac{dy}{dx} = y[\sec^2 x(2\tan x\ \ell n \tan x + \tan x)]$

$\Rightarrow \left.\dfrac{dy}{dx}\right|_{x=\frac{\pi}{4}} = 1(2(1)) = 2$

8. (d) $y = \sin^{-1}\left[\dfrac{\sin\alpha.\sin x}{1-\cos\alpha.\sin x}\right]$

$\Rightarrow \dfrac{dy}{dx} = \dfrac{1}{\sqrt{1 - \dfrac{\sin^2\alpha.\sin^2 x}{1+\cos^2\alpha.\sin^2 x - 2\cos\alpha.\sin x}}}\left(\dfrac{\sin\alpha.\sin x}{1-\cos\alpha.\sin x}\right)'$

$\Rightarrow \dfrac{dy}{dx} = \dfrac{|1-\cos\alpha.\sin x|}{1+\cos^2\alpha.\sin^2 x - 2\cos\alpha.\sin x - \sin^2\alpha\sin^2 x} \times$

$\dfrac{((1-\cos\alpha.\sin x)(\sin\alpha.\cos x) + \cos\alpha.\cos x(\sin\alpha.\sin x))}{(1-\cos\alpha.\sin x)^2}$

Putting $x = 0$ in dy/dx

$\Rightarrow \left.\dfrac{dy}{dx}\right|_{x=0} = \sin\alpha$

9. (b) $f:(-1, 1) \to \mathbb{R}$

$f(0) = -1$

$f'(0) = 1$

Given $g(x) = [f(2.f(x) + 2)]^2$

$\Rightarrow g'(x) = 2[f(2f(x) + 2)] . f'(2f(x) + 2) . 2f'(x)$

$\Rightarrow g'(0) = 2[f(2f(0) + 2)]. f'(2f(0) + 2) . 2f'(0)$

$\Rightarrow 2[f(0)] f'(0).2. f'(0) = -4$

10. **(a)** $f(x) = |x-2| + |x+1| - x$

$\Rightarrow f'(x) = \frac{x-2}{|x-2|} + \frac{x+1}{|x+1|} - 1$

$\Rightarrow f'(-10) = \frac{-12}{12} - \frac{9}{9} - 1 = -3$

11. **(a)** $xy = e^{2(x-y)}$

Taking log both sides, we get $y\,\ell n\,x = 2(x-y)\,\ell n\,e$

$\Rightarrow y\,\ell n\,x = 2(x-y)$ ...(i)

Differentiating both sides, we get $\ell nx\frac{dy}{dx} + \frac{y}{x} = 2 - 2\frac{dy}{dx}$

$\Rightarrow (dy/dx)(\ell n\,x + 2) = 2 - y/x$

$\Rightarrow \frac{dy}{dx} = \frac{2-\frac{y}{x}}{2+\ell nx}$

By (i), we get $y(\ell nx + 2) = 2x$

$\Rightarrow y/x = \left(\frac{2}{\ell nx+2}\right)$ $\Rightarrow dy/dx = \left(\frac{2-\frac{2}{\ell nx+2}}{2+\ell nx}\right)$

$\Rightarrow dy/dx = \frac{2\ell nx+2}{(2+\ell nx)^2}$

12. **(a)** $x^2x - 2xx\cot y - 1 = 0$ ...(i)

Let $P = x^{2x}$

Taking log both side, we get $\ell n\,P = 2x\,\ell n\,x$

$\Rightarrow \frac{1}{P}\frac{dP}{dx} = 2 + 2\,\ell nx$

$\Rightarrow \frac{dP}{dx} = x^{2x}(2+2\ell nx)$ ...(ii)

Let $Q = x^x$

Taking log both side, we get $\ell n\,Q = x\,\ell n\,x$

$\Rightarrow \frac{1}{Q}.\frac{dQ}{dx} = 1 + \ell nx$

$\Rightarrow \frac{dQ}{dx} = x^x(1+\ell nx)$ ...(iii)

Differentiating (i), we get $x^{2x}(2 + 2\ell nx) - 2xx(1 + \ell n\,x)\cot y + 2xx(\text{cosec}^2 y).y' = 0$

$\Rightarrow$ At $x = 1$, $2 - 2(1)(\cot y) + (\text{cosec}^2 y)\,y'(1) = 0$

$\Rightarrow 2 - 2(0) + 2[1]\,y'(1) = 0$

$\Rightarrow y'(1) = -1$

13. **(a)** $y = (\log_{\cos x}\sin x)(\log_{\sin x}\cos x) + \sin^{-1}\frac{2x}{1+x^2}$ which can be written as $\frac{\log\sin x}{\log\cos x} \times \frac{\log\cos x}{\log\sin x} + \sin^{-1}\left(\frac{2x}{1+x^2}\right)$

$\Rightarrow y = \sin^{-1}\left(\frac{2x}{1+x^2}\right) + 1$

Substitute $x = \tan a$; $a \in \left(-\frac{\pi}{2}, \frac{\pi}{2}\right)$

$\Rightarrow y = \sin^{-1}\left(\frac{2\tan a}{1+\tan^2 a}\right)$

$\Rightarrow y = \sin^{-1}(\sin 2a) = 2a$ as $2a \in \left(\frac{-\pi}{4}, \frac{\pi}{4}\right)$

$\Rightarrow y = 2.\tan^{-1} x$ $\Rightarrow y' = \text{——}$

$\Rightarrow$ ' |— ——

14. **(c)** $f(x) = 2^2x - {}^1$

$\ell n(f(x)) = (2x-1)\,\ell n\,2$

$\Rightarrow \frac{f'(x)}{f(x)} = 2\,\ell n\,2$

$\Rightarrow f'(x) = f(x)\,2\,\ell n\,2 = 2^{2x}\,.\,\ell n\,2$ ....(i)

Now, $f(x) = -2x + 2x\,\ell n\,2$

$\Rightarrow f'(x) = -2^x\,\ell n\,2 + 2\,\ell n\,2$

$\Rightarrow 2^{2x}\,\ell n\,2 > -2^x\,\ell n\,2 + 2\,\ell n\,2$ ($\because f'(x) > f'(x)$, given)

$\Rightarrow 2^x\,\ell n\,2(2x+1) > 2\,\ell n\,2$

$\Rightarrow 2^x(2x+1) > 2$ $\Rightarrow (2x)^2 + 2^x - 2 > 0$

$\Rightarrow (2x+2)(2^x-1) > 0$ $\Rightarrow -2 < 2^x < 1$

$\Rightarrow 0 < 2^x < 1$ $\Rightarrow -\infty < x < 0$ i.e., $x < 0$

15. **(d)** $f(x) = \frac{g(x)+g(-x)}{2} + \frac{2}{((h(x)+h(-x)))^{-1}}$ which can be written as $f(x) = \frac{g(x)}{2} + \frac{g(-x)}{2} + 2h(x) + 2h(-x)$

Differentiating, we get $f'(x) = \frac{g'(x)}{2} - \frac{g'(-x)}{2} + 2h'(x) - 2h'(-x)$

$\Rightarrow f'(0) = 0$

16. **(d)** $y = \sec^{-1}(\text{cosec}\,x) + \text{cosec}^{-1}(\sec x) + \sin^{-1}(\cos x) + \cos^{-1}(\sin x)$

$dy/dx = \frac{-\text{cosec}\,x.\cot x}{|\text{cosec}\,x||\cot x|} - \frac{\sec x.\tan x}{|\sec x||\tan x|} - \frac{\sin x}{|\sin x|} - \frac{\cos x}{|\cos x|}$

for all x in the first quadrant

All T-function are positive in Ist quadrant

$\Rightarrow dy/dx = -4$

17. **(d)** $y = \cos^{-1}(\cos x)$

$\Rightarrow \frac{dy}{dx} = \frac{-1}{\sqrt{1-\cos^2 x}}(-\sin x) = \frac{\sin x}{|\sin x|}$

$\Rightarrow \frac{dy}{dx} = -1$ in 3*rd* and 4 quadrant

$= 1$ in 2*nd* and 1*st* quadrant

18. **(a)** Given $x = 2\cos\theta - \cos 2\theta$

$\Rightarrow \frac{dx}{d\theta} = -2\sin\theta + 2\sin 2\theta$

$\Rightarrow y = 2\sin\theta - \sin 2\theta$ $\Rightarrow \frac{dx}{d\theta} = 2\cos\theta - 2\cos 2\theta$

$\Rightarrow \frac{dy}{dx} = \frac{2\cos\theta - 2\cos 2\theta}{2\sin 2\theta - 2\sin\theta}$

$\Rightarrow \frac{dy}{dx} = \frac{\sin\frac{3\theta}{2}.\sin\frac{\theta}{2}}{\sin\frac{\theta}{2}.\cos\left(\frac{3\theta}{2}\right)} = \tan\frac{3\theta}{2}$

19. (a) $f(\tan x) = p$ and $g(\sec x) = q$

$dp/dx = f'(\tan x) . \sec^2 x$

$$\frac{dq}{dx} = g'(\sec x) . \sec x \tan x$$

$$\Rightarrow \frac{dp}{dq} = \frac{f'(\tan x).\sec^2 x}{g'(\sec x).\sec x.\tan x} = \frac{f'(\tan x).\sec x}{g'(\sec x).\tan x}$$

$$\Rightarrow \left.\frac{dp}{dq}\right|_{x=\frac{\pi}{4}} = \frac{f'(1)}{g'(\sqrt{2})}.\sqrt{2} = \frac{\sqrt{2}}{2} = \frac{1}{\sqrt{2}}$$

20. (c) $y = \left(1+\frac{1}{x}\right)\left(1+\frac{2}{x}\right)....\left(1+\frac{n}{x}\right)$

$$\Rightarrow \ell n\, y = \ell n\,(x+1) + \ell n(x+2) + ...+ \ell n(x+n) - n\,\ell n\, x$$

$$\Rightarrow \frac{1}{y}\frac{dy}{dx} = \left(\frac{1}{x+1} + \frac{1}{x+2} + ...+ \frac{1}{x+n} - \frac{n}{x}\right)$$

$$\Rightarrow \frac{dy}{dx} = \frac{(x+1)(x+2).....(x+n)}{x^n}\left[\left(\frac{1}{x+1}+\frac{1}{x+2}+....+\frac{1}{x+n}\right)-\frac{n}{x}\right]$$

$$\Rightarrow \frac{dy}{dx} = \frac{(x+2)(x+3)...(x+n)}{x^n}\left[\left(1+\frac{x+1}{x+2}+....+\frac{x+1}{x+n}\right)-\frac{n}{x}(x+1)\right]$$

$$\Rightarrow \left(\frac{dy}{dx}\right)_{x=-1} = \frac{(1)(2)(3).(n-1)}{(-1)^n}.1$$

$$\Rightarrow \left.\frac{dy}{dx}\right|_{x=-1} = (n-1)!(-1)^n$$

21. (d) Given $y = \log^n x$

$$\Rightarrow \frac{dy}{dx} = \frac{1}{\log^{n-1} x \log^{n-2} x.....x}$$

$\Rightarrow$ x. log x. $\log^2$ x……$\log^n x$ dy/dx = $\log^n x$

22. (a) $x = a(1 + \cos\theta)$

$$\Rightarrow \frac{dx}{d\theta} = -a\sin\theta$$

$y = a(\theta + \sin\theta)$

$$\Rightarrow \frac{dy}{d\theta} = a(1+\cos\theta)$$

$$\Rightarrow \frac{dy}{dx} = \frac{1+\cos\theta}{-\sin\theta} = \frac{2\cos^2\frac{\theta}{2}}{-2\sin\frac{\theta}{2}\cos\frac{\theta}{2}} = -\cot\frac{\theta}{2}$$

$$\Rightarrow \frac{d^2y}{dx^2} = \frac{1}{2}\text{cosec}^2\frac{\theta}{2}\times\frac{d\theta}{dx} = \frac{1}{2}\text{cosec}^2\frac{\theta}{2}\times\frac{-1}{a\sin\theta}$$

$$= \frac{-1}{2^a}.\frac{\text{cosec}^2\frac{\theta}{2}}{2\sin\frac{\theta}{2}\cos\frac{\theta}{2}} = \frac{1}{4a}\text{cosec}^3\frac{\theta}{2}\sec\frac{\theta}{2}$$

$$\Rightarrow \left.\frac{d^2y}{dx^2}\right|_{x=\frac{\pi}{2}} = \frac{-1}{4a}\left(\sqrt{2}\right)^3\left(\sqrt{2}\right) = -\frac{1}{a}$$

23. (b) $y = \sin^{-1}\left(\frac{5x+12\sqrt{1-x^2}}{13}\right)$

Let $x = \sin\theta$ and $5/13 = \cos\omega$

The expression of y reduces to $y = \sin^{-1}(\sin\theta.\cos\omega + \sin\omega\cos\theta)$

$y = \theta + \omega$

$y = \sin^{-1} x + \cos^{-1}(5/13)$

$$\Rightarrow dy/dx = \frac{1}{\sqrt{1-x^2}}$$

24. (c) $f(x) = 1 + nx + \frac{n(n-1)}{2}x^2 \frac{n(n-1)(n-2)}{6}x^3$ +……….+ xn

$f(x)$ can be written as $f(x) = 1 + nC_1\, x + nC_2\, x^2 + nC_3 x^3$ +……..${}^nC_n\, x^n$

$\Rightarrow f(x) = (1 + x)^n$

$\Rightarrow f'(x) = n(1 + x)n - {}^1$

$\Rightarrow f''(x) = n(n - 1)\,(1 + x)n - {}^2$

$\Rightarrow f''(1) = n(n - 1).2n - {}^2$

25. (c) $y = t^{10} + 1$ and $x = t^8 + 1$

$$\Rightarrow \frac{dy}{dt} = 10t^9 \;\&\; \frac{dx}{dt} = 8t^7$$

$$\Rightarrow \frac{dy}{dx} = \frac{5}{4}t^2$$

$$\Rightarrow \frac{d^2y}{dx^2} = \frac{5}{4}(2t)\left(\frac{dt}{dx}\right) = \frac{5}{2}+\left(\frac{1}{8t^7}\right) = \frac{5}{16t^6}$$

$$\Rightarrow \frac{d^2y}{dx^2} = \frac{5}{4}.2t.\frac{1}{8}(x-1)^{-7/8}$$

$$\Rightarrow \frac{d^2y}{dx^2} = \frac{5t}{2.8}.\left(t^8\right)^{-7/8} = \frac{5}{16t^6}$$

26. (c) f: $\mathbb{R} \to \mathbb{R}$ is even

$\Rightarrow f(x) = f(-x)$ $\Rightarrow f'(x) = (f(-x))'$

$\Rightarrow f'(x) = -f'(-x)$ $\Rightarrow f''(x) = f''(-x)$

$\Rightarrow f''(\pi) = f''(-\pi)$ $\Rightarrow f''(-\pi) = 1$

27. (d) $y = e^{2x}$ …(i)

$$\Rightarrow \frac{dy}{dx} = 2e^{2x}$$

$$\Rightarrow \frac{d\;y}{dx} \quad \text{…(ii)}$$

By (i), we get $2x = \ell n\, y$

$$\Rightarrow x = \frac{\ell ny}{2} \qquad \Rightarrow dx/dy = \frac{1}{2y}$$

$$\Rightarrow \frac{d^2x}{dy^2} = \frac{-1}{2y^2} \quad \text{…(iii)}$$

By (ii) & (iii), we get $\frac{d^2y}{dx^2}\times\frac{d^2x}{dy^2} = \frac{-2e^{2x}}{y^2} = \frac{-2}{e^{2x}} = -2e^{-2x}$

28. (d) $y = 2\sin^{-1}\sqrt{1-x} + \sin^{-1} 2\sqrt{x(1-x)}$

Differentiating w.r.t. x, we get $\frac{dy}{dx} = \frac{2}{\sqrt{1-(1-x)}}.\frac{1}{2}\frac{(-1)}{\sqrt{1-x}}$

$$+ \frac{1.2}{\sqrt{1-4(x(1-x))}}.\frac{1}{2}\frac{(1-2x)}{\sqrt{x(1-x)}}$$

$$= \frac{-1}{\sqrt{x}\sqrt{1-x}} + \frac{(1-2x)2}{2\sqrt{x(1-x)}\sqrt{(1-2x)^2}}$$

$$= \frac{-1}{\sqrt{x}\sqrt{1-x}} + \frac{2(1-2x)}{2\sqrt{x(1-x)}|1-2x|}$$

For $x \in (0, 1/2)$

$$\Rightarrow \frac{dy}{dx} = \frac{-1}{\sqrt{x}\sqrt{1-x}} + \frac{1}{\sqrt{x(1-x)}} = 0$$

29. (a) $f(x) = \lambda + \mu|x| + v|x^2|; = \begin{cases} \lambda + \mu x + vx^2 & \text{for } x \ge 0 \\ \lambda - \mu x + vx^2 & \text{for } x < 0 \end{cases}$

Now, $f'(0^-) = \lim_{h\to 0^+} \frac{f(0-h) - f(0)}{-h}$

$$= \lim_{h\to 0^+} \frac{f(-h) - \lambda}{-h} = \lim_{h\to 0^+} \frac{[\lambda - \mu(-h) + vh^2 - \lambda]}{-h}$$

$$= \lim_{h\to 0^+}\left[\frac{\mu h + yh^2}{-h}\right] = \lim_{h\to 0^+} -\mu - vh$$

$\Rightarrow f'(0^-) = -\mu$ ...(i)

Also, $f'(0^+) = \lim_{h\to 0^+} \frac{f(0+h) - f(0)}{h}$

$$= \lim_{h\to 0^+} \frac{f(h) - \lambda}{h} = \lim_{h\to 0^+} \frac{\lambda + \mu h + vh^2 - \lambda}{h}$$

$\Rightarrow f'(0^+) = \mu$ ...(ii)

$\therefore$ $f'(0)$ to exist, $-\mu = \mu \Rightarrow \mu = 0$

30. (a) By the question $f(x) = y$ and $g(y) = x$

Given $f'(x) = dy/dx = \sin x$

$$\Rightarrow g'(x) = \frac{1}{\sin(g(x))} = \text{cosec}(g(x))$$

31. (d) $x = \frac{1+t}{t^3}$ and $y = \frac{3}{2t^2} + \frac{2}{t}$

$$\Rightarrow \frac{dx}{dt} = -\frac{2t+3}{t^4} \text{ and } \frac{dy}{dt} = -\frac{2t+3}{t^3}$$

$\Rightarrow \frac{dy}{dx} = t \quad \Rightarrow y' = t$

$$\Rightarrow f(x) = \frac{1+y'}{(y')^3} = \frac{1+t}{t^3} = x$$

$\Rightarrow f(x) = x$

32. (c) $f(x) = x + \tan x$ ...(1)

$\because$ f is inverse of g

$\Rightarrow$ g is inverse of f i.e., $g = f^{-1}$

Now, $f(f^{-1}(x)) = x$

$\Rightarrow f(g(x)) = x$

$\Rightarrow f'(g(x)).g'(x) = 1$

$$\Rightarrow g'(x) = \frac{1}{f'(g(x))} = \frac{1}{1+\sec^2(g(x))} = \frac{1}{1+(1+\tan^2(g(x))}$$

$$= \frac{1}{2+(f(g(x)) - g(x))^2} = \frac{1}{2+(x-g(x))^2} [\because f(g(x)) = x]$$

33. (b) $5f(x) + 3f\left(\frac{1}{x}\right) = x + 2$ ...(i)

$$5f'(x) + 3f'\left(\frac{1}{x}\right)\left(\frac{-1}{x^2}\right) = 1$$

Put $x = 1$, we get $5f'(1) + 3f'(1)(-1) = 1$

$\Rightarrow 2f'(1) = 1 \quad \Rightarrow f'(1) = 1/2$

Given, $y = x f(x)$

$$\Rightarrow \frac{dy}{dx} = xf'(x) + f(x)$$

Putting $x = 1$ in (i), we get $5f(1) + 3f(1) = 3$

$\Rightarrow 8f(1) = 3 \quad \Rightarrow f(1) = 3/8$

$$\Rightarrow \left.\frac{dy}{dx}\right|_{x=1} = 1.f'(1) + f(1) = 1/2 + 3/8 = \frac{7}{8}$$

34. (c) $y = Ae^{x^2} + Be^{x^2/2}$

$$\Rightarrow \frac{dy}{dx} = Ae^{x^2}(2x) + Be^{x^2/2}(x)$$

$$\Rightarrow \frac{d^2y}{dx^2} = 2Axe^{x^2}(2x) + 2Ae^{x^2} + Bxe^{x^2/2}(2x) + Be^{x^2/2}$$

$$\Rightarrow \frac{d^2y}{dx^2} = 4Ax^2e^{x^2} + 2Ae^{x^2} + 2Bx^2e^{x^2/2} + 2Be^{x^2/2}$$

$$\Rightarrow \frac{d^2y}{dx^2} + 2x^2y = 4Ax^2e^{x^2} + 2Bx^2e^{x^2/2} + 2Ae^{x^2} + 2Be^{x^2/2}$$

$$+ 2x^2Ae^{x^2} + Bx^2e^{x^2/x} = 6x^2Ae^{x^2} + 3Bx^2e^{x^2/2}$$

$$+ 2Ae^{x^2} + Be^{x^2/2} = 3x\left(\frac{dy}{dx}\right) + \frac{1}{x}\frac{dy}{dx}$$

$$\Rightarrow \frac{d^2y}{dx^2} + \left(-3x\frac{dy}{dx} - \frac{1}{x}\right)\frac{dy}{dx} + 2x^2y = 0$$

$\Rightarrow k = -3$

35. (a) $y = \frac{x^2}{2} + \frac{x\sqrt{x^2+1}}{2} + \ell n\sqrt{x\sqrt{x^2+1}}$

$$\Rightarrow \frac{dy}{dx} = x + \frac{1}{2}\left[\frac{x^2}{\sqrt{x^2+1}} + \sqrt{x^2+1}\right]$$

$$+ \frac{1}{2\left(x+\sqrt{x^2+1}\right)} \times \left(1 + \frac{2x}{2\sqrt{x^2+1}}\right)$$

$$= x + \frac{1}{2}\left(\frac{2x^2+1}{\sqrt{x^2+1}}\right) + \frac{1}{2\sqrt{x^2+1}}$$

$$= x + \frac{1}{2\sqrt{x^2+1}} [2(x^2+1)]$$

$\Rightarrow y' = x + \sqrt{x^2+1}$

Also, $2y = x^2 + x\sqrt{x^2+1} + \ell n\left(x + \sqrt{x^2+1}\right)$ (given equation)

$$\Rightarrow 2y = x\left(x+\sqrt{x^2+1}\right) + \ell n\left(x+\sqrt{x^2+1}\right) = x\frac{dy}{dx} + \ell n\left(\frac{dy}{dx}\right)$$

$\Rightarrow k = 2$

36. **(a)** Given $g(x) = (ax^2 + bx + c)\sin x + (dx^2 + ex + f)\cos x$
Differentiating, we get $g'(x) = (2ax + b)\sin x + (ax^2 + bx + c)\cos x + (2dx + e)\cos x - (dx^2 + ex + f)\sin x$ ...(i)
$= \sin x(2ax + b - dx^2 - ex - f) + \cos x(ax^2 + bx + c + 2dx + e)$
Given that $g'(x) = x^2 \sin x$ ...(ii)
Comparing, equation (i) & (ii), $a = 0$, $b = 2$, $c = 0$, $d = -1$, $e = 0$, $f = 2$

37. **(c)** $2f(x) + 3f(-x) = x^2 - x + 1$,
$\Rightarrow 2f'(x) - 3f'(-x) = 2x - 1$
$\Rightarrow 2f'(1) - 3f'(-1) = 1$ ...(1)
and $2f'(-1) - 3f'(-1) = -3$ ...(2)
Equation (1) × 2 + (2) × 3 gives, $4f'(1) - 9f'(1) = 2 + (-3)(3)$
$\Rightarrow -5f'(1) = -7 \qquad \Rightarrow f'(1) = 7/5$

38. **(b)** By sine formula, $\dfrac{a}{\sin A} = \dfrac{b}{\sin B}$

$$\Rightarrow \sin A = \frac{a \sin B}{b}$$

$$\Rightarrow A = \sin^{-1}\left(\frac{a \sin B}{b}\right)$$

$$\Rightarrow \frac{dA}{dB} = \frac{1}{\sqrt{1-\left(\frac{a\sin B}{b}\right)^2}}\cdot\frac{a}{b}\cos B = \frac{a\cos B}{\sqrt{b^2 - a^2\sin^2 B}}$$

$$= \sqrt{\frac{a^2 - b^2\sin^2 A}{b^2 - a^2\sin^2 B}} \quad \left[\begin{array}{l}\because b\sin A = a\sin B \\ \Rightarrow b^2\sin^2 A = a^2\sin^2 B \\ \Rightarrow a^2 - b^2\sin^2 A = a^2\cos^2 B\end{array}\right]$$

39. **(b)** $f(x) = \tan^{-1}\left(\dfrac{1}{\cos^2 x + \cos x + 1}\right) + \tan^{-1}\left(\dfrac{1}{\cos^2 x + 3\cos x + 3}\right)$

$$+ \tan^{-1}\left(\frac{1}{\cos^2 x + 5\cos x + 7}\right)$$

$$+ \tan^{-1}\left(\frac{1}{\cos^2 x + 7\cos x + 13}\right) + \ldots.. + \text{ on terms}$$

$$= \left[\tan^{-1}(\cos x + 1) - \tan^{-1}(\cos x)\right]$$

$$+ \left[\tan^{-1}(\cos x + 2) - \tan^{-1}(\cos x + 1)\right]$$

$$+ \left[\tan^{-1}(\cos x + 3) - \tan^{-1}(\cos x + 2)\right] + \ldots. +$$

$$\left[\tan^{-1}(\cos x + n) - \tan^{-1}(\cos x + \overline{n-1})\right]$$

$$= \tan^{-1}(\cos x + n) - \tan^{-1}(\cos x)$$

$$\Rightarrow f'(x) = \frac{1}{1 + (\cos x + n)^2}[-\sin x] - \frac{1}{1 + \cos^2 x}(-\sin x)$$

$$= \frac{-\sin x}{1 + (\cos x + n)^2} + \frac{\sin x}{1 + \cos^2 x}$$

40. **(b)** Given $(\sin B + \sin A)\, \text{Sin } C + \sin A.\, \sin B = k$
$\Rightarrow (\sin B + \sin A)\sin(A + B) + \sin A.\, \sin B = k$

Differentiating both sides w.r.t A, we get $(\sin B + \sin A).\, \cos(A + B)\left(1 + \dfrac{dB}{dA}\right) + \sin(A+B)\left(\cos B.\dfrac{dB}{dA} + \cos A\right)$

$$+ \sin A.\cos B.\frac{dB}{dA} + \sin B.\cos A = 0$$

$$\Rightarrow \frac{dB}{dA}$$

$$= \frac{-(\sin A + \sin B)\cos(A+B) - \sin(A+B).\cos A - \sin B\cos A}{(\sin A + \sin B)\cos(A+B) + \cos B.\sin(A+B) + \sin A\cos B}$$

$$= \frac{(\sin A + \sin B)\cos C - \sin C\cos A - \sin B\cos A}{-(\sin A + \sin B)\cos C + \cos B\sin C + \sin A\cos B}$$

$$= \frac{-(\sin C\cos A - \cos C\sin A) - \sin B(\cos A - \cos C)}{(\sin C\cos B - \cos C\sin B) + \sin A(\cos B - \cos C)}$$

$$= \frac{-\sin(C - A) - \sin B(\cos A - \cos C)}{\sin(C - B) + \sin A(\cos B - \cos C)}$$

$$A = \frac{\sin(C - A) + \sin B(\cos A - \cos C)}{\sin(B - C) + \sin A(\cos C - \cos B)}$$

41. **(a)** $\begin{vmatrix} x & y & z \\ x' & y' & z' \\ x'' & y'' & z'' \end{vmatrix} = kx^3$

$$\Rightarrow x\begin{vmatrix} 1 & s & t \\ 1 & s + xs' & t + xt' \\ 0 & s' + xs'' + s' & t' + xt'' + t' \end{vmatrix} = kx^3$$

$$\Rightarrow x\begin{vmatrix} 1 & s & t \\ 0 & xs' & xt' \\ 0 & xs'' + 2s' & xt'' + 2t' \end{vmatrix} = kx^3 (R_2 \to R_2 - R_1)$$

$$\Rightarrow x^2\begin{vmatrix} s' & t' \\ xs'' + 2s' & xt'' + 2t' \end{vmatrix} = kx^3$$

$$\Rightarrow x^2\begin{vmatrix} s' & t' \\ xs'' & xt'' \end{vmatrix} = kx^3 (R_2 \to R_2 - 2R_1)$$

$$\Rightarrow x^3\begin{vmatrix} s' & t' \\ s'' & t'' \end{vmatrix} = kx^3 \qquad \Rightarrow k = \begin{vmatrix} s' & t' \\ s'' & t'' \end{vmatrix}$$

$$\Rightarrow k = \begin{vmatrix} \cos x - \sin x & \cos x + \sin x \\ -\sin x - \cos x & -\sin x + \cos x \end{vmatrix}$$

$$\Rightarrow k = (\cos x - \sin x)^2 + (\sin x + \cos x)^2 = 2$$

SECTION–IV: (MORE THAN ONE ARE CORRECT)

1. **(a), (c), (d)**
$f_k(x) = \log_e(f_{k+1}(x)) \ \forall n \in \mathbb{N}$ and $f_1(x) = x$
$\Rightarrow f \ (x) \ \ e^{f\,(x)}$
$\Rightarrow f_2(x) = e^{f_1(x)} = e^x$
$\Rightarrow f_3(x) = e^{f_2(x)} = e^{e^x}$

$\Rightarrow \quad f_4(x) = e^{f_3(x)} = e^{e^{e^x}}$

....

....

$\Rightarrow \quad f_n(x) = e^{e^{e^{e^x}}}$ (e's are (^{n}–1) times)

$\Rightarrow \quad \frac{d}{dx}(f_n(x)) = f_n(x).f_{n-1}(x)f_{n-2}(x)....f_2(x).f_1(x)$

$= f_n(x).\frac{d}{dx}(f_{n-1}(x)) = \prod_{i=1}^{n} f_i(x)$

2. (b), (c), (d)

$f(t) = \log_3 t$

$D = \frac{d}{dx}\left\{\int_{x^2}^{x^3} f(t)dt\right\} = f(x^3).(3x^2) - f(x^2)(2x)$

$= \left(\log 3^{x^3}\right)(3x^2) - \left(\log 3^{x^2}\right)(2x) = 9x^2 \log 3^x - 4x \log 3^x$

Clearly it is not defined for $x = 0$

For $x = 1$, $D = 0$

For $x = \frac{4}{9}, D = 9\left(\frac{16}{81}\right)\log_3\frac{4}{9} - 4\left(\frac{4}{9}\right)\log_3\frac{4}{9}$

$= \left(\frac{16}{9} - \frac{16}{9}\right)\log_3\frac{4}{9} = 0$

For $x = e$, $D = (9e^2 - 4e)\log_3 e = \frac{(9e^2 - 4e)}{\ln 3}$

$\frac{dD}{dx} = 9x^2.\frac{1}{x}.\log_3 e - 4x.\frac{1}{x}\log_3 e + (18x - 4)\log_3 e$

$\left(\frac{dD}{dx}\right)_{x=e} = 9e\log_3 e - 4\log_3 e + (18e - 4)\log_3 e$

$= 27e\log_3 e - 8\log_3 e = \frac{(27e - 8)}{\ln 3}$

3. (a), (b), (c), (d)

$y = \cos^{-1} 2x + \cot^{-1} 5x + \sin^{-1} 2x + \tan^{-1} 5x$

$\Rightarrow \quad y'(x) = \frac{-1.2}{\sqrt{1-4x^2}} - \frac{1.5}{1+25x^2} + \frac{1.2}{\sqrt{1-4x^2}} + \frac{1.5}{1+25x^2} = 0$

$\Rightarrow \quad y'(0) = 0,\ y_1 = y_2 = y_3 = y_4 = y_5 = y_6 = 0$

4. (b), (c) $f(x) = eax \sin(bx + c)$

$\Rightarrow f'(x) = eax.\ a.\sin(bx + c) + eax.\cos(bx + c).b$

Differentiating again, we get $f''(x) = a^2 eax.\sin(bx + c) + abeax.\cos(bx + c) + abeax\cos(bx + c) - b^2 eax \sin(bx + c)$

$\Rightarrow f''(x) = eax \sin(bx + c)[a^2 - b^2] + 2eax.\ ab.\cos(bx + c)]$

$= eax[(a^2 - b^2).\sin(bx + c) + 2ab\cos(bx + c)]$

Dividing throughout by $\sqrt{(a^2 - b^2)^2 + (2ab)^2}$

$= \sqrt{a^4 + b^4 - 2a^2b^2 + 4a^2b^2} = a^2 + b^2$

$\Rightarrow \quad f''(x) = eax(a^2 + b^2)$

$\left(\left(\frac{a^2 - b^2}{a^2 + b^2}\right)\sin(bx + c) + \frac{2ab}{a^2 + b^2}\cos(bx + c)\right)$

which can be written as $f''(x) = eax(a^2 + b^2)$

$\left(\left(\frac{1-(b/a)^2}{1+(b/a)^2}\right)\sin(bx + c) + \frac{2(b/a)}{1+(b/a)^2}\cos(bx + c)\right)$

$= eax(a^2 + b^2)(\cos(2\tan^{-1}b/a).\sin(bx + c) + \cos(bx + c).\sin(2\tan^{-1}b/a) = eax(a^2 + b^2)\sin(bx + c + \phi)$; where

$\phi = 2\tan^{-1}\left(\frac{b}{a}\right)$

Comparing with given $f''(x) = r^2.\sin(bx + \theta).eax$

$\Rightarrow \quad r = \sqrt{a^2 + b^2}$ and $\theta = c + 2\tan^{-1}b/a$

5. (a), (b), (c) $y = \tan x.\tan 2x.\tan 3x$

$\Rightarrow \quad \frac{dy}{dx} = \sec^2 x.\tan 2x.\tan 3x + \sec^2 2x.2.\tan x.\tan 3x + \sec^2 3x.\frac{d}{dx}(3x).\tan x.\tan 2x)$

$= \sec^2 x.\tan 2x.\tan 3x + 2\tan x.\sec^2 2x.\tan(3x) + 3\tan x.\tan 2x.\sec^2 3x$ ....(i)

$\Rightarrow$ Option (a) is correct.

Can also be written by taking $\tan x \tan 2x.\tan 3x$ common $= 2y(\text{cosec } 2x + 3\text{ cosec } 6x + 2\text{ cosec } 4x)$

Also $\tan 3x = \tan(2x + x)$

$\Rightarrow \quad \tan 3x = \frac{\tan 2x + \tan x}{1 - \tan 2x.\tan x}$

$\Rightarrow \quad \tan 3x - \tan 2x - \tan x = \tan 3x.\tan 2x.\tan x = y$

$\Rightarrow \quad \frac{dy}{dx} = 3\sec^2 3x - 2\sec^2 2x - \sec^2 x$

6. (a), (d) $y = \frac{(\sec x + \tan x)}{(\sec x - \tan x)}$

$\Rightarrow \quad \frac{dy}{dx} = \frac{(\sec x - \tan x)(\sec x.\tan x + \sec^2 x) - (\sec x + \tan x)(\sec x \tan x - \sec^2 x)}{(\sec x - \tan x)^2}$

$= \frac{\sec x(\sec x + \tan x)}{\sec x - \tan x} - \frac{(\sec x + \tan x).\sec x(\tan x - \sec x)}{(\sec x - \tan x)^2}$

$= \sec x.(\sec x + \tan x)\left(\frac{1}{\sec x - \tan x} + \frac{1}{\sec x - \tan x}\right)$

$= \frac{2\sec x.(\sec x + \tan x)}{(\sec x - \tan x)}$

Multiplying & dividing by $\sec x + \tan x$

$\Rightarrow \quad dy/dx = 2\sec x.(\sec x + \tan x)^2 = 2(1 + \sin x)^2)\sec^3 x$

7. (a), (c) $f(x) = x^n$; $n \in W$

$\Rightarrow f'(x) = nx^{n-1}$

Given $f'(a + b) = f'(a) + f'(b)$

$\Rightarrow \quad n(a + b)^{n-1} = na^{n-1} + nb^{n-1}$

$\Rightarrow \quad (a + b)^{n-1} = a^{n-1} + bn^{-1}$

$\Rightarrow$ For $n = 2$ and $n = 0$ it holds

8. (a), (b), (c), (d)

$f(x) = (ax + b)\cos x + (cx + d)\sin x$

$f(x) = a\cos x - (ax + b)\sin x + c\sin x + (cx + d)\cos x$

$= \cos x(a + cx + d) + \sin x(c - ax - b)$

Given $f'(x) = x \cos x$ is true $\forall x$

$\Rightarrow$ it is an identify

$\Rightarrow a = 0, b = 1, c = 1, d = 0$

9. (b), (c)

1 is twice repeated root of $ax^3 + bx^2 + bx + d = 0$ (say) $f(x) = 0$

$\Rightarrow f(x) = (x-1)^2 g(x), f'(x) = 3ax^2 + 2bx + b, f(1) = 0, f'(1) = 0, g(1) \square 0$

Now, $f(1) = 0$

$\Rightarrow a + b + b + d = 0 \quad \Rightarrow a + d + 2b = 0;$

$\Rightarrow f'(1) = 0 \quad \Rightarrow 3a + 2b + b = 0$

$\Rightarrow a + b = 0; \quad \Rightarrow b + d = 0$

10. (a), (b), (c), (d)

(a) $f(x) = |x-2|$

$\Rightarrow f(f(x)) = |f(x)-2| = ||x-2|-2|$

$\therefore f(f(x)) = |x-4| = x-4$ for $x > 20$

$\Rightarrow f(f(x))' = 1 \ \forall x > 20$

(b) $f(x) = \dfrac{x}{1+|x|}$

$\Rightarrow f(x) = \dfrac{x}{1-x}$ for $x < 0$

$\Rightarrow f'(x) = \dfrac{(1-x)-x(-1)}{(1-x)^2} = \dfrac{1}{(1-x)^2}$

$\Rightarrow f'(-1) = \dfrac{1}{(1+1)^2} = \dfrac{1}{4}$

(c) $f(0) = 0, f'(0) = b, g(0) = 0$. $(fog)'(0) = c$. (given)

Now $(fog)'(x) = f'(g(x)).\ g'(x)$

$\therefore (fog)'(0) = f'(g(0)).\ g'(0) = f'(0).\ g'(0)$

$c = b.\ g'(0)$

$\Rightarrow g'(0) = c/b$

(d) Let $y = 2\tan^{-x}$ and $z = \sin^{-1}\left(\dfrac{2x}{1+x^2}\right)$ We know that

$$2\tan^{-1} x = \begin{cases} \sin^{-1}\left(\dfrac{2x}{1+x^2}\right) & \text{for } -1 \le x \le 1 \\ -\pi - \sin^{-1}\left(\dfrac{2x}{1+x^2}\right) & \text{for } x < -1 \\ \pi - \sin^{-1}\left(\dfrac{2x}{1+x^2}\right) & \text{for } x > 1 \end{cases}$$

$$\Rightarrow y = \begin{cases} 3 & \text{for } -1 \le x \le 1 \\ -\pi - z & \text{for } x < -1 \\ \pi - z & \text{for } x > 1 \end{cases}$$

$$\Rightarrow y = \begin{cases} 1 & \text{for } -1 < x < 1 \\ -1 & \text{for } x < -1 \\ -1 & \text{for } x > 1 \end{cases}$$

$$\Rightarrow \left(\frac{dy}{dz}\right)_{x=\frac{1}{2}} = 1$$

11. (a), (b), (c), (d)

(a) $f(x) = log(x)$

$f(\log x) = log(\log x)$

$f'(\log x) = \dfrac{1}{\log x.x}$

(b) $y = \log(xx) = x \log x$

$\Rightarrow \dfrac{dy}{dx} = \log x + 1 = = \log_e(ex)$

(c) $y = log_{10} x = \dfrac{\log x}{\log 10}$

$z = log_x 10 = \dfrac{\log 10}{\log x}$

$\Rightarrow \dfrac{dy}{dx} = \dfrac{1}{x \log 10}; \dfrac{dz}{dx} = \dfrac{-\log 10}{(\log x)^2}.\dfrac{1}{x}$

$\Rightarrow \dfrac{dy}{dz} = \dfrac{\dfrac{1/x\log 10}{-\log 10}}{x \log x.\log x} = \dfrac{-x(\log x)^2}{x.(\log 10)^2} = -\left(\dfrac{\log x}{\log 10}\right)^2$

(d) $\because fof^{-1}(x) = x$

$\Rightarrow f(g(x)) = x \qquad \Rightarrow f'(g(x)).\ g'(x) = 1$

$\Rightarrow g'(x) = \dfrac{1}{f'(g(x))} = \dfrac{1}{\sin(g(x))}$

SECTION–V: ASSERTION AND REASON TYPE

1. (d) $y = x^2$

$\Rightarrow \dfrac{dy}{dx} = 2x$

$\Rightarrow \dfrac{d^2y}{dx^2} = 2 \quad$ ...(i)

For f: $[0, \infty) \to [0, \infty)$

$\Rightarrow x = \sqrt{y}$

$\Rightarrow \dfrac{dx}{dy} = \dfrac{1}{2} y^{-1/2}$

$\Rightarrow \dfrac{d^2x}{dy^2} = -\dfrac{1}{4} y^{-3/2} \quad$ ...(ii)

By (i) and (ii), we get $\left(\dfrac{d^2y}{dx^2}\right)\left(\dfrac{d^2x}{dy^2}\right) = \dfrac{-1}{2} y^{-3/2} \ne 1$

$\Rightarrow$ Assertion is incorrect.

$dy/dx = 2x \quad \Rightarrow \dfrac{dx}{dy} = \dfrac{1}{2\sqrt{y}}$

$\Rightarrow \dfrac{dy}{dx} = \dfrac{2x}{2\sqrt{y}} = 1 \quad \Rightarrow$ Reason is correct.

2. (a) $f(x) f(1/x) = f(x) + f(1/x)$

$f(x) = xn + 1$ or $- xn + 1$

if $f(x) = - xn + 1$

$\because f(x).f\left(\dfrac{1}{x}\right) = f(x) + f\left(\dfrac{1}{x}\right)$

$\Rightarrow \ f(x) = \pm x^n + 1$

$f(4) = 65 \quad \Rightarrow f(x) = x^3 + 1$

$\Rightarrow$ Reason is correct

$\Rightarrow f(x) = x^3 + 1 \quad \Rightarrow f'(x) = 3x^2$

$\Rightarrow f'(\ell_1) = 3\ell_1^{\,2}$

$\Rightarrow f'(\ell_2) = 3\ell_2^{\,2} \quad \Rightarrow f'(\ell_3) = 3\ell_3^{\,2}$

$\therefore$ If ℓ_1, ℓ_2, ℓ_3 in G.P. $\Rightarrow 3\ell_1^{\,2}, 3\ell_2^{\,2}, 3\ell_3^{\,2}$ are in G.P.

$\Rightarrow f'(\ell_1), f'(\ell_2), f'(\ell_3)$ are in G.P.

$\Rightarrow$ Assertion is correct

3. (c) $f(x) = (\cos x + i\sin x)(\cos 2x + i\sin 2x)(\cos 3x + i\sin 3x)\ldots\ldots(\cos nx + i\sin nx)$

$= \cos(x + 2x + \ldots.. + nx) + i\sin(x + 2x + \ldots + nx)$

$$= \cos n\left(\frac{n+1}{2}\right)x + i\sin\frac{n(n+1)}{2}$$

$$f'(x) = \frac{n(n+1)}{2}\left[-\sin\frac{n(n+1)}{2}x + i\cos\frac{n(n+1)}{2}x\right]$$

$$\Rightarrow f''(x) = -\left(\frac{n(n+1)}{2}\right)^2 . f(x)$$

$$\Rightarrow f''(1) = -\left(\frac{n(n+1)}{2}\right)^2 f(1) = -\left[n\left(\frac{n+1}{2}\right)\right]^2$$

$$\text{Since } f(x) = \cos\frac{n(n+1)}{2}x + i\sin\left(\frac{n(n+1)}{2}\right)x$$

$\Rightarrow$ *R is incorrect.*

4. (a) $x = \cos\theta + \log\tan(\theta/2)$, $y = \sin\theta$

$$\Rightarrow \frac{dx}{d\theta} = -\sin\theta + \left(\frac{1}{\tan\frac{\theta}{2}}\right).\sec^2\left(\frac{\theta}{2}\right).\frac{1}{2}$$

$$\Rightarrow \frac{dx}{d\theta} = -\sin\theta + \frac{1}{\sin\theta} \Rightarrow \frac{\cos^2\theta}{\sin\theta} \text{ and } \frac{dy}{d\theta} = \cos\theta$$

$$\Rightarrow \frac{dy}{dx} = \tan\theta$$

$$\Rightarrow \frac{d^2y}{dx^2} = \sec^2\theta.\frac{d\theta}{dx} = \sec^2\theta.\left(\frac{\sin\theta}{\cos^2\theta}\right) = \frac{\sin\theta}{\cos^4\theta}$$

$\Rightarrow$ Assertion and reason both are correct

5. (d) $x < 0;\ \dfrac{d}{dx}(\ell n|x|) = \dfrac{1}{|x|}.\dfrac{|x|}{x} = \dfrac{1}{x}$

$\Rightarrow$ Assertion is incorrect.

For $x < 0$; $|x| = -x \quad \Rightarrow$ Reason is correct

SECTION–VI: COMPREHENSION

Passage A:

1. (c) By the question $(f(x).g(x))' = f'(x).g'(x)$

$\Rightarrow f'(x)\,g(x) + f(x)\,g'(x) = f'(x)\,g'(x)$

$\Rightarrow 3x^2.g(x) + x^3.g'(x) = 3x^2.g'(x)$ which is true for $x = 0$

$\Rightarrow 3g(x) + xg'(x) = 3g'(x)$ for $x \neq 0$

$\Rightarrow 3g(x) = (3 - x)\,g'(x)$

$$\Rightarrow \frac{3}{3-x} = \frac{g'(x)}{g(x)};\ \text{for } x \neq 0, 3$$

$$\Rightarrow \ln|g(x)| = -3\ln|3-x| + C$$

$$\Rightarrow |g(x)| = |3-x|^{-3} + \ln C$$

$$\Rightarrow g(x) = \frac{\pm C}{(3-x)^3} \text{ but } g(0) = \frac{1}{3}$$

$$\Rightarrow \frac{1}{3} = \pm\frac{C}{27}$$

$$\Rightarrow g(x) = \frac{9}{(3-x)^3}$$

2. (a) derivative of $\{f(x-3).g(x)\}' = f'(x-3).g(x) + f(x-3).g'(x)$

$$= ((x-3)^3)'\,g(x) + (x-3)^3.\left(\frac{9}{(x-3)^3}\right)'$$

$$= 3(x-3)^2\,g(x) + (x-3)^3\left(\frac{-27}{(x-3)^4}\right)$$

$$= 3(x-3)^2.\frac{9}{(x-3)^3} + \frac{(-27)}{(x-3)} = \frac{27}{x-3} - \frac{27}{x-3} = 0$$

$$\Rightarrow \frac{d}{dx}(\{f(x-3).g(x)\})\Bigg|_{x=100} = 0$$

3. (a)
$$\lim_{x\to0}\frac{f(x).g(x)}{x(1+g(x))} = \lim_{x\to0}\left(\frac{x^3.\dfrac{9}{(x-3)^3}}{x\left(1+\dfrac{9}{(x-3)^3}\right)}\right)$$

$$= \lim_{x\to0}\left(\frac{9x^2}{(x-3)^3\left(1+\dfrac{9}{(x-3)^3}\right)}\right) = \lim_{x\to0}\left(\frac{9x^2}{(x-3)^3+9}\right) = 0$$

Passage B:

By the question $D^*f(x) = \lim\limits_{h\to0}\dfrac{f^2(x+h) - f^2(x)}{h}$

$\Rightarrow D^*f(x) = \lim\limits_{h\to0}\dfrac{f(x+h) - f(x)}{h}.\ [f(x+h) + f(x)]$

$\Rightarrow D^*(f(x)) = f'(x).\ 2.\ f(x)$

4. (b) $u = f(x)$ and $v = g(x)$

$D^*(u\,v) = (u\,v)'\ .2.\ (uv)$

$= (u'\,v + v'\,u)\ 2uv = u^2\,v'\ (2v) + v^2.\ u'(2u)$

$= u^2.\ D^*\,v + v^2\,D^*\,u$

5. (c) $u = f(x)$ and $v = g(x)$

$\Rightarrow D^*\left(\frac{u}{v}\right) = \left(\frac{u}{v}\right)'.2\left[\frac{u}{v}\right] = \left(\frac{vu' - u.v'}{v^2}\right)\frac{2u.v}{v^2}$

$= \frac{v^2 D^* u - u^2 . D^* v}{v^4}$

6. (d) $D^*(\tan x) = (\tan x)'.\ 2\tan x$

$\Rightarrow 2\sec^2 x.\ \tan x$

7. (b) Value of D^* at the point where tangent is parallel to x-*axis*

$\Rightarrow f'(x) = 0$

$\Rightarrow D^* = f'(x).2f(x) = 0$

8. (d) $D^* c = (c)'.\ (2c) = 0\ (2c) = 0$

Passage C:

9. (d) $y = \log x$

$\Rightarrow \frac{dy}{dx} = \frac{1}{x}$ $\qquad \Rightarrow \frac{d^2y}{dx^2} = \frac{-1}{x^2}$

$\Rightarrow \frac{d^3y}{dx^3} = \frac{2}{x^3}$ $\qquad \Rightarrow \frac{d^4y}{dx^4} = \frac{2(-3)}{x^4} = \frac{(-1)^3(3)!}{x^4}$

$\Rightarrow \frac{d^5y}{dx^5} = \frac{2(-3)(-4)}{x^5} = \frac{(-1)^4.4!}{x^5}$

$\therefore$ In general, $\frac{d^ny}{dx^n} = \frac{(-1)^{n-1}.(n-1)!}{x^n}$

10. (d) $y = \frac{1}{1-5x+6x^2}$

$\Rightarrow y = \frac{1}{6x^2-5x+1} = \frac{1}{(2x-1)(3x-1)}$

Let $y = \frac{A}{2x-1} + \frac{B}{3x-1}$

$\Rightarrow 1 = A(3x-1) + B(2x-1)$

For $x = 1/2$; $1 = A\ (1/2)$

$\Rightarrow A = 2$

For $x = \frac{1}{3}$; $1 = B\left(\frac{2}{3} - 1\right)$

$\Rightarrow B = -3$

$\therefore y = \frac{2}{(2x-1)} - \frac{3}{(3x-1)}$

$\Rightarrow y_1 = 2\left[\frac{(-1)(2)}{(2x-1)^2}\right] - 3\left[\frac{(-1)(3)}{(3x-1)^2}\right]$

$\Rightarrow y_2 = 2\left[\frac{(-1)(-2)(2)^2}{(2x-1)^3}\right] - 3\left[\frac{(-1)(-2)(3)^2}{(3x-1)^3}\right]$

$\Rightarrow y_3 = 2\left[\frac{(-1)(-2)(-3)(2)^3}{(2x-1)^4}\right] - 3\left[\frac{(-1)(-2)(-3)(3)^3}{(3x-1)^4}\right]$

$\therefore$ In general, $y_n = 2\left[\frac{(-1)^n(n)!(2)^n}{(2x-1)^{n+1}}\right] - 3\left[\frac{(-1)^n(n)!(3)^n}{(3x-1)^{n+1}}\right]$

$\therefore y_5 = 2\left[\frac{(-1)^5(5!)(2)^5}{(2x-1)^6}\right] - 3\left[\frac{(-1)^5.5!(3)^5}{(3x-1)h6}\right]$

$\Rightarrow y_5 = 120\left[\frac{(3)^6}{(3x-1)^6} - \frac{(2)^6}{(2x-1)^6}\right]$

11. (d) A.T.Q., $n = 4k + 3$

Let $y = \tan^{-1x}$

$\Rightarrow y_1 = \frac{1}{1+x^2}$ $\qquad \Rightarrow y_1(0) = 1 = 0!$

$\Rightarrow (1 + x^2)\,y_1 = 0$ $\qquad \Rightarrow (1 + x^2)y_2 + y_1(2x) = 0$

$\Rightarrow y_2(0) = 0$

Again Differentiate w.r.t. x, we get $(1 + x^2)\,y_3 + y_2(2x) + y_1(2) + 2x\,(y_2) = 0$

$\Rightarrow y_3(0) = -2y_1(0) = -2$

Again different w.r.t. x, we get $(1 + x^2)\,y_4 + y_3(2x) + y_2(2) + 2x\,(y_3) + 2y_2 + 2xy_3 + 2y_2 = 0$

$\Rightarrow (1 + x^2)\,y_4 + 6xy_3 + 6y_2 = 0$

$\Rightarrow y_4(0) = -6y_2(0) = 0$

$\Rightarrow (1 + x^2)\,y_5 + y_4(2x) + 6xy_4 + 6y_3 + 6y_3 = 0$

$\Rightarrow (1 + x^2)\,y_5 + 8xy_4 + 12y_3 = 0$

$\Rightarrow y_5(0) = -12y_3(0) = 24 = 4!$

Again Different, we get $(1 + x^2)\,y_6 + y_5(2x) + 8xy_5 + 8xy_4 + 12y_4 = 0$

$\Rightarrow (1 + x^2)\,y_6 + 10xy_5 + 20y_4 = 0$

$\Rightarrow y_6(0) = -20\,y_4(0) = 0$

Again Different w.r.t. x, $(1 + x^2)\,y_7 + y_6\,(2x) + 10xy_6 + 10y_5 + 20y_5 = 0$

$\Rightarrow (1 + x^2)\,y_7 + 12xy_6 + 30y_5 = 0$

$\Rightarrow y_7(0) = -30y_5(0) = -30(4!) = -6!$

Different again w.r.t. x, we get $(1 + x^2)\,y_8 + y_7\,(2x) + y_7\,(12x) + 12y_6 + 30y_6 = 0$

$\Rightarrow (1 + x^2)\,y_8 + 14xy_7 + 42y_6 = 0$

$\Rightarrow y_8(0) = -42y_6(0) = 0$

$\therefore$ From above, we concludes,

$$y_m(0) = \begin{cases} 0 & \text{for } m = 4n \\ (m-1)! & \text{for } m = 4n+1 \\ 0 & \text{for } m = 4n+2 \\ -(m-1) & \text{for } m = 4n+3 \end{cases}$$

$\therefore y_n - (n-1)!$ for $n = (4k + 3)$; $k \in \mathbb{N}$.

Passage D:

12. (c) Let $y = \log_e x$ or $\ln x$

$\Rightarrow y + \delta y = \log_e(x + \delta x)$

$\Rightarrow \delta y = \ln\,(x + \delta x) - \ln x$ ...(1)

Also, $\delta y = \frac{dy}{dx}.\delta x$

$\Rightarrow \delta y = \frac{1}{x}.\delta x$ ...(2)

Let $x + \delta x = 4.01$ and $x = 4$

$\Rightarrow \delta x = 0.01$ ...(3)

$\therefore$ From (2), $\delta y = \frac{1}{4}(0.01) = 0.0025$ ...(4)

$\therefore$ From (1) and (4), $0.0025 = ln(4.01) - \ln 4$

$\Rightarrow$ $\ln(4.01) = ln4 + 0.0025 = 1.3863 + 0.0025 = 1.3888$

13. (d) $\frac{\delta l}{l} \times 100 = 2$ ...(1) (Given)

Now, $T = 2\pi\sqrt{\frac{l}{g}}$ ...(2)

Let $T = \frac{2\pi}{\sqrt{g}}(l)^{1/2}$ ...(3)

$\Rightarrow$ $\delta T = \frac{2\pi}{\sqrt{g}}\left[(l+\delta l)^{1/2} - (l)^{1/2}\right]$ ...(4)

Also $\delta T = \frac{dT}{dl}.\delta l = \frac{2\pi}{\sqrt{g}}\left(\frac{1}{2\sqrt{l}}\right)(\delta l)$

$\Rightarrow$ $\delta T = \frac{2\pi}{\sqrt{g}}\left(\frac{1}{2\sqrt{l}}\right)\left(\frac{2l}{100}\right)$

$\Rightarrow$ $\frac{\delta T}{T}\times 100 = \frac{\frac{2\pi}{\sqrt{g}}\left(\frac{\sqrt{l}}{100}\right)\times 100}{2\pi\sqrt{\left(\frac{l}{g}\right)}} = 1$

$\Rightarrow$ % age error in $T = 1\%$

14. (a) $\Delta = \sqrt{s(s-a)(s-b)(s-c)}$

$\Rightarrow$ $\ln\Delta = \frac{1}{2}[\ln s + \ln(s-a) + \ln(s-b) + \ln(s-c)]$

$\Rightarrow$ $\frac{1}{\Delta}.\frac{d\Delta}{dc} = \frac{1}{2}\left[\frac{1}{s}.\frac{ds}{dc} + \frac{1}{s-a}.\frac{ds}{dc} + \frac{1}{s-b}.\frac{ds}{dc} + \frac{1}{s-c}.\left(\frac{ds}{dc}-1\right)\right]$

$\Rightarrow$ $\frac{d\Delta}{dc} = \frac{\Delta}{2}\left[\left(\frac{1}{s} + \frac{1}{s-a} + \frac{1}{s-b} + \frac{1}{s-c}\right)\frac{ds}{dc} - \frac{1}{(s-c)} + \frac{1}{s-6}\right]$ ...(1)

Now $\delta\Delta = \frac{d\Delta}{dc}.\delta c$

$\Rightarrow$ $\delta\Delta = \frac{\Delta}{2}\left[\left(\frac{1}{s} + \frac{1}{s-a} + \frac{1}{s-b} + \frac{1}{s-c}\right)\frac{ds}{dc} - \frac{1}{s-c}\right].\delta c$ ...(2)

Also $s = \frac{1}{2}(a+b+c)$

$\Rightarrow$ $\frac{ds}{dc} = \frac{1}{2}$ ...(3)

$\therefore$ From (2) and (3), we get

$\delta\Delta = \delta c.\frac{\Delta}{2}\left[\left(\frac{1}{s} + \frac{1}{s-a} + \frac{1}{s-b} + \frac{1}{s-c}\right)\frac{1}{2} - \frac{1}{s-c}\right]$

$\Rightarrow$ $\delta\Delta = \frac{\Delta}{4}\left[\left(\frac{1}{s} + \frac{1}{s-a} + \frac{1}{s-b} - \frac{1}{s-c}\right)\right].\delta c$

Passage E:

15. (b) $s = 1 + t.e^s$

$\Rightarrow$ $\frac{ds}{dt} = te^s\frac{ds}{dt} + e^s = (s-1)\frac{ds}{dt} + e^s$ ...(1)

$\Rightarrow$ $\frac{d^2s}{dt^2} = (s-1)\frac{d^2s}{dt^2} + \frac{ds}{dt} + e^s\frac{ds}{dt}$

$\Rightarrow$ $\frac{d\ s}{dt}(1-s+1) = (e\ +1).\frac{ds}{dt}$

$\Rightarrow$ $\frac{d^2s}{dt^2} = \frac{e^s+1}{(2-s)}.\frac{ds}{dt}$ ...(2)

From (1), $\frac{ds}{dt} = \frac{e^s}{(2-s)}$ ...(3)

Using (3) in (2), we get $\frac{d^2s}{dt^2} = \frac{e^s(e^s+1)}{(2-s)^2}$

16. (b) $x^2 + y^2 = r^2$ (given).

Put $x = r\cos\theta$, $y = r\sin\theta$

$\Rightarrow$ $\frac{dy}{d\theta} = r\cos\theta$ and $\frac{dx}{d\theta} = -r\cos\theta$

$\therefore$ $\frac{dy}{dx} = -\cot\theta$

$\Rightarrow$ $\frac{d^2y}{dx^2} = \text{cosec}^2\theta\frac{d\theta}{dx}$

$\Rightarrow$ $\frac{d^2y}{dx^2} = \text{cosec}^2\theta\left(\frac{-1}{r\sin\theta}\right) = \frac{-1}{r}\text{cosec}^2\theta$

$\Rightarrow$ $\frac{d^3y}{dx^3} = \frac{-1}{r}(-3\text{cosec}^3\theta\cot\theta)\frac{3\text{cosec}^3\theta.\cot\theta}{r}$

$= \frac{3\cos\theta}{r\sin^4\theta} = \frac{3r\cos\theta.r^2}{(r\sin\theta)^4} = \frac{3r^2x}{y^4}$

SECTION–VII: COLUMN MATCHING

1. **(i)→(d); (ii)→(b); (iii) → (a); (iv) → (b)**

(i) $xy - \log y = 1$

Differentiating both sides w.r.t. x, we get $xy' + y - \frac{1}{y}y' = 0$

or $xyy' + y^2 - y' = 0$

Differentiating again w.r.t. x, we get $xyy' + x(y')^2 + yy' + 2yy' - y' = 0$

$\Rightarrow$ $x(yy' + y'^2) - y' + 3yy' = 0$

$\Rightarrow$ $k = 3$ $\therefore$ **(i)→(d)**

(ii) $x = \sin t$, $y = ae^{t\sqrt{2}} + be^{t\sqrt{2}}$

$\Rightarrow$ $\frac{dx}{dt} = \cos t, \frac{dy}{dt} = \sqrt{2}ae^{\sqrt{2}t} + \sqrt{2}be^{\sqrt{2}t} = \sqrt{2}\left(ae^{\sqrt{2}t} + be^{\sqrt{2}t}\right)$

$\therefore$ $\frac{dy}{dx} = \frac{dy/dt}{dx/dt} = \frac{\sqrt{2}y}{\cos t} = \frac{\sqrt{2}y}{\sqrt{1-\sin^2 t}}\left[\because t \in \left(\frac{-\pi}{2}, \frac{\pi}{2}\right)\right]$

$\Rightarrow$ $\frac{dy}{dx} = \frac{\sqrt{2}y}{\sqrt{1-x^2}}$

$\Rightarrow \left(\sqrt{1-x^2}\right)y' = \sqrt{2}y$

$\Rightarrow (1-x^2)y'^2 = 2y^2$

$\Rightarrow (1-x^2)\,2y'\,y'' - 2xy'^2 = 4yy'$

$\Rightarrow (1-x^2)y'' - xy' = 2y$

$\Rightarrow k = 2 \qquad \therefore$ **(ii)→(b)**

(iii) $F(x) = f(x).\,g(x).\,h(x)\ \forall x \in \mathbb{R}$

$F'(x) = f'(x).\,g(x).\,h(x) + f(x).\,g'(x).\,h(x) + f(x).\,g(x).\,h'(x)$

$\Rightarrow F'(x_0) = f'(x_0).\,g(x_0).\,h(x_0) + f(x_0).\,g'(x_0).\,h(x_0) + f(x_0).\,g(x_0).\,h'(x_0)$

$\Rightarrow 21\,F(x_0) = 4f(x_0).\,g(x_0).\,h(x_0) + f(x_0).\,(-7g(x_0)).\,h(x_0) + f(x_0).\,g(x_0).\,kh(x_0)$

$\Rightarrow 21\,F(x_0) = (4-7+k)\,F(x_0)$

$\Rightarrow k - 3 = 21 \qquad \Rightarrow k = 24$

$\therefore$ **(iii)→(a)**

(iv) $f(x) = x^n,\ n \geq 0$

$f'(x) = nx^{n-1}$

$\therefore f'(a+b) = f'(a) + f'(b);\ \forall a, b > 0$

$\Rightarrow n(a+b)^{n-1} = n(a)^{n-1} + n(b)^{n-1}\ \forall\ a, b > 0$ and $n > 0$

$\Rightarrow (a+b)^{n-1} = a^{n-1} + b^{n-1}\ \forall\ a, b > 0$

$\Rightarrow n - 1 = 1$ or $n = 2$

Also for $n = 0$, $f(x) = 1$

$\Rightarrow f'(x) = 0\ \ \forall x \in \mathbb{R}$

$\therefore$ n has 2 values $\qquad \therefore$ **(iv)→(b)**

2. (i)→(d); (ii)→(c); (iii) → (b); (iv) → (a)

(i) Let $y = f(\tan x)$; $z = g(\sec x)$

$$\Rightarrow \frac{dy}{dz} = \frac{f'(\tan x).\sec^2 x}{g'(\sec x).\sec x.\tan x}$$

$$\Rightarrow \left(\frac{dy}{dz}\right)_{x=\frac{\pi}{4}} = \frac{f'(1).(2)}{g'\left(\sqrt{2}\right).\sqrt{2}} = \frac{(2)(2)}{(4)\sqrt{2}} = \frac{1}{\sqrt{2}}$$

$\therefore$ **(i) → (d)**

(ii) $y = x^3 - 8x + 7;\ x = f(t)$

$$\Rightarrow \frac{dy}{dt} = \frac{dy}{dx} \times \frac{dx}{dt} = (3x^2 - 8) \times f'(t)$$

$\therefore 2 = [3(3)^2 - 8]\,f'(0)$

$\Rightarrow f'(0) = \dfrac{2}{19} \qquad \therefore$ **(ii) → (c)**

(iii) $f(x) = \sin x$, $g(x) = 2x$, $h(x) = \cos x$; $f(x) = [go(fh)]\,(x)$,

$\Rightarrow f'(x) = g'(fh).\,(fh)'\,(x)$

$\Rightarrow f'(x) = 2.\,(fh' + hf')\,(x) = 2[\sin x.\,(-\sin x) + \cos x.\cos x] = 2[\cos^2 x - \sin^2 x] = 2\cos 2x$

$\Rightarrow f''(x) = -4\sin 2x \qquad \Rightarrow \phi''\left(\dfrac{\pi}{4}\right) = -4\sin\dfrac{\pi}{2} = -4$

$\therefore$ **(iii) → (b)**

(iv) $f(x) = \cos^2 x + \cos^2\left(x + \dfrac{\pi}{3}\right) + \sin x.\sin\left(x + \dfrac{\pi}{3}\right);\ g\left(\dfrac{5}{4}\right) = 4:$

$$f(x) = \cos^2 x + \left[\cos x.\frac{1}{2} - \sin x.\frac{\sqrt{3}}{2}\right]^2 + \sin x\left[\sin x\frac{1}{2} + \cos x.\frac{\sqrt{3}}{2}\right]$$

$$= \cos^2 x + \frac{\cos^2 x}{4} + \frac{3}{4}\sin^2 x - \frac{\sqrt{3}}{2}\sin x\cos x + \frac{1}{2}\sin^2 x + \frac{\sqrt{3}}{2}\sin x\cos x$$

$$= \frac{5}{4}\cos^2 x + \frac{5}{4}\sin^2 x = \frac{5}{4}$$

$$\therefore\ gof(x) = g(f(x)) = g\left(\frac{5}{4}\right) = 3$$

$\therefore$ **(iv) → (a)**

SECTION–VIII: INTEGER TYPE

1. $y = \sec^{-1}\left[\dfrac{1}{2x^2-1}\right] : x = \pm\dfrac{1}{\sqrt{2}}$ and $x = \sqrt{1-x^2}$

Put $x = \cos\theta;\ \theta \in \left[0, \dfrac{\pi}{2}\right] - \left\{\dfrac{\pi}{4}\right\}$

$$\Rightarrow y = \sec^{-1}\left(\frac{1}{\cos 2\theta}\right) = \sec^{-1}(\sec 2\theta)$$

$\Rightarrow y = 2\theta$ for $\theta = \cos^{-1}(x)$ and $x \in [0,1] - \left\{\dfrac{1}{\sqrt{2}}\right\}$

$$\Rightarrow \frac{dy}{d\theta} = 2 \qquad \ldots(1)$$

and $z = \sqrt{1-\cos^2\theta} = |\sin\theta|$

$\Rightarrow z = \sin\theta$ for $\theta \in \left[0, \dfrac{\pi}{2}\right]$

$$\Rightarrow \frac{dz}{d\theta} = \cos\theta \text{ for } \theta \in \left[0, \frac{\pi}{2}\right] \qquad \ldots(2)$$

$\therefore \dfrac{dy}{dz} = 2\sec\theta$ for and $\theta = \cos^{-1}x$ and $x \in [0,1] - \left\{\dfrac{1}{\sqrt{2}}\right\}$

$$\Rightarrow \left(\frac{dy}{dz}\right)_{x=\frac{1}{2}} = 2\sec\left(\cos^{-1}\frac{1}{2}\right) = 2\sec\left(\frac{\pi}{3}\right) = 2(2) = 4$$

2. $f(x).\,g(x) = C$

$\Rightarrow f(x).\,g'(x) + g(x).\,f'(x) = 0 \qquad \ldots(1)$

$$\Rightarrow \frac{g'(x)}{g(x)} = -\frac{f'(x)}{f(x)}$$

$$\Rightarrow \frac{g'(x)}{g(x)} + \frac{f'(x)}{f(x)} = 0 \qquad \ldots(2)$$

Differentiating (1) again, $f(x)\,g''(x) + g'(x).\,f'(x) + g(x).\,f''(x) + f'(x).\,g'(x) = 0$

$\Rightarrow f(x).\,g''(x) + g(x).\,f''(x) + 2f'(x).\,g'(x) = 0 \qquad \ldots(3)$

$$\Rightarrow \frac{g''(x)}{g(x)} + \frac{f''(x)}{f(x)} + \frac{2f'(x).g'(x)}{f(x).g(x)} \qquad \ldots(4)$$

Differentiating (3) again, we get $f(x)\,g'''(x) + g'(x)\,f''(x) + g(x)\,f'''(x) + f'(x)\,g''(x) + 2f''(x)\,g'(x) + 2g''(x)\,f'(x) = 0$

$\Rightarrow f(x).\,g'''(x) + g(x).\,f'''(x) + 3f''(x).\,g'(x) + 3g''(x)\,f'(x) = 0$

$$\Rightarrow \frac{g'''(x)}{g(x)}+\frac{f'''(x)}{f(x)}+\frac{3f'(x)g''(x)}{f(x).g(x)}+\frac{3g'(x).f''(x)}{g(x)f(x)}=0 \quad ...(5)$$

$$\Rightarrow \frac{g'''(x)}{g'(x)}.\frac{g'(x)}{g(x)}+\frac{f'''(x)}{f'(x)}.\frac{f'(x)}{f(x)}$$

$$+\frac{3g''(x)}{g(x)}.\frac{f'(x)}{f(x)}+\frac{3f''(x)}{f(x)}.\frac{g'(x)}{g(x)}=0 \quad ...(6)$$

From (2), using $\frac{g'(x)}{g(x)}=-\frac{f'(x)}{f(x)}$ in (6)

$$\Rightarrow -\frac{g''(x)}{g'(x)}+\frac{f'''(x)}{f'(x)}+\frac{3g''(x)}{g(x)}-\frac{3f''(x)}{f(x)}=0$$

$$\Rightarrow \frac{f'''(x)}{f'(x)}-\frac{3f''(x)}{f(x)}-\frac{g''(x)}{g'(x)}+\frac{3g''(x)}{g(x)}=0$$

$\Rightarrow A = 3$

3. $\int_0^y \cos t^2 dt = \int_0^{x^2} \frac{\sin t}{t} dt$

Different both side w.r.t. x,

$$\Rightarrow \cos y^2.\frac{dy}{dx}=\frac{\sin x^2}{x^2}(2x)$$

$$\Rightarrow \cos y^2.\left(\frac{k\sin x^2}{x\cos y^2}\right)=\frac{2\sin x^2}{x}$$

$\Rightarrow k = 2$

4. $\int_e^x t.f(t)dt = \sin x - x\cos x - \frac{x^2}{2} \forall x \in \mathbb{R}-\{0\}$

Different both sides w.r.t. x

$\Rightarrow xf(x) = \cos x + x\sin x - \cos x - x$

$\Rightarrow xf(x) = x\sin x - x \quad \Rightarrow f(x) = \sin x - 1$

$$\Rightarrow f\left(\frac{\pi}{6}\right)=\frac{1}{2}-1=\frac{-1}{2}=\frac{-1}{k} \text{ (given)}$$

$\Rightarrow k = 2$

5. $y = \sin^{-1}\left(\ln\frac{x^2}{2}\right)$ ...(1)

$\Rightarrow \sin y = \ln\left(\frac{x^2}{2}\right)$ ...(2)

$\Rightarrow (\cos y)y' = \frac{2}{x^2}(x) \quad \Rightarrow y' = \frac{2}{x\cos y}$

$\Rightarrow (xy')^2 = \frac{4}{\cos^2 y}$ ...(3)

$$\Rightarrow (xy')^2.\left\{\left(\ln\left(\frac{x^2}{2}\right)\right)^2-1\right\}=\frac{4}{\cos^2 y}\{\sin^2 y-1\}=-4$$

6. $\because \frac{dy}{dx}=\left(\frac{dx}{dy}\right)^{-1}$ ...(i)

$$\Rightarrow \frac{d^2y}{dx^2}=-1\left(\frac{dx}{dy}\right)^{-2}.\frac{d^2x}{dy^2}.\frac{dy}{dx}$$

$$\Rightarrow \frac{d^2y}{dx^2}+\left(\frac{dx}{dy}\right)^{-3}\frac{d^2x}{dy^2}=0\left(\because \frac{dy}{dx}=\left(\frac{dx}{dy}\right)^{-1}\right)$$

$$\Rightarrow \frac{d^2y}{dx^2}+\left(\frac{dy}{dx}\right)^3.\frac{d^2x}{dy^2}=0$$

$\Rightarrow k = 0$

7. $y = (\cot^{-1}x)^2$

$$\Rightarrow \frac{dy}{dx}=2(\cot^{-1}x)\left(\frac{-1}{1+x^2}\right)$$

$\Rightarrow (1+x^2)y_1 + 2\cot^{-1}x = 0$

$$\Rightarrow (1+x^2)y_2 + y_1(2x) - \frac{2}{(1+x^2)}=0$$

$\Rightarrow (1+x^2)^2 y_2 + 2xy_1(1+x^2) - 2 = 0$

$\Rightarrow k = 3$

Application of Derivatives I

CHAPTER 4

RATE OF CHANGE

■ INTRODUCTION

One of the most useful applications of differentiation is found in the problems involving the rate of change of one quantity w.r.t another. For a long time, mathematicians struggled with the development of a method to find the related relation between the rate of change of quantities like the perimeters, areas or volumes of a two dimensional or three dimensional figures when one or more of the variables defining the figure kept changing. It was then, that the theory of related rates was developed with the help of derivatives.

We have always been interested in a wide variety of time rates: the rate at which the speed of a vehicle is increasing, the rate at which the amount of pollutants in the air is increasing, the rate at which the value of a piece of land is increasing and so on.

Now, if y denotes the quantities mentioned above, and is explicitly defined in terms of t, the problem becomes very simple. We just differentiate y w.r.t. t and then evaluate the derivative at the required time.

However, it may so happen that in place of knowing y explicitly in terms of t, we know a relation that connects y with another variable x and that we also know something about $\frac{dx}{dt}$. We may still be able to find $\frac{dy}{dt}$ with the help of $\frac{dx}{dt}$, since y and x are related and that is why the related rates is so useful.

Now, just like the related rates, there can also be developed a relation between the error occurred in the measurement of an independent variable and the resultant error occurred in the measurement of the dependent variable. And thereby, we can find the approximate value of the dependent variable when there is a slight change in the independent variable.

■ DERIVATIVE AS THE RATE OF CHANGE

Instantaneous Rate of Change of Quantities

Theorem: If $y = f(x)$ is a differentiable function of x then $\frac{dy}{dx}$ is called the instantaneous rate of change of y with respect to x.

Proof: Given function $y = f(x)$,

The value of y corresponding to values a and $a + h$ of x are $f(a)$ and $f(a + h)$.

Change in x is h. Corresponding to this change of x, the change in y is $f(a + h) - f(a)$.

$\therefore$ In the range $(a, a + h)$, the average rate of change of y with respect to x is $\frac{f(a+h)-f(a)}{h}$

Here when $h \to 0$, the interval $(a, a + h)$ becomes the point a (instant a, in case of time)

$\therefore$ At $x = a$, the instantaneous rate of change of y with respect to x is given by

$$f'(a) = \lim_{h\to o}\frac{f(a+h)-f(a)}{h}$$

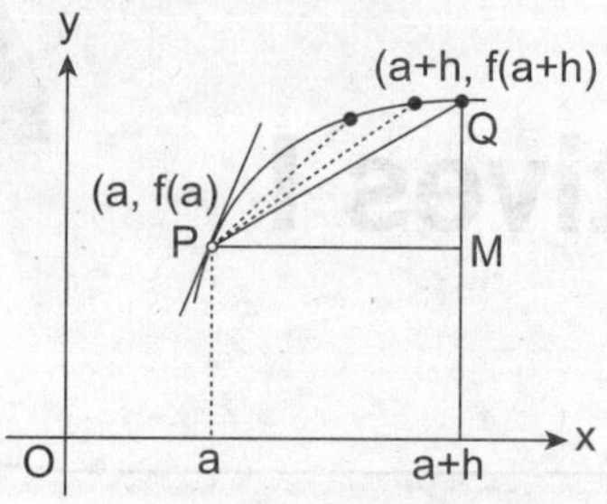

FIGURE 4.1

In general the instantaneous rate of change of y with respect to x is $\frac{dy}{dx}$ or $f'(x)$ when y and x both are function of some other variable.

NOTE:

1. $\frac{dy}{dx} = \frac{(dy/dt)}{(dx/dt)} = \frac{\text{rate of change of } y}{\text{rate of chage of } x}$. *i.e., derivative of y with respect to x is equal to the ratio of the rate change of y w.r.t. time is to the rate of change of x w.r.t. time.*
2. *Suppose* $a + b^2 + c^2 + s^4 = 2h^2$ *be an equation, where a, b, c, h are constants and s is the function of t, then differentiating both sides with respect to t, we get*

   $\therefore\ 0+0+0+4s^3\frac{ds}{dt}=0 \qquad \therefore\ \frac{ds}{dt}=0$ *(is a wrong process)*

   Instead technically correct way of performing the operation is $\frac{da}{dt}+2b\frac{db}{dt}+3c^2\frac{dc}{dt}+4s^3\frac{ds}{dt}=4h\frac{dh}{dt}$

   i.e. $0+0+0+4s^3\frac{ds}{dt}=0 \qquad \Rightarrow \qquad \frac{ds}{dt}=0$

ILLUSTRATION 1: A ladder is resting against a wall making an angle of 30° with the wall. *A* man is ascending the ladder at the rate of 3 ft/sec. His rate of approaching the wall is

(a) 3 ft/sec (b) $\frac{3}{2}$ ft/sec

(c) $\frac{3}{4}$ ft/ sec (d) $\frac{3}{\sqrt{2}}$ ft/ sec

SOLUTION: (b) His rate of approaching the wall = 3 × cos 60° = $\frac{3}{2}$ ft/sec

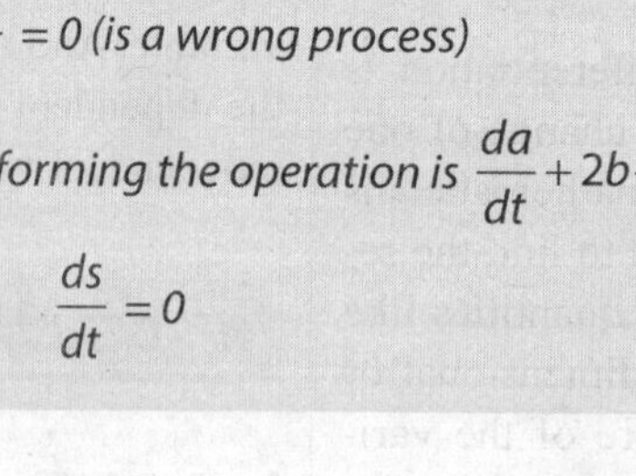

FIGURE 4.2

ILLUSTRATION 2: Two cyclists start from the junction of two perpendicular roads, their velocities being $3\ v$ m/min and $4\ v$ m/min. The rate at which the two cyclists are separating is

(a) $\frac{7}{2}v$ m/min (b) $5v$ m/min

(c) v m/min (d) None of these

SOLUTION: (b) At time t, the distance z between the cyclists is given by

$\Rightarrow\ z^2 = (3\ vt)^2 + (4\ v\ t)^2$ $\therefore\ z = 5vt$

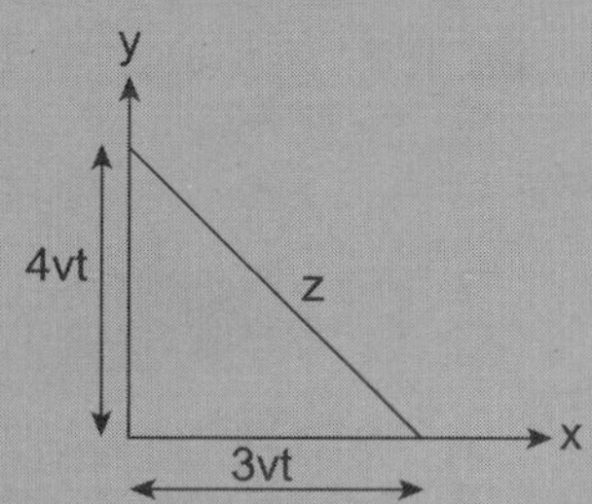

FIGURE 4.3

$$\Rightarrow \frac{dz}{dt} = 5v$$

ILLUSTRATION 3: On the curve $x^3 = 12y$ the abscissa changes at a faster rate than the ordinate. Then x belongs to the interval

(a) $(-2, 2)$ (b) $(-1, 1)$

(c) $(0, 2)$ (d) None of these

SOLUTION: (a) From the question, $\left|\frac{dx}{dt}\right| > \left|\frac{dy}{dt}\right| \Rightarrow \left|\frac{dx}{dy}\right| > 1$. Differentiating $x^3 = 12y$ w.r.t. y, we get

$$\Rightarrow 3x^2\frac{dx}{dy} = 12 \quad \Rightarrow \quad \frac{dx}{dy} = \frac{4}{x^2} \quad \therefore \quad \frac{4}{x^2} > 1 \qquad \left(\because \frac{dx}{dy} > 1\right)$$

$$\Rightarrow x^2 - 4 < 0 \qquad \Rightarrow -2 < x < 2$$

ILLUSTRATION 4: A lamp of negligible height, is placed on the ground 'ℓ' away from a wall. *A* man 'h' m tall is walking at a speed of $\frac{\ell}{10}$ m/sec from the lamp to the nearest point on the wall. When he is midway between the lamp and the wall, the rate of change in the length of this shadow on the wall is

(a) $-\frac{5h}{2}$ m/ sec (b) $-\frac{2h}{5}$ m/ sec

(c) $-\frac{h}{2}$ m/ sec (d) $-\frac{h}{5}$ m/ sec

SOLUTION: (b) Let $BP = x$. From similar Δ's property we get, $\frac{AO}{l}\ \ \frac{h}{x}$

$$\Rightarrow AO = \frac{lh}{x} \Rightarrow \frac{d(AO)}{dt} = \frac{-lh}{x^2}\cdot\frac{dx}{dt}$$

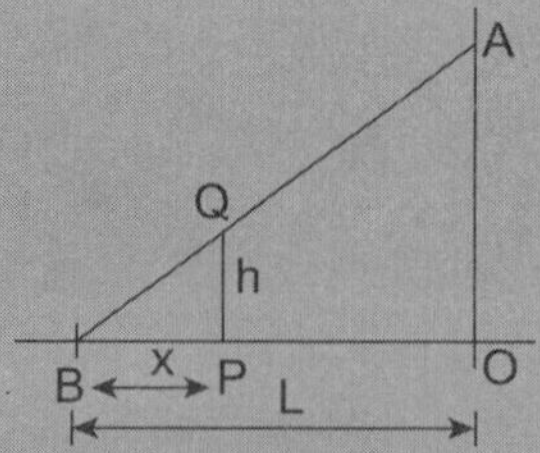

FIGURE 4.4

$$\text{when } x = \frac{l}{2}, \text{ then } \frac{d(AO)}{dt} = -\frac{2h}{5} \text{ m/ sec}$$

$$\left[\because \frac{dx}{dt} = \frac{\ell}{10}\right]$$

ILLUSTRATION 5: A particle moves along the curve $y = \frac{2}{5}x^5 + 3$. Find the point on the curve at which the y-coordinate is changing twice as fast as the x-coordinate.

SOLUTION: $y = \frac{2}{5}x^5 + 3 \Rightarrow \frac{dy}{dx} = \frac{2}{5}5x^4 = 2x^4$

But $\frac{dy}{dx} = 2$ (Given)

$\therefore\ 2x^4 = 2$ $\Rightarrow x^4 = 1 \Rightarrow x = \pm 1$

$\therefore$ when $x = 1,\ y = \frac{2}{5}(1)^5 + 3 = \frac{17}{5}$

when $x = -1,\ y = \frac{2}{5}(-1)^3 + 1 = -\frac{2}{5} + 3 = \frac{13}{5}$

Hence, the required points on the curve are (1, 17/5) and (–1, 13/5).

ILLUSTRATION 6: A man 1.6 m high walks at the rate of 30 meter per minute away from a lamp which is 4 m above ground. How fast is the man's shadow lengthening?

SOLUTION: Let $PQ = 4$ m be the height of pole and, $AB = 1.6$ m be the height of man. Let the end of shadow is R and it is at a distance of l from A, when the man is at a distance x from PQ at some instant 't'.

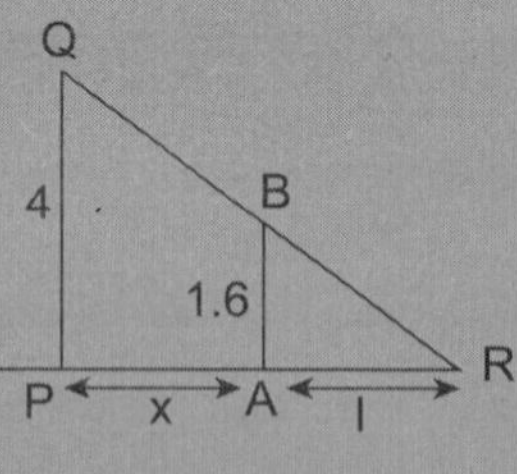

FIGURE 4.5

Since, $\Delta\ PQR$ and $\Delta\ ABR$ are similar, we have

$$\Rightarrow \frac{PQ}{AB} = \frac{PR}{AR}$$

$$\Rightarrow \frac{4}{1.6} = \frac{x+l}{l} \qquad \Rightarrow 2x = 3l$$

$\Rightarrow 2\dfrac{dx}{dt} = 3\dfrac{dl}{dt}$ [given $\dfrac{dx}{dt} = 30$ m/min]

$\Rightarrow \dfrac{dl}{dt} = \dfrac{2}{3}.30$ m/min $= 20$ m/min

ILLUSTRATION 7: A ladder 5 m in length is resting against a vertical wall. The bottom of the ladder is pulled along the ground away from the wall at the rate of 1.5 m/sec. The length of the highest point of the ladder when the foot of the ladder 4.0 m away from the wall decreases at the rate of

(a) 2m/sec (b) 3m/sec

(c) 2.5 m/sec (d) 1.5 m/sec

SOLUTION: (a)

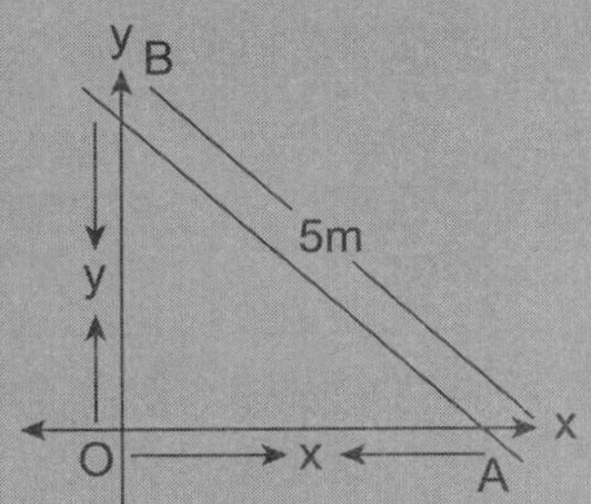

FIGURE 4.6

According to figure $x^2 + y^2 = 25$ ...(i)

Differentiate (i) w.r.t. t, we get $2x\dfrac{dx}{dt} + 2y\dfrac{dy}{dt} = 0$ ...(ii)

Here $x = 4$ and $\dfrac{dx}{dt} = 1.5$

From (i) $4^2 + y^2 = 25 \Rightarrow y = 3$

$\therefore$ From (ii), $2(4)(1.5) + 2(3)\dfrac{dy}{dt} = 0$

So, $\dfrac{dy}{dt} = -2m/\sec$

Hence, length of the highest point decreases at the rate of 2m/sec.

ILLUSTRATION 8: A point on the parabola $y^2 = 18x$ at which the ordinate increases at twice the rate of the abscissa is

(a) $\left(\dfrac{9}{8}, \dfrac{9}{2}\right)$ (b) (2, –4)

(c) $\left(\dfrac{-9}{8}, \dfrac{9}{2}\right)$ (d) (2, 4)

SOLUTION: (a) $y^2 = 18x$; differentiate both sides w.r.t. t, we get $2y\left(\dfrac{dy}{dt}\right) = 18\left(\dfrac{dx}{dt}\right)$

$\Rightarrow 2y\left(2\dfrac{dx}{dt}\right) = 18\left(\dfrac{dx}{dt}\right)$, $\left(\because \dfrac{dy}{dt} = 2\dfrac{dx}{dt}\right)$

$\therefore\ 4y = 18$ or $y = \dfrac{9}{2}$ and $x = \dfrac{y^2}{18} = \dfrac{9}{8}$

Hence the required point is $\left(\dfrac{9}{8}, \dfrac{9}{2}\right)$

ILLUSTRATION 9: The rate of change of $\sqrt{(x^2+16)}$ with respect to $\dfrac{x}{x-1}$ at $x = 3$ is

(a) 2 (b) $\dfrac{11}{5}$

(c) $-\dfrac{12}{5}$ (d) –3

SOLUTION: (c) Let $y = \sqrt{x^2+16}$ and $z = \dfrac{x}{x-1}$

$\Rightarrow\ \dfrac{dy}{dx} = \dfrac{1}{2}\left(x^2+16\right)^{-1/2}(2x)$ and $\dfrac{dz}{dx} = \dfrac{x-1-x}{(x-1)^2} = \dfrac{-1}{(x-1)^2}$

$\therefore\ \dfrac{dy}{dz} = \dfrac{-x}{\sqrt{x^2+16}}\dfrac{1}{(1/(x-1)^2)}$ $\Rightarrow\ \left(\dfrac{dy}{dz}\right)_{x=3} = \dfrac{-3(2)^2}{5} = \dfrac{-12}{5}$

ILLUSTRATION 10: Two men A and B start with velocities v at the same time from the junction of the two roads inclined at 45° to each other. If they travel by different roads, find the rate at which they are being separated.

SOLUTION: Let L and M be the positions of men A and B at any time t after start.

Let $OL = x$ and $LM = y$. Then $OM = x$ and so $\dfrac{dx}{dt} = v$ (given)

from $\Delta\, LOM$, $\cos 45° = \dfrac{OL^2 + OM^2 - LM^2}{2.OL\ OM}$ or $\dfrac{1}{\sqrt{2}} = \dfrac{x^2+x^2-y^2}{2.x.x} = \dfrac{2x^2-y^2}{2x^2}$

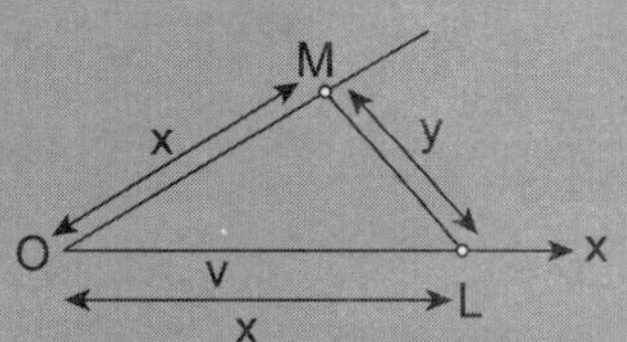

FIGURE 4.7

$\sqrt{2}\ x^2 = 2x^2 - y^2$ or $(2-\sqrt{2})\,x^2 = y^2$

$\Rightarrow\ y = \sqrt{2-\sqrt{2}}\ x$

Differentiating w.r.t. x we get $\dfrac{dy}{dx} = \sqrt{2-\sqrt{2}}$

Now $\because\ \dfrac{dy}{dt} = \dfrac{dy}{dx}.\dfrac{dx}{dt} = (\sqrt{2-\sqrt{2}})\,v$

$\therefore$ They are being separated from each other at the rate $\sqrt{2-\sqrt{2}}v$

ILLUSTRATION 11: x and y are the sides of two squares such that $y = x - x^2$. Find the rate of the change of the area of the second square with respect to the first square.

SOLUTION: Given x and y are sides of two squares thus the area of two squares are x^2 and y^2.

We have to obtain $\dfrac{d(y^2)}{d(x^2)} = \dfrac{2y\dfrac{dy}{dx}}{2x} = \dfrac{y}{x}.\dfrac{dy}{dx}$ ...(i)

where the given curve is, $y = x - x^2$

$\Rightarrow \quad \dfrac{dy}{dx} = 1 - 2x$ ...(ii)

Thus, $\dfrac{d(y^2)}{d(x^2)} = \dfrac{y}{x}(1-2x)$ [From (i) and (ii)]

or $\dfrac{d(y^2)}{d(x^2)} = \dfrac{(x-x^2)(1-2x)}{x}$ $\Rightarrow \dfrac{d(y^2)}{d(x^2)} = (2x^2 - 3x + 1)$

The rate of change of the area of second square with respect to first square is $(2x^2 - 3x + 1)$.

ILLUSTRATION 12: A man is moving away from a tower 85 ft high at a speed of 4ft/sec. Find the rate at which his angle of elevation of the top of the tower is changing, when he is at a distance of 60 ft from the foot of the tower. Assume the eye-level of man to be 5 ft from the ground.

SOLUTION: Let AB be the tower. Let D be at the eye-level of the man. Let x and θ be the distance of the man from the tower and θ be the angle of elevation respectively at time t.

In ΔBDE, $\dfrac{BE}{ED} = \tan\theta$

$\Rightarrow \quad \dfrac{80}{x} = \tan\theta$ $\Rightarrow x = 80\cot\theta$ ...(1)

Speed of man = 4 ft/sec $\therefore \dfrac{dx}{dt} = 4$ ...(2)

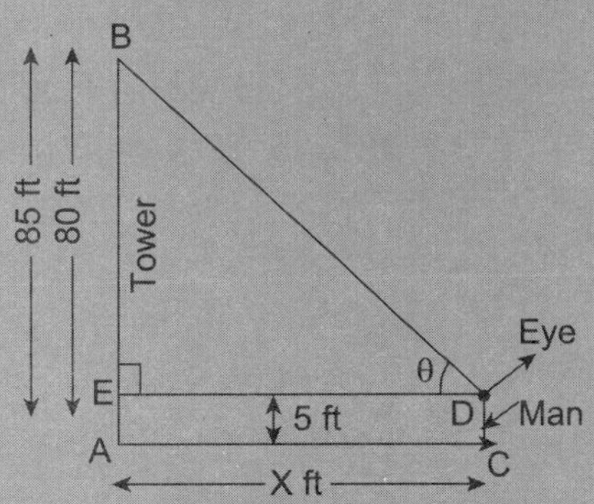

FIGURE 4.8

By Chain rule, $\dfrac{dx}{dt} = \dfrac{dx}{d\theta}.\dfrac{d\theta}{dt}$

$\therefore \quad 4 = \dfrac{d}{d\theta}(80\cot\theta)\dfrac{d\theta}{dt} = -80\,\text{cosec}^2\theta\dfrac{d\theta}{dt}$

$$\therefore \frac{d\theta}{dt} = \frac{4}{-80\operatorname{cosec}^2\theta} = -\frac{\sin^2\theta}{20} = -\frac{1}{20}\left(\frac{BE}{BD}\right)^2$$

$$= -\frac{1}{20}\frac{BE^2}{ED^2} = -\frac{1}{20}\times\frac{(80)^2}{6400+x^2} = \frac{-320}{6400+x^2} \quad (\because BD^2 = BE^2 + ED^2)$$

$\therefore$ When $x = 60$, the rate of change of angle of elevation

$$= \left.\frac{d\theta}{dt}\right|_{x=60} = \frac{-320}{6400+(60)^2} = \frac{-320}{6400+3600}$$

$$= \frac{-320}{10000} = -0.032 \text{ radian/sec}$$

APPLICATION OF DERIVATIVE AS A RATE OF CHANGE

Velocity and Acceleration

Let a particle start moving in a straight line from O and in time 't' it reaches P having covered a distance s and in $t + \delta t$ it reaches Q having covered a distance $s + \delta s$.

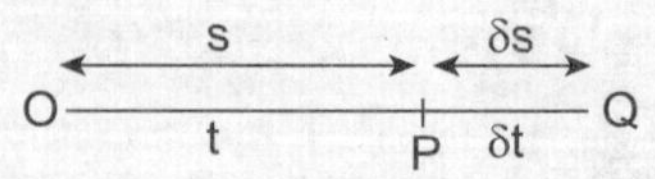

FIGURE 4.9

Now $OP = s$, $OQ = s + \delta s$

$\therefore$ In time δt, average rate of displacement $= \dfrac{\delta s}{\delta t}$

When $\delta t \to 0, \dfrac{\delta s}{\delta t}$ gives the rate of displacement at time t and it is the velocity at time t.

$\therefore$ Velocity at time $t = \lim\limits_{\delta t\to 0}\dfrac{\delta s}{\delta t} = \dfrac{ds}{dt}$.

Hence, $v = \dfrac{ds}{dt}$

NOTE:

1. *Velocity of particle at any point of time can be represented geometrically by the slope of the curve plotted as 's' Vs 't' at that point.*

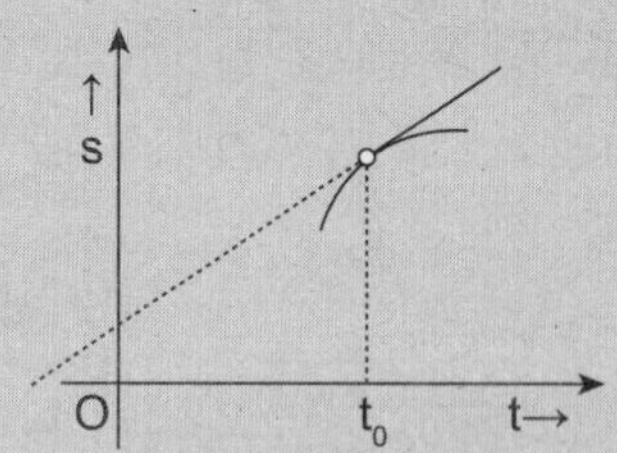

FIGURE 4.10

2. *Velocity is a vector quantity.*
3. *Units of velocity can be meter/sec; cm/sec; km/hr or feet/sec.*
4. *The magnitude of velocity is known as speed (for linear motion) and for non-linear motion velocity and speed are always different.*
5. *Differentiable curve of displacement vs time mean no abrupt change in velocity.*

Now, let v = velocity at time t and $v + \delta v$ = velocity at time $t + \delta t$

$\therefore$ In time δt, change in velocity $= v + \delta v - v = \delta v$

$\therefore$ In time δt, average rate of change in velocity $= \dfrac{\delta v}{\delta t}$

But when $\delta t \to 0, \dfrac{\delta s}{\delta t}$ gives the rate of change of velocity at time t and it is the acceleration at time t.

$\therefore$ Acceleration at time $t = \lim\limits_{\delta t \to 0} \dfrac{\delta v}{\delta t} = \dfrac{dv}{dt} = \dfrac{d}{dt}(v)$

$$= \frac{d}{dt}\left(\frac{ds}{dt}\right) = \frac{d^2 s}{dt^2}.$$

Hence, acceleration $'a' = \dfrac{dv}{dt} = \dfrac{d^2 s}{dt^2}$

NOTE:

1. $a = \dfrac{d^2 s}{dt^2}$ *or* $\dfrac{dv}{dt} = \dfrac{dv}{ds} \times \dfrac{ds}{dt} = v\dfrac{dv}{ds}$
2. *Instantaneous acceleration at a point is a vector quantity*
3. *If the rate of change of velocity is negative, then rate of decrease of velocity is called retardation.*
4. *Units of acceleration can be meter/sec², cm/sec² or feet/sec²*

ILLUSTRATION 13: The distance in seconds, described by a particle in t seconds is given by $s = ae^t + \dfrac{b}{e^t}$. Then acceleration of the particle at time t is

(a) proportional to t (b) proportional to s

(c) s (d) constant

SOLUTION: (c) Given that $s = ae^t + \dfrac{b}{e^t}$

Differentiating w.r.t time t, we get $\dfrac{ds}{dt}$ (velocity) $= ae^t - \dfrac{b}{e^t}$

Again $\dfrac{d^2 s}{dt^2}$ = acceleration $= ae^t + \dfrac{b}{e^t} = s$

ILLUSTRATION 14: If the distance 's' traveled by a particle in time t is $s = a \sin t + b \cos 2t$, then the acceleration at $t = 0$ is

(a) a (b) $-a$

(c) $4b$ (d) $-4b$

SOLUTION: (d) Given $s = a \sin t + b \cos 2t$

$\therefore \dfrac{ds}{dt} = a \cos t - 2b \sin 2t$

$\dfrac{d^2 s}{dt^2} = -a \sin t - 4b \cos 2t$

At $t = 0$, $\dfrac{d^2 s}{dt^2} = -a \sin 0° - 4\, b \cos 0° = -\,4b$

ILLUSTRATION 15: A particle moving according to the formula, $s = 10 + 20t - t^2$, (t measured in seconds and s in meters), starts from a distance of 10 meters from a mark, and moves in a line farther and farther from the mark. How far from the mark does it go, before it starts moving in the opposite direction?

SOLUTION: $s = 10 + 20t - t^2$ ...(i)

$\therefore \quad v = \dfrac{ds}{dt} = 20 - 2t$ ...(ii)

This represents velocity at time t. At the time of start of the movement in the opposite direction, velocity will become zero. Putting $v = 0$ in equation (ii)

we get, $0 = 20 - 2t \quad \Rightarrow t = 10$

$$a = \frac{dv}{dt} = \frac{d}{dt}\left(\frac{ds}{dt}\right) = \frac{d}{dt}(20-2t) = -2$$

$\therefore$ When $t = 10$, $a = -2$ (which is non-zero)

$\therefore$ The direction of particle changes when $t = 10$

$s = 10 + 20(10) - (10)^2 \quad \Rightarrow \quad 10 + 200 - 100 = 110$

Hence the particle goes 110 meter from the mark before it starts moving in the opposite direction.

ILLUSTRATION 16: The velocity of a particle at a time t is given by the relation $\upsilon = 6t - \dfrac{t^2}{6}$. What is the distance traveled in 3 seconds if $s = 0$ at $t = 0$

(a) $\dfrac{39}{2}$ (b) $\dfrac{57}{2}$

(c) $\dfrac{51}{2}$ (d) $\dfrac{33}{2}$

SOLUTION: (c) $\dfrac{ds}{dt} = 6t - \dfrac{t^2}{6}$

Now on integrating both sides $s = 3t^2 - \dfrac{t^3}{18} +$ constant, (where s is distance)

Now put $t = 0$, then $s = 0$ gives constant equal to 0 and putting $t = 3$, we get

$$s = 3(3)^2 - \frac{3^3}{18} = 27 - \frac{27}{18} = \frac{51}{2}$$

Aliter: $\displaystyle\int_0^s ds = \int_0^3\left(6t - \frac{t^2}{6}\right)dt = \frac{51}{2}$

ILLUSTRATION 17: A particle is moving on a straight line, where its position s (in metre) is a function of time t (in seconds) given by $s = at^2 + bt + 6$, $t \geq 0$. If it is known that the particle comes to rest after 4 seconds at a distance of 16 metre, then the retardation in its motion is

(a) -1 m/sec^2 (b) $\dfrac{5}{4}$ m/sec^2

(c) $-\dfrac{1}{2}$ m/sec^2 (d) $-\dfrac{5}{4}$ m/sec^2

SOLUTION: (b) Given equation $s = at^2 + bt + 6$ ...(i)

Differentiating w.r.t. time, we get velocity $(v) = 2at + b$ ...(ii)

After 4 sec, $v = 0$ and distance $s = 16$ meters

$\therefore \quad 0 = 2a \times 4 + b \Rightarrow 8a + b = 0$ ...(iii)

and $16 = 16a + 4b + 6 \Rightarrow 16 = 16a + 4(-8a) + 6$

$\therefore \quad a = -\frac{5}{8}$

But retardation in its motion is, $2a = \frac{-5}{4}$ m/sec^2

$\therefore$ Retardation $= \frac{5}{4}$ m/s^2 (Retardation itself means –ve)

ILLUSTRATION 18: The position of a point in time 't' is given by $x = a + bt - ct^2$, $y = at + bt^2$. Its acceleration at time 't' is

(a) $b - c$
(b) $b + c$
(c) $2b - 2c$
(d) $2\sqrt{b^2 + c^2}$

SOLUTION: (d) Acceleration in direction of x-axis $= \frac{d^2x}{dt^2} = -2c$ and acceleration in direction of y-axis $= \frac{d^2y}{dt^2} = 2b$

Resultant acceleration $= \sqrt{\left(\frac{d^2x}{dt^2}\right)^2 + \left(\frac{d^2y}{dt^2}\right)^2} = \sqrt{(-2c)^2 + (2b)^2} = 2\sqrt{b^2 + c^2}$

ILLUSTRATION 19: If the path of a moving point is the curve $x = at$, $y = b \sin at$, then its acceleration at any instant

(a) is constant
(b) varies as the distance from the axis of x
(c) varies as the distance from the axis of y
(d) varies as the distance of the point from the origin

SOLUTION: (c) $\frac{dx}{dt} = v_x = a \Rightarrow \frac{d^2x}{dt^2} = 0 = a_x$; where a_x is acceleration in x-axis

Similarly $\frac{dy}{dt} = ab \cos at$

$\Rightarrow \quad \frac{d^2y}{dt^2} = -ba^2 \sin at \Rightarrow a_y = -a^2 y$

Hence, a_y changes as y changes

Now, net acceleration $= A = \sqrt{(ax)^2 + (ay)^2} = \sqrt{0^2 + (-a^2y)^2} = |a^2 y|$

Hence, acceleration at any instance varies as the distance from the axis of 'x'.

ILLUSTRATION 20: A man is standing on a straight bridge over a river and another man on a boat is on the river just below the man on the bridge. If the first man starts walking at the uniform speed of 4 m/min and the boat moves perpendicularly to the bridge at the speed of 5 m/min, then at what rate are they separating after x minutes if the height of the bridge above the boat is 3 mt?

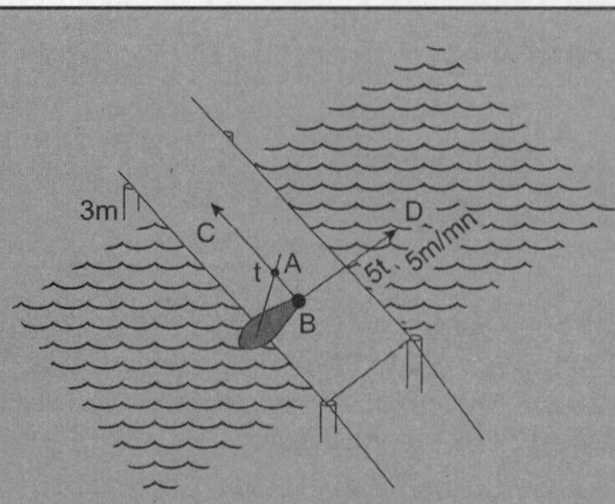

FIGURE 4.11

SOLUTION: Let the initial positions of man (on the bridge) and boat (on the bridge) be A and B, respectively. Now if we observe, initially the distance between A and B is 3 meters (height of the bridge).

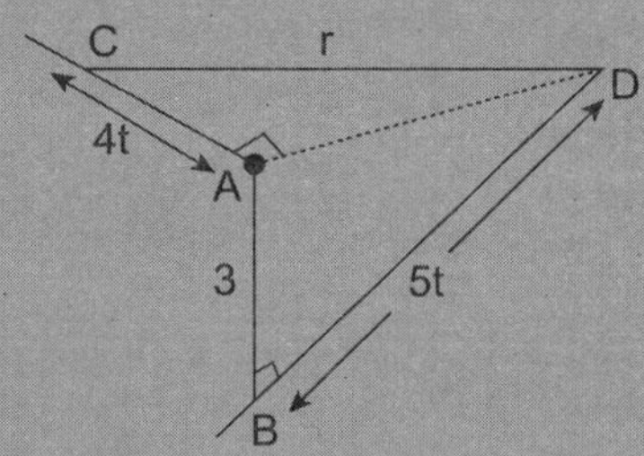

FIGURE 4.12

Let the position of man (on bridge) and the position of boat (on the water) after time 't' be C and D, respectively.

Now $AB \parallel BD$ and $AB \parallel AC$ and as shown in the figure ΔABD and ΔCAD are right angle triangles with right angles at B and A respectively.

$\therefore$ AC is perpendicular to the plane of AB and BD.

$AC \perp AD$

Also, $AC = 4t$(m) and $BD = 5t$ m and $AB = 3mt$

$\therefore$ From the right angled ΔABD, $AD = \sqrt{AB^2 + BD^2} = \sqrt{3^2 + (5t)^2}$

and from the right-angled ΔDAC, $DC = \sqrt{AD^2 + AC^2}$

If $DC = rm$, Then $r = \sqrt{3^2 + (5t)^2 + (4t)^2} = \sqrt{9 + 41t^2}$

$$\therefore \quad \frac{dr}{dt} = \frac{1}{2\sqrt{9+41t^2}}.(41)(2t), \text{ at } t = x \text{ min; } \left(\frac{dr}{dt}\right)_{t=x} = \frac{41x}{\sqrt{9+4x^2}} \text{mt/min}$$

APPLICATION IN TWO DIMENSION

Area and Perimeter of Some Standard Two Dimensional Figures are Listed Below

(a) ***Triangle:*** Area: $\frac{1}{2}ab \sin C$ & Perimeter:$(a + b + c)$

Equilateral triangle: $\angle A = \angle B = \angle C = 60^\circ$ and $BC = CA = AB = a$ (say)

$\therefore$ Area $= \frac{\sqrt{3}}{4}a^2$ and perimeter $= 3a$

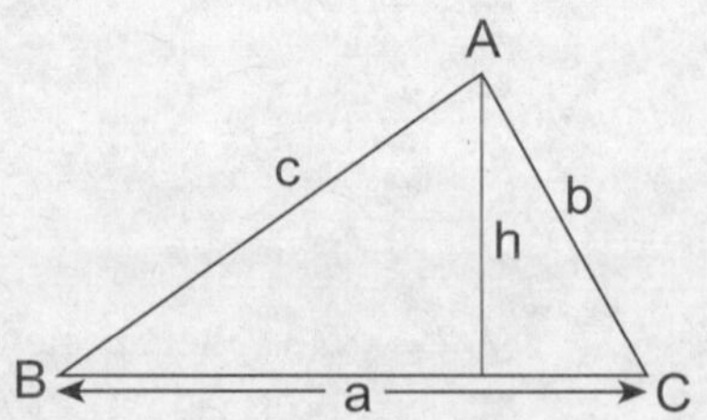

FIGURE 4.13

(b) ***Square:*** In square $\angle A = \angle B = \angle C = \angle D = 90^\circ$ and $AB = DC = BC = AD = a$

$\therefore$ Area $= a^2$ and perimeter $= 4a$

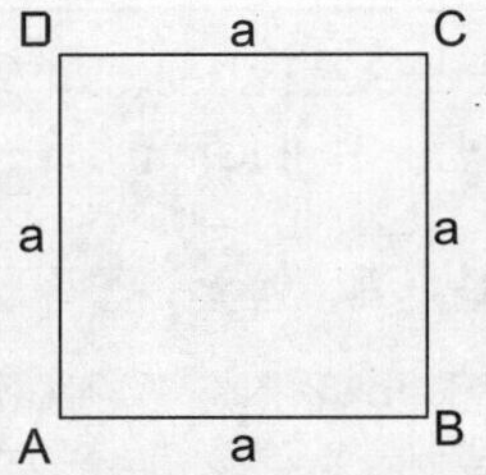

FIGURE 4.14

(c) ***Rectangle:*** In a rectangle $\angle A = \angle B = \angle C = \angle D =$ $90°$ and $AB = DC = a$ and $BC = AD = b$

$\therefore$ Area $= ab$ and perimeter $= 2\ (a + b)$

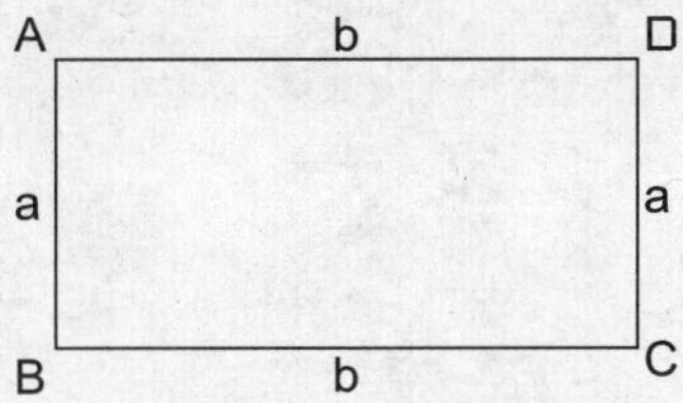

FIGURE 4.15

(d) ***Rhombus:*** Perimeter is $4a$. Area $= \frac{1}{2}d_1d_2$ where d_1 and d_2 are the lengths of the diagonal AC and BD

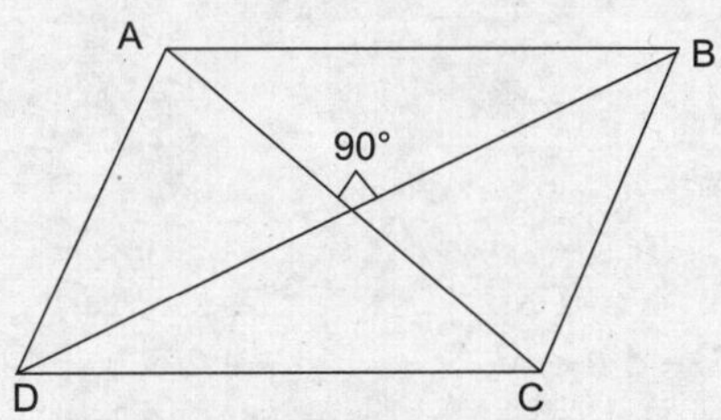

FIGURE 4.16

(e) ***Trapezium:*** In a trapezium AB is parallel to DC and AD and BC are non parallel. If $AB = a$ and $DC = b$ and distance between parallel sides is h, then area $= \frac{1}{2}(a+b)\times h$

(where a and b are length of parallel sides and h is the distance between them).

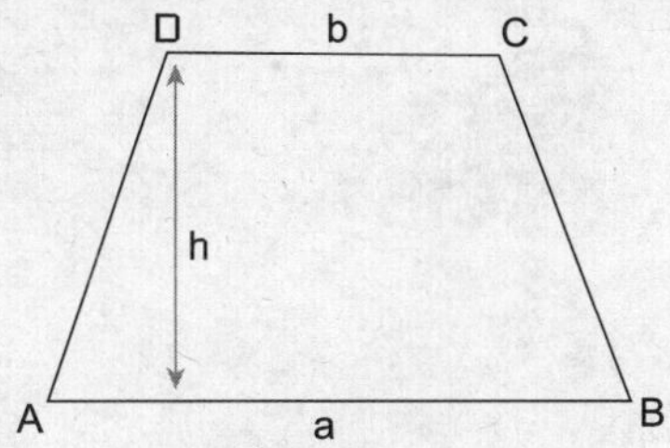

FIGURE 4.17

(f) ***Circle:*** If centre is at O and radius is r

$\therefore$ Area of circle $= \pi r^2$ and perimeter is $2\pi r$. i.e., (circumference)

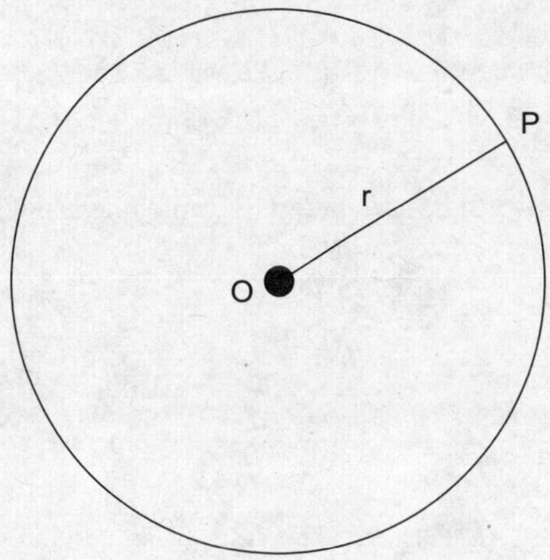

FIGURE 4.18

(g) ***Sector of a circle:*** Area: $\frac{1}{2}r^2\theta$, where θ is in radians and perimeter: $r\ (2 + \theta)$

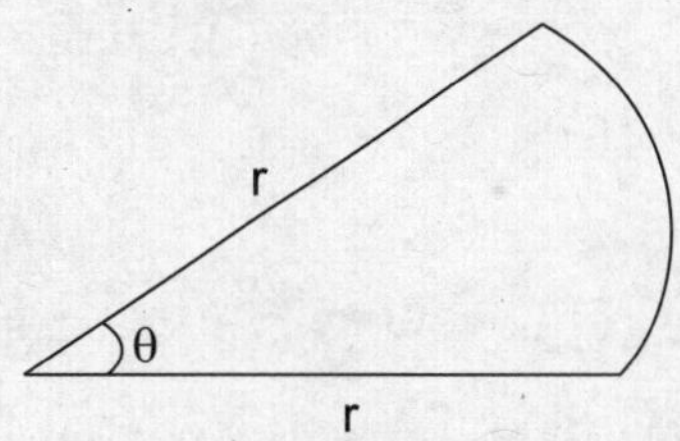

FIGURE 4.19

(h) ***Ellipse:*** If length of major and minor axes are $2a$ and $2b$

$\therefore$ Area $= \pi\ ab$

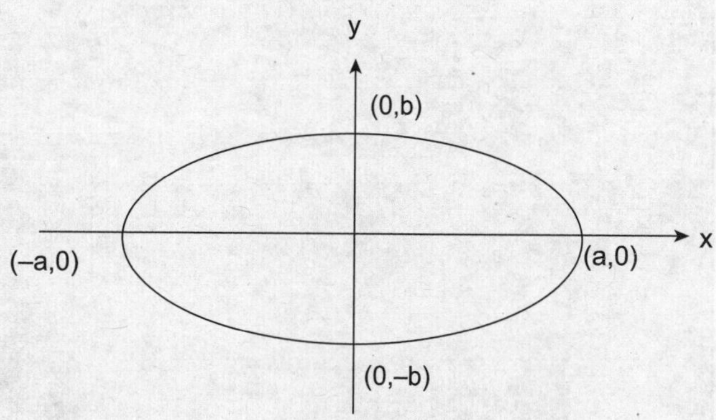

FIGURE 4.20

ILLUSTRATION 21: If by dropping a stone in a quiet lake a wave moves in circle at a speed of 3.5 cm/sec, then the rate of increase of the enclosed circular region when the radius of the circular wave is 10 cm, is $\left(\pi = \frac{22}{7}\right)$

(a) 220 sq. cm/sec
(b) 110 sq.cm/sec
(c) 35 sq.cm/sec
(d) 350 sq.cm/sec

SOLUTION: (a) Given the rate of increasing of the radius $= \frac{dr}{dt} = 3.5\,\text{cm/sec}$ and $r = 10$ cm

Area of circle $= A = \pi r^2$

$$\Rightarrow \frac{dA}{dt} = 2\pi r.\frac{dr}{dt} \Rightarrow \frac{dA}{dt} = 2\pi \times 10 \times 3.5$$

$$\Rightarrow \frac{dA}{dt} = 220\,\text{cm}^2/\text{sec}$$

ILLUSTRATION 22: The sides of an equilateral triangle are increasing at the rate of 2 cm/sec. The rate at which the area increases, when the side is 10 cm is

(a) $\sqrt{3}$ sq unit/sec
(b) 10 sq unit/sec
(c) $10\sqrt{3}$sq unit/ sec
(d) $\frac{10}{\sqrt{3}}$ sq unit/sec

SOLUTION: (c) If x is the length of each side of an equilateral triangle and A is its area,

then $A = \frac{\sqrt{3}}{4}x^2 \Rightarrow \frac{dA}{dt} = \frac{\sqrt{3}}{4}2x\frac{dx}{dt}$

Here, $x = 10$ cm and $\frac{dx}{dt} = 2\,\text{cm/sec}$

$\Rightarrow A = 10\sqrt{3}$ Sq. unit per sec.

ILLUSTRATION 23: A ladder 20 ft. long has one end on the ground and the other end in contact with a vertical wall. The lower end slips along the ground. Show that when the lower end of the ladder is 16 ft. away from the wall, upper end is moving 4/3 times as fast as the lower end.

SOLUTION: Let OC be the wall. Let AB be the position of the ladder at any time t such that $OA = x$ and $OB = y$.

Length of ladder $AB = 20$ ft.

In ΔAOB, $x^2 + y^2 = (20)^2$ ...(1)

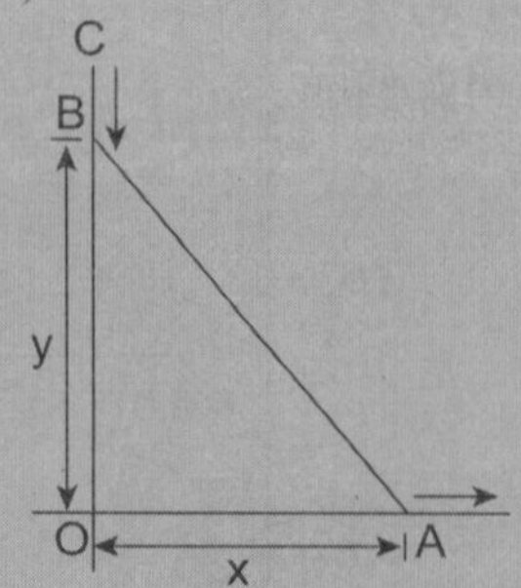

FIGURE 4.21

Differentiating both sides w.r.t. t, we get $2x\frac{dx}{dt}+2y\frac{dy}{dt}=0$

$\therefore \quad \frac{dy}{dt}=-\frac{x}{y}\frac{dx}{dt}=-\frac{x}{\sqrt{400-x^2}}\cdot\frac{dx}{dt}$ {From (1)}

When $x = 16$ ft., then $\frac{dy}{dt}=-\frac{16}{\sqrt{(400-16^2)}}\cdot\frac{dx}{dt}=-\frac{4}{3}\cdot\frac{dx}{dt}$

–ve sign indicates that when x increases with time, y decreases.

Hence the upper end is moving (4/3) times as fast as the lower end.

ILLUSTRATION 24: A kite is moving horizontally at a height of 151.5 metres. If the speed of the kite is 10 m/sec, how fast is the string being let out, when the kite is 250 m from the boy who is flying the kite, the height of the boy being 1.5 m?

SOLUTION: Let the position of the kite at time t be at C.

$\therefore \quad BC = 151.5$ m

Let AD be the boy who is flying the kite.

Let $AD = x = DE$ and $DC = y$

$\therefore \quad CE = BC - BE = 151.5 - 1.5 = 150$ metre

Therefore from the right angled triangle CDE, $y^2 = x^2 + (150)^2$ ...(1)

$\therefore \quad 2y\frac{dy}{dx}=2x\frac{dx}{dt}+0$

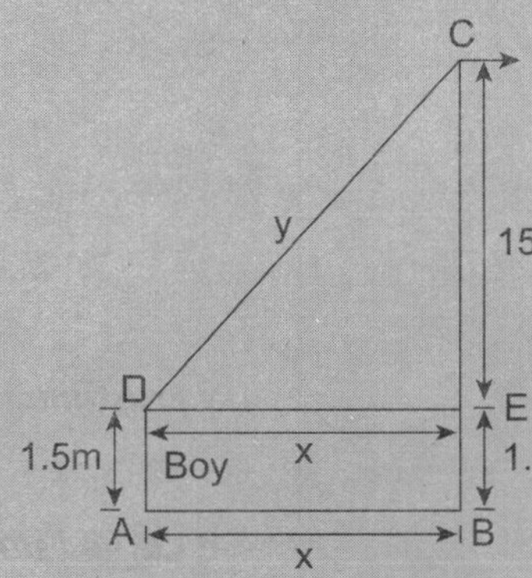

FIGURE 4.22

$\therefore \quad \frac{dy}{dt}=\frac{x}{y}\frac{dx}{dt}=\frac{x}{y}.10$ $\left(\because \frac{dx}{dt}=10\,\text{m/sec}\right)$

$=\frac{10x}{y}=\frac{10\sqrt{(y)^2-(150)^2}}{y}$ {From (1)}

When $y = 250$ m then $\frac{dy}{dt}=\frac{10\sqrt{(250)^2-(150)^2}}{250}=\frac{10\times 200}{250}=8\,\text{m/sec}$

Hence the string is being let out at the rate of 8 m/sec when 250 m of string is out.

APPLICATION IN THREE DIMENSION GEOMETRY

Area and Perimeter of Some Standard Three Dimensional Figures are Listed Below

(a) ***Cube:*** Length of each side = a; Volume = $V = a^3$ and surface area of cube = $S = 6a^2$

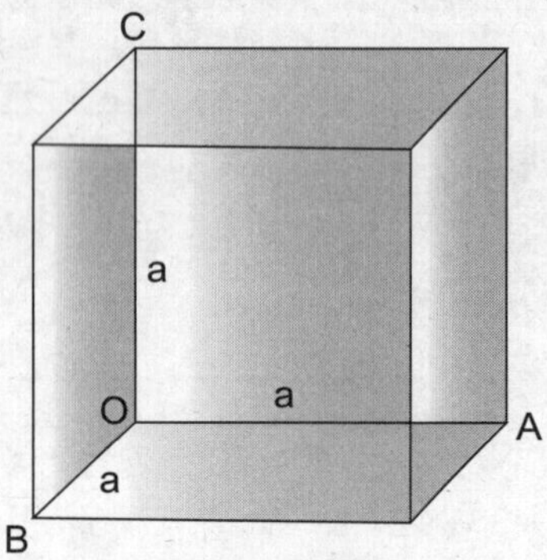

FIGURE 4.23

(b) ***Cuboid:*** Surface area is 2 ($bh + hl + bl$)
Volume: hbl

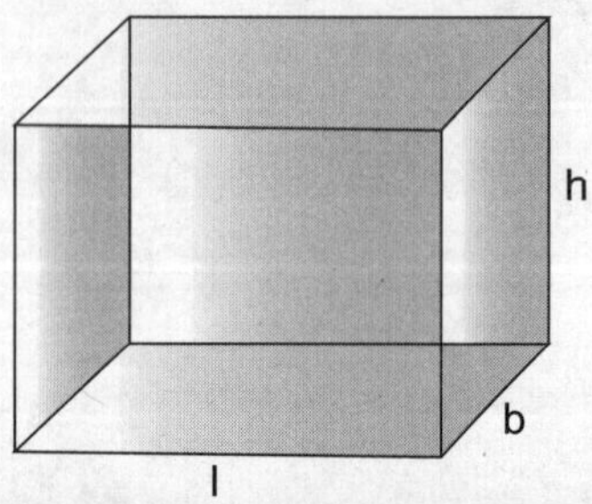

FIGURE 4.24

(c) ***Sphere:*** Surface area is $4\pi r^2$,

Volume = $\frac{4}{3}\pi r^3$

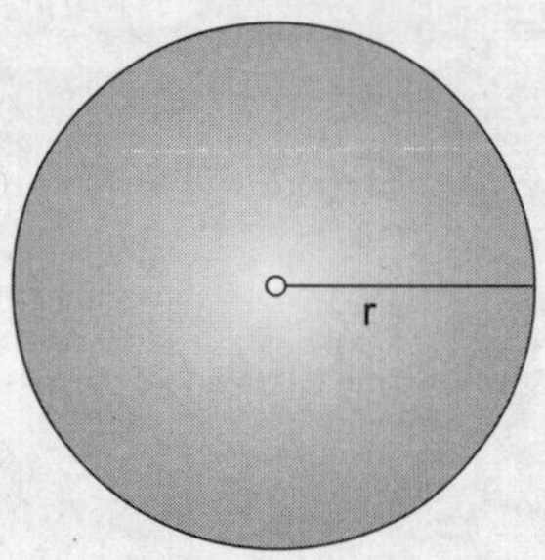

FIGURE 4.25

(d) ***Cone:*** Volume = $\frac{1}{3}\pi r^2 h$

Curved surface area of cone = $\pi r l$

Total surface area = $\pi r l + \pi r^2$

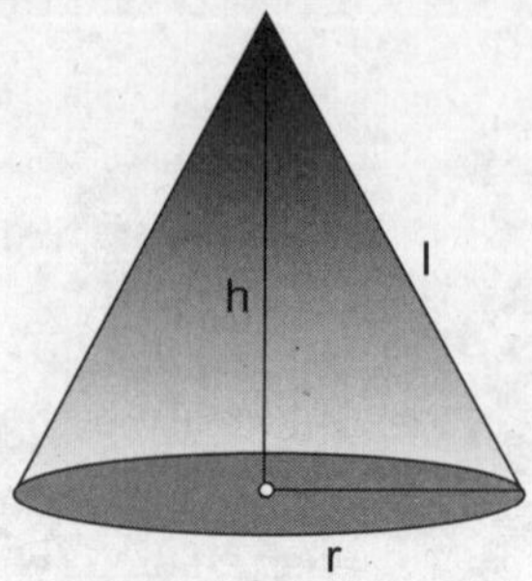

FIGURE 4.26

(e) ***Cylinder:*** Volume is $\pi r^2 h$

Curved surface area: $2\pi r h$

Total surface area is $2\pi rh + 2\pi r^2$

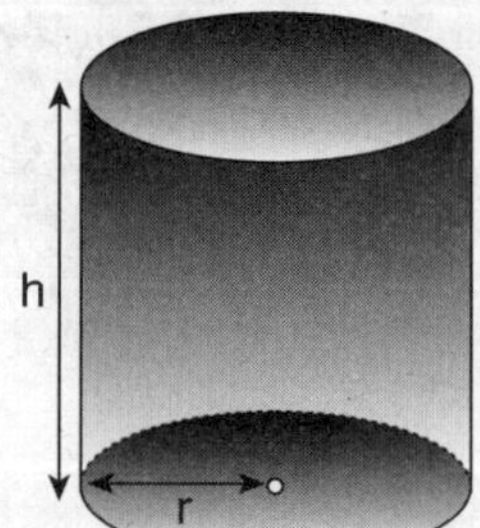

FIGURE 4.27

(f) ***Frustum:*** $V = \frac{1}{3}\pi h\ (R^2 + r^2 + rR)$

Curved surface area: $\pi(R + r)\sqrt{(R - r)^2 + h^2}$

Total surface area: $\pi(R + r)\sqrt{(R - r)^2 + h^2} + \pi(R^2 + r^2)$

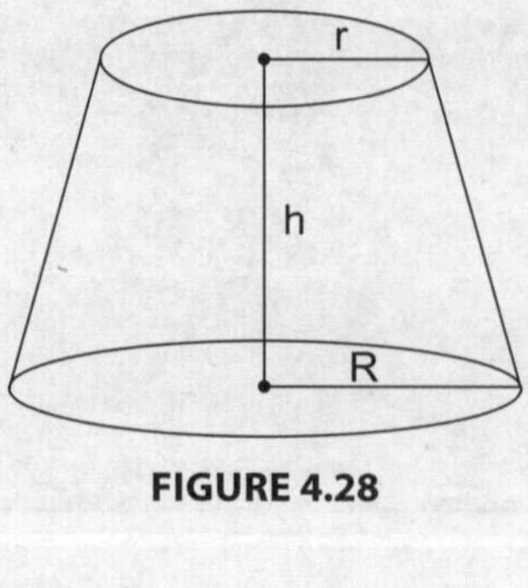

FIGURE 4.28

(g) ***Right triangular prism:*** Lateral Surfaces of a prism are all rectangles. i.e., $ABB'A'$, $ACC'A'$ & $BCC'B'$

Volume of a prism = (area of the base) × (height)

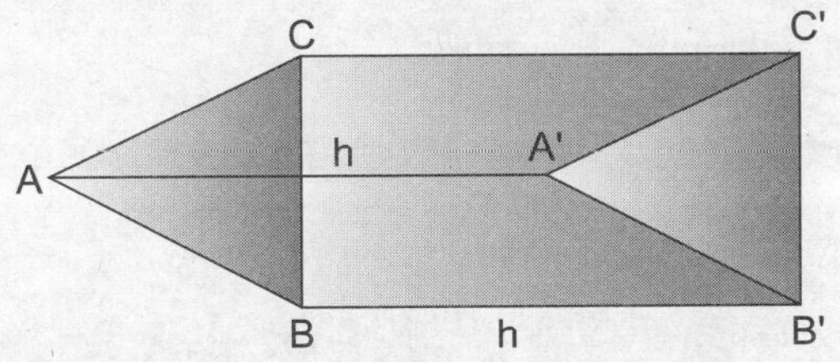

FIGURE 4.29

(h) ***Right Pyramid:***

Volume of pyramid = $\frac{1}{3}$(area of base)×height

Curved surface of a pyramid

$=\frac{1}{2}$(perimeter of the base)× slant height

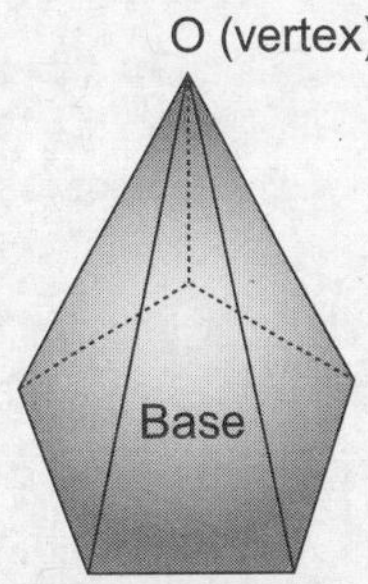

FIGURE 4.30

ILLUSTRATION 25: A cylindrical tank of radius 10 feet is being filled with wheat at the rate of 314 cubic feet per minute. Find the rate of increase of the depth of wheat. (Assume π = 3.14)

SOLUTION: Radius of tank = 10 feet

Let V and h be the volume and depth of wheat at time t.

$\therefore \quad V = \pi(10)^2 h = 100\ \pi h$ cubic ft

$$\therefore \quad \frac{dv}{dt} = 100\pi\frac{dh}{dt} \qquad \ldots(1)$$

Volume of wheat is increasing at the rate of 314 cubic feet per minute

$$\Rightarrow \quad \frac{dv}{dt} = 314$$

$$\therefore \quad (1) \Rightarrow 314 = 100\,\pi\frac{dh}{dt}$$

$$\Rightarrow \quad \frac{dh}{dt} = \frac{314}{100\pi} = \frac{3.14}{\pi} = 1$$

$\therefore$ Depth of wheat is increasing at the rate 1 ft/min

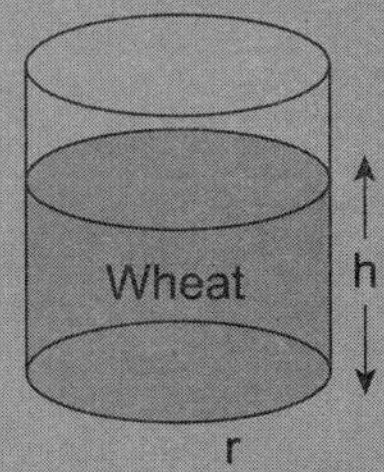

FIGURE 4.31

ILLUSTRATION 26: If water is poured into an inverted hollow cone whose semi-vertical angle is 30°, also known that its depth increases at the rate of 1 cm per sec, then find the rate at which the volume of water is increasing when the depth is 24 cm.

SOLUTION: Let A be the vertex and AO the axis of the cone. Let $O'A = h$ be the depth of water in cone. In $\Delta AO'C$, $\tan 30° = \frac{O'C}{h}$

$$\therefore \quad O'C = \frac{h}{\sqrt{3}} = \text{radius}$$

$$V = \text{volume of water in cone} = \frac{1}{3}\pi(O'C)^2 \times AO' = \frac{1}{3}\pi\left(\frac{h^2}{3}\right)\times h$$

$$\therefore \quad V = \frac{\pi}{9}h^3$$

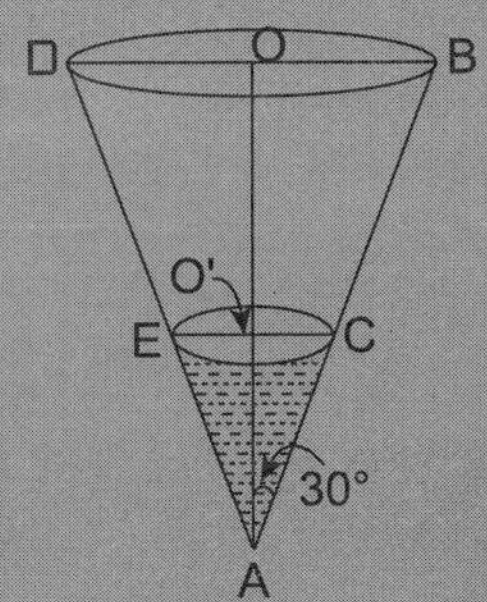

FIGURE 4.32

$$\Rightarrow \frac{dV}{dt} \quad - \quad \frac{dh}{dt} \qquad \ldots(1)$$

but given that depth of water increases at the rate of 1 cm/sec

$\therefore \quad dh/dt = 1$ cm/sec ...(2)

From (1) and (2), $\dfrac{dV}{dt} = \dfrac{\pi h^2}{3}$

When $h = 24$ cm, the rate of increase of volume $= \dfrac{dV}{dt} = \dfrac{\pi(24)^2}{3} = 192\pi\ \text{cm}^3/\text{sec.}$

ILLUSTRATION 27: A cube of ice melts without changing shape at the uniform rate of 4 cm^3/min. The rate of change of the surface area of the cube, in cm^2/min, when the volume of the cube is 125 cm^3, is

(a) -4 (b) $-16/5$

(c) $-16/6$ (d) $-8/15$

SOLUTION: (b) Given $\dfrac{dV}{dt} = -4\text{cm}^3/\text{min}$; and $V = 125\ cm^2$

$V = x^3 \qquad \Rightarrow \dfrac{dV}{dt} = 3x^2 \dfrac{dx}{dt}$

$\Rightarrow -4 = 3x^2 \dfrac{dx}{dt}$ ....(1);

And $S = 6x^2$;

$\Rightarrow \dfrac{dS}{dt} = 12x \dfrac{dx}{dt} \qquad \Rightarrow -4 = 3x^2 \dfrac{dS}{dt} \cdot \dfrac{1}{12x}$

$\Rightarrow \dfrac{dS}{dt} = -\dfrac{16}{x}$; $\qquad$ Now, when $V = 125 = x^3 \Rightarrow x = 5$

$\therefore \dfrac{dS}{dt} = -\dfrac{16}{x}$ cm^2/min $\qquad \Rightarrow \dfrac{dS}{dt} = -\dfrac{16}{5}$ cm^2/min

ILLUSTRATION 28: The radius of a right circular cylinder increases at the rate of 0.1 cm/min, and the height decrease at the rate of 0.2 cm/min. The rate of change of the volume of the cylinders, in cm^3 min, when the radius is 2 cm and the height is 3cm is

(a) -2π (b) $-\dfrac{8\pi}{5}$

(c) $-\dfrac{3\pi}{5}$ (d) $\dfrac{2\pi}{5}$

SOLUTION: (d) Given $V = \pi r^2 h$

Differentiating both sides $\dfrac{dV}{dt} = \pi\left(r^2\dfrac{dh}{dt} + 2r\dfrac{dr}{dt}h\right) = \pi r\left(r\dfrac{dh}{dt} + 2h\dfrac{dr}{dt}\right)$

Given $\dfrac{dr}{dt} = \dfrac{1}{10}$ *and* $\dfrac{dh}{dt} = -\dfrac{2}{10}$

$$\frac{dV}{dt} = \pi r\left(r\left(-\frac{2}{10}\right) + 2h\left(\frac{1}{10}\right)\right) = \frac{\pi r}{5}(-r+h)$$

Thus, when $r = 2$ and $h = 3$, $\dfrac{dV}{dt} = \dfrac{\pi(2)}{5}(-2+3) = \dfrac{2\pi}{5}$

ILLUSTRATION 29: Sand is draining from a conical filter, where height and diameter are both 15 cms, into a cylindrical sand pot of diameter 15 cm. The rate at which sand drains from the filter into the pot is 100 cu cm/min. The rate in cms/min at which the level in the pot is rising at the instant when the sand in the pot is 10 cm, is

(a) $\frac{9}{16\pi}$ (b) $\frac{25}{9\pi}$

(c) $\frac{5}{3\pi}$ (d) $\frac{16}{9\pi}$

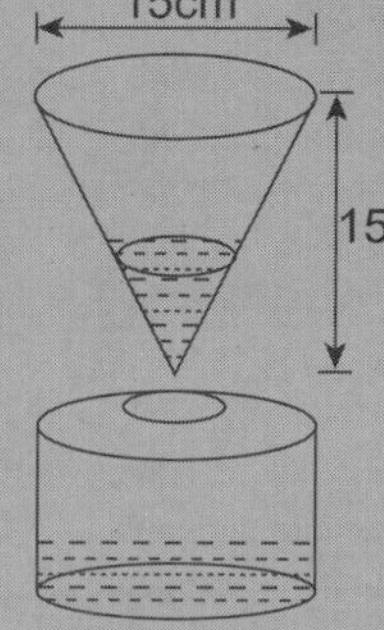

FIGURE 4.33

SOLUTION: (d) For cylindrical pot $V = \pi r^2 h$

$$\frac{dV}{dt} = \pi r^2 \frac{dh}{dt} \qquad \left(r = \text{constant}, \frac{dr}{dt} = 0\right)$$

hence, $100 = \pi r^2 \frac{dh}{dt}$

$$\Rightarrow 100 = \pi \cdot \frac{225}{4} \cdot \frac{dh}{dt} \qquad \left(\because r = \frac{15}{2} \text{ cm}\right)$$

$$\Rightarrow \frac{dh}{dt} = \frac{400}{225\pi} = \frac{400}{225\pi} = \frac{16}{9\pi} \text{ cm/min}$$

ILLUSTRATION 30: A spherical balloon is being inflated so that its volume increases uniformly at the rate of 40 cm^3/min. How fast is its surface area increasing when the radius is 8 cm? Find approximately, how much the radius will increase during the next 1/2 minute.

SOLUTION: Let V be the volume and r the radius of the balloon at any time, then $V = \left(\frac{4}{3}\right)\pi r^3$

$$\therefore \frac{dV}{dt} = \left(\frac{4}{3}\right)(3\pi r^2)\frac{dr}{dt}$$

or $\frac{dV}{dt} = 4\pi r^2 \frac{dr}{dt} = 40$ (given)

$$\therefore \frac{dr}{dt} = \frac{10}{\pi r^2} \qquad \ldots(1)$$

Now let S be the surface area of the balloon when its radius is r, then $S = 4\pi r^2$

$$\therefore \frac{dS}{dt} = 8\pi r \frac{dr}{dt} \qquad \ldots(2)$$

From (1) and (2), $\frac{dS}{dt} = 8\pi r . \frac{10}{\pi r^2} = \frac{80}{r}$

When $r = 8$, the rate of increase of $S = \frac{80}{8} = 10 \text{cm}^2/\text{min}$

$\therefore$ increase of S in $\frac{1}{2}$ minute $= 10 \times \left(\frac{}{}\right) = 5$ cm^2/min

If r_1 be the radius of the balloon after (1/2) min., then $4\pi r_1^2 = 4\pi(8)^2 + 5$ or $r_1^2 - 8^2$

$= \frac{5}{4\pi} = 0.397$ nearly

or $r_1^2 = 64.397$ or $r_1 = 8.025$ nearly

$\therefore$ Required increase in the radius $= r_1 - 8 = 8.025 - 8 = 0.025$ cm

ILLUSTRATION 31: The radius of a right circular cylinder increases at a constant rate. Its altitude is a linear function of the radius and increases three times as fast as radius. When the radius is 1cm the altitude is 6 cm. When the radius is 6cm, the volume is increasing at the rate of 1*cu* cm/sec. When the radius is 36cm, the volume is increasing at a rate of *n* cu. cm/sec. The value of '*n*' is equal to:

(a) 12 (b) 22

(c) 30 (d) 33

SOLUTION: (d) If h and r denotes the height and radius of the cylinder, then $h = ar + b$ where a, b are constant, also $\frac{dh}{dt} = 3\frac{dr}{dt}$ (given)

$\therefore \quad a\frac{dr}{dt} = 3\frac{dr}{dt} \qquad \Rightarrow a = 3$

Hence $h = 3r + b$

when $r = 1$; $h = 6$ $\qquad \Rightarrow 6 = 3 + b \qquad \Rightarrow b = 3$

$\therefore \quad h = 3(r + 1)$

$V = \pi r^2 h = 3\pi r^2(r + 1) = 3\pi(r^3 + r^2)$

$\Rightarrow \quad \frac{dV}{dt} = 3\pi(3r^2 + 2r)\frac{dr}{dt}$ $\qquad$ Where $r = 6$; $\frac{dV}{dt} = 1$ cc/sec

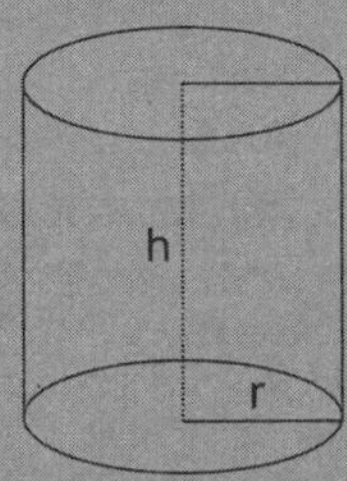

FIGURE 4.34

$\therefore \quad 1 = 3\pi(108 + 12)\frac{dr}{dt}$

$\Rightarrow \quad 360\pi\frac{dr}{dt} = 1 \qquad \Rightarrow \frac{dr}{dt} = \frac{1}{360\pi}$

again when $r = 36$, $\frac{dV}{dt} = n$

$n = 3\pi(3.(36)^2 + 2.36)\frac{dr}{dt} \qquad n = 3\pi.\ 36\ (110).\ \frac{1}{360\pi}$

$n = 33$

ILLUSTRATION 32: An air force plane is ascending vertically at the rate of 100 km/h. If the radius of the earth is r km, how fast is the area of the earth, visible from the plane increasing at earth, then visible from the plane increasing at 3 minutes after it started ascending? It is given that if h is the height of the plane above the earth, the visible area is equal to $\frac{2\pi r^2 h}{r+h}$.

SOLUTION: Let h and A be respectively the height of the plane above the earth and visible area from the planet time t.

$$A = \frac{2\pi r^2 h}{r+h}$$

The height of plane is increasing at the rate of 100 km/h.

$$\therefore \quad \frac{dh}{dt} = 100$$

Rate of change of visible area ($= A$) w.r.t. time $= \frac{dA}{dt} = \frac{dA}{dh} \times \frac{dh}{dt} = 2\pi r^2 \frac{d}{dh}\left(\frac{h}{r+h}\right) \times 100$

$$= 200\pi r^2\left[\frac{(r+h).1 - h(0+1)}{(r+h)^2}\right] = \frac{200\pi r^3}{(r+h)^2}$$

Height of the plane after 3 minutes $=\frac{3}{60}\times 100 = 5$ km

$\therefore$ Rate of increase of visible area w.r.t. after 3 minutes $=\frac{200\pi r^3}{(r+5)^2}$ km²/h.

ILLUSTRATION 33: Water is leaking from a conical funnel at rate of 5cm³/sec. If the radius of the base of the funnel is 5 cm and the altitude is 10cm, find the rate at which the water level is dropping when it is 2.5 cm from the top.

SOLUTION: Let r and h be respectively the radius and the height of the surface of water at time t. Let V be the volume of water in funnel.

$\therefore\ V=\frac{1}{3}\pi r^2 h$ .....(1)

By similar triangles, $\frac{r}{h}=\frac{5}{10}$ $\quad\therefore\ r=\frac{1}{2}h$

$\therefore\ (1)\Rightarrow V=\frac{1}{3}\pi\left(\frac{h}{2}\right)^2=\frac{\pi h^3}{12}$ .....(2)

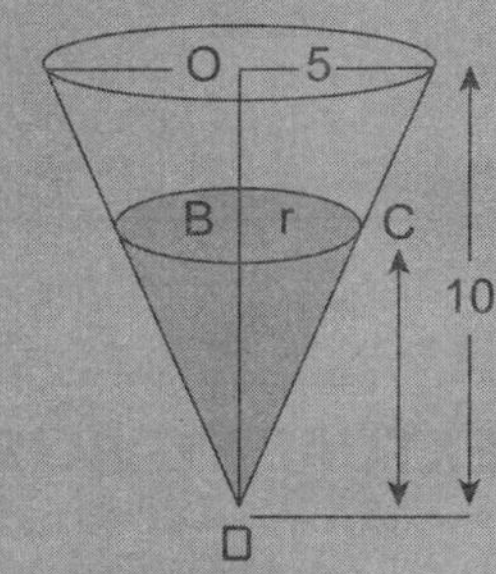

FIGURE 4.35

since water is running out of the funnel at the rate of 5cm³/sec.

$\therefore\ \frac{dV}{dt}=-5\left(\frac{dV}{dt}\text{ is – ve, because } V \text{ decreas as } t \text{ increases}\right)$

$(2)\Rightarrow \frac{dV}{dt}=\frac{d}{dt}\left(\frac{\pi h^3}{12}\right)=\frac{3\pi h^2}{4}\frac{dh}{dt}$

$\Rightarrow \frac{\pi h^2}{4}\frac{dh}{dt}=-5\Rightarrow \frac{dh}{dt}=-\frac{20}{\pi h^2}$

$\therefore$ rate of change of water level (i.e., of h) w.r.t. time $t=\frac{dh}{dt}=-\frac{20}{\pi h^2}$

When water level is 2.5 cm from the top, $h = 10 - 2.5 = 7.5$

$\therefore$ Rate of change of water level w.r.t. t when h is 7.5 $=-\frac{20}{\pi(7.5)^2}=-\frac{16}{45\pi}$ cm/sec.

$\therefore$ Rate of dropping of water level w.r.t. to when h is 7.5 $=\frac{16}{45\pi}$ cm/sec.

■ PROBLEMS BASED ON MARGINAL COSTS AND MARGINAL REVENUE

Working Rule

Use the following results whichever are required

1. Marginal Cost (MC) is the instantaneous rate of change of total cost with respect to the number of items produced at an instant.
2. If total cost when x units is produced is $C(x)$, then marginal cost $=\frac{d(C(x))}{dx}=\frac{dC}{dx}$
3. Marginal revenue (MR) is the instantaneous rate of change of total revenue with respect to the number of times sold at an instant.
4. If $R(x)$ be the total revenue when x units are sold, then marginal revenue $=\frac{d}{dx}\{R(x)\}=\frac{dR}{dx}$

ILLUSTRATION 34: The total cost $C(x)$ associated with the production of x units of an item is given by $C(x) = 0.007x^3 + 0.03x^2 + 15x + 4000$. Find the marginal cost when 7 units are produced.

SOLUTION: Given, $C(x) = 0.007x^3 + 0.003x^2 + 15x + 4000$

Marginal cost is given by $MC(x) = \frac{dC}{dx} = (0.007)3x^2 + (0.003)2x + 15 = 0.021x^2 + 0.006x + 15$

When $x = 17$, $MC(x) = 0.021\ (17)^2 + 0.006 \times 17 + 15$

Hence, $MC\ (17) = 0.021 \times 289 + 0.102 + 15 = 6.069 + 0.102 + 15 = 21.171$

ILLUSTRATION 35: The total revenue received from the sale of x units of a product is given by $R(x) = 13x^2 - 26x + 15$. Find the marginal revenue when $x = 7$

SOLUTION: Given $R(x) = 13x^2 - 26x + 15$

Marginal revenue is given by ...(1)

$$MR(x) = \frac{dR}{dx} = 26x - 26 \quad \text{...(2)}$$

When $x = 7$, $MR(x) = 26 \times 7 - 26 = 26\ (7 - 1) = 26 \times 6 = 156$ $\therefore$ $MR(7) = 156$

TEXTUAL EXERCISE–1: (SUBJECTIVE)

1. If the displacement of a particle is given by $s = \left(\frac{1}{2}t^2 + 4\sqrt{t}\right)m$, where m is in meter. Find the velocity and acceleration at $t = 4$ second.
2. If the displacement of a particle is given by $s = \frac{1}{2}t^3 - 6t$, find the acceleration at the time when the velocity vanishes (i.e., velocity tends to zero).
3. The velocity of a particle moving in the positive direction of x-axis is given by $v = k\sqrt{x}$, where k is a positive constant. Find the acceleration of the particle
4. A particle moves along the curve, $6y = x^3 + 2$. Find the points on the curve at which the y-coordinate is changing 8 times as the x-coordinate.
5. Find the point on the curve $y^2 = 8x$ for which the abscissa and ordinate change at the same rate.
6. The volume of a spherical balloon is increasing at the rate of 25 cm^3/sec. Find the rate of change of its surface area at the instant when radius is 5 cm.
7. The length x of a rectangle is decreasing at the rate of 5 cm/minute and the width y is increasing at the rate of 4 cm/minute. When $x = 8$ cm and $y = 6$ cm, find the rates of change of (i) the perimeter (ii) the area of the rectangle.
8. A circular disc of radius 3 m is being heated. Due to expansion, its radius increases at the rate of 0.05 cm/sec. Find the rate which its area is increasing when radius is 3.2 cm.
9. A car starts from a point P at time $t = 0$ seconds and stops at a point Q. The distance x, in metres, covered by it, in t seconds is given by $x = t^2\left(2 - \frac{t}{3}\right)$. Find the time taken by it to reach Q and also find distance PQ.

Answer Keys

1. $v = 5$m/sec and $a = 7/8$ m/sec^2 **2.** $t = 2$ sec, $a = 6$ unit/sec^2 **3.** $a = k^2/2$ **4.** (4, 11) and (–4, –31/3)
5. (2, 4) **6.** 10cm^2/sec **7.** (i) –2cm/min (ii) 2 cm/min
8. 0.320πcm^2/sec **9.** 4 second, $PQ = \frac{32}{3}m$

TEXTUAL EXERCISE–1: (OBJECTIVE)

1. A stone is dropped into a quite lake and waves move in a circle at a speed of 4 cm/s. At the instant when the radius of the circular wave is 10 cm., the enclosed area increases at the rate

(a) 100π cm²/s (b) 80π cm/s

(c) 40 cm²/sec (d) None of these

2. A balloon is pumped at the rate of a cm³/min. The rate of increase of its surface area when the radius is b cm, is

(a) $2a^2/b^4$ cm²/min (b) $a/2b$ cm²/min

(c) $2a/b$ cm²/min (d) None of these

3. An edge of a variable cube is increasing at the rate of 10cm/s.How fast the volume of the cube will increase when the edge is 5 cm long ?

(a) 750 cm³/s (b) 75 cm³/s

(c) 300 cm³/s (d) 150 cm³/s

4. A stone is thrown vertically upwards from the top of a tower 64 m high according to the law $s = 48t - 16t^2$. The greatest height attained by the stone above ground is

(a) 36m (b) 32m

(c) 100m (d) 64m

5. The diagonal of square is changing at the rate of 0.5 cm/sec. Then the rate of change of area, when the area is 400 cm², is equal to

(a) $20\sqrt{2}\ \text{cm}^2/\text{s}$ (b) $10\sqrt{2}\ \text{cm}^2/\text{s}$

(c) $\frac{1}{10\sqrt{2}}\ \text{cm}^2/\text{s}$ (d) $\frac{10}{\sqrt{2}}\ \text{cm}^2/\text{s}$

6. A particle is moving in a straight line. At time t, the distance between the particle from its starting point is given by $x = t - 6t^2 + t^3$. Its acceleration will be zero at

(a) $t = 1$ unit time (b) $t = 2$ units time

(c) $t = 3$ units time (d) $t = 4$ units time

7. The distance covered by a particle in t second is given by $x = 3 + 8t - 4t^2$. After 1s its velocity will be

(a) 0 unit (b) 3 units

(c) 4 units (d) 7 units

8. The equation of motion of particle moving along a straight line is $s = 2t^3 - 9t^2 + 12t$, where the units of s and t are centimeter and second. The acceleration of the particle will be zero after

(a) $\frac{3}{2}s$ (b) $\frac{2}{3}s$

(c) $\frac{1}{2}s$ (d) 1s

9. A stone is thrown vertically upwards and the height x ft reached by the stone in t seconds is given by $x = 80t - 16t^2$. The stone reaches the maximum height in

(a) 2s (b) 2.5s

(c) 3s (d) 1.5s

10. Gas is being pumped into spherical balloon at the rate of 30ft³/min. Then, the rate at which the radius increases when it reaches the value 15 ft is

(a) $\frac{1}{15\pi}$ ft/min (b) $\frac{1}{30\pi}$ ft/min

(c) $\frac{1}{20}$ ft/min (d) $\frac{1}{25}$ ft/min

11. A spherical balloon is expanding. If the radius is increasing at the rate of 2cm/min, the rate at which volume increase (in cubic centimeters per minute) when the radius is 5 cm is

(a) 10π (b) 100π

(c) 200π (d) 50π

12. A man of 2m height walks at a uniform speed of 6 km/h away from a lamp post of 6m height. The rate at which the length of his shadow increases is

(a) 2 km/h (b) 1km/h

(c) 3 km/h (d) 6 km/h

13. The radius of a cylinder is increasing at the rate of 3 m/s and its altitude is decreasing at the rate of 4 m/s. The rate of change of volume when radius is 4m and altitude is 6m is.

(a) 80π cu m/s (b) 144π cu m/s

(c) 80 cu m/s (d) 64 cu m/s

14. If the radius of circle be increasing at a uniform rate of 2 cm/s. The rate of increase of area of circle, at the instant when the radius is 20 cm, is

(a) 70π cm²/s (b) 70 cm²/s

(c) $80\ \pi$ cm²/s (d) 80 cm²/s

15. OB and OC are two roads enclosing an angle of 120°, X and Y start from 'O' at the same time. X travels along OB with a speed of 4 km/h and Y travels along OC

with a speed of 3km/hr.. The rate at which the shortest distance between X and Y is increasing after 1 h is

(a) $\sqrt{37}\, km/h$ (b) 37 km/h

(d) 13 km/h (d) $\sqrt{13} km/h$

16. A missile, fired from the ground level rises x metres vertically upwards in t seconds where $x = 100t - \frac{25}{2}t^2$. The maximum height reached is

(a) 200 m (b) 125 m
(c) 160 m (d) 190 m

17. A particle moves along a straight line according to the law $s = 16 - 2t + 3t^3$, where s metres is the distance of the particle from a fixed point at the end of t second. The acceleration of the particle at the end of 2 s is

(a) 36 m/s² (b) 34 m/s²
(c) 36m (d) None of these

18. The distance traveled by a motor car in t seconds after the brakes are applied is 's' feet, where $s = 22t - 12t^2$. The distance traveled by the car before it stops, is

(a) 10.08 ft (b) 10 ft
(c) 11 ft (d) 11.5 ft

19. The radius of a circle is increasing at the rate of 0.1 cm/s. When the radius of the circle is 5 cm, the rate of change of its area is

(a) $-\pi$ cm²/s (b) 10π cm²/s
(c) 0.1π cm²/s (d) π cm²/s

20. A spherical balloon is being inflated at the rate of 35 cc/min. The rate of increase of the surface area of the balloon when its diameter is 14 cm, is

(a) 7 sq cm/min (b) 10 sq cm/min
(c) 17.5 sq cm/min (d) 28 sq cm/min

21. A spherical iron ball 10 cm in radius is coated with a layer of ice of uniform thickness that melts at a rate of 50 cm^3/min. When the thickness of ice is 15 cm, then the rate at which the thickness of ice decreases, is

(a) $\frac{5}{6\pi}$ (b) $\frac{1}{54\pi} cm/min$

(c) $-\frac{1}{50\pi} cm/min$ (d) $\frac{1}{36\pi} cm/min$

22. A ladder 10 m long rests against a vertical wall with the lower end on the horizontal ground. The lower end of the ladder is pulled along the ground away from the wall at the rate of 3cm/s. The height of the upper end while it is descending at the rate of 4 cm/s, is

(a) $4\sqrt{3}\, m$ (b) $5\sqrt{3}\, m$
(c) $5\sqrt{2}\, m$ (d) 6 m

23. A particle moves along the curves $y = x^2 + 2x$. Then, the point on the curve such that x and y coordinates of the particle change with the same rate is

(a) (1,3) (b) $\left(\frac{1}{2}, \frac{5}{2}\right)$

(c) $\left(-\frac{1}{2}, -\frac{3}{4}\right)$ (d) (–1,–1)

24. A point is moving on $y = 4 - 2x^2$. The x-coordinate of the point is decreasing at the rate of 5 unit per second. Then the rate at which y coordinate of the point is changing when the point is at (1, 2) is

(a) 5 units (b) 10 units
(c) 15 units (d) 20 units

25. A point moves in a fixed straight path so that $s = \sqrt{t}$; then

(a) acceleration $\propto v^3$
(b) acceleration is negative
(c) velocity is inversely proportional to the distance
(d) None of these

26. A particle describes an ellipse whose semi-axes are 4 mt. and 3 mt. with a constant speed of 1 mt/sec. The velocity of the foot of the perpendicular from the particle on the major axis, when the particle is a distance of 1 meter from the major axis is equal to

(a) 2/11 m/x (b) 11/2 m/s
(c) $\sqrt{(2/11)}$ m/s (d) None of these

27. At a distance of 4000 feet from the launch site, a spectator is observing a rocket being launched. If the rocket lifts off vertically and is rising at a speed of 600 ft/sec when it is at an altitude of 3000 ft, the distance between the rocket and the spectator is changing at that instant at the rate

(a) 300 ft/sec (b) 360 ft/sec
(c) 420 ft/sec (d) 480 ft/sec

28. Let y be the number of people in a village at time t. Assume that the rate of change of the population is proportional to the number of people in the village at any time and further assume that the population never increases in time. Then the population of the village at any fixed time t is given by

(a) $y = e^{kt} + c$, for some constants $c \le 0$ and $k \ge 0$
(b) $y = ce^{kt}$, for some constants $c \ge 0$ and $k \le 0$
(c) $y = e^{ct} + k$ for some constants $c \le 0$ and $k \ge 0$
(d) $y = k\, e^{ct}$, for some constants $c \ge 0$ and $k \le 0$

29. A particle moves along a straight line with the law of motion given by $s^2 = at^2 + 2bt + c$.
Then the acceleration varies as

(a) $\frac{1}{s^3}$ (b) $\frac{1}{s}$

(c) $\frac{1}{s^4}$ (d) $\frac{1}{s^2}$

30. If the distances s covered by a particle in time t is proportional to the cube root of its velocity, then the acceleration is

(a) a constant (b) $\propto s^3$

(c) $\propto \frac{1}{s^3}$ (d) $\propto s^5$

31. A particle moves in a straight line so that $s = \sqrt{t}$, then its acceleration is proportional to

(a) $(\text{velocity})^3$ (b) velocity

(c) $(\text{velocity})^2$ (d) $(\text{velocity})^{3/2}$

32. If a particle moves such that the displacement is proportional to the square of the velocity acquired, then its acceleration is

(a) proportional to s^2

(b) proportional to $\frac{1}{s^2}$

(c) proportional to $\frac{1}{s}$

(d) a constant

33. The rate of change of the surface area of the sphere of radius r when the radius is increasing at the rate of 2cm/s is proportional to

(a) $\frac{1}{r^2}$ (b) $\frac{1}{r}$

(c) r^2 (d) r

34. If the volume of sphere is increasing at a constant rate, then the rate at which its radius is increasing, is

(a) a constant

(b) proportional to the radius

(c) inversely proportional to the radius.

(d) inversely proportional to the surface area.

35. A particle is moving in a straight line such that the distance described s and the time taken 't' are given by $t = as^2 + bs + c, a > 0$. If v is the velocity of the particle at any time t, then acceleration is

(a) $-2av$ (b) $-2av^2$

(c) $-2av^3$ (d) None of these

36. A particle is moving along the curve $x = at^2 + bt + c$. If $ac = b^2$ then the particle would be moving with uniform

(a) rotation (b) velocity

(c) acceleration (d) retardation

37. For a particle moving in a straight line, if time t be regarded as a function of velocity v, then the rate of change of the acceleration a is given by

(a) $a^2 \frac{d^2t}{dv^2}$ (b) $a^3 \frac{d^2t}{dv^2}$

(c) $-a^3 \frac{d^2t}{dv^2}$ (d) None of these

Answer Keys

1. (b)	**2.** (c)	**3.** (a)	**4.** (c)	**5.** (b)	**6.** (b)	**7.** (a)	**8.** (a)	**9.** (b)	**10.** (b)
11. (c)	**12.** (c)	**13.** (a)	**14.** (c)	**15.** (b)	**16.** (a)	**17.** (a)	**18.** (a)	**19.** (d)	**20.** (b)
21. (c)	**22.** (d)	**23.** (c)	**24.** (d)	**25.** (a,b,c)	**26.** (c)	**27.** (b)	**28.** (b)	**29.** (a)	**30.** (d)
31. (a)	**32.** (d)	**33.** (d)	**34.** (d)	**35.** (c)	**36.** (c,d)	**37.** (c)			

ERRORS AND APPROXIMATIONS

Let a function $y = f(x)$ be defined and if Δx be the error occurred while calculating x, then we may also get an error in calculation of y i.e, $f(x)$. The correct value of y should have been $y = (x + \Delta x)$. But the value that we have obtained because of the error in calculation of x will be $y = f(x)$. Therefore $f(x + \Delta x) - f(x)$ will be the error in calculation of y and is denoted Δy

Types of Errors

1. **Absolute errors:** It is deviation of measured value of physical quantity from its actual value i.e error = $\Delta y = f(x + \Delta x) - f(x)$

2. **Relative errors:** It is the ratio of error to the total quantity measured e.g. $\frac{\delta y}{y}$ where δy is absolute error and y is actual value.

3. Percentage errors: It is given by relative error × 100 i.e., $\frac{\delta y}{y}\times 100$

4. Maximum probable error: It is the error encountered in the final measured quantity assuming that all the errors occurring in the measurement of component quantities have same sign. i.e., cumulative in nature e.g. if $z = f(x) + f(y)$ then maximum probable error in $z = |\text{error in } f(x)| + |\text{error in } f(y)|$.

NOTE:

We must be careful to distinguish between derivatives and differentials. They are certainly not the same. When we write $\frac{dy}{dx}$, we are using a symbol for the derivative and when we write dy, we are denoting a differential.

ILLUSTRATION 36: If there is an error of k% in measuring the edge of a cube then the per cent error in estimating its volume is

(a) k (b) $3k$

(c) $k/3$ (d) None of these

SOLUTION: (b) $V = x^3$ and the percent error in measuring $x = \frac{dx}{x}\times 100$

The per cent error in measuring volume $= \frac{dV}{V}\times 100$

Now, $\frac{dV}{dx} = 3x^2$ $\Rightarrow dV = 3x^2\,dx$

$\therefore \frac{dV}{V} = \frac{3x^2 dx}{x^3} = 3\frac{dx}{x}$ $\therefore \frac{dV}{V}\times 100 = 3\frac{dx}{x}\times 100 = 3k\%$

ILLUSTRATION 37: A balloon is in the form of right circular cylinder of radius 1.5 m and length 4 m and is surrounded by hemispherical ends. If the radius is increased by 0.01 m and the length by 0.05 m, find the percentage change in the volume of the balloon.

SOLUTION: If r be the radius and h the height of the cylinder.

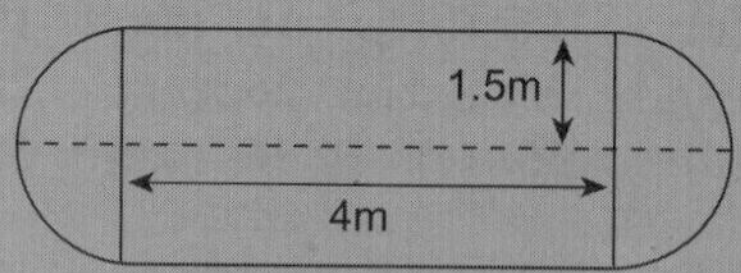

FIGURE 4.36

Volume $V = \pi r^2 h + \frac{2}{3}\pi r^3 + \frac{2}{3}\pi r^3 = \pi r^2 h + \frac{4}{3}\pi r^3$

$\delta V = (\pi r^2)\delta h + h(2\pi r\delta r) + \frac{4}{3}\pi(3r^2)\delta r$

$\therefore \frac{\delta V}{V} = \frac{\pi r(r\delta h + 2h\delta r + 4r\delta r)}{\pi r\left(rh + \frac{4}{3}r^2\right)} = \frac{r\delta h + 2h\delta r + 4r\delta r}{rh + \frac{4}{3}r^2}$

$$= \frac{1.5\times 0.05 + 2\times 4\times 0.01 + 4\times 1.5\times 0.01}{1.5\times 4 + \frac{4}{3}(1.5)^2} = \frac{0.215}{9}$$

$$\therefore \quad \frac{\delta V}{V}\times 100 = \frac{0.215}{9}\times 100 = \frac{21.5}{9} = 2.389\%$$

ILLUSTRATION 38: Find the possible percentage error in computing the parallel resistance R of three resistances R_1, R_2, R_3 from the formula $\frac{1}{R} = \frac{1}{R_1} + \frac{1}{R_2} + \frac{1}{R_3}$, if R_1, R_2, R_3 are each in error by plus 1.2%.

SOLUTION: Given $\frac{1}{R} = \frac{1}{R_1} + \frac{1}{R_2} + \frac{1}{R_3}$ ...(1)

Differentiating both sides, then $-\frac{1}{R^2}dR = -\frac{1}{R_1^2}dR_1 - \frac{1}{R_2^2}dR_2 - \frac{1}{R_3^2}dR_3$

$$\Rightarrow \quad \frac{1}{R}\left(\frac{dR}{R}\times 100\right) = \frac{1}{R_1}\left(\frac{dR_1}{R_1}\times 100\right) + \frac{1}{R_2}\left(\frac{dR_2}{R_2}\times 100\right) + \frac{1}{R_3}\left(\frac{dR_3}{R_3}\times 100\right)$$

$$= \frac{1}{R_1}(1.2) + \frac{1}{R_2}(1.2) + \frac{1}{R_3}(1.2) \qquad \left[\because \frac{dR_i}{R_i}\times 100 = 1.2 \forall i \in \{1,2,3\}\right]$$

$$= 1.2\left(\frac{1}{R_1} + \frac{1}{R_2} + \frac{1}{R_3}\right) = 1.2\left(\frac{1}{R}\right) \qquad \{\text{From (1)}\}$$

$$\therefore \quad \frac{dR}{R}\times 100 = 1.2\%$$

ILLUSTRATION 39: The time T of a complete oscillation of a simple pendulum of length ℓ is given by the equation $T = 2\pi\sqrt{\frac{1}{g}}$, where g is constant. What is the percentage error in T when l is increased by 1%?

SOLUTION: Let Δl be the change in ℓ and ΔT be the corresponding error in T. Then, $\frac{\Delta l}{l}\times 100 = 1$ (Given)

$$\Rightarrow \quad \frac{dl}{l}\times 100 = 1. \text{ Now, } T = 2\pi\sqrt{\frac{1}{g}}$$

$$\Rightarrow \quad \ln T = \ln 2\pi + (1/2)\ln \ell - (1/2)\ln g$$

$$\Rightarrow \quad \frac{1}{T}\frac{dT}{dl} = \frac{1}{2}.\frac{1}{l} \Rightarrow \frac{dT}{dl} = \frac{T}{2l}$$

$$\Rightarrow \quad \frac{dT}{T} = \frac{1}{2\ell}dl$$

$$\Rightarrow \quad \frac{dT}{T}\times 100 = \frac{1}{2}\left(\frac{dl}{l}\times 100\right)$$

$$\Rightarrow \quad \frac{dT}{T}\times 100 = \frac{1}{2} \qquad \left(\because \frac{d\ell}{\ell}\times 100 = 1\right)$$

$$\Rightarrow \quad \frac{\Delta T}{T}\times 100 = \frac{1}{2}$$

So, there is (1/2)% error in calculating the time period T.

APPROXIMATIONS

As the name suggest, the topic approximations is useful to find the approximate value of $y = f(x)$ when a small change in x' has occurred. For example If we need to find the approximate value of $y=\sqrt{0.0037}$ or $y=\sqrt{64.2}$ etc.

Algorithm

Step 1: Define a functional relationship between the independent variable x and dependent variable y by observing the given expression, For example, if we have to find the approximate value of the square root or cube root of a number, then we define $y = x^{1/2}$ or $x^{1/3}$ respectively. Similarly if we have to find the approximate value of logarithmic of a given number, then we consider $y = \log x$.

Step 2: Choose a value of x nearest to the value, at which we have to find y in such a way that either y is given for the chosen x or y can be easily computed for the chosen value of x. For example, if we have to find an approximate value of $(127)^{1/3}$ we take x as 125 because cube root of 125 can be easily calculated.

Step 3: Denote the value of x at which we have to find y by $x + \Delta x$

Step 4: Find Δx and assume that $dx = \Delta x$

Step 5: Find $\frac{dy}{dx}$ from the relation obtained in step I

Step 6: Find the value of $\frac{dy}{dx}$ by putting the value of x chosen in step II.

$$\because \quad f'(x) = \lim_{\delta x \to 0} \frac{f(x+\delta x)-f(x)}{\delta x}$$

Step 7: Find dy by using the relation $dy = \frac{dy}{dx}dx$

i.e., $\frac{dy}{dx} = \lim_{\delta x \to 0} \frac{\delta y}{\delta x}$

Setp 8: Assume that $\Delta y \cong dy$

Setp 9: Find the value of y by putting the value of x chosen in step II in the relation obtained in step I

Setp 10: The approximate value of y is $y + \Delta y$

i.e., if Δx is very small w.r.t then $\frac{dy}{dx} \approx \frac{\delta y}{\delta x} \Rightarrow \delta y = \frac{dy}{dx}\delta x$

$$\because \quad f(x+\delta x) - f(x) = \frac{dy}{dx}.\delta x$$

$$\Rightarrow \quad f(x+\delta x) = f(x) + \frac{dy}{dx}.\delta x$$

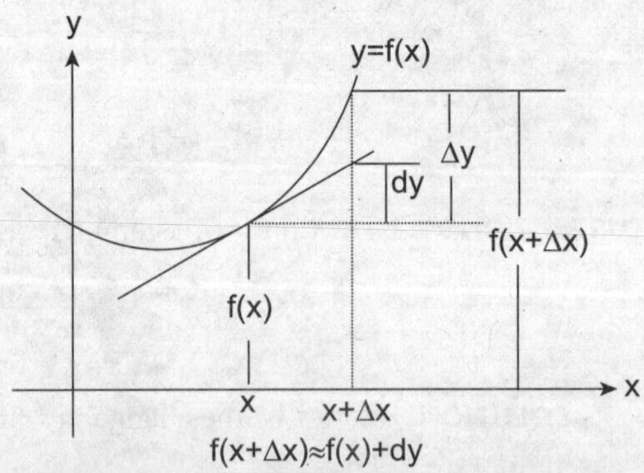

FIGURE 4.37

ILLUSTRATION 40: Find the approximate values of the following by using differentials $\sqrt{0.0037}$

SOLUTION: We write $\sqrt{0.0037} = \sqrt{0.00036+0.0001}$, because $\sqrt{0.0036} = 0.06$

Let $y = \sqrt{x}$ $\qquad \therefore \; y + \Delta y = \sqrt{x+\Delta x}$

Subtracting, we get $\Delta y = \sqrt{x+\Delta x} - \sqrt{x}$

$$\Rightarrow \left(\frac{dy}{dx}\right)\Delta x = \sqrt{x+\Delta x} - \sqrt{x}$$

$$\left(\because \; dy = \left(\frac{dy}{dx}\right)\Delta x \text{ is approx equal to } \Delta y\right) \quad \Rightarrow \quad \frac{1}{2\sqrt{x}}.\Delta x = \sqrt{x+\Delta x} - \sqrt{x}$$

Now, let $x = 0.0036$ and $\delta x = 0.0001$

$$\therefore \ (1) \Rightarrow \frac{0.0001}{2\sqrt{0.0036}} = \sqrt{0.0036+0.0001} - \sqrt{0.0036}$$

$$\Rightarrow \frac{0.001}{2(0.06)} = \sqrt{0.0037} - 0.06$$

$$\Rightarrow \sqrt{0.0037} = 0.06 + 0.00083 = 0.06083$$

ILLUSTRATION 41: Find the approximate value of square root of 25.2.

SOLUTION: Let $f(x) = \sqrt{x} \quad \Rightarrow f'(x) = \frac{1}{2\sqrt{x}}$

Now, $\because f(x+\Delta x) - f(x) = f'(x).\Delta x$ therefore $f(x+\Delta x) - f(x) = \frac{\Delta x}{2\sqrt{x}}$

So we may write as 25.2 = 25 + 0. 2

Taking $x = 25$ and $\Delta x = 0.2$ we have $f(25.2) - f(25) = \frac{0.2}{2\sqrt{25}}$

$$\Rightarrow f(25.2) - f(25) = \frac{0.2}{10} = 0.02 \qquad \Rightarrow f(25.2) = 5.02$$

$$\Rightarrow \sqrt{25.2} = 5.02$$

ILLUSTRATION 42: Find the approximate value of $(0.007)^{1/3}$.

SOLUTION: Let $f(x) = x^{1/3} \quad \Rightarrow f'(x) = \frac{1}{3}x^{-2/3}$

Now $f(x+\Delta x) - f(x) = f'(x).\Delta x = \frac{\Delta x}{3(x^{2/3})}$

We may write, 0.007 = 0.008 – 0.001, taking $x = 0.008$ and $dx = -0.001$,

we have $f(0.007) - f(0.008) = -\frac{0.001}{3(0.008)^{2/3}}$

$$\Rightarrow f(0.007) - (0.008)^{1/3} = -\frac{0.001}{3(0.2)^2}$$

$$\Rightarrow f(0.007) = 0.2 - \frac{0.001}{3(0.04)} = 0.2 - \frac{1}{120} = \frac{23}{120}$$

Hence $(0.007)^{1/3} = \frac{23}{120}$

ILLUSTRATION 43: Find the approximate value of $(1.999)^5$.

SOLUTION: Let $f(x) = x^6$

Now, $f(x + \Delta x) - f(x) = f'(x).\ \Delta x = 6x^5\ \Delta x$

We may write, 1.999 = 2 – 0.001

Taking $x = 2$ and $\Delta x = -0.001$, we have $f(1.999) - f(2) = 6(2)^5 \times -0.001$

$\Rightarrow f(1.999) = f(2) - 6 \times 32 \times 0.001$

$= 64 - 64 \times 0.003 = 64 \times 0.997 = 63.808$ (approx.)

ILLUSTRATION 44: If $y = x^4 - 10$ and if x changes from 2 to 1.99, what is the approximate change in y?

SOLUTION: We have $y = x^4 - 10$

Since, x changes from 2 to 1.99, we have $\Delta x = 1.99 - 2 = 0.01$.

Approximate changes in y i.e., $\Delta y = \left(\frac{dy}{dx}\right)\Delta x$

$= 4x^3\ \Delta x = 4(2)^3 - (-0.01) = -0.32.$

Remark: Actual change in $y = \Delta y = y(1.99) - y(2) = ((1.99)^4 - 10) - ((2)^4 - 10)$

$= 15.682392 - 16 = -0.317608$

ILLUSTRATION 45: Find the approximate value of $f(3.02)$, where $f(x) = 3x^2 + 5x + 3$

SOLUTION: Let $x = 3$ and $x + \Delta x = 3.02$. Then, $\Delta x = 0.02$.

we have, $f(x) = 3x^2 + 5x + 3$

$\Rightarrow f(x) = 3 \times 3^2 + 5 \times 3 + 3 = 45$

Now, $y = f(x)$

$\Rightarrow \Delta y = \frac{dy}{dx}\Delta x$

$\Rightarrow \Delta y = (6x+5)\Delta x = (6(3)+5).(0.02) = 0.46 \qquad \left[\because y = f(x) = 3x^2 + 5x + 3 \Rightarrow \frac{dy}{dx} = 6x + 5\right]$

$\therefore\ f(3.02) = f(x + \Delta x) = y + \Delta y = 45 + 0.46 = 45.46$

Hence, the approximate value of $f(3.02)$ is 45.46

ILLUSTRATION 46: Using differentials find the approximate value of tan 46^0, if it is being given that $1^0 = 0.01745$ radians.

SOLUTION: Let $y = f(x) = \tan x$, $x = 45^0 = (\pi/4)^c$ and $x + \Delta x = 46^0$. Then $\Delta x = 1^0 = 0.01745$ radians

For $x = \pi/4$, we have $y = f(\pi/4) = \tan \pi/4 = 1$

Let $dx = \Delta x = 0.01745$

Now, $y = \tan x \Rightarrow \frac{dy}{dx} = \sec^2 x \Rightarrow \left(\frac{dy}{dx}\right)_{x=\pi/4} = \sec^2 \pi/4 = 2$

$\therefore\ \Delta y = \frac{dy}{dx}\Delta x \Rightarrow dy = 2\ (0.01745) = 0.03490$

$\Rightarrow \Delta y = 0.03490\ [\because \Delta y \cong dy]$

Hence, $\tan 46^0 = y + \Delta y = 1 + 0.03490 = 1.03490$.

ILLUSTRATION 47: If $1° = \alpha$ radians, then the approximate value of cos 60° 2' is

(a) $\frac{1}{2} + \frac{\alpha\sqrt{3}}{60}$ (b) $\frac{1}{2} - \frac{\alpha}{60}$

(c) $\frac{1}{2} - \frac{\alpha\sqrt{3}}{60}$ (d) None of these

SOLUTION: (c) Let $y = \cos x \qquad \Rightarrow \frac{dy}{dx} = -\sin x$

Now, cos 60° 2' = cos 60° + Δy

$$\Delta y = \left(\frac{dy}{dx}\right)_{x=60^\circ} . \Delta x = -\frac{\sqrt{3}}{2}.\Delta x = -\frac{\sqrt{3}}{2}.1' = -\frac{\sqrt{3}}{2} \times \frac{2\alpha}{60}$$

$$\therefore \quad \cos 60^\circ\, 2' = \frac{1}{2} - \frac{\alpha\sqrt{3}}{60}$$

ILLUSTRATION 48: Find the approximate value of $\{(3.92)^2 + 3(2.1)^4\}^{1/6}$.

SOLUTION: Let $f(x, y) = (x^2 + 3y^4)^{1/6}$

Taking $x = 4$, $\Delta x = -0.08$ and $y = 2$, $\Delta y = 0.1$

Differentiating (1) w.r.t. x, treating y as constant,

$$\therefore \quad \frac{\Delta f}{\Delta x} = \frac{1}{6}(x^2 + 3y^4)^{-5/6}(2x)$$

$$= \frac{8}{6}(16+48)^{-5/6} = \frac{4}{3} \times 2^{-5} = \frac{1}{24}$$ and differentiating (1) w.r.t. y treating x as constant,

$$\therefore \quad \frac{\Delta f}{\Delta y} = \frac{1}{6}(x^2 + 3y^4)^{-5/6}(12y^3) = \frac{12(8)}{6}(64)^{-5/6} = 16(2)^{-5} = \frac{1}{2}$$

$$\therefore \quad \text{df} = \frac{\Delta f}{\Delta x}.dx + \frac{\Delta f}{\Delta y}dy = \frac{1}{24} \times -0.08 + \frac{1}{2} \times 0.1 = -\frac{0.01}{3} + \frac{0.1}{2} = 0.466$$

$$\therefore \quad \{(3.92)^2 + 3(2.1)^4\}^{1/6} = f(4, 2) + df = 2 + 0.466 = 2.466$$

ILLUSTRATION 49: The pressure p and the volume v of a gas are connected by the relation $pv^{1.4}$ = const. Find the percentage error in p corresponding to a decrease of 1.2% in v.

SOLUTION: We have, $pv^{1.4} = k$ (constant)

$$\Rightarrow \quad \log p + 1.4 \log v = \log k$$

$$\Rightarrow \quad \frac{1}{p}\frac{dp}{dv} + \frac{1.4}{v} = 0 \Rightarrow \frac{dp}{dv} = -\frac{1.4p}{v}$$

$$\text{Now, } \Delta p = \frac{dp}{dv}\Delta v$$

$$\Rightarrow \quad \Delta p = -\frac{1.4p}{v}\Delta v \Rightarrow \frac{\Delta p}{p} = -1.4\frac{\Delta v}{v}$$

$$\Rightarrow \quad \frac{\Delta p}{p} \times 100 = -1.4\left(\frac{\Delta v}{v} \times 100\right)$$

$$\Rightarrow \quad \frac{\Delta p}{p} \times 100 = -1.4(-1.2) = 0.7 \qquad \left[\because \frac{\Delta v}{v} \times 100 = 1.2, \text{given}\right]$$

TEXTUAL EXERCISE–2: (SUBJECTIVE)

1. The height of a cone increases by k%, its semi-vertical angle remaining the same. What is the approximate percentage increase
   (i) in total surface area, and
   (ii) in the volume, assuming that k is small?

2. Using differentials, find the approximate values of the following:
   (i) $\sqrt{26}$ (ii) $\sqrt{37}$
   (iii) $\sqrt{0.48}$ (iv) $(82)^{1/4}$

3. Find the approximate value of $f(2.01)$, where $f(x) = 4x^2 + 5x + 2$

4. Find the approximate value of $f(5.001)$, where $f(x) = x^3 - 7x^2 + 15$

5. If the radius of a sphere is measured as 9 m with an error of 0.03 m, find the approximate error in calculating its surface area.

6. Find the approximate change in the surface area of a cube of side x meters caused by decreasing the side by 1%.

7. If the radius of a sphere is measured as 7 m with an error of 0.02 m, find the approximate error in calculating its volume.

8. Find the approximate change in the value V of a cube of side x meters caused b increasing the side by 1%.

Answer Keys

1. $2k\%$, $3k\%$ **2.** (i) 5.1 (ii) 6.083 (iii) 0.693 (iv) 3.009
3. 28.21 **4.** –34.995 **5.** $2.16\pi m^2$ **6.** $0.12x^2 m^2$
7. $3.92\pi m^3$ **8.** $0.03x^2 m^3$

TEXTUAL EXERCISE–2: (OBJECTIVE)

1. There is an error of ± 0.04 cm in the measurement of the diameter of a sphere. When the radius is 10 cm, the percentage error in the volume of the sphere is
   (a) ±12 (b) ±10
   (c) ± 0.8 (d) ± 0.6

2. If there is 2 % error in measuring the radius of sphere, then what will be the percentage error in the surface area?
   (a) 3% (b) 1%
   (c) 4% (d) 2%

3. The circumference of a circle is measured as 56 cm with an error 0.02 cm. The percentage error in its area is
   (a) 1/7 (b) 1/28
   (c) 1/14 (d) 1/56

4. If there is an error of 2% in measuring the length of a simple pendulum, then percentage error in its period is
   (a) 1% (b) 2%
   (c) 3% (d) 4%

5. The height of a cylinder is equal to the radius. If an error of $k\%$ is made in the height, then percentage error in its volume is
   (a) $k\%$ (b) $2k\%$
   (c) $k/2\%$ (d) $3k\%$

6. If the ratio of base radius and height of a cone is 1 : 2 and percentage error in radius is $k\%$, then the error in its volume is
   (a) k% (b) 2 k %
   (c) 3 k % (d) None of these

7. The pressure P and volume V of a gas are connected by the relation $PV^{1/4}$ = constant. The percentage increase in the pressure corresponding to a reduction of (1/2)% in the volume is
   (a) $\frac{1}{2}\%$ (b) $\frac{1}{4}\%$
   (c) $\frac{1}{8}\%$ (d) None of these

8. If $y = x^n$, then the ratio of relative errors in y and x is
   (a) 1: 1 (b) 2 : 1
   (c) 1: n (d) n : 1

Answer Keys

1. (d) **2.** (c) **3.** (c) **4.** (a) **5.** (d) **6.** (c) **7.** (c) **8.** (d)

TANGENTS AND NORMALS

INTRODUCTION

Every function of two variables can be represented by a graph in two dimensional space but we are not always able to draw it. After all, for how many different values of the independent variable, can we efficiently find the values of the dependent variable? Yet we are always interested in visualizing what would the graph of the function look like i.e., we are always interested in finding out the behavior of the curve of the function.

Fortunately, many of the properties of the function give a good idea about the behavior of the curve of the function.

The qualitative study of the differential co-efficient or derivative of a function can be used to determine the approximate nature of the curve represented by the function and its various properties. e.g., monotonic nature, maxima/minima, curvature etc. In the previous chapter we have studied that the derivative of a function $y = f(x)$ is the instantaneous rate at which y changes with respect to x, it means that the derivative is the slope of the function's graph at some point (x, y) i.e., the slope of the tangent to the curve at the point (x, y). So the value of derivative at point x on the curve can be used in finding out the tangent to the curve at that point x.

In this section we will discuss in detail the application of derivatives to find out the tangent and normal at the particular points on the curve or to find out the angle at which two curves intersect, the length of tangent, normal, sub-tangent and sub-normal and intercept of the tangent on the axes.

DEFINITION

Tangent at a given point P on a curve is a line which touches the curve at that point and the normal at any point P is a line intersecting the curve at P which is perpendicular to the tangent at P.

Geometrical Interpretation

Given $y = f(x)$ be a continuous curve and $P(x, y)$ and $Q(x + \delta x, y + \delta y)$ be any two points on this curve. Let Q be a point very near to P. Let PT be the tangent to the curve at point P, which makes an angle θ with the positive direction of x-axis and PQ cut OX at M so the angle $\angle QMN = \phi$.

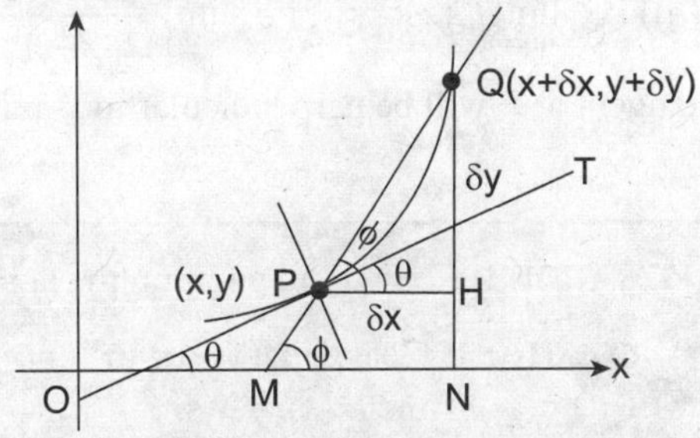

FIGURE 4.38

From Q, draw a perpendicular QN on x-axis and from P draw PH perpendicular to QN respectively. (See the adjacent diagram)

When Q approaches to the point P, the chord QP rotates in the clockwise and tends to becomes tangent at P. (i.e., PT).

Also, when $Q \to P$ then $QH = \delta y \to 0$ and $PH = \delta x \to 0$.

And therefore $\tan\phi = \dfrac{QH}{PH} = \dfrac{\delta y}{\delta x}$ tends to $\dfrac{0}{0}$ form.

Also $\phi \to \theta$ and therefore $\tan\theta = \lim\limits_{\delta x \to 0} \dfrac{\delta y}{\delta x}$ (popularly known as $\dfrac{dy}{dx}$).

Slope of tangent and equation of the tangent:

Case I: If $y = f(x)$ is differentiable for $x = a$ and $P(a, f(a))$ is a point on the curve then the tangent on $y = f(x)$ at point P will be a line with slope $f'(a)$ and hence the equation of the tangent will be given by $y - f(a) = f'(a)(x - a)$

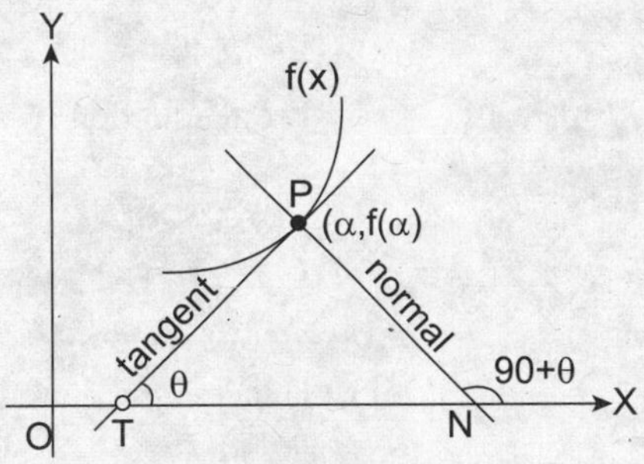

FIGURE 4.39

Case II: If the function $y = f(x)$ has a null derivative at $P(a, f(a))$ i.e., $f'(x) = 0$, then the tangent at P will be parallel to x-axis and its equation is given by $y = f(a)$. Such tangents are known as Horizontal Tangents.

Case III: If the function $y = f(x)$ has an infinite derivative at $P(a, f(a))$ i.e., $\lim_{x\to a}|f'(x)| = \infty$, i.e., $\lim_{x\to a}\left|\frac{f(x)-f(a)}{x-a}\right| = \infty$, then the tangent at P will be perpendicular to x-axis and its equation is given by $x = a$. Such tangents are known as Vertical Tangents.

For example the tangent to the curve $y = x^{1/3}$ at (0, 0) will be given by $x = 0$.

If however, neither (i), (ii) nor (iii) holds, then the graph of $f(x)$ does not have a tangent at the point $P(a, f(a))$

ILLUSTRATION 50: Find the point on the curve $y = x^3 - 3x$ at which tangent is parallel to x-axis.

SOLUTION: The equation of the curve is $y = x^3 - 3x$. Let the point at which tangent is parallel to x-axis be $P(x_1, y_1)$

Then it must lie on curve *i.e.*, $y_1 = x_1^3 - 3x_1$ ...(i)

Also differentiating the equation of the curve *w.r.t.* x,

We get $\frac{dy}{dx} = 3x^2 - 3$ $\Rightarrow \left(\frac{dy}{dx}\right)_{(x_1, y_1)} = 3x_1^2 - 3$

Since, the tangent is parallel to x-axis (given)

$\therefore \left(\frac{dy}{dx}\right)_{x_1, y_1} = 0$

$\Rightarrow 3x_1^2 - 3 = 0$ $\Rightarrow x_1 = \pm 1$ ...(ii)

From (i) and (ii):

When $x_1 = 1$: $y_1 = 1 - 3 = -2$

When $x_1 = -1$: $y_1 = -1 + 3 = 2$

So the points at which tangent is parallel to x-axis are (1, –2) and (–1, 2)

ILLUSTRATION 51: In the curve $3b^2y = x^3 - 3ax^2$, find the points at which the tangent is parallel to the axis of x.

SOLUTION: Equation of the curve is $3b^2 y = x^3 - 3ax^2$ ...(i)

Differentiating *w.r.t.* x, $3b^2 \frac{dy}{dx} = 3x^2 - 6ax$

$\therefore \frac{dy}{dx} = \frac{x^2 - 2ax}{b^2} = \frac{x(x-2a)}{b^2}$ = slope of tangent at (x, y)

If the tangent is parallel to the axis of x, $\frac{dy}{dx} = 0$

$\therefore x = 0, 2a$

From equation (i) $x = 0$ $\Rightarrow y = 0$

$x = 2a$ $\Rightarrow 3b^2 y = 8a^3 - 12^3 = -4a^3$

$\therefore y = \frac{4a^3}{3b^2}$

Hence the required points are (0, 0) and $\left(2a, -\frac{4a^3}{3b^2}\right)$

ILLUSTRATION 52: The curve $y = x^{1/5}$ has at origin (0, 0)

(a) a vertical tangent (b) a horizontal tangent

(c) oblique tangent (d) no tangent

SOLUTION: (a) $\frac{dy}{dx}=\frac{1}{5}x^{-4/5}=\frac{1}{5}.\frac{1}{x^{4/5}}$

$\therefore$ At (0, 0), $\frac{dy}{dx}=\infty$

$\therefore$ Curve has a vertical tangent at (0, 0)

ILLUSTRATION 53: The area of the triangle formed by the co-ordinate axes and a tangent to the curve $xy = a^2$ at the point (x_1, y_1) on it is

(a) $\frac{a^2 x_1}{y_1}$ (b) $\frac{a^2 y_1}{x_1}$

(c) $2a^2$ (d) $4a^2$

SOLUTION: (c) Since $y=\frac{a^2}{x}$

$\Rightarrow \frac{dy}{dx}=-\frac{a^2}{x^2}$

Tangent at (x_1, y_1) to curve $xy = a^2$ is $y - y_1 = -\frac{a^2}{x_1^2}(x - x_1)$

$\Rightarrow x_1^2 y - x_1^2 y_1 = -a^2 x + a^2 x_1$

$a^2x + x_1^2 y = x_1(x_1y_1 + a^2)$ $\quad(\because x_1y_1 = a^2)$

$= x_1(a^2 + a^2) = 2a^2x_1$

This meets x-axis, where $y = 0$ $\Rightarrow a^2x = 2a^2x_1$ $\Rightarrow x = 2x_1$

So, the point on x-axis is $(2x_1, 0)$

Again tangent meets y-axis, where $x = 0 \Rightarrow x_1^2y = 2a^2x_1$, $y=\frac{2a^2}{x_1}$

Point on y-axis is $\left(0, \frac{2a^2}{x_1}\right)$.

$\therefore$ Required area $=\frac{1}{2}(2x_1)\left(\frac{2a^2}{x_1}\right)=2a^2$

ILLUSTRATION 54: Find the co-ordinates of the point on the curve $y = x^2 + 3x + 4$, the tangent at which passes through the origin.

SOLUTION: Equation of the curve is $y = x^2 + 3x + 4$ ....(i)

Differentiating w.r.t. x, $\frac{dy}{dx}=2x+3$

$\therefore$ Equation of the tangent to (i) at (x, y) is

$Y-y=\frac{dy}{dx}(X-x)$ or $Y - y = (2x + 3)(X - x)$

Since it passes through the origin, putting $X = Y = 0$, we get

$-y = (2x + 3)(-x)$ or $y = 2x^2 + 3x$ ...(ii)

From (i) and (ii), $x^2 + 3x + 4 = 2x^2 + 3x$

or $x^2 = 4$ $\therefore x = \pm 2$

When $x = 2$, from (i) $\qquad y = 4 + 6 + 4 = 14$

When $x = -2$, from (ii) $\qquad y = 4 - 6 + 4 = 2$

$\therefore$ (2, 14) and (–2, 2) are the points on (i), the tangents at which pass through the origin.

ILLUSTRATION 55: A function $y = f(x)$ has a second order derivative $f''(x) = 6(x - 1)$. If the graph passes through the point (2, 1) and at this point tangent to the graph is $y = 3x - 1$, then function is:

(a) $(x - 1)^3$ (b) $(x - 1)^2$

(c) $(x + 1)^3$ (d) $(x + 1)^2$

SOLUTION: (a) $y = f(x)$ has a second order derivative of 1st degree and hence it must be a cubic

$\therefore$ Let $f(x) = ax^3 + bx^2 + cx + d$ ...(1)

$\Rightarrow f'(x) = 3ax^2 + 2bx + c = 3$ at (2,1) ...(2)

and $f''(x) = 6ax + 2b = 6(x - 1)$ ...(3)

Comparing the coefficient of x and constant terms in equation (3), we get $a = 1$ and $b = -3$

From (2) we have $3a(4) + 2b(2) + c = 3$ ...(4)

$\therefore$ $12(1) + 4(-3) + c = 3$ $\qquad \therefore$ $c = 3$

Again the point (2,1) lies on $y = f(x)$

$\therefore$ $1 = 8a + 4b + 2c + d$ or $1 = 8, 1 + 4(-3) + 2.3 + d$

$\therefore$ $d = -1$

$\therefore$ $f(x) = x^3 - 3x^2 + 3x - 1 = (x - 1)^3$

ILLUSTRATION 56: Find the tangent lines for the curve $y = \int_0^x 2|t|\,dt$ which are parallel to the bisector of the first coordinate angle.

SOLUTION: We have the given curve, $y = \int_0^x 2|t|\,dt$

Differentiating the curve w.r.t. x we get, $\frac{dy}{dx} = 2|x|$

[Using Leibniz-rule of differentiation under integration]

Since, the tangent lines are parallel to the bisector of the first coordinate angle

We have, $\frac{dy}{dx} = 1$

$\Rightarrow |x| = \frac{1}{2}$ $\qquad \Rightarrow x = \pm\frac{1}{2}$

$\Rightarrow y = 2\int_0^{1/2} t\,dt = 2\left(\frac{t^2}{2}\right)_0^{1/2} = \frac{1}{4}$

Thus the points are (± 1/2, 1/4)

$\Rightarrow$ Equation of tangents are $\frac{y-(1/4)}{x-(\pm 1/2)} = 1$

Therefore, $y = x + \frac{3}{4}$ and $y = x - \frac{1}{4}$ are required equations of the tangents.

ILLUSTRATION 57: Prove that the portion of the tangent to the curve $x^m y^n = a^{m+n}$ intercepted between the axes is divided in the ratio $m : n$ at the point of contact.

SOLUTION: Differentiating the equation to the curve, $mx^{m-1}y^n + nx^m y^{n-1}\frac{dy}{dx} = 0$

$$\Rightarrow \frac{dy}{dx} = -\frac{my}{nx}$$

$\Rightarrow$ Slope of tangent at $(x_1, y_1) = -\frac{my_1}{nx_1}$

Equation of tangent at P is, $y - y_1 = -\frac{my_1}{nx_1}(x - x_1)$

Let the tangent meet x-axis ($y = 0$) at point A

$\Rightarrow -y_1 = \frac{my}{nx}x + \frac{m}{n}y_1 \qquad \therefore\ x = \frac{(m+n)x_1}{m}$

Therefore, the coordinates of A will be $\left(\frac{m \quad n}{\quad},0\right)$ ...(i)

Similarly the tangent meets the y-axis ($x = 0$) at $B\left(0, \frac{m+n}{m}y_1\right)$ ...(ii)

The coordinates of the point which divides BA in the ratio $m : n$ are given by

$$\left(\frac{m\frac{(m+n)}{m}x_1 + 0}{m+n}, \frac{0 + n\frac{(m+n)}{m}y_1}{m+n}\right)$$

$= (x_1, y_1)$ which is the point of contact, P. Hence, the result.

ILLUSTRATION 58: Any tangent at a point $P(x, y)$ to the ellipse $\frac{x^2}{8} + \frac{y^2}{18} = 1$ meets the coordinate axes in the points A and B such that the area of the triangle OAB is least, then the point P is

(a) $(\sqrt{8}, 0)$
(b) $(0, \sqrt{18})$
(c) $(2, 3)$
(d) None of these

SOLUTION: (c) Any point on the ellipse is $(a \cos\theta, b \sin\theta)$ tangent at which is $\frac{x\cos\theta}{a} + \frac{y\sin\theta}{b} = 1$

Its intercepts on the axes are $\frac{a}{\cos\theta}$ and $\frac{b}{\sin\theta}$

$$\Delta = \text{area of } \Delta OAB = \frac{1}{2}OA.OB = \frac{1}{2}\frac{ab}{\cos\theta.\sin\theta} = \frac{ab}{\sin 2\theta}$$

It will be least when $\sin 2\theta$ is greatest so that $2\theta = \frac{\pi}{2}$ or $\theta = \frac{\pi}{4}$

$$\therefore\ P \text{ is} \left(\frac{a}{\sqrt{2}}, \frac{b}{\sqrt{2}}\right) = \left(\frac{\sqrt{8}}{\sqrt{2}}, \frac{\sqrt{18}}{\sqrt{2}}\right) = (2, 3)$$

ILLUSTRATION 59: Prove that $\frac{x}{a} + \frac{y}{b} = 1$ touches the curve $y = be^{-x/a}$ at the point where the curve crosses the axis of y.

SOLUTION: Equation of the curve is $y = be^{-x/a}$ ....(i)

It crosses y-axis, where $x = 0$ $\therefore\ y = be^0 = b$

We are, therefore, required to determine the tangent at the point $(0, b)$.

Differentiating equation (i) both side and with respect to x, $\frac{dy}{dx} = be^{-x/a}\left(-\frac{1}{a}\right) = -\frac{y}{a}$

$\Rightarrow$ Slope of tangent at $(0, b) = \left(\frac{dy}{dx}\right)_{(0,b)} = -\frac{b}{a}$

$\therefore$ Equation of tangent at $(0, b)$ is: $y - b = -\frac{b}{a}(x - 0)$

$\Rightarrow \frac{y}{b} - 1 = -\frac{x}{a}$ $\Rightarrow \frac{x}{a} + \frac{y}{b} = 1$

ILLUSTRATION 60: For the curve $xy = c^2$, prove that the portion of the tangent intercepted between the coordinate axes is bisected at the point of contact.

SOLUTION: Let the point at which the tangent is drawn be (α, β) on the curve $xy = c^2$,

Therefore $\alpha\beta = c^2$ ...(i)

Now, differentiating the given curve, $y =$ —, we get:

We get $\frac{dy}{dx} = -\frac{c^2}{x^2}$

$\Rightarrow \left(\frac{dy}{dx}\right)_{(\alpha,\beta)} = -\frac{c^2}{\alpha^2} = -\frac{\alpha\beta}{\alpha^2} = -\frac{\beta}{\alpha}$ (from (i) $\alpha\beta = c^2$)

Thus, the equation of tangent is, $y - \beta = -\frac{\beta}{\alpha}(x - \alpha)$

$\Rightarrow y\alpha - \alpha\beta = -x\beta + \alpha\beta$ $\Rightarrow x\beta + y\alpha = 2\alpha\beta$

$\Rightarrow \frac{x}{2\alpha} + \frac{y}{2\beta} = 1$

It is clear that the tangent line cuts x and y-axis at $A\ (2\alpha, 0)$ and $B\ (0, 2\beta)$ and the point (α, β) bisects AB.

ILLUSTRATION 61: The curve $y = ax^3 + bx^2 + cx + 5$ touches the x-axis at $P\ (-2, 0)$ and cuts the y-axis at a point Q where its gradient is 3. Then a, b, c are

(a) $-\frac{1}{2}, -\frac{3}{4}, 3$

(b) $3, -\frac{1}{2}, -\frac{3}{2}$

(c) $-\frac{3}{4}, -\frac{1}{2}, 3$

(d) None of these

SOLUTION: (a) The graph cuts y – axis ($x = 0$) at (0,5) and given that $\left.\frac{dy}{dx}\right|_{(0,5)} = 3$

$\Rightarrow 3ax^3 + 2bx + c|_{x=0} = 3$

$\therefore\ c = 3$

Again $\frac{dy}{dx} = 0$ at $P\ (-2,0)$ as it touches x-axis

$\therefore\quad 12a - 4b + c = 0$

or $12a - 4b + 3 = 0$ ...(2)

Also P lies on the curve

$\therefore\quad -8a + 4b - 2c + 5 = 0$ or $-8a + 4b - 1 = 0$ ...(3)

Solving (ii) and (iii), we get $a = -\frac{1}{2}, b - \frac{3}{4}$

GRAPHS WITH VERTICAL TANGENTS

We have already learnt that the tangents which are parallel to the y-axis are known as vertical tangents.

Now, for a tangent to be parallel to y-axis, it is important to understand the following four cases:

(i) $f'(x) = \lim_{\Delta x \to 0} \frac{\Delta y}{\Delta x} = \infty$

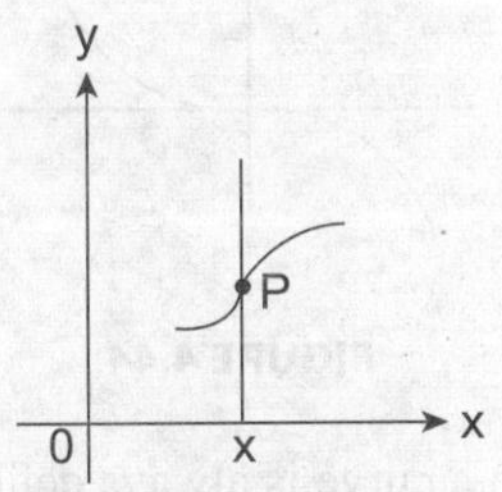

FIGURE 4.40

e.g. $y = (x-1)^{1/5}$ has a vertical tangent at $x = 1$ because $\frac{dy}{dx} \to \infty$ as $x \to 1$.

(ii) $f'(x) = \lim_{\Delta x \to 0} \frac{\Delta y}{\Delta x} = -\infty$

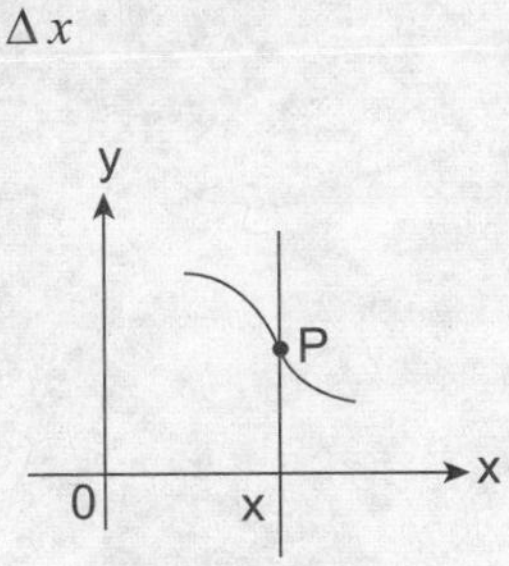

FIGURE 4.41

e.g., $y = -(x-1)^{1/5}$ has a vertical tangent at $x = 1$ because $\frac{dy}{dx} \to -\infty$ as $x \to 1$.

(iii) $f'(x^-) = \lim_{\Delta x \to 0^-} \frac{\Delta y}{\Delta x} = -\infty$; $f'(x^+) = \lim_{\Delta x \to 0^+} \frac{\Delta y}{\Delta x} = \infty$

The left tangent is parallel to the y-axis is directed downward, while the right tangent is parallel to the y-axis and is directed upward

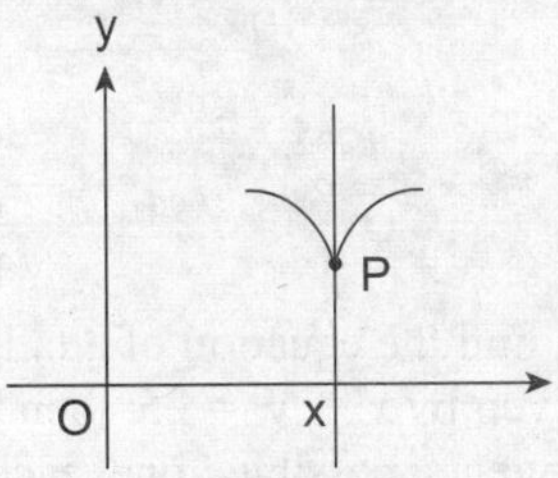

FIGURE 4.42

e.g. $y = (x-1)^{2/5}$ has a vertical tangent at $x = 1$ because $\frac{dy}{dx} \to -\infty$ as $x \to 1^-$ and $\frac{dy}{dx} \to \infty$ as $x \to 1^+$.

(iv) $f'(x^-) = \lim_{\Delta x \to 0^-} \frac{\Delta y}{\Delta x} = \infty$; $f'(x^+) = \lim_{\Delta x \to 0^+} \frac{\Delta y}{\Delta x} = -\infty$

Here, the left tangent is parallel to y-axis and is directed upward, while the right tangent is parallel to the y-axis and is directed downward

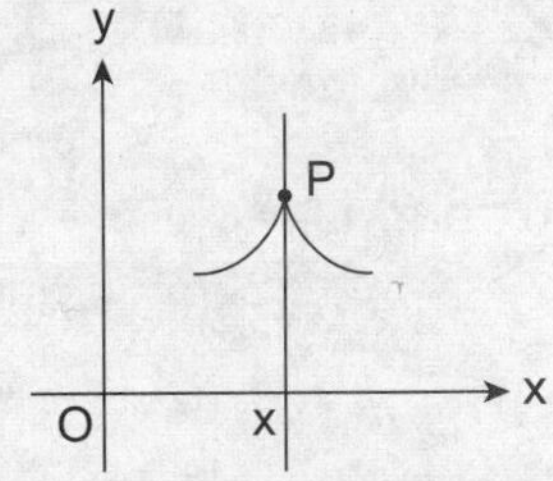

FIGURE 4.43

e.g., $y = -(x-1)^{2/5}$ has a vertical tangent at $x = 1$ because $\frac{dy}{dx} \to \infty$ as $x \to 1^-$ and $\frac{dy}{dx} \to -\infty$ as $x \to 1^+$.

NOTE:

(a) *The basic property of a tangent line is that it indicates the direction of a curve at a point.*

(b) *If tangent is parallel to x-axis,* $\theta = 0° \Rightarrow \tan\theta = \left(\frac{dy}{dx}\right)_{(x_1,y_1)} = 0$

(c) *If tangent is perpendicular to x-axis (or parallel to y-axis) then* $\theta = 90°$

$\Rightarrow \tan\theta = \infty \Rightarrow \cot\theta = \left(\frac{dx}{dy}\right)_{(x_1,y_1)} = 0$ *or* $\left(\frac{dy}{dx}\right)_{(x_1,y_1)} = \infty$

(d) *The value of* θ *always lie between* $-\pi/2$ *to* $\pi/2$

(e) *If the tangent at any point on the curve is equally inclined to both the axes, then* $\frac{dy}{dx} = \pm 1$

(f) *If* $\left(\frac{dy}{dx}\right)_{(x_1,y_1)}$ *fails to exist, even then the tangent can be drawn at* (x_1, y_1)*. e.g.* $\left.\begin{matrix} y = x^{3/5} \\ y = \sqrt{|x|} \end{matrix}\right\}$ *at* $x = 0$

CAUTION

1. If we are to find the equation of a tangent at $x = 3$ on the curve given by $x^2 + y^2 = 25$; then there is not one, but two tangents possible, one each at (3, 4) and (3, –4). And hence, we would need to consider two functions $y = \pm\sqrt{25 - x^2}$, thereby making the curve into two different functions on which the tangents can be found with ease.
2. It is a common mistake to think that the tangent never crosses the curve.

   For example the tangent at origin on the curve $y = x^3$ is $x = 0$

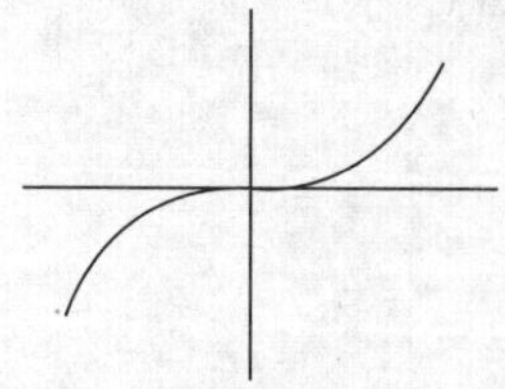

FIGURE 4.44

3. A tangent on a curve is always defined on a point and is irrespective of the fact, whether or not; the tangent touches/cuts the curve at any other point(s).

   For example the line $y = 1$ is a tangent to the curve $y = \cos x$ at $x = 0$, even though it touches the graph at infinite other points.

ILLUSTRATION 62: The curve $y - e^{xy} + x = 0$ has a vertical tangent at the point

(a) (1, 1) (b) at no point

(c) (0, 1) (d) (1, 0)

SOLUTION: (d) Given $y + x = = e^{xy}$ ...(i)

Differentiating both sides w.r.t. x, we get

$y' + 1 = e^{xy}(y + xy')$

$y'(1 - e^{xy}x) = ye^{xy} - 1$

Now $y' = \infty$

$\Rightarrow 1 - xe^{xy} = 0$

$\Rightarrow$ Clearly (1, 0) point satisfies the above equation and hence, the curve $y - e^{xy} + x = 0$ has a vertical tangent at (1, 0)

ILLUSTRATION 63: The triangle formed by the tangent to the curve $f(x) = x^2 + bx - b$ at the point (1, 1) and the co-ordinate axes, lies in the first quadrant. If its area is 2, then the value of b is

(a) –1 (b) 3

(c) –3 (d) 1

SOLUTION: (c) $\frac{dy}{dx} = 2x + b = 2 \; at(1,1)$

Equation of tangent on $f(x)$ at (1, 1) is $y - 1 = (2 + b)(x - 1)$

The x-intercept can be obtained by substituting $y = 0$

Hence $A \equiv \left(\frac{b+1}{b+2}, 0\right)$ $\Rightarrow \; = -\frac{1}{2+b} = \frac{1}{b+2}$

Similarly, the y-intercept can be obtained by substituting $x = 0$

Hence $B \equiv (0, -(b + 1))$ $\Rightarrow y = 1 - (2 + b) = -(b + 1)$

Given that $\Delta = \frac{1}{2} AB = 2$ $\therefore \; AB = 4$

$\Rightarrow -(b + 1)(b + 1) = 4(b + 2)$

or $b^2 + 6b + 9 = 0$ or $(b + 3)^2 = 0$ $\therefore \; b = -3$

ILLUSTRATION 64: The number of points on the curve $x^{3/2} + y^{3/2} = a^{3/2}$ where the tangents are equally inclined to the axes is

(a) 1 (b) 2

(c) 4 (d) None of these

SOLUTION: (a) Given $x^{3/2} + y^{3/2} = a^{3/2}$

Differentiating both sides *w.r.t.* x, we get $\frac{3}{2}x^{1/2} + \frac{3}{2}y^{1/2}y' = 0$

$\Rightarrow \; y' = -\frac{x^{1/2}}{y^{1/2}}$

Now since we require the tangents which are equally inclined to the axes, therefore on equally $y = \pm 1$ we get $y^{1/2} = x^{1/2}$ or $y^{1/2} = -x^{1/2}$

Also $x^{3/2 +} y^{3/2} = a^{3/2}$

$\Rightarrow 2x^{3/2} = a^{3/2}$ or $0 = a^{3/2}$ (not possible) $\Rightarrow x = \frac{a}{2^{2/3}} = y$, hence only one point

ILLUSTRATION 65: The point(s) on the curve $y^3 + 3x^2 = 12y$ where the tangent is vertical, is (are)

(a) $\left(\pm\frac{4}{\sqrt{3}}, -2\right)$ (b) $\left(\pm\sqrt{\frac{11}{3}}, 1\right)$

(c) (0, 0) (d) $\left(\pm\frac{4}{\sqrt{3}}, 2\right)$

SOLUTION: (d) $f(x, y) = y^3 + 3x^2 - 12y = 0$

Slope of tangent is $\frac{dy}{dx} = \frac{f_y}{f_x} = -\frac{6x}{3y^2 - 12}$

If the tangent is vertical $\Rightarrow \frac{dy}{dx} = \infty$

$\Rightarrow y^2 = 4$ $\therefore \; y = \pm 2$

Now $y = -2$ is ruled out as it makes x^2 negative. Hence $y = 2 \;\therefore\; x = \pm\frac{4}{\sqrt{3}}$

ILLUSTRATION 66: Find the equation of a tangent and normal at $x = 0$ if they exist on the curve $y = x^{1/3}(1 - \cos x)$

SOLUTION: $y' = x^{1/3}(\sin x) + (1 + \cos x)\dfrac{1}{3}x^{-2/3}$

which does not exist at $x = 0$ but, Since function is cont. and differentiable at $x = 0$

$$f'(0) = \lim_{h\to 0}\frac{f(0+h)-f(0)}{h} = \lim_{h\to 0}\frac{h^{1/3}(1-\cos h)}{h} = \lim_{h\to 0}\frac{\sin(h/2)}{h/2}.h^{1/3}.\sin\left(\frac{h}{2}\right) = 0$$

$$\Rightarrow \begin{cases}\text{equation of tangent, if } y=0\\ \text{equation of normal, if } x=0\end{cases}$$

ILLUSTRATION 67: The point(s) on the curve $y^3 + 3x^2 = 12y$ where the tangent is vertical, is (are)

(a) $\left(\pm\dfrac{4}{\sqrt{3}}, -2\right)$ (b) $\left(\pm\sqrt{\dfrac{11}{3}}, 1\right)$

(c) $(0, 0)$ (d) $\left(\pm\dfrac{4}{\sqrt{3}}, 2\right)$

SOLUTION: (a) Given, $y^3 + 3x^2 = 12y$

$$\Rightarrow 3y^2\frac{dy}{dx} + 6x = 12\frac{dy}{dx} \quad \text{...(i)}$$

$$\Rightarrow \frac{dy}{dx} = \frac{6x}{12-3y^2} \qquad \Rightarrow \frac{dx}{dy} = \frac{12-3y^2}{6x}$$

For vertical tangent, $\dfrac{dx}{dy} = 0$ $\Rightarrow 12 - 3y^2 = 0 \Rightarrow y = \pm 2$

On putting $y = 2$ in equation (i), we get $x = \pm\dfrac{4}{\sqrt{3}}$ and again putting $y = -2$ in equation (i),

We get $3x^2 = -16$, no real solution.

$\therefore$ The required point is $\left(\pm\dfrac{4}{\sqrt{3}}, 2\right)$.

SLOPE OF NORMAL

We know normal to the curve at $P(a, f(a))$ is a line perpendicular to tangent at $P(a, f(a))$ and passing through P, therefore the slope of the normal will be negative reciprocal of the slope of the tangent at that point.

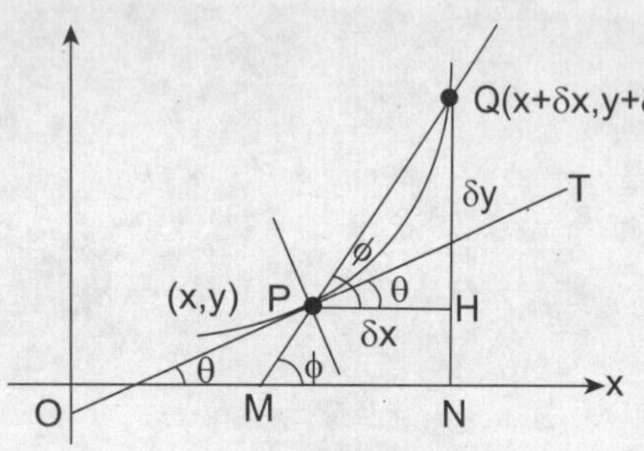

FIGURE 4.45

$\Rightarrow$ Slope of normal at $P(a, f(a)) = -\dfrac{1}{\left(\dfrac{dy}{dx}\right)_{(a,f(a))}}$

$= -\left(\dfrac{dx}{dy}\right)_{(a,f(a))}$ and hence equation of normal is given by

$$y - f(a) = \frac{-1}{f(a)}(x-a)$$ and if slope of tangent $= \infty$, thereby slope of the normal $= 0$

Therefore equation is $y = f(a)$ and if slope of tangent $= 0$, then slope of normal $= \infty$.

Therefore the equation is given by $x = a$.

ILLUSTRATION 68: Find the equation of tangent and normal to the curve $x^2 = 8y + 8$ at the point (0, –1).

SOLUTION: Equation of the curve is $x^2 = 8y + 8$

$\Rightarrow\ y = \dfrac{x^2 - 8}{8}$

Slope of the tangent to the curve at (0, –1) is $\left(\dfrac{dy}{dx}\right)$ at that point

$\because\ \dfrac{dy}{dx} = \dfrac{2x}{8} = \dfrac{x}{4}$ at (0, –1) $\Rightarrow \left(\dfrac{dy}{dx}\right)_{(0,-1)} = 0$

$\therefore$ Equation of tangent at (0, –1) is given by $y - (-1) = 0\ (x - 0)$

$\Rightarrow\ y + 1 = 0(x - 0)$

$\Rightarrow\ y + 1 = 0$

Normal is perpendicular to tangent, so slope of normal $= \dfrac{-1}{dy/dx} = \infty$

(Since $\dfrac{dy}{dx} = 0$) hence the normal will be a line parallel to y-axis and will pass through (0, – 1), therefore the equation of normal at (0, –1) is given by $x = 0$

ILLUSTRATION 69: Find the equation of the normal at (a, a) to the curve $x^2y^3 = a^5$

SOLUTION: Equation of the curve is $x^2y^3 = a^5$. Differentiating both sides w.r.t. x

$2xy^3 + 3x^2y^2\dfrac{dy}{dx} = 0 \qquad \Rightarrow \dfrac{dy}{dx} = -\dfrac{2y}{3x}$

So the value of $\dfrac{dy}{dx}$ at $(a, a) = -\dfrac{2a}{3a} = -\dfrac{2}{3}$

$\therefore$ Slope of tangent at $(a, a) = -\dfrac{2}{3}$

Slope of normal at $(a, a) = \dfrac{3}{2}$

Equation of normal at (a, a) is $y - a = \dfrac{3}{2}(x - a)$ or $3x - 2y - a = 0$

ILLUSTRATION 70: If the slope of the normal to the curve $x^3 = 8a^2 y$, $a > 0$ at a point in the first quadrant is –2/3, then the point is

(a) $(2a, -a)$ (b) $(2a, a)$

(c) $(a, 2a)$ (d) $(-a, a)$

SOLUTION: (b) Let $x^3 = 8a^2y \quad \Rightarrow\ y = \dfrac{x^3}{8a^2}$

$\Rightarrow\ \dfrac{dy}{dx} = \dfrac{3x^2}{8a^2}$

$\therefore$ Slope of normal $= \dfrac{8a^2}{-3x^2} = -\dfrac{2}{3}$ (given)

$\Rightarrow\ 4a^2 = x^2$

$\Rightarrow\ x = 2a$ ($a > 0$, $x > 0$ in Ist quadrant)

$\therefore\ y = \dfrac{x^3}{8a^2} = \dfrac{(2a)^3}{8a^2} = \dfrac{8a^3}{8a^2} = a$ $\therefore$ required point is $(2a, a)$

ILLUSTRATION 71: The area bounded by the axes of reference and the normal to $y = \log_e x$ at the point (1, 0) is

(a) 1 unit^2 (b) 2 unit^2

(c) $\frac{1}{2}$ unit^2 (d) None of these

SOLUTION: (c) $y = \log_e x \Rightarrow \frac{dy}{dx} = \frac{1}{x} \quad \therefore \left(\frac{dy}{dx}\right)_{(1,0)} = 1$

$\therefore$ The equation of the normal at (1, 0) is $y - 0 = \frac{-1}{1}(x - 1)$ or $x + y = 1$

$\therefore$ Area $= \frac{1}{2}.1.1 = \frac{1}{2}$ sq. unit

ILLUSTRATION 72: Find the point on the curve $ay^2 = x^3$ where normal to the curve makes equal intercepts with the axes.

SOLUTION: Let the point at which normal be drawn is (x_1, y_1). Then it must satisfy $ay^2 = x^3$,

i.e., $ay_1^2 = x_1^3$ or $y_1 = \pm\sqrt{\frac{x_1^3}{a}}$

Now, differentiating both sides of the given curve with respect to x we get, $2ay\frac{dy}{dx} = 3x^2$

$$\Rightarrow \left(\frac{dy}{dx}\right)_{(x_1,y_1)} = \frac{3x_1^2}{2ay_1} = \frac{3x_1^2}{2a\sqrt{\frac{x_1^3}{a}}} = \frac{3}{2}\sqrt{\frac{x_1}{a}} \quad ...(i)$$

Thus, slope of normal $= -\left(\frac{dx}{dy}\right)_{(x_1,y_1)} = -\frac{2}{3}\sqrt{\frac{a}{x_1}}$

We know that the slope of the line making equal intercept with the axes $= \pm 1$

$\Rightarrow -\frac{2}{3}\sqrt{\frac{a}{x_1}} = \pm 1 \quad \Rightarrow x_1 = \frac{4a}{9}$

Hence, the required points are $\left(\frac{4a}{9}, \frac{8a}{27}\right)$ and $\left(\frac{4a}{9}, \frac{-8a}{27}\right)$

ILLUSTRATION 73: Find the equation of normal to the curve $x + y = x^y$, where it cuts x-axis.

SOLUTION: Given curve is $x + y = x^y$ ...(i)

at x-axis $y = 0$,

$\therefore x + 0 = x^0 \quad \Rightarrow x = 1$

$\therefore$ Point is A(1, 0)

Now to get slope at (1, 0) of the curve $x + y = x^y$. Take log on both sides we get, $\log(x + y) = y \log x$. Now differentiating with respect of x.

$$\therefore \frac{1}{x+y}\left\{1 + \frac{dy}{dx}\right\} = y\frac{1}{x} + (\log x)\frac{dy}{dx}$$

Putting $x = 1, y = 0$

$\left\{1 + \frac{dy}{dx}\right\} = 0 \quad \Rightarrow \frac{dy}{dx} = -1 \quad \Rightarrow -\left\{\frac{dy}{dx}\right\} = 1$

$\therefore$ Slope of normal = 1

Equation of normal is, $\frac{y - 0}{x - 1} = 1$

$\Rightarrow y = x - 1$

ILLUSTRATION 74: If the line $ax + by + c = 0$ is a normal to the rectangular hyperbola $xy = 1$ then

(a) $a > 0, b > 0$ (b) $a > 0, b < 0$

(c) $a < 0, b > 0$ (d) $a < 0, b < 0$

SOLUTION: (b) and (c) $xy = 1$

$\Rightarrow y = 1/x$ $\Rightarrow \frac{dy}{dx} = -\frac{1}{x^2} < 0$

$\Rightarrow$ Slope of tangent < 0

$\Rightarrow$ Slope of normal > 0 $\Rightarrow \frac{-b}{a} > 0$

$\Rightarrow \frac{b}{a} < 0$

$\Rightarrow$ a and b have opposite sign

Aliter: Differentiating w.r.t. x, $y + x\frac{dy}{dx} = 0$ $\therefore \frac{dy}{dx} = -\frac{y}{x}$

$\therefore$ the equation of the normal at (α,β) is

$y - \beta = \alpha/\beta\,(x - \alpha)$

or $\alpha x - \beta y = \alpha^2 - \beta^2$

The given line is a normal at (α, β) if $\frac{\alpha}{a} = \frac{-\beta}{b} = \frac{\alpha^2 - \beta^2}{-c}$

$\Rightarrow \frac{\alpha}{a} = \frac{\beta}{-b} = \frac{\sqrt{\alpha\beta}}{\sqrt{-ab}} = \frac{1}{\sqrt{-ab}}$ $(\because \alpha\beta = 1)$

$\therefore$ α, β are real if $ab < 0$, i.e., $a > 0, b < 0$ or $a < 0, b > 0$

NOTE:

1. *If normal is parallel to x-axis, then* $-\left(\frac{dx}{dy}\right)_{(a,f(a))} = 0$ *or* $\left(\frac{dx}{dy}\right)_{(a,f(a))} = 0$
2. *If normal is perpendicular to x-axis (or parallel to y-axis), then* $\left(\frac{dy}{dx}\right)_{(a,f(a))} = 0$
3. *If a tangent is parallel to the axis of x then q = 0.* $\therefore \frac{dy}{dx} = \tan\theta = \tan 0 = 0$

   Thus at the point the tangent is parallel to the axis of x we have $\frac{dy}{dx} = 0$
4. *If the tangent is perpendicular to the axis of x, (i.e. parallel to the axis of y) then* $\theta = \pi/2$

   $\therefore \frac{dy}{dx} = \tan\theta = \tan\frac{\pi}{2} = \infty \Rightarrow \frac{dy}{dx} = 0$

   Thus at the point the tangent is perpendicular to the axis of y, we have $\frac{dy}{dx} = 0$
5. *For finding the intercepts on the axes by a tangent, write equation of tangent in intercept form i.e.,* $\frac{x}{a} + \frac{y}{b} = 1$

   $\therefore$ *Intercept on x-axis = a and intercept on y-axis = b.*

ILLUSTRATION 75: Three normal drawn from the point $(c, 0)$ to the curve $y^2 = x$, show that 'c' must be greater than 1/2. One normal is always the x-axis. Find 'c' for which the other two normal are perpendicular to each other.

SOLUTION: The slope form of the normal to the curve $y^2 = 4ax$ is

$y = mx - 2am - am^3$ ....(i)

For the curve given by $y^2 = x$, we have $4a = 1$

$\Rightarrow a = 1/4$

$\therefore$ Equation of normal is $y = mx - \frac{m}{2} - \frac{m^3}{4}$

The equation passes through $(c, 0)$ then

$\therefore \quad 0 = mc - \frac{1}{2}m - \frac{1}{4}m^3$ i.e. $m\left(c - \frac{1}{2} - \frac{m^2}{4}\right) = 0 \quad \therefore \; m = 0, \; \frac{m^2}{4} + \frac{1}{2} - c = 0$

For m = 0, the normal is $y = 0$ which is the x-axis.

The other two values of m are given by $m = \pm 2\sqrt{c - 1/2}$

$\therefore$ for m to be real, $c \neq 1/2$

If $c = 1/2$, then m = 0 which is already considered, so $c > 1/2$

Now, for the other two normal to be perpendicular to each other, we must have

$$\left(2.\sqrt{c - \frac{1}{2}}\right)\left(-2.\sqrt{c - \frac{1}{2}}\right) = -1$$

$\therefore \quad c - 1/2 = 1/4 \qquad \Rightarrow c = 3/4$

ILLUSTRATION 76: The point on the curve where the normal to the curve $9y^2 = x^3$ makes equal intercepts with the axes is

(a) $\left(4, \frac{8}{3}\right)$ (b) $\left(-4, \frac{8}{3}\right)$

(c) $\left(4, -\frac{8}{3}\right)$ (d) None of these

SOLUTION: (a), (c) Given $9y^2 = x^3$

Differentiating both sides, we get $18y\frac{dy}{dx} = 3x^2$.

Since normal makes equal intercepts on the axes therefore $-\frac{1}{dy/dx} = \pm 1$ or $\frac{dy}{dx} = \pm 1$

$\therefore \quad 6y(\pm 1) = x^2$ or $36y^2 = x^4$ or $4x^3 - x^4 = 0$ $(\because 9y^2 = x^3)$

$\therefore \quad x = 4$ and $y = \pm\frac{8}{3}$ ($x = 0$ is excluded as $\frac{dy}{dx}$ becomes zero)

ILLUSTRATION 77: The values of parameter 'a' so that the line $(3 - a)x + ay + a^2 - 1 = 0$ is a normal to the curve $xy = 1$ is/are:

(a) $(3, \infty)$ (b) $(-\infty, 0)$

(c) $(0, 3)$ (d) None of these

SOLUTION: (a, b) $y = \frac{1}{x} \qquad \Rightarrow \frac{dy}{dx} = -\frac{1}{x^2}$

Hence slope of the normal is x^2 which is positive $\forall\, x \in \mathbb{R}$. If $(3 - a)x + ay + a^2 - 1 = 0$ is the normal then slope of normal is given to be $-\frac{3-a}{a} = \frac{a-3}{a}$ and equating $\frac{a-3}{a} = x^2$.

Now, $x^2 \neq 0$

$\Rightarrow \frac{a-3}{a} > 0$ $\Rightarrow a \in (-\infty, 0)$ or $a \in (3, \infty)$

$\Rightarrow a \in (-\infty, 0) \cup (3, \infty)$

CONDITION FOR A GIVEN LINE TO BE TANGENT TO A CURVE

Let us suppose that the line $ax + by + c = 0$ be a tangent to the curve $y = f(x)$ at point $P(x_1, y_1)$.

Then P lies on the curve

$\Rightarrow y_1 = f(x_1)$ ...(i)

And since P also lies on the line

$\Rightarrow ax_1 + by_1 + c = 0$ ...(ii)

Also, slope of the line = slope of tangent to the curve at P

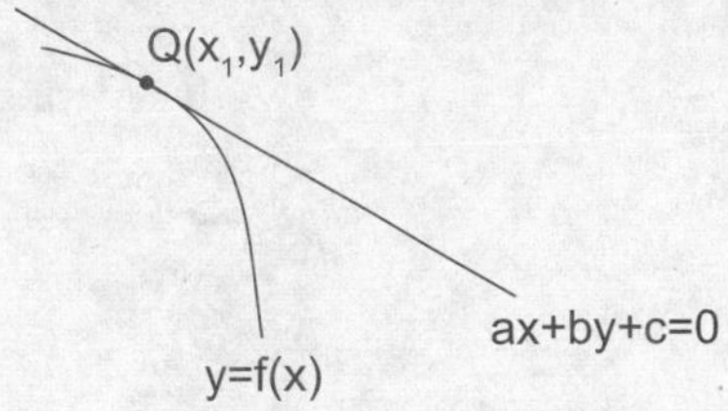

FIGURE 4.46

$\Rightarrow -\frac{a}{b} = \left(\frac{dy}{dx}\right)_{(x_1,y_1)}$ ...(iii)

On eliminating x_1 and y_1 from the equations (i), (ii) and (iii); we can get the required condition for the line $ax + by + c = 0$ to be a tangent to the curve $y = f(x)$.

ILLUSTRATION 78: If the line joining the points (0, 3) and (5, –2) is a tangent to the curve $y = \frac{c}{x+1}$ then the value of c is

(a) 1 (b) –2

(c) 4 (d) None of these

SOLUTION: (c) The equation of the line is $y-3=\frac{3+2}{0-5}(x-0)$, i.e., $x+y-3=0$.

$\Rightarrow y=\frac{c}{x+1}$ $\Rightarrow \frac{dy}{dx}=\frac{-c}{(x+1)^2}$

Let the line touche the curve at (α, β)

$\therefore \alpha + \beta - 3 = 0$ $\Rightarrow \beta = 3 - \alpha$

$\Rightarrow \left.\frac{dy}{dx}\right]_{\alpha,\beta} = \frac{-c}{(\alpha+1)^2} = -1 \ \& \ \beta = \frac{c}{\alpha+1}$

$\therefore \frac{-c}{(c/\beta)^2} = -1$ or $\beta^2 = c$ or $(3-\alpha)^2 = c = (\alpha+1)^2$

$\therefore 3 - \alpha = \pm(\alpha + 1)$ or $3 - \alpha = \alpha + 1$

$\therefore \alpha = 1$. So, $c = (1 + 1)^2 = 4$

ILLUSTRATION 79: The tangent to $y = ax^2 + bx + \frac{7}{2}$ at (1, 2) is parallel to the normal at the point (–2, 2) on the curve $y = x^2 + 6x + 10$. Find the value of a and b.

SOLUTION: $y = ax^2 + bx + \frac{7}{2} \Rightarrow \frac{dy}{dx} = 2ax + b$

$2 = a + b + \frac{7}{2}$ $\qquad \left.\frac{dy}{dx}\right|_{(1,2)} = 2a + b$ (slope of tangent)

$\Rightarrow$ Putting $x = 1, y = 2$

$a + b = -\frac{3}{2}$ ...(1)

Now, considering the curve $y = x^2 + 6x + 10$ ...(2)

$\Rightarrow \frac{dy}{dx} = 2x + 6$

$\Rightarrow \left.\frac{dy}{dx}\right|_{(-2,2)} = 2$ ...(3)

$\therefore$ slope of normal $= -\frac{1}{2}$, then $2a + b = -\frac{1}{2}$ ...(4)

Using (1) and (4), we get $\left.\begin{matrix} a = 1 \\ b = -\frac{5}{2} \end{matrix}\right\}$

■ TANGENTS FROM AN EXTERNAL POINT

Given a point $P(a, b)$ which does not lie on the curve $y = f(x)$, then the equation of possible tangents to the curve $y = f(x)$, passing through (a, b) can be found by first finding the point of contact Q of the tangent with the curve

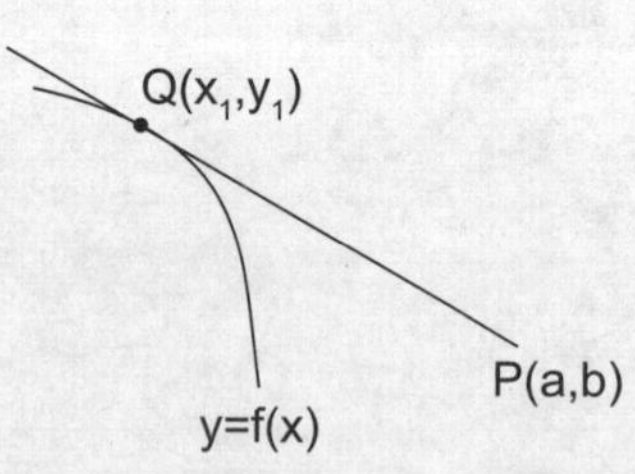

FIGURE 4.47

Let point Q be (x_1, y_1)

Since Q lies on the curve, we have $y_1 = f(x_1)$ ...(1)

Also, the slope of PQ = the slope of the tangent at the point Q on the curve $y = f(x) = \left.\frac{dy}{dx}\right|_{(x_1, y_1)}$

$\therefore$ Slope of $PQ \equiv \frac{y_1 - b}{x_1 - a} = \left.\frac{dy}{dx}\right|_{(x_1, y_1)}$ ...(2)

Solving (1), (2), we can get the point of contact (x_1, y_1)

ILLUSTRATION 80: The equation of the tangents to the curve $y = x^4$ from the point (2, 0) not on the curve, are given by

(a) $y = 0$

(b) $y - 1 = 5(x - 1)$

(c) $y - \frac{4098}{81} = \frac{2048}{27}\left(x - \frac{8}{3}\right)$

(d) $y - \frac{32}{243} = \frac{80}{81}\left(x - \frac{2}{3}\right)$

SOLUTION: (a) and (c) Let (x_0, x_0^4) be the point of tangency.

Then the equation of the tangent will be $y - x_0^4 = \left.\frac{dy}{dx}\right|_{(x_0, x_0^4)} (x - x_0)$

Since this tangent passes through the point (2, 0)

So, we have $-x_0^4 = 4x_0^3(2 - x_0)$,

$\Rightarrow 3x_0^4 - 8x_0^3 = 0$ or $3x_0^4 - 8x_0^3 = 0$

$\Rightarrow x_0 = 0$ or $x_0 = 8/3$,

so that the point of tangency are (0, 0) and (8/3, 4096/81).

Therefore, the equations of the tangents are

$$y = 0 \text{ and } y - \frac{4096}{81} = \frac{2048}{27}\left(x - \frac{8}{3}\right)$$

ILLUSTRATION 81: The tangent to the curve $y = x^2 + 3x$ will pass through the point (0, –9) if it is drawn at the point

(a) (3, 18) (b) (1, 4)

(c) (–4, 4) (d) (–3, 0)

SOLUTION: (a), (d) Let (x_1, y_1) be the point of contact form (0, –9) to the curve $y = x^2 + 3x$.

Then the slope of the tangent can be given by $\frac{y_1+9}{x_1}$, also $\left.\frac{dy}{dx}\right|_{(x_1, y_1)}$ i.e., $(2x_1 + 3)$

$$\Rightarrow \frac{y_1+9}{x_1} = 2x_1 + 3$$

$$\Rightarrow y_1 = 2x_1^2 + 3x_1 - 9 \quad \text{...(i)}$$

Also since x_1, y_1 satisfies the equation of the curve

$$\therefore \quad y_1 = x_1^2 + 3x_1 \quad \text{...(ii)}$$

Comparing (i) and (ii); we get $x_1^2 + 3x_1 = 2x_1^2 + 3x_1 - 9$

$x_1^2 = 9 \Rightarrow x_1 \pm 3$

Point of contact are (3, 18) and (3, 0)

ILLUSTRATION 82: The equations of the tangents to the curve $y = x^4$ from the point (2, 0) not on the curve, are given by

(a) $y = 0$ (b) $y - 1 = 5(x + 1)$

(c) $y - \frac{4098}{81} = \frac{2048}{27}\left(x - \frac{8}{3}\right)$ (d) $y - \frac{32}{243} = \frac{80}{81}\left(x - \frac{2}{3}\right)$

SOLUTION: (a), (c) Let the point of contact of the tangent at (2, 0) at the curve $y = x^4$ meets the curve $y = x^4$

be (h, k) where $k = h^4$ ...(1)

Then the tangent at (h, k) will be $y - k = \frac{dy}{dx}(x - h)$

$\Rightarrow y - k = 4h^3(x - h)$ ...(2)

Now, since it passes through (2, 0)

$\therefore -k = 4h^3(2 - h)$

or $-h^4 = 8h^3 - 4h^4$ (from (1): $k = h^4$)

or $3h^4 - 8h^3 = 0$

$\Rightarrow h = 0$ or 8/3

$\therefore\ k = 0$ or $(8/3)^4$

$\therefore$ Points are (0,0) and $(8/3, (8/3)^4$

$\therefore$ Putting in (2), tangent are $y = 0$ and $y-\left(\frac{8}{3}\right)^4 = 4\left(\frac{8}{3}\right)^3 \times \left(x-\frac{8}{3}\right)$

ILLUSTRATION 83: Find all the lines that pass through the point (1, 1) and are tangent to the curve represented parametrically as $x = 2t - t^2$ and $y = t + t^2$.

SOLUTION: $x = 2t - t^2$ ...(1)

$y = t + t^2$ ...(2)

$\frac{dx}{dt} = 2 - 2t \qquad \frac{dy}{dt} = 1 + 2t$

$\Rightarrow \frac{dy}{dx} = \frac{dy/dt}{dx/dt} = \frac{1+2t}{2-2t}$ ...(3)

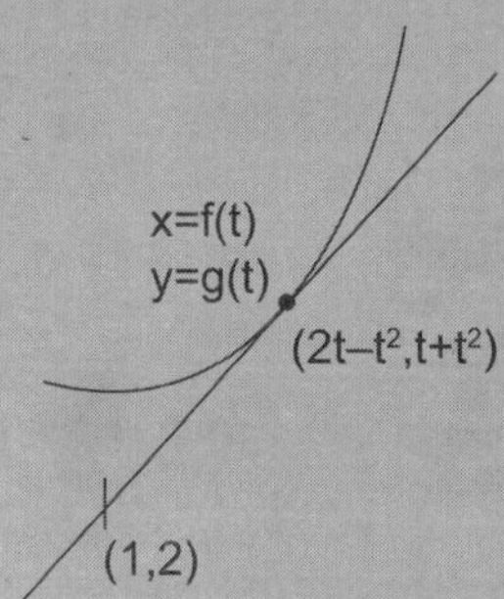

FIGURE 4.48

Slope of the line passing through the points (1, 1) and $(2t - t^2, t + t^2)$ is given by

$m = \frac{t+t^2-1}{2t-t^2-1}$ ...(4)

Equating (3) and (4), we get $\frac{dy}{dx} = \frac{t+t^2-1}{2t-t^2-1}$

$\Rightarrow \frac{1+2t}{2-2t} = \frac{t+t^2-1}{2t-t^2-1}$

$\Rightarrow 2t - t^2 - 1 + 4t^2 - 2t^3 - 2t = 2t + 2t^2 - 2 - 2t^2 - 2t^3 + 2t$

$\Rightarrow 3t^2 - 4t + 1 = 0 \qquad \Rightarrow 3t^2 - 3t - t + 1 = 0$

$\Rightarrow (3t - 1)(t - 1) = 0 \qquad \Rightarrow t = 1$ or $t = 1/3$

Now, when $t = 1$; point $(2t - t^2, t + t^2)$ becomes (1, 1) and hence equation of tangent will be given by

when $t = 1$, then point will be (1, 2) when $t = 1/3$, then point will be $\left(x=\frac{5}{9}, y=\frac{4}{9}\right)$

and $\frac{dy}{dx} = \frac{3}{0}$ for $t = 1$ and $\frac{dy}{dx} = \frac{5}{4}$ for $t = 1/3$

$\therefore$ Equations of tangents, will be $y - 2 = -(x - 1)$ and $y - \frac{4}{9} = \frac{5}{4}\left(x - \frac{5}{9}\right)$; $x = 1$; $5x - 4y - 1$

TANGENTS/NORMALS TO SECOND DEGREE CURVE

1. To find the equation of tangent at (x_1, y_1) substitute xx_1 for x^2, yy_1 for y^2, $\frac{x+x_1}{2}$ for x, $\frac{y+y_1}{2}$ for y and $\frac{xy_1+x_1y}{2}$ for xy and keep the constant as such. This method is applicable only for second degree conics, i.e., $ax^2 + 2hxy + by^2 + 2gx + 2fy + c = 0$

Proof: Differentiating both sides of $ax^2 + 2bxy + by^2 + 2gx + 2fy + c = 0$

We get $2ax + 2hy + 2hxy' + 2byy' + 2g + 2f\,yy' = 0$

$\Rightarrow ax + hy + hxy' + byy' + g + fy' = 0$

$\Rightarrow y' = -\left(\frac{ax+hy+g}{hx+by+f}\right)$

$\therefore$ slope of tangent at (x_1, y_1) is

$$y'\big|_{(x_1,y_1)} = -\left(\frac{ax_1+hy_1+g}{hx_1+by_1+f}\right)$$

$\therefore$ Equation of tangent at (x_1,y_1) is $y - y_1 = y'(x - x_1)$

$\Rightarrow y - y_1 = y'(x - x_1)$

$$\Rightarrow y - y_1 = -\left(\frac{ax_1+hy_1+g}{hx_1+by_1+f}\right)(x-x_1)$$

And on solving the above equations, we get

$$axx_1 + byy_1 + 2h\left(\frac{xy_1+yx_1}{2}\right) + 2g\left(\frac{x+x_1}{2}\right) + 2f\left(\frac{y+y_1}{2}\right) + c = 0$$

2. Easy method to find normal at (x_1, y_1) of second degree conics $ax^2 + 2hxy + by^2 + 2gx + 2fy + c = 0$ .....(i) then according to determinant $\begin{vmatrix} a & h & g \\ h & b & f \\ g & f & c \end{vmatrix}$. Write first two rows $ax + hy + g$ and $hx + by + f$ then equation of normal at (x_1, y_1) of (i) is $\frac{x-x_1}{ax_1+hy_1+g} = \frac{y-y_1}{hx_1+by_1+f}$

Proof: Having already found the slope of tangent at (x_1, y_1) on the curve $ax^2 + by^2 + 2hxy + 2gx + 2fy + c = 0$ as $-\left(\frac{ax_1+hy_1+g}{hx_1+by_1+f}\right)$. Therefore the slope of the normal to the curve at (x_1, y_1) will be $\left(\frac{hx_1+by_1+f}{ax_1+hy_1+g}\right)$

$\therefore$ Equation of normal will be given by

$$(y - y_1) = \left(\frac{hx_1+by_1+f}{ax_1+hy_1+g}\right)(x-x_1)$$

Or $\frac{y-y_1}{hx_1+by_1+f} = \frac{x-x_1}{ax_1+by_1+g}$

ILLUSTRATION 84: Find the equation of the tangent and the normal at the point (2,3) which lies on the curve $x^2 + 3y^2 - 2xy + 4y - 6x - 19 = 0$

SOLUTION: Equation of tangent can be obtained by replacing x^2 by $2x$; y^2 by $3y$, $2xy$ by $3x + 2y$, $2y$ by $(y + 3)$, $2x$ by $(x + 2)$

$\therefore$ Equation of tangent will be $2x + 3(3y) - (3x + 2y) + 2(y + 3) - (x + 2) - 19 = 0$

$\Rightarrow 9y - 4x - 19 = 0$

And the equation of normal can be obtained by using the formula $\frac{x-x_1}{ax_1+hy_1+g} = \frac{y-y_1}{hx_1+by_1+f}$

Where $a = 1, h = -1, g = -3, h = -1, b = 3, f = 2$

$\therefore$ Equation of normal $\frac{x-2}{(1)(2)+(-1)(3)+(-3)} = \frac{y-3}{(-1)(2)+(3)(3)+(2)}$

$\Rightarrow \frac{x-2}{-4} = \frac{y-3}{9}$

$\Rightarrow 9x - 18 = -4y + 12$ $\qquad\qquad \Rightarrow 9x + 4y = 30$

TEXTUAL EXERCISE–1: (SUBJECTIVE)

1. Find the co-ordinates of the points on the curve $2x^2 + 3xy + 4y^2 = 9$ at which the slope is $-7/11$.
2. Show that two tangents can be drawn from the point A$(2a, 3a)$ to the parabola $y^2 = 4ax$. Find the equations of these tangents.
3. Find the equation of the tangent to the curve $y = 2x^3 - x^2 + 3$ at the point (1, 4).
4. Find the condition that the line $ax + by + c = 0$ may be normal to the parabola $y = x^2$.
5. Find the tangents to the curve $y = (x^3 - 1)(x - 2)$ at the points where the curve cuts the x-axis.
6. Find the equation of the normal to the curve $y = (1+x)^y + \sin^{-1}(\sin^2 x)$ at the point $x = 0$.
7. Find the points where the tangent is parallel to x-axis and where it is parallel to y-axis, for the curve $25x^2 + 12xy + 4y^2 = 1$.
8. Find the point on the curve $y = 3x^2 - 2x - 4$ at which tangent is perpendicular to the line $x + 10y - 7 = 0$.
9. Find the point on the curve $2y = 3 - x^2$ the tangent at which is parallel to the line $x + y = 0$.
10. Find the points on the curve $y = x^4 - 6x^3 + 13x^2 - 10x + 5$ where the tangent is parallel to $y = 2x$. Also prove that two of these points have the same tangent.
11. Find the equation of the tangent line to the curve $y = \sqrt{5x-3} - 2$ which is
    (a) parallel to the line $2x - y + 9 = 0$
    (b) perpendicular to the line $5y + 2\sqrt{2}\,x = 13$
12. Prove that the sum of the intercepts on the co-ordinate axes of any tangent to $\sqrt{x} + \sqrt{y} = \sqrt{a}$ is constant.
13. Find equations of tangent and normal to the curve $x + y = x^y$, where the curve cuts x-axis.
14. If the normals drawn to the curve $y = x^2 - x + 1$ at the points A, B and C on the curve are concurrent at the point $P(7/2, 9/2)$, then compute the sum of the slopes of the three normals. Also find their equations and the co-ordinates of the feet of the normals onto the curve.
15. Find the equation of the tangent to the cycloid $x = a(\theta + \sin\theta)$, $y = a(1 - \cos\theta)$ at the point θ.

Answer Keys

1. (1, 1) and (–1, –1)
2. $y = x + a$, $2y = x + 4a$
3. $y = 4x$
4. $2a^2(b + 2c) + b^3 = 0$
5. $3x + y - 3 = 0$ and $7x - y - 14 = 0$
6. $x + y = 1$
7. (1/4, –3/8) and (–1/4, 3/8)
8. (2, 4)
9. (1, 1)
10. (1, 3) (2, 5) (3/2, 65/16)
11. (i) $80x - 40y = 103$ (ii) $2\sqrt{2}y - 5x + 4\sqrt{2} + 1 = 0$
13. $x + y - 1 = 0$ and $x - y - 1 = 0$
14. $\frac{13}{12}; x - y + 1 = 0, (0,1); x - 3y + 10 = 0, (-1,3); 2x + 8y - 43 = 0, \left(\frac{5}{2}, \frac{19}{4}\right)$
15. $x\sin(\theta/2) - y\cos(\theta/2) = a\,\theta\sin(\theta/2)$

TEXTUAL EXERCISE–1: (OBJECTIVE)

1. x and y are the sides of two squares such that $y = x - x^2$. The rate of change of the area of the second square with respect to that of the first square is
   (a) $2(1 - x^2)x$ (b) $2x^2 - 3x + 1$
   (c) $2(2x^2 - 3x + 1)$ (d) None of these
2. Two cyclists start from the junction of two perpendicular roads, their velocities being $3v$ m/min and $4v$/min. The rate at which the two cyclists are separating is
   (a) $(7/2)v$ m/min (b) $5\,v$ m/min
   (c) v m/min (d) None of these

3. Equation of normal to the curve $x + y = x^y$, where it cuts x-axis; is
(a) $x + y - 1 = 0$ (b) $x - y - 1 = 0$
(c) $x + y = 0$ (d) None of these

4. The tangent to the curve $y = e^{2x}$ at the point (0, 1) meets the x-axis at
(a) (0, 0) (b) (2, 0)
(c) (–1/2, 0) (d) None of these

5. The normal at the point (1,1) on the curve $2y = 3 - x^2$ is
(a) $x + y = 0$ (b) $x + y + 1 = 0$
(c) $x - y + 1 = 0$ (d) $x - y = 0$

6. The equation of the tangent to the curve $y = be^{-x/a}$ at point where $x = 0$; is
(a) $\frac{x}{a} - \frac{y}{b} = 1$ (b) $\frac{y}{b} - \frac{x}{a} = 1$
(c) $\frac{x}{a} + \frac{y}{b} = 1$ (d) None of these

7. The slope of the tangent to the curve $y = x^2 - x$ at the point where the line $y = 2$ cuts the curve in the first quadrant is
(a) 2 (b) 3
(c) –.3 (d) None of these

8. If at each point of the curve $y = x^3 - ax^2 + x + 1$ the tangent is inclined at an acute angle with the positive direction of the x-axis, then
(a) $a > 0$ (b) $a \le \sqrt{3}$
(c) $-\sqrt{3} < a < \sqrt{3}$ (d) None of these

9. The points at which the tangent to the curve $ax^2 + 2hxy + by^2 = 1$ is parallel to y-axis are
(a) (0, 0)
(b) where $hx + by = 0$, meet it
(c) where $ax + hy = 0$, meet it
(d) None of these

10. The point of contact at which tangent to $y = e^{-x}$ cuts off equal intercepts is
(a) $(1, e^{-1})$ (b) (0, 1)
(c) $(-1, e)$ (d) None of these

11. The slope of the tangent to the locus $y = \cos^{-1}(\cos x)$ at $x = -\pi/4$ is
(a) 1 (b) 0
(c) 2 (d) –1

12. The equation of tangent to the curve $y = e^{-|x|}$ at the point where the curve cut the line $x = 1$ is
(a) $x + y = e$ (b) $e(x + y) = 1$
(c) $y + ex = 1$ (d) None of these

13. The distance between the origin and the normal to the curve $y = x^2 + e^{2x}$ at $x = 0$ is
(a) $2/\sqrt{3}$ (b) $2/\sqrt{5}$
(c) $\sqrt{3}/2$ (d) $\sqrt{5}/2$

14. The tangent to the parabola $x^2 = 2y$ at the point (1, 1/2) makes with x-axis an angle of
(a) 60° (b) 30°
(c) 45° (d) 0°

15. The point on the curve $y = x^2$, where slope of the tangent is equal to the x-coordinate of the point is
(a) (–1/2, 1/2) (b) (0, 0)
(c) (2, 0) (d) (0, 2)

16. The curve $y - e^{xy} + x = 0$ has a vertical tangent at the point
(a) (1, 0) (b) (0, 0)
(c) (1, 1) (d) at no point

17. The line $x/a + y/b = 1$ touches the curve $y = be^{-x/a}$ at the point
(a) $(a, b/a)$ (b) $(-a, b/a)$
(c) $(a, a/b)$ (d) None of these

18. If $\ell x + my = 1$ is a normal to the parabola $y^2 = 4ax$, then
(a) $a\ell^3 + 2a\ell m^2 = m^2$
(b) $a\ell^3 + 2a\ell m^2 + m^2 = 0$
(c) $a\ell^3 - 2a\ell m^2 - m^2 = 0$
(d) None of these

19. If the tangent to the curve $2y^3 = ax^2 + x^3$ at the point (a, a) cuts off intercepts α, β on co-ordinate axes, where $\alpha^2 + \beta^2 = 61$, then the value of 'a' is equal to:
(a) 20 (b) 25
(c) 30 (d) – 30

20. The equation of the tangent to the curve $\left(\frac{x}{a}\right)^n + \left(\frac{y}{b}\right)^n = 2$ $(n \in \mathbb{N})$ at the point with abscissa equal to 'a' can be:
(a) $\left(\frac{x}{a}\right) + \left(\frac{y}{b}\right) = 2$ (b) $\left(\frac{x}{a}\right) - \left(\frac{y}{b}\right) = 2$
(c) $\left(\frac{x}{a}\right) - \left(\frac{y}{b}\right) = 0$ (d) $\left(\frac{x}{a}\right) + \left(\frac{y}{b}\right) = 0$

21. The equation of the tangent to the curve, $y = \int_{x^2}^{x^3} \frac{dt}{\sqrt{1 + t^2}}$ at $x = 1$ is

(a) $\sqrt{2}y + 1 = x$ (b) $\sqrt{2}y - 1 = x$
(c) $\sqrt{2}y = x$ (d) None

22. The equation of the tangent to the graph of function, $f(x) = | x^2 - | x ||$ at the point with abscissa $x = -2$ is
(a) $3x + y + 4 = 0$ (b) $3x + y - 4 = 0$
(c) $3x - y + 4 = 0$ (d) None

23. The number of values of c such that the straight line $y = 4x + c$ touches the curve $\frac{x^2}{4} + y^2 = 1$ is equal to
(a) 0 (b) 1
(c) 2 (d) infinite

24. The equation of the tangent to the curve $y = 2x^2 + 5x$ at the point where the line $y = 3$ cuts the curve in first quadrant is
(a) $14x - 2y - 1 = 0$ (b) $14x - 2y + 1 = 0$
(c) $14x + 2y - 1 = 0$ (d) None of these

25. The equations of tangents drawn from origin to the circle $x^2 + y^2 - 6x - 6y + 9 = 0$ are
(a) $x = 0$ (b) $x = y$
(c) $y = 0$ (d) $x + y = 0$

26. Sum of the square of the intercepts on the axes cut off by the tangent to $x^{1/3} + y^{1/3} = a^{1/3}$, $a \in \mathbb{R}^+$ at $(a/8, a/8)$ is 2. Then possible values of a is/are
(a) 4 (b) 2
(c) 6 (d) 3

27. The abscissa of the point on the curve $ay^2 = x^3$, the normal at which cuts off equal intercepts from the coordinates axis is
(a) $2a/9$ (b) $4a/9$
(c) $-4a/9$ (d) $-2a/9$

28. Equation of a normal to the curve $y = x^2 - 6x + 6$ which is perpendicular to the straight line joining the origin to the vertex of the parabola is:
(a) $4x - 4y - 1 = 0$ (b) $4x - 4y + 1 = 0$
(c) $4x - 4y - 21 = 0$ (d) $4x - 4y + 21 = 0$

29. The point on the curve $y^3 + 3x^2 = 12y$ where the tangent is vertical, is
(a) $\left(\pm\frac{4}{\sqrt{3}}, -2\right)$ (b) $\left(\pm\frac{11}{\sqrt{3}}, 1\right)$
(c) $(0, 0)$ (d) $\left(\pm\frac{4}{\sqrt{3}}, 2\right)$

30. If a variable tangent to the curve $x^2y = c^3$ makes intercepts a, b on x and y-axis respectively, then the value of a^2b is
(a) $27c^3$ (b) $\frac{4}{27}c^3$
(c) $\frac{27}{4}c^3$ (d) $\frac{4}{9}c^3$

31. The x-intercept of the tangent at any arbitrary point of the curve $\frac{a}{x^2} + \frac{b}{y^2} = 1$ is proportional to:
(a) square of the abscissa of the point of tangency
(b) square root of the abscissa of the point of tangency
(c) cube of the abscissa of the point of tangency
(d) cube root of the abscissa of the point of tangency

Answer Keys

1. (b)	**2.** (b)	**3.** (b)	**4.** (c)	**5.** (d)	**6.** (c)	**7.** (b)	**8.** (c)	**9.** (b)	**10.** (b)
11. (d)	**12.** (d)	**13.** (b)	**14.** (c)	**15.** (b)	**16.** (a)	**17.** (d)	**18.** (a)	**19.** (c, d)	
20. (a, b)	**21.** (a)	**22.** (a)	**23.** (c)	**24.** (a)	**25.** (a, c)	**26.** (a)	**27.** (b)	**28.** (c)	**29.** (d)
30. (c)	**31.** (c)								

■ TANGENT TO PARAMETRIC FUNCTIONS

Given the equation of the curve $x = f(t)$ and $y = g(t)$, then

$$\Rightarrow \frac{dy}{dx} = \frac{\left(\frac{dy}{dt}\right)}{\left(\frac{dx}{dt}\right)} = \frac{g'(t)}{f'(t)}.$$

The equation of tangent at any point 't' on the curve is given by: $y - g(t) = \frac{g'(t)}{f'(t)}(x - f(t))$

The equation of normal at point 't' is given by

$$y - g(t) = -\frac{f'(t)}{g'(t)}(x - f(t))$$

Some common parametric coordinate on a curve are as follows:

(a) For $x^2 + y^2 = a^2$; $x = a\cos\theta$, $y = a\sin\theta$

(b) For $x^2 - y^2 = a^2$; $x = a\sec\theta$, $y = a\tan\theta$

(c) For $\frac{x^2}{a^2} - \frac{y^2}{b^2} = 1$; $x = a\cos\theta$, $y = b\sin\theta$

(d) For $y^2 = 4ax$; $x = at^2$, $y = 2at$

(e) For $\frac{x^2}{a^2} - \frac{y^2}{b^2} = 1$; $x = a\sec\theta$, $y = b\tan\theta$

(f) For $x^{2/3} + y^{2/3} = a^{2/3}$; $x = a\cos^3\theta$, $y = a\sin^3\theta$

(g) For $\sqrt{x} + \sqrt{y} = \sqrt{a}$; $x = a\cos^4\theta$, $y = a\sin^4\theta$

(h) For $\frac{x^n}{a^n} + \frac{y^n}{b^n} = 1$; $x = a(\cos\theta)^{2/n}$, and $y = b(\sin\theta)$

(i) For $\frac{x^n}{a^n} - \frac{y^n}{b^n} = 1$; $x = a(\sec\theta)^{2/n}$, and $y = b(\tan\theta)^{2/n}$

(j) For $c^2(x^2 + y^2) = x^2y^2 \Rightarrow x = c\sec\theta$ and $y = c\operatorname{cosec}\theta$

(k) For $ay^2 = x^3 \Rightarrow x = at^2$ and $y = at^3$

ILLUSTRATION 85: The equation of a curve is given by $x = e^t \sin t$, $y = e^t \cos t$. The inclination of the tangent to the curve at point $t = \pi/4$ is

(a) $\pi/4$ (b) $\pi/3$

(c) $\pi/2$ (d) 0

SOLUTION: $\frac{dy}{dx} = \frac{dy/dt}{dx/dt} = \frac{e^t(\cos t - \sin t)}{e^t(\sin t + \cos t)}$ $\quad \therefore \left.\frac{dy}{dx}\right]_{t=\frac{\pi}{4}} = \frac{\frac{1}{\sqrt{2}} - \frac{1}{\sqrt{2}}}{\frac{1}{\sqrt{2}} + \frac{1}{\sqrt{2}}} = 0$

ILLUSTRATION 86: The normal to the curve $x = a(\cos\theta + \theta\sin\theta)$ $y = a(\sin\theta - \theta\cos\theta)$ at any point θ is such that

(a) it makes a constant angle with x-axis (b) it passes through origin

(c) it is at a constant distance (d) None of these

SOLUTION: (c) Put $\theta = 0$ we get $x = a$, $y = 0$

$$\Rightarrow \frac{dy}{dx} = \frac{dy/d\theta}{dx/d\theta} = \frac{dy(\theta\sin\theta)}{dx(\theta\cos\theta)} = \tan\theta$$

Normal: $y - a(\sin\theta - \cos\theta) = \frac{-\cos\theta}{\sin\theta}[x - a(\cos\theta + \theta\sin\theta)]$

$\Rightarrow \sin\theta.y - x.\cos\theta = a$

Distance from origin = $|a|$, hence constant.

ILLUSTRATION 87: The slope of the tangent to curve $x = a\sin t$, $y = a\left(\cos t + \log\tan\frac{t}{2}\right)$ at the point is

(a) $\tan\frac{t}{2}$ (b) $\cot t$

(c) $\tan t$ (d) None of these

SOLUTION: (b) Slope of tangent $= \frac{dy}{dx} = \frac{dy/dt}{dx/dt}$

$$= \frac{a\left(-\sin t + \frac{1}{\tan t/2}\sec^2\frac{t}{2}.\frac{1}{2}\right)}{a\cos t} = \frac{-\sin t + \frac{1}{2\sin\frac{t}{2}\cos\frac{t}{2}}}{\cos t}$$

$$= \frac{-\sin t + \frac{1}{\sin t}}{\cos t} = \frac{1 - \sin^2 t}{\sin t\cos t} = \frac{\cos^2 t}{\sin t\cos t} = \cot t$$

ILLUSTRATION 88: If p_1 and p_2 be the lengths of perpendiculars from the origin on the tangent and normal to the curve $x^{2/3} + y^{2/3} = a^{2/3}$ respectively, then $4p_1^2 + p_2^2 =$

(a) $4a^2$ (b) $2a^2$

(c) a^2 (d) None of these

SOLUTION: (c) Take the parametric equation as $x = a \sin^3\theta$, $y = a\cos^3\theta$

Tangent is $x \cos\theta + y \sin\theta = (a/2) \sin 2\theta$

Normal is $y \cos\theta - x\sin\theta = a \cos 2\theta$

$$\therefore \quad = \frac{(\ /2)\sin 2}{\sqrt{\left(\cos^2\theta \quad \sin^2\theta\right)}} = -\sin 2$$

$$p_2 = \frac{a\cos 2\theta}{\sqrt{\left(\cos^2\theta + \sin^2\theta\right)}} = a\cos 2\theta$$

$$\therefore \quad 4p_1^2 + p_2^2 = a^2\left(\sin^2 2\theta + \cos^2 2\theta\right) = a^2$$

ILLUSTRATION 89: For the curve $xy = c^2$, prove that

(a) The intercept between the axes on the tangent at any point is bisected at the point of contact.

(b) The tangent at any point makes with the co-ordinate axes a triangle of constant area.

SOLUTION: Let the equation of the curve in parametric form be $x = ct$, $y = c/t$ and the point of contact be $(ct, c/t)$

Equation of tangent is at point (x, y):

$$\Rightarrow Y - c/t = \frac{-c/t^2}{c}.(X - ct) \qquad \Rightarrow t^2Y - ct = -X + ct$$

(a) Let the tangent cut the x and y axes at A and B respectively

Writing the equations as: $\dfrac{X}{2ct} + \dfrac{Y}{2c/t} = 1$

$\Rightarrow x_{\text{intercept}} = 2ct, \; y_{\text{intercept}} = 2c/t$

$\Rightarrow A = (2ct, 0)$ and $B = \left(0, \dfrac{2c}{t}\right)$ and mid point of $AB = \left(\dfrac{2ct+0}{2}, \dfrac{0+2c/t}{2}\right) = (ct, c/t)$

Hence the point of contact bisects AB

(b) If O is the origin then:

Area of triangle $\Delta OAB = \dfrac{1}{2}(OA).(OB)$

$= \dfrac{1}{2}(2ct).\dfrac{2c}{t} = 2c^2$ i.e., constant for all tangents because it is independent of t.

ILLUSTRATION 90: Prove that the segment of the normal to the curve $x = 2a \sin t + a \sin t \cos^2 t$; $y = -a \cos^3 t$ contained between the co-ordinate axes is equal to $2a$.

SOLUTION:
$$\frac{dy}{dx} = \frac{dy/dt}{dx/dt} = \frac{3a\cos^2 t\sin t}{2a\cos t + a\cos^3 t - 2a\sin^2 t\cos t} = \frac{3a\cos^2 t\sin t}{2a\cos t(1-\sin^2 t) + a\cos^3 t}$$

$$= \frac{3a\cos^2 t\sin t}{2a\cos^3 t + a\cos^3 t} = \frac{3a\cos^2 t\sin t}{3a\cos^3 t}; \; \frac{dy}{dx} = \tan t$$

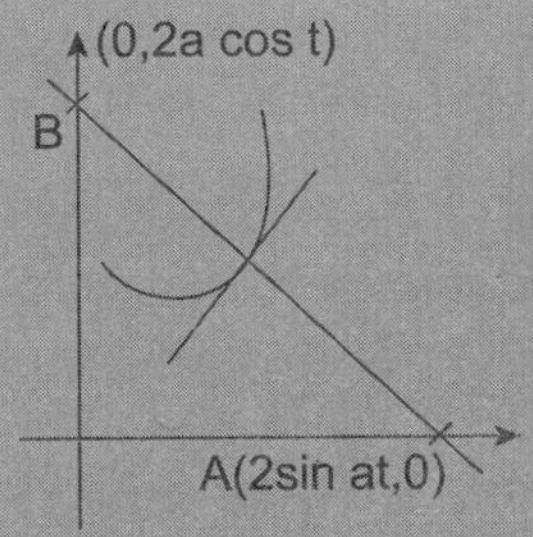

FIGURE 4.49

Equation of normal $y + a\cos^3 t = -\dfrac{\cos t}{\sin t}(x - 2a\sin t - a\sin t\cos^2 t)$

$y\sin t + a\cos^3 t\sin t = -x\cos t + 2a\sin t\cos t + a\sin t\cos^3 t$

$x\cos t + y\sin t = 2a\sin t\cos t$ ...(1)

at $A(2a\sin t, 0)$; $B(0, 2a\cos t)$ then $AB = 2a$

ILLUSTRATION 91: Find the equation of the tangent and normal to the curve $x = a\cos\theta$, $y = b\sin\theta$ at the point 'θ'

SOLUTION: Equation of the curve is:

$x = a\cos\theta$ & $y = b\sin\theta$ ....(i)

Differentiating both x and y with respect to θ.

$\dfrac{dx}{d\theta} = -a\sin\theta$; $\dfrac{dy}{d\theta} = b\cos\theta$

$\therefore \dfrac{dy}{dx} = \dfrac{dy\ d}{dx\ d} = -\dfrac{b\cos\theta}{a\sin\theta}$

Slope of tangent at 'θ' $= \dfrac{b\cos\theta}{a\sin\theta}$

Equation of tangent at 'θ' $(a\cos\theta, b\sin\theta)$ is:

$y - b\sin\theta = -\dfrac{b\cos\theta}{a\sin\theta}(x - a\cos\theta)$

or $ay\sin\theta - ab\sin^2\theta = -bx\cos\theta + ab\cos^2\theta$

or $bx\cos\theta + ay\sin\theta = ab(\sin^2\theta + \cos^2\theta) = ab$

Dividing by ab: $\dfrac{x}{a}\cos\theta + \dfrac{y}{b}\sin\theta = 1$

Slope of normal at 'θ' $= \dfrac{a\sin\theta}{b\cos\theta}$

Equation of normal 'θ' is $y - b\sin\theta = \dfrac{a\sin\theta}{b\cos\theta}(x - a\cos\theta)$

or $\dfrac{y}{\sin\theta} - b = \dfrac{a}{b}\left(\dfrac{x}{\cos\theta} - a\right)$

or $\dfrac{by}{\sin\theta} - b^2 = \dfrac{ax}{\cos\theta} - a^2$

or $\dfrac{ax}{\cos\theta} - \dfrac{by}{\sin\theta} = a^2 - b^2$

ILLUSTRATION 92: Find the equation of the normal at the point 'θ' on the curve $x = 3\cos\theta - \cos^3\theta$, $y = 3\sin\theta - \sin^3\theta$ and show that at the point, where $\theta = \pi/4$, the normal passes through the origin.

SOLUTION: Equation of the curve is $x = 3\cos\theta - \cos^3\theta$ & $y = 3\sin\theta - \sin^3\theta$ ...(i)

$$\frac{dx}{d\theta} = -3\sin\theta - 3\cos^2\theta(-\sin\theta) = -3\sin\theta(1-\cos^2\theta) = -3\sin\theta\sin^2\theta = -3\sin^3\theta$$

$$\frac{dy}{d\theta} = 3\cos\theta - 3\sin^2\theta\cos\theta = 3\cos\theta(1-\sin^2\theta) = 3\cos\theta\cos^2\theta = 3\cos^3\theta$$

$$\frac{dy}{dx} = \frac{dy/d\theta}{dx/d\theta} = \frac{3\cos^3\theta}{-3\sin^3\theta} = -\cot^3\theta$$

Slope of tangent 'θ' $= -\cot^3\theta$

∴ Slope of normal at 'θ' $= \tan^3\theta$

Equation of normal at 'θ' is $y - (3\sin\theta - \sin^3\theta) = \tan^3\theta\,[x - (3\cos\theta - \cos^3\theta)]$

or $y - 3\sin\theta + \sin^3\theta = \dfrac{\sin^3\theta}{\cos^3\theta}[x - 3\cos\theta + \cos^3\theta]$

or $\dfrac{y}{\sin^3\theta} - \dfrac{3}{\sin^2\theta} + 1 = \dfrac{x}{\cos^3\theta} - \dfrac{3}{\cos^3\theta} + 1$

or $x\sec^3\theta - y\,\text{cosec}^3\theta = 3$

$\left[\dfrac{1}{\cos^2\theta} - \dfrac{1}{\sin^2\theta}\right] = 3(\sec^2\theta - \text{cosec}^2\theta)$

At $\theta = \pi/4$ equation of normal is $x\sec^3\dfrac{\pi}{4} - y\,\text{cosec}^3\dfrac{\pi}{4} = 3\left(\sec^2\dfrac{\pi}{4} - \text{cosec}^2\dfrac{\pi}{4}\right)$

or $x(\sqrt{2})^3 - y(\sqrt{2})^3 = 3[(\sqrt{2})^2 - (\sqrt{2})^2]$

or $2\sqrt{2}x - 2\sqrt{2}y = 0$

or $x - y = 0$ which clearly passes through the origin.

ILLUSTRATION 93: Find the length of the portion of the tangent intercepted between the co-ordinate axes at any point of the curve $x = a\cos^3 t$, $y = b\sin^3 t$.

SOLUTION: Equation of the curve are $x = a\cos^3 t$, $y = b\sin^3 t$

$\dfrac{dx}{dt} = -3a\cos^2 t\sin t$, $\dfrac{dy}{dt} = 3b\sin^2 t\cos t$ $\dfrac{dy}{dx} = \dfrac{dy/dt}{dx/dt} = -\dfrac{b\sin t}{a\cos t}$

Equation of tangent at 't' $(a\cos^3 t, b\sin^3 t)$ is $y - b\sin^3 t = -(x - a\cos^3 t)$

or $(a\cos t)y - ab\sin^3 t\cos t = -(b\sin t)x + ab\sin t\cos^3 t$

or $(b\sin t)x + (a\cos t)y = ab\sin t\cos t(\sin^2 t + \cos^2 t) = ab\sin t\cos t$

or $\dfrac{x}{a\cos t} + \dfrac{y}{b\sin t} = 1.$

Intercept on x-axis $= a\cos t$ and Intercept on y-axis $= b\sin t$

∴ Length of the portion of the tangent intercepted between the axes

$$= \left|\sqrt{(\text{intercept on } x-\text{axis})^2 + (\text{intercept on } y-\text{axis})^2}\right| = \sqrt{a^2\cos^2 t + b^2\sin^2 t}$$

ILLUSTRATION 94: Prove that the equation of the tangent at any point 't' to the curves $x = a\dfrac{\varphi(t)}{f(t)}$; $y = a\dfrac{\psi(t)}{f(t)}$

may be written in the form $\begin{vmatrix} x & y & a \\ \varphi(t) & \psi(t) & f(t) \\ \varphi'(t) & \psi'(t) & f'(t) \end{vmatrix} = 0$

SOLUTION: Slope of the tangent is given by $\frac{dy}{dx}=\frac{dy/dt}{dx/dt}=\frac{a.\left[\frac{f(t)\psi'(t)-\psi(t)f'(t)}{(f(t))^2}\right]}{a.\left[\frac{f(t)\phi'(t)-\phi(t)f'(t)}{(f(t))^2}\right]}$

$$\Rightarrow\ m|_{(x,y)}=\left[\frac{f(t)\psi'(t)-\psi(t)f'(t)}{f(t)\phi'(t)-\phi(t)f'(t)}\right]$$

So equation of tangent is $y-\frac{a\psi(t)}{f(t)}=\left[\frac{f(t)\psi'(t)-\psi(t)f'(t)}{f(t)\phi'(t)-\phi(t)f'(t)}\right]\left(x-a\frac{\phi(t)}{f(t)}\right)$ ...(i)

Now expanding the given determinant $\begin{vmatrix} x & y & a \\ \phi(t) & \psi(t) & f(t) \\ \phi'(t) & \psi'(t) & f'(t)\end{vmatrix}=0$ along first row, we get

$$x[\psi(t)f'(t)-\psi'(t)f(t)]-y[\phi(t)f'(t)-\phi'(t)f(t)]+a[\phi(t)\psi'(t)-\phi'(t)\psi(t)]=0 \quad ....(ii)$$

Again expanding equation (i) we get $\{y f(t)-a\psi(t)\}\{f(t)\phi'(t)-\phi(t)f'(t)\}$

$=\{f(t)\psi'(t)-\psi(t)f'(t)\}\{x f(t)-a\phi(t)\}$

Or $x\{\psi(t)f'(t)-f(t)\psi'(t)\}-y\{\phi(t)f'(t)-\phi'(t)f(t)\}+a\{\phi(t)\psi'(t)-\phi'(t)\psi(t)\}=0$ ...(iii)

Equations (ii) and (iii) are same, so given determinant represents the equation of tangent at point *t*.

■ TANGENTS INTERSECTING THE CURVE ITSELF

The tangent at *P* meeting the curve again at Q $\Rightarrow\left(\frac{dy}{dx}\right)_P=\frac{y_2-y_1}{x_2-x_1}$

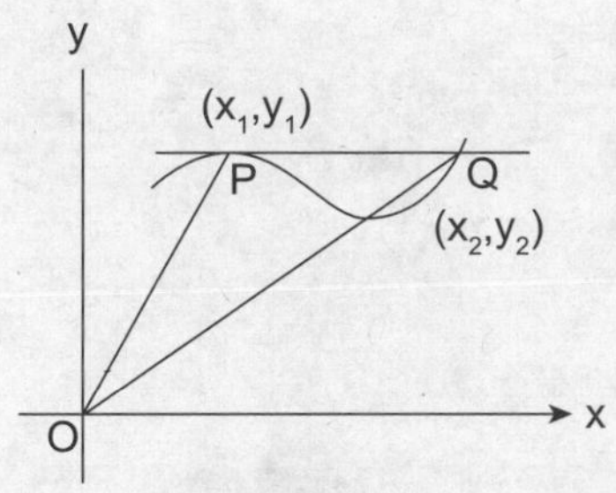

FIGURE 4.50

ILLUSTRATION 95: If the tangent at $P(1, 1)$ on $y^2 = x(2-x)^2$ meets the curve again at Q then the point Q is

(a) $(-1, 2)$

(b) $\left(\frac{9}{4},\frac{3}{8}\right)$

(c) $(4, 4)$

(d) None of these

SOLUTION: (b) Given $y^2 = x(2-x)^2$ Differentiating both sides *w.r.t* x, $2y\,y' = (2-x)^2 - 2x(2-x)$

$\therefore \quad \frac{dy}{dx}$ at $(1,1) = \frac{1-2}{2} = -\frac{1}{2}$

$\therefore$ Tangent is $y - 1 = -1/2\,(x-1)$ or $2y = 3 - x$

Now, solving $2y = 3 - x$ with $y^2 = x(2-x)^2$; we get $\left(\frac{3-x}{2}\right)^2 = x(2-x)^2$

[Putting the value of y]

or $4x^3 - 17x^2 + 22x - 9 = 0$ $\quad\Rightarrow (x-1)(4x^2 - 13x + 9) = 0$

$(x-1)(4x^2 - 13x + 9) = 0$

$\Rightarrow (x-1)(x-1)(4x\ 9) = 0$ $\quad\Rightarrow x = 1$ or $x = \frac{9}{4}$

then $y = \frac{3-x}{2} = \frac{3-\frac{9}{4}}{2} = \frac{12-9}{4\times 9} = \frac{3}{8}$

Hence Q is $\left(\frac{9}{4}, \frac{3}{8}\right)$; Also when $x = 1$, $y = 1$

Hence (1, 1) point is rejected since it is the point p from where tangent is drawn

ILLUSTRATION 96: If the tangent at the point $P(at^2, at^3)$ on the curve $ay^2 = x^3$ meets the curve again at Q whose parameter is t' then $t' =$

(a) $2t$ (b) $-t$
(c) $t/2$ (d) $-t/2$

SOLUTION: (b) The tangent at t is $y - at^3 = \frac{3t}{2}\left(x - at^2\right)$ ...(1)

It meets the curve again at the point Q whose parameter is t' $\therefore$ $Q\,(at'^2, at'^3)$ lies on (1)

$\therefore \quad a\,(t'^3 - t^3) = \frac{3t}{2}\,a(t'^2 - t^2)$

$\therefore \quad (t'^2 + t't + t^2).2 = 3t\,a(t' + t)$ as $t' \neq 1$

$\therefore \quad 2t'^2 - tt' - t^2 = 0$ or $(t' - t)(2t' + 1) = 0$

$\therefore \quad t' = -t/2$

ILLUSTRATION 97: A curve is given by the equations $x = \sec^2\theta$, $y = \cot\theta$. If the tangent at P where $\theta = \pi/4$ meets the curve again at Q, then length PQ =

(a) $\sqrt{15}$ (b) $\frac{3}{2}\sqrt{5}$
(c) $\frac{1}{2}\sqrt{15}$ (d) None of these

SOLUTION: (b) $\frac{dy}{dx} = \frac{dy/d\theta}{dx/d\theta} = \frac{y}{x} = -\frac{1}{2}\cot^3\theta$ when $\theta = \frac{\pi}{4}$; $\frac{dy}{dx} = -\frac{1}{2}\cot^3\left(\frac{\pi}{4}\right) = -\frac{1}{2}$

Now when $\theta = \frac{\pi}{4}$; $x = \sec^2\left(\frac{\pi}{4}\right) = 2$ and $= \cot\left(-\right) = 1$

$\therefore \quad (x, y)|_p = P \equiv (2, 1)$

$T_p \equiv y - 1 = -1/2\,(x-2)$ or $x + 2y - 4 = 0$ ...(1)

Now, the Cartesian equation of the parametric function can be obtained by eliminating θ using the identify $\sec^2\theta - \tan^2\theta = 1$, we get $y^2 = \dfrac{1}{x-1}$ ...(2)

Form (1); we get $y = \dfrac{4-x}{2}$

Substituting this value of y in (2); we get $\left(\dfrac{4-x}{2}\right)^2 = \dfrac{1}{x-1}$

$\Rightarrow$ $x = 2, 5$ and $y = 1$ when $x = 2$ and $y = \dfrac{1}{2}$ when $x = 5$

Hence P is $(2,1)$ (given) and Q is $\left(5, \dfrac{1}{2}\right)$

$\therefore\quad PQ = \sqrt{(5-2)^2 + \left(1 - \dfrac{1}{2}\right)^2} = \sqrt{\dfrac{45}{4}} = \dfrac{3\sqrt{5}}{2}$

ILLUSTRATION 98: If the tangent at the point (x_1, y_1) to the curve $x^3 + y^3 = a^3\,(a \neq 0)$ meets then curve again in (x_2, y_2) then show that $\dfrac{x_2}{x_1} + \dfrac{y_2}{y_1} = -1$

SOLUTION: $x^3 + y^3 = a^3$ ...(1)

$\dfrac{dy}{dx} = -\dfrac{x^2}{y^2}$ ...(2)

$\Rightarrow \left.\dfrac{dy}{dx}\right|_{x_1 y_1} = -\dfrac{x_1^2}{y_1^2}$

Slope of line AB; $\dfrac{dy}{dx} = \dfrac{y_2 - y_1}{x_2 - x_1}$ ..(3)

using (2) and (3) $-\dfrac{x_1^2}{y_1^2} = \left(\dfrac{y_2 - y_1}{x_2 - x_1}\right)$ ...(4)

Now

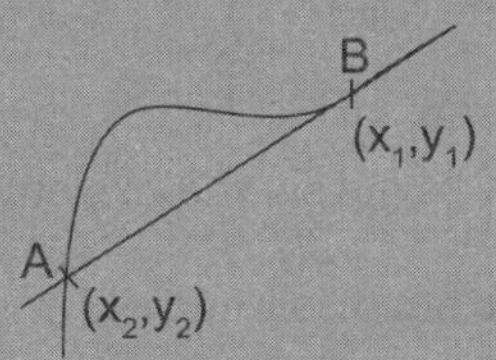

FIGURE 4.51

$$\begin{aligned} x_1^3 + y_1^3 &= a^3 \\ x_2^3 + y_2^3 &= a^3 \\ \hline (x_1^3 - x_2^3) &= -(y_1^3 - y_2^3) \end{aligned} \quad = -(y_1 - y_2)\,(y_1^2 + y_1^{y_2} + y_2^2)$$

$\dfrac{y_2 - y_1}{x_2 - x_1} = -\left(\dfrac{x_1^2 + x_1x_2 + x_2^2}{y_1^2 + y_1y_2 + y_2^2}\right)$ ...(5)

put in (4) $-\dfrac{x_1^2}{y_1^2} = -\left(\dfrac{x_1^2 + x_1x_2 + x_2^2}{y_1^2 + y_1y_1 + y_2^2}\right)$

$x_1^2y_1y_2 + x_1^2y_2^2 - y_1^2x_1x_2 - y_1^2x_2^2 = 0$

$x_1y_1(x_1y_2 - x_2y_1) + (x_1y_2 - y_1x_2)(x_1y_2 + y_1x_2) = 0$

$(x_1y_2 - x_2y_1)(x_1y_1 + x_1y_2 + y_1x_2) = 0$

$\dfrac{x_2}{x_1} + \dfrac{y_2}{y_1} = -1$

ILLUSTRATION 99: The normal to the curve $x = a(\cos\theta + \theta\sin\theta)$, $y = a(\sin\theta, - \theta\cos\theta)$ at any θ is such that

(a) it makes a constant angle with x-axis (b) it passes through the origin

(c) it is at a constant distance from the origin (d) None of these

SOLUTION: (c) $\dfrac{dx}{d\theta} = -a\sin\theta + a\theta\cos\theta + a\sin\theta = a\theta\cos\theta$

$\dfrac{dy}{d\theta} = a\cos\theta - a\cos\theta + a\theta\sin\theta = a\theta\sin\theta$

$\therefore \dfrac{dy}{dx} = \dfrac{y}{x} = \dfrac{\sin\theta}{\cos\theta}$ = slope of tangent

$\therefore$ Slope of normal $= -\dfrac{\cos\theta}{\sin\theta}$

(Now, since slope $= -\cot\theta$ $\therefore$ slope is dependent upon θ. Hence it does not make a constant angle with x-axis)

$\therefore$ Normal is $[y-(a\sin\theta - a\theta\cos\theta)] = -\dfrac{\cos\theta}{\sin\theta}\times[x-(a\cos\theta + a\theta\sin\theta)]$

or $y\sin\theta + x\cos\theta = a(\cos^2\theta + \sin^2\theta) = a$

(Since the constant term in the equation of the normal is not equal to zero,

$\therefore$ the normal does not pass through (0, 0))

Now, its distance from the origin is given by $\dfrac{a}{\sqrt{(\cos^2\theta + \sin^2\theta)}} = a$ i.e., constant

Hence 'c' is the correct answer.

ILLUSTRATION 100: Tangent at a point p_1 [other than (0, 0)] on the curve $y = x^3$ meets the curve again at p_2. The tangent at p_2 meets the curve at p_3 and so on. Show that the abscissa of $p_1, p_2, p_3 \ldots p_n$ a G.P. Also find the ratio $\dfrac{\text{area }(p_1p_2p_3)}{\text{area }(p_2p_3p_4)}$

SOLUTION: curve $\Rightarrow y = x^3$

$\Rightarrow \dfrac{dy}{dx} = 3x^2$ similarly let p_1 on $y = x^3$ be (h, h^3)

$\Rightarrow \left.\dfrac{dy}{dx}\right|_{h,h^2} = 3h^2$ then tangent at $p_1 p^4 = (-8h, -8^3h^3)$

$y - h^3 = 3h^2(x - h)$ ...(1)

it meets $y = x^3$ at p_2 $\dfrac{\Delta\, p_1 p_2 p_3}{\Delta\, p_2 p_3 p_4}$ then put $y = x^3$ in ...(1)

$x^3 - h^3 = 3h^2(x - h)$

$$(x-h)(x^2+xh+h^2) = 3h^2(x-h) = \frac{\frac{1}{2}\begin{vmatrix} h & h^3 & 1 \\ -2h & -8h^3 & 1 \\ 4h & 84h^3 & 1 \end{vmatrix}}{\frac{1}{2}\begin{vmatrix} -2h & -8h^3 & 1 \\ 4h & 64h^3 & 1 \\ -8h & -512h^3 & 1 \end{vmatrix}}$$

$x^2 + xh - 2h^2 = 0$ or $x = h$

$(x - h)(x + 2h) = 0$

$x = h$ or $x = -2h$

Therefore, $x = -2h$ is the point p_2. Which implies $y = -8h^3 = \dfrac{1}{16}$ Ans

Hence $p_2 = (-2h, -8h^3)$

again tangent at p_2 is $y + 8h^3 = 3(-2h)^2(x + 2h)$

it meets $y = x^3$ at p_3

$x^3 + 8h^3 = 12h^2(x + 2h)$

$x = 4h$

then $y = 64h^3$

$p^3 = (4h, 64h^3)$

TANGENT AT ORIGIN

If a rational integral algebraic equation of a curve is passing through origin then the equations of the tangent at the origin is obtained by equating the lowest terms in the equation of curve to be equal to zero.

Proof: Let S: $a_n x^n + a_{n-1}x^{n-1} + \ldots + a_1 x + b_n y^n + b_{n-1} y^{n-1} + \ldots + b_1 y + C_{m,n} x^m y^n + C_{m,n-1} x^m y^{n-1} + \ldots\ldots + C_{1,1} xy = 0$

Then differentiating both sides w.r.t x, we get

$a_n \times n x^{n-1} + a_{n-1}(n-1)x^{n-2} + \ldots + 2a_2 x + a_1 +$
$(b_m \times m y^{m-1} + b_{m-1}(m-1)y^{m-2} + \ldots + 2b_2 y + b_1)y' +$
$C_{m,n}(m x^{m-1} y^n + x^m \times n y^{n-1} \times y_1) + \ldots\ldots + C_{1,1}(y + xy') = 0$

Since, we need to find the slope at origin; therefore putting (x, y) as $(0, 0)$; we get $a_1 + b_1 y' = 0$

$\Rightarrow\ y' = \dfrac{-a_1}{b_1}$

$\therefore$ Equation of tangent at $(0, 0)$ is $y = y'x$

$\Rightarrow\ y = \dfrac{-a_1 x}{b}$

$\Rightarrow\ b_1 y + a_1 x = 0$

e.g.: for the curve $x^2 - 4y^2 + x^4 + 3x^2y + 3x^2y^2 + y^4 = 0$, the tangents at the origin would be given by $x^2 - 4y^2 = 0$

i.e., $x + 2y = 0$ and $x - 2y = 0$

Proof: Differentiating both sides of the equation, we get

$2x - 8y\,y' + 4x^3 + 9x^2y + 3x^3y' + 6xy^2 + 6x^2\,yy' + 4y^3y' = 0$

$$\Rightarrow\ y' = -\frac{2x + 4x^3 + 9x^2y + 6xy^2}{-8y + 3x^3 + 6x^2y + 4y^3}$$

Now for the slope at (0,0); we find

$$\lim_{\substack{x\to 0\\ y\to 0}} y' = \lim_{\substack{x\to 0\\ y\to 0}} -\left(\frac{2x + 4x^3 + 9x^2y + 6xy^2}{-8y + 3x^3 + 6x^2y + 4y^3}\right)$$

$$= \lim_{\substack{x\to 0\\ y\to 0}} -\left(\frac{2x}{-8y}\right) = \lim_{\substack{x\to 0\\ y\to 0}} \left(\frac{x}{4y}\right) = m$$

$\therefore$ Equation of tangent is $y = mx$

$$\Rightarrow\ y = \frac{x}{4y}x \Rightarrow 4y^2 - x^2 = 0$$

$\Rightarrow\ x + 2y = 0$ and $x - 2y = 0$

NOTE:

1. *If the curve* $x^4 + y^4 = x^2 + y^2$, *then the equation of the tangent would be* $x^2 + y^2 = 0$ *which would indicate that the origin is an isolated point on the graph.*
2. *There may exist curves on which one line could be the tangent as well as the normal to a given curve at a given point.*
   e.g. For the curve $x^3 + y^3 - 3xy = 0$ *(Folium of Descartes), the line pair xy=0 is both, a tangent as well as a normal at x =0.*

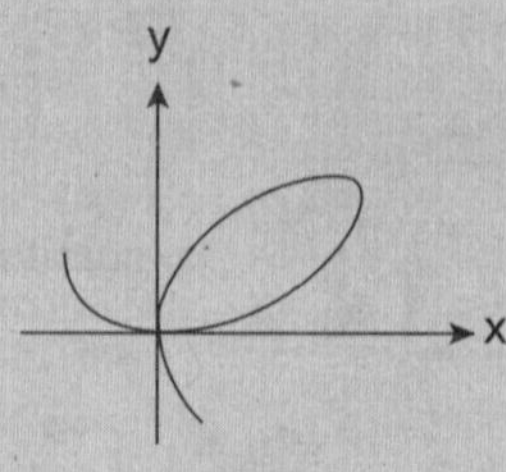

FIGURE 4.52

TEXTUAL EXERCISE–2: (SUBJECTIVE)

1. Find the equation of the tangent and the normal to the curve $y^2 = 4ax$ at the point $(at^2, 2at)$.
2. Find the point on the curve $y = x^3$ where the tangent to it at the point (x_1, x_1^3) intersect the curve again.
3. For the curve $y = 4x^3 - 2x^5$, find all the points at which the tangent passes through the origin.
4. Find the equations of tangent and normal at any point of the curve.
   (a) $x = a\,(t \sin t);\ y = a\,(1 - \cos t)$
   (b) $x = a \sec\theta\ y = b \tan\theta$
   (c) $x = a \cos^3\theta\ y = a \sin^3\theta$
5. Find the angle of intersection of the curves $y^2 = 2ax$ and $y^2 = a^2 - x^2$.
6. If the curve $\frac{x^2}{a^2} + \frac{y^2}{4} = 1$ and $y^3 = 16x$ intersect at right angles show that $a^2 = 4/3$.

Answer Keys

1. $ty = x + at^2;\ y = -tx + 2at + at^3$ **2.** $(-2x_1, -8x_1^3)$ **3.** $(0, 0), (1, 2)$ and $(-1, -2)$ **5.** $\theta = \tan^{-1}\left(\frac{2}{\sqrt{\sqrt{2}-1}}\right)$

TEXTUAL EXERCISE–2: (OBJECTIVE)

1. The tangents to the curve, $x = a(\theta - \sin\theta);\ y = a(1 + \cos\theta)$ at the point $\theta = (2k + 1)\pi,\ (k \in \mathbb{Z})$ are parallel to
   (a) the line $y = x$
   (b) the line $y = -x$
   (c) the x-axis
   (d) the y-axis
2. If the tangent at the point (at^2, at^3) on the curve $ay^2 = x^3$ meets the curve again at P, then P is
   (a) $\left(\frac{at^2}{4}, -\frac{at^3}{8}\right)$ (b) $\left(-\frac{at^2}{4}, \frac{at^3}{8}\right)$
   (c) $\left(\frac{at^2}{4}, \frac{at^3}{8}\right)$ (d) None of these
3. If the parametric equation of a curve is given by $x = e^t \cos t$, $y = e^t \sin t$, then the tangent of the curve at the point $t = \pi/4$ makes with x-axis an angle
   (a) 0 (b) $\pi/4$
   (c) $\pi/3$ (d) $\pi/2$
4. For the curve $x = t^2 - 1;\ y = t^2 - t$, the tangent line is perpendicular to x-axis, then
   (a) $t = 0$ (b) $t = \infty$
   (c) $t = 1/\sqrt{3}$ (d) $t = -1/\sqrt{3}$
5. Sum of squares of intercepts made on coordinate axis by the tangent to the curve $x^{2/3} + y^{2/3} = a^{2/3}$ is
   (a) a^2 (b) $2a^2$
   (c) $3a^2$ (d) $4a^2$

6. If $\frac{x}{a}+\frac{y}{b}=1$ is a tangent to the curve $x = 4t$, $y = 4/t$, $t \in \mathbb{R} - \{0\}$, then
(a) $a > 0, b > 0$ (b) $a > 0, b < 0$
(c) $a < 0, b > 0$ (d) $a < 0, b < 0$

7. The abscissa of the point on the curve $ay^2 = x^3$, the normal at which cuts off equal intercepts from the axes is
(a) 1 (b) $4a/3$
(c) 3 (d) None of these

8. The tangent to the curve $3xy^2 - 2x^2y = 1$ at (1, 1) meets the curve again at the point
(a) $\left(-\frac{16}{5}, -\frac{1}{20}\right)$ (b) $\left(\frac{16}{5}, \frac{1}{20}\right)$
(c) $\left(\frac{1}{20}, \frac{16}{5}\right)$ (d) $\left(-\frac{1}{20}, \frac{16}{1}\right)$

9. If the tangent at P of the curve $y^2 = x^3$ intersects the curve again at Q and the straight lines OP, OQ make angles α, β with the x-axis where 'O' is the origin, then $\frac{\tan\alpha}{\tan\beta}$ has the value equal to:
(a) -1 (b) -2
(c) 2 (d) $\sqrt{2}$

10. The lines $y = -\frac{3}{2}x$ and $y = -\frac{2}{5}x$ intersect the curve $3x^2 + 4xy + 5y^2 - 4 = 0$ at the points P and Q respectively. The tangents drawn to the curve at P and Q:
(a) intersect each other at angle of 45°
(b) are parallel to each other
(c) are perpendicular to each other
(d) None of these

11. Normal to the curve $x = a(2 + \cos\theta)$ and $y = a\sin\theta$ at θ' always passes through the point
(a) $(2a, 0)$ (b) $(0, a)$
(c) (a, a) (d) $(a, 0)$

12. Normal to the curve $x = 3t^2 + 1, y = t^2 - t + 1$ is parallel to x-axis at
(a) $t = \infty$ (b) $t = 0$
(c) $t = 3$ (d) $t = -3$

13. Tangent to the curve $x = t^3 - 6t^2 + 9t$, $y = t^2$ is perpendicular to x – axis at
(a) $t = 1$ (b) $t = 0$
(c) $t = 3$ (d) $t = 4$

14. If the tangent at (1, 1) on $y^2 = x(2 - x)^2$ meets the curve again at P, then the co-ordinates of P are:
(a) $\left(\frac{9}{4}, \frac{3}{8}\right)$ (b) $(3, \sqrt{3})$
(c) (4, 4) (d) None of these

15. Tangent to the curve $x = a\sqrt{\cos 2\theta}\,.\,\cos\theta$; $y = a\sqrt{\cos 2\theta}\,.\,\sin\theta$ at the point corresponding to $\theta = \pi/6$ is:
(a) parallel to x-axis
(b) parallel to y-axis
(c) parallel to the line $y = x$
(d) None of the above

16. Let C be the curve $y = x^3$ (where x takes all real values). The tangent at A meets the curve again at B. If the gradient at B is k times the gradient at A, then k is equal to
(a) 4 (b) 2
(c) -2 (d) $\frac{1}{4}$

17. A curve is represented by the equations $x = \sec^2 t$ and $y = \cot t$ where t is a parameter. If the tangent at the point P on the curve where $t = \pi/4$ meets the curve again at the point Q, then $|PQ|$ is equal to:
(a) $\frac{5\sqrt{3}}{2}$ (b) $\frac{5\sqrt{5}}{2}$
(c) $\frac{2\sqrt{5}}{3}$ (d) $\frac{3\sqrt{5}}{2}$

Answer Keys

1. (c)	2. (a)	3. (d)	4. (a)	5. (a)	6. (a,d)	7. (d)	8. (a)	9. (b)	10. (c)
11. (a)	12. (b)	13. (a,c)	14. (a)	15. (a)	16. (a)	17. (d)			

ANGLES OF INTERSECTION OF TWO CURVES

Let the two curves $C_1: y = f(x)$ and $C_2: y = g(x)$ intersect at $P(x_1, y_1)$ then angle between two curves at P is the angle between their tangents at P. "The angle of intersection of two curves is defined as the angle between the tangents to the two curves at thier common point of intersection."

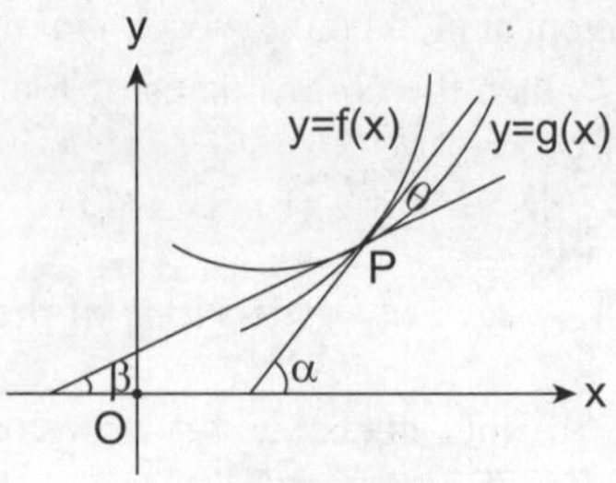

FIGURE 4.53

Hence, if slope of tangents PT and PT' of the two curves at point P be m_1 (tan β) and m_2 (tan α) and θ be the angle between the two curves at P, then $\theta = \alpha - \beta$

$$\Rightarrow \tan\theta = \frac{\tan\alpha - \tan\beta}{1+\tan\alpha\tan\beta} = \left(\frac{m_2 - m_1}{1+m_1m_2}\right)$$

$$\Rightarrow \tan\theta = \left|\frac{m_2 - m_1}{1+m_1m_2}\right|$$

Algorithm

Step 1: Solve both the curves to get point/points of intersection P.

Step 2: Find slope of tangents at P i.e., $m_1 = \frac{dy_1}{dx}$ tanα

and $m_2 = \frac{dy_2}{dx} = \tan\beta$

Step 3: $\beta + \theta = \alpha \Rightarrow \theta = \alpha - \beta$

$$\tan\theta = \tan(\alpha - \beta) = \frac{\tan\alpha - \tan\beta}{1+\tan\alpha\tan\beta}$$

$$\Rightarrow \tan\theta = \frac{m_1 - m_2}{1+m_1m_2}$$

NOTE:

1. *Acute angle of intersection*

   $\Rightarrow$ *qacute* $= \tan^{-1}\left|\frac{m_1 - m_2}{1+m_1m_2}\right|$

2. *If angle of intersection between the curves be 90°, then curves are said to intersect orthogonally*

   i.e. $\left(\frac{dy_1}{dx}\right)_P\left(\frac{dy_2}{dx}\right)_P = -1$ *orthogonally*

3. *Two curves are said to be orthogonal iff* $\left(\frac{dy_1}{dx}\right)\left(\frac{dy_2}{dx}\right) = -1$

4. *If* $\left(\frac{dy_1}{dx}\right)_P\left(\frac{dy_2}{dx}\right)_P = -1$ *but* $\left(\frac{dy_1}{dx}\right)_Q\left(\frac{dy_2}{dx}\right) \neq -1$. *Then the two curves are orthogonal at P but not at Q hence they are not orthogonal.*

5. *The angle of intersection of two curves is the same as the angle between the normals at the point intersection*

   For e.g.: If y = f(x) and y = g(x) intersect at P $\left.\frac{dy_1}{dx}\right|_P = m_1$ *and* $\left.\frac{dy_2}{dx}\right|_P = m_2$ *then angle of intersection*

   $= \theta_{acute} = \tan^{-1}\left|\frac{m_2 - m_1}{1+m_1m_2}\right|$ *and hence the angle between the normals is given by*

$$\phi = \tan^{-1}\left|\frac{\left(\frac{-1}{m_2}\right) - \left(\frac{-1}{m_1}\right)}{1+\left(\frac{-1}{m_1}\right)\left(\frac{-1}{m_2}\right)}\right| = \tan^{-1}\left|\frac{m_2 - m_1}{1+m_1m_2}\right|$$

ILLUSTRATION 101: Find the total number of parallel tangents of $f_1(x) = x^2 - x + 1$ and $f_2(x) = x^3 - x^2 - 2x + 1$.

SOLUTION: Here, $f_1(x) = x^2 - x + 1$ and $f_2(x) = x^3 - x^2 - 2x + 1$

$\Rightarrow \quad f_1'(x) = 2x_1 - 1$ and $f_2'(x) = 3x_2^2 - 2x_2 - 2$

Let tangents drawn to the curves $y = f_1(x)$ and $y = f_2(x)$ at $(x_1, f_1(x_1))$ and $(x_2, f_2(x^2))$ are parallel

$\Rightarrow \quad 2x_1 - 1 = 3x_2^2 - 2x_2 - 2 \qquad \Rightarrow \quad 2x_1 = 3x_2^2 - 2x_2 - 1$

Which is possible for infinite numbers of ordered pairs;

$\therefore$ Infinite Solutions.

ILLUSTRATION 102: Tangent to the curve $y = x^3 + 3x$ at $x = -1$ and $x = 1$ are

(a) parallel
(b) Intersecting obliquely but not at an angle of 45°
(c) intersecting at right angles
(d) intersecting at an angle of 45°

SOLUTION: (a) $\dfrac{dy}{dx} = 3x^2 + 3$

At $x = -1$, $\dfrac{dy}{dx} = 3 + 3 = 6 = (m_1)$ At $x = 1$, $\dfrac{dy}{dx} = 3 + 3 = 6 = (m_2)$

As $m_1 = m_2$ $\therefore$ tangents are parallel

ILLUSTRATION 103: The curves $y = x^2$ and $6y = 7 - x^3$ intersect at the point (1, 1) at an angle

(a) $\pi/4$ (b) $\pi/3$
(c) $\pi/2$ (d) None

SOLUTION: (c) $y = x^2 \quad \Rightarrow \quad \dfrac{dy}{dx} = 2x$

$\Rightarrow \quad \left(\dfrac{dy}{dx}\right)_{(1,\,1)} = 2 \qquad \therefore \quad m_1 = 2$

$6y = 7 - x^3 \qquad \Rightarrow \quad \dfrac{dy}{dx} = -\dfrac{3x^2}{6} = -\dfrac{x^2}{2}$

$\left(\dfrac{dy}{dx}\right)_{(1,1)} = -\dfrac{1}{2} \qquad \Rightarrow \quad m_2 = -\dfrac{1}{2}$

Now $\dfrac{dy}{dx} = \left|\dfrac{m_1 - m_2}{1 + m_1 m_2}\right| = \left|\dfrac{2 + 1/2}{1 + 2(-1/2)}\right| = \left|\dfrac{5/2}{0}\right| \to \infty \qquad \therefore \quad \theta = \pi/2$

ILLUSTRATION 104: If the tangent to the curve $xy + ax + by = 0$ at (1, 1) is inclined at an angle $\tan^{-1} 2$ to axis of x then (a, b) is equal to

(a) (–1, –2) (b) (–1, 2)
(c) (1, –2) (d) (1, 2)

SOLUTION: (c) Now since (1, 1) lies on the curve

$\therefore \quad a + b + 1 = 0$ ...(1)

Given $xy + ax + by = 0$; Differentiating w.r.t. x, $xy' + y + a + by' = 0$ we get

$\Rightarrow \qquad = -\left(\dfrac{a}{x}\,\dfrac{y}{b}\right)$. And given that $\dfrac{dy}{dx} = \tan\theta = 2$

or $-\left(\dfrac{a+y}{x+b}\right)\Bigg|_{(1,1)} = 2$ or $\left(-\dfrac{y+a}{x+b}\right)_{(1,1)} = 2$ $\therefore$ $(1 + a) + 2(1 + b) = 0$

or $a + 2b + 3 = 0$ ...(2)

Solving (1) and (2), we get $a = 1, b = -2$

ILLUSTRATION 105: The curve $y = a^x$ and $y = b^x$ intersect at an angle $\tan^{-1}\left(\dfrac{\log(a/b)}{1+\log a \log b}\right)$ $(a, b > 1)$.

Above statement is

(a) True (b) False

(c) can-not say anything

SOLUTION: (a) Finding point of intersection, P

$a^x = b^x$

$x = 0, y = 1$ $\therefore$ $P = (0,1)$

$\Rightarrow \dfrac{dy}{dx} = a^x \ln a$ $\Rightarrow m_1 = \left(\dfrac{dy}{dx}\right)_P = \ln a$

Similarly $M_2 = \ln b$

$$\tan\phi = \frac{m_1 - m_2}{1+m_1m_2} = \frac{\ln(a/b)}{1+\ln a\ \ln b}$$

$\therefore$ (a) is correct.

ILLUSTRATION 106: Find the angle of intersection between the curves

(a) $y^2 = 2x$ and $x^2 + y^2 = 8$ (b) $y = x^3$ and $6y = 7 - x^2$

SOLUTION: (a) Equation of the curve are $y^2 = 2x$ ...(i)

and $x^2 + y^2 = 8$ ...(ii)

Eliminating, y between (i) and (ii), $x^2 + 2x - 8 = 0$

or $(x + 4)(x - 2) = 0$ $\therefore$ $x = -4, 2$

Of which $x = -4$ gives imaginary values of y and is rejected

when $x = 2, y^2 = 4,$ $\therefore$ $y = \pm 2$

$\therefore$ Points of intersection are (2, 2) and (2, –2)

For the curve (i), $2y\dfrac{dy}{dx} = 2$

$\therefore \dfrac{dy}{dx} = \dfrac{1}{y}$

For the curve (ii), $2x + 2y\dfrac{dy}{dx} = 0$

$\therefore \dfrac{dy}{dx} = -\dfrac{x}{y}$

At (2, 2) slopes of tangents are $\dfrac{1}{2}$ and -1

$$\therefore \tan\theta = \frac{\frac{1}{2}-(-1)}{1+\frac{1}{2}(-1)} = \frac{3/2}{1/2} = 3 \qquad \Rightarrow \theta = \tan^{-1}(3)$$

(b) Equation of curve are $y = x^3$ ...(i)

and $6y = 7 - x^2$ ...(ii)

Eliminating y between (i) and (ii), we get $6x^3 + x^2 - 7 = 0$ ...(iii)

By inspection its one root is 1 and therefore equation (iii) becomes:

$(x - 1)(6x^2 + 7x + 7) = 0$ $\quad \therefore \ x = 1, \dfrac{-7 \pm \sqrt{49-168}}{12}$

The only real value of x is 1 $\quad \therefore$ from equation (i) $y = 1$

The only point of intersection is (1,1)

For the curve (i): $\dfrac{dy}{dx} = 3x^2$

For the curve (ii): $6\dfrac{dy}{dx} = -2x$

or $\dfrac{dy}{dx} = -\dfrac{x}{3}$

At (1, 1) slopes of tangents are 3 and $-\dfrac{1}{3}$

Since these slopes are negative reciprocals of each other. Hence the curves cut orthogonally.

ILLUSTRATION 107: Prove that the curves $xy = 4$ and $x^2 + y^2 = 8$ touch each other.

SOLUTION: Equation of the given curves are $xy = 4$ ...(i)

and $x^2 + y^2 = 8$ ...(ii)

from (i), $1\,y + x\dfrac{dy}{dx} = 0$;

$\therefore \ \dfrac{dy}{dx} = -\dfrac{y}{x}$ ...(iii)

from (ii), $2x + 2y\dfrac{dy}{dx} = 0$;

$\therefore \ \dfrac{dy}{dx} = -\dfrac{x}{y}$ ...(iv)

Putting the value of y from (i) and (ii), we get

$x^2 + \dfrac{16}{x^2} = 8$;

or $x^4 + 16 = 8x^2$

or $x^4 - 8x^2 + 16 = 0$

or $(x^2 - 4)^2 = 0$

or $x^2 - 4 = 0$

or $x^2 = 4$;

$\therefore \ x = \pm 2$

Hence points of intersection of the two curves are (2, 2) and (–2, –2).

Slope of the tangent to the curve (i) at point (2, 2)

$m_1 = -\dfrac{2}{2} = -1$ (from (iii))

Slope of tangent to the curve (ii) at point (2, 2) $m_2 = -\left(\frac{2}{2}\right) = -1$ (from (iv))

$\because$ $m_1 = m_2$, therefore, the curves have a common tangent at (2, 2) i.e., they touch each other at (2, 2).

At point (–2, –2): Slope of tangent to the curve (i), $m_3 = -\left(\frac{-2}{-2}\right) = -1$

Slope of tangent to the curve (ii), $m_4 = -\left(\frac{-2}{-2}\right) = -1$

Since $m_3 = m_4$, hence the two curves touch each other at (–2, –2). Thus curves (i) and (ii) touch each other.

ORTHOGONAL CURVES

If the angle of intersection of two curves is right angle then the two curves are said to be intersecting orthogonally and such curves are called orthogonal curves. e.g. $y = mx$ and $x^2 + y^2 = r^2$ are two orthogonal curves for any value of m and r.

$\therefore$ If the curves are orthogonal then angle of intersection $\theta = \pi/2$

$$\Rightarrow \quad 1 + \left(\frac{dy}{dx}\right)_{C_1}\left(\frac{dy}{dx}\right)_{C_2} = 0$$

$$\Rightarrow \quad \left(\frac{dy}{dx}\right)_{C_1}\left(\frac{dy}{dx}\right)_{C_2} = -1$$

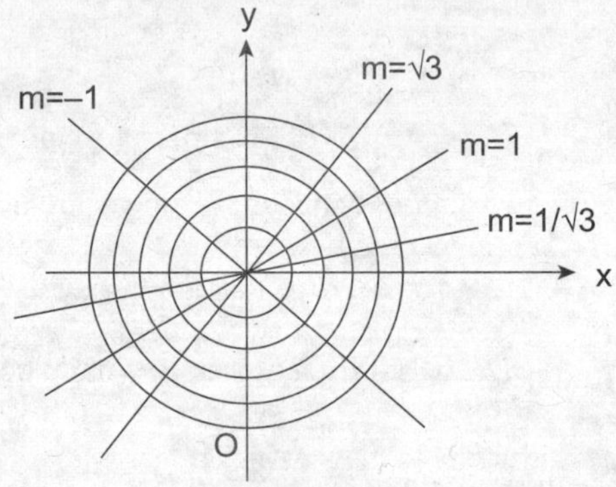

FIGURE 4.54

ILLUSTRATION 108: The curve $x^3 - 3xy^2 + 2 = 0$ and $3x^2y - y^3 - 2 = 0$ cut at an angle of

(a) 45° (b) 60°

(c) 90° (d) 30°

SOLUTION: (c) For the curve $x^3 - 3xy^2 = -2$; we get $3x^2 - 3y^2 - 6xy\frac{dy}{dx} = 0$

$$\Rightarrow \quad \frac{dy}{dx} = \frac{x^2 - y^2}{2xy}$$

And for the curve $3x^2y - y^3 = 2$; we get $3x^2\frac{dy}{dx} + 6xy - 3y^2\frac{dy}{dx} = 0$

$$\Rightarrow \quad \frac{dy}{dx} = \frac{-2xy}{x^2 - y^2}$$

Clearly, $m_1 m_2 = -1$

Hence the curves but each other orthogonally.

ILLUSTRATION 109: The curves $ax^2 + by^2 = 1$ and $a'x^2 + b'y^2 = 1$ intersect orthogonally if

(a) $1/a - 1/b = 1/a' - 1/b'$ (b) $1/a + 1/b = 1/a' + 1/b'$

(c) $1/a + 1/b = 1/a' + 1/b'$ (d) None of these

SOLUTION: (a) For the curve $ax^2 + by^2 = 1$

Differentiating w.r.t x, we get $2ax + 2by\,y' = 0$

$\Rightarrow\ m_1 = y' = \dfrac{-ax}{by}$

And for the curve $a'x^2 + b'y^2 = 1$

$m_1 = y' = \dfrac{-a'x}{b'y}$

If the curves cut orthogonally, then $m_1m_2 = -1$

or $\left(-\dfrac{ax}{by}\right)\left(-\dfrac{a'x}{b'y}\right) = -1$ or $aa'x^2 + bb'y^2 = 0$ ......(1)

Now, we need to find the values of x^2 and y^2 corresponding to the points of intersection of

$ax^2 + by^2 - 1 = 0$ and $a'x^2 + b'y^2 - 1 = 0$

$\therefore\ \dfrac{x^2}{b'-b} = \dfrac{y^2}{a'-a} = \dfrac{1}{ab'-a'b}$

Putting the values of x^2 and y^2 in (1); we get $aa'\dfrac{(b'-b)}{ab'-a'b} + bb'.\dfrac{(a-a')}{ab'-a'b} = 0$

$\Rightarrow\ \dfrac{b'-b}{bb'} + \dfrac{a-a}{aa'} = 0 \Rightarrow \left(\dfrac{1}{b} - \dfrac{1}{b'}\right) + \left(\dfrac{1}{a'} - \dfrac{1}{a}\right) = 0$

or $\dfrac{1}{a} - \dfrac{1}{b} = \dfrac{1}{a'} - \dfrac{1}{b'}$ is the required condition

ILLUSTRATION 110: Which of the following pair(s) of curves is/are orthogonal?

(a) $y^2 = 4ax; y = e^{-x/2a}$ (b) $y^2 = 4ax; x^2 = 4ay$

(c) $xy = a^2, x^2 - y^2 = b^2$ (d) $y = ax; x^2 + y^2 = c^2$

SOLUTION: (a) $y^2 = 4ax, \dfrac{dy}{dx} = \dfrac{4a}{2y} = m_1$

$y = e^{-x/2a}, \dfrac{dy}{dx} = \dfrac{-1}{2a}y = m_2$ $m_1m_2 = \dfrac{4a}{2y} \times \left(-\dfrac{1}{2a}\right)y = -1$

(b) $y^2 = 4ax, \dfrac{dy}{dx} = \dfrac{4a}{2y} = m_1$

$x^2 = 4ay, \dfrac{dy}{dx} = \dfrac{4a}{2a} = m_2$ $m_1m_2 = \dfrac{x}{y}$

(c) $xy = a^2, y + x\dfrac{dy}{dx} = 0$ $\Rightarrow \dfrac{dy}{dx} = -\dfrac{y}{x} = m_1$

$x^2 - y^2 = b^2$ $\Rightarrow \dfrac{dy}{dx} = \dfrac{x}{y} = m_2;\ m_1m_2 = -1$

(d) $y = ax, \dfrac{dy}{dx} = a = m_1$

$x^2 + y^2 = c^2$ $2x + 2y\dfrac{dy}{dx} = 0$ $\Rightarrow \dfrac{dy}{dx} = -\dfrac{x}{y} = m_2$

$m_1m_2 = -\dfrac{ax}{y} = -1$

ILLUSTRATION 111: Show that the curves $\dfrac{x^2}{a^2+k_1} + \dfrac{y^2}{b^2+k_1} = 1$ and $\dfrac{x^2}{a^2+k_2} + \dfrac{y^2}{b^2+k_2} = 1$ intersect orthogonally.

SOLUTION: $\dfrac{x^2}{a^2+k_1} + \dfrac{y^2}{b^2+k_1} = 1$ ...(1)

$$\frac{2x}{a^2+k_1}+\left(\frac{2y}{b^2+k_1}\right)\frac{dy}{dx}=0$$

$$m_1 \Rightarrow \frac{dy}{dx}=-\left(\frac{b^2+k_1}{a^2+k_1}\right)\frac{x}{y} \quad ...(2)$$

$$\frac{x^2}{a^2+k_2}+\frac{y^2}{b^2+k_2}=1 \quad ...(3)$$

$$\frac{2x}{a^2+k_2}+\left(\frac{2y}{b^2+k_2}\right)\frac{dy}{dx}=0$$

$$m_2 \Rightarrow \frac{dy}{dx}=-\left(\frac{b^2+k_2}{a^2+k_2}\right)\frac{x}{y} \quad ...(3)$$

for orthogonally $m_1m_2=-1$ then $\frac{(b^2+k_1)(b^2+k_2)}{(a^2+k_1)(a^2+k_2)}\cdot\frac{x^2}{y^2}=-1$

$$\frac{(b^2+k_1)(b^2+k_2)}{(a^2+k_1)(a^2+k_2)}\frac{x^2}{y^2}=-1 \quad ...(4)$$

using (1) and (2), we get $\frac{x^2}{a^2+k_1}+\frac{y^2}{b^2+k_1}=1$

$$\frac{x^2}{a^2+k_2}+\frac{y^2}{b^2+k_2}=1$$

$$\underline{- \; - \; -}$$

$$x^2\left(\frac{1}{a^2+k_1}-\frac{1}{a^2+k_2}\right)+y^2\left(\frac{1}{b^2+k_1}-\frac{1}{b^2+k_2}\right)=0$$

$$x^2\left(\frac{a^2+k_2-a^2-k_1}{(a^2+k_1)(a^2+k_2)}\right)+-y^2\left(\frac{b^2+k_2-b^2-k_1}{(b^2+k_1)(b^2+k_2)}\right)=0$$

$$x^2\left(\frac{k_2-k_1}{(a^2+k_1)(a^2+k_2)}\right)=-y^2\left(\frac{k_2-k_1}{(b^2+k_1)(b^2+k_2)}\right)$$

$$\frac{(b^2+k_1)(b^2+k_2)}{(a^2+k_1)(a^2+k_2)}=-\frac{y^2}{x^2} \quad ...(5)$$

put the value of $\frac{x^2}{y^2}$ in (4)

$$\left(\frac{(b^2-k_1)(b^2+k_2)}{(a^2+k_1)(a^2+k_2)}\right)\left(\frac{-(a^2+k_1)(a^2+k_2)}{(b^2+k_1)(b^2+k_2)}\right)=-1\,;-1=-1$$

ILLUSTRATION 112: In the two curves $c_1: x=y^2$ and $c_2: xy=k$ cut at right angles find the value of k.

SOLUTION: $x=y^2$ ...(1)

and $xy=k$ ...(2)

$y^3=k$

$y=k^{1/3}$

then $x=k^{2/3}$

point of intersection $(k^{2/3}, k^{1/3})$

using (1)

$$\frac{dy}{dx} = \frac{1}{2y}$$

$$\left.\frac{dy}{dx}\right|_{(k^{2/3},k^{1/3})} = \frac{1}{2k^{1/3}}$$

$$m_1 = \frac{1}{2k^{1/3}}$$

using (2)

$$\frac{dy}{dx} = -\frac{y}{x}$$

$$\left.\frac{dy}{dx}\right|_{(k^{2/3},k^{1/3})} = -\frac{k^{1/3}}{k^{1/3}}$$

$$m_2 = -\frac{1}{k^{1/3}}$$

for orthogonally $m_1 m_2 = -1$

$$-\frac{1}{2.k^{1/3}.k^{1/3}} = -1$$

$$k^{2/3} = \frac{1}{2}$$

$$(k^2) = \left(\frac{1}{2}\right)^3$$

$$k^2 = \frac{1}{8}$$

$$k = \pm\frac{1}{2\sqrt{2}}$$

COMMON TANGENTS

A line which touches two given curves is called a common tangent to the curves. There are two cases:

(i) The point of contact of the common tangent is same for both the curves. Here, the curves touch each other. In such a case the slope of the tangent is equal to the slopes of both the curves at the point of contact.

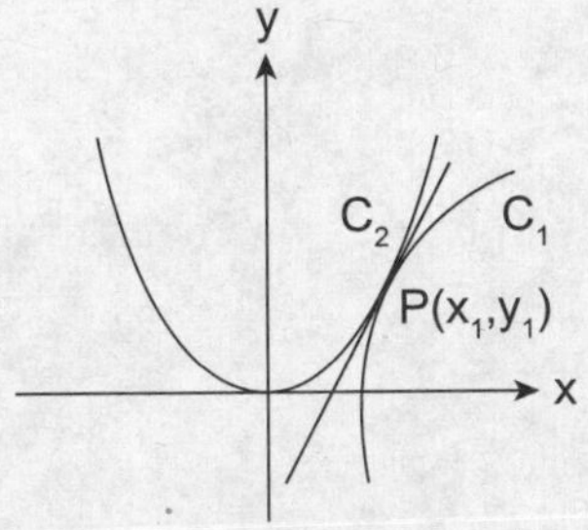

FIGURE 4.55

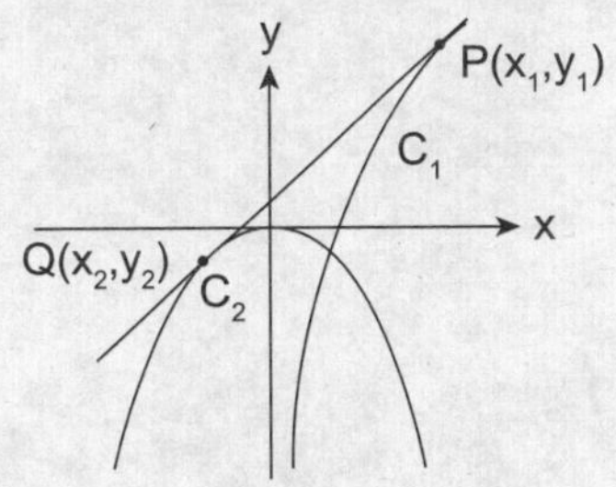

FIGURE 4.56

(ii) The points of contact of the common tangents is different for the two curves. In such a case the slope of the tangent is equal to the slope of the curves at their respective points of contact

i.e., $\left.\frac{dy}{dx}\right|_{(x_1,y_1)}^{C_1} = \left.\frac{dy}{dx}\right|_{(x_2,y_2)}^{C_2} = \frac{y_1 - y_2}{x_1 - x_2}$

ILLUSTRATION 113: Tangent to the curve $y = x^2 + 6$ at point $P(1, 7)$ touches the circle $x^2 + y^2 + 16x + 12y + c = 0$ at a point Q. Then the coordinates of Q are

(a) (–6, –11) (b) (–9, –13)

(c) (–10, –15) (d) (–6, –7)

SOLUTION: The tangent at (1, 7) to the parabola $x^2 = y - 6$ is $x(1) = \frac{1}{2}(y + 7) - 6$

(replacing $x^2 \to xx_1$ and $2y \to y + y_1$)

$\Rightarrow\ 2x = y + 7 - 12$

$\Rightarrow\ y = 2x + 5$ ...(i)

Which is also tangent to the circle $x^2 + y^2 + 16x + 12y + c = 0$

ILLUSTRATION 114: Show that the normals to the curve $x = a(\cos t + t \sin t)$; $y = a(\sin t - t \cos t)$ are tangent lines to the circle $x^2 + y^2 = a^2$.

SOLUTION: $x = a(\cos t + t \sin t)$ ...(1)

$y = a(\sin t - t \cos t)$ ...(2)

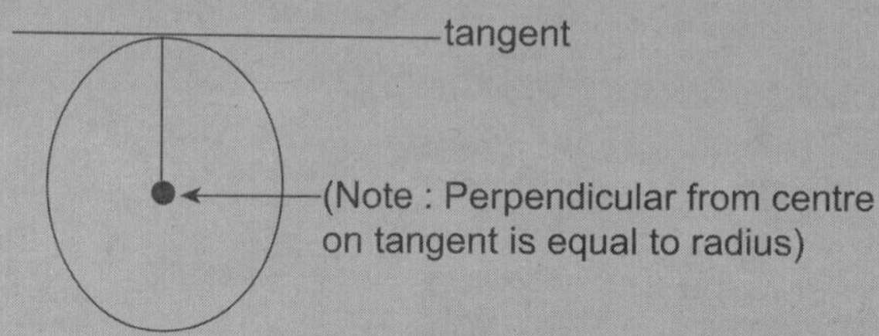

FIGURE 4.57

$$\frac{dy}{dx} = \frac{dy/dt}{dx/dt} = \frac{a(\cos t + t\sin t - \cos t)}{a(-\sin t + t\cos t + \sin t)}$$

$$\frac{dy}{dx} = \tan t \qquad \text{...(3)}$$

ILLUSTRATION 115: Find the gradient of the common tangent to the two curves $y = x^2 - 5x + 6$ and $y = x^2 + x + 1$.

SOLUTION: Let us suppose that $y = ax + b$ is the common tangent to both the curves.

Simultaneously solving $y = ax + b$ and $y = x^2 - 5x + 6$, we get

$ax + b = x^2 - 5x + 6$

Now, since $y = ax + b$ is a tangent, therefore there will be only one point of intersection of the two graphs and hence putting discriminant = 0, we get

$a^2 + 10a + 4b + 1 = 0$ ...(i)

Simultaneously solving $y = ax+b$ and $y = x^2 + x + 1$, we get

$ax + b = x^2 + x + 1$

Now, since $y = ax + b$ is a tangent, therefore there will be only one point of intersection of the two graphs and hence putting Discriminant = 0, we get

$a^2 - 2a + 4b - 3 = 0$ ...(ii)

on solving the equations (i) and (ii), we get $a = -1/3$ and $b = 5/9$

$\Rightarrow$ $3x + 9y = 5$ is the equation of the common tangent.

And solving $3x + 9y = 5$ with the curve $y = x^2 - 5x + 6$,

we get the point of contact as $(7/3, -2/9)$

Similarly solving $3x + 9y = 5$ with the curve $y = x^2 + x + 6$,

we get the point of contact as $(-2/3, 7/9)$.

Equation of Normal

$y - a(\sin t - t\cos t) = -\cot t(x - a(\cos t + t\sin t))$

$x\cos t + y\sin t - a = 0$ then length of perpendicular from the centre of circle (0, 0) upon this normal $\left|\dfrac{0+0-a}{\sqrt{\cos^2 t+\sin^2 t}}\right| = a$

= Radius of circle. Hence normal touches the circle.

Number of Solutions

We know that the equation $f(x) = g(x)$ can be solved by finding the points of intersection of the curves $y = f(x)$ and $y = g(x)$. The concept of tangency between these curves is an important tool in finding the number of roots. The following examples illustrate this method.

ILLUSTRATION 116: Find possible values of p such that the equation $px^2 = \ell nx$ has exactly one solution.

SOLUTION: Two curves must intersect at only one point. Hence

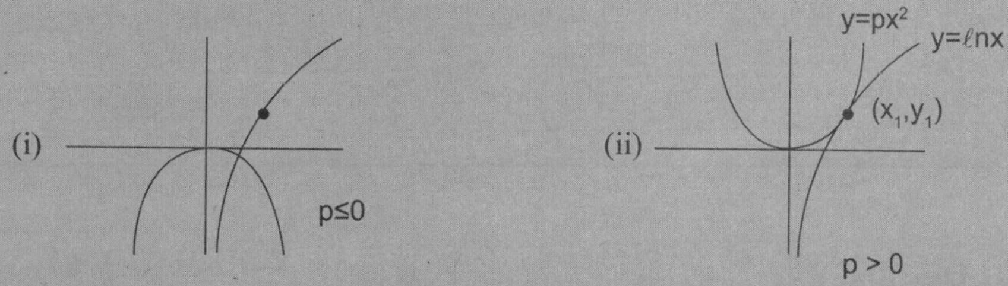

I. if $p \le 0$ then only one solution (see graph)

II. if $p > 0$

then the two curves must only touch each other

i.e., tangent at $y = px^2$ and $y = \ell$nx must have same slope at point (x_1, y_1)

$\Rightarrow 2px_1 = \dfrac{1}{x_1}$

$\Rightarrow x_1^2 = \dfrac{1}{2p}$ ...(i)

also $y_1 = px_1^2$ $\quad \Rightarrow y_1 = p\left(\dfrac{1}{2p}\right)$

$\Rightarrow y_1 = \dfrac{1}{2}$ ...(ii)

and $y_1 = \ell nx_1$ $\quad \Rightarrow \dfrac{1}{2} = \ell nx_1$

$\Rightarrow x_1 = e^{1/2}$ ...(iii)

Hence $x_1^2 = \dfrac{1}{2p}$

$\Rightarrow e = \dfrac{1}{2p}$ $\quad \Rightarrow p = \dfrac{1}{2e}$

Hence possible values of p are $(-\infty, 0] \cup \left\{\dfrac{1}{2e}\right\}$

ILLUSTRATION 117: Find the set of values of p for which the equation $|\ln x| - px = 0$ possess three distinct roots is

SOLUTION: $(y-\beta) = \dfrac{1}{\alpha}(x-\alpha)$

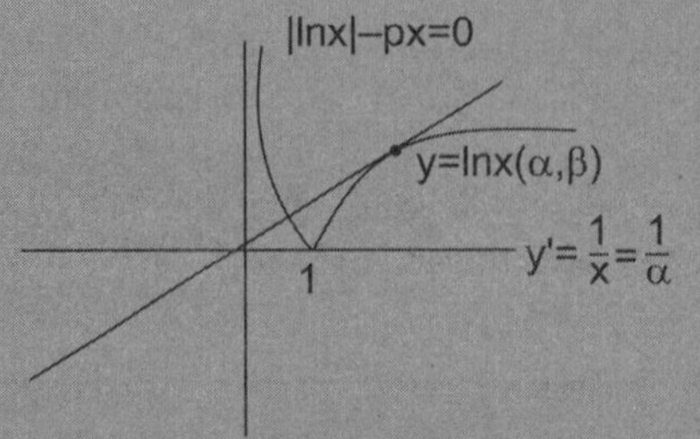

FIGURE 4.58

If it passes the origin

$-\beta = -1$ or $\beta = 1$

$y = px$

or $1 = p.e$ or $p = 1/e$ $\Rightarrow p \in (0, 1/e)$

SHORTEST DISTANCE

The shortest distance between two non-intersecting curves is found along the common normal to the two curves. In fact, if the two curves also have the largest distance between them, then it is also found along the common normal to the two curves. This can be established with the help the concept of maximum minima.

In the figure 4.59 we notice that the shortest distance between the curves is AB and the largest distance between them is

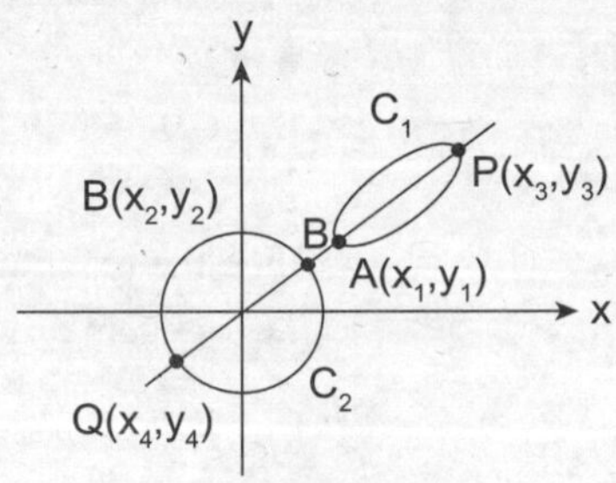

FIGURE 4.59

PQ, both of which are found along a common normal. Note that the common normal may different in two cases.

ILLUSTRATION 118: Find the shortest and the longest distance between the curves $y^2 = 8x$ and $(x-6)^2 + y^2 = 1$

SOLUTION: First of all, let us drawn the two curves

Now, since we know that the shortest and the longest distance are along the common normal, hence, we need to find the normals common to the two curves.

The normal to a centre passes through the centre and hence, every line passing though (6,0) will be a normal to the circle.

Now, we will need to find the normal from (6,0) to $y^2 = 8x$

Equation of normals on parabola from a point (x_1, y_1) is $y_1 = mx_1 - 2am - am^3$

where $(x_1, y_1) = (6,0)$ and $a = 2$

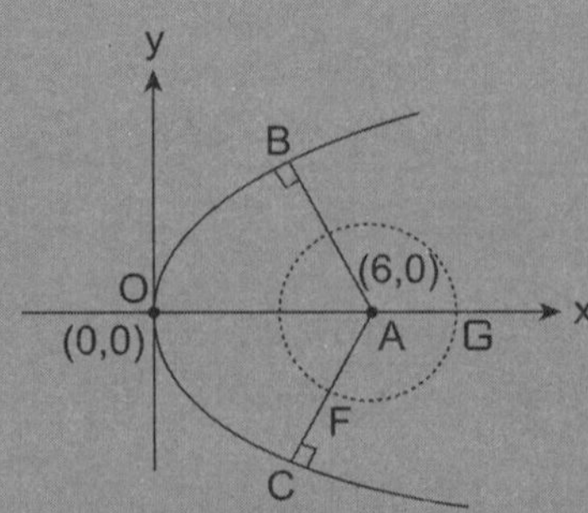

FIGURE 4.60

$\Rightarrow$ $0 = 6m - 4m - 2m^3$

$\Rightarrow$ $2m^3 + 4m - 6m = 0$

$\Rightarrow$ $2m(m^2 - 1) = 0$

$\Rightarrow$ $m(m-1)(m+1) = 0$

$\Rightarrow$ $m = 0$ or 1 or -1

Now any parametric form of the parabola $y^2 = 4ax$ can be written in the terms of slope of the normal as $(am^2, -2am)$

$\therefore$ Points on the parabola $0 \to (0, 0)$ at $m = 0$ i.e. $0 \equiv (0, 0)$

$B \to (a, 2a)$ at $m = -1$ i.e. $B \equiv (2, 4)$

$C \to (a, -2a)$ at $m = 1$ i.e. $C \equiv (2, 4)$

Now $|OA| = 6$

$|OB| = 4\sqrt{2}$

$|OC| = 4\sqrt{2}$

Therefore the shortest distance between the two curves is given by $4\sqrt{2} - 1$ $(BE = CF = 4\sqrt{2} - 1)$

Now, the longest distance should be equal to $|OC| = 6 + 1 = 7$

But the longest distance between these two curves is ∞ when m approaches ∞

$\therefore$ Shortest distance $= 4\sqrt{2} - 1$

NOTE:

1. *The distance along the common normal between the two curves are maximum or minima in their local regions only*
2. *To find the maxima/minima distance; we must also consider the end points of the curve*
3. *More elaboration would be done on the maximum/minimum distance between two curves in the chapter of maxima and minima*
4. *The concepts of coordinate geometry will be used extensively in such problems and hence it is advised to students to make sure that they are through with these concepts. For reference you can use our book of coordinate geometry*

ILLUSTRATION 119: Find the minimum distance of the point (0, 3) from the tangent drawn at the origin to the curve $3x^3 + 7x^3 + 11x^2y + 9xy^2 - 4x^2 - y^2 + xy + 2x - 3y = 0$

SOLUTION: It is important to note that the curve passes through (0, 0) and hence the equation of the tangent at (0, 0) will be $2x - 3y = 0$.

Now minimum distance from (0, 3) to $2x - 3y = 0 \Rightarrow$ the perpendicular distance from (0, 3) to $2x - 3y = 0 = \dfrac{|2\times 0 - 3\times 0|}{\sqrt{2^2 + 3^2}} = \dfrac{9}{\sqrt{13}}$

ILLUSTRATION 120: Find the shortest distance between the line $y = x - 2$ and the parabola $y = x^2 + 3x + 2$.

SOLUTION: Let $P(x_1, y_1)$ be a point closest to the line $y = x - 2$

then $\left.\frac{dy}{dx}\right|_{(x_1, y_1)}$ = slope of line

$\Rightarrow 2x_1 + 3 = 1$

$\Rightarrow x_1 = -1$

$\Rightarrow y_1 = 0$

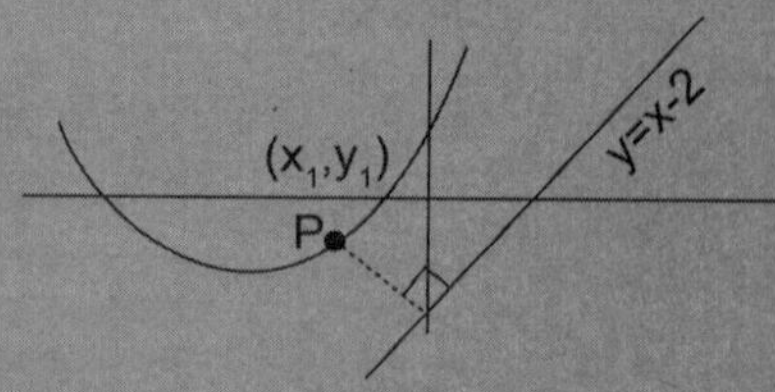

FIGURE 4.61

Hence point (– 1, 0) is the closest and its perpendicular distance from the line $y = x - 2$ will give the shortest distance

$\Rightarrow p = .\frac{3}{\sqrt{2}}$

ILLUSTRATION 121: Find the shortest and the longest between the curve $(x - 6)^2 + y^2 = 1$ and the tangent at (0,0) in the curve $x^3 + y^2 + x^2 = 0$

SOLUTION: The tangent at (0, 0) on the curve $x^3 + y^2 + x^2 = 0$ will be given by $x^2 + y^2 = 0$ which denotes the point (0, 0) only. Hence, we need to find the shortest and the longest distance from the point (0, 0) to the curve $(x - 6)^2 + y^2 = 1$

Common normal to (0, 0) and $(x - 6)^2 + y^2 = 1$ will be $y = 0$ and hence shortest distance = 5 and longest distance = 7

TEXTUAL EXERCISE–3: (SUBJECTIVE)

1. Find the angle of intersection of curves $y = x^2$ and $6y = 7 - x^3$ at (1, 1).
2. Find the angle of intersection of the ellipse $\frac{x^2}{a^2} + \frac{y^2}{b^2} = 1$ and the circle $x^2 + y^2 = ab$ at their point of intersection.
3. Find the angle of intersection of curves $y = [|\sin x| + |\cos x|]$ and $x^2 + y^2 = 5$ where $[x]$ denotes the integral part of number x.
4. Find the angle between the curves $x^3 - 3xy^2 = -2$ and $3x^2y - y^3 = 2$.
5. Find the minimum and maximum values of $[(x + 2)^2 + (y - 1)^2]^{1/2}$, if $(x - 2)^2 + (y + 1)^2 \leq 4$
6. Find the co-ordinates of the point on the curve $x^2 = 4y$ which is at least distance from the line $y = x - 4$
7. Find the shortest distance between curves $xy = 9$ and $x^2 + y^2 = 1$
8. Find the point on hyperbola $3x^2 - 4y^2 = 72$ which is nearest to the straight line $3x + 2y + 1 = 0$

Answer Keys

1. $\pi/2$ **2.** $\tan^{-1}\left(\frac{a-b}{\sqrt{ab}}\right)$ **3.** $\tan^{-1}(2)$ **4.** 90°

5. $2\sqrt{5} - 2, 2\sqrt{5} + 2$ **6.** (2, 1) **7.** $3\sqrt{2} - 1$ **8.** (–6, 3)

TEXTUAL EXERCISE–3: (OBJECTIVE)

1. The angle of intersection of curves $y = x^2$ and $6y = 7 - x^3$ at (1, 1) is
(a) $\pi/4$ (b) $\pi/3$
(c) $\pi/2$ (b) None of these

2. The angle at which the curve $y = ke^{kx}$ intersects the y-axis is
(a) $\tan^{-1}(k^2)$ (b) $\cot^{-1}(k^2)$
(c) $\sin^{-1}\left(\frac{1}{\sqrt{1+k^4}}\right)$ (d) $\sec^{-1}\left(\frac{1}{\sqrt{1+k^4}}\right)$

3. The two curves $x^3 - 3xy^2 + 2 = 0$ and $3x^2y - y^3 = 2$
(a) cut at right angles (b) touch each other
(c) cut at an angle $\pi/3$ (d) cut at an angle $\pi/4$

4. At (0, 0) the curve $y^2 = x^3 + x^2$
(a) makes an angle of 60° with OX.
(b) bisects the angle between the axes.
(c) touches x-axis
(d) None of these

5. The angle of intersection of the two curves $xy = a^2$ and $x^2 + y^2 = 2b^2$ is
(a) $\pi/3$ (b) $\pi/6$
(c) $\pi/4$ (d) None of these

6. The curves $x^3 + pxy^2 = -2$ and $3x^2y - y^3 = 2$ are orthogonal for:
(a) $p = 3$ (b) $p = -3$
(c) no value of p (d) $p = \pm 3$

7. The angle of intersection of the curve $y = x^2$ and $6y = 7 - x^3$ at (1, 1) is:
(a) $\frac{\pi}{5}$ (b) $\frac{\pi}{4}$
(c) $\frac{\pi}{3}$ (d) $\frac{\pi}{2}$

8. The gradient of the common tangent to the two curves $y = x^2 - 5x + 6$ and $y = x^2 + x + 1$ is equal to
(a) $-1/3$ (b) $-2/3$
(c) -1 (d) -3

9. If the curves $a_1x^3 + b_1y^3 = 1$ and $a_2x^3 + b_2y^3 = 1$ are orthogonal, then:
(a) $a_1a_2(b_1 - b_2)^{4/3} + b_1b_2(a_1 - a_2)^{4/3} = 0$
(b) $a_1a_2(b_1 - b_2)^{4/3} - b_1b_2(a_1 - a_2)^{4/3} = 0$
(c) $a_1a_2(a_1 - a_2)^{4/3} + b_1b_2(b_1 - b_2)^{4/3} = 0$
(d) $a_1a_2(a_1 - a_2)^{4/3} - b_1b_2(b_1 - b_2)^{4/3} = 0$

10. If the curves, $\frac{x^2}{a_1} + \frac{y^2}{b_1} = 1$ and $\frac{x^2}{a_2} + \frac{y^2}{b_2} = 1$ cut each other at right angles then:
(a) $a_1 + a_2 = b_1 + b_2$
(b) $a_1 + b_1 = a_2 + b_2$
(c) $a_1 + b_2 = a_2 + b_1$
(d) $a_1a_2(a_1 - b_1) = b_1b_2(a_2 - b_2)$

11. The angle between the tangents to the curve $\frac{x^2}{a^2} + \frac{y^2}{b^2} = 1$ at the points $(a, 0)$ and $(0, b)$ is
(a) $\frac{\pi}{4}$ (b) $\frac{\pi}{2}$
(c) $\frac{\pi}{3}$ (d) None

12. The angle between the tangents to the curves $y = \sin x$ and $y = \cos x$ at a point of intersection is equal to
(a) $\frac{\pi}{4}$ (b) $\tan^{-1} 2\sqrt{2}$
(c) $\tan^{-1}\left(\frac{1}{2\sqrt{2}}\right)$ (d) None of these

13. If two curves $y = a^x$ and $y = e^x$ intersect at an angle α, then $\tan\alpha$ equals
(a) $\left|\frac{1-\log a}{1+\log a}\right|$ (b) $\left|\frac{1+\log a}{1-\log a}\right|$
(c) $\left|\frac{\log a - 1}{\log a + 1}\right|$ (d) None of these

14. The equation of the common tangent to the curves $y^2 = 8x$ and $xy = -1$ is
(a) $3y = 9x + 2$ (b) $y = 2x + 1$
(c) $2y = x + 8$ (d) $y = x + 2$

15. Point on the line $y = 2x + 11$ that is nearest to the circle $16x^2 + 16y^2 + 32x - 8y - 50 = 0$, is
(a) $\left(-\frac{7}{2}, 4\right)$ (b) $\left(-, 2\right)$
(c) $(-3, 5)$ (d) $\left(\frac{1}{2}, 12\right)$

16. The co-ordinates of a point on the parabola $2y = x^3$ which is nearest to the point (0, 3) is:
(a) (2, 2) (b) $(-\sqrt{2}, 1)$
(c) $(\sqrt{2}, 1)$ (d) $(-2, 2)$

17. If curves $\frac{x^2}{a^2} - \frac{y^2}{b^2} = 1$ and $xy = c^2$ intersect orthogonally, then

(a) $a + b = 0$ (b) $a^2 = b^2$

(c) $a + b = c$ (d) None of these

18. The set of values of p for which the equation $|\ln x| - px = 0$ possess three distinct roots is

(a) $\left(0, \frac{1}{e}\right)$ (b) $(0, 1)$

(c) $(1, e)$ (d) $(0, e)$

19. Number of roots of the equation $x^2 . e^{2-|x|} = 1$ is:

(a) 2 (b) 4

(c) 6 (d) zero

Answer Keys

1. (c)	**2.** (b)	**3.** (a)	**4.** (b)	**5.** (c)	**6.** (b)	**7.** (d)	**8.** (a)	**9.** (a)	**10.** (c)
11. (b)	**12.** (b)	**13.** (a,c)	**14.** (d)	**15.** (b)	**16.** (a,d)	**17.** (b)	**18.** (a)	**19.** (b)	

■ LENGTH OF TANGENT, SUB-TANGENT, NORMAL, SUB-NORMAL

Let $P(x, y)$ be any point on curve $\widehat{APB}$ whose equation is $y = f(x)$ and the tangent and the normal at P meet the x-axis in T and N respectively. Drawn a perpendicular PM on the x-axis and if θ be the angle which the tangent at P makes with x-axis.

Then $\angle MPN = 90° - \angle MPT = \angle MTP = \theta$

$$\Rightarrow \tan\theta = \frac{dy}{dx}$$

$$\therefore \cot\theta = \frac{1}{dy/dx} = \frac{dx}{dy}$$

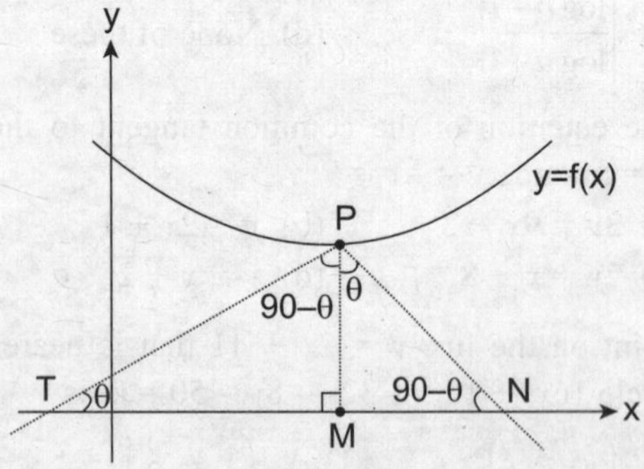

FIGURE 4.62

Length of Tangent

The portion of tangent intercepted between the point of contact and the axis of x is called the length of tangent and is denoted as

L_t ∴ In the right angled triangle PTM: $PT = PM$

$$\text{cosec}\,\theta = PM\sqrt{1+\cot^2\theta}$$

$$L_t = y\sqrt{1+\left(\frac{dx}{dy}\right)^2}$$

Length of Sub-tangent

The sub-tangent for any point (x, y) on the curve is the projection of the tangent on the x-axis.

∴ In the right angled triangle PTM: $MT = PM$

$$\cot\theta = \left(\frac{y}{dy/dx}\right)$$

Length of Normal

The portion of the normal at any point on the curve intercepted between the curve and the axis of x is called the length of the normal.

∴ In the right angled triangle MNP: $PN = PM$

$$\sec\theta = PM\sqrt{1+\tan^2\theta}$$

$$= y\sqrt{1+\left(\frac{dy}{dx}\right)^2}$$

Length of Sub-normal

The sub-normal for any point on the curve is the projection of the normal on the x -axis.

∴ In the right angled triangle MNP: $MN = PM$

$$\tan\theta = y\frac{dy}{dx}$$

ILLUSTRATION 122: The length of the sub-tangent to the curve $x^2 + xy + y^2 = 7$ at $(1, -3)$ is

(a) 3 (b) 5

(c) 15 (d) 3/5

SOLUTION: (c) Length of sub-tangent $= \dfrac{y}{dy/dx}$

Now differentiating both sides of the equation $x^2 + xy + y^2 = 7$;

we get $2x + xy' + y + 2yy' = 0$

$$\Rightarrow\ y' = \frac{-2x+y}{x+2y} \text{ and } \left.\frac{dy}{dx}\right|_{(1,-3)} = -\frac{1}{5} \quad \therefore\ S.T = (-3)(-5) = 15$$

ILLUSTRATION 123: Find the lengths of tangent, sub-tangent, normal and subnormal to $y^2 = 4ax$ at the point $(at^2, 2at)$.

SOLUTION: We have the given curve $y2 = 4ax$ ...(i)

Differentiating equation (i) both sides with respect to x we get $2y\dfrac{dy}{dx} = 4a$

$$\Rightarrow\ \left[\frac{dy}{dx}\right]_{(at^2,2at)} = \frac{4a}{4at} = \frac{1}{t}$$

Now, the length of tangent at $(x_0 = at^2, y_0 = 2at)$ is $= y\sqrt{1+\left(\dfrac{dx}{dy}\right)^2_{(x_0,y_0)}} = 2at\sqrt{1+t^2}$

$\therefore$ Length of normal at $(at^2, 2at)$ is $y\sqrt{1+\left(\dfrac{dy}{dx}\right)^2_{(x_0,y_0)}} = 2at\sqrt{1+1/t^2} = 2a\sqrt{t\quad 1}$

Length of sub-tangent $\dfrac{y_0}{[dy/dx]_{(x_0,y_0)}} = \dfrac{2at}{1/t} = 2at^2$

Length of subnormal $y_0\left[\dfrac{dy}{dx}\right]_{(x_0,y_9)} = 2at.\dfrac{1}{t} = 2a$

ILLUSTRATION 124: Show that the length of the sub-tangent is constant for the curve $y = a^x$.

SOLUTION: Equation of the curve is $y = a^x$ ...(i)

Differentiating $\dfrac{dy}{dx} = a^x \log a = y \log a$ [Using (i)]

Length of the sub-tangent $= y\dfrac{dx}{dy} = y\dfrac{1}{y\log a} = \dfrac{1}{\log a}$

which is clearly a constant.

ILLUSTRATION 125: Show that in the curve $y = be^{x/a}$,

(i) the sub-tangent at any point is of constant length,

(ii) the sub-normal varies as the square of the ordinate.

SOLUTION: Equation of the curve is $y = be^{x/a}$ ...(i)

Differentiating with respect to $\dfrac{dy}{dx} = be^{x/a}\dfrac{1}{a} = \dfrac{y}{a}$ [of (i)]

(i) Sub-tangent $= y\dfrac{dx}{dy} = y\dfrac{a}{y} = a$ which is constant

(ii) Sub-normal $= y\dfrac{dy}{dx} = y\dfrac{y}{a} = \dfrac{y^2}{a} \propto y^2$ i.e., sub-normal varies as the square of the ordinate.

ILLUSTRATION 126: Find the equations of the tangent and normal, the lengths of the tangent and the sub-tangent, the lengths of the normal and sub-normal for the ellipse: $x = a$ cos$t$, $y = b$ sin t; at the point $M(x_1, y_1)$ for which $t = \pi/4$.

SOLUTION: From the given equations, we find that $\frac{dx}{dt} = -a\sin t$; $\frac{dy}{dt} = b\cos t$

$$\frac{dy}{dx} = -\frac{b}{a}\cot t; \left(\frac{dy}{dx}\right)_{t=\pi/4} = -\frac{b}{a}$$

We find the coordinates of the point of tangency M: $x_1 = (x)_{t=\pi/4} = \frac{a}{\sqrt{2}}$, $y_1 = (y)_{t=\pi/4} = \frac{b}{\sqrt{2}}$

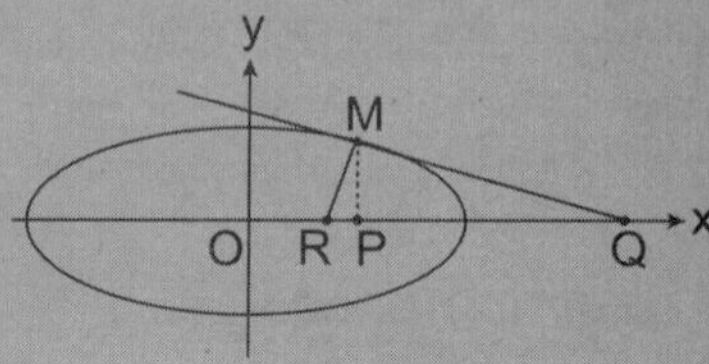

FIGURE 4.63

The equation of the tangent is: $y - \frac{b}{\sqrt{2}} = -\frac{b}{a}\left(x - \frac{a}{\sqrt{2}}\right)$

$\Rightarrow$ $bx + ay - ab\sqrt{2} = 0$

The equation of the normal is: $y - \frac{b}{\sqrt{2}} = \frac{a}{b}\left(x - \frac{a}{\sqrt{2}}\right)$

$\Rightarrow$ $(ax - by)\sqrt{2} - a^2 + b^2 = 0$

The lengths of the sub-tangent and sub-normal are $S_T = \left|\frac{b/\sqrt{2}}{-b/a}\right| = \frac{a}{\sqrt{2}}$

and $S_N = \left|\frac{b}{\sqrt{2}}\left(-\frac{b}{a}\right)\right| = \frac{b^2}{a\sqrt{2}}$

The lengths of the tangent and the normal are $T = \left|\frac{b/\sqrt{2}}{-b/a}\sqrt{(-b/a)^2 + 1}\right| = \frac{1}{\sqrt{2}}\sqrt{a^2 + b^2}$

and $N = \left|\frac{b}{\sqrt{2}}\sqrt{1 + (-b/a)^2}\right| = \frac{b}{a\sqrt{2}}\sqrt{a^2 + b^2}$

ILLUSTRATION 127: Show that in the curve $y = \ell n(x^2 - a^2)$, sum of the length of tangent and sub-tangent varies as the product of the co-ordinates of the point of contact.

SOLUTION: $y = a\,\ell n(x^2 - a^2)$

$$\frac{dy}{dx} = \frac{a.2x}{x^2 - a^2}$$

$$\text{Length of tangent} = \frac{y\sqrt{1 + \left(\frac{dy}{dx}\right)^2}}{dy/dx} = \frac{y\sqrt{1 + \left(\frac{2ax}{x^2 - a^2}\right)^2}}{\left(\frac{2ax}{x^2 - a^2}\right)}$$

$$= \frac{y\sqrt{x^4 + a^4 - 2a^2x^2 + 4a^2x^2}}{2ax} = \frac{y(x^2 + a^2)}{2ax}$$

$$\text{Length of sub-tangent } \frac{y}{dy/dx} = \frac{y(x^2 - a^2)}{2ax}$$

$$LT + ST = \frac{y(x^2 + a^2)}{2ax} + \frac{y(x^2 - a^2)}{2ax} = y.\frac{2x^2}{2ax} = \frac{yx}{a}$$

TEXTUAL EXERCISE–4: (SUBJECTIVE)

1. Show that sub-normal at any point of the curve $y = x \log_e(kx)$ is the fourth proportional for abscissa, ordinate and sum of abscissa and ordinate.

2. Show that the sub-tangnet at any point on the curve $x^a y^b = c^{a+b}$ varies as abscissa.

3. Find the length of the sub-tangent to the curve $y = e^{x/a}$.

4. Show that the curve $ay^2 = (x + b)^3$, the sub-normal varies as the square of the sub-tangent.

5. Show that the sub-tangent and sub-normal of the curve $y^n = a^{n-1}$ are nx and $\dfrac{y^2}{nx}$.

6. Prove that the sub-normal at any point of the curve $y^2x^2 = a^2(x^2 - a^2)$ varies inversely as the cube of its abscissa.

Answer Key

3. a

TEXTUAL EXERCISE–4: (OBJECTIVE)

1. The length of the subnormal to the parabola $y^2 = 4ax$ at any point is equal to
   (a) $a\sqrt{2}$ (b) $2\sqrt{2}a$
   (c) $a/\sqrt{2}$ (d) $2a$

2. If at any point on a curve the sub-tangent and subnormal are equal, the tangent which is equal to
   (a) ordinate (b) $\sqrt{2}$(ordinate)
   (c) $\sqrt{2\text{(ordinate)}}$ (d) None of these

3. Area of triangle formed by the positive x-axis and the normal and the tangent to $x^2 + y^2 = 4$ at $(1, \sqrt{3})$ is
   (a) $2\sqrt{3}$ sq. units (b) $\sqrt{3}$ sq. units
   (c) $4\sqrt{3}$ sq. units (d) None of these

4. The subnormal at any point on the curve $xy^n = a^{n+1}$ is constant for:
   (a) $n = 0$ (b) $n = 1$
   (c) $n = -2$ (d) no value of n

5. If the sub-normal at any point on $y^n = a^{1-n} . x^{n-1}$ is of constant length, then the value of n is
   (a) -2 (b) $1/2$
   (c) 1 (d) 2

6. The length of the normal at 't' on the curve $x = a(t + \sin t)$, $y = a(1 - \cos t)$ is
   (a) a $\sin t$ (b) $2a \sin^3(t/2) \sec(t/2)$
   (c) $2a \sin (t/2)$ (d) $2a \sin (t/2) \tan (t/2)$

Answer Keys

1. (d) 2. (b) 3. (a) 4. (c) 5. (d) 6. (d)

MULTIPLE CHOICE QUESTIONS

SECTION–I

OBJECTIVE SOLVED EXAMPLES

1. Tangent to the folium of descartes $x^3 + y^3 = 3axy$ at the point where it meets the parabola $y^2 = ax$ are parallel to

(a) x-axis (b) y-axis

(c) $y = x$ (d) None of these

Solution: (b) $x^3 + y^3 = 3axy = 0$

or $\frac{dy}{dx} = -\frac{f_x}{f_y} = -\frac{\{x^2 - ay\}}{\{y^2 - ax\}}$

At the point where the curve meets $y^2 = ax$ the value of $\frac{dy}{dx} = \frac{x^2 - ay}{0} = \infty$.

2. If the curve $\left(\frac{x}{a}\right)^n + \left(\frac{y}{b}\right)^n = 2$ touches the straight line $\frac{x}{a} + \frac{y}{b} = 2$, then find the value of 'n'

(a) 2 (b) 3

(c) 4 (d) any real number

Solution: (d) Given $\left(\frac{x}{a}\right)^n + \left(\frac{y}{b}\right)^n = 2$

Differentiating both side w.r.t. x, we get

$$\frac{n}{a}\left(\frac{x}{a}\right)^{n-1} + \frac{n}{b}\left(\frac{y}{b}\right)^{n-1} \times y' = 0$$

$$\Rightarrow \frac{dy}{dx} = -\frac{n}{a}\left(\frac{x}{a}\right)^{n-1} \frac{n}{b}\left(\frac{y}{b}\right)^{n-1} \quad \therefore \quad \frac{dy}{dx} at(a,b) = -\frac{b}{a}.$$

$\therefore$ Tangent is $y - b = -\frac{b}{a}(x - a)$

or $bx + ay = 2ab$ or $\frac{x}{a} + \frac{y}{b} = 2$ for all values of n

$\left(\because \frac{dy}{dx} \text{ is independent of } 'n'\right)$

3. If tangent at any point on the curve $e^y = 1 + x^2$ makes an angle θ with positive direction of x-axis, then

(a) $|\tan \theta| > 1$ (b) $|\tan \theta| < 1$

(c) $\tan \theta > 1$ (d) $|\tan \theta| \leq 1$

Solution: (d) Given $e^y = (1 + x^2)$ Taking $\log_e$ on both the sides, we get $y = \ln(1 + x^2)$

Now, $m = \tan\theta = \frac{dy}{dx} = \frac{2x}{1+x^2}$

$$\Rightarrow |\tan \theta| = \left|\frac{2x}{1+x^2}\right| = \frac{2|x|}{1+|x|^2} \leq 1$$

But we already know that $1+|x|^2 \geq 2|x|$

$(\because AM \neq G.M.) \quad \therefore \quad \frac{2|x|}{1+|x|^2} \leq 1$

4. The value of n for which the area of the triangle formed by the axes of coordinates and any tangent to the curve $x^n y = a^n$ is constant is

(a) 1/2 (b) 2

(c) 3/2 (d) 1

Solution: (d) Given $x^n y = a^n$

Differentiating both side, w.r.t x, we get $nx^{n-1} y + x^n y' = 0$

$$\Rightarrow \frac{dy}{dx} = -\frac{nx^{n-1} y}{x^n} = -\frac{ny}{x}$$

Equation of tangent is $Y - y = -\frac{ny}{x}(X - x)$

If the tangent meets the x-axis at $(A, 0)$ then putting $y = 0$ we can find the value of A

i.e., $A = x\frac{(1+x)}{x}$

And similarly, if the tangent meets the y-axis at (O, B) then putting $x = O$ we get $B = Y(1 + x)$

$$\therefore \quad \Delta = \frac{1}{2}AB = \frac{1}{2}\frac{(1+n)^2}{n}xy = \frac{1}{2}\frac{(1+n)^2}{n}x.\frac{a^n}{x^n}$$

It will be constant if $x^{n-1} = 1$ i.e., $n - 1 = 0$ or $n = 1$

5. The point P on the curve $y = x \tan \alpha - \frac{1}{2}\frac{x^2}{u^2 \cos^2 \alpha}, \alpha \in \left(0, \frac{\pi}{2}\right)$ has a tangent parallel to $y = x + 5$. If the ordinate of P is $\frac{u^2}{4}$ then $\alpha =$

(a) 15° (b) 30°

(c) 45° (d) 60°

Solution: (d) Given $y = x \tan x - \frac{1}{2}\frac{x^2}{u^2 \cos^2 x}$

$$\frac{dy}{dx} = \tan \alpha - \frac{x}{u^2}\sec^2 \alpha \quad \text{...(1)}$$

Now since it is parallel to $y = x + 5$ then $\frac{dy}{dx} = 1$

$\therefore \quad \tan x - \frac{x}{u^2}\sec^2 \alpha = 1$

$\Rightarrow x = (\tan\alpha - 1)u^2 \cos^2 a$ and

$y = \frac{u^2}{4}$ (given)

Put the value of x and y in given equation

$$\Rightarrow y = x\left[\tan\alpha - \frac{1}{2}\frac{x}{u^2\cos^2\alpha}\right]$$

$$\frac{u^2}{4} = (\tan\alpha - 1)u^2\cos^2\alpha\left[\tan\alpha - \frac{1}{2}(\tan\alpha - 1)\right]$$

or $\frac{1}{4} = (\tan\alpha - 1)\cos^2\alpha\left[\frac{\tan\alpha + 1}{2}\right]$

or $\frac{1}{2} = \cos^2\alpha.(\tan^2\alpha - 1) = \sin^2\alpha - \cos^2\alpha$

or $\frac{1}{2} = 1 - 2\cos^2\alpha$ or $\frac{1}{4} = \cos^2\alpha$

$\therefore \quad \cos\alpha = \frac{1}{2}$ only as $\alpha \in \left(0, \frac{\pi}{2}\right)$

$\Rightarrow \alpha = \frac{\pi}{3} = 60^0$

6. The tangent and normal at the point $P(at^2, 2at)$ to the parabola $y^2 = 4ax$ meet the x-axis in T and N respectively, then the angle at which the tangent at P to the parabola is inclined to the tangent at P to the circle through T, P, N is

(a) $\tan^{-1} t^2$ (b) $\cot^{-1} t^2$
(c) $\tan^{-1} |t|$ (d) $\cot^{-1} |t|$

Solution: (c) The tangent to the parabola $y^2 = 4ax$ at (x_1, y_1) i.e., a point on the conic is given by $yy_1 = 2a(x + x_1)$

$\Rightarrow T_p$ is $ty = x + at^2$ ...(1)

And N_p is $y = -tx + 2at + at^3$

Both meet x-axis i.e., $y = 0$ in $T \equiv (-at^2,0)$ and $N \equiv (2a + at^2,0)$

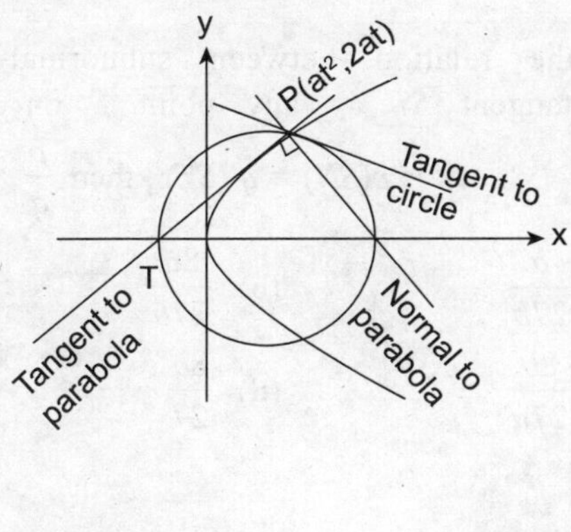

Circle through T,P,N where TP and NP are $\perp$ (being tangent and normal), is a circle on TN as diameter

$\therefore$ Equation of the circle in diametric form can be written as

and $(x + at^2)(x - 2a - at^2) + y^2 = 0$

$x^2 + y^2 - 2ax - at^2(2a + at^2) = 0$

Now tangent to the circle at point (x_1, y_1) can be given as $xx_1 + yy_1 - a(x + x_1) - at^2(2a + at^2) = 0$

Slope of tangent $-\frac{x_1 - a}{y_1} = -\frac{at^2 - a}{2at} = \frac{1 - t^2}{2t}$

Also from (1), slope of tangent to parabola is 1/t

$$\therefore \quad \tan\theta = \left|\frac{\left(\frac{1}{t} - \frac{1-t^2}{2t}\right)}{\left(1 + \frac{1-t^2}{2t^2}\right)}\right| = |t|$$

$\therefore \quad \theta = \tan^{-1}|t|$

7. The points of contact of the tangents drawn from the origin to the curve $y = \sin x$ lie on the curve

(a) $x^2 - y^2 = xy$ (b) $x^2 + y^2 = x^2y^2$
(c) $x^2 - y^2 = x^2y^2$ (d) None of these

Solution: (c) Let the tangent be drawn at the point (x, y). Its equation is $Y - y = \frac{dy}{dx}(X - x)$

But $y = \sin x$

$\therefore \quad \frac{dy}{dx} = \cos x$

$\therefore \quad Y - y = (\cos x)(X - x)$

Since it passes through (0,0), therefore substituting (x, y) by $(0, 0)$ we get $-y = -x\cos x$

or $\frac{y}{x} = \cos x$ and $y = \sin x$

$\therefore \quad \frac{y^2}{x^2} + y^2 = \cos^2 x + \sin^2 x = 1$

or $y^2 + x^2y^2 = x^2$ or $x^2 - y^2 = x^2y^2$

Hence the points of contact lie on $x^2 - y^2 = x^2y^2$

8. If the line $ax + by + c = 0$ is a normal to the curve $xy = 1$, then

(a) $a > 0, b > 0$ (c) $a > 0, b < 0$
(c) $a < 0, b > 0$ (d) $a < 0, b < 0$

Solution: (b), (c) $y = \frac{1}{x}$

$\therefore \quad \frac{dy}{dx} = -\frac{1}{x^2}$

$\therefore$ Slope of normal $= x^2$.
If $ax + by + c = 0$ is normal, then its slope of $-b/a$

$\therefore -\frac{b}{2} = x^2 \quad \Rightarrow \quad -\frac{b}{2} > 0$ or $\frac{b}{a} < 0$

i.e. a and b are of opposite signs

9. The normal to a curve at $P(x, y)$ meets the x-axis at N. If the distance of N from the origin is twice the abscissa of P, then the curve is a:
(a) ellipse (b) parabola
(c) circle (d) hyperbola

Solution: (a, d) $Y - y = \left(\frac{-1}{\frac{dy}{dx}}\right)(X - x)$.

It meets the x-axis ($Y = 0$) at N.

$\therefore N\left(y\frac{dy}{dx} + x, 0\right)$ Given $ON = \pm 2x$

$\therefore y\frac{dy}{dx} + x = \pm 2x$

or $y\,dy = x\,dx$ or $y\,dy = -3x\,dx$

Integrating $\frac{y^2}{2} = \frac{x^2}{2} - \frac{a^2}{2}$ or $\frac{y^2}{2} = -\frac{3x^2}{2} + \frac{k^2}{2}$

or $x^2 - y^2 = a^2$ or $3x^2 + y^2 = k^2$
Above equation represent hyperbola and ellipse respectively

10. A curve C has the property that if the tangent drawn at any point P on C meets the co-ordinate axes at A and B, then P is the mid-point of AB. The curve passes through the point (1, 1). The equation of the curve is
(a) $xy = 1$ (b) $y^2 = 2x - 1$
(c) $x^2 = 2y - 1$ (d) None of these

Solution: (a) Lets suppose $Y - y = \frac{dy}{dx}(X - x)$ is the equation of tangent at $P = (x, y)$

Putting $Y = 0$, we get $X = \frac{x - y}{\frac{dy}{dx}}$ and putting $X = 0$, we get $Y = y - x\frac{dy}{dx}$

$\therefore A \equiv \left(\frac{x - y}{dy/dx}, 0\right)$ and $B \equiv \left(0, y - x\frac{dy}{dx}\right)$

Now given P is the mid-point of AB

$\therefore 2x = \frac{x - y}{\frac{dy}{dx}}$ and $2y = y - x\frac{dy}{dx}$

$\Rightarrow -\frac{y}{x} = \frac{dy}{dx} \quad \Rightarrow xdy + ydx = 0$

[Now, since the portion differentiation of xy is $xdy + y\,dx$]
[$\therefore \int xdy + ydx = xy$]
on integrating both sides, we get $x\,y = \lambda$
It passes through (1, 1)
$\therefore \lambda = 1$
$\therefore xy = 1$ is the required equation of the curve

11. For the curve $y = be^{x/a}$
(a) the sub-tangent is of constant length
(b) the sub-normal is of constant length
(c) the sub-normal varies as the square of ordinate
(d) the sub-tangent varies as the radius vector

Solution: (a), (c) The given curve is $y = be^{x/a}$
Let us consider a point (x_1, y_1) on the curve
Then $y_1 = be^{x_1/a}$ ...(i)
Differentiating the curve $y = be^{x/a}$,
with respect to we get $\frac{dy}{dx} = be^{x/a} \cdot \frac{1}{a}$

$\therefore \left(\frac{dy}{dx}\right)_{(x_1, y_1)} = \frac{b}{a}e^{x_1/a}$ .... (ii)

Thus, the length of sub-tangent $= \left|y_1\left(\frac{dx}{dy}\right)_{(x_1, y_1)}\right|$

$= \left|y_1 \frac{a}{be^{x_1/a}}\right| = \left|be^{x_1/a}\frac{a}{be^{x_1/a}}\right| = a$ (constant) [using (i) and (ii)]

Again, length of subnormal $= \left|y_1\left(\frac{dy}{dx}\right)_{(x_1, y_1)}\right|$

$= \left|be^{x_1/a}\frac{be^{x_1/a}}{a}\right|$

$= \frac{1}{a}\left(be^{x_1/a}\right)^2 = \frac{1}{a}y^2$. Therefore, sub-normal varies as the square of ordinate

12. If the relation between subnormal SN and sub-tangent ST ay any point S on the curve $by^2 = (x + a)^3$ is $p(SN) = q\,(ST)^2$, then $\frac{p}{q} =$

(a) $\frac{a}{27b}$ (b) $\frac{8a}{27b}$
(c) $\frac{8b}{27a}$ (d) $\frac{8b}{27}$

Solution: (d) Here $by^2 = (x + a)^3$, differentiating both sides, we get

$$2by\frac{dy}{dx} = 3(x+a)^2 .1 \Rightarrow \frac{dy}{dx} = \frac{3}{2}\frac{(x+a)^2}{by}$$

∴ Length of subnormal

$$\Rightarrow SN = y\frac{dy}{dx} = \frac{3}{2}\frac{(x+a)^2}{b} \quad ..(1)$$

And length of sub-tangent

$$\Rightarrow ST = y/\frac{dx}{dy} = \frac{2by^2}{3(x+a)^2} \quad ...(2)$$

$$\frac{p}{q} = \frac{(ST)^2}{(SN)} \text{ (given)}$$

$$\Rightarrow \frac{p}{q} = \frac{(2by^2)^2 .2b}{\{3(x+a)^2\}^2 .3(x+a)^2} \text{ \{Using (1) and (2)\}}$$

$$= \frac{8b}{27}\frac{\{(x+a)^3\}^2}{(x+a)^6} \text{ \{Using } by^2 = (x+a)^3\text{\}}$$

$$= \frac{8b}{27}$$

$$\therefore \frac{p}{q} = \frac{8b}{27}$$

13. The angle of intersection of curves, $y = [|\sin x| + |\cos x|]$ and $x^2 + y^2 = 5$ where, [.] denotes the greatest integer function is

(a) $\tan^{-1}(2)$ (b) $\tan^{-1}(1//2)$

(c) $\tan^{-1}(\sqrt{2})$ (d) $\frac{\pi}{2}$

Solution: (a) [Since $(|\sin x| + |\cos x|)^2 = \sin^2 x + \cos^2 x + 2|\sin x| \times |\cos x| = 1 + |\sin 2x| \geq 1$

And $1 + |\sin 2x| \leq 2$

$$\Rightarrow \sqrt{1+|\sin 2x|} \geq 1$$

$$\Rightarrow |\sin x| + |\cos x| \leq \sqrt{2} \text{ and therefore}$$

$$\sqrt{2} \leq |\sin x| + |\cos x| \leq \sqrt{2}$$

∴ $y = [|\sin x| + |\cos x|] = 1 \ \forall \ x \in \mathbb{R}$

Let P and Q be the points of intersection of given curves

Clearly the given curves meet at points where $y = 1$ so, we get $x^2 + 1 = 5$

$x = \pm 2$

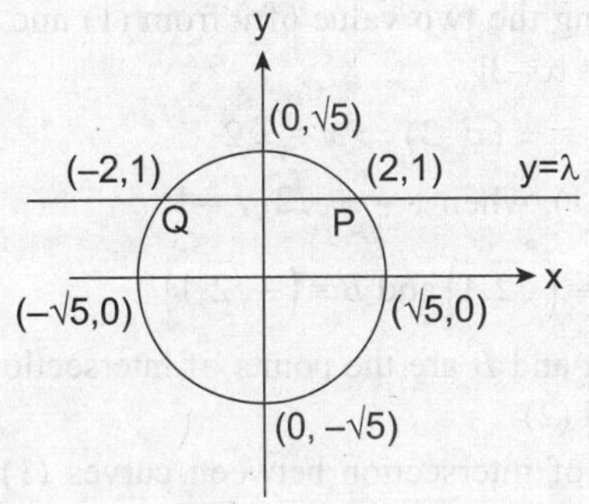

Now P(2,1) and Q (–2,1)

Now, $x^2 + y^2 = 5$

Differentiating the above equation with respect to x, we get $2x + 2y\frac{dy}{dx} = 0 \Rightarrow \frac{dy}{dx} = -\frac{x}{y}$

$$\therefore \left(\frac{dy}{dx}\right)_{(2,1)} = -2 \text{ and } \left(\frac{dy}{dx}\right)_{(-2,1)} = 2$$

Clearly slope of line $y = 1$ is zero and the slope of the tangents at P and Q are (–2) and (2) respectively.

Thus, the angle of intersection is $\tan^{-1}(2)$

14. The acute angles between the curves $y = |x^2 - 1|$ and $y = |x^2 - 3|$ at their points of intersection is

(a) $\tan^{-1}\left(\frac{4\sqrt{2}}{7}\right)$ (b) $\tan\left(\frac{5\sqrt{2}}{7}\right)$

(c) $\tan^{-1}\left(\frac{3\sqrt{2}}{7}\right)$ (d) $\tan^{-1}\left(\frac{2\sqrt{2}}{7}\right)$

Solution: (a) Given curves are $y = |x^2 - 1|$ ...(1)

And $y = |x^2 - 3|$ ...(2)

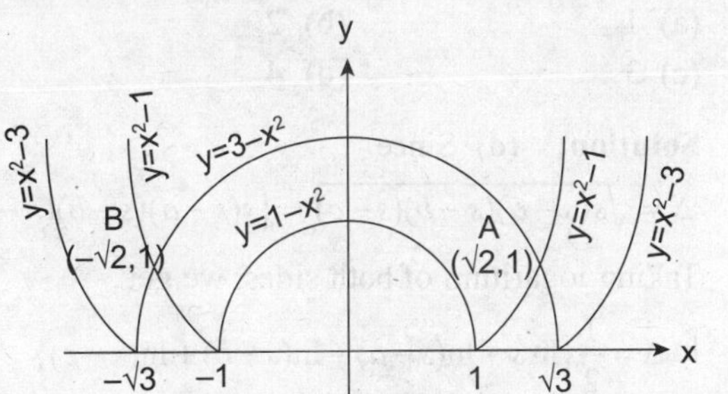

$$y = \begin{Bmatrix} x^2 - 1, \forall |x| \geq 1 \\ 1 - x^2, \forall |x| \leq 1 \end{Bmatrix} \quad ...(3)$$

$$\text{And } y = \begin{Bmatrix} x^2 - 3, \forall |x| \geq \sqrt{3} \\ 3 - x^2, \forall |x| \leq \sqrt{3} \end{Bmatrix} \quad ...(4)$$

Equating the two value of y from (1) and (2), we get
$|x^2-1| = |x^2-3|$
or $x^2-1 = \pm (x^2-3) \Rightarrow x = \pm 2$
From (1), when $x = \pm \sqrt{2}, y = 1$

Let $A \equiv (\sqrt{2},1)$ and $B \equiv (-\sqrt{2},1)$

Here A and B are the points of intersection of curves (1) and (2)

Angle of intersection between curves (1) and (2) at $A(\sqrt{2},1)$:

From (3), $\left(\frac{dy}{dx}\right)_{at(\sqrt{2},1)} = (2x-0) = 2\sqrt{2} = m_1$ (say)

From (4), $\left(\frac{dy}{dx}\right)_{at(\sqrt{2},1)} = (-2x)_{at(\sqrt{2},1)} = -2\sqrt{2} = m_2$ (say)

Let θ be the acute angle between curves (1) and (2) at A, then

$$\tan\theta = \left|\frac{m_1-m_2}{1+m_1m_2}\right| = \left|\frac{2\sqrt{2}+2\sqrt{2}}{1-8}\right| = \frac{4\sqrt{2}}{7}$$

$$\Rightarrow \theta = \tan^{-1}\left(\frac{4\sqrt{2}}{7}\right)$$

15. With the usual meaning for a, b, c and s if Δ be the area of a triangle, if then the error in Δ, *i.e.*, ($\delta\ \Delta$) resulting from a small error in the measurement of c i.e., (δc) is given by $\delta\Delta = \frac{\Delta}{K}\left(\frac{1}{s}+\frac{1}{s-a}+\frac{1}{s-b}-\frac{1}{s-c}\right)\delta c$, then find the value of 'k'

(a) 1 (b) 2
(c) 3 (d) 4

Solution: (d) Since

$$\Delta = \sqrt{s(s-a)(s-b)(s-c)} = \{s(s-a)(s-b)(s-c)\}^{1/2}$$

Taking logarithm of both sides, we get

$$\ln\Delta = \frac{1}{2}\{\ln s + \ln(s-a) + \ln(s-b) + \ln(s-c)\}$$

Differentiating both sides w.r.t 'c', we get

$$\frac{1}{\Delta}\frac{d\Delta}{dc} = \frac{1}{2}\left\{\frac{1}{s}\cdot\frac{ds}{dc} + \frac{1}{(s-a)}\cdot\frac{d(s-a)}{dc} + \frac{1}{(s-b)}\cdot\frac{d(s-b)}{dc}\right\} \quad \text{.... (1)}$$

But $s = \frac{1}{2}(a+b+c)$

$$\therefore \left(\frac{ds}{dc} = \frac{1}{2}\left(\frac{da}{dc}+\frac{db}{dc}+\frac{dc}{dc}\right)\right) \text{ and}$$

$$\because \frac{da}{dc} = \frac{db}{dc} = 0 \text{ and}$$

$$\Rightarrow \frac{dc}{dc} = 1 \qquad \Rightarrow \frac{ds}{dc} = \frac{1}{2}$$

Similarly $\frac{d(s-a)}{dc} = \frac{ds}{dc} - \frac{da}{dc} = \frac{1}{2}$ and

$\frac{d(s-b)}{dc} = \frac{ds}{dc} - \frac{db}{dc} = \frac{1}{2}$ and

$\frac{d(s-c)}{dc} = \frac{ds}{dc} - \frac{dc}{dc} = -\frac{1}{2}$

Therefore from (1),

$$\frac{1}{\Delta}\cdot\frac{\delta\Delta}{\delta c} = \frac{1}{2}\left\{\frac{1}{s}\cdot\frac{1}{2} + \frac{1}{(s-a)}\cdot\frac{1}{2} + \frac{1}{(s-b)}\frac{1}{2} - \frac{1}{(s-c)}\frac{1}{2}\right\}$$

$$\Rightarrow \frac{1}{\Delta}\cdot\frac{\delta\Delta}{\delta c} = \frac{1}{4}\left\{\frac{1}{s} + \frac{1}{(s-a)} + \frac{1}{(s-b)} - \frac{1}{(s-c)}\right\}$$

Therefore $\delta\Delta = \frac{\Delta}{4}\left(\frac{1}{s}+\frac{1}{s-a}+\frac{1}{s-b}-\frac{1}{s-c}\right)\delta c$

16. If the tangent at any point P $(4m^2, 8m^3)$ of $x^3 - y^2 = 0$ is also the equation of the normal to the curve $x^3 - y^2 = 0$ at some other point Q, then 9m^2 is equal to

(a) 1 (b) 2
(c) 3 (d) None of these

Solution: (b) $y^2 = x^3$ ...(1)

$$\Rightarrow 2y \times \frac{dy}{dx} = 3x^2$$

Therefore slope of tangent at

$$P = \left.\frac{dy}{dx}\right|_P = \left.\frac{3x^2}{y^2}\right|_{(4m^2,8m^3)} = 3m$$

$\therefore$ Equation of tangent at P: $y - 8m^3 = 3m(x - 4m^2)$

$y = 3mx - 4m^3$ ...(2)

It cuts curve again at point Q, then solving (1) and (2); we get $x = 4m^2$ or m^2

Now putting $x = 4m^2$; we get $y = 8m^3$ which will give us point P only

Hence put $x = m^2$ in equation (2)

$\Rightarrow y = 3m(m^2) - 4m^3 = -m^3$

$\therefore$ Q is $(m^2, -m^3)$

Slope of tangent at

$$Q = \left.\frac{dy}{dx}\right|_{(m^2-m^3)} = \frac{3(m^4)}{2\times(-m^3)} = \frac{-3}{2}m$$

Slope of normal at $Q = \frac{1}{(-3/2)m} = \frac{2}{3m}$

Since tangent at P is normal at Q

$\therefore$ Equating the slopes of the two lines, we get

$$\frac{2}{3m} = 3m \Rightarrow 9m^2 = 2$$

17. For the curve $x^2 y^3 = c$ (where c is a constant) the portion of the tangent between the axes is divided in the ratio

(a) 3: 5 (b) 2: 5
(c) 3: 2 (d) 1: 5

Solution: (c) Given curve is $x^2y^3 = c$ .... (1)

Differentiating *w.r.t.x*, we get $\frac{dy}{dx} = \frac{-2y}{3x}$

$\Rightarrow$ equation of tangent at general point (x, y) is

$$Y - y = -\frac{2}{3}\frac{y}{x}(X - x)\ B = \left(0, \frac{5}{2}y\right)$$

x - intercept $= \frac{5}{2}x, y - \text{intercept} = \frac{5}{3}y,$

$\Rightarrow A = \left(\frac{5}{2}X, 0\right)$ and Let AP: $PB = k$: 1

$$\Rightarrow P \equiv \left(\frac{5x}{2(k+1)}, \frac{5ky}{3(k+1)}\right)$$

$$\Rightarrow \frac{5ky}{3(k+1)} = x \text{ and } \frac{5ky}{3(k+1)} = y$$

$\Rightarrow k = \frac{3}{2}$ from both equations,

Thus P divies AB in ratio 3: 2

Alternate: For $x^m y^n = c$ $(m, n > 0)$

The portion of tangent between the axes is divided in the ratio n: m.

Therefore required ratio is 3: 2

18. Two curves C_1: $y = x^2 - 3$ and C_2: $y = kx^2, k \in R$ intersect each other at two different points. The tangent drawn to C_2 at one of the points of intersection $A \equiv (a, y_1)$, $(a > 0)$ meets C_1 again at $B(1, y_2)$ $(y_1 \neq y_2)$. The value of 'a' is

(a) 4 (b) 3
(c) 2 (d) 1

Solution: (b) Point $A(a, y_1)$ lies on C_1 and C_2 hence $y_1 = a^2 - 3$ and $y_2 = ka^2$

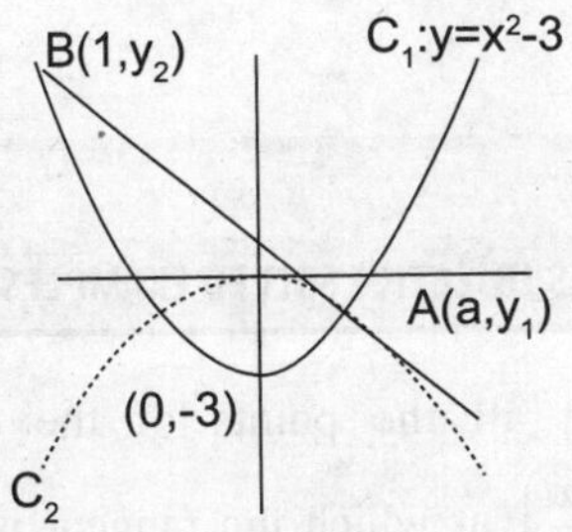

$\Rightarrow a^2 - 3 = ka^2$ ....(1)

now $y = kx^2 \Rightarrow \frac{dy}{dx} = 2kx$

$\therefore \left.\frac{dy}{dx}\right]_{(a, y_1)} = 2ka = \frac{y_2 - y_1}{1-a}$ (But $y_2 = 1 - 3 = -2$)

$$= \frac{-2-(a^2-3)}{1-a}$$

$$\Rightarrow 2ka = \frac{1-a^2}{1-a} = 1 + a$$

$2ka = 1 + a$ .....(2)

Substituting $k =$ ———— from (1) in (2) we get

$$\frac{2a(a^2-3)}{a^2} = 1 + a$$

$\Rightarrow 2a^2 - 6 = a + a^2 \quad \Rightarrow a^2 - a - 6 = 0$

$\Rightarrow a = +3, a = -2$ (rejected)

19. If the side of a triangle vary slightly in such a way that its circum radius remains constant, then, $\frac{da}{\cos A} + \frac{db}{\cos B} + \frac{dc}{\cos C}$ is equal to:

(a) $6R$ (b) $2R$
(c) 0 (d) $2R(dA + dB + dC)$

Solution: (c), (d) Given $\frac{a}{\sin A} = \frac{b}{\sin B} = \frac{c}{\sin C}$

$= 2R$ (say)

$\therefore\ da = 2R \cos A\, dA,\ db = 2R \cos B\, dB$

$dc = 2R \cos C\, dC$

$$\therefore \frac{da}{\cos A} + \frac{db}{\cos B} + \frac{dc}{\cos C}$$

$= 2R\,(dA + dB + dC)$ ....(1)

Also $A + B + C = \pi$

So, $dA + dB + dC = 0$ ....(2)

From equations (1) and (2) we get

$$\frac{da}{\cos A} + \frac{db}{\cos B} + \frac{dc}{\cos C} = 0$$

SECTION–II

SUBJECTIVE SOLVED EXAMPLES

1. Prove that all the points of the curve $y^2 = 4a\left(x + a\sin\frac{x}{a}\right)$ at which the tangent is parallel to the axis of x, lie on a parabola.

Solution: Let (x_1, y_1) be a point on $y^2 = 4a\left(x + a\sin\frac{x}{a}\right)$ ...(i)

the tangent at which is parallel to x-axis

$\therefore\ y_1^2 = 4a\left(x_1 + a\sin\frac{x_1}{a}\right)$ ...(ii)

Differentiating (i), $2y\frac{dy}{dx}$

$= 4a\left(1 + a\cos\frac{x_1}{a}\frac{1}{a}\right)$

or $\frac{dy}{dx} = \frac{2a}{y}\left(1 + \cos\frac{x_1}{a}\right)$

$\therefore$ Slope of tangent at $(x_1, y_1) = \frac{2a}{y_1}\left(1 + \cos\frac{x_1}{a}\right)$

Since tangent at (x_1, y_1) is parallel to x-axis

$\therefore$ Slope of tangent at $(x_1, y_1) = 0$

$\therefore\ \frac{2a}{y_1}\left(1 + \cos\frac{x_1}{a}\right) = 0$

or $1 + \cos\frac{x_1}{a} = 0$

$\cos\frac{x_1}{a} = -1$

$\therefore\ \sin\frac{x_1}{a} = \sqrt{1 - \cos^2\frac{x_2}{a}} = \sqrt{1-1} = 0$

$\therefore$ From (ii), $y_1^2 = 4ax_1$

$\therefore\ (x_1, y_1)$ lies on $y^2 = 4ax$, which is a parabola.

2. The tangent represented by the graph of the function $y = f(x)$ at the point with abscissa $x = 1$ form an angle $\pi/6$ and at the point $x = 2$ an angle of $\pi/3$ and at the point $x = 3$ an angle of $\pi/4$. Then find the value of $\int_1^3 f'(x)\, f''(x)\,dx + \int_2^3 f''(x)\,dx$.

Solution: Given at $x = 1$, $\frac{dy}{dx} = \tan\pi/6 = 1/\sqrt{3}$

or at $x = 1$

$\Rightarrow f'(1) = \tan\pi/6 = 1/\sqrt{3}$

also at $x = 2$ $\qquad \Rightarrow f'(2) = \tan\pi/3 = \sqrt{3}$

and at $x = 3$ $\qquad \Rightarrow f'(3) = \tan\pi/4 = 1$

Then, $\int_1^3 f'(x)\, f''(x)\,dx + \int_2^3 f''(x)\,dx$

Let $f'(x) = t$; $f''(x)\,dx = dt$

$\Rightarrow \int_{f'(1)}^{f'(3)} t\,dt + \left[f'(x)\right]_2^3$

$\Rightarrow \frac{1}{2}\left[t^2\right]_{f'(1)}^{f'(3)} + \{f'(3) - f'(2)\}$

$\Rightarrow \frac{1}{2}\{(f'(3))^2 - (f'(1))^2\} + \{f'(3) - f'(2)\}$

$\Rightarrow \frac{1}{2}\left\{(1)^2 - \left(\frac{1}{\sqrt{3}}\right)^2\right\} + \{1 - \sqrt{3}\}$

$\Rightarrow \frac{1}{2}\left(1 - \frac{1}{3}\right) + (1 - \sqrt{3})$

$\Rightarrow \frac{4}{3} - \sqrt{3} \qquad \Rightarrow \frac{4 - 3\sqrt{3}}{3}$

3. The angles of a triangle are calculated from the sides a, b, c. If small changes δa, δb, δc are made in sides show that approximately $\delta A = \frac{a}{2\Delta}\{\delta a - \delta b.\cos C - \delta c.\cos B\}$ where Δ is the area of the triangle and A, B, C are the angles opposite to a, b, c respectively. Verify that $\delta A + \delta B + \delta C = 0$

Solution: From cosine rule $\cos A = \frac{b^2 + c^2 - a^2}{2bc}$

or $2\cos A = \frac{b^2 + c^2 - a^2}{bc}$ ...(i)

Differentiating both sides, we get $-2\sin A\ \delta A =$

$\frac{bc\{2b\,\delta b + 2c\,\delta c - 2a\,\delta a\} - (b^2 + c^2 - a^2)(b\,\delta c + c\,\delta b)}{(bc)^2}$

$-2bc\sin A.\ \delta A$

$= \frac{(b^2c - c^3 + a^2c)\delta b + (bc^2 - b^3 + a^2b)\delta c - 2abc\,\delta a}{bc}$

$$\Rightarrow\ -2bc\left(\frac{2\Delta}{bc}\right).\delta A$$

$$=\frac{c(a^2-b^2-c^2)\delta b+b(a^2+c^2-b^2)\delta c-2abc\,\delta a}{bc}$$

$$\left\{\ \Delta=-bc\sin A\right\}$$

$$\Rightarrow\ -4\Delta.\delta A$$

$$=\frac{c(2ab\cos C)\delta b+b(2ac\cos B)\delta c-2abc\,\delta a}{bc}$$

$$\therefore\quad \delta A=\frac{a}{2\Delta}\{\delta a-\delta b.\cos C-\delta c.\cos B\} \qquad ...(ii)$$

Similarly, $\delta B=\frac{b}{2\Delta}\{\delta b-\delta c.\cos A-\delta a.\cos C\}$ ...(iii)

and $\delta C=\frac{c}{2\Delta}\{\delta c-\delta a.\cos B-\delta b.\cos A\}$ ...(iv)

Adding (ii), (iii) and (iv) we get

$$\delta A+\delta B+\delta C=\frac{\delta a}{2\Delta}\{a-b\cos C-c.\cos B\}\ +$$

$$\frac{\delta b}{2\Delta}\{b-a\cos C-c.\cos A\}\ +$$

$$\frac{\delta c}{2\Delta}\{c-a\cos B-b.\cos A\}$$

$$=\frac{\delta a}{2\Delta}(a-a)+\frac{\delta b}{2\Delta}(b-b)+\frac{\delta c}{2\Delta}(c-c)=0$$

Hence $\delta A+\delta B+\delta C=0$

4. Find the condition that the line $x\cos\alpha + y\sin\alpha = p$ may touch the curve $\left(\frac{x}{a}\right)^m+\left(\frac{y}{b}\right)^m=1$

Solution: Given equation: $\left(\frac{x}{a}\right)^m+\left(\frac{y}{b}\right)^m=1$

Differentiating the equation of curve with respect to x

we get, m $\left(\frac{x}{a}\right)^{m-1}+m\left(\frac{y}{b}\right)^{m-1}\frac{1}{b}\frac{dy}{dx}=0$

on simplifying we get $\frac{dy}{dx}=\frac{-b^m x^{m-1}}{a^m y^{m-1}}$

Hence, at any point $p\ (x_1, y_1)$ on the curve,

Slope of tangent $=\left(\frac{dy}{dx}\right)_{(x_1,y_1)}=\frac{-b^m x_1^{m-1}}{a^m y_1^{m-1}}$

$\therefore$ Equation of tangent at p is

$$y-y_1=\frac{-b^m x_1^{m-1}}{a^m y_1^{m-1}}(x-x_1)$$

$$\Rightarrow\ \frac{yy_1^{m-1}}{b^m}-\frac{y_1^m}{b^m}=-\frac{x\,x_1^{m-1}}{a^m}+\frac{x_1^m}{a^m}$$

i.e., $\frac{x}{a}\left(\frac{x_1}{a}\right)^{m-1}+\frac{y}{b}\left(\frac{y_1}{b}\right)^{m-1}$

$$=\left(\frac{x_1}{a}\right)^m+\left(\frac{y_1}{b}\right)^m=1$$

(since p lies on the curve at any point)

Hence, the equation of tangent at $P(x_1, y_1)$ on the curve is,

$$\frac{x}{a}\left(\frac{x_1}{a}\right)^{m-1}+\frac{y}{b}\left(\frac{y_1}{b}\right)^{m-1}=1 \qquad ...(i)$$

and $x\cos\alpha + y\sin\alpha = P$ ...(ii)

If equation (ii) is the equation of tangent, then coefficients of (i) and (ii) must be proportional for point (x_1, y_1) i.e., $\frac{\cos\alpha}{\frac{1}{a}\left(\frac{x_1}{a}\right)^{m-1}}=\frac{\sin\alpha}{\frac{1}{b}\left(\frac{y_1}{b}\right)^{m-1}}=\frac{P}{1}$

This gives $\frac{x_1}{a}=\left(\frac{a\cos\alpha}{P}\right)^{\frac{1}{m-1}}$;

$$\frac{y_1}{b}=\left(\frac{b\sin\alpha}{P}\right)^{\frac{1}{m-1}}$$

Since point $P(x_1,\ y_1)$ lies on the curve,

$$\left(\frac{x_1}{a}\right)^m+\left(\frac{y_1}{b}\right)^m=1$$

i.e. $\left(\frac{a\cos\alpha}{P}\right)^{\frac{m}{m-1}}+\left(\frac{b\sin\alpha}{P}\right)^{\frac{m}{m-1}}=1$

i.e., $(a\cos\alpha)^{\frac{m}{m-1}}+(b\sin\alpha)^{\frac{m}{m-1}}=p^{\frac{m}{m-1}}$.

This is the required condition.

5. Show that if $P(x)$ is a polynomial of odd degree greater than 1, then through any point P in the plane, there will be atleast one tangent line to the curve $y = P(x)$. Is this true if $P(x)$ is a curve of even degree?

Solution: If $y = P(x)$, where $P(x)$ is a polynomial of odd degree $d > 1$, then through any point $P\ (a, b)$ there will be atleast one tangent to the curve if and only if $(y - b) = P'(x)\ (x - a)$

or $\{P(x)-b\}=P'(x)\ \{(x-a)\}$ has a real solution

But $xP'(x)-P(x)-aP'(x)+b\ =0$ has a degree 'd' with leading coefficient (d -1) times the leading coefficient of $P(x)$ and by intermediate value theorem it has root (real) i.e., There is a real number x_0 for which tangent to $y = P(x)$ at $\{x_0, P(x_0)\}$ passes through $P(a, b)$. For even degree it may not be true (Consider $y = x^2$).

6. Find the equation of tangents drawn to the curve $y^2 - 2x^2 - 4y + 8 = 0$ from the point (1, 2).

Solution: $y^2 - 2x^2 - 4y + 8 = 0$

$$2y\frac{dy}{dx} - 4x - 4\frac{dy}{dx} = 0$$

$$\therefore \quad \frac{dy}{dx} = \frac{4x}{2y-4}$$

$$\left(\frac{dy}{dx}\right)_{(h,k)} = \frac{4h}{2y-4} = \frac{4h}{2k-4}$$

Equation of tangent $(y - k) = \dfrac{4h}{(2k-4)}(x-h)$

Passes through (1, 2)

$(2 - k)(2k - 4) = 4h(1 - h)$

$4k - 2k^2 - 8 + 4k = 4h - 4h^2$

$4k - k^2 - 4 = 2h - 2h^2$

or $-2h^2 + k^2 + 2h - 4k + 4 = 0$

or $k^2 - 2h^2 - 4k + 8 = 0$

$2h - 4 = 0$ or $h = 2$

$k = 0$ or 4

Equation at (2,0), $y = \dfrac{8}{-4}(x-2)$

Or $y = -2x + 4$ or $2x = 4$

$\therefore$ Equation at (2,4) be $y = 2x$

7. The tangent to curve $y = x - x^3$ at point P meets the curve again at Q. Prove that one point of trisection of PQ lies on y – axis. Find locus of other point of trisection

Solution: $(y - k_1) = (1 - 3h_1^2)(x - h_1)$

$(k_2 - k_1) = (1 - 3h_1^2)(h_2 - h_1)$

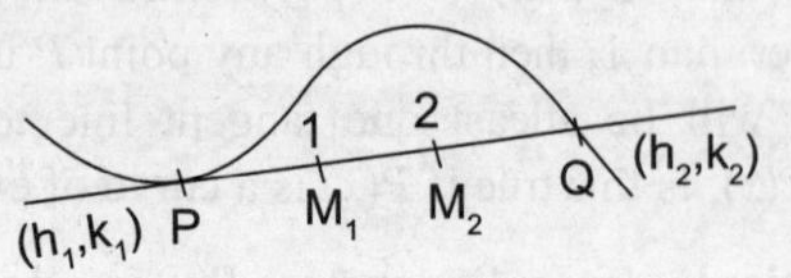

$$(h_2 - h_2^3 - h_1 + h_1^3) = (1 - 3h_1^2)(h_2 - h_1)$$

$$(h_2 - h_1) - (h_2 - h_1)(h_2^2 + h_1^2 + h_1h_2) = (1 - 3h_1^2)(h_2 - h_1)$$

$$1 - h_2^2 - h_2^2 - h_1h_2 = 1 - 3h_1^2$$

$$2h_1^2 - h_2^2 - h_1h_2 = 0$$

$$2h_1^2 - 2h_1h_2 + h_1h_2 - h_2^2 = 0$$

$(h_1 - h_2)(2h_1 + h_2) = 0$

$h_1 = h_{2/2}$

$$M_1\left(\frac{h_2 + 2h_1}{3}, \frac{k_1 + 2k_1}{3}\right)$$

$$M_2\left(\frac{h_1 + 2h_2}{3}, \frac{k_1 + 2k_2}{3}\right)$$

$$k = \frac{h_2}{h} = -h_1$$

$$k = \frac{3h_1 + 15h_1^3}{3} = h - 5h^3 \text{ or } y = x - 5x^3$$

8. A variable ΔABC in the xy plane has its orthocenter at vertex 'B', a fixed vertex 'A' at the origin and the third vertex 'C' restricted to lie on the parabola $y = 1 + \dfrac{7x^2}{36}$. The point B starts at the point (0, 1) at time $t = 0$ and moves upwards along the y axis at a constant velocity of 2cm/sec. How fast is the area of the triangle increasing when $t = \dfrac{7}{2}$ sec.

Solution: $at = 0 \qquad x = 0, y = 1$

$$\frac{dy}{dt} = 2\,\text{cm/sec}$$

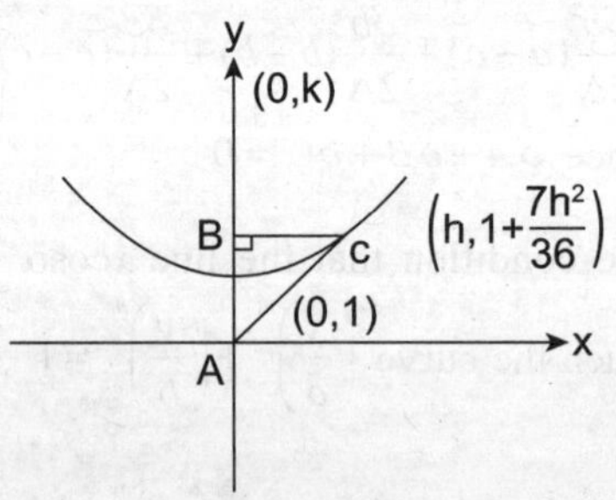

$$A = \frac{1}{2} \times h \times \left(1 + \frac{7h^2}{36}\right)$$

$$\frac{dA}{dt}\left(\frac{1}{2}\left(1 + \frac{7h^2}{36}\right) + \frac{h}{2}\left(\frac{14h}{36}\right)\right)\frac{dh}{dt}$$

$$\frac{dA}{dt} = \left(\frac{1}{2} \times 8 + 3 \times \frac{14 \times 6}{36}\right) \times \frac{6}{7} = (4+7) \times \frac{6}{7}$$

$$= \frac{66}{7}\,\text{cm}^2/\text{sec}$$

9. In an acute triangle ABC if sides a, b be constants and the base angles A and B vary, show that

$$\frac{dA}{\sqrt{a^2 - b^2 \sin^2 A}} = \frac{dB}{\sqrt{b^2 - a^2 \sin^2 B}}$$

Solution: $\dfrac{a}{\sin A} = \dfrac{b}{\sin B}$

or $b \sin A = a \sin B$

$b \cos A \, dA = a \cos B \, dB$

$$\frac{dA}{a\cos B} = \frac{dB}{b\cos A}$$

$$\Rightarrow \frac{dA}{a\sqrt{1-\sin^2 B}} = \frac{dB}{b\sqrt{1-\sin^2 A}}$$

$$\frac{dA}{a\sqrt{1-\dfrac{b^2\sin^2 A}{a^2}}} = \frac{dB}{b\sqrt{1-\dfrac{a^2\sin^2 B}{b^2}}}$$

$$\frac{dA}{\sqrt{a^2-b^2\sin^2 A}} = \frac{dB}{\sqrt{b^2-a^2\sin^2 B}}$$

10. Find the equation of the normal to the curve $y = (1+x)^y + \sin^{-1}(\sin^2 x)$ at $x = 0$.

Solution: given $y = (1+x)^y + \sin^{-1}(\sin^2 x)$

at $x = 0$

$y = (1+0)^y + \sin^{-1}(\sin^2 0)$

$y = 1 + 0 \Rightarrow y = 1$

then the point of intersection (0, 1).

Now, $y = (1+y)^y + \sin^{-1}(\sin^2 x)$

$u = (1+x)^y \Rightarrow \dfrac{dy}{dx} = \dfrac{du}{dx} + \dfrac{dv}{dx}$ ...(1)

$\log u = y \log(1+x)$

$$\frac{1}{u}\frac{du}{dx} = y.\frac{1}{1+x} + \log(1+x).\frac{dy}{dx}$$

$$\frac{du}{dx} = \frac{y(1+x)^y}{1+x} + (1+x)^y.\log(1+x).\frac{dy}{dx}$$

$$\frac{dy}{dx} = y(1+x)^{y-1} + (1+x)^y.\log(1+x).\frac{dy}{dx}$$

and $v = \sin^{-1}(\sin^2 x)$

$\dfrac{dv}{dx} = \dfrac{\sin 2x}{\sqrt{1-\sin^4 x}}$ put in (1)

$$\frac{dy}{dx} = y(1+x)^{y-1} + (1+x)^y$$

$$\log(1+x).\frac{dy}{dx} + \frac{\sin 2x}{\sqrt{1-\sin^4 x}}$$

$$\frac{dy}{dx} = \frac{y(1+x)^{y-1} + \dfrac{\sin 2x}{\sqrt{1-\sin^4 x}}}{1-(1+x)^y.\log(1+x)} \Rightarrow \left.\frac{dy}{dx}\right|_{(0,1)} = 1$$

Hence equation of normal $\Rightarrow y - 1 = -1(x - 0)$

$\Rightarrow x + y = 1$

11. Find the point of the intersecting of the tangents drawn to the curve $x^2y = 1 - y$ at the points where it is intersected by the curve $xy = 1 - y$.

Solution: $xy = x^2y$ ...(1)

$xy(x-1) = 0$

$x = 0, y = 0, x = 1$

$xy = 1 - y$ ...(2)

when $x = 0$ then $y = 1 \Rightarrow (x, y) = (0, 1)$

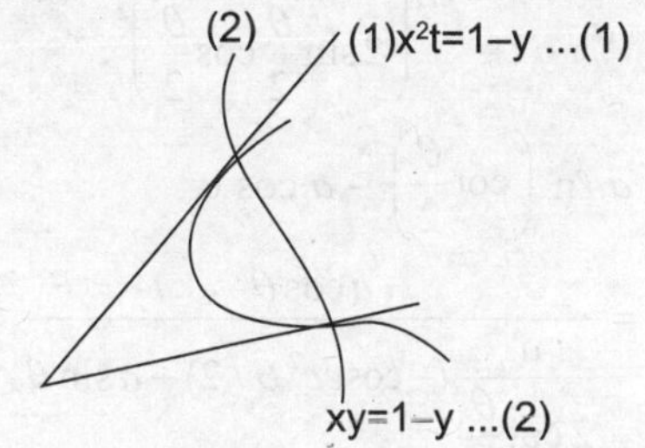

when $x = 1$ then $y = \dfrac{1}{2} \Rightarrow (x, y) = \left(1, \dfrac{1}{2}\right)$

when $y = 0$ then $0 = 1$ (which not possible so reject it)

using (1) and (2), we get $y(x^2 + 1) = 1$

$$y = \frac{1}{x^2+1}$$

$$\frac{dy}{dx} = \frac{-2x}{(1+x^2)^2}$$

$$\left.\frac{dy}{dx}\right|_{(0,1)} = 0$$

Equation of tangent $y - 1 = 0$

$y = 1$ ...(3)

$$\left.\frac{dy}{dx}\right|_{(1,1/2)} = \frac{-2}{4} = \frac{-1}{2}$$

Equation of tangent $y - \dfrac{1}{2} = -\dfrac{1}{2}(x-1)$

$2y - 1 = -x + 1$

$2y + x = 2$ ...(4)

so by using (3) and (4) point of intersection of tangent is (0, 1) Ans

12. A straight line is drawn through the origin and parallel to the tangent to a curve $\dfrac{x+\sqrt{a^2-y^2}}{a} = \ell n\left(\dfrac{a+\sqrt{a^2+y^2}}{y}\right)$ at an arbitrary point *M*. Show that the locus of the point *p* of intersection of the straight line through the origin and the straight line parallel to the x-axis and passing thought the point M is $x^2 + y^2 = a^2$.

Solution: $\dfrac{x+\sqrt{a^2-y^2}}{a} = \ell n\left(\dfrac{a+\sqrt{a^2-y^2}}{y}\right)$

put $y = a\sin\theta$ ...(1)

$$\frac{x+a\cos\theta}{2} = \ell n\left(\frac{a+a\cos\theta}{a\sin\theta}\right)$$

$$\frac{x+a\cos\theta}{a} = \ell n\left(\frac{2\cos^2\frac{\theta}{2}}{2\sin\frac{\theta}{2}\cos\frac{\theta}{2}}\right)$$

$$x = a\,\ell\text{n}\left(\cot\frac{\theta}{2}\right) - a\cos\theta \qquad ...(2)$$

$$\frac{dy}{dx} = \frac{a\cos\theta}{\frac{a}{2\cot\frac{\theta}{2}}(-\text{cosec}^2\,\theta/2) + a\sin\theta}$$

$$\frac{dy}{dx} = \frac{\cos\theta}{-\frac{1}{\sin\theta} + \sin\theta} = \frac{dy}{dx} = -\tan\theta$$

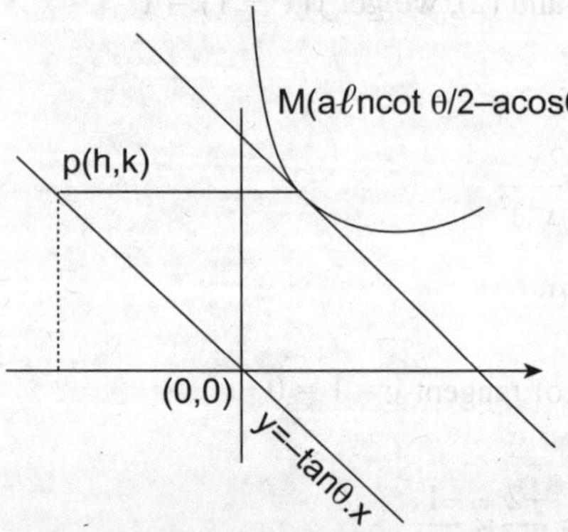

Now $k = -\tan\theta\, h$; $k = -\dfrac{k}{\sqrt{a^2-k^2}}.h$;

$$-h = \sqrt{a^2-k^2}$$

∵ k=asinθ

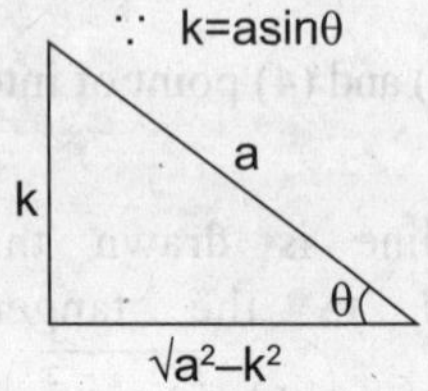

$$a^2 - k^2 = h^2$$

$x^2 + y^2 = a^2$ Ans

13. A line is tangent to the curve $f(x) = \dfrac{41x^3}{3}$ at the point p in the first quadrant, and has a slope of 2009. This line intersects the y-axis at $(0, b)$. Find the value of 'b'.

Solution: $y = \dfrac{41x^3}{3}$ ...(1)

$$\frac{dy}{dx} = 41x^2$$

$$\left.\frac{dy}{dx}\right|_{(\alpha,\beta)} = 41\alpha^2 \qquad ...(2)$$

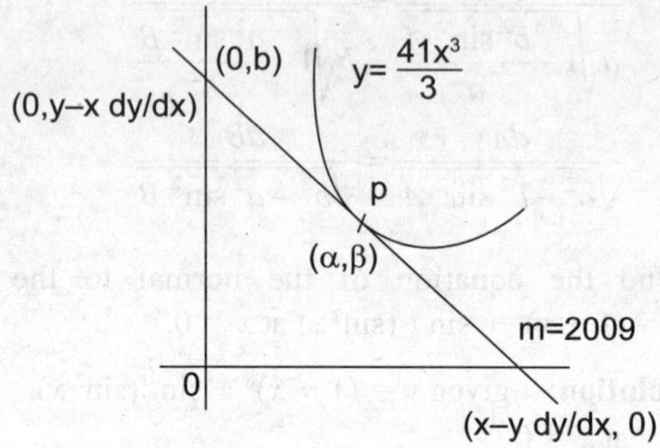

and given m = 2009 ...(3)

equate (2) = (3)

$41\alpha^2 = 2009$

$\alpha = 7$

Now $b = y - x\dfrac{dy}{dx}\left\{\because x = \alpha \text{ then } y = \dfrac{41\alpha^3}{3}\right\}$

$$= \frac{41\alpha^3}{3} - \alpha\, 41\,\alpha^2 = 41\,\alpha^3\left(\frac{1}{3} - 1\right)$$

$$b = -\frac{2}{3}\,41\,\alpha^3$$

∵ $\alpha = 7$ then $b = -\dfrac{82}{3}(7)^3$ Ans

14. A function is defined parametrically by the equations $f(t) = x = \begin{cases} 2t + t^2\sin\frac{1}{t} & ; t \neq 0 \\ 0 & ; t = 0 \end{cases}$ and $g(t) = y = \begin{cases} \frac{1}{t}\sin t^2 & ; t \neq 0 \\ 0 & ; t = 0 \end{cases}$. Find the equation of tangent and normal at the point for $t = 0$ if exist.

Solution: $\dfrac{dy}{dx} = \dfrac{g'(t)}{f'(t)}$ ...(1)

$$g'(t) = \lim_{t\to 0}\left(\frac{g(t) - g(0)}{t - 0}\right) = \lim_{t\to 0}\left(\frac{\frac{1}{t}\sin t^2 - 0}{t}\right) = 1$$

$$f'(t) = \lim_{t\to 0}\left(\frac{f(t)-f(0)}{t-0}\right)$$

$$= \lim_{t\to 0}\frac{2t+t^2\sin\frac{1}{t}}{t} = 2+0=2$$

then $\frac{dy}{dx}=\frac{1}{2}$, so the equation of tangent

$y-0=\frac{1}{2}(x-0)$

$x-2y=0$ Ans

equation of normal $y-0=-2(x-0)$

$2x+y=0$ Ans

15. Find all the tangent to the curve $y=\cos(x+y)$; $-2\pi \le x \le 2\pi$, that are parallel to the line $x+2y=0$.

Solution: $y=\cos(x+y)$ ...(1)

$$\frac{dy}{dx}=-\sin(x+y)\left\{1+\frac{dy}{dx}\right\}$$

$$\frac{dy}{dx}+\sin(x+y).\frac{dy}{dx}=-\sin(x+y)$$

$$\frac{dy}{dx}=\frac{-\sin(x+y)}{1+\sin(x+y)} \quad ...(2)$$

$x+2y=0$ ...(3)

$$\frac{dy}{dx}=-\frac{1}{2} \quad ...(4)$$

equat (2) and (4), we get $\frac{-\sin(x+y)}{1+\sin(x+y)}=-\frac{1}{2}$

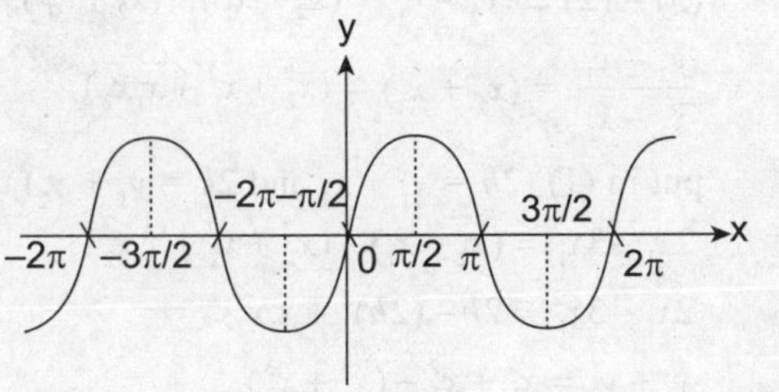

$\sin(x+y)=1$

$x+y=\frac{\pi}{2},-\frac{3\pi}{2}$

put in (1) then points will be $\left(\frac{\pi}{2},0\right),\left(\frac{-3\pi}{2},0\right)$

for $\left(\frac{\pi}{2},0\right)$ for $\left(\frac{-3\pi}{2},0\right)$

equation of tangent

$y-0=-\frac{1}{2}\left(x-\frac{\pi}{2}\right)$

$y-0=-\frac{1}{2}\left(x+\frac{3\pi}{2}\right)$

$x+2y=\frac{\pi}{2}$ Ans

$x+2y=-\frac{3\pi}{2}$ Ans

16. The chord of the parabola $y=-a^2x^2+5ax-4$ touches the curve $y=\frac{1}{1-x}$ at the point $x=2$ and is bisected by that point. Find 'a'.

Solution: $y=\frac{1}{1-x}$ at $x=2$, $y=-1$

$$\frac{dy}{dx}=\frac{1}{(1-x)^2}$$

$$\left.\frac{dy}{dx}\right|_{(2,-1)}=1 \quad ...(1)$$

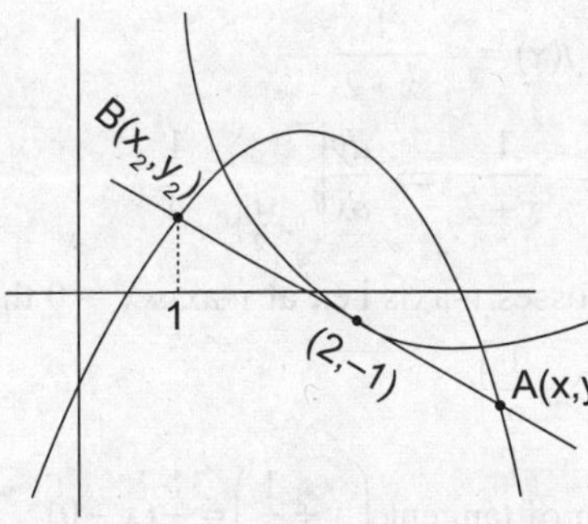

equation of tangent $y+1=1(x-2)$

$y=x-3$ ...(2)

curve $y=-a^2x^2+5ax-4$

$x-3=-a^2x^2+5ax-4$ x_1

$a^2x^2+x(1-5a)+1=0$ x_2

$\frac{x_1+x_2}{2}=2 \Rightarrow x_1+x^2=4$

$x_1+x_2=-\left(\frac{1-5a}{a^2}\right)$

$y_1+y_2=-2$

$4=\frac{5a-1}{a^2} \Rightarrow 4a^2-5a+1=0$

$a=\frac{5\pm\sqrt{25-4.4}}{2.4}$

$a=\frac{5\pm 3}{8}$

$a=1$ Ans

17. Determine a differentiable function $y = f(x)$ which satisfies $f'(x) = [f(x)]^2$ and $f(0) = -\frac{1}{2}$. Find also the equation of the tangent at the point where to curve crosses the y-axis.

Solution: $f'(x) = [f(x)]^2$

$$\frac{f'(x)}{[f(x)]^2} = 1$$

put $f(x) = t \Rightarrow f'(x) = dt$

$$-\frac{1}{f(x)} = x + c$$

$$f(x) = -\frac{1}{x+c}$$

$$x = 0 \Rightarrow f(0) = -\frac{1}{c}$$

$$-\frac{1}{2} = -\frac{1}{c} \Rightarrow c = 2$$

then $f(x) = -\dfrac{1}{x+2}$

$$y = -\frac{1}{x+2} \Rightarrow \left.\frac{dy}{dx}\right|_{\left(0,-\frac{1}{2}\right)} = \frac{1}{4}$$

curve crosses y-axis i.e., at y-axis $x = 0$ then (x, y)

$$= \left(0, -\frac{1}{2}\right)$$

Equation of tangent $\left(y + \frac{1}{2}\right) = \frac{1}{4}(x - 0)$

$$\frac{2y+1}{2} = \frac{x}{4}$$

$x - 4y = 2$ Ans

18. The curve $y = ax^3 + bx^2 + cx + 5$, touches the x-axis at $p(-2, 0)$ and cuts the y-axis at a point Q where its gradient is 3. Find a, b, c.

Solution: $y = ax^3 + bx^2 + cx + 5$

$(-2, 0)$ satisfies the curve

$0 = -8a + 4b - 2c + 5$ ...(1)

Now $\dfrac{dy}{dx} = 3ax^2 + 2bx + c$

$\left.\dfrac{dy}{dx}\right|_{(0,5)} = c$ given $\left.\dfrac{dy}{dx}\right|_{(0,5)} = 3$

then $c = 3$ put in (1) $-8a + 4b = 1$ ...(2)

Also $\left.\dfrac{dy}{dx}\right|_{(-2,0)} = 0$

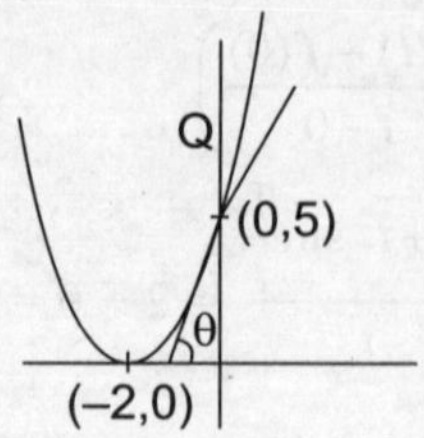

$12a - 4b + 3 = 0$ ...(3)

$(2) + (3) \Rightarrow 4a = -2$

$$\Rightarrow a = -\frac{1}{2}$$

$c = 3$

$b = -\dfrac{3}{4}$ Ans

19. The tangent at a variable point P of the curve $y = x^2 - x^3$ meets again at Q. Show that the locus of the middle point of PQ is $y = 1 - 9x + 28x^2 - 28x^3$

Solution: $y = x^2 - x^3$ ...(1)

$$\frac{dy}{dx} = 2x - 3x^2$$

$y_1 = x_1^2 - x_1^3$ ...(2)

$$\left.\frac{dy}{dx}\right|_{x_1 y_1} = \frac{y_2 - y_1}{x_2 - x_1}$$

$y_2 = x_2^2 - x_2^3$ ...(3)

$$2x_1 - 3x_1^2 = \frac{y_2 - y_1}{x_2 - x_1}$$

$$(3) - (2) \Rightarrow y_2 - y_1 = (x_2^2 - x_1^2) - (x_2^3 - x_1^3)$$

$$\frac{y_2 - y_1}{x_2 - x_1} = (x_2 + x_1) - (x_2^2 + x_1^2 + x_1 x_2)$$

put in (1) ($2h = x_1 + x_2$ and $2k = y_1 + y_2$)

$$2x_1 - 3x_1^2 = (x_2 + x_1) - (x_1^2 + x_2^2 + x_1 x_2)$$

$2x_1 - 3x_1^2 = 2h - (2h)^2 + x_1 x_2$ ...(4)

$$y_1 + y_2 = x_1^2 + x_2^2 - (x_1^3 + x_2^3)$$

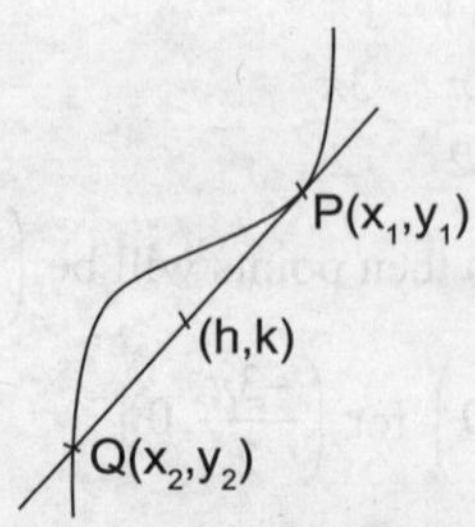

$$2k = (x_1 + x_2)^2 - 2x_1 x_2 - [(x_1 + x_2)^3 - 3x_1 x_2 (x_1 + x_2)]$$

$$2k = 4h^2 - [8h^3 - 3x_1 x_2 (2h)] - 2x_1 x_2$$

20. Show that the distance from the origin of the normal at any point of the curve $x = a\,e^{\theta}\left(\sin\frac{\theta}{2}+2\cos\frac{\theta}{2}\right)$ and $y = ae^{\theta}\left(\cos\frac{\theta}{2}-2\sin\frac{\theta}{2}\right)$ is twice the distance of the tangent at the point from the origin.

Solution: $\frac{dy}{dx} = \frac{dy/d\theta}{dx/d\theta}$

$$= \frac{a\left[e^{\theta}\left(-\sin\frac{\theta}{2}.\frac{1}{2}-2\cos\frac{\theta}{2}.\frac{1}{2}\right)+\left(\cos\frac{\theta}{2}-2\sin\frac{\theta}{2}\right)e^{\theta}\right]}{a\left[e^{\theta}\left(\cos\frac{\theta}{2}.\frac{1}{2}-2\sin\frac{\theta}{2}.\frac{1}{2}\right)+\left(\sin\frac{\theta}{2}+2\cos\frac{\theta}{2}\right)e^{\theta}\right]}$$

$$= \frac{e^{\theta}\left[-\frac{1}{2}\sin\frac{\theta}{2}-\cos\frac{\theta}{2}+\cos\frac{\theta}{2}-2\sin\frac{\theta}{2}\right]}{e^{\theta}\left[\frac{1}{2}\cos\frac{\theta}{2}-\sin\frac{\theta}{2}+\sin\frac{\theta}{2}+2\cos\frac{\theta}{2}\right]}$$

$$= -\frac{5/2\sin\theta/2}{5/2\cos\theta/2} = -\tan\frac{\theta}{2}$$

Equation of normal

$$\Rightarrow\; y - ae^{\theta}\left(\cos\frac{\theta}{2}-2\sin\frac{\theta}{2}\right) = \frac{\cos\theta/2}{\sin\theta/2}\left(x-ae^{\theta}\left(\sin\frac{\theta}{2}+2\cos\frac{\theta}{2}\right)\right)$$

$$\Rightarrow\; y.\sin\frac{\theta}{2} - ae^{\theta}\cos\frac{\theta}{2}\sin\frac{\theta}{2}+2ae^{\theta}\sin^2\frac{\theta}{2} = x\cos\frac{\theta}{2}$$

$$-\,ae^{\theta}\sin\frac{\theta}{2}.\cos\frac{\theta}{2} - 2ae^{\theta}\cos^2\frac{\theta}{2}$$

$$\Rightarrow\; x\cos\frac{\theta}{2} - y\sin\frac{\theta}{2} = 2ae^{\theta}$$

$$\Rightarrow\; x\cos\frac{\theta}{2} - y\sin\frac{\theta}{2} - 2ae^{\theta} = 0$$

its distance from origin $p_1 = \left|\frac{0+0-2ae^{\theta}}{\sqrt{\cos^2\frac{\theta}{2}+\sin^2\frac{\theta}{2}}}\right|$

$p_1 = 2ae^{\theta}$

Similarly find equation of tangent and solve.

21. A curve is given by the equation $x = at^2$ and $y = at^3$. A variable pair of perpendicular lines through the origin '0' meet the curve at P and Q. Show that the locus of the point of intersection of the tangent at P and Q is $4y^2 = 3ax - a^2$.

Solution: $x = at^2$ ...(1)

$y = at^3$ ...(2)

$$\frac{dy}{dx} = \frac{3at^2}{2at}$$

$$\frac{dy}{dx} = \frac{3t}{2} \quad ...(3)$$

Equation of tangent at P is $y - am^3 = \frac{3}{2}\,m(x - am^2)$

$$y = \frac{3}{2}\,mx - \frac{3}{2}\,am^3 + am^3$$

$$y = \frac{3}{2}\,mh - \frac{am^3}{2} \quad ...(4)$$

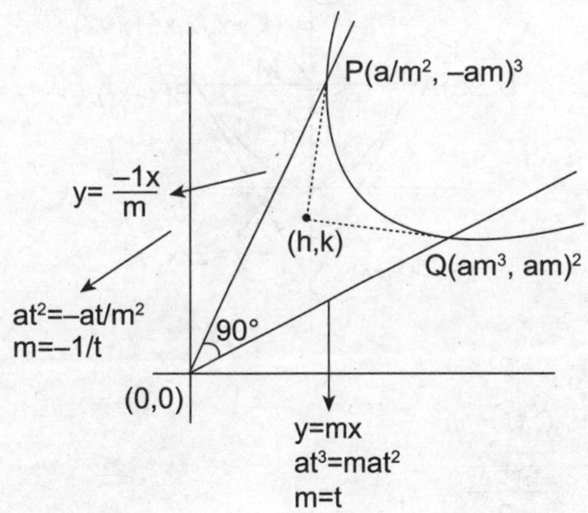

equation of $t \Rightarrow y + \frac{a}{m^3} = -\frac{3}{2m}(x - a/m^2)$

$$y = -\frac{3}{2m}x + \frac{a}{2m^3} \quad ...(5)$$

(4) × (5) and solve (remove m)

22. A and B are points of the parabola $y = x^2$. The tangents at A and B meet at C. The mediam of the triangle ABC from C has length 'm' units. Find the area of the triangle in terms of 'm'.

Solution: $y = x^2$

$$\frac{dy}{dx} = 2x$$

tangent BC $\Rightarrow y - x_1^2 = 2x_1(x - x_1)$

$y = 2xx_1 - x_1^2$ ...(1)

similarly tangent AC

$y = 2xx_2 - x_2^2$ ...(2)

point of intersection (1) and (2) is C

$2xx_1 - x_1^2 = 2xx_2 - x_2^2$

$x = \frac{x_1 + x_2}{2}$ and $y = x_1 x_2$

$$\Delta = \frac{1}{2}\begin{vmatrix} x_1 & x_1^2 & 1 \\ x_2 & x_2^2 & 1 \\ \frac{x_1+x_2}{2} & x_1x_2 & 1 \end{vmatrix} = \frac{1}{2}\begin{vmatrix} x_1 & x_1^2 & 1 \\ x_2 - x_1 & x_2^2 - x_1^2 & 0 \\ \frac{x_2 - x_1}{2} & x_1x_2 - x_1^2 & 0 \end{vmatrix}$$

$$= -(x_2 - x_1)(x_2 - x_1)\begin{vmatrix} 1 & x_2 - x_1 \\ \frac{1}{2} & x_1 \end{vmatrix}$$

$$= \frac{1}{2}(x_2 - x_1)^2\left(x_1 - \frac{1}{2}x_2 - \frac{1}{2}x_1\right) = \frac{1}{4}(x_2 - x_1)^3$$

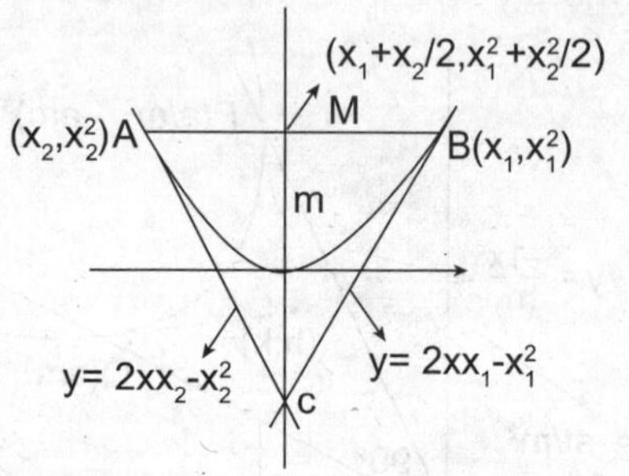

Now

$\because$ $CM = m$

$$\frac{x_1 + x_2}{2} - x_1x^2 = m$$

$$\frac{(x_1 - x_2)^2}{2} = m$$

$$(x_1 - x_2)^2 = 2m$$

$$= \frac{1}{4}(2m)^{3/2} = \frac{m^{3/2}}{\sqrt{2}} \text{ Ans}$$

23. Show that the angle between the tangent at any point 'A' of the curve $\ell n\,(x^2 + y^2) = c\tan^{-1}\left(\frac{y}{x}\right)$ and the line joining A to the origin is independent of the position of A on the curve.

Solution: $\phi = \psi - \theta$

$$\tan\phi = \frac{\tan\psi + \tan\theta}{1 - \tan\psi\tan\theta} = \left(\frac{\frac{2x+cy}{cx-2y} - \frac{y}{x}}{1 + \frac{2x+cy}{cx-2y}\cdot\frac{y}{x}}\right) = \frac{2}{c};\ \frac{dy}{dx}$$

$$\Rightarrow \frac{1}{x^2+y^2}\left(2x + 2y.\frac{dy}{dx}\right) = c\frac{1}{1 + y^2/x^2}\left(\frac{x.\frac{dy}{dx} - y}{x^2}\right)$$

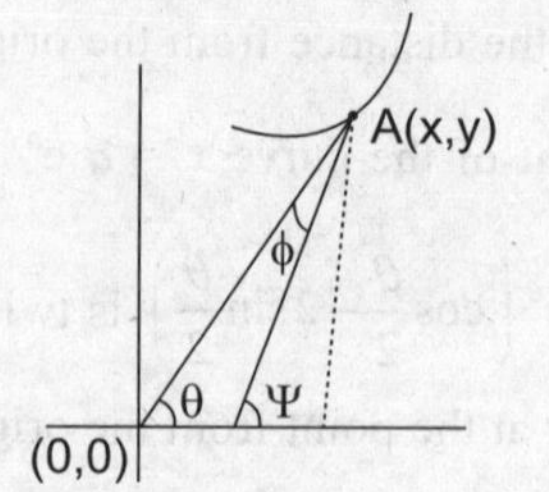

$$\frac{2\left(x + y\frac{dy}{dx}\right)}{x^2 + y^2} = \frac{cx^2}{x^2+y^2}\cdot\frac{1}{x^2}\left(x\frac{dy}{dx} - y\right)$$

$$2x + cy = (cx - 2y)\left(\frac{dy}{dx}\right)$$

$$\frac{dy}{dx} = \frac{2x+cy}{cx-2y}$$

24. Let α be the angle in radians between $\frac{x^2}{36} + \frac{y^2}{4} = 1$ and the circle $x^2 + y^2 = 12$ at their points of intersection. If $\alpha = \tan^{-1}\frac{k}{2\sqrt{3}}$, then find the value of k^2.

Solution: For the points of intersection, we have

$$\frac{12 - y^2}{36} + \frac{y^2}{4} = 1$$

$\Rightarrow$ $y = \pm\sqrt{3}$ and $x = 3$

Consider the point $P(3, \sqrt{3})$

Equation of the tangent at P to the circle is $3x + \sqrt{3}\,y = 12$ slope of this tangent is $-\sqrt{3}$

Equation of the tangent at P to the ellipse is

$$\frac{x}{12} + \frac{\sqrt{3}}{4}y = 1$$

slope of this tangent is $-\frac{1}{3\sqrt{3}}$

if α is angle between these tangents, then $\tan\alpha = \frac{2}{\sqrt{3}}$

$\therefore$ $\alpha = \tan^{-1}\frac{2}{\sqrt{3}}$

$\therefore$ $k = 4$ and hence $k^2 = 16$

25. Prove that there exist exactly two non-similar isosceles triangles ABC such that $\tan A + \tan B + \tan C = 100$.

Solution: Let $A = B$, then $2A + C = 180°$ and $2\tan A + \tan C = 100$

Now $2A + C = 180° \Rightarrow \tan 2A = -\tan C$ ......(1)

Also 2tan A + tan C = 100

$\Rightarrow$ 2tan A – 100 = – tan C ....(2)

From (1) and (2)

$$2\tan A - 100 = \frac{2\tan A}{1-\tan^2 A}$$

Let tan $A = x$, then $\dfrac{2x}{1-x^2} = 2x - 100$

$\Rightarrow x^3 - 50x^2 + 50 = 0$

Let $f(x) = x^3 - 50x^2 + 50$

Then $f'(x) = 3x^2 - 100x$. Thus $f'(x) = 0$ has roots 0, $\dfrac{100}{3}$, Also f(0). $f\left(\dfrac{100}{3}\right) < 0$. Thus $f(x) = 0$ has exactly three distinct real roots. Therefore tan A and hence A has three distinct values. But one of them will be obtuse angle. Hence there exists two non-similar isosceles triangles.

26. Find the shortest distance between the curves $9x^2 + 9y^2 - 30y + 16 = 0$ and $y^2 = x^3$.

Solution: $9x^2 + 9y^2 - 30y + 16 = 0$ can be rewritten as $x^2 + \left(y - \dfrac{5}{3}\right)^2 = 1$

Any point on the curve $y^2 = x^3$ can be taken as (t^2, t^3)

Let l be the distance between the centre of the given circle and the point (t^2, t^3), then $L = l^2 = t^4 + (t^3 - 5/3)^2$.

Now, we calculate the minimum value of l, required distance = l – radius of given circle

Now, $\dfrac{dL}{dt} = 4t^3 + 2\left(t^3 - \dfrac{5}{3}\right)3t^2 = 0$

for maximum or minimum, $t = 0$ or 1

Now, $\dfrac{d^2L}{dt^2} = 12t^2 + 30t^4 - 20t$

$$\left.\frac{d^2L}{dt^2}\right|_{t=0} = 0$$

But, $\left.\dfrac{d^3L}{dt^3}\right|_{t=0} \neq 0$

$\Rightarrow$ there is neither maxima nor minima at $t = 0$

Also, $\dfrac{d^2L}{dt^2} > 0$ at $t = 1$

$\Rightarrow$ L is minimum at $t = 1$

So, shortest distance = (value of l at t = 1) – (radius of the circle) = $\dfrac{\sqrt{13}}{3} - 1$

Column-Matching

27. **Column-I**

(i) The ordinate of the point on the curve $\sqrt{x} + \sqrt{y} = \sqrt{a}$ at which the normal is parallel to the x-axis is

(ii) The length of the perpendicular from the origin to the normal of curve $x = a(\cos\theta + \theta\sin\theta)$, $y = a(\sin\theta + \theta\cos\theta)$, at any point θ is

(iii) The length of sub-tangent to the curve $x^2y^2 = 16a^4$ at the point $(-2a, a)$

(iv) The abscissa of the point on the curve $xy = (a + x)^2$, the normal at which cuts off numerically equal intercepts from the coordinate axis is]

Column-II

(a) a

(b) $2a$

(c) $a/\sqrt{2}$

(d) $\sqrt{2}\,a$

Ans. (i) → (a), (ii) → (a), (iii) → (b), (iv) → (c)

Solution: (i) $\sqrt{x} + \sqrt{y} = \sqrt{a}$

$$\Rightarrow \frac{1}{2\sqrt{x}} + \frac{1}{2\sqrt{y}}y' = 0$$

$$\Rightarrow y' = -\frac{\sqrt{y}}{\sqrt{x}}$$

$m_N = 0 \qquad \Rightarrow m_T = \infty$

$\Rightarrow y' = \infty \qquad \Rightarrow x = 0 \qquad \Rightarrow y = a$

(ii) $\dfrac{dy}{d\theta} = a\theta\sin\theta\,;\ \dfrac{dx}{d\theta} = a\theta\cos\theta\,;\ \dfrac{dy}{dx} = \tan\theta$

Equation of normal $y - a(\sin\theta - \theta\cos\theta) = -\dfrac{\cos\theta}{\sin\theta}(x - a(\cos\theta + \theta\sin\theta))$

$\Rightarrow x\cos\theta + y\sin\theta = a$

$\perp$ distance from (0, 0) = $\left|\dfrac{-a}{\sqrt{\cos^2\theta + \sin^2\theta}}\right| = a$

(iii) $x^2y^2 = 16a^4$

$L_{ST} = \left|\dfrac{y}{x_T}\right| \qquad \Rightarrow xy = 4a^2$

$y + xy' = 0$

$y' = \dfrac{-y}{x}$

$L_{ST} = \left|\dfrac{y}{y/x}\right| = x \qquad \Rightarrow L_{ST} = 2a$

(iv) $xy = (a + x)^2$

$y + xy' = 2(a + x)$

$y' = \pm 1 \qquad y \pm x = 2(a + x)$

$\frac{(a+x)^2}{x} \pm x = 2(aTx)$

$\Rightarrow \pm x = 2(a + x) - \pm x^2 = (2 + x)[x - a]$

$\Rightarrow \pm x^2 = x^2 - a^2$

$2x^2 = a^2 \qquad \Rightarrow x = \pm \frac{a}{\sqrt{2}}$

Solve Comprehension Passage:

A: If y $f(x)$ is curve and if there exists two points A $(x_1, f(x_1))$ and B $(x_2, f(x_2))$ on it such that $f'(x_1) = -\frac{1}{f'(x_2)} = \frac{f(x_2)-f(x_1)}{x_2-x_1}$, then the tangent at x_1 is normal at x_2 for that curve. Now answer the following questions

28. Number of such lines on the curve $y = \sin x$ is

(a) 1 (b) 0
(c) 2 (d) infinite

29. Number of such lines on the curve $y = |\ell n\, x|$ is

(a) 1 (b) 2
(c) 0 (d) infinite

30. Number of such lines on the curve $y^2 = x^3$ is

(a) 1 (b) 2
(c) 3 (d) 0

Solutions:

28. (b) $f(x) = y = \sin x$

$f'(x) = \frac{dy}{dx} = \cos x$

$\therefore \cos x_1 = -\frac{1}{\cos x_2} = \frac{\sin x_2 - \sin x_1}{x_2 - x_1}$

i.e., $\cos x_1 \cos x_2 = -1$

$\therefore \sin x_1 = \sin x_2 = 0 \qquad \therefore$ there is no solution.

29. (c) $f(x) = y = |n\ell\ x|$

$\therefore f(x_1) = -\frac{1}{f'(x_2)} = \frac{f(x_2)-f(x_1)}{x_2-x_1}$

$\Rightarrow \frac{\ell n\, x_1}{x_1|\ell n\, x_1|} = -\frac{x_2|\ell n\, x_2|}{\ell n\, x_2} = \frac{|\ell n\, x_2|-|\ell n\, x_1|}{x_2-x_1}$ ....(i)

$\Rightarrow \ln x_1 . \ln x_2 < 0$

Let $0 < x_1 < 1$, then $1 < x_2$ and $x_1.x_2 = 1$

from (i), we get

$-\frac{1}{x_1} = -x_2 = \frac{\ell n\, x_2 + \ell n\, x_1}{x_2 - x_1} = \frac{\ell n\, x_1x_2}{x_2 - x_1} = 0$ which is possible for infinite many value of x_1, x_2.

30. (b) $y^2 = x^3$

$\therefore y = \sqrt{x^3}$ or $-\sqrt{x^3}$

$2y\frac{dy}{dx} = 3x^2$

$\therefore \frac{3x_1^2}{2y_1} = -\frac{2y_2}{3x_2^2}$

$\Rightarrow \frac{9}{4}x_1^2 x_2^2 = -y_1y_2$

$\therefore y_1y_2 < 0$

Let $y_1 = \sqrt{x_1^3}$ and $y_2 = -\sqrt{x_2^3}$

thus $\frac{3x_1^2}{2\sqrt{x_1^3}} = \frac{2\sqrt{x_2^3}}{3x_2^2} = \frac{-\sqrt{x_2^3}-\sqrt{x_1^3}}{x_2-x_1}$

$\frac{3\sqrt{x_1}}{2} = \frac{2}{3\sqrt{x_2}} = \frac{\sqrt{x_2^3}+\sqrt{x_1^3}}{x_1-x_2}$

$\sqrt{x_1x_2} = \frac{4}{9}$

$3x_1\sqrt{x_1} - 3\sqrt{x_1}\, x_2 = 2\sqrt{x_2^3} + 2\sqrt{x_1^3}$

$3\left(\sqrt{x_1}\right)^3 - \frac{3\times16}{81\sqrt{x_1}} = 2\frac{64}{729\sqrt{x_1^3}} + 2\sqrt{x_1^3}$

$3x_1^3 - \frac{16}{27}x_1 = \frac{128}{729} + 2x_1^3$

$x_1^3 - \frac{16}{27}x_1 = \frac{128}{729}$

$729x_1^3 - 432x_1 - 128 = 0$

Consider $h(t) = 729t^3 - 432t - 128$

$h'(t) = 3 \times 729t^2 - 432 = 0$ gives $t = \pm\frac{4}{9}$

$h\left(-\frac{4}{9}\right) = 0$

$\therefore$ there are two distinct solutions of $729x_1^3 - 432x_1 - 128 = 0$.

B: $a(t)$ is a function of t such that $\frac{da}{dt} = 2$ for all values of t and $a = 0$ when $t = 0$. Further $y = m(t)x + c(t)$ is tangent to the curve $y = x^2 - 2ax + a^2 + a$ at the point whose abscissa 0. Then

31. If the rate of change distance of vertex from the origin with respect to t is k, then k =

(a) 2 (b) $2\sqrt{2}$
(c) $\sqrt{2}$ (d) $4\sqrt{2}$

32. If the rate of change of $c(t)$ with respect to t, when $t = k$ is ℓ, then ℓ =

(a) $16\sqrt{2} - 2$ (b) $8\sqrt{2} + 2$
(c) $10\sqrt{2} + 2$ (d) $16\sqrt{2} + 2$

33. The rate of change of $m(t)$, with respect to t, at $t = \ell$ is

(a) –2 (b) 2
(c) –4 (d) 4

Solution:

$$\frac{da}{dt} = 2 \Rightarrow a = 2t + c$$

$c = 0$ $\{\because a = 0, \text{ when } t = 0)$

$\therefore a = 2t$

$\therefore$ the curve $y = x^2 - 2ax + a^2 + a$ becomes

$y = x^2 - 4tx + 4t^2 + 2t$

if $x = 0$, then $y = 4t^2 + 2t$

$$\frac{dy}{dx} = 2x - 4t$$

$$\therefore \left.\frac{dy}{dx}\right|_{at\,x=0} = -4t$$

$\therefore$ equation of the tangent

$Y - (4t^2 + 2t) = -4t\,(x - 0)$

i.e., $y = -4t\,x + 4t^2 + 2t$

vertex of $y = x^2 - 4t\,x + 4t^2 + 2t$ is $(2t, 2t)$

$\therefore$ distance of vertex from the origin $= 2\sqrt{2}\,t$

$\therefore$ rate of change with respect to $t = 2\sqrt{2}$

i.e., $k = 2\sqrt{2}$

$c(t) = 4t^2 + 2t$

$$\therefore \frac{dc}{dt} = 8t + 2$$

$$\therefore \left.\frac{dc}{dt}\right|_{at\,t=2\sqrt{2}} = 16\sqrt{2} + 2$$

$\therefore \ell\ 16\sqrt{2} + 2$ $m(t) = -4t$

$$\therefore \frac{dm}{dt} = -4 = \left.\frac{dm}{dt}\right|_{at\,t=\ell} = -4$$

Ans: **31.** (b) **32.** (d) **33.** (c)

C: The parametric equation of given curve are $x = a\,(2\cos t + \cos 2t)$, $y = a\,(2\sin t - \sin 2t)$

34. The equation of tangent at any point 't' is

(a) $x\sin\left(\frac{t}{2}\right) + y\cos\left(\frac{t}{2}\right) = a\sin\left(\frac{3t}{2}\right)$

(b) $x\cos\left(\frac{t}{2}\right) + y\sin\left(\frac{t}{2}\right) = a\sin\left(\frac{3t}{2}\right)$

(c) $x\sin\left(\frac{t}{2}\right) + y\cos\left(\frac{t}{2}\right) = 3a\sin\left(\frac{3t}{2}\right)$

(d) $x\cos\left(\frac{t}{2}\right) + y\sin\left(\frac{t}{2}\right) = 3a\sin\left(\frac{3t}{2}\right)$

35. The equation of normal at any point 't' is

(a) $x\cos\left(\frac{t}{2}\right) + y\sin\left(\frac{t}{2}\right) = 3a\cos\left(\frac{3t}{2}\right)$

(b) $x\cos\left(\frac{t}{2}\right) - y\sin\left(\frac{t}{2}\right) = 3a\cos\left(\frac{3t}{2}\right)$

(c) $x\cos\left(\frac{t}{2}\right) + y\sin\left(\frac{t}{2}\right) = 3a\sin\left(\frac{3t}{2}\right)$

(d) $x\cos\left(\frac{t}{2}\right) - y\sin\left(\frac{t}{2}\right) = 3a\sin\left(\frac{3t}{2}\right)$

36. The length of sub tangent at any point 't' is

(a) $|y\tan t|$ (b) $|y\cot t|$
(c) $|y\cot(t/2)|$ (d) $|y\tan(t/2)|$

37. The length of subnormal at any point 't' is

(a) $|y\tan t|$ (b) $|y\cot t|$
(c) $|y\cot(t/2)|$ (d) $|y\tan(t/2)|$

38. If length of perpendiculars from origin on tangent and normal at 't' are p and p_1, respectively, then the value of $9p^2 + p_1^2$ is equal to

(a) $9a^2$ (b) $9a^2\sin^2(t/2)$
(c) $9a^2\cos^2\left(\frac{3t}{2}\right)$ (d) a^2

Solution: $\frac{dx}{dt} = a(-2\sin t - 2\sin 2t)$

$= -2a(\sin t + 2\sin t\cos t) = -2a\sin t\,(1 + 2\cos t)$

$$\frac{dy}{dx} = a(2\cos t - 2\cos 2t) = 2a(\cos t - 2\cos^2 t + 1)$$

$= -2a\,(2\cos^2 t - \cos t - 1)$

$= -2a(2\cos^2 t - 2\cos t + \cos t - 1)$

$= -2a\,(2\cos t + 1)(\cos t - 1)$

$$\text{Now } \left.\frac{dy}{dx}\right|_t = \frac{dy/dt}{dx/dt} = \frac{-2a(\cos t - 1)}{-2a\sin t}$$

$$= \frac{-2\sin^2 t/2}{2\sin t/2\cos t/2} = -\tan(t/2)$$

34. (a) equation of tangent at point 't'

$y - a$ (2 sin$t$ – sin2t)

= – tan(t/2) (x – a(2cos t + cos 2t))

$$\Rightarrow \cos(t/2)\,y+\sin(t/2)\,x$$

$$= \begin{bmatrix} (2\cos t+\cos 2t), \\ \sin(t/2)+\cos\left(\frac{t}{2}\right)(2\sin t-\sin 2t) \end{bmatrix}$$

⇒ RHS = a [(2cos$t$ sin t/2) + (cos 2t sin t/2) + (2sin$t$ cos t/2) (sin2t cos$t$ t/2)]

= a[2(sin (t/2) cos t + cot (t/2) sin t) + (sin t/2 cos2t – sin2t cos t/2)]

= a[2(sin(t + t/2)) + (sin(t/2 – 2t))] = asin(3t/2)

35. (b) Equation of normal

$$(y-a(2\sin t-\sin 2t)) = \frac{1}{\tan(t/2)}(x-a(2\cos t+\cos 2t))$$

⇒ y(sin(t/2)) – x (cos(t/2))

= a[–(2cos t + cos 2t) (cos (t/2)) + (sin (t/2)) (2sin$t$ – sin2t)]

= a[– 2(cos t + cos t/2 – sin t sin t/2) – (cos t/2 cot 2t + sin t/2 sin 2t)]

= a[-2(cos3t/2) – (cos 3t/2)] = –3a cos (3t/2)

⇒ x(cos t/2) – y (sin t/2) = 3a cos (3t/2)

36. (c) The length of subtangent at point 't'

$$= \left|\frac{y}{dy/dx}\right| = \left|\frac{a(2\sin t-\sin 2t)}{-\tan(t/2)}\right|$$

= |y cot (t/2)|

37. (d) The length of subnormal at point 't'

$$= \left|y\frac{dy}{dx}\right| = |y\tan(t/2)|$$

38. (a) Length of perpendicular from (0,0) on the tangent at point 't' is

$$\frac{|0\times\sin(t/2)+0\times\cos(t/2)-a\sin(3t/2)|}{\sqrt{\sin^2(t/2)+\cos^2(t/2)}}$$

⇒ P = |a sin 3t/2|

And length of perpendicular from (0, 0) on the normal at point 't' is

$$\frac{|0\times\cos(t/2)-0\times\sin(t/2)-3a\cos(3t/2)|}{\sqrt{\cos^2(t/2)+\sin^2(t/2)}}$$

⇒ p_1 = |3a cos(3t/2|

$$\therefore\ 9p^2+p_1^2 = 9a^2\sin^2(3t/2)+9a^2\cos^2(3t/2)$$

$= 9a^2$

TUTORIAL EXERCISE

SECTION-III

ONLY ONE CORRECT ANSWER

1. The number of points where the curve $y = \sin x + \frac{1}{2}\sin 2x + \frac{1}{4}\sin 4x$ has a horizontal tangent in the interval $(0, \pi)$ is

(a) 1 (b) 2
(c) 3 (d) 4

2. Total number of parallel tangents of $f_1(x) = x^2 - x + 1$ and $f_2(x) = x^3 - x^2 - 2x + 1$ is equal to

(a) 2 (b) 3
(c) 4 (d) None of these

3. Equation of normal drawn to the graph of the functions defined as $f(x) = \frac{\sin x^2}{x}, x \neq 0$ and $f(0) = 0$ at the origin is

(a) $x + y = 0$ (b) $x - y = 0$
(c) $y = 0$ (d) $x = 0$

4. The line $y = mx + b$ is a tangent to the curve $y = x - x^3$ at the point $P(-1, 0)$. A line through $(-1, 0)$ is also touching the curve at the point $Q(a, c)$. Then

(a) $a = 1/2, b = -2, c = 3/8$ and $m = 2$
(b) $a = 1/4, b = 2, c = 15/64$ and $m = -2$
(c) $a = 1/4, b = -2, c = 15/64$ and $m = -2$
(d) $a = 1/2, b = -2, c = 3/8$ and $m = -2$

5. Consider the curve represented parametrically by the equation $x = t^3 - 4t^2 - 3t$ and $y = 2t^2 + 3t - 5$, where $t \in \mathbb{R}$. If H denotes the number of point on the curve where the tangent is horizontal and V the number of point where the tangent is vertical, then

(a) $H = 2$ and $V = 1$ (b) $H = 1$ and $V = 2$
(c) $H = 2$ and $V = 2$ (d) $H = 1$ and $V = 1$

6. The ordinate of all points on the curve $y = \frac{1}{2\sin^2 x + 3\cos^2 x}$ where the tangent is horizontal, is

(a) Always equal to 1/2
(b) Always equal to 1/3
(c) 1/2 or 1/3
(d) None of these

7. A curve passes through the point $(2a, a)$ and a is such that sum of sub-tangent and abscissa is equal to a. Its equation is

(a) $(x - a)y^2 = a^3$ (b) $(x - a)^2 y = a^3$
(c) $(x - a)y = a^2$ (d) None of these

8. Equation of tangent to the curve $y = \sqrt{101 - \left(\sqrt{-x}\right)^4}$ at the point where the curve intersects another curve $y = \log_{10}|x|$ is

(a) $y + 10x = 101$ (b) $y - 10x = 101$
(c) $x + 10y = 101$ (d) $x - 10y = 101$

9. Let l be the line through origin and tangent to the curve $y = x^3 + x + 16$. The gradient of the line l is

(a) $\frac{13}{2}$ (b) 5
(c) 10 (d) 13

10. Let a curve $y = f(x)$, $f(x) \geq 0 \forall x \in R$ has property that for every point P on the curve length on subnormal is equal abscissa of P. If $f(1) = 3$, then $f(4)$ is equal to

(a) $-2\sqrt{6}$ (b) $2\sqrt{6}$
(c) $3\sqrt{5}$ (d) None of these

11. If at any points on the curve the sub-tangent and sub-normal are equal, then the tangent is equal to

(a) Ordinate (b) $\sqrt{2}$ ordinate
(c) $\sqrt{2(\text{ordinate})}$ (d) None of these

12. The length of the normal to the curve $x = a(\theta + \sin\theta), y = a(1 - \cos\theta)$, at $\theta = \frac{\pi}{2}$ is

(a) $2a$ (b) $a\sqrt{2}$
(c) $a/2$ (d) $a/\sqrt{2}$

13. The beds of two rivers (with in a certain region) are a parabola $y = x^2$ and a straight line $y = x - 2$. These rivers are to be connected by a straight canal. The coordinates of the ends of the shortest canal can be

(a) $\left(\frac{1}{2},\frac{1}{4}\right)$ and $\left(-\frac{11}{8},\frac{5}{8}\right)$

(b) $\left(\frac{1}{2},\frac{1}{4}\right)$ and $\left(\frac{11}{8},-\frac{5}{8}\right)$

(c) (0, 0) and (1, –1)

(d) None of these

14. At (0, 0), the curve $y^2 = x^3 + x^2$

(a) touches x-axis

(b) bisects the angle between the axes

(c) makes an angle of 60^0 with OX

(d) None of these

15. The curve $x + y - \ln(x + y) = 2x - 5$ has a vertical tangent at the point (α,β). Then $\alpha+\beta$ is equal is

(a) –1 (b) 1

(c) 2 (d) –2

16. The number of values of 'k' such that line $x + y = k^2$ becomes tangent to $y = -x^3 - x^2$

(a) 4 (b) 3

(c) 2 (d) None of these

17. The ordinate of $y = (a/2)(e^{x/a} + e^{-x/a})$ is the geometric mean of the length of the normal and the quantity:

(a) $a/2$ (b) a

(c) e (d) None of these

18. If slope of $y = \frac{ax}{b-x}$ at (1, 1) be 2, then b =

(a) 0 (b) 2

(c) 1 (d) None of these

19. One of the points on the curve $f(x) = \frac{x}{1-x^2}$, where the tangent is inclined at an angle of $\frac{\pi}{4}$ to x-axis, is

(a) $\left(2,-\frac{2}{3}\right)$ (b) $\left(3,-\frac{3}{8}\right)$

(c) $\left(-2,\frac{2}{3}\right)$ (d) $\left(-\sqrt{3},\frac{\sqrt{3}}{2}\right)$

20. Tangent of acute angle between the curves $y = |x^2 - 1|$ and $y = \sqrt{7-x^2}$ at their points of intersection is

(a) $\frac{5\sqrt{3}}{2}$ (b) $\frac{3\sqrt{5}}{2}$

(c) $\frac{5\sqrt{3}}{4}$ (d) $\frac{3\sqrt{5}}{4}$

21. S1: The curve $y = 2e^{2x}$ intersects the y-axis at an angle $\tan^{-1}(4)$

S2: Length of normal to a curve at a point is directly proportional to slope of tangent at that points

S3: Length to normal at $(x_1, y_1) = y_1\left(\left.\frac{dy}{dx}\right|_{(x_1,y_1)}\right)$

S4: For the curve $12y = x^3$, ordinate always changes faster than abscissa

(a) FTFF (b) TTTT

(c) FTTF (d) FFFF

22. At a distance of 4000 feet from the launch site, a spectator is observing a rocket being launched. If the rocket lifts off vertically and is rising at a speed of 600 ft/sec when it is at an altitude of 3000 ft, the distance between the rocket and the spectator is changing at that instant at the rate

(a) 300 ft/sec (b) 360 ft/sec

(c) 420 ft/sec (d) 480 ft/sec

23. The tangent to the curve $3xy^2 - 2x^2y = 1$ at (1, 1) meets the curve again at the point

(a) $\left(-\frac{16}{5},-\frac{1}{20}\right)$ (b) $\left(\frac{16}{5},\frac{1}{20}\right)$

(c) $\left(\frac{1}{20},\frac{16}{5}\right)$ (d) $\left(-\frac{1}{20},\frac{16}{1}\right)$

24. The tangent to the graph of the function $y = f(x)$ at the point with abscissa $x = a$ forms with the x-axis an angle of $\pi/3$ and at the point with abscissa $x = b$ at an angle of $\pi/4$, then the value of the integral, $\int_a^b f'(x)$. $f''(x)\,dx$ [Assume $f''(x)$ to be continuous]

(a) 0 (b) 1

(c) –1 (d) None of these

25. The point of contact of the tangents drawn from origin to the curve $y = \cos x$ lies on the curve

(a) $x^2 - y^2 = xy$ (b) $x^2 + y^2 = xy$

(c) $x^2 + y^2 = x^2y^2$ (d) $x^2 - y^2 = x^2y^2$

26. A particle moving on a curve has the position at time t given by $x = f'(t)\sin t + f''(t)\cos t$, $y = f'(t)\cos t - f''(t)\sin t$, where f is a thrice differentiable function. Then the velocity of the particle at time t is

(a) $f'(t)+f''(t)$ (b) $f'(t)-f''(t)$

(c) $f'(t)+f'''(t)$ (d) $f'(t)-f'''(t)$

27. Tangent at an angle increases four times as the angle itself. At that angle, sine of the angle increases at what rate w.r.t. the angle?

(a) $\frac{1}{2}$ units (b) $\frac{1}{\sqrt{2}}$ units

(c) $\frac{\sqrt{3}}{2}$ units (d) None of these

28. The sub-tangent, ordinate and subnormal to the parabola $y^2 = 4ax$ at a point (different from the origin) are in:

(a) G.P. (b) A.P.

(c) H.P. (d) None of these

29. A particle describes an ellipse whose semi-axes are 4m and 3m with centre at origin and a constant speed of 1m/sec. The velocity of the foot of the perpendicular from the particle on the major axis, when the particle is at a distance of 1m from the major axis is equal to

(a) 2/11 m/s (b) 11/2 m/s

(c) $\sqrt{(2/11)}$ m/s (d) None of these

SECTION–IV

MORE THAN ONE ARE CORRECT ANSWER

1. If the curve $\frac{x^2}{a^2}+\frac{y^2}{4}=1$ & $y^3=16x$ intersect at right angles, then values of a is/are

(a) $\frac{2}{\sqrt{3}}$ (b) 2

(c) $-\frac{2}{\sqrt{3}}$ (d) not possible

2. The equation of normal to the curve $\left(\frac{x}{a}\right)^n+\left(\frac{y}{b}\right)^n=2(n\in\mathbb{N})$ at the point with abscissa equal to 'a' can be

(a) $ax + by = a^2 - b^2$ (b) $ax + by = a^2 + b^2$

(c) $ax - by = a^2 - b^2$ (d) $bx - ay = a^2 - b^2$

3. Let the parabolas $y = x^2 + ax + b$ and $y = x(c - x)$ touch each other at the point (1,0).Then

(a) $a = -3$ (b) $b = 1$

(c) $c = 2$ (d) $b + c = 3$

4. For the curve represented paramatrically by the equations, $x = 2\ \ell n\cot t + 1$ & $y = \tan t + \cot t$

(a) tangent at $t = \pi/4$ is parallel to x-axis

(b) normal at $t = \pi/4$ is parallel to y-axis

(c) tangent at $t = \pi/4$ is parallel to the line $y = x$

(d) tangent and normal intersect at the point (2, 1)

5. The angle at which the curve $y = ke^{kx}$ intersects the y-axis is

(a) $\tan^{-1}k^2$ (b) $\cot^{-1}(k^2)$

(c) $\sin^{-1}\left(\frac{1}{\sqrt{1+k^4}}\right)$ (d) $\sec^{-1}\left(\sqrt{1+k^4}\right)$

6. The triangle formed by the normal to the curve $f(x) = x^2 - ax + 2a$ at the point (2, 4) and the coordinate axes lies in second quadrant if its area is 2 sq. units, then a can be

(a) 2 (b) $\frac{17}{4}$

(c) 5 (d) $\frac{19}{4}$

7. If at each point of the curve $y = x^3 - ax^2 + x + 1$, the tangent is inclined at a positive acute angle with positive direction of x-axis, then possible integral value of 'a'

(a) –1 (b) 0

(c) 1 (d) 2

8. For function $f(x) = \frac{\ell nx}{x}$, which of the following statements are true

(a) $f(x)$ has horizontal tangent at $x = e$

(b) $f(x)$ cuts the x-axis only at one point

(c) $f(x)$ is many one function

(d) $f(x)$ has one vertical tangent

9. A tangent drawn to the curve $y = f(x)$ at $P(x, y)$ cuts the x-axis and y-axis at A and B respectively such that $BP: AP = 3: 1$, given that $f(1) = 1$, then

(a) Differential equation of curve is $x\frac{dy}{dx} - 3y = 0$

(b) normal at (1, 1) is $x + 3y = 4$

(c) curve passes through (2, 1/8)

(d) Differential equation of curve is $x\frac{dy}{dx} + 3y = 0$

10. If the tangent to the curve $2y^3 = ax^2 + x^3$ at the point (a, a) cuts off intercepts α, β on co-ordinate axes where $\alpha^2 + \beta^2 = 61$, then the value of a is equal to
(a) 20 (b) 25
(c) 30 (d) –30

11. Two tangents to the graph of function $f(x) = \sqrt{17(1+x^2)}$ intersect at right angles at a certain point on the y-axis. Then equations of tangents is
(a) $y = -x + 4$ (b) $y = x - 4$
(c) $y = x - 4$ (d) $y = 2x + 4$

12. A curve with equation of the form $y = ax^4 + bx^3 + cx + d$ has zero gradient at the point (0, 1) and also touches the x-axis at the point (–1, 0). Then the values of x for which the curve has negative gradient are
(a) $x > -1$ for $a < 0$ (b) $x < 1$
(c) $x < -1$ for $a > 0$ (d) $-1 \le x \le 1$

SECTION–V

ASSERTION REASON TYPE

1. **A:** The tangent at $x = 1$ to the curve $y = x^3 - x^2 - x + 2$ again meets the curve at $x = -2$.
R: When an equation of a tangent solved with the curve, repeated roots are obtained at point of tangency.

2. **A:** On solving the equation of tangent with the equation of circle, we get only one solution.
R: Tangent touches the curve only at one point.

3. **A:** The ratio of length of tangent to length of normal is proportional to the ordinate of the point of tangency at the curve $y^2 = 4ax$.
R: Length of normal and tangent to a curve $y = f(x)$ is $\left|y\sqrt{m}\right|$ and $\left|\frac{y\sqrt{1+m^2}}{m}\right|$, where $m = \frac{dy}{dx}$.

4. **A:** The product of the ordinates of the point of tangency to the curve $(1 + x^2)\, y = 2 - x$, where the tangent makes equal intercept with coordinate axes is equal to 1.
R: Slope of straight line making equal and same sign intercept with coordinate axes is equal to –1.

5. **A:** If S be the area of a circle having radius x and A is the area of an equilateral triangle having side πx at any instant, then $\frac{dA}{dt} > \frac{ds}{dt}$, when $\frac{dx}{dt} > 0$
R: $A > S$

6. **A:** If a quadratic curve passes through (0, 1) and touches the line $y = x$ at the point (1, 1), then the values of x for which the curve has a negative gradient are $x < 1/2$.
R: The equation of the curve is $y = x^2 - x + 1$.

7. **A:** Shortest distance between $|x| + |y| = 2$ and $x^2 + y^2 = 16$ is $4 - \sqrt{2}$
R: Shortest distance between the two smooth curves lies along the common normal

8. **A:** Any tangent to the curve $y = x^7 + 8x^3 + 2x + 1$ makes an acute angle with the positive x-axis.
R: Any tangent to the curve $y = a_0 x^{2n+1} + a_1 x^{2n-1} + a_2 x^{2n-3} + \ldots\ldots + a_n x + 1$ makes an acute angle with the positive x-axis, where $a_1, \ldots\ldots a_{n-1} \ge 0$; $a_0, a_n > 0$ and $n \in \mathbb{N}$.

SECTION–VI

COMPREHENSION PASSAGE

A: Let $f(x) = \frac{1}{1+x^2}$. Let m be the slope, a be the x-intercept and b be the y-intercept of a tangent to $y = f(x)$, then

1. Abscissa of the point of contact of the tangent for which m is greatest
(a) $\frac{1}{\sqrt{3}}$ (b) 1
(c) –1 (d) $-\frac{1}{\sqrt{3}}$

2. Find the greatest value of b

(a) $\frac{9}{8}$ (b) $\frac{3}{6}$

(c) $\frac{1}{8}$ (d) $\frac{5}{8}$

3. Find the abscissa of the point of contact of tangent for which m is smallest

(a) $\frac{1}{\sqrt{3}}$ (b) 1

(c) –1 (d) $-\frac{1}{\sqrt{3}}$

B: Consider the function $f(x) = x^2 f(1) - xf'(2) + f''(3)$, such that $f(0) = 2$

4. The value of $f'(1)$ is

(a) 0 (b) 1

(c) 2 (d) –1

5. Equation of tangent to $y = f(x)$ at $x = 3$ is

(a) $y = x - 7$ (b) $y = \frac{x}{4} - 7$

(c) $y = 4x - 7$ (d) None of these

6. The angle of intersection of $y = f(x)$ and $y = e^{2(x-1)}$ is

(a) $\tan^{-1}\left(\frac{3}{4}\right)$ (b) $\tan^{-1}2$

(c) 0 (b) None of these

C: In second degree curves, a line which once touches the curve can't meet the curve again but in cubic and non-algebraic curves the tangent can meet the curve again. If we solve the equation of tangent and a cubic curve, we will, in general, get three roots, two of which will be equal, since they will correspond to the point where the tangent was initially drawn.

7. If P is a point (β, β^3) different from (0, 0) on the curve $y = x^3$. The tangent at P meets the curve again at Q and tangent at Q meets the curve again at R, then abscissa of the point R must be

(a) 8β (b) -4β

(c) 4β (d) -2β

8. The tangent at $(t, t^2 - t^3)$ on the curve $y = x^2 - x^3$ meets the curve again at Q, and then abscissa of Q must be

(a) $1 + 2t$ (b) $1 - 2t$

(c) $-1 - 2t$ (d) $2t - 1$

9. If the tangent at 't' of the curve $y = 8t^3 - 1$, $x = 4t^2 + 3$ meets the curve at 't' and is normal to the curve at that point, then value of t must be

(a) $\pm\frac{1}{\sqrt{3}}$ (b) $\pm\frac{1}{\sqrt{2}}$

(c) $\pm\frac{\sqrt{2}}{3}$ (d) None of these

D: Let $y = f_1(x)$ and $y = f_2(x)$ be the two curves, meeting at some point $P(x_1, y_1)$, then θ = angle between the two curves at $P(x_1, y_1)$ = *a*ngle between the tangents to the curves at $P(x_1, y_1)$. Clearly, $\theta = \pm(\theta_1 - \theta_2)$. where θ_1 and θ_2 are the inclinations of tangents to the curves $y = f_1(x)$ and $y = f_2(x)$ respectively at the point P. Also, $\tan\theta = \frac{m_1 - m_2}{1 + m_1 m_2}$, where, $m_1 = \left(\frac{dy}{dx}\right)_{(x_1, y_1)}$ for $y = f_1(x) = \tan\theta_1$ and $m_2 = \left(\frac{dy}{dx}\right)_{(x_1, y_1)}$ for $y = f_2(x) = \tan\theta_2$. If the angle of intersection of two curves is a right angle, then the two curves are said to be orthogonal. Therefore for orthogonal curves $\left(\frac{dy}{dx}\right)_{c_1}\left(\frac{dy}{dx}\right)_{c_2} = -1$.

10. The angle between the tangents to the curve $\frac{x^2}{a^2} + \frac{y^2}{b^2} = 1$ at the points $(a, 0)$ and $(0, b)$ is

(a) $\pi/4$ (b) $\pi/2$

(c) $\pi/3$ (d) None of these

11. The angle of intersection of the curves $y = 2\sin^2 x$ and $y = \cos 2x$ at $x = \pi/6$ is

(a) $\pi/4$ (b) $\pi/3$

(c) $\pi/2$ (d) None of these

12. The parabolas $y^2 = 4ax$ and $x^2 = 4by$ intersect orthogonally at the point $P(x_1, y_1)$, where $x_1, y_1 \neq 0$, then

(a) $b = a^2$ (b) $b = a^3$

(c) $b^3 = a^2$ (d) None of these

13. The acute angle between the curves $y = |x^2 - 1|$ and $y = |x^2 - 3|$ at their points of intersection when $x > 0$, is $\tan^{-1}(m)$, where m is equal to

(a) $\frac{2\sqrt{2}}{7}$ (b) $\frac{4\sqrt{2}}{7}$

(c) $\frac{\sqrt{2}}{7}$ (d) None of these

SECTION—VII

COLUMN-MATCHING

1. Match the following

Column-I

(i) Circular plate is expanded by heat from radius 5 cm to 5.06 cm. The approximate increase in area is

(ii) Sides of a cube increasing by 1% then the percentage increase in volume is

(iii) If the rate of decrease of $\frac{x^2}{2} - 2x + 5$ is twice the rate of decrease of x, then x is equal to

(iv) Rate of increase in area of equilateral triangle of side 15 cm, when each side is increasing at the rate of 0.1 cm/s is

Column-II

(a) 4

(b) 0.6π

(c) 7

(d) $\frac{3\sqrt{3}}{2}$

2. Match the following

Column-I

(i) If $f(x)$ is a quadratic expression in x and $6\int_0^1 f(x)\,dx = k f(1) + f(0) + 4f(1/2)$, then k is

(ii) If the sum of the squares of the intercepts on the axes cut off by the tangents to the curve $x^{1/3} + y^{1/3} = a^{1/3}$ $(a > 0)$ at $\left(\frac{a}{8}, \frac{a}{8}\right)$ is 2, then a is

(iii) The distance of the point on $y = x^4 + 3x^2 + 2x$ which is nearest to the line $y = 2x - 1$ is r, then $\sqrt{5}\, r$ is

(iv) If $f(x) = -2\,|\sin x| + ae^{|x|} + 5\,|\tan x|^3$ is differentiable at $x = 0$, then a is

Column-II

(a) 1

(b) 4

(c) 3

(d) 2

3 Let $x = a\cos t + at\sin t$ and $y = a\sin t - at\cos t$. Match the Column-for $t = \pi/4$.

Column-1

(i) Length of sub-tangent

(ii) Length of normal

(iii) Length of intercepts by tangent between co-ordinate axes.

(iv) Perpendicular distance of tangent from origin.

Column-2

(a) $\frac{a\pi}{2}$

(b) $\frac{a}{\sqrt{2}}\left(1 - \frac{\pi}{4}\right)$

(c) $\frac{a\pi}{4}$

(d) $a\left(1 - \frac{\pi}{4}\right)$

4. Column-1

(i) The angle of intersection of $y^2 = 4x$ and $x^2 = 4y$ is $90°$ and $\tan^{-1}\left(\frac{m}{n}\right)$ then $|m + n|$ is equal to (m and n are co-prime)

(ii) The area of triangle formed by normal at the point (1, 0) on the curve $x = e^{\sin y}$ with axes is

(iii) The angle between curve $x^2 y = 1$ and $y = e^{2(1-x)}$

(iv) The length of sub-tangent at any point on the curve $y = be^{x/3}$ is equal to

Column-II

(a) 0

(b) 1/2

(c) 4

(d) 3

SECTION–VIII

NUMERICAL INTEGER TYPE

1. A curve passes through the point (2, –8) and the slope of tangent at any point (x, y) is given by $\frac{x^2}{2} - 6x$. The maximum ordinate on the curve is given by λ, then find (3λ).

2. Find the abscissa of the point on the curve $4y^2 = x^3$, the normal at which cuts intercepts (x-intercept and y-intercept) in the ratio 3:4.

3. Find the least positive integer value of 'α' for which Rolle's Theorem is applicable to function

$$f(x) = \begin{cases} x^{(\alpha^2-4\alpha+3)}.\log x & \text{if } x > 0 \\ 0 & \text{if } x = 0 \end{cases} \text{ in } [0, 1].$$

4. The volume of a moth ball decreases at a rate proportional to its instantaneous surface area. If the diameter of ball decreases from 3cm. to 1cm in 4 month, then how long will it take to disappear completely?

5. A tangent at a point P_1 on the curve $y = x^3$ meets the curve again at P_2 and the tangent at P_2 meets the curve again at P_3 and so on. If co-ordinates of P_1 are (2, 8), then find the abscissa of point P_5.

6. A and B are two tanks, such that the capacity of A is 3 times that of B. Both tanks are completely filled and their inlets are closed. Now water is released from the tanks. The rate of flow of water from each tank is proportional to the water in the tank at that instant. If after 1 hours, the water in time A is 2 times the water in tank B. If both tanks have same quantity of water after time $(\log_{2m}(m))$, then find $\left(\frac{1}{m}\right)$.

7. From a point P on the curve $a^4x + 2b^2y^2 = 0$, tangent PQ and PR are drawn to hyperbola $\frac{x^2}{b^2} - \frac{y^2}{a^2} = 1$. If QR touches a fixed parabola, then find the length of latus rectum of that parabola.

8. A lamp post is of height 50m. A ball is dropped from same height and falls under gravity $(g = 10m/\sec^2)$. If the horizontal distance between the ball and shadow of ball is moving along the ground $\frac{1}{2}$ sec after the ball is dropped.

Answer Keys

SECTION–III

1. (d)	**2.** (d)	**3.** (a)	**4.** (d)	**5.** (b)	**6.** (c)	**7.** (c)	**8.** (b)	**9.** (d)	**10.** (b)
11. (b)	**12.** (b)	**13.** (b)	**14.** (b)	**15.** (b)	**16.** (c)	**17.** (b)	**18.** (b)	**19.** (d)	**20.** (c)
21. (a)	**22.** (b)	**23.** (a)	**24.** (c)	**25.** (d)	**26.** (c)	**27.** (a)	**28.** (a)	**29.** (c)	

SECTION–IV

1. (a, c) **2.** (a, c) **3.** (a, d) **4.** (a, b) **5.** (b, c) **6.** (c) **7.** (a, b, c) **8.** (a, b, c,d) **9.** (a, b)
10. (c, d) **11.** (b, c) **12.** (a, c)

SECTION–V

1. (d) **2.** (c) **3.** (a) **4.** (a) **5.** (a) **6.** (a) **7.** (d) **8.** (a)

SECTION–VI

1. (d) **2.** (a) **3.** (a) **4.** (a) **5.** (c) **6.** (b) **7.** (c) **8.** (b) **9.** (c) **10.** (b)
11. (b) **12.** (d) **13.** (b)

SECTION–VII

1. (i) → (b); (ii) → (c); (iii) → (a); (iv) → (d)
2. (i) → (a); (ii) → (b); (iii) → (a); (iv) → (d)
3. (i) → (b); (ii) → (d); (iii) → (a); (iv) → (c)
4. (i) → (c); (ii) → (b); (iii) → (a); (iv) → (d)

SECTION–VIII

1. 8 **2.** 1 **3.** 4 **4.** 6 **5.** 32 **6.** 3 **7.** 8 **8.** 3200

HINTS AND SOLUTIONS

RATE OF CHANGE TEXTUAL EXERCISE-1: (SUBJECTIVE)

1. $s=\frac{1}{2}t^2+4\sqrt{t}$

$\Rightarrow \frac{ds}{dt}=v=\frac{1}{2}(2t)+\frac{4}{2\sqrt{t}}=t+\frac{2}{\sqrt{t}}$

$\therefore \quad a=\frac{d^2s}{dt^2}=1+2\left(\frac{-1}{2}\right)\left(t\sqrt{t}\right)^{-1}=1-\frac{1}{t\sqrt{t}}$ at $t = 4$s,

$\Rightarrow \frac{ds}{dt}=v=4+\frac{2}{2}=5\ m/s$ and $a=1-\frac{1}{8}=\frac{7}{8}m/s^2$

2. $s=\frac{t^3}{2}-6t \quad \Rightarrow \frac{ds}{dt}=\frac{3t^2}{2}-6=0$

$\Rightarrow t = 2$ sec

$a=\frac{3}{2}(2t)=3t=6\ m/\sec^2$ at $t = 2$sec

3. $v=k\sqrt{x}$; $a=v\frac{dv}{dx} \quad \Rightarrow a=\frac{(k\sqrt{x})k}{2\sqrt{x}}=\frac{k^2}{2}$

4. $6y = x^3 + 2$

$\Rightarrow 6\frac{dy}{dt}=3x^2\frac{dx}{dt}$

A.T.Q, $\frac{dy}{dt}=8\left(\frac{dx}{dt}\right)$

$\Rightarrow 6(8)\frac{dx}{dt}=3x^2\frac{dx}{dt}$

$\Rightarrow x^2 = 16 \quad \Rightarrow x = 4, -4$

$\Rightarrow$ The required point on the curve is (4, 11) and (–4, –31/3)

5. $y^2 = 8x$

$\Rightarrow 2y\frac{dy}{dt}=8\frac{dx}{dt}$

For $\frac{dx}{dt}=\frac{dy}{dt} \quad \Rightarrow 2y = 8,$

$\Rightarrow y = 4, x = 2$

$\therefore$ (2, 4) is the required point

6. $V=\frac{4}{3}\pi R^3$

$\Rightarrow \frac{dV}{dt}=\frac{4}{3}\pi(3R^2)\frac{dR}{dt}=4\pi R^2\frac{dR}{dt}$

$\Rightarrow \frac{dR}{dt}=\left(\frac{dV}{dt}\right)\times\frac{1}{4\pi R^2}$; $A = 4\pi R^2$

$\Rightarrow \frac{dA}{dt}=4\pi(2R).\frac{dR}{dt}=\frac{2}{R}\left(\frac{dV}{dt}\right)$

$\Rightarrow \frac{dA}{dt}=\frac{2}{5}\times 25=10cm^2/s$

7. (i) Perimeter = $P = 2(x + y)$

$\Rightarrow \frac{dP}{dt}=2\left(\frac{dx}{dt}+\frac{dy}{dt}\right)=2(-5+4)=-2$ cm / min

(ii) A = Area = $l \times b = xy$

$\Rightarrow \frac{dA}{dt}=x\frac{dy}{dt}+y\frac{dx}{dt}=8(4)-6(5)=32-30=2$ cm^2 / min

8. $R = 3$m, $A = \pi R^2$; $\frac{dR}{dt}=0.05cm/\sec$

$\Rightarrow \frac{dA}{dt}=2\pi R.\frac{dR}{dt}=2\pi\times 3.2\times 0.05=0.32\pi\ cm^2/s$

9. $t = 0, t = t$

$x=t^2\left(2-\frac{t}{3}\right)=2t^2-\frac{t^3}{3}$

$\Rightarrow \frac{dx}{dt}=4t-\frac{3t^2}{3}=4t-t^2 \quad \therefore \quad 4t - t^2 = 0$

$\Rightarrow t(4 - t) = 0 \quad \Rightarrow t = 0, t = 4s$

$\Rightarrow x=(4)^2\left(2-\frac{4}{3}\right)=16\times\frac{2}{3}=\frac{32}{3}m$

TEXTUAL EXERCISE-1: (OBJECTIVE)

1. (b) $\frac{dr}{dt}=4cm/\sec$, enclosed area $A = \pi r^2$,

Differentiate, w.r.t. t

$\Rightarrow \frac{dA}{dt}=2\pi r.\frac{dr}{dt}$, where r = 10cm

$\Rightarrow \frac{dA}{dt}=2\pi(10)(4) = 80\pi$ cm^2/sec.

2. (c) $\frac{dV}{dt}=a$ cm^3/min

Surface Area $A = 4\pi r^2$, $V=\frac{4}{3}\pi r^3$

$\Rightarrow \frac{dA}{dt}=(4\pi)(2r)\frac{dr}{dt}$ ...(1),

$\Rightarrow \frac{dV}{dt}=\frac{4}{3}\pi(3r^2)\frac{dr}{dt}$

$\Rightarrow \frac{a}{4\pi r^2}=\frac{dr}{dt}$ ...(2),

Put (2) in (1), $\frac{dA}{dt}=(4\pi)(2r)\frac{a}{4\pi r^2}=\frac{2a}{r}$, where $r = b$ cm

$\Rightarrow \frac{dA}{dt}=\frac{2a}{b}cm^2/\min$

3. (a) $\frac{dl}{dt}=10cm/s$

$V = l^3$

$\frac{dV}{dt}=(3l^2)\frac{dl}{dt}$

Where l = 5cm, $\frac{dV}{dt}=3(5)^2(10)=750\ cm^3/\sec$

4. (c) $s = 48t - 16t^2 \Rightarrow \frac{ds}{dt} = 48 - 32t$

$\Rightarrow t = \frac{48}{32} = \frac{3}{2}$

$\Rightarrow s = 48\left(\frac{3}{2}\right) - 16 \times \frac{9}{4} = 72 - 36 = 36m$

Greatest height above ground = 36 + 64 = 100m

5. (b) $\frac{dl}{dt} = 0.5$ and $l = a\sqrt{2}$

$\Rightarrow \frac{l}{\sqrt{2}} = a$ and $A = a^2$

$\Rightarrow A = \frac{l^2}{2}$

$\Rightarrow \frac{dA}{dt} = \frac{1}{2}(2l)\frac{dl}{dt} = l(0.5)$

When A = 400 cm², $\sqrt{400 \times 2} = l$

$\Rightarrow l = 20\sqrt{2}$ cm²

$\Rightarrow \frac{dA}{dt} = 20\sqrt{2} \times \frac{5}{10} = 10\sqrt{2}\ cm^2/s$

6. (b) $x = t - 6t^2 + t^3$

$\Rightarrow v = \frac{dx}{dt} = 1 - 12t + 3t^2$ and $a = \frac{dv}{dt} = -12 + 6t$

$\therefore -12 + 6t = 0 \quad \Rightarrow t = 2$ units

7. (a) $x = 3 + 8t - 4t^2$

$\Rightarrow \frac{dx}{dt} = v = 8 - 8t$, at $t = 1s$

$\Rightarrow v = 8 - 8(1) = 0$

8. (a) $s = 2t^3 - 9t^2 + 12t$

$\frac{ds}{dt} = v = 6t^2 - 18t + 12$ and $\frac{dv}{dt} = a = 12t - 18$

$\therefore 12t - 18 = 0 \quad \Rightarrow t = \frac{18}{12} = \frac{3}{2}s$

9. (b) $x = 80t - 16t^2$

At maximum height, $\frac{dx}{dt} = 0$ i.e., $v = 0$

$\Rightarrow \frac{dx}{dt} = 80 - 32t = 0 \quad \Rightarrow t = \frac{80}{32} = 2.5s$

10. (b) $\frac{dV}{dt} = 30\,ft^3/\min$

$\frac{dr}{dt} = ?$ where $r = 15$ft.

Now, $V = \frac{4}{3}\pi r^3$

$\Rightarrow \frac{dV}{dt} = \frac{4}{3}\pi(3r^2)\frac{dr}{dt} \quad \Rightarrow \frac{dr}{dt} = \frac{dV}{dt} \times \frac{1}{(4\pi r^2)}$

$\Rightarrow \frac{dr}{dt} = (30) \times \frac{1}{4\pi \times (15) \times (15)} ft/\min = \frac{1}{30\pi} ft/\min$

11. (c) $\frac{dr}{dt} = 2cm/\min$

$V = \frac{4}{3}\pi r^3$

$\Rightarrow \frac{dV}{dt} = \frac{4\pi}{3}(3r^2)\frac{dr}{dt} = 4\pi r^2 \frac{dr}{dt}$

$\Rightarrow \frac{dV}{dt} = 4\pi (5)^2 \times 2 = 200\pi$ cm³/min

12. (c) Using similarity of Δs ABC & CDE using B.P.T

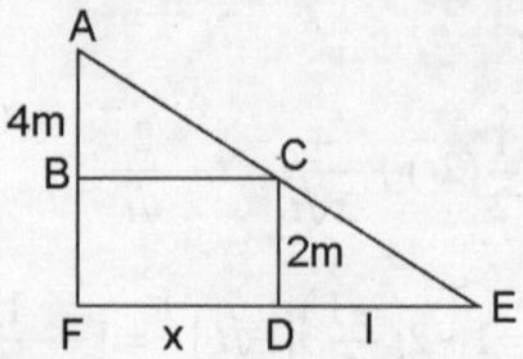

$\frac{AB}{CD} = \frac{BC}{DE} \quad \Rightarrow \frac{4}{2} = \frac{x}{l}$

$\Rightarrow l = \frac{x}{2}$

$\Rightarrow \frac{dl}{dt} = \frac{1}{2}.\frac{dx}{dt}$ and $\frac{dx}{dt} = 6km/hr$

$\Rightarrow \frac{dl}{dt} = \frac{1}{2}(6)$ km / hr $\Rightarrow \frac{dl}{dt} = 3km/hr$

13. (a) $\frac{dr}{dt} = 3m/s$, $\frac{dh}{dt} = -4m/s$

$V = \pi r^2 h$,

$\Rightarrow \frac{dV}{dt} = \pi\left((2rh)\frac{dr}{dt} + r^2.\frac{dh}{dt}\right)$

$\Rightarrow \frac{dV}{dt} = \pi\left((2 \times 4 \times 6)(3) + (4)^2(-4)\right)$

$= \pi(144 - 64) = 80\pi\ m^3/s$

14. (c) $\frac{dr}{dt} = 2cm/\sec$

$A = \pi r^2$

$\Rightarrow \frac{dA}{dt} = \pi(2r)\frac{dr}{dt}$

$\Rightarrow \frac{dA}{dt} = \pi(2 \times 20) \times 2$ cm²/sec = 80π cm²/sec

15. (b) $\frac{dx}{dt} = 4cm/hr$,

$\frac{dy}{dt} = 3cm/hr$, the shortest distance be l using, cosine formula, $\cos(120^\circ) = \frac{x^2 + y^2 - l^2}{2xy}$

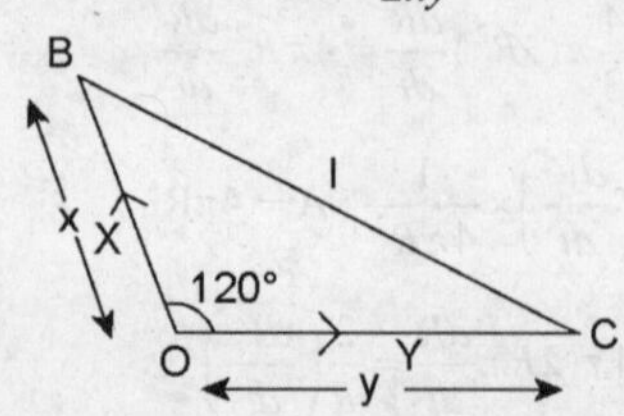

$\Rightarrow \frac{-1}{2}(2xy) = x^2 + y^2 - l^2$

$\Rightarrow \quad l^2 = x^2 + y^2 + xy$

$\Rightarrow \quad (2l).\frac{dl}{dt} = 2x.\frac{dx}{dt} + 2y.\frac{dy}{dt} + x\frac{dy}{dt} + y\frac{dx}{dt}$

After 1 hour, $x = \left(\frac{dx}{dt}\right).t = 4 \times 1 = 4$ km and $y = \left(\frac{dy}{dt}\right).t$

$= 3 \times 1 = 3$ km

$\therefore \quad l = \sqrt{(3)^2 + (4)^2 + 3(4)} = \sqrt{9+16+12} = \sqrt{37}$

$\therefore \quad 2\left(\sqrt{37}\right)\frac{dl}{dt} = 8 \times 4 + 2(3)(3) + 4(3) + 3(4)$

$\Rightarrow \quad 2\sqrt{37}\frac{dl}{dt} = 32 + 18 + 24 = 74$

$\Rightarrow \quad \frac{dl}{dt} = \frac{74}{2\sqrt{37}} = \frac{37}{\sqrt{37}} = \sqrt{37}$ km/hr

16. (a) $x = 100t - \frac{25}{2}t^2$

$\Rightarrow \quad \frac{dx}{dt} = 100 - \frac{25}{2}(2t) = 100 - 25t$

$\Rightarrow \quad 100 - 25t = 0$

$\Rightarrow \quad t = 4$

$\Rightarrow \quad x = 100\,(4) - \frac{25}{2}(16) = 400 - 200 = 200$ m

17. (a) $s = 16 - 2t + 3t^3$

$\Rightarrow \quad \frac{ds}{dt} = -2 + 9t^2 \qquad \Rightarrow \quad \frac{d^2s}{dt^2} = a = 18t$

After $t = 2s$, $a = 36\ m/s^2$

18. (a) $s = 22t - 12t^2$

$\Rightarrow \quad \frac{ds}{dt} = 22 - 24t \qquad \Rightarrow \quad 22 - 24t = 0$

$\Rightarrow \quad t = \frac{22}{24} = \frac{11}{12}$

$\Rightarrow \quad s = 22\left(\frac{11}{12}\right) - 12\left(\frac{11}{12}\right)^2 = \frac{11}{12}(22-11) = \frac{121}{12} = 10.08\,ft$

19. (d) $\frac{dr}{dr} = 0.1$ cm / sec

$A = \pi r^2$

$\Rightarrow \quad \frac{dA}{dt} = \pi.(2r)\frac{dr}{dt}$

$\Rightarrow \quad \frac{dA}{dt} = \pi(2\times 5).\frac{1}{10} = \pi \text{ cm}^2/\text{sec}$

20. (b) $\frac{dV}{dt} = 35 \text{ cm}^3 / \text{min}$

$\therefore \quad V = \frac{4}{3}\pi r^3$, $A = 4\pi r^2$

$\Rightarrow \quad \frac{dV}{dt} = \frac{4}{3}\pi(3r^2)\frac{dr}{dt}, \ \frac{dA}{dt} = (4\pi)(2r).\frac{dr}{dt}$ ...(1)

Put (2) in (1), we get $\frac{dr}{dt} = \left(\frac{dV}{dt}\right)\frac{1}{4\pi r^2}$ ...(2)

$\frac{dA}{dt} = (4\pi)(2r)\left(\frac{dV}{dt}\right) \times \frac{1}{4\pi r^2} = \frac{2}{r}.\frac{dV}{dt} = \frac{2}{7}35 = 10 \text{ cm}^2 / \text{min}$

21. (c) Volume shell, $V = \frac{4}{3}\pi((10+x)^3 - (10)^3)$

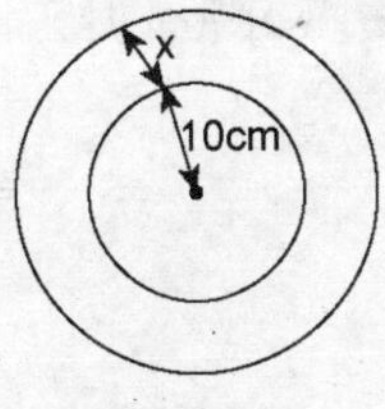

Given, $\frac{dV}{dt} = -50$ cm³/minute

$\Rightarrow \quad \frac{4}{3}\pi\left[3(10+x)^2.\frac{dx}{dt}\right] = -50$

$\Rightarrow \quad \frac{dx}{dt} = \frac{-50}{4\pi(10+x)^2}$

When, $x = 15$, $\frac{dx}{dt} = \frac{-50}{4\pi(25)^2} = \frac{-2}{100\pi} = \frac{-1}{50\pi}$ cm/minute

22. (d) $x^2 + y^2 = 100$

$\Rightarrow \quad 2x\frac{dx}{dt} + 2y.\frac{dy}{dx} = 0 \qquad \Rightarrow \quad x\frac{dx}{dt} + y.\frac{dy}{dt} = 0$

$\Rightarrow \quad x.(3) + y.(-4) = 0$

$\Rightarrow \quad y = \frac{3x}{4} \qquad \Rightarrow \quad x = \frac{4y}{3}$

$\Rightarrow \quad \frac{16y^2}{9} + y^2 = 100 \qquad \Rightarrow \quad \frac{25y^2}{9} = 100$

$\Rightarrow \quad y^2 = \frac{100\times 9}{25} \qquad \Rightarrow \quad y = \frac{10\times 3}{5} = 6m$

23. (c) $y = x^2 + 2x$

$\frac{dy}{dt} = 2x.\frac{dx}{dt} + 2.\frac{dx}{dt}$ ...(i)

Now, $\frac{dx}{dt} = \frac{dy}{dt}$ (Given)

$\Rightarrow \quad 1 = 2x + 2 \qquad \Rightarrow \quad y = \frac{1}{4} + 2\left(\frac{-1}{2}\right) = \frac{-3}{4}, x = \frac{-1}{2}$

$\Rightarrow \quad (x, y) \equiv \left(\frac{-1}{2}, \frac{-3}{4}\right)$

24. (d) $y = 4 - 2x^2$

$\Rightarrow \quad \frac{dy}{dt} = -4x\frac{dx}{dt}$ and $\frac{dx}{dt} = -5$ unit/s

$\Rightarrow \quad \frac{dy}{dt} = -(4)(1).(-5)$ unit/s = 20 unit/ s

25. (a), (b), (c)

$s = \sqrt{t}$

$\Rightarrow \quad \frac{ds}{dt} = \frac{1}{2\sqrt{t}} = v \qquad \Rightarrow \sqrt{t} = \frac{1}{2v}$ ...(i)

$\Rightarrow \quad a = \frac{d^2s}{dt^2} = \frac{1}{2}\left(\frac{-1}{2}\right)t^{-3/2} \quad \Rightarrow \frac{-1}{4t\sqrt{t}} < 0$ ...(ii)

$\therefore \quad a = \frac{-1}{4t\sqrt{t}} = \frac{-1}{4\left(\frac{1}{2v}\right)\left(\frac{1}{2v}\right)^2} = \frac{-8v^3}{4} = -2v^3$

$\Rightarrow a \propto v^3$

$\Rightarrow v = \frac{1}{2\sqrt{t}} \quad \Rightarrow v = \frac{1}{2s}$

$\Rightarrow v \propto \frac{1}{s}$

26. **(c)** $x = 4\cos\theta$ and $y = 3\sin\theta$

$\frac{dx}{dt} = -4\sin\theta.\frac{d\theta}{dt}$ ...(1)

and $\frac{dy}{dt} = 3\cos\theta.\frac{d\theta}{dt}$ ...(2)

Also as $|v| = 1, \quad \Rightarrow \left(\frac{dx}{dt}\right)^2 + \left(\frac{dy}{dt}\right)^2 = 1$

$\Rightarrow \left(\frac{d\theta}{dt}\right)^2 = \frac{1}{16\sin^2\theta + 9\cos^2\theta} = \frac{1}{7\sin^2\theta + 9}$, at $y = 1 =$ 3sinθ

$\Rightarrow \sin\theta = \frac{1}{3}$

$\therefore \left(\frac{d\theta}{dt}\right) = \sqrt{\frac{1}{\frac{7}{9}+9}} = \frac{3}{2\sqrt{22}}$, Put in (1), we get

$\frac{dx}{dt} = \frac{-4}{3}\left(\frac{3}{2\sqrt{22}}\right) = -\sqrt{\frac{2}{11}} m/s$

27. **(b)** $x = 3000$ ft; $y = 5000$ ft;

$y^2 = x^2 + (4000)^2$;

$\frac{dx}{dt} = 600$ft./sec

$\Rightarrow 2y.\frac{dy}{dt} = 2x\frac{dx}{dt}$

$\Rightarrow \frac{dy}{dt} = \frac{x}{y}\frac{dx}{dt}$

$\Rightarrow \left(\frac{dy}{dt}\right) = (600)\left(\frac{3000}{5000}\right) = 120 \times 3 = 360\, ft/\text{sec}$.

28. **(b)** Let y = Number of people at a time t

$\therefore \frac{dy}{dt} \alpha y \quad \Rightarrow \frac{dy}{dt} = ky$

$\Rightarrow \frac{dy}{y} = kdt \quad \Rightarrow \ln y = kt + c$

$\Rightarrow y = e^{kt+c} \quad \Rightarrow y = c'e^{kt}$

$\Rightarrow c' \geq 0$

Since according to question, population never increases i.e., decreasing with time and $\frac{dy}{dt} = ky$

$\Rightarrow k \leq 0$

29. **(a)** $s^2 = at^2 + 2bt + c$,

$\Rightarrow 2s.\frac{ds}{dt} = 2at + 2b$

$\Rightarrow \frac{ds}{dt} = \left(\frac{at+b}{s}\right) = v; \quad \frac{d^2s}{dt^2} = f =$ acceleration and

$s.\frac{ds}{dt} = at + b$

$\Rightarrow s.\frac{d^2s}{dt^2} + \left(\frac{ds}{dt}\right)\left(\frac{ds}{dt}\right) = a$

$\Rightarrow s.f + v^2 = a$

$\Rightarrow f = \frac{a - v^2}{s} = \frac{a - \left(\frac{(at+b)}{s}\right)^2}{s} = \frac{as^2 - a^2t^2 - b^2 - 2atb}{s^2 \times s}$

$= \frac{a^2t^2 + 2abt + ca - a^2t^2 - b^2 - 2atb}{s^3} = \frac{ca - b^2}{s^3}$

$\Rightarrow f \propto \frac{1}{s^3}$

30. **(d)** $s \propto \sqrt[3]{v} \quad \Rightarrow s = k(v)^{\frac{1}{3}}$

$\Rightarrow \frac{ds}{dt} = (k)\frac{1}{3}(v)^{\frac{1}{3}-1}\frac{dv}{dt} \quad \Rightarrow v = \frac{k}{3v^{2/3}}.(a)$

$\Rightarrow \frac{3v^{5/3}}{k} = a \begin{cases} k(v^{1/3}) = s \\ v^{1/3} = \frac{s}{k} \\ v^{5/3} = \frac{s^5}{k^5} \end{cases} \Rightarrow \frac{3.s^5}{k^6} = a$

$\Rightarrow a \propto s^5$

31. **(a)** $s = k\sqrt{t}$

$\Rightarrow \frac{ds}{dt} = \frac{k}{2\sqrt{t}} \quad \Rightarrow v = \frac{k}{2\sqrt{t}}$

$\Rightarrow \sqrt{t} = \frac{k}{2v}$ ...(1)

$\Rightarrow \frac{d^2s}{dt^2} = \frac{k}{2} \times \left(\frac{-1}{2}\right)\left(t\sqrt{t}\right)^{-1} = \frac{-k}{4t\sqrt{t}}$

$\Rightarrow a = \frac{-k}{4t\sqrt{t}}$ ...(2)

$\Rightarrow a = \frac{-k}{4\left(\frac{k^2}{4v^2}\right)^{3/2}} = \frac{-kv^3}{\frac{4}{8}(k)^3} = \frac{-2v3}{k^2}$

$\Rightarrow a \alpha v^3$

32. **(d)** $s = kv^2$,

$\frac{ds}{dt} = k(2v).\frac{dv}{dt}$

$\Rightarrow v = k(2v).(a)$

$\Rightarrow a = \frac{1}{2k}$; which is constant

33. **(d)** $A = 4\pi r^2 \Rightarrow \frac{dA}{dt} = 4\pi(2r)\frac{dr}{dt}$

$\Rightarrow \frac{dA}{dt} = (8\pi \times 2).r = 16\pi r \Rightarrow \frac{dA}{dt} \propto r$

34. **(d)** $\frac{dV}{dt} = c$; c = constant and $V = \frac{4}{3}\pi r^3$

$\Rightarrow \frac{dV}{dt} = \left(\frac{4}{3}\pi\right)(3r^2)\frac{dr}{dt} = 4\pi r^2.\left(\frac{dr}{dt}\right)$

$\Rightarrow \frac{dr}{dt} = \frac{c}{4\pi r^2} \Rightarrow \frac{dr}{dt} \propto \frac{1}{4\pi r^2}$

35. **(c)** $t = as^2 + bs + c$

$\Rightarrow 1 = a\ 2s.\frac{ds}{dt} + b\frac{ds}{dt}$ ...(1)

$\Rightarrow 1 = (2as + b)\,v \Rightarrow v = \frac{1}{2as+b}$

$\Rightarrow 0 = 2a\left(s.\frac{d^2s}{dt^2} + \frac{ds}{dt}.\frac{ds}{dt}\right) + b.\frac{d^2s}{dt^2}$

$2a\,(s.a' + v^2) = -\,ba'$; $a' = \frac{d^2s}{dt^2}$

$\Rightarrow (2as + b)a' = -2av^2 \Rightarrow a' = \frac{-2av^2}{(2as+b)}$

$\Rightarrow a' = -2av^3$

36. **(c), (d)** $x = at^2 + bt + c$

$\Rightarrow \frac{dx}{dt} = 2at + b \Rightarrow \frac{d^2x}{dt^2} = 2a$

37. **(c)** $t = f(v)$ ...(1)

$\Rightarrow 1 = f'(v)\frac{dv}{dt}$

$\Rightarrow \frac{dv}{dt} = \frac{1}{f'(v)} \Rightarrow f'(v) = \frac{1}{a}$

$\Rightarrow f''(v).\frac{dv}{dt} = \frac{-1}{a^2}.\frac{da}{dt}$

$\Rightarrow \frac{da}{dt} = -a^3 f''(v)$ ...(2)

Also $f(v) = t$

$\Rightarrow f'(v) = \frac{dt}{dv}$

$\Rightarrow f''(v) = \frac{d^2t}{dv^2}$ ...(3)

$\therefore$ From (2) and (3), we get $\frac{da}{dt} = -a^3\frac{d^2t}{dv^2}$

TEXTUAL EXERCISE–2: (SUBJECTIVE)

1. $\frac{dh}{h} \times 100 = k$, semi vertical angle doesn't change

$\Rightarrow \frac{h}{r} = t$ (constant) $\Rightarrow h = rt$

(i) Total surface area = $\pi r\,(r + l)$; $l = \sqrt{r^2 + h^2} = r\sqrt{1+t^2}$

$\Rightarrow A = \pi r\left(r + r\sqrt{1+t^2}\right) = \pi r^2\left(1+\sqrt{t^2+1}\right)$

$\therefore A = \frac{\pi h^2}{t^2}\left(1+\sqrt{t^2+1}\right)$

$\Rightarrow \frac{dA}{dh} = \frac{\pi(2h)}{t^2}\left(1+\sqrt{t^2+1}\right)$

$\Rightarrow \frac{dA}{A} = \frac{2}{h}dh$

$\Rightarrow \frac{dA}{A} \times 100 = 2\left(\frac{dh}{h}\right) \times 100$

$\Rightarrow$ % age error $A = 2k\%$

(ii) $V = \frac{1}{3}\pi r^2 h = \frac{1}{3}\pi\frac{h^2}{t^2}.h$

$\Rightarrow \frac{dV}{dh} = \frac{\pi}{3t^2}(3h^2) = \frac{\pi h^2}{t^2}$

$\Rightarrow \frac{dV}{V} = \frac{3\pi h^2}{\pi h^3} = \frac{3}{h}dh$

$\Rightarrow \frac{dV}{V} \times 100 = 3\left(\frac{dh}{h} \times 100\right) = 3k\%$

$\therefore$ % age error in volume = $3k\%$

2. **(i)** Let $f(x) = y = \sqrt{x}$

$\frac{dy}{dx} = \frac{1}{2\sqrt{x}}$

Now, $f(x+\Delta x) = f(x) + \frac{dy}{dx}\Delta x$

Here, $x = 25$, $\Delta x = 1$

$\Rightarrow f(x+\Delta x) = f(26) = \sqrt{25} + \frac{1}{2\sqrt{25}} \times 1 = 5 + 0.1 = 5.1$

(ii) Let $f(x) = \sqrt{x} = y$

$\Rightarrow \frac{dy}{dx} = \frac{1}{2\sqrt{x}}$

Now, $f(x+\Delta x) = f(x) + \frac{dy}{dx}\Delta x$

Here, $x = 36$, $\Delta x = 1$

$\therefore f(37) = \sqrt{36} + \frac{1}{2\sqrt{36}} \times 1 = 6 + \frac{1}{12} = 6.083$ Ans

(iii) $f(x) = \sqrt{x} \Rightarrow \frac{dy}{dx} = \frac{1}{2\sqrt{x}}$

Here, $x = 0.49$, $\Delta x = -\,0.01$

$\therefore f(x+\Delta x) = f(x) + \frac{dy}{dx}\Delta x$

$\Rightarrow f(0.48) = 0.7 + \frac{1}{2\times 0.7} \times (-0.01) = 0.7 - 0.007 = 0.693$

(iv) $(82)^{\frac{1}{4}} = (81+1)^{\frac{1}{4}} = ?$

Let $y = f(x) = (x)^{1/4} \Rightarrow \frac{dy}{dx} = \frac{1}{4}.\frac{1}{(x)^{3/4}}$ ...(1)

Here, $x = 81$, $\Delta x = 1$

$\therefore\ f(x+\Delta x) = f(x)+\dfrac{dy}{dx}\Delta x = (81)^{\frac{1}{4}} + \dfrac{1}{4\times(81)^{\frac{3}{4}}}\times 1$

$= 3+\dfrac{1}{108} = 3.009$

3. Here, $f(x) = 4x^2+5x+2 = y \quad \Rightarrow \quad \dfrac{dy}{dn} = 8x+5$

Now, $f(x+\Delta x) = f(x)+\dfrac{dy}{dx}\Delta x$

Here, $x = 2$, $\Delta x = 0.01$

$\therefore\ f(2.01) = 16 + 10 + 2 + (21)(0.01) = 28.21$

4. $f(5.001) = ?,\ y = f(x) = x^3 - 7x^3 + 15$

Let $x = 5$, $\Delta x = 0.001$

$\Rightarrow f'(x) = 3x^2 - 14x$

$\therefore\ f(x + \Delta x) = f(x) + f'(x).\ \Delta x$

$\Rightarrow f(5.001) = (5)^3 - 7(5)^2 + 15 + [3(5)^2 - 14(5)]\,(0.001)$

$= -35 + 0.005 = -34.995$

5. $\Delta r = 0.03\text{m}$, $r = 9\text{m}$

Area $(A) = 4\pi r^2, \quad \Rightarrow \quad \dfrac{dA}{dr} = 8\pi r$

$\Delta A = \dfrac{dA}{dr}.\Delta r = 8\pi\times 9\times 0.03 = 2.16\pi m^2$

6. $\dfrac{dx}{x}\times 100 = 1\,(\text{Given}) \qquad \ldots(1)$

$A = 6x^2 \quad \Rightarrow \quad \dfrac{dA}{dx} = 12x$

$\therefore\ \Delta A = 12x\times dx = 12x\times\dfrac{x}{100} = \dfrac{12}{100}x^2 = 0.12x^2 m^2$

7. $r = 7\text{m}$, $\Delta r = 0.02\text{m}$

$V = \dfrac{4}{3}\pi r^3 \quad \Rightarrow \quad \dfrac{dV}{dr} = 4\pi r^2$

$\Rightarrow \Delta V = \dfrac{dV}{dr}.\Delta r = 4\pi r^2\times\Delta r = 4\pi\times 49\times 0.02 = 3.92\pi\text{m}^3$

8. $\dfrac{\Delta x}{x}\times 100 = 1 \quad \Rightarrow \quad \Delta x = \dfrac{x}{100}$

Now, $V = x^3 \quad \Rightarrow \quad \dfrac{dV}{dx} = 3x^2$

$\therefore\ \Delta V = 3x^2\times\Delta x = 3x^2\times\dfrac{x}{100} = 0.03x^3 m^3$

TEXTUAL EXERCISE–2: (OBJECTIVE)

1. (d) Let x = diameter of sphere, dx = error in diameter $\pm$ 0.04 cm

V = Volume of sphere $= \dfrac{4}{3}\pi r^3 = \dfrac{4}{3}\pi\dfrac{x^3}{8} = \dfrac{\pi x^3}{6} \qquad \ldots(1)$

$[x = 2r]$, differentiating w.r.t. x on both sides, we get

$\dfrac{dV}{dx} = \dfrac{3\pi x^2}{6} = \dfrac{\pi x^2}{2}$

$\Rightarrow dV = \dfrac{\pi x^2}{2}dx \quad \Rightarrow \quad \dfrac{dV}{V} = \dfrac{\pi x^2}{2}\times\dfrac{dx}{\left(\dfrac{\pi x^3}{6}\right)} = 3\dfrac{dx}{x}$

$\Rightarrow \dfrac{dV}{V}\times 100 = 3\dfrac{dx}{x}\times 100$

$\Rightarrow$ % age error in $V = 3\times\dfrac{(\pm 0.04)}{20}\times 100 = \pm 0.6cm$

2. (c) % age error in measuring radius 'r' $= \dfrac{dr}{r}\times 100 = 2 \qquad \ldots(1)$

Surface area = $A = 4\pi r^2$, differentiating w.r.t. r on both sides, $\dfrac{dA}{dr} = 8\pi r$

$\Rightarrow dA = 8\pi r dr$

$\Rightarrow \dfrac{dA}{A}\times 100 = \dfrac{8\pi r\times dr\times 100}{4\pi r^2} = 2\dfrac{dr}{r}\times 100 = 2\times 2 = 4$

$\Rightarrow$ % age error in measuring surface area = 4%

3. (c) C = circumference of circle = $2\pi r \qquad \ldots(1)$

Different w.r.t. r on both sides, we get $\dfrac{dC}{dr} = 2\pi$

$\Rightarrow dC = 2\pi dr$

$\Rightarrow \dfrac{dC}{C} = \dfrac{2\pi dr}{2\pi r} = \dfrac{dr}{r} \quad \Rightarrow \quad \dfrac{dC}{C}\times 100 = \dfrac{dr}{r}\times 100 \qquad \ldots(2)$

Area = $A = \pi r^2$, different w.r.t. r on both sides, we get $dA = 2\pi r dr$

$\Rightarrow \dfrac{dA}{A}\times 100 = \dfrac{2\pi r dr\times 100}{\pi r^2} = 2\dfrac{dC}{C}\times 100$

$= 2\times\dfrac{0.02}{56}\times 100 = \dfrac{1}{14}$

$\therefore$ % age error in $A = \dfrac{1}{14}$

4. (a) We know that, $T = 2\pi\sqrt{\dfrac{l}{g}}$

Taking log on both sides, $\ln T = \ln 2\pi + \dfrac{1}{2}\ \ln l + \dfrac{1}{2}\ \ln g$,

Different w.r.t. t on both sides, $\dfrac{dT}{T} = 0 + \dfrac{1}{2}\dfrac{1}{l}dl + 0$

$\Rightarrow \dfrac{dT}{T}\times 100 = \dfrac{1}{2}\dfrac{dl}{l}\times 100$

$\Rightarrow$ % age error in $T = -\times 2 = 1\%$

5. (d) Given height (h) = radius (r), $\dfrac{dh}{h}\times 100 = k$

Volume $(V) = \pi r^2 h = \pi h^3$, different w.r.t. h on both sides, $\dfrac{dV}{dh} = 3\pi h^2$

$\Rightarrow \dfrac{dV}{V}\times 100 = \dfrac{3\pi h^2\times dh}{\pi h^3}\times 100 = 3\times\dfrac{dh}{h}\times 100 = 3k$

% age error in volume = $3k\%$

6. (c) $\frac{r}{h}=\frac{1}{2}$

$\Rightarrow$ $2r = h$ ...(1)

Volume (V) $=\frac{1}{3}\pi r^2 h=\frac{1}{3}\pi r^2\times 2r=\frac{2}{3}\pi r^3$;

Different w.r.t. r on both sides, $dV = 2\pi r^2 dr$

$$\Rightarrow \frac{dV}{V}\times 100=\frac{2\pi r^2 dr\times 100}{\frac{2}{3}\pi r^3}=3\frac{dr}{r}\times 100=3k\ \%$$

7. (c) $PV^{\frac{1}{4}}$ = constant = k (say),

Taking log on both sides, $\ln P+\frac{1}{4}\ln V=\ln k$,

Differentiating both sides, $\frac{dP}{P}+\frac{1}{4}\times\frac{1}{V}\times dV=0$

$$\Rightarrow \frac{dP}{P}\times 100=\frac{-1}{4}\times\left(\frac{dV}{V}\times 100\right)=\frac{-1}{4}\times\frac{-1}{2}=\frac{1}{8}$$

$\Rightarrow$ % age error in $P=\frac{1}{8}\%$

8. (d) Relative error in $y=\frac{dy}{y}$ ...(1),

Relative error in $x=\frac{dx}{x}$ ...(2)

$\therefore$ From (1) and (2), $=\frac{\frac{dy}{y}}{\frac{dx}{x}}=\frac{dy}{dx}\times\frac{x}{y}=nx^{n-1}\times\frac{x}{x^n}=n$

$\therefore$ (Relative error in y): (relative error in x) = n : 1

TANGENTS AND NORMALS TEXTUAL EXERCISE–1: (SUBJECTIVE)

1. $\frac{dy}{dx}=-\left(\frac{\partial f}{\partial x}\Big/\frac{\partial f}{\partial y}\right)=-\left(\frac{4x+3y}{8y+3x}\right)=-\frac{7}{11}$

$\Rightarrow x=y$ $\quad\Rightarrow 2x^2+3x.x+4x^2=9$

$\Rightarrow x^2=y^2=1$

$\Rightarrow$ (1, 1), (–1, –1) are the required points

2. Let $(at^2, 2at)$ be a point on parabola, $\frac{dy}{dx}=\frac{2a}{2at}=\frac{1}{t}$ and equation of tangent at $P(at^2, 2at)$ is $t_y=x+at^2$

$\because$ Tangent passes through $(2a, 3a)$

$\Rightarrow 3at=2a+at^2$

$\Rightarrow t^2-3t+2=0$ $\quad\Rightarrow t=1$ or $t=2$

Thus two tangents can be drawn with slope 1 and 1/2, having their equations, $y=x+a$ and $2y=x+4a$

3. $\left(\frac{dy}{dx}\right)_{(1,4)}=6x^2-2x=4$

$\Rightarrow T: (y-4)=4(x-1)$

$\Rightarrow T: y=4x$

4. Equation of Normal to parabola $y=x^2$ is given by $y=mx+\left(\frac{1}{4m^2}+\frac{1}{2}\right)$

Comparing it with $y=-\frac{a}{b}x+\left(\frac{-c}{b}\right)$

$\Rightarrow \frac{-a}{b}=m;\ \frac{1}{4m^2}+\frac{1}{2}=\frac{-c}{b}$

$\Rightarrow \frac{1}{4\left(\frac{a^2}{b^2}\right)}+\frac{1}{2}=\frac{-c}{b}$

$\Rightarrow \frac{b}{4a}+\frac{1}{2}=\frac{c}{b}$

$\Rightarrow \frac{b^2+2a^2}{4a^2}=\frac{-c}{b}$

$\Rightarrow b^3+2a^2b=-4a^2c$

$\Rightarrow 2a^2(b+2c)+b^3=0$, which is the required condition.

5. The curve cuts x-axis at $x = 1, 2$

$\frac{dy}{dx}=(x^3-1)+(x-2)(3x^2)$

$\therefore m_{x=1}=-3;\ m_{x=2}=7$

$\therefore T: y+3x-3=0$ at $x=1, y=0$ and $T: y-7x+14=0$ at $x=2, y=0$

6. $y'=(1+x)^y\left(\ln(1+x)y'+\frac{y}{1+x}\right)+\frac{\sin 2x}{\sqrt{1-\sin^4 x}}$ at $(x = 0)$, $y = 1$ and $y' = 1 + 0 = 1$ and equation of normal will be $y - 1 = -x$

$\Rightarrow x+y=1$

7. $\frac{dy}{dx}=-\left(\frac{50x+12y}{12x+8y}\right)$ as tangent is || to x-axis; $\frac{dy}{dx}=0$

$\Rightarrow 25x=-6y$

$\Rightarrow 25x^2+12\left(-\frac{25x}{6}\right)x+4\left(-\frac{25x}{6}\right)^2=1$

$\Rightarrow 400x^2=9$

$\Rightarrow x=\pm\frac{3}{20}$ and for || to y-axis

$\Rightarrow 12x=-8y$

$\Rightarrow 25x^2+12x\left(-\frac{3}{2}x\right)+4\left(-\frac{3x}{2}\right)^2=1$

$\Rightarrow 16x^2=1$

$\Rightarrow x=\pm\frac{1}{4}$ $\quad\Rightarrow \left(\frac{1}{4},\frac{-3}{8}\right)$ and $\left(\frac{-1}{4},\frac{3}{8}\right)$

8. $\frac{dy}{dx}=6x-2$ and $m_2=-\frac{1}{10}$

$\Rightarrow \frac{dy}{dx}=10=6x-2$

$\Rightarrow$ $12 = 6x \Rightarrow x = 2$

$\Rightarrow$ $y = 3(4) - 2(2) - 4 = 4$

$\Rightarrow$ (2, 4) is the required point

9. $\frac{dy}{dx} = -x\ ;\ m_2 = -1$

$\Rightarrow -x = -1;\ x = 1$

$\Rightarrow\ y = \frac{3-(1)}{2} = 1$

$\Rightarrow$ (1, 1) is the required point.

10. $\frac{dy}{dx} = 4x^3 - 18x^2 + 26x - 10 = 2$

$\Rightarrow (x-1)(4x^2 - 14x + 12) = 0$

$\Rightarrow 2(x-1)(2x^2 - 7x + 6) = 0$

$\Rightarrow 2(x-1)(x-2)(2x-3) = 0$

$\Rightarrow x = 1$ or 2 or 3/2

$\Rightarrow$ (1, 3), (2, 5) (3/2, 65/16)

$\Rightarrow T_{(1,3)}\ (y-3) = 2(x-1)$

$\Rightarrow y = 2x + 1$ and $T_{(2,5)}\ (y-5) = 2(x-2)$

$\Rightarrow y = 2x + 1$

11. $\frac{dy}{dx} = \frac{5}{2\sqrt{5x-3}}$

(a) $m_2 = 2$

$\therefore\ 4\sqrt{5x-3} = 5$

$\Rightarrow 16(5x-3) = 25 \qquad \Rightarrow\ 5x = \frac{25}{16} + 3$

$\Rightarrow x = \frac{73}{80}$

T: $80x - 40y = 103$

(b) $m_2 = -\frac{2\sqrt{2}}{5} \qquad \Rightarrow\ \frac{5}{2\sqrt{5x-3}} = \frac{5}{2\sqrt{2}}$

$\Rightarrow 5x - 3 = 2 \qquad \Rightarrow\ x = 1$

T: $(y - \sqrt{2} + 2) = \frac{5}{2\sqrt{2}}(x-1)$

$\Rightarrow\ 2\sqrt{2}y - 5x + 4\sqrt{2} + 1 = 0$

12. Let $x = a\cos^4\theta$; $y = a\sin^4\theta$

$\frac{dy}{dx} = \frac{-4a\sin^3\theta\cos\theta}{4a\cos^3\theta\sin\theta} = -\tan^2\theta$

T: $(y - a\sin^4\theta) + \tan^2\theta\,(x - a\cos^4\theta) = 0$

$\Rightarrow y\cos^2\theta - a\sin^4\theta\cos^2\theta + x\sin^2\theta - a\cos^4\theta\sin^2\theta = 0$

$\Rightarrow\ \frac{y}{\sin^2\theta} + \frac{x}{\cos^2\theta} = a$

$\Rightarrow$ Sum of intercepts $= a\sin^2\theta + a\cos^2\theta = a =$ constant

13. $x + y = x^y$, Taking log on both sides, $\ln(x+y) = y\ln x$,

Differentiating w.r.t. x

$\Rightarrow\ \frac{1}{x+y}(1+y') = y'\ln x + \frac{y}{x}$

Curve cuts x-axis at (1, 0); $\frac{1}{1}(1+y') = 0$

$\Rightarrow y' = -1$

T: $y + x = 1$

N: $y - x + 1 = 0$

14. Equation of line passing through point $P\left(\frac{7}{2},\frac{9}{2}\right)$ is $\left(y-\frac{9}{2}\right) = m\left(x-\frac{7}{2}\right)$

$\Rightarrow$ Equation of parbola is $y = \left(x^2 - x + \frac{1}{4}\right) + \frac{3}{4}$ or $\left(x-\frac{1}{2}\right)^2 = \left(y-\frac{3}{4}\right)$ …(ii)

Equation of Normal to (ii) is

$\left(y-\frac{3}{4}\right) = m\left(x-\frac{1}{2}\right) + 2\left(\frac{1}{4}\right) + \left(\frac{1}{4}\right).\frac{1}{m^2}$

$\Rightarrow\ y = mx + \frac{5}{4} + \left(\frac{1}{4m^2} - \frac{m}{2}\right)$ …(iii)

Comparing (i) and (iii), we get $\frac{5}{4} + \frac{1}{4m^2} - \frac{m}{2} = \frac{9}{2} - \frac{7m}{2}$

$\Rightarrow 5m^2 + 1 - 2m^3 = 18m^2 - 14m^3$

$\Rightarrow 12m^3 - 13m^2 + 1 = 0$

$\Rightarrow 12m^3 - 12m^2 - m^2 + 1 = 0$

$\Rightarrow 12m^2(m-1) - 1(m^2-1) = 0$

$\Rightarrow (m-1)(12m^2 - m - 1) = 0$

$\Rightarrow (m-1)(3m-1)(4m+1) = 0$

$\Rightarrow m = 1, \frac{1}{3}, \frac{-1}{4}$

$\Rightarrow$ Sum of slopes of Normals $= \frac{13}{12}$

$\therefore$ Eq. of normals will be $\left(y-\frac{9}{2}\right) = \left(x-\frac{7}{2}\right)$, $\left(y-\frac{9}{2}\right) = \frac{1}{3}\left(x-\frac{7}{2}\right)$ and $\left(y-\frac{9}{2}\right) = \frac{-1}{4}\left(x-\frac{7}{2}\right)$

They will intersect the parabola $y = x^2 - x + 1$, at (0, 1) and (2, 3); (– 1, 3) and $\left(\frac{-7}{4},\frac{37}{9}\right)$; $\left(\frac{5}{2},\frac{19}{4}\right)\left(\frac{-7}{4},\frac{93}{16}\right)$

Slope normal at (h, k) is given by $\left(\frac{1}{2h-1}\right)$

For m = 1, $h = 0$

$\Rightarrow$ (0, 1) is root of $\perp$r $\left(y-\frac{9}{2}\right) = \left(x-\frac{7}{2}\right)$

For $m =$ –, $h = -1$

$\Rightarrow$ (– 1, 3) is root of $\perp r$ $\left(y-\frac{9}{2}\right) = \frac{1}{3}\left(x-\frac{7}{2}\right)$

For $m = \frac{-1}{4}, h = \frac{5}{2}$

$\Rightarrow\ \left(\frac{5}{2},\frac{19}{4}\right)$ is the root of $\perp$r $\left(y-\frac{9}{2}\right) = \frac{-1}{4}\left(x-\frac{7}{2}\right)$

$\therefore\ \frac{13}{12}; \left(y-\frac{9}{2}\right) = \left(x-\frac{7}{2}\right), (0,1);$

$\left(y-\frac{9}{2}\right) = \frac{1}{3}\left(x-\frac{7}{2}\right)(-1,3);$

$\left(y-\frac{9}{2}\right) = -\frac{1}{4}\left(x-\frac{7}{2}\right); \left(\frac{5}{2},\frac{19}{4}\right)$

15. $x = a(\theta + \sin\theta)$; $y = a(1 - \cos\theta)$

$\Rightarrow \dfrac{dx}{d\theta} = a(1+\cos\theta); \dfrac{dy}{d\theta} = a(\sin\theta)$

$\therefore$ Slope of tangent $= \dfrac{\sin\theta}{1+\cos\theta} = \dfrac{2\sin\frac{\theta}{2}\cos\frac{\theta}{2}}{2\cos^2\frac{\theta}{2}} = \tan\left(\dfrac{\theta}{2}\right)$

$\therefore$ Equation of tangent at (θ) is $[y - a(1 - \cos\theta)]$

$= \tan\left(\dfrac{\theta}{2}\right)$ $[x - a(\theta + \sin\theta)]$

$\Rightarrow \left[y - a\left(2\sin^2\dfrac{\theta}{2}\right)\right] = \dfrac{\sin\frac{\theta}{2}}{\cos\frac{\theta}{2}}\left[x - a\left(\theta + 2\sin\dfrac{\theta}{2}\cos\dfrac{\theta}{2}\right)\right]$

$\Rightarrow y\ \cos\dfrac{\theta}{2} - 2a\sin^2\dfrac{\theta}{2}\cos\dfrac{\theta}{2}$

$= x\ \sin\dfrac{\theta}{2} - a\sin\dfrac{\theta}{2} - 2a\sin^2\dfrac{\theta}{2}\cos\dfrac{\theta}{2}$

$\Rightarrow x\ \sin\dfrac{\theta}{2} - y\cos\dfrac{\theta}{2} = a\theta\sin\left(\dfrac{\theta}{2}\right)$

TEXTUAL EXERCISE–1: (OBJECTIVE)

1. (b) Area of first square $A_1 = x^2$ and Area of second $A_2 = y^2 = (x - x^2)^2$

$\therefore \dfrac{dA_2/dx}{dA_1/dx} = \dfrac{2(x-x^2)(1-2x)}{2x} = (1 - x)(1 - 2x) = 2x^2 - 3x + 1$

2. (b) Distance covered by them at time $t = 3vt$ and $4vt$ meters respectively.

$\therefore$ Distance (Separation) $= \sqrt{(3)^2 v^2t^2 + (4^2v^2t^2)} = x$ (say)

$\Rightarrow x = 5vt$

$\therefore \dfrac{dx}{dt} = 5vm$/min.

3. (b) on x-axis, $y = 0$

$\Rightarrow x + 0 = x^0 \qquad \Rightarrow x = 1$

Now, $x + y = x^y$ (Given curve)

$\Rightarrow \ln(x + y) = y\ln x$

$\Rightarrow \dfrac{1}{x+y}\left(1+\dfrac{dy}{dx}\right) = \dfrac{y}{x} + \ln x\dfrac{dy}{dx}$

$\Rightarrow \dfrac{1}{x+y} - \dfrac{y}{x} = \dfrac{dy}{dx}\left(\ln \quad - \dfrac{1}{x+y}\right)$

Putting, $x = 1$ and $y = 0$

$\Rightarrow 1 = \dfrac{dy}{dx}(0-1)$

$\Rightarrow \dfrac{dy}{dx} = -1 \qquad \Rightarrow$ Slope of normal = 1

$\Rightarrow$ Equation of normal $y = 1(x - 1)$ or $y - x + 1 = 0$ or $x - y - 1 = 0$

4. (c) $\dfrac{dy}{dx} = m = 2^2e^x$ at $P(0, 1)$; $m = 2$

$\therefore$ Equation of tangent at (0, 1) is $(y - 1) = 2(x - 0)$

$\Rightarrow 2x - y + 1 = 0$

It intersects x-axis, where $y = 0$, i.e., $x = -1/2$

$\therefore \left(-\dfrac{1}{2}, 0\right)$ is the required Point

5. (d) $y = \dfrac{3}{2} - \dfrac{x^2}{2} \quad \Rightarrow \dfrac{dy}{dx} = -x$

$\Rightarrow$ Slope of Normal $= \dfrac{1}{x}$ at (1, 1), $m = 1$

$\therefore$ Equation of normal at (1, 1) is $y - 1 = 1(x - 1)$ or $x - y = 0$

6. (c) $\dfrac{dy}{dx} = \dfrac{-b}{a}e^{-x/a}$ at $x = 0$, $m = -\dfrac{b}{a}$, $y = b$

$\therefore$ Equation of tangent at (0, b) is $y - b = \dfrac{-b}{a}x$ or $ay + bx = ab$ or $\dfrac{x}{a} + \dfrac{y}{b} = 1$

7. (b) $\dfrac{dy}{dx} = 2x - 1$, at $y = 2$,

$2 = x(x - 1) \qquad \Rightarrow x^2 - x - 2 = 0$

$\Rightarrow (x - 2)(x + 1) = 0$

$\Rightarrow x = 2$ or $x = -1$ at $x = 2$, $m = 3$ and at $x = -1$, $m = -3$, but since in first Quadrant

$\Rightarrow x = 2$ and $m = 3$

8. (c) $\dfrac{dy}{dx} = 3x^2 - 2ax + 1$

$\because$ of acute angle, $m > 0$

$\Rightarrow 3x^2 - 2ax + 1 > 0$

$\Rightarrow D < 0 \qquad \Rightarrow 4a^2 - 12 < 0$

$\Rightarrow a \in (-\sqrt{3}, \sqrt{3})$

9. (b) Given curve is $ax^2 + 2hxy + by^2 = 1$

$\Rightarrow 2ax + 2hy + 2hx\dfrac{dy}{dx} + 2by.\dfrac{dy}{dx} = 0$

$\Rightarrow \dfrac{dy}{dx}(2hx + 2by) = -2(ax + hy)$

$\Rightarrow \dfrac{dy}{dx} = \dfrac{-(ax+hy)}{(hx+by)}$, as tangent is || to y-axis

$\Rightarrow m = \infty \qquad \Rightarrow hx + by = 0$

10. (b) $\dfrac{dy}{dx} = -e^{-x}$

$\because$ for equals intercepts, tangent must be of the form $\dfrac{x}{a} + \dfrac{y}{a} = 1$ (line form)

$\Rightarrow$ Slope of tangent $= -1$

$\Rightarrow -1 = -e^{-x} \qquad \Rightarrow e^{-x} = 1$

$\Rightarrow x = 0 \qquad \Rightarrow y = e^{-(0)} = 1$

$\Rightarrow P(0, 1)$ is the required point.

11. (d) $y = \begin{cases} 2\pi + x & ; \ x \in (-2\pi, -\pi) \\ -x & ; \ x \in (-\pi, 0) \\ x & ; \ x \in (0, \pi) \\ 2\pi - x & ; \ x \in (\pi, 2\pi) \end{cases}$

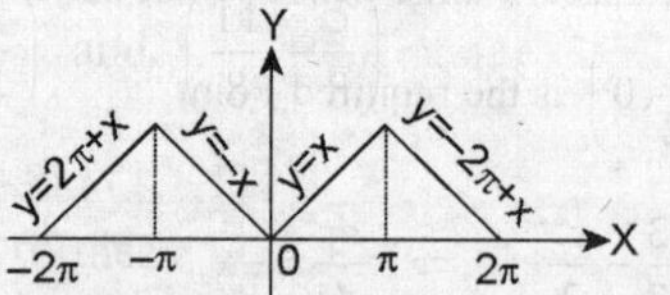

$\therefore \quad \frac{dy}{dx} = \begin{cases} 1 & \text{for } x \in (-2\pi, -\pi) \\ -1 & \text{for } x \in (-\pi, 0) \\ 1 & \text{for } x \in (0, \pi) \\ -1 & \text{for } x \in (\pi, 2\pi) \end{cases}$

$\therefore$ At $x = -\pi/4$, slope tangent $= -1$

12. (d) $y = \begin{cases} e^{-x} & \text{if } x > 0 \\ e^{x} & \text{if } x < 0 \end{cases}$ At $x = 1$, $y = e^{-1}$ and

$\frac{dy}{dx} = \begin{cases} -e^{-x} & \text{if } x > 0 \\ e^{x} & \text{if } x < 0 \end{cases}$

$\therefore$ At $x = 1$, $m = -1/e$

$\therefore$ Equation of tangent at $(1, e^{-1})$ is $(y - 1/e) = \frac{-1}{e}(x - 1)$

$\Rightarrow ey - 1 = 1 - x$

$\Rightarrow ey + x = 2$

$\Rightarrow$ None of these

13. (b) $\frac{dy}{dx} = 2x + 2e^{2x}$

$\therefore$ Slope of tangent at $x = 0$ is $m = 2$

$\Rightarrow$ Slope of tangent at $x = 0 = \frac{-1}{2}$

$\therefore$ Equation of normal at (0, 1) is $y - 1 = \frac{-1}{2}(x)$

or $2y + x = 2$

$\therefore$ Distance between (0, 0) and normal at (0, 1) is given by

$$d = \frac{|2(0) + 0 - 2|}{\sqrt{4+1}} = \frac{2}{\sqrt{5}}$$

14. (c) $\frac{2x}{2} = \frac{dy}{dx} = u \Rightarrow$ Slope of tangent at (1, 1/2) is $m = 1$

$\Rightarrow$ Required angle = 45°

15. (b) $\frac{dy}{dx} = 2x$; A.T.Q.; $2x = x$

$\Rightarrow x = 0$ and $y = 0$

$\Rightarrow P(0, 0)$

16. (a) Given curve is $y - e^{xy} + x = 0$

$\Rightarrow \frac{dy}{dx} - e^{xy}\left(x\frac{dy}{dx} + y\right) + 1 = 0$

$\Rightarrow \frac{dy}{dx}(1 - xe^{xy}) = ye^{xy} - 1$

$\Rightarrow \frac{dy}{dx} = \frac{ye^{xy} - 1}{1 - xe^{xy}}$

For vertical tangent $\frac{dy}{dx} \to \infty$

$\Rightarrow 1 - xe^{xy} = 0$

$\Rightarrow \frac{1}{x} = e^{xy}$ ...(1)

$\therefore$ From given, equation $y - \frac{1}{x} + x = 0$

$\Rightarrow y = \frac{1}{x} - x$ ...(2)

$\therefore$ From (1) and (2); $\frac{1}{x} = e^{x\left(\frac{1}{x} - x\right)}$

$\Rightarrow \frac{1}{x} = e^{1-x^2} = \frac{e}{x^2}$, which holds at $x = 1$ and $y = 0$ i.e., at (1, 0)

17. (d) $bx + ay = ab$

$\Rightarrow y = \frac{ab}{a} - \frac{bx}{a} = -\frac{b}{a}x + b$

$\Rightarrow$ Slope $= \frac{-b}{a}$, Slope of curve $\frac{dy}{dx} = \frac{-b}{a}e^{-x/a}$

$\therefore \frac{-b}{a} = \frac{-b}{a}e^{-x/a} \Rightarrow x = 0$ i.e., at $P(0, b)$

18. (a) $y^2 = 4ax$

$\Rightarrow 2y\frac{dy}{dx} = 4a$

$\Rightarrow \frac{dy}{dx} = \frac{2a}{y}$

$\therefore$ Slope of normal is $m_N = -\frac{y}{2a} = -2\frac{\sqrt{ax}}{2a} = -\sqrt{\frac{x}{a}}$

But $lx + my = 1$ is normal

$\Rightarrow$ Slope $= -\frac{l}{m}$

$\Rightarrow -\frac{l}{m} = -\sqrt{\frac{x}{a}} \Rightarrow x = \frac{al^2}{m^2}$

$\Rightarrow y = 2\frac{al}{m}$

$\Rightarrow l\left(\frac{al^2}{m^2}\right) + m\left(\frac{2al}{m}\right) = 1$

$\Rightarrow al^3 + 2al\, m^2 = m^2$

$\Rightarrow al^2 + 2al\, m^2 = m^2$

19. (c), (d) $6y^2\frac{dy}{dx} = 2ax + 3x^2$

$\Rightarrow \frac{dy}{dx} = \frac{2a^2 + 3a^2}{6a^2} = \frac{5}{6}$ at (a, a)

Let the tangent be $\frac{x}{\alpha} + \frac{y}{\beta} = 1$

$\Rightarrow \beta x + \alpha y = \alpha\beta \quad \Rightarrow m_T = -\dfrac{\beta}{\alpha}$

$\Rightarrow \dfrac{\beta}{\alpha} = \dfrac{5}{6} \quad \Rightarrow \beta = -\dfrac{5}{6}\alpha$

$\Rightarrow \alpha^2 + \dfrac{25}{36}\alpha^2 = 61$

$\Rightarrow \alpha^2 = 36 \quad \Rightarrow \alpha = \pm 6$

$\Rightarrow \beta = \mp 6$

Also $\dfrac{a}{\alpha} + \dfrac{a}{\beta} = 1$ ($\because$ (a, a) lies on $\dfrac{x}{\alpha} + \dfrac{y}{\beta} = 1$)

Case 1: If $\alpha = 6$

$\beta = -5$

$\Rightarrow \dfrac{a}{6} - \dfrac{a}{5} = 1 = 5a - 6a = 30$

$\Rightarrow a = -30$

Case 2: If $\alpha = -6$, $\beta = 5$

$\Rightarrow -\dfrac{a}{6} + \dfrac{a}{5} = 1 \quad \Rightarrow a = 30$

20. (a), (b) $\dfrac{n}{a}\left(\dfrac{x}{a}\right)^{n-1} + \dfrac{n}{b}\left(\dfrac{y}{b}\right)^{n-1}\dfrac{dy}{dx} = 0$

$\dfrac{dy}{du} = -\dfrac{b}{a}\left(\dfrac{bx}{ay}\right)$ ...(1)

When $x = 0$, then $1 + \left(\dfrac{y}{b}\right)^n = 2$ and $y = \pm b$

$\therefore \dfrac{dy}{dx} = -\dfrac{b}{a}(\pm 1) = \mp\dfrac{b}{a}$

Case 1: If $y = b$, then $\dfrac{dy}{dx} = -\dfrac{b}{a}$

$\therefore$ Equation of tangent at (a, b) will be $y - b = -\dfrac{b}{a}(x - a)$

$\Rightarrow ay - ab = -bx + ab$

$\Rightarrow bx + ay = 2ab$

$\Rightarrow \dfrac{x}{a} + \dfrac{y}{b} =$

Case 2: If $y = -b \quad \Rightarrow \dfrac{dy}{dx} = \dfrac{b}{a}$

$\Rightarrow$ Equation of tangent $(a, -b)$ will be $y + b = \dfrac{b}{a}(x - a)$

$\Rightarrow ay + ab = bx - ab \quad \Rightarrow bx - ay = 2ab$

$\Rightarrow \dfrac{x}{a} - \dfrac{y}{b} = 2$

21. (a) $y = \displaystyle\int_{x^2}^{x^3} \dfrac{dt}{\sqrt{1+t^2}}$ at $x = 1$

$\Rightarrow \dfrac{dy}{dx} = \dfrac{3x^2}{\sqrt{1+x^6}} - \dfrac{2x}{\sqrt{1+x^4}}$

$\Rightarrow \left(\dfrac{dy}{dx}\right)_{(1,0)} = \dfrac{3}{\sqrt{2}} - \dfrac{2}{\sqrt{2}} = \dfrac{1}{\sqrt{2}} = m_T$ (Slope of tangent)

$\Rightarrow m_N = -\sqrt{2}$ (Slope of normal)

$\therefore$ Equation of tangent: $y = \dfrac{1}{\sqrt{2}}(x - 1)$

$\Rightarrow \sqrt{2}y + 1 = x$

22. (a) $\dfrac{dy}{dx} = \dfrac{|x^2 - |x||}{x^2 - (x)}\left(2x - \dfrac{|x|}{x}\right)$

$\left(\dfrac{dy}{du}\right)_{x=-2} = \dfrac{|4-2|}{4-2}\left(-4 - \dfrac{2}{-2}\right) = 1(-4+1) = -3$,

$y = |4 - 2| = 2$

$\therefore$ Equation of tangent at $(-2, 2)$ will be $y - 2 = -3(x + 2)$

$\Rightarrow y - 2 = -3x - 6$

$\Rightarrow 3x + y + 4 = 0$

23. (c) At then point of contact, $\dfrac{x^2}{4} + (4x + c)^2 = 1$

$\Rightarrow \dfrac{x^2}{4} + 16x^2 + c^2 + 8cx = 1$

$\Rightarrow 65x^2 + 4\,^2 + 32cx - 4 = 0$; $D = 0$ (for equal roots)

$\Rightarrow (32c)^2 - 4(4)(c^2 - 1)\,65 = 0$

$\Rightarrow c = \pm\sqrt{65}$

$\therefore$ 2 values of c

24. (a) $\dfrac{dy}{du} = 4x + 5$

$\because y = 3 \quad \Rightarrow 2x^2 + 5x - 3 = 0$

$\Rightarrow x = -3, 1/2$

For first quadrant, $x > 0$

$\Rightarrow - \quad \Rightarrow m = 2 + 5 = 7$

$\therefore$ Equation of tangent at $\left(\dfrac{1}{2}, 3\right)$ will be $y - 3 = 7(x - 1/2)$

$\Rightarrow y - 3 = 7x - \dfrac{1}{2} \quad \Rightarrow 14x - 2y - 1 = 0$

25. (a),(c) Given equation of circle can be written as $(x - 3)^2 + (y - 3)^2 = (3)^2$ which has its centre at (3, 3) and radius 3, clearly x-axis and
y-axis are tangents to circle and passing through origin, hence having equations $x = 0$, $y = 0$

26. (a) Curve: $x^{1/3} + y^{1/3} = a^{1/3}$

$\Rightarrow \dfrac{1}{3(\sqrt[3]{x})^2} + \dfrac{1}{3(y)^{2/3}}\dfrac{dy}{dx} = 0$

$\Rightarrow \dfrac{dy}{dx} = -\left(\dfrac{y}{x}\right)^{2/3}$ at $(a/8, a/8) \quad \Rightarrow \dfrac{dy}{dx} = -1$

$\therefore$ Equation of tangent at $(a/8, a/8)$ is $y - \dfrac{a}{8} = -\left(x - \dfrac{a}{8}\right)$

$\Rightarrow y + x = \dfrac{a}{4} \Rightarrow 4x + 4y = a$

$\Rightarrow \dfrac{x}{a/4}+\dfrac{y}{a/4}=1$

$\Rightarrow \dfrac{a^2}{16}+\dfrac{a^2}{16}=2$ (A.T.Q.)

$\Rightarrow \dfrac{a^2}{8}=2 \qquad \Rightarrow a=4$ as $a\in\mathbb{R}^+$

27. (b) Equation of Normal: $\dfrac{x}{a}+\dfrac{y}{a}=1$

$\Rightarrow m_N=-1 \qquad \Rightarrow m_T=1$

Now, $2ay\dfrac{dy}{dx}=3x^2 \quad \Rightarrow \quad \dfrac{dy}{dx}=\dfrac{3x^2}{2ay}$ ...(1)

Also, $ay^2=x^3 \qquad \Rightarrow \sqrt{a}|y|=x^{3/2}$

$\Rightarrow \pm\sqrt{a}y=x^{3/2}$

$\Rightarrow y=\pm\dfrac{x^{3/2}}{\sqrt{a}}$ Putting in (1), we have,

$\dfrac{dy}{dx}=+\dfrac{3x^2}{2\sqrt{a}x^{3/2}}$

$\Rightarrow \dfrac{dy}{dx}=\pm\dfrac{3\sqrt{x}}{2\sqrt{a}} \qquad \Rightarrow \pm\dfrac{3\sqrt{x}}{2\sqrt{a}}=1$

$\Rightarrow x=\dfrac{4a}{9}$

28. (c) $y=(x-3)^2-3$

$\Rightarrow y+3=(x-3)^3$

$\therefore$ Vertex of the parabola = (3, –3)

$\therefore$ Slope of straight line joining vertex and origin

$=m_2=\dfrac{3}{-3}=-1$

$\Rightarrow m_N=1$ and $\dfrac{dy}{dx}=2x-6$

$\Rightarrow m_N=\dfrac{-1}{2x-6}=1 \qquad \Rightarrow x=5/2$ and $y=\dfrac{-11}{4}$

$\therefore$ Equation of normal will be $y+\dfrac{11}{4}=\left(x-\dfrac{5}{2}\right)$ or $4x-4y-21=0$

29. (d) $3y^2\dfrac{dy}{dx}+6x=12\dfrac{dy}{dx}$

$\Rightarrow 6x=(12-3y^2)\dfrac{dy}{dx} \qquad \Rightarrow \dfrac{dy}{dx}=\dfrac{2x}{4-y^2}$

For vertical tangent, $m=\infty=\dfrac{1}{0}$

$\Rightarrow 4-y^2=0 \qquad \Rightarrow y=\pm 2$

Case 1: $y=2$

$\Rightarrow 8+3x^2=24 \qquad \Rightarrow x=\pm\dfrac{4}{\sqrt{3}}$

$\Rightarrow \left(\pm\dfrac{4}{\sqrt{3}},2\right)$ is a required point

Case 2: $y=-2 \qquad \Rightarrow -8+3u^2=-24$

$\Rightarrow 3x^2=-16$ which is impossible

30. (c) $x^2y=c^3$

$\Rightarrow 2xy+x^2y'=0 \qquad \Rightarrow y'=\dfrac{-2y}{x}$

$\therefore$ Equation of tangent at (x, y) is $Y-y=\dfrac{-2y}{x}(X-x)$

$\Rightarrow xY+2yX=3xy \qquad \Rightarrow \dfrac{X}{\frac{3x}{2}}+\dfrac{Y}{3y}=1$

$\Rightarrow a=\dfrac{3x}{2}$ and $b=3y$

$\Rightarrow a^2b=9\dfrac{x^2}{4}3y=\dfrac{27}{4}x^2y=\dfrac{27}{4}c^3$

31. (c) $\dfrac{-2a}{x^3}-\dfrac{2b}{y^3}\dfrac{dy}{dx}=0$

$\Rightarrow \dfrac{dy}{du}=-\dfrac{2a}{x^3}\left(\dfrac{y^3}{2b}\right) \qquad \Rightarrow \dfrac{dy}{du}=\dfrac{-ay^3}{bx^3}$

$\therefore$ Equation of tangent at (x,y) will be $Y-y=-\dfrac{ay^3}{bx^3}(X-x)$

On x-axis, $Y=0 \qquad \Rightarrow -y=\dfrac{-ay^3}{bx^3}(X-x)$

$\Rightarrow \dfrac{-bx^3}{-ay^3}+x=X \qquad \Rightarrow X=\dfrac{-axy^3-bx^3y}{-ay^3}$

$=\dfrac{-xy(ay^2+bx^2)}{-ay^3}=\dfrac{x}{ay^2}(x^2y^2)=\dfrac{x^3}{a}$

$\Rightarrow X\propto x^3$

TEXTUAL EXERCISE–2: (SUBJECTIVE)

1. Given equation is $y^2=4ax$

$T: (y-2at)=-(x-at^2)$

$\Rightarrow yt-x=2at^2-at^2$

$\therefore T: yt-x=at^2$

$N: (y-2at)=-t(x-at^2)$

$\Rightarrow y+xt=2at+at^3$

2. $\left(\dfrac{dy}{dx}\right)_{(x_1,x_1^3)}=3x_1^2$

Let the tangent at $P(x_1, x_1^3)$ intersects the curve again at $Q(x_2, x_2^3)$

$\Rightarrow \left(\dfrac{dy}{dx}\right)_{(x_1,x_1^3)}=\dfrac{y_2-y_1}{x_2-x_1}$

$\Rightarrow 3x_1^2=\dfrac{x_2^3-x_1^3}{x_2-x_1}=x_2^2+x_1^2+x_1x_2$

$\Rightarrow x_2^2+x_1x_2-2x_1^2=0$

$\Rightarrow\ x_2 = \dfrac{-x_1 \pm \sqrt{9x_1^2}}{2} = -2x_1$ or x_1

$\Rightarrow\ x_2 = -2x_1$ i.e., $Q \equiv (-2x_1, -8x_1^3)$

3. $\dfrac{dy}{dx} = 12x^2 - 10x^4$

$T: (Y - y) = (12x^2 - 10x^4)(X - x)$,

Tangent passes through origin $-y = (12x^2 - 10x^4)(-x)$

$\Rightarrow\ -4x^3 + 2x^5 = -x(12x^2 - 10x^4)$

$\Rightarrow\ x = 0, \pm 1$ and $y = 0, 2, -2$

$\therefore$ (0, 0), (1, 2), (–1, –2) are the required points

4. (a) $\dfrac{dy}{dx} = \left(\dfrac{dy}{dt}\Big/\dfrac{dx}{dt}\right) = \dfrac{\sin t}{\sin t + t\cos t}$

$T: (y - a(1 - \cos t)) = \dfrac{\sin t}{\sin t + t\cos t}(x - at\sin t)$

$\Rightarrow\ y(\sin t + t\cos t) - x\sin t = -at\sin^2 t + a\sin t - at\cos^2 t + at\cos t - a\cos t\sin t$

$\Rightarrow\ y(\sin t + t\cos t) - x\sin t = (1 - \cos t)(a\sin t + at\cos t) - at$

$N: (y - a(1 - \cos t)) = -\dfrac{(\sin t + t\cos t)}{\sin t}(x - at\sin t)$

$\Rightarrow\ y\sin t - a\sin t + a\cos t\sin t + x(\sin t + t\cos t) - at\sin^2 t - at^2\cos t\sin t = 0$

$\Rightarrow\ y\sin t + x(\sin t + t\cos t) = a\sin t + at\sin^2 t + (a + at^2)\sin t\cos^t$

(b) $\dfrac{dy}{dx} = \dfrac{b\sec^2\theta}{a\sec\theta\tan\theta} = \dfrac{b}{a}\operatorname{cosec}\theta$

$T: (y - b\tan\theta) = \dfrac{b}{a}\operatorname{cosec}\theta(x - a\sec\theta)$ or $ay\sin\theta - bx$

$= ab\tan\theta\sin\theta - ab\sec\theta = \dfrac{ab(\sin^2\theta - 1)}{\cos\theta}$ or $ay\sin\theta - bx + ab\cos\theta = 0$

$N: b(y - b\tan\theta) = -a\sin\theta(x - a\sec\theta)$

$\Rightarrow\ by + ax\sin\theta = b^2\tan\theta + a^2\tan\theta$

$\Rightarrow\ by + ax\sin\theta = (a^2 + b^2)\tan\theta$

(c) $\dfrac{dy}{dx} = \dfrac{3\sin^2\theta\cos\theta}{-3\cos^2\theta\sin\theta} = -\tan\theta$

$T: (y - a\sin^3\theta) = -\dfrac{\sin\theta}{\cos\theta}(x - a\cos^3\theta)$ or $y\cos\theta + x\sin\theta = a(\sin\theta\cos\theta)$ or $\dfrac{y}{\sin\theta} + \dfrac{x}{\cos\theta} = a$

$N: (y - a\sin^3\theta) = \dfrac{\cos\theta}{\sin\theta}(x - a\cos^3\theta)$

$y\sin\theta - x\cos\theta = a\sin^4\theta - a\cos^4\theta$

$y\sin\theta - x\cos\theta = a(\sin^2\theta - \cos^2\theta)$

5. $2y\dfrac{dy}{dx} = 2a$

$\dfrac{dy}{dx} = \dfrac{2a}{2y} = \dfrac{a}{y} = \pm\dfrac{a}{\sqrt{2ax}}$

$2y\dfrac{dy}{dx} = -2x$

$\Rightarrow\ \dfrac{dy}{dx} = -\dfrac{2x}{2y} = \dfrac{-x}{y} = \dfrac{-x}{\pm\sqrt{a^2 - (x^2)}}$

Solving curves together, $x^2 + 2ax - a^2 = 0$

$\Rightarrow\ x = -a \pm \sqrt{2}a$

Since both curves are symmetric about x axis, we will get same angles for both values of x In 1st Quadrant

$\dfrac{dy_1}{dx} = \dfrac{a}{\sqrt{2a^2(\sqrt{2}-1)}} = \dfrac{1}{\sqrt{2(\sqrt{2}-1)}}$;

$\dfrac{dy_2}{dx} = \dfrac{-(\sqrt{2}-1)a}{\sqrt{2(\sqrt{2}-1)a^2}} = \dfrac{-\sqrt{\sqrt{2}-1}}{\sqrt{2}}$

$$\theta = \tan^{-1}\left|\dfrac{\dfrac{1}{\sqrt{2(\sqrt{2}-1)}} + \dfrac{\sqrt{\sqrt{2}-1}}{\sqrt{2}}}{1 + \dfrac{1}{\sqrt{2\sqrt{2}-1}} \times \dfrac{\sqrt{\sqrt{2}-1}}{\sqrt{2}}}\right|$$

$$= \tan^{-1}\left|\dfrac{2}{\sqrt{2}}\left(\dfrac{1 + \sqrt{2} - 1}{\sqrt{\sqrt{2}-1}}\right)\right| = \tan^{-1}\left(\dfrac{2}{\sqrt{\sqrt{2}-1}}\right)$$

6. Let (α, β) be the point of intersection

For $y^3 = 16x$

$3y^2\dfrac{dy}{dx} = 16 \qquad \Rightarrow\ m_1 = \dfrac{dy}{dx} = \dfrac{16}{3y^2} = \dfrac{16}{3\beta^2}$

For $\dfrac{x^2}{a^2} + \dfrac{y^2}{4} = 1,\ \dfrac{2x}{a^2} + \dfrac{2yy'}{4} = 0$

$\Rightarrow\ m_2 = y' = -\dfrac{4}{y}\left(\dfrac{-x}{a^2}\right) = \dfrac{-4\alpha}{a^2\beta}$

$\because$ Curves intersects at right angle

$\Rightarrow\ m_1 m_2 = -1$

$\Rightarrow\ \dfrac{-64\alpha}{3a^2\beta^3} = -1 \qquad \Rightarrow\ \dfrac{64\alpha}{3a^2(16\alpha)} = 1$

$\Rightarrow\ a^2 = 4/3$

TEXTUAL EXERCISE–2 (OBJECTIVE)

1. (c) $x = a(\theta - \sin\theta)$; $a(1 + \cos\theta)$

$\dfrac{dx}{d\theta} = a(1 - \cos\theta)$; $\dfrac{dy}{dx} = a(-\sin\theta)$

$\Rightarrow\ \dfrac{dy}{dx} = \dfrac{a(0 - \sin\theta)}{a(1 - \cos\theta)} = \dfrac{(-\sin\theta)}{(1 - \cos\theta)}$

$\Rightarrow\ \left(\dfrac{dy}{dx}\right)_{\theta(2k+1)^\pi} = \dfrac{0}{1 - (-1)} = 0$

$\Rightarrow$ Tangent at $x = (2k + 1)\pi$; $k \in \mathbb{Z}$ is parallel to x-axis.

2. (a) $ay^2 = x^3$ has its parametric equations $x = at^2$, $y = at^3$

$\Rightarrow\ \dfrac{dx}{dt} = 2at,\ \dfrac{dy}{dt} = 3at^2$

$\Rightarrow \frac{dy}{dx} = \frac{dy/dt}{dx/dt} = \frac{3t}{2}$

$\therefore$ Equation of tangent to curve at $R(at^2, at^3)$ is $(y - at^3) = \frac{3t}{2}(x - at^2)$

$\Rightarrow 2y - 2at^3 = 3tx - 3at^3 \quad \Rightarrow \quad 2y = 3tx - at^3$

It meets again the curve where $x^3 = ay^2$

$\Rightarrow 4y^2 = (3tx - at^3)^2$

$\Rightarrow 4ay^2 = a(3tx - at^3)^2$

$\Rightarrow 4x^3 = a(9t^2x^2 + a^2t^6 - 6at^4x)$

$\Rightarrow 4x^3 - 9at^2x^2 + 6a^2t^4x - a^3t^6 = 0$

$\Rightarrow x = at^2$ sawflies it

$$\begin{array}{c|cccc} & 4 & -9t^2 & 6a^2t^4 & -a^3t^6 \\ at^2 & & 4at^2 & -5a^2t^4 & a^3t^6 \\ \hline & 4 & -5at^2 & a^2t^4 & 0 \end{array}$$

$\Rightarrow 4x^2 - 5at^2x + a^2t^4 = 0$

$\Rightarrow 4x^2 - 4at^2x - at^2x + a^2t^4 = 0$

$\Rightarrow 4x(x - at^2) - at^2(x - at^2) = 0$

$\Rightarrow x = at^2$ or $x = \frac{at^2}{4}$

$\Rightarrow$ The other point will be $x = \frac{at^2}{4}, y = \frac{3tx}{2} - \frac{at^3}{2}$

$= \frac{3t}{2}\left(\frac{at^2}{4}\right) - \frac{at^3}{2} = \frac{3}{8}at^3 - \frac{at^3}{2} = -\frac{1}{8}at^3$ i.e.,

$\left(\frac{at^2}{4}, -\frac{1}{8}at^3\right)$

3. (d) $x = e^t \cos t$, $y = e^t \sin t$

$\frac{dx}{dt} = e^t(-\sin t) + e^t \cos t$ and $\frac{dy}{dt} = e^t \cos t + e^t \sin t$

$\therefore \frac{dy}{dx} = \frac{\cos t + \sin t}{\cos t - \sin t}$

$\Rightarrow \left(\frac{dy}{dx}\right)_{t=\frac{\pi}{4}} = \frac{\sqrt{2}}{0} = \infty$

$\Rightarrow$ Tangent subtends an angle $\frac{\pi}{2}$ with x-axis.

4. (a) $x = t^2 - 1$; $y = t^2 - 1$

$\frac{dy}{dx} = 2t - 1$, $\frac{dy}{dx} = 2t$

$\therefore \frac{dy}{dx} = \frac{2t-1}{2t}$

$\therefore$ Tangent is $\perp r$ to x-axis

$\Rightarrow \frac{dy}{dx} = \infty \quad \Rightarrow \quad t = 0$

5. (a) Parametric equations of given curve are $x = a\cos^3\theta$, $y = a\sin^3\theta$

$\Rightarrow \frac{dy}{dx} = \frac{3a\sin^2\theta.\cos\theta}{-3a\cos^2\theta\sin\theta} = -\tan\theta$

$\therefore$ Equation of tangent to curve is $(y - a\sin^3\theta) = -\tan\theta(x - a\cos^3\theta)$

$\Rightarrow$ x-intercept $= \frac{a\sin^3\theta}{\tan\theta} + a\cos^3\theta = h$ (say)

$\Rightarrow$ y-intercept $= a\sin^3\theta + a\tan\theta\cos^3\theta = k$ (say)

$\Rightarrow h^2 + k^2 = a^2[(\sin^2\theta\cos\theta + \cos^3\theta)^2 + (\sin^3\theta + \sin\theta.\cos^2\theta)^2]$

$= a^2[\cos^2\theta(\sin^2\theta + \cos^2\theta)^2 + \sin^2\theta(\sin^2\theta + \cos^2\theta)^2]$

$\Rightarrow a^2$

6. (a), (d) $\frac{x}{a} + \frac{y}{b} = 1$ ...(1)

$x = 4t, y = 4/t; t \in \mathbb{R} - \{0\}$

$\Rightarrow \frac{dx}{dt} = 4; \frac{dy}{dt} = \frac{-4}{t^2} \Rightarrow \frac{dy}{dx} = \frac{-1}{t^2}$

$\therefore$ Equation of tangent at 't' is $\left(y - \frac{4}{t}\right) = \frac{-1}{t^2}(x - 4t)$

$\Rightarrow yt^2 - 4t = -x + 4t \quad \Rightarrow \quad x + yt^2 = 8t$

$\Rightarrow \frac{x}{8t} + \frac{y}{8/t} = 1 \quad \Rightarrow \quad a.b > 0$

7. (d) Given curve is $ay^2 = x^3$

$\Rightarrow 2ay\frac{dy}{dx} = 3x^2$

$\Rightarrow$ Slope of normal $= \frac{-2ay}{3x^2}$

$\therefore$ For normal to cut equal intercepts, slope of normal $= \pm 1$

$\Rightarrow \frac{-2ay}{3x^2} = \pm 1 \quad \Rightarrow \quad 2ay = -3x^2$ and $2ay = 3x^2$

$\Rightarrow 4a^2y^2 = 9x^4 \quad \Rightarrow \quad 4a(x^3) = 9x^4$

$\Rightarrow x^3(9x - 4a) = 0 \quad \Rightarrow \quad x = 0$ or $x = 4a/9$

8. (a) $3xy^2 - 2x^2y = 1$

$\Rightarrow 3x(2y)\frac{dy}{dx} + 3y^2 - 2x^2\frac{dy}{dx} - 4xy = 0$

$\Rightarrow (6xy - 2x^2)\frac{dy}{dx} = 4xy - 3y^2$

$\Rightarrow \frac{dy}{dx} = \frac{4xy - 3y^2}{6xy - 2x^2}$

$\therefore$ Slope of tangent at (1, 1) $= \frac{1}{4}$

$\therefore$ Equation of tangent to curve at (1, 1) is $(y - 1) = \frac{1}{4}(x - 1)$

$\Rightarrow y = \frac{1}{4}x + \frac{3}{4}$, It meets the curve where

$3x\left(\frac{x+3}{4}\right)^2 - 2x^2\left(\frac{x+3}{4}\right) = 1$ i.e., $3x(x^2 + 6x + 9) - 8x^2(x + 3) = 16$

$\Rightarrow 3x^3 + 18x^2 + 27x - 8x^3 - 24x^2 = 16$

$\Rightarrow 5x^3 + 6x^2 + 27x + 16 = 0$

$\Rightarrow (x - 1)(x - 1)(5x + 16) = 0$

$\Rightarrow x = 1$ or $x = -\frac{16}{5}$

$\therefore$ The tangent would meet the curve again at $x = \frac{-16}{5}, y = \frac{-1}{20}$

9. (b) $y^2 = x^3 \Rightarrow y = \pm\sqrt{3}$

$\Rightarrow x^3 \geq 0 \Rightarrow x \geq 0$

Let $p(t, t^{3/2})$ be any point on the curve $y^2 = x^3$ ...(i)

$\therefore$ Slope of tangent at p = $\frac{3}{2} t^{1/2}$

$\therefore$ Equation of tangent to curve at P is $(y - t^{3/2}) = \frac{3}{2}t^{1/2}(x-t)$

$\Rightarrow y = \frac{3}{2}t^{1/2}(x-t)+t^{3/2}$

$\Rightarrow y = \frac{3}{2}t^{1/2}x - \frac{3}{2}t^{3/2} + t^{3/2}$

$\Rightarrow y = \frac{3}{2}t^{1/2}x - \frac{1}{2}t^{3/2}$

$\Rightarrow y = \frac{1}{2}\sqrt{t}(3x-t)$ ...(ii)

$\therefore$ At the point of intersection of (i) and (ii), we get $\frac{1}{4}$ $t(3x - t)^2 = x^3$

$\Rightarrow t(9x^2 + t^2 - 6xt) = 4x^3$

$\Rightarrow 4x^3 - 9tx^2 + 6t^2 x - t^3 = 0$

Clearly $(x - t)^2$ is its factor as line (ii) is tangent to curve at $(t, t^{3/2})$

$\Rightarrow (x - t)^2 (4x - t) = 0$

$\Rightarrow$ The tangent will again intersect the curve at Q $\left(\frac{1}{t},\left(\frac{1}{4}\right)^{3/2}\right)$ or $\left(\frac{t}{4}, -\frac{t^{3/2}}{8}\right)$

From (ii), put $x = 1/4$

$\Rightarrow y = \frac{1}{2}\sqrt{t}\left(\frac{3t}{4}-t\right) \Rightarrow y = \frac{1}{2}\sqrt{t}\left(\frac{-t}{4}\right) = -\frac{1}{8}(t)^{3/2}$

$\Rightarrow Q\left(\frac{t}{4}, -\frac{1}{8}(t)^{3/2}\right)$

$\Rightarrow \tan\alpha = t^{3/2} / t = \sqrt{t}$ and $\tan\beta = \frac{-\frac{1}{8}t^{3/2}}{\left(\frac{t}{4}\right)} = \frac{-t^{3/2}}{8} \times \frac{4}{t} = \frac{-1\sqrt{t}}{2}$

$\Rightarrow \frac{\tan\alpha}{\tan\beta} = \frac{\sqrt{t}}{\left(\frac{-1}{2}\sqrt{t}\right)} = -2$

10. (c) $y = -\frac{3}{2}x$ will intersect the curve $3x^2 + 4xy + 5y^2 - 4 = 0$, where $3x^2 - 6x^2 + \frac{45}{4}x^2 - 4 = 0$

$\Rightarrow \frac{33x^2}{4} = 4 \Rightarrow x = \pm\frac{4}{\sqrt{33}}$ i.e.,

at $P\left(\frac{4}{\sqrt{33}}, \frac{-6}{\sqrt{33}}\right)$ and $\left(\frac{-4}{\sqrt{33}}, \frac{6}{\sqrt{33}}\right)$

Next, $y = -\frac{2}{5}$ will intersection curve where

$3x^2 - \frac{8}{5}x^2 + \frac{4}{5}x^2 - 4 = 0$

$\Rightarrow 3x^2 - \frac{4}{5}x^2 = 4 = \frac{11}{5}x^2 = 4$

$\Rightarrow x = \pm 2\sqrt{\frac{5}{11}}$

$\Rightarrow y = -\frac{2}{5}\left(\pm 2\sqrt{\frac{5}{11}}\right)$ i.e., at $\left(2\sqrt{\frac{5}{11}}, \frac{-4}{\sqrt{55}}\right)$ and

$\left(-2\sqrt{\frac{5}{11}}, \frac{4}{\sqrt{55}}\right)$ i.e $Q\left(\frac{10}{\sqrt{55}}, \frac{-4}{\sqrt{55}}\right)$ and $\left(\frac{-10}{\sqrt{55}}, \frac{4}{\sqrt{55}}\right)$

Slope of tangent to curve is given by $6x + 4x\frac{dy}{dx} + 4y + 10y\frac{dy}{dx} = 0$

$\Rightarrow \frac{dy}{dx}(4x + 10y) = -(6x + 4y)$

$\Rightarrow \frac{dy}{dx} = -\frac{(3x \quad 2y)}{(2x \quad 5y)} = -\frac{\left(3- \quad 2\right)}{2 \quad 5}$

y_1 at $P\left(\frac{4}{\sqrt{33}}, \frac{-6}{\sqrt{33}}\right)$ or $\left(\frac{-4}{\sqrt{33}}, \frac{6}{\sqrt{33}}\right)$

$= -\frac{3\left(-\frac{2}{3}\right)+2}{2\left(\frac{-2}{3}\right)+5} = 0$

y_2 at $Q\left(\frac{10}{\sqrt{55}}, -\frac{4}{\sqrt{55}}\right)$ or $\left(\frac{-10}{\sqrt{55}}, \frac{4}{\sqrt{55}}\right)$

$= -\frac{3\left(\frac{-10}{4}\right)+2}{2\left(\frac{-10}{4}\right)+5} = \infty$

$\Rightarrow$ Tangent at P and Q and perpendicular to each other

11. (a) $x = a(2 + \cos\theta), y = a\sin\theta$

$\Rightarrow \frac{dy}{dx} = \frac{a\cos\theta}{a(-\sin\theta)} = -\cot\theta$

$\Rightarrow$ Equation of normal to the curve is $(y - a\sin\theta) = \tan\theta\,[x - a(2 + \cos\theta)]$

$\Rightarrow y - a\sin\theta = x\tan\theta - 2a\tan\theta - a\sin\theta$

$\Rightarrow y = x\tan\theta - 2a\tan\theta$

$\Rightarrow y = (x - 2a)\tan\theta$, which always passes through the point $(2a, 0)$

12. (b) $x = 3t^2 + 1, y = t^2 - t + 1$

$\Rightarrow \frac{dx}{dt} = 6t, \frac{dy}{dt} = 2t - 1$

$\Rightarrow \dfrac{dx}{dy} = \dfrac{6t}{2t-1}$

$\Rightarrow$ Normal is parallel to x-axis for $\dfrac{dx}{dy} = 0$

$\Rightarrow t = 0$

13. (a), (c) $x = t^3 - 6t^2 + 9t, y = t^2$

$\because$ Tangent is $\perp r$ to x-axis

$\Rightarrow \dfrac{dx}{dy} = 0 \quad \Rightarrow \dfrac{3t^2 - 12t + 9}{2t} = 0$

$\Rightarrow t^2 - 4t + 3 = 0 \quad \Rightarrow (t-1)(t-3) = 0$

$\Rightarrow t = 1$ or $t = 3$

14. (a) Given curve is $y^2 = x(2-x)^2$

$\Rightarrow 2y\dfrac{dy}{dx} = x(2)(2-x)(-1) + (2-x)^2$

$\Rightarrow \left(\dfrac{dy}{dx}\right)_{(1,1)} = \dfrac{(-2)+(1)}{2} = \dfrac{-1}{2}$

$\Rightarrow$ Equation of tangent at (1, 1) will be $2(y-1) = (-1)(x-1)$

$\Rightarrow x + 2y = 3$

It again in intersects the curve, where $(3-x)^2 = 4x(2-x)^2$

$\Rightarrow 9 + x^2 - 6x = 4x(4 + x^2 - 4x)$

$\Rightarrow 9 + x^2 - 6x = 16x + 4x^3 - 16x^2$

$\Rightarrow 4x^3 - 17x^2 + 22x - 9 = 0$

$\Rightarrow x = 1, 1, 9/4$

$\Rightarrow$ The co-ordinates of P will be $\left(\dfrac{9}{4}, \pm\dfrac{3}{8}\right)$

15. (a) $x = a\sqrt{\cos 2\theta}.\cos\theta;$

$y = a\sqrt{\cos 2\theta}.\sin\theta;$

$$\frac{dx}{d\theta} = a\sqrt{\cos 2\theta}(-\sin\theta) + a\cos\theta.\frac{1}{2\sqrt{\cos}}(-2\sin 2\theta)$$

$$= \frac{-a\sin\theta\cos 2\theta - a\cos\theta\sin 2\theta}{\sqrt{\cos 2\theta}}$$

$$= \frac{-a[\sin(\theta + 2\theta)]}{\sqrt{\cos 2\theta}} = \frac{-a\sin 3\theta}{\sqrt{\cos 2\theta}} \text{ and}$$

$$\frac{dy}{d\theta} = a\sqrt{\cos 2\theta}(\cos\theta) + a\sin\theta.\frac{1}{2\sqrt{\cos}}(-2\sin 2\theta)$$

$$= \frac{a\cos 2\theta\cos\theta - a\sin\theta\sin 2\theta}{\sqrt{\cos 2\theta}}$$

$$= \frac{a[\cos(2\theta + \theta)]}{\sqrt{\cos 2\theta}} = \frac{a\cos 3\theta}{\sqrt{\cos 2\theta}}$$

$$\Rightarrow \frac{dy}{dx} = \frac{dy/d\theta}{dx/d\theta} = -\cot 3\theta$$

$$\Rightarrow \left(\frac{dy}{dx}\right)_{\theta = \frac{\pi}{6}} = -\cot\frac{\pi}{2} = 0$$

$\therefore$ Equation of tangent to curve at point ($\theta = \pi/6$) will be

$\left(y - \dfrac{a}{\sqrt{2}}.\dfrac{\sqrt{3}}{2}\right) = 0 \Rightarrow y = \dfrac{\sqrt{3}a}{2\sqrt{2}}$ i.e., parallel to x-axis

16. (a) Let $A(a, a^3)$ be point A.

$\therefore$ Equation of tangent at A will be $(y - a^3) = 3a^2(x - a)$ .It meets the curve again.

$\Rightarrow a^3 + 3a^2(x - a) = x^3 \quad \Rightarrow a^3 + 3a^2x - 3a^3 = x^3$

$\Rightarrow 3a^2x - 2a^3 = x^3$

$(x-a)^2$ must be its factor

$\Rightarrow$ The other factor is $x + 2a = 0$

$\Rightarrow x = -2a \quad \Rightarrow y = -8a^3$

$\therefore B = (-2a, -8a^3)$

$\therefore$ Grandant at $B = 3(-2a)^2 = 12a^2$

$\therefore$ A.T.Q; $12a^2 = k(3a^2) \Rightarrow k = 4$

17. (d) $x = \sec^2 t;\ y = \cot t$

At $P \equiv (2, 1)$; $\dfrac{dy}{dx} = \dfrac{-\operatorname{cosec}^2 t}{2\sec^2 t\tan t} = \dfrac{-1}{2}$

$\therefore$ Equation of tangent to curve at $P(2, 1)$ is $(y - 1) = \left(\dfrac{-1}{2}\right)(x-2)$

$\Rightarrow x + 2y = 4$

It again meets the curve $x = 1 + \dfrac{1}{y^2}$

$\Rightarrow 4 - 2y = 1 + \dfrac{1}{y^2} \quad \Rightarrow 4y^2 - 2y^3 = y^2 + 1$

$\Rightarrow 2y^3 - 3y^2 + 1 = 0$

Clearly $y = 1$ satisfies it,

$\Rightarrow 2y^2 - y - 1 = 0 \quad \Rightarrow 2y^2 - 2y + y - 1 = 0$

$\Rightarrow 2y(y-1) + 1(y-1) = 0$

$\Rightarrow y = 1$ or $y = -1/2 \quad \therefore x = 1 + 4 = 5, y = -1/2$

$\Rightarrow Q \equiv \left(5, -\dfrac{1}{2}\right) \quad \Rightarrow |PQ| = \sqrt{9 + \dfrac{9}{4}} = \dfrac{3\sqrt{5}}{2}$

TEXTUAL EXERCISE–3: (SUBJECTIVE)

1. $\left(\dfrac{dy_1}{dx}\right)_{(1,1)} = 2x = 2\left(\dfrac{dy_2}{dx}\right)_{(1,1)} = \dfrac{-3x^2}{6} = \dfrac{-1}{2}$

$\therefore \theta = \tan^{-1}\left|\dfrac{2 + 1/2}{1 - 1/2 \times 2}\right| = \tan^{-1}\left|\dfrac{5/2}{0}\right| = \dfrac{\pi}{2}$

2. Curves are symmetric about axis, so will make same angle at all 4 points of intersection

$y_1^1 = \dfrac{-b^2x}{a^2y};\ y_2^1 = \dfrac{-x}{y}$

$$\therefore \theta = \tan^{-1}\left|\frac{\frac{b^2x}{a^2y} - \frac{x}{y}}{1 + \frac{b^2x^2}{a^2y^2}}\right|$$

Also $\dfrac{x^2}{a^2} + \dfrac{y^2}{b^2} = \dfrac{x^2}{ab} + \dfrac{y^2}{ab} \quad \Rightarrow \dfrac{x^2}{y^2} = \dfrac{a}{b}$

$$\therefore \theta = \tan^{-1}\left|\frac{\frac{b^2}{a^2}\sqrt{\frac{a}{b}} - \sqrt{\frac{a}{b}}}{1 + \frac{b^2a}{a^2b}}\right| = \tan^{-1}\left|\frac{b-a}{\sqrt{ab}}\right|$$

3. $y=\left[|\sin x|+|\cos x|\right]=\begin{cases}\left[\sqrt{2}\sin\left(\frac{\pi}{4}+x\right)\right]=1;\ x\in\left[0,\frac{\pi}{2}\right]\\ \left[\sqrt{2}\sin\left(x-\frac{\pi}{4}\right)\right]=1;\ x\in\left[\frac{\pi}{2},\pi\right]\end{cases}$

$\Rightarrow$ $m = 0$ in 1st quadrant.

At the point of intersection in first quadrant $x^2 + 1 = 5$

$\Rightarrow$ $x^2 = 4;\ x = 2;\ (2, 1)$ and $2x + 2yy' = 0$

$\Rightarrow$ $y' = -x/y = -2$

$\therefore$ $\theta=\tan^{-1}\left|\frac{-2+0}{1-2}\right|=\tan^{-1}2$

Since both functions are symmetric about x and y axis, so angle would be same for other quadrants.

4. $\frac{dy_1}{dx}=-\left(\frac{3x^2-3y^2}{-6xy}\right);\ \frac{dy_2}{dx}=\frac{-(6xy)}{3x^2-3y^2};\ \frac{dy_1}{dx}\times\frac{dy_2}{dx}=-1$

$\Rightarrow$ $\theta = \pi/2$

5. The line AA' joining $A(2, -1)$ and $A'(-2, 1)$ is normal to circle and cuts it at Q $(\neq 0)$

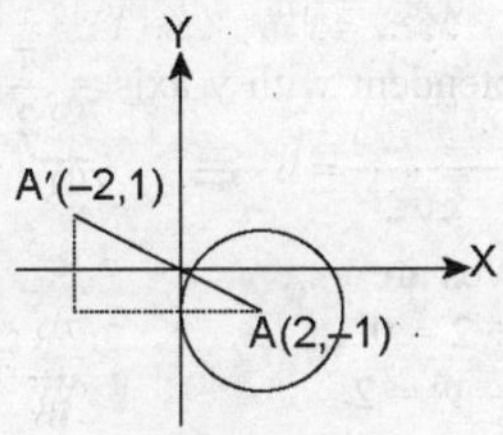

$\therefore$ Minimum value of $[(x + 2)^2 + (y - 1)^2]^{1/2} = (QA')$ and maximum value of $[(x + 2)^2 + (y - 1)^2]^{1/2} = (A'P)$

$\therefore$ Equation of AA' is $y=-\frac{1}{2}x$

$\Rightarrow$ Coordinates of Q and P are given by $(x-2)^2+\left(-\frac{1}{2}x+1\right)^2=4$

$\Rightarrow$ $x^2+4-4x+\frac{1}{4}x^2+1-x=4$

$\Rightarrow$ $\frac{5}{4}x^2-5x+1=0$ $\quad\Rightarrow$ $5x^2-20x+4=0$

$\Rightarrow$ $x=\frac{20\pm\sqrt{400-80}}{10}$ $\quad\Rightarrow$ $x=2\pm\frac{8\sqrt{5}}{10}=2\pm\frac{4}{5}$,

$\Rightarrow$ $y=-1\mp\frac{2}{\sqrt{5}}\Rightarrow P=\left(2+\frac{4}{\sqrt{5}},-1-\frac{2}{\sqrt{5}}\right)$ and

$Q=\left(2-\frac{4}{\sqrt{5}},-1+\frac{2}{\sqrt{5}}\right)$

$\Rightarrow$ Minimum value of $[(x + 2)^2 + (y - 1)^2]^{1/2} = (QA')$

$=\left[\left(4-\frac{4}{\sqrt{5}}\right)^2+\left(-2+\frac{2}{\sqrt{5}}\right)^2\right]^{1/2}$

$=\left[16\left(1+\frac{1}{5}-\frac{2}{\sqrt{5}}\right)+4\left(1+\frac{1}{5}-\frac{2}{\sqrt{5}}\right)\right]^{1/2}$

$=\left[20\left(\frac{6}{5}-\frac{2}{\sqrt{5}}\right)\right]^{1/2}=\left[20\left(\frac{6-2\sqrt{5}}{5}\right)\right]^{1/2}$

$=\sqrt{4\left(6-2\sqrt{5}\right)}=2\sqrt{\left(\sqrt{5}-1\right)^2}=\left(2\sqrt{5}-2\right)$

Maximum value of $[(x + 2)^2 + (y - 1)^2]^{1/2} = A'P$

$=\left[\left(4+\frac{4}{\sqrt{5}}\right)^2+\left(-2-\frac{2}{\sqrt{5}}\right)^2\right]^{1/2}$

$=\left[(16+4)\left(1+\frac{1}{\sqrt{5}}\right)^2\right]^{1/2}=2\sqrt{5}\left(1+\frac{1}{\sqrt{5}}\right)=2\sqrt{5}+2$

6. Clearly, for shortest distance point P tangent must be parallel to line $y = x - 4$ i.e., having slope 1.

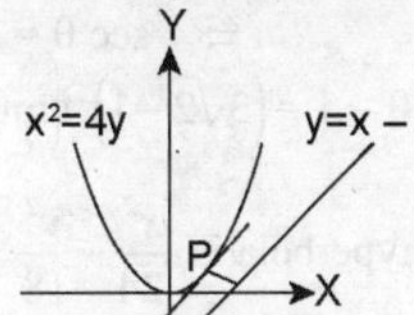

$\therefore$ Equation of tangent to $x^2 = 4y$ of slope 1 is $x=\frac{1}{m}y+$ am or $x=\frac{y}{1}+1$ or $y = x - 1$

Put $y = x - 1$ in $x^2 = 4y$

$\Rightarrow$ $x^2 = 4(x - 1)$ $\quad\Rightarrow$ $x^2 - 4x + 4 = 0$

$\Rightarrow$ $(x - 2)^2 = 0$ $\quad\Rightarrow$ $x = 2, y = 1$

$\therefore$ $P = (2, 1)$

7. Equation of tangent to circle $x^2 + y^2 = 1$ with slope m is $y=mx+\sqrt{m^2+1}$ .....(1)

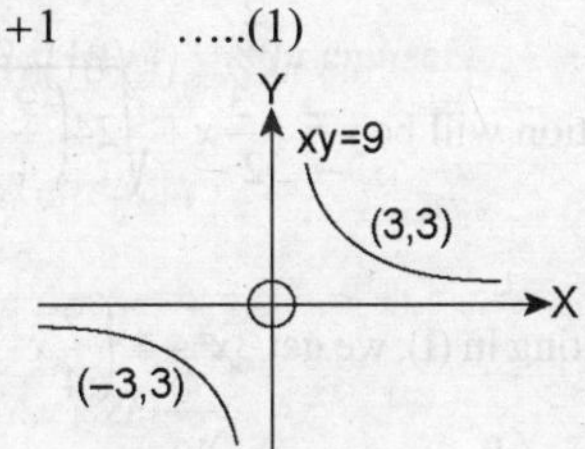

Also slope of tangent C_1: $x^2 + y^2 = 1$

$\Rightarrow$ $2x+2y\frac{dy}{dx}=0$

$\Rightarrow$ $\frac{dy}{dx}=\frac{-x}{y}$

$\Rightarrow$ Slope of normal at Q $(\cos\theta, \sin\theta) \equiv \tan\theta$

C_2: $xy = 9$

$\Rightarrow$ $x\frac{dy}{dx}+y=0$ $\quad\Rightarrow$ $\frac{dy}{dx}=\frac{-y}{x}$

$\Rightarrow$ Slope of Normal at $P\left(3t,\frac{3}{t}\right)=\frac{3t}{3/t}=t^2$

$\therefore$ $\tan\theta=t^2=\frac{\frac{3}{t}-\sin\theta}{3t-\cos\theta}$

$\Rightarrow$ S.D. $= PQ = \sqrt{(3t-\cos\theta)^2 + \left(\frac{3}{t} - \sin\theta\right)^2}$

$= \sqrt{(3t-\cos\theta)^2 + (3t-\cos\theta)^2 .t^4} = (3t - \cos\theta)\ \sqrt{1+t^4}$

$= (3t - \cos\theta)\ .\ \sec\theta = 3t \sec\theta - 1 \mid$

=Also equation of normal to $xy = 9$ at P is

$\left(y - \frac{3}{t}\right) = t^2(x - 3t)$ or $y = t^2 x + \left(\frac{3}{t} - 3t^3\right)$

It paries through h Q (cos θ, sin θ)

$\Rightarrow \sin\theta = \tan\theta.\cos\theta + \frac{3}{t} - 3t^3$

$\Rightarrow \frac{3}{t} - 3t^3 = 0 \quad \Rightarrow \quad t = \pm 1$

$\Rightarrow \tan\theta = 1 \quad \Rightarrow \quad \sec\theta = \sqrt{2}$

$\therefore$ S.D $= 3t \sec\theta - 1 = \left(3\sqrt{2} - 1\right)$ units

8. Equation of hyperbola is $\frac{x^2}{24} - \frac{y^2}{18} = 1$ ...(i)

Let P be the point of (i) atleast distance from $3x + 2y + 1 = 0$

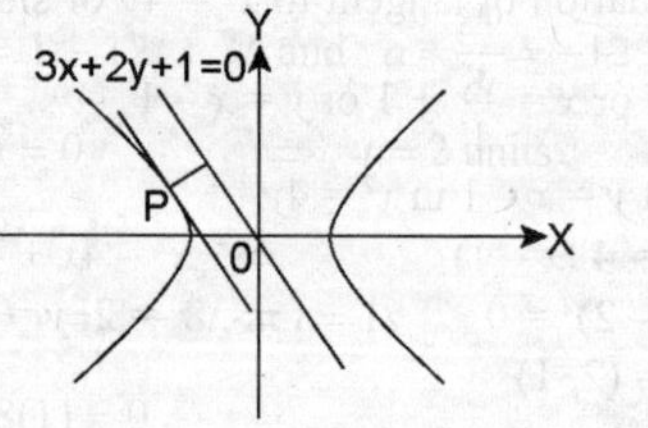

$\Rightarrow$ Slope of tangent at $p = \frac{-3}{2}$

$\therefore$ Its equation will be $y = \frac{-3}{2}x + \sqrt{24\left(\frac{9}{4}\right) - 18}$ or $y = \frac{-3}{2}$ $x \pm 6$

Substituting in (i), we get $3x^2 - 4\left(\frac{9}{4}x^2 + 36 - 18x\right) = 72$

or $3x^2 - 4\left(\frac{9}{4}x^2 + 36 + 18x\right) = 72$

$\Rightarrow 3x^2 - 9x^2 - 144 + 72x = 72$ or $3x^2 - 9x^2 - 144 - 72x = 72$

$\Rightarrow 6x^2 - 72x + 216 = 0$ or $6x^2 + 72x + 216 = 0$

$\Rightarrow (x - 6)^2$ or $(x + 6)^2 = 0$

$\Rightarrow x = 6$ or $-6 \quad \Rightarrow \quad y = -3$ or 3

$\therefore$ Required points are (6, –3) or (–6, 3)

For $P \equiv (6, -3)$; $PM = \frac{|3(6) + 2(-3) + 1|}{\sqrt{9+4}} = \sqrt{13}$

For $P \equiv (-6, 3)$; $PM = \frac{|3(-6) + 2(3) + 1|}{\sqrt{13}} = \frac{11}{\sqrt{13}} = \frac{11}{13}\sqrt{13}$

Clearly $\frac{11}{13}\sqrt{13} < \sqrt{13}$

$\Rightarrow$ (–6, 3) is the required point

TEXTUAL EXERCISE–3: (OBJECTIVE)

1. (c) $y_1 = 2x,\ y_2 = -\frac{1}{2}x^2$

At (1, 1), $y_1 = 2,\ y_2 = \frac{-1}{2}$

$\Rightarrow \tan\theta_1 = 2,\ \tan\theta_2 = \frac{-1}{2}$

$\Rightarrow$ Angle between tangents $= \tan^{-1}\left(\frac{\tan\theta_1 - \tan\theta_2}{1 + \tan\theta_1.\tan\theta_2}\right)$

$= \tan^{-1}\left|\frac{2 + \frac{1}{2}}{1 + 2\left(\frac{-1}{2}\right)}\right| = \frac{\pi}{2}$

2. (b) $y = k_e\ k_x$ ...(i)

$\Rightarrow \frac{dy}{dx} = k^2 e^{kx}$

Curve (i) intersects y-axis at $(0, k)$

$\therefore$ Slope of tangent to curve at $(0, k) = k^2$

$\Rightarrow \tan\alpha = k^2$

$\Rightarrow$ Angle subtendent with y-axis $= \frac{\pi}{2} - \alpha = \frac{\pi}{2} - \tan^{-1}k^2 =$ $\cot^{-1} k^2$

3. (a) Given curves are

$x^3 - 3xy^2 + 2 = 0$ ...(i)

and $3x^2 y - y^3 = 2$ ...(ii)

$\Rightarrow 3x^2 - 3x\left(2y\frac{dy}{dx}\right) - 3y^2 = 0$

$\Rightarrow x^2 - 2xy\frac{dy}{dx} - y^2 = 0$

$\Rightarrow \frac{dy}{dx} = \frac{x^2 - y^2}{2xy}$ ...(iii)

and $3x^2\frac{dy}{dx} + 3y(2x) - 3y^2\frac{dy}{dx} = 0$

$\Rightarrow \frac{dy}{dx} = \frac{6xy}{3y^2 - 3x^2} = \frac{2xy}{y^2 - x^2}$ ...(iv)

$\therefore y_1 y_2 = \left(\frac{x^2 - y^2}{2xy}\right)\left(\frac{2xy}{y^2 - x^2}\right) = -1$ at the point of intersection

4. (b) $y^2 = x^3 + x^2$

$\Rightarrow 2y\frac{dy}{dx} = 3x^2 + 2x$

$\Rightarrow \frac{dy}{dx} = \frac{3x^2 + 2x}{2y} = \frac{3x^2 + 2x}{\pm\sqrt{x^3 + 2}}$

$\Rightarrow \left(\frac{dy}{dx}\right)_{(0,0)} = \lim_{x\to 0}\frac{\pm(3x+2)}{2\sqrt{x+1}} = \pm 1$

$\Rightarrow$ At origin there will be two tangents at angle $\frac{\pi}{4}$ and $\frac{3\pi}{4}$.

5. (c) $xy = a^2$ and $x^2 + y^2 = 2b^2$

$\frac{dy}{dx} = \frac{-a^2}{x^2}$ and $2x + 2y\frac{dy}{dx} = 0$

$\Rightarrow y_1 = \frac{-a^2}{x^2}; y = \frac{-x}{y}$

$\Rightarrow y_1 . y_2 = \frac{a^2}{xy}$ at the point of intersection,

$\Rightarrow y_1 . y_2 = \frac{a^2}{a^2}$ ($\because xy = a^2$ at the point of intersection)

$\Rightarrow \tan\theta = 1 \qquad \Rightarrow \theta = \pi/4$

6. (b) Given curves are

$x^3 + pxy^2 = -2$ ...(i)

and $3x^2 y - y^3 = 2$ ...(ii)

$\Rightarrow 3x^2 + px\left(2y\frac{dy}{dx}\right) + py^2 = 0$

$\Rightarrow y_1 = \frac{dy}{dx} = \frac{-(3x^2 - py^2)}{2pxy}$ ...(iii)

and $3x^2\frac{dy}{dx} + 6xy - 3y^2\frac{dy}{dx} = 0$

$\Rightarrow y_2 = \frac{dy}{dx} = \frac{6xy}{3y^2 - 3x^2} = \frac{2xy}{(y^2 - x^2)}$ ...(iii)

$\therefore$ For orthoginality, $y_1, y_2 = -1$

$\Rightarrow \frac{3x^2 + py^2}{2pxy} \times \frac{2xy}{y^2 - x^2} = 1$

$\Rightarrow 3x^2 + py^2 = p(y^2 - x^2)$

$\Rightarrow 3x^2 = -px^2 \qquad \Rightarrow p = -3$

7. (d) $y = x^2$

$\Rightarrow \frac{dy}{dx} = 2x \qquad \Rightarrow y_1 = 2x$ and $6y = 7 - x^3$

$\Rightarrow \frac{dy}{dx} = \frac{-1}{2}x^2 \Rightarrow y_2 = \frac{-1}{2}x^2$

$\therefore y_1 . y_2 = -x^3$

At (1, 1), $y_1 y_2 = -1$

$\Rightarrow$ Angle of intersection $= \frac{\pi}{2}$

8. (a) $C_1 : y = x^2 - 5x + 6$ ...(i)

$\Rightarrow \frac{dy}{dx} = 2x - 5$

$\Rightarrow y_1 = 2x - 5$ and $C_2 : y = x^2 + x + 1$ ...(ii)

$\Rightarrow \frac{dy}{dx} = 2x + 1 \qquad \Rightarrow y_2 = 2x + 1$

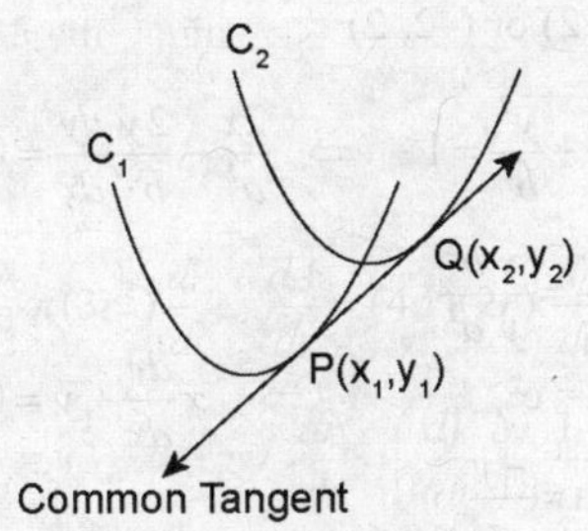

$\therefore$ Slope of common tangent $= 2x_1 - 5 = 2x_2 + 1 = \frac{y_2 - y_1}{x_2 - x_1}$

$\Rightarrow 2x_1 - 5 = 2x_2 + 1 = \frac{(x_2^2 - x_1^2) + (x_2 + 5x_1)}{x_2 - x_1}$

$\Rightarrow x_2 - x_1 = -3$ ...(iii)

and $(x_2 + x_1) + \frac{(x_2 + 5x_1)}{-3} + \frac{5}{3} = 2x_2 + 1$

$\Rightarrow 3x_2 + 3x_1 - x_2 - 5x_1 + 5 = 6x_2 + 3$

$\Rightarrow 4x_2 + 2x_1 = 2$

$\Rightarrow 2x_2 + x_1 = 1$ ...(iv)

Solving (iii) and (iv), we get $x_2 = -2/3$, $x_1 = 7/3$

$\therefore$ Slope of common tangent $= 2x_2 + 1 = 2.\left(\frac{-2}{3}\right) + 1 = \frac{-1}{3}$

9. (a) $a_1 x^3 + b_1 y^3 = 1$ ...(i)

and $a_2 x^3 + b_2 y^3 = 1$ ...(ii)

From (i), $a_1(3x^2) + b_1\left(3y^2\frac{dy}{dx}\right) = 0$

$\Rightarrow y_1 = \frac{dy}{dx} = \frac{-3a_1x^2}{3b_1y^2} = \frac{-a_1x^2}{b_1y^2}$

From (ii), $a_2(3x^2) + b_2\left(3y^2\frac{dy}{dx}\right) = 0$

$\Rightarrow y_2 = \frac{dy}{dx} = \frac{-a_2x^2}{b_2y^2}$

For orthogonality of curves at (h, k)

$y_1 . y_2 = \frac{-a_1h^2}{b_1k^2} \times \frac{-a_2h^2}{b_2k^2} = -1$

$\Rightarrow \frac{a_1a_2}{b_1b_2} . \frac{h^4}{k^4} = -1$ ...(iii)

Also at point of intersection (h, k), $a_1 h^3 + b_1 k^3 = a_2 h^3 + b_2 k^3 = 1$

$\Rightarrow (a_1 - a_2) h^3 = (b_2 - b_1) k^3$

$\Rightarrow \frac{h^4}{k^4}\left[\frac{(b_2 - b_1)}{(a_1 - a_2)}\right]^{4/3}$ ...(iv)

$\therefore$ From (iii) and (iv), $a_1 a_2 (b_2 - b_1)^{4/3} + (a_1 - a_2)^{4/3} b_1 b_2 = 0$

10. (c) $\frac{x^2}{a_1} + \frac{y^2}{b_1} = 1$ and $\frac{x^2}{a_2} + \frac{y^2}{b_2} = 1$ cut each other orthogonality,

$\Rightarrow y_1 = \frac{dy}{dx} = \frac{-h}{k}.\frac{b_1}{a_1}$ and $y_2 = \frac{dy}{dx} = \frac{-h}{k}.\frac{b_2}{a_2}$

$\Rightarrow y_1 . y_2 = \frac{h^2}{k^2}.\frac{b_1b_2}{a_1a_2} = -1$ ...(i)

At point of intersection (h, k), $\frac{h^2}{a_1} + \frac{k^2}{b_1} = \frac{h^2}{a_2} + \frac{k^2}{b_2} = 1$

$\Rightarrow h^2\left(\frac{a_2 - a_1}{a_1a_2}\right) = k^2\left(\frac{b_1 - b_2}{b_1b_2}\right)$

$\Rightarrow \frac{h^2}{k^2} = \frac{b_1 - b_2}{a_2 - a_1}.\frac{a_1a_2}{b_1b_2}$ ...(ii)

From (i) and (ii), we get $y_1\, y_2 = \dfrac{(b_1 - b_2)}{(a_2 - a_1)} = -1$

$\Rightarrow\ b_1 - b_2 = a_1 - a_2 \qquad \Rightarrow\ a_1 + b_2 = a_2 + b_1$

11. (b) $\dfrac{x^2}{a^2} + \dfrac{y^2}{b^2} = 1 \quad \Rightarrow \quad \dfrac{2x}{a^2} + \dfrac{2y}{b^2}\dfrac{dy}{dx} = 0$

$\Rightarrow\ \dfrac{dy}{dx} = \dfrac{-x}{y}.\dfrac{b^2}{a^2}$

$(y_1)\,(a, 0) = \infty$ and $(y_2)\,(0, b) = 0$

$\Rightarrow$ Angle between the tangents is $\dfrac{\pi}{2}$

12. (b) $y = \sin x \quad \Rightarrow \quad \dfrac{dy}{dx}\ \cos x$ …(i)

And $y = \cos x \quad \Rightarrow \quad \dfrac{dy}{dx} = -\sin x$ …(ii)

At the point of intersection $\sin x = \cos x$

$\Rightarrow\ \tan x = 1 \qquad \Rightarrow\ x = n\pi + \dfrac{\pi}{4}; x \in \mathbb{Z}$

$\Rightarrow\ (y_1) = \dfrac{1}{\sqrt{2}}, y_2 = \dfrac{-1}{\sqrt{2}}$ or $(y_1) = -\dfrac{1}{\sqrt{2}}, y_2 = \dfrac{1}{\sqrt{2}}$

$\Rightarrow$ Angle between tangent $= \tan^{-1}\left|\dfrac{\dfrac{1}{\sqrt{2}} + \dfrac{1}{\sqrt{2}}}{1 + \left(-\dfrac{1}{2}\right)}\right|$

$= \tan^{-1}\left(2\sqrt{2}\right)$

13. (a), (c) $y = a^x$

$\Rightarrow\ \dfrac{dy}{dx} = a^x\, \ell n\, a$ …(i)

And $y = e^x \quad \Rightarrow \quad \dfrac{dy}{dx} = e^x$ …(ii)

At point of intersection $a^x = e^x = x = 0$

$\Rightarrow\ y_1 = \ell n\, a,\ y_2 = 1$

Angle between the curves $= \tan^{-1}\left|\dfrac{\ell na - 1}{1 + \ell na}\right|$

14. (d) $C_1 : y^2 = 8x;\ C_2 : xy = 1$

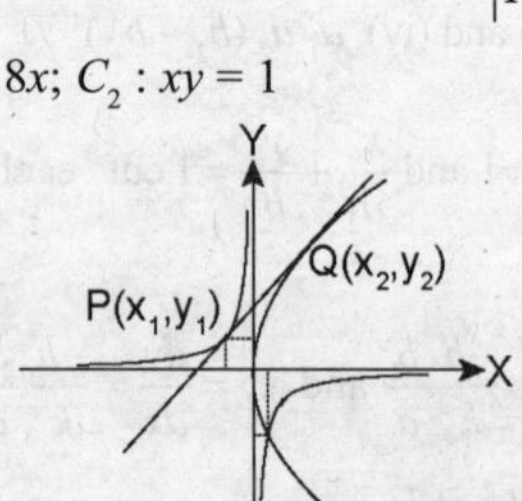

Tangent to C_1 is given by $y = mx + \dfrac{2}{m}$

If it is tangent to $xy = -1$, then $x\left(mx + \dfrac{2}{m}\right) = -1 = -1$ have equal roots

$\Rightarrow\ m^2 x^2 + 2x + m = 0$ has Disc. $= 0$

$\Rightarrow\ 4 - 4m^3 = 0 \qquad \Rightarrow\ m^3 = 1$

$\Rightarrow\ m = 1$

$\Rightarrow$ Equation of common tangent is $y = x + 2$

15. (b) Equation of given circle is $x^2 + y^2 + 2x - \dfrac{1}{2}y - \dfrac{25}{8} = 0$ having its centre at $\left(-1, \dfrac{1}{4}\right)$

$\therefore$ Point on line $y = 2x + 11$ nearest to circle $16x^2 + 16y^2 + 32x - 8y - 50 = 0$ is foot of $\perp r$ from $O\left(-1, \dfrac{1}{4}\right)$ to line

$y = 2x + 11$ i.e., $\dfrac{x+1}{2} = \dfrac{y - \frac{1}{4}}{-1} = \dfrac{-\left(2(-1) - \frac{1}{4} + 11\right)}{4 + (1)}$

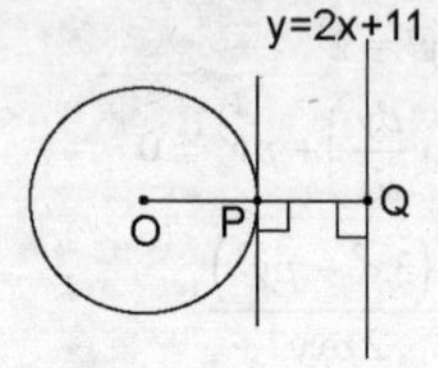

$\Rightarrow\ \dfrac{x+1}{2} = \dfrac{y - \frac{1}{4}}{-1} = \dfrac{-35}{4(5)} = \dfrac{-7}{4}$

$\Rightarrow\ x = -\dfrac{7}{2} - 1,\ y = \dfrac{7}{4} + \dfrac{1}{4}$

$\Rightarrow\ x = -\dfrac{9}{2}, y = 2$ i.e., $\left(-\dfrac{9}{2}, 2\right)$

16. (a), (d) Parametric equation of parabola is $x = t,\ y = \dfrac{1}{2}t^2$

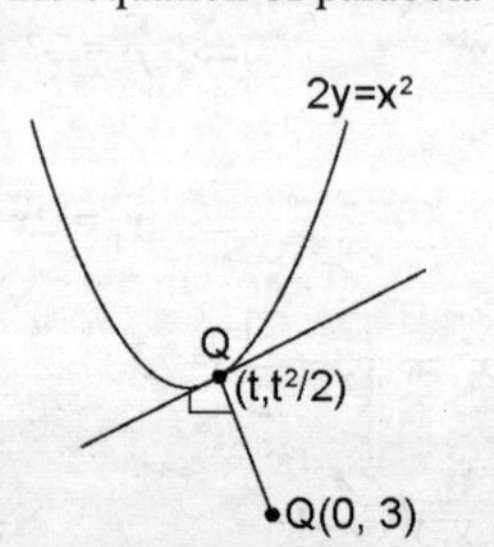

$\Rightarrow$ Slope of normal at $P\left(t, \dfrac{t^2}{2}\right) = -\left(\dfrac{1}{t}\right)$

$\Rightarrow\ \dfrac{\dfrac{t^2}{2} - 3}{t - 0} = \dfrac{-1}{t}$

$\Rightarrow\ \dfrac{t^2}{2} - 3 = -1$

$\Rightarrow\ t^2 = 4 \qquad \Rightarrow\ t = \pm 2$

$\therefore\ P \equiv (2, 2)$ or $(-2, 2)$

17. (b) $C_1 : \dfrac{x^2}{a^2} - \dfrac{y^2}{b^2} = 1 \quad \Rightarrow \quad \dfrac{2x}{a^2} - \dfrac{2y}{b^2}\dfrac{dy}{dx} = 0$

$\Rightarrow\ y_1 = \dfrac{dy}{dx} = \dfrac{x}{y}\dfrac{b^2}{a^2}$ …(i)

$C_2 : xy = c^2 \qquad \Rightarrow\ x\dfrac{dy}{dx} + y = 0$

$\Rightarrow\ y_2 = \dfrac{dy}{dx} = \dfrac{-y}{x}$ …(ii)

$\therefore$ For (i) and (ii) to be orthogonal at point of intersection

(h, k) , $y_1 \cdot y_2 = -\frac{h}{k}.\frac{a^2}{a^2}\times\frac{-k}{h} = -1$

$\Rightarrow b^2 = -a^2 \qquad \Rightarrow a^2 = b^2 = 0$

18. (a) $|\ell n\, x| = px$ ...(i)

Let $f(x) = |\ell n\, x| = \begin{cases} \ell nx;\, x \in [1,\infty) \\ -\ell nx;\, x \in (0,1) \end{cases}$ and $g(x) = px$

Graphically shown below:

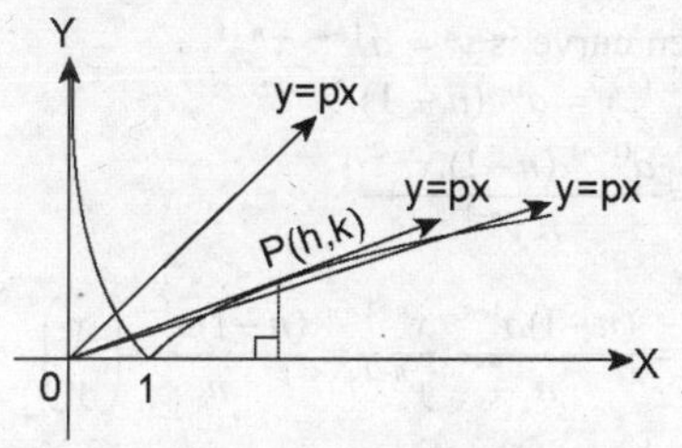

Clearly for three distinct roots of (i); $x > 1$ i.e.,

$\ell n\, x = px;\, x > 1$ ...(ii)

Let $P(h, k)$ be they point tangent of two curves.

$\therefore\ P \equiv (h, k) = (h, \ell n\, h) = (h, ph)$

$\Rightarrow \frac{\ell nh}{h} = p$

But At the point of tangency, $\frac{1}{h} = P \Rightarrow \frac{\ell nh}{h} = \frac{1}{h}$

$\Rightarrow \ell n\, h = 1 \qquad \Rightarrow h = e$

$\therefore\ p = \frac{1}{e}$

$\Rightarrow y = \frac{1}{e}x$ is tangent to $y = \ell n\, x;\, (x > 1)$

$\Rightarrow$ For 3 distinct points of intersection $p \in \left(0, \frac{1}{e}\right)$

19. (b) Let $f(x) = x^2$ and $g(x) = e^{|x|-2}$

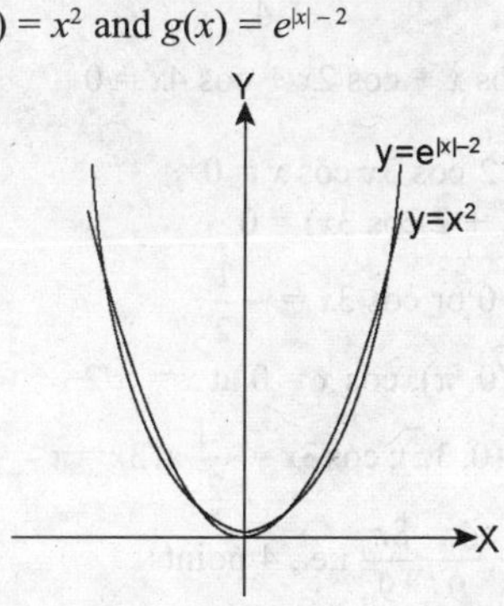

Let $h(x) = f(x) - g(x)$

Clearly, $h(0) = -\frac{1}{e^2} < 0$

$h(2) = 3 > 0$

$h(6) = 36 - e^5 < 0$

$\Rightarrow$ By intermediate theorem there is a root $\in (0, 2)$ and other $(2, 6)$

TEXTUAL EXERCISE-4: (SUBJECTIVE)

1. Length of sub tangent is given by $y\frac{dx}{dy}$ and that of sub normal by $y\frac{dy}{dx}$

Here $y = x\ln(kx)$ ...(1)

$\Rightarrow \frac{dy}{dx} = x\frac{1}{kx}.k + \ln(kx) = 1 + \ln(kx)$

Length of sub-normal

$= y\frac{dy}{dx} = y(1 + \ln kx) = y\left(1 + \frac{y}{x}\right) = \frac{y}{x}(x + y)$ ...(2)

Also if fourth proportion of x, y and $(x + y)$ is t, then

$\frac{x}{y} = \frac{x+y}{t}$

$\Rightarrow t = \frac{y}{x}(x + y)$ ...(3)

$\therefore$ From (2) and (3), the result follows.

2. Given curve is $x^a.y^b = c^{a+b}$

$\Rightarrow b.x^a.y^{b-1}.y' + a.x^{a-1}.y^b = 0$

$\Rightarrow y' = \frac{-ax^{a-1}.y^b}{bx^a.y^{b-1}} = \frac{-a}{b}.\frac{y}{x}$

$\therefore$ Length of sub tangent $= y\frac{dx}{dy} = y.\left(-\frac{bx}{ay}\right) = -\frac{b}{a}(x)$

$\Rightarrow$ Length of sub tangent ∞ (x)

3. Given curve is $y = e^{x/a} \Rightarrow \frac{dy}{dx} = \frac{1}{a}e^{x/a}$

$\Rightarrow$ Length of sub tangent $= y\frac{dx}{dy} = y.\frac{a}{e^{x/a}} = y.\frac{a}{y} = a$

4. $ay^2 = (x + b)^3$

$\Rightarrow 2ayy' = 3(x + b)^2$

$\Rightarrow y' = \frac{3}{2ay}(x + b)^2$ ...(1)

$\therefore$ Length of sub normal

$= yy' = l_1 = \frac{3}{2a}(x+b)^2 = \frac{3}{2a}(ay^2)^{2/3}$ and length of sub

tangent $= \frac{y}{y'} = l_2 = \frac{2ay^2}{3(x+b)^2} = \frac{2ay^2}{3(ay^2)^{2/3}}$

$\therefore\ l_1 = \frac{3}{2a^{1/3}}y^{4/3};\, l_2 = \frac{2a^{1/3}}{3}(y)^{2/3}$

$\Rightarrow l_2^2 = \frac{4a^{2/3}}{9}y^{4/3} = \frac{4a^{2/3}}{9}.\frac{2a^{1/3}}{3}l_1$

$\therefore\ l_2^2 = \frac{8}{27}al_1$

$\Rightarrow l_2^2 \propto l_1$

5. $y^n = a^{n-1}.x$

$\Rightarrow ny^{n-1}y' = a^{n-1} \Rightarrow y' = \frac{a^{n-1}}{n.y^{n-1}}$

$\Rightarrow \quad y.y' = \dfrac{a^{n-1}}{n.y^{n-2}} = \dfrac{y^n}{nxy^{n-2}} = \dfrac{y^2}{nx}$

$\Rightarrow$ Length of sub-normal $= \dfrac{y^2}{nx}$ and

$\dfrac{y}{y'} = y\left(\dfrac{ny^{n-1}}{a^n - 1}\right) = \dfrac{n}{a^{n-1}}.y^n$

$\Rightarrow$ Length of sub tangent $= nx\left[\because \dfrac{y^n}{a^{n-1}} = x\right]$

6. Given curve is $y^2x^2 = a^2(x^2 - a^2)$

$\Rightarrow \quad y^2(2x) + x^2(2yy') = a^2(2x)$

$\Rightarrow \quad 2x^2yy' = 2a^2x - 2xy^2$

$\Rightarrow \quad yy' = \dfrac{a^2 - y^2}{x}$

$\Rightarrow$ Length of sub-normal $= \dfrac{a^2 - \dfrac{a^2}{x^2}(x^2 - a^2)}{x} = \dfrac{a^4}{x^3}$

$\Rightarrow$ Length of sub-normal $\infty \dfrac{1}{x^3}$

TEXTUAL EXERCISE-4: (OBJECTIVE)

1. **(d)** Given curve is $y^2 = 4ax$

$\Rightarrow \quad 2yy' = 4a$

$\Rightarrow \quad yy' = 2a$

$\Rightarrow$ Length of sub-normal $= 2a$

2. **(b)** Given, that $yy' = \dfrac{y}{y'}$

$\Rightarrow \quad y'^2 = 1$

$\therefore$ Length if tangent $= y\sqrt{1 + \left(\dfrac{1}{y'}\right)^2} = y\sqrt{1+1} = \sqrt{2}y$

3. **(a)** Given curve is $x^2 + y^2 = 4$ which is a circle with centre at (0, 0) and radius 2.

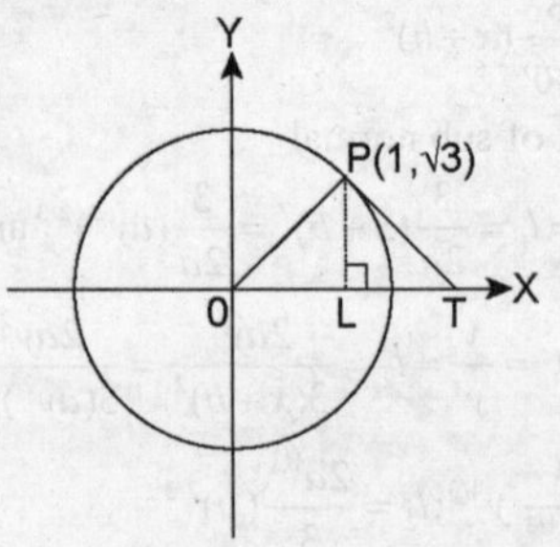

OL = length of sub-normal $= y.y' = \dfrac{-2x}{2} = -x$

$\therefore$ At $P(1, \sqrt{3}) = |-1| = 1$ and LT = sub-tangent

$= \left|\dfrac{y}{y'}\right| = \left|\dfrac{y^2}{-x}\right| = 3$

$\therefore \quad OT = 1 + 3 = 4$

$\therefore$ Area of $\Delta\, OPT = \dfrac{1}{2}(4)(\sqrt{3}) = 2\sqrt{3}$ sq. units

4. **(c)** Given curve is $xy^n = a^{n+1}$

$\Rightarrow \quad x\, ny^{n-1}.y' + y^n = 0$

$\Rightarrow \quad y' = \dfrac{-y^n}{nxy^{n-1}}$

$\Rightarrow \quad yy' = \dfrac{-y^2}{nx} = \dfrac{-y^2.y^n}{na^{n+1}}$

$\Rightarrow \quad yy' = \dfrac{-1}{na^{n+1}}.y^{(n+2)}$

$\Rightarrow$ Length of sub-normal is constant for $n = -2$

5. **(d)** Given curve is $y^n = a^{1-n}.\, x^{n-1}$

$\Rightarrow \quad n.y^{n-1}.\, y' = a^{1-n}(n-1).\, x^{n-2}$

$\Rightarrow \quad y' = \dfrac{a^{(1-n)}.(n-1).x^{n-2}}{n.y^{n-1}}$

$\Rightarrow \quad yy' = \dfrac{(n-1)a^{1-n}}{n}.\dfrac{x^{n-2}}{y^{n-2}} = \dfrac{(n-1)a^{1-n}}{n}\left(\dfrac{x}{y}\right)^{n-2}$

$\Rightarrow$ Length of sub-normal will be constant for $n = 2$ and will be given by $\dfrac{1}{2a}$.

6. **(d)** $x = a\,(t + \sin t)$, $y = a\,(1 - \cos t)$

Length normal at (x, y) is given by $= a\,(1 - \cos t)$

$\sqrt{1 + \left(\dfrac{\sin t}{1 + \cos t}\right)^2} = a\,(1 - \cos t)\sqrt{\dfrac{1+1+2\cos t}{(1+\cos t)^2}}$

$= \dfrac{a(1-\cos t)(\sqrt{2})}{\sqrt{1+\cos t}} = \dfrac{a(2\sin^2 t/2)}{\cos t/2} = 2\,a\,\sin^2 t/2 \sec /2$

$= 2\,a \sin t/2 \tan t/2$

SECTION–III (ONLY ONE CORRECT ANSWER)

1. **(d)** $y = \sin x + \dfrac{1}{2}\sin 2x + \dfrac{1}{4}\sin 4x$

$\Rightarrow \quad \dfrac{dy}{dx} = \cos x + \cos 2x + \cos 4x = 0$

$\Rightarrow \quad \cos x + 2\cos 3x \cos x = 0$

$\Rightarrow \quad \cos x\,(1 + 2\cos 3x) = 0$

$\Rightarrow \quad \cos x = 0$ or $\cos 3x = -\dfrac{1}{2}$

In $x \in (0, \pi)$, $\cos x = 0$ at $x = \pi/2$

In $3x \in (0, 3\pi)$; $\cos 3x = \dfrac{-1}{2}$ at $3x = \pi - \dfrac{\pi}{3}, \pi + \dfrac{\pi}{3}, 3\pi - \dfrac{\pi}{3}$

$\Rightarrow \quad x = \dfrac{2\pi}{9}, \dfrac{4\pi}{9}, \dfrac{8\pi}{9}$ i.e., 4 points

2. **(d)** $f_1(x) = x^2 - x + 1$

$\Rightarrow \quad f_1'(x) = 2x - 1$ and $f_2(x) = x^3 - x^2 - 2x + 1$

$\Rightarrow \quad f_2'(x) = 3x^2 - 2x - 2$

$\therefore \quad f_1'(h_1) = 2h_1 - 1$ and $f_2'(h_2) = 3h_2^2 - 2h_2 - 2$

For parallel tangents, $2h_1 - 1 = 3h_2^2 - 2h_2 - 2$ for some h_1, h_2

$\Rightarrow \quad 2h_1 = 3h_2^2 - 2h_2 - 1$

$\Rightarrow\ 3h_2^2 - 2h_2 - (2h_1 + 1) = 0$

$\Rightarrow\ h_2 = \dfrac{2 \pm \sqrt{4+12(2h_1+1)}}{6}$

$\Rightarrow\ h_2 = \dfrac{2 \pm \sqrt{24h_1+16}}{6}$

$\Rightarrow\ h_2$ is real for $h_1 \geq -\dfrac{2}{3}$

$\Rightarrow\ (h_1, h_2)$, where $h_1\ \dfrac{-2}{3}$ and $h_2 = \dfrac{2 \pm \sqrt{24h_1+16}}{6}$

$\Rightarrow$ Three will be infinitely many parallel tangents.

3. (a) $f(x) = \dfrac{\sin x^2}{x}$; $x \neq 0, f(0) = 0$

$f'(x) = \lim\limits_{h\to 0}\left(\dfrac{f(h)-f(0)}{h}\right) = \lim\limits_{h\to 0}\dfrac{f(h)}{h} = \lim\limits_{h\to 0}\dfrac{\sinh^2}{h^2} = 1$

$\Rightarrow$ Equation of normal to curve at origin is $(y - 0) = -1(x - 0)$

$\Rightarrow\ x + y = 0$

4. (d) $y = x - x^3$

$\Rightarrow\ \dfrac{dy}{dx} = 1 - 3x^2$

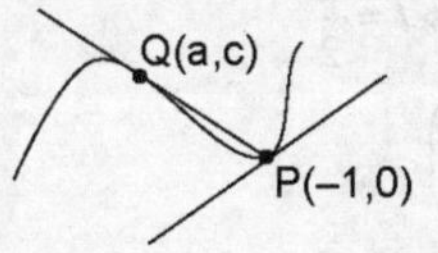

$\therefore$ Slope tangent at $P(-1, 0) = 1 - 3(-1)^2 = -2$

$\therefore$ Equation of tangent to curve at $P(-1, 0)$ is $(y - 0) = (-2)(x + 1)$

$\Rightarrow\ y = -2x - 2$

Comparing with $y = mx + b$

$\Rightarrow\ m = -2, b = -2$

Let $(y - 0) = m'(x + 1)$ be the line though $(-1, 0)$ and touching the curve at $Q(a, c)$

$\Rightarrow\ y = m'(x + 1)$ is tangent to curve at $Q(a, c)$

$\Rightarrow\ m' = 1 - 3a^2$

$\Rightarrow\ y = (1 - 3a^2)(x + 1)$

At the point of intersection $Q(a, c)$

$x - x^3 = (1 - 3a^2)(x + 1)$ has roots $a, a, -1$

$\Rightarrow\ x^3 - 3a^2 x + (1 - 3a^2) = 0$ has roots $a, a, -1$

$\Rightarrow$ Sum of roots $= 2a - 1 = \dfrac{(-1)'(0)}{1} = 0$

$\Rightarrow\ a = 1/2,$

At Q, $y = x - x^3$

$\Rightarrow\ c = a - a^3 = \dfrac{1}{2} - \dfrac{1}{8} = \dfrac{3}{8}$

$\therefore\ a = \dfrac{1}{2}, b = -2, c = \dfrac{3}{8}, m = -2$

5. (b) $x = t^3 - 4t^2 - 3t,\ y = 2t^2 + 3t - 5$

$\Rightarrow\ \dfrac{dy}{dx} = \dfrac{dy/dt}{dx/dt} = \dfrac{4t+3}{3t^2 - 8t}$

$\therefore$ For Horizontal tangents, $\dfrac{dy}{dx} = 0$

$\Rightarrow\ t = -3/4$ and for vertical tangents, $\dfrac{1}{dy/dx} = 0$

$\Rightarrow\ t = 0$ or $t = 8/3$

$\Rightarrow\ H = 1$ and $V = 2$

6. (c) $y = (2\sin^2 x + 3\cos^2 x)^{-1}$

$\Rightarrow\ \dfrac{dy}{dx} = -(2\sin^2 x + 3\cos^2 x)^{-2} \times [4\sin x\cos x - 6\cos x \sin x] = \dfrac{\sin 2x}{(2\sin^2 x + 3\cos^2 x)^2}$

For horizontal tangent, $\dfrac{dy}{dx} = 0$

$\Rightarrow\ \sin 2x = 0 \qquad \Rightarrow\ 2x = n\pi$

$\Rightarrow\ x = \dfrac{n\pi}{2}$; $n \in \mathbb{Z}$

$\therefore\ y\left(at\, x = \dfrac{n\pi}{2}\right) = \dfrac{1}{2}$ for $x = \dfrac{n\pi}{2}$, n = odd and $\dfrac{1}{3}$ at $x = \dfrac{n\pi}{2}$, n = even

7. (c) Length of subtangent is given by $y\,\dfrac{dx}{dy}$

A.T.Q; $x + y\,\dfrac{dx}{dy} = a \Rightarrow\ y\dfrac{dx}{dy} = a - x$

$\Rightarrow\ \dfrac{dx}{a-x} = \dfrac{dy}{y} \qquad \Rightarrow\ \displaystyle\int \frac{dx}{a-x} = \int \frac{dy}{y}$

$\Rightarrow\ -\ell n\,|a - x| = \ell n\, y + \ell n\, k$

$\Rightarrow\ \ell n\, ky\,|a - x| = 0 \qquad \Rightarrow\ ky\,|a - x| = 1$

As it passes through $(2a, a)$

$\Rightarrow\ ka\,|a - 2a| = 1 \qquad \Rightarrow\ k = \dfrac{1}{a|a|}$

$\therefore$ Equation of curve is $\dfrac{1}{a|a|}\, y|a - x| = 1$ or $y^2(a - x)^2 = a^4$

$\Rightarrow\ y(a - x) = \pm\, a^2$ as it passes through $(2a, a)$

$\Rightarrow\ y(a - x) = -a^2$

$\Rightarrow\ y(x - a) = a^2$

8. (b) $y = \sqrt{101 - \left(\sqrt{-x}\right)^4}$

For domain, $101 - \left(\sqrt{-x}\right)^4 \geq 0$

$\Rightarrow\ 101 \geq \left(\sqrt{-x}\right)^4$; $-x \geq 0$

$\Rightarrow\ 101 \geq (-x)^2$; $x \leq 0$

$\Rightarrow\ x^2 \leq 101$; $x \leq 0$

$\Rightarrow\ x \in \left[-\sqrt{101}, 0\right]$ and $y = \sqrt{101 - x^2}$

$\Rightarrow\ \dfrac{dy}{dx} = \dfrac{1}{2\sqrt{101 - x^2}}(-2x)$

$\Rightarrow\ \dfrac{dy}{dx} = \dfrac{-x}{\sqrt{101 - x^2}}$ ...(i)

At the point of intersection of curves, $\sqrt{101-x^2} = \log_{10}(-x)$

$\Rightarrow$ $101 - x^2 = \log^2_{10}(-x) \Rightarrow x = -10$

$\Rightarrow$ Point of intersection of curves is (–10, 1)

$\Rightarrow$ $\left(\dfrac{dy}{dx}\right)_{(-10,1)} = 10$

$\therefore$ Equation of tangent at (–10, 1) is $(y-1) = 10(x+10)$

i.e., $y = 10x + 101$

9. (d) Given curve is $y = x^3 + x + 16$ ....(1)

$\Rightarrow$ $\dfrac{dy}{dx} = 3x^2 + 1$

Let ℓ be given by $y = mx$ and tangent to curve at $P(h, k)$

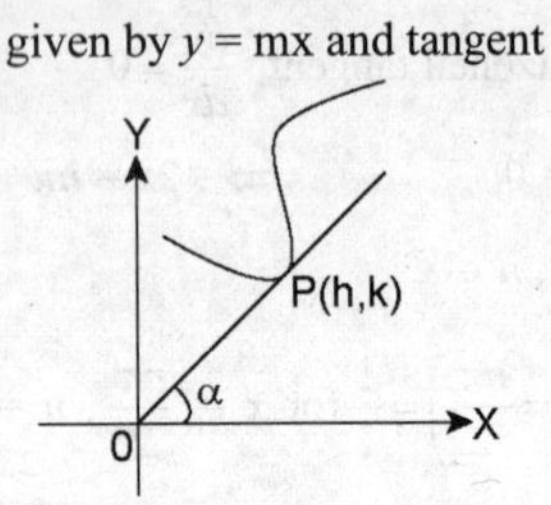

$\Rightarrow$ $m = 3h^2 + 1 = \dfrac{k}{h}$ $\Rightarrow$ $3h^3 + h = k$

$\Rightarrow$ $3h^2 + h = h^3 + h + 16 \Rightarrow 2h^3 = 16$

$\Rightarrow$ $h = 2$

$\Rightarrow$ Slope of tangent line $\ell = 3(h)^2 + 1 = 13$

10. (b) Length of subnormal $= y\dfrac{dy}{dx}$

$\Rightarrow$ ATQ, $y\dfrac{dy}{dx} = x$

$\Rightarrow$ $ydy = xdx$

$\Rightarrow$ $\dfrac{y^2}{2} = \dfrac{x^2}{2} +$ or $y^2 = x^2 + 2k$

$\therefore$ $f(1) = 3$ $\Rightarrow$ $9 = 1 + 2k$

$\Rightarrow$ $k = 4$

$\therefore$ Equation of curve is $y^2 = x^2 + 8$

$\Rightarrow$ $f(4) = \pm\sqrt{24} = \pm 2\sqrt{6}$ but $f(x) \ge 0\ \forall\ x \in \mathbb{R}$

$\Rightarrow$ $f(4) = 2\sqrt{6}$.

11. (b) Subtangent = subnormal

$\Rightarrow$ $y\dfrac{dx}{dy} = y\dfrac{dy}{dx}$ $\Rightarrow$ $\dfrac{dy}{dx} = \pm 1$

$\Rightarrow$ Length of tangent $= y\sqrt{1+\left(\dfrac{dx}{dy}\right)^2} = y\sqrt{2} = \sqrt{2}$ (ordinate)

12. (b) $x = a(\theta + \sin\theta)$, $y = a(1 - \cos\theta)$

Length of normal $= y\sqrt{1+\left(\dfrac{dy}{dx}\right)^2}$

$= a(1-\cos\theta)\sqrt{1+\left(\dfrac{\sin\theta}{1+\cos\theta}\right)^2}$

$= a(1-\cos\theta)\sqrt{\dfrac{1+\cos^2\theta+2\cos\theta+\sin^2\theta}{(1+\cos\theta)^2}}$

$= \dfrac{a(1-\cos\theta)}{(1+\cos\theta)}\sqrt{2(1+\cos\theta)} = \dfrac{a(2\sin^2\theta/2)}{(2\cos^2\theta/2)}2\cos\theta/2$

$= \dfrac{2a\sin^2\theta/2}{\cos\theta/2} = \dfrac{2a\left(\frac{1}{2}\right)}{1/2} = a\sqrt{2}$

13. (b) Given rivers beds are $y = x^2$ and $y = x - 2$

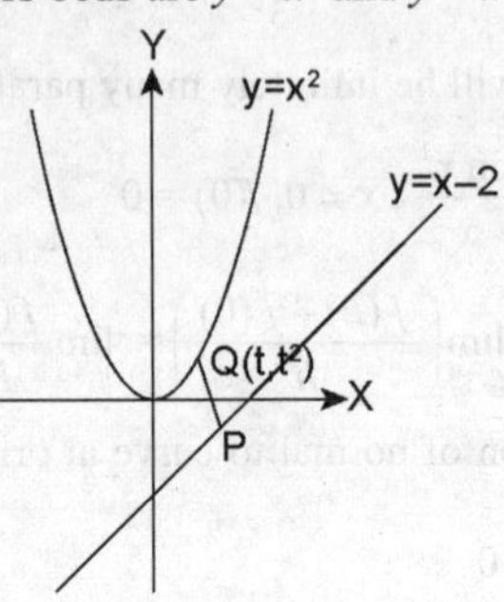

Let QP be the shortest canal

$\Rightarrow$ QP is common normal.

$\Rightarrow$ $-\dfrac{1}{2} = -1 \Rightarrow t = \dfrac{1}{2}$

$\Rightarrow$ $Q \equiv \left(\dfrac{1}{2}, \dfrac{1}{4}\right)$

Also P is foot of $\perp r$ from Q on $y = x - 2$

$\Rightarrow$ co-ordinates of pare given by

$\dfrac{x-\frac{1}{2}}{1} = \dfrac{y-\frac{1}{4}}{-1} = \dfrac{-\left(\frac{1}{2}-\frac{1}{4}-2\right)}{(1)^2+(1)^2}$

$\Rightarrow$ $x = \dfrac{11}{8}, y = \dfrac{-5}{8}$

14. (b) $y^2 = x^3 + x^2$ $\Rightarrow$ $2y\dfrac{dy}{dx} = 3x^2 + 2x$

$\Rightarrow$ $\dfrac{dy}{dx} = \dfrac{3x^2+2x}{2y} = \dfrac{3x^2+2x}{2\sqrt[x]{x+1}}$

$\Rightarrow$ $\lim\limits_{x\to 0}\left(\dfrac{dy}{dx}\right) = \lim\limits_{x\to 0}\dfrac{3x+2}{2\sqrt{x+1}} = 1$

$\Rightarrow$ The curve bisects the angle between the axes.

15. (b) $x + y - \ell n(x + y) = 2x - 5$

$\Rightarrow$ $1+\dfrac{dy}{dx}-\dfrac{1}{(x+y)}\left(1+\dfrac{dy}{dx}\right) = 2$

$\Rightarrow$ $\dfrac{dy}{dx}\left(1-\dfrac{1}{x+y}\right) = 1+\dfrac{1}{x+y}$

$\Rightarrow$ $\dfrac{dy}{dx} = \dfrac{x+y+1}{x+y-1}$ $\Rightarrow$ $\left(\dfrac{dy}{dx}\right)_{(\alpha,\beta)} = \dfrac{\alpha+\beta+1}{\alpha+\beta-1} = \infty$

$\Rightarrow$ $\alpha + \beta - 1 = 0$ $\Rightarrow$ $\alpha + \beta = 1$

16. (c) $y = -x + k^2$ is tangent to $y = -x^3 - x^2$ at $(h, -h^3 - h^2)$

$\Rightarrow -1 = -3h^2 - 2h \Rightarrow 3h^2 + 2h - 1 = 0$

$\Rightarrow 3h^2 + 3h - h - 1 = 0 \Rightarrow (3h-1)(h+1) = 0$

$\Rightarrow h = 1/3$ or $h = -1$

$\therefore$ $y = -x + k^2$ can be tangent to curve at $(-1, 0)$ or at $\left(\frac{1}{3}, \frac{-4}{27}\right)$

If these points lie on $y = -x + k^2$

$\Rightarrow 0 = 1 + k^2$ or $-\frac{4}{27} = \frac{-1}{3} + k^2$

$\Rightarrow k^2 = -1$ or $\frac{1}{3} - \frac{4}{27} = k^2$

$k^2 = -1$ is impossible and $k^2 = 5/27$

$\Rightarrow k = \pm\frac{5}{3\sqrt{3}} \Rightarrow$ Two values of k are possible

17. (b) $y = (a/2) = (e^{x/a} + e^{-x/a})$

$\Rightarrow$ Length of normal $= (\ell) = y\sqrt{1+\left(\frac{dy}{dx}\right)^2}$

Let $y = G.M$ .of ℓ and k

$\Rightarrow y = \sqrt{\ell k}$

$\Rightarrow \left[\frac{a}{2}\left(e^{x/a} + e^{-x/a}\right)\right]^2 = y\sqrt{1+\left(\frac{dy}{dx}\right)^2}.k$

$\Rightarrow y^2 = y\sqrt{1+\frac{1}{2^2}\left(e^{x/a} - e^{-x/a}\right)^2}.k$

$\Rightarrow k = \frac{2y}{\sqrt{\left(e^{x/a} + e^{-x/a}\right)^2}} = \frac{a\left(e^{x/a} + e^{-x/a}\right)}{\left(e^{x/a} + e^{-x/a}\right)} = a$

18. (b) $y = \frac{ax}{b-x}$

$\Rightarrow \frac{dy}{dx} = a\left[\frac{(b-x)(1) - 1(-1)}{(b-x)^2}\right] = a\left[\frac{b+1-x}{(b-x)^2}\right]$

$\Rightarrow$ Slope at $(1, 1) = \frac{a(b)}{(b-1)^2} = 2$ (given)

Also $(1, 1)$ lies on $y = \frac{ax}{b-x}$

$\Rightarrow 1 = \frac{a}{b-1} \Rightarrow a = (b-1)$

$\Rightarrow \frac{b(b-1)}{(b-1)^2} = 2 \Rightarrow \frac{b}{(b-1)} = 2$

$\Rightarrow b = 2$

19. (d) $f(x) = \frac{x}{1-x^2} \Rightarrow f'(x) = \frac{(1-x^2) - x(-2x)}{(1-x^2)^2}$

$\Rightarrow f'(x) = \frac{1+x^2}{(1-x^2)^2}$

$\therefore f'(x) = \tan\frac{\pi}{4} \Rightarrow \frac{1+x^2}{(1-x^2)^2} = 1$

$\Rightarrow x^4 - 3x^2 = 0 \Rightarrow x^2(x^2 - 3) = 0$

$\Rightarrow x = 0$ or $x = \pm\sqrt{3}$

$\Rightarrow$ The required points are $(0,0)$, $\left(\sqrt{3}, -\frac{\sqrt{3}}{2}\right)$ or $\left(-\sqrt{3}, \frac{\sqrt{3}}{2}\right)$

20. (c) $y = |x^2 - 1|$ and $y = \sqrt{7-x^2}$

At the point of intersection $(x^2 - 1)^2 = 7 - x^2$

$\Rightarrow x^4 - x^2 - 6 = 0$

$\Rightarrow (x^2 - 3)(x^2 + 2) = 0$

$\Rightarrow x = \pm\sqrt{3}$

$\Rightarrow$ Point of intersection is $\left(\sqrt{3}, 2\right)$ and $\left(-\sqrt{3}, 2\right)$

Now $y = |x^2 - 1|$

$\Rightarrow y = (x^2 - 1)$ at the point of intersection

$\Rightarrow \frac{dy}{dx} = y_1 = 2x$

$\Rightarrow y_1 = 2\sqrt{3}$ at $\left(\sqrt{3}, 2\right)$ and $y_1 = -2\sqrt{3}$ at $\left(-\sqrt{3}, 2\right)$

Also, $y = \sqrt{7-x^2}$

$\Rightarrow \frac{dy}{dx} = y_2 = \frac{-x}{\sqrt{7-x^2}}$

$\Rightarrow y_2 = -\frac{\sqrt{3}}{2}$ at $\left(\sqrt{3}, 2\right)$ and $y_2 = \frac{\sqrt{3}}{2}$ at $\left(-\sqrt{3}, 2\right)$

$\Rightarrow$ Acute angle between the curves at $\left(\sqrt{3}, 2\right) = \tan^{-1}\left|\frac{y_1 - y_2}{1 + y_1 . y_2}\right| = \tan^{-1}\left|\frac{2\sqrt{3} + \frac{\sqrt{3}}{2}}{1-3}\right| = \tan^{-1}\left(\frac{5\sqrt{3}}{4}\right)$

And at $\left(-\sqrt{3}, 2\right) = \tan^{-1}\left|\frac{-2\sqrt{3} - \frac{\sqrt{3}}{2}}{1-3}\right| = \tan^{-1}\left(\frac{5\sqrt{3}}{4}\right)$

$\Rightarrow \tan\theta = \frac{5\sqrt{3}}{4}$

21. (a) $S_1 : y = 2e^{2x}$. At the point of intersection, on y-axis $P(0, 2)$

Also $\frac{dy}{dx} = 4e^{2x}$

$\Rightarrow \left(\frac{dy}{dx}\right)_{(0,2)} = 4 \Rightarrow \theta = \tan^{-1} 4$

$\Rightarrow$ Curve intersects y-axis at $P(0, 2)$ where the tangent has slope $\theta = \tan^{-1}(4)$

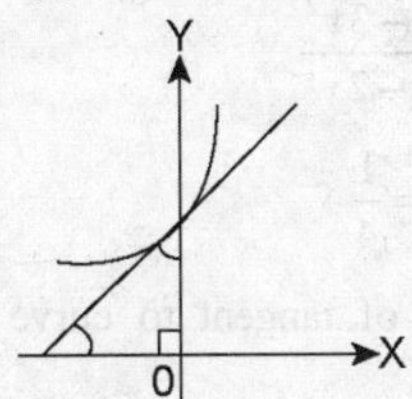

$\Rightarrow \phi = \frac{\pi}{2} - \theta = \frac{\pi}{2} - \tan^{-1}(4) = \cot^{-1}(4)$

$\Rightarrow S_1$ is false (*F*).

S_2: Length normal to curve at a point $P = y_1\sqrt{1+\left(\frac{dy}{dx}\right)^2}$

$\Rightarrow$ Length of normal is proportional to slope of tangent at point *P*.

$\Rightarrow S_2$ is true (*T*)

S_3: Length normal at $P(x_1, y_1) = y_1\sqrt{1+\left(\frac{dy}{dx}\right)^2_{(x_1,y_1)}}$

$\Rightarrow S_3$ is false (*F*)

S_4: $12y = x^3 \quad \Rightarrow 12\frac{dy}{dt} = 3x^2\frac{dx}{dt}$

$\Rightarrow \frac{dy}{dt} = \frac{x^2}{4}.\frac{dx}{dt}$

$\Rightarrow \frac{dy}{dt} > \frac{dx}{dt}$ for $x^2 > 4$ and $\frac{dy}{dt} < \frac{dx}{dt}$ for $x^2 < 4$

$\Rightarrow S_4$ is false (*F*)

$\therefore$ Answer must be FTFF

22. **(b)** $(4000)^2 + (3000 + y)^2 = x^2$

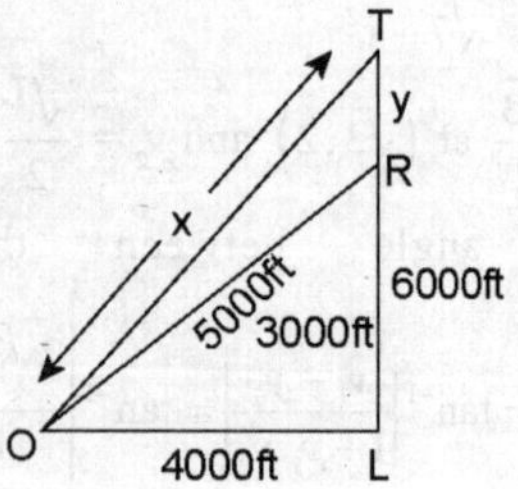

$\Rightarrow 25000 + 6000y + y^2 = x^2$

$\Rightarrow 6000\frac{dy}{dt} + 2y\frac{dy}{dt} = 2x\frac{dx}{dt}$

$\Rightarrow \frac{dx}{dt} = \frac{(3000+y)\frac{dy}{dt}}{x}$

$\Rightarrow$ At *R*; $\frac{dx}{dt} = \frac{(3000+0)}{(5000)} \times 600$

$\Rightarrow \frac{dx}{dt} = 360$ ft./ sec.

23. **(a)** *C*: $3xy^2 - 2x^2y = 1$

$\Rightarrow 3x\left(2y\frac{dy}{dx}\right) + 3y^2 - 2x^2\frac{dy}{dx} - 2y(2x) = 0$

$\Rightarrow 6xy\frac{dy}{dx} - 2x^2\frac{dy}{dx} = 4xy - 3y^2$

$\Rightarrow \frac{dy}{dx} = \frac{4xy-3y^2}{6xy-2x^2}$

$\Rightarrow \left(\frac{dy}{dx}\right)_{(1,1)} = \frac{1}{4}$

$\therefore$ Equation of tangent to curve at (1, 1) is $(y - 1) = \frac{1}{4}(x-1)$

It meets the curve, where $3x\left(\frac{x}{4}+\frac{3}{4}\right)^2 - 2x^2\left(\frac{x}{4}+\frac{3}{4}\right) = 1$

$\Rightarrow 3x(x+3)^2 - 8x^2(x+3) = 16$

$\Rightarrow 3x^3 + 18x^2 + 27x - 8x^3 - 24x^2 - 16 = 0$

$\Rightarrow 5x^3 + 6x^2 - 27x + 16 = 0$

One of its root is $x = 1$

$\Rightarrow$ Other two roots are given by $5x^2 + 11x - 16 = 0$

$\Rightarrow 5x^2 + 16x - 5x - 16 = 0$

$\Rightarrow x(5x+16) - 1(5x+16) = 0$

$\Rightarrow (x-1)(5x+16) = 0$

$\Rightarrow x = -16/5$ is the other point

$\therefore \left(\frac{-16}{5}, \frac{-1}{20}\right)$ and $\left(\frac{-16}{5}, \frac{-25}{12}\right)$

24. **(c)** $f'(a) = \tan - \sqrt{3}$,

$f'(b) = \tan\frac{\pi}{4} = 1;$

$\int_a^b f'(x).f''(x)dx = \left[\frac{[f'(x)]^2}{2}\right]_a^b$

$= \frac{1}{2}[(f'(b))^2 - (f'(a))^2] = \frac{1}{2}[1-3] = -1$

25. **(d)** Equation of line through origin and touching the curve $y = \cos x$ at (h, k) is $y = (-\sin h)x$

At the point of tangency $k = \cos h$ and $k = -h\sin h$

$\Rightarrow k^2 + \frac{k^2}{h^2} = 1 \quad \Rightarrow h^2k^2 + k^2 = h^2$

$\Rightarrow$ Required locus is $x^2y^2 + y^2 = x^2$ or $x^2 - y^2 = x^2y^2$

26. **(c)** $x = f'(t)\sin t + f''(t)\cos t$, $y = f'(t)\cos t - f'(t)\sin t$

$v = \sqrt{\left(\frac{dx}{dt}\right)^2 + \left(\frac{dy}{dt}\right)^2}$

Here $\frac{dx}{dt} = f'(t)\cos t + f'(t)\sin t + f''(t)(-\sin t) + f''(t)$

$\cos t$

$= [f'(t) + f'''(t)](\cos t)$

$\frac{dy}{dt} = f(t)(-\sin t) + f''(t)\cos t - f''(t)\cos t - f'''(t)\sin t$

$= -f'(t)\sin t - f'''(t)\sin t$

$= -[f'(t) + f'''(t)]\sin t$

$\therefore v = \sqrt{(f'(t) + f'''(t))^2} = f(t) + f'''(t)$

27. **(a)** $\frac{d}{dt}(\tan x) = 4\frac{dx}{dt} \quad \Rightarrow \sec^2 x\frac{dx}{dt} = 4$

$\Rightarrow \sec x = \pm 2$

$\therefore \frac{d}{dx}(\sin x) = \cos x = \pm\frac{1}{2}$

$\Rightarrow \sin x$ increase at $\frac{1}{2}$ units rate

28. **(a)** Subtangent $= y\dfrac{dx}{dy} = y.\left(\dfrac{y}{2a}\right) = \dfrac{y^2}{2a}$

Ordinate $= y$,

Subnormal $= y\dfrac{dy}{dx} = 2a$

$\therefore$ $y^2 = (2a)$ (subtangent)

$\Rightarrow$ (Ordinate)^2 = (subnormal) (subtangent)

$\Rightarrow$ G. P

29. **(c)** Let the Equation of ellipse be $\dfrac{x^2}{16} + \dfrac{y^2}{9} =$

$\therefore$ Any point on ellipse in (4 cos θ , 3 sin θ)

$\therefore$ velocity $= \sqrt{(16\sin^2\theta + 9\cos^2\theta)}.\dfrac{d\theta}{dt} = 1$ (given)

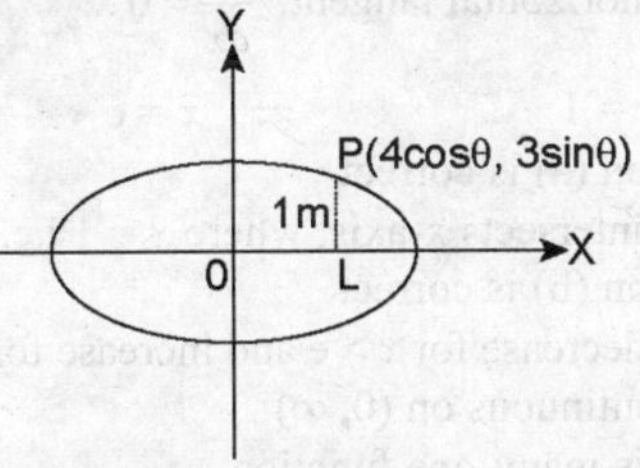

At P, 3 sin θ = 1

$\therefore$ $\dfrac{d}{dt}(4\cos\theta) = -4\sin\theta\dfrac{d\theta}{dt} = -4\left(\dfrac{1}{3}\right)\dfrac{1}{\sqrt{16\sin^2\theta + 9\cos^2\theta}}$

$= -\dfrac{4}{3}\times\dfrac{1}{\sqrt{16\left(\dfrac{1}{9}\right) + 9\left(1 - \dfrac{1}{9}\right)}} = \dfrac{-4}{3}\times\dfrac{1}{\sqrt{\dfrac{16}{9} + \dfrac{72}{9}}}$

$= -\dfrac{4}{3}\times\dfrac{3}{\sqrt{88}} = \dfrac{-4}{2\sqrt{22}} = \dfrac{2}{\sqrt{22}} = \dfrac{\sqrt{2}}{\sqrt{11}}$ (imagination)

SECTION–IV: (MORE THAN ONE CORRECT ANSWER)

1. **(a), (c)** $C_1 : \dfrac{x^2}{a^2} + \dfrac{y^2}{4} = 1$; $C_2 : y^3 = 16x$

For C_1: $\dfrac{2x}{a^2} + \dfrac{2y}{4}\dfrac{dy}{dx} = 0$

$\Rightarrow$ $\dfrac{y}{4}\dfrac{dy}{dx} = \dfrac{-x}{a^2}$ $\Rightarrow$ $\dfrac{dy}{dx} = \dfrac{-4x}{a^2 y}$

$\Rightarrow$ $\left(\dfrac{dy}{dx}\right) = \dfrac{-4h}{a^2 k}$ at (h, k) and $y^3 = 16x$

$\Rightarrow$ $3y^2\dfrac{dy}{dx} = 16 \Rightarrow \dfrac{dy}{dx} = \dfrac{16}{3k^2}$ at (h, k)

$\therefore$ For orthogonal intersection at (h, k), $\left(\dfrac{-4h}{a^2 k}\right)\left(\dfrac{16}{3k^2}\right) = -1$

$\Rightarrow$ $\dfrac{64h}{3a^2k^3} = 1$ …(i)

At (h, k), $\dfrac{h^2}{a^2} + \dfrac{k^2}{4} = 1$ and $k^3 = 16h$

$\therefore$ From (i), $\dfrac{64h}{3a^2(16h)} = 1$

$\Rightarrow$ $\dfrac{4}{3a^2} = 1$ $\Rightarrow$ $a^2 = \dfrac{4}{3}$

$\Rightarrow$ $a = \pm\dfrac{2}{\sqrt{3}}$

2. **(a), (c)** C: $\left(\dfrac{x}{a}\right)^n + \left(\dfrac{y}{b}\right)^n = 2$; $(n \in \mathbb{N})$

$\Rightarrow$ $n\left(\dfrac{x}{a}\right)^{n-1}.\left(\dfrac{1}{a}\right) + n\left(\dfrac{y}{b}\right)^{n-1}.\dfrac{1}{b}.\dfrac{dy}{dx} = 0$

$\Rightarrow$ $\dfrac{dy}{dx} = \dfrac{-x^{n-1}}{y^{n-1}}.\dfrac{b^n}{a^n}$

When $x = a$, $(1)^n + \left(\dfrac{y}{b}\right)^n = 2$

$\Rightarrow$ $\left(\dfrac{y}{b}\right)^n = 1 \Rightarrow \dfrac{y}{b}$ $\Rightarrow$ $y = b$

$\therefore$ $\left(\dfrac{dy}{dx}\right)_{(x=a,\,y=b)} = \dfrac{-a^{n-1}}{b^{n-1}}.\dfrac{b^n}{a^n} = \dfrac{-b}{a}$

$\therefore$ Equation of normal at (a, b) is $(y - b) = \dfrac{a}{b}(x - a)$

$\Rightarrow$ $by - b^2 = ax - a^2$ or $ax - by = a^2 - b^2$

$\Rightarrow$ option (c) is correct .

If n is even, then $\left(\dfrac{y}{b}\right)^n = 1 \Rightarrow \dfrac{y}{b} = \pm 1$

$\Rightarrow$ $y = \pm\, b$

$\therefore$ For $y = -b$, $\left(\dfrac{dy}{dx}\right) = \dfrac{-a^{n-1}}{(-b)^{n-1}}.\dfrac{b^n}{a^n} = \dfrac{a^{n-1}}{b^{n-1}}.\dfrac{b^n}{a^n} = \dfrac{b}{a}$

($\because$ $n - 1$ = odd)

$\Rightarrow$ Equation of normal at $(a, -b)$ will be $(y + b) = \dfrac{-a}{b}(x - a)$

$\Rightarrow$ $ax + by = a^2 - b^2$ $\Rightarrow$ option (a) is correct .

3. **(a), (d)** $C_1 : y = x^2 + ax + b$ and $y = x(c - x)$

At the point of intersection $x^2 + ax + b = cx - x^2$

$\Rightarrow$ $2x^2 + (a - c)x + b = 0$

For tangency at (1, 0), roots must be 1, 1

$\Rightarrow$ $-\dfrac{(a-c)}{2} = 2$ and $\dfrac{b}{2} = 1$

$\Rightarrow$ $a - c = -4$, $b = 2$

Also (1, 0) lies on $y = x(c - x)$

$\Rightarrow$ $0 = 1(c - 1)$ $\Rightarrow$ $c = 1$

$\Rightarrow$ $a = c - 4 = -3$, $b = 2$, $c = 1$

4. **(a), (b)** $x = 2\ \ell n \cot t + 1$; $y = \tan t + \cot t$

$\Rightarrow$ $\dfrac{dx}{dt} = \dfrac{2}{\cot t}.(-\text{cosec}^2 t)$; $\dfrac{dy}{dt} = \sec^2 t - \text{cosec}^2 t$

$\Rightarrow$ $\dfrac{dy}{dx} = \dfrac{\sec^2 t - \text{cosec}^2 t}{-2\text{cosec}^2 t \tan t}$

$\Rightarrow \left(\frac{dy}{dx}\right)_{\text{at } t=\frac{\pi}{4}} = 0$

$\Rightarrow$ Tangent is || to x-axis and normal is || to y-axis.

5. (b), (c) $y = k e^{kx}$

$\Rightarrow \frac{dy}{dx} = k^2 e^{kx}$

At the point of intersection of curve and y-axis, $x = 0$, $y = k$

$\Rightarrow \frac{dy}{dx} = k^2$

$\Rightarrow$ Angle that the curve makes with y-axis $= \frac{\pi}{2} - \tan^{-1}(k^2)$

or $\pi - \left(\frac{\pi}{2} - \tan^{-1} k^2\right)$ i.e., $\phi = \cot^{-1} k^2$

$\Rightarrow \phi = \sin^{-1}\left(\frac{1}{\sqrt{1+k^4}}\right)$

6. (c) $C: y = x^2 - ax + 2a$

$\Rightarrow \frac{dy}{dx} = 2x - a$

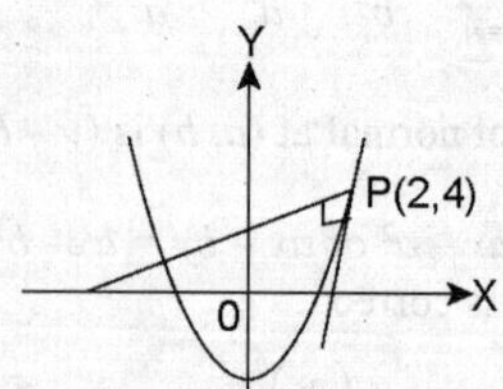

$\Rightarrow$ Slope of normal to curve (c) at $P(2, 4) = -\frac{1}{(4-a)}$

$\therefore$ Equation of normal to curve C at $P(2, 4)$ will be $(y - 4) = \frac{-1}{(4-a)}(x-2)$

It intersect x-axis, where $x = 18 - 4a$ and y-axis where $y = \frac{18-4a}{4-a}$

$\therefore$ Area of $\Delta = \frac{1}{2}(4a-18)\left(\frac{18-4a}{4-a}\right) = 2$

$\Rightarrow (4a - 18)^2 = 4(a - 4)$

$\Rightarrow (2a - 9)^2 = a - 4$

$\Rightarrow 4a^2 - 36a - a + 81 + 4 = 0$

$\Rightarrow 4a^2 - 37a + 85 = 0$

$\Rightarrow a = \frac{37 \pm \sqrt{(37)^2 - 4(4)(85)}}{2(4)}$

$\Rightarrow a = \frac{37 \pm \sqrt{9}}{8}$

$\Rightarrow a = 5$ or $\frac{17}{4}$

But x intercept of normal i.e., $18 - 4a < 0$

$\Rightarrow a = 5$

7. (a), (b), (c) C: $y = x^3 - ax^2 + x + 1$

$\Rightarrow \frac{dy}{dx} = 3x^2 - 2ax + 1 > 0 \ \forall x \in \mathbb{R}$

$\Rightarrow 4a^2 - 12 < 0 \qquad \Rightarrow a^2 < 3$

$\Rightarrow a \in \left(-\sqrt{3}, \sqrt{3}\right)$

$\therefore$ Integral values of $a \in \{-1, 0, 1\}$

8. (a), (b), (c), (d) $y = \frac{\ell n\, x}{x}$

$\Rightarrow \frac{dy}{dx} = \frac{x.\frac{1}{x} - \ell nx.1}{x^2} = \frac{1-\ell nx}{x^2}$

For horizontal tangent, $\frac{dy}{dx} = 0$

$\Rightarrow \ell n\, x = 1 \qquad \Rightarrow x = e$

$\Rightarrow$ option (a) is correct

$f(x)$ intersects x-axis, where $x = 1$ i.e., at $(1, 0)$

$\Rightarrow$ option (b) is correct

$\therefore$ $f(x)$ decrease for $x > e$ and increase for $x \in (0, e)$ and $f(x)$ is continuous on $(0, \infty)$

$\Rightarrow$ $f(x)$ is many-one function

$\Rightarrow$ option (c) is correct

Also $\frac{dy}{dx} = \frac{1-\ell nx}{x^2} \to \infty$ as $x \to 0^+$

$\Rightarrow$ $f(x)$ has one vertical tangent (asymptote)

$\Rightarrow$ option (d) is correct

9. (a), (b) $y = f(x)$

$\Rightarrow$ Equation of tangent at (x, y) is $(Y - y) = \frac{dy}{dx}(\gamma - x)$ ...(i)

It cuts x-axis, where $Y = 0$

$\Rightarrow -y = \frac{dy}{dx}(X - x)$

$\Rightarrow -y\frac{dx}{dy} + x = X \qquad \Rightarrow A \equiv \left(x - y\frac{dx}{dy}, 0\right)$

Further it cuts y-axis, where $X = 0$

$\Rightarrow Y = y - x\frac{dy}{dx} \qquad \Rightarrow B \equiv \left(0, y - x\frac{dy}{dx}\right)$

$\therefore \frac{BP}{AP} = \frac{3}{1} \Rightarrow \frac{\sqrt{x^2 + x^2\left(\frac{dy}{dx}\right)^2}}{\sqrt{y^2\left(\frac{dy}{dx}\right)^2 + y^2}} = \frac{3}{1}$

$\Rightarrow \frac{x\sqrt{1+\left(\frac{dy}{dx}\right)^2}}{y\sqrt{\left(\frac{dy}{dx}\right)^2 + 1}} = \frac{3}{1}$

$\Rightarrow \frac{x}{y\left(\frac{dx}{dy}\right)} = \frac{3}{1} \Rightarrow \frac{x\,dy}{y\,dx} = \frac{3}{1}$

$\Rightarrow$ option (a) is correct

$\Rightarrow \dfrac{dy}{y} = 3\dfrac{dx}{x} \quad \Rightarrow \ell n\, y = \ell n\, x^3 + \ell n\, c$

$\Rightarrow y = cx^3$

$f(1) = 1 \quad \Rightarrow c = 1$

$\Rightarrow y = x^3$

Equation of normal at (1, 1) is $(y - 1) = \left(-\dfrac{1}{3}\right)_{(x-1)}$

$\Rightarrow x + 3y = 4 \quad \Rightarrow$ option (b) is correct

For $x = 2$, $y = x^3 \quad \Rightarrow y = 8$

$\Rightarrow$ Curve passes through (2, 8) and not through (2, 1/8)

10. (c), (d) Given curve is $2y^3 = ax^2 + x^3$

$\Rightarrow 2\left(3y^2\dfrac{dy}{dx}\right) = a(2x) + 3x^2$

$\Rightarrow 6y^2\dfrac{dy}{dx} = 2ax + 3x^2 \quad \Rightarrow \dfrac{dy}{dx} = \dfrac{2ax + 3x^2}{6y^2}$

$\Rightarrow \left(\dfrac{dy}{dx}\right)_{(a,a)} = \dfrac{5}{6}$

$\Rightarrow$ Equation of tangent to curve at (a, a) is $(y - a) = \dfrac{5}{6}(x - a)$

$\Rightarrow 6y - 6a = 5x - 5a \quad \Rightarrow 5x - 6y = -a$

$\Rightarrow \dfrac{x}{(-a/5)} + \dfrac{y}{(a/6)} = 1$

$\Rightarrow \alpha = \dfrac{-a}{5}, \beta = \dfrac{a}{6}$ and $\alpha^2 + \beta^2 = 61$

$\Rightarrow \dfrac{a^2}{25} + \dfrac{a^2}{36} = 61 \quad \Rightarrow 61\, a^2 = 61 \times 25 \times 36$

$\Rightarrow a^2 = 25 \times 36 \quad \Rightarrow a = \pm 30$

$\therefore$ Point (a, a) is (30, 30) or (–30, –30)

11. (b), (c) Let $(y - h) = m(x - 0)$ be tangent drawn through $P(0, h)$

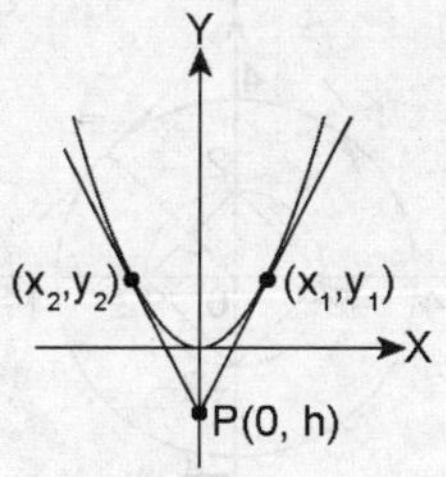

$\Rightarrow y = mx + h$

It intersects curve $y = \sqrt{17(1 + x^2)}$

$\Rightarrow mx + h = \sqrt{17(1 + x^2)}$

$\Rightarrow m^2x^2 + 2mhx + h^2 = 17 + 17x^2$

$\Rightarrow (m^2 - 17)x^2 + 2m\,hx + (h^2 - 17) = 0$

Its Disc. must be zero

$\Rightarrow 4m^2 h^2 - 4(m^2 - 17)(h^2 - 17) = 0$

$\Rightarrow m^2 h^2 - (m^2 h^2 - 17h^2 - 17m^2 + 289) = 0$

$\Rightarrow 17h^2 + 17m^2 - 289 = 0$

$\Rightarrow h^2 + m^2 = 17$

$\Rightarrow m^2 + (h^2 - 17) = 0 \quad \Rightarrow m_1 m_2 = h^2 - 17 = -1$

$\Rightarrow h^2 = 16 \quad \Rightarrow h = \pm 4$

But $h < 0 \quad \Rightarrow h = -4$

$\Rightarrow m^2 = 1 \quad \Rightarrow m = \pm 1$

$\therefore$ Equation of tangent will be $y = x - 4$ and $y = -x - 4$

12. (a), (c) Given curve is $y = ax^4 + bx^3 + cx + d$

$\Rightarrow \dfrac{dy}{dx} = 4ax^3 + 3bx^2 + c$

At (0, 1), $\dfrac{dy}{dx} = 0 \quad \Rightarrow c = 0$

$\Rightarrow y = ax^4 + bx^3 + d$ and $\dfrac{dy}{dx} = 4ax^3 + 3bx^2$

Also $\dfrac{dy}{dx} = 0$ at (–1, 0)

$\Rightarrow -4a + 3b = 0$

$\Rightarrow 3b = 4a$

$\Rightarrow \dfrac{dy}{dx} = 4ax^3 + 4ax^2 < 0$

$\Rightarrow 4ax^2(x + 1) < 0$

Clearly $x = -1$ and $x = 0$ are two of the three critical points as shown below.

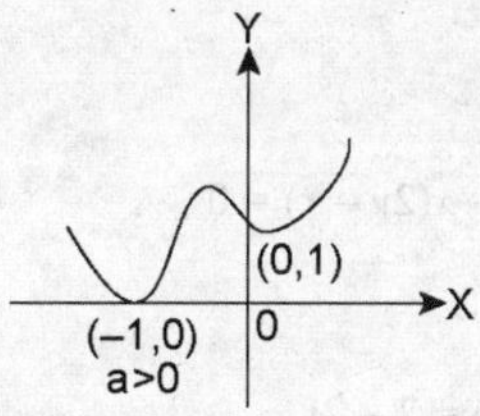

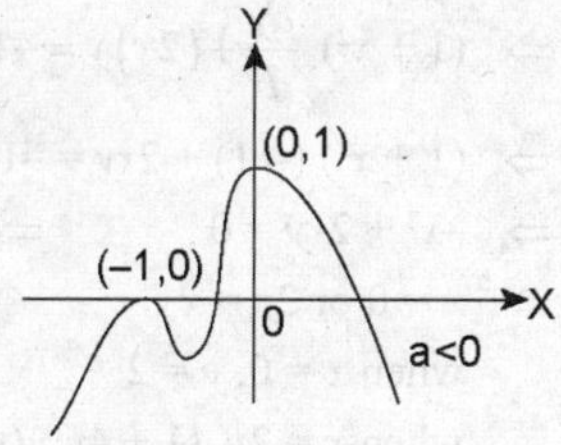

$\therefore \quad 4ax^2(x + 1) < 0$

$\Rightarrow x < -1$ for $a > 0$ and $x > -1$ for $a < 0$

SECTION–V: ASSERTION AND REASON TYPE:

1. (d) $y = x^3 - x^2 - x + 2$

$\Rightarrow \dfrac{dy}{dx} = 3x^2 - 2x - 1$

$\Rightarrow$ Equation of tangent at (1, 1) will be $(y - 1) = 0\,(x - 1)$ i.e., at $y = 1$

$\Rightarrow x^3 - x^2 - x + 2 = 1 \quad \Rightarrow x^3 - x^2 - x + 1 = 0$

$\Rightarrow x^2(x - 1) - 1(x - 1) = 0$

$\Rightarrow (x - 1)^2(x + 1) = 0 \quad \Rightarrow x = 1$ or $x = -1$

$\therefore$ The curve is met by tangent again at $x = -1$

$\Rightarrow$ Assertion is incorrect.

Clearly reason is correct.

2. (c) Let the equationof circle be $x^2 + y^2 = a^2$ and equal of tangent be $y = mx + c$

At the point of intersection $x^2 + (mx + c)^2 = a^2$, which being a quadratic equation would give us repeated single solution.

Thus assertion is correct. But reason is incorrect as if the curve is of degree greater than or equal to 4, then it can have a tangent to curve at two points as shown below.

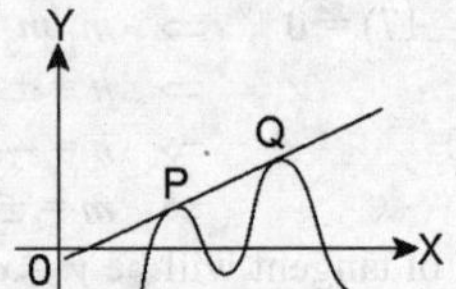

3. (a) Clearly reason is correct and

$$\frac{\text{Length of Tangent}}{\text{Length of Normal}}=\left|\frac{y\sqrt{1+m^2}/m}{y\sqrt{1+m^2}}\right|$$

$$=\left|\frac{1}{m}\right|=\left|\frac{\frac{1}{\frac{dy}{dx}}}{}\right|=\left|\frac{\frac{1}{2a}}{y}\right|=\left|\frac{y}{2a}\right| \text{ i.e., proportional to ordinate}$$

4. (a) Clearly reason is correct that straight line making equal and same sign intercept with co- ordinate axes is $-1 = \tan 135^0$

Substituting $\left(\frac{dy}{dx}\right)=-1$

$\Rightarrow$ $(1+x^2)\frac{dy}{dx}+(2x)y=-1$

$\Rightarrow$ $(1+x^2)(-1)+2xy=-1$

$\Rightarrow$ $-x^2+2xy=0$ $\Rightarrow$ $x(2y-x)=0$

$\Rightarrow$ $x=0$ or $2y=x$

when $x=0$, $y=2$

when $x=2y$, $(1+4y^2)(y)=2-2y$

$\Rightarrow$ $4y^3+3y-2=0$

$\Rightarrow$ $y=\frac{1}{2}$ (only real root)

$\therefore$ Product of ordinates $=2.\frac{1}{2}=1$

5. (a) $S=\pi x^2$ ....(i)

$A=\frac{\sqrt{3}}{4}(\pi x)^2$ .....(ii)

$\Rightarrow$ $\frac{dS}{dt}=2\pi x\frac{dx}{dt}$ and $\frac{dA}{dt}=\frac{\sqrt{3}}{2}\pi x\frac{dx}{dt}$

Clearly $\frac{dS}{dt}>\frac{dA}{dt}$ as $2\pi x>\frac{\sqrt{3}}{2}\pi x$

$\Rightarrow$ Assertion is correct. Also $A>S$

Also S and A are function of the form $y=kx^2$; $x>0$

$\therefore$ If $f(x)=k_1x^2$ and $g(x)=k_2x^2$ such that $k_1>k_2$, then $f'(x)=2k_1x$ and $g'(x)=2k_2x$

$\therefore$ $k_1>k_2$ and $x_0>0$ $\Rightarrow$ $2k_1x_0>2k_2x_0$

$\Rightarrow$ $f'(x_0)>g'(x_0)$.

Thus $f(x_0)>g(x_0)$ $\Rightarrow$ $f'(x_0)>g'(x_0)$

$y=k_1x^2$, $y=k_2x^2$ where $k_1>k_2$

$\Rightarrow$ $x^2=\frac{1}{k_1}y$; $x^2=\frac{1}{k_2}y$ and $\frac{1}{k_1}<\frac{1}{k_2}$

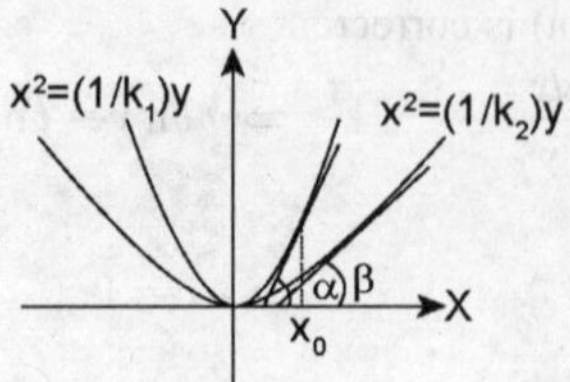

$\therefore$ $f(x_0)=k_1x_0^2$ and $g(x_0)=k_2x_0^2$; $k_1>k_2$

$\Rightarrow$ $f'(x_0)=\tan\alpha>\tan\beta=g'(x_0)$

$\therefore$ Both assertion and reason are correct and reason correctly and explains the assertion

6. (a) Let the curve be $y=ax^2+bx+c$

$\frac{dy}{dx}=2ax+c$

$\Rightarrow$ $\left(\frac{dy}{dx}\right)_{(1,1)}=2a+b=1$ ...(1)

Also curve is passing through (1, 1)

$\Rightarrow$ $1=a+b+c$ ...(2)

$\therefore$ From (1) and (2); $a+(1-c)=1$

$\Rightarrow$ $c=a$

$\therefore$ Curve is $y=ax^2+(1-2a)x+a$

Also curve is passing through (0, 1)

$\Rightarrow$ $1=a$

$\Rightarrow$ Equation of curve is $y=x^2-x+1$ and $\frac{dy}{dx}=2x-1<0$

$\Rightarrow$ $x<\frac{1}{2}$

$\Rightarrow$ Assertion as well as reason both are correct and reason correctly explains the assertion.

7. (d) Obviously reason is correct i.e., shortest distance between two smooth curves lie along the common normal .

Graph of $|x|+|y|=2$ and $x^2+y^2=16$ drawn on same frame of reference is as shown below.

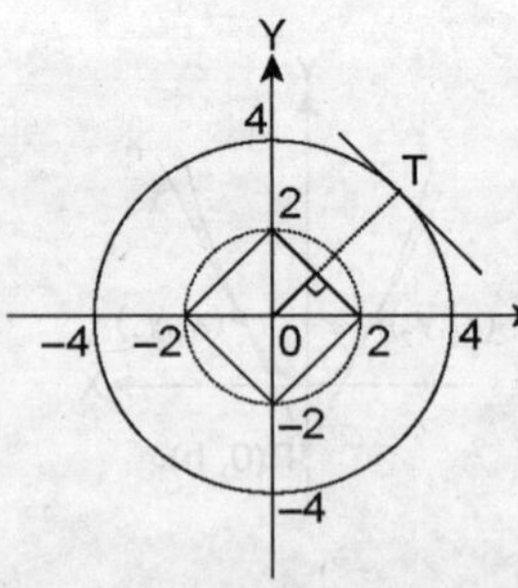

Here the shortest distance between two curves is $AB=2$ and the distance between the common normal $=LT=OT-OL=4-\sqrt{2}>2$

$\Rightarrow$ Assertion is incorrect (As the two curve are not smooth) but reason is correct

8. (a) $y=a_0x^{2n+1}+a_1x^{2n-1}+a_2x^{2n-3}+\ldots\ldots+a_{nx+1}$

$\Rightarrow$ $\frac{dy}{dx}=(2n+1)a_0x^{2n}+(2n-1)a_1x^{2n-2}+\ldots\ldots+a_n>0$

as $a_i\geq 0$ for each $i\in\mathbb{N}$ and $a_n>0$.

⇒ Tangent to curve makes an acute angle with positive x-axis.

⇒ reason is correct

∴ By above reason assertion is also correct

SECTION–VI: (PASSAGE)

Passage A:

$f(x) = \frac{1}{1+x^2}$ $(1 + x^2)^{-1}$

$\Rightarrow f'(x) = \frac{-2x}{(1+x^2)^2} < 0\ \forall\ x > 0$ and $> 0\ \forall\ x < 0$

⇒ Equation of tangent to curve at (x, y) is $(Y - y) = \frac{-2x}{(1+x^2)^2}(Y - x)$ ...(i)

$\Rightarrow a = x + \frac{(1+x^2)^2 y}{2x}, b = y + \frac{2x^2}{(1+x^2)^2}$

1. (d) $f'' = -2\left[\frac{(1+x^2)^2 - x.2(1+x^2)(2x)}{(1+x^2)^4}\right] = -2\ (1 + x^2)$

$\left[\frac{(1+x^2)-4x^2}{(1+x^2)^4}\right] = -2\frac{(1-3x^2)}{(1+x^2)^3} = \frac{2(3x^2-1)}{(1+x^2)^3}$

$f''(x) = 0 \qquad \Rightarrow \quad x = \pm\frac{1}{\sqrt{3}}$

$f'\left(\frac{1}{\sqrt{3}}\right) = \frac{-2/\sqrt{3}}{(4/3)^2} = \frac{-2}{\sqrt{3}} \times \frac{9}{16} = \frac{-9}{8\sqrt{3}}$

$f'\left(\frac{-1}{\sqrt{3}}\right) = \frac{2/\sqrt{3}}{(4/3)^2} = \frac{2}{\sqrt{3}} \times \frac{9}{8\sqrt{3}} = \frac{9}{8\sqrt{3}}$

⇒ Tangent has greatest slope = $\frac{9}{8\sqrt{3}}$ at $x = -\frac{1}{\sqrt{3}}$

2. (a) Graph of $y = \frac{1}{1+x^2}$ is as shown below.

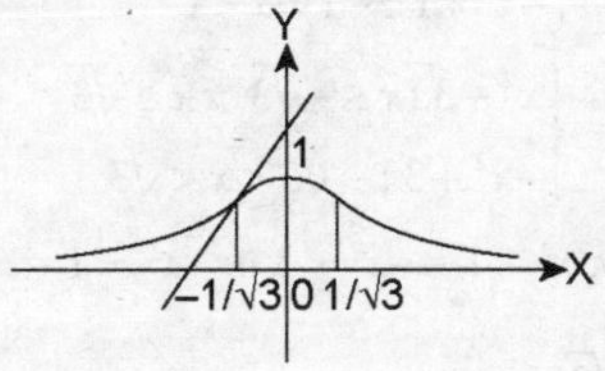

$f(x)$ has greatest slope at $x = -\frac{1}{\sqrt{3}}$ i.e., at point $\left(\frac{-1}{\sqrt{3}}, \frac{3}{4}\right)$

Greatest value of b will occur at same point $\left(\frac{-1}{\sqrt{3}}, \frac{3}{4}\right)$ given by $b = y + \frac{2x^2}{(1+x^2)^2} = \frac{3}{4} + \frac{2/3}{\left(1+\frac{1}{3}\right)^2} =$

$\frac{3}{4} + \frac{2}{3} \times \frac{9}{16} = \frac{3}{4} + \frac{3}{8} = \frac{6+3}{8} = \frac{9}{8}$

3. (a) $'m'$is smallest at $x = \frac{1}{\sqrt{3}}$ and equals $-\frac{9}{8\sqrt{3}}$,

Passage (B):

$f(x) = x^2 f(1) - x f'(2) + f''(3); f(0) = 2$

$\Rightarrow f'(x) = 2x f(1) - f'(2)$ ...(i)

$\Rightarrow f''(x) = 2f(1)$ ...(ii)

$\Rightarrow f''(3) = 2 f(1)$ ...(iii)

Also $f(0) = 2$

$\Rightarrow f''(3) = 2$ ...(iv)

$\Rightarrow f(1) = 1$ (using (iii) and (iv)) from (1) $f'(2) = 4 f(1) - f'(2)$

$\Rightarrow f'(2) = 2f(1) = 2\ (\because f(1) = 1)$

$\Rightarrow f(x) = x^2 - 2x + 2$

4. (a) $f'(x) = 2x - 2 \Rightarrow f'(1) = 0$

5. (c) Equation of tangent at (3, 5) will be $(y - 5) = 4\ (x - 3)$ i.e., $y = 4x - 7$

6. (b) $y = f(x) = x^2 - 2x + 2$

$\Rightarrow y_1 = f'(x) = 2x - 2$ and $y = g(x) = e^{2(x-1)}$

$\Rightarrow y_2 = g'(x) = 2e^{2(x-1)}$

Clearly $x^2 - 2x + 2 = e^{2(x-1)}$ holds at $x = 1$

∴ (1, 1) is the point of intersection of two cures

$\Rightarrow y_1 = 0, y_2 = 2$

$\therefore \tan\theta = \left|\frac{0-2}{1+(0)(2)}\right| = 2$

$\Rightarrow \theta = \tan^{-1}(2)$

Passage (C):

$y = x^3; P \equiv (\beta, \beta^3) \neq (0, 0)$

Equation of tangent at $P(\beta, \beta^3)$ is $(y - \beta^3) = 3\beta^2(x - \beta)$ or $y = 3\beta^2 x - 2\beta^3$

It will intersect the curve $y = x^3$ at Q, where $3\beta^2 x - 2\beta^3 = x^3$

$\Rightarrow x^3 - 3\beta^2 x + 2\beta^3 = 0$

It has two repeated rots $x = \beta$

⇒ $(x - \beta)^2$ is factor of polynomial on L.H.S

$\Rightarrow (x - \beta)^2 (2\beta + x) = 0$

$\Rightarrow x = -2\beta$

$\Rightarrow Q \equiv (-2\beta, -8\beta^3) = (\beta', \beta'^3)$ (say)

∴ The tangent at $Q(\beta', \beta'^3)$ will again intersect the curve at $R \equiv (-2\beta', -8\beta'^3) = (-2(-2\beta), -8(-2\beta)^3) \equiv (4\beta, 64\beta^3)$

7. (c)

8. (b) The tangent at $P(t, t^2 - t^3)$ is given by $y - (t^2 - t^3) = (2(t) - 3t^2)(x - t)$

i.e., $y = (2t - 3t^2)x + (t^2 - t^3) - 2t^2 + 3t^3$

i.e., $y = (2t - 3t^2)x + (2t^3 - t^2) = 0$

It would intersect the curve again at Q where $(2t - 3t^2)x + (2t^3 - t^2) = x^2 - x^3$ i.e., $x^3 - x^2 + (2t - 3t^2)x + (2t^3 - t^2) = 0$

Its two roots are $x = t, t$

⇒ $(x - t)^2$ is a factor of polynomial on L.H.S.

$\Rightarrow (x - t)^2 (x + (2t - 1)) = 0$

⇒ Abscissa of Q will be $x = 1 - 2t$

9. (c) $y = 8t^3 - 1; x = 4t^2 + 3$

Slope of tangent at $t = \frac{24t^2}{8t} = 3t$

$\therefore$ Equation of tangent at 't' is $[y-(8t^3-1)] = 3t[x-(4t^2+3)]$ i.e., $y = 3tx + 8t^3 - 1 - 12t^3 - 9t$ i.e., $y = 3tx + (-4t^3 - 9t - 1)$

$\therefore$ Equation of curve is $\left(\frac{y+1}{8}\right)^2 = \left(\frac{x-3}{4}\right)^3$

$\Rightarrow \left(\frac{3tx-4t^3-9t}{8}\right)^2 = \left(\frac{x-3}{4}\right)^3$ (At the point of intersection)

$\Rightarrow 9t^2x^2 + 16t^6 + 81t^2 - 24t^4x + 72t^4 - 54t^2x = x^3 - 27 - 3x^2(3) + 3x(3)^2$

$\Rightarrow x^3 + (-9-9t^2)x^2 + (27 + 24t^4 + 54t^2)x - 27 - 16t^6 - 81t^2 - 72t^4 = 0$

Its two roots are $x = 4t^2 + 3, 4t^2 + 3$,

$\Rightarrow [x-(4t^2+3)]^2 [x-(3+t^2)] = 0$

$\Rightarrow x = 3 + t^2$

Given that $y = 3tx + (-4t^3 - 9t - 1)$ is normal ...(i)

To curve at $x = 3 + t^2$

$= 3 + 4\left(\frac{t}{2}\right)^2$ or $3 + 4\left(\frac{-t}{2}\right)^2$

$Q \equiv \left(4\left(\frac{\pm t}{2}\right)^2 + 3, \left(\frac{\pm t}{2}\right)^3 - 1\right) = Q\left(\frac{\pm t}{2}\right) = Q(t')$ (say)

when $t' = t/2$ or $-t/2$

$\therefore$ Equation of normal at Q will be $[y-(\pm t^3-1)] = \frac{-1}{3\left(\pm\frac{t}{2}\right)}[x-(3+t^2)]$

$\Rightarrow y = \mp\frac{2}{3t}x + (\pm t^3 - 1) \pm \frac{2}{3t}(3+t^2)$

$\Rightarrow y = \mp\frac{2}{3t}x + (\pm t^3 - 1) \pm \left(\frac{2}{t} + \frac{2t}{3}\right)$

Comparing (i) and (ii) we get, $3t = \frac{-2}{3t}$ or $3t = \frac{2}{3t}$

$\Rightarrow t^2 = \frac{2}{9} \Rightarrow t = \pm\frac{\sqrt{2}}{3}$

Passage: D:

10. (b) $C_1: \frac{x^2}{a^2} + \frac{y^2}{b^2} = 1 \Rightarrow \frac{2x}{a^2} + \frac{2y}{b^2}\frac{dy}{dx} = 0$

$\Rightarrow \frac{dy}{dx} = \frac{-x}{y}\frac{b^2}{a^2} = -b^2x$

$\Rightarrow \tan\theta_1 = \left(\frac{dy}{dx}\right)_{(a,0)} = \left(\frac{-ab^2x}{a^2\sqrt{a^2b^2-b^2x^2}}\right)_{(a,0)}$

$\Rightarrow \theta_1 = \pi/2$ and $\tan\theta_2 = \left(\frac{dy}{dx}\right)_{(0,b)} = 0$

$\Rightarrow \theta_2 = 0^0$

$\Rightarrow$ Angle between tangent $= \pi/2$

11. (b) $y = 2\sin^2 x$; $y = \cos 2x$

$\Rightarrow \left(\frac{dy}{dx}\right) = 4\sin x\cos x = 2\sin 2x$ for C_1 and $\left(\frac{dy}{dx}\right) = -2\sin 2x$ for C_2

$\Rightarrow \tan\theta_1 = 2\sin\pi/3 = \sqrt{3}$, $\tan\theta = \left|\frac{\tan\theta_1 - \tan\theta_2}{1+\tan\theta_1.\tan\theta_2}\right| = \left|\frac{2\sqrt{3}}{-2}\right|$

$\Rightarrow \theta = \pi/3$

12. (d) $C_1: y^2 = 4ax$

$\Rightarrow 2y\frac{dy}{dx} = 4a \Rightarrow \frac{dy}{dx} = \frac{2a}{y}$

$\Rightarrow \left(\frac{dy}{dx}\right)_{(x_1,y_1)} = \frac{2a}{y_1} \Rightarrow \tan\theta_1 = \frac{2a}{y_1}$

$C_2: x^2 = 4by$

$\Rightarrow 2x = 4b\frac{dy}{dx} \Rightarrow \frac{dy}{dx} = \frac{x}{2b}$

$\Rightarrow \left(\frac{dy}{dx}\right)_{(x_1,y_1)} = \frac{x_1}{2b}$

$\therefore$ For orthogonality of curves $\left(\frac{dy}{dx}\right)_{C_1}\cdot\left(\frac{dy}{dx}\right)_{C_2} = -1$

$\Rightarrow \frac{2ax_1}{2by_1} - 1 \Rightarrow \frac{ax_1}{by_1} = -1$ .....(i)

Also (x_1, y_1) lies on $y^2 = 4ax$ and $x^2 = 4by$

$\Rightarrow y_1^2 = 4ax_1$ and $x_1^2 = 4by_1$

$\Rightarrow \left(\frac{x_1^2}{4b}\right)^2 = 4ax_1$

$\Rightarrow x_1^3 = 64ab^2$ $(\because x_1 \neq 0)$

$\Rightarrow x_1 = 4a^{1/3}b^{2/3}$

$\Rightarrow y_1 = \frac{x_1^2}{4b} = 4a^{2/3}b^{1/3}$ .....(ii)

$\therefore$ From (i) and 9ii), we get $\frac{a(4a^{1/3}b^{2/3})}{b(4a^{2/3}b^{1/3})} = -1$

$\Rightarrow \frac{a^{2/3}}{b^{2/3}} = -1 \Rightarrow a^{2/3} = -b^{2/3}$

$\Rightarrow a^2 = -b^2$, which impossible i.e., the above two curves can't intersect orthogonally at any point other than origin.

13. (b) $C_1: y = \begin{cases} x^2-1; x \leq -1 \text{ or } x \geq 1 \\ -x^2+1; -1 < x < 1 \end{cases}$

$C_2: y = \begin{cases} x^2-3; x \leq -\sqrt{3} \text{ or } x \geq \sqrt{3} \\ -x^2+3; -\sqrt{3} < x < \sqrt{3} \end{cases}$

Clearly, $x^2 - 1 = -x^2 + 3$ or $-x^2 + 1 = x^2 - 3$

$\Rightarrow 2x^2 = 4$

$\Rightarrow x = \pm\sqrt{2}$

C_1 and C_2 intersect at $x = -\sqrt{2}$ and at $x = \sqrt{2}$

For $x > 0 \Rightarrow x = \sqrt{2}$

$C_1: y = x^2 - 1$, $C_2: -x^2 + 3$

$\Rightarrow \left(\frac{dy}{dx}\right)_{C_1} = 2x = 2\sqrt{2}$;

$\Rightarrow \left(\frac{dy}{dx}\right)_{C_2} = -2x = -2\sqrt{2}$

$\Rightarrow\ Q = \tan^{-1}\left|\left[\frac{2\sqrt{2}+2\sqrt{2}}{1+(-8)}\right]\right| = \tan^{-1}\left|\left(\frac{4\sqrt{2}}{-7}\right)\right| = \tan^{-1}\left(\frac{4\sqrt{2}}{7}\right)$

$\Rightarrow\ m = \frac{4\sqrt{2}}{}$

SECTION–VII: (COLUMN MATCHING)

1. (i) → b; (ii) → c; (iii) → a; (iv) → d

(i) Given, $r = 5$ cm, $\delta r = 0.06$

$\therefore\ A = \pi r^2$

$\Rightarrow \delta A = 2\pi r\delta r = 10\pi \times 0.06 = 0.6\ \pi$

$\therefore$ **(i) → b**

(ii) Let $V = x^3$ $\quad\Rightarrow\ \delta V = 3x^2\ \delta x$

$\therefore\ \frac{\delta V}{V} \times 100 = 3\frac{\delta x}{x} \times 100 = 3 \times 1 = 3$

$\therefore$ **(ii) → c**

(iii) Since, $(x-2)\ \frac{dx}{dt} = 2\frac{dx}{dt}$

$\Rightarrow x = 4$ $\quad\therefore$ **(iii) → a**

(iv) $A = \frac{\sqrt{3}}{4}x^2$

$\Rightarrow\ \frac{dA}{dt} = \frac{\sqrt{3}}{2}x\frac{dx}{dt} = \frac{\sqrt{3}}{2}.15.\frac{1}{10} = \frac{3\sqrt{3}}{4}$ cm²/s.

$\therefore$ **(iv) → d**

2. (i) →a; (ii) →b; (iii) →a; (iv) →d

(i) $6\int_0^1 (ax^2+bx+c)\,dx = 2a + 3b + 6c$

$= k\,(a+b+c) + c + 4\left(\frac{a}{4}+\frac{b}{2}+c\right)$

$\therefore\ k = 1$

$\therefore$ **(i) →a**

(ii) $\frac{1}{3}x^{-2/3} + \frac{1}{3}y^{-2/3}\ \frac{dy}{dx} = 0$

$\frac{dy}{dx} = -1\ at\ x = \frac{a}{8},\ y = \frac{a}{8}$

Equation of tangent is $y + x = \frac{a}{4}$

$\therefore\ a = 4\ or \frac{x}{a/4}+\frac{y}{a/4} = 1$

$\therefore\ \frac{a^2}{16}+\frac{a^2}{16} = 2$

$\Rightarrow\ a^2 = 16$ $\quad\Rightarrow\ a = 4$

$\therefore$ **(ii) →b**

(iii) $\frac{dy}{dx} = 4x^3 + 6x + 2 = 2$

$2x^3 + 3x = 0 \Rightarrow x = 0, y = 0$

$\therefore$ Point on the curve at the least distance from the line $y = 2x - 1$ is $(0, 0)$

$\Rightarrow$ Least distance $r = \frac{1}{\sqrt{5}}$

$\Rightarrow\ \sqrt{5}r = 1$

$\therefore$ **(iii) → a**

(iv) $f'(0^+) = f'(0^-)$ $\quad\Rightarrow\ -2 + a = 2 - a$

$\Rightarrow\ a = 2$

$\therefore$ **(iv) →d**

3. (i) → b; (ii) → d; (iii) → a; (iv) → c

$x = a$ cost + at sint; $y = a$ sint – at cost

$\Rightarrow\ \frac{dy}{dx} = \frac{a\cos t + at\sin t - a\cos t}{-a\sin t + at\cos t + a\sin t}$

$\Rightarrow\ \frac{dy}{dx} = \tan t$

(i) Length of sub tangent $= \frac{y}{y'} = (a$ sint – at cost). cot $t = a$ cost – at cost cot t

$\therefore$ At, $t = \pi/4$, length of sub tangent

$= \frac{a}{\sqrt{2}} + a\left(\frac{\pi}{4}\right).\frac{1}{\sqrt{2}}(1) = \frac{a}{\sqrt{2}}\left(1-\frac{\pi}{4}\right)$

$\therefore$ **(i) → b**

(ii) Length of normal

$= y\sqrt{1+\left(\frac{dy}{dx}\right)^2} = \left(\frac{a}{\sqrt{2}} - \frac{a\pi}{4\sqrt{2}}\right)\sqrt{1+(1)^2}$

$= \left(\frac{a}{\sqrt{2}} - \frac{a\pi}{4\sqrt{2}}\right)(\sqrt{2}) = a\left(1-\frac{\pi}{4}\right)$

$\therefore$ **(ii) → (d)**

(iii) Equation of tangent at $t = \pi/4$ will be

$Y - \left(\frac{a}{\sqrt{2}} - \frac{a\pi}{4\sqrt{2}}\right) = 1\left(X - \left(\frac{a}{\sqrt{2}} + \frac{a\pi}{4\sqrt{2}}\right)\right)$ on y-axis,

$Y = 0$

$\Rightarrow\ X = \frac{a\pi}{2\sqrt{2}}$ on y-axis, $X = 0$

$\Rightarrow\ Y = \frac{-a\pi}{2\sqrt{2}}$

$\Rightarrow$ Length of intersect of tangent between the axis $= \frac{a\pi}{2}$

$\therefore$ **(iii) → (a)**

(iv) Perpendicular distance of tangent from origin

$= d = \frac{\left|0 - 0 - \frac{a\pi}{2\sqrt{2}}\right|}{\sqrt{2}} = \frac{a\pi}{4}$

$\therefore$ **(iv) → (c)**

4. (i) → (c); (ii) → (b); (iii) → (a); (iv) → (d)

(i) Let the point of intersection be (x_0, y_0)

Now $x^2 = 4y$ $\quad\Rightarrow\ \frac{dy}{dx} = \frac{x}{2}$

$\therefore\ m_1 = \left(\frac{dy}{dx}\right)_{(x_0,y_0)} = \frac{x_0}{2}$ and for $y^2 = 4x$, $\frac{dy}{dx} = \frac{2}{y}$

$\therefore\ m_2 = \left(\frac{dy}{dx}\right)_{(x_0,y_0)} = \frac{2}{y_0}$

$$\therefore\quad \theta=\tan^{-1}\left|\frac{\frac{x_0}{2}-\frac{2}{y_0}}{1+\frac{x_0}{2}\cdot\frac{2}{y_0}}\right|=\tan^{-1}\left|\frac{x_0y_0-1}{2(x_0+y_0)}\right|$$

Clearly $\theta = 90°$ at $x_0 = y_0 = 0$

At the point of intersection $y_0=\frac{x_0^2}{4}$ and $y_0^2 = 4x_0$

$\Rightarrow \frac{x_0^4}{16}=4x_0$

$\Rightarrow x_0 = 0$ or $x_0 = 4, y_0 = 4$

$\Rightarrow \theta=\tan^{-1}\left|\frac{6}{8}\right|=\tan^{-1}\left|\frac{3}{4}\right|$

$\Rightarrow |m+n| = 7$

$\therefore$ **(i) → (c)**

(ii) Given curve is, $x = e^{\sin y}$

$\Rightarrow \ln x = \sin y \quad \Rightarrow \frac{1}{x}=(\cos y)\frac{dy}{dx}$

$\Rightarrow \frac{dy}{dx}=\frac{1}{x}\sec y \quad \Rightarrow \left(\frac{dy}{dx}\right)_{(1,0)}=1$

$\therefore$ Equation of normal at (1, 0) is $(y-0)=-1(x-1)$

$\Rightarrow x+y=1$

$\Rightarrow$ Area of $\Delta=\frac{1}{2}(1)(1)=1/2$ sq. units

$\therefore$ **(ii) → b**

(iii) Given curve is $x^2y = 1$

$\Rightarrow x^2y'+y(2x)=0 \quad \Rightarrow y'=\frac{-2y}{x}$

$\Rightarrow m_1=\frac{-2y_o}{x_0}$ ...(1)

Also, second curve is $y = e^{2(1-x)}$

$\Rightarrow y'=-2e^{2(1-x)}$

$\Rightarrow m_2=-2e^{2(1-x_0)}$ ...(2)

$$\therefore\quad \theta=\tan^{-1}\left|\frac{\frac{-2y_0}{x_0}+2e^{2(1-x_0)}}{1+\frac{4y_0e^{2(1-x_0)}}{x_0}}\right|=\tan^{-1}\left|\frac{2x_0e^{2(1-x_0)}-2y_0}{x_0+4y_0e^{2(1-x_0)}}\right|$$

At the, point intersection, $x_0^2y_0=1$ and $y_0=e^{2(1-x_0)}$

$\Rightarrow x_0=y_0=1$

$\therefore\quad \theta=\tan^{-1}\left|\frac{2x_0y_0-2y_0}{x_0+4y_0^2}\right|=0$

$\therefore$ **(iii) → (a)**

(iv) Given curve is, $y = be^{x/3}$

$\Rightarrow y'=\frac{b}{3}e^{x/3}$

$\Rightarrow \frac{y}{y'}=\frac{y}{\frac{b}{3}e^{x/3}}=\frac{3be^{x/3}}{be^{x/3}}=3$

$\therefore$ **(iv) → (d)**

SECTION–VIII: (NUMERICAL INTEGER TYPE)

1. $\frac{dy}{dx}=$ slope of tangent at

$P(x,y)=\frac{x^2}{2}-6x=\frac{d}{dx}\left(\frac{x^3}{6}-3x^2+c\right)$

$\Rightarrow y=\frac{x^3}{6}-3x^2+c$. Since it passes through (2, –8),

$-8=\frac{4}{3}-12+c$

$\Rightarrow c=\frac{8}{3}$

$\Rightarrow y=\frac{x^3}{6}-3x^2+\frac{8}{3}$

Now, $\frac{dy}{dx}=0 \quad \Rightarrow \frac{x^2}{2}-6x=0$

$\Rightarrow x=0$ or $x=12$ and $\frac{d^2y}{dx^2}=x-6$

$\Rightarrow \left(\frac{d^2y}{dx^2}\right)_{x=0}=-6$ and $\left(\frac{d^2y}{dx^2}\right)_{x=12}=6$

$\Rightarrow$ Ordinate 'y' is maximum at $x=0$, given by $\lambda=\frac{8}{3}$

$\Rightarrow 3\lambda = 8$

2. $4y^2=x^3$

$\Rightarrow$ R.H.S. ≥ 0

$\Rightarrow x\geq 0$ and $y=\pm\sqrt{\frac{x^3}{4}}=\pm\frac{\sqrt{x^3}}{2}$

Let $x=t^2 \quad \Rightarrow y=\pm\frac{\sqrt{t^6}}{2}$

$\Rightarrow y=\pm\frac{t^3}{2}$

Equation of normal to curve at point $\left(t^2,\pm\frac{t^3}{2}\right)$ is

$\left(Y-\left(\pm\frac{t^3}{2}\right)\right)=\left(\mp\frac{4}{3t}\right)(X-t^2)$

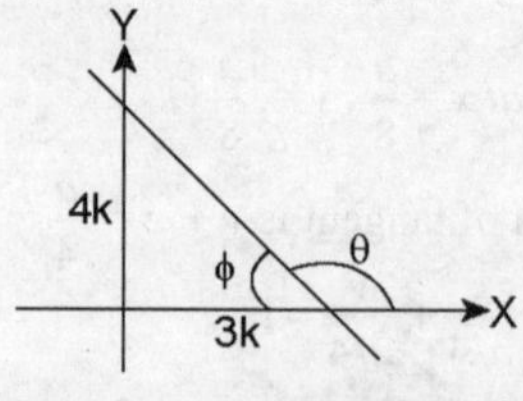

$\tan\theta=\tan(180^0-\phi)=-\tan\phi=-\frac{4}{3}$

$\Rightarrow \mp\frac{4}{3t}=\frac{-4}{3} \quad \Rightarrow t=\pm 1$

$\Rightarrow t^2=1$

$\Rightarrow$ Abscissa of point is $x=t^2=1$

3. $f(0)=0$ and $f(1)=0$

Thus $f(0)=f(1)$

Also $f'(x)=x^{\alpha^2-4\alpha+2}+(\alpha^2-4\alpha+3)x^{\alpha^2-4\alpha+2}.\log x$, which exists finitely in (0, 1) $\forall x\in\mathbb{R}$.

Also $f(x)$ is continuous $\forall x \in (0,1)$.

Thus Rolle's Theorem will be applicable to $f(x)$ in [0, 1] if $\lim_{x\to 0^+} f(x) = f(0) = 0$

$\Rightarrow \lim_{x\to 0^+} x^{(\alpha^2-4\alpha+3)}.\log x = 0$

If $\alpha^2-4\alpha+3=0$, then above is false

If $\alpha^2-4\alpha+3<0$, then $\lim_{x\to 0^+} x^{(\alpha^2-4\alpha+3)}.\log x = -\infty \neq 0$

If $\alpha^2-4\alpha+3>0$, then $\lim_{x\to 0^+} \dfrac{\log x}{x^{-(\alpha^2-4\alpha+3)}}$

$= \lim_{x\to 0^+} \dfrac{\frac{1}{x}}{-(\alpha^2-4\alpha+3)x^{-(\alpha^2-4\alpha+4)}}$

$= \lim_{x\to 0^+} \dfrac{x^{(\alpha^2-4\alpha+4)}}{-(\alpha^2-4\alpha+3} = 0$

$\therefore \alpha^2-4\alpha+3>0$

$\Rightarrow (\alpha-1)(\alpha-3)>0$

$\Rightarrow \alpha \in (-\infty,1)\cup(3,\infty)$

$\Rightarrow$ Least positive integer value of α = 4

4. Given $\dfrac{dV}{dt} \infty - \pi r^2$

$\Rightarrow \dfrac{dV}{dt} = -k\pi r^2 \quad \Rightarrow \dfrac{d}{dt}\left(\dfrac{4}{3}\pi r^3\right) = -k\pi r^2$

$\Rightarrow \dfrac{4}{3}\pi\left(3r^2\dfrac{dr}{dt}\right) = -k\pi r^2$

$\Rightarrow 4\dfrac{dr}{dt} = -k \quad \Rightarrow \dfrac{dr}{dt} = \dfrac{-k}{4}$

$\Rightarrow \dfrac{d}{dt}\left(\dfrac{D}{2}\right) = \dfrac{-k}{4}$

$\Rightarrow dD = \dfrac{-k}{2}dt \quad \Rightarrow D = \dfrac{-k}{2}t + C$

According to Question, when $t=0, D=3$ and when $t=4, D=1$

$\Rightarrow 3 = C$ and $1 = -2k + C$

$\Rightarrow k = 1$

$\therefore D = \dfrac{-t}{2} + 3$

$\therefore$ For $D = 0, \dfrac{t}{2} = 3$

$\Rightarrow t = 6$

5. The parametric equation of curve is (t, t^3).

$\Rightarrow$ Slope tangent = $3t^2$

$\therefore$ Equation of tangent to curve at $P_1(t)$ is given by $\left(y-t^3\right) = 3t^2\left(x-t\right)$.

It meets curve $y = x^3$, where $x^3 - t^3 = 3t^2(x-t)$

$\Rightarrow (x-t)(x^2+tx+t^2) = 3t^2(x-t)$

$\Rightarrow (x-t)(x^2+tx+t^2-3t^2) = 0$

$\Rightarrow (x-t)(x^2+tx-2t^2) = 0$

$\Rightarrow (x-t)[(x-t)(x+2t)] = 0$

$\Rightarrow x = t$ or $x = -2t$

$\Rightarrow$ If $P_1 \equiv (t, t^3)$

$\Rightarrow P_2 \equiv \left(-2t, -2^3 t^3\right),\ P_3 \equiv \left((-2)^2 t, (-2)^6 t^3\right),$

$P_4 \equiv \left((-2)^3 t, (-2)^9 t^3\right)$ and

$P_5 \equiv \left((-2)^4 t, (-2)^{12} t^3\right) \equiv \left(16t, 2^{12} t^3\right)$

Now, if $P_1 \equiv (2,8) \equiv (t, t^3)$

$\Rightarrow t = 2$

$\Rightarrow P_5 \equiv (32, 2^{15})$

$\therefore$ Abscissa of $P_5 = 32$

6. Let V_A and V_B be volume of water in tank at an instant t, then

$\dfrac{dV_A}{dt} = -k_1 V_A$ and $\dfrac{dV_B}{dt} = -k_2 V_B$

$\Rightarrow l_n V_A = -k_1 t + C_1$ and $l_n V_B = -k_2 t + C_2$

Now initially, $t = 0, V_A = V_a$ and $V_B = v_b$

$\Rightarrow l_n\, v_a = C_1$ and $l_n\, v_b = C_2$

$\Rightarrow l_n\left(\dfrac{V_A}{v_a}\right) = -k_1 t$ and $l_n\left(\dfrac{V_B}{v_b}\right) = -k_2 t$

$\Rightarrow V_A = v_a.e^{-k_1 t}$ and $V_B = v_b.e^{-k_2 t}$

After 1 hour, $V_A = 2V_B \quad \Rightarrow \dfrac{V_A}{V_B} = 2$

$\Rightarrow 2 = \dfrac{v_a}{v_b}.\dfrac{e^{-k_1}}{e^{-k_2}}$

$\Rightarrow 2 = 3.\dfrac{e^{-k_1}}{e^{-k_2}} (\because v_a = 3v_b)$

$\Rightarrow \dfrac{2}{3} = e^{(k_2-k_1)}$ .... (1)

Now, if both tanks have same quantity of water after time 't', then $V_A = V_B$

$\Rightarrow v_{ae^{-k_1 t}} = v_{be^{-k_2 t}} \quad \Rightarrow 3\left(e^{(k_2-k_1)t}\right) = 1$

$\Rightarrow 3\left(\dfrac{2}{3}\right)^t = 1$ (Using (1))

$\Rightarrow \left(\dfrac{2}{3}\right)^t = \left(\dfrac{1}{3}\right)$

$\Rightarrow t = \log_{\frac{2}{3}}\left(\dfrac{1}{3}\right) = \log_{2m}(m)$ given

$\Rightarrow m = \dfrac{1}{3}$

$\Rightarrow \dfrac{1}{3} = 3$

7. Given curve is $y^2 = \frac{-a^4}{2b^2}x$, which a parabola is having parametric equation $P\left(-\frac{a^4}{8b^2}t^2, \frac{a^4}{4b^2}t\right)$

$\Rightarrow$ Slope of tangent $= \frac{-a^4/4b^2}{-2a^{4t}/8b^2} = \frac{1}{t}$

$\Rightarrow$ The tangent to hyperbola $\frac{x^2}{b^2} - \frac{y^2}{a^2} = 1$ have points of contact Q and R

$\Rightarrow$ QR is the chard of contact of point P

$\Rightarrow$ Equation of QR will be $\frac{\frac{-a^4}{8b^2}t^2x}{b^2} - \frac{\left(\frac{-a^4}{4b^2}t\right)y}{a^2} = 1$ or $\frac{a^2}{4b^2}ty = 1 + \frac{a^4}{8b^4}t^2x$

$\Rightarrow$ $y = \frac{1}{\left(\frac{a^2}{4b^2}t\right)} + \frac{\frac{a^4}{8b^4}t^2x}{\left(\frac{a^2}{4b^2}t\right)}$ or $y = \frac{1}{\frac{a^2}{4b^2}t} + \frac{a^2tx}{2b^2}$

or $y = \frac{a^2t}{2b^2}x + \frac{2}{\frac{a^2}{2b^2}t}$

Comparing with $y = mx + \frac{a'}{m}$

$\Rightarrow$ Length of latus rectum $= 4a' = 4(2) = 8$

8. Ball is falling under gravity $g = 10m/\sec^2$

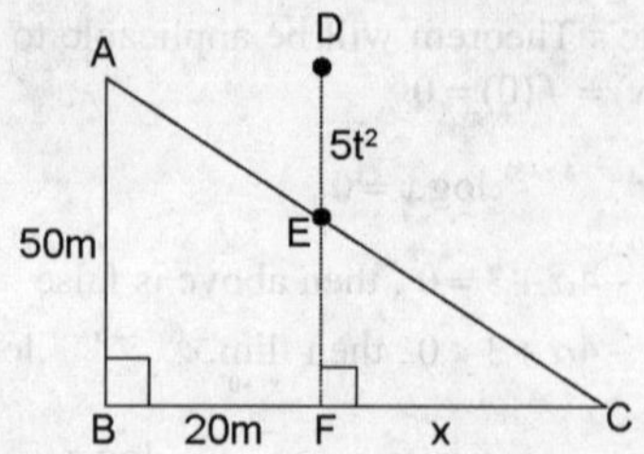

$\therefore$ $s = ut + \frac{1}{2}gt^2;\ u = 0$

$\Rightarrow$ $s = 5t^2$ is the displacement travelled by ball in t seconds.

$\Rightarrow$ $DE = 5t^2$

$\therefore$ $EF = 50 - 5t^2$

In similar Δs, ABC and EFC, $\frac{AB}{EF} = \frac{BC}{FC}$

$\Rightarrow$ $\frac{50}{50-5t^2} = \frac{20+x}{x}$

$\Rightarrow$ $50x = 1000 - 100t^2 + 50x - 5t^2x$

$\Rightarrow$ $x = \frac{200}{t^2} - 20$ $\Rightarrow$ $\frac{dx}{dt} = -\frac{400}{t^3} m/\sec.$

$\Rightarrow$ $\left(\frac{dx}{dt}\right)_{t=\frac{1}{2}\sec.} = -400 \times 8 = -3200 m/\sec,$

Here – ve sign indicates that the image distance from point F is decreasing with time.

Thus in magnitude, shadow of ball is moving with 3200 m/sec.

Application of Derivatives II

5 CHAPTER

MONOTONICITY

■ INTRODUCTION

The word 'monotonicity' derives its meaning from the word 'monotonous' which means without variation so "monotonic functions" are functions which are either strictly increasing or strictly decreasing throughout.

It has great use in practical life e.g. an organization may be interested to know whether after spending 'x' thousand amount for advertising etc. the sale $S(x)$ increases between x from 20 to 50 thousand. Or other company may be interested in knowing the rate of increase in cost or revenue and profit as a function of quantity of production etc.

In the present chapter we are going to study the monotonic nature of different kinds of functions and their applications.

■ MONOTONICITY

'It is study of increasing decreasing/constant behavior of function over an interval as we travel form left to right along its graph'.

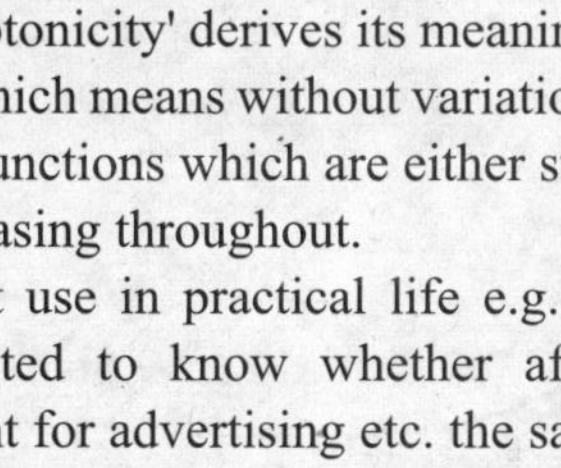

FIGURE 5.1

e.g. The function shown in the figure is decreasing $\forall x \in (-\infty, a)$ and increasing $\forall x \in (a, b)$. Again decreasing $\forall x \in (b, c)$ and remains constant over the interval (c, ∞).

■ MONOTONICITY AT A POINT

If a function $f(x)$ follows any one of the four natures given below, then it is said to be monotonic at $x = a$. Following four terms shall be clearly defined in order to understand monotonicity of $f(x)$ in an interval.

(a) Strictly increasing

(b) Increasing (non-decreasing)

(c) Strictly decreasing

(d) Decreasing (non-increasing)

(a) Strictly increasing functions

A function $f(x)$ is said to be strictly increasing at the point $x = a$. Iff $f(a - h) < f(a) < f(a + h)$, where h is a positive infinitesimal.

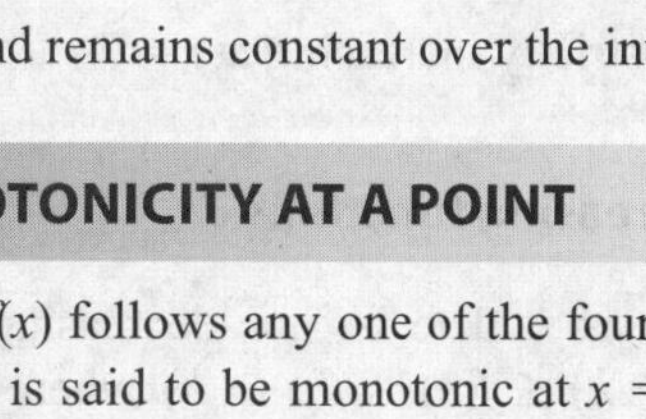

FIGURE 5.2

e.g. $f(x) = e^x$; $f(x) = \ln x$ and $f(x) = 2x + 3$. Similarly observe the function $f(x)$ given below, which is discontinuous at $x = 0$.

$$f(x)=\begin{cases}1-2x^2; & x<0\\ 3+x^2; & x\geq 0\end{cases}$$

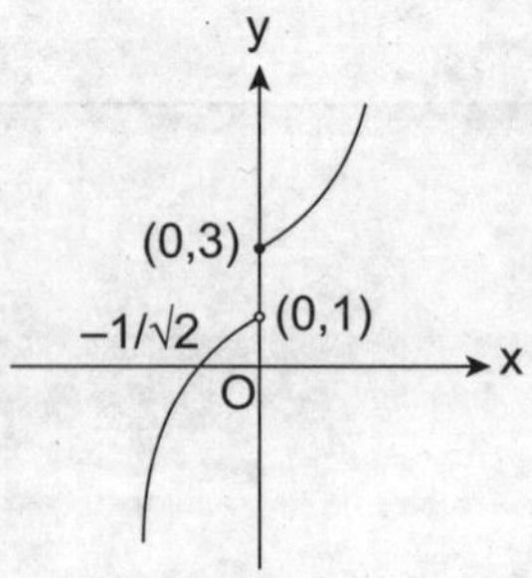

FIGURE 5.3

Clearly $f(0) = 3$

$f(0 - h) < 1$ and $f(0 + h) > 3$

$\therefore\ f(0 - h) < f(0) < f(0 + h)$

$\Rightarrow f(x)$ is strictly increasing at $x = 0$

(b) Non-decreasing functions

A function $f(x)$ is said to be non-decreasing at the point $x = a$ iff $f(a - h) \leq f(a) \leq f(a + h)$ where h is positive infinitesimal.

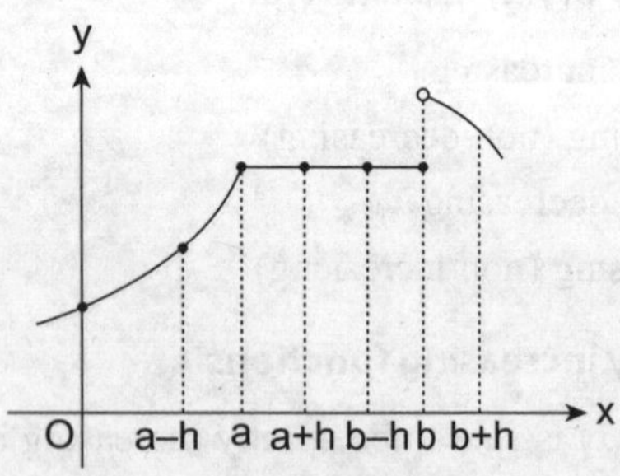

FIGURE 5.4

"We observe that the function shown in above graph is non-decreasing at $x = a$ as well as at $x = b$"

$\because\ f(a-h) < f(a) = f(a+h)$

and $f(b - h) = f(b) < f(b + h)$

(c) Strictly decreasing functions

A function $f(x)$ is said to be strictly decreasing at the point $x = a$ iff $f(a - h) > f(a) > f(a + h)$, where h is positive infinitesimal.

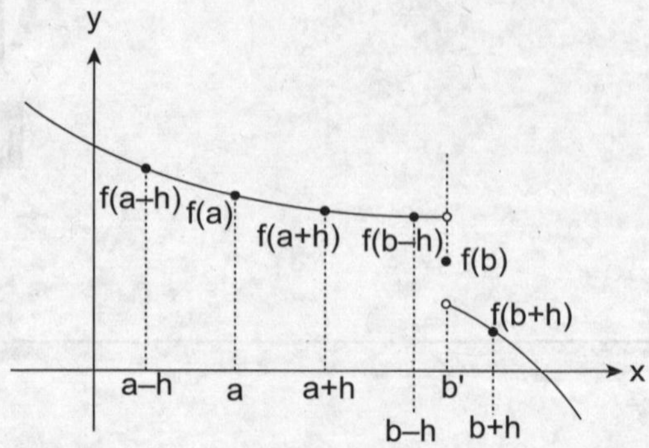

FIGURE 5.5

Also $f(x)$ is strictly decreasing at the point $x = b$, since $f(b - h) > f(b) > f(b + h)$.

e.g. $f(x) = -x^3$; $f(x) = e^{-x}$ and $f(x) = \cot^{-1}(x)$

(d) Non-increasing functions

A function $f(x)$ is said to be non-increasing at the point $x = a$ iff $f(a-h) \geq f(a) \geq f(a+h)$, where h is positive infinitesimal.

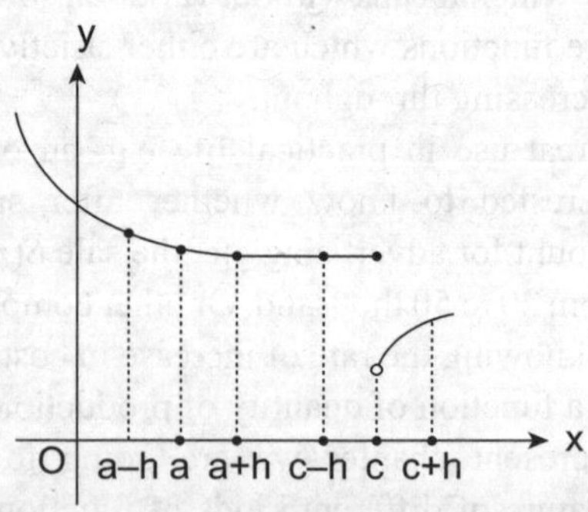

FIGURE 5.6

Important Points to Remember

We can talk of monotonicity of $f(x)$ at $x = a$, only if $x = a$ lies in the domain of f. Continuity and differentiability of $f(x)$ at $x = a$ is not necessary.

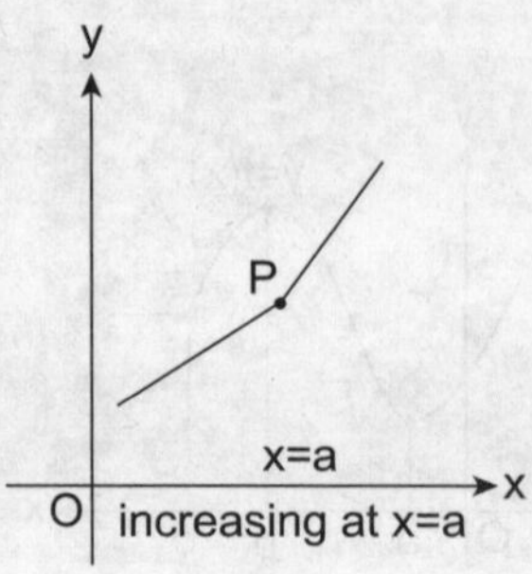

FIGURE 5.7

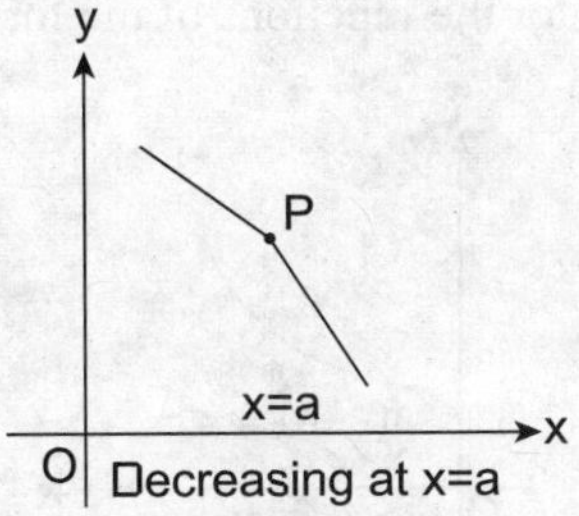

FIGURE 5.8

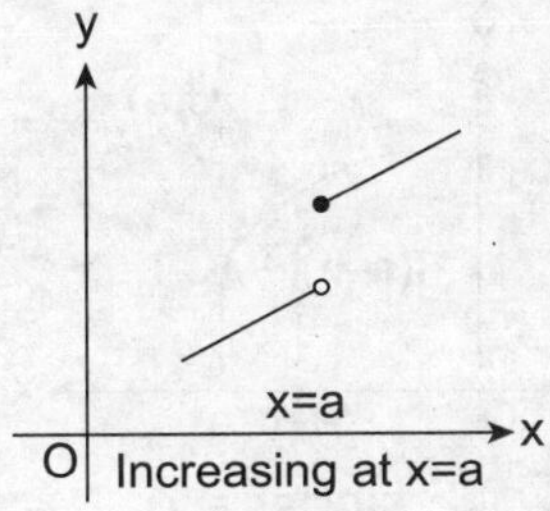

FIGURE 5.9

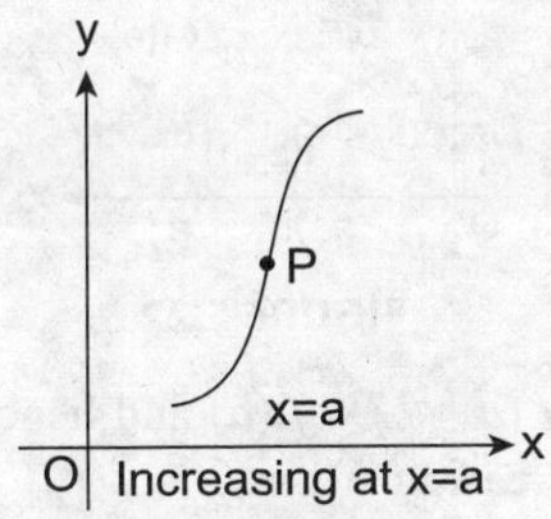

FIGURE 5.10

- If $f(x)$ is constant in the neighborhood of the point $x = a$, then it is called either non-decreasing or non-increasing.
- If $x = a$ is an endpoint, then we use the approximate one-sided inequality to test monotonicity of $f(x)$ at $x = a$.

(i) If $x = a$ is the left endpoint, then we check only the right neighbourhood of a and compare $f(a + h)$ with $f(a)$.
e.g., for the function of the form

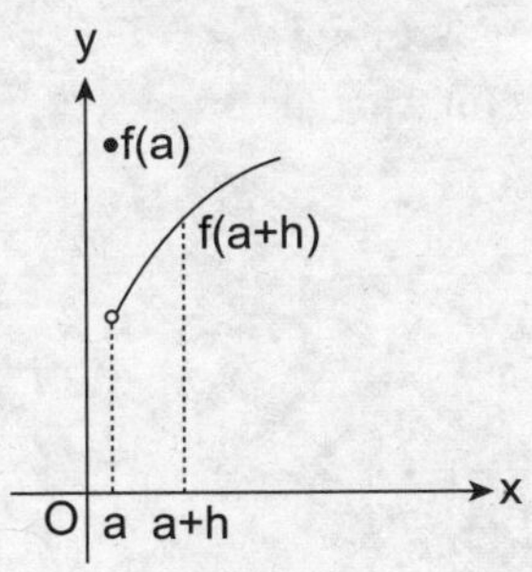

FIGURE 5.11

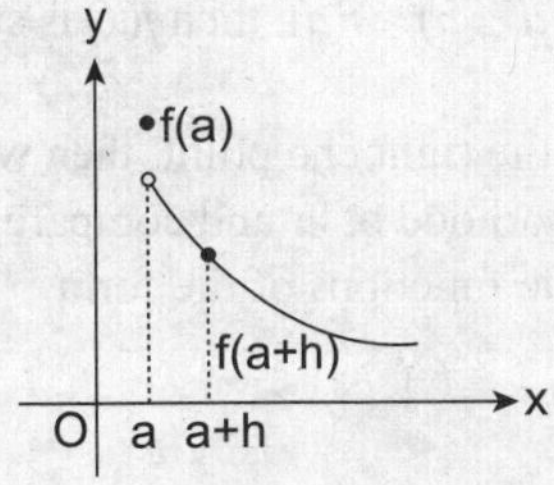

FIGURE 5.12

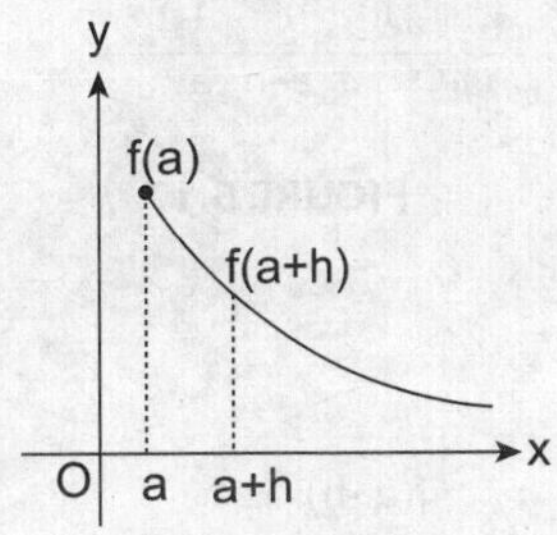

FIGURE 5.13

We have $f(a+h) < f(a)$, and hence $f(x)$ strictly decreasing at $x = a$. And for the functions of the form

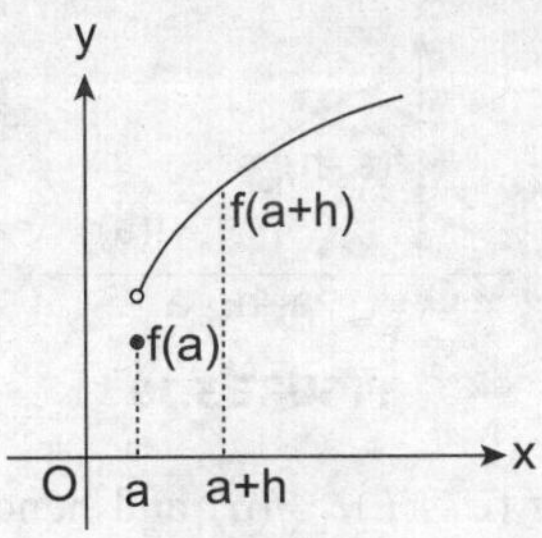

FIGURE 5.14

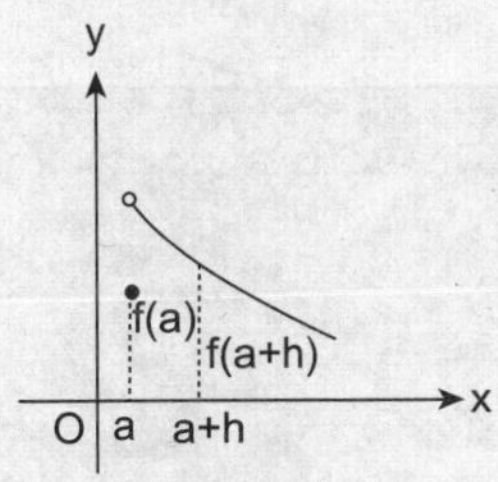

FIGURE 5.15

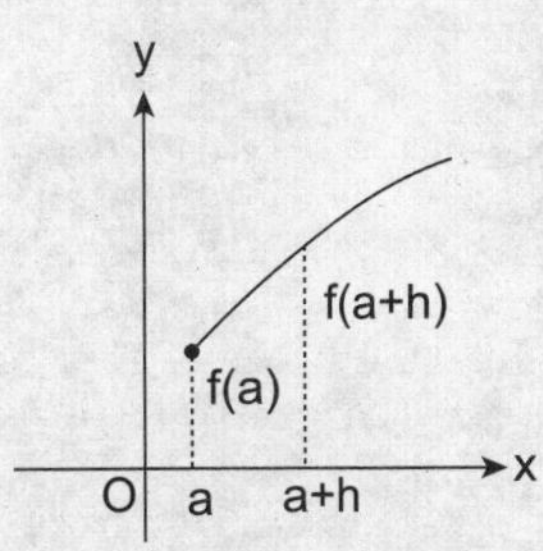

FIGURE 5.16

We have $f(a+h) > f(a)$; then $f(x)$ is strictly increasing at $x = a$.

(ii) If $x = a$ is the right end point, then we check only the left neighborhood of 'a' and compare $f(a-h)$ with $f(a)$ e.g., For the functions of the form

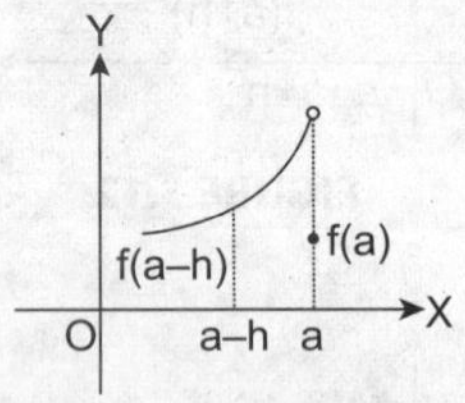

FIGURE 5.17

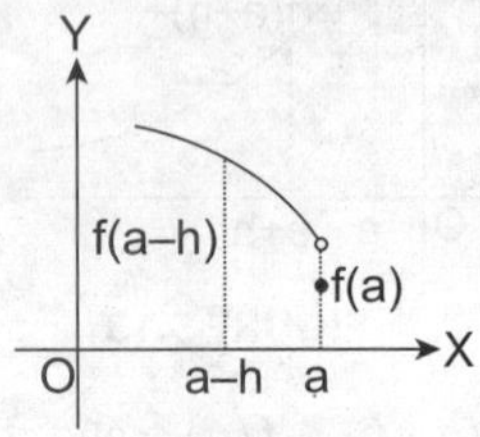

FIGURE 5.18

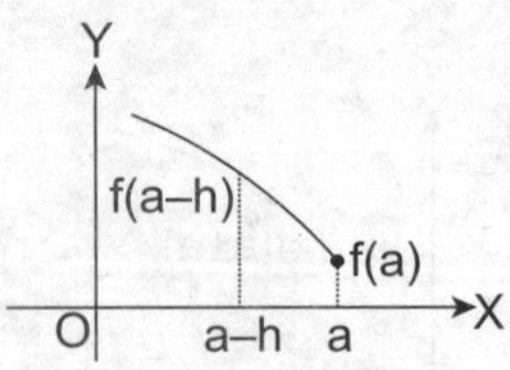

FIGURE 5.19

We have $f(a-h) > f(a)$ and hence the function is strictly decreasing at $x = a$.

Similarly for the functions of the form

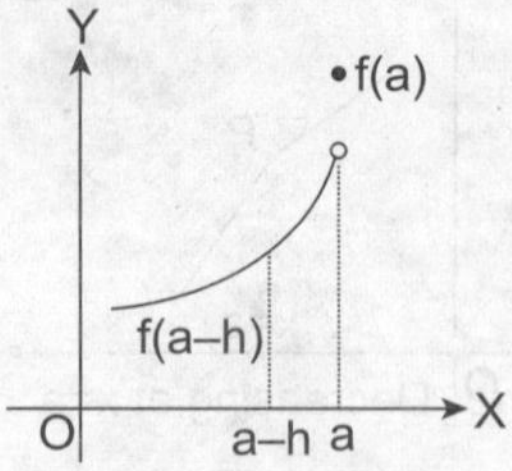

FIGURE 5.20

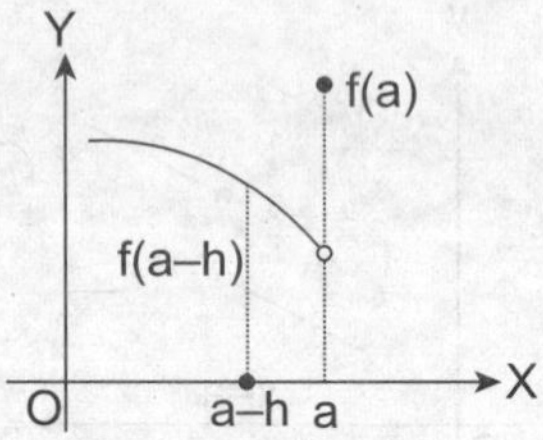

FIGURE 5.21

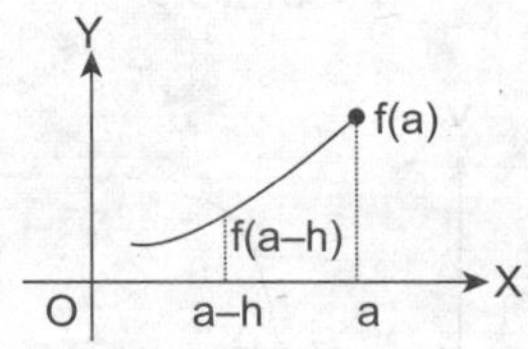

FIGURE 5.22

We have, $f(a-h) < f(a)$ and hence the function is strictly increasing at $x = a$.

$f(x)$ may still be increasing/decreasing at $x = a$ even if $\left(\dfrac{dy}{dx}\right)_{x=a} = 0$.

ILLUSTRATION 1: Examine the behavior of the function $f(x)$ when

(i) $f(x) = x^3$ at the point $x = 0$

(ii) $f(x) = \dfrac{1}{2+x}$ at the point $x = 0$

(iii) $f(x) = \dfrac{1}{1-x^2}$ at the point $x = 0$

(iv) $f(x) = [\sin x]$ at the point $x = \dfrac{\pi}{2}$

SOLUTION: (i) We have $f(x) = x^3$

$f(0-h) = (-h)^3 = -h^3 < 0$ (where h is a positive infinitesimal)

$f(0) = (0)^3 = 0$

$f(0+h) = h^3 > 0$

Since $f(0-h) < f(0) < f(0+h)$

Hence $f(x)$ is a strictly increasing function at $x = 0$

For $y = x^3$; $\dfrac{dy}{dx} = 3x^2$.

At $x = 0$; $\dfrac{dy}{dx} = 0$

∴ If the derivative at a point is zero, even then the function can be monotonic.

i.e., derivatives can be the criterion for determining monotonicity but it is not the sole criterion.

(ii) We have $f(x) = \dfrac{1}{2+x}$

$$f(0-h) = \frac{1}{2+(-h)} = \frac{1}{2-h} > \frac{1}{2} \qquad (\because \text{ if } h > 0 \text{ then } 2 - h < 2 \Rightarrow \frac{1}{2-h} > \frac{1}{2})$$

$$f(0) = \frac{1}{2+0} = \frac{1}{2}$$

$$f(0+h) = \frac{1}{2+(h)} = \frac{1}{2+h} = \frac{1}{2+h} < \frac{1}{2} \qquad (\because \text{ if } h > 0 \text{ then } 2 + h > 2 \Rightarrow \frac{1}{2+h} < \frac{1}{2})$$

Since $f(0 - h) > f(0) > f(0 + h)$

hence $f(x)$ is a strictly decreasing function at $x = 0$.

(iii) $f(x) = \dfrac{1}{1-x^2}$

$$f(0-h) = \frac{1}{1-h^2} > 1$$

$$f(0) = \frac{1}{1-0} = 1$$

$$f(0+h) = \frac{1}{1-h^2} > 1$$

Now $f(0 - h) > f(0)$ and $f(0) < f(0 + h)$ therefore the function is neither increasing nor decreasing at $x = 0$.

(iv) $g(x) = \sin x$

$f(x) = [g(x)] = [\sin x]$

$$f\left(\frac{\pi}{2}-h\right) = \left[\sin\left(\frac{\pi}{2}-h\right)\right] = 0$$

$$f\left(\frac{\pi}{2}\right) = \left[\sin\left(\frac{\pi}{2}\right)\right] = 1$$

$$f\left(\frac{\pi}{2}+h\right) = \left[\sin\left(\frac{\pi}{2}+h\right)\right] = 0$$

Now since $f\left(\frac{\pi}{2}-h\right) < f\left(\frac{\pi}{2}\right)$ and

$$f\left(\frac{\pi}{2}\right) > f\left(\frac{\pi}{2}+h\right)$$

∴ The function is neither increasing nor decreasing at $x = \dfrac{\pi}{2}$

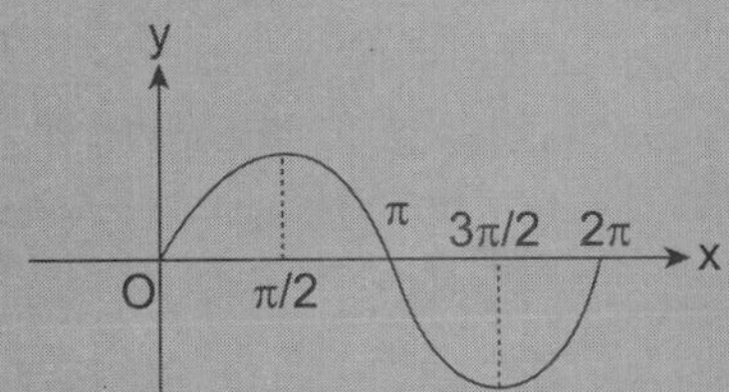

FIGURE 5.23

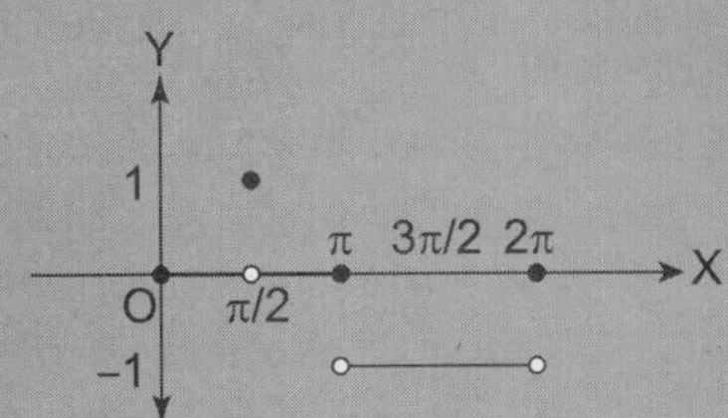

FIGURE 5.24

ILLUSTRATION 2: Find whether the following functions are strictly increasing/strictly decreasing/non-increasing/non-decreasing/neither increasing nor decreasing at $x = a$.

(i) 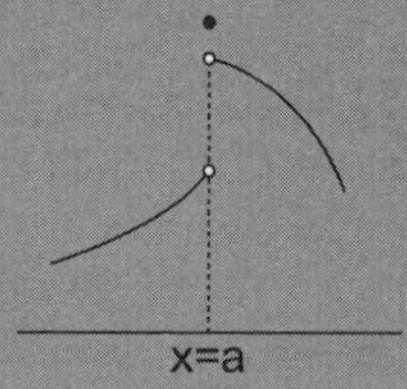

(ii) 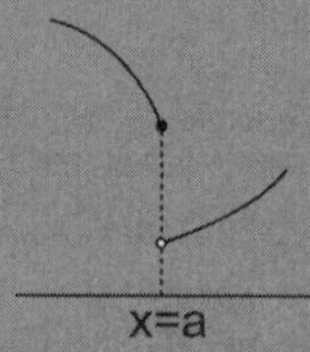

(iii) 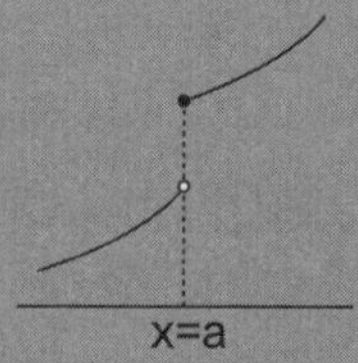

(iv) 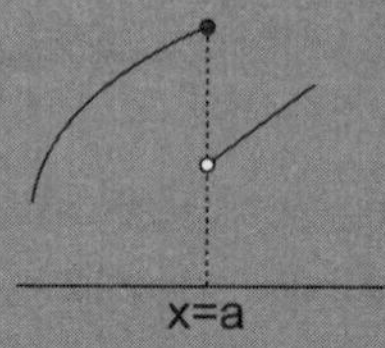

(v) 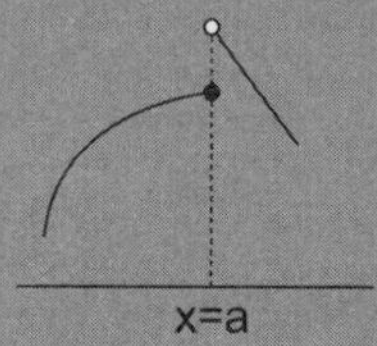

(vi) 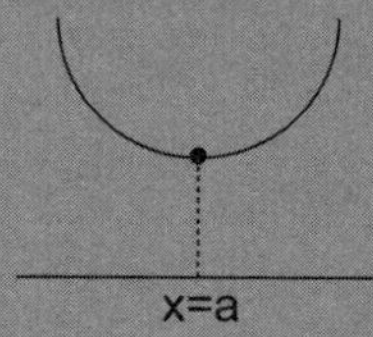

(vii) 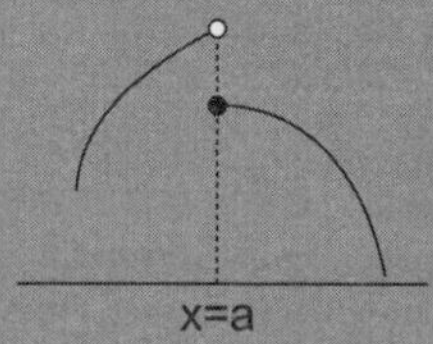

(viii) 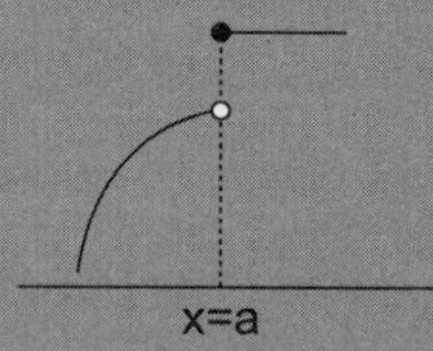

SOLUTION: (i) Neither increasing nor decreasing as $f(a-h) < f(a)$ and $f(a) > f(a+h)$

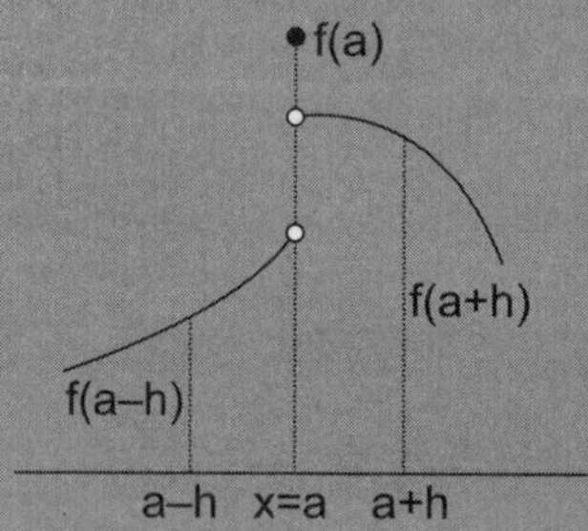

FIGURE 5.25

(ii) Strictly decreasing as $f(a-h) > f(a) > f(a+h)$

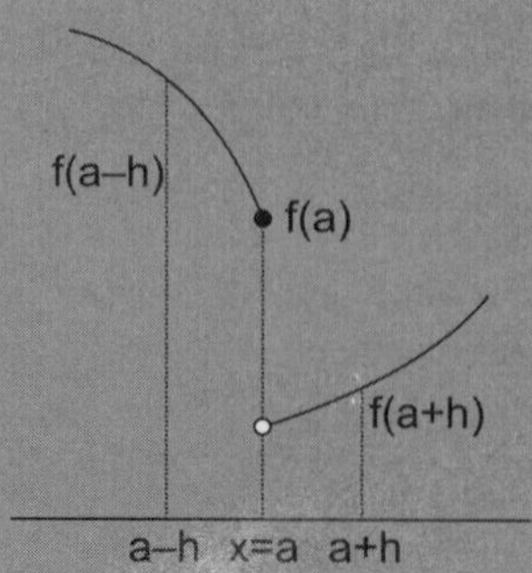

FIGURE 5.26

(iii) Strictly increasing as $f(a-h) < f(a) < f(a+h)$

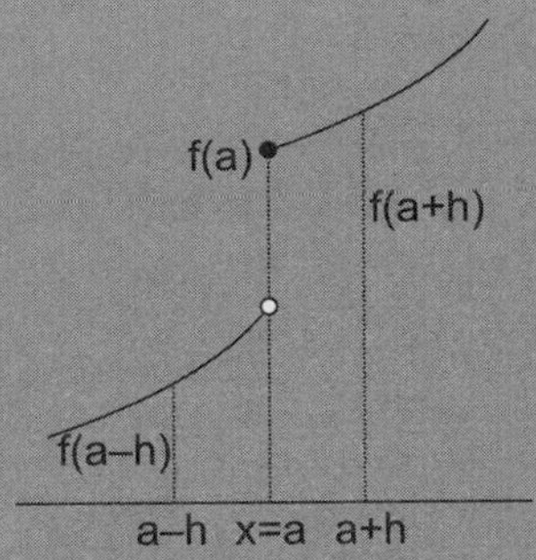

FIGURE 5.27

(iv) Neither increasing nor decreasing as $f(a-h) > f(a)$ and $f(a) < f(a+h)$

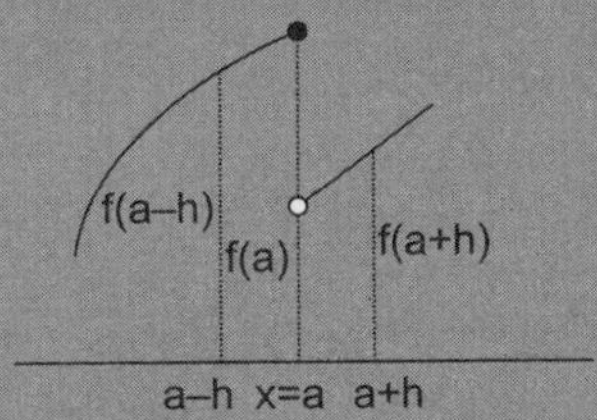

FIGURE 5.28

(v) Strictly increasing as $f(a-h) < f(a) < f(a+h)$

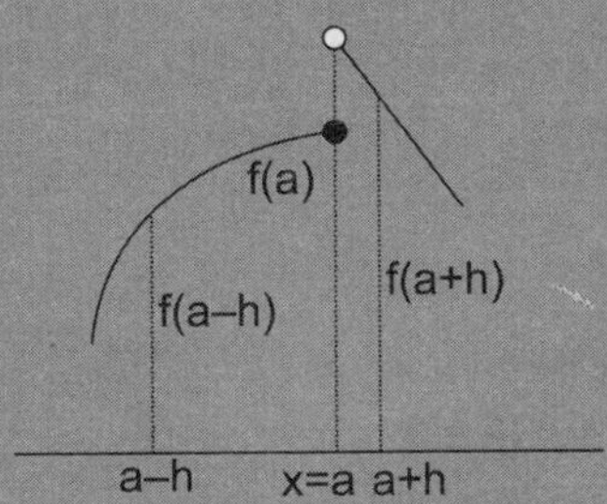

FIGURE 5.29

(vi) Neither increasing nor decreasing as $f(a-h) > f(a)$ and $f(a) < f(a+h)$

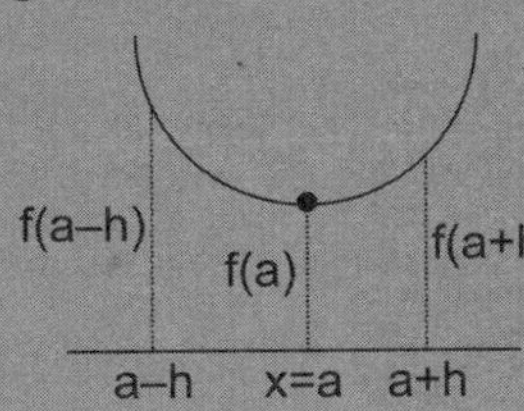

FIGURE 5.30

(vii) Strictly decreasing as $f(a-h) > f(a) > f(a+h)$

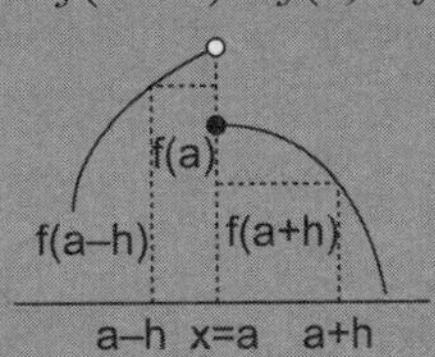

FIGURE 5.31

(viii) non-decreasing as $f(a-h) < f(a)$ and $f(a) = f(a+h)$

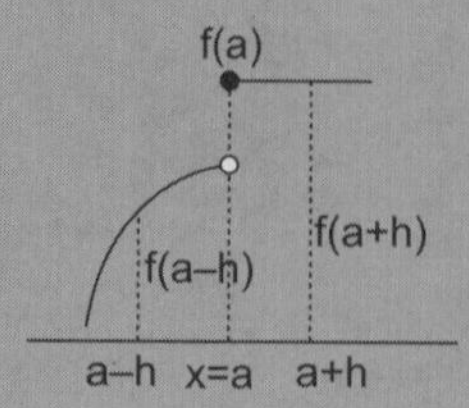

FIGURE 5.32

ILLUSTRATION 3: Check the monotonicity of the following functions at the specified points

(i) $f(x) = sgn(x)$ *at* $x = 0$

(ii) $f(x) = [x]$ at $x = k$, where k is any integer and [.] denotes the greatest integer function.

(iii) $f(x) = -\lceil x \rceil$ at $x = k$, where k is any integer and $\lceil . \rceil$ denotes the least integer function.

SOLUTION: (i) $f(x) = sgn(x)$ at $x = 0$

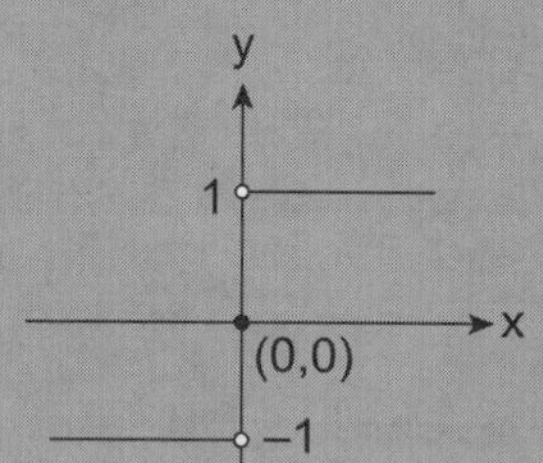

FIGURE 5.33

As is evident from figure 5.33 we have $f(0-h) < f(0) < f(0+h)$

$\therefore$ $f(x)$ is strictly increasing at $x = 0$.

(ii) $f(x) = [x]$ at $x = k$ where k is any integer.

$f(k-h) = [k-h] = (k-1)$

$f(k) = [k] = k$

$f(k+h) = [k+h] = k$

$f(k-h) < f(k)$ but $f(k) = f(k+h)$

$\therefore$ $f(x)$ is non-decreasing at integral values.

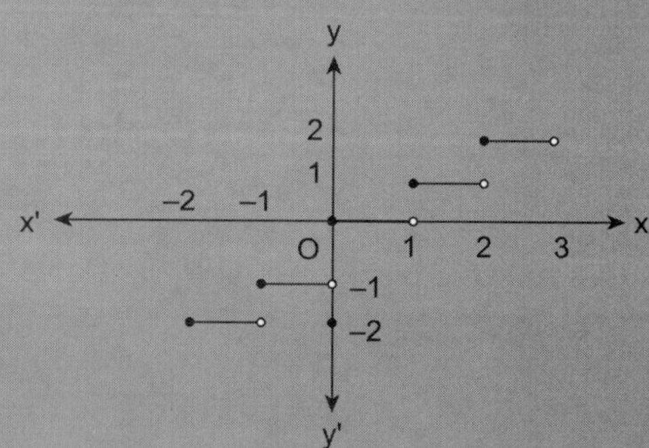

FIGURE 5.34

(iii) $f(x) = -\lceil x \rceil$ at $x = k$ where k is any integer

$f(k-h) = \uparrow -\lceil k-h \rceil = -k$

$f(k) = -\lceil k \rceil = -k$

$f(k+h) = -\lceil k+h \rceil = -k-1$

Now, $f(k-h) = f(k)$ but $f(k) > f(k+h)$

$\therefore$ $f(x)$ is non-increasing at integral values.

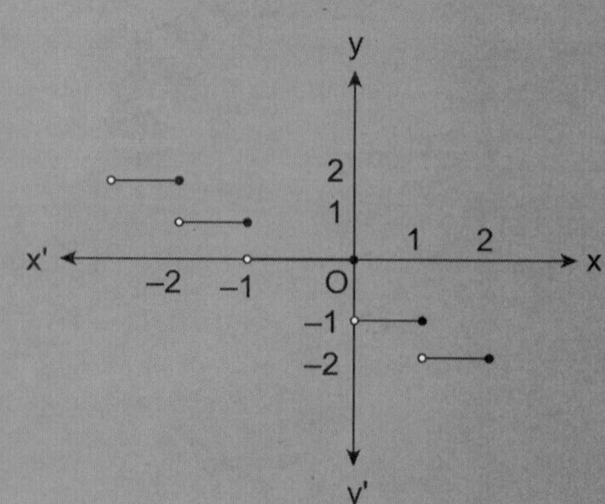

FIGURE 5.35

TEST OF MONOTONICITY AT A POINT

For a differentiable function at $x = a$.

(i) If $f'(a) > 0$, then $f(x)$ is strictly increasing (↑) at $x = a$.

e.g. consider $y = f(x) = x^2$ at $x = 3$, then $f'(x) = 2x$

$\Rightarrow f'(3) = 6 > 0$

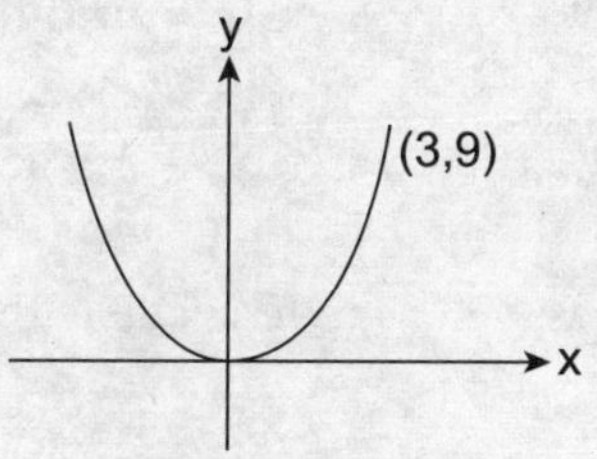

FIGURE 5.36

Therefore $f(x) = x^2$ is strictly increasing (↑) at $x = 3$.

(ii) If $f'(a) < 0$, then $f(x)$ is strictly decreasing (↓) at $x = a$.

e.g. consider $y = f(x) = x^2$ at $x = 3$, then $f'(x) = 2x$

$\Rightarrow f'(-3) = -6 < 0$

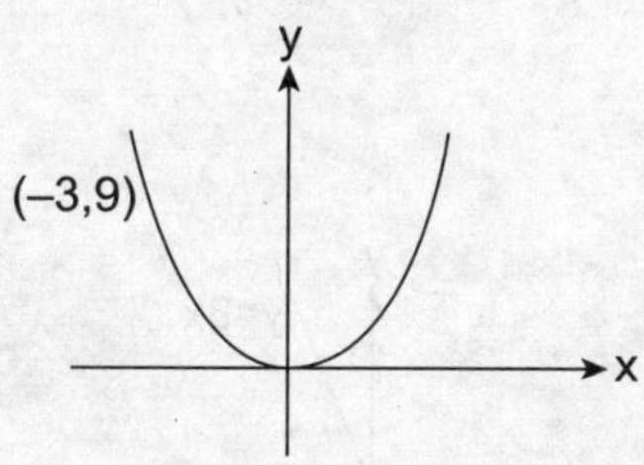

FIGURE 5.37

Therefore $f(x) = x^2$ is strictly decreasing (↓) at $x = -3$

(iii) If $f'(a) = 0$, then examine the signs of $f'(a - h)$ and $f'(a + h)$

(a) If $f'(a - h) > 0$ and $f'(a + h) > 0$ then $f(x)$ is strictly increasing at $x = a$.

Consider $y = f(x) = x^3$ at $x = 0$ then $f'(x) = 3x^2$

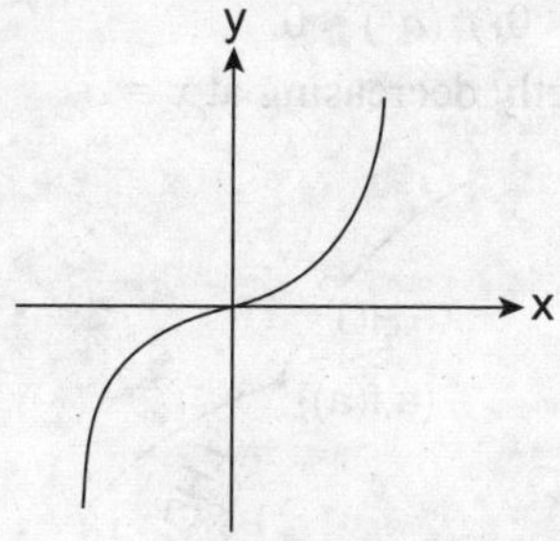

FIGURE 5.38

$\Rightarrow f'(0) = 0$

$f'(0 - h) = f'(-h) = 3(-h)^2 = 3h^2 > 0$

and $f'(0 + h) = f'(h) = 3h^2 > 0$

Now since $f'(0 - h) > 0$ and $f'(0 + h) > 0$

$\therefore$ function is strictly increasing at $x = 0$

(b) If $f'(a - h) < 0$ and $f'(a + h) < 0$ then $f(x)$ is strictly decreasing at $x = a$.

Consider $f(x) = -x^3$

$f'(x) = -3x^2$

$\Rightarrow f'(0) = -3(0)^2 = 0$

$f'(0 - h) = -3(-h)^2 = -3h^2 < 0$

and $f'(0 + h) = -3(h)^2 = -3h^2 < 0$

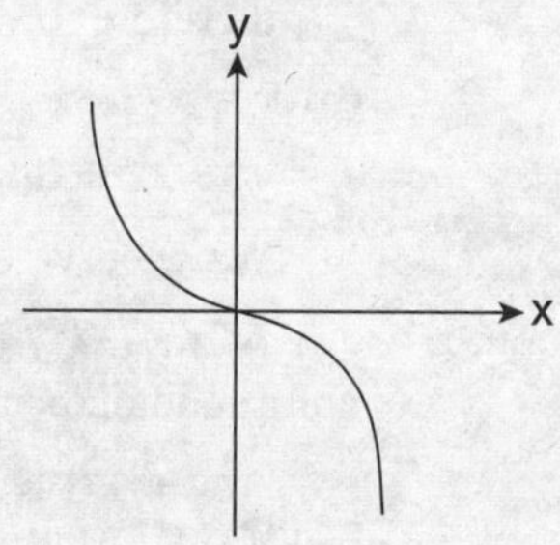

FIGURE 5.39

Now, since $f'(0 - h) < 0$ and $f'(0 + h) < 0$

Therefore $f(x)$ is strictly decreasing at $x = 0$.

(c) If $f'(a - h)$ and $f'(a + h)$ are of opposite sign then $f(x)$ is neither increasing nor decreasing (non-monotonic) at $x = a$.

Consider $f(x) = x^2$ at $x = 0$

$f'(x) = 2x$

$\Rightarrow f'(0) = 2(0) = 0$

$f'(0 - h) = -2h < 0$ and $f'(0 + h) = 2h > 0$

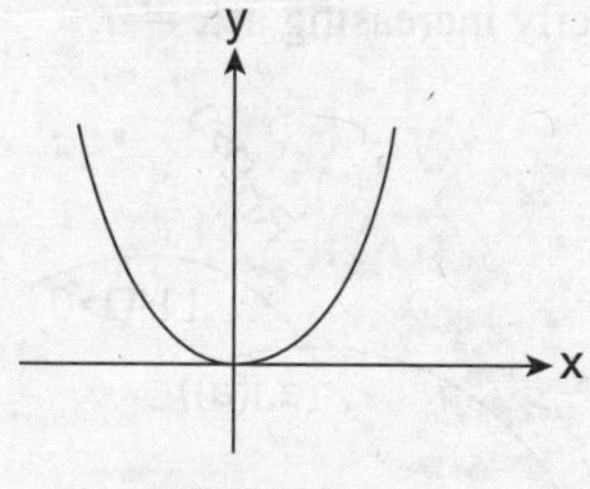

FIGURE 5.40

Since $f'(0 - h) < 0$ and $f'(0 + h) > 0$; therefore $f(x)$ is neither increasing nor decreasing at $x = 0$.

(d) If $f'(a \pm h) = 0$; then $f(x)$ is constant

Consider $f(x) = 5$ at $x = 2$

$f'(2 + h) = 0$ and $f'(2 - h) = 0$

ILLUSTRATION 4: Test the monotonicity of following functions at mentioned points:

(a) $y = x^3 - 3x + 2$ at $x = 0$, 1 and 2

(b) $y = x^3 + 3x^2 + 2$ at $x = -2$ and 1

SOLUTION: (a) $y = x^3 - 3x + 2$

$\Rightarrow y' = 3x^2 - 3 = 3(x-1)(x+1)$

Wavy curve of $f'(x)$ is as shown below

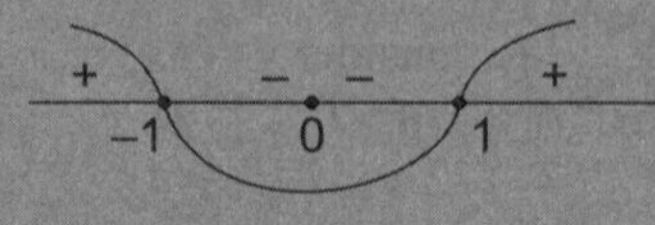

FIGURE 5.41

$f'(x)$ at 0^- is less than 0 and $f'(x)$ at 0^+ is less than 0

Hence $f(x)$ is strictly decreasing at $x = 0$

Also $f'(x)$ changes from negative to positive as it crosses $x = 1$, therefore $f(x)$ is non-monotonic at $x = 1$

And $f'(x)$ is positive on the left neighbourhood as well as right neighbourhood of $x = 2$, therefore $f(x)$ is strictly increasing at $x = 2$

(b) $y = x^3 + 3x^2 + 2$ at $x = -2$ and 1

$y' = 3x^2 + 6x = 3x(x+2)$

Wavy curve of $f'(x)$ is an shown below.

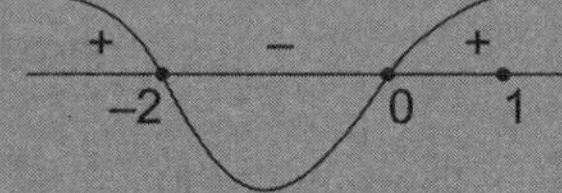

FIGURE 5.42

At $x = -2$; $f'(x)$ goes from negative to positive, hence $f(x)$ is non-monotonic at $x = -2$

And $f'(x)$ is positive in the left as well as the right neighbourhood of $x = 1$, therefore $f(x)$ is strictly increasing at $= 1$

■ NON-DIFFERENTIABLE BUT CONTINUOUS FUNCTION AT $x = a$

Given $f(x)$ is continuous function, not differentiable at 'a' but derivative of $f(x)$ exists in neighborhood of $x = a$

(a) If f is increasing (↑) for $x > a$ as well as for $x < a$ i.e., $f'(a^-) > 0, f'(a^+) > 0$.

$\Rightarrow f$ is strictly increasing at $x = a$.

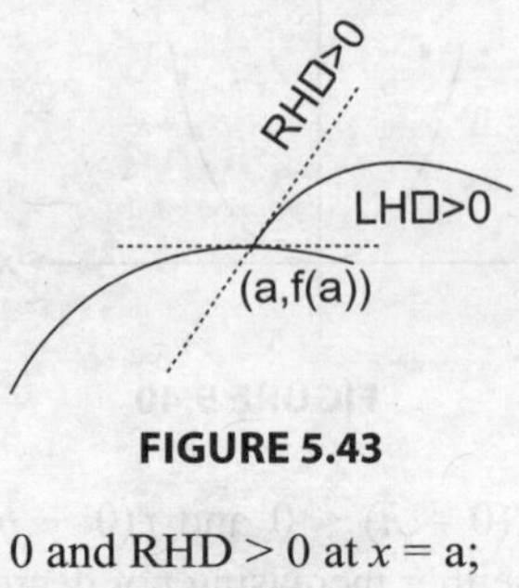

FIGURE 5.43

LHD > 0 and RHD > 0 at $x = a$;

$\therefore f(x)$ is strictly increasing at $x = a$.

e.g., $f(x) = \begin{cases} x; & x \le 0 \\ 3x; & x > 0 \end{cases}$

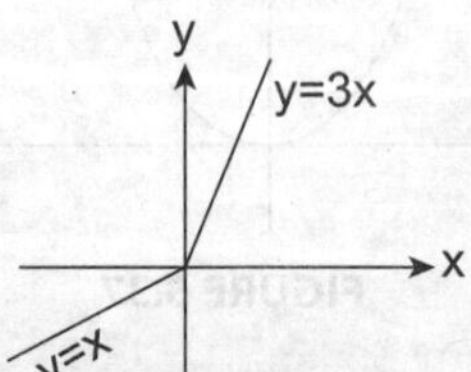

FIGURE 5.44

$f'(0^-) = 1 > 0$

$f'(0^+) = 3 > 0$

$\therefore$ f is increasing for $x > 0$ as well as $x < 0$

(b) If f is decreasing (↓) for $x > a$ as well as for $x < a$. i.e., $f'(a^-) < 0, f'(a^+) < 0$.

$\Rightarrow f$ is strictly decreasing at $x = a$.

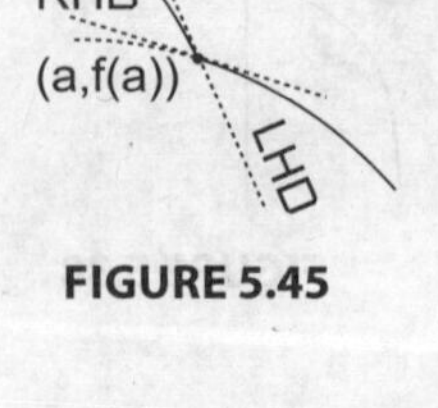

FIGURE 5.45

i.e., At $x = a$; LHD $\neq$ RHD but still LHD and RHD < 0

$\therefore$ $f(x)$ is strictly decreasing at $x = a$.

e.g., $f(x) = \begin{cases} -x; & x \leq 0 \\ -3x; & x > 0 \end{cases}$

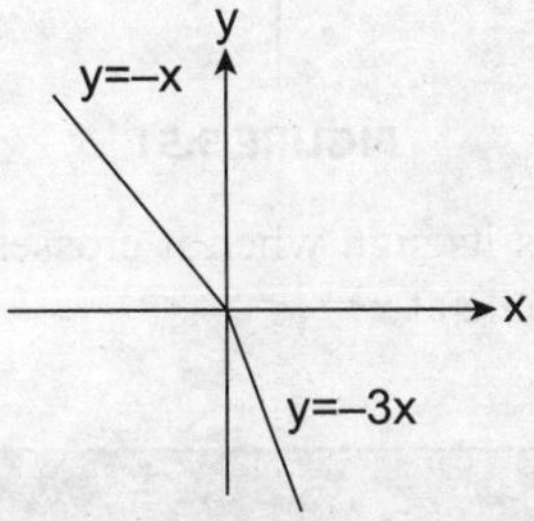

FIGURE 5.46

$f'(0^-) = -1 < 0$

$f'(0^+) = -3 < 0$

$\therefore$ f is decreasing for $x < 0$ as well as $x > 0$

(c) If $f'(a - h) > 0$. $f'(a + h) \geq 0$, $f'(a^+) > 0$ then $f(x)$ is strictly increasing at $x = a$.

Here $f'(a - h)$ represent the derivative at the point on the left of a and $f'(a^-)$ represents the left hand derivative at the point $x = a$

Similarly, $f'(a + h)$ represents the derivative at the point on the right of a and $f'(a^+)$ represents the right hand derivative at the point $x = a$.

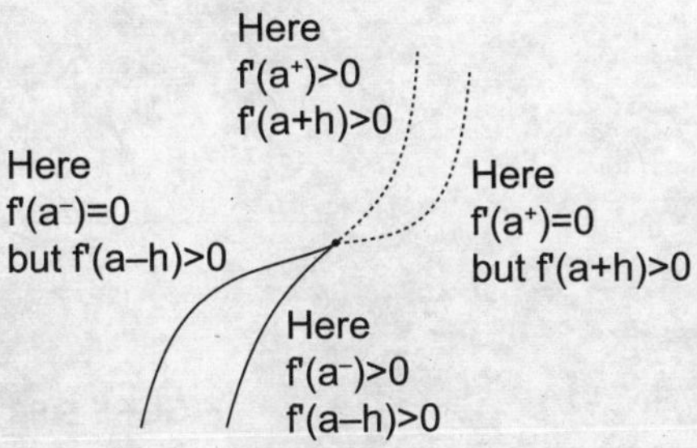

FIGURE 5.47

e.g. $f(x) = \begin{cases} x^3; & x \leq 0 \\ x^5; & x > 0 \end{cases}$

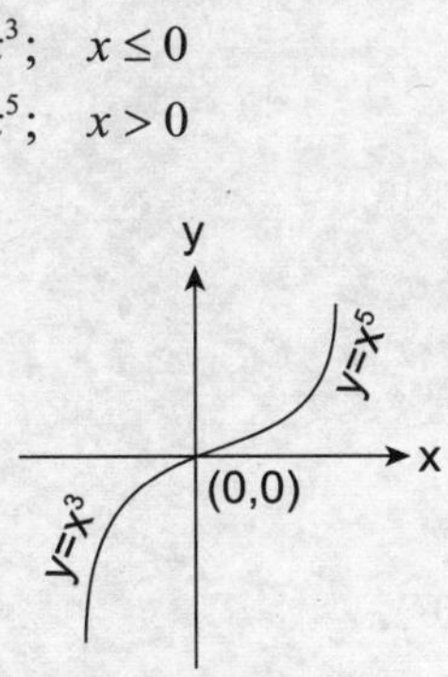

FIGURE 5.48

For $x < 0$

$f'(0) = 3x^2$

$f'(0 - h) = 3(0 - h)^2 = 3h^2 > 0$

Also L.H.D. at $x = 0$ i.e., $f'(0^-) = 0 \geq 0$

Now for $x > 0$

R.H.D. at $x = 0$ i.e., $f'(0^+) = 5x^4 = 0 \geq 0$

$f'(x) = 5x^4$

$f'(0 + h) = 5(0 + h)^4 = 5h^4 > 0$

then $f(x)$ is strictly increasing at $x = 0$.

(d) If $f'(a - h) < 0$. $f'(a^-) \leq 0$, $f'(a + h) < 0$ then $f(x)$ is strictly decreasing at $x = a$.

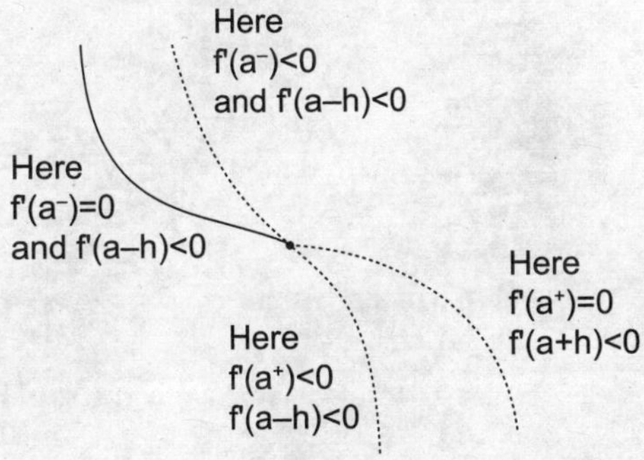

FIGURE 5.49

e.g., Let us consider $f(x) = \begin{cases} -x^3; & x \leq 0 \\ -x^5; & x > 0 \end{cases}$

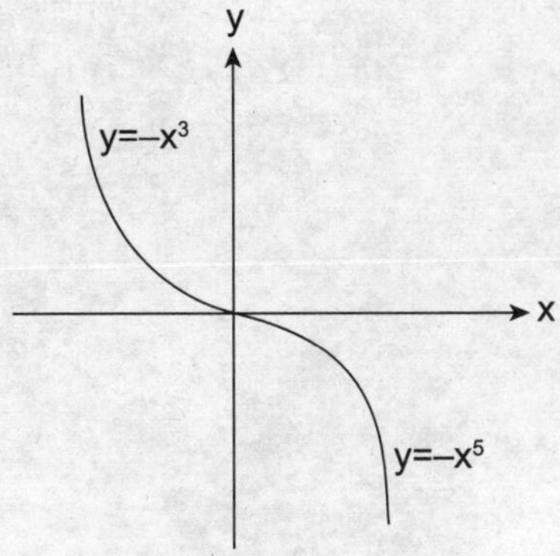

FIGURE 5.50

For $x \leq 0$; $f(x) = -3x^2$

$f'(0 - h) = -3(0 - h)^2 = -3h^2 < 0$

$f'(0^-) = -3(0)^2 = 0 \leq 0$

Similarly for $x > 0$; $f'(x) = -5x^4$

$f'(0 + h) = -5h^4 < 0$

$f'(0^+) = -5(0)^4 = 0 \le 0$

Here $f(x)$ is strictly decreasing at $x = 0$.

(e) If $f'(x)$ changes its sign across $x = a$ then it is non-monotonic at $x = a$.

e.g. Let us consider $f(x) = \begin{cases} -2x; & x \le 0 \\ 3x; & x > 0 \end{cases}$

$f'(0^-) = -2$

$f'(0^+) = 3$

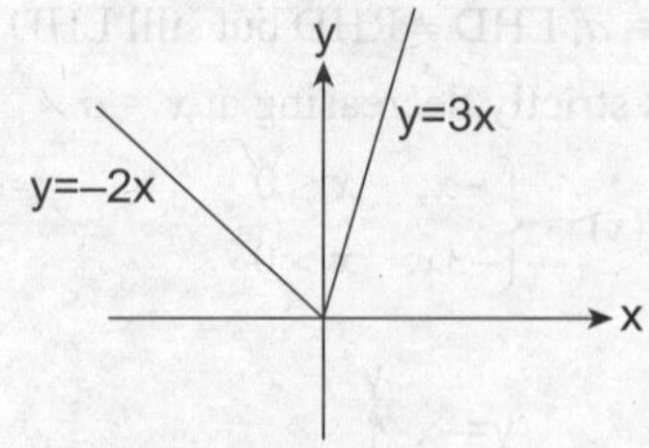

FIGURE 5.51

$\therefore$ $f'(x)$ changes its sign when it crosses $x = a$, then it is non-monotonic at $x = a$.

ILLUSTRATION 5: Test the monotonicity at $x = 0$ for the following functions.

(i) $f(x) = 3x + |2x|$

(ii) $f(x) = \begin{cases} 4x^3; x \le 0 \\ 7x\ ; x > 0 \end{cases}$

(iii) $f(x) = \begin{cases} (x+2)^2; & x \le 0 \\ 4+x; & x > 0 \end{cases}$

SOLUTION: (i) $f(x) = 3x + |2x| = \begin{cases} 5x\ ; x \ge 0 \\ x\ ; x < 0 \end{cases}$

LHD at $x = 0$ is 1

RHD at $x = 0$ is 5

$\therefore$ $f(x)$ is strictly increasing at $x = 0$

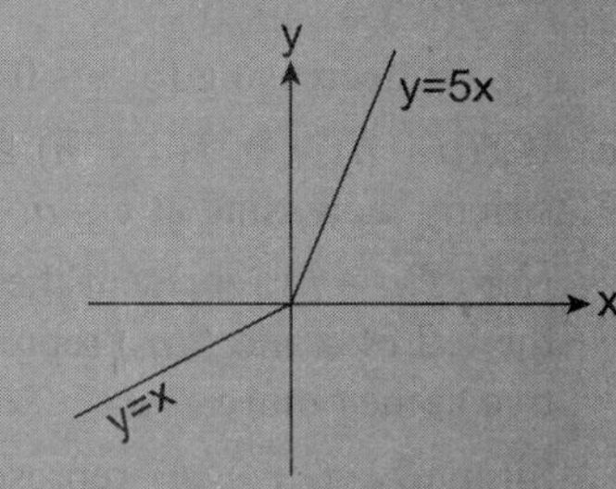

FIGURE 5.52

(ii) LHD at $x = 0$ i.e., $f'(0^-) = 0$

But $f'(0 - h) = 12\,(-h)^2 > 0$

And RHD at $x = 0$ i.e., $f'(0^+) = 7$

$\therefore$ $f(x)$ is strictly increasing at $x = 0$

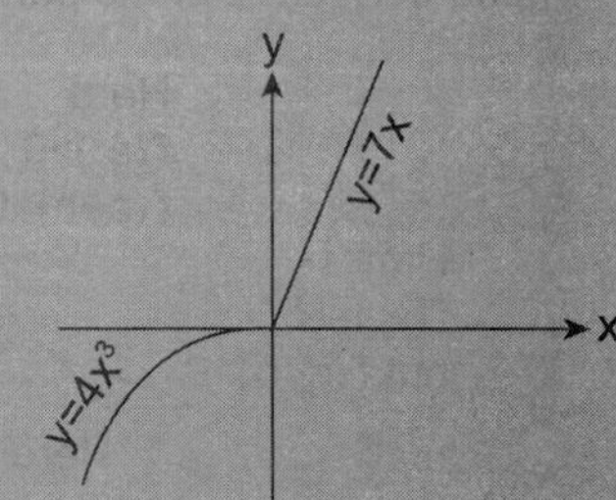

FIGURE 5.53

(iii) LHD at $x = 0$ i.e., $f'(0^-) > 0$

RHD at $x = 0$

i.e., $f'(0^+) > 0$

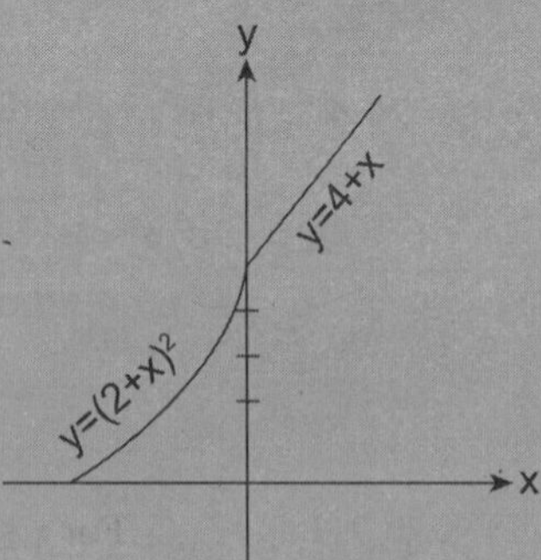

FIGURE 5.54

$\therefore$ $f(x)$ is strictly increasing at $x = 0$

■ NON-DIFFERENTIABLE AND DISCONTINUOUS FUNCTION AT $x = a$

Given $f(x)$ is discontinuous function, not differentiable at $'a'$ but derivative of $f(x)$ exists in neighbourhood of $x = a$

- ❑ $f(a^-) \le f(a) \le f(a^+)$ and $f'(a-h), f'(a+h) > 0$

$\Rightarrow f$ is strictly increasing ($\uparrow$) at $x = 0$

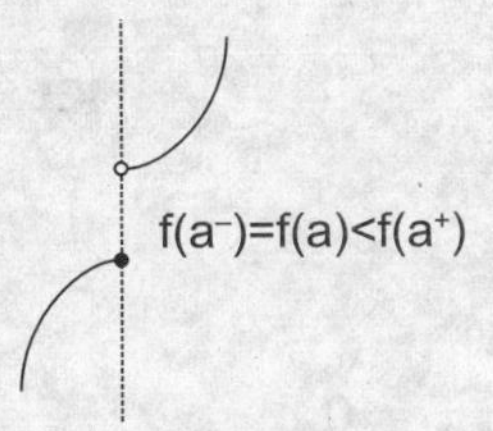

FIGURE 5.55

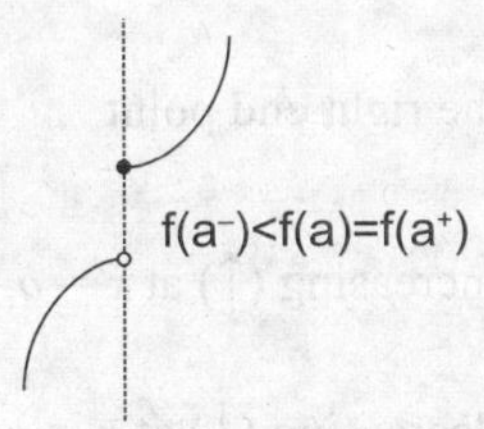

FIGURE 5.56

- ❑ $f(a^-) \ge f(a) \ge f(a^+)$ and $f'(a-h), f'(a+h) < 0$

$\Rightarrow f$ is strictly decreasing ($\downarrow$) at $x = 0$

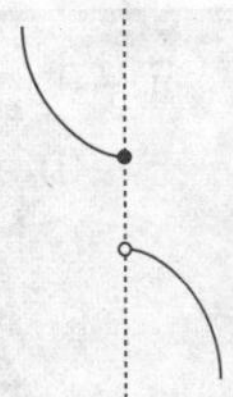

FIGURE 5.57

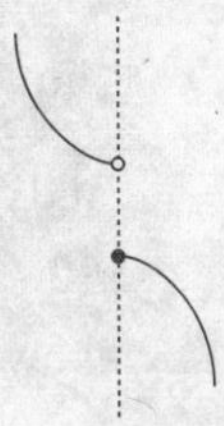

FIGURE 5.58

- ❑ $f(x)$ can be monotonic at $x = a$, even if derivative of $f(x)$ changes its sign across $x = a$ provided basic definition of monotonicity is satisfied.

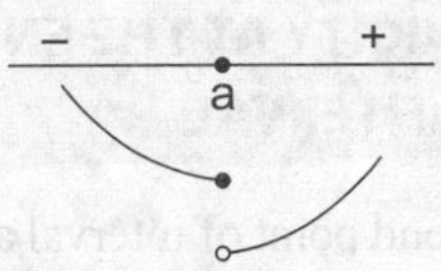

FIGURE 5.59

$f'(a-h) < 0$ and $f'(a+h) > 0$

$f(a-h) > f(a) > f(a+h)$

$\therefore$ at $x = a$; $f(x)$ is strictly decreasing.

ILLUSTRATION 6: Test the monotonicity of following functions at $x = 0$.

(i) $f(x) = \begin{cases} 4 - x^2; & x < 0 \\ 2x + 1; & x \ge 0 \end{cases}$ (ii) $f(x) = \begin{cases} 3 + x^2 e^{-x} & ; x < 0 \\ 2 & ; x = 0 \\ 1 - 2x^2 & ; x > 0 \end{cases}$

(iii) $f(x) = \begin{cases} x^3 + x^2 + 5x; & x < 0 \\ 1 - xe^x; & x \ge 0 \end{cases}$

SOLUTION: (i) $f(0-h) = 4 - (0-h)^2 = 4 - h^2$

$\lim_{h\to 0} f(0-h) = 4$

$f(0) = 1$

$f(0+h) = 2h + 1 > 1$

Now $f(0+h) > f(0)$ and $f(0-h) > f(0)$

$\therefore$ $f(x)$ is neither increasing nor decreasing at $x = 0$ i.e., non-monotonic

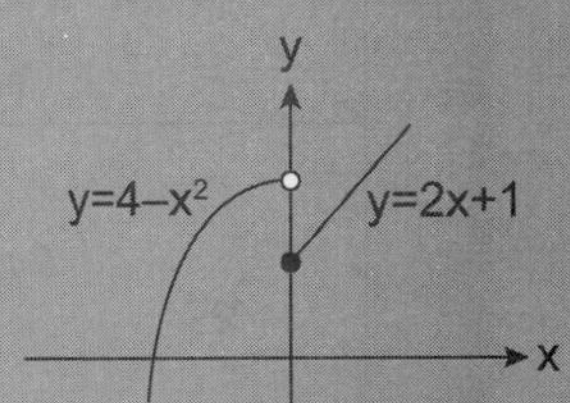

FIGURE 5.60

(ii) $f(0 - h) > 3$

$f(0) = 2$

$f(0 + h) < 1$

Now $f(0 - h) > f(0) > f(0 + h)$

$\therefore$ $f(x)$ is strictly decreasing at $x = 0$

(iii) $\lim\limits_{x \to 0^-} f(x) = \lim\limits_{x \to 0^-} \left(x^3 + x^2 + 5x\right) = 0$

$\lim\limits_{x \to 0^+} f(x) = \lim\limits_{x \to 0^+} (1 - xe^x) = 1$

and $f(0) = 1$

$\therefore$ $f(0 - h) < f(0)$

Now $f(0 + h) = 1 - he^h < 1$

$\Rightarrow$ $f(0 - h) < f(0)$ and $f(0) > f(0 + h)$

$\therefore$ $f(x)$ is neither increasing nor decreasing at $x = 0$

$\Rightarrow$ non-monotonic

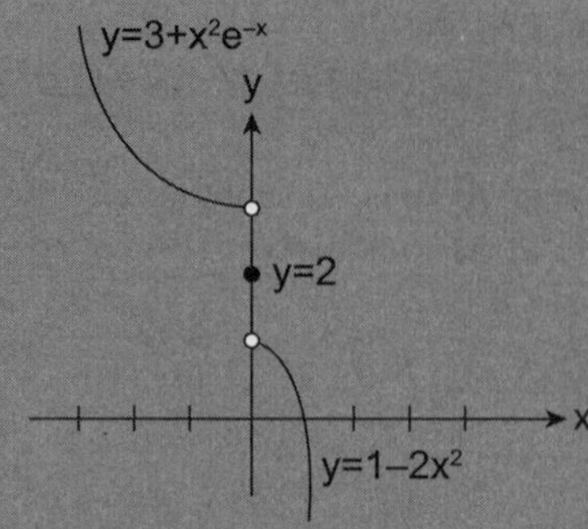

FIGURE 5.61

■ MONOTONICITY AT THE END POINT OF INTERVAL

Given $x = a$ be the end point of interval and $f(x)$ be function, differentiable at $x = a$

❑ If $x = a$ be the left end point

(i) $f'(a^+) > 0$
$\Rightarrow$ f is strictly increasing (↑) at $x = a$.

(ii) $f'(a^+) < 0$
$\Rightarrow$ f is strictly decreasing (↓) at $x = a$.

(iii) $f'(a^+) = 0, f'(a + h) > 0$
$\Rightarrow$ f is strictly increasing (↑) at $x = a$.

(iv) $f'(a^+) = 0, f'(a + h) < 0$
$\Rightarrow$ f is strictly decreasing (↓) at $x = a$.

(v) $f'(a^+) = 0$ and $f'(a + h) = 0$
$\Rightarrow$ f is constant at $x = a$

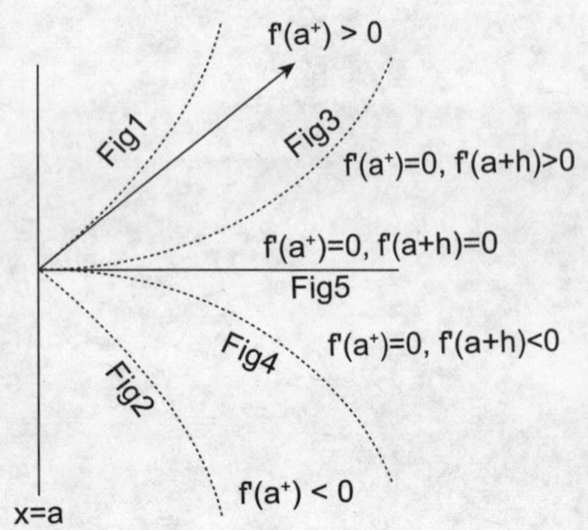

FIGURE 5.62

❑ If $x = a$ be the right end point

(i) $f'(a^-) > 0$
$\Rightarrow$ f is strictly increasing (↑) at $x = a$.

(ii) $f'(a^-) < 0$
$\Rightarrow$ f is strictly decreasing (↓) at $x = a$.

(iii) $f'(a^-) = 0, f'(a - h) > 0$
$\Rightarrow$ f is strictly increasing (↑) at $x = a$.

(iv) $f'(a^-) = 0, f'(a - h) < 0$
$\Rightarrow$ f is strictly decreasing (↓) at $x = a$.

(v) $f'(a^-) = 0$ and $f'(a - h) = 0$
$\Rightarrow$ f is constant at $x = a$

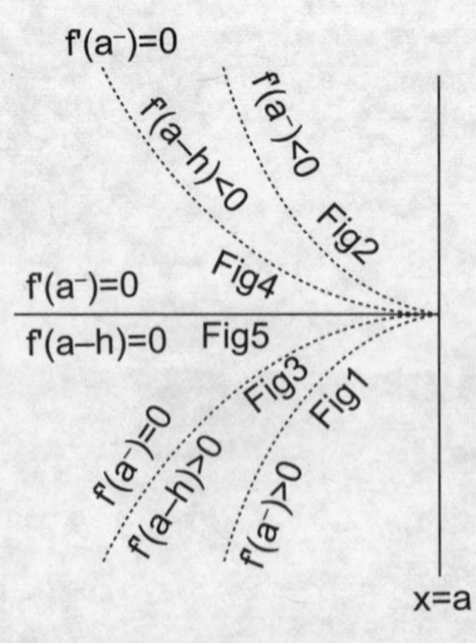

FIGURE 5.63

❑ For function discontinuous at $x = a$ we refer to basic definition of monotonicity.

ILLUSTRATION 7: Test the monotonicity of the function $f(x)$ at $x = -3, 0, 1$; $f(x)=\begin{cases} x^2+3x; & -3\le x<0 \\ \sin^{-1}x; & 0\le x\le 1\end{cases}$

SOLUTION: $f'(x)=\begin{cases} 2x+3 & ;-3\le x<0 \\ \dfrac{1}{\sqrt{1-x^2}} & ;0<x\le 1\end{cases}$

At $x = -3; f'(x) = -3 < 0$

$\therefore$ strictly decreasing at $x = 3$

At $x = 0$; LHL = 0; RHL = 0 $\therefore$ $f(x)$ is continuous

LHD = 3; RHD = 0 $\therefore$ $f(x)$ is non-differentiable

Also $f(0 - h) = h^2 - 3h = h(h - 3) < 0$

$f(0) = 0, f(0 + h) = \sin^{-1}h > 0$

$\Rightarrow f(0 - h) < f(0) < f(0 + h)$ $\therefore$ $f(x)$ is strictly increasing at $x = 0$

At $x = 1; f'(1 - h) > 0$ $\therefore$ strictly increasing at $x = 1$

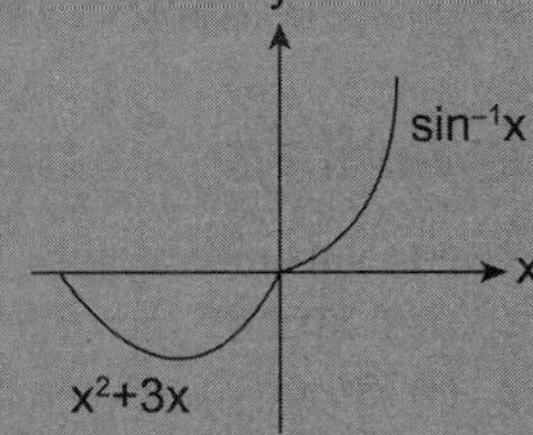

FIGURE 5.64

■ CONCLUSION

1. So we conclude that sign of derivative $f'(x)$ in the neighborhood of the point is sufficient to determine the monotonicity of continuous function $f(x)$ at $x = a$. But for discontinuous functions sign of derivative in the neighborhood of the function concerned is not adequate to decide the monotonicity of function.
2. If a function is monotonic at $x = a$ it cannot have extremum point at $x = a$ and vice versa i.e., A point on the curve can not simultaneously be an extremum as well as monotonic point.

TEXTUAL EXERCISE–1: (SUBJECTIVE)

1. For each of the following graph comment whether $f(x)$ is increasing or decreasing or neither increasing nor decreasing at $x = a$.

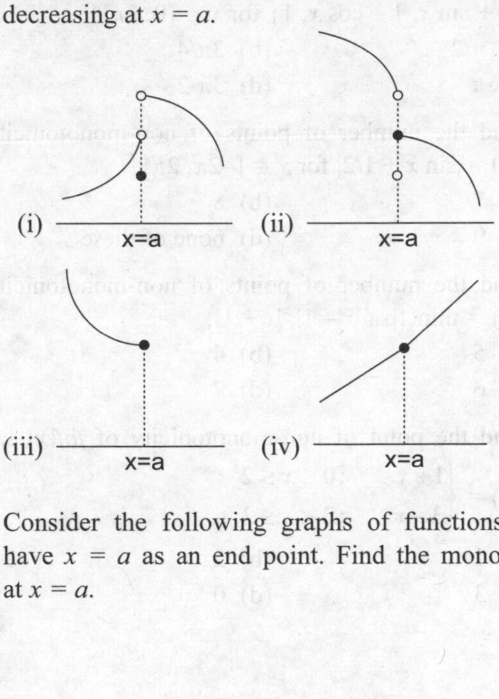

2. Consider the following graphs of functions which have $x = a$ as an end point. Find the monotonicity at $x = a$.

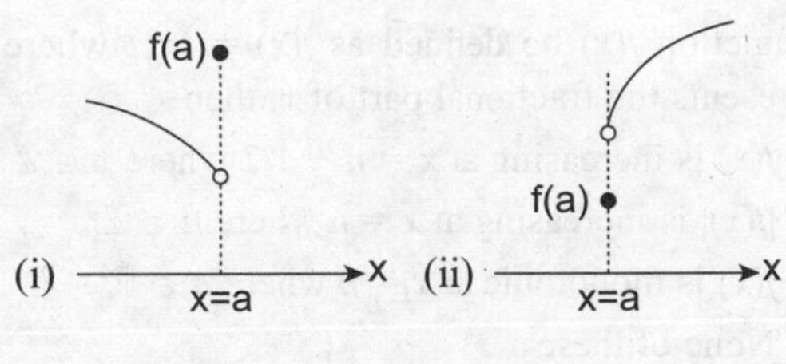

3. Let $f(x) = x^3 - 3x^2 + 3x + 4$. Comment on the monotonic behavior of $f(x)$ at
   (i) $x = 0$
   (ii) $x = 1$
4. Find the monotonicity of the following functions at indicated points:
   (a) $y=(x-2)^5(2x+1)^4$ at $x=0,2$
   (b) $y=x-e^x$ at $x=\dfrac{1}{2}$
   (c) $y=\dfrac{x}{\ln x}$ at $x=\dfrac{1}{e}$, 1, e, e^2

5. Draw the graph of function $f(x)=\begin{cases} x & 0\le x<1 \\ [x] & 1\le x\le 2 \end{cases}$. Comment on the monotonic behavior of $f(x)$ at $x = 0$, 1 and 2.

6. Test the behavior of $f(x) = x\{x\}$ at $x = 0$, where $\{.\}$ represents fractional part function.

Answer Keys

1. (i) Non-monotonic (ii) Strictly decreasing (iii) Strictly decreasing (iv) Strictly increasing
2. (i) Strictly increasing (ii) Strictly increasing
3. (i) Strictly increasing (ii) Strictly increasing
4. (a) Strictly decreasing at $x = 0$, Strictly increasing at $x = 2$ (b) Strictly decreasing (c) Strictly decreasing at $x = 1/e$; non-defined at $x = 1$; non-monotonic at $x = e$, Strictly increasing at $x = e^2$
5. Strictly increasing at $x = 0$, non-decreasing at $x = 1$, $x = 2$.
6. Strictly increasing at $x = 0$

TEXTUAL EXERCISE–1: (OBJECTIVE)

1. Find the possible set of values of k, for which the function $f(x)=\begin{cases} x+1 & ;x<1 \\ k & ;x=1 \\ x^2+x+3 & ;x>1 \end{cases}$ is strictly increasing at $x = 1$
   (a) [1,3] (b) [2,5]
   (c) [1,2] (d) none of these

2. If function $f(x)$ be defined as $f(x) = \{x\}$; where $\{x\}$ represents the fractional part of x; then
   (a) $f(x)$ is increasing at $x = n + 1/2$ where $x \in \mathbb{Z}$
   (b) $|f(x)|$ is increasing at $x = n$ where $n \in \mathbb{Z}$
   (c) $f(x)$ is monotonic at $x = n$ where $n \in \mathbb{R} \sim \mathbb{Z}$
   (d) None of these

3. The number of points in $[0, 2\pi]$ where the function $f(x) = \max\{\sin x, \cos 2x\}$ is non-monotonic is
   (a) 4 (b) 3
   (c) 5 (d) none of these

4. Let function $f(x)$ be defined by $f(x)=\begin{cases} 2x+1 & x\le 1 \\ -x^2+4 & x>1 \end{cases}$.
   Then find the number of points where the function $g(x)$ is non-monotonic, when
   (i) $g(x) = f(x)$
   (a) 1 (b) 2
   (c) 3 (d) 4
   (ii) $g(x) = f(|x|)$
   (a) 1 (b) 2
   (c) 3 (d) 4
   (iii) $g(x) = |f(x)|$
   (a) 2 (b) 3
   (c) 4 (d) 5
   (iv) $g(x) = |f(|x|)|$
   (a) 2 (b) 3
   (c) 4 (d) 5

5. Find the points of non-monotonicity of $f(x) = \max\{1 + \sin x, 1 - \cos x, 1\}$ for $x \in [0, 2\pi]$
   (a) $\pi/2$ (b) $3\pi/4$
   (c) π (d) $3\pi/2$

6. Find the number of points of non-monotonicity of $f(x) = |\sin x + 1/2|$ for $x \in [-2\pi, 2\pi]$
   (a) 7 (b) 8
   (c) 9 (d) none of these

7. Find the number of points of non-monotonicity of $f(x) = \min\{|x|, |x - 1|, |x + 1|\}$
   (a) 5 (b) 4
   (c) 6 (d) 7

8. Find the point of non-monotonicity of $fof(x)$ where $f(x)=\begin{cases} 1+x & ;0\le x\le 2 \\ 3-x & ;2<x\le 3 \end{cases}$
   (a) 1 (b) 2
   (c) 3 (d) 0

9. In the previous question; which of the following statements(s) is/are correct:

(a) $f(f(x))$ is non-monotonic at $x = 1$

(b) $f(f(x))$ is strictly increasing at $x = 0$

(c) $f(f(x))$ is strictly increasing at $x = 2$

(d) $f(f(x))$ is decreasing (but non strictly decreasing) at $x = 3$

10. Let $x_i \ \forall\ i \in \mathbb{N}$ be the values of x for which the function $f(x) = \max\ \{x^2, (1 - x)^2, 2x\ (1 - x)\}$ is non-monotonic; then find $\sum x_i$

(a) 2 (b) –3/2

(c) 1 (d) none of these

Answer Keys

1. (b) **2.** (a, c) **3.** (c) **4.** (i) (a) (ii) (c) (iii) (b) (iv) (d) **5.** (a,b,c) **6.** (b) **7.** (a)

8. (b) **9.** (a, b) **10.** (b)

■ MONOTONIC FUNCTIONS

Functions are said to be monotonic if they are either increasing or decreasing i.e., monotonic in their entire domain.

Monotonicity Over an Interval

A function $y = f(x)$ is called monotonic over its domain (D_f) iff $f(x)$ satisfies any one of the following four conditions.

(i) $f(x)$ is strictly increasing $\forall\ x \in D_f$

i.e., $x_2 > x_1 \Leftrightarrow f(x_2) > f(x_1)\ \forall\ x_1, x_2 \in D_f$

Also known as monotonically/steadily increasing function.

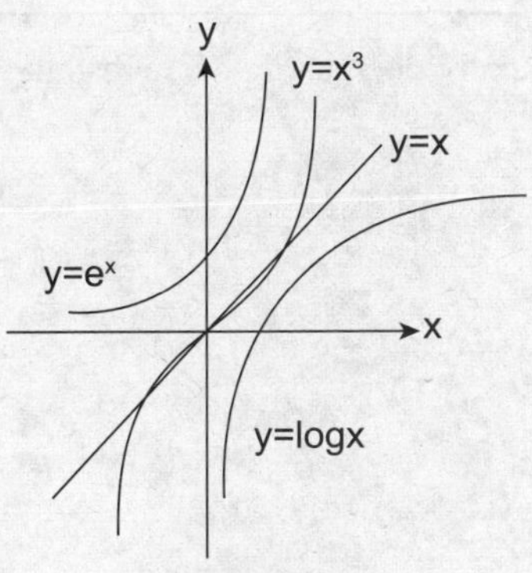

FIGURE 5.65

(ii) $f(x)$ is strictly decreasing $\forall\ x \in D_f$

i.e., $x_2 > x_1 \Leftrightarrow f(x_2) < f(x_1)\ \forall\ x_1, x_2 \in D_f$

Also known as monotonically/steadily decreasing function.

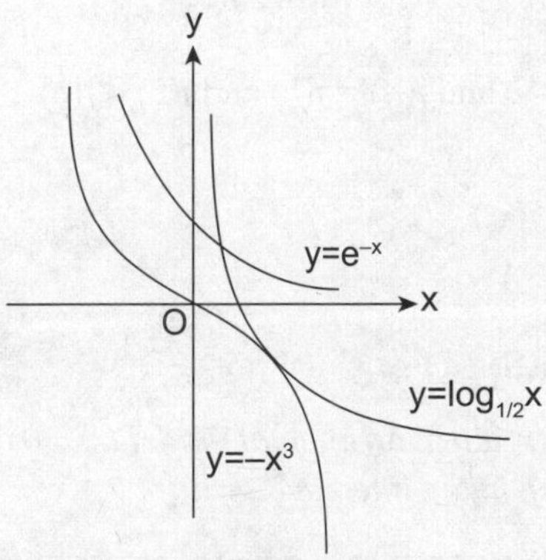

FIGURE 5.66

(iii) $f(x)$ is non-decreasing $\forall\ x \in D_f$

i.e., $x_1 < x_2 \Leftrightarrow f(x_1) \le f(x_2)\ \forall\ x_1, x_2 \in D_f$

e.g. $f(x) = [x]$

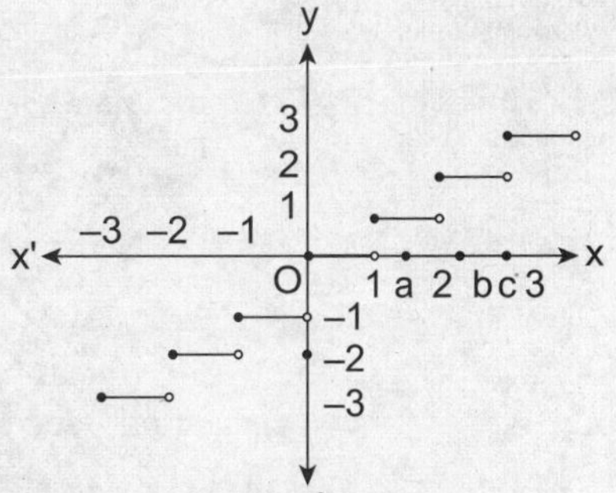

FIGURE 5.67

$a < b < c$

we have, $f(a) < f(b)$ and $f(b) = f(c)$

$\therefore\ x_1 < x_2 \Rightarrow f(x_1) \le f(x_2)$

(iv) $f(x)$ is non-increasing $\forall\ x \in D_f$

i.e., $x_2 > x_1 \Leftrightarrow f(x_2) \le f(x_1)\ \forall\ x_1, x_2 \in D_f$

e.g. $f(x) = -[x]$

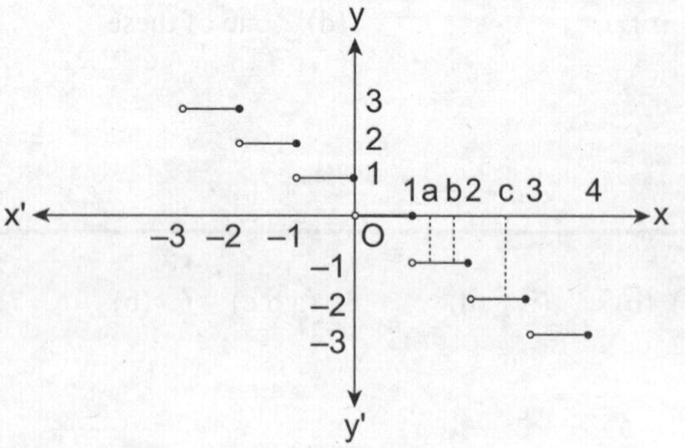

FIGURE 5.68

$a < b < c$ and $f(a) = f(b)$ and $f(b) < f(c)$

$\therefore\ x_1 < x_2$

$\Rightarrow\ f(x_1) \ge f(x_2)$

Monotonicity of Differentiable Functions in an Interval

If for a differentiable function in some interval $\underbrace{x+h-x>0}_{dx>0} \Leftrightarrow \underbrace{f(x+h)-f(x)>0}_{dy>0}$

$\Rightarrow \lim\limits_{h\to 0}\dfrac{f(x+h)-f(x)}{h} > 0 \Leftrightarrow f'(x) > 0$, then f is said to be monotonically (strictly) increasing in that interval. And hence the ratio $\lim\limits_{h\to 0^+} h\sin\dfrac{1}{h} = 0 = \dfrac{f(x+h)-f(x)}{h} > 0$ for increasing function and its limit for $h \to 0$.

i.e., $\lim\limits_{h\to 0}\dfrac{f(x+h)-f(x)}{h} = f'(x) = \dfrac{dy}{dx}$.

Hence $\dfrac{dy}{dx} > 0$ in some interval then y is said to be an increasing function of x in that interval. Similarly if $\dfrac{dy}{dx} < 0$ then y is decreasing in that interval.

REMARKS:

(a) Thus f'(x) ≥ 0 in an interval I with f'(x) = 0 on one or more subintervals of I, then f(x) is said to be a non-decreasing function in the interval I.

(b) But, if f'(x) vanishes at a finite/infinite number of isolated points, provided it be elsewhere uniformly positive, then f(x) will strictly increase.

ILLUSTRATION 8: Find whether the following functions are monotonically decreasing or increasing in the indicated intervals.

(a) $f(x) = x - \tan x$ in $\left(-\dfrac{\pi}{2}, \dfrac{\pi}{2}\right)$ (b) $f(x) = x + \sin x\ \forall x \in \mathbb{R}$

SOLUTION: (a) $f'(x) = 1 - \sec^2 x \le 0\ \left(\dfrac{-\pi}{2}, \dfrac{\pi}{2}\right)$ and $f'(x) = 0$ at $x = 0$ only.

$\Rightarrow f(x)$ is strictly decreasing in $\left(\dfrac{-\pi}{2}, \dfrac{\pi}{2}\right)$

(b) $f(x) = x + \sin x;\ x \in \mathbb{R}$

$\Rightarrow f'(x) = 1 + \cos x = 2\cos^2\dfrac{x}{2} \ge 0\ \forall\ x \in \mathbb{R}$ and $f'(x) = 0$ at $x = (2n+1)\dfrac{\pi}{2}$

$\Rightarrow f(x)$ is strictly increasing $x \in \mathbb{R}$

ILLUSTRATION 9: The length of a longest interval in which the function $f(x) = 3\sin x - 4\sin^3 x$ is increasing, is

(a) $\pi/2$ (b) $\pi/2$

(c) $3\pi/2$ (d) π

SOLUTION: Let $f(x) = 3\sin x - 4\sin^3 x = \sin 3x$ $\Rightarrow f'(x) = 3\cos 3x \geq 0$ for $3x \in \left[2n\pi \frac{-\pi}{2}, 2x\pi + \frac{\pi}{2}\right]$

Thus the longest interval in which sin 3x is increasing, is of length π.

So, the length of largest interval in which $f(x) = \sin 3x$ is increasing, is $\frac{\pi}{3}$.

ILLUSTRATION 10: Find the intervals of monotonocity for the following functions and represent your solution set on the number line.

(a) $f(x) = 2.e^{x^2-4x}$ (b) $f(x) = x^2 e^{-x}$

Also plot the graphs in each case and state their range.

SOLUTION: (a) $f(x) = 2e^{x^2-4x}$

$\Rightarrow$ $f'(x) = 2e^{x^2-4x}(2x-4) = 4e^{x^2-4x}(x-2)$

$\because$ $4e^{x^2-4x} > 0 \ \forall \ x \in \mathbb{R}$

so sign of $f'(x)$ depends only $x - 2$

Now, $f'(x) > 0$ when $x \in (2, \infty)$.

so $f(x)$ is $\uparrow$ on $(2, \infty)$

And $f'(x) < 0$ when $x \in (-\infty, 2)$

so $f(x) \downarrow$ on $(-\infty, 2)$

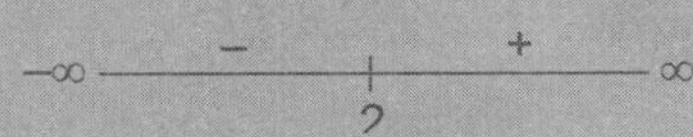

FIGURE 5.69

(b) $f(x) = x^2 e^{-x}$

$f'(x) = -e^{-x}x(x-2)$ $[e^{-x} > 0 \ \forall \ x \in R]$

So, by wavy curve of $f'(x)$

$f'(x) > 0$ when $x \in (0, 2)$ i.e., $f(x) \uparrow$ on $(0, 2)$

and $f'(x) < 0$ when $x \in (-\infty, 0) \cup (2, \infty)$

so $f(x) \downarrow$ on $(-\infty\ 0) \cup (2, \infty)$

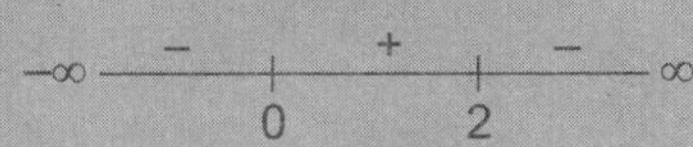

FIGURE 5.70

ILLUSTRATION 11: Find the intervals of monotonocity of the functions in $[0, 2\pi]$

(a) $f(x) = \sin x - \cos x$ (b) $f(x) = \dfrac{4\sin x - 2x - x\cos x}{2 + \cos x}$

SOLUTION: (a) $f(x) = \sin x - \cos x;\ x \in [0, 2\pi]$

$\Rightarrow f'(x) = \sin x + \cos x = \sqrt{2}\sin(x + \pi/4)$

$\because$ $0 \leq x \leq 2\pi$

$\pi/4 \leq x + \pi/4 \leq 9\pi/4$

Now, if $0 < x + \pi/4 < \pi$, then $f'(x) > 0$

$\Rightarrow$ if $-\pi/4 < x < 3\pi/4$ then $f'(x) > 0$

$\Rightarrow$ if $x \in (7\pi/4\ 2\pi] \cup [0, 3\pi/4)$ then $f'(x) > 0$

so $f(x) \uparrow$ on $[0, 3\pi/4) \cup (7\pi/4, 2\pi]$

and if $\pi < x + \pi/4 < 2\pi;\ f'(x) < 0$

$\Rightarrow$ if $3\pi/4 < x < 7\pi/4;\ f'(x) < 0$

so $f(x) \downarrow$ on $(3\pi/4, 7\pi/4)$

(b) $f(x) = \dfrac{4\sin x - 2x - x\cos x}{2+\cos x}$; $x \in [0, 2\pi]$ $\Rightarrow f'(x) = \dfrac{\cos x(4-\cos x)}{(2+\cos x)^2}$

$\because$ $4 - \cos x > 0 \ \forall\ x \in R$ $\quad$ $(2 + \cos x)^2 > 0 \ \forall\ x \in \mathbb{R}$

so sign of $f'(x)$ depend on cos x only $\quad$ $f'(x) > 0$ for $x \in [0, \pi/2) \cup (3\pi/2, 2\pi]$

$f'(x) < 0$ for $x \in (\pi/2, 3\pi/2)$ $\quad$ so $f(x) \uparrow$ on $[0, \pi/2) \cup (3\pi/2, 2\pi]$

and $f(x) \downarrow$ on $(\pi/2, 3\pi/2)$

ILLUSTRATION 12: Find the values of 'a' for which the function $f(x) = \sin x - a \sin 2x - \dfrac{1}{3}\sin 3x + 2ax$ increases throughout the number line.

SOLUTION: $f(x) = \sin x - a \sin 2x - \dfrac{1}{3} \sin 3x + 2ax.$

Now $f'(x) \geq 0$

$\Rightarrow \cos x - 2a \cos 2x - \cos 3x + 2a \geq 0$ $\quad$ $\Rightarrow \cos x - \cos 3x - 2a \cos 2x + 2a \geq 0$

$\Rightarrow 4 \cos x \sin^2 x + 4a \sin^2 x \geq 0$ $\quad$ $\Rightarrow 4 \sin^2 x (\cos x + a) \geq 0$

$\Rightarrow \cos x + a \geq 0 \ \forall\ x \in \mathbb{R}$ $\quad$ $\Rightarrow a \geq 1$

ILLUSTRATION 13: Find the set of values of 'a' for which the function, $f(x) = \left(1 - \dfrac{\sqrt{21-4a-a^2}}{a+1}\right)x^3 + 5x + \sqrt{7}$ is increasing at every point of its domain.

SOLUTION: $f(x) = \left(1 - \dfrac{\sqrt{21-4a-a^2}}{a+1}\right)x^3 + 5x + \sqrt{7}$

Given that $f(x)$ increases $\forall\ x \in R$, therefore $f'(x) > 0$

$\Rightarrow \left(1 - \dfrac{\sqrt{21-4a-a^2}}{a+1}\right) 3x^2 + 5 > 0 \ \forall\ x \in \mathbb{R}$

$\because$ $(ax^2 + bx + c > 0$, then $D < 0)$

$\Rightarrow 0^2 - 4 \times 3 \left(1 - \dfrac{\sqrt{21-4a-a^2}}{a+1}\right) 5 < 0$

$\Rightarrow 1 - \dfrac{\sqrt{21-4a-a^2}}{a+1} \geq 0$ ...(i)

(i) holds in the following cases

Case I: If $a + 1 < 0$ and $21 - 4a - a^2 \geq 0$

$\Rightarrow a < -1$ and $(a + 7)(a - 3) \leq 0$

$\Rightarrow a < -1$ and $-7 \leq a \leq 3$

$\Rightarrow a \in [-7, -1)$ ...(ii)

Case II: if $a + 1 > 0$ $\quad$ $\Rightarrow a \in (-1, \infty)$

$\Rightarrow 21 - 4a - a^2 \geq 0$ and $\dfrac{\sqrt{21-4a-a^2}}{a+1} \leq 1$

$\Rightarrow (a + 7)(a - 3) \leq 0$ and $(a + 1)^2 \geq (21 - 4a - a^2)$

$\Rightarrow -7 \leq a \leq 3$ and $a^2 + 3a - 10 \geq 0$

$\Rightarrow\ a \le -5$ or $a \ge 2$ and $a \in [-7, 3]$

$\Rightarrow\ a \in [2, 3]$ .... (iii)

From (ii) and (iii), we get $a \in [-7, -1) \cup [2, 3]$

ILLUSTRATION 14: If $f(x) = 2e^x - ae^{-x} + (2a + 1)x - 3$ monotonically increases for every $x \in \mathbb{R}$, then find the range of values of 'a'.

SOLUTION: $f(x) = 2e^x - ae^{-x} + (2a + 1)x - 3$

$\because\ f(x)$ increasing for $x \in \mathbb{R}$

$\Rightarrow\ f'(x) \ge 0\ \forall\ x \in \mathbb{R}$

$\Rightarrow\ 2e^x + ae^{-x} + (2a + 1) \ge 0$

$\Rightarrow\ 2e^{2x} + a + (2a + 1)\ e^x \ge 0$

$\Rightarrow\ (e^x + a)(2e^x + 1) \ge 0$

$\Rightarrow\ e^x + a \ge 0 \Rightarrow -e^x\ \forall\ x \in \mathbb{R}$ $\quad [\because 2e^x + 1 > 0\ \forall\ x \in \mathbb{R}]$

$\Rightarrow\ a \ge 0$

ILLUSTRATION 15: If $f(x) = xe^{x(1-x)}$, then $f(x)$ is

(a) increasing on $\left(-\frac{1}{2}, 1\right)$

(b) decreasing on $\left[-\frac{1}{2}, 1\right]$

(c) increasing on R

(d) decreasing on R

SOLUTION: Given, $f(x) = xe^{x(1-x)}$

$\Rightarrow\ f'(x) = e^{x(1-x)} + xe^{x(1-x)}(1 - 2x) = e^{x(1-x)}[1 + x(1 - 2x)] = e^{x(1-x)}(1 + x - 2x^2)$

$= -e^{x(1-x)}(2x^2 - x - 1)$

$= -e^{x(1-x)}(x - 1)(2x + 1)$

Which is positive in $\left(-\frac{1}{2}, 1\right)$ and $f(x) \ge 0$ on $\left[-\frac{1}{2}, 1\right]$

Therefore, $f(x)$ is increasing in $\left[-\frac{1}{2}, 1\right]$

ILLUSTRATION 16: If $f(x) = \sin^4 x + \cos^4 x + bx + c$, then find possible values of b and c such that $f(x)$ is monotonic for all $x \in \mathbb{R}$.

SOLUTION: $f(x) = \sin^4 x + \cos^4 x + bx + c$

$f(x) = 4\sin^3 x\cos x - 4\cos^3 x\sin x + b = 4\sin x\cos x(\sin^2 x - \cos^2 x) + b = -\sin 4x + b$

Hence for $f(x)$ to be monotonic $b \in (-\infty, -1] \cup [1, \infty)$ and $c \in \mathbb{R}$

ILLUSTRATION 17: Find possible values of 'a' such that $f(x) = e^{2x} - (a + 1)\ e^x + 2x$ is monotonically increasing for $x \in \mathbb{R}$.

SOLUTION: $f(x) = e^{2x} - (a + 1)e^x + 2x$

$\Rightarrow\ f(x) = 2e^{2x} - (a+1)\ e^x + 2$

Now, $2e^{2x} - (a+1)\ e^x + 2 \ge 0$ $\quad$ for all $x \in \mathbb{R}$

$\Rightarrow\ 2\left(e^x + \frac{1}{e^x}\right) - (a+1) \ge 0$ $\quad$ for all $x \in \mathbb{R}$

$\Rightarrow\ (a+1) \le 2\left(e^x + \frac{1}{e^x}\right)$ $\quad$ for all $x \in \mathbb{R}$

$\Rightarrow\ a + 1 \le 4$ $\quad \left(\because\ e^x + \frac{1}{e^x} \text{ has minimum value 2}\right)$

$\Rightarrow\ a \le 3$

Aliter: $2e^{2x} - (a+1)e^x + 2 \geq 0$ for all $x \in \mathbb{R}$

Putting $e^x = t$; $t \in (0, \infty)$

$2t^2 - (a+1)t + 2 \geq 0$ for all $t \in (0, \infty)$

Case (i): $D \leq 0$

$\Rightarrow (a+1)^2 - (4)^2 \leq 0$

$\Rightarrow (a+5)(a-3) \leq 0$

$\Rightarrow a \in [-5, 3]$

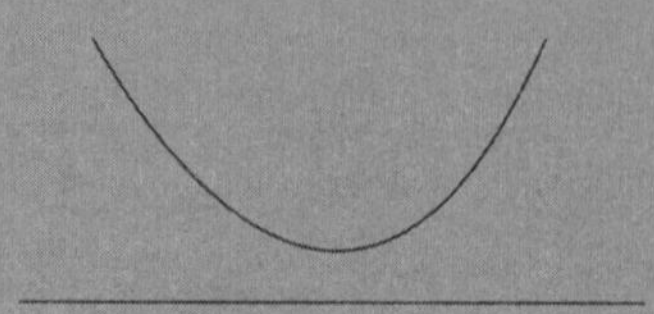

FIGURE 5.71

Or

Case (ii): both roots are non positive $D \geq 0$

and $-\dfrac{b}{2a} < 0$ and $f(0) \geq 0$

$\Rightarrow a \in (-\infty, -5] \cup [3, \infty)$ and $\dfrac{a+1}{4} < 0$ & $2 \geq 0$

$\Rightarrow a \in (-\infty, -5] \cup [3, \infty)$ and $a < -1$ and $a \in R$

$\Rightarrow a \in (-\infty, -5]$

Taking union of (i) and (ii), we get $a \in (-\infty, 3]$

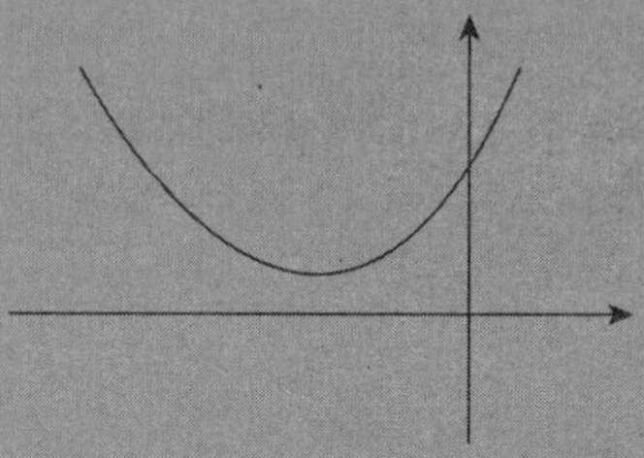

FIGURE 5.72

Monotonicity for Continuous but Non-differentiable Functions in an Interval

Let $f(x)$ is continuous $\forall\ x \in [a,b]$. But not differentiable at finitely many points say a_k; $k = 0, 1, 2, \ldots, n$

$f'(x) > 0\ \forall\ x \in [a,b] \sim \{a_k\}$

$\Rightarrow f(x)$ is strictly increasing (↑)

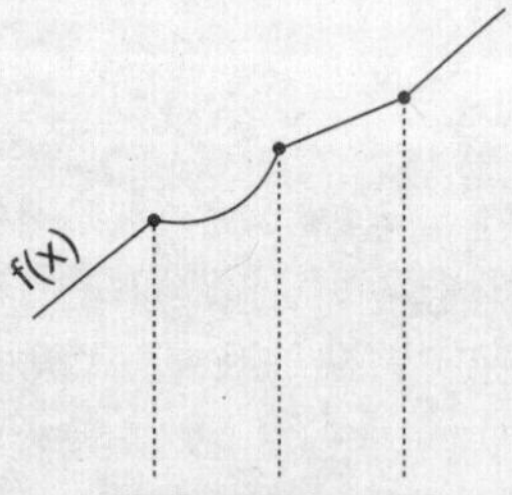

FIGURE 5.73

Clearly, the function is continuous and non-differentiable at $x = a_1, a_2, a_3$ but still the function is strictly increasing at these points.

$f'(x) < 0\ \forall\ x \in [a,b] \sim \{a_k\}$

$\Rightarrow f(x)$ is strictly decreasing (↓)

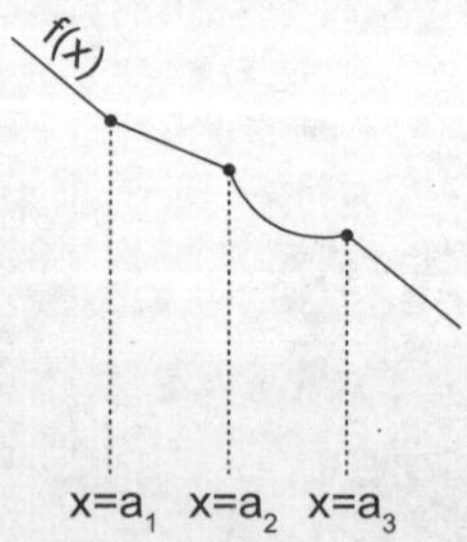

FIGURE 5.74

Clearly, the function is continuous and non-differentiable at $x = a_1, a_2, a_3$ but still the function is strictly decreasing at these points.

ILLUSTRATION 18: Discuss the monotonicity of $f(x) = \begin{cases} 3^x & ; x \leq 1 \\ 4 - x & ; x > 1 \end{cases}$ at $x = 1$

SOLUTION: LHL at $x = 1$; $\lim\limits_{x \to 1^-} f(x) = \lim\limits_{x \to 1^-} \left(3^x\right) = 3$

RHL at $x = 1$; $\lim\limits_{x \to 1^+} f(x) = \lim\limits_{x \to 1^+} (4 - x) = 3$

$f(1) = (3)^1 = 3$

$\therefore$ $f(x)$ is continuous at $x = 1$

$$f'(x) = \begin{cases} 3^x \ell n3 & ; x < 1 \\ -1 & ; x > 1 \end{cases}$$

LHD at $x = 1 = \lim\limits_{x \to 1^-} f'(x) = 3\ell n3$

RHD at $x = 1 = \lim\limits_{x \to 1^+} f'(x) = -1$

Now since $f'(1^-) > 0$ and $f'(1^+) < 0$

$\Rightarrow$ $f(x)$ is non-monotonic at $x = 1$

ILLUSTRATION 19: Let $f(x) = \begin{cases} x^4 - x^3 - x^2 + 3x + 3 & ; x < 0 \\ 3\cos x + x, & ; x \geq 0 \end{cases}$; then check the monotonicity of the function $f(x)$ at $x = 0$

SOLUTION: $f'(x) = \begin{cases} 4x^3 - 3x^2 - 2x + 3 & ; x < 0 \\ -3\sin x + 1 & ; x > 0 \end{cases}$

$\therefore$ $\lim\limits_{x \to 0^-} (f(x)) = \lim\limits_{x \to 0^-} \left(x^4 - x^3 - x^2 + 3x + 3\right) = 3$

and $\lim\limits_{x \to 0^+} (f(x)) = \lim\limits_{x \to 0^+} (3\cos x + x) = 3$

and $f(0) = 3\cos(0) + 0 = 3$

$\therefore$ $f(x)$ is continuous at $x = 0$

Now LHD at $x = 0$ i.e., $f'(0^-) = 3$

RHD at $x = 0$ i.e., $f'(0^+) = -3(\sin 0) + 1 = 1$

Since LHD $\neq$ RHD $\Rightarrow f(x)$ is

non-differentiable at $x = 0$ and since LHD > 0 and RHD > 0

$\Rightarrow$ $f(x)$ is strictly increasing at $x = 0$

Monotonicity for Discontinuous Functions in an Interval

For functions discontinuous at some point a_k in $[a, b]$ monotonicity can't be adequately determined on the basis of sign of derivative, in such cases the basic definition of monotonicity must be followed i.e.,

$$\begin{cases} x_1 > x_2 \Rightarrow f(x_1) > f(x_2) & \text{for strictly } \uparrow \\ x_1 > x_2 \Rightarrow f(x_1) \geq f(x_2) & \text{for non } \downarrow \\ x_1 > x_2 \Rightarrow f(x_1) < f(x_2) & \text{for strictly } \downarrow \\ x_1 > x_2 \Rightarrow f(x_1) \leq f(x_2) & \text{for non } \uparrow \end{cases}$$

ILLUSTRATION 20: Which of the following functions are monotonic in the interval $[a, b]$:

(i)

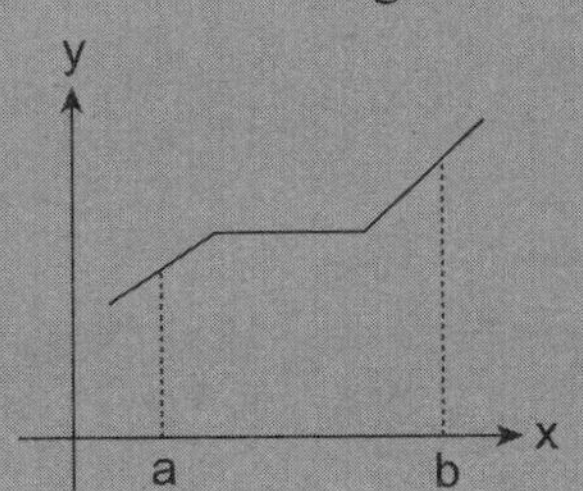

(ii)

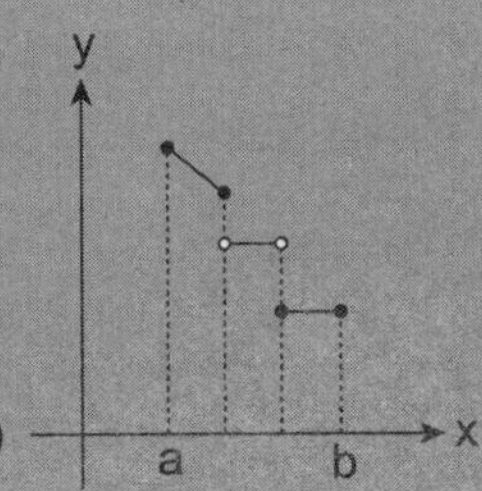

(iii) 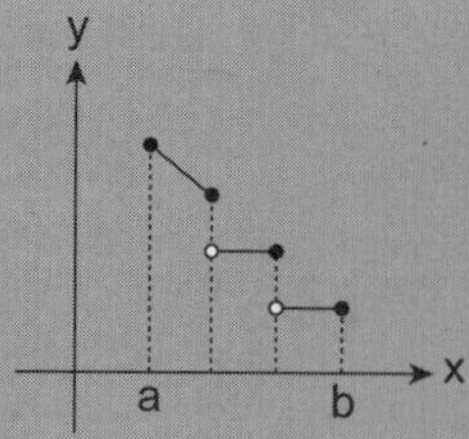

(iv) 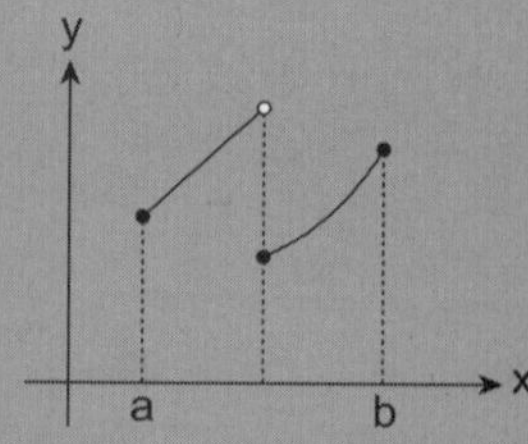

(v) 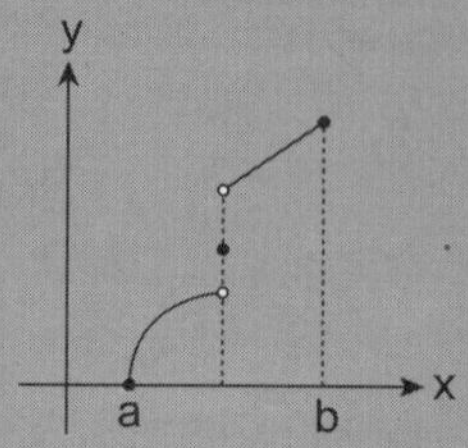

(vi) 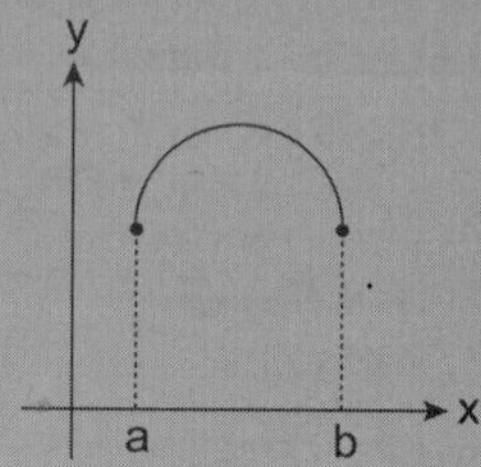

(vii) 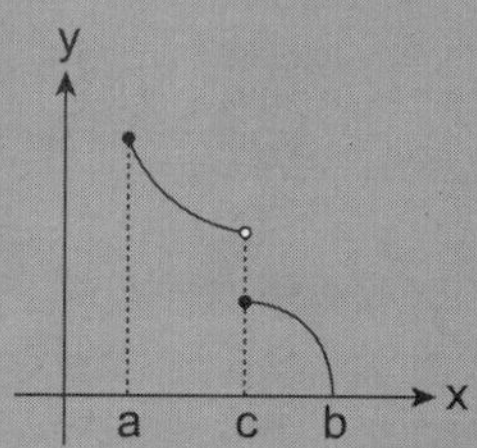

SOLUTION: (i) non-decreasing

(ii) $f(x)$ is a non-increasing function in $[a, b]$

(iii) Monotonic (non-increasing)

(iv) 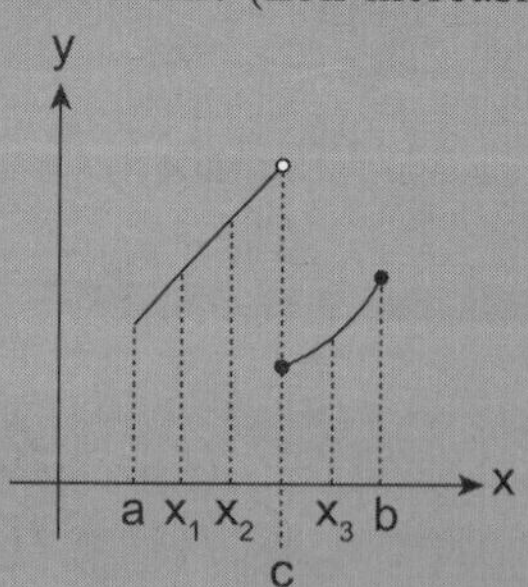

Here, $x_1 < x_2 \Rightarrow f(x_1) < f(x_2)$

and $x_1 < x_3 \Rightarrow f(x_1) > f(x_3)\}$ discrepancy

This can happen only in a discontinuous function.

So, if point, 'c' is not considered, even then also the function can't be called monotonic over $[a, b]$.

(v) Monotonic (strictly increasing)

(vi) non-monotonic

(vii) Strictly decreasing

ILLUSTRATION 21: State which of the following statements are true:

(a) Functions which are increasing as well as decreasing in their domain are said to be non monotonic.

(b) $f(x) = x$- $\sin x$ is monotonically increasing in $(0, 4\pi)$

(c) $f(x) = ax^2 + bx + c$ $(a \neq 0)$ is monotonically increasing in its domain.

(d) $f(x) = |x|$, is non-monotonic in its domain.

(e) $f(x) = \sin x$ is strictly increasing in the interval $\left[0, \frac{\pi}{2}\right]$.

SOLUTION: (a) True (b) True (c) False (d) True (e) True

ILLUSTRATION 22: Find the largest possible real value of k for which the function $f(x) = x^2 - 3kx + 2$ is monotonically increasing $\forall x \in [-3, 9]$.

SOLUTION: $f'(x) \geq 0 \quad \forall x \in [-3, 9]$

$\Rightarrow 2x - 3k \geq 0 \ \forall x \in [-3, 9]$ $\quad \Rightarrow 3k \leq 2x \ \forall x \in [-3, 9]$

And $2x \in [-6, 18]$

But $3k \leq (2x)_{min} = -6$ $\quad \Rightarrow k \leq -2$

$k \in (-\infty, -2]$ and $k_{max} = -2$

ILLUSTRATION 23: Find the range of possible real values of k for which the function $f(x) = x^3 - 2kx^2 + 4x + 2$ is monotonically increasing $\forall x \in \mathbb{R}$.

SOLUTION: $f'(x) = 3x^2 - 4xk + 4 \geq 0 \ \forall x \in \mathbb{R}$

$\Rightarrow D \leq 0$ $\quad \Rightarrow 16k^2 - 48 \leq 0$

$\Rightarrow k^2 \leq 3$ $\quad k \in \left[-\sqrt{3}, \sqrt{3}\right]$

ILLUSTRATION 24: Find the Range of possible real values of b for which the function $f(x) = 2bx - 3\sin x + c$ is monotonically increasing $\forall x \in \mathbb{R}$.

SOLUTION: $2b - 3\cos x \geq 0$

$2b \geq 3\cos x$

$b \geq 3/2$

$b \in \left[\frac{3}{2}, \infty\right)$

TEXTUAL EXERCISE–2: (SUBJECTIVE)

1. Which of the following statements is true/false?
   (a) The function $y = 1 + 3(\log \sin x + \log \operatorname{cosec} x)$ is non-monotonic on $(0, \pi)$
   (b) The function $y = 1 + 3(\log \sin x + \log \operatorname{cosec} x)$ is Monotonic on $(0, \pi)$
   (c) The function $y = \begin{cases} \frac{|\cos x|}{\cos x} & ; \frac{\pi}{2} \neq 0 \\ 0 & ; \frac{\pi}{2} = 0 \end{cases}$ is decreasing for $[0, \pi]$
   (d) The function
   $y = \begin{cases} 1 + 3(\log|\sin x| + log|\cos ecx|, x \neq 0 \\ 0 & , x = 0 \end{cases}$
   is monotonic for $[0, \pi/2]$
   (e) The function $y = \sin^{-1}\left(\frac{2x}{1+x^2}\right)$ is monotonic in $[-1, 1]$
   (f) The function $y = \sin^{-1}\left(\frac{1+x^2}{2x}\right)$ is strictly increasing in its domain
   (g) The function $y = e^{[x]}$, where [.] denotes the greatest integer function is monotonic on $[0, \pi]$

2. Match the functions in Column-I to the intervals of monotocity in Column-II

Column-I	Column-II
(a) $\sin^{-1}(\sin x)$	(i) $[0, \pi]$
(b) $\cos^{-1}(\cos x)$	(ii) $[0, \pi] \sim \{\pi/2\}$
(c) $\tan^{-1}(\tan x)$	(iii) $[-\pi/2, \pi/2] \sim \{0\}$

(d) cosec^{-1} (cosecx) (iv) $(-\pi/2, \pi/2)$
(e) $\sec^{-1}$ (secx) (v) $[\pi/2, 3\pi/2] \sim \{\pi\}$
(f) $\cot^{-1}$ (cotx) (vi) $(0,\pi)$

3. Test whether the following functions are monotonically increasing/decreasing
(a) $\log(3x^3 + 2) + e^{2x-1}$ (b) $\log(x - \sin x) + e^{x + \sin x}$
(c) $e^{2x-1} - e^{1-2x}$

4. For what values of m does the function $f(x) = (m + 2)x^3 - 3mx^2 + 9mx - 1$ strictly decreases for all x.

5. If $f(x) = \left(\dfrac{a^2-1}{3}\right)x^3 + (a-1)x^2 + 2x + 1$ is monotonic increasing for every $x \in \mathbb{R}$, then find the range of values of 'a'.

6. At what values of coefficient a does the function $f(x) = x^3 - ax$ increase along the entire number scale?

7. At what value of b does the function $f(x) = \sin x - bx + c$ decrease along the entire number scale?

Answer Keys

1. (a) F (b) T (c) T (d) T (e) T (f) T (g) T
2. (a) (iii), (iv), (v) (b) (i), (ii), (vi) (c) (iv) (d) (iii), (v) (e) (ii) (f) (vi)
3. (a) increasing (b) increasing (c) increasing
4. $m \in (-\infty, -3]$ 5. $a \in (-\infty, -3] \cup [1, \infty)$ 6. $(-\infty, 0]$ 7. $b \geq 1$

TEXTUAL EXERCISE–2: (OBJECTIVE)

1. The function $f(x) = 2\log(x - 2) - x^2 + 4x + 1$ increases in the interval
(a) $(1, 2)$ (b) $(2, 3)$
(c) $\left(\dfrac{5}{2}, 3\right)$ (d) $(2, 4)$

2. An interval of increases of the function $y = x - 2\sin x$ if $0 \leq x \leq 2\pi$, is
(a) $\left(\dfrac{\pi}{3}, \pi\right)$ (b) $(0,\pi)$
(c) $\left(\dfrac{\pi}{2}, \pi\right)$ (d) $\left(\dfrac{\pi}{3}, \dfrac{5\pi}{3}\right)$

3. The interval of increase of the function $y = x - e^x + \tan\dfrac{\pi}{7}$ is
(a) $(-\infty, -1)$ (b) $(0, \infty)$
(c) $(-\infty, 0)$ (d) $(1, \infty)$

4. $f(x) = \tan^{-1}(\sin x + \cos x)$ is an increasing function in
(a) $(-\pi/2, 0)$ (b) $(0, \pi/2)$
(c) $(-\pi/4, \pi/4)$ (d) None of these

5. For what value of 'a' does the curve $f(x) = x(a^2 - 2a - 1) + \cos x$ is always strictly monotonic $\forall x \in \mathbb{R}$
(a) $a \in \mathbb{R}$
(b) $a > 0$
(c) $1 - \sqrt{2} < a < 1 + \sqrt{2}$
(d) None of these

6. If $f(x) = x^3 + bx^2 + cx + d$ and $0 < b^2 < c$, then in $(-\infty, \infty)$
(a) $f(x)$ is a strictly increasing function
(b) $f(x)$ has a local maxima
(c) $f(x)$ is a strictly decreasing function
(d) $f(x)$ is bounded

7. If $f(x) = \sin x + a^2x + b$ is an decreasing function for all values of x, then
(a) $a \in (-\infty, -1)$ (b) $a \in \mathbb{R}$
(c) $a \in \mathbb{R} - (-1, 1)$ (d) None of these

8. If $f(x) = x^2e^{-x^2/a^2}$ is an increasing function then (for $a > 0$), x lies in the interval
(a) $[a, 2a]$ (b) $(-\infty -a] \cup [0, a]$
(c) $(-a, 0)$ (d) None of these

9. Consider the following behavior of function in $(-1, 1)$
I. Increasing in $[0,1)$ II. Decreasing in $(-1, 0]$
III Continuity IV. Derivability
Which one of the following four function exhibits atleast three of the four mentioned above?
(a) $\max\{x, x^3\}$ (b) $\max\{x, x^2\}$
(c) $\max\{x, |x|\}$ (d) $\max\{x, [x]\}$

10. If the function $f(x) = \left(\dfrac{k\sin x + 2\cos x}{\sin x + \cos x}\right)$ is strictly increasing at all values of x in its domain, then

(a) $k < 1$ (b) $k > 1$
(c) $k < 2$ (d) $k > 2$

11. Let $f(x) = x - [x]$. In which of the following interval $f(x)$ is increasing?
(a) [0, 1) (b) (1, 2)
(c) [2,3] (d) (2, 3]

12. If the function $f(x) = 2x^2 - kx + 5$ is increasing in [1, 2], then 'k' lies in the interval
(a) $(-\infty, 4]$ (b) $(4, \infty)$
(c) $(-\infty, 3)$ (d) $(8, \infty)$

13. If $f(x) = kx^3 - 9x^2 + 9x + 3$ is monotonically increasing in each interval, then
(a) $k < 3$ (b) $k \le 3$
(c) $k > 3$ (d) none of these

14. $f(x) = kx + 2\cos x$ is monotonically decreasing if
(a) $k < 2$ (b) $k > 2$
(c) $k < -2$ (d) $k > -2$

Answer Keys

1. (b, c) **2.** (a, c, d) **3.** (a, c) **4.** (a, c) **5.** (c) **6.** (a) **7.** (c) **8.** (b) **9.** (b, c, d) **10.** (d)
11. (a, b) **12.** (a) **13.** (c) **14.** (c)

INTERVAL OF MONOTONICITY

An interval belonging to the domain of function, in which the function $f(x)$ remains monotonic, is called interval of monotonicity. e.g., for the function $y = x^2 - 3x + 2$

$x \in \left(\frac{3}{2}, \infty\right)$ is interval of monotonic increasing (↑)

$x \in \left(-\infty, \frac{3}{2}\right)$ is interval of monotonic decreasing (↓)

ILLUSTRATION 25: Show that $\frac{\sin x}{x}$ is a decreasing function in the interval $(0, \pi)$ and hence prove that $3\sin 2 > 2\sin 3$.

SOLUTION: $y = \frac{\sin x}{x}$

$\Rightarrow y' = \frac{x\cos x - \sin x}{x^2}$ $\Rightarrow y' = \frac{\cos x(x - \tan x)}{x^2}$

$$\begin{cases} \frac{(+)\quad(-)}{(+)} < 0 & \forall x \in \left(0, \frac{\pi}{2}\right) \\ \frac{(-)\quad(+)}{(+)} < 0 & \forall x \in \left(\frac{\pi}{2}, \pi\right) \end{cases}$$

And hence $\frac{\sin x}{x}$ decreasing uniformly. Now $2 < 3$ and $2, 3 \in (0, \pi)$

$\Rightarrow f(2) > f(3)$

$\Rightarrow \frac{\sin 2}{2} > \frac{\sin 3}{3} \Rightarrow 3\sin 2 > 2\sin 3$

CRITICAL POINTS

- A point belonging to the domain of function $f(x)$ where $f'(x) = 0$ or it is not defined/discontinuous.
- At these points, it is possible that the function may change its monotonicity but it is not always the case.
- The points where $f'(x) = 0$ are known as stationary point.
- The stationary points of $f(x)$ are x–intercepts of the graph of $f'(x)$.

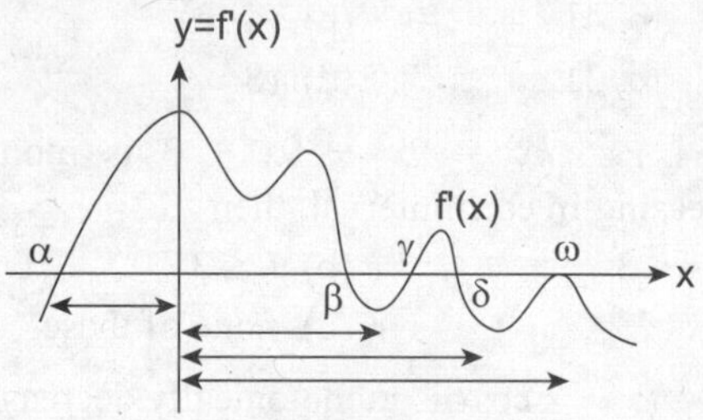

FIGURE 5.75

- If $x = a$ is a critical point of $f(x)$, then it is also a critical point of the function $g(x) = f(x) + k$, where k is a constant. i.e., vertical transformation does not have any effect on the critical points
- If $x = a$ is a critical point of the function $f(x)$, then $x = a + k$ is a critical point of $g(x) = f(x - k)$, where k is a constant.

Similarly $x = a - k$ is a critical point of $h(x) = f(x + k)$, where k is a constant.

ILLUSTRATION 26: Find the critical points of the function $f(x) = x^{3/5}(4 - x)$.

SOLUTION: $f'(x) = x^{3/5}(-1) + (4 - x)\left(\frac{3}{5}\right)\frac{1}{x^{2/5}} = \frac{-5x+12-3x}{5x^{2/5}} = \frac{12-8x}{5x^{2/5}}$

If $f'(x) = 0$

$\Rightarrow\ 8x = 12$

$\Rightarrow\ x = 3/2$

Since $f'(x)$ not defined at $x = 0$, other critical point is $x = 0$

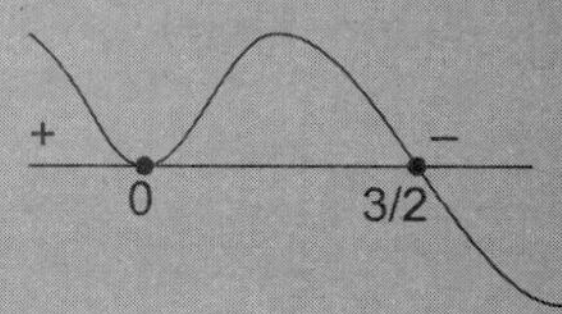

FIGURE 5.76

To find interval of monotonicity for y = f(x)

Given a function $f(x) = x^2 \cdot e^{-x}$.

Step 1: Find Domain

Step 2: Find the derivative of function

$$f'(x) = e^{-x}(2x - x^2) = e^{-x}x(2 - x)$$

Step 3: Find the critical points i.e., $x = 0, 2$.

Step 4: Locate these critical points on real number line.

Find the sign of $f'(x)$ in these intervals obtained.

Step 5: $f'(x) > 0\ \forall\ x \in (0, 2)$ is interval of monotonic increase

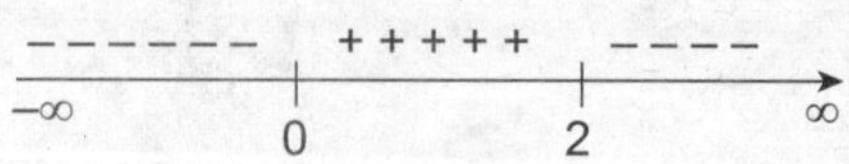

FIGURE 5.77

and $f'(x) < 0\ \forall x \in (-\infty, 0)$ and $(2, \infty)$

$\Rightarrow$ $f(x)$ is monotonically decreasing in $(-\infty, 0)$ and $(2, \infty)$

ILLUSTRATION 27: Find all possible 'b' for which $f(x) = \sin 2x - 8(b + 2)\cos x - (4b^2 + 16b + 6)x$ is monotonic decreasing for $\forall\ x \in \mathbb{R}$ and has no critical point.

SOLUTION: $f'(x) = 2\cos 2x + 8(b + 2)\sin x - (4b^2 + 16b + 6)$

$= 2(1 - 2\sin^2 x) + 8(b + 2)\sin x - (4b^2 + 16b + 6)$

$= -4[\sin^2 x - 2(b + 2)\sin x + (b^2 + 4b + 1)]$

for monotonic decreasing and no critical points $f'(x) < 0\ \forall\ x \in R$

hence $\sin^2 x - 2(b + 2)\sin x + b^2 + 4b + 1 > 0$

$\Rightarrow\ [\sin x - (b + 2)]^2 - (b + 2)^2 + 4b + b^2 + 1 > 0$

$\Rightarrow\ [\sin x - (b + 2)]^2 - \left(\sqrt{3}\right)^2 > 0$

$\Rightarrow\ [\sin x - b - 2 - \sqrt{3}\ ][\sin x - b - 2 + \sqrt{3}\ ] > 0$

$\Rightarrow\ [\sin x - (b + 2 + \sqrt{3})][\sin x - (b + 2 - \sqrt{3})] > 0$

Hence $\sin x > b + (2 + \sqrt{3})$ or $\sin x < (b + 2 - \sqrt{3})$

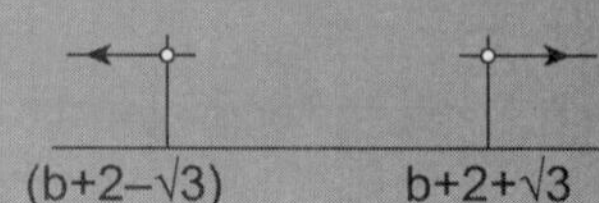

FIGURE 5.78

$\Rightarrow b + (2 + \sqrt{3}) < \sin x \ \forall x \in \mathbb{R}$ or $(b + 2 - \sqrt{3}) > \sin x \ \forall x \in \mathbb{R}$

$\Rightarrow b + (2 + \sqrt{3}) < -1$ or $(b + 2 - \sqrt{3}) > 1$

$\Rightarrow b < -(3 + \sqrt{3})$ or $b > \sqrt{3}$

$\Rightarrow b \in (-\infty, -(3 + \sqrt{3})) \cup (\sqrt{3} - 1, \infty)$

ILLUSTRATION 28: Find all the values of 'a' for which $f(x) = (a^2 - 3a + 2)\cos\left(\frac{x}{2}\right) + (a-1)x$ posses critical points.

SOLUTION: Given, $f(x) = (a^2 - 3a + 2)\cos\frac{x}{2} + (a - 1)x$

$\Rightarrow f'(x) = -\frac{1}{2}(a-1)(a-2)\sin\left(\frac{x}{2}\right) + (a-1)$

$\Rightarrow f'(x) = (a-1)\left[1 - \frac{1}{2}(a-2)\sin\left(\frac{x}{2}\right)\right]$

If $f(x)$ possesses critical points, then $f'(x) = 0$

$\Rightarrow (a-1)\left[1 - \left(\frac{a-2}{2}\right)\sin\left(\frac{x}{2}\right)\right] = 0$ $\quad\Rightarrow a = 1$ and $1 - \left(\frac{a-2}{2}\right)\sin\left(\frac{x}{2}\right) = 0$

$\Rightarrow a = 1$ and $\sin\left(\frac{x}{2}\right) = \frac{2}{a-2}$

$\Rightarrow a = 1$ and $\left|\frac{2}{a-2}\right| \le 1$

$\Rightarrow a = 1$ and $|a - 2| \ge 2$ $\quad\Rightarrow a = 1$ and $a - 2 \ge 2$ or $a - 2 \le -2$

$\Rightarrow a = 1$ and $a \ge 4$ or $a \le 0$ $\quad\Rightarrow a = 1$ and $a \ge 4$ or $a \le 0$

$\Rightarrow a = 1$ and $a \in (-\infty, 0) \cup (4, \infty)$

Therefore, $a \in (-\infty, 0) \cup \{1\} \cup (4, \infty)$

ILLUSTRATION 29: (a) Find the set of all values of the parameter 'a' for which the function, $f(x) = \sin 2x - 8(a + 1)\sin x + (4a^2 + 8a - 14)x$ increases for all $x \in \mathbb{R}$ and has no critical points for all $x \in \mathbb{R}$.

(b) Find all the values of the parameter 'a' for which the function; $f(x) = 8ax - a\sin 6x - 7x - \sin 5x$ increases and has no critical points for all $x \in \mathbb{R}$.

(c) Find the set of values of 'a' for which the function $f(x) = (a^2 + a - 6)\cos 2x + (a - 2)x + \cos 1$ has no critical points.

SOLUTION: (a) $f(x) = \sin 2x - 8(a + 1)\sin x + (4a^2 + 8a - 14)x$

$\Rightarrow f'(x) = 2\cos 2x - 8(a + 1)\cos x + 4a^2 + 8a - 14 = 4\cos^2 x - 2 - 8a\cos x - 8\cos x + 4a^2 + 8a - 14$

$\because f(x) \uparrow \forall x \in \mathbb{R}$ and has no critical points, therefore $f'(x) > 0$

$\Rightarrow \cos^2 x - 2(a + 1)\cos x + (a + 1)^2 - 5 > 0$

$\Rightarrow (\cos x - (a + 1))^2 > 5$

$\Rightarrow \cos x - (a + 1) > \sqrt{5}$ or $\cos x - (a + 1) < -\sqrt{5}$

Case I: $a < -\sqrt{5} - 1 + \cos x$

Now minimum value of $\cos x = -1$

$\Rightarrow$ minimum value of $-\sqrt{5} - 1 + \cos x = -\sqrt{5} - 2$

$\Rightarrow a < -\sqrt{5} - 2$

Case II: $a > \sqrt{5} - 1 + \cos x$

Now maximum value of $\cos x = 1$

$\Rightarrow$ maximum value of $\sqrt{5} - 1 + \cos x = \sqrt{5}$

$\Rightarrow$ $a > \sqrt{5}$

$\therefore$ From (1) and (2); we get $a \in (-\infty, -\sqrt{5} - 2) \cup a \in (\sqrt{5}, \infty)$

(b) $f(x) = 8ax - a\sin 6x - 7x - \sin 5x$

$f'(x) = 8a - 6a\cos 6x - 7 - 5\cos 5x$

$\because$ $f(x)$ increases and has no critical points.

$\therefore$ $f'(x) > 0 \ \forall \ x \in R$

$\Rightarrow$ $8a - 6a \cos 6x - 7 - 5 \cos 5x > 0$

$\Rightarrow$ $8a - 7 - 6a \cos 6x - 5 \cos 5x > 0$

$\Rightarrow$ $8a - 7 > 6a \cos 6x + 5 \cos 5x$

Case (i): For $a > 0$

$8a - 7 > 6a + 5$

$$\begin{bmatrix} \because \text{for } a > 0; \text{ maximum value of} \\ 6a\cos 6x + 5\cos 5x \text{ will be } 6a + 5 \\ \text{at point where } \cos 6x = \cos 5x = 1 \end{bmatrix}$$

$\Rightarrow$ $2a > 12$

$\Rightarrow$ $a > 6$

$\therefore$ $a \in (6, \infty)$ ...... (1)

Case (ii): For $a < 0$

$8a - 7 > -6a + 5$

$$\begin{bmatrix} \because \text{For } a < 0; \text{ maximum value of} \\ 6a\cos 6x + 5\cos 5x \text{ will be } -6a + 5 \text{ at} \\ \text{a point where } \cos 6x = -\cos 5x = -1 \end{bmatrix}$$

$\Rightarrow$ $14a > 12$

$\Rightarrow$ $a > 6/7$ which is impossible as $a < 0$

$\Rightarrow$ $a \in \{\ \}$ ...... (2)

Taking union of (1) and (2); we get $a \in (6, \infty)$

(c) $f(x) = (a^2 + a - 6) \cos 2x + (a - 2)x + \cos 1$

$\Rightarrow$ $f'(x) = -2(a^2 + a - 6) \sin 2x + a - 2$

$\because$ $f(x)$ has no critical points

$\therefore$ $f'(x) \neq 0$

for $f'(x) = 0$; we have

$\Rightarrow$ $-2(a^2 + a - 6) \sin 2x + a - 2 = 0$ $\Rightarrow$ $2(a^2 + a - 6) \sin 2x = a - 2$

$\Rightarrow$ $\sin 2x = \dfrac{a-2}{2(a^2 + a - 6)}$ Now $\sin 2x \in [-1, 1]$

$\Rightarrow$ $-1 \le \dfrac{a-2}{2(a^2 + a - 6)} \le 1$ $\Rightarrow$ $-2 \le \dfrac{a-2}{a^2 + a - 6} \le 2$

Case (i): $\dfrac{a-2}{a^2+a-6} \geq -2$

$\Rightarrow \dfrac{a-2}{a^2+a-6}+2 \geq 0$

$\Rightarrow \dfrac{a-2+2(a^2+a-6)}{a^2+a-6} \geq 0$

$\Rightarrow \dfrac{2a^2+2a-12+a-2}{a^2+a-6} \geq 0$

$\Rightarrow \dfrac{2a^2+3a-14}{a^2+a-6} \geq 0$

$\Rightarrow \dfrac{2a^2+7a-4a-14}{a^2+a-6} \geq 0$

$\Rightarrow \dfrac{(2a+7)(a-2)}{(a+3)(a-2)} \geq 0$

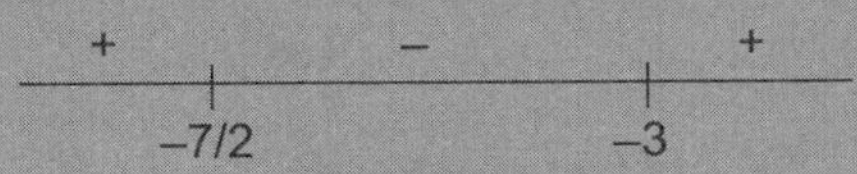

FIGURE 5.79

$\Rightarrow a \in \left(-\infty, \dfrac{-7}{2}\right]$ or $a \in (-3, \infty) - \{2\}$ .... (i)

Case (ii): $\dfrac{a-2}{a^2+a-6} \leq 2$

$\Rightarrow \dfrac{a-2}{a^2+a-6}-2 \leq 0$

$\Rightarrow \dfrac{2(a^2+a-6)-(a-2)}{a^2+a-6} \geq 0$

$\Rightarrow \dfrac{2a^2+2a-12-a+2}{a^2+a-6} \geq 0$

$\Rightarrow \dfrac{2a^2+a-10}{a^2+a-6} \geq 0$

$\Rightarrow \dfrac{(2a+5)(a-2)}{(a-2)(a+3)} \geq 0$

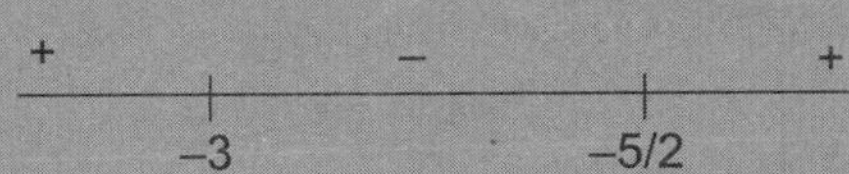

FIGURE 5.80

$\Rightarrow a \in (-\infty, -3) \cup \left[\dfrac{-5}{2}, \infty\right)$ .... (ii)

From (i) and (ii); we get $a \in \left(-\infty, \dfrac{-7}{2}\right] \cup \left[\dfrac{-5}{2}, \infty\right) \sim \{2\}$ .....(iii)

Any $a \in R$ for $f'(x) = 0$ is given in equation (iii)

Hence for no critical points i.e., $f'(x) \neq 0$, $a \in \left(-\dfrac{7}{2}, -\dfrac{5}{2}\right) \cup \{2\}$

as at $x = 2$; $f'(x) = 0$; therefore it is also a critical point.

NOTE:

- ❑ *While expressing the intervals of monotonic increase/decrease, do not use union symbols without taking adequate care.*

$\because$ *it may happen that f (x) decreases in two intervals but fail to behave so in their union.*

Consider $f(x) = x^2 e^{-x}$

Here $f(x) \downarrow$ *for* $(-\infty, 0)$ *and also for* $(2, \infty)$

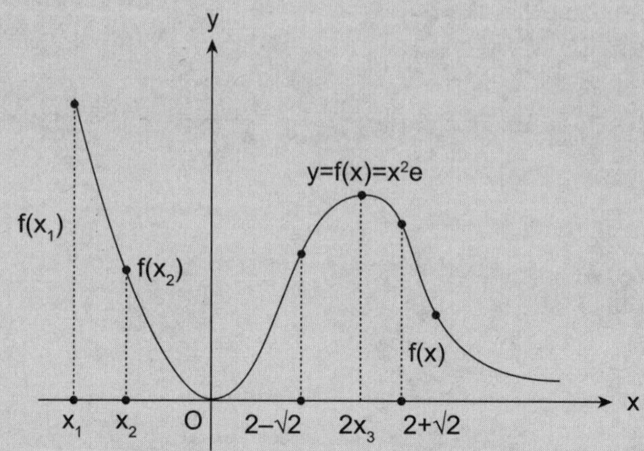

FIGURE 5.81

But as is evident from the graph of the function $x_1 < x_2 \Rightarrow f(x) > f(x_2)$ *but* $x_2 < x_3 \nRightarrow f(x_2) > f(x_3)$

Rather $x_2 < x_3 \Rightarrow f(x_2) < f(x_3)$

$\therefore$ *f(x) is not decreasing on* $(-\infty, 0) \cup (2, \infty)$

- ❑ *Although when f (x) is discontinuous then this may happen that if f(x) increases in [a, b] and [c, d] both, so its also increases in* $[a, b] \cup [c, d]$.

For instance, see the graph function $y = f(x)$

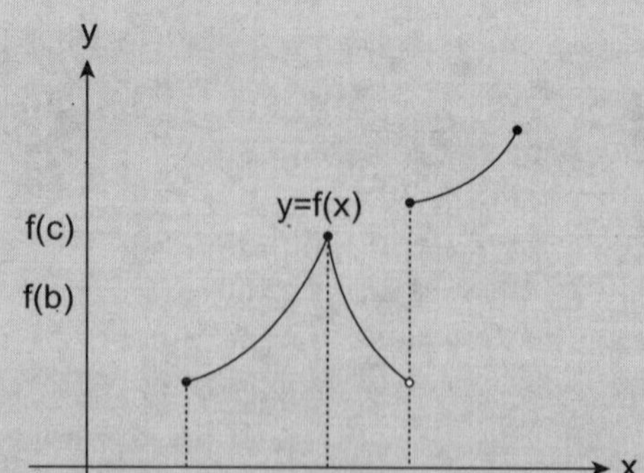

FIGURE 5.82

Here, the function increases in the intervals (a, b), (c, d) and we may proceed to write that it in $(a,b) \cup (c,d)$.

$\because$ *Here we have* $f(b) \geq f(c)$

■ CONCLUSION

1. If $f(x)$ is ↑ in $[a, b]$, decreases in $[c, d]$; again ↑ in $[d, e]$. Then $f(x)$ increases in $[a,b]\cup[d,e]$ is true iff maximum value of $f(x)$ $\forall x \in [a,b]$ should be less than min. value of $f(x)$ $\forall x \in [d,e]$ i.e., $f(b) < f(d)$

   For example consider $f(x)$ as shown in figure 5.83

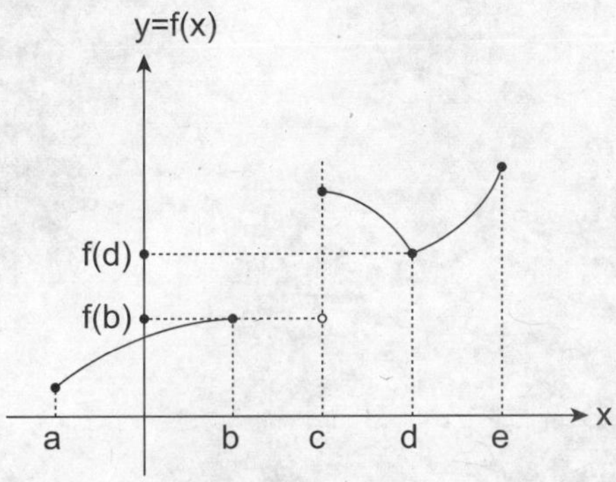

FIGURE 5.83

2. If $f(x)$ is ↓ in $[a, b]$; ↑ in $[c, d]$ and again ↓ in $[d, e]$; then $f(x)$ is decreasing in $[a, b] \cup [d, e]$ iff minimum value of $f(x)$ $\forall x \in [a, b]$ is greater than the maximum value of $f(x)$ $\forall x \in [d, e]$. i.e., $f(b) > f(d)$.

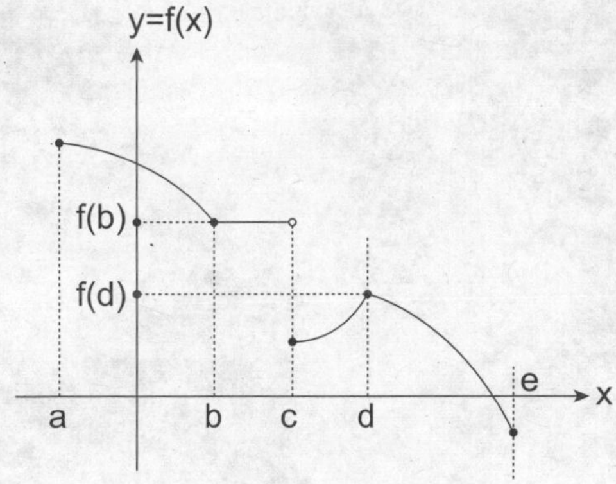

FIGURE 5.84

3. Conventionally interval of monotonicity is expressed using open interval but, ideally use of closed interval is more informative particularly for discontinuous functions.

4. For continuous functions (defined over closed interval) the open intervals of monotonicity can be replaced by closed interval.

ILLUSTRATION 30: If $f(x)$ is increasing in the interval (a, b) and decreasing in the interval (b, c), then for which of the following function, can we say that $f(x)$ increases in the interval $[a, b]$ and decreases in the interval $[b, c]$?

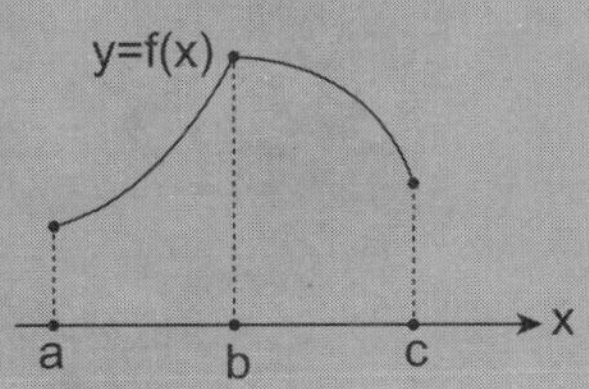

FIGURE 5.85

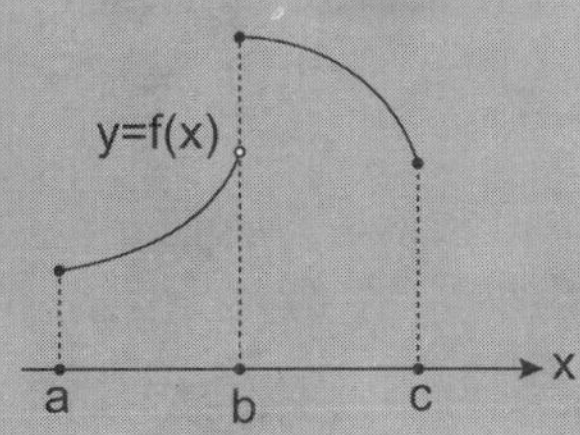

FIGURE 5.86

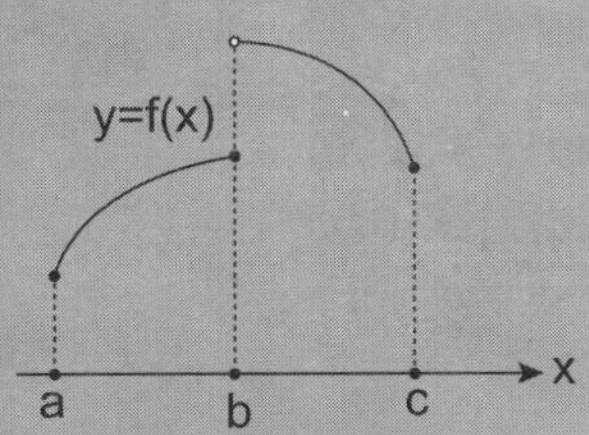

FIGURE 5.87

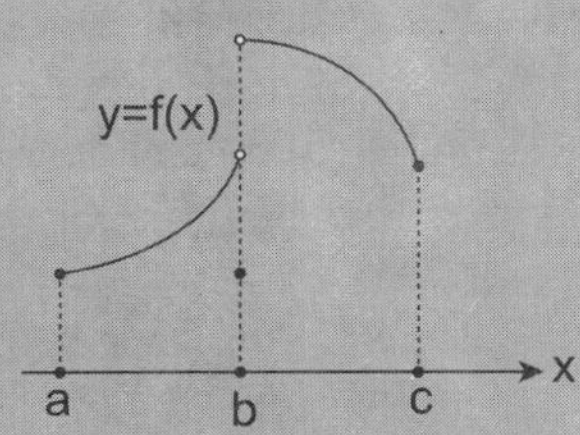

FIGURE 5.88

SOLUTION: 1. Yes, $x_1, x_2 \in [a, b]$ then $x_1 < x_2$ $\Rightarrow f(x_1) < f(x_2)$

and $x_1, x_2 \in [b, c]$

then $x_1 < x_2$ $\Rightarrow f(x_1) > f(x_2)$

$\therefore$ $f(x)$ is strictly increasing in $[a, b]$ and strictly decreasing in $[b, c]$

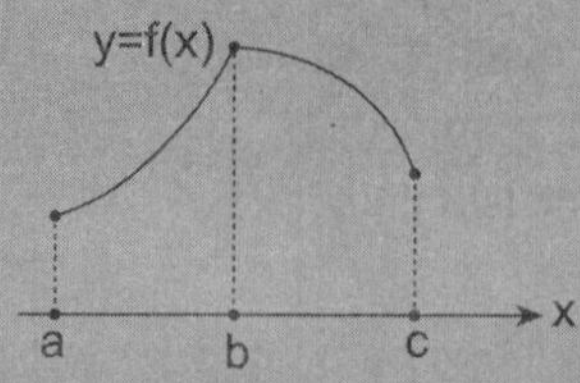

FIGURE 5.89

2. Yes, $x_1, x_2 \in [a, b]$ then $x_1 < x_2 \Rightarrow f(x_1) < f(x_2)$

$\Rightarrow$ $f(x)$ is strictly increasing in $[a, b]$

For $x_1, x_2 \in [b, c]$

Then $x_1 < x_2$

$\Rightarrow$ $f(x_1) > f(x_2)$

$\Rightarrow$ $f(x)$ is strictly decreasing in $[b, c]$

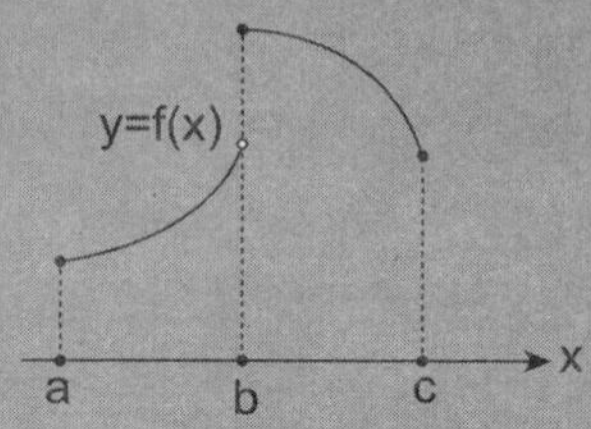

FIGURE 5.90

3. No, For $x_1, x_2 \in [a, b]$

$x_1 < x_2 \Rightarrow f(x_1) < f(x_2)$

$\Rightarrow$ $f(x)$ is strictly increasing for $[a, b]$

For $x_1, x_2, \in [b, c]$

$x_1 < x_2 \nRightarrow f(x_1) > f(x_2)$

$\because$ $b < b + h$ but $f(b) \ngtr f(b + h)$

$\therefore$ $f(x)$ is not strictly decreasing in $[b, c]$

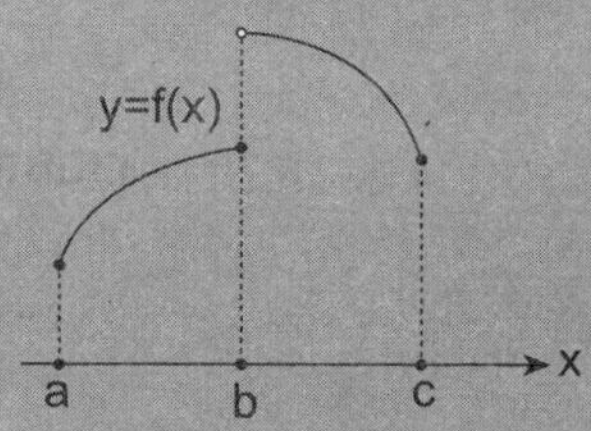

FIGURE 5.91

4. No, For $x_1, x_2 \in [a, b]$

$x_1 < x_2 \nRightarrow f(x_1) < f(x_2)$

$\because$ $b - h < b$ but $f(b - h) > f(b)$

$\therefore$ $f(x)$ is not strictly increasing in $[a, b]$

For $x_1, x_2 \in [b, c]$

$x_1 < x_2 \nRightarrow f(x_1) > f(x_2)$

$\because$ $b < b + h$ but $f(b) < f(b + h)$

$\therefore$ $f(x)$ is not strictly decreasing in $[b, c]$

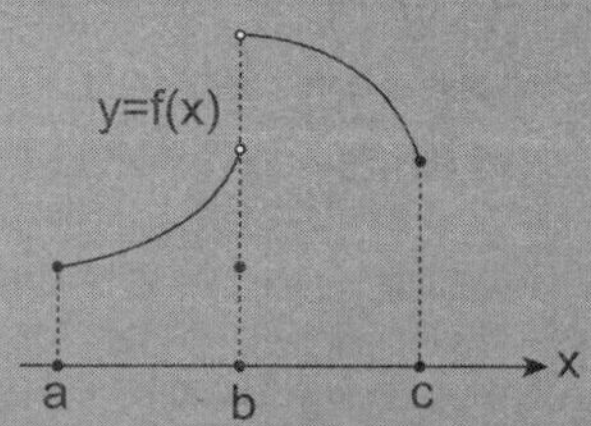

FIGURE 5.92

ILLUSTRATION 31: $f(x) = \int\left(2 - \frac{1}{1+x^2} - \frac{1}{\sqrt{1+x^2}}\right)dx$, then f is

(a) increasing in $(0, \infty)$ and decreasing in $(-\infty, 0)$

(b) increasing in $(-\infty, 0)$ and decreasing in $(0, \infty)$

(c) increasing in $(-\infty, \infty)$

(d) decreasing in $(-\infty, \infty)$

SOLUTION: $f'(x) = 2 - \frac{1}{1+x^2} - \frac{1}{\sqrt{1+x^2}} = \frac{2(1+x^2) - 1 - \sqrt{1+x^2}}{1+x^2}$

$= \frac{1 + 2x^2 - \sqrt{1+x^2}}{1+x^2} > 0 \ \forall x \in R \Rightarrow$ option (c) is correct.

ILLUSTRATION 32: Investigate the behaviour of the following functions for monotonicity in the given intervals,

(i) $f(x) = -\sin^3 x + 3\sin^2 x + 5, x \in [-\pi/2, \pi/2]$

(ii) $f(x) = \sec x - \operatorname{cosec} x,\ x \in (0, \pi/2)$

SOLUTION: (i) $f(x) = -\sin^3 x + 3\sin^2 x + 5, x \in [-\pi/2, \pi/2]$

$\Rightarrow\ f'(x) = -3\sin^2 x.\cos x + 6\sin x.\cos x = 3\sin x\cos x(2 - \sin x)$

For $x \in \left(0, \frac{\pi}{2}\right)$; $\sin x > 0$; $\cos x > 0$ and $2 - \sin x > 0$ $\Rightarrow f(x) > 0$

And for $x \in \left(-\frac{\pi}{2}, 0\right)$; $\sin x < 0$; $\cos x > 0$ and $2 - \sin x > 0$ $\Rightarrow f(x) < 0$

$\Rightarrow$ $f(x)$ is increasing in $(0, \pi/2)$ and decreasing in $(\pi/2, 0)$

(ii) $f(x) = \sec x - \cos ecx, x \in (0, \pi/2)$

$\Rightarrow\ f'(x) = \sec x \tan x + \cos ecx \cot x > 0 \forall x \in (0, \pi/2)$

Thus $f(x)$ is increasing in $(0, \pi/2)$

ILLUSTRATION 33: The interval in which $f(x) = \int_0^x e^t (t-1)(t-2)dt$ is decreasing, is

(a) (1, 2) (b) (1, 3/2)

(c) (1, 3) (d) (1, 4)

SOLUTION: Given $f(x) = \int_0^x e^t (t-1)(t-2)dt$

$\Rightarrow f'(x) = e^x (x-1)(x-2)dt$

For decreasing function $f'(x) < 0$

Hence, $e^x(x-1)(x-2) < 0$

$\Rightarrow (x-1)(x-2) < 0$ i.e., $x \in (1, 2)$

Hence (a), (b) are correct.

ILLUSTRATION 34: The function $f(x) = \sin^4 x + \cos^4 x$ increasing if

(a) $0 < x < \frac{\pi}{8}$ (b) $\frac{\pi}{4} < x < \frac{3\pi}{8}$

(c) $\frac{3\pi}{8} < x < \frac{5\pi}{8}$ (d) $\frac{5\pi}{8} < x < \frac{3\pi}{8}$

SOLUTION: Here $f(x) = \sin^4 x + \cos^4 x$

$\Rightarrow f'(x) = 4\sin^3 x(\cos x) + 4\cos^3 x(-\sin x)$

$\Rightarrow f'(x) = 4\sin x\cos x(\sin^2 x - \cos^2 x)$

$\Rightarrow f'(x) = 2(\sin 2x)(-\cos 2x)$ $\Rightarrow f'(x) = -\sin 4x$

Now $f'(x) > 0$ if $\sin 4x < 0$

$\Rightarrow \pi < 4x < 2\pi$

$\Rightarrow \frac{\pi}{4} < x < \frac{\pi}{2}$

Here (*b*) is only subset i.e., $\left(\frac{\pi}{4}, \frac{\pi}{2}\right)$

ILLUSTRATION 35: The function $y = \frac{x}{1+x^2}$ decreases in the interval

(a) $(-1, 1)$ (b) $[1, \infty)$

(c) $(-\infty, -1]$ (d) $(-\infty, \infty)$

SOLUTION: $y' = \frac{(1+x^2)-2x.x}{(1+x^2)^2} = \frac{1-x^2}{(1+x^2)^2}$

Since $(1+x^2)^2 > 0$ for all x, we have $y' < 0$.

When, $1 - x^2 < 0$, whence $x > 1$ or $x < -1$.

Therefore, $x \in (-\infty, -1)$ or $x \in (1, \infty)$.

Thus $\frac{x}{1+x^2}$ decreases in $(-\infty, -1]$ or $[1, \infty)$.

ILLUSTRATION 36: The function f defined by $f(x) = (x + 2)\, e^{-x}$ is

(a) decreasing for all x

(b) decreasing in $(-\infty, -1)$ and increasing in $(-1, \infty)$

(c) increasing for all x

(d) decreasing $(-1, \infty)$ and increasing in $(-\infty, -1)$

SOLUTION: $f'(x) = -(x + 1)\, e^{-x}$

Obviously $f'(x) < 0$, when $x > -1$ and $f'(x) > 0$ when $x < -1$

Hence $f(x)$ is decreasing in $(-1, \infty)$ and increasing in $(-\infty, -1)$.

ILLUSTRATION 37: The interval of increase of the function $y = x - 2 \sin x$ for $0 \le x \le 2\pi$ is

(a) $\left(\frac{\pi}{3}, \pi\right)$ (b) $(0, \pi)$

(c) $\left(\frac{\pi}{2}, \pi\right)$ (d) $\left(\frac{\pi}{3}, \frac{5\pi}{3}\right)$

SOLUTION: The function increases when its derivative $\frac{dy}{dx} = 1 - 2\cos x$ is greater than zero.

It happens when $\cos x < \frac{1}{2}$ $\Rightarrow x \in \left(\frac{\pi}{3}, \frac{5\pi}{3}\right)$

This is the interval of answer (d), and it includes that of answer (a) and (c).

ILLUSTRATION 38: The function $f(x) = \cos x - 2px$ is monotonically decreasing $\forall\, x \in \mathbb{R}$ for

(a) $p < 1/2$ (b) $p > 1/2$

(c) $p < 2$ (d) $p > 2$

SOLUTION: For $f(x)$ to be monotonically decreasing, $f'(x) < 0\ \forall\, x \in \mathbb{R}$

$\Rightarrow f'(x) = -\sin x - 2p < 0\ \forall\, x \in \mathbb{R}$ $\Rightarrow \frac{1}{2}\sin x + p > 0$

$\Rightarrow p > \frac{1}{2}\sin x\ \forall\, x \in \mathbb{R}$

$\Rightarrow p > \frac{1}{2}$ $\Rightarrow$ option (b) and (d) are correct.

ILLUSTRATION 39: If $a < 0$ and $f(x) = e^{ax} + e^{-ax}$. Suppose that $S = \{x : f(x)$ is monotonically decreasing$\}$ then

(a) $S = \{x : x > 0\}$ (b) $S = \{x : x < 0\}$

(c) $S = \{x : x > 1\}$ (d) $S = \{x : x < 1\}$

SOLUTION: $f'(x) = a\,(e^{ax} - e^{-ax})$.

So f is monotonically decreasing iff $e^{ax} - e^{-ax} > 0$, i.e., $e^{2ax} > 1$, which is true iff $2ax > 0$.

Since $a < 0$, we must have $x < 0$.

ILLUSTRATION 40: If $f(x) = \dfrac{x^2}{2 - 2\cos x}$; $g(x) = \dfrac{x^2}{6x - 6\sin x}$ where $0 < x < 1$, then :

(a) both 'f' and 'g' are increasing functions

(b) 'f' is decreasing and 'g' is increasing function

(c) 'f' is increasing and 'g' is decreasing function

(d) both 'f' and 'g' are decreasing function

SOLUTION: Put $x = \pi/6$ and $\pi/3$ and observe the behaviour of $f(x)$ and $g(x)$.

Alternatively $f'(x) = \dfrac{1}{2}\left[\dfrac{(1-\cos x)\,2x - x^2\sin x}{(1-\cos x)^2}\right]$

$$= \frac{x}{2(1-\cos x)^2}[2(1-\cos x) - x\sin x]$$

$$= \frac{x\left[4\sin^2\frac{x}{2} - 2x\sin\frac{x}{2}\cos\frac{x}{2}\right]}{2(1-\cos)^2}$$ ($\because$ for $\theta \in (0, \pi/2)$ and hence for $\theta \in (0, 1)$, $(\tan\theta)/\theta > 1$)

$$= \frac{2x\sin\frac{x}{2}\cos\frac{x}{2}}{2(1-\cos x)^2}\left[\frac{\tan\frac{x}{2}}{\frac{x}{2}} - 1\right]$$

$\Rightarrow$ Hence f is increasing.

and $g'(x) = \dfrac{1}{6}\left[\dfrac{(x-\sin x)\,2x - x^2(1-\cos x)}{(x-\sin x)^2}\right]$

Consider $x - 2\sin x + x\cos x$, we get

$$2x\cos^2\frac{x}{2} - 4\sin\frac{x}{2}\cos\frac{x}{2}$$

$$= 2x\cos^2\frac{x}{2}\left[1 - \frac{\tan\frac{x}{2}}{\frac{x}{2}}\right] < 0 \left(\because \frac{\tan x/2}{x/2} > 1\right)$$

$\Rightarrow g'(x) < a$ Hence g is decreasing.

ILLUSTRATION 41: If $f(x) = (\tan^{-1}x)^2 + \dfrac{2}{\sqrt{x^2+1}}$, then f is increasing in

(a) $(0, \infty)$ (b) $[1, 10]$

(c) $[3, 5]$ (d) $[2, 5]$

SOLUTION: Given $f(x) = (\tan^{-1}x)^2 + \dfrac{2}{\sqrt{x^2+1}}$

$\Rightarrow f'(x) = \dfrac{2}{1+x^2}\left(\tan^{-1}x - \dfrac{x}{\sqrt{x^2+1}}\right)$

Let $g(x) = \tan^{-1}x - \dfrac{x}{\sqrt{x^2+1}}$

$\Rightarrow g'(x) = \dfrac{1}{x^2+1}\left(1 - \dfrac{1}{\sqrt{x^2+1}}\right) > 0$ for all $x \in \mathbb{R}$

$\Rightarrow g(x)$ is increasing for all $x \in \mathbb{R}$

But $g(0) = 0$ $\Rightarrow g(x) > 0$ for $x > 0$

So, $f'(x) > 0$ for $x > 0$

ILLUSTRATION 42: Find the interval of increase or decrease of the function $f(x) = \int_{-1}^{x}(t^2+2t)(t^2-1)dt$

SOLUTION: $f(x) = \int_{-1}^{x}(t^2+2t)(t^2-1)dt$

$\Rightarrow f'(x) = (x^2+2x)(x^2-1)$

When $f'(x) = 0$ $\Rightarrow x = 0, -2, -1, 1$

Sign scheme for $f'(x)$ is as below

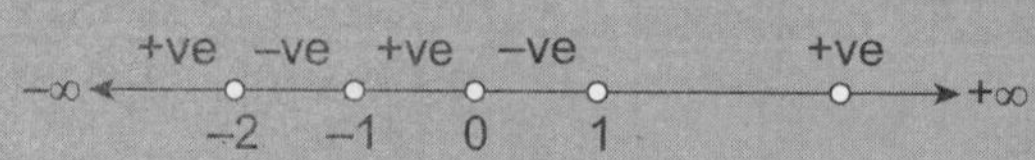

FIGURE 5.93

Clearly, $f'(x) > 0$

When $-\infty < x < -2$ or $-1 < x < 0$ or $1 < x < \infty$

While $f'(x) < 0$

When $-2 < x < -1$ or $0 < x < 1$.

Hence $f(x)$ increases when $-\infty < x < -2$ or $-1 < x < 0$ or $1 < x < \infty$

i.e., in the interval $(-\infty, -2)$, $(-1, 0)$, $(1, \infty)$ and decreases when $-2 < x < -1$ or $0 < x < 1$

i.e., in the interval $(-2, -1)$, $(0, 1)$

ILLUSTRATION 43: Find the interval of monotonicity of the following functions:

(i) $y = \log\left(x + \sqrt{1+x^2}\right)$ (ii) $y = \left(x\sqrt{ax - x^2}\right)$ for $a > 0$

(iii) $y = \dfrac{10}{4x^3 - 9x^2 + 6x}$

SOLUTION: (i) The derivative of the given function,

$$\frac{dy}{dx} = \frac{1}{x+\sqrt{1+x^2}}\left(1 + \frac{x}{\sqrt{1+x^2}}\right) = \frac{1}{\sqrt{1+x^2}}$$

is greater than 0 for all x, showing that y increases on $(-\infty, \infty)$

(ii) Differentiating the given function,

$$\frac{dy}{dx} = \sqrt{ax-x^2} + \frac{x(a-2x)}{2\sqrt{ax-x^2}} = \frac{2(ax-x^2)+ax-2x^2}{2\sqrt{ax-x^2}}; x \in [0, a]$$

$$= \frac{x(3a-4x)}{2\sqrt{ax-x^2}} = \frac{-2x\left(x-\frac{3a}{4}\right)}{\sqrt{ax-x^2}}$$

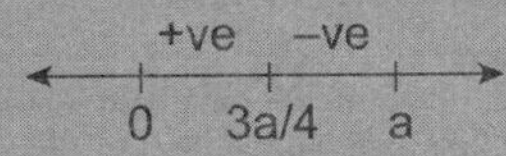

FIGURE 5.94

Thus $dy/dx > 0$ when $0 < x < \frac{3a}{4}$, and less than 0 otherwise. Since the domain of the given function is $[0, a]$, we see that y increases on $\left(0, \frac{3a}{4}\right)$ and decreases on $\left(\frac{3a}{4}, a\right)$.

(iii) The derivative of the given function is $\frac{dy}{dx} = -\frac{10\left(12x^2-18x+6\right)}{\left(4x^3-9x^2+6x\right)}$

$$= -\frac{60\left(2x^2-3x+1\right)}{\left(4x^3-9x^2+6x\right)^2} = -\frac{60(2x-1)(x-1)}{\left(4x^3-9x^2+6x\right)^2}$$

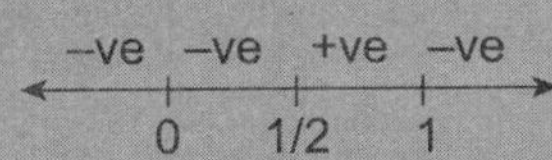

FIGURE 5.95

It is greater than 0 when $\frac{1}{2} < x < 1$, and it is less than 0 for other values of x. Since y is not defined at $x = 0$, we therefore see that it increases on $\left(\frac{1}{2}, 1\right)$ and decreases on $(-\infty, 0)$, $\left(0, \frac{1}{2}\right)$, $(1, \infty)$.

ILLUSTRATION 44: Find the intervals of monotonicity of the function $y = 2x^2 - \log|x|$, $x \neq 0$.

SOLUTION: The given function $y = 2x^2 - \log|x|$, $x \neq 0$ can be re-written as

$$y = \begin{cases} 2x^2 - \log(-x); & x < 0 \\ 2x^2 - \log x; & x > 0 \end{cases}$$

$$\therefore \frac{dy}{dx} = \begin{cases} 4x - \frac{1}{(-x)}(-1) = 4x - \frac{1}{x}; & x < 0 \\ 4x - \frac{1}{x}; & x > 0 \end{cases}$$

i.e., $\frac{dy}{dx} = 4x - \frac{1}{x} = \frac{4}{x}\left(x+\frac{1}{2}\right)\left(x-\frac{1}{2}\right); x \neq 0$ ...(i)

Using the sign rule

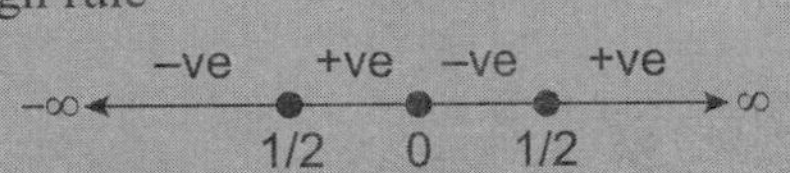

FIGURE 5.96

We have $\frac{dy}{dx} < 0$ for $x < -\frac{1}{2}$ or $0 < x < \frac{1}{2}$ and $\frac{dy}{dx} > 0$ for $-\frac{1}{2} < x < 0$ or $x > \frac{1}{2}$

Hence y is increasing in $\left(-\frac{1}{2}, 0\right), \left(\frac{1}{2}, \infty\right)$

and y is decreasing in $\left(-\infty, -\frac{1}{2}\right), \left(0, \frac{1}{2}\right)$

ILLUSTRATION 45: Let $f(x) = \left(1+\frac{1}{x}\right)^x$; $x > 0$, then prove that $f(x)$ is increasing.

SOLUTION: $f(x) = (1 + 1/x)^x$

$$f'(x) = (1 + 1/x)^x \left[\log(1+1/x) - \frac{1}{x+1}\right] \quad ...(1)$$

The sign of $f'(x)$ depends on $\left(\ln\left(1+\frac{1}{x}\right) - \frac{1}{x+1}\right)$ $\left[\because 1+\frac{1}{x} > 0 \text{ for } x > 0\right]$

Let $\phi(x) = \ln(1 + 1/x) - \frac{1}{x+1}$

$\Rightarrow \phi'(x) = -\frac{1}{x(x+1)^2} < 0 \ \forall \ x > 0$

$\Rightarrow$ so $\phi(x) \downarrow$ on $x > 0$

$\therefore \phi(x) > \lim\limits_{x\to\infty} \phi(x) = 0$

$\Rightarrow \phi(x) > 0 \ \forall \ x > 0$ $\left[\because \lim\limits_{x\to\infty} \phi(x) = 0\right]$

$\Rightarrow \log(1 + 1/x) - \frac{1}{x+1} > 0 \ \forall \ x > 0$

Now, from (1), we can say that $f'(x) > 0 \ \forall \ x > 0$

Hence $f(x)$ increase for $x > 0$

ILLUSTRATION 46: Find the intervals of monotonicity of $f(x) = (3^x - 1)(3^x - 9)^2$.

SOLUTION: $f(x) = (3^x - 1)(3^x - 9)^2$

$\therefore f'(x) = 3^x \ln 3 (3^x - 9)^2 + 2(3^x - 9) \times 3^x \ln(3^x - 1)$

$= 3^x \ln 3 (3^x - 9)[(3^x - 9) + 2(3^x - 1)] = 3^x \ln 3 (3^x - 9)[(3^{x+1} - 11)$

$\therefore f'(x) = 0 \Rightarrow 3^x = 9$ or $3^{x+1} = 11$

$\Rightarrow x = 2$ or $x = \log_3\left(\frac{11}{3}\right)$

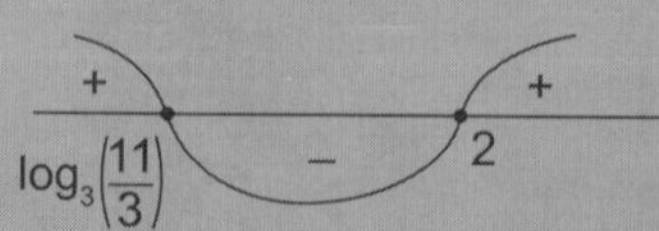

FIGURE 5.97

Thus $f(x)$ is increasing in $\left(-\infty, \log_3\left(\frac{11}{3}\right)\right)$ and $(2, \infty)$

And $f(x)$ is decreasing in $\left(\log_3\left(\frac{11}{3}\right), 2\right)$

ILLUSTRATION 47: Find the intervals of monotonicity of the following functions:

(i) $f(x) = 4x^2 - \ln|x|$ (ii) $f(x) = \dfrac{x^3}{x^4 - 27}$

(iii) $f(x) = \dfrac{|x-3|}{x^2}$

SOLUTION: (i) Given $f(x) = 4x^2 - \ln|x|$

Then $f'(x) = 8x - 1/x = \dfrac{8x^2 - 1}{x} = \dfrac{(2\sqrt{2}x - 1)(2\sqrt{2} + 1)}{x}$

Wavy curve of $f'(x)$ will be

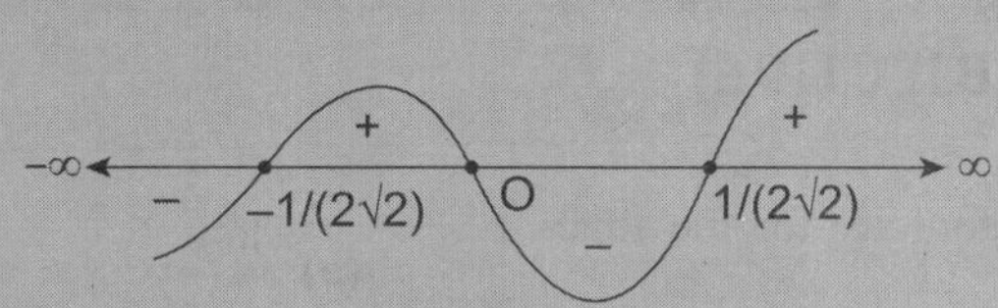

FIGURE 5.98

$\Rightarrow$ $f(x)$ is strictly increasing in $\left(-\dfrac{1}{2\sqrt{2}}, 0\right) and \left(\dfrac{1}{2\sqrt{2}}, \infty\right)$

and $f(x)$ is strictly decreasing in $\left(-\infty, -\dfrac{1}{2\sqrt{2}}\right)$ and $\left(0, \dfrac{1}{2\sqrt{2}}\right)$

(ii) $f(x) = \dfrac{x^3}{x^4 - 27}$, then $f'(x) = \dfrac{3x^2(x^4 - 27) - 4x^3(x^3)}{(x^4 - 27)^2}$

$$\Rightarrow \quad f'(x) = \frac{-(x^6 + 81x^2)}{(x^4 - 27)^2} = \frac{-x^2(x^4 + 81)}{(x^4 - 27)^2} < 0$$

$\therefore$ $f(x)$ is strictly decreasing in its domain i.e., $\mathbb{R} \sim \left\{\sqrt[4]{27}\right\}$

(iii) $f(x) = \dfrac{|x-3|}{x^2}$

$$\therefore \quad f(x) = \begin{cases} \dfrac{x-3}{x^2} & ; x \geq 3 \\ \dfrac{3-x}{x^2} & ; x < 3, x \neq 0 \end{cases} \qquad f'(x) = \begin{cases} \dfrac{x^2 - 2x(x-3)}{x^4} = \dfrac{-x^2 + 6x}{x^4} = \dfrac{6-x}{x^3} ; x \geq 3 \\ \dfrac{-x^2 - 2x(3-x)}{x^4} = \dfrac{x^2 - 6x}{x^4} = \dfrac{x-6}{x^3} ; x < 3, x \neq 0 \end{cases}$$

Clearly, the function $f(x)$ is continuous at $x = 3$ and is non-differentiable at $x = 3$

$\because$ LHD at $x = 3 = \dfrac{-3}{3^3} = \dfrac{-1}{9}$

and RHD at $x = 3 = \dfrac{3}{3^3} = \dfrac{1}{9}$

For $x > 3$

$$f'(x) = -\frac{(x-6)}{x^3}$$

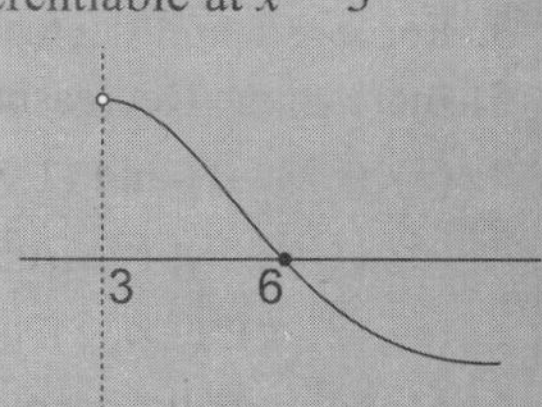

FIGURE 5.99

$\therefore$ Wavy curve of $f'(x)$ is

For $x < 3$; $f'(x) = \frac{(x-6)}{x^3}$

At $x = 3$; $f'(3^-) < 0$ and $f'(3^+) > 0$ is not monotonic at $x = 3$

$\therefore$ $f(x)$ is strictly increasing for $x \in (-\infty, 0)$ and $(3, 6)$

And $f(x)$ is strictly decreasing for $x \in (0, 3)$ and $(6, \infty)$

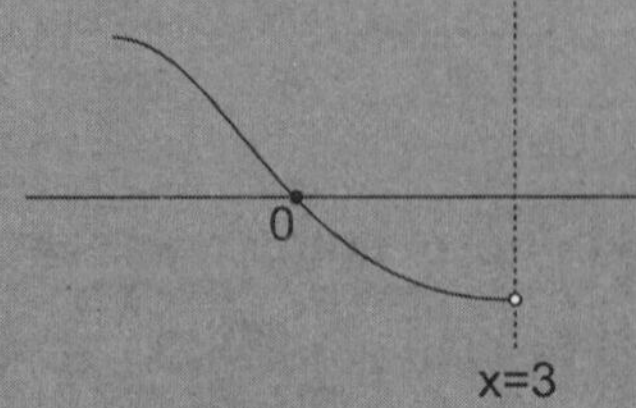

FIGURE 5.100

TEXTUAL EXERCISE–3: (SUBJECTIVE)

1. Compute the intervals of monotonicity for the function $f(x) = x + \ln(1 - 4x)$.
2. Compute the intervals of monotonicity for the function $f(x) = \frac{x}{\ln x}$
3. If the function $f(x) = ax - \sin x$ is monotonic $\forall x \in \mathbb{R}$, then find the range of 'a'.
4. Prove that $f(x) = \int_{x^2}^{x^3} \frac{dt}{\ln t}, (x > 0)$ is always increasing function of x in its domain.
5. Test the monotonicity of the given function and find their intervals of monotonicities.

   (a) $\frac{3x}{1+x^2}$ (b) $\frac{x^2-x+1}{x^2+x+1}$

   (c) $x^{1/x}$ (d) $ex \ln ex$

   (e) $\frac{\ln x}{ex^2}$ (f) $x^3 + x^{-3}$

   (g) $f(x) = 2.e^{x^2-4x}$ (h) $f(x) = x^2e^{-x}$
6. If $\tan(\pi \cos\theta) = \cot(\pi \sin\theta)$, $f(x) = (\cos\theta + \sin\theta)^x$, then determine the interval of monotonicity of $f(x)$.
7. Check whether $f(x) = \cos(\cos x)$ increasing or decreasing in $[0, \pi/2]$.
8. Find the interval in which $f(x) = x^4 - 14x^2 + 24x - 3$ is strictly increasing or strictly decreasing.
9. Find the intervals in which the function $f(x) = 3\cos^4 x + 10\cos^3 x + 6\cos^2 x - 3$, $0 \le x \le \pi$; is monotonically
10. Find the range of values of 'a' for which the function $f(x) = x^3 + (2a+3)x^2 + 3(2a+1)x + 5$ is monotonic in $\mathbb{R}$. Hence find the set of values of 'a' for which $f(x)$ invertible.

Answer Keys

1. in $(-\infty, -3/4]$ and decreasing in $[-3/4, 1/4)$
2. $[e, \infty)$ and decreasing in $(0, 1)$ and $(1, e]$
3. For $a \ge 1$ and decreasing for $a \le -1$
5. Increasing: Decreasing

   (a) $(-\infty, -1]$ and $[1,\infty]$ (b) $(-\infty, -1]$ and $[1,\infty)$; $[-1, 1]$ (c) $(0, e]$; $[e, \infty)$

   (d) $[1/e^2, \infty)$; $(0, 1/e^2]$ (e) $(0, \sqrt{e}]$; $[\sqrt{e}, \infty)$ (f) $(-\infty, -1]$ and $[1,\infty)$; $[-1, 0) \cup (0, 1]$

   (g) $(2, \infty)$; $(-\infty, 2)$ (h) $[0, 2]$; $(-\infty, 0]$ and $[2, \infty)$
6. Monotonically decreasing $\forall x \in \mathbb{R}$
7. increasing
8. Increases on $[-3, 1]$ and $[2, \infty)$; decreases on $(-\infty, -3]$ and $[1, 2]$
9. Increasing in $x \in (\pi/2, 2\pi/3)$ and decreasing in $[0, \pi/2) \cup (2\pi/3, \pi]$
10. $0 \le a \le \frac{3}{2}$

TEXTUAL EXERCISE–3: (OBJECTIVE)

1. A function $g(\theta) = \int_0^{\sin^2\theta} f(x)dx + \int_0^{\cos^2\theta} f(x)dx$; where θ is defined in the interval $\left(-\frac{\pi}{2}, \frac{\pi}{2}\right)$ and $f(x)$ is an increasing function, then $g(\theta)$ is increasing in the interval
(a) $\left(-\frac{\pi}{2}, 0\right)$ (b) $\left(-\frac{\pi}{2}, -\frac{\pi}{4}\right)$
(c) $\left(0, \frac{\pi}{4}\right)$ (d) $\left(-\frac{\pi}{4}, 0\right)$

2. The interval in which the function $f(x)$ = sin $(\ell n\, x) - \cos(\ell n\, x)$ is strictly increasing.
(a) $x \in (e^{2n\pi-\pi/4}, e^{2n\pi+3\pi/4}), n \in \mathbb{Z}$
(b) $x \in [e^{2n\pi-\pi/4}, e^{2n\pi+3\pi/4}], n \in \mathbb{Z}$
(c) $x \in [e^{2n\pi}, e^{(2n+2)\pi}]$
(d) $x \in \mathbb{R}$

3. If $f(x) = a^{\{a^{|x|}\operatorname{sgn} x\}}$; $g(x) = a^{[a^{|x|}\operatorname{sgn} x]}$ for $a > 0$, $a \neq 1$ and $x \in R$, where {} and [] denote the fractional part and integral part functions respectively, then which of the following statements can hold good for the function $h(x)$, where $(\ell n\, a)\, h(x) = (\ell n\,(f(x)) + \ell n(g(x)))$
(a) 'h' is even and increasing
(b) 'h' is odd and decreasing
(c) 'h' is even and decreasing
(d) 'h'is odd and increasing

4. The number of critical points of the function $f(x) = |x|\, e^{-x}$ is
(a) 1 (b) 2
(c) 3 (d) none of these

5. The number of critical points of the function $f(x) = (ax^2 + bx + c)\,|x|$; where $ac < 0$ is
(a) 1 (b) 2
(c) 3 (d) 4

6. The number of critical points of the function $f(x) = (1 - x)\,|x - 3|$ is
(a) 1 (b) 2
(c) 3 (d) 4

7. The critical points of $f(x) = x^2 - 2\,|x|$ are
(a) {0} (b) {–1, 0}
(c) {–1, 0, 1} (d) {0, 1}

8. The number of critical points of $f(x) = (x - 1)(x - 2) + (x - 2)\,|x - 1|$ is
(a) 2 (b) 3
(c) 4 (d) None of these

9. The function $f(x) = 2 \ln |x| - x\,|x|$ decreases over the interval
(a) $(-\infty, -1)$ (b) $(-1, 0)$
(c) $(0, 1)$ (d) $(1, \infty)$

10. $\int_1^x \frac{dt}{t}$ is an increasing function of x for
(a) $x > 0$ (b) $x \geq 0$
(c) $x < 0$ (d) none of these

11. The function $y = \frac{2x - 1}{x - 2}$ $(x \neq 2)$:
(a) is its own inverse
(b) decreases for all values of x
(c) has a graph entirely above x-axis
(d) is bound for all x

12. The values of p for which the function $f(x) = \left(\frac{\sqrt{p+4}}{1-p} - 1\right) x^3 - 3x + \ln 5$ decreases for all real x is:
(a) $(-\infty, \infty)$
(b) $\left[-4, \frac{3-\sqrt{21}}{2}\right] \cup (1, \infty)$
(c) $\left[-3, \frac{5-\sqrt{27}}{2}\right] \cup (2, \infty)$
(d) $[1, \infty)$

13. Let $f(x) = x^3 + ax^2 + bx + 5\sin^2 x$ be an increasing function in the set of real numbers $\mathbb{R}$. Then a and b satisfy the condition:
(a) $a^2 - 3b - 15 > 0$ (b) $a^2 - 3b + 15 < 0$
(c) $a^2 - 3b - 15 < 0$ (d) $a > 0$ and $b > 0$

14. On which of the following intervals, the function $x^{100} + \sin x - 1$ is strictly increasing?
(a) $(-1, 1)$ (b) $(0, 1)$
(c) $(\pi/2, \pi)$ (d) $(0, \pi/2)$

15. In which of the following intervals the function $f(x) = x^2 \log 3x$ is an increasing function

(a) $[0, e]$ (b) $[0, e^{1/2}]$
(c) $(0, e^{-1/2}]$ (d) none of these

16. $f(x) = \tan^{-1}(\sin x + \cos x)^3$ is an increasing function in
(a) $(0, \pi/4)$ (b) $(0, \pi/2)$
(c) $(-\pi/4, \pi/4)$ (d) none of these

17. If the function $f(x) = \cos|x| - 2ax + b$ increases along the entire number scale, the range of values of a is given by
(a) $a \le b$ (b) $a = b/2$
(c) $a \le -1/2$ (d) $a \ge -3/2$

18. The function $f(x) = x - \cot^{-1} x + \log(\sqrt{x^2+1} - x)$ is increasing on
(a) $(-\infty, 0)$ (b) $(0, \infty)$
(c) $(-\infty, \infty)$ (d) $[0, \infty)$

19. The function $\sin^{-1} 2x\sqrt{1-x^2}$ is decreasing on
(a) $\left(-1, -\frac{1}{\sqrt{2}}\right)$ (b) $\left(-\frac{1}{\sqrt{2}}, \frac{1}{\sqrt{2}}\right)$
(c) $\left(\frac{1}{\sqrt{2}}, 1\right)$ (d) $\left[\frac{1}{\sqrt{2}}, 1\right]$

20. The function f defined by $f(x) = (x + 2)e^{-x}$ is
(a) decreasing for all x
(b) decreasing in $(-\infty, -1)$ and increasing $(-1, \infty)$
(c) increasing for all x
(d) decreasing in $(-1, \infty)$ and increasing $(-\infty, -1)$

21. Let $f(x) = x\,e^{x(1-x)}$, then $f(x)$ is
(a) increasing on $[-1/2, 1]$
(b) decreasing on $\mathbb{R}$
(c) increasing on $\mathbb{R}$
(d) decreasing on $[-1/2, 1]$

Answer Keys

1. (d)	**2.** (a,b)	**3.** (d)	**4.** (b)	**5.** (c)	**6.** (b)	**7.** (c)	**8.** (d)	**9.** (a, b, d)	**10.** (a)
11. (a, b)	**12.** (b)	**13.** (b)	**14.** (b,c,d)	**15.** (d)	**16.** (a,c)	**17.** (c)	**18.** (a,b,c,d)	**19.** (a,c,d)	
20. (d)	**21.** (a)								

■ PROPERTIES OF MONOTONIC FUNCTION

By application of increasing (↑) function, the sign of inequality does not change. But the sign of inequality reverses on the application of a decreasing (↓) function. i.e.,

$$\text{if } a \le x \le b; \begin{cases} f(a) \le f(x) \le f(b) & \text{if } f \text{ is } \uparrow \\ f(a) \ge f(x) \ge f(b) & \text{if } f \text{ is } \downarrow \end{cases}.$$

If $f(x)$ is continuous and increasing function for all $x \in [a, b]$ then R_f: $[f(a), f(b)]$.

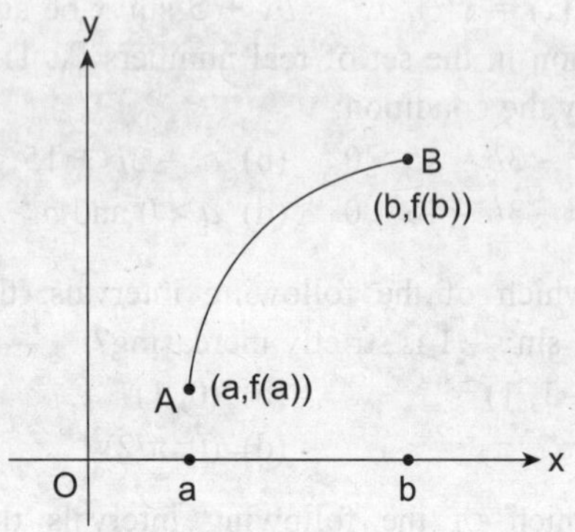

FIGURE 5.101

(i) If $f(x)$ is continuous and decreasing $\forall\ x \in D_f : [a,b]$

Then $R_f : [f(b),\ f(a)]$

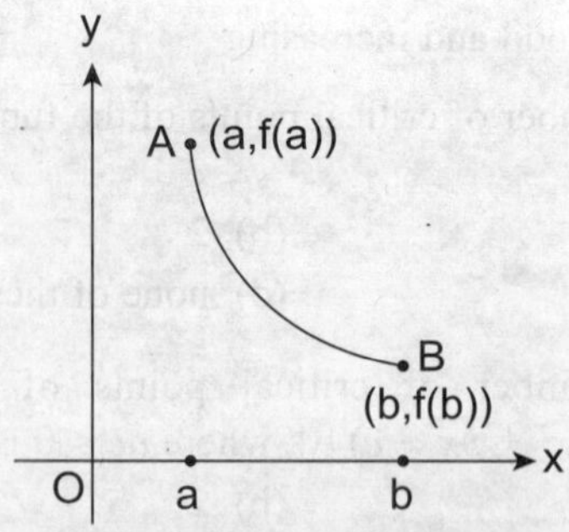

FIGURE 5.102

(ii) If f is increasing for $x \in [a,\alpha)$ & ↓ for $x \in (\alpha, b]$ and $f(x)$ is continuous,

then $R_f : \left[\min\{f(a),\ f(b)\}, f(\alpha)\right]$

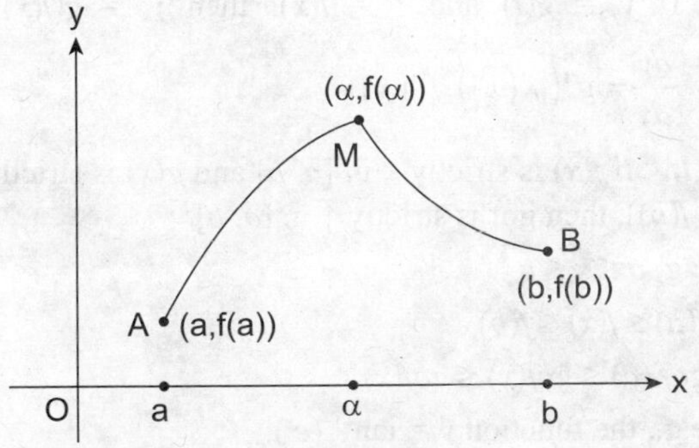

FIGURE 5.103

(iii) If $f(x)$ is monotonically decreasing function $\forall x \in [a, \alpha)$ and increasing function $\forall x \in (\alpha, b]$ and is continuous in $[a, b]$, then $R_f : [f(\alpha), \max\{f(a), f(b)\}]$.

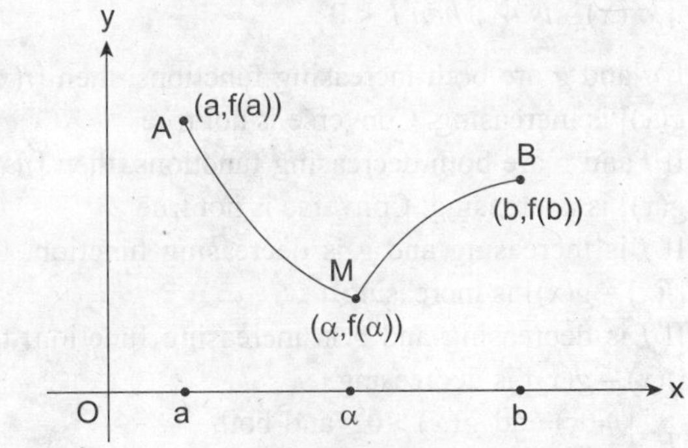

FIGURE 5.104

ILLUSTRATION 48: Find the range of the following function is for indicated domain $f(x) = \ln(x^x + 1)\ \forall x \in (0, 1]$

SOLUTION: $f(x) = \ln(x^x + 1)$. First of all find the range of $(x^x + 1)$

Let $y = x^x$; $\log y = x \ln x$

$\Rightarrow \dfrac{1}{y} \cdot y' = 1 + \ln x$

For $x \in (0, 1]$; $y' = x^x(1 + \ln x)$

Also x^x is always positive

and $1 + \ln x > 0\ \forall x \in \left(\dfrac{1}{e}, 1\right]$

$1 + \ln x < 0\ \forall x \in \left(0, \dfrac{1}{e}\right)$

$1 + \ln x = 0$ at $x = \dfrac{1}{e}$

Let $L = \lim\limits_{x \to 0^+} x^x$; $\ln L = \lim\limits_{x \to 0^+} \dfrac{\ln x}{1/x} = \lim\limits_{x \to 0^+} \dfrac{1/x}{-1/x^2}$

$\Rightarrow \log_e L = 0 \qquad \Rightarrow L = e^0 = 1$

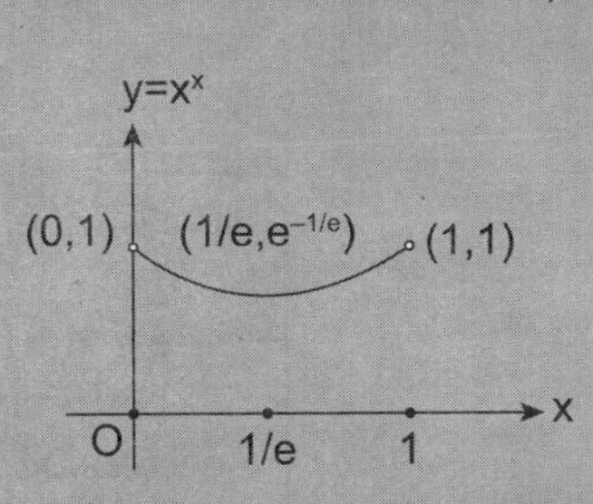

FIGURE 5.105

Range of y: $[e^{-1/e}, 1]$

This is the range of x^x

Now $e^{-1/e} \le x^x \le 1$

$\Rightarrow e^{-1/e} + 1 \le x^x + 1 \le 2 \qquad \Rightarrow \ln(e^{-1/e} + 1) \le (\ln(x^x + 1) \le \ln 2$

Range $\equiv [\ln(e^{-1/e} + 1), \ln 2]$

(iv) If $f(x)$ is monotonically increasing, then $\begin{cases} kf(x) \text{ is } \uparrow \text{ when } k>0 \\ kf(x) \text{ is } \downarrow \text{ when } k<0 \end{cases}$

(v) If f and g are both increasing functions, then $[f(x) + g(x)]$ is increasing. Converse is not true

(vi) If f and g are both decreasing functions, then $[f(x) + g(x)]$ is decreasing. Converse is not true

(vii) If f is increasing and g is decreasing function, then $[f(x) - g(x)]$ is increasing.

(viii) If f is decreasing and g is increasing function, then $[f(x) - g(x)]$ is decreasing.

(ix) If $\begin{cases} f(x) \text{ and } g(x)>0 \text{ and both } \uparrow \\ f(x) \text{ and } g(x)<0 \text{ and both } \downarrow \end{cases}$

$\Rightarrow y = f(x).g(x) \uparrow$. Both converse is not true.

(x) If f is $\uparrow \Rightarrow 1/f$ is decreasing function wherever defined.

(xi) If f and $g > 0$ and f is increasing and g is decreasing

$\Rightarrow \dfrac{f(x)}{g(x)}$ is $\uparrow$

$\because y = \dfrac{f(x)}{g(x)}$

$\Rightarrow y' = \dfrac{f'(x).g(x) - f(x).g'(x)}{g^2(x)}$

$= \dfrac{+(+)-(+)(-)}{+} = +ve$

(xii) Composition of two monotonically increasing function is always an $\uparrow$ function.

If $x_1 > x_2$

$\Rightarrow g(x_1) > g(x_2)$ ($\because g(x)$ is an increasing function)

$\Rightarrow f(g(x_1)) > f(g(x_2))$ ($\because f(x)$ is an increasing function)

$\Rightarrow f(g(x))$ is $\uparrow$ if $f(x)$ and $g(x)$ are $\uparrow$ functions.

(xiii) Composition of two monotonically decreasing functions is always an $\uparrow$ function.

If $x_1 > x_2$

$\Rightarrow g(x_1) < g(x_2)$

($\because g(x)$ is a decreasing function)

$\Rightarrow f(g(x_1)) > f(g(x_2))$

($\because f(x)$ is a decreasing function)

$\Rightarrow f(g(x))$ is $\uparrow$ if $f(x)$ and $g(x)$ are $\downarrow$ function.

(xiv) When f and g have opposite monotonicity, then $f(g(x))$ is a decreasing function.

e.g. $y = f(g(x))$

$y' = f'(g(x)).\, g'(x)$

if $f(x)$ is $\uparrow$ and $g(x)$ is $\downarrow$, then $y' < 0$

($\because f'(g(x)) > 0$ and $g'(x) < 0$)

Similarly if $f(x)$ is $\downarrow$ and $g(x)$ is $\uparrow$, then $y' < 0$

(xv) If $y = g(t)$ and $t = f(x)$, then $y = g(f(x))$ and

$$\frac{dy}{dx} = g'(f(x)).f'(x)$$

Case I: If $f(x)$ is strictly $\uparrow$ in $[a, b]$ and $g(x)$ is strictly $\uparrow$ in $[f(a), f(b)]$, then gof is strictly $\uparrow$ in $[a, b]$.

e.g. $a \le x \le b$

$f(a) \le f(x) \le f(b)$

$gof(a) \le gof(x) \le gof(x)$

e.g., the function $y = \tan^{-1}(e^x)$.

Let $f(x) = e^x$ is strictly increasing and $g(x) = \tan^{-1}(x)$ is strictly increasing $\forall x \in \mathbb{R}$

$\therefore$ $y = g(f(x))$ is strictly increasing.

Case II: If f is strictly decreasing in $[a, b]$ and g is strictly decreasing in $[f(b), f(a)]$, then gof is strictly increasing $\uparrow$ for all x.

e.g.: The function $y = \cot^{-1}(\log_{1/2} x)$

Let $z = \log_{\frac{1}{2}} x$; then z is a decreasing function $\forall x \in (0, \infty)$

$\Rightarrow$ $\log_{1/2} x \in (-\infty, \infty)$ and $\cot^{-1} x$ is strictly decreasing for $x \in \mathbb{R}$

$\Rightarrow$ y is a composition of two decreasing functions

$\Rightarrow$ y is strictly increasing

Case III: If f is strictly increasing in $[a, b]$ and g is strictly decreasing in $[f(a), f(b)]$ then gof is strictly decreasing in $[a, b]$

e.g., $y = \cos(\sin^{-1}x)$ in $[0, 1]$,

$z = \sin^{-1} x$ is increasing in $[0, 1]$

then, range of z in $\left[0, \frac{\pi}{2}\right]$ and $\cos(z)$ is decreasing in $\left[0, \frac{\pi}{2}\right]$

$\therefore$ $y = \cos(\sin^{-1} x)$ is decreasing in $[0, 1]$

Case IV: If f is strictly decreasing in $[a, b]$ and g is strictly increasing in $[f(b), f(a)]$, then gof is strictly decreasing in $[a, b]$

e.g. the function $y = \ln(\cot^{-1}x)$

Let $z = \cot^{-1} x$ is a decreasing function, then $y = ln(z)$ is a decreasing function

(xvi) f and f^{-1} have same monotonic nature. i.e., either both are increasing or both are decreasing.

Proof: If $g(x) = f^{-1}(x)$

$\Rightarrow f(g(x)) = x$

$\Rightarrow f'(g(x)).g'(x) = 1$

$\Rightarrow g'(x) = \dfrac{1}{f'(g(x))}$

$$\Rightarrow \begin{cases} f \text{ is} \uparrow & \Rightarrow g \text{ is} \uparrow \\ f \text{ is} \downarrow & \Rightarrow g \text{ is} \downarrow \end{cases}$$

Now $g'(x)$ has the same sign as $f'(x)$ and hence $g(x)$ has the same monotonocity as that of $f(x)$

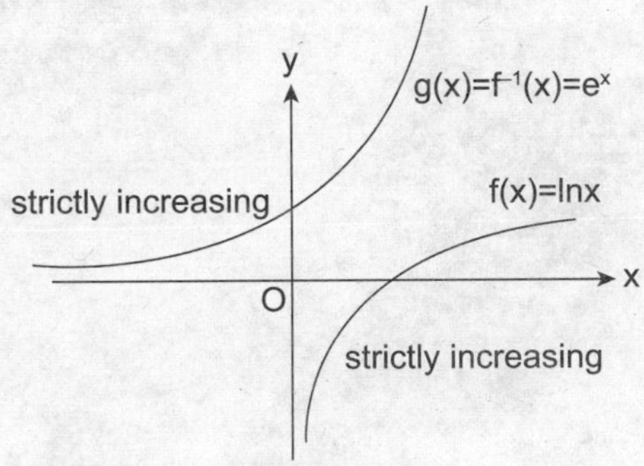

FIGURE 5.106

Similarly if $y = f(x) = -\tan x \ \forall \ x \in (-\pi/2, 0]$ and $g(x) = \tan^{-1}(-x) \ \forall \ x \in [0,\infty)$.

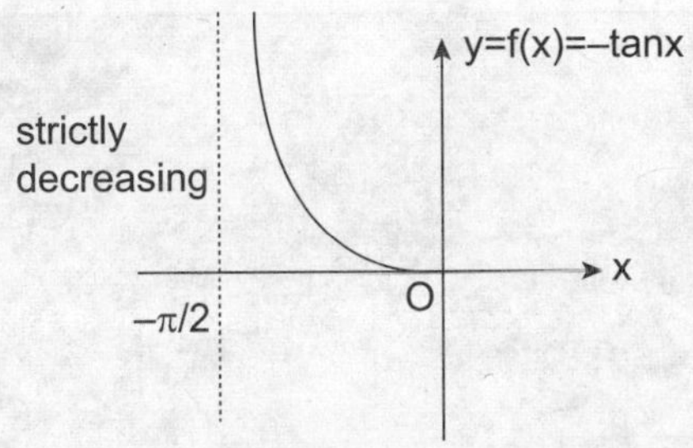

FIGURE 5.107

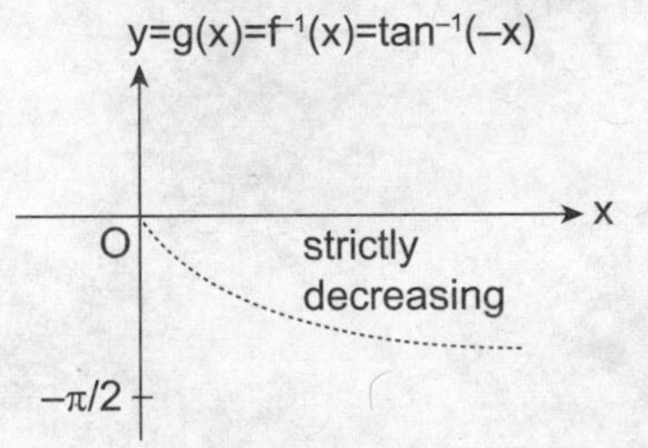

FIGURE 5.108

ILLUSTRATION 49: Let $f(x)$ be an increasing function defined on $(0, \infty)$. If $f(2a^2 + a + 1) > f(3a^2 - 4a + 1)$. Find the range of a.

SOLUTION: Given that $f(x)$ is increasing on $(0, \infty)$ and $f(2a^2 + a + 1) > f(3a^2 - 4a + 1)$

Now, so $2a^2 + a + 1 > 0 \ \forall \ a \in \mathbb{R}$

$[\because$ dis. $< 0 \ \forall \ a \in \mathbb{R}]$ ...(i)

Also $3a^2 - 4a + 1 > 0 \ (\because \ a^2 - 4a + 1) \in D_f$

$\Rightarrow \ (a - 1)(3a - 1) > 0$

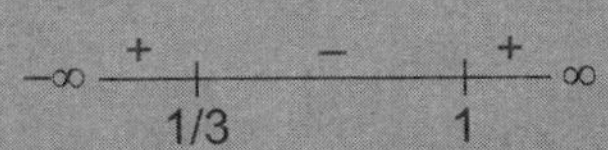

FIGURE 5.109

$\Rightarrow \ a \in (-\infty, 1/3) \cup (1, \infty)$ ...(ii)

And given that $f(x)$ is increasing on $(0, \infty)$

Therefore $f(2a^2 + a + 1) > f(3a^2 - 4a + 1)$

$\Rightarrow \ 2a^2 + a + 1 > 3a^2 - 4a + 1$

$\Rightarrow \ a^2 - 5a < 0$

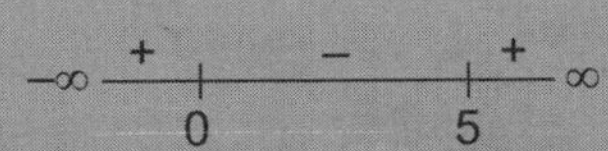

FIGURE 5.110

$\Rightarrow \ a \in (0, 5)$ ...(iii)

From the intersection of (i), (ii) and (iii); we get $a \in (0, 1/3) \cup (1, 5)$

ILLUSTRATION 50: Find the greatest and the least values of the following functions in the given interval if they exist.

(a) $f(x) = \sin^{-1} \frac{x}{\sqrt{x^2+1}} - \ell n x \ in \left[\frac{1}{\sqrt{3}}, \sqrt{3}\right]$ (b) $f(x) = 12x^{4/3} - 6x^{1/3}, x \in [-1, 1]$

(c) $y = x^5 - 5x^4 + 5x^3 + 1$ in $[-1, 2]$

SOLUTION: (a) $f(x) = \sin^{-1}\left(\frac{x}{\sqrt{x^2+1}}\right) - \ln(x)\ ;\ \forall\ x \in \left[\frac{1}{\sqrt{3}}, \sqrt{3}\right]$

$\Rightarrow f'(x) = \frac{1}{1+x^2} - \frac{1}{x} = \frac{x-1-x^2}{x(1+x^2)} = -\left(\frac{x^2-x+1}{x(1+x^2)}\right)$

$\Rightarrow$ For $x > 0$; $x^2 - x + 1 > 0$; $1 + x^2 > 0$

$\Rightarrow f'(x) < 0$

$\Rightarrow f(x)$ is strictly decreasing for $x > 0$

$\Rightarrow f\left(\frac{1}{\sqrt{3}}\right)$ = greatest value and $f(\sqrt{3}) =$ least value

Now $f\left(\frac{1}{\sqrt{3}}\right) = \frac{\pi}{6} + \frac{1}{2}\log 3$ and $f(\sqrt{3}) = \frac{\pi}{3} - \frac{1}{2}\log 3$

$\therefore$ Maximum value $= \frac{\pi}{6} + \frac{1}{2}\log 3$

Minimum value $= \frac{\pi}{3} - \frac{1}{2}\log 3$

(b) $f(x) = 12x^{4/3} - 6x^{1/3}; x \in [-1, 1]$

$\Rightarrow f'(x) = 16x^{1/3} - 2x^{-2/3}$

$\therefore f'(x) > 0 \quad \Rightarrow 16x^{1/3} > 2x^{-2/3}$

$\Rightarrow 16x > 2 \quad \Rightarrow x > \frac{1}{8}$

And $f'(x) < 0 \quad \Rightarrow 16x^{1/3} < 2x^{-2/3}$

$8x < 1 \quad \Rightarrow x < \frac{1}{8}$

$\therefore f(x)$ increases on $\left(\frac{1}{8}, 1\right]$ and decreases on $\left[-1, \frac{1}{8}\right)$

Also $f(1) = 6$

$f(-1) = 18$

$f\left(\frac{1}{8}\right) = -\frac{9}{4}$

$\therefore$ Minimum value $= -\frac{9}{4}$ and Max value $= 18$

(c) $f(x) = x^5 - 5x^4 + 5x^3 + 1\ x \in [-1, 2]$

$f'(x) = 5x^4 - 20x^3 + 15x^2$

$= 5x^2 (x^2 - 4x + 3) = 5x^2 (x - 1)(x - 3)$

Wavy curve of $f'(x)$;

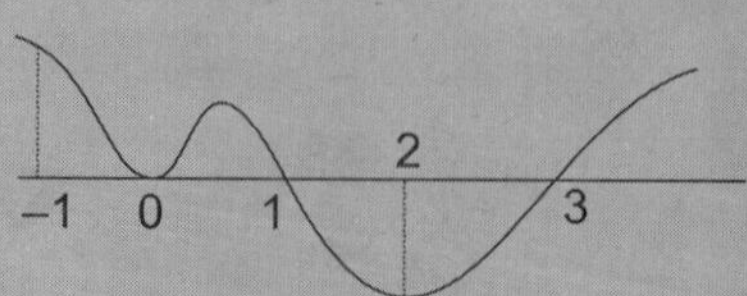

FIGURE 5.111

$\therefore f(x)$ increases on $[-1, 1)$ and decreases on $(1, 2]$

Also $f(1) = 2, f(-1) = -10, f(2) = -7$

$\therefore$ Maximum value $= 2$ and Minimum value $= -10$

ILLUSTRATION 51: Let $a + b = 4$; where $a < 2$ and let $g(x)$ be a differentiable function. If $\frac{dg}{dx} > 0$ for all x, prove that $\int_0^a g(x)dx + \int_0^b g(x)\,dx$ increases as $(b - a)$ increases.

SOLUTION: Let $b - a = k$ and $a + b = 4$

$a = \frac{4-k}{2}$ and $b = \frac{4+k}{2}$

$k > 0$ because $a < 2$ and $b > 2$

Let $\int_0^a g(x)dx + \int_0^b g(x)dx = f(k)$ $\qquad \Rightarrow f(k) = \int_0^{\frac{4-k}{2}} g(x)\,dx + \int_0^{\frac{4+k}{2}} g(x)\,dx$

Differentiating both sides, w.r..t 'k'; we get $f'(k) = \frac{1}{2}\left[g\left(\frac{4+k}{2}\right) - g\left(\frac{4-k}{2}\right)\right]$

Now, given that $g(x)$ is an increasing function

$\therefore \quad \frac{4+k}{2} > \frac{4-k}{2}$ $\qquad \Rightarrow \quad g\left(\frac{4+k}{2}\right) > g\left(\frac{4-k}{2}\right)$

$\Rightarrow \quad f'(k) > 0$

Hence $\int_0^a g(x) + \int_0^b g(x)$ increases if $(b - a)\uparrow$

ILLUSTRATION 52: Let $h(x) = f(x) - \{f(x)\}^2 + \{f(x)\}^3$ for every real number 'x', then :

(a) 'h' is increasing whenever 'f' is increasing

(b) 'h' is increasing whenever 'f' is decreasing

(c) 'h' is decreasing whenever 'f' is decreasing

(d) nothing can be said in general.

SOLUTION: (a), (c) Here $h(x) = f(x) - \{f(x)\}^2 + \{f(x)\}^3$

$\Rightarrow \quad h'(x) = f'(x) - 2f(x)f'(x) + 3\{f(x)\}^2 f'(x)$

$= f'(x)\,[1 - 2f(x) + 3\{f(x)\}^2] = f'(x)\,(3y^2 - 2y + 1)$; where $y = f(x)$

The discriminant of $3y^2 - 2y + 1 = 4 - 12 = -8 < 0$

and so its sign is the same as the co-efficient of y^2 i.e., $3y^2 - 2y + 1 > 0\ \forall\, y \in \mathbb{R}$

$\therefore \quad h'(x) = f'(x)$ (a positive quantity)

$\Rightarrow$ sign of $h'(x)$ is the same as that of $f'(x)$

$\Rightarrow$ either $h'(x) > 0$ and $f'(x) > 0$

or $h'(x) < 0$ and $f'(x) < 0$. Hence $h(x)$ and $f(x)$ increase and decrease together.

ILLUSTRATION 53: Let $f(\sin x) < 0$ and $f''(\sin x) > 0$, $\forall x \in \left(0, \frac{\pi}{2}\right)$ and $g(x) = f(\sin x) + f(\cos x)$, then $g(x)$ is decreasing in

(a) $\left(\frac{\pi}{4}, \frac{\pi}{2}\right)$ $\qquad$ (b) $\left(0, \frac{\pi}{4}\right)$

(c) $\left(0, \frac{\pi}{2}\right)$ $\qquad$ (d) $\left(\frac{\pi}{6}, \frac{\pi}{2}\right)$

SOLUTION: Given $g(x) = f(\sin x) + f(\cos x)$

Differentiating w.r.t. x; we get $g'(x) = f'(\sin x).\cos x - f'(\cos x).\sin x$

Again differentiating w.r.t. x; we get $g''(x) = -f'(\sin x).\sin x + f''(\sin x).\cos^2 x - f'(\cos x).\cos x + f''(\cos x).\sin^2 x$

Now, given $f'(\sin x) < 0 \ \forall x \in \left(0, \frac{\pi}{2}\right)$ ...(i)

$\Rightarrow f'\left(\sin\left(\frac{\pi}{2} - x\right)\right) < 0 \ \forall x \in \left(0, \frac{\pi}{2}\right)$

$\left[\because \text{ If } x \in \left(0, \frac{\pi}{2}\right); \frac{\pi}{2} - x \in \left(0, \frac{\pi}{2}\right)\right]$

$\Rightarrow f'(\cos x) < 0$ ...(ii)

Similarly, given $f''(\sin x) > 0 \ \forall x \in \left(0, \frac{\pi}{2}\right)$ ...(iii)

$\Rightarrow f''\left(\sin\left(\frac{\pi}{2} - x\right)\right) > 0 \qquad \Rightarrow f''(\cos x) > 0$ ...(iv)

$\therefore g''(x) > 0$ (Using equation (i), (ii), (iii) and (iv))

$\Rightarrow g'(x)$ is increasing in $\left(0, \frac{\pi}{2}\right)$. Also $g'\left(\frac{\pi}{4}\right) = 0$

$\Rightarrow g'(x) > 0 \forall x \in \left(\frac{\pi}{4}, \frac{\pi}{2}\right)$ and $g'(x) < 0 \ \forall \ x \in \left(0, \frac{\pi}{4}\right)$. Thus $g(x)$ is decreasing in $\left(0, \frac{\pi}{4}\right)$

ILLUSTRATION 54: Let $f(x)$ be a monotonic polynomial of $(2m - 2)$ degree; where $m \in \mathbb{N}$, then the equation $f(x) + f(3x) + f(5x) + ... + f((2m - 1)x) = 2m - 1$ has

(a) atleast one real root
(b) $(2m - 1)$ real roots
(c) exactly one real root
(d) none of these

SOLUTION: (c). $f(x)$ is monotonic $\Rightarrow f'(x) < 0$ *or* $f'(x) > 0 \ \forall \ x \in R$

$\Rightarrow f'(px) < 0$ or $f'(px) > 0 \ \forall \ x \in R$

$\Rightarrow f(px)$ is also monotonic

$\Rightarrow f(x) + f(3x) + ... + f[(2m-1)x]$ is a monotonic polynomial of odd degree $(2m - 1)$, so it will attain all real values only once.

ILLUSTRATION 55: Given that $f'(x) > g'(x)$ for all real x, and $f(0) = g(0)$, then $f(x) < g(x)$ for all x belonging to

(a) $(0, \infty)$
(b) $(-\infty, 0)$
(c) $(-\infty, \infty)$
(d) none of these

SOLUTION: (b) Let $h(x) = f(x) - g(x)$

$\Rightarrow h'(x) = f'(x) - g'(x) > 0 \ \forall \ x \in \mathbb{R}$

$h(x)$ is an increasing function and $h(0) = f(0) - g(0) = 0$.

Therefore, $h(x) > 0 \ \forall \ x \in (0, \infty)$ and $h(x) < 0 \ \forall \ x \in (-\infty, 0)$

ILLUSTRATION 56: Let domain and range of $f(x)$ and $g(x)$ are $[0, \infty)$. If $f(x)$ be an increasing and $g(x)$ be a decreasing function, also $h(x) = f(g(x))$, $h(0) = 0$ and $p(x) = h(x^3 - 2x^2 + 2x) - h(4)$, then for all x belonging to $(0, 2)$

(a) $p(x)\in(0,-h(4))$ (b) $p(x)\in(-h(4),0)$

(c) $p(x)\in(-h(4),h(4))$ (d) $p(x)\in(h(4),-h(4))$

SOLUTION: (a) Here $h(x)\, f(g(x))$ and $h'(x) = f'(g(x)).g'(x) < 0 \Rightarrow h'(x) < 0\ \forall x \in [0,\infty)$

Also $h(0) = 0$.

Therefore, $h(x) < 0\ \forall\ x \in [0,\infty)$

Now, $p(x) = h(x^3 - 2x^2 + 2x) - h(4)$

$\Rightarrow p'(x) = h'(x^3 - 2x^2 + 2x)(3x^2 - 4x + 2) < 0\ \forall\ x \in (0,2)$

Since $h'(x^3 - 2x^2 + 2x) < 0\ \forall\ x \in (0,\infty)$ and $3x^2 - 4x + 2 > 0\ \forall\ x \in R$

$\Rightarrow$ $p(x)$ is a decreasing function or $p(2) < p(x) < p(0)$ for all $x \in (0,2)$

$\Rightarrow h(4) - h(4) < p(x) < h(0) - h(4)$

$\Rightarrow 0 < p(x) < -h(4)$.

ILLUSTRATION 57: Find a polynomial $f(x)$ of degree 5 which increases in the interval $(-\infty, 2]$ and $[6, \infty)$ and decreases in the interval $[2, 6]$. Given that $f(0) = 3$ and $f'(4) = 0$.

SOLUTION: Since $f'(4) = 0$; therefore $x = 4$ is a repeated root of the polynomial $f(x)$, hence $f(x)$ contains $(x-4)^2$. Also since $x = 2$ and $x = 6$ are critical points, therefore $f'(x)$ must contain $(x-2)$ and $(x-6)$. The wavy cure of derivative will be like

$\Rightarrow f'(x) = k(x-2)(x-4)^2(x-6)$ and $k > 0$

$\Rightarrow f(x) = k\int(x^2 - 8x + 12)(x^2 - 8x + 16)\,dx$

$\Rightarrow f(x) = k\int(x^4 - 16x^3 + 64x^2 + 28(x^2 - 8x) + 192)\,dx$

$\Rightarrow f(x) = k\left(\frac{x^5}{5} - 4x^4 + \frac{92}{3}x^3 - 112x^2 + 192x\right) + c$

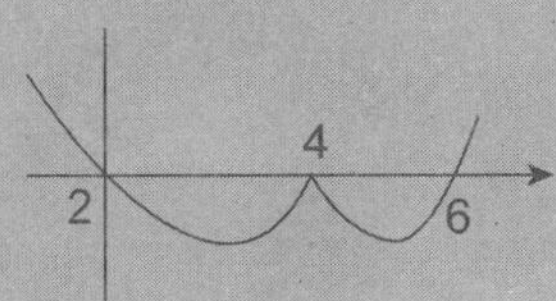

FIGURE 5.112

Now as $f(0) = 3$ $\Rightarrow c = 3$

$$\Rightarrow f(x) = k\left[\frac{x^5}{5} - 4x^4 - \frac{92}{3}x^3 - 112x^2 + 192x\right] + 3,\ k > 0$$

ILLUSTRATION 58: Let $f(x) = \begin{cases} -x^3 + \dfrac{b^3 - b^2 + b - 1}{b^2 + 3b + 2}; & 0 \le x < 1 \\ 2x - 3; & 1 \le x \le 3 \end{cases}$. Find all possible real values of b such that $f(x)$ has the smallest value at $x = 1$

SOLUTION: At $x = 1$, $f(x) = -1$

$\Rightarrow$ Smallest value of $f(x) = -1$

$\Rightarrow$ at all other points of the interval, $f(x) > -1$.

Now, for $x \ge 1$, $f(x) = 2x - 3$

$\Rightarrow f'(x) = 2 > 0 \Rightarrow f(x)$ is an increasing function $\Rightarrow$ least value exists at $x = 1$

Again, for $x < 1$, $f'(x) = -3x^2 < 0 \Rightarrow f(x)$ is decreasing function in the interval $0 \le x < 1$

Therefore, $f(x)$ is smallest at $x = 1$ provided

$$f(1-0) = \lim_{h\to 0} -(1-h)^3 + \frac{b^3-b^2+b-1}{b^2+3b+2} \geq -1$$

$$\Rightarrow -1 + \frac{(b^2+1)(b-1)}{(b+1)(b+2)} \geq -1 \Rightarrow \frac{(b^2+1)(b-1)}{(b+1)(b+2)} \geq 0$$

$$\Rightarrow \frac{(b-1)}{(b+1)(b+2)} \geq 0 \text{ [since } b^2+1 \text{ is always positive]}$$

$\Rightarrow b \in (-2, -1) \cup [1, \infty)$

ILLUSTRATION 59: The number of solutions of the equation $x^3 + 2x^2 + 5x + 2\cos x = 0$ in $[0, 2\pi]$ is

(a) 0 (b) 1

(c) 2 (d) 3

SOLUTION: (a) Let $f(x) = x^3 + 2x^2 + 5x + 2\cos x$

$$\Rightarrow f'(x) = 3x^2 + 4x + 5 - 2\sin x = 3\left(x+\frac{2}{3}\right)^2 + \frac{11}{3} - 2\sin x$$

Now $\frac{11}{3} - 2\sin x > 0 \ \forall x$ (as $-1 \leq \sin x \leq 1$)

$\Rightarrow f'(x) > 0 \ \forall x \Rightarrow f(x)$ is an increasing function.

Now $f(0) = 2 \Rightarrow f(x) > f(0) \Rightarrow f(x) > 2$

$\Rightarrow f(x) = 0$ has no solution in $[0, 2\pi]$

Hence (a) is correct

ILLUSTRATION 60: If $f: [1,10] \to [1, 10]$ is a non-decreasing function and $g: [1, 10] \to [1, 10]$ is a non-increasing function. Let $h(x) = f(g(x))$ with $h(1) = 1$. Then $h(2)$

(a) lies in (1,2) (b) is more than 2

(c) is equal to 1 (d) is not defined

SOLUTION: (c) Since f is non-decreasing and g is non-increasing, so h is a non-increasing function

Now $h(1) = 1$

$\Rightarrow h(x)$ is a constant function $\Rightarrow h(2) = 1$

ILLUSTRATION 61: Let $g(x) = 2f\left(\frac{x}{2}\right) + f(2-x)$ and $f''(x) < 0 \ \forall x \in (0, 2)$. Find the intervals of increase and decrease of $g(x)$.

SOLUTION: We have, $g(x) = 2f\left(\frac{x}{2}\right) + f(2-x)$

$$\Rightarrow g'(x) = 2f'\left(\frac{x}{2}\right)\left(\frac{1}{2}\right) + f'(2-x)(-1)$$

$$\Rightarrow g'(x) = f'\left(\frac{x}{2}\right) - f'(2-x) \quad \text{.....(i)}$$

We are given that $f''(x) < 0, \ \forall x \in (0, 2)$.

It means that $f'(x)$ would be decreasing on (0, 2) which gives arises two cases

Case I: $\frac{x}{2} > (2 - x)$ and $f'(x)$ is decreasing

$\Rightarrow f'\left(\frac{x}{2}\right) < f'(2-x),\ \forall\ x > \frac{4}{3}$

or $g'(x) = f'\left(\frac{x}{2}\right) - f'(2-x) < 0\ \forall\ x \in \left(\frac{4}{3}, 2\right)$

$\therefore$ $g(x)$ is decreasing in $\left(\frac{4}{3}, 2\right)$ ...(ii)

Case II: $\frac{x}{2} < (2 - x)$ and $f'(x)$ is decreasing

$\Rightarrow f'\left(\frac{x}{2}\right) > f'(2-x),\ \forall\ x < \frac{4}{3}$

or $g'(x) = f'\left(\frac{x}{2}\right) - f'(2-x) > 0,\ \forall\ 0 < x < \frac{4}{3}$

$\therefore$ $g(x)$ is increasing in $\left(0, \frac{4}{3}\right)$ ...(iii)

From (ii) and (iii), we conclude that

$g(x)$ is increasing in $\left(0, \frac{4}{3}\right)$ and decreasing in $\left(\frac{4}{3}, 2\right)$

ILLUSTRATION 62: Determine the range of $f(x) = \log_e(2\sin x + \tan x - 3x + 1)$, where $\frac{\pi}{6} \le x \le \frac{\pi}{3}$

SOLUTION: Let $g(x) = 2\sin x + \tan x - 3x + 1$

$\Rightarrow g'(x) = 2\cos x + \sec^2 x - 3$

$= \frac{2\cos^3 x - 3\cos^2 x + 1}{\cos^2 x}$

$\therefore g'(x) > 0$

$\Rightarrow 2\cos^3 x - 3\cos^2 x + 1 > 0$

$\Rightarrow \underbrace{(\cos x - 1)}_{negative}(2\cos^2 x - \cos x - 1) > 0$

$\Rightarrow (2\cos^2 x - \cos x - 1) < 0$

$\Rightarrow (\cos x - 1)(\cos x + 1/2) < 0$

$\Rightarrow \cos x + 1/2 > 0$

$\Rightarrow$ for all $x \in [\pi/6, \pi/3]$

$\Rightarrow g(x)$ is an increasing function of x for $\frac{\pi}{6} \le x \le \frac{\pi}{3}$

$\Rightarrow g\left(\frac{\pi}{6}\right) \le g(x) \le g\left(\frac{\pi}{3}\right)$

$\Rightarrow 2 + \frac{1}{\sqrt{3}} - \frac{\pi}{2} \le g(x) \le 1 + 2\sqrt{3} - \pi$

$\Rightarrow \log_e\left(2 + \frac{1}{\sqrt{3}} - \frac{\pi}{3}\right) \le \log_e g(x) \le \log_e(1 + 2\sqrt{3} - \pi)$

$\therefore$ Range of $f(x)$ is $\left[\log_e\left(2 + \frac{1}{\sqrt{3}} - \frac{\pi}{3}\right), \log_e(1 + 2\sqrt{3} - \pi)\right]$

ILLUSTRATION 63: If $f(x)=\dfrac{\sin x.\cos 3x}{\sin 3x.\cos x}$, then calculate range of $f(x)$.

SOLUTION: $f(x)=\dfrac{\sin x.\cos 3x}{\sin 3x.\cos x}=\dfrac{4\sin^2 x-1}{4\sin^2 x-3}$

Let $g(x)=\dfrac{4x-1}{4x-3}; x\neq 0,\dfrac{3}{4},1; x\in[0,1]$ i.e., $\left(0,\dfrac{3}{4}\right)\cup\left(\dfrac{3}{4},1\right)$

$\therefore\quad g'(x)=\dfrac{-8}{(4x-3)^2}<0$ for all $x\in[0,1]\sim\{3/4, 0\}$

$\Rightarrow$ $g(x)$ is a decreasing function of x

Also $\lim\limits_{x\to(3/4)^-} g(x)=-\infty$ and $\lim\limits_{x\to 3/4^+} g(x)=+\infty$

$\therefore$ Graph of $g(x)$ will be as shown below:

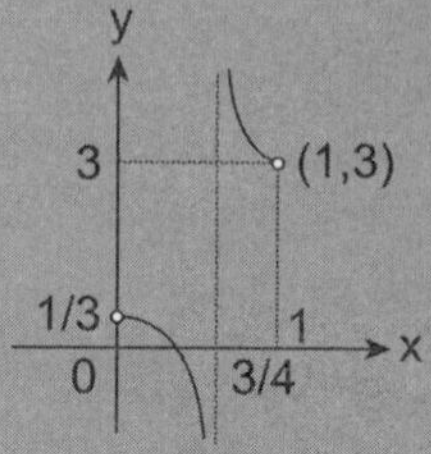

FIGURE 5.113

$\Rightarrow$ $g(x)<1/3$ for $x\in(0, 3/4)$ and $g(x)\geq 3$ for $x\in(3/4, 1)$

$\Rightarrow$ Range of $f(x)$ is $(-\infty, 1/3)\cup(3,\infty)$

ILLUSTRATION 64: Find the set of values of $x\in(0, 2\pi)$ for which the following functions are strictly decreasing.

(a) $2^{x-\sin x}+\log(x+\cos x)$ (b) $\log\left(\cot^{-1}\left((\sin x-\cos x)^5\right)\right)$

SOLUTION: (a) Let $f(x)=x-\sin x$ and $g(x)=(x+\cos x)$

$\Rightarrow$ $f(x)=1-\cos x\geq 0\ \forall x\in\mathbb{R}$

$\Rightarrow$ $f(x)$ is an increasing function $\forall x\in\mathbb{R}$

$\Rightarrow$ $f(x)>f(0)=0\ \forall\ x>0$

$\Rightarrow$ $2f(x)\uparrow x\in(0, 2\pi)$ and $g(x)=x+\cos x$

$\Rightarrow$ $g'(x)=1-\sin x\geq 0\ \forall x\in\mathbb{R}$

$\Rightarrow$ $g(x)$ is an increasing function $\forall x\in\mathbb{R}$

$\Rightarrow$ $g(x)>g(0)=1\ \forall\ x>0$

$\Rightarrow$ $\ln(g(x))\ \forall x\in(0,2\pi)$

$\Rightarrow$ $y=2f(x)+\ln(g(x))$ is an increasing functions $\forall x\in(0, 2\pi)$

(b) $f(x)=\ln(\cot^{-1}(\sin x-\cos x)^5)$

$\Rightarrow$ $f'(x)=\dfrac{1}{\cot^{-1}(\sin x-\cos x)^5}\times\dfrac{1}{1+(\sin x-\cos x)^2}\times 5(\sin x-\cos x)^4\times[\sin x+\cos x]\geq 0$ for

$(\sin x+\cos x)\geq 0$

$\Rightarrow$ $\sqrt{2}\sin\left(x+\dfrac{\pi}{4}\right)\geq 0$

$\Rightarrow$ $\sin\left(x+\dfrac{\pi}{4}\right)\geq 0$, here $x\in(0, 2\pi)$

$\Rightarrow$ $(x+\pi/4)\in(\pi/4, 9\pi/4)$

$\Rightarrow$ $x+\dfrac{\pi}{4}\in\left(\dfrac{\pi}{4},\pi\right]\cup\left[2\pi,\dfrac{9\pi}{4}\right)$

$\Rightarrow$ $x\in\left(0,\dfrac{3\pi}{4}\right]\cup\left[\dfrac{7\pi}{4},2\pi\right)$

ILLUSTRATION 65: Find whether the function cos(sin (cos t)) is increasing or decreasing on the closed interval $[\pi/2, \pi]$?

SOLUTION: As $\frac{\pi}{2} \le t \le \pi$

$\Rightarrow\ 0 \ge \cos t \ge -1$

$\Rightarrow\ 0 \ge \sin(\cos t) \ge -\sin 1$

$\Rightarrow\ 1 \ge \cos(\sin(\cos t)) \ge \cos(\sin 1)$

$\Rightarrow\ y = \cos(\sin(\cos)))$ is a decreasing function

ILLUSTRATION 66: Solve the equation for x: $e^{2x}(x^2+1) = 2x$

SOLUTION: $e^{2x} = \frac{2x}{x^2+1} = \frac{2}{\left(x+\frac{1}{x}\right)}$.

The graph of LHS i.e., e^{2x} will be as shown below:

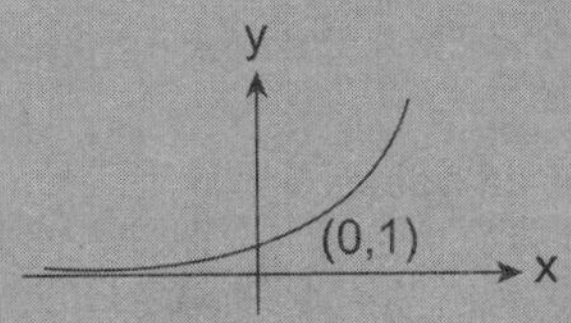

FIGURE 5.114

And the graph of RHS i.e., $\frac{2x}{x^2+1}$ will be as shown below:

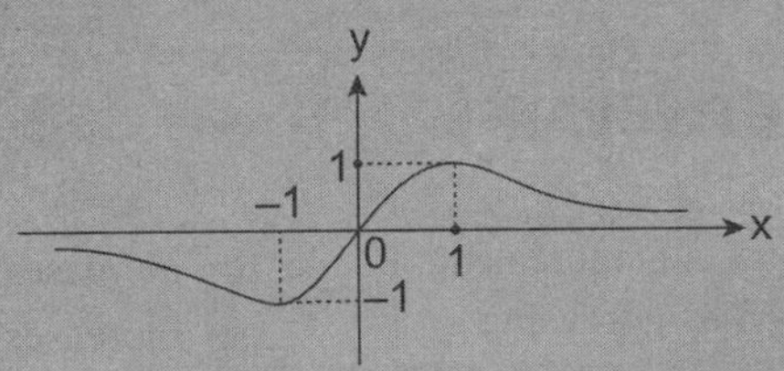

FIGURE 5.115

Thus graph achieves its maximum value (1) at $x = 1$ but the graph of e^{2x} will be greater than 1 for $x > 0$.

Therefore, from the graphs, it is very obvious that $e^{2x}(x^2 + 1) = 2x$ will not have any solution.

ILLUSTRATION 67: Solve the equation $x^4 + 3x^2 - x + 2 = 0$ for x.

SOLUTION: $x^4 + 3x^2 + 2 = x \Rightarrow (x^2 + 1)(x^2 + 2) = x$

$$\Rightarrow\ x^2 + 2 = \frac{x}{x^2+1} = \frac{1}{x+1/x}$$

The minimum value of LHS $= x^2 + 2$ is 2

Where $|x + 1/x| \ge 2 \Rightarrow \frac{1}{\left|x+\frac{1}{x}\right|} \le \frac{1}{2}$

$\Rightarrow\ \frac{1}{x+\frac{1}{x}} \le \frac{1}{2}$ or $\left(\frac{1}{x+\frac{1}{x}}\right) \ge \frac{-1}{2}$

$\Rightarrow\ \frac{1}{x+\frac{1}{x}}$ can never be equal to 2

∴ LHS can never be equal to RHS and hence, no value of x satisfies the equation

Aliter: $x^4 + 2x^2 + 1 = -(x^2 - x + 1)$

LHS is always greater than or equal to 1

And the maximum value of RHS $= -\left(\frac{D}{4a}\right) = -\left(\frac{-(-3)}{4}\right) = -\frac{3}{4}$.

And hence no possible solution.

TEXTUAL EXERCISE–4: (SUBJECTIVE)

1. Let $f(x) = \sin(\cos x)$, then check whether it is increasing or decreasing in $\left[0, \frac{\pi}{2}\right]$.
2. Show that $x^3 - 3x^2 - 9x + 20$ is positive for all values of $x > 4$.
3. Solve for x: $(x + 3)^5 - (x - 1)^5 \geq 244$
4. Find range of
   (a) x^x (b) $\log[(\sin x)^{\sin x} + 1]$
5. Show that $e^{x-1} + x = 2$ has only one real root.

Answer Keys

1. Decreasing 3. $[0, \infty)$
4. (a) $[e^{-1/e}, \infty)$ (b) $[\log(e^{-1/e} + 1), \log 2]$

TEXTUAL EXERCISE–4: (OBJECTIVE)

1. If $f : \mathbb{R} \to \mathbb{R}$ is decreasing and $g : \mathbb{R} \to \mathbb{R}$ is increasing then which of the following functions is increasing
   (a) $f o f$ (b) $g o g$
   (c) $f o g$ (d) $g o f$

2. The function $f(x) = \dfrac{ae^x + be^{-x}}{ce^x + de^{-x}}$ is increasing function of x if
   (a) $ab > cd$ (b) $ad \geq bc$
   (c) $ac > bd$ (d) None of these

3. If the function $f(x)$ increases in the interval (a, b), then the function $\phi(x) = [f(x)]^2$:
   (a) increases in (a, b)
   (b) decreases in (a, b)
   (c) we cannot say that $\phi(x)$ increases or decreases in (a, b)
   (d) None of these

4. Let $g(x) = 2f(x/2) + f(1 - x)$ and $f''(x) < 0$ in $0 \leq x \leq 1$, then $g(x)$:
   (a) decreases in $[0, 2/3]$
   (b) decreases in $[2/3, 1]$
   (c) increases in $[0, 2/3)$
   (d) increases in $(2/3, 1]$

5. If $\phi(x) = f(x) + f(2a - x)$ and $f''(x) > 0$, $a > 0$, $0 \leq x \leq 2a$ then
   (a) $\phi(x)$ increases in $(a, 2a)$
   (b) $\phi(x)$ increases in $(0, a)$
   (c) $\phi(x)$ decreases in $(0, a)$
   (d) $\phi(x)$ decreases in $(a, 2a)$

6. Let f and g be increasing and decreasing functions, respectively from $[0 \cdot \infty)$ to $[0 \cdot \infty)$. Let $h(x) = f[g(x)]$. If $h(0) = 0$, then $h(x) - h(1)$ is:
   (a) always zero (b) strictly increasing
   (c) always negative (d) always positive

7. A function $y = f(x)$ is given by $x = \dfrac{1}{1 + t^2}$ and $y = \dfrac{1}{t(1 + t^2)}$ for all $t > 0$, then f is :
   (a) increasing in $(0, 3/2)$ and decreasing in $(3/2, \infty)$
   (b) increasing in $(0, 1)$
   (c) increasing in $(0, \infty)$
   (d) decreasing in $(0, 1)$

8. The function $f(x) = \dfrac{ax+b}{cx+d}$ is a strictly increasing function for all $x \in \mathbb{R} - \{-d/c\}$, if

(a) $ad - bc < 0$ (b) $ad - bc > 0$

(c) $ad - cd > 0$ (d) $ab - cd < 0$

9. For the positive values of the domain of the function $f(x) = \dfrac{\sin^{-1} x}{\cos^{-1} x}$ is

(a) an increasing function

(b) a strictly increasing function

(c) a decreasing function

(d) a strictly decreasing function

10. The value of a in order that $f(x) = \sqrt{3}\sin x - \cos x - 2ax + b$ decreases for all real values of x, is given by

(a) $a < 1$ (b) $a \geq 1$

(c) $a \geq \sqrt{2}$ (d) $a < \sqrt{2}$

11. If $f(x) = (ab - b^2 - 2)x + \int_0^x (\cos^4\theta + \sin^4\theta)d\theta$ is a decreasing function of x for all $x \in \mathbb{R}$ and $b \in \mathbb{R}$, b being independent of x, then

(a) $a \in (0, \sqrt{6})$ (b) $a \in [-2, 2]$

(c) $a \in (-\sqrt{6}, 0)$ (d) None of these

12. Let $f'(x) > 0$ and $g'(x) < 0$ for all $x \in \mathbb{R}$. Then

(a) $f\{g(x)\} > f\{g(x+1)\}$

(b) $f\{g(x)\} > f\{g(x-1)\}$

(c) $g\{f(x)\} > g\{f(x+1)\}$

(d) $g\{f(x)\} > g\{f(x-1)\}$

13. If $f : [1, 10] \to [1, 10]$ is a decreasing function and $g : [1, 10] \to [1, 10]$ is a non increasing function. Let $h(x) = f(g(x))$ with $h(1) = 1$. Then $h(2)$

(a) lies in (1, 2)

(b) is greater than 2

(c) is greater than or equal 1

(d) is not defined

14. If $\phi(x) = 3f\left(\dfrac{x^2}{3}\right) + f(3 - x^2)$ for all $x \in (-3, 4)$ where $f''(x) > 0$ for all $x \in (-3, 4)$, then $\phi(x)$ is

(a) increasing in [3/2, 4)

(b) decreasing in (–3, –3/2]

(c) increasing in [–3/2, 0]

(d) decreasing in [0, 3/2]

15. For what values of a does the curve $f(x) = x(a^2 - 2a - 2) + \cos x$ is always strictly montonic for all $x \in \mathbb{R}$

(a) $a \in \mathbb{R}$ (b) $a > 0$

(c) $1 - \sqrt{2} < a < 1 + \sqrt{2}$ (d) None of these

16. If f and g are decreasing functions such that *gof* and *fog* are defined, then

(a) *fog* is decreasing (b) *gof* is increasing

(c) *fog* is increasing (d) *gof* is decreasing

17. If $f'(x) = g(x)(x - a)^2$; where $g(a) \neq 0$ and g is continuous at $x = a$, then

(a) $f(x)$ is increasing in the neighbourhood of a if $g(a) > 0$

(b) $f(x)$ is increasing in the neighbourhood of a if $g(a) < 0$

(c) $f(x)$ is decreasing in the neighbourhood of a if $g(a) > 0$

(d) $f(x)$ is decreasing in the neighbourhood of a if $g(a) < 0$

18. Let $g(x) = f(x) + f(1 - x)$ and $f''(x) < 0$, $0 \leq x \leq 1$. Then

(a) $g(x)$ increases on [1/2, 1]

(b) $g(x)$ decreases on [1/2, 1]

(c) $g(x)$ decreases on [0, 1/2]

(d) $g(x)$ increases on [0, 1/2]

19. The function is $\cos^{-1}\left(\dfrac{1-x^2}{1+x^2}\right)$

(a) increasing in $(0, \infty)$

(b) decreasing in $(-\infty, 0)$

(c) decreasing in $(0, \infty)$

(d) increasing in $(-\infty, 0)$

Answer Keys

1. (a, b)	**2.** (b)	**3.** (c)	**4.** (b, c)	**5.** (a, c)	**6.** (a)	**7.** (b,c)	**8.** (b)	**9.** (a,b)
10. (b,c)	**11.** (b)	**12.** (a,c)	**13.** (c)	**14.** (a,b,c,d)	**15.** (a)	**16.** (b,c)	**17.** (a,d)	**18.** (b,d)
19. (a,b)								

APPLICATION OF MONOTONICITY

In order to prove that a function $f(x) \geq k$ for all $x \geq x_0$ it is sufficient to prove that $f(x_0) \geq k$ and $f'(x) \geq 0 \ \forall \ x \geq x_0$.

$\because \ f(x_1) > f(x_2) \ \forall \ x_1 > x_2$

$\therefore \ x \geq x_0 \ \Rightarrow f(x) \geq f(x_0)$

But $f(x_0) \geq k$

$\Rightarrow \ f(x) \geq k \ \forall \ x \geq x_0$

ILLUSTRATION 68: Prove that $(x+2)^5 - (x-1)^5 \geq 33 \ \forall \ x \in (0,\infty)$.

SOLUTION: Let $f(x) = (x+2)^5 - (x-1)^5$

$f'(x) = 5(x+2)^4 - 5(x-1)^4$

For $x \in (0, \infty)$

$x + 2 > x - 1$

$\Rightarrow \ (x+2)^4 > (x-1)^4$

$\Rightarrow \ 5(x+2)^4 - 5(x-1)^4 > 0$ i.e., $f'(x) > 0 \ \forall \ x > 0 \Rightarrow f(x) \geq f(0) \ \forall \ x \geq 0$ and $f(0) : (0+2)^5 - (0-1)^5 = 33$

$\Rightarrow \ f(x) \geq 33 \ \forall \ x \in (0, \infty)$

METHOD OF PROVING INEQUALITY (USING MONOTONICITY)

In order to prove some inequalities any one of the following two methods can be conveniently adopted.

Method I: Rearrange the terms so that LHS and RHS become the value of a function $f(x)$ at two different inputs α, β. i.e., inequality takes the type $f(\alpha) > f(\beta)$ (say), then

it is sufficient to prove that $\begin{cases} f'(x) > 0 \text{ if } \alpha > \beta \\ f'(x) < 0 \text{ if } \alpha < \beta \end{cases}$

ILLUSTRATION 69: Prove that $e^\pi > \pi^e$

SOLUTION: We know that $e < \pi$

Let us suppose that $e^\pi > \pi^e$

$\pi \ \ell ne > e \ \ell n\pi$

$\Rightarrow \ \dfrac{\ell ne}{e} > \dfrac{\ell n\pi}{\pi}$

Let us consider $f(x) = \dfrac{\ell nx}{x}$

Now $f'(x) = \dfrac{\left(\frac{1}{x}\right)x - (\ell nx)}{(x^2)} = \dfrac{1 - \ell nx}{x^2}$

$\Rightarrow \ f'(x) > 0 \ \forall \ x \in (0, e)$ and $f'(x) < 0 \ \forall \ x \in (e, \infty)$

$\therefore$ The function $f(x)$ is a decreasing function for $x \in [e, \infty)$

$\therefore \ e < \pi$

$\Rightarrow f(e) > f(\pi)$

$\Rightarrow \ \dfrac{\ell ne}{e} > \dfrac{\ell n\pi}{\pi}$ $\quad\Rightarrow \pi \ \ln e > e\ln\pi$

$\Rightarrow \ \ln e^\pi > \ln \pi^e$

$\Rightarrow\ e^{\pi} > \pi^{e}$

Therefore our assumption is corrected and $e^{\pi} > \pi^{e}$

Aliter: Consider $h(x) = e^{\pi}$ and $g(x) = \pi^{e}$

$\therefore\ (h(x))^{1/\pi e} = \left(e^{\pi}\right)^{\frac{1}{\pi e}} = e^{1/e}$ and $\left(g(x)\right)^{\frac{1}{\pi e}} = \left(\pi^{e}\right)^{\frac{1}{\pi e}} = \pi^{1/\pi}$

Now let us consider $f(x) = x^{1/x}$

$$\Rightarrow\ \ell n\, f(x) = \frac{\ell n x}{x} \Rightarrow \frac{1}{f(x)} \times f'(x) = \frac{1-\ell n x}{x^{2}}$$

$$\Rightarrow\ f'(x) = \left(x^{1/x}\right)\left(\frac{1-\ell n x}{x^{2}}\right)$$

Now $f'(x) > 0\ \forall x \in (0, e)$ and $f'(x) < 0\ \forall \in (e, \infty)$

$\therefore\ f(x)$ is a decreasing function for $x \in [e, \infty)$

$\therefore$ If $e < \pi$ $\Rightarrow f(e) > f(\pi)$

$\Rightarrow e^{1/e} > \pi^{1/\pi}$ $\Rightarrow e^{\pi} > \pi^{e}$

Method II: To prove $f(x) \geq g(x)$ for all $x \geq a$. Consider the function $h(x) = f(x) - g(x)$

$\therefore\ h'(x) = f'(x) - g'(x)$.

- ❑ Test the monotonicity of $h(x)$. If $h'(x) > 0\ \forall\ x \geq a$ and $h(a) \geq 0$, then $h(x) \geq h(a) \geq 0$

$\Rightarrow h(x) \geq 0\ \forall\ x \geq a$

$\Rightarrow f(x) - g(x) \geq 0\ \forall\ x \geq a$

$\Rightarrow f(x) \geq g(x)\ \forall\ x \geq a$

ILLUSTRATION 70: Prove that $2\sin x + \tan x \geq 3x\ \forall\ x \in \left[0, \frac{\pi}{2}\right)$.

SOLUTION: Let $f(x) = 2\sin x + \tan x\ \forall\ x \in [0, \pi/2)$ and $g(x) = 3x\ \forall\ x \in [0, \pi/2)$

and $h(x) = f(x) - g(x)\ \forall\ x \in [0, \pi/2) = 2\sin x + \tan x - 3x\ \forall x \in [0, \pi/2)$

$h'(x) = 2\cos x + \sec^{2} x - 3$

$$= \frac{2\cos^{3} x - 3\cos^{2} x + 1}{\cos^{2} x}$$

Let $p(x) = 2\cos^{3}x - 3\cos^{2} x + 1$

Now $p'(x) = -6\cos^{2} x \sin x + 6\cos x \sin x$

$\Rightarrow p'(x) = 6\cos x \sin x\,(1 - \cos x)$

For $x \in [0, \pi/2)$

$\cos x > 0$; $\sin x \geq 0$ and $1 - \cos x > 0$

$\Rightarrow p'(x) \geq 0\ \forall x \in \left[0, \frac{\pi}{2}\right)$ $\Rightarrow h'(x) \geq 0\ \forall x \in \left[0, \frac{\pi}{2}\right)$

$\Rightarrow h(x)$ is an increasing function on $\forall x \in \left[0, \frac{\pi}{2}\right)$

$\Rightarrow h(x) = f(x) - g(x)$ is an increasing function on $\forall x \in \left[0, \frac{\pi}{2}\right)$

Now $h(x) \geq h(0) \quad \forall x \in \left[0, \frac{\pi}{2}\right)$

$\Rightarrow f(x) - g(x) > f(0) - g(0) \quad \forall x \in \left[0, \frac{\pi}{2}\right)$

$\Rightarrow f(x) - g(x) \geq 0 \quad \forall x \in \left[0, \frac{\pi}{2}\right)$

$\Rightarrow f(x) \geq g(x)$ on $[0, \pi/2)$ $\qquad \Rightarrow 2\sin x + \tan x \geq 3x \quad \forall x \in \left[0, \frac{\pi}{2}\right)$

ILLUSTRATION 71: Prove that $\frac{\tan}{} > \frac{x}{\sin x}$ for $0 < x < \frac{\pi}{2}$

SOLUTION: We have to show that $\frac{\tan x}{x} > \frac{x}{\sin x}$ for $x \in \left(0, \frac{\pi}{2}\right)$

i.e., $\frac{\tan x \sin x - x^2}{x \sin x} > 0$ for $0 < x < \pi/2$

Since $x \sin x > 0$ for $0 < x < \pi/2$,

it is enough to show that $\tan x \cdot \sin x - x^2 > 0$ for $0 < x < \pi/2$

Let $f(x) = \tan x \sin x - x^2$ for $0 < x < \pi/2$

$f'(x) = \sin x \sec^2 x + \tan x \cos x - 2x = \sin x \sec^2 x + \sin x - 2x$

$f''(x) = \cos x \sec^2 x + \sin x .\, 2 \sec^2 x \tan x + \cos x - 2$

$= \sec x + \cos x - 2 + 2 \sin x \tan x \sec^2 x$

$= \left(\sqrt{\sec x} - \sqrt{\cos x}\right)^2 + 2 \sin x \tan x \sec^2 x > 0$ for $0 < x < \pi/2$

$\therefore$ f' is strictly increasing in $[0, \pi/2)$. Also $f'(0) = 0$

$\Rightarrow f'(x) > 0$ for $0 < x < \pi/2$

$\Rightarrow f$ is strictly increasing in $[0, \pi/2)$. Also $f(0) = 0$

$\Rightarrow f(x) > 0$ for $0 < x <. \pi/2$

$\Rightarrow \tan x \sin x - x^2 > 0$ for $0 < x < \pi/2$.

$\therefore \quad \frac{\tan x \sin x - x^2}{x \sin x} > 0, 0 < x < \pi/2$

$\Rightarrow \quad \frac{\tan x}{x} > \frac{x}{\sin x}$ for $0 < x < \frac{\pi}{2}$.

ILLUSTRATION 72: Establish the inequality of the following by examining the sign of the derivative of an appropriate function:

$$\frac{1}{x + (1/2)} < \ell n\left(1 + \frac{1}{x}\right) < \frac{1}{x} \text{ for } x > 0$$

SOLUTION: Consider $f(x) = \frac{2}{2x+1} - \ell n\left(1 + \frac{1}{x}\right)$;

$$f'(x) = \frac{-4}{(2x+1)^2} - \frac{1}{1+(1/x)} \cdot \left(-\frac{1}{x^2}\right) = \frac{1}{x(x+1)} - \frac{4}{(2x+1)^2} = \frac{1}{x(x+1)(2x+1)^2}$$

which is always +ve for $x > 0$

hence $f(x)$ is $\uparrow$ for $x > 0$

i.e., $f(x) < \lim\limits_{x\to\infty} f(x)$

but $\lim\limits_{x\to\infty} f(x) = \lim\limits_{x\to\infty}\left\{\frac{2}{2x+1} - \ln\left(1+\frac{1}{x}\right)\right\} = 0$

so $f(x) < 0$ i.e., $\frac{2}{2x+1} < \ell n\left(1+\frac{1}{x}\right)$ ....(i)

Similarly consider $g(x) = \ell n\left(1+\frac{1}{x}\right) - \frac{1}{x}$; $g'(x) = \frac{1}{x^2} - \frac{1}{x(x+1)} = \frac{}{x\ (x\ \ 1)} > 0\ \forall\ x > 0$

$g'(x)$ is +ve for $x > 0$ $\Rightarrow$ $g(x)$ is increasing for $x > 0$

so $g(x) < \lim\limits_{x\to\infty} g(x)$ but $\lim\limits_{x\to\infty} g(x) = 0$

so $g(x) < 0$ $\Rightarrow \ln\left(1+\frac{1}{x}\right) < \frac{1}{x}$ .....(ii)

Thus result follows from (i) and (ii).

ILLUSTRATION 73: If $f(x) = \ln(\ln x)$, where $x > e$, prove that $\frac{1}{(m+1)\ln(m+1)} \le f(m+1) - f(m) \le \frac{1}{m\cdot\ln(m)}$ for $m > e$.

SOLUTION: $f(x) = \ln(\ln x)$

$g(x) = f'(x) = \frac{1}{x\ln x}$

$g'(x) = \frac{1}{-(x\ln x)^2}[\ln x + 1] = -\left[\frac{1}{x^2\ln^2 x} + \frac{1}{x^2\ln x}\right]$

< 0 for $x > e$

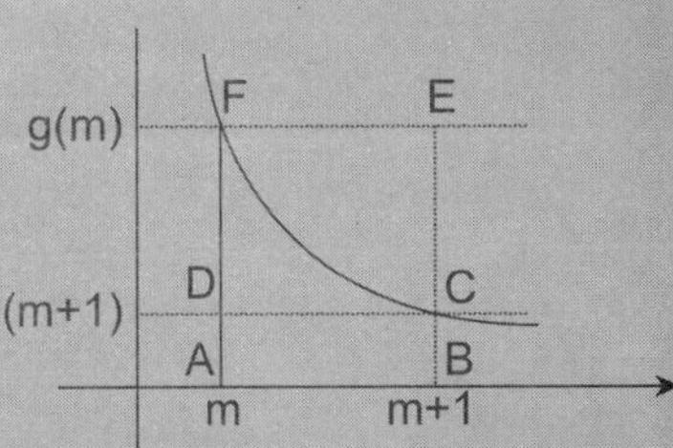

FIGURE 5.116

Hence $g(x)$ is a decreasing function for $x > e$, hence $g(m) > g(m+1)$ for $m > e$

From the graph of $y = g(x)$;

it can be inferred that area of $ABCD$ < area of $ABCF$ < area of $ABEF$

$\Rightarrow g(m+1)(m+1-m) < \int_m^{m+1} g(x)\,dx < g(m)[m+1-m]$

$\Rightarrow g(m+1) \le \int_m^{m+1} f'(x)\,dx \le g(m)$

$\Rightarrow \frac{1}{(m+1)\ln(m+1)} \le f(m+1) - f(m) \le \frac{1}{m\cdot\ln(m)}$

ILLUSTRATION 74: Prove that $\sin x < x < \tan x$, $x \in \left(0, \frac{\pi}{2}\right)$

SOLUTION: Consider $f(x) = \sin x - x$

$\Rightarrow f'(x) = \cos x - 1 = -2\sin^2\frac{x}{2}$

$\Rightarrow f'(x)) < 0$

$\Rightarrow f(x)$ is decreasing $\forall\ x \in \left(0, \frac{\pi}{2}\right)$ i.e., $0 < x < \frac{\pi}{2}$

$\Rightarrow f(0) > f(x) > f\left(\frac{\pi}{2}\right)$ $\Rightarrow f(x) < f(0)$ $\Rightarrow \sin x - x < 0$

$\Rightarrow \sin x < x$ ...(i)

Similarly we can prove $x < \tan x$ ...(ii)

Combining (i) and (ii), we get, $\sin x < x < \tan x$. Hence proved

ILLUSTRATION 75: If $f(x) = \frac{x}{\sin x}$ and $g(x) = \frac{x}{\tan x}$; where $0 < x \le 1$, then in this interval $f(x)$ and $g(x)$ are increasing or decreasing.

SOLUTION: Here $f(x) = \frac{x}{\sin x}$

$\Rightarrow f'(x) = \frac{\sin x.1 - x.\cos x}{\sin^2 x}$ ...(i)

where $\sin^2 x$ is always +ve when $0 < x \le 1$

Method 1: Since $\sin x < x < \tan x$ (as proved in the previous problem)

$\Rightarrow x < \tan x$ $\Rightarrow x < \frac{\sin x}{\cos x}$

$\Rightarrow \sin x - x\cos x > 0$

$\Rightarrow f(x) > 0$, when $0 < x \le 1$

Hence, $f(x)$ is increasing when $0 < x \le 1$.

Method 2: But to check N^r, we again let, $h(x) = \sin(x) - x \cos x$

$\Rightarrow h'(x) = \cos x - 1.\cos x + x \sin x = x \sin x$,

(which is + ve for $0 < x \le 1$)

$\therefore$ $h'(x) > 0$

$\Rightarrow h(x)$ is increasing when $0 < x \le 1$

$\Rightarrow h(0) < h(x)$ $\Rightarrow 0 < \sin x - x\cos x$

$\Rightarrow f(x) > 0$, when $0 < x \le 1$. Hence, $f(x)$ is increasing when $0 < x \le 1$

Again $g(x) = \frac{x}{\tan x}$ (given)

$\Rightarrow g'(x) = \frac{\tan x.1 - x.\sec^2 x}{\tan^2 x}$ ...(ii)

where $\tan^2 x > 0$

for $\tan x - x \sec^2 x$ we let $\phi(x) = \tan x - x \sec^2 x$

$\Rightarrow \phi'(x) = \sec^2 x - \sec^2 x - x(2\sec x).(\sec x \tan x)$

$\Rightarrow \phi'(x) = -2x \sec^2 x \tan x \Rightarrow \phi'(x) < 0$ for $0 < x \le 1$

$\therefore$ $\phi'(x)$ is decreasing when $0 < x \le 1$ $\Rightarrow \phi(0) > \phi(x)$ for $0 < x \le 1$

or $0 < \tan x - x\sec^2 x$ $\therefore$ in (ii), $(\tan x - x\sec^2 x) < 0$

$\Rightarrow g'(x) < 0$, when $0 < x \le 1$

$\therefore$ $g(x)$ is decreasing when $0 < x \le 1$

ILLUSTRATION 76: Show that $1 + x\, ln(x + \sqrt{x^2+1}) \ge \sqrt{1+x^2}$ for all $x \ge 0$.

SOLUTION: Let $f(x) = 1 + x \ln(x + \sqrt{x^2+1}) - \sqrt{1+x^2}$ for all $x \ge 0$.

$$\therefore\ f'(x) = 0 + x\frac{1}{\left(x+\sqrt{x^2+1}\right)}\left(1+\frac{1}{2\sqrt{x^2+1}}2x\right) + \ln\left(x+\sqrt{x^2+1}\right).1 - \frac{1}{2\sqrt{x^2+1}}.2x$$

$$= \frac{x}{\left(x+\sqrt{x^2+1}\right)}\left(\frac{\sqrt{x^2+1}+x}{\sqrt{x^2+1}}\right) + \ln\left(x+\sqrt{x^2+1}\right) - \frac{x}{\sqrt{1+x^2}}$$

$$= \ln\left(x+\sqrt{x^2+1}\right) + \frac{x}{\sqrt{1+x^2}} - \frac{x}{\sqrt{x^2+1}} = \ln\left(x+\sqrt{x^2+1}\right)$$

Since, $x + \sqrt{x^2+1} > 1$ for $x > 0$

$\ln(x + \sqrt{x^2+1}) > \ln 1$ i.e., $f'(x) > 0$ for all $x > 0$

i.e., $f(x)$ increases for $x > 0$

$\therefore\ x \geq 0 \qquad \Rightarrow f(x) \geq f(0)$

$\Rightarrow\ 1 + x\ln\left(x+\sqrt{x^2+1}\right) - \sqrt{1+x^2} \geq 0$

$\Rightarrow\ 1 + x\ln\left(x+\sqrt{x^2+1}\right)$

$\geq\ \sqrt{1+x^2}$ Hence proved.

ILLUSTRATION 77: If $0 < x < \frac{\pi}{2}$ prove that $\cos x > 1 - \frac{x^2}{2}$ $f'(x) = -\sin x + x = x - \sin x$

SOLUTION: Let $f(x) = \cos x - 1 + \frac{x^2}{2}$

$\Rightarrow\ f'(x) = -\sin x + x$

$\Rightarrow\ f''(x) = 1 - \cos x = 2\sin^2\frac{x}{2} \geq 0$

$\Rightarrow\ f'(x)$ is

$\Rightarrow\ f'(x) > f'(0)$ for $x \in (0, \pi/2)$

$\Rightarrow\ f(x)$ for $x \in (0, \pi/2)$

$\Rightarrow\ f(x) > f(0)$ $x \in (0, \pi/2)$

$\Rightarrow\ \cos x - 1 + \frac{x^2}{2} > 0\ \forall x \in (0, \pi/2)$

$\Rightarrow\ \cos x > 1 - \frac{x^2}{2}$ for $x \forall\ (0, \pi/2)$

ILLUSTRATION 78: Prove that for $0 < x_1 < x_2 < \frac{\pi}{2}$, $\frac{\tan x_2}{\tan x_1} > \frac{x_2}{x_1}$.

SOLUTION: We have to prove that $\frac{\tan x_2}{\tan x_1} > \frac{x_2}{x_1}$ for $0 < x_1 < x_2 < \frac{\pi}{2}$

i.e., $x_1 \tan x_2 > x_2 \tan x_1$ for $0 < x_1 < x_2 < \frac{\pi}{2}$

Let $f(x) = x\tan x \qquad \Rightarrow\ f'(x) = x\sec^2 x + \tan x$

$(\sec x, \tan x) > 0$ for $0 < x < \frac{\pi}{2}$

$\therefore\ f'(x) > 0$ for $0 < x < \frac{\pi}{2}$

i.e., $f(x)$ increases in $\left(0, \frac{\pi}{2}\right)$ Hence, $x_2 > x_1$

$\Rightarrow f(x_2) \geq f(x_1)$

i.e., $x_2 \tan x_2 > x_1 \tan x_1$. Hence proved

ILLUSTRATION 79: For all $x \in (0, 1)$

(i) $e^x < 1 + x$ (ii) $\ln(1 + x) < x$

(iii) $\sin x > x$ (iv) $\ln x > x$

SOLUTION: (i) Let $f(x) = e^x - 1 - x$ $\Rightarrow f'(x) = e^x - 1 > 0, \forall x \in (0, 1)$

so, $f(x)$ is increasing, when $0 < x < 1$

$\Rightarrow f(x) > f(0)$ or $e^x - 1 - x > 0$

$\Rightarrow e^x > 1 + x$. Hence (i) is false.

(ii) Let $g(x) = \ln(1 + x) - x$

$\Rightarrow g'(x) = \frac{1}{1+x} - 1 = \frac{-x}{1+x} < 0, \forall x \in (0,1)$

so, $g(x)$ is decreasing, when $0 < x < 1$

$\Rightarrow g(0) > g(x)$ $\Rightarrow \ln(1 + x) < x$. Therefore (ii) is correct

(iii) Let $h(x) = \sin x - x$ $\Rightarrow h'(x) = \cos x - 1 < 0, \forall x \in (0, 1)$

so, $h(x)$ is decreasing, when $0 < x < 1$

$\Rightarrow h(x) < h(0)$ $\Rightarrow \sin x < x$ Hence (iii) is false.

(iv) Let $g(x) = \ln x - x$

$\Rightarrow g'(x)\ \frac{1}{x} - 1 = \frac{1-x}{x} > 0$ for $x \in (0, 1)$

$\therefore\ g'(x) > 0, \forall x \in (0, 1)$ $\Rightarrow g(x)$ is increasing for $x \in (0,1)$

$\Rightarrow g(x) < g(1)$ $\Rightarrow \log x - x < 0$

$\Rightarrow \log x < x$. Hence (iv) is false.

ILLUSTRATION 80: Show that $\frac{x}{1+x} < \ln(1 + x) < x$ for $x > 0$

SOLUTION: Let $f(x) = \ln(1 + x) - \frac{x}{1+x}$ $\Rightarrow$ $f'(x) = \frac{1}{1+x} - \frac{1}{(1+x)^2} = \frac{x}{(1+x)^2}$

Then $f'(x) > 0$ when $x > 0$ and $f(0) = 0$

Thus $f(x)$ is monotonically increasing in the intervals $(0,\infty)$

$\Rightarrow f(x) > f(0) = 0$ when $x > 0$

Hence $f(x)$ is positive for every positive value of x so that

$\ln(1 + x) > \frac{x}{1+x}$ when $x > 0$ ..(i)

Again let $g(x) = x - \ln(1 + x)$

so that $g'(x) = 1 - \frac{1}{1+x} = \frac{x}{1+x} \Rightarrow g'(x) > 0$, when $x > 0$ and equality holds for $x = 0$

Therefore g is monotonically increasing in the intervals $(0,\infty)$

Also $g(0) = 0$ $\therefore$ $g(x) > g(0) = 0$, when $x > 0$

Hence $g(x)$ + ve for + ve values of x, so that $x > \ln(1 + x)$ when $x > 0$ ...(ii)

From (i) and (ii), we have $\dfrac{x}{1+x} < \log(1 + x) < x$ when $x > 0$.

ILLUSTRATION 81: Prove that $x - \dfrac{x^3}{6} < \sin x < x$ for $0 < x \le \dfrac{\pi}{2}$

SOLUTION: we know that $\sin x \le x$ from $0 \le x \le \dfrac{\pi}{2}$ and $\sin x < x$ for $0 \le x \le \dfrac{\pi}{2}$ ...(i)

let $g(x) = x - \dfrac{x^3}{6} - \sin x$

$\therefore$ g is continuous for $0 < x \le \dfrac{\pi}{2}$

$g'(x) = 1 - \cos x - \dfrac{x^2}{2}$ ...(ii)

$\therefore$ g is differentiable for $0 < x \le \dfrac{\pi}{2}$

To find the sign of $g'(x)$ we consider $h(x) = 1 - \cos x - \dfrac{x^2}{2}$

$\therefore$ $h'(x) = 0 - (-\sin x) - \dfrac{1}{2}(2x)$ $\Rightarrow h'(x) = \sin x - x$

From (i), $\sin x < x$ for $0 < x \le \dfrac{\pi}{2}$

$\Rightarrow h'(x) < 0$ for $0 < x \le \dfrac{\pi}{2}$

$\therefore$ h is decreasing for $0 < x \le \dfrac{\pi}{2}$

$\Rightarrow h(0) > h(x) \ge h\left(\dfrac{\pi}{2}\right)$ for $0 < x \le \dfrac{\pi}{2}$

Note that $h(0) = 1 - 1 = 0$ $\Rightarrow h(x) < 0$ for $0 < x \le \dfrac{\pi}{2}$

$\Rightarrow 1 - \cos x - \dfrac{x^2}{2} < 0$ for $0 < x \le \dfrac{\pi}{2}$ ...(iii)

from (ii) and (iii), $g'(x) < 0$ for $0 < x \le \dfrac{\pi}{2}$

$\therefore$ g is decreasing for $0 < x \le \dfrac{\pi}{2}$

$\Rightarrow g(0) > g(x) \ge g\left(\dfrac{\pi}{2}\right)$ for $0 < x \le \dfrac{\pi}{2}$

Note that $g(0) = 0 - 0 - \sin 0 = 0$

$\Rightarrow 0 > x - \dfrac{x^3}{6} - \sin x$ for $0 < x \le \dfrac{\pi}{2}$

$\therefore$ $x - \dfrac{x^3}{6} < \sin x$ for $0 < x \le \dfrac{\pi}{2}$ ...(iv)

From (i) and (iv), we get $x - \dfrac{x^3}{6} < \sin x < x$ for $0 < x \le \dfrac{\pi}{2}$

ILLUSTRATION 82: Show that

(i) $\sin x < x - \frac{x^3}{6} + \frac{x^5}{120}$ for $x > 0$ (ii) $e^x + e^{-x} > 2 + x^2$ for $x \neq 0$

SOLUTION: (i) Let $f(x) = \sin x - x + \frac{x^3}{6} - \frac{x^5}{120}$

$\Rightarrow f'(x) = \cos x - 1 + \frac{x^2}{2} - \frac{x^4}{24}$

$\Rightarrow f''(x) = -\sin x + x - \frac{x^3}{6}$ $\Rightarrow f'''(x) = 1 - \cos x - \frac{x^2}{2}$

$\Rightarrow f''''(x) = \sin x - x$

for $x > 0$, $f''''(x)$ is always negative.

$\Rightarrow f'''(x) \downarrow f'''(0) = 0$

$\Rightarrow f'''(x) < 0$ for $x > 0$

$\Rightarrow f''(x) \downarrow$ for $x > 0$ and $f''(0) = 0$

$\Rightarrow f''(x) < 0$ for $x > 0$

$\Rightarrow f'(x) \downarrow$ for $x > 0$ and $f'(0) = 0$

$\Rightarrow f'(x) < 0$ for $x > 0$

$\Rightarrow f(x) \downarrow$ for $x > 0$ and $f(0) = 0$

$\Rightarrow f(x) < f(0) = 0$ for $x > 0$

$\Rightarrow \sin x < x - \frac{x^3}{6} + \frac{x^5}{120}$ for $x > 0$

(ii) $e^x + e^{-x} > 2 + x^2$ for $x \neq 0$

$f(x) = e^x + e^{-x} - 2 - x^2$ $\Rightarrow f'(x) = e^x - e^{-x} - 2x$

$$= \left[1 + x + \frac{x^2}{\underline{|2}} + \frac{x^3}{\underline{|3}} + \frac{x^4}{\underline{|4}} + \frac{x^5}{\underline{|5}} + ...\right] - \left[1 - x + \frac{x^2}{\underline{|2}} - \frac{x^3}{\underline{|3}} + \frac{x^4}{\underline{|4}} - \frac{x^5}{\underline{|5}} + ...\right] - 2x$$

$$= 2\left[\frac{x^3}{\underline{|3}} + \frac{x^5}{\underline{|5}} + ...\right] \quad ....(i)$$

$\Rightarrow f(x)$ is +ve for $x > 0$ from (i)

$\Rightarrow f(x)$ is increasing for $x > 0$

$\Rightarrow f(x) > f(0)$ for $x > 0$

$\Rightarrow e^x + e^{-x} - 2 - x^2 > 0$ $\Rightarrow e^x + e^{-x} > 2 + x^2$ for $x > 0$ ...(ii)

also $f'(x) = -$ve for all $x < 0$ (from (i))

$\Rightarrow f(x)$ is decreasing for all $x < 0$

$\Rightarrow f(x) > f(0)$ for $x < 0$

$\Rightarrow e^x + e^{-x} - 2 - x^2 > 0$ for all $x < 0$

$\therefore e^x + e^{-x} > 2 + x^2$ ....(iii)

From (ii) and (iii) we have

for all $x \neq 0$; $e^x + e^{-x} > 2 + x^2$

ILLUSTRATION 83: Find the minimum value of the function $f(x) = x^{\frac{3}{2}} + x^{\frac{-3}{2}} - 4\left(x + \frac{1}{x}\right)$ for all permissible real x.

SOLUTION: $f(x) = x^{\frac{3}{2}} + x^{\frac{-3}{2}} - 4\left(x + \frac{1}{x}\right) = x\sqrt{x} + \frac{1}{x\sqrt{x}} - 4\left(x + \frac{1}{x}\right)$

Put $t = \sqrt{x}$; let us say +ve new function as $g(t)$

$$g(t) = t^2 .\, t + \frac{1}{t^2 . t} - 4\left(t^2 + \frac{1}{t^2}\right) = t^3 + \frac{1}{t^3} - 4\left(t^2 + \frac{1}{t^2}\right)$$

$$\Rightarrow\ g(t) = \left(t + \frac{1}{t}\right)^3 - 3.t.\frac{1}{t}\left(t + \frac{1}{t}\right) - 4\left[\left(t + \frac{1}{t}\right)^2 - 2.t.\frac{1}{t}\right]$$

$$\Rightarrow\ g(t) = \left(t + \frac{1}{t}\right)^3 - 4\left(t + \frac{1}{t}\right)^2 - 3\left(t + \frac{1}{t}\right) + 8$$

Put $t + \frac{1}{t} = a$ and $t > 0 \Rightarrow a > 2$

$g(a) = a^3 - 4a^2 - 3a + 8$

$g'(a) = 3a^2 - 8a - 3$

$= 3a^2 - 9a + a - 3$

$= 3a\,(a - 3) + (a - 3) = (3a + 1)\,(a - 3)$

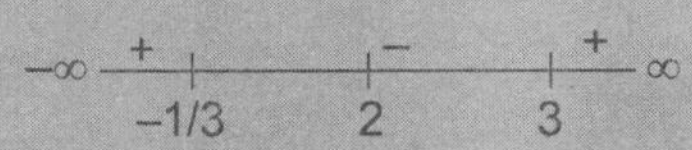

FIGURE 5.117

$g(a)$ decreases from 2 to 3 and increases from 3 to ∞

Hence $g(a)$ has minimum value at $a = 3\ \Rightarrow\ f(a)_{min} = f(3) = -10 = f_{min}(x)$

ILLUSTRATION 84: Prove that $\tan^2 x + 6\ell n \sec x + 2\cos x - 8 + 6\sec x > 0$ for $x \in \left(\frac{3\pi}{2}, 2\pi\right)$.

SOLUTION: $\tan^2 x + 6\ \ell n\ \sec x + 2\cos x + 4 > 6\sec x\ \forall\ x \in \left(\frac{3\pi}{2}, 2\pi\right)$

Let $f(x) = \tan^2 x + 6\ell n\,(\sec x) + 2\cos x + 4 - 6\sec x$

$\Rightarrow\ f'(x) = 2\tan x.\ \sec^2 x + \frac{6}{\sec x}.\ \sec x.\ \tan x - 2\sin x - 6\sec x.\ \tan x$

$= 2\tan x.\ \sec^2 x + 6\tan x - 2\sin x - 6\sec x.\ \tan x$

$= 2\tan x.\ \sec^2 x - 2\sin x + 6\tan x - 6\sec x.\ \tan x$

$= 2\tan x.\ \sec^2 x - 2\tan x.\ \cos x + 6\tan x\,(1 - \sec x)$

$= 2\tan x(\sec^2 x - \cos x) + 6\tan\,(1 - \sec x)$

$f'(x) = 6\tan x\,(1 - \sec x) + 2\tan x\,(\sec^2 x - \cos x)$

for $x \in \left(\frac{3\pi}{2}, 2\pi\right)$;

we have $\tan x < 0$

and $1 - \sec x > 0$

and $\sec^2 x - \cos x > 0$

Now, $f'(x) = \underbrace{6\tan x(1 - \sec x)}_{<0} + \underbrace{2\tan x(\sec^2 x - \cos x)}_{<0}$

$\Rightarrow\ f'(x) < 0$

$\therefore\ f(x) > f(2\pi)\ \forall\ x \in \left(\frac{3\pi}{2}, 2\pi\right)$

$\Rightarrow \tan^2 x + 6\ell n(\sec x) + 2\cos x + 4 - \sec x > 0$

$\therefore \tan^2 x + 6\ell n(\sec x) + 2\cos x + 4 > 6 \sec x$

ILLUSTRATION 85: Find the set of values of x for which the inequality $\ell n\ (1 + x) > x/(1 + x)$ is valid.

SOLUTION: Let $f(x) = \ln(1 + x) - \dfrac{x}{x+1}$; $x \in (-1, \infty) = D_f$

$f'(x) = \dfrac{x}{(x+1)^2}$

$\because f'(x) > 0\ \forall\ x \in (0, \infty)$

so $f(x) \uparrow$ on $(0, \infty)$

$f(x) > f(\min) = 0$ at $x \to 0^+$

$\Rightarrow f(x) > 0\ \forall\ x \in (0, \infty)$ ...(1)

$\Rightarrow \ln(1 + x) > \dfrac{x}{x+1}\ \forall\ x \in (0, \infty)$

Also $f'(x) < 0\ \forall\ x \in (-1, 0)$

$f(x) \downarrow$ on $x \in (-1, 0)$

so $f(x) > f(\min) = 0$ at $x \to 0^-$

$f(x) > 0\ \forall\ x \in (-1, 0)$ ...(ii)

(i) and (ii), we have $f(x) > 0\ \forall\ x \in (-1, 0) \cup (0, \infty)$

$\therefore \ln(1 + x) > \dfrac{x}{1+x}\ \forall\ x \in (-1, 0) \cup (0, \infty)$

ILLUSTRATION 86: Suppose that the function $f(x) = \ln_c \dfrac{x-2}{x+2}$ is defined for all x in the interval $[a, b]$ and is monotonically decreasing. Find the value of 'c' for which there exists 'a' and 'b' $(b > a > 2)$ such that the range of the function is $[\log_c c(b - 1), \log_c c(a - 1)]$.

SOLUTION: Given $f(x) = \log_c \left(\dfrac{x-2}{x+2}\right)$ ...(1)

$c > 0$ and $c \neq 1$

And $\dfrac{x-2}{x+2} > 0 \Rightarrow x \in (-\infty, -2) \cup (2, \infty)$

$$f(x) = \frac{\log_e\left(\dfrac{x-2}{x+2}\right)}{\ln c}$$

or $f(x) = \dfrac{1}{\ln c}[\ln(x - 2) - \ln(x + 2)]$

Differentiating w.r.t. x; we get $f'(x) = \dfrac{4}{(\ln c)(x-2)(x+2)}$

Case I: If $0 < c < 1$; then $\ln c < 0$

Now $f'(x) < 0$

$\Rightarrow \dfrac{4}{(\ln c)(x-2)(x+2)} < 0$

$\Rightarrow \dfrac{4}{(x-2)(x+2)} > 0$ $\Rightarrow x < -2$ or $x > 2$

Case II: If $c > 1$, then $\ln c > 0$

Now $f'(x) < 0$

$\Rightarrow \dfrac{4}{(\ln c)(x-2)(x+2)} < 0$

$\Rightarrow \dfrac{4}{(x-2)(x+2)} < 0 \Rightarrow x \in (-2, 2)$

but for $-2 < x < 2$; $\log_e \dfrac{x-2}{x+2}$ not defined.

Hence Case II must be ignored

Therefore $c \in (0, 1)$ and $x \in (-\infty, -2)$ or $x \in (2, \infty)$ for $f(x)$ to be decreasing

Now given that range of $f = [\log_c c(b-1), \log_c c(a-1)]$

$\therefore$ $f(x)$ is max at $x = a$, min at $x = b$ as $f(x) \downarrow$ and $x \in (a, b) \subset (2, \infty)$

Hence $f_{\min}(x) = f(b) = \log_c c(b-1)$

$\Rightarrow \log_c \dfrac{b-2}{b+2} = \log_c c(b-1)$

Taking antilog on both sides; we get $\dfrac{b-2}{b+2} = c(b-1)$

$\Rightarrow b - 2 = c(b-1)(b+2)$ $\Rightarrow cb^2 + (c-1)b - 2c + 2 = 0$

Now; $D \geq 0$ [$\because b$ is real] $\Rightarrow (c-1)^2 - 4c(-2c+2) \geq 0$

$\Rightarrow 0 < c \leq 1/9$ as $c \in (0, 1)$ according to case analysis (i) and (ii).

ILLUSTRATION 87: Let $f(x)$ and $g(x)$ be two differentiable functions for $x \geq 0$ such that $f(0) = g(0)$ and the slope at any point of $g(x)$ is greater than or equal to the slope at any point of $f(x)$; then prove that $g(x) \geq f(x)\ \forall\ x \geq 0$.

SOLUTION: (Given) $f(0) = g(0)$ and $f'(x) \leq g'(x)\ \forall\ x \geq 0$

$\Rightarrow f'(x) - g'(x) \leq 0\ \forall\ x \geq 0$

Let us consider $h(x) = f(x) - g(x)$

$\Rightarrow h'(x) = f'(x) - g'(x)$

$\therefore h'(x) \leq 0$

$h(x)$ is a decreasing function

$\therefore h(x) \leq h(0)\ \forall\ x \geq 0$

$\Rightarrow f(x) - g(x) \leq f(0) - g(0)\ \forall\ x \geq 0$

$\Rightarrow f(x) - g(x) \leq 0\ \forall\ x \geq 0$

$\therefore f(x) \leq g(x)\ \forall\ x \geq 0$

ILLUSTRATION 88: Show that the equation $x^2 = x \sin x + \cos x$ has exactly two real roots.

SOLUTION: Let us consider a function $f(x)$ such that, $f(x) = x^2 - x \sin x - \cos x$

$\Rightarrow f'(x) = 2x - x \cos x - \sin x + \sin x$

$\Rightarrow f'(x) = x \underbrace{(2 - \cos x)}_{>0}$

$\therefore$ $f(x)$ is a decreasing function on $(-\infty, 0)$ and increasing function on $(0, \infty)$

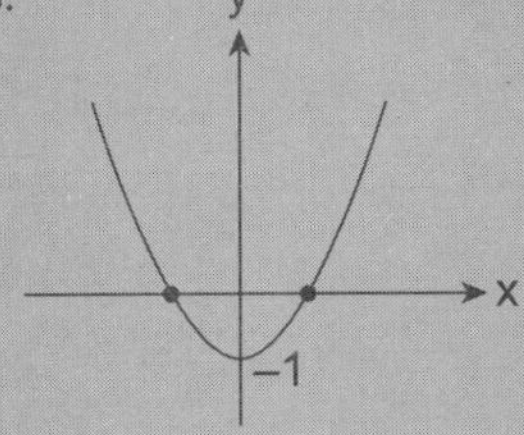

FIGURE 5.118

and $\lim_{x\to\infty} f(x)=\infty$ and $\lim_{x\to-\infty} f(x)=\infty$. Also $f(0) = -1$

hence, $f(x) = 0$ i.e., $x^2 - x\sin x - \cos x = 0$ has exactly two real roots.

ILLUSTRATION 89: Prove that $e^x > 1 + x\ \forall\ x \in \mathbb{R} - \{0\}$

SOLUTION: $f(x) = e^x - 1 - x$

Differentiating w.r.t x; we get $f'(x) = e^x - 1$

$f'(x) > 0\ \forall\ x \in (0, \infty)$ and $f'(x) < 0\ \forall\ x \in (-\infty, 0)$

Case I: $x \in (0, \infty)$

$f(x)$ is an increasing function on $x \in (0, \infty)$

$\therefore\ f(x) > f(0)\ \forall\ x \in (0, \infty)$

$\Rightarrow\ e^x - 1 - x > e^0 - 1 - 0\ \Rightarrow\ e^x > 1 + x\ \forall\ x \in (0, \infty)$

Case II: $x \in (-\infty, 0)$

$f(x)$ is $\downarrow$ function

$\Rightarrow\ f(x) > f(0)\ \forall\ x \in (-\infty, 0)$

$\Rightarrow\ e^x - 1 - x > e^0 - 1 - 0$

$\Rightarrow\ e^x > 1 + x$

$\therefore\ e^x > 1 + x\ \forall\ x \in \mathbb{R} - \{0\}$

ILLUSTRATION 90: Using the relation $2(1 - \cos x) < x^2, x \neq 0$ or otherwise, prove that $\sin(\tan x) \geq x\ \forall\ x \in \left[0, \frac{\pi}{4}\right]$

SOLUTION: Let $f(x) = \sin(\tan x) - x$

$\Rightarrow\ f'(x) = \cos(\tan x).\ \sec^2 x - 1 = \cos(\tan x)(1 + \tan^2 x) - 1$

$= \tan^2 x\ \{\cos(\tan x)\} + \cos(\tan x) - 1$

$> \tan^2 x \cos(\tan x) - \dfrac{\tan^2 x}{2}$

$$\left[\begin{array}{l} \because\ 2(1-\cos x) < x^2;\ x \neq 0 \\ \Rightarrow 1-\cos x < \dfrac{x^2}{2} \\ \Rightarrow 1-\cos(\tan x) < \tan^2 \dfrac{x}{2} \\ \Rightarrow \cos(\tan x) - 1 > -\tan^2 \dfrac{x}{2} \end{array}\right]$$

$\Rightarrow\ f'(x) > \tan^2 x\left[\cos(\tan x) - \dfrac{1}{2}\right]$ $\qquad \Rightarrow\ \tan^2 x\left[\cos(\tan x) - \cos\left(\dfrac{\pi}{3}\right)\right] > 0$

$\Rightarrow\ f(x)$ is increasing function $\forall\ x \in [0, \pi/4]$ $\left(\begin{array}{l} \because\ 0 \leq x \leq \dfrac{\pi}{4} \Rightarrow 0 \leq \tan x \leq 1 < \dfrac{\pi}{3} \\ \Rightarrow \cos(\tan x) > \cos\left(\dfrac{\pi}{3}\right) \end{array}\right)$.

as $f(0) = 0 \Rightarrow f(x) \geq 0,\ \forall\ x \in [0, \pi/4]$

$\Rightarrow\ \sin(\tan x) \geq x\ \forall\ x \in [0, \pi/4]$

TEXTUAL EXERCISE–5: (SUBJECTIVE)

1. Prove the following inequality:
   (a) $2 + \cos 2 < e + \cos e$
   (b) $\ln\left(\pi+\sqrt{\pi^2+1}\right) > \ln\left(3+\sqrt{10}\right)$

2. Prove that the expression $(x - 1)e^x + 1$ is positive for all positive value of x.

3. Prove that $2x > 3 \sin x - x \cos x \ \forall x \in \left[0, \frac{\pi}{2}\right]$.

4. Establish the inequality given below by examining the sign of derivative of an appropriate function:
   $$\frac{1}{x+(1/2)} < \ell n\left(1+\frac{1}{x}\right) < \frac{1}{x} \ for\ x > 0.$$

5. Prove the following inequality:
   $$\frac{\tan x}{x} > \frac{x}{\sin x} \ for\ 0 < x < \frac{\pi}{2}.$$

6. Prove the following results:
   (a) $3 + \sin 3 > e + \sin e$
   (b) $\log(e+\sqrt{e^2+1}) > \log(2+\sqrt{5})$
   (c) $e^\pi > \pi^e$ using $f(x) = x^{1/x}, x > 0$
   (d) $(1/2)^e > 1/e^2$ using $f(x) = (\sin x)^{\sin x} \ \forall\ 0 < x < \pi/2$

7. Prove the following results:
   (a) $e^{\cos x - \sin x} < \dfrac{1-\sin x}{1-\cos x} \ \forall x \in (0, \pi/4)$
   (b) $\sin^2 x < x \sin(\sin x), (0 < x < \pi/2)$
   (c) $x \geq \tan^{-1} x \ \forall x \in [0, \infty)$
   (d) $\left(\tan^{-1}\frac{1}{e}\right)^2 + \dfrac{2e}{\sqrt{e^2+1}} < (\tan^{-1} e)^2 + \dfrac{2}{\sqrt{e^2+1}}$
   (e) $\cos(\sin x) > \sin(\cos x) \ \forall x \in (0, 3\pi/2)$
   (f) $(2\sin x + \tan x) \geq 3x; \ 0 \leq x < \pi/2$
   (g) $e^{\tan^{-1}x}\left(x+\sqrt{1+x^2}\right) < e^{2x} \ \forall x \in (0,\infty)$

8. Prove that, $x^2 - 1 \geq 2x \ln x \geq 4(x - 1) - 2 \ln x$ for $x \geq 1$.

9. If $0 < x \leq 1$, prove that $y = x \ln x - (x^2/2) + (1/2)$ is a function such that $d^2y/dx^2 > 0$. Deduce that $x \ln x > (x^2/2) - (1/2)$.

10. Prove that $0 < x. \sin x - (1/2) \sin^2 x < (1/2)(\pi - 1)$ for $0 < x < \pi/2$.

11. Show that $x^2 \geq (1 + x)[\ln(1 + x)]^2 \ \forall x \geq 0$.

12. Find the set of values of x for which the inequality $\ln(1 + x) > x/(1 + x)$ is valid.

Answer Keys

12. $(-1, 0) \cup (0, \infty)$

TEXTUAL EXERCISE–5: (OBJECTIVE)

1. Which of the following is/are true?
   (a) $e^\pi > \pi^e$
   (b) $(1 + \sin \pi/3)^{1 + \cos \pi/3} > (1 + \cos\pi/3)^{1 + \sin \pi/3}$
   (c) $101^{202} > 202^{101}$
   (d) $(4/3)^{9/4} > (9/4)^{4/3}$

2. For $x > 1$, $y = \ln x$ satisfies the inequality
   (a) $x - 1 > y$ (b) $x^2 - 1 > y$
   (c) $y > x - 1$ (d) $\dfrac{x-1}{x} < y$

3. The set of values of x for which $\ln(1 + x) > \dfrac{x}{1+x}$ is
   (a) $\mathbb{R}$ (b) $\mathbb{R} \sim \{0\}$
   (c) $(0, \infty)$ (d) None of these

4. The set of values of x for which $\sin^2 x < x. \sin(\sin x)$ is
   (a) $\mathbb{R}$ (b) $(2n\pi, 2n\pi + \pi/2); n \in \mathbb{Z}$
   (c) $(0, \pi/2)$ (d) None of these

5. For $x \in (0, \pi/2)$; which of the following is correct?
   (a) $0 < x \sin x - (1/2) \sin^2 x$
   (b) $x \sin x - ½ \sin^2 x < \dfrac{\pi-1}{2}$
   (c) both (a) and (b)
   (d) None of the above

6. $(x + 3)^5 - (x - 1)^5 \geq 244$ is satisfied for
   (a) $[0, \infty)$ (b) $(-\infty, 0]$
   (c) $\mathbb{R}$ (d) None of these

7. Find the range of $y = x^x$

(a) $\mathbb{R}$ (b) $[e^{-1/e},\infty)$
(c) $(0, e^{-1/e})$ (d) None of these

8. Find the range of $y = \ln(\sin x^{\sin x} + 1)$

(a) $[\ln(e^{-1/e}+1), \ln 2]$ (b) $[\ln e^{-1/e}, \ln 2]$
(c) $[\ln e^{-1/e}, \ln 2e]$ (d) None of these

9. Find the range of $y = \ln(x^x + 1)$

(a) $[\ln(e^{-1/e} + 1), \ln 2]$ (b) $[\ln e^{-1/e}, \ln 2]$
(c) $[\ln e^{-1/e}, \ln 2e]$ (d) None of these

10. If $g(x) = \left(x - \dfrac{x^3}{6} - \dfrac{x^5}{120}\right) - \sin x$. Then $\ln\{g(x)\}$, (for $x > 0$), is

(a) Not defined
(b) >0
(c) < 0
(d) defined but can't be estimated > 0 or <0

11. If $f(x) = \ln(1 + x) - \dfrac{\tan^{-1} x}{1+x}$ (for $x > 0$); then sgn $f(x)$ is

(a) 1 (b) -1
(c) 4 (d) None of these

12. Let $g(x) = (\ln(1 + x))^{-1} - x^{-1}, x > 0$, then

(a) $1 < g(x) < 2$ (b) $-1 < g(x) < 0$
(c) $0 < g(x) < 1$ (d) None of these

13. The mapping $f: \mathbb{R} \to \mathbb{R}$ given by $f(x) = x^3 + ax^2 + bx + c$ is bijective if and only if

(a) $a^2 \le 3b$ (b) $a^2 > 3b$
(c) $a^2 - 3b = 0$ (d) None of these

14. If $f: \mathbb{R} \to \mathbb{R}, f(x)$ is a differentiable bijective function, then which of the following may be true ?

(a) $(f(x) - x) f''(x) \le 0\ \forall\ x \in \mathbb{R}$
(b) $(f(x) - x) f''(x) > 0\ \forall\ x \in \mathbb{R}$
(c) If $(f(x) - x) f''(x) > 0$, then $f(x) = f^{-1}(x)$ has no solution
(d) If $(f(x) - x) f''(x) > 0$, then $f(x) = f^{-1}(x)$ has at least one real solution

15. Which of the following is true?

(a) $1 + x\ln\left(x+\sqrt{x^2+1}\right) \ge \sqrt{1+x^2}$ for all $x \ge 0$
(b) $1 + x\ln\left(x+\sqrt{x^2+1}\right) > \sqrt{1+x^2}$ for all $x \ge 0$
(c) $1 + x\ln\left(x+\sqrt{x^2+1}\right) \le \sqrt{1+x^2}$ for all $x \ge 0$
(d) $1 + x\ln\left(x+\sqrt{x^2+1}\right) < \sqrt{1+x^2}$ for all $x \ge 0$

16. Let $f(x) = \dfrac{\sin x}{x}$, where $0 < x < \dfrac{\pi}{2}$, then

(a) $\sin^2 x < x\sin(\sin x)$
(b) $\sin^2 x > x\sin(\sin x)$
(c) $\sin^2 x > 1 + x\sin(\sin x)$
(d) None of these

Answer Keys

1. (a,b,c,d) **2.** (a,b,d) **3.** (c) **4.** (c) **5.** (a,b) **6.** (a) **7.** (b) **8.** (a) **9.** (a) **10.** (a)
11. (a) **12.** (c) **13.** (a) **14.** (a,b,c) **15.** (a) **16.** (a)

■ CURVATURE OF FUNCTION

The curvature can be defined as a measure of rate at which the curve curves (bends). "The rate of bending of curves at a point is known as curvature of the curve at that point."

Given a curve $y = f(x)$ along which slope of tangent at P be $\tan\phi$ and at Q be $\tan(\phi + \delta\phi)$

The change in the direction of the curve is $\delta\phi$ whereas the length of arc to achieve the above change is δs (i.e., $\widehat{PQ}$)

$\therefore$ Average rate of bending (average curvature) $= \left(\dfrac{\delta\phi}{\delta s}\right)$

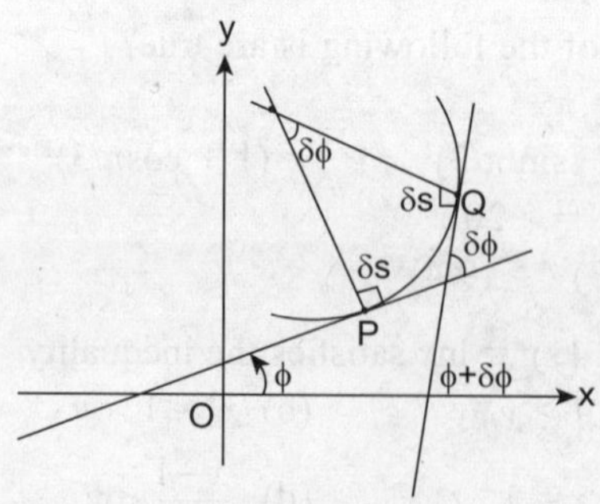

FIGURE 5.119

As $Q \to P$, the arc $\widehat{PQ}$ can be regarded as a circular arc. Also $\delta s \to 0$ and $\delta\phi \to 0$

$\therefore$ Instantaneous rate of bending $= \lim_{\delta s \to 0}\left(\frac{\delta\phi}{\delta s}\right) = \frac{d\phi}{ds}$ is called the curvature of $f(x)$ at point P.

■ CURVATURE OF A CIRCLE

Circle is a curve of fixed curvature and its curvature can be defined as reciprocal of radius (1/r).

Its centre is called centre of curvature.

Proof: For a circle of radius 'r'; we have $\phi = \frac{s}{r} \Rightarrow \frac{\phi}{s} = \frac{1}{r}$

$$\Rightarrow \frac{\delta\phi}{\delta s} = \frac{1}{r}$$

$$\Rightarrow \lim_{\delta s \to 0} \frac{\delta\phi}{\delta s} = \frac{1}{r}.$$ This is constant for a given circle.

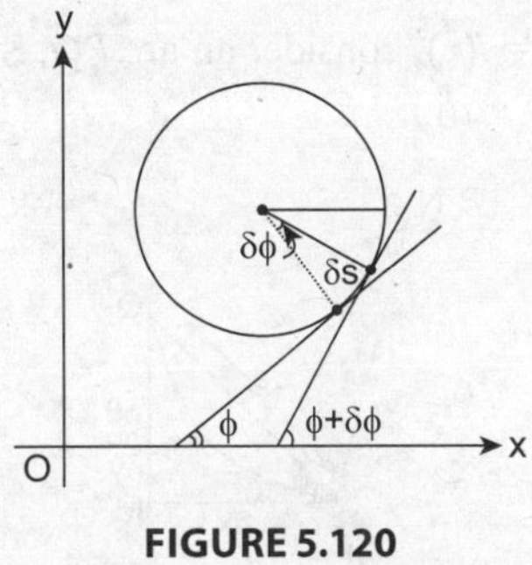

FIGURE 5.120

NOTE

If $\underbrace{radius\ (r) = 0}_{\text{point circle}} \Rightarrow$ *curvature is* ∞.

If $\underbrace{radius\ (r) = \infty}_{\text{straight line}} \Rightarrow$ *curvature is* 0

So curvature of any curve can be measured with the help of a circle.

Let P and Q are two points on the curve y = f(x) and Normal at them intersect at R.

As point Q approaches to P, the point R → N then PN becomes radius of curvature at P.

In Δ PQR:

$$\frac{PR}{\sin\beta} = \frac{PQ}{\sin\delta\phi} \quad \Rightarrow PR = \frac{PQ\sin\beta}{\sin\delta\phi}$$

$[\because$ *when* $Q \to P$; *we get* $\delta s \to 0$ *and* $PQ \to \widehat{PQ}\ ]$

$\Rightarrow \delta\phi \to 0$; $PN \approx PR$ and $\beta \to 90°$

$$\because \ PN = \lim_{Q \to P}(PR) = \lim_{\delta\phi \to 0} \frac{PQ.\sin\beta}{\sin\delta\phi}$$

$$= \lim_{\delta\phi \to 0} \frac{PQ}{\widehat{PQ}} \cdot \frac{\widehat{PQ}}{\delta\phi} \cdot \frac{\delta\phi}{\sin\delta\phi} . \sin\beta$$

$$= \lim_{\delta\phi \to 0} \left(\frac{PQ}{\widehat{PQ}}\right) \cdot \frac{\delta s}{\delta\phi} \cdot \left(\frac{\delta\phi}{\sin\delta\phi}\right) . \sin\beta$$

$$\Rightarrow PN = \lim_{\substack{\delta\phi \to 0 \\ \text{or} \\ \delta s \to 0}} \left(\frac{\delta s}{\delta\phi}\right) = \frac{ds}{d\phi}$$

$$\left[\because \lim_{\delta\phi \to 0}\left(\frac{PQ}{\widehat{PQ}}\right) = 1;\ \lim_{\delta\phi \to 0}\left(\frac{\delta\phi}{\sin\delta\phi}\right) = 1;\ \underbrace{\lim_{\delta\phi \to 0} \sin\beta = 1}_{as\ \beta \to \frac{\pi}{2}}\right]$$

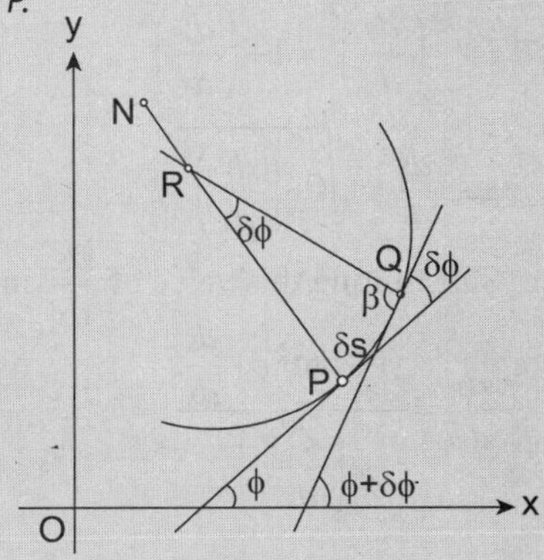

FIGURE 5.121

Radius of curvature (r) = (PN) = $\frac{ds}{d\phi}$. *. Thus curvature at a point P = 1/(radius of curvature at P).*

IF THE FUNCTION IS GIVEN IN CARTESIAN FORM

On the curve $y = f(x)$, consider an arc PQ. Such that $P(x, y)$ and $Q(x + dx, y + dy)$

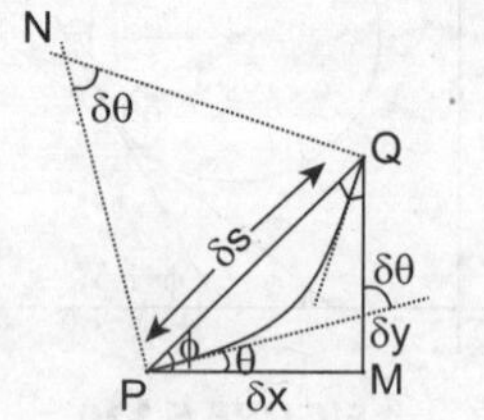

FIGURE 5.122

$$\therefore \quad \tan\phi = \frac{\delta y}{\delta x} \Rightarrow \lim_{Q\to P}\tan\phi = \lim_{\delta x\to 0}\frac{\delta y}{\delta x} \Rightarrow \tan\theta = \frac{dy}{dx}$$

Differentiating both sides with respect to s;

we get $\sec^2\frac{d\phi}{ds} = \frac{d^2y}{dx^2}.\frac{dx}{ds}$ ...(1)

Now; since $(\delta S)^2 = (\delta x)^2 + (\delta y)^2$

$$\Rightarrow \lim_{\delta x\to 0}\left(\frac{\delta s}{\delta x}\right)^2 = \lim_{\delta x\to 0}\left(1+\left(\frac{\delta y}{\delta x}\right)^2\right)$$

$$\Rightarrow \left(\frac{ds}{dx}\right)^2 = 1+\left(\frac{dy}{dx}\right)^2$$

$$\Rightarrow \frac{ds}{dx} = \sqrt{1+\left(\frac{dy}{dx}\right)^2}$$

Substituting this value of $\frac{ds}{dx}$ in (1), we get

$$\frac{ds}{d\phi} = \frac{(1+\tan^2\phi).\frac{ds}{dx}}{\left(\frac{d^2y}{dx^2}\right)}$$

$$= \frac{\left(1+\left(\frac{dy}{dx}\right)^2\right)\sqrt{1+\left(\frac{dy}{dx}\right)^2}}{\left(\frac{d^2y}{dx^2}\right)} = \frac{\left(1+\left(\frac{dy}{dx}\right)^2\right)^{3/2}}{\left(\frac{d^2y}{dx^2}\right)}$$

Conclusion

For any curve $y = f(x)$ at point P(curvature) $= \frac{d\phi}{ds}$ $= \frac{1}{PN} = \frac{1}{\rho}$. where PN = radius of curvature (ρ)

$$= \frac{ds}{d\phi} = \frac{\left(1+\left(\frac{dy}{dx}\right)^2\right)^{3/2}}{\frac{d^2y}{dx^2}}$$

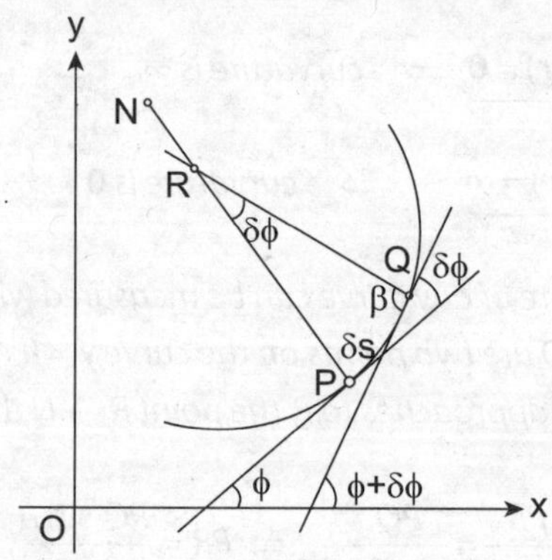

FIGURE 5.123

Clearly the sign of curvature depends on $\frac{d^2y}{dx^2}$

i.e., $\begin{cases} \frac{d^2y}{dx^2} > 0 & \Rightarrow \text{positive curvature} \\ \frac{d^2y}{dx^2} < 0 & \Rightarrow \text{negative curvature} \end{cases}$

NOTE:

- *Since above derivation is independent of choice of axes and depends only on nature of curve, the curvature of the curve remains same by interchanging x and y axes.*

ILLUSTRATION 91: Given a curve with Cartesian equation $y = \sqrt{r^2 - x^2}$, prove that $r = \frac{-\left(1+\left(\frac{dy}{dx}\right)^2\right)^{3/2}}{\left(\frac{d^2y}{dx^2}\right)}$

SOLUTION: $\frac{dy}{dx} = -\frac{x}{\sqrt{r^2 - x^2}}$;

$$\frac{d^2y}{dx^2}=\frac{-\sqrt{r^2-x^2}-(-x).\frac{-x}{\sqrt{r^2-x^2}}}{(r^2-x^2)}=\frac{-(r^2-x^2)-x^2}{(r^2-x^2)\sqrt{r^2-x^2}}=\frac{-r^2}{(r^2-x^2)\sqrt{r^2-x^2}}$$

$$\left(\frac{dy}{dx}\right)^2=\frac{x^2}{r^2-x^2}\Rightarrow\left(1+\left(\frac{dy}{dx}\right)^2\right)^{3/2}=\left(\frac{r^2}{r^2-x^2}\right)^{3/2}$$

Now $\dfrac{\left(1+\left(\frac{dy}{dx}\right)^2\right)^{3/2}}{\frac{d^2y}{dx^2}}=\dfrac{\frac{r^3}{(r^2-x^2)^{3/2}}}{\frac{-r^2}{(r^2-x^2)^{3/2}}}=-r \Rightarrow$ radius of curvature = r and –ve sign shows that curvature is downward.

ILLUSTRATION 92: (a) Find the radius of curvature of the curve $y = x\ln x$ at $x = 1$, also show that its curvature has uniformly positive sign throughout its domain.

(b) Find the radius of curvature of the curve $\frac{x^2}{16}+\frac{y^2}{4}=1.$ at the point $(2, \sqrt{3})$.

SOLUTION: (a) $r=\dfrac{\left(1+\left(\frac{dy}{dx}\right)^2\right)^{3/2}}{\left(\frac{d^2y}{dx^2}\right)}$

For $y = x\ln x$; $x > 0$

$\frac{dy}{dx}=1+\ln x \qquad \Rightarrow \frac{d^2y}{dx^2}=\frac{1}{x}$

Now $r=\dfrac{[1+(1+\ln x)^2]^{3/2}}{\frac{1}{x}}$

Now $x > 0 \qquad \Rightarrow r > 0$

Hence the radius of curvature of the curve $y = x\ln x$ has a uniformly positive sign throughout its domain.

Also $r|_{x=1}=\left.\dfrac{[1+(1+\ln x)^2]^{3/2}}{\frac{1}{x}}\right|_{x=1}=\dfrac{(1+1)^{3/2}}{1}=2\sqrt{2}$

(b) $\frac{x^2}{16}+\frac{y^2}{4}=1 \qquad \Rightarrow x^2 + 4y^2 = 16$

$\Rightarrow 2x + 8y\,y' = 0 \qquad \Rightarrow x + 4yy' = 0$

$\Rightarrow y'=\frac{-x}{4y}$

And $y''=\dfrac{-1(4y)-4y'(-x)}{16y^2}$

$$y''=\frac{-4y+4xy'}{16y^2}=\frac{-y+xy'}{4y^2}=\frac{-y+x\left(\frac{-x}{4y}\right)}{4y^2}=\frac{-(4y^2+x^2)}{16y^3}=\frac{-16}{16y^3}=\frac{-1}{y^3}$$

$$\text{Now } r = \frac{(1+(y')^2)^{3/2}}{y''} = \frac{\left(1+\left(\frac{-x}{4y}\right)^2\right)^{3/2}}{\frac{-1}{y^3}} = \frac{\frac{(16y^2+x^2)^{3/2}}{(4y)^3}}{\frac{-1}{y^3}}$$

$$= \frac{(16y^2+x^2)^{3/2}}{64y^3} \times -y^3 = \frac{-(16y^2+x^2)^{3/2}}{64}$$

Now at $(2, \sqrt{3})$,

$$r = -\frac{(16(3)+4)^{3/2}}{64} = -\frac{(52)^{3/2}}{64} = -\frac{(2\sqrt{13})^3}{64} = -\frac{13\sqrt{13}}{8}$$

Now negative sign shows that the curvature is concave downwards

Hence $|r| = \dfrac{13\sqrt{13}}{8}$

SIGN OF CURVATURE

Nature of bending can be classified in two ways.

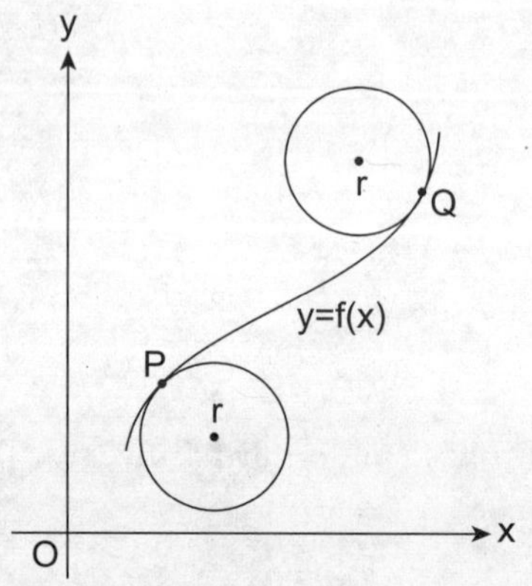

FIGURE 5.124

(a) When the curve bends above its tangent (the sign of curvature is positive).

(b) When the curve bends below its tangent (the sign of curvature is negative).

Concave Upwards (Convex Downwards)

A curve is said to be 'concave upwards' at P iff the curve lies above its tangent in the neighbourhood of P.

Type I: Increasing function with increasing rate of increase i.e., $\dfrac{dy}{dx} > 0$ and $\dfrac{d^2y}{dx^2} > 0$

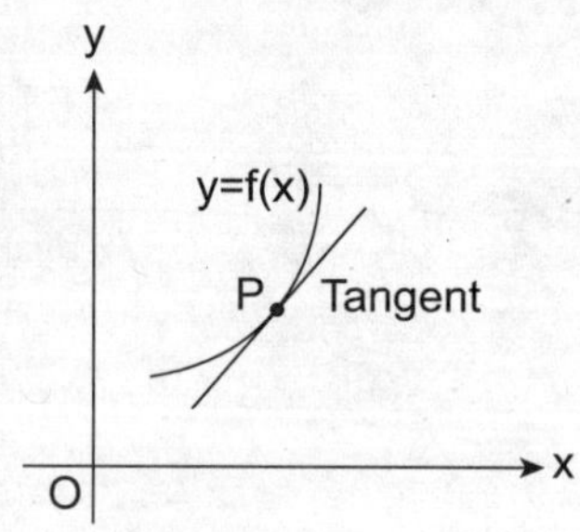

FIGURE 5.125

Type II: Decreasing function with decreasing rate of decrease i.e., $\dfrac{dy}{dx} < 0$ and $\dfrac{d^2y}{dx^2} > 0$

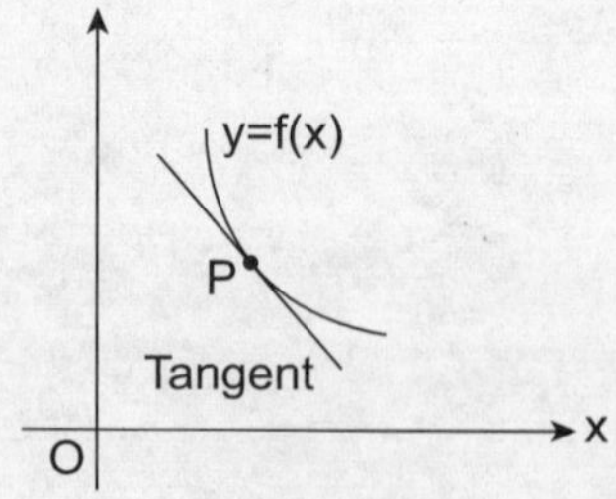

FIGURE 5.126

Concave Downwards (Convex Upwards)

A curve is said to be 'concave downwards' at P iff the curve lies below its tangent in the neighbourhood of P.

Type I: Decreasing function with increasing rate of decrease i.e., $\frac{dy}{dx} < 0$ and $\frac{d^2y}{dx^2} < 0$

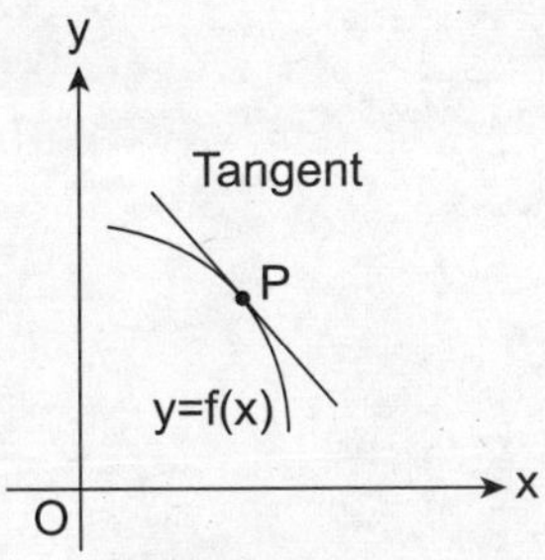

FIGURE 5.127

Type II: Decreasing function with decreasing rate of increase i.e., $\frac{dy}{dx} > 0$ and $\frac{d^2y}{dx^2} < 0$

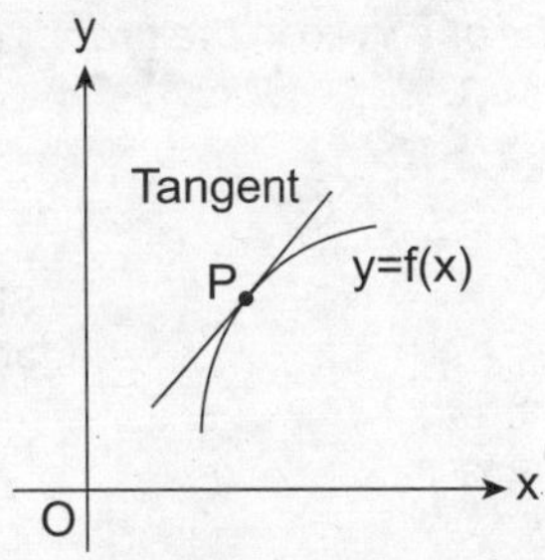

FIGURE 5.128

NOTE

1. *Chord corresponding to the concave upward part of the curves always remains above the curve but for the concave downward curves, it lies below the curve.*
2. *The student can get some help in the identification of the curvature using the BUCKET RULE. If the graph of the function y = f(x) on an interval is concave up then y" > 0; if the graph of the function is concave down, then y" < 0. Writing these inequality in the form* $y" \geq 0$ *and* $y" \leq 0$*, we note that the signs of the inequalities correspond to the directions of concavity of the curve (+ve for upwards, that is the bucket holds water", and -ve for downwards, that is the bucket spills water")*

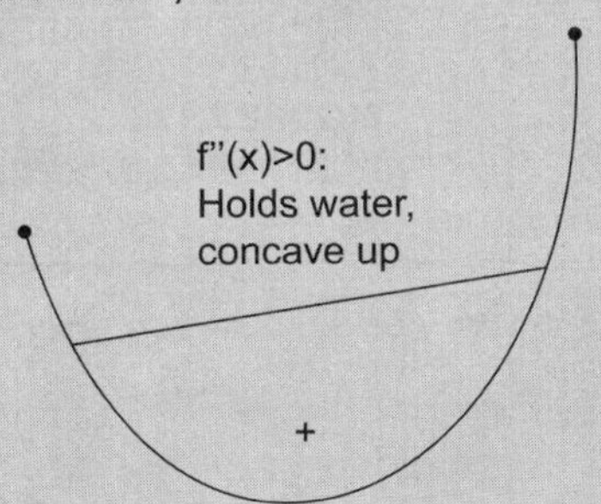

FIGURE 5.129

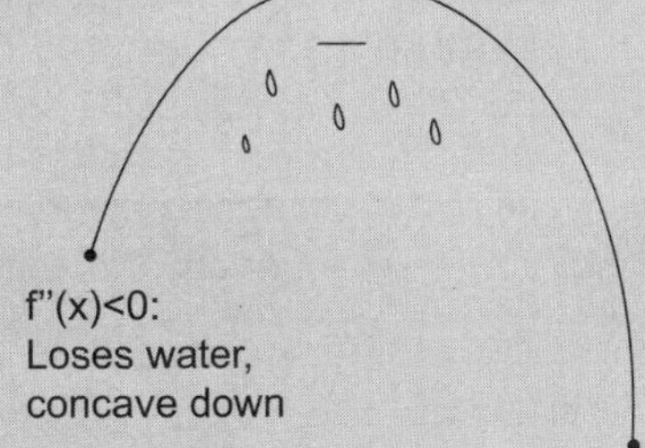

FIGURE 5.130

3. *f and f^{-1} have same monotonic nature i.e., either both increasing or both decreasing but the same can't be said for their curvatures.*

   Proof: *If* $g = f^{-1}$, *then* $f(g(x)) = x \Rightarrow f'(g(x)) \times g'(x) = 1$

   $$\Rightarrow g'(x) = \frac{1}{f'(g(x))}$$

   Now g'(x) has the same sign as f'(x) and hence g(x) has the same monotonocity as f(x), differentiating again; we get $g''(x) = \frac{-1}{(f'(g(x)))^2} \times f''(g(x)) \times g'(x)$

   Now, if f is increasing then g is increasing; therefore g'(x) > 0 and hence g" and f" have opposite signs

   Therefore for increasing functions, the curvature of the inverse graph is opposite to the curvature of the original graph.

However, if f is decreasing, then g is decreasing; therefore g'(x) < 0 and hence g" and f" have same sign.

Therefore for decreasing functions, the curvature of the inverse graph is same as the curvature of the original graph.

This can be observed in the graphs of $f(x) = \ell nx$ and $g(x) = f^{-1}(x) = e^x$

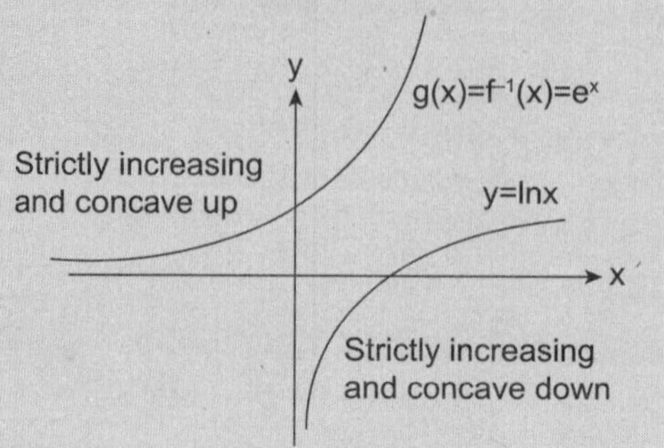

FIGURE 5.131

Now let $y = f(x) = -\tan x;\ x \in (-\pi/2, 0]$ and $g(x) = -\tan^{-1}(x);\ x \in [0, \infty)$

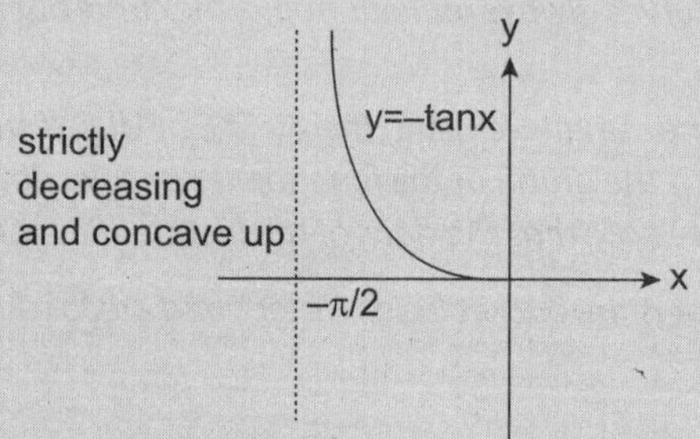

FIGURE 5.132

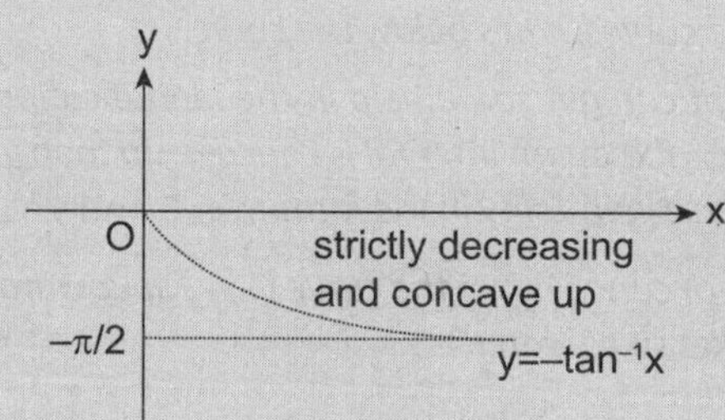

FIGURE 5.133

ILLUSTRATION 93: Establish the intervals of convexity and concavity of the curves represented by the equation

(i) $y = 2 - x^2$ (ii) $y = e^x$

(iii) $y = x^3$

SOLUTION: (i) $y = 2 - x^2$

$\Rightarrow \dfrac{d^2y}{dx^2} = -2 < 0$ for all real x.

$\therefore$ the curve is everywhere convex upwards (concave downwards).

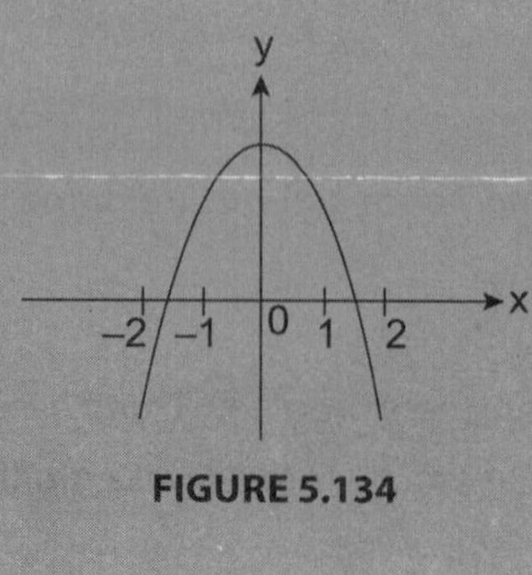

FIGURE 5.134

(ii) $y = e^x$

$\Rightarrow \quad \dfrac{d^2y}{dx^2} = e^x > 0$ for all values of x.

$\therefore$ the curve is everywhere concave upwards (or convex downwards).

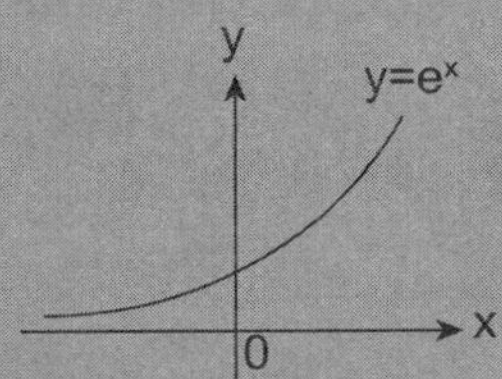

FIGURE 5.135

(iii) $y = x^3$

$$\Rightarrow \quad \frac{d^2y}{dx^2} = 6x \qquad \text{...(i)}$$

Here $\dfrac{d^2y}{dx^2}$ is negative for $x < 0$, and $\dfrac{d^2y}{dx^2}$ is positive for $x > 0$

Hence for $x < 0$, the curve is convex upwards and for $x > 0$ the curve is convex downwards.

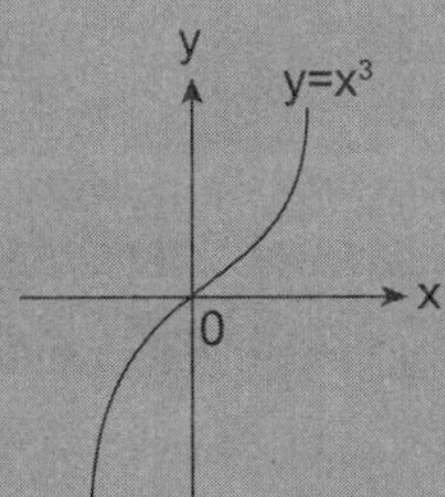

FIGURE 5.136

ILLUSTRATION 94: The curves $y = a(x)$ and $y = b(x)$ are concave on an interval (a, b). Prove that in the given interval

(i) The curve $f(x) = a(x) + b(x)$ is concave

(ii) If $a(x)$ and $b(x)$ are positive and have a common point of minimum, then the curve $y = a(x)\,b(x)$ is concave.

SOLUTION: $y = a(x)\,;\; y = b(x)$

$y'' > 0$

$a''(x) > 0\,;\; b''(x) > 0$ given in the interval (a, b)

(i) $f(x) = a(x) + b(x)$

$\Rightarrow \quad f''(x) = a''(x) + b''(x)$

$f''(x) > 0$

$\because \quad a''(x)\,;\; b''(x) > 0$

$f(x)$ is concave in the given interval (a, b)

(ii) $a(x)$ is +ve; $b(x)$ is +ve both have common point of minimum

$\Rightarrow \quad f(x) = a(x).b(x)$

$\Rightarrow \quad f'(x) = a'(x).b(x) + b'(x).a(x)$

$\Rightarrow \quad f''(x) = a''(x).b(x) + b'(x).a'(x) + b''(x).a(x) + b'(x).a'(x)$

$= a''(x).b(x) + b''(x).a(x) + 2b'(x).a'(x)$

Now, $b''(x) > 0$; $a(x)$ is +ve and $a''(x) > 0$; $b(x)$ +ve.

Also $b'(x).a'(x)$ is + ve. as $x_0 \in (a, b)$ is a common point of minima, then $a'(x)$, $b'(x)$ both simultaneously ↑ or ↓ in (a, x_0) and (x_0, b)

Hence $f''(x) > 0 \ \forall x \in (a, b)$, hence $f(x)$ is concave

ILLUSTRATION 95: Let $P(x)$ be a polynomial with positive coefficients and even exponents. Show that the graph of the function $y = P(x) + ax + b$ is concave everywhere.

SOLUTION: Let $f(x) = P(x) + ax + b$

$\Rightarrow \quad f'(x) = P'(x) + a \qquad [P'(x) \to \text{all odd powers}]$

$\Rightarrow \quad f''(x) = P''(x) \qquad [P''(x) \to \text{all even powers with positive coefficients}]$

$\Rightarrow \quad P''(x) > 0$

So $f''(x) > 0 \qquad \Rightarrow$ graph of $f(x)$ will be concave everywhere.

ILLUSTRATION 96: Prove that if the graph of a function is everywhere convex or everywhere concave, then this function can't have more than one extremum.

SOLUTION: $f''(x) < 0$ for all values of x; $x \in \mathbb{R}$ if graph of function is convex throughout the interval.

$\Rightarrow \quad f''(x)$ is never greater than zero, hence there will be only one extremum i.e., maxima

Similarly $f''(x) > 0$ for all values of x; $x \in \mathbb{R}$ if graph of function is concave throughout the interval

$\Rightarrow \quad f''(x)$ is never less than zero, hence there will be only one extremum i.e., minimum

■ HYPER CRITICAL POINT

In general, a function may be concave up or concave down in different parts of its domain and there may exist infinite/finite such intervals.

Suppose a function 'f' defined in (a, b) is such that it is concave up in (a, c) and concave down in (c, b). Now, the question arises as to what must have happened at $x = c$ and how do we get c. To answer these questions, we should first define the term 'hyper-critical points' or 'critical points of the second kind' or 'second order critical points'

A hyper-critical point of a function 'f' is either the value(s) of x for which $f''(x) = 0$ or the value(s) of x where $f''(x)$ does not exist.

■ POINTS OF INFLEXTION

The point of inflexion is a point which separates the convex portion of the curve from its concave portion.

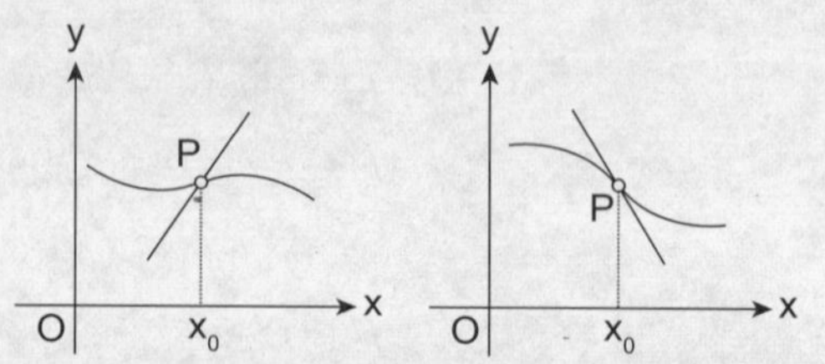

FIGURE 5.137

e.g., consider $y = x^3$

$$\frac{dy}{dx} = 3x^2 \text{ and } \frac{d^2y}{dx^2} = 6x$$

For $x < 0$; $\frac{d^2y}{dx^2} < 0$

$\Rightarrow$ concave downwards

For $x > 0$; $\frac{d^2y}{dx^2} > 0$

$\Rightarrow$ concave downwards

For $x = 0$; $\frac{d^2y}{dx^2} = 0$

$\Rightarrow$ point of infraction

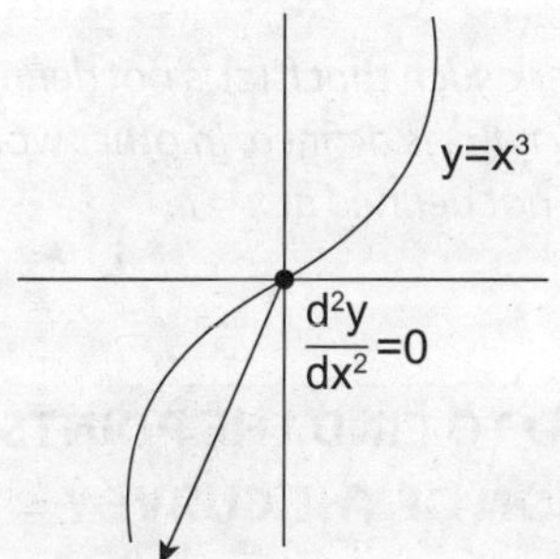

FIGURE 5.138

NOTE:

At the point of inflexion, the tangent line (if it exists) always intersects the curve i.e., the curve crosses its tangent line.

1. *Continuous function 'f' need not have an inflection point at all the points satisfying f''(x) = 0. If f(x) = x^4, we have f''(0) = 0, but the graph of f is always concave up and hence, there is no point inflection.*

   Let us take the function $y = x^5 - 5x^4$.

   Here $y'' = 20x^2(x - 3)$.

   Now y''= 0 for x = 3, the second derivative changes sign, and thus x = 3 is a point of inflection. But when x passes through the point x = 0, the second derivative retains constant sign, and therefore, the origin is not a point of inflection (since the graph of the given function is concave down on both sides of the origin).
2. *If x = c is a point of inflection of a curve y = f(x) and at this point there exists the second derivative f''(c), then f''(c) is necessarily equal to zero (f''(c) = 0).*
3. *The point (1, 0) in $y = (x - 1)^3$, being both a critical point and a point of inflection, is a point of horizontal inflection (Q the tangent at (1, 0) on y is parallel to x-axis).*
4. *If a function f is such that the derivative f''' is continuous at x = c and f''(c) = 0 while f'''(c) ≠ 0, then the curve y = f(x) has a point of inflection for x = c*
5. *It should be noted that a point separating a concave up arc of a curve from a concave down arc; may be such that the tangent at that point is perpendicular to the x-axis i.e., vertical tangent or such that the tangent does not exist This can be demonstrated easily by the behavior of the graph of the function = $\sqrt[3]{x}$ in the vicinity of the origin. In such a case we speak of a point of inflection with vertical tangent*

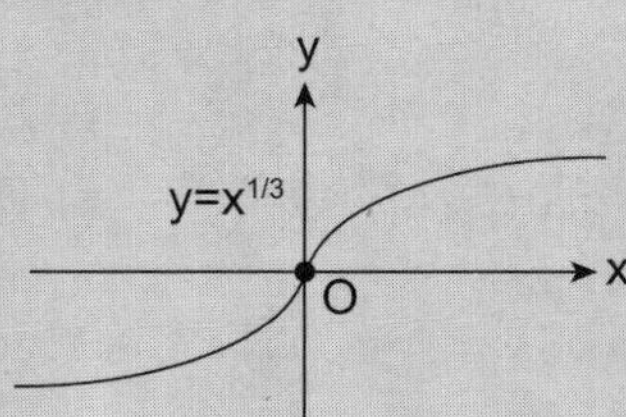

FIGURE 5.139

6. *A number c such that f"(c) is not defined and the concavity of f changes at c will correspond to an inflection point if and only if f(c) is defined. In other words, for a point 'c' to be a point of inflection; f(x) must be defined at x = c; even if f"(x) is not defined at x = c.*

■ METHOD TO FIND THE POINTS OF INFLEXION OF THE CURVE Y = F(X)

Step 1: Find $\frac{d^2y}{dx^2}$ and get all possible x where $\frac{d^2y}{dx^2}=0$ (say $a, b, \ldots$) or where $\frac{d^2y}{dx^2}$ does not exist. (Say $\alpha, \beta, \ldots$)

Step 2: Locate them on real number line and find the sign scheme for $\frac{d^2y}{dx^2}$.

Step 3: The point $x = a$ is a point of inflexion if $\frac{d^2y}{dx^2}$ changes it sign at $x = a$.

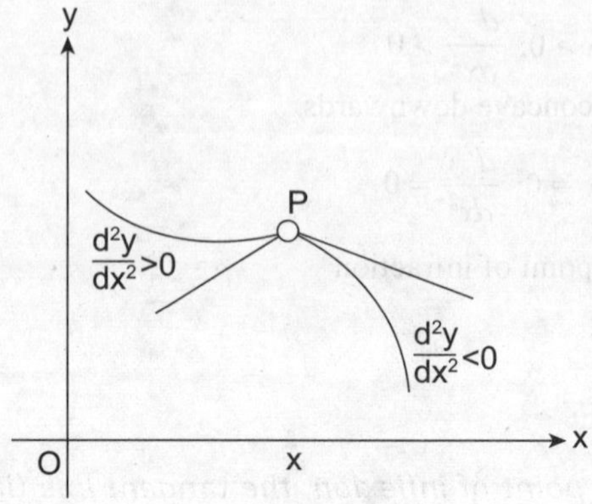

FIGURE 5.141

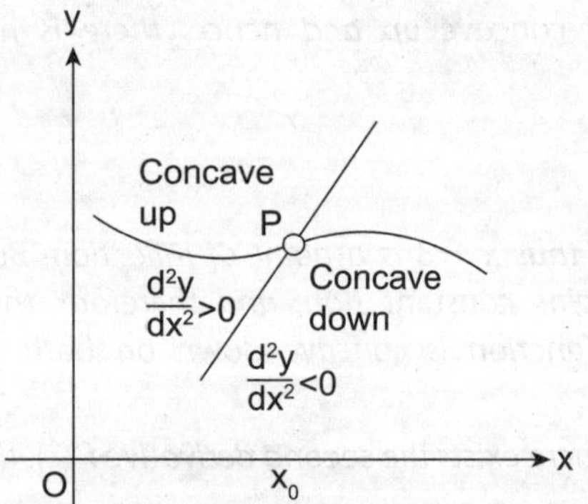

FIGURE 5.140

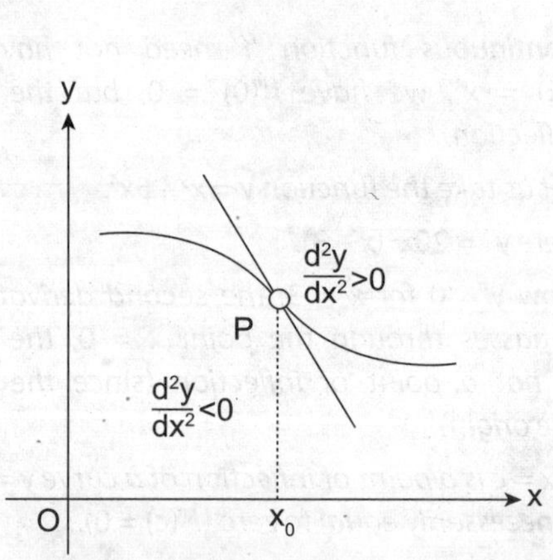

FIGURE 5.142

ILLUSTRATION 97: Examine for convex upwards, concave upwards and points of inflexion of the curve $y = x^4 - 2x^3 + 1$.

SOLUTION: The given curve is $y = x^4 - 2x^3 + 1$

$$\Rightarrow \frac{dy}{dx} = 4x^3 - 6x^2 \text{ and } \frac{d^2y}{dx^2} = 12x^2 - 12x = 12x(x-1)$$

$$\Rightarrow \frac{d^2y}{dx^2} > 0 \text{ for } x \in (-\infty, 0) \cup (1, \infty) \text{ and } \frac{d^2y}{dx^2} < 0 \text{ for } x \in (0,1) \text{ and } \frac{d^2y}{dx^2} = 0 \text{ at } x = 0, 1$$

$\Rightarrow$ $f(x)$ is concave up on $(-\infty, 0) \cup (1, \infty)$ and concave down on $(0, 1)$

Further $x = 0$ and $x = 1$ are the point of inflexion.

ILLUSTRATION 98: Show that every point at which the sine curve $y = c \sin \frac{x}{a}$ meets the axis of x is a point of inflexion of the curve.

SOLUTION: The given sine curve is $y = c \sin \frac{x}{a}$ ...(i)

$$\frac{dy}{dx} = \frac{c}{a}\cos\frac{x}{a};\ \frac{d^2y}{dx^2} = -\frac{c}{a^2}\sin\frac{x}{a} \text{ and } \frac{d^3y}{dx^3} = \frac{-c}{a^3}\cos\frac{x}{a}$$

The given curve (i) meets x-axis at the point where $y = 0$ i.e.,$\sin \frac{x}{a} = 0$

$\Rightarrow \frac{x}{a} = n\pi;\ n \in \mathbb{Z}$ or $x = n\pi\ a;\ n \in \mathbb{Z}$

Now for $x = n\pi a$, $\frac{d^2y}{dx^2} = 0$ and $\frac{d^3y}{dx^3} = \frac{-c}{a^3}\cos n\pi \neq 0$

$\therefore$ $(an\pi, 0)\ n \in \mathbb{Z}$ are the point of inflexion for the curve (i). i.e., every point where the curve meets x-axis is a point of inflextion of the curve.

SOLVING INEQUALITIES USING CURVATURE

Curvature of a graph is highly useful in proving/solving some inequalities, which makes the process easy and time saving.

JENSON'S FUNCTIONAL EQUATION

Equation Jenson observed that for the function '$f(x)$' which are either increasing with a constant rate of increase or decreasing with a constant rate of decrease; $f\left(\frac{mx_1 + nx_2}{m+n}\right) = \frac{mf(x_1) + nf(x_2)}{m+n}$; where m, n are constant real numbers and $x_1, x_2 \in D_f$

Discussion

For increasing function with constant rate of increase.

Let $y = f(x)$ be a function such that $f'(x) > 0$ and $f''(x) = 0\ \forall\ x \in D_f$

The curve is neither concave up, nor concave down $(\because f''(x) = 0)$

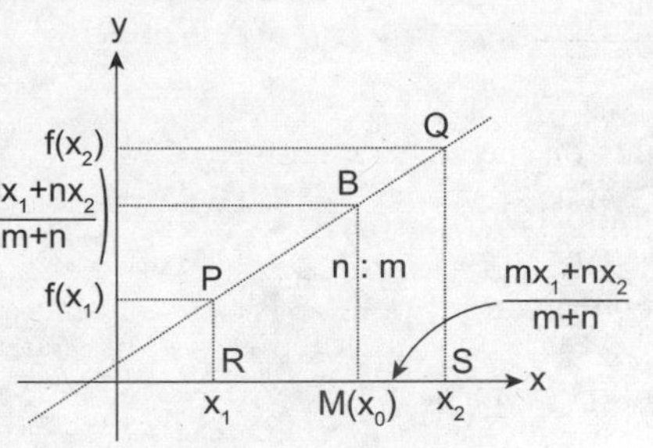

FIGURE 5.143

Let the point B divides the line PQ in the ratio $n : m$

$\therefore$ The foot of perpendicular from B on the x-axis (i.e., M) will divide the line segment joining $(x_1, 0)$ and $(x_2, 0)$ in the ratio $n : m$

$\therefore$ x-coordinate of $M \equiv \frac{mx_1 + nx_2}{m+n} = x_0$ (say)

Similarly y-coordinate of point B will be $\frac{mf(x_1) + nf(x_2)}{m+n}$

And the value of the function $f(x)$ at $x = x_0$ will be $f\left(\frac{mx_1 + nx_2}{m+n}\right)$

And as is evident from the diagram; we get $f\left(\frac{mx_1 + nx_2}{m+n}\right) = \frac{mf(x_1) + nf(x_2)}{m+n}$

Similarly; the same can be derived for decreasing function with constant rate of decrease

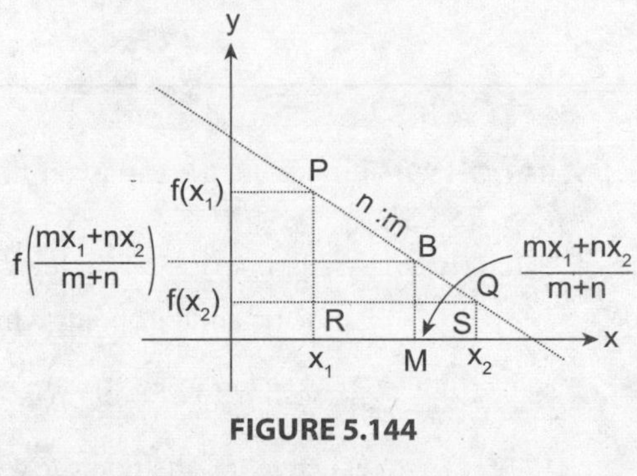

FIGURE 5.144

It is from here that Jenson derived two very useful deductions named as Jenson's inequality

Deduction 1: **For increasing function with decreasing rate of increase:**

If $f'(x) > 0$ and $f''(x) < 0$ for all $x \in D_f$, then the graph of $f(x)$ increases with decreasing rate and remain concave downward ($\because f''(x) < 0$). Therefore chord of the curve lies below the curve. Considering a point B dividing chord PQ in the ratio $n : m$, we get $f\left(\frac{mx_1 + nx_2}{m+n}\right) > \frac{mf(x_1) + nf(x_2)}{m+n}$

($\because AM > BM$)

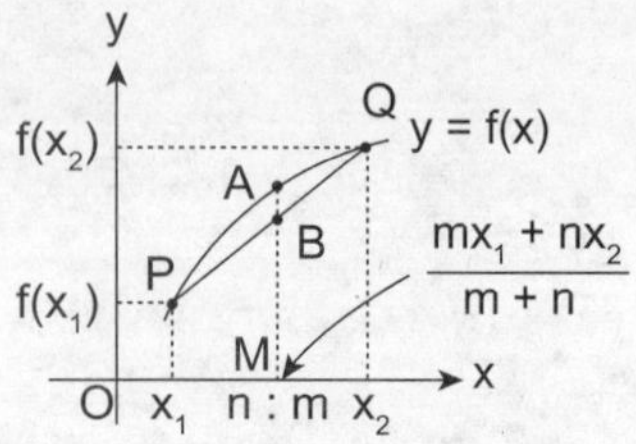

FIGURE 5.145

Similarly for decreasing function with increasing rate of decrease. i.e., $f'(x) < 0$ and $f''(x) < 0$

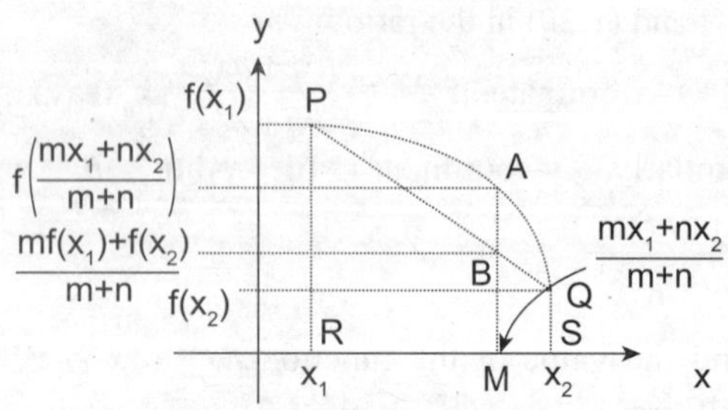

FIGURE 5.146

Deduction 2: **For increasing function with increasing rate of increase**

If $f'(x) > 0$ and $f''(x) = 0$ for all $x \in D_f$ i.e., graph of $f(x)$ increases with increasing rate and remains concave up ($\because f''(x) > 0$). Therefore chord of the curve lies above the curve.

Considering a point B dividing chord PQ in the ratio $n : m$, we get $f\left(\frac{mx_1 + nx_2}{m+n}\right) < \frac{mf(x_1) + nf(x_2)}{m+n}$

($\because AM < BM$) (Similarly you can think of the inequalities for decreasing functions)

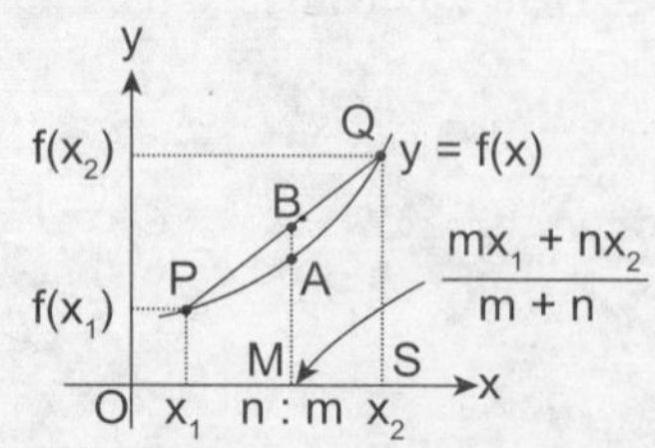

FIGURE 5.147

Similarly for decreasing function with decreasing rate of decrease i.e., $\frac{dy}{dx} < 0$ and $\frac{d^2y}{dx^2} > 0$

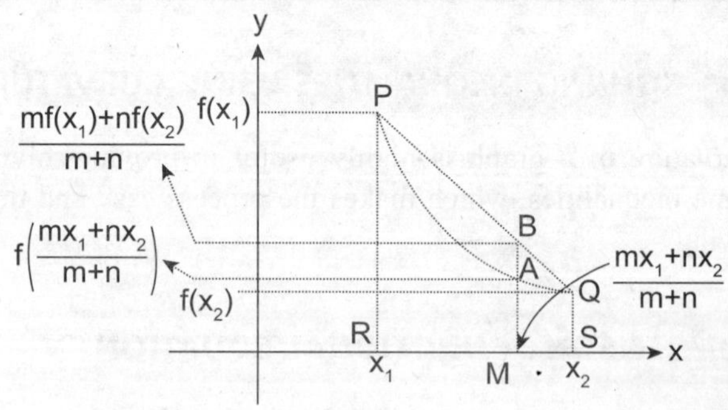

FIGURE 5.148

Conclusion

For concave up curve;

we have $f\left(\frac{mx_1 + nx_2}{m+n}\right) < \frac{mf(x_1) + nf(x_2)}{m+n}$ and for concave down curve; we have $f\left(\frac{mx_1 + nx_2}{m+n}\right) > \frac{mf(x_1) + nf(x_2)}{m+n}$

ILLUSTRATION 99: Prove that for any two number x_1 and x_2, $\frac{2e^{x_1} + e^{x_2}}{3} > e^{\frac{2x_1 + x_2}{3}}$

SOLUTION: Assume $f(x) = e^x$ and let x_1 and x_2 be two points on the curve $y = e^x$

Let R be another point which divides PQ in ratio 1:2

y-coordinate of point R is $\frac{2e^{x_1} + e^{x_2}}{3}$ and y coordinate of point S is $e^{\frac{2x_1 + x_2}{3}}$, since $f(x) = e^x$ is concave up, the point R will always lie above the point S.

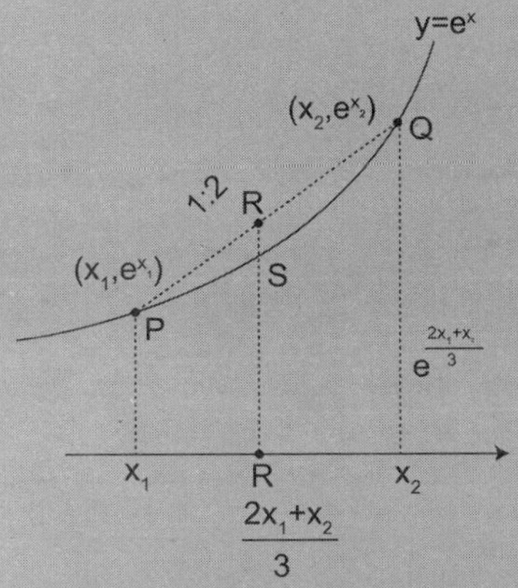

FIGURE 5.149

$$\Rightarrow \quad \frac{2e^{x_1}+e^{x_2}}{3} > e^{\frac{2x_1+x_2}{3}}$$

Aliter: (above inequality could also be easily proved using AM-GM inequality)

ILLUSTRATION 100: If $0 < x_1 < x_2 < x_3 < \pi$, then prove that $\sin\left(\frac{x_1+x_2+x_3}{3}\right) > \frac{\sin x_1+\sin x_2+\sin x_3}{3}$.

Hence show that in a Δ ABC, $(\sin A + \sin B + \sin C) \le \frac{3\sqrt{3}}{2}$

SOLUTION: Point A, B, C form a triangle, y coordinate of centroid G is $\frac{\sin x_1+\sin x_2+\sin x_3}{3}$ and y coordinate of point F is $\sin\left(\frac{x_1+x_2+x_3}{3}\right)$

Hence $\sin\left(\frac{x_1+x_2+x_3}{3}\right) \ge \frac{\sin x_1+\sin x_2+\sin x_3}{3}$

If $A + B + C = \pi$, then $\sin\left(\frac{A+B+C}{3}\right) \ge \frac{\sin A+\sin B+\sin C}{3} \Rightarrow \sin\frac{\pi}{3} \ge \frac{\sin A+\sin B+\sin C}{3}$

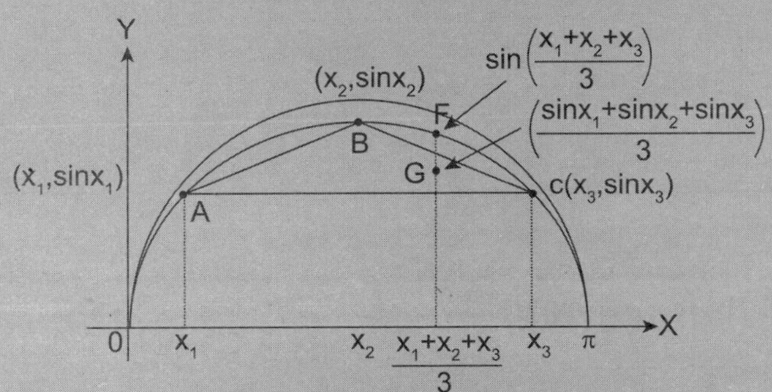

FIGURE 5.150

$$\Rightarrow \quad \frac{3\sqrt{3}}{2} \ge \sin A+\sin B+\sin C$$

$\Rightarrow$ maximum value of $(\sin A + \sin B + \sin C) = \frac{3\sqrt{3}}{2}$

ILLUSTRATION 101: Find the points of inflection of the function $f(x) = \sin^2 x;\ x \in [0, 2\pi]$

SOLUTION: $f(x) = \sin^2 x$

$f'(x) = \sin 2x$

$f''(x) = 2\cos 2x$

$\therefore\ f''(0) \Rightarrow x = \dfrac{\pi}{4}, \dfrac{3\pi}{4}, \dfrac{5\pi}{4}, \dfrac{7\pi}{8}$

All these points are inflection points as sign of $f''(x)$ change on either sides of these points

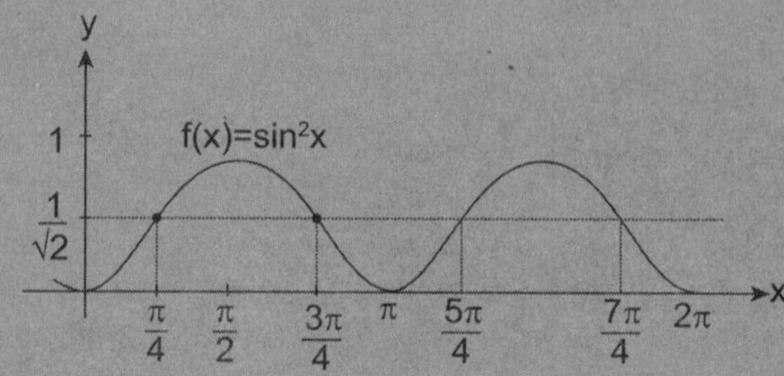

FIGURE 5.151

ILLUSTRATION 102: Find the inflection point of $f(x) = 3x^4 - 4x^3$. Also draw the graph of $f(x)$ giving due importance to maxima, minima and concavity.

SOLUTION: $f(x) = 3x^4 - 4x^3$

$\Rightarrow f'(x) = 12x^3 - 12x^2$

$\therefore\ f'(x) = 0 \Rightarrow x = 0, 1$

examining sign change of $f'(x)$, we have

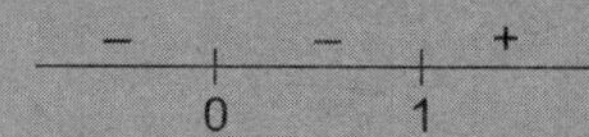

FIGURE 5.152

Thus $x = 1$ is a point of local minima

Also $f''(x) = 12\,(3x^2 - 2x)$

$\therefore\ f''(x) = 0 \Rightarrow x = 0, 2/3$

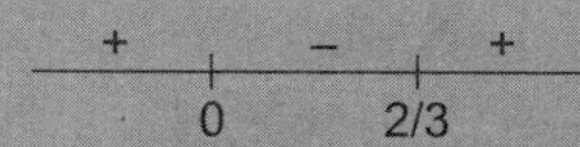

FIGURE 5.153

Again, examining sign of $f''(x)$, we have

Thus $x = 0, 2/3$ are inflection points Hence the graph of $f(x)$ will be as shown below

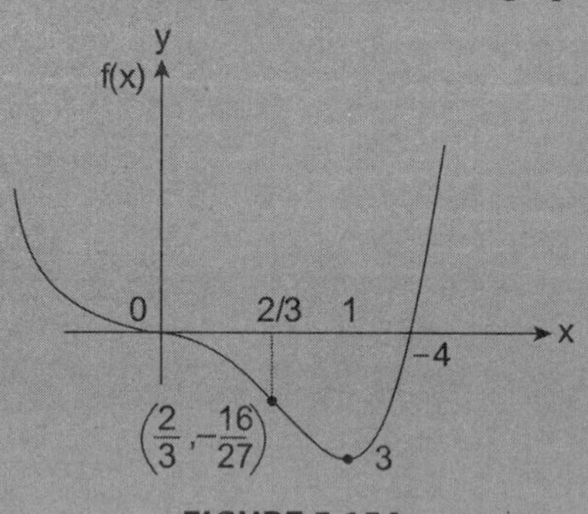

FIGURE 5.154

TEXTUAL EXERCISE–6: (SUBJECTIVE)

1. Test the curvature of the following curves and find the convexity (concavity) and therefore determine the points of inflections, if any.

(a) $f(x) = x^3 - 6x^2$ **(b)** $y = e^x - e^{-x}$

(c) $f(x) = 2x^3 - 3x^2 + 1$ **(d)** $y = 2x^{3/2}$

(e) $y = \dfrac{\ln x}{x}$ **(f)** $y = x \ln x$

2. Let $g(x) = 2f\left(\dfrac{x}{2}\right) + f(2-x)$ and $f''(x) < 0,\ \forall x \in (0, 2)$.

Find the interval of increase and decrease of $g(x)$.

3. Given a function $f(x)$ such that $f''(x) < 0$, $(x_1, f(x_1))$ and $(x_2, f(x_2))$ be two points on $y = f(x)$, then prove that

$f\left(\frac{x_1+x_2}{2}\right) > \frac{f(x_1)+f(x_2)}{2}$ $\forall$ $x_1, x_2 \in$ domain of $f(x)$.

4. If $f(x)$ is monotonicity increasing function $\forall x \in \mathbb{R}$ such that $f''(x) < 0$ & $f^{-1}(x)$ exists, then prove that $\frac{f^{-1}(x_1)+f^{-1}(x_2)+f^{-1}(x_3)}{3} > f^{-1}\left(\frac{x_1+x_2+x_3}{3}\right)$.

5. If $0 < A < \pi/6$, then show $A(\operatorname{cosec} A) < \pi/3$.

6. If $0 < A, B, C < \pi/2$, then show that $A \operatorname{cosec} A + B \operatorname{cosec} B + C \operatorname{cosec} C < \frac{3\pi}{2}$.

7. Test the curvature of following curves and find the interval at which they are concave and draw their graph and also find the points of inflexion, if any:

(a) $y = (x-1)^{1/3}$

(b) $y = x^4 - 2x^3 + 1$

(c) $y = (x-1)(x-2)(x-3)$

(d) $y = (x-1)^2(x-2)$

(e) $y = 3x^2 - 2x^3$ **(f)** $y = \ln \sin x$

(g) $y^2 = x^4 - x^6$ **(h)** $y^2 = x^3$

(i) $y = \frac{e^x - e^{-x}}{2}$ **(j)** $y = \frac{e^x - e^{-x}}{e^x + e^{-x}}$

(k) $y = e^{-x^2}$

8. For an acute angle triangle ABC, prove that

(a) $\sin A + \sin B + \sin C > 2$ for any Δ

(b) $\cos(\pi/4 + A/4) + \cos(\pi/4 + B/4) + \cos(\pi/4 + C/4) \le 3/2$ for any Δ

(c) $\cos A + \cos B + \cos C \le \frac{3}{2}$ for any Δ

(d) $\cos A . \cos B . \cos C \le \frac{1}{8}$ for any Δ

(e) $\sin\frac{A}{2} . \sin\frac{B}{2} . \sin\frac{C}{2} \le \frac{1}{8}$ for any Δ

9. Prove the following inequalities

(i) $\frac{x^2+y^2}{2} \ge \left(\frac{x+y}{2}\right)^2$.

(ii) $\frac{x^2+y^2+z^2}{3} \ge \left(\frac{x+y+z}{3}\right)^2$

(iii) $\frac{x^{2n+1}+y^{2n+1}}{2} \ge \left(\frac{x+y}{2}\right)^{2n+1}, x, y > 0$

10. Find the set of value(s) 'a' for which the function $f(x) = \frac{ax^3}{3} + (a+2)x^2 + (a-1)x + 2$ possess negative point of inflection.

Answers keys

1. **(a)** $x \in (\infty, 2)$ concave downward, $x \in (2, \infty)$ concave upward, $x = 2$ is point of inflection.

(b) Concave downwards for $x < 0$, concave upwards for $x > 0$, Point of inflection $x = 0$

(c) $x \in \left(\infty, \frac{1}{2}\right)$ concave downward, $x \in \left(\frac{1}{2}, \infty\right)$ concave upward $x = 1/2$ is point of inflection

(d) Concave upwards for $x \in (0, \infty)$

(e) Concave downwards on $(0, e^{3/2})$ and concave upwards on $(e^{3/2}, 0)$ and point of inflection $= e^{3/2}$.

(f) Concave upwards on $(0, \infty)$

2. $g(x) \downarrow$ on $(-\infty, 0)$ and on $\left(\frac{4}{3}, \infty\right)$ and $g(x) \uparrow$ on $\left(0, \frac{4}{3}\right]$

7. **(a)** for $x < 1$, $\frac{d^2y}{dx^2} > 0$, the curve is concave upwards; for $x > 1$, $\frac{d^2y}{dx^2} < 0$ the curve is convex up-wards.

(b) concave upward if $x \in (-\infty, 0) \cup (1, \infty)$, point of inflection at $x = 0, 1$

(c) concave up, $\forall x \in (2, \infty)$ **(d)** concave up, $\forall x \in \left(\frac{4}{3}, \infty\right)$

(e) concave up, $\forall x \in \left(-\infty, \frac{1}{2}\right)$ **(f)** concave downward in entire domain

(g) concave up: $x \in \left(-\sqrt{\alpha}, \sqrt{\alpha}\right)$ and $y > 0$, concave down $x \in \left[-1, -\sqrt{\alpha}\right) \cup \left(\sqrt{\alpha}, 1\right]$ and $y > 0$; $\alpha = \frac{9-\sqrt{33}}{12}$;

For y < 0, concavities are opposite in above intervals.

(h) concave up if $x, y > 0$ **(i)** concave up $\forall x > 0$ **(j)** $\forall x < 0$ concave up

(k) $x \in \mathbb{R} \sim \left[-\frac{1}{\sqrt{2}}, \frac{1}{\sqrt{2}}\right]$, it is concave up **10.** $(-\infty, -2) \cup (0, \infty)$

TEXTUAL EXERCISE–6: (OBJECTIVE)

1. For which values of 'a' will the function $f(x) = x^4 + ax^3 + \frac{3x^2}{2} + 1$ will be concave upward along the entire real line
(a) $a \in [0, \infty]$ (b) $a \in (-2, 2)$
(c) $a \in [-2, 2]$ (d) $a \in (0, \infty)$

2. For the cubic, $f(x) = 2x^3 + 9x^2 + 12x + 1$ which one of the following statement, does not hold good?
(a) $f(x)$ is non monotonic
(b) increasing $(-\infty, -2) \cup (-1, \infty)$ and decreasing is $(-2, -1)$
(c) $f: \mathbb{R} \to \mathbb{R}$ is bijective
(d) Inflection point occurs at $x = -3/2$

3. Let h be a twice continuously differentiable positive function on an open interval J. Let $g(x) = \ln(h(x))$ for each $x \in J$ Suppose $(h'(x))^2 > h''(x)(h)(x)$ for each $x \in J$. Then
(a) g is increasing on J
(b) g is decreasing on J
(c) g is concave up on J
(d) g is concave down on J

4. Let $f(x) = \begin{cases} \dfrac{(x-1)(6x-1)}{2x-1} & if\ x \neq \dfrac{1}{2} \\ 0 & if\ x = \dfrac{1}{2} \end{cases}$ then at $x = ½$
(a) f has a local maxima
(b) f has a local minima
(c) f has no inflection point
(d) f has a removable discontinuity

5. Function $f(x)$, $g(x)$ are defined on $[-1, 3]$ and $f''(x) > 0$, $g''(x) > 0$ for all $x \in [-1, 3]$, then which of the following is always true ?
(a) $f(x) - g(x)$ is concave upwards on $[-1,3]$
(b) $f(x)\,g(x)$ is concave upwards on $[-1,3]$
(c) $f(x)\,g(x)$ does not have a critical point $[-1,3]$
(d) $f(x) + g(x)$ is concave upwards on $[-1,3]$

6. Let $p(x)$ be a polynomial of degree 5 and suppose that $p(x)$ has as many inflection points as possible for a polynomial of degree 5. Then the number of inflection points of $p(x)$ is
(a) 5 (b) 4
(c) 3 (d) 2

7. The function $f(x) = (x + 2)^{1/3}$ at $x = -2$
(a) is monotonic
(b) is differentiable
(c) is such that no tangent can be drawn at this point
(d) changes its concavity

8. For the function $f(x) = x^4(12 \ln x - 7)$
(a) the point $(1, -7)$ is the point of inflexion
(b) $x = e^{1/3}$ is the point of minima
(c) the graph is concave downwards in $(0, 1)$
(d) the graph is concave upwards in $(1, \infty)$

9. If f is continuous in $[a, b]$, differentiable in (a, b) and $f(a) = f(b)$, then there exist at least one point $c \in (a, b)$ such that $f'(c) = 0$. This result is known as
(a) Lagrange's theorem (b) Euler's theorem
(c) Rolle's theorem (d) Cauchy's theorem

10. If $f(x) = kx^3 - 9x^2 + 9x + 3$ is monotonically increasing in each interval, then
(a) $k < 3$ (b) $k \leq 3$
(c) $k \geq 3$ (d) none

11. If $f(x)$ is a monotonically decreasing function and have concavity up, then its inverse $f^1(x)$ will be
(a) decreasing and has concavity upwards
(b) decreasing and has concavity downwards
(c) increasing and has concavity downwards
(d) increasing and has concavity upwards.

Answer Keys

1. (c) 2. (a,b,d) 3. (d) 4. (c) 5. (d) 6. (c) 7. (d) 8. (a,b,c,d) 9. (c) 10. (c)
11. (a)

MEAN VALUE THEOREM

ROLLE'S AND MEAN VALUE THEOREM

Rolle's Theorem

Let a function $f(x)$ defined on $[a, b]$ be such that

- it is continuous in the interval $[a, b]$
- it is differentiable in the interval (a, b)
- $f(a) = f(b)$,

then there exist at least one $c \in (a, b)$ such that $f'(c) = 0$

Analytical proof:

Since $f(x)$ is continuous in closed interval $[a, b]$

$\Rightarrow$ $f(x)$ is bounded i.e., $m \le f(x) \le M\ \forall x \in [a, b]$

$\therefore$ $f(a)$ and $f(b)$ are either both maxima (minima) or both are neither maxima nor minima.

So there exist at least one point $c \in (a, b)$, where $f(c) = m$ or M.

Case I:

$M = m$ $\quad \Rightarrow f(x)$ is constant $\forall x \in (a, b)$

$\Rightarrow f(x) = 0\ \forall x \in (a, b)$

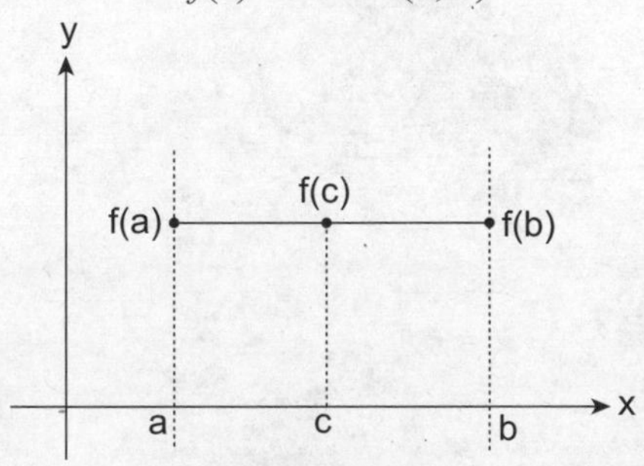

FIGURE 5.155

Case II:

$M \neq m$ and let there lie a point $c \in (a, b)$, where $f(c) = M$.

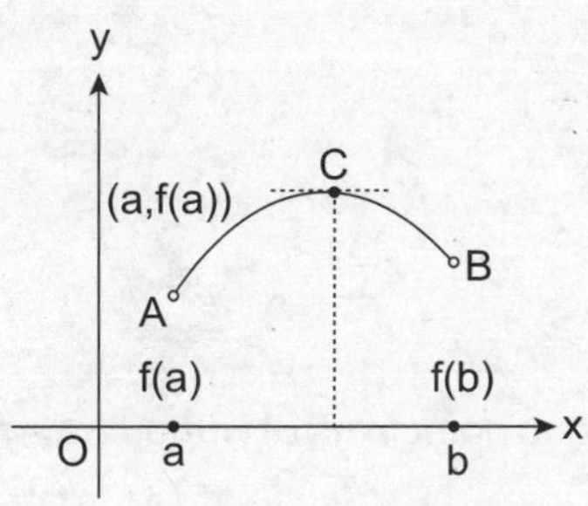

FIGURE 5.156

$\Rightarrow f(c + h) \le f(c)$ and $f(c - h) \le f(c)$

$$\Rightarrow \frac{f(c+h)-f(c)}{h} \le 0 \text{ and } \frac{f(c-h)-f(c)}{-h} \ge 0$$

$$\Rightarrow \lim_{h\to 0}\frac{f(c+h)-f(c)}{h} \le 0$$

$$\text{and } \lim_{h\to 0}\frac{f(c-h)-f(c)}{-h} \ge 0$$

$\Rightarrow f'(c^-) \ge 0$ and $f'(c^+) \le 0$ but $\because f$ is differentiable at c.

$\therefore f'(c^-) = f'(c^+)$

$\Rightarrow f'(c) = 0$

Case III:

$M \neq m$ and let there lie a point $c \in (a, b)$, where $f(c) = m$

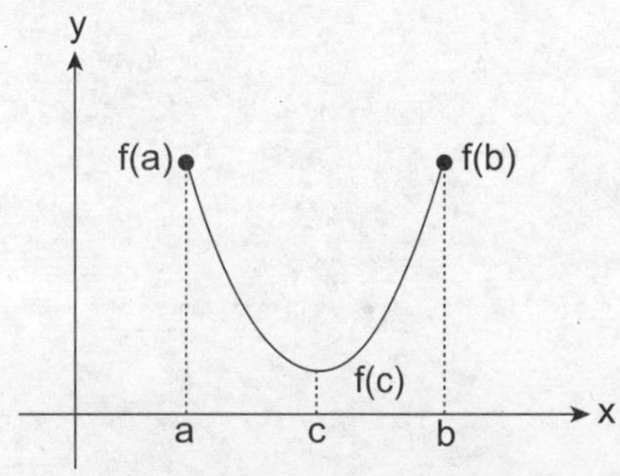

FIGURE 5.157

$\Rightarrow f(c + h) \ge f(c)$ and $f(c - h) \ge f(c)$

$$\Rightarrow \frac{f(c+h)-f(c)}{h} \ge 0$$

$$\text{and } \frac{f(c-h)-f(c)}{-h} \le 0$$

$$\Rightarrow \lim_{h\to 0}\frac{f(c+h)-f(c)}{h} \ge 0$$

$$\text{and } \lim_{h\to 0}\frac{f(c-h)-f(c)}{-h} \le 0$$

$\Rightarrow f'(c^+) \ge 0$ and $f'(c^-) \le 0$

But $\because$ f is differentiable at 'c'

$\therefore f'(c^-) = f'(c^+) = 0 \Rightarrow f'(c) = 0$

Similarly for the function of the type

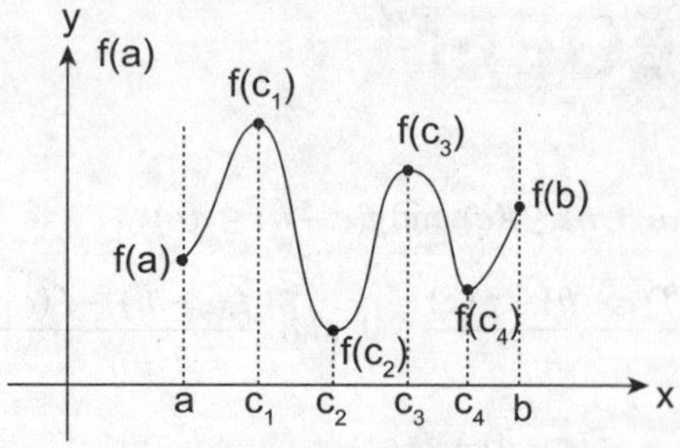

FIGURE 5.158

c_1 and c_3 are the points of local maxima and c_2 and c_4 are the points of local minima.

Hence $f(c_1) = f(c_2) = f(c_3) = f(c_4)$ ....= 0.

Conclusion

There is atleast one point on curve lying between *A* and *B*, the tangent at which is parallel to x-axis.

REMARKS:

- *Rolle's theorem fails for the function which does not satisfy at least one of the three conditions.*

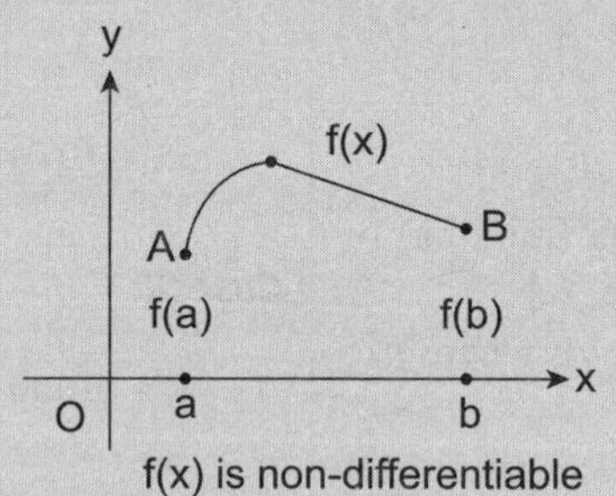

FIGURE 5.159

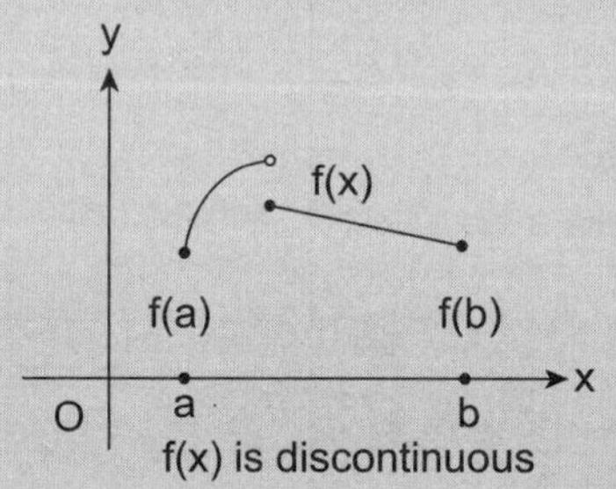

FIGURE 5.160

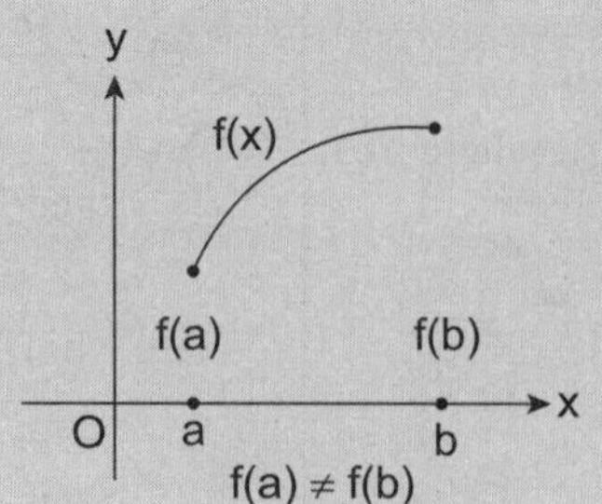

FIGURE 5.161

- *The converse of Rolle's theorem may not be true.* i.e., *f'(c) may be zero at a point in (a, b) without satisfying all the three conditions*

Case I:

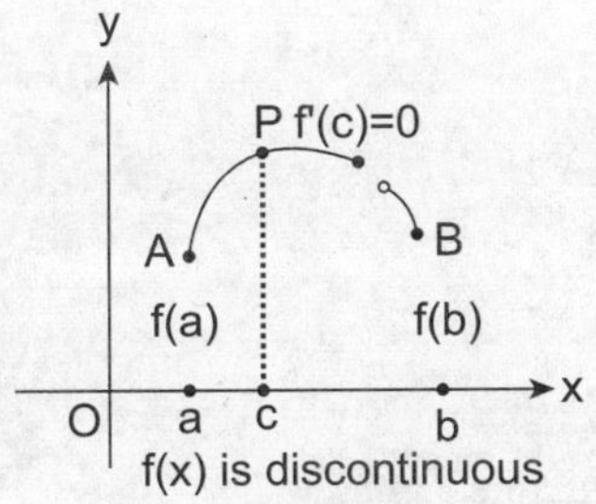

FIGURE 5.162

Case II:

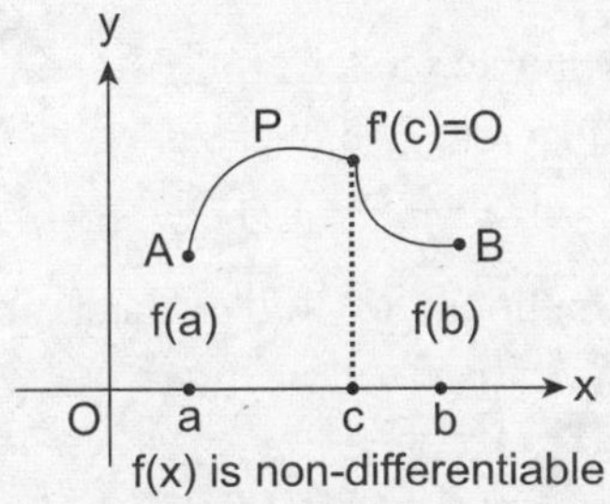

FIGURE 5.163

Case III:

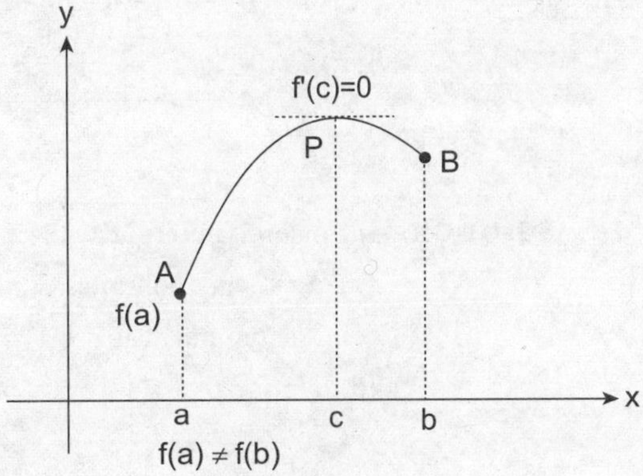

FIGURE 5.164

In all the above there cases, we observed that all the conditions Rolle's theorem are not satisfied because atleast one of the three conditions is being violated. But still, in each of the three cases, there exists a point 'c' such that $c \in (a, b)$ and $f'(c) = 0$

ILLUSTRATION 103: Consider the function $f(x)=\begin{cases} x\sin\dfrac{\pi}{x} & ;x>0 \\ 0 & ;x=0 \end{cases}$, then the number of points in (0, 1) where the derivative $f'(x)$ vanishes, is

(a) 0 (b) 1

(c) 2 (d) infinite

SOLUTION: **(d)** $f(x)$ vanishes at points where $\sin\dfrac{\pi}{x} = 0$ i.e., $\dfrac{\pi}{x} = k\pi$, $k = 1, 2, 3, 4, ...$

hence $x = \dfrac{1}{k}$. Also $f'(x) = \sin\dfrac{\pi}{x} - \dfrac{\pi}{x}\cos\dfrac{\pi}{x}$ if $x \neq 0$

Since the function has a derivative at avery interior point of the interval (0, 1), also continuous in [0,1] and $f(0) = f(1/k)$ hence Rolle's theorem is applicable to each one of the interval S = $\left[\dfrac{1}{2},1\right], \left[\dfrac{1}{3},\dfrac{1}{2}\right], \ldots \left[\dfrac{1}{k+1},\dfrac{1}{k}\right]$, hence $\exists$ some c in each of these interval S where $f'(c) = 0 \Rightarrow$ infinite points.

ILLUSTRATION 104: In which of the following functions Rolle's theorem is applicable?

(a) $f(x)=\begin{cases} x, & 0 \le x < 1 \\ 0, & x = 1 \end{cases}$ on [0, 1]

(b) $f(x)=\begin{cases} \dfrac{\sin x}{x}, & -\pi \le x < 0 \\ 0, & x=0 \end{cases}$ on $[-\pi, 0]$

(c) $f(x)=\dfrac{x^2-x-6}{x-1}$ on $[-2,3]$

(d) $f(x)=\begin{cases}\dfrac{x^3-2x^2-5x+6}{x-1} & \text{if } x\neq 1, \text{ on } [-2,3]\\ -6 & \text{if } x=1\end{cases}$

SOLUTION: (a) discontinuous at $x=1 \Rightarrow$ not applicable

(b) $f(x)$ is not continuous at $x = 0$ hence is not applicable.

(c) discontinuity at $x = 1 \Rightarrow$ not applicable

(d) Notice that $x^3 - 2x^2 - 5x + 6 = (x-1)(x^2 - x - 6)$. Hence, $f(x) = x^2 - x - 6$ if $x \neq 1$ and $f(1) = -6$

$\Rightarrow f$ is continuous at $x = 1$. So $f(x) = x^2 - x - 6$ throughout the interval $[-2,3]$.

Also, note that $f(-2) = f(3) = 0$. Hence, Rolle's theorem is applicable, $f'(x) = 2x - 1$.

$\therefore\ f'(x) = 0 \qquad \Rightarrow x = 1/2$ which lies between -2 and 3.

ILLUSTRATION 105: The function $f(x) = x(x + 3)\,e^{-(1/2)x}$ satisfies the conditions of Rolle's theorem in $[-3, 0]$. The value of c is

(a) 0 (b) –1

(c) –2 (d) –3

SOLUTION: (c) Given $f(x) = (x^2 + 3x)e^{-(1/2)x}$

$\therefore\ f'(x) = (x^2 + 3x)e^{-(1/2)x}\left(-\dfrac{1}{2}\right)+(2x+3)e^{-(1/2)x} = -\dfrac{1}{2}e^{-(1/2)x}\left\{x^2-x-6\right\}$

Since $f(x)$ satisfies the Rolle's theorem

$\therefore\ f'(x) = 0 \Rightarrow -\dfrac{1}{2}e^{-(c/2)}(c^2 - c - 6) = 0 \qquad \Rightarrow f'(c) = 3, -2$

But $c = 3 \notin (-3, 0) \qquad \Rightarrow -2 \in (-3, 0)$

$\therefore\ c = -2$

ILLUSTRATION 106: If $f(x) = \sin x/e^x$ in $[0, \pi]$, then $f(x)$

(a) Satisfies Rolle's theorem and $c=\dfrac{\pi}{4}$, so that $f'\left(\dfrac{\pi}{4}\right)=4$

(b) does not satisfy Rolle's theorem, but $f'\left(\dfrac{\pi}{4}\right)>0$

(c) satisfies Rolle's theorem and $f'\left(\dfrac{\pi}{4}\right)=0$

(d) Satisfies Lagrange's mean value theorem but $f'\left(\dfrac{\pi}{4}\right)\neq 0$

SOLUTION: (c) Given, $f(x)=\dfrac{\sin x}{e^x}$; Here $f(0) = 0, f(\pi) = 0$

Also $f(x)$ is continuous in $[0, \pi]$, Since every exponential function and trigonometric function is continuous in their domain and it is differentiable in the open internal.

Now, $f'(x) = \dfrac{e^x(\cos x-\sin x)}{(e^x)^2}$

$\therefore\ f'(x) = 0$ $\Rightarrow \cos x - \sin x = 0 \Rightarrow x = \dfrac{\pi}{4}$

$\therefore\ f'\left(\dfrac{\pi}{4}\right) = 0$

ILLUSTRATION 107: Verify Rolles theorem for $f(x) = (x - a)^n (x - b)^m$, where m, n are positive real numbers, for $x \in [a, b]$

SOLUTION: Being a polynomial function $f(x)$ is continuous as well as differentiable. Also $f(a) = f(b) = 0$

$\Rightarrow f'(x)=0$ for some $x \in (a, b)$

$\Rightarrow$ 'n' $(x - a)^{n-1} (x - b)^m + m (x - a)^n (x - b)^{m-1} = 0$

$\Rightarrow (x - a)^{n-1} (x - b)^{m-1} [(m + n) x - (nb + ma))] = 0$

$\Rightarrow x = \dfrac{nb+ma}{m+n}$, which lies in the interval (a, b) as m, n are +ve real numbers.

ALGEBRAIC INTERPRETATION OF ROLLE'S THEOREM

Let $f(x)$ be a polynomial having roots 'a' and 'b' where $a < b$, so that we have $f(a) = f(b) = 0$. Also a polynomial function is continuous and differtiable everywhere. Thus $f(x)$ satisfies the conditions of Rolle's Theorem. Consequently, there exists atleast one number $\alpha \in (a, b)$ such that $f'(\alpha) = 0$. In other words $x = \gamma$ is a root of $f'(x) = 0$.

Thus, Rolle's theorem can be interpreted algebraically as between any two roots of a polynomial $f(x)$, there is a always a root of its derivative $f'(x)$.

ILLUSTRATION 108: If $a, b, c \in \mathbb{R}$ such that $2a + 3b + 6c = 0$, show that the quadratic equation $ax^2 + bx + c = 0$ has atleast one real root between 0 and 1.

SOLUTION: Consider the polynomial $f(x) = \dfrac{a}{3}x^3 + \dfrac{b}{2}x^2 + cx$

We have $f(0) = 0$ and $f(1) = \dfrac{a}{3} + \dfrac{b}{2} + c = \dfrac{2a+3b+6c}{6} = 0$ $[\because 2a + 3b + 6c = 0]$

So 0 and 1 are two roots of $f(x) = 0$. Therefore $f'(x) = 0$ i.e., $ax^2 + bx + c = 0$ has atleast one real root between 0 and 1.

APPLICATION OF ROLLE'S THEOREM

If $f(x)$ is a polynomial function, then it is continuous and differentiable in its domain; thereby the following deductions can be made.

1. If all the roots of $f(x) = 0$ are real, then all the roots of $f'(x) = 0$ are also real, and the roots of $f'(x) = 0$ separate the roots of $f(x) = 0$.

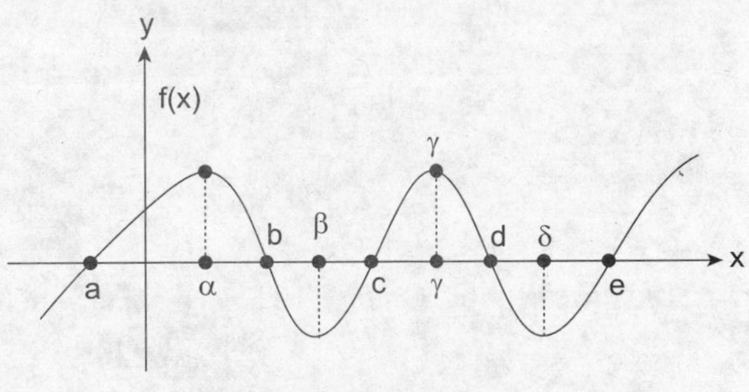

FIGURE 5.165

Here, a, b, c, d, e are the 5 roots of $f(x) = 0$ and $\alpha, \beta, \gamma, \delta$, are the 4 roots of $f'(x) = 0$

2. If $f(x)$ is of degree 'n'; then $f'(x)$ is of degree '$n-1$' and a root of $f'(x) = 0$ exists in each of the $n-1$ intervals between the 'n' roots of $f(x) = 0$ and in such a case, the root of $f''(x) = 0, f'''(x) = 0, \ldots$ are also real and the roots of each of these equations separate those of the preceding equation.
3. Not more than one root of $f(x) = 0$ can lie between two consecutive roots of $f'(x) = 0$.
4. If $f'(x) = 0$ has 'n' real roots, then $f(x) = 0$ can't have more than $(n+1)$ real roots.

   Now, if $f(x) = 0$ has no multiple root, then none of the roots of $f'(x) = 0$ is a root of $f(x) = 0$.

   Here a, b, c are the 3 real roots of $f(x) = 0$ and $\alpha, \beta, \gamma, \delta$ are the 4 roots of $f'(x) = 0$. $f(\alpha) > 0$ and $f(\beta) < 0$

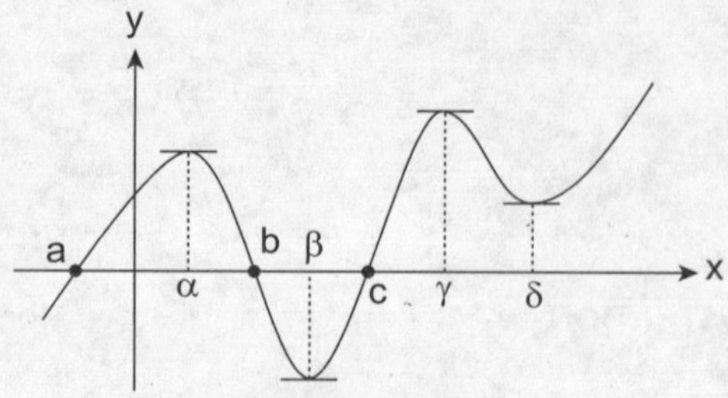

FIGURE 5.166

$\Rightarrow$ there must exists a root of $f(x) = 0$ lying between α and β (and the roots is $x = b$)

Similarly $x = c$ is a root of $f(x) = 0$ lying between two roots of $f'(x) = 0$ i.e., $x = \beta$ and $x = \gamma$

Also, there is no real roots $f(x) = 0$ lying between γ and δ because $f(\gamma).f(\delta) > 0$

NOTE:

Here ;f(x) = 0 will have 5 roots because f'(x) = 0 has 4 roots. However, only 3 of the roots of f(x) = 0 are real.

5. If $f^{(n)}(x)$ is the nth derivative of $f(x)$ and the equation $f^{(n)}(x) = 0$ has some imaginary roots, then $f(x) = 0$ has atleast as many imaginary roots.
6. If all the real roots $\alpha, \beta, \gamma, \delta \ldots$ of $f'(x) = 0$ are known, we can find the number of real roots of $f(x) = 0$ by considering the signs of $f(\alpha), f(\beta)\ldots$.

   A single root of $f(x) = 0$, or no root, lies between α and β according as $f(\alpha)$ and $f(\beta)$ have opposite signs, or the same sign.

ILLUSTRATION 109: If $f(x)$ is a quadratic polynomial satisfies the conditions of Rolle's theorem in [3,5], then $\int_3^5 f(x)\,dx$ equals

(a) 2 (b) –1

(c) 0 (d) –4/3

SOLUTION: (d) Given $f(x)$ satisfy Rolle's theorem in [3, 5]

$\therefore$ $f(x)$ is continuous in [3, 5] and $f(x)$ is differentiable in (3, 5)

and $f(a) = f(b)$ i.e., $f(3) = f(5) = k$ (say)

Let $f(x) = (x-3)(x-5) + k$

$\therefore$ $f(x) = x^2 - 8x + 15$

$$\therefore \int_3^5 (x^2 - 8x + 15 + k)dx = \left[\frac{x^3}{3} - \frac{8x^2}{2} + 15x + kx\right]_3^5$$

$$= \left(\frac{50}{3} - 18\right) = -\frac{4}{3} + 2k, \text{Also } f(4) = -1 + k = -1 \Rightarrow k = 0 \Rightarrow \int_3^5 f(x)dx = -\frac{4}{3}$$

ILLUSTRATION 110: Let $P(x)$ be a polynomial with real coefficients. Let $a, b \in \mathbb{R}$, $a < b$ be two consecutive roots of $P(x) = 0$. Show that there exists'c'such that $a \le c \le b$ and $P'(c) + 100\,P(c) = 0$.

SOLUTION: Consider $f(x) = e^{100x} \cdot P(x)$.

Now $f(a) = f(b) = 0$ $\{$as $P(a) = P(b) = 0\}$

Also as $P(x)$ is polynomial

$\Rightarrow$ $f(x)$ is continuous and differentiable in $[a, b]$

$\Rightarrow$ Rolle's theorem can be applied

$\Rightarrow$ $\exists\, c \in (a, b)$ such that $f'(c) = 0$

Now $f'(x) = e^{100x}(P'(x) + 100 \cdot P(x))$

$\Rightarrow$ $e^{100c}(P'(c) + 100 \cdot P(c)) = 0$

$\Rightarrow$ $P'(c) + 100 \cdot P(c) = 0$ (as $[e^{100c} \neq 0]$), hence proved.

ILLUSTRATION 111: If f and F are continuous in $[a, b]$ and derivable in (a, b) with $F'(x) \neq 0$. Prove that $\exists\, c \in (a, b)$ such that $\dfrac{f'(c)}{F'(c)} = \dfrac{f(b)-f(a)}{F(b)-F(a)}$

SOLUTION: Let $K_1 = f(b) - f(a)$ and $K_2 = F(b) - F(a)$

$\therefore$ To prove : $\dfrac{f'(c)}{F'(c)} = \dfrac{K_1}{K_2}$

Consider a function $\phi(x) = K_1 F(x) - K_2 f(x)$ ....(1)

$\therefore$ $f(x)$ and $F(x)$ are continuous in $[a, b]$ and derivable in (a, b) hence $\phi(x)$ will also be continuous and differentiable

also $\phi(a) = K_1F(a) - K_2 f(a)$ and $\phi(b) = K_1F(b) - K_2f(b)$

now $\phi(a) - \phi(b) = K_1(F(a) - F(b)) - K_2(f(a) - f(b))$

$= [f(b) - f(a)][F(a) - F(b)] - [F(b) - F(a)][f(a) - f(b)]$

$= [f(b) - f(a)]\{F(a) - F(b) + F(b) - F(a)] = 0$

$\Rightarrow$ $\phi(a) = \phi(b)$

Hence Rolles theorem is applicable for $\phi(x)$

$\therefore$ $\exists$ some $c \in (a, b)$, such that, $\phi'(c) = 0$

$= \varphi'(x)]_{x=c} = K_1 F'(x) - K_2 f'(x) = 0]_{x=c}$

or $K_1 F'(c) = K_2 f'(c)$

$\therefore$ $\dfrac{f'(c)}{F'(c)} = \dfrac{K_1}{K_2} = \dfrac{f(b)-f(a)}{F(b)-F(a)}$

ILLUSTRATION 112: Let $f(x)$ be a differentiable function on $[-1, 1]$. If $f(1) = 0$ and $f(x) > 0$ for all x in $(-1, 1)$, prove that the equation $r.\ f(-x) f'(x) = s f'(-x) f(x)$ has solution in $(-1, 1)$ (r and $s \in \mathbb{R}$)

SOLUTION: Let $h(x) = [f(x)]^s.[f(-x)]^r$

$\because$ $f(x)$ is continuous in $[-1, 1]$, so $h(x)$ will be continuous in $[-1, 1]$ and

$\because$ $h'(x) = -1\,[f(x)]^s.r.[f(-x)]^{r-1}.f'(-x) + [f(-x)]^r.s.[f(x)]^{s-1}.f'(x)$ which exists in the open interval $(-1, 1)$.

So $h(x)$ is differentiable function

Now $h(-1) = [f(-1)]^s.f(1)^r = [f(-1)]^s.0 = 0$ $(\because f(1) = 0)$

and $h(1) = f(1)^s.(f(-1))^r = 0.[f(-1)]^r = 0$

$\therefore$ $h(-1) = h(1) = 0$

Thus $h(x)$ satisfies all the three conditions, hence Rolle's theorem is applicable. As such there is atleast one number c in $(-1, 1)$ for which $h'(c) = 0$

Now $h'(c) = 0$

$\Rightarrow -[f(c)]^s.r.[f(-c)]^{r-1}f'(-c)+[f(-c)]^r.s.[f(c)]^{s-1}.f'(c)=0$

$\Rightarrow [f(c)]^{s-1}[f(-c)]^{r-1}[s.f'(c)f(-c)-rf'(-c).f(c)]=0$

$\Rightarrow [s.f'(c)f(-c)-rf'(-c).f(c)]=0 \qquad \because c \in (-1, 1)$ and $f(x) > 0\ \forall\ x \in (-1, 1)$

So $r.f'(x)f(-x)=sf'(-x).f(x)$ has one root in $(-1, 1)$

ILLUSTRATION 113: Find the condition for the polynomial equation $f(x) = 0$ to have a repeated real roots by using Rolle's theorem. Hence or otherwise prove that $\sum_{r=0}^{n}\frac{x^r}{r!}=0$ can't have a repeated root.

SOLUTION: Since $f(x) = 0$ has at least two real roots let be α and β $(\alpha < \beta)$

$\therefore\ f(\alpha) = 0$ and $f(\beta) = 0 \qquad \Rightarrow f(\alpha) = f(\beta) = 0$

and $f(x)$ being a polynomial which is continuous and differentiable everywhere.

By Rolle's theorem $f'(\gamma) = 0$ such that $\gamma \in (\alpha, \beta)$

If $f(x) = 0$ has two real repeated roots, then $f(\alpha) = f(\beta) = f(\gamma) = 0$ and $\alpha = \beta = \gamma$.

i.e., $f(\alpha) = 0$ and $f'(\alpha) = 0$

Now let $g(x) = \sum_{r=0}^{n}\frac{x^r}{r!}=0$

Suppose, if possible $g(x) = 0$ has repeated root α, then $g(\alpha) = 0$ and $g'(\alpha) = 0$

$$\Rightarrow 1+\frac{\alpha}{1!}+\frac{\alpha^2}{2!}+\frac{\alpha^3}{3!}+.....+\frac{\alpha^{n-1}}{(n-1)!}+\frac{\alpha^n}{n!}=0 \qquad ...(i)$$

$$\Rightarrow 0+\frac{1}{1!}+\frac{2\alpha}{2!}+\frac{3\alpha^2}{3!}+.....+\frac{n\alpha^{n-1}}{n!}=0$$

$$\Rightarrow 1+\frac{\alpha}{1!}+\frac{\alpha^2}{2!}+.....+\frac{\alpha^{n-1}}{(n-1)!}=0 \qquad ...(ii)$$

Subtracting (ii) from (i), we get $\frac{\alpha^n}{n!}=0$

$\therefore\ \alpha = 0$

$\therefore$ The repeated root must be zero.

But $\alpha = 0$ is not a root of (i) $\qquad (\because 1 \neq 0)$

Hence equation (i) can not have a repeated root.

ILLUSTRATION 114: If a, b, c be non-zero real numbers such that

$\int_0^1(1+\cos^8 x)(ax^2+bx+c)dx = \int_0^2(1+\cos^8 x)(ax^2+bx+c)dx=0$ then equation $ax^2 + bx + c = 0$ will have one root between 0 and 1 and other root between 1 and 2.

SOLUTION: Let $f(x)=\int_0^x(1+\cos^8 x)(ax^2+bx+c)dx \qquad ......(i)$

$\Rightarrow f'(x)=(1+\cos^8 x)(ax^2+bx+c) \qquad ....(ii)$

From given conditions, $f(1) = f(2) = 0$, Also $f(0) = 0 \Rightarrow f(0) = f(1) = f(2) = 0$

$\therefore$ By Rolle's theorem, for $f(x)$ in [0, 1]

$f'(\alpha) = 0$ for at least one α such that $0 < \alpha < 1$ and by Rolle's theorem for $f(x)$ in [1, 2]

$f'(\beta) = 0$ for at least one β such that $1 < \beta < 2$

Now from (ii) $f'(\alpha) = 0$

$\Rightarrow \quad (1+\cos^8\alpha)(a\alpha^2+b\alpha+c) = 0$

$\Rightarrow \quad a\alpha^2 + b\alpha + c = 0 \qquad \because \quad 1+\cos^8\alpha \neq 0$

Similarly, β is a root of the equation $ax^2 + bx + c = 0$

$\Rightarrow$ Equation $ax^2 + bx + c = 0$ has one root α between 0 and 1,

and other root β between 1 and 2.

ILLUSTRATION 115: Let $f(x) = (x - a)(x - b)(x - c)$, $a < b < c$. Show that $f'(x) = 0$ has two roots one belonging to (a, b) and other belonging to (b, c)

SOLUTION: Here, $f(x)$ being a polynomial is continuous and differentiable for all real values of x.

We also have $f(a) = f(b) = f(c)$

If we apply Rolle's theorem to $f(x)$ in $[a, b]$ and $[b, c]$ we would observe that $f'(x) = 0$ would have atleast one root in (a, b) and atleast one root in (b, c)

But $f'(x) = 0$ is a polynomial of degree two, hence $f'(x) = 0$ can't have more than two roots.

It implies that exactly one root of $f'(x) = 0$ would lie in (a, b) and exactly one root of $f'(x) = 0$ would be in (b, c).

TEXTUAL EXERCISE–1: (SUBJECTIVE)

1. Show that $f(x) = 4x^3 - 6x^2 + 4x - 1$ has at least one root in (0, 1).

2. If equation $ax^3 + bx^2 + cx + d = 0$ has one real root then prove that the equation $\frac{ax^4}{4}+\frac{bx^3}{3}+\frac{cx^2}{2}+dx+e=0$ can't have more than 2 distinct real root.

3. If equation $ax^4 + bx^3 + cx^2 + dx + k = 0$ has three distinct real roots, then prove that the equation $4ax^3 + 3bx^2 + 2cx + d = 0$ will have atleast 2 distinct real roots.

4. Let $f(x)$, $g(x)$ be differentiable in $[a, b]$ and $f(a) = g(a)$ and $f(b) = g(b)$. Show that there exists at least one c in (a, b) such that $f'(c) = g'(c)$; will the statement be true if $f(a) = f(b)$ and $g(a) = g(b)$.

5. If $f(x)$ and $g(x)$ are differentiable functions for $0 \le x \le 1$ such that $f(0) = 5$, $g(0) = 1$, $f(1) = 10$, $g(1) = 3$, then show that there exists atleast one c satisfying $0 < c < 1$ where $2f'(c) = 5g'(c)$.

6. Suppose that the second derivative of f exists everywhere and that $f(x_1) = f(x_2) = f(x_3) = 0$ where $x_1 < x_2 < x_3$. Show that $f''(c) = 0$ for some no. c with $x_1 < c < x_3$.

7. If $f(x)$ is differentiable functions $\forall\, x \in [a, b]$ such that a and b are both positive, then show that there exists atleast one $c \in (a, b)$ where $2\sqrt{c}\, f'(c) = \frac{f(b) - f(a)}{\sqrt{b}-\sqrt{a}}$.

8. Show that between any two roots of the equation $e^x \cos x = 1$ there exists at least one root of $e^x \sin x - 1 = 0$.

9. Are the conditions of Rolle's theorem satisfied for the following functions:
   (a) $f(x) = |9 - x^2|$ in $[-3, 3]$
   (b) $f(x) = \ln\{(x^2 + ab)/[(a + b)x]\}$ in $[a, b]$; $ab > 0$
   (c) $f(x) = x^3 - 3x^2 + 2x$ in [0, 2]
   (d) $f(x) = e^x(\sin x - \cos x)$ in $[\pi/4, 5\pi/4]$
   (e) $f(x) = (x - a)^m (x - b)^n$ in interval $[a, b]$; where $m, n \in \mathbb{N}$.

10. If $f(x) = x^4 - 2x^3 + 2x^2 - x$, then prove by Rolle's theorem that the equation $4x^3 - 6x^2 + 4x - 1 = 0$ has

atleast one real root in (0, 1) and hence/otherwise prove that $f(x)$ has exactly one real root $\in$ (0, 2).

11. If $c_0+(c_1/2)+(c_2/3)+\ .....\ +(c_n/n+1)=0$, where $c_0, c_1, c_2, ...c_{n+1} \in R$, then prove that the equation $c_0+c_1x+c_2x^2+.........+c_nx^n=0$, has atleast one real root in (0, 1).

12. Show that the equation $(x-a)^3+(x-b)^3+(x-c)^3+(x-d)^3=0$, where $a, b, c, d \in \mathbb{R}$ are not all equal, has only one real root.

13. Prove that the equation $3x^5+15x-8=0$ has only one real root.

14. Discuss the nature of roots of the equation $x^3-6x^2+9x-2=0$ and locate them.

15. Let f'' exists for all $x \in [ab]$. Let $\phi(x)=f(x)+(b-x)f'(x)+A(b-x)^2$ where A is constant so chosen that $\phi(b)=\phi(a)$. Apply Rolle's theorem to calculate that $f(b)=f(a)+(b-a)f'(a)+[f''(c)/2](b-a)^2$ for some $c \in (ab)$.

Answer Keys

4. yes **9.** Condition of Rolle's theorem are satisfied for (a), (b), (c), (d) and (e)

14. All the roots are real, one belongs to (0, 1)
Second root = 2, third lies between 3 and 4.

TEXTUAL EXERCISE–1: (OBJECTIVE)

1. Rolle's theorem is not applicable to the function $f(x)=|x|$ for $-2 \le x \le 2$ because

(a) f is continuous for $-2 \le x \le 1$
(b) f is not derivable for $x=0$
(c) $f(-2)=f(2)$
(d) f is not a constant function

2. If $f(x)=x^a\log x$ and $f(0)=0$, then the value of a for which Rolle's theorem can be applied in [0, 1] is

(a) –2 (b) –1
(c) 0 (d) 1/2

3. If Rolle's theorem holds for the function $f(x)=x^3+bx^2+ax+5$ on [1, 3] with $c=[2+1/\sqrt{3}]$, then (a, b) is

(a) (3, –5) (b) (6, –11)
(c) (11, –6) (d) (11, 6)

4. To which of the following Rolle's theorem can be applied?

(a) $f(x)=\tan x$ in $[0, \pi]$
(b) $f(x)=\cos(1/x)$ in [–1, 1]
(c) $f(x)=x^2$ in [2, 3]
(d) $f(x)=x(x+3)e^{-x/2}$ in [–3, 0]

5. The c of Rolle's theorem for the function $f(x)=\sin x$ in $[0, \pi]$ is

(a) 0 (b) $\frac{1}{6}\pi$
(c) $\frac{1}{3}\pi$ (d) $\frac{1}{2}\pi$

6. Polynomial $x^3+3x-10$ has

(a) at least one real root
(b) exactly one real root
(c) two real roots
(d) all the three roots are equal

7. The function in which Rolle's theorem is verified is

(a) $f(x)=\log\left(\frac{x^2+ab}{(a+b)x}\right)$ in $[a, b]$ where $(0<a<b)$
(b) $f(x)=(x-1)(2x-3)$ in (1, 3)
(c) $f(x)=2+(x-1)^{2/3}$ in [0, 2]
(d) $f(x)=\cos(1/x)$ in [–1, 1]

8. If $a+b+c=0$, then the quadratic equation $3ax^2+2bx+c=0$ has

(a) imaginary roots
(b) at least one real root in (0,1)
(c) one root in [2, 3] and other in [3, 6]
(d) none of these

9. Of the equation $x^4-x^3-x+1=0$, 1 is a

(a) double root (b) simple root
(c) triple root (d) None of these

10. The equation $3x^2+4ax+b=0$ has at least one root in (0,1) if :

(a) $4a+b+3=0$ (b) $2a+b+1=0$
(c) $b=0, a=-4/3$ (d) None of these

11. If $f(x) = (x-1)(x-2)(x-3)(x-4)$, then out of the three roots of $f'(x) = 0$
(a) three are positive
(b) three are negative
(c) two are imaginary
(d) three are real, some positive, some negative

12. If the function $f(x) = x^3 - 6x^2 + ax + b$ defined on [1,3] satisfies the Rolle's theorem for $c = \frac{(2\sqrt{3}+1)}{\sqrt{3}}$ then:
(a) $a = 11, b = 6$ (b) $a = -11, b = 6$
(c) $a = 11, b \in \mathbb{R}$ (d) None of these

13. Using Rolle's theorem equation $a_0x^n + a_1x^{n-1} + \ldots + a_n = 0$ has at least one root between 0 and 1, if :
(a) $\frac{a_0}{n} - \frac{a_1}{n-1} + \ldots + a_{n-1} = 0$
(b) $\frac{a_0}{n-1} + \frac{a_1}{n-2} + \ldots + a_{n-2} = 0$
(c) $na_0 + (n-1)a_1 + \ldots + a_{n-1} = 0$
(d) $\frac{a_0}{n+1} + \frac{a_1}{n} + \ldots + a_n = 0$

14. The number of values of a for which the equation $x^3 - 3x + a = 0$ has two distinct real roots lying in the interval (0, 1) are:
(a) 2 (b) 3
(c) 0 (d) infinite

15. Number of roots of the equation $x^n - a = 0$, in (0, 1) is
(a) 1 (b) at most 1
(c) 0 (d) nothing can be said

16. In (0, 1) the equation $x^4 + 2x^2 - 2 = 0$ has:
(a) one root (b) two roots
(c) no root (d) nothing can be said

17. In which of the following functions, Rolle's theorem is applicable?
(a) $f(x) = |x|$ in $-2 \le x \le 2$
(b) $f(x) = \tan x$ in $0 \le x \le \pi$
(c) $f(x) = 1 + (x-2)^{2/3}$ in $1 \le x \le 3$
(d) $f(x) = x(x-2)^2$ in $0 \le x \le 2$

18. The Rolle's theorem is applicable in the interval $-1 \le x \le 1$ for the function
(a) $f(x) = x$ (b) $f(x) = x^2$
(c) $f(x) = 2x^3 + 3$ (d) $f(x) = |x|$

19. If the function $f(x) = ax^3 + bx^2 + 11x - 6$ satisfies the condition of Rolle's theorem in [1, 3] and $f'\left(2 + \frac{1}{\sqrt{3}}\right) = 0$, then the values of a, b are respectively
(a) $-1, 6$ (b) $-2, 1$
(c) $1, -6$ (d) $-1, \frac{1}{2}$

Answer Keys

1. (b)	**2.** (d)	**3.** (c)	**4.** (d)	**5.** (d)	**6.** (a,b)	**7.** (a)	**8.** (b)	**9.** (a)	**10.** (b)
11. (a)	**12.** (c)	**13.** (d)	**14.** (c)	**15.** (b)	**16.** (a)	**17.** (d)	**18.** (b)	**19.** (c)	

■ LAGRANGE'S MEAN VALUE THEOREM

If a function $f(x)$ defined on $[a, b]$ is such that it is
- ❑ Continuous over the interval $[a, b]$
- ❑ Differentiable in the interval (a, b), then $\exists$ at least one $c \in (a, b)$ where $f'(c) = \frac{f(b) - f(a)}{b - a}$

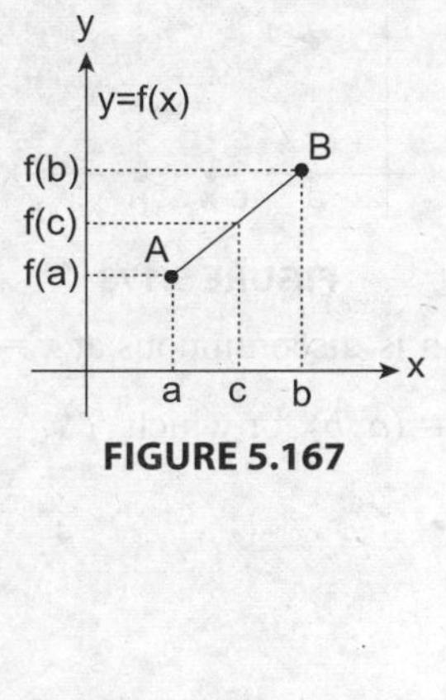

FIGURE 5.167

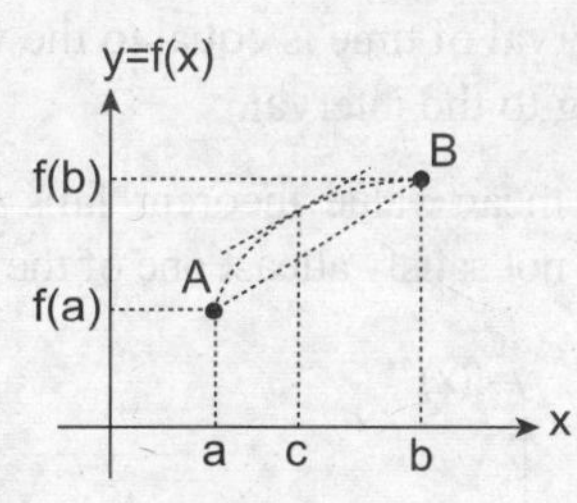

FIGURE 5.168

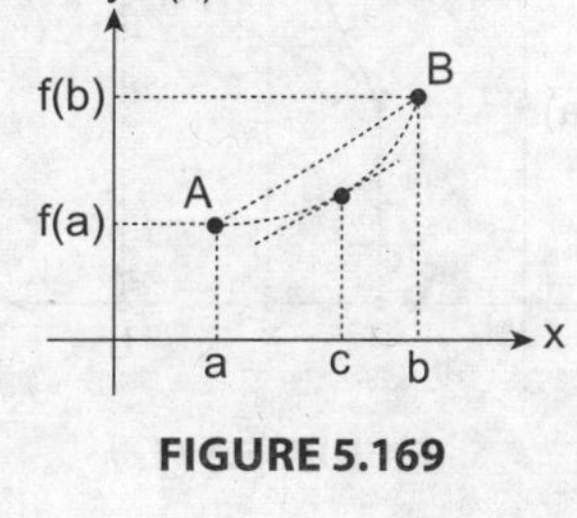

FIGURE 5.169

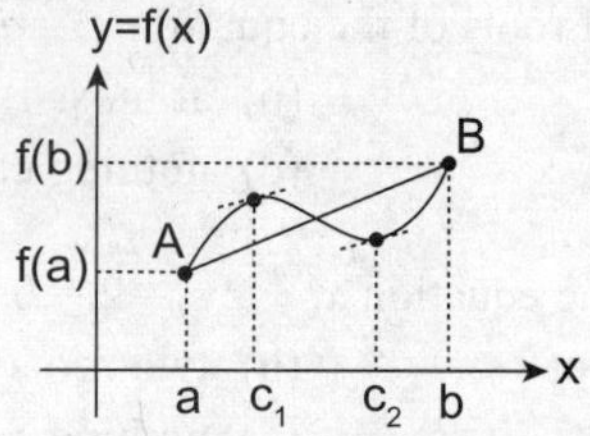

FIGURE 5.170

i.e., where slope of tangent becomes equal to slope of the chord AB.

Proof: Considering functions like $F(x) = f(x) + Ax$ ...(i)

or $F(x) = f(x) - f(a) - (x - a)A$

or $F(x) = f(x) + (x - a)A$

where A is an unknown constant, such that they satisfy the condition of Rolle's theorem

Clearly $F(x)$ is continuous on $[a, b]$ and differentiable on (a, b). [$F(x)$ taken as in equation (i)]

For $F(a) = F(b)$, we need $f(b) - f(a) + (b - a)A = 0$

$\Rightarrow$ $A = \dfrac{-(f(b)-f(a))}{b-a}$

$\Rightarrow$ $F(x) = f(x) - \dfrac{(f(b)-f(a))x}{b-a}$ satisfies all conditions of Rolle's theorem

$\Rightarrow$ atleast one $c \in (a, b)$ such that $F'(c) = 0$

$\Rightarrow$ $F'(c) = f'(c) - \dfrac{f(b)-f(a)}{b-a} = 0$

$\Rightarrow$ $f'(c) = \dfrac{f(b)-f(a)}{b-a}$

REMARKS:

Rolle's theorem is a special case of LMVT since f(a) = f(b) $\Rightarrow f'(c) = \dfrac{f(b)-f(a)}{b-a}$ $\Rightarrow f'(c) = \dfrac{0}{b-a} = 0$

■ PHYSICAL SIGNIFICANCE

$\because$ $\dfrac{f(b)-f(a)}{b-a}$ is average rate of change of function $f(x)$ on the interval $[a, b]$ and $f'(c)$ is the instantaneous rate of change of the function at $x = c$.

Thus, the average rate of change of a function over an interval is also the actual rate of change of the function at some point of the interval".

In particular, for instance, the average velocity of a particle over an interval of time is equal to the velocity at some instant belonging to the interval.

❑ Lagrange's mean value theorem fails for the function which does not satisfy atleast one of the two conditions.

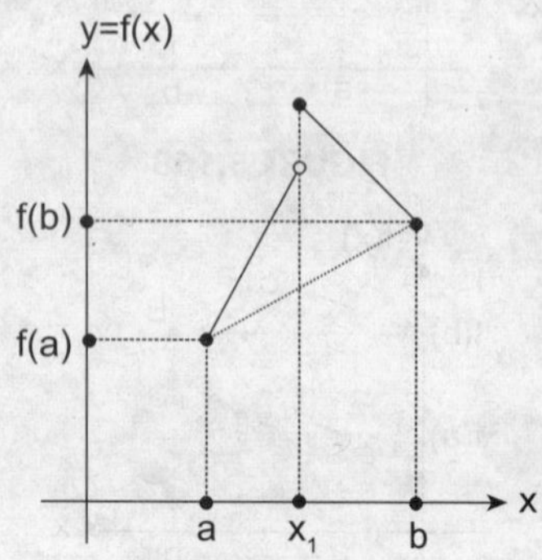

FIGURE 5.171

The function is discontinuous at $x = x_1$

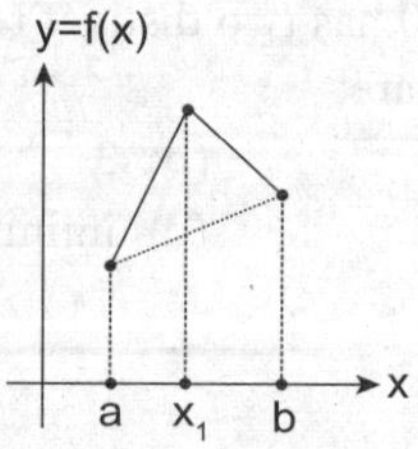

FIGURE 5.172

The function is non-differentiable at $x = x_1$

❑ The converse of L.M.V.T. may not be true i.e., $f(x)$ may be equal to $\dfrac{f(b)-f(a)}{b-a}$ at a point c in (a, b) without satisfying both the conditions of L.M.V.T.

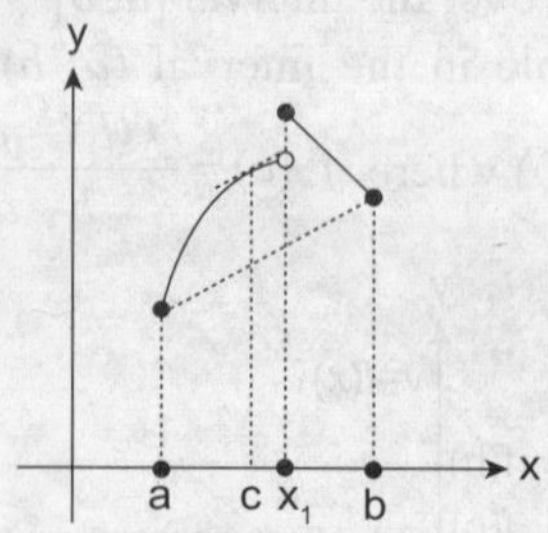

FIGURE 5.173

The function is discontinuous at $x = x_1$; but still there exists at 'c' $\in (a, b)$ for which $f'(c) = \dfrac{f(b)-f(a)}{b-a}$

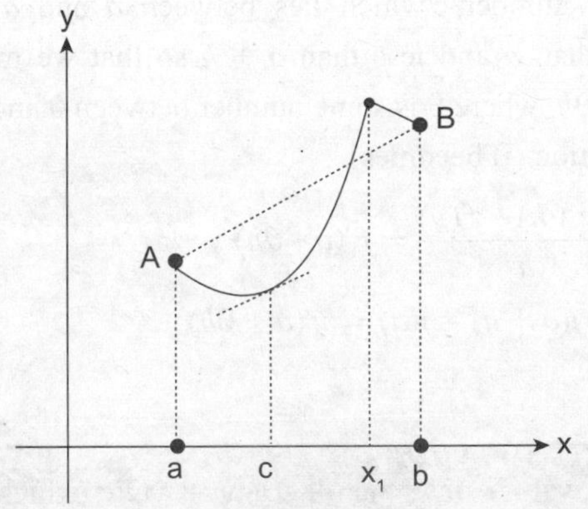

FIGURE 5.174

The function is non-differentiable at $x = x_1$; but still there exists $c' \in (a, b)$ for which $f'(c) = \dfrac{f(b)-f(a)}{b-a}$

ILLUSTRATION 116: Find a point on $y = (x-2)^2$ where the tangent is parallel to the chord joining (2, 0) and (4, 4)

SOLUTION: The given function $f(x) = (x-2)^2$ is continuous on [2, 4] and differentiable on (2, 4). Therefore, it satisfies the Lagrange's mean value theorem, there exists $c \in (a, b)$ and such that

$$f'(c) = \frac{f(b)-f(a)}{b-a}$$

$$\Rightarrow f'(c) = \frac{4-0}{4-2} = 2$$

Now, $f'(x) = 2(x-2)$

$\Rightarrow f'(c) = 2(c-2)$

Now, $f'(c) = 2$ $\qquad \Rightarrow 2(c-2) = 2$

$\Rightarrow c = 3$

$\therefore$ Point on the curve is (c, f(c)) is (3, 1).

ILLUSTRATION 117: Find a point on the curve $f(x) = \sqrt{x-2}$ in [2, 3] when the tangent is parallel to the chord joining the end points.

SOLUTION: The given function $f(x) = \sqrt{x-2}$ is continuous on [2, 3] and is differentiable on (2, 3).

Therefore, it satisfies the Lagrange's mean value theorem, there exist $c \in (a, b)$ such that

$$f'(c) = \frac{f(b)-f(a)}{b-a}$$

$$\Rightarrow f'(c) = \frac{f(3)-f(2)}{3-2} = \frac{\sqrt{3-2}-\sqrt{2-2}}{3-2} = 1$$

Now, $f'(x) = \dfrac{1}{2} \times \dfrac{1}{\sqrt{x-2}}$ $\qquad \Rightarrow f'(c) = \dfrac{1}{2\sqrt{x-2}}$

Now $f'(c) = 1$ $\qquad \Rightarrow \dfrac{1}{2\sqrt{c-2}} = 1$

$\Rightarrow \sqrt{c-2} = \dfrac{1}{2}$ $\qquad \Rightarrow c-2 = \dfrac{1}{4}$

$\Rightarrow c = \dfrac{9}{4}$

$\therefore$ point on the curve is (c, f(c)). i.e., $\left(\dfrac{9}{4}, \dfrac{1}{2}\right)$

ALTERNATIVE FORM OF LMVT

If a function $f(x)$ is continuous in a closed interval $[a, a+h]$ and derivable in the open interval $(a, a+h)$, then there exists at least one number 'θ'$\in (0, 1)$ such that $f(a+h) = f(a) + h f'(a+\theta h)$.

Proof: Substitute $b - a = h$

So that h denotes the length of the interval $[a, b]$

The number,'c'which lies between a and $a+h$, is greater than a and less than $a+h$ so that we may write $c = a + \theta h$, where θ is some number between 0 and 1. Thus the equation (i) becomes

$$\frac{f(a+h)-f(a)}{h} = f'(a+\theta h)$$

$$\Rightarrow f(a+h) = f(a) + hf'(a+\theta h)$$

ILLUSTRATION 118: Suppose that $f(0) = -3$ and $f'(x) \le 5$ for all values of x, then the largest value which $f(2)$ can attain is

(a) 7 (b) –7

(c) 13 (d) 8

SOLUTION: (a) Using LMVT in [0, 2]

$$\frac{f(2)-f(0)}{2-0} = f'(c) \text{ where } c \in (0, 2)$$

$$\frac{f(2)+3}{2} \le 5 \qquad \Rightarrow f(2) \le 7$$

ILLUSTRATION 119: Given: $f(x) = 4 - \left(\frac{1}{2}-x\right)^{2/3}$; $g(x) = \begin{cases} \frac{\tan[x]}{x} & , x \ne 0 \\ 1 & , x = 0 \end{cases}$ $4 - \left(\frac{1}{2}-x\right)^{2/3}$

$h(x) = \{x\}$ $k(x) = 5^{\log_2(x+3)}$

then in [0, 1]. Lagranges mean value theorem is NOT applicable to

(a) f, g, h (b) h, k

(c) f, g (d) g, h, k

SOLUTION: (a) f is not differentiable at $x = \frac{1}{2}$ $\Rightarrow$ L.M.V.T is not applicable to f

g is not continuous in [0, 1] at $x = 0$ $\Rightarrow$ L.M.V.T is not applicable to g

h is not continuous in [0, 1] at $x = 1$ and 0 $\Rightarrow$ L.M.V.T is not applicable to h

$k(x) = (x+3)^{\ln_2 5} = (x+3)^p$ where $2 < p < 3$, is continuous and differentiable in [0, 1] and (0, 1) respectively and hence, LMVT is applicable to k.

ILLUSTRATION 120: Let $f(x) = x^3$, use mean value theorem to write $\frac{f(x+h)-f(x)}{h} = f'(x+\theta h)$, with $0 < \theta < 1$. If $x \ne 0$, then $\lim\limits_{h\to 0} \theta$ is equal to

(a) –1 (b) –0.5

(c) 0.5 (d) 1

SOLUTION: Given, $f(x) = x^3$

$\Rightarrow f(x+h) = (x+h)^3$

Now, $f'(x) = 3x^2$

$\therefore f'(x+\theta h) = 3(x+\theta h)^2$

Given, $\frac{f(x+h)-f(x)}{h}=f'(x+\theta h)$

$\Rightarrow \frac{(x+h)^3-x^3}{h}=3(x+\theta h)^2$

$\Rightarrow \frac{x^3+h^3+3xh(x+h)-x^3}{h}=3(x^2+\theta^2h^2+2x\theta h)$

$\Rightarrow h^2+3x^2+3xh=3x^2+3\theta^2h^2+6x\theta h$

$\Rightarrow h+3x=3\theta^2 h+6x\theta$

Taking limit on both sides, we get $\lim_{h\to 0}(h+3x)=\lim_{h\to 0}(3\theta^2h+6x\theta)$

$\Rightarrow 3x=6x\lim_{h\to 0}\theta$ $\Rightarrow \lim_{h\to 0}\theta=\frac{1}{2}=0.5$

ILLUSTRATION 121: If the mean value theorem is $F(b)-f(a)=(b-a)f'(c)$. Then , for the function $x^2-2x+3in$ $\left[1,\frac{3}{2}\right]$ the value of c is

(a) 6/5 (b) 5/4

(c) 4/3 (d) 4/6

SOLUTION: Let $f(x)=x^2-2x+3$

Since, $f'(c)=\frac{f\left(\frac{3}{2}\right)-f(1)}{\frac{3}{2}-1}$ [given]

$\Rightarrow 2c-2=\frac{\frac{9}{4}-\frac{6}{2}+3-(1-2+3)}{\frac{3}{2}-1}$ $\Rightarrow c=\frac{5}{4}\in\left[1,\frac{3}{2}\right]$

ILLUSTRATION 122: The value of c, in Lagrange's mean value theorem for the functions $f(x)=x(x-1)(x-2)$ in the interval [0, 1/2] is

(a) $\frac{1}{4}$ (b) $1-\frac{\sqrt{21}}{6}$

(c) $\frac{9}{8}$ (d) $1+\frac{\sqrt{21}}{6}$

SOLUTION: **(b)** Given, $f(x)=x^3-3x^2+2x$

$\Rightarrow f'(x)=3x^2-6x+2$

Now $f(a)=f(0)=0$ and $f(b)=f\left(\frac{1}{2}\right)=\frac{1}{2}\left(\frac{1}{2}-1\right)\left(\frac{1}{2}-2\right)=\frac{3}{8}$

By Lagrange's mean value theorem $\frac{f(b)-f(a)}{b-a}=f'(c)$ $\Rightarrow \frac{\frac{3}{8}-0}{\frac{1}{2}-0}=3c^2-6c+2$

$\Rightarrow 12c^2-24c+5=0$

$\Rightarrow c = \dfrac{24 \pm \sqrt{576-240}}{24} = 1 \pm \dfrac{\sqrt{21}}{6}$

But c lies between 0 and $\dfrac{1}{2}$ $\therefore$ We take, $c = 1 - \dfrac{\sqrt{21}}{6}$

ILLUSTRATION 123: Let $f: [-1, 2] \to R$ be differentiable such that $0 \le f'(t) \le 1$ for $t \in [-1, 0]$ and $-1 \le f'(t) \le 0$ for $t \in [0, 2]$. Then

(a) $-2 \le f(2) - f(-1) \le 1$
(b) $1 \le f(2) - f(-1) \le 2$
(c) $-3 \le f(2) - f(-1) \le 0$
(d) $-2 \le f(2) - f(-1) \le 0$

SOLUTION: (a) $0 \le f'(t) \le 1$ for $t \in [-1, 0]$ (given)

$\Rightarrow 0 \le \int_{-1}^{0} f'(t)\,dt \le 1;\ 0 \le f(0) - f(-1) \le 1$ ....(1)

Also $-1 \le f'(t) \le 0$ for $t \in [0, 2]$ (given)

$\Rightarrow -2 \le \int_{0}^{2} f'(t)\,dt \le 0$

$\Rightarrow -2 \le f(2) - f(0) \le 0$ ....(2)

$\therefore$ (1) + (2) gives

$-2 \le f(2) - f(-1) \le 1$

ILLUSTRATION 124: Consider $f(x) = |1 - x|;\ 1 \le x \le 2$ and $g(x) = f(x) + b \sin \dfrac{\pi}{2} x,\ 1 \le x \le 2$. Then which of the following is correct?

(a) Rolles theorem is applicable to both f, g and $b = \dfrac{3}{2}$

(b) LMVT is not applicable to f and Rolles theorem if applicable to g with $b = \dfrac{1}{2}$

(c) LMVT is applicable to f and Rolles theorem is applicable to g with $b = 1$

(d) Rolles theorem is not applicable to both f, g for any real b.

SOLUTION: $f(x) = x - 1,\ 1 \le x \le 2$

$g(x) = x - 1 + b \sin \dfrac{\pi}{2} x,\ 1 \le x \le 2$

$f(1) = 0;\ f(2) = 1$

$\Rightarrow$ Rolle's theorem is not applicable to 'f' but LMVT is applicable to f.

($\because$ $x - 1$ is continuous and differentiable in [1, 2] and (1, 2) respectively)

Now $g(1) = b$; $g(2) = 1$ and

Function $x - 1$, $\sin \dfrac{\pi}{2} x$ are both continuous in [1, 2] and (1, 2)

$\therefore$ For Rolle's theorem to be applicable to g, we must have $b = 1$

ILLUSTRATION 125: Suppose that f is differentiable for all x and that $f'(x) \le 2$ for all x. If $f(1) = 2$ and $f(4) = 8$ then $f(2)$ has the value equal to

(a) 3
(b) 4
(c) 6
(d) 8

SOLUTION: **(b)** Using LMVT for f in [1, 2]

$\exists\, c \in (1, 2)$ such that $\dfrac{f(2)-f(1)}{2-1} = f'(c) \le 2$ ($\because f'(x) \le 2\ \forall\ x$)

$\Rightarrow f(2) - f(1) \le 2 \quad \Rightarrow f(2) \le 4$ ....(1)

Again using LMVT in [2, 4]

$\exists\, d \in (2, 4)$ such that $\dfrac{f(4)-f(2)}{4-2} = f'(d) \le 2$

$\therefore\ f(4) - f(2) \le 4 \Rightarrow 8 - f(2) \le 4 \Rightarrow 4 \le f(2) \quad \Rightarrow f(2) \ge 4$ ....(2)

From (1) and (2), $f(2) = 4$

ILLUSTRATION 126: If the function $f: [0, 4] \to R$ is differentiable, then show that

(i) $f^2(4) - f^2(0) = 8 f'(a) f(b)$ for $a, b \in (0, 4)$

(ii) $\int_0^4 f(t)dt = 2[\alpha f(\alpha^2) + \beta f(\beta^2)],\ \forall\ 0 < \alpha, \beta < 2$

SOLUTION: **(i)** Since f is differentiable on [0, 4] so it is continuous also. Hence by LMVT,

$\exists$ some $a \in (0, 4)$ such that $f'(a) = \dfrac{f(4)-f(0)}{4-0}$ ....(1)

again, by intermediate value theorem for continuous functions,

$\exists\, b \in (0, 4)$ such that $f(b) = \dfrac{f(0)+f(4)}{2}$ ....(2)

from (1) and (2) $f'(a) \cdot f(b) = \dfrac{f^2(4) - f^2(0)}{8}$

(ii) $\int_0^4 f(t)dt = 2[\alpha f(\alpha^2) + \beta f(\beta^2)],\ \forall\ 0 < \alpha, \beta < 2$. (To prove)

Consider a function $g(x) = \int_0^{x^2} f(t)dt$; $x \in [0, 2)$

$\Rightarrow g'(x) = 2x f(x^2)$

apply LMVT in [0, 1], $\exists$ some $\alpha \in (0, 1)$, such that $g'(\alpha) = \dfrac{g(1)-g(0)}{1-0} = g(1)$ ....(1)

again applying LMVT in [1, 2), $\exists\, b$ such that $g'(\beta) = \dfrac{g(2)-g(1)}{2-1} = g(2) - g(1)$ ....(2)

Adding (1) and (2), $g'(\alpha) + g'(\beta) = g(2)$ i.e., $2[\alpha f(\alpha^2) + \beta f(\beta^2)] = \int_0^4 f(t)dt$

ILLUSTRATION 127: Use Mean value theorem to prove $e^x \ge 1 + x,\ \forall\ x \in \mathbb{R}$

SOLUTION: Consider the function $f(x) = e^x - 1$ in $[0, x]$ where $x > 0$

$\therefore\ f$ is continuous and differentiable hence using LMVT $\exists$ some $c \in (0, x)$

Such that $f'(c) = \dfrac{(e^x-1)-0}{x} = \dfrac{e^x-1}{x}$

but $f'(c) = e^c$; hence $\dfrac{e^x-1}{x} = e^c > 1$, for $x > 0$

$\therefore\ e^x - 1 > x \quad \Rightarrow e^x > x + 1$ for $x > 0$ ....(1)

again consider the function $f(x) = e^x - 1$ in $[x, 0]$, where $x < 0$

using LMVT $\exists$ some $c \in (x, 0)$ such that $f'(c) = \dfrac{0-(e^x-1)}{-x} = \dfrac{e^x-1}{x}$

but $f'(c) = e^c$, hence $\frac{e^x - 1}{x} = e^c < 1$ for $c < 0$

Hence $\frac{(e^x - 1)}{x} < 1$ for $x < 0$ $\Rightarrow (e^x - 1) > x$ $\Rightarrow$ (as x is –ve)

$\Rightarrow e^x - 1 - x > 0$ for $x < 0$ ....(2)

From (1) and (2), we get $e^x > x + 1$ for $x \neq 0$

$\therefore$ for $x = 0$ equality holds $\therefore$ $e^x \geq x + 1$ for $x \in R$]

ILLUSTRATION 128: Verify LMVT for $f(x) = -x^2 + 4x - 5$ and $x \in [-1, 1]$

SOLUTION: $f(1) = -2; f(-1) = -10$

$\Rightarrow f'(c) = \frac{f(1) - f(-1)}{1-(-1)}$ $\Rightarrow -2c + 4 = 4 \Rightarrow c = 0$

ILLUSTRATION 129: Using Lagrange's mean value theorem, prove that if $b > a > 0$, then $\frac{b-a}{1+b^2} < \tan^{-1} b - \tan^{-1} a < \frac{b-a}{1+a^2}$

SOLUTION: Let $f(x) = \tan^{-1} x$; $x \in [a, b]$, applying LMVT

$f'(c) = \frac{\tan^{-1} b - \tan^{-1} a}{b-a}$ for some c such that $a < c < b$ and $f'(x) = \frac{1}{1+x^2}$

Now $f'(x)$ is a monotonically decreasing function, hence if $a < c < b$ $\Rightarrow f'(b) < f'(c) < f'(a)$

$\Rightarrow \frac{1}{1+b^2} < \frac{\tan^{-1} b - \tan^{-1} a}{b-a} < \frac{1}{1+a^2}$ Hence proved.

TEXTUAL EXERCISE–2: (SUBJECTIVE)

1. Using LMVT prove that $|\cos a - \cos b| \leq |a - b|$
2. If $a <$ b, show that a real number 'c' can be found in (a, b) such that $3c^2 = a^2 + ab + b^2$.
3. Use LMVT to prove that $\tan x \geq x$ for $x \in \left[0, \frac{\pi}{2}\right)$.
4. Let a, b, c be 3 real number *s.t.* $a < b < c$, $f(x)$ is continuous in $[a, c]$ and differentiable in (a, c). Also $f'(x)$ is strictly increasing in (a, c). Prove that $(b - c) f(a) + (c - a) f(b) + (a - b) f(c) < 0$.
5. Using the function $\phi(x) = f(x) - f(a) - \frac{x-a}{b-a}[f(b) - f(a)]$ or $F(x) = f(x) + Ax$ or $F(x) = f(x) - f(a) + A(x - a)$. State and prove LMVT assuming $f(x)$ to be continuous and differentiable in $[a, b]$.
6. Verify the following functions for LMVT and find the lagrange's mean value c:

   (a) $\ln x$ in $[1, e]$

   (b) x^3 in $[a, b]$

   (c) $x + 1/x$ in $[1/2, 2]$
7. Using Lagrange's mean value theorem or otherwise, prove that

   (a) $|\sin x - \sin y| \leq |x - y| \; \forall x, y \in R$.

   (b) $\frac{\beta-\alpha}{1+\beta^2} < \tan^{-1}\beta - \tan^{-1}\alpha < \frac{\beta-\alpha}{1+\alpha^2}$ where $\beta > \alpha > 0$.

   (c) $(b - a) \sec^2 a < \tan b - \tan a < (b - a) \sec^2 b$ where $0 < a < b < \pi/2$
8. Let f, g, h be three continuous functions in the interval $[a, b]$ and differentiable in the interval (a, b). Show that there exists a number $c \in (a, b)$ such that $\begin{vmatrix} f'(c) & g'(c) & h'(c) \\ f(a) & g(a) & h(a) \\ f(b) & g(b) & h(b) \end{vmatrix} = 0$.

9. Are the conditions of LMVT satisfied for $f(x)=\left[x^4(x-1)\right]^{1/5}$ on $[-1/2, 1/2]$. If yes, then find the value of c appearing in the theorem.

10. If $f(x)$ is quadratic polynomial and a, b are any 2 numbers, show that $(a + b)/2$ is the only value of c which satisfies the LMVT in (a, b).

Answer Keys

6. **(a)** $(e-1)$ **(b)** $c=\begin{cases}\sqrt{\dfrac{a^2+ab+b^2}{3}}; a\geq 0\\ -\sqrt{\dfrac{a^2+ab+b^2}{3}}; b\leq 0\\ \pm\sqrt{\dfrac{a^2+ab+b^2}{3}}; a<0 \text{ and } b>0\end{cases}$ **(c)** 1 **9.** Not satisfied

TEXTUAL EXERCISE–2: (OBJECTIVE)

1. A value of c for which the conclusion of mean value theorem holds for the function $f(x) = \log_e x$ on the interval [1, 3] is

(a) $2 \log_3 e$ (b) $\frac{1}{2}\log_e 3$

(c) $\log_3 e$ (d) $\log_e 3$

2. The approximate value of c of the mean value theorem for the function $f(x) = x(x-1)(x-2)$ in $[0, 1/2]$ is

(a) 0.5 (b) 0.3

(c) 0.2 (d) None of these

3. If a function $f(x)$ is continuous in the closed interval [2, 4] and differentiable in the open interval (2, 4) and $f(2) = 5$, $f(4) = 13$, if at least one point c in (2, 4) then $f'(c)$ is

(a) 2 (b) 3

(c) 4 (d) 6

4. If f is continuous in $[a, b]$ and differentiable (a, b), then there exists at least one point c in (a, b) such that $f'(c)$ is equal to

(a) $\dfrac{f(b)+f(a)}{b+a}$ (b) $\dfrac{f(b)-f(a)}{b+a}$

(c) $\dfrac{f(b)-f(a)}{b-a}$ (d) $\dfrac{f(b)+f(a)}{b-a}$

5. Let $f(x) = e^x$, $x \in [0, 1]$, then a number c in the Lagrange's mean value theorem is

(a) $\log(e-1)$ (b) $\log(e+1)$

(c) $\log e$ (d) None of these

6. Let $f(x)$ satisfy the requirements of Lagrange's mean value theorem in [0, 2]. If $f(0) = 0$ and $|f'(x)| \leq 1/2$ for all x in [0, 2], then

(a) $f(x) \leq 2$

(b) $|f(x)| \leq 1$

(c) $f(x) = 2x$

(d) $f(x) = 3$ for at least one x in [0,2]

7. For $f(x) = (x-1)^{2/3}$, mean value theorem is applicable in the interval

(a) (1, 2) (b) (0, 2)

(c) any finite interval (d) None of these

8. In [0, 1], Lagrange's mean value theorem is NOT applicable to

(a) $f(x)=\begin{cases}\frac{1}{2}-x, & x<\frac{1}{2}\\ \left(\frac{1}{2}-x\right)^2 & x\geq\frac{1}{2}\end{cases}$

(b) $f(x)=\begin{cases}\dfrac{\sin x}{x}, & x\neq 0\\ 1 & x=0\end{cases}$

(c) $f(x) = x\,|x|$

(d) $f(x) = |x|$

9. The value of c of the mean value theorem, if $f(x) = 2x^2 + 3x + 4$ in [1, 2] is:

(a) 1 (b) 2

(c) 3/2 (d) 2/3

10. If f be the quadratic function defined on $[a, b]$ by $f(x) = \alpha x^2 + \beta x + \gamma, \alpha \neq 0$, then the real '$c$' guaranteed by the Lagrange's mean value theorem is equal to:

(a) $\frac{1}{2}(a+b)$ (b) $(a|b + b|a)$

(c) $2ab/(a + b)$ (d) $\sqrt{(ab)}$

11. Let $f(x)$ and $g(x)$ be differentiable in $[0, 1]$ such that $f(0) = 2$, $g(0) = 0$, $f(1) = 6$ by LMVT. Let there exist a real number c in $(0,1)$ such that $f'(c) = 2g'(c)$, then $g(1) =$

(a) 1 (b) –1

(c) 2 (d) –2

12. Let $f(x) = 1/x^2$, $g = 1/x$ on $[a, b]$, $0 < a < b$. Let $\frac{f(b)-f(a)}{g(b)-g(a)} = \frac{f'(c)}{g'(c)}$ for some $a < c < b$. Then c is

(a) A.M. of a and b (b) G.M. of a and b

(c) H.M. of a and b (d) None of these

13. If $f(x)$ is twice differentiable polynomial function such that $f(1) = 1, f(2) = 4, f(3) = 9$, then :

(a) $f''(x) = 2 \forall x \in \mathbb{R}$

(b) there exist at least one $x \in (1, 2)$ such that $f'(x) = 3$

(c) there exist at least one $x \in (2, 3)$ such that $f'(x) = 5 = f''(x)$

(d) there exist at least one $x \in (1, 3)$ such that $f'(x) = 2$

14. Let $f(x)$ be a non-constant twice differentiable function defined on $(-\infty, \infty)$ such that $f(x) = f(1 - x)$ and $f'\left(\frac{1}{4}\right) = 0$. Consider the following statements:

(i) $f'(x)$ vanishes at least twice on $[0, 1]$

(ii) $f'\left(\frac{1}{2}\right) = 0$, $f''(x) = 0$ at least once in $\left(\frac{1}{4}, \frac{1}{2}\right)$ and $\left(\frac{1}{2}, \frac{3}{4}\right)$

(iii) $\int_{-1/2}^{1/2} f\left(x+\frac{1}{2}\right)\sin x\, dx = 0$

(iv) $\int_{-1/2}^{1/2} f(t)e^{\sin \pi t}dt = \int_{1/2}^{1} f(1-t)e^{\sin \pi t}dt$, then only

(a) (i) and (ii) are true

(b) (ii) and (iii) are true

(c) (i), (ii) and (iii) are true

(d) All of the above

15. The value of c in $(0,2)$ satisfying the mean value theorem for the function $f(x) = x(x - 1)^2$, $x \in [0,2]$ is equal to

(a) $\frac{3}{4}$ (b) $\frac{4}{3}$

(c) $\frac{1}{3}$ (d) $\frac{2}{3}$

16. If the mean value theorem is $f(b) - f(a) = (b - a) f'(c)$. Then, for the function $x^2 - 2x + 3$ in $\left[1, \frac{3}{2}\right]$, the value of c is

(a) 6/5 (b) 5/4

(c) 4/3 (d) 7/6

17. If $f(x) = \sin x/e^x$ in $[0, \pi]$, then $f(x)$

(a) satisfies Rolle's theorem and $c = \frac{\pi}{4}$, so that $f'\left(\frac{\pi}{4}\right) = 4$

(b) does not satisfy Rolle's theorem but $f'\left(\frac{\pi}{4}\right) > 0$

(c) satisfies Rolle's theorem and $f'\left(\frac{\pi}{4}\right) = 0$

(d) satisfies Langranges mean value theorem but $f'\left(\frac{\pi}{4}\right) \neq 0$

18. If $f(x) = x^2 - 2x + 4$ on $[1,5]$, then the value of a constant c such that $\frac{f(5)-f(1)}{5-1} = f'(c)$, *is*

(a) 0 (b) 1

(c) 2 (d) 3

19. In the mean value theorem $f(b) - f(a) = (b - a) f'(c)$, if $a = 4$, $b = 9$ and $f(x) = \sqrt{x}$, then the value of c is

(a) 8.00 (b) 5.25

(c) 4.00 (d) 6.25

Answer Keys

1. (b)	**2.** (c)	**3.** (c)	**4.** (c)	**5.** (a)	**6.** (b)	**7.** (a)	**8.** (a)	**9.** (c)	**10.** (a)
11. (c)	**12.** (c)	**13.** (b)	**14.** (d)	**15.** (b)	**16.** (b)	**17.** (c)	**18.** (d)	**19.** (d)	

MAXIMA AND MINIMA

■ INTRODUCTION

You may not be interested but one who looks after the supply and management of a power to a city always tries to know exactly when the demand (power consumption) is maximum or minimum so that the according arrangements can be done. Similarly the people who deal with shares want to exactly know as to when the value of a particular share will be minimum so that they can purchase and when will it be the maximum so that they can sell it. The value of a share is actually a variable dependent upon so many variables. Applications of derivative (i.e., maxima/ minima is done almost in all walks of life e.g., botany, environmental sciences, politics, designing of water tanks, dams, grains silos and various storage tanks in the industries. It is extremely useful in surface designing of aircrafts, spaceships, missile etc.

So even if we know in a function, how one dependent variable varies with respect to one or more independent variables, yet the question remains how to find out the extreme values of dependent variable and for what respective values of independent variable/variables it occur.

It is logically understandable that for a curve represented by the function $y = f(x)$ in a given interval, at some point the slope of tangent will become zero which implies that the derivative becomes zero, i.e., the curve ceases to increase or decrease. So a point where the slope of the curve becomes zero is a natural choice for considering whether there is a maximum or minima there. But several complications arise. If the slope of a given point is zero, does that point have to be a maxima or minima? If the slope never becomes zero in an interval will it not have a maxima or minima? If it will, then how can we find it?

In this section we will try to find the answers to the above and other related questions and see how the concept of differentiation and other related concepts can be used.

■ MAXIMA AND MINIMA

- The notion of optimising functions is used in almost every sphere of life including geometry, business, trade, industries, economics, medicines etc. In this chapter we shall see how calculus defines the notion of maxima and minima and distinguishes it from the greatest and least value or global maxima and global minima of a function.
- Since most of the functions which we encounter within practical world are differentiable hence we continue our discussion with such functions only unless otherwise stated.

■ RELATIVE (LOCAL) MAXIMA AND MINIMA

A function $f(x)$ is said to have a local maxima at $x = a$ if $f(a)$ is greater than every other value assumed by $f(x)$ in the immediate neighbourhood of $x = a$.

$$\left.\begin{aligned} f(a) &\geq f(a+h) \\ f(a) &\geq f(a-h) \end{aligned}\right\} \text{ for a sufficiently small positive } h.$$

$\Rightarrow$ $x = a$ gives maxima

In other words, a function $f(x)$ is said to have a local maximum at $x = a$ if $f(a) \geq f(x)\ \forall\ x \in (a - h, a + h)$, where h is a small positive arbitrary number.

A function $f(x)$ is said to have a minima at $x = b$ if

$$\left.\begin{aligned} f(b) &\leq f(b+h) \\ f(b) &\leq f(b-h) \end{aligned}\right\} \text{ for a sufficiently small positive } h.$$

In other words, a function $f(x)$ is said to have a local minimum at $x = b$ if $f(b) \leq f(x)\ \forall\ x \in (b - h, b + h)$, where h is a small positive arbitrary number.

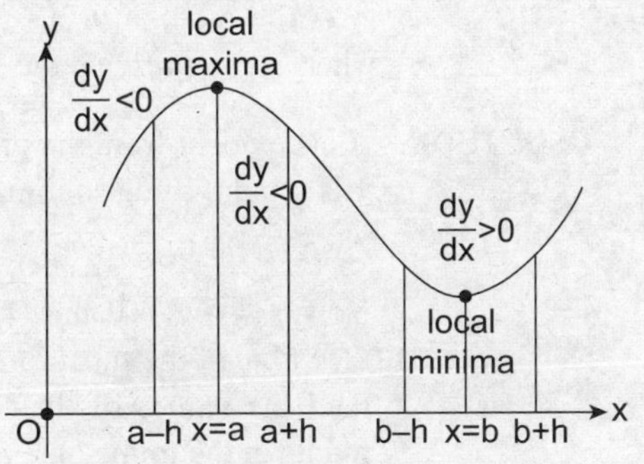

FIGURE 5.175

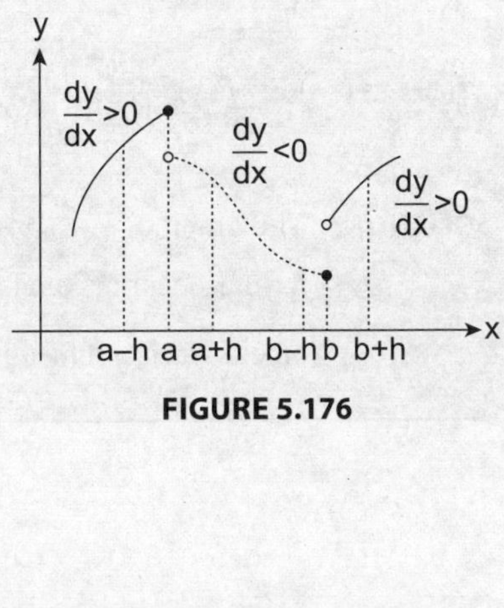

FIGURE 5.176

Being the greatest and least values of the function in the neighbourhood of the point in question, these are also known as local/relative extrema.

- The term 'extremum' or 'extremal' or 'turning value' is used both for maximum/minimum value.
- The above definition is applicable to all functions continuous or discontinuous, differentiable or non-differentiable at $x = a$.
- If the graph of a function f attains a local maximum at the point $(a, f(a))$, then $x = a$ is called the point of local maximum and $f(a)$ is called the local maximum value. A similar terminology is used for local minimum.
- A function can have several local maximum and minimum values.
- If a function is strictly increasing or strictly decreasing at an interior point $x = a$ it can't have an extremum at $x = a$ and vice versa.

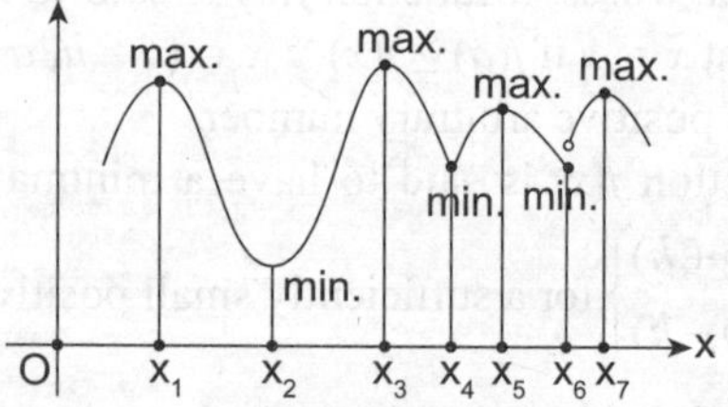

FIGURE 5.177

Here x_1, x_3, x_5 and x_7 are the points of local maxima and x_2, x_4 and x_6 are the points of local minima.

- A local maximum (local minimum) value of a function may not be the greatest (least) value in a finite interval. A local minimum value may be greater than a local maximum value.

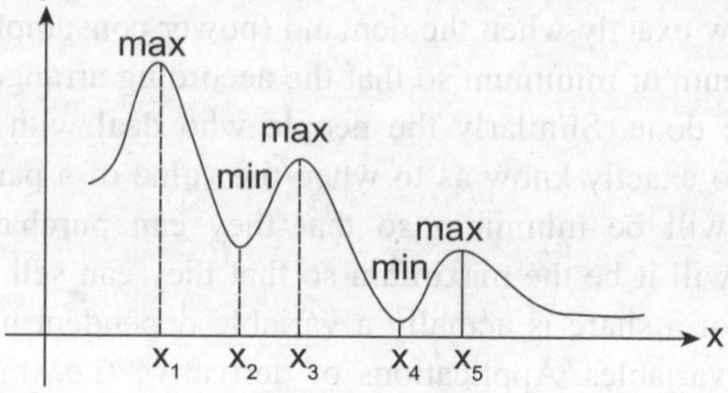

FIGURE 5.178

Here $f(x)$ at x_2 (point of local minima) is more than $f(x)$ at x_5 (point of local maxima).

For a continuous function; there must exist one local minima between any two local maxima and vice-versa. However; this may or may not be the case for discontinuous functions.

ILLUSTRATION 130: Test the function $f(x) = \{x\}$ for the existence of a local maximum and minimum at $x = 1$, where $\{.\}$ represents the fractional part function

SOLUTION: As is evident from the graph, $x = 1$ is a point of discontinuity

Also $f(1) = 0$

Now, $f(1 - h) > 0$ and $f(1 + h) > 0$ i.e., the value of the function at $x = 1$ is less than the values of the function at the points in the immediate neighbourhood of 1. Thus, $x = 1$ is the point of local minimum.

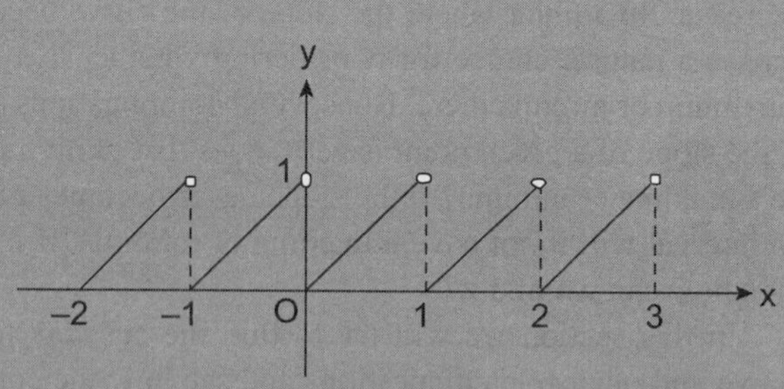

FIGURE 5.179

ILLUSTRATION 131: Let $f(x) = \begin{cases} |x|; 0 < |x| \le 2 \\ \frac{1}{2}; x = 0 \end{cases}$. Examine the behavior of $f(x)$ at $x = 0$

SOLUTION: The graph of $y = f(x)$ is shown below

$f(x)$ has local maxima at $x = 0$ because $f(0) = \frac{1}{2}$ is greater than every other values assumed by $f(x)$ in the immediate neighborhood of $x = 0$.

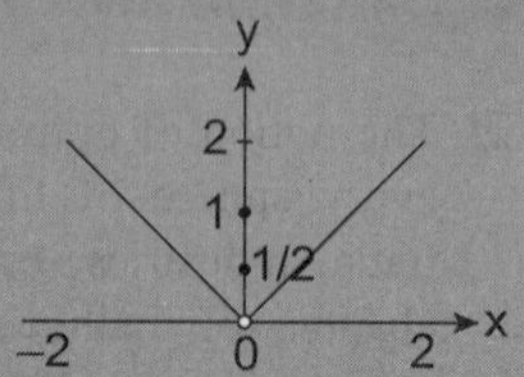

FIGURE 5.180

ILLUSTRATION 132: Let $f(x)=\begin{cases}1-x+a & \text{if } x\le 1\\ 2x+3 & \text{if } x>1\end{cases}$ If $f(x)$ has local minimum at $x = 1$, then $a \le$

(a) 2 (b) 3

(c) 5 (d) None of these

SOLUTION: (c) We have $f(x)=\begin{cases}x-1+a & \text{if } x\le 1\\ 2x+3 & \text{if } x>1\end{cases}$

Since $y = 1 - x + a$ is decreasing function and $y = 2x + 3$ is increasing function $f(x)$ will have a local minimum at $x = 1$

If $f(1) \le f(x)$ for $x > 1$ or if $a \le 2x + 3$ for $x > 1$

$\Rightarrow a \le 5$

ILLUSTRATION 133: For a function $f(x)=\begin{cases}1\,; x=1\\ 2\,; x=2\end{cases}$; is it correct to say that $x = 2$ is a point of local maxima and $x = 1$ is a point of local minima

SOLUTION: No, it is false to say so because local maxima and minima are properties of interval and not of an isolated point.

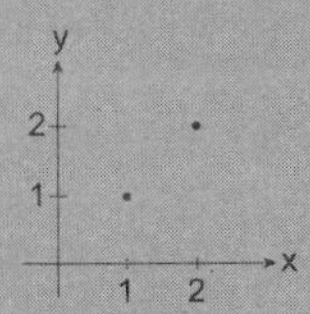

FIGURE 5.181

ILLUSTRATION 134: Consider $f(x) = [\sin x]$ for $x \in [0, 2\pi]$, where [.] denotes the greatest integer function. Then is it correct to say that $x = \pi/2$ is a point of local maxima?

SOLUTION: Yes, it is correct to say so, because in the immediate neighborhood of $x = \pi/2$; there is no values of x for which $f(\pi/2) < f(x)$

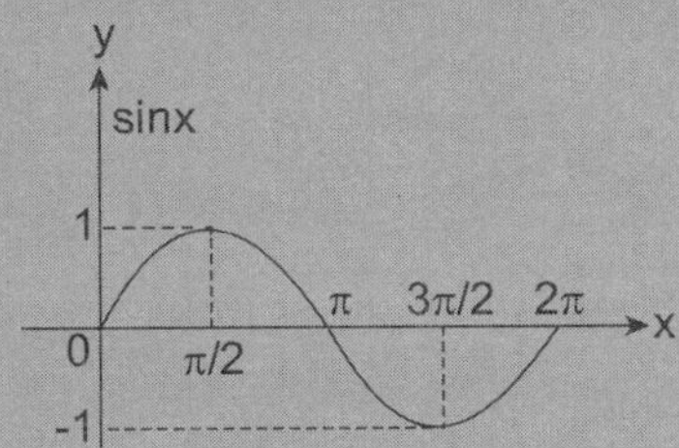

FIGURE 5.182

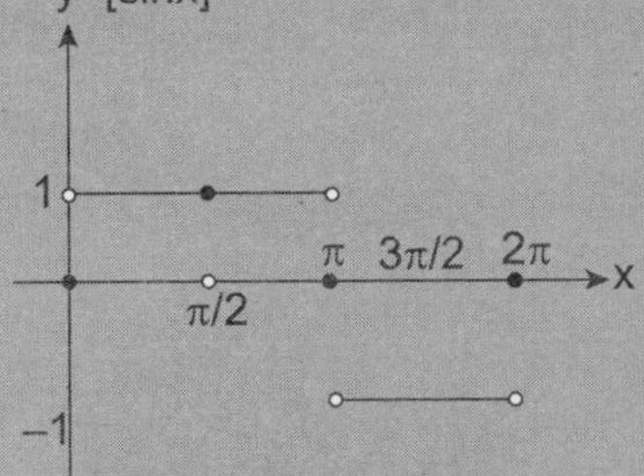

FIGURE 5.183

ILLUSTRATION 135: Find the number of points of local maxima and also the number of points of local minima for $y = ||x^2| - 2|x| - 3|$

SOLUTION: As we know the graph for $y = x^2 - 2x - 3$ and $y = x^2 + 2x - 3$ are as shown below:

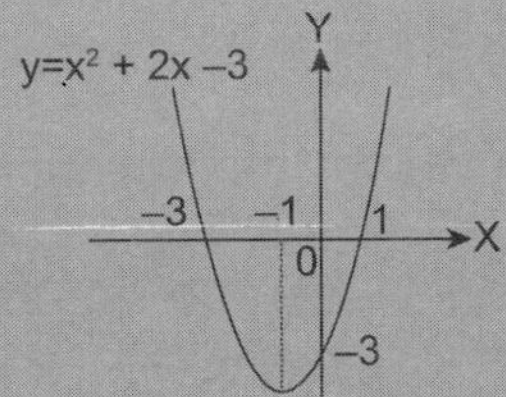

FIGURE 5.184

(i) For $x \ge 0$, $y = |x^2 - 2x - 3|$ $\Rightarrow y=\begin{cases}x^2-2x-3 & \text{for } x\ge 3\\ -(x^2-2x-3) & \text{for } 0\le x<3\end{cases}$

(ii) For x < 0, y = |x² + 2x – 3| $\Rightarrow y = \begin{cases} x^2+2x-3 & \text{for } x \le -3 \\ -(x^2+2x-3) & \text{for } -3 < x < 3 \end{cases}$

The above cases are represented graphically by following figure

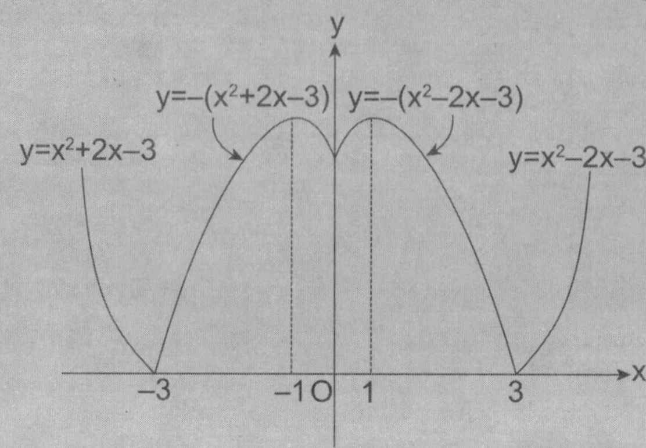

FIGURE 5.185

Now as evident from the graph; we have 2 points of local maxima ($x = -1, 1$) and 3 points of local minima ($x = 3, 0, 3$).

ILLUSTRATION 136: Find the points of local maxima/minima for $x \in [0, 4.5]$ the function $y = |x-1| + |x-2| + |x-3| + |x-4|$; where $x \in [0, 4.5]$

SOLUTION: $y = |x-1| + |x-2| + |x-3| + |x-4|$

$$y = \begin{cases} 10-4x \ ; & x < 1 \\ 8-2x \ ; & 1 \le x < 2 \\ 4 \ ; & 2 \le x < 3 \\ 2x-2 \ ; & 3 \le x < 4 \\ 4x-10 \ ; & x \ge 4 \end{cases}$$

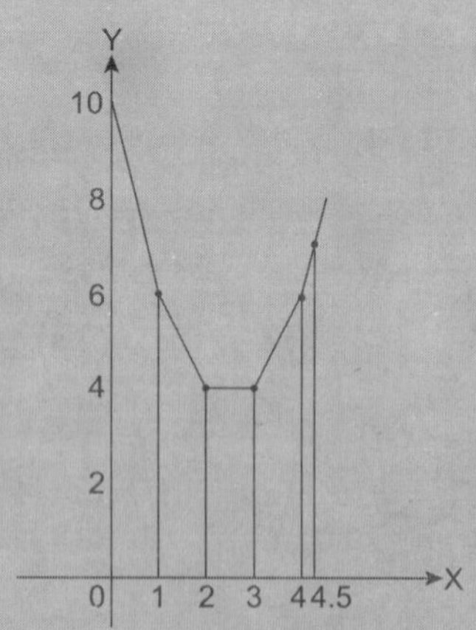

FIGURE 5.186

Now $x = 0$ and $x = 4.5$ are the points of local maxima and points $x = 2, 3$ are points of local minima. The points in the interval (2, 3) can be referred to as neither the points of local maxima nor the points of local minima, since the function $f(x)$ is constant for $x \in (2, 3)$.

Necessary and Sufficient Conditions for Local Maxima and Minima (For Differentiable Functions)

If $x = a$ is maxima.

$$\Rightarrow \begin{cases} f(a) \ge f(a+h) \\ f(a) \ge f(a-h) \end{cases}$$

$$\Rightarrow \begin{cases} \lim_{h\to 0}\left(\dfrac{f(a+h)-f(a)}{h}\right) \le 0 \\ \lim_{h\to 0}\left(\dfrac{f(a-h)-f(a)}{-h}\right) \ge 0 \end{cases}$$

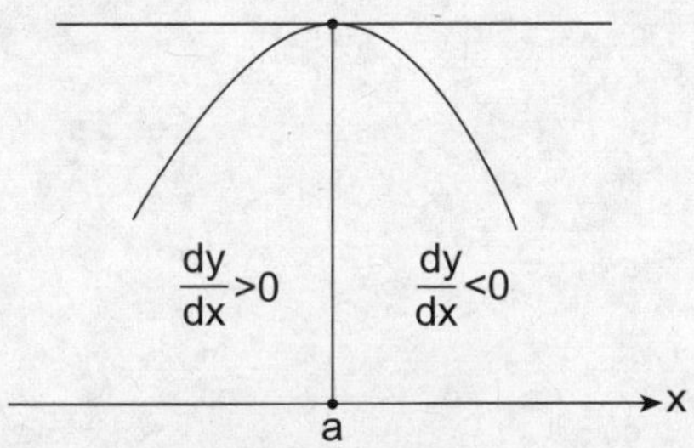

FIGURE 5.187

Clearly $\forall\, x \in (a-h, a)$: $\dfrac{dy}{dx} > 0$

$\Rightarrow$ $f(x)$ is increasing

Clearly $\forall\, x \in (a, a+h,)$: $\dfrac{dy}{dx} < 0$

$\Rightarrow$ $f(x)$ is decreasing

$\Rightarrow$ $\dfrac{dy}{dx} = 0$ at $x = a$ and it changes its sign as we move from non-negative to non-positive.

If $x = b$ is minima

$$\Rightarrow \begin{cases} f(b) \le f(b+h) \\ f(b) \le f(b-h) \end{cases}$$

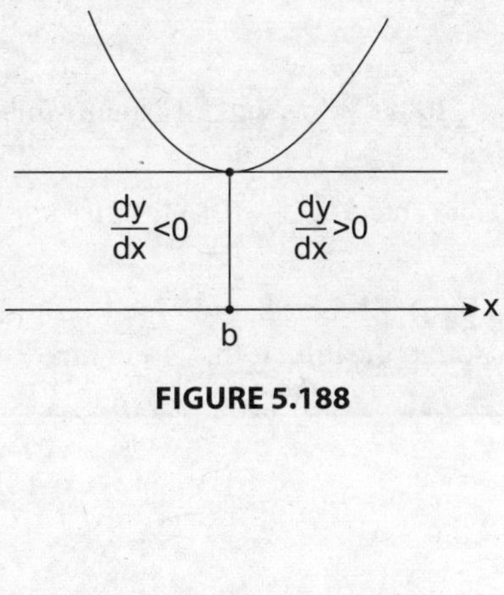

FIGURE 5.188

$$\Rightarrow \begin{cases} \lim_{h\to 0}\left(\dfrac{f(b+h)-f(b)}{h}\right) \ge 0 \\ \lim_{h\to 0}\left(\dfrac{f(b-h)-f(b)}{-h}\right) \le 0 \end{cases}$$

$\Rightarrow$ Clearly $\forall\, x \in (b-h, b)$: $\dfrac{dy}{dx} < 0$

$\Rightarrow$ $f(x)$ is decreasing

$\Rightarrow$ Clearly $\forall\, x \in (b, b+h)$: $\dfrac{dy}{dx} > 0$

$\Rightarrow$ $f(x)$ is increasing

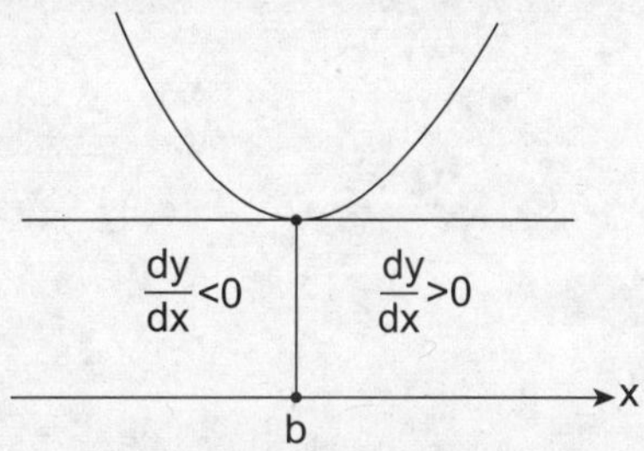

FIGURE 5.189

$\Rightarrow$ $\dfrac{dy}{dx} = 0$ at $x = b$ and it changes its sign from non-positive to non-negative as we move from $b - h$ to $b + h$ across b.

■ FERMAT THEOREM

If $x = a$ is a point in an open interval in the domain of a differentiable function f, such that $f(a)$ exists, and if $(a, f(a))$ is a point of local extremum (either a maximum or a minimum), then $f'(x) = 0$.

Geometrically, Fermat theorem says that if there is a tangent at a highest point or lowest point of the graph of a differential function and further if the point of contact is not an end point of the graph, then the tangent line is necessarily horizontal.

Proof: We shall prove the above theorem only in the case that $(a, f(a))$ is a local maximum point, since a similar proof (with the inequalities reversed) is valid for a local minimum point.

Since $(a, f(a))$ is a local maximum point, $f(a-h) \le f(a)$ and $f(a+h) \le f(a)$ for all positive h in some open interval containing a.

Thus $f(a-h) - f(a) \le 0$

Since h is positive, $\frac{f(a-h)-f(a)}{-h} \geq 0$ and $\lim_{h\to 0}\frac{f(a-h)-f(a)}{-h} \geq 0$

Similarly; $\lim_{h\to 0}\frac{f(a+h)-f(a)}{h} \leq 0$

Since $f'(a)$ exists, the above two limits must have a common value which is $f'(a)$. Thus $f'(a)$ is both greater than or equal to zero and also less than or equal to zero. The only number which satisfies both of these conditions is zero, hence $f'(a) = 0$.

Hence, slope of the tangent at the extreme point in an open interval of a differentiable function is horizontal.

ILLUSTRATION 137: Suppose $x^3 + ax^2 + bx + c$ satisfies $f(2) = 10$ and takes the extreme value 4 where $x = 1$. Find the value of a, b and c.

SOLUTION: $f(x) = x^3 + ax^2 + bx + c$

Given $f(2) = 8 + 4a + 2b + c = 10$

$\Rightarrow 4a + 2b + c - 2 = 0$ ...(1)

Also $f'(x) = 3x^2 + 2ax + b$ and $f(x)$ has extrema at $x = 1$

$\Rightarrow f'(1) = 0$ (by Fermat theorem)

$\Rightarrow 3 + 2a + b = 0$ ...(2)

Also $f(1) = 4$ $\Rightarrow a + b + c = 3$ ...(3)

On solving (1), (2) and (3); we get $a = 2$; $b = -7$; $c = 8$

ILLUSTRATION 138: Given that the function $f(x) = (x - a)^2 + (x - b)^2 + (x - c)^2$ has a minimum, find the corresponding values of x

SOLUTION: We have $f(x) = (x - a)^2 + (x - b)^2 + (x - c)^2$ ...(1)

It is a differentiable function for $x \in (-\infty, \infty)$. Hence by Fermat theorem, a minimum can be attained when $f'(x) = 0$

Differentiating (1) w.r.t x, we get $f'(x) = 2(x - a) + 2(x - b) + 2(x - c)$ ...(2)

$f'(x) = 0 \Rightarrow 2(x - a) + 2(x - b) + 2(x - c) = 0$

$\Rightarrow 3x - (a + b + c) = 0 \Rightarrow x = \frac{1}{3}(a+b+c)$

Since a single value of x is obtained and $f(\pm\infty) = \infty$, without further investigation, we can say the minimum is attained at $x = \frac{1}{3}(a+b+c)$.

ILLUSTRATION 139: Check whether the function $f(x) = 2 + 3x^2$, $x \in [-1, 0]$ satisfies the conditions of Fermat theorem.

SOLUTION: $f(x) = 2 + 3x^2$ $\Rightarrow f'(x) = 6x$

Also $f'(x) < 0 \ \forall \ x \in (-1, 0)$

$\therefore$ The given function is strictly decreasing in $[-1, 0]$ and consequently attains maximum at $x = -1$ and minimum at $x = 0$.

Since, these points are not interior points of the interval $[-1, 0]$ we can't apply Fermat theorem.

In fact $f'(-1) = -6$ and $f'(0) = 0$. We see that $f'(0) = 0$ but this inference could not have been drawn using Fermat theorem (which is not applicable in this problem).

ILLUSTRATION 140: If $f(x) = x^3 + ax^2 + bx + c$ has stationary point at $x = -1$ and $x = 3$. Find a, b, c

SOLUTION: Since $f(x)$ has stationary point at $x = -1$ and $x = 3$

$\Rightarrow f'(-1) = 0$ and $f'(3) = 0$

Now, $f'(x) = 3x^2 + 2ax + b$

$\Rightarrow f'(-1) = 3 - 2a + b = 0$

And $f'(3) = 27 + 6a + b = 0$

Simultaneously solving; we get $a = -3$, $b = -9$, $c \in R$

ILLUSTRATION 141: If $f(x) = a \ln |x| + bx^2 + x$ has extremum at $x = 1$ and $x = 3$, then

(a) $a = -3/4$, $b = -1/8$
(b) $a = 3/4$, $b = -1/8$
(c) $a = -3/4$, $b = 1/8$
(d) None of these

SOLUTION: Around $x = 1, 3$ we have $|x| = x$.

$\therefore\ f(x) = a \ln x + bx^2 + x,\qquad \Rightarrow\ f'(x) = \frac{a}{x} + 2bx + 1$

From the question, $f'(1) = 0, f'(3) = 0$, we have $a + 2b + 1 = 0,\ \frac{a}{3} + 6b + 1 = 0$

Solving we get $a = -3/4$ and $b = -1/8$

ILLUSTRATION 142: Let $f(x) = x^3 - 6x^2 + 12x - 3$. Then at $x = 2$, $f(x)$ has

(a) a maximum
(b) a minimum
(c) both a maximum and a minimum
(d) neither a maximum nor a minimum

SOLUTION: (d) $f'(x) = 3x^2 - 12x + 12 = 3(x - 2)^2$

$\therefore\ f'(2) = 0; f'(2 - \varepsilon) = 3\varepsilon^2 > 0; f'(2 + \varepsilon) = 3\varepsilon^2 > 0$

$\Rightarrow f'(2 \pm \varepsilon) = 3\varepsilon^2 > 0$ for any real number $\varepsilon > 0$

Hence, $f(x)$ has neither a minimum nor a maximum at $x = 2$

ILLUSTRATION 143: Let $P(x) = a_0 + a_1x^2 + a_2x^4 + \ldots + a_nx^{2n}$ be a polynomial in a real variable x, with $0 < a_0 < a_1 < a_2 < \ldots < a_n$. Then function $P(x)$ has

(a) neither a maximum nor a minimum
(b) only one maximum
(c) only one minimum
(d) None of these

SOLUTION: $P(x) = a_0 + a_1x^2 + a_2x^4 + \ldots + a_nx^{2n}$

$\Rightarrow P'(x) = 2a_1x + 4a_2x^3 + \ldots + 2n\,a_n\,x^{2n-1}$

$= 2x(a_1 + 2a_2x^2 + \ldots + na_n\,x^{2n-2})$

Here $x = 0$ is only critical point as $a_1 + 2a_2x^2 + \ldots + na_nx^{2n-2}$ is always positive. And sign of $P'(x)$ changes from –ve to +ve at $x = 0$. So this is the point of minimum.

ILLUSTRATION 144: If the function $f(x) = \frac{t + 3x - x^2}{x - 4}$, where '$t$' is a parameter has a minimum and a maximum then the range of values of 't' is

(a) $(0, 4)$
(b) $(0, \infty)$
(c) $(-\infty, 4)$
(d) $(4, \infty)$

SOLUTION: $f(x) = \dfrac{t+3x-x^2}{x-4}$; $f'(x) = \dfrac{(x-4)(3-2x)-(t+3x-x^2)}{(x-4)^2}$

for maximum or minimum, $f'(x) = 0$

$\Rightarrow -2x^2 + 11x - 12 - t - 3x + x^2 = 0$

$\Rightarrow -x^2 + 8x - (12 + t) = 0$

for maxima and minima to exist; the above equation must have two real and distinct roots.

$\therefore\ D > 0 \qquad \Rightarrow 64 - 4(12 + t) > 0 \qquad \Rightarrow t < 4$

CONCLUSION

- The necessary condition for maxima or minima for a differentiable function at a point belonging to an open interval is $\dfrac{dy}{dx} = 0$
- The points where $\dfrac{dy}{dx} = 0$ are known as stationary points as the instantaneous rate of change of function momentarily ceases at these points.
- But if $\dfrac{dy}{dx}$ changes sign from non-positive to non-negative as x advances through x_0 and $\left(\dfrac{dy}{dx}\right)_{x_0} = 0$; there is a minimum at $x = x_0$.
- And if $\dfrac{dy}{dx}$ changes sign from non-negative to non-positive as x advances through x_0 and $\left(\dfrac{dy}{dx}\right)_{x_0} = 0$; there is a maximum at $x = x_0$.
- If $\dfrac{dy}{dx}$ does not change sign while passing through x_0 and $\left(\dfrac{dy}{dx}\right)_{x_0} = 0$, then $f(x)$ is neither a maximum nor a minimum. Such points are called Inflection Points.

ILLUSTRATION 145: Find the critical points for the following functions:

(a) $f(x) = x^{2/3}$

(b) $f(x) = \dfrac{ax}{1+x^2}$

(c) $f(x) = \dfrac{x^2 - x + 1}{x^2 + x + 1}$

(d) $f(x) = x^2 e^{-x}$

(e) $f(x) = x^2 \ln x$

(f) $f(x) = x(\ln x)^2$

SOLUTION: (a) $f(x) = x^{2/3}$

$\Rightarrow f'(x) = \dfrac{2}{3}x^{-1/3} = \dfrac{2}{3\sqrt[3]{x}}$ which is never zero

$\Rightarrow f'(x) \to -\infty$ when $x \to 0^-$ $\qquad \Rightarrow f'(x) \to +\infty$ when $x \to 0^+$

i.e., $f'(x)$ does not exist at $x = 0$ $\qquad$ So $x = 0$ is the only critical point

(b) $f(x) = \dfrac{ax}{1+x^2}$

$\Rightarrow f'(x) = \dfrac{a(1+x^2) - ax(2x)}{(1+x^2)^2} = \dfrac{a(1-x^2)}{(1+x^2)^2} = 0$ at $x = \pm 1$

Clearly $f'(x)$ always exists finitely and never discontinuous but $f'(x) = 0$ at $x = \pm 1$.

So $x = -1$ and $x = 1$ are two stationary points (critical points)

(c) $f(x) = \dfrac{x^2 - x + 1}{x^2 + x + 1}$

$\Rightarrow f'(x) = \dfrac{(2x-1)(x^2+x+1) - (2x+1)(x^2-x+1)}{(x^2+x+1)^2} = \dfrac{2(x^2-1)}{(x^2+x+1)^2}$

$\Rightarrow \dfrac{2(x^2-1)}{(x^2+x+1)^2} = 0$ when $x = \pm 1$

Since there are no such points when $f'(x)$ does not exist, so only two stationary points $x = \pm 1$

(d) $f(x) = x^2 e^{-x}$ $\Rightarrow f'(x) = -x^2 e^{-x} + 2xe^{-x} = 0$

$\Rightarrow f'(x) = xe^{-x}[2 - x] = 0$

$\Rightarrow x = 0$ or $x = 2$ are two stationary points

(e) $f(x) = x^2 \ln x$ $\Rightarrow f'(x) = \dfrac{x^2}{x} + 2x \ln x$

$\Rightarrow f'(x) = x(1 + 2\ln x) = 0$

$\Rightarrow x = 0$ or $\log x = -1/2$ $\Rightarrow x = \dfrac{1}{\sqrt{e}}$

Apparently two stationary points but $x = 0$ do not lie in the domain of $f(x)$ so only stationary point is $x = \dfrac{1}{\sqrt{e}}$

(f) $f(x) = x(\ln x)^2$ $\Rightarrow f'(x) = \dfrac{x.2\ln x}{x} + (\ln x)^2$

$\Rightarrow f'(x) = \ln x(2 + \ln x) = 0$

$\Rightarrow x = 1$ or $x = 1/e^2$ are two stationary points

ILLUSTRATION 146: Find the points of inflexion of the curve $x = e^t$, $y = \sin t$.

SOLUTION: $x = e^t$, $y = \sin t$.

$dx = e^t\, dt$; $dy = \cos t\, dt$

$\Rightarrow \dfrac{dy}{dx} = \dfrac{\cos t}{e^t}$ $\Rightarrow \dfrac{d}{dx}\left(\dfrac{dy}{dx}\right) = \dfrac{d}{dt}\left(\dfrac{\cos t}{e^t}\right)\dfrac{dt}{dx}$

$= \left[\dfrac{-\sin t.e^t - e^t \cos t}{e^{2t}}\right] \cdot \dfrac{1}{e^t}$

$\Rightarrow \dfrac{d^2y}{dx^2} = -\left[\dfrac{\sin t + \cos t}{e^{2t}}\right]$

$\Rightarrow \dfrac{d^2y}{dx^2} = 0$; when $\sin t + \cos t = 0$

$\Rightarrow \sin(t + \pi/4) = 0$

$\Rightarrow \sin(t + \pi/4) = \sin(0)$ $\Rightarrow t + \dfrac{\pi}{4} = n\pi + (-1)^n(0) \Rightarrow t = \left(n\pi - \dfrac{\pi}{4}\right); n \in \mathbb{Z}$

ILLUSTRATION 147: At what values of a and b does the point (1, 3) serve as the point of inflection of the curve $y = ax^3 + bx^2$?

SOLUTION: Let $f(x) = ax^3 + bx^2$

$\Rightarrow f'(x) = 3ax^2 + 2bx$

$\Rightarrow f''(x) = 6ax + 2b$, for (1, 3) to be point of inflection $f''(1) = 0$

$\Rightarrow 6a.1 + 2b = 0$ ...(i)

$\Rightarrow 3a + b = 0$ and $f(1) = 3 = a(1)^3 + b(1)$

$\Rightarrow 3 = a + b$ ......(ii)

Solving (i) and (ii), we get $b = \frac{9}{2}$ and $a = -\frac{3}{2}$

CONTINUOUS AND NON-DIFFERENTIABLE FUNCTIONS

If $f(x)$ is continuous but non-differentiable at $x = a$, then necessary and sufficient condition **for maxima**

(i) $f'(x) \geq 0 \ \forall \ x \in (a-h, a)$;

(ii) $f'(x) \leq 0 \ \forall \ x \in (a, a+h)$, where $h \to 0$

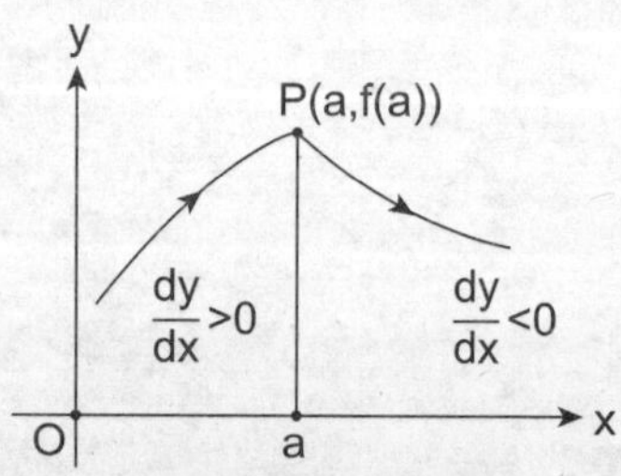

FIGURE 5.190

for maxima

(i) $f'(x) \leq 0 \ \forall \ x \in (a-h, a)$;

(ii) $f'(x) \geq 0 \ \forall \ x \in (a, a+h)$ where $h \to 0$

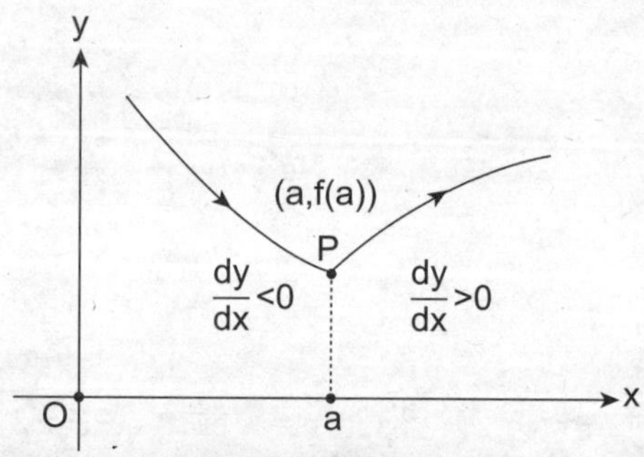

FIGURE 5.191

Where $h \to 0$

NOTE:

f'(a) = 0 is not a necessary condition if the function is non-differentiable at x = a:

ILLUSTRATION 148: Find the local or local maxima for the following functions

(a) $f(x) = |x|$

(b) $f(x) = |x^2 - 2x - 3|$

(c) $f(x) = \left|e^{-|x|} - 1/2\right|$

(d) $f(x) = \begin{cases} -x \ ; x \leq 0 \\ x^3 \ ; \ x > 0 \end{cases}$

SOLUTION: (a) As is evident from the graph of $f(x) = |x|$ as shown below

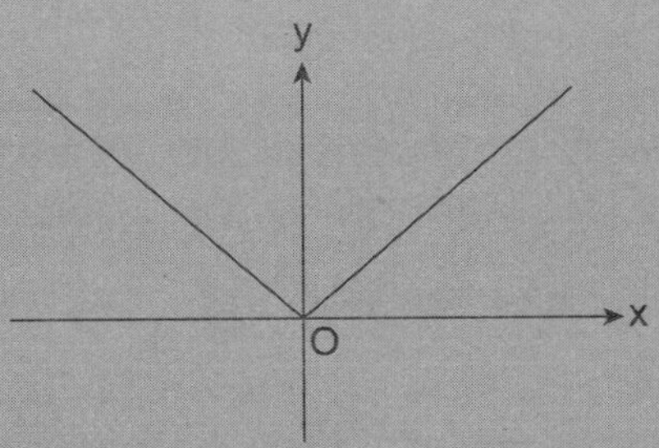

FIGURE 5.192

$f'(0 - h) \leq -1$ and $f'(0 + h) \geq 1$

$\Rightarrow$ $x = 0$ is a point of local minima

(b) As is evident form the graph, $f(x) = |x^2 - 2x - 3|$ as shown below

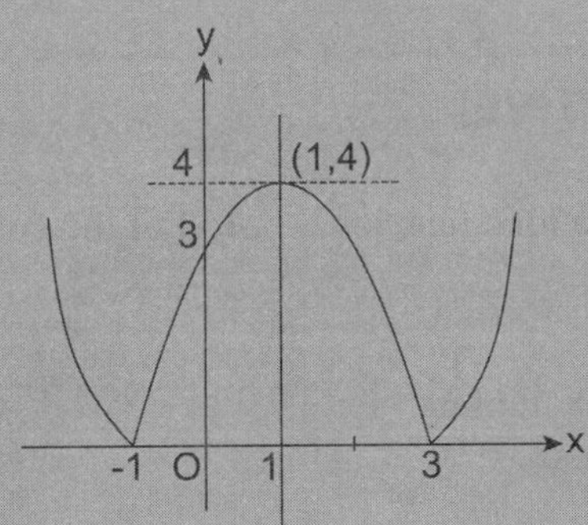

FIGURE 5.193

$\Rightarrow$ $f'(1 - h) \leq 0$ and $f'(-1 + h) \geq 0$

$\Rightarrow$ $x = -1$ is a point of local minima.

Also $f'(3 - h) \leq 0$ and $f'(3 + h) \geq 0$

$\Rightarrow$ $x = 3$ is a point of local minima.

Similarly $f'(1 - h) \geq 0$ and $f'(1 + h) \leq 0$

$\Rightarrow$ $x = 1$ is a point of local maxima

(c) The graph of $y = |e^{-|x|} - 1/2|$ is as shown below

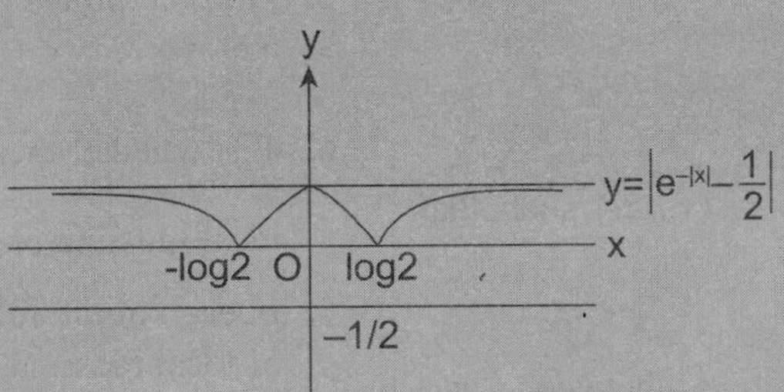

FIGURE 5.194

Here $f'(-\ln 2 - h) \leq 0$ and $f'(-\ln 2 + h) \geq 0$

$\Rightarrow$ $x = -\ln 2$ is a point of local minima.

Also $f'(\ln 2 - h) \le 0$ and $f'(\ln 2 - h) \ge 0$

$\Rightarrow$ $x = \ln 2$ is a point of local minima.

Similarly $f'(0 - h) \ge 0$ and $f'(0 + h) \le 0$ $\Rightarrow$ $x = 0$ is a point of local maxima

(d) $f(x) = f(x) = \begin{cases} -x\,; x \le 0 \\ x^3\,; x > 0 \end{cases}$

$\Rightarrow$ $f'(x) = \begin{cases} -1\;;\; x < 0 \\ 3x^2\;;\; x > 0 \end{cases}$

Now at $x = 0$

$f'(0 - h) = -1 < 0$ and $f'(0 + h) = 3h^2 > 0$

$\Rightarrow$ $x = 0$ is a point of local minima

TEXTUAL EXERCISE–1: (SUBJECTIVE)

1. Find the points of local maxima/minima for a function $y = f(x) = \dfrac{x^4}{4} - 3x^3 + \dfrac{23}{2}x^2 - 15x + 1$.

2. Find the points of local maxima/minima for the function $y = f(x) = \sin x + \cos x \;\forall\; 0 < x < \pi/2$

3. Check for following graphs of $y = f(x)$ (twice differentiable everywhere) $f'(x_1) = f'(x_2) = f'(x_3) = 0$

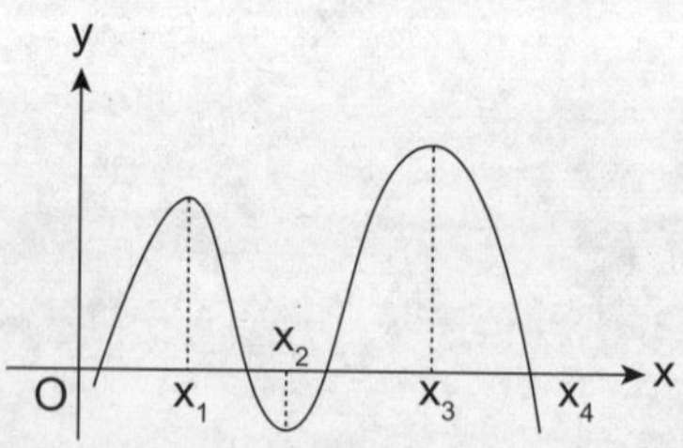

FIGURE 5.195

(a) $f(x_1).f'(x_1) = ...$ (+ve/–ve)

(b) There exists exactly one $c \in (x_1, x_2)$ such that $f''(c) = 0$ (True/False)

(c) $f'(x_3).f'(x_4) = ...$ (+ve/–ve)

(d) For a differentiable function, between two consecutive local minima, there is always a local maxima (True/False)

(e) Local maximum value is always greater than the local minimum value for any function $f(x)$ (True/False)

4. For the given function:

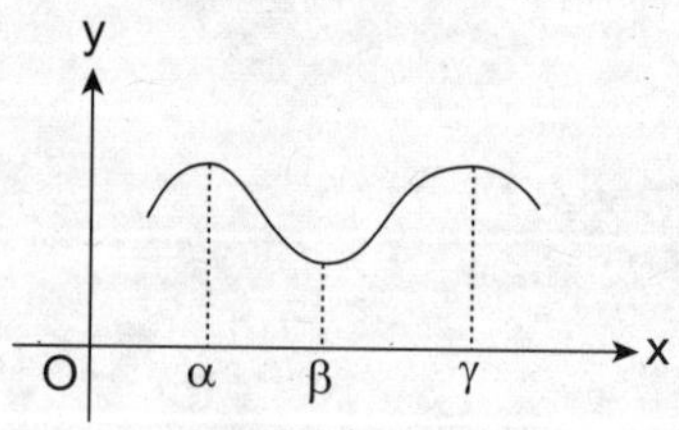

FIGURE 5.196

(i) $f'(\beta) = ...$ (zero/positive/negative)

(ii) $[f'(\alpha - h)][f'(\gamma + h)] = ...$ (zero/positive/negative); $h > 0$

(iii) $[f'(\alpha + h)][f'(\beta - h)] = ...$ (zero/positive/negative); (where $h > 0$ and $h \to 0$)

5. Find the points of local maxima/minima for function $f(x) = x^3/3 - x + 1$.

6. Test whether the function $f(x) = \begin{cases} 1 - 2x; & x \le 0 \\ x^2\;; & x > 0 \end{cases}$ has local maxima or local minima at $x = 0$

7. In each of the following case identify if $x = a$ is point of local maxima, minima or neither

(i)

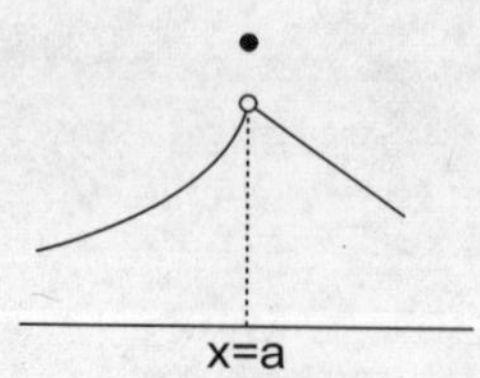

(ii) 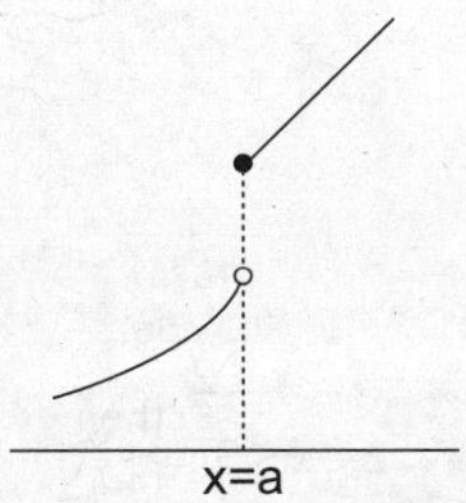

(iii) 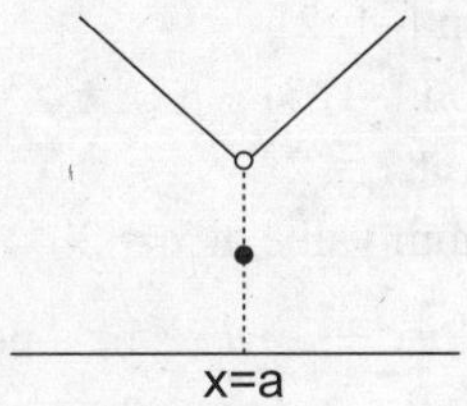

8. Draw the graph of function $f(x) = 2\,|x - 2| + 5\,|x - 3|$ $(x \in \mathbb{R})$. Also identify points of local maxima/minima and also global maximum/minimum values.

9. Examine the graph of the following functions in each case and identify the points of global maximum/minimum and local maximum/minimum.

(i) 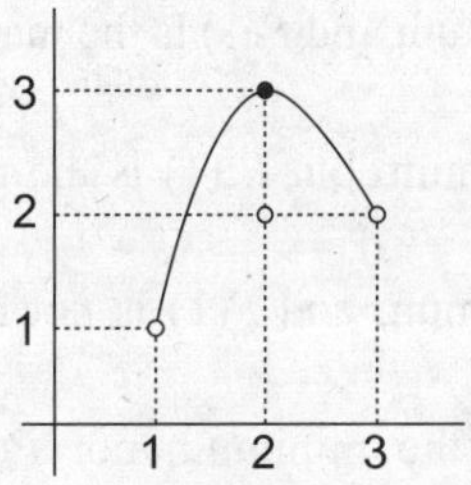

(ii) 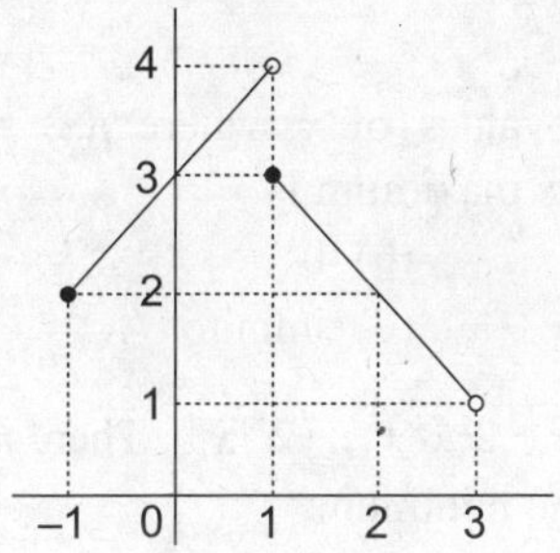

(iii) 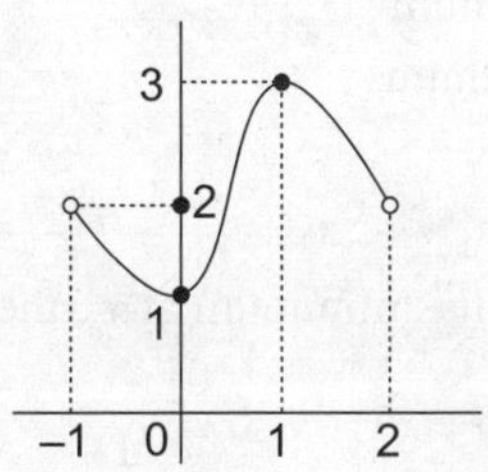

Answer Keys

1. local minima at $x = 1, 5$; local maxima at $x = 3$
2. Local maximum at $x = \pi/4$
3. (a) –ve (b) true (c) +ve (d) True (e) False
4. (i) zero (ii) negative (iii) positive
5. Local maxima at $x = -1$ and Local minima at $x = 1$
6. Local minima
7. (i) Maxima (ii) Neither maxima nor minima (iii) Minima
8. Local minima at $x = 3$, Global minimum value 2 at $x = 3$, No point of local maximum, Global maximum value is not defined.
9. (i) Local maxima at $x = 2$, Local minima at $x = 3$, Global maximum at $x = 2$
   (ii) Local minima at $x = -1$, No point of Global minimum, no point of local or Global maxima
   (iii) Local and Global maximum at $x = 1$, Local and Global minimum at $x = 0$.

TEXTUAL EXERCISE–1: (OBJECTIVE)

1. Let $f: \mathbb{R} \to \mathbb{R}$ be defined by $f(x) = \begin{cases} k - 2x, & \text{if } x \le -1 \\ 2x + 3, & \text{if } x > -1 \end{cases}$

If f has a local minimum at $x = -1$, then a possible value of k is

(a) 1 (b) 0

(c) $-\dfrac{1}{2}$ (d) –1

2. The minimum value of $f(x) = e^{(x^4 - x^3 + x^2)}$ is

(a) e (b) –e

(c) 1 (d) –1

3. Given $P(x) = x^4 + ax^3 + bx^2 + cx + d$ such that $x = 0$ is the only real root of $P'(x) = 0$.

If $P(-1) < P(1)$, then in the interval $[-1, 1]$

(a) $P(-1)$ is the minimum and $P(1)$ is the maximum of P
(b) $P(-1)$ is not minimum but $P(1)$ is the maximum of P
(c) $P(-1)$ is the minimum and $P(1)$ is not maximum of P
(d) Neither $P(-1)$ is the minimum nor $P(1)$ is the maximum of P

4. The number of values of x, where $f(x) = \cos x + \cos\sqrt{2}x$ attains its maximum is
(a) 1 (b) 0
(c) 2 (d) infinite

5. Let $f(x) = 1 + 2x^2 + 2^2x^4 + \ldots + 2^{10}x^{20}$. Then, $f(x)$ has
(a) more than one minimum
(b) exactly one minimum
(c) at least one maximum
(d) None of the above

6. If $f(x) = \sum_{n=1}^{m}(x-n)^2$; has minimum at x_0, then x_0 is
(a) $(m!)^{1/m}$ (b) $\dfrac{1}{\dfrac{1+\frac{1}{2}+\frac{1}{3}+\ldots+\frac{1}{m}}{m}}$
(c) $(m+1)/2$ (d) None of these

7. Suppose that f is continuous on the closed interval A. Also B is a closed interval such that $B \subseteq A$. Choose the correct statement(s)
(a) $\min_B f \le \min_A f$
(b) $\max_B f \le \min_A f$
(c) $\min_B f \le \max_A f$
(d) $\max_B f \le \max_A f$

8. If $f(x) = \begin{cases} 3x^2+12x-1; & -1 \le x \le 2 \\ 37-x; & 2 < x \le 3, \end{cases}$ then
(a) $f(x)$ is increasing on $[-1, 2]$
(b) $f(x)$ is continuous on $[-1, 3]$
(c) $f'(x)$ does not exist at $x = 2$
(d) $f(x)$ has the maximum value at $x = 2$

9. Let $P(x) = a_0 + a_1x^2 + a_2x^4 + \ldots + a_nx^{2n}$ be a polynomial in a real variable x with $0 < a_0 < a_1 < a_2 < \ldots < a_n$. The function $P(x)$ has
(a) neither a maximum nor a minimum
(b) only one maximum
(c) only one minimum
(d) only one maximum and only one minimum

10. If λ, μ be real numbers such that, $x^3 - \lambda x^2 + \mu x - 6 = 0$ has its roots real and positive, then the minimum value of μ, is:
(a) $3(6)^{1/3}$ (b) $3(6)^{2/3}$
(c) $(6)^{1/3}$ (d) $(6)^{2/3}$

11. Let $f(x) = 4\tan x - \tan^2 x + \tan^3 x$, $x \ne n\pi + \dfrac{\pi}{2}$ has:
(a) only one point of local maxima
(b) only one point of local minima
(c) neither local minima nor maxima
(d) None of the above

Answer Keys

1. (d) **2.** (c) **3.** (b) **4.** (a) **5.** (b) **6.** (c) **7.** (c,d) **8.** (a,b,c,d) **9.** (c)
10. (b) **11.** (c)

FIRST DERIVATIVE TEST (CONTINUOUS FUNCTIONS)

Let $f(x)$ be defined and continuous on a certain interval (a, b) and have a derivative everywhere in the interval (a, b) except possibly at a finite number of points, and have a finite number of stationary points. Then, in order to find the extrema of the function, the following steps should be followed:

Step I: Differentiate the function and find out the critical points.

Step II: Locate these critical points on the real number line and test the monotonicity of the function in the intervals so obtained.

Step III: At a critical point $x = a$:

Case: I If LHD ≤ 0 and RHD ≥ 0; then $x = a$ is a point of local minima.

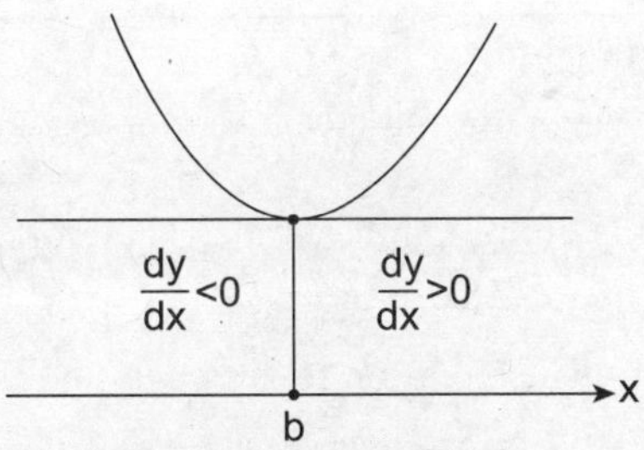

FIGURE 5.197

Case II: If LHD ≥ 0 and RHD ≤ 0; then $x = a$ is a point of local maxima.

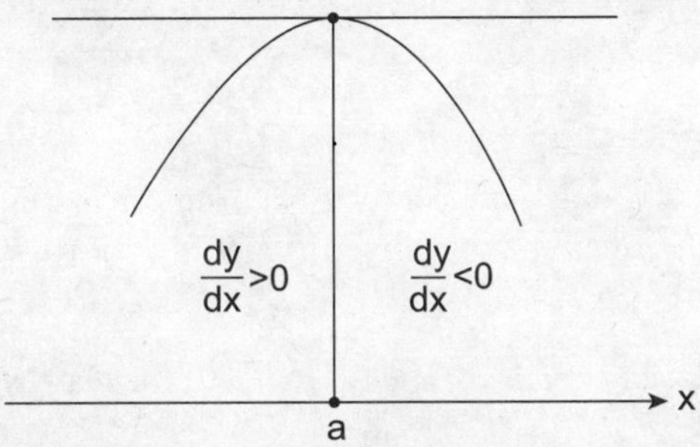

FIGURE 5.198

Case III: If LHD < 0 and RHD < 0; then $x = a$ is a point of inflection.

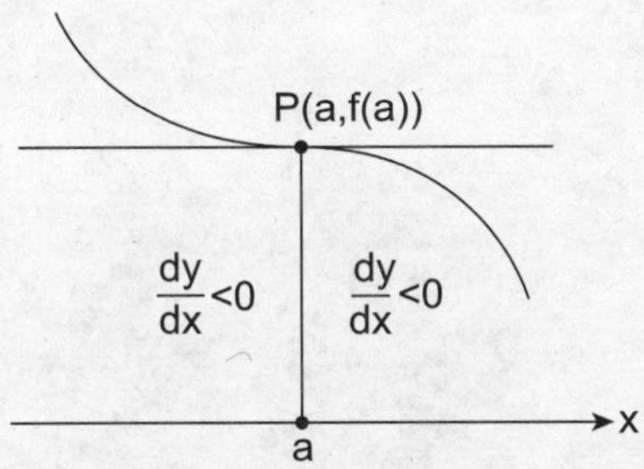

FIGURE 5.199

Case IV: If LHD > 0 and RHD > 0; then $x = a$ is a point of inflection.

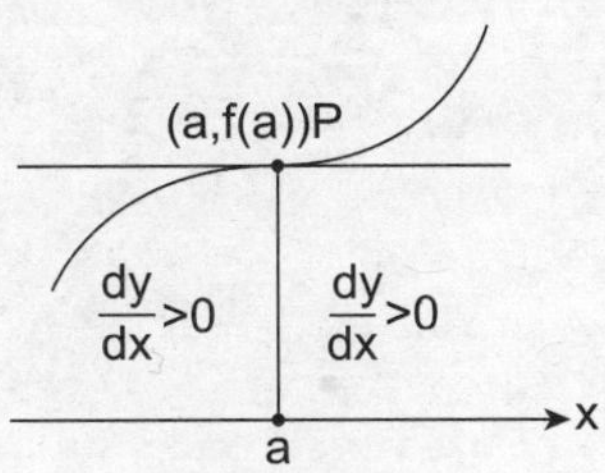

FIGURE 5.200

Step IV: At the left end point 'a'

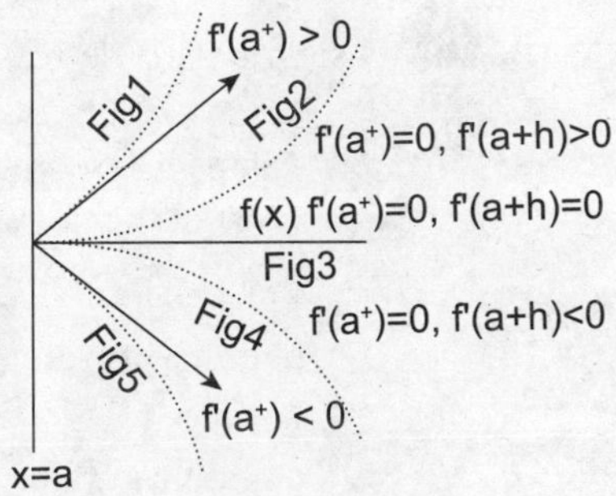

FIGURE 5.201

Fig 1: If $f'(a^+) > 0$, then $x = a$ is a point of local minima

Fig 2: If $f'(a^+) = 0$, and $f'(a + h) > 0$, then $x = a$ is a point of local minima

Fig 3: If $f'(a^+) = 0$ and $f'(a + h) = 0$; then $x = a$ can either be called a point of local minima or a point of local maxima

Fig 4: If $f'(a^+) = 0$ and $f'(a + h) < 0$; then $x = a$ is a point of local maxima

Fig 5: If $f'(a^+) < 0$; then $x = a$ is a point of local maxima

At the right end point 'b'

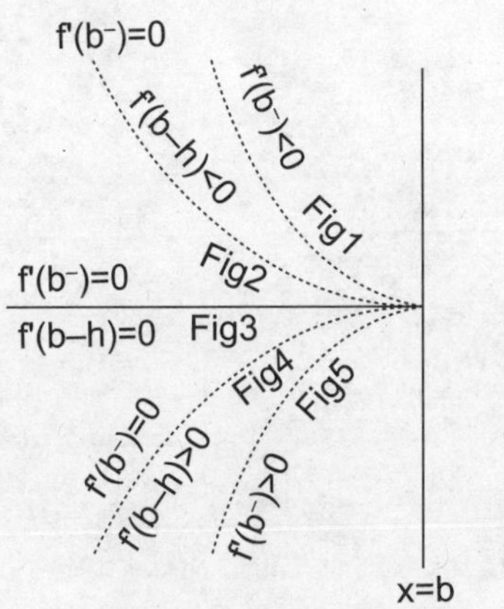

FIGURE 5.202

Fig 1: If $f'(b^-) < 0$; then $x = b$ is a point of local minima

Fig 2: If $f'(b^-) = 0$ and $f'(b - h) < 0$. Then $x = b$ is a point of local minima

Fig 3: If $f'(b^-) = 0$ and $f'(b - h) = 0$; then $x = b$ can either be called a point of local maxima or a point of local minima

Fig 4: If $f'(b^-) = 0$ and $f'(b - h) > 0$; then $x = b$ is a point of local maxima

Fig 5: If $f'(b^-) > 0$; then $x = b$ is a point of local maxima.

ILLUSTRATION 149: Using the first derivative, find the extrema of the function $f(x)=\frac{3}{4}x^4 - x^3 - 9x^2 + 7$.

SOLUTION: The function is defined and differentiable over the entire number scale. Therefore, only the real roots of the derivative equation $f'(x)=3x^3-3x^2-18x=0$

$\Rightarrow$ $3x(x+2)(x-3)$ are critical points. Equating this expression to zero, we find the critical points: $x_1=-2$, $x_2=0$, $x_3=3$ (they should always be arranged in an increasing order). Let us now investigate the sign of the derivative in the neighbourhood of each of these points. Wavy curve of $f'(x)$ is as shown below:

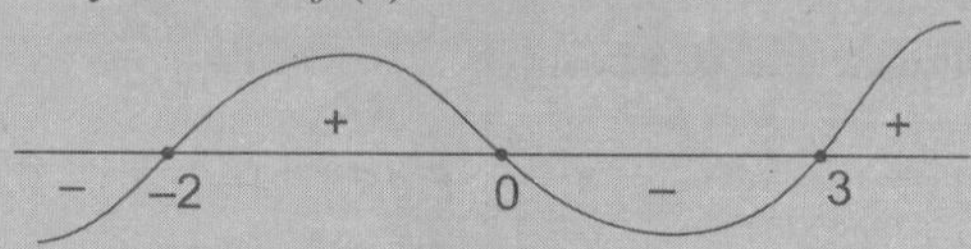

FIGURE 5.203

The derivative at all the points $x < -2$ has one and the same sign i.e., it is negative. Analogously, in the interval (–2, 0), the derivative is positive, in the interval (0, 3) it is negative and for at $x > 3$, it is positive. Hence at the points $x_1 = -2$ and $x_3 = 3$ we have local minima and the local minimum values are $f(-2) = -9$ and $f(3) = -40\frac{1}{4}$ and at the point $x_2 = 0$, there is a local maxima and the local maximum value is given by i.e., $f(0) = 7$.

ILLUSTRATION 150: The function $\frac{\sin(x+\alpha)}{\sin(x+\beta)}$ has no maximum or minimum if

(a) $\beta - \alpha = k\pi$ (b) $\beta - \alpha \neq k\pi$

(c) $\beta - \alpha = 2k\pi$ (d) None of these

SOLUTION: (b) Let $f(x)=\frac{\sin(x+\alpha)}{\sin(x+\beta)}$, so that

$$f'(x)=\frac{\sin(x+\beta)\cos(x+\alpha)-\sin(x+\alpha)\cos(x+\beta)}{\sin^2(x+\beta)}=\frac{\sin(\beta-\alpha)}{\sin^2(x+\beta)}$$

Thus $f(x)$ has no maximum or minimum if $f'(x) \neq 0$, i.e., $\sin(\beta - \alpha) \neq 0$, equivalently $\beta - \alpha \neq k\pi$.

ILLUSTRATION 151: Find the extrema of the function $3\sqrt[3]{x^2} - x^2$ using first derivative.

SOLUTION: The function is defined and continuous throughout the number scale.

Let us find the derivative, $f'(x)=2\left(\frac{1}{\sqrt[3]{x}}-x\right)$

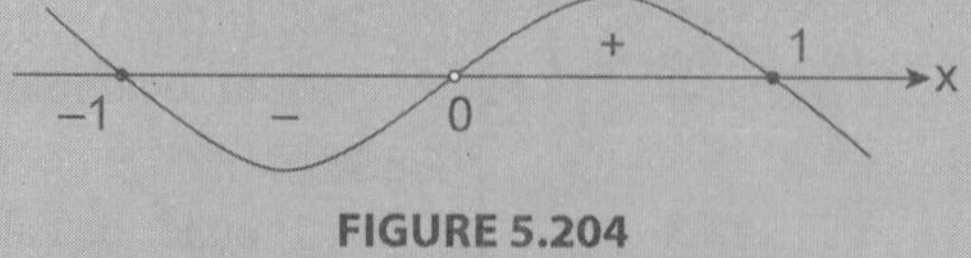

FIGURE 5.204

From the equation $f'(x)=0$ we find the roots of the derivative $x = \pm 1$.

Furthermore the derivative goes to infinity at the point $x = 0$.

Thus, the critical points are $x_1=-1$, $x_2=0$, $x_3=1$.

The results of investigating the sign of the derivative in the neighbourhood of these points are given in figure.

The investigation shows that the function has two maxima: $f(-1) = 2$; $f(1) = 2$ and a minimum $f(0) = 0$.

ILLUSTRATION 152: Find the sides of a rectangle with the greatest possible perimeter inscribed in a semicircle of radius R.

SOLUTION: $AO = x$; $AB = (R^2 - x^2)^{1/2}$

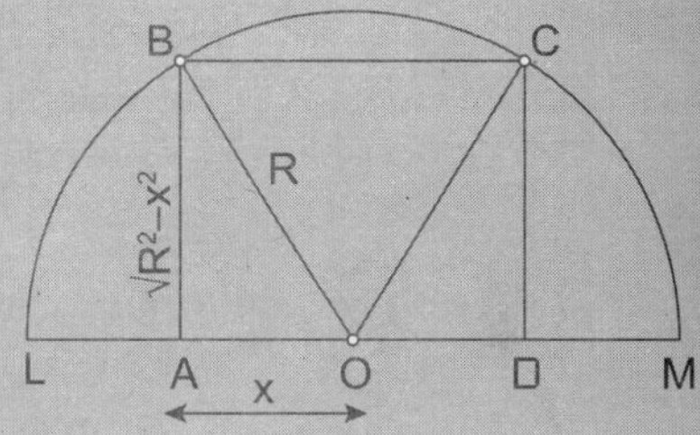

FIGURE 5.205

Perimeter of $ABCD$ be $AB + BC + CD + DA$

$$\Rightarrow P(x) = 2(R^2 - x^2)^{1/2} + 4x$$

$$\Rightarrow P'(x) = 2.\frac{1}{2}.\frac{-2x}{\sqrt{(R^2 - x^2)}} + 4$$

Now, $P'(x) = 0$

(condition for greatest possible perimeter)

$$\Rightarrow 0 = \frac{-2x + 4\sqrt{R^2 - x^2}}{\sqrt{(R^2 - x^2)}} \qquad \Rightarrow 2x = 4\sqrt{R^2 - x^2}$$

$$\Rightarrow 4x^2 = 16(R^2 - x^2) \qquad \Rightarrow 20x^2 = 16R^2$$

$$\Rightarrow x^2 = \frac{16R^2}{20} \qquad \Rightarrow x = \frac{4R}{2\sqrt{5}}$$

$$\Rightarrow x = \frac{2R\sqrt{5}}{5} \qquad \Rightarrow 2x = \frac{4\sqrt{5}R}{5} = AD = BC$$

$$\Rightarrow AB = CD = \frac{R\sqrt{5}}{5}$$

ILLUSTRATION 153: Find the altitude of a right circular cone having the least volume circumscribed about a sphere of radius R.

SOLUTION: $CD = CO = r$, in $\Delta\, LCD$, $LC = CD$ cosecθ $= r$ cosecθ.

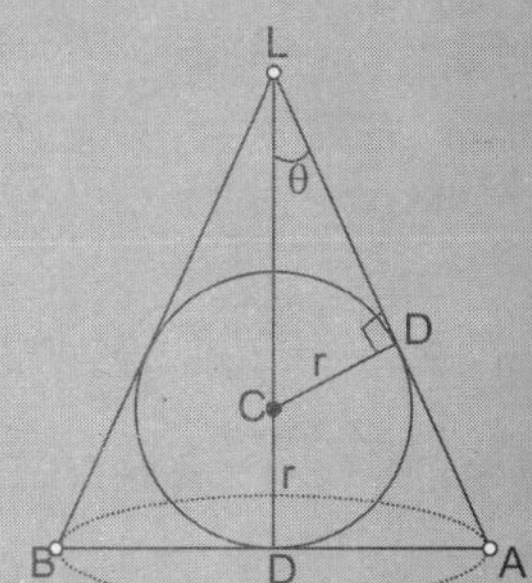

FIGURE 5.206

$\therefore$ Height of cone $LO = LC + CO = r\,\text{cosec}\,\theta + r$

Radius of cone $BO = LO \tan\theta = r(\text{cosec}\,\theta + 1).\tan\theta$

$$\therefore \text{ Volume of cone} = \frac{1}{3}\pi\,[r(\text{cosec}\,\theta + 1).\tan\theta]^2[r\,\text{cosec}\,\theta + r]$$

$$\Rightarrow V(\theta) = \frac{1}{3}\pi\,\tan^2\theta\, r^3(1 + \text{cosec}\,\theta)^3$$

$$\Rightarrow V'(\theta) = 0$$

[condition for least volume]

$$\Rightarrow V'(\theta) = \frac{1}{3}\pi r^3\,[2\tan\theta\sec^2\theta(1 + \text{cosec}\,\theta)^3 + \tan^2\theta.\, 3(1 + \text{cosec}\,\theta)^2(-\text{cosec}\,\theta.\cot\theta)]$$

$$\Rightarrow V'(\theta) = \frac{1}{3}\pi r^3\,\tan\theta(1 + \text{cosec}\,\theta)^2[2\sec^2\theta\,(1 + \text{cosec}\,\theta) - 3\,\text{cosec}\,\theta]$$

$\therefore\ V'(\theta)=0 \Rightarrow (3\sin\theta-1)(\sin\theta+1)=0$

$\Rightarrow \sin\theta=\frac{1}{3}$ and altitude of cone $= r(1+\operatorname{cosec}\theta)=r(1+3)=4r$

ILLUSTRATION 154: Find the altitude of a cone of the least volume which can be drawn around a hemisphere of radius R(the centre of the base of the cone falls on the centre of the sphere)

SOLUTION: $AO=H;\ BO=r$ $\Rightarrow \frac{r}{H}=\tan\theta$

$\Rightarrow r=H\tan\theta;\ \frac{R}{H}=\sin\theta;\ \frac{R}{\sin\theta}=H$

$\Rightarrow r=\frac{R}{\sin\theta}.\tan\theta=\frac{R}{\cos\theta}$

$\Rightarrow V(\theta)=\frac{1}{3}\pi\left(\frac{R}{\cos\theta}\right)^2.\frac{R}{\sin\theta}=\frac{1}{3}\pi R^3\frac{1}{\cos^2\theta}.\frac{1}{\sin\theta}$

$\Rightarrow V'(\theta)=0$ [condition for least volume]

$\Rightarrow V'(\theta)=\frac{2\sin^2\theta.\cos\theta-\cos^3\theta}{(\cos 2\theta.\sin\theta)^2}$ $\therefore\ V'(\theta)=0$

$\Rightarrow 0=\cos\theta[2\sin^2\theta-\cos^2\theta]$ $\Rightarrow V'(\theta)=\cos\theta[-3\sin^2\theta+1]$

$\Rightarrow 0=\cos\theta[3\sin^2\theta-1]$ $\Rightarrow \sin\theta=\frac{1}{\sqrt{3}}$

$\Rightarrow H=\frac{R}{\sin\theta}=R\sqrt{3}$

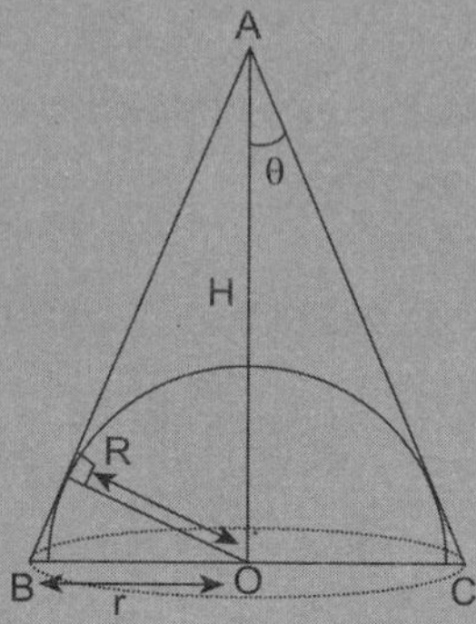

FIGURE 5.207

ILLUSTRATION 155: The function $f(x)=\int_{-1}^{x} t(e^t-1)(t-1)(t-2)^3(t-3)^5\,dt$ has local minimum at $x=$

(a) 0 (b) 1

(c) 2 (d) 3

SOLUTION: **(b), (d)** $\int_{-1}^{x} t(e^t-1)(t-1)(t-2)^3(t-3)^5\,dt$

$\Rightarrow f'(x)=x(e^x-1)(x-1)(x-2)^3(x-3)^5$ (Using Leibnitz rule)

At $x=1, 3$ slope will change from –ve to +ve

$\Rightarrow x=1, 3$ is the point of local minima.

ILLUSTRATION 156: If m and n are positive integers and $f(x)=\int_{1}^{x}(t-a)^{2n}(t-b)^{2m+1}\,dt$, a > b, then

(a) $x=b$ is a point of local minimum (b) $x=b$ is a point of local maximum

(c) $x=a$ is a point of local minimum (d) $x=a$ is a point of local maximum.

SOLUTION: **(a)** $f'(x)=(x-a)^{2n}(x-b)^{2m+1}$.

Obviously $f'(a^-),\ f'(a^+)>0$

while $f'(b^-)<0$ and $f'(b^+)>0$

Hence $x=b$ is a point of local minima.

ILLUSTRATION 157: Let $f(x) = x^{n+1} + a.x^n$, where be 'a' is a positive real number. Then $x = 0$ is a point of

(a) local minimum for any integer n (b) local maximum for any integer n

(c) local minimum if n is an even integer (d) local minimum if n is an odd integer

SOLUTION: $f'(x) = x^{n-1}[(n+1)x + na]$. If n is even, then $f'(0^-) < 0$ and $f'(0^+) > 0$

Hence '0' is a point of minimum when n is even.

ILLUSTRATION 158: The function $f(x) = \int_1^x \{2(t-1)(t-2)^3 + 3(t-1)^2(t-2)^2\}\, dt$ attains its maximum at $x =$

(a) 1 (b) 2

(c) 3 (d) 4

SOLUTION: We have $f(x) = \int_1^x [2(t-1)(t-2)^3 + 3(t-1)^2(t-2)^2]dt$

$= \int_1^x (t-1)(t-2)^2[2(t-2) + 3(t-1)]\,dt$

$= \int_1^x (t-1)(t-2)^2(5t-7)dt$

$\therefore \quad f'(x) = (x-1)(x-2)^2(5x-7)$

Now for maximum or minimum, $f'(x) = 0$. This gives $x = 1, 2, 7/5$

(i) Consider $x = 1$

For $x < 1$; $\frac{dy}{dx} > 0$ and for $x > 1$; $\frac{dy}{dx} < 0$

$\therefore$ y is max. at $x = 1$

(ii) Consider $x = 7/5$

It will be min. as $\frac{dy}{dx}$ changes sign from –ive to +ive

(iii) At $x = 2$, $\frac{dy}{dx}$ does not change sign so $f(x)$ is neither max. nor min at $x = 2$.

ILLUSTRATION 159: If $f(x) = (x^2 - 1)^{n+1}(x^2 + x + 1)$, $n \in N$ and $f(x)$ has a local extremum at $x = 1$, then $n =$

(a) 2 (b) 3

(c) 4 (d) 5

SOLUTION: $\frac{dy}{dx} = (x^2-1)^{n+1}(2x+1) + (n+1)(x^2-1)^n . 2x(x^2+x+1)$

$= (x^2-1)^n[(x^2-1)(2x+1) + 2x(n+1)(x^2+x+1)]$

Since $f(x)$ has a local extremum; $\frac{dy}{dx}$ must change sign i.e., $f(1^+)$ and $f(1^-)$ should be of opposite signs.

Now we know that $x^2 + x + 1$ is always positive ($b^2 - 4ac$ = negative) and the first term tends to zero as $x \to 1$

$\Rightarrow$ Hence the sign of $\frac{dy}{dx}$ will depend upon $(x^2-1)^n$. If n is even then $f(1^+)$ and $f(1^-)$ will have the same sign, but they must be of opposite sign for the existence of extremum. Hence n must be odd. Hence (b) and (d) are the correct choices.

ILLUSTRATION 160: In a printed book the text must occupy S sq. cm of each page, the top and bottom margins must be a cm each and the right and left hand margins b cm each. If we are interested only in saving paper, then what must be the size of the printed page.

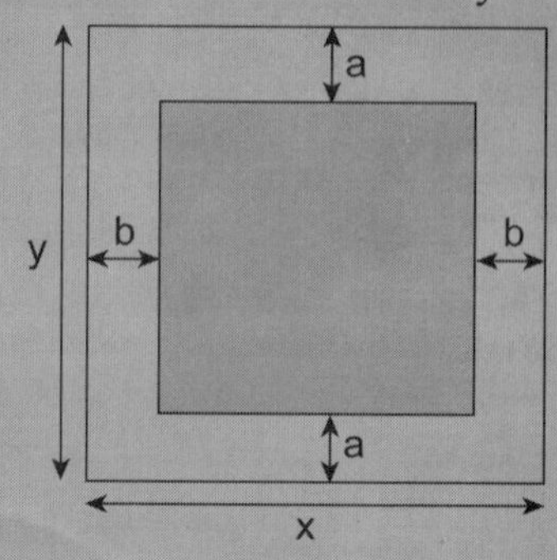

FIGURE 5.208

SOLUTION: $S=(x-2b)(y-2a)$

$\Rightarrow S=-2ax-2by+xy+4ab$

$\Rightarrow xy=S+2ax+2by-4ab$

$= S+2ax+2b\left[\dfrac{S}{x-2b}+2a\right]-4ab$

$\Rightarrow A(x)=S+2ax+2b\left[\dfrac{S}{x-2b}+2a\right]-4ab$

$\therefore A'(x)=0,$ [condition for saving paper]

$\Rightarrow A'(x)=2a-\dfrac{2bS}{(x-2b)^2}$ $\Rightarrow A'(x)=0$

$\Rightarrow x=2b+\sqrt{\dfrac{bS}{a}}$. Similarly $y=2a+\sqrt{\dfrac{Sa}{b}}$

ILLUSTRATION 161: A covered box of volume 73 cm^3 and the base sides in a ratio of 1 : 2 is to be made. What must the lengths of all sides be so that the total surface area is the least possible?

SOLUTION: Volume $= l \times b \times h$

Let $l = x$, $b = 2x$, $h = y$

$\Rightarrow 72cm^3 = x.2x.y$ $\Rightarrow 72=2x^2.y$

Total surface area $= 2\,[\,lb + bh + hl\,] = 2\,[x.2x+x.y+2x.y]$

$\Rightarrow f(x)=2\left[2x^2+3x.\dfrac{72}{2x^2}\right]$ $\Rightarrow f(x)=4x^2+\dfrac{6\times 72}{2x}$

$\Rightarrow f'(x)=8x-\dfrac{6\times 72}{2x^2}=0$ $\Rightarrow 8[x^3-27]=0$ $\Rightarrow x=3$

Therefore $b = 3$ cm, $l = 6$ cm, $h = 4$ cm.

SADDLE POINT

Consider the two curves; $y = x^3$ and $y = x^{1/3}$

For $f(y) = x^3$

$f'(x) = 3x^2$ Now $f'(x)|_{x=0} = 0$

And $f''(x) = 6x$, now $f''(0-h) = -6h < 0$ and

$f''(0+h) = 6h > 0$

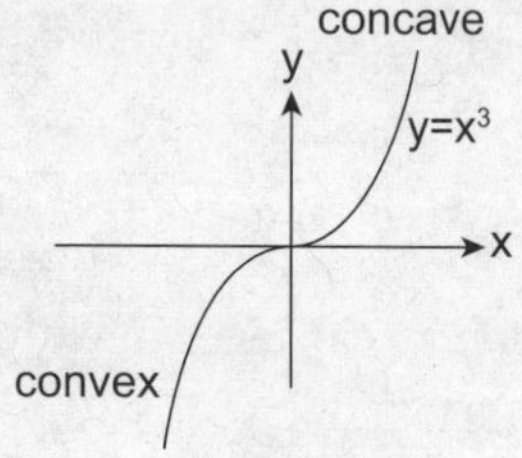

FIGURE 5.209

Here $f''(x)$ changes sign from positive to negative as it crosses $x = 0$; hence the curvature changes from convex to concave or in other words, $x = 0$ is a point of inflection. Also the tangent at $x = 0$ is $y = 0$ (Horizontal tangent)

Now for $f(x) = x^{1/3}$; $f'(x) = \dfrac{1}{3}\dfrac{1}{x^{2/3}}$ and

$f''(x) = \dfrac{1}{3}\left(\dfrac{-2}{3}\right)\times\dfrac{1}{x^{5/3}} = \dfrac{-2}{9}\dfrac{1}{x^{5/3}}$

$f''(0+h) = \dfrac{-2}{9}\dfrac{1}{h^{5/3}} < 0$ and $f''(0-h) = \dfrac{-2}{9}\dfrac{1}{(-h)^{5/3}} > 0$

Hence curvature of the graph changes from concave to convex as it crosses $x = 0$. Hence $x = 0$ is a point of inflection. But the tangent $f(x)$ at $x = 0$ is $x = 0$ i.e., vertical tangent (non-horizontal tangent).

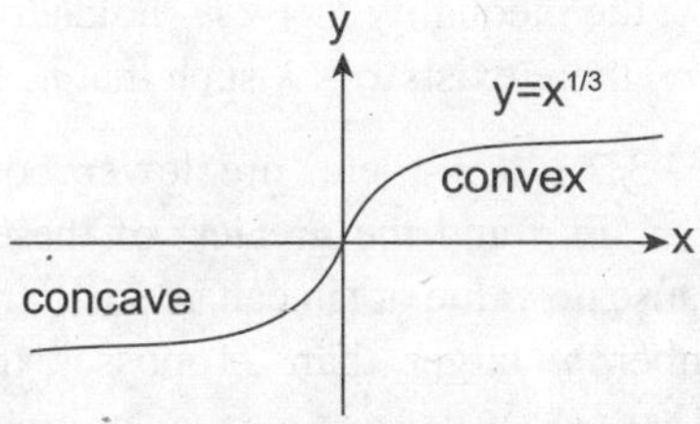

FIGURE 5.210

Now a saddle point is defined as a point where an increasing/decreasing graph can be envisioned to have a temporary resting spot i.e., a point of inflection where $f'(x) = 0$.

Therefore A saddle point is a special case of the point of inflection.

Hence; in the above mentioned two cases $x = 0$ is a saddle point for $f(x) = x^3$ and not for $f(x) = x^{1/3}$

ILLUSTRATION 162: Consider the curve $y = \dfrac{x}{1+x^2}$; find the points of inflection and the saddle points

SOLUTION: Given $f(x) = \dfrac{x}{1+x^2}$

$$\Rightarrow \; f'(x) = \frac{1(1+x^2)-2x(x)}{(1+x^2)^2} = \frac{1-x^2}{(1+x^2)^2}$$

$$\text{And } f''(x) = \frac{-2x(1+x^4+2x^2)-(1-x^2)\times 2(1+x^2)\times 2x}{(1+x^2)^4}$$

$$= \frac{-2x\left[(1+x^4+2x^2)+(2-2x^4)\right]}{(1+x^2)^4}$$

$$= -2x\frac{(-x^4+2x^2+3)}{(1+x^2)^4} = 2x\frac{(x^4-2x^2-3)}{(1+x^2)^4} = \frac{2x(x^2-3)}{(1+x^2)^3}$$

Wavy curve of $f'(x)$

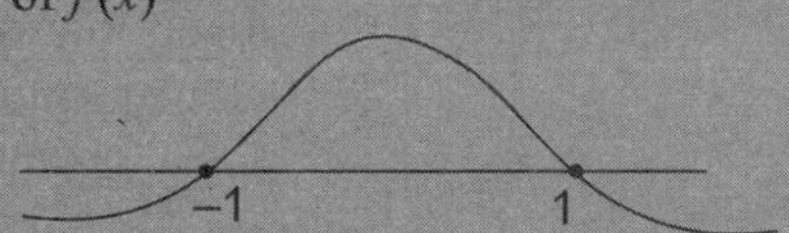

FIGURE 5.211

Wavy curve of $f''(x)$

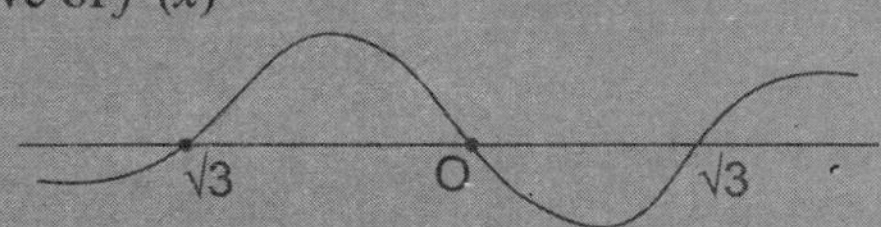

FIGURE 5.212

Now as $f'(-1) = 0$ and $f'(1-h) < 0$ and $f'(-1+h) > 0$; then $x = -1$ is a point of local minima

And as $f'(1) = 0$ and $f'(1-h) > 0$ and $f'(1+h) < 0$; then $x = 1$ is a point of local maxima

And the curve changes from concave down to concave up as it crosses $x = -\sqrt{3}$; hence $x = -\sqrt{3}$ is a point of inflection.

Similarly $x = 0$ and $x = \sqrt{3}$ are also points of inflection.

Now; since there is no point of inflection at which $f'(x) = 0$ (i.e., tangent to the curve is horizontal); hence no saddle point.

■ BOUNDEDNESS

A function $f(x)$ whose values lie between two real and finite numbers for all possible inputs that can be given to it is called bounded function. *e.g.*, $f(x)$ = sin x, cos x, $\frac{1}{x^2+1}, \frac{2x}{x^2+1}, \frac{x^2-1}{x^2+1}$ etc.

An expression of x say $f(x)$ is said to be bounded if we can find two real and finite numbers m and M. such that all the possible values of function lie between them. *i.e.*, $m < f(x) < M$ or $m \le f(x) \le M \;\forall\; x \in D_f$ (domain of $f(x)$). The m is called lower bound of the expression where as M is called upper bound of the expression. The least such number M(sayM_0), is called maximum value of the function and greatest value of m (say m_0) is called minimum value of the function. Following are the properties of lower and upper bound:

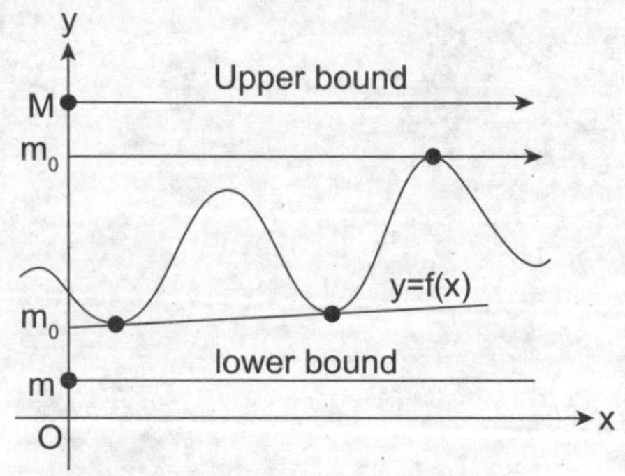

FIGURE 5.213

Existence of one lower bound (m) mean existence of infinitely many lower bounds m_k where k = 1, 2, 3,.... i.e., $< m_2 < m_1 < m <$ .... $< m_0 \le f(x)$ at $x = x_0$ then $y = m_0$ is greatest of all the lower bounds called GLB and if $f(x) = m_0$ for some $x_0 \in D_f$, then $f(x_0) = m_0$ is the minimum value of $f(x)$ i.e., $f_{minimum} = m_0 \le f(x)$.

Existence of one upper bound mean existence of inifinitly many upper bounds, so $f(x) \le M_0 < M < M_1 < M_2 < M_3 <$ ....so $y = M_0$ is least upper bound and if $M_0 = f(x_0)$ for some $x_0 \in D_f$ then M_0 is called maximum value of $f(x)$.

Greatest Lower Bound

The greatest of all lower bounds is called G.L.B. (m_0) and if $f(x) = m_0$ for some $x_0 \in D_f$ then $f(x_0)$ is called minimum value of $f(x)$.

To number m_0 is called the greatest lower bound of the function $y = f(x)$ on a set x if

(i) $\forall\; x \in X$; the inequality $f(x) \ge m_0$ holds true

(ii) $\forall\; m > m_0$ there exists $x \in X$ such that $f(x) < m$

e.g., –3, –2, –3/2, ..., –1 etc. are lower bound for the function $f(x)$ = sin x and the greatest of these is –1 (i.e., $m_0 = -1$), because no value of sin can be smaller than –1 and no such number m larger than –1 posses this property $(i.e. \sin x > m \;\forall\; x \in \mathbb{R})$ therefore –1 is known as greatest lower bound (GLB) for sin x.

Also for any number $m > -1$; there exists real solutions for the inequality sinx < m, i.e., if $m = -0.9$; then there exists real solutions for the inequality sinx < –0.9.

Lowest Upper Bound

The smallest of all upper bounds is called L.U.B. (M_0) and if $f(x) = M_0$ for some $x_0 \in D_f$ then $f(x_0)$ is called maximum value of $f(x)$.

The number M_0 is called the least upper bound of the function $y = f(x)$ on a set X if

(i) $\forall\; x \in X$ the inequality $f(x) \le M_0$ holds true,

(ii) $\forall\; M' < M$ there exists. $x' \in X$ such that $f(x') > M'$.

e.g. Any real number larger than 1 is upper bound for sin x and 1 is the smallest such number called as least upper bound (LUB (M_0) = 1) because no value of sinx can exceed 1 and no number (M) smaller than 1 has this property $(i.e. \sin x < M \;\forall\; x \in \mathbb{R})$.

Also for any number $m < 1$; there exists real solutions for the inequality sin $x < m$ i.e., if, = 0.9; then there exists real. Solutions for the inequality sin $x > 0.9$

Since sin x assumes the above two values, –1 at x = $x = (4k-1)\frac{\pi}{2}$ & *at* $x = (4k+1)\frac{\pi}{2}$ where $k \in \mathbb{Z}$ therefore –1 is called minimum value and 1 is called maximum value of the function sin x.

■ GLOBAL MAXIMA AND GLOBAL MINIMA

Let $y = f(x)$ be a given function in an interval $[a, b]$ and $\alpha_1, \alpha_2, \alpha_3, \ldots, \alpha_4$ be the critical points and $f(\alpha_1), f(\alpha_2), f(\alpha_3), \ldots f(\alpha_n)$ be the values of the function at critical points.. The Greatest/largest/global maximum/absolute maximum values of a function in a closed interval $[a, b]$ is given by $M = \max\{f(a), f(\alpha_1), f(\alpha_2), f(\alpha_3), \ldots f(\alpha_n), f(b)\}$ and the least/smallest/Global minimum/absolute minimum of the function $f(x)$ in $[a, b]$ is given by $m = \min\,\{f(a), f(\alpha_1), f(\alpha_2), f(\alpha_3), \ldots f(\alpha_n), f(b)\}$. Let $y = f(x)$ be a given function in an interval (a, b).

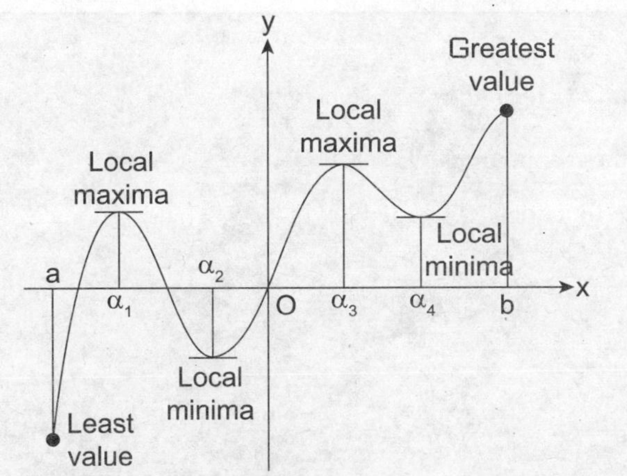

FIGURE 5.214

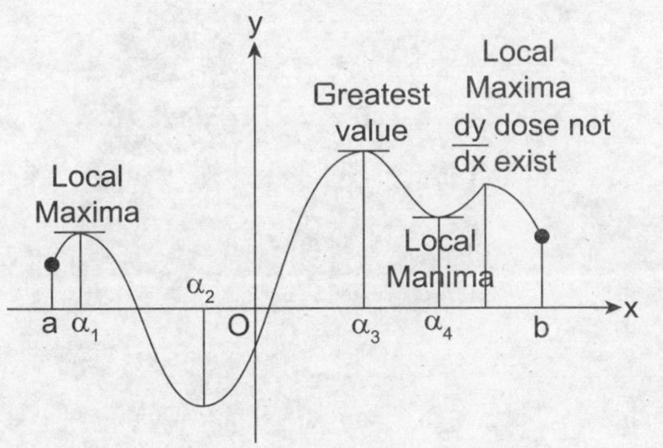

FIGURE 5.215

The Greatest/largest/global maximum/absolute maximum values of a function in an open interval (a, b) is given by M = max $\{f(a^+), f(\alpha_1), f(\alpha_2), f(\alpha_3), \ldots, f(\alpha_n), f(b^-)\}$ the least/smallest/Global minimum/absolute minimum of the function $f(x)$ in $[a, b]$ is given by m = max $\{f(a^+), f(\alpha_1), f(\alpha_2), f(\alpha_3), \ldots, f(\alpha_n), f(b^-)\}$

■ CAUTION

If M or m happen to be $f(a^+)/f(b^-)$ then we conclude that $f(x)$ does not attain the respective global maximum/minimum value. and the range remains the open interval. e.g., for the function $f(x) = x \ \forall\ x \in [1, 2]$; the graph of the function is as shown below.

Here $f(1)$ is the absolute minima and $f(2)$ is the absolute maxima.

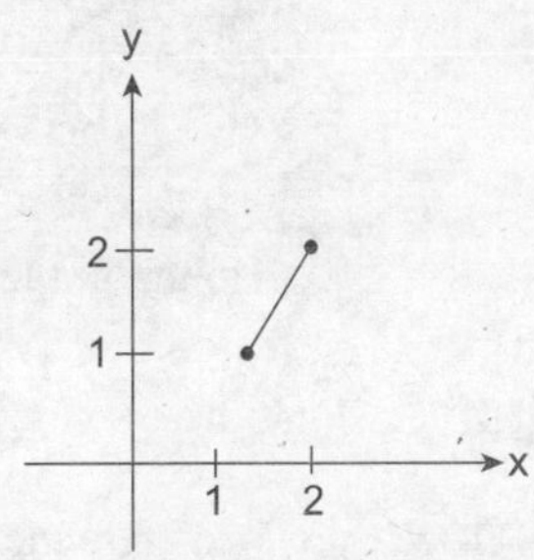

FIGURE 5.216

However if the function is defined on an open interval i.e., $f(x) = x \ \forall\ x \in (1, 2)$; then graph of the function is as shown below

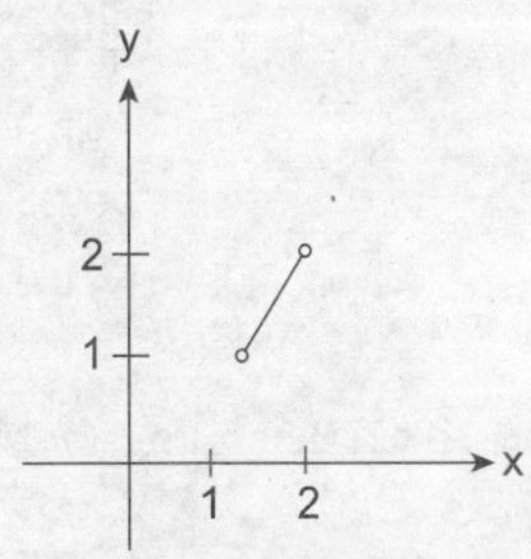

FIGURE 5.217

There $f(1)^+$ *is* the local minima and $f(2^-)$ is the local maxima; thereby we conclude that $f(x)$ does not attain the respective global maxima as well as the global minima and the range of the function will be (1, 2)

ILLUSTRATION 163: The image of the interval [– 1, 3] under the mapping $f(x) = 4x^3 - 12x$ is

(a) [– 2, 0]
(b) [– 8, 72]
(c) [– 8, 0]
(d) None of these

SOLUTION: To find the image of the given interval, we must find the set of values of $f(x)$ for $x \in [-1, 3]$.

By virtue of the continuity of $f(x)$, the images is the interval $\left[\min\limits_{x\in[-1,3]} f(x), \max\limits_{x\in[-1,3]} f(x)\right]$

The critical points of $f(x)$ are given by $f'(x) = 12x^2 - 12 = 12(x^2 - 1) = 0$

That is, $x = \pm 1$, so that $f(1) = 4(1) - 12 = -8$, $f(-1) = -4 + 12 = 8$ and

$f(3) = 4(27) - 12(3) = 108 - 36 = 72.$

$\therefore \max_{x \in [-1, 3]} f(x) = f(3) = 72$ and $\min_{x \in [-1, 3]} f(x) = f(1) = -8$

Hence the image of $[-1, 3]$ under the mapping $f(x)$ is $[-8, 72]$.

ILLUSTRATION 164: Find the greatest and least values of the function $x^3 - 18x^2 + 96x$ in $[0, 9]$

SOLUTION: Let $f(x) = x^3 - 18x^2 + 96x$

For maximum or minimum of $f(x)$

$\Rightarrow f'(x) = 3x^2 - 36x + 96 = 0$

$\Rightarrow 3(x-4)(x-8) = 0 \qquad \Rightarrow x = 4, 8$

Now, we have $f(0) = 0, f(4) = 160, f(8) = 128, f(9) = 135.$

Hence in the given interval: greatest value of $f(x) = 160$ and least value of $f(x) = 0$

ILLUSTRATION 165: Find the maximum and minimum value of $f(x) = \dfrac{e^x + e^{-x}}{2}$ for all $x \in [-\ln 2, \ln 7]$

SOLUTION: $f(x)$ is differentiable at all x in its domain

$\therefore f(x) = 0 \qquad \Rightarrow \dfrac{e^x - e^{-x}}{2} = 0 \qquad \Rightarrow x = 0$

We need to check the values of $f(x)$ at $x = 0$, and at the end points.

$x = -\ln 2$, and $x = \ln 7$.

The values of f are $f(0) = 1$,

$f(-\ln 2) = 5/4$

$f(\ln 7) = 25/7$

Clearly, the function has greatest value 25/7 at $x = \ln 7$, and the smallest value of 1 at $x = 0$.

ILLUSTRATION 166: Determine the greatest and the least values of the following piece wise defined function

$$f(x) = \begin{cases} 2x^2 + \dfrac{2}{x^2} & \text{for} \quad -2 \le x < 0;\ 0 < x \le 2 \\ 1 & \text{for} \quad x = 0 \end{cases}$$

SOLUTION: In the present case $f(x)$ is not continuous at $x = 0$

Hence our method of finding the absolute extrema will vary slightly

Equating $f'(x) = 0$, we have $4(x - 1/x^3) = 0$

$\Rightarrow x = \pm 1$

Now $f(-2) = 17/2 = f(2); f(-1) = 4 = f(1); f(0) = 1$

Generally students reply that the greatest value of $f(x) = 17/2$ and least value of $f(x) = 1$ but it is however not true. We have already mentioned that $f(x)$ is discontinuous at $x = 0$. We can see that when $x \to 0; f(x) \to \infty$. Thus, greatest value of $f(x)$ is not defined however the least value of $f(x) = 1$ is true.

ILLUSTRATION 167: If $f(x) = \int_x^{x^2} (t-1)\, dt$, $1 \le x \le 2$, then global maximum value of $f(x)$ is:

(a) 1 (b) 2

(c) 4 (d) 5

SOLUTION: Let $f'(x) = 2x^3 - 3x + 1$

$\Rightarrow f''(x) = 6x^2 - 3 > 0$ for $x > 1$

$\Rightarrow f'(x)$ is increasing in (1, 2]

$\Rightarrow f'(x) > f'(1)\ \forall\ x \in (1, 2]$

$\Rightarrow f'(x) > 0$

$\Rightarrow f(x)$ is increasing in (1, 2]

$\Rightarrow$ Max $f(x) = f(2)$

ILLUSTRATION 168: Find the greatest and least values, if any, of the following functions $f(x) = \sin(\sin x)$, $x \in R$.

SOLUTION: Here $f(x) = \sin(\sin x)$, $x \in R$

We know that $-1 \le \sin x \le 1$ for all $x \in R$

$\therefore\ \sin(-1) \le \sin(\sin x) \le \sin 1$,

for all $x \in R$

[sinx is an increasing function on [–1, 1]]

$\Rightarrow -\sin 1 \le f(x) \le \sin 1$ for all $x \in R$

Hence the greatest value of $f(x)$ in sin1 and its least value is –sin1

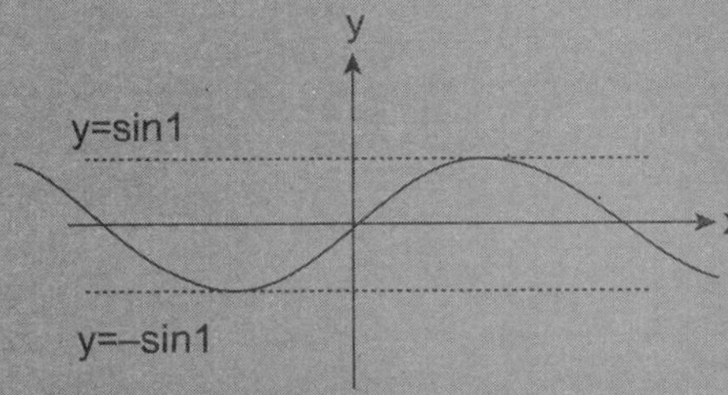

FIGURE 5.218

ILLUSTRATION 169: Discuss maxima and minima of $f(x) = |x^2 - 9|$ on [–5, 5]

SOLUTION: $f(x) = \begin{cases} x^2 - 9 & : \ -5 \le x < -3 \\ 9 - x^2 & : \ -3 \le x < 3 \\ x^2 - 9 & : \ 3 \le x \le 5 \end{cases}$

Clearly $f(x)$ is continuous everywhere

$f(x) = \begin{cases} 2x & : -5 \le x < -3 \\ \text{does not exists} & : x = -3 \\ -2x & : -3 \le x < 3 \\ \text{does not exists} & : x = 3 \\ 2x & : 3 < x \le 5 \end{cases}$

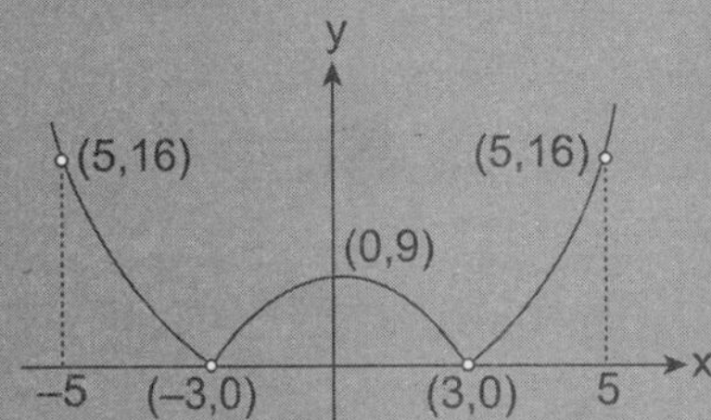

FIGURE 5.219

$f(x) = 0$ at $x = 0$ when $f(x) = -2x$, $-3 < x < 3$ and at $x = -3$ and 3, $f(x)$ is continuous but not differentiable so critical points are – 3, 0, 3. From the graph, it is clear that the (0, 9) is the point of maxima and (0, –3), (0, 3) are the points of minima.

x	-5	-3	0	3	5
$f(x)$	16	0	9	0	16
Result	Greatest	Local minima and also absolute minimum	Local minima not greatest	Local minima and also absolute minimum	Greatest

ILLUSTRATION 170: Show that the function $x^3 - 3x^2 + 6x + 4$ has neither a maximum nor minimum.

SOLUTION: Let $y = f(x) = x^3 - 3x^2 + 6x + 4$ ...(i)

$\therefore\ \dfrac{dy}{dx} = 3x^2 - 6x + 6 = 3(x^2 - 2x + 2)$

For maximum or minimum value of y, $\frac{dy}{dx} = 0$

$\therefore \quad 3x^2 - 6x + 6 = 0 \qquad \therefore \quad x = \frac{6 \pm \sqrt{36-72}}{6} = \frac{6 \pm 6i}{6} = 1 \pm i$

$\therefore \quad \frac{dy}{dx} \neq 0$ for any real value of x and $\frac{dy}{dx}$ exists at all x.

Therefore, y has neither a maximum nor a minimum value.

ILLUSTRATION 171: Find the greatest and least values of the following functions on the indicated intervals:

(a) $f(x) = 2x^3 - 3x^2 - 12x + 1$ on [–2, 5/2] (b) $f(x) = x^2 \ln x$ on [1, e]

SOLUTION: (a) Let $f(x) = 2x^3 - 3x^2 - 12x + 1$

$\Rightarrow \quad f'(x) = 6x^2 - 6x - 12$

It vanishes at two points: $x_1 = -1$ and $x_2 = 2$. They both lie inside the indicated interval [–2, 5/2]; consequently both of them must be taken into consideration. To find the extreme values of the function it is necessary to compute its values at the points x_1 and x_2 and also at the end points of the segment.

$f(-2) = -3, f(-1) = 8;\ f(2) = -19,\ f(5/2) = -16\frac{1}{2}$

Hence the greatest value is $f(-1) = 8$ and the least $f(2) = 19$.

(b) Find the critical points: $f'(x) = x(1 + 2\ln x)$. The derivative $f'(x)$ does not vanish inside the given interval [1, e]. Therefore there are no critical points inside the indicated interval. It now remains to compute the values of the function at the end-points of the interval [1, e]; $f(1) = 0; f(e) = e^2$.

Thus $f(1) = 0$ is the least value of the function and $f(e) = e^2$, the greatest.

ILLUSTRATION 172: Find the greatest and the least value of the function $f(x) = \tan^{-1}\frac{1-x}{1+x}$ on the intervals [0, 1].

SOLUTION: Let $f'(x) = \frac{1}{1+\left(\frac{1-x}{1+x}\right)^2} \cdot \left[\frac{-(1+x)-(1-x)}{(1+x)^2}\right] = \frac{(1+x)^2}{2(1+x^2)} \cdot \frac{(-2)}{(1+x)^2} = -\frac{1}{1+x^2} < 0$

$\Rightarrow f(0) = \tan^{-1}(1)$

$\Rightarrow$ $f(x)$ is monotonically decreasing function in $0 \leq x \leq 1$

$\Rightarrow \quad f(0) \geq f(x) \geq f(1)$

$\Rightarrow \quad f_{max} = f(0) = \tan^{-1}(1) = \frac{\pi}{4}$

$\Rightarrow \quad f_{min} = f(1) = \tan^{-1}(0) = 0$

ILLUSTRATION 173: Find the greatest and the least value of the function $f(x) = \frac{a^2}{x} + \frac{b^2}{1-x}$ on the intervals (0, 1). ($a > 0, b > 0$)

SOLUTION: Let $f'(x)=\dfrac{-a^2}{x^2}+\dfrac{b^2}{(1-x)^2}$

Now $f'(x)=0$ $\Rightarrow \dfrac{a^2}{b^2}=\dfrac{x^2}{(1-x)^2}$

$\Rightarrow \pm\dfrac{a}{b}=\dfrac{x}{1-x}$ $\Rightarrow \pm\dfrac{a}{b}=\dfrac{x-1+1}{1-x}$

$\Rightarrow \pm\dfrac{a}{b}=-1+\dfrac{1}{1-x}$ $\Rightarrow 1\pm\dfrac{a}{b}=\dfrac{1}{1-x}$

$\Rightarrow \dfrac{b\pm a}{b}=\dfrac{1}{1-x}$ or $1-x=\dfrac{b}{b\pm a}$

$\Rightarrow x=\dfrac{b\pm a-b}{b\pm a}$ or $x=\dfrac{\pm a}{b\pm a}$

$f(0)=$ function does not exist and $\lim\limits_{x\to 0^+} f(x)\to\infty$

$f(1)=$ function does not exist and $\lim\limits_{x\to 1^-} f(x)\to\infty$

$$f\left(\frac{\pm a}{b\pm a}\right)=\frac{a^2(b\pm a)}{\pm a}+\frac{b^2.(b\pm a)}{b}=\pm a\,(b\pm a)+b(b\pm a)$$

$=(b\pm a)(b\pm a)=(b\pm a)^2$ i.e., least value

ILLUSTRATION 174: If $f(x)$ $\cos x+\dfrac{1}{2}\cos 2x-\dfrac{1}{3}\cos 3x$ then the difference between the greatest and least values of the function is

(a) $\dfrac{3}{8}$ (b) $\dfrac{8}{7}$

(c) $\dfrac{9}{4}$ (d) $\dfrac{2}{3}$

SOLUTION: The function is periodic with period 2π. Hence the required difference is the difference between greatest and least values in the interval $[0, 2\pi]$.

$$\frac{dy}{dx}=-(\sin x+\sin 2x-\sin 3x)$$

$$=-\left(2\sin\frac{3x}{2}\cos\frac{x}{2}-2\sin\frac{3x}{2}\cos\frac{3x}{2}\right)$$

$$=-2\sin\frac{3x}{2}\left(\cos\frac{x}{2}-\cos\frac{3x}{2}\right)=-2\sin\frac{3x}{2}.2\sin x.\sin\frac{x}{2}$$

$\dfrac{dy}{dx}=0$ at $x=0,\dfrac{2\pi}{3}$, π, 2π in $[0, 2\pi]$

Corresponding values of y at the above points are $y=\dfrac{7}{6},\dfrac{-13}{12},\dfrac{-1}{6},\dfrac{7}{6}$ respectively

Hence greatest value is $\dfrac{7}{6}$ and least is $\dfrac{-13}{12}$; then the difference is $\dfrac{7}{6}-\left(\dfrac{-13}{12}\right)=\dfrac{27}{12}=\dfrac{9}{4}$

ALGEBRA OF GLOBAL EXTREMA

I. If $y = f(x)$ has a local maximum at $x = a$ then $y = -f(x)$ has a local minimum at $x = a$ and vice-versa.

For example, $y = \sin(x)$ has local maximum at $x = \dfrac{\pi}{2}$.

Hence $y = -\sin(x)$ has a local minimum at $x = \dfrac{\pi}{2}$

Similarly, $y = e^{|x|}$ has a local minimum at $x = 0$.

Hence, $y = -e^{|x|}$ has a local maximum at $x = 0$.

If two functions f and g attain their greatest (least) value at $x = a$ then $y = f(x) + g(x)$ also attains its greatest (least) value at $x = a$.

Proof: If $f(a - h) < f(a) < f(a + h)$
$g(a - h) < g(a) < g(a + h)$
then $f(a - h) + g(a - h) < f(a) + g(a) > f(a + h) + g(a + h)$

For example, the greatest value of $y = \cos^2 x + \dfrac{1}{x^4+1}$ is 2 when $x = 0$, since both $\cos^2 x$ and $\dfrac{1}{x^4+1}$ attain their greatest values at $x = 0$.

ILLUSTRATION 175: Find the minimum value of the function $f(x) = 8^x + 8^{-x} + 4(4^x + 4^{-x})$, $\forall x \in \mathbb{R}$.

SOLUTION: $f(x) = \left(8^x + \dfrac{1}{8^x}\right) + 4\left(4^x + \dfrac{1}{4^x}\right)$

Both the functions $8^x + \dfrac{1}{8^x}$ and $4^x + \dfrac{1}{4^x}$ attain the least values at $x = 0$

Hence, the minimum values of $f(x) = 1 + 1 + 4(1 + 1) = 10$.

II. If f and g are non-negative function which attain their greatest (least) values at $x = a$, then $y = f(x)\,g(x)$ also attains its greatest (least) values at $x = a$. For example, $y = (1 + \sin^2 x)\sin^3 x$ attains the maximum value 2 at $x = \pi/2$, since both $(1 + \sin^2 x)$ and $\sin^3 x$ attains their greatest value at $x = \dfrac{\pi}{2}$.

III. If f is such that $f(x)$ is maximum (minimum) at $x = a$ provided $f(a) \neq 0$; then $\dfrac{k}{f(x)}$ is minimum (maximum) at $x = a$ (where k is a positive constant) and if k is a negative constant, then $\dfrac{k}{f(x)}$ is maximum/minimum at the point $x = a$ where $f(x)$ is maximum/minimum (provided $f(a) \neq 0$). i.e.,

k	f(x) at x = a	k/f(x) at x = a
Positive	maximum	minimum
	minimum	maximum
Negative	maximum	maximum
	minimum	minimum

IV. If f is non-negative and g is positive so that f attains its greatest (least) value at $x = a$ and g attains its least (greatest) value at $x = a$ then $y = \dfrac{f(x)}{g(x)}$ attains its greatest (least) value at $x = a$. For example $y = \dfrac{1+|\cos x|}{3+\cos x}$ attains the maximum value of 1 at $x = \pi$.

Similarly $y = \dfrac{|\sin x| + |\operatorname{cosec} x|}{3+\cos 4x}$ attains the minimum values at $x = \dfrac{\pi}{2}$ and the minimum values is $\dfrac{2}{3+1} = \dfrac{1}{2}$

V. If $f(x)$ is continuous on $[a, b]$ and $g(x)$ is continuous on $[m, M]$, where m and M are the absolute minimum and the absolute maximum of f on $[a, b]$, then max gof = max $g(x)$

$x \in [a, b]; x \in [m, M]$ and min gof = min $g(x)$

$x \in [a, b]; x \in [m, M]$

EVEN/ODD FUNCTION

(i) An even function has an extremum at $x = 0$; provided it is defined in the immediate neighbourhood of $x = 0$

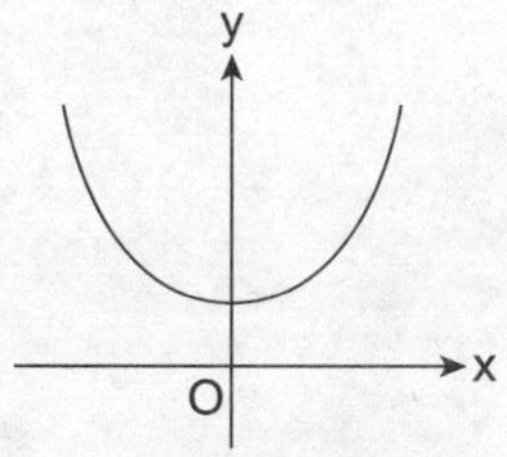

FIGURE 5.220

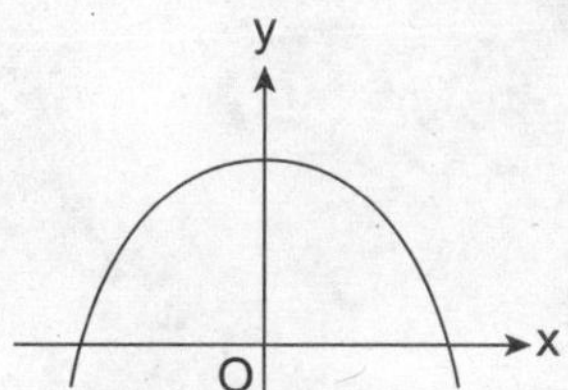

FIGURE 5.221

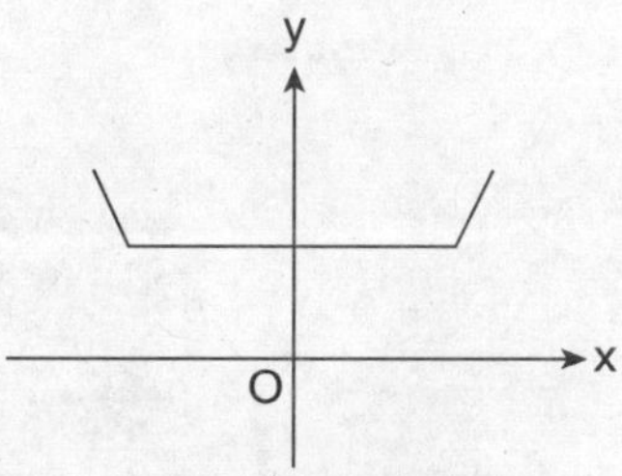

FIGURE 5.222

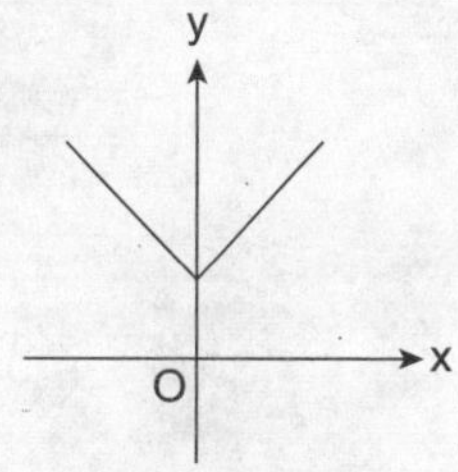

FIGURE 5.223

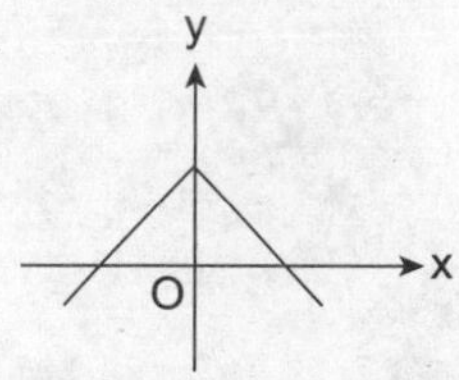

FIGURE 5.224

(ii) If an even function f has a local maximum (minimum) at $x = a$ then it also has a local maximum (minimum) at $x = -a$.
For example, $y = x^4 - 8x^2$ has local minimum at $x = \pm 2$ and a local maximum at $a = 0$.
Also $y = \cos x$ has a local minimum at $x = \pm\frac{\pi}{2}$ and maximum at $x = 0$.

(iii) If an odd function f has a local maximum (minimum) at $x = a$ then it has a local minimum (maximum) at $x = -a$. For example, $y = \sin x$ has a local maximum at $x = \pi/2$ and a local minimum at $x = -\pi/2$.

ILLUSTRATION 176: Find the greatest and the least value of the function $F(x) = \frac{\sin 2x}{\sin(x+\pi/4)}$ on the interval $\left[0, \frac{\pi}{2}\right]$

SOLUTION: Clearly function $F(x)$ is continuous and differentiable on $[0, \pi/2]$.

Given $F(x) = \frac{\sin 2x}{\sin\left(x+\frac{\pi}{4}\right)}$

$$\Rightarrow \quad F'(x) \frac{2\cos 2x \ \sin\left(x+\frac{\pi}{4}\right) - \sin 2x \cos\left(x+\frac{\pi}{4}\right)}{\left(\sin\left(x+\frac{\pi}{4}\right)\right)^2}$$

Now for greatest or least value; we equate $F'(x) = 0$

$\Rightarrow$ $2\cos 2x \sin(x + \pi/4) = \sin 2x \cos(x + \pi/4)$

If $x \neq \pi/4$; then we can say $2\tan\left(x+\frac{\pi}{4}\right) = \tan 2x$

$\Rightarrow 2\left(\frac{1-\tan x}{1+\tan x}\right)=\frac{1-\tan^2 x}{1+\tan^2 x}$ $\Rightarrow \frac{2}{1+\tan x}=\frac{1+\tan x}{1+\tan^2 x}$

$\Rightarrow$ 2 + 2tan²x = 1 + tan²x + 2 tanx

$\Rightarrow$ tan²x – 2tanx + 1 = 0

$\Rightarrow$ tanx = ± 1 $\Rightarrow$ x = ± π/4 (Rejected)

Clearly there is one value of x (i.e π/4) satisfying $F'(x) = 0$

∴ Critical point = π/4

Now, $F(0) = 0$

F(π/4) = 1

F(π/2) = 0

∴ greatest value = 1 and least value 0

Aliter: Using sin(A + B) = sinA cosB + cosA sinB; we can say that $\sin\left(\frac{\pi}{4}+x\right)=\frac{1}{\sqrt{2}}$ (sinx + cos x)

Also sin2x = (sin x + cos x)² – 1

Now, we represent the given function as a composite function $F(x) = f(g(x))$

Where $y = g(x) = \sin x + \cos x$ and $f(y)=\frac{y^2-1}{\frac{1}{\sqrt{2}}y}$

Let us find the greatest and the least value of $g(x)$. The critical points of $g(x)$ are the roots of the equation cosx – sinx = 0 where only $x = \pi/4$ lies in the interval [0, π/2].

Now, g(0), g(π/4) and g(π/2), implies that the range of $g(x)$ is [1, √2].

Now, $f'(y)=\sqrt{2}\left(1+\frac{1}{y^2}\right)>0$ for $y \in [1, \sqrt{2})$. Consequently, the function $f(y)$ increases on the interval [1, √2] and attains its greatest and least values at the right and left endpoints of the interval, respectively

$$\therefore \quad \min_{y\in[1,\sqrt{2}]} f(y) = f(1) = 0 \text{ and } \max_{y\in[1,\sqrt{2}]} f(y)=f(\sqrt{2})=\sqrt{2}\left(\frac{(\sqrt{2})^2-1}{\sqrt{2}}\right)=1$$

Therefore the greatest value of $f(x) = 1$ and least value of $f(x) = 0$.

ILLUSTRATION 177: Find the extrema of the following functions:

(a) $f(x)=\frac{50}{3x^4+8x^3-18x^2+60}$ **(b)** $f(x)=\sqrt{e^{x^2}-1}$

SOLUTION: **(a)** $f(x)=\frac{50}{3x^4+8x^3-18x^2+60}$

Here it is simpler to find the extrema of the function $g(x)=3x^4+8x^3-18x^2+60$.

Since $g'(x)=12x^3+24x^2-36x=12x(x^2+2x-3)$; Now, g'(x) = 0 $\Rightarrow$ $x = -3, 0, 1$

and $g''(x)=12(3x^2+4x-3)$

the critical points are $x_1=-3,\ x_2=0,\ x_3=1$ and the character of the extrema is readily determined from the sign of the second derivative $g''(-3)>0$.

Hence at the point $x_1 = -3$ the function $f_1(x)$ has minimum and the given function $f(x)$ obviously has a maximum i.e., $f(-3) = -2/3$

$\Rightarrow$ $g''(0) < 0$ hence at the point $x_2 = 0$ the function $g(x)$ has a maximum and $f(x)$ has a minimum

i.e., $f(0) = 5/6$; $g''(1) > 0$

Therefore at the point $x_3 = 1$; the function $g(x)$ has a minimum and $f(x)$ has a maximum i.e., $f(1) = 50/53$.

(b) In this case it is easier to find the points of extremum of the radicand; Let $g_1(x) = e^{x^2} - 1$ which coincide with the points of extremum of the function $f(x)$.

Let us find the critical points of $g(x)$

$$g'(x) = 2xe^{x^2}$$

$\Rightarrow$ $g'(x) = 0$ at the point $x = 0$.

Determine the sign of the second derivative at the point $x = 0$.

$$g''(x) = 2e^{x^2}(1 + ex^2) \qquad \Rightarrow g''(0) = 2 > 0$$

Therefore, the point $x = 0$ is a minimum of the function $g(x)$; it will also be a minimum of the given function $f(x)$; i.e., $f(0) = 0$.

ILLUSTRATION 178: Find the local maximum and minimum values of the function $f(x) = \dfrac{100}{x^4 - 6x^3 + 12x^2 + 4}$; also find its range.

SOLUTION: Here it is simpler to find the extrema of the function $g(x) = x^4 + 6x^3 + 12x^2 + 4$

$g'(x) = 4x^3 - 18x^2 + 24x = 2x(2x^2 - 9x + 12)$

$(\because 2x^2 - 9x + 12 > 0 \ \forall \ x \in \mathbb{R})$

The critical points are $x = 0$

$\Rightarrow$ $g''(x) = 12(x^2 - 3x + 2)$

$\Rightarrow$ $g''(x)\big|_{x=0} > 0$

$\because$ $g''(0) > 0$; hence, at the point $x_2 = 0$ the function $g(x)$ has a minima and hence $g_{min} = 4$

$\Rightarrow$ $f_{max} = 25$

Also, $g_{max} = \infty$ $\qquad \Rightarrow f_{min} \to 0$

$\therefore$ range of $f(x) = (0, 25]$

ILLUSTRATION 179: Find the minimum values of the function $f(x) = x^{\frac{3}{2}} + x^{\frac{-3}{2}} - 4\left(x + \dfrac{1}{x}\right)$ for all permissible real x

SOLUTION: Domain for $f(x)$ is $x > 0$

$$f(x) = x^{3/2} + x^{-3/2} - 4\left(x + \frac{1}{x}\right)$$

$$f(x) = \left(\sqrt{x} + \frac{1}{\sqrt{x}}\right)^3 - 3\left(\sqrt{x} + \frac{1}{\sqrt{x}}\right) - 4\left[\left(\sqrt{x} + \frac{1}{\sqrt{x}}\right)^2 - 2\right]$$

Let $\sqrt{x} + \dfrac{1}{\sqrt{x}} = y$

Clearly $y=\sqrt{x}+\frac{1}{\sqrt{x}}\geq 2$ for $x>0$

$\Rightarrow$ $y \in [2, \infty]$

Let $g(y) = y^3 - 3y - 4y^2 + 8$

Now $g(y) = y^3 - 4y^2 - 3y + 8$ where $y \in [2, \infty]$

$g'(y) = 3yt^2 - 8y - 3 = (y - 3)(3y + 1)$

$\therefore$ $g'(y) = 0$

$\Rightarrow$ $y = 3$ $\quad (\because y \neq -1/3)$

And $g''(y) = 6y - 8$

$\Rightarrow$ $g''(3) = 10 > 0$

$\Rightarrow$ $g(3)$ is the absolute minimum

$g(3) = 27 - 9 - 36 + 8 = -10$

Hence $f_{\min} = g(3) = -10$

MISCELLANEOUS METHOD

Many problems of maxima/minima/range can be solved using elementary methods and without using calculus. It is essential for a student to know these methods as it may reduce the calculations and hence speedúp your solution.

As an example, it is obvious that if $f(x)=\frac{|x|}{1+x^2}$, then $f(x)=\left|\frac{1}{x+\frac{1}{x}}\right|$; $f(1)=\frac{1}{2}$ is the only maximum value of f, which is achieved when $x = \pm 1$.

It is to be noticed that some important problems of maxima and minima can be solved by elementary algebraical methods, without recourse to calculus.

ILLUSTRATION 180: Find the minimum value of $f(x) = 2x^2 + 3x + 4$.

SOLUTION: $f(x) = 2(x^2 + 3x/2 + 2) = 2(x + 3/4)^2 + 23/16$

Hence the function has the minimum value 23/16, corresponding to $x = -3/4$

ILLUSTRATION 181: Find the least value of $y = a^2x + b^2/x \ \forall \ x > 0$.

SOLUTION: The function $a^2x + b^2/x$ may be written in the form $\left(\sqrt{a^2x}-\sqrt{\frac{b^2}{x}}\right)^2+2\sqrt{a^2b^2}$, it is obvious that the expression can never be less than $2|ab|$ and this value is attained when $\sqrt{ax}=\sqrt{\frac{b}{x}}$, or $x=\sqrt{\frac{b}{a}}$

ILLUSTRATION 182: Find the range of $-3x^2 + 4x - 5$ for $x \in (0,2]$

SOLUTION: $f(0) = -5$ $\quad \because x \neq 0$ and only approaching towards 0

$\Rightarrow$ $\lim_{x\to 0} f(x) = -5$ and $f(2) = -3(2)^2 + 4(2) - 5 = -9$

$\frac{-b}{2a}=\frac{-4}{2\times(-3)}=\frac{2}{3}$

$\because \frac{2}{3} \in (0,2]$

$\therefore f\left(\frac{-b}{2a}\right)=\frac{-D}{4a}=\frac{-11}{3}$

$\therefore$ min value = –9 and max value = –11/3

$\Rightarrow$ Range [–9,–11/3]

ILLUSTRATION 183: Find the range of $y=\frac{x+2}{2x^2+3x+6}$, if x is real

SOLUTION: $y=\frac{x+2}{2x^2+3x+6}$

$\Rightarrow 2yx^2+3yx+6y=x+2$

$\Rightarrow 2yx^2+(3y-1)x+6y-2=0$ .....(i)

Case (i): If $y \neq 0$, then equation (i) is quadratic in x

$\because$ x is real

$\Rightarrow D \geq 0$

$\Rightarrow (3y-1)^2-8y(6y-2) \leq 0$ $\Rightarrow (3y-1)^2(13y+1) \leq 0$

$y \in \left[-\frac{1}{13},\frac{1}{3}\right]-\{0\}$

Case (ii): If $y = 0$, then equation becomes $x = -2$ which is possible as x is real

$\therefore$ Range $=\left[-\frac{1}{13},\frac{1}{3}\right]$

ILLUSTRATION 184: Find the range of the expression $\frac{x^2-4x+3}{x^2-7x+6}$, *for* $x \in \mathbb{R}$

SOLUTION: $\frac{x^2-4x+3}{x^2-7x+6}=\frac{(x-1)(x-3)}{(x-1)(x-6)},\ x \neq 1,6 = \frac{x-3}{x-6},\ x \neq 1,6$

Let $y=\frac{x-3}{x-6} \Rightarrow x-3=xy-6y$

$\Rightarrow x=\frac{3-6y}{1-y} \Rightarrow y \in R-\{1\}$

For $x=1$, $y=\frac{1-3}{1-6} \Rightarrow y=\frac{2}{5}$

Hence range of expression will be $R-\left\{1,\frac{2}{5}\right\}$

ILLUSTRATION 185: For $x \geq 0$, find the smallest value of the function $f(x)=\frac{4x^2+8x+13}{36(1+x)}$

SOLUTION: We have $f(x)=\frac{4x^2+8x+13}{36(1+x)}=\frac{4(x+1)^2+9}{36(1+x)}$

$\frac{1}{9}(x+1)+\frac{1}{4(x+1)} \geq \sqrt{\frac{1(x+1)}{9}\times\frac{1}{4(x+1)}}$ [$\because$ A.M $\geq$ G.M]

Equality occurs when $(x+1)^2 = \frac{9}{4}$ $\Rightarrow \frac{x+1}{9} + \frac{1}{4(x+1)} \geq 2 \times \frac{1}{2\times 3} = \frac{1}{3}$

$\Rightarrow x+1 = \frac{3}{2}$ *i.e* $x = \frac{1}{2}$ $x+1 = \frac{3}{2}$ *i.e* $x = \frac{1}{2}$ and the minimum value of $f(x)$ is $\frac{1}{3}$

ILLUSTRATION 186: If $a_1, a_2, \ldots\ldots a_n$ are positive real numbers whose product is a fixed number e, the minimum value of $a_1 + a_2 + a_3 + \ldots\ldots a_{n-1} + 2a_n$ is

(a) $n(2e)^{1/n}$
(b) $(n+1)e^{1/n}$
(c) $2ne^{1/n}$
(d) $(n+1)(2e)^{1/n}$

SOLUTION: $\because$ AM $\geq$ G.M

$$\frac{a_1 + a_2 + a_3 + \ldots.. + 2a_n}{n} \geq (a_1 a_2 a_3 \ldots.. 2a_n)^{1/n}$$

$$a_1 + a_2 + a_3 + \ldots. + 2a_n \geq n(2a_1 a_2 \ldots. a_n)^{1/n}$$

$$a_1 + a_2 + a_3 + \ldots\ldots + 2a_n \geq n(2e)^{1/n}$$

ILLUSTRATION 187: Divide 64 into two parts such that sum of the cubes of two parts is minimum.

SOLUTION: Let x and y be two positive numbers such that $x + y = 64$ ....(i)

Let $u = x^3 + y^3$ ....(ii)

Eliminate x from (ii) with the help of (i), then $u = (64 - y)^3 + y^3$

$\therefore \quad \frac{du}{dy} = 3(64-y)^2 + 3y^2$ ....(iii)

and $\frac{d^2u}{dy^2} = 6(64-y) + 6y = 384 > 0$ ....(iv)

For maximum or minimum of u, $\frac{du}{dy} = 0$

Then $3(64)(2y - 64) = 0$ $\therefore \; y = 32$

From (i) $x = 32$

It is clear from (iv), u is minimum

Hence $x = 32, y = 32$

ILLUSTRATION 188: Find two positive numbers x and y such that $x + y = 60$ and xy^3 is maximum.

SOLUTION: $x + y = 60$

$\Rightarrow x = 60 - y$ $\Rightarrow xy^3 = (60-y)y^3$

Let $f(y) = (60 - y)y3;\ y \in (0, 60)$ for maximizing $f(y)$ let us find critical points

$f'(y) = 3y^2(60 - y) - y^3 = 0$

$f'(y) = y^2(180 - 4y) = 0$

$\Rightarrow y = 45$

$f'(45^+) < 0$ and $f'(45^-) > 0$. Hence local maxima at $y = 45$.

So $x = 15$ and $y = 45$.

Aliter: $x + \frac{x}{3} + \frac{y}{3} = 60$ and $\frac{x + 3(y/3)}{9} \geq \sqrt{x\left(\frac{y}{3}\right)^3}$ $(\because \text{AM} \geq \text{GM})$

Equality occurs with $x = y/3$ $\Rightarrow x = 15$ and $y = 45$.

ILLUSTRATION 189: As a result of n measurements of an unknown quantity x the numbers $x_1, x_2, \ldots\ldots\ldots, x_n$ are obtained. It is required to find at what value of x the sum of the squares of the errors $f(x)=(x-x_1)^2+(x-x_2)^2+\ldots\ldots+(x-x_n)^2$ will be the least.

SOLUTION: Compute the derivative $f'(x)=2(x-x_1)+2(x-x_2)+\ldots\ldots+2(x-x_n)$

The only root of the derivative is $x=\dfrac{x_1+x_2+\ldots..+x_n}{n}$

Then for all x we have $f''(x)=2n>0$. Therefore the function $f(x)$ has its minimum at the point $x=\dfrac{x_1+x_2+\ldots+x_n}{n}$

Being the only minimum it coincides with the least value of the function.

And so the best (in the sense of the principle of the minimum squares) approximate value of an unknown quantity x is the arithmetic mean of the values $x_1, x_2, \ldots, x_n$.

ILLUSTRATION 190: If $a+b+c+d$ be constant, then find the condition for which $abcd$ have its maximum value.

SOLUTION: So long as any two, say a and b, are unequal we can without altering c and d (and thus keeping $a+b$ constant) increase ab, and therefore also $abcd$ by making a and b equal. Hence $abcd$ does not attain its maximum value until $a=b=c=d$. This is true by the virtue of symmetry.

ILLUSTRATION 191: If $x+y+z=a$, find the maximum value of xy^2z^3.

SOLUTION: $xy^2z^3=2^2\,3^3\,.x.\dfrac{y}{2}.\dfrac{y}{2}.\dfrac{z}{3}.\dfrac{z}{3}.\dfrac{z}{3}$ and its to be a maximum, where $x+\dfrac{y}{2}+\dfrac{y}{2}+\dfrac{z}{3}+\dfrac{z}{3}+\dfrac{z}{3}=a$; and for the greatest value of xy^2z^3, we equate $\dfrac{x}{1}=\dfrac{y}{2}=\dfrac{z}{3}=\dfrac{a}{6}$. Therefore the maximum value is $\dfrac{2^2.3^3.a^6}{6^6}=\dfrac{a^6}{2^4.3^3}$

ILLUSTRATION 192: What are the greatest and least values of $a\sin x+b\cos x$?

SOLUTION: $F(x)=a\sin x+b\cos x=\sqrt{a^2+b^2}\left(\dfrac{a}{\sqrt{a^2+b^2}}\sin x+\dfrac{b}{\sqrt{a^2+b^2}}\cos x\right)$

Let $\cos\alpha=\dfrac{a}{\sqrt{a^2+b^2}}$ & $\sin\alpha=\dfrac{b}{\sqrt{a^2+b^2}}$

$\Rightarrow\ f(x)=\sqrt{a^2+b^2}\sin(x+\alpha)$

And as the greatest and least values of a sine are 1 and –1, the maximum and minimum values required are $\sqrt{a^2+b^2}$ and $-\sqrt{a^2+b^2}$ respectively.

ILLUSTRATION 193: If λ, μ be real numbers such that $x^3-\lambda x^2+\mu x-6=0$ has its roots real and positive, then the minimum value of μ is

(a) $3\times\sqrt[3]{36}$ (b) 11

(c) 0 (d) None of these

SOLUTION: Let a, b, c be the roots. Then $ab+bc+ca=\mu$, $abc=6$.

Dividing, $\dfrac{1}{a}+\dfrac{1}{b}+\dfrac{1}{c}=\dfrac{\mu}{6}$.

$AM > GM$ $\Rightarrow\ \dfrac{\frac{1}{a}+\frac{1}{b}+\frac{1}{c}}{3}\geq\sqrt[3]{\dfrac{1}{abc}}$

or $\mu \geq 18.\sqrt[3]{\frac{1}{abc}} = 3.6^{2/3}$

$\therefore$ the minimum value of $\mu = 3.6^{2/3}$.

ILLUSTRATION 194: If $x, y \in \mathbb{R}$ and satisfy the equation $xy(x^2 + y^2) = x^2 - y^2$, where $x \neq 0$, then find the minimum possible value of $x^2 + y^2$.

SOLUTION: If $x = r\cos\theta$ and $y = r\sin\theta$, then $x^2 + y^2 = r^2$.

Hence we have to minimize r^2.

Now in the given equation substituting; $x = r\cos\theta$ and $y = r\sin\theta$

$\Rightarrow r^2\sin\theta\cos\theta\,(r^2\cos^2\theta + r^2\sin^2\theta) = r^2\cos^2\theta - r^2\sin^2\theta$

$\Rightarrow \frac{r^2}{2}\sin 2\theta \times r^2 = r^2\cos 2\theta$

$\Rightarrow \frac{r^2}{2}\sin 2\theta = \cos 2\theta$

$\Rightarrow \frac{r^2}{2} = \cot 2\theta$

$\Rightarrow r^2 = 2\cot 2\theta$

$\Rightarrow 0 < \cot 2\theta < \infty$

Now, $-\infty < \cot 2\theta < \infty$ but $r^2 > 0$

When $\theta = \frac{\pi}{4}$, minimum value of r^2 does not exist but greatest lower bond is 0.

ILLUSTRATION 195: Suppose that the power (P) at every point (x, y) in the plane Cartesian is defined by the formula $P = 1 - x^2 + 2y^2$

Show that the minimum power along the line $x + y = 1$ is -1.

SOLUTION: $P = 1 - x^2 + 2y^2$ where $x + y = 1$

Substituting $y = 1 - x$ in (P); we get

$\Rightarrow P = 1 - x^2 + 2(1 - x)^2 = 1 - x^2 + 2(1 + x^2 - 2x)$

$\Rightarrow P = x^2 - 4x + 3 = (x - 2)^2 - 1$

$\Rightarrow P_{min} = -1$

ILLUSTRATION 196: The range of the function $f(x) = \sqrt{9 - x^2} + \sqrt{x^2 - 4}$

SOLUTION: Let $x^2 = 9\cos^2\theta + 4\sin^2\theta$

Then $9 - x^2 = 9 - (9\cos^2\theta + 4\sin^2\theta)$

$= 9\sin^2\theta - 4\sin^2\theta$

$= 5\sin^2\theta$ and

$X^2 - 4 = 9\cos^2\theta + 4\sin^2\theta - 4$

$= 5\cos^2\theta$

$\therefore f(x) = \sqrt{5}\,|\sin\theta| + \sqrt{5}\,|\cos\theta|$

$\Rightarrow y_{min} = \sqrt{5}$ and $y_{max} = \sqrt{5}\left(\frac{1}{\sqrt{2}} + \frac{1}{\sqrt{2}}\right) = \sqrt{10}$

Hence the range of $f(x)$ is $\left[\sqrt{5}, \sqrt{10}\right]$.

ILLUSTRATION 197: A particle is moving on the curve defined parametrically by the system of equation $x = 1 - 2\cos^2 t$ and $y = \cos t$. If the particle is close to the origin when $t = \cos^{-1}(\alpha)$ for $0 \le t \le \pi/2$, then find the value of 'α'.

SOLUTION: Distance'd' from the origin is $= \sqrt{x^2 + y^2}$

$$\Rightarrow d = \sqrt{(1-2\cos^2 t)^2 + \cos^2 t}$$

$$\Rightarrow d = \sqrt{4\cos^4 t - 3\cos^2 t + 1}$$

$$\Rightarrow d = 2\sqrt{\left(\cos^2 t - \frac{3}{8}\right)^2 + \frac{16}{14} - \frac{9}{64}} \qquad \Rightarrow d = 2\sqrt{\left(\cos^2 t - \frac{3}{8}\right)^2 + \frac{7}{64}}$$

This is a quadratic in $\cos^2 t$, and will be minimum when $\cos^2 t = \frac{3}{8}$

$$\Rightarrow \cos t = \frac{\sqrt{3}}{2\sqrt{2}} \qquad \Rightarrow \cos t = \frac{\sqrt{6}}{4} \qquad \Rightarrow \alpha = \frac{\sqrt{6}}{4}$$

ILLUSTRATION 198: Find the minimum value of $f(x, y) = x^2 - 2x + y^2 + 4y$ when x and y are subjected to the restrictions $0 \le x \le 1$ and $0 \le y \le 1$

SOLUTION: We have $f(x, y) = x^2 + y^2 - 2x + 4y$

Let $(x, y) = (\cos\theta, \sin\theta)$, then $\theta \in [0, \pi/2]$ and $f(x, y) = f(\theta) = \cos^2\theta + \sin^2\theta - 2\cos\theta + 4\sin\theta = 1 - 2\cos\theta + 4\sin\theta$

$f'(\theta) = 4\cos\theta + 2\sin\theta > 0 \ \forall \ \theta \in [0, \pi/2]$

$\therefore \ f(\theta)$ is strictly increasing in $[0, \pi/2]$

$\therefore \ f(\theta)_{min} = f(0) = 1 - 2 = -1$

Alternative: $f(x, y) = (x-1)^2 + (y+2)^2 - 5$

So, to minimize f over the unit square is the same as minimizing the distance from a point in this square to the point of coordinates $(1, -2)$

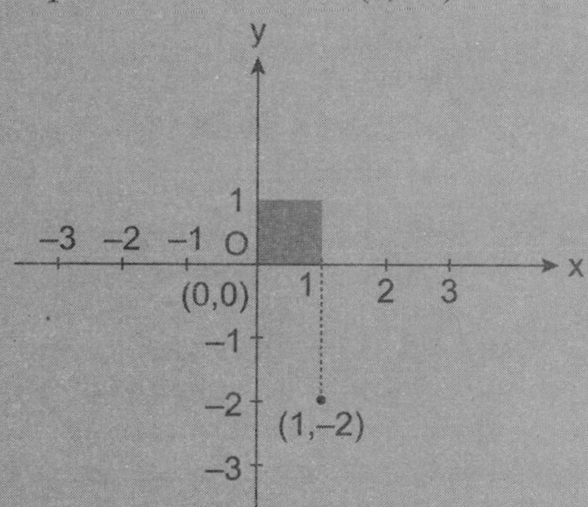

FIGURE 5.225

The nearest point to $(1, -2)$ in the square is then $(1, 0)$

So $f(1, 0) = -1$ must be the minimum value.

ILLUSTRATION 199: Find the least and the greatest value of $f(x, y) = x^2 + y^2 - xy$, where x and y are connected by the relation $x^2 + 9y^2 = 9$

SOLUTION: Here $x^2 + 9y^2 = 9$

$\Rightarrow$ —+ =

Let $x = 3\cos\theta$, $y = \sin\theta$

Hence, $f(x, y) = x^2 + y^2 - xy = 9\cos^2\theta + \sin^2\theta - 3\sin\theta\cos\theta$

$$= 9\left(\frac{1+\cos 2\theta}{2}\right) + \frac{1}{2}(1-\cos 2\theta) - \frac{3}{2}\sin 2\theta = 4\cos 2\theta - \frac{3}{2}\sin 2\theta + 5$$

Since we know that $a\sin\theta + b\cos\theta$ lies in between $-\sqrt{a^2+b^2}$ and $\sqrt{a^2+b^2}$

$\therefore$ the maximum/minimum values of $\left(4\cos 2\theta - \frac{3}{2}\sin 2\theta\right)$ are $\sqrt{\left(\frac{3}{2}\right)^2 + 4^2}$ and $-\sqrt{\left(\frac{3}{2}\right)^2 + 4^2}$

i.e., $\frac{\sqrt{73}}{2}$ and $-\frac{\sqrt{73}}{2}$

Hence, the greatest value of $f(x, y)$

$= \frac{\sqrt{73}}{2} + 5 = \frac{10+\sqrt{73}}{2}$ and the least value of $f(x, y) = -\frac{\sqrt{73}}{2} + 5 = \frac{10-\sqrt{73}}{2}$

ILLUSTRATION 200: Find the maximum and minimum values of $x^2 + y^2$ where, $ax^2 + 2hxy + by^2 = 1$

SOLUTION: Let $x = r\cos\theta$, $y = r\sin\theta$.

Then $x^2 + y^2 = r^2$,

Substituting these values of x and y in $ax^2 + 2hxy + by^2 = 1$; we get $r^2(a\cos^2\theta + 2h\sin\theta\cos\theta + b\sin^2\theta) = 1$

Now the problem reduces to that of finding the extreme values of r^2,

where $\frac{1}{r^2} = a\cos^2\theta + 2h\sin\theta\cos\theta + b\sin^2\theta$

Let us now define a function f as

$f(\theta) = a\cos^2\theta + 2h\sin\theta\cos\theta + b\sin^2\theta$ for $\theta \in [0, 2\pi]$ ...(1)

Since r^2 has a maximum or minimum according as $1/r^2$ has a minimum or a maximum, therefore, the extreme value of r^2 are the same as the extreme values of f, a maximum value of r^2 being a minimum value of f, and a minimum value of r^2 being maximum value of f.

We can write (1) as

$$f(\theta) = \frac{1}{2}(a+b) + \frac{1}{2}(a-b)\cos 2\theta + h\sin 2\theta \quad ...(2)$$

Now, maximum/minimum value of $\frac{1}{2}(a-b)\cos 2\theta + h\sin 2\theta$ is $\pm\sqrt{\left(\frac{1}{2}(a-b)\right)^2 + h^2}$

respectively.

The extreme values of 'f' are given by $\frac{1}{2}(a+b) \pm \frac{1}{2}\{(a-b)^2 + 4h^2\}^{1/2}$

Hence the maximum values of $x^2 + y^2$ i.e., r^2 is $\left[\frac{1}{2}(a+b) - \frac{1}{2}\{(a-b)^2 + 4h^2\}^{1/2}\right]^{-1}$ and the minimum value of $x^2 + y^2$ is $\left[\frac{1}{2}(a+b) + \frac{1}{2}\{(a-b)^2 + 4h^2\}^{1/2}\right]^{-1}$

TEXTUAL EXERCISE–2: (SUBJECTIVE)

1. Find the greatest (M) and least (m) values of the following functions on the indicated intervals:
   (a) $f(x) = xe^{-x}$ on $[0, \infty)$
   (b) $f(x) = \sqrt{(1-x^2)(1+2x^2)}$ on $[-1, 1]$
2. Find the greatest and least values of the functions
   (a) $y = arc\ \cos x^2$ on $\left[-\sqrt{1/2}, \sqrt{1/2}\right]$
   (b) $y = x + \sqrt{x}$ on $[0, 4]$
3. Find the greatest and least values of the functions
   (a) $f(x) = arc\tan x - \frac{1}{2}\ln x$ on $\left[\frac{1}{\sqrt{3}}, \sqrt{3}\right]$
   (b) $f(x) = 2\sin x + \sin 2x$ on $\left[0, \frac{3}{2}\pi\right]$
   (c) $f(x) = \begin{cases} 2x^2 + \frac{2}{x^2}; & -2 \le x < 0;\ 0 < x \le 2 \\ 1 & ; x = 0 \end{cases}$
   (d) $f(x) = x - 2\ln x$ on $[1, e]$
4. Find the local maxima/local minima of the function $f(x)$ and also the image of interval
   (a) [0, 3] (b) [0, 4]
   under the mapping $f(x) = x^5 - 5x^4 + 5x^3 + 1$.
5. A point P is moving on a circle $x^2 + y^2 = a^2$. Find the max. area of ΔOPM. Also find its maximum perimeter.

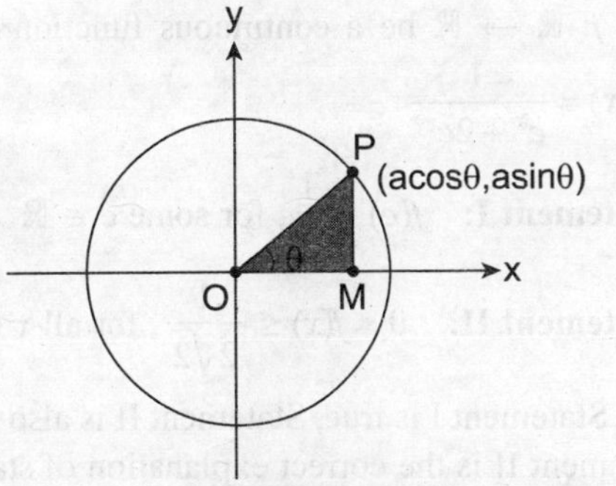

FIGURE 5.226

6. Find the points of local maxima and local minima of the function $f(x) = (x-1)^3 (x+1)^2$. Find also the local maximum and local minimum values.
7. A ship of an enemy is moving along the curve $y = x^2 + 2$. A soldier is at the point (3, 2). Find the minimum distance between the soldier and the ship.
8. Divide a no. 4 into two positive numbers such that the sum of the square of first and the cube of the second is a minimum.
9. Using the first derivative, find the extrema of the function $f(x) = \frac{x^2 - 3x + 2}{x^2 + 2x + 1}$
10. Find the extrema of function $f(x) = \sqrt[3]{(x-1)^2} + \sqrt[3]{(x+1)^2}$

Answer Keys

1. (a) $M = 1/e$, m = does not exist; glb = 0 (b) $M = 3/\sqrt{8}$, $m = 0$
2. (a) $M = \pi/2$, $m = \pi/3$ (b) $M = 6$, $m = 0$
3. (a) $M = \pi/6 + 0.25\ ln3$, $m = \pi/3 - 0.25 \ln 3$ (b) $M = 3\sqrt{3}/2$, $m = -2$
   (c) $m = 1$, M does not exist (d) $M = 1$, $m = 2 - \ln 4$
4. (a) [–26, 2] (b) [–26, 65]
5. Maxima at $\frac{\pi}{4}, \frac{3\pi}{4}, \frac{5\pi}{4}, \frac{7\pi}{4}$.; Maximum area $= \frac{1}{2}a^2$, Maximum perimeter $= \left(\sqrt{2}+1\right)a$
6. $f_{max} = f(-1) = 0$; $f_{min} = f\left(-\frac{1}{5}\right) = \frac{-3456}{3125}$
7. $\sqrt{5}$ unit
8. 8/3, 4/3
9. $f_{min}(7/5) = -1/24$
10. $f_{min}(\pm 1) = \sqrt[3]{4}$, f_{max} does not exist, local maximum values $f(0) = 2$

TEXTUAL EXERCISE-2: (OBJECTIVE)

1. Let $f: \mathbb{R} \to \mathbb{R}$ be a continuous function defined by $f(x) = \frac{1}{e^x + 2e^{-x}}$

Statement I: $f(c) = \frac{1}{3}$, for some $c \in \mathbb{R}$

Statement II: $0 < f(x) \le \frac{1}{2\sqrt{2}}$, for all $x \in \mathbb{R}$.

(a) Statement I is true, Statement II is also true, Statement II is the correct explanation of statement I.
(b) Statement I is true, Statement II is also true, Statement II is not the correct explanation of Statement I.
(c) Statement I is true, Statement II is false.
(d) Statement I is false, Statement II is true

2. The function $f(x) = x^3 + ax^2 + bx + c$, $a^2 \le 3b$ has
(a) one maximum value
(b) one minimum value
(c) no extreme value
(d) one maximum and one minimum value

3. If $y = \frac{\sin(x+a)}{\sin(x+b)}$, $a \ne b$, then y has
(a) minima at $x = 0$
(b) maxima at $x = 0$
(c) neither minima nor maxima at $x = 0$
(d) None of the above

4. The difference between the greatest and least values of function $f(x) = \cos x + \frac{1}{2}\cos 2x - \frac{1}{3}\cos 3x$ is
(a) $\frac{2}{3}$ (b) $\frac{8}{7}$
(c) $\frac{3}{8}$ (d) $\frac{9}{4}$

5. The minimum value of $x^2 + \frac{1}{1+x^2}$ is at
(a) $x = 0$ (b) $x = 1$
(c) $x = 4$ (d) $x = 3$

6. If $ax^2 + bx + 4$ attains its minimum value -1 at $x = 1$; then the values of a and b are respectively ($a \ne 0$)
(a) 5, –10 (b) 5, –5
(c) 10, 10 (d) 10, –5

7. The minimum value of $e^{(2x^2-2x+1)\sin^2 x}$ is
(a) 0 (b) 1
(c) 2 (d) 3

8. If $y = a \ln x + bx^2 + x$ has its extremum at $x = -1$ and $x = 2$, then
(a) $a = 2,\ b = \frac{1}{2}$ (b) $a = 2,\ b = -\frac{1}{2}$
(c) $a = \frac{1}{2},\ b = 2$ (d) $a = -\frac{1}{2}, b = 2$

9. The maximum slope of the curve $y = -x^3 + 3x^2 + 2x - 27$ is
(a) 5 (b) –5
(c) 1/5 (d) None of these

10. On the interval [0, 1] the function $x^{25}(1-x)^{75}$ takes its maximum value at the point.
(a) 0 (b) 1/4
(c) 1/2 (d) 1/3

11. The function $f(x) = a \sin x + \frac{1}{3}\sin 3x$ has maximum value at $x = \frac{\pi}{3}$. The value of a is
(a) 3 (b) 1/3
(c) 2 (d) 1/2

12. The absolute maximum of $x^{40} - x^{20}$ on the interval [0,1] is
(a) –1/4 (b) 0
(c) 1/4 (d) 1/2

13. The extreme values of $4\cos(x^2)\cos\left(\frac{\pi}{3}+x^2\right)\cos\left(\frac{\pi}{3}-x^2\right)$ over R, are
(a) –1, 1 (b) –2, 2
(c) –3, 3 (d) –4, 4

14. Tangent is drawn to ellipse $\frac{x^2}{27} + y^2 = 1$ at $(3\sqrt{3}\cos\theta, \sin\theta)$ (where $\theta \in (0, \pi/2)$). Then the value of θ such that sum of intercepts on axes made by this tangent is minimum is
(a) π/3 (b) π/6
(c) π/8 (d) π/4

15. Let $p(x)$ be a real polynomial of least degree which has a local maximum at $x = 1$ and a local minimum at $x = 3$. If $p(1) = 6$ and $p(3) = 2$, then $p'(0)$ is

(a) 9 (b) 10
(c) 11 (d) None of these

16. Let $f: R \to R$ be defined as $f(x) = |x| + |x^2 - 1|$. The total number of points at which f attains either a local maximum or local minimum is

(a) 5 (b) 6
(c) 7 (d) 8

17. Maximum value of the function $f(x) = \frac{x}{8} + \frac{2}{x}$ on the interval [1, 6] is

(a) 1 (b) $\frac{9}{8}$
(c) $\frac{13}{12}$ (d) $\frac{17}{8}$

Answer Keys

1. (a)	**2.** (c)	**3.** (c)	**4.** (d)	**5.** (b)	**6.** (a)	**7.** (b)	**8.** (b)	**9.** (a)	**10.** (b)
11. (c)	**12.** (b)	**13.** (a)	**14.** (b)	**15.** (a)	**16.** (a)	**17.** (d)			

■ SECOND/HIGHER ORDER DERIVATIVE TEST

Step I: Find the derivative of the function and find the root of $f'(x) = 0$ (Say $x = x_0, x_1, x_2, \ldots$)

Step II: Now find $f''(x)$ at $x = x_0$ then following cases may arise:

- ☐ If $f''(x_0) < 0$, then $f(x)$ is maximum at $x = x_0$.
- ☐ If $f''(x_0) > 0$, then $f(x)$ is minimum at $x = x_0$
- ☐ If $f''(x_0) = 0$, then second derivative test fails to conclude.

Step III: Now find $f'''(x)$ at $x = x_0$ and following two cases may arise:

- ☐ If $f'''(x_0) \neq 0$, then $f(x)$ has neither maximum nor minimum (inflexion point) at $x = x_0$.
- ☐ But if $f'''(x_0) = 0$, then go for next higher derivative test.

Step IV: Find $f^{iv}(x_0)$ and analysing the following cases:

- ☐ If $f^{iv}(x_0) = 0$, then similar analysis of higher derivative continues.
- ☐ If $f^{iv}(x_0)$ = *positive* then $f(x)$ is minimum at $x = x_0$
- ☐ If $f^{iv}(x_0)$ = *negative* then $f(x)$ is maximum at $x = x_0$

In general, let $f'(x_0) = f''(x_0) = \ldots = f^{(n-1)}(x_0) = 0, f^{(n)}(x_0) \neq 0$. If n is odd, then there is neither maximum nor minimum at $x = x_0$ and if n is even then $f^{(n)}(x_0) > 0$

$\Rightarrow$ min. at x_0 and $f^{(n)}(x_0) < 0$

$\Rightarrow$ max. at x_0.

Proof: This proof is not required). Let h be a very small positive number

Sign of {f(a + h) – f(a)}	Sign of {f(a – h) – f(a)}	Conclusion
+ve $\Rightarrow f(a+h) > f(a)$	+ve $\Rightarrow f(a-h) > f(a)$	$f(x)$ has min at $x = a$
–ve $\Rightarrow f(a+h) < f(a)$	–ve $\Rightarrow f(a-h) < f(a)$	$f(x)$ has max. at $x = a$
+ve $\Rightarrow f(a+h) > f(a)$	–ve $\Rightarrow f(a-h) < f(a)$	$f(x)$ has neither max. nor min value at $x = a$
–ve $\Rightarrow f(a+h) < f(a)$	+ve $\Rightarrow f(a-h) > f(a)$	$f(x)$ has neither max. nor min value at $x = a$

By Taylor's expansion, $f(a+h) = f(a) + \frac{h}{1!}f'(a) + \frac{h^2}{2!}f''(a) + \frac{h^3}{3!}f'''(a) + ..$

or $f(a+h) - f(a) = \frac{h}{1!}f'(a) + \frac{h^2}{2!}f''(a) + \frac{h^3}{3!}f'''(a) + \frac{h^4}{4!}f^{iv}(a) + \ldots$ ...(1)

and $f(a-h) - f(a) = -\frac{h}{1!}f'(a) + \frac{h^2}{2!}f''(a) - \frac{h^3}{3!}f'''(a) + \frac{h^4}{4!}f^{iv}(a) - \ldots$ ....(2)

A. If $f'(a) \neq 0$, then from (1) and (2), we have

$$f(a+h) - f(a) = \frac{h}{1!}f'(a) \quad \ldots(3)$$

and $f(a-h)-f(a)=-\frac{h}{1!}f'(a)$ (neglecting other terms) ...(4)

From (3) and (4), it is clear that,

$f(a+h)-f(a)$ and $f(a-h)-f(a)$ have opposite signs, therefore $f(x)$ has neither maximum nor minimum value at $x=a$

B. If $f'(a)=0$ and $f''(a)\neq 0$, then (1) and (2), we have

$$f(a+h)-f(a)=\frac{h^2}{2!}f''(a)$$

and $f(a-h)-f(a)=\frac{h^2}{2!}f''(a)$ (neglecting other terms)

From (5) and (6) it is clear that

(i) If $f''(a)<0$, then $f(a+h)-f(a)<0$ and $f(a-h)-f(a)<0$ and therefore, $f(x)$ has maximum value at $x=a$

(ii) If $f''(a)>0$, then $f(a+h)-f(a)>0$ and $f(a-h)-f(a)>0$ and therefore, $f(x)$ has minimum value at $x=a$

C. If $f'(a)=0, f''(a)=0$ and $f'''(a)\neq 0$, then from (1) and (2), we have

$$f(a+h)-f(a)=\frac{h^3}{3!}f'''(a) \quad ...(7)$$

$$\text{and } f(a-h)-f(a)=-\frac{h^3}{3!}f'''(a) \quad ...(8)$$

(neglecting other terms)

From (7) and (8) it is clear that,

$f(a+h)-f(a)$ and $f(a-h)-f(a)$ have opposite signs and hence $f(x)$ has neither maximum nor minimum value at $x=a$

D. If $f'(a)=0, f''(a)=0, f'''(a)=0$ and $f^{iv}(a)\neq 0$,

Then from (i) and (ii), we have $f(a+h)-f(a)=\frac{h^4}{4!}f^{iv}(a)$ and $f(a-h)-f(a)=\frac{h^4}{4!}f^{iv}(a)$

(i) if $f^{iv}(a)<0$, then $f(x)$ has maximum value at $x=a$

(ii) if $f^{iv}(a)>0$, then $f(x)$ has minimum value at $x=a$

We can proceed in this way for higher derivatives till they become non zero.

e.g consider $f(x)=x^5$

then $f'(x)=5x^4$ and $f'(x)=0\Rightarrow x=0$

$f''(x)=20x^3$ and $f''(x)|_{x=0}=0$

$f'''(x)=60x^2$ and $f'''(x)|_{x=0}=0$

$f^{iv}(x)=120x$ and $f^{iv}(x)|_{x=0}=0$

$f^{v}(x)=120\neq 0$

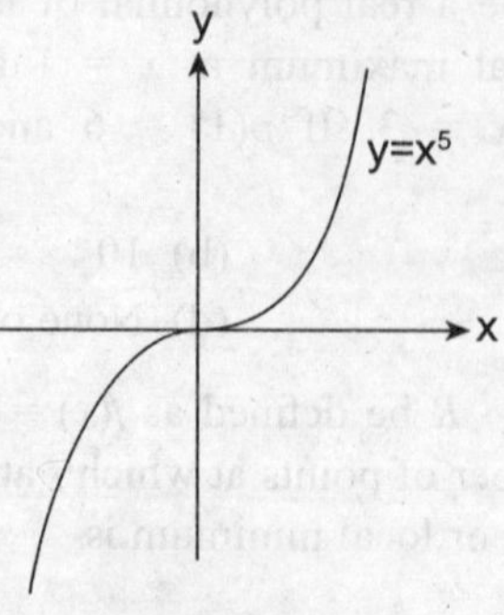

FIGURE 5.227

Now as mentioned above; n 5 is odd; then there is neither maxima nor minima at $x=0$

Similarly for the function $f(x)=x^6$

We have $f'(x)=6x^5$ and $f'(x)=0\Rightarrow x=0$

$f''(x)=30x^4$ and $f^{ii}(x)|_{x=0}=0$

$f'''(x)=120x^3$ and $f^{iii}(x)|_{x=0}=0$

$f^{iv}(x)=360x^2$ and $f^{iv}(x)|_{x=0}=0$

$f^{v}(x)=720x$ and $f^{v}(x)|_{x=0}=0$

$f^{vi}(x)=720\neq 0$

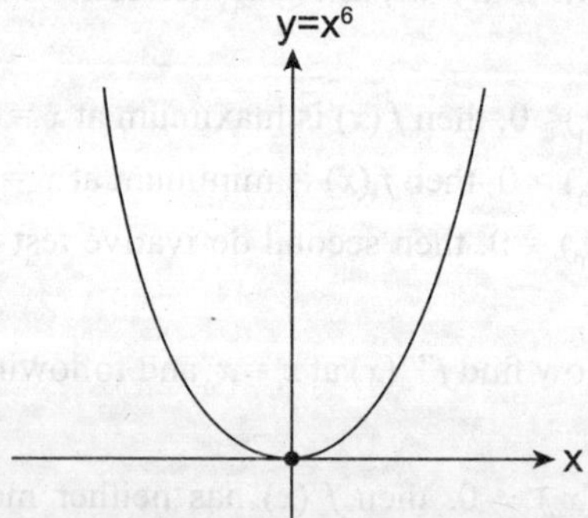

FIGURE 5.228

Now, as mentioned above; $n=6$ is even; then there is either a maxima or a minima at $x=0$

Now; in order to find whether it is a minima or a maxima at $x=0$; we will need to use the first order derivative and compare the values of $f(0-h)$; $f(0)$ and $f(0+h)$

$f(0-h)=(-h)^6=h^6>0$

$f(0)=0$

$f(0+h)=h^6>0$

Now since $f(0-h)>f(0)$ and $f(0+h)>f(0)$ hence; $f(x)$ is minimum at $x=0$.

ILLUSTRATION 201: Find the maximum and minimum values of the following functions.

(i) $f(x) = x\,(x - 1)^2$

(ii) $f(x) = x^2 - 3x^{2/3}$

SOLUTION: (i) **Ist derivative test:** The function is defined and continuous for all x

The derivative of $f(x)$ is $1.\,(x-1)^2 + 2\,x.\,(x-1) = (x-1)\,(3x-1)$

For maximum and minimum values of $f(x)$; Put $f'(x) = 0$

$\therefore\ x = 1,\ 1/3$ (critical points)

Sign scheme for $f'(x)$ is as:

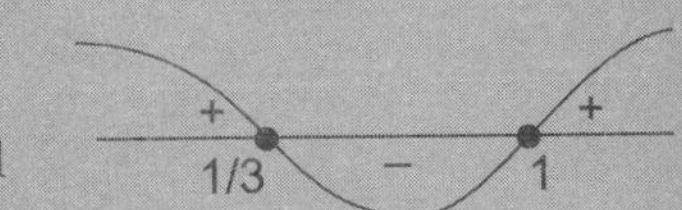

FIGURE 5.229

Thus $f(x)$ is maximum at $x = 1/3$ and minimum at $x = 1$

and max. $f(x) = f(1/3) = \dfrac{1}{3}\left(\dfrac{1}{3} - 1\right)^2 = \dfrac{4}{27}$

while minimum $= f(1) = 0$

2nd derivative test: $f(x) = 6x - 4$

Since $f''(1/3) = 6.\,\dfrac{1}{3} - 4 = -2 < 0$

$\therefore$ function $f(x)$ has local maxima at $x = 1/3$ and $f''(1) = 2 > 0$

$\therefore$ function $f''(x)$ has local minimum at $x = 1$

(ii) This function is also defined and continuous for all real x

The derivative is $f'(x) = 2x - 3.\,\dfrac{2}{3}\,.\,x^{-1/3}$

$\Rightarrow\ f'(x) = 2(x - 1/x^{1/3})$

From the equation $f(x) = 0$, we have the roots $x = \pm 1$

Furthermore, $f(x)$ is undefined when $x = 0$.

Thus the critical points are $x = -1, 0, 1$

Now, the sign scheme for $f(x)$ is as:

It is clear that $f(x)$ has two minima at $x = -1$ and $x = 1$

$f(-1) = -2;\ f(1) = -2$ and a maximum $f(0) = 0$

ILLUSTRATION 202: Let $f(x) = \displaystyle\int_1^x \frac{\sin t}{t}\,dt \quad \left(x > \frac{\pi}{2}\right)$, then

(a) $f(x)$ has local maxima at $x = 2n\pi$ where $(n \in N)$

(b) $f(x)$ has local minima at $x = 2n\pi$ where $(n \in N)$

(c) $f(x)$ has local maxima at $x = (4n + 1)\dfrac{\pi}{2}$ where $(n \in N)$

(d) None of these

SOLUTION: $\Rightarrow\ f'(x) = \dfrac{\sin x}{x} = 0$

$\Rightarrow\ x = n\,\pi\ (n \in N)$

$\Rightarrow\ f''(x) = \dfrac{x\cos x - \sin x}{x^2}$

$\Rightarrow\ f''(n\pi) = \dfrac{\cos n\pi}{n\pi} = -\dfrac{1}{n\pi}$ if n is odd and $\dfrac{1}{n\pi}$ if n is even.

ILLUSTRATION 203: Using the second derivative, find the extrema of the function $y = 2\sin x + \cos 2x$.

SOLUTION: Since the function is a periodic one we may confine ourselves to the interval $[0, 2\pi]$.

Find the first and second derivatives:

$y' = 2\cos x - 2\sin x = 2\cos x\,(1 - 2\sin x)$

$y'' = -2\sin x - 4\cos 2x$

from the equation $2\cos x\,(1 - 2\sin x) = 0$ determine the critical points on the interval $[0, 2\pi]$

$x_1 = \frac{\pi}{6};\ x_2 = \frac{\pi}{2};\ x_3 = \frac{5\pi}{6};\ x_4 = \frac{3\pi}{2}$

Now find the sign of the second derivative at each critical point:

$y''(\pi/6) = -3 < 0$; hence we have a maximum $y(\pi/6) = 3/2$ at the point $x_1 = \pi/6$.

$y''(\pi/2) = 2 > 0$; hence we have a minimum $y(\pi/2) = 1$ at the point $x_2 = \pi/2$.

$y''(5\pi/6) = -3 < 0$; hence we have a maximum $y(5\pi/6) = 3/2$ at the point $x_3 = 5\pi/6$.

$y''(3\pi/2) = 6 > 0$; hence we have a minimum $y(3\pi/2) = -3$ at the point $x_4 = 3\pi/2$.

ILLUSTRATION 204: Show that there is one maximum and one minimum value of $x + 1/x$, but the maximum is less that the minimum. What is its reason?

SOLUTION: Let $f(x) = x + \frac{1}{x}$

$\therefore\ f(x) = 1 - \frac{1}{x^2} = \frac{x^2 - 1}{x^2}$

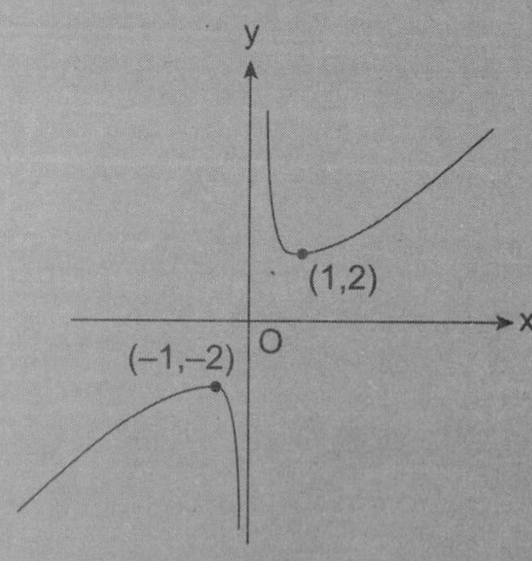

FIGURE 5.230

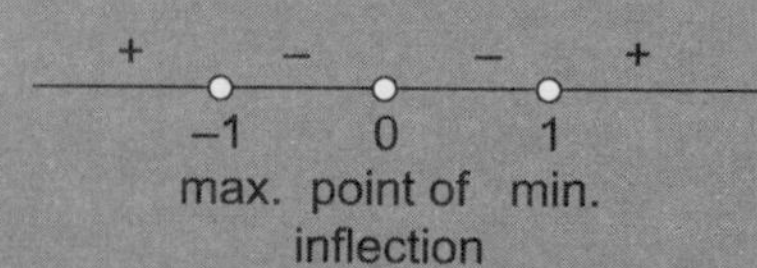

FIGURE 5.231

Sign scheme for $\frac{dy}{dx}$, where $x^2 - 1 = 0$ i.e., $x = \pm 1$

Put $x^2 = 0$, $(x = 0)$ is a repeated root.

From the graph it is clear $x = -1$ is a point of maxima and $x = 1$ is a point of minima.

Maximum value $= -2$, minimum value $= 2$. Hence maximum is less that minimum.

ILLUSTRATION 205: Maximum and minimum values of the function, $f(x) = \frac{2 - x}{\pi}\cos \pi\,(x + 3) + \frac{1}{\pi^2}\sin \pi\,(x + 3)$ $0 < x < 4$ occur respectively at :

(a) $x = 1$ (b) $x = 2$

(c) $x = 3$ (d) $x = \pi$

SOLUTION: $\frac{dy}{dx} = -(2 - x)\sin\pi(x + 3) = 0$

$\Rightarrow x = 1, 2, 3$

$\Rightarrow \left.\frac{d^2y}{dx^2}\right] = -(2 - x)\,\pi\cos\pi(x + 3) + \sin\pi(x + 3);$

$\Rightarrow \left.\frac{d^2y}{dx^2}\right]_{x=1} = -\pi$ $\Rightarrow \left.\frac{d^2y}{dx^2}\right]_{x=2} = 0$

$\Rightarrow \left.\frac{d^2y}{dx^2}\right]_{x=3} = \pi$

ILLUSTRATION 206: For the function $f(x) = \begin{cases} 7-x^2 & : x<2 \\ x^2-6x+17 & : x \le 2 \end{cases}$ show that maximum is less than the minimum value.

SOLUTION: Since $f(2) = 9, f(2^+) = 9, f(2^-) = 3$

$f(x)$ is discontinuous at $x = 2$

Also $f'(x) = \begin{cases} -2x & : x<2 \\ \text{not exist} & : x=2 \\ 2x-6 & : x>2 \end{cases}$

$f'(x) = 0$ at $x = 3$ for $f'(x) = 2x - 6$ and $f''(3) = 2 > 0$ so there is minima at $x = 3$ and minimum value at $x = 3$ is 8. Also $f'(x) = 0$ at $x = 0$ for $f'(x) = -2x$ and $f''(0) = -2 < 0$ so there is maxima at $x = 0$ and $f(0) = 7$. Thus value at minima > value at maxima

This becomes possible due to the fact that $f(x)$ has a discontinuity at $x = 2$ between the critical points $x = 0$ and 3.

NOTE:

It can easily be seen that f(x) have no greatest and least values.

ILLUSTRATION 207: Break up the number 8 into two summands such that the sum of their cubes is the least possible.

SOLUTION: Let two numbers be x and $8 - x$

Let $f(x) = x^3 + (8-x)^3$

$\Rightarrow f'(x) = 3x^2 - 3(8-x)^2 = 3[x^2 - (8-x)^2] = 3[[x-(8-x)][x+8-x]]$

$\Rightarrow f'(x) = 3[2x-8][8]$

$\Rightarrow f'(x) = 0$ at $x = 4$

$\Rightarrow f''(x) = 48 > 0 \Rightarrow x = 4$ is the point of minima $\Rightarrow$ Required summands are 4, 4

ILLUSTRATION 208: Decompose the number 36 into two factors such that the sum of their squares is the least possible.

SOLUTION: Let one number be x, other be $36/x$.

$$\Rightarrow \quad f(x) = x^2 + \left(\frac{36}{x}\right)^2$$

$$\Rightarrow \quad f'(x) = 2x + 2\left(\frac{36}{x}\right)\cdot\left(\frac{-36}{x^2}\right)$$

$$\therefore \quad f'(x) = 0 \Rightarrow x^4 = (36)^2 \Rightarrow x = 6$$

$$\text{And } f''(x) = 2 + \frac{2(36)^2(3)}{x^4}$$

$$\Rightarrow \quad f''(x) > 0 \text{ at } x = 6 \text{ (Point of minima)}$$

ILLUSTRATION 209: Discuss maxima and minima of the function $\sin^p\theta \cos^q\theta$; $p, q > 0$, $0 < \theta < \pi/2$.

SOLUTION: $y = \sin^p\theta \cos^q\theta$, $p, q > 0$, $0 < \theta < \pi/2$

$z = \ln y = p \ln \sin\theta + q \ln \cos\theta$

We know that y and $\ln y$ have same nature regarding max/min. for $y > 0$.

$$\frac{dz}{d\theta} = p\cot\theta - q\tan\theta \Rightarrow \frac{dz}{d\theta} = 0 \quad \Rightarrow \tan\theta = \sqrt{p/q} \qquad [\because \tan\theta > 0]$$

and $\dfrac{d^2z}{d\theta^2} = -p\,\text{cosec}^2\theta - q\sec^2\theta < 0$

$\therefore$ z i.e., $\ln y$ i.e., y has maxima (local) at $\theta = \tan^{-1}\sqrt{p/q}$

$$\text{and greatest value} = \left\{\frac{\sqrt{p}}{\sqrt{(p+q)}}\right\}^p \left\{\frac{\sqrt{q}}{\sqrt{p+q}}\right\}^q = \left[\frac{p^p q^q}{(p+q)^{p+q}}\right]^{1/2}$$

ILLUSTRATION 210: The function $S(x) = \int_0^x \sin\left(\frac{\pi t^2}{2}\right)dt$ has two critical points in the interval [1, 2.4]. One of the critical points is a local minimum and the other is a local maximum. The local minimum occurs at $x =$

(a) 1 (b) $\sqrt{2}$

(c) 2 (d) $\dfrac{\pi}{2}$

SOLUTION: $S(x) = \int_0^x \sin\left(\frac{\pi t^2}{2}\right)dt$; $S'(x) = \sin\left(\frac{\pi x^2}{2}\right) = 0$

$\dfrac{\pi x^2}{2} = n\pi \Rightarrow x^2 = 2n$ ($1 \le x^2 \le 5.76$ as is given)

Hence $n = 1$ or $2 \Rightarrow x = \sqrt{2}$ or $x = 2$; $S''(x) = \cos\left(\frac{\pi x^2}{2}\right).\ \pi x$

and $S''(\sqrt{2}) < 0$ and $S''(2) > 0 \Rightarrow$ minima at $x = 2$

ILLUSTRATION 211: The perimeter of an isosceles triangle is equal to $2p$. What must be its sides be so that the volume of the solid generated by revolving the triangle about its base is greatest possible?

SOLUTION: When the given triangle is rotated about its base ($BC = 2a$); a circular cone will be formed.

Their radius will be $AD = \sqrt{c^2 - a^2}$ and height $= CD = BD = a$

Hence, the volume of the solid generated $V = 2.\ \frac{1}{3}\pi.AD^2.CD = \frac{2\pi}{3}(c^2 - a^2)a$

But perimeter $2p = 2c + 2a$ $\Rightarrow p = c + a$

$\therefore\ V = \frac{2\pi}{3}a\{(p-a)^2 - a^2\} = \frac{2\pi}{3}a\{p^2 - 2p\} = \frac{2\pi}{3}\{ap^2 - 2a^2p\}$

$\therefore\ \frac{dV}{da} = \frac{2\pi}{3}\{p^2 - 4ap\} = 0$ $\Rightarrow a = p/4$

$\therefore$ Base $= 2a = p/2$ and $c = p - a = 3p/4$

Also $\frac{d^2V}{da^2} = \frac{2\pi}{3}\{-4p\} < 0$. Thus V is maximum

ILLUSTRATION 212: If $P(x)$ be a polynomial of degree 3 satisfying $P(-1) = 10$, $P(1) = -6$ and $P(x)$ has maximum at $x = -1$ and $P'(x)$ has minima at $x = 1$. Find the distance between the local maximum and local minimum of the curve.

SOLUTION: Given $P(x)$ be a polynomial of degree 3

$\therefore$ Let $P(x) = ax^3 + bx^2 + cx + d$

Given $P(-1) = 10$

$\Rightarrow -a + b - c + d = 10$ ...(1)

And $P(1) = -6$

$\Rightarrow a + b + c + d = -6$ ...(2)

Also given $P(x)$ has max. at $x = -1$

$\Rightarrow P'(-1) = 0$

$\Rightarrow 3a - 2b + c = 0$ ...(3)

And $P'(x)$ has min at $x = 1$

$\Rightarrow P''(1) = 0$

$\Rightarrow 6a + 2b = 0$ ...(4)

Solving (1), (2), (3), (4), we get $a = 1$, $b = -3$, $c = -9$, $d = 5$

So $P(x) = x^3 - 3x^2 - 9x + 5$

$\Rightarrow P'(x) = 3x^2 - 6x - 9 = 0$

$\Rightarrow P'(x) = 3(x + 1)(x - 3) = 0$

Now $x = -1$ is point of max. (given)

And $x = 1$ is point of min. ($\because f''(1) > 0$)

$\therefore$ local maxima point $(-1, 10)$ and local minima point $(3, -22)$

$\Rightarrow$ distance $= \sqrt{(3+1)^2 + (-22-10)^2} = 4\sqrt{65}$

ILLUSTRATION 213: A particle is moving in a straight line such that its distance at any time t is given by $s = \frac{t^4}{4} - 2t^3 + 4t^2 + 7$. Then

(a) velocity is max. at $t = (6 - 2\sqrt{3})/3$ (b) acceleration is min. at $t = 2$

(c) min. distance is at $t = 0, 4$ (d) None of these

SOLUTION: Given $s = \frac{t^4}{4} - 2t^3 + 4t^2 + 7$

$\Rightarrow \; v = \frac{ds}{dt} = t^3 - 6t^2 + 8t$

$\Rightarrow \; a = \frac{dv}{dt} = 3t^2 - 12t + 8$

At $= t = 2$; $\frac{d^2s}{dt^2} = \frac{dv}{dt} < 0$ $\Rightarrow$ maxima at $t = 2$

At $t = 4$; $\frac{d^2s}{dt^2} = \frac{dv}{dt} > 0$ $\Rightarrow$ minima at $t = 4$

Now; $s(0) = 7$ and $s(4) = 7$

$\therefore$ minimum distance is at $t = 0, 4$

For maximum velocity; $\frac{dv}{dt} = 0$ $\Rightarrow 3t^2 - 12t + 8 = 0$

$\Rightarrow \; t = \frac{12 \pm \sqrt{144 - 12 \times 8}}{6} = \frac{12 \pm \sqrt{12 \times 4}}{6} = \frac{12 \pm 4\sqrt{3}}{6} = \frac{6 \pm 2\sqrt{3}}{3}$

Now $\frac{d^2v}{dt^2} = 6t - 12$

At $= t = \frac{6+2\sqrt{3}}{3}$; $\frac{d^2v}{dt^2} > 0 \Rightarrow$ minimum

At $t = \frac{6-2\sqrt{3}}{3}$; $\frac{d^2v}{dt^2} < 0 \Rightarrow$ maximum

$\therefore$ maximum velocity is at $t = \frac{6-2\sqrt{3}}{3}$

For minimum acceleration

$\frac{da}{dt} = 0 \Rightarrow 6t - 12 = 0 \Rightarrow t = 0$ and $\frac{d^2a}{dt^2} = 6 > 0$ $\Rightarrow$ minimum

$\Rightarrow$ minimum acc. is at $t = 2$

ILLUSTRATION 214: Investigate the function $y = \cos x - 1 + \frac{x^2}{2!} - \frac{x^3}{3!}$ for an extremum at the point $x = 0$.

SOLUTION: $y' = -\sin x + x - \frac{x^2}{2}$ $\Rightarrow y'(0) = 0$

$\Rightarrow \; y'' = -\cos x + 1 - x$ $\Rightarrow y''(0) = 0$

And $y''' = \sin x - 1$ $\Rightarrow y'''(0) = -1 \neq 0$

And so the first non-zero derivative at the point $x = 0$ is a derivative of the third order, i.e., of an odd order; this means that there is no extemum at the point $x = 0$.

ILLUSTRATION 215: Find the area of the right angled triangle of least area that can be drawn so as to circumscribe a rectangle of sides 'a' and 'b', the right angle of the triangle coinciding with one of the angles of the rectangle.

SOLUTION: As shown in the diagram; let the rectangle $BDEF$ be inscribed in the triangle ABC.

$\therefore \; \Delta AEF \sim \Delta EDC$

$\Rightarrow \frac{y}{b} = \frac{a}{x}$ $\Rightarrow xy = ab$ ...(1)

Now, area of $\Delta ABC = A = \frac{1}{2}(a+x)(b+y) \Rightarrow A = \frac{1}{2}(a+x)\left(\quad \frac{ab}{}\right)$

Equating $\frac{dA}{dx} = 0$; we have $\frac{1}{2}\left[(a+x)\left(-\frac{ab}{x^2}\right)+\left(b+\frac{ab}{x}\right)\right]=0$

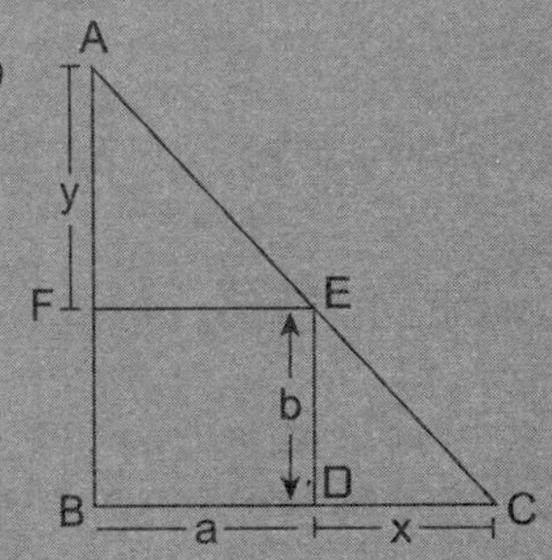

FIGURE 5.232

$\Rightarrow -a^2b - abx + bx^2 + abx = 0$

$\Rightarrow bx^2 = a^2b \Rightarrow x = a$

Putting $x = a$ in (i); we get $y = b$

Now, $\frac{dA}{dx} = \frac{1}{2}\left(\frac{-a^2b}{x^2}+b\right)$

$\Rightarrow \frac{d^2A}{dx^2} = \frac{1}{2}\left(\frac{2a^2b}{x^3}\right)$

And $\left.\frac{d^2A}{dx^2}\right|_{x=a} = \frac{a^2b}{a^3} = \frac{b}{a} > 0$ So A is min at $x = a$ and $y = b$

$\Rightarrow A_{min} = \frac{1}{2}(2a)(2b) = 2ab$

ILLUSTRATION 216: Let $f(x) = \begin{cases} e^x & ,0 < x \le 1 \\ 2-e^{x-1} & ,1 < x \le 2 \\ x-e & ,2 < x \le 3 \end{cases}$ and $g(x) = \int_0^x f(t)\,dt$, then :

(a) $g(x)$ has local minima at $x = e$ and local maxima at $x = 1 + in2$

(b) $g(x)$ has local maxima at $x = 1$ and local minima at $x = 2$

(c) $g(x)$ does not have local maxima

(d) $g(x)$ does not have local minima

SOLUTION: $g'(x) = f(x) = \begin{cases} e^x & ,0 < x \le 1 \\ 2-e^{x-1} & ,1 < x \le 2 \\ x-e & ,2 < x \le 3 \end{cases}$

For max. or min, of $g(x)$ we have $g'(x) = 0$

Since e^x is always greater than zero.

$\therefore$ $g'(x) = 0$

when $2 - e^{x-1} = 0$ or $x - 1 = \log 2$ or $x = 1 + \log 2$, $1 < x \le 2$

Also $x - e = 0$ when $x = e$, $2 < x \le 3$

$g''(x) = \begin{cases} -e^{x-1} & ,1 < x \le 2 \\ 1 & ,2 < x \le 3 \end{cases}$ $\therefore$ $g''(1 + \log 2) = -e^{\log 2} = -2 < 0$, i.e., $-ive$

$\therefore$ $g(x)$ is max. at $x = 1 + \log 2$ Also $g''(e) = 1 > 0$, i.e., $+ ive$

$\therefore$ $g(x)$ is min at $x = e$

EXTREMA OF PARAMETRIC FUNCTION

Consider a function defined parametrically: $x = x(t)$, $y = y(t)$. Suppose that we are interested in finding the points of extrema of this function. We can eliminate the parameter 't' to get y as a function of x. For example, consider $x = t + 1,\ y = \begin{cases} 2t+2, & t \le 0 \\ 3-3t, & t > 0 \end{cases}$

On elimination of t, we get $y = \begin{cases} 2x, & x \le 1 \\ 6-3x, & x > 1 \end{cases}$

If we draw the graph of $y = f(x)$ we can apply the basic definition of local maximum to claim that the function has a local maximum at $x = 1$.

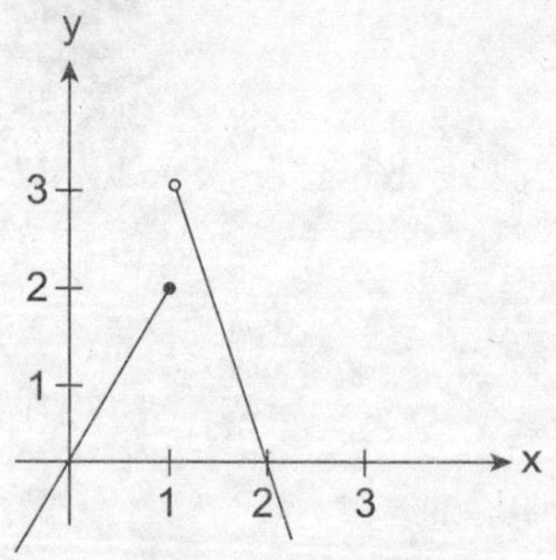

FIGURE 5.233

FIRST DERIVATIVE TEST FOR PARAMETRIC FUNCTIONS

Assume that the function is continuous, the following steps should be followed:

1. Find the critical points: $\dfrac{dy}{dx} = \dfrac{dy/dt}{dx/dt}$
2. Find values of t, where dy/dx is zero or does not exist.
3. Find the sign scheme of dy/dx on the number line of t.
4. Now, convert the sign scheme of dy/dx on the number line of x.
5. If $x = x(t)$ is a strictly increasing function t, then the sign scheme in x is the same as the sign scheme in t.
6. If $x = x(t)$ is a strictly decreasing function of t, then the sign scheme in x is obtained by reversing the number line in t.

Consider $x = t^3 - 3t$, $y = t^3 + 3t + 2$; $\dfrac{dy}{dx} = \dfrac{t^2+1}{t^2-1}$

Now, $\dfrac{dy}{dx} \ne 0\ \forall\, t \in \mathbb{R}$

But $\dfrac{dy}{dx}$ does not exist at $t = \pm 1$ or at $x = \mp 2$

Sign scheme of dy/dx in t:

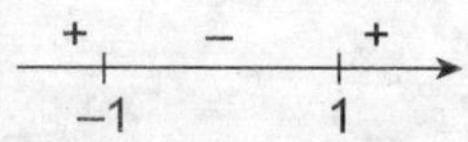

FIGURE 5.234

$x = t^3 - 3t$ is a strictly increasing function of t, $x(-1) = -2$, $x(1) = -2$

Sign scheme of dy/dx in x:

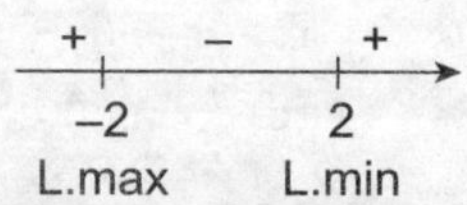

FIGURE 5.235

Hence, $x = -2$ is a point of local maximum and $x = 2$ is a point of local minimum.

ILLUSTRATION 217: If a function is defined parametrically as $x = 3 - 2t^3$ and $y = 6t + t^2$; then find the values of x for which the function attains local maxima or local minima.

SOLUTION: $\dfrac{dy}{dx} = \dfrac{2(3+t)}{-6t^2}$

The critical points in terms of t are -3 and 0.

Sign scheme of dy/dx in t:

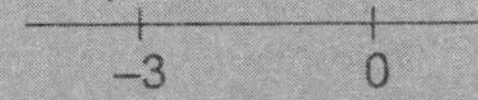

FIGURE 5.236

Now, at $t = -3$; $x = 57$ and at $t = 0$; $x = 3$

Also, $x = x(t)$ is a strictly decreasing function of t.

Sign scheme of dy/dx in x:

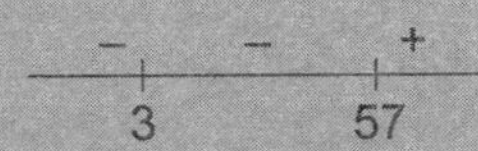

FIGURE 5.237

Hence, it is clear that $x = 3$ is not a point of extremum and $x = 57$ is a point of local minima.

ILLUSTRATION 218: If a function is defined parametrically as $x = -4t + \cos\dfrac{\pi t}{2}$, $y = t^4 - 6t^2 + 8t$ then find the values of 'x' for which the function attains local maxima or local minima.

SOLUTION: $\dfrac{dy}{dx} = \dfrac{4(t-1)^2(t+2)}{4 - \dfrac{\pi}{2}\sin\dfrac{\pi t}{2}}$

The critical points are $t = -2, 1$

sign scheme of dy/dx in t:

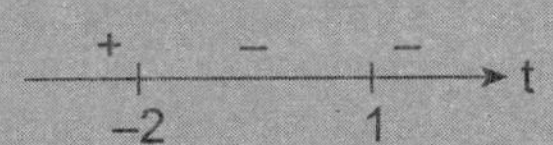

FIGURE 5.238

Sign scheme of dy/dx in x :

Clearly $x = -2$ is not a point of extremum and $x = 3$ is a point of local minimum

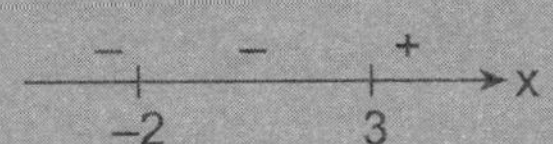

FIGURE 5.239

SECOND DERIVATIVE TEST FOR PARAMETRIC FUNCTION

Assume that the function is differentiable $\dfrac{dy}{dx} = \dfrac{dy/dt}{dx/dt}$.

First we get the stationary points: we find the values of $t = t_c$ where $\dfrac{dy}{dt} = 0$ but $\dfrac{dx}{dt} \neq 0$. If $\dfrac{dx}{dt} = 0$, then this test is not applicable.

Now $\dfrac{d^2y}{dx^2} = \dfrac{\ddot{y}\dot{x} - \ddot{x}\dot{y}}{(\dot{x})^3} \Rightarrow \left.\dfrac{d^2y}{dx^2}\right|_{t=t_c} = \left.\dfrac{\ddot{y}\dot{x} - \ddot{x}\dot{y}}{(\dot{x})^3}\right|_{t=t_c} = \left.\dfrac{\ddot{y}}{(\dot{x})^2}\right|_{t=t_c}$

Now $\left.\dfrac{d^2y}{dx^2}\right|_{t=t_c} > 0$, *if* $\left.\dfrac{d^2y}{dt^2}\right|_{t=t_c} > 0$, then $x = x(t_c)$ is a point of local minimum.

Further $\left.\dfrac{d^2y}{dx^2}\right|_{t=t_c} < 0$, if $\left.\dfrac{d^2y}{dt^2}\right|_{t=t_c} < 0$,

then $x = x(t_c)$ is a point of local maximum.

Consider $x = \tan^{-1}t + 1$, $y = \ell n(4 - t^2)$

$\dfrac{dy}{dt} = 0 \Rightarrow t = 0$

We confirm that at $t = 0$, $\frac{dx}{dt} \neq 0$

The sign of $\left.\frac{d^2y}{dx^2}\right|_{t=0}$ is same as sign of $\left.\frac{d^2y}{dt^2}\right|_{t=0}$

$$\therefore \quad \frac{d^2y}{dt^2} = -\left.\frac{2(t^2+4)}{(4-t^2)^2}\right|_{t=0} < 0$$

Hence, $x = x(0) = 1$ is a point of local maximum.

ILLUSTRATION 219: Find the extrema of the function $y = f(x)$ represented parametrically as $\begin{cases} x = \alpha(t) = t^5 - 5t^3 - 20t + 7 \\ y = \beta(t) = 4t^3 - 3t^2 - 18t + 3(-2 < t < 2) \end{cases}$

SOLUTION: We have $\alpha'(t) = 5t^4 - 15t^2 - 20$

In the interval $(-2, 2)$, $\alpha'(t) \neq 0$

Now, we find $\beta'(t)$ and equate it to zero

$\beta'(t) = 12t^2 - 6t - 18 = 0$

Whence $t_1 = -1$ and $t_2 = 3/2$

These roots are interior points of the given interval of the parameter t.

Further, $\beta''(t) = 24t - 6$;

$\Rightarrow \beta''(-1) = -30 < 0, \beta''(3/2) = 30 > 0$

Consequently, the function $y = f(x)$ has a local maximum $y = 14$ at $t = -1$ (i.e., at $x = 31$) and a local

Minimum at $y = -69/4$ at $t = 3/2$(i.e., at $x = -1033/32$)

ILLUSTRATION 220: The function $y = f(x)$ is represented parametrically:

$\begin{array}{l} x(t) = t^3 + 3t + 1 \\ y(t) = t^3 - 3t + 1 \end{array}$. Find the extrema of this function:

SOLUTION: For the given functions $x(t) = t^3 + 3t + 1$; $y(t) = t^3 - 3t + 1$

$$\frac{dx}{dt} = 3t^2 + 3; \; \frac{dy}{dx} = \frac{3(r^2-1)}{3(r^2+1)} \qquad \frac{dy}{dt} = 3t^2 - 3; \; \frac{dy}{dx} = 0 \qquad \text{at } t = \pm 1$$

$$\frac{d^2y}{dx^2} = \frac{d}{dx}\left(\frac{dy}{dx}\right) = \frac{d}{dt}\left(\frac{dy}{dx}\right)\frac{dt}{dx}$$

$$= \frac{d}{dt}\left(\frac{t^2-1}{t^2+1}\right) \cdot \frac{dt}{dx} = \left[\frac{2t(t^2+1) - 2t(t^2-1)}{(t^2+1)^2}\right]\frac{1}{3(t^2+1)} = \frac{1}{3}\left[\frac{4t}{(t^2+1)^3}\right]$$

$$\Rightarrow \frac{d^2y}{dx^2} = 0 \text{ at } t = 0$$

$\Rightarrow x(-1) = -1 - 3 + 1 = -3$; $y(-1) = -1 + 3 + 1 = 3$ $\qquad \Rightarrow x(1) = 5$; $y(1) = -1$

$(-3, 3)$ is a point of maxima $t = -1$; $\frac{d^2y}{dx^2} < 0$

$(5, 1)$ is a point of minima $t = \pm 1$; $\frac{d^2y}{dx^2} > 0$

$(1, 1)$ is point of inflection at $t = 0$.

DARBOUX THEOREM

If $f(x)$ is differentiable for $a \le x \le b, f(a) = \alpha, f(b) = \beta$, and γ lies between α and β, then there is a ξ between a and b for which $f'(\xi) = \gamma$

Proof: Let γ be such that; $\alpha < \gamma < \beta$ and let $\psi(x) = f(x) - \gamma(x - a)$

Then $\psi(x)$ is continuous, and therefore attains its lower bound in (a, b) at some point ξ of (a, b).

The point ξ can't be a or b, because $\psi'(a) = \alpha - \gamma < 0, \psi'(b) = \beta - \gamma > 0$

Hence $\psi(x)$ has a minimum at some ξ between a and b, and $\psi'(\xi) = 0$, i.e., $f'(\psi) = \gamma$

FORK EXTREMUM THEOREM

If f is a continuous function defined on a finite or infinite interval I such that f has a unique local extremum in I, then that local extremum is also an absolute extremum on I.

Proof: Let us consider that the function 'f' has unique extremum, a local maximum at $x = a$. Consider any other number b in I. The graph moves downward on both sides of a. So if $f(b)$ were greater than $f(a)$, then by the extreme value theorem for the closed interval with endpoints a and b, f would have an absolute minimum at some point α between a and b. (α can not be equal to a or b). Then f would have a local minimum at α, contradicting our hypothesis that f has only one local extremum. We can extend this argument to the case where f has a local minimum at 'a' on similar concept.

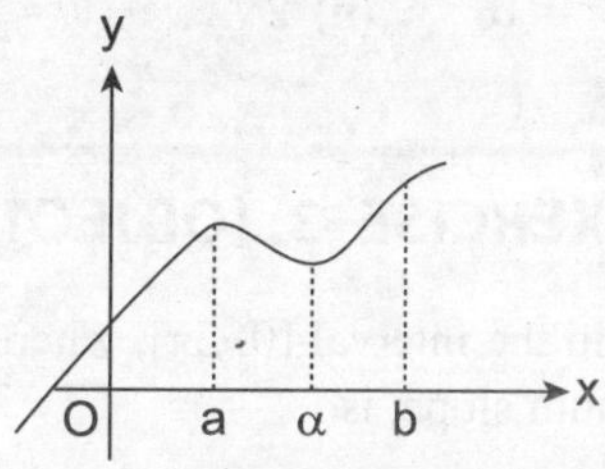

FIGURE 5.240

REMARK:

If we want to maximize or minimize the function f on the open interval I, and we find that f has only one critical point in I, a number α at which $f'(\alpha) = 0$.

If $f''(x)$ has the same sign at all points of I, then the above theorem implies that $f(\alpha)$ is an absolute extremum of on I.

A minimum at x if $f''(x) > 0$ and a maximum if $f''(x) < 0$. (The function is concave up or concave down respectively).

TEXTUAL EXERCISE–3: (SUBJECTIVE)

1. Using the second derivative, find the extrema of the function $f(x) = 2x^3 - 15x^2 - 84x + 8$

2. Investigate the following functions for extrema

   (a) $f(x) = x^4 e^{-x^2}$ **(b)** $f(x) = \sin 3x - 3\sin x$

3. Show that a triangle of max. area that can be inscribed in a circle of radius a is an equilateral triangle.

4. Show that the height of the cylinder of maximum volume that can be inscribed in a sphere of radius a is $2a/\sqrt{3}$.

5. Find the coordinates of the point P on the curve $\frac{x^2}{8} + \frac{y^2}{18} = 1$ in the 1st quadrant so that the area of the triangle formed by the tangent at P and the coordinate axes is minimum.

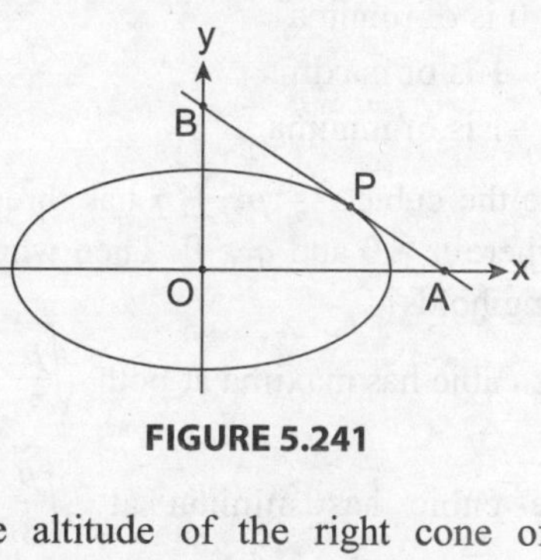

FIGURE 5.241

6. Find the altitude of the right cone of maximum volume that can be inscribed in a sphere of radius $\mathbb{R}$.

7. Find the altitude of the right circular cylinder of maximum volume that can be inscribed in a given right circular cone of height 'h'.

8. Find the equation of a line through (1,8) cutting the positive semi axes at A and B if

(i) The area of ΔOAB is minimum

(ii) Sum of its intercept on the coordinates axes is minimum.

(iii) Its intercept between the coordinate axes is minimum.

Answer Keys

1. $f_{max}(-2) = 100, f_{min}(7) = -629$ 2. (a) max $= 4/e^2$, min $=0$ (b) max $= 4$, min $= -4$

5. (2, 3); $x = 2\sqrt{2}\cos\theta, y = 3\sqrt{2}\sin\theta$ 6. $4R/3$ 7. $h/3$

8. (i) $8x + y = 16$ (ii) $2\sqrt{2}\,x + y = 8 + 2\sqrt{2}$ (iii) $2x + y = 10$; min. intercept $5\sqrt{5}$, .

TEXTUAL EXERCISE-3: (OBJECTIVE)

1. The point in the interval $[0, 2\pi]$, where $f(x) = e^x \sin x$ has maximum slope, is

(a) $\frac{\pi}{4}$ (b) $\frac{\pi}{2}$

(c) π (d) $\frac{3\pi}{2}$

2. If $f(x) = x^2 + 4x + 1$, then

(a) $f(x) = f(-x)$, for all x

(b) $f(x) \neq 1$, for any $x \in \mathbb{R}$

(c) $f''(x) > 0$, for all x

(d) $f(x) > 1$, for $x \leq 4$

3. The maximum value of function $f(x) = \sin x(1 + \cos x)$, $x \in \mathbb{R}$ is

(a) $\frac{3^{3/2}}{4}$ (b) $\frac{3^{5/3}}{4}$

(c) $\frac{3}{2}$ (d) $\frac{3^{7/5}}{4}$

4. For the function $f(x) = xe^x$ the point

(a) $x = 0$ is of maxima

(b) $x = 0$ is of minima

(c) $x = -1$ is of maxima

(d) $x = -1$ is of minima

5. Suppose the cubic $x^3 - px + q$ has three distinct real roots where $p > 0$ and $q > 0$. Then which one of the following holds?

(a) The cubic has maxima at both $\sqrt{\frac{p}{3}}$ and $-\sqrt{\frac{p}{3}}$

(b) The cubic has minima at $\sqrt{\frac{p}{3}}$ and maxima at $-\sqrt{\frac{p}{3}}$

(c) The cubic has minima at $-\sqrt{\frac{p}{3}}$ and maxima at $\sqrt{\frac{p}{3}}$

(d) The cubic has minima at both $\sqrt{\frac{p}{3}}$ and $-\sqrt{\frac{p}{3}}$

6. If $f(x) = 2x^3 - 21x^2 + 36x - 30$, then which one of the following is correct

(a) $f(x)$ has minimum at $x = 1$

(b) $f(x)$ has maximum at $x = 6$

(c) $f(x)$ has maximum at $x = 1$

(d) $f(x)$ has no maxima or minima

7. The maxima value of $\frac{\ln x}{x}$ in $(2, \infty)$ is

(a) 1 (b) $2/e$

(c) e (d) $1/e$

8. If m and M respectively denote the minimum and maximum of $f(x) = (x - 1)^2 + 3$ for $x \in [-3, 1]$, then the ordered pair (m, M) is equal to

(a) (–3, 19) (b) (3, 19)

(c) (–19, 3) (d) (–19, –3)

9. The greatest value of $f(x) = (x + 1)^{1/3} - (x - 1)^{1/3}$ on [0, 1] is

(a) 0 (b) 1

(c) 2 (d) –1

10. The function $x\sqrt{1-x^2}$, $(x > 0)$ has

(a) a local maxima

(b) a local minima

(c) neither a local maxima nor a local minima
(d) None of the above

11. The function $f(x) = x + \frac{1}{x}$ has
(a) a local maxima at $x = 1$ and a local minima at $x = -1$
(b) a local minima at $x = 1$ and a local maxima at $x = -1$
(c) absolute maxima at $x = 1$ and absolute minima at $x = -1$
(d) absolute minima at $x = 1$ and absolute maxima at $x = -1$

12. The maximum value of $f(x) = \frac{x}{4 + x + x^2}$ on [–1, 1] is
(a) $-\frac{1}{3}$ (b) $-\frac{1}{4}$
(c) $\frac{1}{4}$ (d) $\frac{1}{6}$

13. Observe the statements given below
Assertion (A): $f(x) = xe^{-x}$ has the maximum at $x = 1$
Reason (R): $f'(1) = 0, f''(1) < 0$
Which of the following is correct?
(a) Both (A) and (R) are true and (R) is the correct reason for (A)
(b) Both (A) and (R) are true, but (R) is not the correct reason for (A)
(c) (A) is true, (R) is false
(d) (A) is false, (R) is true

14. The function $f(x) = x^2 e^{-2x}, x > 0$. Then, the maximum value of $f(x)$ is
(a) $\frac{1}{e}$ (b) $\frac{1}{2e}$
(c) $\frac{1}{e^2}$ (d) $\frac{4}{e^4}$

15. If the function $f(x) = 2x^3 - 9ax^2 + 12a^2 x + 1$; $a > 0$ attains its maximum and minimum at p and q respectively such that $p^2 = q$, then a equals
(a) 0 (b) 1
(c) 2 (d) None of these

16. A population $p(t)$ of 1000 bacteria introduced into nutrient medium grows according to the relation $p(t) = 1000 + \frac{1000t}{100 + t^2}$. The maximum size of this bacterial population is
(a) 1100 (b) 1250
(c) 1050 (d) 5250

17. The maximum value $x^{1/x}$ is
(a) $1/e^e$ (b) e
(c) $e^{1/e}$ (d) $1/e$

18. If $f(x)$ ——— for every real number x, then minimum value of $f(x)$
(a) does not exist (b) is equal to 1
(c) is equal to 0 (d) is equal to –1

19. The largest value of $2x^3 - 3x^2 - 12x + 5$ for $-2 \le x \le 4$ occurs at x is equal to
(a) –4 (b) 0
(c) 1 (d) 4.

20. The minimum value of $4e^{2x} + 9e^{-2x}$ is
(a) 11 (b) 12
(c) 10 (d) 14

21. The maximum value $x^3 - 3x$ in the interval [0,2] is
(a) –2 (b) 0
(c) 2 (d) 1

22. If for a function $f(x)$, $f'(a) = 0$ $f''(a) = 0$, $f'''(a) > 0$, then at $x = a$, $f(x)$ is
(a) minimum
(b) maximum
(c) not an extreme point
(d) extreme point

23. A minimum value of $\int_0^x te^{t^2} dt$ is
(a) 0 (b) 1
(c) 2 (d) 3

24. Let $a, b, \in \mathbb{R}$ be such that the function f given by $f(x) = \log|x| + bx^2 + ax, x \ne 0$ has extreme values at $x = -1$ and $x = 2$
Statement 1: f has local maximum at $x = 2$ and local minima at $x = -1$.
Statement 2: $a = \frac{1}{2}$ and $b = \frac{-1}{4}$
(a) Statement – 1 is false, statement 2 is true
(b) Statement – 1 is true, statement 2 is true; statement 2 is a correct explanation for statement 1
(c) Statement – 1 is true, statement 2 is true; statement 2 is not a correct explanation for statement 1
(d) Statement 1 is true, statement 2 is false

25. Find the local maxima of the function defined parametrically as $x = (t + 1)$ and $y = t^3 - t^2$

(a) (1, 0) (b) (0, 1)
(c) (2/3, 5/3) (d) None of these

26. In the above question; the local maxima will be attained when t is equal to

(a) 2 (b) 0
(c) 2/3 (d) None of these

27. Find the difference between the minimum and maximum values of 'y' where $y = (1 - t)^{3/2}$ and $x = t^{3/2}$

(a) 2 (b) 1
(c) 3 (d) None of these

28. For the function defined parametrically as $x = \dfrac{t^2}{1-t^2}$ and $y = \dfrac{1}{1+t^2}$; answer the questions that follow

(i) The maximum value of the function is achieved when x =

(a) 1/2 (b) –1
(c) 1 (d) 0

(ii) The minimum value of the function is achieved when x =

(a) 1/2 (b) –1
(c) 1 (d) 0

(iii) The range of the function will be given by

(a) (0, 1] ~{1/2}
(b) (0, 1]
(c) (0, 1] ~{1/3, 1/2}
(d) None of these

(iv) The function $y = f(x)$ is decreasing for $x \in$

(a) $(-\infty, -1)$
(b) $(-1, 0)$
(c) $(-\infty, 0)$
(d) None of these

(v) The function $y = f(x)$ is increasing $x \in$

(a) $(0, \infty)$ (b) (0, 1]
(c) $[0, \infty)$ (d) None of these

Answer Keys

1. (b)	**2.** (c)	**3.** (a)	**4.** (d)	**5.** (b)	**6.** (c)	**7.** (c)	**8.** (b)	**9.** (c)	**10.** (a)
11. (b)	**12.** (d)	**13.** (a)	**14.** (c)	**15.** (c)	**16.** (c)	**17.** (c)	**18.** (d)	**19.** (d)	**20.** (b)
21. (c)	**22.** (c)	**23.** (a)	**24.** (c)	**25.** (a)	**26.** (b)	**27.** (b)	**28. (i)** (d)	**(ii)** (b)	**(iii)** (a)
(iv) (a)	**(v)** (d)								

■ EXTREMA OF DISCONTINUOUS FUNCTIONS

❑ Minimum at
$x = a$: $f(a) < f(a-h)$ & $f(a) < f(a+h)$

❑ Maximum at
$x = a$: $f(a) > f(a-h)$ & $f(a) > f(a+h)$

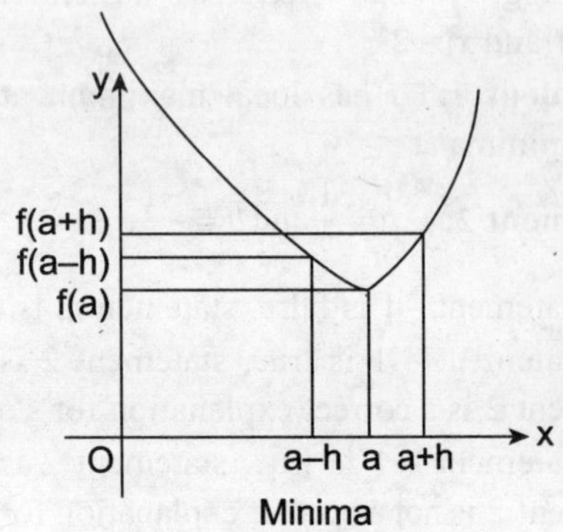

FIGURE 5.242

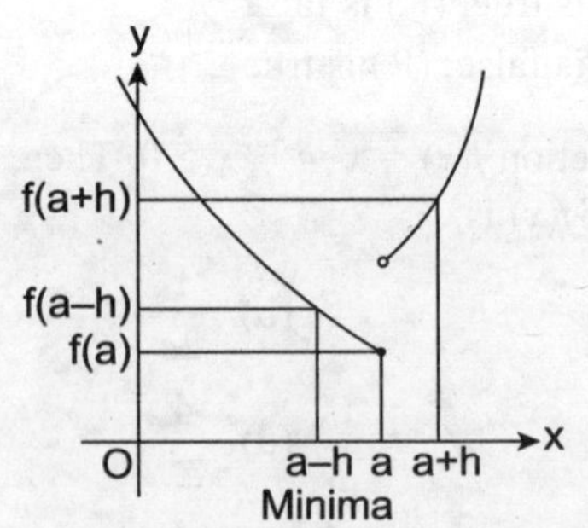

FIGURE 5.243

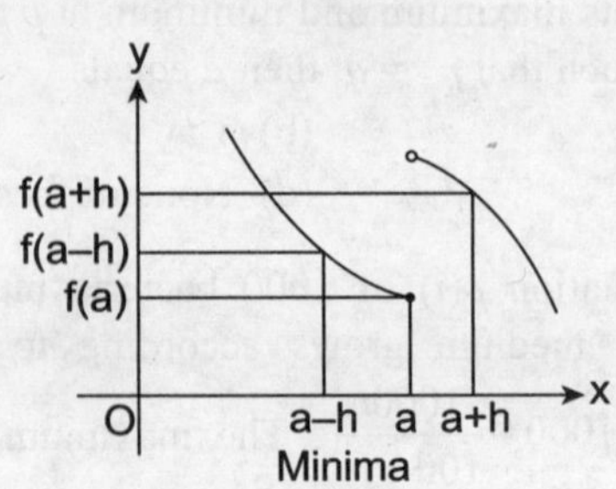

FIGURE 5.244

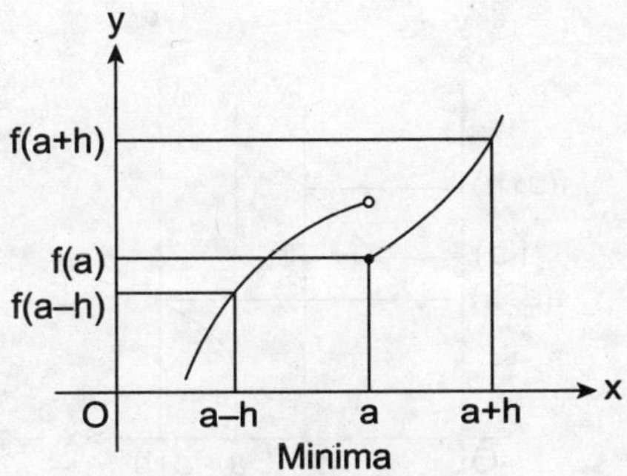

FIGURE 5.245

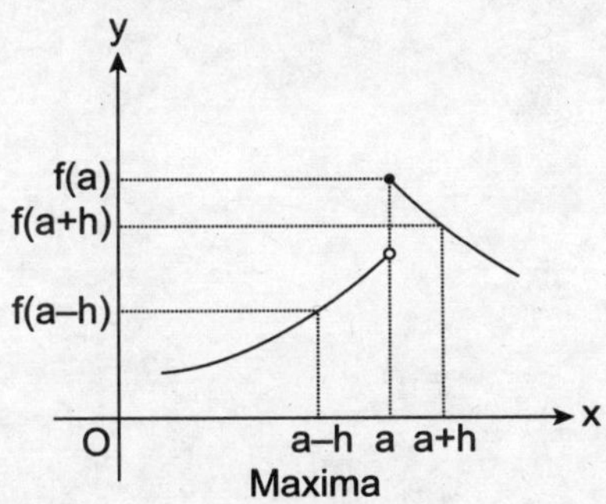

FIGURE 5.246

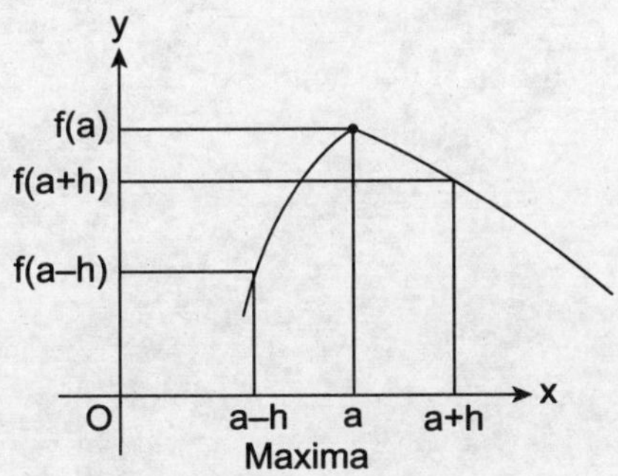

FIGURE 5.247

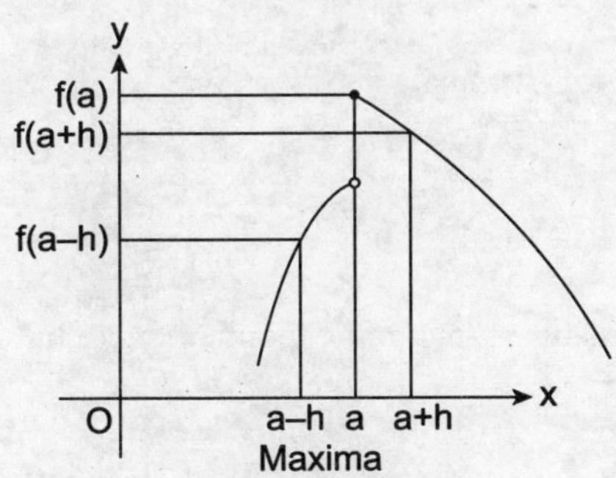

FIGURE 5.248

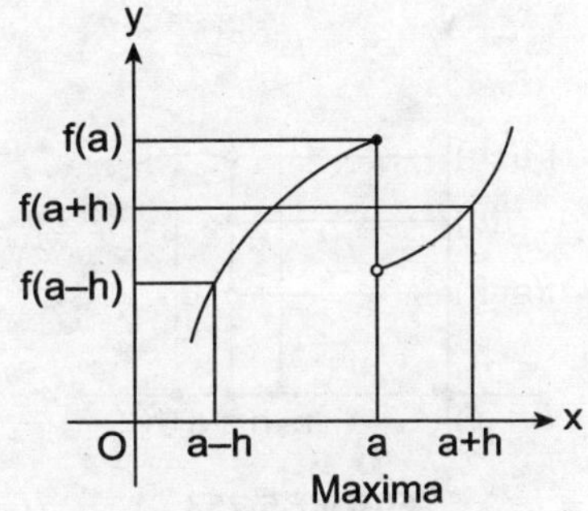

FIGURE 5.249

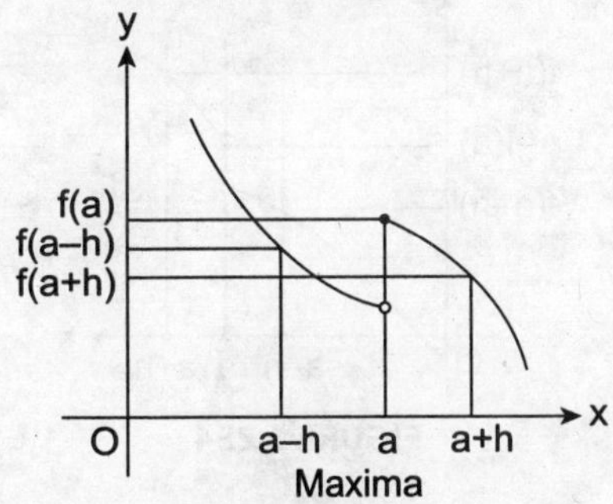

FIGURE 5.250

- Neither maximum nor minimum at $x = a$: $f(a-h) < f(a) < f(a+h)$ or

  or $f(a-h) > f(a) > f(a+h)$

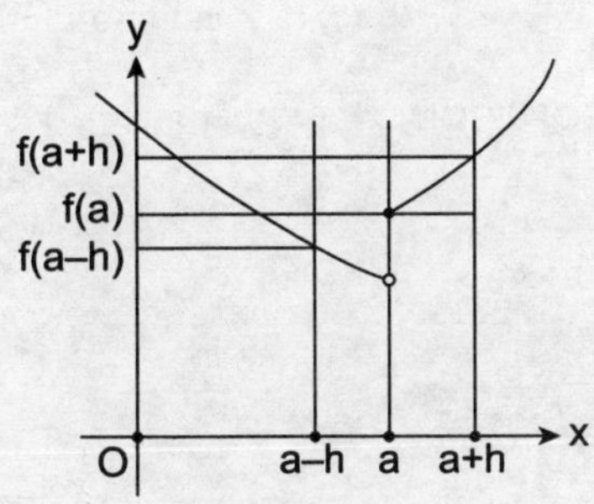

FIGURE 5.251

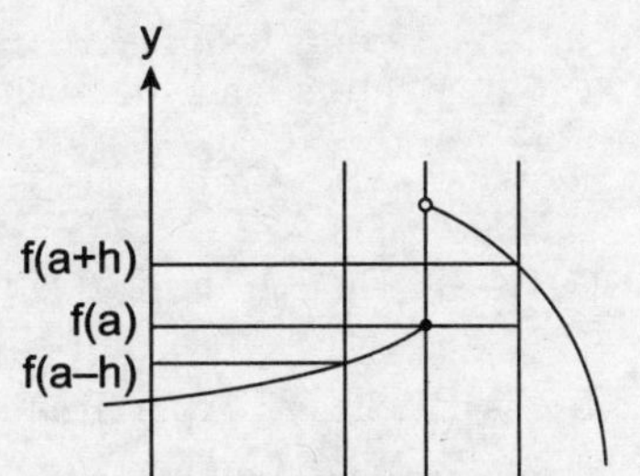

FIGURE 5.252

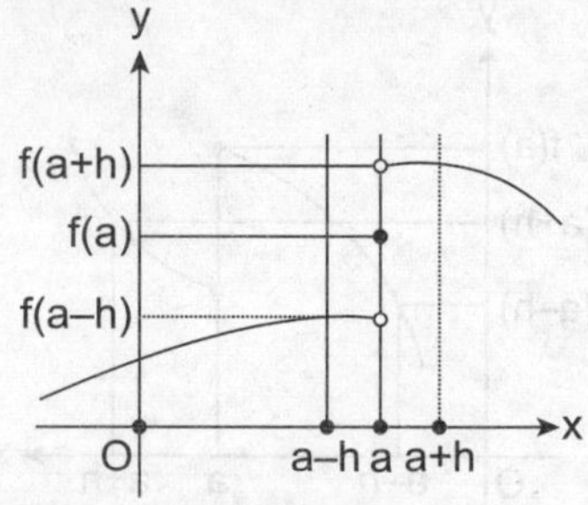

FIGURE 5.253

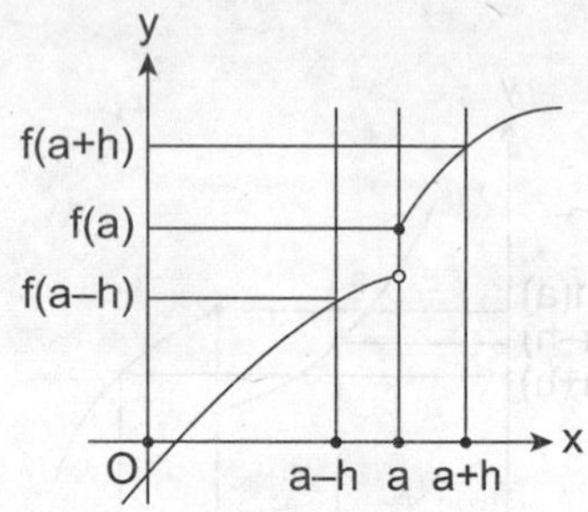

FIGURE 5.254

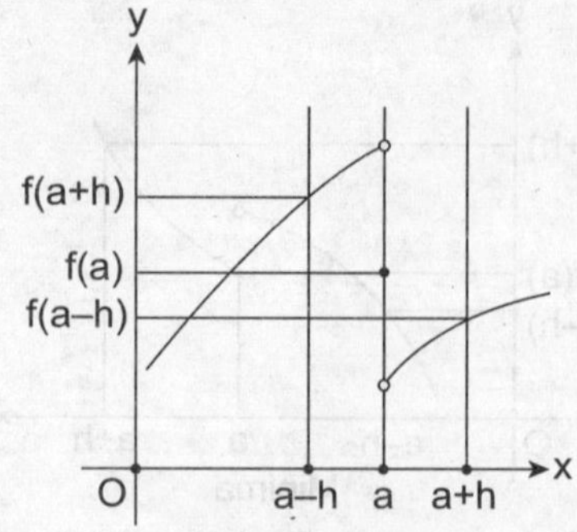

FIGURE 5.255

ILLUSTRATION 221: Let $f(x) = \begin{bmatrix} |x| \; for \; 0 < |x| \le 2 \\ 1 \quad for \; x = 0 \end{bmatrix}$. Then at $x = 0$, 'f' has :

(a) a local maximum (b) no local maximum

(c) a local minimum (d) no extremum.

SOLUTION: It is clear at $x = 0$ is local maxima

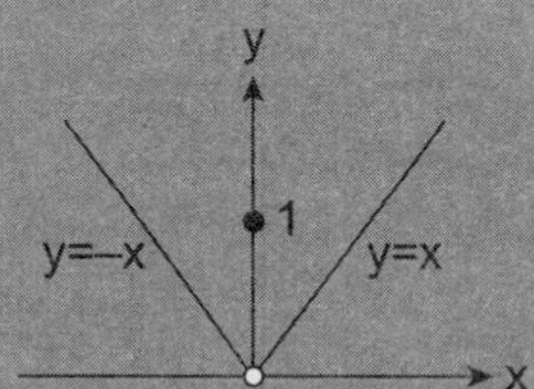

FIGURE 5.256

ILLUSTRATION 222: Investigate the function $f(x) = \begin{cases} -2x \quad ; \; x < 0 \\ 3x + 5; \; x \ge 0 \end{cases}$ for extrema.

SOLUTION: Though the derivative $f'(x) = \begin{cases} -2 \quad ; x < 0 \\ 3 \quad ; x > 0 \end{cases}$ exists at all points except the point $x = 0$ and changes sign from minus to plus when passing through the point $x = 0$ there is no minimum here:

$\Rightarrow f(0) = 5 > f(x)$ at $-1 < x < 0$

This is explained by the fact that the function is discontinuous at the point $x = 0$.

ILLUSTRATION 223: Find the maximum or minimum value of

$f(x)$ at $x = 1$ if $f(x) = \begin{cases} \dfrac{x^2-1}{x-1}, & x \neq 1 \\ 4, & x = 1 \end{cases}$

SOLUTION: Given $f(x) = \begin{cases} \dfrac{x^2-1}{x-1}, & x \neq 1 \\ 4, & x = 1 \end{cases}$

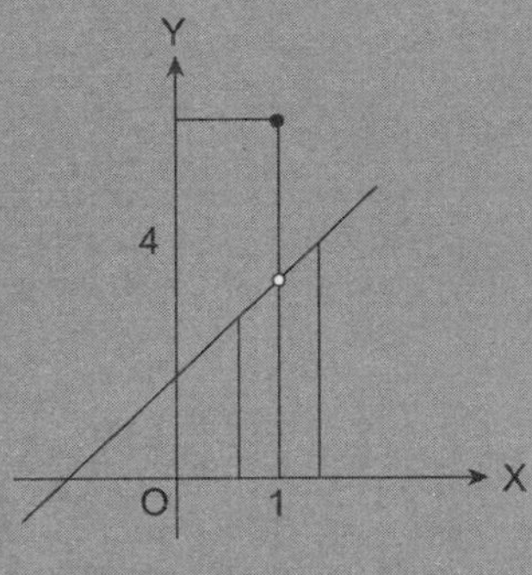

FIGURE 5.257

$f(x)$ is discontinuous at $x = 1$

Hence maximum value of $f(x)$ at $x = 1$ is 4 and minimum value does not exist.

ILLUSTRATION 224: Let $f(x) = \begin{cases} 1+\sin x, & x < 0 \\ x^2 - x + 1, & x \geq 0 \end{cases}$. Then

(a) f has a local maximum at $x = 0$ (b) f has a local minimum at $x = 0$

(c) f is increasing every where (d) f is decreasing everywhere

SOLUTION: (c) $\lim\limits_{x\to 0} x^n \sin(1/x^2) = 0$ for $n > 0$. Thus (a) and (b) are false.

$f(0) = \lim\limits_{x\to 0} \dfrac{f(x) - f(0)}{x - 0} = \lim\limits_{x\to 0} x^{n-1} \sin(1/x^2)$, which exists for $n > 1 \Rightarrow$ (c) is true.

ILLUSTRATION 225: If $f(x) = \begin{cases} x^2 + 4x, & -3 \leq x \leq 0 \\ -\sin x, & 0 < x \leq \pi/2 \\ -\cos x - 1, & \pi/2 < x \leq \pi \end{cases}$, then

(a) $x = -2$ is the point of global minima (b) $x = \pi$ is the point of global minima

(c) $f(x)$ is differentiable at $x = \pi/2$ (d) $f(x)$ is discontinuous at $x = 0$

SOLUTION: From above figure it is clearly shown that $x = -2$ is the point of global minima.

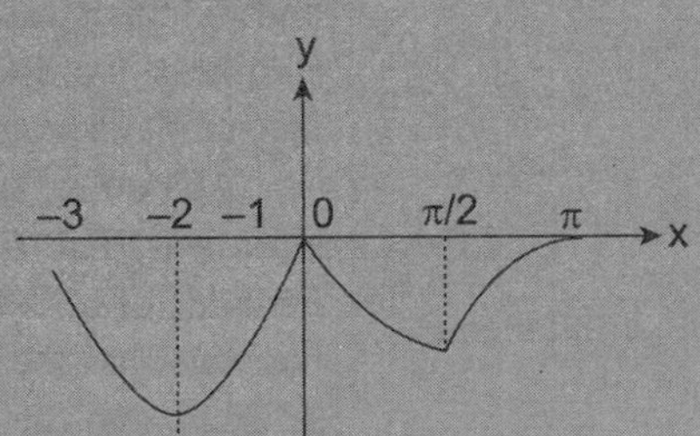

FIGURE 5.258

ILLUSTRATION 226: Let $f(x) = \begin{cases} x^2 + x; & -1 \le x < 0 \\ \lambda; & x = 0 \\ \log_{1/2}\left(x + \frac{1}{2}\right); & 0 < x < \frac{3}{2} \end{cases}$. Discuss global maxima, minima for $\lambda = 0$ and $\lambda = 1$.

For what values of λ does $f(x)$ has global maxima

SOLUTION: Graph of $y = f(x)$ for $\lambda = 0$

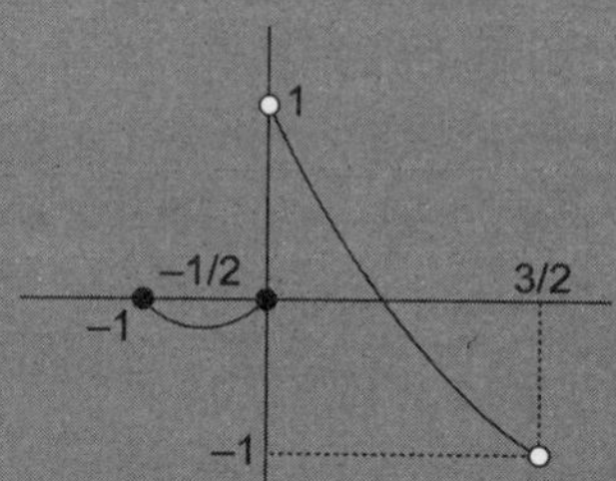

FIGURE 5.259

No global maxima, minima

Graph of $y = f(x)$ for $\lambda = 1$

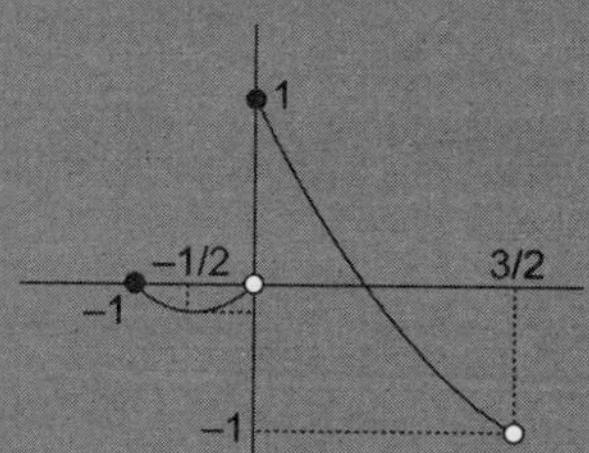

FIGURE 5.260

Global maxima is 1, which occurs at $x = 0$

Global minima does not exists

$\lim_{x\to 0^-} f(x) = 0, \ \lim_{x\to 0^+} f(x) = 1, \ f(0) = \lambda$

For global maxima to exists $f(0) \ge 1$

$\Rightarrow \lambda \ge 1.$

■ MAXIMA AND MINIMA OF FUNCTIONS OF SEVERAL VARIABLES

We give a few indications concerning the extension of some of the preceding results to functions of two or more independent variables.

In the first place let us seek for the maxima and minima of a function $u = \phi(x, y)$. ...(1)

A first condition is that we must have simultaneously

$$\frac{\partial \phi}{\partial x} = 0, \frac{\partial \phi}{\partial y} = 0 \qquad ...(2)$$

where the differential coefficients are "partial".

For if u be greater (or less) than any other value of the function obtained by varying x, y within certain limits, u will be maximum (or minimum) when y is kept constant and x alone is varied. This requires in general that $\partial f/\partial x = 0$. Similarly, u must be a maximum (or minimum) when x kept constant and y alone varies; this requires that $\partial f/\partial x = 0$.

As before, these conditions, though necessary, are not sufficient. The further examination of the question, in its general form, is beyond the scope of the text; but it often happens that the existence of maxima and minima can be inferred, and the discrimination between them effected, by independent consideration. The conditions (2) then supply all that is analytically necessary.

ILLUSTRATION 227: Find the cuboids of the least surface area for a given volume

SOLUTION: Let x, y, z be the edges, and a^3 the given volume. Since $xyz = a^3$ ...(1)

The function to be made minimum is

$$u = xy + yz + zx = xy + \frac{a^3}{x} + \frac{a^3}{y} \quad ...(2)$$

The conditions $\partial u/\partial x = 0$, $\partial u/\partial y = 0$ give $x^2y = a^3$, $xy^2 = a^3$ the only real solution of which is $x = y = a$, which implies $z = a$

It appears from (2) that x and y being essentially positive in this problem, there is a lower limit to the surface area of the parallelepiped. And the above investigative shows that this limit is not attained unless the figure be a cube.

MAXIMUM AND MINIMUM FOR DISCRETE VALUED FUNCTIONS

Discrete values function: A real valued function whose domain is a finite or countable set is called discrete valued function. Since the function can give exactly one image of every point of domain, range of discrete valued functions is also finite or countable.

For example function defined by

(i) $f(n) = n^2$; $n \in \mathbb{N}$ is a discrete function with domain $\mathbb{N}$ set of natural numbers and range $= \{n^2; n \in \mathbb{N}\} = \{1, 4, 9, 16, \ldots\}$

(ii) $f(x) = \frac{2n}{n+1}; n \in \{1,2,3,.....10\}$ is a discrete function with domain set $= \{1,2,3,\ldots 10\}$

and range $= \left\{1, \frac{4}{3}, \frac{3}{2}, \frac{8}{5}, \frac{5}{3}, \frac{12}{7}, \frac{7}{4}, \frac{16}{9}, \frac{9}{5}, \frac{20}{21}\right\}$

The graphs of discrete functions are discontinuous. Let us study the maxima/minima of such functions with the help of the following illustrations:

ILLUSTRATION 228: Find the largest term in the sequence

$$a_n = \frac{n}{n^2+90} (n \in \mathbb{N})$$

SOLUTION: Consider the function $f(x) = \frac{x}{x^2+90}, x > 0$

Then $f'(x) = \frac{(x^2+90) - 2x^2}{(x^2+90)^2}$

$= \frac{-(x+\sqrt{90})(x-\sqrt{90})}{(x^2+90)^2} > 0$ for $x \in \left(-\sqrt{90}, \sqrt{90}\right)$ and < 0 for $x < -\sqrt{90}$ or $x > \sqrt{90}$

$\Rightarrow$ $f(x)$ is strictly increasing in $\left(0, \sqrt{90}\right)$

And Strictly decreasing in $\left(\sqrt{90}, \infty\right)$

$\Rightarrow$ $f(x)$ has greatest value at $x = \sqrt{90} \approx 9.48$

Hence, the given sequence has the greatest value either at $x = 9$ or $n = 10$

Now, we compare $a_9 = \frac{1}{19}$ and $a_{10} = \frac{1}{19}$

Thus, $a_9 = a_{10} = \dfrac{1}{19}$ are the largest terms of the given sequence

ILLUSTRATION 229: Find the largest term in the sequence $a_n = \dfrac{n^2}{(n^3+200)^2}$

SOLUTION: Consider the function $f(x) = \dfrac{x^2}{(x^3+200)^2}$ in the interval $(1, \infty)$

Since the derivative $f'(x) = \dfrac{x(400-x^3)}{(x^3+200)^2}$

It is positive at $0 < x < \sqrt[3]{400}$ and negative at $x > \sqrt[3]{400}$, the function $f(x)$ increases at $0 < x < \sqrt[3]{400}$ and decreases at $x > \sqrt[3]{400}$.

From the inequality $7 < \sqrt[3]{400} < 8$ it follows that the largest term in the sequence can be either a_7 or a_8.

Since $a_7 = \dfrac{49}{543} > a_8 = \dfrac{8}{89}$, the largest term in the given sequence is $a_7 = \dfrac{49}{543}$

ILLUSTRATION 230: In how many positive parts should an integer $N \geq 5$ be dissected, so that the product of the parts is maximized.

SOLUTION: Let $x_1, x_2, \ldots x_n > 0$ be real numbers such that $x_1 + x_2 + x_3 + \ldots x_n = N$

Using A.M. ≥ G.M; we get $\dfrac{x_1 + x_2 + \ldots + x_n}{n} \geq (x_1.x_2....x_n)^{1/n}$

$\Rightarrow \quad x_1.x_2......x_n \leq \left(\dfrac{x_1 + x_2 + ...x_n}{n}\right)^n$

Therefore maximum value of $x_1. x_2. x_3 \ldots\ldots x_n$ is obtained when $x_1 = x_3 = x_3 = \ldots\ldots = x_n$

($\because$ Maximum value of G.M is obtained when all parts are equal)

Now $x_1 + x_2 + x_3 + \ldots x_n = N$ and $x_1 = x_2 = \ldots\ldots x_n$

$\Rightarrow \quad x_1 = x_2 = \ldots\ldots = x_n = \dfrac{N}{n}$

Now, function to be maximized $x_1 = x_2 = x_3 = x_n$ i.e., $\left(\dfrac{x_1 + x_2 + \ldots + x_n}{n}\right)$ which is a discrete function of n. In order to arrive at some possible neighborhood we make it continuous and differentiable.

Thus changing the variables from n to y, we write $f(y) = \left(\dfrac{N}{y}\right)^y$

For maxima; $f'(y) = 0$ i.e., $f'(y) = f(y)\left(\ell n\left(\dfrac{N}{y}\right) - 1\right)$ $f'(y) = 0$ for $\dfrac{N}{y} = e$ or $y = \dfrac{N}{e}$

The nearest integer to $y = \dfrac{N}{n}$ is $\left[\dfrac{N}{e}\right]$ or $\left[\dfrac{N}{e}\right] + 1$ where [.] denotes the greatest integer function.

Now, we need to compare $f\left(\left[\dfrac{N}{e}\right]\right)$ and $f\left(\left[\dfrac{N}{e}\right]+1\right)$ to get the maximum value.

ILLUSTRATION 231: A manufacturer determines that the demand for 'n' lamps priced at p rupees each is given by the function $n = f(p) = 80 - \frac{1}{2}p$ where p is an even integer, $0 \le p \le 160$. The range of $f(p)$ is a set of integers that are on the interval $0 \le n \le 80$. Suppose that the lamp manufacturer has determined that the cost of producing n lamps is $(200 + 25n)$ rupees. How many lamps should be manufactured to maximize profit ?

SOLUTION: The total profit $f(n)$ obtained by producing n lamps at p rupees is

$f(n) = np - (200 + 25n)$

$= n(160 - 2n) - (200 + 25n)$

$= -2n^2 + 135n - 200$

We consider the function $g(x) = -2x^2 + 135x - 200$, $0 \le x \le 80$ and observe that whenever x is an integer, n, $g(n) = f(n)$, and thus all points $(n, f(n))$ are on the graph $g(x)$.

Observe also that $g\left(\frac{1}{2}\right) = -133$, but $f\left(\frac{1}{2}\right)$ is undefined.

Now, since $G'(x) = -4x + 135$

Then $g'(x) > 0$ if $x < \frac{135}{4}$, and $g'(x) < 0$ if $x > \frac{135}{4}$, we see that $g(x)$ is increasing in $0 \le x \le \frac{135}{4}$ and is decreasing in $\frac{135}{4} \le x \le 80$

Hence, g has its maximum at $x = \frac{135}{4}$

Now, nearest integer to $\frac{135}{4}$ are 33 and 34.

We find $g(33) = f(33) = 2077$ and $f(34) = g(34) = 2078$. Since $g(34)$ is larger, a maximum profit of 2078 rupees results from the production of 34 sets.

ILLUSTRATION 232: A joy ride which can hold maximum 45 people to groups of 30 or more is such that, if a group contains exactly 30 people, each person pays 55 rupees and in larger groups, everybody's fare is reduced by 1 rupee for each person in excess of 30. Determine the size of the group for which the revenue per ride will be the greatest.

SOLUTION: We wish to maximize the revenue

Revenue = (Number of people in the group) (Fare per person)

Let x be the number of people in excess of 30 who take the trip. Then

Number of people in the group = $30 + x$; Fare per person = $55 - x$

Let $R(x)$ be the revenue for the bus company:

$R(x) = (30 + x)(55 - x) = 1650 + 25x - x^3$

Next, find the domain: we note that there must be at least 30 people ($x = 0$) and at most 40 people ($x = 10$); thus $0 \le x \le 15$, but because x represents the number of people it must be an integer.

The critical numbers are found by solving $R'(x) = 25 - 2x = 0$

Because the derivative exists throughout the interval, the only critical number is $x = 12.50$. But x must be an integer, so $x = 12.5$ is not in the domain. To find the optimal integer solution observe that R is increasing on (0,12.5) and decreasing on (12.5, 15).

It follows that the optimal integer values of x is either $x = 12$ or $x = 13$, because $R(12) = 1806$ and $R(13) = 1,806$.

We conclude that the bus company's revenue will be greatest when the group contains either 12 or 13 people in excess of 35, for groups of 47 or 48. In either case, the maximum revenue will be 2,256 rupees.

ILLUSTRATION 233: Find the least and greatest values of the function $f(x) = \sin(\cos(\sin x))$ on the closed interval $[\pi/2, \pi]$

SOLUTION: $\because$ $\sin x$ decreases on $\left[\frac{\pi}{2}, \pi\right]$; therefore if $\pi/2 \le x_1 < x_2 \le \pi$, then $0 \le \sin x_2 < \sin x_1 \le 1$, and the points $\sin x_1$, $\sin x_2$ lie in the fist quadrant since $1 < \pi/2$.

Also, we know that the function $\cos x$ decreases on the interval $[0, \pi/2]$, hence we have $0 < \cos(\sin x_1) < \cos(\sin x_2) \le 1$.

But the points $\cos(\sin x_1)$, $\cos(\sin x_2)$ also lie in the first quadrant and the function $\sin x$ increases on the interval $[0, \pi/2]$, therefore $0 < \sin(\cos(\sin x_1)) < \sin((\cos(\sin x_2)) < 1$.

Now, the function $f(x) = \sin((\cos(\sin x))$ is increasing on the interval $[\pi/2, \pi]$, consequently, the minimum value of $f(x)$ on this interval is equal to $f(\pi/2) = \sin(\cos 1)$, whereas the maximum value to $f(\pi) = \sin(\cos 0) = \sin 1$.

ILLUSTRATION 234: The fuel charges for running a train are proportional to the square of the speed generated in miles per hour and costs × 48 per hour at 16 miles per hour. The most economical speed if the fixed charges i.e., salaries etc. amount to × 300 per hour

(a) 10 (b) 20

(c) 30 (d) 40

SOLUTION: Let the speed of the train be v and distance to be covered be s so that total time taken is s/v hour.

Cost of fuel per hour $= kv^2$ (k is constant)

Also $48 = k.16^2$ by given condition

$\therefore$ $k = 3/16$

$\therefore$ Cost of fuel per hour $= \frac{3}{16}v^2$

Other charges per hour are 300.

$\therefore$ Charges per hour are $\frac{3}{16}v^2 + 300$

$\therefore$ Total expenses for the journey

$$E = \left(\frac{3}{16}v^2 + 300\right)\frac{S}{v} \text{ or } E = S\left(\frac{3}{16}v + \frac{300}{v}\right)$$

$$\frac{dE}{dV} = s\left(\frac{3}{16} - \frac{300}{v^2}\right) = 0$$

$\therefore$ $v^2 = 1600$ or $v = 40$

$$\frac{d^2E}{dv^2} = S\left(\frac{600}{v^3}\right) = +\text{ve for } v = 40$$

And hence E is minimum at $v = 40$.

TEXTUAL EXERCISE–4: (SUBJECTIVE)

1. Investigate the function $f(x)=\begin{cases}2x^2+3; & x\neq 0\\ 4 & ; x=0\end{cases}$ for extrema.

2. If $f(x)=\begin{cases}1+x; & 0\le x\le 2\\ 3-x; & 2<x\le 3\end{cases}$, then find the points of local maxima, local minima, global maxima and global minima for $f(x)$.

3. Find extrema for the function $f(x)=\sqrt{2-x^2}$

4. Find global minima for $f(x)=\log_{\frac{1}{4}}\left(x-\frac{1}{4}\right)+\frac{1}{2}\log_4$ $(16x^2-8x+1)$

5. Find global extrema for $f(x)=\tan^{-1}\left(\frac{3x-x^3}{1-3x^2}\right)$

6. Find the points for global extrema for $f(x)=\tan^{-1}\left(\frac{2x}{1-x^2}\right)$

7. Let $f(x)=\begin{cases}\sqrt{x+2}; & -2\le x<0\\ |x-1|; & 0\le x\le 3\end{cases}$. State which of the following is/are true.
   (i) The function $f(x)$ has a maximum at $x = 0$
   (ii) The function $f(x)$ does not have maximum at $x = 0$
   (iii) The function $f(x)$ has maximum at $x = 3$
   (iv) The function $f(x)$ has global as well as local minimum at $x = -2$ and 1

8. Suppose $f(x)=\begin{cases}-x^3+k^2-3k+2; & 0\le x<1\\ 2x-3 & ; 1\le x\le 3\end{cases}$. If $f(x)$ is the smallest at $x = 1$, then find the interval of k.

9. If a function $f(x)$ is defined as $f(x)=\begin{cases}2x+\dfrac{b^3+b^2+7b+3}{b^2+3b+2}; & 0\le x\le 1\\ 6-2x & ; 1<x\le 3\end{cases}$, then find the values of 'b' for which $f(x)$ is greatest at $x = 1$.

Answer Keys

1. Function is discontinuous at $x = 0$, no extrema, g.l.b $= 3$
2. Local maxima $\rightarrow x = 2$
   Local minima $\rightarrow x = 0, 3$
   Global maxima $\rightarrow x = 2$
   Global minima $\rightarrow x = 3$
3. Minima $\rightarrow f(x) = 0$ at $x=\pm\sqrt{2}$
   Maxima $\rightarrow f(x) = \sqrt{2}$ at $x = 0$
4. $f(x) = 1$; $x\in\left(\frac{1}{4},\infty\right)$ i.e., a constant function
5. No point of global extrema
6. No point of extrema
7. (ii), (iii), (iv)
8. $k \le 1$ or $k \ge 2$
9. $b \in (-2, -1)$ or $[1, \infty)$

TEXTUAL EXERCISE–4: (OBJECTIVE)

1. Let $f(x)=\begin{cases}\sin\dfrac{\pi x}{2}; & 0\le x<1\\ 3-2x: & x\ge 1\end{cases}$; then
   (a) $f(x)$ has local maximum at $x = 1$
   (b) $f(x)$ has local minimum at $x = 1$
   (c) $f(x)$ does not have local extremum at $x = 1$
   (d) $f(x)$ has global minimum at $x = 1$

2. If $f(x)=\begin{cases}7-x^2; & x<2\\ 11-x; & x\ge 2\end{cases}$; then
   (a) $f(x)$ has local maxima at $x = 0$
   (b) $f(x)$ has local maxima at $x = 2$
   (c) $f(x)$ has local maxima at $x = 11$
   (d) None of these

3. If $f(x)=\begin{cases}3x^2+12x-1; & -1\le x\le 2\\ 37-x; & 2<x\le 3\end{cases}$; then

(a) $f(x)$ is increasing on [–1, 2]
(b) $f(x)$ is continuous on [–1, 3]
(c) $f'(2)$ does not exist
(d) $f(x)$ has the maximum value at $x = 2$

4. Check the function for local extrema at $x = 0$, where

$f(x)=\begin{cases}4-x^2; & x<0\\ 2x+1; & x\ge 0\end{cases}$

(a) local maxima (b) local minima
(c) point of inflection (d) None of these

5. Check the function for local extrema at $x = 0$, where

$f(x)=\begin{cases}3+x^2e^{-x}; & x<0\\ 2; & x=0\\ 1-2x^2; & x>0\end{cases}$

(a) local maxima (b) local minima
(c) point of inflection (d) None of these

6. Check the function for local extrema at $x = 0$, where

$f(x)=\begin{cases}x^3+x^2+5x; & x<0\\ 1-xe^x; & x\ge 0\end{cases}$

(a) local maxima (b) local minima
(c) point of inflection (d) None of these

7. If $f(x)=\begin{cases}1+x^2-3x, x<0\\ \cos x+2x, x\ge 0\end{cases}$, then the global maximum and local minimum values of $f(x)$ for $x \in [-2,2]$ are respectively.

(a) 4 + cos 2, 1 (b) 11, 1
(c) Dose not exist (d) None of these

8. Let $f(x)=\begin{cases}\sin^{-1}\alpha+x^2, 0<x<1\\ 2x, & x\ge 1\end{cases}$, then $f(x)$ can have a minimum at $x = 1$, if the value of α is

(a) 1 (b) –1
(c) 0 (d) None of these

9. Let $f(x)=\begin{cases}x^3-x^2+10x-5, x\le 1\\ -2x+\log_2(b^2-2), x>1\end{cases}$, the set of values of b for which $f(x)$ has greatest value at $x = 1$ is given by

(a) $1\le b\le 2$ (b) $b = \{1,2\}$
(c) $b\in(-\infty,-1)$ (d) None of these

10. Let $f(x)=\begin{cases}x^2+3x, & -1\le x<0\\ -\sin x, & 0\le x<\pi/2\\ -1-\cos x, & \frac{\pi}{2}\le x\le\pi\end{cases}$.

Then global maxima of $f(x)$ and global minima of $f(x)$ are equals

(a) –1 (b) 0
(c) –3 (d) –2

11. If $f(x)=\begin{cases}e^x & ,0\le x\le 1\\ 2-e^{x-1} & ,1<x\le 2\\ x-e & ,2<x\le 3\end{cases}$ and

$g(x) = \int_0^x f(t)dt, x\in[1,3]$ Then $g(x)$ has

(a) Local maxima at $x = 2$ and local minima at $x = 1$
(b) Local maxima at $x = 1 + \ln 2$ and local minima at $x = e$
(c) No local maxima
(d) No local minima

12. The total number of local maxima and local minima of the function $f(x)=\begin{cases}(2+x)^3, -3<x\le -1\\ x^{2/3} & ,-1<x<2\end{cases}$ is :

(a) 0 (b) 1
(c) 2 (d) 3

13. Let the function $f(x)$ be defined as $f(x)=\begin{cases}\tan^{-1}\alpha-3x^2, 0<x<1\\ -6x, & x\ge 1\end{cases}$, $f(x)$ can have a maximum at $x = 1$ if the value of α is

(a) 0 (b) 2
(c) 1 (d) None of these

15. Let $f(x) = \cos 2\pi x + x - [x]$, where [.] denotes the greatest integer function. Then the number of points in [0,10] at which $f(x)$ assumes its local maximum value is

(a) 10 (b) 9
(c) 1 (d) infinite

Answer Keys

1. (a) **2.** (a,b) **3.** (a,b,c,d) **4.** (b) **5.** (d) **6.** (a) **7.** (b) **8.** (d) **9.** (d)
10. (b,d) **11.** (b) **12.** (c) **13.** (d) **14.** (c)

AREA AND PERIMETER OF SOME STANDARD TWO DIMENSIONAL FIGURES ARE LISTED BELOW

(a) Triangle: Area: $\frac{1}{2}ab\sin C$ and perimeter: $(a+b+c)$

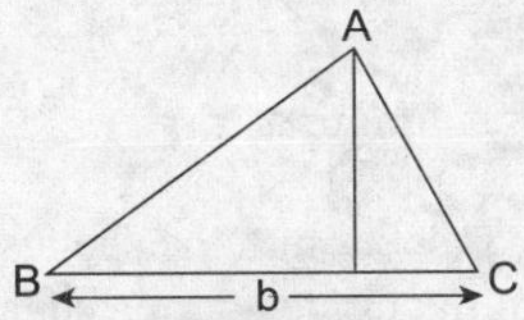

FIGURE 5.261

Equilateral triangle: $\angle A+\angle B+\angle C=60^{\circ}$ and BC $= CA = AB = a$ (say)

$\therefore$ Area $=\frac{\sqrt{3}}{4}a^2$ and perimeter $= 3a$.

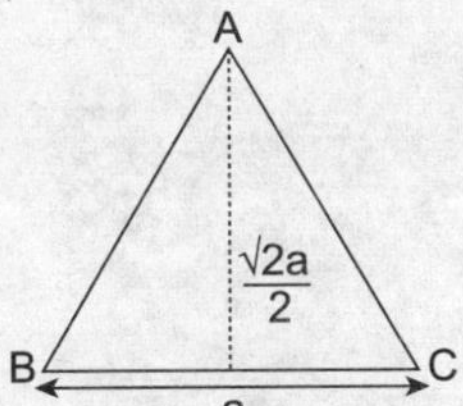

FIGURE 5.262

(b) Sector of a Circle: Area: $\frac{1}{2}r^2 d\theta$ where θ is in radians

and Perimeter : $r(2 + d\theta)$

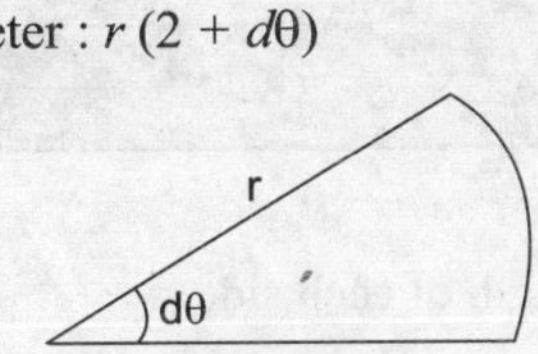

FIGURE 5.263

(c) Rectangle: In a rectangle $\angle A+\angle B+\angle C+\angle D=90^{\circ}$ $AB = DC = a$ and $BC = AD = b$

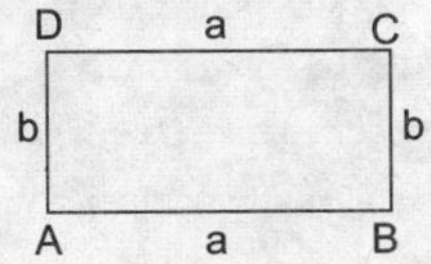

FIGURE 5.264

$\therefore$ Area $= ab$ and perimeter $= 2(a+b)$

(d) **Rhombus:** Perimeter is $4a$

Area $= a^2\sin\theta$

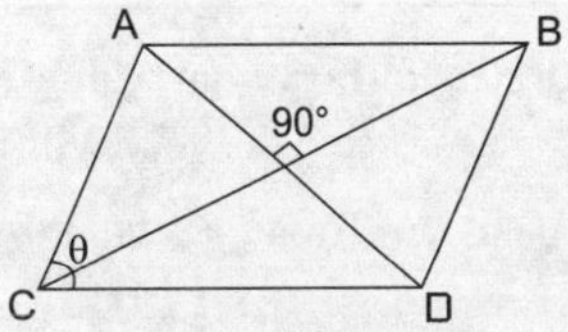

FIGURE 5.265

(e) Ellipse: If length of major and minor axes are $2a$ and $2b$ $\therefore$ Area $= \pi ab$

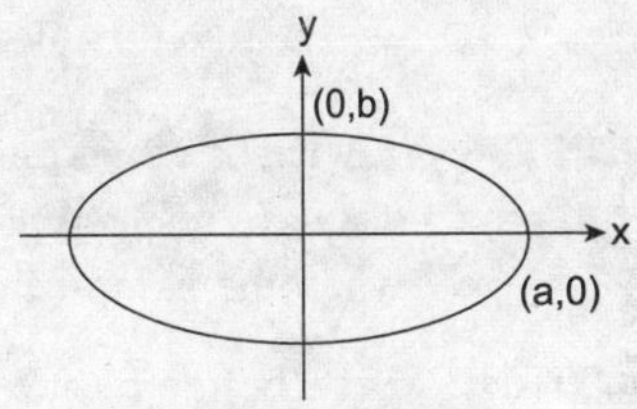

FIGURE 5.266

(f) Trapezium: In a trapezium AB is parallel to DC and AD and BC are not parallel.

If $AB = a$ and $DC = b$ and distance between parallel sides is h, then area $=\frac{1}{2}(a+b)\times h$

where a and b are parallel sides and h is distance between them

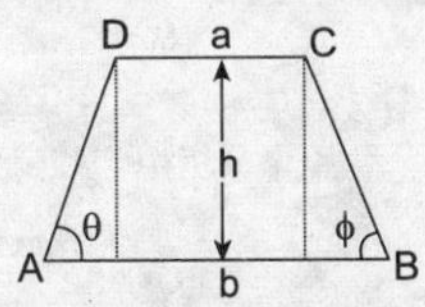

FIGURE 5.267

(g) Circle: If centre is at O and radius is r, then

$\therefore$ Area of sector $OPQ=\frac{1}{2}r^2\theta$ and arc length $(PQ) = r.\theta$.

Area of circle πr^2, circumference of circle = 2πr

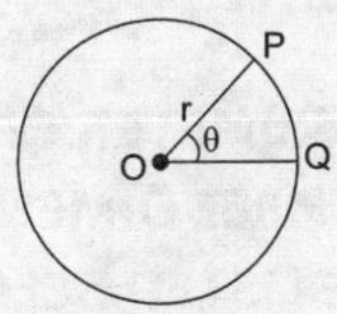

FIGURE 5.268

(h) Square: In square $\angle A=\angle B=\angle C=\angle D=90^{\circ}$ and $AB = DC = BC = AD = a$

$\therefore$ Area $= a^2$ and perimeter $= 4a$

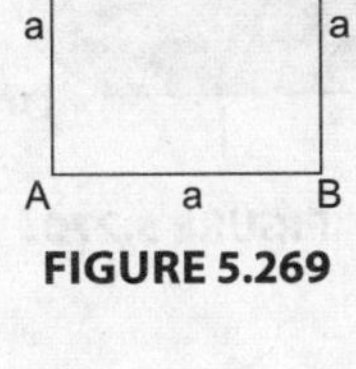

FIGURE 5.269

ILLUSTRATION 235: For what value of x the area of rectangle whose length and breadth are $2x$ and $(15 - 2x)$ respectively will be maximum?

SOLUTION: Area of rectangle = Length × Breadth

$\therefore \quad A = 2x(15-2x) = 30x - 4x^2$

$\therefore \quad \frac{dA}{dx} = 30 - 8x$ and $\frac{d^2A}{dx^2} = -8 < 0$ ....(i)

For maximum or minimum $\frac{dA}{dx} = 0 \quad \Rightarrow x = \frac{15}{4}$

Hence it is clear from (i) that area of rectangle is maximum at $x = \frac{15}{4}$

ILLUSTRATION 236: A wire of given length l is cut into two portions which are bent into the shapes of a circle and a square respectively. Show that the sum of the areas of the circle and the square will be least when the side of the square is equal to the diameter of the circle.

SOLUTION: Let r be the radius of the circle and x be the side of the square.
Then l = sum of perimeters of the circle and the square $l = 2\pi r + 4x$ ...(i)

If S be the sum of the areas of the circle and the square, then $S = \pi r^2 + x^2$

$= \pi\left(\frac{l-4x}{2\pi}\right)^2 + x^2$ from (i)

$= \frac{1}{4\pi}(l-4x)^2 + x^2$

$\therefore \quad \frac{dS}{dx} = \frac{2}{4\pi}(l-4x)(-4) + 2x = -\frac{2}{\pi}(l-4x) + 2x$

and $\frac{d^2S}{dx^2} = \frac{8}{\pi} + 2 > 0 \qquad \therefore \; S$ is least

For maximum or minimum $\frac{dS}{dx} = 0 \Rightarrow l - 4x - \pi x = 0$ or $x = \frac{l}{4+\pi}$ ....(ii)

$4x + \pi x = 2\pi r + 4x$ (from (i) and (ii))

$\Rightarrow x = 2r$

$\Rightarrow$ Each side of square = Diameter of circle

AREA AND PERIMETER OF SOME STANDARD THREE DIMENSIONAL FIGURES ARE LISTED BELOW

(a) Cuboid: Surface area is 2 $(bl + hl + bh)$

Volume: hbl

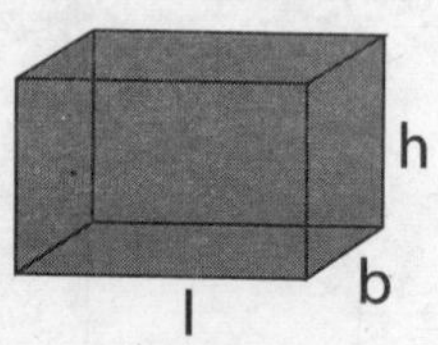

FIGURE 5.270

(b) Cube: Length of each side = a

Volume $V = a^3$

and surface area of cube $S = 6a^2$

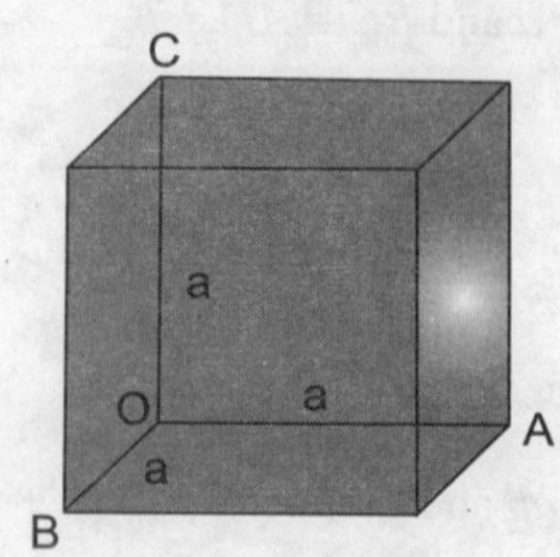

FIGURE 5.271

(c) Sphere: Surface area is $4\pi r^2$,

Volume $= \dfrac{4}{3}\pi r^3$

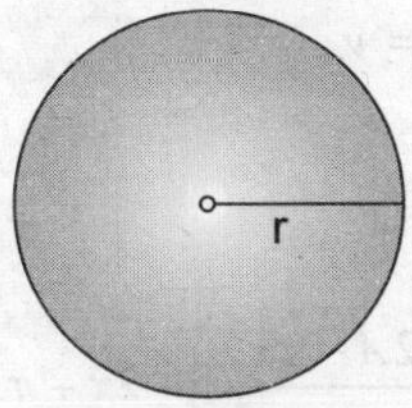

FIGURE 5.272

(d) Cone: Volume $= \dfrac{1}{3}\pi r^2 h$

Curved surface area of cone $= \pi r l$

Total surface area $= \pi r l + \pi r^2$

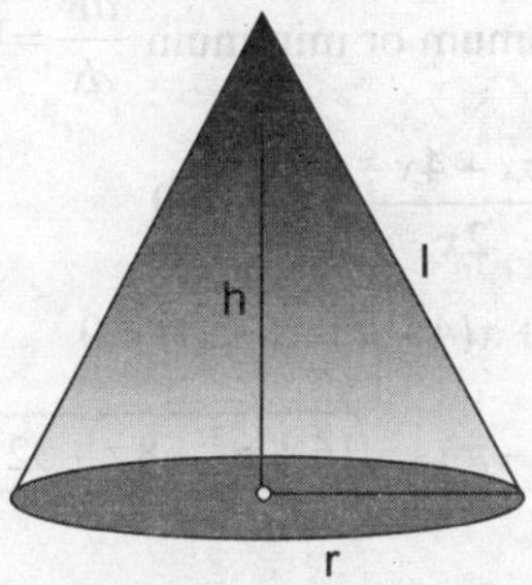

FIGURE 5.273

(e) Cylinder: Volume is $\pi r^2 h$ and

Curved Surface area: $2\pi r h$

Total surface area is $2\pi rh + 2\pi r^2$

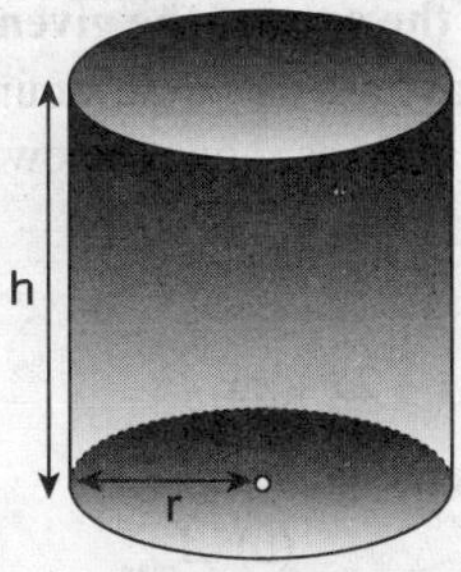

FIGURE 5.274

(e) Right Triangular Prism: Lateral surfaces of a prism are all rectangles

i.e. $ABB'A'$, $ACC'A'$ & $BCC'B'$

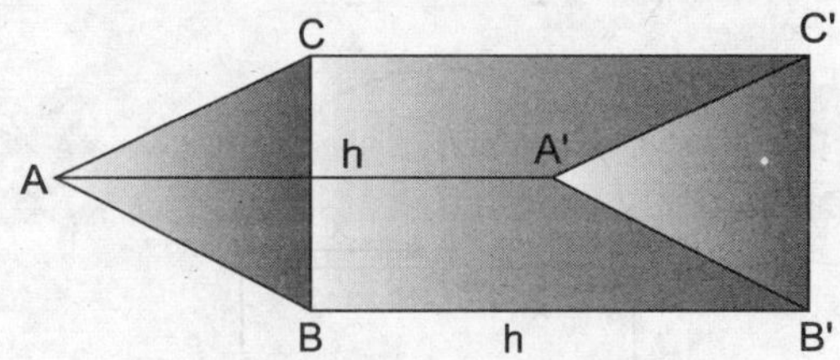

FIGURE 5.275

Volume of a prism = (area of the base) × (height)

NOTE:

If base is equilateral triangle with side a and height of prism is h, then volume = $\left(\dfrac{\sqrt{3}}{4}a^2\right) \times h$

Lateral surface area of a prism = perimeter of the base × height

Total surface area of a prism = Lateral surface area + 2 area of the base

(f) Right Pyramid: Slant surfaces of a pyramid are triangles.

Volume of pyramid $= \dfrac{1}{3}$(area of base)×height

Curved surface of a pyramid

$= \dfrac{1}{2}$(perimeter of the base)× slant height

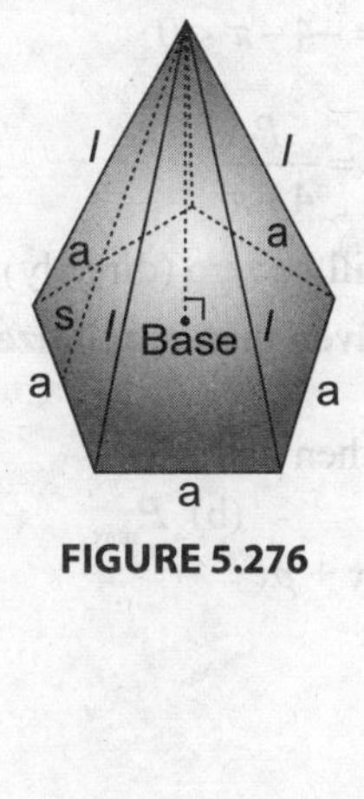

FIGURE 5.276

SOME IMPORTANT CASES

1. (i) If perimeter is given, then maximize and minimize the area of the given figure:

Here we have a semi-circle mounted on a rectangle.

Let diagram be as shown below:

$\therefore \quad A = 2xy + \frac{1}{2}\pi x^2$ ...(i)

and $P = 2y + 2x + \pi x$ ...(ii)

If P is given then find

(a) A_{min} (b) A_{max}

From equation (ii) $\frac{P - 2x - \pi x}{2} = y$

Putting in equation (i) we get,

$$A = 2x\left(\frac{P - 2x - \pi x}{2}\right) + \frac{1}{2}\pi x^2 = Px - 2x^2 - \frac{\pi x^2}{2}$$

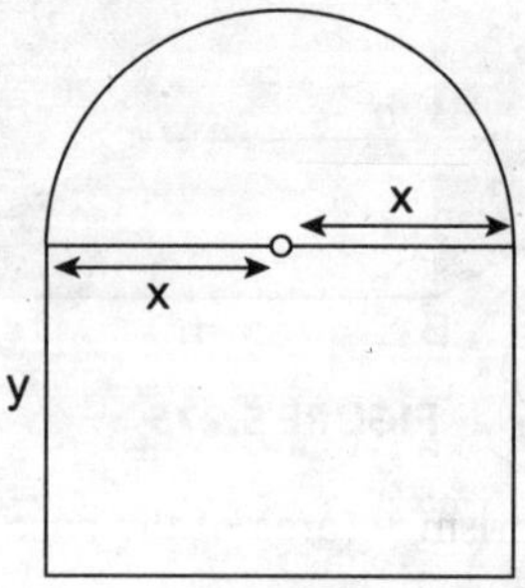

FIGURE 5.277

For max or min $\frac{dA}{dx} = 0$

$\Rightarrow \frac{dA}{dx} = P - 4x - \frac{2\pi x}{2}$

$\Rightarrow P - (4 + \ )x = 0$

$\Rightarrow x = \frac{P}{4 + \pi}$

And $\frac{d^2A}{dx^2} = -4 - \pi < 0$

$\Rightarrow$ For A_{max}; $x = \frac{P}{4 + \pi}$

And A_{min} will be zero (directly), when $x = 0$

(ii) If area is given then maximize and minimize the perimeter.

A is given then find

(a) P_{min} (b) P_{max}

$P = 2y + 2x + px^2$

and $A = 2xy + \frac{1}{2}\pi x^2$

$\Rightarrow \frac{A - \frac{1}{2}\pi x^2}{2x} = y$

$\Rightarrow \frac{2A - \pi x^2}{4x} = y$

So $P = 2\left(\frac{2A - \pi x^2}{4x}\right) + 2x + \pi x^2$

$= \frac{A}{x} - \frac{\pi x}{2} + 2x + \pi x^2$

$\Rightarrow \frac{dP}{dx} = -\frac{A}{x} - \frac{\pi}{2} + 2 + 2\pi x$

for maximum or minimum $\frac{dP}{dx} = 0$

$\Rightarrow \frac{-2A - \pi x + 4x + 4\pi x^2}{2x} = 0$

$\Rightarrow x^2(4\pi) + x(4 - \pi) + (-2A) = 0$

$\Rightarrow x = \frac{-(4 - \pi) + \sqrt{16 + \pi^2 - 8\pi + 32A}}{8\pi} = x_0 \text{ (say)}$

$\Rightarrow$ At $x = x_0$, $\frac{d^2P}{dx^2} > 0$

$\therefore$ P is minimum at $x = x_0$.

Also $\lim_{x \to 0} P = \infty$ $(\because$ when $x \to 0; y \to \infty)$

$\Rightarrow P_{max}$ cannot be found

2. (i) Maximize the area of the triangle (with fixed base) inscribed in a circle of given radius r.

FIGURE 5.278

For a given base, area of triangle is maximum when its altitude is maximum. i.e., when it is an isosceles triangle.

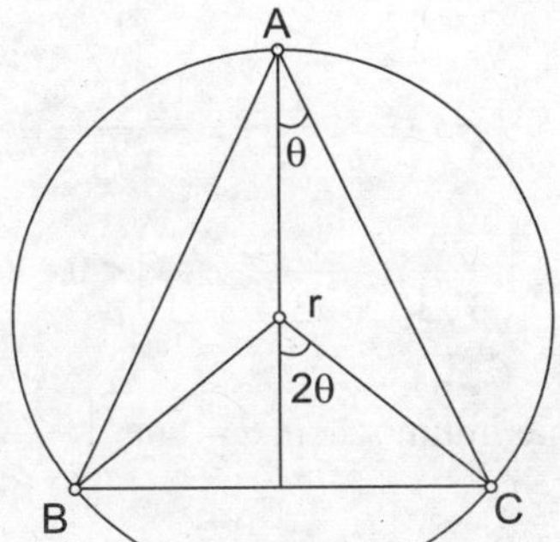

FIGURE 5.279

$\therefore$ For isosceles ΔABC, area

$\Rightarrow S = \frac{1}{2} \times (BC) \times (AD)$

$\Rightarrow S = \frac{1}{2}(2r\sin 2\theta) \times r(1+\cos 2\theta)$

$\Rightarrow S = r^2 \sin 2\theta(1+\cos 2\theta)$

For minimum or maximum; $\frac{dS}{d\theta} = 0$

$\Rightarrow r^2[\sin 2\theta(-\sin 2\theta \times 2) + (\cos 2\theta + 1)\cos 2\theta \times 2] = 0$

$\Rightarrow (\cos^2 2\theta - \sin^2 2\theta) + \cos 2\theta = 0$

$\Rightarrow \cos 4\theta + \cos 2\theta = 0$

$\Rightarrow 2\cos 3\theta \cos\theta = 0$

$\Rightarrow 3\theta = \frac{\pi}{2}$ or $\theta = \frac{\pi}{2}$ (rejecting)

$\therefore \theta = \frac{\pi}{6}$ i.e., area of the triangle is maximum when it is equilateral.

(ii) Maximize the area of triangle in a given ellipse one of its vertex is at extremity of major axis:

S = area ABC = $\frac{1}{2} \times (2b\sin\phi) \times a(1+\cos\phi)$ = $ab\sin\phi(1+\cos\phi) = ab\sin\phi(1+\cos\phi)$

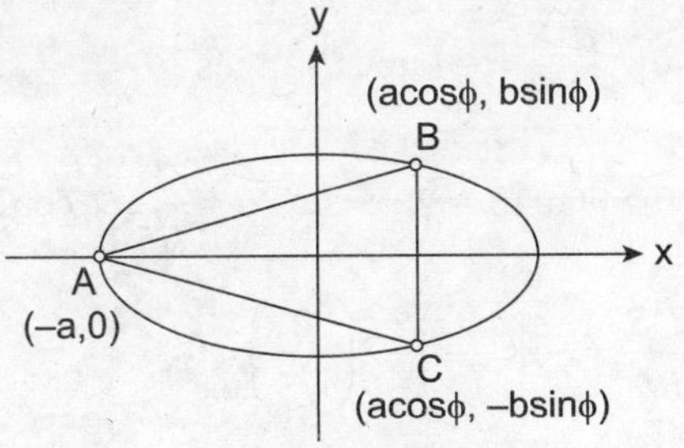

FIGURE 5.280

$\Rightarrow \frac{dS}{d\phi} = 0$

$\Rightarrow ab[\cos\phi(1+\cos\phi) + \sin\phi(-\sin\phi)] = 0$

$\Rightarrow ab(\cos\phi + \cos 2\phi) = 0$

$\Rightarrow ab(2\cos 2\phi + \cos\phi - 1) = 0$

$\Rightarrow \cos\phi = 1/2$; $\cos\phi = -1$ (rejected)

At $\cos\phi = 1/2$; $\frac{d^2S}{d\phi^2} < 0$

$\Rightarrow$ Maximum area = $\frac{3\sqrt{3}}{4}$ and minimum area = 0

3. (a) Minimizing/maximizing the area of a triangle circumscribed around a circle:

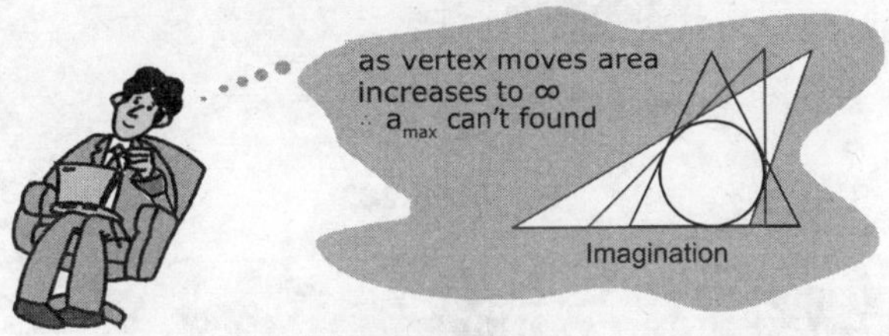

FIGURE 5.281

For a given height the triangle of minimum area is the isosceles triangle

For a circumscribed isosceles ΔABC

(easily observerd using symmetry)

$AD = R + R + \text{cosec}\theta$

$BC = 2CD = 2(AD\tan\theta) = 2R(1+\text{cosec}\theta)\tan\theta$

So area of the triangle is

$S = \frac{1}{2}R(1+\text{cosec}\theta) \times 2R(1+\text{cosec}\theta)\tan\theta$

For maximum or minimum $\frac{dS}{d\theta} = 0$

$\frac{dS}{d\theta} = R^2\sec^2\theta(1+\text{cosec}\,\theta)^2 + R^2\tan\theta \times 2(1+\text{cosec}\,\theta)(-\text{cosec}\,\theta\cot\theta)$

Now, $\frac{dS}{d\theta} = 0$

$\Rightarrow 1 + \text{cosec}\theta = 0$ (rejected)

or $\sec 2\theta(1+\text{cosec}\,\theta) = 2\text{cosec}\,\theta$

$\Rightarrow \frac{1}{\cos^2\theta}\left(\frac{\sin\theta+1}{\sin\theta}\right) = \frac{2}{\sin\theta}$

$\Rightarrow -2\cos 2\theta + \sin\theta + 1 = 0$

$\Rightarrow 2\sin^2\theta + \sin\theta - 1 = 0$

$\Rightarrow 2\sin^2\theta + 2\sin\theta - \sin\theta - 1 = 0$

$\Rightarrow \sin\theta = -1$(rejected) or $\sin\theta = 1/2$

For $\sin\theta = 1/2$; $\frac{d^2S}{d\theta^2} > 0$

$\Rightarrow$ Minimum at $\theta = \frac{\pi}{6}$

$\Rightarrow$ Minimum area $= 3\sqrt{3}R^2$

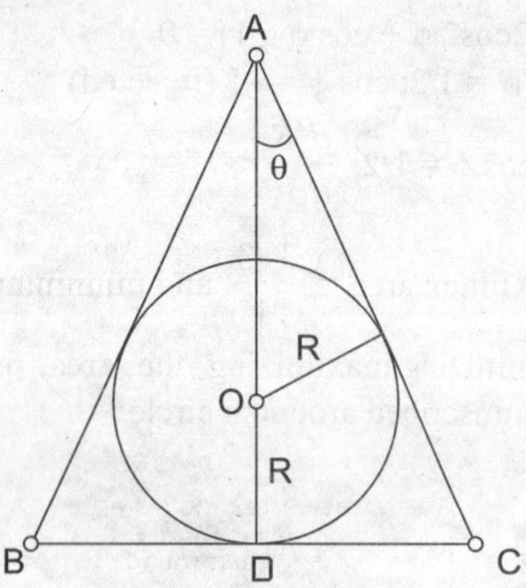

FIGURE 5.282

■ INSCRIBED FIGURES

(a) Right circular cylinder in sphere

Given, radius of sphere is R; we need to find the maximum/minimum volume and surface area of inscribed right circular cylinder

Let radius of the base of the cylinder be 'r' and its height be 'h'.

V (Volume of the cylinder)

$= \pi r^2 h = \pi (R\cos\theta)^2(2R\sin\theta)$

$= 2\pi R^3 \sin\theta\cos^2\theta = V(\theta)$

For maximum/minimum

$\frac{dV}{d\theta} = 0$

$\Rightarrow 2\pi R^3(\cos^3\theta - \sin^2\theta \times 2\cos\theta) = 0$

$\Rightarrow \cos\theta = 0$ or $\cos^2\theta = 2\sin^2\theta$

$\Rightarrow \tan^2\theta = \frac{1}{2} \Rightarrow \tan\theta = \frac{1}{\sqrt{2}}$

Now $\frac{d^2V}{d\theta^2}$

$= 2\pi R^3(3\cos^2\theta(-\sin\theta) - 2(-\sin\theta\sin^2\theta + 2\sin\theta\cos^2\theta))$

$= 2\pi R^3(-3\cos^2\theta\sin\theta - 2(-\sin^3\theta + 2\sin\theta\cos^2\theta))$

Now when $\cos\theta = 0$; $\sin\theta = 1$

$\Rightarrow \frac{d^2V}{d\theta^2} = 4\pi R^2 > 0$

$\Rightarrow$ V is minimum when $\cos\theta = 1$

And when $\tan\theta = \frac{1}{\sqrt{2}}$; $\sin\theta = \frac{1}{\sqrt{3}}$; $\cos\theta = \frac{\sqrt{2}}{\sqrt{3}}$

Now

$$\frac{d^2V}{d\theta^2} = 2\pi R^3\left(-3\times\frac{2}{3}\times\frac{1}{\sqrt{3}} + 2\times\frac{1}{3\sqrt{3}} - 4\times\frac{1}{\sqrt{3}}\times\frac{2}{3}\right)$$

$$= 2\pi R^3\left(\frac{-6}{3\sqrt{3}} + \frac{2}{3\sqrt{3}} - \frac{8}{3\sqrt{3}}\right) < 0$$

$\Rightarrow$ V is maximum when $\theta = \tan^{-1}\left(\frac{1}{\sqrt{2}}\right)$

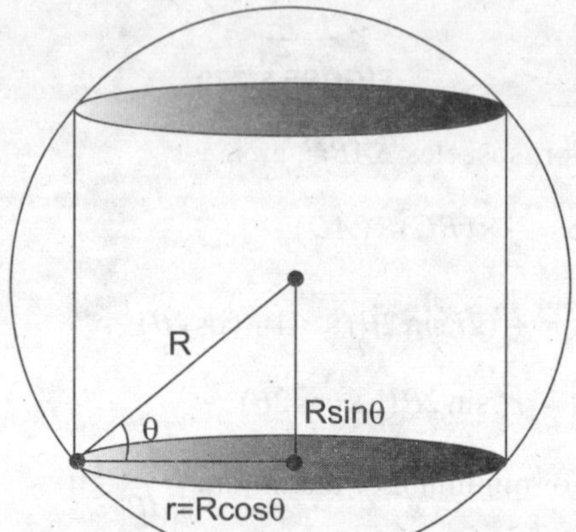

FIGURE 5.283

S(surface area) $= 2\pi rh + \pi r^2$

$= 2\pi r\cos\theta(R\sin\theta + 2R\cos\theta)$

$= 2\pi R^2\cos\theta(\cos\theta + 2\sin\theta) = S(\theta)$

For maximum/minimum surface area: equate

$\frac{dS}{d\theta} = 0$

$\Rightarrow -\sin\theta(\cos\theta + 2\sin\theta) + \cos\theta(-\sin\theta + 2\cos\theta) = 0$

$\Rightarrow -2\sin\theta\cos\theta - 2\sin^2\theta + 2\cos^2\theta = 0$

$\Rightarrow 2\cos 2\theta - \sin 2\theta = 0$

$\Rightarrow \tan 2\theta = 2 \Rightarrow \theta = \frac{\tan^{-1}2}{2}$

Now $\frac{d^2S}{d\theta^2} = -4\sin 2\theta - 2\cos 2\theta$

When $\tan 2\theta = 2 \Rightarrow \sin 2\theta = \frac{1}{\sqrt{5}}$ & $\cos 2\theta = \frac{2}{\sqrt{5}}$

$\Rightarrow \frac{d^2S}{d\theta^2} = -4\left(\frac{1}{\sqrt{5}}\right) - 2\left(\frac{2}{\sqrt{5}}\right) < 0$

$\Rightarrow$ Surface area is maximum when $\theta = \frac{\tan^{-1}2}{2}$

Also surface area will be minimum when $\theta = \pi$ i.e., the base of cylinder has a zero radius.

(b) Right circular cone in sphere

Given, radius of sphere is *R*; we need to find the maximum/minimum volume and surface area of inscribed right circular cone.

Let radius of the base of the cone be '*r*' and its height be '*h*'.

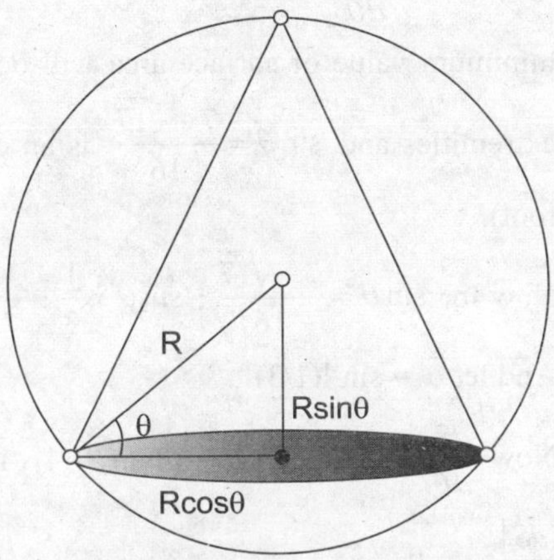

FIGURE 5.284

V (volume of the cylinder)

$$= \frac{1}{3}\pi r^2 h = \frac{1}{3}\pi\ (R\cos\theta)^2 (R + R\sin\theta)$$

$$= \frac{\pi R^3}{3}\cos^2\theta\ (1+\sin\theta)$$

For V to be maximum/minimum; we equate

$$\frac{dV}{d\theta} = \frac{\pi R^3}{3}\times\left[2\cos\theta(-\sin\theta)(1+\sin\theta)+\cos^3\theta\right]$$

$$= \frac{\pi R^3}{3}[-2\sin\theta\cos\theta - 2\sin^2\theta\cos\theta + \cos^3\theta]$$

$$= \frac{\pi R^3}{3}\cos\theta\ [(1-\sin^2\theta) - 2\sin^2\theta - 2\sin\theta]$$

$$= \frac{\pi R^3}{3}\cos\theta[-3\sin^2\theta - 2\sin\theta + 1]$$

$$= \frac{\pi R^3}{3}\cos\theta[-3\sin^2\theta - 3\sin\theta + \sin\theta + 1]$$

$$= \frac{\pi R^3}{3}\cos\theta[(-3\sin\theta+1)(\sin\theta+1)]$$

$$\frac{dV}{d\theta} = 0 \Rightarrow \cos\theta = 0 \text{ or } \sin\theta = \frac{1}{3} \text{ or } \sin\theta = -1$$

$\Rightarrow$ $\theta = \pi/2$ or $\theta = \sin^{-1}(1/3)$

or $\theta = \dfrac{3\pi}{2}$ (Rejected)

Now when $\theta = \pi/2-$; $\dfrac{dV}{d\theta} < 0$

$\Rightarrow$ $\theta = \pi/2$ is a point of minima

$$\theta = \frac{\pi}{2}^+;\ \frac{dV}{d\theta} > 0$$

$\Rightarrow$ Minimum volume = 0

and when $\theta = \left(\sin^{-1}\left(\frac{1}{3}\right)\right)^-;\ \dfrac{dv}{d\theta} > 0$

and $\theta = \left(\sin^{-1}\left(\frac{1}{3}\right)\right)^+;\ \dfrac{dv}{d\theta} < 0$

$\Rightarrow$ $\theta = \sin^{-1}(1/3)$ is a point of maxima

$$\Rightarrow V_{max} = \frac{\pi R^3}{3}\times\frac{8}{9}\left(1+\frac{1}{3}\right) = \frac{32\pi R^3}{81}$$

Aliter:

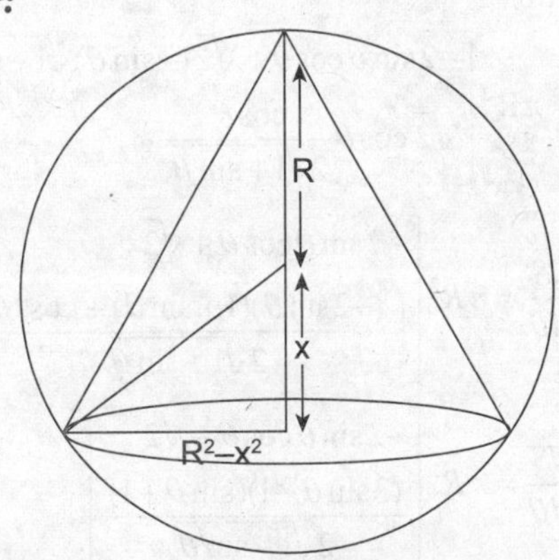

FIGURE 5.285

$$V = \frac{1}{3}\pi(R^2 - x^2)(R + x)$$

$$= \left(\frac{1}{3}\pi\right)[-x^3 - Rx^2 + R^2x + R^3]$$

$$\frac{dV}{dx} = 0 \Rightarrow -3x^2 - 2Rx + R^2 = 0$$

$$\Rightarrow 3x^2 + 2Rx - R^2 = 0$$

$$x = \frac{-2R \pm \sqrt{4R^2 + 12R^2}}{6}$$

$$\Rightarrow x = \frac{-2R \pm 4R}{6} = \frac{R}{3} \text{ or } -R \text{ (rejected)}$$

$$\Rightarrow \text{Now } \frac{d^2V}{dx^2} = \frac{1}{3}\pi\left[-3x^2 - 2Rx + R^2\right]$$

$$\left.\frac{d^2V}{dx^2}\right|_{x=R/3} < 0$$

$\Rightarrow$ max volume $= \dfrac{1}{3}\pi\left(R^2 - \dfrac{R^2}{9}\right)\left(R + \dfrac{R}{3}\right)$

$= \dfrac{1}{3}\pi\dfrac{8R^2}{9}\times\dfrac{4r}{3} = \dfrac{32\pi R^3}{81}$

S(surface area) $= \pi r\sqrt{r^2+h^2} + \pi r^2$

$= \pi R\cos\theta\,[R\cos\theta + \sqrt{(R\cos\theta)^2 + (R + R\sin\theta)^2}\,]$

For maximum/minimum surface area; $\dfrac{dS}{d\theta} = 0$

Now

$S = \pi R^2\left[(\cos\theta(\cos\theta + \sqrt{\cos^2\theta + 1 + \sin^2\theta + 2\sin\theta})\right]$

$\Rightarrow\ S = \pi R^2\left[\cos^2\theta + \sqrt{2}\cos\theta\sqrt{1+\sin\theta}\right]$

Now $\dfrac{dS}{d\theta}$

$$= \pi R^2\begin{bmatrix} -2\sin\theta\cos\theta + \sqrt{2}(-\sin\theta)\sqrt{1+\sin\theta} + \\ \sqrt{2}\cos\theta\dfrac{\cos\theta}{2\sqrt{1+\sin\theta}} \end{bmatrix}$$

$$\Rightarrow\ \frac{dS}{d\theta} = \pi R^2\begin{bmatrix} -2\sin\theta\cos\theta + \sqrt{2} \\ \left(\dfrac{(-2\sin\theta)(1+\sin\theta) + \cos^2\theta}{2\sqrt{1+\sin\theta}}\right) \end{bmatrix}$$

$$\Rightarrow\ \frac{dS}{d\theta} = \pi R^2\begin{bmatrix} -2\sin\theta\cos\theta - \sqrt{2} \\ \dfrac{(3\sin\theta - 1)(\sin\theta + 1)}{2\sqrt{1+\sin\theta}} \end{bmatrix}$$

$$\Rightarrow\ \frac{dS}{d\theta} = \pi R^2\begin{bmatrix} -2\sin\theta\cos\theta + \\ \dfrac{1}{\sqrt{2}}(1 - 3\sin\theta)\sqrt{1+\sin\theta} \end{bmatrix}$$

$\dfrac{dS}{d\theta} = 0 \Rightarrow (1 - 3\sin\theta)\sqrt{1+\sin\theta} = 2\sqrt{2}\sin\theta\cos\theta$

$\Rightarrow$ $(1 + 9\sin^2\theta - 6\sin\theta)(1 + \sin\theta) = 8\sin^2\theta(1 - \sin^2\theta)$

$\Rightarrow$ $8\sin^4\theta + 9\sin^3\theta + 9\sin^2\theta - 6\sin^2\theta - 8\sin^2\theta + \sin\theta - 6\sin\theta + 1 = 0$

$\Rightarrow$ $8\sin^4\theta + 9\sin^3\theta - 5\sin^2\theta - 5\sin\theta + 1 = 0$

Clearly; $\sin\theta = -1$ satisfies

$\Rightarrow\ \dfrac{dS}{d\theta} = (\sin\theta + 1)(8\sin^3\theta + \sin^2\theta - 6\sin\theta + 1) = 0$

$\sin\theta = -1$ or $8\sin^3\theta + \sin^2\theta - 6\sin\theta + 1 = 0$

Now $\sin\theta = -1$; satisfied $8\sin^3\theta + \sin^2\theta - 6\sin\theta + 1 = 0$

$\Rightarrow\ \dfrac{dS}{d\theta} = (\sin\theta + 1)^2\ (8\sin^2\theta - 7\sin\theta + 1)$

$\sin\theta = -1 \Rightarrow \theta = 3\pi/2$ (not possible)

$\Rightarrow$ $8\sin^2\theta - 7\sin\theta + 1 = 0$

$\Rightarrow\ \sin\theta = \dfrac{7 \pm \sqrt{49 - 32}}{16} = \dfrac{7 \pm \sqrt{17}}{16}$

Now $\sin\theta \neq \dfrac{7 + \sqrt{17}}{16}$ ($\because \dfrac{7 + \sqrt{17}}{16} > \dfrac{1}{3}$ and for $\sin\theta > 1/3$; $\dfrac{dS}{d\theta} < 0$ and hence; the maximum/minimum value of surface area will occur at the extremities and $\sin\theta = \dfrac{7 + \sqrt{17}}{16}$ is an extraneous root).

Now for $\sin\theta = \dfrac{7 - \sqrt{17}}{16}$; $\sin\theta < \dfrac{1}{3}$

And let $\alpha = \sin^{-1}(1/3)$

Now $\dfrac{dS}{d\theta} = -\pi R^2\left[\sin 2\theta + (3\sin\theta - 1)\sqrt{1+\sin\theta}\right]$

$\left.\dfrac{dS}{d\theta}\right|_{\theta=\alpha} = 0$

Consider $f(x) = \sin 2x + (3\sin x - 1)\sqrt{1+\sin x}$

Now $f(\alpha) = 0$

And $f'(x)$ is an increasing function when $x \in (0, \pi/4)$

Now $\alpha = \sin^{-1}\left(\dfrac{7 - \sqrt{17}}{16}\right) \in \left(0, \dfrac{\pi}{6}\right)$

$\Rightarrow$ $f(x) > f(\alpha)$ for $x > \alpha$

And $f(x) < f(\alpha)$ for $x < \alpha$

$\Rightarrow\ \left.\dfrac{ds}{d\theta}\right|_{\alpha<\theta<\pi/4} < 0$ and $\left.\dfrac{ds}{d\theta}\right|_{0<\theta<\alpha} > 0$

$\therefore$ $\theta = \alpha$ is a point of maxima

$\Rightarrow\ \sin\theta = \dfrac{7 - \sqrt{17}}{16}$ is a point of maxima

Aliter:

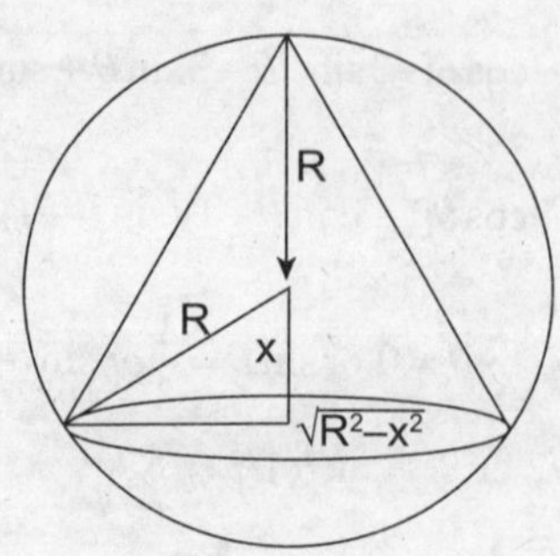

FIGURE 5.286

$S = \pi rl + \pi r^2$

$$= \pi\left(\sqrt{R^2 - x^2}\right)\left(\sqrt{(R+x)^2 + \left(\sqrt{R^2 - x^2}\right)^2} + \sqrt{R^2 - x^2}\right)$$

$$= \pi\sqrt{R^2 - x^2}\left(\sqrt{2R}\times\sqrt{R+x} + \sqrt{R^2 - x^2}\right)$$

$$= \pi\left(\sqrt{2R}\times\sqrt{R-x}\times(R+x) + (R^2 - x^2)\right)$$

$$= \frac{ds}{dx} = 0$$

$$\Rightarrow \sqrt{2R}\times\frac{-1}{2\sqrt{R-x}}\times(R+x) + \sqrt{2R}\times\sqrt{R-x} - 2x = 0$$

$$\Rightarrow \frac{-R\sqrt{2R} - x\sqrt{2R} + 2\times\sqrt{2R}(R-x) - 4x\sqrt{R-x}}{2\sqrt{R-x}} = 0$$

$$\Rightarrow \sqrt{2R}\,(R-x) = 4x\left(\sqrt{R-x}\right)$$

$$\Rightarrow \sqrt{2R}\ \sqrt{R-x} = 4x \text{ (For } x \neq R)$$

Squaring; we get $R(R - x) = 8x^2$

$\Rightarrow 8x^2 + Rx - R^2 = 0$

$$\Rightarrow x = \frac{-R \pm \sqrt{R^2 + 32R^2}}{16} = \frac{-R \pm \sqrt{33}\,R}{16}$$

$$\Rightarrow x = \frac{\left(\sqrt{33} - 1\right)R}{16}$$

$$\frac{dS}{dR} = \frac{\sqrt{2R}(R-x) - 4x\sqrt{R-x}}{2\sqrt{R-x}}$$

$$= \sqrt{\frac{R}{2}}\times\sqrt{R-x} - 2x$$

$$\frac{d^2S}{dR^2} = \sqrt{\frac{R}{2}}\times\frac{-1}{2\sqrt{R-x}} - 2 < 0$$

$\therefore$ S is maximum when $x = \frac{\left(\sqrt{33} - 1\right)R}{16}$

(c) Right circular cylinder in cone

Given, radius of right circular cone is 'R' and height of right circular cone is 'H'; we need to find the maximum/minimum volume and curved surface area of inscribed right circular cylinder.

Let radius of the base of the cylinder be 'r' and its height be 'h'.

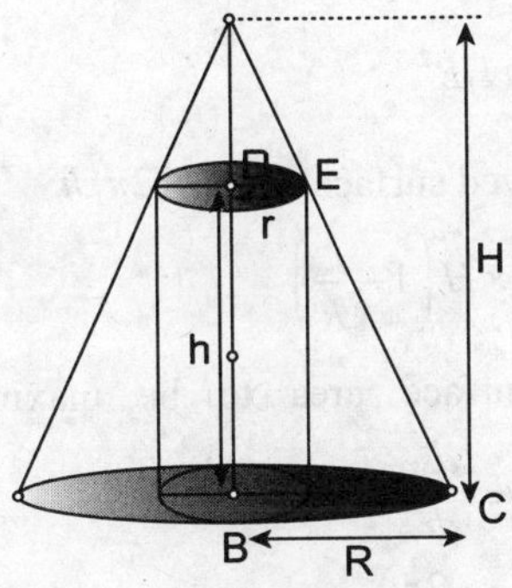

FIGURE 5.287

$$\frac{AD}{DE} = \frac{AB}{BC}$$

$$\Rightarrow \frac{H - h}{r} = \frac{H}{R}$$

$$\Rightarrow h = H\left(1 - \frac{r}{R}\right)$$

V (Volume of the cylinder)

$$= \pi r^2 h = \pi r^2 H\left(1 - \frac{r}{R}\right) = g(r)$$

For volume to be maximum/minimum; we have

$$\frac{dV}{dr} = 0\text{; where } V = \pi H\left(r^2 - \frac{r^3}{R}\right)$$

$$\Rightarrow \pi H\left[2r - \frac{3r^2}{R}\right] = 0$$

$$\Rightarrow r = 0 \text{ or } 2 = \frac{3r}{R}$$

$$\Rightarrow r = \frac{2R}{3}$$

Now; $\frac{d^2V}{dr^2} = \pi H\left[2 - \frac{6r}{R}\right]$

$$\left.\frac{d^2V}{dr^2}\right|_{r=0} > 0$$

$\Rightarrow r = 0$ is the condition for minimum

$$\left.\frac{d^2V}{dr^2}\right|_{r=\frac{2R}{3}} = \pi H\left[2 - \frac{6\times 2R}{3R}\right] < 0$$

$\Rightarrow r = \frac{2R}{3}$ is the condition for maximum

$\therefore$ minimum volume

$$= \pi H\left(\frac{4R^2}{9} - \frac{8R^3}{27R}\right) = \pi HR^2\times\frac{4}{9}\left(1 - \frac{2}{3}\right)$$

$= \frac{4}{27}\pi HR^2$

S (curved surface area) $= 2\pi rh$

$= 2\pi r \times H\left(1-\frac{r}{R}\right)$

For surface area to be maximum/minimum;

we have $\frac{ds}{dr}=0$

$\Rightarrow \; 2\pi H\left(1-\frac{2r}{R}\right)=0$

$\Rightarrow \; r=\frac{R}{2}$

Now; $\frac{d^2S}{dr^2}=2\pi H\left(\frac{-2}{R}\right)<0$

⇒ $r = R/2$ is the point of maxima

⇒ Maximum curved surface area

$= 2\pi H\times\frac{R}{2}\left(1-\frac{R/2}{R}\right)=2\pi H\times\frac{R}{2}\times\frac{1}{2}=\frac{\pi RH}{2}$

EXCRIBED FIGURES

(a) Cone around sphere

Given, radius of sphere is 'R'; we need to find the maximum/minimum volume and surface area of excribed right circular cone.

Let radius of the base of the cone be 'r' and its height be 'h'.

Let, the semi-vertical angle of the cone be 'θ', then we have

$h = R + R\,\mathrm{cosec}\,\theta$

$r = R(1+\mathrm{cosec}\,\theta)\tan\theta$

V (volume of the sphere) $= \frac{1}{3}\pi r^2 h$

$= \frac{\pi R^3}{3}\tan^2\theta\,(1+\mathrm{cosec}\,\theta)^3$

For volume to be max/min., we have $\frac{dV}{d\theta}=0$

$$\Rightarrow \frac{\pi R^3}{3}\begin{bmatrix}2\tan\theta\sec^2\theta(1+\mathrm{cosec}\theta)^3+\\ 3(1+\mathrm{cosec}\theta)^2\times(-\mathrm{cosec}\theta\cot\theta).\tan^2\theta\end{bmatrix}=0$$

⇒ $2\tan\theta\,(1+\mathrm{cosec}\theta)^2\,[\sec^2\theta(1+\mathrm{cosec}\,\theta)+3(-\mathrm{cosec}\theta)]=0$

Now $\tan\theta = 0$ (not possible)

and $\mathrm{cosec}\theta = -1$ (not possible)

⇒ $\sec^2\theta\,(1+\mathrm{cosec}\,\theta) - 3\mathrm{cosec}\theta = 0$

$\Rightarrow \frac{1}{\cos^2\theta}\left(1+\frac{1}{\sin\theta}\right)=\frac{3}{\sin\theta}$

$\Rightarrow \frac{(1+\sin\theta)}{(\sin\theta)(1-\sin^2\theta)}=\frac{3}{\sin\theta}\Rightarrow\frac{1}{3}=1-\sin\theta$

⇒ $\sin\theta = 2/3$ ($\because \sin\theta \neq 0,-1$)

Now $\tan\theta=\frac{2}{\sqrt{5}}$; $\cos\theta=\frac{\sqrt{5}}{3}$

$\sec\theta=\frac{3}{\sqrt{5}}$; $\mathrm{cosec}\theta=\frac{3}{2}$

Using First derivatives test; we have

$\alpha<\left(\sin^{-1}\left(\frac{2}{3}\right)\right)$;

⇒ $\sin\alpha < 2/3$; $\tan\alpha < \frac{2}{\sqrt{5}}$; $\mathrm{cosec}\,\alpha > 3/2$

$\Rightarrow f'\left(\sin^{-1}\left(\frac{2}{3}\right)\right)^{-}<0$ and $\sec\alpha<\frac{3}{\sqrt{5}}$

and for $\beta > (\sin^{-1}(2/3))$

$\sin\beta > 2/3$; $\tan\beta > \frac{2}{\sqrt{5}}$;

$\mathrm{cosec}\,\beta < 3/2$ and $\sec\beta > \frac{3}{\sqrt{5}}$

$\Rightarrow f'(\sin^{-1}(2/3))^{+}>0$

⇒ $\theta = \sin^{-1}(2/3)$ is the point of minima

$\Rightarrow$ minimum volume $=\frac{\pi R^3}{3}\times\frac{4}{5}\times\left(1+\frac{3}{2}\right)^3$

$=\frac{\pi R^3\times 4}{3\times 5}\times\frac{125}{8}=\frac{\pi R^3\times 25}{6}=\frac{25}{6}\pi R^3$

By observation; Maximum volume will be ∞ (when $\theta \to \pi/2$)

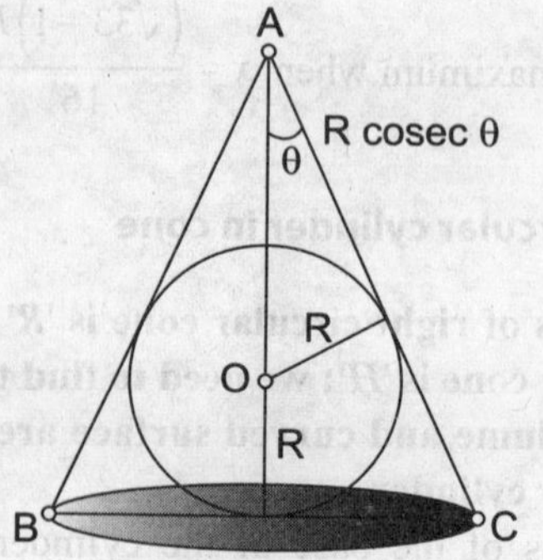

FIGURE 5.288

S (Surface area) $= \pi r\sqrt{r^2+h^2}+\pi r^2$

$= \pi(R+R\operatorname{cosec}\theta)^2.\tan\theta(\sec\theta+\tan\theta)$

$$S=\pi R^2(1+\sin\theta)^3\times\frac{1}{\sin\theta\cos\theta}$$

For surface area to be max/min; we have

$$\frac{dS}{d\theta}=0\Rightarrow\left[\frac{3(1+\sin\theta)^2\times\cos\theta(\sin\theta\cos\theta)-(\cos^2\theta-\sin^2\theta)(1+\sin\theta)^3}{(\sin\theta\cos\theta)^2}\right]=0$$

$\Rightarrow$ $3(1+\sin\theta)^2\times\cos^2\theta\times\sin\theta=(1+\sin\theta)^3(\cos^2\theta-\sin^2\theta)$

$\Rightarrow$ Either $(1+\sin\theta)=0$ (Not possible)

or $3\times\cos^2\theta\times\sin\theta=(1+\sin\theta)(\cos^2\theta-\sin^2\theta)$

$\Rightarrow$ $3(1-\sin^2\theta)\times\sin\theta=(1+\sin\theta)(1-2\sin^2\theta)$

Let $\sin\theta=a$

$\Rightarrow$ $3a-3a^3=1+a-2a^2-2a^3$

$\Rightarrow$ $a^3-2a^2-2a+1=0$

$\Rightarrow$ $(a+1)(a^2-3a+1)=0$

$\Rightarrow$ $a^2-3a+1=0\quad(\because a+1\neq 0)$

$\Rightarrow$ $a=\frac{3\pm\sqrt{9-4}}{2}=\frac{3+\sqrt5}{2}$ or $\frac{3-\sqrt5}{2}$

$\therefore$ $\sin\theta=\frac{3-\sqrt5}{2}\quad\left(\because\sin\theta\neq\frac{3+\sqrt5}{2}\right)$

Now $\frac{dS}{d\theta}=\pi R^2\left(\frac{-(1+\sin\theta)^2(\sin^2\theta-3\sin\theta+1)}{(\sin\theta\cos\theta)^2}\right)$

Now consider $f(\theta)=\sin^2\theta-3\sin\theta+1$

$$f(\theta)=\left(\sin\theta-\left(\frac{3-\sqrt5}{2}\right)\right)\left(\sin\theta-\left(\frac{3+\sqrt5}{2}\right)\right)$$

$\Rightarrow$ $f(\theta)$ is negative for $\theta<\sin^{-1}\left(\frac{3-\sqrt5}{2}\right)$

$\Rightarrow$ $\frac{dS}{d\theta}>0$ for $\theta<\sin^{-1}\left(\frac{3-\sqrt5}{2}\right)$

And $f(\theta)$ is positive for $\theta>\sin^{-1}\left(\frac{3-\sqrt5}{2}\right)$

$\Rightarrow$ $\frac{dS}{d\theta}<0$ for $\theta>\sin^{-1}\left(\frac{3-\sqrt5}{2}\right)$

$\therefore$ S is maximum at $\theta=\sin^{-1}\left(\frac{3-\sqrt5}{2}\right)$

Also S will be minimum when $R=0$

(b) Cone around cylinder

Given, radius of right circular cone is '*R*' and height of right circular cone is '*H*'; we need to find the maximum/minimum volume and surface area of excribed right circular cone.

Let radius of the base of the cone be 'r' and its height be 'h'.

Let, the semi-vertical angle of the cone be '$90-\theta$', then we have

V (Volume of the sphere) $=\frac{1}{3}\pi r^2 h$

$=\frac{1}{3}\pi(H+R\tan\theta)^3.\cot^2\theta$

$=\frac{\pi\cot^2\theta(H+R\tan\theta)^3}{3}$

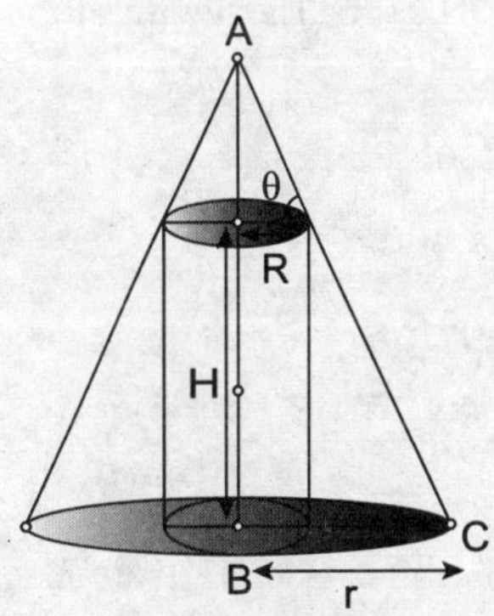

FIGURE 5.289

For V to be maximum/minimum we have $\frac{dv}{d\theta}=0$

$$\frac{dV}{d\theta}=\frac{\pi}{3}\left[2\cot\theta\times(-\operatorname{cosec}^2\theta)(H+R\tan\theta)^3+3(H+R\tan\theta)^2\times R\sec^2\theta\times\cot^2\theta\right]$$

$=\frac{\pi}{3}(H+R\tan\theta)^2\times\cot\theta$

$\left[-2\operatorname{cosec}^2\theta(H+R\tan\theta)+3\times R\sec^2\theta\times\cot\theta\right]$

Now $H+R\tan\theta\neq 0$ and $\cot\theta\neq 0$

$\therefore$ $2\operatorname{cosec}^2\theta(H+R\tan\theta)=3R\sec^2\theta\times\cot\theta$

$\Rightarrow$ $2\times\frac{1}{\sin^2\theta}\left(H+R\frac{\sin\theta}{\cos\theta}\right)=3\times R\times\frac{1}{\cos^2\theta}\times\frac{\cos\theta}{\sin\theta}$

$\Rightarrow$ $2(H\cos\theta+R\sin\theta)=3R\sin\theta$

$[\because\cos\theta\neq 0$ and $\sin\theta\neq 0]$

$\Rightarrow$ $H\cos\theta+R\sin\theta=3/2\,R\sin\theta$

$\Rightarrow$ $H\cos\theta=\frac{R}{2}\sin\theta$

$\Rightarrow \quad \tan\theta = \left(\dfrac{H}{R/2}\right)$

$$\frac{dv}{d\theta} = \frac{\pi}{3}(H + R\tan\theta)^2 \times \cot\theta \times \frac{1}{\sin^2\theta} \times (R\tan\theta - 2H)$$

Now; we need to find whether we get a maxima or minima at $\theta = \tan^{-1}(H/2R)$

Now; In the left neighborhood of $\theta = \tan^{-1}\left(\dfrac{H}{R/2}\right)$

$\tan\alpha < \tan\theta \Rightarrow \tan\alpha < H/R/2 \Rightarrow \tan\alpha < 2H/2$

$\Rightarrow \quad \left.\dfrac{dV}{d\theta}\right|_{\theta<\tan^{-1}\left(\frac{2H}{R}\right)} < 0$ and In the right neighborhood;

We have $\left.\dfrac{dV}{d\theta}\right|_{\theta>\tan^{-1}\left(\frac{2H}{R}\right)} > 0$

Hence; $\theta = \tan^{-1}\left(\dfrac{2H}{R}\right)$ is a point of minima

$\therefore$ Minimum volume $= \dfrac{\pi}{3}\left(\dfrac{R}{2H}\right)^2\left(H + R\times\dfrac{2H}{R}\right)^3$

$= \dfrac{\pi}{3}\times\dfrac{R^2}{4H^2}\times(3H)^3 = \dfrac{\pi R^2}{3\times4\times H^2}\times 27H^3$

$= \dfrac{9\pi R^2 H}{4}$

For maximum; $\theta \to 0$;

$\therefore$ Max volume $\to \infty$

ILLUSTRATION 237: The height of the cylinder of max. volume that can be inscribed in a sphere of radius 'R' is

(a) $\dfrac{2R}{\sqrt{3}}$ (b) $\dfrac{R}{\sqrt{2}}$

(c) $\dfrac{5R}{4}$ (d) None of these

SOLUTION: If r be the radius and h the height, then from the figure

$R + (h^2/4) = R^2$

$\therefore \quad h^2 = 4(R^2 - r^2)$

Now $V = \pi r^2 h = \pi\left(R^2 - \dfrac{1}{4}h^2\right)h = \pi\left(R^2 h - \dfrac{1}{4}h^3\right)$

$\therefore \quad \dfrac{dV}{dh} = \pi\left(R^2 - \dfrac{3}{4}h^2\right) = 0$ for max or min

This gives $h = (2/\sqrt{3})R$

$d^2V/dh^2 = -6h/h < 0$

Hence V is max, when $h = 2R/\sqrt{3}$

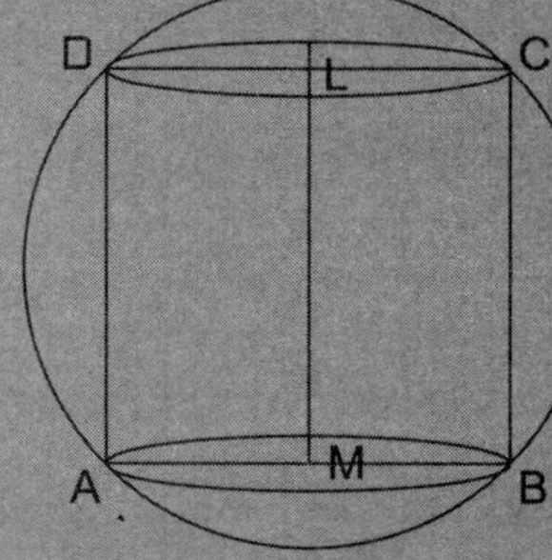

FIGURE 5.290

ILLUSTRATION 238: The altitude of a right circular cone minimum volume circumscribed about a sphere of radius r is

(a) $2r$ (b) $3r$

(c) $5r$ (d) None of these

SOLUTION: Let R be the radius of cone, ℓ its slant height and h be the height $V = \dfrac{1}{3}\pi R^2 h$

We have to make V a function of single variable $\dfrac{r}{h-r} = \dfrac{R}{1} = \sin\alpha$

or $\dfrac{r}{h-r} = \dfrac{R}{\sqrt{R^2+h^2}}$

$\therefore \quad r^2(R^2 + h^2) = R^2(h^2 - 2hr + r^2)$

$$\therefore \quad R^2 h = \frac{r^2h^2}{h-2r} \qquad ...(2)$$

$$\therefore \quad V = \frac{1}{3}\pi\frac{r^2h^2}{h-2r} \text{ where } r \text{ is given}$$

$$\therefore \quad V = \frac{1}{3}\pi\frac{r^2}{\frac{1}{h}-\frac{2r}{h^2}}$$

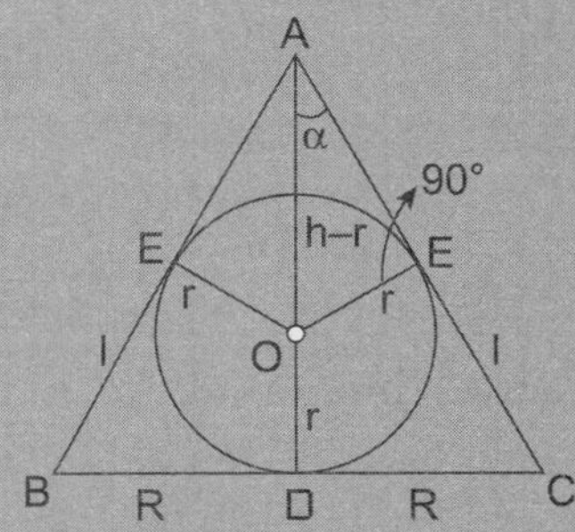

FIGURE 5.291

Now V will be minimum if $z = \frac{1}{h} - \frac{2r}{h^2}$ is max

$$\frac{dz}{dh} = \frac{-1}{h^2} + \frac{4r}{h^3} = 0 \qquad \therefore \ h = 4r$$

$$\frac{d^2z}{dh^2} = \frac{2}{h^3} - \frac{12r}{h^4} = \frac{2}{h^3}\left[1-\frac{6r}{h}\right] = \frac{2}{h^3}\left(1-\frac{6}{4}\right) = -ive$$

$\therefore$ z is max and hence V is minimum when $h = 4r$

$$\therefore \quad \sin\alpha = \frac{r}{h-r} = \frac{1}{3} \qquad \because \ h = 4r \text{ by}(1)$$

ILLUSTRATION 239: Find the relation between height and radius of conical tent of given capacity so that the least amount of canvas is used.

SOLUTION: $V = \frac{1}{3}\pi r^2 h$ (given)

$\therefore$ $h^2 = 9V^2/\pi^2 r^4$

Hence because of the tent, we are concerned only with the curved surface πrl and not that of the base $S = \pi rl$

$\therefore$ $S^2 = z = \pi^2 r^2 l^2 = \pi^2 r^2 (r^2 + h^2)$

or $z = \pi^2 r^2 \left[r^2 + \frac{9V^2}{\pi^2 r^4}\right] = \pi^2 r^4 + \frac{9V^2}{r^2}$

$$\frac{dz}{dr} = 4\pi^2 r^3 - \frac{18V^2}{r^3} \qquad \Rightarrow \qquad r^6 = \frac{9V^2}{r^2}$$

$$\frac{dz}{dr} = 4\pi^2 r^3 - \frac{18V^2}{r^3} \qquad \Rightarrow \qquad r^6 = \frac{9V^2}{2\pi^2}$$

Also $\frac{d^2z}{dr^2} = 12\pi^2 r^2 + \frac{54V^2}{r^4} = \frac{12\pi^2 r^6 + 54V^2}{r^4}$

$= \frac{6(9V^2) + 54V^2}{r^2} = +ive$ when $r^6 = \frac{9V^2}{2\pi^2}$

Hence z i.e., S^2 is minimum or S is minimum when $2\pi^2 r^6 = 9V^2$

or $2\pi^2 r^2 = 9\ 9.\frac{1}{9}\pi^2 r^4 h^2$

or $2r^2 = h^2$ or $h = r\sqrt{2}$

ILLUSTRATION 240: Rectangles are inscribed inside a semi-circle of radius r. Find the rectangle with maximum area.

SOLUTION: Let sides of rectangle be x and y

$\Rightarrow A = xy$

Here x and y are not independent variables and are related by Pythagoras theorem with r

$\frac{x^2}{4} + y^2 = r^2 \qquad \Rightarrow y = \sqrt{r^2 - \frac{x^2}{4}}$

$A(x) = x\sqrt{r^2 - \frac{x^2}{4}}$

$A(x) = \sqrt{x^2r^2 - \frac{x^4}{4}}$

Let $f(x) = r^2x^2 - \frac{x^4}{4}$; $\in (0, r)$

Now $A(x)$ is maximum when $f(x)$ is maximum

Hence $f'(x) = x(2r^2 - x^2) = 0$

$\Rightarrow x = r\sqrt{2}$

also $f'\left(r\sqrt{2^+}\right) < 0$ and $f'\left(r\sqrt{2^-}\right) > 0$

confirming at $f(x)$ is maximum when $x = r\sqrt{2}$ and $y = \frac{r}{\sqrt{2}}$.

$\Rightarrow A = xy = r^2$

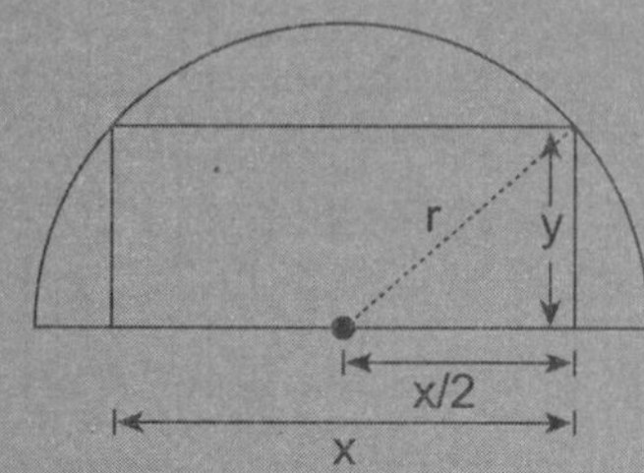

FIGURE 5.292

Aliter: Let use choose coordinate system with origin as centre of circle $A = xy$

$\Rightarrow A = 2\,(r\cos\theta)\,(r\sin\theta)$

$\Rightarrow A = r^2 \sin 2\theta \quad \theta \in \left(0, \frac{\pi}{2}\right)$

Clearly A is maximum when $\theta = \frac{\pi}{2}$

$\Rightarrow x = r\sqrt{2}$ and $y = \frac{r}{\sqrt{2}}$.

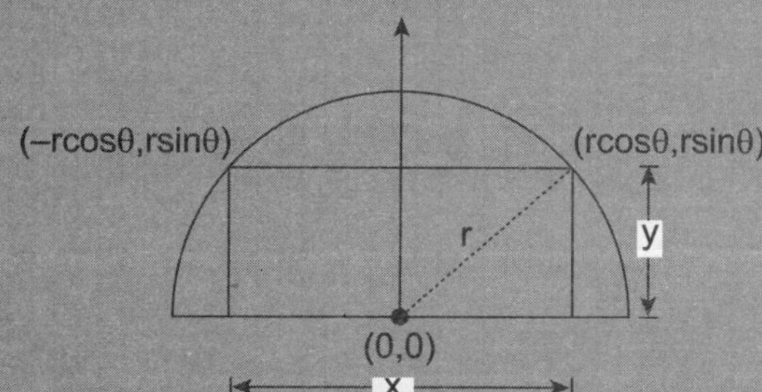

FIGURE 5.293

ILLUSTRATION 241: A sheet of area 40 m^2 in used to make an open tank with square base. Find the dimensions of the base such that volume of this tank is maximum.

SOLUTION: Let length of base be x m and height be y m.

$V = x^2y$

again x and y are related to surface area of this tank which is equal to 40 m^2.

$\Rightarrow x^2 + 4xy = 40$

$\Rightarrow y = \frac{40 - x^2}{4x}$; $x \in \left(0, \sqrt{40}\right)$

$V(x) = x^2\left(\frac{40 - x^2}{4x}\right)$

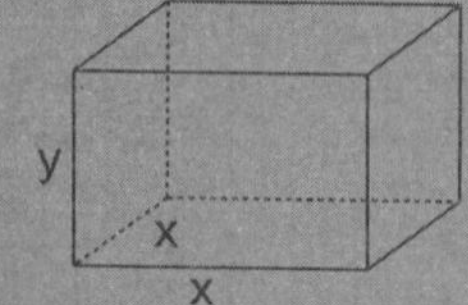

FIGURE 5.294

$$V(x) = \frac{(40x - x^3)}{4}$$

Maximizing volume, we get $V'(x) = \frac{(40x - 3x^2)}{4} = 0$

$\Rightarrow \; x = \sqrt{\frac{40}{3}} m$ $\qquad \Rightarrow \; V''(x) = -\frac{3x}{2}$

$\Rightarrow \; V''\left(\sqrt{\frac{40}{3}}\right) < 0$

Confirming that volume is maximum at $x = \sqrt{\frac{40}{3}} m$.

ILLUSTRATION 242: Among all regular square pyramids of volume $36\sqrt{2}\ cm^3$. Find dimensions of the pyramid having least lateral surface area.

SOLUTION: Let the length of a side of base be x cm and y be the perpendicular height of the pyramid

$V = \frac{1}{3}$ area of base × height

$V = \frac{1}{3} x^2 y = 36\sqrt{2}$

$y = \frac{108\sqrt{2}}{x^2}$ and $S = \frac{1}{2}$ perimeter of base x slant height $= \frac{1}{2}(4x).l$

$l = \sqrt{\frac{x^2}{4} + y^2}$

$S = 2x\sqrt{\frac{x^2}{4} + y^2} = \sqrt{x^4 + 4x^2 y^2}$

$S = \sqrt{x^4 + 4x^2\left(\frac{108\sqrt{2}}{x^2}\right)^2}$

$S(x) = \sqrt{x^4 + \frac{8.(108)^2}{x^2}}$

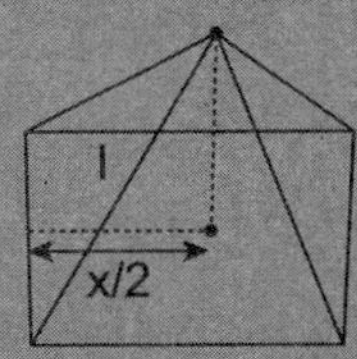

FIGURE 5.295

Let $f(x) = x^4 + \frac{8.(108)^2}{x^2}$ for minimizing $f(x)$

$\Rightarrow \; f(x) = 4x^3 - \frac{16(108)^2}{x^3} = 0$

$\Rightarrow \; f'(x) = 4\frac{(x^6 - 6^6)}{x^3} = 0$

$\Rightarrow \; x = 6$, which a point of minima. Hence $x = 6$ cm and $y = 3\sqrt{2}$.

ILLUSTRATION 243: Show that the volume of the greatest cylinder which can be inscribed in a cone of height 'h' and semi-vertical angle α is $\frac{4}{27}\pi h^3 \tan^2 \alpha$

SOLUTION: Let PQ, RS be a cylinder of radius x inscribed in the cone ABC of height h and semi-vertical angle α. From the figure, $AM\, x \cot \alpha$

$\therefore$ height of the cylinder $PQRS = MO = h - x \cot\alpha$

If V be the volume of the cylinder PQRS then

$V = \pi x^2 (h - x \cot\alpha)$

$= \pi h x^2 - \pi \cot\alpha\, x^3$ which is to be maximized

We have $\dfrac{dV}{dx} = 2\pi hx - 3\pi \cot\alpha\, x^2$

For a maximum or minimum of V, we must have $\dfrac{dV}{dx} = 0$

$\Rightarrow \pi x (2h - 3(\cot\alpha) x) = 0$

$\Rightarrow 2h - 3(\cot\alpha)x = 0\ [x \neq 0]$

$\Rightarrow x = \dfrac{2h}{3}\tan\alpha$

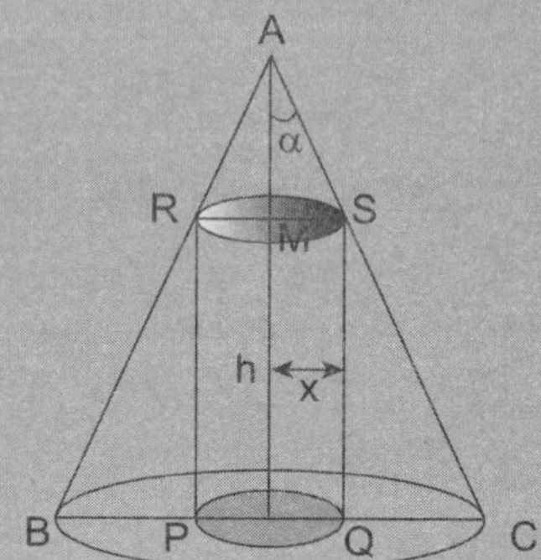

FIGURE 5.296

Now $\dfrac{d^2V}{dx^2} = 2\pi h - 6\pi \cot\alpha\, x$

$= 2\pi h - 6\pi \cot\alpha.\ \dfrac{2h}{3}\tan\alpha$, when $x = \dfrac{2h}{3}\tan\alpha$

$= -2\pi h < 0$

$\therefore$ V is maximum when $x =$ —tan

The maximum value of $V = \pi.\left(\dfrac{2h}{3}\tan\alpha\right)^2\left(h - \dfrac{2h}{3}\tan\alpha.\cot\alpha\right)$

$= \dfrac{4}{27}\pi h^3 \tan^2\alpha$

ILLUSTRATION 244: A given quantity of metal is to be cast into half cylinder i.e., with a rectangular base and semi-circular end. Show that in order that the total surface area may be minimum, the ratio of the height of the cylinder to the diameter of the semi-circular ends is $\pi : (\pi + 2)$.

SOLUTION: Let x be the radius and y the height of the cylinder.

Volume of the half cylinder $= \dfrac{1}{2}\pi x^2 y = V$ (given) ...(i)

Total surface area of half cylinder,

$\Rightarrow S =$ Curved surface of half cylinder

+ area of two semi-circular ends + area of rectangular base $ABCD$

$= \dfrac{1}{2}(2\pi xy) + 2\left(\dfrac{1}{2}\pi x^2\right) + 2x.y$

$= \pi xy + \pi x^2 + 2xy = (\pi + 2)xy + \pi x^2$

$= (\pi + 2).\dfrac{2V}{\pi x} + \pi x^2$ ((From (i))

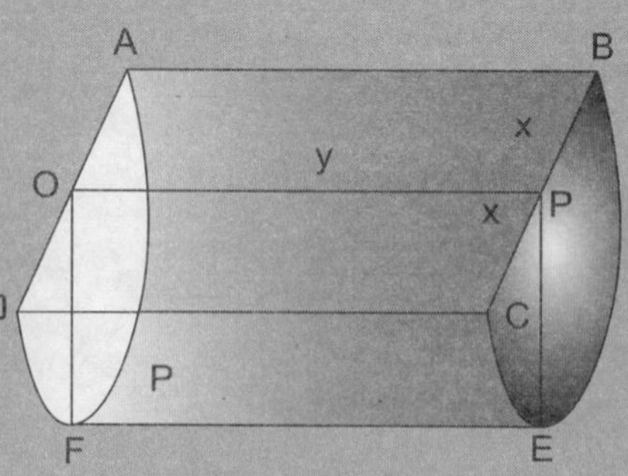

FIGURE 5.297

$\therefore \dfrac{dS}{dx} = -\dfrac{2V(\pi + 2)}{\pi x^2} + 2\pi x$ and $\dfrac{d^2S}{dx^2} = \dfrac{4V(\pi + 2)}{\pi x^3} + 2\pi$ ...(ii)

For max or min of S, $\frac{dS}{dx} = 0$

$\therefore \quad -2V(\pi+2)+2\pi^2 x^3 = 0$

$\Rightarrow \quad \pi x^3 = \frac{V(\pi+2)}{\pi}$

From (ii), $\frac{d^2S}{dx^2} = 4\pi + 2\pi = 6\pi > 0$. Hence S is minimum

$\Rightarrow \quad -\pi x^2 y(\pi+2)+2\pi^2 x^3 = 0$ (From (i))

$\Rightarrow \quad \frac{y}{2x} = \frac{\pi}{\pi+2}$

$y : 2x = \pi : (\pi+2)$ which is the required ratio

ILLUSTRATION 245: The sum of lengths of the hypotenuse and another side of a right angled triangle is given. The area of the triangle will be maximum if the angle between them is:

(a) $\frac{\pi}{6}$ (b) $\frac{\pi}{4}$

(c) $\frac{\pi}{3}$ (d) $\frac{5\pi}{12}$

SOLUTION: (c) $A = \frac{x\sqrt{c^2-2cx}}{2}$

$f(x) = 4A^2 = x^2(c^2 - 2cx)$

$f'(x) = x^2(-2c) + 2x(c^2 - 2xc)$

$\Rightarrow f'(x) = 2xc^2 - 6cx^2$

$\therefore f'(x) = 0$

$\Rightarrow 2xc(c - 3x) = 0$

$\Rightarrow x = 0$ *or* $x = c/3$

And $f''(x) = 2c^2 - 12cx$

$f''(0) = 2c^2 > 0$ and $f''(c/3) = -2c^2 < 0$

$\therefore f(x)$ is maximum for $x = c/3$

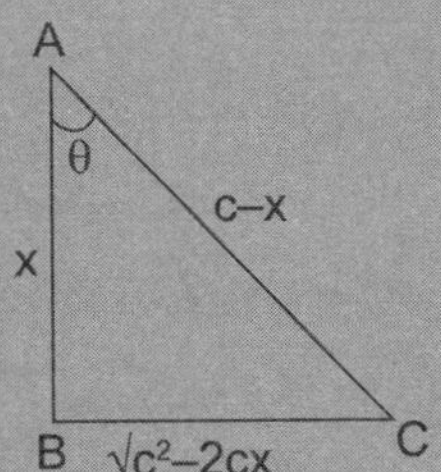

FIGURE 5.298

$\Rightarrow \cos\theta = \frac{1}{2}$ $\Rightarrow \theta = \frac{\pi}{3}$

ILLUSTRATION 246: A rectangle with one side lying along the x-axis is to be inscribed in the closed region of the xy plane bounded by the lines $y = 0$, $y = 3x$, and $y = 30 - 2x$. The largest area of such a rectangle is

(a) $\frac{135}{8}$ (b) 45

(c) $\frac{135}{2}$ (d) 90

SOLUTION: $A = (x_2 - x_1)y$ where y is the of the rectangle. Also $y = 3x_1$ and $y = 30 - 2x_2$

Now, $A(y) = y\left(\frac{30-y}{2} - \frac{y}{3}\right)$

$\Rightarrow 6A(y) = (90 - 3y - 2y)y = 90y - 5y^2$

$\Rightarrow 6A'(y) = 90 - 10y = 0$

$\Rightarrow y = 9; A''(y) = -10 < 0$

$\therefore x_1 = 3;$

$x_2 = \dfrac{21}{2}$

$A_{max} = \dfrac{15 \cdot 9}{2} \; 9 = \dfrac{15 \cdot 9}{2} = \dfrac{135}{2}$

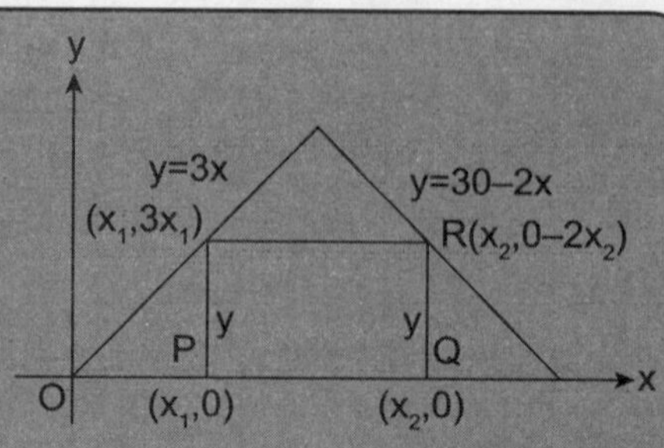

FIGURE 5.299

ILLUSTRATION 247: The coordinates of the points $P(x, y)$ lying in the first quadrant on the elllipse $x2/8 + y2/18 = 1$ so that the area of the triangle formed by the tangent at P and the coordinate axes is the smallest, are given by

(a) (2, 3) (b) (√8, 0)

(c) (√18, 0) (d) None of these

SOLUTION: Any point on the ellipse is given by (√8 cos θ, √18 sin θ)

Now $\dfrac{2x}{8} + \dfrac{2}{18} y \dfrac{dy}{dx} = 0$

$\Rightarrow \dfrac{dy}{dx} = -\dfrac{9x}{4y}$

$\Rightarrow \left.\dfrac{dy}{dx}\right|_{(\sqrt{8}\cos\theta, \sqrt{18}\sin\theta)} = -\dfrac{9\sqrt{8}\cos\theta}{4\sqrt{18}\sin\theta} - \dfrac{\sqrt{9}}{2}\cot\theta$

Hence the equation of the tangent at (√8 cos θ, √18 sin θ) is

$\Rightarrow y - \sqrt{18}\sin\theta = -\dfrac{\sqrt{9}}{2}\cot\theta(x - \sqrt{8}\cos\theta)$

Therefore, the tangent cuts the coordinate axes at the points $\left(0, \dfrac{\sqrt{18}}{\sin\theta}\right)$ & $\left(\dfrac{\sqrt{8}}{\cos\theta}, 0\right)$

Thus the area of the triangle formed by this tangent and the coordinate axes is

$\Rightarrow A = \dfrac{1}{2}\sqrt{18}.\sqrt{8}\dfrac{1}{\cos\theta\sin\theta} = \dfrac{6}{\cos\theta\sin\theta} = 12\operatorname{cosec}2\theta$

But cosec 2θ is smallest when θ = π/4. Therefore A is smallest when θ = π/4.

Hence the required point is $\left(\sqrt{8}.\dfrac{1}{\sqrt{2}}, \sqrt{18}.\dfrac{1}{\sqrt{2}}\right) = (2,3)$

ILLUSTRATION 248: A conical vessel is to be prepared out of a circular sheet of gold of unit radius. How much sectorial area is to be removed from the sheet so that the vessel has maximum volume?

SOLUTION: Sectorial area AOB is removed and the remaining part be folded into a cone of height h and radius r.

$\because \theta = \text{Angle} = \dfrac{\text{Arc } AB}{\text{radius of gold sheet}} = \dfrac{\text{Arc } AB}{1} = \text{Arc } AB$

$\therefore 2\pi r = \theta$ ..(i)

and $r^2 + h^2 = 1$ ...(ii)

$\therefore$ Volume of cone $V = \dfrac{1}{3}\pi r^2 h = \dfrac{1}{3}\pi r^2(\sqrt{1 - r^2})$

$$\Rightarrow\ V^2 = \frac{\pi^2 r^4 (1-r^2)}{9}$$

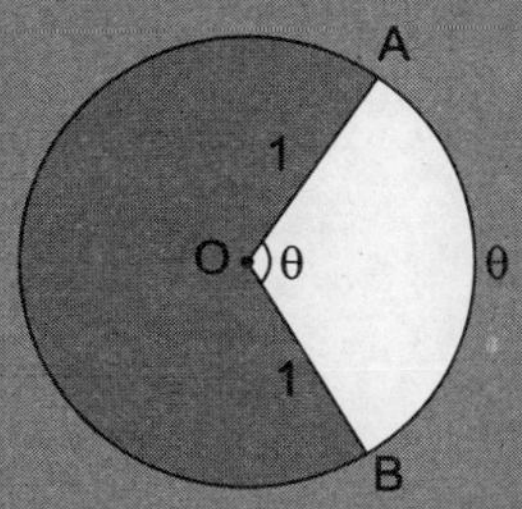

Circular Sheet

FIGURE 5.300

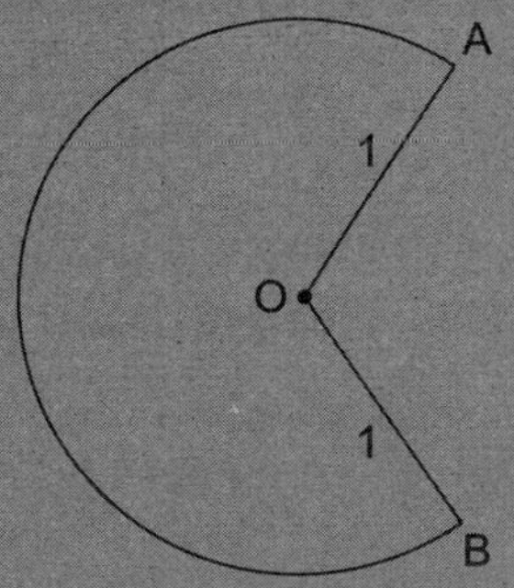

After Removed part

FIGURE 5.301

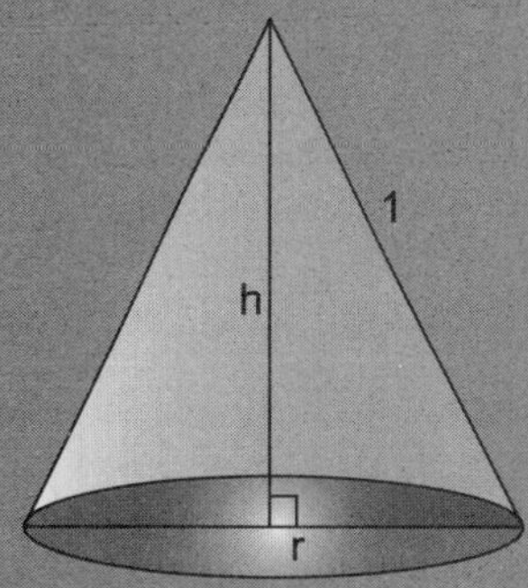

Conical Vassel

FIGURE 5.302

Let $y = V^2 = \dfrac{\pi^2 (r^4 - r^6)}{9}$

$$\therefore\ \frac{dy}{dr} = \frac{\pi^2}{9}(4r^3 - 6r^5) \text{ and } \frac{d^2y}{dr^2} = \frac{\pi^2}{9}(12r^2 - 30r^4)$$

For max. or min of y, $\dfrac{dy}{dx} = 0$

$$\therefore\ r = \sqrt{\frac{2}{3}}$$

Then $\left.\dfrac{d^2y}{dx^2}\right|_{r=\sqrt{2/3}} = \dfrac{\pi^2}{9}\left(12.\dfrac{2}{3} - 30.\dfrac{4}{9}\right) = -\dfrac{16}{27}\pi^2$

$\therefore$ y is maximum then V is also maximum at $r = \sqrt{\dfrac{2}{3}}$

$\therefore$ Required sectorial area $= \dfrac{1}{2}.(1)^2.\theta = \dfrac{1}{2}\theta = \pi r = \pi\sqrt{\dfrac{2}{3}}$

GENERAL CONCEPT (SHORTEST DISTANCE OF A POINT FROM A CURVE)

Given a fixed point $A(a, b)$ and a moving point $P(x, f(x))$ on the curve $y = f(x)$. Then AP will be maximum or minimum if it is normal to the curve at P.

Proof: $F(x) = (x - a)^2 + (f(x) - b))^2$

$$\Rightarrow F'(x) = 2(x - a) + 2(f(x) - b) \cdot f'(x)$$

$$\therefore\ F'(x) = 0 \ \Rightarrow f'(x) = -\frac{(x-a)}{f'(x) - b}$$

Also $m_{AP} = \dfrac{f(x) - b}{x - a}$.

Hence $f'(x) \cdot m_{AP} = -1$.

$\Rightarrow$ $AP \perp$ tan gent *to* $f(x)$ at P.

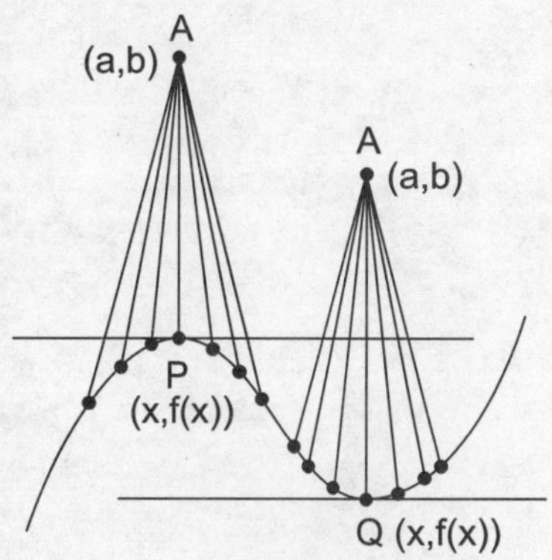

FIGURE 5.303

ILLUSTRATION 249: Find a point on the curve $x^2 + 2y^2 = 6$ whose distance from the line $x + y = 7$, is minimum.

SOLUTION: The given curve $\frac{x^2}{6} + \frac{y^2}{3} = 1$

Any point on it will be given by $(\sqrt{6}\cos\theta, \sqrt{3}\sin\theta)$

The distance of this point from the line $x + y = 7$ is given by $D = \frac{\sqrt{6}\cos\theta + \sqrt{3}\sin\theta - 7}{\sqrt{2}}$ for

min D, $\frac{dD}{d\theta} = 0$

$\Rightarrow \sqrt{6} - \sin\theta + \sqrt{3}\cos\theta = 0$

$\Rightarrow \tan\theta = \frac{1}{\sqrt{2}}$

$\Rightarrow \cos\theta = \frac{\sqrt{2}}{\sqrt{3}}$ and $\sin\theta = \frac{1}{\sqrt{3}}$

$\therefore$ Point is given by (2, 1)

ILLUSTRATION 250: The coordinates of the point on the parabola $y^2 = 8x$ which is at minimum distance from the circle $x^2 + (y + 6)^2 = 1$ are

(a) (2, –4) (b) (18, –12)

(c) (2, 4) (d) None of these

SOLUTION: Let $P(2t^2, 4t)$ be any point on the parabola.

The centre of the given circle is $O(0, -6)$ and the radius is 1.

$OP^2 = 4t^4 + (4t + 6)^2 = 4[t^4 + 4t^2 + 9 + 12t]$

$= 4s$ where $s = t^4 + 4t^2 + 12t + 9$

$\frac{dS}{dt} = 4t^3 + 8t + 12 = 4(t^3 + 2t + 3) = 4(t + 1)(t^2 - t + 3)$

Now $\frac{dS}{dt} = 0$

$\Rightarrow t = -1$ (other roots are imaginary)

So $\frac{d^2S}{dt^2} = 4(3t^2 + 2)$

$\Rightarrow \left.\frac{d^2s}{dt^2}\right|_{t=-1} > 0.$

Hence OP^2 is minimum at $t = -1$. But if A is any point on the circle and on OP(min), then AP will be minimum when OP is minimum as $AP = OP -$ (radius of circle).

Thus the required point is $P(2(-1))^{2,} 4(-1)) = (2, -4)$

ILLUSTRATION 251: (i) Find the point on the hyperbola $3x^2 - 4y^2 = 72$ which is nearest to the line $3x + 2y + 1 = 0$

(ii) Find the shortest distance between the curves $9x^2 + 9y^2 - 30y + 16 = 0$ and $y^2 = x^3$.

SOLUTION: (i) Slope of the given line $= -3/2$. First of all we try to locate the points on the curve at which the tangent is parallel to the give line

Differentiating $3x^2 - 4y^2 = 72$. w.r.t, x, we get $6x - 8y\frac{dy}{dx} = 0$

$\Rightarrow \frac{dy}{dx} = \frac{3y}{4y} = -\frac{3}{2} \Rightarrow \frac{x}{y} = -2$

Also, $3\left(\frac{x}{y}\right)^2 - 4 = \frac{72}{y^2} \Rightarrow \frac{72}{y^2} = 3,4-4, = 8 \Rightarrow y^2 = 9 \Rightarrow y = 3,-3$

The required points are (–6, 3) and (6, –3)

Distance of (–6, 3) from the given line $= \frac{|-18+6+1|}{\sqrt{3}} = \frac{11}{\sqrt{13}}$

And the distance of (6, –3) from the given line $= \frac{|18-6+1|}{\sqrt{13}} = \frac{13}{\sqrt{13}} = \sqrt{13}$

Clearly the required point is (–6, 3)

(ii) $9x^2 + 9y^2 - 30y + 16 = 0$ can be rewritten as $x^2 + \left(y - \frac{5}{3}\right)^2 = 1$

Any point on the curve $y^2 = x^3$ can be taken as (t^2, t^3).

Let d be the distance between the centre of the given circle and the point (t^2, t^3), then $K = d^2 = t^4 + (t^3 - 5/3)^2$

Now, we calculate the minimum value of L. Required distance = d – radius of given circle.

Now, $\frac{dK}{dt} = 4t^3 + 2\left(t^3 - \frac{5}{3}\right)3t^2 = 0$

For maximum or minimum, $t = 0$ or 1

Now, $\frac{dK}{dt^2} = 12t^2 + 30t^4 - 20t; \left.\frac{d^2K}{dt^2}\right|_{t=0} = 0$

But, $\left.\frac{d^3K}{dt^3}\right|_{t=0} \neq 0$

$\Rightarrow$ There is neither maxima nor minima at $t = 0$

Also, $\frac{d^2K}{dt^2} > 0$ at $t = 1$

$\Rightarrow$ d^2 is minimum at $t = 1$ i.e., d is minimum at $t = 1$

So, shortest distance = (value of d at $t = 1$) – (radius of the circle) $= \frac{\sqrt{13}}{3} - 1$

ILLUSTRATION 252: The points on the curve $5x^2 - 8xy + 5y^2 = 4$ whose distance from the origin is maximum or minimum are

(a) $\left(\sqrt{2}, \sqrt{2}\right)$ (b) $\left(-\sqrt{2}, -\sqrt{2}\right)$

(c) $\left(\frac{\sqrt{2}}{3}, -\frac{\sqrt{2}}{3}\right)$ (d) $\left(-\frac{\sqrt{2}}{3}, \frac{\sqrt{2}}{3}\right)$

SOLUTION: Let (r, θ) be the polar co-ordinates of any point P on the curve where r is the distance of the point from origin

$\therefore$ $x = r\cos\theta$ and $y = r\sin\theta$

$\Rightarrow r^2[5(\cos^2\theta + \sin^2\theta) - 8\sin\theta.\cos\theta] = 4$

$\Rightarrow r^2 = \dfrac{4}{5 - 4\sin 2\theta}$

Now, r^2 is max. when $5 - 4\sin 2\theta$ is minimum $= 5 - 4 = 1$ when $\sin 2\theta = 1$

$\Rightarrow 2\theta = 90^0$ $\quad\Rightarrow \theta = 45^0$

$\therefore\ r = \pm 2, \theta = 45^0$

Again r^2 is minimum when $5 - 4\sin 2\theta$ is maximum $= 5 + 4 = 9$ when $\sin 2\theta = -1$

$\therefore\ 2\theta = \dfrac{3\pi}{2}$ $\quad\therefore\ \theta = \dfrac{3\pi}{4}$

$\therefore\ r = \pm\dfrac{2}{3}, \theta = \dfrac{3\pi}{4}$

Hence the points are $(r\cos\theta, r\sin\theta)$ where r, θ are given by (1) and (2). Thus we get the four points given in (a), (b), (c), (d).

ILLUSTRATION 253: The largest distance of the point $(a, 0)$ from the curve $2x^2 + y^2 - 2x = 0$ is given by

(a) $\sqrt{1+2a+2a^2}$ (b) $\sqrt{1+2a-a^2}$

(c) $\sqrt{1-2a+2a^2}$ (d) $\sqrt{1-2a+a^2}$

SOLUTION: Let D be the distance of $(a, 0)$ from (x, y) on the curve then $D = \sqrt{(x-a)^2 + y^2}$

If D is to be the maximum $\quad\Rightarrow D^2$ is maximum

Now, $D^2 = (x - a)^2 + y^2$

$\Rightarrow D^2 = (x - a)^2 + 2x - 2x^2 = -x^2 + 2x(1 - a) + a^2$

$\Rightarrow \dfrac{dD^2}{dx} = -2x + 2(1-a)$

Now, $\dfrac{dD^2}{dx} = 0$ $\quad\Rightarrow x = 1 - a$

By change of sign rule, D^2 is maximum or else $\dfrac{d^2D^2}{dx^2} = -ive$ putting $x = 1 - a$

$D^2 = -(1 - a)^2 + 2(1 - a)^2 + a^2 = 1 - 2a + 2a^2$

$\therefore\ D = \sqrt{1-2a+2a^2}$

ILLUSTRATION 254: The co-ordinates of a point of the parabola $y = x^2 + 7x + 2$ which is closest to the straight line $y = 3x - 3$ is

(a) $(-2, \infty)$ (b) $(-2, -8)$

(c) $(2, -8)$ (d) None of these

SOLUTION: Let (x, y) be one the parabola $y = x^2 + 7x + 2$ its distance from the line $y = 3x - 3$ or $3x - y - 3 = 0$ is

$$D = \left|\frac{3x-y-3}{\sqrt{(10)}}\right| = \left|\frac{3x-(x^2+7x+2)-3}{\sqrt{(10)}}\right| = \left|\frac{-x^2-4x-5}{\sqrt{(10)}}\right|$$

$$D=\left|\frac{x^2+4x+5}{\sqrt{(10)}}\right|=\left|\frac{(x+2)^2+1}{\sqrt{10}}\right|=\frac{(x+2)^2+1}{\sqrt{(10)}}$$

Now, $\frac{dD}{dx}=\frac{2(x+2)}{\sqrt{(10)}}=0$

$\Rightarrow x=-2$

And hence y is -8 i.e., point is $(-2, -8)$

$\frac{d^2D}{dx^2}=\frac{2}{\sqrt{(10)}}=+ive$

And hence min. at $(-2,-8)$

ILLUSTRATION 255: The parabola $y = x^2 + px + q$ cuts the straight line $y = 2x - 3$ at a point with abscissa 1. If the distance between the vertex of the parabola and the x-axis is least then:

(a) $p = 0$ and $q = -2$

(b) $p = -2$ and $q = 0$

(c) least distance between the parabola and $x-$axis is 2

(d) least distance between the parabola and $x-$axis is 1

SOLUTION: When $x = 1$; $y = -1$ (from the line)

This must lie on the parabola $y = x^2 + px + q$

$\Rightarrow -1 = 1 + p + q$

$\Rightarrow p + q = -2$

$\therefore$ Now distance of the vertex of the parabola from the x-axis is

$$d=f\left(-\frac{p}{2}\right)=\frac{p^2}{4}-\frac{p^2}{2}+q=q-\frac{p^2}{4}$$

Substituting $q = -2 - p$ here

$$f(p)=-2-p-\frac{p^2}{4}$$

Hence $f'(p)=-1-\frac{p}{2}=0$

$\Rightarrow p=-2$

Hence $q = 0$

Note that least distance of the vertex from x-axis is 1

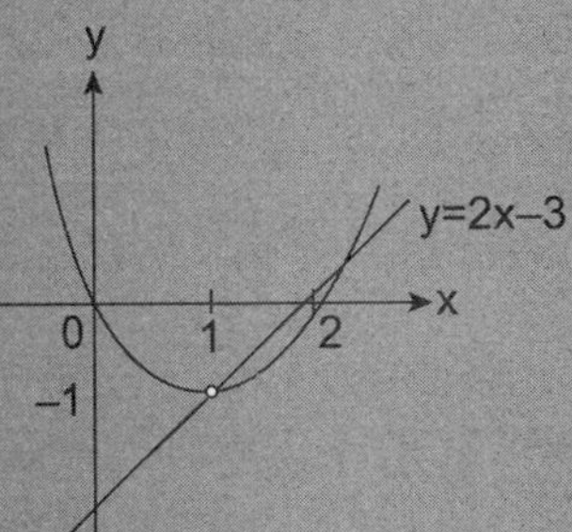

FIGURE 5.304

ILLUSTRATION 256: Find the minimum value of $(x_1-x_2)^2+\left(\sqrt{2-x_1^2}-\frac{9}{x_2}\right)^2$ where $x_1\in(0,\sqrt{2})$ and $x_2\in R^+$.

SOLUTION: Let $y_1=\sqrt{2-x_1^2}$ *and* $y_2=\frac{9}{x_2}\Rightarrow x_1^2+y_1^2=2$ *and* $x_2\ y_2=9$

Hence given expression represents the distance between points $P_1(x_1,y_1)$ *and* $P_2(x_2,y_2)$ lying on the curves $x^2+y^2=2$ and $xy = 9$ respectively in the first quadrant.

Thus in order to find the least value of the given expression we must find the least distance between the indicated curves.

For $xy = 9$, $\frac{dy}{dx} = -\frac{y}{x} = -\frac{9}{x^2}$.

Hence slope of normal to $xy = 9$ at $P_2(x_2, y_2)$ is $\frac{x_2^2}{9}$ and the equation of normal at P_2 is;

$(y - y_2) = \frac{x_2^2}{9}(x - x_2)$

It must pass through the origin (as we are interested in common normal)

$\Rightarrow 0 - \frac{9}{x_2} = \frac{x_2^2}{9}(0 - x_2) \Rightarrow x_2^4 = 81$

$\Rightarrow \; x_2 = 3 \Rightarrow y_2 = 3.$

Thus least distance between the curves is $\sqrt{9+9} - \sqrt{2} = 2\sqrt{2}$.

Hence the least value of the expression is 8.

ILLUSTRATION 257: Find the shortest distance between the line $y = x - 2$ and the parabola $y = x^2 + 3x + 2$.

SOLUTION: Let $P(x_1, y_1)$ be a point closet to the line $y = x - 2$

Then $\left.\frac{dy}{dx}\right|_{(x_1, x_2)} = \text{slope of line}$

$\Rightarrow 2x_1 + 3 = 1 \qquad \Rightarrow x_1 = -1$

$\Rightarrow y_1 = 0$

Hence point (–1, 0) is the closest and its perpendicular distance from the line $y = x - 2$ will give the shortest distance

$\Rightarrow \; p = \frac{3}{\sqrt{2}}$

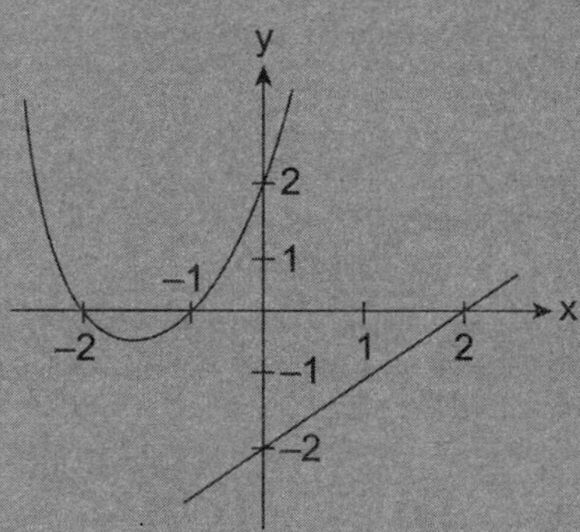

FIGURE 5.305

ILLUSTRATION 258: The point (0,5) is closest to the curve $x^2 = 2y$ at

(a) $(2\sqrt{2},0)$ (b) (0,0)

(c) (2,2) (d) None of these

SOLUTION: If $x = t$, then $y = t^2/2$ are the parametric equations of the parabola, any point on it is $\left(t, \frac{t^2}{2}\right)$ and if its distance from (0, 5) be D.

then $Z = D^2 = t^2 + \left(\frac{t^2}{2} - 5\right)^2$

$\therefore \; \frac{dZ}{dt} = 2t + 2t\left(\frac{t^2}{2} - 5\right) = 0$

$\therefore \; \frac{t}{2}(t^2 - 8) = \frac{1}{2}(t^3 - 8t) = 0 \qquad \Rightarrow t = 0, \pm 2\sqrt{2}$

Now, $\frac{d^2Z}{dt^2} = \frac{1}{2}(3t^2 - 8)$

It is $+ive$ for $t = \pm 2\sqrt{2}$

$\therefore$ D is min. when $t = \pm 2\sqrt{2}$, $y = \frac{t^2}{2} = 4$

Points are $(\pm 2\sqrt{2}, 4)$

ILLUSTRATION 259: The co-ordinates of a point on the parabola $y^2 = 8x$ whose distance from the circle $x^2 + (y + 6)^2 = 1$ is minimum is

(a) (2, 4) (b) (2, –4)

(c) (18, –12) (d) (8, 8)

SOLUTION: Any point on the parabola $y^2 = 8x$ ($4a = 8$ or $a = 2$) is $(at^2, 2at)$ or $(2t^2, 4t)$. Its distance from the circle means its distance from the centre (0, –6) of the circle. If D be the distance, then

$$Z = D^2 = (2t^2)^2 + (4t + 6)^2 = 4(t^4 + 4t^2 + 12 + 9)$$

$$\therefore \frac{dz}{dt} = 4(4t^3 + 8t + 12) = 0 \Rightarrow 16(t^3 + 2t + 3) = 0$$

or $16(t + 1)(t^2 - t - 3) = 0 \Rightarrow \quad t = -1$

Now, $\frac{d^2z}{dt^2} = 16(3t^2 + 2) =$ positive, hence minimum

$\therefore$ Point is (2,-4)

TEXTUAL EXERCISE–5: (SUBJECTIVE)

1. Towns A and B are situated on the same side of a straight road at distances a and b respectively, from it. Perpendicular drawn from A and B meet the road at the points C and D, respectively. The distance between C and D is c. A hospital is to be built at a point P on the road such that the distance APB is minimum. Find the position of P.

2. A lantern must be hanged directly above a circular plaza of radius R. At what height it must be installed to provide the best lighting form the road around the plaza? (the intensity of illumination of a surface is directly proportional to the cosine of the angle of incidence of the rays and indirectly proportional to the square of the distance from the source of light).

3. What must be the dimensions of a symmetrical cross of maximum area that can be removed from a circular disc of given radius 'a'? (see figure)

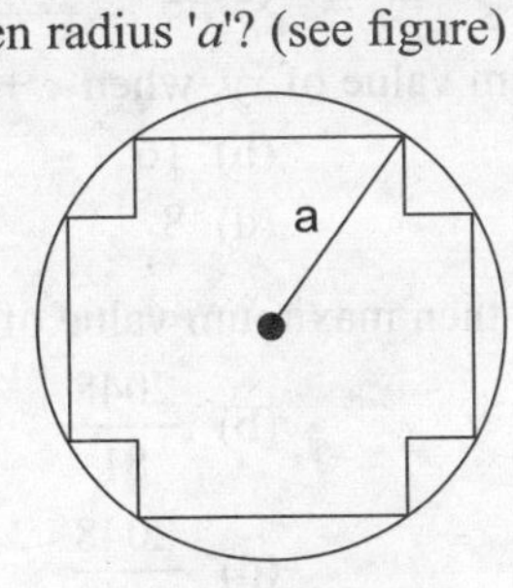

FIGURE 5.306

4. A manufacturer plans to construct a cylindrical cane to hold one cubic meter of liquid. If the cost of constructing the top and bottom of the cane is twice the cost of constructing the sides, what are the dimensions of the most economical cane?

5. The shape of a hole bored by a drill is cone surmounted by a cylinder. If the cylinder be of height 'h' and radius 'r' and semi-vertical angle of the cone be α where $\tan \alpha = h/r$, show that for a total height H of the hole, volume removed is maximum if $h = H(\sqrt{7} + 1)/6$

6. A factory D is to be connected by a road with a straight railway line on which a town 'A' is situated. The distance DB of the factory to the railway line is $5\sqrt{3}$ km., length AB of the railway line is 20 km. Freight charges on road are twice the charges on the railway. At what point $P(AP < AB)$ on the railway line should the road DP be so as to ensure minimum freight charges from the factory to the town?

7. Find the coordinates of a point on the parabola $y = x^2 + 7x + 2$ which is closest to the straight line $y = 3x - 3$.

8. Find the point of the hyperbola $\frac{x^2}{24} - \frac{y^2}{18} = 1$ which is closest to the straight line $3x + 2y + 1 = 0$. Compute

the distance between the point and the line.

9. Find the point on $p^2x^2 + 9y^2 = 9p^2$, $9 < p^2 < 18$, that is farthest from the point (–3, 0).

10. Prove that the minimum intercept made by the axes on the tangent to the ellipse $\frac{x^2}{a^2}+\frac{y^2}{b^2}=1$ is $a + b$. Prove further that it is divided at the point of contact into parts which are equal to semi-axes, respectively.

11. Find the point (α, β) on the ellipse $4x^2 + 3y^2 = 12$ in the first quadrant, so that the area enclosed by the lines $y = x$, $y = \beta$, $x = \alpha$ and the x-axis is maximum.

12. N is the foot of the ⊥r drawn from the centre O on to the tangent at a point P on the ellipse $(a > b)$. Prove that the maximum area of the triangle OPN is $\frac{1}{4}(a^2 - b^2)$ and find the maximum length of PN.

Answer Keys

1. At distance $x = \frac{ac}{a+b}$ from C.
2. $\frac{R}{\sqrt{2}}$
3. $\sqrt{\frac{10-2\sqrt{5}}{5}}a; \frac{\sqrt{5-2\sqrt{5}}}{5}a$
4. $r = \frac{1}{(4\pi)^{\frac{1}{3}}}.m; h = \left(\frac{16}{\pi}\right)^{\frac{1}{3}}.m$
6. At distance $x = 5$ km from B
7. (–2, –8)
8. (–6, 3), $\frac{11}{\sqrt{13}}$
9. (3, 0)
11. $\left(\frac{3}{2}, 1\right)$
13. $(a - b)$

TEXTUAL EXERCISE–5: (OBJECTIVE)

1. The shortest distance between the line $y - x = 1$ and the curve $x = y^2$ is
(a) $\frac{3\sqrt{2}}{8}$ (b) $\frac{2\sqrt{3}}{8}$
(c) $\frac{3\sqrt{2}}{5}$ (d) $\frac{\sqrt{3}}{4}$

2. If θ is the semi vertical angle of a cone of maximum volume and given slant height, then $\tan\theta$ is given by
(a) 2 (b) 1
(c) $\sqrt{2}$ (d) $\sqrt{3}$

3. A circular sector of perimeter 60 m with maximum area is to be constructed. The radius the circular arc in metre must be
(a) 20 (b) 5
(c) 15 (d) 10

4. Divide 12 into two parts such that the product of the square of one part and fourth power of the second part is maximum, are
(a) 6, 6 (b) 5, 7
(c) 4, 8 (d) 3, 9

5. The minimum value $2x + 3y$, when $xy = 6$ is
(a) 9 (b) 12
(c) 8 (d) 6

6. The maximum area of the rectangle that can be inscribed in a circle of radius r, is
(a) πr^2 (b) r^2
(c) $\pi r^2/4$ (d) $2r^2$

7. The perimeter of a sector is a constant. If its area is to be maximum, the sectorial angle is
(a) $\frac{\pi^c}{6}$ (b) $\frac{\pi^c}{4}$
(c) 4^c (d) 2^c

8. The maximum value of xy, when $x + 2y = 8$ is
(a) 20 (b) 16
(c) 24 (d) 8

9. If $x + y = 8$, then maximum value of x^2y is
(a) $\frac{2048}{9}$ (b) $\frac{2048}{81}$
(c) $\frac{2048}{3}$ (d) $\frac{2048}{27}$

10. If $x - 2y = 4$, the minimum value of xy is

(a) –2 (b) 0

(c) 0 (d) –3

11. The sum of two numbers is 20. If the product of the square of one number and cube of the other is maximum, then the numbers are

(a) 12, 8 (b) 3, 4

(c) 9, 12 (d) 15, 18

12. If $a^2x^4 + b^2y^4 = c^6$, then maximum value of xy is

(a) $\frac{c^2}{\sqrt{ab}}$ (b) $\frac{c^3}{ab}$

(c) $\frac{c^3}{\sqrt{2ab}}$ (d) $\frac{c^3}{2ab}$

13. The point (0, 5) is closer the curve $x^2 = 2y$ at

(a) $(2\sqrt{2},0)$ (b) (0, 0)

(c) (2, 2) (d) None of these

14. If P is a point on $\frac{x^2}{a^2}+\frac{y^2}{b^2}=1$ with focii S and S', then the maximum value of $\Delta SPS'$ is

(a) ab (b) abe^2

(c) abe (d) ab/e

Answer Keys

1. (a)	**2.** (c)	**3.** (c)	**4.** (c)	**5.** (b)	**6.** (d)	**7.** (d)	**8.** (d)	**9.** (d)	**10.** (a)
11. (a)	**12.** (c)	**13.** (d)	**14.** (c)						

MULTIPLE CHOICE QUESTIONS

SECTION–I

OBJECTIVE SOLVED EXAMPLE

1. Let three degree polynomial function $f(x)$ has local maximum at $x = -1$ and $f(-1) = 2, f(3) = 18, f'(x)$ has a minima at
$x = 0$, then:

(a) The distance between $(-1, 2)$ and $(a, f(a))$ where a denotes point where function has local max/min is $2\sqrt{5}$

(b) The function decreases from 1 to $2\sqrt{5}$

(c) The function increases from 1 to $2\sqrt{5}$

(d) The function decreases from -1 to 1

Solution: (a) Let $f(x) = ax^3 + bx^2 + cx + d$

$f(-1) = 2, f(3) = 18, f'(x)$ has a min. at $x = 0$, so that $f''(x) = 0$ at $x = 0, f(x)$ has a local max, at $x = -1$

$\therefore\ f'(-1) = 0$

$\therefore$ These conditions imply $-a + b - c + d = 2$

$27a + 9b + 3c + d = 18$

$\therefore\ 28a + 8b + 4c = 16$

$f'(x) = 3ax^2 + 2bx + c, f''(x) = 6ax + 2b$

$f'(-1) = 0$

$\Rightarrow 3a - 2b + c = 0, f''(0) = 0$

$\Rightarrow b = 0$

Putting $b = 0, 7a + c = 4, 3a + c = 0$

$\therefore\ a = 1, c = -3, b \therefore d = 0$

Hence $f(x) = x^3 - 3x$

$\therefore\ f'(x) = 3(x^2 - 1), f''(x) = 6x$

Now, $f'(x) = 0$

$\Rightarrow x = 1, -1; y = -2, 2$ respectively

$\therefore\ (1, -2)$ or $(-1, 2) = (a, f(a))$

Now, $f''(x) = 6x = 6$ at $x = 1, = -6a t\ x = -1$

$\therefore$ at $(1, -2)$, $f(x)$ is min. and at$(-1,2)$, $f(x)$ is max.

$\therefore\ d^2 = \sqrt{4+16} = 2\sqrt{5}$

2. The set of values of λ for which the function $f(x) = (4\lambda - 3)(x + \log 5) + 2(\lambda - 7).\ \cot\frac{x}{7}\sin^2\frac{x}{2}$ does not posses critical point is:

(a) $[1, \infty)$ (b) $(2, \infty)$

(c) $(-\infty, -4/3)$ (d) $(-\infty, -1)$

Solution: (b, c) $2\cot\frac{x}{2}\sin^2\frac{x}{2} = 2\cos\frac{x}{2}\sin\frac{x}{2} = \sin x$

$\therefore\ f(x) = (4\lambda - 3)(x + \log 5) + (\lambda - 7)\sin x$

$f'(x) = (4\lambda - 3) + (\lambda - 7)\cos x = 0$ ..(i)

$\therefore\ \cos x = \frac{4\lambda - 3}{\lambda - 7}$ ...(ii)

Now $-1 \le \cos x \le 1$

$\therefore\ -1 \le \frac{4\lambda - 3}{\lambda - 7} \le 1$; Above gives us two inequalities

$-1 - \frac{4\lambda - 3}{\lambda - 7} \le 0$ or $\frac{4\lambda - 3}{\lambda - 7} \le 0$

$\Rightarrow \frac{-5\lambda + 10}{\lambda - 7} \le$ or $\frac{3\lambda + 4}{\lambda - 7} \le 0$

$\Rightarrow \frac{5(\lambda - 2)}{\lambda - 7} \ge 0$ *or* $\frac{3(\lambda + 4/3)}{\lambda - 7} \le 0$

Above are the conditions for $f(x)$ to have critical points. But the function does not posses critical points. Therefore we must have

$\frac{5(\lambda - 2)}{\lambda - 7} < 0$ or $\frac{3(\lambda + 4/3)}{\lambda - 7} > 0$

$\Rightarrow \frac{5(\lambda - 2)(\lambda - 7)}{(\lambda - 7)^2} < 0$

$\Rightarrow \frac{3(\lambda + 4/3)(\lambda - 7)}{(\lambda - 7)^2} > 0$

$\therefore\ \lambda \in (2, 7)$ or $\lambda < -4/3$ or > 7

$\therefore\ \lambda \in (2, 7)$ or $\lambda \in (-\infty, -4/3)$ or $(7, \infty)$

$\therefore\ \lambda \in (2, 8)$ or $\lambda \in (-\infty, -4/3)$

3. The greatest value of the function $f(x) = \frac{\sin 2x}{\sin\left(\pi + \frac{\pi}{4}\right)}$ on the interval $\left[0, \frac{\pi}{2}\right]$ is

(a) $\frac{1}{\sqrt{2}}$ (b) $\sqrt{2}$

(c) 1 (d) $-\sqrt{2}$

Solution: (c) $f(x) = \frac{(\sin x + \cos x)^2 - 1}{\frac{1}{\sqrt{2}}(\sin x + \cos x)} = \sqrt{2}\frac{t^2 - 1}{t}$

(Putting $\sin x + \cos x = t$)

or $f(x) = \phi(t) = \sqrt{2}\left(t - \frac{1}{t}\right)$

where $t = g(x) = \sin x + \cos x$, $x \in [0, \pi/2]$

$g'(x) = \cos x - \sin x = 0 \Rightarrow \tan x = 1$

$\Rightarrow x = \pi/4$ and $g''(x) < 0$

$\therefore$ $g(x)$ is max, when $x = \pi/4$

At $x = 0$, $t = 1$ $\therefore$ $t \in [1, \sqrt{2}]$

Now $\phi(t) = \sqrt{2}\left(t - \frac{1}{t}\right)$ where $t \in [1, \sqrt{2}]$

$\phi'(t) = \sqrt{2}\left(1 + \frac{1}{t^2}\right) > 0$

$\therefore$ $\phi(t)$ is increasing

Hence $\phi(t)$ is greatest at the end point of interval $[1, \sqrt{2}]$ i.e. $t = \sqrt{2}$

$\therefore$ $f(x) = \phi(t) = \sqrt{2}\left[\sqrt{2} - \frac{1}{\sqrt{2}}\right] = 1$

4. The least value of a for which the equation $\frac{4}{\sin x} + \frac{1}{1 - \sin x} = a$ has at least one solution on the interval $(0, \pi/2)$ is

(a) 9 (b) 4

(c) 8 (d) 1

Solution: (a) Since $a = \left(\frac{4}{\sin x} + \frac{1}{1 - \sin x}\right)$, a is least

$$\therefore \frac{da}{dx} = \left[-\frac{4}{\sin^2 x} + \frac{1}{(1 - \sin x)^2}\right]\cos x = 0$$

We have to find the values of x in the interval $(0, \pi/2)$.

$\therefore$ $\cos x \neq 0$ and the other factor when equated to zero give:

$\Rightarrow \sin x = 2/3$

$$\therefore \frac{d^2a}{dx^2} = \left[\frac{8}{\sin^3 x} + \frac{2}{(1 - \sin x)^3}\right]$$

Put $\sin x = \frac{2}{3}$

or $\cos^2 x = 1 - \frac{4}{9} = \frac{5}{9}$

$$\therefore \frac{d^2a}{dx^2} = \left[\frac{8}{8/27} + 227\right] = 81$$

$\therefore$ a is minimum and its value is

$$\frac{4}{2/3} + \frac{1}{1 - (2/3)} = 6 + 3 = 9$$

5. The set of all values of k for which the function

$f(x) = (k^2 - 3k + 2)\left(\cos^2 \frac{x}{4} - \sin^2 \frac{x}{4}\right) + (k - 1)x + \sin 1$

does not posses critical points is

(a) $[1, \infty)$ (b) $(0,1) \cup (1,4)$

(c) $(-2,4)$ (d) $(1,3) \cup (3,5)$

Solution: (b) Replacing $\cos^2 \frac{x}{4} - \sin^2 \frac{x}{4}$ by $\cos \frac{x}{2}$; we get

$$\frac{dy}{dx} = -\frac{1}{2}(k^2 - 3k + 2)\sin\frac{x}{2} + (k - 1)$$

$$= -\frac{1}{2}(k - 1)(k - 2)\sin\frac{x}{2} + (k - 1)$$

$$= -\frac{(k - 1)}{2}\left[(k - 2)\sin\frac{x}{2} - 2\right] \neq 0$$

Because the function does not posses critical points $k - 1 \neq 0$ and $\sin\frac{x}{2} = \frac{2}{k - 2}$ does not posses any solution

$\Rightarrow k \neq$ and $\left|\frac{2}{k - 2}\right| > 1$ as $\left|\sin\frac{x}{2}\right| \leq 1$

$\Rightarrow k \neq$ and $|k - 2| < 2$

$\Rightarrow k \neq 1$ and $-2 < (k - 2) < 2$ or $0 < k < 4$

Thus k lies in the interval $(0,4)$ but $k \neq 1$

i.e. $k \in (0,1) \cup (1,4)$

6. Rectangle of maximum area that can be inscribed in an equilateral triangle of side a will have area =

(a) $\frac{a^2\sqrt{3}}{2}$ (b) $\frac{a^2\sqrt{3}}{4}$

(c) $\frac{a^2\sqrt{3}}{8}$ (d) None of these

Solution: (c) Let the side $BC = a$ be chosen along $x - axis$ and altitude AD be along $y - axis$

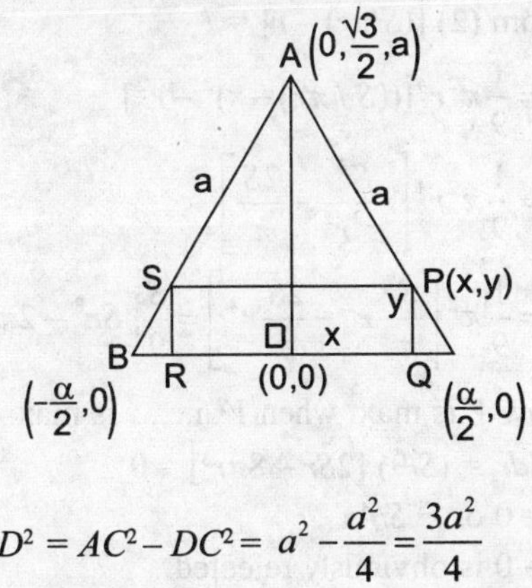

$$AD^2 = AC^2 - DC^2 = a^2 - \frac{a^2}{4} = \frac{3a^2}{4}$$

$\therefore \quad AD = \dfrac{a\sqrt{3}}{2}$

Let $QPRS$ be the rectangle inscribed in the triangle. If A be its area, then $A = 2xy$ where (x, y) are the coordinates of vertex P which lies on line AC whose equation by intercepts form is

$$\frac{x}{a/2} + \frac{y}{\sqrt{3}a/2} = 1 \; or \; \frac{2x}{a} + \frac{2y}{a\sqrt{3}} = 1 \quad .....(i)$$

Area $A = 2xy = x\left(1 - \dfrac{2x}{a}\right) a\sqrt{3}$ by (1)

$$\frac{dA}{dx} = a\sqrt{3}\left(1 - \frac{4x}{a}\right) = 0$$

$\therefore \quad x = \dfrac{a}{4}$

$\dfrac{d^2A}{dx^2} < 0$ and A is maximum

$\therefore \quad A = \dfrac{a}{4}\left(1 - \dfrac{1}{4}\right)a\sqrt{3} = \dfrac{a^2\sqrt{3}}{8}$

7. The semi-vertical angle of a right cone of given total surface (including area of base) and max. volume is

(a) $\sin^{-1}\dfrac{1}{3}$ (b) $\sin^{-1}\left(\dfrac{1}{\sqrt{3}}\right)$

(c) 45^0 (d) 30^0

Solution: (a) $s = \pi r (r + l)$ = constant

$V = \dfrac{1}{3}\pi r^2 h$

$\therefore \quad z = V^2 = \dfrac{1}{9}\pi^2 r^4 h^2$

or $z = \dfrac{1}{9}\pi^2 r^4 (l^2 - r^2)$

Hence z is a function of two variables r and l and we will eliminate l with the help of (2) in order to make z (i.e., V^2) a function of a single variable.

From (2) $[(S/\pi r) - r] = l$

$\therefore \quad z = \dfrac{1}{9}\pi^2 r^4 [((S/\pi r) - r)^2 - r^2]$

or $\quad z = \dfrac{1}{9}\pi^2 r^4 \left[\dfrac{S^2}{\pi^2 r^2} - \dfrac{2S}{\pi}\right]$

or $\quad z = \dfrac{1}{9}\pi^2 \left[\dfrac{S^2}{\pi^2} r^2 - \dfrac{2S}{\pi} r^4\right] = \dfrac{S}{9}\left[Sr^2 - 2\pi r^4\right]$

Now V is max. when V^2 i.e., z is max

$\therefore \quad dz/dr = (S/9)\,[2Sr - 8\pi r^3] = 0$

$\therefore \quad r = 0$ or $r^2\; S/4\pi$

$r = 0$ is obviously rejected

Now $d^2z/dr^2 = (S/9)[2S - 24\pi r^2]$

$= (S/9)\,[2S - 6S] = -(4S^2/9) < 0$

When $r^2 = S/4\pi$. Hence z i.e. V^2 is max or V is max

Now $r^2 = S/4\pi$ or $4\pi r^2 = S = \pi r^2 + \pi rl$

$3\pi r^2 = \pi rl$

$\therefore \quad \dfrac{r}{1} = \dfrac{1}{3}$ or $\sin a = \dfrac{1}{3}$

$\therefore \quad \alpha = \sin^{-1}\dfrac{1}{3}$

8. The ratio of altitude of the cone of greatest volume which can be inscribed in a given sphere to the diameter of the sphere is

(a) 2/3 (b) 3/4

(c) 1/3 (d) ¼

Solution: (a) Let h be the height of the cone and r be its radius.

$\therefore \quad h = CL = CO + OL = a + OL$

$\therefore \quad OL = h - a$

$R = LA = \sqrt{(OA^2 - OL^2)}$

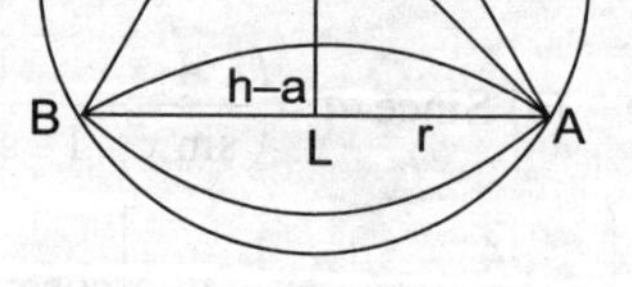

or $\quad r = \sqrt{\{a^2 - (h-a)^2\}} = \{2ah - h^2\}$

$V = \dfrac{1}{3}\pi r^2 h = \dfrac{1}{3}\pi(2ah - h^2)h$

$= \dfrac{1}{3}\pi(2ah^2 - h^3)$

$dV/dh = (\pi/3)\,(4ah - 3h^2) = 0$

$\therefore \quad h = 0$ or $4a/3$

$h = 0$.(rejected)

$\therefore \quad h = 4a/3 = (2/3)\,(2a)$

$h = \dfrac{2}{3}$ (diameter)

9. Global minimum value of $f(x) = x^8 + x^6 - x^4 - 2x^3 - x^2 - 2x + 9$ is

(a) 0 (b) 1

(c) 5 (d) 9

Solution: (c) $f(x) = x^8 + x^6 - x^4 - 2x^3 - x^2 - 2x + 9$

If we represent $f(x) = (\text{real number})^2 + c$. Then c will be minimum.

$f(x) = (x^8 - 2x^4 + 1) + (x^6 - 2x^3 + 1) + (x^4 - 2x^2 + 1) + (x^2 - 2x + 1) + 5$
$= (x^4 - 1)^2 + (x^3 - 1)^2 + (x^2 - 1)^2 + (x - 1)^2 + 5$

Obviously at $x = 1$ all square term will be zero

$\Rightarrow f(x)_{min} = 5$ at $x = 1$

10. The minimum value of $\left(1+\dfrac{1}{\sin^n \alpha}\right)\left(1+\dfrac{1}{\cos^n \alpha}\right)$ for $\alpha \in \left(0, \dfrac{\pi}{2}\right)$ is given by

(a) 1 (b) 2
(c) $(1 + 2^{n/2})^2$ (d) None of these

Solution: (c) Let $f(\alpha) = \left(1+\dfrac{1}{\sin^n \alpha}\right)\left(1+\dfrac{1}{\cos^n \alpha}\right)$

$f(\alpha) = (1 + \text{cosec}^n\alpha)(1 + \sec^n\alpha)$

$\Rightarrow f'(\alpha) = (n\,\text{cosec}^{n-1}\alpha)(-\cot^2\alpha)(1 + \sec^n\alpha) + (1 + \text{cosec}^n\alpha)(n \sec^{n-1}\alpha \tan^2\alpha)$

$\Rightarrow f'(\alpha) = \left(-n\dfrac{1}{\sin^{n-1}\alpha}\times\dfrac{\cos^2\alpha}{\sin^2\alpha}\right)\left(1+\dfrac{1}{\cos^n\alpha}\right) + \left(1+\dfrac{1}{\sin^n\alpha}\right)\left(n\dfrac{1}{\cos^{n-1}\alpha}\times\dfrac{\sin^2\alpha}{\cos^2\alpha}\right)$

$\Rightarrow f'(\alpha) = -n\left(\dfrac{\cos^2\alpha}{\sin^{n+1}\alpha}\right)\left(\dfrac{\cos^n\alpha+1}{\cos^n\alpha}\right) + \left(\dfrac{\sin^n\alpha+1}{\sin^n\alpha}\right) n\left(\dfrac{\sin^2\alpha}{\cos^{n+1}\alpha}\right)$

Now $f'(\alpha) = 0$

$\Rightarrow \dfrac{(\cos^n\alpha+1)(\cos^3\alpha)}{\sin^{n+1}\alpha\cos^{n+1}\alpha} = \dfrac{(\sin^n\alpha+1)(\sin^3\alpha)}{\sin^{n+1}\alpha\cos^{n+1}\alpha}$

$\Rightarrow \cos^{n+3}\alpha + \cos^3\alpha = \sin^{n+3}\alpha + \sin^3\alpha$

$\Rightarrow (\cos^{n+3}\alpha - \sin^{n+3}\alpha) + \cos^3\alpha - \sin^3\alpha = 0$

$\Rightarrow (\cos\alpha - \sin\alpha)\,[\cos^{n+2}\alpha + \cos^{n+1}\alpha \sin\alpha + \cos^n\alpha\sin^2\alpha + \ldots + \sin^{n+2}\alpha + \cos^2\alpha + \cos\alpha.\sin\alpha + \sin^2\alpha]$

$\Rightarrow (\cos\alpha - \sin\alpha)\,[\cos^{n+2}\alpha\,(1 + \tan\alpha + \tan^2\alpha + \ldots + \tan^{n+2}\alpha) + \cos^2\alpha\,(1 + \tan\alpha + \tan^2\alpha)] = 0$

Now for $\alpha \in (0, \pi/2)$;

$[\cos^{n+2}\alpha\,(1 + \tan\alpha + \ldots\ \tan^{n+2}\alpha) + \cos^2\alpha\,(1 + \tan\alpha + \tan^2\alpha)] > 0$

$\Rightarrow$ only solution of $f'(\alpha) = 0 \Rightarrow \cos\alpha = \sin\alpha$

$\Rightarrow \alpha = \pi/4$

For $\alpha \to \pi/4^-$; $\cos\alpha - \sin\alpha > 0 \Rightarrow f'(\alpha) < 0$

and $\alpha \to \pi/4^+$; $\cos\alpha - \sin\alpha < 0 \Rightarrow f'(\alpha) > 0$

$\alpha = \pi/4$ is a point of minima

And $f\left(\dfrac{\pi}{4}\right) = \left(1+\dfrac{1}{(1/\sqrt{2})^n}\right)^2 = (1+2^{n/2})^2$

11. $f(x)$ is cubic polynomial which has local maximum at $x = -1$, If $f(2) = 18$, $f(1) = -1$ and $f'(x)$ has local minima at $x = 0$, then

(a) the distance between point of maxima and minima is $2, \sqrt{5}$.
(b) $f(x)$ is increasing for $x \in [1, 2, \sqrt{5})$
(c) $f(x)$ has local minima at $x = 1$
(d) the value of $f(0) = 5$

Solution: (b, c) Since $f(x)$ has local maxima at $x = -1$ and $f'(x)$ has local minima at $x = 0$.

$\therefore f''(x) = \lambda x$

$f'(x) = \lambda\dfrac{x^2}{2} + c$ $[f'(-1) = 0]$

$\dfrac{\lambda}{2} + c = 0$

$\Rightarrow \lambda = -2c$ ...(1)

again, Integrating both sides we get

$f(x) = \lambda\dfrac{x^3}{6} + cx + d$ ...(2)

$f(2) = \lambda\left(\dfrac{8}{6}\right) + 2c + d = 18$ and

$f(1) = \dfrac{\lambda}{6} + c + d = -1$

$\therefore$ using (i),(ii) and (iii), we get

$f'(x) = \dfrac{1}{4}(57x^2 - 57) = \dfrac{57}{4}(x-1)(x+1)$

(using number line rule)

$\therefore f(x)$ is increasing for $[1, 2, \sqrt{5}]$ and $f(x)$ has local maximum at $x = -1$ and $f(x)$ has local minimum at $x = 1$ also, $f(0) = \dfrac{34}{4}$.

12. Number of solution(s) satisfying the equation, $3x^2 - 2x^3 = \log_2(x^2 + 1) - \log_2 x$ is:

(a) 1 (b) 2
(c) 3 (d) None of these

Solution: (a) Compare the greatest value of the function appearing on the left hand side of the equation with the least value appearing on the right hand side. $\Rightarrow x = 1$

Note that L.H.S. has a maximum value 1 at $x = 1$ but R.H.S. side has a minimum value at $x = 1$

$\Rightarrow x = 1$ is the only solution

13. A right triangle is drawn in a semicircle of radius $\frac{1}{2}$ with one of its legs along the diameter. The maximum area of the triangle is

(a) $\frac{1}{4}$ (b) $\frac{3\sqrt{3}}{32}$

(c) $\frac{3\sqrt{3}}{16}$ (d) $\frac{1}{8}$

Solution: (b) Construct an altitude from B to AC meeting the diameter AC at D and produced BD intersect circle at E.

$(BD)(DE) = x(1 - x)$ (property of circle) $[AD = x; CD = 1 - x]$

but $BD = DE$

$\therefore\ BD = \sqrt{x(1-x)}$

$$\text{Area} = A = \frac{x\sqrt{x-x^2}}{2}$$

$(\frac{1}{2} \times \text{Base} \times \text{Height})$

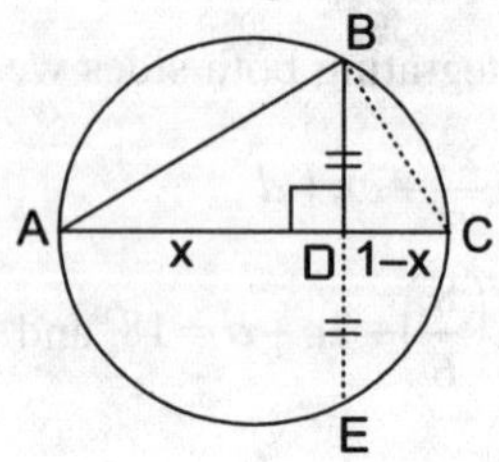

$$\Rightarrow A = \frac{\sqrt{x^3 - x^4}}{2}$$

$$\Rightarrow A^2 = \frac{x^3 - x^4}{2};\ \text{Now } \frac{dA^2}{dx} = 0$$

$$\Rightarrow \frac{3x^2 - 4x^3}{4} = 0$$

$\Rightarrow x^2(3 - 4x) = 0$

$\Rightarrow x = 0$ or $x = 3/4$

$$\frac{d^2(A^2)}{dx^2} = \frac{6x - 12x^2}{4}$$

$\frac{d^2(A^2)}{dx^2} = 0$ at $x = 0$ and < 0 at $x = 3/4$

$\therefore$ maximum area of triangle is achieved when

$$x = \frac{3}{4} \text{ and } A_{\max} = \frac{3}{4} \times \frac{\sqrt{\frac{3}{4} - \frac{9}{16}}}{2}$$

$$= \frac{3}{8} \times \sqrt{\frac{12-9}{16}} = \frac{3\sqrt{3}}{32}$$

9. Let N be any four digit number say $x_1 x_2 x_3 x_4$. Then maximum value of $\frac{N}{x_1 + x_2 + x_3 + x_4}$ is equal to

(a) 1000 (b) $\frac{1111}{4}$

(c) 800 (d) None of these

Solution: (a)

$$\frac{N}{x_1 + x_2 + x_3 + x_4} = \frac{1000x_1 + 100x_2 + 10x_3 + x_4}{x_1 + x_2 + x_3 + x_4}$$

$$= 1000 - \frac{(900x_2 + 990x_3 + 999x_4)}{(x_1 + x_2 + x_3 + x_4)}$$

$\Rightarrow$ maximum value of $\frac{N}{x_1 + x_2 + x_3 + x_4} = 1000$

14. Suppose x_1 and x_2 are the point of maximum and the point of minimum respectively of the function $f(x) = 2x^3 - 9ax^2 + 12a^2x + 1$ respectively, then for the equality $x_1^2 = x_2$ to be true, the value of 'a' must be

(a) 0 (b) 2

(c) 1 (d) 1/4

Solution: (b) $f'(x) = 6(x^2 - 3ax + 2a^2)$

$= 6(x - 2a)(x - a) = 0 \Rightarrow x = 2a$ or a

$f''(x) = 6(2x - 3a)$

$$\left.\begin{array}{l} f''(2a) = a \\ f''(a) = -a \end{array}\right];\ \text{Now}$$

Case I: If $a > 0$ then $x_1 = a$

$x_2 = 2a$

Now $x_1^2 = x_2 \Rightarrow a^2 = 2a \quad \Rightarrow a = 2$

Case II: If $a < 0$ then $x_1 = 2a$

$x_2 = a$

Now $x_1^2 = x_2$ but LHS > 0 and RHS < 0

$\therefore$ not possible

15. Point 'P' lies on the curve $y = e^{-x^2}$ and has the coordinate (x, e^{-x^2}) where $x > 0$. Point Q has the coordinates $(x, 0)$. If 'O' is the origin then the maximum area of the triangle POQ is

(a) $\frac{1}{\sqrt{2e}}$ (b) $\frac{1}{\sqrt{4e}}$

(c) $\frac{1}{\sqrt{e}}$ (d) $\frac{1}{\sqrt{8e}}$

Solution: (d) Area $= A = \frac{xe^{-x^2}}{2}$

$$\Rightarrow A' = \frac{1}{2}\left[e^{-x^2} - 2x^2 \cdot e^{-x^2}\right]$$

$$= \frac{e^{-x^2}}{2}\left[1-2x^2\right] = 0$$

$$\Rightarrow x = \frac{1}{\sqrt{2}} \text{ gives } A_{\max.}$$

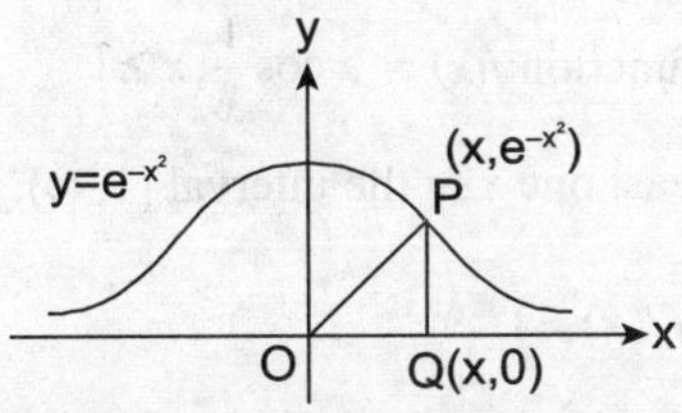

$$A_{\max} = \frac{e^{-1/2}}{2\sqrt{2}} = \frac{1}{\sqrt{8e}}$$

16. The minimum value of $\dfrac{\tan\left(x+\frac{\pi}{6}\right)}{\tan x}$ is:

(a) 0 (b) 1/2
(c) 1 (d) 3

Solution: (d) $f(x)$ has a period equal to π and can take values (−∞, ∞)
⇒ 3 is the local minimum value.

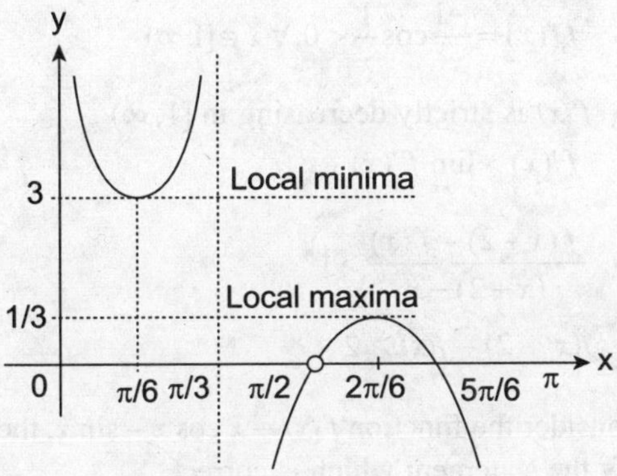

$$y = \frac{2\sin\left(x+\frac{\pi}{6}\right)\cos x}{2\sin x\cos\left(x+\frac{\pi}{6}\right)} = \frac{\sin\left(2x+\frac{\pi}{6}\right)+\sin\frac{\pi}{6}}{\sin\left(2x+\frac{\pi}{6}\right)-\sin\frac{\pi}{6}}$$

$$= 1 + \frac{1}{\sin\left(2x+\frac{\pi}{6}\right)-\sin\frac{\pi}{6}}$$

y is minimum if $\sin\left(2x+\frac{\pi}{6}\right)-\sin\frac{\pi}{6}$ is maximum

$$\Rightarrow 2x+\frac{\pi}{6} = \frac{\pi}{2}$$

$$\Rightarrow x = \frac{\pi}{6}$$

$$\Rightarrow y_{\min} = 1+\frac{1}{\sin\frac{\pi}{2}-\sin\frac{\pi}{6}} = 1+2 = 3$$

17. Let $f(x) = \dfrac{\tan^n x}{\sum_{r=0}^{2n}\tan^r x}$, $n \in N$, where $x \in \left[0, \frac{\pi}{2}\right)$

(a) $f(x)$ is bounded and it takes both of it's bounds and the range of $f(x)$ contains exactly one integral point.
(b) $f(x)$ is bounded and it takes both of it's bounds and the range of $f(x)$ contains more than one integral point.
(c) $f(x)$ is bounded but minimum and maximum does not exists.
(d) $f(x)$ is not bounded as the upper bound does not exist.

Solution: (a) Let $\tan x = t$

$$\Rightarrow f(x) = \frac{t^n}{1+t+....+t^4+....+t^{2n}}$$

$$= \frac{1}{\left(t^n+\frac{1}{t^n}\right)+\left(t^{n-1}+\frac{1}{t^{n-1}}\right)+.......+\left(t+\frac{1}{t}\right)+1}$$

$$\le \frac{1}{2n+1}$$

[Equality holds at $x = \pi/4$]

also $f(0) = 0 \Rightarrow$ range of $f(x)$ is $\left[0, \frac{1}{2n+1}\right]$

18. (a) Let $f(x) = (1 + b^2)x^2 + 2bx + 1$ and let $m(b)$ be the minimum value of $f(x)$. As b varies, the range of $m(b)$ is

(a) [0, 1] (b) $\left(0, \frac{1}{2}\right]$
(c) $\left[\frac{1}{2}, 1\right]$ (d) (0, 1]

Solution: (a) $f(x) = (1 + b^2)x^2 + 2bx + 1$
∵ $1 + b^2 > 0$ so upward parabola

$$\min f(x) = m(b) = -\frac{D}{4a}$$

$$m(b) = -\frac{4b^2-4(1+b^2)}{4(1+b^2)}$$

$$m(b) = \frac{1}{1+b^2}$$

for $1 + b^2 \geq 1$ and $\dfrac{1}{1+b^2} > 0$

$$\frac{1}{1+b^2} \leq 1$$

so $0 < \dfrac{1}{1+b^2} \leq 1$

$0 < m(b) \leq 1$

19. If $P(x)$ is a polynomial of degree less than or equal to 2 and S is the set of all such polynomials so that $P(0) = 0$, $P(1) = 1$ and $P'(x) > 0\ \forall\ x \in [0,1]$, then

(a) $S = \phi$

(b) $S = ax + 1\ (1 - a)\ x^2\ \forall\ a \in (0, 2)$

(c) $S = ax + (1 - a)\ x^2\ \forall\ a \in (0, \infty)$

(d) $S = ax + (1 - a)\ x^2\ \forall\ a \in (0, 1)$

Solution: (b) Let the polynomial be $P(x) = ax^2 + bx + c$

Given $P(0) = 0$ and $P(1) = 1 \Rightarrow c = 0$ and $a + b = 1$

$\Rightarrow a = 1 - b$

$\therefore P(x) = (1 - b)\ x^2 + bx$

$\Rightarrow P'(x) = 2\ (1 - b)x + b$

Given $P'(x) > 0,\ \forall\ x \in [0,1]$

$\Rightarrow 2(1 - b)\ x + b > 0$

$\Rightarrow$ When $x = 0$, $b > 0$ and when $x = 1$, $b < 2$

$\Rightarrow 0 < b < 2$

$\therefore S = \{(1 - a)x^2 + ax,\ \alpha \in \in 0, 2)\}$

20. The tangent to the curve $y = e^x$ drawn at the point (c, e^c) intersects the line joining the points $(c. - 1, e^{c-1})$ and $(c + 1, e^{c+1})$

(a) on the left of $x = c$ (b) on the right of $x = c$

(c) at no point (d) at all points

Solution: The equation of tangent to the curve $y = e^x$ at (c, e^c) is $y - e^c = e^c\ (x - c)$

and equation of line joining $(c - 1, e^{c-1})$ and $(c + 1, e^{c+1})$ is

$$y - e^{c-1} = \frac{e^{c+1} - e^{c-1}}{(c+1)-(c-1)}[x-(x-1)]$$

$$\Rightarrow y - e^{c-1} = \frac{e^c(e-e^{-1})}{2}[x-(c+1)] \quad \ldots(2)$$

Subtracting equation (1) and (2), we get

$$e^c - e^{c-1} = e^c(x-c)\left[\frac{e-e^{-1}-2}{2}\right] + e^c\left(\frac{e-e^{-1}}{2}\right)$$

$$\Rightarrow x - c = \frac{\left[1-e^{-1}-\left(\dfrac{e-e^{-1}}{2}\right)\right]}{\dfrac{e-e^{-1}-2}{2}} = \frac{2-e-e^{-1}}{e-e^{-1}-2}$$

$$= \frac{e+e^{-1}-2}{2(e-e^{-1})} = \frac{\dfrac{e+e^{-1}}{2}-1}{1-\dfrac{e-e^{-1}}{2}} = \frac{+ve}{-ve} = -ve$$

$\Rightarrow x - c < 0 \Rightarrow x < c$

$\therefore$ The two lines meet on the left of line $x = c$

21. For the function $f(x) = x\cos\dfrac{1}{x}, x \geq 1$

(a) for least one x in the interval $[1, \infty)$, $f(x + 2) - f(x) < 2$

(b) $\lim\limits_{x\to\infty} f'(x) = 1$

(c) for all x in the interval $[1, \infty)$, $f(x + 2) - f(x) > 2$

(d) $f'(x)$ is strictly decreasing in the interval $[1, \infty)$

Solution: (b, c, d) we have, $f(x) = x\cos\dfrac{1}{x}, x \geq 1$

$$\therefore f'(x) = \cos\frac{1}{x} + \frac{1}{x}\sin\frac{1}{x}$$

$$\lim_{x®¥} f'(x) = \cos 0 + (0) \times (\text{some finite value})$$

$$\lim_{x\to\infty} f'(x) = 1$$

Also $f''(x) = \dfrac{1}{x^2}\sin\dfrac{1}{x} - \dfrac{1}{x^2}\sin\dfrac{1}{x} - \dfrac{1}{x^3}\cos\dfrac{1}{x}$

$$\Rightarrow f''(x) = \frac{-1}{x^3}\cos\frac{1}{x} < 0, \forall x \in [1,\infty)$$

$\Rightarrow f'(x)$ is strictly decreasing in $[1, \infty)$

$$\therefore f'(x) > \lim_{x\to\infty} f'(x)$$

$$\Rightarrow \frac{f(x+2)-f(x)}{(x+2)-x} > 1$$

$\Rightarrow f(x + 2) - f(x) > 2$

22. Consider the function $f(x) = x\cos x - \sin x$, then identify the statement which is correct.

(a) f has a minima at $x = 0$

(b) f is monotonic decreasing at $x = 0$

(c) f has a maxima at $x = \pi$

(d) f is monotonic increasing at $x = \pi$

Solution: (b) $f'(x) = -x\sin x = 0$ when $x = 0$

or π $\left.\begin{array}{l} f'(0^-) = (-)(-)(-) < 0 \\ f'(0^+) = (-)(+)(+) < 0 \end{array}\right]$ no sign change;

$f(x)$ does not have a minima at $x = 0$.

This also implies that f is decreasing at $x = 0$

$\Rightarrow$ (b) is correct

$$\left.\begin{array}{l} f'(x) = -(x\sin x) \\ f'(\pi^+) = (-)(+)(-) > 0 \\ f'(\pi^-) = (-)(+)(+) < 0 \end{array}\right\} \text{sign change from positive to negative}$$

$f(x) = -(x \sin x)$

Therefore $f(x)$ has maxima at $x - \pi$. Thus also means that $f(x)$ is non-monotonic at $x = \pi$.

23. Let $f(x)$ and $g(x)$ be two continuous functions defined from $R \to R$, such that $f(x_1) > f(x_2)$ and $g(x_1) < g(x_2)$, $\forall x_1 > x_2$, then solution set of $f\left(g(\alpha^2 - 2\alpha)\right) > f\left(g(3\alpha - 4)\right)$ is

(a) R (b) ϕ

(c) $(1, 4)$ (d) $R - [1, 4]$

Solution: (c) Obviously f is increasing and g is decreasing in (x_1, x_2)

Hence $f\left(g(\alpha^2 - 2\alpha)\right) > f\left(g(3\alpha - 4)\right)$

Now, as f is increasing; we get $g(\alpha^2 - 2\alpha) > g(3\alpha - 4)$

$\therefore\ \alpha^2 - 2\alpha < 3\alpha - 4$ (as g is decreasing)

$\alpha^2 - 5\alpha + 4 < 0$

$(\alpha - 1)(\alpha - 4) < 0$

$\Rightarrow a \in (1, 4)$

24. A function $y = f(x)$ is given by $x = \dfrac{1}{1+t^2}$ and $y = \dfrac{1}{t\left(1+t^2\right)}$ for all $t > 0$ then f is:

(a) increasing in $(0, 3/2)$ and decreasing in $(3/2, \infty)$

(b) increasing in $(0, 1)$

(c) increasing in $(0, \infty)$

(d) decreasing in $(0, 1)$

Solution: (b) $\dfrac{dx}{dt} = -\dfrac{2t}{(1+t)^2}$

$$\frac{dy}{dt} = -\frac{1+3t^2}{t^2(1+t^2)^2}$$

$$\frac{dy}{dx} = \frac{1+3t^2}{2t^3} > 0 \quad \text{for } t > 0$$

$\therefore$ y is increasing for every $x \in (0, 1)]$

25. If $f(x) = \displaystyle\int_{x^2}^{x^3} \frac{dt}{\ln t}, x > 0, \neq 1$ then

(a) $f(x)$ is an increasing function

(b) $f(x)$ has a minima at $x = 1$

(c) $f(x)$ is a decreasing function

(d) $f(x)$ has a maxima at $x = 1$

Solution: $f(x) = \displaystyle\int_{x^2}^{x^3} \frac{dt}{\ln t}$

For increasing or decreasing function,

$$f'(x) = \frac{1}{\ln x^3}.3x^2 - \frac{1}{\ln x^2}.2x \quad \text{(using Leibniz formula)}$$

$$= \frac{1}{\ln x}(x^2 - x)$$

sign of $f'(x)$

$$\begin{array}{ccc} + & & + \\ 0 & \text{———} & 1 \end{array}$$

Since $f'(x) > 0$ for $x > 0, x \neq 1$ hence $f(x)$ is increasing function

Hence (a) is correct

26. $f:[1, \infty) \to R$: $f(x)$ is a monotonic and differentiable function and $f(1) = 1$, then number of possible solutions of the equation $f(f(x)) = \dfrac{1}{x^2 - 2x + 2}$ is/are

(a) 2 (b) 1

(c) infinite (d) zero

Solution: (b) $g(x) = f(f(x))$

$g'(x) = f'(f(x))\, f'(x) > 0$

$g(1) = f(f(1)) = f(1) = 1$

$g(x) \geq 1$

Also RHS $= f\{g(x)\} > f\{g(x-1)\}$

$\therefore\ f(f(x) = \dfrac{1}{x^2 - 2x + 2}$; we can infer that the LHS is ≥ 1 where RHS is ≤ 1

$\therefore$ Only one solution is possible i.e when both sides are equal to 1

27. Suppose $f'(x)$ exists for each x and $h(x) = f(x) - (f(x))^2 + (f(x))^3$ for every real number x. Then.

(a) h is increasing whenever f is increasing

(b) h is increasing whenever f is decreasing

(c) h is decreasing whenever f is decreasing

(d) nothing can be said in general

Solution: (a,c) We have

$h'(x) = f'(x) - 2f'(x)\, f(x) + 3\, f'(x)\, f(x)^2$

$$= 3f'(x)\left[f(x)^2 - \frac{2}{3}f(x) + \frac{1}{3}\right]$$

$= 3\, f'(x)\, [(f(x) - 1/3)^2 + 2/9]$

Thus, $h'(x) > 0$ if $f'(x) > 0$

and $h'(x) < 0$ if $f'(x) < 0$

Therefore, h increases (decreases) whenever f increases (decreases).

28. The maximum value of $F(x) = \int_{7\pi/6}^{x} (a\sin t + b\cos t)\,dt$, $a, b \in R^+, x \in \left[\frac{7\pi}{6}, \sqrt{21}\right]$ is

(a) $a + b$ (b) $a\sqrt{21} - b\frac{7\pi}{6}$

(c) 0 (d) None of these

Solution: (c) Let $F'(x) = a \sin x + b \cos x < 0 \;\forall\; x \in \left[\pi, \frac{3\pi}{2}\right]$

$\Rightarrow F(x)$ is decreasing in $\left[\frac{7\pi}{6}, \sqrt{21}\right]$

so, $F(x)$ is maximum at $x = \frac{7\pi}{6}$ which is 0.

29. Let $g(x) = \int_0^x f(t)dt$ and $f(x)$ satisfies the equation $f(x + y) = f(x) + f(y) + 2xy - 1$ for all $x, y \in \mathbb{R}$ and $f'(0) = 2$, then

(a) g increases on $(0, \infty)$ and decreases on $(-\infty, -0)$

(b) g increases on $(0, \infty)$

(c) g decreases on $(-\infty, \infty)$

(d) g increases on $(-\infty, \infty)$

Solution: (d) $g(x) = \int_0^x f(t)dt$

$\Rightarrow g'(x) = f(x)$

Now given $f(x + y) = f(x) + f(y) + 2xy - 1$

Putting $x = 0, y = 0$; we get

$f(0) = f(0) + f(0) + 0 - 1$

$\Rightarrow f(0) = 1$

Also given that $f'(0) = 2$

Now; $f(x) = \lim_{h\to 0} \frac{f(x+h) - f(x)}{h}$

$= \lim_{h\to 0} \frac{f(x) + f(h) + 2xh - 1 - f(x)}{h}$

$= \lim_{h\to 0} \frac{f(h) + 2xh - 1}{h}$

Applying L'Hospital Rule, we get

$f'(x) = \lim_{h\to 0} f'(h) + 2x$

$= f'(0) + 2x = 2x + 2$

$\therefore f(x) = x^2 + 2x + c \quad \because f(0) = 1 \Rightarrow c = 1$

$\Rightarrow f(x) = (x + 1)^2 \quad \Rightarrow g'(x) > 0$

$\Rightarrow g(x)$ is an increasing function. Hence $g(x)$ increases $(-\infty, \infty)$

30. The function $f(x) = \frac{\log(\pi + x)}{\log(e + x)}$ is

(a) increasing on $[0, \infty)$

(b) decreasing on $[0, \infty)$

(c) increasing on $[0, \pi/e]$ and decreasing on $[\pi/e, \infty)$

(d) decreasing on $[0, \pi/e]$ and decreasing on $[\pi/e, \infty)$

Solution: $f(x) = \frac{\log(\pi + x)}{\log(e + x)}$

$\therefore f'(x) = \frac{\left(\frac{1}{\pi + x}\right)^{\log(e+x)} - \left(\frac{1}{e + x}\right)^{\log(\pi+x)}}{(\log(e + x))^2}$

Let $h(x) = \frac{\log(e + x)}{\pi + x} - \frac{\log(\pi + x)}{e + x}$

Let us cosigner $g(x) = x\, lnx$

$\Rightarrow g'(x) = x \times -+ \ell nx = +\ell nx$

$g'(x) > 0 \;\forall\; x \in (1/e, \infty)$ and $g'(x) < 0 \;\forall\; x \in (0, 1/e)$

Now $e < \pi$

$\Rightarrow e + x < \pi + x \;\forall\; x \in (0, \infty)$

$\Rightarrow g(e + x) < g(\pi + x)$

[$\because g(x)$ is an increasing function for $x > 1/e$]

$\Rightarrow (e + x)\ell(e + x) < (\pi + x)\, ln\, (\pi + x)$

$\Rightarrow \frac{\ell x(e + x)}{\pi + x} < \frac{\ell n(\pi + x)}{e + x}$

$\Rightarrow \frac{\ell n(e + x)}{\pi + x} - \frac{\ell n(\pi + x)}{e + x} < 0$

$\Rightarrow h(x) < 0$

$\therefore f'(x) = \frac{h(x)}{(\ell n(e + x))^2} < 0 \;\forall\; x \in [0, \infty)$

Hence $f(x)$ decreases for $[0, \infty)$

31. $f(x)$ is cubic polynomial which has local maximum at $x = -1$, If $f(2) = 18$, $f(1) = -1$ and $f'(x)$ has local minima at $x = 0$, then

(a) the distance between point of maxima and minima is $2\sqrt{5}$

(b) $f(x)$ is increasing for $x \in \left[1, 2\sqrt{5}\right]$

(c) $f(x)$ has local minima at $x = 1$

(d) the value of $f(0) = 5$

Solution: (b), (c) Since $f(x)$ has local maxima at $x = -1$ and $f'(x)$ has local minima at $x = 0$

$\therefore f''(x) = \lambda x$

$f'(x) = \lambda\frac{x^2}{2}+c \qquad \{f'(-1) = 0\}$

$\Rightarrow \frac{\lambda}{2}+c=0$

$\Rightarrow \lambda = -2c$ ...(i)

again, integrating both sides we get

$f(x)=\lambda\frac{x^3}{6}+cx+d$ ...(ii)

$f(2)=\lambda\left(\frac{8}{6}\right)+2c+d=18$

and $f(1) = —+c+d = –$ .....(iii)

∴ Using (i), (ii) and (iii) we get

$f(x)=\frac{1}{4}(19x^3-57x+34)$

∴ $f'(x)=\frac{1}{4}\left(57x^2-57\right)$

$=\frac{57}{4}(x-1)(x+1)$ (using number line rule)

∴ $f(x)$ is increasing for $\left[1,2\sqrt{5}\right]$

and $f(x)$ has local maximum at $x = -1$ and $f(x)$ has local minimum at $x = 1$

also, $f(0)=\frac{34}{4}$

32. A truck is to be driven 300 km on a highway at a constant speed of x kmph. Speed rules of the highway required that $30 \le x \le 60$. The fuel costs Rs 10 per litre and is consumed at the rate of $2+\frac{x^2}{600}$ liters per hour. The wages of the driver are Rs. 200 per hour. The most economical speed to drive the truck, in kmph, is

(a) 30 (b) 60

(c) $30\sqrt{3.3}$ (d) $20\sqrt{3.3}$

Solution: (b) Time taken by the truck $=\frac{300}{x}$ hours

petrol consumed $=\left(2+\frac{x^2}{600}\right)\frac{300}{x}$ litre expenses on travelling

$E = 200\frac{300}{x}+\left(2+\frac{x^2}{600}\right)\frac{3000}{x}$

$=\frac{60000}{x}+\frac{6000}{x}+5x$

$=\frac{66000}{x}+5x$

∴ $\frac{dE}{dx}=-\frac{66000}{x^2}+5<0$ for all $x \in [30, 60]$

∴ most economical speed is 60 kmph.

33. The curve $y=\frac{2x}{1+x^2}$ has

(a) exactly three points of inflection separated by a point of maximum and a point of minimum

(b) exactly two points of inflection with a point of maximum lying between them

(c) exactly two points of inflection with a point of minimum lying between them

(d) exactly three points of inflection separated by two points of maximum

Solution: (a) Graph of $y=\frac{2x}{1+x^2}$ is

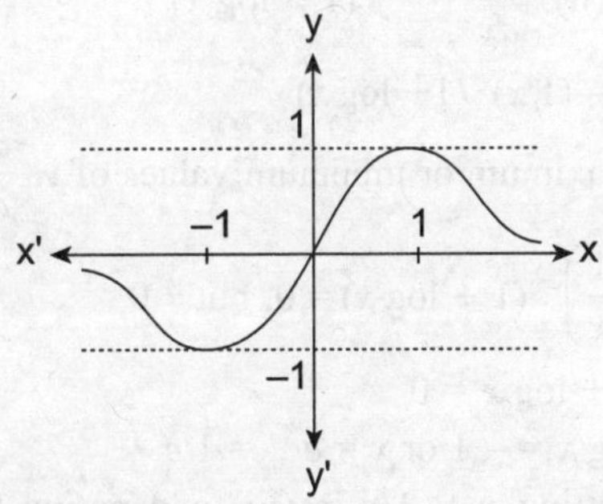

Figure from the graph it is clear that there are three points of inflection separated by a point of minimum and a point of maximum

Aliter: $\frac{dy}{dx}=\frac{2(1+x^2)-2x.2x}{(1+x^2)^2}=\frac{2(1-x^2)}{(1+x^2)^2}$

$x = -1$ is a minimum and $x = 1$ is a maximum

$\frac{d^2y}{dx^2}=\frac{\left(1+x^2\right)^2(-4x)-2\left(1-x^2\right)2\left(1+x^2\right)2x}{(1+x^2)^4}$

$=\frac{-4x(1+x^2)-8x(1-x^2)}{(1+x^2)^3}$

$=\frac{-4x-4x^3-8x+8x^3}{(1+x^2)^3}=\frac{-12x+4x^3}{(1+x^2)^3}=\frac{4x(x^2-3)}{(1+x^2)^3}$

there are 3 points of inflection:

$x = 0, -\sqrt{3}, \sqrt{3}$

($\because \frac{d^2y}{dx^2}$ changes sign while x passes through these points)

SECTION–II

SUBJECTIVE SOLVED EXAMPLE

1. Show that the maximum value of $(1/x)^x$ is $e^{1/e}$.

Solution: Let $y = (1/x)^x$ ..(i)

Then $\log y = x \log(1/x) = -x \log x$

Differentiating both sides with respect to x, we get

$$\frac{1}{y}\frac{dy}{dx} = -\log x - x.\frac{1}{x} = -(1+\log x) \quad ..(ii)$$

Differentiating again with respect to x, we get

$$-\frac{1}{y^2}\left(\frac{dy}{dx}\right)^2 + \frac{1}{y}.\frac{d^2y}{dx^2} = -\frac{1}{x} \quad ...(iii)$$

From (ii), $\frac{dy}{dx} = -y\,(1 + \log x)$

$= -(1/x)^x\,(1 + \log x)$ ...(iv)

For maximum or minimum values of y, $\frac{dy}{dx} = 0$

$\therefore \left(\frac{1}{x}\right)^x (1 + \log x) = 0$, but $\neq 0$

$\therefore$ $1 + \log x = 0$

$\therefore$ $\log x = -1$ or $x = e^{-1} = 1/e$

Putting $x = 1/e$ in (iii) and noting that for this value of x

$\Rightarrow \frac{dy}{dx} = 0$, we get,

$$\frac{d^2y}{dx^2} = \left[-\frac{1}{x}.y\right]_{x=1/e} = \left[-\frac{1}{x}.\left(\frac{1}{x}\right)^x\right]_{x=1/e}$$

$= e\,(e)^{1/e} < 0$

$\therefore$ at $x = 1/e$, y has maximum value and the maximum value of y is $e^{1/e}$.

2. Let $f(x) = \sin^3 x + \lambda \sin^2 x, -\frac{\pi}{2} < x < \frac{\pi}{2}$. Find the intervals in which λ should lie in order that $f(x)$ has exactly one minimum and exactly one maximum.

Solution: $f(x) = \sin^3 x + \lambda \sin^2 x, \; -\frac{1}{2}\pi < x < \frac{1}{2}\pi$

$f'(x) = 3\sin^2 x \cos x + 2\lambda \sin x \cos x$

$= \sin x \cos x\,(3\sin x + 2\lambda)$

For max. or min. of $f(x)$,

$\Rightarrow f(x) = 0$

$\Rightarrow \sin 2x = 0$

$\therefore$ $x = \frac{n\pi}{2}, n \in I$

or $3\sin x + 2\lambda = 0$

$\therefore \sin x = -\frac{2\lambda}{3}$,

which is defined only if $-1 \le -\frac{2\lambda}{3} \le 1$

or $-\frac{3}{2} \le \lambda \le \frac{3}{2}$

But $-\frac{1}{2}\pi < x < \frac{1}{2}\pi$

$\therefore$ the only values of x for which $f(x) = 0$ are $x = 0$ and $x = \sin^{-1}\left(-\frac{2\lambda}{3}\right), -\frac{3}{2}, \lambda \neq 0$.

Here $\lambda \neq 0$. as then we have only one critical point.

Now $f(x) = \cos 2x.\,(3\sin x + 2\lambda) + \frac{1}{2}\sin 2x.\,3\cos x$

When $x = 0, f''(x) = 2\lambda$

Which is + ve or – ve according as $\lambda >$ or < 0 respectively.

$\therefore$ When $x = 0$, $f(x)$ is max. if $\lambda < 0$ and minimum if $\lambda > 0$.

Also when $x = \sin^{-1}\left(-\frac{2\lambda}{3}\right)$

i.e. $\sin x = -\frac{2\lambda}{3}, -\frac{3}{2} < \lambda < \frac{3}{2}, \lambda \neq 0$

$\Rightarrow f''(x) = (1 - 2\sin^2 x)(3\sin x + 2\lambda) + 3\sin x\,(1 - \sin^2 x)$

$$= -\frac{8}{9}\lambda\left[\frac{9}{4} - \lambda^2\right] = \frac{8}{9}\lambda\left(\lambda + \frac{3}{2}\right)\left(\lambda - \frac{3}{2}\right)$$

Obviously, $f''(x)$ is + ve if $-3/2 < \lambda < 0$

$\therefore$ in this case $f(x)$ is minimum

and $f(x)$ is – ve, if $0 < \lambda < 3/2$

$\therefore$ in this case $f(x)$ is maximum

Hence $f(x)$ has exactly one minimum and exactly one maximum if

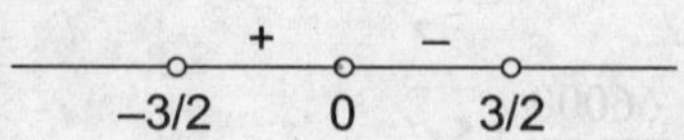

$-3/2 < \lambda < 0$ or $0 < \lambda < 3/2$

3. The function $y = \dfrac{ax+b}{(x-1)(x-4)}$ has turning point at P (2, – 1). Find the values of a and b and that y is maximum at P.

Solution: We have $y = \dfrac{ax+b}{(x-1)(x-4)}$ ...(i)

so that $\dfrac{dy}{dx} = \dfrac{a(x^2-5x+4)-(ax+b)(2x-5)}{(x^2-5x+4)^2}$ ...(ii)

Since $P(2, -1)$ is the turning point,

$\therefore$ P lies on (i) and at P, $\dfrac{dy}{dx} = 0$

$\because$ $P(2, -1)$ lies on (i)

$\therefore$ Substituting $x = 2, y = -1$ in (i)

Also at P (2, – 1),

$\Rightarrow \dfrac{dy}{dx} = \dfrac{-2a+(2a+b)}{4} = 0$

$\Rightarrow b = 0$

$\therefore$ From (iii) we get $a = 1$

Hence $a = 1, b = 0$

Putting $a = 1, b = 0$ in (i), we get

$y = \dfrac{x}{x^2-5x+4} = \dfrac{1}{x-5+4/x} = \dfrac{1}{z}$ (say)

where $z = x - 5 + 4/x$

$\Rightarrow \dfrac{dz}{dx} = 1 - \dfrac{4}{x^2}, \dfrac{d^2z}{dx^2} = \dfrac{8}{x^3}$

For max. or min. of z. $\dfrac{dz}{dx} = 0$

$\Rightarrow x = \pm 2$

when $x = 2, y = -1$

When $x = 2, y = -1$

and $\dfrac{d^2z}{dx^2} = 1$ (+ve)

$\Rightarrow$ z is minimum at P(2, – 1)

Hence $y = 1/z$ is max. at P (2, – 1)

4. Find all the values of the parameter a for which the points of minima of the function $f(x) = 1 + a^2x - x^3$ satisfy the inequality $\dfrac{x^2+x+2}{x^2+5x+6} < 0$.

Solution: $f(x) = 1 + a^2x - x^3$

Since points of minima of $f(x)$ satisfy the inequality $\dfrac{x^2+x+2}{x^2+5x+6} < 0$.

We should consider the solution set of the inequality as domain of $f(x)$

Now $\dfrac{x^2+x+2}{x^2+5x+6} = \dfrac{(1+1/2)^2+7/4}{(x+2)(x+3)} < 0$

$\Rightarrow (x+2)(x+3) < 0$

$\Rightarrow -3 < x < -2$ ...(i)

$\Rightarrow f'(x) = a^2 - 3x^2 = 0$

$\Rightarrow x = \pm\dfrac{a}{\sqrt{3}}$

Case I: $x = \dfrac{a}{\sqrt{3}}$ then $-3 < \dfrac{a}{\sqrt{3}} < -2$

so $3\sqrt{3} < a < -2/\sqrt{3}$

$\therefore f''\left(\dfrac{a}{\sqrt{3}}\right) = -\dfrac{6a}{\sqrt{3}} > 0$

$\therefore \dfrac{a}{\sqrt{3}}$ is point of minima of $-3\sqrt{3} < a < -2/\sqrt{3}$

Case II: $x = -\dfrac{a}{\sqrt{3}}$, then $-3 < -\dfrac{a}{\sqrt{3}} < -2$

or $2\sqrt{3} < a < 3\sqrt{3}$

Hence $a \in (-3\sqrt{3}, -2\sqrt{3}) \cup (2\sqrt{3}, 3\sqrt{3})$

5. Find real values of x for which $27^{\cos 2x} . 81^{\sin 2x}$ is minimum. Also find this minimum values.

Solution: Let $y = 27^{\cos 2x} . 81^{\sin 2x} = 3^{3\cos 2x + 4\sin 2x}$

Now, y will be minimum when 3 cos $2x$ + 4 sin$2x$ is minimum

Let $u = 3\cos 2x + 4\sin 2x$

Putting $3 = r\cos\theta$, $4 = r\sin\theta$

then $r = \sqrt{(3^2+4^2)} = 5$; $\tan\theta = 4/3$

$\theta = \tan^{-1}(4/3)$

$\sin\theta = 4/5$, $\cos\theta = 3/5$

$\Rightarrow \theta \in Q$

$\therefore u = 5\cos(2x - \theta)$

$\Rightarrow -5 \le u \le 5$

min. $u = -5$

$\Rightarrow y = 3^{-5} = \dfrac{1}{243}$

Also u (so y) will be minimum when $\cos(2x - \theta) = -1$

$\Rightarrow 2x - \theta = 2n\pi + \pi$

$\Rightarrow x = n\pi + \pi/2 + \dfrac{1}{2}\tan^{-1}\dfrac{4}{3}$

Hence, y will be minimum when $x = n\pi + \pi/2 + \dfrac{1}{2}\tan^{-1}\dfrac{4}{3}$

and $y_{min} = \dfrac{1}{243}$

6. Show that (α – 1/α – x) (4 – 3 x^2) has just one maximum and one minimum value. Show also that the difference between then is $\frac{4}{9}(\alpha+1/\alpha)^3$.

Solution: Let $f(x) = (\alpha - 1/\alpha - x)(4 - 3x^2)$

$\therefore\ f'(x) = 9x^2 - 6(\alpha - 1/\alpha)x - 4$

This is a quadratic in x, and hence $f(x) = 0$ gives one value, which is maximum and another value which is minimum. The two roots are

$$\therefore\ x = \frac{6(\alpha-1/\alpha)\pm\sqrt{36(\alpha-1/\alpha)^2+144}}{18}$$

$$= \frac{2\alpha}{3} \text{ or } -\frac{2}{3\alpha}$$

The difference between the values of $f(x)$ at $x = -\frac{2}{3\alpha}$ and $x = \frac{2\alpha}{3}$ is

$$= \left(\alpha-\frac{1}{\alpha}+\frac{2}{3\alpha}\right)\left(4-\frac{4}{3\alpha^2}\right)-\left(\alpha-\frac{1}{\alpha}+\frac{2\alpha}{3}\right)\left(4-\frac{4\alpha^2}{3}\right)$$

$$= 4\left(\alpha-\frac{1}{\alpha}\right)-\frac{4}{3\alpha^2}\left(\alpha-\frac{1}{\alpha}\right)+\frac{8}{3\alpha}-\frac{8}{9\alpha^3}$$

$$4\left(\alpha-\frac{1}{\alpha}\right)+\frac{4\alpha^3}{3}\left(\alpha-\frac{1}{\alpha}\right)+\frac{8\alpha}{3}-\frac{8\alpha^3}{9}$$

$$= \frac{8}{3}\left(\alpha+\frac{1}{\alpha}\right)+\frac{4}{3}\left(\alpha-\frac{1}{\alpha}\right)\left(\alpha^2-\frac{1}{\alpha^2}\right)-\frac{8}{9}\left(\alpha^3-\frac{1}{\alpha^3}\right)$$

$$= \frac{1}{9}\left(\alpha+\frac{1}{\alpha}\right)\left[24+12\left(\alpha-\frac{1}{\alpha}\right)-8\left(\alpha+\frac{1}{\alpha}-1\right)\right]$$

$$= \frac{4}{9}\left(\alpha+\frac{1}{\alpha}\right)^3$$

7. Obtain the maximum and minimum values of the expression $\frac{x^2 - 2x\cos\alpha+1}{x^2-2x\cos\beta+1}$, $x \in R$ and $0 < \beta < \pi/2$.

Solution: Let $f(x) = \frac{x^2-2x\cos\alpha+1}{x^2-2x\cos\beta+1}$

$$\Rightarrow\ f'(x) = \frac{2(x^2-1)(\cos\alpha-\cos\beta)}{(x^2-2x\cos\beta+1)^2}$$

$$= \frac{2(1-x^2)(\cos\beta-\cos\alpha)}{(x^2-2x\cos\beta+1)^2} \quad (\because 0<\beta<\alpha<\pi/2)$$

For maximum or minimum of $f(x)$; $f'(x) = 0$

$\therefore\ x = \pm 1$

$$\therefore\ f''(x) = \frac{4(\cos\beta-\cos\alpha)(x^3-3x+2\cos\beta)}{(x^2-2x\cos\beta+1)^3}$$

$\Rightarrow f''(1) < 0$ and $f''(-1) > 0$

$\Rightarrow f(x)$ is maximum at $x = 1$ and minimum at $x = -1$

$\Rightarrow$ Hence maximum and minimum values of $f(x)$ are $f(1)$ and $f(-1)$

or $\frac{2-2\cos\alpha}{2-2\cos\beta}$ and $\frac{2+2\cos\alpha}{2+2\cos\beta}$

i.e. $\frac{\sin^2\alpha/2}{\sin^2\beta/2}$ and $\frac{\cos^2\alpha/2}{\cos^2\beta/2}$

8. Show that $\log y$ lies between $\frac{2(y-1)}{y+1}$ and $\frac{y^2-1}{y}$ for all $y > 0$

Solution: If $g(y) = \frac{2(y-1)}{y+1} - \log y$,

$g'(y) = -\frac{(y-1)^2}{y(y+1)^2} < 0$ for all $y > 0$

Thus $g(y)$ is a decreasing function for all $y > 0$ and as $g(1) = 0$, $g(y) < 0$ for all $y > 1$.

If $h(y) = \frac{y^2-1}{y} - \log y$, $h'(y) = 1 - \frac{1}{y} + \frac{1}{y^2} > 0$ for all $y > 1$.

$h(1) = 0$ and $h(y)$ is increasing for all $y > 1$ so that $h(y) > 0$, $y > 1$

$\therefore$ for all $y > 1$, $\frac{2(y-1)}{y+1} < \log y < \frac{y^2-1}{y}$

When $0 < y < 1$, one can introduce $y' = \frac{1}{y} > 1$ and

then $\frac{2(y'-1)}{y'+1} < \log y' < \frac{y'^2-1}{y'}$

$$\Rightarrow\ \frac{2\left(\frac{1}{y}-1\right)}{\frac{1}{y}+1} < \log\frac{1}{y} < \frac{\frac{1}{y^2}-1}{\frac{1}{y}}$$

$$\Rightarrow\ \frac{-2(y-1)}{y+1} < -\log y < -\frac{y^2-1}{y}$$

$$\Rightarrow\ \frac{y^2-1}{y} < \log y < \frac{2(y-1)}{1+y}$$

9. The sum of the surfaces of a cube and a sphere is given; show that when the sum of their volume is least, the diameter of the sphere is equal to the edge of the cube.

Solution: Let x be side of the cube and r be radius of the sphere

Surface area $= 6x^2 + 4\pi r^2 = k$ ....(i)

Volume $= V = x^3 + \pi r^3$ ....(ii)

$\Rightarrow \dfrac{dV}{dx} = 3x^2 + 4\pi r^2 \dfrac{dr}{dx}$ ...(iii)

Differentiating (i) with respect to x, we get

$\Rightarrow 12x + 8\pi r \dfrac{dr}{dx} = 0$

$\Rightarrow \dfrac{dr}{dx} = -\dfrac{3x}{2\pi r}$

equation (iii) becomes,

$\dfrac{dV}{dx} = 3x^2 + 4\pi r^2 \left(-\dfrac{3x}{2\pi r}\right) = 3x(x - 2r)$ ....(iv)

For local maxima/minima, $\dfrac{dV}{dx} = 0$

$\Rightarrow x = 0$ or $x = 2r$

Differentiating (iv) w.r.t. x we get

$\dfrac{d^2V}{dx^2} = 6x - 6r - 6x \dfrac{dr}{dx}$

$= 6x - 6r - 6x\left(-\dfrac{3x}{2\pi r}\right)$

$= V''(0) = -ve$

$\Rightarrow V''(2r) = 12r - 6r + \dfrac{18(2r)^2}{2\pi r} = +ve$

$\therefore$ sum of volume of cube and sphere is least when $x = 2r$

10. Choose a and b such that the point A(2, 2.5) becomes a point of inflection of the curve $x^2 y + \alpha x + \beta y = 0$. Will it have some more points of inflection? What are they?

Solution: $x^2 y + \alpha x + \beta y = 0$

$\Rightarrow y = \dfrac{-\alpha x}{(x^2 + \beta)}$

$\Rightarrow y' = \dfrac{-\alpha(\beta - x^2)}{(x^2 + \beta)^2}$

$\Rightarrow y'' = \dfrac{-\alpha(x^2 + \beta)[2x^2 - 6x\beta]}{(x^2 + \beta)^4}$; $y'' = 0$ condition for point of inflection

$\Rightarrow 2x^3 - 6x\beta = 0$ at point (2, 2.5)

$\Rightarrow 2(2)^3 - 6(2)\beta = 0$

$\Rightarrow \beta = 4/5$

$\Rightarrow x^2 y + \alpha x + \beta y = 0$

$\Rightarrow 4.\dfrac{5}{2} + \alpha.2.\dfrac{4}{3}.\dfrac{5}{2} = 0$

$\Rightarrow 2\alpha = -\dfrac{10}{3} - 10$

$\Rightarrow 2\alpha = -\dfrac{40}{3}$

$\Rightarrow \alpha = -\dfrac{20}{3}$

And $y'' = 0$

$\Rightarrow 2x^3 - 6x\beta = 0$

$\Rightarrow x(2x^2 - 6\beta) = 0$

$\Rightarrow x = 0, x = \pm\sqrt{3\beta} = \pm 2$

$\therefore$ Points (–2, – 2.5); (0, 0) are also point of inflection

11. A firm has a branch store in each of the three cities A, B and C. A and B are 320 km. apart and C is 200 km. from each of them. A go down is to be built equi-distant from A and B. In order to minimize the time of transportation it should be located so that sum of the distances from the godown to each of the cities is minimum. Where should the godown be built.

Solution: At G where $GA = GB = 320/\sqrt{3}$ and G is on the perpendicular bisector of AB

Let G be the position of go down at a distance x each from A and B.

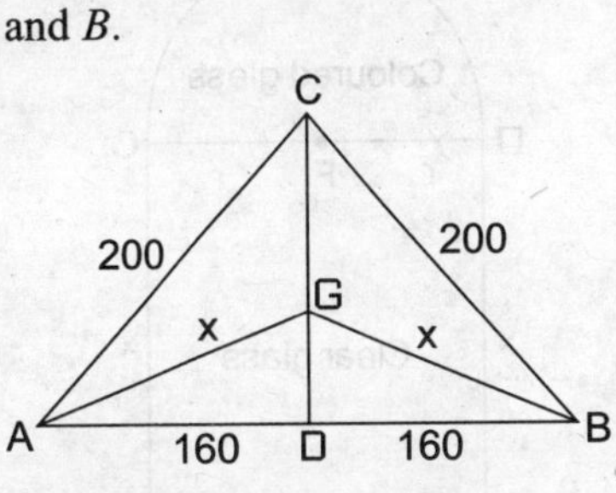

Also $CD = \sqrt{(200^2 - 160^2)} = 120$

$GD = \sqrt{(x^2 - 160^2)}$

$\therefore$ $GC = DG - DG = 120 - \sqrt{(x^2 - 160^2)}$

If $y = GA + GB + GC$, then

$y = 2x + 120 - \sqrt{(x^2 - 160^2)}$

$\dfrac{dy}{dx} = 2 - \dfrac{1}{2\sqrt{(x^2 - 160^2)}}.2x = 0$ for max. /min.

$\therefore \dfrac{2}{x} = \dfrac{1}{\sqrt{(x^2 - 160^2)}}$ ...(i)

or $4(x^2 - 160^2) = x^2$ $\therefore x = \dfrac{320}{\sqrt{(3)}}$

$\dfrac{d^2y}{dx^2} = -\left[1.\dfrac{1}{\sqrt{(x^2 - 160^2)}} + x.\dfrac{-1}{2(x^2 - 160^2)^{3/2}}.2x\right]$

$= -\left[\frac{2}{x} - x^2 \cdot \frac{8}{x^3}\right]$ by (1)

$= \frac{6}{x} > 0$

$\therefore$ y is minimum when $x = \frac{320}{\sqrt{(3)}}$ and G is on the perpendicular bisector of AB.

12. A window of fixed perimeter (inducing the base of the arc) is in the form of a rectangle surmounted by a semi-circle. The semi-circular portion is fitted with coloured glass while the rectangular part is fitted with clear glass. The clear glass transmits three times as much light per square meter as the coloured glass does. What is the ratio of the sides of the rectangle so that the window transmits the maximum light?

Solution: Let $2r$ be the diameter of circular arc and x be length the other side of rectangular portion

Total perimeter $= 2(2r + x) + \pi r = k$, say ...(i)

Let the amount of light per square meter for the coloured glass be c: then for the clear glass it is $3c$ per square metre. Let S denote the total amount of light

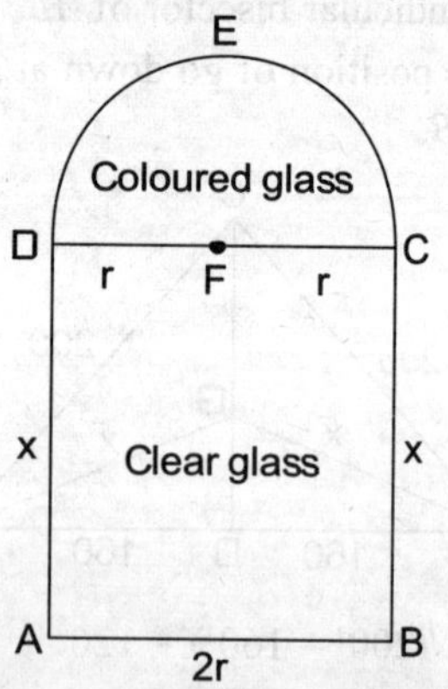

Then $S = (2rx)3c + \frac{1}{2}\pi r^2 . c = \frac{c}{2}\left[12rx + \pi r^2\right]$

$= \frac{c}{2}\left[6r(k - 4r - \pi r) + \pi r^2\right]$

$= \frac{c}{2}\left[6rk - 24r^2 - 5\pi r^2\right]$

$\therefore \quad \frac{dS}{dr} = \frac{c}{2}\left[6k - 48r - 10\pi r\right] = 0$

$\therefore \quad r = \frac{6k}{48 + 10\pi}$ .....(2)

$\therefore \quad \frac{d^2S}{dr^2} = \frac{c}{2}\left[-48 - 10\pi\right] < 0$

$\therefore$ Max

$\therefore$ $48r + 10\pi r = 6[4r + 2x + \pi r]$ by (1) and (2)

$r(24 + 4\pi r) = 12x$ $\therefore$ $2r(6 + \pi) = 6x$

$\therefore$ Ratio $= \frac{2r}{x} = \frac{6}{6+\pi}$

13. Find the point on the curve $4x^2 + a^2y^2 = 4a^2$; $4 < a^2 < 8$ that is farthest from the point $(0, -2)$.

Solution: The given equation is $\frac{x^2}{a^2} + \frac{y^2}{4} = 1$, which represents an ellipse on which any point may be taken an $(a \cos\phi, 2\sin\phi)$.

If d be its distance from $(0, -2)$, then let $z = d^2 = a^2 \cos^2\phi + 4(1 + \sin\phi)^2$

$\frac{dz}{d\phi} = -2a^2 \cos\phi \sin\phi + 8(1 + \sin\phi)\cos\phi = 0$ ...(i)

$= (4 - a^2)\sin 2\phi + 8\cos\phi$

From (1), we get $\cos\phi = 0$

Or $\sin\phi = \frac{4}{a^2 - 4} = \frac{1}{a^2/4 - 1} > 1$

By the given condition $4 < a^2 < 8$ or $1 < a^2/4 < 2$ and this value is rejected.

We choose $\cos\phi = 0$

$\therefore$ $\phi = \pi/2$

So the point becomes $(0, 2)$

Also $\frac{d^2z}{d\phi^2} = (4 - a^2)2\cos 2\phi - 8\sin\phi$

$= (4 - a^2)(-2) - 8 = 2(a^2 - 8) = -ive$ as $4 < a^2 < 8$

Hence $z = d^2$ is maximum when $\phi = \frac{\pi}{2}$

$\Rightarrow$ Point $= (0, 2)$

14. A tall electric pole is to be kept in vertical position by a stretched straight wire from the pole to the ground. The wire has to clear a wall 6 meter high and 4m from the pole. The least length of the wire that can be used between the pole and the ground is

Solution: Let $y = OP$ and $\angle POQ = \theta$. Then from the figure, it is clear that $y = 6 \operatorname{cosec}\theta + 4\sec\theta$

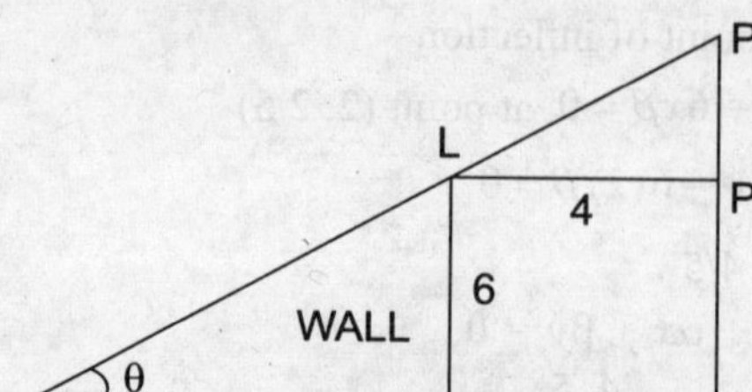

$\therefore \quad \frac{dy}{d\theta} = -6 \text{ cosec } \theta \cot \theta + 4 \sec \theta \tan \theta = 0$

For max. or min

$\Rightarrow \tan^3\theta = 6/4 = 3/2$

$\therefore \tan\theta = 3^{1/3}/2^{1/3}$

$\frac{d^2y}{d\theta^2} = 6 \text{cosec}\theta \cot^2\theta + 6\text{cosec}^3\theta + 4 \sec\theta \tan^2\theta$

$+ 4\sec^3\theta > 0$

Since θ is an acute angle. Hence is minimum when $\tan\theta = 3^{1/3}/2^{1/3}$

$\therefore$ Min. value of y is given by

$$y = \sqrt{2^{2/3} + 3^{2/3}}\left[\frac{3.2}{3^{1/3}} + \frac{2.2}{2^{1/3}}\right]$$

$$= 2(2^{2/3} + 3^{2/3})^{3/2}$$

15. From a variable point of an ellipse $\frac{x^2}{a^2} + \frac{y^2}{b^2} = 1$ normal is drawn to the ellipse. The maximum distance of the normal from the centre is ellipse is ...

Solution: Any normal to the ellipse is ax sec t – by cosec $t = a^2 - b^2$

If p be the length of perpendicular from (0, 0), then

$$p = \frac{a^2 - b^2}{\sqrt{(a^2 \sec^2 t + b^2 \text{cosec}^2 t)}}$$

Now p will be maximum if its denominator $\sqrt{(a^2 \sec^2 t + b^2 \text{cosec}^2 t)}$ is minimum as its numerator is constant

Now, let $K = \frac{a^2}{\cos^2 t} + \frac{b^2}{\sin^2 t}$

$$\frac{dK}{dt} = 2a^2 \sec^2 t \tan t - 2b^2 \text{cosec}^2 t \cot t = 0$$

$\Rightarrow \tan^2 t = \frac{b}{a}$

$\therefore K = (a + b)2$

$\therefore$ minimum value of $\sqrt{K}$ is $(a + b)$

$\therefore$ Maximum value of $p = (a^2 - b^2)/(a + b) = a - b$

16. Two towns located on the same side of the river agree to construct a pumping station and filtration plant at the river's edge, to be used jointly to supply the towns with water. If the distances of the two towns from the river are 'a' and 'b' and the distance between them is 'c', Show that the pipe lines joining them to the pumping station is atleast as great as $\sqrt{c^2 + 4ab}$.

Solution: $L = AP + PB$

$$L = \sqrt{a^2 + x^2} + \sqrt{(K - x)^2 + b^2}$$

$$\frac{dL}{dx} = \frac{2x}{2\sqrt{a^2 + x^2}} - \frac{2(K - x)}{2\sqrt{(K - x)^2 + b^2}}$$

for maximum or minimum $\frac{dL}{dx} = 0$

$$\frac{x}{\sqrt{a^2 + x^2}} = \frac{K - x}{\sqrt{(K - x)^2 + b^2}}$$

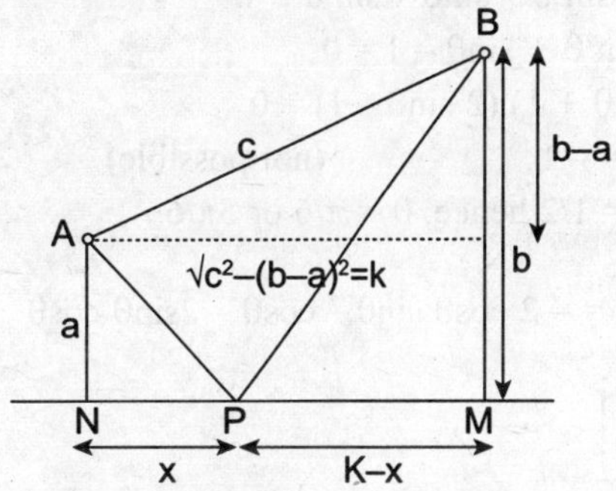

$x^2 [(K - x)^2 + b^2)] = (K - x)^2 (a^2 + x^2)$

$b^2 x^2 = a^2 (K - x)^2$

$bx = a (K - x)$

$x (a + b) = aK$

$x = \frac{Ka}{a + b} \qquad (K - x = \frac{Kb}{a + b})$

$L|_{x = \frac{Ka}{a+b}}$

$$= \sqrt{a^2 + \frac{K^2a^2}{(a + b)^2}} + \sqrt{b^2 + \frac{K^2b^2}{(a + b)^2}}$$

$$= \frac{a}{a + b}\sqrt{(a + b)^2 + K^2} + \frac{b}{a + b}\sqrt{(a + b)^2 + K^2}$$

$$= \frac{\sqrt{(a + b)^2 + K^2}}{a + b}(a + b)$$

$$= \sqrt{(a + b)^2 - c^2 - (a - b)^2}$$

$$= \sqrt{c^2 + 4ab}$$

17. A point P is given on the circumference of a circle of radius r. Chords QR are parallel to the tangent at P. Determine the maximum possible area of the triangle PQR.

Solution: Ar. of $\Delta PQR = \frac{2r\cos\theta(r + r\sin\theta)}{2}$

$A(\theta) = r^2 \cos\theta (1 + \sin\theta)$

$A'(\theta) = r^2 [\cos\theta . \cos\theta - (1 + \sin\theta) \sin\theta]$

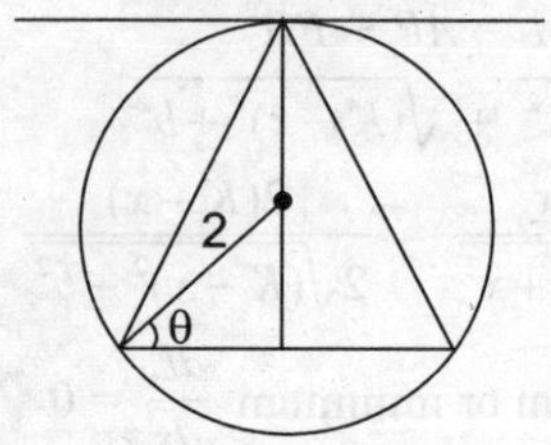

for maximum or minimum $A'(\theta) = 0$

$\cos^2\theta - \sin\theta\,(1 + \sin\theta) = 0$

$= 1 - \sin^2\theta - \sin\theta - \sin^2\theta = 0$

$= 2\sin^2\theta + \sin\theta - 1 = 0$

$= (\sin\theta + 1)(2\sin\theta - 1) = 0$

$\sin\theta = -1$ (not possible)

$\sin\theta = 1/2$ hence, $\theta = \pi/6$ or $5\pi/6$

$$\frac{d^2A}{d\theta^2} = -2\cos\theta\sin\theta - \cos\theta - 2\sin\theta\cos\theta$$

$$\left.\frac{d^2A}{d\theta^2}\right]_{\theta=\pi/6} = -ve$$

$\Rightarrow$ A is maximum

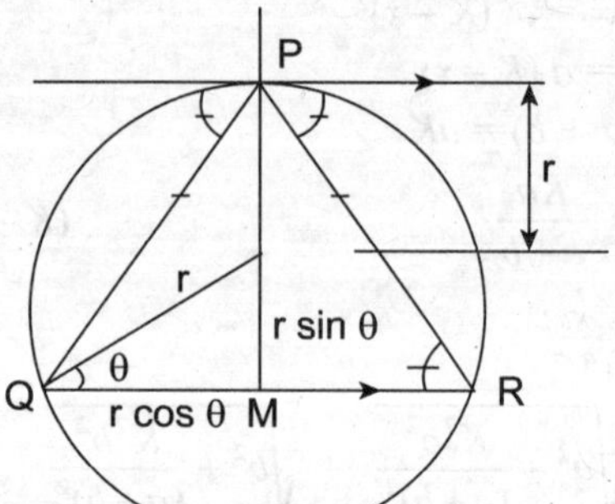

$$A_{max} = 2r^2\,\frac{\sqrt{3}}{2}\left(1+\frac{1}{2}\right)\frac{1}{2}$$

$$\Rightarrow A_{max} = \frac{3\sqrt{3}}{4}r^2$$

18. Find the value of a and b where $a < b$, for which the integral $\int_a^b (24-2x-x^2)^{1/2}\,dx$ has the largest value.

Solution: $I = \int_a^b [25-(x+1)^2]^{1/2}\,dx$

for I to be largest $(x + 1)^2$ must be minimum

$\Rightarrow x = -1$ i.e. $a = -1$

$\therefore\ I = \int_{-1}^{b} (24-2x-x^2)\,dx$

For maxima, $\frac{dI}{db} = 24 - 2b - b^2 = 0$

$\Rightarrow b^2 + 2b - 24 = 0$

$\Rightarrow (b + 6)(b - 4) = 0$

As $b \neq -6$ hence $b = 4$

Hence $I = \int_{-1}^{4} (25-(x+1)^2)^{1/2}\,dx$

put $x + 1 = 5\sin\theta$

$$= 24\int_0^{\pi/2} \cos^2\theta\,d\theta = \frac{25\pi}{4}$$

Ans. Hence $a = -1$; $b = 4$; $I_{max} = \frac{25\pi}{4}$

19. If f and F are continuous in [a, b] and derivable in (a, b) with $F'(x) \neq 0\ \forall\, x\in(a,b)$. Prove that $\exists\, c \in (a, b)$ such that $\frac{f'(c)}{F'(c)} = \frac{f(b)-f(a)}{F(b)-F(a)}$.

Solution: Let $K_1 = f(b) - f(a)$ and $K_2 = F(b) - F(a)$

$\Rightarrow \frac{f'(c)}{F'(c)} = \frac{K_1}{K_2}$

Consider a function $\phi(x) = K_1F(x) - K_2f(x)$ ....(1)

$\therefore$ f (x) and $F(x)$ are continuous in $[a, b]$ and derivable in (a, b) hence $\phi(x)$ will also be continuous and differentiable

also $\phi(a) = K_1F(a) - K_2 f(a)$

and $\phi(b) = K_1F(b) - K_2f(b)$

now $\phi(a) - \phi(b) = K_1(F(a) - F(b)) - K_2(f(a) - f(b))$

$= [f(b) - f(a)]\,[F(a) - F(b)] - [F(b) - F(a)]\,[f(a) - f(b)]$

$= [f(b) - f(a)]\,\{F(a) - F(b) + F(b) - F(a)\} = 0$

$\Rightarrow \phi(a) = \phi(b)$

Hence rolles theorem is applicable for $\phi(x)$

$\therefore$ $\exists$ some $c \in (a, b)$, such that, $\phi'(c) = 0$

$\varphi'(x)]_{x=c} = K_1F'(x) - K_2f'(x) = 0$

or $K_1F'(c) = K_2f'(c)$

$$\therefore\ \frac{f'(c)}{F'(c)} = \frac{K_1}{K_2} = \frac{f(b)-f(a)}{F(b)-F(a)}$$

20. Use the mean value theorem to prove $e^x \geq 1 + x$, $\forall\, x \in \mathbb{R}$,

Solution: Consider the function $f(x) = e^x - 1$ in $[0, x]$ where $x > 0$

$\therefore$ f is continuous and differentiable hence using $LMVT$ $\exists$ some $c \in (0, x)$

$$f'(c) = \frac{(e^x-1)-0}{x} = \frac{e^x-1}{x}$$

$$\left[f'(c) = \frac{f(x)-f(0)}{x-0}\right]$$

but $f'(c) = e^c$; hence $\frac{e^x-1}{x} = e^c > 1$, for $x > 0$

$\therefore\ e^x - 1 > x$

$\therefore\ e^x > x + 1$ for $x > 0$ ....(1)

again consider the function

$f(x) = e^x - 1$ in $[x, 0]$ where $x < 0$

using *LMVT* $\exists$ some $c \in (x, 0)$ such that

$$f'(c) = \frac{0-(e^x-1)}{-x} = \frac{1-e^x}{-x} = \frac{e^x-1}{x}$$

but $f'(c) = e^c$ hence $\frac{e^x-1}{x}$

$= e^c < 1$ for $c < 0$

hence $\frac{(e^x-1)}{x} < 1$ for $x < 0$

$(e^x - 1) > x$ (as x is $-ve$)

$e^x - 1 - x > 0$ for $x < 0$ ....(2)

from (1) and (2)

$e^x > x + 1$ for $x \neq 0$

$\therefore$ for $x = 0$ equality holds

$\therefore\ e^x \geq x + 1$ for $x \in R$

21. Find extrema of $f(x) = 3x^4 + 8x^3 - 18x^2 + 60$. Draw graph of $g(x) = \frac{40}{f(x)}$ and comment on its local and global extrema.

Solution: $f'(x) = 0$

$\Rightarrow 12x\,(x^2 + 2x - 3) = 0$

$\Rightarrow 12x\,(x - 1)(x + 3) = 0$

$\Rightarrow x = -3, 0, 1$

$f'(x) = 12(x + 3)\,x(x - 1)$

$-$ -3 $+$ 0 $-$ 1 $+$

local minima occurs at $x = -3, 1$

local maxima occurs at $x = 0$

$f(-3) = -75$, $f(1) = 53$ are local minima

$f(0) = 60$ is local maxima

$\lim_{x\to\infty} f(x) = \infty$, $\lim_{x\to-\infty} f(x) = \infty$

Hence global maxima does not exists: Global minima is -75

$$g'(x) = \frac{-40}{(f(x))^2} f'(x)$$

$\Rightarrow$ $g(x)$ has same critical points as that of $f(x)$.

A rough sketch of $y = f(x)$ is

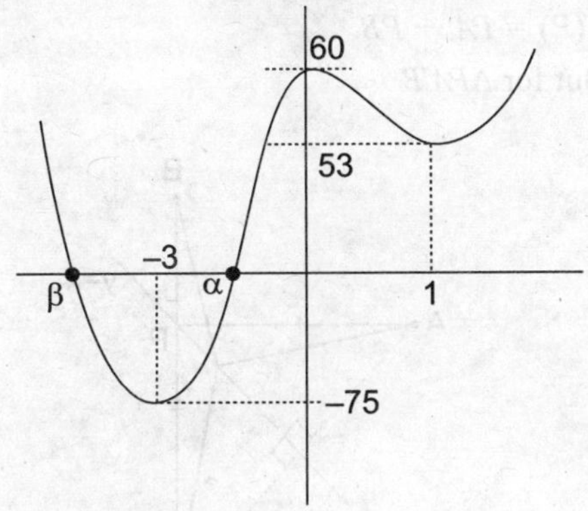

Let zeros of $f(x)$ be α, β

$\Rightarrow$ $g(\alpha)$, $g(\beta)$ are undefined,

Now since $\lim_{x\to\beta^-} g(x) = \infty$, $\lim_{x\to\beta^+} g(x) = -\infty$,

$\lim_{x\to\alpha^-} g(x) = -\infty$, $\lim_{x\to\alpha^+} g(x) = \infty$

$\Rightarrow x = \alpha, x = \beta$ are asymptotes of $y = g(x)$.

Also $\lim_{x\to\infty} g(x) = 0$, $\lim_{x\to-\infty} g(x) = 0$

$\Rightarrow y = 0$ is also an asymptote.

$\Rightarrow x = -3, x = 1$ are local minima of $y = f(x)$

$\Rightarrow x = -3, x = 1$ are local maxima of $y = g(x)$

Similarly, $x = 0$ is local minima of $y = g(x)$. Global extrema of $g(x)$ does not exists.

A rough sketch of $y = g(x)$ is

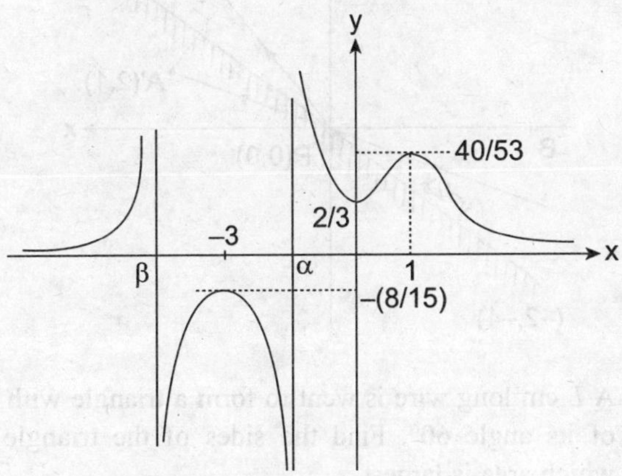

22. Let $A(1, 2)$ and $B(-2, -4)$ be two fixed points. A variable point P is chosen on the straight line $y = x$ such that perimeter of ΔPAB is minimum. Find coordinates of P.

Solution: Since distance AB is fixed so for minimizing the perimeter of ΔPAB, we basically have to minimize $(PA + PB)$

Let A' be the mirror image of A in the line $y = x$.

$F(P) = PA + PB$

$F(P) = PA' + PB$

But for $\Delta PA'B$

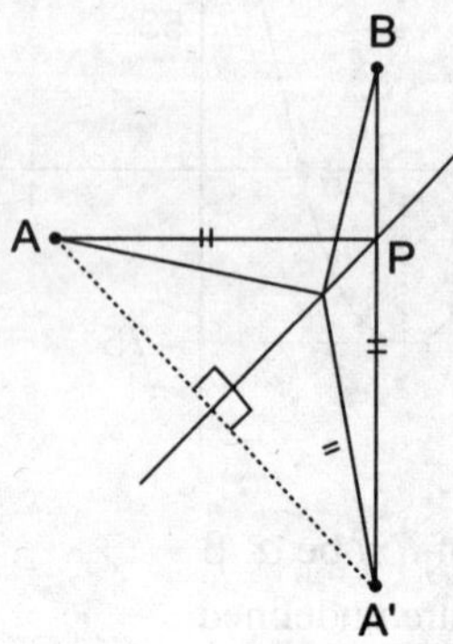

$PA' + PB \geq A'B$ and equality hold when P, A' and B becomes collinear. Thus for minimum path length point P is that special point for which PA and PB be come incident and reflected rays with respect to the mirror $y = x$.

Equation of line joining A' and B is $y = 2x$ intersection of this line with $y = x$ is the point P.

Hence $P \equiv (0, 0)$.

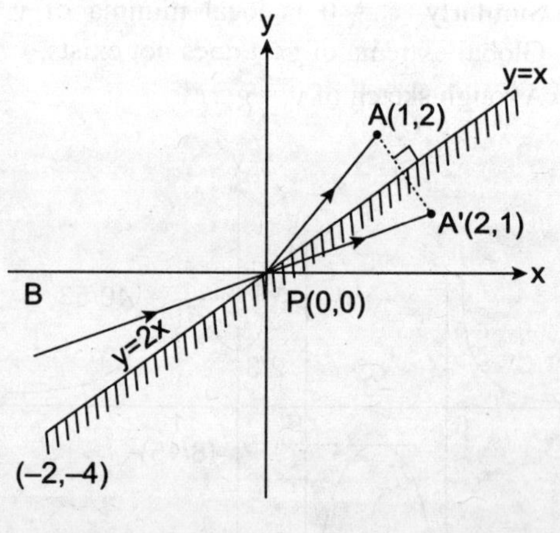

23. A L cm long wire is went to form a triangle with one of its angle 60°. Find the sides of the triangle for which area is largest.

Solution: Let the sides be a, b, c and $\angle A = \pi/3$

$$\cos\frac{\pi}{3} = \frac{b^2+c^2-a^2}{2bc}$$

$$\Rightarrow b^2+c^2-a^2 = bc$$

$$\Rightarrow (b+c)^2 - a^2 = 3bc$$

Also $a + b + c = L \Rightarrow b+c = L-a$

$$\Rightarrow (L-a)^2 - a^2 = 3bc \text{ or } bc = \frac{1}{3}L(L-2a)$$

Now the area of triangle

$$\Delta = \frac{1}{2}bc\sin 60^o = \frac{1}{4\sqrt{3}}L(L-2a) \Rightarrow \frac{d\Delta}{da} = -\frac{1}{2\sqrt{3}}$$

Thus Δ is a decreasing function of a. We have

$$b + c = \frac{1}{3}L - a \text{ and } bc = L(L-2a)$$

$$\Rightarrow (b-c)^2 = (b+c)^2 - 4c \geq 0$$

$$\Rightarrow (L-a)^2 \geq \frac{4}{3}L(L-2a)$$

$$\Rightarrow 3L^2 + 3a^2 - 6aL \geq 4L^2 - 8La$$

$$\Rightarrow 3a^2 + 2aL - L^2 \geq 0$$

$$\Rightarrow (3a-L)(a+L) \geq 0 \Rightarrow a \geq \frac{L}{3}$$

Thus least value of a is 1/3 and 'a' attains this value when $b = c$

$\Rightarrow$ when $a = L/3, b = c = L/3$

Now Δ is maximum when a is least. Hence for maximum area, sides of the triangle must be equal and must be equal to $L/3$ each.

24. If a, b, c be non-zero real numbers such that $\int_0^1 (1+\cos^8 x)(ax^2+bx+c)dx$

$= \int_0^2 (1+\cos^8 x)(ax^2+bx+c)dx = 0$, then equation $ax^2 + bx + c = 0$ will have one root between 0 and 1 and other root between 1 and 2.

Solution: Let $f(x) = \int_0^x (1+\cos^8 x)(ax^2+bx+c)dx$

$\therefore \quad f'(x) = (1+\cos^8 x)(ax^2+bx+c)$

From given conditions

$f(1) = f(0) = 0$

$\Rightarrow f(0) = f(1)$ and $f(2) - f(0) = 0$

$\Rightarrow f(0) = f(2)$

From (ii) and (iii), we get $f(0) = f(1) = f(2) = 0$

By Rolle's theorem for $f(x)$ in [0, 1]

$f'(\alpha) = 0$ at least one α such that $0 < \alpha < 1$

By Rolle's theorem for $f(x)$ in [1, 2]

$f'(\beta) = 0$ at least one β such that $1 < \beta < 2$

Now from (i), $f'(\alpha) = 0$

$\Rightarrow \quad (1+\cos^8 x)(ax^2+bx+c) = 0 \qquad \because 1+\cos^8\alpha \neq 0$

$\therefore\ a\alpha^2+\beta\alpha+c=0$

Similarly, β is a root of the equation $ax^2 + bx + c = 0$

But equation $ax^2 + bx + c = 0$ has one root α between 0 and 1, and other root β between 1 and 2.

25. If λ, μ be real numbers such that $x^3 - \lambda x^2 + \mu x - 6 = 0$ has its roots real and positive, then the minimum value of μ is

Solution: Let $f(x) = x^3 - \lambda x^2 + \mu x - 6 = 0$

Let α, β, γ be the roots.

$\Rightarrow \alpha+\beta+\gamma=\lambda$ ...(i)

and $\alpha\beta+\beta\gamma+\gamma\alpha=\mu$ ...(ii)

$\Rightarrow \alpha\beta\gamma=6$ ...(iiii)

from (ii) and (iii), we get $\dfrac{\alpha\beta+\beta\gamma+\gamma\alpha}{\alpha\beta\gamma}=\dfrac{\mu}{6}$

$\Rightarrow \dfrac{1}{\alpha}+\dfrac{1}{\beta}+\dfrac{1}{\gamma}=\dfrac{\mu}{6}$ ...(iv)

As we know $AM > GM$

$$\Rightarrow \frac{\frac{1}{\alpha}+\frac{1}{\beta}+\frac{1}{\gamma}}{3}\ge\left(\frac{1}{\alpha}\cdot\frac{1}{\beta}\cdot\frac{1}{\gamma}\right)^{1/3}$$

$$\Rightarrow \frac{\mu/6}{3}\ge\left(\frac{1}{6}\right)^{1/3} \quad \text{(using (iii) and (iv))}$$

$$\Rightarrow \mu\ge 18\left(\frac{1}{6}\right)^{1/3} \quad \text{or} \quad \mu\ge\frac{18}{6}6^{2/3}$$

$\therefore\ \mu\ge 3(6^{2/3})$

26. For all x in [0, 1], let the second derivative $f''(x)$ of a function $f(x)$ exist and satisfy $|f''(x)| \le 1$. If $f(0) = f(1)$, then show that $|f'(x)| < 1$ for all in [0, 1].

Solution: $f''(x)$ exists for all x in [0, 1]

$\therefore$ $f(x)$ and $f'(x)$ are differentiable and continuous in [0, 1].

Now $f(x)$ is continuous in [0,1] and differentiable in (0, 1) and $f(0) = f(1)$

$\therefore$ By Rolle's theorem there is at least one c such that $f'(c) = 0$

where $0 < c < 1$.

Case I: Let $x = c$ then $f'(x) = f'(c) = 0$

$\therefore\ |f'(x)| = |0| = 0 < 1$

Case II: Let $x > c$. By Lagrange's mean value theorem for $f'(x)$ in $[c, x]$

$$\frac{f'(x)-f'(c)}{x-c}=f''(\alpha) \text{ for at least one } \alpha,\ c<\alpha<x$$

$(\because f'(c)=0)$

or $f'(x)=(x-c)f''(\alpha)$

or $|f'(x)|=|(x-c)||f''(\alpha)|$

But $x \in [0, 1]$, $c \in (0, 1)$

$\therefore\ |x-c|<1-0$ or $|x-c|<1$

and $|f''(x)|$ given 1 for all $x \in [0, 1]$

$\therefore\ |f''(\alpha)|\le 1$

$\therefore\ |f'(x)|<1.1 \quad (\because |f'(x)|=|(x-c)||f''(\alpha)|)$

or $|f'(x)| < 1$ for all [0, 1]

Case III: Let $x < c$ then $\dfrac{f'(c)-f'(x)}{c-x}=f''(\alpha)$

$\therefore\ |-f'(x)|=|c-x||f''(\alpha)|$

$\Rightarrow |f'(x)|<1.1$

or $|f'(x)|<1$

Combining all cases, we get

$|f'(x)| < 1$ for all $x \in [0, 1]$

27. If f is an increasing function from $R \to R$ such that $f(x) > 0$, $f(x) \neq 0$ and f^{-1} exists, then show that $\dfrac{d^2(f^{-1}(x))}{dx^2}<0$.

Solution: Let f be an increasing function

$\Rightarrow f'(x)>0$ and $f''(x)>0$ ...(i)

(given)

Let $g(x)=f^{-1}(x)$ ...(ii)

Then $f'(g(x)).\ g'(x) = 1$

$\Rightarrow g'(x)=\dfrac{1}{f'(g(x))}$ ...(iii)

Again differentiating both sides with respect to x, we get

$$g''(x)=-\frac{1}{\{f'(g(x))\}^2}f''(g(x)).g'(x) \quad \text{...(iv)}$$

Let $g(x) = f^{-1}(x) = y$

$\Rightarrow x = f(y)$

$\Rightarrow 1 = f'(y)\dfrac{dy}{dx}$

$\Rightarrow \dfrac{dy}{dx}=\dfrac{1}{f'(y)}>0$

$\Rightarrow g'(x)>0$

From equation (iv), we have

$$\frac{d^2}{dx^2}=(g(x))<0 \quad [\because f(g(x))>0]$$

or $$\frac{d^2(f^{-1}(x))}{dx^2}<0 \quad [\because g(x)=f^{-1}(x)]$$

28. Let $f(x)=(x-a)(x-b)(x-c), a<b<c$. Show that $f'(x)=0$ has two roots one belonging to (*a*, *b*) and other belonging to (*b*, *c*)

Solution: Here, *f* (*x*) being a polynomial is continuous and differentiable for all real values of *x*.

We also have $f(a)=f(b)=f(c)$

If we apply Rolle's theorem to *f* (*x*) in [*a*, *b*] and [b, c] we would observe that $f'(x)=0$ would have atleast one root in (*a*, *b*) and atleast one root in (*b*, *c*)

But $f'(x)=0$ is a polynomial of degree two, hence $f'(x)=0$ cannot have more than two roots.

It implies that exactly one root of $f'(x)=0$ would lie in (*a*, *b*) and exactly one root of $f'(x)=0$ would be in (*b*, *c*).

29. If the function of *f*: [0, 4] → *R* is differentiable, then show that,

(i) $(f(4))^2 - (f(0))^2 = 8f'(a)f(b)$ for *a*, *b* ∈ (0, 4)

(ii) $\int_0^4 f(t)\,dt = 2\{\alpha f(\alpha^2)+\beta f(\beta^2)\}$ for all 0 < α, β < 2

Solution: (i) Since *f* is differentiable

⇒ *f* is continuous also

Thus by lagrange's mean value theorem a ∈ (0, 4) such that

$$f'(a)=\frac{f(4)-f(0)}{4-0}=\frac{f(4)-f(0)}{4} \quad ...(i)$$

Also by intermediate mean value theorem there exists *b* ∈ (0, 4) such that

$$f(b)=\frac{f(4)+f(0)}{2} \quad ....(ii)$$

from (i) and (ii), we get

$$\Rightarrow f'(a)f(b)=\frac{f(4)-f(0)}{4}\times\frac{f(4)+f(0)}{2}$$

$$\Rightarrow f'(a)f(b)=\frac{(f(4))^2-(f(0))^2}{8}$$

$\Rightarrow 8f'(a)f(b)=(f(4))^2-(f(0))^2$ for some *a*, *b* ∈ (0, 4)

(ii) Putting $t = z^2$ we have $\int_0^4 f(t)\,dt=\int_0^2 2z\,f(z^2)dz$

Consider the function of ϕ (*t*) is given by $\int_0^t f(t)\,dt$

$$\Rightarrow \phi(t)=\int_0^t 2z\,f(z^2)dz,\ t\in[0,2]$$

Clearly, ϕ (t) being an integral function of a continuous function, is continuous and differentiable on [0, 2]

$$\therefore \frac{\phi(2)-\phi(0)}{2-0}=\phi'(c)$$

$$\Rightarrow \frac{\int_0^2 2z\,f(z^2)\,dz-\int_0^0 2z\,f(z^2)\,dz}{2-0}=2cf(c^2)$$

(using $\phi'(t)=2t\,f(t^2)$)

$$\Rightarrow \int_0^2 2z\,f(z^2)\,dz=4c\,f(c)^2 \quad ...(i)$$

Also by intermediate mean value theorem for *c* ∈ (0, 2) there exists α, β ∈ (0, 2) such that

$$\Rightarrow \frac{\phi'(\alpha)+\phi'(\beta)}{2}=\phi'(c) \text{ where } 0<\alpha<c<\beta<2$$

$$\Rightarrow 2\alpha f(\alpha^2)+2\beta f(\beta^2)=2\{2c\,f(c^2)\} \quad ...(ii)$$

from (i) and (ii)

$$\int_0^2 2z\,f(z^2)dz=2\alpha f(\alpha^2)+2\beta f(\beta^2)$$

for all 0 < α, β < 2

30. The curves $y=a(x)$ and $y=b(x)$ are concave on an interval (*a*, *b*). Prove that in the given interval

(i) the curve $f(x)=a(x)+b(x)$ is concave

(ii) if *a*(*x*) and *b*(*x*) are positive and have a common point of minimum, then the $y=a(x)b(x)$ curve is concave.

Solution: $y = a(x)$; $y = b(x)$; $y'' > 0$

$a''(x)>0$; $b''(x)>0$

given in the interval (*a*, *b*)

(i) $f(x)=a(x)+b(x)$

$\Rightarrow f''(x)=a''(x)+b''(x)$

$f''(x)>0$

$\because a''(x)$; $b''(x)$

f(*x*) is concave in the given interval (*a*, *b*)

(ii) *a*(*x*) is +ve; *b*(*x*) is +ve both have common point of minimum

$\Rightarrow f(x)=a(x).b(x)$

$\Rightarrow f'(x)=a'(x).b(x)+b'(x).a(x)$

$\Rightarrow f''(x)=a''(x).b(x)+b'(x).a'(x)+b''(x).a(x)+b'(x).a'(x)$

$= a''(x).b(x)+b''(x).a(x)+2b'(x).a'(x)$

$= b''(x)>0$; $a(x)$ is +ve

$\Rightarrow a''(x) > 0;$

$a(x)$ is +ve.

So $b'(x).a'(x)$ is +ve.

Hence $f''(x) > 0$

So $f''(x)$ is positive, hence $f(x)$ is concave

31. Prove that if the relationship $|f(x)| \geq |\theta'(x)|$ is valid in the interval $[a, b]$ and $\phi'(x)$ does not vanish, then the $|\Delta f(x)| \geq |\Delta\theta(x)|$ relationship is also valid, where $\Delta f(x) = f(x+\Delta x) - f(x)$, $\Delta\phi(x) = \phi(x+\Delta x) - \phi(x)$ and x and $x + \Delta x$ are arbitrary points of the interval $[a, b]$.

Solution: If $f(x)$, $\phi(x)$ be two functions defined in an interval $[a, b]$

$$\Rightarrow \frac{f(b)-f(a)}{\phi(b)-\phi(a)} = \frac{f'(c)}{\phi'(c)}$$

Let $a = x$; $b = x + \Delta x$

$$\Rightarrow \frac{f(x+\Delta x)-f(x)}{\phi(x+\Delta x)-\phi(x)} = \frac{f'(c)}{\phi'(c)}$$

$$\Rightarrow \frac{\Delta f(x)}{\Delta\phi(x)} = \frac{f'(c)}{\phi'(c)}$$

$$\Rightarrow |f'(x)| \geq |\phi'(x)| \quad \text{(given)}$$

$$\Rightarrow |f'(c)| \geq |\phi'(c)|$$

$$\frac{|f'(c)|}{|\phi'(c)|} \geq 1$$

$$\Rightarrow \frac{|\Delta f(x)|}{|\Delta\phi(x)|} \geq 1 \quad \text{(from (i))}$$

Applying modulus both sides of (i),

we get $|\Delta f(x)| \geq |\Delta\phi(x)|$

32. A cubic $f(x)$ vanishes at $x = -2$ and has local minimum and local maximum at $x = -1$ and $x = 1/3$ respectively. If $\int_{-1}^{1} f(x)dx = \frac{14}{3}$, find the cubic $f(x)$.

Solution: Now, since $f(x)$ is a cubic polynomial, hence $f'(x)$ is a quadratic polynomial and given that $f(x)$ has its local minima at $x = -1$ and local maxima at $x = 1/3$.

$$\therefore f'(x) = a(x+1)\left(x-\frac{1}{3}\right)$$

$$f'(x) = a\left(x^2+\frac{2}{3}x-\frac{1}{3}\right)$$

Integrating $f(x) = a\left(\frac{x^3}{3}+\frac{x^2}{3}-\frac{x}{3}\right)+c$

$\because f(-2) = 0$

$$\Rightarrow 0 = a\left(\frac{-8}{3}+\frac{4}{3}+\frac{2}{3}\right)+c$$

$$\Rightarrow c = \frac{2a}{3}$$

$$\therefore f(x) = a\left(\frac{x^3}{3}+\frac{x^2}{3}-\frac{x}{3}+\frac{2}{3}\right)$$

Given that $\int_{-1}^{1} f(x) = \frac{14}{3}$

$$\Rightarrow \frac{a}{3}\int_{-1}^{1}(x^3+x^2-x+2)dx = \frac{14}{3}$$

$$\Rightarrow \frac{a}{3}\left[\frac{x^4}{4}+\frac{x^3}{3}-\frac{x^2}{2}+2x\right]_{-1}^{1} = \frac{14}{3}$$

$$\Rightarrow \frac{a}{3}\left[\frac{2}{3}+4\right] = \frac{14}{3}$$

$$\Rightarrow \frac{a}{3}\left[\frac{14}{3}\right] = \frac{14}{3}$$

$\Rightarrow a = 3$

Hence $f(x) = x^3 + x^2 - x + 2$

33. Investigate for maxima and minima for the function $f(x)$ where

$$f(x) = \int_1^x [2(t-1)(t-2)^3 + 3(t-1)^2(t-2)^2]dt$$

Solution:

$$f(x) = \int_1^x [2(t-1)(t-2)^3 + 3(t-1)^2(t-2)^2]dx$$

By Newton Leibnitz's Rule; we get

$f'(x) = 2(x-1)(x-2)^3 + 3(x-1)^2(x-2)$

$= (x-1)(x-2)^2(5x-7)$

Now, sign convention of $f'(x)$ is as shown below:

$-\infty$ ——(+)—— 1 ——(−)—— 7/5 ——(+)—— 2 ——(+)—— ∞

Max. at $x = 1$; $f(1) = 0$

Min. at $x = 7/5$; $f(7/5) = -\frac{108}{3125}$

34. Find the greatest and least value for the function $y = x + \sin 2x$, $0 \leq x \leq 2\pi$

Solution: $y = x + \sin 2x \quad x \in [0, 2\pi]$

Equating $\frac{dy}{dx} = 0$; we get $1 + 2\cos 2x = 0$

$\cos 2x = -\frac{1}{2} = \cos\frac{2\pi}{3}$

$\Rightarrow 2x = 2n\pi \pm \left(\frac{2\pi}{3}\right)$

$2x = \frac{2\pi}{3}, \frac{4\pi}{3}, \frac{8\pi}{3}, \frac{10\pi}{3}$

$x = \frac{\pi}{3}, \frac{2\pi}{3}, \frac{4\pi}{3}, \frac{5\pi}{3}$

Now, the greatest value (M) and the least value (m) will be given by

$$\max\left\{ f(0), f\left(\frac{\pi}{3}\right), f\left(\frac{2\pi}{3}\right), f\left(\frac{4\pi}{3}\right), f\left(\frac{5\pi}{3}\right), f(2\pi)\right\}$$

and

$$\min\left\{ f(0), f\left(\frac{\pi}{3}\right), f\left(\frac{2\pi}{3}\right), f\left(\frac{4\pi}{3}\right), f\left(\frac{5\pi}{3}\right), f(2\pi)\right\}$$

respectively

$F(0) = 0; f(2\pi) = 2\pi;$

$f\left(\frac{\pi}{3}\right) = \frac{\pi}{3} + \frac{\sqrt{3}}{2};\ f\left(\frac{4\pi}{3}\right) = \frac{4\pi}{3} + \frac{\sqrt{3}}{2};$

$f\left(\frac{2\pi}{3}\right) = \frac{2\pi}{3} - \frac{\sqrt{3}}{2};\ f\left(\frac{5\pi}{3}\right) = \frac{5\pi}{32} - \sqrt{3}$

$\therefore$ $M = 2\pi$ achieved at $x = 2\pi$ and $m = 0$ achieved at $x = 0$.

35. Suppose $f(x)$ is a function satisfying the following conditions:

(i) $f(0) = 2, f(1) = 1$

(ii) f has a minimum value at $x = \frac{5}{2}$ and

(iii) for all x,

$$f'(x) = \begin{vmatrix} 2ax & 2ax-1 & 2ax+b+1 \\ b & b+1 & -1 \\ 2(ax+b) & 2ax+2b+1 & 2ax+b \end{vmatrix}$$

Where a, b are some constants. Determine the constants a, b and the function $f(x)$.

Solution:

$$f'(x) = \begin{vmatrix} 2ax & 2ax-1 & 2ax+b+1 \\ b & b+1 & -1 \\ 2(ax+b) & 2ax+2b+1 & 2ax+b \end{vmatrix}$$

On applying $C_2 \to C_2 + C_3 - C_1$; we get

$$f'(x) = \begin{vmatrix} 2ax & 2ax+b & 2ax+b+1 \\ b & 0 & -1 \\ 2(ax+b) & 2ax+b+1 & 2ax+b \end{vmatrix}$$

On applying $R_3 \to R_3 - R_1$; we get

$$f'(x) = \begin{vmatrix} 2ax & 2ax+b & 2ax+b+1 \\ b & 0 & -1 \\ 2b & 1 & -1 \end{vmatrix}$$

On applying $R_3 \to R_3 - 2R_2$; we get

$$f'(x) = \begin{vmatrix} 2ax & 2ax+b & 2ax+b+1 \\ b & 0 & -1 \\ 0 & 1 & 1 \end{vmatrix}$$

On applying $C_3 \to C_3 - C_2$; we get

$$f'(x) = \begin{vmatrix} 2ax & 2ax+b & 1 \\ b & 0 & -1 \\ 0 & 1 & 1 \end{vmatrix}$$

$\Rightarrow f'(x) = 2ax + b$

Now, $f'\left(\frac{5}{2}\right) = 0$

$\Rightarrow 5a + b = 0$ ...(1)

Substituting $b = -5a$ in $f'(x)$; we get

$f'(x) = 2ax - 5a$

$\Rightarrow f'(x) = a(2x - 5)$

Integrating both sides; we get

$f(x) = a(x^2 - 5x) + c$

Given $f(0) = 2$ and $f(1) = 1$

Solving the above equations; we get $c = 2$ and $a = \frac{1}{4}$

$\Rightarrow f(x) = \frac{1}{4}(x^2 - 5x) + 2$

Now $f'(x) = \frac{1}{4}(2x-5) = \frac{x}{2} - \frac{5}{4}$

$b = -\frac{5}{4}$ and $b = \frac{1}{4}$

36. Suppose $f(x)$ is a real valued polynomial function of degree 6 satisfying the following conditions;

(a) f has minimum value at $x = 0$ and 2

(b) f has maximum value at $x = 1$

(c) for all x, $\lim_{x\to 0} \frac{1}{x} \ell n \begin{vmatrix} \frac{f(x)}{x} & 1 & 0 \\ 0 & \frac{1}{x} & 1 \\ 1 & 0 & \frac{1}{x} \end{vmatrix} = 2.$

Determine $f(x)$.

Solution: $\lim_{x\to 0}\frac{1}{x}\log_e\begin{vmatrix}\frac{f(x)}{x} & 1 & 0\\ 0 & \frac{1}{x} & 1\\ 1 & 0 & \frac{1}{x}\end{vmatrix}=2$

$\Rightarrow \lim_{x\to 0}\frac{1}{x}\log_e\left\{\frac{f(x)}{x^3}+1\right\}=2$

$\Rightarrow \lim_{x\to 0}\log_e\left\{\frac{f(x)}{x^3}+1\right\}^{1/x}=2$

Let $f(x) = ax^6 + bx^5 + cx^4 + dx^3 + ex^2 + fx + g$

For the $\lim_{x\to 0}\ell n\left(\frac{f(x)}{x^3}+1\right)^{1/x}$ to be finite $\lim_{x\to 0}\frac{f(x)}{x^3}$ must be zero.

$\Rightarrow \lim_{x\to 0} ax^3+bx^2+cx+d+\frac{e}{x}+\frac{f}{x^2}+\frac{g}{x^3}=0$

$\Rightarrow d = e = f = g = 0$

$\Rightarrow f(x) = ax^6 + bx^5 + cx^4$

Now, $\lim_{x\to 0}\log_e\left[\frac{f(x)}{x^3}+1\right]^{1/x}$

$\Rightarrow \lim_{x\to 0}\ell n\left(1+\frac{f(x)}{x^3}\right)^{\frac{1}{\frac{f(x)}{x^3}}\times\frac{\frac{f(x)}{x^3}}{x}}$

$\Rightarrow \lim_{x\to 0}\ell n e^{\frac{f(x)}{x^4}}=\lim_{x\to 0}\frac{f(x)}{x^4}$

$\Rightarrow \lim_{x\to 0}\frac{f(x)}{x^4}=2$

$\Rightarrow \lim_{x\to 0} ax^2 + bx + c = 2$

$\Rightarrow c = 2$

$\Rightarrow f(x) = ax^6 + bx^5 + 2x^4$

$\Rightarrow f'(x) = 6ax^5 + 5bx^4 + 8x^3$

Now given that $f'(1) = 0$ and $f'(2) = 0$

$\Rightarrow 6a + 5b = -8$ ...(i)

and $24a + 10b = -8$ ...(ii)

Solving; we get $a=\frac{2}{3}$ and $b=-\frac{12}{5}$

$\Rightarrow f(x) = \frac{2}{3}x^6 - \frac{12}{5}x^5 + 2x^4$

37. Find the maximum perimeter of a triangle on a given base 'a' and having the given vertical angle α.

Solution: $R=\frac{a}{2\sin\alpha}=\frac{b}{2\sin\beta}=\frac{c}{2\sin c}$

P(perimeter) $= a + b + c$

$P = a + 2R\sin B + 2R\sin C$

$= a + 4R\sin\frac{B+C}{2}\cos\frac{B-C}{2}$

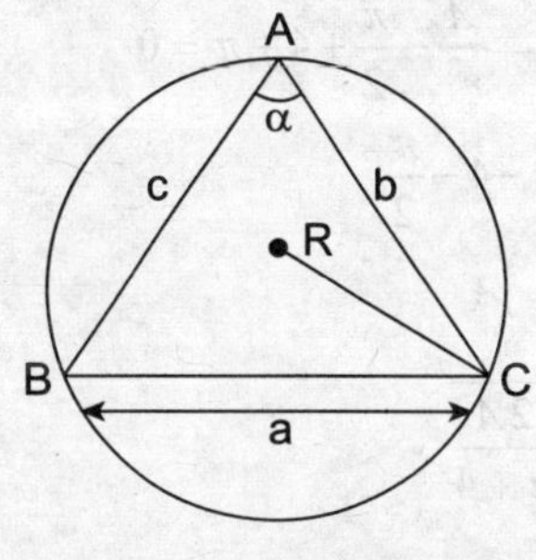

$P = a + 4R\cos\frac{\alpha}{2}\cos\frac{B-C}{2}$

P is max when $\cos\left(\frac{B-C}{2}\right)=1$

$\Rightarrow B = C$ $\therefore P_{max} = a + 4R\cos\frac{\alpha}{2}$

$= a+4\frac{a}{2\sin\alpha}\cos\frac{\alpha}{2}$

$= a + a\operatorname{cosec}\frac{\alpha}{2}$

38. The plan view of a swimming pool consists of a semicircle of radius r attached to a rectangle of length '$2r$' and width 's'. If the surface area A of the pool is fixed, for what value of 'r' and 's' the perimeter 'P' of the pool is minimum.

Solution: Area of swimming pool = area of rectangle + area of semi-circle

$\Rightarrow A = 2rS + \frac{\pi r^2}{2}$

$\Rightarrow S = \frac{A-\frac{\pi r^2}{2}}{2r}$ ...(1)

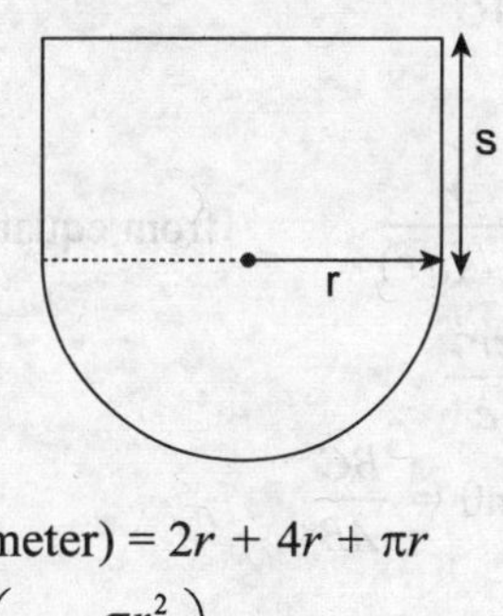

P(perimeter) $= 2r + 4r + \pi r$

$P = 2\left(\frac{A-\frac{\pi r^2}{2}}{2r}\right) + 2r + \pi r$

$$P = \frac{A}{r} - \frac{\pi r}{2} + 2r + \pi r$$

Equating $\frac{dP}{dr} = 0$;

we get $-\frac{A}{r^2} - \frac{\pi}{2} + 4 + \pi = 0$

$\Rightarrow\ -\frac{A}{r^2} = -4 - \frac{\pi}{2}$

$\Rightarrow\ \frac{2A}{\pi + 4} = r^2$

$\Rightarrow\ r = \sqrt{\frac{2A}{\pi + 4}}$

39. For a given curved surface of a right circular cone when the volume is maximum, prove that the semi vertical angle is $\sin^{-1}\frac{1}{\sqrt{3}}$.

Solution: Let the radius of right circular cone is r and semi vertical angle is θ.
According to question, curved surface area of right circular cone is given.
So, Let curved surface area $= c$ (constant)

$\Rightarrow\ \pi r\ell = c$

$\Rightarrow\ r\ell = \frac{c}{\pi}$ ...(i)

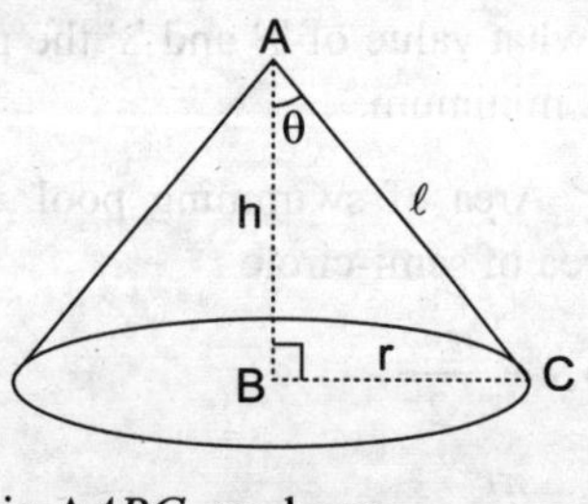

Now, in ΔABC, we have

$\sin\theta = \frac{BC}{AC}$

$\Rightarrow\ \sin\theta = \frac{r}{\ell}$

$\Rightarrow\ \sin\theta = \frac{r}{c/(\pi r)}$ [from equation (i) $\ell = \frac{c}{\pi r}$]

$\Rightarrow\ \sin\theta = \frac{\pi r^2}{c}$ ...(ii)

Again $\tan\theta = \frac{BC}{AB}$

$\Rightarrow\ \tan\theta = \frac{r}{h}$

$\Rightarrow\ h = \frac{r}{\tan\theta} = r\cot\theta$

∴ volume of right circular cone

$V = \frac{1}{3}\pi r^2 h$

$\Rightarrow\ V(\theta) = \frac{1}{3}\pi r^2 . r\cot\theta$

$= \frac{1}{3}\pi r^3 \cot\theta$

$= \frac{1}{3}\pi\left(\frac{c\sin\theta}{\pi}\right)^{3/2}\cot\theta$

from equaton (*ii*) $r = \left(\frac{c\sin\theta}{\pi}\right)^{1/2}$

$V(\theta) = \left(\frac{1}{3}\frac{\pi c^{3/2}}{\pi^{3/2}}\right).\sin^{3/2}\theta.\cot\theta$

$= k.\ \sin\theta.\ \sin^{1/2}\theta.\ \frac{\cos\theta}{\sin\theta}$ $\left(\text{Let } k = \frac{1}{3}\frac{c^{3/2}}{\pi^{1/2}}\right)$

$= k\ \sin^{1/2}\theta.\ \cos\theta$

$\because\ \frac{dV(\theta)}{d\theta} = k.\left[\frac{1}{2\sqrt{\sin\theta}}\cos\theta.\cos\theta - \sin^{1/2}\theta\sin\theta\right]$

$= k\left[\frac{\cos^2\theta}{2\sqrt{\sin\theta}} - \sin^{3/2}\theta\right]$

$= \frac{k}{2\sqrt{\sin\theta}}\ [\cos^2\theta - 2\sin^2\theta]$

$= \frac{k}{2\sqrt{\sin\theta}}[1 - \sin^2\theta - 2\sin^2\theta]$

$= \frac{k}{2\sqrt{\sin\theta}}[1 - 3\sin^2\theta]$

For the volume to be maximum; we must have $\frac{dV(\theta)}{d\theta} = 0$

$\Rightarrow\ 1 - 3\sin^2\theta = 0$

$\Rightarrow\ \sin^2\theta = 1/3$

$\Rightarrow\ \sin\theta = \frac{1}{\sqrt{3}}$

$\Rightarrow\ \theta = \sin^{-1}\left(\frac{1}{\sqrt{3}}\right)$

Now, $V'(\theta) = \underbrace{\frac{k}{2\sqrt{\sin\theta}}}_{>0}\ \underbrace{(1 - \sqrt{3}\sin\theta)(1 + \sqrt{3}\sin\theta)}_{>0}$

∴ The sign convention of $V'(\theta)$ is as shown below

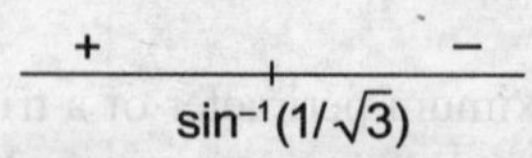

So, $V(\theta)$ i.e., volume has maximum vlaue at $\theta = \sin^{-1}\left(\frac{1}{\sqrt{3}}\right)$

40. Of all the lines tangent to the graph of the curve $y = \frac{6}{x^2+3}$, find the equations of the tangent lines of minimum and maximum slope.

Solution: Equation of curve is $y = \frac{6}{x^2+3}$ since, we have to find the equation of tangents lines of maximum and minimum slope i.e. we have to maximise/minimise $f'(x)$.

$f(x) =$ ———

$$\Rightarrow f'(x) = -\frac{6}{(x^2+3)^2}.2x$$

$$\Rightarrow f'(x) = g(x) = -12\frac{x}{(x^2+3)^2}$$

$$g'(x) = -12\left[\frac{(x^2+3)^2.1 - 2x(x^2+3).2x}{(x^2+3)^4}\right]$$

$$= -12\left[\frac{(x^2+3)^2 - 4x^2(x^2+3)}{(x^2+3)^4}\right]$$

$$= -12\,(x^2+3)\left[\frac{x^2+3-4x^2}{(x^2+3)^4}\right]$$

$$= -12\frac{3-3x^2}{(x^2+3)^3}$$

$$= 36.\frac{x^2-1}{(x^2+3)^3}$$

$$= 36\frac{(x-1)\,(x+1)}{(x^2+3)^3}$$

Now; sign convention of $g'(x)$ is as shown below

$$\begin{array}{ccccc} + & & - & & + \\ \hline & -1 & & 1 & \end{array}$$

So, $g(x)$ has maximum value at $x = -1$ and minimum value of $x = 1$

$$g_{\text{max.}} = g(-1) = -12\frac{-1}{(1+3)^2} = \frac{12}{16} = \frac{3}{4}$$

$\Rightarrow$ maximum slope = 3/4 at the point $x = -1$

The y – *coordinate of* $f(x)$ at $x = -1$ can be obtained by

Substituting $x = -1$ in $y = \frac{6}{x^2+3}$

$$\therefore\ y|_{x=-1} = \frac{6}{1+3} = \frac{6}{4}$$

$\therefore$ Equation of tangent line passes through point $\left(-1, \frac{6}{4}\right)$ with maximum slope 3/4 is

$$y - 6/4 = 3/4\,(x+1)$$

$$\Rightarrow 4y - 6 = 3x + 3$$

$$\Rightarrow 3x - 4y + 6 + 3 = 0$$

$$\therefore\ 3x - 4y + 9 = 0$$

Similarly $g_{\text{min.}} = g(+1) = -\frac{12.1}{(1+3)^2} = -\frac{12}{16}$

$\therefore$ minimum slope = – 3/4 achieved at $x = 1$

And at the point $x = 1$; we have

$$y = \frac{6}{x^2+3} = \frac{6}{1+3} = \frac{6}{4}$$

hance equation of tangent line passes through point $\left(1, \frac{6}{4}\right)$ and minimum slope $\frac{-3}{4}$, is.

$$y - \frac{6}{4} = -\frac{3}{4}(x-1)$$

$$\Rightarrow 4y - 6 = -3x + 3$$

$$\Rightarrow 4y - 6 + 3x - 3 = 0$$

$$\therefore\ 3x + 4y - 9 = 0$$

41. Prove that $\sin x + 2x \geq \frac{3x.(x+1)}{\pi}\ \forall x \in \left[0, \frac{\pi}{2}\right]$. (Justify the inequality, if any used).

Solution: Let us consider $f(x) = \sin x + 2x - \frac{3x(x+1)}{\pi}$

$$f'(x) = \cos x + 2 - \frac{3}{\pi}\,(2x+1)$$

$f''(x) = -\sin x - \frac{6}{\pi} < 0\ \forall\ x \in \left[0, \frac{\pi}{2}\right]$ $f'(x)$ decreasing function ...(i)

Also $f'(0) = 3 - \frac{3}{\pi} > 0$ ....(ii)

$f'\left(\frac{\pi}{2}\right) = 2 - \frac{3}{\pi}(\pi+1) = -1 - \frac{3}{\pi} < 0$ ...(ii)

(1), (ii) (iii) there exist certain value $x \in \left[0, \frac{\pi}{2}\right]$ for which $f'(x) = 0$ and this point must be a point of maxima of $f(x)$ since the sign of $f'(x)$ changes *+ve to –ve*

Also we can sec that $f(0) = 0$ and $f\left(\frac{\pi}{2}\right) = \frac{\pi}{4} - \frac{1}{2} > 0$

Let $x = p$ be the pt at which the max. of $f(x)$ occurs in $\left[0, \frac{\pi}{2}\right]$ since $f'(x) = 0$ in only once in $\left[0, \frac{\pi}{2}\right]$

Consider $x \in [O, P]$

$\Rightarrow f(x) \geq 0$

$\Rightarrow f(x)$ is an increasing function

Also $x \in \left[P, \frac{\pi}{2}\right]$

$\Rightarrow f'(x) < 0$

$\Rightarrow f(0) \le f(x)\ [0 \le x] \quad \Rightarrow f(x) \ge 0$

$f(x)$ is decreasing

for $x < \frac{\pi}{2}$

$\Rightarrow f(x) > f\left(\frac{\pi}{2}\right) > 0$

Hence $f(x) \ge 0\ \forall\ x \in \left[0, \frac{\pi}{2}\right]$

42. Find the greatest rectangle that can be inscribed in a circle $x^2 + y^2 = R^2$

Solution: Area of rectangle $ABCD = (2x_A).(2y_A)$

$f(x_A) = (\text{Area})^2 = 16x^2_A\,(R^2 - x^2_A)$

$$\frac{df(x_A)}{dx_A} = 16\left[2x_A(R^2 - x_A^2) + x_A^2(-2x_A)\right]$$

$$= 16\left[2R^2x_A - 4x_A^3\right]$$

$$\Rightarrow \frac{d^2 f(x_A)}{dx_A^2} = 16[2R^2 - 12x_A^2]$$

for maxima/minima, $\frac{df(x_A)}{dx_A} = 0$

$\Rightarrow x_A = 0$ or $x_A = \frac{R}{\sqrt{2}}$

$$f''\left(\frac{R}{\sqrt{2}}\right) = 16\left[2R^2 - 12.\frac{R^2}{2}\right] = -ve$$

$\therefore\ x_A = \frac{R}{\sqrt{2}}$ is a point of local maxima.

$$y_A = \sqrt{R^2 - x_A^2} = \sqrt{R^2 - \frac{R^2}{2}} = \frac{R}{\sqrt{2}} = x_A$$

$\therefore$ Rectangular with maximum area is a square and area of greatest rectangle (square) $= (2x_A)(2y_A) = 2R^2$

43. Analyze the graph of $f(x) = x + \frac{1}{x}$. Prove that local maxima value is less then local minima value.

Solution: $f'(x) = 1 - \frac{1}{x^2}$ ...(1)

$f''(x) = \frac{2}{x^3}$ ...(2)

For points of local maxima/minima

$f'(x) = 0 \Rightarrow x = \pm 1$

$f''(-1) = -ve$

$\Rightarrow x = -1$ is a point of local maxima and local maximum value is –2.

Also $f''(1) = +ve$

$x = 1$ is a point of local minima and local minimum value is $f(x) = 2$

We further observe that $f(x) = x + \frac{1}{x}$ is discontinuous at $x = 0$

Also, (i) $\lim_{x \to 0^+} f(x) = \infty$ (Asymptotic to $y - a$xis)

(ii) $\lim_{x \to 0^-} f(x) = -\infty$ (Asymptotic to $y - a$xis)

(iii) $\lim_{x \to \infty} f(x) = \infty$ (Asymptotic to $y = x$)

(iv) $\lim_{x \to \infty} f(x) = -\infty$ (Asymptotic to $y = x$)

(v) $f'(x) > 0\ \forall\ |x| > 1$ i.e., $\forall\ x > 1$ and $x < -1$.

$\Rightarrow f(x)$ is increasing $\forall |x| > 1$ otherwise decreasing

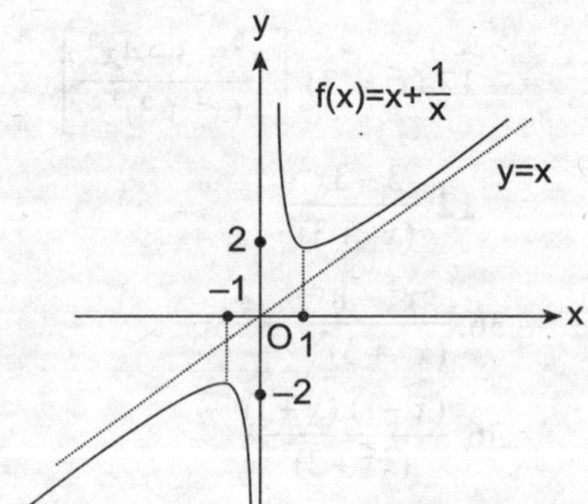

From the above information, we can draw the graph of $f(x)$ as shown in figure.

Note: A line is asymptote to a graph (curve) if curve approaches to that line in the limiting case

44. Find the value of a and b, if $y = a \log x + bx^2 + x$ has local maxima and minima at $x = -1$ and $x = 2$ respectively.

Solution: Since $x = -1$ and $x = 2$ are points of local maxima and minima respectively

So $\frac{dy}{dx}$ should vanish at these two values

$$\frac{dy}{dx} = \frac{a}{x} + 2bx + 1$$

$$\left(\frac{dy}{dx}\right)_{x=-1} = -a - 2b + 1 = 0 \quad \text{...(i)}$$

$$\left(\frac{dy}{dx}\right)_{x=2} = \frac{a}{2} + 4b + 1 = 0 \quad \text{...(ii)}$$

On solving (i) and (ii), we get
$a = 2, b = -1/2$.

45. Prove that the least perimeter of an isosceles triangle in which a circle of radius r can be inscribed is $6r\sqrt{3}$.

Solution: Let α be the semi – vertical angle of the ΔABC

$$\left.\begin{aligned} AE &= r\cot\alpha \\ IA &= r\operatorname{cosec}\alpha \end{aligned}\right\} \quad \ldots\text{(i)}$$

$\therefore\ AD = AI + ID$
$= r \operatorname{cosec}\alpha + r = r(\operatorname{cosec}\alpha + 1)$
$BD = AD\tan\alpha$
$= r\tan\alpha\,(1 + \operatorname{cosec}\alpha)$
$= r\tan\alpha + r\sec\alpha$
Since ΔABC is isosceles, AD bisects BC
$\Rightarrow BD = CD$

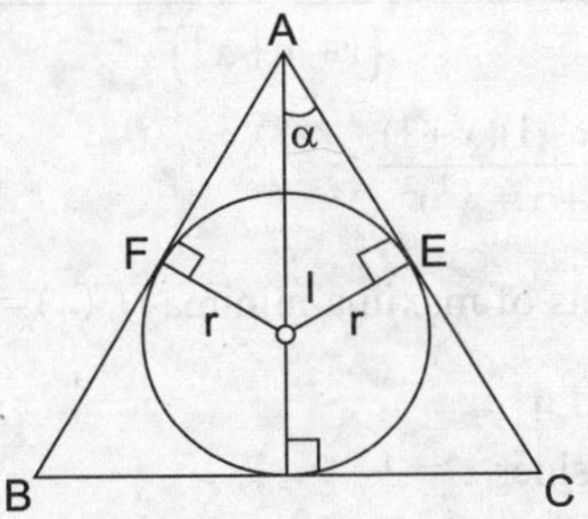

Recall: ***Length of*** **tangents to** a ***circle from outside points are equal in magnitude***

$\therefore\ CD = CE$ and $BD = BF$
Perimeter $= 2(AE + BD + CD) = P$(say)
$\Rightarrow P = (AE + 2BD) \times 2$
Or $P = [r\cot\alpha + 2r(\tan\alpha + \sec\alpha)] \times 2$

$$= 2r\frac{(1+\sin^2\alpha + 2\sin\alpha)}{\sin\alpha\cos\alpha}$$

$$\Rightarrow \frac{dP}{d\alpha} = \frac{2r(1+\sin\alpha)^2(2\sin\alpha - 1)}{(\sin\alpha\cos\alpha)^2}$$

for maxima and minima $\dfrac{dP}{d\alpha} = 0$

$\Rightarrow \sin\alpha = -1$ or $\sin\alpha = 1/2$

$\Rightarrow$ Not possible or $\alpha = \dfrac{\pi}{6}$

To prove that $\alpha = \dfrac{\pi}{6}$ is a point of local minima, we can use the first derivative test or second derivative test. Which one should be prefer? Think, before you proceed further.

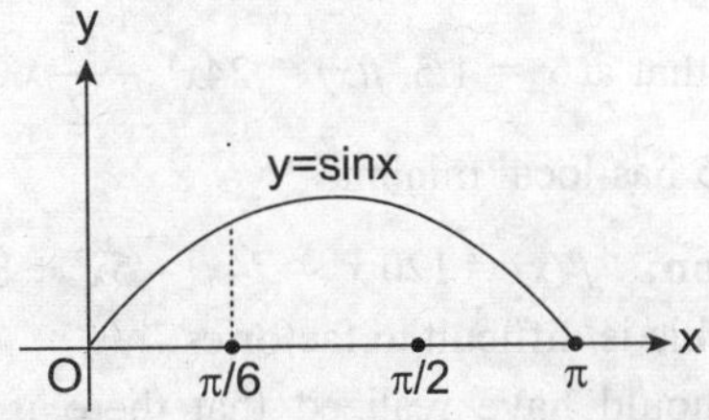

$$P'\left(\frac{\pi}{6} - h\right) = -ve\left(\because \sin\left(\frac{\pi}{6} - h\right) < \frac{1}{2}\right)$$

$$P'\left(\frac{\pi}{6} + h\right) = +ve\left(\because \sin\left(\frac{\pi}{6} + h\right) > \frac{1}{2}\right)$$

$\Rightarrow \alpha = \dfrac{\pi}{6}$ is a point of local minima

$$\Rightarrow P_{\min.} = P\left(\frac{\pi}{6}\right) = \left(\frac{2r\left[1+\sin^2\frac{\pi}{6} + 2\sin\frac{\pi}{6}\right]}{\sin\frac{\pi}{6}\cos\frac{\pi}{6}}\right) = 6\sqrt{3}r.$$

46. Find the maximum surface area of a cylinder that can be inscribed in a given sphere of radius R.

Solution: Let r be the radius and h be the height of cylinder. Consider the right triangle shown in figure $r = R\cos\theta$ and $h = 2R\sin\theta$.
Surface area of the cylinder $S(\theta) = 2\pi r h + 2\pi r^2$

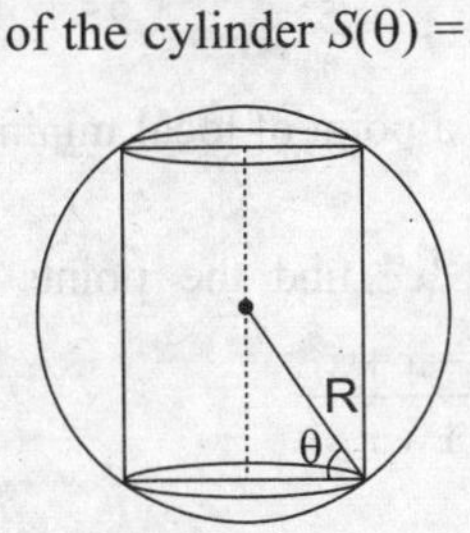

$\Rightarrow S(\theta) = 4\pi R^2\sin\theta\cos\theta + 2\pi R^2\cos^2\theta$
$\Rightarrow S(\theta) = 2\pi R^2\sin 2\theta + 2\pi R^2\cos^2\theta$
$\Rightarrow S'(\theta) = 4\pi R^2\cos 2\theta - 2\pi R^2\sin 2\theta$
Equating $S'(\theta) = 0 \Rightarrow 2\cos 2\theta - \sin 2\theta = 0$
$\Rightarrow \tan 2\theta = 2$

$$\Rightarrow \theta = \frac{1}{2}\tan^{-1}2$$

S ∀ (θ) $= -8\pi R^2\sin^2\theta - 4\pi R^2\cos 2\theta$

$$S''(\theta) = -8\pi R^2\left[\frac{2}{\sqrt{5}}\right] - 4\pi R^2\left[\frac{1}{\sqrt{5}}\right] < 0$$

Hence surface area is maximum for $\theta = \dfrac{1}{2}\tan^{-1}2$

$S_{\max} = 2\pi R^2\sin 2\theta + 2\pi R^2\cos^2\theta$

$$S_{\max} = 2\pi R^2\left[\frac{2}{\sqrt{5}}\right] + 2\pi R^2\left[\frac{\sqrt{5}+1}{2\sqrt{5}}\right] = \pi R^2(1+\sqrt{5})$$

47. Prove that at $x = 1/5$, $f(x) = 24x^5 - \frac{37}{2}x^4 - \frac{5}{3}x^3 + 4x^2 - x + 5$ has local minima

Solution: $f'(x) = 120x^4 - 74x^3 - 5x^2 + 8x - 1$

Well, this is difficult to factories

You should have realized that there is no need to factories, you just need to verify that $f'\left(\frac{1}{5}\right)$ is zero

$$f'\left(\frac{1}{5}\right) = 120.\left(\frac{1}{5^4}\right) - 74\left(\frac{1}{5^3}\right) - 5\left(\frac{1}{5^2}\right) + 8\left(\frac{1}{5}\right) - 1$$

$$= \frac{1}{5^3}(24 - 74 - 25 + 200 - 125) = 0$$

at $x = 1/5$, there could be a local maxima/minima

Think before proceeding further:

Should we use first derivative test or second derivative test

It is difficult to find $f'\left(\frac{1}{5} - h\right)$ or $f'\left(\frac{1}{5} + h\right)$, so we find $f''\left(\frac{1}{5}\right)$.

$\Rightarrow f''(x) = 480x^3 - 222x^2 - 10x + 8$

$$\therefore \quad f''\left(\frac{1}{5}\right) = 480.\frac{1}{5^3} - 222\left(\frac{1}{25}\right) - 2 + 8 = +ve$$

$\therefore \quad x = \frac{1}{5}$ is a point of local minima

48. For all real 'x', find the points of local maxima/minima of $\frac{1 - x + x^2}{1 + x + x^2}$.

Solution:

Method 1: The equation can be rewritten as

$$y = \frac{(1 + x + x^2) - 2x}{1 + x + x^2}$$

Or $y = 1 - \frac{2x}{(1 + x + x^2)}$ Or $y = 1 - \frac{2}{\frac{1}{x} + 1 + x}$

Let $z = \frac{1}{x} + 1 + x$

We have $y = 1 - \frac{2}{z}$

If for $x = x_1$, z has local maxima, then for $x = x_1$, y has local maxima

If for $x = x_2$, z has local minima, then for $x = x_2$ y has local minima

Now we have to simply find maximas and minimas of 'z'

$$\frac{dz}{dx} = -\frac{1}{x^2} + 1$$

$\frac{dz}{dx} = 0$ (for maxima/minima)

$\Rightarrow x^2 = 1$ or $x = \pm 1$ $\qquad \frac{d^2z}{dx^2} = \frac{2}{x^3}$

Now $\left(\frac{d^2z}{dx^2}\right)_{x=1} = 2 > 0$ (minima)

Again $\left(\frac{d^2z}{dx^2}\right)_{x=-1} = -2 < 0$ (maxima)

So $y = \frac{1 - x + x^2}{1 + x + x^2}$ has a minima at $x = 1$ and its corresponding value is $f(1) = 0$ and has a maxima at $x = -1$ and its corresponding value is $f(-1) = 3$

Method 2: $y = \frac{1 - x + x^2}{1 + x + x^2}$ ($f(x)$ say)

$$\frac{dy}{dx} = \frac{(1 + x + x^2)(2x - 1) - (1 - x + x^2)(1 + 2x)}{(1 + x + x^2)^2}$$

$$= \frac{2(x - 1)(x + 1)}{(1 + x + x^2)^2}$$

For points of maxima minima $f'(x) = \frac{dy}{dx} = 0$

$\Rightarrow x = \pm 1$

Consider $x = 1$

Left hand derivative at $x = 1$

$$f'(1 - h) = \frac{2(1 - h - 1)(1 - h + 1)}{(+ve)} = \frac{2(-h)(2 - h)}{(+ve)}$$

$$= \frac{2(-ve)(+ve)}{(+ve)} = -ve$$

Right hand derivative at $x = 1$

$$f'(1 + h) = \frac{2(1 + h - 1)(1 + h + 1)}{(+ve)} = \frac{2(+ve)(+ve)}{(+ve)} = +ve$$

(note) $h \to 0$, $h > 0$)

$\Rightarrow x = 1$ is a point of local minima and its minima value is $f(1) = \frac{1}{3}$

Consider $x = -1$

Left hand derivative at $x = -1$

$$f(-1 - h) = \frac{2(-1 - h - 1)(-1 - h + 1)}{+ve}$$

$$= \frac{2(-2 - h)(-h)}{+ve} = \frac{2(-ve)(-ve)}{(+ve)}$$

$= +ve$ (where $h > 0$, $h \to 0$)

Right hand derivative at $x = -1$

$$f'(-1+h) = \frac{2(-1+h-1)(-1+h+1)}{(+ve)}$$

$$= \frac{2(-2+h)(h)}{(+ve)} = \frac{2(-ve)(+ve)}{(+ve)}$$

$= -ve$

$\Rightarrow$ $x = -1$ is a point of local maxima and its local maximum value is $f(-1) = 3$

Can we say $\frac{1}{3} \le \frac{1-x+x^2}{1+x+x^2} \le 3$

Think before you proceed further:

Method 3: Let $y = \dfrac{1-x+x^2}{1+x+x^2}$

$y + xy + x^2y = 1 - x + x^2$

$\Rightarrow x^2(y-1) + x(y+1) + (y-1) = 0$

Since, x is real, $D \ge 0$

$\Rightarrow (y+1)^2 - 4(y-1)(y-1) \ge 0$

$\Rightarrow (y+1)^2 - (2y-2)^2 \ge 0$

$\Rightarrow (y+1-2y+2)(y+1+2y-2) \ge 0$

$\Rightarrow (3-y)(3y-1) \ge 0$

$\Rightarrow (y-3)\left(y-\frac{1}{3}\right) \le 0$

$\Rightarrow \frac{1}{3} \le y \le 3$

Well let us return to method 2. We have proved that at $x = -1$, we have a point of local maxima and its value is 3 and at $x = 1$, we have a point of local minima and its value is $\frac{1}{3}$. One possible graph of the given function based on this information could be.

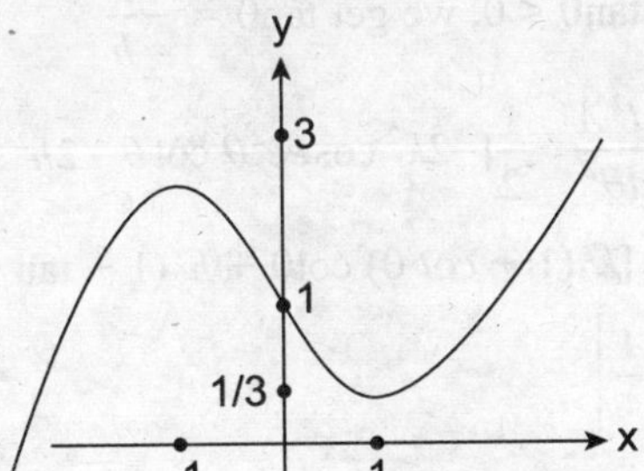

But according to method 3, absolute minimum of the function is $\frac{1}{3}$ and absolute maximum of the function is 3. So, let us analyze the problem further using calculus.

$f(0) = 1$

$$\lim_{x\to\infty} f(x) = \lim_{x\to\infty} \frac{x^2\left(\frac{1}{x^2}-\frac{1}{x}+1\right)}{x^2\left(\frac{1}{x^2}+\frac{1}{x}+1\right)} = \frac{0-0+1}{0+0+1} = 1$$

$$\lim_{x\to-\infty} f(x) = \lim_{x\to-\infty} \frac{x^2\left(\frac{1}{x^2}-\frac{1}{x}+1\right)}{x^2\left(\frac{1}{x^2}+\frac{1}{x}+1\right)} = \frac{0+0+1}{0-0+1} = 1$$

Further we observe that $f'(x) = \dfrac{2(x^2-1)}{(x^2+x+1)^2}$ is positive $\forall\ x \in (-\infty, -1) \cup (1, \infty)$ i.e., in this interval $f(x)$ is increasing and $\forall\ -1 < x < 1$, $f'(x)$ is negative i.e. in this interval, $f(x)$ a decreasing function

Using this information, we can draw the graph of $f(x) = \dfrac{1-x+x^2}{1+x+x^2}$ as follows

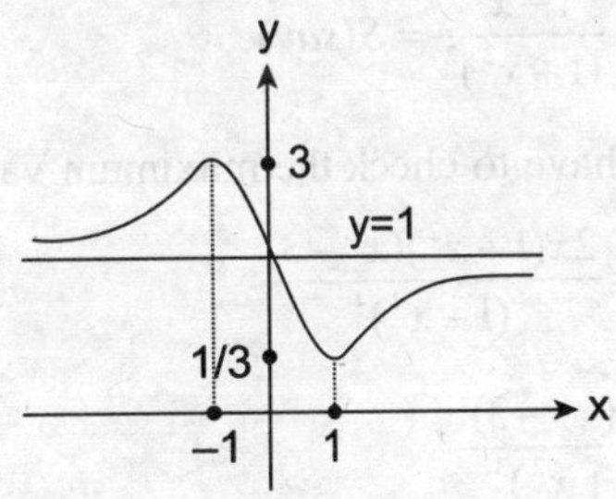

49. Prove that $\dfrac{x}{1+x\tan x}$ is maximum when $x = \cos x$, for $0 \le x \le \pi/2$

Solution: Given $y = \dfrac{x}{1+x\tan x} (= f(x)\,say)$

y can be rewritten as $y = \dfrac{1}{\frac{1}{x} - \tan x} = \dfrac{1}{z}$ where $z = \dfrac{1}{x} + \tan x$

$\Rightarrow$ 'y' is maximum when 'z' is minimum and 'y' is minimum when 'z' is maximum

So, to find maximum of y, we find minimum of z.

$$\frac{dz}{dx} = -\frac{1}{x^2} + \sec^2 x$$

$\dfrac{dz}{dx} = 0$ for points of local maximum/minima

$\Rightarrow x = \pm \cos x$

$\Rightarrow x = \cos x \quad \left(\because x \in \left(0, \frac{\pi}{2}\right)\right)$

Note: In this problem, we are required to find absolute maximum or minimum. So we should not find second derivative. We should find value of the function at the end points as well as at the points, where there is a possibility of local maxima/minima.

$$f(\cos x) = \frac{\cos x}{1 + \cos x \tan(\cos x)} = +ve$$

$(\because x = \cos x \in [0, 1])$

$\left(\because x \in \left(0, \frac{\pi}{2}\right)\right)$ $\quad f(0) = 0 \quad (-)$

$x = \cos x$ is a point of absolute maximum for $f(x)$.

50. Find the co-ordinates of the point on the curve $y = \frac{x}{1+x^2}$, where tangent to the curve has greatest slope?

Solution: It is important to note that it is not the value of 'y' which is maximum rather it is value of $\frac{dy}{dx}$

So, $\frac{dy}{dx} = \frac{1-x^2}{(1+x^2)^2} = S(say)$

Now we have to check the maximum value S.

So, $\frac{dS}{dx} = \frac{2x(1+x^2)(x^2-3)}{(1+x^2)^4}$

$$= \frac{2x(x^2-3)}{(1+x^2)^3}$$

Equation $\frac{dS}{dx} = 0$ for points of local maxima/minima, we get $x = 0$ or $\pm\sqrt{3}$

It can be checked that $\frac{dS}{dx}$ changes sign from (+)ve to (–)ve about $x = 0$, so maxima at $x = 0$

And at $x = \pm\sqrt{3}$ slope changes from (–) ve to (+)ve, so minima at both points.

When $x = 0$, y is equal to 0.

So the co – ordinate at which curve $y = \frac{x}{1+x^2}$ has greatest value of slope of tangent is origin.

51. Let (h, k) be a fixed point, where $h > 0$, $k > 0$. A straight line passing through this point cuts the positive direction of the coordinate axes at the point P and Q. Find the minimum area of the triangle OPQ, O being the origin.

Solution: Equation of any line through the point (h, k) is $y - k = m(x - h)$

For this line to intersect the positive direction of two axes, $m = \tan\theta < 0$.

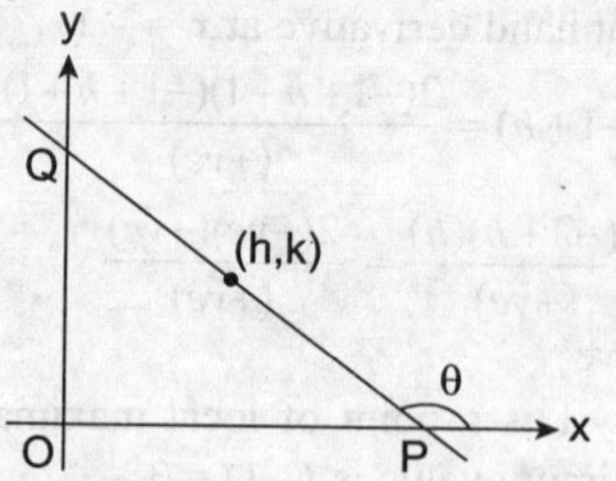

The line (1) meets x-axis in $P\left(h - \frac{k}{m}, 0\right)$ and y-axis in $Q(0, k - mh)$

Let A = Area of triangle OPQ

$$= \frac{1}{2}(OP)(OQ) = \frac{1}{2}\left(h - \frac{k}{m}\right)(k - mh)$$

$$= -\frac{1}{2m}(k - mh)^2$$

$$= -\frac{1}{2\tan\theta}(k - h\tan\theta)^2$$

$$= -\frac{1}{2\tan\theta}[k^2 + h^2\tan^2\theta - 2hk\tan\theta]$$

$$= \frac{1}{2}[2hk - k^2\cot\theta - h^2\tan\theta]$$

$$\frac{dA}{d\theta} = \frac{1}{2}[-k^2(-\operatorname{cosec}^2\theta) - h^2\sec^2\theta]$$

Now,

To obtain minimum value of A, we put $\frac{dA}{d\theta} = 0$,

This implies $k^2 \operatorname{cosec}^2\theta - h^2\sec^2\theta = 0$

$$\frac{k^2}{\sin 2\theta} = \frac{h^2}{\cos^2\theta}$$

$\Rightarrow \tan\theta = \pm k/h$

As $\tan\theta < 0$, we get $\tan\theta = -\frac{k}{h}$

Next, $\frac{d^2A}{d\theta^2} = \frac{1}{2}[-2k^2\operatorname{cosec}^2\theta\cot\theta - 2h^2\sec^2\theta\tan\theta]$

$= -[k^2(1 + \cot^2\theta)\cot\theta + h^2(1 + \tan^2\theta)\tan\theta]$

$$\Rightarrow \left.\frac{d^2A}{d\theta^2}\right]_{\tan\theta = -k/h}$$

$$= -\left[k^2\left(1 + \frac{h^2}{k^2}\right)\left(-\frac{h}{k}\right) + h^2\left(1 + \frac{k^2}{h^2}\right)\left(-\frac{k}{h}\right)\right]$$

$$= (h^2 + k^2)\left(\frac{h}{k} + \frac{k}{h}\right) > 0$$

Thus, A is least when $\tan\theta = -\frac{k}{h}$. Also the least value of A is

$$A_{min} = \frac{1}{2}\left[2hk - k^2\left(-\frac{k}{h}\right) - h^2\left(-\frac{k}{h}\right)\right]$$

$$A_{min} = \frac{1}{2}[2hk + hk + hk] = 2hk$$

Method 2: $\tan\theta = \frac{k}{MP}$

$\Rightarrow k = MP\tan\theta$

$\Rightarrow MP = k\cot\theta$

$$\text{Area} = \frac{1}{2}\times(h + k\cot\theta)(k + h\tan\theta)$$

$$= \frac{1}{2}(2hk + h^2\tan\theta + k^2\cot\theta)$$

$$\frac{dA}{d\theta} = \frac{1}{2}[h^2\sec^2\theta - k^2\operatorname{cosec}^2\theta]$$

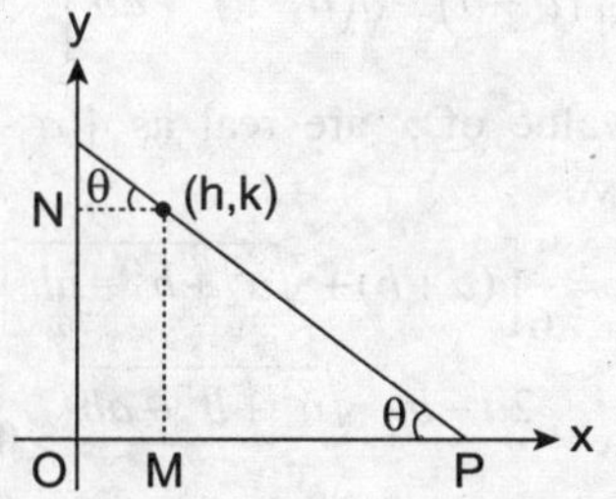

For local maxima/minima $\frac{dA}{d\theta} = 0$

$$\Rightarrow \frac{h^2}{\cos^2\theta} = \frac{k^2}{\sin^2\theta}$$

$$\Rightarrow \tan^2\theta = \left(\frac{k}{h}\right)^2$$

$$\tan\theta = \pm\left(\frac{k}{h}\right)$$

Since, θ is acute and $h > 0$, $k > 0$

$$\Rightarrow \tan\theta = \pm\frac{k}{h}$$

$$\frac{d^2A}{d\theta^2} = \frac{1}{2}\ [h^2(2\sec\theta\tan\theta) + k^2(2\operatorname{cosec}\theta\cot\theta)] >$$

$0\ \forall\ \theta \in \left(0, \frac{\pi}{2}\right)$ (see figure)

$\therefore \tan\theta = \frac{k}{h}$ is point of local minima.

Think before proceeding further:

Use first derivative to prove that $\tan\theta = \frac{k}{h}$ is a point of local minima

$$\frac{dA}{d\theta} = \left[\frac{1}{2}\frac{h^2}{(\sin\theta)^2}\left(\tan\theta + \frac{k}{h}\right)\right]\left(\tan\theta - \frac{k}{h}\right)$$

Let at $\theta = \theta_0$, $\tan\theta_o = \frac{k}{h}$

$$A'(\theta_o - \Delta\theta) = [+\text{ve}]\left(\tan(\theta_0 - \Delta\theta) - \frac{k}{h}\right) = -ve$$

$$\left(\because \tan(\theta_o - \Delta\theta) < \frac{k}{h}\right)$$

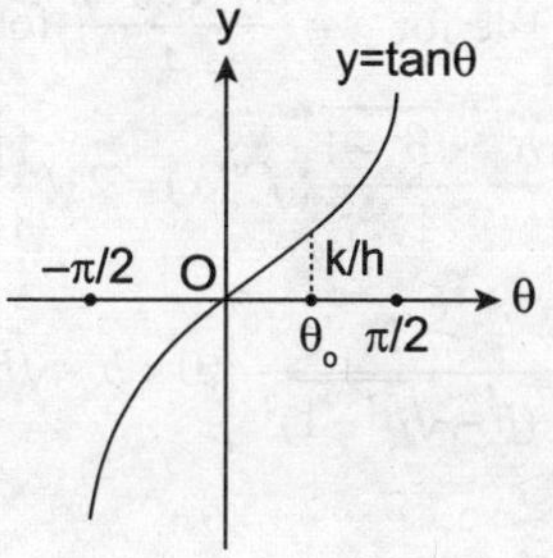

$$A'(\theta_o + \Delta\theta) = [+\text{ve}]\left(\tan(\theta_0 + \Delta\theta) - \frac{k}{h}\right) = +ve$$

$$\left(\because \tan(\theta_o + \Delta\theta) > \frac{k}{h}\right)$$

$$(\text{Area})_{min} = \frac{1}{2}\left(h + \frac{hk}{k}\right)\left(k + \frac{hk}{h}\right)$$

$$= \frac{1}{2}(2h)(2k) = 2hk$$

52. Determine the points of maxima and minima of the function $f(x) = \frac{1}{8}\ln x - bx + x^2$, $x > 0$ where $b \geq 0$ is constant

Solution: Note that $f(x)$ is differentiable for each $x > 0$

Thus, critical points of $f'(x) = 0$ are solutions we have

$$f'(x) = \frac{1}{8x} - b + 2x$$

For critical points, we solve $f'(x) = 0$

Now since equation $f'(x) = 0$ is quadratic in x, so on solving $\frac{1}{8x} - b + 2x = 0$, we get $x = \frac{b \pm \sqrt{b^2 - 1}}{4}$

For x to be real, $b^2 - 1 \geq 0$; $b \leq -1$ or $b \geq 1$

but $b \geq 0$ is given, so $b \geq 1$

$$f''(x) = -\frac{1}{8x^2} + 2$$

At $x = \frac{b + \sqrt{b^2 - 1}}{4}$; $f''(x) = 2 - \frac{1}{8}\left[\frac{+16}{(b + \sqrt{(b^2 - 1)})^2}\right]$

$$= 2\left[1 - \frac{1}{(b + \sqrt{b^2 - 1})^2}\right] \text{ as } b > 1$$

$\Rightarrow b+\sqrt{b^2+1}>1$

$\Rightarrow \left(b+\sqrt{b^2-1}\right)^2>1$

$\dfrac{1}{\left(b+\sqrt{b^2-1}\right)^2}<1$

$f'(x)=$ +ve for $x=\dfrac{b+\sqrt{b^2-1}}{4}$ for $b>1$

At $x=\dfrac{b-\sqrt{b^2-1}}{4}$; $f''(x)=2-\dfrac{1}{8}\left[\dfrac{16}{(b-\sqrt{b^2-1})^2}\right]$

$=2\left[1-\dfrac{1}{(b-\sqrt{b^2-1})^2}\right]$; $0<b-\sqrt{b^2-1}<1$ for $b>1$

$f''(x)=-$ ve

(i) For $b>1$, $f'(x)$ has maxima at $x=\dfrac{b-\sqrt{b^2-1}}{4}$ and minima at $x=\dfrac{b+\sqrt{b^2-1}}{4}$

For $b=1, f'(x)=0,\ f'''(x)=\dfrac{2}{8x^3}=\dfrac{1}{4x^3}$

So $f'''(x)=\dfrac{1}{4(1/4)^3}\neq 0$ for $b=1, x=\dfrac{1}{4}$

$\therefore$ If $b=1$ then function has neither maxima nor minima at any x.

Note: For $b=1$

$f'(x)=\dfrac{1}{8x}+2x-1=\dfrac{(4x-1)^2}{8x}>0\ \forall x>0$

$\therefore$ $f(x)$ is strictly increasing function

53. A rectangular sheet of metal has four equal square portions removed at the corner and the sides are then turned up so as to form an open rectangular box. Show that when the volume contained in the box is maximum, the depth will be $\dfrac{1}{6}\left\{(a+b)-\sqrt{a^2-ab+b^2}\right\}$, Where a, b are the sides of the original rectangle.

Solution: Let x be the length of each side of the squares removed at the corner. Then the dimension of the box are $(a-2x)$, $(b-2x)$ and x, see figure

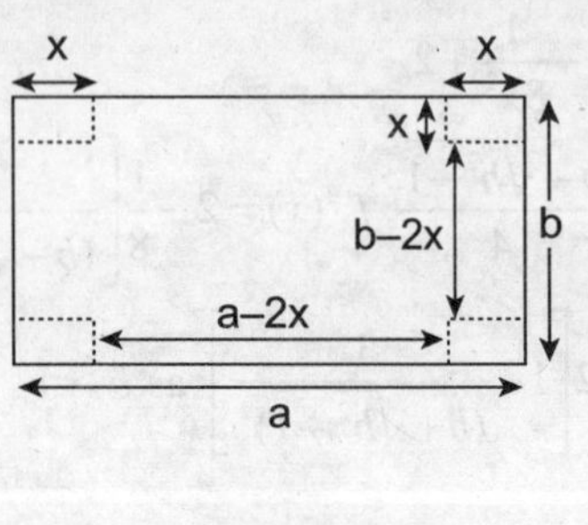

$\therefore$ V be the volume containing in the box, then

$V=(a-2x)(b-2x)x$

$V=4x^3-2x^2(a+b)+abx$ ...(i)

$\therefore \dfrac{dV}{dx}=12x^2-4x(a+b)+ab;$ ...(ii)

$\dfrac{d^2V}{dx^2}=24x-4(a+b)$ ...(iii)

Equation $\dfrac{dV}{dx}$ to zero, we get

$12x^2-4x(a+b)+ab=0$

or $x=\dfrac{4(a+b)\pm\sqrt{16(a+b)^2-48ab}}{24}$

$x=\dfrac{1}{6}\left[(a+b)\pm\sqrt{(a+b)^2-3ab}\right]$

$x=\dfrac{1}{6}\left[(a+b)\pm\sqrt{(a-b)^2+ab}\right]$

The value of x are real as $\{(a-b)^2+ab\}$ is positive

Let $x=\dfrac{1}{6}\left[(a+b)+\sqrt{a^2+b^2-ab}\right]$

$a-2x=\dfrac{2a-b-\sqrt{a^2+b^2-ab}}{3}>0$ ...(iv)

(Should be greater than zero) similarly,

$b-2x=2b-a-\sqrt{a^2+b^2-ab}>0$ ...(v)

Adding (iv) and (v), we get $a+b>2\sqrt{a^2+b^2-ab}$

Squaring and simplifying, we get $(a-b)^2<0$ which is false

$\Rightarrow x=\dfrac{1}{6}\left[(a+b)+\sqrt{a^2+b^2-ab}\right]$ is rejected

Also $\dfrac{d^2V}{dx^2}=24x-4(a+b)$

$=-4\sqrt{a^2+b^2-ab}$ for $x=\dfrac{1}{6}\left[a+b-\sqrt{a^2+b^2-ab}\right]$

$\therefore$ Volume is maximum for this value x, i.e. depth of the box

54. Assuming the petrol burnt (per hour) in driving a motor boat varies as the cube of its velocity, show that most economical speed when going against a current of c km per hour is $\left(\dfrac{3c}{2}\right)$ kms/hour.

Solution: Let the velocity of the motor boat be v km/hour

Then velocity of the boat relative to the current $=(v-c)$ km per hour

Let the total distance to be covered be 'a' k

Also we are given that petrol that burns in covering 'a' kms is given by

$$P = K\frac{a}{v-c}.v^3 \text{ (K is proportional constant)}$$

$$\frac{dP}{dv} = ak\left[\frac{(v-c)^3v^2 - v^3(1)}{(v-c)^2}\right] = \frac{ak(2v^3-3cv^2)}{(v-c)^2} \quad \text{and}$$

$$\frac{d^2p}{dv^2} = \frac{ak}{(v-c)^4}\{(v-c)^2(6v^2-6vc)-(2v^3-3cv^2)2(v-c)\}$$

$$= \left\{\frac{ak}{(v-c)^3}\right\}\left[6v(v-c)^2 - 2v^2(2v-3c)\right]$$

Equating $\frac{dP}{dv}$ to zero, we get $2v^3 - 3cv^2 = 0$

Which gives wither $v = 0$ or $\left(\frac{3}{2}\right)c$

If $v = \frac{3c}{2}, \frac{d^2p}{dv^2}$ = Positive i.e., P is minimum

$\therefore$ Petrol burnt is minimum when $v = \frac{3c}{2}$

i.e. the most economical speed is $\left(\frac{3c}{2}\right)$ km/hour

56. The sum of the surfaces of a cube and a sphere is given; show that when the sum of their volume is least, the diameter of the sphere is equal to the edge of the cube.

Solution: Let x be side of the cube and r be radius of the sphere

Surface Area $= 6x^2 + 4\pi r^2 = k$ (constant) …(1)

Volume $= V = x^3 + \frac{4}{3}\pi r^3$ …..(2)

If we substitute the value of r from the equation (1) to equation (2) proceed further, then the calculations become complicated. Try it. Before proceeding further think, what else can be done?

$\frac{dV}{dx} = 3x^2 + 4\pi r^2\frac{dr}{dx}$ (from (2)) …..(3)

Differentiating (1) with respect to x, we get

$12x + 8\pi r\frac{dr}{dx} = 0 \Rightarrow \frac{dr}{dx} = -\frac{3x}{2\pi r}$

equation (3) becomes, $\frac{dV}{dx} = 3x^2 + 4\pi r^2\left(-\frac{3x}{2\pi r}\right)$

$= 3x(x - 2r)$ …(4)

For local maxima/minima,

$\frac{dV}{dx} = 0 \Rightarrow x = 0 \; or \; x = 2r$

Differentiating (4) w.r.t x we get

$$\frac{d^2V}{dx^2} = 6x - 6r - 6x\frac{dr}{dx}$$

$$= 6x - 6r - 6x\left(-\frac{3x}{2\pi r}\right)$$

$V''(0) = -$ ve

$V''(2r) = 12r\;6r + \frac{18(2r)^2}{2\pi r} = +ve$

$\therefore$ Sum of volume of cube and sphere is least when $x = 2r$.

57. Determine the least value of the function $f(x) = (x + a + b)(x + a - b)(x - a + b)(x - a - b)$, where a and b are real constant

Solution: This problem can be solved easily without using calculus as follows:

$f(x) = (x + (a + b))(x - (a + b))(x + (a - b))(x - (a - b))$

$= (x^2 - (a + b)^2)(x^2 - (a - b)^2)$

$= t^2 - t((a + b)^2 + (a - b)^2) + (a^2 - b^2)^2$ where $t = x^2$

$= t^2 - 2t(a^2 + b^2) + (a^2 - b^2)^2$

$= (t - (a^2 + b^2))^2 - (a^2 + b^2)^2 + (a^2 - b^2)^2$

$= (x^2 - (a^2 + b^2))^2 - 4a^2b^2$

$f_{min} = -4a^2b^2$ when $x^2 = a^2 + b^2$.

$f(x)$ has local minima's at $x = \pm\sqrt{a^2 + b^2}$

Because of symmetry, $f(x)$ should have local maxima at $x = 0$. And its local maxima value is

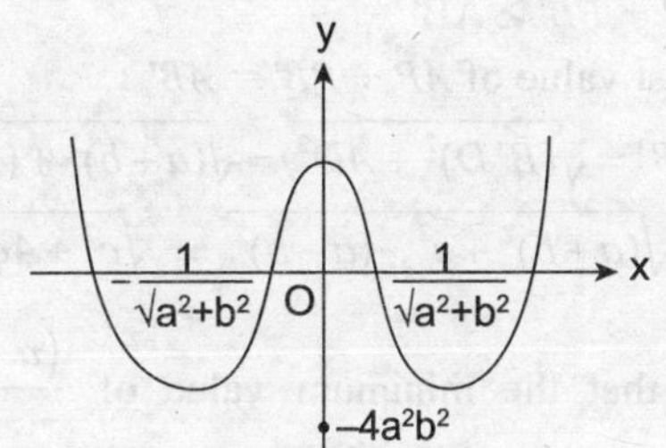

$f(0) = (a + b)(a - b)(b - a)(-a - b)$

$= (a + b)^2(a - b)^2 = (a^2 - b^2)^2$

Method 2: $f(x) = (x^2 - (a + b)^2)(x^2 - (a - b)^2)$

$f'(x) = (x^2 - (a + b)^2).(2x) + (x^2 - (a - b)^2).2x = 4x[x^2 - (a^2 + b^2)]$

For points of local maxima/minima

$f'(x) = 0 \Rightarrow x[x^2 - (a^2 + b^2)] = 0$

$\Rightarrow x = 0$ or $x = \pm\sqrt{a^2 + b^2}$

$f''(x) = 3x^2 - (a^2 + b^2)$

$f''(0) = -(a^2 + b^2) = -ve$

$\Rightarrow$ x = 0 is point of local maxima

$f''(\pm\sqrt{a^2+b^2}) = 2(a^2+b^2) = \pm ve$

$\Rightarrow x = \pm\sqrt{a^2+b^2}$ are points of local minima's.

58. Two towns, located on the same side of a straight river, agree to construct a pumping station and filling plant at the river's edge to be used jointly to supply the towns with water. If the distances of the two towns from the river are 'a' and 'b' and the distances between them is 'c', show that the sum of the lengths of the pipe line joining them to the pumping station is at least as great as $\sqrt{c^2+4ab}$

Solution: Well, this problem can easily be solved using concepts of plain geometry, instead of calculus. We have to minimize $AP + BP$

Let $BM = MB'$ and BB' be perpendicular to LM.

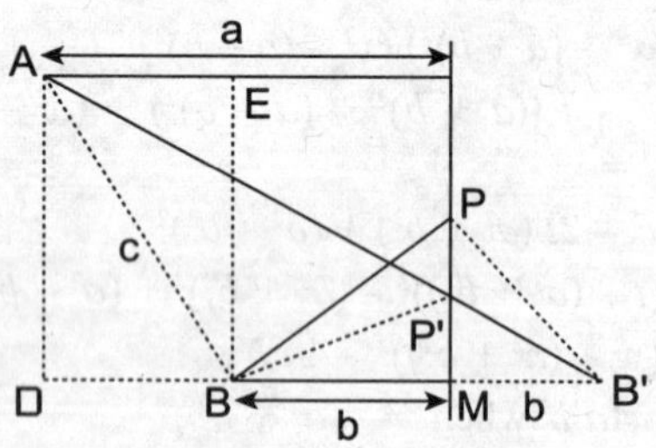

$\therefore$ we have to minimize $AP + PB'$

$\therefore$ ($\because PB = PB'$)

$\because$ Sum of two sides of a triangle $\geq$ third side

$\Rightarrow AP + PB' \geq AB'$

$\Rightarrow$ least value of $AP + PB' = AB'$

$\Rightarrow AB' = \sqrt{(B'D)^2 + AD^2} = \sqrt{(a+b)^2 + (BE)^2}$

$= \sqrt{(a+b)^2 + c^2 - (a-b)^2} = \sqrt{c^2+4ab}$

59. Prove that the minimum value of $\dfrac{(a+x)(b+x)}{c+x}$, $x > -c$ is $\left(\sqrt{a-c}+\sqrt{b-c}\right)^2$, $a > c, b > c$

Solution: There are various ways by which this problem can be solved.

Method 1: $y = \dfrac{(a+x)(b+x)}{c+x}$

Let $c + x = t$

$$y = \frac{[(a-c)+t][(b-c)+t]}{t}$$

$$= t + (a-c) + (b-c) + \frac{(a-c)(b-c)}{t}$$

$$= t + \frac{(a-c)(b-c)}{t} + 2\sqrt{(a-c)(b-c)} + (\sqrt{a-c})^2 + (\sqrt{b-c})^2 - 2\sqrt{(a-c)(b-c)}$$

$$= \left(\sqrt{t} + \sqrt{\frac{(a-c)(b-c)}{t}}\right)^2 + \left(\sqrt{a-c} - \sqrt{b-c}\right)^2$$

$\Rightarrow y_{\min} = \left(\sqrt{a-c} - \sqrt{b-c}\right)^2$

when $\sqrt{t} + \sqrt{\dfrac{(a-c)(b-c)}{t}} = 0$

Well, *I* think we have gone wrong. Can you locate the mistake Think before you proceed further?

$x > -c \Rightarrow x + c > 0$

$\Rightarrow t > 0$

$\Rightarrow$ For no value of t; $\sqrt{t} + \sqrt{\dfrac{(a-c)(b-c)}{t}}$ can be zero

$\therefore$ y can also be written as

$$y = \left(\sqrt{t} - \sqrt{\frac{(a-c)(b-c)}{t}}\right)^2 + \left(\sqrt{a-c} + \sqrt{b-c}\right)^2$$

$\therefore y_{\min} = \left(\sqrt{a-c} + \sqrt{b-c}\right)^2$ when

$\sqrt{t} - \sqrt{\dfrac{(a-c)(b-c)}{t}} = 0$

Method 2: $y = \dfrac{(a+x)(b+x)}{c+x} = \dfrac{ab + (a+b)x + x^2}{c+x}$

$$\frac{dy}{dx} = \frac{(c+x)((a+b)+2x) - (ab+(a+b)x+x^2)}{(c+x)^2}$$

$$= \frac{x^2 + 2cx - ab + bc + ca}{(c+x)^2}$$

For points of local maxima/minima

$f'(x) = 0 \Rightarrow x = \dfrac{-2c \pm 2\sqrt{(a-c)(b-c)}}{2}$

Since $x > -c$

$\Rightarrow x = -c + \sqrt{(a-c)(b-c)}$

$$f'(x) = \frac{(x+c-\sqrt{(a-c)(b-c)})(x+c+\sqrt{(a-c)(b-c)})}{(c+x)^2}$$

$$f'(-c+\sqrt{(a-c)(b-c)} - h) = \frac{(-h)(+ve)}{+ve} = -ve$$

$$f'(-c+\sqrt{(a-c)(b-c)} + h) = \frac{(h)+(+ve)}{(+ve)} = +ve$$

$\therefore x = -c + \sqrt{(a-c)(b-c)}$ is a point of local minima or local minimum value of the function is

$$f\left(-c+\sqrt{(a-c)(b-c)}\right)$$

$$=\frac{\left(a-c+\sqrt{(a-c)(b-c)}\right)\left(b-c+\sqrt{(a-c)(b-c)}\right)}{\sqrt{(a-c)(b-c)}}$$

$$= (a-c) + (b-c) + 2\sqrt{(a-c)(b-c)}$$

$$= \left(\sqrt{a-c}+\sqrt{b-c}\right)^2$$

Note: In this problem, finding second derivative would be more cumbersome.

Method 3: Let $y = \dfrac{(a+x)(b+x)}{c+x}$

$\Rightarrow cy + xy = ab + (a+b)x + x^2$

$\Rightarrow x^2 + (a+b-y)x + (ab-cy) = 0$

Since x is real $\Rightarrow D \geq 0$

$\Rightarrow (a+b-y)^2 - 4(ab-cy) \geq 0$

$\Rightarrow (a+b)^2 + y^2 - 2(a+b)y - 4ab + 4cy \geq 0$

$\Rightarrow y^2 + 2(2c-a-b) + (a-b)^2 \geq 0$

$\Rightarrow y \geq \left(\sqrt{a-c}+\sqrt{b-c}\right)^2 \; (\because x + c > 0)$

60. If $ax^2 + \dfrac{b}{x} > c$ for all x, where $a > 0$ and $b > 0$. Show that $27\,ab^2 \geq 4c^3$

Solution: Well, if you think, you may get the idea that if $ax^2 + \dfrac{b}{x} > c \ni\ni x \in R$ then $\left(ax^2+\dfrac{b}{x}\right)_{\text{minimum}} > c$

Let $f(x) = ax^2 + \dfrac{b}{x}$ $f'(x) = 2ax - \dfrac{b}{x^2}$ $f''(x) = 2a + \dfrac{2b}{x^3}$

for points of maxima/minima $f'(x) = 0$

$\Rightarrow 2ax - \dfrac{b}{x^2} = 0 \Rightarrow x = \left(\dfrac{b}{2a}\right)^{1/3}$

$f''\left(\left(\dfrac{b}{2a}\right)^{1/3}\right) = +ve$

$\therefore \; x = \left(\dfrac{b}{2a}\right)^{1/3}$ is a point of local minima

$\Rightarrow f\left(\left(\dfrac{b}{2a}\right)^{1/3}\right) > c \qquad (\because f(x) > c\, \forall x \in \mathbb{R})$

$27ab^2 > 4c^3$

61. A variable line through the point (a, b) meets the positive x-axis and positive y-axis in the points A and B. Find the minimum perimeter of the triangle OPQ.($a > 0$, $b > 0$).

Solution: $P = OA + OB + AB$

$= (a + b\cot\theta) + (b + a\tan\theta) + \sqrt{(a+b\cot\theta)^2 + (b+a\tan\theta)^2}$

$= a + b + a\tan\theta + b\cot\theta + \sqrt{(a\sec\theta + b\,\mathrm{cosec}\,\theta)^2}$

$= a\left(1+\dfrac{\sin\theta}{\cos\theta}+\dfrac{1}{\cos\theta}\right) + b\left(1+\dfrac{\cos\theta}{\sin\theta}+\dfrac{1}{\sin\theta}\right)$

$= (1 + \sin\theta + \cos\theta)(a\sec\theta + b\,\mathrm{cosec}\,\theta)$

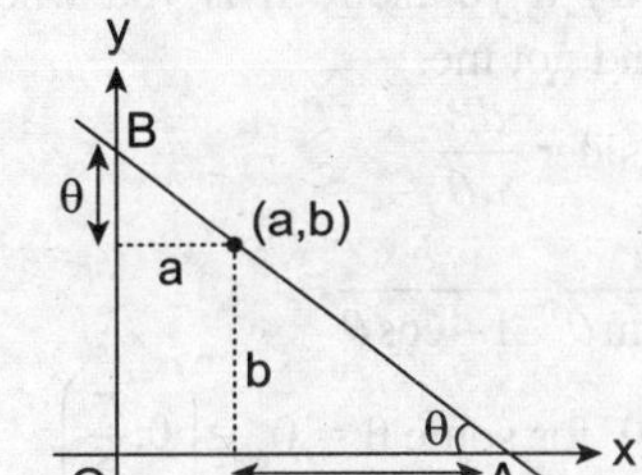

$\dfrac{dp}{d\theta} = a(\sec^2\theta) + b(-\mathrm{cosec}^2\theta) + a\sec\theta\tan\theta - b\,\mathrm{cosec}\,\theta\cot\theta$

$= a\left(\dfrac{1+\sin\theta}{\cos^2\theta}\right) - b\left(\dfrac{1+\cos\theta}{\sin^2\theta}\right)$

For points of maxima/minima $\dfrac{dP}{d\theta} = 0 \Rightarrow \dfrac{a}{b} = \dfrac{1-\sin\theta}{1-\cos\theta}$

$\Rightarrow \dfrac{a}{b} = \dfrac{\left(\sin\frac{\theta}{2}-\cos\frac{\theta}{2}\right)^2}{2\sin^2\frac{\theta}{2}} = \dfrac{1}{2}\left(1-\cot\dfrac{\theta}{2}\right)^2$

$1-\cot\dfrac{\theta}{2} = \pm\sqrt{\dfrac{2a}{b}} \quad \cot\dfrac{\theta}{2} = 1 \mp \sqrt{\dfrac{2a}{b}}$

Well, do you think that we are doing right? Think again before *I* correct the mistake that is commonly committed by the students.

Again consider, $\dfrac{a}{b} = \dfrac{\left(\sin\frac{\theta}{2}-\cos\frac{\theta}{2}\right)^2}{2\sin^2\frac{\theta}{2}}$

$\Rightarrow \pm\sqrt{\dfrac{a}{b}} = \dfrac{\cos\frac{\theta}{2}-\sin\frac{\theta}{2}}{\sqrt{2}\sin\left(\frac{\theta}{2}\right)} \qquad \text{...(i)}$

$\because \; \theta \in \left(0, \dfrac{\pi}{2}\right)$ for ΔOPQ to be formed.

$\Rightarrow \dfrac{\theta}{2} \in \left(0, \dfrac{\pi}{4}\right) \Rightarrow \cos\dfrac{\theta}{2} > \sin\dfrac{\theta}{2}$

$\Rightarrow$ Right Hand Side of (i) is positive

$$\Rightarrow \frac{\cos\frac{\theta}{2}-\sin\frac{\theta}{2}}{\sqrt{2}\sin\frac{\theta}{2}}=+,\sqrt{\frac{a}{b}}$$

$$\Rightarrow \cot\frac{\theta}{2}-1=\sqrt{\frac{2a}{b}} \Rightarrow \cot\left(\frac{\theta}{2}\right)=1+\sqrt{\frac{2a}{b}}$$

Note: Well, now the problem is how to prove that it is a point of local minima and not local maxima. Why don't you try it yourself? It is you who has to clear IIT–JEE and not me.

Let us consider $\frac{dP}{d\theta}$

$$\frac{dP}{d\theta}=\frac{a}{1-\sin\theta}-\frac{b}{1-\cos\theta}.$$

Let $\frac{dP}{d\theta}=0$ for some $\theta=\theta_0\in\left(0,\frac{\pi}{2}\right)$

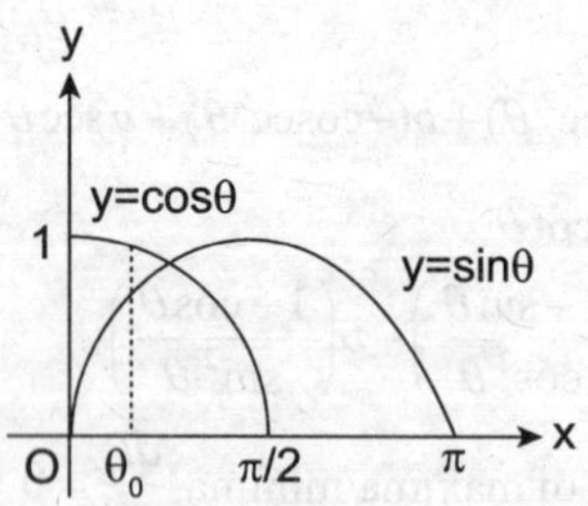

At $\theta=\theta_o-h$, $\sin\theta<\sin\theta_0$; $\cos\theta>\cos\theta_0$

$$\Rightarrow \frac{a}{1-\sin\theta}<\frac{a}{1-\sin\theta_o} \text{ and } \frac{b}{1-\cos\theta}>\frac{b}{1-\cos\theta_o}$$

$\Rightarrow P'(\theta_o-h)=$ –ve, Similarly, $P'(\theta_0+h)=$ +ve

$\therefore$ $\theta-\theta_0$ can only be a point of local minim and minimum perimeter is given by

$$P=(1+\sin\theta\cos\theta)\left(\frac{a}{\cos\theta}+\frac{b}{\sin\theta}\right)$$

$$=\left(2\cos^2\frac{\theta}{2}+2\sin\frac{\theta}{2}\cos\frac{\theta}{2}\right)\left(\frac{a}{2\cos^2\frac{\theta}{2}-1}+\frac{b}{2\sin\frac{\theta}{2}\cos\frac{\theta}{2}}\right).$$

Since, $\cot\frac{\theta}{2}=\frac{\sqrt{b}+\sqrt{2a}}{\sqrt{b}}$

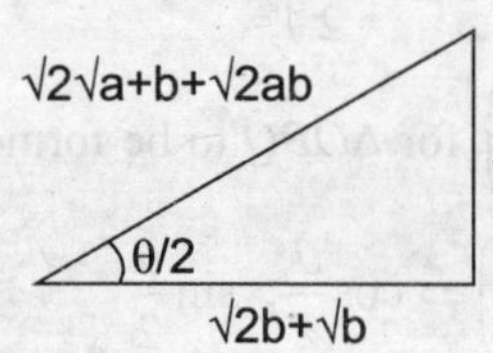

$$\Rightarrow P=2\cos\frac{\theta}{2}\left(\cos\frac{\theta}{2}+\sin\frac{\theta}{2}\right)\left(\frac{a}{2\cos^2\frac{\theta}{2}-1}+\frac{b}{2\cos\frac{\theta}{2}\sin\frac{\theta}{2}}\right)$$

$$=2\left(\frac{a+b+\frac{3}{2}\sqrt{2ab}}{a+b+\sqrt{2ab}}\right)\times\frac{\left(a+b+\sqrt{2ab}\right)^2}{\left(a+b+\frac{3}{2}\sqrt{2ab}\right)}$$

$$=2\left(a+b+\sqrt{2ab}\right)$$

$y=a^4\sec^2x+b^4\operatorname{cosec}^2x$

$\Rightarrow y'=a^4\times 2\sec^2x\tan x+b^4\times 2\operatorname{cosec}x(-\operatorname{cosec}x\cot x)$

Now for maxima/minima; we should have $y'=0$

$\Rightarrow a^4\sec^2x\tan x=b^4\operatorname{cosec}^2x\cot x$

$$\Rightarrow a^4\frac{\sin x}{\cos^3x}=b^4\frac{\cos x}{\sin^3x}$$

$$\Rightarrow \tan x^4 x=\frac{b^4}{a^4}\Rightarrow \tan^2x=\frac{b^2}{a^2}$$

$$\Rightarrow \sec^2x=\frac{a^2+b^2}{a^2} \;\&\; \operatorname{cosec}^2x=\frac{a^2+b^2}{b^2}$$

Now $y''=2a^4\times 2\sec x(\sec x\tan x)\tan x+2a^4\times 2\sec^2x(\sec^2x)$

$-2b^4\times 2\operatorname{cosec}x(-\operatorname{cosec}x\cot x)\cot x$

$-2b^4\times 2\operatorname{cosec}^2x(-\operatorname{cosec}^2x)$

$=4[a^4(\sec^2x(\sec^2x+\tan^2x))+b^4(\operatorname{cosec}^2x(\operatorname{cosec}^2x+\cot^2x)]>0\ \forall\ \tan^2x=b^2/a^2$

$\Rightarrow y$ has a minima when $\tan^2x=b^2/a^2$

$$\text{Now } y_{\min}=a^4\left(\frac{a^2+b^2}{a^2}\right)+b^4\left(\frac{a^2+b^2}{b^2}\right)$$

$$=(a^2+b^2)^2$$

62. Determine the points of maxima and minima of the function $f(x)=\frac{1}{8}\ell nx-bx+x^2, x>0$, where $b\ge 0$ is a constant.

Solution: $f(x)=\frac{1}{8}\ell nx-bx+x^2, x>0, b\ge 0$

$$f'(x)=\frac{1}{8x}-b+2x \quad\quad .....(1)$$

$f'(x)=0\Rightarrow 16x^2-8bx+1=0$ (for max.or min)

$$\therefore\quad x=\frac{1}{4}\left[b\pm\sqrt{b^2-1}\right] \quad\quad ...(2)$$

Above will give real values of x if $b^2-1\ge 0$ i.e., $b\ge 1$ or $b\le -1$. But b is given to be +ve. Hence we choose $b\ge 1$

If $b=1$ then $x=\frac{1}{4}$; If $b>1$ then $x=\frac{1}{4}\left[b\pm\sqrt{b^2-1}\right]$

$$f''(x)=-\frac{1}{8x^2}+2=\frac{16x^2-1}{8x^2}$$

Its sign will depend on N^r $16x^2-1$ as $8x^2$ is +ve.

We shall consider its sign for $x=\frac{1}{4}$ and $x=\frac{1}{4}\left[b\pm\sqrt{b^2-1}\right]$

Note this step:

$f''(x)=0$ at $x=1/4$

$\therefore$ Neither max. nor min. as $f''(x)=0$

N^r of $f''(x)=16x^2-1=\left[b+\sqrt{b^2+1}\right]^2-1$

$=$ +ve for $b>1$

$\therefore$ minima

or N^r of $f''(x)=\left[b-\sqrt{b^2-1}\right]^2-1=$ –ve for $b>1$

$\therefore$ maxima

63. Suppose $p(x)=a_0+a_1x+a_2x^2\ldots.a_nx^n$. If $|p(x)|\le|e^{x-1}-1|$ for all $x\ge0$, prove that $|a_1+2a_2+\ldots.na_n|\le1$

Solution: Given that

$p(x)=a_0+a_1x+a_2x^2+\ldots..+a_nx^n$ ...(i)

and $|p(x)|\le|e^{x-1}-1|,\ \forall\ x\ge0$ ...(ii)

To prove that $|a_1+2a_2+\ldots.+na_n|\le1$

It can be clearly seen that in order to prove the result it is sufficient to prove that $|p'(1)|\le1$

We know that,

$$|p'(1)|=\lim_{h\to0}\left|\frac{p(1+h)-p(1)}{h}\right|\le\lim_{h\to0}\frac{|p(1+h)|+|p(1)|}{|h|}$$

[Using equation (2) for $x=1$]

But $|p(1)\le|e^0-1|$

[Using equation (2) for $x=1$]

$\Rightarrow$ $|p(1)|\le0$

But being absolute value, $|p(1)|\ge0$

Thus we must have $|p(1)|=0$

Also $|p(1+h)|\le|e^h-1|$

(Using equation (2) for $x=1+h$)

Thus $|p'(1)|\le\lim_{h\to0}\frac{|e^h-1|}{|h|}=1$

or $|p'(1)|\le1$

$\Rightarrow$ $|a_1+2a_2+\ldots+na^n|\le1$

64. Let $-1\le p\le1$. Show that the equation $4x^3-3x-p=0$ has a unique root in the interval [1/2,1] and identify it.

Solution: Given that $-1\le p\le1$

Consider $f(x)=4x^3-3x-p=0$

Now, $f(1/2)=\frac{1}{2}-\frac{3}{2}-p=-1-p\le0$ as $(-1\le p)$

Also $f(1)=4-3-p=1-p\ge0$ as $(p\le1)$

$\therefore$ $f(x)$ has at least one real root between [1/2,1]

Also $f'(x)=12x^2-3>0$ on [1/2,1]

$\Rightarrow$ f is increasing on [1/2,1]

$\Rightarrow$ f has only one real root between [1/2,1]

To find the root, we observe $f(x)$ contains $4x^3-3x$ which is multiple angle formula of $\cos3\theta$ if we put $x=\cos\theta$

$\therefore$ Let req. root be $\cos\theta$ then,

$4\cos^3\theta-3\cos\theta-p=0$

$\Rightarrow$ $\cos3\theta=p$

$\Rightarrow$ $3\theta=\cos^{-1}p$

$\Rightarrow$ $\theta=\frac{1}{3}\cos^{-1}(p)$

$\therefore$ Root is $\cos\left(\frac{1}{3}\cos^{-1}(p)\right)$

65. Using Rolle's theorem, prove that there is at least one root in $(45^{1/100},46)$ of the polynomial $p(x)=51x^{101}-2323(x)^{100}-45x+1035$

Solution: We are given

$P(x)=51x^{101}-2323x^{100}-45x+1035$

To show that at least one root of $P(x)$ lies in $(45^{1/100},46)$, using Rolle's theorem, we consider anti – derivative of $P(x)$

i.e., $F(x)=\frac{x^{102}}{2}-\frac{2323x^{101}}{101}-\frac{45x^2}{2}+1035x$

Then being a polynomial function $F(x)$ is continuous and differentiable

Now, $F(45^{1/100})=\frac{(45)^{\frac{102}{100}}}{2}-\frac{2323(45)^{\frac{101}{100}}}{101}-\frac{45.(45)^{\frac{2}{100}}}{2}+1035(45)^{\frac{1}{100}}$

$=\frac{45}{2}(45)^{\frac{2}{100}}-23\times45(45)^{\frac{1}{100}}-\frac{45.(45)^{\frac{2}{100}}}{2}+1035(45)^{\frac{1}{100}}=0$

And

$$F(46)=\frac{(46)^{102}}{2}-\frac{2323(46)^{101}}{101}-\frac{45(46)^2}{2}+1035(46)$$

$= 23(46)^{101} - 23\ (46)^{101} - 23 \times 45 \times 46 + 1035 \times 46 = 0$

$\therefore\ F'\left(45^{\frac{1}{100}}\right) = F(46) = 0$

$\therefore$ Rolle's theorem is applicable

Hence, there must exist at least one root of $F'(x) = 0$

i.e., $P(x)$ = in the interval $\left(45^{\frac{1}{100}}, 46\right)$

66. If $|f(x_1) - f(x_2)| < (x_1 - x_2)^2$, for all $x_1, x_2 \in R$. Find the equation of tangent to the curve $y = f(x)$ at the point (1,2)

Solution: Given that $|f(x_1) - f(x_2)| < (x_1 - x_2)^2$, $x_1, x_2 \in R$

Let $x_1 = x + h$ and $x_2 = x$ then we get

$|f(x + h) - f(x)| < h^2$

$\Rightarrow |f(x + h) - f(x)| < |h|^2$

$\Rightarrow \left|\frac{f(x+h)-f(x)}{h}\right| < |h|$

Taking limit as $h \to 0$ on both sides, we get

$\lim_{h\to 0}\left|\frac{f(x+h)-f(x)}{h}\right| < \delta$ (a small + ve number)

$\Rightarrow |f'(x)| < \delta \qquad \Rightarrow f'(x) = 0$

$\Rightarrow f(x)$ is a constant function. Let $f(x) = k$ i.e., $y = k$

As $f(x)$ passes through $(1, 2) \Rightarrow y = 2$

$\therefore$ Equation of tangent at (1, 2) is,

$y - 2 = 0\ (x - 1)$ i.e., $y = 2$

67. For a twice differentiable function $f(x)$, $g(x)$ is defined as $g(x) = [(f'(x)^2] + (f''(x) \times f(x))$ on $[a, e]$.

If for $a < b < c < d < e$, $f(a) = 0$, $f(b) = 2$, $f(x) = -1$, $f(d) = 2$, $f(e) = 0$ then find the minimum number of zeros of $g(x)$.

Solution: $g(x) = (f'(x))^2 + f''(x)f(x) = \frac{d}{dx} f(x)\,f'(x))$

Let $h(x) = f(x)\,f'(x)$

Then $f(x) = 0$ has four roots namely a, α, β, e

Where $b < \alpha < c$ and $c < \beta < d$.

And $f'(x) = 0$ at three point k_1, k_2, k_3

Where $a < k_1 < \alpha, \alpha < k_2 < \beta, \beta < k_3 < e$

[$\because$ Between any two roots of a polynomial function $f(x) = 0$ there lies atleast one root of $f'(x) = 0$]

$\therefore$ There are atleast 7 roots $f(x).f'(x) = 0$

$\Rightarrow$ There are atleast 6 roots of $\frac{d}{dx}(f(x)f'(x)) = 0$

i.e., of $g(x) = 0$.

68. Let f be a function defined on R (the set of all real numbers) such $f'(x) = 2010\ (x - 2009)\ (x - 2010)^2\ (x - 2011)^3\ (x - 2012)^4$ for all $x \in R$. If g is a function defined on R with values in the interval $(0, \infty)$ such that $f(x)$ ln $(g(x))$, for all $x \in R$ then the number of points in R at which g has a local maximum is

Solution: We have, $F'(x) = 2010\ (x - 2009)\ (x - 2010)^2\ (x - 2011)^3\ (x - 2012)^4$

As $f(x) = \ln g(x)$

$\Rightarrow g(x) = e^{f(x)}$

$\Rightarrow g'(x) = e^{f(x)}\cdot f'(x)$

For max/min, $g'(x) = 0$

$\Rightarrow f'(x) = 0$

Out of two points one should be a point of maxima and other that of minima

$\therefore$ There is only one point of local maxima

69. For all $x \in [0, 1]$, let second derivative $f''(x)$ of a function $f(x)$ exists for and satisfy $|f''(x)| \le 1$. If $f(0) = f(1)$, then show that $|f'(x)| < 1$ for all $x \in [0, 1]$.

Solution: As $f(0) = f(1)$, by the Roll's theorem there exists $\alpha \in (0,1)$ such that $f'(\alpha) = 0$

Let $x \in [0, 1]$ and $x \neq \alpha$. Applying Lagrange's mean value theorem to $[x, \alpha]$ if $0 \le x < \alpha$ or $[\alpha, x]$ if $\alpha < x \le 1$, we get there exists β lying between α and x

such that $\frac{f'(x) - f'(\alpha)}{x - \alpha} = f''(\beta)$

$\Rightarrow f'(x) = (x - \alpha)\, f''(\beta) \qquad [\because f'(\alpha) = 0]$

$\Rightarrow |f'(x)| = |x - \alpha|\ |f''(\beta)| \le |x - \alpha|\ (1) < 1$

$[\because x, \alpha \in [0, 1], x \neq \alpha]$

But $|f'(\alpha)| = 0$

Thus, $|f'(x)| < 1\ \forall\ x \in [0, 1]$

70. Show that the function $f(x) = \log(1 + x) - \frac{2}{2+x}$ is an increasing function

Solution: We have $f(x) = \log(1 + x) - \frac{2}{2+x}$ whose domain is $(-1, \infty)$

Now $f'(x) = \frac{1}{1+x} - \frac{2(2+x) - 2x.1}{(2+x)^2}$

$= \frac{1}{1+x} - \frac{x^2}{(2+x)^2} = \frac{(2+x)^2 - 4(1+x)}{(1+x)(2+x)^2}$

$= \frac{4 + 4x + x^2 - 4 - 4x}{(1+x)(2+x)^2} = \frac{x^2}{(1+x)(2+x)^2}$

We observe that $f'(x) > 0$ for all $x > -1$ except at $x = 0$ where its value is zero.

Hence, $f(x)$ is an increasing function in $[-1, \infty)$.

Since, $f(x)$ is increasing throughout its domain, so its is an increasing function.

71. Show that $f(x) = \log \sin x$ is increasing in $\left(0, \frac{\pi}{2}\right)$ and decreasing in $\left(\frac{\pi}{2}, \pi\right)$

Solution: We have $f(x) = \log \sin x$

$\therefore\ f'(x) = \frac{1}{\sin x} \cos x = \cot x$

When $x \in \left(0, \frac{\pi}{2}\right)$ i.e., when $0 < x < \frac{\pi}{2}$, we have $\cot x > 0$

Thus, $f'(x) > 0$ for all x in $\left(0, \frac{\pi}{2}\right)$ and so $f(x)$ is increasing in $\left(0, \frac{\pi}{2}\right)$.

Again when $x \in \left(\frac{\pi}{2}, \pi\right)$ i.e., when $\frac{\pi}{2} < x < \pi$, we have $\cot x < 0$

Thus $f(x) < 0$ for all x in $\left(\frac{\pi}{2}, \pi\right)$ and so $f(x)$ is decreasing in. $\left(\frac{\pi}{2}, \pi\right)$

72. Let $f(x) =$

$$\frac{2}{\sqrt{3}} \tan^{-1}\left(\frac{2x+1}{\sqrt{3}}\right) - \log(x^2 + x + 1) + (b^2 - 5b + 3)x + C$$

If $f(x)$ is a decreasing function of x for all $x \in R$, find permissible values of parameter b.

Solution: $f'(x) = \frac{2}{\sqrt{3}}\left\{\frac{1}{1 + \left((2x+1)/\sqrt{3}\right)^2}\right\}$

$$\left(\frac{2}{\sqrt{3}}\right) - \frac{(2x-1)}{x^2+x+1} + (b^2 - 5b + 3)$$

$$= \frac{4}{3}\left(\frac{3}{4x^2+4x+4}\right) - \frac{(2x-1)}{x^2+x+1} + (b^2 - 5b + 3)$$

$$= \frac{-2x}{x^2+x+1} + (b^2 - 5b + 3)$$

$f'(x) < 0$ for all $x \in \mathbb{R}$

$$\Rightarrow b^2 - 5b + 3 < \frac{2x}{x^2+x+1}$$

Let $\frac{2x}{x^2+x+1} = y$

$\Rightarrow yx^2 + (y-2)x + y = 0$

$\Rightarrow (y-2)^2 - 4y^2 \geq 0 \quad (\because\ x \in \mathbb{R})$

$\Rightarrow (3y-2)(y+2) \leq 0$

$\Rightarrow -2 \leq y \leq 2/3$

$\Rightarrow \left.\frac{2x}{x^2+x+1}\right]_{\min} = -2$

$\therefore\ b^2 - 5b + 3 < -2$

$\Rightarrow b^2 - 5b + 5 < 0$

$\Rightarrow b \in \left[\frac{5-\sqrt{5}}{2}, \frac{5+\sqrt{5}}{2}\right]$

73. If $ax + \left(\frac{b}{x}\right) \geq c$ for all positive values of x, where a, b, c are positive constants, show that $ab \geq \left(\frac{\quad}{\quad}\right)$

Solution: Let $y = f(x) = ax + \frac{b}{x} - c$,

Differentiating w.r.t., $x\ \frac{dy}{dx} = a - \frac{b}{x^2}$

If $\frac{dy}{dx} \geq 0$ i.e., $a \geq \frac{b}{x^2}$ or $x^2 \geq \frac{b}{a}$ or $x \geq \sqrt{\left(\frac{b}{a}\right)}$ or x is positive since a and b both are positive; then the given function increases.

Thus the function $f(x)$ is strictly increasing for $x > \sqrt{\left(\frac{b}{a}\right)}$

Thus $y = f(x) \geq 0$ for all $x \geq \sqrt{\left(\frac{b}{a}\right)}$

$\Rightarrow ax + \frac{b}{x} - c \geq 0$ for $x = \sqrt{\left(\frac{b}{a}\right)}$

$\Rightarrow ax + \frac{b}{x} \geq c$ i.e., $a^2x^2 + + 2ab \geq c^2$ for $x^2 = \sqrt{\left(\frac{b}{a}\right)}$

i.e., $x^2 + \frac{b}{x} - \frac{b^2}{\left(\frac{b}{a}\right)} - ab \geq c^2$ i.e., $4ab \geq c^2$

74. Find the value of a in order that $f(x) = \sqrt{3} \sin x - \cos x - 2ax + b$ decreases for all real values of x

Solution: Let $f(x) = \sqrt{3} \sin x - \cos x - 2ax + b$

$\Rightarrow f(x) = 2\left(\frac{\sqrt{3}}{2} \sin x - \frac{1}{2} \cos x\right) - 2ax + b$

$\Rightarrow f(x) = 2\left(\cos\frac{\pi}{6}\sin x \frac{\pi}{6}\cos x\right) - 2ax + b$

$\Rightarrow f(x) = 2\sin\left(x - \frac{\pi}{6}\right) - 2ax + b$

$\Rightarrow f(x) = 2\left[\sin\left(x - \frac{\pi}{6}\right) - ax\right] + b$

$\Rightarrow \sin\left(x - \frac{\pi}{6}\right) < ax$ for $f(x)$ to be decreasing.

Therefore, it gives $a \geq 1$.

75. Find the set of all values of a for which the function $f(x) = \left(\frac{\sqrt{a+4}}{1-a} - 1\right)x^5 - 3x + \log 5$ decreases for all real x.

Solution: $f'(x) = \left(\frac{\sqrt{a+4}}{1-a} - 1\right)5x^4 - 3$; For $f(x)$ to be decreasing x, we must have $f'(x) < 0 \; \forall \; x$

$\Rightarrow \left(\frac{\sqrt{a+4}}{1-a} - 1\right)x^4 < \frac{3}{5}$ ∀ real values of x. This is possible only if $\frac{\sqrt{a+4}}{1-a} - 1 \leq 0$

This inequality is always true if $a > 1$ ....(i)

i..e $a \in (1, \infty)$.

We must have $a \geq -4$ ...(ii)

for $\sqrt{a+4}$ to be real.

Therefore we have $\frac{\sqrt{a+4}}{1-a} \leq 1$

$\Rightarrow \sqrt{a+4} \leq 1 - a$

$\Rightarrow a + 4 \leq 1 + a^2 - 2a$

$\Rightarrow a \leq \frac{3-\sqrt{21}}{2}$ ...(iii)

So combining (i) and (ii) we get

$\Rightarrow a \in \left[-4, \frac{3-\sqrt{21}}{2}\right] \cup (1, \infty)$ ..(iv)

then concluding (i) and (iv)

76. Find the values of x for which $f(x) + g(x)$ is strictly increasing/decreasing for $0 < x < 1$ where $f(x) = \frac{x^2}{2 - 2\cos x}$ & $g(x) = \frac{x^2}{6x - 6\sin x}$

Solution: $f'(x) = \frac{1}{2}\left[\frac{(1-\cos x)2x - x^2 \sin x}{(1-\cos x)^2}\right]$

Now consider the numerator as

$p(x) = 2(1 - \cos x) - x \sin x$

$= 4\sin^2\frac{x}{2} - 2x\sin\frac{x}{2}\cos\frac{x}{2}$

$= 2x\sin\frac{x}{2}\cos\frac{x}{2}\left[\frac{\tan\frac{x}{2}}{\frac{x}{2}} - 1\right] > 0$

$\Rightarrow f'(x) > 0$

$\Rightarrow f$ is strictly increasing

Now $g'(x) = \frac{1}{6}\left[\frac{(x - \sin x)2x - x^2(1 - \cos x)}{(x - \sin x)^2}\right]$

Again, consider the numerator as

$q(x) = x - 2\sin x + \cos x$

$= 2x\cos^2\frac{x}{2} - 4\sin\frac{x}{2}\cos\frac{x}{2}$

$= 2x\cos^2\frac{x}{2}\left[1 - \frac{\tan\frac{x}{2}}{\frac{x}{2}}\right] < 0$

$\Rightarrow g'(x) < 0 \Rightarrow g$ is strictly decreasing

Now $f'(x) + g'(x)$

$= 2x\left(1 - \frac{\tan x/2}{x/2}\right) \times \cos x/2 \times \left(\cos\frac{x}{2} - \sin\frac{x}{2}\right)$

$x > 0 \; \forall \; x \in (0, 1)$

and $\tan x > x \; \forall \; x \in (0, \pi/2)$

For $x \in (0, 1)$; $x/2 \in (0, 1/2)$

$\Rightarrow \tan x/2 > x/2$

$\Rightarrow \frac{\tan x/2}{x/2} > 1$

$\Rightarrow 1 - \frac{\tan x/2}{x/2} < 0$ ...(2)

Now, for $x \in (0, \pi/2)$; $\cos x/2 > \sin x/2$

$\Rightarrow$ for $x \in (0, 1)$; $\cos x/2 > \sin x/2$

Now; $f'(x) + g'(x) < 0 \; \forall \; x \in (0, 1)$

And hence $f(x) + g(x)$ is strictly decreeing in (0, 1)

77. Let $f(x) = 1 - x - 4x^3$; find all real values of x satisfying the inequality $1 - f(x) - 4(f(x))^3 > f(1 - 3x)$

Solution: $f(x) = 1 - x - 4x^3$

$\Rightarrow f(f(x)) = 1 - f(x) - 4(f(x))^3$

Also $f'(x) = -1 - 12x^2 < 0$

$\therefore$ $f(x)$ is strictly decreasing for $x \in R$

$\therefore$ $(f(x)) > f(1.3x)$

$\therefore$ $f(x) < 1 - 3x$ ($\because f(x)$ is a decreasing function)

$\Rightarrow 1 - x - 4x^3 < 1 - 3x$

$\Rightarrow 2x - 4x^3 < 0$

$\Rightarrow 2x(1 - 2x^2) < 0$

$\Rightarrow x(2x^2 - 1) > 0$

$$\Rightarrow x\left(x-\frac{1}{\sqrt{2}}\right)\left(x+\frac{1}{\sqrt{2}}\right)>0$$

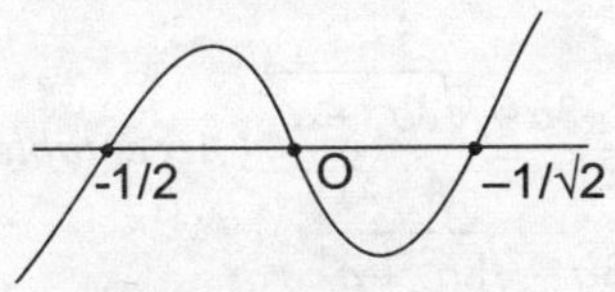

The values of x satisfying the above inequality are

$$\left(-\frac{1}{\sqrt{2}},0\right)\cup\left(\frac{1}{\sqrt{2}},0\right)$$

78. Find the set of all values of 'a' for which $f(x) = \left(\frac{\sqrt{a+8}}{2-a}-1\right)x^5 - 7x + \log_3 4$ decreases for all x

Solution: $f'(x) = 5\left(\frac{\sqrt{a+8}}{2-a}-1\right)x^4 - 7$

Since $f(x)$ decreases for all x, $f'(x) \le 0$

$$\Rightarrow 5\left(\frac{\sqrt{a+8}}{2-a}-1\right)x^4 - 7 \le 0$$

$$\Rightarrow 5\left(\frac{\sqrt{a+8}}{2-a}-1\right) \le \frac{7}{x^4}$$

The LHS should be less than equal to the least values of RHS

$$\Rightarrow 5\left(\frac{\sqrt{a+8}}{2-a}-1\right) \le 0$$

$$\Rightarrow \frac{\sqrt{a+8}}{2-a} \le 1$$

Now; $a + 8 \ge 0$

$\Rightarrow a \ge -8$

Case I: If $2 - a > 0$ then $a < 2$

And $\sqrt{a+8} \le 2-a$

Squaring; we get

$a + 8 \le 4 + a^2 - 4a$

$a^2 - 5a - 4 \ge 0$

$$a = \frac{5\pm\sqrt{25+16}}{2} = \frac{5\pm\sqrt{41}}{2}$$

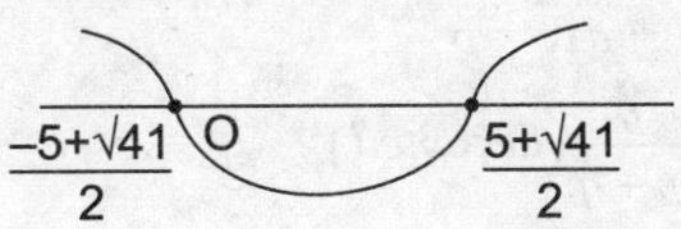

$$\Rightarrow a \in \left(-\infty, \frac{5-\sqrt{41}}{2}\right] \cup \left[\frac{5+\sqrt{41}}{2}, \infty\right) \quad \ldots(3)$$

Taking intersection of (1) and (3); we get

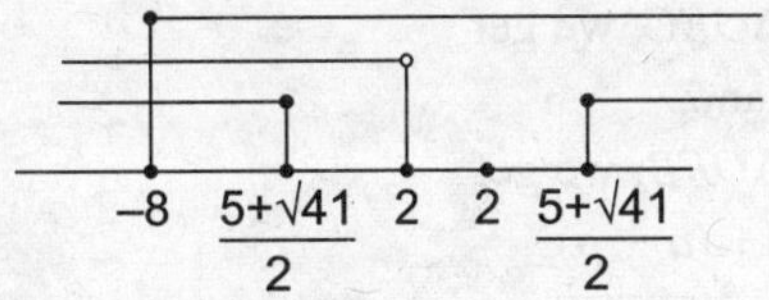

$$a \in \left[-8, \frac{5-\sqrt{41}}{2}\right] \quad \ldots\ldots(4)$$

Case II: If $2 - a < 0 \Rightarrow a > 2$ .....(5)

Then $\frac{\sqrt{a+8}}{2-a} \le 1$ is

Always true since LHS < 0 and RHS ≥ 1

∴ Taking intersection of (4) and (5); we get

$$a \in \left[-8, \frac{5-\sqrt{41}}{2}\right] \text{ and } (2, \mu)$$

79. Prove that $2\sin x + \tan x \ge 3x \ \forall\ x \in (0, \pi/2)$

Solution: Let $f(x) = 2\sin x + \tan x \ \forall\ x \in (0, \pi/2)$

and $g(x) = 3x \ \forall\ x \in (0,\pi/2)$

and $h(x) = f(x) - g(x) \ \forall\ x \in (0,\pi/2)$

$= 2\sin x + \tan x - 3x \ \forall x \in (0,\pi/2)$

$h'(x) = 2\cos x + \sec^2 - 3$

$= 2\cos^3 x - 3\cos^2 x + 1 \cos^2 x$

Let $p(x) = 2\cos^3 x - 3\cos^2 x + 1$

Now $p'(x) = -6\cos^2 x \sin x + 6\cos x \sin x$

$\Rightarrow p'(x) = 6\cos x \sin x(1 - \cos x)$

For $x \in (0,\pi/2)$

$\cos x > 0$; $\sin x > 0$ and $1 - \cos x > 0$

$\Rightarrow p'(x) > 0$

$\Rightarrow h'(x) > 0$

$\Rightarrow h(x)$ is an increasing function

$\Rightarrow f(x) - g(x)$ is an increasing function

Now $h(x) > h(0)$

$\Rightarrow f(x) - g(x) > f(0) - g(0)$

$\Rightarrow f(x) - g(x) \ge 0$

$\Rightarrow f(x) \ge g(x)$

$\Rightarrow 2\sin x + \tan x \ge 3x$

80. A sector of angle ∀θ" is circular ring bounded by the cut from a curve C where C: $x^2 + y^2 = r^2$ ($a \le r^2 \le b^2$). Find the value of ∀θ" which is just sufficient enough to contain the rectangle with the maximum area that can be carved out of this circular ring.

Solution: Let the dimensions of the rectangle of maximum area be p and $2q$ (as shown in the diagram)

From ΔOEC, we get

$q = a \tan\alpha$

From ΔOFB; we get

$b^2 = q^2 + (a+p)^2$

$\Rightarrow p = \sqrt{b^2 - q^2} - a$

Now Area of rectangle $= A = 2qp$

$= 2\left(\sqrt{b^2-q^2} - a\right)q$

$$\frac{dA}{dq} = 0 \Rightarrow \left(\sqrt{b^2-q^2} - a\right) + q.\frac{-2q}{2\sqrt{b^2-q^2}}$$

$$\Rightarrow \sqrt{b^2-q^2} - a = \frac{q^2}{\sqrt{b^2-q^2}}$$

$$\Rightarrow b^2 - q^2 - a\sqrt{b^2-q^2} = q^2$$

$$\Rightarrow -a\sqrt{b^2-q^2} = 2q^2 - b^2$$

$$\Rightarrow a\sqrt{b^2-q^2} = b^2 - 2q^2$$

Squaring

$$\Rightarrow a^2\left(b^2-q^2\right) = b^4 + 4q^4 - 4b^2q^2$$

$$\Rightarrow a^2b^2 - a^2q^2 = b^4 + 4q^4 - 4b^2q^2$$

$$\Rightarrow -4q^4 + q^2(4b^2 - a^2) + b^2(a^2 - b^2) = 0$$

$$q^2 = \frac{-\left(4b^2-a^2\right) \pm \sqrt{16b^4 + a^4 - 8b^2a^2 + 16a^2b^2 - 16b^4}}{-8}$$

$$q^2 = \frac{-4b^2 + a^2 \pm \sqrt{a^4 + 8a^2b^2}}{-8}$$

$$q^2 = \frac{4b^2 - a^2 \mp a\sqrt{a^2 + 8b^2}}{8}$$

$$q^2 = \frac{4b^2 - a^2 + a\sqrt{a^2+8b^2}}{8} (\text{Rejected } \because q^2 < b^2)$$

$$\text{or } q^2 = \frac{4b^2 - a^2 - a\sqrt{a^2+8b^2}}{8} (\text{Acceptable balue of } q)$$

Now $q = a\tan\alpha$

$$\Rightarrow \theta = 2\alpha = 2\tan^{-1}\sqrt{\frac{4b^2 - a^2 - a\sqrt{a^2+8b^2}}{8a^2}}$$

Aliter: $b^2 = q^2 + (a+p)^2$

$\Rightarrow q^2 = b^2 - (a+p)^2 = b^2 - a^2 - p^2 - 2ap$

Area$^2 = 4q^2p^2 = 4(b^2 - a^2 - p^2 - 2ap)\,p^2$

$= 4(b^2p^2 - a^2p^2 - p^4 - 2ap^3)$ $\quad \dfrac{d(Area)^2}{dP} = 0$

$\Rightarrow 2b^2p - 2pa^2 - 4p^3 - 6ap^2 = 0$

$\Rightarrow 2p(b^2 - a^2 - 2p^2 - 3ap) = 0$

either $p = 0$ or $b^2 - a^2 - 2p^2 - 3ap = 0$

or $2p^2 + 3ap + a^2 - b^2 = 0$

$$\Rightarrow p = \frac{-3a \pm \sqrt{9a^2 - 8a^2 + 8b^2}}{4} = \frac{-3a \pm \sqrt{8b^2+a^2}}{4}$$

$$= p = \frac{-3a + \sqrt{8b^2+a^2}}{4} (\textit{Acceptable value of } p)$$

$$\text{or } p = \frac{-3a - \sqrt{8b^2+a^2}}{4} (\textit{rejected})$$

($\because p$ cannot be less than 0)

$$q^2 = b^2 - \left(a - \frac{3a}{4} + \frac{\sqrt{8b^2+a^2}}{4}\right)^2$$

$$= b^2 - \left(\frac{a}{4} + \frac{\sqrt{8b^2+a^2}}{4}\right)^2$$

$$= \frac{16b^2 - a^2 - \left(8b^2 + a^2\right) - 2a\sqrt{8b^2+a^2}}{16}$$

$$= \frac{4b^2 - a^2 - a\sqrt{8b^2+a^2}}{8}$$

$$\text{Therefore } \theta = 2\alpha = 2\tan^{-1}\sqrt{\frac{4b^2 - a^2 - a\sqrt{8b^2+a^2}}{8a^2}}$$

81. Find the maximum value of $f(x) = |x|^p\,|x-1|^q$ for all x $\in$ where $p, q, \in$

$$f(x) = \begin{cases} (-1)^{p+q}\,x^p(x-1)^q & ;x<0 \\ 0 & ;x=0 \\ (-1)^q\,x^p(x-1)^q & ;0<x<1 \\ 0 & ;x=1 \\ x^p(x-1)^q & ;x>1 \end{cases}$$

Solution:

$$f'(x) = \begin{cases} (-1)^{p+q}\,[x^{p-1}(p)(x-1)^q + qx^p(x-1)^{q-1}]; & x<0 \\ 0 & ;x=0 \\ (-1)^q[px^{p-1}(x-1)^q + qx^p(x-1)^{q-1}]; & 0<x<1 \\ 0 & ;x=1 \\ px^{p-1}(x-1)^q + qx^p(x-1)^{q-1} & ;x>1 \end{cases}$$

$$\therefore f'(x) = 0 \Rightarrow \left(\left(x^{p-1}\right)\left(x-1\right)^{q-1}\right)\left(P(x-1) + qx\right) = 0$$

Now $x = 0$ (Rejected) or $x = 1$ (rejected)

or $(p+q)x = p$

$$\Rightarrow x = \frac{p}{p+q} (\textit{accepted})$$

∴ For maxima

$$f\left(\frac{p}{p+q}\right)=\left(\frac{p}{p+q}\right)^p\left|\frac{p}{p+q}\right|^2$$

$$\left[\because \frac{p}{p+q}>0 \ \& \frac{p}{p+q}-1<0\right]$$

$$\Rightarrow f\left(\frac{p}{p+q}\right)=\frac{p^p+q^q}{(p+q)^{p+q}}$$

82. A regular hexagonal cardboard with side length = 'a' is to be converted into an open box of maximum volume (with an hexagonal base). Find the volume.

Solution: Let $AB = x$; then $BC = x\sin 60^0$ and $B = a - x$

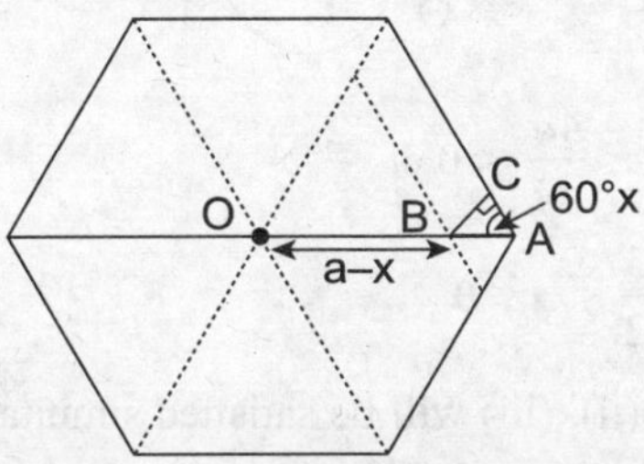

Now volume of hexagonal cardboar*d* = *A*rea of base × height

$$=\left(\left(\frac{\sqrt{3}}{4}\right)\times(OB)^2\times 6\right)\times x\sin 60^0$$

For volume to be maximum/minimum; we equate

$$V=6.\frac{3}{8}\left(a^2x+x^3-2ax^2\right)$$

$$\frac{dV}{dx}=0\Rightarrow a^2+3x^2-4ax=0$$

$$\Rightarrow 3x^2-3ax-ax+a^2=0\Rightarrow 3x(x-a)-a(x-a)=0$$

$\Rightarrow x = a$ (Rejected) or $x = a/3$

$$V=6.\frac{3}{8}.\frac{a}{3}\left(\frac{2a}{3}\right)^2=\frac{a^3}{6}.6=a^3$$

83. A cylinder is obtained by revolving a rectangle about the x-axis, the base of the rectangle lying on the x-axis and the entire rectangle lying in the region between the centre $y=\dfrac{x}{x^2+1}$ and the x-axis.

Find the maximum possible volume of the cylinder.

Solution: $y=\dfrac{x}{x^2+1}$; $\dfrac{dy}{dx}=\dfrac{(x^2+1)-2x^2}{(x^2+1)^2}=\dfrac{1-x^2}{(1+x^2)^2}$

Now dy/dx = 0 ⇒ x = 1 or – 1

Now $v = \pi y^2 (x_2 - x_1)$

Since the ordinate at A and B have to be equal

hence $\dfrac{x_1}{x_1^2+1}=\dfrac{x_2}{x_2^2+1}$

or $x_1x_2^2+x_1=x_2x_1^2+x_2$

or $x_1x_2(x_2-x_1)-(x_2-x_1)=0$

$\Rightarrow (x_2-x_1)(x_1x_2-1)=0$

$\Rightarrow x_2=\dfrac{1}{x_1}$ as $(x_1\neq x_2)$

Hence $v=\dfrac{\pi x_1^2}{\left(1+x_1^2\right)^2}\left(\dfrac{1}{x_1}-x_1\right)=\dfrac{\pi x_1(1-x_1^2)}{\left(1+x_1^2\right)}$

$\therefore\ v(x)=\dfrac{\pi x}{(1+x^2)^2}$

$V'(x) = \pi\ [(1 + x^2)^2 (1 - 3x^2) - (x - x^3)2 (1 + x^2)2x] = 0$

On simplifying $x^4 - 6x^2 + 1 = 0$

$$=\frac{6\pm\sqrt{32}}{2}=3\pm 2\sqrt{2}$$

+ sign is rejected as $x=\sqrt{3+2\sqrt{2}}=\sqrt{2}+1$ which is greater than 1

Hence $x=\sqrt{3-2\sqrt{2}}=\sqrt{2}-1$

$$\therefore\ v_{\max}=\frac{\pi\left(\sqrt{2}-1\right)\left(1-\left(3-2\sqrt{2}\right)\right)}{\left(1+3-2\sqrt{2}\right)^2}$$

$$=\frac{\pi\left(\sqrt{2}-1\right)\left(2\sqrt{2}-2\right)}{\left(4-2\sqrt{2}\right)^2}=\frac{2\pi\left(3-2\sqrt{2}\right)}{4\left(2-\sqrt{2}\right)^2}$$

$$=\frac{2\pi}{8}\frac{3-2\sqrt{2}}{\left(\sqrt{2}-1\right)^2}=\frac{\pi}{4}\ \text{(Ans)}$$

Assertion and Reason

84. A: The function $f(x) = 2\sin x + \cos 2x$ $(0 \le x \le 2\pi)$ has minimum at $x = \pi/6$ and maximum at $5\pi/6$.

R: The function $f(x)$ above decreases on $(0, \pi/6)$, increases on $(\pi/6, 5\pi/6)$ and decreases on $(5\pi/6, 2\pi)$

Solution: $f(x) = 2\sin x + \cos 2x$; $x \in [0,2\pi]$

$\therefore\ f'(x) = 2\cos x - 2\sin 2x$

$= 2\cos x\,(1 - 2\sin x)$

$\cos x > 0$ for $x \in [0, \pi/2) \cup [3\pi/2, 2\pi]$

and $\cos x < 0$ for $x \in (\pi/2, 3\pi/2)$

and $1 - 2\sin x > 0$ for $x \in [0, \pi/6) \cup (5\pi/6, 2\pi]$
and $1 - 2\sin x < 0$ for $x \in (\pi/6, 5\pi/6)$
for $x \in$
$\therefore$ $f'(x) > 0$ for $x \in [0, \pi/6)$ and
$(\pi/2, 5\pi/6)$ and $(3\pi/,2\pi]$

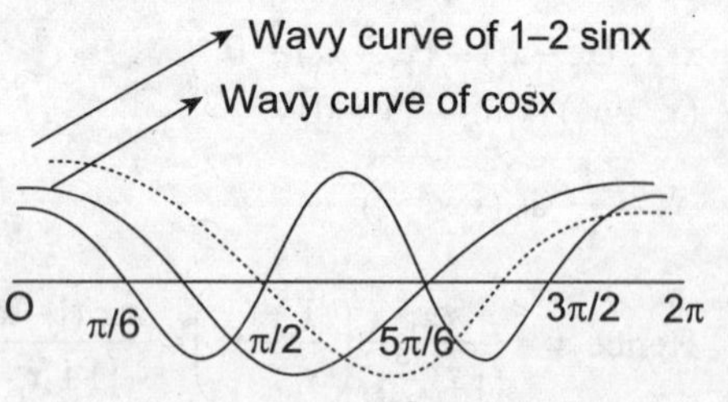

$f'(x) < 0$ for $x \in (\pi/6, \pi/2)$ and $(5\pi/6, 3\pi/2)$
Now at $x = \pi/6$; LHD > 0 and RHD < 0
and since $f(x)$ is a trigonometric function of sinx and cosx, therefore $f(x)$ is a continuous function in $[0,2\pi]$
Hence; $f(x)$ has its minima at $x = \pi/6$
Similarly; at $x = 5\pi/6$; LHD > 0 and RHD < 0 and hence another minima at $x = 5\pi/6$
At $x = \pi/2$; LHD < 0 and RHD > 0
$\therefore$ maxima at $x = \pi/2$
Similarly $x = 3\pi/2$; LHD < 0 and RHD > 0
$\therefore$ maxima at $x = 3\pi/2$
$\therefore$ Now of the statement is correct

85. A: Let $f:[0, \infty) \to [0, \infty)$ and $g:[0, \infty) \to [0, \infty)$ be non-increasing and non-decreasing functions respectively and $h(x) = g(f(x))$. If f and g are differentiable for all points in their respective domains and $h(0) = 0$ then $h(x)$ is constant function.

R: $g(x) \in [0, \infty) \Rightarrow h(x) \geq 0$ and $h'(x) \leq 0$

Solution: (A) $h(x) = g(f(x))$ and $f(x) \in [0, \infty)$
$\therefore$ $h(x) \geq 0$ ....(1)
and $h(0) = 0$ ....(2)
Also $h'(x) = g'(f(x)) f'(x) \leq 0$ ....(3)
$\therefore$ from (1), (2) and (3)
$h(x)$ is constant function.

86. A: The equation $3x^2 + 4ax + b = 0$ has at least one root in (0, 1), if $3 + 4a = 0$

R: $f(x) = 3x^2 + 4ax + b$ is continuous and differentiable in the interval (0, 1)

Solution: (D) A
Case 1: for case 1
$f(0) f(1) < 0$
$b(3 + 4a + b) < 0$

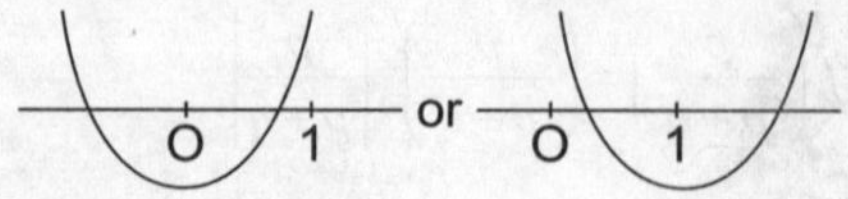

Case 2: for case 2
$f(0) > 0$
$\Rightarrow b > 0$ ...(i)
And $f(1) > 0$
$\Rightarrow 3 + 4a + b > 0$ ...(ii)
Also $0 < -\frac{4a}{6} < 1$

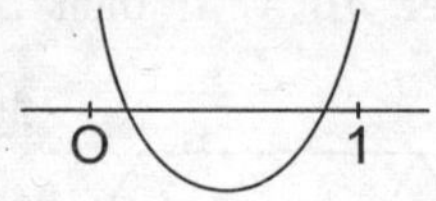

$\Rightarrow -1 < \frac{4a}{6} < 0$
$\Rightarrow -\frac{3}{2} < a < 0$ ...(iii)
(i), (ii), (iii) will be satisfied simultaneously
$\therefore$ statement – 1 is false
Statement – 2 is obviously true.

87. A: $f(x)$ is increasing function with concavity upwards, then concavity of $f^{-1}(x)$ is also upwards.

R: If $f(x)$ is decreasing function with concavity upwards, then concavity of $f^{-1}(x)$ is also upwards.

Solution: (d) Let $g(x)$ be the inverse function of $f(x)$. Then $f(g(x)) = x$.
$\therefore$ $f'(g(x)).g'(x) = 1$
i.e., $g'(x) = \frac{1}{f'(g(x))}$
$\therefore$ $g''(x) = -\frac{1}{f''(g(x))}.g'(x)$
In statement – 1 $f''(g(x)) > 0$ and $g'(x) > 0$
$\therefore$ $g''(x) < 0$ and so the concavity of $f^{-1}(x)$ is downwards
$\therefore$ statement is false
In statement – 2 $f''(g(x)) > 0$ and $g'(x) < 0$
$\therefore$ $g''(x) > 0$ and so the concavity of $f^{-1}(x)$ is upwards
$\therefore$ statement is true

Column Matching

88. **Column I**

(i) A rectangle is inscribed in an equilateral triangle of side 4 cm. Maximum area of such a rectangle is

(ii) The greatest distance between $x^2 + y^2 - 2x - 2y + 1 = 0$, $x^2 + y^2 - 10x + 4y + 20 = 0$ is 3λ then λ is

(iii) Maximum value of $x^3 - 3x^2 - x + 3$ when $x \in [0, 4]$ is $5k$, then value of k is

(iv) Minimum value of $\cos 4x - 6 \cos 2x + 5$ is

Column II

(a) $2\sqrt{3}$

(b) 0

(c) 32

(d) 3

Ans. **(i) → (a); (ii) → (d);**
(iii) → (d); (iv) → (b)

Solution: **(i)** Let $PQ = x$

Then $BP = \dfrac{4-x}{2}$

In ΔBPS

$\therefore \quad PS = \dfrac{4-x}{2}\tan 60^0 = \dfrac{\sqrt{3}(4-x)}{2}$

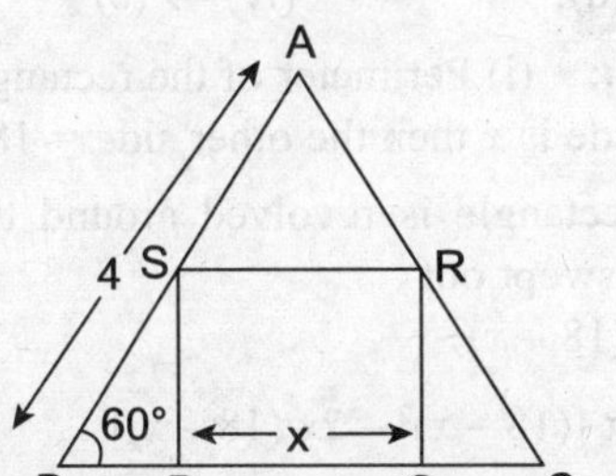

$\therefore$ Area A of rectangle = $PS.PQ$

$= \dfrac{\sqrt{3}}{2}(4-x)x$

$\dfrac{dA}{dx} = \dfrac{\sqrt{3}}{2}(4-2x) = 0 \quad \Rightarrow \quad x = 2$

$\dfrac{d^2A}{dx^2} = -\sqrt{3} < 0$

$\therefore$ A is maximum, when $x = 2$

$\therefore$ maximum area $= \dfrac{\sqrt{3}}{2} 2.2 = 2\sqrt{3}$

(ii) $S_1 = x^2 + y^2 - 2x - 2y + 1 = 0$

$\Rightarrow C_1: (1, 1); R_1 = 1$

$S^2 = x^2 + y^2 - 10x + 4y + 20 = 0$

$\Rightarrow C_2: (5, -2); R_2: 3$

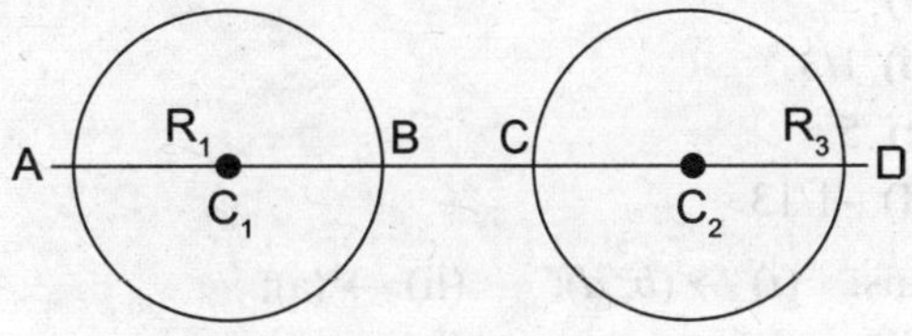

Greatest distance is AD

$= C_1C_2 + R_1 + R_2$

$= 5 + 1 + 3 = 9$

(iii) $y = x^3 - 3x^2 - x + 3$

$\Rightarrow y' = 3x2 - 6x - 1$

$y' = 0$, we get $3x2 - 6x - 1 = 0$

Equating $y' = 0$, we get $3x^2 - 6x - 1 = 0$

$\Rightarrow \quad x = \dfrac{6+4\sqrt{3}}{6}, \dfrac{6-4\sqrt{3}}{6}$

Now $y' = 3\left(x - \left(\dfrac{6+4\sqrt{3}}{6}\right)\right)\left(x - \left(\dfrac{6-4\sqrt{3}}{6}\right)\right)$

wavy curve of y' is as shown below

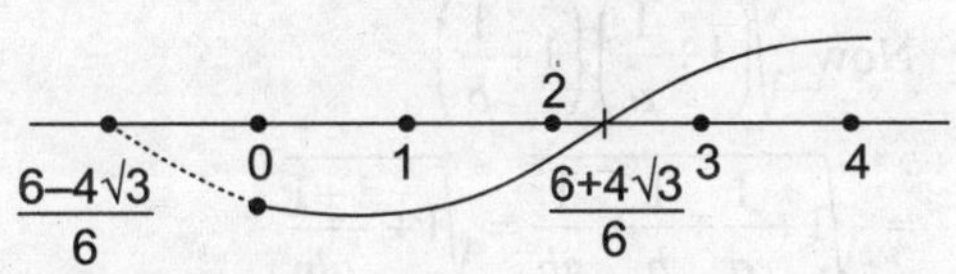

Hence; we see that y attains its maximum values at the end points only

$f(0) = 3, f(4) = 15$

$\Rightarrow$ Maximum is 15

$\Rightarrow 5k = 15 \qquad \Rightarrow k = 3$

(iv) $y = \cos^4 x - 6 \cos^2 x + 5$. Let $\cos^2 x = t$

$y = t^2 - 6t + 5; 0 \le t \le 1$

for $t \in [0, 1]$ min occurs at $t = 1$

y min = 0.

89. **Column I**

(i) If x is real, then the greatest and least value of the expression $\dfrac{x+2}{2x^2+3x+6}$ is

(ii) If $a + b = 1$; $a > 0$, $b > 0$, then the minimum value of $\sqrt{\left(1+\dfrac{1}{a}\right)\left(1+\dfrac{1}{b}\right)}$ is

(iii) The maximum value obtained by $y = 10 - |x - 10|; -9 \le x \le 9$, is

(iv) If $P(t^2, 2t)$, $t[0, 2]$ is an arbitrary point on parabola $y^2 = 4x$. Q is foot of perpendicular from focus S on the tangent at P, then maximum area of triangle PQS

Column II

(a) 3

(b) 1/3

(c) 5

(d) –1/13

Ans. (i) → (*b*, *d*); (ii) → (a);
(iii) → (a); (iv) → (c)

Solution: (i) $y = \dfrac{x+2}{2x^2+3x+6}$

$\Rightarrow 2yx^2 + 3xy + 6y = x + 2$

$2yx^2 + x(3y - 1) + 6y - 2 = 0$

$D \ge 0$

$\Rightarrow (3y-1)^2 - 8y(6y-2) \ge 0$

$9y^2 - 6y + 1 - 48y^2 + 16y \ge 0$

$\Rightarrow -39y^2 + 10y + 1 \ge 0 \Rightarrow 39y^2 - 10y - 1 \ge 0$

$\Rightarrow (13y+1)(3y-1) \ge 0$

$\dfrac{-1}{13} \le y \le \dfrac{1}{3}$

(ii) $a + b = 1$

Now $\sqrt{\left(1+\dfrac{1}{a}\right)\left(1+\dfrac{1}{b}\right)}$

$= \sqrt{1+\dfrac{1}{a}+\dfrac{1}{b}+\dfrac{1}{ab}} = \sqrt{1+\dfrac{1+1}{ab}}$

Also $\sqrt{ab} < \dfrac{a+b}{2} = \dfrac{1}{2}$

$\therefore\ ab < \dfrac{1^2}{4} \qquad \Rightarrow \dfrac{1}{ab} > \dfrac{4}{1^2}$

$\therefore\ \sqrt{\left(1+\dfrac{1}{a}\right)\left(1+\dfrac{1}{b}\right)} \ge \sqrt{1+\dfrac{4(1+1)}{1^2}} = 3$

(iii) $y = 10 - |x - 10|$

$-9 \le x \le 9$

$-19x - 10 - 1 < 0$

$\therefore\ y = 10 - (10 - x) = x$

$\therefore$ maximum value of $y = 9$

(iv) Equation of tangent at P is $ty = x + t^2$

it intersects the line $x = 0$ at Q

$\therefore$ coordinates of Q are $(0, t)$

area of $\Delta PQS = \dfrac{1}{2}\begin{vmatrix} 0 & t & 1 \\ 1 & 0 & 1 \\ t^2 & 2t & 1 \end{vmatrix}$

$= \dfrac{1}{2}[-t(1-t^2) + 2t] = \dfrac{1}{2}(t + t^3)$

$\dfrac{dA}{dt} = \dfrac{1}{2}(3t^2 + 1) > 0\ \forall\ t \in [0,2]$

Area is maximum for $t = 2$

max area $= \dfrac{1}{2}[2 + 8] = 5.$

90. Column I

(i) The dimensions of the rectangle of perimeter 36 cm, which sweeps out the largest Volume when revolved about one of its sides, are

(ii) Let $A(-1, 2)$ and $B(2, 3)$ be two fixed points, a point P lying on $y = x$ such that perimeter of triangle PAB is minimum, then sum of the abscissa and ordinate of point P, is

(iii) If x_1 and x_2 are abscissa of two points on the curve $f(x) = x - x^2$ in the interval [0, 1] then maximum value of expression $(x_1 + x_2) - (x_1^2 + x_2^2)$ is

(iv) The number of non – zero integral values of 'a' for which the function $f(x) = x^4 + ax^3 + \dfrac{3x^2}{2} + 1$ is concave upward along the entire real line is

Column II

(a) 6

(b) 12

(c) 4

(d) 1/2

Ans. (i) → (*b*, *a*); (ii) → (c);
(iii) → (d); (iv) → (c)

Solution: (i) Perimeter of the rectangle = 36 cm

If one side is x then the other side $= 18 - x$

If the rectangle is revolved around the side x then volume swept out

$V = \pi x(18 - x)^2$

$\dfrac{dV}{dx} = \pi[(18-x)^2 - 2x(18-x)]$

$= \pi(18 - x)(18 - x - 2x)$

$x = 6$ and $y = 12$

(ii) $A(-1, 2)$, $B(2, 3)$ and P in a point on $y = x$

perimeter of ΔPAB is minimum when $PA + PB$ is minimum

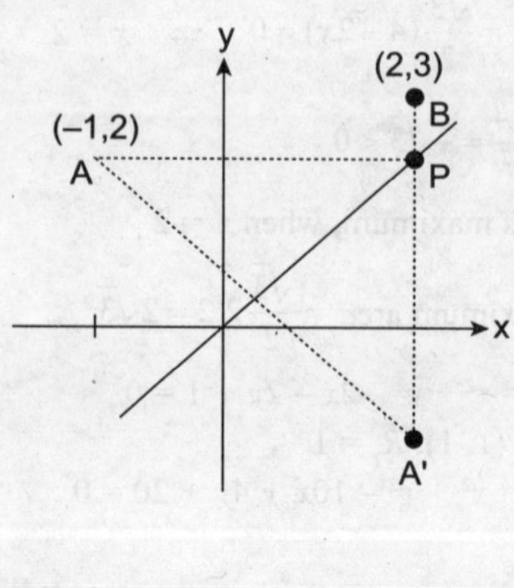

image of A(–1, 2) in the line $y = x$ is $A'(2, -1)$
Equation of $A'B$ is $x = 2$
hence P is (2, 2)

(iii) Let (x_1, y_1) and (x_2, y_2) are two points.
$\therefore\ y_1 + y_2 = (x_1 + x_2) - (x_1^2 + x_2^2)$
Now $y = x - x^2 = -\left(x - \frac{1}{2}\right)^2 + \frac{1}{4}$
$\therefore\ (y_1 + y_2)_{max.} = 2 \times \frac{1}{4} = \frac{1}{2}$

(iv) $f''(x) = 12x^2 + 6ax + 3 \geq 0 \geq x \in R$
$\Rightarrow a \in [-2, 2]$
$\Rightarrow$ No. of non-zero integer values of 'a' is 4.

91. **Column I**

(i) A function f is differentiable in [0, 5] such that $f(0) = 4$ and $f(5) = -1$. If $g(x) = \frac{f(x)}{x+1}$, then there exists some $c \in (0,5)$ such that $g'(c)$ is equal to

(ii) Let $f(x)$ and $g(x)$ be differentiable for $0 \leq x \leq 1$ $f(0) = 2$, $g(0)$, $f(1) = 6$. Let there exists a real number c∈ (0,1) such that $f'(x) = 2g'(x)$, Then $g(1)$ is equal to

(iii) Let Lagrange's mean value theorem is satisifed fot $f(x) = \sqrt{25 - x^2}$ and $c \in (1, 5)$. Then the value of c^2 is

Column II

(a) 3
(b) –5/6
(c) 15
(d) 2

Ans. (i) → (b), (ii) → (d),
(iii) → (c)

Solution: Using *LMVT*

$$g'(c) = \frac{g(5) - g(0)}{5} = \frac{-1/6 - 4}{5} = -\frac{5}{6}$$

(ii) → (b)
Let $\phi(x) = f(x) - 2g(x), x \in [0, 1]$
$\Rightarrow \phi(x) = 2, (1) = 6 - 2g(1)$
Now $\phi'(x) = f'(x) - 2g'(x)$
$\Rightarrow \phi(x)$ satisfies condition of LMVT on [0, 1]
$\Rightarrow \phi(0) = \phi(1)$
$\Rightarrow \phi\ 2 = 6 - 2g(1)$
$\Rightarrow \phi\ g(1) = 2$
(iii) → (c)

$$f'(c) = \frac{f(5) - f(1)}{5 - 1}$$

$$\Rightarrow \frac{-c}{\sqrt{25 - c^2}} = \frac{-\sqrt{6}}{2}$$

$\Rightarrow c^2 = 15$

92. Match the internal with function which are increasing int eh interval

Column I

(i) $(-\infty, 0)$
(ii) $(0, \infty)$
(iii) R
(iv) $(-1, 5)$

Column II

(a) $f(x) = \frac{e^{2x} - 1}{e^{2x} + 1}$
(b) $f(x) = -x^3 + 6x^2 + 15x + 5$
(c) $f(x) = 1 - x^3 - x^5$
(d) $f(x) = x^3 + bx^2 + cx + d, 0 < b^2 < c$

Ans. (i) → (a), (c), (d), (ii) → (a), (c), (d),
(iii) → (a), (c), (d), (iv) → (a), (b), (c), (d)

Solution: $f(x) = \frac{e^{2x} - 1}{e^{2x} + 1}$

$$\Rightarrow f'(x) = \frac{4e^{2x}}{\left(e^{2x} + 1\right)^2} > 0\ \forall\ x \in R$$

$\Rightarrow$ P → A,B,C,D
$f(x) = -x^3 + 6x^2 + 15x + 5$
$\Rightarrow f'(x) = -3x^2 + 12x + 15$
$\Rightarrow$ Q → D
$f'(x) > 0 \qquad \Rightarrow x \in (-1, 5)$
$f(x) = 1 + x^3 + x^5$
$\Rightarrow f'(x) = 3x^2 + 5x^4 \geq 0\ \forall\ x \in R$
$\Rightarrow$ R → A, B, C, D
$f(x) = x^3 + bx^2 + cx + d$
$\Rightarrow f'(x) = 3x^2 + 2bx + c > 0\ x \in R$ as $b^2 < c$
$\Rightarrow$ S → A, B, C, D

Comprehension Passage

A: Consider a function $f(x) = \left(\alpha - \frac{1}{\alpha} - x\right)(4 - 3x^2)$ where 'α' is a positive parameter

93. Number of points of extrema of $f(x)$ for a given value of α is

(a) 0 (b) 1
(c) 2 (d) 3

Solution: (c) $f(x) = \left(\alpha - \frac{1}{\alpha} - x\right)(4-3x^2)$

$$f'(x) = -(4-3x^2) + \left(\alpha - \frac{1}{\alpha} - x\right)$$

$$(-6x) = 9x^2 - 6\left(\alpha - \frac{1}{\alpha}\right)x - 4$$

$$D = 36\left(\alpha - \frac{1}{\alpha}\right)^2 + 144 > 0$$

$\therefore$ there are two critical points are given by

$$x = \frac{6\left(\alpha - \frac{1}{\alpha}\right) \pm 6\sqrt{\left(\alpha - \frac{1}{\alpha}\right)^2 + 4}}{18}$$

$$= \frac{6\left(\alpha - \frac{1}{\alpha}\right) \pm 6\left(\alpha + \frac{1}{\alpha}\right)}{18} = \frac{2\alpha}{3}, -\frac{2}{3\alpha}$$

$x = -\frac{2}{3\alpha}$ is point of local maximum and $x = \frac{2\alpha}{3}$ is point of local minimum.

94. Absolute difference between local maximum and local minimum values of *f(x)* in terms of α is

(a) $\frac{4}{9}\left(\alpha + \frac{1}{\alpha}\right)^3$ (b) $\frac{2}{9}\left(\alpha + \frac{1}{\alpha}\right)^3$

(c) $\left(\alpha + \frac{1}{\alpha}\right)^3$ (d) independent of α

Solution: $f\left(\frac{2\alpha}{3}\right) = \left(\alpha - \frac{1}{\alpha} - \frac{2\alpha}{3}\right)\left(4 - 3.\frac{4\alpha^2}{9}\right)$

$$= \left(\frac{\alpha}{3} - \frac{1}{\alpha}\right)\left(4 - \frac{4\alpha^2}{3}\right)$$

$$= 4\frac{\alpha^2-3}{3\alpha}\left(\frac{3-\alpha^2}{3}\right) = \frac{4}{9\alpha}(\alpha^2-3)(3-\alpha^2) = -\frac{4(\alpha^2-3)^2}{9\alpha}$$

$$f\left(-\frac{2}{3\alpha}\right) = \left(\alpha - \frac{1}{\alpha} + \frac{2}{3\alpha}\right)\left(4 - \frac{4}{3\alpha^2}\right)$$

$$= 4\left(\alpha - \frac{1}{3\alpha}\right)\left(\frac{3\alpha^2-1}{3\alpha^2}\right) = \frac{4(3\alpha^2-1)}{9\alpha^3}$$

$$\therefore \quad f\left(-\frac{2}{3\alpha}\right) - f\left(\frac{2\alpha}{3}\right) = \frac{4(3\alpha^2-1)^2}{9\alpha^3} + \frac{4(\alpha^2-3)^2}{9\alpha}$$

$$= \frac{4(3\alpha^2-1)^2 + 4\alpha^2(\alpha^2-3)^2}{9\alpha^3}$$

$$= \frac{4}{9\alpha^3}\left[9\alpha^4 - 6\alpha^2 + 1 + \alpha^6 - 6\alpha^4 + 9\alpha^2\right]$$

$$= \frac{4}{9\alpha^3}(\alpha^6 + 3\alpha^4 + 3\alpha^2 + 1)$$

$$= \frac{4(\alpha^2+1)^3}{9\alpha^3} = \frac{4}{9}\left(\alpha + \frac{1}{\alpha}\right)^3$$

95. Least possible value of the absolute difference between local maximum and local minimum values of *f(x)* is

(a) $\frac{32}{9}$ (b) $\frac{16}{9}$

(c) $\frac{8}{9}$ (d) $\frac{1}{9}$

Solution: Least value $= \frac{32}{9}$

B: For the cubic $f(x) = \frac{x^3}{3} - (m-3)\frac{x^2}{2} + mx + 3 = 0$; find the value of '*m*' for which it has

96. positive point of maximum

(a) (0,1] (b) $(-\infty,1] \cup [9,\infty)$

(c) $[9,\infty)$ (d) None of these

97. negative point of minimum

(a) (0,1] (b) $(-\infty,1] \cup [9,\infty)$

(c) $[9,\infty)$ (d) None of these

98. positive point of minimum

(a) (0,1] (b) $(-\infty,0] \cup [9,\infty)$

(c) $[9,\infty)$ (d) None of these

99. negative point of maximum

(a) $(-\infty,1]$ (b) $(-\infty,1] \cup [9,\infty)$

(c) $[9,\infty)$ (d) None of these

100. negative point of inflection

(a) (0,1] (b) $(-\infty,1] \cup [9,\infty)$

(c) $(-\infty,3]$ (d) None of these

101. positive point of inflection

(a) $(3, \infty)$ (b) $(-\infty,1] \cup [9,\infty)$

(c) $[9,\infty)$ (d) None of these

Solution: Given $f(x) = \frac{x^3}{3} - (m-3)\frac{x^2}{2} + mx + 3$

$\Rightarrow f'(x) = x^2 - (m-3)x + m$ and $f''(x) = 2x - (m-3)$

96 (c) For positive point of maximum; both roots of $f'(x) = 0$ must be positive

$\therefore$ Discriminate of $f'(x) = 0$ must be ≥ 0 and sum of roots > 0 and product of roots > 0

$\Rightarrow D \geq 0 \Rightarrow m \in (-\infty,1] \cup [9,\infty)$

Sum $> 0 \Rightarrow$, $m > 3$

Product $> 0 \Rightarrow m > 0$

Taking intersection; we get $m \in [9,\infty)$

97. (a) For negative point of minimum; both roots of $f'(x) = 0$ must be negative

$\therefore$ Discriminate of $f'(x) = 0$ must be ≥ 0

and sum of roots < 0 and product of roots > 0

$\Rightarrow D \geq 0 \Rightarrow m \in (-\infty, 1] \cup [9, \infty)$

and $m - 3 < 0$ and $m > 0$

$\Rightarrow m \in (0,1]$

98. (b) For positive point of minimum; atleast one root of $f'(x) = 0$ must be positive

$\Rightarrow$ Discriminate of $f'(x) = 0$ must be ≥ 0

Also; either both roots of $f'(x) = 0$ must be positive OR; both roots of $f'(x) = 0$ must be opposite in sign

Case I: Both roots of $f'(x)$ are positive $\Rightarrow m \in [9,\infty)$

Case II: Both roots of $f'(x) = 0$ are opposite in sign

$\Rightarrow f(0) \leq 0$ and product of roots ≤ 0

$\Rightarrow m \leq 0$; Also $D \geq 0$

$\Rightarrow m \in (-\infty, 0]$ $\quad \therefore m \in (-\infty, 0] \cup [9, \infty)$

99. (a) For negative point of maximum; atleast one root of $f'(x) = 0$ must be negative

$\therefore$ Discriminate of $f'(x) = 0$ must be ≥ 0 Also; both roots should not be positive

$\Rightarrow m \in (-\infty, 1]$

100. (c) Negative point of inflection:

$\Rightarrow$ The value of x for which $\dfrac{d^2y}{dx^+}$ = 0 must be negative.

$\Rightarrow f''(x) = 0 \Rightarrow m = (m-3)$ Now $x < 0$

$\Rightarrow m - 3 < 0 \Rightarrow m < 3$

101. (a) Positive point of inflection

$\Rightarrow$ The value of x for which $\dfrac{d^2y}{dx^2}$ = 0 must be positive

$f''(x) = 0 \Rightarrow 2x = m - 3$

Now $x > 0 \Rightarrow m - 3 > 0 \Rightarrow m > 3$

C: A sector of angle θ is cut from a circular ring bounded by the curve C represented by $x^2 + y^2 = r^2$ where $a^2 \leq r^2 \leq b^2$. A right circular frustum is made of this sector (curved surface only) in a usual manner. Then answer the questions that follow.

102. The angle θ for which the volume of the frustum generated is the maximum is

(a) $\dfrac{2\pi}{\sqrt{3}}$ (b) $\dfrac{2\sqrt{2}\pi}{\sqrt{3}}$

(c) $\sqrt{2}\pi$ (d) $\sqrt{3}\pi$

Solution: Let the radii of the frustum be a' and b' where $a' < b'$

Now, $b\theta = 2\pi b'$

$$\Rightarrow b' = \frac{b\theta}{2\pi}$$

Similarly $a' = \dfrac{a\theta}{2\pi}$

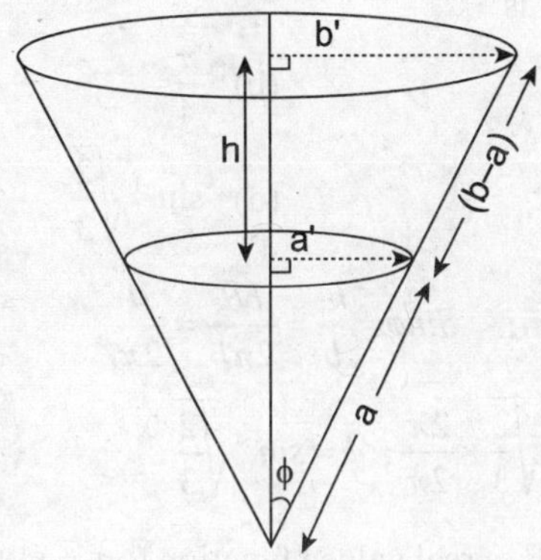

$$V_{frustum} = V_{bigger\ cone} - V_{smaller\ cone}$$

$$\frac{1}{3}\pi(b')^2\sqrt{b^2-(b')^2} - \frac{1}{3}\pi(a')^2\sqrt{a^2-(a)^2}$$

$$= \frac{1}{3}\pi\frac{b^2\theta^2}{4\pi^2}\sqrt{b^2-\frac{b^2\theta^2}{4\pi^2}} - \frac{1}{3}\pi\frac{a^2\theta^2}{4\pi^2}\sqrt{a^2-\frac{a^2\theta^2}{4\pi^2}}$$

$$= \frac{1}{12\pi}\left(b^3-a^3\right)\left(\theta^2\sqrt{1-\frac{\theta^2}{4\pi^2}}\right)$$

= Differentiating and equating $\dfrac{dV}{d\theta}$ *frustum* = 0

$$2\theta\sqrt{1-\frac{\theta^2}{4\pi^2}} + \theta^2 \times \frac{-2\theta}{4\pi^2} \times \frac{1}{2\sqrt{1-\frac{\theta^2}{4\pi^2}}} = 0$$

$\Rightarrow$ either θ = 0 (rejected)

$$\text{or} \quad \left(\sqrt{1-\frac{\theta^2}{4\pi^2}}\right)^2 = \frac{\theta^2}{8\pi^2}$$

$$\Rightarrow \frac{\theta^2}{\pi^2}\left(\frac{1}{8}+\frac{1}{4}\right) = 1 \Rightarrow \theta = \frac{8}{3}\pi^2$$

$$\Rightarrow \theta = \sqrt{\frac{2}{3}} \times 2\pi$$

103. Find the maximum volume of the cone

(a) $\dfrac{1}{6}\pi R^3$ (b) $\dfrac{\sqrt{2}\pi\left(b^3-a^3\right)}{9\sqrt{3}}$

(c) $\dfrac{2\pi\left(b^3-a^3\right)}{9\sqrt{3}}$ (d) None of these

Solution:

$$\max V = \frac{1}{12\pi}(b^3 - a^3)\left(\frac{2}{3}\times 4\pi^2\sqrt{1-\frac{2}{3}\times\frac{4\pi^2}{4\pi^2}}\right)$$

$$= \frac{8}{12.3\sqrt{3}.\pi}.(b^3-a^3)\pi = \frac{2\pi}{9\sqrt{3}}(b^3-a^3)$$

104. The semi-vertical angle of the cone with the maximum volume is

(a) $\frac{\pi}{6}$ (b) $\frac{\pi}{4}$

(c) $\frac{\pi}{3}$ (d) $\sin^{-1}\sqrt{\frac{2}{3}}$

Solution: $Sin\phi = \frac{b'}{b} = \frac{b\theta}{2\pi b} = \frac{\theta}{2\pi}$;

$\sin\phi = \sqrt{\frac{2}{3}}\times\frac{2\pi}{2\pi}$; $\phi = sin^{-1}\sqrt{\frac{2}{3}}$

D: For $x \in \mathbb{R}$, a real valued function $f(x) = x^4 + Ax^3 + Bx^3 + Cx + D$ is having distinct positive root in *AP* (α being the smallest root), where the sum and the product of the roots is 24 and 945 respectively

On the basis of the information provided above, answer the questions that follows.

105. The graph of $f(x)$ is symmetric about x =

(a) 3 (b) 4

(c) 5 (d) 6

106. For all real x, then function $f(x)$ will observe the property

(a) $f(x) = f(6 - x)$ (b) $f(x) = f(12 - x)$

(c) $f(x) = f(18 - x)$ (d) None of these

107. The function achieves, one of its local minima in the interval

(a) (α, α + 1) (b) (α + 1, α + 2)

(c) (α +4, α + 5) (d) (α + 5, α + 6)

108. If local maxima is achieved at $x = x_1$, then the distance between the two local minima, will be

(a) $2\sqrt{x_1}$ (b) $2\sqrt{x_1 - 1}$

(c) $2\sqrt{x_1 + 1}$ (d) None of these

109. The steepest slope of tangent (s) will occur for x belong to the interval

(a) (α+1, α+2) (b) (α + 2, α + 3)

(c) (α + 4, α + 5) (d) (α + 6, ∞)

Ans: 1. (d) 2. (b)

3. *(a, d)* 4. (b)

5. (a)

Solution: $f(x) = (x - 3)(x - 5)(x - 7)(x - 9)$
$= x^4 - 24x^3 + 206x^2 - 744x + 945$ wavy curve of $f(x)$

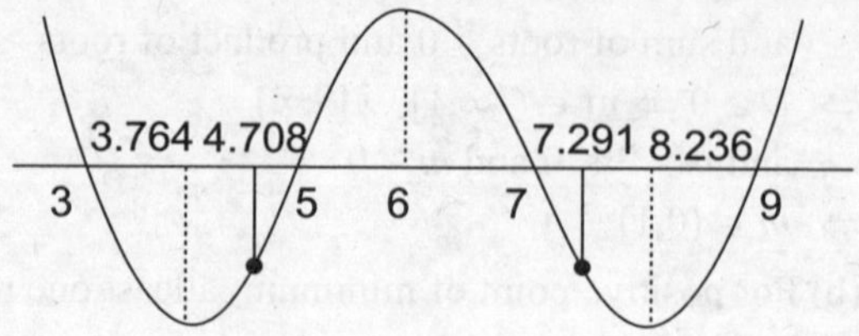

$f'(x) = (x - 3)(x - 5)(x - 7) + (x - 3)(x - 7)(x - 9) + (x - 3)(x - 5)(x - 9) + (x - 5)(x - 7)(x - 9)$

$f'(3) < 0; f'(5) > 0; f'(7) < 0;$

$f'(9) > 0\ f'(4) > 0; f'(6) = 0; f'(8) < 0$

$f'(x) = 0 \Rightarrow x^3 - 18x^2 + 103x - 186 = 0$

Now, we know that $x - 6$ is a factor of $f'(x)$=0.

Therefore by long division method, we can factorize $x^3 - 18x^2 + 103x - 186 = 0$ to get

$(x - 6)(x^2 - 12x + 31) = 0 \Rightarrow x = 6$ or $x = 6 \pm \sqrt{5}$ 8.236 and 3.764

For, x = 6, the function wil have its local maxima

And, for $x = 6 \pm \sqrt{5}$, the function will achieve its local minima.

and $f''(x) = 3x^2 - 36x + 103 = 0$

$\Rightarrow$ x 7.291 and 4.70833

at x = 7.291, the graph has the minimum slope

And at x = 4.70833, the graph has the maximum slope.

E: A park is in the shape of a trapezium *ABCD* length of three sides of a trapezium (including two non-parallel sides) are equal to 100 *m* i.e., *AD* = *BC* = *DC* =100*m*.The fourth side is such that the area of trapezium *ABCD* is maximum. Four persons namely *P, Q, M, N* are standing at positing *A, B, C, D* respectively. Based on the above information, answer the questions that follow

110. What is the area of the trapezium?

(a) 7500 m^2 (b) 7500 $\sqrt{3}$ m^2

(c) 2500 $\sqrt{3}m^2$ (d) None of these

111. *P* and *Q* move towards each other along *AB* with a speed of 1*m*/sec each *N* and *M* move towards each other along *CD* with a speed of 1/2 m/sec. Assuming that they all start simultaneously, each find the rate of change of area quadrilateral *PQMN* after 25 seconds

(a) $-7500\sqrt{3}$ m^2/sec (b) -7500 m^2/sec

(c) $-2500m^2$/sec (d) $-2500\sqrt{3}$ m^2/sec

112. N starts moving towards M and Q starts moving towards P at the rate of 1 m/sec respectively. Assuming all start moving simultaneously, find the rate of change of area of ΔPQN after 50 seconds.

(a) $-25\sqrt{3}\ m^2/sec$ (b) $-50\sqrt{3}\ m^2/sec$

(c) $-150\sqrt{3}\ m^2/sec$ (d) $-100\sqrt{3}\ m^2/sec$

113. P and M approach each other via the shortest distance possible at speeds of $\sqrt{3}/2$ m/sec, similarly for Q and N. If they all start simultaneously, find the rate of change of area of quadrilateral $PQMN$, 50 seconds after they start

(a) $50\sqrt{3}\left(1-\sqrt{3}\right)$ (b) $100\sqrt{2}(1-\sqrt{3})$

(c) $100\sqrt{3}(1-\sqrt{3})$ (d) None of these

114. In the previous question, find the rate of change of area the circle circumscribing the quadrilateral $PQMN$, 50 seconds after start.

(a) $\pi(25-50\sqrt{3})$ (b) $\pi(75-100\sqrt{3})$

(c) -100π (d) None of these

Solutions:

110. Let x be the height of the trapezium

$$\therefore \quad Area=\left(\frac{1}{2}\times x\times\sqrt{100^2-x^2}\right)2+100\times x$$

For area to be maximum; we have $\frac{dArea}{dx}=0$

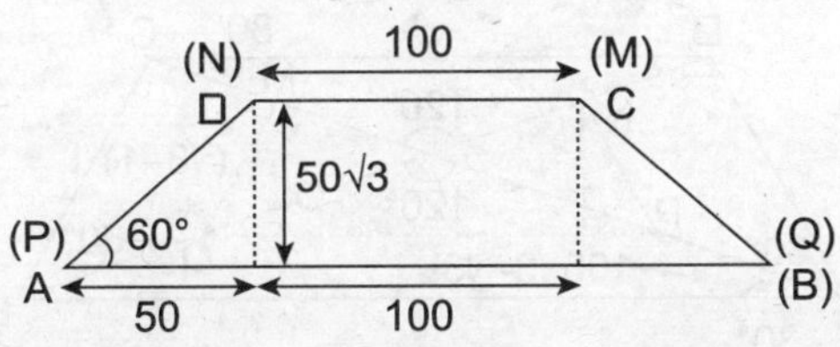

$$\sqrt{100^2-x^2}+x\times\frac{-x}{\sqrt{100^2-x^2}}+100=0$$

$\Rightarrow 100^2-x^2+\frac{x^4}{100^2-x^2}-2x^2=10000$

$\Rightarrow (100^2-x^2)(-3x^2)+x^4=0$

$\Rightarrow 4x^4-3\times 100^2\times x^2=0$

$\Rightarrow x=0$ or $4x^2=3\times(100)^2$

$\Rightarrow x=50\sqrt{3}$

Aliter: $Area=\frac{a\sin\theta}{2}\times(a+a+2a\cos\theta)$

$=a^2\sin\theta\,(1+\cos\theta)$

For Area to be maximum/minimum; we have $\frac{d(Area)}{d\theta}=0$

$\Rightarrow 2a^2[\cos\theta\,(1+\cos\theta)+\sin\theta\,(-\sin\theta)]=0$

$\Rightarrow \cos\theta+\cos 2\theta=0$

$\Rightarrow \cos 2\theta=-\cos\theta=\cos(\pi-\theta)$

$\Rightarrow 2\theta=2n\pi\pm(a-\theta)$

Case I: $2\theta=2n\pi+(\pi-\theta)$

$\Rightarrow 3\theta=2n\pi+\pi$

For $\theta\in(0,\pi/2)$; $\theta=\pi/3$

Case II: $2\theta=2n\pi-(\pi-\theta)$

$\theta=(2n-1)\pi$

Not possible

Hence maximum area $=100^2\times\frac{\sqrt{3}}{2}\left(1+\frac{1}{2}\right)$

$=\frac{3\sqrt{3}\times 100^2}{4}=$ when height $50\sqrt{3}$

111. The height of the quadrilateral (trapezium) remains same

Now Area $=\frac{1}{2}\times((100-t)+2(200-2t))\times 50\sqrt{3}$

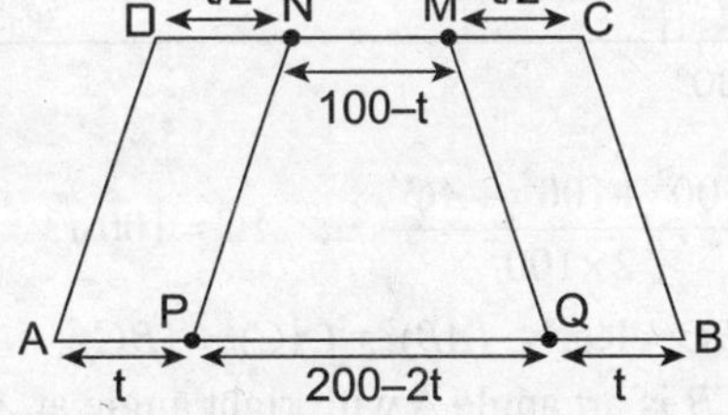

[∵ Distance between N and M after 't' seconds $=100-t$. Distance between P and Q and after 't' seconds $=200-2t$]

Now $\frac{d(Area)}{dt}=\frac{d}{dt}\left[\frac{3}{2}(100-t)\times 50\sqrt{3}\right]=75\sqrt{3}\times(-1)$

$=-75\sqrt{3}\ m^2/\sec$

112. Let coordinates of A be $=(0,0)$

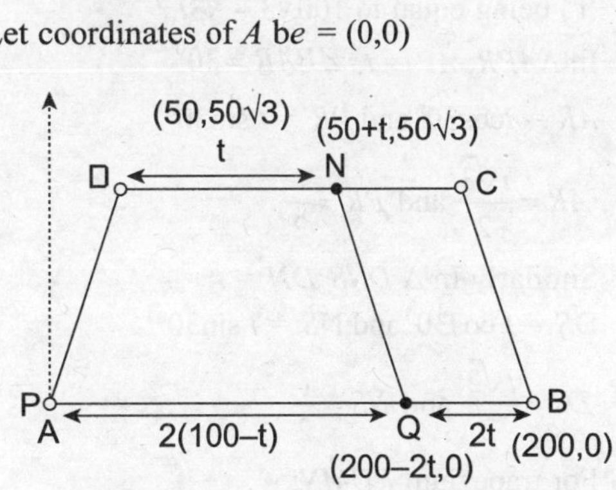

After 't' seconds; coordinates of $N=(50+t,50\sqrt{3})$

After 't' seconds; coordinates of $Q=(2(100-t),0)$

$$Area=\frac{1}{2}\begin{vmatrix} 0 & 0 \\ 50+t & 50\sqrt{3} \\ 2(100-t) & 0 \\ 0 & 0 \end{vmatrix}=\frac{1}{2}.2.50\sqrt{3}.(100-t)$$

Now $\frac{d(Area)}{dt}=-50\sqrt{3}$

Aliter: Area = $\frac{1}{2}\times Base\times Height$

$$=\frac{1}{2}\times 2(100-t)\times 50\sqrt{3}$$

$$\frac{d(Area)}{dt}=-50\sqrt{3}$$

113. In ΔACD; we have $\cos D=\frac{AD^2+CD^2-AC^2}{2\times AD\times CD}$

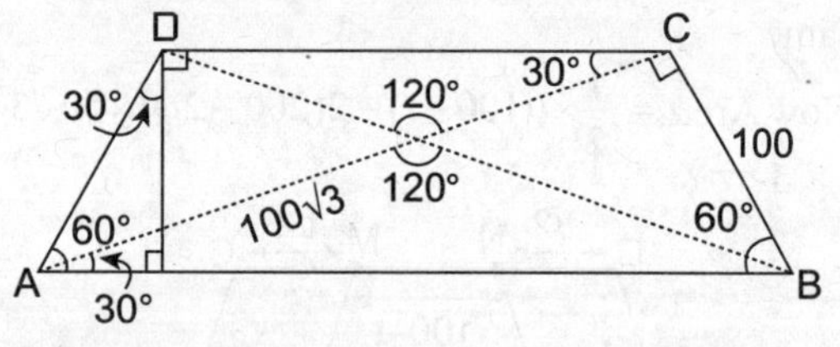

$$\frac{-1}{2}=\frac{100^2+100^2-AC^2}{2\times 100^2}\Rightarrow AC=100\sqrt{3}$$

In ΔABC; clearly; $(AB)^2=(AC)^2+(BC)^2$

$\Rightarrow$ *ACB* is art.angle Δ with right angle at $\angle C$

$\therefore$ $\angle CAB=30^0$

Now since *P* and *Q* are moving a long diagonals AC andBD with the same speed

$\therefore$ at any point of time, *PQ* is always parallel to *AB*

Similarly *MN* is always parallel to *CD*

$\therefore$ PQMN is a trapezium with each diagonal (at time 't') being equal to $100\sqrt{3}-\sqrt{3}t$.

In ΔAPR; $AP=t$, $\angle PAR=30^0$

$\Rightarrow$ $AR=t\cos 30^0$ and $PR=t\sin 30^0$

$\Rightarrow$ $AR=\frac{t\sqrt{3}}{2}$ and $PR=\frac{t}{2}$

Similarly In Δ *DNS*: $DN=t$;

$\Rightarrow$ $DS=t\cos 30^0$ and $NS=t\sin 30^0$

$\Rightarrow$ $Ds=\frac{t\sqrt{3}}{2}$ and $NS=\frac{t}{2}$

$\therefore$ For trapezium *PQMN*;

$$PQ=AB-2(AR)=200-2\left(\frac{t\sqrt{3}}{2}\right)=200-t\sqrt{3}$$

and height of trapezium *PQMN* =

Height of trapezium *ABCD* – (*PR* + *NS*)

$=50\sqrt{3}-t$

and $MN=CD-2(DS)=100-2\left(\frac{t\sqrt{3}}{2}\right)$

$=100-t\sqrt{3}$

Now Area of trapezium (*PQMN*) [After time '*t*'] is

$$\frac{1}{2}\times(PQ+MN)\times height$$

$$=\frac{1}{2}\times[(200-\sqrt{3}t)+(100-\sqrt{3}t)]\times(50\sqrt{3}-t)$$

$$=\frac{1}{2}(300-2\sqrt{3}t)\times(50\sqrt{3}-t)$$

$$=(150-\sqrt{3}t)(50\sqrt{3}-t)$$

Now; $\frac{d(Area)}{dt}$

$=-\sqrt{3}(50\sqrt{3}-t)-1(150-\sqrt{3}t)$

$=-150+\sqrt{3}t-150+\sqrt{3}t$

$=2(\sqrt{3}t-150)$

$\therefore$ $\left.\frac{d(Area)}{dt}\right|_{t=50}=2(50\sqrt{3}-150)$

$=100\sqrt{3}(1-\sqrt{3})\ m^2/sec$

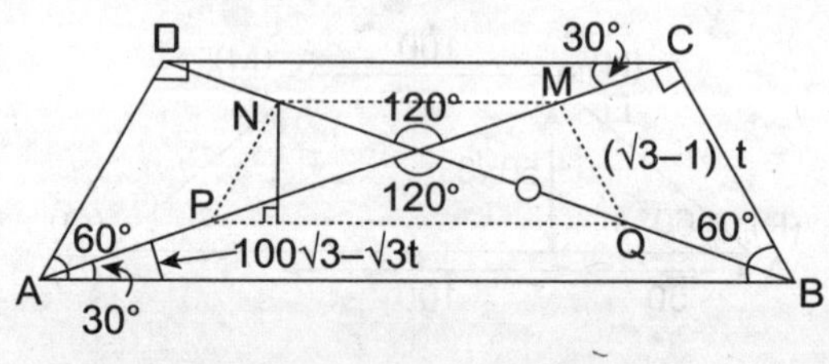

114. $\because$ $\angle PMQ$ & $\angle PNQ$ are 90^0 each

$\therefore$ *PQ* is the diameter of the circle

Let 'O' be the centre

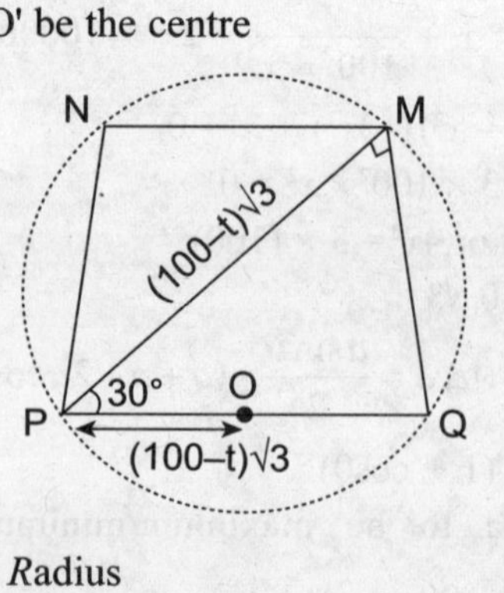

$\Rightarrow$ PO = *Radius*

$\Rightarrow$ Area = π *x* (Radius)^2

And radius $= 100 - \frac{\sqrt{3}}{2}t$

$\therefore$ Area $= \pi\left(100 - \frac{\sqrt{3}}{2}t\right)^2$

$$\frac{d(Area)}{dt} = \pi \times 2\left(100 - \frac{\sqrt{3}}{2}t\right)$$

$$= \sqrt{3}\pi\left(100 - \frac{\sqrt{3}}{2}t\right)$$

$$\left.\frac{d(Area)}{dt}\right|_{t=50}$$

$= \sqrt{3}\pi\ (100 - 25\sqrt{3})$
$= \pi\ (75 - 100\sqrt{3})$

F: $f : D \to R, f(x) = \frac{x^2 + bx + c}{x^2 + b_1x + c_1}$, where α, β are the roots of the equation $x^2 + bx + c = 0$ and α_1, β_1 are the roots of $x^2 + b_1x + c_1 = 0$. Now answer the following questions for *f(x)*. Now answer the following questions based in the above comprehension ∀

115. If $\alpha_1 < \alpha < \beta_1 < \beta$, then
(a) *f(x)* is increasing in $(\alpha_1 \beta_1)$
(b) *f(x)* is increasing in (α, β)
(c) *f(x)* is decreasing in (β_1, β)
(d) *f(x)* is increasing in $(-\infty, \alpha)$

116. If $\alpha_1 < \beta_1 < \alpha < \beta$, then
(a) *f(x)* has a minima in (α, β) and a minima in (α, β)
(b) *f(x)* has a minima in (α, β) and a maxima in (α_1, β_1)
(c) *f′(x)* > 0 where ever defined
(d) *f′(x)* < 0 where ever defined

117. Given that $b \neq b_1$ and the equations $x^2 + bx + c = 0$ and $x^2 + b_1x + c_1 = 0$ do not have real roots, then
(a) *f′(x)* = 0 has real and distinct roots
(b) *f′(x)* = 0 has real and equal roots
(c) *f′(x)* = 0 has imaginary roots
(d) nothing can be said

118. In the above problem $\lim_{x\to\infty}[f(x)] \lim_{x\to-\infty}[f(x)]$ (where [.] denotes the greatest integer function) is equal to
(a) 1 (b) 0
(c) – 1 (d) does not exists

119. In the last problem if $b > b_1$, then
(a) *x* coordinate of point in minima is greater than *x* coordinate of point of maxima
(b) *x* coordinate of point in minima is greater than *x* coordinate of point of maxima
(c) it also depend upon *c* and c_1
(d) nothing can be said

120. If $b = b_1$ and $c \neq c_1$; and $x^2 + bx + c = 0$ and $x^2 + b_1x + c_1 = 0$ does not have real roots; then
(a) *f(x)* = 0 will have real and equal roots
(b) *f(x)* = 0 will have a local maxima at $x = 0$ if $c < c_1$
(c) *f(x)* = 0 will have a local minima at $x = 0$ if $c < c_1$ maxima at $x = -b/2$ if $c > C_1$
(d) None of these

Solution:
The graph of $x^2 + bx + c$ will be as shown below

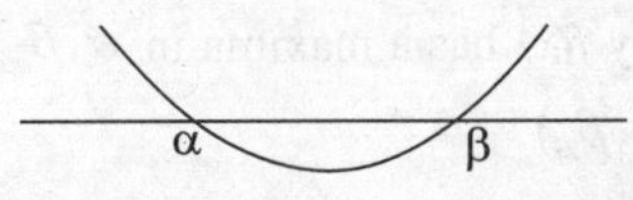

(assuming α < β)

And the graph of $x^2 + b_1x + c_1$ will be as shown below

(assuming $\alpha_1 < \beta_1$)

Therefore the graph of $\frac{1}{x^2 + b_1x + c_1}$ will be as shown below

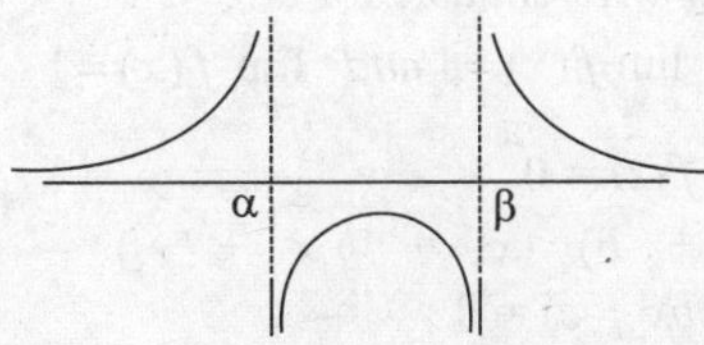

115. If $\alpha_1 < \alpha < \beta_1 < \beta$ then graph of *f(x)* will be as show below

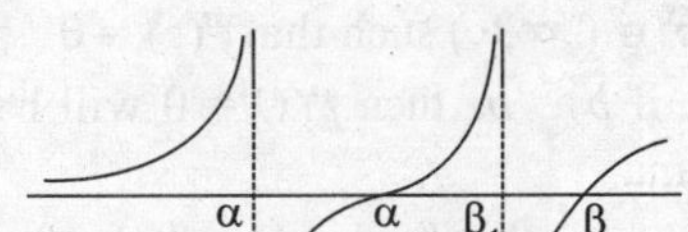

[∵ *f(x)* will have vertical asymptotes at $x = \alpha_1, \beta_1$ and *f(x)* > 0 ∀ $(-\infty, \alpha_1)$ and (α, β_1) and (β, ∞)
Also *f(x)* < 0 ∀ (α_1, α) and (β,β) with *f*(α) and *f*(β) = 0
Graph of *f(x)* is shown.Clearly *f(x)* is increasing in (α_1, β_1).

116. If $\alpha_1 < \beta_1 < \alpha < \beta$

$\Rightarrow f(x) = \dfrac{(x-\alpha)(x-\beta)}{(x-\alpha_1)(x-\beta_1)}$

Wavy curve of $f(x)$ =

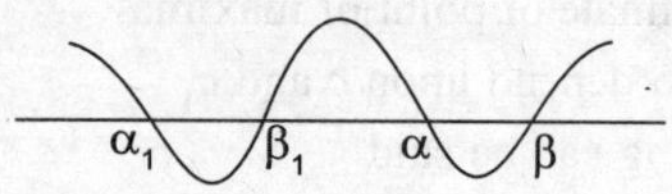

Now $f(x) > 0 \;\forall\; x \in (-\infty,\alpha_1) \cup (\beta, \alpha) \cup (\beta,\infty)$
and $f(x) < 0 \;\forall\; x \in (\alpha_1,\beta_1) \cup (\alpha,\beta)$~
The graph of $f(x)$ will be as shown below

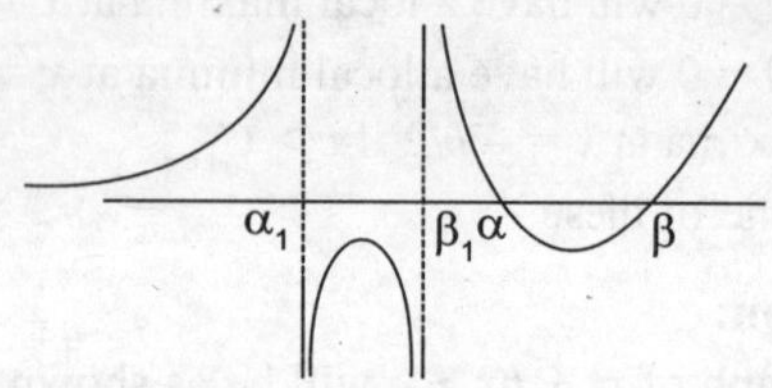

Clearly $f(x)$ has a maxima in α, β and a minima in (α_1, β_2)

117. If $x^2 + bx + c = 0$ and $x^2 + b_1x + c_1 = 0$ do not have real roots; then

$$f(x) = \frac{x^2+bx+c}{x^2+b_1x+c_1} > 0 \;\forall\; x \in \mathbb{R}$$

And

$$f'(x) = \frac{(2x+b)(x^2+b_1x+c_1)-(2x+b_1)(x^2+bx+c)}{(x^2+b_1x+c_1)^2}$$

Now $f(x)$ is a rational function where denominator $\neq 0$

$\Rightarrow f(x)$ is differentiable for all $x \in \mathbb{R}$

Now $\lim\limits_{x\to\infty} f(x) = 1$ *and* $\lim\limits_{x\to-\infty} f(x) = 1$

Now $f'(x) = 0$

$\Rightarrow (2x + b)\ (x^2 + b_1x + c_1) - (2x + b_1)(x^2 + bx + c) = 0$

Which is a quadratic and can have two roots

Now, Since $\lim\limits_{x\to\pm\infty} f(x) = 1$

$\Rightarrow \exists$ a 'c' $\in (-\infty,\infty)$ such that $f'(c) = 0$

Now, if $b = b_1$; then $f'(x) = 0$ will have only one extrema

Here, given that $b \neq b_1$; then $f'(x) = 0$ will have real and distinct roots $f(x)$ has one of the two graphs

$\Rightarrow f'(x) = 0$ has real and distinct roots.

118. As explained earlier; $\lim\limits_{x\to\infty} f(x) = \lim\limits_{x\to-\infty} f(x) = 1$

$\Rightarrow \lim\limits_{x\to\infty} f(x) \times \lim\limits_{x\to-\infty} f(x) = 1$

Clearly $\lim\limits_{x\to\infty}[f(x)] \lim\limits_{x\to-\infty}[f(x)] = 0$

119. $f(x) = \dfrac{x^2+bx+c}{x^2+b_1x+c_1} = 1 + \dfrac{(b-b_2)x+c-c_1}{x^2+bx+c_1}$

$$= 1 + \frac{\dfrac{(b-b_1)}{x} + \dfrac{c-c_1}{x^2}}{1+\dfrac{b_1}{x}+\dfrac{c_1}{x^2}}$$

for $b > b_1$

$\lim\limits_{x\to\infty} f(x) \to 1^+$

$\Rightarrow$ point of maxima is greater than point of minima.

120. $f(x) = \dfrac{x^2+bx+c_1+(c-c_1)}{x^2+bx+c_1}$ $(\because b_1 = b)$

$\Rightarrow f(x) = 1 + \dfrac{c-c_1}{x^2+bx+c_1}$

Now; $f(x)$ will be maximum when $\dfrac{c-c_1}{x^2+bx+c_1}$ is maximum

If $c > c_1$; then $f(x)$ will be maximum when $x^2 + bx + c_1$ is minimum

i.e., at $x = -b/2$

If $c < c_1$; then $f(x)$ will be maximum when $x^2 + bx + c_1$ is maximum i.e., at $x \to \pm\infty$

Also; we already know that when $b = b_1$; $f'(x) = 0$ will have real and equal roots hence; (a) and (d) options are corrects

G: Let $f'(\sin x) < 0$ and $f''(\sin x) > 0 \;\forall\; x \in \left(0, \dfrac{\pi}{2}\right)$

Now consider a function $g(x) = f(\sin x) + f(\cos x)$

121. $g(x)$ decreases if x belongs to

(a) $\left(0,\dfrac{\pi}{4}\right)$ (b) $\left(\dfrac{\pi}{4},\dfrac{\pi}{2}\right)$

(c) $\left(\dfrac{\pi}{6},\dfrac{\pi}{3}\right)$ (d) None of these

122. $g(x)$ increase if x belongs to

(a) $\left(0,\dfrac{\pi}{4}\right)$ (b) $\left(\dfrac{\pi}{4},\dfrac{\pi}{2}\right)$

(c) $\left(\dfrac{\pi}{8},\dfrac{\pi}{3}\right)$ (d) $\left(\dfrac{\pi}{6},\dfrac{\pi}{3}\right)$

123. The set of critical points of $g(x)$ is

(a) $\left\{\dfrac{\pi}{8},\dfrac{\pi}{6}\right\}$ (c) $\left\{\dfrac{\pi}{8},\dfrac{\pi}{6},\dfrac{\pi}{3}\right\}$

(c) $\left\{\dfrac{\pi}{8},\dfrac{\pi}{6},\dfrac{\pi}{4}\right\}$ (d) None of these

Solution:

$f'(\sin x) < 0\ \forall\ x \in \left(0, \frac{\pi}{2}\right)$ ...(1)

$\Rightarrow f'\left(\sin\left(\frac{\pi}{2} - x\right)\right) < 0\ \forall\ x \in \left(0, \frac{\pi}{2}\right)$

$\Rightarrow f'(\cos x) < 0\ \forall\ x \in \left(0, \frac{\pi}{2}\right)$ ...(2)

Similarly as $f''(\sin x) > 0$ ...(3)

$\Rightarrow f''(\cos x) > 0\ \forall\ x \in \left(0, \frac{\pi}{2}\right)$ ...(4)

Now $g'(x) = f'(\sin x).\cos x - f'(\cos x).\sin x$

$\Rightarrow g''(x) = f''(\sin x).\cos^2 x - f'(\sin x).\sin x - f''(\cos x)(-\sin^2 x) - f'(\cos x)\cos x$

$\Rightarrow g''(x) > 0\ \forall\ x \in \left(0, \frac{\pi}{2}\right)$

{using (1), (2), (3) and (4)}

$\Rightarrow g'(x)$ is increasing fn. $x \in \left(0, \frac{\pi}{2}\right)$ with $g'(x)$

$\Rightarrow x = \pi/4$

$\Rightarrow g'(x) < 0$ for $\forall\ x \in \left(0, \frac{\pi}{4}\right)$

$\Rightarrow g(x)$ is decreasing for $(0, \pi/4)$

and $g'(x) > 0$ for $x \in \left(\frac{\pi}{4}, \frac{\pi}{2}\right)$

$\Rightarrow g(x)$ is increasing of r $\left(\frac{\pi}{4}, \frac{\pi}{2}\right)$

121. (a)

122. (b)

123. (d)

H: Let f and g are two functions such that f and y are continuous in $[a, b]$ and differentiable in (a, b) then $\exists$ at least one $c \in (a, b)$ such that

(i) $f'(c) = \frac{f(b) - f(a)}{b - a}$

(ii) If $f(a) = f(b)$ but $a \neq b$, then $f'(x) = 0$

(iii) If $g'(x) \neq 0$, then $\frac{f(b) - f(a)}{f(b) - g(a)} = \frac{f'(c)}{g'(c)}$ (Cauchy theorem)

124. The set of values of k, for which equation $x^3 - 3x + k = 0$ has two distinct roots in (0,1) is

(a) $k \in (1, 4)$ (b) $k \in (0, \infty)$
(c) $k \in (0, 1)$ (d) $k \in \phi$

125. Which of the following is true?

(a) $|\tan^{-1}x - \tan^{-1}y| \leq |x - y|\ \forall\ x, y \in R$
(b) $|\tan^{-1}x - \tan^{-1}y| \geq |x - y|\ \forall\ x, y \in R$
(c) $|\sin x - \sin y| \geq |x - y|\ \forall x, y \in R$
(d) None of these

126. Let $0 < \alpha < \theta < \beta < \frac{\pi}{2}$, then $\frac{\sin\alpha - \sin\beta}{\cos\beta - \cos\alpha}$ is equal to

(a) $\tan\theta$ (b) $-\tan\theta$
(c) $\cot\theta$ (d) $-\cot\theta$

Solutions:

124. (d) Let $0 < \alpha < \theta < \beta < 1$, and α, β are the roots of $f(x) = x^3 - 3x + k = 0$

$\Rightarrow f(\alpha) = f(\beta) = 0$

$\Rightarrow f(x)$ satisfies LMVT

$\Rightarrow f'(c) = 0 \Rightarrow 3c^2 = 0$

$\Rightarrow c = \pm 1$

but c must be lies between α and β.

Hence $k \in \phi$

125. (a) Let $f(x) = \tan^{-1}x$

then for some $a \in (x, y)$, $f'(\alpha) = \frac{\tan^{-1}y - \tan^{-1}x}{y - x}$ (LMVT)

$\Rightarrow \left|\frac{1}{1+\alpha^2}\right| = \left|\frac{\tan^{-1}x - \tan^{-1}y}{x - y}\right| \leq 1$

$\Rightarrow |\tan^{-1}x - \tan^{-1}y| \leq |x - y|$

126. (d) Let $f(x) = \sin x$ and $g(x) = \cos x$, Also $\sin x \neq 0$ for $x \in 0, \left(0, \frac{\pi}{2}\right)$ then by cauchy's theorem

$$\frac{f(\beta) - f(\alpha)}{g(\beta) - g(\alpha)} = \frac{f'(\theta)}{g'(\theta)}$$

$$\Rightarrow \frac{\sin\beta - \sin\alpha}{\cos\beta - \cos\alpha} = \frac{\cos\beta}{-\sin\alpha} = -\cot\theta$$

I: There is a parabola $y = x^2 + x + a$, where a be a parameter which changes at a constant rate such that $\frac{da}{dt} =$ 5. If $a = 0$ when $t = 0$. let $A(t)$ be the area bounded by $y = x^2 + x + a$, x-axis, y-axis and $x = a$ at the time t.

127. $A(2) =$

(a) $\frac{1450}{3}$ (b) $\frac{475}{6}$
(c) $\frac{a^2}{3} + \frac{3a^2}{2}$ (d) None of these

128. Maximum value of $A(t)$ when $t \in [0,2]$

(a) $\dfrac{475}{6}$ (b) $\dfrac{1450}{3}$

(c) $\dfrac{1950}{3}$ (d) $\dfrac{2575}{6}$

129. Maximum value of $A'(t)$ when $t[0, 2]$

(a) $\dfrac{1450}{3}$ (b) $\dfrac{475}{6}$

(c) 650 (d) 1350

Solution:

127. (a) $\dfrac{da}{dt} = 5$

$\therefore \; a = 5t + c$

$\therefore \; a = 5t \qquad \{\because a = 0, \text{ when } t = 0\}$

$\therefore \; y = x^2 + x + 5t$

Now $I = \int_0^{10} \left(x^2 + x + 10\right) dx$

$$\Rightarrow \; I = \left(\frac{x^3}{3} + \frac{x^2}{2} + 10x\right)\Bigg|_0^{10} = \frac{1000}{3} + \frac{100}{2} + 100$$

$$= \frac{1000 + 450}{3} = \frac{1450}{3}$$

128. (b) $\int_0^{5t} \left(x^2 + x + 5t\right) dt = \left(\dfrac{x^3}{3} + \dfrac{x^2}{2} + 5tx\right)_0^{5t}$

$$A(t) = \frac{125t^3}{3} + \frac{25t^2}{2} + 25t^2$$

$A'(t) = 125t^2 + 25t + 50t > 0$

$\therefore$ maximum value of $A(t) = \dfrac{1000}{3} + \dfrac{1000}{2} + 100 = \dfrac{1450}{3}$

129. (c) $A''(t) = 250t + 75 > 0$

$\therefore$ max. value of $A'(t) = 500 + 50 + 100 = 650$

TUTORIAL EXERCISE

SECTION-III

ONLY ONE CORRECT ANSWER

1. The function $f(x) = \dfrac{ax+b}{cx+d}$ is a strictly increasing function $\forall\ x \in R - \{-d/c\}$, if

(a) $ad - bc < 0$ (b) $ad - bc > 0$
(c) $ab - cd > 0$ (d) $ab - cd < 0$

2. If $f(x) = x^2$ is an increasing function, then (here $a > 0$)

(a) $x \in [a, 2a)$ (b) $x \in (-\infty, -a] \cup [0, a]$
(c) $x \in (-a, 0)$ (d) None of these

3. The interval in which $f(x) = \cot^{-1} x + x$ increases, is

(a) $\mathbb{R}$ (b) $(0, \infty)$
(c) $\mathbb{R} - \{n\pi\}$ (d) None of these

4. If $f(x) = ax^3 + bx^2 + cx + d$, where a,b,c,d are real numbers and $3b^2 < c^2$, is an increasing cubic function and $g(x) = af'(x) + bf''(x) + c^2$, then

(a) $\int_a^x g(t)\,dt$ is a decreasing function

(b) $\int_a^x g(t)\,dt$ is an increasing function

(c) $\int_a^x g(t)\,dt$ is a neither increasing nor decreasing function

(d) None of the above

5. If $f(x) = \ln(1+x) - \dfrac{\tan^{-1} x}{1+x}$ (for $x > 0$); then sgn $f(x)$ is

(a) 1 (b) -1
(c) 4 (d) None of these

6. If $f''(x) > 0$ and $f'(1) = 0$ such that $g(x) = f(\cot^2 x + 2\cot x + 2)$, where $0 < x < \pi$, then the interval in which $g(x)$ is decreasing is

(a) $(0, \pi)$ (b) $\left(\dfrac{\pi}{2}, \pi\right)$
(c) $\left(\dfrac{3\pi}{4}, \pi\right)$ (d) $\left(0, \dfrac{3\pi}{4}\right)$

7. Let $f(x) = \dfrac{\sin x}{x}$, where $0 < x < \dfrac{\pi}{2}$, then:

(a) $\sin^2 x < x \sin(\sin x)$
(b) $\sin^2 x > x \sin(\sin x)$
(c) $\sin^2 x > 1 + x \sin(\sin x)$
(d) None of these

8. Let $f(x)$ be a differentiable function such that, $f'(x) = \dfrac{1}{\log_3[\log_{1/4}(\cos x + a)]}$. If $f(x)$ is increasing for all values of x, then:

(a) $a \in (5, \infty)$ (b) $a \in \left(1, \dfrac{5}{4}\right)$
(c) $a \in \left(\dfrac{5}{4}, 5\right)$ (d) None of these

9. If $\phi(x) = f(x) + f(2a - x)$ and $f''(x) > 0$, $a > 0$, $0 \le x \le 2a$, then

(a) $\phi(x)$ increases in $(a, 2a)$
(b) $\phi(x)$ increases in $(0, a)$
(c) $\phi(x)$ decreases in $(a, 2a)$
(d) None of these

10. Let $f'(x) > 0$ and $f''(x) < 0$, where $x_1 < x_2$, then which of the following is true

(a) $f\left(\dfrac{x_1 + 2x_2}{3}\right) > \dfrac{f(x_1) + 2f(x_2)}{3}$

(b) $f\left(\dfrac{x_1 + 2x_2}{3}\right) < \dfrac{f(x_1) + 2f(x_2)}{3}$

(c) $f\left(\dfrac{x_1 + 2x_2}{3}\right) = \dfrac{f(x_1) + 2f(x_2)}{3}$

(d) None of these

11. If $0 < A < \pi/6$, then which of the following is correct

(a) A (cosec A) $< \pi/3$ (b) $\sin(A)/A > \pi/3$
(c) A (cosec A) $< \pi/6$ (d) $\sin(A)/A > \pi/6$

12. If $f''(x) < 0$ for all $x \in (a, b)$, then $f'(x) = 0$

(a) exactly once in (a, b)
(b) at most once in (a, b)
(c) atleast once in (a, b)
(d) None of these

13. If a, b, c be non-zero real numbers such that $\int_0^1 (1+\cos^8 x)(ax^2+bx+c)dx$

$= \int_0^2 (1+\cos^8 x)(ax^2+bx+c)dx,$

Then the equation $ax^2 + bx + c = 0$ will have
(a) atleast one root $\in (1, 2)$
(b) both roots between 0 and 1
(c) both roots between 1 and 2
(d) None of these

14. Let f: $[2, 7] \to [\mathbb{R}]$ be a continuous and differentiable function. Then the value of $(f(7) - f(2))$ $\frac{(f(7))^2 + (f(2))^2 + f(2).f(7)}{3}$, is (where $c \in (2, 7)$)
(a) $3f^2(c) f'(c)$ (b) $5f^2(c).f(c)$
(c) $5f^2(c).f'(c)$ (d) None of these

15. The equation $\sin x + x \cos x = 0$ has at least one root in the interval
(a) $\left(-\frac{\pi}{2}, 0\right)$ (b) $(0, \pi)$
(c) $\left(-\frac{\pi}{2}, \frac{3\pi}{2}\right)$ (d) None of these

16. Let $f(x) = ax^5 + bx^4 + cx^3 + dx^2 + ex$, where $a, b, c, d, e \in \mathbb{R}$ and $f(x) = 0$ has a positive root α, then
(a) $f'(x) = 0$ has root α_1 such that $0 < \alpha_1 < \alpha$
(b) $f''(x) = 0$ has at least one real root
(c) $f'(x) = 0$ has at least two real roots
(d) all of the above

17. $f(x)$ is a polynomial of degree 4 with real coefficients such that $f(x) = 0$ is satisfied by $x = 1, 2, 3$ only, then $f'(1). f'(2). f'(3)$ is equal to:
(a) 0 (b) 2
(c) –1 (d) none of these

18. If $f(x)$ is a polynomial of degree 5 with real coefficients such that $f(|x|) = 0$ has 8 real roots, then $f(x) = 0$ has:
(a) 4 real roots only
(b) 5 real roots (one – ve other + ve)
(c) 3 real roots
(d) nothing can be said

19. If the function $f(x) = |x^2 + a\,|x| + b|$ has exactly three points of non-differentiability, then which of the following can be true?
(a) $b \le 0, a < 0$ (b) $b < 0, a \in \mathbb{R}$
(c) $b > 0, a \in \mathbb{R}$ (d) all of these

20. The point of the curve $3x^2 - 4y^2 = 72$ which is nearest to the line $3x + 2y - 1 = 0$ is:
(a) (–6, 3) (b) (6, – 3)
(c) (6, 6) (d) (6, 5)

21. The equation $3x^2 + 4ax + b = 0$ has at least one root in (0,1) if
(a) $4a + b + 3 = 0$ (b) $2a + b + 1 = 0$
(c) $b = 0, a = -4/3$ (d) none of these

22. The point on the curve $y = x^3$, where the tangent is parallel to the chord joining (1,1) and (3,27) is
(a) $\left(\frac{\sqrt{39}}{3}, \frac{13\sqrt{39}}{3}\right)$ (b) $\left(\frac{\sqrt{39}}{3}, \frac{13\sqrt{39}}{9}\right)$
(c) $\left(\frac{\sqrt{39}}{3}, \frac{\sqrt{39}}{18}\right)$ (d) none of these

23. If $f(x) = (ab - b^2 - 2)x + \int_0^x (\cos^4\theta + \sin^4\theta)d\theta$ is a decreasing function of x for all $x \in \mathbb{R}$ and $b \in \mathbb{R}$, b being independent of x, then
(a) $a \in (0, \sqrt{2}]$ (b) $a \in [-2, 2]$
(c) $a \in [-\sqrt{2}, 0)$ (d) None of these

24. The angle between the tangent lines to the graph of the function $f(x) = \int_2^x (2t-5)\,dt$ at the points where the graph cuts the x-axis is
(a) $\pi/6$ (b) $\pi/4$
(c) $\pi/3$ (d) $\pi/2$

25. In which of the following functions Rolle's Theorem is applicable?
(a) $f(x) = \begin{cases} x, & 0 \le x < 1 \\ 0, & x = 1 \end{cases}$ on [0, 1]
(b) $f(x) = \begin{cases} \frac{\sin x}{x}, & -\pi \le x < 0 \\ 0, & x = 0 \end{cases}$ on $[-\pi, 0]$
(c) $f(x) = \frac{x^2 - x - 6}{x - 1}$ on [–2, 3]
(d) $f(x) = \begin{cases} \frac{x^3 - 2x^2 - 5x + 6}{x - 1} & \text{if } x \ne 1, \text{ on } [-2, 3] \\ -6 & \text{if } x = 1 \end{cases}$

26. Let $f(x)$ and $g(x)$ be two differentiable function in $\mathbb{R}$ and $f(2) = 8$, $g(2) = 0$, $f(4) = 10$ and $g(4) = 8$ then
(a) $g'(x) > 4f'(x)\ \forall\ x \in (2, 4)$
(b) $3g'(x) = 4f'(x)$ for at least one $x \in (2,4)$

(c) $g(x) > f(x)\ \forall\ x \in (2, 4)$
(d) $g'(x) = 4f'(x)$ for at least one $x \in (2, 4)$

27. For the cubic, $f(x) = 2x^3 + 9x^2 + 12x + 1$ which one of the following statement, does not hold good?
(a) $f(x)$ is non monotonic
(b) Increasing in $(-\infty, -2)$ and $(-1, \infty)$ and decreasing is $(-2, -1)$
(c) $f: \mathbb{R} \to \mathbb{R}$ is bijective
(d) Inflection point occurs at $x = -3/2$

28. The set of value(s) of 'a' for which the function $f(x) = \dfrac{ax^3}{3} + (a + 2)x^2 + (a - 1)x + 2$ possess a negative point of inflection.
(a) $(-\infty, -2) \cup (0, \infty)$ (b) $\{-4/5\}$
(c) $(-2, 0)$ (d) empty set

29. Consider $f(x) = |1 - x|$; $1 \le x \le 2$ and $g(x) = f(x) + b \sin\dfrac{\pi}{2}x$; $1 \le x \le 2$, then which of the following is correct?
(a) Rolles theorem is applicable to both f, g and $b = 3/2$
(b) LMVT is not applicable to f and Rolles theorem is applicable to g with $b = 1/2$
(c) LMVT is applicable to f and Rolles theorem is applicable to g with $b = 1$
(d) Rolles theorem is not applicable to both f, g for any real b.

30. Consider $f(x) = \displaystyle\int_0^x \left(t + \frac{1}{t}\right) dt$ and $g(x) = f'(x)$ for $x \in \left[\dfrac{1}{2}, 3\right]$. If P is a point on the curve $y = g(x)$ such that the tangent to this curve at P is parallel to a chord joining the points $\left(\dfrac{1}{2}, g\left(\dfrac{1}{2}\right)\right)$ and $(3, g(3))$ of the curve, then the coordinates of the point P
(a) can't be found out (b) $\left(\dfrac{7}{4}, \dfrac{65}{28}\right)$
(c) $(1, 2)$ (d) $\left(\sqrt{\dfrac{3}{2}}, \dfrac{5}{\sqrt{6}}\right)$

31. For the function $f(x) = x + \sin x$, $x \in [1, 2]$, the value of c for the L.M.V. theorem is applicable
(a) $\cos^{-1}\left(2\cos\dfrac{3}{2}\cos\dfrac{1}{2}\right)$
(b) $\cos^{-1}\left(2\cos\dfrac{3}{2}\right)$
(c) $\cos^{-1}\left(2\cos\dfrac{3}{2}\sin\dfrac{1}{2}\right)$
(d) None of these

32. Let f be differentiable for all x. If $f(1) = -3$ and $f'(x) \ge 2$ for $x \in [1, 6]$, then
(a) $f(6) \ge 8$ (b) $f(6) \ge 7$
(c) $f(6) < 4$ (d) $f(6) = 5$

33. If a function $f(x)$ has $f'(a) = 0$ and $f''(a) = 0$, then
(a) $x = a$ is a maximum for $f(x)$
(b) $x = a$ is a minimum for $f(x)$
(c) It is difficult to say (a) and (b)
(d) $f(x)$ is necessarily a constant function

34. Let f and g be increasing and decreasing functions, respectively from $[0, \infty)$ to $[0, \infty)$. Let $h(x) = f[g(x)]$. If $h(0) = 0$, then $h(x) - h(1)$ is:
(a) always zero
(b) strictly increasing
(c) always negative
(d) always positive

35. The set of all values of 'a' for which the function, $f(x) = (a^2 - 3a + 2)\left(\cos^2\dfrac{x}{4} - \sin^2\dfrac{x}{4}\right) + (a - 1)x + \sin 1$ does not possess critical points is:
(a) $[1, \infty)$ (b) $(0, 1) \cup (1, 4)$
(c) $(-2, 4)$ (d) $(1, 3) \cup (3, 5)$

36. If $f(x) = 1 + x + \displaystyle\int_1^x \left(\ln^2 t + 2\ln t\right) dt$, then $f(x)$ increases in
(a) $(0, \infty)$ (b) $(0, e^{-2}) \cup (1, \infty)$
(c) no value (d) $(1, \infty)$

37. $f(x) = x^9 + 3x^7 + 6$ is increasing for
(a) all positive real x (b) all negative real x
(c) all $x \in \mathbb{R}$ (d) None of these

38. Let $f(x) = \begin{cases} \sin\dfrac{\pi x}{2}; & 0 \le x < 1 \\ 3 - 2x; & x \ge 1 \end{cases}$; then
(a) $f(x)$ has local maximum at $x = 1$
(b) $f(x)$ has local minimum at $x = 1$
(c) $f(x)$ does not have local extremum at $x = 1$
(d) $f(x)$ has global minimum at $x = 1$

39. A function $g(\theta) = \int_0^{\sin^2\theta} f(x)dx + \int_0^{\cos^2\theta} f(x)dx$ is defined in the interval $\left(-\frac{\pi}{2}, \frac{\pi}{2}\right)$, where $f(x)$ is an increasing function, then $g(\theta)$ is increasing in the interval

(a) $\left(-\frac{\pi}{2}, 0\right)$ (b) $\left(-\frac{\pi}{2}, -\frac{\pi}{4}\right)$
(c) $\left(0, \frac{\pi}{4}\right)$ (d) $\left(-\frac{\pi}{4}, 0\right)$

40. Let $f'(x) > 0$ and $g'(x) < 0\ \forall\ x \in \mathbb{R}$. Then
(a) $f(g(x)) < f(g(x+1))$ (b) $g(f(x)) > g(f(x-1))$
(c) $f(g(x)) > f(g(x-1))$ (d) $g(f(x)) > g(f(x+1))$

41. From a fixed point P on the circumference of a circle of radius a, the perpendicular PR is drawn to the tangent at Q(a variable point). The maximum area of ΔPQR is ka^2. Then k is

(a) $\frac{3\sqrt{3}}{4}$ (b) $\frac{3\sqrt{3}}{8}$
(c) $\frac{2\sqrt{3}}{5}$ (d) $\frac{2\sqrt{2}}{3}$

42. If $f''(x) + f'(x) + f^2(x) = x^2$ be the differential equation of a curve and let P be the point of maxima, then number of tangents which can be drawn from P to $x^2 - y^2 = a^2$ is/are
(a) 2 (b) 1
(c) 0 (d) either 1 or 2

43. If m and n are positive integers and $f(x) = \int_1^x (t-a)^{2n}(t-b)^{2m+1}\,dt,\ a \neq b$ then:
(a) $x = b$ is a point of local minimum
(b) $x = b$ is a point of local maximum
(c) $x = a$ is a point of local minimum
(d) $x = a$ is a point of local maximum

44. Point 'A' lies on the curve $y = e^{-x^2}$ and has the coordinate (x, e^{-x^2}), where $x > 0$. Point B has the coordinates $(x, 0)$. If 'O' is the origin, then the maximum area of the triangle AOB is

(a) $\frac{1}{\sqrt{2e}}$ (b) $\frac{1}{\sqrt{4e}}$
(c) $\frac{1}{\sqrt{e}}$ (d) $\frac{1}{\sqrt{8e}}$

45. The vertices of a triangle are $(0, 0)$, $(x, \cos x)$ and $(\sin^3 x, 0)$, where $0 < x < \frac{\pi}{2}$. The maximum area for such a triangle in sq. units, is.

(a) $\frac{3\sqrt{3}}{32}$ (b) $\frac{\sqrt{3}}{32}$
(c) $\frac{4}{32}$ (d) $\frac{6\sqrt{3}}{32}$

46. A rectangle with one side lying along the x-axis is to be inscribed in the closed region of the xy plane bounded by the lines $y = 0$, $y = 3x$, and $y = 30 - 2x$. The largest area of such a rectangle is.

(a) $\frac{135}{8}$ (b) 45
(c) $\frac{135}{2}$ (d) 90

47. Which of the following statements is true for the function $f(x) = \begin{cases} \sqrt{x}; & x \geq 1 \\ x^3; & 0 \leq x \leq 1 \\ \frac{x^3}{3}; & x < 0 \end{cases}$

(a) It is monotonic increasing $\forall\ x \in R$
(b) $f'(x)$ fails to exist for 3 distinct real values of x
(c) $f'(x)$ changes its sign twice as x varies from $(-\infty, \infty)$
(d) function attains its extreme values at x_1 and x_2, such that $x_1, x_2 > 0$

48. Give the correct order of initials T or F for following statements. Use T if statement is true and F if it is false.

Statement 1: If $f: \mathbb{R} \to \mathbb{R}$ and $c \in \mathbb{R}$ is such that f is increasing in $(c - \delta, c)$ and f is decreasing in $(c, c + \delta)$, then f has a local maximum at c. Where δ is a sufficiently small positive quantity.

Statement 2: Let $f: (a, b) \to \mathbb{R}$, $c \in (a, b)$. Then f can not have both a local maximum and a point of inflection at $x = c$.

Statement 3: The function $f(x) = x^2 |x|$ is twice differentiable at $x = 0$.

Statement 4: Let $f: [c - 1, c + 1] \to [a, b]$ be bijective map such that f is differentiable at c, then f^{-1} is also differentiable at $f(c)$.

(a) FFTF (b) TTFT
(c) FTTF (d) TTTF

49. The sum of the terms of an infinitely decreasing geometric progression is equal to the greatest value of the function $f(x) = x^3 + 3x - 9$ on the interval $[-2, 3]$. If the difference between the first and the second term of the progression is equal to $f'(0)$, then the common ratio of the G.P. is

(a) 1/3 (b) 1/2
(c) 2/3 (d) 3/4

50. The lateral edge of a regular rectangular pyramid is 'a' cm long. The lateral edge makes an angle α with the plane of the base. The value of α for which the volume of the pyramid is greatest, is:

(a) $\frac{\pi}{4}$ (b) $\sin^{-1}\sqrt{\frac{2}{3}}$
(c) $\cot^{-1}\sqrt{2}$ (d) $\frac{\pi}{3}$

51. Let $f(x) = \begin{cases} x^{3/5} & \text{if } x \le 1 \\ -(x-2)^3 & \text{if } x > 1 \end{cases}$. Then the number of critical points on the graph of the function is.

(a) 1 (b) 2
(c) 3 (d) 4

52. A curve with equation of the form $y = ax^4 + bx^3 + cx + d$ has zero gradient at the point (0, 1) and also touches the x-axis at the point (–1, 0), then the values of x for which the curve has a negative gradient are.

(a) $x > -1$ (b) $x < 1$
(c) $x < -1$ (d) $-1 \le x \le 1$

53. The function 'f' is defined by $f(x) = x^p (1-x)^q$ for all $x \in \mathbb{R}$, where p, q are positive integers, has a maximum value, for x equal to:

(a) $\frac{pq}{p+q}$ (b) 1
(c) 0 (d) $\frac{p}{p+q}$

54. Let $f(x) = \begin{cases} \frac{(x-1)(6x-1)}{2x-1} & \text{if } x \ne \frac{1}{2} \\ 0 & \text{if } x = \frac{1}{2} \end{cases}$, then at $x = \frac{1}{2}$

(a) f has a local maxima
(b) f has a local minima
(c) f has an inflection point
(d) f has a removable discontinuity

55. If $f(x) = \int_x^{x^2} (t-1)\, dt$, $1 \le x \le 2$, then global maximum value of $f(x)$ is:

(a) 1 (b) 2
(c) 4 (d) 5

56. A right triangle is drawn in a semicircle of radius 1/2 with one of its legs along the diameter. The maximum area of the triangle is

(a) $\frac{1}{4}$ (b) $\frac{3\sqrt{3}}{32}$
(c) $\frac{3\sqrt{3}}{16}$ (d) $\frac{1}{8}$

57. P and Q are two points on a circle of centre C and radius α, the angle PCQ being 2θ, then the radius of the circle inscribed in the triangle CPQ is maximum when.

(a) $\sin\theta = \frac{\sqrt{3}-1}{2\sqrt{2}}$ (b) $\sin\theta = \frac{\sqrt{5}-1}{2}$
(c) $\sin\theta = \frac{\sqrt{5}+1}{2}$ (d) $\sin\theta = \frac{\sqrt{5}-1}{4}$

58. Two sides of a triangle are to have lengths 'a' cm and 'b' cm. If the triangle is to have the maximum area, then the length of the median from the vertex containing the sides 'a' and 'b' is.

(a) $\frac{1}{2}\sqrt{a^2+b^2}$ (b) $\frac{2a+b}{3}$
(c) $\sqrt{\frac{a^2+b^2}{2}}$ (d) $\frac{a+2b}{3}$

59. Let $f(x) = \int_1^x \left(t\ln(t) - \frac{\ln t}{t} \right) dt$; $(x > 1)$, then

(a) $f(x)$ has one point of maxima and no point of minima.
(b) $f(x)$ has two distinct roots
(c) $f(x)$ has one point of minima and no point of maxima
(d) $f(x)$ is monotonic

60. Suppose that f is a polynomial of degree 3 and that $f''(x) \ne 0$ at any of the stationary point. Then

(a) f has exactly one stationary point.
(b) f must have no stationary point.
(c) f must have exactly 2 stationary points.
(d) f has either 0 or 2 stationary points.

61. The coordinate of the point on $y^2 = 8x$, which is closest from $x^2 + (y+6)^2 = 1$ is/are

(a) (2, – 4) (b) (18, – 12)
(c) (2, 4) (d) none of these

62. Let $f(x) = 1 + 2x^2 + 2^2x^4 + \ldots + 2^{10}x^{20}$. Then $f(x)$ has

(a) more than one minimum
(b) exactly one minimum

(c) atleast one maximum
(d) None of the above

63. A differentiable function $f(x)$ has a relative minimum at $x = 0$, then the function $y = f(x) + ax + b$ has a relative minimum at $x = 0$ for
(a) all a and all b (b) all b if $a = 0$
(c) all $b > 0$ (d) all $a > 0$

64. Let $f: [a, b] \to \mathbb{R}$ be a function such that $c \in (a, b)$, $f'(c) = f''(c) = f'''(c) = f^{iv}(c) = f^{v}(c) = 0$, then
(a) f has local extremum at $x = c$
(b) f has neither local maximum nor local minimum at $x = c$
(c) f is necessarily a constant function
(d) it is difficult to say whether (a) or (b)

65. If $f(x) = 1 + 2x^2 + 4x^4 + 6x^6 + ... + 100x^{100}$ is a polynomial in a real variable x, then $f(x)$ has :
(a) neither a maximum nor a minimum
(b) only one maximum
(c) only one minimum
(d) None of these

66. If $f(x) = \frac{x^2 - 1}{x^2 + 1}$ for every real x, then the minimum value of f
(a) does not exist because f is unbounded
(b) is not attained even though f is bounded
(c) is equal to 1
(d) is equal to – 1

67. The equation $x + e^x = 0$ has
(a) no real root (b) one real positive root
(c) two real roots (d) one real negative root

68. The greatest values of the function $f(x) = \frac{\sin 2x}{\sin(x + x/4)}$ on the interval $\left[0, \frac{\pi}{2}\right]$ is equal to
(a) $\frac{1}{\sqrt{2}}$ (b) 2
(c) 1 (d) $-\sqrt{2}$

69. The minimum value $3x + 4y$, when $xy = r^2$ and $x > 0$ is
(a) $4\sqrt{3}\,r$ (b) $24\sqrt{r}$
(c) $12r$ (d) None of these

70. The function $f(x) = x^3 + 24x^2 + ax - 10$ attains its relative minimum value at $x = 1$. Then the value of a is
(a) 51 (b) – 51
(c) – 45 (d) None of these

71. The minimum value of x^x is attained when x is equal to:
(a) e (b) e^{-1}
(c) 1 (d) e^2

72. The values of constants a and b for which the function, $y = a \log_e x + bx^2 + x$ has a local minimum at $x = 1$ and local maximum at $x = 2$ are:
(a) $a = \frac{2}{3}, b = -\frac{1}{6}$ (b) $a = \frac{2}{3}, b = \frac{1}{6}$
(c) $a = -\frac{2}{3}, b = \frac{1}{6}$ (d) $a = -\frac{2}{3}, b = -\frac{1}{6}$

73. The maximum slope of the curve $y = -x^3 + 3x^2 + 2x - 27$ will be:
(a) –165/8 (b) – 27
(c) 5 (d) None of these

74. At $x = a$, there is minimum for a given function $f(x)$, then:
(a) $\lim_{x\to a^-} f'(x) = \lim_{x\to a^+} f'(x)$
(b) $\lim_{x\to a^-} f'(x) > 0$, $\lim_{x\to a^+} f'(x) < 0$
(c) $\lim_{x\to a^-} f'(x) < 0$, $\lim_{x\to a^+} f'(x) > 0$
(d) Nothing can be said

75. A closed vessel tapers to a point both at its top E and its bottom F and is fixed with EF vertical when the depth of the liquid in it is x cm, the volume of the liquid in it is, $x^2(15 - x)$ cu. cm. The length EF is:
(a) 7.5 cm (b) 8 cm
(c) 10 cm (d) 12 cm

76. The lateral edge of a regular hexagonal pyramid is 1cm. If the volume is maximum, then its height must be equal to:
(a) 1/3 (b) 2/3
(c) $\frac{1}{\sqrt{3}}$ (d) 1

77. Let $f(x) = \begin{cases} x^3 - x^2 + 10x - 5, & x \le 1 \\ -2x + \log_2(b^2 - 2), & x > 1 \end{cases}$ the set of values of b for which $f(x)$ have greatest value at $x = 1$ is given by:
(a) [1, 2] (b) {1, 2}
(c) $(-\infty, -1)$ (d) None of these

78. The least area of a circle circumscribing any right triangle of area S is:
(a) πS (b) $2\pi S$
(c) $\sqrt{\pi S}$ (d) $4\pi S$

79. Equation of a straight line passing through (1, 4) if the sum of its positive intercepts on the co-ordinate axes is the smallest is:

(a) $2x + y - 6 = 0$ (b) $x + 2y - 9 = 0$

(c) $y + 2x - 6 = 0$ (d) None of these

80. Two points $A(1, 4)$ and $B(3, 0)$ are given on the ellipse $2x^2 + y^2 = 18$. The co-ordinates of a point on the ellipse such that the area of the triangle ABC is greatest is equal to

(a) $(\sqrt{6}, \sqrt{6})$ (b) $(-\sqrt{6}, \sqrt{6})$

(c) $(\sqrt{6}, -\sqrt{6})$ (d) $(-\sqrt{6}, -\sqrt{6})$

81. Let f: $(0, \pi) \to \mathbb{R}$ be a function defined by $f(x) = \max\{\sin 2x, \cos 2x\}$, then set of points of which $f(x)$ has local maxima or minima is equal to

(a) $\left\{\frac{\pi}{4}, \frac{\pi}{2}\right\}$ (b) $\left\{\frac{\pi}{2}, \frac{3\pi}{4}\right\}$

(c) $\left\{\frac{\pi}{8}, \frac{\pi}{4}, \frac{5\pi}{8}\right\}$ (d) None of these

82. The point(s) of minimum of the function, $f(x) = 4x^3 - x|x - 2|, x \in [0, 3]$ is

(a) $x = 0$ (b) $x = 1/3$

(c) $x = 1/2$ (d) $x = 2$

83. If the function $y = \frac{ax+b}{(x-4)(x-1)}$ has an extremum at $P(2, -1)$, then the values of a and b are

(a) $a = 0, b = 1$ (b) $a = 0, b = -1$

(c) $a = 1, b = 0$ (c) $a = 1, b = 0$

84. The minimum value of $2\log_{10} x - \log_x .01$, $x > 1$ is

(a) 1 (b) –1

(c) 2 (d) None of these

85. The maximum value of $x^{2/3} + (x-2)^{2/3}$ is

(a) 0 (b) 2

(c) $2^{2/3}$ (d) None of these

86. The minimum value of the function $f(x) = \frac{x^p}{p} + \frac{x^{-q}}{q}$ where $\frac{1}{p} + \frac{1}{q} = 1, p > 1$ is equal to

(a) 1 (b) 0

(c) 2 (d) None of these

87. Let $P(x) = a_o + a_1x^2 + a_2x^4 + a_3x^6 + ...a_nx^{2n}$ be a polynomial in a real variable x with $0 < a_o < a_1 < a_2 < ...... < a_n$. The function $P(x)$ has

(a) neither a max nor a min.

(b) only one max

(c) both max. and min.

(d) only one min.

88. If M be the greatest value and m be the least value of $f(x) = 2x^3 - 3x^2 - 12x + 1$ for $-1 \le x \le 3/2$, then the ordered pair (M, m) is

(a) (8, – 19) (b) (8, 17)

(c) (–17, – 19) (d) None of these

89. Let $P(x) = a_1x + a_2x^3 + a_3x^5 + ... + a_nx^{2n-1}$ be a polynomial in a real variable x with $0 < a_1, a_2,...., a_n$ then the function $P(x)$ has

(a) No extremum (b) One minimum

(c) One maximum (d) More than one extreme

90. The function $f(x) = \cos|x| - 2ax + b$ increases along the entire number scale, the range of values of a is given by

(a) $a \le b$ (b) $a = \frac{b}{2}$

(c) $a \le \frac{-1}{2}$ (d) $a \ge \frac{-3}{2}$

91. If $a^2x^4 + b^2y^4 = c^6$, then the maximum value of xy is

(a) $\frac{|c|^3}{2|ab|}$ (b) $\frac{|c|^3}{\sqrt{2|ab|}}$

(c) $\frac{|c|^3}{|ab|}$ (d) $\frac{|c|^3}{\sqrt{|ab|}}$

92. The minimum area bounded by $y = \left[\frac{x^2}{64} + 2\right]$, $y = x - 1, x = 0$, above the x – axis, (where [.] is greatest integer function) is equal to

(a) 1 (b) 2

(c) 3 (d) 4

93. Suppose x_1 and x_2 are the point of maximum and the point of minimum respectively of the function $f(x) = 2x^3 - 9ax^2 + 12a^2x + 1$ respectively, then for the equality $x_1^2 = x_2$ to be true the value of 'a' must be:

(a) 0 (b) 2

(c) 1 (d) 1/4

94. The local minimum value of $\frac{\tan(x + \pi/6)}{\tan x}$ is:

(a) 0 (b) 1/2

(c) 1 (d) 3

95. The radius of a right circular cylinder of greatest curved surface which can be inscribed in a given right circular cone is:

(a) one third that of the cone

(b) $\frac{1}{\sqrt{2}}$ times that of the cone

(c) $\frac{2}{3}$ that of the cone

(d) $\frac{1}{2}$ that of the cone

96. The lengths of the hypotenuse of a right angled triangle is given the area of the triangle will be maximum if the angle between hypotenuse and base is

(a) $\frac{\pi}{6}$ (b) $\frac{\pi}{4}$

(c) $\frac{\pi}{3}$ (d) $\frac{5\pi}{12}$

97. The first and the second derivatives of a function $f(x)$ exists at all points in (a, b) with $f'(c) = 0$ where $a < c < b$. Further more if $f'(x) < 0$ at all points on the immediate left of c and $f'(x) > 0$ for all points on the immediate right of c then at $x = c$, $f(x)$ has a:

(a) local maximum (b) point of inflexion

(c) local minimum (d) global maximum

98. The least value of $'a'$ for which the equation, $\frac{4}{\sin x} + \frac{1}{1 - \sin x} = a$ has atleast one solution on the interval $(0, \pi/2)$ is:

(a) 3 (b) 5

(c) 7 (d) 9

99. The set of all values of $'a'$ for which the function, $f(x) = (a^2 - 3a + 2)\left(\cos^2\frac{x}{4} - \sin^2\frac{x}{4}\right) + (a - 1)x + \sin 1$ does not possess critical points is

(a) $[1, \infty)$ (b) $(0, 1) \cup (1, 4)$

(c) $(-2, 4)$ (d) $(1, 3) \cup (3, 5)$

100. The least value of the function $f(x) = \int_{5\pi/3}^{x} (6\cos t - 2\sin t)dt$ in $\left[\frac{5\pi}{3}, \frac{7\pi}{4}\right]$ is:

(a) $3\sqrt{3} - 2\sqrt{2} - 1$ (b) $3\sqrt{3} - 2\sqrt{2} + 1$

(c) $3\sqrt{3} + 2\sqrt{2} - 1$ (d) zero

101. For all $a, b \in \mathbb{R}$ the function $f(x) = 3x^4 - 4x^3 + 6x^2 + ax + b$ has:

(a) no extremum

(b) exactly one extremum

(c) exactly two extremum

(d) three extremum.

102. Let $f(x) = \int_0^x \frac{\cos t}{t}\, dt$, $x > 0$. Then $f(x)$ has

(a) maxima at $x = n\pi$ when $n = -2, -4, -6,.....$

(b) maxima at $x = (2n + 1)\pi/2$ when $n = -1, -3, -5,...$

(c) minima at $x = (2n + 1)\pi/2$ when $n = 0, 2, 4,....$

(d) minima at $x = (2n + 1)\pi/2$ when $n = 1, 3, 5,....$

103. The number of solutions of the equation, $a^{f(x)} + g(x) = 0$, when $a > 0$, $g(x) \neq 0$ and $g(x)$ has a minimum value 1/2 is:

(a) one (b) two

(c) infinite (d) zero

104. On the interval $\left[\frac{5\pi}{4}, \frac{4\pi}{3}\right]$ the least value of the function $f(x) = \int_{5\pi/4}^{x} (3\sin t + 4\cos t)\, dt$ is equal to

(a) 0 (b) $-2\sqrt{3} + \frac{3}{2} + \frac{1}{\sqrt{2}}$

(c) $-2\sqrt{2} + \frac{2}{3} + \frac{1}{\sqrt{3}}$ (d) None of these

SECTION–IV

MORE THAN ONE ARE CORRECT

1. $f(x) = (x^9 + 3x^7 + 6)^{97}$ is increasing for

(a) All positive real x

(b) All $x \in \mathbb{R} - \{0\}$

(c) All negative real x

(d) None of these

2. If $f(x)$ and $g(x)$ are two positive and increasing functions, then

(a) $(f(x))g(x)$ is always increasing

(b) If $(f(x))^{g(x)}$ is decreasing, then $f(x) \leq 1$,

(c) If $(f(x))^{g(x)}$ is decreasing, then $f(x) > 1$,

(d) If $f(x) > 1$, then $(f(x))^{g(x)}$ is increasing

3. If f: $\mathbb{R} \to \mathbb{R}$, $f(x)$ is a differentiable bijective function, then which of the following may be true?
(a) $(f(x) - x)f''(x) < 0\ \forall\ x \in \mathbb{R}$
(b) $(f(x) - x)f''(x) > 0\ \forall\ x \in \mathbb{R}$
(c) If $(f(x) - x)f''(x) > 0$, then $f(x) = f^{-1}(x)$ has no solution
(d) If $(f(x) - x)f''(x) > 0$, then $f(x) = f^{-1}(x)$ has at least one real solution

4. Which of the following statements is true about the monotonocity of $Q(x)$; where $Q(x) = 2f\left(\frac{x^2}{2}\right) + f(6 - x^2)\ \forall\ x \in R$.
If it is given that $f''(x) > 0\ \forall\ x \in R$.
(a) $Q(x)$ is increasing in $x \in (-2,0)\cup(2,\infty)$
(b) $Q(x)$ is decreasing in $x \in (-\infty,-2)\cup(0,2)$
(c) $Q(x)$ is increasing in $x \in (-\infty,-2)\cup(-2,0)$
(d) $Q(x)$ is decreasing in $x \in (-2,0)\cup(2,\infty)$

5. If $\phi(x) = 3f\left(\frac{x^2}{3}\right) + f(3-x^2)\ \forall\ x \in (-3, 4)$ where $f''(x) > 0\ \forall\ x \in (-3, 4)$, then $\phi(x)$ is
(a) increasing in $\left(\frac{3}{2}, 4\right)$
(b) decreasing in $\left(-3, -\frac{3}{2}\right)$
(c) increasing in $\left(-\frac{3}{2}, 0\right)$
(d) decreasing in $\left(0, \frac{3}{2}\right)$

6. If $0 < A, B, C < \pi/2$, then which of the following is correct
(a) $A \operatorname{cosec} A + B \operatorname{cosec} B + C \operatorname{cosec} C < \frac{3\pi}{2}$
(b) $A \operatorname{cosec} A + B \operatorname{cosec} B + C \operatorname{cosec} C > \frac{3\pi}{2}$
(c) $\sin A + \sin B + \sin C > 2$
(d) None of these

7. Let $f(x) = \sin x + ax + b$, then $f(x) = 0$ has
(a) only one real root which is positive if $a > 1, b < 0$
(b) only one real root which is negative if $a > 1, b > 0$
(c) only one real root which is negative if $a < -1$, $b < 0$,
(d) None of these

8. At $x \to 0^+$, all of these function $\frac{1}{x}, \frac{1}{x^2}, \frac{1}{\sqrt{x}}$ become infinite. Which of these increases most rapidly:
(a) $\frac{1}{x}$ (b) $\frac{1}{x^2}$
(c) $\frac{1}{\sqrt{x}}$ (d) all increase with equal rate

9. The function $f(x) = x - \cot^{-1} x + \log(\sqrt{x^2+1} - x)$ is increasing on
(a) $(-\infty, 0)$ (b) $(0, \infty)$
(c) $(-\infty, \infty)$ (d) $[0, \infty)$

10. The function is $\cos^{-1}\left(\frac{1-x^2}{1+x^2}\right)$
(a) increasing in $(0, \infty)$ (b) decreasing in $(-\infty, 0)$
(c) decreasing in $(0, \infty)$ (d) increasing in $(-\infty, 0)$

11. If $f(x) = \frac{x}{\sin x}$ and $g(x) = \frac{x}{\tan x}$; where $0 < x \le 1$, then in the interval
(a) both $f(x)$ and $g(x)$ are increasing
(b) both $f(x)$ and $g(x)$ are decreasing
(c) $f(x)$ is increasing
(d) $g(x)$ is decreasing

12. The function $f(x) = \int_0^x \sqrt{1 - t^4}\, dt$ is such that:
(a) it is defined on the interval $[-1, 1]$
(b) it is an increasing function
(c) it is an odd function
(d) it is an even function

13. If $f(x) = \begin{cases} 7 - x^2; & x < 2 \\ 11 - x; & x \ge 2 \end{cases}$, then
(a) $f(x)$ has local maxima at $x = 0$
(b) $f(x)$ has local minima at $x = 2$
(c) $f(x)$ has local maxima at $x = 11$
(d) None of these

14. If $f(x) = \begin{cases} 3x^2 + 12x - 1; & -1 \le x \le 2 \\ 37 - x; & 2 < x \le 3 \end{cases}$; then
(a) $f(x)$ is increasing on $[-1,2]$
(b) $f(x)$ is continuous on $[-1,3]$
(c) $f'(2)$ does not exist
(d) $f(x)$ has the maximum value at $x = 2$

15. Let S be the set of real values of parameter λ for which the equation $f(x) = 2x^3 - 3(2 + \lambda)x^2 + 12\lambda x$ has exactly one local maximum and exactly one local minimum. Then S is a super set of

(a) $(-4,\infty)$ (b) $(-3,3)$
(c) $(3,\infty)$ (d) $(-\infty, 0)$

16. The function $f(x) = \sin x - x\cos x$ is:
(a) maximum or minimum for all integral multiple of π
(b) maximum if x is an odd positive or even negative integral multiple of π
(c) minimum if x is an even positive or odd negative integral multiple of π
(d) None of these

17. For the function $f(x) = x^4 (12\ln x - 7)$
(a) the point $(1, -7)$ is the point of inflection
(b) $x = e^{1/3}$ is the point of minima
(c) the graph is concave downwards in $(0,1)$
(d) the graph is concave upwards in $(1, \infty)$

18. In which of the following graphs $x = c$ is the point of inflection.

(a) 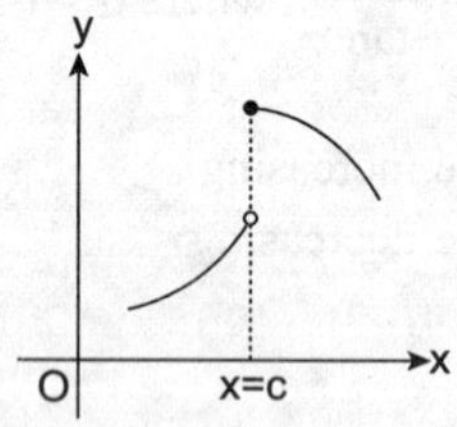

(b) 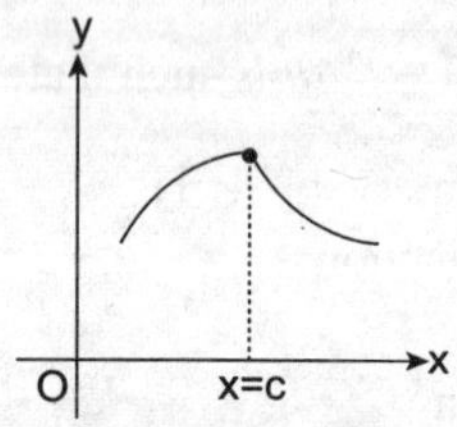

(c) 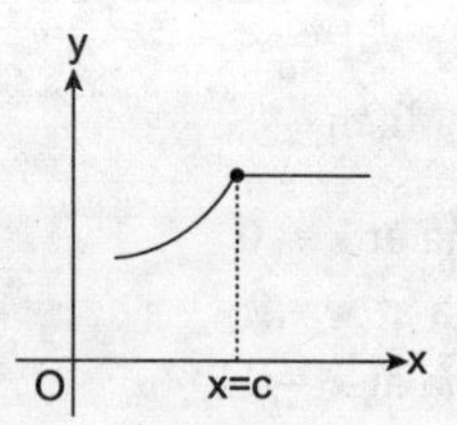

(d) 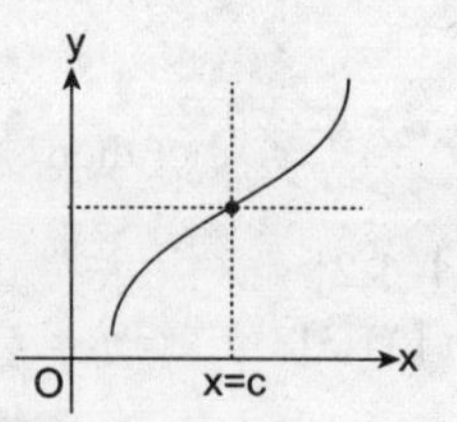

19. Let $f(x) = \dfrac{x-1}{x^2}$, then which of the following is correct.
(a) $f(x)$ has minima but no maxima.
(b) $f(x)$ increases in the interval $(0, 2)$ and decreases in the interval $(-\infty, 0) \cup (2, \infty)$
(c) is concave down in $(-\infty, 0) \cup (0, 3)$
(d) $x = 3$ is the point of inflection.

20. Suppose $F(x) = \int_0^{\sqrt{9-x^2}} e^{\frac{t^2}{2}}\,dt$. Then,
(a) $F(x)$ is increasing for $x \in (-3, 0)$
(b) $F(x)$ is decreasing for $x \in (0, 3)$
(c) $F(0)$ is the maximum value of $F(x)$
(d) $F'(x)$ is an odd function.

21. Let $f(x) = ax^3 + bx^2 + cx + 1$ have extrema at $x = \alpha, \beta$ such that $\alpha\beta < 0$ and $f(\alpha).f(\beta) < 0$. Then the equation $f(x) = 0$ has
(a) three equal real roots
(b) three distinct real roots
(c) one positive root if $f(\alpha) < 0$ and $f(\beta) > 0$
(d) one negative root if $f(\alpha) > 0$ and $f(\beta) < 0$

22. The function $f(x) = x^2 + \dfrac{\lambda}{x}$ has a
(a) minimum at $x = 2$ if $\lambda = 16$
(b) maximum at $x = 2$ if $\lambda = 16$
(c) maximum for no real value of λ
(d) point of inflection at $x = 1$ if $\lambda = -1$

23. If $f(x) = \sin^6 x + \cos^6 x$, then
(a) $f(x) \le 1$ (b) $f(x) \le 2$
(c) $f(x) > \dfrac{1}{4}$ (d) $f(x) > \dfrac{1}{8}$

24. The extremum of the function, $f(x) = |x^2 + 2x - 3| + \dfrac{3}{2}\ln x$, $x \in \left[\dfrac{1}{2}, 4\right]$ occur at:
(a) $x = 1$ (b) $x = 3$
(c) $x = 1/2$ (d) $x = 4$

25. The parabola $y = x^2 + px + q$ cuts the straight line $y = 2x - 3$ at a point with abscissa 1. If the distance between the vertex of the parabola and the x-axis is least then:
(a) $p = 0$ and $q = -2$
(b) $p = -2$ and $q = 0$
(c) least distance between the parabola and x-axis is 2
(d) least distance between the parabola and x-axis is 1

26. If $f(x) = a\sin x + 1/3\sin 3x$ has an extremum at $x = \dfrac{2\pi}{3}$, then:
(a) $a = 2$
(b) $f(2\pi/3)$ is maximum for $a = 2$
(c) $f(\pi/2)$ is minimum for $a = 2$
(d) there are three critical points between $(0, \pi)$

27. Let $y = f(x)$ be the equation of a parabola which is touched by the line $y = x$ at the point where $x = 1$. Then
(a) $f'(0) = f'(1)$
(b) $f'(1) = 1$
(c) $f(0) + f'(0) + f''(0) = 1$
(d) $2f(0) = 1 - f'(0)$

28. Let $f(x) = (x - 1)^4 \cdot (x - 2)^n, n \in \mathbb{N}$. Then $f(x)$ has
(a) a maximum at $x = 1$ if n is odd
(b) a maximum at $x = 1$ if n is even
(c) a minimum at $x = 2$ if n is even
(d) a maximum at $x = 2$ if n is odd

29. Let $f(x) = \phi(2 - x) + \phi(x)$ and $\phi''(x) < 0$ for $x \in [0, 2]$. Then
(a) $f(x)$ is increasing in [0,1]
(b) $f(x)$ is decreasing in [0,1]
(c) $f(x)$ is decreasing in [1, 2]
(d) $f(x)$ is increasing in [1,2]

30. The value of x for which the function $f(x) = \int_0^x (1-t^2)\, e^{-t^2/2} dt$ has an extremum is equal to
(a) 0 (b) 1
(c) -1 (d) None of these

31. The function sin $^{1}2x\sqrt{1\ \ x^2}$
(a) has $x = -\dfrac{1}{\sqrt{2}}$ as a point of minimum
(b) has $x = \dfrac{1}{\sqrt{2}}$ as a point of maximum
(c) attains its least value at $x = 0$
(d) attains its least value at $x = 1$.

32. If a differentiable function $f(x)$ has a relative minimum at $x = 0$, then the function $y = f(x) + ax^2 + bx + c$ has a relative minimum at $x = 0$ for
(a) $b = 0$, all a (b) $b = 0, a > -\dfrac{1}{2} f''(0)$
(c) $a = 0, b = 0$ (d) $a = 0, b = 0, c = 2$

33. If $f(x) = \sin^{-1}\left(\dfrac{2x}{1+x^2}\right)$, then
(a) $f'(1)$ does not exist
(b) $f'(-1)$ does not exist
(c) $x = 1$ is a local maximum for $f(x)$
(d) $x = 1$ is a local minimum for $f(x)$

34. Let $f(x) = (x - 1)^{p} \cdot (x - 2)^q$ where $p > 1, q > 1$. Each critical point of $f(x)$ is a point of extremum when
(a) $p = 3, q = 4$ (b) $p = 4, q = 2$
(c) $p = 2, q = 3$ (d) $p = 2, q = 4$

35. The point (0, 3) is closest to the curve $x^2 = 2y$ at
(a) $(2\sqrt{2}, 0)$ (b) (0, 0)
(c) (2, 2) (d) (–2, 2)

36. An extremum value of $y = \int_0^x (t-1)(t-2)\,dt$ is equal to
(a) 5/6 (b) 2/3
(c) 1 (d) 2

37. An extremum value of the function $f(x) = (\text{arc}\sin x)^3 + (\text{arc}\cos x)^3$ is:
(a) $\dfrac{7\pi^3}{8}$ (b) $\dfrac{\pi^3}{8}$
(c) $\dfrac{\pi^3}{32}$ (d) $\dfrac{\pi^3}{16}$

38. If $f(x) = 4x^3 - x^2 - 2x + 1$ and $g(x) = \begin{cases} \min\{f(t): 0 \le t \le x\} & ; 0 \le x \le 1 \\ 3 - x & ; 1 < x \le 2 \end{cases}$ then $g\left(\dfrac{1}{4}\right) + g\left(\dfrac{3}{4}\right) + g\left(\dfrac{5}{4}\right)$ has the value equal to
(a) $\dfrac{7}{4}$ (b) $\dfrac{9}{4}$
(c) $\dfrac{13}{4}$ (d) $\dfrac{5}{2}$

39. Let $f(x) = (x^2 - 1)^n (x^2 + x + 1)$, then $f(x)$ has local extremum at $x = 1$, when:
(a) $n = 2$ (b) $n = 3$
(c) $n = 4$ (d) $n = 6$

40. If $f(x) = \begin{cases} x+2 & -1 \le x < 0 \\ 1 & x = 0 \\ x/2 & 0 < x \le 1 \end{cases}$ then on [–1, 1], this function has
(a) a minimum
(b) a maximum
(c) either a maximum or a minimum
(d) neither a maximum nor a minimum

41. The extremum value of the function $f(x) = \dfrac{1}{\sin x + 4} - \dfrac{1}{\cos x - 4}$, where $x \in \mathbb{R}$ is:
(a) $\dfrac{4}{8-\sqrt{2}}$ (b) $\dfrac{2\sqrt{2}}{8-\sqrt{2}}$
(c) $\dfrac{2\sqrt{2}}{4\sqrt{2}+1}$ (d) $\dfrac{4\sqrt{2}}{8+\sqrt{2}}$

SECTION–V

ASSERTION AND REASON

1. A: Both $\sin x$ and $\cos x$ are decreasing function in the interval $(\pi/2, \pi)$.

R: If a differentiable function decreases in an interval (a,b), then its derivative also decreases in (a,b).

2. Let $f(x) = 2 + \cos x$ for all real x

A: For each real t, there exists a point 'c' in $[t, t + \pi)$ such that $f'(c) = 0$.

R: $f(t) = f(t + 2\pi)$ for each real t.

3. A: The greatest of the numbers $1, 2^{1/2}, 3^{1/3}, 4^{1/4}, 5^{1/5}, 6^{1/6}, 7^{1/7}$ is $3^{1/3}$.

R: $x^{1/x}$ is increasing for $0 < x < e$ and decreasing for $x > e$

4. A: Let f: $[0,\infty) \to [0,\infty)$ and g: $[0,\infty) \to [0,\infty)$ be non-increasing and non-decreasing functions respectively and $h(x) = g(f(x))$. If f and g are differentiable for all points in their respective domains and $h(0) = 0$, then $h(x)$ is constant function.

R: $g(x) \in [0, \infty) \Rightarrow h(x) \ge 0$ and $h'(x) \le 0$

5. A: $f(x)$ is increasing function with concavity upwards, then concavity of $f^{-1}(x)$ is also upwards.

R: If $f(x)$ is decreasing function with concavity upwards, then concavity of $f^{-1}(x)$ is also upwards.

6. Let $f(x)$: $\mathbb{R} \to \mathbb{R}$ is differentiable and strictly increasing function throughout its domain

A: If $|f(x)|$ is also strictly increasing function, then $f(x) = 0$ has no real roots.

R: At $-\infty$, $f(x)$ may approach to 0, but can not be equal to zero.

7. A: If $g(x)$ is a differentiable function and Rolles theorem is not applicable to $f(x) = \frac{x^2-1}{g(x)}$ in $[-1,1]$, then $g(x)$ has atleast one root in $(-1,1)$.

R: If $f(a) = f(b)$, then Rolles theorem is applicable for $x \in (a, b)$.

8. A: Let $f(x) = 1 + 3x^2 + 3^2x^4 + 3^3x^6 + \ldots + 3^{30}x^{60}$ has exactly one point of local minima.

R: $f'(x)$ changes sign at $x = 0$ only.

9. A: Let $f(x) = 5 - 4(x-2)^{2/3}$, then at $x = 2$, the function $f(x)$ attains neither least value nor greatest value.

R: $x = 2$ is the only critical point of $f(x)$

10. A: Shortest distance between $|x| + |y| = 2$ and $x^2 + y^2 = 16$ is $4 - \sqrt{2}$.

R: Shortest distance between the two smooth curves lies along the common normal.

11. A: If $f(x)$ is a continuous function in its domain, then between any two consecutive maxima there always lies one minima.

R: If $f(x)$ is continuous then, for existence of maxima at $x = c$, $f'(x) > 0$ where $x < c$ and $f'(x) < 0$ where $x > c$, where as for minima at $x = c$. $f'(x) < 0$ at $x < c$ and $f'(x) > 0$ if $x > c$.

12. A: If $f(x) = \max\{x^2 - 2x + 2, |x-1|\}$ the greatest value of $f(x)$ on the interval $[0, 3]$ is 5

R: Greatest value $= f(3) = \max\{5, 2\} = 5$.

13. A: The graph $y = x^3 + ax^2 + bx + c$ has no extermum, if $a^2 < 3b$

R: y is either increasing or decreasing $\forall\, x \in \mathbb{R}$.

14. A: The least value of the function $f(x) = -x^2 + 4x + 1 + \sin^{-1} x$ on the interval $[-1, 1]$ is $-4 - \frac{\pi}{2}$.

R: $f(x)$ is increasing function having range $\left[-4 - \frac{\pi}{2}, 4 + \frac{\pi}{2}\right]$

15. A: The greatest value of abc for positive values of a, b, c subject to the condition $ab + bc + ca = 12$ is 8

R: $ab = bc = ca$

16. A: The function $f(x) = x^2 + \frac{16}{x}$ has a minimum value 12 at $x = 2$.

R: As x increases through 2, $f'(x)$ changes sign from positive to negative.

SECTION–VI

COMPREHENSION PASSAGE

A: $f: \mathbb{R} \to \mathbb{R}$, $f(x)$ is a differentiable function such that all its successive derivatives exist. $f'(x)$ can be zero at discrete points only and $f(x).f''(x) \le 0\ \forall\ x \in \mathbb{R}$.

1. If $f(a) = 0$, then which of the following is correct

(a) $f(a + h) f''(a - h) < 0$
(b) $f(a + h) f'(a - h) > 0$
(c) $f(a + h) f'(a - h) < 0$
(d) $f(a + h) f''(a - h) < 0$

2. If α and β are two consecutive roots of $f(x) = 0$, then

(a) $f'(\gamma) = 0; \gamma \in (\alpha, \beta)$ for some γ
(b) $f''(\gamma) = 0; \gamma \in (\alpha, \beta)$ for some γ
(c) $f'''(\gamma) = 0; \gamma \in (\alpha, \beta)$ for some γ
(d) $f''''(\gamma) = 0; \gamma \in (\alpha, \beta)$ for some γ

3. If $f'(x) \ne 0$, then maximum number of real roots of $f''(x) = 0$ is/are

(a) no real root (b) one
(c) two (d) three

B: If $f(x)$ is a differentiable function wherever it is continuous and $f'(c_1) = f'(c_2) = 0$, $f''(c_1).f''(c_2) < 0$, $f(c_1) = 5$, $f(c_2) = 0$ and $(c_1 < c_2)$.

4. If $f(x)$ is continuous in $[c_1, c_2]$ and $f''(c_1) - f''(c_2) > 0$, then minimum number of roots of $f'(x) = 0$ in $[c_1 - 1, c_2 + 1]$ is

(a) 2 (b) 3
(c) 4 (d) 5

5. If $f(x)$ is continuous in $[c_1\ c_2]$ and $f''(c_1) - f''(c_2) < 0$, then minimum number of roots of $f'(x) = 0$ in $[c_1 - 1, c_2 + 1]$ is

(a) 1 (b) 2
(c) 3 (d) 4

6. If $f(x)$ is continuous in $[c_1.\ c_2]$ and $f''(c_1) - f''(c_2) > 0$, then minimum number of roots of $f(x) = 0$ in $[c_1 - 1, c_2 + 1]$ is

(a) 2 (b) 3
(c) 4 (d) 5

C: Let $y = 2\sqrt{x} + bx$ be curve, $(2x - y) + \lambda(2x + y - 4) = 0$ be family of lines.

7. If curve has slope 1/6 at (9,0) then a tangent belonging to family of lines is

(a) $x + 2y - 5 = 0$ (b) $x - 2y + 3 = 0$
(c) $3x - y - 1 = 0$ (d) $3x + y - 5 = 0$

8. A line of the family cutting positive intercepts on axes and forming triangle with coordinate axes, then minimum length of the line segment between axes is

(a) $(2^{2/3} - 1)^{3/2}$ (b) $2\sqrt{5}$
(c) $7^{3/2}$ (d) 27

9. Two perpendicular chords of curve $y^2 - 4x - 4y + 4 = 0$ belonging to family of lines form diagonals of a quadrilateral. Minimum area of quadrilateral is

(a) 16 (b) 32
(c) 64 (d) 50

D: If a continuous function f defined on the real line R, assumes positive and negative values in R, then the equation $f(x) = 0$ has a root in R. For example, if it is known that a continuous function f on R is positive at some point and its minimum value is negative then the equation $f(x) = 0$ has a root in R.

Consider $f(x) = ke^x - x$ for all real x where k is a real constant.

10. The line $y = x$ meets $y = ke^x$ for $k \le 0$ at

(a) no point (b) one point
(c) two points (d) more than two points

11. The positive value of k for which $ke^x - x = 0$ has only one root is

(a) 1/e (b) 1
(c) e (d) $\log_e 2$

12. For $k > 0$, the set of all values of k for which $ke^x - x = 0$ has two distinct roots is

(a) (0, 1/e) (b) (1/e, 1)
(c) (1/e,) (d) (0, 1)

E: Suppose you do not know the function $f(x)$, however some information about $f(x)$ is listed below. Read the following carefully before attempting the questions

(i) $f(x)$ is continuous and defined for all real numbers

(ii) $f'(-5) = 0$; $f'(2)$ is not defined and $f'(4) = 0$

(iii) (–5, 12) is a point which lies on the graph of $f(x)$

(iv) $f''(2)$ is undefined, but $f''(x)$ is negative everywhere else.

(v) the signs of $f'(x)$ is given below

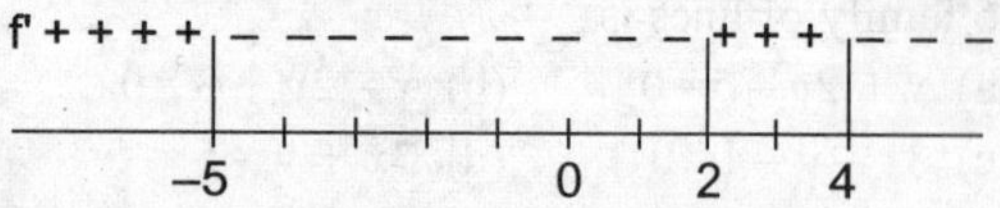

13. On the possible graph of $y = f(x)$ we have
(a) $x = -5$ is a point of relative minima.
(b) $x = 2$ is a point of relative maxima.
(c) $x = 4$ is a point of relative minima.
(d) graph of $y = f(x)$ must have a geometrical sharp corner.

14. From the possible graph of $y = f(x)$, we can say that
(a) There is exactly one point of inflection on the curve.
(b) $f(x)$ increases on $-5 < x < 2$ and $x > 4$ and decreases on $-\infty < x < -5$ and $2 < x < 4$.
(c) The curve is always concave down.
(d) Curve always concave up.

15. Possible graph of $y = f(x)$ is

(a)
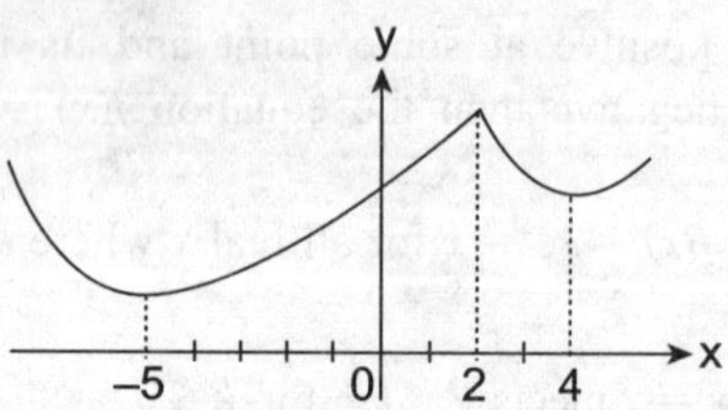

(b)
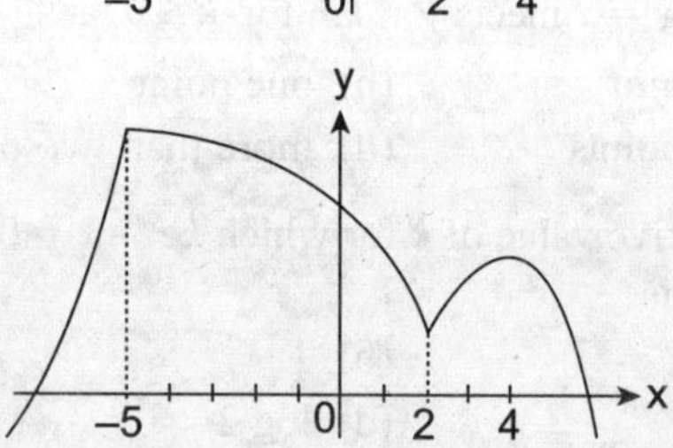

(c)
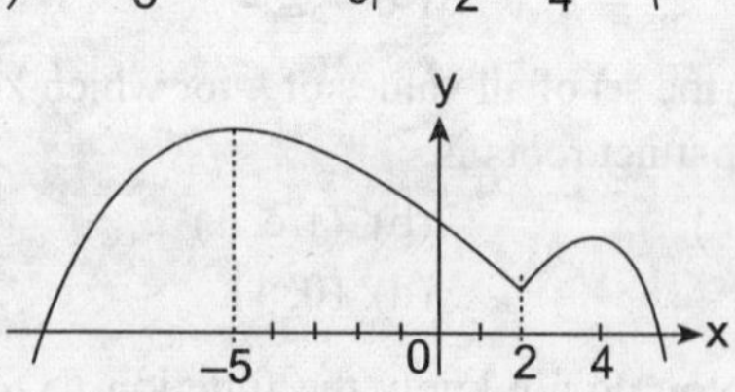

(d)
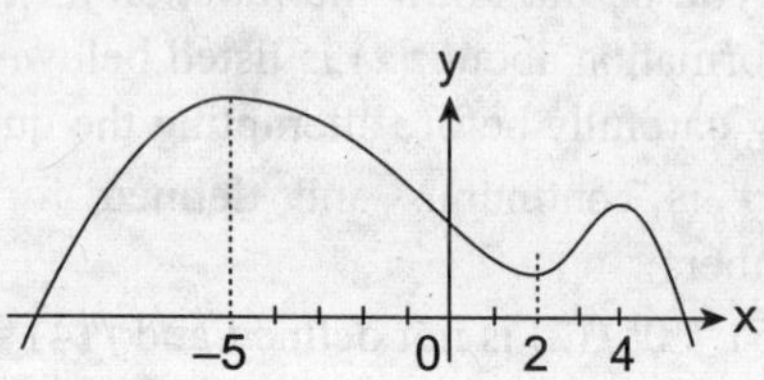

F: The greatest (or least) values of a continuous function $f(x)$ on an interval $[a, b]$ is attained either at the critical points, or at the end points of the interval. To find the greatest (or least) value of the function we have to compute its values at all the critical points on the interval $[a, b]$, the values $f(a)$, $f(b)$ of the function at the end-points of the interval and choose the greatest (or least) one out of numbers obtained.

16. For which value of x this function $f(x) = \sqrt{(1-x^2)(1+2x^2)}$ on $[-1, 1]$ possess maximum value is
(a) 1/2 (b) 1/4
(c) –1/2 (d) –1/4

17. The largest term in the sequence $a_n = \left(\dfrac{n^2}{n^3+200}\right)$ is
(a) $\dfrac{59}{435}$ (b) $\dfrac{1}{12}$
(c) $\dfrac{49}{543}$ (d) $\dfrac{59}{434}$

18. The function $f(x) = ax + \dfrac{b}{x}$ $(a, b, x > 0)$, consists of two summands, one summand is proportional to the independent variable x, the other inversely proportional to it. Then the least value of function is at x is equal to
(a) $\sqrt{ab}$ (b) $\sqrt{\dfrac{b}{a}}$
(c) $\sqrt{\dfrac{a}{b}}$ (d) $\sqrt{\dfrac{1}{ab}}$

19. The least value of the function $f(x) = arc\tan x - \dfrac{1}{2}$. In x on $\left[\dfrac{1}{\sqrt{3}}, \sqrt{3}\right]$ is
(a) $\dfrac{\pi}{6} + 0.25\ In\ 3$ (b) $\dfrac{\pi}{3} - 0.25\ In\ 3$
(c) $\dfrac{\pi}{6} - 0.25\ In\ 3$ (d) $\dfrac{\pi}{3} + 0.25\ In\ 3$

G: Consider the function
$f(x) = \max\ \{x^2, (1-x)^2, 2x(1-x)\}$
where $0 \le x \le 1$

20. The interval in which $f(x)$ is increasing in
(a) $\left(\dfrac{1}{3}, \dfrac{2}{3}\right)$ (b) $\left(\dfrac{1}{3}, \dfrac{1}{2}\right)$
(c) $\left(\dfrac{1}{3}, \dfrac{1}{2}\right)$ and $\left(\dfrac{1}{2}, \dfrac{2}{3}\right)$ (d) $\left(\dfrac{1}{3}, \dfrac{1}{2}\right)$ and $\left(\dfrac{2}{3}, 1\right)$

21. The interval in which $f(x)$ is decreasing is

(a) $\left(\frac{1}{3},\frac{2}{3}\right)$ (b) $\left(\frac{1}{3},\frac{1}{2}\right)$

(c) $\left(0,\frac{1}{2}\right)$ and $\left(\frac{1}{2},\frac{2}{3}\right)$ (d) $\left(\frac{1}{3},\frac{1}{2}\right)$ and $\left(\frac{2}{3},1\right)$

22. Let Rolle's theorem is applicable for $f(x)$ on $[a, b]$, then $a + b + c$ is (where c is p.t. $f'(x) = 0$)

(a) 2/3 (b) 1/3

(c) 1/2 (d) 3/2

H: If f: $\mathbb{R} \to \mathbb{R}$ is a function defined by $f(x) = 2\sin^2 2x + \frac{3}{4}\sin 4x + ax$, $\mathbb{R}$ is the set of real numbers and a is real. Then

23. Complete set of value of a for which $f(x)$ is strictly increasing for all $x \in \mathbb{R}$.

(a) $(-\infty, -5)$ (b) $(-5, \infty)$

(c) $[5, \infty)$ (d) $(-\infty, 5]$

24. Complete set of value of a for which $f(x)$ is strictly decreasing for all $x \in \mathbb{R}$.

(a) $(-\infty, -5]$ (b) $(-5, \infty)$

(c) $[5, \infty)$ (d) $(-\infty, 5]$

25. Complete set of values of a for which $f(x)$ is onto is

(a) $(-\infty,\infty) - \{0\}$

(b) $(-5, \infty)$

(c) $[5, \infty)$

(d) None of these

I: Let $f(x, y) = \tan^4 x + \tan^4 y + 3\cot^2 x \cot^2 y$

$g(x, y) = 3 + \sin^2(x + y)$

26. The minimum value of $f(x, y)$ can be given as

(a) 4 (b) $\sqrt{6}$

(c) $2\sqrt{6}$ (d) 3

27. The range of $g(x, y)$ can be given as

(a) $[0, 4]$ (b) $[3, 4]$

(c) $[-3, 3]$ (d) $[0,3]$

28. The number of solutions of the equation $f(x, y) = g(x, y)$ are

(a) 0 (b) 1

(c) 2 (d) 3

SECTION–VII

COLUMN MATCHING

1. **Column I**

(i) The number of the distinct real roots of the equation $(x + 1)^5 = 2(x^5 + 1)$ is

(ii) The absolute maximum value of the function $f(x)=\dfrac{(x+1)^4}{x^4-x^3+x^2-x+1}$ is

(iii) Let $f(x) = ab\sin x + \sqrt{1-a^2}\cos x + c$, where $|a|$, $|b| < 1$. then difference of maximum and minimum value of $f(x)$ is

(iv) If $u = \sqrt{4\cos^2\theta + \sin^2\theta} + \sqrt{4\sin^2\theta + \cos^2\theta}$ then the difference between maximum and minimum value of u^2 is

Column II

(a) 16

(b) 3

(c) 1

(d) 2

2. **Column I**

(i) A function f is differentiable in $[0, 5]$ such that $f(0) = 4$ and $f(5) = -1$. If $g(x) = \dfrac{f(x)}{x+1}$, then there exists some $c \in (0, 5)$ such that $g'(c)$ is equal to

(ii) Let $f(x)$ and $g(x)$ be differentiable for $0 \le x \le 1$ $f(0) = 2$, $g(0) = 0$, $f(1) = 6$. Let there exists a real number $c \in (0,1)$ such that $f'(c) = 2g'(c)$, Then $g(1)$ is equal to

(iii) Let f be differentiable $\forall\, x$, if $f(1) = -2$, $f'(x) \ge 2$ $\forall\, x \in [1, 6]$, then $f(6)$ has least possible value

(iv) Let Lagrange's mean value theorem is satisifed for $f(x) = \sqrt{25-x^2}$ and $c \in (1, 5)$. Then the value of c^2 is

Column II

(a) 8

(b) –5/6

(c) 15

(d) 2

3. In the following $[x]$ denotes the greatest integer less than or equal to x.

Column I

(i) $x\,|x|$

(ii) $\sqrt{|x|}$

(iii) $x + [x]$

(iv) $|x - 1| + |x + 1|$

Column – II

(a) continuous in $(-1,1)$

(b) differentiable in $(-1,1)$

(c) strictly increasing in $(-1,1)$

(d) non differentiable at least at one point in $(-1, 1)$

4. **Column I**

(i) If the greatest and least values of the function $f(x)=\begin{cases} 2x^2+\dfrac{2}{x^2}, x\in[-2,2]\sim\{0\} \\ 1\ , x=0 \end{cases}$ are G and L respectively on $[1, 2]$, then

(ii) If the greatest and least values of the function $f(x)=x^3-6x^2+9x+1$ on $[0, 3]$ are G and L respectively, then

(iii) If the greatest and least values of the function $f(x) = arc\ \tan x - \dfrac{1}{2}\ \ln x$ on $\left[\dfrac{1}{\sqrt{3}}, \sqrt{3}\right]$ are G and L respectively, then

Column II

(a) $[G + L] = 1$ where [.]= greatest integer function

(b) $[G + L] = 6$ where [.] = greatest integer function

(c) $[G+L] = 12$ where [.] = greatest integer function

(d) $(G+ L)= 5$ where (.) = Least integer function

(e) $(G + L) =10$ (.) Least integer function.

SECTION–VIII

1. Let $f:[-1,2]\to(-\infty,\infty)$ be given by $f(x)=\dfrac{x^4+3x^2+1}{x^2+1}$, then find value of $[\ _{\text{max.}}]$ in $[-1, 2]$; where [.] is gint function:

2. A channel of length 27m wide falls at right angle into another channel of length 64m wide. Then find the smallest length of the log that can't be floated along the system.

3. The interval to which λ belong so that the function $f(x)=\left(1-\dfrac{\sqrt{21-4\lambda-\lambda^2}}{\lambda+1}\right)x^3+5x+7$ is increasing at every point of its domain is $(a, b) \cup [c, d]$, then find $|a+b+c+d|$

4. The perimeter of a rectangle is 20 cm (constant). If length 'l' of rectangle is increasing at rate 2cm/sec, then find the length l beyond which if length is increased, area of rectangle decreases.

5. A circular sheet has radius $\sqrt{6}$ units. A Sector is cut and the remaining part of sheet is used to form a cone by joining the edges. Let V_0 be the maximum volume of which the cone can be formed, then evaluate $\tan^2\left(\dfrac{V_0}{8\sqrt{2}}\right)$.

6. Let P be the perimeter of rectangle of maximum area which can be inscribed inside ellipse $\dfrac{x^2}{25}+\dfrac{y^2}{16}=1$, then evaluate $\log_{3\sqrt{2}}(3P)$.

7. The height of a cylinder is increasing at rate of 1 unit / sec and radius is decreasing at rate $\dfrac{1}{2}$ unit / sec. Then find the least integer greatest, then the value of the ratio of rate of change of volume to rate of change of curved surface area at the instant $h = 10$ units and $r = 12$ units.

8. Let $f(x)$ be a function such that $f(x + y) = f(x) + f(y) + 2xy - 1\ \forall\ x, \in \mathbb{R}$ and $f'(0) = 2$. Further let $g(x) = \int_0^x f(t)dt$, then find the maximum value of $g(x)$ in $[1, 3]$.

9. If $y=ax^4+bx^3+cx^2+dx+e$ has critical points and $\log\left[-3b^4+12b^2-32ac+8ab^2c\right]$ is defined, then find the greatest possible value of 'b'.

10. If $f(x)$ is a twice differentiable function in $\mathbb{R}$ such that $f(a) = 0, f(b) = -2, f(c) = 3, f(d) = -1, f(e) = 0$; $a < b < c$, then find the minimum number of roots of equation $g(x) =0$, where $g(x) = (f'(x))^2 + f(x).f''(x)$.

11. An enemy helicopter if flying on a curve having its equation given by $y = x^2 + 4$. A soldier is waiting at a point (3, 4) to hit the helicopter as soon as it is at nearest distance to him. The distance between the helicopter and the soldier at the time, he hits the helicopter is '*d*', then find [d]; where [.] is greatest integer function.

12. If $a, b > 0$ such that $a^2 + b = 2^{5/3}.3^{1/3}$, then find the maximum value of term independent of x in the expansion of $\left(\frac{a}{2}x^{1/6} + \frac{b}{3}x^{-1/3}\right)^9$.

13. If $f(x) = \begin{cases} 5\tan^{-1}\alpha - 3x^2; 0 < x < 1 \\ 5x - 3; \quad x \geq 1 \end{cases}$, then find the least integer value of α for which $f(x)$ has minima at $x = 1$

14. For x to be real, find the maximum value of $f(x) = 6(\cos x - x)\left(x + \sqrt{x^2 + \sin^2 x}\right)$.

15. From a given solid cone of height H, another cone of height h is carved out such that its volume is maximum, then find $H : h$.

Answer Keys

SECTION–III

1. (b) 2. (b) 3. (a) 4. (a) 5. (a) 6. (d) 7. (a) 8. (d) 9. (a) 10. (a)
11. (a) 12. (b) 13. (a) 14. (c) 15. (b) 16. (d) 17. (a) 18. (b) 19. (a) 20. (b)
21. (b) 22. (b) 23. (b) 24. (d) 25. (d) 26. (d) 27. (c) 28. (a) 29 (c) 30. (d)
31. (c) 32. (b) 33. (c) 34. (a) 35. (b) 36. (a) 37. (c) 38. (a) 39. (d) 40. (d)
41. (b) 42. (a) 43. (a) 44. (a) 45. (a) 46. (c) 47. (a) 48. (a) 49. (c) 50. (c)
51. (b) 52. (c) 53. (d) 54. (c) 55. (c) 56. (b) 57. (b) 58. (a) 59. (d) 60. (d)
61. (a) 62. (b) 63. (b) 64. (d) 65. (c) 66. (d) 67. (d) 68. (c) 69. (a) 70. (b)
71. (b) 72. (d) 73. (c) 74. (c) 75. (c) 76. (c) 77. (d) 78. (a) 79. (a) 80. (d)
81. (c) 82. (b) 83. (c) 84. (c) 85. (b) 86. (a) 87. (d) 88. (b) 89. (a) 90. (c)
91. (b) 92. (d) 93. (b) 94. (d) 95. (d) 96. (b) 97. (c) 98. (d) 99. (b) 100. (d)
101. (b) 102. (d) 103. (d) 104. (b)

SECTION–IV

1. (a, c) 2. (a,b,d) 3. (b,c) 4. (a,b) 5. (a,b,c,d) 6. (a) 7. (a,b,c) 8. (b)
9. (a,b,c,d) 10. (a,b) 11. (c,d) 12. (a,b,c) 13. (a,b) 14. (a,b,c,d) 15. (c,d)
16. (a,b,c) 17. (a,b,c,d) 18. (a,b,c,d) 19. (b,c,d) 20. (a,b,c,d) 21. (b,c,d) 22. (a,c,d)
23. (a,b,d) 24. (a,c,d) 25. (b,d) 26. (a,b,c,d) 27. (b,d) 28. (a,c) 29. (b,c) 30. (b,c)
31. (a,b) 32. (b,c,d) 33. (a,b,c) 34. (b,d) 35. (b,c,d) 36. (c,d) 37. (a,c) 38. (d) 39. (a,c,d)
40. (a,b) 41. (a,c)

SECTION–V

1. (c) 2. (b) 3. (a) 4. (a) 5. (d) 6. (a) 7. (c) 8. (a) 9. (d) 10. (d)
11. (a) 12. (b) 13. (a) 14. (a) 15. (b) 16. (c)

SECTION–VI

1. (b) 2. (b) 3. (b) 4. (c) 5. (b) 6. (a) 7. (b) 8. (b) 9. (b) 10. (b)
11. (a) 12. (a) 13. (d) 14. (c) 15. (c) 16. (a, c) 17. (c) 18. (b) 19. (b) 20. (d)
21. (c) 22. (d) 23. (c) 24. (a) 25. (a) 26. (c) 27. (b) 28. (a)

SECTION–VII

1. (i) → (b); (ii) → (a); (iii) → (d); (iv) → (c)
2. (i) → (b); (ii) → (d); (iii) → (a); (iv) → (c)
3. (i) → (a, b, c); (ii) → (a, d); (iii) → (c, d); (iv) → (a, b)
4. (i) → (c, d); (ii) → (b); (iii) → (a)

SECTION–VIII

1. 5 **2.** 125 **3.** 3 **4.** 5 **5.** 3 **6.** 3 **7.** 2 **8.** 21 **9.** 2 **10.** 6
11. 2 **12.** 7 **13.** 2 **14.** 3 **15.** 3

HINTS AND SOLUTIONS

TEXTUAL EXERCISE-1: (SUBJECTIVE)

1. (i) $f(a-h) > f(a)$ and $f(a+h) > f(a)$

$\Rightarrow f(x)$ is non-monotonic at $x = a$

(ii) $f(a-h) > f(a) > f(a+h)$

$\Rightarrow f(x)$ is strictly decreasing at $x = a$

(iii) $f(a-h) > f(a)$

$\Rightarrow f(x)$ is strictly decreasing at $x = a$

(iv) $f(a-h) < f(a) < f(a+h)$

$\Rightarrow f(x)$ is strictly increasing at $x = a$

2. (i) $f(a-h) < f(a)$

$\Rightarrow f(x)$ is strictly increasing at $x = a$

(ii) $f(a) < f(a+h)$

$\Rightarrow f(x)$ is strictly increasing at $x = a$

3. $f(x) = x^3 - 3x^2 + 3x + 4$

$f(x)$ being a polynomial function is continuous and differentiable on $\mathbb{R}$.

$f'(x) = 3x^2 - 6x + 3 = 3(x^2 - 2x + 1)$
$= 3(x-1)^2 \geq 0 \ \forall x \in \mathbb{R}$.

$\Rightarrow f(x)$ is strictly increasing $\forall x \in \mathbb{R}$

$\Rightarrow f(x)$ is strictly increasing at

(*i*) $x = 0$ and (ii) at $x = 1$.

4. (a) $y = (x-2)^5 (2x+1)^4$

$\Rightarrow f'(x) = 8(x-2)^5 (2x+1)^3 + 5(2x+1)^4 (x-2)^4$

$\Rightarrow f'(x) = (2x+1)^3 (x-2)^4 [8(x-2) + 5(2x+1)]$

$\Rightarrow f'(x) = (18x - 11)(2x+1)^3 (x-2)^4$

$\Rightarrow f'(0) = (-11)(1)(16) < 0$

$\Rightarrow f(x)$ is strictly decreasing at $x = 0$

$\Rightarrow f'(2) = (25)(5)^3(0) = 0$

$\Rightarrow f'(2-h) = (25 - 18h)(5 - 2h)^3(-h)^4 = (+)(+)(+) = +ve$

$\Rightarrow f'(2+h) = (25 + 18h)(5 + 2h)^3(h)^4 = (+)(+)(+) = +ve$

$\Rightarrow f(x)$ is strictly increasing at $x = 2$

(b) $y = x - e^x$

$\Rightarrow f'(x) = 1 - e^x$

$\Rightarrow f'\left(\frac{1}{2}\right) = 1 - e^{1/2} < 0$ as $e = 2.7183$

$\Rightarrow f(x)$ is a decreasing function at $x = \frac{1}{2}$.

(c) $f(x) = \frac{x}{\ell nx}$ at $x = \frac{1}{e}, 1, e, e^2$

$$\Rightarrow f'(x) = \frac{(\ell nx).1 - x.\frac{1}{x}}{(\ell nx)^2} = \frac{\ell nx - 1}{(\ell nx)^2}$$

$$\Rightarrow f'\left(\frac{1}{e}\right) = \frac{\ell ne^{-1} - 1}{(\ell ne^{-1})^2} = -2 < 0$$

$\Rightarrow f(x)$ is decreasing at $x = 1/e$.

$\because$ Function is not defined at $x = 1$.

$$\Rightarrow f'(e) = \frac{\ell ne - 1}{(\ell ne)^2} = 0$$

$$\Rightarrow f'(e-h) = \frac{\ell n(e-h) - 1}{[\ell n(e-h)]^2} < 0 \text{ and } f'(e+h) = \frac{\ell n(e+h) - 1}{(\ell n(e+h))^2} > 0$$

$\Rightarrow f'(e)$ in stationary point i.e., non- monotonic at $x = e$

$$\Rightarrow f'(e^2) = \frac{\ell ne^2 - 1}{(\ell ne^2)^2} = \frac{1}{4} > 0$$

$\Rightarrow f(x)$ is increasing at $x = e^2$

5. $f(x) = \begin{cases} x\,; 0 \leq x < 1 \\ [x]; 1 \leq x \leq 2 \end{cases} = \begin{cases} x\,; 0 \leq x < 1 \\ 1; 1 \leq x < 2 \\ 2\,; x = 2 \end{cases}$

$\Rightarrow f'(x) = \begin{cases} 1; 0 < x < 1 \\ 0; 1 < x < 2 \end{cases}$

Graph of $f(x)$ is as shown below.

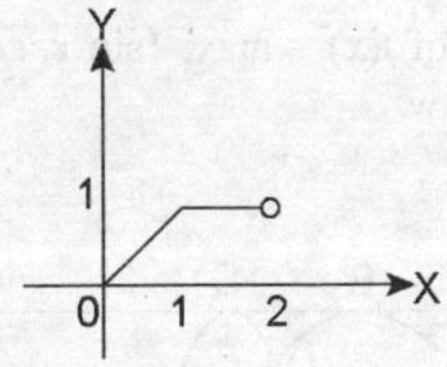

$f'(0) = f'(0^+) = 1 > 0$

$\Rightarrow f(x)$ is strictly increasing at $x = 0$.

$\Rightarrow f'(1^-) = 1; f'(1^+) = 0$

$\Rightarrow f'(1)$ is not defined.

Also $f(1-h) < f(1) = 1 = f(x) \ \forall x \in (1, 2)$

$\Rightarrow f(x)$ is increasing (not strictly at $x = 1$)

$\Rightarrow f(x)$ is discontinuous at $x = 2$ and $f(2-h) = 1 < f(2) = 2$

$\Rightarrow f(x)$ is increasing at $x = 2$

6. $f(x) = x\{x\} = x(x - [x])$

$f(0-h) = (-h)(-h - [-h])$
$= (-h)(-h - (-1))$
$= (-h)(-h + 1) = (-)(+) = -ve$

$f(0) = 0, f(0+h) = (h)(h - [h])$
$= (h)(h - 0) = h^2 = +ve$

$\Rightarrow f(0-h) < f(0) < f(0+h)$

$\Rightarrow f(x)$ is strictly increasing at $x = 0$

TEXTUAL EXERCISE-1: (OBJECTIVE)

1. (b) $f(x) = \begin{cases} x+1\,; x < 1 \\ k\,; x = 1 \\ x^2 + x - 3\,; x > 1 \end{cases}$

$\Rightarrow f'(x) = \begin{cases} 1; x < 1 \\ 2x + 1\,; x > 1 \end{cases}$

$\Rightarrow$ $f(x)$ is strictly increasing in $(-\infty, 1)$ and in $(1, \infty)$.

$\therefore$ $f(x)$ to be strictly increasing at $x = 1$,

$\lim\limits_{x \to 1^-} f(x) \le k \le \lim\limits_{x \to 1^+} f(x)$

$\Rightarrow$ $\lim\limits_{x \to 1^-} (x + 1) \le k \le \lim\limits_{x \to 1^+} (x^2 + x + 3)$

$\Rightarrow$ $2 \le k \le 5$

$\therefore$ $f(x)$ will be strictly increasing for k belonging to every subset of $[2, 5]$

2. (a), (c) $f(x) = \{x\} = x - [x]$

$\Rightarrow$ $f(x) = x - n$ for $x \in [n, n + 1)$

$\Rightarrow$ $f'(x) = 1$ for $x \in (n, n + 1)$

$\Rightarrow$ $f(x)$ is strictly increasing at $x = n + \dfrac{1}{2}$

$\Rightarrow$ $|f(x)| = |\{x\}| = \{x\}$ as $\{x\} \in [0, 1)$

$\because$ $|f(n - h)| = \{n - h\} = (n - h) - (n - 1) = 1 - h$

$\Rightarrow$ $|f(n)| = \{x\} = 0$, $|f(n + h)| = \{n + h\} = (n + h) - n = h$

$\therefore$ $|f(n - h)| > |f(n)|$ and $|f(x + h)| > |f(n)|$

$\Rightarrow$ $|f(x)|$ is non-monotonic at $x = n \in \mathbb{Z}$

From above, we have $f'(x) = 1\ \forall\ x \in (n, n + 1)$; $n \in \mathbb{Z}$

$\Rightarrow$ $f(x)$ is strictly increasing at $x = n$; $x \in \mathbb{R} - \mathbb{Z}$.

3. (c) The graph of $f(x) = \max. \{\sin x, \cos 2x\}$ in $[0, 2\pi]$ is as shown below.

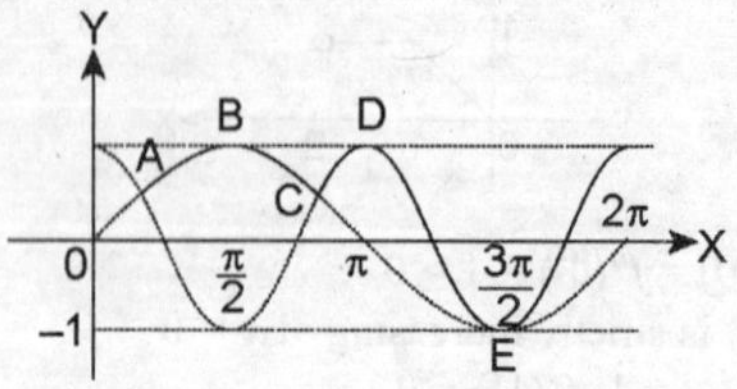

$f(x)$ is non-monotonic at points A, B, C, D and E i.e., at 5 points

4. $f(x) = \begin{cases} 2x + 1\ ; x \le 1 \\ -x^2 + 4\ ; x > 1 \end{cases}$

(i) (a) $g(x) = f(x) = \begin{cases} 2x + 1\ ; x \le 1 \\ -x^2 + 4\ ; x > 1 \end{cases}$

$\Rightarrow$ $g'(x) = \begin{cases} 2\ ; x < 1 \\ -2x\ ; x > 1 \end{cases}$

$\Rightarrow$ $g(x)$ increases for $x < 1$ and decreases for $x > 1$

$\Rightarrow$ $\lim\limits_{x \to 1^-} = \lim\limits_{x \to 1^-} (2x + 1) = 3$ and $\lim\limits_{x \to 1^+} g(x) = \lim\limits_{x \to 1^+} (-x^2 + 4) = 3$;

$f(1) = 3$

$\Rightarrow$ $g(x)$ is a continuous function which increase on $(-\infty, 1)$ and decreases on $(1, \infty)$.

$\Rightarrow$ $x = 1$ is only point of non-monotonicity

(ii) (c) $g(x) = f(|x|)$

$\Rightarrow$ $g(x)$ is symmetric about origin

$\Rightarrow$ $g(x)$ has 3 points of non-monotonicity $x = -1$, $x = 0$ and $x = 1$ i.e., 3 points.

(iii) (b) $g(x) = |f(x)|$

Graph of $y = g(x)$ is as shown below

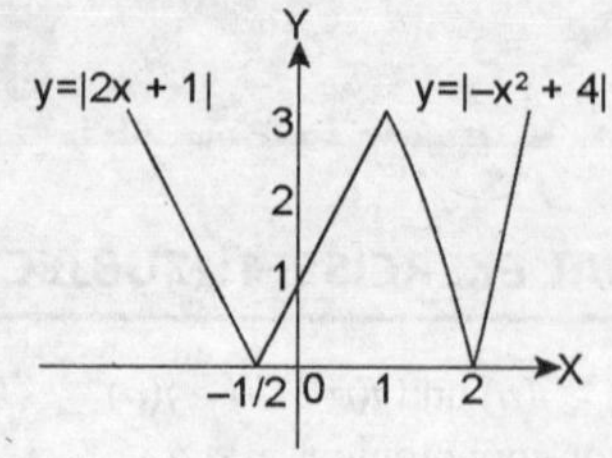

Clearly $f(x)$ is non-monotonic at $x = \dfrac{-1}{2}$, $x = 1$ and at $x = 2$ i.e., at 3 points .

(iv) (d) $g(x) = |f(|x|)|$

The graph of $y = g(x)$ will be as shown below.

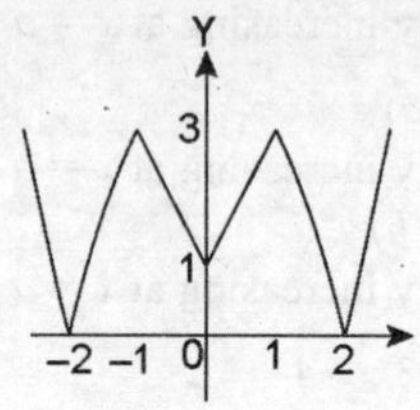

Clearly $g(x)$ is non-monotonic at $x = -2$, $x = -1$, $x = 0$, $x = 1$, $x = 2$ i.e., at 5 points.

5. (a), (b), (c)

$f(x) = \{1 + \sin x\ ,\ 1 - \cos x,\ 1\}$; $x \in [0, 2\pi]$

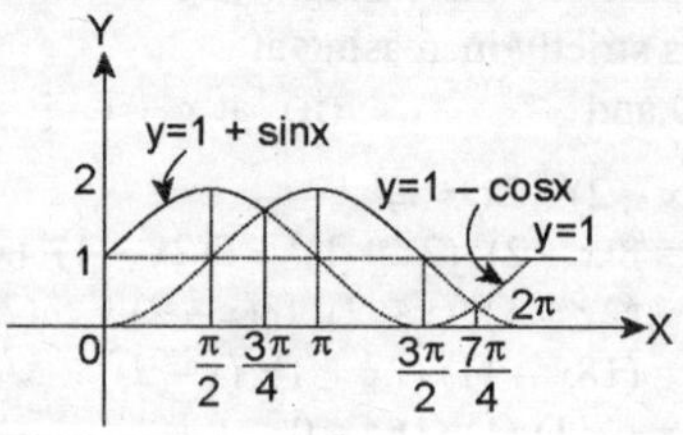

Clearly $f(x)$ is non-monotonic at $x = \dfrac{\pi}{2}, \dfrac{3\pi}{4}, \pi$

6. (b) $f(x) = |\sin x + 1/2|$ for $x \in [-2\pi, 2\pi]$

The graph of $y = f(x)$ is as shown below.

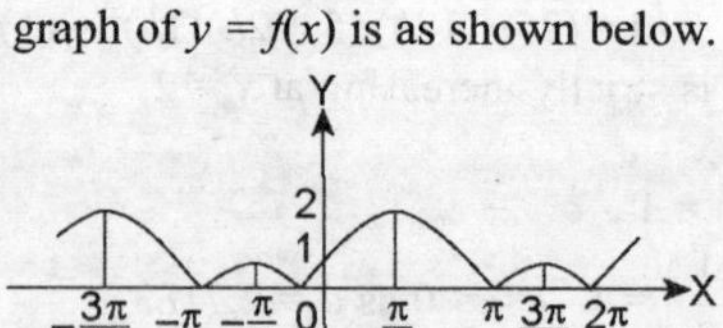

Clearly $f(x)$ is non-monotonic at $x =$

$\dfrac{-3\pi}{2}, -\pi + \dfrac{\pi}{6}, \dfrac{-\pi}{2}, \dfrac{-\pi}{6}, \dfrac{\pi}{2}, \pi + \dfrac{\pi}{6}, \dfrac{3\pi}{2}, 2\pi - \dfrac{\pi}{6}$

i.e., at $x = \dfrac{-3\pi}{2}, \dfrac{-5\pi}{6}, \dfrac{-\pi}{2}, \dfrac{7\pi}{6}, \dfrac{3\pi}{2}, \dfrac{11\pi}{6}$ i.e., at 8 points.

7. (a) $f(x) = \min. \{|x|, |x - 1|, |x + 1|\}$

The graph of $y = f(x)$ is as shown below.

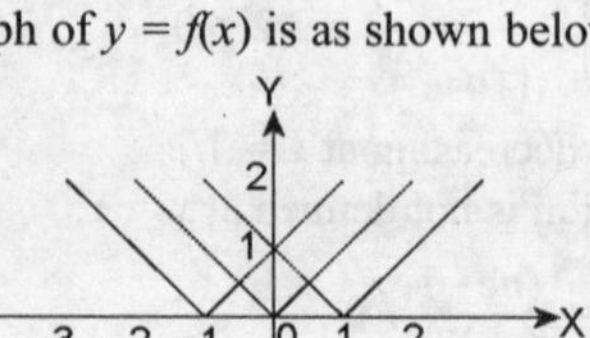

Clearly $f(x)$ is non-differentiable at $x = -1, -\frac{1}{2}, 0, \frac{1}{2}, 1$

i.e., at 5 points

8. (b) $f(x) = \begin{cases} 1+x\ ; 0 \le x \le 2 \\ 3-x\ ; 2 < x \le 3 \end{cases}$

$\Rightarrow fof(x) = \begin{cases} 1+f(x); 0 \le x \le 2 \\ 3-f(x); 2 < f(x) \le 3 \end{cases}$

$= \begin{cases} 1+(1+x); 0 \le x \le 2; 0 \le x \le 2 \\ 1+(3-x); 0 \le 3-x \le 2; 2 < x \le 3 \\ 3-(1+x); 2 < 1+x \le 3; 0 \le x \le 2 \\ 3-(3-x); 2 < 3-x \le 2 < x \le 3 \end{cases}$

$= \begin{cases} 2+x\ ; -1 \le x \le 1; 0 \le x \le 2 \\ 4-x\ ; 1 \le x \le 3; 2 < x \le 3 \\ 2-x\ ; 1 < x \le 2; 0 \le x \le 2 \\ x\ ; 0 \le x < 1; 2 < x \le 3 \end{cases} = \begin{cases} 2+x\ ; 0 \le x \le 1 \\ 4-x\ ; 2 < x \le 3 \\ 2-x\ ; 1 < x \le 2 \end{cases}$

The graph of $fof(x)$ will be as shown below.

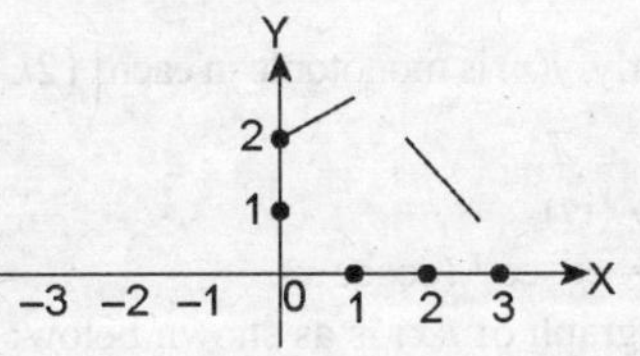

Here $fof(1-h) < fof(1) > fof(1+h)$

$\Rightarrow$ $fof(x)$ is non-monotonic at $x = 1$

Also $fof(2-h) > fof(2) < fof(2+h)$ for $h \to 0$

$\Rightarrow$ $fof(x)$ is non-monotonic at $x = 2$

$\therefore$ $fof(x)$ is non-monotonic at two points.

9. (a), (b) In view of figure shown in Q. 8

$fof(x)$ is strictly increasing on [0, 1) and is strictly decreasing on (1, 2) and on (2, 3] and non-monotonic at $x = 1$ and at $x = 2$

10. (b) $f(x) = \max.\ \{x^2, (1-x)^2, 2x(1-x)\}$.

The graph of $f(x)$ will be as shown below.

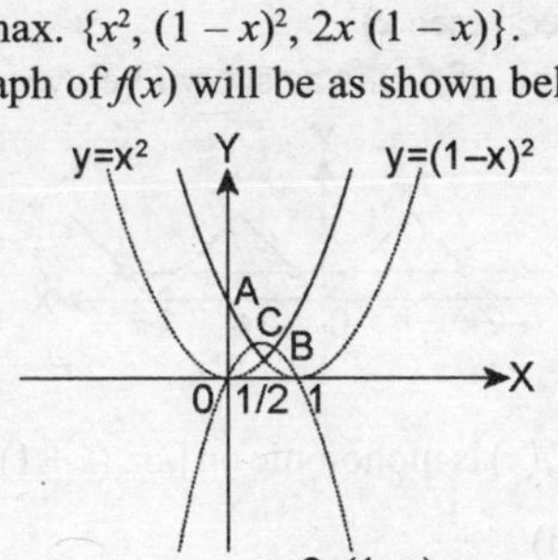

Clearly $x = \frac{1}{3}, \frac{1}{2}, \frac{2}{3}$ are the only point of non-monotonicity.

$\Rightarrow$ Sum of abscissae of points of non- monotonicity = $\sum x_i = \frac{1}{3} + \frac{1}{2} + \frac{2}{3} = \frac{3}{2}$

TEXTUAL EXERCISE–2: (SUBJECTIVE)

1. (a) $f(x) = 1 + 3(\log \sin x + \log \operatorname{cosec} x);\ x \in (0, \pi)$

$\Rightarrow f(x) = 1 + 3(\log (\sin x . \operatorname{cosec} x)$

$\Rightarrow f(x) = 1 + 3 \log 1$

$\Rightarrow f(x) = 1\ \forall\ x \in (0, \pi)$

$\Rightarrow$ $f(x)$ is monotonic (*constant*) on $(0, \pi)$

$\Rightarrow$ (*a*) is false

(b) True

(c) $y = \begin{cases} \frac{|\cos x|}{\cos x}; x \ne \frac{\pi}{2} \\ 0\ ; x = \frac{\pi}{2} \end{cases}$

$\Rightarrow y = \begin{cases} 1\ ; & x \in \left[0, \frac{\pi}{2}\right) \\ 0\ ; & x = \frac{\pi}{2} \\ -1\ ; & x \in \left(\frac{\pi}{2}, \pi\right] \end{cases}$

$\Rightarrow$ $f(x)$ is a decreasing function $[0, \pi]$

$\Rightarrow$ (c) is true ,

(d) $y = \begin{cases} 1+3(\log|\sin x| + \log|\operatorname{cosec} x|; x \ne 0 \\ 0\ ; x = 0 \end{cases}$

$\Rightarrow y = \begin{cases} (1+3 \log 1)\ ; x \ne 0 \\ 0\ ; x = 0 \end{cases}$

$\Rightarrow y = \begin{cases} 1\ ; x \ne 0 \\ 0\ ; x = 0 \end{cases}$

$\Rightarrow$ $f(x)$ is monotonically increasing (not strictly) on $[0, \pi/2]$

$\Rightarrow$ (d) is True.

(e) $y = \sin^{-1}\left(\frac{2x}{1+x^2}\right)$

We know, $2\tan^{-1} x = \begin{cases} \sin^{-1}\left(\frac{2x}{1+x^2}\right); -1 \le x \le 1 \\ -\pi - \sin^{-1}\left(\frac{2x}{1+x^2}\right); x < -1 \\ \pi - \sin^{-1}\left(\frac{2x}{1+x^2}\right); x > 1 \end{cases}$

$\Rightarrow \sin^{-1}\left(\frac{2x}{1+x^2}\right) = \begin{cases} 2\tan^{-1} x; 1 \le x \le 1 \\ -\pi - 2\tan^{-1} x\ ; x < -1 \\ \pi - 2\tan^{-1} x\ ; x > 1 \end{cases}$

$\Rightarrow$ $\sin^{-1}\left(\frac{2x}{1+x}\right)$ is continuous function and

$\frac{d}{dx}\left(\sin^{-1}\left(\frac{2x}{1+x^2}\right)\right) = \begin{cases} \frac{2}{1+x^2}; -1 < x < 1 \\ \frac{-2}{1+x^2}\ ; x < -1 \\ \frac{-2}{1+x^2}\ ; x > 1 \end{cases}$

$\Rightarrow$ $f(x)\downarrow$ for $x < -1$, for $x \in (-1, 1)$ and $\downarrow$ for $x > 1$.

$\Rightarrow$ $f(x)$ is monotonically increasing on $[-1, 1]$

$\Rightarrow$ (e) is True.

(f) $f(x) = \sin^{-1}\left(\dfrac{1+x^2}{2x}\right)$

$\dfrac{1+x^2}{2x} = y$

$\Rightarrow x^2 - 2xy + 1 = 0$

$\Rightarrow x = \dfrac{2y \pm \sqrt{4y^2-4}}{2}$

$\Rightarrow x = y \pm \sqrt{y^2-1}$

$\Rightarrow y \le -1$ or $y \ge 1$

$\Rightarrow \dfrac{1+x^2}{2x} \le -1$ or ≥ 1

$\therefore$ $f(x) = \sin^{-1}\left(\dfrac{1+x^2}{2x}\right)$ is defined for $\dfrac{1+x^2}{2x} = -1$ or 1

$\Rightarrow (x+1)^2 = 0$ or $(x-1)^2 = 0$

$\Rightarrow x = 1$ or $x = -1$

$\Rightarrow$ $f(x)$ is defined only at $x = -1$ and 1

$\therefore$ $D_f = \{-1, 1\}$

$\Rightarrow f(-1) = \sin^{-1}(-1) = -\dfrac{\pi}{2}$ and $f(1) = \sin^{-1}(1) = \dfrac{\pi}{2}$

$\therefore$ $-1 < 1$

$\Rightarrow \sin^{-1}(-1) < \sin^{-1}(1)$

$\Rightarrow$ $f(x)$ is monotonically increasing in its domain

$\Rightarrow$ (f) is true.

(g) $y = e^{[x]} = \begin{cases} 1 \text{ for } x \in [0,1) \\ e \text{ for } x \in [1,2) \\ e^2 \text{ for } x \in [2,3) \\ e^3 \text{ for } x \in [3,\pi] \end{cases}$

Clearly $f(x)$ is constant on each of the intervals $[0, 1)$, $[1, 2)$, $[2, 3)$ and $[3, \pi]$ and at the point of discontinuity $k \in \{1, 2, 3\}$,

$f(k-h) < f(k) = f(k+h)$ for $h \to 0^+$

$\Rightarrow$ $f(x)$ is monotonically increasing on $[0, \pi]$

$\Rightarrow$ (g) is true .

2. (a) $\sin^{-1}(\sin x) = \begin{cases} -(x+\pi); & -\dfrac{3\pi}{2} \le x < -\dfrac{\pi}{2} \\ x; & -\dfrac{\pi}{2} \le x \le \dfrac{\pi}{2} \\ -x+\pi; & \dfrac{\pi}{2} < x \le \dfrac{3\pi}{2} \end{cases}$

$\Rightarrow$ $f(x)$ is monotonic in $\left((2k+1)\dfrac{\pi}{2}, (2k+3)\dfrac{\pi}{2}\right)$ for each $k \in \mathbb{Z}$

$\Rightarrow$ (a)→ (iv) , (v)

Also monotonicity on $\left[\dfrac{-\pi}{2}, \dfrac{\pi}{2}\right] \sim \{0\}$ means monotonicity on $\left(\dfrac{-\pi}{2}, \dfrac{\pi}{2}\right) - \{0\}$ and

$f\left(\dfrac{-\pi}{2}\right) < f\left(\dfrac{-\pi}{2}+h\right) \;\&\; f\left(\dfrac{\pi}{2}-h\right) < f\left(\dfrac{\pi}{2}\right)$

where $h \to 0^+$

$\Rightarrow$ (iii) also holds

$\Rightarrow$ (a)→(iii), (iv), (v)

(b) $f(x) = \cos^{-1}(\cos x)$

Graph of $f(x) = \cos^{-1}(\cos x)$ is as shown below.

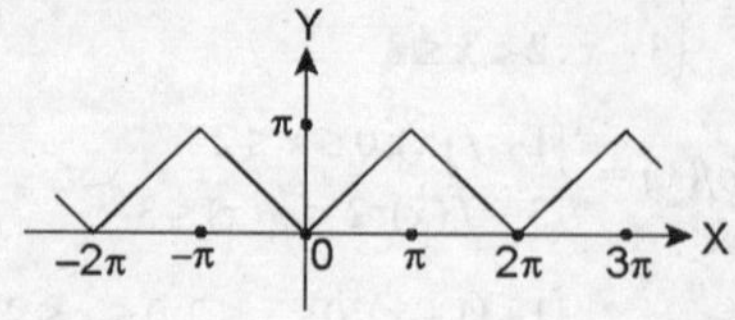

Clearly $f(x)$ is monotonic on $\pi, (n+1)\pi]$ and on $(n\pi, (n+1)\pi)$ for each $n \in \mathbb{Z}$.

$\Rightarrow$ (b)→(i), (ii) and (vi) are true.

(c) $f(x) = \tan^{-1}(\tan x)$

Graph of $f(x) = \tan^{-1}(\tan x)$ is as shown below.

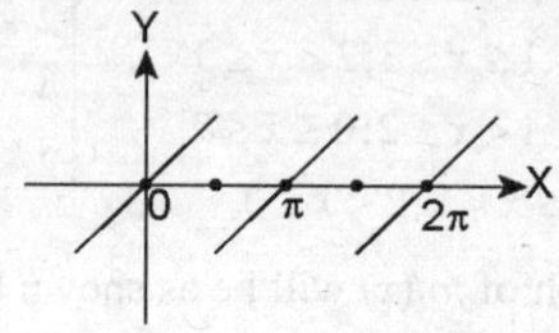

Clearly, $f(x)$ is monotonic in each $\left((2k+1)\dfrac{\pi}{2}, (2k+3)\dfrac{\pi}{2}\right)$ for $k \in \mathbb{Z}$

$\Rightarrow$ (c)→ (iv)

(d) $f(x) = \text{cosec}^{-1}(\text{cosec } x)$

The graph of $f(x)$ is as shown below:

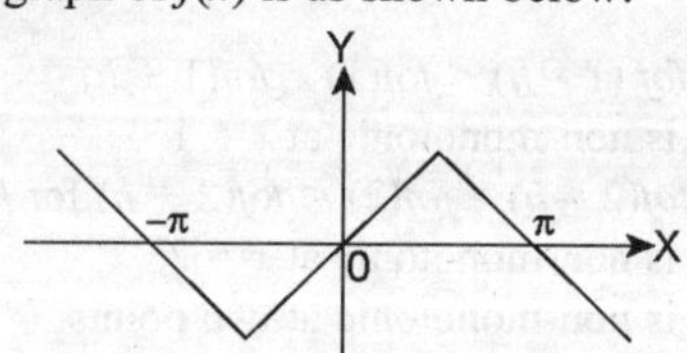

$\Rightarrow$ $f(x)$ is monotonic on $\left[(2k+1)\dfrac{\pi}{2}, (2k+3)\dfrac{\pi}{2}\right] - \{(k+1)\pi\}$

$\Rightarrow$ (d) → (iii), (v) .

(e) $f(x) = \sec^{-1}(\sec x)$

The graph of $f(x)$ is as shown below:

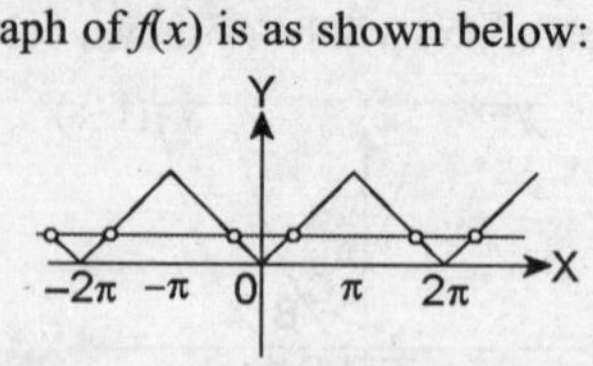

Clearly $f(x)$ is monotonic on $[k\pi, (k+1)\pi - \left\{\left(k+\dfrac{1}{2}\right)\pi\right\}$

$\Rightarrow$ (e)→ (ii)

(f) $f(x) = \cot^{-1}(\cot x)$

The graph of $f(x)$ is as shown below.

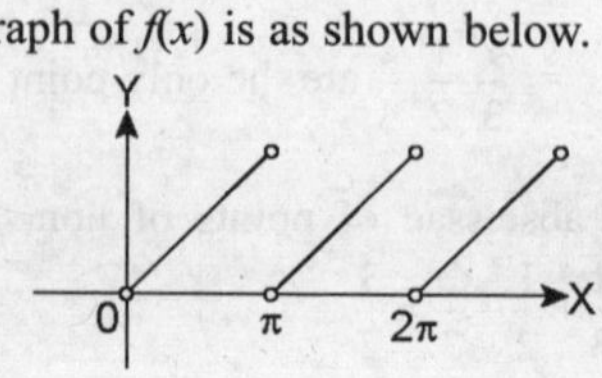

Clearly $f(x)$ is monotonic on $(k\pi, (k+1)\pi)$ for each $k \in \mathbb{Z}$.

$\Rightarrow$ (f)→ (vi)

3. (a) $f(x) = \log(3x^2 + 2) + e^{2x-1}$

$\Rightarrow f'(x) = \dfrac{9x^2}{3x^2+2} + 2\left(e^{2x-1}\right)$

$\Rightarrow Df = \{x : x \in \mathbb{R} \text{ and } 3x^2 + 2 > 0\}$

$\Rightarrow f(x)$ is increasing function .

(b) $f(x) = \log(x - \sin x) + e^{x + \sin x}$

$\Rightarrow f'(x) = \dfrac{1-\cos x}{(x-\sin x)} + (1 + \cos x)\, e^{x+\sin x}$

Clearly, $Df = \{x: x \in \mathbb{R} \text{ and } x > \sin x\} = \{x > 0\}$

$\Rightarrow f'(x) > 0\ \forall\ x \in \mathbb{R}$

$\Rightarrow f(x)$ is an increasing function .

(c) $f(x) = e^{2x-1} - e^{1-2x}$

$\Rightarrow f'(x) = 2e^{2x-1} + 2\, e^{1-2x} > 0\ \forall\ x \in \mathbb{R}$

$\Rightarrow f(x)$ is an increasing function .

4. $f(x) = (m+2)x^3 - 3\, mx^2 + 9\, mx - 1$

$\Rightarrow f'(x) = 3(m+2)x^2 - 6\, mx + 9\, m$

$\therefore$ $f(x)$ decrease for all $x \in \mathbb{R}$

$\Rightarrow (m+2) < 0,\ 36\, m^2 - 108\, m\, (m+2) \le 0$

$\Rightarrow m < -2,\ m^2 - 3m\,(m+2) \le 0$

$\Rightarrow m < -2,\ -2m^2 - 6m \le 0$

$\Rightarrow m < -2,\ m^2 + 3m \ge 0$

$\Rightarrow m < -2,\ m \in (-\infty, -3] \cup [0, \infty)$

$\Rightarrow m \in (-\infty, -3]$

5. $f(x) = \left(\dfrac{a^2-1}{3}\right)x^3 + (a-1)\,x^2 + 2x + 1$

$\Rightarrow f'(x) = (a^2 - 1)\,x^2 + 2(a-1)\,x + 2$

For $a^2 - 1 = 0$, $f'(x) = 2(a-1)\,x + 2$

For $a = 1$, $f'(x) = 2 > 0$

$\Rightarrow f(x)$ is increasing $\forall\ x \in \mathbb{R}$

For $a = 1$

For $a = -1$, $f'(x) = -4x + 2$

$\Rightarrow f(x)$ is not increasing $\forall\ x \in \mathbb{R}$

Now for $a^2 - 1 > 0$ and $4(a-1)^2 - 8(a^2-1) \le 0$; $f'(x) > 0\ \forall\ x \in \mathbb{R}$

$\Rightarrow a \in (-\infty, -1) \cup (1, \infty)$ and $4(a-1)\,(a - 1 - 2a - 2) \le 0$

$\Rightarrow a \in (-\infty, -1) \cup (1, \infty)$ and $a \in (-\infty, -3] \cup [1, \infty)$

$\Rightarrow a \in (-\infty, -3] \cup (1, \infty)$

Also $a = 1$ is permissible

$\Rightarrow a \in (-\infty, -3] \cup [1, \infty)$

6. $f(x) = x^3 - ax$

$\Rightarrow f'(x) = 3x^2 - a$

For $f'(x) \ge 0\ \forall\ x \in \mathbb{R}$

$3x^2 \ge a\ \forall\ x \in \mathbb{R}$

$\Rightarrow a \le 3x^2\ \forall\ x \in \mathbb{R}$

$\Rightarrow a \le 0$

$\Rightarrow a \in (-\infty, 0]$

7. $f(x) = \sin x - bx + c$

$\Rightarrow f'(x) = \cos x - b$

$\therefore$ $f(x)$ decreasing $\forall\ x \in \mathbb{R}$

$\Rightarrow f'(x) \le 0\ \forall\ x \in \mathbb{R}$

$\Rightarrow b \ge 1$

$\Rightarrow b \in [1, \infty)$

TEXTUAL EXERCISE-2: (OBJECTIVE)

1. (b), (c) $f(x) = 2\log(x-2) - x^2 + 4x + 1$

$\Rightarrow f'(x) = \dfrac{2}{(x-2)} - 2x + 4 = \dfrac{-2x^2+8x-6}{(x-2)}$

$= \dfrac{-2\left(x^2-4x+3\right)}{(x-2)} = \dfrac{-2(x-1)(x-3)}{(x-2)}$

$f(x)$ increasing

$\Rightarrow f'(x) > 0$

$\Rightarrow \dfrac{(x-1)(x-3)}{(x-2)} < 0$

$\Rightarrow x \in (-\infty, 1) \cup (2, 3)$ but $Df = (2, \infty)$

$\therefore$ $f(x)$ increase in $(2, 3) \supseteq \left(\dfrac{5}{2}, 3\right)$

2. (a), (c), (d)

$y = x - 2\sin x;\ 0 \le x \le 2\pi$

$f'(x) = 1 - 2\cos x$ for $f(x)$ to be increasing

$\Rightarrow \cos x \le \dfrac{1}{2}$

$\Rightarrow x \in \left[\dfrac{\pi}{3}, 2\pi - \dfrac{\pi}{3}\right]$

$\Rightarrow x \in \left[\dfrac{\pi}{3}, \dfrac{5\pi}{3}\right]$

3. (a), (c) $y = x - e^x + \tan\dfrac{\pi}{7}$

$\Rightarrow f'(x) = 1 - e^x \ge 0$

$\Rightarrow e^x \le 1$

$\Rightarrow x \le 0$

$\Rightarrow x \in (-\infty, 0]$

4. (a), (c) $f(x) = \tan^{-1}(\sin x + \cos x)$

$f'(x) = \dfrac{1}{1+(\sin x+\cos x)^2} \times [\cos x - \sin x]$

$= \dfrac{\cos x - \sin x}{2 + 2\sin x\cos x} = \dfrac{(\cos x - \sin x)}{2 + \sin x}$

Clearly denominator is +ve

$\therefore$ $\cos x \ge \sin x$

$\Rightarrow x \in \left[2n\pi - \dfrac{3\pi}{4}, 2n\pi + \dfrac{\pi}{4}\right];\ n \in \mathbb{Z}$

$\Rightarrow f(x)$ is increasing function in $(-\pi/4, \pi/4)$

5. (c) $f(x) = x(a^2 - 2a - 2) + \cos x$

$\Rightarrow f'(x) = (a^2 - 2a - 2) - \sin x$

$\therefore$ For $f(x)$ to be always strictly monotonic, $f'(x) > 0$ or $f'(x) < 0\ \forall\ x \in \mathbb{R}$

$\Rightarrow f'(x) \ge 0\ \forall\ x \in \mathbb{R}$ or $f'(x) \le 0\ \forall\ x \in \mathbb{R}$

$\Rightarrow$ $(a^2 - 2a - 2) \geq \sin x$ or $(a^2 - 2a - 2) \leq \sin x\ \forall\ x \in \mathbb{R}$
$\Rightarrow$ $(a^2 - 2a + 1) - 3 \geq \sin x$ or $(a^2 - 2a + 1) - 3 \leq \sin x\ \forall\ x \in \mathbb{R}$
$\Rightarrow$ $(a - 1)^2 \geq \sin x + 3$ or $(a - 1)^2 \leq \sin x + 3$
$\Rightarrow$ $(a - 1)^2 \geq 4$ or $(a - 1)^2 \leq 2$
$\Rightarrow$ $(a - 1) \in (-\infty, -2] \cup [2, \infty)$ or $(a - 1) \in \left[\ \sqrt{2}, \sqrt{2}\right]$
$\Rightarrow$ $a \in (-\infty, -1] \cup [3, \infty)$ or $a \in \left[1-\sqrt{2}, 1+\sqrt{2}\right]$

6. **(a)** $f(x) = x^3 + bx^2 + cx + d;\ 0 < b^2 < c,$
$\Rightarrow$ $f'(x) = 3x^2 + 2bx + c$
Disc. $= 4b^2 - 4(3)(c)$
$= 4(b^2 - 3c)$
$= 4(b^2 - c) - 8c < 0$ $[\because b^2 - c < 0$ and $c > 0]$
$\Rightarrow$ $f'(x) > 0\ \forall\ x \in \mathbb{R}$
$\Rightarrow$ $f(x)$ is strictly increasing function.

7. **(c)** $f(x) = \sin x + a^2 x + b$
$\Rightarrow$ $f'(x) = \cos x + a^2$
$\therefore$ for $f(x)$ to be increasing, $\cos x + a^2 \geq 0$
$\Rightarrow$ $a^2 \geq -\cos x\ \forall\ x \in \mathbb{R}$
$\Rightarrow$ $a^2 \geq 1$
$\Rightarrow$ $a \in (-\infty, -1] \cup [1, \infty)$
$\Rightarrow$ $a \in \mathbb{R} - (-1, 1)$

8. **(b)** $f(x) = x^2 - x^{-x^2/a^2}$

$$\Rightarrow f'(x) = x^2\left(\frac{-2x}{a^2}\right)e^{-x^2/a^2} + (2x)e^{-x^2/a^2} = 2x\ e^{-x^2/a^2}\left[1 - \frac{x^2}{a^2}\right]$$

$$= \frac{2xe^{-x^2/a^2}\left(a^2 - x^2\right)}{a^2}$$

For $f(x)$ to be increasing, $f'(x) \geq 0$
$\Rightarrow$ $x\,(a^2 - x^2) \geq 0$
$\Rightarrow$ $x(x + a)\,(x - a) \leq 0$
$\Rightarrow$ $x \in (-\infty, -a]\ [0, a]$

9. **(b), (c), (d)**
(a) $f(x) = \max.\ \{x, x^3\}$

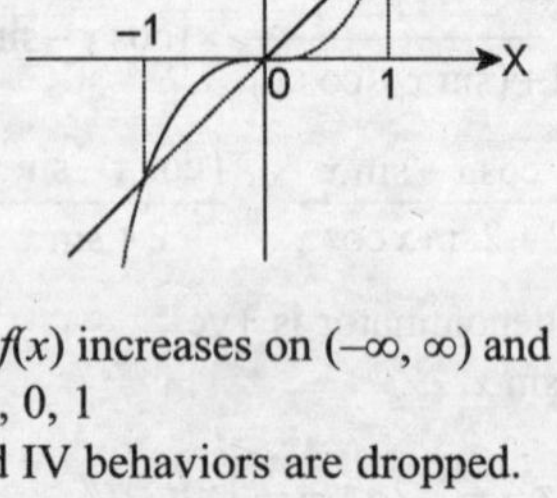

Clearly $f(x)$ increases on $(-\infty, \infty)$ and non-differentiable at $x = 1, 0, 1$
$\Rightarrow$ IInd and IV behaviors are dropped.
(b) $f(x) = \max.\ \{x, x^2\}$

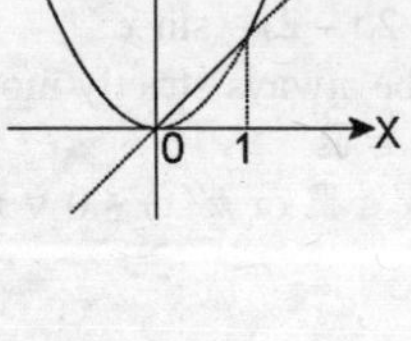

Clearly $f(x)$ decreases on $(-\infty, 0]$ and hence on $(-1, 0]$, $f(x)$ is increasing on $[0, 1)$
Also $f(x)$ is continuous but non-differentiable at $x = 0$ and at $x = 1$
$\Rightarrow$ $f(x)$ exhibits 3 behaviors.
(c) $f(x) = \max\ \{x, |x|\}$

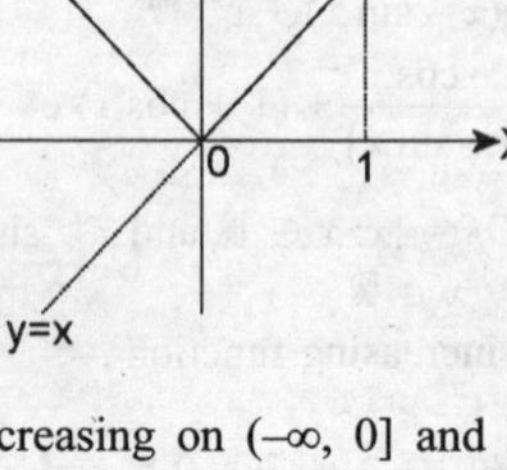

$\Rightarrow$ $f(x)$ is decreasing on $(-\infty, 0]$ and hence on $(-1, 0]$, increasing on $[0, \infty)$ and hence on $[0, 1)$.
Also $f(x)$ is non-differentiable at $x = 0$ but continuous
$\Rightarrow$ $f(x)$ exhibits 3 behaviors.
(d) $f(x) = \max\ \{x, [x]\} = x$ as $[x] = \leq x\ \forall\ x \in \mathbb{R}$

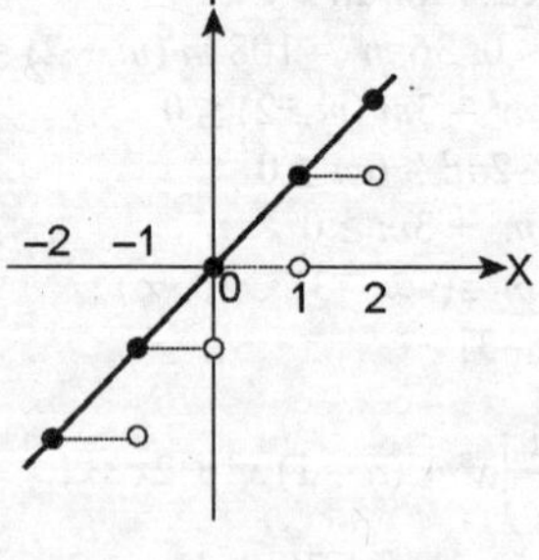

Clearly $f(x) = x$
$\Rightarrow$ $f(x)$ is increasing on $[0, 1)$ continuous and differentiable i.e., exhibits 3 behaviors.

10. **(d)** $f(x) = \dfrac{k\sin x + 2\cos x}{\sin x + \cos x}$

$$\Rightarrow f(x) = \frac{2\sin x + 2\cos x + (k-2)\sin x}{(\sin x + \cos x)}$$

$$\Rightarrow f(x) = 2 + \frac{(k-2)\sin x}{(\sin x + \cos x)}$$

$$\Rightarrow f'(x) = (k-2)\left[\frac{(\sin x + \cos x)\cos x - \sin x(\cos x - \sin x)}{(\sin x + \cos x)^2}\right]$$

$$\Rightarrow f'(x) = (k-2)\left[\frac{1}{(\sin x + \cos x)^2}\right]$$

$\Rightarrow$ $f'(x) > 0\ \forall\ k > 2$ and $\forall\ x \in D_f$

11. **(a), (b)** $f(x) = x - [x] = \{x\}$
$\Rightarrow$ $f(x)$ is increasing in $(k, k + 1)$ for each $k \in \mathbb{Z}$. Also in $[k, k + 1)$

12. **(a)** $f(x) = 2x^2 - kx + 5$
$\Rightarrow$ $f'(x) = 4x - k$
For $x \in [1, 2]$, $4x - k \in [4 - k, 8 - k]$

$\therefore\ f'(x) \geq 0$

$\Rightarrow\ 4 - k \geq 0$

$\Rightarrow\ k \leq 4$

$\Rightarrow\ k \in (-\infty, 4]$

13. (c) $f(x) = kx^3 - 9x^2 + 9x + 3$

$f'(x) = 3kx^2 - 18x + 9$

$= 3(kx^2 - 6x + 3)$

$\therefore$ $f(x)$ is monotonically increasing

$\Rightarrow\ kx^2 - 6x + 3 \geq 0\ \forall x \in \mathbb{R}$

$\Rightarrow\ k > 0$ and $(-6)^2 - 12k \leq 0$

$\Rightarrow\ k > 0$ and $k \geq 3$

14. (c) $f(x) = kx + 2\cos x$

$\Rightarrow\ f'(x) = k - 2\sin x \leq 0$

$\Rightarrow\ k \leq 2\sin x$

$\Rightarrow\ k \leq -2$

$\therefore$ if $k < -2$, then $f(x)$ is monotonically decreasing

TEXTUAL EXERCISE-3: (SUBJECTIVE)

1. $f(x) = x + \ell n(1 - 4x)$

For $f(x)$ to be defined $1 - 4x > 0$

$\Rightarrow\ x < 1/4$

$\Rightarrow\ D_f = (-\infty, 1/4)$

$\Rightarrow\ f'(x) = 1 - \dfrac{4}{(1-4x)} = \dfrac{-4x-3}{1-4x}$

$\therefore$ For $f(x)$ to be increasing $(-4x - 3) \geq 0$ i.e., $x \leq -3/4$ i.e., $x \in (-\infty, -3/4]$ and for $f(x)$ to be decreasing $(-4x - 3) \leq 0$

i.e., $x \geq \dfrac{-3}{4}$ i.e., $x \in \left[\dfrac{-3}{4}, \dfrac{1}{4}\right)$

2. $f(x) = \dfrac{x}{\ell nx}; x > 0, x \neq 1$

$\Rightarrow\ f'(x) = \left(\dfrac{\ell nx - x.\frac{1}{x}}{(\ell nx)^2}\right)$

$\Rightarrow\ f'(x) = \left(\dfrac{\ell nx - 1}{(\ell nx)^2}\right)$

$\therefore$ For $f(x)$ to be increasing $f'(x) \geq 0$

$\Rightarrow\ \ell n\,x \geq 1$

$\Rightarrow\ x \geq e$

$\Rightarrow\ x \in [e, \infty)$ and for $f(x)$ to be decreasing $f'(x) \leq 0$

$\Rightarrow\ \ell n\,x \leq 1$

$\Rightarrow\ x \in (-\infty, e]$ but $x > 0, x \neq 1$

$\Rightarrow$ $f(x)$ is decreasing for $x \in (0, 1)$ and for $x \in (1, e]$

3. $f(x) = ax - \sin x$

$\Rightarrow\ f'(x) = a - \cos x$

$\Rightarrow$ $f(x)$ is monotonically increasing $\forall x \in \mathbb{R}$

$\Rightarrow\ a - \cos x \geq 0$

$\Rightarrow\ \cos x \leq a$

$\Rightarrow\ a \geq 1$

For $f(x)$ to be monotonically decreasing $\forall x \in \mathbb{R}$

$a - \cos x \leq 0$

$\Rightarrow\ \cos x \geq a$

$\Rightarrow\ a \leq -1$

4. $f(x) = \displaystyle\int_{x^2}^{x^3} \frac{dt}{\ell nt}, (x > 0)$

$\Rightarrow\ f'(x) = \dfrac{1}{\ell nx^3}.(3x^2) - \dfrac{1}{\ell nx}(2x) = \dfrac{3x^2}{3\ell nx} - \dfrac{2x}{2\ell nx} = \left(\dfrac{x}{\ell nx}\right)$

$(x - 1)$

For $0 < x < 1$, $\ell n\,x < 0$

$\therefore$ For $f(x)$ to be increasing $x\,(x - 1) < 0$

$\Rightarrow\ x \in (0, 1)$, which is true.

For $x > 1$, $\ell n\,x > 0$

$\Rightarrow\ x(x - 1) > 0$

$\Rightarrow\ x \in (-\infty, 0) \cup (1, \infty)$

$\Rightarrow\ x \in (1, \infty)$

Thus $f(x)$ increase on $(0, 1)$ and on $(1, \infty)$

5. (a) $f(x) = \dfrac{3x}{1+x^2}$

$\Rightarrow\ f'(x) = \dfrac{(1+x^2)(3) - 3x(2x)}{(1+x^2)^2}$

$\Rightarrow\ f'(x) = \dfrac{3-3x^2}{(1+x^2)^2}$

$\Rightarrow$ $f(x)$ is monotonically increasing

$\Rightarrow\ 1\ x^2 \geq 0$

$\Rightarrow\ x \in [-1, 1]$ and $f(x)$ is monotonically decreasing

$\Rightarrow\ 1 - x^2 \leq 0$

$\Rightarrow\ x \in (-\infty, -1] \cup [1, \infty)$

$\therefore$ Interval of M.I. is $[-1, 1]$ and intervals of M.D. are $(-\infty, -1]$ and $[1, \infty)$

(b) $f(x) = \dfrac{x^2 - x + 1}{x^2 + x + 1}$

$\Rightarrow\ f'(x) = \dfrac{(x^2+x+1)(2x-1) - (x^2-x+1)(2x+1)}{(x^2+x+1)^2}$

$= \dfrac{2(x^2-1)}{(x^2+x+1)^2}$

$\Rightarrow$ $f(x)$ is M.I. on $(-\infty, -1]$ and $[1, \infty)$ and $f(x)$ is M.D. on $[-1, 1]$

(c) $f(x) = (x)^{1/x}$; $x > 0$

$\Rightarrow\ \ell n\,f(x) = \dfrac{1}{x}\ell nx$

$\Rightarrow\ \dfrac{1}{f(x)}.f'(x) = \dfrac{1}{x^2} - \dfrac{1}{x^2}\ell nx$

$\Rightarrow\ f'(x) = \dfrac{x^{1/x}}{x^2}(1 - \ell nx)$

$\Rightarrow$ $f(x)$ is M.I for $\ell n\,x \leq 1$ i.e., on $(0, e]$ and $f(x)$ is M.D for $\ell n\,x \geq 1$ i.e., on $[e, \infty)$

(d) $f(x) = ex\,\ell n\,ex$; $x > 0$

$\Rightarrow\ f(x) = ex\,[1 + \ell n\,x]$

$\Rightarrow\ f'(x) = e\,[1 + 1 + \ell n\,x]$

$\Rightarrow$ $f(x)$ is M.I. on $x \in [e^{-2}, \infty)$ and $f(x)$ is M.D. on $x \in (0, e^{-2}]$

(e) $f(x) = \dfrac{\ell nx}{ex^2}$; $x > 0$

$\Rightarrow f'(x) = \dfrac{1}{e}\left[\dfrac{x - 2x\ell nx}{x^4}\right]$; $x > 0$

$= \dfrac{1}{e}\left[\dfrac{1-2\ell nx}{x^3}\right]$; $x > 0$

$\Rightarrow f(x)$ is M.I. for $\ell n\, x < \dfrac{1}{2}$ i.e., $x \in \left(0, \sqrt{e}\right]$ and $f(x)$ is M.D. for $\ell n\, x > \dfrac{1}{2}$ i.e., $x \in \left[\sqrt{e}, \infty\right)$

(f) $f(x) = x^3 + x^{-3}$

$\Rightarrow f'(x) = 3x^2 + (-3)\, x^{-4} = 3\left[x^2 - \dfrac{1}{x^4}\right] = 3\left[\dfrac{x^6 - 1}{x^4}\right]$

$= \dfrac{3(x^2-1)(x^4+x^2+1)}{x^4}$

$\therefore$ $f(x)$ is M.I. for $x^2 - 1 \geq 0$ i.e., on $(-\infty, -1]$ and $[1, \infty)$ and $f(x)$ is M.D. for $x^2 - 1 \leq 0, x \neq 0$ i.e., on $[-1, 0)$ and $(0, 1]$

(g) $f(x) = 2\, e^{x^2-4x}$

$\Rightarrow f'(x) = 2\left[e^{x^2-4x}\right].[2x-4] = 4(x-2)\, e^{x^2-4x}$

$\Rightarrow f(x)$ is M.I. on $[2, \infty)$ and $f(x)$ is M.D. on $(-\infty, 2]$

(h) $f(x) = x^2\, e^{-x}$

$\Rightarrow f'(x) = -x^2\, e^{-x} + 2x\, e^{-x} = xe^{-x}\,(2-x)$

$\Rightarrow f(x)$ is M.I. for $x\,(2-x) \geq 0$ i.e., on $[0, 2]$ and $f(x)$ is M.D. for $x(2-x) \leq 0$ i.e., on $(-\infty, 0] \cup [2, \infty)$

6. $\tan(\pi \cos\theta) = \cot(\pi \sin\theta)$,

$\Rightarrow \tan(\pi\cos\theta) = \tan\left[(2n+1)\dfrac{\pi}{2} - \pi\sin\theta\right]$

$\Rightarrow \pi\cos\theta = m\pi + (2n+1)\,\dfrac{\pi}{2} - \pi\sin\theta$

$\Rightarrow \cos\theta + \sin\theta = m + \dfrac{(2n+1)}{2}$; m, $n \in \mathbb{Z}$

$\therefore$ $f(x) = (\cos\theta + \sin\theta)^x$

$\Rightarrow f(x) = \left[\dfrac{2(\text{m+n})+1}{2}\right]^x$; $2(m+n)+1 > 0$

Also $(\cos\theta + \sin\theta) \in \left[-\sqrt{2}, \sqrt{2}\right]$

$\Rightarrow \dfrac{2(m+n)+1}{2} \in \left(0, \sqrt{2}\right]$

$\Rightarrow (m+n) + \dfrac{1}{2} \in \left(0, \sqrt{2}\ \right]; m, x \in \mathbb{Z}$

$\Rightarrow m + n = 0$

$\Rightarrow (\cos\theta + \sin\theta) = \dfrac{1}{2}$

$\Rightarrow f(x) = \left(\dfrac{1}{2}\right)^x$

$\Rightarrow f'(x) = \left(\dfrac{1}{2}\right)^x \ell n\left(\dfrac{1}{2}\right)$

$\Rightarrow f'(x) = -\left(\dfrac{1}{2}\right)^x \ell n\, 2 < 0\ \forall\, x \in \mathbb{R}$

$\Rightarrow f(x)$ is a decreasing function $\forall\, x \in \mathbb{R}$

7. $f(x) = \cos(\cos x)$

$\Rightarrow f'(x) = \sin(\cos x).\sin x$

In $x \in [0, \pi/2]$, $\sin x \geq 0$ and $\cos x \in [0, 1]$

$\Rightarrow \sin(\cos x) \in [\cos 1, 1]$

$\Rightarrow f'(x) \geq 0\ \forall\, x \in [0, \pi/2]$

$\Rightarrow f(x)$ is monotonically increasing on $[0, \pi/2]$.

8. $f(x) = x^4 - 14x^2 + 24x - 3$

$\Rightarrow f'(x) = 4x^3 - 28x + 24 = 4(x^3 - 7x + 6) = 4(x-1)(x^2 + x - 6) = 4(x-1)(x+3)(x-2)$

$\Rightarrow f(x)$ is M.I. for $x \in [-3, 1]$ and $[2, \infty)$ and $f(x)$ is M.D. for $x \in (-\infty, -3]$ and $[1, 2]$

9. $f(x) = 3\cos^4 x + 10\cos^3 x + 6\cos^2 x - 3$; $0 \leq x \leq \pi$.

$\Rightarrow f'(x) = -12\cos^3 x\sin x - 30\cos^2 x\sin x - 12\cos x\sin x$

$= (-6\cos x\sin x)\,(2\cos^2 x + 5\cos x + 2)$

$= (-6\sin x\cos x)\,(2\cos x + 1)\,(\cos x + 2)$

$= -3\sin 2x\,(2\cos x + 1)\,(\cos x + 2)$

$\Rightarrow f'(x) \leq 0$ for $x \in \left[0, \dfrac{\pi}{2}\right], x \in \left[\dfrac{2\pi}{3}, \pi\right]$ and $f'(x) \geq 0$ for $x \in \left[\dfrac{\pi}{2}, \dfrac{2\pi}{3}\right]$

$\therefore$ $f(x)$ is increase on $\left[\dfrac{\pi}{2}, \dfrac{2\pi}{3}\right]$ and decreasing on $\left[0, \dfrac{\pi}{2}\right]$ and $\left[\dfrac{2\pi}{3}, \pi\right]$

10. $f(x) = x^3 + (2a+3)\, x^2 + 3(2a+1)\, x + 5$

$\Rightarrow f'(x) = 3x^2 + 2(2a+3)\, x + 3(2a+1)$

$\therefore$ For $f(x)$ to be monotonic on $\mathbb{R}$, $f'(x) \geq 0\ \forall\, x \in \mathbb{R}$ i.e., $4(2a+3)^2 - 36(2a+1) \leq 0$

$\Rightarrow (2a+3)^2 - 18a - 9 \leq 0$

$\Rightarrow 4a^2 - 6a \leq 0$

$\Rightarrow 2a\,(2a-3) \leq 0$

$\Rightarrow a \in [0, 3/2]$

Also $f'(x) \geq 0\ \forall\, x \in \mathbb{R}$ and $a \in [0, 3/2]$

$\Rightarrow f(x)$ is injective for $a \in [0, 3/2]$

$\Rightarrow f(x)$ is invertible for $a \in [0, 3/2]$

TEXTUAL EXERCISE–3: (OBJECTIVE)

1. (d) $g(\theta) = \displaystyle\int_0^{\sin^2\theta} f(x)dx + \int_0^{\cos^2\theta} f(x)dx$

$\Rightarrow g'(\theta) = f(\sin^2\theta)\,[2\sin\theta\cos\theta] + f(\cos^2\theta)\,[-2\cos\theta\sin\theta]$

$= (\sin 2\theta)\,[f(\sin^2\theta) - f(\cos^2\theta)\,]$

For $\theta \in \left(\dfrac{-\pi}{2}, \dfrac{\pi}{2}\right), 2\theta \in (-\pi, \pi)$

$\Rightarrow \sin 2\theta < 0$ for $2\theta \in (-\pi, 0)$ i.e., $\theta \in \left(\dfrac{-\pi}{2}, 0\right)$ and $\sin 2\theta > 0$ for $2\theta \in (0, \pi)$ i.e., $\theta \in \left(0, \dfrac{\pi}{2}\right)$

Case (i): $\theta \in \left(\dfrac{-\pi}{2}, \dfrac{-\pi}{4}\right)$

$\Rightarrow \sin 2\theta < 0$ and $\sin^2\theta > \cos^2\theta$

$\Rightarrow f(\sin^2\theta) - f(\cos^2\theta) > 0$ $\quad(\because f$ is $\uparrow)$

$\Rightarrow g'(\theta) < 0$ i.e., $g(\theta)$ is decreasing

Case (ii): $\theta \in \left(\frac{-\pi}{4}, 0\right)$

$\Rightarrow$ $\sin 2\theta < 0$ and $\sin^2 \theta < \cos^2 \theta$

$\Rightarrow$ $f(\sin^2 \theta) - f(\cos^2 \theta) < 0 \quad (\because f \text{ is } \uparrow)$

$\Rightarrow$ $g'(\theta) > 0$ i.e., $g(\theta)$ is increasing

Case (iii): $\theta \in \left(0, \frac{\pi}{4}\right)$

$\Rightarrow$ $\sin 2\theta > 0$ and $\sin^2 \theta < \cos^2 \theta$

$\Rightarrow$ $f(\sin^2 \theta) - f(\cos^2 \theta) < 0$

$\Rightarrow$ $g'(\theta) < 0$ i.e., $g(\theta)$ is decreasing

Case (iv): $\theta \in \left(\frac{\pi}{4}, \frac{\pi}{2}\right)$

$\Rightarrow$ $\sin 2\theta > 0$ and $\sin^2 \theta > \cos^2 \theta$

$\Rightarrow$ $f(\sin^2 \theta) - f(\cos^2 \theta) > 0$

$\Rightarrow$ $g'(\theta) > 0$ i.e., $g(\theta)$ is increasing

2. (a), (b) $f(x) = \sin(\ell n\, x) - \cos(\ell n\, x)$

$\Rightarrow f'(x) = \frac{1}{x}.[\cos(\ell n\, x) + \sin(\ell n\, x)];\ x > 0$

For $f(x)$ to be strictly increasing $f'(x) \geq 0$

$\Rightarrow$ $\cos(\ell n\, x) + \sin(\ell n\, x) \geq 0$

$\Rightarrow$ $\cos(\ell n\, x) \geq -\sin(\ell n\, x)$

$\Rightarrow$ $\ell n\, x \in \left[2n\pi - \frac{\pi}{4}, (2n+1)\pi - \frac{\pi}{4}\right]; n \in \mathbb{Z}$

$\Rightarrow$ $x \in \left[e^{2n\pi - \pi/4}, e^{2n\pi + 3\pi/4}\right]; n \in \mathbb{Z}$

3. (d) $f(x) = a^{\{a^{|x|}.\text{sgn}\, x\}}; g(x) = a^{[a^{|x|}.\text{sgn}\, x]}$; $a > 0, a \neq 1, x \in \mathbb{R}$.

$(\ell n\, a)\, h(x) = (\ell n(f(x)) + \ell n(g(x))$

$\Rightarrow$ $h(x) = \frac{\ell n(f(x).g(x))}{\ell n(a)} = \frac{1}{\ell n(a)}.\ell n\left(a^{\{a^{|x|}\text{sgn}\, x\} + [a^{|x|}\text{sgn}\, x]}\right)$

$= \frac{1}{\ell n(a)}.\ell n\left(a^{a^{|x|}.\text{sgn}\, x}\right) = \frac{1}{\ell n(a)}.a^{|x|}.\text{sgn}\, x.\ell n(a) = a^{|x|\,\text{sgn} x}$

$$\Rightarrow h(x) = \begin{cases} -a^{(-x)} & \text{for } x < 0 \\ 0 & \text{for } x = 0 \\ a^x & \text{for } x > 0 \end{cases}$$

$\therefore$ $h(-x) = -a^{(x)}$ for $x > 0$

$= -ax = -h(x)$ and $h(-x) = a^{-x}$ for $x < 0$

$= -(-a^{-x}) = -h(x)$

Thus $h(x)$ is an odd function.

Also $h'(x) = \begin{cases} a^{-x} & \text{for } x < 0 \\ a^x & \text{for } x > 0 \end{cases}$

$\Rightarrow$ $h'(x) \geq 0\ \forall\ x \in \mathbb{R}$

$\Rightarrow$ $h(x)$ is increasing

4. (b) $f(x) = |x|e^{-x}$

$$\Rightarrow f(x) = \begin{cases} -xe^{-x} & \text{for } x < 0 \\ xe^{-x} & \text{for } x \geq 0 \end{cases}$$

$$\Rightarrow f'(x) = \begin{cases} xe^{-x} - e^{-x} & \text{for } x < 0 \\ -xe^{-x} + e^{-x} & \text{for } x > 0 \end{cases} = \begin{cases} (x-1)e^{-x} & \text{for } x < 0 \\ e^{-x}(1-x) & \text{for } x > 0 \end{cases}$$

$\Rightarrow$ $f(x) \downarrow$ for $x < 0$, $\uparrow$ for $0 < x < 1$ and $\downarrow$ for $x > 1$

$\Rightarrow$ $x = 0$ and $x = 1$ are two critical points.

5. (c) $f(x) = (ax^2 + bx + c).|x|$; where $ac < 0$

$$= \begin{cases} -x(ax^2 + bx + c); x < 0 \\ x(ax^2 + bx + c); x \geq 0 \end{cases} = \begin{cases} -ax^3 - bx^2 - cx; x < 0 \\ ax^3 + bx^2 cx; x \geq 0 \end{cases}$$

$$\Rightarrow f'(x) = \begin{cases} -3ax^2 - 2bx - c; x < 0 \\ 3ax^2 + 2bx + c; x > 0 \end{cases}$$

Disc. of above quadratics $= 4b^2 - 12ac > 0$ as $ac < 0$

For $x < 0$, Product of roots $= \frac{-c}{-3a} = \frac{c}{3a} < 0$ as $ac < 0$

$\Rightarrow$ There is exactly one $-ve$ real root (α(*say*))

For $x > 0$, product of roots $= \frac{c}{3a} < 0$ as $ac < 0$

$\Rightarrow$ There is exactly one +ve real root (β(*say*))

The graph of $f(x)$ will be as shown below.

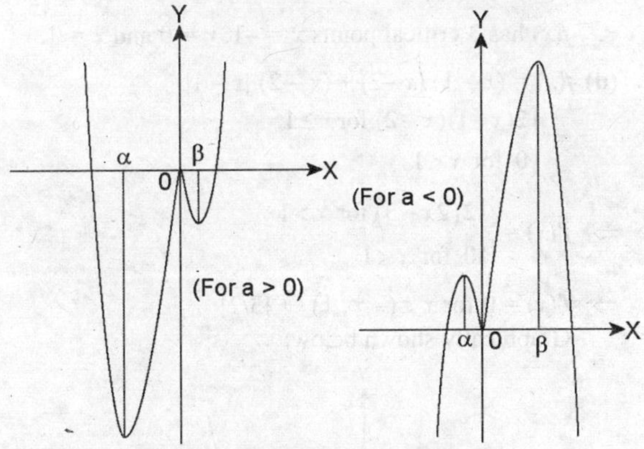

Thus there are true critical points α, 0, β

6. (b) $f(x) = (1 - x)\,|x - 3|$

$$\Rightarrow f(x) = \begin{cases} (x-1)(x-3) \text{ for } x < 3 \\ -(x-1)(x-3) \text{ for } x \geq 3 \end{cases}$$

$$\Rightarrow f(x) = \begin{cases} x^2 - 4x + 3 \text{ for } x < 3 \\ -x^2 + 4x - 3 \text{ for } x \geq 3 \end{cases}$$

$$\Rightarrow f'(x) = \begin{cases} 2x - 4 \text{ for } x < 3 \\ -2x + 4 \text{ for } x > 3 \end{cases}$$

$\Rightarrow$ $f'(x) < 0$ for $x < 2$ and $x > 3$ and $f'(x) > 0$ for $2 < x < 3$ and $f'(x) > 0$ at $x = 2$

Graphically,

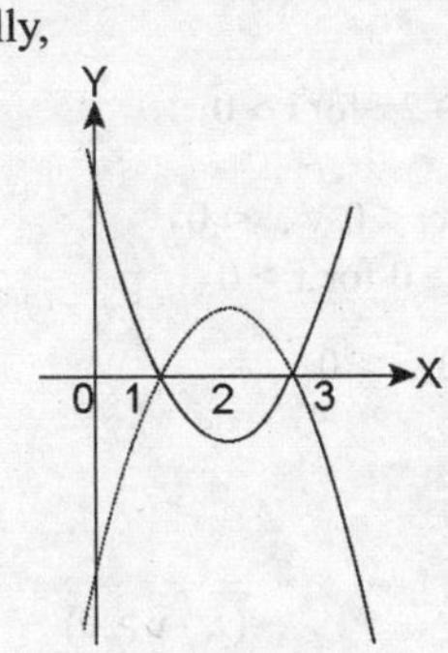

$\Rightarrow$ $f(x)$ has 2 critical points namely $x = 2$ and $x = 3$.

7. (c) $f(x) = x^2 - 2|x| = |x|^2 - 2|x| = (|x|)(|x| - 2)$

$\Rightarrow f(x) = 0$ for $|x| = 0$ or $|x| = 2$

$\Rightarrow x = 0$ or $x = \pm 2$ and $f(x) = \begin{cases} x^2 + 2x \text{ for } x < 0 \\ x^2 - 2x \text{ for } x \geq 0 \end{cases}$

$\Rightarrow f'(x) = \begin{cases} 2x + 2 \text{ for } x < 0 \\ 2x - 2 \text{ for } x > 0 \end{cases}$

$\Rightarrow f'(x) = 0$ at $x = -1$ and at $x = 1$

Also $f'(x) < 0$ for $x < -1$ and $x \in (0, 1)$ and $f'(x) > 0$ for $x \in (-1, 0)$ and $x \in (1, \infty)$

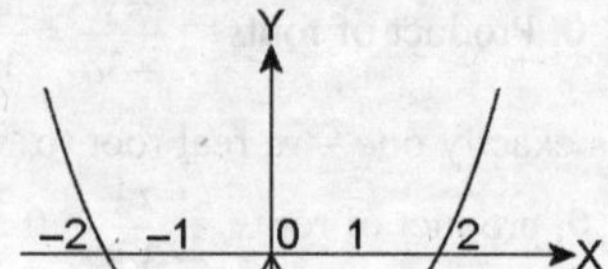

$\therefore$ $f(x)$ has 3 critical points $x = -1$, $x = 0$ and $x = 1$.

8. (d) $f(x) = (x - 1)(x - 2) + (x - 2)|x - 1|$

$= \begin{cases} 2(x-1)(x-2) \text{ for } x \geq 1 \\ 0 \text{ for } x < 1 \end{cases}$

$\Rightarrow f'(x) = \begin{cases} 2(2x-3) \text{ for } x > 1 \\ 0 \text{ for } x < 1 \end{cases}$

$\Rightarrow f'(x) = 0$ for $x \in (-\infty, 1) \cup \{3/2\}$

Graphically shown below:

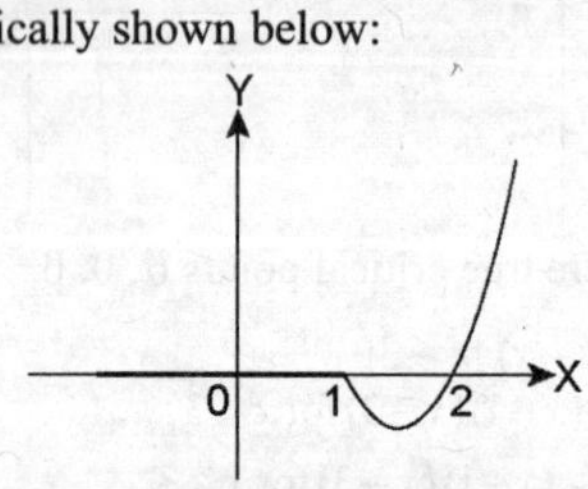

$\therefore$ $f(x)$ has infinitely many critical points

9. (a), (b), (d)

$f(x) = 2\,\ell n\,|x| - x\,|x|$

$\Rightarrow f(x) = \begin{cases} 2\ell n(-x) + x^2 \text{ for } x < 0 \\ 2\ell n x - x^2 \text{ for } x > 0 \end{cases}$

$\Rightarrow f'(x) = \begin{cases} \dfrac{2}{x} + 2x \text{ for } x < 0 \\ \dfrac{2}{x} - 2x \text{ for } x > 0 \end{cases}$

Clearly $f'(x) < 0\ \forall\ x < 0$

Now $f'(x) > 0$ for $x > 0$

$\Rightarrow \dfrac{2}{x} - 2x > 0;\ x > 0$

$\Rightarrow \dfrac{2 - 2x^2}{x} > 0$

$\Rightarrow 2 - 2x^2 > 0 \qquad (\because x > 0)$

$\Rightarrow x^2 - 1 < 0$

$\Rightarrow x \in (0, 1)$

$\therefore$ $f(x) \downarrow$ for $x \in (-\infty, 0)$ and $(1, \infty)$ and $f(x) \uparrow$ for $x \in (0, 1)$

10. (a) $f(x) = \displaystyle\int_1^x \frac{dt}{t} \Rightarrow f'(x) = \frac{1}{x}$

$\Rightarrow$ $f(x)$ is increasing function for $x > 0$

11. (a), (b) $y = \dfrac{2x-1}{x-2} (x \neq 2)$

$\Rightarrow xy - 2y = 2x - 1$

$\Rightarrow x(y - 2) = 2y - 1$

$\Rightarrow x = \dfrac{2y-1}{y-2}$

$\Rightarrow f^{-1}(x) = \dfrac{2x-1}{x-2}$

$\Rightarrow$ $f(x)$ is inverse of it self.

Range of $f(x) = \mathbb{R} - \{2\}$

Also $f'(x) = \dfrac{(x-2)(2)-(2x-1)(1)}{(x-2)^2}$

$\Rightarrow f'(x) = \dfrac{-3}{(x-2)^2} < 0$

$\Rightarrow$ $f(x)$ is a decreasing function on $\mathbb{R} - \{2\}$

12. (b) $f(x) = \left(\dfrac{\sqrt{P+4}}{1-p} - 1\right) x^5 - 3x$

$\Rightarrow f'(x) = \left(\dfrac{\sqrt{P+4}}{1-p} - 1\right)(3x^2) - 3$

$\therefore$ For $f(x)$ decreasing, $\left(\dfrac{\sqrt{P+4}}{1-p} - 1\right)x^2 - 1 \leq 0 \forall x \in \mathbb{R}$

Case (i): $\dfrac{\sqrt{P+4}}{1-p} - 1 \leq 0$, then $f'(x) \leq 0$ i.e., $\dfrac{\sqrt{P+4}}{1-p} \leq 1$

which is true for $p > 1$

Now for $p < 1$ and $p \geq -4$

$\dfrac{\sqrt{p+4}}{1-p} \leq 1$ (*Both sides non-negative*)

$\Rightarrow \dfrac{p+4}{(1-p)^2} \leq 1$

$\Rightarrow p + 4 \leq p^2 - 2p + 1$

$\Rightarrow p^2 - 3p - 3 \geq 0$

$\Rightarrow p = \left(-\infty, \dfrac{3-\sqrt{21}}{2}\right] \cup \left[\dfrac{3+\sqrt{21}}{2}, \infty\right)$

$\Rightarrow p \in \left[-4, \dfrac{3-\sqrt{21}}{2}\right]$

$\therefore \left(\dfrac{\sqrt{p+4}}{1-p} - 1\right)x^2 - 1 \leq 0$

For $p \in \left[-4, \dfrac{3-\sqrt{21}}{2}\right] \cup (1, \infty)$

Case (ii): $\left(\dfrac{\sqrt{p+4}}{1-p}\right)-1\geq 0$

$\Rightarrow \dfrac{\sqrt{p+4}}{1-p}\geq 1, -4\leq p<1$ and $p+4\geq p^2-2p+1; p<1$

$\Rightarrow p^2-3p-3\leq 0; p<1$

$\Rightarrow p\in\left[\dfrac{3-\sqrt{21}}{2},1\right)$, then $f'(x)\leq 0$

$\Rightarrow x\in\left[\dfrac{p-1}{\sqrt{p+1}},\dfrac{1-p}{\sqrt{p+1}}\right]$

$\therefore$ $f(x)$ decrease for $\forall x\in\mathbb{R}$, when $P\in\left[-4,\dfrac{3-\sqrt{21}}{2}\right]\cup(1,\infty)$

13. (b) $f(x)=x^3+ax^2+bx+5\sin^2 x$

$f'(x)=3x^2+2ax+b+10\sin x\cos x$

$=3x^2+2ax+b+5\sin 2x$

$f'(x)\geq 0\ \forall x\in\mathbb{R}$

$\Rightarrow (2a)^2-4(3)(b+5\sin 2x)\leq 0$

$\Rightarrow a^2-3(b+5\sin 2x)\leq 0$

$\Rightarrow a^2-3b\leq 15\sin 2x$

$\Rightarrow a^2-3b\leq -15$

$\Rightarrow a^2-3b+15\leq 0$

14. (b), (c), (d)

$f(x)=x^{100}+\sin x-1$

$f'(x)=100x^{99}+\cos x$ for $f(x)$ to be increasing $100x^{99}+\cos x\geq 0$ i.e., $100x^{99}\geq -\cos x\geq -1$

$\therefore$ $100x^{99}\geq -1$

$\Rightarrow f(x)\uparrow$

$\Rightarrow x\geq\left(\dfrac{-1}{100}\right)^{99}$

$\Rightarrow f(x)$ is increasing in$(0, 1)$, $\left(\dfrac{\pi}{2},\pi\right)$ and $\left(0,\dfrac{\pi}{2}\right)$

15. (d) $f(x)=x^2\log 3x; x>0$

$\Rightarrow f'(x)=3x^2.\dfrac{1}{3x}+(\log 3x)(2x)$

$\Rightarrow f'(x)=x+2x\log 3x$

$=x(1+2\log 3x)$ for $f(x)$ increasing, $(1+2\log 3x)\geq 0$

$\Rightarrow 2\log 3x\geq -1$

$\Rightarrow \log 3x\geq -1/2$

$\Rightarrow 3x\geq e^{-1/2}$

$\Rightarrow x\geq\dfrac{1}{3}e^{-1/2}$

$\Rightarrow x\in\left[\dfrac{1}{3}e^{-1/2},\infty\right)$

16. (a), (c) $f(x)=\tan^{-1}(\sin x+\cos x)^3$

$\Rightarrow f'(x)=\dfrac{3(\sin x+\cos x)^2.(\cos x-\sin x)}{1+(\sin x+\cos x)^6}$

$\therefore$ $f(x)$ increase

$\Rightarrow \sin x=-\cos x$ or $\cos x-\sin x\geq 0$

$\Rightarrow x\in\left[2n\pi-\dfrac{\pi}{4},2n\pi+\dfrac{\pi}{4}\right]; n\in\mathbb{Z}$

17. (c) $f(x)=\cos|x|-2ax+b$

$\Rightarrow f'(x)=-\sin x-2a$

$\therefore$ $f'(x)\geq 0\ \forall x\in\mathbb{R}$

$\Rightarrow -\sin x-2a\geq 0\ \forall x\in\mathbb{R}$

$\Rightarrow -2a\leq\sin x\ \forall x\in\mathbb{R}$

$\Rightarrow 2a\leq -1$

$\Rightarrow a\leq\dfrac{-1}{2}$

18. (a), (b), (c), (d)

$f(x)=x-\cot^{-1}x+\log\left(\sqrt{x^2+1}-x\right)$

$\Rightarrow f'(x)=1+\dfrac{1}{\sqrt{1+x^2}}+\dfrac{1}{\left(\sqrt{x^2+1}-x\right)}\times\left[\dfrac{x}{\sqrt{x^2+1}}-1\right]$

$=1+\dfrac{1}{\sqrt{1+x^2}}+\left(\dfrac{-1}{\sqrt{x^2+1}}\right)=1$

$\Rightarrow f(x)$ is increasing function $\forall x\in(-\infty,\infty)$

19. (a), (c), (d)

$f(x)=\sin^{-1}\left(2x\sqrt{1-x^2}\right)$

$$\Rightarrow 2\sin^{-1}x=\begin{cases}\sin^{-1}\left(2x\sqrt{1-x^2}\right); \dfrac{-1}{\sqrt{2}}\leq x\leq\dfrac{1}{\sqrt{2}}\\ -\pi\sin^{-1}\left(2x\sqrt{1-x^2}\right); -1\leq x\leq\dfrac{-1}{\sqrt{2}}\\ \pi-\sin^{-1}\left(2x\sqrt{1-x^2}\right); \dfrac{1}{\sqrt{2}}\leq x\leq 1\end{cases}$$

$$\Rightarrow f(x)=\begin{cases}2\sin^{-1}x; \dfrac{-1}{\sqrt{2}}\leq x\leq\dfrac{1}{\sqrt{2}}\\ -\pi-2\sin^{-1}x; -1\leq x\leq\dfrac{-1}{\sqrt{2}}\\ \pi-2\sin^{-1}x; \dfrac{1}{\sqrt{2}}\leq x\leq 1\end{cases}$$

$$\Rightarrow f'(x)=\begin{cases}\dfrac{2}{\sqrt{1-x^2}}; \dfrac{-1}{\sqrt{2}}<x<\dfrac{1}{\sqrt{2}}\\ \dfrac{-2}{\sqrt{1-x^2}}; x\in\left(-1,\dfrac{-1}{\sqrt{2}}\right)\cup\left(\dfrac{1}{\sqrt{2}},1\right)\end{cases}$$

20. (d) $f(x)=(x+2)e^{-x}$

$\Rightarrow f'(x)=-(x+2)e^{-x}+e^{-x}$

$=e^{-x}(-x-1)=-(x+1)e^{-x}\leq 0$ for $x\geq -1$ and ≥ 0 for $x\leq -1$

$\Rightarrow f(x)$ is increasing on $(-\infty,-1]$ and decreasing on $[-1,\infty]$

21. (a) $f(x)=x\,e^{x(1-x)}$

$f'(x)=x\,e^{x(1-x)}.[1-2x]+e^{x(1-x)}.1$

$=e^{x(1-x)}[-2x^2+x+1]$

$=e^{x(1-x)}[-2x^2+2x-x+1]$

$=e^{x(1-x)}[-2x(x-1)-1(x-1)]$

$=e^{x(1-x)}[(x-1)(-2x-1)]$

$\Rightarrow f'(x)\geq 0$

$\Rightarrow (x-1)(2x+1)\leq 0$

$\Rightarrow x\in\left[\dfrac{-1}{2},1\right]$ and $f'(x)\leq$ for $x\in\left(-\infty,\dfrac{-1}{2}\right]\cup[1,\infty)$

TEXTUAL EXERCISE-4: (SUBJECTIVE)

1. $f(x) = \sin(\cos x)$,

$f'(x) = (-\sin x) \cos(\cos x)$

For $x \in \left[0, \frac{\pi}{2}\right]$, $\sin x \in [0, 1]$, $\cos x \in [0, 1]$

$\Rightarrow$ $\cos(\cos x) \in [\cos 1, 1]$

$\Rightarrow$ $f'(x) \le 0 \ \forall\ x \in [0, \pi/2]$

$\Rightarrow$ $f(x)$ is decreasing on $[0, \pi/2]$

2. $f(x) = x^3 - 3x^2 - 9x + 20$

$\Rightarrow$ $f'(x) = 3x^2 - 6x - 9$

$\Rightarrow$ $f'(x) = 3(x^2 - 2x - 3) = 3[(x-3)(x+1)]$

$\Rightarrow$ $f'(x) > 0$ for $x \in (-\infty, -1) \cup (3, \infty)$ and $f'(x) < 0$ for $\in (-1, 3)$, $f'(x) = 0$ at $x = -1, 3$

$\Rightarrow$ $f(x) \uparrow$ on $(3, \infty)$ $\qquad \Rightarrow$ $f(x) > f(4)\ \forall\ x > 4$

$\Rightarrow$ $f(x) > 0$ $\qquad [\because f(4) = 0]\ \forall\ x \in (4, \infty)$

3. $(x+3)^5 - (x-1)^5 \ge 244$

Let $f(x) = (x+3)^5 - (x-1)^5 - 244$

$\Rightarrow$ $f'(x) = 5(x+3)^4 - 5(x-1)^4$

$= 5[(x+3)+(x-1)][(x+3)-(x-1)][(x+3)^2+(x-1)^2]$

$= 5(2x+2)(4)[(x+3)^2+(x-1)^2]$

$= 40(x+1)[(x+3)^2+(x-1)^2]$

$\Rightarrow$ $f'(x) \le 0$ for $x \le -1$ and $f'(x) \ge 0$ for $x \ge -1$

$\Rightarrow$ $f(x) \uparrow$ on $[-1, \infty)$

$\Rightarrow$ $f(x) \ge f(0)\ \forall\ x \in [0, \infty)$

$\Rightarrow$ $f(x) \ge 0\ \forall\ x \in [0, \infty)$ $\quad [\because f(0) = 0]$

$\Rightarrow$ $(x+3)^5 - (x-1)^5 \ge 244\ \forall\ x \in [0, \infty)$

4. (a) $f(x) = x^x$

$\Rightarrow$ $\ell n f(x) = x\, \ell n\, x$

$\Rightarrow$ $f'(x) = x^x(1 + \ell n\, x)$; $x > 0$

$\Rightarrow$ $f'(x) \le 0$ for $x \le -$ and $f'(x) \ge 0$ for $x \ge \frac{1}{e}$ and $f(x) \to \infty$ as $x \to \infty$

$\Rightarrow$ $f(x) \in \left[f\left(\frac{1}{e}\right), \infty\right)$

$\Rightarrow$ Range $= [(1/e)^{1/e}, \infty) = [(e)^{-1/e}, \infty)$

(b) Let $g(x) = (\sin x)^{\sin x}$

Domain of $g(x) = [2n\pi, (2n+1)\pi]$

$\ln g(x) = (\sin x).\ \ln \sin x$

$\Rightarrow$ $\frac{1}{g(x)}.g'(x) = \sin x.\frac{1}{\sin x}.\cos x + (\ln \sin x)\cos x$; $x \in (2n\pi, (2n+1)\pi) = (\cos x)(1 + \ln \sin x)$

$\Rightarrow$ $g'(x) = (\sin x)^{\sin x}.\ \cos x\,(1 + \ln \sin x)$

For $n = 0$

$$\Rightarrow \begin{cases} g'(x) < 0 \text{ for } x \in \left(0, \sin^{-1}\frac{1}{e}\right) \\ g'(x) > 0 \text{ for } x \in \left(\sin^{-1}\frac{1}{e}, \frac{\pi}{2}\right) \\ g'(x) < 0 \text{ for } x \in \left(\frac{\pi}{2}, \pi - \sin^{-1}\frac{1}{e}\right) \\ g'(x) > 0 \text{ for } x \in \left(\pi - \sin^{-1}\frac{1}{e}, \pi\right) \end{cases}$$

$\therefore$ $g(0) = 1$, $g\left(\sin^{-1}\frac{1}{e}\right) = \left(\frac{1}{e}\right)^{1/e}$, $g\left(\frac{\pi}{2}\right) = 1$, $g\left(\pi - \sin^{-1}\frac{1}{e}\right) = \left(\frac{1}{e}\right)^{1/e}$, $g(\pi) = 1$

$\Rightarrow$ Range of $g(x) = \left[\left(\frac{1}{e}\right)^{1/e}, 1\right]$

$\Rightarrow$ Range of $\left[(\sin x)^{\sin x} + 1\right]$ is $\left[\left(\frac{1}{e}\right)^{1/e} + 1, 2\right]$

Range of $\ln\left((\sin x)^{\sin x} + 1\right)$ is $\left[\ln\left(1 + \left(\frac{1}{e}\right)^{1/e}\right), \ln 2\right]$

5. $e^{x-1} + x = 2$

$\Rightarrow$ $e^{x-1} = 2 - x$

Let $f(x) = e^{x-1}$ and $g(x) = 2 - x$

$\Rightarrow$ $f'(x) = e^{x-1}$ and $g'(x) = -1$

$\Rightarrow$ $f'(x) > 0\ \forall x \in \mathbb{R}$ and $g'(x) < 0\ \forall x \in \mathbb{R}$

$\Rightarrow$ $f(x)$ is strictly increasing and $g(x)$ is strictly decreasing functions.

$\Rightarrow$ $f(x)$ and $g(x)$ will intersect at exactly one point

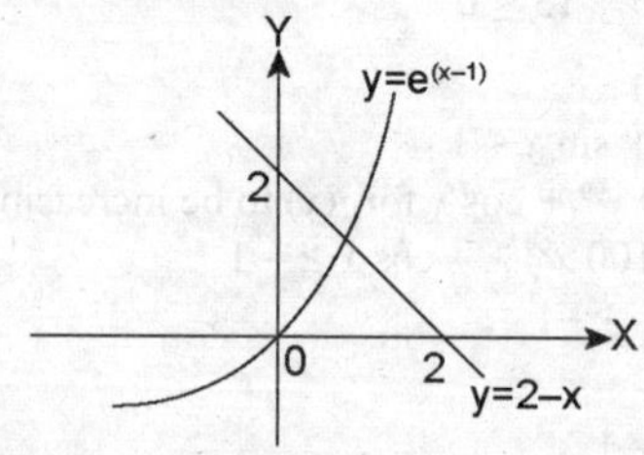

$\Rightarrow$ $f(x) = g(x)$ has exactly one real root which is $x = 1$

TEXTUAL EXERCISE-4: (OBJECTIVE)

1. (a), (b) $f: \mathbb{R} \to \mathbb{R}, f \downarrow$

$g: \mathbb{R} \to \mathbb{R}$, $g \uparrow$

$(fog)'(x) = f'g(x)\ .\ g'(x) = (\le 0).(\ge 0)$

$\Rightarrow$ $(fog)'(x) \le 0$

$\Rightarrow$ $fog(x)$ is $\downarrow$

$(gof)'(x) = g'(f(x))\ .\ f'(x) = (\ge 0).(\le 0)$

$\Rightarrow$ $(gof)'(x) \le 0$

$\Rightarrow$ $gof(x)$ is $\downarrow$

$(fof)'(x) = f'(f(x))\ .\ f'(x) = (\le 0)(\le 0)$

$\Rightarrow$ $(fof)'(x) \ge 0$

$\Rightarrow$ $fof(x)$ is $\uparrow$ and $(gog)'(x) = g'(g(x)).\ g'(x) = (\ge 0).(\ge 0)$

$\Rightarrow$ $gog(x)$ is $\uparrow$

Thus fof and gog are increasing functions.

2. (b) $f(x) = \frac{ae^x + be^{-x}}{ce^x + de^{-x}}$

$\Rightarrow$ $f'(x)$

$= \frac{(ce^x + de^{-x})(ae^x - be^{-x}) - (ae^x + be^{-x})(ce^x - de^{-x})}{(ce^x + de^{-x})^2}$

$\Rightarrow\ f'(x) = \dfrac{\left(ace^{2x} - bde^{-2x} - be + ad\right) - \left(ace^{2x} - bde^{-2x} + bc - ad\right)}{\left(ce^{x} + de^{-x}\right)^2}$

$= \dfrac{2(ad - bc)}{\left(ce^{x} + de^{-x}\right)^2}$

$\Rightarrow$ $f(x)$ increase for ad $\geq$ bc

3. **(c)** $\phi(x) = [f(x)]^2$

$\Rightarrow\ \phi'(x) = 2[f(x)].f'(x)$

As $f(x)$ increase in interval (a, b)

$f'(x) \geq 0$ in (a, b) but $f(x)$ can take non-negative or non-positive values

$\Rightarrow$ $\phi(x)$ can be increasing or decreasing or non-monotonic in (a, b)

4. **(b), (c)** $g(x) = 2f(x/2) + f(1 - x)$ and $f''(x) < 0$ for $x \in [0, 1]$

$\Rightarrow$ $f'(x)$ is decreasing on [0, 1]

Now, $g'(x) = 2.\dfrac{1}{2}f'(x/2) - f'(1 - x)$

$\Rightarrow\ g'(x) = f'(x/2) - f'(1 - x)$

For $g(x)$ increasing $g'(x) \geq 0$

$\Rightarrow\ f'(x/2) \geq f'(1 - x)$

$\Rightarrow\ x/2 \leq 1 - x$

$\Rightarrow\ \dfrac{3}{2}x \leq 1$

$\Rightarrow\ x \leq \dfrac{2}{3}$

$\therefore$ $g(x)$ increase on $\left[0, \dfrac{2}{3}\right]$ and decrease on $\left[\dfrac{2}{3}, 1\right]$

5. **(a), (c)** $\phi(x) = f(x) + f(2a - x)$; $0 \leq x \leq 2a$

$\Rightarrow\ \phi'(x) = f'(x) - f'(2a - x);\ 0 \leq x \leq 2a$

Here $-2a \leq -x \leq 0$

$\Rightarrow\ 0 \leq 2a - x \leq 2a$

$\because\ f''(x) > 0\ \forall\ 0 \leq x \leq 2a$

$\Rightarrow\ f'(x) \uparrow \forall\ 0 \leq x \leq 2a$

$\therefore\ \phi(x) \uparrow$

$\Rightarrow\ \phi'(x) \geq 0$

$\Rightarrow\ f'(x) \geq f'(2a - x)$

$\Rightarrow\ x \geq 2a - x \quad \Rightarrow x \geq a$

$\therefore$ $\phi(x) \uparrow$ on [a, 2a] and $\phi(x) \downarrow$ on [0, a]

6. **(a)** $f: [0, \infty) \to [0, \infty) : \uparrow$

$g: [0, \infty) ; \downarrow$

$h(x) = f[g(x)];\ h(0) = 0,\ h(x) - h(1) = ?$

$h'(x) = f'(x)\,(g(x))\,.\,g'(x) \leq 0$

But Range of $h(x) = [0, \infty)$ and $h(x) \leq h(0)\ \forall\ x \geq 0$

$\Rightarrow\ h(x) \leq 0\ \forall\ x \geq 0$

$\Rightarrow\ h(x) = 0\ \forall\ x \geq 0$

$\Rightarrow\ h(1) = 0$

$\Rightarrow\ h(x) - h(1) = 0$

7. **(b), (c)** $x = \dfrac{1}{1+t^2}$ and $y = \dfrac{1}{t\left(1+t^2\right)}\ \forall t > 0$

$\Rightarrow\ x = (1 + t^2)^{-1};\ y = (t + t^3)^{-1}$

$\Rightarrow\ \dfrac{dx}{dt} = \dfrac{-1}{\left(1+t^2\right)^2}(2t);\ \dfrac{dy}{dt} = \dfrac{-1}{\left(t+t^3\right)^2}\left(1+3t^2\right)$

$\Rightarrow\ \dfrac{dy}{dx} = \dfrac{\left(1+3t^2\right)}{t^2(2t)} = \dfrac{1+3t^2}{2t^3} > 0$ as $t > 0$

$\Rightarrow$ f is increasing in (0, 1) and (0, ∞)

8. **(b)** $f(x) = \dfrac{ax+b}{cx+d}$; $x \in \mathbb{R} - \{d/c\}$

$\Rightarrow\ f'(x) = \dfrac{(cx+d)(a) - (ax+b)(c)}{(cx+d)^2}$

$= \dfrac{ad - bc}{(cx+d)^2}$; $x \in \mathbb{R} - \{d/c\}$

$\Rightarrow$ $f(x)$ is strictly increasing function for $ad - bc \geq 0$

9. **(a), (b)** $f(x) = \dfrac{\sin^{-1} x}{\cos^{-1} x}$

$D_f = [-1, 1)$

$\Rightarrow$ Positive values of domain of function is the set (0, 1)

$\Rightarrow\ f'(x) = \dfrac{\left(\cos^{-1} x\right).\dfrac{1}{\sqrt{1-x^2}} + \left(\sin^{-1} x\right)\dfrac{1}{\sqrt{1-x^2}}}{\left(\cos^{-1} x\right)^2}$

$\Rightarrow\ f'(x) = \dfrac{\left(\cos^{-1} x + \sin^{-1} x\right)}{\left(\sqrt{1-x^2}\right)\left(\cos^{-1} x\right)^2}$

$\Rightarrow\ f'(x) = \dfrac{\pi}{2\sqrt{1-x^2}\left(\cos^{-1} x\right)^2}\ \forall\ x \in (0, 1)$

$\Rightarrow$ $f(x)$ is strictly increasing function

10. **(b), (c)** $f(x) = \sqrt{3}\sin x - \cos x - 2ax + b$

$\Rightarrow\ f'(x) = \sqrt{3}\cos x + \sin x - 2a$

$f(x)$ decreases $\forall\ x \in \mathbb{R}$ if $\sqrt{3}\cos x + \sin x - 2a \leq 2a\ \forall\ x \in \mathbb{R}$ i.e., $\sqrt{3}\cos x + \sin x \leq 2a\ \forall\ x \in \mathbb{R}$

$\Rightarrow\ \sqrt{3+1} \leq 2a$

$\Rightarrow\ a \geq 1$

11. **(b)** $f(x) = (ab - b^2 - 2)\,x + \int_0^x \left(\cos^4\theta + \sin^4\theta\right)d\theta$

$\Rightarrow\ f'(x) = (ab - b^2 - 2) + (\cos^4 x + \sin^4 x)$

$= (ab - b^2 - 2) + (1 - 2\sin^2 x \cos 2x)$

$= (ab - b^2 - 2) + \left(1 - \dfrac{1}{2}\sin^2 2x\right)$

$= ab - b^2 - 1 - \dfrac{1}{2}\sin^2 2x$

$\because$ $f(x)$ is decreasing function $\forall\ x \in \mathbb{R}$

$\Rightarrow\ ab - b^2 - 1 - \dfrac{1}{2}\sin^2 2x \leq 0\ \forall\ x \in \mathbb{R}$

$\Rightarrow\ 2(ab - b^2 - 1) \leq \sin^2 2x\ \forall\ x \in \mathbb{R}$

$\Rightarrow\ 2(ab - b^2 - 1) \leq \min.(\sin^2 2x)$

$\Rightarrow\ 2(ab - b^2 - 1) \leq 0$

$\Rightarrow\ 2b^2 - 2ab + 2 \geq 0$ for $\forall\ b \in \mathbb{R}$

$\Rightarrow$ Disc. ≤ 0

$\Rightarrow\ 4a^2 - 4(2)(2) \leq 0$

$\Rightarrow\ a^2 - 4 \le 0$

$\Rightarrow\ a \in [-2, 2]$

12. **(a), (c)** $f'(x) > 0$ and $g'(x) < 0\ \forall\ x \in \mathbb{R};\ x < x + 1$

$\Rightarrow\ f(x) < f(x+1)$ [as $f(x)\uparrow$]

$\Rightarrow\ g(f(x)) > g(f(x+1))$ [as $g(x)\downarrow$]

$\Rightarrow$ (*d*) is incorrect

Now, $x < x + 1$

$\Rightarrow\ g(x) > g(x+1)$ [as $g(x)\downarrow$]

$\Rightarrow\ f(g(x)) > f(g(x+1))$ [as $f(x)\uparrow$]

$\Rightarrow$ (*a*) is correct and (*b*) is incorrect

Also $x < x + 1$

$\Rightarrow\ f(x) < f(x+1)$

$\Rightarrow\ g(f(x) > g(f(x+1))$

$\Rightarrow$ option (*c*) is correct

13. **(c)** $f: [1, 10] \to [1, 10]$ is $\downarrow$,

$g: [1, 10] \to [1, 10]$ is $\downarrow$,

$h(x) = f(g(x));\ h(1) = 1$

$h'(x) = f'(g(x)).\ g'(x)$

$= (\le 0).(\le 0) \ge 0$

$\Rightarrow\ h(x)\uparrow$

$\Rightarrow\ h(x) \ge h(1)\ \forall\ x \ge 1$

$\Rightarrow\ h(x) \ge 1\ \forall\ x \ge 1$

$\Rightarrow\ h(2) \ge 1$ (*In particular*)

14. **(a), (b), (c), (d)**

$\phi(x) = 3f\left(\dfrac{x^2}{3}\right) + f(3 - x^2)\ \forall\ x \in (-3, 4)$ and $f''(x) > 0$

$\forall\ x \in (-3, 4)$

$\Rightarrow\ \phi'(x) = 3\left(\dfrac{1}{3}\right)(2x) f'\left(\dfrac{x^2}{3}\right) - 2x f'(3 - x^2)$

$\Rightarrow\ \phi'(x) = 2x\left[f'\left(\dfrac{x^2}{3}\right) - f'(3 - x^2)\right]\ \forall\ x \in (-3, 4)$ ...(*i*)

$\because\ f''(x) > 0\ \forall\ x \in (-3, 4)$

$\Rightarrow\ f'(x)\uparrow\ \forall\ x \in (-3, 4)$

$\therefore$ For $\phi(x)$ to be increasing $\phi'(x) \ge 0$ i.e.,

$2x\left[f'\left(\dfrac{x^2}{3}\right) - f'(3 - x^2)\right] \ge 0$

Case (i): $-3 < x \le 0$, then $f'\left(\dfrac{x^2}{3}\right) - f'(3 - x^2) \le 0$

$\Rightarrow\ f'\left(\dfrac{x^2}{3}\right) \le f'(3 - x^2)$

$\Rightarrow\ \dfrac{x^2}{3} \le 3 - x^2$

$\Rightarrow\ \left(1 + \dfrac{1}{3}\right)x^2 \le 3$

$\Rightarrow\ x^2 \le \dfrac{9}{4}$

$\Rightarrow\ \dfrac{-3}{2} \le x \le \dfrac{3}{2}$

$\therefore$ For case restriction, $x \in \left[\dfrac{-3}{2}, 0\right]$

Case (ii): $0 \le x < 4$, then $f'\left(\dfrac{x^2}{3}\right) - f'(3 - x^2) \ge 0$

$\Rightarrow\ \dfrac{x^2}{3} \ge 3 - x^2$

$\Rightarrow\ x^2 \ge \dfrac{9}{4}$

$\Rightarrow\ x \in \left(-\infty, \dfrac{-3}{2}\right] \cup \left[\dfrac{3}{2}, 4\right)$

For $\phi(x)$ to be decreasing

Case (i): $-3 < x \le 0$, then $f'\left(\dfrac{x^2}{3}\right) - f'(3 - x^2) \ge 0$

$\Rightarrow\ x \in \left(-\infty, \dfrac{-3}{2}\right] \cup \left[\dfrac{3}{2}, \infty\right)$

For case restriction, $x \in \left(-3, \dfrac{-3}{2}\right]$

Case (ii): $0 \le x < 4$, then $f'\left(\dfrac{x^2}{3}\right) - f'(3 - x^2) \le 0$

$\Rightarrow\ x \in \left[\dfrac{-3}{2}, \dfrac{3}{2}\right]$

For case restriction, $x \in \left[0, \dfrac{3}{2}\right]$

15. **(a)** $f(x) = x(a^2 - 2a + 2) + \cos x$

$\Rightarrow\ f'(x) = (a^2 - 2a + 2) - \sin x$

For $f(x)$ to be strictly monotonically increasing $\forall\ x \in \mathbb{R}$, $f'(x) \ge 0\ \forall\ x \in \mathbb{R}$

$\Rightarrow\ a^2 - 2a + 2 - \sin x \ge 0\ \forall\ x \in \mathbb{R}$

$\Rightarrow\ a^2 - 2a + 2 \ge \sin x\ \forall\ x \in \mathbb{R}$

$\Rightarrow\ a^2 - 2a + 2 \ge \max.[\sin x]$

$\Rightarrow\ a^2 - 2a + 2 \ge 1$

$\Rightarrow\ a^2 - 2a + 1 \ge 0$

$\Rightarrow\ (a - 1)^2 \ge 0$

$\Rightarrow\ a \in \mathbb{R}$

For $f(x)$ to be strictly monotonically decreasing $\forall\ x \in \mathbb{R}$, $f'(x) \le \forall\ x \in \mathbb{R}$

i.e., $(a^2 - 2a + 2) \le \sin x\ \forall\ x \in \mathbb{R}$

i.e., $(a^2 - 2a + 2) \le \min.(\sin x)$

i.e., $a^2 - 2a + 2 \le -1$

$\Rightarrow\ a^2 - 2a + 3 \le 0$, which false for every $a \in \mathbb{R}$.

$\therefore\ f(x)$ is always strictly increasing $\forall\ a \in \mathbb{R}$

16. **(b), (c)** $f, g\downarrow$

$(fog)'(x) = f'(g(x)).g'(x) = (\le 0).(\le 0) \ge 0$

$(gof)'(x) = g'(f(x)).f'(x) = (\le 0).(\le 0) \ge 0$

17. **(a), (d)** $f'(x) = g(x)(x - a)^2;\ \lim\limits_{x \to a} g(x) = g(a)$

$f'(a - h) = g(a - h)(a - h - a)^2;\ h \to 0^+$

$\Rightarrow\ f'(a - h) = g(a - h)(h^2);\ h \to 0^+$

$\Rightarrow\ f'(a - h) = g(a)\,h^2;\ h \to 0;\ g(a) \ne 0$

$\Rightarrow\ f'(a - h) > 0$ for $g(a) > 0$

Also, $f'(a + h) = g(a + h)(a + h - a)^2$

$\Rightarrow\ f'(a + h) = g(a + h)(h)^2;\ h \to 0^+$

$\Rightarrow\ f'(a + h) = g(a).\ h^2;\ h \to 0^+$

$\Rightarrow f'(a+h) > 0$ for $g(a) > 0$

$\Rightarrow f(x)$ is increasing in neighbourhood of a for $g(a) > 0$ and decreasing for $g(a) < 0$

18. **(b), (d)** $g(x) = f(x) + f(1-x)$ and $f''(x) < 0;\ 0 \le x \le 1.$

$\Rightarrow g'(x) = f'(x) - f'(1-x);\ 0 \le x \le 1$

$\because f''(x) < 0\ \forall\ 0 \le x \le 1$

$\Rightarrow f'(x) \downarrow$ for $x \in [0, 1]$

$\Rightarrow g(x)$ will increase when $g'(x) \ge 0$ i.e., $f'(x) - f'(1-x) \ge 0$ i.e., $x \le 1 - x$

$\Rightarrow 2x \le 1$

$\Rightarrow x \le \dfrac{1}{2}$

$\therefore$ $g(x)$ increase on $\left[0, \dfrac{1}{2}\right]$ and decrease on $\left[\dfrac{1}{2}, 1\right]$.

19. **(a), (b)** $2\tan^{-1} x = \begin{cases} \cos^{-1}\left(\dfrac{1-x^2}{1+x^2}\right) \text{for } x \ge 0 \\ -\cos^{-1}\left(\dfrac{1-x^2}{1+x^2}\right) \text{for } x < 0 \end{cases}$

$\Rightarrow f(x) = \cos^{-1}\left(\dfrac{1-x^2}{1+x^2}\right) = \begin{cases} 2\tan^{-1} x \text{ for } x \ge 0 \\ -2\tan^{-1} x \text{ for } x < 0 \end{cases}$

$\Rightarrow f'(x) = \begin{cases} \dfrac{2}{1+x^2} \text{ for } x > 0 \\ \dfrac{-2}{1+x^2} \text{ for } x < 0 \end{cases}$

$\Rightarrow f(x) \uparrow$ for $x > 0$ and $\downarrow$ for $x < 0$

TEXTUAL EXERCISE–5: (SUBJECTIVE)

1. **(a)** Let $f(x) = x + \cos x$

$\Rightarrow f'(x) = 1 - \sin x \ge 0$

$\Rightarrow f(x)$ is an increasing function

$\Rightarrow f(2) < f(e)$

$\begin{bmatrix} \because f'(x) \ne 0 \text{ on any interval} \\ \Rightarrow f(a) \ne f(b) \text{ for } a \ne b \end{bmatrix}$

$\Rightarrow 2 + \cos 2 < e + \cos e$

(b) Let $f(x) = \ell n\left(x + \sqrt{x^2+1}\right)$

$\Rightarrow f'(x) = \left(1 + \dfrac{x}{\sqrt{x^2+1}}\right)\left(\dfrac{1}{x+\sqrt{x^2+1}}\right)$

$\Rightarrow f'(x) = \dfrac{1}{\sqrt{x^2+1}} > 0 \forall x \in \mathbb{R}$

$\Rightarrow f(x)$ is an increasing function.

$\Rightarrow f(\pi) > f(3)$

$\Rightarrow \ell n\left(\pi + \sqrt{\pi^2+1}\right) > \ell n\left(3 + \sqrt{10}\right)$

2. Let $f(x) = (x-1)e^x + 1$

$\Rightarrow f'(x) = (x-1)e^x + e^x = x > 0\ \forall\ x > 0$

$\Rightarrow f(x)$ is an increasing function for $x > 0$

$\Rightarrow f(x) > f(0)$ for $x > 0$

$\Rightarrow f(x) > 0\ \forall\ x > 0$

$\Rightarrow (x-1)e^x + 1$ is positive $\forall\ x > 0$

3. Let $f(x) = 2x + x\cos x - 3\sin x > 0$

$\Rightarrow f'(x) = 2 + (-x\sin x) + (\cos x) - 3\cos x$

$\Rightarrow f'(x) = 2 - x\sin x - 2\cos x = 2\left(2\sin^2\dfrac{x}{2}\right) - x\left(2\sin\dfrac{x}{2}\cos\dfrac{x}{2}\right)$

$= \left(2\sin\dfrac{x}{2}\right)\left(2\sin\dfrac{x}{2} - x\cos\dfrac{x}{2}\right)$ .....*(i)*

Let $g(x) = 2\sin\dfrac{x}{2} - x\cos\dfrac{x}{2}$

$\Rightarrow g'(x) = \cos\dfrac{x}{2} + \dfrac{x}{2}\sin\dfrac{x}{2} - \cos\dfrac{x}{2} = \dfrac{x}{2}\sin\dfrac{x}{2} \ge 0 \forall x \in \left[0, \dfrac{\pi}{2}\right]$

$\Rightarrow g(x)$ is $\uparrow$ for $x \in \left[0, \dfrac{\pi}{2}\right]$

$\Rightarrow g(x) > g(0)\ \forall\ x \in [0, \pi/2]$

$\Rightarrow g(x) > 0\ \forall\ x \in \left[0, \dfrac{\pi}{2}\right]$ as $g(0) = 0$

$\therefore$ From (1), $f'(x) > 0\ \forall\ x \in [0, \pi/2]$

$\Rightarrow f(x)$ is $\uparrow$ for $x \in [0, \pi/2]$

$\Rightarrow f(x) > f(0)\ \forall\ x \in [0, \pi/2]$

$\Rightarrow 2x + x\cos x - 3\sin x > 0\ \forall\ x \in \left[0, \dfrac{\pi}{2}\right]$

$\Rightarrow 2x > 3\sin x - x\cos x\ \forall\ x \in \left[0, \dfrac{\pi}{2}\right]$

4. Let $f(x) = \dfrac{1}{x + \left(\dfrac{1}{2}\right)} - \ell n\left(1 + \dfrac{1}{x}\right);\ x > 0$

$\Rightarrow f'(x) = \dfrac{-1}{\left(x+\dfrac{1}{2}\right)^2} - \dfrac{x}{(x+1)} \times \left(\dfrac{-1}{x^2}\right) = \dfrac{-1}{\left(x+\dfrac{1}{2}\right)^2} + \dfrac{1}{x(x+1)}$

$= \dfrac{-x(x+1) + \left(x+\dfrac{1}{2}\right)^2}{x(x+1)\left(x+\dfrac{1}{2}\right)^2} = \dfrac{\dfrac{1}{4}}{x(x+1)\left(x+\dfrac{1}{2}\right)^2} > 0\ \forall\ x > 0$

$\Rightarrow f(x)$ is $\uparrow\ \forall\ x > 0$

$\Rightarrow f(x) < f(\infty)$ for $0 < x < \infty$

$\Rightarrow \dfrac{1}{\left(x+\dfrac{1}{2}\right)} - \ell n\left(1+\dfrac{1}{x}\right) < 0$

$\Rightarrow \dfrac{1}{x+\dfrac{1}{2}} < \ell n\left(1+\dfrac{1}{x}\right)$ ...(1)

Next, Let $g(x) = \ell n\left(1+\dfrac{1}{x}\right) - \dfrac{1}{x}$

$\Rightarrow g'(x) = \dfrac{x}{x+1} + \dfrac{1}{x^2} > 0\ \forall\ x > 0$

$\Rightarrow g(x)$ is $\uparrow\ \forall\ x > 0$

$\Rightarrow g(x) < g(\infty)$ for $0 < x < \infty$

⇒ $\ell n\left(1+\frac{1}{x}\right)-\frac{1}{x}<0\ \forall\ 0<x<\infty$

⇒ $\ell n\left(1+\frac{1}{x}\right)<\frac{1}{x}\ \forall\ x>0$ ...(2)

Combining (1) and (2), we get $\frac{1}{\left(x+\frac{1}{2}\right)}<\ell n\left(1+\frac{1}{x}\right)<\frac{1}{x}$

$\forall\ x>0$

5. Let $f(x) = \sin x \tan x - x^2$ for $x \in [0, \pi/2)$

⇒ $f'(x) = \sin x.\ \sec^2 x + \tan x\ .\ \cos x - 2x$

⇒ $f'(x) = \sin x\ .\ \sec^2 x + \sin x - 2x$

$f''(x) = \sin x\ .\ 2\sec^2 x \tan x + \sec^2 x \cos x + \cos x - 2$

$= 2\sin^2 x \sec^3 x + \sec^2 x \cos x + \cos x - 2$

$= 2 \sec x.\ \tan^2 x + \sec x + \cos x - 2$

$= 2 \sec x.\ \tan^2 x + \left(\cos x+\frac{1}{\cos x}\right)-2$

For $x \in [0, \pi/2)$ $\left(\because x+\frac{1}{x}\geq 2\forall x>0\right)$

$f''(x) \geq 0\ \forall\ x \in [0, \pi/2)$

⇒ $f'(x)$ is ↑ for $x \in [0, \pi/2)$

$f'(x) \geq f'(0)\ \forall\ x \in [0, \pi/2)$

⇒ $f'(x) \geq 0\ \forall\ x \in [0, \pi/2)$ as $f'(0) = 0$

⇒ $f(x)$ ↑ $\forall\ x \in [0, \pi/2)$

⇒ $f(x) \geq f(0)\ \forall\ x \in [0, \pi/2)$

⇒ $\sin x \tan x - x^2 \geq 0\ \forall\ x \in [0, \pi/2)$

⇒ $\sin x \tan x - x^2 > 0\ \forall\ x \in (0, \pi/2)$ as $\sin x \tan x - x^2$ is increasing and not a constant function in any interval.

⇒ $\frac{\tan x}{x}>\frac{x}{\sin x}\forall x\in(0,\pi/2)$

6. (a) Let $f(x) = x + \sin x$

⇒ $f'(x) = 1 + \cos x \geq 0\ \forall\ x \in \mathbb{R}$

⇒ $f(x)$ is an increasing function $\forall\ x \in \mathbb{R}$

⇒ $f(3) > f(e)$

⇒ $3 + \sin 3 > e + \sin e$

(b) $f(x) = \log\left(x+\sqrt{x^2+1}\right)$

⇒ $f'(x)=\frac{1}{x+\sqrt{x^2+1}}\left(1+\frac{x}{\sqrt{x^2+1}}\right)=\frac{1}{\sqrt{x^2+1}}>0\forall x\in\mathbb{R}$

⇒ $f(x)$ is ↑ $x \in \mathbb{R}$

⇒ $f(e) > f(2)$ as $e \simeq 2.7183$

⇒ $\log\left(e+\sqrt{e^2+1}\right)>\log\left(2+\sqrt{5}\right)$

(c) $f(x) = (x)^{1/x}$, $x > 0$

⇒ $\ell n\, f(x) = \frac{1}{x}\ell n$ x

⇒ $\frac{1}{f(x)}.f'(x)=\frac{1}{x^2}+\ell nx\left(\frac{-1}{x^2}\right)$

⇒ $f(x) = (x)^{1/2}\,[1 - \ell n\, x].\frac{1}{x^2}$

⇒ $f(x)$ ↑ for $1 \geq \ell n\, x$ i.e., $0 < x \leq e$ and $f(x)$ ↓ for $x \geq e$

⇒ $f(e) > f(\pi)$ ⇒ $e^{1/e} > \pi^{1/\pi}$

⇒ $e\pi > \pi^e$

(d) Let $f(x) = (\sin x)^{\sin x}\ \forall\ 0 < x < \pi/2$

⇒ $\ell n\, f(x) = (\sin x)\, \ell n\, (\sin x)$

⇒ $\frac{f'(x)}{f(x)}$ = cos x + cos x . ℓn sin x

⇒ $f'(x) = (\sin x)^{\sin x}$. cos x. (1 + ℓn sin x)

⇒ $f(x)$ for ℓn sin x ≥ −1 i.e., for sin x ≥ 1/e

⇒ $\sin^{-1}(\sin x) \geq \sin^{-1}(1/e)$ $\left[\because \sin^{-1}x \text{ is an increasing function on } [-1,1]\right]$

⇒ $x \geq \sin^{-1}(1/e)$

Now $e > 2$

⇒ $0<\frac{1}{e}<\frac{1}{2}$

⇒ $\sin^{-1}\left(\frac{1}{e}\right)<\sin^{-1}\left(\frac{1}{2}\right)$

⇒ $f\left(\sin^{-1}\left(\frac{1}{e}\right)\right)<f\left(\sin^{-1}\left(\frac{1}{2}\right)\right)$

⇒ $\left(\frac{1}{e}\right)^{1/e}<\left(\frac{1}{2}\right)^{1/2}$

⇒ $\left(\frac{1}{2}\right)^{e}>\left(\frac{1}{e}\right)^{2}$

7. (a) $e^{\cos x-\sin x}<\frac{1-\sin x}{1-\cos x}\forall x\in\left(0,\frac{\pi}{4}\right)$ or

$\frac{e^{\cos x}}{e^{\sin x}}<\frac{1-\sin x}{1-\cos x};\forall x\in\left(0,\frac{\pi}{4}\right)$ or $e^{\cos x}(1 - \cos x) <$

$e^{\sin x}(1 - \sin x)\ \forall\ x \in (0, \pi/4)$ ...(1)

Let $f(x) = e^x(1 - x)$

⇒ $f'(x) = e^x - (x\, e^x + e^x)$

⇒ $f'(x) = e^x - (xe^x + e^x)$

⇒ $f'(x) = -xe^x$; $x \in (0, \pi/4)$

⇒ $f(x)$ ↓ for $x \in (0, \pi/4)$

In $x \in (0, \pi/4)$, cos x > sin x

⇒ $f(\cos x) < f(\sin x)$

⇒ $e^{\cos x}(1 - \cos x) < e^{\sin x}(1 - \sin x)$ or $e^{\cos x-\sin x}<\frac{1-\sin x}{1-\cos x}$

$\forall\ x \in (0, \pi/4)$.

(b) $\sin^2 x < x \sin(\sin x)$; $0 < x < \pi/2$ or $\frac{\sin x}{x}<\frac{\sin(\sin x)}{\sin x}$;

$0 < x < \pi/2$

Let $f(x)=\frac{\sin x}{x}$

⇒ $f'(x)=\frac{x\cos x-\sin x1}{x^2}$

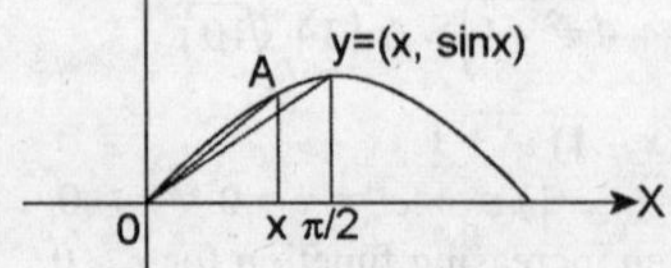

Here $\frac{\sin x}{x}$ is the slope of chord OA on sine curve where $A(x, \sin x)$ is a point on $y = \sin x$ curve for $x \in (0, \pi/2)$

Clearly as $x \uparrow$, Slope $\left(=\frac{\sin x}{x}\right)\downarrow$

$\Rightarrow f(x) = \frac{\sin x}{x}$ is a decreasing function on $(0, \pi/2)$

Also from graph given below

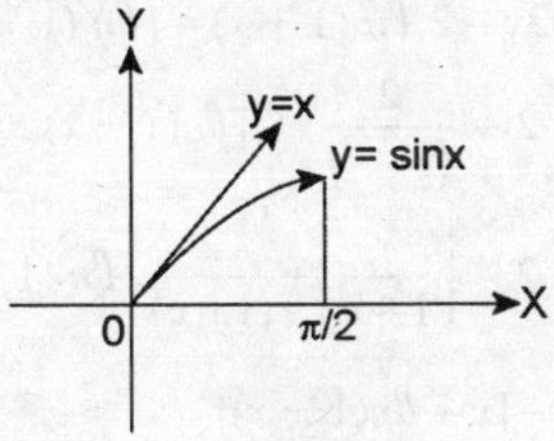

We note that $\sin x < x$ for $x \in (0, \pi/2)$

$\Rightarrow f(\sin x) > f(x)$

$\Rightarrow \frac{\sin(\sin x)}{\sin x} > \frac{\sin x}{x}$ for $x \in (0, \pi/2)$ i.e., $\sin^2 x < x \sin(\sin x)$ for $x \in (0, \pi/2)$

(c) Let $f(x) = x - \tan^{-1} x$; for $x \in [0, \infty]$

$\Rightarrow f'(x) = 1 - \frac{1}{1+x^2} = \frac{x^2}{1+x^2} \geq 0\ \forall\ x \in [0, \infty)$

$\Rightarrow f(x)$ is $\uparrow\ \forall\ x \in [0, \infty)$

$\Rightarrow f(x) > f(0)\ \forall\ x \in [0, \infty)$

$\Rightarrow x - \tan^{-1} x > 0\ \forall\ x \in [0, \infty)$

$\Rightarrow x > \tan^{-1} x\ \forall\ x \in [0, \infty)$

(d) Let $f(x) = (\tan^{-1} x)^2 + \frac{2}{\sqrt{1+x^2}}$

$$\Rightarrow f'(x) = \frac{2\tan^{-1} x}{(1+x^2)} + \left(\frac{-2x}{(1+x^2)\sqrt{1+x^2}}\right)$$

$$= \frac{2}{(1+x^2)}\left[\tan^{-1} x - \frac{x}{\sqrt{1+x^2}}\right] \quad \ldots(1)$$

Now, let $g(x) = \tan^{-1} x - \frac{x}{\sqrt{1+x^2}}$

$$\Rightarrow g'(x) = \frac{1}{1+x^2} - \left[\frac{\sqrt{1+x^2} - x\frac{x}{\sqrt{1+x^2}}}{(1+x^2)}\right]$$

$$= \frac{1}{1+x^2} - \left[\frac{1}{(1+x^2)\sqrt{1+x^2}}\right] = \left(\frac{1}{1+x^2}\right)\left(1 - \frac{1}{\sqrt{1+x^2}}\right) >$$

$0\ \forall\ x \in \mathbb{R}$ as $1 > \frac{1}{\sqrt{1+x^2}}$

$\Rightarrow g(x)\uparrow$

$\Rightarrow g(x) > g(0)\ \forall\ x \in [0, \infty)$

$\Rightarrow g(x) > 0\ \forall\ x \in [0, \infty)$

$\therefore$ Form (1), we get $f'(x) > 0\ \forall\ x \in [0, \infty)$

$\Rightarrow f(x)\uparrow$

$\Rightarrow f\left(\frac{1}{e}\right) < f(0)$

$$\Rightarrow \left(\tan^{-1}\frac{1}{e}\right)^2 + \frac{2e}{\sqrt{e^2+1}} < \left(\tan^{-1} e\right) + \frac{2}{\sqrt{1+e^2}}$$

(e) $\cos(\sin x) > \sin(\cos x)$

i.e., $\cos(\sin x) > \cos\left(\frac{\pi}{2} - \cos x\right)$

$\because\ \sin x + \cos x \leq \sqrt{2} < \frac{\pi}{2}$

$\Rightarrow \sin x < \frac{\pi}{2} - \cos x$ as $\forall\ x \in \left[0, \frac{3\pi}{2}\right]$

$\sin x \in [0, 1]$ and $\cos x \in [-1, 1]$

$\therefore\ \frac{\pi}{2} - \cos x \in \left(\frac{\pi}{2} - 1, \frac{\pi}{2} + 1\right)$, where $\cos x$ is $\downarrow$ function

$\Rightarrow \cos(\sin x) > \cos\left(\frac{\pi}{2} - \cos x\right)$

$\Rightarrow \cos(\sin x) > \sin(\cos x)$

(f) Let $f(x) = 2\sin x + \tan x - 3x$; $x \in [0, \pi/2)$

$\Rightarrow f'(x) = 2\cos x + \sec^2 x - 3$; $x \in [0, \pi/2)$

$\Rightarrow f''(x) = -2\sin x + 2\sec^2 x \tan x$; $x \in [0, \pi/2)$

$\Rightarrow f''(x) = -2\sin x + 2\sec^3 x \cdot \sin x$

$\Rightarrow f''(x) = (2\sin x)(\sec^3 x - 1) \geq 0\ \forall\ x \in [0, \pi/2)$

$\Rightarrow f'(x)\ \forall\ x \in [0, \pi/2)$

$\Rightarrow f'(x) \geq f'(0)\ \forall\ x \in [0, \pi/2)$

$\Rightarrow f'(x) \geq 0\ \forall\ x \in [0, \pi/2)$

$\Rightarrow 2\sin x + \tan x \geq 3x\ \forall\ x \in [0, \pi/2)$

(g) $e^{\tan^{-1} x}\left(x + \sqrt{1+x^2}\right) < e^{2x}\ \forall\ x \in (0, \infty)$

i.e., $\tan^{-1} x + \ln\left(x + \sqrt{1+x^2}\right) < 2x$

Thus consider $f(x) = \tan^{-1} x + \ln\left(x + \sqrt{1+x^2}\right) - 2x$

$\Rightarrow f'(x) = \frac{1}{1+x^2} + \frac{1}{\sqrt{1+x^2}} - 2 < 0$

Thus $f(x)$ is strictly $\downarrow$ function $\forall x \in \mathbb{R}$ and since $f(0) = 0$

$$\Rightarrow \begin{cases} \text{If } x > 0 & \Rightarrow f(x) < f(0) = 0 \\ & \Rightarrow f(x) < 0 \\ & \Rightarrow \tan^{-1} x + \ln\left(x + \sqrt{1+x^2}\right) < 2x \\ \text{If } x < 0 & \Rightarrow f(x) > f(0) = 0 \\ & \Rightarrow f(x) > 0 \\ & \Rightarrow \tan^{-1} x + \ln\left(x + \sqrt{1+x^2}\right) > 2x \end{cases}$$

8. Let $f(x) = x^2 - 1 - 2x\,\ln x$; $x \geq 1$

$\Rightarrow f(x) = 2x - 2 - 2\ln x$; $x \geq 1$

$\Rightarrow f''(x) = 2 - \frac{2}{x} = 2\left(1 - \frac{1}{x}\right)$; $x \geq 1$

$\Rightarrow f'''(x) = 2\left(\frac{1}{x^2}\right) > 0\ \forall\ x \geq 1$

$\Rightarrow f''(x)\uparrow \forall x \geq 1$
$\Rightarrow f''(x) \geq f''(1)\ \forall x \geq 1$
$\Rightarrow f''(x) \geq 0\ \forall x \geq 1$
$\Rightarrow f'(x)\uparrow x \geq 1$
$\Rightarrow f'(x) \geq f'(1)\ \forall x \geq 1$
$\Rightarrow f'(x) \geq 0\ \forall x \geq 1$
$\Rightarrow f(x) \uparrow \forall x \geq 1$
$\Rightarrow f(x) \geq f(1)\ \forall x \geq 1$
$\Rightarrow f(x) \geq 0\ \forall x \geq 1$
$\Rightarrow x^2 - 1 \geq 2x\ \ell n\, x\ \forall x \geq 1$ ...(1)

Let $g(x) = 2x\ \ell n - 4(x-1) + 2\ \ell n\, x;\ x \geq 1$

$\Rightarrow g'(x) = 2 + 2\ \ell n\, x - 4(1) + \dfrac{2}{x};\ x \geq 1$

$\Rightarrow g''(x) = \dfrac{2}{x} - \dfrac{2}{x^2};\ x \geq 1$

$\Rightarrow g''(x) = \dfrac{2}{x}\left(1 - \dfrac{1}{x}\right);\ x \geq 1$

$\Rightarrow g''(x) = \dfrac{2}{x}\left(\dfrac{x-1}{x}\right);\ x \geq 1$

$\Rightarrow g''(x) = \dfrac{2(x-1)}{x^2};\ x \geq 1$

$\Rightarrow g''(x)\ \forall x \geq 1$
$\Rightarrow g'(x)\uparrow \forall x \geq 1$
$\Rightarrow g'(x) \geq g'(1)\ \forall x \geq 1$
$\Rightarrow g'(x) \geq 0\ \forall x \geq 1$
$\Rightarrow g(x)\uparrow \forall x \geq 1$
$\Rightarrow g(x) \geq g(1)\ \forall x \geq 1$
$\Rightarrow 2x\ \ell n\, x - 4(x-1) + 2\ \ell n\, x \geq 0\ \forall x \geq 1$ ...(2)

$\therefore$ From (1) & (2), we get

$x^2 - 1 \geq 2x\ell nx \geq 4(x-1) - 2\ell nx\ \forall x \geq 1$

9. For $0 < x \leq 1$

$\Rightarrow y = x\ \ell n\, x - \dfrac{x^2}{2} + \dfrac{1}{2}$

$\Rightarrow \dfrac{dy}{dx} = 1 + \ell n\, x - x$

$\Rightarrow \dfrac{d^2y}{dx^2} = \dfrac{1}{x} - 1 = \left(\dfrac{1-x}{x}\right) > 0$ as $x \in (0, 1)$

$\Rightarrow \dfrac{dy}{dx} \uparrow$ for $x \in (0, 1)$

$\Rightarrow \left(\dfrac{dy}{dx}\right)_{x\in(0,1]} \leq 0$

$\Rightarrow y \downarrow$ for $x \in (0, 1]$
$\Rightarrow f(x) \geq f(1)\ \forall x \in (0, 1]$

$\Rightarrow x\ \ell n\, x - \dfrac{x^2}{2} + \dfrac{1}{2} \geq 0$

10. Let $f(x) = x \sin x - \dfrac{1}{2}\sin^2 x$

$f'(x) = x \cos x + \sin x - \sin x \cos x = (x - \sin x)\cos x + \sin x > 0$

$\forall x \in \left(0, \dfrac{\pi}{2}\right)$ as $x > \sin x$

$\Rightarrow f(x)$ is$\uparrow$ function when $x \in \left(0, \dfrac{\pi}{2}\right)$

$\therefore\ 0 < x < \dfrac{\pi}{2}$

$\Rightarrow f(0) < f(x) < f\left(\dfrac{\pi}{2}\right) \Rightarrow 0 < x\sin x - \dfrac{1}{2}\sin^2 x < \dfrac{\pi}{2} - \dfrac{1}{2}$

11. Let $f(x) = x^2 - (1 + x)\,[\ell n(1 + x)]^2\ \forall x \geq 0$

$\Rightarrow f'(x) = 2x - (1 + x)\,.\,2\,[\ell n(1 + x)].\ \dfrac{1}{(1+x)} - [\ell n(1+x)]^2$

$\Rightarrow f'(x) = 2x - 2\ \ell n\,(1 + x) - [\ell n\,(1 + x)]^2$

$\Rightarrow f''(x) = 2 - \dfrac{2}{(1+x)} - 2[\ell n(1 + x)\,.\,\dfrac{1}{(1+x)}$

$\Rightarrow f''(x) = 2 - \left[\dfrac{x}{1+x}\right] - \dfrac{2}{(1+x)}\ \ell n\,(1 + x)$

$= \dfrac{2}{(1+x)}\,[x - \ell n(1 + x)]$ ...(1)

Let $g(x) = x - \ell n(1 + x)$

$\Rightarrow g'(x) = 1 - \dfrac{1}{1+x} = \dfrac{x}{1+x} \geq 0\ \forall x \geq 0$

$\Rightarrow g(x) \geq g(0)\ \forall x \geq 0$
$\Rightarrow g(x) \geq 0$ ...(2)
$\therefore$ From (1) & (2), we get $f''(x) \geq 0\ \forall x \geq 0$
$\Rightarrow f'(x)\uparrow \forall x \geq 0$
$\Rightarrow f'(x)\uparrow \geq f'(0)\ \forall x \geq 0$
$\Rightarrow f'(x) \geq 0\ \forall x \geq 0$
$\Rightarrow f(x)\ \forall x \geq 0$
$\Rightarrow f(x) \geq f(0)\ \forall x \geq 0$
$\Rightarrow f(x) \geq 0\ \forall x \geq 0$
$\Rightarrow x^2 \geq (1 + x)\,[\ell n(1 + x)]^2\ \forall x \geq 0$

12. $f(x) = \ell n(1 + x) - \dfrac{x}{(1+x)};\ x > -1$

$\Rightarrow f'(x) = \dfrac{1}{1+x} - \dfrac{[(1+x) - x.1]}{(1+x)^2} = \dfrac{1}{(1+x)} - \dfrac{1}{(1+x)^2}$

$= \dfrac{x}{(1+x)^2} \geq 0 \forall x \geq 0$

$\Rightarrow f(x)$ for $x \geq 0$
$\Rightarrow f(x) \geq f(0) \uparrow \forall x \geq 0$

$\Rightarrow \ell n(1 + x) - \dfrac{x}{1+x} \geq 0$

$\Rightarrow \ell n(1 + x) \geq \dfrac{x}{1+x}\ \forall x \geq 0$

Also $f(x)$ being injective and $\ell n(1 + x) - \dfrac{x}{1+x} = 0$ at $x = 0$

$\Rightarrow \ell n\,(1 + x) > \dfrac{x}{(1+x)} \forall x > 0$ ...(1)

Also $f'(x) \downarrow$ for $x \in (-1, 0]$
$\Rightarrow f(x) > f(0)\ \forall x \in (-1, 0)$

$\Rightarrow \ell n(1 + x) - \dfrac{x}{(1+x)} > 0\ \forall x \in (-1, 0)$ ...(2)

$\therefore$ From (1) & (2), we get $\ell n\,(1 + x) - \dfrac{x}{(1+x)} > 0\ \forall x \in (-1, 0) \cup (0, \infty)$

TEXTUAL EXERCISE-5: (OBJECTIVE)

1. (a), (b), (c), (d)

(a) Let $f(x) = (x)^{1/x}$; $x > 0$

$\Rightarrow \ell n\, f(x) = \frac{1}{x}\ell nx$

$\Rightarrow \frac{1}{f(x)}.f'(x) = \frac{1}{x^2} - \frac{1}{x^2}\ell n$

$\Rightarrow f'(x) = \frac{f(x)}{x^2}(1 - \ell n\, x)$

$\Rightarrow f(x) \uparrow$ for $0 < x \le \frac{1}{e}$ and $f(x) \downarrow$ for $x \ge \frac{1}{e}$

$\therefore\ f\left(\frac{1}{\pi}\right) < f\left(\frac{1}{e}\right) \left(\begin{matrix}\because \pi > e \\ \Rightarrow \frac{1}{\pi} < \frac{1}{e}\end{matrix}\right)$

$\Rightarrow \left(\frac{1}{\pi}\right)^{\pi} < \left(\frac{1}{e}\right)^{e}$

$\Rightarrow e^e < \pi^\pi$ and $f(e) > f(\pi)$

$\Rightarrow e^{1/e} > \pi^{1/\pi}$

$\Rightarrow e^\pi > \pi^e$

$\Rightarrow$ (a) is true .

(b) Let $f(x) = (1 + x)^{1/1+x}$

$\Rightarrow \ell n\, f(x) = \frac{1}{(1+x)}\ell n(1+x)$

$\Rightarrow \frac{1}{f(x)}.f'(x) = \frac{1}{(1+x)}.\frac{1}{(1+x)} - \frac{1}{(1+x)^2}\ell n(1+x)$

$\Rightarrow f'(x)\ \frac{(1+x)^{1/1+x}}{(1+x)^2}.[1-\ell n(1+x)]$

$\therefore$ $f(x) \uparrow$ for $1 - \ell n(1 + x) \ge 0$ i.e., for $(1 + x) \le e$, i.e., $x \le e - 1$

Now, $\left(\sin\frac{\pi}{3} > \cos\frac{\pi}{3}\right) < e - 1$

$\Rightarrow f\left(\cos\frac{\pi}{3}\right) < f\left(\sin\frac{\pi}{3}\right)$

$\Rightarrow \left(1+\sin\frac{\pi}{3}\right)^{\frac{1}{1+\sin\frac{\pi}{3}}} > \left(1+\cos\frac{\pi}{3}\right)^{\frac{1}{1+\cos\frac{\pi}{3}}}$

$\Rightarrow \left(1+\sin\frac{\pi}{3}\right)^{1+\cos\frac{\pi}{3}} > \left(1+\cos\frac{\pi}{3}\right)^{1+\sin\frac{\pi}{3}}$

$\Rightarrow$ (b) is true

(c) Let $f(x) = x^{1/x}$, $x > 0$

$\Rightarrow f(x) \uparrow$ for $0 < x \le \frac{1}{e}$ and $\downarrow$ for $x \ge \frac{1}{e}$

Now, $101 < 202$ and both $> \frac{1}{e}$

$\Rightarrow f(101) > f(202)$

$\Rightarrow f(101)^{1/101} > (202)^{1/202}$

$\Rightarrow (101)^{202} > (202)^{101}$

$\Rightarrow$ (c) is true

(d) $\frac{1}{e} < \frac{4}{3} < \frac{9}{4}$

$\Rightarrow f\left(\frac{4}{3}\right) > f\left(\frac{9}{4}\right)$

$\Rightarrow \left(\frac{4}{3}\right)^{3/4} > \left(\frac{9}{4}\right)^{4/9}$

$\Rightarrow \left(\frac{4}{3}\right)^{9/4} > \left(\frac{9}{4}\right)^{4/3}$

$\Rightarrow$ (d) is true .

2. (a), (b), (d)

(a) Let $f(x) = \ell n\, x - x + 1$; $x > 1$

$\Rightarrow f'(x) = \frac{1}{x} - 1 = \frac{1-x}{x} < 0$ for $x > 1$

$\Rightarrow f(x) \downarrow$ for $x > 1$

$\Rightarrow f(1) > f(x)\ \forall\ x > 1$

$\Rightarrow 0 > \ell n\, x - x + 1\ \forall\ x > 1$

$\Rightarrow \ell n\, x < x - 1\ \forall\ x > 1$

$\Rightarrow y < (x - 1)\ \forall\ x > 1$

$\Rightarrow$ (a) is correct

(b) Again from above $f(1) > f(x^2)\ \forall > 1$

$\Rightarrow 0 > 2\ \ell n\, x - x^2 + 1$

$\Rightarrow x^2 - 1 > 2\ \ell n\, x > \ell n$ x

$\Rightarrow x^2 - 1 > y\ \forall\ x > 1$

$\Rightarrow$ (b) is correct

(c) $\because$ (a) is true

$\Rightarrow$ (c) is false .

(d) Let $f(x) = \ell n\, x + \frac{1}{x} - 1$

$\Rightarrow f'(x) = \frac{1}{x} - \frac{1}{x^2} = \left(\frac{x-1}{x^2}\right) > 0$ for $x > 1$

$\Rightarrow f(x) \uparrow$ for $x > 1$

$\Rightarrow f(x) > f(1)\ \forall\ x > 1$

$\Rightarrow \ell n\, x + \frac{1}{x} - 1 > 0\ \forall\ x > 1$

$\Rightarrow \ell n\, x > 1 - \frac{1}{x}$

$\Rightarrow \ell n\, x > \frac{x-1}{x} \Rightarrow y > \frac{x-1}{x} \forall x > 1$

3. (c) $f(x) = \ell n\,(1 + x) - \frac{x}{(1+x)}$; $x > -1$

$\Rightarrow f'(x) = \frac{1}{(1+x)} - \frac{(1+x)-x}{(1+x)^2}$; $x > -1$

$\Rightarrow f'(x) = \frac{1}{1+x} - \frac{1}{(1+x)^2} = \frac{(1+x)-1}{(1+x)^2} = \frac{x}{(1+x)^2}$

$\Rightarrow f(x) \uparrow\ \forall\ x \ge 0$

$\Rightarrow f(x) \ge f(0)\ \forall\ x \ge 0$

$\Rightarrow f(x) > f(0)\ \forall\ x > 0$

$\Rightarrow \ell n\,(1 + x) > \frac{x}{(1+x)}\ \forall\ x > 0$

4. (c) Let $f(x) = \frac{\sin x}{x}$

We know that $\frac{\sin x}{x}$ is a decreasing function for $x \in \left(2n\pi, 2n\pi + \frac{\pi}{2}\right]$; $x \in W$ and in above intervals $x > \sin x$

$\Rightarrow f(x) < f(\sin x)$

$\Rightarrow \frac{\sin x}{x} < \frac{\sin(\sin x)}{\sin x}$

$\Rightarrow \sin^2 x < x \sin(\sin x)$

5. (a), (b) Let $f(x) = x \sin x - \left(\frac{1}{2}\right) \sin^2 x$

$\Rightarrow f'(x) = x \cos x + \sin x - \frac{1}{2}(2 \sin x \cos x)$

$= x \cos x + \sin x - \sin x \cos x$

$= x \cos x + \sin x (1 - \cos x)$

> 0 for $x \in (0, \pi/2)$

$\Rightarrow f(x)\uparrow$ on $(0, \pi/2)$

$\Rightarrow f(x) > f(0)\ \forall\ x \in (0, \pi/2)$

$\Rightarrow x \sin x - \frac{1}{2} \sin^2 x > 0\ \forall\ x \in (0, \pi/2)$

$\Rightarrow$ option (*a*) is correct

Also $f(x) < f(\pi/2)\ \forall\ x \in (0, \pi/2)$

$\Rightarrow x \sin x - \frac{1}{2}(\sin^2 x) < \frac{\pi}{2} - \frac{1}{2}$

$\Rightarrow$ option (*b*) is correct

6. (a) Let $f(x) = (x + 3)^5 - (x - 1)^5 - 244$

$\Rightarrow f'(x) = 5(x + 3)^4 - 5(x - 1)^4$

$= 5[(x + 3)^2 + (x - 1)^2].[(x + 3)^2 - (x - 1)^2]$

$= 5[(x + 3)^2 + (x - 1)^2] [(x + 3) - (x - 1)] [(x + 3) + (x - 1)]$

$= 5[(x + 3)^2 + (x - 1)^2] [4] [2x + 2]$

$= 40(x + 1) [(x + 3)^2 + (x - 1)^2] \geq 0\ \forall\ x \geq -1$

$\Rightarrow f(x)\uparrow\ \forall\ x \geq -1$

$\Rightarrow f(x) \geq f(0)\ \forall \geq 0$

$\Rightarrow (x + 3)^5 - (x - 1)^5 - 244 \geq 0\ \forall\ x \geq 0$

$\Rightarrow (x + 3)^5 - (x - 1)^5 \geq 244\ \forall\ x \geq 0$

7. (b) $y = x^x, x > 0$

$\Rightarrow \ell n\, y = x\, \ell n\, x$

$\Rightarrow \frac{1}{y}\frac{dy}{dx} = x.\frac{1}{x} + \ell n x \quad \Rightarrow \frac{dy}{dx} = x^x(1 + \ell n x)$

$\Rightarrow f(x)\downarrow$ for $x \in (0, e^{-1})$ and $f(x)\uparrow$ for $x \in [e^{-1}, \infty)$

$\Rightarrow$ Range of $f(x) = [f(e^{-1}), f(\infty)) = \left[\left(e^{-1}\right)^{e^{-1}}, \infty\right) = [e^{-1/e}, \infty)$

8. (a) $y = \ell n(\sin x^{\sin x} + 1)$

$y = \ell n\, u;\ u = (\sin x)^{\sin x} + 1$

$\Rightarrow \frac{dy}{dx} = \frac{1}{\left[(\sin x)^{\sin x} + 1\right]}\left(\frac{du}{dx}\right)$

$= \frac{1}{(\sin x)^{\sin x} + 1}\left[\frac{d}{dx}(\sin x)^{\sin x}\right]$ ...(1)

Let $t = (\sin x)^{\sin x}$; $\sin x > 0$

$\Rightarrow \ell n\, t = (\sin x).\ \ell n \sin x$

$\Rightarrow \frac{1}{t}\frac{dt}{dx} = \sin x.\frac{1}{\sin x}.\cos x + (\ell n \sin x).\cos x$

$\Rightarrow \frac{dt}{dx} = (\sin x)^{\sin x}[\cos^x(1 + \ell n \sin x)]$ ...(2)

$\therefore$ From (1) & (2), we get $\frac{dy}{dx} = \frac{1}{\left[(\sin x)^{\sin x} + 1\right]}.(\sin x)^{\sin x}.$

$\cos x\,(1 + \ell \sin x)$

$f(x)$ is defined on $(0, \pi)$, $(2\pi, 3\pi)$, ...and attains its range values in each of these intervals .

$\Rightarrow f'(x) \geq 0$ for $\cos x.(1 + \ell n \sin x) \geq 0$

Now $1 + \ell n(\sin x) \geq 0$

$\Rightarrow \ell n(\sin x) \geq -1$

$\Rightarrow \sin x \geq e^{-1}$

$\Rightarrow 1 + \ell n(\sin x) \leq 0$ for $\sin x \in \left(0, \frac{1}{e}\right]$ and $1 + \ell n(\sin x)$

≥ 0 for $\sin x \in \left[\frac{1}{e}, 1\right]$

$$\Rightarrow f'(x)\begin{cases} <0 & \text{for } x \in \left(0, \sin^{-1}\frac{1}{e}\right] \\ >0 & \text{for } x \in \left[\sin^{-1}\frac{1}{e}, \frac{\pi}{2}\right] \\ <0 & \text{for } x \in \left(\frac{\pi}{2}, \pi - \sin^{-1}\left(\frac{1}{e}\right)\right] \\ >0 & \text{for } x \in \left[\pi - \sin^{-1}\left(\frac{1}{e}\right), \pi\right) \end{cases}$$

$\lim_{x\to 0^+} f(x) = \lim_{x\to 0^+} \ell n(\sin x^{\sin x} + 1)$

Let $L = \lim_{x\to 0^+}(\sin x)^{\sin x}$

$\Rightarrow \ell n\, L = \lim_{x\to 0^+}(\sin x)\ell n(\sin x) = \lim_{x\to 0^+}\frac{\ell n(\sin x)}{\operatorname{cosec} x}$

$= \lim_{x\to 0^+}\frac{\left(\frac{1}{\sin x}\right)(\cos x)}{-\operatorname{cosec} x.\cot x} = \lim_{x\to 0^+}(-\sin x) = 0$

$\Rightarrow L = e^0 = 1$

$\therefore \lim_{x\to 0^+} \ell n(\sin x^{\sin x} + 1) = \ell n\, 2$,

$f\left(\sin^{-1}\frac{1}{e}\right) = \ell n\left(\left(\frac{1}{e}\right)^{1/e} + 1\right)$,

$f(\pi/2) = \ell n(2)$,

$f\left(\pi - \sin^{-1}\frac{1}{e}\right) = \ell n\left(\left(\frac{1}{e}\right)^{1/e} + 1\right)$

$f(\pi^{-1}) = \ell n\, 2$

$\therefore$ Range of $f(x) = \left[\ell n\left(\left(\frac{1}{e}\right)^{1/e} + 1\right), \ell n 2\right]$

$= [\ell n(e^{-1/e} + 1), \ell 2]$

9. (a) $y = \ell n(x^x + 1), x > 0$

$f'(x) = \frac{1}{x^x + 1}.\frac{d}{dx}(x^x)$ ...(1)

Let $u = x^x$

$\Rightarrow \ell n\, u = x\, \ell n\, x$

$\Rightarrow \dfrac{1}{u}\dfrac{dy}{dx} = 1 + \ell nx$

$\Rightarrow \dfrac{dy}{dx} = x^x(1 + \ell n\, x)$ …..(2)

$\therefore\ f'(x) = \dfrac{1}{(x^2+1)}.x^x(1+\ell nx)$

$\Rightarrow f'(x)\downarrow$ for $x \in (0, e^{-1})$ and $f'(x)\uparrow$ for $x \in [e^{-1}, \infty)$

$\lim\limits_{x\to0^+} f(x) = \lim\limits_{x\to0^+} = x^x L$

$\Rightarrow \ell n\, L = \lim\limits_{x\to0^+} x\ell nx = \lim\limits_{x\to0^+}\left(\dfrac{\ell nx}{1/x}\right)\left(\dfrac{\infty}{\infty} form\right)$

$\Rightarrow \ell n\, L = \lim\limits_{x\to0^+}\left(\dfrac{1/x}{-1/x^2}\right) = \lim\limits_{x\to0^+}(-x)$

$\Rightarrow L = e^0 = 1$

$\Rightarrow \lim\limits_{x\to0^+} \ell n\,(x^x + 1) = \ell n\, 2$ and $f(e^{-1}) = \ell n\left(\left(e^{-1}\right)^{e^{-1}} + 1\right) = \ell n\,(e^{-1/e} + 1)$

$\therefore$ Range $f(x) = [\ell n(e^{-1/e} + 1), \ell n\, 2]$

10. (a) $g(x) = \left(x - \dfrac{x^3}{6} - \dfrac{x^5}{120}\right) - \sin x$

$\Rightarrow g'(x) = 1 - \dfrac{x^2}{2} - \dfrac{x^4}{24} - \cos x$

$\Rightarrow g''(x) = -\dfrac{x}{1} - \dfrac{x^3}{6} + \sin x$

$\Rightarrow g''(x) = -1 - \dfrac{x^2}{2} + \cos x = -(1 - \cos x) - \dfrac{x^2}{2} < 0\ \forall\, x > 0$

$\Rightarrow g''(x) \downarrow$ for $x > 0$

$\Rightarrow g''(x) < g''(0)\ \forall\, x > 0$

$\Rightarrow g''(x) < 0\ \forall\, x > 0$

$\Rightarrow g'(x) \downarrow$ for $x > 0$

$\Rightarrow g'(x) < g'(0)\ \forall\, x > 0$

$\Rightarrow g'(x) < 0\ \forall\, x > 0$

$\Rightarrow g(x) \downarrow \forall\, x > 0$

$\Rightarrow g(x) < g(0)\ \forall\, x > 0$

$\Rightarrow x - \dfrac{x^3}{6} - \dfrac{x^5}{120} - \sin x < 0\ \forall\, x > 0$

$\Rightarrow \ell n\left(x - \dfrac{x^3}{6} - \dfrac{x^5}{120} - \sin x\right)$ is not defined for $x > 0$

11. (a) $f(x) = \ell n(1 + x) - \dfrac{\tan^{-1} x}{1+x}$; $x > 0$

$\Rightarrow f'(x) = \dfrac{1}{(1+x)} - \left[\dfrac{(1+x).\dfrac{1}{1+x^2} - \tan^{-1} x}{(1+x)^2}\right]$

$= \dfrac{1}{(1+x)} - \dfrac{1}{(1+x)^2(1+x^2)} + \dfrac{\tan^{-1} x}{(1+x)^2}$

$= \dfrac{1}{(1+x)} - \left[\dfrac{(1+x)(1+x^2)-1}{(1+x)^2(1+x^2)}\right] + \dfrac{\tan^{-1} x}{(1+x)^2}$

$= \dfrac{x+x^2+x^3}{(1+x)^2(1+x^2)} + \dfrac{\tan^{-1} x}{(1+x)^2} = \dfrac{x(1+x+x^2)}{(1+x)^2(1+x^2)} + \dfrac{\tan^{-1} x}{(1+x)^2} > 0$

$\forall\, x > 0$

$\Rightarrow f(x) \uparrow \forall\, x > 0$

$\Rightarrow f(x) > f(0)\ \forall\, x > 0$

$\Rightarrow \ell n(1 + x) - \dfrac{\tan^{-1} x}{1+x} > 0\ \forall\, x > 0$

$\Rightarrow f(x) > 0\ \forall\, x > 0$

$\Rightarrow \text{sgn}\,(f(x)) = 1\ \forall\, x > 0$

12. (c) $g(x) = [\ell n(1 + x)]^{-1} - (x)^{-1}; x > 0$

$= \dfrac{1}{\ell n(1+x)} - \dfrac{1}{x}, x > 0$

$\Rightarrow g'(x) = \dfrac{-1}{[\ell n(1+x)]^2}.\dfrac{1}{(1+x)} + \dfrac{1}{x^2}, x > 0$

$= \dfrac{(1+x)[\ell n(1+x)]^2 - x^2}{x^2(1+x)\ell n(1+x)}$

Let $f(x) = \dfrac{(x)}{\sqrt{(x+1)}} - \ell n(1+x)$;

$\Rightarrow f'(x) = \left(\dfrac{\sqrt{x+1} - (x).\dfrac{1}{2\sqrt{x+1}}}{(x+1)}\right) - \left(\dfrac{1}{1+x}\right)$

$= \left(\dfrac{2(x+1).-x}{2\sqrt{x+1}} - 1\right).\dfrac{1}{(1+x)}$

$= \left(\dfrac{x+2}{2\sqrt{x+1}} - 1\right).\dfrac{1}{(1+x)}$

$= \left[\dfrac{1}{2}\left\{\dfrac{x+1+1}{\sqrt{x+1}}\right\} - 1\right].\dfrac{1}{(x+1)}$

$= \left[\dfrac{1}{2}\left\{\sqrt{x+1} + \dfrac{1}{\sqrt{x+1}}\right\} - 1\right].\dfrac{1}{(x+1)}$

$\because\ \sqrt{x+1} + \dfrac{1}{\sqrt{x+1}} > 2$

$\Rightarrow \dfrac{1}{2}\left\{\sqrt{x+1} + \dfrac{1}{\sqrt{x+1}}\right\} > 1$

$\Rightarrow f'(x) > 0$

$\Rightarrow f(x) \uparrow \forall\, x > -1$

$\Rightarrow f(x) > f(0)\ \forall\, x > -1$

$\Rightarrow \dfrac{x}{\sqrt{x+1}} - \ell n\,(1 + x) > 0\ \forall\, x > -1$

$\Rightarrow \dfrac{x}{\sqrt{x+1}} > \ell n\,(1 + x)\ \forall\, x > -1$

For $-1 < x < 0$,

$\left(\dfrac{x}{\sqrt{x+1}}\right)^2 < (\ell n(1 + x))^2$ ($\because$ both sides use –ve) i.e., $\dfrac{x^2}{(x+1)} < [\ell n(1+x)]^2$

$\Rightarrow$ $x^2 < (x+1)\,[\ell n(1+x)]^2$

$\Rightarrow$ $(x+1)\,[\ell n(1+x)]^2 - x^2 > 0$

$\Rightarrow$ $\dfrac{(x+1)[\ell n(1+x)]^2 - x^2}{x^2(1+x)\ell n(1+x)} < 0 \left[\begin{matrix}\because \ell n(1+x) < 0\\ \text{for} -1 < x < 0\end{matrix}\right]$

$\Rightarrow$ $g'(x) < 0$

For $0 < x < 1$

$\dfrac{x}{\sqrt{x+1}} > \ell n(1+x)$

$\Rightarrow$ $\left(\dfrac{x}{\sqrt{1+x}}\right)^2 > [\ell n(1+x)]^2$

$\Rightarrow$ $x^2 > (x+1)\,[\ell n(1+x)]^2$

$\Rightarrow$ $(x+1)\,[\ell n(x+1)]^2 - x^2 < 0$

$\Rightarrow$ $\dfrac{(x+1)[\ell n(x+1)]^2 - x^2}{x^2(1+x)\ell n(1+x)}$

$\Rightarrow$ $g'(x) < 0$

$\Rightarrow$ $g(x)$ is a decreasing function for $x \in (-1, \infty) - \{0\}$

Also $g(-1^+) = 0^- + 1 = 1^-$

Also $g(x) = \dfrac{x - \ell n(1+x)}{x\ell n(1+x)}; x > 0$

Let $h(x) = x - \ell n(1+x)$

$\Rightarrow$ $h'(x) = 1 - \dfrac{1}{1+x} = \dfrac{x}{1+x}$

$\Rightarrow$ $h'(x) > 0$ for $x > 0$

$\Rightarrow$ $h(x) \uparrow$ for $x > 0$

$\Rightarrow$ $h(x) > h(0)\ \forall\ x > 0$

$\Rightarrow$ $h(x) > 0\ \forall\ x > 0$

$\Rightarrow$ $g(x) > 0\ \forall\ x > 0$

Thus $g(x)$ is continuously decreasing function with $g(-1^+) = 1^-$ and $g(x) > 0\ \forall\ x > 0$

$\Rightarrow$ $0 < g(x) < 1$

13. (a) $f(x) = x^3 + ax^2 + bx + c$

$f'(x) = 3x^2 + 2ax + b$.

For bijective function, $f'(x) \geq 0\ \forall\ x \in \mathbb{R}$

$\Rightarrow$ $4a^2 - 4(3)(b) \leq 0$

$\Rightarrow$ $a^2 \leq 3b$

14. (a), (b), (c)

(a) If $f(x) = x + \sin x$

$\Rightarrow$ $f'(x) = 1 + \cos x \geq 0\ \forall\ x \in \mathbb{R}$

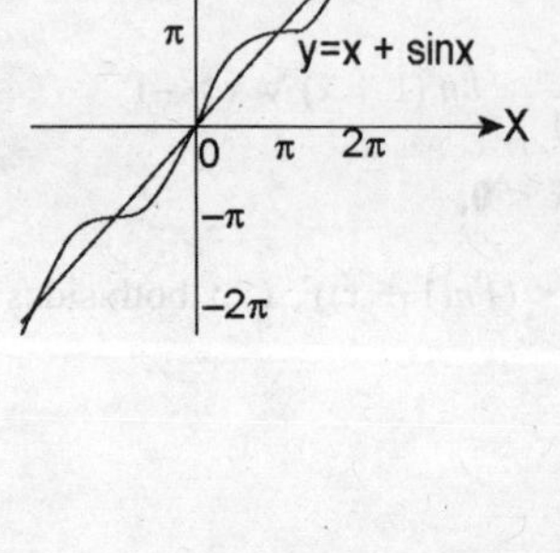

$\Rightarrow$ $f(x)$ is bijective from $\mathbb{R}$ to $\mathbb{R}$,

Here $(f(x) - x).f''(x) < 0\ \forall\ x \in \mathbb{R}$

$\Rightarrow$ Option (*a*) may be true.

(b) If $f(x) = e^x > 0\ \forall\ x \in \mathbb{R}, f'(x) = e^x > 0\ \forall\ x \in \mathbb{R}$ and $f(x)$ is bijective from $\mathbb{R}$ to $\mathbb{R}$

$\Rightarrow$ $f(x) - x = ex - x > 0\ \forall\ x \in \mathbb{R}$

and $f''(x) = e^x > 0\ \forall\ x \in \mathbb{R}$

$\left[\begin{matrix}\because \text{for } x \leq 0, e^x > 0, -x \geq 0 \Rightarrow e^x - x > 0\\ \text{and for } x > 0, e^x - x = 1 + \dfrac{x^2}{2!} + \dfrac{x^3}{3!} + \ldots > 0\end{matrix}\right]$

$\Rightarrow$ $(f(x) - x)\,.\,f''(x) > 0\ \forall\ x \in \mathbb{R}$

$\Rightarrow$ Option (*b*) may be true

(c) If $(f(x) - x).f''(x) > 0$

$\Rightarrow$ $f(x) - x > 0, f''(x) > 0\ \forall\ x \in \mathbb{R}$ or $f(x) - x < 0, f''(x) < 0\ \forall\ x \in \mathbb{R}$

Note that in this case $(f(x) - x) > 0, f''(x) > 0$ for some part of domain, can't hold as otherwise $f''(x)$ has to be zero at the concavity i.e., $(f(x) - x).f''(x) = 0$

$\therefore$ for $(f(x) - x)\,.\,f''(x) > 0$

Either $f(x)$ remains concave upwards and above line $y = x$ or $f(x)$ remains concave downwards and below line $y = x\ \forall\ x \in \mathbb{R}$

$\Rightarrow$ $f(x) \neq x$ for any $x \in \mathbb{R}$

$\Rightarrow$ $f(x) = f^{-1}(x)$ has no solution

$\Rightarrow$ (*c*) is correct and hence (*d*) incorrect

15. (a) $f(x) = 1 + x\,\ell n\left(x + \sqrt{x^2+1}\right) - \sqrt{1+x^2}$

$\Rightarrow$ $f'(x) = \dfrac{x}{\left(x+\sqrt{x^2+1}\right)}\left(1 + \dfrac{x}{\sqrt{x^2+1}}\right) + \ell n$

$\left(x+\sqrt{x^2+1}\right) - \dfrac{x}{\sqrt{1+x^2}}$

$= \dfrac{x}{\sqrt{x^2+1}} + \ell n\left(x+\sqrt{x^2+1}\right)\dfrac{-x}{\sqrt{x^2+1}}$

$= \ell n\left(x+\sqrt{x^2+1}\right) \geq 0 \forall x \geq 0$

$\Rightarrow$ $f(x) \uparrow\ \forall\ x \geq 0$

$\Rightarrow$ $f(x) \geq f(0)\ \forall\ x \geq 0$

$\Rightarrow$ $1 + x\,\ell n\left(\sqrt{x+1} + x\right) \geq \sqrt{1+x^2}\ \ \forall\ x \geq 0$

16. (a) $f(x) = \dfrac{\sin x}{x}, 0 < x < \dfrac{\pi}{2}$

It is a decreasing function, being slope of chord joining origin to any point of $y = \sin x$ for $x \in (0, \pi/2)$

$\Rightarrow$ $f(\sin x) > f(x)\ \forall\ x \in (0, \pi/2)$ as for $x \in (0, \pi/2)$, $\sin x < x$

$\Rightarrow$ $\sin(\sin x) > \dfrac{\sin x}{x}$

$\Rightarrow$ $\sin^2 x < x\sin(\sin x)$ $\left[\begin{matrix}\because x, \sin x > 0\\ \text{for } x \in \left(\dfrac{\pi}{2}\right)\end{matrix}\right]$

TEXTUAL EXERCISE-6: (SUBJECTIVE)

1. **(a)** $f(x) = x^3 - 6x^2$

$\Rightarrow f'(x) = 3x^2 - 12x$

$\Rightarrow f''(x) = 6x - 12$

$\Rightarrow f''(x) = 0$ for $x = 2$

$\Rightarrow f(x)$ is concave downwards for $x < 2$, concave upwards for $x > 2$ and point of inflexion at $x = 2$.

(b) $y = e^x - e^{-x}$

$\Rightarrow f'(x) = e^x + e^{-x}$

$\Rightarrow f''(x) = e^x - e^{-x} = \dfrac{e^{2x}-1}{e^{2x}}$

$\therefore$ e^{2x} is ↑ function

$\Rightarrow e^{2x} \le e^0 \ \forall\ x \le 0$

$\Rightarrow e^{2x} - 1 \le 0 \ \forall\ x \le 0$

$\Rightarrow f''(x) \le 0 \ \forall\ x \le 0$ and $e^{2x} \ge e^0 \ \forall\ x \ge 0$

$\Rightarrow e^{2x} - 1 \ge 0 \ \forall\ x \ge 0$

$\Rightarrow f''(x) \ge 0 \ \forall\ x \ge 0$

$\Rightarrow f(x)$ is concave downwards for $x < 0$, concave upwards for $x > 0$,

(c) $f(x) = 2x^3 - 3x^2 + 1$

$\Rightarrow f'(x) = 6x^2 - 6x$

$\Rightarrow f''(x) = 12x - 6 = 0$ for $x = 1/2$

$\Rightarrow f(x)$ is concave downwards for $x < \dfrac{1}{2}$, concave upwards for $x > \dfrac{1}{2}$, Point of inflexion $x = \dfrac{1}{2}$

(d) $f(x) = 2x^{3/2};\ x > 0$

$\Rightarrow f'(x) = 2\left(\dfrac{3}{2}\right)x^{1/2} = 3x^{1/2}$

$\Rightarrow f''(x) = \dfrac{3}{2(x)^{1/2}} > 0 \ \forall\ x > 0$

$\Rightarrow f(x)$ is concave upwards for $x \in (0, \infty)$

(e) $y = \dfrac{\ell nx}{x};x > 0$

$\Rightarrow f'(x) = \dfrac{x.\frac{1}{x} - \ell nx.1}{x^2} = \dfrac{1-\ell nx}{x^2}$

$\Rightarrow f''(x) = \dfrac{x^2\left(-\frac{1}{x}\right) - (1-\ell nx)(2x)}{x^4}$

$\Rightarrow f''(x) = \dfrac{-x - 2x + 2x\ell nx}{x^4}$

$\Rightarrow f''(x) = \dfrac{2x\ell nx - 3x}{x^4}$

$\Rightarrow f''(x) = \dfrac{2\ell nx - 3}{x^3} = 0$ at $x = e^{3/2}$, < 0 for $x < e^{3/2}$ and > 0 for $e^{3/2}$

$\Rightarrow f(x)$ is concave downwards on $(0, e^{3/2})$ concave upwards on $(e^{3/2}, \infty)$ and having point of inflexion at $x = e^{3/2}$

(f) $f(x) = x\,\ell n\,x;\ x > 0$

$\Rightarrow f'(x) = x.\dfrac{1}{x} + \ell n\,x\,.\,1$

$\Rightarrow f'(x) = 1 + \ell n\,x$

$\Rightarrow f''(x) = \dfrac{1}{x} > 0$ for $x > 0$

$\Rightarrow f(x)$ is concave upwards for $x \in (0, \infty)$.

2. $g(x) = 2f\left(\dfrac{x}{2}\right) + f(2 - x),$

$g'(x) = 2.\dfrac{1}{2}f'\left(\dfrac{x}{2}\right) - f'(2-x)$

$\Rightarrow g'(x) = f'\left(\dfrac{x}{2}\right) - f'(2-x)$ ...(i)

$\because$ $f''(x) < 0 \ \forall\ x \in (0, 2)$

$\Rightarrow f'(x)$ ↑ on $(-\infty, 0]$ and on $[2, \infty)$ and $f'(x)$ ↓ on $(0, 2)$

Let $g'(x) \ge 0$

From (i), we get $f'\left(\dfrac{x}{2}\right) \ge f'(2 - x)$

Case (i): $f'(x)$ ↑

$\Rightarrow \dfrac{x}{2} \ge 2 - x \quad \Rightarrow \dfrac{3}{2}x \ge 2 \Rightarrow x \ge \dfrac{4}{3}$

But $f'(x)$ ↑ on $(-\infty, 0]$ and on $[2, \infty)$

$\Rightarrow \dfrac{x}{2}$ and $2 - x \ge 2$

$\Rightarrow x \ge 4$ and $x \le 0$, which is impossible .

Case (ii): $f'(x)$ ↓

$\Rightarrow \dfrac{x}{2} \le 2 - x \Rightarrow x \le \dfrac{4}{3}$

But $f'(x)$ ↓ on $(0, 2)$

$\Rightarrow \dfrac{x}{2}, (2 - x) \in (0, 2)$

$\Rightarrow x \in (0, 4)$ and $x \in (0, 2)$

$\therefore$ For $x \in (0, 2)$, $\dfrac{x}{2}$, $(2 - x) \in (0, 2)$ and in $(0, 2)$, $f'(x)$ ↓

and for $x \in \left(0, \dfrac{4}{3}\right]$, $\dfrac{x}{2} \le (2 - x)$

$\Rightarrow f'\left(\dfrac{x}{2}\right) \ge f'(2-x) \quad \Rightarrow g'(x) \ge 0$

$\therefore$ $g(x)$ ↑ on $\left(0, \dfrac{4}{3}\right]$ and $g(x)$ ↓ on $(-\infty, 0]$ and on $\left(\dfrac{4}{3}, \infty\right)$

3. Clearly if A_1 is mid point A_2A_3, then L will be mid point AB (By application of B.P.T. Theorem)

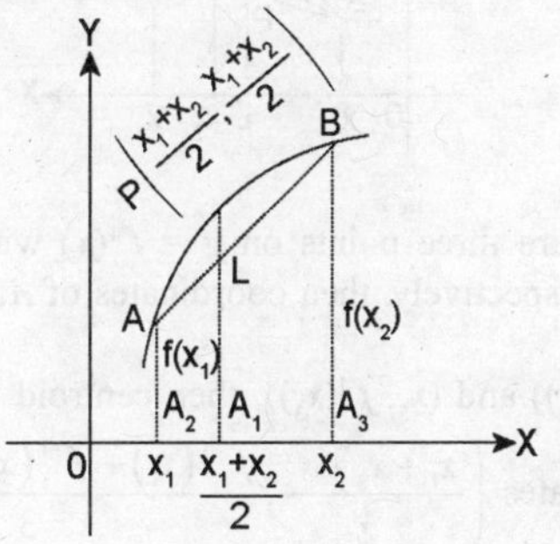

$\Rightarrow\ A_1L = \dfrac{AA_2 + BA_3}{2} = \dfrac{f(x_1)+(x_2)}{2}$ and co-ordinates of L

will be $\left(\dfrac{x_1+x_2}{2}, \dfrac{f(x_1)+f(x_2)}{2}\right)$

Also $A_1P = f\left(\dfrac{x_1+x_2}{2}\right)$

Obviously $A_1P > A_1L$

$\Rightarrow\ f\left(\dfrac{x_1+x_2}{2}\right) > \dfrac{f(x_1)+f(x_2)}{2}\ \forall\ x_1, x_2 \in$ Domain of $f(x)$

4. $f(x) \geq 0\ \forall\ x \in \mathbb{R}, f''(x) < 0$ and $f^{-1}(x)$ exists.

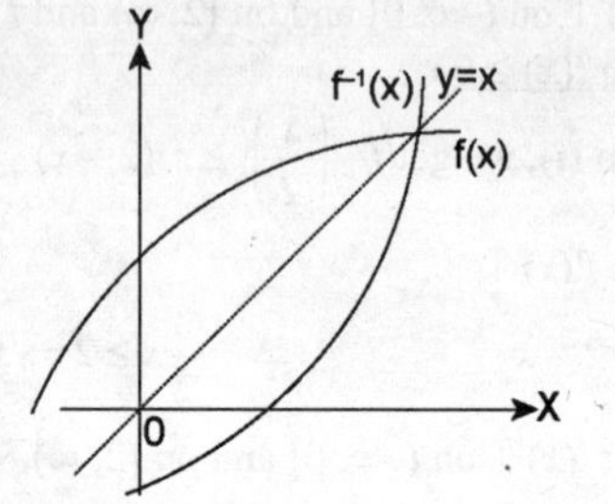

$\because$ Let $y = f^{-1}(x)$

$\Rightarrow\ x = f(y)$

$\Rightarrow\ \dfrac{dy}{dx} = f'(y)$

$\Rightarrow\ dy/dx = \dfrac{1}{f'(y)}$

$\Rightarrow\ \dfrac{d}{dx}(f^{-1}(x)) = \dfrac{1}{f'(f^{-1}(x))} > 0$ as $f'(x) \geq 0\ \forall\ x \in \mathbb{R}$

$\Rightarrow\ f^{-1}(x)$ is monotonically increasing function.

Also $\dfrac{d^2}{dx^2}(f^{-1}(x))$

$= \dfrac{-1}{\left[f'(f^{-1}(x))\right]^2}.f''(f^{-1}(x)).\times\dfrac{1}{f'(f^{-1}(x))}$

$= (-)(-)(+) = +ve$

$\Rightarrow\ f^{-1}(x)$ has concavity upwards.

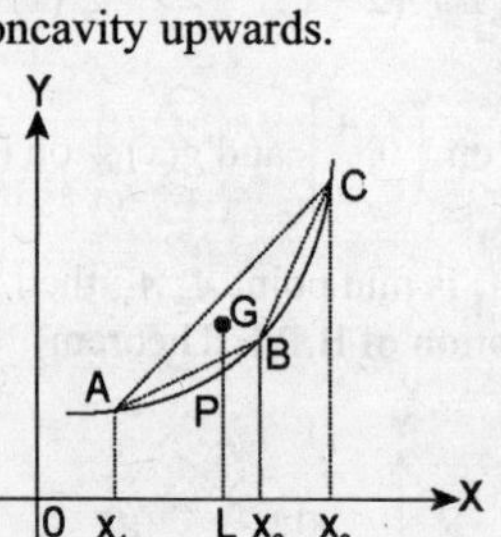

If ABC are three points on $y = f^{-1}(x)$ with abscissa x_1, x_2 and x_3 respectively, then coordinates of A, B, C will be $(x_1, f^{-1}(x_1))$.

$(x_2, f^{-1}(x_2))$ and $(x_3, f^{-1}(x_3))$, then centroid G of triangle has co-ordinates $\left(\dfrac{x_1+x_2+x_3}{3}, \dfrac{f^{-1}(x_1)+f^{-1}(x_2)+f^{-1}(x_3)}{3}\right)$.

which lies below AC but above the curve $y = f^{-1}(x)$

$\Rightarrow\ LG > PG$

$\Rightarrow\ \dfrac{f^{-1}(x_1)+f^{-1}(x_2)+f^{-1}(x_3)}{3} > f^{-1}\left(\dfrac{x_1+x_2+x_3}{3}\right)$

5. Let $f(x) = \dfrac{\sin x}{x}$; $0 < x < \pi/2$

Clearly $f(x)$ is a decreasing function $f(A) > f(\pi/6)$ for $0 < A < \dfrac{\pi}{6}$

$\Rightarrow\ \dfrac{\sin A}{A} > \dfrac{1/2}{\pi/6}$

$\Rightarrow\ \dfrac{1}{A(\operatorname{cosec} A)} > \dfrac{3}{\pi}$

$\Rightarrow\ A \operatorname{cosec} A < \pi/3$

6. Let $f(x) = \dfrac{\sin x}{x}$; $0 < x < \dfrac{\pi}{2}$

$\because\ f(x)$ is decreasing function

$\Rightarrow\ f(x) > f(\pi/2)\ \forall\ 0 < x < \pi/2$

$\Rightarrow\ \dfrac{\sin x}{x} > \dfrac{1}{\frac{\pi}{2}}$

$\Rightarrow\ \dfrac{1}{x \operatorname{cosec} x} > \dfrac{1}{\frac{\pi}{2}}$

$\Rightarrow\ 0 < x \operatorname{cosec} x < \pi/2$

$\therefore$ For $A, B, C, \in (0, \pi/2)$

$A \operatorname{cosec} A$, $B \operatorname{cosec} A$, $\operatorname{cosec} A \in \left(0, \dfrac{\pi}{2}\right)$

$\Rightarrow$ A $\operatorname{cosec} A + B \operatorname{cosec} A + C \operatorname{cosec} A < \dfrac{3\pi}{2}$

7. (a) $y = (x-1)^{1/3}$

$\Rightarrow\ \dfrac{dy}{dx} = \dfrac{1}{3}(x-1)^{-2/3}$

$\Rightarrow\ \dfrac{d^2y}{dx^2} = \dfrac{-2}{9}(x-1)^{-5/3}$

$\Rightarrow\ \dfrac{d^2y}{dx^2} > 0$ for $x < 1$ and $\dfrac{d^2y}{dx^2} < 0$ for $x > 1$

$\Rightarrow$ Curve is concave upwards for $x < 1$ and concave downwards for $x > 1$ and having no point of inflexion.

(b) $y = x^4 - 2x^3 + 1$

$\Rightarrow\ \dfrac{dy}{dx} = 4x^3 - 6x^2$

$\Rightarrow\ \dfrac{d^2y}{dx^2} = 12x^2 - 12x = 12x(x-1)$

$\therefore\ \dfrac{d^2y}{dx^2} < 0$ for $x \in (0, 1)$ and $\dfrac{d^2y}{dx^2} > 0$ for $x \in (-\infty, 0) \cup (1, \infty)$ and point of inflexion are $x = 0, 1$

i.e., concave downwards for $x \in (0, 1)$ and concave upwards for $x \in (-\infty, 0)$ and for $x \in (1, \infty)$.

(c) $y = (x-1)(x-2)(x-3)$

$\Rightarrow y = (x^2 - 3x + 2)(x-3)$

$\Rightarrow y = x^3 - 3x^2 + 2x + 9x - 6$

$\Rightarrow y = x^3 - 6x^2 + 11x - 6$

$\Rightarrow \dfrac{dy}{dx} = 3x^2 - 12x + 11$ and $\dfrac{d^2y}{dx^2} = 6x - 12 = 0$ at $x = 2$

$\Rightarrow f(x)$ is concave downwards for $x \in (-\infty, 2)$ and concave upwards for $x \in (2, \infty)$ point of inflexion is $x = 2$

(d) $y = (x-1)^2 (x-2)$

$\Rightarrow y = (x^2 - 2x + 1)(x-2)$

$\Rightarrow y = x^3 - 2x^2 + x - 2x^2 + 4x - 2$

$\Rightarrow y = x^3 - 4x + 5x - 2$

$\Rightarrow \dfrac{dy}{dx} = 3x^2 - 8x + 5$

$\Rightarrow \dfrac{d^2y}{dx} = 6x - 8 = 2(3x-4) = 0$ at $\dfrac{4}{3}$

$\Rightarrow f(x)$ is concave downwards for $x < 4/3$, concave upwards for $x > 4/3$, point of inflexion at $x = 4/3$.

(e) $y = 3x^2 - 2x^3$

$\Rightarrow \dfrac{dy}{dx} = 6x - 6x^2$

$\Rightarrow \dfrac{d^2y}{dx^2} = 6 - 12x = 6(1-2x) = 0$ at $x = 1/2$,

$\Rightarrow \dfrac{d^2y}{dx^2} < 0$ for $x > \dfrac{1}{2}$ and > 0 for $x < \dfrac{1}{2}$

$\Rightarrow f(x)$ is concave upwards for $x < \dfrac{1}{2}$, point inflexion $= \dfrac{1}{2}$

(f) $y = \ell n(\sin x); x \in (2n\pi, (2n+1)); x \in \mathbb{Z}$

$\Rightarrow \dfrac{dy}{dx} = \dfrac{1}{\sin x}\cos x = \cot x$

$\Rightarrow \dfrac{d^2y}{dx^2} = -\operatorname{cosec}^2 x < 0\ \forall\ x \in (2n\pi, (2n+1)\pi)$;

$\Rightarrow f(x)$ is concave downwards $\forall\ x \in (2n\pi, (2n+1)\pi)$; $n \in \mathbb{Z}$.

(g) $y^2 = x^4 - x^6$ ...(*i*)

$\Rightarrow y = \pm\sqrt{x^4 - x^6}$

$\Rightarrow y = \pm x^2\sqrt{1-x^2}$

$\Rightarrow$ Equation (*i*) represents a many-many relation with its domain $[-1, 1]$

$\Rightarrow \dfrac{dy}{dx} = \pm\left(x^2 . \dfrac{1}{2\sqrt{1-x^2}}(-2x) + 2x\sqrt{1-x^2}\right)$

$\Rightarrow \dfrac{dy}{dx} = \pm\left(\dfrac{-x^3 + 2x(1-x^2)}{\sqrt{1-x^2}}\right)$

$\Rightarrow \dfrac{dy}{dx} = \pm\left(\dfrac{2x - 3x^3}{\sqrt{1-x^2}}\right)$

$$\therefore \frac{dy}{dx} = \begin{cases} \dfrac{2x-3x^3}{\sqrt{1-x^2}} \text{ for } y > 0 \\ \dfrac{-(2x-3x^3)}{\sqrt{1-x^2}} \text{ for } y < 0 \end{cases}$$

$$\therefore \frac{d^2y}{dx^2} = \begin{cases} \dfrac{6x^4 - 9x^2 + 2}{(1-x^2)^{3/2}} \text{ for } y > 0 \\ \dfrac{-(6x^4 - 9x^2 + 2)}{(1-x^2)^{3/2}} \text{ for } y < 0 \end{cases}$$

$\therefore \dfrac{d^2y}{dx^2} = 0$ at $x^2 = \dfrac{9 \pm \sqrt{81-48}}{12}$ i.e.,

$x^2 = \dfrac{3}{4} \pm \dfrac{\sqrt{33}}{12} = \dfrac{9 \pm \sqrt{33}}{12} = \alpha, \beta (say)$

$$\Rightarrow \frac{d^2y}{dx^2} = \begin{cases} < 0 \text{ for } x^2 \in (\alpha, \beta) \text{ for } y > 0 \\ > 0 \text{ for } x^2 \in (0, \alpha) \cup (\beta, \infty) \text{ for } y > 0 \\ > 0 \text{ for } x^2 \in (\alpha, \beta) \text{ for } y < 0 \\ < 0 \text{ for } x^2 \in (0, \alpha) \cup (\beta, 1) \text{ for } y < 0 \end{cases}; \text{ But } 0 < \alpha$$

$< 1 < \beta$ and $x^2 \in [0, 1]$

$$\Rightarrow \frac{d^2y}{dx^2} = \begin{cases} \left.\begin{matrix} < 0 \text{ for } x^2 \in (\alpha, 1] \\ > 0 \text{ for } x^2 \in (0, \alpha) \end{matrix}\right\} \text{for } y > 0 \\ \left.\begin{matrix} > 0 \text{ for } x^2 \in (\alpha, 1] \\ < 0 \text{ for } x^2 \in (0, \alpha) \end{matrix}\right\} \text{for } y < 0 \end{cases}$$

<u>For $y > 0$</u>

The curve is concave upwards for $x \in (-\sqrt{\alpha}, \sqrt{\alpha})$; where $\alpha = \dfrac{9-\sqrt{33}}{12}$; concave downwards for $x \in [-1, -\sqrt{\alpha}) \cup (\sqrt{\alpha}, 1]$

<u>For $y < 0$</u>

The curve is concave downwards for $x \in (-\sqrt{\alpha}, \sqrt{\alpha})$; $\alpha = \dfrac{9-\sqrt{33}}{12}$; concave upwards for $x \in [-1, -\sqrt{\alpha}) \cup (\sqrt{\alpha}, 1]$.

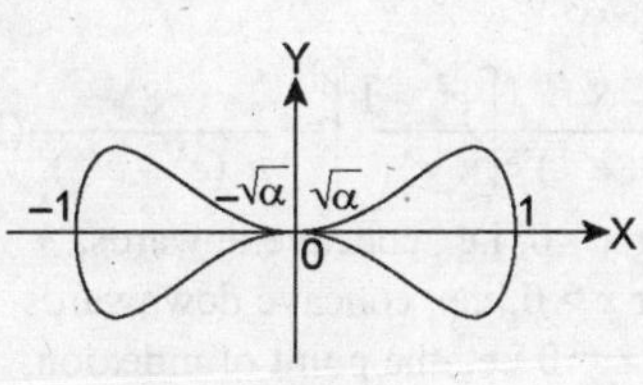

(h) $y^2 = x^3; x \geq 0$ ...(*i*)

$\Rightarrow y = \pm(x)^{3/2}$

Equation (*i*) represents a one-many relation with domain $[0, \infty)$

$$\Rightarrow \frac{dy}{dx} = \begin{cases} \dfrac{3}{2}\sqrt{x} \text{ for } y > 0 \\ -\dfrac{3}{2}\sqrt{x} \text{ for } y < 0 \end{cases}$$

$$\Rightarrow \frac{d^2y}{dx^2} = \begin{cases} \dfrac{3}{4\sqrt{x}} \text{ for } y > 0 \\ -\dfrac{3}{4\sqrt{x}} \text{ for } y < 0 \end{cases}$$

$\Rightarrow \dfrac{d^2y}{dx^2} > 0 \ \forall\ x \in [0, \infty)$ and $y > 0$ and $\dfrac{d^2y}{dx^2} < 0 \ \forall\ x \in (0, \infty)$ and $y < 0$

$\Rightarrow f(x)$ is concave upwards for $y > 0$ and $f(x)$ is concave downwards for $y < 0$

Graphically shown below:

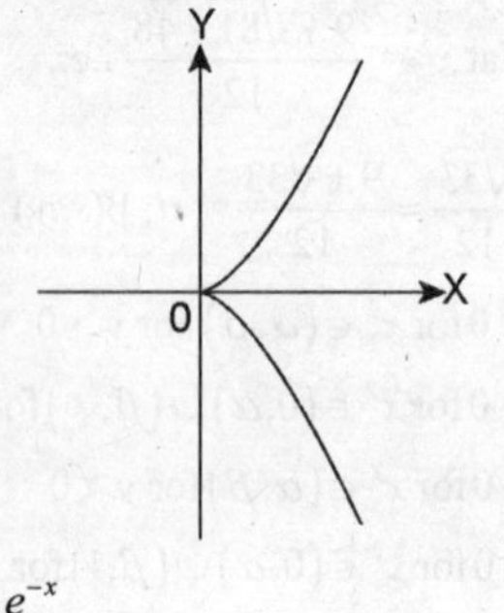

(i) $y = \dfrac{e^x - e^{-x}}{2}$

$\Rightarrow \dfrac{dy}{dx} = \dfrac{e^x + e^{-x}}{2}$

$\Rightarrow \dfrac{d^2y}{dx^2} = \dfrac{e^x - e^{-x}}{2} = \dfrac{e^{2x} - 1}{2e^x}$

< 0 for $x > 0$ and > 0 for $x > 0 = 0$ at $x = 0$

$\Rightarrow f(x)$ is concave downwards for $x < 0$, concave upwards for $x > 0$ and having point of inflexion at $x = 0$

(j) $y = \dfrac{e^x - e^{-x}}{e^x + e^{-x}}$

$\Rightarrow \dfrac{dy}{dx} = \dfrac{(e^x + e^{-x})(e^x + e^{-x}) - (e^x - e^{-x})^2}{(e^x + e^{-x})^2}$

$\Rightarrow \dfrac{dy}{dx} = \dfrac{4}{(e^x + e^{-x})^2}$

$\Rightarrow \dfrac{(-8)}{(e^x + e^{-x})^3}(e^x - e^{-x})$

$= \dfrac{-8}{(e^x + e^{-x})^3} \cdot \left[\dfrac{e^{2x} - 1}{e^x}\right] = \dfrac{8}{e^x(e^x + e^{-x})^3}(1 - e^{2x})$

> 0 for $x < 0$, i.e., concave upwards,

< 0 for $x > 0$, i.e., concave downwards

$= 0$ at $x = 0$ i.e., the point of inflexion,

(k) $y = e^{-x^2}$

$\Rightarrow \dfrac{dy}{dx} = -2xe^{-x^2}$

$\Rightarrow \dfrac{d^2y}{dx^2} = 4x^2e^{-x^2} + e^{-x^2}(-2)$

$\Rightarrow \dfrac{d^2y}{dx^2} = (4x^2 - 2)e^{-x^2} = 2(2x^2 - 1)e^{-x^2}$

< 0 for $x \in \left(\dfrac{-1}{\sqrt{2}}, \dfrac{1}{\sqrt{2}}\right)$ i.e., concave downwards,

> 0 for $x \in \left(-\infty, \dfrac{-1}{\sqrt{2}}\right) \cup \left(\dfrac{1}{\sqrt{2}}, \infty\right)$ i.e., concave upwards,

$= 0$ at $x = \pm\dfrac{1}{\sqrt{2}}$ i.e., points of inflexion,

8. (a) Clearly from the diagram slope of chords OS, OR, OQ, OP are in increasing order

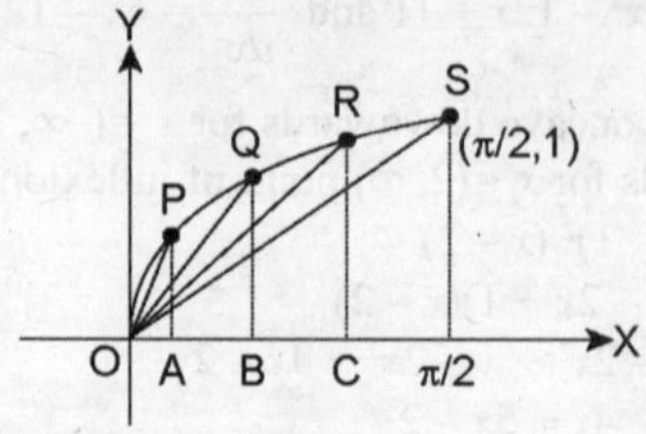

$\Rightarrow m_{OP} > m_{OS}$, $m_{OQ} > m_{OS}$, Also $m_{OR} > m_{OS}$

$\Rightarrow \dfrac{\sin A}{A} > \dfrac{2}{\pi}$ and $\dfrac{\sin B}{B} > \dfrac{2}{\pi}$ Also $\dfrac{\sin C}{C} > \dfrac{2}{\pi}$

$\Rightarrow \sin A > \dfrac{2A}{\pi}, \sin B > \dfrac{2B}{\pi}, \sin C > \dfrac{2C}{\pi}$

$\Rightarrow \sin A + \sin B + \sin C > \dfrac{2(A + B + C)}{\pi}$

$\Rightarrow \sin A + \sin B + \sin C > 2$

(b) Let $f(x) = \cos x$

$\Rightarrow f'(x) = -\sin x$

$\Rightarrow f''(x) = -\cos x < 0$ for $x \in \left(0, \dfrac{\pi}{2}\right)$

$\Rightarrow f(x)$ has concavity downwards for $0 < x < \dfrac{\pi}{2}$

$\because$ A, B, C are angle of Δ, $\dfrac{A}{4} + \dfrac{\pi}{4}$ etc $< \dfrac{\pi}{2}$

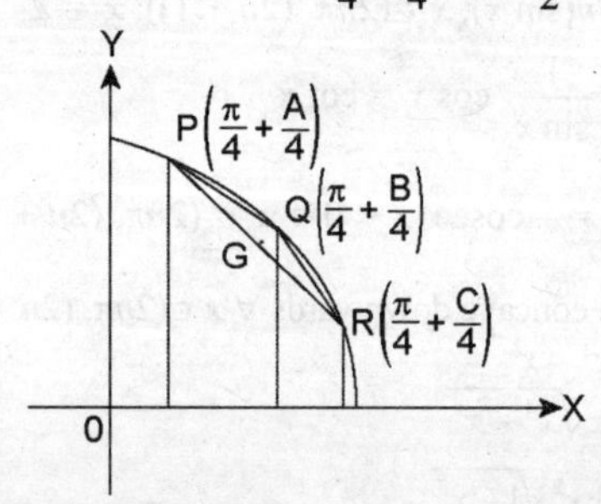

$$G\left(\dfrac{\dfrac{3\pi}{4} + \dfrac{A + B + C}{4}}{3}, \dfrac{\cos\left(\dfrac{\pi}{4} + \dfrac{A}{4}\right) + \cos\left(\dfrac{\pi}{4} + \dfrac{B}{4}\right) + \cos\left(\dfrac{\pi}{4} + \dfrac{C}{4}\right)}{3}\right)$$

where G is the centroid of ΔPQR.

$$\Rightarrow f\left(\dfrac{\pi}{4} + \dfrac{\pi}{12}\right) \geq \left(\dfrac{\cos\left(\dfrac{\pi}{4} + \dfrac{A}{4}\right) + \cos\left(\dfrac{\pi}{4} + \dfrac{B}{4}\right) + \cos\left(\dfrac{\pi}{4} + \dfrac{C}{4}\right)}{3}\right)$$

$$\Rightarrow 3f\left(\dfrac{\pi}{3}\right) \geq \cos\left(\dfrac{\pi}{4} + \dfrac{A}{4}\right) + \cos\left(\dfrac{\pi}{4} + \dfrac{B}{4}\right) + \cos\left(\dfrac{\pi}{4} + \dfrac{C}{4}\right)$$

$$\Rightarrow \dfrac{3}{2} \geq \cos\left(\dfrac{\pi}{4} + \dfrac{A}{4}\right) + \cos\left(\dfrac{\pi}{4} + \dfrac{B}{4}\right) + \cos\left(\dfrac{\pi}{4} + \dfrac{C}{4}\right)$$

(c) Let $f(x) = \cos x$ and PQR be $a\ \Delta$ with vertices P, Q and R on curve $y = \cos x$

G is the centroid of $\Delta\ PQR$, given by

$$\left(\frac{A+B+C}{3}, \frac{\cos A+\cos B+\cos C}{3}\right)$$

Clearly $f\left(\frac{A+B+C}{3}\right) \geq \frac{\cos A+\cos B+\cos C}{3}$

$\Rightarrow\ 3.\cos\frac{\pi}{3} \geq \cos A + \cos B + \cos C$

$\Rightarrow\ \cos A + \cos B + \cos C \leq \frac{3}{2}$

(d) $\because$ For +ve real numbers A.M $\geq$ G.M

$\Rightarrow\ \frac{\cos A+\cos B+\cos C}{3} \geq \sqrt[3]{\cos A \cos B . \cos C}$

$\Rightarrow\ \cos A \cos B \cos C \leq \left(\frac{\cos A+\cos B+\cos C}{3}\right)^3$

$\Rightarrow\ \cos A . \cos B . \cos C \leq \left(\frac{3}{2(3)}\right)^3$

$\left[\because \text{In part (c) already proved, } \cos A+\cos B+\cos C \leq \frac{3}{2}\right]$

$\Rightarrow\ \cos A . \cos B . \cos C \leq \frac{1}{8}$

(e) $\cos A + \cos B + \cos C$

$= 2\cos\frac{A+B}{2}\cos\frac{A-B}{2} + \cos\left(\pi-(A+B)\right)$

$= 2\cos\frac{A+B}{2}\cos\frac{A-B}{2} + \left(-\cos(A+B)\right)$

$= 2\cos\frac{A+B}{2}\cos\frac{A-B}{2} - \left(2\cos^2\frac{A+B}{2} - 1\right)$

$= 2\cos\frac{A+B}{2}\left[\cos\frac{A-B}{2} - \cos\frac{A+B}{2}\right] + 1$

$= 2\cos\frac{A+B}{2}\left[2\sin\frac{A}{2}\sin\frac{B}{2}\right] + 1$

$= 4\sin\frac{A}{2}\sin\frac{B}{2}\sin\frac{C}{2} + 1 \because \cos A + \cos B + \cos C \leq 3/2$

$\Rightarrow\ 4\sin\frac{A}{2}\sin\frac{B}{2}\sin\frac{C}{2} + 1 \leq \frac{3}{2}$

$\Rightarrow\ 4\sin\frac{A}{2}\sin\frac{B}{2}\sin\frac{C}{2} \leq \frac{1}{2} \Rightarrow \sin\frac{A}{2}\sin\frac{B}{2}\sin\frac{C}{2} \leq \frac{1}{8}$

9. (i) Let $f(x) = x^2$

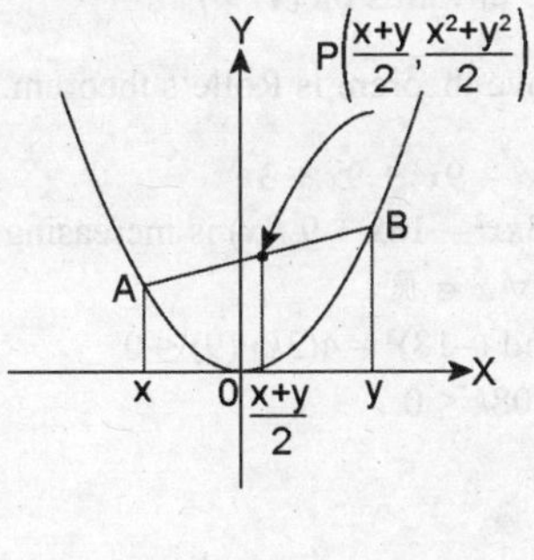

where P is mid-point of AB

$\Rightarrow\ \frac{x^2+y^2}{2} \geq f\left(\frac{x+y}{2}\right) = \left(\frac{x+y}{2}\right)^2$

(ii)

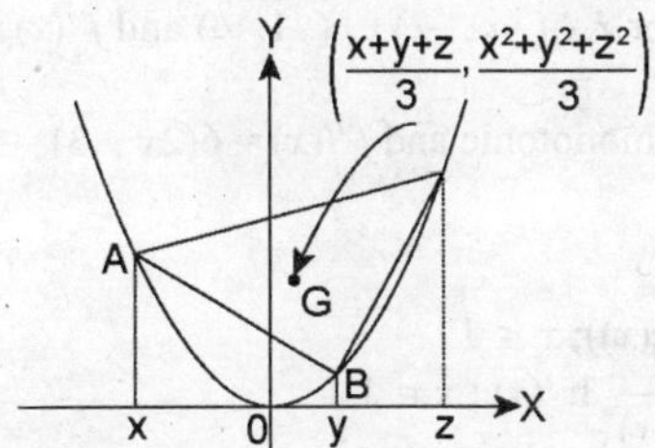

Where G is centroid of ΔABC

$\Rightarrow\ \frac{x^2+y^2+z^2}{3} \geq f\left(\frac{x+y+z}{3}\right) = \left(\frac{x+y+z}{3}\right)^2$

(iii) Let $f(x) = x^{2x+1}$; $x > 0, x \in W$

$\Rightarrow\ f(x) = (2n+1)\,x^{2n}$

$\Rightarrow\ f''(x) = (2n+1)(2n)\,x^{2x-1} > 0\ \forall\ x > 0$

$\Rightarrow\ f(x)$ is concave upwards $\forall\ x > 0$

$\therefore$ If A, B are 2 points on curve $y = f(x)$, then mid points AB i.e., M has coordinates *(say)* $\left(\frac{x+y}{2}, \frac{x^{2x+1}+y^{2x+1}}{2}\right)$

$\Rightarrow\ \frac{x^{2x+1}+y^{2x+1}}{2} \geq f\left(\frac{x+y}{2}\right)$

$\Rightarrow\ \frac{x^{2x+1}+y^{2x+1}}{2} \geq \left(\frac{x+y}{2}\right)^{2x+1}$; $\forall\ x, y > 0, x \in W$

10. $f(x) = \frac{ax^3}{3} + (a-2)\,x^2 + (a-1)\,x + 2$

$\Rightarrow\ f(x) = \frac{a}{3}(3x^2) + 2(a+2)\,x + (a-1)$

$\Rightarrow\ f'(x) = ax^2 + 2(a+2)\,x + (a-1)$

$\Rightarrow\ f''(x) = 2ax + 2(a+2)$

$\therefore\ f''(x) = 0$

$\Rightarrow\ x = \frac{-x(a+2)}{a} < 0$

$\Rightarrow\ -(a+2)\,(2) < 0$

$\Rightarrow\ a\,(a+2) > 0$

$\Rightarrow\ a < -2$ or $a > 0$

$\Rightarrow\ a \in (-\infty, -2) \cup (0, \infty)$.

TEXTUAL EXERCISE-6: (OBJECTIVE)

1. (c) $f(x) = x^4 + ax^3 + \frac{3x^2}{2} + 1$

$\Rightarrow\ f(x) = 4x^3 + 3ax^2 + 3x$

$\Rightarrow\ f''(x) = 12x^2 + 6ax + 3$

$= 3(4x^2 + 2ax + 1)$

$\Rightarrow\ f(x)$ will be concave upwards for $4x^2 + 2ax + 1 \geq 0\ \forall\ x \in \mathbb{R}$

$\Rightarrow\ (2a)^2 - 4(4)(1) \leq 0$

$\Rightarrow\ a^2 + 4 \leq 0$

$\Rightarrow\ a \in [-2, 2]$

2. (a), (b), (d)
$f(x) = 2x^3 + 9x^2 + 12x + 1$
$\Rightarrow f'(x) = 6x^2 + 18x + 12 = 6(x^2 + 3x + 12)$
$= 6(x + 1)(x + 2)$
$\Rightarrow f'(x) > 0$ for $x \in (-\infty, -2) \cup (-1, \infty)$ and $f'(x) < 0$ for $x \in (-2, -1)$
$\Rightarrow f(x)$ is non-monotonic and $f''(x) = 6(2x + 3) = 12x + 18 = 0$
$\Rightarrow x = -3/2$

3. (d) $g(x) = \ell n(h(x));\ x \in J$
$\Rightarrow g'(x) = \dfrac{1}{h(x)}.h'(x)\ ;\ x \in J$
$\Rightarrow g''(x) = \dfrac{h(x)h''(x) - [h'(x)]^2}{(h(x))^2}$
$\because (h'(x))^2 > h''(x)\, h(x)$
$\Rightarrow g''(x) < 0$
$\Rightarrow g(x)$ is concave down on J.

4. (c) $f(x) = \begin{cases} \dfrac{(x-1)(6x-1)}{2x-1} & ; x \neq \dfrac{1}{2} \\ 0 & ; x = \dfrac{1}{2} \end{cases}$ then, $f(x)$ has infinite discontinuity at $x = \dfrac{1}{2}$

$$f'(x) = \begin{cases} \dfrac{(2x-1)(12x-7) - (6x^2 - 7x + 7)(2)}{(2x-1)^2} \text{ for } x \neq \dfrac{1}{2} \end{cases}$$

$$= \begin{cases} \dfrac{24x^2 - 26x + 7 - 12x^2 + 14x - 2}{(2x-1)^2} \text{ for } x \neq \dfrac{1}{2} \end{cases}$$

$$= \begin{cases} \dfrac{12x^2 - 12x + 5}{(2x-1)^2} \text{ for } x \neq \dfrac{1}{2} \end{cases}$$

$\Rightarrow f'(x) > 0\ \forall\ x \neq \dfrac{1}{2}$
$\Rightarrow f(x)$ has no local maxima and local minima point .

$$\Rightarrow f''(x) = \begin{cases} \dfrac{(2x-1)^2(24x-12) - (12x^2 - 12x + 5)(4)(2x-1)}{(2x-1)^4} \text{ for } x \neq \dfrac{1}{2} \end{cases}$$

$$= \begin{cases} \dfrac{96x^3 - 96x^2 - 48x^2 + 24x + 48x - 12 - 96x^3 + 48x^2 + 96x^2 - 40x - 48x + 20}{(2x-1)^4} \text{ for } x \neq \dfrac{1}{2} \end{cases}$$

$$= \dfrac{-16x + 8}{(2x-1)^4} \text{ for } x \neq \dfrac{1}{2}$$

$\Rightarrow f''(x) \neq 0$ on $\mathbb{R} - \left\{\dfrac{1}{2}\right\}$; but $\left\{\dfrac{-8(2x-1)}{(2x-1)^4} \text{ for } x \neq \dfrac{1}{2}\right.$

$$= \begin{cases} \dfrac{-8}{(2x-1)^3} \text{ for } x \neq \dfrac{1}{2} \end{cases}$$

$\Rightarrow f(x)$ has no inflexion point .

5. (d) $F_1(x) = f(x) - g(x)$
$\Rightarrow F_1'(x) = f'(x) - g'(x)$
$\Rightarrow F_1''(x) = f''(x) - g''(x)$
$\therefore f''(x), g''(x) > 0\ \forall\ x \in [-1, 3]$
$f''(x) - g''(x) > 0$ or < 0 at any $x \in [-1, 3]$
Similarly $F_2(x) = f(x) + g(x)$
$\Rightarrow F_2''(x) = f''(x) + g''(x) > 0\ \forall\ x \in [-1, 3]$
$\Rightarrow f(x) + g(x)$ is concave upwards $\forall\ x \in [-1, 3]$
Now $F_3(x) = f(x) \,.\, g(x)$
$\Rightarrow F_3'(x) = f(x) \,.\, g'(x) + g(x) \,.\, f'(x)$
$\Rightarrow F_3''(x) = f(x) \,.\, g''(x) + g'(x) f'(x) + g(x) f''(x) + f'(x).g'(x)$
Then nothing can be said about its concavity and critical points on $[-1, 3]$

6. (c) If $p(x)$ is of degree 5, then $p''(x)$ is of degree = 3
$\Rightarrow p''(x) = 0$ has at most 3 roots .
$\Rightarrow$ At most 3 points of inflexion.

7. (d) $f(x) = (x + 2)^{1/3}$ at $x = -2$
$\Rightarrow f'(x) = \dfrac{1}{3}(x + 2)^{-2/3} > 0\ \forall\ x \neq -2$
$\Rightarrow f''(x) = -\dfrac{2}{9}(x + 2)^{-5/3}$
$\Rightarrow f''(x) = \dfrac{-2}{9(x+2)^{5/3}} > 0$ for $x < -2$ and $f''(x) < 0$ for $x > -2$
$\therefore f(x)$ changes its concavity at $x = -2$

8. (a), (b), (c), (d)
$f'(x) = x^4(12\ \ell n\, x - 7);\ x > 0$
$f'(x) = x^4\left(\dfrac{12}{x}\right) + (12\ \ell n\, x - 7) \,.\, 4x^3$
$= 12x^3 + 4x^3(12\ \ell n\, x - 7)$
$= 48x^3\ \ell n\, x - 16x^3$
$= 16x^3(\ell n x^3 - 1)$
$= 0$ at $x = 0$ or at $x = e^{1/3}$
But $x > 0$
$\Rightarrow x = e^{1/3}$ is a critical point and $f''(x) = 16x^3\left(\dfrac{1}{x^3}(3x^2)\right) + (\ell n x^3 - 1)(48x^2)$
$\Rightarrow f''(x) = 48x^2(\ell n x^3) = 144x^2\ \ell n\, x$
$\Rightarrow f''(x) < 0$ for $x \in (0,1)$,
$f''(x) = 0$ at $x = 1$,
$f''(x) > 0$ for $x \in (1, \infty)$
$\Rightarrow x = e^{1/3}$ is point of minima, point $(1, -7)$ is point of in flexion, the curve is concave downwards on $(0, 1)$ and concave upwards on $(1, \infty)$

9. (c) The above theorem is Rolle's theorem.

10. (c) $f(x) = kx^3 - 9x^2 + 9x + 3$
$\Rightarrow f'(x) = 3kx^2 - 18x + 9$ $f(x)$ is increasing $\forall\ x \in \mathbb{R}$
$\Rightarrow f'(x) \geq \forall\ x \in \mathbb{R}$
$\Rightarrow k > 0$ and $(-18)^2 - 4(3k)(9) \leq 0$
$\Rightarrow 324 - 108k \leq 0$
$\Rightarrow k \geq 3$

11. **(a)** Let $y = f^{-1}(x)$

$\Rightarrow x = f(y) \quad \Rightarrow \quad \frac{dx}{dy} = f'(y)$

$\Rightarrow \frac{dy}{dx} = \frac{1}{f'(y)} < 0$ as $f(x)$ is a decreasing function.

$\Rightarrow f^{-1}(x)$ is a decreasing function and $\frac{d^2y}{dx^2} = \frac{-1}{[f'(y)]^2}$.

$f''(y)\frac{dy}{dx} \geq 0$ as $f(x)$ has its concavity up ($f''(y) \geq 0$)

and $f'(y) \leq 0$

$\Rightarrow \frac{d^2y}{dx^2} \geq 0 \ \forall x \in$ Domain $\Rightarrow f^{-1}(x)$ is concave upwards.

MEAN VALUE THEOREM TEXTUAL EXERCISE–1: (SUBJECTIVE)

1. Let $f'(x) = 4x^3 - 6x^2 + 4x - 1, x \in (0, 1)$

$\Rightarrow f(x) = x^4 - 2x^3 + 2x^2 - x + c$

$\Rightarrow f(0) = c, f(1) = c$

$\therefore$ $f(x)$ satisfies the conditions of applicability of Rolle's theorem in (0, 1)

$\Rightarrow f'(x)$ has at least one root in (0, 1) i.e., $4x^3 - 6x^2 + 4x - 1 = 0$ has at least root in (0, 1).

2. Let if possible $f(x) = \frac{ax^4}{4} + \frac{bx^3}{3} + \frac{cx^2}{2} + dx + e = 0$ has 3 and hence 4 distinct real roots (*say*) α, β, γ, δ.

$\Rightarrow f(\alpha) = f(\beta) = f(\gamma) = f(\delta)$

$\therefore$ By Rolle's theorem, $f'(x) = 0$ has at least one roots in each interval (α, β), (β, γ) and (γ, δ), but $f'(x) = ax^3 + bx^2 + cx + d$

$\therefore$ $ax^3 + bx^2 + cx + d = 0$ has 3 distinct real roots, which is contrary to the given condition that $ax^3 + bx^2 + cx + d = 0$ has exactly one root.

Hence $f(x)$ can't have more than 2 distinct real roots.

3. If $f(x) = ax^4 + bx^3 + cx^2 + dx + k$

$\Rightarrow f'(x) = 4ax^3 + 3bx^2 + 2cx + d$

Let α, β, γ be 3 real and distinct roots of $f(x) = 0$

$\Rightarrow f(\alpha) = f(\beta) = f(\gamma) = 0$

$\therefore$ By Rolle's theorem $f'(x) = 0$, will have at least one root in each of the intervals (α, β) and (β, γ) i.e., $4ax^3 + 3bx^2 + 2cx + d = 0$ has at least 2 real and distinct roots.

4. Let $F(x) = f(x) - g(x)$.

Since $f(x)$, $g(x)$ are differentiable in [a, b]

$\Rightarrow F(x)$ is also differentiable in [a, b], Further $f(a) = g(a)$

$\Rightarrow F(a) = 0$ and $f(b) = g(b)$

$\Rightarrow F(b) = 0$

$\therefore$ $F(a) = F(b)$

$\Rightarrow$ By Rolle's theorem

$f'(c) = 0$ for at least some $c \in (a, b)$ i.e., $f'(c) = g'(c)$ for some $c \in (a, b)$.

The statement will remain true if $f(a) = f(b)$ and $g(a) = g(b)$ as in this case too we get $F(a) = F(b)$.

5. Let $F(x) = 2f(x) - 5g(x)$

$F(0) = 2f(0) - 5g(0)$

$= 2(5) - 5(1) = 5$ and $F(1) = 2f(1) - 5g(1) = 2(10) - 5(3) = 5$

$\therefore$ $F(0) = F(1)$

$\Rightarrow$ By Rolle's theorem $\exists\ c \in (0, 1)$ s.t. $F'(c) = 0$

$\Rightarrow 2f'(c) = 5g'(c)$ for some $c \in (0, 1)$

6. Since $f(x_1) = f(x_2) = f(x_3) = 0$

$\Rightarrow$ By Rolle's theorem, $\exists\, c_1 \in (x_1, x_2)$ and $c_2 \in (x_2, x_3)$ such that $f'(c_1) = 0$ and $f'(c_2) = 0$.

Again $f(x)$ is differentiable twice

$\Rightarrow \exists\ c \in (c_1, c_2)$ such that $f''(c) = 0$ i.e., $f''(c) = 0$ for $x_1 < c_1 < c < c_2 < x_3$ i.e., $f''(c) = 0$ for $x_1 < c < x_3$

7. Let $g(x) = \frac{\sqrt{x}}{2\sqrt{x}}$; $x \in (a, b)$, then $\exists\ c \in (a, b)$ s.t.

$$\frac{f'(c)}{g'(c)} = \frac{f(b) - f(a)}{g(b) - g(a)} = \frac{f(b) - f(a)}{\sqrt{b} - \sqrt{a}}$$

$\Rightarrow 2\sqrt{c}\, f'(c) = \frac{f(b) - f(a)}{\sqrt{b} - \sqrt{a}}$ for some $c \in (a, b)$

8. Let $f(x) = e^{-x} - \cos x$ has two consecutive roots α, β

Clearly it is root continuous and differentiable function $\forall x \in \mathbb{R}$

Thus in [α, β], so by rolls theorem

∃ Atleast one root $\gamma \in (\alpha, \beta)$ where $f'(\gamma) = 0$

$\Rightarrow (\sin x - e^{-x})$ at $x = \gamma = 0$

$\Rightarrow e^{-\gamma} - \sin\gamma = 0$ i.e., $1 = e^{\gamma}\sin\gamma$

$\therefore$ $e^{x}\sin x - 1 = 0$ has atleast one root $\gamma \in (\alpha, \beta)$)

9. **(a)** $f(x) = |9 - x^2|$; $x \in [-3, 3]$

Clearly $f(-3) = f(3) = 0$;

$f(x)$ is continuous on [–3, 3] and $f(x) = \{9 - x^2$ for $x \in [-3, 3]$

$\Rightarrow f'(x) = -2x$ for $x \in (-3, 3)$

$\Rightarrow f(x)$ is differentiable in (–3, 3)

$\Rightarrow$ Rolle's theorem is applicable.

Put $f'(c) = 0$

$\Rightarrow -2c = 0 \quad \Rightarrow c = 0$

$\therefore$ $f'(0) = 0$ and $0 \in (-3, 3)$

$\Rightarrow$ Rolle's theorem is satisfied

(b) $f(x) = \ell n\{(x^2 + ab)/[(a + b)x]\}$; $x \in [a, b]$; $ab > 0$

$f(a) = \ell n\left\{\frac{a^2 + ab}{a^2 + ab}\right\} = \ell n\ 1 = 0$ and $f(b) = \ell n\left\{\frac{b^2 + ab}{ab + b^2}\right\} = \ell n 1 = 0$

Also for $x \in [a, b]$; $ab > 0$,

$g(x) = \frac{x^2 + ab}{(a+b)x}$ is continuous

$\Rightarrow \ell n\{g(x)\}$ is also continuous in [a, b] and $f'(x)$

$$= \frac{(a+b)x}{(x^2+ab)} \cdot \left[\frac{(a+b)x(2x) - (x^2+ab)(a+b)}{((a+b)x)^2}\right]$$

$$= \frac{(a+b)x}{(x^2+ab)} \cdot \left[\frac{ax^2 + bx^2 - a^2b - ab^2}{(a+b)^2 x^2}\right]$$

$$= \frac{\left[a(x^2 - ab) + b(x^2 - ab)\right]}{(a+b)x(x^2+ab)}$$

$$= \frac{(a+b)(x^2-ab)}{(a+b)x(x^2+ab)} = \frac{x^2-ab}{x(x^2+ab)} \text{ which exists } \forall\, x$$

$\in (a, b)$

$\Rightarrow$ $f(x)$ satisfies the conditions of Rolle's theorem.

(c) $f(x) = x^3 - 3x^2 + 2x$; $x \in [0, 2]$

$\Rightarrow$ $f(0) = f(2) = 0$ and $f(x)$ being a polynomial function is continuous on [0, 2] and differentiable on(0, 2)

$\Rightarrow$ $f(x)$ satisfies Rolle's conditions.

(d) $f(x) = e^x(\sin x - \cos x)$; $x \in \left[\frac{\pi}{4}, \frac{5\pi}{4}\right]$

$\Rightarrow$ $f(x)$ being a product of two continuous functions is also continuous on $\left[\frac{\pi}{4}, \frac{5\pi}{4}\right]$

Also, $f'(x) = e^x(\cos x + \sin x) + e^x(\sin x - \cos x) = 2ex \sin x$

Which exists $\forall\, x \in \left(\frac{\pi}{4}, \frac{5\pi}{4}\right)$

Also $f\left(\frac{\pi}{4}\right) = e^{\pi/4}\left(\sin\frac{\pi}{4} - \cos\frac{\pi}{4}\right) = 0$ and

$$f\left(\frac{5\pi}{4}\right) = e^{5\pi/4}\left(\sin\frac{5\pi}{4} - \cos\frac{5\pi}{4}\right) = e^{5\pi/4}\left[\frac{-1}{\sqrt{2}} + \frac{1}{\sqrt{2}}\right] = 0$$

$\therefore$ All the conditions of Rolle's theorem are satisfied.

(e) $f(x) = (x - a)^m (x - b)^n$; $x \in [a, b]$

$f(x)$ being a polynomial function, is continuous on $[a, b]$.

Also $f'(x) = n(x - a)^m (x - b)^{n-1} + m(x - a)^{m-1} (x - b)^n$ which is continuous and hence $f(x)$ is derivate $\forall\, x \in (a, b)$.

Also, $f(a) = f(b) = 0$

$\Rightarrow$ Conditions of Rolle's Theorem are satisfied.

10. $f(x) = x^4 - 2x^3 + 2x^2 - x$

$f(0) = 0$ and $f(1) = 0$

$\therefore$ By Rolle's Theorem, $f'(x) = 0$ has at least one root in (0, 1) i.e., $4x^3 - 6x^2 + 4x - 1 = 0$ has at least one root in (0, 1) say α,

$\Rightarrow$ $0 < \alpha < 1$.

Let $g(x) = 4x^3 - 6x^2 + 4x - 1 = 0$ has another root β such that $1 < \beta < 2$ as 1 and 2 are not roots of $4x^3 - 6x^2 + 4x - 1 = 0$ (*verify*)

$\therefore$ $g(\alpha) = g(\beta) = 0$

$\Rightarrow$ $g'(x) = 0$ has a root in (α, β) (*By* Rolle's theore*m*)

$\Rightarrow$ $12x^2 - 12x + 4 = 0$ has a root in (α, β)

$\Rightarrow$ $3x^2 - 3x + 1 = 0$ has a root in (α, β) but $3x^2 - 3x + 1 = 0$ has no real root

($\because$ Disc. $= 9 - 12 = -3 < 0$)

$\therefore$ $4x^3 - 6x^2 + 4x - 1 = 0$ has exactly one root in (0, 2)

11. $f(x) = C_0x + C_1\frac{x^2}{2} + C_2\frac{x^3}{3} + C_3\frac{x^4}{4} + \ldots\ldots + C_n\frac{x^{n+1}}{n+1}$, then $f(0)$ $= 0$ and $f(1) = C_0 + \frac{C_1}{2} + \frac{C_2}{3} + \ldots + \frac{C_n}{n+1} = 0$ (Given)

$\therefore$ By Rolle's Theorem $f'(x) = 0$ has a root in (0, 1)

$\Rightarrow$ $C_0 + C_1 + C_2x^2 + C_3x^3 + \ldots C_nx^n = 0$ has a root in (0, 1).

12. $f(x)$ being a polynomial of odd degree ha sat least one root .

Let $f(x) = (x - a)^3 + (x - b)^3 + (x - c)^3 + (x - d)^3 = 0$

$\Rightarrow$ Let if possible $f(x)$ has 2 real root α and β

$\Rightarrow$ $f(\alpha) = f(\beta) = 0$

$\Rightarrow$ $f'(x)$ = has at least one root in (α, β) i.e., $3[(x - a)^2 + (x - b)^2 + (x - c)^2 + (x - d)^2] = 0$ has at least one root in (α, β).

But above is true when $x = a = b = c = d$ which is false as a, b, c, d are not all equal.

$\therefore$ Our supposition was wrong and hence $f(x) = 0$ has only real root.

13. $f(x) = 3x^5 + 15x - 8 = 0$

$f(x) = 0$ is a polynomial equation of odd degree, hence has at least one real root.

Let α, β be two roots of $f(x) = 0$

$\Rightarrow$ $f(\alpha) = f(\beta) = 0$

$\therefore$ By Rolle's theorem $f'(x) = 0$ has at least one real root in (α, β).

$\Rightarrow$ $15x^4 + 15 = 0$ has a real root in (α, β) , which is false as $x^4 + 1 = 0$ has no real root.

14. Let $f(x) = x^3 - 6x^2 + 9x - 2$

$f(x)$ being a polynomial equation of odd degree has at least one root .

Let if possible $f(x)$ has 2 real roots α and β

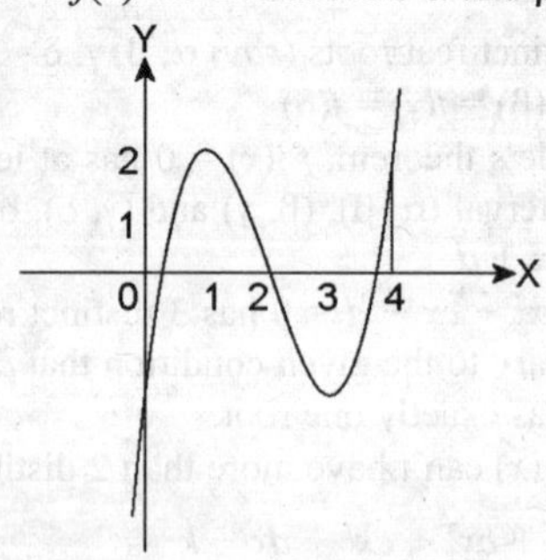

$\Rightarrow$ $f(\alpha) = f(\beta) = 0$

$\therefore$ By Rolle's theorem $f'(x) = 0$ has at least one root in (α, β) i.e., $3x^2 - 12x + 0 = 0$ and hence $x^2 - 4x + 3 = 0$ has a root in (α, β)

But $x = 1$ and $x = 3$ are its two roots

$\Rightarrow$ $f(x) = 0$ has one root $x = 2$, and two real roots each one in(0, 1) and other in (3, 4)

15. $\phi(x) = f(x) + (b - x)f'(x) + A(b - x)^2$; where A is constant so that $\phi(b) = \phi(a)$

$\Rightarrow$ $f(b) = f(a) + (b - a)f'(a) + A(b - a)^2$

$$\Rightarrow \frac{f(b) - f(a) - (b-a)f'(a)}{(b \quad a)}$$

$\Rightarrow$ By Rolle's Theorem, $\phi'(c) = 0$ for some $c \in (a, b)$ i.e.,

$\phi'(c) = f(c) + (b - c)f'(c) + A(b - c)^2 = 0$

$\Rightarrow$ $f(c) + (b - c)f'(c) + A(b - c)^2 = 0$

$\Rightarrow$ $f'(c) + (b - c)f''(c) - f'(c) - 2A(b - c) = 0$

$\Rightarrow$ $(b - c)f''(c) - 2A(b - c) = 0$

$$\Rightarrow \frac{f(b) - f(a) - (b-a)f'(a)}{(b-a)^2} = \frac{f''(c)}{2}$$

$\Rightarrow$ $f(b) = f(a) + (a-b)f'(a) + \dfrac{f''(c)}{2}(b-a)^2$ for some $c \in (a, b)$

TEXTUAL EXERCISE–1: (OBJECTIVE)

1. (b) $f(x) = |x|;\ x \in [-2, 2]$

$f(x)$ is continuous on $[-2, 2]$ and $f(-2) = f(2) = 2$

But not differentiable at $x = 0 \in (-2, 2)$

Hence Rolle's Theorem is not applicable in $[-2, 2]$

2. (d) $f(x) = x^a \log x;\ f(0) = 0;\ x \in [0, 1]$

$f(0) = 0 = f(1)$

Clearly $f(x)$ is continuous $\forall\ a > 0$ and $x \in (0, 1]$ except possibility at $x = 0$.

For $a > 0$:

Now $\lim\limits_{x\to 0^+} f(x) = \lim\limits_{x\to 0^+} x^a \log x = \lim\limits_{\to} \dfrac{\log}{} ....\left(\dfrac{\infty}{\infty}\text{ form}\right)$

$= \lim\limits_{x\to 0^+} \dfrac{\frac{1}{x}}{-ax^{-a-1}} = \lim\limits_{x\to 0^+}\left(\dfrac{x^a}{-a}\right) = 0 = f(0) = 0$

$\therefore$ $f(x)$ is continuous for $\forall\ a > 0$ and $x \in [0, 1]$.

For $a = 0$:

$f(x) = \log x$

$\lim\limits_{x\to 0^+} f(x) = -\infty,\ f(0) = 0$

$\Rightarrow$ $f(x)$ is discontinuous at $x = 0$ for $a = 0$ and hence Rolle's Theorem is not applicable.

For $a < 0$:

$f(x) = \left(\dfrac{\log x}{x^{-a}}\right);\ x \in (0, 1)$ which is continuous except possible at $x = 0$

$\lim\limits_{x\to 0^+} f(x) = \lim\limits_{x\to 0^+} \dfrac{\log x}{x^{-a}} = -\infty \times \infty = -\infty \neq f(0)$

$\therefore$ Rolle's Theorem is not applicable for $a \leq 0$ and hence can be applicable for $a > 0$

Now $f(x) = x^a \log x;\ a > 0$

$\Rightarrow$ $f'(x) = x^a.\dfrac{1}{x} + \log x\left(x^a\right)$

$\Rightarrow$ $f'(x) = x^{a-1} + x^a \log x$ which exists $\forall\ x \in (0, 1)$ as $f'(x)$ is a continuous function for $x \in (0, 1)$

$\Rightarrow$ Roll's theorem can be applied for $a > 0$ i.e., at $a = \dfrac{1}{2}$, not for $a = -2, -1, 0$

3. (c) $f(x) = x^3 + bx^2 + ax + 5;\ x \in [1, 3]$

$c = \left(2 + \dfrac{1}{\sqrt{3}}\right)$, $(a, b) =?$ and $f(1) = f(3)$

$\Rightarrow$ $1 + b + a + 5 = 27 + 9b + 3a + 5$

$\Rightarrow$ $a + b + 1 = 3a + 9b + 27$

$\Rightarrow$ $2a + 8b = -26$

$\Rightarrow$ $a + 4b = -13$ ...(1)

Now $f'(x) = 3x^2 + 2bx + a$

$f'(c) = 0$

$\Rightarrow$ $3c^2 + 2bc + a = 0$ ...(2)

$\because$ $c = 2 + \dfrac{1}{\sqrt{3}}$ is a root of equation (2)

$\Rightarrow$ $c = 2 - \dfrac{1}{\sqrt{3}}$ is also a root of equation (2)

$\Rightarrow$ $\dfrac{-2b}{3} = 4;\ 4 - \dfrac{1}{3} = \dfrac{a}{3}$

$\Rightarrow$ $a = 11,\ b = -6$

$\Rightarrow$ $(a, b) = (11, -6)$

4. (d)

(*a*) $f(x) = \tan x$ is discontinuous in $[0, \pi]$, having discontinuity at $\pi/2$

$\Rightarrow$ $f(x) = \tan x$ can't be so.

(*b*) Next, $f(x) = \cos(1/x);\ x \in [-1, 1]$

$f(x)$ has discontinuity (*oscillating at* $x = 0$,

(*c*) $f(x) = x^2$ in $[2, 3]$

$f(2) = 4 \neq f(3) = 9$

(*d*) $f(x) = x(x + 3)\, e^{-x/2}$ in $[-3, 0]$

$f(-3) = f(0) = 0$,

$f(x)$ is continuous $\forall\ x \in [-3, 0]$,

Also $f(x)$ is differentiable $\forall\ x \in (-3, 0)$.

Hence Rolle's theorem is applicable

5. (d) $f(x) = \sin x;\ x \in [0, \pi]$

$f(0) = f(\pi) = 0$,

Also $f(x) = \sin x$ is continuous on $[0, \pi]$ and differentiable on $(0, \pi)$

$\Rightarrow$ $f'(c) = \cos c = 0$

$\Rightarrow$ $c = \pi/2$ in $[0, \pi]$

6. (a), (b) $f(x) = x^3 + 3x - 10$

$f'(x) = 3x^2 + 3 \neq 0$ for any $x \in \mathbb{R}$

Also $f'(x) > 0\ \forall\ x \in \mathbb{R}$ and $f(x)$ being polynomial of odd degree has exactly one root (*real*)

7. (a)

(*a*) $f(x) = \log\left(\dfrac{x^2 + ab}{(a+b)x}\right);\ x \in [a, b];\ (a < a < b)$

$f(a) = \log\left(a\dfrac{(a+b)}{(a+b)}\right) = \log 1 = 0;\ f(b) = \log\left(\dfrac{(b^2 + ab)}{(a+b)b}\right)$

$= \log 1 = 0$

$f'(x) = \dfrac{(a+b)x}{(x^2 + ab)}\left\{\dfrac{(a+b)x(2x) - (x^2 + ab)(a+b)}{[(a+b)x]^2}\right\}$

$= \dfrac{[(a+b)x^2 - (ab)(a+b)]}{(a+b)x.(x^2 + ab)}$

$= \dfrac{x^2 - ab}{x(x^2 + ab)}$ which exist $\forall\ x \in (a, b)$; where $0 < a < b$.

Also $f(x)$ being composition of two continuous function on $[a, b]$; $0 < a < b$ is also continuous on $[a, b]$

$\Rightarrow$ Rolle's Theorem is applicable to $f(x)$

(*b*) $f(x) = (x - 1)(2x - 3);\ x \in (1, 3)$.

$f(1) = 0,\ f(3) = (2)(3) = 6$

∴ $f(1) \neq f(3)$

⇒ Rolle's Theorem is not applicable.

(*c*) $f(x) = 2 + (x-1)^{2/3}$ in [0, 2],

$f(0) = 2 + 1 = 3, f(2) = 3$

Also $f(x)$ is continuous on [0, 2] and $f'(x) = \frac{2}{3}\cdot\frac{1}{(x-1)^{1/3}}$

which does not exist at $x = 1$.

⇒ Rolle's Theorem is not applicable.

(*d*) $f(x) = \cos(1/x)$; $x \in [-1, 1]$

∵ $f(x)$ has oscillating discontinuity at $x = 0$

⇒ Rolle's Theorem is not applicable.

8. **(b)** Let $f(x) = ax^3 + bx^2 + cx$

⇒ $f(0) = f(1) = a + b + c = 0$

∴ By Rolle's Theorem, $f'(\alpha) = 0$ for at least one $\alpha \in (0, 1)$

⇒ $3ax^2 + 2bx + c = 0$ has at least one root in (0, 1).

9. **(a)** Let $f(x) = x^4 - x^3 - x + 1$

Clearly $x = 1$ is a root of $f(x) = 0$

Also $f'(x) = 4x^3 - 3x^2 - 1$

⇒ $x = 1$ is a root of $f'(x) = 0$ and $f''(x) = 12x^2 - 6x$

⇒ $x = 1$ is a twice root of $f(x) = 0$

10. **(b)** Let $f(x) = x^3 + 2ax^2 + bx$

⇒ $f'(x) = 3x^2 + 4ax + b$

⇒ $f(0), f(1) = 1 + 2a + b$

∴ $f'(x) = 0$ i.e., $3x^2 + 4ax + b = 0$ has at least one root in (0, 1) if $2a + b + 1 = 0$

11. **(a)** $f(x) = (x-1)(x-2)(x-3)(x-4)$,

$f(1) = f(2) = f(3) = f(4) = 0$

⇒ $f'(x) = 0$ has a root $\alpha \in (1, 2)$, $\beta \in (2, 3)$ and $\gamma \in (3, 4)$ i.e., all three positive roots

12. **(c)** $f(x) = x^3 - 6x^2 + ax + b$; $x \in [1, 3]$.

$f(1) = f(3)$

⇒ $1 - 6 + a + b = 27 - 54 + 3a + b$

⇒ $a + b - 5 = 3a + b - 27$

⇒ $2a = 22$

⇒ $a = 11$

$f'(x) = 3x^2 - 12x + a$

$f'(x) = 3x^2 - 12x + 11 = 0$

$$\Rightarrow x = \frac{12 \pm \sqrt{144-132}}{6}$$

$$\Rightarrow x = \frac{12 \pm \sqrt{12}}{6}$$

$$\Rightarrow x = \frac{12 \pm 2\sqrt{3}}{6} = \frac{4\times\sqrt{3}\times\sqrt{3} \pm 2\sqrt{3}}{2\sqrt{3}\sqrt{3}}$$

$$\Rightarrow x = \frac{2\sqrt{3} \pm 1}{\sqrt{3}}$$

$$\therefore c = \frac{2\sqrt{3}+1}{\sqrt{3}} \in \left(1, \sqrt{3}\right)$$

∴ Rolle's Theorem holds for $a = 11$, $b \in \mathbb{R}$ and $c = \frac{2\sqrt{3}+1}{\sqrt{3}}$

13. **(d)** Let $f'(x) = a_0 x^n + a_1 x^{n-1} + \ldots\ldots a_n$ and $f(x) = \frac{a_0 x^{n+1}}{n+1} + \frac{a_1 x^n}{n} + \ldots\ldots + a_n(-x)$

$$\Rightarrow f(0) = 0 \text{ and } f(1) = \frac{a_0}{n+1} + \frac{a_1}{n} + \ldots + \frac{a_{n-1}}{2} + a_n$$

∴ $f'(x) = 0$ will have at least one root in (0, 1) if $f(1) = 0$

i.e., $\frac{a_0}{n+1} + \frac{a_1}{n} + \ldots + \frac{a_{n-1}}{2} + a_n = 0$

14. **(c)** Let $f(x) = \frac{x^4}{4} - \frac{3x^2}{2} + ax$

$f(0) = 0, f(1) = \frac{1}{4} - \frac{3}{2} + a$

∴ $f'(x) =$ has at least one root in (0, 1)

if $f(1) = 0$ i.e., $a = \frac{3}{2} - \frac{1}{4} = \frac{5}{4}$ i.e., $x^3 - 3x + a = 0$ has at least one root (0, 1) for $a = \frac{5}{4}$

Let α be that root in (0, 1)

If β is any other root in (0, 1) i.e., $f'(\alpha) = f'(\beta) = 0$; $\alpha, \beta \in (0, 1)$

⇒ $f''(x) = 0$ has a root in (α, β) i.e., $3x^2 - 3 = 0$ has a root in (α, β)

⇒ $x^2 - 1 = 0$ has a root in (α, β)

But its roots are $\pm 1 \notin (\alpha, \beta)$

∴ $x^3 - 3x + a = 0$ can't have two distinct real roots for any real 'a'.

15. **(b)** Let $f'(x) = x^n - a$; $x \in (0, 1)$ and let $f(x) = \frac{x^{n+1}}{(n+1)} - ax$

$$\Rightarrow f(0) = 0, f(1) = \frac{1}{n+1} - a$$

∴ $f'(x) = 0$ i.e., $x^n - a = 0$ has at least one root in (0, 1) if $a = \frac{1}{(n+1)}$.

Let if possible α, β ($\alpha < \beta$) be two roots in (0, 1) i.e., $f'(\alpha) = f'(\beta) = 0$

⇒ $f''(x) = 0$ has a root in (α, β) i.e., $nx^{n-1} = 0$ has a root in $(\alpha, \beta) \subset (0, 1)$

But its real root is $0 \notin (0, 1)$

∴ $f'(x) = 0$ can't have 3 real roots i.e., $x^n - a = 0$ has at most 1 root in (0, 1)

16. **(a)** Let $f(x) = \frac{x^5}{5} + \frac{2x^3}{3} - 2x$

⇒ $f'(x) = x^4 - 2x^2 - 2$

Now, $f'(0) = -2, f'(1) = 1$

⇒ $f'(x) = 0$ has a root in (0,1).

Let if possible $f'(x) = 0$ has two roots α, β in(0, 1) ; $\alpha < \beta$

⇒ $f'(\alpha) = f'(\beta) = 0$, $(\alpha, \beta) \subset (0, 1)$

∴ By Rolle's theorem, $f''(x) = 0$ has a root in $(\alpha, \beta) \subset (0, 1)$ i.e., $4x^3 + 4x = 0$ has a root in (α, β)

⇒ $x(x^2 + 1) = 0$ has a root in $(\alpha, \beta) \subset (0, 1)$, which is impossible

⇒ $f'(x) = 0$ has Exactly one root in (0, 1)

17. (d)

(*a*) $f(x) = |x|; -2 \le x \le 2$

$\because$ $f(x)$ is non-differentiable at $x = 0 \in (-2, 2)$. Rolle's theorem is not applicable.

(*b*) $f(x) = \tan x; 0 \le x \le \pi$,

$\because$ $f(x)$ is discontinuous at $x = \pi/2 \in [0, \pi]$. Rolle's theorem is not applicable.

(*c*) $f(x) = 1 + (x - 2)^{2/3}; 1 \le x \le 3$

$f(1) = f(3) = 2$,

$f(2^-) = 1 = f(2^+) = f(2)$

$\Rightarrow$ $f(x)$ is continuous in [1, 3]

$$f'(2^-) = \lim_{h\to 0^+}\frac{f(2-h)-f(2)}{-h} = \lim_{h\to 0^+}\frac{\left[1+(-h)^{2/3}\right]-[1]}{(-h)}$$

$$= \lim_{h\to 0^+}(-h)^{-1/3} = -\infty;$$

$$f'(2^+) = \lim_{h\to 0^+}\frac{f(2+h)-f(2)}{h}$$

$$= \lim_{h\to 0^+}\frac{1+(h)^{2/3}-1}{h} = \lim_{h\to 0^+}\frac{1}{(h)^{1/3}} = \infty$$

$\Rightarrow$ $f(x)$ is not differentiable at $x = 2 \in (1, 3)$, hence Rolle's Theorem is not applicable .

(*d*) $f(x) = x(x - 2)^2$

$\because$ $f(0) = f(2) = 0$, $f(x)$ being a polynomial function is continuous in [0, 2] and differentiable in (0, 2), hence Rolle's theorem is applicable .

18. (b)

(*a*) $f(-1) \ne f(1)$

(*b*) $f(-1) = f(1) = 1$ and $f(x) = x^2$ being polynomial function is continuous and differentiable and hence Rolle's theorem is applicable .

(*c*) $f(-1) = 1, f(1) = 5$

$\Rightarrow$ $f(-1) \ne f(1)$

(*d*) $f(x) = |x|$; which is not differentiable at $x = 0 \in (-1, 1)$

19. (c) $f(x) = ax^3 + bx^2 + 11x - 6$ satisfies conditions of Rolle's theorem in [1, 3]

$\Rightarrow$ $a + b + 11 - 6 = 27a + 9b + 33 - 6$

$\Rightarrow$ $26a + 8b + 22 = 0$

$\Rightarrow$ $13a + 4b + 11 = 0$ ...(1)

$\Rightarrow$ $f'(x) = 3ax^2 + 2bx + 11$

$$\therefore\ f'\left(2+\frac{1}{\sqrt{3}}\right) = 0$$

$$\Rightarrow\ \left(2+\frac{1}{\sqrt{3}}\right)+\left(2-\frac{1}{\sqrt{3}}\right)=\frac{-2b}{3a} \text{ and}$$

$$\left(2+\frac{1}{\sqrt{3}}\right)\left(2-\frac{1}{\sqrt{3}}\right)=\frac{11}{3a}$$

$\Rightarrow$ $12a = -2b$

$$\Rightarrow\ b = -6a \text{ and } \left(4-\frac{1}{3}\right)=\frac{11}{3a} \Rightarrow a = 1 \text{ and } b = -6$$

TEXTUAL EXERCISE-2: (SUBJECTIVE)

1. Let $f(x) = \cos x; x \in [a, b]$

$\therefore$ By L.M.V.T, $f'(x) = -\sin x = \dfrac{\cos b - \cos a}{b-a}$

For some $x \in (a, b)$

$$\Rightarrow\ \left|\frac{\cos b - \cos a}{b-a}\right| \le 1$$

$\Rightarrow$ $|\cos b - \cos a| \le |b - a|$ or $|\cos a - \cos b| \le |a - b|$

2. Let $f(x) = x^3; x \in [a, b]$

$\therefore$ By L.M.V.T, $\exists\ c \in (a, b)$ such that, $3c^2 = \dfrac{f(b)-f(a)}{b-a}$

i.e., $3c^2 = \dfrac{b^3-a^3}{b-a}$ or $3c^2 = b^2 + ab + a^2$

3. Let $f(x) = \tan x - x; x \in [0, c]; c < \dfrac{\pi}{2}$

$\therefore$ By L.M.V.T, $f'(k) = \dfrac{f(c)-f(0)}{c-0}$ for some $k \in (0, c)$

$$\Rightarrow\ \sec^2 k - 1 = \frac{\tan c - c - 0}{c}$$

$\Rightarrow$ $(\tan c - c) = c(\sec^2 k - 1) \ge 0$

$\Rightarrow$ $\tan c - c \ge c\ \forall\ 0 < c < \pi/2$

$\Rightarrow$ $\tan x \ge 2x \ge x\ \forall\ 0 < x < \pi/2$

$\Rightarrow$ $\tan x \ge x\ \forall\ 0 \le x < \pi/2$

Hence $\tan x \ge x\ \forall\ x \in [0, \pi/2)$.

4. $a, b, c \in \mathbb{R}$ such that $a < b < c$,

$f(x)$ is continuous in [a, c] and differentiable in (a, c).

$f'(x)$ is strictly monotonic (a, c).

By L.M.V.T, $\exists\ c_1 \in (a, b)$ and $c_2 \in (b, c)$ such that $f'(c_1)$

$$= \frac{f(b)-f(a)}{b-a} \text{ and } f'(c_2) = \frac{f(c)-f(b)}{c-b}$$

Since $f'(x)$ is strictly increasing and $c_1 < c_2$

$\Rightarrow$ $f'(c_1) < f'(c_2)$

$$\Rightarrow\ \frac{f(b)-f(a)}{b-a} < \frac{f(c)-f(b)}{(c-b)}$$

$\Rightarrow$ $(c - b)(f(b)) + (b - c) f(a) < (b - a)(f(c)) - (b - a) f(b)$

$\Rightarrow$ $(-b + c + b - a) f(b) + (b - c) f(a) + (a - b) f(c) < 0$

$\Rightarrow$ $(b - c) f(a) + (c - a) f(b) + (a - b) f(c) < 0$

5. (i) $\phi(x) = f(x) - f(a) - \dfrac{(x-a)}{(b-a)} \times [f(b) - f(a)]$ ...(*i*)

$\phi(a) = f(a) - f(a) = 0$ and $\phi(b) = [f(b) - f(a)] - [f(b) - f(a)] = 0$

$\therefore$ By Rolle's theorem, $\exists\ c \in (a, b)$ such that $\phi'(c) = 0$ i.e.,

$$f'(c) - \frac{(1)}{(b-a)}[f(b) - f(a)] = 0$$

$\Rightarrow$ $f'(c) = \dfrac{f(b)-f(a)}{(b-a)}$ which is the result of L.M.V.T

(ii) $F(x) = f(x) + Ax$; such that $F(a) = F(b)$ and A = constant

$\Rightarrow$ $f(a) + Aa = f(b) + ab$

$$\Rightarrow\ A = \frac{f(b)-f(a)}{a-b}$$

$\therefore\ F(x) = f(x) + \dfrac{f(b)-f(a)}{a-b}.x$

$\therefore$ By Rolle's Theorem $\exists\, c \in (a, b)$ such that $F'(c) = 0$ i.e.,

$f'(c) + \dfrac{f(b)-f(a)}{a-b} = 0$

i.e., $f'(c) = \dfrac{f(b)-f(a)}{(b-a)}$, which is the result of L.M.V.T.

(iii) Let $F(x) = f(x) - f(a) + A(x - a)$, where A = constant such that $F(a) = F(b)$

$\Rightarrow f(a) - f(a) + A(a - a) = f(b) - f(a) + A(b - a)$

$\Rightarrow A = \dfrac{f(b)-f(a)}{(a-b)}$

$\therefore\ F(x) = f(x) - f(a) + \dfrac{(f(b)-f(a))}{(a-b)}(x-a)$

$\therefore$ By Rolle's theorem, $\exists\, c \in (a, b)$ such that $F'(c) = 0$

$\Rightarrow f'(c) + \dfrac{[f(b)-f(a)]}{(a-b)} = 0$

$\Rightarrow f'(c) = \dfrac{f(b)-f(a)}{b-a}$, which is the result of L.M.V.T

6. (a) $f(x) = \log_e x$ in $[1, e]$

By L.M.V.T; $f'(c) = \dfrac{f(b)-f(a)}{b-a}$ i.e., $\dfrac{1}{c} = \dfrac{1-0}{e-1}$ for $c \in [1, e)$

$\Rightarrow c = e - 1$

(b) $f(x) = x^3$; $x \in [a, b]$

By L.M.V.T, $3c^2 = \dfrac{b^3-a^3}{b-a}$

$\Rightarrow 3c^2 = b^2 + ab + a^2$

$\Rightarrow c = \pm\sqrt{\dfrac{b^2+ab+a^2}{3}}$

$\therefore\ c = \sqrt{\dfrac{b^2+ab+a^2}{3}}$ for $a \geq 0$ and $c = -\sqrt{\dfrac{b^2+ab+a^2}{3}}$

for $b \leq 0$ and $c = \pm\sqrt{\dfrac{b^2+ab+b^2}{3}}$ for $a < 0$ and $b > 0$

(c) $f(x) = x + \dfrac{1}{x}; x \in \left[\dfrac{1}{2}, 2\right]$

$f'(x) = 1 - \dfrac{1}{x^2}$,

By L.M.V.T, $1 - \dfrac{1}{c^2} = \dfrac{\left(2+\frac{1}{2}\right)-\left(\frac{1}{2}+2\right)}{\left(2-\frac{1}{2}\right)}$

$\Rightarrow 1 - \dfrac{1}{c^2} = 0$

$\Rightarrow c^2 = 1$

$\Rightarrow c = \pm 1$

$\therefore\ c = 1 \in \left(\dfrac{1}{2}, 2\right)$

7. (a) Let $f(x) = \sin x$; $x \in [a, b]$

$\therefore$ By L.H.V.T, $f'(c) = \dfrac{f(b)-f(a)}{b-a}$ for some $c \in (a, b)$

$\Rightarrow \cos c = \dfrac{\sin b - \sin a}{b-a}$

$\Rightarrow \left|\dfrac{\sin b - \sin a}{b-a}\right| = |\cos c| \leq 1$

$\Rightarrow |\sin b - \sin a| \leq |b - a|$

$\Rightarrow |\sin x - \sin y| \leq |x - y|\ \forall\, x\, y \in \mathbb{R}$

(b) Let $f(x) = \tan^{-1} x$; $x \in [\alpha, \beta]$; $\alpha > 0$; $\beta > 0$

$\therefore$ By L.M.V.T, $\dfrac{1}{1+c^2} = \dfrac{\tan^{-1}(\beta)-\tan^{-1}(\alpha)}{\beta-\alpha}$ for $c \in (\alpha, \beta)$

But $\dfrac{1}{1+x^2}$ is a decreasing function on $\mathbb{R}^+$ hence $\alpha < c < \beta$

$\Rightarrow \dfrac{1}{1+\beta^2} < \dfrac{1}{1+c^2} = \dfrac{\tan^{-1}\beta-\tan^{-1}\alpha}{\beta-\alpha} < \dfrac{1}{1+\alpha^2}$

$\Rightarrow \dfrac{\beta-\alpha}{1+\beta^2} < \left(\tan^{-1}\beta-\tan^{-1}\alpha\right) < \dfrac{\beta-\alpha}{1+\alpha^2}$

(c) Let $f(x) = \tan x$; $x \in [a, b]$; $a > 0$, $b < \dfrac{\pi}{2}$

By L.M.V.T, $\sec^2 x = \dfrac{\tan b - \tan a}{(b-a)}$ for some $c \in (a, b)$

$\because\ \sec^2 x$ is an increasing function on $\left[0, \dfrac{\pi}{2}\right)$ i.e., also in (a, b)

$\Rightarrow \sec^2 a < \sec^2 c < \sec^2 b$

$\Rightarrow \sec^2 a < \dfrac{\tan b - \tan a}{b-a} < \sec^2 b$

$\Rightarrow (b - a)\sec^2 a < \tan b - \tan a < (b - a)\sec 2b$; where $0 < a < b < \pi/2$

8. Let $F(x) = \begin{vmatrix} f(x) & g(x) & h(x) \\ f(a) & g(a) & h(a) \\ f(b) & g(b) & h(b) \end{vmatrix}$; $x \in [a, b]$

$\therefore$ By L.M.V.T, $F'(c) = \begin{vmatrix} f'(c) & g'(c) & h'(c) \\ f(a) & g(a) & h(a) \\ f(b) & g(b) & h(b) \end{vmatrix}$

$= \dfrac{F(b)-F(a)}{b-a} = \dfrac{0-0}{b-a} = 0$

$\Rightarrow \begin{vmatrix} f'(c) & g'(c) & h'(c) \\ f(a) & g(a) & h(a) \\ f(b) & g(b) & h(b) \end{vmatrix} = 0$

9. $f(x) = [x^4(x - 1)]^{1/5}$; $x \in \left[\dfrac{-1}{2}, \dfrac{1}{2}\right]$

$f(x) = x^{4/5}(x - 1)$ which is continuous on $\left[\dfrac{-1}{2}, \dfrac{1}{2}\right]$

$f'(0^-) = \lim\limits_{h\to 0^+} \dfrac{(-h)^{4/5}(-h-1)^{1/5} - 0}{(-h)}$

$= \lim_{h\to 0^+} \frac{(-h-1)^{1/5}}{(-h)^{1/5}} = \lim_{h\to 0^+}\left[\frac{1+h}{h}\right]^{1/5} = \infty$ and $f'(0^+)$

$= \lim_{h\to 0^+} \frac{(h)^{4/5}(h-1)^{1/5}}{h}$

$= \lim_{h\to 0^+} \frac{(h-1)^{1/5}}{(h)^{1/5}} = \lim_{h\to 0^+}\left(\frac{h-1}{h}\right)^{1/5} = -\infty$

⇒ $f(x)$ is not differentiable at $x = 0$ and hence non-differentiable on $\left(\frac{-1}{2}, \frac{1}{2}\right)$

⇒ L.M.V.T' *S* conditions are not satisfied on $\left[\frac{-1}{2}, \frac{1}{2}\right]$.

10. Let $f(x) = px^2 + qx + r$; $x \in [a, b]$

∴ By L.M.V.T, $f'(c) = \frac{f(b)-f(a)}{b-a}$ for some $c \in (a, b)$

i.e., $(2pc + q) = \frac{p(b^2-a^2)+q(b-a)}{(b-a)}$ or $2pc + q = p(b + a) + q$

⇒ $2pc = p(a + b)$

⇒ $c = \frac{a+b}{2}$

∴ $c = \frac{a+b}{2}$ is the only value of 'c' satisfying L.M.V.T

TEXTUAL EXERCISE-2: (OBJECTIVE)

1. (b) $f(x) = \ell n\, x$; $x \in [1, 3]$

By L.M.V.T, $f'(c) = \frac{f(3)-f(1)}{3-1}$ for some $c \in (1, 3)$

⇒ $2f'(c) = \ell n\, 3 - \ell n\, 1 = \ell n\, 3$

⇒ $f'(c) = \frac{1}{2}\ell og_e 3$

2. (c) $f(x) = x(x-1)(x-2)$; $x \in [0, 1/2]$

$= x^3 - 3x^2 + 2x$

By L.M.V.T, $f'(c) = \frac{f\left(\frac{1}{2}\right) - f(0)}{\left(\frac{1}{2} - 0\right)}$ for some $c \in (0, 1/2)$

⇒ $(3c^2 - 6c + 2) = \frac{\left(\frac{1}{2}\right)\left(\frac{-1}{2}\right)\left(\frac{-3}{2}\right)}{\frac{1}{2}} = \frac{3}{4}$

⇒ $12c^2 - 24c + 5 = 0$

⇒ $c = \frac{24 \pm \sqrt{576-240}}{24}$

⇒ $c = \frac{24 \pm \sqrt{336}}{24}$ for $c \in \left(0, \frac{1}{2}\right), c = \frac{24-\sqrt{336}}{24}$ i.e.,

$c = 1 - 4\frac{\sqrt{21}}{24}$

⇒ $c = \frac{24-4(4.8)}{24}$

⇒ $c \approx 1 - 0.8 = 0.2$

3. (c) By L.M.V.T,

$f'(c) = \frac{f(4)-f(2)}{4-2}$ for some $c \in (2, 4)$ i.e., $f'(c) = \frac{13-5}{2} = 4$

4. (c) By Result L.M.V.T, $f'(c) = \frac{f(b)-f(a)}{(b-a)}$

5. (a) $f(x) = e^x$; $x \in [0, 1]$,

By L.M.V.T, $\exists\, c \in (0, 1)$, such that $f'(c) = \frac{f(1)-f(0)}{1-0}$

⇒ $e^c = e - 1$

⇒ $c = \ell n\,(e - 1)$

6. (b) By L.M.V.T, $\exists\, c \in (0, 2)$ such that $f'(c) = \frac{f(2)-f(0)}{2-0}$

i.e., $f'(c) = \frac{f(2)}{2}$

∵ $|f'(x)| \le 1/2\ \forall\, x \in [0, 2]$

⇒ $|f'(c)| \le \frac{1}{2}$

⇒ $\left|\frac{f(2)}{2}\right| \le \frac{1}{2}$

⇒ $|f(2)| \le 1$

Similarly applying L.M.V.T on $[0, x]$; where $x \in (0, 2]$, we see $|f(x)| \le 1\ \forall\, x \in (0, 2]$

Also $|f(0)| = 0$

⇒ $|f(x)| \le 1\ \forall\, x \in [0, 2]$

7. (a) $f(x) = (x-1)^{2/3}$

(*i*) $f(x)$ is continuous function on $[a, b]\ \forall\, a, b \in \mathbb{R}$ and $a < b$.

(*ii*) $f'(x) = \frac{2}{3(x-1)^{1/3}}$ which is discontinuous at $x = 1$

⇒ $f(x)$ is non-differentiable in every open interval containing 1

⇒ Lagrange's mean values theorem is applicable on (1, 2).

8. (a) For $x \in [0, 1]$,

(*a*) $f(x) = \begin{cases} \left(\frac{1}{2} - x\right), x < \frac{1}{2} \\ \left(\frac{1}{2} - x\right)^2, x \ge \frac{1}{2} \end{cases}$; $f(x)$ is continuous on [0, 1].

$f'(x) = \begin{cases} -1; x < \frac{1}{2} \\ -2\left(\frac{1}{2} - x\right); x > \frac{1}{2} \end{cases}$

⇒ $f'(x)$ is discontinuous at $x = \frac{1}{2}$

⇒ $f(x)$ is non-differentiable at $x = \frac{1}{2}$

⇒ L.M.V.T is not applicable.

(*b*) $f(x) = \begin{cases} \dfrac{\sin x}{x}; x \neq 0 \\ 1 \ ; x = 0 \end{cases}$

$\lim_{x \to 0} f(x) = 1$ i.e., $f(x)$ is continuous on [0, 1],

$f'(x) = \left\{ \dfrac{x\cos x - \sin x}{x^2}; x \neq 0 \right.$ which is continuous on(0, 1) i.e., $f(x)$ is differentiable on (0, 1)

⇒ L.M.V.T is applicable

(*c*) $f(x) = x\,|x| = \begin{cases} x^2 \ ; x \geq 0 \\ -x^2 \ ; x < 0 \end{cases}$

Which is continuous on [0, 1] and $f'(x) = \begin{cases} 2x \ ; x > 0 \\ -2x \ ; x < 0 \end{cases}$ which is continuous on (0, 1)

⇒ L.M.V.T is applicable

(*d*) $f(x) = |x| = \begin{cases} x ; x \geq 0 \\ -x \ ; x < 0 \end{cases}$

which is continuous $\forall\, x \in [0, 1]$ and $f'(x) = \begin{cases} 1 \ ; x > 0 \\ -1 \ ; x < 0 \end{cases}$

⇒ $f(x)$ is non-differentiable at $x = 0$ but it is differentiable in (0, 1).

⇒ L.M.V.T is applicable on [0, 1].

9. (c) $f(x) = 2x^2 + 3x + 4;\ x \in [1, 2]$.

By L.M.V.T, $f'(c) = \dfrac{f(2) - f(1)}{2 - 1}$ for some $c \in (1, 2)$

i.e., $4c + 3 = \dfrac{18 - 9}{1} = 9$

⇒ $4c = 6$

⇒ $c = 3/2 \in (1, 2)$

10. (a) Let $f(x) = \alpha x^2 + \beta x + \gamma;\ \alpha \neq 0$

By L.M.V.T, $f'(c) = \dfrac{f(b) - f(a)}{b - a}$ for some $c \in (a, b)$

i.e., $2\alpha c + \beta = \dfrac{\alpha\left(b^2 - a^2\right) + \beta(b - a)}{(b - a)}$ i.e., $2\alpha c + \beta = \alpha(b + a) + \beta$

⇒ $c = \dfrac{a + b}{2}$

11. (c) $f(0) = 2g(0) = 0, f(1) = 6$

Let $F(x) = f(x) = 2g(x)$

⇒ $F(x)$ is continuous on [0, 1] and differentiable on (0, 1).

∴ By L.M.V.T $\exists\ c \in (0, 1)$

Such that $F'(c) = \dfrac{F(1) - F(0)}{1 - 0}$ i.e., $f'(c) - 2g'(c) = [f(1) - 2g(1)] - [f(0) - 2g(0)]$

⇒ $0 = 6 - 2g(1) - 2 + 0$ ⇒ $g(1) = 2$

14. (c) $f(x) = 1/x^2,\ g(x) = 1/x;\ x \in [a, b];\ 0 < a < b$.

By given condition, $\dfrac{\dfrac{1}{b^2} - \dfrac{1}{a^2}}{\dfrac{1}{b} - \dfrac{1}{a}} = \dfrac{\dfrac{-2}{c^3}}{\dfrac{-1}{c^2}};\ a < c < b$

⇒ $\dfrac{a^2 - b^2}{a^2 b^2} \times \dfrac{ab}{a - b} = \dfrac{2}{c^3} \times \dfrac{c^2}{1}$

⇒ $\dfrac{a + b}{ab} = \dfrac{2}{c} \Rightarrow c = \dfrac{2ab}{a + b}$

⇒ C is H.M of 'a' and 'b'

13. (b) By L.M.V.T on [1, 2] $\exists\ x \in (1, 2)$ such that $f'(x) = \dfrac{f(2) - f(1)}{2 - 1} = 4 - 1 = 3$ $\exists\ x \in (1, 2)$ such that

$f''(x) = \dfrac{f'(2) - f'(1)}{2 - 1} = f'(2) - f'(1)$

Similarly, by L.M.V.T on [2, 3] $\exists\ x \in (2, 3)$ such that $f'(x) = \dfrac{f(3) - f(2)}{3 - 2} = \dfrac{9 - 4}{1} = 5$ and $\exists\ x \in (2, 3)$ such that

$f''(x) = \dfrac{f'(3) - f'(2)}{3 - 2} = f'(3) - f'(2)$.

Also by L.M.V.T on [1, 3] $\exists$

$x \in (1, 3)$ such that $f'(x) = \dfrac{f(3) - f(1)}{3 - 1} = \dfrac{9 - 1}{2} = 4$

14. (d) $f(x) = f(1 - x)$

Replacing x by $\left(\dfrac{1}{2} - x\right)$ gives

$f\left(\dfrac{1}{2} - x\right) = f\left(1 - \left(\dfrac{1}{2} - x\right)\right)$

⇒ $f\left(\dfrac{1}{2} - x\right) = f\left(\dfrac{1}{2} + x\right)$

⇒ $f(x)$ is symmetric about line $x = \dfrac{1}{2}$ and $f'\left(\dfrac{1}{4}\right) = 0$

Means tangent to curve at $x = \dfrac{1}{4}$ is || to x-axis.

Now $f\left(\dfrac{1}{2} - x\right) = f\left(\dfrac{1}{2} + x\right)$

⇒ $-f'\left(\dfrac{1}{2} - x\right) = f'\left(\dfrac{1}{2} + x\right)$

Put $x = 1/4$

⇒ $-f'\left(\dfrac{1}{4}\right) = f'\left(\dfrac{3}{4}\right)$ but $f'\left(\dfrac{1}{4}\right) = 0 \Rightarrow f'\left(\dfrac{3}{4}\right) = 0$

⇒ $f'(x)$ vanishes at least twice in [0, 1]

⇒ (*i*) is true

Now, as $f'\left(\dfrac{1}{2} - h\right) = -f'\left(\dfrac{1}{2} + h\right)$; $h \to 0^+$ and $f(x)$ is differentiable on [0, 1]

⇒ $f'\left(\dfrac{1^-}{2}\right) = f'\left(\dfrac{1^+}{2}\right) = f'\left(\dfrac{1}{2}\right) = k$ (*say*)

⇒ $k = -k$

⇒ $k = 0$

⇒ $f'\left(\dfrac{1}{2}\right) = 0$

Again by Rolle's Theorem, $f''(x) = 0$ at least once in $\left(\frac{1}{4},\frac{1}{2}\right)$ and in $\left(\frac{1}{2},\frac{3}{4}\right)$

$\Rightarrow$ (*ii*) is true

Now $\int_{-1/2}^{1/2} f\left(x+\frac{1}{2}\right)$ sin *x* dx

Let $G(x) = f\left(x+\frac{1}{2}\right)$ sin x

$G(-x) = f\left(-x+\frac{1}{2}\right)\sin(-x)$

$\Rightarrow G(-x) = -f\left(x+\frac{1}{2}\right)\sin x \quad \left(\because f\left(\frac{1}{2}-x\right)=f\left(\frac{1}{2}+x\right)\right)$

$\Rightarrow G(x) = -G(-x)$

$\Rightarrow G(x)$ is an odd function.

$\Rightarrow \int_{-1/2}^{1/2} f\left(x+\frac{1}{2}\right)\sin dx = 0$

$\Rightarrow$ (*iii*) is correct

Next, $\int_{-1/2}^{3/2} f(t)e^{\sin \pi t}dt = \int_{1/2}^{3/2} f(t)e^{\sin \pi t}dt$

($\because f(x)$ is symmetric about $x = 1/2$)

$= \int_{1/2}^{3/2} f(1-t)e^{\sin \pi t}dt$

15. (b) $f(x) = x(x-1)^2; x \in[0, 2]$

By L.M.V.T, $f'(c) = \dfrac{f(2)-f(0)}{(2-0)}$ for some $c \in (0, 2)$

i.e., $3c^2 - 4c + 1 = \frac{2}{2} = 1$

$\Rightarrow c(3c-4) = 0$

$\Rightarrow c = 0$ or $c = 4/3 \quad \because \quad c = \frac{4}{3} \in [0, 2]$

16. (b) $f(x) = x^2 - 2x + 3; x \in\left[1,\frac{3}{2}\right]$

By L.M.V.T, $f'(c) = \dfrac{f\left(\frac{3}{2}\right)-f(1)}{\frac{3}{2}-1} = \dfrac{\left[\left(\frac{9}{4}-3+3-(2)\right)\right]}{\frac{1}{2}}$

$\Rightarrow (2c-2) = \frac{1}{4}\times\frac{2}{1} = \frac{1}{2}$

$\Rightarrow 2c = \frac{5}{2}$

$\Rightarrow c = 5/4$

17. (c) $f(x) = \dfrac{\sin x}{e^x}; x \in[0, \pi]$.

$f(0) = 0; f(\pi) = \dfrac{\sin}{}$

$\therefore$ By Rolle's Theorem, $f'(c) = 0$

$\Rightarrow \dfrac{e^x\cos x-(\sin x)e^x}{e^{2x}} = 0$ for $x = c$

$\Rightarrow \dfrac{\cos c-\sin c}{e^c} = 0$

$\Rightarrow c = \dfrac{\pi}{4}$

18. (d) $f(x) = x^2 - 2x + 4; x \in[1, 5]$,

$f'(c) = \dfrac{f(5)-f(1)}{5-1}$

$\Rightarrow 2c-2 = \dfrac{(25-10+4)-(3)}{5-1}$

$\Rightarrow 2c-2 = \dfrac{16}{4} = 4$

$\Rightarrow 2c = 6 \quad \Rightarrow c = 3$

19. (d) $f(x) = \sqrt{x}, x \in[4, 9]$

By L.M.V.T, $f'(c) = \dfrac{f(b)-f(a)}{b-a}$ for some $c \in(4, 9)$

$\Rightarrow \dfrac{1}{2\sqrt{c}} = \dfrac{3-2}{9-4}$

$\Rightarrow \dfrac{1}{2\sqrt{c}} = \dfrac{1}{5} \Rightarrow \sqrt{c} = 5/2 \quad \Rightarrow c = \dfrac{25}{4} = 6.25$

MAXIMA AND MINIMA TEXTUAL EXERCISE–1: (SUBJECTIVE)

1. $f(x) = \dfrac{x^4}{4} - 3x^2 + \dfrac{23}{2}x^2 - 15x + 1$

$f'(x) = x^3 - 9x^2 + 23x - 15$

For $f'(x) = 0$

$[(x-1)(x^2) - 8x(x-1) + 15(x-1)] = 0$

$\Rightarrow (x-1)(x^2 - 8x + 15) = 0$

$\Rightarrow (x-1)(x-3)(x-5) = 0$

$\therefore x = 1, 3, 5$ are critical points and $f''(x) = 3x^2 - 18x + 23$ and $f''(1) = 8, f''(3) = -4\ f''(5) = 8$

$\Rightarrow$ Points of local maximum $\to$ 3 and points of local minima $\to$ 1, 5

2. $f(x) = \sin x + \cos x\ \forall\ 0 < x < \pi/2$

$f'(x) = \cos x - \sin x = 0$

$\Rightarrow x = \pi/4$ and $f''(\pi/4) = \dfrac{-2}{\sqrt{2}} = -\sqrt{2} < 0$

$\Rightarrow f(x)$ has *a* local maxima at $x = \pi/4$.

3. $f'(x_1) = f'(x_2) = f'(x_3) = 0$ (*Given*)

Clearly x_1 and x_3 are points of local maxima and x_2 is a point of local maxima.

(a) $f(x_1) \cdot f''(x_1) = (+)(-) = -ve$.

(b) $\because f'(x_1) = f'(x_2) = 0$ and $f(x)$ is twice differentiable, by Rolle's Theorem $\exists$ $c \in (x_1, x_2)$ such that $f''(c) = 0$, thus true.

(c) $f''(x_3) \cdot f'(x_4) = (-)(-) = +ve$.

(d) True (standard result).

(e) Local maxima value can be smaller than local minimum value as is clear from the graph given below.

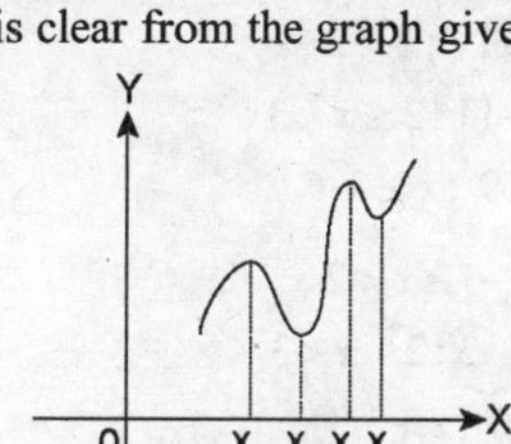

Clearly $f(x_4) > f(x_1)$

$\Rightarrow$ Given statement is false.

4. (i) $f'(\beta) = 0$ ($\because$ β is point of local minima)

(ii) $[f'(\alpha - h)]\,[f'(\gamma + h)] = (+)\,(-) = -\,ve$

($\because$ $(\alpha - h)$ lies on increasing portion and $(\gamma + h)$ lies on decreasing portion)

(iii) $[f'(\alpha + h)]\,[f'(\beta - h)]$; $h > 0, h \to 0$

$= (-)\,(-) = +\,ve$ as $(\alpha + h)$ as well as $(\beta - h)$ lies on decreasing potion.

5. $f(x) = \dfrac{x^3}{3} - x + 1$

$\Rightarrow f'(x) = (x^2 - 1) = 0$

$\Rightarrow x = \pm 1$

$\Rightarrow f''(x) = 2x$

$\Rightarrow f''(1) = 2, f''(-1) = -2$

$\Rightarrow f(x)$ has local maxima at $x = -1$ and local minima at $x = 1$.

6. $f(x) = \begin{cases} 1 - 2x \;; x \le 0 \\ x^2 \;; x > 0 \end{cases}$

$\Rightarrow f'(x) = \begin{cases} -2 \;; x < 0 \\ 2x \;; x > 0 \end{cases}$

$\Rightarrow f'(x) < 0$ for $x < 0$ and $f'(x) > 0$ for $x > 0$ and $f(x)$ has discontinuity at $x = 0$

$\Rightarrow f(x)$ has a point of local minima at $x = 0$.

7. (i) since $f(a - h) < f(a) > f(a + h)$ for $h > 0$ and $h \to 0^+$

$\Rightarrow f(x)$ has point of local maxima at $x = a$

(ii) $\because$ $f(a - h) < f(a + h)$; for $h \to 0^+$

$\Rightarrow$ $x = a$ is neither a point of local maxima nor a point of local minima.

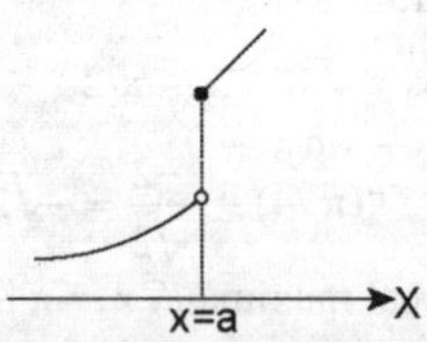

(iii) $f(a - h) > f(a) < f(a + h)$; $h \to 0^+$

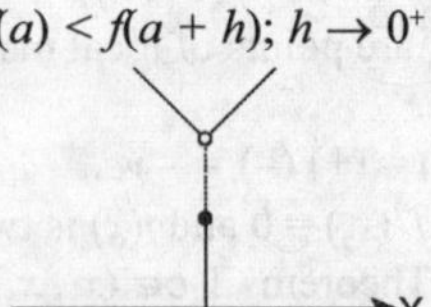

$\Rightarrow$ $x = a$ is a point of local minima.

8. $f(x) = 2|\,x - 2| + 5\,|x - 3|$; $x \in \mathbb{R}$

$= \begin{cases} -7x + 19 \;; x < 2 \\ -3x + 11 \;; 2 \le x < 3 \\ 7x - 19 \;; x \ge 3 \end{cases}$

$\Rightarrow f'(x) = \begin{cases} -7 \;; x < 2 \\ -3 \;; 2 < x < 3 \\ 7 \;; x > 3 \end{cases}$

The graph of $y = f(x)$ as is shown below.

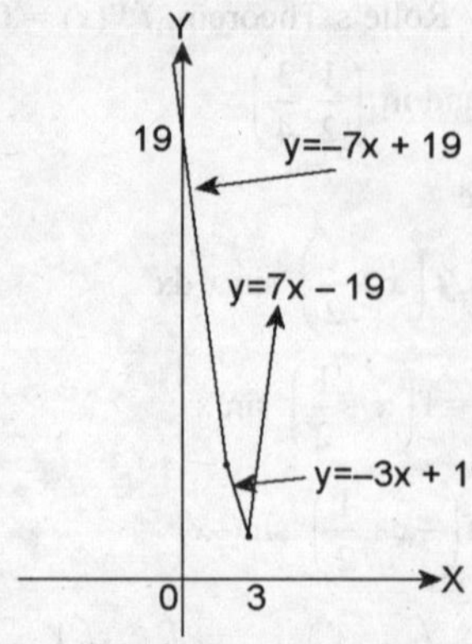

Clearly $f(x)$ has point of local minima and Global minima at $x = 3$ and the local minimum/global minimum value is $f(3)$ $= 7(3) - 19 = 2$

Also there is no point of local minima and global minima.

9. (i) $f(x)$ has a point of local maxima as well global maxima at $x = 2$.

$x = 3$ is the point of local minima as $f(3 - h) > f(3)$ for $h > 0$ and $h \to 0$

(ii) $x = -1$ is point of local minima,

No point of local maxima and no points of global minima and global maxima.

(iii) $x = 0$ is the point of local minima as well as global minima.

$x = 1$ is the point of local maxima as well as global maxima.

TEXTUAL EXERCISE–1: (OBJECTIVE)

1. (d) $f\!: \mathbb{R} \to \mathbb{R}$; $f(x) = \begin{cases} k - 2x, x \le -1 \\ 2x + 3, x > -1 \end{cases}$

$\Rightarrow f'(x) = \begin{cases} -2 \;; x < -1 \\ 2 \;; x > -1 \end{cases}$

$\Rightarrow f(x)$ has *a* local at $x = -1$ provided $f(-1) \le 2(-1) + 3$

$\Rightarrow k + 2 \le 1$

$\Rightarrow k \le -1$

2. (c) $f(x) = e^{(x^4 - x^3 + x^2)}$

$\Rightarrow f'(x) = e^{(x^4 - x^3 + x^2)}.(4x^3 - 3x^2 + 2x) = e^{(x^4 - x^3 + x^2)}.x(4x^2 - 3x + 2)$

Clearly $4x^2 - 3x + 2 > 0 \;\forall\; x \in \mathbb{R}$

$\Rightarrow f'(x) \ge 0 \;\forall\; x \ge 0$ and $f'(x) \le 0 \;\forall\; x \le 0$

$\Rightarrow f(x)$ is decreasing $\forall\; x \le 0$ and $f(x)$ is increasing $\forall\; x \ge 0$

$\Rightarrow f(x)$ has a local minima at $x = 0$ with minimum value $=$ $f(0) = 1$.

3. (b) $p(x) = x^4 + ax^3 + bx^2 + cx + d$

$p'(x) = 4x^3 + 3ax^2 + 2bx + c$

$p'(0) = 0$ and $x = 0$ is only root of $p'(x) = 0$

$\Rightarrow c = 0$

$\Rightarrow p'(x) - 4x^3 + 3ax^2 + 2bx$ and $4x^3 + 3ax^2 + 2bx = 0$

$\Rightarrow$ $4x^2 + 3ax + 2b = 0$ has no real root

$\Rightarrow$ $4x^2 + 3ax + 2b > 0 \ \forall \ x \in \mathbb{R}$

$\Rightarrow$ $p'(x) = x(4x^2 + 3ax + 2b) < 0$ for $x < 0$ and > 0 for $x > 0$

$\Rightarrow$ $p(x)$ has a point of local minima at $x = 0$, given by $p(0) = d$

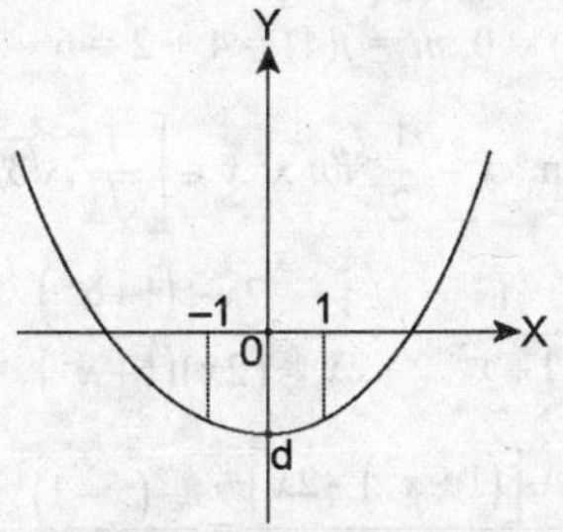

$\therefore$ In interval $[-1, 1]$, $p(1)$ is maximum and $p(0)$ is minimum and $p(-1)$ is not minimum.

4. (a) $f(x) = \cos x + \cos \sqrt{2x}$

Period of $\cos x = 2\pi$,

Period of $\cos \sqrt{2x} = \dfrac{2\pi}{\sqrt{2}} = \dfrac{\pi}{\sqrt{2}}$

If $f(x)$ is periodic, then its period = L.C.M $\left(2\pi, \dfrac{\pi}{\sqrt{2}}\right)$

$= \pi$. L.C.M $\left(2, \dfrac{1}{\sqrt{2}}\right)$, which does not exist

$\Rightarrow$ $f(x)$ is not *a* periodic function i.e., $f(x) = f(x + T)$ is never possible for any real T and maximum value of $f(x) = 2$ at $x = 0$, and would be attained only once

5. (b) $f(x) = 1 + 2x^2 + 2^2 x^4 + \ldots + 2^{10} . x^{20}$

$\Rightarrow$ $f'(x) = 2(2x) + 2^2 (4x^3) + \ldots + 2^{10} (20 x^{19}) < 0$ for $x < 0$ and > 0 for $x > 0$ and $= 0$ at $x = 0$

$\Rightarrow$ $f(x)$ has *a* local minima at $x = 0$

6. (c) $f(x) = \sum_{n=1}^{m} (x-n)^2$

$$f'(x) = \sum_{n=1}^{m} 2(x-n) = 2\sum_{n=1}^{m}(x-n) = 2\left[\sum_{n=1}^{m} x - \sum_{n=1}^{m} n\right]$$

$$= 2\left(mx - \frac{m(m+1)}{2}\right) = 2\,mx - m(m+1)$$

$\Rightarrow$ $f'(x) = 0$ at $x = \dfrac{m+1}{2}$

Also $f''(x) = 2m > 0$

$\Rightarrow$ $f(x)$ ahs *a* local minima at $x = \dfrac{m+1}{2}$.

7. (c), (d) Let $m = \min. f_A$

$\Rightarrow$ $f(x) \geq \min. f_A \ \forall \ x \in A$

In particular, $\min. f_B \geq \min f_A$ ...(i)

And $\max. f_B \geq \min. f_A$ ...(2)

Also $f(x) \leq \max. f_A \ \forall \ x \in A$

$\therefore$ In particular, $\min. f_B \leq \max. f_A$ ...(3)

And $\max f_B \leq \max. f_A$ ...(4)

8. (a), (b), (c), (d)

If $f(x) = \begin{cases} 3x^2 + 12x - 1; -1 \leq x \leq 2 \\ 37 - x; 2 < x \leq 3 \end{cases}$

Clearly $f(x)$ is continuous in $[-1, 3]$

$\Rightarrow$ $f'(x) = \begin{cases} 6x + 12; -1 < x < 2 \\ -1; 2 < x < 3 \end{cases}$

$\Rightarrow$ $f'(x) > 0$ for $x \in (-1, 2)$ and < 0 for $x \in (2, 3)$

$\Rightarrow$ $f(x)$ is increasing on $[-1, 2]$ and $f(x)$ is decreasing on $[2, 3]$.

Also $f'(2^-) = 24, f'(2^+) = -1$

$\Rightarrow$ $f'(x)$ does not exist at $x = 2$

$\Rightarrow$ $f(x)$ has maximum value at $x = 2$

9. (c) $p(x) = a_0 + a_1 x^2 + a_2 x^4 + \ldots + a_n x^{2n}$

$\Rightarrow$ $p'(2x) = 2a_1 x + 4a_2 x^3 + \ldots + 2n\, a_n x^{2n-1}$

Since, $0 < a_0 < a_1 < a_2 < \ldots < a_n$

$\Rightarrow$ $p'(x) < 0$ for $x < 0$, $p'(0) = 0$ and $p'(x) > 0 \ \forall \ x > 0$

$\Rightarrow$ $p(x)$ has only one minima and no maxima.

10. (b) Let $\lambda_1, \lambda_2, \lambda_3$ be roots of $x^3 - \lambda x^2 + \mu x - 6 = 0$, $\lambda_1, \lambda_2, \lambda_3 > 0$

$\Rightarrow$ $\lambda_1 + \lambda_2 + \lambda_3 = (-1)^1 \left(\dfrac{-\lambda}{1}\right) = \lambda, \lambda_1 \lambda_2 + \lambda_2 \lambda_3 + \lambda_3 \lambda_1 =$

$(-1)^2 \left(\dfrac{\mu}{1}\right) = \mu$ and $\alpha_1.\alpha_2.\alpha_3 = (-1)^3 \left(\dfrac{-6}{1}\right) = 6$

$\Rightarrow$ $\dfrac{6}{\lambda_3} + \dfrac{6}{\lambda_1} + \dfrac{6}{\lambda_2} = \mu$

$\Rightarrow$ $\dfrac{1}{\lambda_1} + \dfrac{1}{\lambda_2} + \dfrac{1}{\lambda_3} = \dfrac{\mu}{6}$

$\because$ $\alpha_1, \alpha_2, \alpha_3$ are $+ve$

$\Rightarrow$ $\dfrac{1}{\lambda_1} + \dfrac{1}{\lambda_2} + \dfrac{1}{\lambda_3} \geq 3\sqrt[3]{\dfrac{1}{\lambda_1} . \dfrac{1}{\lambda_2} . \dfrac{1}{\lambda_3}}$

$\Rightarrow$ $\dfrac{1}{\lambda_1} + \dfrac{1}{\lambda_2} + \dfrac{1}{\lambda_3} \geq 3\sqrt[3]{\dfrac{1}{6}}$

$\Rightarrow$ $\dfrac{\mu}{6} \geq 3 . \sqrt[3]{\dfrac{1}{6}}$

$\Rightarrow$ $\mu \geq 18 . \dfrac{1}{\sqrt[3]{6}}$

$\Rightarrow$ $\mu \geq 3(6) . \dfrac{1}{\sqrt[3]{6}}$

$\Rightarrow$ $\mu \geq 3(6)^{2/3}$

11. (c) $f(x) = 4 \tan x - \tan^2 x + \tan^3 x$; $x \neq n\pi + \dfrac{\pi}{2}$

$\Rightarrow$ $f'(x) = (4 - 2 \tan x + 3 \tan^2 x) \sec^2 x$

$\because$ $x \neq n\pi + \dfrac{\pi}{2}$

$\Rightarrow$ $\sec^2 x \geq 1$ and $f'(x) = 0$

$\Rightarrow$ $3 \tan^2 x - 2 \tan x + 4 = 0$ but $3 \tan^2 x - 2 \tan x + 4 > 0$ $\forall \ x \neq n\pi + \pi/2$

$\Rightarrow$ $f'(x) > 0 \ \forall \ x \neq n\pi + \pi/2$

$\Rightarrow$ $f(x)$ is neither local minima, nor local maxima.

TEXTUAL EXERCISE–2:(SUBJECTIVE)

1. (a) $f(x) = x.\, e^{-x}$ on $[0, \infty)$

$f'(x) = -x\, e^{-x} + e^{-x}\,.\,1 = e^{-x}(1 - x)$

$\Rightarrow f'(x) < 0$ for $x > 1$

$\Rightarrow f'(x) = 0$ at $x = 1$ and $f'(x) > 0$ for $x < 1$

$\Rightarrow$ $x = 1$ is a point of local maximum as well as global maxima at $x = 1$.

$\Rightarrow$ Greatest value of function $f(x) = f(1) = e^{-1} = 1/e$ and least value does not exists.

However $g.l.b = \lim\limits_{x\to\infty} f(x) = \lim\limits_{x\to\infty} x.e^{-x} = \lim\limits_{x\to\infty}\frac{x}{e^x}$

$= \lim\limits_{x\to\infty}\frac{1}{e^x} = 0$ *(using L.H Rule)*

(b) $f(x) = \sqrt{(1-x^2)(1+2x^2)}$ on $[-1, 1]$

$\Rightarrow f'(x) = \frac{1}{2\sqrt{(1-x^2)(1+2x^2)}}$

$\times\left[\frac{(1-x^2)(4x)+(1+2x^2)(-2x)}{1}\right]$

$= \left[\frac{-8x^3+2x}{2\sqrt{(1-x^2)(1+2x^2)}}\right] = \frac{x(1-4x^2)}{\sqrt{(1-x^2)(2x^2+1)}}$

$\Rightarrow f'(x) < 0$ for $\frac{-1}{2} < x < 0$ and $x > 1/2$ and $f'(x) > 0$ for $0 < x$ $1/2$ and $-1 < x < \frac{-1}{2}$, $f'(x) = 0$ at $x = 0$, $1/4$

$\Rightarrow f(x)$ has a local minima at $x = 0$ and local maxima at x $\pm 1/2$.

Now $f(-1) = 0, f(0) = 1, f(-1/2) = \sqrt{\frac{3}{4}+\frac{3}{2}} = \frac{3}{2\sqrt{2}} = \frac{3\sqrt{2}}{4}$

and $f(1) = 0$

$\therefore$ Greatest value $(M) = \frac{3\sqrt{2}}{4}$ or $\frac{6}{4\sqrt{2}} = \frac{3}{2\sqrt{2}} = \frac{3}{\sqrt{8}}$ and

Least value $(m) = 0$.

2. (a) $y = arc\cos x^2$ i.e., $y = \cos^{-1}(x^2)$; $\frac{-1}{2} \le x^2 \le \frac{1}{2}$

But $x^2 \ge 0$

$\therefore$ $y = \cos^{-1}(x^2)$; $0 \le x^2 \le \frac{1}{2}$; $\frac{-1}{\sqrt{2}} \le x \frac{1}{\sqrt{2}}$

Clearly $f(x)$ is an even function and $f(x)$ is a continuous and $f'(0^+) = 0$

$\Rightarrow f'(0^-) = 0$

Further $f'(x) = \frac{-2x}{\sqrt{1-x^4}}$

$\Rightarrow f'(x) < 0$ for $x > 0$ and $f'(x) > 0$ for $x < 0$

$\Rightarrow f(x)$ increase in $\left(\frac{-1}{\sqrt{2}}, 0\right)$ and decreases on $\left(0, \frac{1}{\sqrt{2}}\right)$,

$f'(0) = 0$

$\Rightarrow M = f(0) = \cos^{-1}(0) = \pi/2$ and

$m = f\left(\pm\frac{1}{\sqrt{2}}\right) = \cos^{-1}\left(\frac{1}{2}\right) = \frac{\pi}{3}$

(b) $y = x + \sqrt{x}$ on $[0, 4]$

$\Rightarrow f'(x) = 1 + \frac{1}{2\sqrt{x}} = \frac{2\sqrt{x}+1}{2\sqrt{x}} > 0\ \forall\ x \in [0, 4]$

$\Rightarrow f(x)$ increases on $[0, 4]$

$\Rightarrow m = f(0) = 0$, $m = f(4) = 4 + 2 = 6$

3. (a) $f(x) = \tan^{-1} x - \frac{1}{2}\ \ell n\, x$; $x \in \left[\frac{1}{\sqrt{3}}, \sqrt{3}\right]$

$f'(x) = \frac{1}{1+x^2} - \frac{1}{2x} = \frac{2x-(1+x^2)}{(2x)(1+x^2)}$

$= \frac{-\left[(1+x^2)-2x\right]}{2x(1+2x)} = \frac{-(x-1)^2}{2x(1+x^2)} < 0\ \forall\ x \in \left[\frac{1}{\sqrt{3}}, \sqrt{3}\right]$

$\Rightarrow f(x)$ is a decreasing function on $\left[\frac{1}{\sqrt{3}}, \sqrt{3}\right]$

$\Rightarrow M = f\left(\frac{1}{\sqrt{3}}\right) = \tan^{-1}\left(\frac{1}{\sqrt{3}}\right) + \frac{1}{2}\ell n\sqrt{3} = \frac{}{6}\ \frac{}{4}$ and

$m = f\left(\sqrt{3}\right) = \tan^{-1}\sqrt{3} - \frac{1}{2}\ell n\sqrt{3} = \frac{\pi}{3} - \frac{1}{4}\ell n3$

(b) $f(x) = 2\sin x + \sin 2x$; $x \in \left[0, \frac{3}{2}\pi\right]$

$\Rightarrow f'(x) = 2\cos x + 2\cos 2x = 2\left[2\cos\frac{3x}{2}\cos\frac{x}{2}\right] = 4\cos\frac{3x}{2}\cos\frac{x}{2}$

$\because$ $0 \le \frac{3x}{2} \le \frac{9\pi}{4}; 0 \le \frac{x}{2} \le \frac{3}{4}\pi,$

$\therefore$ $f'(x) = 0$

$\Rightarrow$ $\frac{3x}{2} = \frac{\pi}{2}, \frac{3\pi}{2}$ or $\frac{x}{2} = \frac{\pi}{2}$

$\Rightarrow$ $x = \frac{\pi}{3}, \pi$

For $x \in \left[0, \frac{\pi}{3}\right]; \frac{3x}{2} \in \left[0, \frac{\pi}{2}\right]$ and $\frac{x}{2} \in \left[0, \frac{\pi}{6}\right]$

$\Rightarrow$ $\cos\frac{3x}{2} \ge 0, \cos\frac{x}{2} \ge 0$

$\Rightarrow f'(x) \ge 0,$

For $x \in \left[\frac{\pi}{3}, \pi\right]; \frac{3x}{2} \in \left[\frac{\pi}{2}, \frac{3\pi}{2}\right]$ and $\frac{x}{2} \in \left[\frac{\pi}{6}, \frac{\pi}{2}\right]$

$\Rightarrow$ $\cos\frac{3x}{2} \le 0, \cos\frac{x}{2} \ge 0$

$\Rightarrow f'(x) \le 0$

For $x \in \left[\pi, \frac{3\pi}{2}\right]; \frac{3x}{2} \in \left[\frac{3\pi}{2}, \frac{9\pi}{4}\right]$ and $\frac{x}{2} \in \left[\frac{\pi}{2}, \frac{3\pi}{4}\right]$

$\Rightarrow$ $\cos\frac{3x}{2} \ge 0, \cos\frac{x}{2} \le 0$

$\Rightarrow f'(x) \le 0$

$\Rightarrow\ M = f(\pi/3) = 2\sin\dfrac{\pi}{3} + \sin\dfrac{2\pi}{3}$

$= 2\left(\dfrac{\sqrt{3}}{2}\right) + \dfrac{\sqrt{3}}{2} = \dfrac{3\sqrt{3}}{2}$ and $m = \min\{f(0), f(3\pi/2)\}$

$= \min.\{0, -2\} = -2$

(c) $f(x) = \begin{cases} 2x^2 + \dfrac{2}{x^2}, -2 \le x < 0; 0 < x \le 2 \\ 1 \quad ; \quad x = 0 \end{cases}$

$\Rightarrow\ f'(x) = \left\{4x + 2\left(\dfrac{-2}{x^3}\right)\right\}; -2 < x < 0 \text{ or } 0 < x < 2$

Now $f'(x) > 0$

$\Rightarrow\ x - \dfrac{1}{x^3} > 0 \qquad \Rightarrow\ \dfrac{x^4 - 1}{x^3} > 0$

$\Rightarrow\ x(x^4 - 1) > 0 \qquad \Rightarrow\ x(x^2 + 1)(x^2 - 1) > 0$

$\Rightarrow\ x(x^2 - 1) > 0 \qquad \Rightarrow\ (x + 1)x(x - 1) > 0$

$\Rightarrow\ x \in (-1, 0) \cup (1, 2)$ and $f'(x) < 0$ for $x\ (-2, -1) \cup (0, 1)$

$\Rightarrow\ f(x)$ has points of local minima at $x = -1$ and at $x = 1$ and $f(0^+) = \infty = f(0^-)$

$\Rightarrow\ M = \min\{f(-1), f(1), f(0)\} = \min\{4, 4, 1) = 1$

(d) $f(x) = x - 2\ \ell n\ x; x \in [1, e]$

$\Rightarrow\ f'(x) = 1 - \dfrac{2}{x}$

$\Rightarrow\ f'(x) < 0$ for $1 \le x < 2$ and $f'(x) > 0$ for $x > 2$

$\Rightarrow\ f(x)$ has a point of local minima at $x = 1$.

$\Rightarrow\ m = f(2) = 2 - 2\ \ell n\ 2 = 2 - \ell n\ 4$ and $M = \max.\{f(1), f(e)\} = \max.\{1, e - 2\} = 1$

$\therefore\ m = 2 - \ell n\ 4, m = 1$

4. $f(x) = x^5 - 5x^4 + 5x^3 + 1$

$f'(x) = 5x^4 - 20x^3 + 15x^2$

$f'(x) = 0$

$\Rightarrow\ 5x^2(x^2 - 4x + 3) = 0 \quad \Rightarrow\ 5x^2(x - 1)(x - 3) = 0$

$\Rightarrow\ x = 0$ or 1 or 3

$f'(x) < 0$

$\Rightarrow\ x \in (1, 3)$

$f'(x) > 0$

$\Rightarrow\ x \in (-\infty, 1) \cup (3, \infty)$

$\Rightarrow\ f(x)$ has a local maxima at $x = 1$ and $f(x)$ has a local minima at $x = 3$

$\because$ Local maximum value $= f(1) = 2$ and local minimum value $= f(3)$

(a)

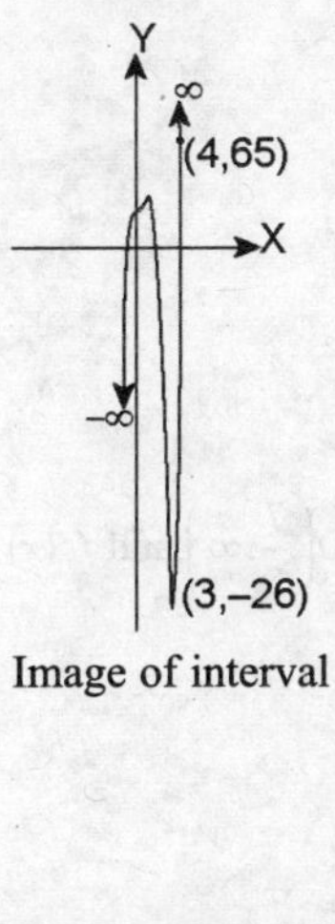

$\therefore$ Image of interval [0, 3] undefined is [– 26, 2]

(b) Image of interval [0, 4];

$f(4) = (4)^5 - 5(4)^4 + 5(4)^3 + 1$

$= (4)^4(-1) + 5(4)^3 + 1$

$= (4)^3[-4 + 5] + 1 = 65$

$\Rightarrow$ Image of interval [0, 4] under $f = [-26, 65]$

5. $x^2 + y^2 = a^2$

$A(\theta) = \dfrac{1}{2}|(OM)(PM)| = \dfrac{1}{2}|a\cos\theta . a\sin\theta|$

$= \dfrac{1}{2}a^2|(\sin\theta\cos\theta)|$

$\Rightarrow\ A(\theta) = \dfrac{1}{4}a^2|\sin 2\theta|$

$\Rightarrow\ A = \begin{cases} \dfrac{1}{4}a^2\sin 2\theta; 0 \le \theta < \dfrac{\pi}{2} \\ \dfrac{-1}{4}a^2\sin 2\theta; \dfrac{\pi}{2} < \theta < \pi \\ \dfrac{1}{4}a^2\sin 2\theta; \pi \le \theta \le \dfrac{3\pi}{2} \\ \dfrac{-1}{4}a^2\sin 2\theta; \dfrac{3\pi}{2} < \theta \le 2\pi \end{cases}$

$\Rightarrow\ \dfrac{dA}{d\theta} = \begin{cases} \dfrac{a^2}{2}\cos 2\theta; 0 < \theta < \dfrac{\pi}{2} \text{ and } \pi < \theta < \dfrac{3\pi}{2} \\ -\dfrac{a^2}{2}\cos 2\theta; \dfrac{\pi}{2} < \theta < \pi \text{ and } \dfrac{3\pi}{2} < \theta < 2\pi \end{cases}$

$\therefore\ \dfrac{dA}{d\theta} > 0$ for $\theta \in (0, \pi/4) \cup$

$\left(\pi, \dfrac{5\pi}{4}\right) \cup \left(\dfrac{\pi}{2}, \dfrac{3\pi}{4}\right) \cup \left(\dfrac{3\pi}{2}, \dfrac{7\pi}{4}\right)$ and $\dfrac{dA}{d\theta} < 0$ for $\theta \in$

$\left(\dfrac{\pi}{4}, \dfrac{\pi}{2}\right) \cup \left(\dfrac{3\pi}{4}, \pi\right) \cup \left(\dfrac{5\pi}{4}, \dfrac{3\pi}{2}\right) \cup \left(\dfrac{7\pi}{4}, 2\pi\right)$

$\Rightarrow$ Max. $\left\{A\left(\dfrac{\pi}{4}\right), A\left(\dfrac{3\pi}{4}\right), A\left(\dfrac{5\pi}{4}\right) A\left(\dfrac{7\pi}{4}\right)\right\}$ = Max

$\left\{\dfrac{1}{4}a^2, \dfrac{1}{4}a^2, \dfrac{1}{4}a^2, \dfrac{1}{4}a^2\right\} = \dfrac{1}{4}a^2$

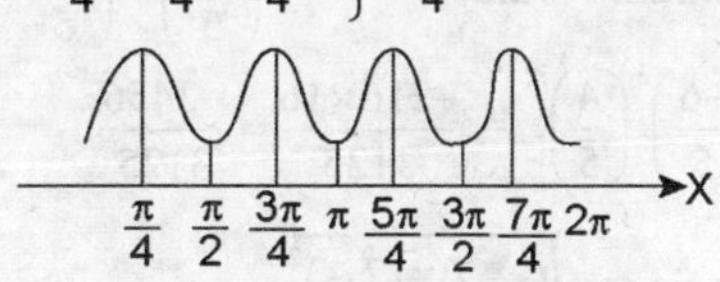

$\therefore$ Maximum area $= \dfrac{1}{4}a^2$ when $\theta = \pi/4$

$\therefore$ Perimeter $P(\theta) = a + a|\cos\theta| + a|\sin\theta|$

$\Rightarrow\ p(\theta) = \begin{cases} a + a\cos\theta + a\sin\theta; 0 \le \theta \le \dfrac{\pi}{2} \\ a - a\cos\theta + a\sin\theta; \dfrac{\pi}{2} < \theta \le \pi \\ a - a\cos\theta - a\sin\theta; \pi < \theta < \dfrac{3\pi}{2} \\ a + a\cos\theta - a\sin\theta; \dfrac{3\pi}{2} \le \theta \le 2\pi \end{cases}$

$$\Rightarrow p'(\theta) = \begin{cases} -a\sin\theta + a\cos\theta; 0 < \theta < \dfrac{\pi}{2} \\ a\sin\theta + a\cos\theta; \dfrac{\pi}{2} < \theta < \pi \\ a\sin\theta - a\cos\theta; \pi < \theta < \dfrac{3\pi}{2} \\ -a\sin\theta - a\cos\theta; \dfrac{3\pi}{2} < \theta < 2\pi \end{cases}$$

$\therefore$ $p'(\theta) = 0$ at $\theta = \pi/4, 3\pi/4, 5\pi/4, \dfrac{7\pi}{4}$

Also $p'(\theta) > 0$ for $\theta \in (0, \pi/4)$

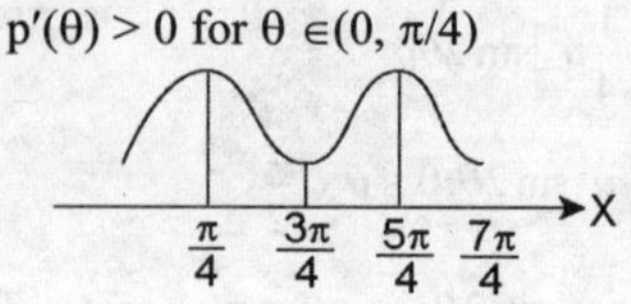

$\Rightarrow$ $p(\theta)_{max.}$ = max. $\{p(\pi/4), p(5\pi/4)\}$

$= \max. \left\{a + \dfrac{a}{\sqrt{2}} + \dfrac{a}{\sqrt{2}}, a + \dfrac{a}{\sqrt{2}} + \dfrac{a}{\sqrt{2}}\right\}$

$= a + \sqrt{2a} = \left(\sqrt{2}+1\right)a$

6. $f(x) = (x-1)^3(x+1)^2$

$\Rightarrow$ $f'(x) = (x-1)^3 . 2(x+1) + (x+1)^2 (3)(x-1)^2 = (x-1)^2 (x+1)[2(x-1) + 3(x+1)] = (x-1)^2(x+1)(5x+1)$

$\therefore$ $f'(x) = 0$

$\Rightarrow$ $x = -1, \dfrac{-1}{5}$ or 1

Also $f'(x) < 0$ for $x \in \left(-1, \dfrac{-1}{5}\right)$ and $f'(x) > 0$ for $x \in (-\infty, -1) \cup \left(\dfrac{-1}{5}, \infty\right)$

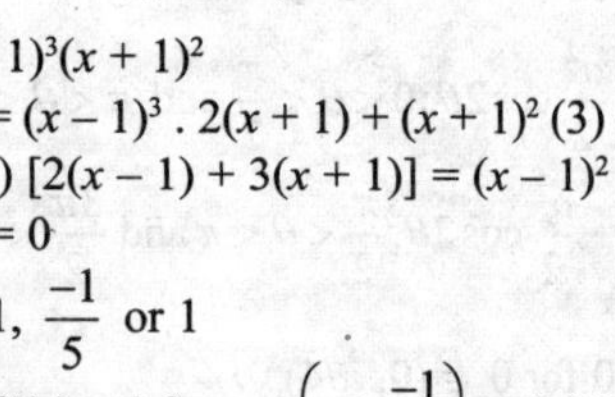

$\Rightarrow$ $f(x)$ has local maximum value $= f(-1) = 0$ and local minimum value $= f\left(\dfrac{-1}{5}\right) = \left(\dfrac{-1}{5} - 1\right)^3 \left(\dfrac{-1}{5} + 1\right)^2$

$= \left(\dfrac{-6}{5}\right)^3 \left(\dfrac{4}{5}\right)^2 = \dfrac{-216 \times 16}{3125} = \dfrac{-3456}{3125}$

7. Let $f(t) = SA = \sqrt{(t-3)^2 + (t^2)^2}$

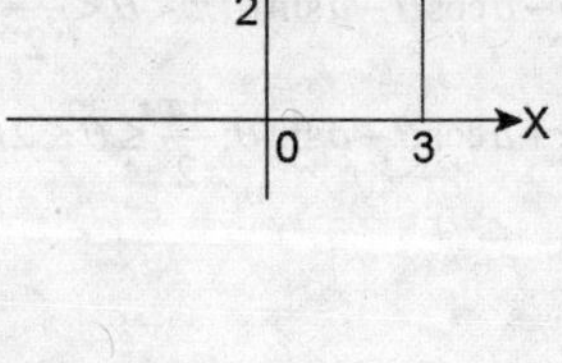

$\Rightarrow$ $f'(t) = \dfrac{2(t-3) + 4t^3}{2\sqrt{(t-3)^2 + t^4}}$

For Maximum/Minimum of $f(t)$, $f'(t) = 0$

$\Rightarrow$ $2t^3 + t - 3 = 0$

$\Rightarrow$ $2(t-1)t^2 + 2(t-1)t + 3(t-1) = 0$

$\Rightarrow$ $(t-1)(2t^2 + 2t + 3) = 0$

$\Rightarrow$ $t = 1$ is the only root.

$\therefore$ $f(t)_{min} = f(1) = \sqrt{(-2)^2 + (1^2)^2} = \sqrt{5}$ units .

8. Let $x + y = 4$ ...(1)

Let $S = x^2 + y^3$

$\Rightarrow$ $S = x^2 + (4-x)^3$

$\Rightarrow$ $\dfrac{ds}{dx} = 2x + 3(4-x)^2(-1)$

$= 2x - 3(4-x)^2 = -3x^2 + 26x - 48$

For max./ min. of S, put $\dfrac{ds}{dx} = 0$

$\Rightarrow$ $3x^2 - 26x + 48 = 0$ and $\dfrac{d^2s}{dx^2} = -6x + 26$ and $\dfrac{ds}{dx} = 0$

$\Rightarrow$ $x = \dfrac{26 \pm \sqrt{(-26)^2 - 12 \times 48}}{6}$

$\Rightarrow$ $x = \dfrac{26 \pm 10}{6} = 6 \text{ or } \dfrac{8}{3}$

$\therefore$ $\left(\dfrac{d^2s}{dx^2}\right)_{x=6} = -10$ and $\left(\dfrac{d^2s}{dx^2}\right)_{x=\frac{8}{3}} = 10$

$\Rightarrow$ S will be minimum for $x = \dfrac{8}{3}$ and y = y/3

$\therefore$ $\dfrac{8}{3}, \dfrac{4}{3}$

9. $f(x) = \dfrac{x^2 - 3x + 2}{x^2 + 2x + 1}$ and $f'(x)$

$= \dfrac{(x^2+2x+1)(2x-3) - (x^2-3x+2).(2x+2)}{(x^2+2x+1)^2}$

$= \dfrac{5x^2 - 2x - 7}{(x^2+2x+1)^2}$

$\Rightarrow$ $f'(x) = \dfrac{5x^2 - 2x - 7}{\left(x^2+2x+1\right)^2}$

$\Rightarrow$ $f'(x) = \dfrac{5x^2 - 7x + 5x - 7}{\left(x^2+2x+1\right)^2}$

$\Rightarrow$ $f'(x) = \dfrac{x(5x-7) + 1(5x-7)}{\left(x^2+2x+1\right)^2}$

$\Rightarrow$ $f'(x) = \dfrac{(x+1)(5x-7)}{\left(x^2+2x+1\right)^2}$

$\Rightarrow$ $f'(x) > 0$ for $x \in (-\infty, -1) \cup \left(\dfrac{7}{5}, \infty\right)$ and $f'(x) < 0$ for $x \in \left(-1, \dfrac{7}{5}\right)$

$\Rightarrow$ $f(x)$ has a local minima at $x = \frac{7}{5}$ and the local minimum value is given by, $f\left(\frac{7}{5}\right) = \frac{\left(\frac{7}{5}-1\right)\left(\frac{7}{5}-2\right)}{\left(\frac{7}{5}+1\right)^2}$

$$= \frac{\left(\frac{2}{5}\right)\left(\frac{-3}{5}\right)}{\frac{144}{25}} = \frac{-6}{25} \times \frac{25}{144} = -\frac{1}{24}$$

Hence $f_{\min} = f\left(\frac{7}{5}\right) = -\frac{1}{24}$

10. $f(x) = \sqrt[3]{(x-1)^2} + \sqrt[3]{(x+1)^2} = (x-1)^{2/3} + (x+1)^{2/3}$

$\Rightarrow f'(x) = \frac{2}{3}(x-1)^{-1/3} + \frac{2}{3}(x+1)^{-1/3}$

$\Rightarrow f'(x) = \frac{2}{3(x-1)^{1/3}} + \frac{2}{3(x+1)^{1/3}} = 0$ at $x = 0$ and $f(0) = 2$

$\Rightarrow f''(x) = \frac{2}{3}\left(\frac{-1}{3}\right)\left(\frac{1}{(x-1)^{4/3}} + \frac{1}{(x+1)^{4/3}}\right)$

$\Rightarrow f''(x) = -\frac{2}{9}\left[\frac{1}{(x-1)^{4/3}} + \frac{1}{(x+1)^{4/3}}\right] < 0\ \forall x \in \mathbb{R}$; $f(\pm1) = (4)^{1/3}$

$\Rightarrow$ Also $f'(\pm1)$ does not exist and rough graph will be of the form as shown below.

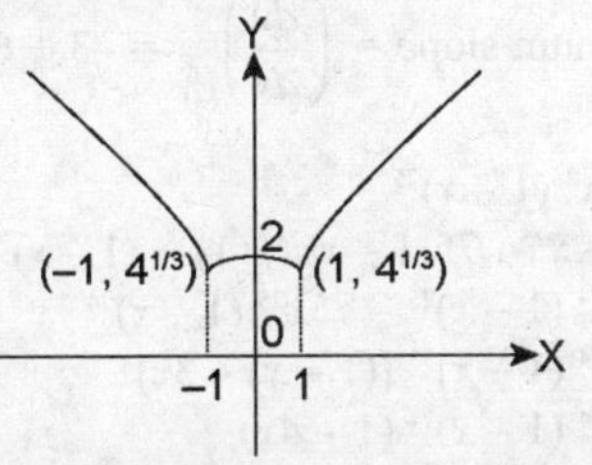

Thus $f_{\min} = f(\pm1) = (4)^{1/3}$ and $f_{\max}$ does not exist and local maximum value $= f(0) = 2$

TEXTUAL EXERCISE-2: (OBJECTIVE)

1. (a) $f: \mathbb{R} \to \mathbb{R}; f(x) = \frac{1}{e^x + 2e^{-x}}$

$\Rightarrow f(x) = \frac{e^x}{e^{2x}+2}$

$\Rightarrow f'(x) = \frac{(e^{2x}+2)e^x - e^x(2e^x)}{(e^{2x}+2)^2}$

$\Rightarrow f'(x) = \frac{2e^x - e^{3x}}{(e^{2x}+2)^2} > 0\ \forall x \in \mathbb{R}$

$\Rightarrow f'(x) > 0$ for $2e^x - e^{3x} > 0$ i.e., for $2 > e^{2x}$

$\Rightarrow 2x < \ell n\, 2$

$\Rightarrow x < \frac{1}{2}\ell n2$ and $f'(x) < 0$ for $x > \frac{1}{2}\ell n2$

$\therefore$ $f(x) \uparrow x < \frac{1}{2}\ell n2$ and $f(x) \downarrow$ for $x > \frac{1}{2}\ell n2$

$\therefore$ $f_{\max} = f\left(\frac{1}{2}\ell n2\right) = \frac{1}{e^{\ell n\sqrt{2}} + 2e^{\ell n\left(\frac{1}{\sqrt{2}}\right)}}$

$$= \frac{1}{\sqrt{2} + 2\left(\frac{1}{\sqrt{2}}\right)} = \frac{1}{2\sqrt{2}}$$

$\Rightarrow \lim_{x\to-\infty} f(x) = 0$ and $\lim_{x\to\infty} f(x) = 0$

$\Rightarrow$ Range of $f(x) = \left(0, \frac{1}{2\sqrt{2}}\right]$

Also $f(x)$ is continuous and hence attains each value in between 0 and $\frac{1}{2\sqrt{2}}$ and hence $f(c) = \frac{1}{3}$ for some $c \in \mathbb{R}$.

2. (c) $f(x) = x^3 + ax^2 + bx + c$, $a^2 \le 3b$

$\Rightarrow f'(x) = 3x^2 + 2ax + b$

Disc. $= 4a^2 - 12b$

$= 4(a^2 - 3b) \le 0$ as $a^2 \le 3b$

$\Rightarrow f'(x) \ge 0\ \forall x \in \mathbb{R}$

$\Rightarrow$ $f(x)$ is an increasing function $\forall\, x \in \mathbb{R}$.

$\Rightarrow$ $f(x)$ has no extreme values.

3. (c) $y = \frac{\sin(x+a)}{\sin(x+b)}, a \ne b$

$$\frac{dy}{dx} = \frac{\sin(x+b)\cos(x+a) - \sin(x+a)\cos(x+b)}{[\sin(x+b)]^2}$$

$$= \frac{\sin[(x+b)-(x+a)]}{[\sin(x+b)]^2} = \frac{\sin(b-a)}{[\sin(x+b)]^2}\begin{cases} >0 \text{ for } b>0 \\ <0 \text{ for } b<a \end{cases}$$

$\Rightarrow$ $f(x)$ has neither maxima nor a minima at $x = 0$

4. (d) $f(x) = \cos x + \frac{1}{2}\cos 2x - \frac{1}{3}\cos 3x$

$\Rightarrow f'(x) = -\sin x - \sin 2x + \sin 3x$

$\Rightarrow f'(x) = (\sin 3x - \sin x) - \sin 2x$

$\Rightarrow f'(x) = 2\cos 2x \sin x - 2\sin x \cos x$

$= (2\sin x)(\cos 2x - \cos x) = -4\sin x \,.\, \sin\frac{3x}{2}.\sin\frac{x}{2}$

$\therefore$ $f'(x) = 0$

$\Rightarrow$ $\sin x = 0$ or $\sin\frac{3x}{2} = 0$ or $\frac{x}{2} = 0$

$\Rightarrow$ $x = n\pi$ or $= \frac{2n\pi}{3}$

$f(x)$ is periodic with period $=$ L. C. M $\left(2\pi, \pi, \frac{2\pi}{3}\right) = 2\pi$

$\therefore$ In $[0, 2\pi]$; $f'(x) = 0$ at $x = 0, \pi, 2\pi, \frac{2\pi}{3}, \frac{4\pi}{3},$

$\therefore$ $f(0) = 1 + \frac{1}{2} - \frac{1}{3} = \frac{3}{2} - \frac{1}{3} = \frac{9-2}{6} = \frac{7}{6}$

$f(\pi) = -1 + \frac{1}{2}+\frac{1}{3} = -\frac{1}{2}+\frac{1}{3} = \frac{-3+2}{6} = \frac{-1}{6}$

$\left(\frac{2\pi}{3}\right) = \frac{-1}{2}+\frac{1}{2}\left(\frac{-1}{2}\right)-\frac{1}{3} = \frac{-1}{2}-\frac{1}{4}-\frac{1}{3} = \frac{-13}{12}$

$f\left(\frac{4\pi}{3}\right) = -\frac{1}{2}+\frac{1}{2}\left(\frac{-1}{2}\right)-\frac{1}{3}(1) = \frac{-13}{12}$

$\therefore$ Difference between greatest and least $= \frac{7}{6}+\frac{13}{12} = \frac{27}{12} = \frac{9}{4}$

5. (b) $f(x) = x^2 + \frac{1}{1+x^2} = \left[(1+x^2)+\frac{1}{(1+x)}\right]-1$

$\because x + \frac{1}{x} \geq 2 \ \forall\, x \geq 0$

$(1 + x^2) + \frac{1}{(1+x^2)} \geq 2$ and equality holds at $x = 0$

$\Rightarrow f(x) \geq (2 - 1)$ i.e., $f(x) \geq 1$

$\Rightarrow$ Minimum value of $f(x) = 1$

6. (a) $ax^2 + bx + 4$ has its minimum value $= \frac{-D}{4a}$

$= -\frac{(b^2-16a)}{4(a)}$ at $x = \frac{-b}{2a}$

$\Rightarrow \frac{-D}{4a} = -1$ and $-\frac{b}{2a} = 1$

$\Rightarrow D = 4a;\ b = -2a$

$\Rightarrow b^2 - 4ac = 4a;\ b = -2a$

$\Rightarrow b^2 - 16a\,(4) = 4a,\ b = -2a$

$\Rightarrow 4a^2 = 20\,a$

$\Rightarrow a = 5,\ b = -10$

$\therefore (a, b) \equiv (5, -10)$

7. (b) $f(x) = e^{(2x^2-2x+1)\sin^2 x} = e^{\left[2\left(x^2-x+\frac{1}{4}\right)-\frac{1}{2}+1\right]\sin^2 x} = e^{\left[2\left(x-\frac{1}{2}\right)^2+\frac{1}{2}\right]\sin^2 x}$

$\because$ Exponential function is an increasing function and $\left[2\left(x-\frac{1}{2}\right)^2+\frac{1}{2}\right]\sin^2 x \geq 0$ and equality holds at $x = n\pi$

$\Rightarrow$ Minimum value of $f(x) = f(0) = 1$

8. (b) $y = a\,\ell nx + bx^2 + x;\ x > 0$

$\Rightarrow \frac{dy}{dx} = \frac{a}{x} + 2bx + 1$

$\therefore \frac{dy}{dx} = 0$

$\Rightarrow \frac{2bx^2+x+a}{x} = 0$

$\Rightarrow 2bx^2 + x + a = 0$

$\Rightarrow x = \frac{-1\pm\sqrt{1-8ab}}{4b}$

$\therefore x = \frac{-1\pm\sqrt{1-8ab}}{4b}$ and $x = \frac{-1+\sqrt{1-8ab}}{4b}$ are points of extremem.

$\Rightarrow \frac{-1-\sqrt{1-8ab}}{4b} = -1$ and $\frac{-1+\sqrt{1-8ab}}{4b} = 2$

$\Rightarrow -1-\sqrt{1-8ab} = -4b$ and $-1+\sqrt{1-8ab} = -4b = 8b$

$\Rightarrow 4b = -2$

$\Rightarrow b = -1/2$

$\Rightarrow -1+\sqrt{1+4a} = -4$

$\Rightarrow \sqrt{1+4a} = -3$, which is impossible

$\therefore \frac{-1-\sqrt{1-8ab}}{4b} = 2$ and $\frac{-1+\sqrt{1-8ab}}{4b} = -1$

$\Rightarrow -2 = 4b$

$\Rightarrow b = -1/2$ and $-1-\sqrt{1-8ab} = 8b$

$\Rightarrow -1-\sqrt{1+4a} = -4$

$\Rightarrow -\sqrt{1+4a} = -3$

$\Rightarrow 1 + 4a = 9$

$\Rightarrow 4a = 8$

$\Rightarrow a = 2$

9. (a) $y = -x^3 + 3x^2 + 2x - 27$

$\frac{dy}{dx} = -3x^2 + 6x + 2$

$\frac{d^2y}{dx^2} = -6x + 6$

For max/min slope $\left(\frac{dy}{dx}\right), \frac{d^2y}{dx^2} = 0$

$\Rightarrow x = 1$

$\therefore$ Maximum slope $= \left(\frac{dy}{dx}\right)_{x=1} = -3 + 6 + 2 = 5$

10. (b) $f(x) = x^{25}(1-x)^{75}$

$\Rightarrow f'(x) = x^{25} \,.\, 75(1-x)^{74}(-1) + (1-x)^{75} \,.\, 25\,x^{24}$

$= 25x^{24}(1-x)^{75} - 75x^{25}(1-x)^{74}$

$= 25x^{24}(1-x)^{75}[(1-x) - 3x]$

$= 25x^{24}(1-x)^{74}(1-4x)$

< 0 for $x < \frac{1}{4}$ and > 0 for $x < \frac{1}{4}$

$\Rightarrow f(x) \uparrow$ on $\left(0, \frac{1}{4}\right)$ and $\downarrow$ on $\left(\frac{1}{4}, 1\right)$

$\Rightarrow f_{\max} = f\left(\frac{1}{4}\right) = \left(\frac{1}{4}\right)^{25}\left(1-\frac{1}{4}\right)^{75}$ at $x = 1/4$

11. (c) $f(x) = a\sin x + \frac{1}{3}\sin 3x$

$f'(x) = a\cos x + \cos 3x$

$= a\cos x + [4\cos^3 x - 3\cos x]$

$= 4\cos^3 x + (a-3)\cos x$

$= (\cos x)[4\cos^2 x + (a-3)]$

$f''(x) = 12\cos^2 x(-\sin x) - (a-3)\sin x$

$= -[12\cos^2 x + (a-3)]\sin x$

$f(x)$ has maximum at $x = \pi/3$

$\Rightarrow f'(\pi/3) = 0$

$\Rightarrow \frac{1}{2}\left[4\left(\frac{1}{4}\right)+(a-3)\right]=0$

$\Rightarrow a = 2$

12. (b) $f(x) = x^{40} - x^{20};\ x \in [0, 1]$

$\Rightarrow f'(x) = 40x^{39} - 20x^{19}$

$= 20x^{19}(2x^{20} - 1)$

$\therefore f'(x) = 0$ at $x^0 = 0$ or at $x = \left(\frac{1}{20}\right)^{1/20}$

Also $f'(x) < 0$ on $\left(0, \left(\frac{1}{2}\right)^{1/20}\right)$ and $f'(x) > 0 \left(\left(\frac{1}{2}\right)^{1/20}, 1\right]$

$\Rightarrow f(x)$ has a local minima at $x = \left(\frac{1}{2}\right)^{1/20}$

$\therefore$ Absolute maximum value of $f(x) = \max.\{f(0), f(1)\} = \max.\{0, 0\} = 0$

13. (a) $f(x) = 4\cos(x^2)\cos\left(\frac{\pi}{3}+x^2\right)\cos\left(\frac{\pi}{3}-x^2\right)$

$\Rightarrow f(x) = 4\cos x^2\left[\cos^2\frac{\pi}{3} - \sin^2 x^2\right]$

$\Rightarrow f(x) = \cos x^2 - 4\cos^2 \sin^2 x^2$

$\Rightarrow f(x) = \cos x^2\,[1 - 4\sin^2 x^2] - \cos x^2\,[1 - 4(1 - \cos^2 x^2)]$

$= \cos x^2\,[-3 + 4\cos^2 x^2]$

$= 4\cos^3 x^3 - 3\cos x^2$

$= \cos 3x^2$ having minimum value -1 and maximum value $= 1$ on $\mathbb{R}$.

14. (b) Given ellipse is $\frac{x^2}{27}+\frac{y^2}{1}=1$ ...(1)

$P \equiv \left(3\sqrt{3}\cos\theta, \sin\theta\right);\ 0 < \theta < \pi/2$

$\therefore$ Equation of tangent to (1) at p is $\frac{x\left(3\sqrt{3}\cos\theta\right)}{27} + \frac{y\sin\theta}{1} = 1$ or $\frac{x}{\left(\frac{27}{3\sqrt{3}}\sec\theta\right)} + \frac{y}{(\operatorname{cosec}\theta)} = 1$

<u>A.T.Q:</u> To minimize $S = \frac{27}{3\sqrt{3}}\sec\theta + \operatorname{cosec}\theta$ i.e., $S = 3\sqrt{3}\sec\theta + \operatorname{cosec}\theta$

$\therefore \frac{ds}{d\theta} = 3\sqrt{3}\sec\theta\tan\theta - \operatorname{cosec}\theta \cdot \cot\theta$

$\therefore \frac{ds}{d\theta} = 0 \Rightarrow 3\sqrt{3}\sec\theta\tan\theta = \operatorname{cosec}\theta\cot\theta$

$\Rightarrow 3\sqrt{3}\frac{\sin\theta}{\cos^2\theta} = \frac{\cos\theta}{\sin^2\theta}$

$\Rightarrow 3\sqrt{3}\sin^3\theta = \cos^3\theta \quad \tan^3 = \frac{1}{3\sqrt{3}} = \left(\frac{1}{\sqrt{3}}\right)^3$

$\Rightarrow \tan\theta = \frac{\pi}{6}$ for $\theta \in \left(0, \frac{\pi}{2}\right)$

$\therefore \frac{ds}{d\theta} < 0$ for $\theta \in \left(0, \frac{\pi}{6}\right)$ and $\frac{ds}{d\theta} > 0$ for $\theta \in \left(\frac{\pi}{6}, \frac{\pi}{2}\right)$

$\therefore f_{\min} = f\left(\frac{\pi}{6}\right) = \frac{27}{3\sqrt{3}}\sec\frac{\pi}{6} + \operatorname{cosec}\frac{\pi}{6} = 3\sqrt{3}\left(\frac{2}{\sqrt{3}}\right) + 2$

$= 8$ at $\theta = \pi/6$

15. (a) $p'(1) = 0;\ p'(3) = 0$

Let $p(x) = ax^3 + bx^2 + cx + d$

$\Rightarrow p'(x) = 3ax^2 + 2bx + c$

$\Rightarrow 3ax^2 + 2bx + c = 3a(x - 1)(x - 3)$

$\Rightarrow 3ax^2 + 2bx + c = 3ax^2 + (-3a - 9a)x + 9a$

$\Rightarrow 2b = -12a,\ c = 9a$

$\Rightarrow b = -6a,\ c = 9a$

$\therefore p'(x) = 3ax^2 - 12ax + 9a$

$\Rightarrow p(x) = ax^3 - 6ax^2 + 9ax + d$

Now $p(1) = 6$

$\Rightarrow a - 6a + 9a + d = 6$

$\Rightarrow 4a + d = 6 \quad \Rightarrow d = 6 - 4a$

$\therefore p(x) = ax^3 - 6ax^2 + 9ax + 6 - 4a$

Also $p(3) = 2$

$\Rightarrow 27a - 54a + 27a + 6 - 4a = 2$

$\Rightarrow a = 1$

$\therefore p(x) = x^3 - 6x^2 + 9x + 2$

$\Rightarrow p'(x) = 3x^2 - 12x + 9 \Rightarrow p'(0) = 9$

16. (a) $f: \mathbb{R} \to \mathbb{R}$

$$f(x) = |x| + |x^2 - 1| = \begin{cases} -x + x^2 - 1 \text{ for } x < -1 \\ -x - x^2 + 1 \text{ for } -1 \le x < 0 \\ x - x^2 + 1 \text{ for } 0 \le x < 1 \\ x + x^2 - 1 \text{ for } x \ge 1 \end{cases}$$

$$\Rightarrow f'(x) = \begin{cases} 2x - 1 \text{ for } x < -1 \\ -2x - 1 \text{ for } -1 < x < 0 \\ -2x + 1 \text{ for } 0 < x < 1 \\ 2x + 1 \text{ for } x > 1 \end{cases}$$

$\Rightarrow f'(-1^-) = -3,\ f'(-1^+) = 1,\ f'(0^-) = -1,\ f'(0^+) = 1,\ f'(1^-) = -1,\ f'(1^+) = 3,\ f'(x) = 0$ at $x = -\frac{1}{2}$ and at $x = \frac{1}{2}$

$$\text{And } f''(x) = \begin{cases} 2 \text{ for } x < -1 \\ -2 \text{ for } -1 < x < 0 \\ -2 \text{ for } 0 < x < 1 \\ 2 \text{ for } x > 1 \end{cases}$$

Thus $f(x)$ is points of non-differentiability at $x = -1$, 0 and 1

The graphs of $f(x)$ will be of the form as shown below.

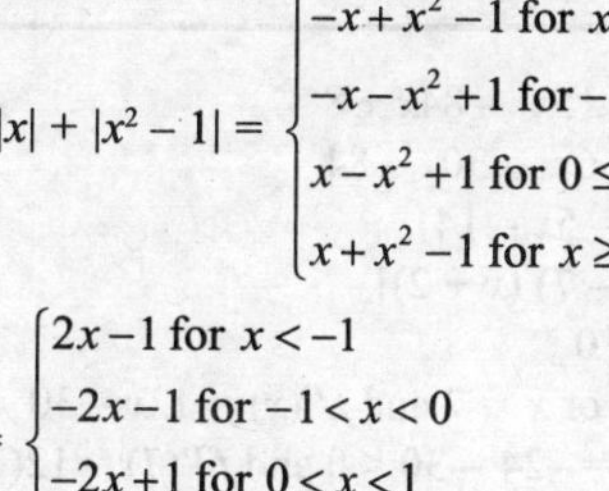

$\therefore f(x)$ has 5 points of local maximum or minimum .

17. (d) $f(x) = \frac{x}{8}+\frac{2}{x}; x \in [1, 6]$

$\Rightarrow f'(x) = \frac{1}{8}+\left(\frac{-2}{x^2}\right)=\frac{1}{8}-\frac{2}{x^2}=\left(\frac{x^2-16}{8x^2}\right)$

$\therefore f'(x) = 0$

$\Rightarrow \frac{2}{x^2}=\frac{1}{8}$

$\Rightarrow x^2 = 16$

$\Rightarrow x = \pm 4$ and $f''(x) = -2\left(\frac{-2}{x^3}\right)=\frac{4}{x^3}$

$\Rightarrow f''(4) = \frac{1}{16} > 0$ and $f''(-4) = \frac{-1}{16} < 0$

$\Rightarrow f'(x) < 0$ for $x \in [1, 4)$ and $f'(x) > 0$ for $x \in (4, 6]$

$\Rightarrow f(x)$ has maximum value = max. $\{f(1), f(6)\}$

$= \text{max.}\left\{\frac{1}{8}+2, \frac{6}{8}+\frac{2}{6}\right\}$

$= \text{max.}\left\{\frac{17}{8}, \frac{13}{12}\right\}=\frac{17}{8}$

TEXTUAL EXERCISE-3: (SUBJECTIVE)

1. $f(x) = 2x^3 - 15x^2 - 84x + 8$

$\Rightarrow f'(x) = 6x^2 - 30x - 84$

$= 6[x^2 - 5x - 14)$

$= 6[(x - 7)(x + 2)]$

$\therefore f'(x) = 0$

$\Rightarrow x = -2$ or $x = 7$ and $f''(x) = 12x - 30$

$\therefore f'(-2) = -24 - 30 < 0$ and $f''(7) = 12(7) - 30 > 0$

$\Rightarrow f(x)$ has a local maxima at $x = -2$ and local minima at $x = 7$ and the local maximum value $= f(-2) = -629$

2. (a) $f(x) = x^4 e^{-x^2}$

$\Rightarrow f'(x) = x^4(-2x(e^{-x^2} + e^{-x^2}(4x^3) = e^{-x^2}(4x^3 - 2x^5)$

$\therefore f'(x) = 0$

$\Rightarrow 4x^3 - 2x^5 = 0$

$\Rightarrow 2x^3(2 - x^2) = 0$ and $f''(x) = e^{-x^2}(12x^2 - 10x^4) + (4x^3 - 2x^5)$

$= e^{-x^2}[12x^2 - 10x^4 - 8x^4 + 4x^6]$

$= 2e^{-x^2}(2x^4 - 9x^2 + 6)x^2$

$= 2x^2 e^{-x^2}(2x^4 - 9x^2 + 6)$

$\therefore f''(0) = 0, f''\left(\pm\sqrt{2}\right) = 2(2)e^{-2}(8 - 18 + 6) < 0$

Here second derivate test fails to conclude for maximum/minimum at $x = 0$, thus we will use first derivation test.

$f'(-0.1) = e^{-(-0.1)^2}(4(-0.1)^3 - 2(-0.1)^5)$

$= -e^{-(0.1)^2}(2)(0.1)^3\left[2-(0.1)^2\right]$

And $f'(0.1) = e^{-(0.1)^2}[4(0.1)^3 - 2(0.1)^5] = 2(0.1)^3 e^{-(0.1)^2}[2 - 0.1)^2]$

$\Rightarrow x = 0$ is a point of local minima.

$\therefore f(x)$ has local maximum value at $x = \pm\sqrt{2}$ given by $f\left(\pm\sqrt{2}\right) = 4/e^2$ and $f(x)$ ha s a local at $x = 0$ given by $f(0) = 0$

(b) $f(x) = \sin 3x - 3 \sin x$

$\Rightarrow f'(x) = 3 \cos 3x - 3 \cos x$

$= 3[4 \cos^3 x - 3 \cos x] - 3 \cos x$

$= 12 \cos^3 x - 12 \cos x$

$= (12 \cos x)(\cos^2 x - 1)$

$\therefore f'(x) = 0$

$\Rightarrow \cos x = 0$ or $\cos x \pm 1$

$\Rightarrow x = (2n + 1)\frac{\pi}{2}, x = n\pi$ and $f''(x) = -9 \sin + 3 \sin x$

$= -9(3 \sin x - 4 \sin^3 x) + 3 \sin x$

$= 36 \sin^3 x - 24 \sin x$

$= 12 \sin x(3 \sin^2 x - 2)$

$\therefore f''\left((2n+1)\frac{\pi}{2}\right) = 12 \sin x(1)$

> 0 for $x = (4n + 1)\frac{\pi}{2}; x \in \mathbb{Z}$

< 0 for $x = (4n + 3)\frac{\pi}{2}; x \in \mathbb{Z}$

$f''(n\pi) = 0, f'(2n\pi - h) < 0, f'(2n\pi + h) < 0,$

$f'((2n + 1)\pi - h) > 0, f'(2n\pi + h) > 0$

$\Rightarrow x = n\pi$ are points of inflexion and $x = (4n + 1)\frac{\pi}{2}$ are points of local minima and $x = (4n + 3)\frac{\pi}{2}$ are points of local maxima.

Hence local minimum value of $f(x) = f\left((4n+1)\frac{\pi}{2}\right) = -1 - 3(1) = -4$ and local maximum value $f(x)$

$= f\left((4n+3)\frac{\pi}{2}\right) = 1 - 3(-1) = 4$

$\therefore$ Local minimum value of function $= -4$ and Local maximum value of function $= 4$.

3. Area of $\Delta ABC = \frac{1}{2}bh$ ...(1)

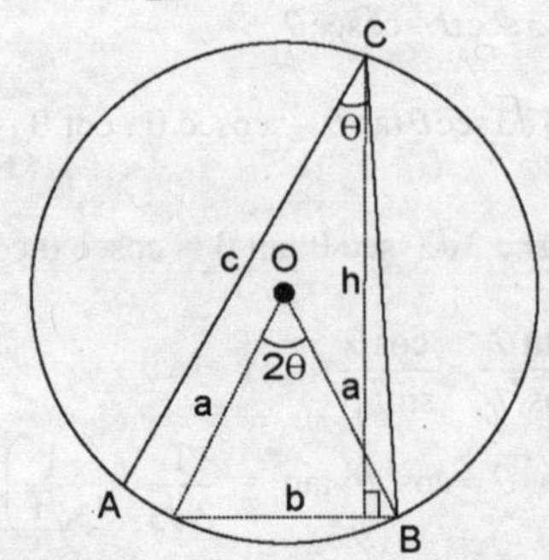

Clearly for maximum area, and fixed b, h must be greatest, Thus C must be at the top of O vertically above as shown below.

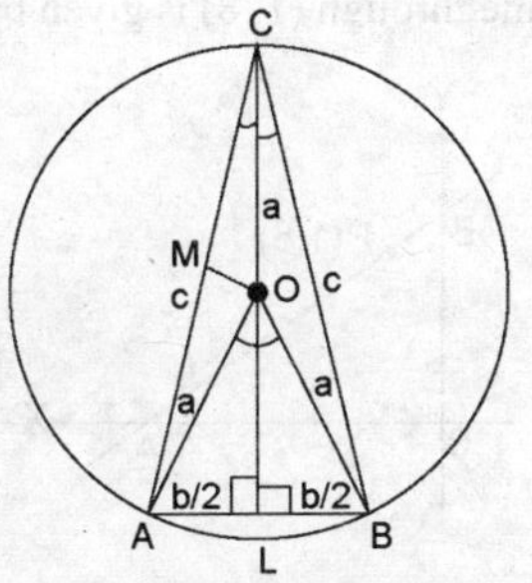

Clearly $\Delta ACL \cong \Delta BCL$

$\Rightarrow$ $AC = BC = C$(say)

$\therefore$ ar. $\Delta ABC = 2(ar\ \Delta ACL)$

$= 2\left(\frac{1}{2}\left(\frac{b}{2}\right)(CL)\right) = \frac{b}{2} . c \sin\theta$

$= \frac{1}{2}\ bc \sin\theta$ ....(2)

Also, $\angle AOB = 360^\circ - 4\theta$

$\Rightarrow$ $\angle AOL = 180^\circ - 2\theta$,

$\Rightarrow$ $\sin(180^\circ - 2\theta) = \frac{b/2}{a}$

$\Rightarrow$ $b = 2a \sin 2\theta$ ...(3)

In Δ COM, $\cos(90^0 - \theta) = \frac{c/2}{a}$

$\Rightarrow$ $c = 2a \sin\theta$ ...(4)

Using (3) & (4) in (2), we get $\Delta = \frac{1}{2}(2a \sin 2\theta)(2a \sin\theta) \sin\theta$

$\Rightarrow$ $\Delta = 2a^2 \sin 2\theta . \sin^2\theta$

$= 2a^2(2 \sin\theta \cos\theta) \sin^2\theta$

$= 4a^2 \sin^3\theta \cos\theta$

$\therefore$ For maximum area $\frac{d\Delta}{d\theta} = 0$

$\Rightarrow$ $-4a^2 \sin^3\theta \sin\theta + 4a^2 \cos\theta(3 \sin^2\theta \cos\theta) = 0$

$\Rightarrow$ $-\sin^4\theta + 3\sin^2\theta\cos^2\theta = 0$

$\Rightarrow$ $\sin^2\theta = 0$ or $3\cos^2\theta = \sin^2\theta$

$\Rightarrow$ $\sin\theta = 0$ or $\tan\theta = \sqrt{3}$

$\Rightarrow$ $\theta = 0$ or $\theta = \pi/3$

$\Rightarrow$ Area of Δ will be maximum for $\theta = 60^0$

i.e., ΔABC is an equilateral with maximum area $= 4a^2$

$\left(\frac{\sqrt{3}}{2}\right)^3\left(\frac{1}{2}\right) = \frac{3\sqrt{3}\,a^2}{4}$

4. Volume of cylinder $(V) = \pi r^2 h = \pi\left(a^2 - \frac{h^2}{4}\right)h$

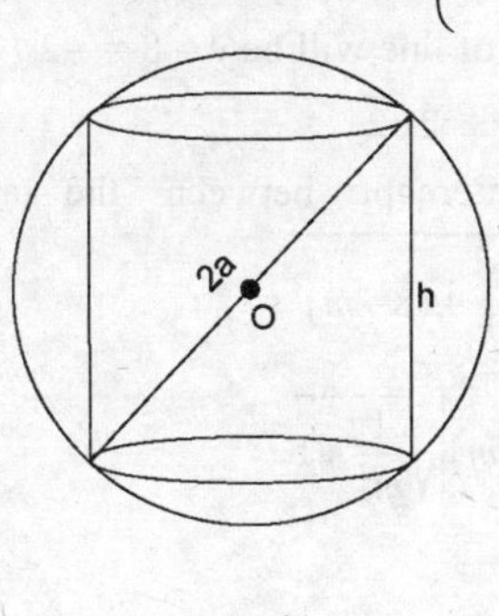

$\left[\because 4a^2 = (2r)^2 + h^2 \Rightarrow \ell^2 = a^2 - \frac{h^2}{4}\right]$

i.e., $V = \pi a^2 h - \frac{\pi h^3}{4}$

$\therefore$ For maximum volume, $(dv/dh) = 0$ i.e., $\pi a^2 - \frac{\pi}{4}(3h^2) = 0$

$\Rightarrow$ $\frac{3}{4}h^2 = a^2$

$\Rightarrow$ $h = \frac{2}{\sqrt{3}}a.$

5. Let the co-ordinates of P be $(2\sqrt{2}\cos\theta, 3\sqrt{2}\sin\theta)$; $0 < \theta < \pi/2$

$\therefore$ Equation of tangent to ellipse at P will be $\frac{(2\sqrt{2}\cos\theta)x}{8} + \frac{(3\sqrt{2}\sin\theta)y}{18} = 1$

$\therefore$ Area of Δ formed by above tangent with co- ordinates axes

$A = \frac{1}{2}\left(\frac{8}{2\sqrt{2}\cos\theta}\right)\left(\frac{18}{3\sqrt{2}\sin\theta}\right) = \frac{6}{\sin\theta\cos\theta} = \frac{12}{\sin 2\theta}$

$= 12 \operatorname{cosec} 2\theta$

$\therefore$ $\frac{dA}{d\theta} = -24\ (\operatorname{cosec} 2\theta . \cot 2\theta)$

For maximum/minimum of A, $\frac{dA}{d\theta} = 0$

$\Rightarrow$ $\cot 2\theta = 0$

$\Rightarrow$ $\cos 2\theta = 0$

$\Rightarrow$ $2\theta = \pi/2$

$\Rightarrow$ $\theta = \pi/4$

$\therefore$ Maximum area $= 12 \operatorname{cosec} \pi/2 = 12$ sq. units and the corresponding co-ordinates of will be $\equiv (2, 3)$

6. $\Delta ADB \sim \Delta ABL$

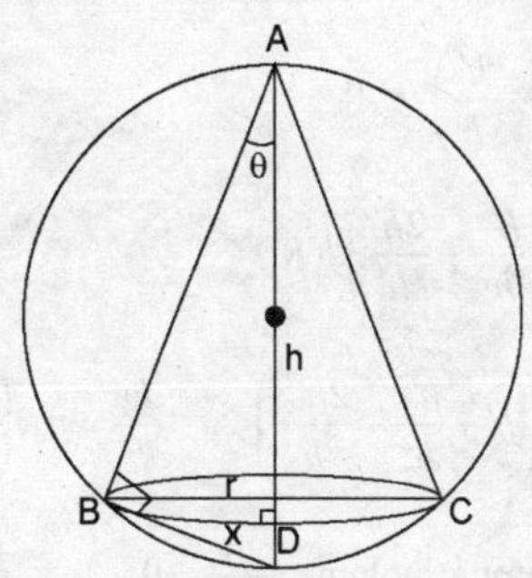

$\Rightarrow$ $\frac{h}{AB} = \frac{r}{x} = \frac{AB}{2R}$

$\Rightarrow$ $\frac{h}{\sqrt{h^2 + r^2}} = \frac{r}{x} = \frac{\sqrt{h^2 + r^2}}{2R}$

$\Rightarrow$ $2Rh = h^2 + r^2$ ...(1)

Volume of cone $(V) = \frac{1}{3}\pi r^2 h$

$V = \frac{1}{3}\pi\,(2Rh - h^2)h$ (from (1))

$\Rightarrow \quad V = \frac{2}{3}\pi Rh^2 - \frac{1}{3}\pi h^3$

$\Rightarrow \quad \frac{dv}{dh} = \frac{2}{3}\pi R(2h) - \frac{1}{3}(3h^2)$

$\therefore$ For maximum volume, $\frac{dv}{dh} = 0$

$\Rightarrow \quad \frac{4\pi}{3} Rh = \pi h^2$

$\Rightarrow \quad h = \frac{4}{3}R$

7. $\Delta ALM \sim \Delta ABD$

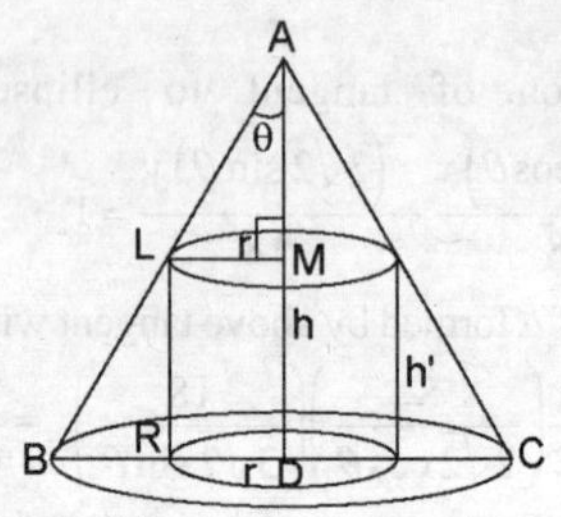

$\Rightarrow \quad \frac{AL}{AB} = \frac{LM}{BD} = \frac{AM}{AD}$

$\Rightarrow \quad \frac{AL}{AB} = \frac{r}{R} = \frac{h-h'}{h}$

$\Rightarrow \quad r = \left(\frac{h-h'}{h}\right)R$

Volume of cylinder $= V = \pi r^2 h'$

$\Rightarrow \quad V = \pi\left(\frac{h-h'}{h}\right)^2 h'.R$

$\Rightarrow \quad V = \pi\left(1-\frac{h'}{h}\right)^2 h'.\text{R}$

$\Rightarrow \quad V = \left(1+\frac{h'^2}{h^2}-\frac{2h'}{h}\right).h'R$

$\Rightarrow \quad V = \pi R\left(h'+\frac{h'^3}{h^2}-\frac{2h'^2}{h}\right) \quad \therefore \quad \frac{dv}{dh'} = \pi R\left(1+\frac{3h'^2}{h^2}-\frac{4h'}{h}\right)$

For maximum volume, $\frac{dv}{dh'} = 0$

$\Rightarrow \quad 1 + \frac{3h'^2}{h^2} - \frac{4h'}{h} = 0$

$\Rightarrow \quad h^2 + 3h'^2 - 4hh' = 0$ or $3h'^2 - 4hh' + h^2 = 0$

$\Rightarrow \quad 3h'^2 - 3hh' - hh' + h^2 = 0$

$\Rightarrow \quad 3h'(h' - h) - h(h' - h) = 0$

$\Rightarrow \quad (3h' - h)(h' - h) = 0$

$\Rightarrow \quad h' = \frac{h}{3}$ or $h' = h$

$\therefore$ For maximum volume of cylinder $h' = \frac{h}{3}$

8. Equation of line through (1, 8) is given by $(y - 8) = m(x - 1)$

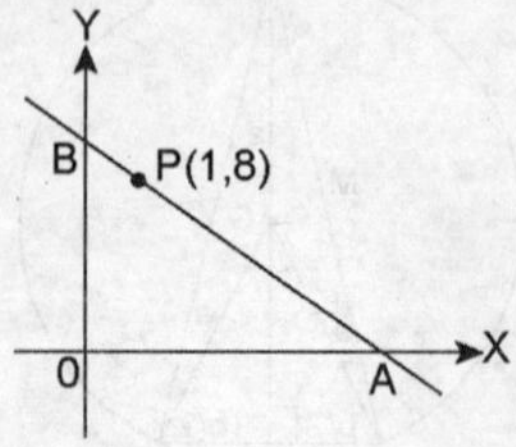

It intersect x-axis where $x = \frac{-8}{m}+1$ and y-axis where $x = 0$ i.e., $y = -m + 8$

$\therefore$ Area of Δ OAB $= A = \frac{1}{2}\left(\frac{m-8}{m}\right)(8-m)$ i.e., $A = \frac{-1}{2}\frac{(m-8)^2}{m}$

(i) For minimum area, $\frac{dA}{dm} = 0$

$\Rightarrow \quad -\frac{1}{2}\left[\frac{m.2(m-8)-(m-8)^2.1}{m^2}\right] = 0$

$\Rightarrow \quad (m - 8)(m + 8) = 0$

$\Rightarrow \quad m = \pm 8$ but $m < 0$ as x and y intersect are $+ve$

$\therefore$ Equation of line will be $y - 8 = -8(x - 1)$

i.e., $8x + y = 16$ Ans

(ii) S = (x-intercept) + (y-intercept)

$\Rightarrow \quad S = \left(\frac{m-8}{m}\right) + (8-m)$

$= (m-8)\left(\frac{1-m}{m}\right) = \frac{(m^2-9m+8)}{m}$

$\therefore \quad \frac{ds}{dm} = -\left[\frac{m(2m-9)-(m^2-9m+8)}{m^2}\right]$

$\Rightarrow \quad \frac{ds}{dm} = -\left[\frac{m^2-8}{m^2}\right]$

$\therefore$ For minimum of S, $\frac{ds}{dm} = 0$

$\Rightarrow \quad m^2 - 8 = 0$

$\Rightarrow \quad m = \pm 2\sqrt{2}$

For x and y-intercept positive, $m = -2\sqrt{2}$

$\therefore$ Equation of line will be $y - 8 = -2\sqrt{2}\,(x - 1)$ or $2\sqrt{2}\,x + y = 8 + 2\sqrt{2}$

(iii) L = Intercept between the axes = AB = $\sqrt{\left(\frac{m-8}{m}\right)^2+(8-m)^2}$

$L = \left|(8-m)\right|\sqrt{\frac{1}{m^2}+1}$

But $m < 0$

$\Rightarrow 8 - m > 0$

$\Rightarrow L = \frac{8-m}{|m|}\sqrt{1+m^2}$

$\Rightarrow L = \frac{(m-8)}{m}\sqrt{1+m^2}$ ($\because m < 0$)

$\therefore \frac{dL}{dm} = \frac{(m-8)}{m}\left[\frac{2m}{2\sqrt{1+m^2}}\right] + \sqrt{1+m^2} \cdot \frac{d}{dm}\left(\frac{m-8}{m}\right)$

$\Rightarrow \frac{dL}{dm} = \frac{m-8}{\sqrt{1+m^2}} + \sqrt{1+m^2}.\left[\frac{m-(m-8).1}{m^2}\right]$

$= \frac{m-8}{\sqrt{1+m^2}} + \frac{8\sqrt{1+m^2}}{m^2} = \frac{m^2(m-8)+8(1+m^2)}{m^2\sqrt{1+m^2}}$

$= \frac{m^3+8}{m^2\sqrt{1+m^2}}$

$\therefore \frac{dL}{dm} = 0$

$\Rightarrow m = -2$

$\therefore$ Equation of line will be $y - 8 = -2(x - 1)$ i.e., $2x + y = 10$ and the minimum value of intercept

$= \sqrt{\left(\frac{-2-8}{-2}\right)^2 + (8+2)^2} = \sqrt{125} = 5\sqrt{5}$

TEXTUAL EXERCISE–3: (OBJECTIVE)

1. (b) $f(x) = e^x \sin x; x \in [0, 2\pi]$

$f(x) = e^x \cos x + \sin e^x = e^x [\sin x + \cos x]$

$f'(x) = 0$ for $\tan x = -1$

$\Rightarrow x = \frac{3\pi}{4}, \frac{7\pi}{4}$

$f''(x) = e^x[\cos x - \sin x] + [\sin x + \cos x]\, e^x$

$= e^x[2 \cos x] = 2e^x \cos x$

Also $f''(x) = 0$

$\Rightarrow 2e^x \cos x = 0$

$\Rightarrow x = \pi/2$ or $3\pi/2$ and $f'''(x) = 2[e^x(-\sin x) + \cos x .e^x] = 2e^x [\cos x - \sin x]$

$f'''(\pi/2) = 2e^{\pi/2} [0 - 1] < 0$ and $f'''(3\pi/2) = 2\, e3^{\pi/2}[0 + 1] > 0$

$\therefore f'(x)$ has maximum slope at $x = \pi/2$

2. (c) $f(x) = x^2 + 4x + 1$;

$f(x) = x^2 + 4x - 3 = (x + 2)^2 - 3$

$\Rightarrow f(x) \in [-3, \infty)$

$\Rightarrow f(x) = 1$ at $x = 0$ and $f(x) \neq f(-x)$

Also $f'(x) = 2x + 4$ and $f''(x) = 2 > 0\ \forall\ x \in \mathbb{R}$.

Since $f(-1) = 1 - 4 + 1 = -2 < 1$

$\therefore f(x) > 1\ \forall\ x \leq 4$ is false.

3. (a) $f(x) = \sin x(1 + \cos x)$; $x \in \mathbb{R}$

$\Rightarrow f(x) = \sin x + \frac{1}{2}\sin 2x$

$\Rightarrow f'(x) = \cos x + \cos 2x$

$\Rightarrow f'(x) = 2\cos\left(\frac{3x}{2}\right)\cos\left(\frac{x}{2}\right)$

$\therefore f'(x) = 0$

$\Rightarrow \cos\frac{3x}{2} = 0, \cos\frac{x}{2} = 0$

$\Rightarrow \frac{3x}{2} = (2n+1)\frac{\pi}{2}$ or $\frac{x}{2} = (2n+1)\frac{\pi}{2}$

$\Rightarrow 3x = (2n + 1)\pi$ or $x = (2n + 1)\pi$

$\Rightarrow x = (2n + 1)\pi$ or $x = \frac{(2n+1)\pi}{3}$

$f''(x) = -\sin x - 2 \sin 2x = -\sin x - 4\sin x \cos x = -\sin x\,(1 + 4 \cos x)$

$\therefore f''\left(\frac{\pi}{3}\right) = -\left(\frac{\sqrt{3}}{2}\right)\left(1+4\left(\frac{1}{2}\right)\right) < 0$

$\Rightarrow f(x)$ has a maxima at $x = \pi/3$ and the maximum value $= f(\pi/3)$

$= \left(\sin\frac{\pi}{3}\right)\left(1+\cos\frac{\pi}{3}\right) = \frac{\sqrt{3}}{2}\left(1+\frac{1}{2}\right) = \left(\frac{\sqrt{3}}{2}\right)\left(\frac{3}{2}\right) = \frac{3\sqrt{3}}{4}$

4. (d) $f(x) = xe^x$

$\Rightarrow f'(x) = xe^x + e^x$

$\Rightarrow f'(x) = 0$ for $x = -1$ and $f''(x) = xe^x + e^x + ex = (x + 2)\, e^x$

$f''(-1) = e^{-1} > 0$

$\Rightarrow f(x)$ has a minima at $x = -1$ given by $f(-1) = -e^{-1} = -1/e$

5. (b) $f(x) = x^3 - px + q; p > 0, q > 0$.

$f'(x) = 3x^2 - p = 0$

$\Rightarrow x = \pm\sqrt{\frac{p}{3}}$

$f''(x) = 6x$

$\therefore f''\left(\sqrt{\frac{p}{3}}\right) = 6\sqrt{\frac{p}{3}} > 0$ and $f''\left(-\sqrt{\frac{p}{3}}\right) = -6\sqrt{\frac{p}{3}} < 0$

$\therefore f(x)$ has a local maxima at $-\sqrt{\frac{p}{3}}$ and a local minima at $\sqrt{\frac{p}{3}}$.

6. (c) $f(x) = 2x^3 - 21x^2 + 36x - 30$

$\Rightarrow f'(x) = 6x^2 - 42x + 36 = 6(x^2 - 7x + 6) = 6(x - 1)(x - 6)$

$\therefore f'(x) = 0$

$\Rightarrow x = 1$ or $x = 6$

And $f''(x) = 6(2x - 7) = 12x - 42$

$\therefore f''(1) = 12 - 42 = -30 < 0$ and $f''(6) = 72 - 42 = 30 > 0$

$\therefore f(x)$ has a maxima at $x = 1$, where as a local minima at $x = 6$

7. (c) $f(x) = \frac{\ell nx}{x}; x \in (2, \infty)$

$\Rightarrow f'(x) = \frac{(1-\ell nx)}{x^2}$

$\therefore f'(x) = 0$ at $x = e$ and $f''(x) = \frac{x^2\left(\frac{-1}{x}\right) - (1-\ell nx)(2x)}{x^4}$

$\Rightarrow f''(x) = \dfrac{-x-2x+2x\ell nx}{x^4}$

$\Rightarrow f''(x) = \dfrac{2\ell nx-3}{x^3}; x \in (2,\infty)$

$\Rightarrow f''(e) = \dfrac{2-3}{3} = \dfrac{-1}{e^3} < 0$

$\Rightarrow f(x)$ has a local maxima at $x = e$

8. (b) $f(x) = (x-1)^2 + 3; x \in [-3, 1]$

$\Rightarrow f'(x) = 2(x-1)$

$\therefore f'(x) = 0$

$\Rightarrow x = 1$ and $f''(x) = 2$

$\Rightarrow f(x)$ has a local minima at $x = 1$

$\therefore f(x)$ has minima value $m = f(1) = 3$ and $f(x)$ has maximum value M

$= \max.\{f(-3), f(1)\}$

$= \max.\{19, 3\} = 19.$

$\therefore (m, M) \equiv (3, 19)$

9. (c) $f(x) = (x+1)^{1/3} - (x-1)^{1/3}; x \in [0, 1]$

$\Rightarrow f'(x) = \dfrac{1}{3(x+1)^{2/3}} - \dfrac{1}{3(x-1)^{2/3}} = \dfrac{1}{3}\left[\dfrac{(x-1)^{2/3}-(x+1)^{2/3}}{(x+1)^{2/3}(x-1)^{2/3}}\right]$

$= 0$ at $x = 0$

And $f''(x) = \left(\dfrac{1}{3}\right)\left(\dfrac{-2}{3}\right)\cdot\dfrac{1}{(x+1)^{5/3}} + \dfrac{1}{3}\left(\dfrac{2}{3}\right)\cdot\dfrac{1}{(x-1)^{5/3}}$

$\therefore f''(0) = -\dfrac{2}{9} - \dfrac{2}{9} = \dfrac{-4}{9} < 0$

$\therefore f(x)$ has a local maxima at $x = 0$

$\therefore$ The greatest value $f(x) = f(0)$

$= -1(-1)^{1/3} = 2$

10. (a) $f(x) = x\sqrt{1-x^2}; (x>0)$

$\Rightarrow f'(x) = x. \dfrac{1(-2x)}{2\sqrt{1-x^2}} + \sqrt{1-x^2}$

$\Rightarrow f'(x) = \dfrac{-x^2+1-x^2}{\sqrt{1-x^2}} = \dfrac{1-2x^2}{\sqrt{1-x^2}}$

$\therefore f'(x) = 0$ at $x = \pm\sqrt{\dfrac{1}{2}}$ and $f''(x)$

$= \dfrac{\sqrt{1-x^2}(-4x) - (1-2x^2)\dfrac{-2x}{2\sqrt{1-x^2}}}{1-x^2}$

$\Rightarrow f''(x) = \dfrac{-4x\sqrt{1-x^2} + \dfrac{x(1-2x^2)}{\sqrt{1-x^2}}}{(1-x^2)}$

$\Rightarrow f''(x) = \dfrac{-4x(1-x^2)+x-2x^3}{(1-x^2)\sqrt{1-x^2}}$

$= \dfrac{-3x+2x^3}{(1-x^2)\sqrt{1-x^2}} = \dfrac{x(2x^2-3)}{(1-x^2)^{3/2}}$

$\therefore f''\left(-\sqrt{\dfrac{1}{2}}\right) = \dfrac{\left(-\dfrac{1}{\sqrt{2}}\right)(1-3)}{\left(\dfrac{1}{2}\right)^{3/2}} > 0$ and f''

$\left(\sqrt{\dfrac{1}{2}}\right) = \dfrac{\left(\dfrac{1}{\sqrt{2}}\right)(1-3)}{(1/2)^{3/2}} < 0$

$\therefore f(x)$ has a local maxima for $x > 0$ i.e., at $x = \sqrt{\dfrac{1}{2}}$

11. (b) $f(x) = x + \dfrac{1}{x}$

$\Rightarrow f'(x) = 1 - \dfrac{1}{x^2}$

$\therefore f'(x) = 0$

$\Rightarrow x^2 = 1$

$\Rightarrow x = \pm 1$ and $f''(x) = \dfrac{2}{x^3}$

$\therefore f''(-1) = -2 < 0$ and $f''(1) = 2 > 0$

$\therefore f(x)$ has a local maxima at $x = -1$ and a local minima at $x = 1$.

12. (d) $f(x) = \dfrac{x}{x^2+x+4}; x \in [-1,1]$

$f'(x) = \dfrac{(x^2+x+4) - x(2x+1)}{(x^2+x+4)}$

$\Rightarrow f'(x) = \dfrac{-x^2+4}{(x^2+x+4)}$

$\therefore f'(x) = 0 \qquad \Rightarrow x = \pm 2$

And $f''(x) = \dfrac{(x^2+x+4)(-2x) - (-x^2+4)}{(x^2+x+4)^2}$

$= \dfrac{-2x^3-2x^2-8x+x^2-4}{(x^2+x+4)^2} = \dfrac{-2x^3-x^2-8x-4}{(x^2+x+4)^2}$

$\therefore f''(2) < 0, f''(-2) => 0$

$\therefore f(x)$ has a maxima at $x = 2$

$\therefore$ Maximum of $f(x)$ in $[-1, 1]$

$= \text{Max.}\{0, f(-1), f(1)\}$

$= \text{Max.}\left\{\dfrac{-1}{4}, \dfrac{1}{6}\right\} = \dfrac{1}{6}$

13. (a) $f(x) = xe^{-x}$

$\Rightarrow f'(x) = -x\,e^{-x} + e^{-x} = e^{-x}(1-x)$

Clearly $f'(x) > 0$ for $x < 1$,

$f'(x) = 0$ at $x = 1$ and $f'(x) < 0$ for $x > 1$

$\Rightarrow f(x)$ has a local maxima and hence absolute maxima at $x = 1$

$\Rightarrow$ Assertion is true

$f''(x) = e^{-x}(-1) + (1-x)(-e^{-x}) = e^{-x}(-1-1+x) = e^{-x}(x-2)$

$\therefore f''(1) = -e < 0$

$\therefore$ Reason is also true and is the correct explanation of reason

14. (c) $f(x) = x^2 e^{-2x}, x > 0$

$\Rightarrow f'(x) = x^2(-2e^{-2x}) + e^{-2x}(2x) = 2x\,e^{-2x}(1-x)$

$\therefore f'(x) = 0$ at $x = 0$ or at $x = 1$

$f'(x<0) < 0, f'(0<x<1) > 0, f'(x>1) < 0$

$\Rightarrow f(x)$ has a local minima at $x = 0$ and a local maxima at $x = 1$and the local maximum value $= f(1) = 1/e^2$

15. (c) $f(x) = 2x^3 - 9ax^2 + 12a^2x + 1$

$\Rightarrow f'(x) = 6x^2 - 18ax + 12a^2 = 6(x^2 - 3ax + 2a^2)$

$\therefore f'(x) = 0$

$\Rightarrow x^2 - 2ax - ax + 2a^2 = 0$

$\Rightarrow x(x-2a) - a(x-2a) = 0$

$\Rightarrow (x-2a)(x-a) = 0$

$\Rightarrow x = a$ or $x = 2a$

$f''(x) = 6(2x - 3a) = 12x - 18a$

$f''(a) = 12a - 18a = -6a$ and $f''(2a) = 24a - 18a = 6a$

$\therefore f(x)$ has a local maxima at $a = p$ and $f(x)$ has a local minima at $2a = q$

Now A.T.Q, $p^2 = q$

$\Rightarrow a^2 = 2a$

$\Rightarrow a(a-2) = 0$

$\Rightarrow a = 0$ or $a = 2$

But $a > 0$

$\Rightarrow a = 2$

16. (c) $p(t) = 1000 + \dfrac{1000t}{100+t^2}$

$$\Rightarrow \frac{dp}{dt} = \frac{(100+t^2)(1000) - (1000t)(2t)}{(100+t^2)^2}$$

$$= \frac{10^5 + 10^3t^2 - 2\times10^3t^2}{\left(100+t^2\right)^2} = \frac{10^5 - 10^3t^2}{\left(100+t^2\right)^2} = \frac{10^3\left(10^2 - t^2\right)}{\left(100+t^2\right)^2}$$

$\Rightarrow \dfrac{dp}{dt} > 0$ for $t \in (-10, 10)$ and $\dfrac{dp}{dt} < 0$ for $t < -10$ or $t > 10$

$\Rightarrow$ P will be maximum at $t = 10$ and P_{max} given by $P(10)$

$= 1000 + \dfrac{10^4}{200} = 1000 + 50 = 1050$

17. (c) $f(x) = (x)^{1/x}; x > 0$

$\Rightarrow \ell n\, f(x) = \dfrac{1}{x}\ell nx$

$$\Rightarrow \frac{1}{f(x)}.f'(x) = \frac{1}{x^2} + (\ell nx)\left(\frac{-1}{x^2}\right)$$

$\Rightarrow f'(x) = (x)^{1/x} . \dfrac{1}{x^2}(-\ell n\,x + 1)$

$\Rightarrow f'(x) = 0$ at $x = e$

$\Rightarrow f'(x) < 0$ for $x > e$ and $f'(x) > 0$ for $x < e$

$\Rightarrow f(x)$ has *a* maximum at $x = e$

$\therefore f_{max}(x) = f(e) = e^{1/e}$

18. (d) $f(x) = \dfrac{x^2-1}{x^2+1}; x \in \mathbb{R}$

$$\Rightarrow f'(x) = \frac{\left(x^2+1\right)(2x) - \left(x^2-1\right)(2x)}{\left(x^2+1\right)^2}$$

$$\Rightarrow f'(x) = \frac{2x^3 + 2x - 2x^3 + 2x}{\left(x^2+1\right)^2}$$

$\Rightarrow f'(x) = \dfrac{4x}{(x^2+1)^2} < 0$ for $x < 0$ and > 0 for $x > 0, f(0) = 0$

$\Rightarrow f(x)$ has a local minimum and hence absolute minimum at $x = 0$, given by $f(0) = -1$

19. (d) $f(x) = 2x^3 - 3x^2 - 12x + 5; -2 \le x \le 4$

$\Rightarrow f'(x) = 6x^2 - 6x - 12 = 6(x^2 - x - 2)$

$\Rightarrow f'(x) = 6(x-2)(x+1)$

$\Rightarrow f'(x) = 0$ at $x = -1$ and $x = 2$ and $f'(x) > 0$ for $x < -1$ and $x > 2$ and $f'(x) < 0$ for $-1 < x < 2$

$\Rightarrow f(x)$ has a local maxima at $x = -1$ and local minima at $x = 2$

$\therefore f_{max} = \max.\{f(-1), f(4)\}$

$= \max\{12, 37\} = 37$ at $x = 4$

20. (b) $f(x) = 4e^{2x} + 9e^{-2x}$

$\Rightarrow f'(x) = 8e^{2x} - 18e^{-2x} = 2(4e^{2x} - 9e^{-2x})$

$\therefore f'(x) = 0$

$\Rightarrow 4e^{2x} = 9e^{-2x}$ $\qquad \Rightarrow 4e^{4x} = 9$

$\Rightarrow e4x = 9/4$ $\qquad \Rightarrow 4x = 2\,\ell n(3/2)$

$\Rightarrow x = \dfrac{1}{2}\ell n\left(\dfrac{3}{2}\right)$ and $f''(x) = 2(8e^{2x} + 18e^{-2x}) > 0\ \forall\, x \in \mathbb{R}$

$\therefore f(x)$ has a point of minima at $x = \dfrac{1}{2}\ell n\left(\dfrac{3}{2}\right)$ and the minimum value is given by $f\left(\dfrac{1}{2}\ell n\dfrac{3}{2}\right) = 4\left(\dfrac{3}{2}\right) + 9\left(\dfrac{2}{3}\right)$

$= 12$

21. (c) $f(x) = x^3 - 3x; x \in [0, 2]$

$\Rightarrow f'(x) = 3x^2 - 3 = 3(x^2 - 1)$

$\therefore f'(x) = 0$

$\Rightarrow x = \pm 1$ and $f''(x) = 6x$

Also $f''(1) = 6 > 0$

$\Rightarrow f(x)$ has a local minima at $x = 1$, thus maximum value of $f(x)$ is given by $f_{max.} = \max.\{f(0), f(2)\} = \max.\{0, 2\} = 2$

22. (c) $\because f'(a) = 0, f''(a) = 0$ and $f'''(a) \ne 0$

$\Rightarrow x = a$ is neither a point of maxima nor a point of minima

23. (a) $f(x) = \int_0^x te^{t^2}\,dt$

$\Rightarrow f'(x) = x\ e^{x^2} = 0$

$\Rightarrow x = 0$ and $f''(x) = x(2x)\ e^{x^2} + e^{x^2}(1) = e^{x^2}(2x^2 + 1) > 0\ \forall\, x \in \mathbb{R}$

$\Rightarrow f(x)$ has a minimum value of $x = 0 = f(0) = 0$

24. (c) $f(x) = \log|x| + bx^2 + ax, x \ne 0$

$$= \begin{cases} \log x + bx^2 + ax, x > 0 \\ \log(-x) + bx^2 + ax, x < 0 \end{cases}$$

$$\Rightarrow f'(x) = \begin{cases} \dfrac{1}{x} + 2bx + a, x > 0 \\ \dfrac{1}{x} + 2bx + a, x < 0 \end{cases}$$

$\therefore\ f'(x) = 0$

$\Rightarrow\ 2bx^2 + ax + 1 = 0$

$\Rightarrow\ x = \dfrac{-a \pm \sqrt{a^2 - 4(2b)}}{4b}$

For Extreme values at $x = -1$ and $x = 2$,

$\dfrac{-a-\sqrt{a^2-8b}}{4b} = 1, \dfrac{-a+\sqrt{a^2-8b}}{4b} = 2$

$\Rightarrow\ a + \sqrt{a^2-8b} = 4b$ and $a - \sqrt{a^2-8b} = -8b$

$\Rightarrow\ 2a = -4b$

$\Rightarrow\ a = -2b$

$\therefore\ \sqrt{a^2+4a} = -2a - a = -3a$

$\Rightarrow\ a^2 + 4a = 9a^2$

$\Rightarrow\ 8a^2 = 4a$

$\Rightarrow\ a = 0$ or $\dfrac{1}{2}$

For $a = 0$, $b = 0$ (*impossible*)

$\therefore\ a = \dfrac{1}{2}$

$\Rightarrow\ b = \dfrac{-1}{4}$

$\Rightarrow$ Statement (1) is correct.

$f''(x) = \left\{\dfrac{-1}{x^2} + 2b \text{ for } x \neq 0\right.$ and $f''(-1) = 1 + 2b = 1 - \dfrac{1}{2} = \dfrac{1}{2} > 0,$

$f''(2) = \dfrac{-1}{4} - \dfrac{1}{2} = \dfrac{-3}{4} < 0$

Thus $f(x)$ has a local maxima at $x = 2$ and local minima at $x = -1$

25. **(a)** $x = (t + 1)$ and $y = t^3 - t^2$

$\Rightarrow\ \dfrac{dx}{dt} = 1,\ \dfrac{dy}{dt} = 3t^2 - 2t$

$\Rightarrow\ \dfrac{dy}{dt} = 3t^2 - 2t$

For maxima/minima, $\dfrac{dy}{dt} = 0$

$\Rightarrow\ t(3t - 2) = 0$

$\Rightarrow\ t = 0$ or $t = 2/3$ and $\dfrac{d^2y}{dx^2} = \dfrac{d^2y}{dt^2}\dfrac{dt}{dx} = (6t - 2)(1) = 6t - 2$

$\therefore\ \left(\dfrac{d^2y}{dx^2}\right) = -2$ at $t = 0$ and 2 at $t = 2/3$

$\Rightarrow\ y = f(x)$ has a local maxima at $t = 0$ i.e., at $(1, 0)$

26. **(b)** In the above question the local maxima is attained at $t = 0$

27. **(b)** $y = (1 - t)^{3/2}$ and $x = t^{3/2}$; $0 < t < 1$

$\Rightarrow\ \dfrac{dy}{dt} = \dfrac{-3}{2}(1-t)^{1/2}, \dfrac{dx}{dt} = \dfrac{3}{2}t^{1/2}$

$\therefore\ \dfrac{dy}{dx} = \dfrac{dy/dt}{dx/dt} = \dfrac{-(1-t)^{1/2}}{t^{1/2}}$

$\therefore$ For maxima/minima $\dfrac{dy}{dx} = 0$

$\Rightarrow\ t = 1$

$\Rightarrow\ \dfrac{d^2y}{dx^2} = \dfrac{-\left[t^{1/2}\left(\dfrac{-1}{2(1-t)^{1/2}}\right) - (1-t)^{1/2}\dfrac{1}{2t^{1/2}}\right]}{t}$

$= \left(\dfrac{t^{1/2}}{2(1-t)^{1/2}} + \dfrac{(1-t)^{1/2}}{2t^{1/2}}\right) \div t = \left[\dfrac{t+1-t}{2(1-t)^{1/2} + t^{1/2}}\right] \times \dfrac{1}{t}$

$= \dfrac{1}{2t^{3/2}(1-t)^{1/2}}$

Which does not exist at $t = 1$

So let's go back to first derivate tests, $f'(0 < t < 1) < 0$

$\therefore\ \dfrac{dy}{dx} < 0$ for $0 < t < 1$

$\Rightarrow\ y = f(x)$ is a decreasing function for $0 < t < 1$.

Thus y_{max}. $y(t = 0) = 1$ and $y_{min} = y(t = 1) = 0$

$\therefore\ |Y_{max} - Y_{min}| = 1$

28. $x = \dfrac{t^2}{1-t^2}, y = \dfrac{1}{1+t^2}$

Here for $x \in \mathbb{R}$; $\dfrac{t^2}{1-t^2} \in \mathbb{R}$

$\Rightarrow\ 1 - t^2 \neq 0$

$\Rightarrow\ t \neq \pm 1$

Also $x - xt^2 = t^2$

$\Rightarrow\ x = (1 + x)t^2$

$\Rightarrow\ t^2 = \dfrac{x}{1+x} \geq 0$

$\Rightarrow\ x < -1$ or $x \geq 0$

$\therefore\ D_f = (-\infty, -1) \cup [0, \infty)$ and

$y = f(x) = \dfrac{x+1}{(2x+1)}; x \in (-\infty, -1) \cup [0, \infty)$

$\Rightarrow\ f(x) = \left[\dfrac{(2x+1)-(x+1)(2)}{(2x+1)^2}\right] = \left[\dfrac{-1}{(2x+1)^2}\right] < 0$

$\therefore\ f(x)$ is a decreasing function

$\therefore\ f(-\infty) = \lim\limits_{x\to-\infty}\left(\dfrac{x+1}{2x+1}\right) = \lim\limits_{x\to-\infty}\left(\dfrac{1+1/x}{2+1/x}\right) = \dfrac{1}{2}$

$f(-1^-) = 0, f(0) = 1,\ f(\infty) = \lim\limits_{x\to0}\left(\dfrac{x+1}{2x+1}\right) = \dfrac{1}{2}$

(i) **(d)**

$\Rightarrow\ f(x)$ has a maxima at $x = 0$,

(ii) **(b)**

$\Rightarrow\ f(x)$ has a minimum value at $x = -1$

(iii) **(a)** The range of function is

$\left(\dfrac{1}{2}, 0\right) \cup \left[1, \dfrac{1}{2}\right) = (0,1) - \left\{\dfrac{1}{2}\right\}$

(iv) **(a)** The function $y = f(x)$ is a decreasing function for $x \in (-\infty, -1)$ and on $[0, \infty)$

(v) **(d)** $f(x)$ is a decreasing function on $(-\infty, -1)$ and on $[0, \infty)$

TEXTUAL EXERCISE– 4 : (SUBJECTIVE)

1. $f(x) = \begin{cases} 2x^3+3\,;x\neq 0 \\ 4\;\;;x=0 \end{cases}$

$\Rightarrow f'(x) = \{4x\;;x\neq 0$

$\Rightarrow f'(x) < 0$ for $x < 0$ and $f'(x) > 0$ for $x > 0$ and $f'(0^-) = 3, = f'(0^+)$ and $f(0) = 4$

$\Rightarrow f(x)$ has a removable discontinuity at $x = 0$

Also $\lim\limits_{x\to 0} f(x) = 3 < f(0) = 4$

$\Rightarrow$ There is no extreme however g.l.b of $f(x) = 3$

2. $f(x) = \begin{cases} 1+x\,;0\le x\le 2 \\ 3-x\,;2<x\le 3 \end{cases}$

$f(2^-) = 3; f(2^+) = 1$

$\therefore$ $f(x)$ is discontinuous at $x = 2$

Now, $f'(x) = \begin{cases} 1\;;0<x<2 \\ -1\;;2\le x<3 \end{cases}$

$\Rightarrow f(x)$ increase for $x \in(0, 2)$ and $f(x)$ decrease for $x \in(2, 3)$

$\therefore$ $f(0) = 1, f(2^-) = 3,$

$f(2^+) = 1, f(3) = 0$

$\therefore$ $f(x)$ has local minima at $x = 0$ at $x = 3$,

$f(x)$ has local maxima at $x = 2$ as well as global maxima at $x = 2$

Also $f(x)$ has global minima at $x = 3$

3. $f(x) = \sqrt{2-x^2}; -\sqrt{2}\le x\le\sqrt{2}$

$\Rightarrow f'(x) = \dfrac{-2x}{2\sqrt{2-x^2}} = \dfrac{-x}{\sqrt{2-x^2}}; x\in\left[-\sqrt{2},\sqrt{2}\right]$

$\therefore$ $f(x)\downarrow$ for $x \in \left[0,\sqrt{2}\right]$ and $f(x)$ for $x \in \left[-\sqrt{2},0\right]$

$\therefore$ $f(x)$ has a local (*global*) maxima at $x = 0$ given by $f(0) = \sqrt{2}$ and local (*global*) minima at $x = \pm\sqrt{2}$ given by $f\left(\pm\sqrt{2}\right) = 0$

4. $f(x) = \log_{1/4}\left(x-\dfrac{1}{4}\right)+\dfrac{1}{2}\log_4(16x^2-8x+1)\,;\;\dfrac{4x-1}{4}>0$

$f(x) = \log_{1/4}\left(x-\dfrac{1}{4}\right)+\dfrac{1}{2}\log_4(4x-1)^2$

$= \log_{1/4}\left(x-\dfrac{1}{4}\right)+\dfrac{1}{2}(2).\dfrac{1}{2}\log_2|4x-1|$

$= \dfrac{-1}{2}\log_2\left(x-\dfrac{1}{4}\right)+\dfrac{1}{2}\log_2|4x-1|$

$= \dfrac{1}{2}\log_2\left|\dfrac{(4x-1)}{(4x-1)}\times 4\right| = \dfrac{1}{2}\log_2(4) = 1$

$\therefore$ $f(x) = 1; x \in\left(\dfrac{1}{4},\infty\right)$

Thus $f(x)$ is a constant function for $x \in\left(\dfrac{1}{4},\infty\right)$

5. $f(x) = \tan^{-1}\left(\dfrac{3x-x^3}{1-3x^2}\right)$

We know that $3\tan^{-1}x \begin{cases} \tan^{-1}\left(\dfrac{3x-x^3}{1-3x^2}\right) \text{ for } \dfrac{-1}{\sqrt{3}}<x<\dfrac{1}{\sqrt{3}}, \\ -\pi+\tan^{-1}\left(\dfrac{3x-x^3}{1-3x^2}\right) \text{ for } -\infty<x<\dfrac{1}{\sqrt{3}} \\ \pi+\tan^{-1}\left(\dfrac{3x-x^3}{1-3x^2}\right) \text{for } x>\dfrac{1}{\sqrt{3}} \end{cases}$

$\Rightarrow f(x) = \begin{cases} 3\tan^{-1}x \text{ for } \dfrac{-1}{\sqrt{3}}<x<\dfrac{1}{\sqrt{3}} \\ \pi+3\tan^{-1}x \text{ for } x<-\dfrac{1}{\sqrt{3}} \\ -\pi+3\tan^{-1}x \text{ for } x>\dfrac{1}{\sqrt{3}} \end{cases}$

$\Rightarrow f'(x) = \begin{cases} \dfrac{3}{1+x^2} \text{ for } \dfrac{-1}{\sqrt{3}}<x<\dfrac{1}{\sqrt{3}} \\ \text{for } x<-\dfrac{1}{\sqrt{3}} \\ \text{and for } x>\dfrac{1}{\sqrt{3}} \end{cases}$ and hence $f(x)$ is an function on $\left(-\infty,-1\sqrt{3}\right)$ on $\left(-\dfrac{1}{\sqrt{3}},\dfrac{1}{\sqrt{3}}\right)$ and on $\left(\dfrac{1}{\sqrt{3}},\infty\right)$

i.e., there is no point of extrema.

6. $f(x) = \tan^{-1}\left(\dfrac{2x}{1-x^2}\right)$

We know that $2\tan^{-1}x = \begin{cases} \tan^{-1}\left(\dfrac{2x}{1-x^2}\right);-1<x<1 \\ -\pi+\tan^{-1}\left(\dfrac{2x}{1-x^2}\right);x<-1 \\ \pi+\tan^{-1}\left(\dfrac{2x}{1-x^2}\right);x>1 \end{cases}$

$\Rightarrow f(x) = \begin{cases} 2\tan^{-1}x;-1<x<1 \\ 2\tan^{-1}x+\pi\,;x<-1 \\ 2\tan^{-1}x-\pi\,;x>1 \end{cases}$

$\Rightarrow f'(x) = \dfrac{2}{1+x^2}$ for $x \in(-1, 1), (-\infty, -1)$ and on $(1, \infty)$

$\Rightarrow f(x)\uparrow$ on $(-\infty, -1)$, $(-1, 1)$ and on $(1, \infty)$

Thus there is no point of extreme.

7. $f(x) = \begin{cases} \sqrt{x+2}\;\;;-2\le x<0 \\ |x-1|\;;0\le x\le 3 \end{cases}$

$\Rightarrow f'(x) = \begin{cases} \dfrac{1}{2\sqrt{x+2}};-2<x<0 \\ -1\;;0<x<1 \\ 1\;\;;1<x<3 \end{cases}$

Also $f(0^-) = \sqrt{2}$, $f(0^+) = 1$ and $f(0) = 1$

$\Rightarrow$ $f(x)$ is discontinuous at $x = 0$ and $f(x) \uparrow$ for $x \in (-2, 0)$, $\downarrow$ for $x \in (0, 1)$ and for $x \in (1, 3)$

$f(-2) = 0, f(0) = 1, f(1) = 0, f(3) = 2$

$\therefore$ $f(x)$ has maximum value at $x = 3$

$\Rightarrow$ (*i*) is false

(ii) is true

(iii) is true

Also $f(x)$ has local minima as well as global minima at $x = 1$ as well at $x = -2$

$\Rightarrow$ (*iv*) is true

8. $f(x) = \begin{cases} -x^3 + k^2 - 3k + 2; 0 \le x < 1 \\ 2x - 3\ ; 1 \le x \le 3 \end{cases}$

$f(1^-) = -1 + k^2 - 3k + 2 = k^2 - 3k + 1$

$f(1) = f(1^+) = -1; f'(x) = 2$ for $1 < x < 3$

$f'(x) = -3x^2$ for $0 < x < 1$

$\therefore$ For $f(x)$ to have smallest value at 1, $f(x) \ge -1\ \forall\ 0 \le x \le 1$

$\Rightarrow -x^3 + k^2 - 3k + 2 \ge -1\ \forall\ 0 \le x \le 1$ i.e., $-x^3 + k^2 - 3k + 3 \ge 0\ \forall\ 0 \le x \le 1$

$\Rightarrow k^2 - 3k + 3 \ge x^3\ \forall\ x \in [0, 1]$

$\Rightarrow k^2 - 3k + 3 \ge 1 \qquad \Rightarrow k^2 - 3k + 2 \ge 0$

$\Rightarrow (k-2)(k-1) \ge 0 \qquad \Rightarrow k \le 1$ or $k \ge 2$

9. $f(x) = \begin{cases} 2x + \dfrac{b^3 + b^2 + 7b + 3}{b^2 + 3b + 2}; 0 \le x \le 1 \\ 6 - 2x\ ; 1 < x \le 3 \end{cases}$

$\Rightarrow f'(x) = \begin{cases} 2;\ 0 < x < 1 \\ -2; 1 < x < 3 \end{cases}$

$\Rightarrow f(x) \uparrow$ for $0 < x < 1$ and $\downarrow$ for $1 < x < 3$

Also $f(1) = 2 + \dfrac{b^3 + b^2 + 7b + 3}{b^2 + 3b + 2}$ and $f(1^+) = 4$

$\therefore$ For $f(x)$ to have maximum at $x = 1$, $f(1) \ge 4$

$\Rightarrow 2 + \dfrac{b^3 + b^2 + 7b + 3}{b^2 + 3b + 2} \ge 4$

$\Rightarrow \dfrac{b^3 + b^2 + 7b + 3}{b^2 + 3b + 2} \ge 2$

$\Rightarrow \dfrac{b^3 + b^2 + 7b + 3 - 2b^2 - 6b - 4}{b^2 + 3b + 2} \ge 0$

$\Rightarrow \dfrac{b^3 - b^2 + b - 1}{b^3 + 3b + 2} \ge 0 \quad \Rightarrow \dfrac{(b^2 + 1)(b - 1)}{(b + 1)(b + 2)} \ge 0$

$\Rightarrow (b - 1)(b + 1)(b + 2) \ge 0; b \ne -1, -2$

$\Rightarrow b \in (-2, -1) \cup [1, \infty)$

TEXTUAL EXERCISE–4: (OBJECTIVE)

1. (a) $f(x) = \begin{cases} \sin\dfrac{\pi x}{2}; 0 \le x < 1 \\ 3 - 2x\ ; x \ge 1 \end{cases}$

$\Rightarrow f'(x) = \begin{cases} \dfrac{1}{2}\cos\dfrac{\pi x}{2}; 0 < x < 1 \\ -2\ ; x > 1 \end{cases}$

$\Rightarrow f(x) \uparrow$ for $0 < x < 1$ and $\downarrow$ for $x > 1$

Also $f(1^-) = \sin\left(\dfrac{\pi}{2}\right) = 1$ and $f(1) = f(1^+) = 1$

$\Rightarrow f(x)$ is a continuous at $x = 1$

$\Rightarrow f(x)$ has a local as well as global maxima at $x = 1$

2. (a), (b) $f(x) = \begin{cases} 7 - x^2\ ; x < 2 \\ 11 - x\ ; x \ge 2 \end{cases}$

$\Rightarrow f'(x) = \begin{cases} -2x\ ; x < 2 \\ -1\ ; x > 2 \end{cases}$

$\Rightarrow f(x) \uparrow$ for $x \le 0$, $\downarrow$ for $0 < x < 2$ and then $\downarrow$ for $x > 2$ with a discontinuity at $x = 2$ and a point of non-differentiability at $x = 2$

$\Rightarrow f(x)$ has a local maxima at $x = 0$ and a local maxima well as point of global maxima at $x = 2$

3. (a), (b), (c), (d)

$f(x) = \begin{cases} 3x^2 + 12x - 1; -1 \le x \le 2 \\ 37 - x;\ 2 < x \le 3 \end{cases}$

$\Rightarrow f'(x) = \begin{cases} 6x + 12\ ; -1 < x < 2 \\ -1\ ; 2 < x < 3 \end{cases}$

$\Rightarrow f(x) \uparrow$ for $x \in (-1, 2)$ and $\downarrow$ for $x \in (2, 3)$ and $f(x)$ is continuous at $x = 2$

$\Rightarrow f(x)$ has a point of local as well as global maxima at $x = 2$

Also $f'(2^-) = 24$ and $f'(2^+) = -1$

$\Rightarrow f'(x)$ does not exist at $x = 2$

4. (b) $f(x) = \begin{cases} 4 - x^2\ ;\ x < 0 \\ 2x + 1\ ; x \ge 0 \end{cases}$

$\Rightarrow f(0^-) = 4; f(0^+) = f(0) = 1$

$\Rightarrow f(x)$ is discontinuous at $x = 0$

Also $f'(x) = \begin{cases} -2x;\ x < 0 \\ 2\ ; x > 0 \end{cases}$

$\Rightarrow f(x) \uparrow \forall\ x \in \mathbb{R}$ but $f(0^-) = 4 > f(0) = 1 < f(x)$ for $\forall\ x > 0$

$\Rightarrow f(x)$ has a local minima at $x = 0$.

5. (d) $f(x) = \begin{cases} 3 + x^2 e^{-x}\ ; x < 0 \\ 2\ ;\ x = 0 \\ 1 - 2x^2\ ; x > 0 \end{cases}$

$\Rightarrow f(0^-) = 3; f(0) = 2, f(0^+) = 1$ and $f'(x)$

$= \begin{cases} -x^2 e^{-x} + 2xe^{-x}; x < 0 \\ -4x\ ; x > 0 \end{cases}$

$\Rightarrow f'(x) = \begin{cases} xe^{-x}(2 - x); x < 0 \\ -4x; x > 0 \end{cases}$

$\Rightarrow f(x)$ is a $\downarrow$ function $\forall\ x \in \mathbb{R}$ but discontinuous at $x = 0$ and $f(0^-) = 3 > f(0) = 2 > f(0^+) = 1$

$\Rightarrow x = 0$ is not a point of extreme and $f''(x) = -4\ \forall\ x > 0$

$\Rightarrow f(x)$ is not a point of inflexion.

6. (a) $f(x) = \begin{cases} x^3+x^2+5x\ ; x<0 \\ 1-xe^x\ ;\ x\ge 0 \end{cases}$; $f(0^-) = 0; f(0) = f(0^+) = 1$

⇒ $f(x)$ is discontinuous at $x = 0$

⇒ $f'(x) = \begin{cases} 3x^2+2x+5\ ; x<0 \\ -xe^x - e^x\ ; x>0 \end{cases}$

⇒ $f'(x) > 0$ for $x < 0$ and $f'(x) < 0$ for $x > 0$ and $f(0^-) = 0 < f(0) = f(0^+) = 1 > f(x)\ \forall\ x > 0$

⇒ $x = 0$ is a point of local maxima.

7. (b) $f(x) = \begin{cases} 1+x^2-3x\ ; x<0 \\ \cos x + 2x\ ; x\ge 0 \end{cases}$; $f(0^-) = 1; f(0) = f(0^+) = 1$

⇒ $f(x)$ is a continuous function.

Also, $f'(x) = \begin{cases} 2x-3\ ; x<0 \\ 2-\sin x\ ; x<0 \end{cases}$

⇒ $f(x) \downarrow$ for $x < 0$ and $f(x) \uparrow$ for $x > 0$

⇒ $x = 0$ is a point of local minima at $x = 0$ and the local minimum value $= f(0) = 1$ and the global maximum value $= \max.\{f(-2), f(2)\} = \max.\ \{11, \cos 2 + 4\} = 11$

∴ (11, 1) is the required ordered pair.

8. (d) $f(x) = \begin{cases} \sin^{-1}\alpha + x^2, 0<x<1 \\ 2x\ ,\ x\ge 1 \end{cases}$; $f(1^-) = \sin^{-1}\alpha + 1 = \sin^{-1}\alpha + 1; f(1^+) = f(1) = 2$

⇒ $f(x)$ is discontinuous at $x = 1$

Also $f'(x) = \begin{cases} 2x\ ; 0<x<1 \\ 2\ ; x>1 \end{cases}$

⇒ $f(x)$ is an increasing function

Now $x = 1$ will be a point of local minima if $f(1^-) > f(1)$

⇒ $\sin^{-1}\alpha + 1 > 2$

⇒ $\sin^{-1}\alpha > 1$ which is impossible

9. (d) $f(x) = \begin{cases} x^3-x^2+10x-5, x\le 1 \\ -2x+\log_2(b^2-2), x>1 \end{cases}$; $f(1^-) = 5 = f(1); f(1^+) = \log_2(b^2-2) - 2$ and $f'(x) = \begin{cases} 3x^2-2x+10; x<1 \\ -2\ ; x>1 \end{cases}$

⇒ $f(x) \uparrow$ for $x < 1$ and $\downarrow$ for $x > 1$ and $f(x)$ is discontinuous at $x = 1$, such that $f(1^-) = f(1) = 5$ and for $f(x)$ to have greatest value at $x = 1, f(1) \ge f(1^+)$

⇒ $5 \ge \log_2(b^2-2) - 2$ ⇒ $7 \ge \log_2(b^2-2)$

⇒ $0 < b^2 - 2 \le 128$ ⇒ $2 < b^2 \le 130$

⇒ $b \in \left[-\sqrt{130}, \sqrt{2}\right) \cup \left(\sqrt{2}, \sqrt{130}\right]$

10. (b), (d) $f(x) = \begin{cases} x^2+3x\ ; -1\le x<0 \\ -\sin x; 0\le x<\dfrac{\pi}{2} \\ -1-\cos x; \dfrac{\pi}{2}\le x\le \pi \end{cases}$; $f(0^-) = 0, f(0^+) = 0, f(0)$; $f\left(\dfrac{\pi}{2}^-\right) = -1; f\left(\dfrac{\pi}{2}^+\right) = -1; f\left(\dfrac{\pi}{2}\right)$

⇒ $f(x)$ is a continuous function in $[-1, \pi]$

Also $f'(x) = \begin{cases} 2x+3\ ; -1<x<0 \\ -\cos x\ ; 0<x<\dfrac{\pi}{2} \\ \sin x\ ; \dfrac{\pi}{2}<x<\pi \end{cases}$

⇒ $f(x) \uparrow$ for $-1 < x < 0$, $\downarrow$ for $0 < x < \pi/2$ and $\uparrow$ for $\dfrac{\pi}{2} < x < \pi$

⇒ Global maxima of $f(x)$ in $[-1, \pi]$ $= \max.\{f(0), f(\pi)\} = 0$ and global minima of $f(x)$ in $[-1, \pi]$ $= \min.\{f(-1), f(\pi/2)\} = -2$

11. (b) $f(x) = \begin{cases} e^x ; 0\le x\le 1 \\ 2-e^{x-1} ; 1<x\le 2 \\ x-e;\ 2<x\le 3 \end{cases}$; $f(1^-) = e = f(1); f(1^+) = 2 - e^0 = 1$ and $f(2^-) = 2 - e = f(2)$ and $f(2^+) = 2 - e$

⇒ $f(x)$ is discontinuous at $x = 1$ in[0, 3]

Here $g(x) = \int_0^x f(t)dt\ ; x \in [1,3]$

Also $f(x)$ is discontinuous at $x = 1$

∴ $g(x) = \begin{cases} \int_0^x f(t)dt \text{ for } x=1 \\ \int_0^1 f(t)dt + \int_1^x f(t)dt \text{ for } 1<x\le 3 \end{cases}$

⇒ $g'(x) = \begin{cases} f(x) \text{ for } x=1 \\ 0+f(x)\ ; 1<x\le 3 \end{cases}$

⇒ $g'(x) = \begin{cases} f(1) = e \text{ for } x = 1 \\ 2-e^{x-1} ; 1<x\le 2 \\ x-e\ ; 2<x\le 3 \end{cases}$

∴ $g(x) \uparrow$ for $x \in [1, (\ell n\ 2) + 1]$; $\downarrow$ for $x \in [(\ell n\ 2) + 1, e]$; $\uparrow$ for $x \in [e, 3]$ and $g(x)$ is continuous on [1, 3]

∴ $g(x)$ has a local maxima at $x = 1 + \ell n\ 2$ and local minima at $x = e$

12. (c) $f(x) = \begin{cases} (2+x)^3 ; -3<x\le -1 \\ x^{2/3} ; -1<x<2 \end{cases}$; $f(-1) = f(-1^-) = 1; f(-1^+) = 1$

⇒ $f(x)$ is a continuous function in (–3, 2) and $f'(x) = \begin{cases} 3(2+x)^2 ; -3<x<-1 \\ \dfrac{2}{3}(x)^{-1/3} ; -1<x<2 \end{cases}$

⇒ $f(x) \uparrow$ for $x \in (-3, -1)$ and then $\downarrow$ for $x \in (-1, 0)$ and then $\uparrow$ for $x \in (0, 2)$

⇒ $f(x)$ has a local maxima at $x = -1$ and a local minima at $x = 0$

∴ 2 local maxima and minima are there.

13. (d) $f(x) = \begin{cases} \tan^{-1}\alpha - 3x^2, 0<x<1 \\ -6x,\ x\ge 1 \end{cases}$

$f(1^-) = \tan^{-1}\alpha - 3$;

$f(1^+) = f(1) = -6$

$\therefore$ $f(x)$ is discontinuous at $x = 1$ and $f'(x) = \begin{cases} -6x \text{ for } 0 < x < 1 \\ -6 \text{ for } x > 1 \end{cases}$

$\Rightarrow$ $f(x)$ is a $\downarrow$ function

Thus for $f(x)$ to have maxima at x= 1, $f(1^-) < f(1)$

$\Rightarrow$ $\tan^{-1}\alpha - 3 < -6$

$\Rightarrow$ $\tan^{-1}\alpha < -3$

Which is never possible as $\tan^{-1}\alpha > -\pi/2$ for every real α

14. (c) $f(x) = \cos 2\pi x + x - [x]$;

$\Rightarrow$ $f(x) = \cos 2\pi x + \{x\}$

$\Rightarrow$ $f(x)$ is a periodic function with period 1 and $f(x) = \begin{cases} 1 \text{ at } x = 0 \\ x + \cos 2\pi x \text{ for } 0 < x < 1 \\ 1 \text{ at } x = 1 \end{cases}$

Graphically $y = f(x)$ is as shown below.

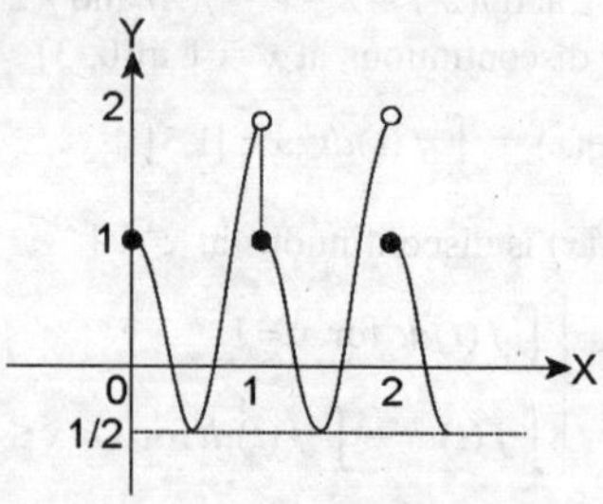

$\therefore$ In [0, 10], $f(x)$ attains its local maximum value only at $x = 0$ i.e., only once.

TEXTUAL EXERCISE–5: (SUBJECTIVE)

1. APB = AP + $PB \geq$ AB,

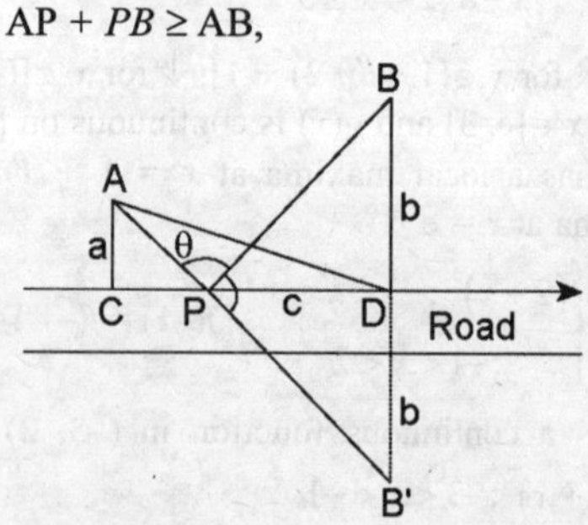

Also AP + PB = AP + PB', where B′ is the image of B on CPD and AP + $PB' \geq$ AB′ equality holds when APB′ is a straight line.

Let us suppose that CDE is x-axis and BDB′ be y-axis with D as origin, then coordinates of B′ ≡ (0, –b) and that of A ≡ (–c, a)

Equation of line joining A and B′ i.e., AB′ is given by $(y + b) = a + b\ (x - 0)$

It intersect x-axis where $y = 0$

$\Rightarrow$ $b = -(a + b)\ x/c$

$\Rightarrow$ $x = \dfrac{-bc}{(a+b)}$

$\therefore$ Distance of P from $C = CD - |PD| = C - \dfrac{bc}{a+b} = \dfrac{ac+bc-bc}{a+b} = \dfrac{ac}{a+b}$

2. $I = k.\dfrac{\cos\theta}{(h^2+R^2)}$; k = constant proportionality

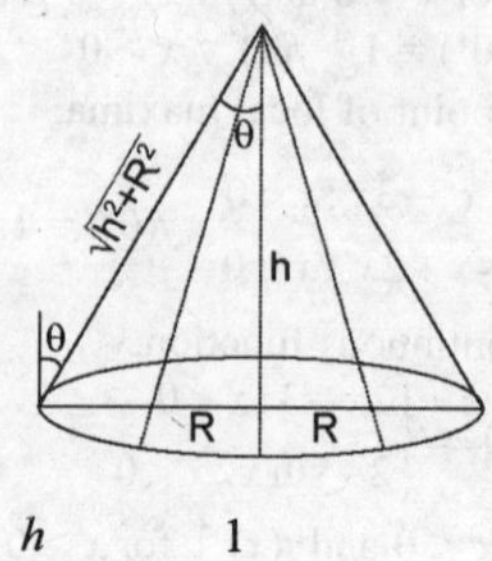

$$I = k.\frac{h}{\sqrt{h^2+R^2}}.\frac{1}{(h^2+R^2)}$$

$$\Rightarrow I = \frac{kh}{(h^2+R^2)^{3/2}}$$

$$\therefore \frac{dI}{dh} = k\left[\frac{(h^2+R^2)^{3/2}.1 - h.\frac{3}{2}(2h)(h^2+R^2)^{1/2}}{(h^2+R^2)^3}\right] = k$$

$$\left[\frac{(h^2+R^2)^{1/2}}{(h^2+R^2)^3}\left[\frac{(h^2+R^2)-3h^2}{1}\right]\right] = \frac{k(R^2-2h^2)}{(h^2+R^2)^{5/2}}$$

$\therefore$ For max./min. of I, $\dfrac{dI}{dh} = 0$

$\Rightarrow$ $R^2 = 2h^2$

$\Rightarrow$ $h = R/\sqrt{2}$. Also

$$\frac{d^2I}{dh^2} = k\left[\frac{(h^2+R^2)^{5/2}(-4h) - (R^2-2h^2).\frac{5}{2}(h^2+R^2)^{3/2}(2h)}{(h^2+R^2)^5}\right]$$

$$\Rightarrow \left(\frac{d^2I}{dh^2}\right)_{h=R/\sqrt{2}} = k\left[\frac{(h^2+R^2)^{3/2}\left[-4h(h^2+R^2) - 5h(R^2-2h^2)\right]}{(h^2+R^2)^5}\right]$$

$$= \frac{-4kh}{(h^2+R^2)^{5/2}} < 0$$

Thus I will be maximum when $h = R/\sqrt{2}$.

3. Area of symmetrical cross $= 2\left[\frac{1}{2}(b)(2x+b) + xb\right] = b^2(2x + b) + 2bx = b^2 + 4bx$ ...(1)

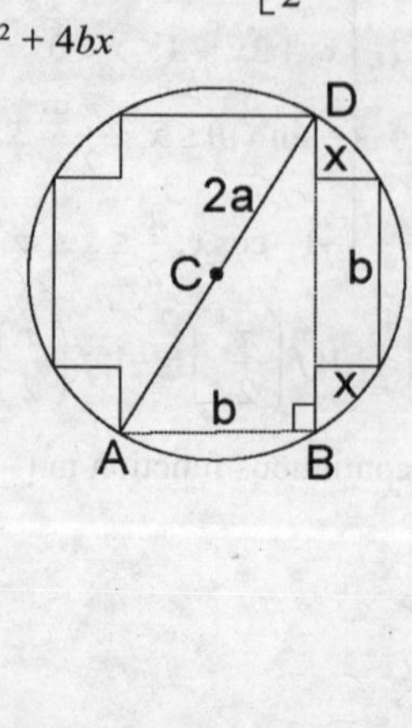

Also, in rt. ∠d Δ ABD, $4a^2 = b^2 + (b + 2x)^2$ i.e., $4a^2 = b^2 + b^2 + 4x^2 + 4bx$ or $4a^2 = 2b^2 + 4x^2 + 4bx$

$\Rightarrow 2a^2 = b^2 + 2x^2 + 2bx$

$$\Rightarrow a^2 = \frac{b^2}{2} + x^2 + bx \quad \text{...(2)}$$

$$\Rightarrow a^2 = \frac{b^2}{2} + x^2 + bx + \frac{b^2}{4} - \frac{b^2}{4}$$

$$\Rightarrow a^2 = \frac{b^2}{4} + \left(x + \frac{b}{2}\right)^2$$

$$\Rightarrow \left(x + \frac{b}{2}\right)^2 = \frac{4a^2 - b^2}{4}$$

$$\Rightarrow x + \frac{b}{2} = \frac{\sqrt{4a^2 - b^2}}{2}$$

$$\Rightarrow x = \frac{\sqrt{4a^2 - b^2} - b}{2} \quad \text{........(3)}$$

Using (2) in (1) we get, $A = b^2 + 4b\left(\frac{\sqrt{4a^2 - b^2} - b}{2}\right)$

$$\Rightarrow A = b^2 + 2b\left(\sqrt{4a^2 - b^2} - b\right)$$

$$\Rightarrow A = 2b\sqrt{4a^2 - b^2} - b^2$$

$$\Rightarrow \frac{dA}{db} = 2b.\frac{1}{2\sqrt{4a^2 - b^2}}(-2b) - 2b + 2\sqrt{4a^2 - b^2}$$

$$\Rightarrow \frac{dA}{db} = \frac{-2b^2}{\sqrt{4a^2 - b^2}} - 2b + 2\sqrt{4a^2 - b^2}$$

$$= \frac{-2b^2 - 2b\sqrt{4a^2 - b^2} + 2\left(4a^2 - b^2\right)}{\sqrt{4a^2 - b^2}}$$

$$= \frac{8a^2 - 4b^2 - 2b\sqrt{4a^2 - b^2}}{\sqrt{4a^2 - b^2}}$$

From max, $\frac{dA}{db} = 0$

$\Rightarrow 8a^2 - 4b^2 = 2b\sqrt{4a^2 - b^2}$

$\Rightarrow 4a^2 - 2b^2 = b\sqrt{4a^2 - b^2}$

$\Rightarrow (4a^2 - 2b^2)^2 = b^2(4a^2 - b^2)$

$\Rightarrow 16a^4 + 4b^4 - 16a^2 b^2 = 4a^2 b^2 - b^4$

$\Rightarrow 16a^4 + 5b^4 - 20\, a^2 b^2 = 0$

$\Rightarrow 16a^4 - 20a^2 b^2 + 5b^4 = 0$

$$\Rightarrow b^2 = \frac{20a^2 \pm \sqrt{400a^4 - 20 \times 16a^4}}{2 \times 5}$$

$$\Rightarrow b^2 = \frac{20a^2 \pm 4\sqrt{5}\, a^2}{10}$$

$$\Rightarrow b^2 = \frac{10a^2 \pm 2\sqrt{5}\, a^2}{5}$$

$$\Rightarrow b = \frac{\sqrt{10 - 2\sqrt{5}}}{5} a$$

$$\Rightarrow \begin{bmatrix} \because b^2 < 2a^2 \\ \text{from (2)} \end{bmatrix} \text{ and } \frac{\sqrt{4a^2 - b^2} - b}{2} = x$$

$$\Rightarrow x = \frac{\sqrt{4a^2 - \left(\frac{10a^2 - 2\sqrt{5}\, a^2}{5}\right)} - b}{2}$$

$$\Rightarrow x = \frac{a\left(\sqrt{\frac{10 + 2\sqrt{5}}{5}} - \sqrt{\frac{10 - 2\sqrt{5}}{5}}\right)}{2}$$

$$\Rightarrow x = \frac{a}{2\sqrt{5}}\left(\sqrt{10 + 2\sqrt{5}} - \sqrt{10 - 2\sqrt{5}}\right)$$

Now $\left(\sqrt{10 + 2\sqrt{5}} - \sqrt{10 - 2\sqrt{5}}\right)^2 = 20 - 2\sqrt{100 - 20} = 20 - 2\sqrt{80} = 20 - 8\sqrt{5}$

$$\Rightarrow \left(\sqrt{10 + 2\sqrt{5}} - \sqrt{10 - 2\sqrt{5}}\right) = \sqrt{20 - 8\sqrt{5}} = 2\sqrt{5 - 2\sqrt{5}}$$

$$\therefore \quad x = \frac{a}{2\sqrt{5}}\left(2.\sqrt{5 - 2\sqrt{5}}\right)$$

$$\Rightarrow x = \frac{\sqrt{5 - 2\sqrt{5}}}{\sqrt{5}} a \text{ or } x = \frac{\sqrt{5 - 2\sqrt{5}}}{5} a$$

$\therefore$ Dimension are $\sqrt{\frac{10 - 2\sqrt{5}}{5}} a$ and $\sqrt{\frac{5 - 2\sqrt{5}}{5}} .a$

4. $V = 1\ m^3 = \pi r 2h$ ...(1)

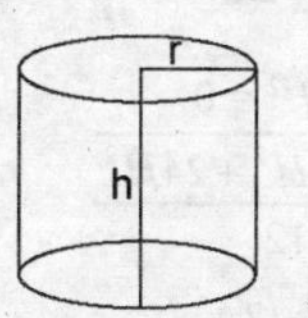

Let the cost per m^2 of curved surface $= x$ Rs.

$\therefore$ The cost per m^2 of base and top surface $= 2x$ Rs.

$\therefore$ Total cost $C = (2\pi rh)(x) + (2\pi r^2)(2x)$

$= 2\pi rh\, x + 4\, \pi r^2 x$

$$= 2\pi r\left(\frac{V}{\pi r^2}\right)x + 4\pi r^2 x$$

$$\Rightarrow C = \left(\frac{2V}{r} + 4\pi r^2\right)x$$

$$\Rightarrow \frac{dC}{dr} = 2Vx\left(\frac{-1}{r^2}\right) + 4\pi x(2r)$$

For minimum cost $\frac{dC}{dr} = 0$

$$\Rightarrow 8\pi r = \frac{2V}{r^2}$$

$$\Rightarrow r^3 = \frac{V}{4\pi} \Rightarrow r = \left(\frac{V}{4\pi}\right)^{1/3}$$

$\therefore \quad V = 1$

$$\Rightarrow r = \left(\frac{1}{4\pi}\right)^{1/3} m \text{ and } h = \frac{1}{\pi r^2} = \left(\frac{16}{\pi}\right)^{1/3} .m$$

5. tan α = h/r

V_{max} at $h = H\left(\sqrt{7}+1\right)/6$

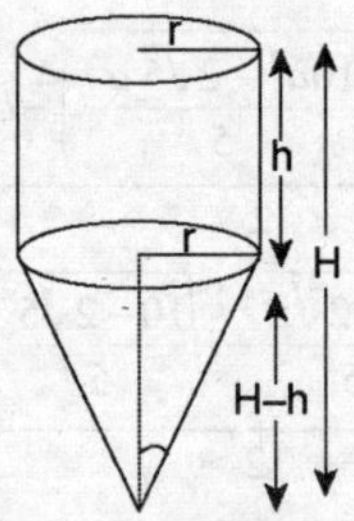

$$V = \frac{1}{3}\pi r^2 (H-h) + \pi r^2 h \qquad \ldots(1)$$

$$\tan\alpha = \frac{r}{H-h} = \frac{h}{r} \text{ (given)}$$

$$\Rightarrow r^2 = h(H-h) \qquad \ldots(2)$$

Using (2) in (1), we get $V = \frac{\pi}{3}(H-h)^2 h + \pi h^2(H-h)$

$$\Rightarrow V = \frac{\pi}{3}(H^2 h + h^3 - 2H h^2) + \pi H h^2 - \pi h^3$$

$$\Rightarrow \frac{dV}{dh} = \frac{\pi}{3}(H^2 + 3h^2 - 2H(2h)) + \pi H(2h) - 3\pi h^2$$

$$= \frac{1}{3}H^2 + h^2 - \frac{4}{3}Hh + 20\,Hh - 30\,h^2$$

For maximum volume, $\frac{dV}{dh} = 0$

$$\Rightarrow \frac{1}{3}H^2 + \frac{2}{3}Hh = 2h^2$$

$$\Rightarrow 6h^2 - 2H h - H^2 = 0$$

$$\Rightarrow h = \frac{2H \pm \sqrt{4H^2 + 24H^2}}{12}$$

$$\Rightarrow h = \frac{2H \pm 2H\sqrt{7}}{12}$$

$$\Rightarrow h = \frac{H + \sqrt{7}H}{6} = \left(\sqrt{7}+1\right)\frac{H}{6}$$

6. Let the fright changes on railway = p Rs/km.

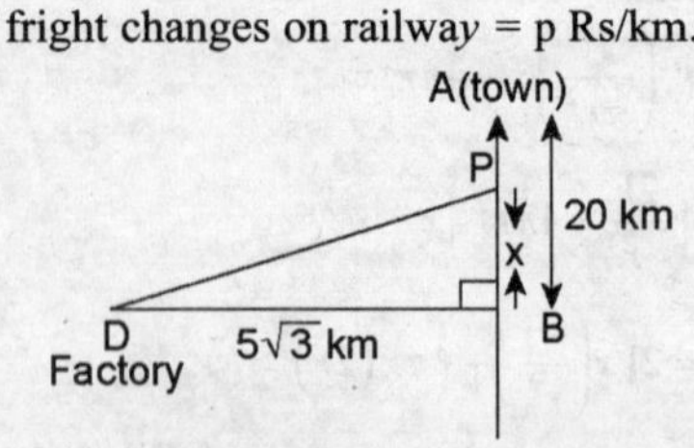

∴ That on road = 2p Rs /km.

∴ Total fright changes $C = (DP) \times 2P + (AP) \times p$

$$= \left(2\sqrt{\left(5-\sqrt{3}\right)^2 + x^2} + (20-x)\right)p$$

$$\therefore \frac{dC}{dx} = \left[\frac{2(2x)}{2\sqrt{75+x^2}} + (-1)\right]p = \left[\frac{2x}{\sqrt{75+x^2}} - 1\right]p$$

∴ For minimum C, $\frac{dC}{dx} = 0$

$$\Rightarrow 2x = \sqrt{75+x^2}$$

$$\Rightarrow 4x^2 = 75 + x^2$$

$$\Rightarrow 3x^2 = 75$$

$$\Rightarrow x^2 = 25$$

$\Rightarrow x = 5$ km from B.

7. For minimum of AP, tangent at A is || to $y = 3x - 3$

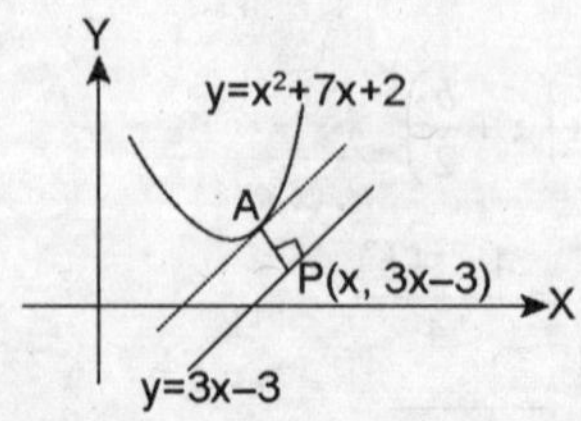

$$\Rightarrow (2x_0 + 7) = 3$$

$$\Rightarrow 2x_0 = -4$$

$$\Rightarrow x_0 = -2$$

$$\Rightarrow A = (-2, -8)$$

8. $\frac{x^2}{24} - \frac{y^2}{18} = 1 \qquad \ldots(1)$

Let P $\left(\sqrt{24}\sec\theta, \sqrt{18}\tan\theta\right)$ be the required point on (1), for which be parallel to line $3x + 2y + 1 = 0$

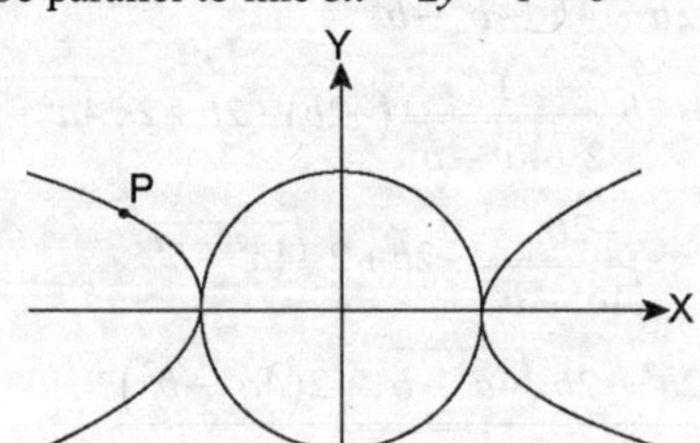

Figure correction

$$\Rightarrow \frac{\sqrt{18}\sec^2\theta}{\sqrt{24}\sec\theta.\tan\theta} = \frac{-3}{2}$$

$$\Rightarrow \frac{3\sqrt{2}\sec\theta}{2\sqrt{6}\tan\theta} = \frac{-3}{2}$$

$$\Rightarrow \frac{1}{\sqrt{3}} \text{ cosec } \theta = -1$$

$$\Rightarrow \text{cosec } \theta = -\sqrt{3}$$

$$\Rightarrow \cot^2\theta = 2$$

$$\Rightarrow \cot\theta = \pm\sqrt{2} \text{ and } \tan\theta = \pm\frac{1}{\sqrt{2}}, \sec\theta = \pm\sqrt{\frac{3}{2}}$$

∵ Point must line IInd quadrant, sec θ < 0, tan θ > 0

$$\Rightarrow \sec\theta = -\frac{\sqrt{3}}{2}, \tan\theta = \frac{1}{\sqrt{2}}$$

∴ $p = (-6, 3)$

∴ Minimum distance between p and the line $3x + 2y + 1 = 0$ is given by $\frac{|3(-6) + 2(+3) + 1|}{\sqrt{9+4}} = \frac{11}{\sqrt{13}}$

9. Given equation is $p^2 x^2 + 9y^2 = 9p^2$; $9 < p^2 < 18$

$\Rightarrow \dfrac{x^2}{9}+\dfrac{y^2}{p^2}=1$

Let the required point be p(3 cos θ, p sin θ), its distance from θ(–3, 0) is given by $p\theta=\sqrt{(3\cos\theta+3)^2+(p\sin\theta)^2}$

= D (say)

$\Rightarrow (P\theta)^2 = 9(\cos\theta + 1)^2 + p^2\sin^2\theta$

$\Rightarrow \dfrac{dD^2}{d\theta} = 9(2)(1+\cos\theta)(-\sin\theta) + 2p^2\sin\theta\cos\theta$

$= -18\sin\theta - 18\sin\theta\cos\theta + 2p^2\sin\theta\cos\theta$

$= \sin\theta.(2p^2\cos\theta - 18\cos\theta - 18)$

$\therefore$ Form max, D^2, $\dfrac{dD^2}{d\theta}=0$

$\Rightarrow \sin\theta = 0$ or $2p^2\cos\theta = 18\cos\theta + 18$

$\Rightarrow \cos\theta = \dfrac{18}{2p^2-18}$

$\Rightarrow \cos\theta = \dfrac{9}{p^2-9}$ $\quad\because\ 9 < p^2 < 18$

$\Rightarrow 0 < p^2 - 9 < 18$

$\Rightarrow \dfrac{9}{p^2-9} > 1$, which is impossible as $\cos\theta \le 1$.

$\therefore \sin\theta = 0$

$\Rightarrow$ p ≡ (3, 0)

Also (–3, 0) is the left end point major axis of ellipse, the point (3, 0) i.e., right end point of major axis is the point lying on ellipse at farthest distance .

10. Let the equation of tangent point p(a cos θ, b sin θ) be $\dfrac{x\cos\theta}{a}+\dfrac{y\sin\theta}{b}=1$

It intersect x-axis, where y = 0 i.e., x = a sec θ and y-axis, where x = 0 i.e., y = b cosec θ

$\therefore A \equiv (a\sec\theta, 0)$ and $B \equiv (0, b\sec\theta)$

$\therefore AB = \sqrt{a^2\sec^2\theta+b^2\operatorname{cosec}^2\theta} = D$ (say)

$\Rightarrow D^2 = a^2\sec^2\theta + b^2\operatorname{cosec}^2\theta$

$\therefore$ For max./min.; $\dfrac{dD^2}{d\theta}=0$

$\Rightarrow \dfrac{dD^2}{d\theta} = a^2(2\sec^2\theta\tan\theta) + b^2(-2\operatorname{cosec}^2\theta\cot\theta)$

$\Rightarrow 2a^2\sec^2\theta\tan\theta = 2b^2\operatorname{cosec}^2\theta\cot\theta$

$\Rightarrow \dfrac{a^2}{\cos^3\theta}.\sin\theta = \dfrac{b^2}{\sin^3\theta}.\cos\theta$

$\Rightarrow a^2\sin^4\theta - b^2\cos^4\theta = 0$

$\Rightarrow \tan^4\theta = \dfrac{b^2}{a^2} \Rightarrow \tan^2\theta = \dfrac{b}{a}$

$\Rightarrow \tan\theta = \pm\sqrt{\dfrac{b}{a}} \Rightarrow \sec^2\theta = 1+\dfrac{b}{a}$ & cosec2θ = 1 + $\dfrac{a}{b}=\dfrac{b+a}{b}$

$\therefore$ Minimum intersect $D_{\min} = \sqrt{a^2\left(\dfrac{b+a}{a}\right)+b^2\left(\dfrac{a+b}{a}\right)} =$

$\sqrt{(a+b^2)} = |a+b| = (a+b)$

11. Let the point P(α, β) be ($\sqrt{3}$ cosθ, sinθ) on the ellipse $\dfrac{x^2}{3}+\dfrac{y^2}{3}=1$

As shown in the figure the Area (s) enclosed is trapezium OMPB

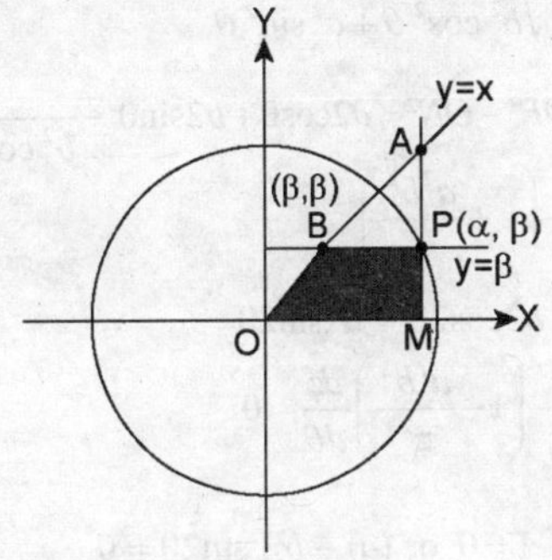

$S=\dfrac{1}{2}(OM+BP)\times PM$

$S=\dfrac{1}{2}(2\alpha-\beta)\beta=\dfrac{1}{2}(2\sqrt{3}\cos\theta-2\sin\theta)2\sin\theta$

$S = \sqrt{3}\sin2\theta + \cos2\theta - 1$

$\Rightarrow \dfrac{dS}{d\theta} = 2(\sqrt{3}\cos2\theta - \sin2\theta) = 0$

$\Rightarrow \tan2\theta = \sqrt{3}$

$\Rightarrow 2\theta = \dfrac{\pi}{3}$

Thus $\theta = \dfrac{\pi}{6}$

$\dfrac{d^2S}{d\theta^2} = -4(\sqrt{3}\sin2\theta+\cos2\theta) = -8$ at $\theta = \dfrac{\pi}{6}$

$\therefore \dfrac{d^2S}{d\theta^2} < 0$

$\Rightarrow$ Maxima at $\theta = \dfrac{\pi}{6}$

$\Rightarrow$ For maximum are point P is $\left(\dfrac{3}{2},1\right)$

Aliter: $\because S = \sqrt{3}\sin2\theta + \cos2\theta - 1 = 2(\cos2\theta.\cos\pi/3 + \sin2\theta\sec\pi/3) - 1 = 2\cos(2\theta - \pi/3) - 1$

For $S_{\max}$ $2\theta = \dfrac{\pi}{3}$

$\Rightarrow \theta = \dfrac{\pi}{6}$

12. Equation of tangent $\dfrac{x}{a}\cos\theta+\dfrac{y}{b}\sin\theta=1$ i.e., $bx\cos\theta + ay\sin\theta - ab = 0$

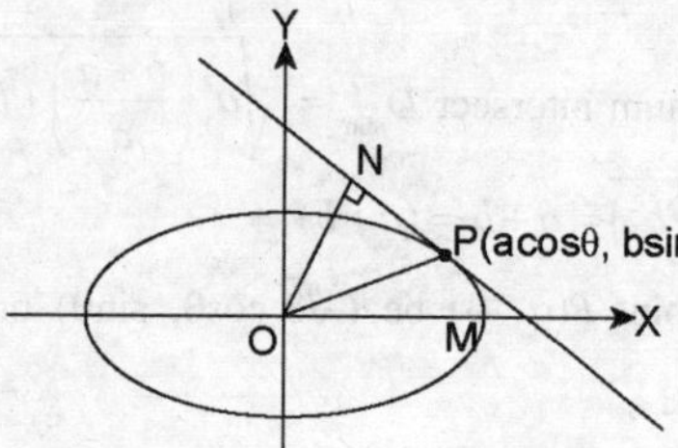

$\Rightarrow$ $ON = \dfrac{ab}{\sqrt{b^2\cos^2\theta + a^2\sin^2\theta}}$ ...(1)

$S = PN^2 = OP^2 - ON^2 = a2\cos\theta + b2\sin\theta - \dfrac{a^2b^2}{b^2\cos^2\theta + a^2\sin^2\theta}$

$= a^2 + b^2 - \left(z + \dfrac{a^2b^2}{z}\right)$ ...(2)

Where $z = b2\cos2\theta + a2\sin2\theta$

$\dfrac{ds}{d\theta} = -\left(1 - \dfrac{a^2b^2}{z^2}\right)\dfrac{dz}{d\theta} = 0$

$\Rightarrow$ $\dfrac{a^2b^2}{z^2} - 1 = 0$ or $(a^2 - b^2)\sin2\theta = 0$

$\Rightarrow$ $\sin2\theta = 0$

$\Rightarrow$ $\theta = 0$ or π for minima

$\Rightarrow$ For $S_{\max}$

$\Rightarrow$ $z = ab$

$\Rightarrow$ $b^2\cos^2\theta + a^2\sin^2\theta = ab$

$\Rightarrow$ $(b^2 - a^2)\cos^2\theta = ab - a^2$

$\Rightarrow$ $\cos^2\theta = \dfrac{a}{b+a}$

$\Rightarrow$ $\sqrt{S_{\max}} = \sqrt{a^2 + b^2 - 2ab}$

$\Rightarrow$ $(PN)_{\max} = (a - b)$ ...(3)

Area Δ OPN $= \dfrac{1}{2}\dfrac{ab}{\sqrt{z}}\sqrt{a^2 + b^2 - z - \dfrac{a^2b^2}{z}}$

$= \dfrac{ab}{2}\sqrt{\dfrac{a^2+b^2}{z} - \dfrac{a^2b^2}{z^2} - 1}$

For let $T = \dfrac{a^2+b^2}{z} - \dfrac{a^2b^2}{z^2}$

$\dfrac{dT}{d\theta} = \left(-\dfrac{(a^2+b^2)}{z^2} + \dfrac{2a^2b^2}{z^3}\right)(a^2 - b^2)\sin2\theta$

$= \dfrac{a^2 - b^2}{z^3}\sin2\theta(2a^2b^2 - z(a^2+b^2)) = 0$

$\Rightarrow$ $z = \dfrac{2a^2b^2}{a^2+b^2}$

Area of $(\Delta OPN)_{max}$

$= \dfrac{ab}{2}\sqrt{(a^2+b^2) \times \dfrac{(a^2+b^2)}{2a^2b^2} - \dfrac{a^2b^2}{4a^4b^4}(a^2+b^2)^2 - 1}$

$= \dfrac{ab}{2}\sqrt{\dfrac{(a^2+b^2)}{2a^2b^2} - \dfrac{(a^2+b^2)^2}{4a^2b^2} - 1}$

$= \dfrac{ab}{2}\sqrt{\dfrac{1}{4(a^2b^2)}(a^2+b^2)^2 - 1} = \dfrac{ab}{2}\dfrac{(a^2-b^2)}{2ab} = \dfrac{1}{4}(a^2 - b^2)$

TEXTUAL EXERCISE–5:(OBJECTIVE)

1. (a) $y = x + 1$ will be || to tangent at $P(y_0^2, y_0)$ on $x = y^2$

$\Rightarrow$ $\dfrac{1}{2y_0} = 1 \Rightarrow y_0 = \dfrac{1}{2}$

$\Rightarrow$ $P\left(\dfrac{1}{4}, \dfrac{1}{2}\right)$

$\Rightarrow$ ⊥r distance of line from P $\equiv \dfrac{\left|\frac{1}{4} - \frac{1}{2} + 1\right|}{\sqrt{(1)^2 + (-1)^2}} = \dfrac{3/4}{\sqrt{2}} =$

$\dfrac{3}{4\sqrt{2}} = \dfrac{3\sqrt{2}}{8}$

2. (c) $V = \dfrac{1}{3}\pi r^2 h = \dfrac{1}{3}\pi r^2\left(\sqrt{\ell^2 - r^2}\right)$

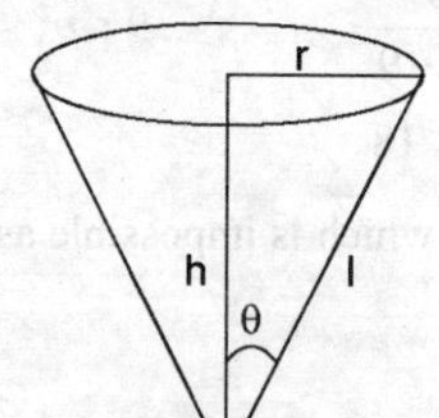

$\therefore$ $\dfrac{dV}{dr} = \dfrac{\pi}{3}\left[r^2\left(\dfrac{-2r}{2\sqrt{\ell^2 - r^2}}\right) + 2r\sqrt{\ell^2 - r^2}\right]$

$= \dfrac{\pi}{3}\left[\dfrac{-r^3 + 2r(\ell^2 - r^2)}{\sqrt{\ell^2 - r^2}}\right] = \dfrac{\pi}{3}\left[\dfrac{2r\ell^2 - 3r^3}{\sqrt{\ell^2 - r^2}}\right]$

$\Rightarrow$ For maximum volume $\dfrac{dV}{dr} = 0$

$\Rightarrow$ $r(2\ell^2 - 3r^2) = 0$

$\Rightarrow$ $\dfrac{\ell^2}{r^2} = \dfrac{3}{2} \Rightarrow \dfrac{\ell}{r} = \sqrt{\dfrac{3}{2}}$

$\Rightarrow$ cosec θ = $\sqrt{3/2}$

$\Rightarrow$ cot θ = $\dfrac{1}{\sqrt{2}} \Rightarrow \tan\theta = \sqrt{2}$

3. (c) $P = 60^0 = \ell + 2r$ ...(1)

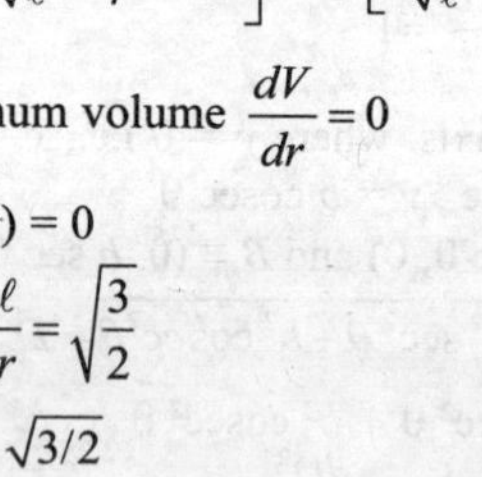

Also $A = \dfrac{1}{2} = \ell r = \dfrac{1}{2}(60 - 2r)r$

$\Rightarrow$ $A = 30r - r^2$

$\Rightarrow$ $\dfrac{dA}{dr} = 30 - 2r$ and $\dfrac{d^2A}{dr^2} = -2$

$\therefore \quad \frac{dA}{dr} = 0$

$\Rightarrow \ \ell = 15$

$\therefore$ Maximum Area for $\ell = 15$

4. (c) $x + y = 12$ .....(1)

$P = x^2 .(y)^4$

$\Rightarrow P = y^4(12 - y)^2$

$\Rightarrow \frac{dP}{dy} = y^4(2)(12 - y)(-1) + (12 - y)^2 . 4y^3$

$\therefore \quad \frac{dP}{dy} = 0$

$\Rightarrow 2(12 - y). y^3 (24 - 2y - y) = 0$

$\Rightarrow 2(12 - y) . y^3 (24 - 3y) = 0$

$\Rightarrow y = 0$ or 12 or 8

$\Rightarrow y$ must be 8

$\Rightarrow$ Two parts will be 4 and 8

5. (b) $S = 2x + 3y$; $xy = 6$

$\Rightarrow S = 2x + 3\left(\frac{6}{x}\right) = 2x + \frac{18}{x}$

$\therefore \quad \frac{dS}{dx} = 2 + 18\left(\frac{-1}{x^2}\right)$

$\therefore \quad \frac{dS}{dx} = 0 \Rightarrow 1 = \frac{9}{x^2}$

$\Rightarrow x = 3$ or -3

$\frac{d^2S}{dx^2} = \frac{36}{x^3}$ which > 0 for $x = 3$

$\Rightarrow x = 3, y = 2$

$\Rightarrow S_{min} = 2(3) + 3(2) = 12$

6. (d) Area of rectangle, $A = \ell b$ or $A = \ell.\sqrt{4r^2 - \ell^2}$

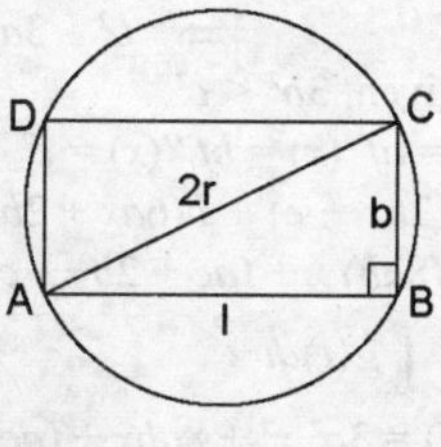

$\Rightarrow \frac{dA}{d\ell} = \frac{\ell(-2\ell)}{2\sqrt{4r^2 - \ell^2}} + \sqrt{4r^2 - \ell^2}$

$= \frac{-\ell^2 + 4r^2 - \ell^2}{\sqrt{4r^2 - \ell^2}} = \frac{4r^2 - 2\ell^2}{\sqrt{4r^2 - \ell^2}}$

$\therefore \quad \frac{dA}{d\ell} = 0 \quad \Rightarrow 4r^2 = 2\ell^2$

$\Rightarrow \ell^2 = 2r^2 \qquad \therefore \ A = \sqrt{2}r\sqrt{2r^2} = 2r^2$

7. (d) $P = 2r + \ell = 2r + r\theta = (2 + \theta)r$

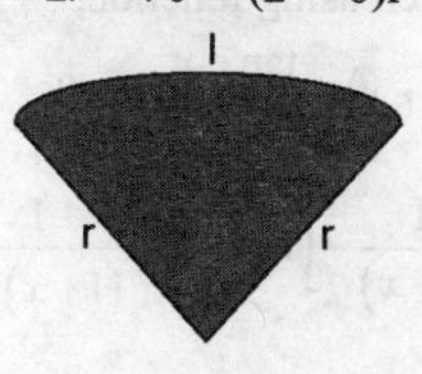

$A = \frac{\theta.r^2}{2} = \frac{\theta}{2}\left(\frac{p}{2+\theta}\right)^2$; p = constant

$\Rightarrow \frac{dA}{d\theta} = \frac{1}{2}p^2\left(\frac{\theta}{(2+\theta)^2}\right) = \frac{1}{2}p^2\left[\frac{(2+\theta)^2 - \theta.2(2+\theta)}{(2+\theta)^4}\right]$

$= \frac{1}{2}p^2\left[\frac{(2+\theta)(2+\theta-2\theta)}{(2+\theta)^4}\right] = \frac{1}{2}p^2 = \frac{(2-\theta)}{(2+\theta)^3} = 0$

$\Rightarrow \theta = 2^c$

8. (d) $P = xy$; $x + 2y = 8$

$\Rightarrow p = (y)(8 - 2y) = 8y - 2y^2$

$\Rightarrow \frac{dp}{dy} = 8 - 4y = 0$

$\Rightarrow y = 2$

$\Rightarrow x = 4$

$\therefore$ Maximum of $xy = (4)(2) = 8$

9. (d) $x + y = 8$; $p = x^2 y$

$\Rightarrow p = x^2(8 - x) = 8x^2 - x^3$

$\Rightarrow \frac{dp}{dx} = 16x - 3x^2 = x(16 - 3x) = 0$

$\Rightarrow x = 0$ or $x = 16/3$

$\therefore$ Maximum value of $x^2 y = \left(\frac{16}{3}\right)^2\left(8 - \frac{16}{3}\right) = \frac{2048}{27}$

10. (a) $x - 2y = 4$; $p = xy$

$\Rightarrow p = y(4 + 2y) = 4y + 2y^2$

$\Rightarrow \frac{dp}{dy} = 4 + 4y = 0$

$\Rightarrow y = -1$ & $\frac{d^2p}{dy^2} = 4$

$\Rightarrow P$ will be minimum for $y = -1$ and the minimum value of $p = xy = (4 - 2)(-1) = -2$

11. (a) $S = x + y = 20$ ...(1)

$P = x^2 . y^3 = y^3(20 - y)^2$

$\Rightarrow \frac{dp}{dy} = y^3(2)(-1)(20 - y) + 3y^2(20 - y)^2$

$= y^2(20 - y)[3(20 - y) - 2y]$

$= y^2(20 - y)(60 - 5y)$

$\therefore \quad \frac{dp}{dy} = 0$

$\Rightarrow y = 0$ or $y = 20$ or $y = 12$

$\therefore$ For the product to be maximum, $y = 12$ and $x = 8$

12. (c) $a^2 x^4 + b^2 y^4 = c^6$ ...(1)

$P = xy$;

P will be maximum if p^4 is maximum,

$\therefore \quad P^4 = x^4 y^4 = \frac{1}{b^2}x^4\left(b^2y^4\right)$

$P^4 = \frac{x^4}{b^2}(c^6 - a^2 x^4)$

$P^4 = \frac{c^6}{b^2}x^4 - \frac{a^2}{b^2}x^8$

$\Rightarrow \quad \frac{d(p^4)}{dx} = \frac{c^6}{b^2}(4x^3) - \frac{a^2}{b^2}(8x^7)$

$\therefore \quad \frac{dp^4}{dx} = 0 \Rightarrow 4x^3\left(\frac{c^6}{b^2} - 2\frac{a^2}{b^2}x^4\right)$

$\Rightarrow \; x = 0$ or $x^4 = \frac{c^6}{2a^2}$ ...(2)

$\Rightarrow x = \left(\frac{c^6}{2a^2}\right)^{1/4} = \frac{c^{3/2}}{(2)^{1/4}a^{1/2}}$ and $b^2y^4 = c^6 - \frac{c^6}{2} = \frac{c^6}{2}$

$\Rightarrow y^4 = \frac{c^6}{2b^2}$ ...(3)

$\therefore \; x^4y^4 = \frac{c^{12}}{4a^2b^2} \Rightarrow xy = \frac{c^3}{(4a^2b^2)^{1/4}} = \frac{c^3}{\sqrt{2ab}} = P_{max}$

13. **(d)** Let $p\left(x_0, \frac{x_0^2}{2}\right)$ be the point on curve and A (0, 5)

$\Rightarrow D^2 = (AP)^2 = x_0^2 + \left(\frac{x_0^2}{2} - 5\right)^2$

$\therefore \quad \frac{dD^2}{dx_0} = 2x_0 + 2\left(\frac{x_0^2}{2} - 5\right)(x_0)$

$= 2x_0\left[1 + \frac{x_0^2}{2} - 5\right] = 2x_0\left[\frac{x_0^2}{2} - 4\right] = 0$

$\Rightarrow x_0 = 0; x_0^2 = 8$

$\Rightarrow x_0 = \pm\sqrt{2}$ & $\frac{d^2D^2}{dx_0^2} = 3x_0^2 - 8$

$\therefore \quad \left(\frac{d^2D^2}{dx_0^2}\right)_{x_0 = 2\sqrt{2}} = 3(8) - 8 = 16 > 0$

& $\left(\frac{d^2D^2}{dx_0^2}\right)_{x_0 = -2\sqrt{2}} = 16 > 0$

$\Rightarrow D^2$ and hence D will be minimum for $x_0 = \pm 2\sqrt{2}$ i.e., at point $(2\sqrt{2}, 4)$ and $(-2\sqrt{2}, 4)$

14. **(c)** $\Delta = \frac{1}{2}(ss')(b\sin\theta)$

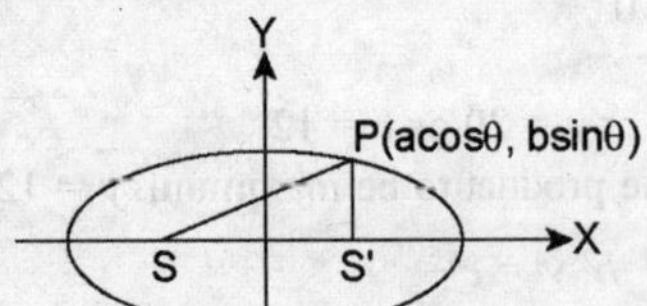

$= \frac{1}{2}$ (2ae) (b sin θ)

= ae b sin θ

$\therefore \quad \frac{d\Delta}{d\theta}$ = ae b cos θ = 0

$\Rightarrow \theta = \pi/2$

$\Rightarrow p \equiv (\theta, b)$

$\Rightarrow$ Max. $\Delta = aeb$

SECTION–III: SINGLE CORRECT ANSWER)

1. **(b)** $f(x) = \frac{ax+b}{cx+d}; x \in \mathbb{R} - \left\{\frac{d}{c}\right\}$

$\Rightarrow f'(x) = \frac{(cx+d)(a) - (ax+b)(c)}{(cx+d)^2} = \frac{acx + ad - acx - bc}{(cx+d)^2}$

$= \frac{ad - bc}{(cx+d)^2}$

$\Rightarrow f'(x) > 0$ for $ad - bc > 0$

2. **(b)** $f(x) = x^2\, e^{-x^2/a^2}$; $a > 0$

$f'(x) = x^2 \,.\, e^{\frac{-x^2}{a^2}}\left(\frac{-2x}{a^2}\right) + e^{-x^2/a^2}(2x)$

$= 2x \,.\, e^{-x^2/a^2}\left(1 - \frac{x^2}{a^2}\right)$

$\therefore \; f'(x) \geq 0 \quad \Rightarrow \quad x(a^2 - x^2) \geq 0$

$\Rightarrow (x + a)(x)(x - a) \leq 0 \Rightarrow x \in (-\infty, -a] \cup [0, a]$

3. **(a)** $f(x) = \cot^{-1}x + x$

$\Rightarrow f'(x) = \frac{-1}{1+x^2} + 1 = \frac{-1+1+x^2}{1+x^2} = \frac{x^2}{1+x^2} \geq 0 \forall x \in \mathbb{R}$

$\Rightarrow x \in \mathbb{R}$

4. **(a)** $f(x) = ax^3 + bx^2 + cx + d$

Let $f'(x) = 3ax^2 + 2bx + c$

Now, Disc. of $f'(x) = 4b^2 - 4(3a)(c)$

$= 4(b^2 - 3ac)$

$\because \; f(x)$ is given to be an increasing cubic function

$\Rightarrow f'(x) \geq 0 \quad \Rightarrow \quad b^2 - 3ac \leq 0, a > 0$

Also it is given, $3b^2 < c^2$

Now, $g(x) = af'(x) = bf''(x) = c^2$

$= a(3ax^2 + 2bx + c) + b(6ax + 2b) + c^2$

$= 3a^2x^2 + (8ab)x + (ac + 2b^2 + c^2)$

Let $F(x) = \int_a^x g(t)dt$

$\Rightarrow F'(x) = g(x) = 3a^2x^2 + 8abx + (ac + 2b^2 + c^2)$

Disc. of $g(x) = (8ab)^2 - 4(3a^2)(ac + 2b^2 + c^2)$

$= 64a^2b^2 - 12a^2(ac + 2b^2 + c^2)$

$= 40a^2b^2 - 12a^3c - 12a^2c^2$

$= 4a^2(10b^2 - 3ac - 4c^2)$

$= 4a^2(4(3b^2 - c^2) - 2b^2 - 3ac)$

$\left[\begin{array}{l}\because b^2 - 3ac \leq ac \geq 0 \Rightarrow ac \geq 0 \\ \text{and } 3b^2 - c^2 < 0 (given)\end{array}\right]$

$\Rightarrow$ Disc. of $g(x) \leq 0 \quad \Rightarrow \quad F'(x) = g(x) \leq 0$

$\Rightarrow F(x)$ is a decreasing function.

5. **(a)** $f(x) = \ell n(1+x) - \frac{\tan^{-1}x}{1+x}; x > 0$

$f'(x) = \frac{1}{(1+x)} - (\tan^{-1}x)\left(\frac{-1}{(1+x)^2}\right) - \frac{1}{(1+x)} \cdot \frac{1}{1+x^2}$

$\Rightarrow\ f'(x) = \dfrac{1}{1+x} + \dfrac{\tan^{-1} x}{(1+x)^2} - \dfrac{1}{(1+x)(1+x^2)}$

$= \dfrac{1}{(1+x)}\left[1 - \dfrac{1}{1+x^2}\right] + \dfrac{\tan^{-1} x}{(1+x)^2}$

$= \dfrac{x^2}{(1+x)(1+x)} + \dfrac{\tan^{-1} x}{(1+x)^2} > 0\ \forall\, x > 0$

$\Rightarrow$ f (x) is an increasing function for $x > 0$

$\Rightarrow f(x) > f(0)\ \forall\, x > 0$

$\Rightarrow \ell(1+x) - \dfrac{\tan^{-1} x}{1+x} > 0$

$\Rightarrow f(x) > 0\ \forall\, x > 0 \quad \Rightarrow$ sgn $(f(x)) = 1$

6. (d) $f''(x) > 0, f'(1) = 0;$

$g(x) = f(\cot^2 x + 2 \cot x + 2);\ 0 < x < \pi$

$\Rightarrow g'(x) = f'(\cot^2 x + 2 \cot x + 2)\ .\ [2 \cot x\,(-\operatorname{cosec}^2 x) + 2(-\operatorname{cosec} 2x)]$

$= f'(\cot 2x + 2\cot x + 2)\,(-2 \operatorname{cosec}^2 x)\,(1 + \cot x)$

Now $f''(x) > 0$

$\Rightarrow f'(x)$ is an increasing function

$\Rightarrow f'(x) \geq f'(1)\ \forall\, x \geq 1$

$\Rightarrow f'(x) \geq 0\ \forall\, x \geq 1$ and $\cot^2 x + 2\cot x + 2 = (\cot^2 x + 1)^2 + 1 \geq 1$

$\Rightarrow f'(\cot 2x + 2 \cot x + 2) \geq 0\ \forall\, x \in (0, \pi)$

$\therefore\ g(x)$ will be decreasing provided $\cot x + 1 \geq 0$

$\Rightarrow \cot x \geq -1$

$\Rightarrow x \in \left(0, \dfrac{3\pi}{4}\right]$

7. (a) $f(x) = \dfrac{\sin}{\quad};0< \ <-$

$\because\ f(x) = \dfrac{\sin}{\quad}$ represents the slope of chord joining the point p$(x, \sin x)$ on the graph of $y = \sin x$ and origin, which decrease for $0 < x < \pi/2$

$\Rightarrow f(x) = \dfrac{\sin x}{x};0<x<\pi/2$ is a decreasing function.

Also $\sin x < x$ for $0 < x < \pi/2$

$\Rightarrow f(\sin x) > f(x);\ 0 < x < \pi/2$

$\Rightarrow \dfrac{\sin(\sin x)}{\sin x} > \dfrac{\sin x}{x}$

$\Rightarrow x \sin(\sin x) > \sin^2 x$

8. (d) $f'(x) = \dfrac{1}{\log_3\left[\log_{1/4}(\cos x + a)\right]}$

$\because\ f(x)$ is ↑

$\Rightarrow f'(x) > 0$

$\Rightarrow \log_3[\log_{1/4} (\cos x + a)] > 0$

$\Rightarrow \log_{1/4}(\cos x + a) > 1$

$\Rightarrow 0 < (\cos x + a) < \dfrac{1}{4}$

$\Rightarrow -a < \cos x < \dfrac{1}{4} - a$

$\Rightarrow -a < -1$ and $1 < \dfrac{1}{4} - a$

$\Rightarrow a > 1$ and $a < -3/4$, which is impossible simultaneously i.e., $a \in \phi$

9. (a) $\phi(x) = f(x) + f(2a - x)$ and $f''(x) > 0$, $a > 0$, $0 \leq x \leq 2a$,

$f''(x) > 0$

$\Rightarrow f'(x) \uparrow\ \forall\, x \in [0, 2a]$

Now $\phi'(x) = f'(x) + f'(2a - x)\,(-1)$

$= f'(x) - f'(2a - x)$

For $\phi(x)$ to be increasing $x \geq 2a - x \geq 0$

$\Rightarrow 4a \geq 2x \geq 2a \quad \Rightarrow 2a \geq x \geq a$

$\Rightarrow x \in [a, 2a]$

Similarly for $\phi(x)$ to be decreasing $x \in [0, a]$

10. (a) $f'(x) > 0, f''(x) < 0, x_1 < x_2$

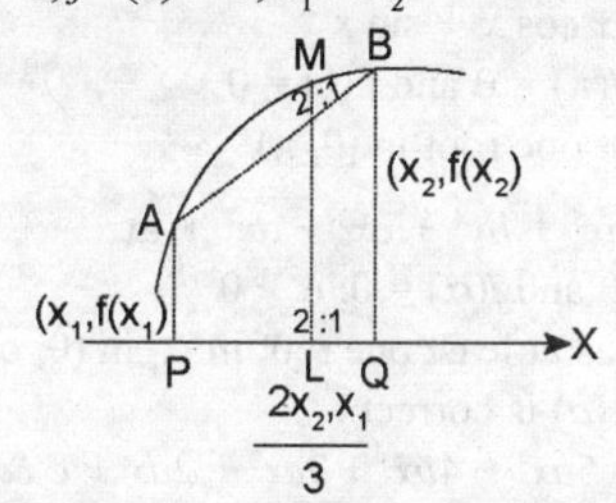

Co-ordinates of P $\equiv \left(\dfrac{2x_2 + x_1}{3}, \dfrac{2f(x_2) + f(x_1)}{3}\right)$

Now $LP < LM$

$\Rightarrow \dfrac{2f(x_2) + f(x_1)}{3} < f\left(\dfrac{2x_2 + x_1}{3}\right)$

11. (a) If $0 < A < \pi/6$,

$\because\ f(x) = \dfrac{\sin x}{x}$ is a decreasing function

$\Rightarrow g(x) = x$ is an increasing function for $0 < x < \pi/6$

$\Rightarrow g(A) < g(\pi/6)$ for $0 < A < \pi/6$

$\Rightarrow$ A cosec $A < \dfrac{\pi}{6}$cosec$\dfrac{\pi}{6}$

$\Rightarrow$ A cosec $A < \dfrac{\pi}{3}$

12. (b) $f''(x) < 0\ \forall\, x \in (a, b)$

$\Rightarrow f'(x) \downarrow\ \forall\, x \in (a, b) \quad \Rightarrow f'(x) \leq 0\ \forall\, x \in (a, b)$

Also $f'(x)$ being decreasing and continuous is injective function

$\Rightarrow f'(x) = 0$ at most once in (a, b)

13. (a) $\int_0^1 \left(1 + \cos^8 x\right)\left(ax^2 + bx + c\right)dx$

$= \int_0^2 \left(1 + \cos^8 x\right)\left(ax^2 + bx + c\right)dx$

$\Rightarrow \int_1^2 \left(1 + \cos^8 x\right)\left(ax^2 + bx + c\right)dx = 0$

$\because\ (1 + \cos^8 x) \geq 1$

$\Rightarrow ax^2 + bx + c > 0\ \forall\, x \in (1, 2)$

$\Rightarrow ax^2 + bx + c < 0$ in a sub-interval of $(1, 2)$

$\Rightarrow ax^2 + bx + c = 0$ has two real and distinct roots at least one of which must lie in $(1, 2)$

14. (c) $\frac{(f(7)-f(2))}{1}\cdot\frac{(f(7)^2+f(2)^2+f(2).f(7))}{3}$

$=\frac{(f(7))^3-(f(2))^3}{3}$

Let $g(x) = (f(x))^3$

$\Rightarrow$ $g'(c)=\frac{(f(7))^3-(f(2))^3}{(7-2)}$

$\Rightarrow$ $3(f(c))^2 . f'(c)=\frac{(f(7))^3-(f(2))^3}{5}$

$\Rightarrow$ $\frac{(f(7))^3-(f(2))^3}{3}=5(f(c))^2 f'(c)$

15. (b) Let $f(x) = x \sin x$

$\Rightarrow$ $f'(x) = x \cos x + \sin x$

$\therefore$ $f(0) = f(\pi) = 0$ and $f'(x) = 0$

$\Rightarrow$ At least one root in $(0, \pi)$

16. (d) $f(x) = ax^5 + bx^4 + cx^3 + dx^2 + ex$

$f(0) = 0$ and $f(\alpha) = 0$; $\alpha > 0$

$\Rightarrow$ $f'(x)$ has at least one root in α_1 in $(0, \alpha)$

$\Rightarrow$ option (*a*) is correct.

$f'(x) = 5ax^4 + 4bx^3 + 3cx^2 + 2dx + e$ & $f''(x) = 20ax^3 + 12bx^2 + 6cx + 2d$ which being cubic (odd degree) has at least one root

$\Rightarrow$ option (*b*) is correct.

$\because$ $f'(x)$ is a polynomial of even degree and has a real root α_1, then it must have another real root α_2 as the complex roots always occur in conjugate pairs.

$\Rightarrow$ option (*c*) is also correct i.e., all the given options are correct .

17. (a) $\because f(x) = 0$ is satisfied by only $x = 1$, $x = 2$ and $x = 3$

$\Rightarrow$ one of $x = 1, 2$ or 3 must be a repeated root without loss of generality

Let $x = 1$ is a repeated root

$\Rightarrow$ $f(x) = k(x-1)^2 (x-2)(x-3)$

$\Rightarrow$ $f'(x) = k[(x-1)^2 (2x-5) + (x-2)(3x^2-10x+7) + (x-3)(3x^2-8x+5)]$

$\Rightarrow$ $f'(1) = 0$

$\Rightarrow$ $f'(1) . f'(2) . f'(3)$ = similarly if $x = 2$ or $x = 3$ is a repeated root, then $f''(2) = 0$ and $f'''(3) = 0$

$\Rightarrow$ $f'(1) . f'(2) . f'(3) = 0$

18. (b) $\because f(|x|) = 0$ has eight real roots i.e., $\pm\alpha_1, \pm\alpha_2, \pm\alpha_3, \pm\alpha_4$ (*say*) where $\alpha_i > 0$

$\Rightarrow$ $f(x) = 0$ has 4 positive real roots $\alpha_1, \alpha_2, \alpha_3, \alpha_4$ and 1 negative

19. (a) $f(x)=\begin{cases}x^2+a|x|+b \text{ for } x^2+a|x|+b\ge 0\\ -(x^2+a|x|+b) \text{ for } x^2+a|x|+b<0\end{cases}$

$=\begin{cases}x^2+ax+b \text{ for } x^2+ax+b\ge 0 \text{ for } x\ge 0\\ x^2+ax+b \text{ for } x^2-ax+b\ge 0 \text{ for } x<0\\ -(x^2+ax+b) \text{ for } x^2+ax+b<0 \text{ for } x\ge 0\\ -(x^2-ax+b) \text{ for } x^2-ax+b<0 \text{ for } x<0\end{cases}$

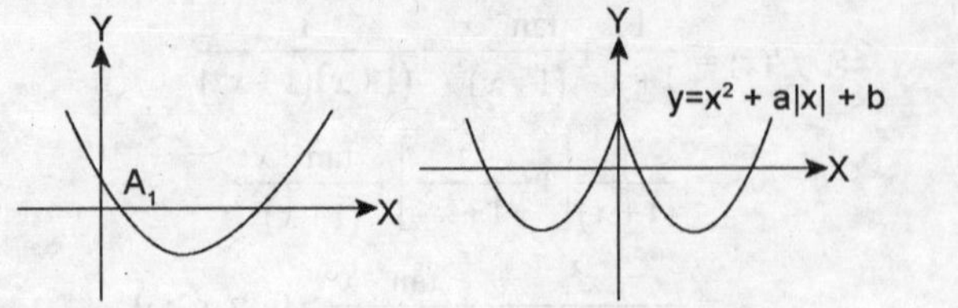

But above has 5 points of non-differentiability

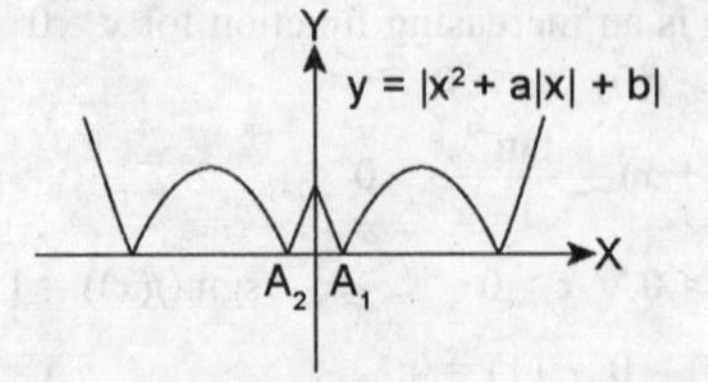

$\therefore$ For 3 points non-differentiability, A_1 and A_2 should be absent

$\Rightarrow$ $f(x) = x^2 + ax + b$ must be of the from as shown below

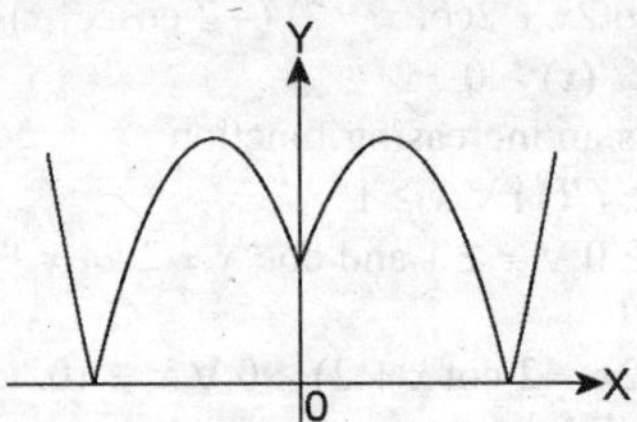

$\Rightarrow$ $\frac{-a}{2}>0, b\le 0$

$\Rightarrow$ $a < 0, b \le 0$

20. (b) $\frac{x^2}{24}-\frac{y^2}{18}=1$ .....(1)

Let (x_1, y_1) be the point on (1) which is nearest to line $3x + 2y - 1 = 0$

$\Rightarrow$ $\frac{1}{24}(2x_1)-\frac{1}{18}(2y_1).\frac{dy}{dx}=0$

$\Rightarrow$ $\frac{y_1}{18}\frac{dy}{dx}=\frac{x_1}{24}\Rightarrow\frac{dy}{dx}=\frac{3}{4}\frac{x_1}{y_1}$, which must be same as slope of line i.e., $-3/2$

$\therefore$ $\frac{3}{4}\frac{x_1}{y_2}=\frac{-3}{2}$

$\Rightarrow$ $2x_1 = -4y_1$ or $x_1 = -2y_1$

$\Rightarrow$ $\frac{x_1^2}{24}-\frac{x_1^2}{72}=1$

$\Rightarrow$ $x_1 = \pm 6$

$\therefore$ $P \equiv (6, -3)$ or $(-6, 3)$

Now Distance P (6, –3)

$=\frac{|3(6)+2(-3)-1|}{\sqrt{9+4}}=\frac{11}{\sqrt{13}}$ and distance of $P(-6, 3)$

$=\left|\frac{3(-6)+2(-3)-1}{\sqrt{9+4}}\right|=\frac{25}{\sqrt{13}}$

$\therefore$ Point (6, –3) is nearest point

21. **(b)** Let $F(x) = x^3 + 2ax^2 + bx$, then $F'(x) = 3x^2 + 4ax + b$
It will have at least one root in (0, 1) if $= F(0) = F(1)$
i.e., $0 = 1 + 2a + b$

22. **(b)** By L.M.V.T, $f'(c) = \dfrac{f(b)-f(a)}{b-a}$

$\Rightarrow\ 3c^2 = \dfrac{27-1}{3-1} = 13$

$\Rightarrow\ c = \pm\sqrt{\dfrac{13}{3}}$

$\therefore$ Points on the curve will be

$\left(-\sqrt{\dfrac{13}{3}}, \dfrac{-13}{3}\sqrt{\dfrac{13}{3}}\right)$ and $\left(\sqrt{\dfrac{13}{3}}, \dfrac{13}{3}\sqrt{\dfrac{13}{3}}\right)$

$\equiv \left(-\dfrac{\sqrt{39}}{3}, \dfrac{-13\sqrt{39}}{9}\right)$ and $\left(\dfrac{\sqrt{39}}{3}, \dfrac{13\sqrt{39}}{9}\right)$

23. **(b)** $f(x) = (ab - b^2 - 2)\,x + \int_0^x (\cos^4\theta + \sin^4\theta)\,d\theta$

$\Rightarrow\ f'(x) = (ab - b^2 - 2) + (\cos^4 x + \sin^4 x) \le 0$

$\Rightarrow\ \cos^4 x + \sin^4 x + ab - b^2 - 2 \le 0\ \forall\ x \in \mathbb{R}$ and $b \in \mathbb{R}$

$\Rightarrow\ 1 - 2\sin^2 x\cos 2x + ab - b^2 - 2 \le 0$

$\Rightarrow\ -b^2 + ab - 1 \le \dfrac{1}{2}\sin^2 2x\ \forall\ x, b \in \mathbb{R}$

$\Rightarrow\ b^2 - ab + 1 \ge \dfrac{-1}{2}\sin^2 2x\ \forall\ x, b \in \mathbb{R}$

$\Rightarrow\ b^2 - ab + 1 \ge 0\ \forall\ b \in \mathbb{R}$

$\Rightarrow\ (-a)^2\ 4 \le 0$

$\Rightarrow\ a \in [-2, 2]$

24. **(d)** $f(x) = \int_2^x (2t-5)\,dt$

$\Rightarrow\ f'(x) = (2x - 5)$

The graph will intersect x-axis where $f(x) = 0$

$\Rightarrow\ \left[t^2 - 5t\right]_2^x = 0$ i.e., $(x^2 - 5x) - (4 - 10) = 0$

$\Rightarrow\ x^2 - 5x + 6 = 0$

$\Rightarrow\ x = 2$ or 3

$\therefore\ m_1 = f'(2) = -1,\ m_2 = f'(3) = 1$

$\therefore$ Angle between the tangents $= \pi/2$

25. **(d)**

(a) $f(x) = \begin{cases} x\ ; 0 \le x < 1 \\ 0\ ;\ \ 1 \end{cases}$

$\because\ f(x)$ is discontinuous at $x = 1$, Rolle's theorem is not applicable

(b) $f(x) = \begin{cases} \dfrac{\sin x}{x}; -\pi \le x < 0 \\ 0;\ x = 0 \end{cases}$

$\Rightarrow\ f(x)$ is discontinuous at $x = 0$

(c) $f(x) = \dfrac{x^2 - x - 6}{(x-1)}\ ;\ x \in [-2, 3]$

$\Rightarrow\ f(x)$ is discontinuous at $x = 1$

(d) $f(x) = \begin{cases} \dfrac{x^3 - 2x^2 - 5x + 6}{x-1}; x \ne 1 \\ -6\ ; x = 1 \end{cases}$

$\Rightarrow\ \lim\limits_{x\to1} f(x) = \lim\limits_{x\to1}\dfrac{(x-1)(x+2)(x-3)}{(x-1)} = -6 = f(1)$

$\therefore\ f(x)$ is continuous in $[-2, 3]$
Again $f(x)$ being a rational function is differentiable
Also $f(-2) = 0 = f(3)$

$\Rightarrow$ Rolle's theorem is applicable

26. **(d)** Let $F(x) = g(x) - 4(x)$

$F(2) = g(2) - 4f(2) = 0 - 4(8) = -32$

$F(4) = g(4) - 4f(4) = 8 - 4(10) = -32$

$\because\ F(2) = F(4)$, by Rolle's theorem $\exists\ x \in (2, 4)$ s.t. $F'(x) = 0$ i.e., $g'(x) - 4f'(x) = 0$ for some $x \in (2, 4)$

27. **(c)** $f(x) = 2x^3 + 9x^2 + 12x + 1$

$f'(x) = 6x^2 + 18x + 12$

$= 6(x^2 + 3x + 12) = 6(x + 1)(x + 2)$

$\Rightarrow\ f(x)$ is non-monotonic

$\Rightarrow$ (a) is correct.

$f'(x) > 0$ for $x < -2$ or $x > -1$ and $f'(x) < 0$ for $x \in (-2, -1)$

$\Rightarrow$ (b) is correct.

$\because\ f(x)$ is non-monotonic

$\Rightarrow$ it is not bijective

$\Rightarrow$ (c) is incorrect.

$f''(x) = 6\,(2x + 3) = 0$

$\Rightarrow\ x = -3/2$

$\Rightarrow\ x = -3/2$ is a point of inflexion

$\Rightarrow$ (d) is correct.

28. **(a)** $f(x) = \dfrac{ax^3}{3} + (a + 2)\,x^2 + (a - 1)\,x + 2$

$\Rightarrow\ f'(x) = ax^2 + 2(a + 2)\,x + (a - 1)$ and $f''(x) = 2ax + 2(a + 2) = 0$

$\Rightarrow\ x = -\dfrac{(a+2)}{a}$ for negative point of inflection

$\Rightarrow\ \dfrac{a+2}{a} > 0$

$\Rightarrow\ a(a + 2) > 0$

$\Rightarrow\ a < -2$ or $a > 0$

$\Rightarrow\ a \in (-\infty, -2) \cup (0, \infty)$

29. **(c)** $f(x) = |1 - x|;\ 1 \le x \le 2$ and $g(x) = f(x) + b\sin\dfrac{\pi}{2}x;\ 1 \le x \le 2,$

(i) $f(1) = 0, f(2) = 1$

$\Rightarrow$ Rolle's Theorem not applicable and $f(x)$ is non-differentiable at $x = 1$, but differentiable in (1, 2)

$\Rightarrow$ L.M.V.T is applicable.

(ii) $g(1) = f(1) + b\sin\dfrac{\pi}{2} = b$ and $g(2) = f(2) + b\sin\pi = 1$

$\Rightarrow$ Rolle's Theorem is applicable in (1, 2) for $b = 1$ and L.M.V.T is applicable for $\forall\ b \in \mathbb{R}$

30. **(d)** $f(x) = \int_0^x \left(t + \dfrac{1}{t}\right)dt$ and $g(x) = f'(x)\ \forall\ x \in \left[\dfrac{1}{2}, 3\right]$

$\therefore\ g(x) = \left(x + \dfrac{1}{x}\right)\forall x \in \left[\dfrac{1}{2}, 3\right]$

$\Rightarrow$ $g'(x) = 1 - \dfrac{1}{x^2} = \dfrac{g\left(\frac{1}{2}\right) - g(3)}{\frac{1}{2} - 3}$

$\Rightarrow$ $1 - \dfrac{1}{x^2} = \dfrac{\left(\frac{1}{2}+2\right) - \left(3+\frac{1}{3}\right)}{-5/2}$

$\Rightarrow$ $1 - \dfrac{1}{x^2} = \dfrac{\left(\frac{5}{2} - \frac{10}{3}\right)}{-5/2}$

$\Rightarrow$ $1 - \dfrac{1}{x^2} = -1 + \dfrac{4}{3}$

$\Rightarrow$ $\dfrac{1}{x^2} = 2 - \dfrac{4}{3} = \dfrac{2}{3}$

$\Rightarrow$ $x^2 = 3/2$

$\Rightarrow$ $x = \pm \sqrt{3/2}$

But $x \in \left[\frac{1}{2}, 3\right] \Rightarrow x = \sqrt{\frac{3}{2}}$ and $y = x + \frac{1}{x} = \sqrt{\frac{3}{2}} + \sqrt{\frac{2}{3}} = \frac{5}{\sqrt{6}}$

$\therefore$ $P = \left(\sqrt{\frac{3}{2}}, \frac{5}{\sqrt{6}}\right)$

31. **(c)** $f(x) = x + \sin x, x \in [1, 2]$

$\Rightarrow$ $f'(x) = 1 + \cos x$

By L.M.V.T., on [1, 2], $f'(C) = \dfrac{f(2) - f(1)}{2-1}$

$\Rightarrow$ $1 + \cos C = (2 + \sin 2) - (1 + \sin 1)$

$\Rightarrow$ $1 + \cos C = \sin 2 - \sin 1$

$\Rightarrow$ $\cos C = 2 \cos \frac{3}{2} \sin \frac{1}{2}$

$\Rightarrow$ $C = \cos^{-1}\left(2 \cos \frac{3}{2} \sin \frac{1}{2}\right)$

32. **(b)** $f(1) = -3$ and $f'(x) \geq 2\ \forall\ x \in [1, 6]$

By L.M.V.T $\exists$ a point 'c' in (1, 6) for which $f'(c) = \dfrac{f(6) - f(1)}{6-1}$

$\Rightarrow$ $f'(c) = \dfrac{f(6)+3}{5}$ but $f'(x) \geq 2\ \forall\ x \in [1, 6]$

$\Rightarrow$ $f'(c) \geq 2$

$\Rightarrow$ $\dfrac{f(6)+3}{5} \geq 2$

$\Rightarrow$ $f(6) + 3 \geq 10$

$\Rightarrow$ $f(6) \geq 7$

33. **(c)** Let $f(x) = x^3$

$\Rightarrow$ $f'(x) = 3x^2$ and $f''(x) = 6x$

$\Rightarrow$ $f'(0) = 0, f''(0) = 0$

Graphically, shown below

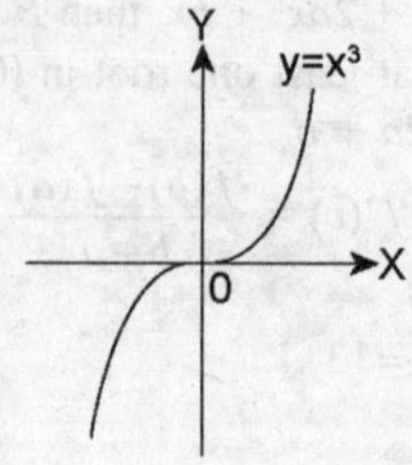

Clearly $x = 0$ is neither a point of maxima nor a point minima, i.e., a point of inflexion.

Now consider $f(x) = x^4$

$\Rightarrow$ $f'(x) = 4x^3$

$\Rightarrow$ $f''(x) = 12x^2$

$\Rightarrow$ $f'(0) = 0, f''(0) = 0$

Graphically, shown below

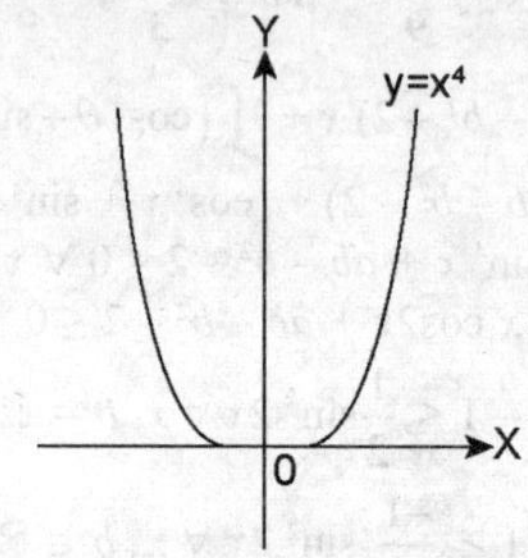

Now, $x = 0$ is a point of minima,

Similarly for $y = -x^4$, $x = 0$ will be a point of maxima, i.e., if $f'(a) = 0$ and $f''(a) = 0$, then it is difficult to (*say*) whether $x = a$ is a point of maxima or minima.

34. **(a)** $h'(x) = \underbrace{f'(g(x))}_{(+)} . \underbrace{g'(x)}_{(-)}$

$\Rightarrow$ $h'(x) \leq 0\ x \in [0, \infty)$

$\Rightarrow$ $h(x)$ is a decreasing function $\forall\ x \in [0, \infty)$

$\Rightarrow$ $h(x) \leq h(0)\ \forall\ x \geq 0$

$\Rightarrow$ $h(x) \leq 0\ \forall\ x \in [0, \infty)$ but $h(x) \in [0, \infty)$

$\Rightarrow$ $h(x) = 0\ \forall\ x \in [0, \infty)$

35. **(b)** $f(x) = (a^2 - 3a + 2)\left(\cos^2 \frac{x}{4} - \sin^2 \frac{x}{4}\right)$

$\Rightarrow$ $f(x) = (a-1)(a-2)\left(\cos \frac{x}{2}\right) + (a-1)x + \sin 1;\ a \neq 2$

$\Rightarrow$ $f'(x) = (a-1)(a-2)\left(\frac{1}{2}\right)\left(-\sin \frac{x}{2}\right) + (a-1) = (a-1)\left[1 - \frac{1}{2}(a-2)\sin \frac{x}{2}\right]$

For no critical points, $a \neq 1$, $(a-2)\sin \frac{x}{2} \neq 2\ \forall\ x \in \mathbb{R}$

$\Rightarrow$ $a \neq 1$, $\sin \dfrac{x}{2} \neq \dfrac{2}{a-2}\ \forall x \in \mathbb{R}$

$\Rightarrow$ $a \neq 1$; $\dfrac{2}{a-2} < -1$ or $\dfrac{2}{a-2} > 1$

$\Rightarrow$ $a \neq 1$; $\dfrac{2+a-2}{a-2} < 0$ or $\dfrac{2-a+2}{a-2} > 0$

$\Rightarrow a \neq 1 ; \dfrac{a}{a-2} < 0$ or $\dfrac{4-a}{a-2} > 0$

$\Rightarrow a \neq 1$; $a \in (0, 2)$ or $a \in (2, 4)$

$\Rightarrow a \in (0, 4) - \{1, 2\}$

If $a = 2$, $f(x) = (x) + \sin 1$

$\Rightarrow f'(x) = 1 \ \forall x \in \mathbb{R}$

$\Rightarrow f(x)$ has no critical point for $a \in (0, 4) - \{1\}$

36. (a) $f(x) = 1 + x + \int_1^x \left(\ell n^2 t + 2\ell n t\right) dt,$

$\Rightarrow f'(x) = 1 + \ell n^2 x + 2\,\ell n x = (\ell n\, x + 1)^2$

$\Rightarrow f'(x) \geq 0 \ \forall x > 0$

37. (c) $f(x) = x^9 + 3x^7 + 6$

$\Rightarrow f'(x) = 9x^8 + 21x^6 \geq 0 \ \forall x \in \mathbb{R}$

$\Rightarrow f(x)$ is increasing $\forall x \in \mathbb{R}$

38. (a) $f(x) = \begin{cases} \sin\dfrac{\pi x}{2} ; 0 \leq x < 1 \\ 3 - 2x ; x \geq 1 \end{cases}$

$\Rightarrow f'(1^-) = 1 = f(1^+) = f(1)$

$\Rightarrow f(x)$ is a continuous function and

$f'(x) = \begin{cases} \dfrac{\pi}{2}\cos\dfrac{\pi}{2}x ; 0 < x < 1 \\ -2 \ ; x > 1 \end{cases}$

$\Rightarrow f'(1^-) = 0; f'(1^+) = -2$ and $f'(1-h) = \dfrac{\pi}{2}\cos\dfrac{\pi}{2}(1-h) > 0$

$\Rightarrow f(x)$ has a point of non-differentiability at $x = 1$ and also having point of maxima there

39. (d) $g(\theta) = \int_0^{\sin^2\theta} f(x)dx + \int_0^{\cos^2\theta} f(x)dx$

$\Rightarrow g'(\theta) = f(\sin^2\theta)(\sin 2\theta) + f(\cos^2\theta)(-\sin 2\theta) = (\sin 2\theta)[f(\sin^2\theta) - f(\cos^2\theta)]$

$\therefore g'(\theta) \geq 0$

$\Rightarrow (\sin 2\theta)[f(\sin^2\theta) - f(\cos^2\theta)] \geq 0$

$\because$ f is increasing

$\Rightarrow f(\sin^2\theta) - f(\cos^2\theta) \geq 0$ and $\sin 2\theta \geq 0$

$\Rightarrow \theta \in \left[\dfrac{-\pi}{2}, \dfrac{-\pi}{4}\right] \cup \left[\dfrac{\pi}{4}, \dfrac{\pi}{2}\right]$ and $\theta \in \left[0, \dfrac{\pi}{2}\right]$

$\Rightarrow \theta \in \left[\dfrac{\pi}{4}, \dfrac{\pi}{2}\right]$ or $f(\sin^2\theta) - f(\cos^2\theta) \leq 0$ and $\sin 2\theta \leq 0$

$\Rightarrow \theta \in \left[\dfrac{-\pi}{4}, \dfrac{\pi}{4}\right]$ and $\theta \in \left[\dfrac{-\pi}{2}, 0\right] \Rightarrow \theta \in \left[\dfrac{-\pi}{4}, 0\right]$

$\therefore$ f is increasing in $\left[\dfrac{-\pi}{4}, 0\right]$ and $\left[\dfrac{\pi}{4}, \dfrac{\pi}{2}\right]$

40. (d) $f'(x) > 0$ and $g'(x) < 0 \ \forall x \in \mathbb{R}$

$F(x) = f(g(x))$

$\Rightarrow F'(x) = f'(g(x)) \,.\, g'(x) = (+)(-) = -$ve

$\therefore f(g(x))$ is ↓ and $G(x) = g(f(x))$

$\Rightarrow G'(x) = g'(f(x)).\, f'(x) = (-)(+) = -$ve

$\Rightarrow g(f(x))$ is ↓

$\Rightarrow g(f(x)) > g(f(x + 1))$

41. (b) area of Δ PQR $= \dfrac{1}{2} QR \times PR$

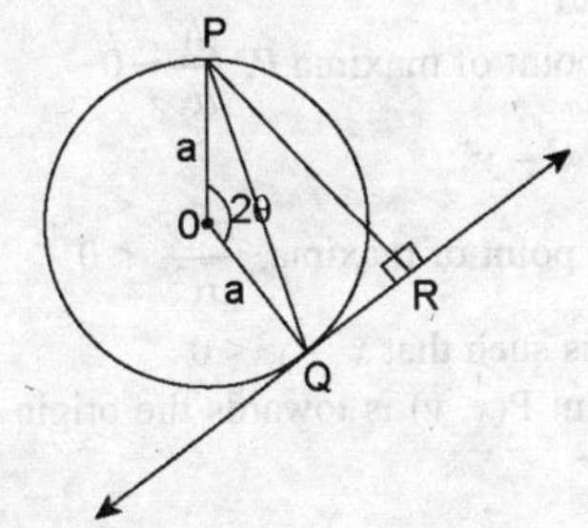

$A = \dfrac{1}{2}(QP)\cos\theta \,.\, (QP)\sin\theta$

$= \dfrac{1}{2}(QP)^2 \cos\theta \sin\theta$ ...(1)

Also by cos in formula, $\cos 2\theta = \dfrac{a^2 + a^2 - (QP)^2}{2a^2}$

$\Rightarrow 2a^2 \cos 2\theta = 2a^2 - QP^2$

$\Rightarrow QP^2 = 2a^2(1 - \cos 2\theta)$ ...(2)

From (1) and (2), we get $A = \dfrac{1}{2}(2a^2)(1 - \cos 2\theta)\cos\theta \sin\theta$

$\Rightarrow A = \dfrac{a^2}{2}(1 - \cos 2\theta)\sin 2\theta$

$\Rightarrow A = \dfrac{a^2}{2}[\sin 2\theta - \sin 2\theta \cos 2\theta]$

$\Rightarrow \dfrac{dA}{d\theta} = \dfrac{a^2}{2}[2\cos 2\theta = 2\sin^2 2\theta - 2\cos 2\theta \cos 4\theta]$

$= \dfrac{a^2}{2}[2\cos 2\theta + 2(1 - \cos^2 2\theta) - 2\cos 2\theta(2\cos^2 2\theta - 1)]$

$= \dfrac{a^2}{2}[-4\cos^3 2\theta - 2\cos^2 2\theta + 4\cos 2\theta + 2]$

$\therefore \dfrac{dA}{d\theta} = 0$

$\Rightarrow 2\cos^3 2\theta + \cos^2 2\theta - 2\cos 2\theta - 1 = 0$

$\Rightarrow (\cos 2\theta - 1)(2\cos^2 2\theta + 3\cos 2\theta + 1) = 0$

$\Rightarrow (\cos 2\theta - 1)(2\cos 2\theta + 1)(\cos 2\theta + 1) = 0$

$\Rightarrow \cos 2\theta = 1$ or $\cos 2\theta = \dfrac{-1}{2}$ or $\cos 2\theta = -1$

$\because \theta$ is acute

$\Rightarrow \theta \in (0, \pi/2)$

$\Rightarrow \cos 2\theta = \dfrac{-1}{2}$, so that $\theta = \pi/3$

$\therefore A_{max} = \dfrac{a^2}{2}\left(1 - \cos^2\dfrac{\pi}{3}\right)\sin\dfrac{2\pi}{3} = \dfrac{a^2}{2}\left(1 + \dfrac{1}{2}\right)\left(\dfrac{\sqrt{3}}{2}\right)$

$= \dfrac{3\sqrt{3}}{8}a^2$

$\Rightarrow k = \dfrac{3\sqrt{3}}{8}$

42. (a) $f''(x) = f'(x) + f^2(x) = x^2$

$\Rightarrow \quad \dfrac{d^2y}{dx^2} + \dfrac{dy}{dx} + y^2 = x^2$

At the point of maxima P, $\dfrac{dy}{dx} = 0$

$\Rightarrow \quad \dfrac{d^2y}{dx^2} = x^2 - y^2$

$\because$ P is the point of maxima, $\dfrac{d^2y}{dx^2} < 0$

$\Rightarrow$ $P(x, y)$ is such that $x^2 - y^2 < 0$

$\Rightarrow$ The point P(x, y) is towards the origin of hyperbola $x^2 - y^2 = a^2$

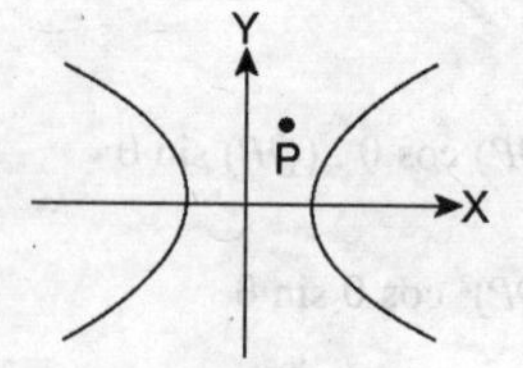

$\Rightarrow$ Two tangents can be drawn from P

43. (a) $m, n \in \mathbb{N}$,

$f(x) = \int_a^x (t-a)^{2n} (t-b)^{2m+1}\, dt$, $a \neq b$,

$\Rightarrow f'(x) = (x - a)2n\ (x - b)2m^{+1}$

$\therefore\ f'(x) = 0$

$\Rightarrow\ x = a$ or $x = b$

Case (i Let $a < b$;

$f'(a - h) = (a - h - a)^{2n} (a - h - b)^{2m+1}$

$= (+) (-) = -\text{ve}$

$f'(a + h) = (a + h - a)^{2n} (a + h - b)^{2m+1}$

$= (+) (-) = -\text{ve}$

'a' is not a critical point

$f'(b - h) = (b - h - a)^{2n} (b - h - b)^{2m+1}$

$= (+) (-) = -\text{ve}$

$f'(b + h) = (b + h - a)^{2n} (b + h - b)^{2m+1}$

$= (+) (+) = +\ ve$

$\Rightarrow\ x = b$ is a point of local minimum.

Case(ii): $b < a$

$f'(a - h) = (a - h - a)^{2n} (a - h - b)^{2m+1}$

$= (+) (+) = +\text{ ve}$

$f'(a + h) = (a + h - a)^{2n} (a + h - a)^{2m+1}$

$= (+) (+) = +\ ve$

$f'(b - h) = (b - h - a)^{2n} (b - h - b)^{2m+1}$

$= (+) (-) = -\text{ve}$

$f'(b + h) = (b + h - a)^{2n} (b + h - b)^{2m+1}$

$= (+) (+) = +\ ve$

$\Rightarrow\ x = b$ is a point of local maximum

44. (a) $y = e^{-x^2}$

$y' = -2x\ e^{-x^2} < 0$ for $x > 0$ and > 0 for $x < 0$

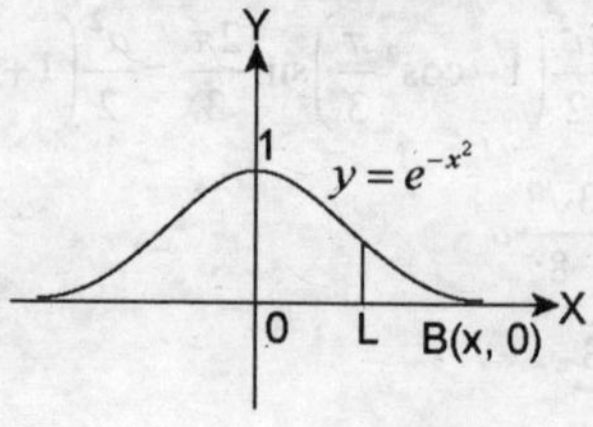

$y''(x) = -2\left[x(-2x)e^{-x^2} + e^{-x^2}\right]$

$= -2[1 - 2x^2]\ e^{-x^2} = 2(2x^2 - 1)\ e^{-x^2}$

$\Rightarrow\ y''(x) < 0$ for $x \in \left(\dfrac{-1}{\sqrt{2}}, \dfrac{1}{\sqrt{2}}\right)$ and > 0 for $x \in \left(-\infty, \dfrac{-1}{\sqrt{2}}\right) \cup \left(\dfrac{1}{\sqrt{2}}, \infty\right)$

Area of $\Delta\ AOB = \dfrac{1}{2}(OB) \times (AL)$

$A = \dfrac{1}{2}(x)\left(e^{-x^2}\right)$

$\therefore\ \dfrac{dA}{dx} = \dfrac{1}{2}x(-x)e^{-x^2} + \dfrac{1}{2}e^{-x^2} = \dfrac{1}{2}e^{-x^2}\left(1 - 2x^2\right)$

$\therefore\ \dfrac{dA}{dx} = 0 \Rightarrow x = \pm\dfrac{1}{\sqrt{2}}$ But $x > 0 \Rightarrow x = \dfrac{1}{\sqrt{2}}$

$\therefore\ A_{max.} = \dfrac{1}{2}\left(\dfrac{1}{\sqrt{2}}\right)e^{-1/2} = \dfrac{1}{2\sqrt{2}}e^{-1/2} = \dfrac{1}{\sqrt{8e}}$

45. (a) Area of $\Delta\ OAB = \dfrac{1}{2}(OB) \times (AL)$

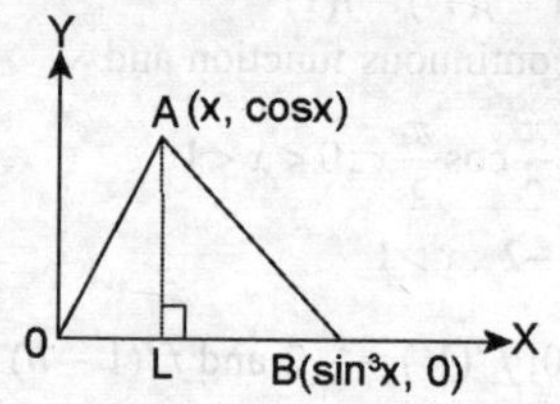

$\Rightarrow\ A = \dfrac{1}{2}(\sin^3 x)(\cos x)$

$\Rightarrow\ \dfrac{dA}{dx} = \dfrac{1}{2}\sin^3 x(-\sin x) + \dfrac{1}{2}\cos^2 x.(3\sin^2 x) = \sin^2 x$

$\left[\dfrac{3}{2}\cos^2 x - \dfrac{1}{2}\sin^2 x\right] = (\sin^2 x)\left[\dfrac{3}{2}\cos^2 x + \dfrac{1}{2}\cos^2 x - \dfrac{1}{2}\right]$

$= (\sin^2 x)\left(2\cos^2 x - \dfrac{1}{2}\right)$

$\therefore$ For max./min. of A, $\dfrac{dA}{dx} = 0$

$\Rightarrow\ \sin^2 x = 0$ or $\cos^2 x = \dfrac{1}{4}$ $\Rightarrow\ \cos x = \dfrac{1}{2}$

$\therefore\ A_{max.} = \dfrac{1}{2}\left(\dfrac{\sqrt{3}}{2}\right)^3\left(\dfrac{1}{2}\right) = \dfrac{3\sqrt{3}}{32}$

46. (c) $\therefore$ Area of $\Delta\ KLMN$

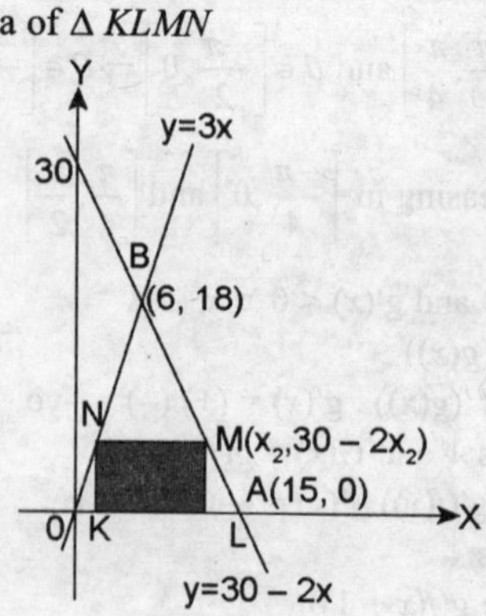

$= A = (KL) \times (ML)$

$= [(x_2 - x_1)] \times 3x_1$ ...(1)

Also $3x_1 = 30 - 2x_2$

$\Rightarrow 2x_2 = 30 - 3x_1$

$\Rightarrow x_2 = 15 - \frac{3}{2}x_1$ ...(2)

Using (2) in (1), we get $A = \left(15 - \frac{3}{2}x_1 - x_1\right) \times 3x_1$

$\Rightarrow A = \left(15 - \frac{5}{2}x_1\right) \times 3x_1 \Rightarrow A = 45x_1 - \frac{15}{2}x_1^2$

$\therefore \frac{dA}{dx_1} = 45 - \frac{15}{2}(2x_1) = 45 - 15x_1$

$\therefore$ For maximum A, $\frac{dA}{dx_1} = 0$

$\Rightarrow x_1 = 3$

$\therefore A_{max.} = \left[15 - \frac{5}{2}(3)\right](9) = \frac{15}{2} \times 9 = \frac{135}{2}$

47. (a) $f(x) = \begin{cases} \sqrt{x} & ; x \ge 1 \\ x^3 & ; 0 \le x \le 1 \\ \frac{x^3}{3} & ; x < 0 \end{cases}$; $f(1^-) = f(1) = f(1^+) = 1; f(0^-) = f(0)$

$= f(0^+) = 0$

$\Rightarrow f(x)$ is a continuous function on $\mathbb{R}$.

Also, $f'(x) = \begin{cases} \frac{1}{2\sqrt{x}} & ; x > 1 \\ 3x^2 & ; 0 < x < 1 \\ x^2 & ; x < 0 \end{cases}$

Clearly $f'(x) > 0 \ \forall x \in \mathbb{R}$

$\Rightarrow f(x)$ is monotonically increasing $\forall x \in \mathbb{R}$.

$f'(0^-) = f'(0^+) = 0, f'(1^-) = 3, f'(1^+) = \frac{1}{2}$

$\Rightarrow f'(x)$ does not exists at exactly one point i.e., $x = 1$

$\because f'(x) \ge 0 \ \forall x \in \mathbb{R}$.

$\Rightarrow f'(x)$ does not change its sign in $(-\infty, \infty)$.

$\because f(x)$ is continuous and increasing function, it does not attains its extreme values.

48. (a) **Statement 1:** is true only when $f(x)$ is continuous at $x = c$ or $f(c) > f(c + h)$; $h \in (0, \infty)$ if discontinuous at c, i.e., statement 1 is False.

Statement 2: is false as illustrated by following function discontinuous at $c \in (a, b)$

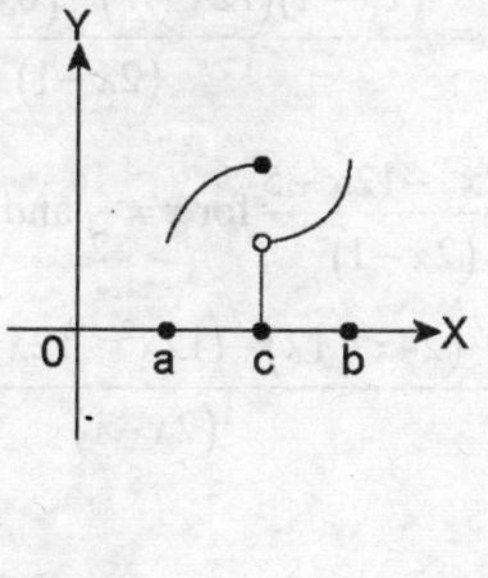

Statement 3: $f(x) = x^2 |x| = \begin{cases} x^3 ; x \ge 0 \\ -x^3 ; x < 0 \end{cases}$

$\Rightarrow f'(x) = \begin{cases} 3x^2 ; x > 0 \\ -3x^2 ; x < 0 \end{cases} \Rightarrow f''(x) = \begin{cases} 6x ; x > 0 \\ -6x ; x < 0 \end{cases}$

Clearly $f(x)$ is twice differentiable at $x = 0$

$\Rightarrow$ Statement (3) is true

Statement (4): is false, consider $f(x) = x^3$ in $[-1, 1]$; $c = 0$, then $f'(x) = 3x^2$ and $f''(x) = 6x$ but $f^{-1}(x) = (x)^{1/3}$

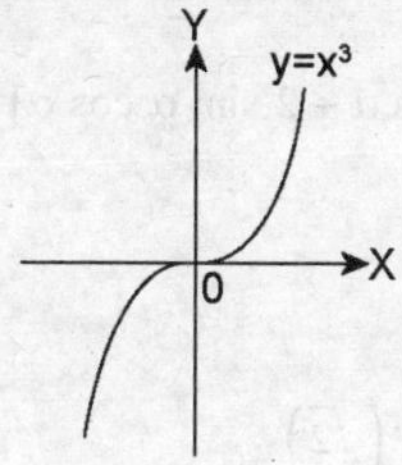

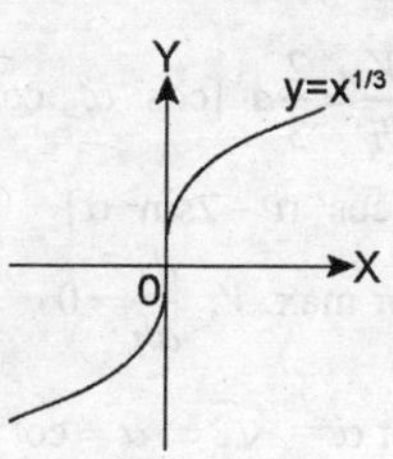

$\Rightarrow \frac{d}{dx}\left(f^{-1}(x)\right) = \frac{1}{3}x^{-2/3} = \infty$ at $x = 0$

$\Rightarrow f^{-1}(x)$ is non-differentiable at $x = 0$

49. (c) $S = \frac{a}{1-r} = f_{max}$ for $x \in [-2, 3]$, $f(x) = x^3 + 3x - 9$

$\Rightarrow f'(x) = 3x^2 + 3 = 3(x^2 + 1)$

$\Rightarrow f(x)$ is an increasing function.

$\Rightarrow f_{max.} = f(3) = 27 + 9 - 9 = 27$

$\therefore 27 = \frac{a}{1-r}$ ....(1)

$a - ar = 3(0)^2 + 3$

$\Rightarrow a(1 - r) = 3$

$\Rightarrow \frac{1}{1-r} = \frac{a}{3}$ ....(2)

$\therefore$ From (1) and (2), $27 = \frac{a^2}{3} \Rightarrow a = 9, -9$

$\Rightarrow 1 - r = \frac{3}{a} = \frac{1}{3}$ or $\frac{-1}{3}$ for $a = 9, -9$

$\Rightarrow r = \frac{2}{3}$ or $r = \frac{4}{3}$ for $a = 9, -9$

But for decreasing infinite G.P., $|r| < 1$

$\Rightarrow r = \frac{2}{3}$ and $a = 9$

50. (c) Volume $= V = \frac{1}{3}$(area ABCD) $\times h$

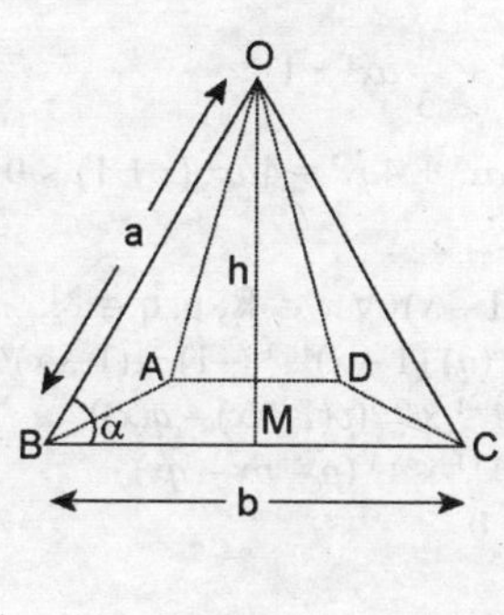

Here $h = a \sin \alpha$;

$BL = \sqrt{a^2 - h^2} = a \cos \alpha$

$\therefore\ 4a^2 \cos^2 \alpha = 2b^2$

$\Rightarrow\ b^2 = 2a^2 \cos^2 \alpha$

$\Rightarrow\ b = \sqrt{2}\, a \cos\alpha$

$\therefore\ V = \frac{1}{3}(b)^2 \times h = \frac{1}{3}\left(\sqrt{2}\, a\cos\alpha\right)^2 .a\sin\alpha$

$\Rightarrow\ V = \frac{2}{3}a^3 \cos^3\alpha \sin\alpha$

$\Rightarrow\ \frac{dV}{dh} = \frac{2}{3}a^3\,[\cos^2\alpha \,.\, \cos\alpha - 2\sin^2\alpha\cos\alpha] = \frac{2}{3}a^3 \cos$ $\alpha[\cos^2\alpha - 2\sin^2\alpha]$

$\therefore$ For max. V, $\frac{dv}{dh} = 0$

$\Rightarrow\ \cot\alpha = \sqrt{2} \Rightarrow \alpha = \cot^{-1}\left(\sqrt{2}\right)$

51. (b) $f(x) = \begin{cases} x^{3/5} & ; x \le 1 \\ -(x-2)^3 & ; x > 1 \end{cases}$

$f(1^-) = 1$; $f(1^+) = 1$ and $f(1) = 1$

$f'(x) = \begin{cases} \frac{3}{5}x^{-2/5} & ; x < 1 \\ -3(x-2)^2 & ; x > 1 \end{cases}$

$\therefore\ f'(1^-) = \frac{3}{5}; f'(1^+) = -3$

$\therefore$ $f(x)$ is non-differentiable at $x = 1$

Also $f'(x) > 0$ for $x \in (1, 1 + h)$ and $f'(x) < 0$ for $x \in (1, 1 + h)$

$\Rightarrow$ $x = 1$ is a point of local maxima, where $f'(x)$ does not exist, also $f'(2) = 0$

$\Rightarrow$ $x = 2$ is also a critical point.

$\therefore$ There are exactly 2 critical points $x = 1$ and $x = 2$

52. (c) $y = ax^4 + bx^3 + cx + d$

$\Rightarrow\ f'(x) = 4ax^3 + 3bx^2 + c = 0$ at $(0, 1)$

$\Rightarrow\ c = 0, f(0) = 1$

$\Rightarrow\ d = 1$

Also $f'(x) = 0$ at $x = (-1, 0)$

Also $f(-1) = 0$ and $f'(-1) = 0$

$\Rightarrow\ a - b + 1 = 0$ and $-4a + 3b = 0$

$\Rightarrow\ b = -$

$\therefore\ f(x) = ax^4 + \frac{4}{3}ax^3 + 1$

$\Rightarrow\ f'(x) = 4ax^3 + 4ax^2 = 4ax^2(x + 1) < 0$

$\Rightarrow\ x < -1$

53. (d) $f(x) = x^p(1 - x)^q\ \forall\ x \in \mathbb{R}$; $p, q \in \mathbb{N}$,

$\Rightarrow\ f'(x) = x^p(q)(1 - x)^{q-1}(-1) + (1 - x)^q \,.\, p. x^{p-1}$

$= (1 - x)^{q-1} x^{p-1}(p(1 - x) - q(x))$

$= (1 - x)^{q-1} x^{p-1}(p - px - qx)$

$= f'(x) = 0$

$\Rightarrow\ x = 1$ or 0 or $\frac{p}{p+q}$

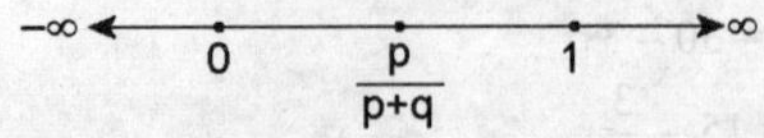

Case (i): p = even, q = even

$\Rightarrow\ f'(x) = (-1)^q (x)^{p-1}((p + q)x - p)(x - 1)^{q-1}$

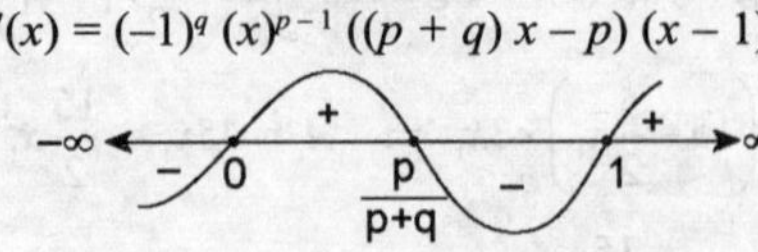

$\Rightarrow\ x = \frac{p}{p+q}$ is a point of local maxima

Case(ii): p = odd, q = even

$\Rightarrow\ x = \frac{p}{p+q}$ is a point of local maxima

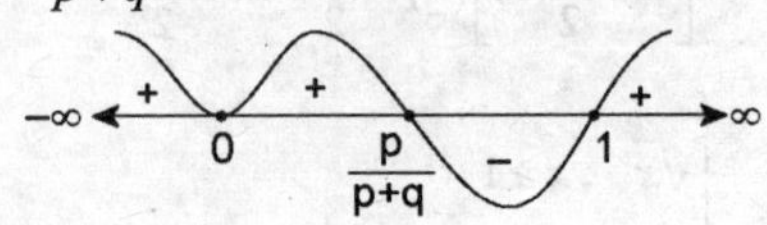

case(iii): p = odd, q = odd

$\Rightarrow\ x = \frac{p}{p+q}$ is a point local maxima.

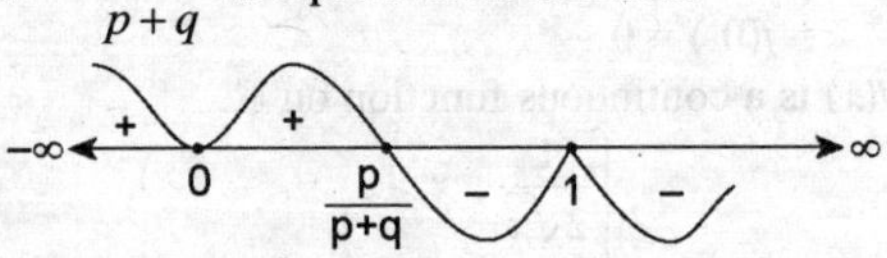

case(iv): p = even, q = odd

$\Rightarrow\ x = \frac{p}{p+q}$ is a point of local maxima.

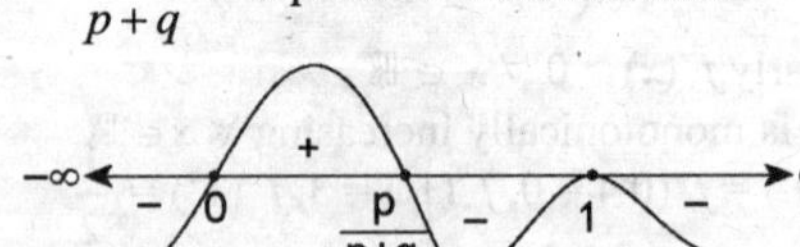

54. (c) $f(x) = \begin{cases} \frac{(x-1)(6x-1)}{(2x-1)} & ; x \ne \frac{1}{2} \\ 0 & ; x = \frac{1}{2} \end{cases}$

$f\left(\frac{1^-}{2}\right) = +\infty, f\left(\frac{1^+}{2}\right) = -\infty$

$\Rightarrow$ $f(x)$ has infinite discontinuity at $x = \frac{1}{2}$

Also $f'(x) = \frac{(2x-1)(12x-7) - (6x^2 - 7x + 1)(2)}{(2x-1)^2}$

$\Rightarrow\ f'(x) = \frac{12x^2 - 12x + 5}{(2x-1)^2}$ for $x \ne \frac{1}{2}$ and $f''(x)$

$= \frac{(2x-1)^2(24x-12) - (12x^2 - 12x + 5)(2)(2x-1)(2)}{(2x-1)^4}$

$$\Rightarrow f''(x) = \frac{(2x-1)^3(12) - 4(2x-1)(12x^2-12x+5)}{(2x-1)^4}$$

$$= \frac{12(2x-1)^2 - 4(12x^2-12x+5)}{(2x-1)^3}$$

$$= \frac{-48x+12+48x-20}{(2x-1)^3} = \frac{-8}{(2x-1)^3}$$

$$\Rightarrow f''(x) = \begin{cases} >0 \text{ for } x < \frac{1}{2} \\ <0 \text{ for } x > \frac{1}{2} \end{cases}$$

$\Rightarrow x = \frac{1}{2}$ is a point of inflexion.

55. **(c)** $f(x) = \int_x^{x^2} (t-1)\,dt;\ 1 \le x \le 2,$

$f'(x) = (x^2-1)(2x) - (x-1)(1)$

$\Rightarrow f'(x) = 2x^3 - 3x + 1$

$\Rightarrow f'(x) = (x-1)(2x^2+2x-1)$

$\therefore f'(x) = 0$

$\Rightarrow x = 1$ or $x = \frac{-2 \pm \sqrt{4+8}}{2(2)}$ i.e., $x = 1,\ x = \frac{-1 \pm \sqrt{3}}{2}$

$\therefore x = 1$, in $x \in [1, 2]$

$f''(x) = 6x^2 - 3 = 3(2x^2 - 1)$

$\Rightarrow f''(1) = 3 > 0$

$x = 1$ is a point of local minima

$\Rightarrow$ The global maximum value function [1; 2] will be $f(2)$

$$= \int_2^4 (t-1)\,dt = \left[\frac{t^2}{2} - t\right]_2^4 = [(8-4) - (2-2)] = 4$$

56. **(b)** Clearly $x \ge 0$ and $x < \frac{1}{2}$

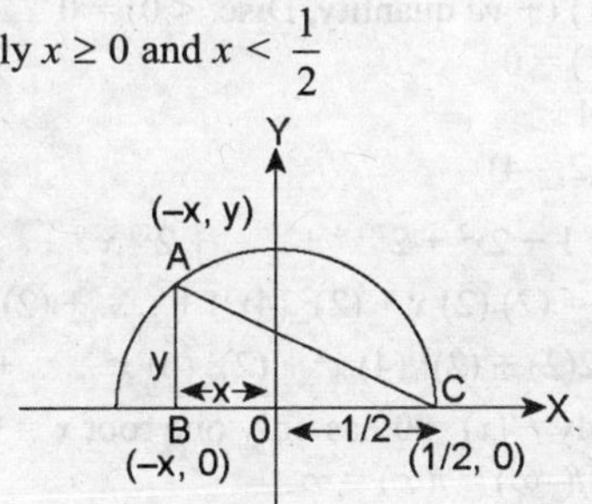

$\therefore$ Area of $\Delta ABC = \frac{1}{2}\left(x + \frac{1}{2}\right) \cdot y$ ...(1)

$\because$ Point $A(-x, y)$ lies on circle $x^2 + y^2 = \frac{1}{4}$

$$\Rightarrow y = \sqrt{\frac{1}{4} - x^2}$$

$$\Rightarrow \Delta = \frac{1}{2}\left(x + \frac{1}{2}\right)\sqrt{\frac{1}{4} - x^2}$$

$$\Rightarrow \Delta = \left(\frac{1}{2}x + \frac{1}{4}\right)\sqrt{\frac{1}{4} - x^2}$$

$$\Rightarrow \frac{dA}{dx} = \left(\frac{1}{2}x + \frac{1}{4}\right) \cdot \frac{1}{2} \times \frac{2(-2x)}{\sqrt{1-4x^2}} + \sqrt{\frac{1}{4} - x^2}\left(\frac{1}{2}\right)$$

$$= \frac{(2x+1)}{4}\left(\frac{-2x}{\sqrt{1-4x^2}}\right) + \frac{\sqrt{1-4x^2}}{4}$$

$$= \frac{-2x(2x+1) + (1-4x^2)}{4\sqrt{1-4x^2}} = \frac{-8x^2 - 2x + 1}{4\sqrt{1-4x^2}}$$

$$\therefore \frac{dA}{dx} = 0$$

$\Rightarrow 8x^2 + 2x - 1 = 0$

$\Rightarrow (2x+1)(4x-1) = 0$

$\Rightarrow x = \frac{-1}{2}$ or $x = \frac{1}{4}$, But $x \ge 0$

$\Rightarrow x = \frac{1}{4}$

$$\therefore A_{max.} = \frac{1}{2}\left(\frac{1}{4} + \frac{1}{2}\right)\sqrt{\frac{1}{4} - \frac{1}{16}} = \frac{1}{2}\left(\frac{3}{4}\right)\left(\sqrt{\frac{4-1}{16}}\right)$$

$$= \frac{3}{8}\frac{\sqrt{3}}{4} = \frac{3\sqrt{3}}{32}$$

57. **(b)** In ΔPCN, $PM + MC = \alpha$

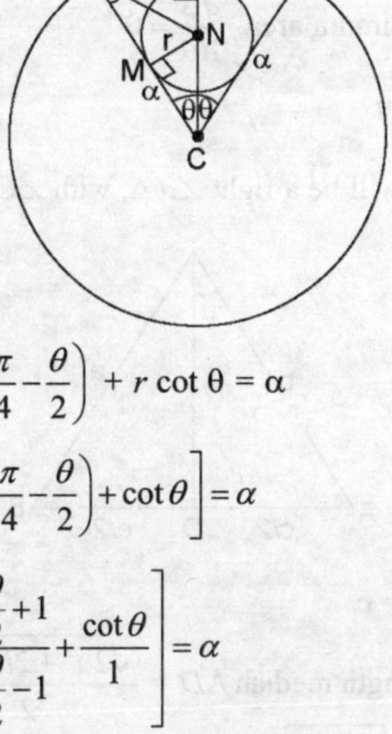

$$\Rightarrow r \cot\left(\frac{\pi}{4} - \frac{\theta}{2}\right) + r \cot\theta = \alpha$$

$$\Rightarrow r\left[\cot\left(\frac{\pi}{4} - \frac{\theta}{2}\right) + \cot\theta\right] = \alpha$$

$$\Rightarrow r\left[\frac{\cot\frac{\theta}{2} + 1}{\cot\frac{\theta}{2} - 1} + \frac{\cot\theta}{1}\right] = \alpha$$

$$\Rightarrow r\left[\frac{\cos\frac{\theta}{2} + \sin\frac{\theta}{2}}{\cos\frac{\theta}{2} - \sin\frac{\theta}{2}} + \frac{\cot\theta}{1}\right] = \alpha$$

$$\Rightarrow r\left[\frac{1 + \sin\theta}{\cos\theta} + \cot\theta\right] = \alpha$$

$\Rightarrow r[\sec\theta + \tan\theta + \cot\theta] = \alpha$

$$\Rightarrow r = \frac{\alpha}{\sec\theta + \tan\theta + \cot\theta}$$

$$\Rightarrow r = \frac{\alpha}{\left(\frac{1}{\cos\theta} + \frac{\sin\theta}{\cos\theta} + \frac{\cos\theta}{\sin\theta}\right)}$$

$\Rightarrow r = \dfrac{\alpha \sin\theta\cos\theta}{(\sin\theta + 1)}$

$\Rightarrow r = \dfrac{\alpha}{2}.\dfrac{\sin 2\theta}{(1+\sin\theta)}$

$\Rightarrow \dfrac{dr}{d\theta} = \dfrac{\alpha}{2}.\dfrac{(1+\sin\theta)(2\cos 2\theta) - \sin 2\theta\cos\theta}{(1+\sin\theta)^2}$

$\therefore \dfrac{dr}{d\theta} = 0$

$\Rightarrow (1 + \sin\theta)(2 - 4\sin^2\theta) - 2\sin\theta\cos^2\theta$

$\Rightarrow (1 + \sin\theta)[2 - 4\sin^2\theta - 2\sin\theta(1 - \sin\theta)]$

$\Rightarrow (1 + \sin\theta)(-2\sin^2\theta - 2\sin\theta + 2) = 0$

$\Rightarrow \sin\theta = -1$ or $\sin^2\theta + \sin\theta - 1 = 0$

$\Rightarrow \sin\theta = \dfrac{-1\pm\sqrt{1+4}}{2}$

$\Rightarrow \sin\theta = \dfrac{\sqrt{5}-1}{2}$

58. (a) $\Delta = \dfrac{1}{2}$ ab sin θ

$\Rightarrow \dfrac{d\Delta}{d\theta} = \dfrac{1}{2}ab\cos\theta$

$\therefore$ For maximum area, $\dfrac{d\Delta}{d\theta} = 0$

$\Rightarrow \cos\theta = 0$

$\Rightarrow \theta = \pi/2$

$\Rightarrow \Delta\, ABC$ will be a right $\angle d\, \Delta$, with $\angle C = \pi/2$

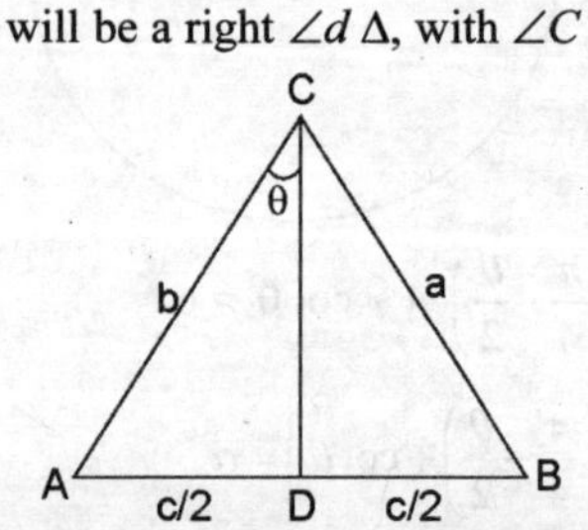

$\Rightarrow a^2 + b^2 = c^2$ .....(1)

Also, length median $AD = \dfrac{\sqrt{2a^2+2b^2-c^2}}{2} = \dfrac{\sqrt{c^2}}{2} = \dfrac{c}{2}$

$\Rightarrow AD = \dfrac{\sqrt{a^2+b^2}}{2}$

59. (d) $f(x) = \int_1^x \left(t\ell nt - \dfrac{\ell nt}{t}\right)dx;\ x > 1$

$\Rightarrow f(x) = x\,\ell nx - \dfrac{\ell nx}{x}$

$\therefore f'(x) = 0$

$\Rightarrow (\ell n\, x)\left(x - \dfrac{1}{x}\right)$

$\Rightarrow \ell n\, x = 0$ or $x - \dfrac{1}{x} = 0$

$\Rightarrow x = 1$ or $x^2 - 1 = 0$

$\Rightarrow x = 1$ or $x = \pm 1$

But $x > 1$

$\Rightarrow$ f has no stationary point

$\because \left(x - \dfrac{1}{x}\right) = \dfrac{x^2-1}{x} > 0$

$\Rightarrow (x^2 - 1)(x) > 0$

$\Rightarrow x^2 - 1 > 0$ as $x > 1$

$\Rightarrow (x + 1)(x - 1) > 0$

$\Rightarrow x > 1$

Also, $\ell n\, x$ for $x > 1$

$\therefore f'(x) > 0\ \forall\ x > 1$

$\Rightarrow f'(x)$ is monotonically increasing function for $x > 1$.

60. (d) Let $f(x) = ax^3 + bx^2 + cx + d$

$\Rightarrow f'(x) = 3ax^2 + 2bx + c$

$\Rightarrow f''(x) = 6ax + 2b$

If $f'(x_0) = 0$ and $f''(x_0) = 0$, then x_0 will be a repeated root of $f'(x) = 0$

$\Rightarrow f'(x) = 3a(x - x_0)^2$

$\Rightarrow f(x)$ has exactly one stationary point.

Now, it is given that if $f'(x_0) = 0$, then $f''(x_0) \neq 0$

$\Rightarrow f'(x) = 0$ do not have repeated roots i.e., either no root or two distinct real roots.

Thus either 0 or 2 stationary points.

61. (a) Let $P(2t^2, 4t)$; slope of normal

$\Rightarrow$ Equation of normal at P is $y = -xt + 2at + at^3$ i.e., $y = -tx + 4t + 2t^3$

It passes through the centre of circle $(x)^2 + (y + 6)^2 = 1$

$\Rightarrow -6 = -t(0) + 4t + 2t^3$

$\Rightarrow 2t^3 + 4t + 6 = 0$

$\Rightarrow t^3 + 2t + 3 = 0$

$\Rightarrow (t + 1)(t^2 - t + 3) = 0$

$\Rightarrow (t + 1)$(+ *ve* quantity, Disc. < 0) = 0

$\Rightarrow (t + 1) = 0$

$\Rightarrow t = -1$

$\therefore P = (2, -4)$

62. (b) $f(x) = 1 + 2x^2 + 2^2 x^4 + \ldots.. + 2^{10} x^{20}$

$\Rightarrow f'(x) = (2)(2)\,x + (2)^2 (4x^3) + \ldots.. + (2)^{10} (20)\, x^{19}$

$= x\,[2(2) + (2)^2 (4)\, x^2 + (2)^3 (6)\, x^4 \ldots.. + (2)^{10} (20)\, x^{18}]$

Clearly $f'(x) = 0$ has only one root $x = 0$,

Also $f(-\infty) = f(\infty) = \infty$

$\Rightarrow x = 0$ is the point of minima.

63. (b) $f'(0) = 0$ …(1) and $f''(0) > 0$ …(2)

$y = f(x) + ax + b$

$\Rightarrow \dfrac{dy}{dx} = f'(x) + a$

$\therefore \left(\dfrac{dy}{dx}\right)_{x=0}\ f'(0) + a = a$

$\Rightarrow \left(\dfrac{dy}{dx}\right)_{x=0} = 0$ for $a = 0$ and $\forall\ b \neq 0$ and $\dfrac{d^2y}{dx^2}$

$= f''(x) > 0$

$\Rightarrow x = 0$ is a point of minima for $a = 0$

64. (d) $\because f'(c) = 0$

$f''(c) > 0$

$\Rightarrow$ c is a point of local minima,

$f''(c) < 0$

$\Rightarrow$ c is a point of local maxima.

$f''(c) = 0$, then, we find $f'''(c)$, if $f'''(c) \neq 0$, then $x = c$ is a point of inflexion i.e., neither maxima, nor minima and if

$f'''(c) = 0$, then we find $f^{iv}(c)$, if $f^{iv}(c) > 0$

$\Rightarrow x = c$ is a part minima and if $f^{iv}(x) < 0$

$\Rightarrow x = c$ is a part of maxima and so on.

So, $f'(c) = f'(c) = f''(c) = f^{iv}(c) = 0$

$\Rightarrow x = c$ may be a point of extremum or point of inflection.

65. (c) $f(x) = 1 + 2x^2 + 4x^4 + 6x^6 + \ldots + 100x^{100}$

$\Rightarrow f'(x) = 2(2x) + 4(4x^3) + 6(6x^5) + \ldots + 100(100x^{99})$

$= x\,[(2)^2 + (4)^2 x^2 + (6)^2 x^4 + \ldots\ldots + (100)^2 x^{98}] = 0$ only at $x = 0$

Also $f(-\infty) = f(\infty) = \infty$

$\Rightarrow x = 0$ is the only point of minima.

66. (d) $f(x) = \dfrac{x^2-1}{x^2+1} = \dfrac{x^2+1-2}{(x^2+1)} = 1 - \dfrac{2}{(x^2+1)}$ ...(1)

Now, $x^2 + 1 \le 1$

$\Rightarrow 0 < \underline{\quad\quad} \le$

$\Rightarrow -2 \le \dfrac{-2}{x^2+1} < 0$

$\Rightarrow -1 \le \left(1 - \dfrac{2}{x^2+1}\right) < 1$

$\therefore$ $Rf = [-1, 1)$

$\Rightarrow f(x)$ is a bounded function.

Again $f'(x) = -2\left[\dfrac{-1}{(x^2+1)^2}(2x)\right] = \dfrac{4x}{(x^2+1)^2} < 0$ for $x <$ 0 and > 0 for $x > 0$ and $= 0$ at $x = 0$

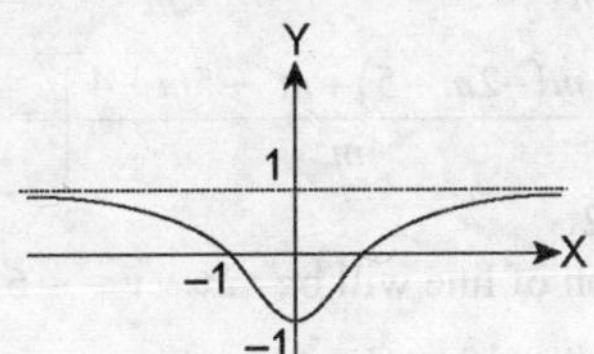

$\Rightarrow$ Minimum value of $f(x) = -1$

67. (d) $x + ex = 0$; Let $f(x) = x + e^x$

$\Rightarrow f'(x) = 1 + e^x > 1\ \forall\ x \in \mathbb{R}$

$\Rightarrow f(x)$ is an increasing function $\forall\ x \in \mathbb{R}$ and also continuous

$\Rightarrow f(x) = 0$ has exactly one root given by $x = -ex < 0$

Which is negative.

68. (c) $f(x) = \dfrac{\sin 2x}{\sin\left(x + \dfrac{\pi}{4}\right)}; x \in \left[0, \dfrac{\pi}{2}\right]$

$\Rightarrow f'(x) = \dfrac{\sin\left(x+\frac{\pi}{4}\right)2\cos 2x - \sin 2x.\cos\left(x+\frac{\pi}{4}\right)}{\sin^2\left(x+\frac{\pi}{4}\right)}$

$\therefore$ $f'(x) = 0$

$\Rightarrow \tan\left(x + \dfrac{\pi}{4}\right) = \dfrac{\tan 2x}{2}; x \neq \dfrac{\pi}{4}$

$\Rightarrow \dfrac{1+\tan x}{1-\tan x} = \dfrac{1}{2}\left(\dfrac{2\tan x}{1-\tan^2 x}\right), x \neq \dfrac{\pi}{4}, \dfrac{\pi}{2}$

$\Rightarrow 1 + \tan x = \dfrac{\tan x}{1+\tan x}; x \neq \dfrac{\pi}{4}, \dfrac{\pi}{2}$

$\Rightarrow 1 + \tan^2 x + \tan x = 0$

$\Rightarrow$ which is impossible.

At $x = \dfrac{\pi}{4}, f'\left(\dfrac{\pi}{4}\right) = \dfrac{(1)(0)-(1)(0)}{1} = 0$

Also $f(0) = 0, f(\pi/4) = 1, f(\pi/2) = 0$

$\Rightarrow x = \pi/4$ is a point of maxima and the maximum value is 1.

69. (a) $xy = r^2$ and $x > 0$

$\Rightarrow y \ge 0$

$\therefore$ $x>0, y>0$, By A.M-G.M inequality, $\dfrac{3x+4y}{2} \ge \sqrt{(3x)(4y)}$

$= \sqrt{12xy} = \sqrt{12r^2} = 2r\sqrt{3}$

$\Rightarrow 3x + 4y \ge 4\sqrt{3}r$

$\Rightarrow$ Minimum value of $3x + 4y = 4\sqrt{3}r$

70. (b) $f(x) = x^3 + 24x^2 + ax - 10$

$\Rightarrow f'(x) = 3x^2 + 48x + a$

$\Rightarrow f'(1) = 0$

$\Rightarrow 3 + 48 + a = 0$

$\Rightarrow a = -51$

71. (b) $y = x^x$

$\Rightarrow \ell n\, y = \ell n\, x^x$

$\Rightarrow \ell n\, y = x\, \ell n\, x$

$\Rightarrow \dfrac{1}{y}y' = 1 + \ell n\, x$

$\Rightarrow y' = x^x(1 + \ell n\, x)$ $\therefore$ $y' = 0$ at $x = e^{-1}$

Also $y' > 0$ for $x > e^{-1}$ and < 0 for $x \in (0, e^{-1})$

$\Rightarrow f(x)$ has minimum value at e^{-1}

72. (d) $f(x) = a\,\ell n\, x + bx^2 + x$

$\Rightarrow f'(x) = \dfrac{a}{x} + 2bx + 1$

$\Rightarrow f'(1) = 0$ and $f'(2) = 0$

$\Rightarrow a + 2b + 1 = 0$ and $\dfrac{a}{2} + 4b + 1 = 0$

$\Rightarrow a + 2b + 1 = 0$ and $a + 8b + 2 = 0$

$\Rightarrow b = \dfrac{-1}{6}$ and $a = \dfrac{-2}{3}$

73. (c) $y = -x^3 + 3x^2 + 2x - 27$

$\Rightarrow y' = -3x^2 + 6x + 2$

$\Rightarrow$ $y'' = -6x + 6$

For maximum slope $y'' = 0$

$\Rightarrow$ $x = 1$ and is given by $y'(1) = -3 + 6 + 2 = 5$

74. (c) At $x = a$, $f(x)$ will have a minima if $f(x)$ is a decreasing function in $(a - \delta, a)$ and increasing function in $(a, a + \delta)$ for $\delta \to 0$,

$\Rightarrow$ $\lim_{x\to a^-} f'(x) < 0$ and $\lim_{x\to a} f'(x) > 0$

75. (c) $V = x^2(15 - x) = 15x^2 - x^3$

$$\frac{dV}{dx} = 30x - 3x^2 = 3x(10 - x)$$

For maximum/minimum volume $x = 0$ or $x = 10$ & $\frac{d^2V}{dx^2} = 30 - 6x$ & $\left(\frac{d^2V}{dx^2}\right)_{x=0} = 30 > 0$ and $\left(\frac{d^2V}{dx^2}\right)_{x=10} = -30 < 0$

$\therefore$ V will be maximum when $x = 10$

Also $\frac{dV}{dx} < 0$ for $x > 10$ and $\frac{dV}{dx} > 0$ for $x < 10$

$\Rightarrow$ $EF = 10$ cm.

76. (c) $h^2 + x^2 = 1$ ...(1)

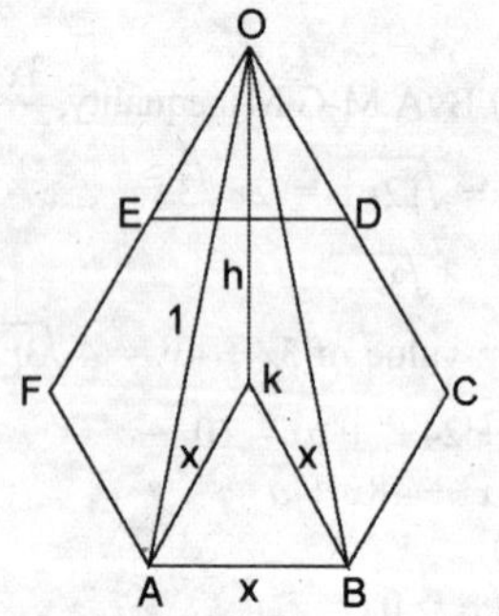

$$V = \frac{1}{3}\left(\frac{\sqrt{3}}{4}x^2\right) \times h = \frac{1}{4\sqrt{3}}.h(1-h^2)$$

$$V = \frac{1}{4\sqrt{3}}(h - h^3)$$

$$\Rightarrow \frac{dV}{dh} = \frac{1}{4\sqrt{3}}(1 - 3h^2)$$

For maximum volume, $\frac{dV}{dh} = 0$

$$\Rightarrow h = \frac{1}{\sqrt{3}}$$

77. (d) $f(x) = \begin{cases} x^3 - x^2 + 10x - 5, x \le 1 \\ -2x + \log_2(b^2 - 2), x > 1 \end{cases}$

$f(1^-) = 5 = f(1)$; $f(1^+) = \log_2(b^2 - 2) - 2$

For $f(x)$ to have greatest value at $x = 1$

$\log_2(b^2 - 2) - 2 \le 5$

$\Rightarrow$ $\log_2(b^2 - 2) \le 7 = 0 < b^2 - 2 \le 128$

$\Rightarrow$ $2 \le h^2 \le 130$

$\Rightarrow$ $h \in [-\sqrt{130}, \sqrt{2}] \cup [\sqrt{2}, \sqrt{130}]$

78. (a) Area of circle $= \pi r^2$ and Area of $\Delta = \frac{1}{2}\cos(2r\sin\theta)$

$= 2r^2 \sin\theta \cos\theta$

$\Delta = r^2 \sin 2\theta = S$ (*Given*)

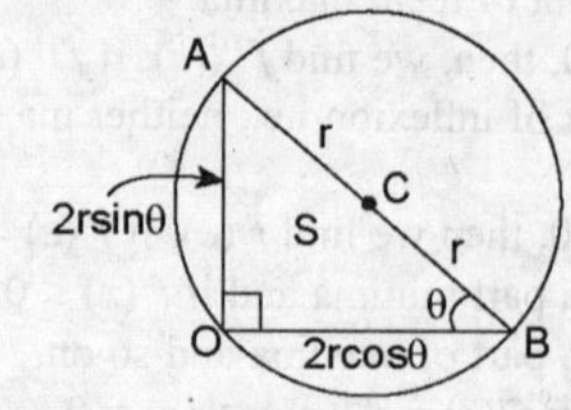

$\Rightarrow$ $r^2 = \frac{S}{\sin 2\theta} = S \text{ cosec } 2\theta$

$\therefore$ Area of circle $A = \pi$ (S cosec 2θ)

$\therefore$ For least/Area of circle, $\frac{dA}{d\theta} = 0$

$\Rightarrow$ $\pi S(-2 \text{ cosec } 2\theta \cot 2\theta) = 0$

$\Rightarrow$ $\frac{1}{\sin 2\theta}.\frac{\cos 2\theta}{\sin 2\theta} = 0$

$\Rightarrow$ $\cos 2\theta = 0$

$\Rightarrow$ $2\theta = \pi/2$

$\Rightarrow$ $\theta = \pi/4$

$\Rightarrow$ Area of circle $= A = \pi S(\text{cosec } \pi/2) = \pi S$

79. (a) Equation of line passing through (1, 4) is $(y - 4) = m(x - 1)$

$\Rightarrow$ $mx - y = m - 4$

$$\Rightarrow \frac{x}{\left(\frac{m-4}{m}\right)} + \frac{y}{(4-m)} = 1$$

Clearly for line through (1, 4) and positive intercepts, $m < 0$,

$\Rightarrow$ $\frac{m-4}{m}$, $4 - m > 0$

$$\Rightarrow S = \frac{m-4}{m} + 4 - m = \frac{-m^2 + 5m - 4}{m}$$

$$\Rightarrow \frac{dS}{dm} = \left[\frac{m(-2m+5) + m^2 - 5m + 4}{m^2}\right] = \left[\frac{-m^2 + 4}{m^2}\right] = 0$$

$\Rightarrow$ $m = -2$

$\therefore$ Equation of line will be $-2x - y = -6$ or $2x + y - 6 = 0$

80. (d) Given ellipse is $2x^2 + y^2 = 18$

$$\Rightarrow \frac{x^2}{9} + \frac{y^2}{18} = 1 \quad .....(1)$$

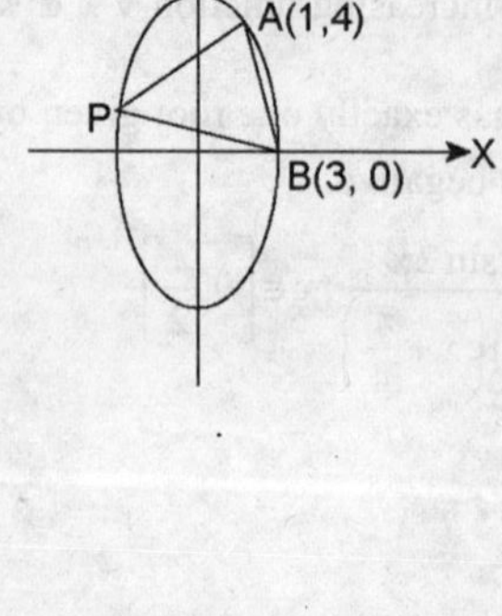

Let the $P \equiv (3\cos\theta, 3\sqrt{2}\sin\theta)$

$\therefore$ Area of $\Delta ABP = A = \left|\frac{1}{2}\begin{vmatrix}1 & 4 & 1\\ 3 & 0 & 1\\ 3\cos\theta & 3\sqrt{2} & 1\end{vmatrix}\right|$

$= \frac{1}{2}\left|6\sqrt{2}\sin\theta + 12\cos\theta - 12\right|$

$A = \pm\left(3\sqrt{2}\cos\theta - 6\sin\theta\right)$

$\Rightarrow \frac{dA}{d\theta} = \pm\left(3\sqrt{2}\cos\theta - 6\sin\theta\right)$

$\therefore$ For maximum/minimum area A, $\frac{dA}{d\theta} = 0$,

$\Rightarrow 3\sqrt{2}\cos\theta - 6\sin\theta = 0$

$\Rightarrow 3\sqrt{2}\cos\theta = 6\sin\theta$

$\Rightarrow \tan\theta = \frac{3\sqrt{2}}{6} = \frac{1}{\sqrt{2}}$

$\Rightarrow \sec^2\theta = 1 + \frac{1}{2} = 3/2$

$\Rightarrow \cos\theta = \pm\sqrt{\frac{2}{3}}; \sin\theta = \pm\sqrt{\frac{1}{3}}$

$\therefore P \equiv \left(3\sqrt{\frac{2}{3}}, 3\sqrt{2}\sqrt{\frac{1}{3}}\right)$ or $\left(-3\sqrt{\frac{2}{3}}, -3\sqrt{2}\sqrt{\frac{1}{3}}\right)$ or

$P \equiv \left(\sqrt{6}, \sqrt{6}\right)$ or $\left(-\sqrt{6}, -\sqrt{6}\right)$

But P should not be in Ist quadrant, hence,

$P \equiv \left(-\sqrt{6}, -\sqrt{6}\right)$

81. (c) $f: (0, \pi) \to \mathbb{R}$;

$f(x) = \max.\{\sin 2x, \cos 2x\}$

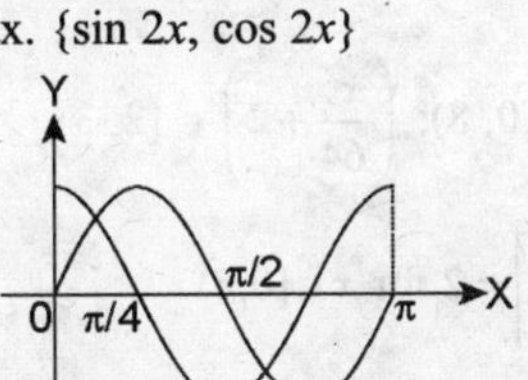

$\Rightarrow f(x) = \begin{cases}\cos 2x; 0 < x \le \frac{\pi}{8}\\ \sin 2x; \frac{\pi}{8} \le x \le \frac{5\pi}{8}\\ \cos 2x; \frac{5\pi}{8} \le x < \pi\end{cases}$

$\Rightarrow f(x)$ has local maxima at $x = \frac{\pi}{4}$ and local minima at $x = \frac{\pi}{8}, \frac{5\pi}{8}$

82. (b) $f(x) = 4x^3 - x\,|x - 2|; x \in [0, 3]$

$\Rightarrow f(x) = \begin{cases}4x^3 + x^2 - 2x; 0 \le x < 2\\ 4x^3 - x^2 + 2x; 2 \le x \le 3\end{cases}$

$\Rightarrow f'(x) = \begin{cases}12x^2 + 2x - 2; 0 < x < 2\\ 12x^2 - 2x + 2; 2 < x < 3\end{cases}$

$\Rightarrow f'(x) = \begin{cases}(2x+1)(6x-2); 0 < x < 2\\ > 0 \quad ; \quad 2 < x < 3\end{cases}$

$\Rightarrow f'(x) = 0$ at $x = \frac{1}{3}$ and $f'(x) < 0$ for $x \in \left(0, \frac{1}{3}\right)$ and $f'(x) > 0$ for $x \in \left(\frac{1}{3}, 3\right)$

$\Rightarrow f(x)$ has a point of minimum at $x = \frac{1}{3}$.

83. (c) $y = \frac{ax+b}{(x-4)(x-1)}$

$\Rightarrow f'(x) = \frac{(x-4)(x-1)(a) - (ax+b)(2x-5)}{\left[(x-4)(x-1)\right]^2}$

$= \frac{a\left(x^2 - 5x + 4\right) - (ax+b)(2x-5)}{\left[(x-4)(x-1)\right]^2}$

$= \frac{x^2(a - 2a) + x(-5a + 5a - 2b) + (4a + 5b)}{\left[(x-4)(x-1)\right]^2}$

$= \frac{-ax^2 - 2bx + 4a + 5b}{\left[(x-4)(x-1)\right]^2}$

At $P(2, -1)$; $f'(x) = 0$

$\Rightarrow -4b - 4b + 4a + 5b = 0$

$\Rightarrow b = 0$

$\Rightarrow y = \frac{ax}{(x-4)(x-1)}$

$\Rightarrow -1 = \frac{2a}{(-2)(1)}$

$\Rightarrow a = 1 \qquad \therefore a = 1, b = 0$

84. (c) $y = 2\log_{10} x - \log_x .01, x > 1$

$\Rightarrow y = 2\log_{10} x - \log_x 10^{-2}$

$\Rightarrow y = 2\log_{10} x + 2\log_x 10$

$\Rightarrow y = 2\left[\log_{10} x + \frac{1}{\log_{10} x}\right] \ge 2$

$\Rightarrow$ Minimum value $f(x) = 2$

85. (b) $f(x) = x^{2/3} + (x - 2)^{2/3}$

$\Rightarrow f'(x) = \frac{2}{3}(x)^{-1/3} + \frac{2}{3}(x-2)^{-1/3} = \frac{2}{3}\left[\frac{1}{x^{1/3}} + \frac{1}{(x-2)^{1/3}}\right]$

$\therefore f'(x) = 0$

$\Rightarrow x^{-1/3} = -(x - 2)^{-1/3}$

$\Rightarrow x - 2 = -x$

$\Rightarrow 2x = 2$

$\Rightarrow x = 1$

$f''(x) = \frac{2}{3}\left[\left(\frac{-1}{3}\right)x^{-4/3} + \left(\frac{-1}{3}\right)(x-2)^{-4/3}\right]$

$\Rightarrow f''(1) = \frac{2}{3}\left[\frac{-1}{3} - \frac{1}{3}\right] = \frac{-4}{9} < 0$

$\Rightarrow$ $f(x)$ has a local maxima at $x = 1$ and the maximum value of $f(x)$

$= f(1) = 1 + (1-2)^{2/3} = 2$

86. (a) $f(x) = \frac{x^p}{p} + \frac{x^{-q}}{q}; \frac{1}{p} + \frac{1}{q} = 1, p > 1$

$\Rightarrow f'(x) = x^{p-1} - x^{-q-1}$

$\therefore f'(x) = 0$

$\Rightarrow x^{p-1} = x^{-q-1}$

$\Rightarrow x^{p-1} = \frac{1}{x^{q+1}}$

$\Rightarrow x^{p+q} = 1$

$\Rightarrow x = 1$ and $f''(x) = (p-1)\,x^{p-2} + (q+1)\,x^{-q-2}$

$\Rightarrow f''(1) = (p-1) + (q+1) = p + q$

$= pq \left(\because \frac{1}{p} + \frac{1}{q} = 1\right)$

$\therefore\ p + q = pq$

$\Rightarrow q(1-p) = -p$

$\Rightarrow q = \frac{p}{p-1} [\because p > 1 \Rightarrow q > 0]$

$\therefore f''(1) = pq > 0$

$\Rightarrow$ $f(x)$ has a minima at $x = 1$

$\Rightarrow$ Minimum value of $f(x) = \frac{1}{p} + \frac{1}{q} = 1$ (*given*)

87. (d) $p(x) = a_0 + a_1 x^2 + a_2 x^4 + a_3 x^6 + \ldots\ldots + a_n x^{2n}; 0 < a_0 < a_1 < a_2 < \ldots\ldots < a_n$

$\Rightarrow p'(x) = 2\,a_1\,x + 4\,a_2\,x^3 + 6\,a_3\,x^5 + \ldots\ldots + 2n\,a_n\,x2^{n-1}$

$\Rightarrow p'(0) = 0$ and $p''(x) = 2a_1 + 12\,a_2\,x^2 + 30\,a_3\,x^4 + \ldots\ldots\ldots + 2n\,a_n\,(2x-1)\,x2x^{-2}$

$\Rightarrow p''(0) = 2a_1 > 0$

$\Rightarrow$ $p(x)$ has exactly one local minima at $x = 0$

88. (b) $f(x) = 2x^3 - 3x^2 - 12x + 1; -1 \le x \le 3/2,$

$f'(x) = 6x^2 - 6x - 12$

$\Rightarrow f'(x) = 6\,[x^2 - x - 2]$

$\Rightarrow f'(x) = 6(x-2)\,(x+1)$

$\Rightarrow$ $f(x) \uparrow$ for $x \in (-\infty, -1)\ (2, \infty)$ and $f(x) \downarrow$ for $x \in (-1, 2)$ and $f'(x) = 0$ at $x = -1, 2$

$\Rightarrow$ In $[-1, 3/2]$, $f(x)$ has maximum value at $x = -1$

$\Rightarrow M = f(-1)$

$= -2 - 3 + 12 + 1 = 8$ and $m = f(3/2)$

$= 2\left(\frac{27}{8}\right) - 3\left(\frac{9}{4}\right) - 12\left(\frac{3}{2}\right) = \frac{27}{4} - \frac{27}{4} - 18 + 1 = -17$

$\therefore\ M = 8, m = -17$

89. (a) $p(x) = a_1\,x + a_2\,x^3 + a_3\,x^5 + \ldots\ldots + a_n\,x^{2n-1}$ and $0 < a_1, a_2, \ldots, a_n$.

$\Rightarrow p'(x) = a_1 + 3a_2\,x^2 + 5a_3\,x^4 + \ldots\ldots + (2n-1)\,a_n\,x^{2n-2} > 0$ as $a_i, x^{2i} \ge 0$ for each i

$\Rightarrow$ $p(x)$ is an increasing function and hence has no extremum.

90. (c) $f(x) = \cos|x| - 2ax + b$

$\Rightarrow f(x) = \cos x - 2ax + b$

$[\because \cos(-x) = \cos x \Rightarrow \cos|x| = \cos x]$

$\Rightarrow f'(x) = -\sin x - 2a \ge 0\ \forall\ x \in \mathbb{R}$ (Given)

$\Rightarrow \sin x \le -2a\ \forall\ x \in \mathbb{R}$

$\Rightarrow 1 \le -2a\ \forall\ x \in \mathbb{R}$

$\Rightarrow a \le -\frac{1}{2}$

91. (b) $a^2 x^4 + b^2 y^4 = c^6$ (*Given*)

By A.M.-G.M. inequality of non-negative real numbers

$\frac{a^2x^4 + b^2y^4}{2} \ge \sqrt{a^2x^4.b^2y^4}$

$\Rightarrow \frac{c^6}{2} \ge \sqrt{a^2b^2x^4y^4}$

$\Rightarrow \frac{c^6}{2} \ge |a||b|\,x^2\,y^2$

$\Rightarrow x^2\,y^2 \le \frac{c^6}{2|a|\,|b|}$

$\Rightarrow \frac{-|c^3|}{\sqrt{2|a||b|}} \le xy \le \frac{|c^3|}{\sqrt{2|a||b|}}$

$\Rightarrow$ Maximum value of $xy = \frac{|c^3|}{\sqrt{2|ab|}}$

92. (d) $y = \left[\frac{x^2}{64} + 2\right]$; $[x]$ is gint x

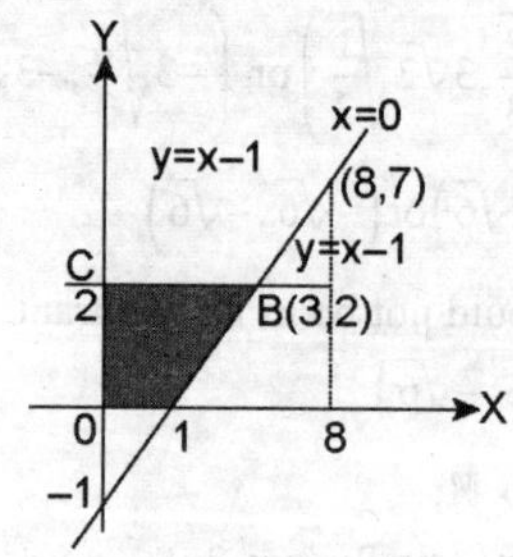

For $x \in [0, 8)$; $\left(\frac{x^2}{64} + 2\right) \in [2, 3)$

$\Rightarrow \left[\frac{x^2}{64} + 2\right] = 2$ for $x \in [0, 8)$

$\therefore$ Required Area = area of trapezium OABC

$= \frac{1}{2}[1+3](2) = 4$

93. (b) $f(x) = 2x^3 - 9ax^2 + 12a2x + 1$

$f(x_1) = 0, f(x_2) = 0$

$\Rightarrow 6x_1^{\,2} - 18ax_1 + 12a^2 = 0$ and $6x_2^{\,2} - 18ax_2 + 12a^2 = 0$

$\Rightarrow x_1 + x_2 = -(-3a) = 3a$ and $x_1\,x_2 = 2a^2$

$\Rightarrow x_1 = 2a, x_2 = a$ or $x_1 = a, x_2 = 2a$

Also $f''(x) = 12x - 18a$

$f''(a) = -6a$ and $f''(2a) = 6a$

$\because\ x = x_1$ is the point of maxima and $x = x_2$ is the point of minima.

$\Rightarrow \begin{cases} x_1 = a, & x_2 = 2a \text{ for } a > 0 \\ x_1 = 2a, & x_2 = a \text{ for } a < 0 \end{cases}$ [$\because$ a $\neq$ 0 as otherwise $f(x)$ $= 2x^3 + 1$, which has no point of maxima and minima]

For a > 0:

$x_1 = a, x_2 = 2a$

$\therefore \quad x_1^2 = x_2$

$\Rightarrow \quad a^2 = 2a$

$\Rightarrow \quad a(a-2) = 0$

$\Rightarrow \quad a = 0 \text{ or } a = 2 \qquad \therefore \quad a = 2$

For a < 0:

$x_1^2 = x_2$ is impossible as $x_1 = 2a$ and $x_2 = a$

$\Rightarrow \quad x_1^2 = 4a^2$ and $x_2 < a$

$\Rightarrow \quad x_1^2 > 0$ and $x_2 < 0$

$\Rightarrow \quad x_1^2 = x_2$ is impossible

94. **(d)** $f(x) = \dfrac{\tan(x+\pi/6)}{\tan} = \left(\dfrac{\dfrac{\tan x + \dfrac{\pi}{\sqrt{3}}}{1+(\tan x).\dfrac{\pi}{\sqrt{3}}}}{(\tan x)}\right)$

$$= \frac{\sqrt{3}\tan x + 1}{\left(\sqrt{3}-\tan x\right)}.\frac{1}{\tan x} = \frac{\sqrt{3}+\cot x}{\sqrt{3}-\tan x}$$

$$\Rightarrow \quad f'(x) = \frac{\left(\sqrt{3}-\tan x\right)(-\text{cosec}^2 x) - \left(\sqrt{3}+\cot x\right)(-\sec^2 x)}{\left(\sqrt{3}-\tan x\right)^2}$$

$\Rightarrow \quad f'(x) = 0$

$\Rightarrow \quad \left(\sqrt{3}+\cot x\right)(\sec^2 x) = \left(\sqrt{3}-\tan x\right)(\text{cosec}^2 x)$

$\Rightarrow \quad \left(\sqrt{3}+\cot x\right).\dfrac{1}{\cos^2 x} = \left(\sqrt{3}-\tan x\right).\dfrac{1}{\sin^2 x}$

$\Rightarrow \quad \sqrt{3}\sin^2 x + \cos x.\sin x = \sqrt{3}\cos^2 x - \sin x \cos x$

$\Rightarrow \quad \sqrt{3}\cos 2x - \sin 2x = 0$

$\Rightarrow \quad \tan 2x = \sqrt{3}$

$\Rightarrow \quad 2x = n\pi + \dfrac{\pi}{3}; n \in \mathbb{Z}$

$\Rightarrow \quad x = \dfrac{n\pi}{2} + \dfrac{\pi}{6}; n \in \mathbb{Z}$

$\Rightarrow \quad f\left(\dfrac{\pi}{6}\right) = \dfrac{\tan\left(\dfrac{\pi}{3}\right)}{\tan\left(\dfrac{\pi}{6}\right)} = \dfrac{\sqrt{3}}{\dfrac{1}{\sqrt{3}}} = 3$ and

$$f\left(-\frac{\pi}{3}\right) = \frac{\tan\left(\dfrac{-\pi}{3}+\dfrac{\pi}{6}\right)}{\tan\left(-\dfrac{\pi}{3}\right)} = \frac{\tan\left(\dfrac{-\pi}{6}\right)}{\tan\left(-\dfrac{\pi}{3}\right)} = \frac{1}{3}$$

$\therefore \quad f(x)(\min) = \dfrac{1}{3}$

$\because \quad f(0^+) = +\infty, f\left(\dfrac{\pi}{6}\right) = 3, f\left(\dfrac{\pi}{3}\right) = +\infty$ and $f'\left(\dfrac{\pi}{6}\right) = 0$

$\Rightarrow \quad x = \dfrac{\pi}{6}$ is the point of local minima.

$\Rightarrow$ Local minimum value of $f(x) = 3$

95. **(d)** Curved surface area of cylinder $= S = 2\pi r l$ ...(1)

Also $\dfrac{r}{R} = \dfrac{L-l}{L}$

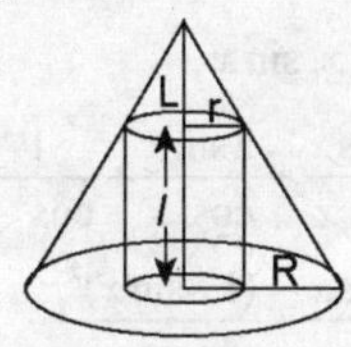

$\Rightarrow \quad r = R\left(1-\dfrac{l}{L}\right)$ ...(2)

$\therefore \quad S = 2\pi l R\left(1-\dfrac{l}{L}\right)$

$S = 2\pi l R - \dfrac{2\pi R l^2}{L}$

$\therefore \quad \dfrac{dS}{dl} = 2\pi R - \dfrac{2\pi R}{L}(2l)$ $\qquad \dfrac{\tan(x+\pi/6)}{\tan x}$

For max. S, $\dfrac{dS}{dl} = 0$

$\Rightarrow \quad 2\pi R\left(1-\dfrac{2l}{L}\right) = 0$

$\Rightarrow \quad 1 = 2l/L$

$\Rightarrow \quad 2l = L$

$\therefore \quad \dfrac{r}{R} = \dfrac{2l-l}{2l} = \dfrac{1}{2}$

$\Rightarrow \quad r = R/2$

96. **(b)** Let the length of hypotenuse $= \ell$ and angle between hypotenuse and base $= \theta$.

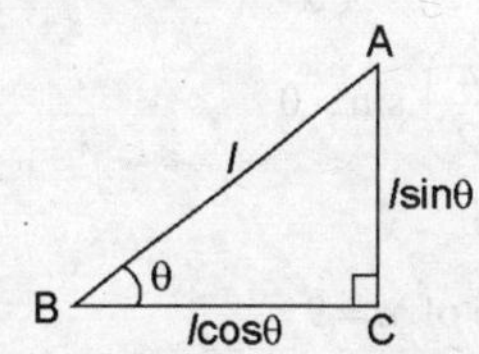

$\Rightarrow \quad A = \dfrac{1}{2}\ell\cos\theta.\ell\sin\theta$

$\Rightarrow \quad A = \dfrac{1}{4}\ell^2\sin 2\theta$

$\Rightarrow \quad \dfrac{dA}{d\theta} = \dfrac{\ell^2}{4}(2)\cos^2\theta$

For maximum/minimum $\dfrac{dA}{d\theta} = 0 \Rightarrow \theta = \dfrac{\pi}{4}$

97. **(c)** Clearly f (x) has a local minimum at $x = c$ as $f'(c-\delta) < 0$ and $f'(c+\delta) > 0$ for $\delta \to 0$ and $f'(c) = 0$

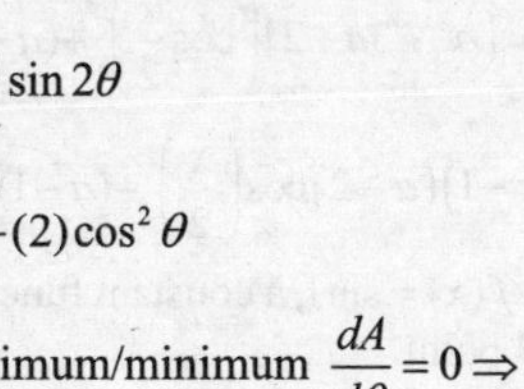

98. (d) $f(x)=\frac{4}{\sin x}+\frac{1}{1-\sin x}=a; \sin x\neq 0,1$

$\Rightarrow f'(x)=4(-\operatorname{cosec}x\ \cot x)+2\sec^2 x\ \tan x+\sin^3 x$

$+\tan^2 x\ \sin x$

$\Rightarrow f'(x)=-\frac{4\cos x}{\sin^2 x}+\frac{2\sin x}{\cos^3 x}+\frac{1}{\cos^3 x}+\frac{\sin^2 x}{\cos^3 x}$

$\Rightarrow f'(x)=-\frac{4\cos x}{\sin^2 x}+\frac{(1+\sin x)^2}{\cos^3 x}$

$\Rightarrow f'(x)=0\Rightarrow \frac{(1+\sin x)^2}{\cos^3 x}=\frac{4\cos x}{\sin^2 x}$

$\Rightarrow (1+\sin x)^2=\frac{4\cos^4 x}{\sin^2 x}$

$\Rightarrow (1+\sin x)=\pm\frac{2\cos^2 x}{\sin x}$

$\Rightarrow \sin x+\sin^2 x=\pm\ 2\cos^2 x$

$\Rightarrow \sin^2 x+\sin x=\pm\ 2(1-\sin^2 x)$

$\Rightarrow 3\sin^2 x+\sin x-2=0$ or $\sin^2 x-\sin x-2=0$

$\Rightarrow (3\sin x-2)(\sin x+1)=0$ or $(\sin x-2)(\sin x+1)=0$

$\Rightarrow \sin x=\frac{2}{3}$ or $\sin x=-1$ or $\sin x=2$ but $\sin x\neq 2$

$\Rightarrow \sin x=\frac{2}{3}$ or $\sin x=-1$

$\therefore\ f(x)\min.=\min.\left\{\frac{4}{\frac{2}{3}}+\frac{1}{1-\frac{2}{3}},\frac{4}{-1}+\frac{1}{2}\right\}=\min.\left\{9,-\frac{7}{2}\right\}$

But for $x\in\left(0,\frac{\pi}{2}\right), \sin>0$

$\Rightarrow f(x)_{\min}=9$

$\Rightarrow$ Least value of $a=9$

99. (b) $f(x)=\left(a^2-3a+2\right)\left(\cos^2\frac{x}{4}-\sin^2\frac{x}{4}\right)+(a-1)x+\sin 1$

Or $f(x)=\left(a^2-3a+2\right)\left(\cos\frac{x}{2}\right)+(a-1)x+\sin 1$

$\Rightarrow f(x)=(a-1)(a-2)\cos\left(\frac{x}{2}\right)+(a-1)x+\sin 1$

For $a=1, f(x)=\sin 1$, a constant function, hence having no critical point.

For $a=2, f(x)=x+\sin 1 = f'(x)=1$, having no critical point.

For $a\neq 1,\neq 2,\ f(x)=(a-1)(a-2)\cos\frac{x}{2}$

$+(a-1)x+\sin 1$

$\Rightarrow f'(x)=-\frac{1}{2}\left(\sin\frac{x}{2}\right)(a-1)(a-2)+(a-1)$

$=(a-1)\left[1-\frac{1}{2}(a-2)\sin\frac{x}{2}\right]$

For no critical point $(a-2)\sin\frac{x}{2}\neq 2$

$\Rightarrow \sin\frac{x}{2}\neq\frac{2}{(a-2)}$

$\Rightarrow \frac{2}{a-2}<-1$ or >1

$\Rightarrow \frac{2}{a-2}+1<0$ or $\frac{2}{a-2}-1>0$

$\Rightarrow \frac{a}{a-2}<0$ or $\frac{4-a}{a-2}>0$

$\Rightarrow a(a-2)<0$ or $(a-2)(a-4)<0$

$\Rightarrow a\in(0,2)$ or $a\in(2,4)$.

$\Rightarrow a\in(0,4)-\{1\}$

$\Rightarrow a\in(0,1)\cup(1,4)$

100. (d) $f(x)=\int_{5\pi/3}^{x}(6\cos t-2\sin t)dt$

$\Rightarrow f'(x)=(6\cos x-2\sin x)$

$\therefore\ f'(x)=0\Rightarrow 6\cos x-2\sin=0$

$\Rightarrow \tan x=3$

In $\left[\frac{5\pi}{3},\frac{7\pi}{4}\right]$; $\cos x>0$, and $\sin x<0$

$\Rightarrow f'(x)>0 \qquad \Rightarrow f(x)$ is$\uparrow$

$\Rightarrow$ least value of $f(x)$ will be at $n=\frac{5\pi}{3}$ i.e., $f\left(\frac{5\pi}{3}\right)$

$=\int_{5\pi/3}^{5\pi/3}(6\cos t-2\sin t)dt = 0$

101. (b) $f(x)=3x^4-4x^3+6x^2+ax+b$

$\Rightarrow f'(x)=12x^3-12x^2+12x+a=12x(x^2-x+1)+a$

$\Rightarrow f''(x)=36x^2-24x+12=12(3x^2-2x+1)$

Disc. of $3x^2-2x+1=4-12=-8<0$

$\Rightarrow f''(x)>0\ \forall x\in\mathbb{R}$

$\Rightarrow f(x)$ is always concave upwards and $f(-\infty)=f(\infty)=\infty$

$\Rightarrow f(x)$ has exactly one extremum i.e., minima.

102. (d) $f(x)=\int_0^x\frac{\cos t}{t}dt; x>0$

$\Rightarrow f''(x)=\frac{\cos x}{x}=0$ at $x=(2n+1)\frac{\pi}{2}; n\in\mathbb{Z}$

$\Rightarrow f''(x)=\frac{x(-\sin x)-\cos x}{x^2}$

$\Rightarrow f''(x)=\frac{x\sin x-\cos x}{x^2}$ at $x=(2n+1)\frac{\pi}{2}$

$\Rightarrow f''(x)=\frac{-\sin(2n+1)\frac{\pi}{2}}{x}$

$\Rightarrow f''(x)=\frac{-1}{(2n+1)\frac{\pi}{2}}$ for n = even integer.

$\Rightarrow\ f''(x) = \dfrac{-1}{(2n+1)\dfrac{\pi}{2}}$ for n = odd integer.

$\Rightarrow\ f(x)$ has maxima for $x = (2n+1)\dfrac{\pi}{2};\ n \in \{0, 2, 4, \ldots\ldots\}$ $\cup \{-1, -2, -3, \ldots\ldots\}$

$\Rightarrow\ f(x)$ has minima for $x = (2n+1)\dfrac{\pi}{2};\ n \in \{-1, -2, -3, \ldots\ldots\} \cup \{0, 1, 2, 3, \ldots\ldots\}$

103. (d) $a^{f(x)} + g(x) = 0$

$\because\ g(x) \geq \dfrac{1}{2}$ and $a^{f(x)} > 0\ \forall x \in \mathbb{R}$ because $a > 0$

Thus $a^{f(x)} + g(x)$ can never be zero

Hence the above equation has no real solution.

104. (b) $x \in \left[\dfrac{5\pi}{4}, \dfrac{4\pi}{3}\right]$, $f(x) = \int_{5\pi/4}^{x}(3\sin t + 4\cos t)dt$

$f'(x) = (3\sin x + 4\cos x)$

$\Rightarrow$ In $x \in \left[\dfrac{5\pi}{4}, \dfrac{4\pi}{3}\right]$, $\sin < 0$ and $\cos x < 0$

$\Rightarrow\ f'(x) < 0\ \forall x \in \left[\dfrac{5\pi}{4}, \dfrac{4\pi}{3}\right]$

$\Rightarrow\ f(x)$ is a creasing function an $\left[\dfrac{5\pi}{4}, \dfrac{4\pi}{3}\right]$

$\Rightarrow\ f(x)$ has its least value at $x = \dfrac{4\pi}{3}$ given by $f\left(\dfrac{4\pi}{3}\right)$

$$= \int_{5\pi/4}^{4\pi/3}(3\sin t + 4\cos t)\,\mathrm{dt} = [3(-\cos t)]_{5\pi/4}^{4\pi/3} + 4[\sin t]_{5\pi/4}^{4\pi/3}$$

$$= -3\left[\left(-\frac{1}{2}\right) - \left(-\frac{1}{\sqrt{2}}\right)\right] + 4\left[\frac{-\sqrt{3}}{2} + \frac{1}{\sqrt{2}}\right]$$

$$= \frac{3}{2} - \frac{3}{\sqrt{2}} - \frac{4\sqrt{3}}{2} + \frac{4}{\sqrt{2}} = \frac{3}{2} - 2\sqrt{3} + \frac{1}{\sqrt{2}}$$

SECTION–IV: (MORE THAN ONE CORRECT ANSWER)

1. (a), (c) $f(x) = (x^9 + 3x^7 + 6)^{97}$

$\Rightarrow\ f'(x) = (97)[x^9 + 3x^7 + 6)^{96}(9x^8 + 7x^6) \geq 0\ \forall x \in \mathbb{R}$

$\Rightarrow\ f(x)$ is increasing $\forall x \in \mathbb{R}$.

2. (a), (b), (d) $f(x) > 0, g(x) > 0, f'(x) \geq 0, g'(x) \geq 0$

$\Rightarrow\ (f(x).g(x))' = f'(x).g(x) + f(x).g'(x) \geq 0\ \forall x \in \mathbb{R}$

$\Rightarrow\ f(x).g(x) \uparrow\ \forall x \in \mathbb{R}$

$\Rightarrow$ Option (a) is correct

$\Rightarrow$ Let $F(x) = (f(x))^{g(x)}$

$\Rightarrow\ \ln F(x) = g(x).\ln f(x)$

$\Rightarrow\ \dfrac{1}{F(x)}.F'(x) = \dfrac{g(x)}{f(x)}.f'(x) + g'(x)\ln f(x)$

$\Rightarrow\ F(x) = F(x) = \left[\dfrac{g(x).f'(x)}{f(x)} + g'(x)\ln f(x)\right]$

Clearly if $\ln f(x) > 0$ i.e., $f(x) > 1$, then $F'(x) \geq 0$ i.e., $F(x)$ is increasing

$\Rightarrow$ option (b) is correct

Thus if $F(x)$ is decreasing, then $\ln f(x) \leq 0$ i.e., $f(x) \leq 1$

$\Rightarrow$ option (d) is correct

3. (b), (c) $\because\ f(x) = x^3$ is bijective function, with

$(f(x) - x)f''(x) = (x^3 - x)(6x) = 6x^2(x^2 - 1)$

> 0 for $x \in (-\infty, -1) \cup (1, \infty)$ and < 0 for $x \in (-1, 1)$ i.e., all bijective functions do not follow option (a) and (b)

However option (b) may be true for function which are strictly above the line $y = x$, strictly increasing and having concavity upwards e.g. $y = e^x = 1 + x + \dfrac{x^2}{2!} + \dfrac{x^3}{3!} + \ldots..$

$\Rightarrow\ e^x - x = \dfrac{x^2}{2!} + \dfrac{x^3}{3!} + \ldots...$

$\Rightarrow\ f(x) - x = e^x - x > 0\ \forall x \in \mathbb{R}$ and

$f''(x) = e^x > 0 \forall x \in \mathbb{R}$

$\Rightarrow\ (f(x) - x)(f''(x)) > 0\ \forall x \in \mathbb{R}$

Now $(f(x) - x)f''(x) > 0$

$\Rightarrow\ y = x$ and $y = f(x)$ do not intersect and either $f(x) > x$ and $f''(x) > 0$ or $f(x) < x$ and $f''(x) < 0$ i.e., function is above line $y = x$ and concave upwards or function is below line $y = x$ and concave downwards.

$\Rightarrow\ f(x) = f^{-1}(x)$ has no solution

4. (a), (b) $Q(x) = 2f\left(\dfrac{x^2}{2}\right) + f(6 - x^2)\ \forall x \in \mathbb{R}$

$\Rightarrow\ Q'(x) = 2 \times \dfrac{1}{2}(2x)f'\left(\dfrac{x^2}{2}\right) + (-2x)f'(6 - x^2)$

$\because\ f''(x) > 0\ \forall x \in \mathbb{R}$

$\Rightarrow\ f'(x)$ is increasing $\forall x \in \mathbb{R}$

$\Rightarrow\ Q'(x) \geq 0$ for $2x\left(f'\left(\dfrac{x^2}{2}\right) - f'(6 - x^2)\right) \geq 0$

$\Rightarrow\ Q(x)$ is increasing either for $x \geq 0)$ and $\dfrac{x^2}{2} \geq 6 - x^2$ or $x \leq 0)$ and $\dfrac{x^2}{2} \leq 6 - x^2$ i.e.. for $x \geq 0$ and $x^2 \geq 4$ or $x \leq 0$ and $x^2 \leq 4$ i.e., for $x \in [-2, 0] \cup [2, \infty)$

$\therefore\ f(x)$ increasing on $[-2, 0] \cup [2, \infty)$ and decreasing on $(-\infty, -2) \cup (0, 2)$

5. (a), (b), (c), (d) $\phi(x) = 3f\left(\dfrac{x^2}{3}\right) + f(3 - x^2)\ \forall x \in \mathbb{R}(-3, 4)$

$f''(x) > 0\ \forall x \in (-3, 4)$

$\phi'(x) = 3 \times \dfrac{2x}{3}f'\left(\dfrac{x^2}{3}\right) - 2xf'(3 - x^2)\ \forall x \in (-3, 4)$

$\therefore$ $\phi(x)$ is increasing for either

$x \ge 0, \dfrac{x^2}{3} \ge 3 - x^2, x \in (-3,4)$ or $x \le 0, \dfrac{x^2}{3} \le 3 - x^2, x \in (-3,4)$

i.e., either $x \ge 0,\ x^2 \ge \dfrac{9}{4}, x \in (-3,4)$ or

$x \le 0,\ x^2 \le \dfrac{9}{4}, x \in (-3,4)$

$\Rightarrow$ $\phi(x)$ increasing for $x \in \left[-\dfrac{3}{2}, 0\right]$ and $\left[\dfrac{3}{2}, 4\right]$ and $\phi(x)$ decreasing for $x \in \left(-3, -\dfrac{3}{2}\right)$ and $\left(0, \dfrac{3}{2}\right)$

6. (a) $0 < A$, B, $C < \pi/2$,

A cosec A + B cosec B + C cosec C

$$= \frac{A}{\sin A} + \frac{B}{\sin B} + \frac{C}{\sin C} \quad \ldots(1)$$

Let $f(x) = \dfrac{x}{\sin x}$

$$\Rightarrow f'(x) = \frac{\sin x - x\cos x}{\sin^2 x} = \frac{g(x)}{\sin^2 x} \text{ (say)} \quad \ldots(2)$$

Now, $g'(x) = \dfrac{\cos x + x\sin x - \cos x}{\sin^2 x} = \dfrac{x}{\sin x} > 0\ \forall x \in \left(0, \dfrac{\pi}{2}\right]$

$\Rightarrow$ $g(x)$ is an increasing function $\forall x \in \left(0, \dfrac{\pi}{2}\right]$

$\Rightarrow$ $g(x) > g(0)\ \forall x \in \left[0, \dfrac{\pi}{2}\right]$

$\Rightarrow$ $g(x) > 0\ \forall x \in \left(0, \dfrac{\pi}{2}\right]$ ...(3)

$\therefore$ From (2) and (3), $f'(x) > 0\ \forall x \in \left(0, \dfrac{\pi}{2}\right]$

$\Rightarrow$ $f(x)$ is an increasing function $\forall x \in \left(0, \dfrac{\pi}{2}\right]$

$$\Rightarrow \frac{A}{\sin A}, \frac{B}{\sin B}, \frac{C}{\sin C} < \frac{\pi/2}{\sin \pi/2}\ \forall A, B, C \in \left(0, \frac{\pi}{2}\right)$$

$$\Rightarrow \frac{A}{\sin} + \frac{B}{\sin B} + \frac{C}{\sin C} < \frac{\pi}{2}\ \forall A, B, C, \in \left(0, \frac{\pi}{2}\right)$$

$$\Rightarrow \frac{A}{\sin} + \frac{B}{\sin B} + \frac{C}{\sin C} < \frac{3\pi}{2}$$

$\Rightarrow$ A cosec A + B cosec B + C cosec $C < \dfrac{3\pi}{2}$

$\Rightarrow$ option (*a*) is correct

Option (*c*) is false e.g., if $A, B, C \in \left(0, \dfrac{\pi}{6}\right)$

$\Rightarrow$ $\sin A, \sin B, \sin C < \dfrac{1}{2}$

$\Rightarrow$ $\sin A + \sin B + \sin C < \dfrac{3}{2}$

7. (a), (b), (c) $f(x) = \sin x + ax + b$,

$\Rightarrow$ $f'(x) = \cos x + a$

$\Rightarrow$ $f(x) \uparrow$ for $\cos \ge -a$ which is true $\forall x \in \mathbb{R}$ provided $-a \le -1$ i.e., $a \ge 1$ and $f(x) \downarrow$ for $\cos x \le -a$ which is true $\forall x \in \mathbb{R}$ provided $-a \ge 1$ i.e., $a \le -1$

Thus for unique solution of $\sin x = x$, $a \in (-\infty, -1] \cup [1, \infty)$ and Range of $f(x)$ must contain 0.

$\Rightarrow$ $\sin x + ax + b = 0$ for some $x \in \mathbb{R}$

$\Rightarrow$ $-\sin x = ax + b$

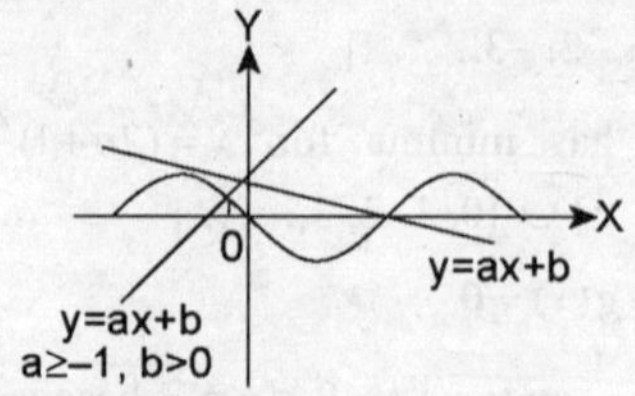

Thus $f(x) = 0$ is always possible for $a \in (-\infty, -1] \cup [1, \infty)$,

But being monotonic function $f(x) = 0$ has exactly one real root, x.

$\Rightarrow$ For +ve real root, $a \le -1, b > 0$ or $a \ge 1, b < 0$ and for –ve real root $a \ge 1, b > 0$ or $a \le -1, b < 0$

8. (b) Let $f(x) = \dfrac{1}{x}, g(x) = \dfrac{1}{x^2}, h(x) = \dfrac{1}{\sqrt{x}}$

$$\Rightarrow f'(x) = \frac{-1}{x^2}, g'(x), = \frac{-2}{x^3}, h'(x) = \frac{-1}{2x\sqrt{x}}$$

$$\therefore f'(x) = \frac{-1}{x^2}, g'(x) = \frac{-2}{x^3}, h'(x) = \frac{-1}{2(x)^{3/2}}$$

For $\rightarrow x \rightarrow 0^+$, $x^3 < x^2 < x^{\frac{3}{2}}$

$$\Rightarrow \frac{1}{x^3} > \frac{1}{x^2} > \frac{1}{x^{3/2}} > 0$$

$$\Rightarrow \frac{-1}{x^3} < \frac{-1}{x^2} < \frac{-1}{x^{3/2}} \quad \ldots(i)$$

Also $\dfrac{-2}{x^3} < \dfrac{-1}{x^3}$ ...(ii)

and $-\dfrac{1}{x^{3/2}} < \dfrac{-1}{2x^{3/2}}$ ...(iii)

From (*i*), (*ii*) and (*iii*), we have $-\dfrac{2}{x^3} < \dfrac{-1}{x^2} < \dfrac{-1}{2x^{3/2}} < 0$

$\Rightarrow$ $g'(x) < f'(x), h'(x) < 0$

$\Rightarrow$ $|g'(x)| > |f'(x)| > |h'(x)|$

$\Rightarrow$ $g(x)$ decreases most rapidly when $x > 0$ and increases

$\Rightarrow$ $g(x)$ increases most rapidly when $x \rightarrow 0^+$ i.e., $\dfrac{1}{x^2}$

9. (a), (b), (c), (d) $f(x) = x - \cot^{-1} x + \log\left(\sqrt{x^2+1} - x\right)$

$$\Rightarrow f'(x) = 1 + \frac{1}{1+x^2} + \frac{\left(\dfrac{x}{\sqrt{x^2+1}} - 1\right)}{\left(\sqrt{x^2+1} - x\right)}$$

$$\Rightarrow f'(x) = 1 + \frac{1}{1+x^2} + \left(\frac{-1}{\sqrt{x^2+1}}\right)$$

$\Rightarrow \quad f'(x) = 1 + \dfrac{1}{(x^2+1)} - \dfrac{-1}{\sqrt{x^2+1}}$

$\Rightarrow \quad f'(x) = \left(1 - \dfrac{1}{\sqrt{x^2+1}}\right) + \dfrac{1}{x^2+1} \qquad \because x^2+1 \geq 1$

$\Rightarrow \quad \sqrt{x^2+1} \geq 1$

$\Rightarrow \quad \dfrac{1}{\sqrt{x^2+1}} \leq 1 \Rightarrow 1 - \dfrac{1}{\sqrt{x^2+1}} \geq 0$

$\Rightarrow \quad f'(x) > 0 \ \forall x$ for which $\sqrt{x^2+1} > x$

$\Rightarrow \quad f'(x) > 0 \ \forall x \in \mathbb{R}$

10. (a), (b) $f(x) = \cos^{-1}\left(\dfrac{1-x^2}{1+x^2}\right)$

$\cos^{-1}$ is a deceasing function for $x \in [-1,1]$

$\Rightarrow \quad \left(\dfrac{1-x^2}{1+x^2}\right) \in [-1,1]$

$\Rightarrow \quad -1 \leq \dfrac{1-x^2}{1+x^2} \leq 1$

$\Rightarrow \quad -(1+x^2) \leq (1-x^2) \leq (1+x^2)$

$\Rightarrow -1 - x^2 \leq 1 - x^2 \leq 1 + x^2$

$\Rightarrow \quad -1 \leq 1$ and $2x^2 \geq 0$ Which holds $\forall x \in \mathbb{R}$

Now $f'(x) = \dfrac{-1}{\sqrt{1-\left(\dfrac{1-x^2}{1+x^2}\right)}} \times \left(\dfrac{(1+x^2)(-2x)-(1-x^2)(2x)}{(1+x^2)^2}\right)$

$\Rightarrow \quad f'(x) = \dfrac{-1}{\sqrt{\dfrac{2x^2}{1+x^2}}} \times \left(\dfrac{-4x}{(1+x^2)^2}\right)$

$\Rightarrow \quad f'(x) = \dfrac{4x}{\sqrt{2}|x|(1+x^2)^{3/2}}$

$\Rightarrow \quad f'(x) = \dfrac{-2\sqrt{2}}{(1+x^2)^{3/2}} < 0$ for $x < 0$ and

$f'(x) = \dfrac{2\sqrt{2}}{(1+x^2)^{3/2}} > 0 \ \forall x \in > 0$

$\Rightarrow \quad f(x)$ decreases for $x \in (-\infty, 0)$ and $f(x)$ increases for $x \in (0, \infty)$

11. (c), (d) $f'(x) = \dfrac{x}{\sin x}$ and $g(x) = \dfrac{x}{\tan x}; 0 < x \leq 1.$

$\Rightarrow \quad f'(x) = \dfrac{\sin x - x\cos x}{\sin^2 x} = \dfrac{h(x)}{\sin^2 x} \qquad \ldots(i)$

where $h(x) = \sin x - x\cos x$

$\Rightarrow \quad h'(x) = \cos x + x\sin x - \cos x$

$\Rightarrow \quad h'(x) = x\sin x > 0 \ \forall x \in (0,1]$

$\Rightarrow \quad h(x) > h(0) \ \forall x \in (0,1]$

$\Rightarrow \quad h(x) > 0 \ \forall x \in (0,1] \qquad \ldots(ii)$

$\therefore$ From (*i*) and (*ii*), $f'(x) > 0 \ \forall x \in (0,1]$

$\Rightarrow \quad f(x)$ increases $\forall x \in (0, 1]$.

Now $g'(x) = \dfrac{\tan x - x\sec^2 x}{\tan^2 x} = \dfrac{k(x)}{\tan^2 x}$ (*say*); where

$k'(x) = \tan x - x\sec^2 x$

$\Rightarrow \quad k'(x) = \sec^2 x - x(2\sec^2 x \ \tan x) - \sec^2 x$

$\Rightarrow \quad k'(x) = -2x \ \sec^2 x \ \tan x < 0 \ \forall x \in (0,1]$

$\Rightarrow \quad k(1) \leq k(x) < k(0) \ \forall \ 0 < x \leq 1$

$\Rightarrow \quad k(x) < 0 \ \forall x \in (0, 1]$

$\Rightarrow \quad g'(x) < 0 \ \forall x \in (0, 1]$

$\Rightarrow \quad g(x)$ is a decreasing function $\forall x \in (0,1]$

12. (a), (b), (c) $f(x) = \int_0^x \sqrt{1-t^4}\,dt \qquad \ldots(i)$

$\Rightarrow \quad f'(x) = \left(\sqrt{1-x^4}\right) \qquad \ldots(ii)$

For $f(x)$ to be defined $1 - t^4 \geq 0 \Rightarrow t^4 \leq 1$

$\Rightarrow \quad t^2 \leq 1$

$\Rightarrow \quad t \in [-1,1]$

$\Rightarrow \quad x \in [-1,1]$

$\Rightarrow$ Option (*a*) is correct

From (*ii*); $f''(x) \geq 0$ is an increasing function

$\Rightarrow$ option (*b*) is correct

Also $f(-x) = \int_0^{-x} \sqrt{1+t^4}\,dt$

Put $t = -u \Rightarrow dt = -du$

$\because f(-x) = \int_0^u \sqrt{1-u^4}\,(-du) = -\int_0^u \sqrt{1-u^4}\,du$

$= -\int_0^x \sqrt{1-x^4}\,dx = f(x)$

$\Rightarrow \quad f(x)$ is an odd function

$\Rightarrow$ option (*c*) is correct

13. (a), (b) $f(x) = \begin{cases} 7-x \ ; x < 2 \\ 11-x \ ; x \geq 2 \end{cases}$

$\Rightarrow \quad f'(x) = \begin{cases} -2x \ ; x < 2 \\ -1 \quad ; x > 2 \end{cases}$

$\Rightarrow \quad f'(x) = \begin{cases} +ve \text{ for } x < 0 \\ -ve \text{ for } 0 < x < 2 \\ -1 \text{ for } \quad x > 2 \end{cases}$

Also $f(2^-) = 3, f(2^+) = 9$

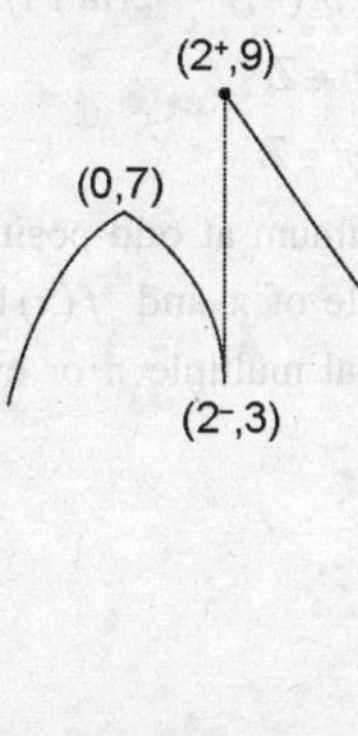

$\Rightarrow$ $f(x)$ has a local maxima at $x = 0$ and local minima at $x = 2$

14. (a), (b), (c), (d) $f(x) = \begin{cases} 3x^2 + 12x - 1; & -1 \le x \le 2 \\ 37 - x; & 2 < x \le 3 \end{cases}$

$\Rightarrow$ $f'(x) = \begin{cases} 6x + 12; & -1 < x < 2 \\ -1; & 2 < x < 3 \end{cases}$

$\Rightarrow$ $f'(x) = \begin{cases} +ve; & -1 < x < 2 \\ -ve; & 2 < x < 3 \end{cases}$

Also $f(2^-) = 35, f(2^+) = 35 = f(2)$

$\Rightarrow$ $f(x)$ is continues on [–1, 3]

$\Rightarrow$ Option (*b*) is correct and $f(x)$ has a local maxima at $x = 2$

$\Rightarrow$ Option (*d*) is correct
$f'(2^-) = 24, f'(2^+) = -1$

$\Rightarrow$ $f'(2)$ does not exist

$\Rightarrow$ Option (*c*) is correct
Also $f(x)$ is increasing on [–1, 2]

$\Rightarrow$ Option (*a*) is correct
Thus option (*a*), (*b*), (*c*) and (*d*) are correct

15. (c), (d) $f(x) = 2x^3 - 3(2+\lambda)x^2 + 12\lambda x$

$\Rightarrow$ $f'(x) = 6x^2 - 6(2+\lambda)x + 12\lambda$

Now, $f(x)$ has exactly one-local maxima one-local minima

$\Rightarrow$ $f'(x) = 0$ has two district real roots.

$\Rightarrow$ Disc. > 0

$\Rightarrow$ $36(2+\lambda)^2 - 24(12\lambda) > 0$

$\Rightarrow$ $3(2+\lambda)^2 - 24\lambda > 0$

$\Rightarrow$ $(2+\lambda)^2 - 8\lambda > 0$

$\Rightarrow$ $\lambda^2 - 4\lambda + 4 > 0$

$\Rightarrow$ $(\lambda - 2)^2 > 0$

$\Rightarrow$ $\lambda \ne 2$

$\Rightarrow$ $S = \mathbb{R} - \{2\}$

$\Rightarrow$ S is a super set of (3, ∞) and (–∞, 0)

16. (a), (b), (c) $f(x) = \sin x - x\cos x$

$\Rightarrow$ $f'(x) = \cos x + x\sin x - \cos x$

$\Rightarrow$ $f'(x) = x\sin x$

$\Rightarrow$ $f''(x) = x\cos x + \sin x$

$\therefore$ $f'(x) = 0$ for $x = n\pi;\ n \in \mathbb{Z}$ for $x = (2m+1)\pi;\ m \in \mathbb{Z}$

$\Rightarrow$ $f''(x) = (2m+1)\pi(-1) = -2(m+1)\pi; m \in \mathbb{Z}$

For $x = 2m\pi;\ m \in \mathbb{Z}$

$f''(x) = 2m\pi;\ m \in \mathbb{Z}$

$\therefore$ $f(x)$ has maximum at odd positive or even negative integeal multiple of π and $f(x)$ has minimum at odd negative integeal multiple π or even positive integeal multiple of π.

17. (a), (b), (c), (d) $f(x) = x^4(12\ln x - 7); x > 0$

$\Rightarrow$ $f'(x) = x^4\left(\frac{12}{x}\right) + 4x^3(12\ln x - 7)$

$\Rightarrow$ $f'(x) = 12x^3 + 4x^3(12\ln x - 7)$

$\Rightarrow$ $f'(x) = 4x^3(3 + 12\ln x - 7)$

$\Rightarrow$ $f'(x) = 4x^3(12\ln x - 4)$

$\Rightarrow$ $f'(x) = 16x^3(3\ln x - 1)$

$\therefore$ $f'(x) = 0\ e^{1/3} (\because x > 0)$ and

$f''(x) = 16x^3\left(\frac{3}{x}\right) + (3\ln x - 1)(48x^2)$

$\Rightarrow$ $f''(x) = 48x^2 + 48x^2(3\ln x - 1)$

$\Rightarrow$ $f''(x) = (48x^2)(1 + 3\ln x - 1)$

$\Rightarrow$ $f''(x) = 144x^2 \ln x$

$\Rightarrow$ $f''(e^{1/3}) = 48e^{2/3} > 0$

$\Rightarrow$ $x = e^{1/3}$ is a point of minima Also $f''(x) = 0$ at $x = 1$

$\Rightarrow$ (1, –7) is the point of inflection.
Also $f''(x) > 0$ for $\ln x > 0$ i.e., $x > 1$

$\Rightarrow$ $f(x)$ is concave upwards for $x \in (1, \infty)$ and concave downwards for $x \in (0, 1)$.

18. (a), (b), (c), (d) Since in each of the graphs given in figures (*a*), (*b*) (*c*), (*d*), concavity of curve is changing at $x = c$, hence $x = c$ is the point of inflection in each graph.

19. (b), (c), (d) $f(x) = \frac{x-1}{x^2} = \frac{1}{x} - \frac{1}{x^2}; x \ne 0$

$\Rightarrow$ $f'(x) = \frac{-1}{x^2} + \frac{2}{x^3}$

$\Rightarrow$ $f'(x) = 0 \Rightarrow \frac{2}{x^3} = \frac{1}{x^2}; x \ne 0$

$\Rightarrow$ $x = 2; f(0^-) = f(0^+) = -\infty$

$\Rightarrow$ $f'(x) > 0 \Rightarrow \left(\frac{2-x}{x3}\right) > 0$ and $(x-2)x^3 < 0; x \ne 0$

$\Rightarrow$ $x \in (0, 2)$

$\Rightarrow$ $f(x)$ increases for $x \in (0, 2)$ and $f(x)$ decreases for $x \in (-\infty, 0) \cup (2, \infty)$

$\Rightarrow$ $f(x)$ has a local maxima at $x = 2$.

Also $f''(x) = \frac{2}{x^3} - \frac{6}{x^4} = \left(\frac{2x-6}{x^4}\right) = 0$ at $x = 3 \Rightarrow x = 3$ is a point of inflection.

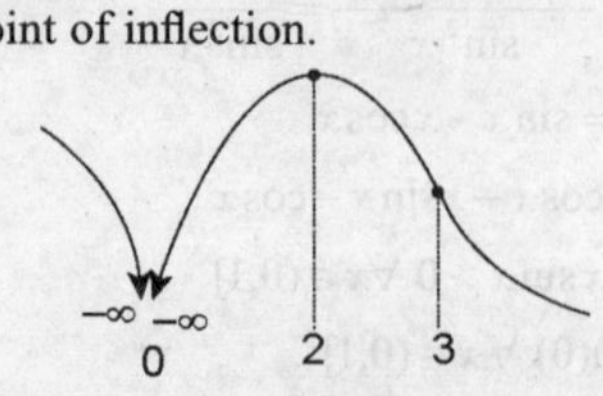

Also $f''(x) > 0$ for $x > 3$ and $f''(x) < 0$ for $x < 3$

20. (a), (b), (c), (d) $F(x)=\int_0^{\sqrt{9-x^2}} e^{\frac{t^2}{2}}dt;$

$\Rightarrow\ F'(x)=e^{(9-x^2)/2}.\dfrac{1}{2\sqrt{9-x^2}}.(-2x)$

$\Rightarrow\ F'(x)=\dfrac{-x}{\sqrt{9-x^2}}.e^{(9-x^2)/2}$

$\Rightarrow\ F'(x)>0$ for $x\in(-3,0)$ and $F'(x)<0$ for $x\in(0,3)$

$\Rightarrow\ F'(x)=0$ at $x=0$ and $F(0)=\int_0^3 e^{\frac{t^2}{2}}dt$ is the maxima value of $F(x)$

$\Rightarrow\ F'(-x)=-F'(x)$

$\Rightarrow\ F'(x)$ is an odd function

21. (b), (c), (d) $f(x)=ax^3+bx^2+cx+1$

$f'(\alpha)=f'(\beta)=0$ and $\alpha.\beta<0$

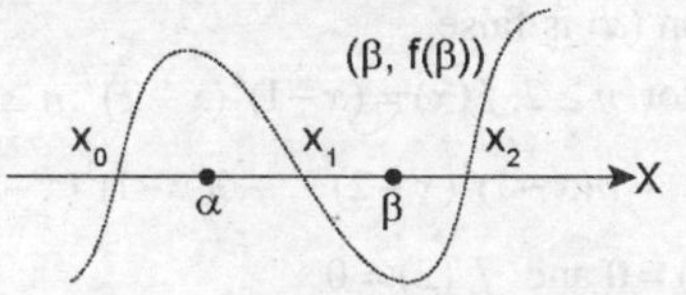

$\Rightarrow$ α and β are of opposite signs and $f(\alpha).f(\beta)<0$

$\Rightarrow\ f(\alpha)$ and $f(\beta)$ are of opposite signs.

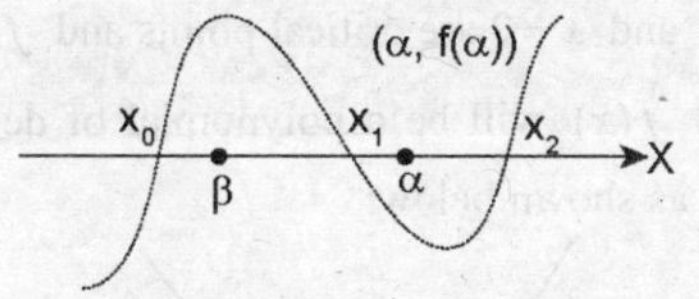

$\Rightarrow\ f(x)$ has three district real root x_0, x_1, x_2, one negative (x_0) and other two (x_1 and x_2) positive if $f(\alpha)>0, f(\beta)<0$

$\Rightarrow$ one +ve and 2 –ve real roots if $f(\alpha)>0$ and $f(\beta)<0$.

22. (a), (c), (d) $f(x)=x^2+\dfrac{\lambda}{x}$

$\Rightarrow\ f'(x)=2x-\dfrac{\lambda}{x^2}$

$\Rightarrow\ f''(x)=2+\dfrac{2\lambda}{x^3}$

Now, $f'(x)=0\Rightarrow 2x^3-\lambda=0\Rightarrow x=\left(\dfrac{\lambda}{2}\right)^{1/3}$

and $f''\left(\left(\dfrac{\lambda}{2}\right)^{1/3}\right)=2+\dfrac{2\lambda}{\lambda/2}=6>0$

$\Rightarrow\ f(x)$ has a minimum at $x=2$ if $\lambda=16$.

For maxima, $f''\left(\left(\dfrac{\lambda}{2}\right)^{1/3}\right)<0$, but it is impossible as $f''\left(\left(\dfrac{\lambda}{2}\right)^{1/3}\right)$ is +ve

Now, $f''(x)=0\Rightarrow x=-(\lambda)^{1/3}$

$\Rightarrow\ f(x)$ has a point of inflection at $x=1$ if $\lambda=-1$

23. (a), (b), (d) $f(x)=\sin^6 x+\cos^6 x$

$\Rightarrow\ (\sin^2 x+\cos^2 x)^3-3\sin^2 x\cos^2 x(\sin^2 x+\cos^2 x)$

$\Rightarrow\ 1-\dfrac{3}{4}\sin^2 2x\ \in\left(\dfrac{1}{4},1\right]$

$\Rightarrow\ f(x)\ge\dfrac{1}{4}$ and $f(x)\le 1$

24. (a), (c), (d) $f(x)=|x^2+2x-3|+\dfrac{3}{2}\ln x; x\in\left[\dfrac{1}{2},4\right]$

$\Rightarrow\ f(x)=|(x+3)(x-1)|+\dfrac{3}{2}\ln x$

$$\Rightarrow\ f(x)=\begin{cases}-(x+3)(x-1)+\dfrac{3}{2}\ln x & \text{for } x\in\left[\dfrac{1}{2},1\right]\\ (x-3)(x-1)+\dfrac{3}{2}\ln x & \text{for } x\in[1,4]\end{cases}$$

$$\Rightarrow\ f'(x)=\begin{cases}-2x-2+\dfrac{3}{2x} & \text{for } x\in\left(\dfrac{1}{2},1\right)\\ 2x+2+\dfrac{3}{2x} & \text{for } x\in(1,4)\end{cases}$$

Now $-2x-2+\dfrac{3}{2x}<0$

$\Rightarrow\ \dfrac{-4x^2-4x-3}{2x}<0$

$\Rightarrow\ (4x^2+4x-3)(2x)>0$

$\Rightarrow\ (2x+3)(2x-1)(2x)>0;\ x\in\left(\dfrac{-3}{2},0\right)\cup\left(\dfrac{1}{2},\infty\right)$

$$\Rightarrow\ f'(x)=\begin{cases}-ve \text{ for } x\in\left(\dfrac{1}{2},1\right)\\ +ve \text{ for } x\in(1,4)\end{cases}$$

$\Rightarrow\ x=1$ is a point of local minima and $x=\dfrac{1}{2}$ and $x=4$ are point of local maxima.

25. (b), (d) $y=x^2+px+q$ …(1)

Cuts the straight line $y=(2x-3)$, where $x=1$ i.e., $y=-1$

$\Rightarrow$ (1, –1) lies an (1)

$\Rightarrow\ -1=1+p+q\Rightarrow p+q=-2$ …(2)

Vertex of parabola is $\left(\dfrac{-p}{2},\dfrac{-(p^2-4q)}{4}\right)\equiv\left(\dfrac{-p}{2},\dfrac{-p^2+4q}{4}\right)$

Distance between vertex and x-axis

$=\dfrac{|p^2-4q|}{4}=\dfrac{1}{4}|p^2-4(-2-p)|=\dfrac{1}{4}|p^2+4p+8|$

$=\dfrac{p^2+4p+8}{4}$ as $p^2+4p+8>0$

Let $L=\frac{1}{4}(p^2+4p+8)$

$\Rightarrow \quad \frac{dL}{dp}=\frac{1}{4}(2p+4)=\frac{p}{2}+1$

For least value of $L, \frac{dL}{dp}=0$

$\Rightarrow \quad \frac{}{}+1=0 \Rightarrow \quad =-2$

Also $p+q=-2$

$\Rightarrow \quad q=-2-p=-2+2=0$

$\therefore \quad p=-2,\ q=0$ and least distance $=\frac{1}{4}(4-8+8)=1$

26. (a), (b), (c), (d) $f(x)=a\sin x+\frac{1}{3}\sin 3x$

$\Rightarrow \quad f'(x)=a\cos x+\frac{1}{3}(3\cos 3x)$

$\Rightarrow \quad f'(x)=a\cos x+\cos 3x$

$\Rightarrow \quad f'(x)=4\cos^3-3\cos x+a\cos x$

$\Rightarrow \quad f'(x)=(\cos x)\left[4\cos^2 x+(a-3)\right]$

$\therefore \quad f'(x)=0 \Rightarrow \cos x=0$ or $\cos^2 x=\frac{3-a}{4}$

$\because \quad n=\frac{2\pi}{3}$ is a point of extremum

$\Rightarrow \quad f'\left(\frac{2\pi}{3}\right)=0 \Rightarrow \frac{1}{4}=\frac{3-a}{4} \Rightarrow a=2$

$\therefore \quad f'(x)=(\cos x)[4\cos^2 x-1]$

Also $f''(x)=-2\sin x-3\sin 3x$

$\Rightarrow \quad f''\left(\frac{2\pi}{3}\right)=-2\left(\frac{\sqrt{3}}{2}\right)-3(0)=-\sqrt{3}<0$

$\Rightarrow \quad x=\frac{2\pi}{3}$ is point of maxima for $a=2$

Also $f''\left(\frac{\pi}{2}\right)=-2-3(-1)=1>0$

$\Rightarrow \quad x=\frac{\pi}{2}$ is point of minima for $a=2$

Also $\cos^2 x=\frac{3-a}{4}=\frac{3-2}{4}=\frac{1}{4}$

$\Rightarrow \quad \cos x=\pm\frac{1}{2}$

$\therefore \quad f'(x)=0 \Rightarrow x=\frac{\pi}{3},\frac{\pi}{2},\frac{2\pi}{3}$

$\Rightarrow \quad f(x)$ has 3 critical points in $(0, \pi)$

27. (b), (d) $\because y=x$ is a line tangent to $y=f(x)$ at $x=1$ i.e., at (1, 1)

$\Rightarrow \quad f'(1)=1$ and $f(1)=1$

Let the equation of parabola $y=ax^2+bx+c$

$\Rightarrow \quad f'(x)=2ax+b$

$\Rightarrow \quad f(1)=a+b+c=1$ and $f'(1)=2a+b=1$

$\Rightarrow \quad a-c=0 \Rightarrow c=a$

$\therefore \quad f(x)=ax^2+(1-2a)x+a$

$\Rightarrow \quad f(0)=a, f'(0)=(1-2a); f''(0)=0$

$\Rightarrow \quad f(0)+f'(0)+f''(0)=1-a\neq 1$

Also $2f(0)=2a$ and $1-f'(0)=1-(1-2a)=2a$

$\therefore \quad 2f(0)=1-f'(0)$

28. (a), (c) For $n=1,\ f(x)=(x-1)^4(x-2)$

$\Rightarrow \quad f'(x)=(x-1)^4+(x-2).4(x-1)^3$

$\Rightarrow \quad f'(1)=0$ and $f'(2)=1$

$\Rightarrow \quad x=2$ is not a critical point $\forall$ odd integer n

$\Rightarrow$ option (*d*) is false,

But for $n\geq 2, f(x)=(x-1)^4(x-2)^n; n\geq 2$

$f'(x)=n(x-1)^4(x-2)^{n-1}+4(x-1)^3(x-2)^n$

$\Rightarrow \quad f'(1)=0$ and $f'(2)=0$

$\Rightarrow \quad x=1$ and $x=2$ are critical points $\forall n\geq 2$

For n = even natural no., $n\geq 2$

$\Rightarrow \quad n-1$ and $x=2$ are critical points and $f(1)=f(2)=0$

Then $f(x)$ will be a polynomial of degree $(n+4)=$ even as shown below:

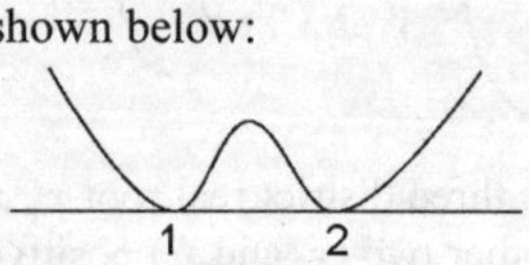

$\Rightarrow \quad x=1$ and $x=2$ are point of minima for $n=$ even.

$\Rightarrow$ Option (*c*) is correct and option (*b*) is incorrect

For n = odd natural number

$x=1$ is a critical point and $f(x)$ is a polynomial of odd degrees $(n+4)$ as shown below:

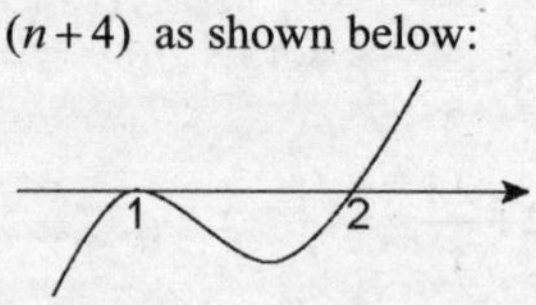

$\Rightarrow \quad x=1$ is a point of local maxima for $n=$ odd

$\Rightarrow$ option (*a*) is correct

29. (b), (c) $f(x)=\phi(2-x)+\phi(x)$

$\Rightarrow \quad f'(x)=-\phi'(2-x)+\phi'(x)$ ...(i)

Now $\phi''(x)<0\ \forall x\in[0,2]$

$\Rightarrow \quad \phi'(x)$ is a decreasing function an $x\in[0,2]$

Now for $x\in[0,1]; (2-x)\geq x$

$\Rightarrow \quad \phi'(2-x)\leq\phi'(x)$

$\Rightarrow \quad \phi'(x)-\phi'(2-x)\geq 0$ ...(ii)

$\therefore$ From (i) & (ii) $f'(x) \geq 0 \ \forall x \in [0,1]$ and hence, $f'(x) \leq 0 \ \forall x \in [1,2]$

$\Rightarrow$ $f(x)$ is increasing an $[0,1]$ and decreasing an $[1,2]$

30. (b), (c) $f(x) = \int_0^x (1-t^2)e^{-\frac{t^2}{2}} dt$

$\Rightarrow$ $f'(x) = (1-x^2)e^{-\frac{x^2}{2}} = 0 \Rightarrow x = \pm 1$

31. (a), (b) $y = \sin^{-1}\left(2x\sqrt{1-x^2}\right)$

Let $\theta = \sin^{-1} x \ \Rightarrow \ \theta \in \left[\frac{-\pi}{2}, \frac{\pi}{2}\right]; x \in [-1,1]$

$\Rightarrow$ $x = \sin\theta \ \Rightarrow \ \cos\theta = \sqrt{1-x^2}$

$$\Rightarrow y = \sin^{-1}(\sin 2\theta) = \begin{cases} -(2\theta+\pi); 2\theta \in \left[-\pi, \frac{-\pi}{2}\right] \\ 2\theta; \quad 2\theta \in \left[\frac{-\pi}{2}, \frac{\pi}{2}\right] \\ -(2\theta-\pi); 2\theta \in \left[\frac{\pi}{2}, \pi\right] \end{cases}$$

$$= \begin{cases} -2\sin^{-1}x - \pi; \ \theta \in \left[\frac{-\pi}{2}, \frac{-\pi}{4}\right]; x \in \left[-1, \frac{1}{\sqrt{2}}\right] \\ 2\sin^{-1}x; \quad \theta \in \left[\frac{-\pi}{4}, \frac{-\pi}{4}\right]; x \in \left[\frac{-1}{\sqrt{2}}, \frac{1}{\sqrt{2}}\right] \\ -2\sin^{-1}x + \pi; \ \theta \in \left[\frac{\pi}{4}, \frac{\pi}{2}\right]; x \in \left[\frac{1}{\sqrt{2}}, 1\right] \end{cases}$$

$$\Rightarrow f'(x) = \begin{cases} \frac{-2}{\sqrt{1-x^2}}; \ x \in \left[-1, \frac{-1}{\sqrt{2}}\right] \\ \frac{2}{\sqrt{1-x^2}}; \ x \in \left[\frac{-1}{\sqrt{2}}, \frac{1}{\sqrt{2}}\right] \\ \frac{-2}{\sqrt{1-x^2}}; \ x \in \left[\frac{1}{\sqrt{2}}, 1\right] \end{cases}$$

$\Rightarrow$ $f(x)\downarrow$ on $x \in \left[-1, \frac{-1}{\sqrt{2}}\right]$ and $\uparrow$ on $x \in \left[\frac{-1}{\sqrt{2}}, \frac{1}{\sqrt{2}}\right]$ and $\downarrow$ on $\left[\frac{1}{\sqrt{2}}, 1\right]$

$\Rightarrow$ $f(x)$ has local maxima at $x = -1, \frac{1}{\sqrt{2}}$ and local minima at $n = -\frac{1}{\sqrt{2}}, 1$

Clearly $f(x)$ has its least value at $x = \frac{-1}{\sqrt{2}}$ or $x = 1$

$\Rightarrow$ $f\left(\frac{-1}{\sqrt{2}}\right) = \sin^{-1}\left(-\sqrt{2} \times \frac{1}{\sqrt{2}}\right) = -\frac{\pi}{2}$ and $f(1) = 0$

$\Rightarrow$ $f(x)$ has its least value of $x = -\frac{1}{\sqrt{2}}$

32. (b), (c), (d) $f(x)$ has a relative minimum at $x = 0$

$\Rightarrow$ $f'(0) = 0$ and $f''(0) > 0$

Now $y = f(x) + an^2 + bx + c$

$\Rightarrow$ $y' = f'(x) + 2ax + b$

$\Rightarrow$ $y'(0) = f'(0) + 2a(0) + b + b = 0$

$\therefore$ $y = f(x) + ax^2 + c$

$\Rightarrow$ $y''(x) = f''(x) + 2a$

For relative minima, $y''(0) > 0$

$\Rightarrow$ $f''(0) + 2a > 0$

$\Rightarrow$ $a > \frac{-1}{2} f''(0)$

$\Rightarrow$ Option (a) is incorrect

$\Rightarrow$ Option (b) is correct

Also, $f''(0) > 0$ and $\frac{-1}{2} f''(0) < 0$

$\Rightarrow$ $a = 0$ is permitted

$\therefore$ Option (c) is correct,

Since C can take any value

$\Rightarrow$ Option (d) is also correct

33. (a), (b), (c) $f(x) = \sin^{-1}\left(\frac{2x}{1+x^2}\right)$

$$= \begin{cases} 2\tan^{-1}x; \ x \in [-1,1] \\ 2\tan^{-1}x + \pi; \ x \in (-\infty, -1) \\ 2\tan^{-1}x - \pi; \ x \in (1, \infty) \end{cases}$$

$\Rightarrow$ $f'(x) = \left\{\frac{2}{1+x^2} \forall x \in \mathbb{R}\right.$

$\Rightarrow$ $f(x)$ is strictly increasing function $\forall x \in \mathbb{R}$

$\Rightarrow$ $f'(1^-) = \lim\limits_{x \to 1^-} \frac{f(x) - f(1)}{(x-1)} = \lim\limits_{x \to 1^-} \frac{2\tan^{-1}x - \frac{\pi}{2}}{(x-1)}$

$= \lim\limits_{x \to 1^-} \left(\frac{2}{1+x^2}\right) = 1$ and $f'(1^+) = \lim\limits_{x \to 1^+} \frac{f(x) - f(1)}{x-1}$

$= \lim\limits_{x \to 1^+} \frac{2\tan^{-1}x - \pi - \frac{\pi}{2}}{x-1} = \lim\limits_{x \to 1^+} \frac{2\tan^{-1}x - \frac{3\pi}{2}}{x-1} = -\infty$

$\Rightarrow$ $f'(1)$ does not exist.

$\because$ $f(x)$ is an odd function.

$f'(-1)$ does not exist.

$f(1^-) = \frac{\pi}{4}, f(1^+) = -\frac{\pi}{2}$

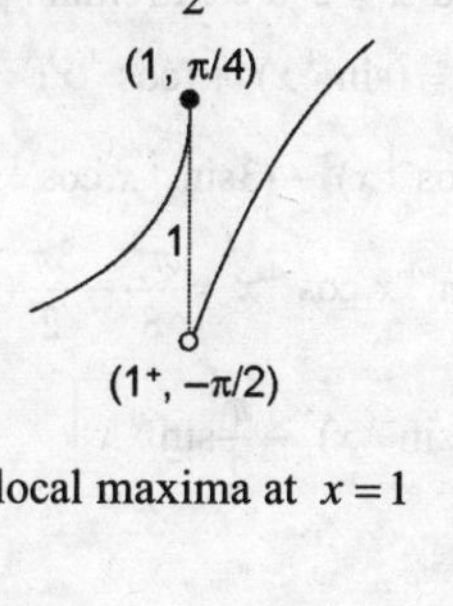

$\Rightarrow$ (x) has a local maxima at $x = 1$

34. (b), (d) $f(x)=(x-1)^p.(x-2)^q$; where $p>1, q>1$

$\because$ $p\geq 2, q\geq 2, f(x)$ is a polynomial at degree greats than or equal to 4 having $x=1$ root repeated p times and $x=2$ root repeated q times.

$\Rightarrow$ $f'(x)=(x-1)^p.q(x-2)^{q-1}+(x-2)^q.p(x-1)^{p-1}$

$=(x-1)^{p-1}(x-2)^{q-1}[q(x-1)+p(x-2)]$

$=(x-1)^{p-1}(x-2)^{q-1}[(p+q)x-(2p+q)]=0$

Critical points are $x=1, x=2$ and $x=\dfrac{2p+q}{p+q}$

Exactly critical point will be an extremum if the polynomial is of even degree. i.e., p + q = even and $p, q>2$

$\Rightarrow$ $p=4, q=2$ and $p=2, q=4$ are possible

35. (b), (c), (d) $P\left(x_1,\dfrac{x_1^2}{2}\right)$ Let be the point on the curve $x^2=2y$ such that P is closed to $Q(0,3)$.

Then $\left(\dfrac{dy}{dx}\right)_{\text{at P}}=-\left(\dfrac{x_1-0}{\dfrac{x_1^2}{2}-3}\right)$

$\Rightarrow$ $x_1=-\left(\dfrac{x_1}{\dfrac{x_1^2}{2}-3}\right)$

$\Rightarrow$ $x_1=0$ or $x_1^2=4$

$\Rightarrow$ $x_1=0$ or $x_1=\pm 2$

$\Rightarrow$ $P\equiv(0,0)$ or $(-2,2),(2,2)$

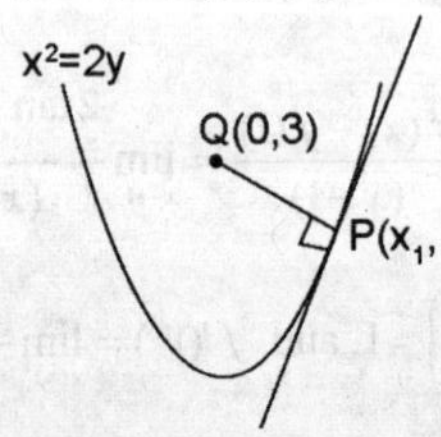

36. (c), (d) $y=\int_0^x (t-1)(t-2)dt$

$y'=(x-1)(x-2)=x^2-3x+2$

$y'=0\Rightarrow x=1$ or $x=2$

$\Rightarrow$ $y''=2x-3$

$\Rightarrow$ $y''(1)=-1, y''(2)=1$

$\Rightarrow$ $x=1$ and $x=2$ are extremum points

37. (a), (c) $f(x)=(\sin^{-1}x)^3+(\cos^{-1}x)^3$

$=(\sin^{-1}x+\cos^{-1}x)^3-(3\sin^{-1}x.\cos^{-1}x)(\sin^{-1}x+\cos^{-1}x)$

$=\dfrac{\pi^3}{8}-\dfrac{3\pi}{2}\sin^{-1}x.\cos^{-1}x=\dfrac{\pi^3}{8}-\dfrac{3\pi}{2}(\sin^{-1}x)\left(\dfrac{\pi}{2}-\sin^{-1}x\right)$

$=\dfrac{\pi^3}{8}+\dfrac{3\pi}{2}\left[(\sin^{-1}x)^2-\dfrac{\pi}{2}\sin^{-1}x\right]$

$=\dfrac{\pi^3}{8}+\dfrac{3\pi}{2}\left[(\sin^{-1}x)^2-\dfrac{\pi}{2}\sin^{-1}x+\dfrac{\pi^2}{16}-\dfrac{\pi^2}{16}\right]$

$=\dfrac{\pi^3}{8}+\dfrac{3\pi}{2}\left[\left(\sin^{-1}x-\dfrac{\pi}{4}\right)^2-\dfrac{\pi^2}{16}\right]$

$=\dfrac{\pi^3}{8}+\dfrac{3\pi}{2}\left(\sin^{-1}x-\dfrac{\pi}{4}\right)^2-\dfrac{3\pi^3}{32}$

$\Rightarrow$ $f(x)=\dfrac{\pi^3}{8}-\dfrac{3\pi^3}{32}+\dfrac{3\pi}{2}\left(\sin^{-1}x-\dfrac{\pi}{4}\right)^2$

$\Rightarrow$ $f(x)=\dfrac{\pi^3}{32}+\dfrac{3\pi}{2}\left(\sin^{-1}x-\dfrac{\pi}{4}\right)^2$

$\Rightarrow$ $f(x)_{\text{min.}}=\dfrac{\pi^3}{32}$ at $\sin^{-1}x=\dfrac{\pi}{4}$ and

$f(x)_{\text{max.}}=\dfrac{\pi^3}{32}+\dfrac{3\pi}{2}\left(-\dfrac{\pi}{2}-\dfrac{\pi}{4}\right)^2$

$=\dfrac{\pi^3}{32}+\dfrac{3\pi}{2}\left(\dfrac{9\pi^2}{16}\right)=\dfrac{7\pi^3}{8}$

38. (d) $f(x)=4x^3-x^2-2x+1$ and

$g(x)=\begin{cases}\min\{f(t):0\leq t\leq x\}; 0\leq x\leq 1\\ 3-x \quad ; 1<x\leq 2\end{cases}$

$\Rightarrow$ $f'(x)=12x^2-2x-2=0$

$\Rightarrow$ $6x^2-x-1=0$

$\Rightarrow$ $(3x+1)(2x-1)=0$

$\Rightarrow$ $x=-\dfrac{1}{3}$ or $x=\dfrac{1}{2}$

$\Rightarrow$ $f(x)\uparrow$ on $x\in\left(-\infty,-\dfrac{1}{3}\right]\cup\left[\dfrac{1}{2},\infty\right)$ and

$f(x)\downarrow$ an $x\in\left(-\dfrac{1}{3},\dfrac{1}{2}\right)$

$\Rightarrow$ $g(x)=\begin{cases}f(x); & 0\leq x\leq\dfrac{1}{2}\\ f\left(\dfrac{1}{2}\right); & \dfrac{1}{2}<x\leq 1\\ 3-x \;; & 1<x\leq 2\end{cases}$

$\Rightarrow$ $g(x)=\begin{cases}4x^3-x^2-2x+1; & 0\leq x\leq\dfrac{1}{2}\\ \dfrac{1}{4}; & \dfrac{1}{2}<x\leq 1\\ 3-x; & 1<x\leq 2\end{cases}$

$\Rightarrow$ $g\left(\dfrac{1}{4}\right)+g\left(\dfrac{3}{4}\right)+g\left(\dfrac{5}{4}\right)=\dfrac{1}{2}+\dfrac{1}{4}+\dfrac{7}{4}=\dfrac{10}{4}=\dfrac{5}{2}$

39. (a), (c), (d) $f(x)=(x^2-1)^n(x^2+x+1)$

Repeated roots of $f(x)=0$ are $-1,1$

If n is eve, then $f(x)$ will be a polynomial of even degree and $f(x)\geq 0\ \forall x\in\mathbb{R}$ $n=1$ and $x=-1$ will become the points of extremum.

If n is odd, then $f(0)<0$, then $x=1$ and $x=-1$ will remain no longer points of extremum.

$\Rightarrow\ n\neq$ odd

$\Rightarrow\ n=2$ or 4 or 6

40. (a), (b) $f(x)=\begin{cases}x+2\ ;-1\leq x<0\\ 1\ ;x=0\\ x/2\ ;0<x\leq 1\end{cases}$

$f(0^-)=2,\ f(0)=1,\ f(0^+)=0$

$x=0$ is not an extremum point, $f'(x)=\begin{cases}1;\ -1<x<0\\ \dfrac{1}{2};\ 0<x<1\end{cases}$

$\Rightarrow f(x)$ is on increasing function, however discontinuous at $x=0$, graphically dream below.

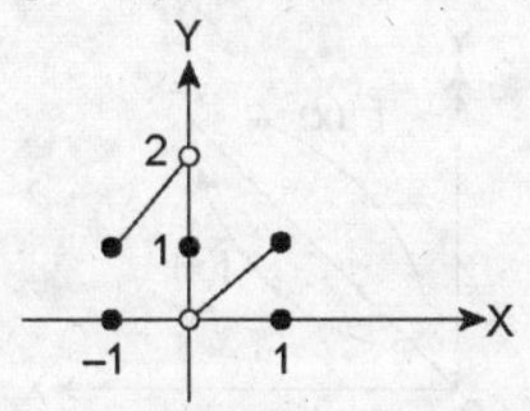

$x=-1$ is a point of minima and $x=1$ is a point of maxima.

41. (a), (c) Let $y=f(x)=\dfrac{1}{\sin x+4}-\dfrac{1}{\cos x-4}$

$$=\frac{(\cos x-\sin x)-8}{4(\cos x-\sin x)+\sin x\ \cos x-16}$$

$$=\frac{(\cos x-\sin x)-8}{4(\cos x-\sin x)-\frac{1}{2}[1-2\sin x\ \cos x-1]-16}$$

$$=\frac{(\cos x-\sin x)-8}{4(\cos x-\sin x)-\frac{1}{2}[(\cos x-\sin x)^2]-16+\frac{1}{2}}$$

Put $\cos x-\sin x=t\in\left[-\sqrt{2},\sqrt{2}\right]$

$\Rightarrow\ y=g(t);\ t=h(x);$

where $g(t)=\dfrac{2t-16}{8t-t^2-31}=\dfrac{16-2t}{t^2-8t+31};$

$$\therefore\ \frac{dy}{dx}=\frac{dy}{dt}\times\frac{dt}{dx}=g'(t)\times[\sin x-\cos x]$$

$$=\frac{(t^2-8t+31)(-2)-(16-2t)(2t-8)}{(t^2-8t+31)^2}\times(-\sin x-\cos x)$$

$$=\frac{\left(2t^2-32t+66\right)}{\left(t^2-8t+31\right)^2}\times(-\sin x-\cos x)$$

$$=\frac{-2\left[t-\left(8-\sqrt{31}\right)\right]\left[t-\left(8+\sqrt{31}\right)\right](\sin x+\cos x)}{\left(t^2-8t+31\right)^2}$$

$\therefore\ \dfrac{dy}{dx}=0$

$\Rightarrow\ t=8-\sqrt{31}$ or $8+\sqrt{31}$ or $\sin x+\cos x=0$ but $t\in\left[-\sqrt{2},\sqrt{2}\right]\ \Rightarrow\ t\neq 8\pm\sqrt{31}$

$\therefore$ Critical points are the only solutions of $\sin x+\cos x-0$

$\Rightarrow\ \sqrt{2}\left(\cos\left(x-\dfrac{\pi}{4}\right)\right)=0\ \Rightarrow\ \left(x-\dfrac{\pi}{4}\right)=(2n+1)\dfrac{\pi}{2}$

$\Rightarrow\ x=n\pi+\dfrac{3\pi}{4}$ or equivalently $x=\left(n\pi-\dfrac{\pi}{4}\right);\ n\in\mathbb{Z}$

Since $f(x)$ is continuous and periodic function, extremum values will occur only at $x=n\pi-\dfrac{\pi}{4};\ n\in\mathbb{Z}$

Now $f\left(n\pi-\dfrac{\pi}{4}\right)=\dfrac{1}{\sin\left(n\pi-\dfrac{\pi}{4}\right)+4}-\dfrac{1}{\cos\left(n\pi-\dfrac{\pi}{4}\right)-4}$

$$=\begin{cases}\dfrac{1}{\frac{-1}{\sqrt{2}}+4}-\dfrac{1}{\frac{1}{\sqrt{2}}-4} & \text{for } n=\text{ even}\\[2ex] \dfrac{1}{\frac{1}{\sqrt{2}}+4}-\dfrac{1}{\frac{-1}{\sqrt{2}}-4} & \text{for } n=\text{ odd}\end{cases}$$

$$=\begin{cases}\dfrac{2\sqrt{2}}{4\sqrt{2}-1} & \text{for } n=\text{even}\\[2ex] \dfrac{2\sqrt{2}}{4\sqrt{2}+1} & \text{for } n=\text{ odd}\end{cases}$$

$$=\begin{cases}\dfrac{4}{8-\sqrt{2}} & \text{for } n=\text{even}\\[2ex] \dfrac{4}{8+\sqrt{2}}\ \text{or}\ \dfrac{2\sqrt{2}}{4\sqrt{2}+1} & \text{for } n=\text{ odd}\end{cases}$$

Aliter: $y=\dfrac{16-2t}{t^2-8t+31};\ t\in\left[-\sqrt{2},\sqrt{2}\right]$ and

$$y'(t)=\frac{2(t^2-16t+33)}{(t^2-8t+31)^2}=\frac{2[t^2-16t+64-31]}{(t^2-8t+31)^2}$$

$$=\frac{2\left[(t-8)^2-31\right]}{(t^2-8t+31)^2}=0$$

$\Rightarrow\ t=8\pm\sqrt{31}>\sqrt{2}$

$\Rightarrow\ y(t)$ is monotonic in $\left[-\sqrt{2},\sqrt{2}\right]$

$\Rightarrow$ Extremum will be

$$f\left(-\sqrt{2}\right)=\frac{16+2\sqrt{2}}{33+8\sqrt{2}}=\frac{2\sqrt{2}\left(4\sqrt{2}+1\right)}{\left(4\sqrt{2}+1\right)^2}=\frac{2\sqrt{2}}{4\sqrt{2}+1}$$

And

$$f\left(\sqrt{2}\right)=\frac{16-2\sqrt{2}}{33-8\sqrt{2}}=\frac{2\sqrt{2}\left(4\sqrt{2}-1\right)}{\left(4\sqrt{2}-1\right)^2}=\frac{2\sqrt{2}}{4\sqrt{2}-1}=\frac{4}{8-\sqrt{2}}$$

SECTION–V: (ASSERTION – REASON)

1. (c) Clearly, assertion is correct i.e., $\sin x$ and $\cos x$ decreases on $\left(\frac{\pi}{2},\pi\right)$.

Reason is incorrect as for a decreasing function having concave upwards graph, $f'(x)<0$ but $f''(x)>0$

$\Rightarrow f(x)\downarrow$ but $f'(x)\uparrow$ e.g., $f(x)=\cos x; x\in\left(\frac{\pi}{2},\pi\right)$

$\Rightarrow f'(x)=-\sin x<0$ and $f''(x)=-\cos x>0$

$\Rightarrow f(x)\downarrow$ but $f'(x)\uparrow$

2. (b) $f(x)=2+\cos x;\ x\in\mathbb{R}$

$\Rightarrow f'(x)=-\sin x=0$ for $x=n\pi;\ n\in\mathbb{Z}$

$\Rightarrow f'(x)=0$ once in each interval $[t,t+\pi)$.

If $t=m\pi$ for some fixed $m\in\mathbb{Z}$, then $f'(m\pi)=0$ i.e., $f'(t)=0$ and if $t\neq m\pi;\ m\in\mathbb{Z}$, then $t\in(m\pi,(m+1)\pi)$; for some $m\in\mathbb{Z}$, then $f''((m+1)\pi)=0$ i.e., $f'(c)=0$ and $c=(m+1)\pi\in[t,t+\pi)$

$\Rightarrow$ Assertion is true

Clearly, reason is correct as $f(x)=2+\cos$ is periodic with period 2π, but does not explains the assertion.

3. (a) $y=f(x)=(x)^{1/x}$

$\Rightarrow \ln y=\frac{1}{x}\ln x$

$\Rightarrow \frac{1}{y}.\frac{dy}{dx}=\frac{1}{x^2}+(\ln x)\left(\frac{-1}{x^2}\right)$

$\Rightarrow \frac{dy}{dx}=(x)^{1/x}\left[\frac{1-\ln x}{x^2}\right]$

$\Rightarrow f(x)\uparrow$ for $x\in(0,e)$ and l, for $x\in(e,\infty)$

$\Rightarrow$ Reason is correct

$\therefore\ (1)^{1/1}<(2)^{1/2}<(e)^{1/e}>(3)^{1/3}>(4)^{1/4}>(5)^{1/5}>(6)^{1/6}>(7)^{1/7}$

$\Rightarrow$ Clearly either $2^{1/2}$ or $3^{1/3}$ is greatest

Now $2^{1/2}<3^{1/3}\Leftrightarrow 2^{3/2}<3\Leftrightarrow 2\sqrt{2}<3\Leftrightarrow 2.828<3$

which is true.

Thus $(3)^{1/3}$ is greatest

$\Rightarrow$ Assertion is correct and is supported by reason.

4. (a) f: $[0,\infty)\rightarrow[0,\infty)$;

g: $[0,\infty)\rightarrow[0,\infty)$;

$\therefore\ f'(x)\le 0$ and $g'(x)\ge 0$ and $h(x)=g(f(x))$

$\Rightarrow h'(x)=g'(f(x)).f'(x)=(\ge 0).(\le 0)\le 0$

$\therefore\ h'(x)\le 0$ but $h(0)=0$ and

$h(x)=g(f(x)):[0,\infty)\rightarrow[0,\infty)$

$\Rightarrow h(x)$ is a non-increasing function with $h(0)=0$ and having range $[0,\infty)\Rightarrow h(x)=0\ \forall x\in[0,\infty)$

$\Rightarrow h(x)$ is a constant function. Thus both assertion and reason are correct and assertion is supported by reason.

5. (d) Let $y=f^{-1}(x)$

$\Rightarrow f(y)=x$

$\Rightarrow f'(y)=\frac{dx}{dy}$

$\Rightarrow \frac{dy}{dx}=\frac{1}{f'(y)}=(f'(y))^{-1}$

$\Rightarrow \frac{d}{dx}\left(f^{-1}(x)\right)=\frac{1}{f'(y)}$ ...(*i*) and

$\frac{dy^2}{dx^2}=\frac{-1}{(f'(y))^2}.\frac{f''(y)}{f'(y)}$ ...(*ii*)

$\therefore$ If $f(x)$ is increasing function with concavity upwards

$\Rightarrow f'(y)>0$ and $f''(y)>0$

$\Rightarrow$ From (*i*); $f^{-1}(x)\uparrow$ and $\frac{d^2}{dx^2}\left(f^{-1}(x)\right)<0$

$\Rightarrow f^{-1}(x)$ increases and has concavity downwards

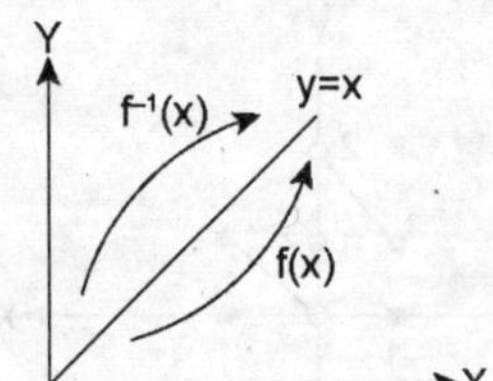

$\Rightarrow$ Assertion is incorrect.

On the other hand, if $f(x)\downarrow$ i.e., $f'(x)<0$ and $f''(x)>0$,

then from (*i*) $f^{-1}(x)\downarrow$ and from (*ii*) $\frac{d^2}{dx^2}\left(f^{-1}(x)\right)>0$

$\Rightarrow f^{-1}(x)\downarrow$ with concavity upwards

$\Rightarrow$ Reason is correct

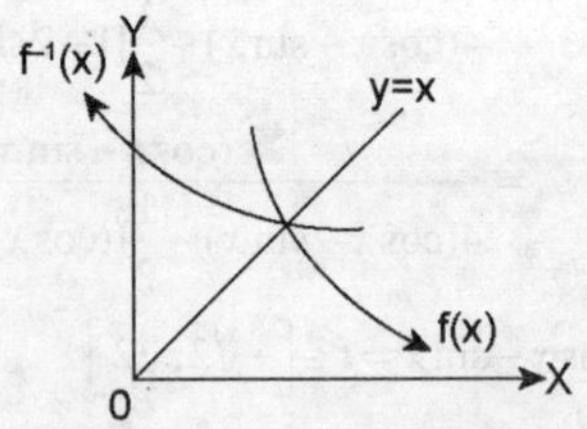

6. (a) $f(x):\mathbb{R}\rightarrow\mathbb{R}$ is differentiable and strictly increasing function in domain. If $f(x)$ is strictly increasing function, then it is not necessary that $|f(x)|$ is also increasing. However $|f(x)|$ will be an increasing function if $f(x)\forall x\in\mathbb{R}$

e.g., $f(x)=e^x$,

$\Rightarrow f(x)=0$ has no real root

$\Rightarrow$ Assertion is correct.

Reason is correct, as if $f(x)=0$ at $x=c$ (*say*), then $f(x)<0$ for $x<c$

$\Rightarrow$ $|f(x)|$ will be a decreasing an function an $(-\infty,c)$ and increasing an (c,∞)

$\Rightarrow$ At $-\infty, f(x)\to 0$, but can't be equal zero

$\Rightarrow$ Reason is correct and supports assertion

7. (c) Reason is incorrect, as Rolle's theorem is applicable if $f(a)$ and $f(b)$ and when $f(x)$ is continuous an $[a,b]$ and derivable an (a,b).

$f(-1)=f(1)=0$ if $g(-1),g(1)\neq 0$

Further it $g(x)\neq 0$ at any point in [–1, 1], then $g(x)$ is differentiable

$\Rightarrow$ $f(x)$ is also differentiable and hence continuous

$\Rightarrow$ Rolle's theorem will be applicable, hence for non-applicability of Rolle's theorem an $f(x)$, $g(x)=0$ at least once in $[-1,1]$.

$\Rightarrow$ Assertion is correct

8. (a) $f(x)=1\dfrac{((3x^2)^{31}-1)}{(3x^2-1)}$

$\Rightarrow$ $f'(x)=6x+3^2(4x^3)+3^3(6x^5)+.....+3^{30}(60x^{59})$

$\Rightarrow$ $f'(x)=x(6+3^2(4)x^2+3^3(6)(x^4)+.......+3^{30}(60)x^{58}]$

$=0$ only at $x=0$ i.e., $f'(x)$ changes its sign only at $x=0$ and $f'(x)<0$ for $x<0$ and $f(x)>0$ for $x>0$

$\Rightarrow$ $f(x)$ has a local minima at $x=0$

9. (d) $f(x)=5-4(x-2)^{2/3}$

$\Rightarrow$ $f'(x)=-4\left(\dfrac{2}{3}\right)(x-2)^{-1/3}=\dfrac{-8}{3(x-2)^{1/3}}$

$\Rightarrow$ $f'(x)$ does not exist at $x=2$

$\Rightarrow$ $x=2$ is a critical point of $f(x)$

Also $f'(x)>0$ for $x<2$ and $f'(x)<0$ for $x>2$

$\Rightarrow$ $x=2$ is a point of local maxima or absolute maxima at $x=2$

$\Rightarrow$ Assertion is incorrect, but reason is correct

10. (d) Obviously, reason is correct,

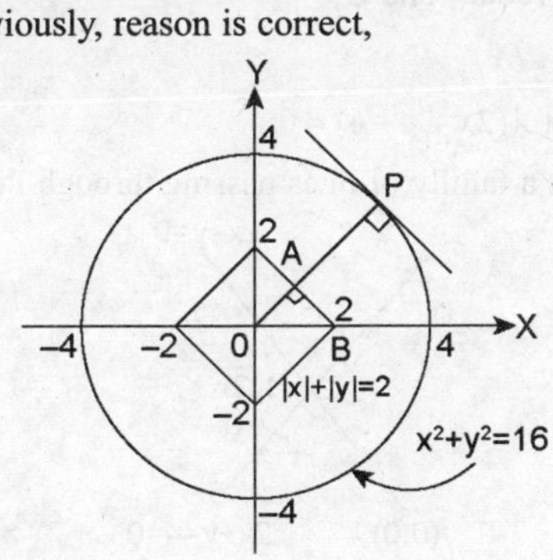

$\therefore$ AP = OP – OA $=4-\sqrt{2}$ and BC = Shortest distance between two curves $=2<\left(4-\sqrt{2}\right)$

$\because$ Circle is smooth curve but $|x|+|y|=2$ is not smooth through out

$\Rightarrow$ Assertion is incorrect

11. (a) Clearly assertions is true. Also reason explains the assertion, as if $x=a$ and $x=b$ are two consecutive maximas, then

$f'(x)<0$ for $x\in(a,a+\delta);\delta\to 0^+$ and $f'(x)>0$ for $x\in(b-\delta;b);\delta^1\to 0^+$ but $f(x)$ is a continuous function

$\Rightarrow$ $\exists\ c\in(a,b)$ such that $f'(x)<0$ for $x\in(c-\in,c),\in\Rightarrow 0^+$ and $f'(x)>0$ for $x\in(c,c+\in'),\in'\to 0^+$

$\Rightarrow$ $x=c$ is a point of minima and $a<c<b$. Thus option (*a*) is correct.

12. (b) $f(x)=\max.\{x^2-2x+2,|x-1|\}$

$=\max.\{(x-1)^2+1,|x-1|\}$

$=\max\{|x-1^2+1,|x-1|$ for $x\in[0,2),(x-1)\in[-1,1)$

$\Rightarrow$ $|x-1|\in(0,1]$

$\Rightarrow$ $|x-1|^2\in(0,1]$

$\Rightarrow$ $|x-1|^2+1\in(1,2]$

$\Rightarrow$ $|x-1|^2+1>|x-1|$ for $x\in[0,2)$ and for $x\in[2,3],|x-1|\in[1,2]$

$\Rightarrow$ $|x-1|^2\geq|x-1|\Rightarrow|x-1|^2+1>|x-1|$ for $x\in[2,3]$

Thus $|x-1|^2+1>|x-1|\ \forall x\in[0,3]$

$\therefore$ $f(x)=|x-1|^2+1$ for $x\in[0,3]$

$\Rightarrow$ $f(x)_{\max}=\max.\{(x-1)^2+1\};x\in[0,3]$

$=(3-1)^2+1=5=f(3)$

$\Rightarrow$ Assertion is correct

Also greatest value $=f(x)=\max.\{5,2\}=5$

$\Rightarrow$ Reason is correct, but does not explain the assertion

13. (a) $f(x)=x^3+ax^2+bx+c$

$f'(x)=3x^3+2ax+b.$

Disc. $=4a^2-12b=4(a^2-3b)<0$ if $a^2<3b$

$\Rightarrow$ $f'(x)>0\ \forall x\in\mathbb{R}$

$\Rightarrow$ $f(x)$ is strictly increasing $\forall x\in\mathbb{R}\Rightarrow f(x)$ has no extremum i.e., assertion is correct.

$\Rightarrow$ Reason is correct and correctly explains the assertion.

14. (a) $f(x)=(-x^2+4x+1)+\sin^{-1}x;\ x\in[-1,1]$

$f'(x)=(-2x+4)+\dfrac{1}{\sqrt{1-x^2}}$

For $x\in[-1,1],(-2x+4)\in[2,6]$

$\Rightarrow$ $f'(x)>0\ \forall x\in[-1,1]$

$\Rightarrow$ $f(x)$ is increasing on $[-1,1]$

$\Rightarrow$ Least value of

$f(x) = f(-1) = (-(1)-4+1) + \sin^{-1}(-1) = -4 - \dfrac{\pi}{2}$

$\Rightarrow$ Assertion is correct, also reason is correct and correctly explains the assertion

15. (b) $\because$ a, b, c, > 0

$\Rightarrow$ ab, bc, ca, > 0

$\therefore$ By A.M. $\geq$ G.M., $ab+bc+ca \geq 3.\sqrt[3]{(ab.bc.ca)}$

$\Rightarrow$ $ab+bc+ca \geq 3.\sqrt[3]{a^2b^2c^2}$

$\Rightarrow$ $ab+bc+ca \geq 3(abc)^{2/3}$

$\Rightarrow$ $12 \geq 3(abc)^{2/3}$

$\Rightarrow$ $(abc)^{2/3} \leq 4$

$\Rightarrow$ $(abc) \leq (4)^{3/2} = 8$

$\Rightarrow$ Greatest value of $(abc) = 8$ and will occur it

$ab = bc = ca = 4$

$\Rightarrow$ Assertion as well as reason both are correct, but reason does not correctly explains the assertion.

16. (c) $f(x) = x^2 + \dfrac{16}{x}$

$\Rightarrow$ $f'(x) = 2x - \dfrac{16}{x^2}$

$\Rightarrow$ $f'(x) = 0$

$\Rightarrow$ $2(x^3-8) = 0 \Rightarrow x = 2$ and $f'(x) < 0$ for $x < 2$ and $f'(x) > 0$ for $x > 2$

$\Rightarrow$ $f'(x)$ changes its sign through 2 from –ve to +ve.

$\Rightarrow$ $f'(x)$ has minimum value $= f(2) = 4+8 = 12$ at $x = 2$

$\Rightarrow$ Assertion is correct, but reason is incorrect.

SECTION–VI: PASSAGES

A: $f(x).f''(x) \leq 0 \;\; \forall\, x \in \mathbb{R}$

$\therefore$ $f(x) \leq 0 \Rightarrow f''(x) \geq 0$ and $f(x) \geq 0 \Rightarrow f''(x) \leq 0$ and $f'(x) = 0$

$\therefore$ Graph of $f'(x) = 0$ will be of the type.

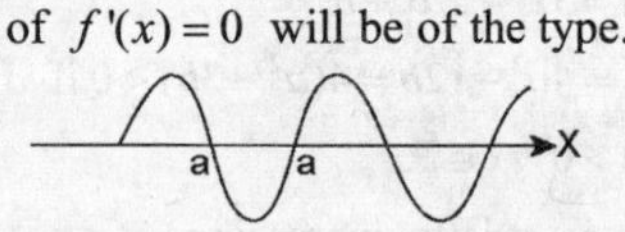

Clearly $f(x)$ changes its concavity on x-axis.

$\therefore$ $f(a) = 0 \Rightarrow$ $(a, 0)$ is a point where $f''(a) = 0$

Now $f(a+h).f''(a-h) = (-)(-) = +ve$ or $(+)(+) = +ve$

$\Rightarrow$ Option (*a*) is incorrect

$\Rightarrow$ $f(a+h).f''(a-h) > 0$

$\Rightarrow$ Option (*b*) is correct

Further $f'(a+h).f''(a-h)$

$= (-)(-) = +$ ve or $(+)(+) = +$ ve

$\Rightarrow$ Option (*c*) is incorrect

Next, $f(a+h).f''(a-h) = (+)(+) = +ve$ or $(-)(-) = +ve$

$\Rightarrow$ Option (*d*) is incorrect

1. (b)

2. (b) Clearly $f''(\gamma) < 0$ or $f''(\gamma) > 0$ for $\gamma \in (\alpha, \beta)$.

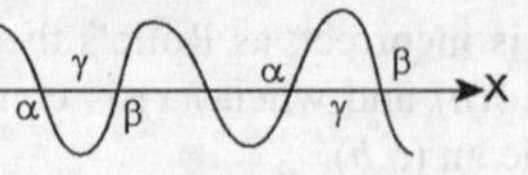

However $f''(\alpha) = 0$ and $f''(\beta) = 0$ i.e., α , β are two consecutive roots of $f''(x) = 0$, hence by Rolle's theorem

$\exists\, \gamma \in (\alpha, \beta)$

such that $f'''(\lambda) = 0$

3. (b) If $f'(x) \neq 0$ i.e., curve takes no turn and $f(x)$ is differentiable and hence is continuous

$\Rightarrow$ $f'(x) > 0\ \forall x \in \mathbb{R}$ or $f'(x) < 0\ \forall x \in \mathbb{R}$

Also $f(x).f''(x) < 0$

$\Rightarrow$ $y = f(x)$ has at most one real root

B: $f(x)$ is differentiable wherever continuous and $f'(C_1) = f'(C_2) = 0$, $f'(C_1).f''(C_2) < 0$, $f(C_1) = 5$, $f(C_2) = 0$ and $C_1 < C_2$

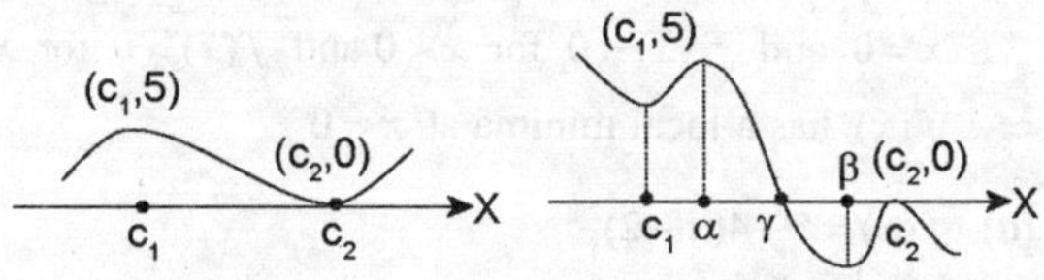

Fig (i) Fig(ii)

4. (c) In figure (*i*), $f''(C_1) - f''(C_2) < 0$; where as figure (*ii*), $f''(C_1) - f''(C_2) > 0$

$\Rightarrow$ $f'(x) = 0$ has at least 4 roots in $[C_1 - 1, C_2 + 1]$ C_1, C_2, α, β

5. (b) In figure (*i*), $f''(C_1) - f''(C_2) < 0$

$\Rightarrow$ $f'(x) = 0$ has at least 2 roots C_1, C_2 in $[C_1 - 1, C_2 + 1]$

6. (a) In figure (*ii*), $f''(C_1) - f''(C_2) > 0$, then $f(x) = 0$ has at least 2 roots γ and C_2

C: $y = 2\sqrt{x} + bx$ ...(*i*)

$(2x - y) + \lambda(2x + y - 4) = 0$ ...(*ii*)

i.e., (2) is a family of lines passing through P(1, 2)

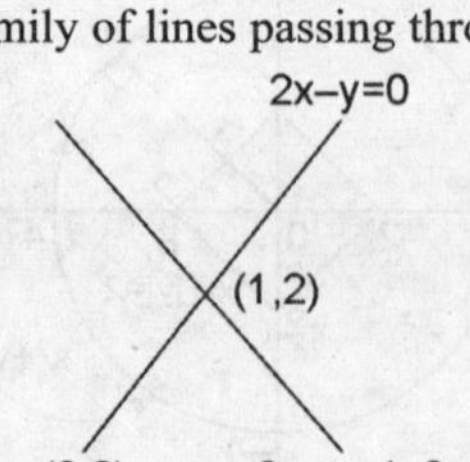

$\Rightarrow$ $y = 2\sqrt{x} + bx$

$\Rightarrow$ $\dfrac{dy}{dx} = \dfrac{1}{\sqrt{x}} + b$

7. **(b)** Slope of curve at (9, 0) is 1/6

$\Rightarrow \frac{1}{3}+b=\frac{1}{6}\Rightarrow b=\frac{-1}{6}$

$\Rightarrow y=2\sqrt{x}-\frac{1}{6}x$

Now equation of line through (1, 2) is $(y-2)=m(x-1)$

or $y=mx+(2-m)$

Now it is tangent to curve $y=2\sqrt{x}+\left(\frac{-1}{6}\right)x$

$\Rightarrow mx+(2-m)=2\sqrt{x}-\frac{1}{6}x$ or

$6mx+(2-m)(6)=12\sqrt{x}-x$ or

$(6m+1)x-12\sqrt{x}+6(2-m)=0$ has equal roots, Disc. $=0$

$\Rightarrow 144-24(6m+1)(2-m)=0$

$\Rightarrow 6-(6m+1)(2-m)=0$

$\Rightarrow 6-[12m-6m^2+2-m]=0$

$\Rightarrow 6m^2-11m+4=0$

$\Rightarrow 6m^2-8m-3m+4=0$

$\Rightarrow 2m(3m-4)-1(3m-4)=0$

$\Rightarrow (2m-1)(3m-4)=0$

$\Rightarrow m=\frac{1}{2}$ or $m=\frac{4}{3}$, but roots should be +ve

$\Rightarrow \frac{12}{6m+1}>0, \frac{6(2-m)}{6m+1}>0\Rightarrow m=\frac{1}{2}$ or $\frac{4}{3}$

$\Rightarrow$ Required equation will be

$(y-2)=\frac{1}{2}(x-1)$ or $(y-2)=\frac{4}{3}(x-1)$

$\Rightarrow x-2y+3=0$ or $4x-3y+2=0$

8. **(b)** Let the equation of line be $(y-2)=m(x-1)$ .....(*i*)

Or $mx-y=m-2$ or $\frac{m}{m-2}x-\frac{y}{m-2}=1$ or

$\frac{x}{\left(\frac{m-2}{m}\right)}+\frac{y}{(2-m)}=1$

Area of Δ formed by line (*i*) with coordinate axes

$A=\frac{1}{2}\left(\frac{m-2}{m}\right)(2-m)$

$\Rightarrow A=\frac{-(m-2)^2}{2m}$

$\Rightarrow \frac{dA}{dm}=-\frac{1}{2}\left[\frac{2m(m-2)-(m-2)^2}{m^2}.1\right]$

$\Rightarrow \frac{dA}{dm}=0\Rightarrow (m-2)(2m-m+2)=0$

$\Rightarrow m=2$ or $m=-2$, but for forming Δ with +ve co-ordinate axis, $m<0\Rightarrow m=-2$

$\therefore$ required line is $(y-2)=-2(x-1)$ or $2x+y-4=0$

$\Rightarrow \frac{x}{2}+\frac{y}{4}=1$

Least length $=\sqrt{4+16}=\sqrt{20}$

9. **(b)** Given parabola is $(y-2)^2=4x$ .....(*i*), having its vertex at (0, 2) and focus at S(1, 2) and the two chards pass through (1, 2) i.e., chords are focal chords and perpendicular to each other.

Let the origin be shifted at (0, 2), hence (*i*) becomes $Y^2=4aX;\ a=1$,

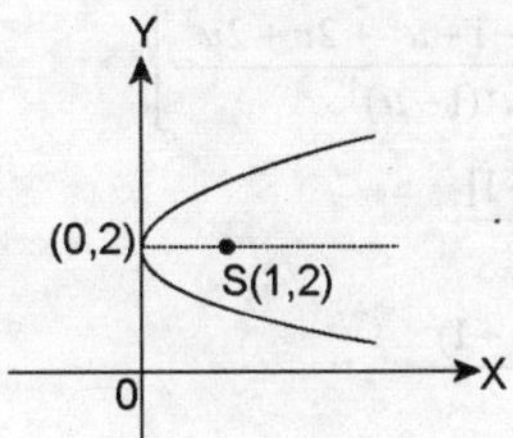

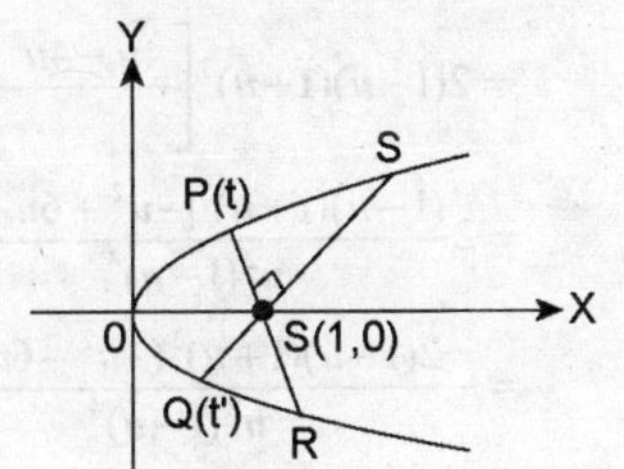

Equation of focal chard at P(*t*) is $y=\frac{2t}{t^2-1}(x-a);\ a=1$ and that at Q (t') is $y=\frac{2t'}{t'^2-1}(x-a);\ a=1$ and length focal chard at

P (*t*) is given by PR $=a\left(t+\frac{1}{t}\right)^2=\left(t+\frac{1}{t}\right)^2$ and at Q (t') is given by QS $=a\left(t'+\frac{1}{t'}\right)^2=\left(t'+\frac{1}{t'}\right)^2$

$\therefore$ Area of Quadrilateral PQRS $-(PR\times QS)$

$\Rightarrow \Delta=\frac{1}{2}\left(t+\frac{1}{t}\right)^2\left(t'+\frac{1}{t'}\right)^2$ .....(*i*) ; where (*Slope* of PR) $\times$ (*Slope* of QS) $=-1$

$\Rightarrow \left(\frac{2t}{t^2-1}\right).\left(\frac{2t'}{t'^2-1}\right)=-1$

$\Rightarrow \frac{t'^2-1}{t'}=\frac{-4t}{t^2-1}$

$\Rightarrow \left(t'-\frac{1}{t'}\right)^2=\frac{-4t}{t^2-1}$

$\Rightarrow \left(t'+\frac{1}{t'}\right)^2=\left(t'-\frac{1}{t'}\right)^2+4=\left(\frac{-4t}{t^2-1}\right)^2+4$

$\Rightarrow \left(t'+\frac{1}{t'}\right)^2=\frac{16t^2+4(t^4-2t^2+1)}{(t^2-1)^2}$ .....(2)

Using (2) in (1), we get $\Delta=\frac{1}{2}\left(t+\frac{1}{t}\right)^2\left[\frac{4t^4+8t^2+4}{(t^2-1)^2}\right]$

$\Rightarrow \Delta=\frac{4}{2}\left(\frac{(t^2+1)^2}{t^2}\right)\left(\frac{(t^2+1)^2}{(t^2-1)^2}\right)$

$\Rightarrow \Delta=2\left[\frac{(t^2+1)^4}{t^2(t^2-1)^2}\right]\to\infty$ as $t\to\infty$ Put $t^2=u\geq 0$

$\Rightarrow\ \Delta = \dfrac{2(1+u)^4}{4(1-u)^2};\ u \ge 0$

$\Rightarrow\ \dfrac{d\Delta}{du} = 2\left[\dfrac{u(1-u)^2.4(1+u)^3 - (1+u)^4(1-u)^2 + u.2(1-u)(1+u)^4}{u^2(1-u)^4}\right]$

$= \dfrac{2(1-u)(1+u)^3}{u^2(1-u)^4}\left[\dfrac{4u(1-u)-(1-u^2)+2u(1+u)}{u^2(1-u)^4}\right]$

$= 2(1-u)(1+u)^3\left[\dfrac{4u-4u^2-1+u^2+2u+2u^2}{u^2(1-u)^4}\right]$

$= 2\dfrac{(1-u)(1+u)^3[-u^2+6u-1]}{u^2(1-u)^4}$

$= -\dfrac{2(1-u)(1+u)^3(-u^2-6u+1)}{u^2(1-u)^4}$

$= \dfrac{-2(1+u)^3(u^2-6u+1}{u^2(1-u)^3} = 0$ for $u = -1$ or $\dfrac{6 \pm \sqrt{36-4}}{2}$

But $u \ge 0$

$\Rightarrow\ u = 3 \pm 2\sqrt{2}$

Now $\Delta\left((u = 3+2\sqrt{2}\right) = \dfrac{2\left(u+2\sqrt{2}\right)^4}{\left(3+2\sqrt{2}\right)\left(2+2\sqrt{2}\right)^2}$

$= \dfrac{2\left(2\sqrt{2}\right)^4\left(1+\sqrt{2}\right)^4}{\left(\sqrt{2}+1\right)^2(2)^2\left(1+\sqrt{2}\right)^2}$

$= \dfrac{128}{4}\dfrac{\left(1+\sqrt{2}\right)^4}{\left(1+\sqrt{2}\right)^4} = 32$

And $\Delta\left(u = 3-2\sqrt{2}\right) = \dfrac{2\left[4-2\sqrt{2}\right]^4}{\left(3-2\sqrt{2}\right)\left(2-2\sqrt{2}\right)^2}$

$= \dfrac{2\left(2\sqrt{2}\right)^4\left(\sqrt{2}-1\right)^4}{\left(\sqrt{2}-1\right)^2(2)^2\left(\sqrt{2}-1\right)^2} = 32$

$\therefore$ Minimum value of Δ = 32 squares

D:

10. (b) At the point of intersection of $y = x$ and $y = ke^x, k \le 0$

$ke^x - x = 0;\ k \le 0$

Let $f(x) = ke^x - x;\ k \le 0$

$f'(x) = ke^x - 1;\ k \le 0$

$\Rightarrow\ f'(x) < 0\ \ \forall x \in \mathbb{R}$

$\Rightarrow\ f(x)$ is a decreasing function

$\Rightarrow\ f(x) = 0$ has a unique solution

11. (a) $f(x) = ke^x - x;\ k > 0$

$f'(x) = ke^x - 1$

$f''(x) = ke^x > 0\ \forall\ x \in \mathbb{R}$

$\Rightarrow\ y = f(x)$ is concave upwards

$\therefore$ For unique roots of $f(x) = 0$, $f(x_0) = f'(x_0) = 0$ for some $x_0 \in \mathbb{R}$

$\Rightarrow\ ke^{x_0} = 1$ and $ke^{x_0} - 1 = 0$

$\Rightarrow\ ke^{x_0} = 1\ \Rightarrow\ k = \dfrac{1}{e}$

12. (a) $f(x) = ke^x - x;\ k > o$

$\Rightarrow\ f'(x) = ke^x - 1$

$\Rightarrow\ f''(x) = ke^x > 0\ \forall x \in \mathbb{R}$

$\Rightarrow\ y = f(x)$ is concave upwards $\forall x \in \mathbb{R}$ for two roots of $f(x) = 0$, $\exists\ x_0 \in \mathbb{R}$ such that $f'(x_0) = 0$ and $f(x_0) < 0$

$\Rightarrow\ ke^{x_0} - 1 = 0$ and $ke^{x_0} - x_0 < 0$

$\Rightarrow\ e^{x_0} = \dfrac{1}{k}$ and $1 - x_0 < 0$

$\Rightarrow\ e^{x_0} = \dfrac{1}{k}$ and $x_0 > 1$

$\Rightarrow\ e^{x_0} > e^1\ \Rightarrow\ \dfrac{1}{k} > e\ \Rightarrow\ k < \dfrac{1}{e}$

Also $k > 0\ \Rightarrow\ k \in (0, 1/e)$

E: From the given information, we conclude following.

(i) $f(x)$ is a continuous function on $\mathbb{R}$

(ii) $f''(x) < 0\ \forall x \in \mathbb{R} - \{2\}$

$\Rightarrow\ f(x)$ has its concavity downwards

(iii) $f''(2)$ is not defined

(iv) $f(x)$ is increasing on $(-\infty, -5)$, decreasing on $(-5, 2)$, increasing on $(2, 4)$, decreasing on $(4, \infty)$

(v) $x = -5$ is a point of local maxima, $x = 2$ is a point local minima and sharp turning point, $x = 4$ is a point of local maxima. The graph of $y = f(x)$ will be as shown below.

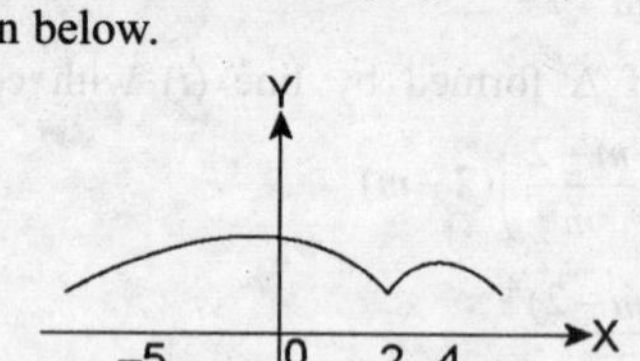

13. (d) Clearly $y = f(x)$ has a sharp corner at $x = 2$

14. (c) Clearly $f''(x) < 0\ \forall x \in \mathbb{R} - \{2\}$

$\Rightarrow$ Curve is always concave downwards

15. (c) Clearly graph of $y = f(x)$ can be of the shape as represented by option (c)

F:

16. (a), (c) $f(x)=\sqrt{\left(1-x^2\right)\left(1+2x^2\right)}$

$$\Rightarrow\ f'(x)=\frac{1}{2\sqrt{\left(1-x^2\right)\left(1+2x^2\right)}}$$

$$\times\left[\left(1-x^2\right)(4x)+\left(1+2x^2\right)(-2x)\right]=0$$

$\Rightarrow\ (2x)\left[2-2x^2-1-2x^2\right]=0$

$\Rightarrow\ x=0$ or $4x^2=1$

$\Rightarrow\ x=0$ or $x=\pm-$

$\therefore\ x=0,\pm\frac{1}{2},\pm1,$ are critical point.

$\Rightarrow\ f(0)=1, f\left(\pm\frac{1}{2}\right)=\sqrt{\left(\frac{3}{4}\right)\left(\frac{3}{2}\right)}=\frac{3}{2\sqrt{2}},$

$\Rightarrow\ f(\pm1)=0$

$\Rightarrow\ f(x)$ has maximum value $=\frac{3}{2\sqrt{2}}$ at $x=\pm\frac{1}{2}$

17. (c) $f(x)=a_n=\frac{n^2}{n^3+200};\ n\in\mathbb{N}$

$$\Rightarrow\ f'(x)=\frac{\left(n^3+200\right)(2n)-n^2\left(3n^2\right)}{\left(n^3+200\right)^2}$$

$$\Rightarrow\ f'(x)=\frac{2n^4+400n-3n^4}{\left(n^3+200\right)^2}$$

$$\Rightarrow\ f'(x)=\frac{n\left(400-n^3\right)}{\left(n^3+200\right)^2}=0$$

$\Rightarrow\ n=(400)^{1/3}\in(7,8)$

$\Rightarrow\ f'(x)>0$ for $n<[400]^{1/3}$ and $f'(x)<0$ for $n>(400)^{1/3}$

$\Rightarrow\ f(n)_{\max}=\max.\{f(7),f(8)\}=\max\left\{\frac{49}{543},\frac{64}{712}\right\}=\frac{49}{543}$

18. (b) $f(x)=ax+\frac{b}{x};\ a,\ b,\ x>0$

$\Rightarrow\ f'(x)=a-\frac{b}{x^2}=0\ \Rightarrow\ x^2=\frac{b}{a}\ \Rightarrow\ x=\sqrt{\frac{b}{a}}$

$\Rightarrow\ f'(x)<0\ \Rightarrow\ a<\frac{b}{x^2}\ \Rightarrow x^2<\frac{b}{a}$

$\Rightarrow\ x\in\left[0,\sqrt{\frac{b}{a}}\right)$ and $f'(x)>0\ \Rightarrow\ x\in\left(\sqrt{\frac{b}{a}},\infty\right)$

$\Rightarrow\ f(x)$ has its least value at $x=\sqrt{\frac{b}{a}}$

19. (b) $f(x)=\tan^{-1}x-\frac{1}{2}\ln x;\ x\in\left[\frac{1}{\sqrt{3}},\sqrt{3}\right]$

$$f'(x)=\frac{1}{1+x^2}-\frac{1}{2x}=0$$

$$\Rightarrow\ \frac{2x-1-x^2}{2x(1+x^2)}=0$$

$\Rightarrow\ x^2+1-2x=0$

$\Rightarrow\ (x-1)^2=0\ \Rightarrow\ x=1$ and

$f'(x)=-(x-1)^2\le 0\ \forall x\in\left[\frac{1}{\sqrt{3}},\sqrt{3}\right]$

$\Rightarrow\ f(x)$ is a decreasing function

$\Rightarrow$ Least value of $f(x)$ in $\left[\frac{1}{\sqrt{3}},\sqrt{3}\right]$ will be $=f\left(\sqrt{3}\right)$

$=\tan^{-1}\sqrt{3}-\frac{1}{2}\ln\sqrt{3}=\frac{\pi}{3}-\frac{1}{4}\ln 3$

G: $f(x)=\max.\{x^2,(1-x)^2,2x(1-x)\};\ 0\le x\le 1$

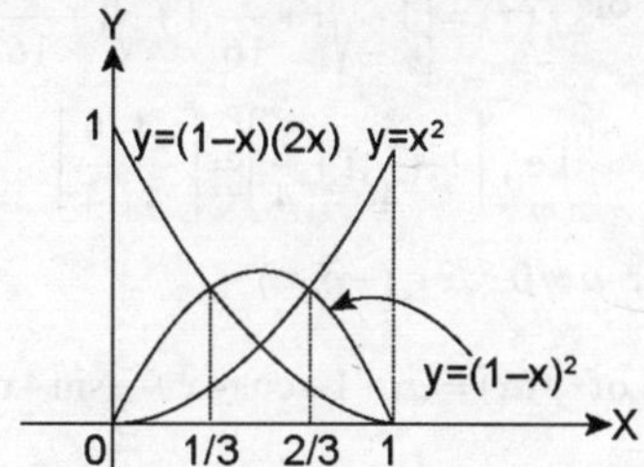

$$\Rightarrow\ f(x)=\begin{cases}(1-x)^2 & \text{for } 0\le x\le\frac{1}{3}\\ 2x(1-x) & \text{for } \frac{1}{3}\le x\le\frac{2}{3}\\ x^2 & \text{for } \frac{2}{3}\le x\le 1\end{cases}$$

20. (d) $f(x)$ increases in $\left(\frac{1}{3},\frac{1}{2}\right)$ and $\left(\frac{2}{3},1\right)$

21. (c) $f(x)$ decreases in $\left(0,\frac{1}{3}\right)$ and $\left(\frac{1}{2},\frac{2}{3}\right)$

22. (d) Rolle's theorem is applicable on $\left[\frac{1}{3}+h,\frac{2}{3}-h\right];\ h\in\left[0,\frac{1}{6}\right)$

$\Rightarrow\ a=\frac{1}{3}+h,\ b=\frac{2}{3}-h$ and $f'(x)\left(\frac{1}{2}\right)=0\ \Rightarrow\ c=\frac{1}{2}$

$\therefore\ a+b+c=\left(\frac{1}{3}+h\right)+\left(\frac{2}{3}-h\right)+\frac{1}{2}=\frac{3}{2}$

H: $f:\mathbb{R}\to\mathbb{R};\ f(x)=2\sin^2 2x+\frac{3}{4}\sin 4x+ax$

$\Rightarrow\ f'(x)=8\sin 2x\ \cos 2x+\frac{3}{4}(4)\cos 4x+a$

$\Rightarrow\ f'(x)=4\sin 4x+3\cos 4x+a$

$\Rightarrow\ f'(x)\in[a-5,\ a+5]$

23. (c) $f(x)$ strictly increasing $\forall x\in\mathbb{R}$

$\Rightarrow\ f'(x)\ge 0\ \ \forall x\in\mathbb{R}$

$\Rightarrow\ a-5\geq 0$

$\Rightarrow\ a\in[5,\infty)$

24. (a) $f(x)$ is strictly decreasing $\forall x\in\mathbb{R}$

$\Rightarrow\ f'(x)\leq 0\ \forall x\in\mathbb{R}$

$\Rightarrow\ a+5\leq 0\ \forall x\in\mathbb{R}$

$\Rightarrow\ a\leq -5\ \forall x\in\mathbb{R}$

$\Rightarrow\ a\in(-\infty,-5]$

25. (a) Clearly for $a=0, f(x)=2\sin^2 2x+\frac{3}{4}\sin 4x$

$=1-\cos 4x+\frac{3}{4}\sin 4x$

$\Rightarrow$ Range of $f(x)=\left[1-\sqrt{1+\frac{9}{16}},1+\sqrt{1+\frac{9}{16}}\right]$

i.e., $\left[1-\frac{5}{4},1+\frac{5}{4}\right]=\left[\frac{-1}{4},\frac{9}{4}\right]$

and for $a\neq 0$, $ax\in(-\infty,\infty)$

$\Rightarrow$ Range of $f(x)=ax+1-\cos 4x+\frac{3}{4}\sin 4x$ is $(-\infty,\infty)$

$\Rightarrow\ f(x)$ is onto for $a\in(-\infty,\infty)-\{0\}$

I: $f(x,y)=\tan^4 x+\tan^4 y+3\cot^2 x\ \cot^2 y$ and $g(x,y)=3+\sin^2(x+y)$.

26. (c) $f(x,y)=\tan^4 x+\tan^4 y+3\cot^2 x\ \cot^2 y$

$=\tan^4 x+\tan^4 y+\frac{3}{2}\cot^2 x\ \cot^2 y+\frac{3}{2}\cot^2 x.\ \cot^2 y$

$\therefore$ By A.M. $\geq$ G.M. of non-negative real numbers.

$\Rightarrow\ f(x,y)\geq 4\sqrt[4]{\frac{9}{4}}$

$\Rightarrow\ f(x,y)\geq 4\sqrt{\frac{3}{2}}=4\frac{\sqrt{3}}{\sqrt{2}}=2\sqrt{2}\sqrt{3}$

$\Rightarrow\ f(x,y)\geq 2\sqrt{6}$ and it occurs when each of

$\tan^4 x=\tan^4 y=\frac{3}{2}\cot^2 x\ \cot^2 y=\sqrt{\frac{3}{2}}$

$\Rightarrow\ \tan^2 x=\left(\frac{3}{2}\right)^{1/4}=\tan^2 y$

and $\cot^2 x=\left(\frac{2}{3}\right)^{1/4}, \cot^2 y=\left(\frac{2}{3}\right)^{1/4}$

27. (b) $\because\ \sin^2(x+y)\in[0,1]$

$\Rightarrow\ 3+\sin^2(x+y)\in[3,4]$

$\Rightarrow\ g(x,y)\in[3,4]$

$\Rightarrow$ Range of $g(x,y)=[3,4]$

28. (a) $f(x,y)=g(x,y)$

$\because$ Range of $f(x,y)=\left[2\sqrt{6},\infty\right)$ and range of $g(x,y)=[3,4]$ and $2\sqrt{6}>4$

$\Rightarrow\ [3,4]\cap\left[2\sqrt{6},\infty\right)=\phi$

$\Rightarrow\ f(x,y)=g(x,y)$ has no solution

SECTION–VII: (COLUMN – MATCHING)

1. (i) → (b); (ii) → (a); (iii) → (d); (iv) → (c)

(i) Let $f(x)=(x+1)^5-2(x^5+1)$

$\Rightarrow\ f'(x)=5(x+1)^4-2(5x^4)=5\left[(x+1)^4-2x^4\right]$

$f'(x)=0$

$\Rightarrow\ \left(\frac{x+1}{x}\right)^4=2$

$\Rightarrow\ 1+\frac{1}{x}=\pm(2)^{1/4}$

$\Rightarrow\ \frac{1}{x}=-1\pm\sqrt[4]{2}$

$\Rightarrow\ x=\frac{1}{\left(-1\pm\sqrt[4]{2}\right)}$ i.e., $\frac{1}{-1-(2)^{1/4}}$ and $\frac{1}{-1+(2)^{1/4}}=\alpha,\beta$

(Say)

And $f(-\infty)=\lim\limits_{x\to-\infty}(x+1)^5-2(x^5+1)$

$=\lim\limits_{x\to-\infty}x^5\left[\left(1+\frac{1}{x}\right)^5-2\left(1+\frac{1}{x^5}\right)\right]=\lim\limits_{x\to-\infty}x^5[1-2]=\infty$

$\Rightarrow\ f(\infty)=-\infty;\ f(0)=-1, f(-1)=0$

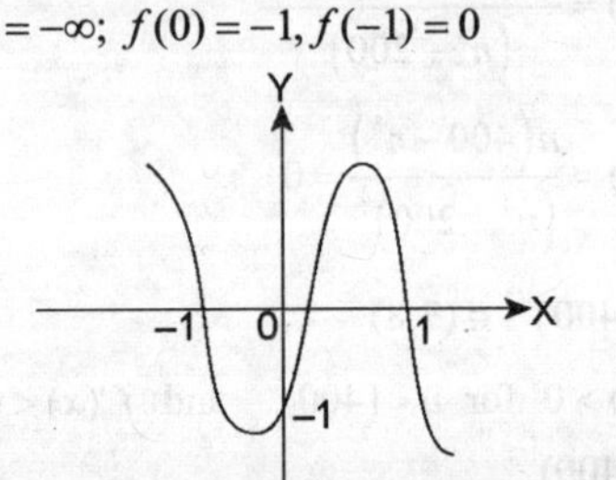

$\because\ f'(x)=0$ has two real roots & $f(x)$ is a polynomial of 5th degree and $f'(\alpha)=f'(\beta)=0$ but $f'(\alpha)\neq 0, f(\beta)\neq 0$

$\Rightarrow\ f(x)=0$ has exactly 3 distinct real roots.

$\therefore$ **(i) → (b)**

(ii) $f(x)=\frac{(x+1)^4}{x^4-x^3+x^2-x+1}=\frac{(x+1)^4}{\left(\frac{1-(-x)^5}{1-(-x)}\right)}=\frac{(x+1)^5}{(1+x^5)}$

$\Rightarrow\ f'(x)=\frac{(x^5+1)5(x+1)^4-(x+1)^5(5x^4)}{(x^5+1)^2}$

$=\frac{5(x+1)^4[x^5+1-x^4(x+1)]}{(x^5+1)^2}=\frac{5(x+1)^4[1-x^4]}{(x^5+1)^2}$

$=\frac{5(x+1)^4(1-x)(1+x)(1+x^2)}{(1+x^5)^2}$

$\Rightarrow f'(x)=0$ at $x=-1,1$

Also $f(x)=0$ at $x=-1$ and $f(x)\ge 0$

$f'(x)<0$ for $x\in(-\infty,-1)\cup(1,\infty)$ and $f'(x)>0$ for $x\in(-1,1)$

$\therefore f_{max}$ (absolute) $=\max\{f(-\infty), f(1), f(\infty)\}$

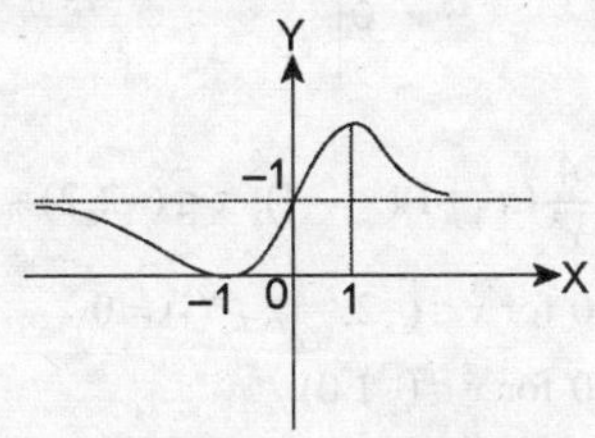

But $f(-\infty)=f(\infty)=1$ and $f(1)=16$

$\Rightarrow$ $f_{max}(absolute) = 16$ $\therefore$ **(ii) → (a)**

(iii) $f(x)=ab\,\sin x+\sqrt{1-a^2}\,\cos x+c;\ |a|<1,$

$f(x)\in\left[c-\sqrt{a^2b^2+(1-a^2)},c+\sqrt{a^2b^2+(1-a^2)}\right]$

$\Rightarrow (f_{\max}-f_{\min})=2\sqrt{a^2b^2+(1-a^2)}=2\sqrt{^2(b^2-1)+1}$

Now $a^2(b^2-1)+1\le -\dfrac{\left[(0)^2-4(b^2-1)(1)\right]}{4(b^2-1)}$

$\left(\because ax^2+bx+c\le\dfrac{-D}{4a}\text{for } a<0\right]$

$\Rightarrow a^2(b^2-1)+1\le 1$ at $a=0$

$\Rightarrow (f_{\max}-f_{\min})\le 2$ $\therefore$ **(iii) → (d)**

(iv) $u^2=(4+1)+2\sqrt{4\cos^4\theta+4\sin^4\theta+17\sin^2\theta\cos^2\theta}$

$\Rightarrow u^2=5+2\sqrt{4(\sin^2\theta+\cos^2\theta)^2+9\sin^2\theta\cos^2\theta}$

$\Rightarrow u^2=5+2\sqrt{4+\dfrac{9}{4}\sin^2 2\theta}$

$\Rightarrow {u^2}_{\min}=5+2(2)=9$ and ${u^2}_{\max}$

$=5+2\sqrt{4+\dfrac{9}{4}}=5+2\left(\dfrac{5}{2}\right)=10$

$\Rightarrow \left(u^2_{\max}-u^2_{\min}\right)=(10-9)=1$ $\therefore$ **(iv) → (c)**

2. (i) → (b); (ii) → (d); (iii) → (a); (iv) → (c)

(i) f is differentiable in [0,5]; $f(0)=4, f(5)=-1$

$\Rightarrow g(x)=\dfrac{f(x)}{x+1},\ g(0)=\dfrac{f(0)}{0+1}=\dfrac{4}{1}=4,\ g(5)=\dfrac{f(5)}{5+1}=\dfrac{-1}{6}$

$\therefore$ By L.M.V.T, $\dfrac{g(5)-g(0)}{5-0}=g'(c)$ for some $c\in(0,5)$

$\Rightarrow g'(c)=\dfrac{\frac{-1}{6}-4}{5-0}=\dfrac{-25}{6\times 5}=\dfrac{-5}{6}$

$\therefore$ **(i) → (b)**

(ii) $f(x)$ and $g(x)$ are differentiable for $0\le x\le 1$, $f(0)=2,\ g(0)=0,\ f(1)=6.$

$\because f'(c)-2g'(c)=0$ for some $c\in(0,1)$

$\Rightarrow f(0)-2g(0)=f(1)-2g(1)$

$\Rightarrow 2-2(0)=6-2g(1)$

$\Rightarrow 2g(1)=4$

$\Rightarrow g(1)=2$ $\therefore$ **(ii) → (d)**

(iii) By L.M.V.T, on [1, 6], $\dfrac{f(6)-f(1)}{6-1}=f'(c)$ for at least one $c\in(1, 6)$ but $f'(x)\ge 2\,\forall x\in[1,6]$

$\Rightarrow f'(c)\ge 2$

$\Rightarrow \dfrac{f(6)-(-2)}{5}\ge 2$

$\Rightarrow f(6)\ge 8$

$\Rightarrow$ Least possible value of $f(6)=8$

$\therefore$ **(iii) → (a)**

(iv) $f(x)=\sqrt{25-x^2};\ c\in(1,5)$

By L.M.V.T. $f'(c)=\dfrac{f(5)-f(1)}{5-1}$

$\Rightarrow \left|\dfrac{1(-x)}{\sqrt{25-x^2}}\right|_{x-c}=\dfrac{0-\sqrt{24}}{4}$

$\Rightarrow \dfrac{-c}{\sqrt{25-c^2}}=\dfrac{-\sqrt{6}}{2}$

$\Rightarrow 2c=\sqrt{6}\,\sqrt{25-c^2}$

$\Rightarrow 4c^2=6\,(25-c^2)$

$\Rightarrow 10c^2=150$

$\Rightarrow$ 15 $\therefore$ **(iv) → (c)**

3. (i) → (a), (b), (c); (ii) → (a), (d); (iii) → (c), (d); (iv) → (a), (b)

(i) $f(x)=x|x|=\begin{cases}-x^2 & \text{for } x<0\\ x^2 & \text{for } x\ge 2\end{cases}$

$\Rightarrow f'(x)=\begin{cases}-2x & \text{for } x<0\\ 2x & \text{for } x>0\end{cases}$

$\Rightarrow \lim\limits_{x\to 0^-}f'(x)=0=\lim\limits_{x\to 0^+}f'(x)$ and $f(0^-)=f(0^+)$

Also $f'(x)\ \ge 0$ for $\forall x\in\mathbb{R}$

$\Rightarrow f(x)$ is continuous, differentiable Strictly increasing on $\mathbb{R}$ $\therefore$ **(i) → (a), (b), (c).**

(ii) $f(x)=\sqrt{|x|}=\begin{cases}\sqrt{x} & \text{for } x\ge 0\\ \sqrt{-x} & \text{for } x<0\end{cases}$

$\Rightarrow f(0^-)=0, f(0^+)=0=f(0)$

$\Rightarrow f(x)$ is continuous on $\mathbb{R}$, $f'(x)=\begin{cases}\dfrac{-1}{2\sqrt{-x}} & \text{for } x<0\\ \dfrac{1}{2\sqrt{x}} & \text{for } x>0\end{cases}$

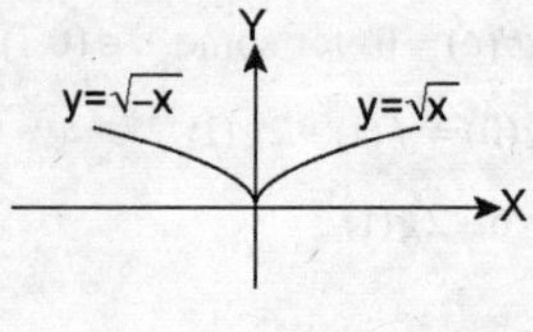

Clearly $f'(0^-)=-\infty$ and $f(0^+)=\infty$

$\Rightarrow$ $f(x)$ is non-differentiable at $x=0$ and hence and $f'(x)>0$

Also $f'(x)<0$ for $x<0$ and $f'(x)>0$

$\therefore$ **(ii) → (a), (d)**

(iii) $f(x)=x+[x]$

$f(x)$ is continuous in (–1, 1) except possibly at $x=0$.

Now, $\lim\limits_{x\to0^-} f(x)=\lim\limits_{x\to0^-} x+[x]=0-1=-1$ and

$\lim\limits_{x\to0^+} f(x)=\lim\limits_{x\to0^+} x+[x]=0+0=0$

$\Rightarrow$ $f(x)$ is discontinuous in $(-1,1)$ and hence $f(x)$ is non-differentiable in $(-1,1)$

Now $f(x)=\begin{cases} x-1 & \text{for } x\in(-1,0) \\ x & \text{for } x\in(0,1) \end{cases}$

$\Rightarrow$ $f'(x)=1>0$ for $x\in(-1,0)\cup(0,1)$ and $f(0^-)=-1$ and $f(0)=0, f(0^+)=0$

$\Rightarrow$ $f(0^-)<f(0)=f(0^+)$

$\Rightarrow$ $f(x)$ is Strictly increasing in $(-1,1)$

$\therefore$ **(iii) → (c), (d)**

(iv) $f(x)=|x-1|+|x+1|=\begin{cases} -x+1-x-1 & \text{for } x<-1 \\ -x+1+x+1 & \text{for } x\in(-1,1) \\ x-1+x+1 & \text{for } x>1 \end{cases}$

$=\begin{cases} -2x & \text{for } x<-1 \\ 2 & \text{for } -1<x<1 \\ 2x & \text{for } x>1 \end{cases}$

$\therefore$ For $x\in(-1,1)$, $f(x)=2$

$\Rightarrow$ $f(x)$ is continuous and derivable on $(-1,1)$

$\therefore$ **(iv) → (a), (b)**

4. (i) → (c), (d); (ii) → (b); (iii) → (a)

(i) $f(x)=\begin{cases} 2x^2+\dfrac{2}{x^2};\ x\in[-2,2]-\{0\} \\ 1\ ;\ x=0 \end{cases}$

$\Rightarrow$ $f'(x)=\left\{4\left(x-\dfrac{1}{x^3}\right);\ x\in(-2,2)-\{0\}\right.$

$\Rightarrow$ $f'(x)=\left\{4\left(\dfrac{x^4-1}{x^3}\right);\ x\in(-2,2)-\{0\}\right.$

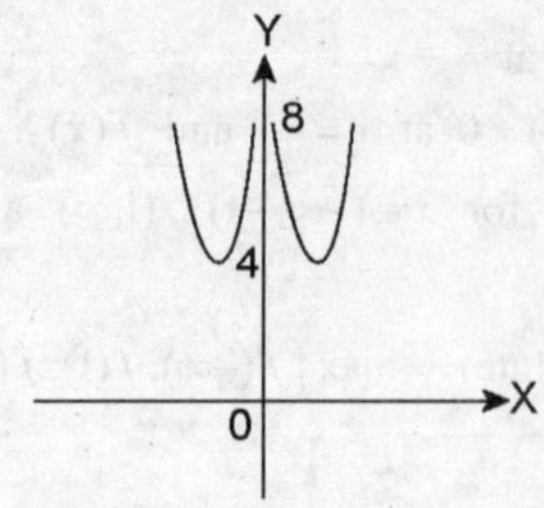

$\Rightarrow$ $f'(x)=\dfrac{4}{x^3}(x^2+1)(x^2-1);\ x\in(-2,2)-\{0\}$

$\Rightarrow$ $f'(x)<0$ for $x\in(-2,-1), f'(1)=0$

$\Rightarrow$ $f'(x)>0$ for $x\in(-1,0)$

$\Rightarrow$ $f'(x)<0$ for $x\in(0,1)$,

$\Rightarrow$ $f'(1)=0$ and $f'(x)>0$ for $x>1$

Now in [1, 2]

$\Rightarrow$ L $=f(1)=2+\dfrac{2}{1}=4$

$\Rightarrow$ G $=f(2)=8+\dfrac{2}{4}=8.5$

$\Rightarrow$ G – L $=(8.5-4)=4.5$

$\Rightarrow$ $(G-L)=5$, where [ ] is greater integer function.

$\therefore$ **(i) → (c)**

(ii) $f(x)=x^3-6x^2+9x+1$

$\Rightarrow$ $f'(x)=3x^2-12x+9=3(x^2-4x+3)=3(x-1)(x-3)$

$\Rightarrow$ $f'(x)<0$ for $x\in(1,3)$, and $f'(x)>0$ for $x\in(-\infty,1)$ and $(3,\infty)$ and $f'(x)=0$ at $x=1$ and $x=3$

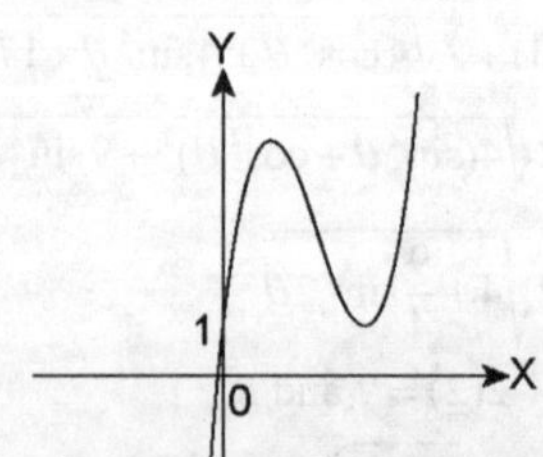

$\Rightarrow$ $f(3)=27-54+27+1=1$

$\Rightarrow$ $G=f(1)=1-6+9+1=5$ and $L=f(3)=1$

$\Rightarrow$ $[G+L]=6$ on, $(G-L)=4$

$\therefore$ **(ii) → (b)**

(iii) $f(x)=\tan^{-1}x-\dfrac{1}{2}\ln x;\left[\dfrac{1}{\sqrt{3}},\sqrt{3}\right]$

$\Rightarrow$ $f'(x)=\dfrac{1}{1+x^2}-\dfrac{1}{2x}=\dfrac{2x-(1+x^2)}{2x(1+x^2)}=\dfrac{-(x-1)^2}{2x(x^2+1)}$

$\Rightarrow$ $f'(x)>0$ for $x>0$

$\Rightarrow$ $f'(x)>0$ on $\left[\dfrac{1}{\sqrt{3}},\sqrt{3}\right]$

$\Rightarrow \ L = f\left(\frac{1}{\sqrt{3}}\right) = \tan^{-1}\frac{1}{\sqrt{3}} - \frac{1}{2}\ln\left(\frac{1}{\sqrt{3}}\right)$

$\Rightarrow \ L = \frac{\pi}{6} + \frac{1}{2} \times \frac{1}{2}\ln 3 = \frac{\pi}{6} + \frac{1}{4}\ln 3$ and G

$= \tan^{-1}\sqrt{3} - \frac{1}{2}\ln\sqrt{3} = \frac{\pi}{3} - \frac{1}{4}\ln 3$

$\Rightarrow \ L + G = \frac{\pi}{2}$

$\Rightarrow \ [L + G] = \left[\frac{\pi}{2}\right] = 1$ and $[G + L] = 1$, $(G - L)$

$= \left(\frac{\pi}{6} - \frac{1}{2}\ln 3\right) \ \left(\because \frac{\pi}{6}, \frac{1}{2}\ln 3 \in \left(\frac{1}{2}, 1\right)\right)$

$\Rightarrow \ (G - L) \in \left(\frac{-1}{2}, \frac{1}{2}\right)$

$\Rightarrow \ (G - L) \neq 5$, where () is least integer function.

$\therefore$ **(iii) → (a)**

SECTION–VIII: (NUMERICAL INTEGER TYPE)

1. Let $x^2 = t$; $y = g(t)$ and $t = h(x)$ where $= \frac{t^2 + 3t + 1}{t + 1}, t = x^2$

$\therefore \ \frac{dy}{dx} = \frac{dg}{dt} \times \frac{dt}{dx} = \frac{(t+1)(2t+3) - (t^2 + 3t + 1)}{(t+1)^2} \times 2x$

$\therefore \ \frac{dy}{dx} = \frac{t^2 + 2t + 2}{(t+1)^2} \times (2x) = 0$

$\Leftrightarrow \ x = 0$ and $\frac{dy}{dx} < 0$ for $x < 0$ and $\frac{dy}{dx} > 0$ for $x > 0$

$\Rightarrow \ f(x)$ decreases on $[-1, 0)$ and increases on $(0, 2]$

Also $f(x)$ is even function.

$\Rightarrow \ f_{\max} = f_{\max}$ in $[0, 2] = f(2) = \frac{16 + 12 + 1}{4 + 1} = \frac{29}{5}$

$\Rightarrow \ [f_{\max.}] = \left[\frac{29}{5}\right] = 5$

2. The log which can't be flown along the system will be in a situation shown below.

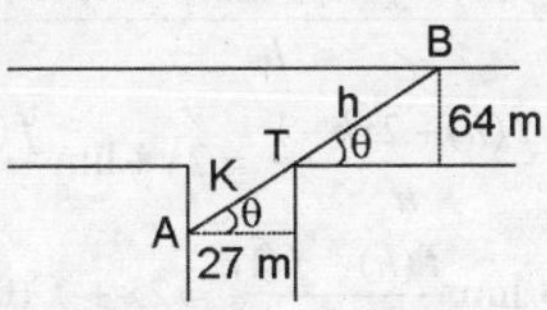

Let $AB = l = AT + TB$

$\Rightarrow \ l = k + h$

$\Rightarrow \ l = 27 \sec\theta + 64 \operatorname{cosec}\theta$

$\Rightarrow \ \frac{dl}{d\theta} = 27 \sec\theta \tan\theta - 64 \operatorname{cosee}\theta . \cot\theta$

$\therefore \ \frac{dl}{d\theta} = 0$

$\Rightarrow \ 27\frac{\sin\theta}{\cos^2\theta} - \frac{64\cos\theta}{\sin^2\theta} = 0$

$\Rightarrow \ 27\sin^3\theta = 64\cos^3\theta$

$\Rightarrow \ \tan^3\theta = \frac{64}{27}$

$\Rightarrow \ \tan\theta = \frac{4}{3}$

$\Rightarrow \ \sec\theta = \frac{5}{3}$ and $\frac{d^2l}{d\theta^2} = 27\sec^3\theta + 27\tan^2\theta\sec\theta +$ $64\operatorname{cosee}^3\theta + 64\cot^2\theta\cos\theta$

$\left(\frac{d^2l}{d\theta^2}\right)_{\theta = \tan^{-1}\frac{4}{3}} > 0$

$\Rightarrow$ Minimum value of l required to form above situation

$= 27\left(\frac{5}{3}\right) + 64\left(\frac{5}{4}\right) = 45 + 80 = 125m$

$\therefore$ A log of minimum length $125m$ can't be flown

3. $f'(x) = 3\left(1 - \frac{\sqrt{21 - 4\lambda - \lambda^2}}{\lambda + 1}\right)x^2 + 5 \geq 0$

$\Leftrightarrow \ 0 - 60\left(1 - \frac{\sqrt{21 - 4\lambda - \lambda^2}}{\lambda + 1}\right) \leq 0$ (*i.e.*, Disc. ≤ 0)

$\Rightarrow \ \left(1 - \frac{\sqrt{21 - 4\lambda - \lambda^2}}{\lambda + 1}\right) \geq 0$

It is trivially true for $\lambda + 1 < 0$ i.e., $\lambda \in (-\infty, -1)$ and $\lambda^2 + 4\lambda - 21 \leq 0$

$\Rightarrow \ \lambda \in (-\infty, -1)$ and $\lambda \in [-7, 3)$

$\Rightarrow \ \lambda \in [-7, -1)$

For $\lambda + 1 > 0$ and $\lambda \in [-7, 3]$ i.e., $\lambda \in (-1, 3]$;

$1 \geq \frac{\sqrt{21 - 4\lambda - \lambda^2}}{\lambda + 1}$

$\Rightarrow \ \lambda + 1 \geq \sqrt{21 - 4\lambda - \lambda^2}$

$\Rightarrow \ \lambda^2 + 2\lambda + 1 \geq 21 - 4\lambda - \lambda^2$

$\Rightarrow \ 2\lambda^2 + 6\lambda - 20 \geq 0$

$\Rightarrow \ \lambda^2 + 3\lambda - 10 \geq 0$

$\Rightarrow \ (\lambda + 5)(\lambda - 2) \geq 0$

$\Rightarrow \ \lambda \in (-\infty, -5] \cup [2, \infty)$,

But $\lambda \in (-1, 3]$

$\Rightarrow \ \lambda \in (2, 3]$

$\therefore \ f(x)$ increases for $\lambda \in [-7, -1) \cup [2, 3] = [a, b) \cup [c, d]$

$\Rightarrow \ a = -7, \ b = -1, \ c = 2, \ d = 3$

$\therefore \ |a + b + c + d| = |-7 - 1 + 2 + 3| = 3$

4. Perimeter $= 2(l + b) = 20$

$\Rightarrow \ l + b = 10$

$\Rightarrow \ \frac{dl}{dt} + \frac{db}{dt} = 0$

$\Rightarrow \dfrac{dp}{dt} = -\dfrac{dl}{dt} = -2cm/\sec$

Now $A = l.b$

$\Rightarrow \dfrac{dA}{dt} = l\dfrac{db}{dt} + b.\dfrac{dl}{dt}$

$\Rightarrow l(-2) + b(2) = -2(l-b)$

Now, $\dfrac{dA}{dt} \le 0$

$\Rightarrow -2(l-b) \le 0$

$\Rightarrow l \ge b$

$\Rightarrow l \ge (10-l)(\because l+b=10)$

$\Rightarrow 2l \ge 10$

$\Rightarrow l \ge 5$

$\therefore$ When $l = 5cm$, area of rectangle start decreasing:

5. Let 'h' be the height of cone and r be its radius. Clearly, $\sqrt{6}$ will be the slant height of the cone.

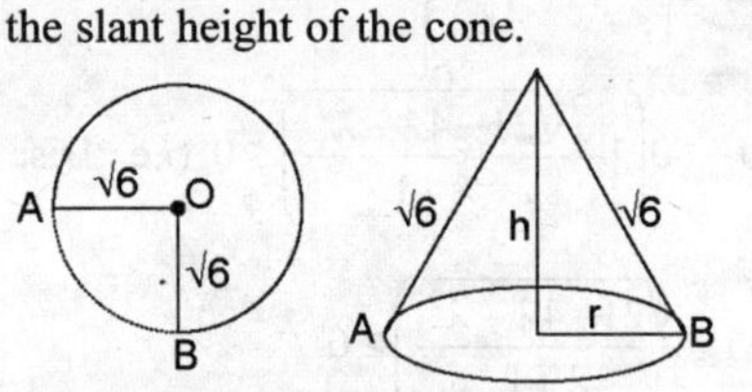

Thus, $h^2 + r^2 = 6$ .... (1)

Now, volume of cone is given by,

$V = \dfrac{4}{3}\pi r^2 h = \dfrac{4}{3}\pi(6-h^2)h$

$\therefore \dfrac{dV}{dh} = \dfrac{4}{3}\pi(6-3h^2) = 0$

$\Rightarrow h^2 = 2$

$\Rightarrow \dfrac{d^2V}{dh^2} = \dfrac{4}{3}\pi(-6h) = -8\pi h < 0$

$\Rightarrow$ V will be maximum for $h = \sqrt{2}$

$\therefore V_{\max.} = V_0 = \dfrac{4}{3}\pi(6-2)\sqrt{2}$

$\Rightarrow V_0 = \dfrac{16\sqrt{2}\pi}{3} = 8\sqrt{2}\left(\dfrac{2\pi}{3}\right)$

$\Rightarrow \dfrac{V_0}{8\sqrt{2}} = \dfrac{2\pi}{3}$

$\Rightarrow \tan^2\left(\dfrac{V_0}{8\sqrt{2}}\right) = \tan^2\left(\dfrac{2\pi}{3}\right) = \tan^2\dfrac{\pi}{3} = 3$

6. Let the coordinate of C be (5cosθ, 4cosθ), then area of rectangle = (10cosθ) (8cosθ) = 40 (sin2θ), which will be maximum for $2\theta = \dfrac{\pi}{2}$ i.e., $\theta = \dfrac{\pi}{4}$.

$\Rightarrow$ Length of rectangle $= 10\cos\theta = \dfrac{10}{\sqrt{2}}$ and breadth $= 8\sin\theta = \dfrac{8}{\sqrt{2}}$

$\therefore$ Perimeter

$P = 2(l+b) = 2\left(\dfrac{10}{\sqrt{2}} + \dfrac{8}{\sqrt{2}}\right) = 2\left(\dfrac{18}{\sqrt{2}}\right) = 18\sqrt{2}$

$\Rightarrow 3P = 54\sqrt{2} = (27)\left(2\sqrt{2}\right)$

$\Rightarrow 3P = \left(3\sqrt{2}\right)^3$

$\Rightarrow \log_{3\sqrt{2}}(3P) = \log_{3\sqrt{2}}\left(3\sqrt{2}\right)^3 = 3$

7. Volume of cylinder $= V = \pi r^2 h$

$\Rightarrow \dfrac{dV}{dt} = \pi\left(r^2\dfrac{dh}{dt} + 2rh\dfrac{dr}{dt}\right)$

$\Rightarrow \left(\dfrac{dV}{dt}\right) = \pi\left(r^2(1) + 2rh\left(\dfrac{-1}{2}\right)\right) = \pi(r^2 - rh)$

$\Rightarrow \left(\dfrac{dV}{dt}\right)_{h=10,r=12} = \pi(144-120) = 24\pi$

$S = 2\pi rh$

$\Rightarrow \dfrac{dS}{dt} = 2\pi\left(r\dfrac{dh}{dt} + h\dfrac{dr}{dt}\right) = 2\pi\left(r + h\left(\dfrac{-1}{2}\right)\right)$

$\Rightarrow \dfrac{dS}{dt} = 2\pi\left(r - \dfrac{h}{2}\right)$

$\therefore \left(\dfrac{dS}{dt}\right)_{h=10,r=12} = 2\pi(12-5) = 14\pi$

$\Rightarrow \dfrac{dV/dt}{ds/dt} = \dfrac{24\pi}{14\pi} = \dfrac{12}{7} = 1\dfrac{5}{7}$

$\Rightarrow$ Least integer greater than $\dfrac{12}{7} = 2$

8. $g(x) = \int_0^x f(t)dt$

$\Rightarrow g'(x) = f(x)$ ...(*i*)

and $g(0) = 0$ ...(*ii*)

Now, $f'(x) = \lim\limits_{h\to 0}\dfrac{f(x+h) - f(x)}{h}$

$= \lim\limits_{h\to 0}\dfrac{f(x) + f(h) + 2xh - 1 - f(x)}{h}$

$= \lim\limits_{h\to 0}\dfrac{f(h) + 2xh - 1}{h} = 2x + \lim\limits_{h\to 0}\dfrac{f(h)-1}{h}$

$= 2x + \lim\limits_{h\to 0}\dfrac{f(h) - f(1)}{h} = 2x + f'(0) = 2x + 2$

$\left[\begin{array}{l}\because \text{ put } x = y = 0 \\ \Rightarrow f(0) = f(0) + f(0) - 1 \\ \Rightarrow f(0) = 1\end{array}\right]$

$\therefore f'(x) = 2(x+1)$

$\Rightarrow f(x) = 2\left[\dfrac{x^2}{2} + x\right] + C$

$\Rightarrow f(x) = x^2 + 2x + C$

$\therefore \quad f(0)=1$

$\Rightarrow \quad C=1$

$\Rightarrow \quad f(x)=(x+1)^2$ .... (iii)

$\therefore$ From (i) and (iii), $g'(x)=(x+1)^2 \geq 0 \ \forall x \in \mathbb{R}$

$\Rightarrow$ $g(x)$ is an increasing function and $g(x)=\int (x+1)^2 dx$

$\Rightarrow \quad g(x)=\frac{(x+1)^3}{3}+C_1$

Also $g(0)=0$

$\Rightarrow \quad C_1=-\frac{1}{3}$

$\Rightarrow \quad g(x)=\frac{(x+1)^3}{3}-\frac{1}{3}$

$\Rightarrow$ g max. in [1, 3] $=g(3)=\frac{(4)^3}{3}-\frac{1}{3}=\frac{63}{3}=21$

9. Let $f(x)=ax^4+bx^3+cx^2+dx+e$

$\Rightarrow \quad f'(x)=4ax^3+3bx^2+2cx+d$

$\Rightarrow \quad f''(x)=12ax^2+6bx+2c$

For $f(x)$ to have critical points

$f''(x)=0$ must have real roots and sign of $f''(x)$ must change across the neighbour hood of these roots.

$\Rightarrow$ $f''(x)=0$ must have real and distinct roots.

$\Rightarrow$ Disc. > 0

$\Rightarrow \quad (6b)^2-4(12a)(2c)>0$

$\Rightarrow \quad 36b^2-96ac>0$

$\Rightarrow \quad 12(3b^2-8ac)>0$

$\Rightarrow \quad 3b^2-8ac>0$ ...(1)

Now, $\log\left[-3b^4+12b^2-32ac+8ab^2c\right]$ is defined

$\Rightarrow \quad -3b^4+12b^2-32ac+8ab^2c>0$

$\Rightarrow \quad -3b^2(b^2-4)-8ac(4-b^2)>0$

$\Rightarrow \quad (b^2-4)(8ac-3b^2)>0$

$\Rightarrow \quad (b^2-4)(3b^2-8ac)<0$ ...(2)

From (1) and (2), $b^2-4<0$

$\Rightarrow \quad b\in[-2,2]$

$\Rightarrow$ Greatest possible value of $b=2$

10. Since $f(x)$ is twice differentiable, $f(x)$ and $f'(x)$ are continuous function and by the given information, the rough graph will be as shown below:

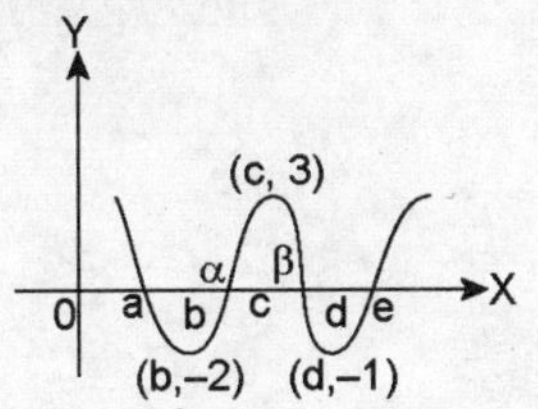

$g(x)=\left(f'(x)\right)^2+f(x).f''(x)=\frac{d}{dx}\left(f(x).f'(x)\right)=\frac{dh}{dx}$

where $h(x)=f(x).f'(x)$ ...(i)

Clearly $f(x)=0$ has at least 4 roots $a,\alpha\in(b,c)$, $\beta\in(c,d),e$ and $f'(x)=0$ has at least 3 roots (3 stationary points).

$\Rightarrow$ $h(x)=f(x).f'(x)=0$ has at least 7 roots as roots of $f(x)=0$ and that of $f'(x)=0$ are different.

$\Rightarrow$ By Rolle's theorem $h'(x)=g(x)=0$ has at least 6 roots, at least one root between two consecutive roots of $h(x)=0$

$\therefore$ Ans: 6

11. Equation of parabola is $y=x^2+4$. Its parametric equation is $\left(\frac{1}{2}t,4+\frac{1}{4}t^2\right)$, let it be Q (*nearest point to P*)

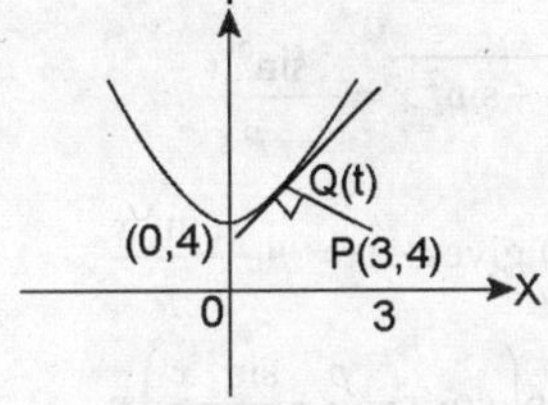

$\Rightarrow$ (*Slope of tangent at Q*) × (*Slope of PQ*) = −1

$\Rightarrow \quad (t)\times\left(\frac{\frac{1}{4}t^2}{\frac{1}{2}t-3}\right)=-1$

$\Rightarrow \quad \frac{t^3}{t-6}=-2$

$\Rightarrow \quad t^3+2t-12=0$

$\Rightarrow \quad t=2$

$\Rightarrow \quad Q\equiv(1,5)$

$\Rightarrow \quad PQ=\sqrt{(3-1)^2+(4-5)^2}=\sqrt{5}$

$\Rightarrow \quad d=\sqrt{5}$

$\Rightarrow \quad [d]=2$

12. $T_{r+1}={}^9C_r\left(\frac{a}{2}x^{1/6}\right)^{9-r}.\left(\frac{b}{3}x^{-1/3}\right)^r={}^9C_r\frac{(a)^{9-r}}{(2)^{9-r}}.\frac{(b)^r}{(3)^r}.(x)^{\frac{9-r}{6}-\frac{r}{3}}$

For term independent of $x, \frac{9-r}{6}-\frac{r}{3}=0$

$\Rightarrow \quad r=3$

$\therefore \quad T_4={}^9C_3\frac{(a)^6}{(2)^6}.\frac{(b)^3}{(3)^3}=\frac{9\times8\times7}{6\times(2)^6(3)^3}.a^6.b^3$

$=\frac{7}{144}a^6b^3=\frac{7}{144}(a^2b)^3=\frac{7}{144}\left(\sqrt{a^2b}\right)^6\leq\frac{7}{144}\left(\frac{a^2+b}{2}\right)^6$

$=\frac{7}{144}\left(\frac{(2)^{5/3}.(3)^{1/3}}{2}\right)^6=\frac{7}{144}\left((2)^{2/3}.(3)^{1/3}\right)^6$

$\therefore \quad T_4\leq\frac{7}{144}\times(2)^4(3)^2 \quad \Rightarrow \quad T_4\leq 7$

$\therefore$ Maximum value of $T_4=7$

13. For $0<x<1, f'(x)=-6x<0$ and for $x>1, f'(x)=5>0$

$\Rightarrow$ $f(x)$ is decreasing for $x\in(0,1)$ and increasing for $x\in(1,\infty)$.

$\therefore$ For $f(x)$ to be minima at $x=1$, $5\tan^{-1}\alpha-3\geq f(1)$

$\Rightarrow 5\tan^{-1}\alpha-3\geq 2$

$\Rightarrow \alpha\geq\tan 1>\tan\frac{\pi}{4}=1$

$\Rightarrow \alpha>1$

$\Rightarrow$ Least integer value of $\alpha>2$

14. Let $x+\sqrt{x^2+\sin^2 x}=p$ ...(i)

$\Rightarrow -\sin^2 x=p\left(x-\sqrt{x^2+\sin^2 x}\right)$

$\Rightarrow x-\sqrt{x^2+\sin^2 x}=-\frac{\sin^2 x}{p}$ ...(ii)

$\therefore$ (i) + (ii) gives, $2x=p-\frac{\sin^2 x}{p}$ ...(iii)

$\therefore f(x)=6\left(\cos x-\frac{p}{2}+\frac{\sin^2 x}{2p}\right)p$

$\Rightarrow f(x)=3\left(2p\cos x-p^2+\sin^2 x\right)$

$=3\left(2p\cos x-p^2+1-\cos^2 x\right)$

$=3\left[1-(p^2+\cos^2 x-2p\cos x)\right]$

$=3\left[1-(p-\cos x)^2\right]\leq 3$

$\Rightarrow$ Maximum value of $f(x)=3$

Remark: one can verify that $f(x)=3$ holds $p=\cos x$ i.e., $\sqrt{x^2+\sin^2 x}=\cos x-x$

$\Rightarrow 2x\cos x=\cos 2x$

$\Rightarrow \frac{\cos 2x}{\cos x}=2x$

15. In Similar Δs ADE and AFC, $\frac{r}{R}=\frac{H-h}{H}$

$\Rightarrow r=\frac{R}{H}(H-h)$ ...(i)

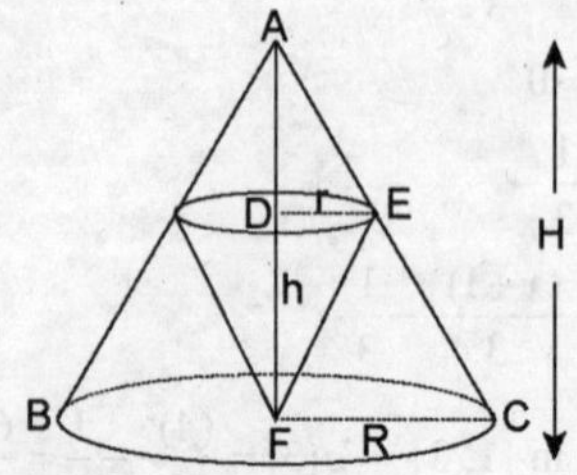

Now, volume of small cone

$V=\frac{1}{3}\pi r^2 h=\frac{1}{3}\pi\frac{R^2}{H^2}(H-h)^2 h$

$\Rightarrow V=\frac{\pi R^2}{3H^2}(H^2 h+h^2-2Hh^2)$

$\Rightarrow \frac{dV}{dh}=\frac{\pi R^2}{3H^2}(H^2+3h^2-4Hh)$

$\therefore$ For maximum volume, $\frac{dV}{dh}=0$

$\Rightarrow H^2+3h^2-4Hh=0$

$\Rightarrow H^2-3hH-hH+3h^2=0$

$\Rightarrow H(H-3h)-h(H-3h)=0$

$\Rightarrow H=h$ or $H=3h$

But $H = h$ is impossible, hence $H = 3h$ for maximum volume thus H: $h = 3$